W9-AUR-508

ENCYCLOPEDIA OF THE
ENLIGHTENMENT

ENCYCLOPEDIA OF THE
ENLIGHTENMENT

VOLUME 1
A–L

Editor
MICHEL DELON

Adviser to the English-Language Edition
PHILIP STEWART

Translation Editor
GWEN WELLS

FITZROY DEARBORN PUBLISHERS
CHICAGO • LONDON

Fitzroy Dearborn Publishers gratefully acknowledges financial assistance provided by the French Ministry of Culture-Centre National du Livre for the translation of this book.

Originally published as *Dictionnaire européen des Lumières*
Copyright © Presses Universitaires de France, 1997

Copyright © 2001
FITZROY DEARBORN PUBLISHERS

FITZROY DEARBORN PUBLISHERS
919 North Michigan Avenue, Suite 760
Chicago, IL 60611
USA

or

FITZROY DEARBORN PUBLISHERS
310 Regent Street
London W1R 5AJ
UK

British Library and Library of Congress Cataloging in Publication Data are available.

ISBN 1-57958-246-x

First published in the USA and UK 2001

Typeset by Andrea Rosenberg
Printed by Edwards Brothers, Ann Arbor, Michigan
Index by Fred Leise, Between the Lines Indexing and Editorial Services, Ann Arbor, Michigan
Cover design by Peter Aristedes, Chicago Advertising and Design, Chicago, Illinois

Cover Art: Jacques-Louis David, *Portrait d'Antoine-Laurent Lavoisier et de sa femme* (1788). The Metropolitan Museum of Art, Purchase, Mr. and Mrs. Charles Wrightsman Gift, in honor of Everett Fahy, 1977. (1977.10) Photograph © 1986 The Metropolitan Museum of Art

CONTENTS

Preface to the French Edition — *page* vii

Preface to the English Edition — xi

Note on Usage and Style — xv

Contributors — xvii

Translators, Translation Reviewers, Copy Editors — xxi

Acknowledgments — xxiii

General Bibliography — xxv

List of Entries — xxvii

Encyclopedia of the Enlightenment, A–L — I

PREFACE TO THE FRENCH EDITION

This *Encyclopedia* makes no claim to map systematically a field that is clearly defined and delimited once and for all. The Enlightenment simultaneously denotes (1) a historically specific intellectual movement, (2) the period during which this movement came to the fore, but during which it was never dominant in quantitative (or even in qualitative) terms, (3) the issues that we have inherited from it, and (4) a system of values that remains—or is today reemerging as—a subject of debate. These four definitions are connected, often in competition and sometimes in contradiction with one another. While it made possible the development of conceptually linked philosophical theories, the "philosophy" of the Enlightenment, situated between theory and action, abstraction and literature, never resolved itself into a system. Its period of development varied from country to country, from the turn of the 18th century in England and France until the mid–19th century in some parts of Eastern Europe. The Enlightenment's questions about a universal model of mankind, about humanity's perfectibility, and about the progress of society are once again being raised today, indicating both the continuity of these issues and the lack of irrevocable attainments. No encyclopedia, as a fixed collection of articles, can hope to bring closure to what remains a subject of historical research and ideological discussion. The discontinuous and alphabetical form was one of the Enlightenment's favorite genres with which to criticize and sometimes even harass tradition, and to bring together and make accessible ideas long restricted to different disciplines and professional groups. An encyclopedia of the Enlightenment written today is not a new encyclopedic whole such as the 18th century might have envisaged: our current perspective is not to be confused with the situation of more than two centuries ago— the intersection of knowledge and ideological combat cannot be naively perpetuated.

There currently exists a proliferation of reference works in which the need to redraw a map of knowledge is mingled with the desire to go back to positive facts, an awareness of epistemological changes, and a fear of glib arguments. In this context, a critical appraisal of the Enlightenment seems necessary for at least four reasons. First of all, 18th-century studies have undergone considerable development throughout the world during the last 25 years, as witness the foundation of national societies and an international society for the study of the period, the success of conferences on the Enlightenment and numerous similar exchanges, and myriad specialized journals, collections, databases, and websites. Research has become institutionalized and systematized, and has also found new objects and points of view. The appearance of new fields of investigation calls for a summing-up, however provisional, an outlining of trends, a singling out of principal themes, and also from time to time an indication of omissions.

Second, the renewal of research into the period is linked to the opening up of viewpoints and the dialogue among researchers from different disciplines and countries. An encyclopedia of the Enlightenment is obliged to be interdisciplinary and international in its subject matter as much as in its approach, while accepting that this objective cannot be achieved in every article, that it represents a direction and an intention, and that a great deal remains to be done in this field. It has often been stressed that the French *Lumières* are neither the Enlightenment, nor the *Aufklärung*, nor the *Illuminismo*. Enlightenment Europe was characterized by tensions between universalism and a French model of society; the French Enlightenment itself was marked by a contradiction between worldliness and refinement, on the one hand, and rationalism and anthropological optimism, on the other. Just as Enlightenment thought in French-speaking countries was deepened by the schism between Jean-Jacques Rousseau and the Encyclopedists, so too the European Enlightenment developed through competition between an expansion of French language and culture and a rejection of this model in the name of national values. The initiative and direction of the present work are French, but its advisory board and contributors are European.

The third reason for this *Encyclopedia* is that France does not have the same tradition of dictionaries of concepts and ideas as does Germany. The French have innumerable dictionaries of proper names, whether of writers, philosophers, artists, scholars or historical figures, and there is no lack of reference works focused on events or periods, such as the rich syntheses devoted to the *Grand Siècle,* the ancien régime, the French Revolution, and the Empire. A few works attempting to cover the Enlightenment exist in other languages, but these either concentrate mainly on proper names or restrict themselves to the categories of Enlightenment philosophy. The present *Encyclopedia of the Enlightenment* is intended to be conceptual in the widest sense of the word, running from philosophical and scientific concepts to literary and artistic categories. Individual figures active during the Enlightenment are not the subjects of separate articles; their names, however, are indexed, enabling the reader to locate them in the various articles. The only proper names found in the titles of articles are those of a few mythological or allegorical figures relevant to an overview of concepts. Thus, the Enlightenment is neither reduced to its philosophy, nor identified with the 18th century alone: each country and each discipline is allowed its own chronological account.

The final justification for this *Encyclopedia* concerns the ideological situation at the close of the 20th century, which saw the disappearance of the opposition between the two great systems of thought inherited from the Enlightenment, liberalism and socialism. This historic shift has brought the fundamental values of the Enlightenment back under discussion—in the best and the worst sense of discussion. In the best sense, since we must now take a pluralistic view of categories such as reason and progress that have been monopolized respectively by the model of the exact sciences and by that of quantifiable economic development: rationality and progress cannot be reduced to a single definitive norm; instead, they must be related to the debates that marked their appearance and evolution and put into the context of the contradictions and anxieties of our own era. However, the calling into question of the Enlightenment's attainments becomes a matter of grave consequence when it bears on respect for the individual, the consistency of the principle of reason in relation to each person, or faith in exchanges and in the possibility of change. The 18th century's optimism, rationalism, and cosmopolitanism are often blamed for all our woes. *The Encyclopedia of the Enlightenment,* gathering together information, issues, and inquiries from diverse perspectives, does not aim to sidestep these contemporary debates. We had allowed for the possibility of contradictory statements about a single concept; and in the end we have opted for multiple entries that intersect and overlap in order to allow different or even discordant voices to be heard. Different contributions on a single subject occasionally follow one another so as to emphasize the diversity of points of view.

Comprising the main strands in the web of interrelated articles are syntheses dealing with the countries or cultural regions that to varying degrees were centers of the Enlightenment—Germany, England, the Balkans, Scotland, Spain, etc.—and the regions or cultures with which Europe was in dialogue (Africa, America, China, Japan, Islam, etc), as well as the major scientific and artistic disciplines and fields of intellectual activity (astronomy, chemistry, music, painting, etc.). To this first series of major articles is added a second, dealing with political, economic, legal, and above all cultural institutions (academies, libraries, salons); literary and artistic genres (comedy, the novel, opera, portraiture, landscape); philosophical categories (prejudice, progress, reason); religious categories (Jansenism, Pietism); and aesthetic categories (the baroque, the beautiful, the grotesque, ugliness, the rococo, the sublime). A third series of articles introduces anthropological categories (love, the body, tears, rumor, work) that allow cross-disciplinary viewpoints, as well as shorter notes on more limited elements characteristic of the Enlightenment, of the sensibilities or worldliness of the age, that serve as symptoms, cultural indices, or counterpoints (night, persiflage, reverie).

Each article is conceived less as an exhaustive survey or synthesis than as an overview, or even an exploration, of issues; both the further reading list and the cross-references guide the reader to a fuller consideration and supplementary information. The authors have been allowed considerable freedom of tone and complete independence of opinion; they have signed and take responsibility for their contributions. The chronological limits and the ideological center of gravity of the Enlightenment are thus presented in different ways according to place, subject, and interpretation. In some instances the Enlightenment appears as a long-term movement of ideas and sensibilities. In others, it is envisaged as a more precise moment in European history. The approach adopted by individual contributors sometimes includes the French Revolution and the tumult of the Napoleonic era, and sometimes it does not. Opposing points of view find expression from one article to another, while complementary points of view juxtapose national and cultural experiences in the context of a single entry. Standardization has been brought to bear only at the level of material presentation and general balance. The *Encyclopedia of the Enlightenment* was not conceived on the model of the French Republic's division into *départements* or the Napoleonic administration of occupied Europe.

The further readings can only be a partial list of relevant works: they have often had to be shortened from the authors' original suggestions. From article to article they complement one another; repetition of titles has been generally avoided, although not forbidden. The further readings are somewhat oriented toward the French-speaking world as far as the initial investigation of a subject is concerned, but they also allow for the possibility of further study in other European languages. Articles from the great dictionaries of ideas and concepts have not been systematically cited, although they always offer a useful complement, providing as they do a wider view of history and issues. The general bibliography lists the titles that could have been cited for a great many articles, as well as a few key research tools of 18th-century studies. The recent and ongoing proliferation of published material precludes any attempt to be exhaustive, which could only be achieved by means of constantly updated computer databases. The aim of the present work is to provide the basic elements of research and to offer new interconnections, interdisciplinary cross-references, and further lines of inquiry to specialists of various disciplines and various nationalities. Some entries are presented provocatively as a simple series of references and bibliographical information. The book's flexible format, and a dynamic that computer programs have taught us to refer to as interactive—between the unity of each contribution and the potential for free-ranging consultation, between the fixed character of print and the meandering aspect of all research—match the refusal to define or limit the Enlightenment.

More than 200 contributors have been gathered together, representing some 15 nationalities. A balance has been sought between established and universally recognized researchers and newcomers to 18th-century studies. The diversity of voices was chosen to accommodate both information on known facts and the opening-up of new viewpoints, the presence of both necessary or expected entries and suggestive, more surprising articles. The majority of articles were originally written in French, about a quarter in German, and a few in English, Danish, or Italian. The *Encyclopedia of the Enlightenment* aims to be a varied, restless, sometimes unsettling work, willfully incomplete and resolutely "in progress." Reproduced on the cover, Jacques-Louis David's portrait of the chemist Antoine-Laurent de Lavoisier and his wife offers us an image of the 18th century that links scientific research, artistic creation, political involvement, and moral and social life. Far from being isolated within a self-enclosed sphere of knowledge, Lavoisier is presented to us as a man of the world, attentive to the presence of his wife and collaborator, taking pains over the surroundings in which he lives. He can handle a pen just as well as instruments of measurement and experimentation. In the background, a sketchbook recalls the artistic talents of Madame Lavoisier, who may have been taught by David himself. The painting is dated 1788: it invites us to consider the Enlightenment on either side of the break represented by the Revolution, both in itself and in its relation to the event of the Revolution. There is an interplay between the transparency of the glass instruments and the couple's intelligence, between the rigor of scientific observation and the warmth of a loving gaze. The Enlightenment is not to be appropriated by any group or any nationality: it bursts out beyond the history of philosophy or literature and overflows the national boundaries of England, France, or Germany. We trust that in the following articles the reader will find its intellectual vigilance and its passionate dilettantism, its moral rigor, and its taste for life.

Michel Delon
University of Paris IV–Sorbonne

PREFACE TO THE ENGLISH EDITION

The French title of this volume, *Dictionnaire européen des Lumières* (European Dictionary of the Enlightenment), stands for the vision and ideal that inspired the book while also incorporating part of an inherent problem. One cannot undertake any kind of account of what we call the Enlightenment without taking stock of matters of terminology: for it is not quite the same thing to say "Enlightenment," *Aufklärung,* or *Lumières.* Although they have quite different histories and thus convey different subtleties, the words "Enlightenment" and *Aufklärung* denote processes and are very close semantically. *Lumières,* on the other hand, is more abstract, often used interchangeably with *les philosophes,* both being plural. Thus, one literally cannot construct the same sentences using *Lumières* that one can with *Aufklärung* or "Enlightenment." Here arises a problem of equivalences among the different languages: *Lumières* cannot perfectly be translated by "Enlightenment" nor "Enlightenment" by *Lumières.*

It is helpful to bear in mind that "Enlightenment" is not a native term at all in English, and that when it was introduced it was highly pejorative. Etymologically related expressions such as "this enlightened age" were certainly to be found in the 18th century, but the term "Enlightenment" itself was not used to describe the era; there were other semantically similar terms independent of the light metaphor, the best known being "the Age of Reason," apparently coined by Thomas Paine. The 1944 edition of the *Oxford Universal Dictionary,* which dates the first attested instance of "Enlightenment" in that same sense from 1865, still offers this most instructive definition: "Shallow and pretentious intellectualism, unreasonable contempt for authority and tradition, etc.; applied esp. to the spirit and aims of the French philosophers of the 18th c." Perhaps that is why English-speaking historians of Europe well into the 20th century were in the habit of referring neither to "Enlightenment" nor to an "age" at all but to "the *philosophes*" in the plural. That the English word *philosophes* is borrowed from another language is, of course, also significant.

Period labels in art and literature are frequently applied after the fact, but it bears noting that the use of metaphors relating in some way or another to "enlightening" derives from the 18th century's own discourse, even if the way it works varies according to the context of different national languages. In fact, if we are to believe Charles Sorel, the metaphor was already current in 1671, when he wrote *De la connaissance des bons livres* (On the Knowledge of Worthy Books):

> This century is well enlightened, for all we hear is *lumières.* The word crops up in all sorts of places where we would formerly have found *esprit* or *intelligence,* and it sometimes happens that those who use the word apply it so ineptly that, with all their *lumières,* one could say they are completely in the dark.

At that point the term lacked the specificity it was progressively to acquire; early in the 18th century the movement that would become the Enlightenment was referred to rather as *la nouvelle philosophie* (the new philosophy)—although this phrase principally referred to what later was simply called science. The reference was ultimately shortened to just *philosophie,* with the label *les philosophes* designating its partisans, a moniker well enough established that a satirical play by that name, Charles Palissot's *Les philosophes,* was mounted to some acclaim at the Comédie-Française in 1760.

Doubtless the growing use of light metaphors owed something not only to their rich biblical overtones—an ever-present rhetorical staple in Christian countries—but also to the central role of optics in the early phases of the new philosophy and important achievements in that domain by some of its principal figureheads, particularly René Descartes and Sir Isaac Newton. The transition from scientific to abstract meanings attributed to *lumière(s)* can be seen in the series of definitions offered in Antoine Furetière's *Dictionnaire universel* (Universal Dictionary) in 1690, which includes the following:

> *Lumière,* a subtle, quick, and elusive body that causes brightness, illuminates, gives color to all things, and makes objects visible. . . . Colors are nothing but different reflections of *lumière.* God made *lumière* on the first day of creation and made the sun, which is the source and father of *lumière,* on the fourth; its excessive *lumière* is blinding to the eye. During its eclipse, it has but a feeble and somber *lumière.* The Moon, Venus, etc., borrow their *lumière* from the Sun's. . . .
>
> *Lumière* is also used figuratively in matters spiritual and moral, and signifies sight, knowledge, penetration. . . . The *lumières* of Faith and the Gospel have dissipated the shadows and the blindness of humankind. . . . The pagans knew God only by means of natural *lumière;* they abused *lumières,* knowledge that they acquired through study. . . . One says, in this sense, that a man has little *lumière* to mean his mind has limited range. . . .
>
> *Lumière* is also said of the beginnings of a proof, an indication, something that helps to make a discovery or come to a conclusion. Such-and-such witness has furnished us *lumières* to convict such-and-such accused. Judges have particular *lumières* for deciding a case; Lawyers often furnish them nothing but false *lumières.*

I have retained the French word rather than attempting to translate it here in order to show the variations in meaning (light, revelation, information, insight) and the complex interplay between singular and plural, literal and metaphorical usages.

The French use of *lumière(s)* was well established after 1750, no longer just as a kind of generic term for intellectual progress but to denote a specific contemporary transformation. In 1754 Claude Crébillon referred to "this century of enlightenment and philosophy." At about the same time in the *Encyclopédie,* Denis Diderot alluded to "the sound philosophy, the light of which is spreading abroad" while the baron d'Holbach considered the "progress of enlightenment that, in the last 50 years, has rapidly spread from one end of Europe to the other." In German, *Aufklärung* was in the air by the 1780s, soon to be followed by the more sarcastic *Aufklärerei* (around 1800). The English term, finally, derives from the German *Aufklärung.* There are similar variants in other languages. However, *Aufklärung* does not really enter the domain of literary history until the end of the 19th century, and *Siècle des Lumières* was not commonly used until at least the late 1950s. Jacques Roger wrote in 1967 that "it is current today to speak in French of *lumières* to designate the 18th century," but he added that this usage seemed recent and "certainly results from foreign influences, that of the English *Enlightenment* and even more of the German *Aufklärung.*"

All told, the Enlightenment had throughout the 19th century a rather bad reputation, the proof of its excesses lying precisely in the Revolution of 1789—the conventional wisdom about the Revolution being that which was reflected in a popular song: "C'est la faute à Voltaire, c'est la faute à Rousseau" (It's Voltaire's fault; it's Rousseau's fault). Many a book in England and France purported to protect the innocent against the noxious legacy of the previous century, sporting titles such as E. Grosse's *Dictionnaire d'antiphilosophisme, ou Réfutation des erreurs du XVIIIe siècle* (1856; Antiphilosophical Dictionary; or, Refutation of the Errors of the 18th Century). Great umbrage was taken by the *bien-pensants* (right-thinking men) especially in England, with regard to everything deriving from, or smacking of, Enlightenment. One late 19th-century English biographer, John Lord, concluded a blanket condemnation of Rousseau by denouncing in the same breath Rousseau's novel *La nouvelle Héloïse* (1761; Julie, or the New Héloïse) and his *Du contrat social* (1762; The Social Contract). In the novel, Lord asserted, Rousseau "undermines virtue as he had undermined truth and law. Here reprobation must become unqualified, and he appears one of the very worst men who ever exercised a commanding influence on a wicked and perverse generation." Even Rousseau, that anti-*philosophe* so enamored of virtue, could not escape this overwhelming 19th-century curse on the 18th. It was even worse for Voltaire, who was positively demonized, especially by the religious press.

But the quarrels of one century are not those of the next, and we have come to a point where the once-decried Enlightenment has come to be taken often as shorthand for the 18th century. So Enlightenment it is, although it is still misleading to use the term to designate, as some often do, an entire historical period. No single label can properly encapsulate the 18th century, or any other era. The Enlightenment is more properly thought of as a movement (or "Enlightenment project," as it is now sometimes called) operating throughout the century, one that begins among a small number of scholars and gradually reaches a wider and wider audience. It certainly had its effect over time, but it probably never reached the consciousness of most inhabitants of 18th-century Europe. Despite considerable rehabilitation, the *philosophes* could hardly stand immune from the philosophical and political currents of the 20th century; I will not repeat here what Michel Delon says about these in his preface.

The production of the present volume was not motivated by the need for a new defense or apology of the Enlightenment; instead, it was inspired by new perspectives and new research. Although it still manifests in many ways the residual traditional francocentrism of Enlightenment history and studies, the *Encyclopedia of the Enlightenment* also seeks to remold that traditional approach by intentionally embracing as much of Europe as possible, stressing not only problematics that were similar (or different) in various countries but also the multiple networks that linked people of learning throughout Europe and beyond.

Like the great *Encyclopédie* of 1751–65, this work is a compendium, and like that earlier project, this *Encyclopedia* was written, one might say, by a *société de gens de lettres* (community of scholars) who represent no single institution, country, or methodology. For that reason one might appropriately quote from the *Encyclopédie*'s own editors, Diderot and Jean le Rond D'Alembert, who declared in 1752:

> The job of the editors, as editors, is limited to assembling and publishing the work of other authors along with their own; but they have never pretended to commit themselves, nor reform articles written by others, nor go back to the sources from which they might have been drawn.

This is another way of saying that the *Encyclopedia of the Enlightenment* represents a collaboration, but a loose one, with no attempt to create a seamless work with a uniform point of view. And so, in a way, it is a worthy tribute, 250 years later, to the *Encyclopédie* that epitomized the Enlightenment, and the broad community of endeavor it symbolized.

Philip Stewart
Duke University

NOTE ON STYLE AND USAGE

Ambitious in scope and, among modern dictionaries, innovative in its concepts-based approach, the *Dictionnaire européen des Lumières*, edited by Michel Delon, drew accolades from reviewers in both the scholarly and the general press in France when it appeared in 1997. Fitzroy Dearborn Publishers is pleased to make this exceptional reference work available to English-speaking readers.

In producing the *Encyclopedia of the Enlightenment*, the English-language editors have eliminated a handful of entries found in the French original, deeming them so specialized or local as to be inaccessible to most English-language readers. Throughout the volume occasional brief glosses have been discreetly inserted into the text to help identify historical figures or events. Philip Stewart of Duke University, editorial adviser to the English-language edition, has contributed a preface to complement that of Michel Delon. Professor Stewart also has expanded the Coffeehouse entry to include information on the emergence of that social institution in London, and he has prepared a fine essay on the Revolutionary Calendar expressly for the present volume. The Further Readings that follow each entry have been culled from the bibliographies in the original French edition; many of the original contributors provided a list of supplementary reference works in English for inclusion in the present volume. A single, comprehensive index has been substituted for the two indices (one of proper names, the other of themes) found in the French edition. Apart from these changes, the *Encyclopedia of the Enlightenment* is a translation of the French original; as such, it reflects the predominantly France-centered focus of that work.

By design, in terms of both content and format, this portrait of the Enlightenment is modeled on that emblematic Enlightenment venture, Diderot and D'Alembert's *Encyclopédie*. Just as appropriately, given the Enlightenment ideal of intellectual liberty, the more than 200 contributors to this *Encyclopedia*—mostly French, but also including specialists from Germany, Italy, Switzerland, Sweden, Denmark, and the United Kingdom—clearly benefited from complete editorial freedom in writing their entries. Both factual and interpretive, these essays reflect the wide variety of approaches and theoretical perspectives current in European scholarship, ranging from aesthetics to philology to cultural critique inspired by the work of Michel Foucault, and so on. The entries are just as diverse on the level of style. The translators have made every effort to preserve contributors' individual styles, although the very process of translation into fluent and idiomatic English has inevitably entailed the loss of some stylistic idiosyncrasies.

Readers may benefit from a few words of explanation on some further points of usage and style. Out of respect for linguistic diversity, titles of literary, philosophical, and other 18th-century works are given in the original language whenever possible, followed by a parenthesis containing the original date of publication and a courtesy translation (which in some cases corresponds to a published translation). As an exception to this general policy, it has been deemed unnecessary to provide a courtesy translation in the case of Diderot and D'Alembert's *Encyclopédie*, which is referred to in French only throughout the volume. No courtesy translation is provided for the titles of periodicals, but these are followed, when possible, by a parenthesis showing the run dates for the publication. In order to avoid potential confusion among the numerous royal academies, royal societies, and the like in different countries, names of institutions are given in the original language when possible, followed by a courtesy translation in parentheses. The salient exception to this policy is the Berlin Academy, which for simplicity's sake is cited in English (the institution was renamed—once in French, once in German—and restructured twice during the 18th century).

The cross-references in the French edition have been "imported" directly into the English edition and, in a very few cases, slightly augmented. The comprehensive index in the English-language edition includes headings corresponding to each entry (for which page runs are indicated in boldface type within the entry), and many other headings for important individuals, works, institutions, and concepts. In writing their entries, a great many contributors have referred to definitions of words given in the *Encyclopédie,* the Jesuit-compiled *Dictionnaire de Trévoux,* or other significant 18th-century reference works—to such an extent that indexing such occurrences would result in a long series of meaningless page numbers. Such reference works are therefore cited in the index only when the text contains a substantive discussion of them.

CONTRIBUTORS

Jean-Christophe ABRAMOVICI, François-Rabelais University, Tours

Sylviane ALBERTAN-COPPOLA, University of Rouen

Anne AMEND, University of Giessen

Lise ANDRIES, Centre National de la Recherche Scientifique

Wolfgang ASHOLT, University of Osnabrück

Sylvain AUROUX, Centre National de la Recherche Scientifique; École Normale Supérieure de Fontenay-Saint-Cloud

François AZOUVI, Centre National de la Recherche Scientifique; École des Hautes Études en Sciences Sociales

Margherita AZZI VISENTINI, Polytechnic School of Milan

Antoine de BAEQUE, University of Saint-Quentin-en-Yvelines

Patrice BAILHACHE, University of Nantes

Bernard BALAN

Françoise BARGUILLET, Lycée Montaigne, Bordeaux

Michel BARIDON, University of Bourgogne

Jean BART, University of Bourgogne

Gérard BEAUR, Centre National de la Recherche Scientifique; member of the editorial board of the journal *Histoire et sociétés rurales*

Annie BECQ, University of Caen

Bruno BELHOSTE, Institut National de Recherche Pédagogique

Georges BENREKASSA, University of Paris VII–Denis-Diderot

Bernadette BENSAUDE-VINCENT, University of Paris X–Nanterre

Jean-Claude BERCHET, University of Paris III–Sorbonne-Nouvelle

Dietrich BERDING, University of Bayreuth

Marcel BERNOS, University of Provence

Michael BERNSEN, University of Ruhr, Bochum

Jean-Paul BERTAUD, University of Paris I–Panthéon-Sorbonne

Gilles BERTRAND, Pierre-Mendès-France University, Grenoble II

Helen BIERI

Michaël BIZIOU, University of Paris X–Nanterre

Sven BJÖRKMAN, University of Uppsala

Rudolf BKOUCHE, University of Lille

Michel BLAY, Centre National de la Recherche Scientifique

Christine BLONDEL, Centre National de la Recherche Scientifique

Brenno BOCCADORO, University of Geneva

Jean-Michel BOEHLER, University of Human Sciences at Strasbourg

Olivier BONFAIT

Philippe BORDES, University of Paris X–Nanterre

Michel BOTTIN, University of Nice–Sophia-Antiopolis

Dominique BOUREL, Jerusalem Center for French Research

Marie-Noëlle BOURGUET, University of Paris VII; Institut Universitaire de France

Patrick BRASART, University of Paris VIII–Saint-Denis

Béatrice BRAUD, École des Hautes Études en Sciences Sociales, in collaboration with the Institut d'Histoire Moderne et Comtemporaine; École Normale Supérieure

Thierry BRESSAN, University of Paris VII–Denis-Diderot

Éric BRIAN, École des Hautes Études en Sciences Sociales

Numa BROC, University of Perpignan; Comité de Travaux Historiques et Scientifiques, Paris

Christophe BRUN, University of Versailles–Saint-Quentin-en-Yvelines

Else Marie BUKDAHL, Royal Academy of Fine Arts, Copenhagen

Paul BUTEL, University of Bordeaux III–Michel-de-Montaigne

Danielle BUYSSENS, Geneva Public and University Library

Alain CABANTOUS, University of Paris X–Nanterre

Claude CAILLY, University of Bordeaux III–Michel-de-Montaigne

Mara CAIRA-PRINCIPATO, University Institute of Modern Languages, Milan

Jean-Daniel CANDAUX, Geneva Public and University Library

Olivier CHALINE, École Normale Supérieure, Paris

Serge CHASSAGNE, Lumière University–Lyon II

Louis CHÂTELLIER, Institut Universitaire de France; University of Nancy II

Guy CHAUSSINAND-NOGARET, École des Hautes Études en Sciences Sociales

Pierre CHESSEX, editor, *Dictionnaire historique de la Suisse*

Jean-Philippe CHIMOT, University of Paris I–Panthéon-Sorbonne

Claudine COHEN, École des Hautes Études en Sciences Sociales

Monique COTTRET, University of Paris X–Nanterre

Marcel COURDURIÉ, Marseille-Provence Chamber of Commerce and Industry

Mauro CHRISTOFANI, University of Naples Federico II; Institute for Etruscan-Italian Archaeology of the National Council of Research, Rome

Laurence CROQ, Haut-Mesnil College, Montrouge

Jean DAGEN, University of Paris IV–Sorbonne

Otto DANN, University of Cologne

Frédéric DASSAS

François de GANDT, University of Lille III

Marc DELEPLACE, Institute for the History of the French Revolution; University of Paris I–Panthéon-Sorbonne

Didier DELEULE, University of Paris X–Nanterre

Michel DELON, University of Paris IV–Sorbonne

René DEMORIS, University of Paris III–Sorbonne-Nouvelle

Jean DEPRUN, University of Paris I–Panthéon-Sorbonne

Sylvie DERVAUX, University of Paris X–Nanterre

Robert DESCIMON, Centre National de la Recherche Scientifique (Centre de Recherches Historiques–École des Hautes Études en Sciences Sociales)

Jean DHOMBRES, École des Hautes Études en Sciences Sociales

Jacques DOMENECH, University of Nice–Sophia-Antiopolis

George DULAC, Centre National de la Recherche Scientifique

Jean DUMA, University of Poitiers

Jacques DUPÂQUIER, member, Academy of Moral and Political Sciences and Institut Universitaire de France

Pascal DURIS, Victor-Segalen University, Bordeaux

François-Xavier EMMANUELLI

Walter FÄHNDERS, University of Osnabrück

Catherine FARAGGI

Arlette FARGE, Centre National de la Recherche Scientifique (Centre de Recherches Historiques–École des Hautes Études en Sciences Sociales)

Danielle FAUQUE, Laboratoire d'Histoire des Sciences (Centre National de la Recherche Scientifique– Groupe d'Histoire et de Diffusion des Sciences d'Orsay), University of Paris XI–Orsay

Ernst FEIL, University of Munich

Nathalie FERRAND, University of Orléans

Gonthier Louis FINK, University of Human Sciences at Strasbourg

Jean-Louis FISCHER, Centre National de la Recherche Scientifique; Alexandre-Koyré Center; Museum of Natural History

Laurence FONTAINE, European University Institute, Florence

Pierre FRANTZ, University of Franche-Comté

Daniela GALLINGANI, University of Bologna

Petra GEKELER, University of Saar

Gérard GENGEMBRE, University of Caen

Florence GETREAU, National Museum of Arts and Popular Traditions, Paris; Centre National de la Recherche Scientifique, and National Superior Conservatory of Music of Paris

Jean-Marcel GOGER, University of Perpignan

Gianliugi GOGGI, University of Pisa

Gabriel GOHAU, University of Paris VII–Denis-Diderot

Angelica GOODDEN, Oxford University; St. Hilda's College, Oxford

Jean-Marie GOULEMOT, François-Rabelais University, Tours, Institut Universitaire de France

Patrick GRAILLE, University of Paris X–Nanterre

Jean-Pierre GUICCIARDI, Camille-Sée College; University of Paris VII–Denis-Diderot

Édouard GUITTON, University of Rennes II–Haute-Bretagne; Society of the Friends of Roucher and André Chénier

Fritz-Peter HAGER, University of Zurich

William HAUPTMAN, University of Lausanne

Jürgen HEIDEKING, University of Cologne

Carole HERZOG, University of Lausanne

François HINCKER, University of Paris I–Panthéon-Sorbonne

Marian HOBSON, Queen Mary and Westfield College, University of London

Joachim Christian HORN, Regensburg University

Heinrich HUDDE, Erlangen-Nuremberg University

Jean-Marcel HUMBERT, Hôtel de Salm, Paris

Nicole JACQUES-CHAQUIN, École Normale Supérieure de Fontenay-Saint-Cloud

Philippe JUNOD, University of Lausanne

Philippe KAENEL, University of Lausanne

Didier KAHN, Centre National de la Recherche Scientifique; University of Paris IV–Sorbonne

Annette KEILHAUER, University of Saar

Hans-Otto KLEINMANN, University of Cologne; Institute of Latin American and Iberian History

Diethelm KLIPPEL, University of Bayreuth

Béla KÖPECZI, University Eötvös, Budapest

Walter KUHFUSS, Trèves High School, Trier

Peter KUHRMANN

Yves LAISSUS, Committee of Historic and Scientific Work, Natural History Museum, Paris

Catherine LARRÈRE, University of Bordeaux III–Michel-de-Montaigne

Jean-Pierre LE GOFF, Institut Universitaire de Formation des Maîtres, Caen; Institut de Recherche sur l'Enseignement des Mathématiques de Basse-Normandie

René LE MÉE, Centre National de la Recherche Scientifique (Centre de Recherches Historiques–École des Hautes Études en Sciences Sociales) Laboratoire de Démographie Historique

Sophie LE MÉNAHÈZE-LEFAY, University of Reims–Champagne-Ardenne

Véronique LE RU, Institut Universitaire de Formation des Maîtres, Reims; University of Reims

Erik LEBORGNE, University of Paris III–Sorbonne-Nouvelle

François LEBRUN, University of Rennes II–Haute-Bretagne

André LESPAGNOL, University of Rennes II–Haute-Bretagne

Zdzislaw LIBERA, University of Warsaw; Institute for Literary Research at the Academy of Sciences

Robert LOCQUENEUX, University of Sciences and Technologies, Lille I; Center for Research on the Analysis of Knowledge Theory, Centre National de la Recherche Scientifique, Department of Philosophy at the University Charles-de-Gaulle–Lille III

Laurent LOTY, University of Rennes II–Haute Bretagne

Hans-Jürgen LÜSEBRINK, University of Saar

André MAGNAN, University of Paris X–Nanterre

Jean-Rémy MANTION, University of Bordeaux III–Michel-de-Montaigne

Dominique MARGAIRAZ, University of Paris I–Panthéon-Sorbonne

Francine MARKOVITS, University of Paris X–Nanterre

Didier MASSEAU, University of Valenciennes

Nicole MASSON, École Normale Supérieure, Paris

Antony MCKENNA, Centre National de la Recherche Historique; Jean-Monnet de Saint-Étienne University

Claude MICHAUD, University of Paris I–Panthéon-Sorbonne

Christian MICHEL, University of Paris X–Nanterre

Vincent MILLIOT, University of Orléans; Institut d'Histoire Moderne et Comtemporaine

Philippe MINARD, University of Lille III

Nadia MINERVA, University of Bologna

Jean MONDOT, University of Bordeaux III–Michel-de-Montaigne

Marie-France MOREL, École Normale Supérieure de Fontenay–Saint-Cloud

Roland MORTIER, Free University of Brussels

Monique, MOSER-VERREY, Laval University, Quebec

Hisayasu NAKAGAWA, National Museum of Kyoto; Academy of Japan; University of Kyoto

Barbara de NEGRONI, La Bruyère College, Versailles

Hugues NEVEUX, University of Paris X–Nanterre

Michel NOIRAY, Centre National de la Recherche Scientifique, University of Paris IV–Sorbonne

Dolf OEHLER, University of Bonn

Marc PARMENTIER, University of Lille III

Jean-Noël PASCAL, University of Perpignan

Claude-Yves PETITFRÈRE, François-Rabelais University, Tours

Nicholas PHILLIPSON, University of Edinburgh

Colette PIAU-GILLOT, University of Paris XI–Orsay

Antoine PICON, École des Ponts et Chaussées, Paris

Madeleine PINAULT SØRENSEN, Louvre Museum

Pierre PINON, School of Architecture of Paris-Belleville

Édouard POMMIER, Honorary General Inspector of the Museums of France

Charles PORSET, Centre National de la Recherche Scientifique, University of Paris IV–Sorbonne

Roy PORTER, Wellcome Institute for the History of Medicine, London

Jean-Pierre POUSSOU, University of Paris IV–Sorbonne

Stéphane PUJOL, University of Paris X–Nanterre

Jean QUENIART, University of Rennes II–Haute-Bretagne

Daniel RABREAU, University of Paris I–Panthéon-Sorbonne

Patricia RADELET DE GRAVE, Catholic University of Louvain

Rolf REICHARDT, University of Mainz

Pierre RETAT, Lumière University–Lyon II

Ulrich RICKEN, University of Leipzig; University of Halle

Giuseppe RICUPERATI, University of Turin

Antonella ROMANO

Hanna ROOSE, University of Heidelberg

Suzanne ROTH

Jean-Marie ROULIN, University of Pennsylvania, Philadelphia

Jean-Michel ROY, Institute of Modern and Contemporary History, Centre National de la Recherche Scientifique– École Normale Supérieure

Martin RUEFF, University of Paris IV–Sorbonne

Baldine SAINT GIRONS, University of Paris X–Nanterre

Michèle SAJOUS D'ORIA, University of Bari

Gerhard SAUDER, University of Saar

Philipp SCHÄFER, University of Passau

Jochen SCHLOBACH, University of Saar;
International Society for Eighteenth-Century
Studies

Werner SCHNEIDERS, University of Westfälische
Wilhelms, Münster

Hans Ulrich SEIFERT, University of Trier

Catriona SETH

Jean SGARD, University of Grenoble

Bent SØRENSEN

Jürgen von STACKELBERG, University of Göttingen

Isabelle STENGERS, Free University of Brussels

Udo STRÄTER, University of Halle

Madeleine Van STRIEN-CHARDONNEAU,
University of Leiden; University of Utrecht

Anthony STRUGNELL, University of Hull; Director
of *Studies on Voltaire and the Eighteenth
Century*

Fabienne STURM, Curator of the Museum of
Watchmaking and Enamel, Geneva

Pierre SWIGGERS, Faculty of Humanities, Leuven

Jean TARRADE, University of Poitiers

Heinz THOMA, Martin-Luther University, Halle-
Wittenberg; Center for Interdisciplinary
Research on the Enlightenment in Europe;
Academy of Sciences of Saxony

Ann THOMSON, University of Caen

Alain TOUWAIDE

Raymond TROUSSON, Free University of Brussels

Lydia VASQUEZ, University of the Basque Country,
Vitoria, Spain

Jean-Pierre VERDET, Paris Observatory

Alain VIALA, University of Paris III–Sorbonne-
Nouvelle

Gabrijela VIDAN, University of Zagreb

Florence VIOT

Bernhard von WALDKIRCH, Kunsthaus Zurich

Françoise WAQUET, Centre National de la
Recherche Scientifique, University of Paris IV–
Sorbonne

Jean WEISGERBER, Free University of Brussels;
Briije University, Brussels

Siegfried WIEDENHOFER, Marquette University,
Milwaukee

Sylvie WUHRMANN, University of Lausanne

Carsten ZELLE, University of Siegen

TRANSLATORS, TRANSLATION REVIEWERS, COPY EDITORS

Translators
Alison Anderson
Pamela Buck
Marjolin De Jager
Graham Falconer
Vera Grayson
Christina Kotchemidova
Monique Lamontagne
Kathryn Nanovic-Morlet
Virginia Phillips
Pauline Pocknell
Nidra Poller
Marijke Rijsberman
César Rouben
Molly Stevens
Richard Sundt
Robert Sykes

Translation Reviewers
Janet Battiste
Élisabeth Caron
Teresa Fagan
Graham Falconer
Theodore Kendris
Elizabeth Nishiura
Pauline Pocknell
Marijke Rijsberman
Cathy Shapiro
Nataša Vukičević

Copy Editors
Christopher Abbott
Patrick Heenan
Robert Huber

ACKNOWLEDGMENTS

Fitzroy Dearborn Publishers wishes to extend sincere thanks to the individuals and institutions whose support has been invaluable in bringing the *Encyclopedia of the Enlightenment* to completion. We gratefully acknowledge financial support in the form of a translation grant provided by the Centre National du Livre, a part of the French Ministry of Culture. Kathryn Nanovic-Morlet, managing director of the French Publishers' Agency in New York, handled translation rights, and she and her staff also cheerfully provided sound advice on many other matters. We are also indebted to the Presses Universitaires de France, especially Marion Colas, director of foreign rights at the press, for their collegiality and cooperation. Michel Delon, editor of the French edition, provided some extremely valuable feedback and personally reviewed a number of the translations. We are grateful to him and to the French contributors for their vision and expertise. Special thanks go to Philip Stewart, who went far beyond the call of duty in his capacity as adviser to the English edition: he was exceptionally generous in reviewing material and providing comments, and he also contributed his scholarly expertise by writing new material. Theodore Kendris, the original commissioning editor for the project, did a superb job of organizing it and overseeing its early stages. We are also indebted to our staff bibliographer, Anne-Marie Bogdan, her assistant, Thad King, and a sizeable team of freelance researchers for their skill in handling the bibliographic challenges that arose during the project. Last, but by no means least, we thank the translation reviewers, translators, copy editors, and proofreaders who worked on the project for all their hard work, and we commend them on a job well done.

GENERAL BIBLIOGRAPHY

Reference Works

Black, Jeremy, and Roy Porter, editors, *A Dictionary of Eighteenth-Century World History*, Oxford and Cambridge, Massachusetts: Blackwell, 1994; as *The Penguin Dictionary of Eighteenth-Century History*, London and New York: Penguin, 1996; as *Dictionary of Eighteenth-Century History*, London: Penguin, 2001

Ferrone, Vincenzo, and Daniel Roche, editors, *L'Illuminismo: Dizionario storico*, Rome: Laterza, 1997

Reichardt, Rolf, and Hans-Jürgen Lüsebrink, editors, *Handbuch politisch-sozialer Grundbegriffe in Frankreich, 1680–1820*, Munich: Oldenbourg, 1985–

Schneiders, Werner, editor, *Lexikon der Aufklärung: Deutschland und Europa*, Munich: Beck, 1995

Viguerie, Jean de, *Histoire et dictionnaire du temps des Lumières*, Paris: Laffont, 1995

Yolton, John W., et al., *The Blackwell Companion to the Enlightenment*, Oxford and Cambridge, Massachusetts: Blackwell, 1992

General Studies

Cassirer, Ernst, *The Philosophy of the Enlightenment*, translated by Fritz C.A. Koelln and James P. Pettegrove, Princeton, New Jersey: Princeton University Press, 1951 (original German edition, 1932)

Chaunu, Pierre, *La Civilisation de l'Europe des Lumières*, Paris: Arthaud, 1971; new edition, Paris: Flammarion, 1982

Gay, Peter, *The Enlightenment: An Interpretation*, 2 vols., London: Weidenfeld and Nicolson, 1966; New York: Knopf, 1966–69

Goodman, Dena, *The Republic of Letters: A Cultural History of the French Enlightenment*, Ithaca, New York: Cornell University Press, 1994

Gusdorf, Georges, *Les principes de la pensée au siècle des Lumières*, Paris: Payot, 1971

Gusdorf, Georges, *Dieu, la nature, l'homme au siècle des Lumières*, Paris: Payot, 1972

Habermas, Jürgen, *The Structural Transformation of the Public Sphere: An Inquiry into a Category of Bourgeois Society*, translated by Thomas Burger and Frederick Laurence, Cambridge, Massachusetts: MIT Press, 1989 (original German edition, 1962)

Hampson, Norman, *The Enlightenment*, London: Penguin, 1968; as *A Cultural History of the Enlightenment*, New York: Pantheon, 1968

Hazard, Paul, *The European Mind: The Critical Years, 1680–1715*, translated by J. Lewis May, New Haven, Connecticut: Yale University Press, 1953 (original French edition, 1935)

Hazard, Paul, *European Thought in the Eighteenth Century, from Montesquieu to Lessing*, translated by J. Lewis May, London: Hollis and Carter, and New Haven, Connecticut: Yale University Press, 1954 (original French edition, 1946)

Im Hof, Ulrich, *The Enlightenment*, translated by William E. Yuill, Oxford and Cambridge, Massachusetts: Blackwell, 1994 (original German edition, 1993)

Jacob, Margaret C., *The Radical Enlightenment: Pantheists, Freemasons, and Republicans*, London and Boston: Allen and Unwin, 1981

Kant, Immanuel, *Foundations of the Metaphysics of Morals: and, What Is Enlightenment?*, Upper Saddle River, New Jersey: Prentice Hall, 1997

Mortier, Roland, *Clartés et ombres du siècle des Lumières: Études sur le 18ᵉ siècle littéraire*, Geneva: Droz, 1969

Pomeau, René, *L'Europe des Lumières: Cosmopolitisme et unité européenne au XVIIIᵉ siècle*, Paris: Stock, 1966

Porter, Roy, *Enlightenment: Britain and the Creation of the Modern World*, London: Allen Lane, and Penguin, 2000; as *The Creation of the Modern World: The Untold Story of the British Enlightenment*, New York: Norton, 2000

Roche, Daniel, *Les Républicains des lettres: Gens de culture et Lumiéres au XVIIIᵉ siècle*, Paris: Fayard, 1988

Roger, Philippe, editor, *L'homme des Lumières, de Paris à Petersbourg*, Naples: Vivarium, 1995

Soboul, Albert, Guy Lemarchand, and Michèle Fogel, *Le siècle des Lumières*, 2 vols., Paris: Presses Uuniversitaires de France, 1977–97

Spencer, Samia I., editor, *French Women and the Age of Enlightenment*, Bloomington: Indiana University Press, 1984

Venturi, Franco, *Settecento riformatore,* 5 vols. in 7, Turin, Italy: Einaudi, 1969–90

Vierhaus, Rudolf, *Was war Aufklärung?* Wolfenbüttel, Germany: Lessing-Akademie, and Göttingen, Germany: Wallstein, 1995

Vovelle, Michel, editor, *L'homme des Lumières,* Paris: Seuil, 1996

Periodicals and Collections

British Journal for Eighteenth-Century Studies (1978–)

Dix-huitième siècle (1969–)

The Eighteenth Century: Theory and Interpretation (1979–)

Eighteenth-Century Fiction (1988–)

Eighteenth-Century Life (1974–)

Eighteenth-Century Studies (1967–)

International Directory of Eighteenth-Century Studies (1987–)

Recherches sur Diderot et sur l'Encyclopédie (1986–)

Studies in Eighteenth-Century Culture (1971–)

Studies on Voltaire and the Eighteenth Century (1956–) (a series of some 400 titles, including many independent monographs)

LIST OF ENTRIES

VOLUME 1
Academic Movement
Académie Française
Académie Royale des Sciences de Paris
Academies, Provincial
Acoustics
Actor
Adventurer
Aesthetics
Affinity
Africa
Agriculture: Agronomy
Agriculture: Typology
Alchemy
Algebra
Anarchy
Anatomy
Ancients and the Moderns, Quarrel of the
Anti-Enlightenment
Antiquity
Apologetics
Archeology
Architecture
Army
Art Academies
Art Criticism
Artist
Astronomy
Atheism
Authority, Government, and Power
Autobiography
Automaton

Balkans
Ballistics
Ballooning
Barbarian and Savage: Overview
Barbarian and Savage: Representations
Baroque
Beautiful
Bible
Bibliophilism
Body, Representations of

Books and Reading
Boudoir
Bouffons, Quarrel of the
Bourgeoisie, Professional
Bureaucracy

Calendar, French Revolutionary
Canal
Capitalism
Caricature
Castrati
Catholicism
Censorship
Chance and Necessity
Charity
Chemistry
Childbirth
Children
China
Citizen
City: Planning
City: Urbanization
Civilization and Civility
Clandestine Literature
Classicism
Classification
Clergy: Catholic
Clergy: Regular and Secular
Cloth
Coffeehouse
Collections and Curiosities
Colonialism
Color
Comedy
Commedia dell'arte
Confraternity
Conversation
Corpuscle
Correspondence: Overview
Correspondence: Literary
Cosmopolitanism
Counterpoint
Counter-Revolution

Court, French Royal
Credit and Banking
Criticism

Dance
Death
Decoration
Deism
Demography
Denmark
Devil
Dialogue
Dictionary
Dilettante
Doubt, Scepticism, and Pyrrhonism
Drama
Drawing
Dream
Dynamics

Earth, Shape of the
Eclecticism
Education, Instruction, and Pedagogy
Egyptomania
Electricity
Eloquence
Empiricism
Encyclopedia
Energy
England
Engraving
Enlightenment, Representations of
Enthusiasm
Epicurianism
Equality and Inequality
Eroticism
Essay
Etruscan
Europe
Evil, Representations of
Exchange
Exclusivity System

Fable: Overview
Fable: Critique
Fairground Theatre
Fairs and Markets
Fanaticism
Fatherhood
Festival
Feudalism
Finance
Food
Force
Fortification
France
Freemasonry
Function
Furniture

Garden
Gas
Genius
Geography
Geology
Geometry
Germany
Germany and the Holy Roman Empire
God
Grammar
Grand Tour
Grotesque
Guild

Happiness
Harmony and Melody
Heat
Hero, Representations of
History, Philosophy of
Holland
Hospital
Hungary
Hydrography and Navigation

Idea
Ideal
Ideology and Ideologues
Idolatry
Illuminism
Illustration
Imagination
Imitation
Industrialization
Inspiration
Intendancy System
Interest
Irony
Islam
Italy

Jansenism
Japan
Jardin du Roi (French Royal Botanical Garden)
Jesuits
Judaism
Justice and Prisons

Landscape
Language
Latin America
Law, Public
Liberalism
Libertinism
Library
Love
Luxury

VOLUME 2
Magnetism
Map

Mask
Materialism
Mathematics
Mechanics, Analytic
Mechanism
Medicine
Melancholy
Mesmerism
Metaphysics
Migration
Mineralogy
Miniature
Moderation
Monadism
Monarch, Enlightened
Monster
Monument
Mountain
Museum
Music: Overview
Music: Criticism
Music: Musical Instruments
Mysticism

Nation
Natural History
Natural Law and the Rights of Man
Nature
Newspapers and Journalism
Newtonianism
Night
Nobility
Nobility, Commercial
North America
Novel
Novel, Gothic

Observatories and Observation Instruments
Opera
Opera, Comic
Optics and Light
Optimism and Pessimism
Orders and Classes
Orient and Orientalism
Originality

Painting: Overview
Painting: Exhibitions
Palladianism
Pantomime
Parade
Paradox
Parlements, French
Parody
Passions
Passions, Representations of
Patriotism
Peasantry
Peddler
People

Persiflage
Perspective
Philosophes
Philosophy, German
Phlogiston
Physics, Experimental
Physiocracy
Physiognomy
Physiology
Picturesque
Pietism
Poetry
Poland
Police
Political Economy
Popular Culture
Portraiture
Ports
Prejudice: Overview
Prejudice: German Philosophy
Printing
Prison
Probability Theory
Progress
Prometheus
Property
Protestantism
Proverb
Providence
Pygmalion

Reason
Religion, Popular
Remedies
Reproduction
Republic of Letters
Reverie
Revolution
Rococo
Ruins
Rumor
Russia

Salon
Satire
Science: Collections
Science: Dissemination and Popularization
Scotland
Sculpture
Secularization and Dechristianization
Sensationalism
Sensibility
Servant
Sexuality, Representations of
Siècle
Silhouette and Découpage
Slavery
Sociability
Social Contract
Socrates

Soldier
Song
Spain and Portugal
Species
Stars
State
Studio
Sublime
Sun and the Solar System
Surgery
Sweden
Switzerland

Tale
Taste
Tears
Technical Instruction
Technology
Terror
Theatre and Staging
Theology, German
Thermometry
Toleration
Tomb

Trade
Tradition
Tragedy
Translation
Transport Systems
Travel

Ugliness and Deformity
Uneasiness
Utility
Utopia

Vaudeville
Village Communities
Virtue
Volcano

War and Peace
Watchmaking
Weights and Measures
Witchcraft
Women Writers and Feminism
Words, Abuse of
Work

A

Absolutism. *See* Monarch, Enlightened

Academic Movement

According to Bernard Le Bovier de Fontenelle, the end of the 17th century marked the dawn of a new era for academies. A few years later, the chevalier de Jaucourt confirmed this prognosis and wrote the following remarks in the *Encyclopédie* article "Académie": "Most nations have academies at present, even Russia." It is therefore no surprise that historiographers have described the 18th century as the "age of academies" throughout Europe (see Hahn).

At the time of Fontenelle's writing, the academies had already enjoyed a long history that, in modern times, had started with the Accademia Platonica (Platonic Academy) in Florence. Numerous academies had been founded during the 16th and 17th centuries, particularly in the Italian peninsula, and prestigious institutions had been born, such as the Royal Society in London (1662) and, in Paris, the Académie Française (1634) and the Académie Royale des Sciences (1666). The academic movement continued to flourish during the 18th century, and scientific societies in particular enjoyed steady growth, according to studies. The first half of the century saw the birth of numerous institutions. Some of them enjoyed an exceptional reputation, such as the Societas Regia Scientiarum (Royal Society of Sciences) in Berlin (1700), the Istituto delle Scienze (Institute of Sciences) in Bologna (1711), and the Academia Scientiarum Imperialis Petropolitanae (Imperial Academy of Sciences of Saint Petersburg, 1724). In the second half of the century, the academies that had been founded earlier grew and expanded. New institutions were also born, more numerous but also smaller than those founded in the earlier half of the century. Every state's capital city had its own academy, sometimes several, but there also were academies in areas other than the seat of government. France boasted some 30 officially incorporated provincial academies, and Tuscany had a population of 1,500 Academicians. Western and central Europe (west of a line joining Uppsala to Messina) had the majority of institutions; some areas had a particularly dense concentration of academies. According to the *Encyclopédie,* Italy, where some 500 then existed, had "more academies than in all the rest of the world." The growth in the number of academies was a continuous phenomenon that went beyond specific areas or countries to become a truly European phenomenon. Academies also flourished in the overseas colonies, including those of Britain (the American Philosophical Society of Philadelphia, 1768); Holland (the Bataviaasch Gnootschap van Kunsten en Wetenschappen [Batavian Society of Arts and Sciences, 1778]); France (the Société Royale des Sciences et des Arts du Cap Français [Royal Society of Arts and Sciences of Cap Français] in Santo Domingo, 1784); and Spain (numerous Sociedades Económicas de Amigos del

Pais [Economic Society of Friends of Peace], the first created in Manila in 1781).

Although there were local variations, official academies tended to share characteristics borrowed from one of two main models: the Royal Society in London and the various royal academies in Paris. The London model had several distinctive characteristics: creation through private initiative, a large membership, relatively loose ties with the state, and autonomous financing. The Parisian model was from the outset that of a state institution, with state financing, closer supervision, and fewer members. According to James E. McClellan, the Parisian model predominated, in a ratio of around five to one, in the case of scientific societies; that model prevailed on the Continent in absolute and centralized monarchic systems and in Catholic countries. The London model was adopted mainly in England, the Netherlands, the American colonies, Protestant countries, and states that were less centralized (see McClellan).

The world of the European academies was fundamentally united by common practices and discourses. Many academies had honorary or corresponding members and thus extended their influence outside the limits of their city or country, sometimes to great distances. For example, the Accademia Etrusca (Etruscan Academy) in the small city of Cortone admitted more than 100 honorary members during the 18th century. The network of academies was further strengthened by the presence of members belonging to several institutions. Evrard Titon du Tillet, for example, was affiliated with some 30 academies, some in France and others in Italy, Spain, and Portugal. Such multiple memberships held by the same individual were not unusual, especially for people of great talent, and this pattern contributed to the creation and consolidation of an international scholarly community. The academic election of nonresidents resulted in exchanges of letters and services and helped disseminate learned contributions. For example, the foreign members of the Accademia Etrusca were required to send their essays on a subject from ancient times to Cortona for reading in public sessions. Some scientists pursued their entire career in the academic world. For example, the mathematician Joseph-Louis Lagrange (1736–1816) went from Turin's scientific academy to that of Berlin, and was finally called to Paris by Louis XVI to sit as a member of the Académie Royale des Sciences. Such cases were in fact rare, but they nonetheless attest to the truly European character of the academic world.

The international dimension of the scholarly world is also evidenced in the epistolary exchanges that the academies maintained with one another. Such exchanges, which had been initiated in the previous century—for instance, Henry Oldenburg's correspon- dence conducted on behalf of the Royal Society— became a normal aspect of academic life. The Academia Scientiarum in Saint Petersburg was thus in contact with more than 20 other institutions. Certain academies, such as the American Philosophical Society of Philadelphia, included in their statutes the obligation to correspond with other learned societies elsewhere in the world. This policy was meant to encourage the exchange of news and publications, to help disseminate individual work and discoveries, and to keep members abreast of activities in other academies—in short, to provide exposure to a larger audience than that afforded by a city or a region. Competitions, which probably originated in the mathematical challenges launched in the previous century, became an established fact of life in the 18th-century academies, if only on account of their sheer numbers. In France competitions generated ever-growing enthusiasm, as evidenced in their increase in number from 48 during the decade 1700–09 to 618 in the 1780s. For the societies that sponsored them, these scholarly contests were the token of "maximum opening, of dialogue with the 'Republic of Letters,' of response to outside solicitations, and of a new public that made them partially relax limits on recruitment" (see Roche); in fact, out of the 92 prizes awarded by the Académie Royale des Sciences de Paris between 1720 and 1793, at least 47 were awarded to foreigners.

The pan-European solidarity of the academies manifested itself with particular brilliance in projects that were carried out jointly, especially in the sciences. Thus, the transits of Venus in 1761 and 1769 mobilized approximately 500 observers around the globe, under the aegis of the French Académie des Sciences and London's Royal Society, with the support of many other institutions. Similarly, in 1781 the Societas Meteorologica (Meteorological Society) of Mannheim launched a systematic program of meteorological observations, for which it approached around 30 other academies.

There is nothing surprising, therefore, in the fact that plans were made to bring a concrete unity to the world of the academies, perhaps in imitation of the great dreams that Mersenne, Oldenburg, and Leibniz had cherished. In the 1780s the chevalier Quesnay de Beaurepaire, a grandson of the Physiocrat François Quesnay, devised a plan to unite all the scientific societies in the world. He asked for the *philosophes'* support and enlisted Benjamin Franklin's help, but despite some early successes he was unable to carry out his project to complete fruition. The attempt by the Patriotic Society of Hesse-Hamburg (1775–81) to establish a network of correspondence bureaus connected to a central committee was more successful. The society approached numerous academies, particularly in northern and central Europe, with the aim of improving the dissemination of scientific information. The same goal was also at the core of the projects devised by the abbé Rozier and Pahin de La Blancherie during these same years, for which they sought the academies' support.

Shared practices—such as the adoption of similar rules and rituals—encouraged relations among academies, uniting them in a vast community of scholars. Beyond these practices, a universalist discourse developed in these institutions, imparting to members a cosmopolitan feeling and the belief that they belonged to an international society that transcended the constraints of political and religious barriers. Thus, when the "American" Arthur Lee resigned from London's Royal Society during the war between the American colonies and England (he was the only one to do so), the chairman of the English academy chastised him for forgetting that he belonged to the universal fraternity of knowledge. The solidarity uniting the Academicians of the world was based on a fiction, namely that of a society of equals pursuing a common goal. Widespread praise of the academic enterprise contributed to the formation of a universal model of *homo academicus*: this model combined sociability with the notion of altruistic pursuit of humanity's common good, devoid of any individual interest. As the academic phenomenon increased throughout Europe, tireless efforts were made to strengthen the ways in which academies functioned, and speeches praising the Academicians and their work nourished belief in the academic ideal. All these factors were inseparable from a general sense of trust and faith in this type of institution. This trust was based in a double tradition: first, the humanist ideology of the Renaissance, with its insistence on the sociable character of human beings and on the cognitive function of conversation ("knowledge is born through conversation and ends in conversation," in the words of S. Guazzo); and second, Francis Bacon's teaching, with its recommendation regarding the pooling of talents in the service of useful knowledge. These two currents of thought bore their finest fruits in the optimistic climate of the Enlightenment.

It is therefore quite justifiable to speak of a "Europe of academies." However, it is also important to emphasize the qualitative differences that existed among these institutions. In addition to the official academies—which were the most enduring and, for that very reason, the best known—there were numerous private societies that held meetings of a more or less formal nature and depended on the initiative and activities of a single individual or group. The existence of such societies was ephemeral and they had limited influence. In a hierarchy of the official academies, those at the top of the pyramid were the royal institutions of Paris, London, Berlin, Saint Petersburg, and Stockholm. Vincenzo Ferrone has emphasized the preeminence of the

Académie Royale des Sciences de Paris, confirming the assessment made by Enlightenment thinkers such as the comte de Lagrange, who, in 1787, declared the institution to be the "foremost tribunal for the sciences." The great state academies worked for the glory of the princes who financed them and of the countries to which they belonged, and this occasionally gave rise to fierce competition. For instance, the patronage that England's Royal Society and France's Académie des Sciences generously granted to the expeditions into the Pacific Ocean from the 1760s on was an extension of the general rivalry between those two countries. The spirit of fraternity and cosmopolitanism that characterized the academic world was shattered in the face of national interests and a policy of prestige that was sufficient to lure away even the best talents. Thus, for instance, Frederick II of Prussia offered Leonhard Euler, whom he wanted to attract to Berlin, a much more tempting pension than the one that the illustrious mathematician was receiving in Saint Petersburg. Finally, there was the difference in status: in fact, there could be no common measure between the major institutions, such as the Académie Royale des Sciences de Paris, and the provincial academies. The former was endowed with great financial means and a first-rate membership, while the latter had limited resources and a more modest membership. The provincial academies in France admitted many amateurs as members; this was a perceived flaw that the Académie Royale des Sciences, concerned with the preservation of its elitist character, always took great pains to avoid.

The contribution of the provincial institutions was generally less one of creation than of propagation of ideas and models developed elsewhere, and, predictably, they usually lagged behind the capital cities' academies and had less influence. Among provincial scholars, this situation nourished feelings of inferiority in comparison with the "important gentlemen" of Paris, coupled with strong demands for equality. Montesquieu echoed these sentiments when, in a speech at the Bordeaux academy, he urged his fellow townsmen to rid themselves "of this prejudice that the provinces are not in a position to perfect the sciences and that academies can flourish only in capital cities." The interests of provincial societies were often limited in scope and were usually restricted to the preoccupations of a small geographical area, such as its history, botany, and agronomy. In fact, some academies were specifically created to solve local or regional problems. The numerous *sociedades económicas* (economic societies) that were founded in the Spanish world—approximately 70 between 1770 and 1820—were specifically intended to solve the crisis of the Spanish economy by using relevant ideas the Enlightenment had generated in Europe (see Shafer). Similarly, the economic societies that were created in the Germanic countries during the second half of the 18th century—85 of them between 1760 and 1784—were a typical example of an almost exclusive interest in the "little fatherland," as indicated by the frequent incorporation of the words *Land* or *Vaterland* in the names of these societies. These academies implemented studies, drew up inventories, and established plans for the development of the economy, all at the local or regional level. They found their inspiration and their common denominator in patriotism, that is, in a set of civic and social ideals based on pietism and on the moral philosophy of the early Enlightenment (see Lowood).

The disciplines pursued by the academies constituted another dividing line between them. Some of these institutions were encyclopedic in nature, such as those in the French provinces that dealt with the belles lettres, the sciences, and the arts. However, specialized academies were much more numerous owing to an epistemological shift that had started around the middle of the 17th century. The diversity was extreme, going from a whole discipline to a single subject. Many institutions were devoted to the belles lettres and some—such as Accademia della Crusca (Academy of the Cross) in Florence (1583), the Académie Française in Paris, or the Real Academia Española (Royal Spanish Academy) in Madrid (1713)—were exclusively given to the study of language and worked in particular on the compilation of dictionaries. Sacred history inspired the founding of many institutions in Italy, some of which were extremely specialized, such as the three academies established in Rome by Benedict XIV in 1740 for the study of church councils, ecclesiastical history, and liturgy. Secular history was equally fruitful, as evidenced, in the case of France, by the numerous volumes of *Mémoires* (Reports) published by the Académie des Inscriptions et Belles Lettres (Academy of Inscriptions and Letters). Interest in the history of the nation or a locality was the source of many new academies throughout Europe. In Italy alone, for example, the Accademia Etrusca in Cortone (1727) and the Accademia Ercolanense (Herculanean Academy) in Naples (1755) were devoted to regional history. The fine arts and their various branches—architecture, painting, sculpture, and music—gave birth to academies everywhere; Nikolaus Pevsner documents more than 100 of them (see Pevsner). Germany and Italy offered the highest concentrations of fine-arts institutions, while France, England, and Spain boasted the most prestigious ones: France, with the Académie Royale de Peinture et de Sculpture (Royal Academy of Painting and Sculpture, 1648) and the Académie Royale d'Architecture (1671); England, with the Royal Academy (1768); and Spain, with the Academia de Nobles Artes (Academy of the Noble Arts) and then the Academia de Bellas Artes de

San Ferdinando (1744; Academy of Fine Arts of San Ferdinando). The sciences gave birth to a rising number of institutions devoted to one or all of the scientific disciplines—medicine, surgery, the mechanical arts, and, particularly during the second half of the 18th century, botany, meteorology, and agriculture.

The academies fulfilled an important social function. They were a privileged forum for debates, conversations, and exchanges. They welcomed foreign travelers. For example, Montesquieu and Charles de Brosses were received in academies when they traveled in Italy even though they were not members of them. Academies provided the setting for prestigious encounters, such as the historic meeting of Voltaire and Franklin at the Académie des Sciences in Paris. The abbé André Morellet, evoking in advance the sadness that would grip him and his colleagues on the day that the Académie Française closed, recalled the pleasure that they had drawn from "meeting three times a week with respectable people brought together by the same tastes." The pleasure of the Academicians' meetings was occasionally enhanced either by prestigious meeting places or by gardens that re-created the small wood near Athens where Plato and his disciples had met, the foundation and sanctuary of all civilization. Thus, the Roman Arcades held their meetings, during the summer months, in the Bosco Parrasio, a simple and charming site in harmony with the poetic reform proposed by these pastoral scholars. Sometimes, however—above all in smaller cities or with certain private academies—the social function prevailed over literary or scientific endeavors and the meetings became no more than elegant conversations in a leisurely context. In these circumstances the academy took on the appearance of a club.

The 18th century was undoubtedly the age of academies, but throughout Europe other new forms of associations competed with the academies: salons, reading groups, societies of connoisseurs, and above all Masonic lodges, which often combined with academies and rapidly formed an imposing international network with a distinctive cultural identity. Beyond these rival organizations, the academies had to contend with the criticism that grew as the century progressed. In the article "Science" in the *Encyclopédie,* Jaucourt draws up a list of "vices" harmful to these institutions:

Here, inequality of rank is set by the statutes of the prince, whereas only the superiority of genius should be recognized. Instead, there is a perpetual tribute of fastidious praise, the shameful language of servitude. Often, in these very academies, the reward of merit is taken away by intrigue or hypocrisy. Cupidity, vanity, jealousy, and scheming have taken root in our literary societies, more than the ambition to distinguish oneself through one's talents; sagacity has turned into self-conceit, love of beauty into false wit.

This denunciation, however, was not categorical; it was aimed at the membership and at those who governed the institutions rather than at the academies per se. The *Supplément* to the *Encyclopédie* also published two speeches by Jean-Henri-Samuel Formey that highlight the "advantages of the academies."

The French Revolution gave a sharper spin to the disputes that had been ongoing during the last decades of the ancien régime. Such disputes had arisen within the academies themselves, which deplored the intervention of the authorities in the election of members. Criticism was also brought to bear from outside the institutions, by candidates who had been unsuccessful in their bid for membership or by writers whose hopes of obtaining the approval of these higher authorities for their labors or their discoveries had been disappointed. In the view of their detractors, the academies were consubstantial with an ancient and obsolete political order: despotism. This charge predated the Revolution. In fact, as early as 1782 Jacques-Pierre Brissot had pointed out in *De la vérité* (On Truth) that a modern country such as England had few academies, whereas they abounded in "states full of superstitions and ignorance," as exemplified in the Italian peninsula. Bound to an old political order, the academies inevitably infringed on the principles of the new society. The non-egalitarian aspects of these institutions, in particular the differences in status among members, were decried. Moreover, the academies were accused of harboring "literary aristocracies," for whom the limited number of seats became a stratagem to keep out those talented people who might otherwise have overshadowed them. The Academicians were also denounced for their privileges, huge pensions showered on them by the public treasury that were deemed to be an insult to "meritorious, poverty-stricken people."

In addition, the academies reflected an institutional order based on corporate entities. They had already been attacked on these grounds under the ancien régime by critics inspired by Physiocracy, who had denounced them as obstacles to freedom, as intermediate bodies erected between the individual and the nation. These arguments were reignited during the revolutionary period and they carried some weight in the abolition of the academies in France. On 8 August 1793, the day of the fateful vote, the abbé Grégoire denounced the "guildsmen" in these institutions who had "pretensions to arrogate to themselves the exclusive privilege of talent." It was argued that the academies were lacking in intellectual quality because corruption, rather than merit, determined the results of membership elections;

it followed that many Academicians and their works were mediocre. In the view of disparagers, the academies were structured in a manner radically contrary to the progress of knowledge. According to Jean-Paul Marat, in *Les charlatans modernes ou Lettres sur le charlatanisme académique* (1791; The Modern Charlatans; or, Letters on Academic Charlatanism), they were not the "refuge of new truths" but the "asylum of old prejudices." More generally, it was felt that "great individuals do more than large institutions." Critics used concrete examples to elaborate wider views, clearly inspired by Rousseauistic ideas that linked independence, originality, and creativity. True genius could not be found in academies; moreover, these institutions corrupted talent and stifled enthusiasm.

On 8 August 1793, the Convention voted to abolish the academies in France: that date symbolically marked the end of a great era during which these institutions had been considered the privileged trustees of a three-fold mission: the glory of the monarch or the state, the progress of knowledge, and the happiness of all. The discredit that the words "academic" and "academicism" endured during the 19th century shows that the vitality and creativity that, since the Renaissance, had established and legitimized the academy had been decisively erased from the collective memory.

FRANÇOISE WAQUET

See also Académie Française; Academies, Provincial; Antiquity; Art Academies

Further Reading

Daston, Lorraine, "The Ideal and Reality of the Republic of Letters in the Enlightenment," *Science in Context* 4, no. 2 (1991)

Hahn, Roger, "The Age of Academies," in *Solomon's House Revisited: The Organization and Institutionalization of Science,* edited by Tore Frängsmyr, Canton, Massachusetts: Science History, 1990

Lowood, Henry Ernest, *Patriotism, Profit, and the Promotion of Science in the German Enlightenment: The Economic and Scientific Societies, 1760–1815,* New York: Garland, 1991

McClellan, James E., III, *Science Reorganized: Scientific Societies in the Eighteenth Century,* New York: Columbia University Press, 1985

McClellan, James E., III, "L'Europe des académies," *Dix-huitième siècle* 25 (1993)

Pevsner, Nikolaus, *Academies of Art, Past and Present,* Cambridge: University Press, and New York: Macmillan, 1940

Roche, Daniel, *Le siècle des Lumières en province: Académies et Académiciens provinciaux, 1680–1789,* Paris: Mouton, 1978

Schlereth, Thomas J., *The Cosmopolitan Ideal in Enlightenment Thought: Its Form and Function in the Ideas of Franklin, Hume, and Voltaire, 1694–1790*, Notre Dame, Indiana: University of Notre Dame Press, 1977

Shafer, Robert Jones, *The Economic Societies in the Spanish World, 1763–1821*, Syracuse, New York: Syracuse University Press, 1958

Académie Française

History of an Institution

The Académie Française was founded in 1635 on the initiative of Cardinal Richelieu, minister of state during the reign of Louis XIII. The minister's goal was to enrich France with an institution for intellectual exchange that would be comparable, and even superior, to the academies that had flourished in Italy since the 16th century. The idea was not a new one. In the 16th century Jean-Antoine de Baïf had attempted to create a royal academy, but it had been short-lived. Richelieu's innovation was twofold: he emphasized the political stakes underlying the creation of the Académie, and also assigned it a specialized function. Unlike the Italian models and Baïf's academy, the Académie Française was to restrict itself to questions concerning language and literature. (Baïf's academy had been conceived to deal with poetry and music, while the Italian models embraced, to varying degrees, all intellectual and artistic domains.) The Académie was political in its intent, for its objective was to establish norms for the French language that would to the linguistic and cultural unification of the country. This was reflected in the institution's charter, which stipulated:

> Statute XXIV—The principal function of the Académie will be to work with the utmost possible diligence to endow our language with exact rules and make it pure, eloquent, and capable of treating subjects in the arts and the sciences.

The new assembly was therefore entrusted with a mission that was of the utmost importance to national interests. However, the Académie was explicitly excluded from the right to debate religious, social, and political matters:

> Statute XXIX—Matters concerning religion and theology will not be debated in the Académie; matters political and moral shall be treated in the

Académie in conformity with the authority of the Prince, the state of the government, and the laws of the realm.

The Académie was thus empowered to give official sanction to cultural practices, but remained subject to governmental authority.

After considering taking the name "Académie Royale," the new institution decided instead to incorporate into its name the adjective *français* to make explicit its principal goal of promoting the French language. And in fact, the mission of linguistic standardization unquestionably dominated the first 50 years of the institution's existence. Treatises on poetics and on rhetoric were planned but never produced, an indication that the codification of the rules of the French language was an ever-increasing concern. Some preparatory work was done to create a *Grammaire* (Grammar) and that work was used as the source for Vaugelas's *Remarques* (1647; Comments on the French Language). The fact Vaugelas decided to publish these preliminary findings suggests he had despaired of ever seeing the Académie complete its work on the project. (The *Grammaire* in question, incidentally, finally materialized only in 1932, and it was brutally criticized by Ferdinand Brunot among others.) Increasingly, the issue of the *Dictionnaire* (1694; Dictionary) generated conflicts and debates. The Academicians were working so slowly that in 1671 Jean-Baptiste Colbert, minister under Louis XIV, reorganized the assembly's working methods, introducing a system of attendance tokens to spur members on. Conflicts escalated to such a degree that whereas the initial project had called for a single dictionary unifying the French language, three separate dictionaries were eventually produced. In one faction, the Academician Patru and a few young authors around him believed that the models considered by the Académie were too archaic (particularly the classification of words according to etymological roots); so they decided to work on a resolutely modern dictionary, which was published (in Switzerland) in 1680 under the name of *Richelet* (Richelet's Dictionary). In another faction, Antoine Furetière, who found the central project too exclusively literary, quarreled openly with the other Academicians and launched into the preparation of his own dictionary, which was completed by Pierre Bayle and published in 1690; it covers all the aspects of vocabulary, including technical, familiar, and obsolete words.

The Académie finally delivered its dictionary (1694), but it was so poorly done that a first printing had to be pulped. It had been restricted to terms from "elegant language"; as a result, the Académie had to commission Thomas Corneille to prepare a complementary *Dictionnaire des sciences* (1694; Dictionary of Sciences) on a rush basis. This marked a new phase of the Académie's history: from then on, the institution would place more emphasis on the other aspect of its raison d'être, namely sociability and literary consecration, while maintaining activity on the dictionary at a reduced pace.

From Legitimization to Academicism

Among people of letters (writers, but also more generally literate persons from various fields of knowledge), the impulse to get together, to discuss their activities, and to show each other their respective works is very old. The first academy in France, the Jeux Floraux (Floral Games) of Toulouse, was founded in the Middle Ages. After the Wars of Religion, the general upsurge in sociability and the marked increase in erudition produced a plethora of intellectual circles and private gatherings of friends, often associated with salons. One of these circles gathered around Jean Chapelain and Conrart in the 1630s; its activities appeared to be an extension of François de Malherbe's teachings and served as the foundation on which Richelieu built the new official institution. The issuing of the letters patent of the Académie Française (January 1635), followed by their official registration (which was delayed until 1637 owing to the Parlement's distrust of the new institution), marked the time when the writer's status in society began to be recognized, at least in terms of serving as a linguistic role model. The new institution thus played a major role in the nascent literary culture. The Académie represented a threefold advantage for literary sociability. First, the new institution imparted legitimacy to literary gatherings. Second, protection by the authorities, even if it implied some limitations on freedom, offered writers a channel of communication with the people who had power and money, and who were thus sources of financial support and means of subsistence. Third, peer recognition, so vital to the making of a writer's reputation, found an elite, emblematic expression in the new institution.

The Académie was fully established by 1639, when elections brought membership to 40 as stipulated by the charter (the number of Academicians at the outset had been 27), and the administrative system was in place (director and chancellor elected for three months, and a permanent secretary). Logically enough, the "founding members" comprised the private circle that had been at the source of the project, along with a few of Richelieu's protégés. According to the regulations, however, it was through a voting process by the Academicians that new members were to be chosen. Being elected and having access to the French spheres of influence became an endeavor that was as much political as it was aesthetic.

During its first two generations the institution was essentially a place for the promotion of new ideas—a cautious but real innovation. The few illustrious writers who had difficulty in gaining admission were examples of political obstacles rather than of rejection on aesthetic grounds (Jean de La Fontaine had been Fouquet's protégé, while Pierre Corneille had been on tense terms with Richelieu). On the other hand, the Académie was truly innovative in its proposals for the social recognition of writers. Particularly noteworthy initiatives included the creation of literary prizes for eloquence and poetry (Prix d'Éloquence, 1671; Prix de Poésie, 1701); and support for women's access, if not to membership in the institution, at least to places in the audience (1671) and even to the rank of laureate, as was achieved by Madeleine de Scudéry in 1671.

This movement of literary sociability went hand in hand with the shaping of the French intellectual world through the creation of other academies specializing in related fields: the Académie Royale de Peinture et de Sculpture (1648; Royal Academy of Painting and Sculpture), the Académie des Inscriptions et Belles-Lettres (1663; Academy of Inscriptions and Letters), the Académie Royale des Sciences de Paris (1666; French Royal Academy of Science), and so on. The members of the Académie Française played an important part as promoters and collaborators in the establishment of the latter two academies and in the creation of the first periodicals, in particular the *Mercure galant* and the *Journal des savants*, which had ties to the Académie des Sciences. The writers who were members of the Académie thus played an important role in the general consecration of French artists and intellectuals in the 17th century.

At the same time, the social makeup of the Académie Française was slowly changing. In the initial composition of the institution, the members were writers recruited on the basis of their literary merit. Most of them came from the bourgeoisie, a small number from the lower and poorer segment of the nobility, none from the higher aristocracy. Beginning in the 1670s, however, another kind of recruitment developed: membership in the Académie came to be coveted as a sign of prestige and good taste by members of high society, even those with few literary pretensions. In 1667 Colbert himself agreed to join the ranks of the Academicians. Bishops and aristocrats (some belonged to both clergy and aristocracy) vied for admission and were elected. Being an Academician became a means of displaying one's status as part of the cultured and distinguished world, as well as a means of showing that one enjoyed the patronage of the current authorities.

This new social structure inherent in the Académie was echoed in a wider movement, on the national scale, that would gain momentum throughout the Enlightenment. Daniel Roche has convincingly analyzed this phenomenon, showing how the Académie Française helped promote the spread of the academic model throughout France (see Roche). It started in 1661–66 with the establishment of an academy in Arles. The avowed goal, in this city whose population spoke *langue d'oc* (Occitan), was the promotion of French. The way to provide a solid foundation to the new academy was to "affiliate" it: the fledgling institution in Arles asked to be a dependent of the Académie Française. The Parisians were initially reluctant to accede to the wishes of the provincials but eventually agreed, and the movement took hold and grew. From the end of the 17th century and throughout the 18th, a whole network of local societies spread the "French academic model" throughout the country, sometimes officially and at other times by adopting the existing model for their statutes and working methods. That model soon spread across national borders: Prussia, England, Spain, and Austria created their own national academies on models inspired from the French. As a great political power, France was a model, particularly in cultural matters, and the Académie Française was at the vanguard of a movement that had national as well as international scope. The Académie's crucial role in the propagation of ideas, knowledge, and literature explains the prestige that increasingly attracted the higher strata of society.

Modernism and Enlightenment

The recruitment of the social elite encouraged academicism, but it also had another paradoxical effect. The Académie Française was an arena for aesthetic disputes, and the famous Quarrel of the Ancients and the Moderns split the institution into two factions, starting in 1687. The controversy did not end in a decisive swing to one side or the other, but the moderns were in a majority: the increasingly numerous aristocrats in the Académie tended be attracted by a more "worldly" culture and were anxious to please the king; they were therefore inclined to champion the superiority of the *siècle de Louis le Grand* (the age of Louis the Great)

over all the previous great centuries. This victory on the part of the moderns encouraged the gradual introduction of Enlightenment ideas in the Académie. The notions of progress and rationalism, championed by the moderns, gained considerable support within the institution.

In aesthetic matters, however, the Académie remained a bastion of conservatism: the poetics set forth by Nicolas Boileau-Despréaux in the 17th century was formally adopted as the norm, and the 18th-century literati made no call for a different model. The Academicians also remained conservative regarding religious, political, and moral matters, as required by their statutes. The abbé de Saint-Pierre was denied admission on these grounds, while Montesquieu, author of the *Lettres persanes* (1721; Persian Letters), and Voltaire, annoyed by this state of affairs, fired squibs at the Académie. However, the revival of salon life during the first part of the 18th century had an impact on the institution: the support of the salons gave considerable leverage to those seeking election. The Académie was thus an important force in the propagation, or even the creation, of public opinion. Gradually, the *philosophes* won more space in the ranks of the assembly. Montesquieu was elected thanks to the salon of Madame de Lambert; then, in turn, came Marivaux and Voltaire (both in 1746), followed by the abbé Duclos (1747), who went on to become secretary of the Académie in 1755, and by D'Alembert. In time, a conflict took shape, manifesting itself openly in 1760: the supporters of the *philosophes'* views confronted the traditionalists and prevailed over them. Thus, although some major figures of the Enlightenment (Diderot, Rousseau, and Beaumarchais, for example) did not join the Académie, the institution reflected the enlightened opinions of the *philosophes,* as Rousseau reminds us at the beginning of the *Lettre à D'Alembert* (1758; Letter to M. D'Alembert on Theatre). This does not mean that the Académie was entirely on the side of the *philosophes:* for one thing, the institution never questioned the monarchical state or the principle of religion; moreover, ideological differences among the Academicians split the institution with respect to various issues. Still, the Académie was active in the intellectual debates of the era, and the provincial academies (Dijon, Bordeaux) were even more audacious in the spread of modern ideas.

The role of the Académie should not be overestimated, however. Since its early days, it had been subjected to criticism of all kinds. Notably, some aristocratic and independent thinkers viewed the Académie as a pack of mangy poets (for example, Saint-Évremond, as early as 1637, in his *Comédie des Académistes* [Comedy of the Academicists]). In the 18th century, there were any number of sarcastic comments on the Academicians' lethargy, on the slow pace of their dictionary, and on the uselessness of their institution (including Voltaire's remarks in his *Lettres philosophiques* [1734; Philosophical Letters]). The situation of the Académie was in fact paradoxical: the assembly, whose ostensible purpose was the promotion of writers, was not generating creative energy. Despite its prestige, the Académie was the object of derision because it served as a mere relay station echoing received ideas rather than as a center of invention.

Dissolution and Reconstitution

The shockwaves generated by the French Revolution reinforced the criticisms that had been made of the Académie. It was taken to task for its conservatism, in spite of its inclination toward Enlightenment ideas, and it was reproached above all for its uselessness. The charge of uselessness was aimed not only at the Académie Française but at the whole system of state academies in France. In fact, these criticisms are somewhat surprising given that the Académie had welcomed the Estates General, as speeches by Félix Vicq d'Azyr or Stanislas-Jean de Boufflers attest. However, attacks on the ideological machine of the ancien régime were at that point becoming more and more virulent. Chamfort was one of the most active participants in these attacks, and the title of a pamphlet dated September 1789 explicitly states the goal of the *Suppression de toutes les académies comme onéreuses à l'état et nuisibles aux sciences, à la littérature et aux arts* (Abolition of All Academies As Institutions Costly for the State and Detrimental to Sciences, Literature, and the Arts). The "Carmagnole of the Muses"—to cite the evocative title of a work by Jean-Claude Bonnet—attacked the academies in general and the Académie Française in particular. The assembly's very composition—with some members unknown to the greater public, whose merits could therefore not be judged, alongside writers of varying repute and aristocrats—made it suspect. The fact that it had been founded by the very minister who had promoted absolute monarchy made the Académie look like a symbol of despotism, and Jean-Paul Marat bluntly accused it of charlatanism. On 8 August 1793 it was decided, at the abbé Henri Grégoire's urging, to abolish it.

There was, however, some pleading in favor of the academies, with emphasis (Talleyrand, Condorcet) on the fact that national interests were served by providing state financing to institutions that at least functioned as repositories of knowledge. Beginning in 1790 Malesherbes had been proposing reorganization, rather than abolition, of the Académie, and the Academicians followed this suggestion. Thus, shortly after Thermidor the assembly was reorganized and reconstituted as the Institut de France, with the Académie Française incorporated as a part of it. The Académie was assigned a new mission, that of conservatory of the cultural heritage, in addition to the missions already entrusted to the institution at the time of its founding. (For the sake of anecdotal and symbolic interest, let us note that it was under the Consulate that the Academicians adopted the green robe; prior to that time they had dressed in their normal city attire.)

The Académie Française thus played only a limited, and even then paradoxical, role in the spread of Enlightenment ideas. And yet, despite the critics of the revolutionary era who considered it a bastion of reactionary thinking, it was not a hotbed for the constant fight against new ideas. An innovative institution under Louis XIII, and then, under Louis XIV, a politically and aesthetically conservative institution as well as a partisan of "modernism," the Académie during the 18th century was in effect a sounding board for Enlightenment ideas. Finally, following its reorganization, the institution reappeared in the form that reflected its new function: a true conservatory.

ALAIN VIALA

See also Académie Royale des Sciences de Paris; Ancient and the Moderns, Quarrel of the; Dictionary

Further Reading

Albert-Buisson, François, *Les quarante au temps de Lumières*, Paris: Fayard, 1960

Fumaroli, Marc, *Trois institutions littéraires*, Paris: Gallimard, 1994

Roche, Daniel, *Le siècle des Lumières en province: Académies et académiciens provinciaux, 1670–1789*, Paris: Mouton, 1978

Viala, Alain, *Naissance de l'écrivain: Sociologie de la littérature à l'âge classique*, Paris: Éditions de Minuit, 1985

Académie Royale des Sciences de Paris

The period from 1699, when the official statutes of the Académie Royale des Sciences de Paris (French Royal Academy of Science) were first put into effect, to the institution's abolition (as an entity linked to the monarchy) in 1793, marked a golden age in the history of science. During that period of institutional stability the Académie des Sciences was the hegemonic center of French scientific activity. In the larger European context the Académie des Sciences was one of the poles in a system of scientific exchanges that was fairly independent of governmental authorities. Whether we consider the dissemination of Sir Isaac Newton's theories to the Continent, the impact of Gottfried Wilhelm Leibniz's calculus in France, the growth of mathematical analysis, the mathematization of mechanics, or the emergence of the new chemistry, all of these fundamental advances in the history of science were fostered by the Académie des Sciences. The Academicians' role in the long process of compiling the comprehensive *Description et perfection des arts et métiers* (1761; Description and Perfection of the Arts and Trades), along with their continual work to evaluate new discoveries, made this learned society a veritable crossroads of the numerous avenues making up the history of technology in the 18th century. The Academicians also attached great importance to the teaching of science, their courses, and their textbooks, and they were leaders in the formulation of projects for public education during the Revolution. In short, the Académie des Sciences was a significant laboratory for pedagogic experiments, the results of which should interest modern historians of teaching. Finally, the history of this scientific society has an interesting political dimension: from the moment of its creation in 1666 by Jean-Baptiste Colbert, the institution worked to further absolutism. During the last decades of the ancien régime, the Académie became the center of intense activity aimed at reforming the monarchy—which it ultimately outlived. Despite its temporary abolition in 1893, the institution was reconstituted in a more democratic form after the Revolution and still exists today. The history of the academy thus has much to reveal about the history of the French state.

Historiography amply covers the many aspects of the academy's story. The institution's main statutes have been published and analyzed, and virtually all of the Academicians have been identified. The body of scientific knowledge that left a mark on the history of the Académie has been noted and unceasingly examined. The major trends in academic life during the 18th century have been described in monographs and in quantitative and comparative analyses. The concrete terms and conditions under which the Académie des Sciences operated are well known, thanks to historians' careful examination of evidence related to the scholarly practices of the times, and the places and materials involved have been studied. The impact of the institution's organization on the scientific practices of the time has been assessed in different ways, and the academic language of science has been scrutinized. The Académie's involvement in the monarchical system has been the topic of several studies.

The 1699 statutes reveal a great deal about the main characteristics of the Académie des Sciences at the end of the 17th century—characteristics that would change during the course of the 18th century. The 1699 text reflects the experience acquired by the Académie des Sciences since its creation. The absence of formal statutes between 1666 and 1699 should be interpreted as what it actually was: a deliberate means of denying the Academicians the comfort of a guaranteed annuity. Colbert wanted to make members solely dependent on the generosity of his bonuses, and he had left the Académie des Sciences without statutes so that its members would have no recourse to any legally binding document. In 1699, during a period characterized by the general expectation that the duc de Bourgogne would succeed Louis XIV and by the prospect of reforms in scientific teaching, the abbé Bignon prepared an updated version of the academy's statutes. His objectives in this were to rejuvenate the Académie des Sciences, to eliminate the secrecy surrounding the work of the Academicians, and to better ensure them a reliable income. (In the 30-year period from 1666 to 1699, the ostensibly "arbitrary" bonus payments had in fact given way to regular payments through sheer force of custom.) The main purpose of the 1699 regulations, however, was not to bring order to an assembly that until that time had been left to its own devices, but instead to establish rules for governing what from then on would be a state body.

Fourteen articles in the statutes of 1699 set forth the structure of the Académie des Sciences as a strict hierarchy, with ten honorary members at the top rank, followed by twenty pensioners, then twenty associates, and finally twenty students. Only native-born French subjects were eligible to become honorary members. These top-ranking Academicians were elected and their names were subsequently submitted to the monarch for approval, on the strength of the fact that "their intelligence in mathematics and in physics made them commendable." In most cases, honorary members were court dignitaries—active or retired ministers. Honorary members did not do much in the way of work. Instead, they constituted a pool of candidates from whom, as stipulated in the statues, the king annually selected a chair and a vice chair. As moderator of debates within the society, the chair (most often Bignon in the Académie's early years) essentially served as the king's eye (of surveillance) and arm (of authority) in the institution. Beginning in 1700 the posts of chair and vice chair were supplemented by a director and an assistant director chosen from among the pensioners—that is to say, from the ranks of the scientists. The 1699 statutes provided ample scope for a man as ambitious as Bignon, who served 32 times as chair or vice chair between 1699 and 1734. Beginning with René-Antóine Ferchault de Réaumur, who served as director or assistant director 21 times between 1713 and 1753, the directors gradually superseded the chairs in terms of actually wielding authority over the Académie des Sciences. Antoine-Laurent de Lavoisier's decisive role as director during the reform of 1785 attests to this growth of the director's power (in marked contrast to Jean le Rond D'Alembert's failed attempts at reform in 1769, when he was the director). Further evidence of this trend toward granting greater authority to scientists can be seen in the fact that in 1793, the year the Académie des Sciences was abolished, a pensioner had actually become chair.

From the 1730s onward, the posts of secretary and treasurer—which were filled on a perpetual rather than an annual basis—were held by pensioners, and these permanent officers provided the sole assurance of continuity in the leadership of the Académie des Sciences. Over the course of the 18th century, certain names dominated these positions: Couplet the Elder and then Couplet the Younger served as permanent treasurer from 1699 to 1743; thereafter, the comte de Buffon served in that capacity from 1744 to 1788. Bernard Le Bovier de Fontenelle was permanent secretary from 1697 to 1740. After an interlude, Grandjean de Fouchy succeeded him, serving from 1744 to 1776. The marquis de Condorcet, who had acted as Fouchy's substitute from 1773 to 1776, took over from Fouchy and served as secretary until 1793.

With the exception of the honorary members, the Academicians, each of whom had a particular area of expertise, were grouped into categories or "classes" determined by area of specialization. However, it would be an anachronism to speak in terms of academic disciplines, since at that time scientific training did not correspond to the notion of disciplines as we understand them today. The itineraries followed by some Academicians, such as Buffon and D'Alembert, who moved from one class to another as they threaded their way up through the curricular hierarchy, show us that although these scholars had specialized knowledge, it is not possible to maintain that they fell within the rigorously precise disciplinary boundaries. This absence of stable disciplinary limits is also apparent from rethinking of

curricular categories that was a part of the reorganization of 1785.

The classes were oriented toward either mathematics or physics, and it was only rarely that Academicians crossed this divide during the course of their career. The opposition between mathematics and physics, which is evident in documents from 1666 onward, structured many of the Académie des Sciences' customs, notably that of ensuring that representatives from these two groups were equally represented on committees of general interest. At the time the word "physics" referred to sciences related to the three kingdoms present in nature: animals, minerals and plants, which were investigated by "anatomists," "chemists," and "botanists," respectively. Finer degrees of specialization could be added to these basic categories. The anatomists, for example, were often physicians, and the task of dissecting animals was their responsibility, while among the botanists there were a fair number of apothecaries. These latter Academicians were frequently officeholders in the Jardin du Roi (French Royal Botanical Garden), a teaching institution and a repository for medicinal plant specimens.

The field of mathematical sciences included "geometers," "astronomers," and "mechanical engineers." Of these three groups, only geometers would be considered "mathematicians" today. The field of geometry continued to expand throughout the century owing to the importance accorded first of all to differential calculus and then to related conceptual and technical developments, which not only led to refinements in calculus itself but also increased the extent of its applications. In principle, mechanical engineers were concerned with machinery; notable practitioners include Réaumur and Jacques de Vaucanson, for example. Article XXXI of the 1699 statutes discussed mechanical engineering—the only field of scientific study whose representatives were charged with specific daily activities under the king's orders. The article stipulated that these Academicians were responsible for inspecting the machines whose inventors had requested a *privilège d'exploitation* (royal permission to market their machines) and for conducting tours of inspection in factories. Beginning in the 1730s, various Academicians held these positions. However, mechanical engineering, like other categories of scientific knowledge, could not remain fixed in the face of the constant discoveries and innovations of the 18th century. During the last two-thirds of the century, a competent geometer, even one not particularly well versed in machines and automatons, could hold a post as a mechanical engineer. Among the "astronomers," on the other hand (even though some crossover into other mathematical fields can be discerned), there existed veritable dynasties that monopolized that branch of science, including the Cassini-

Maraldi family, the Delisle-Buaches, and the La Hires. The highly technical nature of the practice of astronomy, along with the increasing importance of the Observatoire de Paris (Paris Observatory) and cartography were determining factors in consolidating that area of study.

One may wonder about the reasons for this initial division of the sciences into six categories, with geography, optics, and mineralogy not being granted independent places. In 1699 the Académie's objective was not to establish a philosophical system, but instead to determine the limits of those sciences that might be useful to the monarchy. In each of the sciences this notion of utility, which itself changed as the century advanced, took on particular forms appropriate to the field of study. Beyond the improvements brought to areas such as machinery, cartography, and pharmacy, "utility" was sometimes defined as a contribution to the monarch's glory. Beginning in the 1720s, numerous Academicians could be counted among the inspectors of the royal establishments. This trend would lead to a particular relationship between the sciences and political authority that was to prevail at the end of the ancien régime. This relationship entailed a system of exchanges. The scientists supplied the government with instruments of all kinds, while in return the government granted the Academicians privileges of various types; university chairs, as well as civil service posts, were created, and a number of teaching institutions and scientific establishments were reformed. Other factors, stemming as much from changes in the practice of science itself as from the relationship between the Académie des Sciences and the government, or the Académie's place within the Republic of Letters, had a bearing on the meaning of the word "utility" in the context of the sciences. Beginning in the middle of the century, several attempts were made to reconsider or revise the Académie's curricular categories. This movement culminated in the 1785 reorganization of the institution, resulting in the establishment of eight classes: geometry; astronomy; mechanics; general physics; anatomy; chemistry and metallurgy; botany and agriculture, and natural history and mineralogy.

In 1699 each class included three Parisian pensioners, two associates who were French nationals, and Parisian students working under a particular pensioner. The 1716 regulation changed the students' status, making them assistants, and stipulated that their number should be 12 (2 per class). Residence in Paris was a formal requirement for pensioners and students, as were probity and high moral standards. In 1699 members of the regular clergy could be appointed only as honorary members of the Académie. In 1716 a new statute abolished this restriction and reserved associateships "unrelated to any science" to be assigned to "a few [members of the regular] clergy." These clergymen eventually

came to be called "free associates." However, they were barred from access to pensions, and this sidelining of the regular clergy freed the Académie from the influence of the most active of the religious congregations. That was a point on which the geometer D'Alembert found support for his pleading, half a century later, in favor of the Jesuits' expulsion.

According to the 1699 statutes, pensioners and associates had to be at least 25 years old. They also had to be known "for the publication of an important piece of work, the brilliant teaching of a course, the invention of a machine, or for some sort of special discovery." Students had to be at least 21 years old, and the nominations made by the king were based on a list of candidates produced by means of a vote taken among the Academicians, with an explicit proviso concerning the promotion of students or associates. Pensioners, meanwhile, were required to inform the Académie des Sciences of their work in progress and to participate actively in the institution's meetings. Associates were invited to do the same. The Académie des Sciences was also obligated to undertake the regular publication of its activities—and even to publish retrospectively the papers produced during the first phase of its existence (1666–98).

Further provisions of the 1699 statutes included instituting the nomination of eight foreign associates. These were not assigned to any particular class. In 1716 the number of associates not affiliated with any particular class was increased to 12, when, in addition to the eight associate memberships given to foreigners, four associate positions were created for members of the regular clergy, as noted above. None of these associates was entitled to a pension. From 1731 to 1765 there were eight "foreign associates." The number of "free associates" rose from four in 1716 to six in 1731, and subsequently to eight in 1762 and twelve in 1765. The statutory revisions of 1785 maintained the numbers of foreign associates at eight and free associates at twelve.

Finally, from very early on, the Académie des Sciences maintained a network of correspondents. By 4 March 1699, 85 correspondents had been designated, but it was not until 1753 that there was a precise statute spelling out the criteria for their appointment and for the kind of follow-up to the exchanges established with them.

Organization is not everything. The 1699 statutes did ensure some stability for the Académie des Sciences, but, as we have just seen, a number of measures had to undergo significant adjustment. The Académie did in fact experience profound transformations over the course of the 18th century. Some of these transformations, such as the advances in mathematics and chemistry were specifically science-related. Other transformations were the result of administrative decisions. The statutes of 1699—the last set to be issued by the Sun King to the Académie des Sciences—put an end to any doubts about its permanence as an institution. The revised statutes of 1785, issued on the eve of the Revolution, reflected the first reorganization initiated by reform-minded scientists. Other transformations also played an important role in shaping the Académie des Sciences. There was a spectacular boom in science books, marked especially by Denis Diderot and D'Alembert's encyclopedic enterprise, and also by Buffon's work. At the end of the century, the success of the sciences, the enthusiasm for balloons, or for discoveries useful to the public good were important factors, as was the increase in the number of protests against the existing academic order. In the final analysis, it seems that all the transformations of academic activities in 18th-century France reflected the same characteristic process: that of centralization of official scientific sanction in a circumscribed social milieu. This tendency toward centralization and monopoly of the scientific realm was bolstered by the Académie's official statutes and by the place the institution occupied in the monarchical system. The Académie was charged with evaluating new techniques, and to this end it had at its disposal censorship privileges. The institution's privileged position raises the interesting question of the correlation between known tendencies (centralization, censorship, and so forth) that might be called contextual, and concrete transformations in the Académie's activities.

Throughout the 18th century the Academicians continued to evaluate reports, procedures, and machines. This was the scientists' task and they fulfilled a useful social function by performing it, since it was on the basis of their judgments that marketing and publication rights were granted. During the first half of the century the Academicians' social status continued to grow. However, in the middle of the century, we can identify an important cultural shift, as the two basic types of Parisian scientist recognized in the early 1700s—the priest-mathematician and the faculty physician—lost their preeminence to the geometrician and the naturalist (as personified by D'Alembert and Buffon, respectively). Also in the middle of the century, there was a relative increase in the number of members coming from the nobility, a sign of the Académie des Sciences' integration into the Parisian elite.

The Académie des Sciences evolved as an institution in the more general context of a flourishing of learned societies throughout Europe and a gradual strengthening of a well-educated elite, both in Paris and in other parts of France. Over the course of the 18th century, this movement was accompanied by an increase in the numbers of books and periodicals being published. As the keystone of this whole system, the Académie des Sciences had to take into account the large increase in both learned publications and works intended for the layperson. As the century progressed, the Académie des Sciences also had to enlarge its interests to include nascent disciplines that had not come within its original purview: economics, for example. During the 1780s the Académie had to face severe criticism from those in the Republic of Letters who were excluded from its ranks; such critics, for example, used Mesmer's theory of magnetism and a symbol for science freed from the guardianship of the Académie.

In 1699 the Académie des Sciences brought together groups of scientists under the same patronage, with each scientist having his own area of expertise. But by 1785 the Académie had evolved into a homogeneous institution integrated into a network of administrative authorities; it was a state apparatus suffering from a grave financial crisis but running smoothly nonetheless. It is thus possible to catch a glimpse of the conditions that led simultaneously to the abolition of the Académie Royale des Sciences, to the action of its members during the Revolution, and to the creation of the First Class in the more democratic Institut de France. The same kind of logic explains the fact that this First Class contributed to the survival of the Académie des Sciences after the Revolution, that it restored the institutional link between science and state, and that it gave this link a radically new form. The historical phenomenon of the Académie Royale des Sciences thus touches on the history of scientific theories, the institutional and cultural history of science, and the history of the state in France.

ÉRIC BRIAN

See also Science: Dissemination and Popularization

Further Reading

Biagioli, Mario, *Galileo, Courtier: The Practice of Science in the Culture of Absolutism*, Chicago: University of Chicago Press, 1993

Brian, Éric, *La mesure de l'État: Administrateurs et géomètres au XVIIIᵉ siècle*, Paris: Albin Michel, 1994

Brian, Éric, and Christiane Demeulenaere-Douyère, editors, *Histoire et mémoire de l'Académie des sciences: Guide de recherches*, London, Paris, and New York: Tec and Doc, 1996

Crosland, Maurice P., *Science under Control: The French Academy of Sciences, 1795–1914*, Cambridge and New York: Cambridge University Press, 1992

Gillispie, Charles Coulston, *Science and Polity in France at the End of the Old Regime*, Princeton, New Jersey: Princeton University Press, 1980

Hahn, Roger, *The Anatomy of a Scientific Institution: The Paris Academy of Sciences, 1666–1803*, Berkeley: University of California Press, 1971

McClellan, James E., *Science Reorganized: Scientific Societies in the Eighteenth Century*, New York: Columbia University Press, 1985

Roche, Daniel, *Le siècle des Lumières en province: Académies et académiciens provinciaux, 1680–1789*, 2 vols., Paris: Mouton, 1978

Salomon-Bayet, Claire, *L'institution de la science et l'expérience du vivant: Méthode et expérience à l'Académie royale des sciences, 1666–1793*, Paris: Flammarion, 1978

Shapin, Steven, *A Social History of Truth: Civility and Science in Seventeenth-Century England*, Chicago: University of Chicago Press, 1994

Shapin, Steven, and Simon Schaffer, *Leviathan and the Air-Pump: Hobbes, Boyle, and the Experimental Life*, Princeton, New Jersey: Princeton University Press, 1985

Stroup, Alice, *A Company of Scientists: Botany, Patronage, and Community at the Seventeenth-Century Parisian Royal Academy of Sciences*, Berkeley: University of California Press, 1990

Sturdy, David J., *Science and Social Status: The Members of the Académie des Sciences, 1666–1750*, Woodbridge, Suffolk, and Rochester, New York: Boydell Press, 1995

Taton, René, "Die Akademien," in *Die Philosophie des 17. Jahrhunderts*, edited by Jean-Pierre Schobinger, vol. 2, Basel: Schwabe, 1993

Academies, Provincial

The academic movement originated within the "Republic of Letters," an entity both real and mythical, which was based on the notion that equality exists among men of letters, over and above any differences in social background, status, or nationality that might divide them. That dream, we should recall, had obsessed humanist scholars during the Renaissance. In the 15th century Marsilio Ficino and Giovanni Pico della Mirandola founded in Florence the Accademia Platonica (Platonic Academy), inspired by the Greek model of the Akademia (the garden where Plato taught). The Accademia Platonica was a meeting place for philosophers and scholars who corresponded with their learned counterparts elsewhere in Europe. Sixteenth-century Italy saw the birth of a large number of academies founded on the model of a humanistic culture opposed to the Scholasticism of the universities; by the 1530s there were some 500 of them (56 in Rome, 70 in Bologna, others in Venice, in Verona, and in Naples).

The Republic of Letters became more tightly consolidated during the first half of the 17th century. At the time, the upper echelons of the European intelligentsia were united by several factors: the rise of rationalism, a keen and shared interest in the emerging sciences, and, despite a facade of conformism, a tendency to distance themselves from religious orthodoxy. In 1603 the celebrated Accademia dei Lincei (Academy of Lynxes) was established in Rome; its influence was to become quite strong in the following century. In Paris the circles gathered around the brothers Pierre and Jacques Dupuy and around Father Marin Mersenne established solid ties with other European academies. In England rising interest in the sciences resulted in the creation of the Royal Society, established as a private institution in 1645; Charles II later made it an official academy in 1662.

The academic movement that flourished in Europe during the second half of the 17th century was markedly different from the academicism of the preceding decades, although there were certain elements of continuity. The cultural world had changed substantially: knowledge was no longer the exclusive monopoly of an extremely restricted number of initiates but was reaching broader strata of a population eager to be informed of advances of human knowledge. The large European cities were no longer the only centers to have "intellectual" circles in their midst. Over a period of many years and with considerable variation as to scope and ambition, scholarly associations and learned societies were formed in midsize cities. Their aim was to develop an interest in literature, the sciences, and new technologies and to collect all knowledge of local, national, or universal importance; their activity thus paralleled that of the great national academies emerging during the same period. The foundation in 1635 of the Académie Française by Cardinal Richelieu, minister of state under Louis XIII, and the subsequent creation of various sister royal academies during the reign of Louis XIV provided a model for the institutionalization of knowledge that was to be adopted by other European sovereigns. Members of the provincial academies, motivated by a powerful desire for legitimacy, in turn requested official state sanction. This new cultural configuration was the result of many factors.

One important factor was the sense that encyclopedic knowledge had accumulated to such a degree that it was necessary to find more efficient ways to manage it; one way to do this was to call widely on the local elites, as individual, piecemeal initiatives were deemed to be insufficient or invalid. It should be noted that this period in the institutionalization of the cultural field dates back to the closing decades of the 17th century, a period that Paul Hazard characterized, in 1935, as the "crisis of European consciousness." And unquestionably, the establishment of an academic network was connected with a general cultural anxiety: the advent of new knowledge was accompanied by the sense, whether well-founded or illusory, that previous knowledge, however solidly established, was being called into question. The conflict in worldviews is exemplified in the great Gottfried Wilhelm Leibniz, who was among the last metaphysicians to construct a rational system incorporating the existence of God and accounting for the world as a whole, and who was, at the same time, a mathematician very much attracted to scientific modernity and a scholar who dreamed of reunifying the Republic of Letters through European academicism. The provincial academies could not recruit such prestigious personalities as Leibniz and could not cultivate philosophical ambitions to the same extent, but the same desire for unity motivated their activities. Local societies, concerned with maintaining cultural traditions, provided a structure for what were originally meetings of friends dedicated to the pleasures of social life and to the cultivation of belles lettres, and their existence as institutions imparted a more scholarly tone to their activities. The safeguarding of the cultural heritage and the shift in policy toward scientific knowledge should not therefore be considered as irreconcilable tendencies.

Another determining factor in the new cultural configuration was the rise to power of an elite that was more demanding in its desire to absorb new knowledge. From this perspective, the provincial academies attest to the massive pedagogical efforts made throughout the 18th century, often neglected or underestimated by historians of culture, who have tended to focus too exclusively on the large urban centers. Daniel Roche's admirable study has definitively put an end to this injustice by revealing the extraordinary richness of provincial intellectual life in 18th-century France (see Roche).

Yet another factor in the cultural shift was the need for new ways of granting official recognition to the elites in a Europe that was undergoing radical intellec-tual transformation and where new scientific knowledge was perceived as an indispensable source of progress. Clearly, the idea of official recognition, which has ended up being considered to be one of the essential components of the Enlightenment, did not become entrenched with equal strength or at the same time in every part of 18th-century Europe. There was, however, a principle common to all the countries that were open to academicism: the large academies alone were not sufficient to respond to cultural needs, and a whole system of relays was necessary; hence the indispensable creation of provincial academies.

We should make a distinction between provincial societies and the great European academies, whether we are speaking of France's Académie Française, its Académie Royale des Sciences, and, to a lesser extent, its Académie des Inscriptions et Belles-Lettres (Academy of Inscriptions and Letters); of England's Royal Society and Royal Society of Arts; of Germany's famous Berlin Academy, reestablished in 1743 by Frederick II; or of Italy's Permanent Academy of Sciences in Turin and its Academy of Sciences and Belles-Lettres in Naples, developed by Bernardo Tanucci in 1779. All these institutions recruited renowned intellectuals, leading state dignitaries, or personalities endowed with an aura of celebrity, whereas few of the provincial Academicians reached such levels of charisma. The Masonic lodges that were also spreading throughout Europe were motivated by the same egalitarian desire as their academic sister institutions, but their recruitment standards were more open socially: small traders and craftsmen appeared in their ranks. Moreover, these lodges were spurred on by an ideology of mutual aid and virtue, an ideology that did not exist with the same intensity or in the same forms in the provincial academies. Also worthy of note are the learned institutions, the numerous agricultural societies in England and France toward the end of the ancien régime, and the societies dealing with medicine or with natural history, which differed from other models by virtue of their quest for specialized knowledge.

Current research provides us with few clues as to what provincial academicism was like from a European perspective. Originally, private groups—jurists, physicians, professors with a great love for belles lettres or for local history—asked powerful and titled protectors to vouchsafe the seriousness of their endeavors and to intercede with the central authorities in support of their applications for letters patent. For example, in Nîmes at the end of the 17th century such appeals were made to Chancellor Le Tellier, the governor of Languedoc (the duc du Maine), and the lieutenant general of the province (the duc de Noailles). The names of powerful noble families are similarly present at Soissons: Estrées, Rohan, and Orléans in particular. In the same town,

Pellisson and the lawyer Patru, both members of the Académie Française, received requests for patronage. The provincial movement in France benefited from the reorganization of the royal academies, even though, as Roche points out, the provincial societies were being established without any coordinated plan. The state authorities wished to use the cultural network as a post of observation—if not one of control—over the regions of France. The Academicians' general obedience to the monarch could only encourage the sovereign in this direction, and yet relations between the provincial societies and the academy responsible for them were still characterized by a certain amount of tension. Some of these societies, faithful to the egalitarian dream of the Republic of Letters, refused to submit and proclaimed their independence; but most of the time the attraction exerted by the great Parisian academies, or the vague hope of belonging to them some day, became an incentive for allegiance. There were some national differences. In England, for example, there was a more pronounced trend toward privatization. In general, however, the model of allegiance to a central institution dominated the academies of 18th-century Europe.

Let us sketch an outline of the history of the academic movement, beginning with its earliest phase. It would be inaccurate to speak of "the Italian provinces," since Italy at that time had not yet become a nation, but we should note that in most of the small states of the peninsula the academic movement was solidly established at an early date. The movement in Italy benefited from a scholarly and artistic tradition that had gone uninterrupted since humanism and the great period of scientific investigation in the 17th century: the Accademia del Cimento (Florence, 1657), the Accademia degli Investiganti (Naples, 1678), and the Accademia degli Inquieti (Academy of the Uneasy) founded in Bologna in 1690 by the astronomer Estachio Manfredi. The first Portuguese academies were created in the second half of the 17th century, but academies in that country only really developed in number and influence at the beginning of the 18th century, when John V founded the Royal Academy of History (1720), based on the model of the royal academies of France and Italy. There were eight societies in France prior to 1700: those of Avignon (1658), Castres (1660–80), Arles (1669), Soissons (1674), Nîmes (1682), Angers (1685), and Villefranche-en-Beaujolais (1695), and the Jeux Floraux in Toulouse (1695).

The second phase of academicism (1720–60) was the most creative: some 20 academies were founded in France after the Regency, most of them before 1750. Many of them manifested a clear scientific orientation well before the publication of the *Encyclopédie*, and they worked to compensate for the shortcomings of universities, where traditional methods continued to

dominate. Eminent physicists and chemists such as the abbé Jean-Antoine Nollet in Bordeaux, the baron Guyton de Morveau in Dijon, and Jean-Antoine-Claude Chaptal in Montpellier conducted experiments that were widely discussed, both locally and at the national level. Botany was also a subject of study, but medicine more rarely. In mid–18th century Spain, the academic movement bestowed a new fame on cities such as Vitoria, Saragossa, Seville, and Barcelona. The movement also flourished in Portugal, with the creation of a number of academies: the Laureados (Laureates) in Santarém (1721), the Problemática in Setúbal (1721), and the Vimaranense (1724) were followed by the Unidos, the Torre de Moncorvo (1731), the Bracarense (1731), and the Seminário in Viseu, which was founded by Bishop Julio de Oliveira in 1747. We should also recall the linguistic and literary vocation of the academic movement: it aimed at promoting national languages by boosting the publication of new dictionaries and shaping the language of the elites through the adoption of the terms required for scientific discourse. These were measures that central authorities usually encouraged, public finances permitting. During this period, academies generally maintained good relations with the regional authorities, which were anxious to provide protection that would reflect well on themselves. Tensions, however, appeared here and there: Monseigneur de Belsunce, the bishop of Marseille, considered the academy of that city to be an "assembly of Jansenists and freethinkers." In France the bishops agreed to support the academies only on the condition that they clearly state their philosophical and religious neutrality.

During its final phase (1760–89), the academic movement in France was clearly losing momentum, for academies were established in only four cities during those years: Agen (1776), Grenoble (1780), Valence (1784), and Orléans (1784). The situation was complex. The sense that the Republic of Letters was in a state of crisis was expressed in a desire for unification. At the very same time, however, specialized and competing academies were founded, including government-sponsored royal agricultural societies; reading rooms; and institutions "dedicated to the Muses," or societies for teaching the fine arts. The government showed increasing interest in the academic movement in the hope of uniting knowledge and power, at precisely the same time that academic institutions were coming into intellectual maturity.

Although the French academic model served as an example to other countries, academic culture developed differently in different contexts. The expansion of the Spanish academies was reinforced, despite the fear of decadence and the distrust generated during the Inquisition. There were 95 applications for letters patent on behalf of academies, including one in Madrid (1775) and another in Saragossa (1776). Three societies were founded in the Canary Islands, and there were also applications from less prestigious places such as Alba de Tormes (1776), Baza (1779), and San Clemente (1783). In Hungary the development of the academic movement came later: prior to the 1770s, only a few isolated aristocrats had maintained cultural relations with one another, following traditional models. It was only later, with the creation of intellectual societies headed by new social leaders (military officers, civil servants, teachers), that a significant transformation occurred. In a number of European monarchies, the French Revolution threw the world of academicism into disarray: many societies were suspected of promoting liberal ideas, and academies in Austria, Hungary, and Spain, for example, had to reduce their activities.

Some specific national traits are worthy of mention. For example, academies in Italian cities retained their scientific orientation throughout the 18th century, their emphasis on technology aimed at the industrialization and improvement of agricultural practices. There was also an established artistic tradition in Italy, often accompanied by teaching, as at the Accademia Musicale Chigiana in Siena.

In Spain the Sociedades Económicas de Amigos del País (Economic Societies of Friends of the Country) attest to a systematic desire for the modernization of technology, which sets them apart from the Royal Academies of Language and of Sciences created in 1714 and 1774, respectively. Thus, Pedro Rodríguez Campomanes published his *Idea segura para extender y adoptar en España los conocimentos verdaderos de la agricultura* (1763; The Only Way to Extend and Adopt in Spain True Knowledge on Agriculture), a work that he further developed in 1774 with *El discurso sobre el fomento de la industria popular* (Discourse on the Development of Popular Industry). The Spanish societies responded to this appeal by adopting the organizational model of the first among them, the Real Sociedad Vascongada de los Amigos del Pais (Royal Basque Society of Friends of the Country), established in 1765 in accordance with the Project for the Creation of an Economic Society or Academy of Agriculture, Sciences, Useful Arts, and Commerce, a plan that had been worked out a few years earlier by the Count of Peñaflorida and his friends the Caballeritos (little knights) of Azcoitia. The plan was divided into several sections devoted to agriculture, industry, commerce, architecture, animal husbandry, and domestic economy, but the techniques that were most useful received the most attention. The activities of the societies included numerous and varied experiments; foreign books were imported (Peñaflorida bought the *Encyclopédie*); contacts were established with foreign scholars; and scholarship recipients were sent abroad. The Basque Society also created an education center, El Seminario Patriotico (the Patriotic Seminary), in Vergara. In spite of the suspicions of the Inquisitors, these societies were active and, more often than not, enjoyed royal protection. Their decline caused sufficient anxiety to prompt a royal decree demanding an investigation of the situation. The matter was debated, the activities of the societies were supported, and reform projects were proposed.

Portuguese academicism asserted itself against Spanish dominance though foreign influences, notably those coming from England and France. There were numerous signs of this tendency: the decline of Spanish as a second language; the increase in the number of French, Italian, and Dutch grammars; and the study of foreign cultures in the academies. Most revealing of this particular situation is the fact that the Academia Cirurgica Prototipo-Lusitanica Portuense (the Prototypical Portuguese Surgical Academy), established in Oporto and later converted into a society of medicine, was the only institution to welcome Spanish Academicians in its midst.

English, French, and Italian academies were open to all forms of knowledge, with a clear shift of emphasis toward the applied sciences in the last few decades of the 18th century. In northern Italy (Milan, Turin, Udine), academies dedicated to agriculture, claiming to follow the physiocratic movement, formed a vast network supported by the local authorities.

One of the main functions of the academic movement was to provide hospitality to men of letters, scientists, art lovers, and, more generally, the scholarly elite who crisscrossed the European cultural space in order to satisfy their intellectual curiosity. In the course of their visit to Italy, Montesquieu and Charles de Brosses, although not members, were welcomed in several academies. Travel accounts and the first tourist guides, such as those of the German Heinrich Reichard, provide a sense of the importance of provincial academicism: distinguished travelers enjoyed the possibility of associating with the academic circles of the host city and, above all, were assured they would be welcomed in the actual headquarters of the society. These privileges were perceived as signs of recognition among peers. The ritual of ceremonial welcome was often followed by a visit to a "cabinet of curiosities," or scientific collection, belonging to one of the honorable members of the institution. It is to be noted, as a proof of this ritual, that the local academies are systematically mentioned in Reichard's *Guide des voyageurs en France* (1810; Travelers' Guide to France).

There was no academic life without ritual: speeches and eulogies reflected the desire to celebrate the academies themselves and to impress upon the local population the seriousness of the institution's activities. This rhetorical pomp caused academicism to become deeply entrenched in a tradition that bestowed honor and prestige on those who excelled in the art of eloquence, demonstrating their perfect mastery of the conventional poetic heritage of the schools and universities. Provincial ceremonial traditions were different, however, from those practiced in the great academies of the large European cities. In the provinces, eulogies were meant to celebrate the moral qualities of modest scholars rather than to pay homage to first-class intellectuals. In France the organization of provincial academies was modeled on the Académie Française and, to a lesser extent, on the Académie Royale des Sciences or the Académie des Inscriptions et Belles-Lettres. Equality among members was proclaimed, and recognition was granted exclusively for talent, although these principles were not unanimously respected. There were internal distinctions among ordinary, honorary, and associate (or corresponding) members, with honorary membership often being bestowed upon persons of high social rank, such as magistrates or bishops. This return to an internal hierarchy could be a source of tensions (in Bordeaux, for instance), or it could be rejected by those societies that from the outset had proclaimed the strictest equality among members.

Lacking systematic subsidies from the central authorities, the societies had to negotiate constantly with mayors, deputy mayors, *intendants* (magistrates), and governors in order to obtain subsidies. There were two other sources of revenue: sponsorship and individual contributions, which helped to reinforce the place of societies in local life and enhanced their dedication to a public role. Academies were consulted on hospitals, town planning, or regional festivals, and they did their best to ensure their city's cultural influence in the rest of the country. The connections between academicism and the world of collectors and "curiosities" should again be emphasized. Affluent members of academies, who often had curiosity cabinets containing precious stones, coins, and antiquities, engaged in a policy of purchases for the societies to which they belonged and sometimes even bequeathed to those societies part of their collections. Additionally, in France the academies had educational ambitions: at a time when technical instruction was too weak to meet the professional needs of the country, some of the provincial societies provided free courses in applied drawing, whereas the royal academies maintained their monopoly on the training of the great artists of the country.

Academicism was an urban phenomenon. In France, according to Roche, the total for all cities that had an academy was no more than 23,000 people, and they accounted for no more than 2 percent of the general population. Out of this already very low figure, the number of Academicians was still smaller: approximately 1,000 people in the early years of the 18th century; 2,500 to 3,000 on the eve of the French Revolution; and 6,000 in total for the entire century. Keeping in mind that the educated elite comprised 13,000 to 15,000 people, it can only be concluded that intellectual societies were very restrictive in their recruitment. However, the very rigorous selection procedure bestowed an unquestionable prestige upon those who were elected. Success in an academic competition was a sign of cultural recognition for those who were not privileged from birth, and was even enough to launch a writer's career. The case of Jean-Jacques Rousseau, making his stunning entrance into the world of literature after the remarkable award he received from the Dijon Academy for his *Discours sur les sciences et les arts* (1750; Discourse on the Sciences and Arts), is well known. However, such successes were infrequent, and the hopes of less-affluent prizewinners were often disappointed, particularly at the end of the century, when the number of applications exceeded the number of careers offered by civil society. In France the Academicians' social origins, as well as the places that the three estates occupied respectively within the academies, reveal an unquestionable conservatism: 20 percent of the nation's Academicians belonged to the clergy, 37 percent to the nobility, and 43 percent were commoners. The nobility enjoyed a strong proportional representation within the academies, but the clergy was underrepresented in comparison to its urban influence—a sign of cultural secularization that can also be observed in other European countries. Moreover, the large number of cultural leaders (physicians, teachers, magistrates) among Academicians was obviously reached at the expense of traders and manufacturers; wage earners and shopkeepers were excluded from the intellectual elite.

Finally, provincial academicism must also be placed in the context of a wider history of culture. The increase and diversification of knowledge in Europe from 1680 to 1789 forced the elites had to consolidate their ties, expand their frame of reference, and invent new social structures for imparting legitimacy and recognition. They also had to organize a system for promoting talent in order to compensate for the deficiencies in the traditional universities. Still, the academic world remained conservative in nature, and its rituals and internal hierarchy reflected, apart from a few minor differences, the very structure of society.

DIDIER MASSEAU

See also Académie Française

Further Reading

Roche, Daniel, *Le siècle des lumières en province: Académies et académiciens provinciaux, 1670–1789*, Paris: Mouton, 1978

Academies of Art. *See* Art Academies

Acoustics

Understood today as the science of vibrations, their production, propagation, and effects, acoustics acquired its scientific status in the 17th century. The new science owed a particular debt to the work of Sir Isaac Newton, who demonstrated the role of elasticity in the formation and transmission of sound waves. In the 18th century two major themes preoccupied scholars: on the one hand, the mathematical understanding of physical phenomena such as the propagation of sound in a fluid or the vibration of strings, and, on the other hand, the most scientific study possible of musical sound and, consequently, of music itself. The development of scientific interest in music as a whole is explained, at least in part, by the fact that tonal harmony had become the norm in nearly all musical compositions.

In 1700 Joseph Sauveur invented the term *acoustique* (acoustics) to designate the science of sounds. Sauveur's investigations concentrated essentially on three areas: the production of sound at a specific frequency; the vibration of strings and air in musical instruments; and the organization of musical sounds into a rational system accompanied by a new notation. Having gleaned from Father Marin Mersenne's work that the frequency of the beats of two organ pipes was equal to the difference in their respective frequencies, Sauveur extrapolated a method for producing a sound of a given frequency (100 Hertz) and reported his findings to the Académie Royale des Sciences de Paris (French Royal Academy of Sciences): "If the pitch at the Paris Opera is determined with respect to a fixed sound, we can be certain to have precisely the same pitch in China." However, this method was to prove highly imprecise in practice. Scientists of the 18th century preferred direct application of the formula giving the frequency of a string's fundamental tone as a function of its physical characteristics (density, tension, etc.). (It may be noted in passing that Sauveur, by recognizing the role played by beat frequency in dissonance, paved the way for Helmholtz's physiological analysis of musical sound.)

Vibrations of Strings and Propagation of Sound

At the very beginning of the 18th century, Sauveur discovered experimentally the possibility of various modes of harmonic vibration of strings and coined the terms *noeuds* (nodes) and *ventres* (antinodes) to describe his results. (Incidentally, he was also the first to use the term *harmonique* [harmonics] in a systematic way.) Sauveur outlined a logical explanation of the phenomenon. If a taut string on a violin, guitar or other stringed instrument is separated by a bridge into two parts, one of which is one-quarter of the length of the other, then the shortest section (which is one-fifth of the total length) yields the fifth harmonic of the fundamental note produced by the whole string. This shorter part transmits its movement across the bridge to the neighboring part, which cannot vibrate with a period of four-fifths of the fundamental—which would be its own note—but instead has to take on the motion of the shorter section. Thus, the longer section subdivides itself into four equal parts, each part being equal in length to the shorter section, thereby forming three nodes beyond the bridge.

To understand the progress made in comparison to the 17th century, it should be emphasized that Mersenne, in his *Harmonie universelle* (1636; Universal Harmony), had no other explanation—or conception—of the vibration of strings than the one that Beeckman had provided in 1615 in his *Journal*: assuming that a string takes the form of an isosceles triangle, of which the apex of the equal sides is the middle of the string, then a string half as long, but with the same composition and form, will be subject to an equal tension. The restoring force toward the position of equilibrium will therefore be the same for both two strings, as will the velocity. (Here, Beeckman and Mersenne were applying the Aristotelian law that velocity is proportional to force.) Because the shorter string has just half the distance to travel, it will vibrate twice as fast as the other one. This explanation suffers from at least two serious errors: it imposes on the strings a form that is clearly contrary to experience, and it excludes from consideration all vibrations that are not fundamental, even though Mersenne could certainly hear the harmonic overtones. Moreover, although he had not gone into detail, Wallis had reported in 1677 an experimental study by two Englishmen of the vibration of strings, with nodes and antinodes. Sauveur's analysis was more detailed, but it was still inadequate—in both experimental and mathematical terms—because it did not envisage the combination of several modes of vibration, nor did it contain any pertinent dynamic calculation.

The mathematical analysis of the motion of strings would be considerably developed in the 18th century, giving rise to what became known as the "querelle des cordes vibrantes" (debate over the vibration of strings), which was definitively resolved only with Fourier's series. This scientific dispute can be summed up as follows. In 1716 Brook Taylor wrote the equation of motion: assuming that the restoring force on each point of a string is proportional to its distance from its position of equilibrium, the curve is then the fundamental sinusoid—the only kind of vibration that Taylor found—and it determines the frequency. In 1728 Jean Bernoulli considered first of all the specific case of a string reduced to 1, 2, . . . , *n* equidistant masses and applied the principle of the conservation of energy. He arrived at the same results as Taylor. Twenty years later, in his *Recherches sur la courbe que forme une corde tendue mise en vibration* (1747; Research on the Curve Formed by a Taut String Set in Vibration) and *Addition au mémoire sur la courbe que forme une corde tendue mise en vibration* (1750; Additional Comments to the Paper about the Curve Formed by a Taut String Set in Vibration), Jean le Rond D'Alembert created a stir by proposing a "direct" and general method entirely different from Taylor's. Applying a change of variables, D'Alembert integrated the partial differential equation known today as the "vibrating strings equation," which he had formulated. In the sinusoidal case, D'Alembert perfected it so as to lead to the process of the separation of variables, which is well known today. The difficulty was that two apparently arbitrary functions appeared in the solution, but D'Alembert refused to believe that the functions were absolutely arbitrary. In 1748 Leonhard Euler went even further, admitting that the function representing a solution at the initial instant could correspond to a curve "freely traced by hand." Daniel Bernoulli took up Taylor's solution again in 1753, generalizing its application to a mixture of harmonics, which are infinite in number if the string has an infinite number of points—a sort of Fourier series ahead of its time. Euler would not accept this solution, claiming that not all types of curves could be represented by infinite series of harmonics. It was then that the young Lagrange, at the beginning of his career, brought every-

one into harmony (to use Montucla's felicitous phrase) by repeating the results of Daniel Bernoulli and Euler with a direct, dynamic study of the motion of each of the points on the string (*Recherches sur la nature et la propagation du son* [1759; Research on the Nature and Propagation of Sound]; *Nouvelles recherches sur la nature et la propagation du son* [1760–61; New Research . . .]; *Additions aux premières recherches sur la nature et la propagation du son* [1760–61; Additions to the First Research . . .]). The transition from the finite case to the infinite case was thus the precursor to Fourier's integral.

At the end of the 18th century, E.F. Chladni performed many experiments on the vibrations of various bodies such as strings, rods, membranes, and bells (*Entdeckungen über die Theorie des Klanges* [1787; Discoveries about the Theory of Sound]). Transposed into two dimensions, Chladni's technique of sprinkling sand on vibrating plates (the sand gathered in nodal lines) resembles Sauveur's technique of hanging paper tabs on the strings so as to make nodes and antinodes visible (these tabs moved toward the nodes as the strings vibrated).

The theoretical study of the propagation of sound waves made little significant progress during the Enlightenment. Conceiving of sound as a succession of collisions progressing from one molecule to the next, in his *Philosophiae Naturalis Principia Mathematica* (1687; Mathematical Principles of Natural Philosophy) Newton had calculated that the speed of sound is proportional to the quotient of the square root of the elasticity divided by the density. Euler and Lagrange adopted this formula, believing that equations for the motion of aerial "fibers" were of the same sort as those for vibrating strings, with elasticity replacing tension. But in the case of spherical waves, no one knew how to integrate these equations. The results were also in conflict with experimental evidence, as scientists were thinking in terms of isothermal compressibility without realizing that sonic compressions occur too rapidly for thermic equilibrium to be established between one fiber and the next, or that the phenomenon relates to adiabatic compressibility (which Pierre-Simon Laplace would learn in 1826). In contrast, the experimental study of the propagation of sound did make some progress. The speed of sound in the air was determined with greater precision than in the 17th century; further, it was found that the speed of sound is compounded by wind speed, that it is independent of pressure, and that it increases with the temperature. Enlightenment scientists also learned that sound travels in liquids (the abbé Jean Antoine Nollet, *Leçons de physique expérimentale* [1743–48; Lectures in Experimental Physics]). Chladni extended his experiments to explore the propagation of sound in solids and various gases.

Musical Acoustics

It is usually argued that physical acoustics became independent of musical theory with the birth of modern mechanics in the 17th century. In the 18th century, the advent of the new tonal music led to the appearance of a body of excellent and quite original work in the field of musical acoustics.

Around the beginning of the 18th century, well before Helmholtz, Sauveur (who was probably more of a physicist than he was a mathematician) intuitively grasped the role played by beats in musical aesthetics. Beat tones are unpleasant; they account for the dissonance of the chords that produce them and the consonance of those that do not. (Sauveur's observation was merely qualitative; he did not quantify dissonance as a function of beat frequency.) However, although the structure of the inner ear was still unknown and the phenomenon of sound had not been studied in physiological terms, a purely numeric analysis of the phenomenon of music was still possible. Sauveur therefore devoted much of his effort to defining what he called a "system" (or "temperament") of music, which he accompanied by an astute use of base-ten logarithms and an original notation that he hoped to see supplant the traditional *do, re, mi,* and so on. (In fact, Sauveur's system of notation did not catch on.) With the benefit of hindsight, it is clear that the question of "temperament"—the approximation by a limited set of fixed notes of the profuse set of proper notes in every possible key—belonged to the 17th century. Mersenne, Christiaan Huygens, Gottfried Wilhelm Leibniz, and their contemporaries had their fixed opinions on the subject—sometimes very elegant ones, as in the case of Huygens and Sauveur. However, the definitive and nearly universal adoption of equal temperament would soon make this sort of thinking fade from the scientific scene. The purely numerical approach to music persisted longer, as exemplified by the young Euler's *Tentamen Novae Theoriae Musicae* (1739; An Attempt at a New Theory of Music).

The prevailing theory in the 17th century was what we call the "coincidence of pulses." A musical sound comprises a regular succession of "pulses," and a chord of two sounds is the more harmonious to the extent that their respective frequencies are synchronous; thus, in the octave, the quintessential consonant interval, one pulse in two of the higher-pitched sound coincides with each pulse of the lower-pitched sound. Euler adopted this concept, which he justified by the beauty of order; it was almost the only nonmathematical notion that enabled him to reduce the aesthetic problem to numeric analysis. However, the true originality of Euler's work lay not so much in this aesthetic aspect as in the extraordinary arithmetical demonstration that he gave to his theory. Beginning with two sounds having frequencies that can be represented by two prime numbers, p and q, Euler estimated their degree on the musical scale at $p + q - 1$. Remarkably, this purely arithmetical reasoning led him to the same estimate provided in the 17th century by the theory of the coincidence of pulses. For more complex cases, Euler took the degree of the lowest common multiple of the number of reduced vibrations (i.e., reduced by their highest common factor). In this way, he managed to encode the ordered "beauty" of the chords of any number of sounds, as well as successions of two chords and even of any number of chords—in other words, of an entire piece of music. His method also enabled him to classify the succession of notes that we call "scales" (limiting himself to those where powers of two, three, and five occur).

Situated at nearly the opposite pole from Euler's numerical approach was that of Jean-Philippe Rameau and D'Alembert. In the latter's *Éléments de musique théorique et pratique suivant les principes de M. Rameau* (1752; Elements of Theoretical and Practical Music Following the Principles of Monsieur Rameau), the mathematician clearly restricts musical theory to the status of a branch of physics, based on two physical phenomena. The first is that all sonorous objects cause to be heard, "apart from the principal and its octave, two other very high-pitched sounds . . . the octave of the fifth . . . [and] . . . the double octave of its major third." The second is that of the similarity of a note and its octaves. Naturally, D'Alembert was perfectly aware that the notes in the first of these cases (including the first octave) correspond respectively to notes with frequencies two, three, and five times that of the fundamental. These observations marked the beginning of the harmonic series; D'Alembert did not extend it since he meant to limit himself to experience, to that which can be heard. Moreover, it was this limitation that enabled him to identify the consonant chords. The inclusion of all partial sounds would have opened the floodgates to cacophony. The combination of the two phenomena immediately provided justification for the perfect major chord, consisting of the fundamental, major third, and fifth: "This chord is the work of nature." The other chords, the scales, and the successions of chords are deduced from the same basic phenomena, but by making use of auxiliary principles of "conformity" (or conventions). For this reason, the laws of harmonics seem to be demonstrated with much less certainty than in Euler's case. Nevertheless, D'Alembert's treatise—which introduced the fundamental bass, the *basso continuo,* and other truly musical concepts—remains much closer to the world of music than Euler's work. D'Alembert was able to impart to Rameau's ideas all the clarity and rigor they had previously lacked. At the beginning of the collaboration between the two men all went well. Before long, however, Rameau claimed to have found in sonorous objects the basis of all science, including mathematics. D'Alembert was obliged to curb this extravagance and answer unjustified criticisms.

Another approach to musical theory was still in its infancy during the Enlightenment. It was the approach that introduced *sons résultants* (combination tones), discovered by the German organist Georg Andreas Sorge in 1740. Italian violinist Guiseppe Tartini discussed such sounds (although he was mistaken with respect to their pitch) in a work that was as confused as those of Euler and D'Alembert were clear and well constructed. Combination tones occur when two simple sounds are emitted with enough intensity so that their "combination" is not linear. The most intense combination tone—virtually the only one to be perceptible—is that for which the frequency is equal to the difference between the frequencies of the initial sounds. (However, the combination tone is not to be confused with any beats that might be produced by the same initial sounds.) In the 19th century Helmholtz would show how combination tones play a part in the consonance or dissonance of chords.

PATRICE BAILHACHE

See also Function; Music

Further Reading

Euler, Leonhard, *Leonhardi Euleri Opera Omnia*, Leipzig and Berlin: Teubner, 1911–

Lagrange, Joseph Louis, *Oeuvres de Lagrange*, vol. 1, Paris: Gauthier-Villars, 1867

Rameau, Jean Philippe, *Nouveau système de musique théorique*, Paris: Ballard, 1726; reprint, Bourg-la-Reine, France: Zurfluh, 1996

Taylor, Brook, *Methodus Incrementorum Directa et Inversa*, London: Pearson, 1715

Truesdell, C., *The Rational Mechanics of Flexible or Elastic Bodies, 1638–1788: Introduction to Leonhardi Euleri Opera Omnia, vol. X et XI Seriei Secundae*, Zurich: Orell Füssli, 1960

Actor

In the Europe of the Enlightenment, recognition of the distinctive art of acting coincided with actors' achievement of social status. In Catholic countries, from the 17th century onward, there was a flagrant contradiction between the cultural prestige of the theatre and its condemnation by the religious authorities, who were especially severe in France and in some cases went so far as to excommunicate actors. In practice, ecclesiastical attitudes were sometimes more tolerant, yet even such widely renowned French actors as Molière or Adrienne Lecouvreur could not be given religious (or indeed, even respectable) funerals, whereas English actor David Garrick was interred with great pomp in London's Westminster Abbey. In France actors did not achieve full status as citizens until the Revolution, when, to varying degrees, some of them, such as Jean-Marie Collot d'Herbois or Talma, became politically active. In contrast, in England and Germany, actors were socially acceptable throughout the 18th century.

The status of touring or provincial actors compared adversely to that of the most prominent actors established in the capital. More generally, the social status of actors in France reflected an extreme polarization of cultural attitudes. On the one hand, actors enjoyed celebrity and the power to fascinate; on the other, they were relegated to the margins of society. They thus became the victims of contempt, sometimes even from those who generally tended to defend them: the *philosophes* of the Enlightenment. Actors were still considered—and often considered themselves—court entertainers rather than professionals, and acting was even seen as a form of prostitution. The scandalous personal lives of some actors cast a shadow over the entire profession, clothing them, in the eyes of the public, in the splendor of vice. However, because of their skills, the depth of their thinking, their actions, and their relationships, a certain number of actors (such as Garrick in England; Mademoiselle Clairon, Lekain, and Talma in France; and August Wilhelm Iffland in Germany) can be considered authentic intellectuals of the Enlightenment. Others continued to live as touring actors or nomadic artists at fairs and in the streets, keeping alive a very different, popular theatrical tradition.

Several notable actors played a significant role in bringing about the theatrical reforms that the *philosophes* of the Enlightenment sought. Garrick, Molé, and Eckhof—an international celebrity who acted in George Lillo's *The London Merchant* (1731) and Denis

Diderot's *Le père de famille* (1758; Father of a Family) as well as in Gotthold Ephraim Lessing's *Emilia Galotti* (1772)—upheld the modern dramatic repertoire. Caroline Neuber lent her support to Johann Christoph Gottsched in the creation of a literary theatre in Germany, and Lekain's collaboration and exchange of views with Voltaire greatly contributed to the evolution of dramatic writing, which increasingly took into account the design of the stages on which plays would be produced. On the Continent, the combined influence of famous actors and the *philosophes* led to the expulsion of privileged spectators from the stage. In England this same reform was also carried out by Garrick, who exercised enormous influence as manager of the Drury Lane Theatre over a period of three decades. However, the "reform of the theatre" could not be initiated by actors or by managers of acting companies. For example, Francesco Antonio Riccoboni did all he could as a manager to endow the theatre with moral and artistic dignity, but the outcome was not decisive. The requirement of unity in dramatic action also affected the manner in which actors played their roles. At the end of the century, the collaboration of Marie-Joseph Chénier, Talma, and David led to a remarkably coherent dramatic aesthetic. It was then that it became possible to develop approaches to theatre that integrated all the components of theatrical art.

In France, as in other European countries, theorists and critics agreed on the need for naturalism, expressiveness, "fire," elegance, and clear diction from actors. Prior to the publication of Rémond de Sainte-Albine's treatise *Le comédien* (1745; The Comedian), theatrical acting had not been deemed worthy of study a specific topic. The art of the great actor was considered to be the same as that of an orator making or "performing" a speech, and the great Roman orators Quintilian and Cicero were cited as theoretical models. While Saint-Albine accepted this rhetorical tradition in his text, he reinterpreted it in terms of the art of the actor. The treatise aroused a controversy, reflected in such texts as Riccoboni's *L'art du théâtre* (1750; The Art of Theatre), Servandoni d'Hannetaire's *Observations sur l'art du comédien* (1774; Observations on the Art of the Comedian), and Diderot's *Paradoxe sur le comédien* (1773; Paradox on the Comedian). These debates were echoed in Germany, through the writings of Lessing and Eckhoff, and culminated in Johann Jakob Engel's treatise *Idées sur le geste et l'action théâtrale* (1795; Ideas on Gesture and Dramatic Action), which is a true semiological study of theatrical gesture. The most vigorously debated question concerned the role of sincerity in the art of a great actor. Diderot held that a great actor is an objective one, who creates a character based on an ideal model that he alone has conceived. Language and its origins also posed problems for the Enlightenment.

Diderot had already addressed these issues in his *Lettre sur les sourds et les muets* (1751; Letter on the Deaf and Mute). The art of the actor seemed to him to be torn between a language governed by conventions and a language of "natural" expressiveness. If, in effect, gesture and inflection were the distinguishing marks of "original" or "natural" language, then dramatic art could free itself from conventions and return to the sources of natural energy. In principle, the emotions of the spectator should thereby be intensified. In Diderot's opinion, the aim was to break with both the rhetorical conventions of acting and the theoretical positions that subordinated dramatic acting to the Logos (the word), thus reducing acting to the status of mere illustration. Theatrical reform thus entailed going to extremes in giving independence to dramatic language. However, Diderot's opinions were subject to change, depending on whether he adopted the point of view of the actor or that of the spectator. When he adopted the spectator's vantage point, Diderot wanted violent, natural, sublime emotions; when he imagined the actor's point of view, he could not avoid the question of art and its duplicity: hence the "paradox" treated in his *Paradoxe sur le comédien*.

It is very difficult to determine the extent to which these theories exercised an active influence on dramatic acting. Diderot's *Paradoxe sur le comédien* was unknown in the 18th century, although its central thesis was known, as it had appeared in "Observations sur une brochure intitulée Garrick ou les acteurs anglais" (1770; Observations on a Booklet Entitled "Garrick; or, the English Actors"), an article published in Friedrich Melchior von Grimm's *Correspondance littéraire*. While it may be said that no "revolution" took place in acting as a result of the various theoretical positions taken up by one group or another, it is still possible to speak of an "evolution" in acting. It is likely, for example, that Diderot and Voltaire did have some influence on the way Lekain and Mademoiselle Clairon performed their roles. A style of acting emerged that, compared to past styles, was more active, more physical, and more naturalistic in its codes. Voltaire was deeply affected by this tendency toward physicality and naturalism, which he had helped to stimulate, but which also alarmed his more conservative tastes. He had advocated gestures and physical presence but was embarrassed when Mademoiselle Clairon abandoned the proprieties far too obviously. In this regard Diderot was more consistent than Voltaire: he defended even the most daring innovations that the great *comédienne* had introduced.

Changes in the style of acting were part of the more general evolution of the theatre and of dramatic genres, but acting styles in turn helped shape developments in theatre and contributed to the emergence of new genres.

Until the 18th century, differences between tragic and comic acting had been clearly defined by tradition; during the age of the Enlightenment, the quest for intermediate genres presented new problems for actors. Because tragic acting was more closely bound by convention than was comic acting, the former was more difficult to reform. The frequent use of lilting or chanting when speaking dramatic verse was far removed from the natural tone that the reformers sought, and it seemed extremely difficult to introduce a greater degree of physicality into the performance while maintaining the dignity that was expected of tragedy. Garrick, who was experienced in all the dramatic genres, was justly celebrated in Europe, and especially in France, because he offered an alternative to the conventional French style of tragic acting: those who saw him could catch a glimpse of something of the "Shakespearean sublime." The art of the brilliant tragedian Talma may have been influenced by the years that he had spent in England in his youth.

The traditions of comic acting were less constricting and more diverse than those of tragic acting. In Paris, for example, the tradition of the Théâtre-Français coexisted with the Italian tradition, in which boldly stylized acting was nevertheless perceived to be livelier and less formal than the conventional French style. The acting style of high comedy served as the primary point of reference for drama—a new, more flexible alternative to tragedy that came to incorporate both tragic theatricality and Italian verve. However, nothing in the develop-

ment of this emergent genre indicates that there was any corollary "intermediate" style of acting, although it seems that these experiments took something from the origins of melodramatic performance. Actors such as Molé in France and Iffland in Germany laid the foundations for this style of acting. Europe has rarely known so many actors of unquestionable genius, and without them the 18th century could never have been seen as a golden age of theatre.

PIERRE FRANTZ

See also Drama; Fairground Theatre; Pantomime; Paradox

Further Reading

Barnett, Dene, *The Art of Gesture: The Practices and Principles of 18th-Century Acting,* Heidelberg: Winter, 1987

Iffland, August Wilhelm, *Meine theatralische Laufbahn,* Leipzig: Goschen, 1798; reprint, Stuttgart: Reclam, 1976.

Price, Cecil, *Theatre in the Age of Garrick,* Oxford: Blackwell, and Totowa, New Jersey: Rowman and Littlefield, 1973

Rougement, Martine de, *La vie théâtrale en France au XVIIIe siècle,* Paris: Champion, 1988

West, Shearer, *The Image of the Actor: Verbal and Visual Representation in the Age of Garrick and Kemble,* London: Pinter, and New York: St. Martin's Press, 1991

Administration. *See* Bureaucracy

Adventurer

In the 18th century the word "adventurer" lost its military or gallant connotations and took on new meanings in the majority of European languages. However, the notion of the adventurer remained vague, as elusive as the type of person it denoted. There appear to have been four characteristics that, taken together, help us to

define the adventurer. First, he had no stable resources and no fixed place in society, meaning that he had to make do by living on his wits. Second, sooner or later he broke the law, thus running specific, concrete risks such as duels, prison, or exile. Third, he was by choice or by necessity a traveler, going from country to country, nearly always within Europe. Fourth, he had received the basic formal education common to all these countries, allowing him to infiltrate the aristocratic or bourgeois worlds in which he sought his livelihood. However, we should note that these four characteristics could be present in varying proportions and that it was rare for anyone to be a lifelong adventurer: many alternated between phases of adventure and calm, or settled down when it was time to do so.

It was generally a social disparity that made someone turn into an adventurer. Lack of money could drive a young man from a good family to seek out—by whatever means he could—the lifestyle that he believed should be his. Or, in a different scenario of social disparity, the educated son of an artisan or a tradesman could make an attempt to improve his station by fraudulent means. In the latter instance, the adventurer would often spend time as a monk or a soldier of fortune in the Church or the army, before escaping from an unbearable discipline into a life of crime. Other adventurers were social misfits from birth. Casanova, for example, was the son of an actress and spent his whole life in close proximity to the world of the theatre, which was by definition outside any social hierarchy.

How did one cease being an adventurer? In many cases, death stopped the adventurer in mid-career: Chevrier died in Rotterdam, Maubert de Gouvest in Altona, and the chevalier de Mainvilliers in the vicinity of Danzig. Others chose to end their lives themselves: Tilly shot himself in the head, Albergoni hanged himself, Stiepan Zannowich bled himself to death. Still others rotted away until death liberated them: Théodore de Neuhof in prison for debt, Afflisio in the galleys, du Laurens in a monastery, Cagliostro in an Italian dungeon, Vincent Gaudio in prison, and then, having gone mad, in an asylum in Amsterdam. Beyond a certain age, they could no longer be adventurers. As Casanova wrote at the age of 58: "Whenever I consider becoming an adventurer again, I look at myself in the mirror and start to laugh." The luckiest ones finally managed to settle down, usually in stages, after more or less extended relapses into their former way of life.

As long as they were in good health, adventurers were travelers first and foremost. It was often necessity that spurred them on after they had been banished because of some scandal or other. In such a case, a journey could entail a change in identity. Adventurers assumed a sort of social virginity, starting over by taking another name, laying claim to a title such as baron, count, or prince, whichever seemed the most useful. But necessity was joined with pleasure, and an adventurer who had enough money could travel all over Europe as a dilettante, using French as his lingua franca. Preferred itineraries developed along the main travel routes, and a very specific travel guide took shape, in which the great

cosmopolitan cities, such as London, Paris, Amsterdam, Naples, and Venice, shone brightly. However, Madrid was not recommended, since it was too zealously religious, while Vienna was said to be spoiled by the prudishness of the Empress Maria Theresa. Smaller cities could be favored if their rulers willingly listened to men with ideas—such rulers included, for example, King Stanislas of Poland; Cobenzl, the Austrian Minister in Brussels; and the Prince of Hesse. Preferred locations also included the cities of great conferences, such as Utrecht or Augsburg; and those known for their spas, such as Aachen, Plombières, or Spa itself, where highly varied but transient societies were favorable to profitable encounters. In all their travels, adventurers frequented the same places. Inns were centers for the cosmopolitan intermingling of people from all walks of life, and theatres offered the same advantages, as well as the entertaining company of actors and the merry glitter of appearances.

Throughout their wanderings the adventurers' dream was to make a success of their lives, even if it meant going from one profession to another to do so. As swindlers they dealt in false bills of exchange; as impostors they passed themselves off as princes. Stiepan Zannowich, for example, used the name "Castriotto of Albania" and managed to win the hospitality and support of two kings, Stanislas of Poland and Frederick William of Prussia. Still more astonishing was the success of Théodore de Neuhof, who ended up becoming king of Corsica. In truth, what brought the adventurers the most success was to take advantage of their knowledge of the world and profit from their ability to please. To begin with, this meant pleasing women, either vulgarly, as did Tiretta, a personage who appears in Casanova's account, or more subtly, as when Tilly capitalized on his American divorce. Above all, however, it meant pleasing the powerful, starting with the kings who dispensed jobs and rewards. If a prince was not available, ministers and lords were very useful to those who knew how to beg elegantly, that is, in enough of an offhand manner to seem not to be in need. Failing a post or a large sum, an ornate snuffbox with a portrait of a lord could serve as a letter of introduction in the next adventure. At least, this was the game that top-flight adventurers played, skillfully adopting a tone of respect without sycophancy and familiarity without impudence.

Other adventurers, rejected or treated as subordinates, were glad to make money from undergoing conversions (some perhaps sincere) in line with the wishes of dominant religions. In London, Psalmaanaazaar used more than a little imagination, claiming to be a Formosan victim of the French Jesuits; he invented a language for his supposedly native Formosa and even succeeded in teaching it to future missionaries.

However, religion was less profitable than gambling, where the gold flowed freely as long as one was not overly scrupulous about how one went about attaining it. Ange Goudar was able to publish *L'histoire des Grecs, ou de ceux qui corrigent la fortune au jeu* (1757; The History of the Greeks; or, Those Who Mitigate Fortune with Gambling), in which he revealed a certain number of the tools of his trade, including the use of his wife to lure his victims. A skillful player could make a living from gambling, provided that he did not go too far. Although the morality of the age was indulgent on this point, a cheat who was recognized as such would have to leave the game and, in any case, would no longer be able to find anyone with whom to gamble. Another advantage of gambling was that it could be used as a social passport, allowing adventurers to penetrate circles that would otherwise have remained closed to them. In those circles, they exploited the gullibility of the public by becoming merchants of dreams, or charlatans. Cagliostro and Saint-Germain made themselves out to be initiates and grand masters of the cabala. Casanova pretended to be protected by a spirit that passed all sorts of secrets to him by way of a mysterious pyramid. He used it to fascinate the wealthy Mademoiselle d'Urfé and thus extract enormous sums of money from her. But in order for the imposture to last, he had to have genuine information. Casanova knew enough chemistry to perform certain scientific conjuring tricks and enough cryptography to make his supernatural contacts plausible; and what he did not know, he invented. He was skilled at improvising from small clues and at passing off his prudent silences as though they were profound.

Adventurers sometimes tried their hand at genuine professions as merchants, engineers, manufacturers, panners for gold, managers of lotteries, organizers of shows, and so on. But they would burn their fingers when such undertakings became prolonged, for their preferred terrain was that of grand and fabulous projects: they were not interested in realizing them or in making a success of them. If they placed themselves at the service of the state, it was usually in gangs that dealt in secret diplomacy or espionage. Adventurers approached the intellectual professions as more or less genuine secretaries, nominal librarians, or occasional tutors, but they generally gave up such inferior positions in order to make themselves accepted as equals in the world of their employers. In general, adventurers rejected hard work and self-improvement in favor of brilliant but selective improvisation.

Nevertheless, some adventurers became writers and left a body of work to posterity, albeit reluctantly, renouncing both the ambition of a true adventurer, because the writing profession was not respected at all, and the pleasures of adventure, since writing a life prevented one from living it. To be an amateur of belles lettres, tossing off the occasional little verses, madrigals, or drawing-room comedies was all very well: to earn a living by writing was quite another matter. It was as a side effect of their careers that some adventurers, driven by necessity, had recourse to writing, except in those cases where it served as a means to make oneself noticed by the rich and powerful. If, therefore, some adventurers have to be included among the greatest writers of the century, this was doubtless despite their best intentions. Pierre-Augustin Caron de Beaumarchais put as much energy into selling guns as in writing for the theatre. The abbé Prévost appears to have given up writing once his struggle to survive became less arduous. One finds this pattern even in Jean-Jacques Rousseau's career, with his decided contempt for the "profession of author" and his desire to settle down once he had reached middle age. As for Casanova, he always had a taste for literature, but it was only when he was getting along in years that he resigned himself to being recognized as an author and published conciliatory works in the hope of securing his return to Venice. It was at Dux, in the final years of his life, that he undertook his *Histoire de ma vie* (The Story of My Life), in order to relive his former happiness through writing. The nature of the life of an adventurer, the impulses that led him to such a lifestyle, and the incoherence inherent in the adventurous life give the works of these authors a distinctive tone, even if, as far as the thoughts they expressed are concerned, adventurers were less inventive than one might have expected. They were too concerned with reassuring, and with being accepted by those in power, to risk presenting innovative ideas.

Finally, it may be asked why adventurers had such an easy time in the Europe of the Enlightenment. First, it is necessary to keep in mind the prestige of the traveler who inspired the curiosity and dispelled the boredom of a bored and blasé society. Adventurers not only came from other places and exploited their exoticism, but also brought with them a sense of vitality and a contagious taste for happiness because they lived intensely, enjoying the moment. In a cosmopolitan Europe, they also exploited the prestige of the French, whose language they spoke. In addition, adventurers made use of the networks of Freemasonry, since their own networks were fairly unstable. Adventurers often knew each other and sometimes collaborated, but they always kept a watchful eye on one another. Finally, the hierarchical order of the old society was still solid enough not to fear these unclassifiable individuals but was already weakened enough to appreciate their originality: adventurers were felt to be more entertaining than dangerous. Favored by this amused tolerance, the adventurers of Europe were the secret explorers of the social ladder, bringing information about foreign customs, transplanting ideas, and thus stimulating a process of questioning of which they themselves were often unaware.

SUZANNE ROTH

See also Autobiography

Further Reading

Casanova, Giacomo, *History of My Life*, 12 vols., translated by Willard R. Trask, New York: Harcourt, Brace and World, 1966–71; London: Longmans, 1967–71 (original French edition, 1826–38)

Roth, Suzanne, *Les aventuriers au XVIIIe siècle*, Paris: Éditions Galilée, 1980

Aesthetics

In his *Kritik der reinen Vernunft* (1781; Critique of Pure Reason), Immanuel Kant justifies his appropriation of the term "aesthetics" to designate "the science of all the a priori principles of sensibility" by explaining that, "only the Germans now use the word 'aesthetics' to designate what others call the 'critique of taste.'" Although Kant eventually abandons the Greek etymological sense of "aesthetics" (in his *Kritik der Urteilskraft* [1790; Critique of Judgment]), his temporary redefinition nonetheless set the course for the development of the modern meaning of the word. Throughout *Kritik der reinen Vernunft,* Kant attempts to develop the concept of sensory knowledge, that is, knowledge that combines experience (knowledge of objects) and knowledge gained by understanding (intellectual activity). He argues that sensory knowledge is not an amalgamation of sensations, but is instead endowed with a priori "forms" through which understanding conditions our reception of objects; reason, in contrast, attempts to find its bearings by means of "ideas"—by seeking a unity that is inaccessible through experience.

This separation of the concepts on which theoretical knowledge is based, on the one hand, and the concepts of reason, on the other, would leave us torn between necessity and freedom if these two types of knowledge were not brought together by the faculty of judgment. Kant attempts to explain this process of reconciliation in the *Kritik der Urteilskraft,* in which he makes judgment the key faculty joining understanding and reason. Robert Klein has shown that the faculty of judgment also takes over the role formerly attributed to the imagination in ancient epistemology, becoming the locus where sensibility and thought converge (see Klein). Judgment does not work according to universal principles that would necessarily determine its object. On the

contrary, judgment is active; it is endowed with an inherent principle that allows it to unify particular phenomena by attributing to them a finality that resides in its way of perceiving, and not in the things themselves. Although we cannot understand the precise process through which judgments are formed, the faculty of judgment essentially involves positing a harmonious congruence between our faculties and nature. Through this congruence, we reach a subjective state that becomes the basis for our sense of pleasure. Although this state is subjective, it is nonetheless universal and common to all human beings. This state is a judgment of taste, an aesthetic judgment that does not correspond to the satisfaction of a desire; it is therefore a disinterested judgment. This state does not depend on a sensation—it is the form of the object, not the object's substance, that is important to us—nor does the judgment depend on a concept: it is not even necessary to know the nature of the object that we judge to be beautiful. Aesthetic judgment is a judgment that can be exercised on both natural objects and on works of art. Kant's definitions thus render inoperable two of the principal criteria used to define beauty in the 18th century—pleasantness and utility—by excluding them from aesthetic judgment proper.

Kant locates aesthetic judgment in a specific area of mental activity in which "free play" between the faculty of understanding and the imagination occurs. This activity is somewhat paradoxical, because while it might seem to be governed by a law, it actually remains free, and while it might seem to attribute a certain finality to objects, their specific purpose is actually unknown. The foundation of this activity is too general to be useful to understanding; it is the idea that a subjective conformity exists between nature and our faculties, that it is our very humanity that controls the possibility of aesthetic judgment. Kant solves the problem of the status of aesthetic judgment that preoccupied the whole of the 18th century by separating the issue of taste from morality and from pleasure, thus paving the way for the establishment of autonomy in the field of art. At the same time, however, by virtue of the role that he assigns to our humanity, he perpetuates the conception of art as the expression of moral ideas—a notion that was already well entrenched in thinking on art throughout the 18th century.

In his letters "on aesthetic education" (1793–95), Friedrich von Schiller develops the notion of "play" in a discussion that makes aesthetics the focus of the social domain. He takes up Jean-Jacques Rousseau's position, denouncing the dangers of an intellect forced to function on an abstract plane imposed by the modern state. However, Schiller is writing after the Reign of Terror. Therefore, in opposition to Rousseau's *Du contrat social* (1762; The Social Contract), he makes art rather than government the agent of regeneration: its pedagogical mission is to restore to us the totality of our nature, which the arts of social life have disturbed. Formal and sensual drives are reconciled in the *Spieltrieb* (drive to play), which is concerned with beauty and which, as a "living form," is neither action nor passion, neither abstraction nor pure impression. According to Schiller, in human society the dynamic mental state that overpowers nature comes first and is followed by the ethical plane, which gives nature a morality. Finally, the aesthetic state subordinates the individual will to the general will. In this way, the aesthetic state perfects the general will through the nature of the individual and brings true society into being. Only beauty can bring forth the social character of human beings; only taste can generate harmony in society, because taste is the source of harmony in the individual. The pleasure of sensation is purely individual; the pleasure of knowledge belongs only to the species; and only the pleasure given by beauty combines sensibility and understanding and reunites us simultaneously as individuals and as species.

In his lectures of 1823 and 1826, Georg Wilhelm Friedrich Hegel adopts this idea of the role of aesthetics in human development and accords it higher importance than art: "Art no longer has the high purpose for us that it once did"; "art, far from being the noblest form of the mind, only reaches its real crowning point in knowledge" (*Vorlesungen über die Aesthetik* [1835–38; Introduction to Aesthetics]). According to Hegel, aesthetic beauty is the first step toward reconciling pure thought and the external and the transitory; but beauty remains inferior to thought in that beauty does not penetrate the mind completely, nor does beauty create an idea from the conception of forms. On the other hand,

aesthetics is necessarily modern because it corresponds to the progress of the mind: beyond art as a living experience, we have reached a stage where thinking about art has priority. Aesthetics surpasses art and beauty becomes the Idea of beauty. Thus, Hegel attributes the late emergence of the term "aesthetics" to the high degree of consciousness and reflection attained in general by his own era. Aesthetics, as a global reflection on art rooted in philosophy, therefore manifested itself later than the more confused remarks by experts on taste or by theoreticians concerned with beauty. In order to make this leap, art had to attain, or at least had to envisage, a civic role; it could no longer develop according to the commands or the tastes of individuals, no matter how well educated those individuals might be (see Crow).

The term "aesthetics" in its modern sense is used for the first time by Alexander Baumgarten in his *Meditationes Philosophicae de Nonnulis ad Poema Pertinentibus* (1735; Reflections on Poetry) and then in *Aesthetica* (1750–58; Aesthetics). As Kant said, the word "aesthetics" was at that time used only by German writers. Baumgarten tackles an important problem in 18th-century epistemology, that of the nature of sensory experience and of its relationship to artistic form. He further develops Gottfried Wilhelm Leibniz's contrast between distinct (or logical) knowledge, on the one hand, and sensory (or aesthetic) knowledge, on the other. In so doing, Baumgarten refers not only to philosophical schools but also to the paths of aesthetic thought of the age. One theory conceives of art in terms of how its effects on our senses—a subjective version of the social practice of seeking to refine the senses and educate the emotions. Another theory of beauty—often more academic than the first—attempts to base beauty on the objectivity of forms. A third line, joining together objectivity and subjectivity, addresses the ideal that is or is not present in a work of art; the viewer or reader can observe the traces of this ideal, particularly in rough drafts.

By stressing the fact that our knowledge is rooted in the senses and by linking all sensation to the pleasure or the pain that accompanies it, John Locke paves the way for theories that aim to communicate both the pleasure of art and the pleasure received by the senses. All pleasure derives from the satisfaction of a lack. According to the abbé Jean-Baptiste Dubos, in his *Réflexions critiques sur la poésie et sur la peinture* (1719; Critical Reflections on Poetry and Painting), the human mind needs constant stimulation; people "need to be busy in order to avoid boredom," and this fact explains "the attraction human beings feel for lively passions." Pleasure or displeasure cause the emotions to rebound onto the person who feels it; this type of theory implies that self-awareness is present in any reaction. Therefore, sensation and emotion cannot be entirely distinguished from one another: a sensation accompanies each surge of feeling. According to Dubos, the life of the emotions needs to be constantly nourished and art provides this nourishment with the least danger. The consciousness we have of the movement of our inner life and of the pleasure we take in that consciousness is reinforced by our realization that we are in front of a painting or at the theatre and that we are not confronted by a real danger. The effect that a work of art has upon us—and not the work itself—determines the work's value; neither formal rules nor the three traditional unities can guarantee its quality: "The reasoning of others can easily convince us of the contrary of what we think, but not of the contrary of what we feel." Dubos is thus able to include in his theory effects that not only have nothing to do with intellectual knowledge, but that go far beyond it: music, for example, has "an analogy with our passions, a certain power to depict them that words alone can never attain." Dubos cites the *Spectator,* in which Joseph Addison, in articles on "the pleasures of the imagination" (1711), had insisted on the subjectivity of these pleasures. Addison contends that an imaginative person "often feels more satisfaction at the sight of fields and meadows than would someone else who owned them." He thus confirms the mediating role of the imagination between sensation and knowledge: "the pleasures of the imagination, taken in their widest sense, are neither as vulgar as those of the senses nor as refined as those of the understanding." He asserts that the most important and most powerful sense is sight: "By the pleasures of the imagination, I mean only those pleasures that originate in sight." Dubos agrees: "sight has more power over the soul than the other senses." This theory leads, especially for Dubos, to a comparison between poetry and painting that takes into consideration the factor of time, along with status of signs—natural for painting, "arbitrary" and "artificial" for poetry—as integral parts of the experience of the work of art.

The contribution of each of the senses differs in quality—or, according to Kant, in "form." The sculptor of the *Laocoön* group hides ugliness from our view by avoiding the grimace and the mouth open in suffering, while the poet transforms the ugliness of the forms by presenting them in succession (Gotthold Ephraim Lessing, *Laokoon* [1766; Laocoön: An Essay upon the Limits of Painting and Poetry]). Taste serves as a model for distinguishing between pleasures; taste "binds us to something through feeling" (Montesquieu), but the term can also be applied to intellectual things, because the mind acquires knowledge both through ideas and through feelings: "Although we contrast ideas with feelings, when the mind understands something, it feels it."

Since taste does not follow rules, it "is not a theoretical knowledge," and for that reason judgments of taste risk being eccentric. This risk of eccentricity explains the efforts to ascribe taste only to a particular social class: "If [talent] has more to do with a certain refined pleasure shared by high society, it is known as taste." The same risk also explains satirical works such as Alexander Pope's *Epistle to the Right Honourable Earl of Burlington* (1731), which attacks extravagant taste, or David Hume's essay "Of the Standard of Taste," or the book by the painter William Hogarth, *The Analysis of Beauty: Written with a View of Fixing the Fluctuating Ideas of Taste* (1753). Again, it is Kant who explains how subjectivity and universality exist simultaneously in making judgments of taste.

Authors of essays and treatises about beauty attempted to break the vicious circle: is something beautiful because it is pleasurable, or does it please because it is beautiful? To this end, they described what Jean-Pierre de Crousaz terms "the real and natural characteristics of beauty" (*Traité du beau* [1715; Treatise on Beauty]), valid everywhere and for everyone: variety, unity, order, and proportion. "Beauty" could be applied to customs, governments, colors—and especially to virtue. According to Francis Hutcheson the Elder, our sense of beauty is like a sixth sense that responds to uniformity within variety. That response functions as the objective "purpose" in the object that is being contemplated, and toward which this sense is directed. Love of beauty and love of virtue come together because of the benevolent favor of Providence. (In his analysis of finality without purpose, and in the care he takes to differentiate the role of each concept, Kant untangled the problem of taste, morality, and pleasure, and created aesthetics as an independent area of inquiry.) However, a more concrete theory of the beautiful emerges not only with Denis Diderot, in his article "Beau" (Beauty) in the *Encyclopédie,* but with the architect Charles-Étienne Briseux, for example, who refers to the work of D'Alembert. Briseux limits his discussion to a theory of proportion; on the other hand, Diderot elaborates this theory to explain not only the instinct of the artist seeking a beautiful form but also the development of art in history. Great masters have developed by means of "lengthy observation, consummate experience . . . a quiet, secret sense of analogy acquired after an infinite number of observations of which the memory fades but the impression remains" (Diderot, *Salon de 1767* [1767 Exhibition]). According to these thinkers, beauty resides in "the perception of relationships." They are thus able to make progress toward an ideal that has never in fact been fully realized and that is perhaps better grasped in a sketch full of energy that leaves the viewer free to complete the finished form.

In fact, the 18th century saw the development of a whole series of aesthetic theories. Diderot himself, great critic that he was, contributed to the dissemination of a great number of them: the practical aesthetics of artists, gleaned from his relations with Jean-Baptiste Siméon Chardin, Étienne-Maurice Falconet, and Jacques-Germain Soufflot; a moral aesthetics, arising from his position as leader of the Encyclopedists; a civic aesthetics, born from his desire to make art an instrument of social reform; and, lastly, a formal aesthetics, defined by his ability as a great thinker, an intellectual before that term was even coined. Nevertheless, it was not until Kant that aesthetics became a field in its own right.

MARIAN HOBSON

See also Art Criticism; Beautiful; Ideal; Imagination; Sublime; Taste

Further Reading

Becq, Annie, *Genèse de l'esthétique française moderne: De la raison classique à l'imagination créatrice, 1680–1814*, Pisa: Pacini, 1984

Crousaz, Jean-Pierre de, *Traité du beau*, Amsterdam: Honoré, 1715

Crow, Thomas E., *Painters and Public Life in Eighteenth-Century Paris*, New Haven, Connecticut: Yale University Press, 1985

Hobson, Marian, *The Object of Art: The Theory of Illusion in Eighteenth-Century France*, Cambridge and New York: Cambridge University Press, 1982

Klein, Robert, *Form and Meaning: Essays on the Renaissance and Modern Art*, New York: Viking Press, 1979 (original French edition, 1970)

Nivelle, Armand, *Les théories esthétiques en Allemagne de Baumgarten à Kant*, Paris: Les Belles Lettres, 1955

Affinity

It is exceedingly difficult to pinpoint the origins of the notion of affinity. Medieval alchemists used the term to refer to a far more ancient idea, already considered to be self-evident when Empedocles explained the perpetual transformation of the cosmos in terms of a rivalrous and complementary relationship between love (a unifying force) and hate (a separating force). Historically, the notion of affinity was not limited to any particular discipline. Like many of the terms that come down to us from alchemy, the concept of affinity survived in two areas that are widely divergent today—the science of chemistry and the metaphoric "chemistry" of emotional relationships between human beings. Johann Wolfgang Goethe's novel *Die Wahlverwandtschaften* (1809; Elective Affinities) takes up this dual meaning of the word "affinity," in a double opposition between, on the one hand, amorous passion and the civil laws of marriage, and, on the other, as analogues, chemical activity and mechanical behavior. Today novelists, poets, or sometimes psychologists are the only ones who think in terms of emotional or spiritual affinities between people. Chemical affinity, in contrast, has had a genuine history marked by a succession of sudden developments, in which the relationship between chemistry and physics came into play at certain crucial points. This article will thus focus exclusively on the history of the concept of chemical affinity.

For "corpuscularists" such as Robert Boyle, the already traditional notion of affinity was typical of the kind of fictitious ideas that endowed chemical substances and elements with the appearance of being alive and possessing feeling or even knowledge. Affinity had no place in the theories of those scientists who recognized in matter only "primary" properties that can be derived from the form and motion of the final components. On the other hand, for Georg Ernst Stahl, the chemist who at the beginning of the 18th century fought against corpuscular mechanism, the concept of affinity had a precise meaning, "the attraction of like by like," and it offered an explanation of chemical reactions. In his view the fact that nitric acid attacks metals attested to the two substances sharing the same principle, which Stahl named "combustible" or "phlogistic earth."

However, it was by losing its association with the theme of attraction of likes that affinity would become one of the key notions of 18th-century chemistry. The starting point for this development is "Question 31" of Sir Isaac Newton's *Opticks* (1704), in which Newton introduces the relative force of attraction of a series of reagents for a particular substance. The order of the series is determined by the capacity of one of the reagents in the series to displace and replace another reagent in the series associated with the substance in question. In 1718 the French chemist Étienne-François Geoffroy presented to the Académie Royale des Sciences (French Royal Academy of Sciences) a table that incorporated Newton's ordering principle. In a context dominated by Cartesian thought, Geoffroy made no direct reference to "forces" and spoke instead in terms of "relationships." Before long, chemists were saying "relationship" and "affinity" indiscriminately, and the construction of ever more comprehensive, ever more precise tables, became one of the classic tasks of chemists all across Europe. Thus, when Scottish chemist Joseph Black identified "fixed air" (carbon dioxide) in 1756, he proudly added a column to the existing tables, ordering the reagents that displaced one another in their association with the newly identified gas.

At the heart of 18th-century chemistry, affinity (in the sense of a relationship or an elective attraction) thus held a key position. The concept offered chemists everywhere the prospect of a systematic enrichment of their science, a veritable common "research project" that accompanied implementation of a new concept of the chemical reaction as "displacement." But affinity also promised a theoretical understanding of "displacement," and on that account became a field for controversy between those who wanted to subordinate chemistry to Newtonian forces and those for whom affinity symbolized the idea that chemical activity could not be reduced to the interplay of mechanical masses.

Roger Boscovich and the comte de Buffon were the main champions of the theory based on Newtonian forces. They maintained that it was the minute distance over which the forces act that caused the complication of chemical activity and the specificity of chemical properties. According to Boscovich, when the distance was small, the force could be either attractive or repellent. In Buffon's view these distances required taking into account the configurations of bodies, an added complication. Contrary to Boscovich, who believed that chemistry, having become intelligible in principle, would remain empirical in practice, Buffon was convinced that his "great-nephews" (i.e., scientists of the future) would be able to calculate the progress of chemical reactions as Newton had calculated the progress of the planets.

In the other camp, "Enlightenment chemists" in France took up Stahl's fight against the imperialism of "mechanics"—that is, the science of masses, whether defined in Cartesian or Newtonian terms. Thus, Gabriel-François Venel, author of the article "Chimie" (1753; Chemistry) in the *Encyclopédie*, presents affinity as the "knot" or binding factor operating in mixed bonds, which he contrasts to the aggregative bonding—explained by simple proximity—posited by the mechanists.

The quarrel applied not only to ideas but also to the very meaning of the tables and the chemical reactions that they arrayed. In the view of "Enlightenment chemists" such as Pierre Joseph Macquer, author of the *Dictionnaire de chimie* (1766; Dictionary of Chemistry), affinity characterized the "principles" or "elements" quantitatively, in terms of their interrelations. In other words, the object of chemistry was first of all to characterize qualitative properties intrinsic to substances, affinity being an instrument for approximating the strength of each reagent, which was considered one of that reagent's properties. In contrast, "Newtonian" chemists viewed affinity as a purely relational property. Any substance taken independently of others was considered to be devoid of chemical property, just as an isolated mass is devoid of acceleration. As a corollary, affinity was not the way to characterize the properties of a substance. It explained those properties and made sense both of the bond and the transformation of bonds brought about by a reaction. As a result, from an empirical standpoint, affinity constituted the main goal of a chemistry in need of a theory that would enable chemists to deduce the chemical reactions that the tables had arranged in order.

Swedish chemist Torbern Bergman's Newtonian views prompted him to undertake the monumental task of studying and putting all possible chemical reactions into tables (published between 1775 and 1783). By doing so, Bergman was to transform the very notion of chemical reaction. The only chemical reactions known and explored until then those that were "interesting" from the points of view both of the laboratory and of the artisan. In modern terms these were "complete" reactions—the ones that allowed the laboratory chemist to isolate and identify substances and offered artisans the processes needed for the creation of new products. For Bergman, in contrast, any and all reactions were of interest and were deemed worthy of experimental investigation. Bergman's comprehensive experimentation led him to encounter problems that, until then, had been unknown: a number of the reactions were incomplete and led to a mixture of reagents. However, Bergman viewed such reactions as anomalies. By definition, affinity, which he called "elective attraction," was an all-or-nothing concept: he believed that the strongest reagent, in its association with another like reagent, completely expelled the weakest reagent. Nevertheless, the "elective" property, accepted as self-evident by all chemists of the 18th century, was explicitly challenged from then on. Another unresolved issue was that the "circumstances" Bergman had to invoke—the "physical factors" that were an obstacle to a true chemical attraction—created a conceptual distance between Newtonian chemistry and the astronomical model.

This relationship between "circumstances" and the invincible force of attractions is dramatized in Goethe's novel. Edward and Odile have already met, and their mutual indifference has reassured Edward and Charlotte when they make the decision to take Odile into their household. However, passion, like chemistry, is an "art of circumstances," in which everything depends on the way in which the bodies come into contact with one another. Whether in the field of human passions or chemical reactions, each encounter is an adventure that escapes rational prediction. Edward and Odile will fall passionately in love.

What was normal and what was abnormal? In *La statique chimique* (1803; The Chemical Equilibrium), Claude Louis Berthollet proposes to reverse the interpretation of Bergman's tables. What physical circumstances explain, he argues, is none other than the complete reaction. (A product of reaction escapes from the reactive process as it occurs, whether by precipitation in solid form or volatilization in gaseous form.) The general case is an evolution toward a mixture in which reagents and the products of reaction coexist, in proportions that can be determined by the chemist. The affinity evidenced by the reaction means that chemistry does not follow the logic of celestial mechanics, but rather the laws of statics, the science of mechanical equilibriums. Statics entails the study of the state of equilibrium produced by a chemical reaction and the possibilities for modifying it.

However, Berthollet retained for affinity the double interpretative role that it possessed in the 18th century—the capacity to explain both "chemical bonds" and their modification through chemical reactions. However, if affinities had ceased to be "elective," governed by an all-or-nothing logic in the context of reactions, how can the same be so where compounds are concerned? Berthollet concludes that what we call a chemical compound also derives from a mixture and that the relative proportions of simple substances entering into a compound (which analytic chemistry had begun to evaluate systematically) are only average proportions. This must be true if affinity is a complex expression of Newtonian forces, since these cannot justify a qualitative "election"—a mutually exclusive choice—but only quantitative proportions susceptible to continual variation.

What exactly, then, is affinity from the point of view of the chemist? According to Berthollet, affinity is the sole factor entering into the definition of equilibrium that the chemist cannot manipulate, and it defines the "chemical mass" as such. By varying temperature, pressure, or the concentration of reagents, the chemist can influence the course of a reaction or even force it to reverse its "natural"—which is to say, usual—direction, but he cannot modify the "chemical mass." Apart from this, affinity is no more than one of the factors involved in the "conditions of reaction."

For the first time, with Berthollet, affinity ceased to be the privileged conceptual instrument of chemists, uniting them despite their differences. Berthollet's "Newtonian" affinity actually called into question the very practice on which 18th-century chemistry was based and which at the same time extended artisanal procedures and renewed their meaning and objectives: the purification of substances and their identification. Scientists now knew that the same compound could be obtained by way of different paths of reaction and owed its properties only to its composition. Moreover, the nomenclature devised by Lavoisier, Guyton de Morveau, Antoine Fourcroy, and Berthollet himself had, in 1787, endowed that knowledge with the additional power of assigning names to compounds. But if Berthollet was right, the idea of a pure substance no longer made sense. The chemical compound lost its identity and became a mixture, the composition of which depended on the conditions of reaction.

Chemistry in the first decades of the 19th century was associated with the "triumph of analysis." Berthollet had therefore been defeated. This outcome, with the undoing of the components of the affinity of 18th-century chemists and its consequences, would also be the end of "Enlightenment chemistry" as a source of cultural inspiration offering a scientific alternative to the dominant mechanistic theory.

In fact, affinity had offered Enlightenment thinkers such as Denis Diderot the apparently stable example of an access to matter that did not submit it to the homogeneity of masses and the uniformity of force, the example of qualitatively differentiated "forces" creating qualitatively new compounds. At the time, affinity authorized attributing to "living" matter other properties that were still less mechanistic, such as sensitivity (which Diderot opposed to the perceptions, desires, memories, and aversions of Pierre-Louis Moreau de Maupertuis). The notion of affinity created the possibility of a coherent continuity, whereas Newton's concept of "blind and uniform" attractions meant viewing life as a kind of fortuitous miracle.

From this point of view, the last thinker of the Enlightenment was Georg Wilhelm Friedrich Hegel. In the "Theory of Measurement," which is part of his *Wissenschaft der Logik* (Science of Logic), Hegel closely analyzes Berthollet's thesis, according to which the elective character of affinity was merely an appearance depending on physical circumstances. Hegel does not attach much importance to the specifics of the attempts made, at about the same time, by the Swedish chemist Jöns Jakob Berzélius to "salvage" the possibility that compounds are characterized by the fixed proportions of their constituents. (Berzélius, like Michael

Faraday and Sir Humphry Davy, explained the chemical bond by electrical forces rather than Newtonian ones.) What Hegel (like Berzélius) finds important is the supposition that affinity is merely the result of a quantitative difference. Hegel asserts that such speculations lead to the building of structures without foundations, made up of invalid categories. Only elective chemical affinity takes into account the efficient experimental practice of chemists and, accordingly, prevents the logic of nature from being reduced to mere quantitative logic.

With Hegel, the concept of affinity, on which so much in 18th-century chemistry depended, apparently achieved definitive status; by interrupting the "little-by-little" process of quantitative variation, it confirmed the appearance of a new qualitative entity. Nonetheless, it was in the same period that affinity lost its importance in the eyes of chemists themselves. Berthollet's proposition had led to a lengthy controversy involving the chemist Joseph Louis Proust, an advocate of the identity of chemical compounds in terms of the fixed proportions of their constituents; this controversy finally ended in general indifference. While the protagonists (analyzing what to us is a blend of various oxides, which the techniques of the period could not clearly differentiate) accused one another of insincerity, the notion of fixed proportion was in fact preserved and from then on used explicitly as the basis of analytic reasoning. In 1832 Louis Joseph Gay-Lussac finally established the distinction, which prevails today, between the "mixture" produced by a chemical reaction and the constituent parts of that mixture, which are subject to fixed proportions.

The notion of affinity in effect brought together two separate problems, that of the chemical bond and that of the modification of chemical bonds. The problem of the chemical bond was eventually disassociated from that of affinity, and each of these entities would be investigated following two different paths. Both would ultimately be incorporated into physics, but into two very different branches of that science. The problem of chemical bonds would be a part of the discovery of the molecular structures explored by organic synthesis; the problem would later become the theory of valences; finally, chemical bonds would be interpreted in physical terms, in the context of a physics that was no longer mechanical but dealt in quanta. In a sense, this epilogue vindicated Hegel, since the central feature of quantum physics is a discontinuity foreign to mechanics, that of the quantum of action. At the beginning of the 18th century, the notion of affinity had excluded the assumption of the attraction of likes, and the idea that one molecule could be constituted of two like atoms had been rejected as absurd during the first half of the 19th century. It is thus no small irony that the simplest chemical bond—the one that quantum chemistry would put into equations—is the one that unites two (similar) atoms of hydrogen.

What chemists today still call "affinity" remains confined to a domain where it can no longer be described as "elective." As Berthollet had insisted, it characterizes the composition of the mixture produced by a reaction and the manner in which a chemist can influence the direction of chemical reactions. Like the problem of chemical bonds, these questions do not pertain to the realm of contemporary physics, in relation to the mechanism of forces, but instead are addressed in the field of thermodynamics. In effect, affinity represents a direct translation into chemical terms of the consequences of the second law of thermodynamics. In a sense, the dual outcomes of the problems of chemical bonds and chemical reactions vindicates those who saw in chemical activity a domain that resisted the domination of forces and masses, although they would no doubt have been disappointed in the manner of vindication. History usually tells the story of the winner, it would be the science of physics that, in transforming itself, came to incorporate and "finally define, in a rigorous fashion," the knowledge of chemists.

ISABELLE STENGERS

See also Chemistry; Corpuscle

Further Reading

Bensaude-Vincent, Bernadette, and Isabelle Stengers, *A History of Chemistry,* translated by Deborah van Dam, Cambridge, Massachusetts: Harvard University Press, 1996 (original French edition, 1993)

Holmes, Frederic Laurence, "From Elective Affinities to Chemical Equilibrium: Berthollet's Law of Mass Action," *Chymia* 8 (1962)

Holmes, Frederic Laurence, *Eighteenth-Century Chemistry As an Investigative Enterprise,* Berkeley: University of California Press, 1989

Knight, David, *Atoms and Elements: A Study of Theories of Matter in England in the Nineteenth Century,* London: Hutchinson, 1970

Stengers, Isabelle, "Ambiguous Affinity: The Newtonian Dream of Chemistry in the Eighteenth Century," in *A History of Scientific Thought,* edited by Michel Serres, Oxford and Cambridge, Massachusetts: Blackwell, 1995 (original French edition, 1989)

Thackray, Arnold, *Atoms and Powers: An Essay on Newtonian Matter-Theory and the Development of Chemistry,* Cambridge, Massachusetts: Harvard University Press, and London: Oxford University Press, 1970

Africa

During the Enlightenment the term "terra incognita" (unknown land) often appeared on European maps representing the interior of the African continent. Europeans had considered Africa inhospitable since their first explorers reached its shores at the dawn of the Renaissance and the continent remained unknown, largely unexplored because of its vastness and the many insurmountable obstacles presented by its terrain and inhabitants. From the European perspective, Africa was an imaginary territory, seen through the prism of myths and legends as the realm of monsters. Jean-Jacques Rousseau, in the sixth note of his *Discours sur l'origine et les fondements de l'inégalité parmi les hommes* (1755; Discourse on the Origins of Inequality) observes that "the whole of Africa and its numerous inhabitants, as distinctive for their character as for their color, have yet to be investigated." In general, the rare accounts published by those cautious travelers—sailors, traders, colonial officials, soldiers, and missionaries—who undertook to introduce the continent to others were limited to the particular interests of their respective authors. Commerce between Africa and Europe took place along the coasts. Goods such as ebony, rubber, sugar, spices, ostrich feathers, gold, ivory, and, above all, slaves were brought to the Western trading companies by means of direct collaboration between indigenous traders and European criminals who had become mercenaries.

According to the German philosopher Heeren, in his *Ideen über die Politik, den Verkehr und den Handel der vornehmsten Völker der alten Welt: Afrikanische Völker* (1793; Historical Researches into the Politics, Intercourse, and Trade of the Carthaginians, Ethiopians, and Egyptians), "to date, no explorer has penetrated far enough into the interior of Africa to make his own observations." Europeans of the time therefore had to rely on what Heeren calls "the reports of the ignorant inhabitants." In reality there were few contacts with Africans that went beyond the slave trade, wars, raids, and religious conversions. Even those contacts were burdened by the prejudices from ancient tales that were revived in the compilations and fictions of the 18th century, which continued to attribute countless vices to the black race: laziness, lack of discipline, low intelligence, vanity, cowardice, insensitivity, cruelty, lechery, jealousy, treachery, hypocrisy, fanaticism, atheism, fetishism, idolatry, polygamy—or, in two words widely used in the period, savagery and degeneracy. Thus, for example, the English authors who published a vast panorama of the continent in Volume 14 of *The Universal History* (1760) state in their preface: "It is a common saying that all the peoples of the world have some good qualities and some bad ones, with the exception of Africans. It is difficult to find among them anything that is not bad." Similar assertions can be found in the writings of John Locke, David Hume, George Berkeley, Voltaire, the comte de Buffon, Benjamin Franklin, Georg Wilhelm Friedrich Hegel, Immanuel Kant, and others.

Such contempt was rooted in a long-standing religious and scientific tradition. Some theologians still traced the descent of black people either from Cain, whose skin God had blackened as punishment for murdering his brother Abel, or from Ham, who had been chastised for revealing the nakedness of his father Noah. The scientific tradition is illustrated by the abbé Demanet, who, in his *Nouvelle histoire de l'Afrique française* (1707; A New History of French Africa), explains the pigmentation of Africans through climatic influences. Physiologists debated the existence of a blackish "coating" or a specific gelatinous substance between the skin and the flesh. However, the worst scientific interpretation was based on the school of thought initiated in the *Systema Naturae* (1735; A General System of Nature) by the Swedish Lutheran naturalist Carolus Linnaeus, who established a meticulous hierarchy of human types and traced the genealogy of the black race back to the pongo and the orangutan. This genealogy also left its imprint on Buffon's *Histoire naturelle* (1765; Natural History), in the article "Nomenclature des singes" (Nomenclature of the Apes), and in Christoph Meiners's *Grundriss der Geschichte der Menschheit* (1786; History of Humankind). The relationship established between a dark complexion (perceived as indicative of the hostility attributed to all subterranean worlds) and the superstitious aspects of Christianity prevailed. Blackness was believed to augur evil, corruption, and diabolism. In his *Mélanges intéressants et curieux* (1765; Interesting and Odd Miscellanies), Rousselot de Surgy makes use of this elementary color symbolism connection with the Scriptures to legitimize both his aversion toward "a nation whose soul is as black as its body" and the use, by divine right as it were, of the whip.

The so-called enlightened public disseminated this imagery, which had become a cultural tradition, so that the dominant ideology emanating from travel narratives was reflected in the beginnings of African exoticism—a theme that was gradually introduced into 18th-century literature. Initially represented as a new fictional territory available for the wanderings of heroes, Africa was almost invariably reduced to a few Eurocentric clichés stripped of any local detail. All Africans were described in the same manner regardless of their different roots, and they were even confused with the native peoples of the Americas. Western ignorance of the countries of Africa was reflected in a general misunderstanding of their indigenous inhabitants. The dominant, cliché-ridden atmosphere reinforced traditional views that were both superficial and artificial. The most serious shortcoming in these works is the lack of psychological depth and character development in the portrayals of Africans. It was as if there were a threatening taboo that precluded considering the richness and diversity of African civilizations.

Two peoples in particular captured the imagination of Europeans and served as a foil for Western fantasies: the Jaga of Angola and the Hottentots. The Jaga, wandering through the kingdom of Matamba, had terrified and repelled Europeans ever since they had been described by three writers: the English adventurer Andrew Battell (*The Strange Adventures of Andrew Battell* [1625]); the Flemish Olfert Dapper (*Naukeurige beschrijvinge der Africanische gewesten* [1668; Description of Africa]); and Giovanni Antonio Cavazzi, a Dominican friar from Italy (*Istorica descrizione* [1687; Historical Description]). Inspired by these books, which had been compiled and augmented with various Portuguese accounts by Jean-Baptiste Labat (*Relation historique de l'Ethiopie occidentale* [1732; Historical Description of Western Ethiopia]), Jean-Louis Castilhon places the Jaga cannibals at the center of his novel *Zingha, reine d'Angola* (1769; Zingha, Queen of Angola), attributing their barbarity to religious and political causes: "No people was ever more cruel or more ferociously superstitious than the Jaga, for their inhumanity is ordained by religion, and powerfully authorized by law."

The Hottentots are mentioned in nearly all compilations on black Africa that are based upon the German work *Caput Bonae Spei Hodiernum* (1719; The Present State of the Cape of Good Hope) by a colonial official, Peter Kolb. Horror or disgust were inspired by the Hottentot women's *tablier charnel* (the elongation of the labia, a practice referred to as the "Hottentot apron"), the men's removal of one testicle, and their customs of anointing themselves with oil and draping animal entrails around their legs, their "filth," and the "clicks" (glottal stops) that were part of their language.

Fortunately, the trend toward genuine interest in the African continent, sparked by more characteristic Enlightenment attitudes, bespoke a new vision of the world that helped counter the myth of a hostile land and the stereotype of the evil savage. Depictions of delightful landscapes and virtuous inhabitants began to appear. A series of works propagated idyllic representations and celebrated the "good Negro" or the "Generous Slave"—an expression inspired by the *Esclave généreux,* an unpublished play by the comtesse Boufflers. According to Rousseau, the countess's play was a plagiarism of *Oroonoko; or, The Royal Slave* (1688), a successful novel by the Englishwoman Aphra Behn that had been translated and adapted by Pierre-Antoine de La Place in 1745. Among other texts, the *Histoire naturelle du Sénégal* (1757; A Voyage to Senegal, the Isle of Goree, and the River Gambia) by the explorer Michel Adanson was motivated by a scientific desire to emphasize the primitivism of Africa and to inspire admiration of "the most perfect image of pure Nature." The innocent and peaceful tribes had evolved on their fertile native soil in a state of gentle oblivion, unaware of need or the sorrow of loss, the disappointments of ambition or the devouring heat of passion, as if in a golden age, free and happy in the lightness of their hearts and consciences.

Through the mirror of literature, the wisdom of the Senegalese was placed in contrast to the identity of the civilized Europeans, an identity that was dissatisfied because it was counterfeit. In spite of their lack of accuracy, these reassuring Rousseauesque images of natural nobility represented a break with three centuries of indifference and militant hatred. "What a beautiful land Madagascar is!" Gommermon wrote to Joseph-Jérôme Lefrançois de Lalande in 1771. "Nature seems to have settled there, as if in a private sanctuary, to work on other models than those she has used in other places: one encounters there the most wonderful and unusual forms at every step."

Of course, not all descriptions were inspired by praiseworthy motives. Many involved pure fabrication, particularly the French narratives and essays published after the Seven Years' War that called for explorers to venture into the true African interior. The Treaty of Paris in 1763 weakened France considerably: it lost its colonies in Canada and India to the benefit of Prussia and, above all, England, which along with Spain became the leading colonial power in the world. From that point on, the ethical problems raised by the slave trade and by the notion of servitude deeply influenced public debate. However, humanitarian considerations were far from being the only issue. There was a primary concern with the economic necessity of finding better ways to manage the region and the immense resources of a territory that had been significantly depopulated by slave traders. A period of commercial reconstruction then began, through the revival of a more or less explicit policy of expansionism. On the one hand, colonial administrators and traders pondered the best methods for exploiting the treasures and the peoples scattered throughout the interior of Africa. On the other hand, the *philosophes* and the Physiocrats denounced the loss of earnings inherent in slavery, a system that was crippled by the lack of motivation to work among those who had been displaced and that had been built upon a scaffolding of inhumanity.

A period of polemics arose between the cynical reasoning of European businessmen and a handful of writers who were not always free from contradiction themselves. As a forerunner in this debate, Montesquieu took up the ideas of the slave traders in order to demonstrate their absurdity. In Chapter 5 of *De l'esprit des lois* (1748; The Spirit of Laws), which emphasizes the hypocrisy of whites and the ineptitude of their policies, Montesquieu writes:

> having exterminated the peoples of America, the Europeans have had to enslave those of Africa in order to clear all that land . . . It is impossible for us to imagine that the people of Africa are human beings, because if we did so we would begin to believe that we ourselves are not Christians. Petty minds exaggerate the injustice that has been done to Africans. For, if that injustice were as great as they claim, would it not have occurred to the princes of Europe, who form so many pointless agreements among themselves, to form a general agreement in favor of mercy and pity?

This model of humanitarian protest is reinforced by Voltaire in both his *Essai sur les moeurs et l'esprit des nations* (1756; An Essay on Universal History, and the Manners and Spirit of Nations) and *Candide* (1759; Candide); by Claude-Adrien Helvétius in *De l'esprit* (1758; Essays on the Mind and Its Several Faculties); and by Rousseau in *La nouvelle Héloïse* (1761; Julie; or, The New Heloise) and later in *Du contrat social* (1762; The Social Contract). The increasing vehemence and radicalism of this protest is clearly discernable in the chapter devoted to this theme in Volume I of *L'Arétin moderne* (1763; The Modern Aretino) by the abbé Dulaurens, cynically entitled "Negroes: We Are in the Wrong, But We Need Sugar." Another example can be found in the note on Africa in the section entitled "Winter" in the great poem *Les saisons* (1769; The Seasons) by the marquis de Saint-Lambert:

> I enter into the heart of this beautiful land; everywhere I find war; I see the gentlest of men, who should have nothing to fight about in a region where the land lavishes everything upon them, I see them intent on harming one another, on massacring one another, on enslaving one another. I learn that the Negroes once lived in peace, but that the English, the French, and the Portuguese, with infernal cunning, sow and cultivate divisions among these peoples, who sell them their prisoners of war. And I know how such prisoners are treated on our sugar islands, and in the colonies of the Portuguese and the Spanish.

Also written in 1769, the 12th letter of the *Voyage à l'Île de France* (1769; A Trip to the Île de France) by Bernardin de Saint-Pierre, one of the few writers knowledgeable about Africans, expresses similar compassion for the oppressed as well as resentment and indignation toward the West:

> I am angry that the philosophers who fight abuses with so much courage have hardly spoken about the slavery of blacks, except to make jokes about it. They avert their eyes. They speak of the Massacre of Saint Bartholomew, or the massacre of the Mexicans by the Spanish, as if this crime did not occur in our own time, and in which half of Europe has participated . . . The beautiful colors of pink and flame our ladies wear, the cottons that line their skirts, the sugar, coffee, and chocolate they consume at breakfast, the rouge they use to highlight their paleness—the hands of unfortunate blacks have prepared all this for them. Sensitive women, you weep at tragedies, yet the sources of your own pleasures are wet with tears and tainted with the blood of men.

Such reproaches became more common and increasingly pointed in relating the triumph of the Enlightenment to the disappearance of colonies and their arbitrary governments. In Volume 1 of Louis-Sébastien Mercier's futuristic novel *L'an 2440: Rêve s'il en fut jamais* (1771; Astraea's Return; or, The Halcyon Days of France in the Year 2440: A Dream), the hero, as he travels around a reformed Paris, contemplates a monument representing the repentance of the murderous countries and a majestic statue erected to the glory of the "avenger of the New World," the black instigator of an unstoppable general uprising. The traveler thus discovers the history of the slaves who "spilled the blood of their tyrants. French, Spanish, English, Dutch, Portuguese, all were the victims of the sword, of poison and of fire . . . The natives repossessed their indefeasible rights since they were the rights of Nature." Mercier's "exterminating angel" becomes an instrument of divine justice, guiding humanity toward a better future. Having failed in his role as a guide, the white man moves into an inferior position.

This sublime image of a hero aware of his liberating and civilizing mission reappears in the second edition of the *Histoire philosophique et politique des établissements et du commerce des Européens dans les deux Indes* (first edition 1770; A Philosophical and Political History of the Settlements and Trade of the Europeans in the East and West Indies), written by the abbé Raynal and Denis Diderot. This work, a true anticolonialist survey of the age, reinforces the subversive dream that only a violent revolution can respond to the institutionalized barbarity of despotism, that the promise of a great and lasting good justifies recourse to a great but transient wrong. Hoping and praying for the appearance of a "Spartacus" who could free the Africans from their chains (but not, as in Mercier's novel, the whole of humanity), in Volume 3 of the *Histoire* Diderot legitimizes the right to revolt and to slay tyrants: "Then the *Code noir* (Black Code) will disappear, and how terrible will be the *Code blanc* (White Code) if the victor considers only his right to reprisals."

Admittedly, there were less virulent protests that helped to increase public sensitivity and to defeat the racism in European minds. The primitivist trend among the Protestants had drawn a great deal of attention to the goodness of the blacks, and to the wickedness of their masters, ever since the egalitarian *Directions to Slaveholders* (1673) by the Quaker Baxter and the moving lessons of *Ooronoko*. In his *Thoughts on Slavery* (1774), John Wesley, the father of the Methodist Church and one of the most respected figures in England, caused a scandal with his view that Angolans possessed the same natural rights as the English. Wesley declared that he preferred honest poverty to riches bought with the tears, sweat, and blood of other humans. In this polemical vein, *L'Afrique hollandaise* (1783; Dutch Africa) depicts the decadence of the Dutch West India Company at Cape Town, its corrupt administration, and its cruel and greedy officials: "Unfortunately, to a master, his slaves are the same as his bulls, his cows, and all his domestic animals. The word 'slave' alone makes all reasonable men tremble; but until the slave trade is abolished by the unanimous consent of all civilized nations, the master who owns them can treat them however he wishes."

An Italian compilation, *Africa* (1784), drew a more general portrait of a continent ravaged and wounded by the slave traders. Recounting the stages of this "detestable commerce," it offers a rare numerical evaluation of the costs of its formidable growth: "During 1768 alone, 104,100 slaves were taken from Africa. The English bought 53,100 for service in the West Indies, and 63,000 for their colonies in North America, while the French bought 23,500, the Dutch 11,300, the Portuguese 8,700, and the Danes 1,200." Even omitting some countries from his calculations, the author estimates that a total of four million Africans had "perished in America to enrich Europeans" during the 18th century.

Modern historians come closer to the truth in putting forward a total of 100 million people deported from Africa from the 16th century until the abolition of slavery. Abolition had been demanded unconditionally by the philanthropists, travelers, and writers of the Société des Amis des Noirs (Society of the Friends of Blacks; founded by Brissot on 19 February 1788, on the model of the British Society for the Abolition of the Slave Trade). Among its most illustrious members were the marquis de Mirabeau, the marquis de Lafayette, Jacques Necker, Petion, the abbé Sieyès, the marquis de Condorcet, and above all the abbé Grégoire, who spent 40 years defending Africans. In October 1790 Grégoire was hanged in effigy by the planters of Santo Domingo for having proclaimed too loudly the hope to which enlightened Europe could not fail to respond: "no longer will the rays of the heavenly body that gives us light fall on the chains of slaves." After the abolition of slavery by the Convention (1794) and its reestablishment by Napoleon (1802), European awareness of Africa only truly made progress when the dream of equality finally came true.

PATRICK GRAILLE

See also Colonialism; Slavery

Further Reading

Hair, P.E.H., *Africa Encountered: European Contacts and Evidence, 1450–1700,* Aldershot, Hampshire and Brookfield, Vermont: Variorum, 1997

Hoffmann, Léon-François, *Le nègre romantique: Personnage littéraire et obsession collective,* Paris: Payot, 1973

Mercier, Roger, *L'Afrique noire dans la littérature française: Les premières images, XVIIᵉ–XVIIIᵉ siècles,* Dakar: Université de Dakar, Faculté des Lettres et Sciences Humaines, 1962

Newton-King, Susan, *Masters and Servants on the Eastern Cape Frontier, 1760–1803,* Cambridge and New York: Cambridge University Press, 1999

Reader, John, *Africa: A Biography of the Continent,* London: Hamish Hamilton, 1997; New York: Knopf, 1998

Seeber, Edward Derbyshire, *Anti-Slavery Opinion in France during the Second Half of the Eighteenth Century,* Baltimore, Maryland: Johns Hopkins Press, and London: Oxford University Press, 1937

Vissière, Isabelle and John-Louis, *La traite des noirs au siècle des Lumières: Témoignages de négriers,* Paris: Métailié, 1982

Agriculture

Agronomy

Never has agriculture been so discussed and written about as it was in 18th-century Europe. It was of course not a new concern: from time immemorial, agriculture had been the basic activity for most Europeans, providing the lion's share of revenues and dominating the overall economy. Interest in this economic sector had waned somewhat during the 17th century. However, beginning at the turn of the 18th century that interest was rekindled in enlightened circles, and it eventually increased to the point of triggering a veritable "agromania."

Agromania and Anglomania

Research into the best ways of implementing improvements in agricultural production had certainly not been lacking in the period preceding the Enlightenment, and a number of texts intended to spread the good word had been published during that time. Olivier de Serres's *Théâtre d'agriculture et ménage des champs* (1600; The Theatre of Agriculture and the Rural Household) or Estienne and Liébaut's *L'agriculture et la maison rustique* (1570; Agriculture and the Rustic House) are but two examples. After 1750, however, the movement to improve agriculture became ubiquitous and gained momentum. While "classic" instructional texts were supplemented and brought up to date through successive editions, and new books appeared. France, for example, saw the publication of the *Traité de la culture des terres, suivant les principes de M. Tull* (1753–61; Treatise on the Cultivation of Lands Following M. Tull's Principles); the *Éléments d'agriculture* (1762; Elements of Agriculture) by Henri-Louis Duhamel de Monceau, and the *Essai sur l'amélioration des terres* (1763; Essay on the Improvement of Lands) by Patullo. To some extent, these texts represent the starting point of French agronomic research based on observation and systematic experimentation. Similarly, studies by the baron Guyton de Morveau, the comte de Fourcroy, and Jean-Antoine-Claude Chaptal advanced the chemical study of soils, while other research focused on nutrition for plants. France's first veterinary schools were established in Lyon and Alfort in the middle of the 18th century.

Naturally, this movement was connected to the development of physiocratic theory, which considered agriculture the mainspring of the economy. According to the Physiocrats, agriculture was the only activity that produced real wealth, and farmers were the only truly productive class. The agronomy/Physiocracy combination helps to explain the enthusiasm for working the land that began to affect the enlightened elite. Periodicals and manuals proliferated, spreading new ideas everywhere and publicizing experiments that had been conducted in various places. The first examples were the French *Annales d'agriculture* and the English *Farmer's Magazine*. The articles and plates in the *Encyclopédie* that dealt with agricultural problems also helped to disseminate new ideas.

Information was also transmitted by other channels, notably the agricultural societies that were formed throughout Europe. In France, the first such society was founded in 1757 in Brittany; the Paris association was established in 1761. By the end of the 18th century there were more than 300 agricultural societies in Germany, with particularly dense concentrations of them in Saxony, Prussia, and Bavaria. In England these organizations began to emerge late in the 18th century, beginning only in 1775, but the movement flourished from that point on. Generally speaking, the members of agricultural societies included aristocrats and also representatives of other social groups, including large farmsteaders, who met to compare their experimental results. It became fashionable not only to talk about agronomy but to conduct tests on estates that essentially became model farms in the process. Among the most famous of these experiments were those carried out by the duc de La Rochefoucauld-Liancourt on his Liancourt estate (in what was to become the department of Oise) and those conducted by Antoine-Laurent de Lavoisier at Freschines (in what would become the department of Loir-et-Cher). The French state soon began to manifest its interest in agricultural experimentation by providing subsidies and other forms of encouragement, such as publicizing the new innovations. The creation of the Société Royale d'Agriculture (Royal Society of Agriculture) in 1778 was another important example of state support. Other institutions emerged, such as the Board of Agriculture in England founded by Arthur Young in 1793, which was devoted to agricultural progress throughout the kingdom.

Throughout Europe, English innovation was the unique driving force behind the feverish intensity of agromania. Initiatives undertaken on the Continent were essentially inspired by the changes that had taken place in England over the past several decades. In this respect, Jethro Tull's book *The New Horse Hoeing Husbandry; or, An Essay on the Principles of Tillage and Vegetation,* published in 1731, was extremely influential and served as an important reference work for decades. Tull advocated deep plowing and a complex system of crop rotation, and also emphasized the importance of cultivating fodder plants and plants with roots; on the other hand, he opposed fallowing. There was nothing revolutionary in any of this. Tull was influenced by the Dutch example, with which he was well acquainted, and he developed ideas put forth by his 17th-century predecessors in England, who had shared his fascination with Dutch agricultural prowess. Holland had long since adopted the intensive techniques recommended by agronomists, but had not won over many followers from other countries. By adopting Dutch methods and expanding them to a larger scale, England was able to pilot a system of experimental agriculture.

The English aristocracy, then the gentry, became enamored of agronomy very early on. In Norfolk, beginning in 1730, Charles, Second Viscount Townshend of Raynham began the most famous project of the period. On his Raynham estate, Townshend started a crop rotation system that ensured that the land would never be unproductive, giving priority to winter fodder and artificial meadows. The Norfolk system, based on the combination of turnips, barley, clover, and wheat, and popularized by the man who was nicknamed "Turnip" Townshend, enjoyed great success. It was imitated by other members of the aristocracy and became a model system whose merits were universally praised. With Townshend following on the heels of Arthur Young, the image of the gentleman farmer was born. At the same time, there emerged a class of large-scale farmer-capitalists who systematically sought to maximize profit. Among them were Thomas Coke, who experimented with new equipment on his Holkham estate, and Robert Bakewell, who practiced selective breeding to improve his livestock. Breeding became an essential activity during the 18th century, coinciding with an increase in speculative farming that was ever more open to the markets stimulated by increasing demand emanating from urban centers. Farmers had changed. The enclosure movement led to the concentration of farms and land consolidation and, from there—at least, so it was argued on both sides of the English Channel—to better yields and the development of animal husbandry.

These successes explain the Anglomania that affected a large part of Europe. In France, in particular, everyone praised the triumphs of English agriculture and began to discount French farming methods as archaic. On the eve of the French Revolution, Young's *Travels in France* (1792) gave substance to the idea that French agriculture lagged behind the times. It was claimed that French yields were inferior to English yields by one

third. Agronomists and Physiocrats alike proposed a variety of remedies for this handicap, including the adoption of complex crop-rotation systems, the elimination of fallowing and of collective constraints, and providing incentives for large-scale farming.

Traditional Agriculture

Throughout Europe, the cultivation of grains traditionally dominated agriculture. Bread, porridge, and pancakes were the main dietary staples, and wheat, to borrow the time-honored expression, represented "a necessary evil" (see Mulliez). However, this seemingly restricted general view was subject to some important regional variations. Although it is quite clear that the problem of grain supply was not negligible, two erroneous ideas must be discarded: first, the idea that the cultivation of grains was a completely hegemonic practice, and second, the notion that agriculture was limited to subsistence levels, inward-looking and cut off from markets. Although self-sufficiency was a consistent goal among farmers, it is clear that it was an ideal that very few households were able to achieve. Few farms produced enough to meet the needs of the families that worked them and rare were the regions that did not produce a surplus of one crop, only to face a deficit of wheat. The primacy of grains thus imposed considerable constraints.

Prior to the 18th century, in order to avoid depleting and eventually exhausting the soil, fields had never been cultivated continuously. In order to maintain a viable level of nutrients, land needed lie fallow for varying amounts of time. In reality, the timeframe and methods for this fallow period differed considerably from one area to another. In some instances, fields were simply left uncultivated for a certain period of time until they were ready for a new crop. In other instances regular crop rotation, requiring a strict alternation between fallowing and planting, was implemented. The first system was reserved for areas where the soil was poor, and the method required very little fertilizer. This system was used in some mountainous regions and in the vast territories of eastern Europe—on some of the plains of Russia, for example, where crop rotation had not yet taken hold. The second system required better soil and involved less extensive farming.

In a similar manifestation of regional variety, there were two major kinds of crop rotation. One was known as triennial rotation, in which a cycle of winter crops, spring crops (March crops, such as oats), and fallow was planted. This system was predominant on the large plains surrounding Paris Basin and beyond, on the great plains of northern Europe. The second crop-rotation scheme, known as biennial, was used chiefly in the Mediterranean and was based on a simple alternation of wheat and fallowing. In all cases, some portion of the land remained uncultivated each year—a state of affairs that drew unanimous protests from agricultural reformers. However, one should not infer from this that the fallowing period was an inactive time in the farming calendar—quite the contrary. In all the major agricultural regions farmers adopted many methods, for example, plowing two, three, even four successive times in order to prepare the land for the two successive harvests it would later yield.

No matter which crop rotation system was used, the land needed to be fertilized, and most fertilizer came from animals. The problem of livestock was therefore crucial, and crop yields varied depending on the size of the herd. The number of animals was often limited by fodder resources, particularly during the winter, and by the amount of land left for grass. At the same time, it was often greatly tempting to farmers to sacrifice meadows to the plow in order to produce the maximum amount of grain for human consumption. Clearly, ancien régime agriculture was generally caught in a vicious circle. Under these circumstances, apart from the fields reserved for grazing, there were three sources of food for animals: common lands reserved for grazing, penned areas of fallow land, or fields left vacant after harvest (where grazing was at best meager). This last method required that all animals have access to the whole of the community's plowable land once the harvest had been brought in. It was considered a reactionary practice that discouraged private initiative, and as such was roundly condemned by advocates of agricultural reform and agrarian individualism, as well as by advocates of large-scale farming.

Yet large-scale farmers were in reality far from being penalized by the practice of common grazing after harvest, since they alone owned the large herds of sheep for which the stubble fields were an essential source of food. In Beauce, for example, only farms of over 150 acres had real herds. In fact, large-scale farmers resisted giving their harvested fields over to common grazing because they wanted to reserve their fields for their own herds, which could number in the hundreds. Yet, despite all these sheep, large-scale farmers did not always have enough manure for their land—far from it. Manure shortages were obviously far worse for small-scale farmers who did not have nearly as much livestock. Shortages of this type were prevalent in the area around Paris, for example, and, in most intensive farming regions. However, such shortages did not necessarily affect other regions where the same dominant configuration of wheat and sheep existed. On landed estates in Andalusia and Castile, as well as in Sicily and southern Italy, the most common pattern consisted of nomadic livestock farming alongside extensive farming that used little manure. And we do not propose even to attempt to address, in the context of this article, the complexities of land use on the enormous farms of the Polish and Russian plains.

We should not conclude that grain farming prevailed everywhere, despite the priority afforded to self-sufficiency. Mountain economies were shaped by other demands: there, livestock farming played a primary role, providing dairy products, cheeses, and smoked meats, while forestry made use of other resources. In the wet areas of western France, cattle were predominant and meadowlands were much more extensive than fields devoted to grains. Finally, wherever climatic conditions and terrain permitted and a market was accessible, vineyards emerged, mobilizing large numbers of winegrowers who mainly produced for the market—even if it forced the growers themselves to buy almost all their food. The vineyards around Paris, which supplied the capital, and the Saintonge vineyards, which concentrated on the production of spirits, both attest to the integration of viticulture into the commercial economy. This trend was even more pronounced in vineyards that had newly acquired prestige, such as those that produced champagne in France, sherry in Spain, or port in Portugal. Cities played a fundamental role in the rise of viticulture as a commercial concern, and also triggered the development of farms to supply the markets on their peripheries. London and Paris, in this respect, are obvious examples. There were, therefore, other areas of specialization and methods of intensive agriculture in addition to the well-known achievements of Dutch and Flemish farms, with their complex systems for rotating crops over a cycle that might last eight to 12 years. Owing to innovations such as these, the 18th century is generally considered a decisive period in the modernization of agriculture.

Agricultural Revolution or Agricultural Transition?

The 18th-century agricultural "revolution" is generally understood as having originated in England, with a second wave following in rural France (albeit with a noticeable time lag). While this view is not false, it needs to be qualified somewhat. Recent historiography has tended to relativize the performance of English farmers and to reassess conventional accounts of the "revolution" in agriculture. Norfolk alone cannot stand for the whole of Great Britain's agriculture, and Young's opinions may be somewhat biased. Perhaps the French, so ready to admire the methods adopted on the other side of the English Channel, succumbed to a sort of hero worship so prevalent that it even had a name based on the word "idolatry": *youngolâtrie*.

It has been suggested that there were in effect two agricultural revolutions. One was based on improved farming techniques; it is said to have taken place, to a large extent, during the 17th century and eventually to have resulted in increased production and yield. The other revolution is said to have resulted from enclosures. Carried out for the most part during the 18th century, the widespread construction of fences would have had little effect on production, but quite a large impact on productivity (see Allen, 1991). Increases in grain production created surpluses until the middle of the century, when a period of consistent grain shortages began. This discrepancy clearly shows that even the rapid expansion of agricultural production could not perfectly keep pace with the concomitant rapid growth in population.

In France the debate continues over whether or not a true agricultural revolution occurred in that country. The growth in French agricultural production during the 18th century seems irrefutable, even if its extent can still be debated. How else, in the absence of agricultural progress, would it have been possible to feed a population that had grown 25 percent, while famines (and the deaths that usually accompanied them) were in decline? In fact, any analysis of the issue must take into account two problems. First, it must be determined whether growth in agricultural production was only a return to previous levels of production, or whether, on the other hand, it indicates an unprecedented degree of progress. Second, we must also determine whether there was a growth in consumption and, as an indirect result, in per capita production—in other words, whether the French ate better and production levels were able to keep pace with population growth. With regard to the first problem, it is difficult to deny that at the end of the century population levels had climbed beyond the previous maximum population levels reached during the 14th or 16th centuries; therefore, the volume of overall production was certainly greater than it had ever been before. The second problem raises certain contradictions. On the one hand, the tensions that reemerged from time to time in the agricultural market seem to argue against a substantial increase in available and stockable surpluses. On the other hand, the diminished intensity and frequency of food shortage crises suggests that there was no appreciable decline in production. It seems reasonable to conclude that overall, the increase in production paralleled the population growth, which was estimated to have risen approximately 25 to 30 percent in the course of the 18th century.

Is it appropriate, then, to speak of an agricultural revolution in France? The change was spectacular, unprecedented, and irreversible. However, it was not violent, abrupt, or radical. Instead, the changes seem to have occurred in the context of long-term progress as a series of processes, a succession of experiments. It might therefore be preferable to use a less dramatic concept than revolution—perhaps the notion of "transition."

Any assessment depends on one's point of view and the vocabulary one chooses. In any event, during the 18th century crises in subsistence, which had periodically rocked most European societies, generally subsided. The fact that harvests became less irregular was obviously fundamental, but was there a corresponding amount of progress in terms of yield? It is difficult to formulate a viable theory on this point. The variety of local situations and the persistent disparity in their circumstances prevent us from drawing firm conclusions. The only thing that we can assert is that yields in France undoubtedly increased, but not at an explosive rate, and that, as in every other part of Europe, agricultural progress should also be measured in other terms, such as the expansion of farmland through land clearing. This practice was limited in France—despite measures taken by the state in 1760 to encourage clearing and land reclamation through tax exemptions—but land clearing brought about important changes wherever forests, fallow land, or marshes still took up large areas. The economic exploitation of the commons in England and the drainage schemes undertaken on the plains of northern Germany—and pursued in the regions around Milan and in Venetia (in combination with irrigation work)—contributed to an increase in the total area of cultivable land. Farming system reforms, intensification procedures, and increased specialization offered other alternatives.

American corn (or maize) was introduced onto the Iberian Peninsula in the 16th century. From there it rapidly crossed the Pyrenees and was eventually planted throughout much of southwestern France. In the 18th century maize was also grown in eastern France and northern Italy, where it was used to make polenta. This plant had an essential virtue: it offered a seed yield that was much greater than that of wheat. Yet the geographic spread of corn cultivation seemed to be blocked in the 18th century, and at certain points there was even a decline in the planting of corn in favor of wheat. On the plain of the Po, rice was the crop with the fastest rate of increase in popularity. The most significant change of all, however, was undoubtedly the introduction of the potato. Although its caloric value was relatively low, the potato had two benefits: an exceptional seed yield and the capacity to adapt to the most barren soil. Despite initial reactions of hostility, potatoes met with increased acceptance at an irregular rhythm following food shortages, from which it offered relatively quick relief. Potatoes played a larger and larger role in northern and eastern France, in the Austrian Netherlands, and above all in Germany. Elsewhere, its emergence and expansion came even sooner—for instance, as early as 1694 in the Vivarais region of France.

In regions characterized by large-scale farming, farmers had long since acquired the habit of practicing "refreshment" on fallow land in order to increase production. The increase in production of nitrogen-fixing leguminous plants (peas, vetches, etc.) helped to revitalize the soil and lengthen the intervals between fallow periods, while artificial fodder plants became more and more important. Sainfoin and then alfalfa were introduced onto land that was not part of the rotation, and these, along with clover integrated into the crop rotation system, provided more food for livestock. The introduction of Spanish merino sheep into France at the very end of the 18th century and the creation of the Rambouillet sheep farm in 1786 progressively improved the quality of sheep breeding in France. The increasing use of urban fertilizers (in the form of "night soil") and manure from the aristocratic stables allowed for better fertilization of the soil. Even in regions of small-scale farming such as the Kochersberg district of Alsace and parts of Germany, the introduction of fodder or industrial plants (madder, flax, etc.) brought undisputed benefits.

Owing to market pressures, specialization became more pronounced. Despite the repeated ban on planting land with grapes, vineyards clearly continued to expand in 18th-century France. A portion of viticultural activity was dedicated to the pursuit of quality: determination on the part of some major landowners led to the creation of the first great vintages, beginning with the Médoc area in the Bordeaux region. Farmers in Normandy began to cultivate grass, which reflected the growing priority given to livestock farming over grain production. Other products, including mulberries, olives, and the fruit trees of the Mediterranean regions, were planted for speculative purposes and enjoyed considerable success. It would be some time before European societies moved from a situation of chronic shortage to one of overproduction. While it would be wrong to suppose that no improvements had occurred prior to the 18th century, it was at that point that change became truly perceptible. In a sense, this change can be viewed as the sum of a whole series of small advances—or rather, the result of many small advances occurring simultaneously. Under these circumstances, to what agents should credit be given for the dissemination of new plants, new methods, and new techniques? Undoubtedly, this process of dissemination owed a great deal to a sort of contagion effect, based on the examples offered by various pioneers. Was Voltaire, then, deliberately exaggerating when he penned the ironic statement, "Useful things have been written on agriculture; everyone read them except farm workers"?

GÉRARD BÉAUR

See also Agriculture: Typology

Further Reading

Allen, Robert C., "The Two English Agricultural Revolutions, 1450–1850," in Bruce M.S. Campbell and Mark Overton, editors, *Land, Labour, and Livestock: Historical Studies in European Agricultural Productivity*, Manchester: Manchester University Press, 1991

Allen, Robert C., *Enclosure and the Yeoman,* Oxford: Clarendon Press, and New York: Oxford University Press, 1992

Bourde, André J., *Agronomie et agronomes en France au XVIIIe siècle,* 3 vols., Paris: S.E.V.P.E.N., 1967

Braudel, Fernand, and Ernest Labrousse, editors, *Histoire économique et sociale de la France*, 4 vols., Paris: Presses Universitaires de France, 1970–82; see especially vol. 2 (1970)

Le bulletin de la S.H.M.C. (1999) (special issue entitled "Le paysan et la terre")

Finberg, H.P.R., et al., editors, *The Agrarian History of England and Wales*, London: Cambridge University Press, 1967–; see especially vol. 5, pt. 2, and vol. 6, 1985–89

Hoffman, Philip T., *Growth in a Traditional Society: The French Countryside, 1450–1815,* Princeton, New Jersey: Princeton University Press, 1996

Le Roy Ladurie, Emmanuel, and Joseph Goy, *Tithe and Agrarian History from the Fourteenth to the Nineteenth Centuries: An Essay in Comparative History,* Cambridge and New York: Cambridge University Press, 1982

Moriceau, Jean Marc, "Au rendez-vous de la 'révolution agricole' dans la France du XVIIIe siècle: À propos des régions de grande culture," *Annales, histoire, sciences sociales* 49 (1994)

Mulliez, J., "Du blé, mal nécessaire: Réflexions sur les progrès de l'agriculture de 1750 à 1850," *Revue d'histoire moderne et contemporaine* (January–March 1979)

Overton, Mark, *Agricultural Revolution in England: The Transformation of the Agrarian Economy, 1500–1850,* Cambridge and New York: Cambridge University Press, 1996

Agriculture

Typology

To what extent can the Enlightenment be credited with the changes that occurred in European agriculture in the 18th century? Responding to this question is made difficult by both the geographic diversity of existing conditions, rendering any typology uncertain, and the problems of interpretation raised by the available sources, ranging from the registers of tithes and annuities that Slicher van Bath, Marczewski, and Toutain used to produce their quantitative historical study of official surveys to the painstaking examination of notarial acts.

The Problematic: Incentives and Obstacles to Agricultural Transformation

In an effort to find rigorous causality, historians may be tempted to attribute the transformations of agriculture in the 18th century to the convergence of four more or less determinant factors: natural constraints, the effects of the relationship between population and prices, legal and social structures, and, finally, the dominant ideology, or "spirit of the times."

Natural Constraints

Even though "famines" gradually gave way to "scarcities," northern Europe still experienced periods of exceptional cold or rain (1740–52, 1767–73, 1785–89) that apparently had a more catastrophic impact than the hot, dry summers of the south. These cold, rainy periods were responsible for poor harvests and the resulting shortages and high cost of grain. Agriculture continued to be more at the mercy of these meteorological fluctuations than of long-term variations in climate. While the climate as a whole was becoming increasingly mild, cold periods continued to occur; the "little ice age" that began around 1550 was to continue until the mid–19th century. Northern and mountainous regions of Europe found themselves particularly vulnerable to unfavorable climatic conditions (see Pfister). The situation became critical where these conditions were combined with poor soil, as in Ireland, Scandinavia, and Russia, where a quarter of the land was considered to be sterile, necessitating either clearing or intermittent use of the land.

However, the stimulus of population growth, the lure of profit, and human ingenuity combined to ensure that adverse natural conditions could be overcome. The acquisition of new land—whether by clearing, drainage (in the British fens and the Flemish polders), or irrigation (in the Mediterranean region)—often recovered the most mediocre of soils, cultivation of which was only marginally profitable. Bringing some relief to "hunger for land" seems to have been easier on the eastern and southern margins of Europe, where new acquisitions were still possible through colonial settlements, than in western Europe, where the peasantry often could count only on reserves consisting of communal property, and only at the risk of creating economic imbalances among forests, pasturage, and cultivation, as well as grave social conflicts.

The Population/Price Binomial

Given that the essential preoccupation of the older agrarian economy was to feed people, it is necessary to examine demographic trends: the population supplied not only the mouths to be fed but the labor power available to feed them. Europeans were twice as numerous at the end of the 18th century as at the beginning, rising in numbers from fewer than 100 million to nearly 200 million. Broken down according to country, this demographic upsurge amounted to increases of 30 percent in France; 40 to 60 percent in Spain, Italy, and England; and more than 100 percent in the Netherlands and the Rhineland, as well as in central and eastern Europe. Behind this upsurge lay a slight and belated drop in death rates coupled with continued high birthrates, the latter testifying to the existence of prolific and dynamic younger generations.

Demographic pressures and increasing population density, from 30 to 50 inhabitants per square kilometer, were factors that stimulated both the availability of work, often inseparable from increased farming, and the demand for agricultural products. The question of antecedence thus arises. Was demographic growth preceded by an increase in agricultural production, as suggested by Paul Bairoch in light of the case of today's underdeveloped countries? Or, on the contrary, did the growth of the population both precede and determine higher levels of agricultural production through its effect on demand? Even if high population densities do not necessarily lead to agrarian progress (see Morineau), they could be a stimulus for innovation (as Esther Boserup explains) and incite men to take up the demographic challenge. It seems that we must abandon the mechanistic conception of demography that reduces it to a variable dependent on and dictated by subsistence. Another analysis made by Jean Meuvret and Pierre Goubert, following Ernest Labrousse and based on registers of local market prices, shows that the slow rise in prices (on the order of 60 percent for grain in France between 1726–41 and 1771–89) cannot be explained exclusively in monetarist terms, namely by the influx of precious metals from the Americas, which provoked a moderate and salutary inflation (see Meuvret, 1971, 1977–88; Goubert). The rise in prices also stemmed from the increased number and improved living standards of potential consumers. By virtue of this centuries-old upward trend, agricultural production—which had been a necessity for a rural population trying to feed itself—began to be shaped by a temptation to accumulate tradable surpluses ready for sale to nonproducers in the city. If the alimentary imperative sometimes yielded to speculation, it was because land rents were soaring, increasing by about 100 percent for tithes and rents in France, overtaking the rise in prices as well as enhancing the lure of profit.

Legal and Social Structures

For this agricultural speculation to succeed, certain legal and social conditions had to occur simultaneously. The farmer who worked the land had to be its "proprietor," or at least "be in possession of" it under advantageous conditions (Vogt). Farmers had to become producer-vendors, able to dispose of marketable surpluses over and above the bare minimum. They had to give up the mentality of the *rentier* (tenant farmer) who views the land primarily as a source of steady income, adopting instead a capitalist spirit of enterprise and investment, which implies the availability of capital and a penchant for risk. Such was far from being the case throughout Europe, where the system of manorial or crown lands, the proliferation of small farms, or the absence of a dynamic bourgeoisie could act as very effective brakes on agricultural progress.

The Spirit of the Age

Physiocratic propaganda, disseminated by agricultural societies and buttressed by official studies, invariably insisted on a double imperative: on the one hand, access to ownership, preferably of a large estate or farm considered capable of yielding a negotiable surplus and making progress; on the other hand, the freedom to cultivate and sell produce for a substantial profit. Production would be encouraged by the reduction in lands left fallow and by the abolition of such communal "constraints" as obligatory crop rotation and common pasture. Commerce would benefit from the unrestricted circulation of grain and free export. With their progressive, individualistic, and liberal tendencies, the Physiocrats joined in the euphoria and optimism of a period in which the "theories of penury" (see Léon) that had been associated with mercantilism were replaced by "theories of abundance" befitting a liberal economy and times of relative prosperity.

However, while the notion of agricultural progress was desirable, was such progress really possible? In order to find out, one must descend from the ivory towers of the Physiocrats and examine the practical accomplishments of the agronomists, whether in the systematic codification of agricultural theory, based upon global philosophies of the economy and society, or in the practical progress made by the farmers themselves. In this experimental context, reflecting the spirit of the age, it is useful to distinguish between an affected and snobbish "agromania" and, among the "agronomic" models proposed, those practices that could actually be adopted by some or all of the peasantry. In 1756 the Parlement of Toulouse declared: "The park of Versailles," where seed experiments were conducted under the aegis of Madame de Pompadour, "will not decide the fate of our land." The same might be said of the sheepfold of Rambouillet, where Marie-Antoinette, adorned in potato blossoms, would play shepherdess, feeding and milking her sheep with her own hands. Other royal "farmers" included Joseph II of Austria, who, for purposes of propaganda, was occasionally seen behind a plow, and George III of England, whose nickname "Farmer George" would be passed on to posterity on account of his keen interest in his property at Windsor.

At the same time, there emerged around Henri-Louis Duhamel du Monceau, the duc de La Rochefoucauld-Liancourt, the marquis de Turbilly, and many others an "aristocracy of agronomy" whose members were able to extend cultivable land by clearing, by improvement, or by rearranging the layout of fields. They were also able to reduce fallowing in favor of improved methods of crop rotation, equivalent to methods used in Germany or in England (the Norfolk system). These experimental farmers also succeeded in adopting "new" crops (corn, potatoes, and speculative or forage plants), practicing enclosure, and placing animal husbandry, a key to the new agriculture because it provided manure, in the service of intensified cultivation.

Nonetheless, in western Europe at the end of the 18th century, fallow fields still made up an average of 30 to 50 percent of the cultivable land. Raw agricultural productivity had increased by only some 0.5 to 1 percent a year on average, and grain yields had remained static, at an average ratio of seed to harvest of 1:4, 1:5, or 1:6. This was hardly the "agricultural revolution" imagined by the "drawing room agronomists." Too many factors opposed such a revolution, including legal factors (insufficient and fragmented land, as well as the precariousness of lease farming); financial and technical factors (the cost of experiments with unpredictable results, heavy exactions, and archaic farm implements); and social factors (attachment to traditional cultures and communal practices, the force of "habit").

However, does the existence of obstacles allow us to dismiss, purely and simply, any notion of agricultural progress in the 18th century? In order to understand the situation, one must avoid seeing the world through the eyes of the agronomists of the period, much less through those of the Physiocrats, those unconditional partisans of "great and rich agriculture." The fact is that the agricultural "revolution" was hardly perceptible, in the sense that it evolved over a period of centuries, between the 16th and the 19th. But the Enlightenment was indeed a pivotal period, both a recuperation from the inertia and destruction of the 17th century and a bridge to the growth of the 19th, in the wake of three revolutions: the social-political revolution of 1789 in France, the commercial revolution stemming from dramatically improved road and rail systems, and, finally, the industrial revolution, which, while furnishing agriculture with machines and fertilizer, also absorbed the overpopulation of the countryside.

Nevertheless, redefining "agricultural revolution" as a long-term process is one thing, demythologizing the concept is another. The peasantry did not need ideological arguments to make, sometimes unwittingly, gradual progress toward diversification and intensification of agriculture through minor experiments and discoveries in their own gardens. This process has been described as "the culmination of slow progress from the earliest times" (see Bloch); as "small changes that yielded a rich harvest" (Étienne Juillard); and as "minor modifications that had a snowball effect" (Emmanuel Le Roy Ladurie). Such transformations occurred because of a considerable investment in human effort and as a consequence of day-to-day ingenuity, not because of some technological upheaval. Apart from isolated instances of innovation, historians do not always find progress where it might rightly be expected. It would be a mistake to draw a contrast between a Europe of large-scale cultivation, committed to the way of progress, and a Europe of small-scale cultivation, a prisoner of tradition and routine.

Overview of European Agriculture: Four Scenarios

The British Model

The originality of British agronomy was twofold. First of all, it meant that the ruling classes would appropriate a substantial portion of agricultural production and maintain control of the land. Second, it consisted of using on the resulting large farms the improved equipment made available by the industrial revolution, which, quite opportunely, accompanied this agricultural revolution. The goal was to orient production toward sales through the integration of agriculture in the monetary economy.

The disintegration of the traditional manorial system is explained both by the secularizations of the Reformation in the 16th century and by the confiscations, often to the benefit of the commoners, that accompanied the political revolution of 1688 (see Marx, 1970, 1980). Seigniorial reserves dwindled early on, but, while the lord no longer administered justice over his tenants, the leases themselves had become very precarious. The system of freeholding—with its free, perpetual, and easily transmissible rents and its light and immutable taxes—gave way either to leases that were hereditary (copyholding) but burdened with very heavy exactions for entry and transmission, or, increasingly, to temporary leases that exposed the tenant to eviction without compensation. A new, less feudal and more capitalist gentry was taking the place of the traditional landed aristocracy; the new gentry profited both from the indebtedness of the freeholders from the end of the 16th century onward, and from the more draconian conditions of tenancy, as rich landowners rounded out their estates by the reattachment of free leases to their own reserves.

Furthermore, communal holdings could not resist the acquisitiveness of the new clan of landowners. Ever since the 15th century, initially by private agreement and then by virtue of Acts of Parliament, this immense reserve of land had been melting away. In the 18th century, with the complicity of a Parliament dominated by the gentry, enclosures reached their peak. They were often put forward as an extension of cultivable land (through reclamation or draining) or a redistribution of common fields, but they could also be created by outright expropriation and consolidation. Whatever the means, the enclosures benefited those highly individualistic agrarian entrepreneurs otherwise known as "gentleman farmers."

Economically, such enterprises met with undeniable success. Single-tenant farms, freed from seigniorial charges and collective constraints, allowed for the rationalization of a capitalist type of agriculture conducive to modern methods. The value of the land increased at the same time as land rent improved. Emphasis was put on the development of animal husbandry (Robert Bakewell and the selection of breeds), which in turn produced manure, and on the extension of forage crops (the turnips of Lord Townshend), making possible complex and accelerated crop rotations (Norfolk type) that progressively eliminated the need for fallow land. In the county of Norfolk the Colke family implemented a number of innovations, including the stabling of cattle in sheds, the use of manure and various fertilizers (e.g., bone meal), the introduction of new plants (rutabaga, sugar beets), and advanced techniques (seeders). This evolution occurred in the context of an industrial revolution that furnished ever more efficient harrows and plows, allowing deeper and repeated tilling (Jethro Tull), as well as mechanical seeders and threshing machines beginning in the 1780s (Meikle), then tedders and steam-driven mowers, tested in 1794. Accompanying this technological progress was an ideological atmosphere (fostered by agricultural societies and academies, specialized newspapers and reviews, and, beginning in 1793, a Board of Agriculture with Arthur Young as its secretary) favorable to the development of economic liberalism. The result was an increase in both production and productivity on the order of one-third to one-half, with yields ranging from 1:7 to 1:10. This increase met the needs of a large and growing population, with a high proportion of nonproducers (35 percent) and wages higher than in France. It also responded to the demand for grain to export, with more than 100,000 tons shipped annually from what was at the time considered to be the "granary of Europe."

The other side of the coin was to be found in the proletarianization of peasant society. While its magnitude has been exaggerated, a rural exodus did occur very early in England, where the proportion of the active population engaged in agriculture fell from 70 to 40 percent during the 18th century. The effects of this depopulation of the countryside, following the consolidation of land ownership, were softened by the emergence of urban industry. However, one must not underestimate either the steady liquidation of the English peasantry, in the traditional sense, or the exacerbation of social distinctions. Those who were "dominant" in both the political and economic spheres were recruited from the noble and bourgeois elite, while the "dominated" came from the peasantry, hurt by the redistribution of land and the mechanization of farming and progressively deprived of both land and grazing rights. Distinctions were drawn as well between the yeomen, free peasants who were relatively well off, and the cottagers, peasants without land, threatened by poverty and the rural exodus. A redistribution of the amount of work available compensated for the harsh law of profit. Cottagers became laborers and farm workers, the fact that they remained indispensable for such work as weeding and tending the animals reduced their risk of unemployment. The policy of assistance to the indigent (the Poor Laws), for which credit must go to the gentry, provided another form of compensation.

A similar pattern of a concentration of property at the expense of the peasantry occurred in the case of Ireland, which resembled that of England (although it was aggravated by the effects of English conquest and the brutal dispossession of the old property owners by English landlords). Economic and social conditions were another matter, however. Ireland was largely a place of mountains, forests, and bogs, and the Irish were perilously dependent on the English demand for their livestock while relying on massive importation of grain. Periodic famines stimulated the cultivation of potatoes as an alternative. British agriculture was unique and would serve as a reference model for those parts of Europe tempted by large-scale agriculture.

From the Channel to the Elbe: The Diversity of Western Europe

The transition from feudalism to capitalism, a favorite theme of German historians, is fundamental to the understanding of the history of agriculture. However, it seems to apply more to Britain than to the rest of western Europe, which, in contrast, was characterized by a diversity of natural and legal conditions. At the risk of oversimplification, the common denominator for so many different conditions arguably lies in the relationship between the nobility and a peasantry that was seeking emancipation.

Major changes in the traditional nobility are indeed characteristic of the modern era. "No land without a lord" or "No lord without a title"? The first formula sums up the situation in the Netherlands, the greater part of France, western Germany, northern Italy, and northern Spain, where nobility depended both on land (as much on leaseholds cultivated by peasants as on the "reserve" farmed directly by the lord) and on the rights deriving from the ancient privileges of fief and sovereignty, which took on a significance that was increasingly economic. In regions where activity was less developed and monarchic authority was remote, from the Auvergne, Burgundy, and the Franche-Comté to Bavaria, the last vestiges of servitude (mortmain) continued to reinforce the lords' position. But more often, in taking from 25 to 35 percent of the gross yield of the land (tithe included), nobility became more a means of extracting wealth than a form of authority, which was becoming increasingly challenged. As a matter of fact, within the sphere of influence of Roman law ("No lord without a title"), land without a lord, the allodium, flourished. The "French model" was characterized by the extent of the seigniorial reserve, which was either bitterly defended or obstinately reconstituted after the crises brought on by an active policy of reallocation and the consolidation of farms conferred upon large landholders (see Moriceau; Moriceau and Postel-Vinay). In contrast, in the northwestern part of the German-speaking lands, from the Rhineland to Lower Saxony, the near absence of estates based upon the French model led to smaller seigniorial properties and a more widespread breaking up of landholdings. Ownership de jure in the Roman sense of the term was completed by ownership de facto owing to a very favorable system of possession. The precarious leases common in France (hierarchical tenant-farming in the Île-de-France, share-cropping in western France, and, in Brittany, estates that could be terminated by the landlord) were replaced by lifetime or hereditary leases called *Erblehen*. This was accomplished by means of *Erbzins*, nearly immutable fees centered around the *Hof* as farming unit, or even by various kinds of term leases based on a contract with the tenant. Whatever the type of lease, the main concern of the lord in this region was to ensure the productive capacity of the peasant leasehold.

Against the reaction of the nobles in France in the years 1760 to 1770, the peasantry put up a resistance that was all the more fierce because it was integrated into well-organized communities with a certain degree of autonomy. These groups willingly rebelled against the seigniory, which was seen as having played the role of usurper in the edicts of enclosure, or the seizure of communal property by forcible occupation or preemption. While peasant ownership was threatened by the townsmen's offensive in France and the Netherlands, the peasantry was consolidating its independence in many other European countries (Germany, Norway, Sweden, Denmark).

Augmented by prevailing inheritance practices, the extreme fragmentation of land often necessitated a reallocation of property (the *Storskifte* in Sweden and Finland during the 1780s). Was this compatible with agricultural progress? As an alternative to the large-scale physiocratic cultivation found in the Île-de-France, the Rhenish and Flemish regions practiced a kind of "handicraft farming" that was flexible and intensive, similar to gardening, and based essentially upon manual labor. German cameralism (Johann Beckmann, Albert Thaer, Jean-Christian Schubart), with its practical and experimental tendencies, attempted to reconcile, on the one hand, the preoccupation with the common good and strengthening of absolute power within the framework of the territorial state directed by the *Landesherr* (for example, the margrave Charles Frederick of Baden), with, on the other hand, the French physiocratic theories based on natural order, liberty, and profit. Such a policy, concerned both with intervention and forecasting, was halfway between liberalism and mercantilism and was not exempt from ulterior motives of profit.

Progress lay less in the difficult expansion of arable land (only a 1 to 2 percent increase in France during the 18th century) than in research into intensified cultivation. A system of mixed farming prevailed on the plains of Europe, with grains predominant, corresponding to eating habits. This system was continually enriched by the development of new types of farming—for example, the production of materials for textiles or dyestuffs (linen, hemp, madder, pastel woad, tobacco, hops). Farming was further intensified through the growing importance of livestock, which fed on forage plants and provided manure for cultivation. Specialization in livestock was concentrated in those mountainous regions that were ideal for grazing, as in the Alps and the Jura, or in the north, where animal husbandry was readily integrated with international trade. The opportunities for exporting meat, as well as the rising price of butter during the 18th century, thus worked in favor of Danish agriculture.

Farming Systems in Eastern Europe: Resistance to Change

Southwestern Germany, Lower Saxony and Bavaria formed a bridge between two worlds extending on either side of the Elbe. From a "full world," that of western Europe, with its high population densities and chronic shortages of land, grain, and timber, one passed progressively into eastern Europe, a world characterized by underpopulation and low population density, its lands ready for colonization and its grain ripe for export. The *Grundherrschaf* (manorial system), which had been based on the levy of rents and fees by a lord who acted as both landlord and dispenser of justice, gave way to *Gutherrschaft,* a system based on the exploitation by a landowning aristocracy of both a piece of property and the people who occupied it. As one advanced toward the east, traveling from Prussia to Russia, passing through the Baltic provinces, Mecklenburg, Pomerania, Silesia, Austria, Hungary, Bohemia, Moravia, and Poland, the taxes and fees imposed grew more onerous, individual liberty diminished, and hereditary possession disappeared.

Compared to the seigniory of western Europe, the eastern domain was characterized first of all by an extraordinary concentration of land—hundreds, indeed thousands of hectares in the *dominical* of Bohemia, the Polish *folwark,* and the Russian *pomestye*—in the hands of the state, the Church, and the nobility. The central power sought to assure the fidelity of the nobility (Prussian *Junkers,* Polish *zlachta*) through the concession of land, which constituted most of their revenue, plus the grant of a portion of administrative authority. The magnates, such as the Potockis and Radziwills in Poland, the Schwarzenbergs in Moravia, or the Orloffs and Potemkins in Russia, ended up monopolizing the land to the detriment of peasant ownership, which tended to disappear.

Made profitable by their stewards, such holdings were the basis of a massive production of grain, which, benefiting from rising prices in the 18th century, was quite capable of supplying international wheat markets, particularly through the Baltic ports located at the mouths of the great navigable waterways. Sometimes sustained by the economic liberalism of rulers such as Catherine II, with her support for freedom of trade, these marketable surpluses were over and above what was necessary for the daily needs of a growing population, provided for the most part by the production of rye. In fact, the population of Prussia doubled in the second half of the century, while that of Russia rose between 1724 and 1789 from 14 million to 30 million, of whom more than 95 percent lived in the countryside. However, the great magnitude of production, explained more by the expansion of farmland than by the productivity of the soil (seed-to-harvest yields were on the order of 1:3, 1:4, or sometimes even 1:5), implies no significant technical development. The system, a veritable machine for exploiting manpower, was based on the employment of unpaid manual labor, in the context of an extensive agriculture founded on a traditional three-year rotation even though the latter system was severely criticized in Russia by the "Free Economic Society."

In fact, the noble farmer-proprietor, preferring to live on his land rather than invest his revenues in it, was more interested in the amount of work performed than in the extent of cultivation itself. Cultivation was always extendable through the development of unoccupied lands (as with the development of 200,000 hectares under Frederick-William I, which was carried out by draining the marshes of the Oder and the Warthe), by developing sterile lands in Pomerania and East Prussia, and by settling German-speaking colonists in the Hungarian Banat and on the lower course of the Volga. In fact, there was a flagrant disproportion between the extent of lands to colonize and the relative shortage of the manpower that the nobility tried to attach to the soil. As a consequence, the lord exercised an almost unlimited authority, not only over the lands constituting his estate but also over the "souls" attached to it. The wealth of an estate could be measured in thousands of *arpents* or in *deciatines* (an archaic measure of land), or in tens or hundreds of villages, with the lord asserting himself as both landowner and supreme dispenser of justice. The system depended not on rent in kind or in money, as in the West, but on payment in labor. The lord exacted this payment all the more harshly since he benefited from the passivity, indeed the complicity, of enfeebled governments. With the increase during the second half of the 18th century of *bartchina* (unpaid labor) relative to *obrok* (payment in money), the small-scale free peasants of Russia found their position waning.

However, subjugation took on a wide range of forms. The agrarian system was particularly oppressive in lands bordering the Baltic Sea: Schleswig-Holstein,

Denmark, Swedish Pomerania, and Lithuania. *Leibeigenschaft* (servitude) developed with the help of the noble's right to buy, sell, trade, or transfer his serfs (for example, to the East, for colonization). The serfs were forbidden to lodge a complaint or to leave the estate. The loss of liberty was often manifested in the lord's right to restrict a male serf's marriage options to a woman with the same status and on the same estate and to confiscate a serf's possessions upon his death (mortmain); in *Gesindedienst,* the obligation of the serf's children to work for the lord as servants; and a primitive feudal exaction that took the form of unpaid labor and that could occupy the serf's time from two to six days a week. In these conditions, all attempts at progress risked being thwarted by social stagnation, with the peasants' lack of freedom leading to a total lack of interest.

Although serfdom was becoming less harsh in Bavaria, despite persistence of mortmain, it was reinforced from Prussia to Russia beginning in the 16th century, in what has been termed "refeudalization" or a "second serfdom." In the 18th century, enlightened despotism brought about some improvements. In Poland the agrarian reforms of Stanislaus-Augustus Poniatowski resulted in the partial abolition of personal servitude and the limitation of obligatory unpaid labor in 1781. Under the Austro-Hungarian monarchy, a cadastral survey was tentatively established (1747–85) as a basis for a fairer sharing of taxes and more secure property rights. However, nothing of the sort occurred in Russia where, for political and economic reasons, Catherine II placated her nobles by making serfdom harsher and extending it, in the very heart of the Enlightenment. Serfdom was seen as the foundation of the Russian monarchy (hence the aggravation of the conditions of the serfs and the extension of serfdom into Little Russia and Ukraine between 1765 and 1783); it was also seen as the basis of the traditional social equilibrium (as evidenced in the Charter of the Nobility of 1785).

The absence of an enlightened bourgeoisie that, as in the West, would have been capable of imposing a revolutionary course, further accounts for the inertia and archaism of the system. Nonetheless, peasant liberation movements had begun to spring up by the end of the century. Opposition could not get started, however, within the *mir,* a form of collective organization that was subject to the pressures of the landed aristocracy. Based on the periodic redistribution of land, the Russian *mir,* unlike the village communities of the West, never became either a framework for peasant ownership or a means for contesting seigniorial authority. Even so, the agrarian troubles in the Baltic provinces, the peasant uprisings in Poland in the second half of the century (from the tentative efforts of Celina Bobinska to the Kosciusko insurrection in 1794), the uprising of the Don cossacks led by Pugachev in 1773, and the Raditchev protests in 1790 all attest to the peasants' aspiration for liberty and to the depths of the economic and social malaise that the French Revolution would only partially correct.

Mediterranean Contrasts

In reviewing the distinctions between agrarian systems on one side of the Elbe and the other, we must bear in mind the fundamental differences between agriculture in the north of Europe and that in the south, which was characterized by marked contrasts (see the research by Maurice Aymard on southern Italy, by Jacques Revel on the Roman countryside, and by Pierre Ponsot on Andalusia). The natural contrasts were related to underutilization of the soil in the south: immense areas were either mountainous or wooded, and the cultivable zone was restricted. In the rare pockets of intensive cultivation in the Mediterranean region, rice, vegetables, and fruit were often grown on irrigable land surrounding the towns. There were other natural contrasts in the uses to which the soil was put, as illustrated by the age-old opposition between sedentary farmers practicing *cultura promiscua*—growing the traditional crops of wheat, grapes, or olives—and the herders of transhumant sheep, who were grouped within a powerful corporation called the *Mesta*. Overall, only one-third of the agricultural land, and even less in Apulia and in Calabria, benefited from regular exploitation, with uncultivated land covering the remaining two-thirds. There was a world of difference, however, between the wheat granary of Sicily and the diversified and intensive agriculture on the hills of Tuscany. Above all, there were contrasts in the socioeconomic structures imposed by the system of latifundia. Most of the land belonged to a minority of major landowners—monarchs, the Church, the nobility—who carved out large domains that were rented en bloc to a local squire or bourgeois according to a system of sharecropping. Sometimes parcels would be sublet to peasants whom the master had previously installed following the archaic formula of *colonat,* under precarious leases characterized by short terms and onerous levies. This "refeudalization," especially in the Italian Mezzogiorno, resulted in a certain inertia with regard to improving the land, together with the survival of archaic techniques, and the persistence of derisory yields made unreliable by extremes of weather (catastrophic droughts and torrential rains). In contrast, in Spain the *Reconquista* of the Andalusian plain and the Castilian plateau, as well as the colonization of the land, led to a redistribution of land that benefited peasant ownership, which became hereditary and free of exactions. However, while the peasants preserved their personal liberty, in contrast to the countries of eastern Europe, they did not escape economic loss. Because of the scarcity and high cost of arable land, peasants were often reduced to the position of agricultural laborers.

With few exceptions, these conditions taken together called for an extensive agricultural and pastoral economy in all but the northern parts of the Italian and Iberian peninsulas. Nevertheless, the image of a vast grain-growing estate, coupled with great transhumant herds requires some modification. The grains consisted chiefly of wheat with optimal yields of 1:4 or 1:5, and there were greater numbers of sheep than of cattle; corn appeared from the 16th century onward, and potatoes a short time later, at the end of the 18th century. The agrarian reforms advocated by economists and stewards alike went to the root of the problem; they aimed to expand cultivable lands and, with the establishment of an equitable cadastre, sought to bring about a better distribution of these lands and, eventually, to alleviate the harsher aspects of the feudal system. The urban bourgeoisie deserves credit for the emergence of a more modern and "capitalist" agriculture, for which Tuscany provides a model. The fact that the land still belonged to a minority did not necessarily constitute a handicap for these regions. Yet, it would have to be an enlightened and dynamic minority, open to progress, and the benefits of the arrangement would be felt by rural society as a whole. It must be said, however, that in the Mediterranean ecosystem, sociolegal obstacles combined with natural and technical constraints to keep agriculture in a state of persistent mediocrity.

Did the economic and technical changes observed in European agriculture clear the way for social change? Although it must be admitted that the overall output of the land increased during the 18th century, as is attested by tithing records, it is probable that high population growth caused a reduction in the average product per capita (see Morineau). This latter finding implies that progress seems to have worked exclusively in favor of the upper layer of rural society. Growth or well-being? In the countries affected by agricultural progress, one may observe, in the years leading up to 1789, a growing polarization between the minority of great landowners, comfortably provided with capital, lands, and equipment, and the mass of dependent peasants, whose only recourse for subsistence was to be found in agricultural wages or the rural craft industry. In France the revolutions of 1789–93 and 1848 made possible the emancipation of the peasants by delivering a fatal blow to the seigniorial system and estate servitude, but they hardly succeeded in establishing social justice in the rural regions of Europe.

JEAN-MICHEL BOEHLER

See also Agriculture: Agronomy; Demography; Feudalism; Food; Peasantry; Physiocracy; Village Communities

Further Reading

Bloch, Marc, *French Rural History: An Essay on Its Basic Characteristics*, London: Routledge and Paul, and Berkeley: University of California Press, 1966 (original French edition, 1931)

Cipolla, Carlo M., editor, *Fontana Economic History of Europe*, 6 vols., London: Fontana, 1972

Goubert, Pierre, *The French Peasantry in the Seventeenth Century*, translated by Ian Patterson, Cambridge and New York: Cambridge University Press, 1986 (original French edition, 1982)

Léon, Pierre, *Économies et sociétés préindustrielles*, vol. 2, *1650–1780*, Paris: Colin, 1970

Marx, Roland, *La révolution industrielle en Grande-Bretagne, des origines à 1850*, Paris: Colin, 1970

Marx, Roland, *Histoire de la Grande-Bretagne*, Paris: Colin, 1980

Meuvret, Jean, *Études d'histoire économique: Recueil d'articles*, Paris: Colin, 1971

Meuvret, Jean, *Le problème des subsistances à l'époque Louis XIV*, 3 vols., Paris: Mouton, 1977–88

Moriceau, Jean Marc, "Au rendez-vous de la 'révolution agricole' dans la France du XVIIIe siècle: À propos des regions de grande culture," *Annales, histoire, sciences sociales* 49 (1994)

Moriceau, Jean-Marc, and Gilles Postel-Vinay, *Ferme, entreprise, famille: Grande exploitation et changements agricoles: Les Chartier, XVIIe–XIXe siècle*, Paris: Éditions de l'École des Hautes Études en Sciences Sociales, 1992

Morineau, Michel, *Les Faux-semblants d'un démarrage économique, agriculture et démographie en France au XVIIIe siècle*, Paris: Colin, 1971

Pfister, Christian, *Das Klima der Schweiz von 1525–1860 und seine Bedeutung in der Geschichte von Bevölkerung und Landwirtschaft*, 2 vols., Bern: Haput, 1984

Ponsot, Pierre, *Atlas de historia económica de la baja Andalucía: Siglos XVI–XIX*, Seville: Editoriales Andaluzas Unidas, 1986

Slicher van Bath, Bernard H., *The Agrarian History of Western Europe, 500–1850*, London: Arnold, 1963

Alchemy

Contrary to a fairly widespread misconception, the age of the Enlightenment did not mark the eclipse of alchemy. It would be more accurate to speak of its permanence and vitality throughout the 18th century. Alchemy's many avatars were part of a varied, little-studied spectrum that needs to be resituated, without preconceived notions, in a century rich in contradictions.

Chemistry and Alchemy

Up until the end of the Renaissance no distinction was made between chemistry and alchemy. In the 17th century both were closely related to medicine thanks to the promotion, by Paracelsians of all nationalities, of *chimie spagyrique*, a medical alchem(istr)y that was influenced by hermetic and mystical speculations. (Thus, in the eyes of many of these *chimistes* God was the first alchemist, he who separated the pure from the impure, the waters above from the waters below.) Alchemy's main purpose was the preparation of medicines, but also, in certain cases, the search for the philosopher's stone. For J.B. Van Helmont (1577–1664) or J.-J. Becher (1635–82), there was no difference between chemistry and alchemy. This "chemistry" was watered down over the course of the 18th century, gradually separating from medicine to become an independent science and, with Antoine-Laurent de Lavoisier (1743–94), a discipline closely resembling modern chemistry. Alchemy, meanwhile, went its own way, but not without some degree of overlap that persisted at least until the middle of the century. In 1702 the terminological ambiguity between "chemistry" and "alchemy" is apparent in the very title of Manget's *Bibliotheca Chemica Curiosa*. After midcentury the two notions became more distinct. Various articles on the subject in the *Encyclopédie*, from 1751 to 1776, clearly separate the respective disciplines: "Alchimie" (Alchemy), "Chimie" (Chemistry), "Philosophie Hermétique" (Hermetic Philosophy), "Pierre philosophale" (Philosopher's Stone), "Azote" (Nitrogen), etc. The same is true of Lenglet-Dufresnoy's *Histoire de la philosophie hermétique* (1742; History of Hermetic Philosophy). In contrast, up to the early 19th century in Germany, alchemy was often designated as *höhere Chemie* (higher chemistry).

In the 18th century alchemy was still very actively practiced and it keenly interested many rulers. Jean Erhard and Sylvain Matton (see Matton 1987, 1995), following Figuier and Hermann Kopp (see Kopp), document the era's many notorious charlatans. Fontenelle (*Histoire de l'Académie des sciences, année 1722* [History of the Academy of Sciences, Year 1722]) and Montesquieu (*Lettres persanes* [1721; The Persian Letters]), among others, cite Paris, Spain, and Vienna as the gathering places of European alchemists. Even after Lavoisier, the chemist Fourcroy, in the article "Alchimie" in the *Encyclopédie méthodique* (1792; Methodical Encyclopedia), was still denouncing this dangerous mania that had brought to ruin so many credulous men. More than 20 years earlier, the chevalier de Jaucourt, picking up on Fontenelle's remarks (1722), was already using the same language in the article "Pierre philosophale" in the *Encyclopédie*. These discussions of alchemy attest to the prestige alchemy still enjoyed in scientific circles, although this status diminished perceptibly over the course of the century, weakened by ever more frequent accusations of moral and social fraud. Although it was often proclaimed that no one had ever succeeded in making gold, in 1722 even Fontenelle did not dare to deny the theoretical possibility of the transmutation. A renowned academic such as the learned theologian J.F. Buddeus (1667–1729), who could hardly be suspected of pronounced occultist sympathies, studied the question of transmutation and recognized that it was impossible to prove philosophically that it would be unnatural. His opinion was shared by a large number of his scientific and scholarly contemporaries. In 1711, when the physician F. Pousse published in Paris a severely critical *Examen des principes des alchimistes* (An Examination of the Principles of Alchemists), the reviews that appeared in publications as varied as the *Journal des savants* (1665), the *Mémoires de Trévoux,* and the *Mercure galant* all agreed that the theoretical impossibility of alchemy could not be demonstrated. Indeed, great chemists such as Georg Ernst Stahl (1660–1734), Hermann Boerhaave (1668–1738), and Guillaume-François Rouelle (1703–70) could also, on occasion, admit without embarrassment their belief in the theoretical possibility of alchemy, but not their interest in its practice. Similarly, the physician Cromwell Mortimer, secretary of London's Royal Society and a former student of Boerhaave, in dedicating Volume 40 of the *Philosophical Transactions* to the astronomer John Winthrop, (1714–79) in 1741, assured him that his exceptional knowledge of the profound mysteries of the most secret hermetic science would forever earn him the respect of scientists and educated men. Stahlian chemist J.F. Henckel (1679–1744), in his definition of

chemistry, went as far as to specify that "its most sublime part" is "alchemy or chemistry par excellence, the art of making base metals noble" (Baron d'Holbach, *Textes choisis* [1957; Selected Texts]). Even the *Encyclopédie méthodique* attests to only a gradual change in mentality in the wake of Lavoisier's discoveries. For example, Fourcroy (1755–1809), a close collaborator of Lavoisier, in his 29-page article "Alchimie" (1792) echoed Pierre-Joseph Macquer (1766), acknowledging that the phrase "the impossibility of making gold has not been demonstrated," is sufficient to constitute "an argument that many men use against detractors of this so-called art, and that can be answered only by the failure of researchers." It was not until the article "Métallisation" (1808; Metallization) that Fourcroy would adopt a more decisive tone and position.

The Literature of Alchemy

The alchemy that flourished in England, Spain, and Italy up to the end of the 17th century is still not well known to scholars. Alchemy in those countries appears to have produced much less new work after the 1730s. In contrast, there was a spectacular growth in alchemical publications in the German-speaking countries, which was clearly the result of their demographic and cultural revival but also of the teaching of chemistry in German universities, which was in advance of the rest of Europe. (The first Italian university chair, at Bologna, was not established until 1737.) This development was subject to three main influences: theosophists and followers of Jakob Boehme's mysticism, among whom the best known was Georg von Welling, an adept both of theurgy and of the cabala; the Rosicrucian myth (often associated with the cult of the "Germanic Hermes," Paracelsus), which attracted renewed interest from midcentury; and Freemasonry, which provided an ideal focal point for the first two influences. In France the volume of publications on alchemy had certainly decreased since the 17th century, but this noticeable decline was partially compensated by the deluge of manuscripts on alchemy that inundated not only France but the whole of Europe.

Alchemy in the age of the Enlightenment was primarily a continuation of the movement of the 16th and 17th centuries: countless translations and new editions were published in western Europe during the first third of the 18th century. The *Novum Lumen Chymicum* (1604; A New Light of Alchemy) by the "Cosmopolitan" (M. Sendivogius) was republished in German in 1718 (and again in 1750 and 1766), in English in 1722, and in French in 1723. Another classic, the *Introitus Apertus ad Occlusum Regis Palatium* (1667; Secrets Revealed; or, An Open Entrance to the Sealed Palace of the King Containing the Greatest Treasure in Chemistry

Never Yet So Plainly Discovered), by "Eirenaeus Phila-lethes" (George Starkey), reappeared in German in 1705 (then in subsequent editions in 1748 and later), in English in 1709, in Spanish in 1727, and in French in 1742 and 1754. It was also during this period—following Manget's monumental anthology of the most famous medieval Latin and modern texts in alchemy, *Bibliotheca chemica curiosa* (1702; Library of Chemical Curiosities)—that the bookseller Friedrich Roth-Scholtz had a German equivalent prepared, his enormous *Deutsche Theatrum Chemicum* (1728–32; Library of German Chemists). France did not lag behind: the *Bibliothèque des philosophes chimiques* (1740–54; Library of Chemical Philosophers), which had first appeared at the end of the 17th century, was republished in a significantly amplified version by Mangin de Richebourg. Lenglet-Dufresnoy's *Histoire de la philosophie hermétique* (1742; History of Hermetic Philosophy) came out at the same time. The alchemical interpretation of mythology, which was very common in the 16th and 17th centuries, was also continued, notably with A.J. Pernety's *Les fables égyptiennes et grecques dévoilées* (1758, 1786; The Egyptian and Greek Fables Revealed)—a new version of M. Maier's *Arcana Arcanissima* (1614; Most Secret Secrets)—and the *Dictionnaire mytho-hermétique* (1787; Mytho-Hermetic Dictionary), which served as an index to his *Fables*; similarly, in German, authors such as Naxagoras or Hermann Fictuld, were fascinated by the myth of the Golden Fleece. Finally, alchemical iconography continued to produce some very fine works, including manuscript copies of the great iconographic cycles of the Middle Ages and the Renaissance (*Donum Dei*; *Splendor solis*), as well as new creations, such as the *Hermaphroditisches Sonn- und Monds-kind* (1752; The Hermaphrodite Child of the Sun and Moon) by a certain L.C.S., or the *Geheime Figuren der Rosenkreutzer* (Secret Symbols of the Rosicrucians), inspired by G. von Welling and published in 1785–88 by the Gold- und Rosenkreutzer (Gold and Rose Cross) sect, after a long period of circulating in manuscript form.

The newest trends arose in the field of mystical alchemy. Jakob Boehme and G. von Welling, not to mention the Christian cabala, were important influences in Germany as well as in Russia, where the Freemason I.V. Lopukhin (1756–1816) was engaged in extensive publishing activities in which alchemy played an important role. A hermetic interpretation of nature was presented in the astonishing *Aurea Catena Homeri* (1723; Homer's Gold Chain) by A.J. Lorcjweger, which was frequently republished, in particular by the Gold- und Rosenkreutzer under the title *Annulus Platonis oder physikalisch-chymische Erklärung der Natur* (1781; Annulus Platonis; or, Physico-Chemical Explanation of Nature). A French translation of this work

was published in 1772 as *La nature dévoilée* (Nature Revealed), but French manuscript versions had been circulating since 1749. The Gold- und Rosenkreutzer circle also brought forth the superb and dense *Compass der Weisen* (Compass of the Wise), edited by "Ketmia Vere" (C. Goldman von Jäger) in 1779. The young Johann Goethe would be fascinated by all this literature, which he discovered around 1768–69.

One of the most notable innovations of the 18th century was the collusion between alchemy and Freemasonry and the integration of alchemy into many Masonic rites. From the middle of the century onward, alchemy spread into such orders as the Strict Templar Observance, the Asiatic Brothers, and the lodge of United Friends. It also found a place in virtually all the mystical lodges, including those of eastern Europe, not to mention the para-Masonic sects, such as the Gold-und Rosenkreutzer or, in France, the "hermetic rite" of the Illuminés of Avignon, led by Pernety beginning in 1779. In 1766 the baron de Tschoudy, whose interest was mainly limited to recopying 17th-century alchemical writings, proclaimed in *L'Étoile flamboyante, ou la société des francs-maçons* (The Blazing Star; or, The Society of Freemasons) that the ultimate aim of Masonry was none other than that of alchemy. His book was translated and republished up until 1810, when it appeared with a dedication to the glory of the "great Napoleon."

Finally, it should be noted that some alchemical works were closely related to the scientific or literary currents of the time. Fabre du Bosquet, in his *Concordance mytho-physico-cabalo-hermétique* (Mytho-Physico-Cabalo-Hermetic Concordance), then circulating in manuscript form, provides a rare example of phlogistic alchemy (published in Barcelona, 1986). In *Le diadème des sages* (1781; The Diadem of the Sages), while the diplomat O.-H. de Loos (1725–85), a fervent defender of the myth of Nicolas Flamel, attacked Saint-Martin's famous work *Des erreurs et de la vérité* (1775; On Errors and Truth). However, the publication of Lavoisier's *Méthode de nomenclature chimique* (Method of Chemical Nomenclature) in 1787 and his *Traité élémentaire de chimie* (Elements of Chemistry) in 1789 marked a decisive turning point in the history of the discipline. A few alchemists stubbornly held their ground, particularly in Germany and in eastern Europe, where Lavoisier's work met with nationalistic resistance, but there was a spectacular decline in the number of printed works on alchemy, and even in manuscript works, within the space of a few years.

Alchemy and "Enlightenment"

Given its recognized scientific status, alchemy did not appear in J.-B. Thiers's *Traité des superstitions* (1679; A

Treatise on Superstitions)—a text frequently republished in the 18th century—because it did not correspond to any of the criteria given in Chapter IX of Thiers's classification, which was inspired by the Scholastic tradition. Alchemy was not a favorite target for Enlightenment thinkers and did not necessarily inspire unanimous opposition from enlightened Europe, even though the advocates of "common sense" tended spontaneously to place it in the ranks of fantasy. As Herwig Buntz has shown, in a progressive Bavarian periodical, the *Parnassus Boicus* (1722–40), the treatment of alchemy evolved in line with the ideas of its contributors. At first rather favorable to alchemy, the *Parnassus Boicus* became clearly hostile by 1725, and then the topic disappeared from its columns, to be replaced by new subjects related to the natural sciences. In 1758 the Bavarian Academy of Sciences was founded, explicitly in the wake of the *Parnassus Boicus,* for the advancement of the sciences and liberal arts, among which only chemistry was included. The *Parnassus Boicus* also helped to separate chemistry from alchemy in the minds of progressive thinkers, at a time when even the great German dictionaries persisted in expounding the potential and the interest of the objectives of alchemy in the three realms of nature. In 1758 and in 1761, a controversy arose between the alchemist Pernety and the abbé Villain over Nicolas Flamel. Villain, evidence in hand, claimed that Flamel was not an alchemist. Fréon's *L'année littéraire* twice opened its columns to Pernety, whereas the *Journal encyclopédique* (15 April 1758) was hostile to him. In the second half of the century, the Rosicrucianism that was flourishing in Germany was clearly oriented against the spread of the Enlightenment, and in Prussia in the 1770s the Gold- und Rosekreutzer sect was sometimes used in the repression of free thought.

However, the borders between alchemy and chemistry were not always so clearly drawn. In his memoir for the Académie Royale des Sciences de Paris (French Royal Academy of Science), *Des supercheries concernant la pierre philosophale* (1722; On Hoaxes Related to the Philosopher's Stone), the chemist Étienne-François Geoffroy borrowed substantially from an alchemist, Michel Maier (*Examen fucorum pseudo-chymicorum detectorum et in gratiam veritatis amantium succincte refutatorum* (1617). Further, a manuscript in the library of the chemist Jean Hellot (1685–1766) is none other than a Latin translation (also by Geoffroy) of *Alchimia denudata* (1716; Alchemy Revealed), by the German Naxagoras (1708). By the same token, the abbé Le Mascrier (1697–1760) who was involved in the dissemination of clandestine philosophical texts (see Moureau) also translated the *Chansons intellectuelles sur la résurrection du phénix* (1622, 1758; Intellectual Songs on the Rise of the Phoenix), a treatise by the alchemist Michel Maier, and, if Mascrier is to be believed, several other alchemical texts. In Germany even a man such as Georg Foster (1754–94), who had been won over to Enlightenment thought, allowed himself to be seduced by Rosicrucianism. Denis Diderot tells us that his chemistry teacher Rouelle—who also taught Gabriel-François Venel, Holbach, and even Lavoisier, inspired the chemistry of the *Encyclopédie,* and no doubt unwittingly influenced Diderot's own philosophy—ended his course every year by demonstrating the reality of alchemy "in fact and in principle" and even considered working on alchemy "in his final years." Brumore, the charlatan who animated the oracle of the "Holy Word" in Pernety's circle of Illuminés in Avignon, was none other than J.B.P. Guyton de Morveau, the brother of the chemist who collaborated with Lavoisier and initiated the project of a new chemical nomenclature.

Alchemy was also sometimes used for political ends. In his *Chrysomander* (1783), the Russian Freemason Nicolaï Novikov (1744–1818), who was influenced by theosophical currents of thought and adhered to an essentially Christian Enlightenment, portrayed a magician named Hyperion, more illuminated than enlightened, who uses alchemy to govern better his empire (see Faivre). Just as paradoxically, the Order of the Illuminati of Bavaria (1776–87), conceived by J.A. Weishaupt to serve the most radical wing of the German Enlightenment, hid its true objectives under a facade of theosophy and occultist Freemasonry in order both to maintain confidentiality and to increase recruitment. Not even the members knew about the subterfuge, which ultimately led to the Order's collapse. Its organizer, Adolf von Knigge, was himself a deserter from occultist Freemasonry who had taken up a radical version of the German Enlightenment. In this case, occultism was a strange ploy used by the faction that had the strongest ideological opposition to it. As was noted, however, in the *Journal* of Bourrée de Corberon (1748–1810), a diplomat with a passion for the occult, "for some years, the spirit of philosophy, while rejecting the beliefs of the pious, has not opposed otherworldly knowledge" (Viatte, *Les sources occultes du romantisme: Illuminisme–théosophie* [1928; The Occult Sources of Romanticism: Illuminism and Theosophy]).

There were even deeper affinities between these two apparently antithetical currents of thought. For example, the unusual (and surprising) interest that Henri de Boulainviller (1658–1722) took in Paracelsus can be explained by his ties to the alchemist F.-M.-P. Colonna, the author of an *Abrégé de la doctrine de Paracelse* (1724; A Summary of Paracelsus's Doctrine), in which J. Ehrard has suggested "the occult sources of Diderot's thinking" should be sought. More generally, as A. Mothu has recently pointed out, certain themes from

17th-century Paracelsian doctrines, such as the universal spirit reappear in the clandestine philosophical literature of the Enlightenment (see Mothu). This copresence of seemingly contradictory ideas is less surprising when we recall that Paracelsianism, from the 16th century onward, had acted as an objective and involuntary ally of irreligion by way of its naturalism, a fact of which P. Garasse, in his *La doctrine curieuse des beaux esprits de ce temps* (1625; The Curious Doctrine of the Great Minds of This Time), is perfectly aware. This objective alliance was still operative in the 18th century. As J. Ehrard has shown in the case of Diderot, recourse to the doctrines of Paracelsian alchem(istr)y was a strategy that some Enlightenment thinkers still found useful at a time when these ideas were not yet discredited.

Diderot had rather mixed feelings toward alchemy. His amused toleration of Rouelle's alchemical convictions is in line with his position on Paracelsus and Van Helmont expressed in his article "Théosophes" in the *Encyclopédie* (1765). In the article Diderot demonstrates a love for chemistry equal only to his hatred of metaphysics and obscure language. But, while viewing theosophy sympathetically from a safe distance, Diderot was in no way inclined to give it precedence over "the spirit of discovery and research" of the Encyclopedists. We may smile over the "cyclometry" by which he tried to solve the squaring of the circle; but chemistry was far too central to his philosophy for him to embrace its distorted, alchemical form.

More than Diderot, whose thinking cannot be reduced to unequivocal or preestablished schemes, the baron d'Holbach is a perfect example of an Enlightenment thinker for whom the fracture between chemistry and alchemy had a solid basis in ideology. While he contributed a great deal to the introduction of the chemical and mineralogical sciences from the German-speaking countries into France, he was careful not to import their obscure older sister, alchemy, along with them. Holbach treated the subject in several highly critical articles in the *Encyclopédie*: "Élévation (alchimie)" (1775; Elevation [Alchemy]); "Mercure ou Vif-argent" (Mercury or Quicksilver); "Or (Histoire naturelle, minéralogie et chimie)" (Gold [Natural History, Mineralogy, and Chemistry]); "Régule d'antimoine" (Regulus of Antimony); "Soufre" (1765; Sulfur). Writing on the virtues attributed to the regulus of antimony by alchemists, he says: "We shall not pause here to refute these completely unfounded and fanciful ideas." Although Malouin's article "Alchimie" (1751) shows some approval for a "real science to which sensible, honest people can apply themselves," the *Encyclopédie* as a whole was clearly hostile to alchemy once Malouin had been ousted by Venel (1753). Venel's article "Hermétique (Philosophie)" (1765; Hermetic Philosophy),

apparently intended to correct Malouin's article, gives no ground to the defenders of alchemy:

> Even if this mysterious apparatus were not in itself irksome . . . it is certainly not to the taste of our century or our nation; our philosophy is communicative and favors proof . . . I know perfectly well that many great chemists will accuse this judgment of laziness or of ignorance, but we will still reply that such is the taste of our century . . . We therefore dare to be disgusted even by the works of second-class alchemists (the most useful ones), the Lulles, the Paracelsuses, etc., while admitting nonetheless that the true masters of the art must drink from these primary sources, no matter how troubled and bitter they may be.

Eleven years later, the anonymous article "Azote" (Nitrogen) even more outspoken, relegating transmutation to the "land of chimeras": every substance, including the metals, has its own seed; a man cannot lay an egg nor produce watercress. This was the typical Aristotelian argument, widely debated since the Middle Ages and here summarily propounded. If we add to this verdict the judgments of Holbach, the case seems to be closed, in spite of Diderot's article "Théosophes," which should not be put on the same level. As for Malouin's embarrassing article "Alchimie," its refutation would be among Fourcroy's avowed objectives in his article of the same title in the *Encyclopédie méthodique* (Methodical Encyclopedia).

DIDIER KAHN

See also Chemistry; Corpuscle; Freemasonry; Illuminism

Further Reading

Debus, Allen G., *The French Paracelsians: The Chemical Challenge to Medical and Scientific Tradition in Early Modern France*, Cambridge and New York: Cambridge University Press, 1991

Faivre, Antoine, *Eckartshausen et la théosophie chrétienne*, Paris: Klincksieck, 1969

García Font, Juan, *Historia de la alquimia en España*, Madrid: Editora Nacional, 1976

Kopp, Hermann, *Die Alchemie in älterer und neuerer Zeit*, 2 vol., Heidelberg: Winter, and Leipzig: Tränker, 1886; reprint, Hildesheim: Olms, 1962

Martels, Z.R.W.M. von, editor, *Alchemy Revisited*, Leiden and New York: Brill, 1990

Matton, Sylvain, "Une autobiographie de Jean Vauquelin des Yveteaux: Le traité de la Pierre philosophale," *Chrysopoeia* 1 (1987)

Matton, Sylvain, "L'interprétation alchimique de la mythologie," *Dix-huitième siècle* 27 (1995)

McIntosh, Christopher, *The Rose Cross and the Age of Reason: Eighteenth-Century Rosicrucianism in Central Europe and Its Relationship to the Enlightenment*, Leiden and New York: Brill, 1992

Mothu, A., "Hermétisme et 'libre pensée': Note sur l'esprit universel," *La Lettre Clandestine* 1 (1992)

Moureau, François, *De bonne main: La communication manuscrite au XVIIIe siècle*, Paris: Universitas, and Oxford: Voltaire Foundation, 1993

Algebra

In the *Encyclopédie* article entitled "Algèbre," Jean le Rond D'Alembert refuted the views of those who would define algebra as "the art of resolving mathematical problems," not because that definition lacks specificity, but because it implies analysis and would be more appropriate for defining the objectives of the analytic art. Nevertheless, D'Alembert—appealing, as he often does, to common sense—wrote in the entry entitled "Analyse" (Analysis) that "these two words, 'analysis' and 'algebra,' are also often regarded as synonyms." He thus avoided any discussion that might threaten the unity of mathematics. After declaring that algebra is a "sort of arithmetic"—a subtle distinction that seems to require further explanation, but also one of the commonplaces of the period—he merely reproduced a history of algebra written by the abbé Jean-Paul de Gua de Malves. D'Alembert failed to mention that although Gua represented the very lively tradition of Cartesian algebra, that tradition was not the whole of algebra. Gua had set out to draw battle lines in a way that could not be stated more clearly than in the title of the book that brought him fame: *Usages de l'analyse de Descartes pour découvrir, sans le secours du calcul différentiel, les propriétés, ou affections principales des lignes géométriques de tous les ordres* (1740; Uses of Descartes's Analysis to Discover, without the Aid of Differential Calculus, the Properties or Principal Affections of Geometric Lines of All Degrees). Enlightenment algebra was indispensable to all the mathematics of the moderns; it was conceptually unified, yet it had more than one purpose.

The achievement of unity in mathematics was the ambition of (among others) Joseph-Louis Lagrange, who wanted to place all mathematics in the category of algebra. Fortunately, this proposition did nothing to prevent the emergence, during the closing decades of the 18th century, of a remarkable and distinctive style of algebra that clearly led to the structural algebra of Évariste Galois and Niels Henrik Abel in the 19th century. Moreover, to a greater extent than infinitesimal analysis, at least after 1730, algebra as a language of the sciences inspired the *philosophes*, particularly Étienne Bonnot de Condillac, who used it as material for his theory of knowledge. Algebra penetrated deeper than any other part of 18th-century mathematics into the general culture, although its impact was still not profound if one judges by the contents of the undergraduate honors examinations in mathematics at Cambridge University around 1795, in which equations of the second degree appear as the most difficult material, or even by the observations made around the same time concerning the lack of algebraic knowledge among first-year students at the École Polytechnique (Polytechnical School) in Paris.

High-Risk Combinations of Signs

The representation of variables by the letters of the alphabet generally seemed to be the defining characteristic of algebra, permitting instant recognition of the field but also making it "unpleasant because of the novelty of the terms and the characters that it uses, and the dryness of the matters that it deals with," as Thomas Fantet de Lagny explained in his *Nouveaux éléments d'arithmétique et d'algèbre* (1697; New Principles of Arithmetic and Algebra). In the foreword to his *Mémoires sur différents sujets de mathématiques* (1748; Notes on Various Mathematical Subjects), Denis Diderot expressed the same feeling, set out to expound as many "interesting" topics in mathematical physics as he can, and protested, "I have had no other recourse than to place my xs and ys in such a way that those who have no knowledge of algebra may omit them, without detriment to either the flow or the clarity of the discussion."

This aversion to abstract symbols was still pervasive in 1796, when Pierre-Simon Laplace, in his *Exposition du système du monde* (The System of the World), managed to avoid writing a single equation, even though he proved that if a planet obeys the law of areas on its orbit (equality in a given interval of time of areas described by a line joining the planet to a fixed point), it is attracted by that point in inverse proportion to the square of the distance. Precisely because it is a language that has no spoken form, algebra was a mystery to Enlightenment thinkers, and it is not certain whether Nicholas Saunderson, the blind mathematician from Cambridge, resolved that mystery with his declaration that letters represent quantities in algebra exactly as they represent people in the ordinary course of life (1740; *The Elements of Algebra in Ten Books* [translated into French in 1756]). In algebra there is no need to specify the nature of the quantities in question—numbers, fractions, geometric quantities, etc. Indeed, this indeterminacy is what gives algebra its advantage and establishes it as a practice.

Lagny, an expert calculator, appropriately characterized algebra, holding that it is just as useful in the synthetic methods that follow the ancient models—that is, Greek geometry—as it is in the analytic methods of the moderns. Above all, it was advantageous for those questions that depend "precisely and immediately on combinations." This remark is rich in implications, suggesting the multiplicity of solutions to a problem—an equation that summarizes a given problem can present several solutions—as well as the diversity in systems of classification and the possibility of eliminating obscure sequences of reasoning. However, this ambitious perspective did not prevent Lagny from setting decisive limits for algebra: "The resolution of equations is the purpose and the goal of the whole of algebra." All 18th-century mathematicians accepted these parameters, but only in the sense that they believed that ideally, one could reduce any problem to an equation and even, more often than not, to a polynomial equation.

There was a contradiction between this limited view of algebra and the purpose that was envisaged for it. More was expected from algebra, as is clear from reading the remarks of Saunderson, a devotee who wrote very elegantly about algebra as "the logic of the mathematician" (in the introduction to *The Elements of Algebra in Ten Books*). This characterization means that algebra is a new logic, replacing Aristotelian logic. The latter was discredited or reduced to insignificance by Leonhard Euler, who explained his reasoning with spatial schemas of inclusion in his *Lettres à une princesse d'Allemagne* (1768–72; Letters of Euler to a German Princess, on Different Subjects in Physics and Philosophy), a highly inventive popularization of mathematics.

At the very beginning of the 18th century, algebra had disappointed—or rather dismayed—mathematicians such as Michel Rolle, who wanted to make algebra the sole means of access to geometric curves. His interesting *Traité d'algèbre* (1690; Treatise on Algebra) had led him to the Académie Royale des Sciences de Paris, where he continually sought to identify the difficulties in differential methods, and did so only in order to quarrel with other scholars. He had to be reminded of the courtesies that the Academicians had included in their protocols, and, finally convinced in 1706, he turned against what he had excessively praised.

Algebra caused disappointment once again at the end of the century. In his thesis of 1799, Carl Friedrich Gauss showed that his "fundamental theorem" called for a demonstration that algebra alone could not provide. It was necessary, he contended, to study the intersections of curves, to use arguments in which continuity plays a role, and therefore to consider infinitesimal methods. While the history of this theorem pervaded the history of algebra in the 18th century before arriving at this point, let us first consider yet another disappointment caused by algebra, which appears in the abbé de Condillac's *Langue des calculs* (Language of Calculations). Condillac's book remained unfinished because such a project is by definition impossible to finish, but it had tremendous pedagogical impact and was published posthumously in 1798. The resounding declaration with which the work opens was certainly received with unanimous enthusiasm among men of science: "Every language is an analytic method, and every analytic method is a language." However, Condillac's thesis that invention consists in following the natural development of language was just as rapidly rejected. This thesis presents algebra as a paradigm for the project of "giving to all the sciences the exactitude that has been thought to be the exclusive property of mathematics." Under the cover of science, Condillac was thinking just as much about metaphysics. He set forth the following argument: "Algebra is a well-made language, and it is the only one: nothing in it appears to be arbitrary. Analogy, which is inescapably present, leads us logically from expression to expression." This assertion leads to a reductive judgment: "The method of invention is none other than analogy itself." Condillac was responding, of course, to one of the deep anxieties of the age of the Enlightenment—how to maintain enlightenment and take it further in practice—but people were well aware that in algebra the analogy was not given but constructed, and the "perfected" state of the language of algebra is not in any sense a cause, but a consequence. What, then, was the nature of the knowledge that algebra provided? Augmenting previous explanations of a priori synthetic judgments, Immanuel Kant's comprehensive analysis represented the culmination of a century of inquiry and, in combination with Lagrange's activities, denied any specificity to algebra.

Moreover, the excessive flexibility of the word "analogy" should have alerted Condillac to be more prudent, since "analogies" in the mathematical sense—derived from the theory of proportions in the fifth book of Euclid's *Elements*—essentially permit mathematicians to work with variables designated by letters, without any need to specify the nature of those variables. There was a price to be paid for this understanding of analogy—a price often overlooked in French and German books about algebra, but frequently mentioned by the Cambridge mathematicians, notably Saunderson, who pointed out the ontological argument inherent in algebra. This "amnesia" on the part of the Continental mathematicians led to the emergence of a distinctive, autonomous mathematical culture there.

The Unattainable Perfection of Algebra

A problem of classification within integral calculus led D'Alembert to propose an early demonstration of the "fundamental theorem." In fact, following in the footsteps of Jean Bernoulli, D'Alembert sought to determine the form of all the primitives of rational fractions (that is, the quotients of two polynomials), on which a large number of resources had been expended, from calculations based on changing the variables to some surprising manipulations. D'Alembert understood that the classification depended exclusively on the factorization in the polynomial of the denominator of the rational fraction. In short, could any polynomial—that is, a sum of the monomials $a_k x^k$—be reduced to a product of the factors of the first degree $(x - x_k)$.

René Descartes had already asked this question and had answered it in the affirmative, as clear and distinct thought seemed to him to demand. However, in order to do so, Descartes had introduced fictional numbers that he called, appropriately enough, "imaginary" numbers. Thus, in order to reduce $x^2 + 1$ to the product of two numbers, he had "imagined" a number i such that $(x + i)(x - i) = x^2 + 1$. This i is necessarily imaginary, and not a number like the others, because when the terms of the preceding equation are broken down power by power, the inevitable result is $i^2 = -1$, a negative square. Thus, by way of the idea of polynomial analysis, Descartes had limited the horizon of algebra with his appeal to imaginary numbers, which became indispensable. Although D'Alembert accepted Cartesian algebra without argument, for the purposes of integral calculus he had to specify the nature of the "fictions." They appeared, in the form x_k, among the factors of the first degree of decomposition of a polynomial. The theorem that D'Alembert established was thus a reduction that permitted integral calculus, for the "fictions" that Descartes had found necessary are all of the same form. They are complex numbers—that is, every x_k is $a_k + ib_k$ where a_k and b_k are docile "real" numbers, and essentially only one imaginary i is needed, which is precisely the square root of -1.

In fact, with this analytic objective D'Alembert performed the work of an algebraist. He structured complex numbers as a field—that is, as an ensemble of elements that remained stable when subjected to operations of addition, subtraction, multiplication, and division. But he went beyond algebra, at least in the sense in which it was understood in the 19th century, by also stabilizing exponentiation within this field (α^β is still a complex number when α and β are complex numbers). With considerable clarity, the comte de Bougainville accounted for this explanation in his *Traité de calcul intégral pour servir de suite à l'analyse des infiniment petits de M. le marquis de l'Hôpital* (1754; Treatise on Integral Calculus to Serve as Sequel to the Analysis of Infinitesimals by M. the Marquis de l'Hôpital).

It was within the framework of algebra that first Euler and then Lagrange—in 1749 and 1769, respectively—provided the proof for D'Alembert's theorem. They worked on the polynomials and ingeniously juggled the symmetric functions of the roots rationally expressible by means of the coefficients of the polynomial. They also perfected the purely algebraic theory of elimination that Étienne Bézout adapted for the structuring of plane curves. (Bézout had demonstrated that two algebraic curves of respective degrees m and n have mn points of intersection.) However, these demonstrations were difficult, and they were not included in any algebra textbook. Lagrange did not include such a proof in his *Éléments d'algèbre* (1774; Elements of Algebra), the French translation of Euler's *Vollständige Anleitung zur Algebra* (1770; Complete Instructions on Algebra); he preferred to add indeterminate analysis. Like mathematics itself, algebra had two systems.

The change of rhythm that Laplace introduced in 1795 in one of his most brilliant lectures at the École Normale Supérieure is therefore surprising, for his demonstration takes up less than two pages and he presented it in front of a large audience. The fact that Laplace, who was approaching the age of 50, did not work within algebra as if it were a privileged domain is already a sign that the theorem, through his inspiration, belonged to another kind of mathematics. This is evident from his recourse to the results of the intermediate values, a proposition (taken from the field of mathematical analysis rather than from algebra) on the cancellation of a polynomial that takes positive and negative values. Lagrange and Euler had already made use of this proposition, but Laplace emphasized its particular importance in a lecture on algebra. Jean-Robert Argand, 11 years later, and soon after him Augustin-Louis Cauchy, maintained the simplicity of the proof of the theorem by shifting its meaning into analysis through a careful study of the local behavior of a power of a complex number.

Meanwhile, in 1799 Gauss had provoked the collapse of the minimalist conception of algebra, instantly eliminating the Cartesian "imaginary" numbers, for while he regarded the existence of such numbers as normal, it remained to be proved that they formed a field, or that they obeyed the usual laws of algebra. A new level of algebra became indispensable.

Toward Algebraic Structures

This new algebra emerged abruptly but had been in gestation throughout the 18th century in two main forms. Cartesian geometry was maintained and developed into a truly algebraic geometry. For very good reasons, Sir Isaac Newton, in the *Philosophiae Naturalis Principia Mathematica* (1687; Mathematical Principles of Natural Philosophy), had replaced Descartes's "geometric curves" with "algebraic curves," their implicit equation being provided by a polynomial of two variables. Descartes had proved that curves of the second degree correspond to all the plane sections of the cone. In order to classify curves of the third degree, Newton used differential calculus in his *Enumeratio LinearumTertii Ordinis* (1711; Enumeration of Lines of the Third Order), which appeared as an appendix to his *Opticks* (1704). He also took a projective approach, similar to that of Girard Desargues, to the problem of the perspective of such curves.

In 1740 Gua contested the absence of algebraic logic in the inventory of such curves. He also remarked that there is a body of algebraic doctrine in the transformation of equations, to which he restricted himself in order to complement Newton's demonstrations. Euler, and after him Gaspard Monge, pursued the same line of thought and succeeded in creating an analytic geometry, as well as rules for changing reference coordinates; those rules were the first steps in linear algebra, extending it to quadratic forms. In 1850 Gérard Cramer of Geneva used algebra to address the problem of curves, and he proudly described his approach in his *Analyse des lignes courbes algébriques* (Analysis of Algebraic Curved Lines), giving a form to Newton's method of the parallelogram for the study of singularities.

A different line of thought, which developed out of a similar inspiration and at a later stage, essentially focused on equations. At the end of the 1760s, Étienne Bézout wrote a six-volume *Cours de mathématiques* (Course in Mathematics) that established the standard for the training of military engineers in France. He then went on to analyze methods for resolving equations of the third and fourth degrees. His ideas were quickly taken up in numerous articles published in Turin and then in Berlin by Lagrange, who then addressed the symmetric functions of roots, which he regarded as structured ensembles. In England, meanwhile, the Oxford mathematician Waring had already expounded in his *Meditationes Algebraicae* (1770; Algebraic Meditations), in a style that is still used today, the rational expression of these functions based on the coefficients of the equation.

By generalizing the form of the solutions given to equations of the third degree, and following in this way the precise analytic movement of algebra, Alexandre-Théophile Vandermonde proposed to introduce the complex roots of unity in order to put into linear form expressions capable of producing all the roots of a general equation. With this method of "Lagrange's resolvents," Vandermonde succeeded at least in rationally expressing the roots of the equation $x^{11} - 1 = 0$, reducing it first to an equation of the fifth degree. Lagrange deployed enough explanations to make it appear that the general equation of the fifth degree could not be rationally resolved. In Modena in 1798 Paolo Ruffini published what he thought was a general proof, but it was in fact flawed. When a proof finally came 30 years later, algebra was completely transformed.

JEAN DHOMBRES

See also Function; Geometry; Language; Mathematics

Further Reading

Condillac, Étienne Bonnot de, *La langue des calculs,* Paris: Houel, 1798; reprint, edited by Anne-Marie Chouillet, Lille, France: Presses Universitaires de Lille, 1981

Derrida, Jacques, *L'archéologie du frivole,* Paris: Denoël/Gouthier, 1976

Dhombres, Jean, editor, *Leçons de mathématiques,* Paris: Dunod, 1992; see especially appendices 4–8

Nový, Luboš, *Origins of Modern Algebra,* Prague: Academia, and Leiden: Noordhoff International, 1973

Vuillemin, Jules, *La philosophie de l'algèbre,* Paris: Presses Universitaires de France, 1962; 2nd edition, 1993

Allegory. *See* Fable

Anarchy

During the second half of the 18th century the concept of anarchy developed in four types of discourse: political philosophy, institutional theory, political polemics, and social discourse. This conceptualization began with a movement away from the etymological meaning of the word—absence of government—toward the idea, expressed in Volume 1 of the *Encyclopédie* (1751), that anarchy is "a disorder within the state in which no one has sufficient authority to govern or to enforce laws, so that the people conduct themselves as they wish, without subordination and without police discipline." (A similar definition can be found in Volume 1 of Chambers's *Cyclopaedia*, published in England in 1728.)

Early on, this perception of anarchy as essentially linked to disorder and disorganization was incorporated into theories about the formation and evolution of political societies. Like the notion of despotism, the concept of anarchy introduced into these theories the idea of the degeneration of established political forms. In Book 3, Chapter 10 of *Du contrat social* (1764; The Social Contract), Jean-Jacques Rousseau asserts, "when the state is dissolved, the abuse of government, whatever it may be, commonly takes the name of anarchy." The same idea is found in Volume 1 of the baron de Bielfeld's *Institutions politiques* (1760; Political Institutions). Anarchy thus had a place in linear and ternary models of political evolution, as an intermediate period between an original established state, generally republican, and a tyranny born out of anarchy (see Gabriel Bonnot de Mably's *Droits et devoirs du citoyen* [1758; Rights and Duties of the Citizen]).

However, anarchy also appeared in circular models of political development, no longer as a precursor of despotism, but as both the original political condition and the inevitable outcome of the process of political evolution (see Linguet's *Oeuvres* [1774; Works]). In both types of models, a particular relationship was posited between anarchy and despotism; that relationship in theory became gradually stronger and ultimately established anarchy as the equivalent of tyranny. (This latter model was prevalent in the political debates around the events of Thermidor in 1795 and in Schlegel's work in 1796, although in Germany at that time there was an overall conceptual split between despotism and anarchy.) In this perspective, anarchy, having originally been seen as the harbinger of tyranny, later became its alter ego, and was finally conflated with tyranny altogether.

The reverse relationship could also be assumed to exist between anarchy and tyranny. For example, in his preface to the first edition of *Kritik der reinen Vernunft* (1784; Critique of Pure Reason), Immanuel Kant argues: "In the beginning, under the reign of the dogmatists . . . power was despotic. But inasmuch as the laws of power still bore the mark of ancient barbarism, the metaphysics of dogmatism gradually declined into complete anarchy as a result of internal conflicts, and from time to time the sceptics—who are like nomads, terrified of settling permanently on any plot of land—broke the bonds of society." However, in the *Deutsche Enzyklopädie* (1778; German Encyclopedia), this degenerate form of anarchy is contrasted to the premise of a positive anarchy, understood as an egalitarian society that preceded the formation of states.

Alongside these theoretical reflections, the concept of anarchy was placed in historical context—a process that led to its being identified as a determinate form of government. Ever since Montesquieu's *Considérations sur les causes de la grandeur des Romains et de leur décadence* (1734; Considerations on the Causes of the Grandeur and Decadence of the Romans), ancient Rome under the triumvirate had been cited in connection with the idea of anarchy. Anarchy took a more contemporary turn, however, when it surfaced in Sweden under Gustav III, or in Poland, which called the best "physicians" of constitutions, such as Rousseau and Linguet, to its side to rid the nation of its endemic anarchy. Within this historical framework, the idea of anarchy met with its greatest success through studies of "feudal anarchy" during the Middle Ages, although reticence on the part of German scholars meant that dictionaries in that language did not include the term *Feudalanarchie;* moreover, there was a great deal of chronological imprecision: it was never clear whether "feudal anarchy" referred to the Merovingian period, Carolingian decadence, or the High Middle Ages.

The notion of feudal anarchy provided an early historical model in which anarchy was identified with a specific form of government: the aristocracy. However, there was some hesitation about how that anarchy should be interpreted. Some writers, such as the comte de Mirabeau in his *Essai sur le despotisme* (1775; Essay on Despotism), saw feudal anarchy as the matrix of representative government, which was thought to have developed from the assemblies convened by the Merovingian and Carolingian monarchs every March and May. In contrast, other thinkers, including Linguet (as cited above), praised the ability of the monarchy to keep anarchy in check.

This belief in monarchies' capacity to thwart anarchy remained the dominant position at the beginning of the French Revolution. Accordingly, the Republic was condemned as a vector of anarchy, and tyranny itself could sometimes appear to act as a remedy against anarchy. For example, in his *Letter to a Member of the National Assembly* (January 1791), Edmund Burke declared that Oliver Cromwell had saved Britain from the evils of anarchy and that, although Cromwell's government was military and despotic, it had been methodical and ruled by law. However, in France the republican offensive of 1791 and the events of 10 August 1792—when Louis XVI's guards were massacred, the monarchy suspended, and the king himself arrested—swept the monarchy up in the wake of anarchy for some time, while the Republic, absolved of any suspicion of anarchy, was triumphant.

However, this republican triumph was a fragile one, since it was limited to France alone. Burke maintained the validity of monarchy as the only bulwark against anarchy in his *Reflections on the Revolution in France* (1790), and as early as 1792 Christoph Martin Wieland, in writings included in *Sämmtliche Werke,* Volume 31 (1857) of his *Complete Works,* expressed his dread of the anarchic state in which France found itself. The triumph of the Republic was challenged as soon as the Republic, forgetful of the virtues of representative government, slid toward a "democracy" that was irreversibly stained by the vice of anarchy, as in Year II of the Revolution (1793–94). Having been identified with the aristocracy (by way of the concept of "feudal anarchy") and then with the Republic, anarchy was given its most lasting institutional image when it was identified with democracy, and in particular with the French revolutionary government of Year II. In this context, it was once again directly linked to despotism. For example, in 1789 Jean-Joseph Mounier described anarchy as "the despotism of the multitude," which he abhorred even more than the despotism of an individual.

The beginning of the French Revolution marks a turning point as regards the importance of the conceptual work involving the notion of anarchy, which had repercussions beyond French borders. The reversal of the respective positions of the monarchy and the Republic as they related to the concept of anarchy occurred during the great debates concerning institutions of government, beginning in 1789. In the course of these debates the notion of anarchy was invoked with considerable flux in its meaning—by those who defended the royal prerogative, notably the monarchists under the National Constituent Assembly (1789–91), then by the Girondins in 1793, and finally, in Year III (1794–95), by those who advocated a moderate republicanism—before gradually crystallizing during the last of the constitutional debates, in 1795.

This development of the idea of anarchy in connection with institutions was centered on the questions of the royal veto and the hereditary nature of monarchic power. The defenders of royal prerogative, led by the abbés Maury and Augustin Barruel, insisted that if the king were deprived of the veto and thus of his legislative power, the Constitution would be establishing a de facto Republic, a true anarchy. Similarly, in the name of the need for stable executive leadership—the sole bulwark against anarchy—supporters of the monarchy defended the principle of hereditary succession. However, the veto was unacceptable to the opponents of royal prerogative, such as La Vicomterie, because the monarch's right to veto contradicted the principle of a separation of powers. There was general agreement that any failure to keep the powers separate was synonymous with anarchy, because it would mean the absence of any delimitation—and thus of any limitation—of power, and unlimited power is by nature arbitrary. This concept of arbitrary power was employed during the debates in Year III among those who attacked both the Constitution of 1793 and the revolutionary government as being anarchic—the former because it was based on unicameralism, the latter because it had increased the number of arbitrary acts by creating revolutionary committees and tribunals.

However, anarchy could not always be so easily detected in unlimited nature of a given entity. Such was the case involving two great principles derived from the concept of natural law: liberty and equality. Monarchists and Girondins, from Malouet to Brissot, issued continual vehement warnings against the anarchic dangers of unlimited political liberty that knew no legal boundaries. The Girondins, however, were just as vehement in denouncing anarchy from the moment they identified it with the will to undermine the unlimited exercise of property rights and, more generally, the unlimited freedom of economic activity. In 1789 the marquis de Condorcet, for example, had seen restrictions of commerce as one of the principal causes of anarchy (see Volume 9 of his *Oeuvres* [1847–49; Works]).

Equality went beyond the bounds of anarchy in the opposite direction. Unlimited equality in the economic and social domains—which was in reality anarchy—in those realms wore the guise of the *loi agraire* (agrarian law), whereas anarchy was recognized as such in the political domain. As for the principle of hereditary succession, it was attacked as being contrary to the principle of the sovereignty of the nation. Those who upheld this latter principle saw the power to enact laws as a fundamental attribute of the state and believed that the hereditary principle thwarted the right to legislate by binding future generations, thus depriving them of the full exercise of their sovereignty.

This final institutional debate on the idea of anarchy, which had begun with the Revolution, did not end until Year III. It was based above all on the recognition of the principle of national sovereignty, which was not easily disassociated from the accusation of anarchy so strongly formulated by Barruel and Mounier. Once the legitimacy of this principle had been assured in 1792, the issue of how it would be exercised became the main locus of the debates in Year III. Direct democracy, which was seen as decidedly anarchic because it validated recourse to insurrection when circumstances warranted it, was rejected in favor of a representative government, which was seen as the sole guarantor against anarchy. At the same time, "revolution," which had been discussed alongside anarchy in texts published before 1789, was once again associated with anarchy. From then on, anarchy was condemned in the same way as the "revolutionary government" was, by the triumph of "constitutional government." (The development of the notion of anarchy within the institutional realm was above all a French phenomenon. In 1795 Mounier, exiled from France, continued to identify the Republic with anarchy, while Burke was equally consistent in maintaining a similar position, and Wieland saw France as being in an anarchic condition after 1792.)

In contrast to this relatively flexible understanding of anarchy in theoretical discussion and in institutional debates, the notion provoked a markedly less equivocal discourse as soon as it entered the arena of political confrontation. The Jacobins had appeared incapable of using the vocabulary of anarchy except within the limits defined by their adversaries, which explains why this terminology temporarily disappeared from official political discourse in Year II. It was at this point that the term "anarchist" appeared and was immediately applied to the Jacobins in an anonymous pamphlet, *Grands remerciements aux Jacobins* (28 February 1791; Great Thanks Offered to the Jacobins). Its first appearance in German was in Wieland's *Divine Discourses* (1793). The Jacobins were joined by the "Republicans" but the consequences of the events of 10 August 1792 rapidly drove them into the camp of the

opponents of anarchy (at least in France). In addition to the Jacobins, a succession of other groups were deemed incarnations of anarchy: the Montagnards (1792); the "Maratistes," or supporters of Marat (1793); the *sans-culottes,* supporters of the Terror (1793–94); the monarchists (1795); and, finally, the Babouvistes, or followers of Babeuf (1796). Of all these appellations, that of "Jacobin," first formulated by the Girondins and then revived during the Thermidorian debates, was the most stable (Wieland was still calling the Jacobins "anarchists" in 1793, and that designation persisted as late as 1800 in Genoa).

The royalists' intervention at the side of the Jacobins and the *sans-culottes* in 1795 corresponded to the emergence of the "Thermidorian" form of anarchy—the most coherent model available at the time. It succeeded in fusing the various constituent elements of a negative anarchy, setting it up as a social "antimodel." This conception marked the passage from a view of politics as a dichotomy between "friends" and "enemies" of anarchy to a ternary division of the political domain, the center of which was occupied by the supporters of the Constitution of Year III and the two wings by its Jacobin and royalist opponents, both camps being designated as "anarchists." The earlier dichotomy was thus maintained. This new configuration was expressed in the phrase found in the civil oath of Year V (1796–97): "Contempt for anarchy, contempt for royalty, fidelity to the Constitution of Year III."

However, in this period the term "anarchist" occasionally attained a certain autonomy. In 1793 Brissot used it briefly in his *Patriote français* without any accompanying reference. The anarchist was described as a creature of darkness: the darkness of his clandestine activity (after the end of the Terror, which was a veritable institutionalized anarchy) and the darkness of his ignorance. He was also described as a young unmarried man, without property, an isolated and asocial individual—traits that explained his perseverance in advocating agrarian law and the equal distribution of all wealth. More distinctively, but also more rarely, the social image of the anarchist embodied a more concrete reality, as when the *Mercure de France* (18 September 1790) denounced the workers of Angers who had unfurled the red flag as anarchistic troublemakers.

It is this "social" dimension of the concept of anarchy formulated in Year III that has proved to be its most lasting feature. This dimension had been expressed even before Year III, to the extent that "disorder," which constituted the permanent conceptual background of anarchy, had early on taken on a clearer meaning, especially in France after 1789, whether because of fears of civil war or the "disorganization of society." (The civil wars of ancient Rome were understood in terms of anarchy.) The taxes and requisitions imposed by the revolutionary government in Year II revealed the full extent of the anarchist plot against the rich and the owners of property. Even more than the notion of "anarchy" itself, the designation "anarchist" carried negative connotations. It should be noted that in France, the word *anarchisme* (anarchism) was very rarely used, and even then only as an equivalent of *anarchie* (anarchy); it thus did not yet designate any specific political tendency. This did not prevent attempts, even fruitless ones, to turn the tables, above and beyond the simple act of turning the insult "anarchist" upon those who had first used it. Thus, in the month of Thermidor in Year VII (July 1799), Jourdan, speaking in the Council of the 500, went so far as to claim the epithet of "anarchist," as soon as it had been demonstrated that royalists could use that epithet to vilify the true republicans.

MARC DELEPLACE

See also Authority, Government, and Power

Further Reading
Deleplace, Marc, "La notion d'anarchie pendant la Révolution française (1789–1801)," *Annales historiques de la Révolution française* 68, no. 1 (1992)
Freeman, Michael, *Edmund Burke and the Critique of Political Radicalism*, Chicago: University of Chicago Press, and Oxford: Blackwell, 1980

Anatomy

The *Encyclopédie* article "Anatomie" (Anatomy), dating from 1751, defines its topic as the art of dissection carried out in order to attain "a knowledge of the solid parts comprising the bodies of animals." In that article, these body parts were distinguished as similar, dissimilar, or organic, in accordance with Aristotelian tradition. However, in the article "Organe" (Organ), dating from 1765, Denis Diderot was able to categorizes the parts as "primary and secondary organs" because the inherent functional value of similar parts—bone, nerve, muscle, and so on—had by that time been recognized. Anatomical knowledge remained essentially contemplative, and was considered useful only insofar as it could contribute to medicine and surgery: "He who best knows a clock is the workman most able to repair it." In this context, the task of the 18th-century anatomist was to progress from an "unproductive examination of solid parts" to a physiological comprehension of the action of these solid parts on the fluid parts, with a view to understanding the mechanical workings of the human body as a static and hydraulic machine.

In the same article on organs, Diderot drew a distinction between human anatomy and comparative anatomy. For him, as for most of his contemporaries, the idea of comparative anatomy was limited to the study of the relationship between organic structure and function in animals "in order to achieve—by a comparison of that which occurs in them with that which occurs in us—a more perfect knowledge of the human body." This type of comparative approach had been central to anatomical research since the times of Galen. Comparative anatomy in this vein was reinvigorated in the modern period, first by Andreas Vesalius, then by William Harvey, who relied on the concept of *mechanica* set forth by Francis Bacon in the 17th century. During the 18th century, the anatomy inspired by Bacon's mechanistic theory of the body moved toward the microscopic observation of ever smaller parts. Special attention was paid to the capillaries, using the injection technique that had made Frederik Ruysch famous at the beginning of the 18th century. But this anatomy dealing with fine structures continued to be carried out in the same theoretical framework that viewed the body as a machine. It was assumed that with better information about the solid parts and the nature of humors, "the laws of mechanics" could be engaged to reveal that respiration, the distribution of "nerve juices," the function of the spleen, and so on "could be deduced from the simplest principles." Ideally, according to Hermann Boerhaave, that information could then serve as the foundation for medicine.

In *Praelectiones Academicae in Proprias Institutions Rei Medicae* (1739–44; Academical Lectures on the Theory of Physic), Boerhaave applied mechanical principles to transform physiology into an *anatomia animata* (anatomy in motion), arguing that function is the organ's power to act and depends on its *fabrica* (structure). Sickness, on the other hand, was understood in terms of dysfunction. In the *Encyclopédie* article "Maladie" (1765; Malady), Diderot described illness as a disturbance of the organs "that causes a lesion that is more or less noticeable in the exercise of one or several functions."

Given the prevalence of this model in the 18th century, anatomical dissection performed on cadavers came to be seen as "the sole light of medicine" (Giovanni Battista Morgagni, *De sedibus et causis morborum per anatomen indagatis* [1761; The Seats and Causes of Diseases, Investigated by Anatomy]). Dissection was thought to permit symptomatic diagnosis of the disturbance or destruction of functions, and belief in the diagnostic value of the practice ultimately led to experiments on the living and even to vivisection of those condemned to death. The recognized "usefulness" of dissection guaranteed it would become widespread—to such an extent that early on, Diderot envisaged its institutional proliferation: "In a well-ordered society, priests should only receive cadavers from the hands of an anatomist and . . . there should be a law forbidding the burial of a body before it has been opened" (*Encyclopédie*, "Cadavre" [1751; Cadaver]).

A clear example of the scope and limits of the confluence of anatomy, medicine, and physiological experimentation (including dissection) is found in the 19th Letter of Morgagni's book, which deals with the topic of suffocation—in particular suffocation caused by hanging. Morgagni relates how, in the course of examining the cadavers of executed criminals, he tried first of all to distinguish the effects of strangulation from possible traces of previous illnesses, the symptoms of which he investigates. He then discusses the results of experiments on the compression and ligature of nerves, blood, and air passages passing from the head to the chest. From these results, he speculates upon the mechanics of death by strangulation and singles out the anatomical signs of suffocation that—by extrapolation to deaths by drowning, asphyxia, or other causes—might have medical and legal value. Morgagni hypothesizes that these same signs may account for certain diseases of the throat or chest, to which physicians should pay particular attention. Of course, death by "inhalation of air [that is] too thick or thin" (that is, the halting of gaseous exchanges at the level of tissues) remained unexplained until discoveries in the field of chemistry at the end of the century. On that topic, Morgagni was satisfied either to suspend his judgment or to call upon traditional 18th-century medical theories.

Although physiological experimentation on animals necessarily depended upon anatomical knowledge, the information gleaned was not sufficient to allow for the development of an independent science of comparative anatomy in the modern period. In 1727 Sir Hans Sloane wished for the creation of a "sort of comparative anatomy of bones" in order to identify fossil remains ("Mémoire sur les dents et autres ossements de

l'éléphant trouvés en terre," *Mémoires de l'Académie des Sciences* [1727; Report on the Teeth and Other Elephant Fossils Found in the Ground, Reports of the Académie des Sciences]) and, in 1768, Jean Étienne Guettard lamented the fact that such an anatomy still did not exist (*Mémoires sur différentes parties des sciences et des arts* [Reports on the Different Branches of the Sciences and the Arts). Osteology had, however, begun to emerge as a branch of study distinct from medicine and was given its own entry in Buffon's *Histoire naturelle générale et particulière* (1749; Natural History, General and Particular), in a section that Buffon entrusted to Louis-Jean-Marie Daubenton, in 1749. Nonetheless, writing in the *Encyclopédie méthodique* (1792; Methodical Encyclopedia) Félix Vicq d'Azyr argued, "it is the comparison of organs considered at different intervals in a creature's system that will shed the most light upon the mechanism and use of its components." However, Vicq d'Azyr added that "this comparison . . . [has] barely begun," and he proposed to define a program for making such comparisons systematically.

According to Vicq d'Azyr, natural history classifies animals according to the relationships between their exterior traits while comparative anatomy "limits its research to the internal structure." These sciences must be made to work together in an order defined by "the progressive combination of the organs in the various animal classes." However, Vicq d'Azyr proposed to begin with the most complex class of animals, reversing the proposed order of research, because, while humans and the viviparous quadrupeds are the most complex organisms, they were also the best known. In anatomical analysis, the study of organs remained inseparable from their functional importance and their place in the overall activity of the system living in its natural environment. Thus, Vicq d'Azyr was able to observe that "certain constant relationships exist between the structure of a carnivore's teeth and the structure of that animal's muscles, fingers, fingernails, tongue, stomach, and intestines." In fact, by 1788 the young scientist Georges Cuvier had already described the tree-creeper, a bird that feeds on arboreal insects and whose legs, tail, beak, tongue, and stomach are organized in a manner that is adapted to its particular diet (letter of 17 November 1788, in *Lettres de Georges Cuvier à C.M. Pfaff* [1858; Letters of Georges Cuvier to C.M. Pfaff]). Anatomical structure therefore continued to be understood as the expression of the "laws of animal economy," taking into account the animal's place in "the natural economy."

Vicq d'Azyr remains best known for having instituted a second form of comparative anatomy, namely "the in-depth examination and comparison of organs in the same kind of animals and their comparison." This method allowed him to establish the similarity of anterior and posterior limbs in quadrupeds. From this similarity, he deduced that "nature appears . . . to follow a type or general model not only in the structure of the various animals . . . but in their various organs, as well"—an assertion confirmed by the 1779 discovery of the intermaxillary bone in human beings. Johann Wolfgang von Goethe made corresponding discoveries in 1782. Until the end of the 18th century, the supposed absence of an intermaxillary in humans was considered proof of their position at the head of the animal kingdom; the discovery of this bone abolished that privilege and made Man a *Primus inter pares* (first among equals), thus forcing a reappraisal of traditional anthropocentrism. Humans retained their preeminence, but all "organized bodies" would henceforth be taken into account in a "science of organization." That science was the direct precursor to modern biology, which emerged 1802. The science of organization also led to the emergence of "general anatomy" (Xavier Bichat, *Anatomie générale, appliquée à la physiologie et à la médecine* [1801; General Anatomy, Applied to Physiology and Medicine]), which later evolved still further into histology (Karl Friedrich von Heusinger, *System der Histologie* [1822; System of Histology]), thanks to a shift in focus from the heart (the machine's motor) and the brain (the expression of the directive power of the soul) toward the glands and tissues.

BERNARD BALAN

See also Automaton; Medicine; Physiognomy; Surgery

Further Reading

Cole, F.J., *A History of Comparative Anatomy, from Aristotle to the Eighteenth Century*, London: Macmillan, 1944

Knight, Bernard, *Discovering the Human Body*, New York: Lippincott and Crowell, and London: Heinemann, 1980

Sakka, Michel, *Histoire de l'anatomie humaine*, Paris: Presses Universitaires de France, 1997

Ancients and the Moderns, Quarrel of the

A monumental study by Chantal Grell has recently highlighted the omnipresence of the theme of classical antiquity in 18th-century France. The education system, the Académie des Inscriptions et Belles-Lettres (Academy of Inscriptions and Letters), the Académie de Peinture et de Sculpture (Academy of Painting and Sculpture), curricula within still other academies, and archeological and philological studies all reveal the extent to which awareness of the "ancients"—as the peoples of the classical civilizations were then known—remained at the heart of basic cultural instruction during the Enlightenment. On some crucial points, however, antiquity was no longer held up as an absolute model, as it had been among the humanists of the Renaissance and the writers of the 17th century. The confrontation between two antithetical positions concerning the role and value of classical antiquity gave rise to what became known as the "Quarrel of the Ancients and the Moderns"—a polemics that divided European intellectuals for decades, particularly during the period 1687 to 1715. The Quarrel contributed to the emergence of a wide-reaching modernist consciousness. Champions of modernity initially proclaimed the modern age as equal in value to antiquity, and later as superior to it. From then on, the notion of "the modern," which had previously been a simple synonym for "contemporary" (in contrast to the notion of "the past," as it had been understood during the Middle Ages and the Renaissance), came to refer to the idea of a specific historical era. The plural "moderns" referred to the authors and artists of this period, which was defined as beginning with the Renaissance and extending to encompass the present and the future (expectations about its duration varied from author to author). The term "ancients," meanwhile, referred to the Greek and Roman authors and artists of a well-defined period, separated from the contemporary era by the Middle Ages. The age of the Enlightenment, in France and throughout Europe, is in fact inseparable from this challenge to the perceived superiority of the cultures of classical antiquity.

It was no coincidence that the debate between the unconditional supporters of antiquity and the partisans of the moderns became heated at a time when it was generally agreed that French literature and civilization had reached their apogee in classicism, and when it was becoming increasingly difficult to reconcile the remarkable advances in the sciences, the arts, and literature with the principle of slavish imitation of ancient models. The superiority attributed to the moderns had political implications that soon became apparent. On 27 January 1687 Charles Perrault read before the assembled company of the Académie Française a text that, in both content and form, reflected a modernist movement. "Le siècle de Louis le Grand" (The Age of Louis the Great) was a panegyric poem that offered justification for the contemporary period and, at the same time, for the French monarchy. Most of the classical authors in attendance considered the reading of this poem to be a provocation.

However, the opposition between antiquity and the modern era was not invented in the 17th century: that opposition was already the basis of the historical thought of Renaissance humanists. According to the cyclical theory of history, the grandeur of antiquity, after its decline, was followed by the dark period of the Middle Ages, but that grandeur was subsequently reborn in a second historical cycle in the new age. In this schema, reference to the artists of antiquity was extremely positive, and the translation of the ancients' works into various national languages was valorized as an intrinsically creative process. With the exception of Italy, this process contributed to the development of the unique characteristics of different national cultures. By imitating the ancients, it was argued, each civilization could raise itself to a comparable level of glory. According to the humanist aesthetic, the ancient models had achieved perfection, but modern civilizations would catch up with them in the future. On the basis of this theory of cycles, Italian Renaissance thinkers had already presented a systematic comparison between the works of the two periods. Benedetto Accolti's *De praestantia virorum sui aevi dialogos* (1460; Dialogues on the Excellence of Men in Their Age) and Sperone Speroni's *Dialogo delle lingue* (1530; Dialogue on Languages) had reevaluated their own era and their national language, which they considered to be as suitable as Latin for expressing the knowledge and discoveries of the human mind. There was a direct connection between Speroni's work and Joachim Du Bellay's *Défense et illustration de la langue française* (1549; Defense and Illustration of the French Language). In France comparisons between the ancients and the moderns had been actively pursued since Henri Étienne's *Traité de la conformité du langage français avec le grec* (1565; Treatise on the Conformity of the French Language with Greek). Étienne still referred to "conformity" between French and Greek, but later the duc de Béthune, alluding to Plutarch, preferred the term "parallel," as in the title of his *Parallèles de César et de Henri le Grand* (1615; Parallels between Caesar and Henri the Great). In 1688, with the publication of Perrault's *Parallèle des Anciens et des Modernes* (Parallel between the Ancients and the Moderns), this comparative

approach was explicitly presented as the very basis of the Quarrel.

Born out of the cyclical theory of the Renaissance, the hypothesis of a new period of grandeur was not unanimously accepted in the era of the Counter-Reformation and of the baroque. In Italy, in particular, there was an overwhelming sense of pessimism. During the first half of the 17th century, the parallel between the ancients and the moderns was used to counter the notion of irreversible decadence over the course of history. That strategy is evident, for example, in Alessandro Tassoni's *Paragone degl'ingegni antichi e moderni* (1620; Comparison of Spirits of the Ancients and the Moderns), and Secondo Lancellotti's *L'hoggidì overo il mondo non peggiore ne piú calamitoso del passato* (1623; The Present; or, This World Is neither Worse nor More Calamitous than the Past One). Similarly, in England there was a debate that pitted those theologians who upheld a model of pure decadence against those who defended the contemporary era (see Jones). In France Gabriel Naudé's *Additions à l'histoire de Louis XI* (1630; Addenda to the History of Louis XI) and, above all, Rampalle's *Erreur combattue, discours académique où il est curieusement prouvé que le monde ne va point de mal en pis* (1649; Error Refuted, an Academic Discourse in Which It Is Curiously Proven That the World Is Not Going from Bad to Worse) attempted to revive the theory of cycles—and their own period along with it. Perrault's poem provoked a decisive turn in the debate. His primary objective was to invalidate the hypothesis of corruption, but the poem deals with the unfolding of history in general, and it paved the way for a modern vision of the world and of history.

The Quarrel of the Ancients and the Moderns had an enormous impact on two essential realms of Enlightenment thought: historical thought, where the theory of indefinite progress became a schema that could be applied to future of humanity; and aesthetics and poetics, where the idea of an absolutely definable point of perfection was challenged though the rejection of the dogma of imitating the ancients.

Toward New Conceptions of History

The cyclical theory of history, which was the basis of the schema of Antiquity/Middle Ages/Modern Times, and which was the foundation of the historical reflections of Renaissance humanists and thinkers of the 17th century, provided a useful way to explain what was seen as an ascending period in history. The theory was also useful for inspiring literary and artistic creations capable of leading society to new cultural heights and to perfection in all areas of knowledge. However, the schema also predicted that decadence would inevitably follow periods of greatness. At a time when contemporaries believed that France had arrived at a peak of grandeur, the question was naturally raised as to whether decadence was inevitable, or whether, on the contrary, the increase in knowledge would guarantee indefinite progress. While the admirers of the ancients replied to such questions by maintaining their attachment to the cyclical model—and some of them even evoked decadence on a global scale, a general corruption of humanity—the partisans of the moderns unanimously challenged all theories of decadence. The two camps thus represented two fundamentally different schools of thought.

In his *Parallèle des Anciens et des Modernes,* Perrault argued in favor of a variation of the theory of cycles in which different countries experience cultural perfection, but in which modern cycles are capable of surpassing those of the ancients. This theory allowed for ebbs and flows, but it held that perceptible progress would be the overall pattern, with French civilization and the French monarchy leading the way—for the "age of Louis the Great" was at the time surpassing all the glorious eras of other civilizations. The abbé Dubos, and later Voltaire, adopted Perrault's version of the cyclical theory. But the limits of this cyclical model could already be clearly discerned in the first dialogue of Perrault's text, in the announcement of the decadence to come:

I rejoice to see that our age has, in some ways, reached the peak of perfection. And since for many years progress has marched onward at a slightly slower pace, and appears almost imperceptible, just as the days seem not to get longer as they approach the solstice, I still have the joy of thinking that we likely do not have many things to envy of those who come after us.

In the 18th century the lament of decadence became almost a commonplace, one that could adequately be explained by this variation of the cyclical theory.

However, the debates in the ongoing Quarrel also inspired a new historical model that took center stage in 18th-century discussions: the theory of linear progress. Bernard Le Bovier de Fontenelle laid the foundations for this theory in his *Digression sur les Anciens et les Modernes* (1688; Digression on the Ancients and the Moderns), his first contribution to the debate. Beginning with a rejection of the concept of a gradual depletion of nature—a theme constantly rehashed by partisans of the ancients—Fontenelle suggested that the people of antiquity were, by nature, neither better nor worse than those of his own time; the constant growth of human knowledge seemed to him to guarantee lasting progress. Challenging the traditional comparison between the evolution of humanity and that of a single individual, Fontenelle moved beyond the theory of

cycles. In his view, humankind is not comparable to a human being in its evolution. Humanity, he argued, had passed through childhood and adolescence to enter a period of "virility," but, unlike human individuals, humanity would not experience old age:

The comparison . . . between all men throughout the centuries and a single man can be applied to our question of the ancients and the moderns. . . . The timeless man will not experience an old age; he will always be capable of doing those things he did in his youth, and will even be more capable of doing so. . . . This means, leaving this allegory aside, that mankind will never degenerate and that the sound views of all the good minds to come will be added onto the other.

However, unlike certain simplifiers of the theory of progress who came after him, Fontenelle did not foresee constant progress in all areas. The increase in knowledge seemed to him to make philosophy the standard of reference for assessing his own era. This new emphasis prefigured the idea of a hierarchy of epochs since the Renaissance (scholarship, literature, philosophy)—a hierarchy that Jean le Rond D'Alembert would include at the beginning of the *Encyclopédie* in his "Discours préliminaire" (1751; Preliminary Discourse). In *Sur l'histoire* (On History), a text most likely written between 1691 and 1699 but not published until 1758, Fontenelle added an important nuance to his theory. In addition to the increase in intellectual knowledge, or to the diminution of errors (which amounts to the same thing in his view), and to "true history," which deals with human passions, he discerned "a third thing that results from both the opinions of the mind and the passions of the heart: the mores of men, their customs, their different usages." This third domain evolves according to a complex law, combining cyclical changes in taste and an overall ascendant movement that enables one to speak of progress even in aesthetic matters "by conserving whatever was good in those tastes."

Fontenelle's theory of history, a direct result of the Quarrel, is clearly important: it was the first time that history had been presented as an all-encompassing method that made it possible to define the evolution of humanity and to explain all the sciences and the arts through a necessary historical sequence.

Nevertheless, it would be wrong to reduce the Quarrel's effects on the historical thinking of the Enlightenment to a simple statement that the moderns were victorious. The supporters of the ancients (Nicolas Boileau-Despréaux, Racine, Jean de La Fontaine, Jean de La Bruyère, Arnault, Pierre-Daniel Huet, and others) had good reasons to oppose the euphoria with which their adversaries regarded the present. With regard to the 18th century, it is extremely important to remember that reference to the ancients went hand in hand with an ideal of simplicity and integrity, and therefore with an underlying criticism of the cultural policies and the ostentatious pomp of the monarchy. In his *Réflexion critique sur quelques passages du rhéteur Longin* (1693; Critical Reflection on Certain Passages by the Rhetorician Longinus), Boileau replied to Perrault's criticism of Homer by idealizing

> the mores of that ancient age that Hesiod called the Age of Heroes. . . . Monsieur P[errault] triumphs in showing how far removed that simplicity is from our indolence and luxury, which he regards as one of the great gifts that God has made to men, and yet they are the origin of all our vices.

In his *Discours sur Théophraste* (1688; Discourse on Theophrastus), La Bruyère had previously contrasted the former utopia of Greek antiquity to the corruption of French court life under Louis XIV:

> Athens was free, it was the center of a republic, its citizens were equal, they felt no shame whatever in relation to one another. . . . There was something simple and popular in their mores, which, I admit, bear little resemblance to ours; yet, in general, what a people the Athenians were, and what a city Athens was! What laws! What order! What values! What discipline! What perfection in all the arts!

In the final phase of the Quarrel, when Anne Dacier upheld the superiority of the ancients in her book *Des causes de la corruption du goût* (1714; On the Causes of the Corruption of Taste) and Houdard de la Motte became the spokesman of the moderns in his *Réflexions sur la critique* (1715; Reflections on Criticism), the endless debates on the Homeric style, its metaphors and epithets, its composition, and its flawed taste, also implied a sort of bygone utopia, the dream of a natural antiquity that was simple, naive, and uncorrupted (see Hepp). These arguments were taken up again later in the 18th century, in the great debates on luxury, the state of nature, and the ancient republics of Greece and Rome.

The Problem of the Middle Ages

An important period in history was, in a sense, the victim of both sides of the Quarrel of the Ancients and the Moderns: everyone essentially concurred in their negative assessment of the Middle Ages. The idea of an intermediate period between the fall of the Roman Empire and the Renaissance had already appeared in the writings of Petrarch, because, in the cyclical theory of history, it was a corollary to the concept of the Renaissance. The expression *Moyen Âge* (Middle Ages) was still rare in 18th-century France. In Germany it was used for the first time by Cellarius, in his *Historia Universalis in Antiquam, Medii Aevi ac Nouam Divisa* (1685–96; Universal History Divided into Antiquity, the Middle Ages, and the New), and the expression very quickly became commonplace in German (as *Mittlere Zeit* or *Mittelalter*). In France the concept of the Middle Ages already existed in the 18th century, but it became established as a term of historical periodization only at the end of the century (see Voss).

For the supporters of the moderns and the theorists of progress in the 18th century, the Middle Ages posed an important problem because, envisaged as a period of darkness after the brilliance of antiquity, the medieval period seemed to prove the possibility of a retrograde movement of history. In the 17th century the Middle Ages were criticized on aesthetic grounds, for their lack of good taste and order, while Enlightenment intellectuals viewed the Middle Ages as a period of ignorance and intolerance (as evidenced, notably, in the Church's abuse of power, with its Inquisition and torture).

Fontenelle had already noted in his *Digression* that it would be difficult to apply the new theory of progress to the Middle Ages. As we have seen, he rejected the comparison between the aging of a person and that of humankind, as far as the final phases of old age and death are concerned. Nevertheless, he arrived at an explanation of this retrograde movement in the past:

> The centuries of barbarism that followed the age of Augustus and preceded the present age provide the supporters of antiquity with what seems to come closest to a good argument among so many others. How was it, they ask, that in those times ignorance was so deep-rooted and so pervasive? It was because [people] no longer understood the Greek and Latin texts, which they no longer read: but as soon as those excellent models were once again placed before them, reason and good taste were reborn.

While not denying that the Middle Ages were a time of ignorance, Fontenelle also challenged the theory of cycles, the logical consequence of which is to place antiquity on a pedestal that he considered far too lofty. He thus compared the Middle Ages to a sickness—to a temporary amnesia that did not prevent the convalescent from resuming his education at the point where it had been interrupted.

Anne-Robert-Jacques Turgot, in Chapter IX of his *Recherches sur les causes des progrès et de la décadence des sciences et des arts* (1748; Studies on the Causes of Progress and Decadence in the Sciences and Arts), compared the Middle Ages to "those rivers that flow underground for part of their course but reappear further along, swollen with a large quantity of water that has been filtered through the ground." The same disdain for the Middle Ages appears in the third section of the marquis de Condorcet's *Esquisse des progrès de l'esprit humain* (1794; Outlines of an Historical View of the Progress of the Human Mind), where—by spatial analogy to the etymology of the word "progress" as "forward motion"—Condorcet negatively characterized the period as "a disgraceful immobility" in which "all progress in the sciences ceased." These different images indicate how difficult it was to fit a condemnation of the Middle Ages into a progressivist vision of history.

This is why one also finds a cautious rehabilitation of the medieval period in the writing of several of the supporters of the moderns. Fontenelle himself praised the poetry of medieval troubadours in his *Histoire du Romieu de Provence* (History of Romieu of Provence), long before those works were rediscovered by the romantics. Specialists in history or in medieval literature were well aware that the categorical condemnation of the period was open to debate. La Curne de Sainte-Palaye implored the members of the Académie des Sciences et Belles-Lettres (Academy of Science and Letters) "to study modern antiquities, above all those of our nation" (as cited in Voss). The second half of the century witnessed a partial rehabilitation of the Middle Ages with the success throughout Europe of James Macpherson's *Poems of Ossian* (1765). In France, publication of the work of the Benedictines of Saint-Maur and adaptations of medieval romances by the comte de Tressan produced similar revitalizing effects. This rehabilitation of medieval culture in turn prepared the way for romantics' admiration of the Middle Ages, which they considered an integral part of the modern era.

Challenging the Aesthetics of Perfection

In true Renaissance tradition, the Quarrel of the Ancients and the Moderns was primarily a debate over the arts and literature: above all, it concerned the aesthetic value of human creation. According to the dogma of *imitatio,* the ancients had already achieved aesthetic perfection. For the admirers of antiquity, beauty was therefore a value definable by norms, and absolute beauty did exist. The classical doctrine had attempted to set forth in detail the rules of good taste. Challenging this system with an aesthetics of relative beauty, one of the principal results of the Quarrel was to pave the way for the great debates of the 18th century and the romantic period, in which all art and all literature were

evaluated exclusively in their historical context and in terms of their specific value (see Jauss).

Detailed comparisons between the works produced by the ancients and those created by the moderns resulted in the distinguishing of different aesthetic domains, each evaluated according to its own particular historical trajectory. For all the authors involved in the Quarrel, it was undeniable that some of these domains had achieved perfection very early on, during antiquity: poetry and rhetoric were constantly cited as examples of this. As early as 1670, Desmarets de Saint-Sorlin, in his *Comparaison de la langue et de la poésie françaises avec la grecque et la latine* (Comparison of French Language and Poetry with Those in Greek and Latin), arrived at an important distinction by which he attempted to explain poetry's precocious attainment of perfection: "There is a great difference between works that imitate nature, such as paintings or statues, and works of invention, such as great poetry." The poet was given value, "elevated above all science or reading, productive and fertile in himself," and, for that reason, he was capable of freeing himself from imitation of the ancients. In contrast, according to Fontenelle's *Digression,* if poetry were able to reach the heights of perfection in antiquity, it was because it required no more than "a certain number of fairly limited views." Owing to their "lively imagination," argued Fontenelle, the ancients were able to achieve poetic perfection in a short amount of time—an approach that allowed poetry to be relativized and ranked just below philosophy. In the third dialogue of his *Parallèle,* Perrault resolved the problem of the rapid perfection of poetry in antiquity by suggesting that progress among modern authors was evinced in their aptitude for subtle psychological analysis: "There are a thousand delicate sentiments about each [of the passions] in the works of our authors, in their moral treatises, in their tragedies, in their novels, and in their exercises in rhetoric, that are not found among the ancients." From this debate on the precocious perfection achieved by the ancients, Perrault drew a crucial distinction for the future between two sorts of beauty that exist in all things: "Universal and absolute beauty, which is pleasing to all people, at all times, and in all places; [and] another [beauty], particular and relative, which is pleasing only to certain people, in certain places, and at certain times."

The questioning of the aesthetics of perfection was even more extreme among other authors, who discovered the historical dimension of art. Thus, in his *Sur les poèmes des Anciens* (1685; On the Poems of the Ancients), Charles de Marguetel de Saint Denis de Saint-Évremond declared:

There is no one who has more admiration than I for the works of the ancients. I admire their design, their economy, their elevation of the mind, the range of their knowledge; but religion, government, mores, and manners have changed so greatly in the world that we need a new art to enter into the taste and genius of the age in which we live.

On the aesthetic level, therefore, the indirect outcome of the Quarrel—an outcome that was, however, important for the age of the Enlightenment—was a reconsideration on both sides of the classical normative aesthetic, leading to the discovery of relative beauty.

Effects of the Quarrel throughout Europe

The Quarrel had lasting repercussions throughout all of Europe, albeit with national differences regarding the ancients and the way in which they were judged. It is very clear that Perrault's advocacy of the moderns was based on claims that French civilization had reached a level of perfection comparable to that of the age of Augustus. The reactions of various European countries to the Quarrel during the 18th century were largely determined by whether they accepted or rejected the French claim to universalism. "Modernity" went hand in hand with this French spirit, while reference to the ancients, and above all to Greek civilization, served to legitimize the national cultures and literatures of other European countries.

In England William Temple was decidedly on the side of the ancients in his treatise *Upon the Ancient and Modern Learning* (1690). Most English writers adopted classicist positions, including, for example, Alexander Pope, in his *Essay on Criticism* (1711). But in *The Advancement and Reformation of Modern Poetry* (1701), John Dennis challenged the aesthetics of imitation and insisted on the potential for enthusiasm and passion that characterized poets. Dennis thus launched a movement that had crucial repercussions for 18th-century aesthetics. Original genius, engaged in spontaneous creation free from an imitation of the ancients, was promoted through Edward Young's *Conjectures on Original Composition* (1759), and this position was echoed widely throughout Europe.

In Germany involvement in the Quarrel was marked by the fact that French language and culture were dominant among the aristocratic elite in many of the princely courts. As a result, German literature had to be defined by reference not only to antiquity but also to France, which was presented as a new model for modern times. In the first half of the 18th century, Johann Christoph Gottsched's spontaneous approval of Perrault's thesis did not prevent him from referring to the ancients when he attempted to establish rules for German literature in his *Versuch einer kritischen Dicht-*

kunst vor die Deutschen (1730; Attempt at a Critical Poetics for the German People) (see Martini).

In the second half of the 18th century, the return to Greek antiquity was very clearly motivated by a rejection of French and Francophile versions and interpretations of antiquity. Against these, Johann Joachim Winckelmann proposed the ideal of an *edle Einfalt und stille Grösse* (noble simplicity and calm grandeur) in Greek art. In *Gedanken über die Nachahmung der griechischen Werke in der Malerei und Bildhauerkunst* (1755; Reflections on the Painting and Sculpture of the Greeks), Winckelmann argued that "the imitation of the ancients is the only way for us to become great, and even, if possible, inimitable." Greek art, he asserted, was even superior to nature, in that it achieved what nature has never been able to achieve and because it embodied ideas through universal and typical methods. Winckelmann strongly influenced the classicism of Weimar and initiated its tendency to aestheticize history. In contrast to the situation in France in 1687, where emancipation of national literature was expressed through a critique of the ancients, classic German literature began with a return to antiquity. The contrast could not have been greater between this idealization of Greek art and the speculations of the Francophile writers at the Prussian court who, around 1750, hoped to follow Perrault and discover the crowning glory of German culture by imitating the age of Louis XIV.

In the 1770s the central issues of the Quarrel were discussed again in Germany, this time with reference to the theory of progress, which German classicism tried to harmonize with its admiration for antiquity. In his *Kritische Wälder* (1768–69; Critical Forests; or, Reflections on the Science and Art of the Beautiful), Johann Gottfried von Herder rejected not only the rules of French classicism but also the idealization of antiquity, which was different from the contemporary world. In his *Auch eine Philosophie der Geschichte zur Bildung der Menschheit* (1774; Yet Another Philosophy of History for the Education of Humanity) Herder revealed "his great subject," the "outline for the progress" of humankind. The idea of progress that was not linear but was characterized by significant stages became fairly widespread among German philosophers and historians. Thus, Immanuel Kant defined progress as a moral requirement in his *Welches sind die wirklichen Fortschritte, die die Metaphysik seit Leibnitzens und Wolf's Zeiten in Deutschland gemacht hat?* (1791; What Real Progress Has Metaphysics Made in Germany since the Time of Leibniz and Wolff?), and he linked it to the idea of freedom in his *Ideen zu einer allgemeinen Geschichte in weltbürgerlicher Absicht* (1786; Idea for a Universal History with a Cosmopolitan Intent). Isaak Iselin, in *Über die Geschichte der Menschheit* (1768; On the History of Mankind), also conceived of history as a progressive movement, advancing step by step. The French Revolution did not contradict this progressivist interpretation of history, but in Kant's view, as expressed in *Erneute Frage, ob das menschliche Geschlecht im beständigen Fortschreiten zum Besseren sei* (1798; Renewed Question, If Humankind Is in Constant Progress to the Better), it seemed to show that "the state must be reformed by seeking to evolve rather than seeking revolution in order to make continual progress."

The delayed appearance of the Quarrel of the Ancients and the Moderns in Germany, at the end of the 18th century, produced some significant attempts to synthesize hopes for future progress with a positive interpretation of antiquity. Friedrich von Schiller saw two great eras in universal history, as defined in the title of his work *Über naive und sentimentalische Dichtung* (1795–96; On the Naive and Sentimental in Literature). Although he supported the position of the defenders of the moderns in the Quarrel, Schiller found his ideal for the future neither in the natural state of ancient Greece nor in the modern state of a conscious ("sentimental") art, but in a synthesis of the two, toward which humankind was progressing. This philosophy of history, obeying purely aesthetic criteria, has sometimes been construed as a response by the classicists of Weimar to the French Revolution, and as a sort of escape from historical reality into the autonomy of art.

The tendency to harmonize nature and culture, so evident in the German approach to the Quarrel, is also manifested in the interpretation of the Rousseauist critique of alienation—the ostensible result of the sciences, the arts, and social inequality (see Schröder). Herder, Kant, and Fichte saw no contradiction between Rousseau's central thesis and a future progress that would go beyond the premise of the Quarrel of the Ancients and the Moderns. In *Über die Bestimmung des Gelehrten* (1794; The Purpose of Higher Education), Fichte declared:

> For Rousseau, retrograde movement [*Rückkehr*] is progress [*Fortgang*]; for him the lost state of nature is the final goal that humanity, now corrupted and deformed, must attain. He therefore does what we do: he works to cultivate mankind in his own way, and to make it progress toward its final, supreme goal.

At the end of the 18th century, therefore, the Quarrel of the Ancients and the Moderns resulted in a distant but important echo. The new vision of history for which Fontenelle had opened the way was now devel-oped into an intellectual synthesis that led directly to the great achievements in the philosophy of history during the 19th century.

JOCHEN SCHLOBACH

See also Architecture; Classicism; Criticism; History, Philosophy of; Progress; Siècle

Further Reading

Baron, H., "The 'Querelle' As a Problem for Renaissance Scholarship," *Journal of the History of Ideas* 20 (1959)

Gossman, Lionel, *Medievalism and the Ideologies of the Enlightenment: The World and Work of LaCurne de Sainte-Palaye,* Baltimore, Maryland: Johns Hopkins Press, 1968

Grell, Chantal, *Le dix-huitième siècle et l'antiquité en France (1680–1789),* 2 vols., Oxford: Voltaire Foundation, 1995

Guyer, F.E., "The Dwarf on the Giant's Shoulders," *Modern Language Notes* 45 (1930)

Hepp, Noémi, *Homère en France au XVIIIᵉ siècle,* Paris: Klincksieck, 1968

Jauss, H.R., "Ästhetische Normen und geschichtliche Reflexion in der 'Querelle des Anciens et des Modernes,'" in *Parallèle des Anciens et des Modernes en ce qui regarde les arts et les sciences,* by Charles Perrault, Munich: Eidos Verlag, 1964

Jones, Richard Foster, *Ancients and Moderns: A Study of the Background of the Battle of the Books,* St. Louis, Missouri: Washington University, 1936; 2nd edition, 1961

Keller, Barbara G., *The Middle Ages Reconsidered: Attitudes in France from the Eighteenth Century through the Romantic Movement,* New York: Peter Lang, 1994

Martini, F., "Modern, Die Moderne," in *Reallexikon der deutschen Literaturgeschichte,* 2nd edition, by Paul Merker and Wolfgang Stammler, edited by Werner Kohlschmidt and Wolfgang Mohr, vol. 2, Berlin: De Gruyter, 1965

Schlobach, Jochen, *Zyklentheorie und Epochenmetaphorik: Studien zur bildlichen Sprache der Geschichtsreflexion in Frankreich von der Renaissance bis zur Frühaufklärung,* Munich: Fink, 1980

Schröder, Winfried, "Querelle des Anciens et des Modernes," in *Europäische Enzyklopädie zu Philosophie und Wissenschaften,* edited by Hans Jörg Sandkühler, vol. 3, Hamburg: Meiner, 1990

Voss, Jürgen, *Das mittelalter im historischen Denken Frankreichs,* Munich: Fink, 1972

Anti-Enlightenment

Arguably, Gottfried Wilhelm Leibniz's polemical opposition, in his *Essais de Théodicée* (1710; Theodicy), to the views set forth in Pierre Bayle's *Dictionnaire historique et critique* (1697; A Historical and Critical Dictionary) and to what Voltaire called Bayle's "paradox"—the possible existence of a society of virtuous atheists posited in Bayle's *Réponses aux questions d'un provincial* (1703; Answers to the Questions of a Provincial)—marked the beginning of a battle of ideas that would last more than a century. Bayle's work provoked numerous more orthodox polemics, and the list of his adversaries was long and diverse: the Protestant Jurieu in Geneva; Bernard and Jean Leclerc, both refugees in the Netherlands; Jacquelot, a refugee in Berlin who also answered to Bernard Le Bovier de Fontenelle; the eminent Anglicans Ralph Cudworth, Thomas Sherlock, William King, and John Tillotson; and the Jansenists Antoine Arnauld and Pierre Nicole were only the first. However, beyond the names cited above, one fact is obvious: whatever the chosen criteria—religious, metaphysical, ethical, or political—the clash that accompanied the coming of the Enlightenment resonated throughout Europe. Enlightenment thought presented a new vision of the world, transforming culture throughout the entire Continent and even in the Americas. But backlash against the new ideas was no less widespread. Across Europe, the defense systems of those institutions and individuals opposed to or threatened by the considerable transformations underway were activated, sometimes after a certain delay. These defensive reactions can be discerned both philosophically and geographically. Seeking to refute John Locke, the Italian cardinal Gerdil published in Turin his French-language text, the *Défense du sentiment du Père Malebranche sur la nature et l'origine des idées contre l'examen de M. Locke* (1748; In Defence of Father Malebranche's Opinion on the Nature and the Origin of Ideas, As Opposed to M. Locke's Examination). The philosophers of Greco-Roman antiquity also formed a focal point in the battle of ideas. In his *Démonstration de l'existence de Dieu, tirée de la connaissance de la nature et proportionnée à la faible intelligence des plus simples* (1713–18; A Demonstration of the Existence, Wisdom, and Omnipotence of God, Drawn from the Knowledge of Nature, Particularly of Man, and Fitted to the Meanest Capacity), François de Salignac de la Mothe-Fénelon attacked both Baruch Spinoza and the atomism of Epicurus and Lucretius. Cardinal de Polignac wrote his *Anti-Lucretius, sive De Deo et Natura, Libri Novem* (1747; Anti-Lucretius of God and Nature: A Poem) against Lucretius and Epicurus. This refutation, which appeared in part in 1716, was published posthumously in 1747 and translated into French in 1749. The cardinal based his arguments on Cartesian physics and metaphysics, attacking both atheism and Spinoza. How, then, should we interpret the notion of "anti-Enlightenment thinkers"? As they resisted the cultural changes underway, anti-Enlightenment thinkers, just like advocates of the Enlightenment, were characterized by diversity and their differences from one another: what did Fénelon, Louis-Claude de Saint-Martin, and the marquis de Sade have in common?

To a great extent, the concept of "Anti-Enlightenment" is simply a by-product of the fierce polemics common during the age of the Enlightenment; the term provided a category in which all the thinkers who did not come within the sphere of influence of the *philosophes* could be conveniently lumped together. This classification would include the authors of works inspired by the metaphysics of René Descartes, Leibniz, or Nicolas de Malebranche, whose systems continued to be associated with the Christian religion of their time. Religious thought was the main factor in the rift between enlightened thinkers and their adversaries. There were many writers who refused to accept the increasing role of reason and the covert or open appearance of criticism of Christian faith, of the mysteries of miracles, and of the Bible. On one side stood the Catholic or Protestant tradition embodied in thinkers such as Jacques-Bénigne Bossuet, Father Pierre-Daniel Huet, Malebranche, Jacques Abbadie, Bernard Lamy, and Fénelon. O the opposite side stood modernity heralded by Spinoza, its way prepared by Bayle and Fontenelle, Locke, and the Enlightenment *philosophes*. As Jean Deprun has written: "Mercier's 'moral sun,' a collective beacon and human enterprise, stands in opposition to the fixed star of eternal light" (see Deprun). This image suits all those who defended religious orthodoxy in all its forms, and it applies equally well to illuminist beliefs. But would it be apt as a characterization of the marquis de Sade, who was a plagiarist of the Enlightenment and a blaspheming catechumen? The image of a black sun would be more appropriate in his case. In any event, before moving to a consideration of the points of opposition between the two camps, it should be stressed that the history of ideas still holds some surprises for us. Sometimes a few heterodox ingredients were sufficient to divert the apologetic line of reasoning from its usual path or subvert it entirely.

In his *Traité de morale* (1684; Treatise on Ethics), Malebranche declared "the love of order is not merely the principal moral virtue, it is the only virtue"; this idea was to inspire the marquis de Mirabeau, in his *Philosophie rurale* (1763; Rural Philosophy) and his *Les économiques* (1769; Economics), just as it would inspire Denis Diderot in *Le fils naturel* (1757; The Natural Son) and the *Entretiens sur "Le fils naturel"* (1757; Discussions on "Le fils naturel"). Malebranche's opinion, and more specifically the Augustinian idea of order, became "the love of order" in the works of Mirabeau and "the taste for order" in those of Diderot—that is to say, a secular foundation of the Enlightenment's moral philosophy. The author of the *Traité de la vérité de la religion chrétienne* (1684; Treatise on the Truth of the Christian Religion) and of the *Traité de la divinité de N.S. Jésus-Christ* (1689; Treatise on the Divinity of Our Lord Jesus Christ), two great authoritative apologetic works, was the Protestant pastor Abbadie. He laid the groundwork for Jean-Jacques Rousseau and the marquis de Vauvenargues in their development of the idea of *amour de soi* (self-love), which is different from *amour-propre* (self-centeredness), in an original expression of the morality of feeling, when he defined "the natural love of respect, the love of ourselves, looking after our self-preservation, the desire for our happiness" in *L'art de se connaître soi-même ou la recherche des sources de la morale* (1692; The Art of Self-Knowledge; or, The Search for the Sources of Morality). Similarly, the concept of the beautiful that Father Yves-Marie André (who was influenced by Malebranche) proposed in his *Traité du Beau* (1741; A Treatise on the Beautiful) made its mark on the century and inspired Diderot, particularly in the article "Beau" (Beautiful) in the *Encyclopédie*. More generally, the atheist Claude-Adrien Helvétius spoke for many *philosophes* when he confirmed that he had received "the divine unction that emanates from the maxims in the Gospel" (*De l'esprit* [1758; Essays on the Mind and Its Several Faculties]) in order to establish the humanist ethics of the Enlightenment.

Nevertheless, we should recall that in France and elsewhere in Europe, the great majority of the Enlightenment's implacable adversaries were apologists of the Christian religion, including a great number of Catholics as well as some eminent Protestant figures. It is all but impossible to name all those who defended orthodoxy against the Enlightenment *philosophes*. From the moment they were published, various individual works by the *philosophes* provoked numerous apologetic refutations. Devotion to the dogmas of Christianity and affinity with its ethics guided the defenders of the faith. The man who believed in original sin and the man of the Enlightenment represented anthropologies and cosmologies that were at odds with one another. The apologists loudly proclaimed that without the biblical God men were doomed to fall into immorality, and Sade provided an opportune if rather extreme confirmation of this thesis by rejecting outright every premise of Enlightenment ethics. But what weight did the apologist's arguments carry? From Blaise Pascal to François-

René de Chateaubriand, not a single apologist, with the exception of Fénelon, won glory and fame. Although some of them published significant work, these apologists tend to be known only to experts in the field. Ordinary readers are more likely to remember the nonentities—"Nonnotte, Patouillet, and associates"—so loudly decried by Voltaire. Yet there were countless adversaries of the Enlightenment and some of them were formidable polemicists. The sense that the Church and its dogmas were in great danger lent their diatribes against the *philosophes* considerable harshness. Throughout Europe, the Jesuits in particular attacked the new ideas; however, the suppression of the Society of Jesus gave no respite to the confrontation that became much more generalized and exacerbated just before 1760. The entire Catholic Church, over and above its institutions, rose up against a body of ideas that threatened its major role in ancien régime society. The Protestants did not lag behind, even if their number seemed relatively small in comparison to the defense battalions of the Catholics.

Anti-Enlightenment and Apologetics before the "Encyclopédie"

France, the land of the Enlightenment, was quite naturally the preferred battleground for the struggle between religious orthodoxy and the *philosophes*. Before referring to what was written and published in other countries (sometimes in French), it is important first to single out a few names and tendencies that either strengthened or weakened Christian apologetics in defense of their dogmas against the assaults of an advancing philosophy. Albert Monod has compiled a list of approximately 750 apologetic works published between 1715 and the beginning of the French Revolution (see Monod). More than two-thirds of these were published in the second half of the century, after the *Encyclopédie* had begun to appear. The years that passed between the severe crisis of the affair of the abbé de Prades and the fallout from the reception of the *Encyclopédie*'s initial volumes, on the one hand, and the tumult unleashed by the baron d'Holbach's *Système de la nature, ou, Des lois du monde physique et du monde moral* (1770; The System of Nature; or, The Laws of the Moral and Physical World), on the other, coincide with the period of the largest number of publications, and the end of this period signals the desire for renewal.

One problem encountered in the process of evaluating such a vast production involves deciding on a criterion for selecting those works that enjoyed success, were frequently reprinted, and thus accomplished their mission, and eliminating from consideration those that today might merit only a passing reference in the history of ideas. Many of the authors who came after Father Fénelon and his substantial work, which was to inspire a philosophical current with its own particularities, may appear mediocre today. However, this period included some formidable apologists, such as the Oratorian Claude-François Houteville, author of *La vérité de la religion chrétienne prouvée par les faits* (1722; The Truth of the Christian Religion Proven by Facts). Still, as Diderot remarked, Houteville's inordinate desire to prove miracles and prophecies in that book merely demonstrated the weaknesses of a historical method of proof through facts.

Several works by Jean-Pierre de Crousaz—*Traité du beau* (1715; A Treatise on the Beautiful), *Examen du traité de la liberté de penser de Collins* (1718; An Examination of Collins's Treatise on the Freedom of Thought), *Cinq sermons sur la vérité de la religion chrétienne* (1722; Five Sermons on the Truth of the Christian Religion), and *Examen du pyrrhonisme ancien et moderne* (1733; An Examination of Ancient and Modern Pyrrhonism)—attest to a particularly rigorous Christianity as much as to sincere open-mindedness when faced with questions raised by the Enlightenment. In his *Traité de l'esprit humain* (1741; Treatise on the Human Mind), Crousaz criticized Alexander Pope as well as the optimism of Leibniz and Christian Wolff.

Le spectacle de la nature ou Entretiens sur les particularités de l'histoire naturelle qui ont paru les plus propres à rendre les jeunes gens curieux et à leur former l'esprit (Nature Displayed: Being Discourses on Such Particulars of Natural History As Were Thought Most Proper to Excite the Curiosity, and Form the Minds of Youth) by the abbé Noël-Antoine Pluche appeared in 1732, and enjoyed significant success in France and elsewhere in Europe. Pluche's work was a popularized presentation of scientific material in 11 volumes with engravings, calculated to impart knowledge and, at the same time, to appease Christian minds intrigued by the new ideas. The reference in the subtitle to Pluche's *Entretiens sur la pluralité des mondes* (1686; Conversations on the Plurality of Worlds) became a symbol of renewal. Pluche attacked mythology and Scholasticism in particular, but in a supplementary work, the *Histoire du ciel* (1738; The History of the Heavens), he refuted both Cartesian physics and Newtonian gravitation. The very title of Father Claude Buffier's *Cours de sciences sur des principes nouveaux et simples pour former le langage, l'esprit et le cœur dans l'usage ordinaire de la vie* (1732; A Science Course on New and Simple Principles Aimed at Developing Language, the Mind, and the Heart in the Ordinary Circumstances of Life) shows that this Jesuit had a similar desire to educate and edify. Buffier's work dealt with grammar, metaphysics, music, and politics, among other topics. Whether or not it was a conscious aim, the desire to shape minds through such

works, intended for a readership that was vast for the period, was becoming manifest. Translated into several languages and reprinted many times during the 18th century, Pluche's work, at least, was to have an enormous impact, as attested by Rousseau's *La profession de foi du vicaire savoyard* (1762; The Creed of a Priest of Savoy).

Many books appeared in refutation of Voltaire's *Lettres philosophiques* (1734; Philosophical Letters) and, as an indirect consequence, these works also challenged Locke. Among them is a work by the Protestant David-Renaud Boullier, entitled *Réflexions sur quelques principes de la philosophie de M. Locke à l'occasion des "Lettres philosophiques" de M. de Voltaire* (1735; Reflections on a Few Principles of Mr. Locke's Philosophy on the Occasion of the Publication of M. de Voltaire's "Lettres philosophiques"). Boullier renewed his attack in 1741 with his *Défense des "Pensées" de Pascal contre la critique de M. de Voltaire* (In Defense of Pascal's "Pensées" against M. de Voltaire's Criticism). He was to pursue a career as a tenacious apologist, notably with an *Apologie de la métaphysique à l'occasion du "Discours préliminaire de l'Encyclopédie"* (1753; An Apology of Metaphysics on the Occasion of the Publication of the "Discours preliminaire de l'Encyclopédie") and another work, the *Pièces philosophiques et littéraires* (1759; Philosophical and Literary Writings), in which he refuted Étienne Bonnot de Condillac's sensationalism. The Oratorian Father Joseph Adrien Lelarge de Lignac set about writing a book against the most widespread work of the 18th century of Enlightenment inspiration in his *Lettres à un Amériquain sur l'"Histoire naturelle générale et particulière" de M. de Buffon* (1751; Letters to an American on M. de Buffon's "Histoire naturelle générale et particulière"). To combat Helvétius, Lignac wrote an *Examen sérieux et comique des discours sur l'esprit* (1759; A Serious and Comic Examination of the Discourses on the Mind), from which Rousseau was to learn a great deal. In 1753 Lignac wrote his *Éléments de métaphysique tirés de l'expérience* (Elements of Metaphysics Derived from Experience), a critique of Locke, and in 1760, in the same spirit, he authored *Le témoignage du sens intime et de l'expérience opposé à la foi profane et ridicule des fatalistes modernes* (The Testimony of Inmost Sense and Experience As Opposed to the Secular and Ridiculous Faith of Modern-Day Fatalists), in which he attacked the Encyclopedists and determinism. Alongside these texts, we should not omit to mention the poem "La Religion" (1742; Religion) by Louis Racine, which attaches a famous name to the attacks against Locke, Bayle, and Pope in particular. The poem, which is infused with a sometimes rather unorthodox form of Malebranche's thinking, saw a great many reprints and translations. Some of the works mentioned were immediate refutations, others a posteriori reactions, such as Les "Lettres persanes" convaincues d'impiété (The "Persian Letters" Convicted of Impiety), published by the abbé Gaultier in 1751.

Anti-Enlightenment Thinkers and Apologetics after the "Encyclopédie"

The abbé Gauchat, in his impressive apologetic opus Lettres critiques ou analyse et réfutation de divers écrits modernes contre la religion (1755–63; Critical Letters; or, An Analysis and Refutation of Several Modern Writings against Religion), refuted the work of Bayle as condensed by de Marsy in his Analyse raisonnée des oeuvres de Bayle (1755; A Reasoned Analysis of Bayle's Works), which had earned de Marsy a stint in the Bastille (1755). Gauchat also responded to Diderot's Pensées philosophiques (Philosophical Thoughts) in Volume 1 of his Lettres critiques (1755), and, with his Catéchisme du livre "De l'esprit" (Catechism of the Book "De l'esprit"), in Volume 12 of the Lettres critiques (1758), Gauchat offered his response to Helvétius's work. "L'infâme" (Voltaire's term for the philosophes' enemy) had in his own way learned a lesson from the scandalous affair of the abbé de Prades. It should be emphasized that the Church turned to the secular arm for support as long as it was able to—that is to say, until the French Revolution. Upon the indictment by Omer Joly de Fleury before the Parlement of Paris, the ban on Helvetius's De l'esprit—followed by the suspension of the continued publication of the Encyclopédie in 1759—preceded the barbaric acts against Calas and the chevalier de la Barre. The severity of the repression against the philosophes in general, and against some individuals in particular, was proportionate to the peculiar theoretical weakness of the apologists. The eight volumes of Abraham Joseph de Chaumeix's Préjugés légitimes et réfutation de l'"Encyclopédie" avec un examen critique du livre "De l'esprit" (1758; Legitimate Prejudices and Refutation of the "Encyclopédie," with a Critical Examination of the Book "De l'esprit") provided intellectual support for the repression, but Chaumeix's work was capable of swaying only the members of the party of the devout. With his acceptance speech as a new member in the Académie Française, approved by the king, Father Jean-Georges Lefranc de Pompignan, poet and author of La dévotion réconciliée avec l'esprit (1754; Devotion Reconciled with the Mind), unleashed a storm against the spirit of the philosophes, one that turned against him in the end: readers still laugh at Voltaire's and André Morellet's gibes against Lefranc. As the Jesuits, with their periodical Journal de Trévoux, and the Jansenists, with their Nouvelles ecclésiastiques, frequently skirmished with one another, they did not provide revealed religion with the support it so badly needed.

All that is remembered of this disappointing period of Catholic apologetics is the names of those to whom Voltaire gave a certain notoriety by relentlessly targeting them, including Chaumeix; Louis Stanislas Fréron and his Année littéraire (Literary Yearbook); and Father Guillaume-François Berthier, editor of the Journal de Trévoux, whom Voltaire "buried" 22 years before his actual death in his Relation de la maladie, de la confession, de la mort et de l'apparition du jésuite Berthier (An Account of the Jesuit Berthier's Illness, Confession, Death, and Apparition). Among the other Catholic apologists who owed the greater part of their notoriety to Voltaire were Patouillet, with his Histoire du Pélagianisme (1767; History of Pelagianism), and Nonnotte, who was to enjoy success among the "right-thinking" conformists with his Erreurs de Voltaire (1762; Voltaire's Errors), reprinted several times during the 18th and 19th centuries. However, the Church's recourse to the secular branch revealed the state of the forces at work: Catholic apologetics was short of clever scholars—of philosophers, in a word. The Encyclopedists did not really find any adversaries of their own caliber and institutions constituted the safest defense of dogmas. This lack of philosophical aptitude was precisely what the famous Christophe de Beaumont, archbishop of Paris, illustrated in the Mandement (Pastoral Letter) denouncing Rousseau's Émile, ou, De l'education (1762; Émile; or, Concerning Education).

Apart from the fratricidal quarrels between Jesuits and Jansenists—which were also found in Spain with the lampoon Delación de la doctrina de los intitulados Jesuítas (1768; Denunciation of the Doctrine of the Jesuits), attributed to Enrique Florez—considerable confusion seems to have reigned at the time in the very heart of the Church. The writings by the Catholic apologists, hardly suspected of heresy, were above all characterized by their retrograde spirit and the mediocrity of their argumentation. The concern with the defense of the dogmas of the Catholic religion went well beyond the borders of the kingdom of France thanks to Salchli, a professor in Lausanne and the author of the Lettres sur le Déisme (1759; Letters on Deism), and even thanks to the king of Poland, Stanislas Leszczinscki, who wrote L'incrédulité combattue par le simple bon sens (1760; Unbelief Fought with Simple Common Sense). In 1761, the Hungarian Protestant Teleky de Szek published an Essai sur la faiblesse des esprits forts (Essay on the Weakness of Rational Minds), in which he explains that miracles are performed in order to reestablish the divine order. He criticizes Bayle, Voltaire, Diderot, and the Encyclopedists, as well as Frederick II of Prussia.

Neither the number of works devoted to the defense of orthodoxy nor their subsequent editions were able to mask the general decline of apologetics. How could the apologists hope to counter the fighting spirit of deism in Voltaire's *Dictionnaire philosophique* (1764; Philosophical Dictionary), or Holbach's audacious advocacy of atheism in *Le système de la nature, ou Des lois du monde physique et du monde moral* (1770; The System of Nature; or, On the Laws of the Physical World and of the Moral World)? The defenders of the faith had to redouble their efforts, as did Father Fidèle de Pau, author of the *Philosophe dithyrambique* (1765; The Dithyrambic Philosopher). In this zealous defense of Catholicism, Father Fidèle accused the *philosophes,* from Montesquieu to Helvétius, of being "the cause of the calamities on Earth." The same year, the abbé Bergier, a more levelheaded soul, published *Le Déisme réfuté par lui-même* (Deism Refuted by Itself), which is directed against Rousseau. This Catholic apologist always put forward his arguments carefully and with definite pertinence. However, Bergier's intelligence was perhaps deceptive; in the conclusion of the fifth letter, "Sur la tolérance" (On Toleration), he reveals a very narrow mind-set:

> With the fine system of toleration, France would have become a refuge for all the visionaries and all the libertines in the Universe, who are always ready to gain entry here. We would be reduced to tolerating atheism and to living among monsters. . . . Having learned from the example of our neighbors and from our own dangers, we thank God for having saved both religion and morality through the same miracle.

Bergier exalted the alliance forged between throne and altar even in that area which constituted for Rousseau and Voltaire the worst fault in the century of the *philosophes:* that is, intolerance. In a work representing an identical spirit, the *Lettres de quelques juifs portugais, allemands et polonais, à M. de Voltaire* (1769; Letters from Some Portuguese, German, and Polish Jews to Monsieur Voltaire), the abbé Guénée sought to produce a systematic refutation of Voltaire's writings, specifically addressing his *Traité sur la tolérance* (1763; A Treatise on Toleration). Following Nonnotte and Bergier, Guénée fiercely attacked the concept of toleration: "Toleration . . . was not only a grave sin against conscience, a blameworthy violation of one of the first laws of nature, it was also a public offense and the public offense most deserving of punishment." Taking up as an example the Jewish Question, so dear to Voltaire, Guénée proved himself to be a theoretician specializing in intolerance.

Despite the condemnations and the censorship, it was exceedingly difficult thereafter to halt the popularization of the *philosophes'* ideas. During this period, when the philosophy of the Enlightenment triumphed, up until the French Revolution, the anti-*philosophes* still tried to take up the challenge. However, in the wake of the publication of Holbach's *Système de la nature,* they found they even had to borrow some of Voltaire's and Rousseau's own arguments. Countless apologetic works tried to combat the theses in Holbach's book. The abbé Bergier responded rapidly to those theses with his *Examen du matérialisme ou Réfutation du "Système de la nature"* (1771; Examination of Materialism; or, Refutation of the "Système de la nature"). However, in this dense work no argument measured up to the author's personal conviction that feeling contributes to the rationality of man. Thus, Bergier became indebted to Rousseau, whom he had earlier refuted, since, in his concern to demonstrate God's existence he appealed to feeling as a means of proof. The *Réflexions philosophiques sur "Le système de la nature"* (1772; Philosophical Reflections on "Le système de la nature") by the German Protestant philosopher Holland appeared during the same period.

Before Chateaubriand came into the field, some precursors of an apparently more flexible apologetics became outrageously opportunistic in their polemics against the *philosophes.* These apologists understood how to take advantage of Rousseau's work and, more generally, of the contradictory views that existed among the *philosophes,* especially after Holbach's *Système de la nature* had appeared. Rousseau's thinking was reviewed, corrected, and adjusted to the requirements of the defense of revelation. Nor did these apologists shy away from occasionally quoting Voltaire. Inspired by the success of *La nouvelle Héloïse* (1761; Julie; or, The New Héloïse), the epistolary novels of the abbé Gérard and the abbé Barruel were imitations of a novel by the Protestant minister Jacob Vernes, who was the true inventor of this strange compromise, or rather of apologetic plagiarism, with *La confidence philosophique* (1771; Philosophical Confidence). That work was followed by the abbé Gérard's *Le comte de Valmont ou les égarements de la raison* (1774; The Count of Valmont; or, The Caprices of Reason) and later by the abbé Barruel's *Les Helviennes ou Lettres provinciales philosophiques* (1781; The Helviennes; or, Provincial Philosophical Letters), works that offered immoralism as the only alternative to the biblical God. In these epistolary novels, young and likable heroes appear, such as the comte de Valmont or, in the *Helviennes,* the chevalier de . . . and the baronne de. . . . Such characters are sensitive to the mind-set of the times and feel attracted to the new philosophy, which eventually leads them astray into the worst trials and tribulations. After numerous letters recounting the protagonists' transgressions and answers to these from characters who have remained devout—answers that are essentially sermons against all of the ideas of Enlightenment philosophy—the hero and heroine rediscover the straight path in the bosom of religion. For example, in the abbé Gérard's novel, Valmont finds on the bedside table of Lausane—his friend and imagined rival, who has been ruined by philosophy—a bogus piece of philosophical writing, *Le grand oeuvre* (The Great Work), in which Gérard caricatures the spirit of the Enlightenment by attacking Holbach's *Système de la nature*.

In their controversies the apologists thus forged proofs in order to better condemn the immoralism of their adversaries. Embedding arguments in fiction, especially in novels, was a favored form of Christian apologetics before the French Revolution. These novels see the birth of negative heroes who imitate the essential themes of Enlightenment philosophy in their speeches. With their supposedly philosophical words and the loosest of morals, they are, oddly enough, paving the way for the fictions of Sade. We know that Sade had read Bergier, and it is very likely that the highly successful works of Vernes, Barruel, and Gérard had also passed through his hands. Was the work of the divine marquis then not to a great extent the fruit of his instructive reading? In its determination to fight the philosophy of the Enlightenment, did Christian apologetics paradoxically contribute to the emergence of a disturbing immoralism? Did these upright abbés have offspring that were as unexpected as they were shameful?

In Liège a Jesuit priest, François-Xavier Feller, published a *Catéchisme philosophique, ou recueil d'observations propres à défendre la religion chrétienne contre ses ennemis* (1773; A Philosophical Catechism; or, A Collection of Observations That Will Defend the Christian Religion against Its Enemies). Before the French Revolution, from 1781 onward, on the initiative of D'Alembert, the Académie Française (which supported the *philosophes* at that time) devised a competition for the plan of a nondenominational catechism. The defenders of Catholicism reacted, and in 1787 Stéphanie Ducrest de Saint-Aubin, the comtesse de Genlis, published her book with the programmatic title *La religion considérée comme l'unique base du bonheur* (Religion As the Only Basis for Happiness). In the book *De l'excellence de la religion* (1786; On the Excellence of Religion), frequently reprinted during the French Revolution and under the Empire, La Luzerne affirmed the success of disbelief and predicts the end of religion and the downfall of France.

In Spain anti-Enlightenment thinkers attempted to avert the progress of *las luces* (the Enlightenment) and of *enciclopedismo* (Encyclopedism). In 1771 in Madrid,

the Portuguese writer Luis Jose Pereira published his *Theodicea* (Theodicy), in which he tried specifically to link sensationalist philosophy to the principles of revealed religion. Cevallos y Mier, to cite another example, published a voluminous *Falsa filosofia* (1774–76; False Philosophy), a refutation of atheism and deism, subversive doctrines he considers crimes of state. The Italian jurist Cesare Bonesana Beccaria had reason to complain about Cevallos, insofar as the latter's *Analisis del libro intitulado "Delitos y penas"* (Analysis of the Book Entitled "Crimes and Punishments") contributed to the condemnation Beccaria's book by the Inquisition in 1777. In 1786 Forner—the most acerbic polemicist of his time—published his *Oración apologética por la España y su merito literario* (Apologetic Oration for Spain and Its Literary Merit), in which "the Rousseaus, the Voltaires, and the Helvétiuses" were discredited.

In England, Anglican apologists refuted the arguments of Enlightenment philosophers, especially those of Hume. The controversy against Hume is illustrated by three theologians who were shocked by his attacks against their faith. George Campbell wrote *A Dissertation on Miracles* (1763), which for a long time was thought to be the best criticism of the English philosopher; Hume responded to Campbell with a letter. In the same vein, William Adams wrote an *Essay on Hume* (1752). John Douglas published *The Criterion; or, Miracles Examined* (1754), in which he argued against recent miracles without grasping the dangerous implications of his arguments for the sanctity of past miracles. These three apologists tended to avoid as much as possible having recourse to miracles. Their doctrine was characterized by a kind of semirationalism, even though they remained deeply Christian. One of the most original Anglican apologists was William Paley, who taught morality, metaphysics, and theology at Christ's College in Cambridge. He wrote *The Principles of Moral and Political Philosophy* in 1785. Paley's most original work remains *Horae Paulinae; or, The Truth of the Scripture History of St. Paul Evinced* (1790). He also wrote *A View of the Evidences of Christianity* (1794). In order to defend the apologetic thesis contained in this work, Paley used the legacy of Nathaniel Lardner as support, namely the *Credibility of the Gospel History*, which represented a prime example of orthodoxy. Finally, Paley's *Natural Theology; or, Evidences and Attributes of the Deity Collected from the Appearances of Nature* (1802) appeared in Italian translation in 1808 and in Spanish in 1825. Paley asserted that we might be able to affirm the existence of God scientifically in some way if we had a sixth sense, which in fact man lacks. Is there is a hint of a compromise with rationalism in this representation of divine transcendence? One might imagine that a person such as Helvétius would regard the notion of feeling with a certain irony, but Paley's method was quite clever. Through his original approach and his mild judgments in the defense of faith, Paley appeared to express himself more as a theologian close to the tradition of English latitudinarianism than as the Anglican equivalent of the French and Spanish apologists.

Side by side with orthodox Christianity appeared the illuminism of Martinès de Pasqually and his disciple Louis-Claude de Saint-Martin, the "unknown philosopher." Should Saint-Martin's book *Des erreurs et de la vérité* (1775; On Errors and Truth) be seen as the mystical antithesis of the *Système de la nature*? The contrast was great between the then-triumphant key ideas of the Enlightenment and the spiritualism of Saint-Martin, who once again took up the idea of the Fall of man in his *Tableau naturel des rapports qui existent entre Dieu, l'homme et l'univers* (1782; A Natural Depiction of the Relations That Exist among God, Man, and the Universe). Saint-Martin claimed to be a follower of the philosophy of Jakob Boehme, whose works he translated; Saint-Martin also published *L'homme de désir* (1790; The Man of Desire). The latter was surely read by Rétif de La Bretonne, author of the *Philosophie de Monsieur Nicolas* (1796; Monsieur Nicolas's Philosophy), followed by Holbach's *Histoire critique de Jésus-Christ; ou Analyse raisonnée des Évangiles: Ecce homo* (1770; Ecce Homo! or, A Critical Inquiry into the History of Jesus of Nazareth) and Saint-Martin's *Le nouvel homme* (1792; The New Man). Defender of the innate and of metaphysics, Rétif consigned his polemic regarding Condillac's philosophy to his *Discours en réponse au citoyen Garat, professeur d'entendement humain aux écoles normales sur l'existence d'un sens moral* (1801; A Discourse in Response to Citizen Garat, Professor of Human Understanding in the Normal Schools, on the Existence of a Moral Sense). An advocate of theocracy, Rétif de la Bretonne proved himself to be a traditionalist who foreshadowed the theories of Joseph de Maistre and of Louis, vicomte de Bonald, in his *Lettre à un ami sur la Révolution française* (1795; Letter to a Friend on the French Revolution) and *L'éclair sur l'association humaine* (1797; Light on Human Association). Rétif's *Ministère de l'homme esprit* (1802; Ministry of Human Spirit) contained an altogether original Martinist critique of *Le génie du Christianisme, ou Beautés de la religion chrétienne* (1802; The Genius of Christianity; or, The Spirit and Beauties of the Christian Religion). Together with the work of Emmanuel Swedenborg, Rétif's work was to be read by Honoré de Balzac and Charles-Augustin Sainte-Beuve, in particular. Martinism, imprinted with a religiosity that was above all a gnosis for illuminated initiates, would have a decided influence on the romantics.

In the works of Antoine Adrien Lamourette—who was the constitutional bishop of Lyon before ending up on the scaffold—the author's temperament made a reconciliation between the Church of the ancien régime and post-Revolutionary France seem almost possible. Lamourette's writings were an inspiration to Chateaubriand. In the *Pensées sur la philosophie de l'incrédulité* (1786; Thoughts on the Philosophy of Unbelief), Lamourette recalled being moved by the sight of the common people in church. In 1788 Lamourette published *Les délices de la religion ou le pouvoir de l'Evangile pour nous rendre heureux* (The Delights of Religion; or, The Power of the Gospel to Make Us Happy), in which, predating Chateaubriand, he evoked images of nature that inspire piety and make one accept the idea of religion. The title of the work he published in 1789 clearly shows Lamourette's preoccupations as well as his very original contribution to resolving certain contradictions: *Pensées sur la philosophie de la foi, ou le système du Christianisme entrevu dans son analogie avec les idées naturelles de l'entendement humain* (Thoughts on the Philosophy of Faith; or, The System of Christianity Considered through Its Analogy with the Natural Ideas of the Human Understanding). Far removed from Pascal but concerned with remaining faithful to Christianity, Lamourette developed a new cosmology, an innovative theology for which he deserves to be seen as more than a precursor of Chateaubriand. Did Lamourette betray the Church or should he be considered an innovator of the same caliber as Pierre Teilhard de Chardin? Lamourette's *Prônes civiques, ou le pasteur patriote* (Civic Sermons; or, The Patriotic Pastor), which appeared in 1790–91, show his conception of a social Christianity, a perspective that had been nurtured by his reading of both the *philosophes* and Malebranche. Lamourette's tragic destiny makes this original attempt at reconciling faith in the Church with the ideals of the French Revolution very moving. The other apologetic writings that appeared after 1789 were both antiphilosophical and antirevolutionary. Among these are the works of Barruel, such as *Le patriote véridique ou discours sur les vraies causes de la Révolution actuelle* (1789; The Truthful Patriot; or, Discourse on the True Causes of the Present Revolution); Joseph de Maistre's *Considérations sur la France* (1796; Considerations on France); and, finally, Bonald's *Théorie du pouvoir politique et religieux dans la société civile* (1796; Theory of Political and Religious Power in Civil Society).

And then came Chateaubriand, whose apologetic oeuvre should not be allowed to eclipse the rebirth of apologetics before him, for he was but one of the agents of that rebirth—although certainly the most famous among them. In 1801 Ballanche published *Du sentiment considéré dans ses rapports avec la littérature et les arts* (On Feeling, Considered in Its Relationship with Literature and the Arts). Also noteworthy was a supposedly Rousseauist catechism entitled the *Théorie du bonheur* (1801; Theory of Happiness) by the abbé Gérard, which was, however, primarily antiphilosophical and antirevolutionary. It was a sequel to the *Comte de Valmont,* also published by the abbé Gérard in 1801—that is, before his *Génie du Christianisme* (1802; The Genius of Christianity). Chateaubriand, author of the *Essai sur les révolutions* (1797; An Historical, Political, and Moral Essay on Revolutions, Ancient and Modern), which took the legacy of the *philosophes* into account, had certainly read Ballanche and the abbé Gérard, and he was familiar with the abbé Pluche's *Le spectacle de la nature.* With definite opportunism and a great deal of talent, Chateaubriand renewed Christian apologetics, thanks to the aesthetics of romanticism that he promoted in his work, more as an artist than as a philosopher.

In 1817 Félicité Robert de Lamennais published the first part of his *Essai sur l'indifférence en matière de religion* (Essay on Indifference As Regards Religion), in which he shows himself to be a formidable heir to the apologists of the 18th century. The sequel was to appear in 1820. Lamennais confirmed a great devotion to the orthodox dogmas of the Church. Proclaiming his faith in a God of vengeance and retribution, he scoffed at all morality that does not receive divine sanction: "The only guarantor for public safety will be the executioner, and justice will be proclaimed in the name of death, since people have been unwilling to proclaim it in the name of God." The development of this unusual thinker falls outside the period covered here, but it reflects the contradictions of the anti-Enlightenment legacy. Did the Church win its struggle against the Enlightenment given that France has clearly remained a Catholic country? Or, on the contrary, should one conclude that the philosophy of the Enlightenment, along with the French Revolution and its Declaration of the Rights of Man and Citizen, definitively put an end to an ancient world that saw throne and altar as one—a concept abolished forever after throughout Europe in the mind if not in fact?

Without answering either question affirmatively, one may well wonder about the evolution of a Christianity maintained or restored throughout Europe. Jean Étienne Marie Portalis, who was minister of religion from 1801 onward, in his *De l'usage et de l'abus de l'esprit philosophique durant le XVIIIe siècle* (1820; On the Use and Abuse of the Philosophical Spirit during the Eighteenth Century), rejected both the "sterile and turbulent metaphysics of *Du contrat social* [The Social Contract]" of Rousseau and Immanuel Kant's *Kritik der reinen Vernunft* (1781; Critique of Pure Reason), while appreciating "the admirable *Essais* [Essays] of Nicole and the excellent *Traités* [Treatises] of Bossuet and Fénelon." Was the message of the anti-Enlighten-

ment thinkers so poor that Jacques Necker's *De l'importance des opinions religieuses* (1788; On the Importance of Religious Opinions) remained the only work worth remembering? Jean-Étienne-Marie Portalis in a sense erased a century of apologetics when he showed disdain for the Enlightenment, both in France and in Germany. However, is there not a wealth of lessons to be learned from recalling the destiny that, after 1820, befell the emblematic figures of the Anti-Enlightenment, such as Chateaubriand and Lamennais? What a contrast with the serried ranks of the apologetics of the 18th century, broken only by Lamourette! Without necessarily spurning orthodoxy, as Madame de Staël did so strikingly in her *Réflexions sur le suicide* (1813; Reflections on Suicide), the age of romanticism inherited elements from both the Enlightenment and the Anti-Enlightenment. Those thinkers who were marginal, such as the illuminists, were an inspiration for the energy of Balzac and so many others. Seen in historical perspective, the anti-Enlightenment thinkers often seem to be the hidden side of the Enlightenment, drawing the essence of their substance from the works of the *philosophes,* exploiting every alleged weakness of the adversary. With Chateaubriand these thinkers were finally ennobled, and with style. This glorification proves that it would be as unproductive as it would be absurd to disregard those who maintained a passionate debate with the *philosophes* around the key ideas of the Enlightenment. Passionate debate, after all, is what created the entire wealth of the history of 18th-century thought.

JACQUES DOMENECH

See also Apologetics; Catholicism; Charity; Counter-Revolution; Prejudice; Virtue

Further Reading

Crocker, Lester G., *An Age of Crisis: Man and World in Eighteenth-Century French Thought,* Baltimore, Maryland: Johns Hopkins Press, 1959

Delon, Michel, *L'idée d'énergie au tournant des Lumières (1770–1820),* Paris: Presses Universitaires de France, 1988

Deprun, Jean, "Les Anti-Lumières," in *Histoire de la philosophie,* volume 2, *De la Renaissance à la révolution kantienne,* edited by Yvon Belaval, Paris: Gallimard, 1973

Domenech, Jacques, *L'éthique des Lumières: Les fondements de la morale dans la philosophie française du XVIIIe siècle,* Paris: Vrin, 1989

Monod, Albert, *De Pascal à Chateaubriand: Les défenseurs français du Christianisme de 1670 à 1802,* Paris: Alcan, 1916; reprint, New York: Franklin, 1971

Pomeau, René, editor, *Voltaire en son temps,* 5 vols., Oxford: Voltaire Foundation, 1985–94; revised edition, 2 vols., Paris: Fayard, and Oxford: Voltaire Foundation, 1995

Stephen, Leslie, *History of English Thought in the Eighteenth Century,* 2 vols., London: Smith, and New York: Putnam, 1876; reprint, New York: Harcourt, Brace and World, 1962

Antiquity

The notion of antiquity, which was central to a whole set of problems in the 18th century, seems simple as it is defined, for example, in Antoine-Joseph Pernety's *Dictionnaire portatif de peinture, sculpture et gravure* (1757; A Portable Dictionary of Painting, Sculpture, and Engraving): "The word 'antiquity'covers all works of painting, sculpture, and architecture created in Greek and Roman times." The definition continues, "antique figures should serve as rule and model." This art, the very expression of ideal beauty, was associated with a perfect, supreme, "classical" art (in one of its meanings, the word "classical" was a synonym for "antiquity"). Antique art did acquire a new dimension in the 18th century, but its status as a primary source was already established in the history of Western art; artists had sought to imitate or even surpass the art of the ancients since the Italian Renaissance. The story of Michelangelo being able to sell his *Cupido* as an authentic antique was sometimes retold in the 18th century (for example, it was recounted in both the *Encyclopédie* and Pernety's *Dictionnaire portatif*). In the days of Louis XIV, there was even a vast project to reconstruct part of ancient Rome at Versailles. In 1666 the Académie de France was founded in Rome in order to allow direct contact with the masterpieces of antiquity (and the Renaissance) and, concretely, to allow French artists to make copies of ancient art for the royal court. A century later, the collection at the gardens of Versailles, composed of "all that is beautiful in Italy," still had an impact on the aesthetics of Johann Gottfried von Herder, as expressed in his *Plastik: Einige Wahrnehmungen über Form und Gestalt aus Pygmalions bildendem Traume* (1778; Sculpture: Certain Observations on Form and Shape from Pygmalion's Graphic Dream). The need to reinforce practice with theory was not overlooked. The Académie Royale de Peinture et de Sculpture (Royal Academy of Painting and Sculpture) in Paris offered many courses in antique sculpture in the third quarter of the century, which included Anguier's lectures on the Farnese *Hercules* and the *Laocoön;* Marsy's comments on the Belvedere Torso; Buyster's lectures on the *Gladiator;* and Regnaudin's analyses of the antique Bacchus, the *Venus de Medici,* and the *Borghese Gladiator.* Copies and casts of the most famous works were also acquired by other European courts, notably in England and Spain.

In fact, the confrontation of 18th-century art with antique forms came through an "inheritance" of past references to antiquity that had essentially been uninterrupted since the Renaissance. More accurately than the French *retour* (literally, "return,"), the English word "revival" conveys the extent of artistic engagement with classical sources. Further, it would hardly be possible to reduce all the perceptible changes in artistic theory and expression in the latter half of the century to the discoveries at Herculaneum (1738), Pompeii (1748), and Stabies (1749) or to the publication of Johann Joachim Winckelmann's *Gedanken über die Nachahmung der Griechischen Werke in der Malerei und der Bildhauerkunst* (1755; Reflections on the Painting and Sculpture of the Greeks). Winckelmann was of course at the forefront of the movement, controversially labeled "neoclassicism," that captivated all of Europe at the end of the century. But above and beyond these specific influences, "antiquity" corresponded to the spirit of the times and the needs of the Enlightenment. The antique model was seen as an effective weapon in the struggle against the rococo, which was considered politically, morally, and aesthetically decadent. Whereas the entourage of Winckelmann, Alessandro Albani, and Anton Raphael Mengs focused on the aesthetic value of antique art, the comte de Caylus studied the works from a more technical or documentary angle. In France interest in antique models later took on political significance and became an important aspect of the art of the Revolution. In this "return"—to origins, to simplicity, to nature—the reference to antiquity was somewhat eclectic. Antiquity can be perceived in all sorts of artistic works: art adapted to the lighthearted taste of the period, such as Joseph-Marie Vien's *La marchande d'amours* (1763; Merchant of Love) or Mengs's *Le jugement de Pâris* (c. 1757; The Judgment of Paris);

moralistic art, such as Jacques-Louis David's *Bélisaire demandant l'aumône* (1781; Belisarius Begging for Alms) or Gavin Hamilton's *Andromache Weeping over the Corpse of Hector* (1762); works bathed in melancholy sentiment, such as Hubert Robert's paintings of ruins; the "archeological" drawings of Giambattista Piranesi; the sculptures of Edme Bouchardon (*La Fontaine de Grenelle* [1739–45]); or furniture "in the Greek style" made by Louis-Joseph Le Lorrain (1757). However, this article will not focus on 18th-century art itself, whether of Greek, Etruscan, Roman, or Egyptian influence, but rather, on the wide-ranging contacts that artists established with the art of antiquity during the age of the Enlightenment.

Artists and Approaches to Antiquity

Perhaps one of the simplest ways to immerse oneself in the principles of antique art during the Enlightenment was by studying the abundant series and collections of engravings that had been in circulation since the Renaissance (Antonio Lafreri [1540–1580], Cavalleriis [1561–94], Ulisse Aldrovandi [1556], Perrier [1638], Charles Perrault [1673], Joachim von Sandrart [1680], Desgodetz [1682], Bartoli [1695]). In the early 18th century, authors such as Alessandro Maffei (1704), Bernard de Montfaucon (1719), and Jonathan Richardson (1722) published more methodical works that were used as reference works. For example, an English translation of Montfaucon's work published between 1721 and 1725 influenced works by English potter and manufacturer Josiah Wedgwood in the third quarter of the century—although most of the images in Wedgwood's considerable repertory were derived from significant works published in the middle of the century, such as the baron d'Hancarville's illustrated *Collection of Etruscan, Greek, and Roman Antiquities from the Cabinet of Honourable William Hamilton* (1766–76; bilingual edition English/French); Piranesi's *Della introduzione e del progresso delle belle arti* (1765; On the Beginnings and Progress of Fine Arts), which inspired Hamilton's book; Winckelmann's *Monumenti Antichi inediti* (1767; Previously Unpublished Ancient Monuments); Caylus's *Recueil d'antiquités égyptiennes, étrusques, grecques, romaines et gauloises* (1752–67; A Collection of Egyptian, Etruscan, Greek, Roman, and Gallic Antiquities); and the official publication of the excavations at Herculaneum, *Le pitture antiche d'Ercolano e contorni* (1757–62; Antique Paintings from Herculaneum and Vicinity). Many other artists were influenced by these images; borrowings from *Le pitture antiche d'Ercolano* and Caylus's *Recueil* are commonly recognized in such works as Vien's *Une prêtresse brûle de l'encens sur un trépied* (1762; Priestess Burning Incense on a Tripod); Mengs's *Le Parnasse* (1761; Par-

nassus) and *Auguste et Cléopâtre* (1760; Augustus and Cleopatra); West's *William Penn's Treaty with the Indians* (1771); David's *Pâris et Hélène* (1788; Helen and Paris); Robert Adam's interior motifs; and Georges Jacob's furniture. In architecture, an exceptional number of books, with a wealth of illustrations of antique monuments, appeared from the middle of the century onward. These included Piranesi's *Prima parte di architetture e prospettive* (1743; Architecture and Perspectives, Part 1) and *Antichità romane* (1756; Roman Antiquity); Julienne-David Leroy's *Ruines des plus beaux monuments de la Grèce* (1758; Ruins of the Most Beautiful Monuments of Greece); James Stuart and Nicholas Revett's *The Antiquities of Athens* (1762–1816); James Dawkins and Robert Wood's *The Ruins of Palmyra* (1753); Adam's *Ruins of the Palace of the Emperor Diocletian at Spalatro in Dalmatia* (1764); and Charles-Louis Clérisseau's *Antiquités de la France* (1778; Antiquities of France). Most of these works were the fruit of study tours.

In fact, such tours were no longer reserved for solely for youths taking the grand tour; artists from all disciplines increasingly took the opportunity to get a closer look at antique art. In France these artists were encouraged by the director of the Bâtiments du Roi (Royal Buildings), the marquis de Marigny, who awarded scholarships, as well as by the comte de Caylus, who insisted in his lectures on the importance of this type of travel, positing that "going away effaces the prejudices of school and studio, and a certain national taste that is always hard to eliminate" ("Vie de Simon Guillain," in *Vies d'artistes du XVIIIe siècle* [1750; Life of Simon Guillain, in Lives of Eighteenth-Century Artists]). Many artists went abroad to create works on-site, often in the company of a patron (Cochin and Soufflot with the marquis de Marigny and the abbé Le Blanc; Wood with Dawkins). Architects, artists, and sculptors were attracted by the various new discoveries of the era. For example, Laurent Guiard, the author of numerous copies of antiques destined for private Parisian clients, seized the occasion in 1756 to accompany the abbé Barthélemy and the president de Cotte on their trip to Naples. There, in spite of the Bourbons' close surveillance of the site, which prevented the circulation of good images of the excavations for a long time, Guiard was able to sketch the "Equestrian Balbi" and later make a small bronze reproduction. These sketches were also used to illustrate the monument in *Le voyage pittoresque* (1781–86; The Picturesque Voyage) by the abbé Saint Non.

Nevertheless, before traveling to the archeological sites of Naples, or even to Greece or the Levant, artists traditionally first made their most fruitful and promising stop—at the Eternal City, a virtual "Academy of Europe." Some artists traveled to Rome at their own expense (Dejoux, Guerne, Jean-Baptiste Lemoyne, Pierre Patte, Jean-Baptise Pigalle), following the example of 17th-century predecessors (Anguier, Sarrazin). Other, more fortunate artists found patrons or were financed by institutions such as the Society of Dilettanti in London, which paid, for example, for Richard Chandler's expedition to the Levant in 1764–66. Alessandro, the cardinal Albani, the 18th-century "Hadrian" and undeniably the most powerful patron in Italy, financed Winckelmann and Mengs, figures who are emblematic of this new interest in antiquity. The list of artists, mainly foreigners, who benefited from Albani's protection and goodwill is long: Charles-Louis Clérisseau, Peter Joseph Krahe, Caroline Pichler, Peter Anton von Verschaffelt, William Chambers, Patch, Richard Wilson, Joseph Wilton. Artists who followed an institutional program of study had access to the most organized structures, such as the Accademia del Disegno (Academy of Drawing) in Florence and its associated establishment in Rome. The Académie de France in Rome, however, had the best system, because for four years it hosted the winners of the Grands Prix. The advantages artists received from this kind of system were obvious: visits and opportunities to study the city's antique monuments and collections, contacts with collectors and dealers, and an introduction to the artistic "avant-garde." Piranesi, in particular, had a decisive influence on the generation of French architects in residence at the Académie de France in the 1740s and 1750s (Clérisseau, Louis-Jean Desprez, Charles de Wailly, Jean Petitot).

The residents' first and perhaps easiest contact with antiquity, however, was in working with the collection of casts housed at the Palazzo Mancini. The collection of nearly 100 plaster casts was admired by visitors to the Académie; these casts were often used foremost as decoration, particularly under Wleughel's directorship. Nevertheless, we know that the program of the Académie included courses in work "in the antique fashion," which was also the case at the other great institution in Rome, the Accademia di San Luca (Saint Luke's Academy). The educational function of such collections was widely acknowledged (Caylus, Charles de Brosses, Mengs). Johann Georg Sulzer, in his *Allgemeine Theorie der schönen Künste* (1771–74; General Theory of Fine Arts) considered the collections to be indispensable for training the eye and the taste for beautiful forms. Gotthold Ephraim Lessing, visiting Mannheim in 1777, observed that the "antiquities room"—a term used indiscriminately both for authentic antiquities and, as in this case, for copies and casts— was more useful to artists than working on-site. In fact, the collection's fame, though short-lived (1769–1803), attracted such personalities as Johann Wolfgang von Goethe, Friedrich von Schiller, Johann Gottfried von Herder, and Henrich Heine, who were charmed by it. One of the most important artists of the period maintained that plaster casts were an essential working tool. In 1753 Mengs opened his own rich collection of casts (gathered the moment he arrived in Rome) to young artists and even held classes there. To extend its educational mission, the collection was later dispersed among the academies of Madrid, Turin, Dijon, and Dresden. Mengs also provided cases full of plaster casts for the new Akademie Augsburg (Academy of Augsburg), to which he and Winckelmann both belonged as of 1757, although it was sometimes very difficult to obtain good casts of certain works (for example the *Laocoön* or the Apollo Belvedere).

Students, or more precisely sculptors, of the Académie de France in Rome assumed an additional task inherited from their 17th-century predecessors: making replicas of antiques for the king. True, the days when hundreds of Italian masterpieces were brought to France to furnish Versailles were past, but the existence of copies—some celebrated, some now lost—is recorded. These included Bouchardon's copy of the Barberini *Faun* (1732), Adam's copy of *Mars at Rest* (1730), Francin's copy of the *Woman Playing Jacks* (1736), Jean-Baptiste Boudard's copy of the *Man Pulling out a Thorn* (1740), Saly's copy of *Antinoüs* (1747), and Challes's copy of the *Torlonia Antinoüs* (1752). In the third quarter of the century, however, the practice of copying tended to be replaced by the extensive study of drawing and was later resumed only under the direction of Angiviller: replicas made later in the 18th century included, for example, Bornier's copy of the *Antinoüs* (1787–91), Chinard's copy of the *Dying Gladiator* (1784–87), and Fortin's copy of the *Woman Playing Jacks* (1787).

Under ideal conditions, instruction in the art of antiquity was supplemented by classes in theory, but unfortunately this was not the case at the Académie de France in Rome. In Paris, on the other hand, there was a renewed program of such lectures, starting in 1747, thanks to the first royal painter, Charles Antoine Coypel, and supported by the royal buildings director, Lenormant de Tournehem, and the comte de Caylus. The latter was by far the most active member of the Académie, notably as the author of numerous essays— such as *Sur la peinture des anciens* (1753; On the Paintings of the Ancients), *Sur les peintres grecs* (1754; On Greek Painters), *Sur les sculpteurs grecs* (1754; On Greek Sculptors), and *Parallèle de la peinture et de la sculpture* (1759; Parallel between Painting and Sculpture)—and, notably, a collection of his works entitled *Recueil* (Collection). The count was also well known for the awarding of prizes—for example, for the "study of heads and the expression of the passions" (1760) or for perspective (1763). Caylus also worked directly with artists with the goal of helping them to learn more about antiquity. In this way, he attempted to revive the ancient technique of encaustic painting, which had been described by Pliny, and which was illustrated by Vien at the 1755 Salon with his *Tête de Minerve* (Head of Minerva). Caylus also worked with Le Lorrain at re-creating a Homeric mood by reciting the description of Achilles's shield to the painter, who then transformed the words into drawings. Despite Caylus's efforts, there were only a limited number of lectures analyzing the art of antiquity. The practice seemed to be reserved for the École Royale des Élèves Protégés (Royal School for Sponsored Students), inaugurated in 1749 to prepare students for residence in Rome where theoretical and practical study of antiquity was required.

Caylus also commissioned drawings of Roman antiquities from Edme Bouchardon and Hubert Robert so that he might have a vast collection of images available. A similar commission favoring the study of antiquity can be found in Richard Topham's exceptional collection; the drawings were done in the first third of the 18th century by a team of at least 35 Italian artists, including the young Pompeo Battoni and the highly accomplished Giovanni Domenico Campiglia, who became a professional engraver for other English collectors (Sir Charles Frederick, Sir Roger Newdigate, William Cock).

The Artist's Activities during the "Revival" of Antiquity

Generally speaking, the relationship between artists and collectors was an important and perhaps even a determining factor in the interest that arose for in antiquities. From the middle of the century onward, the art market, still centered in Rome despite the discovery of sites buried by Mount Vesuvius, was swamped by foreign collectors; particularly ubiquitous were Britons, for whom the grand tour had almost become an obligation. It was not by mere chance that Matthew Brettingham, Gavin Hamilton, Thomas Jenkins, Joseph Nollekens, Piranesi, and Bartolomeo Cavaceppi took the opportunity to become independent dealers. Jenkins began as a serious artist and then completely abandoned artistic creation to become one of the most influential dealers of his time, although his reputation was somewhat tainted. The most interesting example is Hamilton. He initially wanted to become a painter, creating pictures with Homeric subjects (for example, the *Farewell of Hector and Andromache* [c. 1770]); he then became an antiquarian—through excavations at the Villa Adriana in Tivoli, in Ostia, in Gabies, and at other sites—and a dealer, being the principal purveyor for the collections of Charles Townley, marquess of Lansdowne. In this capacity, Hamilton discovered and sold famous statues such as a version of *Cincinnatus,* Gabies's *Diana,* and

the Townley *Venus,* a statue that figures prominently in John Zoffany's portrait of Townley in his library (1770). Other artist-dealers took part in excavations of archeological sites. Competing with Hamilton and Jenkins, Piranesi also searched for antiquities. He specialized in decorative objects: candelabras and urns that could be exported more easily than statues and busts. One aspect of Piranesi's *Diverse Maniere d'adornare i cammini* (1769: Fireplace Ornamentation) can be seen as an advertisement for antiquities, which Piranesi was reputed to sell at high prices. Following Cavaceppi's example, Piranesi even published a sort of sales catalogue—*Vasi, candelabri, cippi, sarcophagi, tripodi, Lucerne et ornamenti antichi* (1778; Vases, Candelabra, Memorial Stones, Sarcophagi, Tripods, Lamps, and Antique Ornaments)—in which some of the illustrated pages were devoted to potential buyers. Other architects, such as Moreau or Wailly, took part in excavations without seeking financial gain. Their reconstruction of the Diocletian Thermes provided a large part of the material for Peyre's *Oeuvres d'architecture* (1765; Works of Architecture).

The combination of excavation and art dealing gave rise to a third profession: the artist-restorer. To satisfy the taste and demands of the period, thousands of restorations, copies, casts, and counterfeits were handled by Nollekens, Pompeo Savini, Pietro Bracci, Cavaceppi, Angelini, and many other artists, under the direction of Hamilton, Jenkins, or Mengs. Restorations were not always carried out in the spirit of "scientific reconstruction." Nollekens and Jenkins did not hesitate to take fragments from different objects and put them together to make "complete antiques." Piranesi was also very imaginative in his "restorations," as was evidenced by two candelabras bought by Newdigate that also inspired interiors by Robert Adam. A typical example that characterizes this period was the torso found by Hamilton at Tivoli in 1772 and mistakenly restored as the *Diomedes* because the restorers did not recognize the bust's true subject, which was only revealed a short time later by the discovery of the *Discus Thrower* on the Esquiline Hill in Rome in 1781. Of all these restorers, the most renowned was Bartolomeo Cavaceppi, a friend of Winckelmann's and the chief employee of the pope and of Cardinal Albani. Strangely enough, Cavaceppi's own creations, notably his portraits, were barely influenced by the antique spirit. He produced *Raccolta d'antiche statue* (1768–72; Collection of Antique Statues), a three-volume work with illustrations and commentaries on the "creations" of his studio, some of which were available for purchase. Other examples of artist-restorers who did not carry over the "classical" style into their personal creations can be found among sculptors from the early 18th century, such as Massimiliano Soldani, Giovan Battista Foggini, Filippo della

Valle, and Maini, who all distributed antique models in bronze. By the 1760s, however, the market for bronze statuettes was no longer dominated by sculptors but had been taken over by bronzers: Zoffoli, Luigi Valadier, Righetti, and Boschi. Their production was probably more helpful in disseminating images than in increasing the contact between artists and antiquity.

Naturally, the majority of important artists of the period also collected antiques, though they did not all draw the same lessons from them. Lambert-Sigisbert Adam, a sculptor renowned for his contributions to the French baroque, inherited or bought from Cardinal Polignac almost 70 antique statues, which are described in Adam's *Recueil de sculptures antiques grecques et romaines* (1754; A Collection of Ancient Greek and Roman Sculptures). Adam thoroughly restored those sculptures in anticipation of an eventual sale. However, the works appeared on an inventory of the sculptor's possessions compiled after his death and were later dispersed. The architect, draftsman, archeologist, dealer, and collector Piranesi exhibited a large part of his personal collection in his own "museum," a sort of art gallery that occupied several rooms of his home. When Piranesi died, the collection included more than 300 objects ;it was later purchased by Gustav III of Sweden. The exceptionally rich Mengs collection also included antiques; the most remarkable items, a collection of what were thought to be Etruscan vases, were partially included in Winckelmann's *Descriptions des pierres gravées* (1760; Description of Engraved Stones) and *Monumenti antichi inedit, i* but the artist later exchanged these vases for engravings. A few small busts, reliefs, statuettes, and cameos made up another series in Mengs' collection of antiquities. However, these objects were quite modest when compared to the paintings, drawings, and engravings in his collection, and its true wealth lay in the casts used for educational purposes, as mentioned above.

The opening of private collections for educational purposes, and the desire to return inaccessible works to the public were inherent in the Enlightenment mentality. In this spirit, Caylus encouraged artists (Bouchardon, Vassé) to work on his collection of antiquities, exhorting "those who collect monuments to communicate them to the public" (*Recueil* [1752]). In Rome the reorganization of the Capitol in the 1730s and the acquisition of Cardinal Albani's first collection led to the opening of the Musei Capitolini in 1734. This museum clearly favored contact with the art of antiquity, even if it is difficult to know exactly who actually visited the museum. A drawing by Giovanni Domenico Campiglia, published in Giovanni Gaetano Bottari's *Musei Capitolini* (1755), shows artists drawing sketches based on casts of antiquities in the collection. The Villa Albani, on the Via Salaria, where the cardinal's rich collection was housed, also opened its doors, but it was more of an art gallery than a museum, catering particularly to well-to-do collectors for whom Albani would procure the "desired" antiquities. The Museum Herculaneum was created in 1758, but this institution was hardly conducive to research because drawing was forbidden there. The projects that most directly involved artists were the foundation of the Museo Clementino, in 1771, and, a few years later, the foundation of the museum named for Pius VI, both in the Vatican (now known jointly as the Museo Pio-Clementino). Piranesi, Cavaceppi, Angelini, Jenkins, Hamilton, and many other art dealers contributed their energies to these projects. The two new museums, seeking to prevent the exportation of Roman treasures abroad, acquired works of Roman sculpture through these dealers, obtaining in particular recent discoveries from excavations currently underway. Cavaceppi offered the museums more than a hundred works from his own studio, which was often referred to as a "museum" in itself, in particular by Winckelmann.

Opening antique collections to the public was an important step—although its impact was less important in Rome, a city already filled with ancient art and monuments, than in Paris. In the French capital the impact of public access to antiquities was especially noticeable after the signing of the Treaty of Tolentino at the end of the century, when the majority of Italian masterpieces were brought on extended loan to the recently created Musée du Louvre.

CAROLE HERZOG

See also Archeology; Architecture; Decoration; Etruscan; Ruins

Further Reading

Beck, Herbert, and Peter C. Bol, editors, *Forschungen zur Villa Albani: Antike Kunst und die Epoche der Aufklärung,* Berlin: Mann, 1982

Boime, Albert, *Art in an Age of Revolution, 1750–1800,* Chicago: University of Chicago Press, 1987

Brunel, Georges, editor, *Piranèse et les Français,* Rome: Edizioni dell'Elefante, 1978

Chevallier, Raymond, editor, *L'antiquité gréco-romaine vue par le siècle des Lumières,* Tours: Centre de Recherches A. Piganiol, 1987

Eriksen, Svend, *Early Neo-Classicism in France,* edited by Peter Thornton, London: Faber, 1974

Haskell, Francis, and Nicholas Penny, *Taste and the Antique: The Lure of Classical Sculpture, 1500–1900,* New Haven, Connecticut: Yale University Press, 1981

Honour, Hugues, "After the Antique: Some Italian Bronzes of the Eighteenth Century," *Apollo* 77 (March 1963)

Howard, Seymour, "An Antiquarian Handlist and Beginnings of the Pio-Clementino," *Eighteenth-Century Studies* 7 (1973–74)

Howard, Seymour, *Antiquity Restored: Essays on the Afterlife of the Antique*, Vienna: IRSA, 1990

Irwin, D., "Gavin Hamilton: Archaeologist, Painter, and Dealer," *Art Bulletin* 44 (June 1962)

Pfotenhauer, Helmut, Markus Bernauer, and Norbert Miller, editors, *Frühklassizismus: Position und Opposition: Winckelmann, Mengs, Heinse*, Frankfurt: Deutscher Klassiker Verlag, 1995

Ramage, N.H., "Piranesi's Decorative Friezes: A Source for Neoclassical Border Patterns," *Ars Ceramica* 8 (1991)

Reilly, Robin, *Josiah Wedgwood, 1730–1795*, London: Macmillan, 1992

Scott, Jonathan, *Piranesi*, London: Academy Editions, and New York: St. Martin's Press, 1975

Apologetics

French Catholic Apologetics

The practice of apologetics in defense of the Christian faith goes back to the beginnings of Christianity. Originally intended to combat paganism, this theological discipline has throughout history proved remarkably capable of evolving along with changes in society. During the Enlightenment, apologetics concentrated on defending Christianity against the objections of deists and materialists, even though most of the apologists' arguments in these disputes had already been formulated by the Church Fathers. Catholic apologists were only too ready to point this strategy out to support their view of the *philosophes* as simply updated versions of Celsus and Porphyrus, rehashing worn-out objections that had already been crushed by the first apologists. And indeed, it was by modifying their methods of argument and their strategies, rather than offering new proofs in defense of religion, that Catholic apologists of the 18th century managed to conform to the spirit of the times. For example, the arguments of atheists were countered with praise of the marvels of Creation, according to the traditional belief in *coeli enarrant gloriam Dei* (the heavens declare the glory of God). At the same time, the Enlightenment's infatuation with the sciences inspired arguments drawn from progress in the field of physics, giving both an agreeably modern twist and a solid footing to age-old apologetics. In his desire to conform to the Enlightenment world view, the abbé Noël-Antoine Pluche went so far as to write an apology for Christianity in the form of a scientific textbook. His *Le spectacle de la nature ou entretiens sur les particularités de l'histoire naturelle qui ont paru les plus propres à rendre les jeunes gens curieux et à leur former l'esprit* (1732–50; Nature Displayed: Being Discourses on Such Particulars of Natural History As Were Thought Most Proper to Excite the Curiosity and Form the Minds of Youth), a nine-volume sequel to *Entretiens sur les particularités de l'histoire naturelle qui ont paru les plus propres à rendre les jeunes gens curieux et à leur former l'esprit* (Discourses on Such Particulars of Natural History As Were Thought Most Proper to Excite the Curiosity and Form the Minds of Youth), takes the form of both a catechism and an encyclopedia of natural science. It contains everything that was necessary to a scientific education, including plates with illustrations on botany, geology, and zoology.

In an age that set great store by the lessons of experience, Enlightenment apologists countered the arguments of the deists, who were more numerous than the atheists, by citing a series of "facts" that demonstrated the truth of the Christian faith. The Oratorian Claude-François Houteville opened the way to historical apologetics in 1722, with his *Vérité de la religion chrétienne prouvée par les faits* (Truth of the Christian Religion Proven by Facts). Starting from the principle that there is "nothing more palpable, more incisive, more persuasive" than facts, he gave a new twist to the traditional proof by miracles by applying the logic of secular criticism to the marvels recounted in Holy Scripture. Various apologies of this sort appeared in the course of the 18th century. C.-J.-B. d'Agneaux Devienne, L. François, and R.F. Du Breil de Pontbriand popularized Houteville's arguments, while presenting them with somewhat less vigor. In 1747 the grammarian Nicolas Beauzée even offered an "abridged version" of these historical proofs.

Beauzée, known for his participation in the *Encyclopédie*, is typical of the more enlightened Catholic apologists of the 18th century. While it is true that the defenders of the faith included a number of mediocre minds, writers with no talent who simply repeated borrowed arguments, many apologists were totally unlike the earnest obscurantists lampooned by Voltaire's vengeful quill. They understood that in an age when reason was so highly valued it was necessary to philosophize if one wanted to be convincing. They did not hesitate to cast off their theologian's robes and speak the language of the *philosophes*. If they were to prove the falsity of materialist systems and the insufficiency of natural religion, they had to call those who held these doctrines into a court of reason and not before a tribunal of the Church's authority. Thus, in *Le philosophe moderne ou l'incrédule condamné au tribunal de la raison* (1759; The Modern Philosopher; or, The Unbeliever Condemned in the Court of Reason), D. Le Masson des Granges fought the *philosophes* on their own ground by attempting to show the incoherences and absurdities in their theories. In *La religion vengée de l'incrédulité par l'incrédulité elle-même* (1770; Religion Avenged for Unbelief by Unbelief Itself), Bishop Jean-Georges Lefranc de Pompignan attempted to locate contradictions in the arguments of the adversaries of the Church and thus to set them against each other, rather than using Holy Scripture against them.

But were these attempts to adapt apologetics to enlightened ways of thinking enough to convince a reader who was already set against Christianity? To disarm anti-Christian assaults, religion itself had to be subjected to reasoned criticism. This was the approach chosen by the abbé G. Gauchat in an aptly and characteristically titled work, *Accord du christianisme et de la raison* (1768; Agreement between Christianity and Reason). Weary of hearing from enemies of the Church the "eternal reproach . . . of prejudice and blind faith based on neither conviction or principle," Gauchat set out to examine all the elements of Catholic faith in the light of reason. The abbé Joseph Adrien Lelarge de Lignac, a somewhat eccentric disciple of Malebranche who was imbued with sensationalism, carried this logic of secularization to the limits in his *Présence corporelle de l'homme en plusieurs lieux, prouvée possible par les principes de la bonne philosophie* (1764; Physical Presence of Man in Several Places Proved Possible by the Principles of Good Philosophy), in which he attempted to demonstrate that the Eucharist is compatible with the laws of physics. He based his proof of the Christian mystery on a scientific experiment that showed that when a worm is cut in half, the two separate pieces continue to live and move. Consequently, nothing could logically preclude that the soul of a man, and therefore the soul of Jesus could survive in the same way and be present in different hosts. Lelarge was not the only apologist who tried to reconcile religion with science. G.F.A. de Forbin, a mathematician and physicist, published the *Accord de la foi avec la raison dans la manière de présenter le système physique du monde et*

d'expliquer les différents mystères de religion (1757; Agreement of Faith with Reason in the Manner of Presenting the Physical System of the World and Explaining the Various Mysteries of Religion). These examples show the determination of Catholic apologists to adjust their methods to match the rationalist and scientific demands of their times. However, in so doing, they had to remove faith from the sphere of the sacred and, on their adversaries' ground, fight a battle that had already been lost. Georg Wilhelm Friedrich Hegel, in Part 6 of his *Phänomenologie des Geistes* (1807; The Phenomenology of Mind), provides a very perceptive analysis of this aspect of the age of Enlightenment: Faith let itself be invaded by Reason and did not recognize the danger until it was too late.

Protestant Apologetics in French

Faced by the rising tide of disbelief, Catholics and Protestants tried to forget their differences. While some Catholics wrote articles criticizing the reformed churches for encouraging deism by spreading the spirit of free inquiry, other Catholics, making use of whatever arguments came to hand, did not hesitate to appeal to Protestant apologetics to make their case. One of their sources was Pastor Jacques Abbadie's *Traité de la vérité de la religion chrétienne* (1684–89; Treatise on the Truth of the Christian Religion), which throughout the 18th century offered apologists of both persuasions a simple, well-organized set of proofs that never sacrificed the call of the heart to the language of reason. This brand of psychological apologetics, exalting the inner benefits of faith and the beauties of Christianity, seems to have been more developed among Protestant writers. The work of Marie Huber is typical of this type of apologetics that sought to appeal to the heart as much as to the mind. Resolutely turning her back on proof by facts, in her *Lettres sur la religion essentielle à l'homme* (1738–39; Letters on the Religion Essential to Man) she asserted the superiority of the authority derived from religion itself over that which comes only from external proofs such as miracles or prophecies. Citing Marie Huber's religious fervor combined with her total freedom of thought, scholar Albert Monod sees her as a figure of the "religious rationalism" of Protestant apologists in the age of the Enlightenment. Combining science and piety, Turettin and his successor Joseph Vernet produced, between 1730 and 1788, a *Traité de la vérité de la religion chrétienne* (Treatise on the Truth of the Christian Religion) that offers a perfect balance between internal and external proofs of religion.

Aside from these comprehensive apologetic compendiums, Protestants were present and influential in the daily battle waged by Christians against ever-bolder irreligious writings. David-Renaud Boullier, a Dutch pastor of French origin, expressed himself on most of the important controversies of the century. When Voltaire's *Lettres philosophiques* (1734; Philosophical Letters) was published in 1734, Boullier brought out his *Réflexions sur quelques principes de la philosophie de M. Locke à l'occasion des "Lettres philosophiques" de M. de Voltaire* (Reflections on Some Principles of the Philosophy of Locke on the Occasion of the Publication of Voltaire's "Lettres philosophiques") raising many relevant issues, particularly those related to the attributes of matter. Boullier also responded to the "Discours préliminaire" (Preliminary Discourse) of the *Encyclopédie* and went into battle against the thesis of the abbé de Prades, as well as attacking materialism after the publication of Claude Adrien Helvetius's book *De l'esprit* (1758; Essays on the Mind and Its Several Faculties). Then there was Allamand, the Waldensian pastor who wrote a refutation of Denis Diderot entitled *Pensées anti-philosophiques* (1751; Anti-Philosophical Thoughts), and another book attacking the baron d'Holbach, *L'anti-Bernier ou Nouveau Dictionnaire de théologie* (1770; The Anti-Bernier; or, New Dictionary of Theology). In 1749 the Berliner Jean-Henri-Samuel Formey attacked both Diderot and Toussaint in his *Pensées raisonnables opposées aux pensées philosophiques, avec un essai de critique sur le livre intitulé "Les moeurs"* (Reasonable Thoughts As Opposed to Philosophical Thoughts, with a Critical Essay on the Book Entitled "Les moeurs"). Similarly, Formey attempted to reconcile religion and science in *Le philosophe chrétien* (1750; The Christian Philosopher), following that work with an *Essai sur la nécessité de la révélation* (1754; Essay on the Necessity of Revelation) another essay on *Les preuves de l'existence de Dieu ramenées aux notions communes* (1758; The Proofs of the Existence of God Reduced to Common Notions), and finally two refutations: *L'anti-Sans Souci ou la philosophie des nouveaux philosophes naturalistes, déistes et autres impies dépeinte au naturel* (1760; The Anti-Sans Souci; or, The Philosophy of the New Naturalist Philosophers, Deists, and Other Unbelievers Portrayed As They Really Are) and *L'anti-Émile* (1763).

Beyond the Borders of France

The above examples from outside France show that it is futile to attempt to draw clear geographic demarcations within 18th-century apologetics, as is also the case when trying to map the spread of the Enlightenment. The zones of influence of antiphilosophical publications were determined by language rather than by nationality. For example, if Poland played a role in the defense of the Christian faith, it did so beyond its own national borders. The exiled king of Poland, Stanislas Leckzinscki, was living in Nancy when, admittedly with the help of P. Menoux, he wrote in French *L'incrédulité combattue par le simple bon sens* (1760; Unbelief Fought with Simple Common Sense). The Hungarian Count Joseph Teleky of Szek helped in the fight against impiety by publishing his *Essai sur la faiblesse des esprits forts* (1761; Essay on the Weakness of Freethinkers) in Amsterdam.

In other parts of Enlightenment Europe, notably in Spain and Italy, translations of French leaders in the defense of the faith, such as Nonnotte, the abbé Nicolas-Sylvestre Bergier, or Guénée, were more common than apologetic works by local authors. The case of the Savoyard, Cardinal Sigismondo Gerdil, who was a professor in Italy, is particularly interesting: while his devotional texts were written in Italian, he seems to have reserved French for his militant apologetic works, such as *L'immortalité de l'âme démontrée contre Locke* (1747; The Immortality of the Soul Demonstrated against Locke). Just as Enlightenment ideas circulated throughout Europe, the field of apologetics was characterized by important cultural exchanges, the true extent of which, however, is hard to determine from the current state of research.

On the other hand, specific aspects of apologetics in different parts of Europe were closely linked to national traits. Obviously, in those countries where Enlightenment ideas were late in coming, an authentic national apologetics was equally tardy, if not nonexistent. Apologetics in Spain in the late 18th and early 19th centuries tended to be more a defense of the representatives of religion than of religion itself. Thus, Brother Velez, in his attempt to defend priests against attacks from all sides, minimized the prelates' resources and emphasized the heavy taxes imposed on the Spanish Church in his *Apologia del altar y del trono* (1818; Apologia for the Altar and the Throne). In addition to such "clerical" apologetics, there was also an abundant literature of refutation in Spain during this period—often in the form of pamphlets—that condemned the *philosophes* and their systems of thought. Two authors stand out: Brother F. de Cavallos, who wrote against the marchese di Beccaria, Jean-Jacques Rousseau, and Voltaire in *Juicio final de Voltaire* (Final Judgment of Voltaire), begun in 1778; and F. Aragones, the author of antiphilosophical *Cartas* (Letters).

Naturally, the situation of apologetics in England, which engaged in two-way exchanges with the French Enlightenment, was altogether different. England, which had been affected by deism before France, produced a significant body of apologetic demonstrations, often completely translated into French, upon which French apologists drew extensively. Early in the century, the sermons of John Tillotson, archbishop of Canterbury, were translated, along with the treatises of Thomas Sherlock, bishop of London, notably the *Trial of the Witnesses of the Resurrection of Jesus, Examined and Judged according to the Rules of the Bar* (1729; translated into French in 1733), an original work that influenced many apologists.

Germany had a number of innovative theologians who were careful to reassure readers that they could be enlightened without being atheists, to the point that it was possible to speak of a Catholic *Aufklärung*—an enlightened religion that had no equivalent in France, where attempts to adapt apologetics to Enlightenment mentality were limited to modernizing methods of proof without any change in the essential dogma. This enlightened Catholicism also influenced the Austrian Netherlands (now Belgium), where—according to R. Mortie—one could find minds that were open and yet attached to revealed truth. C.F. de Nelis is an example of this sort of Christian *philosophe*, who existed alongside such virulent apologists such as François-Xavier Feller; in his article "Littérature de langue française" (Literature in French—published in *Belgique autrichienne* (Austrian Belgium)—Feller defined the *philosophes* as nothing less than the incarnation of evil on Earth.

Conclusion

From this overall survey of 18th-century apologetics, several major points emerge. First, during this period there was an exceptional abundance of literature in defense of religion. These works have since fallen into an oblivion that does not do justice to the extraordinary efforts made by tireless writers who were often talented and sometimes remarkably knowledgeable and intelligent, such as the abbé Bergier, or capable of scathing humor, such as the abbé Guénée. It seemed to the apologists that the ship of Christianity was sinking fast and they had to run back and forth from stem to stern, vainly trying to bail it out. Indeed, no sooner was one impious work refuted than another appeared, and then another even more audacious. Bergier had no sooner handed over the manuscript of a work opposing Rousseau, *Le déisme réfuté par lui-même* (1765; Deism Refuted by Itself), than he had to fend off Holbach, in an *Apologie de la religion chrétienne contre l'auteur du "Christianisme dévoilé"* (1769; Apologia for the Christian Religion against the Author "Le christianisme dévoilé"), and then find a riposte to Voltaire's more insidious mockery of Holy Scripture, in his *Suite de l'Apologie de la religion chrétienne contre l'auteur du "Christianisme dévoilé" ou Réfutation des principaux articles du "Dictionnaire philosophique"* (Sequel to the Apologia for the Christian Religion against the Author of "Le christianisme dévoilé"; or, Refutation of the Main Articles in the "Dictionnaire philosophique"). Christianity was truly shielded on all sides by support-

ers who strove valiantly to parry every blow that was aimed at it.

Another feature that clearly emerges from a survey of the defense of religion is the relationship between apologetics and politics. The religious reaction against new ideas that endangered the faith was accompanied, on a European scale, by an anti-French resistance. Those who were called *Volteristas* in Spain or *Voltaireschi* in Italy were seen as emulators of the French *philosophes*. This view was carried over into the Revolutionary period and continued under the First Empire, when the Catholic reaction against progressive ideas in Spain tended to be combined with opposition to the French Revolution and resistance against the French invader. An outright political challenge paralleled the purely intellectual opposition between Enlightenment and anti-Enlightenment ideas. Throughout the 18th century the argument used in favor of Christianity was that religion could serve as a safeguard both by controlling the excesses of the people and by limiting the power of their monarch. After 1770 the social utility of Christianity actually became the key term in apologetics. Instead of being summoned to appear before the court of reason, religion was brought before the tribunal of politics. The abbé d'Arnavon, who clearly understood this, summed up the problem poignantly in his *Discours apologétique de la religion chrétienne, au sujet de plusieurs assertions du "Contrat social"* (1773; Apologetic Discourse on the Christian Religion, with Regard to Several Assertions in "Du contrat social"), where he asked:

> Does Christian law fit in with politics or does it not? Is it favorable or indifferent to civic interests? Does it strengthen or weaken the constitution of empires? In short, is it helpful or harmful? This is the essential question, the new battlefield where our *philosophes* are skirmishing, and their last line of defense.

The best representative of this "social" apologetics on the eve of the Revolution was the abbé Antoine Adrien Lamourette, who would later become a bishop under the Constitution of 1790.

Consequently, apologetic literature serves as an excellent indication of changing mentalities to the extent that it reflects the ideals of the age. For example, Bishop Lefranc de Pompignan revealed the spirit of the period by devoting an entire work to the subject, *La dévotion réconciliée avec l'esprit* (1754; Devotion Reconciled with the Mind). Basing his argument on the Gospel parable of the talents, he concluded that, since Christ taught that a man should not hide his natural talent, it follows that all the arts are perfectly reconcilable with religious practice. Eighteenth-century apologists sought to demonstrate that the true place of a Christian is indeed in this world and that respect for the precepts of the Church does not prevent one from living with the times. Similarly, apologetics expressed the aspiration to happiness of the age as a whole when it promised the inner joys of the Christian in this world, together with a guarantee of salvation.

In the final analysis, however, it must be recognized that no matter what line of defense was adopted, Enlightenment apologetics ultimately failed. Some of the apologists, primarily among the Protestants but including some Catholics, developed a form of Christianity that had been adjusted to current fashion by diluting religious doctrine in the general movement of the Enlightenment, in which case apologetics retained the basic principles of Christianity but lost its identity as a faith. Others clung to their positions and engaged in a direct battle with the Enlightenment that they were doomed to lose because it is impossible to demonstrate by reason that which depends on faith. In this sense, 18th-century Christian apologetics was indeed a child of the Enlightenment.

SYLVIANE ALBERTAN-COPPOLA

See also Anti-Enlightenment; Catholicism; Eloquence; Protestantism

Further Reading

Albertan-Coppola, Sylviane, "Recherches sur la littérature apologétique catholique en France de 1730 à 1770," *Revue de l'histoire des religions* (April–June 1988)

Everdell, William R., *Christian Apologetics in France, 1730–1790: The Roots of Romantic Religion,* Lewiston, New York: Mellen Press, 1987

Hulliung, Mark, *The Autocritique of Enlightenment: Rousseau and the Philosophes,* Cambridge, Massachusetts: Harvard University Press, 1994

McManners, John, *Death and the Enlightenment: Changing Attitudes to Death among Christians and Unbelievers in Eighteenth-Century France,* Oxford: Clarendon Press, and New York: Oxford University Press, 1981

Monod, Albert, *De Pascal à Chateaubriand: Les défenseurs français du Christianisme de 1670 à 1802,* Paris: Alcan, 1916; reprint, Geneva: Slatkine Reprints, 1970; New York: Franklin, 1971

O'Keefe, Cyril B., *Contemporary Reactions to the Enlightenment (1728–1762),* Geneva: Slatkine, 1974

Palmer, Robert, *Catholics and Unbelievers in Eighteenth-Century France,* Princeton, New Jersey: Princeton University Press, 1939

Pappas, John, *Berthier's Journal de Trévoux and the Philosophes,* Geneva: Institut et Museé Voltaire, 1957

Archeology

The science of archeology emerged at the end of the 17th century, when new historical methods were being developed. Alternatively, it could be argued that the birth of archeology was itself one of the marks of the renewal of methodological approaches. Scholars began to draw distinctions between secondary sources (the historians' narratives) and primary sources (nonliterary evidence). As Jacob Spon, a physician from Lyon, wrote in his *Recherches des antiquités et curiosités de la ville de Lyon* (1673; Research on Antiquities and Curious Sites in the City of Lyons), it was necessary to "show outsiders that the stones speak all over our streets, teaching us how the city was under Roman domination." Objects—for example, inscriptions, coins, works of art, ruins, or articles used in daily life—were sources that could compensate for silences or obscurities in written texts, for these objects provided information about different aspects of ancient civilizations. Moreover, objects could be studied more directly than texts, since language was not an issue in their interpretation. This interest in the material aspects of archeology led to the development of a whole new literature, ranging from Catherinot's modest observations on urban sedimentation in 1685 to Bianchini's groundbreaking attempt at a comparative iconography in 1697. Numismatics, epigraphy, and the archeology of monuments were developed as specialized areas of study, each with its own modern challenges. This development occurred through the work of a new brand of authors, who were not only academics specializing in ancient texts but also doctors, artists, architects, engineers, and other eminent members of society—in short, educated amateurs and antiquarians. These scholars were not merely collectors shut up in their private *cabinets* (rooms filled with artifacts); on the contrary, they were open to scientific methods and, in the spirit of the advice offered by Baudelot de Dairval in his *De l'utilité des voyages et de l'avantage que la recherche des antiquités procure aux savants* (1686; On the Usefulness of Traveling and the Advantage that the Search for Antiquities Procures for Scientists), they traveled and did field work.

The antiquarian approach encouraged, and even made possible, the exploration of the historical and geographic parameters of the classical world. Scholars from non-Mediterranean countries took interest in their own national, pre-historic antiquities; Italians studied the pre-Roman past of the peninsula, and scholars from all over Europe turned toward the "Orient" of Greece and Egypt.

This development naturally came into conflict with the vision of those historians among the *philosophes* who scorned material artifacts, which they considered to be mere details—historically specific details, perhaps, but insignificant ones nevertheless. The fact that the *philosophes* (Montesquieu, Voltaire, Denis Diderot, the Encyclopedists) held archeology and "antiquity-mania" in contempt was not the least of the paradoxes of the Enlightenment. This dismissive attitude was all the more unjustified given that the *philosophes* had a passion for technique and the material aspects of civilization (as evidenced, for example, in the entries on the various professions that appear in the *Encyclopédie*), and, like the antiquarians, they embraced the idea of classification, which included the new possibilities offered by representation and engraving. The *philosophes* were also among the 18th century's admirers of antiquity. Diderot, for example, greatly admired the paintings of Herculaneum.

Archeological Sites

The focus of European archeology in the 18th century was not limited to Europe, although it was concentrated there. In fact, three types of sites should be distinguished. The great interest in the classical world made Italy a privileged area for research; archeological excavations there attracted local scholars and learned travelers alike. Northern Europe—logically enough, given the absence of classical material—was chiefly of interest to local scholars pursuing research on the origins of their own nations. By contrast, during this period, the Greek and Egyptian Orient were of interest only to visiting scholars.

Since at least the 16th century, Rome had been the center of research into antiquity—a place where local scholars and antiquarians from all over Europe collaborated. Rome boasted world's the most impressive classical ruins and the greatest number of works of art awaiting study. Foreigners who visited Rome stayed for

years and pursued very different projects. Artists sought models and collectors sought works of art, while antiquarians looked for coins and inscriptions and, more generally, for objects that provided some kind of historical evidence. Beginning in the 16th century a great many scholars and artists took an interest in the visible vestiges of art or works of art yielded by excavations; the idea of protecting national heritage developed only slowly.

Growing interest in artifacts gave shape to a new scholarly tradition—a truly archeological approach—represented in 18th-century Italy by the writers Ficorini, Venuti, Visconti, Guattani, and Fea. Foreign antiquarians also flocked to Rome, consolidating that city's position as the center of European archeological research. The founding of the Institute for Archeological Correspondence at the beginning of the 19th century signaled Rome's importance in the world of archaeology.

Most of the great aristocratic Italian families (Albani, Borghese, Barberini), as well as cardinals, and ambassadors felt an obligation to own a collection of ancient objects. Excavations proliferated on Palatine Hill, on the Appian Way, and at Hadrian's Villa. In order to keep up with the supply of artifacts intended for study or the galleries of foreign enthusiasts, increasing numbers of self-interested archeologists raided tombs and the ruins of ancient villas. At the end of the 18th century, British scholars such as Gavin Hamilton, Thomas Jenkins, and R. Fagan specialized in this kind of commercial archeology. In Athens the French consul Fauvel, along with Lord Elgin's representative Lusieri, both educated artists, dismembered monuments—a relatively brutal method of rescuing a site's most beautiful pieces. It was not until after the publication of Quatremère de Quincy's *Lettres à Miranda sur le déplacement des monuments de l'art de l'Italie* (1796; Letters to Miranda on the Moving of the Artistic Monuments of Italy) that the idea that sculptures lost their meaning when they were separated from their context gradually gained currency. In the meantime, Bernardino Drovetti, Giovanni Battista Belzoni, Rifaud, and others continued the practice of removing artifacts from sites in Egypt until late in the 19th century, in the belief—not entirely unfounded because tomb-robbing was also practiced by some Egyptians—that they were doing good.

The Near East had long been difficult to reach and it was explored by Europeans only at the end of the 17th century, with most of the archeological work commencing only in the second half of the 18th century. Even then, knowledge of ancient Greece remained essentially limited to literature—for example, the abbé Barthélemy's *Voyage du jeune Anacharsis en Grèce* (1788; Young Anacharsis's Journey across Greece). The first travelers to visit Greece with scientific ambitions went there at the dawn of the Enlightenment. *Journey into Greece* (1678), by the English botanists Spon and Wheeler, contains the first accurate description of the ruins of Athens, which they visited in 1676.

It was only later, as a result of a journey made by the architect Nicholas Revett and the painter James Stuart (1751–53), that detailed geometric drawings were made, based on surveys of the monuments of Athens—including the Acropolis, even though that monument had been bombarded by the Venetians in 1687. Fortunately, drawings of the Acropolis sculptures, attributed to Jacques Carrey, had been made prior to an earlier bombing in 1674. However, Revett and Stuart were not the first to publish their drawings (*The Antiquities of Athens, Measured and Delineated* [1762–1816]). Beginning in 1758, the French architect David Le Roy, who had been to Athens in 1752, published his *Ruines des plus beaux monuments de la Grèce* (The Ruins of the Most Beautiful Greek Monuments), a series of prints that were more picturesque than accurate. Once again, it was two architects, Haller von Hallerstein from Germany and Cockerell from England, who, in 1811, carried out the excavations and surveys for two crucial discoveries: the Temples of Aigina and Bassai.

Scholars who planned excavations in the East made the search for the site of Troy a high priority in their expeditions to the East. In his *Voyage dans la Troade ou Tableau de la plaine de Troie dans son état actuel* (1799; A Journey in Trojan Land; or, A Depiction of the Troy Plain in Its Current State), Le Chevalier worked out a system that designated one site in the Troad (Pinarbasi) as the location of the city of Priam—a conclusion accepted as authoritative until the discoveries made by Heinrich Schliemann.

Egypt was not unknown to Europeans during the age of the Enlightenment, owing to the publications of scholars such as Father Sicard (1726), Benoît de Maillet (1735), Richard Pococke (*A Description of the East and Some Other Countries* [1743–45]), and Frederick Norden (1753). However, the fantastic visions of Egypt presented in the work of Athanasius Kircher still dominated popular perceptions of that country. Napoleon's expedition to Egypt early in the 19th century included scholars and artists, such as Vivant Denon; these archeologists provided the first detailed surveys of the monuments of the pharaohs, in the *Description de l'Égypte* (1809–22; Description of Egypt), with important consequences for both the arts and the sciences.

Northern Europe concealed a wellspring of less "artistic" archeological treasures. It was perhaps the challenge posed by simple but mysterious objects such as tools or weapons made of stone, bronze, and iron, as well as plainly decorated ceramics, that led to methodological innovations by northern European scholars, liberated as they were from the cultural fascination with the Greco-Roman classical world. At the end of the 17th century and the beginning of the 18th, Scandinavian, British, and German scholars who were engaged in research into their national origins (such as Olaus Wormius, a Danish physician) developed systems of interpretation that took into account all available data, including objects, landscapes, and historic knowledge. As scholars (for example, John Aubrey and Thomas Browne in England) set about creating a "comparative antiquity"—that is, a comparative approach to archaic cultures—they devoted themselves to concrete topographical and chronological studies. Their attempts at classification culminated in Olof Rudbeck's invention of stratigraphic observation; this Swedish scholar's innovation is detailed in his *Atlantica* (1697). From the beginning of the 18th century, classification even became typological, as exemplified by the approach taken by German scholar Rhode in his *Cimbrisch-Holsteinische Antiquitäten Remarques* (Remarks on Cimbrian-Holstein Antiquities). In Britain William Stukeley's topographical research established a tradition that directly paved the way for the work of the military engineer Roy on "Roman camps," undertaken in the middle of the 18th century.

The revival of interest in peoples such as the ancient Germans (as represented in Keysler's *Antiquitates Selectae Septentrionales et Celtica* [1720; Selected Antiquities of the Northern and Celtic Regions], among other works) and the Gauls (owing to exploration of their archeological remains) allowed scholars to trace the antiquity of the northern nations even further back in time than the date ascribed to those cultures in Greek and Roman texts. In 18th-century France there was a resurgence of interest in the Gauls, who, since the 16th century, had been regarded as the mythical founders of both the French monarchy and ancient French cities. Beginning in the age of the Enlightenment, the Gauls were presented as the actual ancestors of the French, seamlessly integrated into the lineage of the Franks. An abundant literature was dedicated to the Gauls, but archeology played only a feeble role in it, despite the idea—put forth by Pierre Laureau de Saint-André in his *Histoire de France avant Clovis* (1789; The History of France before Clovis)—that the traces of the Gauls preserved in the earth constituted "the most beautiful of libraries." Studies by the comte de Caylus, who shared Laureau's conviction, and those by de La Sauvagère (*Recueil d'antiquités dans les Gaules* [1770; A Collection of Antiquities from the Gauls]) were based on chance discoveries that could not be dated. Prehistoric flint tools, megaliths, and objects from the Bronze and Iron Ages were attributed to the Gauls as well as to the Franks.

Interest in archeology as it related to national origins also affected areas in which the classical heritage was present, notably Italy, but the focus was limited to the pre-Roman dimension of ancient cultures. Scholars became fascinated by the mysterious Etruscans, who, according to most ancient authors (apart from Denys of Halicarnassus), had come from the East. The 18th century saw numerous excavations, at sites such as Volterra, Cortone, and Tarquinia (modern Corneto), that unearthed tombs containing paintings and abundant funerary furnishings. Texts summarizing these discoveries, such as Antonio Francesco Gori's *Museum Etruscum* (1737–43; Etruscan Museum), were published rapidly. However, the intermingling of Greek and Etruscan art caused some confusion: vases that were said to be Etruscan were not recognized as actually being Greek, imported from Attica, until the very end of the 18th century (Lanzi, *Saggio di lingua etrusca e di altre antiche d'Italia* [1789; Essay on the Etruscan Language and Other Languages Spoken in Ancient Italy]). During this period, archeological investigation of the Etruscans, as of the Gauls, and of all the other ancient peoples linked to "ethnic" origins, remained in its infancy.

Themes and Methods

From the end of the 17th century onward, the requisite elements for a positive approach to the traces left by past civilizations were in place. Comparison was followed by classification, in order to arrive at an interpretation. Objects were arranged according to their materials, their uses, and their meanings. To reach this stage in the development of their discipline, antiquarians improved their organizational models and perfected their methods. Over the course of the 18th century, antiquarians were no longer content merely to enrich their personal collections or to keep their correspondents informed through the exchange of letters. Numerous academies were established: in France, the Académie des Inscriptions et Belles-Lettres (Academy of Inscriptions and Letters), several provincial academies, and then later Académie Celtique (Celtic Academy), founded at the beginning of the 19th century; in Italy, the Accademia Etrusca (Etruscan Academy) in Cortone and the Accademia Ercolanese (Herculanean Academy) in Naples; and, in Britain, the Society of Dilettanti in London. Each of these academies was at the center of a network of informants. Museums came next: the Museo Maffeiano in Verona; the royal museum of Portici which was transferred to the Palazzo degli Studi in Naples in 1787; the Museo Guarnacci in Volterra; the Museo Pio-Clementino in the Vatican; and even the small museum of Arles at Les Alyscamps.

Knowledge of classical antiquity continued to dominate the field of archeology, usually to the detriment of prehistoric or protohistoric cultures. A refusal to accept how far back the "natural history of humanity" went

often prevented the correct interpretation of the most ancient artifacts. Nevertheless, all aspects of life in antiquity, including everyday life, were scrutinized by juxtaposing texts and objects. The first great summaries of archeology were published, often in the then-fashionable form of anthologies. In France, for example, such anthologies included Bernard de Montfaucon's *L'antiquité expliquée et représentée en figures* (1719; Antiquity Explained and Illustrated) and Caylus's *Recueil d'antiquités égyptiennes, étrusques, grecques, romaines et gauloises* (1752–67; A Collection of Egyptian, Etruscan, Greek, Roman, and Gallic Antiquities). Paintings of the sites on Mount Vesuvius were published in *Le pitture antiche d'Ercolano e contorni* (1757–62; Ancient Paintings in Ercolanum and Vicinity). Guattani published what was certainly the first archeological periodical, the *Monumenti antichi inediti: Ovvero, Notizie sulle antichità e belle arti di Roma* (1784–1805).

By the end of the age of the Enlightenment, two new fundamental methods had emerged in the field of archeology: acquiring knowledge through drawing and surveying sites, and gleaning information from the excavation of artifacts. Both cases required extreme precision, in terms of knowledge of either visual details or material context. The quality of the layouts and reproductions in Antoine Babuty Desgodetz's *Les édifices antiques de Rome dessinés et mesurés très exactement* (1682; The Ancient Buildings of Rome Accurately Measured and Delineated) assured that work's enduring success. Beaumesnil, an amateur antiquarian, astonished academics with the richness of the drawings that he had made throughout France (1739–87). As soon as the Etruscan paintings were discovered at Tarquinia, Byres commissioned the Polish artist Franciszek Smuglewicz to reproduce in a series of illustrations (1764–66).

Apart from isolated experiments like the 1582 excavation of the theatre at Augst (Switzerland), the first full-scale archeological excavation was that of Herculaneum, buried beneath the town of Resina to the south of Naples. Following a number of accidental discoveries, some houses and the *cavea* (tiers) of a theatre were unearthed in 1738–39, under the direction of the engineer Alcubierre. The excavation, which started out from galleries dug out of the lava, was almost all subterranean. Visiting scholars found it difficult to visit the site, and they generally regretted that the excavations had been so limited. However, as Winckelmann pointed out, in order to uncover more of the remains, it "would have been necessary to sacrifice a well-constructed and well-populated town." At Pompeii (then known as Civita), where the ancient layer of soil was closer to the surface and there were no modern buildings covering the site, more extensive excavation was possible. But to facilitate the excavation process and because there was more interest in works of art than in architectural structures, the trenches were progressively filled in as they were explored. Excavations led by Karl Jakob Weber (from 1755), then by La Vega, uncovered the area around the theatre (1764–69) and revealed a number of structures, including the Villa of Diomedes (1771–74); the gate of Herculaneum; and the Via Consolare. Beginning in about 1811, under the regime of Joachim Murat, the earth from the sections that had been excavated was taken outside the city. Aubin-Louis Millin publicized the new program of excavation in his *Description des tombeaux qui ont été découverts à Pompéi dans l'année 1812* (1813; A Description of the Tombs Unearthed in Pompeii in 1812):

> Today they [the excavators] wish to understand the extent of the city before they set about completely uncovering it, and digging has begun around its outer walls. When these have been exposed, the excavators will then proceed along the various streets and penetrate into the houses that stand beside them.

For a long time, however, this approach remained unique to Pompeii. When excavations began at Ostia at the very beginning of the 19th century, Petrini, the architect in charge of the site, rejected the idea of completely opening it up. The original style of archeological survey, which had emerged in the 16th and 17th centuries, continued to be the most common kind of exploration until the beginning of the 20th century. There was, however, one exception at a more modest site at Châtelet (Haute-Marne), where excavation took place between 1772 and 1774. An ironmaster, Pierre-Clement Grignon, began a large-scale excavation of a minor Romano-Gallic town. His initial, exploratory digging led to the discovery of a collection of streets, houses, workshops, and shrines that he was able to map very precisely, since the earth was removed beyond the excavated area. He was the first archeologist to work out the organization of a site and to determine in advance the tools to be used. He also maintained a precise logbook of the excavation, going so far as to sift the soil in order to determine the location of wooden structures by the traces they had left in the earth. The excavations were initially subsidized by King Louis XV, but they were stopped because of the reaction of those who could not understand Grignon's interest in gathering and studying simple iron nails or fragments of pottery. Grignon was also the first to publish excavation reports (*Bulletins des fouilles* [1774–75; Reports on Excavations]) and to have drawings of objects made as they were discovered.

Archeology and Art

Beginning in the middle of the 18th century, art during the age of the Enlightenment was replete with references to antiquity. Charles-Nicolas Cochin's journey to Rome in 1750 is generally considered to be a landmark in the development of neoclassicism, but the phenomenon of imitation was complex and ambiguous. No artist was prepared to admit that he had slavishly copied ancient art. In this context, Winckelmann's contributions in *Geschichte der Kunst des Altertums* (1764; History of Ancient Art) were crucial, as they placed the antiquarian knowledge in a new historic and artistic light. To the extent that artists were inspired by ancient cultures, they became archeologists. Neoclassical architects (Charles-Louis Clérisseau, Pâris, Robert Adam) took part in research, while engineers who constructed roads and aqueducts in the Roman fashion also collaborated with antiquarians (notably, in France, with Caylus).

However, the brand of archeology practiced by artists did not require the philological precision sought by antiquarians. Neoclassical taste helped promote knowledge, but simultaneously presented some obstacles to it. In the second edition of *Ruines des plus beaux monuments de la Grèce* (1770; Ruins of the Most Beautiful Monuments of Greece), Le Roy responded from an artistic perspective to the criticisms that Stuart and Revett had made regarding his lack of precision. All sorts of issues, including nationality, were mixed up in these debates. Ancient Greek art, as an ideal of simplicity and purity, was exalted by Le Roy and then by the engraver Pierre-Jean Mariette and by Winckelmann. In response to those views, Roman art was defended by the architect and engraver Giambattista Piranesi (*Della magnificenza ed architettura dei Romani* [1761; On the Magnificence of the Architecture of the Romans]). Piranesi declared that Roman architecture, which expressed both effectiveness in construction and a spirit of civic awareness, owed nothing to the Greeks. Rather, Roman construction continued the Italic tradition of the Etruscans and could inspire national unity in Italy. His praise for inventiveness did not prevent Piranesi from dedicating his life to the study of Roman architecture or from regretting that the contemporary order of things did not allow it to re-create its past grandeur.

During the 19th century archeology gradually put artistic priorities aside. However, the ideological objectives of archeology would never be completely abandoned.

PIERRE PINON

See also Antiquity; Architecture; Collections and Curiosities; Decoration; Egyptomania; Etruscan; Ruins

Further Reading

Chevallier, Raymond, editor, *L'antiquité gréco-romaine vue par le siècle des Lumières,* Tours: Centre de Recherche A. Piganiol, 1987

Étienne, Roland, and Françoise Étienne, *The Search for Ancient Greece,* New York: Abrams, 1992 (original French edition, 1990)

Moatti, Claude, *In Search of Ancient Rome,* translated by Anthony Zielonka, New York: Abrams, 1993 (original French edition, 1989)

Momigliano, Arnaldo, "Ancient History and the Antiquarian," in *Problèmes d'historiographie ancienne et moderne,* Paris: Gallimard, 1983

Parslow, Christopher Charles, *Rediscovering Antiquity: Karl Weber and the Excavation of Herculaneum, Pompeii, and Stabiae,* Cambridge and New York: Cambridge University Press, 1995

Pinon, Pierre, *La Gaule retrouvée,* Paris: Gallimard, 1991

Schnapp, Alain, *The Discovery of the Past,* translated by Ian Kinnes and Gillian Varndell, London: British Museum Press, 1996; New York: Abrams, 1997 (original French edition, 1993)

Thuillier, Jean-Paul, *Les Étrusques: La fin d'un mystère?* Paris: Gallimard, 1990

Vercoutter, Jean, *The Search for Ancient Egypt,* New York: Abrams, 1992 (original French edition, 1986)

Architecture

Two great French architects of the revolutionary era—Claude-Nicolas Ledoux (1736–1806), a prolific builder and the prophet of an architectural poetics, and Étienne-Louis Boullée (1728–99) founder of the Grands Prix of the Académie Royale d'Architecture—both stated at the end of their careers that architecture was still "in its infancy." This assertion is indicative of the astonishing belief in the perfectibility of art that existed two centuries ago.

Symbolized by the *Encyclopédie,* widely circulated in the press and in the specialized literature of art criticism, theory, and philosophy, and then in classical art history, the Enlightenment ideal of progress heralded a desire to break with the immediate past or, rather, with certain creative and formal traditions that were considered obsolete. Stigmatizing the routine-mindedness and the errors of the architects of his time, Pierre Patte (1723–1812), one of the architectural theorists who became influential after 1760, shared the view expressed by Jean le Rond D'Alembert in his *Discours préliminaire* (Preliminary Discourse). Up until that time, Patte asserts, architecture had been no more than the "decorated mask of one of our most basic needs." And yet the entries written by Jacques-François Blondel for the *Encyclopédie,* as well as the images that illustrate them, seem quite conventional given the context of the time, with its militant advocacy of a "regeneration" of architecture and of the arts more generally. This apparent conventionality may be one of the reasons why historians of classical architecture did not until relatively recently accept the idea of "Enlightenment architecture," to be understood not only as testament to the era but as a vehicle for reform and progressive thought, just as literature and the sciences were.

The convergence of ideal and practice, of theory and application in the domain of the "art of building" appears not to have become a reality until the last few decades of the 18th century, when architecture's designation as an art was rightly challenged. Boullée viewed the art of building as only "a secondary art . . . the scientific part of architecture." He understood architecture itself as a "product of the mind," for conception precedes execution. From that time on, architects would count themselves among the masters of the liberal arts, and the scientific activity that related to their profession would be governed by the same morality or ethic that safeguarded the notion of a "public" that emerged during the Enlightenment. One generation's hopes in the 1750s were finally realized in the 1780s. The regeneration of the arts appeared to have come about; it was perceived as an accelerated trend, as an amplification of the dynamic of progress dear to a society that had come into its own imbued with the philosophical spirit. From 1789 on the political revolution combined with the revolution in mores that innovative local magistrates, town planners, and architects had sought since the reign of Louis XV. The improvement in public mores may have been the corollary of an ideal characterized by a strongly utilitarian idea of happiness and by a new awareness of civic and patriotic duty.

Voltaire's tragedies with their historical heroism and Denis Diderot's dramas both adopted in the theatre a maudlin and sentimental style that corresponded in painting, sculpture, and music to the "virtuous" style of Jacques-Louis David, Jean-Baptiste Greuze, Jean-Baptiste Pigalle, Jean-Antoine Houdon, and Christoph Willibald von Gluck. A similar psychological and dramatic flair and a similar didactic function seem to characterize the work of architects of the period. In Paris, the architect Nicolas Le Camus de Mézières published a successful work, *Le génie de l'architecture ou l'analogie de cet art avec nos sensations* (1780; The Genius of Architecture; or, The Analogy of This Art with Our Sensations). The book, which was translated into German in 1789, shows how the concerns of architects had come to resemble those of the men of letters and the artists who called themselves citizens and *philosophes*.

For Le Camus de Mézières, the origins of architecture, revisited through the myth of Vitruvius's primitive hut, revealed new values through a naturalistic structural perception of the ancient orders. The imitation of nature was to guide the use of the square and the compass. As in the other arts, this concept of imitation was related to the sensationalist philosophy formulated by John Locke and Étienne Bonnot de Condillac. Sensitive to the poetry of light and shadow, aroused by the contours of pure geometric forms, which he commends for their effects on the soul, Boullée attributes therapeutic or even cathartic virtues to the art of architecture, declaring in his *Essai sur l'art* (ca. 1790; Essay on Art) that architecture "is a beneficent art that overwhelms our senses through all the impressions that it communicates to them." In a later work, *L'architecture considérée sous le rapport de l'art, des moeurs et de la législation* (1804; Architecture Considered in Relation to Art, Morals, and Legislation), Ledoux formulates the educational and social applications of what his contemporaries called "character" in architecture:

> If the example of virtues does more to advance the progress of all good impulses than the finest dialogue, the monuments that sanctify them have the greatest impact on the laboring classes, who do not have the time to read.

Against Rocaille: Imagining in the "Antique" Style

Patronage by enlightened monarchs went through an unprecedented period of artistic splendor in Enlightenment Europe. It became an instrument of power, identity, and education for the peoples who were subject to new states, new authorities, and the politics of alliance among the ruling courts. After the death of Louis XIV the myth of Versailles, just like the French language (adopted as the language of Europe), encouraged emulation in art, language, and church ceremonial. Both Papal Rome and the powerful Counter-Reformation

societies whose baroque militancy had triumphed in the 17th century extended their influence to Austria, Bohemia, and the German-speaking Catholic countries. Through the influence of the Iberian Peninsula they also affected the colonies in the Americas. Baroque style dominated Western architecture for several decades, although not without variations in scale, form, and character.

However, beginning in the 1720s the more prosperous countries, France and England, along with certain circles that were resistant to both Roman rhetoric and the hegemony Italian art had enjoyed since the Renaissance turned their backs on the persuasive grandiloquence of the baroque masters and produced an art freed from academic norms and based on a completely unprecedented ornamental repertory and structural implementation. In the era of the painters Antoine Watteau and Tiepolo, rococo architecture, whether secular or religious, symbolized a new expression of "modern times." Concerned with progress and integration and acutely aware of Europe's constantly expanding horizons, the Nordic kingdoms and Russia launched policies for prestigious building projects that became occasions for inviting foreign artists to train their architects on site.

Standards of taste that transcended national boundaries came into being as artists, philosophers, men of letters, scientists, and even certain princes and rulers undertook journeys for the sake of "study." The circulation of works of art, the development of drawing, engraving, and books, and the establishment of new collections, academies, and schools of art or engineering considerably broadened the choice and use of models. A certain cosmopolitan intelligentsia considered Paris, the headquarters of the Republic of Letters, the crucible of radical changes in taste.

Rejecting the solemn weightiness of the 17th century without sacrificing its sumptuous mode of expression, the new style of the French Regency was based on values that were recognizable in the most cultivated social circles: lightness, grace, flexibility, mobility, and clarity. Bourgeois art, which found external expression in the cities through refined domestic architecture, reflected the prosperity of a society in which trade and the professions were thriving concerns, and members of those sectors appropriated for themselves the signs of aristocracy while adapting them to their own circumstances.

In this context of rocaille and rococo, French architects remained faithful in monumental art, whether secular or religious, to the monarchic or "grandiose" classicism that Jules Hardouin-Mansart had heralded. In numerous urban projects R. de Cotte and G. Boffrand, creators of rocaille moldings, varied and lightened the use of prescribed patterns intended to soothe the eye. E. Héré, a disciple of Boffrand at the court of

Lorraine, created in Nancy (1751–60) sumptuous squares punctuated with fountains, statues, trophies, arcades, and a triumphal arch. In these squares the orders of antiquity serve as settings for rocaille ornamentation and as background for J. Lamour's wrought-iron gates. The theme of the royal square, inherited from the 17th century, expanded during the 18th century owing to local magistrates' priorities. The French example, followed in Lisbon, Berlin, Brussels, and Copenhagen, became the very symbol of Enlightenment city planning. Between 1733 and 1745, J.-N. Servandoni, a Parisian by adoption, created at Saint-Sulpice the first great church facade endowed with a powerful and dynamic classicism directly inspired by his drawings of scenery in the antique style. This variety of expression, whether in the grandiose genre promoted by the Académie Royale d'Architecture, the elegant classicism appreciated at court, or rocaille in general, gave French architecture in the first half of the 18th century a suppleness of interpretation that favored its wide diffusion beyond French borders, notably in the German-speaking countries.

English architects did not disregard these various trends, but they largely avoided them. The two-fold influence of Roman baroque and Versailles classicism can certainly be found in the work of Sir Christopher Wren at the end of the 17th century, but rocaille hardly affected England and came late to English decorative arts. Up until the middle of the 18th century in both town and country, at court as in religious art, British architecture oscillated between two secular tendencies from the Continent: classicism inspired by Andrea Palladio (1508–80) and late mannerism. Two artists were very clearly dominant, both in the great country residences of the aristocracy and in the churches being rebuilt in the City of London. They were John Vanbrugh and Nicholas Hawksmoor, who created a type of austere baroque that varied in its treatment of pure external volumes, and they integrated into their buildings a number of Gothic or Elizabethan traits. Vanbrugh's Castle Howard and Blenheim Palace (1705–24) and Hawksmoor's Christ Church, Spitalfields, and Saint George, Bloomsbury (1716–31) are masterpieces of the modern style in England. J. Gibbs, a Scot and a Catholic who was trained in Rome by C. Fontana, illustrated the return to antique elegance in his Church of Saint Martin-in-the-Fields in London (1721–26), while Lord Burlington, along with William Kent and C. Campbell, reaffirmed the preeminence of Palladianism in Chiswick House (1720–25). Palladianism would spread across Europe in the second half of the century, as well as to North America.

In Italy, from Milan to the Kingdom of the Two Sicilies, enthusiasm for the baroque persisted until the middle of the 18th century, and the fascination that Rome exerted did not wane during the entire century. Among the nations drawn to the Eternal City, Great Britain provided the largest numbers of artists, future members of the Society of Dilettanti, aristocrats, discriminating connoisseurs, and snobs whose education was incomplete without the "grand tour" of Europe, culminating in a stay in Rome. French artists who had won the Grands Prix spent several years at the Académie de France in Rome, where an authentic cosmopolitanism reigned as people mingled around the same centers of interest: landscapes and archeological sites, great monuments, and the artworks of the Renaissance.

The discovery and systematic excavation of the buried sites of Herculaneum (1709–38) and Pompeii (1748), followed by publications about them, provided a new and relative context for knowledge of Greek and Roman civilization. It was deemed essential to revisit Rome with its temples and its population of statues. Meanwhile, the antiquities of other European nations and the history of non-European nations became potential critical sources that enthralled scholars and artists. In Paris Bernard de Montfaucon published *L'antiquité expliquée* (1719–24; Antiquity Explained) and the comte de Caylus published his *Recueil d'antiquités égyptiennes, étrusques, grecques, romaines et gauloises* (7 volumes, 1752–67; A Collection of Egyptian, Etruscan, Greek, Roman, and Gallic Antiquities). Johann Bernhard Fischer von Erlach, an Austrian architect who trained in Rome for 15 years, wrote and illustrated the first *Entwurf einer historischen Architektur* (1721; Groundings for a History of Architecture). Its text, in German and French, compared evidence that encompassed the East and the West, Rome, Greece, and Egypt as well as the most remote periods. A new dramaturgy of the history of artistic creation was obviously called for. Lovers of antiquity—dealers in antiquities, historians, and visionary artists—moved in succession into the field. Propelled by Johann Joachim Winckelmann, Giovanni Paolo Pannini, and Giambattista Piranesi, an axis that linked Rome, Paris, and London provided guidelines for an antique revival set in opposition to the freedoms of rocaille, which were deemed irrational and uncontrollable (see Charles-Nicolas Cochin's "Supplication aux orfèvres," (Plea to the Goldsmiths) in the *Mercure de France,* December 1754).

In literature, the aura of Father Fénelon's *Les aventures de Télémaque* (1699; The Adventures of Telemachus) shone brightly throughout the century through numerous editions. The epic tale had a belated but frenetic sequel in the abbé Barthélemy's celebrated *Voyage du jeune Anacharsis en Grèce* (1788; Travels of Anacharsis the Younger in Greece). Fiction seems to have managed to anchor itself in concrete visions of the Greek world, at long last observed and directly linked to the sites—themselves the source of anthropological and ethnographic discourses on the nature of excavations and on the character of their inhabitants. Robert Wood published accounts of his journeys to Palmyra (1753) and Baalbek (1757), J.-D. Le Roy published *Les ruines des plus beaux monuments de la Grèce* (1758; The Ruins of the Most Beautiful Greek Monuments), and G.-P.-M. Dumont published the reliefs of Paestum done by his friend Jacques-Germain Soufflot (1764) in competition with the work of two Englishmen, James Stuart and Nicholas Revett, in *The Antiquities of Athens, Measured and Delineated* (1762–1816). Numerous "picturesque voyages" to Sicily and around the Mediterranean found their way into print.

In his *Della magnificenza ed architettura dei Romani* (1761; On the Magnificence of the Architecture of the Romans), Piranesi sets out to contrast the new Doric Greek model to the Etruscan style of his native Tuscany, but it was above all his personal and dreamlike vision of ruins that Piranesi depicted in his engravings, as well as in his fantasy drawings (*Carceri d'Invenzione* [1750–61; The Dark Prisons]) that launched a liberating movement in architectural drawing. In the style of the theatrical perspectives of the famous Galli Bibiena, which had become European, Piranesi transformed the *veduta* (view) into a true architectural fiction that was both picturesque and illusionist. An entire Piranesi-inspired school developed among English and French artists trained in Rome. Their success indicates the extent of the crisis in architecture and in theory, which was unprecedented in its breadth and which found expression throughout the closing years of the ancien régime.

Theory and the Crisis of Classical Architecture

The crisis of classical architecture reached its peak in the 1720s and 1730s. First manifested in the building of private dwellings, it also affected the realm of public and religious buildings. It was borne out in the changing theories of the beautiful that multiplied during this period, notably in France. Detached from metaphysics and strongly influenced by English empiricism, French discourse on architecture was linked to the domains of scientific and experimental knowledge and was integrated into broader reflections on the nature and the role of the fine arts, initially through the works of the abbé Dubos, then in such works as Father Yves André's *Essai sur le beau* (1751; Essay on the Beautiful) and the abbé Batteux's *Les Beaux-Arts réduits à un même principe* (1746; Fine Arts Reduced to a Common Principle), and on up to the work of the Encyclopedists.

Particularly in the field of the art of building, rejection of the secular rules of classicism was based on the relativity of the new archeological knowledge and on the spirit of experimentalism in the physical and social sciences. The primacy of the hierarchic system of the ancient orders faded away, and the animist doctrine of the divine harmonic proportions was superseded by concerns about understanding and behavior, whether individual or collective. It is also important to note that theorizing involved different or even opposing conceptions of society and of the discipline that served or illustrated it. Such oppositions came into play, for example, when it came to defining the power relations between patrons and creators and the degree of autonomy or influence held by the creators compared to that of the consumers of architecture—that is, the new patrons from the financial or intellectual bourgeoisie, which constituted the "enlightened public" of the great cities. The ethics of an artistic "profession" whose relations with the "crafts" of building remained uncertain was outlined as the century went on. The French state, meanwhile, succeeded in defining and directing a national taste based on a balance between the imitation of nature and the imitation of antiquity. In France in particular, the powerful institutions that controlled architecture—the Académie Royale d'Architecture, the Direction des Bâtiments du Roi (Royal Buildings Administration), the *intendants* and engineers in the fiscal administrative districts—were solidly rooted in the ideal of progress that validated the new theories.

Before 1750 the Quarrel of the Ancients and the Moderns, in which François Blondel had opposed the Perrault brothers at the end of the 17th century, led theorists increasingly to take up positions in favor of either the ancients or the moderns, or to attempt to reduce their divergences through a critical reexamination of the arguments in that debate. Within the framework of Cartesian rationalism, Blondel had tried to establish a scientific aesthetic in which the ancient orders, taken as norms as Vitruvius had urged, expressed ideal and intangible harmonic proportions. Against this "absolute" or "essential" beauty, inherent in nature and revealed by the ancients, Claude Perrault had advocated a standard of "relative" or "acquired" beauty derived from custom—as the development of taste seemed to prove—but perfectible by education. Perrault and other champions of the moderns revealed the influence of Locke's sensationalist philosophy in their attempts to demonstrate physical (natural) laws for the art of building and for the rules of convention or custom upon which judgments of taste depend. As in the perspective endorsed by Voltaire, Montesquieu, and Diderot, it was the analysis of this feeling, or perfectible faculty of taste that made it possible to define architecture in an experimental manner, deriving it from anthropology and no longer exclusively from the formal and symbolic anthropomorphism that had been in force since the Renaissance.

Writers on architecture had traditionally been pragmatic when it came to transmitting their main ideas about construction—solidity, materials, stonecutting, elevations, and customary techniques—but some of them began trying to ground the analysis of architectural concepts in a new visual logic that placed a premium on the relationships among different types of effects. For example, Michel de Frémin, in his *Mémoires critiques d'architecture* (1702; Critical Reports on Architecture), and J.-L. de Cordemoy, in his *Nouveau traité de toute l'architecture* (1706; A New Treatise on Architecture as a Whole), were among the first to follow Perrault and rehabilitate the principles of lightness, technical aptitude, and economy in Gothic buildings, even as they expounded the expressive beauty of the free classical order (load-bearing columns contrasted with pillars embellished with pilasters). Simplicity, linked to the dogma of the imitation of nature, became a dominant aesthetic value, with effects both on the relationship between spatial layout and decoration and on that between symmetry and character. Charles Briseux, in his *L'art de bâtir des maisons de campagne* (1743; The Art of Building Country Houses), and Jacques-François Blondel, in his *De la distribution des maisons de plaisance* (1737–38; On the Arrangement of Leisure Houses), were more obviously attuned to their time, when domestic architecture was becoming more diverse and increasingly focused on convenience and comfort. They set forth the laws on *distribution* (arrangement), which seemed at that time the most progressive element of French architecture and was widely exported. (Jacques-François Blondel [1705–74] should not be confused with François Blondel [1618–86], mentioned above.)

At the turn of the century, in the context of astonishingly varied programs of urban architecture that expressed a "mania for building" (Louis-Sébastien Mercier) and the expansion of cities, the notion of architectural "character" became a hobbyhorse for theorists. Important collections such as Jacques-François Blondel's *L'architecture française* (1752–56; French Architecture) and Patte's *Les monuments érigés en France à la gloire de Louis XV* (1765; Monuments Erected in France to the glory of Louis XV) are more descriptive than theoretical, but they are masterly demonstrations of the idea of a French taste (or of the "grand genre," in reference to the age of Louis XIV). This idea of French style, maintained by the monarchy in Paris as in the capital cities of the French provinces, became a model for exportation. Blondel was thus responding to the Europe-wide success of C. Campbell's *Vitruvius Britannicus* (1715–25).

Blondel and Platte were the two best-known architect-writers in Europe. They were influential theorists, very well informed about variations in taste, and anxious to impose a rational order on architectural knowledge and to achieve a balance between the Vitruvian ideal and modern relativism. Patte published his *Mémoires sur les objets les plus importants de l'architecture* (1769; Reports on the Most Important Objects of Architecture) in 1769. Blondel published the first four volumes of *Cours d'architecture* (Course in Architecture) between 1771 and 1772; Patte continued the last two volumes of this work (1777). Blondel transformed the theory of character into a detailed and quasi utilitarian system that incorporated the fixed language of the ancient orders, and he was dogmatic in his role as a professor at the Académie Royale d'Architecture and the École des Ponts et Chaussées (School of Civil Engineering). The *Cours d'architecture*, a major survey of knowledge and a monument to the academic tradition, appeared at a time when the revival of "antique" classicism, influenced by Piranesi and archeology, was infiltrating official training in architecture. Blondel was disenchanted by the attitude of the new generation of architects born in the 1730s, whom he had very largely helped to train but who had been "perverted" by the fervor for antiquity and by ideas emanating from sensationalist philosophy, and he sought to preserve the system of ideal, essential rules for future generations. Blondel wrote the entries on architecture in the *Encyclopédie,* but in the volumes of plates in the *Supplément* of 1777 the works of one of his most brilliant but dissident pupils, Charles De Wailly, are put forward as exemplary. Ten years later still, Antoine Quatremère de Quincy wrote an entirely new dictionary of architecture as part of Volume I of the *Encyclopédie méthodique* (1788; A Methodical Encyclopedia) published by Charles Joseph Panckoucke.

The theorist who mounted the most effective opposition to Blondel's conservatism was M.-A. Laugier. His works promoted a program for learning taste and reason that was addressed as much to connoisseurs and critics as to practicing architects, and they enjoyed considerable success. His *Essai sur l'architecture* (1753; An Essay on Architecture) was reissued with a polemical preface and a dictionary in 1755, and translated into English in the same year and into German in 1756. It was followed by *Observations sur l'architecture* (1765; Observations on Architecture), which supplemented the *Essai* by explaining the more experimental buildings of the age, such as J.-G. Soufflot's basilica of Sainte-Geneviève (1757–80; now called the Panthéon). Laugier's approach is based on analysis of the senses and feelings and a rejection of the experience of custom (habit) in imitation. He calls for the education of the faculty of judgment through contact with nature. Nevertheless, taste, the basis for the recognition and affirmation of character, should not be used to justify arbitrary preferences. He writes:

No further progress can be hoped for in the Arts if they are all restricted to imitation of created things; the criticism that is so necessary to their improvement has no role to play unless one has rules that are founded not upon what is, but upon what should be.

Laugier's rationalism was much more relativistic than J.-F. Blondel's but is no less dependent upon respect for a founding principle. In Laugier's view, that principle was the existence of an essential beauty, external to human beings but perceptible within the logic of structures imitated from nature—the original beauty of the orders invented by the Greeks on the basis of the primitive hut evoked by Vitruvius. Genius must invent forms adapted to its time—and why not a "French order"?—but it would avoid caprice if it submitted to the immutable laws of nature. Laugier, like Cordemoy, admired the expressive and functional structure of Gothic buildings, even though their character and proportions seemed to him to be barbaric, and he believed that the architecture of his day should be renewed through the beautiful and simple stability of Greek architecture. For him, the truth of the precept, which metaphorically symbolizes a return to the mythical hut, lays the foundations of the architectural and urban ethic desired by bourgeois society.

In Italy the theoretical movement in architecture developed initially in Venetia around the teaching of Carlo Lodoli. Strongly influenced by the ideas of Perrault, Cordemoy, and Frézier, Lodoli carried to extremes the rationalist approach of the moderns. However, the ideal harmony that he recommended between architectonic forms and construction materials made him a functionalist, a precursor of some of the theories of Palladian neoclassicism. He also placed a high value on the role of mathematics in recommending the expressive use of pure geometric forms. Directly readable volumes formed the basis of architectural effects for Lodoli, to the detriment of decoration and, in particular, of ornamentation, whose excessive use he denounced.

Lodoli's teaching was transmitted by two of his disciples in books that were widely distributed in Europe: Francesco Algarotti's *Saggio sopra l'architettura* (1757, Essay on Architecture) and A. Memmo's *Elementi dell'architettura Lodoliana,* (1786, Elements of Lodoli's Architecture). These works, which were augmented with ideas from Laugier and from British empiricist philosophers, became the basis of the theories of the most celebrated Italian writer and architectural critic of the second half of the 18th century, Francesco Milizia. Milizia, who moved in the same Roman circles as Winckelmann and Anton Rafael Mengs, was the author of numerous works written in a polemical vein that

assured their success: the *Principi di architettura civile* (1781; Principles of Civil Architecture), *Del teatro* (1773; On Theatre), and *Memorie di architetti antichi e moderni* (1785; The Lives of Celebrated Architects, Ancient and Modern) among others.

From Poetics to Eloquence in Architecture

Diderot writes in Friedrich Melchior von Grimm's *Correspondance littéraire* (15 January 1763) that "giving the fine arts a place in the art of governing the nations means giving the arts an importance that must be felt in what is produced." Architects who adhered to this maxim had first of all to get architecture included in the ranks of the liberal arts. This ran counter to the dominant idea, perfectly expressed by the abbé Batteux, that architecture had no place among the fine arts—the arts of imitation such as poetry, painting, and sculpture—for, unlike those arts, the art of building did not imitate nature but instead put into use nature's raw materials.

The refutation of this conventional wisdom relied on three arguments. First, that architecture, like other manual arts, was an art of design (the pure forms of geometry could also be found in nature). Second, judgments of taste concerning architecture showed its aptitude for moving those who saw it and who could appreciate the relations between style and convenience. Here, style was assimilated to taste, which could be simple, medium, or sublime. According to Jacques-François Blondel, style could become sacred, heroic, pastoral, regular, irregular, symmetrical, varied, and so on. Third, the very origins of architecture, as related by Vitruvius through the myth of the rustic hut, or as one could observe them in the structure of Gothic buildings (see Laugier), demonstrated that the logic of forms and their combinations was inspired by the nature of the materials or by the constitution of plants and animals. As for architectural character (nuanced by decoration), it was analogous to human nature, which had itself been expressed poetically by mythology since ancient times.

The return to Horace's *Ars poetica* (The Art of Poetry) and the transposition to architecture of the old theme of *ut pictura poesis* (as in painting, so in poetry) offered definitive support for the theory of character. Better still, it culminated at the end of the century in the concept of "eloquent architecture" (*l'architecture parlante*) that illustrated the thesis of art as language in terms of Condillac's sensationalist analysis. Before Laugier and Blondel, the architect Germain Boffrand, a leading builder and unrivaled authority throughout the first half of the century, had undoubtedly been the first to campaign for poetic illustration in architecture. In his *Livre d'architecture* (1745; Book of Architecture) he states:

[Architecture] is open to various genres that cause its parts to be animated by the various characteristics it evokes. Through its composition, a building expresses, as in a theatre, whether a scene is pastoral or tragic, whether it is a temple or a palace, a public building ordained for certain uses, or a private house. Through the style in which they are decorated, these different buildings must announce their purpose to the viewer and, if they do not, they sin against expression and are not what they should be.

Diderot, in "Le monument de la place de Reims" (1760; The Monument in the Square at Reims) agrees with this principle: "I would demand . . . of those who are to construct a building that one should be able to guess its purpose as soon as one catches sight of it." In his *Essai sur la peinture* (1766; Essay on Painting), Diderot insists on the conceptual labor of the architect-artist, which must contribute to progress by emulating the other arts. He advises: "Although architecture gave birth to painting and sculpture, it is to these two arts that architecture owes its great perfection, and I advise you not to place your trust in the talent of any architect who is not a great draftsman."

Boullée and Ledoux, two great visionary architects of the period, also address this theme. Ed io anche son pittore" (And I too am a painter), writes Boullée, in a pastiche of Corregio's declaration of faith on discovering the art of Raphael, while Ledoux affirms that "you who wish to become an architect should begin by being a painter." The drawing of architectural fictions in the style of Piranesi or the picturesque (De Wailly, Boullée) became the basis for the theory of "the architecture of the brush," which authorized megalomaniacal stagings and imperious chiaroscuro effects. On paper, wash and watercolor modeled stone, clouds, and the natural landscape surrounding architecture. Drawing freed the imagination from the conventions of usefulness and propriety and, with a view to exalted feeling, offered genius an unlimited palette of effects. Enlightenment architecture tended toward the expression of grand emotions. Like the poetry and the fine arts of the period, architecture was infiltrated by the philosophy of the sublime that English thinkers, in particular, had conveyed to artists. Ledoux, a notorious Anglophile, often expressed himself in the style of Edmund Burke on the integration of natural phenomena into the effect of the monumental sublime (see Saint-Girons, 1990).

"Greek" Taste and the Classical Revival

In England in the second half of the 18th century, the rural habitat of the nobility witnessed the development of sumptuous country houses, administrative centers, and other prestigious buildings constructed in the style of the antique villas by Palladio that adorned the hinterland of Venetia in the middle of the 16th century. British Palladianism, introduced at the start of the 17th century by Inigo Jones, became widespread in the 18th century and in its turn became an influential force in world architecture, from Russia to the New World. The Scotsman Charles Cameron and the Americans Thomas Jefferson and B.-H. Latrobe are among the best representatives of this international trend. William Chambers and Robert Adam, the two most celebrated architects of the period, were open to a broad range of influences. They were respectful of indigenous traditions but also steeped in French aesthetic theories and enthralled by the revival of archeology.

A great traveler in his youth, a pupil of Blondel in Paris, and a disciple of Laugier, Chambers later became one of the founders of England's Royal Academy (1768) and architect to George III. His publications include drawings of buildings made in China (1757), a *Treatise on Civil Architecture* (1759), and the plans and blueprints for Kew Gardens (1763), the crowning work in the development of the landscape gardens that in France are also called "Anglo-Chinese." A follower of Piranesi, Chambers became a Palladian in order to launch his career as an architect. He introduced the French taste for Greek style (see below) into Great Britain in the casino of Marino, near Dublin (1758). His masterpiece is Somerset House (1776–86), the immense palace with accommodations for government offices that towers over a section of the banks of the Thames in London. Somerset House is a display of powerful orders, arcades, and bossed facings that recall the repertoire of Piranesi, used here in the service of state architecture.

Robert Adam and his brother James were indefatigable in their "up-to-the-minute" renovations of the interior spaces of old residences, on whose exteriors they amalgamated ancestral (sometimes Gothic or Elizabethan) values with the style of the classical revival. The Adam brothers published countless drawings in their *Works in Architecture* (1773–79). Adapting the "Pompeian" (sometimes called "Etruscan") style for the walls, ceilings, and furnishings of sumptuous salons, galleries, and vestibules, they provided a pared-down, elegant, and inventive version of the "arabesque," or "grotesque," style at Syon House in Middlesex (1762–69), Saint James's Square in London (1772), and Osterley Park in Middlesex (1775–79). James Wyatt, Henry Holland, George Dance the Younger, Thomas Harrison, and John Soane, among many other first-rate architects, were no less inventive or prolific. They defined a new, distinctively British classicism, admirably adapted to the landscape style of the great natural spaces that were inspired by the paintings of Poussin and the Italian *vedutisti* (painters of panoramic views).

In France a second "Louis XV" style appeared during the last 20 years of the king's reign and was dubbed "Grecian." Refined and varied, it persisted into the reign of Louis XVI and underwent further refinement from the end of the 1780s through the French Directory before finally disappearing under the First Empire, when it was eclipsed by a more ostentatious eclecticism.

One Frenchman's journey, modeled on the English grand tour but officially organized, had an especially significant impact on architecture and the decorative arts in France. In 1750 Monsieur de Vandières, a brother of Madame de Pompadour, traveled to Rome. At the time Vandières was just assuming his appointment as successor to his uncle as director general of royal buildings, a post he held from 1751 to 1774 under the name of the marquis de Marigny. The architects Soufflot and Dumont and the draftsman-engraver Cochin were his enlightened mentors.

Paris was the home not only of Cochin but also of such famous scholars, antiquaries, collectors, and polymaths as Caylus, Pierre-Jean Mariette, and the architect and archeologist Le Roy. The French capital thus became the principal center of new output in the decorative arts, inspired by recently discovered ancient objects and fragments of monuments. Among the volumes of engravings that were most widely distributed throughout Europe were F. de Neufforge's *Recueil élémentaire d'architecture* (1757–68; Elementary Anthology of Architecture) and J.-C. Delafosse's *Nouvelle iconologie historique* (1767–85; A New Historical Iconology). These volumes introduced the new decorative vocabulary to architects, decorators, and master masons from Bordeaux to Lille and from Brussels to Stockholm.

The architecture that Marigny sought to promote under Louis XV would be illustrated by Soufflot and his followers, young disciples of Piranesi who, in the years from 1745 to 1760, had won the Grands Prix at the Académie Royale d'Architecture. This resolutely "modern" policy was pursued under Louis XVI by Marigny's successor, the comte d'Angiviller, a friend of Turgot's. The first royal architect, A.-J. Gabriel, influenced in his final projects by N.-M. Potain, his chief assistant, made some concessions to the taste for "Grecian" style both in Versailles, in the construction of the Petit Trianon (1761–70) and in his work on the Opéra (1770), and, in Paris, in the Place Louis XV (now the Place de la Concorde) and the chapel of the École Militaire (Military School). In the domain of religious architecture, the most important French building of the age was Soufflot's basilica of Sainte Geneviève in Paris.

Capital circulated once again throughout France, thanks to the Peace Treaty of 1763, and a boom in private construction projects fostered the spread of the new style in bourgeois and noble circles alike. *Hôtels particuliers* (private mansions) and, for the first time, rental buildings were tricked out in "antique" décor. After returning from Rome, L.-F. Trouard, J.-F.-T. Chalgrin, P.-L. Moreau-Desproux, M.-J. Peyre, Charles De Wailly, and P.-A. Pâris created a new formal repertoire along with other young architects starting their brilliant careers, including C.-N. Ledoux, E.-L. Boullée, F.-J. Bélanger, and A.-T. Brongniart. In mansions that were isolated like temples at the heart of picturesque gardens, these architects combined free layouts with monumental sculpture and pure geometric forms and finished the structures with varied bossed frontages or split facings. Hubert Robert and Charles-Louis Clérisseau invented decorative schemes based on landscapes or arabesques that equaled anything in the new English style. The pavilion of Bagatelle, built by Bélanger for the comte d'Artois (later Charles X) in the Bois de Boulogne (1777), was a masterpiece of the genre in Paris that epitomized the art of suburban follies.

English, Anglo-Chinese, or landscape gardens dotted with Greek, Turkish, Chinese, or Egyptian structures—as in the parks of the Désert de Retz, Monceau, Méréville, or the Petit Trianon, with its Rousseauesque hamlet—expressed a nostalgia for Arcadia and a dream of escape conducive to the imaginative framework of the antique r the exotic. The city of Paris itself was opened up to nature. Courtyards planted with elms or lime trees, avenues, promenades, and monumental quays replaced the obsolete city walls and the muddy riverbanks. Urban dwellers of the Enlightenment, lovers of *vedute* (vistas) and architectural fictions, discovered the landscape inherent in the city itself. From that point onward, the art of building had to take into account the specific places in which the public assembled or obtained services.

Picturesque drawing led architects to try out new plastic or spatial solutions and to captivate the public. Drawing, linked to the realization of vast urban development programs, played a dominant role in the instruction given at the Académie Royale d'Architecture, whose prestige was unrivalled either in France or elsewhere in Europe. Leading artists such as M. Crucy or L. Combes—recipients of the Premier Grand Prix in 1774 and 1781 respectively—made their careers in their hometowns after returning from Rome. As a result, Nantes and Bordeaux came to resemble enormous building sites. The many foreigners who came to Paris for training in the last few decades of the 18th century also launched very successful careers after returning to their home countries.

Along with Peyre, Chalgrin, and Boullée, Charles De Wailly was one of the Academicians who had the greatest influence in the training of young architects and who made the greatest impact on the public. As a professor De Wailly was sought out by Russian pupils in particular. To the public he was the architect of the new Comédie-Française theatre (1768–82, now the Odéon theatre). During the Revolution De Wailly's major projects, including the Théâtre des Arts, the palace of the Assemblée Nationale (National Assembly), and the Artists' Plan for the refurbishing of Paris, set the standards. These projects indicate that even in that troubled period there was an interest in symbolic architecture (see A.-G. Kersaint's *Discours sur les monuments publics, prononcé le 15 décembre 1791 à l'Assemblée Nationale* [1792; Speech on Public Monuments, Given at the National Assembly on 15 December 1791]).

A more general notion of "revolutionary architecture" can be seen at work in the anticlassical character of a whole range of buildings produced in the final decades of the century. Boullée and Ledoux were the leaders of this tendency, which exemplifies the utopia of art in the service of society.

In his great project drawings, which in themselves are megalomaniacal because of the unlimited program that they express, Boullée affirmed the primacy of nature, physical and human, in the art of conceiving architecture. The geometric purity in the drawings, the simple strength of elevations placed before immense vistas, and the use of mythological motifs all reveal the theatricality of the urban life dreamed of by the lovers of antiquity. The Revolution, after all, was played out under the banner of democracy and the Roman and Athenian republics. The Cirque de la Fédération (The Circus of the Federation), located on the Champs-de-Mars in Paris, like many other settings or spaces for public festivities, whether in Paris or the provinces, expressed this aspiration toward "virtuous" architecture.

Ledoux was responsible for several functional and formal revolutionary buildings under the ancien régime, including the Royal Saltworks of Arc-et-Senans (1775–79), the Hôtel Thélusson in Paris (1781), and the tax offices at the wall of the headquarters of the Fermiers Généraux in Paris (1785–89). In Ledoux's works, the art of powerful contrasts and the poetry of light and shadow subjected to the geometric or sculptural arrangement of masses were realized in stone.

Ledoux's 1804 book on architecture, magnificently illustrated with engravings, offered a message to posterity that was seemingly not understood in France in the 19th century. Nevertheless, from the reign of Louis XVI on, many of the students of the Académie Royale, some of Ledoux's colleagues, and, in particular, some major artists outside France who themselves tended toward Piranesian principles, were responsive to the liberating example that Ledoux had set.

John Soane in London, G.-A. Selva in Venetia, and S. Perez in Spain joined a new international trend that found its most spectacular expressions in the northern countries and in Russia. L.-J. Desprez, a disciple of De Wailly employed by the Swedish court, transposed his Piranesian and historicist visions of architecture to the theatre. Ledoux's pupil T. de Thomon built a commercial exchange in Saint Petersburg that is as solid as a temple at Paestum. De Wailly, Ledoux, and Clérisseau sent their own designs to Catherine II and Paul I. Meanwhile, new Russian architects trained in Paris and Rome developed an original style that was grandiose and very florid. Its lyricism was tempered, however, by the example of Anglo-Italian Palladianism, which was directly represented in Saint Petersburg by C. Cameron and G. Quarenghi. Chalgrin and De Wailly's Russian students, among others, perpetuated the aesthetic of Enlightenment architecture on the banks of the Neva River into the middle of the 19th century. B.-J. Bajenov, J.-E. Starov, and A.-D. Zakharov succeeded each other as the leading figures in this transformation.

In Italy and Germany, the classical revival began in the 1780s and 1790s. F. Gilly, a revolutionary architect who was very much influenced by France, became the symbol of a brilliant German school in which, under the influence of Winckelmann and Johann Wolfgang von Goethe, a neo-Hellenic nationalism dominated the romantic art of the 19th century. From C.-G. Langhans's Brandenburg Gate in Berlin (1789–91) to the masterpieces of F. Weinbrenner, K.-F. Schinkel, and L. von Klenze in Berlin and Munich, German architects spread an increasingly archeological imitation of the art of antiquity all the way to Greece itself, which was newly liberated from the Turks. Finally, while architecture in Spain was dominated by Italian and French influences throughout the 18th century, and was resolutely baroque, it too underwent a tardy classical revival. The Academy of San Fernando in Madrid broke new theoretical ground and fostered the outstanding career of J. de Villanueva (1785–1819), the creator of the Museo del Prado (Prado Museum) in that city.

DANIEL RABREAU

See also Antiquity; Baroque; City: Urbanization; Decoration; Drawing; Justice and Prisons; Monument; Palladianism; Rococo

Further Reading

Braham, Allan, *Architecture of the French Enlightenment*, London: Thames and Hudson, 1980

Chouillet, Jacques, *L'esthétique des Lumières*, Paris: Presses Universitaires de France, 1974

Gallet, Michel, *Paris Domestic Architecture of the 18th Century*, London: Barrie and Jenkins, 1972

Kaufmann, Emil, *Architecture in the Age of Reason*, Cambridge, Massachusetts: Harvard University Press, 1955

Pevsner, Nikolaus, *A History of Building Types*, London: Thames and Hudson, 1976

Rabreau, Daniel, "Architecture et art urbain" (bibliography), in *L'Europe à la fin du XVIIIe siècle, vers 1780–1802: Scandinavie, Empire russe et Empire ottoman exclus,* by Jean Bérenger et al., Paris: SEDES, 1985

Rykwert, Joseph, *The First Moderns: The Architects of the Eighteenth Century,* Cambridge, Massachusetts: MIT Press, 1980

Saint Girons, Baldine, *Esthétiques du XVIIIe siècle: Le modèle français,* Paris: Sers, 1990

Summerson, John Newenham, *Architecture in Britain, 1530–1830,* London and Baltimore, Maryland: Penguin, 1953

Vidler, Anthony, *L'espace des Lumières: Architecture et philosophie de Ledoux à Fourier,* Paris: Picard, 1995

Army

In recent years the history of armies in the modern era has been transformed by the research of such scholars as André Corvisier. For these scholars, the army is no longer to be considered a simple historical appendage to the modern state. Instead, the army is viewed as an institution that reflects or even explains a state's economy, its social and intellectual systems, and the formation of that state's structure. Many scholars in English-speaking countries speak of a "military revolution," a seismic event that affected all these structures. As the use of firearms and shock tactics became prevalent in warfare, the numbers of military personnel were by necessity increased, leading to the training of professionals capable of carrying out orders quickly and decisively. Increased staffing requirements in turn entailed an increase in the cost of armies, which was addressed by establishing military-bureaucratic states that essentially destroyed the decentralized feudal order that had dominated for centuries. Because of their demands, armies were among the driving forces in the formation of the modern state.

The growing importance of firearms in the 18th century accelerated an evolution in the military that had begun three centuries earlier. Modern warfare required planning. Private entrepreneurs had provided *soudards* (fighting men) to states, but from then on states were in need of *soldats* (soldiers), technicians recruited and given defined status by the rulers who employed them. Monarchs served as both recruiters and commanders of their own armies, which were constituted through two different modes of recruitment—one voluntary (for career military men), the other involuntary (conscription into the militia).

Voluntary enlistment, with commitments of three to eight years or longer, provided men with a career of sorts. Whether they were considered local men or for-eigners, soldiers were drawn into the rank and file by any number of factors: hunger, a need to evade the law, a taste for adventure, or state compulsion. The German state of Hesse, as well as Ireland, Italy, and Hungary, provided regiments to the states of Europe. Switzerland was a veritable soldier factory. Through a system known as "capitulation," the Swiss cantons provided heads of state with regiments with their own leaders and their own rules of conduct. The proportion of foreign soldiers remained high in the armies of England (60 percent) and Prussia (50 percent) but declined in France (from 30 percent to about 10 percent).

The militias complemented the regular armies. In France the royal militia (1719) was drawn from the peasantry, chosen by lot from among unmarried men between 16 and 40 years old, who then underwent military training in their local area. In wartime, these militiamen replaced or reinforced the professionals in military strongholds. The French militia, which was 50,000 strong in 1789, was criticized for its inegalitarian character. Spain copied the French royal militia, but not without some problems. The English militia (the New Militia, 1769) was composed of fusiliers operating outside their counties of origin. In Sweden the *Indelta* (1683), a force that was essential to the state, was manned and maintained by groups of *rotars* (farmers). In Prussia the *Kantonsystem* (1733) allowed noble officers to recruit men from their own cantons; after being enrolled at the age of 10, these recruits were given military instruction for two years, starting at the age of 18, and they served for two to three months in the units of their territorial lords. In Russia, the army initially obtained its troops through levies conducted throughout the empire, based on the infantry system, with the *starosts* (elders) choosing one man for every 100 plows. From 1726 onward, Peter the Great mobilized one man for every 250 counted in the first official census (conducted in 1721), and each district provided one regiment. Military service was for life. After the death of Peter the Great, the levying of soldiers passed into the control of governors and noble landowners, with the latter taking advantage of their authority by exempting the best workers among their serfs. The army of the Holy Roman Empire, in Germany, was heterogeneous. In their role as rulers over several states, the emperors had access to the services of German regiments (which they attempted to standardize), as well as to the services of regiments recruited in the Netherlands or in the military borderlands, which provided a livelihood for soldier-farmers. The German emperors had nominal command of the army raised by the Diet in the ten circles of the Empire. All the imperial vassals—whether secular princes, ecclesiastical princes, or free cities—had to provide contingents of soldiers. This army, which sometimes exceeded 100,000 men, was of poor quality because the princes invested greater effort in organizing their own armies than they dedicated to the imperial regiments. In Poland the kings had available to them peasant militias and military units raised by the cities. In this feudal state, the elected sovereign did not succeed in establishing a strong army capable of either impeding the activities of the magnates, who were divided into factions, or opposing the partition undertaken by Poland's powerful neighbors.

The burden of military recruitment on the populations of Europe is difficult to calculate. It has been estimated that on the eve of the French Revolution, the proportion of personnel in the regular armies to members of the general population was around 1:145 in France (180,000 soldiers), 1:96 in the territories of the Habsburg monarchy (240,000), 1:29 in Prussia (190,000), 1:310 in Britain (51,000), 1:64 in Russia (220,000), and 1:45 in Sweden (45,000). The burden of military expenditure was heavy in France, Austria, and Prussia, but England devoted more money to its navy than to its army. In France military spending constituted 26 percent of the budget, after having risen to 45 percent during the American War of Independence. In Austria military expenditure was around 35 percent of the budget, having been approximately 90 percent during the wars against Louis XIV and the Ottomans. In Prussia 60 percent of the state's expenditure went to the army in 1770, and during the Seven Years' War the king received money from England, as well as contributions from the occupied countries. Over the course of the 18th century, rulers sought to limit as much as possible the portion of their budgets that was devoted to war. This was especially the case in France, where, in order to realize savings, the king was forced to cut the number of soldiers, while improving their training, intensifying their drills, and developing new tactics.

In the largest states in Europe, armies had become the property of the rulers, serving as administrative departments and assisting heads of state in their councils. In France the Secrétaire d'État de la Guerre (Secretary of State for War), who also performed civilian tasks in the frontier provinces, controlled six departments charged with separate functions, including training and regulation, officers' commissions, inspections, and subsistence allowances. These departments also supervised the activity of the department of fortifications, the corps of geographic engineers, and repositories of archival materials and relief maps. In the provinces, the *intendants* of the army, the commissioners of war, and the inspectors of war were gradually militarized—following the example set by the creation of the post of secretary of war in 1758—and formed the link between the central administration and the troops. In order to make decisions about the conduct of operations, the king surrounded himself with advisers recruited from among the military leaders and then, in 1788, he established a Conseil de la Guerre (War Council) composed of eight generals and chaired by the secretary of war. In Austria the *Generalkrieg-kommissariat* (General Department of War) and the *Hofkriegsrat* (High Council of War) led the army. The Haugwitz reforms of 1752 carefully outlined the tasks of these two bodies: to the former were allocated problems related to pay, discipline, and training, while the latter was responsible for problems of command. The Prussian king, who dedicated most of his time to military affairs, could count on the assistance of a leading staff secretary, aides-de-camp, and a confidential military Chancellery. The General Directory of Finance, War, and State Lands linked the various administrations in order to make them collaborate as harmoniously as possible on solutions for military problems. In England the Board of General Officers was responsible for command, while administration was split between the Secretary of War (responsible for the infantry and cavalry), the Board of Ordnance (responsible for the artillery), the Paymaster, and the Comptroller of the Army and Accounts.

In France, England, and some of the German states, rulers, in their capacity as masters of the armies, were confronted with the problem of venality, in the form of purchases of commissions by those seeking appointment as subordinate officers (captains) or as senior officers (colonels); such commissions divided the nobility and created conflict. In France impoverished noble officers blamed the defeat in the Battle of Rossbach on aristocratic commissioned officers or on recently ennobled individuals who were the proprietors of their units but had little military experience. In 1776 the French monarchy made venality illegal, and that problem would gradually disappear through a series of structural changes in the French military. Venality persisted, however, in England and Germany, where its effects were less far-reaching.

In both France and Prussia the recruitment and promotion of officers was based increasingly on the criterion of birth, and it became difficult for a commoner to win his epaulets and move up through the military hierarchy. This state of affairs arose both from pressure exerted by the nobles on the rulers—the chevalier d'Arc testified to this pressure in his book *La noblesse militaire* (1756; The Military Nobility)—and from the desire of some rulers (in Austria, for example) to have a foreign aristocracy attached to them. In 1789, in France, where there was 1 officer for every 17 soldiers, 88 percent of the officers were noblemen; in Prussia, where there was 1 officer for every 25 men, 90 percent of the officers belonged to the aristocracy. In France the Edict of Ségur (1781), which denied a career as an officer to those who could not prove three degrees of nobility, was only the culmination of an aristocratic reaction that had begun very early on in the 18th century. Whether they were veterans or young trained men, any number of petty officers saw their legitimate aspirations for promotion thwarted. On the eve of the French Revolution, such men listened attentively to those "patriots" who advocated equal access to all the offices of the state.

There was also a deep malaise among the officers of higher rank. Poor and provincial nobles had given impetus to the aristocratic reaction within the army, but they wanted to add criteria of talent and merit to that of birth. These aristocrats were fully trained and had served the monarchy for a long time, yet their advancement up the ranks was slow. By contrast, noblemen of the court made rapid progress and ultimately came to monopolize the army's highest ranks and offices. Officers from the lesser nobility thus turned toward the advocates of reform, if not of revolution. Some of these officers joined Masonic lodges and occasionally visited salons where they were exposed to the liberal ideas of the Enlightenment; the salons influenced them even more than their military service during the fighting in North America. Like French civil society, French military society was in crisis. In 1788 and 1789, at the moment of revolt, the army did not offer the support that the monarchy was entitled to expect.

Rulers wanted to give high-quality military instruction to the soldiers they employed. Schools preparing men for a military career or for military command were opened in Austria, France, and Prussia. In France 12 military schools were created in 1776, including those at Sorrèze and Brienne. They received the best candidates, including Napoleon Bonaparte. Until 1788 a competition permitted the most talented to enter the École de Guerre (School of War) in Paris. The school at

Mézières trained the best military engineers in Europe: Nicholas-Léonard Carnot completed his studies there in 1777. In Prussia, beginning in 1765, the 12 best students in the cadet corps took courses at the Académie des Nobles (Academy of Nobles). High-quality military schools were also opened at Wiener-Neustadt (1752), Saint Petersburg, and Munich. The transformation of warfare over the course of the 18th century made improvements in military training indispensable.

Rational Warfare

The 18th century was a period when civilians and military personnel competed to transform the art of war and to make it into a true science, in which the relationships among bodies of troops, movements, positions, time, and space could be anticipated through calculation. Previously, battles had been military operations that, in wars of position (wars relying on controlling strongholds), weakened the opposing force and, through skillful action, drove it to flee the battlefield. The cavalry took the offensive role, opening breaches in the enemy's ranks that allowed the infantry, which was initially deployed in defensive squares, to rush into battle. War was costly, its duration had to be cut. Moreover, the development of artillery and the invention of the rifle had changed things: the cannon and the rifle had improved firing rates (two to three shots per minute), which created a wall of fire that pinned down the enemy. The infantry was stretched out in several lines, six rows deep, and it took a very long time for the men to get into battle formation. As a result, the infantry was exposed to enemy fire and its movements were too slow to hold the enemy back. This drawback led to the idea of using a deeper battle formation deploying columns of infantrymen. This technique allowed for shock attacks using with bayonets attached to rifle barrels, but the deep formation reduced the infantry's firing power, and it was also difficult for the soldiers to move from deep battle formation to a shallower configuration. Frederick William I of Prussia discovered one possible maneuver for surmounting this problem. His army arrived on the battlefield in columns, with each company formed into lines beforehand and separated from the one ahead by a distance equal to its front. A revolving motion around a fixed pivot deployed the line into three ranks, which marched upon the enemy, rather than running toward them, firing regular salvos before attacking with bayonets. His son Frederick II changed the parallel formation into an oblique formation: his regiments approached enemy lines from an angle. The Prussian army took on the form of a set of stacked groups, preventing the enemy from judging the depth of their deployment. The part of the army that was responsible for the main offensive was reinforced by concealed reserves; the remainder of the army, in reserve echelons, prevented the enemy from modifying their battle formation. This marked the inauguration of the modern form of battle, which aimed to concentrate the maximum force on a given point in order to gain the advantage of numbers.

In the second half of the century, the French were unrivalled in their ability to devise tactics superior to those of the armies that had defeated them. Among military thinkers, the comte de Guibert was one of the most famous tacticians. He published his *Essai général de tactique* (General Essay on Tactics) in 1772 and his *La défense du système de guerre moderne* (Defense of the Modern System of War) in 1779. Based on the initial premise that, by temperament, the French were ill-suited to the Prussian-style training that enabled armies to remain implacable in the face of fire, Guibert recommended the use of short lines, which could be formed rapidly and could concentrate their fire heavily on one specific point in the enemy's lines; meanwhile the light infantry in column formation would deal the decisive blow. Guibert revived the idea of breaking up the army into divisions, composed of infantry and light artillery, that would remain in contact with the rest of the army in order to separate, immobilize, attack, and destroy the enemy. French military leaders spent a long time debating which new maneuvers would best combine the advantages of both the shallow and deep formations. In 1778 leaders experimented with such new maneuvers at the military camp in Vaussieux. The cannon designed by Gribeauval permitted the rapid deployment of the artillery on the battlefield, wherever the infantry—the "queen of battles"—had need of it, and the design assured the success of Guibert's system. His reforms, issued in 1791, were adopted by the revolutionary army.

Like other military thinkers, Guibert did not reflect on war only in terms of tactics or the organization of armies; like the jurists, the philosophers, and the utopians of his time, he pondered both the rules of war and human rights. Such questions had long been debated and had been raised anew by Grotius (1624) and Samuel von Pufendorf (1672), as well as by Thomas Hobbes and John Locke. The latter had a profound influence on the thinkers of the 18th century—from Montesquieu to Voltaire; from Christian Wolff to Emmerich de Vattel; and from Jean-Jacques Rousseau to the Encyclopedists—as they considered the problem of the use of armed force. According to Locke, human beings evolved from the state of nature into a civil society by modeling their relations on recognition of natural law; in contrast, relations between nations were not codified but remained anarchic. In order to progress from this primitive state, nations would have to create a juridical bond, the law of nations, which would be based on natural law; however, only a federal authority could establish such a law. Until an international law was drawn up, making possible universal peace and ensuring the common good, wars would persist. In a Lockean international system, war could be justified only by self defense, and, in order to avoid the horrors of war, an entire body of positive norms could be set in place and recognized by all. In "humanized" wars, conquered countries paid tribute, with the agreement of their rulers, and in return the conquering power guaranteed that its soldiers, being better disciplined, would not commit pillage. The very existence of prisoners of war meant that exchanges could be organized; besieged populations that surrendered were no longer subjected to systematic reprisals.

However, if war were understood only as a means of defense or of achieving universal peace, would not the nature of armies be changed? In reality, they all too often remained instruments of internal repression in the hands of rulers. As Voltaire declared, the first person to issue an order was a victorious general, and Jean-Paul Marat was by no means alone in pointing out that armies were bearers of "the chains of despotism." Joseph Servan de Gerbey asked whether military society could be reconciled with civil society and whether the soldier could not be a citizen by accomplishing tasks in the general interest. Denis Diderot declared that it was necessary for citizens, whatever their station, to have two suits of clothing—the garments appropriate to their rank in society and a military uniform. Rousseau added that "every citizen must be a soldier out of duty, but none by profession," and that "citizens march into combat without sorrow; without a passion for victory, they know better how to die than how to conquer." This statement echoes the views of Guibert, who condemned the use of vagabonds and foreigners driven by necessity to serve under the flag. The national conscript army was at the heart of the democratic project. In 1792 war rapidly produced "the armed revolution"—the war of the masses that Guibert had foreseen.

JEAN-PAUL BERTAUD

See also Ballistics; Migration; Nobility; Soldier

Further Reading

Bacot, Guillaume, *La doctrine de la guerre juste,* Paris: Economica, 1989

Black, Jeremy, *A Military Revolution? Military Change and European Society, 1550–1800,* Atlantic Highlands, New Jersey: Humanities Press, and London: Macmillan, 1991

Corvisier, André, *Armies and Societies in Europe, 1494–1789,* Bloomington: Indiana University Press, 1979 (original French edition, 1976)

Kennet, Lee B., *The French Armies in the Seven Years' War: A Study in Military Organization and Administration,* Durham, North Carolina: Duke University Press, 1967

Scott, Samuel F., *The Response of the Royal Army to the French Revolution: The Role and Development of the Line Army, 1787–93,* Oxford: Clarendon Press, 1978

Art Academies

Origins, Models, and Developments

Academies of art were first established in 16th-century Italy. Based on the model of the humanistic societies that had started to emerge toward the end of the 15th century, these institutions took the name "academies" in reference to the gardens of Akademos, where Plato taught, and to the school of philosophy he founded. The Accademia del Disegno (Academy of Drawing), founded in Florence by Cosimo de Medici in 1563 on the initiative of the painter, architect, and art historian Giorgio Vasari, represented a fundamental step in the definition and development of academies of art. The most famous Florentine artists of the time became members of this academy, which was given a double mission: the improvement of the artists' social status and the teaching of students. The Accademia di San Luca (Saint Luke's Academy) was founded by Pope Gregory XIII in Rome in 1577, and was reorganized in 1593 by Cardinal Federico Borromeo and the painter Federico Zuccari. It transformed the principles that had been adopted in Florence into a formal educational program. At the same time, some small private academies were emerging, their meetings held in artists' studios or in patrons' residences. Such was the case of the Accademia degli Incamminati (Academy of the Progressives), founded around 1582 by the Carraccis of Bologna. Whether an academy was under the protection of a sovereign or was a private society, these institutions devoted to the study of art were part of the broader academic movement that occurred in a growing number of disciplines throughout the 16th century.

The art academies of Florence and Rome were the prototypes of modern art schools, but the real model for the establishments that appeared up until the end of the 18th century was the prestigious academy founded in Paris at the behest of the royal court, modeled on the Italian societies. Established in 1648, the Académie Royale de Peinture et de Sculpture (Royal Academy of Painting and Sculpture) was part of an important academic movement that began with the creation of the Académie Française (1635). That movement intensified from 1661 onward, spurred by the policies of Jean-Baptiste Colbert, comptroller general of finances under Louis XIV. Colbert's model became the ideal followed throughout Europe, and his doctrine spread rapidly thanks to the appointment of artists trained in Paris at the helm of some European academies. For example, Josef Werner, Antoine Pesne, and Nicolas Le Sueur all served as director at Berlin's Kunstakademie (Art Academy), while other Paris-trained artists led schools in cities in the French provinces: Jean-Baptiste Descamps at Rouen, Jean-Baptiste Oudry at Beauvais, etc. With the creation of the Académie Royale de Peinture et de Sculpture, Paris eclipsed Rome as the artistic capital of Europe. The founding of the academy consecrated the entry of painting into the ranks of the liberal arts and paved the way for the modern understanding of the fine arts as distinct from the applied arts and the sciences because their objective was pleasure. The eventual creation of "academies of fine art" signaled the gradually narrowing focus of the "fine arts" on drawing. Out of the 25 academies of art in 1740, as inventoried by Nikolaus Pevsner, only about ten followed (on a smaller scale) the model established in Florence and Rome and later followed in Paris. The creation and the reorganization of this kind of institution escalated during the second half of the 18th century, and as a result in 1790 well over 100 fine-arts academies existed (see Pevsner). This growth was particularly noticeable in France, where some 30 schools or academies of art, in principle affiliated with and dependent on the Académie Royale in Paris, were created in various provincial cities between 1726 (Toulouse) and 1786 (Orléans, Toulon).

Training

In his statement "sculpture and painting are in fact twin sisters, born simultaneously from the same father, namely drawing" (*Le vite de' piu eccellenti pittori, scultori e architettori* [1568; Lives of the Most Eminent Painters, Sculptors, and Architects]), Vasari encapsulates the essential role drawing would play in academies of art. In fact, his association of drawing with invention, with the idea, with "sensitive expression, and with the explicit formulation of some notion present in the mind" greatly influenced the orientation given to the young artists' academic training. The Accademia del Disegno in Florence provided for the appointment of "visitors" entrusted with the task of spending time in the studios in order to correct beginners' drawings. At the Accademia di San Luca in Rome, Zuccari tried to systematize the Florentine teaching program, parts of which had never actually been put into effect. Zuccari's recommendations included organizing regular gatherings where young artists could draw from works from classical antiquity, the works of the great masters, or a live model, all under the supervision of a faculty member.

Drawing from a live model was introduced at the academy founded by Federico Borromeo in Milan in 1620, among other institutions. It was practiced regularly in private academies and it became the keystone of academic teaching. The Académie Royale in Paris elevated that practice to the status of the ultimate stage in the rigorous training of students to represent the human body. Training involved three steps. Young artists began by copying from works by ancient and contemporary masters, initially drawing parts of bodies, then the entire body. They then tackled three-dimensional drawing by copying plaster casts of ancient statues. "Having been bored out of his mind working day after day, also night after night with a lamp, in front of a still life" (Jean-Baptiste Siméon Chardin, quoted by Denis Diderot, *Salon de 1765* [The 1765 Exhibition]), the student was finally promoted to life drawing, which involved a live model, naked or partly draped, posing in a way chosen by the professor. In this final stage of training, the study of facial expressions conveying emotion was also part of the program.

This curriculum, which took the novice "step by step from the simplest rudiments to the most complex aspects of drawing" (*Encyclopédie, Recueil de planches* [Collection of Plates], Book II, article "Dessin" [Drawing]), was adopted by most of the academies, sometimes in a simplified format or a more diversified one, but always with the utmost attention devoted to life drawing. For example, in 1754 Pope Benedict XIV created in the Capitol an Accademia del Nudo (Academy of the Nude), affiliated with the Accademia di San Luca and devoted exclusively to the study of the human figure. The use of the word "academic" in the *Encyclopédie* to designate drawings based on the live model shows the extent to which the academies were identified with that practice. However, the relevance of academic drawing was questioned, in particular by Diderot, who in his *Essais sur la peinture* (1796; Essays on Painting) criti-

cizes it for feeding the imagination of the students with "actions, positions, and artificial, fussy, affected subjects [that are] ridiculous and cold" and for creating a kind of "mannerism." This criticism heralded the negative connotation that the adjective "academic" would have in the 19th century. In the last quarter of the 17th century, the Quarrel of the Ancients and the Moderns provoked a split over the merits of drawing versus color within the Académie Royale de Peinture et de Sculpture. Despite the victory of the colorists' party, which was led by Roger de Piles, actual academic training generally left out the problem of color in the belief that skill in this area came with experience. The science of model making was similarly neglected. It was therefore outside the academy, in their master's studio, that students learned about the techniques of color and sculpture.

In addition to studio courses, academies of art provided a theoretical curriculum. Professors offered courses in geometry, perspective, and anatomy that formed the essential nucleus of the program; there were also occasional lectures delivered by the Academicians. This theoretical teaching was sometimes pushed further for some privileged students, chosen among the best in a competitive examination. In 1666 Louis XIV established the Académie de France in Rome. From then on, the Parisian Académie Royale sent to Rome a dozen students who had won prizes in their respective disciplines; they received a pension from the king for several years and were assigned the duty of copying the city's masterpieces. In 1748 Lenormant de Tournehem created the École Royale des Élèves Protégés (Royal School for Privileged Students), where, before departing for Rome, the Grand Prix recipients were required to take an intensive program consisting of courses in history, mythology, literature, and geography. In 1673, following the example of the Parisian institution, the Florentine Accademia del Disegno opened a subsidiary in Rome. Other schools, such as the Danish royal academy of the fine arts, provided their students with scholarships allowing them to travel in Europe.

Artisans and Artists

From the 16th century to the end of the 18th, the development of academies was directly linked with artists' aspiration to professional status. The establishment of this new form of professional association freed them from the guilds, the organizations of artisans that had regulated the practice of trades, including painting and sculpture, since the Middle Ages. During the Renaissance painting and sculpture were still considered mechanical arts. Because of the pigments they used, the painters of Florence belonged to the same guild as physicians, apothecaries, and notions dealers. The Accademia del Disegno there was the first institution to break away from the medieval system. In 1571 a decree exempted Florentine painters and sculptors from the obligation to belong to the guild. In Rome sculptors had already obtained the same freedom in 1539, thanks to an initiative led by Michelangelo. Roman painters, meanwhile, had to wait for the creation of the Accademia di San Luca in 1577. In France the Académie Royale was created at the request of several artists who wished to free themselves from the jurisdiction of the guild, in order to get away from "the traditional and small-minded milieu of the mechanical trades" (see Heinich, 1993). The guild reacted to this attack against its monopoly by creating the Académie de Saint-Luc (Saint Luke's Academy); it was first associated with the royal undertaking, but it very quickly parted ways with it. Quarrels between the new institution and the old guild lasted more than a century, until 1776, when guilds and similar corporate bodies were abolished by royal edict. In fact, art academies were seldom created without having to fight against the local guilds. In this respect, the Royal Academy of London (1768) was an exception, as was the Academy of Antwerp (1663), which was an offshoot of the guild itself.

The academic movement elevated painting and sculpture to places among the liberal arts, but it did not necessarily separate them from the mechanical arts. "It is up to the Liberal Arts to pull the Mechanical Arts from the degradation in which prejudice has kept them for so long," Diderot asserts in his 1751 article "Art" in the *Encyclopédie*. This plea in favor of the mechanical arts constituted an innovative position, but in fact, from very early on the art academies also participated in artisans' training. This trend began in Germany and it was only later that it spread to France, growing mainly during the latter half of the 18th century. As early as 1704 the Kunstakademie in Berlin, anxious to promote cooperation between artists and artisans, chose to change its name to the Akademie der Künste und der Mechanischen Wissenschaften (Academy of the Arts and Mechanical Sciences). When he reorganized the Dresden Academy in 1764, Christian Ludwig von Hagedorn assigned it the mission of encouraging not only the arts but also commerce. He believed that providing factory artisans and workers with drawing courses would help improve their taste and, as a consequence, the quality of industrial products. In 1771 the Royal Academy of Copenhagen showed its own initiative in this regard by opening an elementary drawing course for artisans; that example was followed eight years later by Stockholm. As this movement spread to most of the art academies, numerous schools of drawing were created. These schools were meant to provide a practical program for the professional accreditation of tradesmen. They were often private and tuition-free, and they were encouraged and sometimes run by the academies. The schools

had high attendance rates and helped "to spread a utilitarian and aesthetic ideal" (see Roche). In France, Descamps founded the first establishment of this kind in Rouen in 1741; a dozen such schools were created in the course of the following decades. The École Royale Gratuite de Dessin (Royal Free School of Drawing), founded in 1767 in Paris by Jean-Jacques Bachelier, was one of them. Similar initiatives were taken elsewhere in Europe from midcentury on. In 1742 the Dublin Society created a school of drawing to encourage the arts and, more importantly, to improve factory production. Robert Foulis's Academy in Glasgow, also a private institution, was founded in 1753 for the same reason; it was open to artisans as well as artists. In Geneva in 1751, Pierre Subeyran created an École de Dessin (School of Drawing) aimed at developing only the local art industries, such as jewelry making and watch-making.

Hierarchies and Monopolies

The Académie Royale de Peinture et de Sculpture in Paris gave Europe a model of academic life entirely turned toward what was at the time a predominant part of artistic production: history painting. That category encompassed "any work with a subject borrowed from a historical or literary book, and showing one or several characters, authentic or not" (see Locquin). In 1668 André Félibien, in one of the first publications of the Académie Royale, stated clearly that not all the subjects used in painting had a right to the same consideration. This fundamental principle, inherited from the Italian Renaissance, led him to group subjects in categories (the "genres") and to rank them on a scale of values (from inanimate to animate subject, and from animals to human beings) that led from still life to allegory (the noblest part of history painting). A "hierarchy of genres," based of course on the subjects of the painted works, was thus codified. This hierarchy labeled artists according to their production, in effect giving them a title. The painter of historical scenes occupied the highest rank in the academic hierarchy, and the structure of the Académie Royale in Paris reflected this supremacy down to the last detail. Any artist could hope to become an Academician, but only history painters were allowed to teach students. Posts as "officers," such as those of professor or director, were in theory reserved for history painters. A painter of seascapes, for instance, had absolutely no chance of pursuing an academic career. Finally, it was the "noble genre" of historical painting that regularly received commissions from the state because it was deemed more capable than any other genre of expressing the king's majesty.

Just as the guilds had held a monopoly on the practice of specific crafts, the Académie Royale claimed the exclusive right to teach in France. Courses focused above all on the demands of history painting; the curriculum was entirely organized around the representation of the human body and aimed at preparing young artists to paint nudes and to depict drapery. This type of art "could hardly be done other than in paintings of ancient history, mythology, or allegory" (see Heinich, 1993). Institutions that devoted some attention to the painting of landscapes, animals, or flowers, as was the case with the Dresden Academy from 1764 on, were rare. As a matter of course, the major prizes were awarded to future history painters and allowed them to go to Rome in order to copy Raphael, Domenichino, the Carraccis, and of course ancient art.

In England the Royal Academy of Arts was established in 1768. Although under royal patronage, it was an entirely private establishment. The Academy organized annual exhibitions that became fundamental to the institution as a source of income. The first official exhibition of the French Académie Royale had taken place in 1667. From 1725 onward, this event was held in the Salon Carré at the Louvre; the regular occurrence of these exhibitions, which came to be called "Salons," nourished art criticism in its infancy. The Académie Royale de Peinture et de Sculpture exercised a quasi monopoly on the public exhibition of works of art. Only Academicians and accredited artists had the right to exhibit their paintings in the Salons, and the layout of the exhibition was a clear indication that the organizers respected the hierarchy of genres. The catalog, as well as the places given to the paintings, reflected the preeminent position the "historian" occupied within the institution. Two arguments that were often mentioned in the artistic literature of the 18th century supported this privilege. First, history painting was said to encompass all the other genres (it was the total genre), and second, it required a vast amount of erudition and skill on the part of the painter (it was a scholarly genre).

Challenges to the relevance of this academic doctrine began as early as the second half of the 18th century. Artists, theorists, and critics began to protest against the discrimination practiced against painters who specialized in genres other than history painting. Although he does not go so far as to challenge the validity of the hierarchy of genres, Claude-Henri Watelet attempts to keep things in perspective in his 1757 Encyclopédie article "Genre (peinture)" (Genre [Painting]). Like so many others before him, Watelet uses the ancient comparison between "the main genres in the art of painting and the different genres in poetry," but he does so only in order to hold forth on "the likeness of the practice" of both arts. This comparison had been used in the past to raise the art of painting to the level of the liberal arts, but in this case Watelet uses the Horatian topos of *ut pictura poesis* (as in poetry, so in painting) to uphold a new cause: it allows him to invoke the dignity of poetry in order to "give the world a nobler idea of the artists we call *genre painters.*"

SYLVIE WUHRMANN

See also Academic Movement; Art Criticism; Artist; Drawing; Painting; Studio

Further Reading

Boschloo, Anton W.A., et al., editors, *Academies of Art: Between Renaissance and Romanticism,* The Hague: SDU Uitgeverij, 1989

Crow, Thomas E., *Painters and Public Life in Eighteenth-Century Paris,* New Haven, Connecticut: Yale University Press, 1985

Fontaine, André, *Les doctrines d'art en France: Peintres, amateurs, critiques, de Poussin à Diderot,* Paris: Laurens, 1909; reprint, Geneva: Slatkine, 1970

Hargrove, June, editor, *The French Academy: Classicism and Its Antagonists,* Newark: University of Delaware Press, and London: Associated University Presses, 1990

Heinich, Nathalie, "Académies," in *Encyclopaedia universalis,* vol. 1, Paris: Encyclopaedia Universalis, 1990

Heinich, Nathalie, "De l'apparition de l''artiste' à l'invention des 'beaux-arts,'" *Revue d'histoire moderne et contemporaine* 37 (January–March 1990)

Heinich, Nathalie, *Du peintre à l'artiste: Artisans et académiciens à l'âge classique,* Paris: Editions de Minuit, 1993

Kristeller, Paul Oskar, "The Modern System of the Arts," in *Renaissance Thought and the Arts: Collected Essays,* Princeton, New Jersey: Princeton University Press, 1980; expanded edition, 1990

Locquin, Jean, *La peinture d'histoire en France de 1747 à 1785: Étude sur l'évolution des idées artistiques dans la seconde moitié du XVIIIe siècle,* Paris: Laurens, 1912; reprint, Paris: ARTHENA, 1978

Pevsner, Nikolaus, *Academies of Art, Past and Present,* Cambridge: University Press, and New York: Macmillan, 1940

Roche, Daniel, *Le siècle des Lumières en province: Académies et académiciens provinciaux, 1680–1789,* Paris: Mouton, 1978

Art Criticism

Definitions

Its diverse meanings make it difficult to give a single universal definition of art criticism. In the broad sense the expression sometimes seems to cover all writing about art. In a far stricter sense, however, it designates a specific literary genre that was born in France in the 18th century—the famous "Salon." In fact, the notion varies in its meaning as well as in its breadth depending on both geographic and historical parameters, since the terms themselves do not describe the same reality from one language to another. In France art criticism is generally understood to be a review of a temporary public exhibition of contemporary works of art. Many writers from Denis Diderot to Guillaume Apollinaire distinguished themselves within this renowned tradition, including Stendhal, Alfred de Musset, Charles Baudelaire, Théophile Gautier, the Goncourts, Emile Zola, and Joris-Karl Huysmans. Exceptions do exist: Jean Ehrard devoted a book to Montesquieu as an art critic (see Ehrard), although Montesquieu never wrote a word about a Salon, and his notes, jotted down during the course of his travels, dealt for the most part with artists and monuments of the past.

In Germany the weight of philosophical tradition, the precocious status of the history of art in the universities, and the success of *Kunstwissenschaft* (the science of art), which developed from both positivism and formalism, conferred on the word *Kunstkritik* (art criticism) a meaning closer to that of the French *théorie de l'art* (the theory of art) or *science de l'art* (the science of art). The German influence most likely explains the orientation toward aesthetics found in the Italian concept of *critica d'arte,* whose history Lionello Venturi attempted to write (see Venturi). The Spanish term's meaning seems to correspond to the Italian. As for the English term "art criticism," even though it has different sources, it too is strongly theoretical, the empirical tradition counterbalancing the importation of German idealism.

Although in its narrow sense the term *critique d'art* was indeed invented in France during the Enlightenment, it was nonetheless heralded by a long tradition. Thus, as a specific genre its relationship to the more general genre of writings about art should first be examined. The broader category of writings about art includes documents that are extremely diverse in nature, function, and status. For example, Julius von Schlosser's indispensable inventory of 1924, the monumental *Kunstliteratur* (Art Literature) contains material written by artists, art lovers, historians, philosophers, theologians, men of letters, etc., while the range of genres represented encompasses everything from the treatise to the poem, including manuals, newspaper columns, biographies, novels, correspondence, dialogues, essays, memoirs, guidebooks, and travel diaries. Contracts, inventories, court transcripts, and still other genres could also be added. In its own way, each of these documents informs us about the history of taste. Some presuppose, explicitly or implicitly, a certain concept of art or even a system of values. But only those documents that include opinions about a particular work of art come under the category of art criticism proper (a term derived from the Greek *krinein* [to judge]).

Nevertheless, the fields of criticism, aesthetics, and art theory are tightly interlocked. Any value judgment is based on at least an implicit definition of the status of an art object or on criteria of quality. Aesthetics, a discipline whose name did not appear until the 18th century in the writings of Alexander Gottlieb Baumgarten, was usually understood as a general commentary of philosophical inspiration on art or on "beauty," while artistic theory first developed in the statements of artists themselves concerning their artistic activity.

Historically, speculation about "the beautiful" and the conditions governing its manifestation preceded the critical examination of particular works of art. Antiquity, when art criticism in the modern sense was unknown, saw the development of the elements of a philosophical aesthetics. These philosophical elements, in combination with the theoretical bases that were worked out simultaneously in the studios, paved the way for the future emergence of criticism in its narrower sense. Art theory, whose development presupposed an awareness of the autonomy and specificity of artistic values, resurfaced and evolved during the Renaissance. Closer to the practice of art than was aesthetics, which was concerned only with the nature of the beautiful, art theory was nonetheless distinct from art criticism in that theory was meant to precede creation, which it envisaged from the standpoint of principles. Eminently normative, even didactic, art theory laid down rules and precepts meant to guide the execution of the work of art. Art criticism, on the other hand, necessarily followed the creative act, since it was used to judge a particular work's conformity to those principles, whether or not they were stated explicitly. The subtitle of André Félibien's book *Idée du peintre parfait* (1707; Idea of the Perfect Painter) expresses this relationship very clearly: "To serve as a yardstick for judgments about the work of painters." No art criticism could therefore exist in the absence of underlying theories or aesthetics; and as both of these branches could also refer to examples of created works, the inevitable interconnection of theory, aesthetics and criticism—from a perspective that is both historical and logical—becomes clear. The questions "What is art?"; "How does one create art?"; and "Is this work successful?" are therefore highly interdependent.

Categories and Critical Tools

The theoretical foundations and the formal prototypes of art criticism must be sought in the speculative effervescence of the Italian Renaissance. Leon Alberti, Leonardo da Vinci, Giorgio Vasari, and Giovanni Paolo Lomazzo, among many others, enriched Western thought about art for several centuries.

Alongside the proliferation of academies of art (more than 100 of which existed by the end of the 18th century), a wave of doctrinal inspiration spread throughout Europe. A new genre, that of the talk or lecture, appeared and met with decided success in Paris, where Italian and French paintings, especially those by Nicolas Poussin, were analyzed and commented on regularly. In 1668 Charles Le Brun, defender of the superiority of drawing, reworked the rules of a theory of the representation of the passions, or "affects." Le Brun's influence would be felt far beyond 1759, the year in which the comte de Caylus founded a special prize (a competition called *de la tête d'expression* [the expressive head]). It would extend up to the time of the founding of physiognomy by Johann Caspar Lavater. In 1667 Félibien codified the famous hierarchy of genres, which would long constitute an essential point of reference.

It was within the same framework, after the victory of the partisans of Rubens over those of Poussin, that a new conception of color developed, color then being defined as the specificity of painting. Roger de Piles, author of the *Cours de peinture par principes* (1708; A Course in Painting Based on Principles), became its chief proponent. Champion of the "unity of effect" and of the "economy of the whole," which he sought in the harmony of coloring and in the chiaroscuro, Piles tried to work out systematic criteria of judgment, which he schematized in his famous "Balance des peintres" (The Painter's Scale). But his numerous writings contributed above all to the enrichment of a specific terminology and transmitted to future art criticism elements of appreciation of the pictorial creation in itself, elements that the theoreticians of Venetian painting, such as Paolo Pino or Marco Boschini, had begun to develop. Diderot, among others, would be their heir.

Aesthetic speculation in the 18th century wavered between the poles of reason and feeling, of innateness and empiricism, of an objective definition of beauty and a subjective concept of taste. In turn, David Hume's associationism, George Berkeley's idealism, Étienne Bonnot de Condillac's sensationalism, and Jean-Jacques Rousseau's primitivism all influenced art criticism. And although the classical notions of harmony, proportion, composition, and perspective continued to be discussed, the concepts of genius, enthusiasm, imagination, naïveté, or effect won more and more ground. In France the leaders of the debate were Jean Pierre de Crousaz (*Traité du Beau* [1715; Treatise on the Beautiful]), the abbé Dubos (*Réflexions critiques sur la poésie et sur la peinture* [1719; Critical Reflections on Poetry and Painting]), Father Yves-Marie André (*Essai sur le beau* [1741; Essay on the Beautiful]), and Charles Batteux (*Les Beaux-Arts réduits à un même principe* [1746; Fine Arts Reduced to a Common Principle]). In England there were the noteworthy contributions of Joseph Addison (*Essays on Taste; or, The Pleasures of the Imagination* [1712]), the earl of Shaftesbury (*A Letter concerning Enthusiasm* [1708] and *A Letter concerning the Art or Science of Design* [1712]), Francis Hutcheson (*An Inquiry into the Origin of Our Ideas of Beauty and Virtue* [1725]), William Hogarth (*The Analysis of Beauty* [1753]), Daniel Webb (*An Inquiry into the Beauties of Painting* [1760]), and Sir Joshua Reynolds (*Discourses* [1769–90]). Germany's contribution was also considerable, and included Johann Joachim Winckelmann (*Gedanken über die Nachahmung der griechischen Werke in der Malerei und Bildhauerkunst* [1755; Reflections on the Painting and Sculpture of the Greeks]), Christian Ludwig von Hagedorn (*Betrachtungen über die Malerey* [1762; Observations on Painting]), R. Mengs (*Gedanken über die Schönheit und den Geschmack in der Malerey* [1762; Thoughts on Beauty and Taste in Painting]), Gotthold Ephraim Lessing (*Laokoon* [1766; Laocoön: An Essay upon the Limits of Painting and Poetry]), Johann Georg Sulzer (*Allgemeine Theorie der schönen Künste* [1771–74; General Theory of Fine Arts]), and Karl Philipp Moritz (*Über die bildende Nachahmung des Schönen* [1788; Concerning the Creative Imitation of the Beautiful]).

The common postulate in every consideration of art remained the principle of the imitation of nature, which was not to be dethroned by the principle of subjective expression until the romantic era. But critics still had to agree on the meaning given to those terms, and the divergence between the Platonic and Aristotelian traditions still provoked some lively quarrels, as exemplified by Diderot's preamble to his *Salon de 1767* (1767 Exhibition). The search for a compromise between illusionism and ideal imitation, exactness and verisimilitude, the literal copy of nature ("just as it is") and a selective interpretation of it ("as it should be") continued to fuel the debate.

Derived from the principle of mimesis, or imitation, the principle of decorum also had roots in antiquity. Borrowed from Vitruvius, who had defined it as architecture's conformity to its symbolic and practical functions, the principle of decorum was then applied to painting. Classicists like Fréart de Chambray renamed it "costume" or "custom" and reinterpreted it in the ethical sense of decency, the social sense of appropriateness, or in the archeological sense of respect for historical truth or local color. For example, in his *Manière de bien juger des ouvrages de peinture* (1771; How to Appreciate the True Worth of Paintings), Laugier denounced the "anachronisms and parachronisms that in a great many good pictures reveal the dumb ignorance of the painter." On the other hand, in *Les misotechnites aux enfers* (1763; The Misotechnites in the Underworld), Charles-Nicolas Cochin pleaded for "license" and "a costume more in accordance with the rules of taste than with historical accuracy."

The criterion that a picture be faithful to the text it illustrated also turned up from time to time in the writings of 18th-century critics, who were attempting in this way to defend their domain against the artists, who claimed the exclusive right to judge what Diderot was to call "technique." The extension to the realm of literature of the quarrel concerning the *paragona*, or a comparison of the arts, which had been introduced during the Renaissance, had led to the dogma of *ut pictura poesis* (as in painting, so in poetry), which would scarcely be challenged before the publication of Lessing's *Laokoon*. The kinship between the verbal and pictorial arts thus made possible the borrowing of categories of analysis from literary criticism or rhetoric. Charles-Antoine Coypel, author of the discourses *Sur l'art de peindre en le comparant à l'art de bien dire* (1749; On the Art of Painting Compared to the Art of Elocution) and *Parallèle de l'éloquence et de la peinture* (1751; Parallels between Eloquence and Painting), became the spokesman for this perspective. First invoked by painters in order to justify their admission into the select world of the liberal arts, the notion was later used by writers to bolster their claim to competence in judging paintings.

The forms and genres of criticism also derived from a long tradition, even if their diversification increased in the second half of the 18th century. *Ekphrasis,* or literary description, which goes back to Philostratus and even to Homer, sometimes (in Diderot, for example) took the form of a narrative account of a dream or of an imaginary walk inside a painting. Also back in vogue were the dialogue form (used by Father Fénelon, Coypel, and Cochin) and the epistolary form (used by La Font de Saint-Yenne and Bachaumont). The pride of place conquered anew by academic lecturers (Coypel, François Desportes, Jean-Baptiste Oudry, and Cochin) generated a deluge of eloquence. Caylus delivered at least 33 lectures. Traditional genres such as the poem (Claude-Henri Watelet, Marsy, and Lemierre); biogra-

phies (Dézallier d'Argenville); essays (Bachaumont); letters (Baillet de Saint-Jullien, Le Blanc, and Mathon de La Cour); courses (Piles); speeches (Duperron); memoirs, treatises, theses, interviews, dialogues, considerations, observations, and other reflections continued to flourish. In addition, there developed a genre first introduced by Baldinucci in the 17th century: the dictionary (Pierre-Jean Mariette, Pernety, A.L. Millin) and even the encyclopedia (Watelet). The burlesque, satiric, or parodic vein found its expression in epigrams, lampoons, and broadsides or in vaudevilles (satiric sketches). And caricatures, which would prove enormously successful in the next century with the "Salons pour rire" (Humorous Salons), were just making their first appearance.

The Salons

The very term *salonnier,* coined in the 19th century to describe the writer or journalist who reviews a Salon, proves how closely the emergence of art criticism proper was bound to the institution of the Salon. The temporary public exhibition of contemporary works of art at regular intervals seemed indeed to be both a requirement and a factor that shaped the genre. As early as 1564 the idea had been launched as a function of the Accademia di Disegno (Academy of Drawing), founded in Florence by Vasari. In France Article XXV of the statutes of the Académie Royale de Peinture et de Sculpture (Royal Academy of Painting and Sculpture), promulgated by Jean-Baptiste Colbert in 1663, envisaged a private exhibition on the first Saturday in July, on the occasion of the annual general assembly. At first, exhibitions took place at irregular intervals, but from the time of Louis XV's reign onward the scheduled recurrence of these events fluctuated between once every other year to once a year, while the length of each exhibition increased: a show that had lasted two weeks in 1667 was soon extended to a whole month. Organized first at the Palais-Royal, then later at the Grande Galerie du Louvre, the shows from 1725 onward were held in the Salon Carré, which gave its name to both the exhibition and the commentaries on it. This double usage of the term *salon* confirms the link between the institution and the new literary genre.

The growing success of the Salons, entry to which was free, is confirmed by the steady increase in the sale of the catalogs, whose print runs grew from 8,000 in 1755 to 20,000 in 1783. In 1765 Diderot estimated there were 20,000 visitors. The spectacular proliferation of pamphlets, brochures, and broadsides about the Salon Carré exhibit provides another indication of its audience, a proliferation paralleled by a flourishing press coverage. An increasing number of reviews appeared in the *Avant-coureur,* the *Observateur lit-*

téraire, the *Année littéraire,* the *Mercure de France,* the *Journal encyclopédique,* the *Journal de Trévoux,* and the *Journal de Paris,* among other periodicals. To these must be added such publications as the abbé Raynal's *Nouvelles littéraires,* Grimm's *Correspondance littéraire,* and Bachaumont's *Mémoires secrets.* All in all, from 1737 until the end of the century there were more than 600 reviews.

If there were ever a domain in which the social history of art brought about a drastic change in ideas, it was the history of criticism. First viewed as literary history, studies of criticism had often concentrated on the great writers. Thus Diderot, who is sometimes wrongly described as the creator of the genre, monopolized the attention of scholars for a long time. Today the field of research has expanded considerably, revealing a large body of anonymous writings by forgotten authors included in the Deloynes collection kept at the Bibliothèque Nationale. New points of view have brought to light the importance of social, political, and economic factors in the examination of the objectives and strategies of an art criticism that was born within an eminently polemical context.

For example, before Thomas Crow, Jürgen Habermas drew attention to the Salon's role in the creation of a new public forum that was defined as much in the press as in society drawing rooms, cafés, or theatre stalls. In the context of an ideology of progress founded on freedom of speech, the critic sometimes claimed to be the spokesman, sometimes the educator of the people or even of the painter. His role was to teach "the artists what they must do, and art-lovers what they should admire," Millin argued in his *Dictionnaire des Beaux-Arts* (1806; Dictionary of Fine Arts). The layman's claim to his right to judge, first made by Piles and Dubos, provoked passionate reactions from the artists and administrators of the Académie Royale, who strove mightily to impose control over public opinion, even to discredit it. For criticism was seen at that time as doubly subversive insofar as it attacked simultaneously both the tastes of the aristocratic clientele and the established authorities. An attack on the obscurity of the allegory or on the frivolous mythology of the art seen in rococo boudoirs represented both a denunciation of society's corruption and a threat to the market. The importance of these issues explains the violence of the polemics that in 1747 followed La Font de Saint-Yenne's first contribution to the genre. Its true founder, he ultimately ceased writing reviews after 1754. The artists counterattacked. Cochin flew to Boucher's defense, wielding both broadsides and caricatures. Until that time the Académie Royale de Peinture et de Sculpture, whose membership was by invitation only, had been the only authority of legitimization and had held the monopoly on official commissions for works of art.

Criticism of its products, considered to be an indirect challenge to the institution and its advantages, naturally upset its beneficiaries. Antoine and Coypel as well as Cochin reacted by denouncing the incompetence of amateurs. Élie Catherine Fréron and Friedrich Melchior von Grimm, on the contrary, defended ordinary art-lovers whom Jean-Étienne Liotard in 1781 dubbed the "ignorarts," asserting that they "are sometimes very good judges."

In this atmosphere the creation in 1748 of a Salon Jury appeared as a sort of preemptive defense against attacks. In 1749 the Salon was canceled because the artists refused to submit themselves to public appraisal. In 1759 a proposal to found a journal of art criticism, presented by the abbé Laugier, was rejected by the marquis de Marigny on Cochin's advice. In 1767 Cochin asked that all reviews bear a signature. And in 1769 Fréron was imprisoned for an article that was considered insulting.

As a result of the pressure of censorship, the greater part of the reviews published in French periodicals in the 18th century were anonymous, and of the 150 satirical writings published before 1789, very few bore official "approval." On the contrary, the majority listed a fictitious place of publication or were published abroad and signed by pseudonyms, which spurred many attempts to guess at their authorship. In the 1770s and 1780s the debate became increasingly politicized, and art criticism became tinged with an oppositional radicalism, especially in reviews by Mathon de La Cour, Gorsas, Carmontelle, Marat, and Mercier. With the emergence of the *feuilleton,* or literary serial, the phenomenon recurred under the Consulate and the Empire, since the same causes produced the same effects and since censorship banished political debate to the aesthetic field. But this was a reactionary yearning, a nostalgia for the age of Louis XIV, which, in Boutard's case, conveyed his opposition to Napoleon, which he expressed by means of criticism of the emperor's official painters, while Chaussard and Geoffroy invoked tradition in order to demonstrate their allegiance to the regime.

In addition, subversion was practiced on a formal level. Bernadette Fort has shown convincingly how, in what she has called the "democratic" side of criticism, recourse to burlesque and parody, and borrowing from light comedy and popular culture constitute clear demonstrations of opposition to established rules and accepted conventions (see Fort). By means of devious strategies, the many bizarre titles that flourished in pamphlets long ignored by historians invoked, in turn, the authority of such figures as Cassandra, Nostradamus, Figaro, Harlequin, Gilles, Scapin, Marlborough, Janot Muggins, Gaspard, Lustucru, and Merlin. They also include "an idler"; Monsieur Bonhomme (Goodfellow);

Monsieur Badigeon (Daub); Marie Jeanne, the flower girl; Jérôme, the snuff grinder; a young lady of 14; cousin Jacques; and even a monkey. For laymen to speak in this way was totally in keeping with the strategy of a discourse that mimics madness, ignorance, or simple common sense. In response to a reproach artists frequently made to critics, there were also many references to blindness—such as in caricatures depicting critics with white cane, dog, magnifying glass, or lorgnette. The famous dead were also invoked. Apelles, Raphael, Michelangelo, Guido Reni, Rubens, and Colbert are among the authorities depicted as witnesses whose task it was to condemn contemporary decadence in the fine arts.

We must now resituate the monument represented by Diderot's nine *Salons* (1759–81) within this broadened arena. Although Diderot did not create the genre (Saint-Yves, La Font de Saint-Yenne, Raynal, Bachaumont, Le Blanc, and Grimm were his forerunners), he certainly gave it respectability. Indeed, the prestige of Diderot's texts is exceptional, especially since, being written for Grimm's *Correspondance* littéraire (which circulated in manuscript copies), the readership they enjoyed at that time was as restricted as it was aristocratic. Their considerable influence on the history of criticism was only felt, therefore, after their publication in the 19th century. In addition to the literary quality that guarantees them an important position among Diderot's work, these *Salons,* given the author's erudition, constitute an essential summa that encapsulates the aesthetic debates of the time. Drawing on diverse French, Italian, English, and German sources, and even in his own contradictions, as fruitful as they are abundant, Diderot reflected the tensions between sensationalism and rationalism, relativism and idealism, preromanticism and neoclassicism, painting and literature, genre and history, modern and ancient. The importance of Diderot's contribution lies in the convergence of a theoretical speculation at work in several essays and his connoisseur's experience, which he acquired by visiting studios. Through his reflections on the position and functions of criticism, his frequent use of comparison and analytic description, Diderot laid the foundations of a method that would serve as model for a long time to come.

Countries and Genres Outside of France

Although the prestige of the Salon is linked to France, other countries did produce notable reviews of exhibitions. However, the genre developed later, and on a less spectacular scale, outside France. Other countries lacked a Diderot to found a tradition and above all to attract the attention of historians. Yet the growth of public exhibitions did not fail to provoke written reactions.

In England, the best known area thanks to Johannes Dobai's monumental study (see Dobai), the art shows of the Society of Artists held from 1760 onward, and the annual show (which required an admission fee) of England's Royal Academy, beginning in 1769, encouraged the appearance of criticism that, as in France, was published in brochures and newspapers (*The Spectator, The Monthly Review, The Morning Post,* and later *The Artist*). The satiric and farcical vein flourished in England too, at the expense of official authority. The chief authors were Henry Bate-Dudley, John Wolcot, and John Williams. But it was not until the next century that the great names of English criticism appeared, with figures such as William Hazlitt and John Ruskin, among others.

In Germany too the academies organized exhibitions—for instance, as early as 1764 in Dresden, 1767 in Düsseldorf, 1778 in Kassel, and 1786 in Berlin. And the press kept pace with this activity—with the *Der teutsche Merkur* in Weimar (to which Johann Heinrich Merck contributed) and the *Deutsche Kunstblätter* in Dresden. But political fragmentation kept the phenomenon within modest bounds in Germany, and the absence of any systematic analysis means we have little knowledge of the history of German criticism from this period, except for the Schlegels' *Athenäeum* (1798–1800) and Johann Wolfgang von Goethe's *Propyläen,* together with the competitions that Goethe organized in Weimar from 1798 on.

The situation was the same in Italy, despite the existence of periodicals (*Giornale delle belle*) and *Memorie per le belle arti;* these have never been the object of systematic study. As for Geneva, recent studies have revealed the production of critical, often anonymous, reviews inspired by the exhibitions of the Société des Arts, inaugurated in 1789.

Meanwhile, literature about art was flourishing throughout 18th-century Europe, and much of it became available to readers in France. Although Lessing's *Laokoon* (1766) was not translated into French until 1802, Winckelmann's *Gedanken über die Nachahmung* was available in France as early as 1756, one year after its German publication, and the French translation of his *Geschichte der Kunst des Altertums* (History of Ancient Art) followed two years after its initial publication in 1764. Sulzer's *Allgemeine Theorie der schönen Künste* (1771–74; General Theory of Fine Arts) was published in the *Supplément* of the *Encyclopédie* in 1776, and Salomon Gessner's *Brief über die Landschaftsmalerey an Herrn Füsslin* (1762; A Letter to Mr. Füessli, on Landscape Painting) appeared in French in 1773. Jonathan Richardson's *An Essay on the Theory of Painting* (1715) was translated into French in 1728, Edmund Burke's *A Philosophical Enquiry into the Origin of Our Ideas of the Sublime and Beautiful* (1757) was translated in 1765, and Burke's influence was discernable in Diderot's *Salon* of 1767. The other category of aesthetics imported from Great Britain, the picturesque (about which William Gilpin expressed his theories in 1792), traveled across the Channel with the vogue for landscapes and for writing about gardens.

PHILIPPE JUNOD

See also Aesthetics; Beautiful; Color; Imitation; Painting; Ugliness and Deformity

Further Reading

Becq, Annie, *Genèse de l'esthétique française moderne: De la raison classique à l'imagination créatrice, 1680–1814,* 2 vols., Pisa: Pacini, 1984

Crow, Thomas E., "The Oath of the Horatii in 1785: Painting and Pre-Revolutionary Radicalism in France," *Art History* 1 (1978)

Crow, Thomas E., *Painters and Public Life in Eighteenth-Century Paris,* New Haven, Connecticut: Yale University Press, 1985

Crow, Thomas E., "La critique des Lumières dans l'art du dix-huitième siècle," *Revue de l'art* 73 (1986)

Dobai, Johannes, *Die Kunstliteratur des Klassizismus und der Romantik in England,* 4 vols., Bern: Benteli, 1974–84

Ehrard, Jean, *Montesquieu, critique d'art,* Paris: Presses Universitaires de France, 1965

Fort, Bernadette, "Voice of the Public: The Carnivalization of Salon Art in Prerevolutionary Pamphlets," *Eighteenth-Century Studies* 22 (1989)

Lee, R.W., "Ut Pictura Poesis: The Humanistic Theory of Painting," *Art Bulletin* (1940)

McWilliam, Neil, editor, *A Bibliography of Salon Criticism in Paris from the Ancien Régime to the Restoration, 1699–1827,* Cambridge and New York: Cambridge University Press, 1991

Orwicz, Michael R., editor, *Art Criticism and Its Institutions in Nineteenth-Century France,* Manchester and New York: Manchester University Press, 1994

Pevsner, Nikolaus, *Academies of Art, Past and Present,* Cambridge: Cambridge University Press, and New York: Macmillan, 1940

Venturi, Lionello, *History of Art Criticism,* translated by Charles Marriott, New York: Dutton, 1936; new, revised edition, 1964

Wrigley, Richard, "Censorship and Anonymity in Eighteenth-Century French Art Criticism," *Oxford Art Journal* 2 (1983)

Wrigley, Richard, *The Origins of French Art Criticism: From the Ancien Régime to the Restoration,* Oxford: Clarendon Press, and New York: Oxford University Press, 1993

Artist

The modern European concept of the artist began to emerge during the Renaissance. While that concept evolved at a pace that differed from nation to nation, the cultural forces that shaped it were the same everywhere: plastic artists, particularly painters, strongly desired to create a distinction between themselves and mere craftsmen. The term "artist" essentially consecrated that distinction, and its meaning was later expanded to include other practitioners of the fine arts, such as sculptors, architects, musicians, and poets. The category of the "fine arts" can itself be linked to the long process of the "liberation" of workers from the "shackles" of the guilds. That process was marked by significant events—including the founding of the great art academies and the creation of the Salons (the first public exhibitions of art)—and occurred during a period in which the system of state patronage (whether

monarchic or national) was beginning to coexist with the more anonymous forms of demand generated by commercial art markets. The "shackles" of the guilds thus gave way to different types of constraints, which fostered in the public imagination the hard-won image of the artist as a professional in the liberal arts, and, over and above that image, the idea of the exceptional individual responding to a vocation. All of these factors contributed to the emergence of new notions of the studio and of art. As successor to the plural term "the arts," understood up to that time as techniques requiring "thoughtful intelligence" or as quasi sciences with wider aims than that of creating beauty, the prestigious word "art," used in the singular, signified a gift for reaching the essence of the ideal, for fulfilling a moral or civic mission. The term described a human activity par excellence insofar as it attested to the artist's freedom and creative capacities, revealing the uniqueness of an individual who devoted himself entirely to his creative work.

The new concepts of the artist and art had first flourished in 16th-century Italy. During the Enlightenment, France essentially took over center stage in the revision of the notions of the artist and art. That country's vast network of academies had served as a model throughout Europe beginning in the second half of the 17th century. France was somewhat late to adopt the noun *esthétique* (aesthetics), but the concept was well represented in French thinkers' general reflections on the beautiful, which had been infused with German and British theories on the topic, and which had proved capable of encompassing under the single idea of "art" the different activities that produced beauty. For this reason, the term "artist" will be explored in this article based on the French example—an example that mirrors and shows the results of the multiple transformations that affected institutional structures and representations during this period.

Archaic Usages

Derived from the medieval Latin word *artista*, the French word *artiste* first appeared at the end of the 14th century in the language of university scholars. Examples taken from 16th-century texts show complexity both in meaning and function. The word was used as both adjective and a noun. In its adjectival function, *artiste* meant "made with skill," as in *un artiste monumen* (a skillfully crafted monument); in its nominal function it designated a student or master in the Faculté des Arts (Faculty of Arts), as in the meaning attributed by Charles Du Cange to the late Latin term in the didactic context of the liberal arts, or in the meaning of the medieval French word *artien* (one who has studied the arts). Du Cange's term did not supplant the classical Latin word *artifex* (one who practices an art or craft). The adverb *artistement* (artistically) meant "in the manner of a craftsman," that is to say, "by means of machines and tools," as opposed to *divinement* (by divine creation), *miraculeusement* (miraculously), or *habilement* (skillfully, in the sense of "by means of artifice or guile"). A French-Latin dictionary of 1630 gives both *artiste* and *artisan* (craftsman) as synonyms of *artifex*. The shift in focus, during the 17th century, toward purely human abilities—albeit brilliant ones—that led to the extension of meaning of the term, either as an adjective or as a noun, to refer to either a "thing" (a watch or a machine) "that is extremely well wrought" (Antoine Furetière's *Dictionnaire*), or to designate the worker (Furetière; César-Pierre Richelet's *Dictionnaire* [1680]; *Dictionnaire de l'Académie Française* [1762; Dictionary of the Académie

Française]), provided that he worked with "thoughtful intelligence," "great skill," or "facility." The term applied in particular to the worker "who is well versed in applying chemical processes," (Furetière; *Dictionnaire de l'Académie Française*).

Both the latter meaning and the academic definition appear in the first edition of the *Dictionnaire de Trévoux* (1704; Dictionary of Trévoux) and these usages persisted into the 18th century. The first meaning, "a well-wrought thing," appears in the *Encyclopédie* and in the *Dictionnaire de l'Académie Française* and is still included in the last edition of the *Dictionnaire de Trévoux* (1771), which relegates that meaning to the category of *autrefois* (archaism), although the dictionary still mentions—but as the last definition listed—the second meaning (someone who has studied the liberal arts), which the other dictionaries omit. Nor do the other dictionaries retain the mention of the adjectival function, about which Trévoux had doubts, since "good writers" did not use *artiste* in this way. The primary meaning of the term, according to the *Dictionnaire de Trévoux,* is "someone who excels in the mechanical arts that presuppose thoughtful intelligence." That category would include clockmakers, for example, who were *grands artistes* (great artists) if they were *habiles* (skillful). In contrast, cobblers (*ne sutor ultra crepidam* [let the shoemaker stick to his last]), even if they were "good," remained "craftsmen. In addition—but mentioned secondarily—some "painters, sculptors, architects," were called *artistes;* with regard to this category, the dictionary provides a cross-reference to the entry "Arts libéraux" (Liberal Arts). The concept of the liberal arts had itself fluctuated since the days of the medieval *trivium* and *quadrivium* (bachelors' and masters' courses of study). Traditionally, the *trivium* comprised grammar, rhetoric, and dialectics, while the *quadrivium* included arithmetic, geometry, astronomy, and music—and, by extension, came to embrace the fine arts. It is not at all clear whether the use of the word *artiste*, without the qualifying adjective *grand*, indicated a case that was distinct from the that of the clockmaker, whose expertise was indicated only when an adjective was used, whereas when it was a matter of art in the modern sense, the use of the noun *artiste* alone was sufficient to attest to the latter's excellence. According to Jacques Lacombe, the author of a dictionary devoted to the fine arts, in the 1750s the custom of "adding some epithet to the word artist in order to describe the talents of the person to whom it is applied" was still "quite common."

The abbé Jean-Baptiste Dubos employs the method of adding adjectives in his *Réflexions critiques sur la poésie et sur la peinture* (1719; Critical Reflections on Poetry and Painting). Yet his hyperbolic modifiers, following a usage seen in the 17th century, enhance the term "artisan"; further, in his famous opening remarks, the abbé asks the artists' forgiveness—not for defining them as craftsmen, but for having omitted the meliorative adjective, which, if used too often, would have made his text unwieldy. Dubos thus did not feel that he possessed a term that, used alone, was capable of expressing the idea of excellence; the French language at that time apparently lacked a generic term, a sign of the recognition of a category distinct from that of the craftsmen among whom the meliorative adjective brought prestige and singled out only the exceptional cases. The term *artiste* would become the word capable of adding connotations of refinement to the crafts and emphasizing the change in status of the creators of images. Admittedly, Pierre Bayle had uses the noun *artiste* 20 years earlier in connection with the classical Greek painter Apelles, but along with it he used a reinforcing adjective ("the most consummate artists"); and the fact that it is applied to a painter indicates not so much the recognition of a specific category as the inclusion of painters of images in the group of elite manual workers who used "thoughtful intelligence and skill," in exactly the way in which Richelet's dictionary (1680) had defined artists.

Skilled Practitioners

The first meaning of *artiste*—"skilled practitioner"—predominated during at least the first half of the 18th century, and from that time on coexisted with the tendency to reserve the term for *imageurs* (makers of likenesses). This is necessarily the case in Lacombe's dictionary, which is restricted in scope to the fine arts (1759) but which nonetheless features as its first definition of the artist "a person from the liberal arts," before applying the term "particularly" to painters, sculptors, and engravers. As for the *Encyclopédie,* the entry "Artiste" (without signature or asterisk), far from restricting this term to those who draw or paint, follows the traditional practice of designating "workers who excel in those mechanical arts that require thoughtful intelligence." The rest of the entry emphatically confirms that the term *artiste* sufficed to indicate excellence, specifying that, "the word *artiste* is always a form of praise." However, *artiste* seems to have been a term of praise applied to mechanical arts worthy of intellectual respect, because this first definition is contrasted with second definition, which is another traditional usage. The second definition gives the example of the chemist, in the context of "those half-practical, half-speculative sciences" (what the classical lexicon called *art*). In such cases, the definition explains, one would call "a good artist" someone who is "capable of skill-fully executing the procedures that others have invented," and therefore, someone who understands very well "the practical aspect," but who is limited to that aspect. In the *Encyclopédie* then, *artiste* refers to "that subordinate section of the profession" and is assigned a qualifier in the case of the worker who is worthy of esteem but who lacks creativity. The meliorative connotation of the single word *artiste* remains limited to the sphere of the mechanical, and the artist's links to execution and manipulation exclude him from creativity, even when he belongs to the realm of the liberal arts.

In the same way that, as we have seen, the subjects included within the liberal arts tended to become more specialized so that the fine arts could become a part of the category as a whole, the fine arts themselves were defined by the fact that unlike both the mechanical arts and the sciences, the fine arts existed for the production of pleasure (Jean-François Marmontel, in the "Arts Libéraux" [Liberal Arts] article in the *Supplément* to the *Encyclopédie* [1776]) or because they satisfied a "need for feeling" (Claude-Henri Watelet's dictionary, left unfinished in 1786 and completed by Lévêque, to become the entry "Beaux-Arts" [Fine Arts] in the *Encyclopédie méthodique* [1788; A Methodical Encyclopedia]). The definition of *artiste* in the latter dictionary—"a man who practices a liberal profession"—restricts the term to the domain of the fine arts, while accentuating its difference from the term *artisan,* and adds the reminder that both terms had been used "indiscriminately" until that time.

Nonetheless, the artist continued to be confused with the artisan, because both categories involved "manual work." In principle, the category of the artist was restricted to painters, sculptors, and engravers, excluding poets and musicians, who made use of "conventional signs." Watelet's text from the last decades of the century certainly takes into account the progress achieved in the plastic arts, especially in the area of painting, whose diverse aspects Nathalie Heinich has studied in connection with the rise of academies from the middle of the 17th century (see Heinich). Heinich notes their acquisition of competency through the transmission of theoretical knowledge; the kinds of remuneration they received, halfway between those of the producer-tradesman and those of "the creator," who profited from his "renown" through the distribution channels of the merchants, shifting the emphasis from *opus* (the work) to *virtus* (qualities); and their personalization of the badges of excellence: signatures, biographies, and their serving as models of behavior (which, during that period, meant being considered "good company"—that is, among those whose manners the comte de Caylus, from 1748, and Watelet thought it advisable to adopt).

Creative Genius

However, Watelet's article also reveals the ambiguity of the status of these "artists," since the materials that they handled prevented their being grouped in the same category as those who used symbolic systems. A privileged position in the realm of the beautiful, defined by the title "artist," remained limited to plastic artists. Hence the distinction between the artist and the craftsman, repeated endlessly in the literature of art in the second half of the century, took on new life with the contrast between the machine and the human body, which was destined for a brilliant career in Germany. This debate moved to the very core of the realm of painting, helping to create the distinction between the painters whose works nourish the soul and those whose paintings nourish the eye. An equally lively polemics took place over the issue of drawing versus color. Ultimately the art of painting was credited for its ability to make a purely spiritual use of material means in order to speak to the soul. For this reason, the article signed by Lévêque, "Peintre" (Painter) in the *Encyclopédie méthodique,* calls the painter "a poet," following in the wake of those who since the end of the 1740s had kept alive the discourse on ideal beauty and the eminent dignity of art and artists—topics that had enthused poets since the classical era.

A seminal article by Paul Oskar Kristeller long ago established the importance, in the history of the modern system of fine arts, of Father Charles Batteux's treatise *Les Beaux-Arts réduits à un même principe* (1746; Fine Arts Reduced to a Common Principle), which was widely distributed republished and eventually reprinted. In Part 3, Chapter 3 of this treatise, Batteux encompasses painters, musicians, poets, dancers, and others in his definition of artists and uses the term "art," in the singular, to describe their diverse activities, while emphasizing constantly that art is "only created in order to deceive." He argues that enthusiasm (or a strong, purely human emotion), under whose sign he groups all artistic producers, is absolutely distinct from ordinary feelings, since it springs not from a real object but from "a forceful idea that strikes the artist" (*Principes de la littérature* [Principles of Literature])—in other words, from a representation created by the imagination. Art operates in the realm of the artificial—with no pejorative connotations—and its materials are "signs": words, notes, colors, or gestures (*Les Beaux-Arts réduits à un même principe*). The modern sense of the word "art" was thus already present. In *Du sentiment* (1801; On Emotion), Pierre-Simon Ballanche even considers the term "artist" to be less comprehensive than the term "poet"—a clear indication of creativity as the common characteristic of the two terms. The word "artist" sufficed to confer value, because, as Louis-Sebastien Mercier complains in the "Artiste" entry in *Néologie ou vocabulaire de mots nouveaux, à renouveler ou pris dans des acceptions nouvelles* (1801; Neology; or, A Vocabulary of New Words, Words to Be Redefined or Words Considered according to New Meanings), in the aftermath of the French Revolution the term had been used to ennoble the ventriloquist, the barber—and even the boot scraper. How can "geniuses," endowed with this powerful enthusiasm, force themselves to "produce the beautiful on a fixed date, just as a coat is duly promised?" protests Charles-Antoine Coypel in a letter dating from 1739. In a similar spirit, Elie Fréron asks with regard to Jean-Baptiste-Siméon Chardin, "Have they no right to idleness? Have they not transferred their very souls onto the canvas or into the poem, thus making the works priceless?" Stimulated by the obligations of patronage or by production for the marketplace, awareness of the singularity of genius went hand in hand with an undefined social position, or "classless status," that was already keenly felt during the age of the Enlightenment. An attempt to remedy this lack of defined status is reflected in the constant references—which were strongly reactivated by Johann Winckelmann and which were to inspire the Revolutionaries—to those mythical Greek cities capable of acknowledging and employing, in ways far surpassing the perspective of individual enjoyment, the civilizing virtues of art.

ANNIE BECQ

See also Aesthetics; Beautiful; Dilettante; Drawing; Enthusiasm; Imitation; Inspiration; Studio; Sublime

Further Reading

Becq, Annie, *Genèse de l'esthétique française moderne: De la raison classique à l'imagination créatrice, 1680–1814,* Paris: Pacini, 1984

Heinich, Nathalie, *Être artiste: Les transformations du statut des peintres et des sculpteurs,* Paris: Klincksieck, 1996

Rey, A., "Le nom d'artiste," *Romantisme* 55 (1987)

Astronomy

The Triumph of Newtonian Physics

One essential achievement sums up astronomy in the age of the Enlightenment: the creation of analytic celestial mechanics. The term shows clearly how much the development of this branch of astronomy is inseparable from mathematical analysis. The most immediate result of this close tie was the triumph of the concepts of Sir Isaac Newton (1643–1727) over those of René Descartes (1596–1650). Although slow in coming, the Newtonian victory was total and irrevocable. Once the two-body system was studied analytically, astronomers immediately abandoned their faith in Descartes's vortices of subtle matter, which were impervious to calculation. Another seemingly paradoxical result was that the torch was passed over to continental Europe, which for so long had turned a deaf ear to the Newtonian message, while English science began to flag, as though crushed by the weight of Newton's great work. In fact, just as in the era of astronomy in Alexandria, most 18th-century astronomers were mathematicians— "geometers," since they defined themselves by that term; most Enlightenment geometers were French or Swiss.

In England itself, Newtonian physics spread only slowly. Newton's short course of lectures at Cambridge was sparsely attended. According to William Whiston (1667–1752), who was to succeed to Newton's chair, this lack of attendance came about because Newton's lectures were too difficult to understand. The basis of the curriculum was still the *Traité de physique* (1672; A System of Natural Philosophy) by the orthodox Cartesian Jacques Rohault (1620–75), translated first into Latin, then into English. In the 1723 English edition of Rohault's treatise, however, Samuel Clarke (1675–1729) supplemented the text with notes that are either quotations from Newton or commentaries, and which constitute a thorough refutation of Rohault's Cartesian physics. Newton's philosophy thus seems to have infiltrated Cambridge under the cover of a Cartesian. In France itself and in the Netherlands—with the exception of the physicists Willem Jacob s'Gravesande (1688–1742) and Petrus Musschenbroek (1692–1761)—the Cartesians vehemently rejected Newton's physics, since the Newtonian concept of attraction seemed less clear to them than Descartes's vortices and it reminded them disagreeably of the occult nature of scholastic physics.

In France the leaders of the anti-Newtonian forces were members of the Académie Royale des Sciences de Paris (French Royal Academy of Science). Among them was Bernard Le Bovier de Fontenelle (1657–1757), the author of *Entretiens sur la pluralité des mondes* (1686; Conversations on the Plurality of Worlds); that work's reputation was diminished when Leonhard Euler's (1701–83) *Lettres à une princesse d'Allemagne, sur divers sujets de physique et de philosophie* (1768–72; Letters of Euler to a German Princess, on Different Subjects in Physics and Philosophy) was published. Another anti-Newtonian member of the Académie—and an ardent defender of Descartes—was Jacques Cassini (1677–1756), known as Cassini II. (His father, Jean-Dominique Cassini [1625–1712], known as Cassini I, was the first director of the Observatoire de Paris [Paris Observatory].) Jacques Cassini opposed the theory of the flattening of the Earth at the poles, which Pierre-Louis Moreau de Maupertuis (1698–1759) defended. It was not until 1740 that, understanding the futility of this rearguard action, Jacques Cassini gradually abandoned his scientific activities and left to his son and successor, César-François Cassini (1714–84), the responsibility of pursuing the family's work: the drawing up of the map of France and administration of the observatory. Credit for introducing Newtonianism into Académie des Sciences properly belongs to Maupertuis, who, in his *Discours sur les différentes figures des astres* (1732; Treatise on the Different Configurations of Heavenly Bodies), took Newton's side. It is true that in 1728 Maupertuis had made a trip to London, at the time when Voltaire was beginning to write his "English letters," which he eventually published under the title *Lettres philosophiques* (1734; Philosophical Letters). Letter XIV reveals the shock that any Frenchman versed in science or philosophy would experience on arrival there:

> A Frenchman who arrives in London will find philosophy, like every thing else, very much changed there. He had left the world a *plenum*, and he now finds it a *vacuum*. At Paris the universe is seen, composed of vortices of subtile matter; but nothing like it is seen in London. . . . According to your Cartesians, every thing is performed by an impulsion, of which we have very little notion; and according to Sir Isaac Newton, 'tis by an attraction, the cause of which is as much unknown to us. At Paris you imagine that the Earth is shaped like a melon, or of an oblique figure; at London it has an oblate one.

Voltaire published his *Éléments de la philosophie de Newton* (The Elements of Sir Isaac Newton's Philosophy) in 1738; he was also responsible for the preface to the French translation (by the marquise du Châtelet

[1706–49], in collaboration with Alexis Clairaut [1713–65]), of Newton's *Philosophiae Naturalis Principia Mathematica* (1689; Mathematical Principles of Natural Philosophy). As Jean Le Rond D'Alembert (1717–83) observes in the *Encyclopédie*:

> It took more than half a century to pacify the academies of continental Europe with respect to attraction. It remained shut up on its island; or if it crossed the water, it seemed to be nothing but the reappearance of a monster that had just been banished; we were congratulating ourselves so heartily for having done away with occult elements from philosophy, we were so afraid that these elements would creep back into it again; we were so pleased with having introduced an apparent mechanism into a description of nature that we rejected the true mechanism that had just been revealed without granting it a hearing. . . . Maupertuis was the first among us to have dared openly to proclaim himself a Newtonian. He thought that one could be a good citizen without blindly adopting the physics of one's country, and in order to attack this physics required a courage for which we owe him a debt of gratitude.

In 1734 the Académie des Sciences awarded a prize to Daniel Bernoulli (1700–82) for a report, conceived in 1732, devoted to the two-body problem; there, for the first time, the analytic translation of Newton's theories appeared. Then, in 1736, Euler published his *Mechanica sive Motus Scientia Analytice Exposita* (A Scientific Analysis Expounding the Mechanics of Motion), in which, despite the retention of many characteristic traits of the old geometric methods, he deals analytically with the kinematics and dynamics of an affected point of a mass. He first studies the free motion of such a point in a vacuum and then in a resistant medium; he then considers the forced movement of this same point. He obtains three equations of motion in space by the projection of the force onto the axes of a mobile trihedron. Colin Maclaurin (1698–1746), in his *A Complete System of Fluxion* (1742), was to take a necessary step forward by resolving the forces on three fixed axes, thereby producing a much clearer and more symmetrical calculation.

The Founding of Celestial Mechanics

In 1743 D'Alembert published his famous *Traité de dynamique* (Treatise on Dynamics), which provides a general and direct method of putting into equation form all the problems of dynamics. He bases mechanics on three principles: inertia, compound motion, and the equilibrium between two bodies. Following Newton's

lead, D'Alembert calls inertial force that property of bodies consisting of continuation in a state of either rest or motion as long as some cause does not occur to produce motion or to change it. D'Alembert recognizes only two types of such causes. Those of the first kind appear at the same time as the effect that they produce: these are the causes that have their origin in the observable and mutual action of the bodies and are a consequence of their impenetrability. Such causes therefore amount to impetus and several other actions that derive from it. All the other causes are perceptible only through their effects, and D'Alembert admits to not knowing their nature. They are the causes that make heavy objects fall toward the center of the Earth and hold the planets in their orbits. D'Alembert states the problem of compound motion in these terms: just as the motion of a body that changes direction can be considered to be composed of its initial motion and of the new motion that it has acquired, so the body's initial motion can be considered to be composed of the new motion it has taken on and of another motion that it has lost. It follows that the laws of a motion modified by an obstacle of any kind depend solely on the laws of the motion destroyed by these same obstacles. In order to determine the laws of a motion modified by obstacles, it is sufficient to have carefully noted the laws of equilibrium. It remained therefore to specify the principle of equilibrium. According to D'Alembert, although every geometer agrees that two bodies moving in opposite directions are in equilibrium when their masses are in inverse proportion to the velocity with which they tend to move, it is difficult to demonstrate this rigorously. The majority of geometers therefore preferred to consider this law to be an axiom, rather than trying to prove it. D'Alembert proposes a method of remedying this. All things considered, there is only one single case where equilibrium is clearly and distinctly manifested: this occurs when the masses of two bodies are equal and their velocities are equal and opposite. Accordingly, the only step that D'Alembert needs to take to prove equilibrium in other cases is to reduce them to this first simple and obvious case.

In the preliminary discourse of his *Traité de dynamique*, D'Alembert concludes the presentation of his three principles in the following way:

> The principle of equilibrium, together with those of inertia and compound motion, thus leads us to the solution of all problems having to do with the motion of a body, insofar as it can be altered by a mobile and impenetrable obstacle, that is to say, by another body to which it must necessarily communicate some motion in order to conserve at least part of its own. From these combined principles, one can easily deduce the laws of the motion

of bodies that come into collision, or that attract each other by means of some body placed between them and to which they are attached. If the principles of inertial force, compound motion, and equilibrium are essentially different from each other, as one cannot fail to agree; and if, moreover, these three principles are sufficient for mechanics, then this science has been reduced to the least possible number of principles, because all the laws of motion of bodies, in any circumstances whatsoever, are founded on these three principles. This is what I have attempted to do in this treatise.

The combining of the principle of compound motion with that of equilibrium was to take the name of "D'Alembert's Principle." Joseph Louis Lagrange (1736–1813) explains it in this way:

> If one imparts to several bodies motions that they may be forced to change on account of their mutual actions, it is clear that one can consider these motions to be composed of the motions the bodies will assume in reality and of other motions that are destroyed; whence it follows that the latter motions must be such that the bodies propelled by these motions alone are in equilibrium.

Although D'Alembert's principle is extremely clear, it necessitates some very laborious mathematical operations. However, this principle proved particularly useful for solving the difficult problem of the precession of the equinoxes.

In 1758, as the last stage of the final victory of Newtonian mechanics, Clairaut revisited the problem of the return of Halley's comet, forecast for that very year, and he applied the theory of planetary perturbations to the comet. He found that Halley's comet would return to its perihelion not in 1758 but rather, owing to delays in its movement caused by the action of Jupiter and Saturn, in mid-April 1759. Having omitted some small factors from his calculations, he added that the margin of error for this event was about a month. As if to mark the spectacular victory of analytic celestial mechanics, the comet reached its perihelion on 12 March 1759. A few years earlier, Clairaut had been the first to tackle the tricky three-body question and to apply it to the motions of the Moon, publishing his *Théorie de la lune* (Theory of the Moon) in 1752 and his *Tables de la lune* (Lunar Tables) in 1754. Although the analytic solution of the motion of two bodies is relatively straightforward, the introduction of a third, fairly massive body fairly close to the two others makes the latter solution almost impossible to arrive at. This three-body configuration is of course the case of the system formed by the Sun, the Earth, and the Moon. Even today, we still have only a semianalytic theory of the motion of these bodies.

Lagrange's *Méchanique analytique* (Analytic Mechanics), published for the first time in 1788, was the crowning achievement of the work undertaken by the great 18th-century geometers. The aims of this remarkable treatise are:

> to reduce the theory of mechanics and the art of reducing its related problems to general formulae, whose simple development will provide all the equations necessary for the solution of every problem. To collect and present from a single point of view the different principles so far discovered that facilitate the solving of the problems of mechanics, to show their mutual dependence, and to make them available for a judgment of their correctness and their range.

Lagrange underscores the essentially analytic nature of his approach:

> No diagrams will be found in this work. The methods I expound here require neither constructions nor geometrical or mechanical reasoning, but only algebraic operations performed in a regular and consistent manner. Those who like analysis will be pleased to see mechanics become a new branch of it and will be grateful to me for having thus broadened the field.

Newton's mechanics were indeed purely geometric. He developed his theorems by deducing proof from hypotheses, using constructions and diagrams. His method was purely synthetic, consisting of drawing the consequences of given hypotheses. In contrast, Lagrange's method, in which algebra was applied to geometry, was entirely analytic. He looked for the conditions of existence of a theorem or of the properties of the diagram. Euler and Maclaurin had already laid down the basic principles of analytic mechanics, but it was Lagrange who took analytic mechanics to its highest level of development. He endeavored in his mechanics to provide, once and for all, every necessary proof and to bring as many things as possible together in a single formula. His aim is to deal with all the individual cases of mechanics through a purely intellectual operation, based on a general, simple, and clear schema. In his earliest work, this method had enabled Lagrange to relate the phenomena of sound to the theory of vibrating strings. It was also this method that, in the last work he presented to the mathematics section of the Académie des Sciences, enabled him to simplify to a remarkable degree his theory of variations in the elements of the planets, and to propose a general method for the solution of all the problems of mechanics in cases where the forces of interference are relatively small in comparison to the main forces. Although Lagrange by and large made the most effective efforts to generalize a solution or to exhaust a subject, he sometimes created new difficulties where none existed, needlessly applying his skillful and erudite methods to the solution of elementary problems that required no more than the simplest of constructions. For instance, on the occasion of the transit of Venus, he took an analytic approach to the simple geometric problem of the planet's solar entrance and exit curves for the various points on the Earth.

Another result of the clash between the Cartesian and Newtonian systems was the birth of a new discipline, geodesy. Since the spherical form of the Earth did not provide a solution to the problem of the relative equilibrium of a homogeneous mass in uniform rotation, Newton had concluded that the Earth is not spherical and that it must have the form of an ellipsoid of revolution. Then, combining the centrifugal force and the mutual attraction of the particles, he had shown that this ellipsoid is affected by a flattening of $1/230$. For purely philosophical reasons, some people took offense at the idea that the Earth was not a perfect sphere. Others had already postulated that it had the form of an elongated ellipsoid. In fact, before Newton's *Principia* appeared, a French astronomer, Jean Richer (1630–96), had observed a variation in gravity between that found in Paris and a measurement that had been made during an expedition in Cayenne in 1672. (Richer had discovered that he had to shorten the length of the pendulums of his clocks so that they would continue to mark seconds.) In any given place, weight results from gravity and from the radial component of centrifugal force. According to a well-known law, centrifugal force increases as one approaches the equator. Once Richer had taken his measurements, the differences found between the theoretical variations and the observed variations made it possible to discover the effects of the variation of the terrestrial radius but not to determine the precise shape of the Earth. For this reason, astronomers preferred to study directly the curvature of the meridian based on the measurement of the linear distance separating two places on the same meridian and on the measurement of their angular difference in latitude. If the Earth were spherical, the curvature of the arcs measured in different places would be identical. If not, this curvature would vary: the length of the degree—that is, the length of the arc whose latitudes at their extremities vary by one degree—would increase the greater the weaker the curvature, and therefore the given section under study would be all the more flattened. The interpretation of measurements led to an error on the part of some scientists, including Jean-Dominique Cassini and his son Jacques, who confused the angle of the verticals and the angle of directions joining the points in question at the center of the Earth. This confusion, which lasted until 1713, led Jacques Cassini to maintain that the Earth had the form of an elongated ellipsoid. The unfortunate victim of an unlucky circumstance, he upheld this assertion well beyond 1713. From the year 1683, the astronomers at the Observatoire de Paris had undertaken to extend as far as Dunkirk and Collioure the arc of the meridian that the abbé Jean Picard (1620–82) had measured between Paris and Amiens in 1670. In 1720 Jacques Cassini published and analyzed the results of this vast enterprise. The length of an arc of a degree seemed to him greater for the arc of 6° to the south of Paris than for the arc of 2° to the north. In reality, the difference was insignificant, given the order of magnitude of errors in measurement. Yet Cassini felt authorized to state that the ellipsoid of the Earth was elongated, and all the Cartesians fell into step with him. Nevertheless, by 1735, when the Académie des Sciences decided to organize two expeditions, to Lapland and Peru respectively, to measure the arcs of the meridian near the equator and near the North Pole, Jean Bernoulli (1667–1748) was the only mathematician who still clung to Jacques Cassini's thesis. The Peruvian expedition, led by Charles Marie de la Condamine (1701–74) and joined by Pierre Bouguer (1698–1758), worked for eight years in extremely uncomfortable conditions, which Bouguer's determination managed to overcome. The Lapland expedition, led by Maupertuis and joined by Clairaut, set off in 1736 and succeeded in measuring one degree of a meridian in less than one year. From 1737 onward, well before the completion of the measurements at the equator, the results of the Lapland expedition made it possible to settle the argument by comparing the arc-length of a degree in the polar region to the arc-length of a degree in Paris: the Earth really does have the form of a flattened ellipsoid. This agreement between the calculations based on Newton's theory of gravity and a series of geodesic measurements was confirmed in 1751 by an estimate of a degree of a meridian made by Nicolas Louis de Lacaille (1713–62) at the Cape of Good Hope.

Pierre Simon Laplace and William Herschel

During the course of the 18th century three new fields of astronomy developed: analytic celestial mechanics, astrometry, and geodesy. Methods were created and instruments developed in each of these fields, and new data had begun to emerge. Two astronomers were to dominate the end of the age of the Enlightenment: Pierre Simon Laplace (1749–1827) and William Herschel (1738–1822). Laplace's work concerned primarily celestial mechanics, and Herschel's extended to all the fields of astronomy.

From the age of 20, at the time when he had just arrived in Paris and had received D'Alembert's support, Laplace set himself a precise, rigorous, and ambitious program, to which he adhered throughout his life and—amazingly—succeeded in bringing to completion. As his first objective, Laplace aimed to demonstrate conclusively, through increased precision, the equivalence of the constantly evolving astronomical observations and the results of the theoretical deductions possible within the strict framework of Newtonian theory. He showed exemplary persistence in working toward this goal, setting himself the task of justifying the secular acceleration of the Moon solely by means of the laws of Newtonian mechanics. D'Alembert and Clairaut had already failed in such an endeavor, and Lagrange would also fail, but Laplace was to succeed. On 19 December 1787 he presented the solution in a session of the Académie des Sciences. Laplace's second objective was to reduce the gap between the laws of motion and the laws of gravity, which involved, on the one hand, consolidating the philosophical and empirical bases of the theory of gravity and, on the other, establishing its universality by showing that it applied just as much to the motion of the heavenly bodies as to their shapes, just as much to celestial motion as to terrestrial motion.

Laplace's first two projects in no way diverged from Newton's ideas. The last two projects in Laplace's program, in contrast, were not only more ambitious but were opposed to Newton's very philosophy. Laplace sought to show that the stability of the observed cosmic systems could be explained and predicted by the theory of gravitation. He also proposed that the laws that preserve this order are also capable of creating it. (Newton, in diametrical opposition, thought that the terrestrial system was unstable, to the point that God had to intervene at very long but inevitable and regular intervals, and that a gravitation incapable of maintaining order in the world could not, a fortiori, explain its origin.) Laplace's greatness was that he reached the goal that he had set in his youth: his monumental *Mécanique céleste* (1805; Celestial Mechanics) fulfills the first three goals and his *Exposition du système du monde* (1796; The System of the World) achieves the last one.

In addition to the fortuitous discoveries of Uranus and the Sun's movement toward the apex, astronomy owes to William Herschel an impressive series of inventories of the objects that exist in the universe. At a period when all other astronomers were preoccupied with constructing telescopes of modest dimensions but endowed with greater and greater precision, Herschel launched himself into the construction of larger and larger telescopes. As early as 1783, with the help of his 12-inch-diameter telescope, he continued his systematic search for double stars but added to these the search for the nebulae that Charles Messier (1730–1817) had begun to catalog in 1780. This 20-year-long program permitted him to catalog 2,500 nebulae. Herschel's project was more ambitious than that of a simple catalog; he intended nothing less than to reveal the "constitution of the heavens"—a goal that would never be reached but that would lead to a remarkable harvest of results. For instance, his research established the distinction between nebulae, in the precise meaning of the term (gaseous clouds), and groups of stars. Herschel was the first to define the flat structure of the Milky Way, (which Thomas Wright (1711–86) had intuited in 1750), and to observe that several kinds of nebulae, which he described as "spotted," had the potential of being reduced to stars (William Parsons, the 3rd earl of Rosse, confirmed this finding in 1845). Herschel's ambition to reveal the constitution of the heavens led him to devise a method of using standards, which, even though it was to fail, remains the seed of today's statistical methods. He divided the sky into small zones, in each of which he counted the number of stars of each magnitude. Unfortunately, this method cannot provide access to the structure of the starry sky because the apparent brightness of the stars depends not only on their distances but also on their intrinsic luminosity, which varies from star to star.

In 1789 Herschel put into service his largest telescope: 48 inches in diameter with a focal length of 40 feet. Eleven years later he published the first of his four large studies devoted to cosmology. In this first report, Herschel presented and classified all the forms of nebulae he had observed in his earlier pamphlet, *Account of Some Observations Tending to Investigate the Construction of the Heavens;* the study was a morphological classification intended to show how the forms are linked one to the other, with the hope of gaining insight into the evolution of these nebulae. Herschel's other three reports devoted to the constitution of the heavens were eventually published over the course of the 19th century. The results remain spectacular, but Herschel's total confidence in his telescopes, whose power was supposed to lead him to the ends of the universe, was shaken: ambiguous objects exist whose nature he could not determine, and worse, it was probable that a more powerful telescope than his most powerful one, even if it did resolve the image of one obscure object, would only discover still other, even more obscure objects. Nevertheless, however great the sense of failure felt by Herschel at the end of his life, he remains one of the greatest observers in the history of astronomy.

JEAN-PIERRE VERDET

See also Earth, Shape of the; Newtonianism; Observatories and Observation Instruments; Optics and Light; Science: Dissemination and Popularization; Stars; Sun and the Solar System

Further Reading

Hoskin, Michael A., *William Herschel and the Construction of the Heavens,* London: Oldbourne, 1963

Mach, Ernst, *The Science of Mechanics: A Critical and Historical Exposition of Its Principles,* Chicago: Open Court, 1893; 6th edition, LaSalle, Illinois: Open Court, 1974 (original German edition, 1883)

Merleau-Ponty, Jacques, *La science de l'univers à l'âge du positivisme: Étude sur les origines de la cosmologie contemporaine,* Paris: Vrin, 1983

Verdet, Jean-Pierre, *Une histoire de l'astronomie,* Paris: Seuil, 1990

Atheism

The Idea and Its History

The word "atheism" comes from the Greek *atheos* and served in antiquity to describe the attitude of all those who adhered to a religion other than that of the Greeks (for example, Christianity) and did not participate in the official cult. The Epicurean doctrine—according to which any representation of the divine emanates from the fear felt by a powerless humanity—constituted the first attempt to interpret religion according to its function, and later champions of atheism would take up this form of explanation for belief in deities. Within European cultures, the perceived need for a specific term by which to designate "unbelievers"—that is, non-Christians—diminished during the Middle Ages but resurfaced at the outset of the modern era and during the Reformation. Certain of the designations for nonbelievers that emerged throughout history have since fallen into disuse ("Epicurean" and "Lucianist," for example), while others (such as "deist," "atheist") have survived since antiquity, and still others (such as "materialist," "pantheist," or "freethinker") did not appear until the end of the 17th or the beginning of the 18th century.

As is the case with the notion of materialism, the concept of atheism appeared frequently in apologetic texts, where it was often used in a very broad and polemical sense in order to combat what were judged to be heterodox opinions. In the context of the struggle waged against free thought and libertinism, it was fairly common for those charged with atheism also to find themselves reproached for leading a life deemed to be immoral because it was nonconformist. Dictionaries of the 17th and 18th centuries confirm this conflation of ideas by grouping the terms "atheist," "freethinker," "voluptuary," and "vagabond" under the same heading—"libertine"—thereby associating intellectual and moral subversion with social marginality. It was only in the 18th century, at the time when French materialism was proudly proclaimed to be a form of atheism, that the term regained its true meaning.

From the 16th Century to the Atheism of the Enlightenment

The atheism of the Enlightenment unfolded at the end of a long process that had been underway in various cultural centers since the beginning of the modern era. This process was marked by an increasing detachment from the Christian faith (especially Scholasticism), and by the gradual appearance of various forms of Protestantism. Several phases, sometimes concomitant, marked the transition from deism to pantheism and even, in the case of some writers, to atheistic positions. At the same time, scepticism emerged—a form of agnosticism whose proponents avoided all noumenal speculation and refused even to broach the question of a Creator. Finally, the annals of the Inquisition, attesting to a widespread reserve concerning the doctrine of transubstantiation, prove the existence of a grassroots form of atheism supported by practical arguments.

In the modern era, atheist thought first emerged in Italy during the 16th and early 17th centuries, when it was fomented by repeated challenges to the traditional truths and dogmas of the Church. The creation of the world, the immortality of the soul, the miracles performed by Christ, his divinity—these were the issues that fueled intellectual discussions of that era. The rediscovery of the manuscript of Poggio Bracciolini's *De rerum natura* (1417; On the Nature of Things) takes on a special importance here, for this text caused a lengthy debate on atomism and the question of the creation of the world. Other works cited in the debate included Bernardino Telesio's *De rerum natura* (1565; On the Nature of Things) and Giordano Bruno's *De l'infinito* (1591; On the Infinite Universe and Worlds). The same Bracciolini manuscript also provoked the publication of texts denouncing atheism, such as Benito Pereira's *De communibus omnium rerum naturalium principiis et affectionibus* (1579; On the Universal Origin and Condition of All Natural Things) or Fausto Sozzini's *Contra atheos* (Against Atheists), published before 1598. One of the most extreme representatives of atheistic thought was Giulio Cesare Vanini, who in *De Admirandis Naturae Reginae Deaeque Mortalium Arcanis* (1616; On the Arcane Admiration of the Queen; or, Nature and the Goddess of Mortals) affirmed that matter is eternal and doubted that God had been the cause of the Creation—opinions that cost him his life at the stake in 1619.

During this period there was no atheism, in the strict sense of the word, in England, although the "religious atheism" presented in Thomas Hobbes's *Leviathan* (1651) essentially contributed to the secularization of English political thought. The most radical English advocates of politico-religious thinking—the "Levelers," for instance—related their reading of the Bible to natural law, as occurs in the works of William Walwyn or Clement Writer, for example. Freethinkers such as John Toland (*Christianity Not Mysterious* [1696]) or John Collins (*Discourse of Freethinking* [1713]) made possible the breakthrough of deism. Richard Bentley's text *Matter and Motion Cannot Think; or, A Confutation of Atheism* (1692) set off a controversy over the immortality of the soul, a dispute that was pursued throughout the 18th century.

Similarly, atheism remained an exception in the German-speaking countries. Neither those first exposed to Spinozist pantheism (Martin Knutzen, Friedrich Wilhelm Stosch, Theodor Ludwig Lau, and Johann Christian Edelmann, for example) nor the thinkers of the later stages of the *Aufklärung* who engaged in criticism of religion (Hermann Samuel Reimarus, and Carl Friedrich Bahrdt, among others) went beyond their often bitterly anticlerical positions and critiques of orthodox ideas. Even when these thinkers rejected all theology—as did Abt or Georg Christoph Lichtenberg, for example—they stopped just short of atheism. Only J.H. Schulz, in his *Philosophische Betrachtungen* (1786), and J.A. Einsiedel adopted more decisive positions. The supposed "quarrel over atheism" (1788–89), provoked by two essays by F.K. Forberg that appeared in the *Philosophische Journal* edited by Johann Gottlieb Fichte and Friedrich Immanuel Niethammer, testified, as far as atheism was concerned, less to the existence of a true atheism than to the susceptibility and vigilance of the government of the Electorate of Saxony.

In France atheist tendencies first emerged with the freethinking movement of the 17th century. That movement drew ideas from many sources, including Aristotelianism as understood by Averroës, Italian naturalism (Tommaso Campanella), and scepticism, in both its ancient and modern forms (Michel Eyquem de Montaigne or Pierre de Charron in *De la sagesse* [1601; On Wisdom]). The freethinkers endorsed the idea of a secularization of morality based on relativism and scepticism; their system of thought was also characterized by a pessimistic understanding of human nature and a naturalism that bordered on cynicism. Two main currents can be discerned within this movement's shifting composition: one inspired by the aristocracy, whether social or intellectual; the other, scholarly, as expressed in the anonymous *Theophrastus Redivivus* (1659; Theophrastus Renewed), a text that attacked religion and theology, thus laying the theoretical foundations of atheism during the age of the Enlightenment. The Jewish tradition and its critique of Christianity, as found in the works of Baruch Spinoza, for example, also played a significant role in the gradual disintegration of Christian orthodoxy. However, it was Pierre Bayle's *Dictionnaire historique et critique* (1697; An Historical and Critical Dictionary) that contributed the most to propagating a radical scepticism well into the 18th century, since, by citing biblical texts with contradictory meanings, Bayle pitted reason against faith and thus relativized all the bases of religion. Bernard Le Bovier de Fontenelle's *Histoire des oracles* (1687; History of Oracles) followed the same trend.

Scientific progress and discoveries during the 18th century were also instrumental in the dissolution of the theological interpretation of the world. An impassioned debate had brought the Church and the natural sciences into conflict over the heliocentric view of the world (Johannes Kepler, Galileo). Sir Isaac Newton, with his *Philosophiae Naturalis Principia Mathematica* (1687; Mathematical Principles of Natural Philosophy) and the formulation of the law of gravity, advanced a step further on the path toward a scientific approach to the cosmos. However, while Newton sought to reconcile his views with religion, Immanuel Kant and Pierre-Simon Laplace (author of *Mécanique céleste* [1805; Celestial Mechanics]), in formulating their theory of the "nebula," demonstrated that the theory of the creation of the world was untenable. Lalande concluded that although we cannot prove the existence of God, we can explain everything without him.

Not only the macrocosm but also the microcosm—that is, humankind—were subjected to scientific analysis. Increasingly precise scientific studies (by Boyle, Hermann Boerhaave, Abraham Tremblay, René-Antoine Ferchault de Réaumur, and others) stressing the intrinsic cohesion of all living things would in time undermine the dualism of body and soul that was the mainstay of the Christian view of humanity. Finally, scientific discoveries made in the course of voyages by explorers such as the comte de Bougainville, James Cook, and Forster, by making possible comparisons between different evolutionary stages in natural and social history, not only undermined the credibility of Genesis and Christian chronology but also destroyed the theological view of history.

One of the characteristics of the 18th century was that scientific data and experimental results enjoyed unprecedented circulation. Already, at the end of the 17th century, Fontenelle could confidently expect that his *Entretiens sur la pluralité des mondes* (1686; Conversations on the Plurality of Worlds) would have a fairly large, if worldly, readership. In comparison, Voltaire's popularization of Newton's thought (*Éléments de la philosophie de Newton* [1738; The Elements of Sir Isaac Newton's Philosophy]) reached a far wider public, and finally, the *Encyclopédie*, despite the constraints imposed by censorship, broadened even further the gap between all the branches of knowledge and the theological interpretation of the world, creating an immense stir among the literate bourgeoisie.

Materialist philosophers in France during the age of the Enlightenment gave atheism a militant form. Julien Offroy de La Mettrie was following the Epicurean conception of the function of religion when he affirmed that achieving freedom from anxiety about death is a prerequisite for achieving freedom from superstition—that is to say, from all religion. Delving into psychology (*Histoire naturelle de l'âme* [1745; The Natural History of the Soul]), physiology (*L'homme machine* [1748; Man, a Machine]), and morality (*Discours sur le bonheur* [1748; Discourse on Happiness]), La Mettrie's principal texts rehabilitate the flesh and explain the mind and soul as physical attributes. Adopting a resolutely polemical tone, La Mettrie aims to prove that theology and reason, philosophy and Christian morality are irreconcilable (*Discours préliminaire* [1751; Preliminary Discourse]). His texts elaborate a natural morality based on physiology and are uniquely preoccupied with earthly concerns. According to this morality, the supreme good, as stated by Claude-Adrien Helvétius in *De l'esprit* (1758; Essays on the Mind and Its Several Faculties), is the happiness of humanity—a happiness attainable thanks to the unfettered development of the physical and mental attributes of the individual. Evil is not inherent in human nature. When it exists, it is simply the result of either a defective physical organism or a bad upbringing.

When he took up the defense of Calas and Sirven around 1760, Voltaire revealed his virulent anticlericalism. However, he did not propose to abrogate religion—which in his view was an efficient way to socially integrate the lower classes; hence, "If there were no God, we would have to invent him." Meanwhile, the materialists who had rallied around the baron d'Holbach tried to systematize and politicize both materialism and atheism. The first part of Holbach's *Système de la nature; ou, Des lois du monde physique et du monde moral* (1770; The System of Nature; or, The Laws of the Moral and Physical World) deals with matter, while the second addresses religious representations and their function. In that second part Holbach develops a systematic refutation of theism, deism, pantheism, optimism, and all proofs of the existence of God. He argues that knowledge of nature and the application of reason are indispensable prerequisites for the destruction of religion: "While ignorance of nature gave birth to the gods, knowledge of nature will serve to destroy them." Holbach also cautions against the fatal bond uniting despotism and priestly domination: "Ambition, imposture, and tyranny are in league to make joint use [of God], so as to blind the people and keep them under the yoke." Nonetheless, just as in the works of Epicurus, a quietist attitude would ultimately prevail in Holbach's work. This attitude in evident in his reference—which markedly weakens the force of his overall argument—to a possible reign of toleration, which, as in England, would make atheism unnecessary, and also by his affirmation that atheism is worthless to the masses, whom he suspects of being incapable of getting rid of religious imagery.

This elitist attitude—which, as an element of its critique of religion, emphasizes the imposture of priests—in combination with a limited rationalism, certainly characterizes the atheism of the *Système de la nature,* while simultaneously limiting the scope of Holbach's argumentation. These limits would be passed only by the critiques of religion (by David Friedrich Strauss, Ludwig Feuerbach, and Karl Marx, among others) that emerged in the 19th century.

HEINZ THOMA

See also Doubt, Scepticism, and Pyrrhonism; Epicureanism; Fanaticism; Libertinism; Materialism; Secularization and Dechristianization

Further Reading

Delon, Michel, "Débauche, libertinage," in *Handbuch politisch-sozialer Grundbegriffe in Frankreich, 1680–1820,* edited by Rolf Reichardt and Hans-Jürgen Lüsebrink, vol. 13, Munich: Oldenbourg, 1992

Hunter, Michael, and David Wooton, editors, *Atheism from the Reformation to the Enlightenment,* Oxford:

Clarendon Press, and Oxford and New York: Oxford University Press, 1992

Kors, Alan Charles, *Atheism in France, 1650–1729,* vol. 1, Princeton, New Jersey: Princeton University Press, 1990

Popkin, Richard H., *The History of Scepticism from Erasmus to Descartes,* Assen, Netherlands: Van Gorcum, 1960; revised and expanded edition, as *The History of Scepticism from Erasmus to Spinoza,* Berkeley: University of California Press, 1979

Attraction. *See* Newtonianism

Authority, Government, and Power

Sources and Modalities of an Ideological Confrontation

Authority, government and power were three key concepts in the ideological confrontation between the forces of conservatism and the forces of progress, a confrontation that pervaded Europe in the 18th century and culminated in the crisis of 1789. Within any single state this clash raised the question of who held political authority and, as a result, had the right to govern and legitimately to exercise power. The conservative and progressive political camps had already taken up their positions in the 17th century. The conservatives appealed to divine right, and the progressives appealed to natural law and the notion of contract. The concept of divine right, which had originated in the Middle Ages, was used to justify the absolutism of Louis XIV in France and the absolutist ambitions of the Stuarts in England and Scotland. It was the Stuarts, above all, who triggered the reaction of the defenders of the rights of the people; this led to a reinforcement of the tradition that traced the notion of political authority to a contract agreed upon between a people and its prince.

John Locke, the apologist of English parliamentary constitutionalism and a supporter of the House of Orange, was the model for Enlightenment intellectuals who argued that political authority should be dependent on the idea of a contract. This idea also owed much to Hugo Grotius and Samuel von Pufendorf, the most illustrious representatives of the great German-Dutch school of *Naturrecht* (natural law). It was from Grotius, as absolutist as he may have been, that the progressives derived the principle of the natural socia-bility of human beings—the essential condition for the contract and the negation of the intrinsic egoism of humanity—upon which Thomas Hobbes, in particular, based his apologia for absolutism. From Pufendorf came the idea of a freely undertaken contract between the sovereign and the people, in which the people had an obligation to obey from which they could not free themselves for any reason. Here, whereas both Grotius and Pufendorf remained cautious about the implications of natural law, leaving to their readers the main task of harmonizing political theory and practice, Locke boldly shifted the terms of the debate to the *fons et origo* (source and origin) of political authority by stipulating that the contract gave the people an inalienable right to rebel against the established power if that power excessively infringed natural law. Locke's constitutional liberalism provided the touchstone for the two parties that, in the 18th century, would take over from both the defenders of divine right and the defenders of natural law—that is, supporters of either enlightened despotism or popular sovereignty. Both groups presented themselves as the successors to the doctrine of monarchic absolutism upheld by the Catholic Church, a doctrine that was well on the way to losing all intellectual credibility.

The Debate on Sovereignty

It was Montesquieu who imported Locke's principle of the right to resist, based on the theory of the contract, from England to France. Montesquieu accompanied it with an analysis of the English constitution, which brings out the idea of a balance of powers. According to Montesquieu, himself a lawyer, "it defies common sense to insist that the authority of the prince should be sacred and that the authority of the Law should not be so" *Mes pensées* (1752; My Thoughts). Despotism is no more than arbitrariness raised to the status of a law, the end result of a long-running abuse of power that threatens all the peoples of Europe. The best remedy is to preserve national sovereignty and therefore to guarantee political freedom by preventing the concentration of power in the hands of a single individual or group.

Those who have commented on the famous sixth chapter in Book XI of Montesquieu's *De l'esprit des lois* (1748; The Spirit of Laws), which is about the English constitution, have long sought to demonstrate that, inspired by his experience in England, Montesquieu was trying to base political freedom on a rigorous separation of the legislative, executive, and judicial powers. However, since Louis Althusser published *Montesquieu: La politique et l'histoire* (1964; Politics and History: Montesquieu, Rousseau, Hegel, and Marx), this so-called separation of powers has been recognized as an imaginary theoretical model elaborated at the end of the 19th century and the beginning of the 20th.

A close reading of Montesquieu's text reveals that it is the sharing of power by the king, the nobility, and the people—rather than the separation of power among them—that protects the nation against all forms of despotism, including the despotism of the people. The text also reveals Montesquieu's stance in favor of a moderate regime in which his own social class, the nobility, acts as a counterweight to the people and as a moral example for them. These contradictory interpretations of the chapter may be explained by the fact that Montesquieu's method of exposition straddles both deductive analysis and empirical research. The rigorous principles on which the myth of the separation of powers has been constructed appear ahead of the detailed description of the actual functioning of the English constitution. This method also explains why it was possible for Montesquieu to influence, directly or indirectly, both the doctrine of enlightened despotism and that of popular sovereignty. These doctrines were elaborated most notably by Frederick II of Prussia and Catherine II of Russia (on the side of enlightened despotism), and by Diderot and Rousseau (on the side of popular sovereignty).

However, it is important to emphasize that at least at the outset, these were not doctrines based on fundamentally antithetical concepts of political authority. Rulers and philosophers alike were convinced that they were providing similar solutions to similar problems. Even certain aspects of the ideas of Rousseau, the most radically committed of all to the will of the people as the source of political authority, are in some respects comparable to the imperious thought of the rulers, who, moreover, were increasingly open to the conviction that they were no more than the servants of their subjects.

This ambiguity is nowhere more evident than in the essay that marks Diderot's first foray into the field of political theory, the article "Autorité politique" (1751; Political Authority) written for the *Encyclopédie*. Diderot's article reflects the admixture of audacity and caution characteristic of Montesquieu's writings, but he focuses on maintaining the integrity of authority rather than dispersing that authority among the component parts of the state. Diderot's concern with maintaining authority shows that he had diverged from the path laid out by Montesquieu, for whom he nonetheless avowed an unfailing admiration. Like Montesquieu in his analysis of the English constitution, Diderot proclaims his main principles at the start of his article, but he then considerably weakens their force by linking them to a historical model that seems to contradict them. He begins with this lapidary statement: "No human being has received from nature the right to command others." He then eliminates any doubt about the source of political legitimacy: "The prince receives from his subjects themselves the *authority* that he has over them." To ensure that there is no ambiguity on the issue, he adds: "The crown, the government, and public *authority* are possessions that belong to the body of the nation, and princes are their usufructuaries, ministers, and trustees."

Popular sovereignty seems to be a right about which there can be no compromise. In fact, however, the very opposite is true. By using the example of Henri IV of France in order to throw some historical light on his principles, Diderot deflects his readers toward enlightened despotism, a name that he does not dare to speak, and quotes the beloved king admonishing his people: "My will must be reason enough; an obedient state never asks its ruler what his will is. I am King. I speak to you as a king. I want you to obey me." Although there is a contract between ruler and people, the people cannot terminate it, by resisting the sovereign, if the monarch has justice on his side. Even in the case of an unjust king, the people can do nothing but submit, while bending God's ear with their prayers. It was only when the romantic figure of Henri IV was replaced by the harsh realism of Catherine II that Diderot changed his mind on this point.

Voltaire, in *La Henriade* (1723; the Henriade) expresses a similar admiration for Henri IV. More historian than political theorist, Voltaire extended this admiration to Frederick II and to Catherine II, whose enlightened opposition to the clergy seemed to him also to advance the interests of their peoples, despite their occasional offenses against freedom. In effect, Frederick replaced monarchy by divine right with a secular doctrine of royal authority, largely inspired by the theory of the social contract. According to the Prussian king, the consent of the people was the foundation of royal power, imposing on the monarch a permanent moral obligation to watch over the welfare of his citizens and to be accountable to them in his administration. However, like Diderot's depiction of Henri IV, this "first servant of the state" lost none of his authority by this shift. On the contrary, according to Frederick's own *Essai sur les formes de gouvernement et sur les devoirs des souverains* (Essay on the Forms of Government and on the Duties of Rulers), paternal authority alone permits the prince to be for society "what the head is for the body. The prince must see, think, and act for the whole community, in order to procure all possible benefits for it."

In Germany few voices were raised to contradict such ideas, because unlike in France and England, there were virtually no bourgeois supporters of the Enlightenment. Instead, the members of the German intellectual elite fairly easily came to terms with a monarchic absolutism presented in a modernizing and liberal guise. However, this controlled freedom, the gift of the ruler, no longer suited Diderot. He had learned from experience to view Frederick, the absurdly self-proclaimed *philosophe,* as a cynic who belittled the people's abilities to shape their own well-being. Diderot displays the same distrust of rulers in his commentary on the *Instruction* (1767) issued by that other great despot, Catherine II, whose eloquence and culture had made Enlightenment Europe believe that she would be a defender of freedom. Faced with this empress, who had made a strange adaptation of Montesquieu's *De l'esprit des lois* (a text Diderot considered sacred) by forcing it toward the defense of despotism, Diderot reveals in his *Observations sur le Nakaz* (Observations on Catherine the Great's "Nakaz") that he is irrevocably committed to popular sovereignty. His riposte in that text to Catherine's assertion that the sovereign is the source of all political and civil power is that the real source of such power is "the consent of the nation represented by their deputies or by an assembly as a body."

It would be correct to see this text as Diderot's equivalent to Rousseau's *Du contrat social* (1762; The Social Contract). The crucial difference is that for Diderot theory cannot be separated from practice. Diderot therefore turns his gaze toward Russia and, later, toward America, at a time when the greatest experiment in popular sovereignty was unfolding—an experiment that he evokes enthusiastically in his contributions to Raynal's *Histoire philosophique et politique des établissements et du commerce des Européens dans les deux Indes* (1770; A Philosophical and Political History of the Settlements and Trade of the Europeans in the East and West Indies).

For all his daring in applying popular sovereignty to the actual political circumstances of his day, Diderot was merely following in the wake of Rousseau and *Du contrat social.* Proud of the rights that he had been granted, at least in his own imagination, through being a citizen of Geneva, Rousseau sought to ground those rights in unshakable political principles. Freedom is the first and by far the most important of these rights. It is an absolute political value, and it requires a conceptual basis that can withstand any test. Paradoxically, Rousseau finds such a foundation in the ideas of Hobbes, who had also sought to defend political authority in the state against any abuse, although with different ends in mind. Like his contemporaries, Rousseau pays tribute to the doctrine of contract, but he renovates it by borrowing from Hobbes the notion of an indivisible sovereignty. Contrary to Hobbes, however, Rousseau locates this sovereignty exclusively in the people, who cannot in any circumstances transfer it into the hands of those who govern. This transformation implies a radical reevaluation of the pact that founds a society. The traditional pact of submission, which Rousseau regards as contrary to natural law and to the equality that is the essential condition of freedom, is replaced by a pact of association. This agreement is made between the body of the people and individuals—that is, between the sovereign power and its subjects. However, once the individual has consented to the association, he cannot in any way retrieve his natural freedom; otherwise, the authority of the state—the sovereignty of the people—would run the risk of being contested at any moment.

How, then, can one speak of freedom? Rousseau's answer resolves the apparent contradiction in a brilliantly concise manner. In *Du contrat social* he holds that the pact implies a form of association "by which each one, uniting himself to all, nonetheless obeys only himself and remains as free as he was before." The individual gains access to this superior freedom by alienating all his natural rights to the keeping of the community, a gesture that serves to transform those rights into civil ones and makes the individual into a citizen. In submitting to the general will of the sovereign body, of which the individual is a member, the citizen merely obeys laws that are the acts by which this will is expressed in concrete terms. In the constitution of the state based on the social contract, popular sovereignty is manifested in the legislative function. The executive function of government, entrusted to magistrates, must be strictly subordinated for fear that the magistrates might usurp sovereignty, thereby breaking the social contract. Similarly, Rousseau declares representative systems unacceptable because they alienate and dilute popular sovereignty. In later texts, however, he had to bow to reality by formulating a system of representation in which the deputies are obliged to express the will of the people through imperative mandates.

What should be said of England, the home of the spirit of Locke that inspired a revolution in Continental Europeans' perception of political authority? It must be acknowledged that debate on such questions had been marginalized after the Glorious Revolution of 1688 had brought about political stability through a compromise among the royal, aristocratic, and parliamentary powers. This debate continued to run implicitly through public life in the writings of John Toland, the radical Whigs, and the Dissenters, only to come to the forefront again during the struggle of the American colonies for independence. However, this renaissance was short-lived in England. The antirepublican reaction led by Edmund Burke and provoked by the French Revolution gave birth to a political tradition that was far removed from progressive Enlightenment ideas about political authority. Burke replaced the concepts of political right and contract, advocated by Locke and carried to the democratic extreme by Rousseau, with the values of obedience and duty, reinventing for modern times the premises of the conservative camp in the debate on the legitimacy of power.

ANTHONY STRUGNELL

See also Natural Law and the Rights of Man; Sociability; Social Contract; State

Further Reading

Althusser, Louis, *Politics and History: Montesquieu, Rousseau, Hegel, and Marx*, translated by Ben Brewster, London: NLB, 1972; 2nd edition, 1977 (original French edition, 1964)

Antoine, Gérald, *Liberté, égalité, fraternité, ou, Les fluctuations d'une devise*, Paris: UNESCO, 1981; 2nd edition, 1989

Cobban, Alfred, *Edmund Burke and the Revolt against the Eighteenth Century: A Study of the Political and Social Thinking of Burke, Wordsworth, Coleridge, and Southey*, London: Allen and Unwin, and New York: Macmillan, 1929; 2nd edition, London: Allen and Unwin, and New York: Barnes and Noble, 1960

Dickinson, H.T., *Liberty and Property: Political Ideology in Eighteenth-Century Britain*, London: Weidenfeld and Nicolson, and New York: Holmes and Meier, 1977

Gough, J.W., *John Locke's Political Philosophy*, Oxford: Clarendon Press, 1950; 2nd edition, 1973

Hoffmann, Paul, *Théories et modèles de la liberté au XVIIIe siècle*, Paris: Presses Universitaires de France, 1996

Schneiders, Werner, editor, *Lexikon der Aufklärung: Deutschland und Europa*, Munich: Beck, 1995

Starobinski, Jean, *The Invention of Liberty, 1700–1789*, translated by Bernard C. Swift, Geneva: Skira, 1964 (original French edition, 1964)

Strugnell, Anthony, *Diderot's Politics*, The Hague: Nijhoff, 1973

Autobiography

Although descended from a rich and ancient tradition, autobiography, in the modern sense of the term, only began to emerge as a genre during the Enlightenment. The term itself was coined somewhat later, at the beginning of the 19th century and only came into general use in the mid–19th century. Some historians claim 1782, the year in which the first six books of Jean-Jacques Rousseau's *Confessions* appeared, as the official birth date of the genre. It would be excessive to regard Rousseau as the sole originator of autobiography, for there were after all a whole series of founding texts, from Augustine's *Confessions* (397–401) to a handful of important works of the Renaissance: Enea Silvio Piccolomini's *Commentarii* (1584; The Commentaries of Pius II); Teresa of Avila's *Libro de su vida* (1588; The

Book of Her Life); Benvenuto Cellini's *Vita* (1558; A Life); Cardan's *De propria vita liber* (The Book of My Life), written around 1576; and Michel Eyquem de Montaigne's *Essais* (1580–95; Essays). There were also works such as Abélard's *Historia calamitatum mearum* (written ca. 1136; The Story of My Misfortunes), Dante's *La vita nuova* (ca. 1293; The New Life), and Petrarch's *Secretum meum* (written 1342–58; My Secret), to name only the most celebrated. We may nevertheless safely assert that autobiography was a key genre throughout the Enlightenment and that Rousseau's work was by far the most original and influential example of this kind of writing.

The development of autobiography coincided with the period often referred to as the "turning point of the

Enlightenment," from 1770 to 1820–30. More than any other genre, autobiography marked this change of direction in which intellectual energy focused on the self as microcosm instead of aspiring to knowledge of the entire universe. If encyclopedias and dictionaries, travel literature, and systematic essays on forms of government or the history of mores were the types of expression that corresponded to the triumphant Enlightenment, autobiography, as an integral, encyclopedic, and methodical narrative of the self, corresponded perfectly to that period in European history when the Enlightenment took on a romantic coloring, if not a romantic orientation. Writers discovered the charms of introspection, memory (above all of childhood), dream and reverie, solitude, and nature, and in much of the literature of this period, the voice of the heart outweighed that of reason.

Yet these tendencies, which seemed to threaten the ideology of the Enlightenment, were made to conform to its intellectual and moral requirements. Far from abandoning themselves to the fascination of the different conditions of their souls, writers of autobiography aimed to explore what it means to be human. They wanted to understand the human species by recounting their own lives and by giving form to the mass of their own experiences. Aspiring to knowledge of the self, the modern autobiographer sought to contribute to a science that had yet to be founded; in Alexander Pope's words, "The proper study of mankind is man." Contemporary autobiographers would add that writers who wanted to study humankind should study themselves and that autobiographical writing was the best way to do so. In Rousseau's view, "no one can write the life of a man but himself." He designated autobiography as a royal path that leads us not only toward the understanding of the individual but, at the same time, toward the understanding of the human species as a whole, so long as readers undertake their portion of the task and use the self of the autobiographer as a "type for comparison."

The history of the editions, imitations, translations, and proliferation of autobiographies confirms that these grandiose claims of autobiography immediately struck a very resonant chord among the European public. As evidence of autobiography's widespread popularity, one could cite Nikolay Mikhaylovich Karamzin's comment in his *Pisma russkago puteshestvennika* (1791–92; Letters of a Russian Traveler) that he preferred Rousseau's *Confessions,* Johann Heinrich Jung-Stilling's *Heinrich Stillings Jugend* (1777; Heinrich Stilling's Youth) and Karl Philipp Moritz's *Anton Reiser: Ein psychologischer Roman* (1785–90; Anton Reiser: A Psychological Novel) to "all the psychological systems in the world." Written in 1791, Karamzin's comment shows that the Russian elite, not surprisingly, had not only read the

Confessions in the original text, well before it was translated into Russian in 1797 (a version close to the original), but were also familiar with apparently minor texts of German literature and fully understood the spiritual élan that characterized the collective enterprise of the autobiographers in the last third of the 18th century. The history of the development of autobiography, therefore, accurately reflects the creative energy of the genre.

For strategic reasons—because their authority and credibility were not yet established—writers presented their autobiographies as scientific or philosophical works rather than as literary works. In earlier times, anyone writing a confession had to reassure the reader that it was for religious, pedagogical, or apologetic motives—never for aesthetic reasons. Autobiography did not aim for a place in the system of genres; authors even feigned a certain contempt for style and form in the belief that the absence of these elements would convince readers of the author's concern for truth. Sometimes this contempt for style was sincere and the text suffered accordingly. Many autobiographers, above all Rousseau, insisted on sacrificing fine language, as if the use of the art of rhetoric immediately undermined the whole autobiographical project. In the preamble to the Neuchâtel manuscript, Rousseau declares:

> If I try to take care in writing . . . I will not paint myself, I will disguise myself. . . . I therefore come to terms with style as with other things. . . . I will always adopt the style that occurs to me, I will change it according to my mood without scruple, I will tell everything as I feel it as I see it, without self-questioning or embarrassment; without fine phrases. . . . My unequal and natural style, sometimes rapid and sometimes diffuse, sometimes wise and sometimes crazy, sometimes serious and sometimes cheerful, will itself become part of my story.

This is the paradox of autobiography: the absence of style guarantees the sincerity of the work, but the very lack of style is the story, originating in the author himself. For similar reasons, autobiographers avoided every form of narrative that too closely resembled fiction, which, by definition, was the opposite of truth. Rétif de La Bretonne promises that in his work "the truth will be stripped of the cheap rhetoric of fable and fiction will no longer conceal it," brilliantly mimicking the citizen of Geneva (i.e., Rousseau), whom he reproaches for having "made a novel," although he had promised the contrary. Not without some unintentional comedy, Rétif—the author of *La philosophie de Monsieur Nicolas* (1796; Monsieur Nicolas's Philosophy)—also expresses the ambition of the new autobiography: "by this painful anatomy to give to my nation the most useful of books, to illuminate my times, to benefit posterity, which perhaps will not have anyone so courageously truthful." Rousseau took this inherent tendency of the genre to the limits when he proposed to "say everything." Such was the categorical imperative of autobiography which all the autobiographers at the turning point of the Enlightenment, as well as their successors, would come up against.

To say everything is to confess everything, and Rousseau, in his *Rêveries du promeneur solitaire* (1782; The Reveries of the Solitary Walker), thought that he *had* said everything; yet those who emulated him, such as Rétif, claimed that true autobiography was still to be written and that they were the ones who were going to do it. Others disputed the assumptions of the Rousseauist program and accepted an element of fiction as the regrettable but unavoidable part of the autobiographical project. Johann Wolfgang von Goethe even put a grain of irony into an all too elegantly balanced title: *Aus meinem leben: Dichtung und Wahrheit* (1811–22; From My Life: Truth and Fiction).

Nevertheless, what made Rousseauist autobiography innovative was precisely its bias toward complete sincerity. The supremely indiscreet author of autobiography no longer insisted—as for example in the case of memoirs—on protecting his private and intimate life. By announcing that they were baring their own hearts, autobiographers invited their readers to be indiscreet. Exhibitionism on display without fear of taboos or scandals was certainly not the least of the attractions of the genre. Generally, this perilous exercise was reserved for certain privileged beings, famous people who knew themselves to be in the eyes of the public. The first use of the term "autobiography" in Germany is significant in this regard. It appears in the anthology entitled *Selbstbiographien berühmter Männer* (1796; Autobiographies of Famous Men), which was edited by Seybold, an associate of Johann Gottfried von Herder.

Rare indeed were those nameless men and (especially) women who embarked upon the new direction in autobiography, understood as a unique account of a unique individual with a unique destiny. Indeed, it is hard to imagine a woman of the classical age of autobiography directly adopting Rousseau's tone, admitting the faults of her childhood or adolescence, and claiming the right, as Rousseau did, to present such a book to God the Father in person! Women who wanted to be writers were restricted to traditional forms of autobiography—memoirs or letters—as well as novels, in which they could camouflage their personal experiences. The self-important autobiography remained a masculine prerogative. (Certain important exceptions to this rule did exist, notably in the form of professional autobiographies of prostitutes, such as that of Con Phillips in

England, who wrote *Apology for the Conduct* (1748), a frankly cynical text resembling the novels *Moll Flanders* (1722), *Fanny Hill: Memoirs of a Woman of Pleasure* (1749), and *Thérèse Philosophe* (1748; Thérèse As Philosopher). The exception that proved the rule was Madame Roland's *Mémoires particuliers* (1793; Particular Memoirs). The extraordinary frankness of this work shocked its greatest admirers, including Sainte-Beuve, yet today the text appears at times to be a model of feminine writing and of enlightened autobiography. Perhaps the despair of a prisoner destined for the guillotine was required for a woman to dare to ignore the taboos of propriety, to surpass even her idol Rousseau in the subtle sobriety of her self-analysis, while lacking his unbridled and ostentatious narcissism and his propensity for self-pity.

Male autobiographers—champions of sincerity, men celebrated for their lives and their work—were solicited by their publishers or by their associates to defend themselves against harmful and untruthful biographies by revealing the truth of their own lives. They did not disdain their women readers, nor did they address themselves only to their equals; their discourses were not esoteric, for they wanted to be heard by the whole of humanity. Autobiography, which depicted the private life of a public man, was therefore a genre as all-embracing as the novel and was indeed in direct competition with the novel in terms of audience and success. Although autobiographers claimed to disdain fiction, many of them had first established a literary reputation based on a novel—or even on a novel written in the first person. This was the case with Rousseau and Rétif, and also with Jean-Paul Richter and Goethe, who can hardly be accused of those grandiloquent gestures of sincerity that affected so many of Rousseau's direct successors. Almost all the great writers of autobiography and of memoirs with autobiographical tendencies (as opposed to those who wrote memoirs under the ancien régime) had careers as men of letters behind them. These included playwrights, such as Carlo Goldoni (1707–93), Carlo Gozzi (1720–1806), and Vittorio Alfieri (1749–1803) in Italy; Colley Cibber (1671–1757) in Britain; Ludvig Holberg (1684–1754) and Johannes Ewald (1743–81) in Denmark; and Denis Ivanovich Fonvizin (1745–92) in Russia. Others were poets, such as Carl Michael Bellmann (1740–95) in Sweden; Christian Friedrich Daniel Schubart (1739–91) in Germany; and William Cowper (1731–1800), William Wordsworth (1770–1850), and Samuel Taylor Coleridge (1772–1834) in Britain; or scholars and philosophers, such as Giambattista Vico (1668–1744), Johann Georg Hamann (1730–88), David Hume (1711–76), Edward Gibbon (1737–94), and Salomon Maimon (1753–1800); or polymaths, such as Diego de Torres Villarroel (1693–1770) in Spain, Andrei Timofeevich Bolotov (1738–1833) in Russia, and Adolf von Knigge (1752–96), the German translator of Rousseau's *Confessions*. Almost all the great autobiographers of the Enlightenment could rely on a long experience of writing, and even Casanova was not a literary novice when he set out to write his *Memoirs* (1789–98). Autobiographical writing became part of the professional writer's purview in the bourgeois era. As the poet Charles Baudelaire would observe in the 19th century: "we make our confessions pay handsomely."

During this period when modern autobiography was still in gestation, critics considered the autobiographical genre to be related either to religious exercises or to historiography. Samuel Johnson, the greatest writer of biographies in England, formulated his biographical credo in two essays that appeared, respectively, in *The Rambler*, number 60 (1751), and in *The Idler*, number 84 (1759). Johnson assigned a new field to the biographies of the Enlightenment and proclaimed the superiority of autobiography. In his view, because biography is always partial, and always dependent on hypotheses, whoever writes his own life is in a better position to know for certain what concerns him and to make the whole truth known to his readers. Here we see already a topos of post-Rousseauist autobiography, which will recur in such authors as Gibbon, Rétif, Alfieri, and Richter. Some historians have insisted on the profoundly democratic aspect of this new conception of biography. Johnson declared the right of every person to recount his or her own life, each account of a life having its own interest and utility. He also affirmed that each individual is capable of understanding any biography, since all human beings have essentially the same experiences. Further, Johnson, who himself left some fragments of an account of his childhood, valued the "minutes of life" that had already been defended by John Aubrey in his *Lives of Eminent Men* (1680).

The same ideas later inspired others who thought about the status of both biography and autobiography. In Germany, at the time when Rousseau's *Émile, ou, De l'éducation* (1762; Émile; or, Concerning Education) appeared, these concepts were taken up by Thomas Abbt, in Letter 211 of his *Briefe, die Neueste Literatur betreffend* (1762; Letters concerning the Newest Literature), and contested by Herder, the great promoter of reflections on autobiography, who emphasized the profound singularity of every individual experience in his *Über Thomas Abbts Schriften* (1768; On Thomas Abbt's Writings). Herder was among those who were sometimes sceptical and sometimes optimistic about the capacity of autobiography to promote knowledge of the self. In the end he preferred "practico-historical" autobiographies, which he distinguished from confessions or histories of the soul. It was logical that *The Private Life of the Late Benjamin Franklin* (1793) became the

model that he recommended—rather than Rousseau's *Confessions*—as "a school of work, wisdom, and morality," in the first letter of the first volume of his *Humanitätsbriefe* (1793; Letters on Humanity). Like Herder, Immanuel Kant, Friedrich von Schlegel, and Goethe expressed reservations about Rousseau's autobiographical program, although they remained—or had once been—assiduous readers of his book. Kant challenged even the possibility of knowledge of the self in his *Anthropologie in pragmatischer Hinsicht* (1798; Anthropology from a Pragmatic Point of View), and Goethe, who was of the same opinion, never ceased repeating that reflection on the self does not lead very far and that human beings can know themselves only through the *vita activa* (active life).

Schlegel, using the concept of "pure autobiography" in the 196th fragment in the *Athenäum-Fragmente* (1798; Athenaeum Fragments) places neurotics like Rousseau, "with their eyes eternally fixed on the self," in the same category as "born historians . . . who use their own lives to feed their historiographical art," pedants who wish to put their lives in order before they disappear, "coquettes casting longing eyes on posterity," and those whom he calls "autopsists." Finally, Schleiermacher, in the 336th fragment, ridicules "the boring frankness of the enthusiasts," while E.T.A. Hoffmann, through the intermediary of his cat Murr, mocks the mania "for the detailed circumstances of all the events of [their] youth" that haunted contemporary autobiographers.

Rousseau's *Confessions* represents for the history of autobiography what the year 1789 does for French history as a whole: a decisive and irrevocable turning point. Accordingly, in the 18th century there was a period "before Rousseau" and a period "after Rousseau." However, under what we might call the "ancien régime" of autobiography, an informed observer could have seen some indications, especially in England, that the account of one's own life was to take on a new shape, that the era of autobiographies of the religious or humanistic type was over, and that the genre would be used from then on as a true quest for the self—a self conscious of its own worth and freed from feudal or religious bonds.

Just as Protestantism had paved the way for the French Revolution, so Puritan and Pietist techniques of self-analysis prepared the ground for the new interrogation of the self. In England those who recounted their every deed and gesture with an unprecedented frankness drew directly or indirectly on a spiritual tradition that attached importance to the slightest manifestations of the soul. Here one may cite Cibber, George Anne Bellamy, and other heirs of this tradition, as well as the newer tradition of the family chronicle, which culminated in John Bunyan's autobiographical work, *Grace*

Abounding to the Chief of Sinners (1666). Misch has called Bunyan's book "a new type of religious history of the soul" (see Misch). Bunyan's writing provides the earliest example in this genre of the premise of a simple style, denuded of all rhetoric. *Apology*—the title of texts by both Cibber (1740) and Miss Bellamy (1785)—was in itself revelatory. It is true that the tone of the apology changed completely from that of a religious apology to that of the artist who entertains as much as he instructs, or who demonstrates, as Cibber does, a personality ready to mock himself and his own vanity while confessing his follies with a smile. In Germany too, Pietist confession, following August Hermann Francke's model (1690–91), prepared the way for modern self-analysis. A curious document of the early *Aufklärung* is significant in this respect. In Adam Bernd's *Eigene Lebens-Beschreibung* (1738; *His Own Life Described*), the banished pastor's confession of sins gives way to a maniacal inventory of his illnesses and neuroses. Bernd presents himself to the scientists of his time as a medical and psychic sphinx, and he details his weaknesses with all the zeal of a seducer listing his conquests or a convert confessing his former faults. This was a radical change of paradigm compared to that of Bunyan, the "chief of sinners." It is clear that the pride inherent in Bernd's consciousness of his miserable originality prefigures that of Rousseau, who would find another way of exorcising his demons, fixated as he was on the idea of his own primal innocence and the limpidity of his heart.

A second text that gave a new form and meaning to Pietist autobiography was *Heinrich Stillings Jugend*, written by Johann Heinrich Jung—who was known as Jung-Stilling—and published by Goethe in 1777. Like many 18th-century autobiographers, Jung came from a modest background and was self-educated. He was associated at Strasbourg with the Sturm und Drang movement led by Goethe. Under the latter's influence he stressed the literary character of his own "true history." Jung-Stilling's somewhat mawkish tone tends to obscure his edifying message. The second part of this idyllic autobiography, the social ascent of a child of the common people, did not enjoy the enormous success of the first.

The life of Karl Philipp Moritz (1756–93) has some similarities to Jung-Stilling's, but his *Anton Reiser*, subtitled *Ein psychologischer Roman* (A Psychological Novel), was a much more penetrating and modern text. The son of a quietist, Moritz wrote of himself as "oppressed from the cradle," educated in fear of the doctrines of Madame de Guyon and the victim of "the hell of poverty" throughout a childhood characterized by emotional deprivation. Despite his manic-depressive constitution, Moritz had an astonishing career, becoming a Freemason, a friend of Moses Mendelssohn, and

an intimate of the *Aufklärer*, the leaders of the German Enlightenment who gathered in Henriette Herz's salon in Berlin. Goethe considered Moritz a brother and rated his works highly, as did Schiller. The romantics would see him as a precursor, and Heine would designate *Anton Reiser* as "one of the great monuments of its time." Forgotten or neglected for many years, *Anton Reiser* appears today to be the only autobiography of the Enlightenment comparable to the *Confessions*, and even superior to Rousseau's work in the depth and minutiae of its social and psychological analysis. Casting autobiographical material in the mold of the novel (without, however, disowning his ambition to know and to make known his inner being), Moritz succeeded in getting beyond one of the great contradictions of the genre, summarized in Phillipe Lejeune's careful analysis of the "autobiographical pact" (see Lejeune, 1975). Conscious of the fate of "pure" autobiography, which promises us the truth about the writer's self by speaking in the first person but deceives itself and the reader at the same time, Moritz chose the opposite method. In order to escape from the novelistic lie, he made himself into a hero of a novel with a highly symbolic name, Anton the *Reiser* (traveler)—a hero, or rather an anti-hero, whose experiences he related and commented upon in a precise but somewhat drab style. By his sobriety he seems to prefigure Gustave Flaubert's impersonal style. For Moritz, as for Rousseau, autobiography had an anthropological goal. Although less ostentatious and radical than the author of the *Confessions*, Moritz too wanted to make known the whole truth about a human being. To this end, he meticulously reconstructed the concatenation of small causes and large effects of a psychic life. Yet there is a bizarre lacuna in this book that is both an essay and a bildungsroman: sexuality. It seems as if all of Anton's libido were invested in his indomitable desire to learn the truth about himself. In reality, Moritz was obliged to censor himself by the fact that homosexual inclinations were inadmissible during his time, even by a partisan of the *Aufklärung*. Despite its sense of propriety, *Anton Reiser*, a true novel, was destined to serve as a counterpart to the *Magazin zur Erfahrungsseelenkunde*, which the writer edited from 1783 to 1793. A child of the Fourth Estate, Moritz addressed himself to the common people, desiring to educate them and promote their emancipation. His life would remain incomplete, like his *Anton Reiser*; and, unlike his two idols, Rousseau and Goethe, he was unable to achieve his full stature. The autobiographer Moritz, an enthusiastic student of experimental psychology, was one of the writers who prepared the ground for the psychoanalytic revolution.

Rousseau, Geneva's famed Protestant son, introduced autobiography into French literature, where other forms of autobiographical writing—essays, portraits, memoirs, letters, and novels in the first person—had previously prevailed. His *Confessions* were written between 1762 and 1770 and published posthumously in 1782 and 1788. The book emphatically renounced the Christian tradition of autobiography established by Saint Augustine and sought to initiate a new era. These *Confessions* of a neglected and persecuted philosopher claimed both to clear his name, out of respect for public opinion, and to liberate the exemplary individual from Christian morality through the epic affirmation of a naturally virtuous nature. Moreover, this author, who was so sincere, nourished the secret yet barely concealed ambition to give the public nothing less than a Bible of the Self. Rousseau's opening gesture in his autobiography—sounding the last trumpet in order to gather his audience together—was, to say the least, Promethean beneath its exterior of faith. It is as if, in giving an account of himself, Rousseau was re-creating or reinventing the human species.

Rousseau's grandiose project was balanced and enlivened by his remarkable candor. Never doubting himself, his judgment, or his memory, he believed that he knew what he felt in his heart and had the "chain of sentiments" at his disposal as a "faithful guide." This extreme candor had many advantages. It inspired the autobiographer to set out on a quest for his childhood and gave him the means to evoke it. With Rousseau, the Enlightenment's interest in origins became a passion for childhood; and it is to him that we owe the discovery of childhood, the major achievement of autobiography. Since Rousseau, childhood has been the soul of autobiography and its narrative substance. As soon as autobiographers set out to recount their adult lives, they risk becoming merely writers of memoirs, which is why so many writers publish only their memories of childhood and youth. Rousseau avoided this pitfall in that he pictured himself as the eternal, incorrigible child, "poor Jean-Jacques," ashamed to the point of incontinence, faced with the great world that wanted to render homage to his genius. To discover childhood, and invent it as a subject for writing, was to be interested in internal and social phenomena that had previously been considered insignificant or derisory—the "puerile stupidities" for which rationalists, such as La Harpe, reproached the author of the *Confessions*. Rousseau had shown that the true nature of adult human beings, or indeed of great persons, is to be found in their original smallness, and that the sublime caliber of their true character is already—in the midst of actions that may appear ridiculous or trivial—better revealed when they are small than in their maturity. Childhood seems to be the autobiographer's main source of freshness and élan. The autobiographical drive resembled that of the Enlightenment in general, as when the Third Estate, which wanted to be the whole nation, claimed the right of free speech, since what they had to say was just as worthy as what was said by highest in the land. As Rousseau declared in the preamble to the Neuchâtel manuscript: "In whatever obscurity I may have lived, if I have thought more and better than kings, the history of my soul is more interesting than the history of theirs."

To make such a claim is to apply the ideas of the *drame bourgeois* (contemporary dramas depicting middle-class situations) to autobiography. Rousseau was the only great protagonist of the Enlightenment to have written "the secret history of [his] soul, " and his prodigiously eloquent history had an enormous seductive power, despite the pathological tendencies that disfigure it and the author's declared intention to leave the final word to the reader's judgment. In introducing the autobiographical genre into France, Rousseau also invented the theory that he inscribed in his text in the course of elaborating it. Having defined his autobiographical ideal in the *Confessions*—an ideal based on the postulates of absolute sincerity and transparency—Rousseau came up against the problems of autobiography. This led to a change of method and to the rehabilitation of fiction within the authentic discourse in his later writings, *Rousseau, juge de Jean-Jacques: Dialogues* (1780–82; Rousseau, Judge of Jean-Jacques: Dialogues) and *Rêveries du promeneur solitaire* (1782; The Reveries of the Solitary Walker).

Rousseau, the true Narcissus of the Enlightenment, never stopped pursuing the reflection of his ego, just as Achilles never stopped running after the tortoise. Lacking the power to grasp this reflection once and for all, the autobiographer managed to invent it, while assuring the reader of the perfect likeness of his self-portrait. Among those who denounced the utopian character of the Rousseauist project, one of the most perceptive was Jean-Paul Richter, who wrote in the *Vorschule zur Ästhetik* (1804; School for Aesthetics): "In general, self-regard does not yield true vision, it perceives only the reflected and fragmented eye. And the mirror does not reflect itself. Were we to know ourselves completely, we would be our own boundless creator." According to Richter, who placed Rousseau at the head of the category of "borderline and feminine geniuses," the essential part of the individual is contained in the unconscious, the existence of which was totally unknown to Rousseau and his peers—Alfieri, Moritz, and Novalis.

With the works of Rétif (1734–1806) and Giacomo Casanova (1725–98), autobiographies increased in size and range. In length they rivaled memoirs, such as those of the duc de Saint-Simon, and their passionate adventures paralleled those of novels. Rétif stated that he had begun writing the 16 volumes of *Monsieur Nicolas ou Le cœur humain dévoilé* (1794–97; Monsieur Nicolas; or, The Human Heart Laid Bare) before he had read the

Confessions, yet he wrote a sort of pastiche, which is especially striking in the programmatic passages and in the addresses to the reader, even though some of them are decidedly original: "I am a living book, my reader! Read me!" Clearly, the obligation to confess the error of one's ways was already one of the established topoi of autobiography, as were the numerous warnings to the prudish reader and the emphasis on moral and educational purpose. Like Casanova, Rétif included in his autobiography a number of amorous adventures, narrating them with all the brio of a consummate storyteller. Indeed, Rétif moved from autobiography disguised as fiction to overt autobiography by way of his journal, *Mes inscriptions* (1889; My Inscriptions). Having had more than 700 mistresses, most of whom were commoners or prostitutes, this former typographer, who printed his texts himself, was as tireless in his loquacious prose as in his pursuit of love: polygamy, or polymorphy, and polygraphy were, in his case, mutually enriching. As a result, the autobiographical enterprise led to a veritable galaxy of texts in which *Monsieur Nicolas* was the central star. Schiller, one of the first and most avid readers of Rétif's autobiography, strongly recommended it to Goethe and compared its power to that of Cellini's autobiography, which Goethe had translated. For a long time, however, France repudiated the writer whom Sainte-Beuve would call "the disgusting Rétif."

Casanova's *Mémoires* are even more valuable as a document of the history of morals in the Europe of the Enlightenment. Casanova was a Venetian adventurer whose career seems more romantic than that of any hero of a romantic novel. The text was written in French between 1789 and 1798, but the complete manuscript was published only in 1960–61 by the German publisher Brockhaus, which had acquired it in 1820 (it was published in France by Plon). Readers in the 19th century had access to only abridged and bowdlerized versions of Casanova's magnificent text but were nevertheless scandalized by it. It was considered an autobiography because of its intimate revelations, but it also belonged to a genre bordering on memoirs. This is not so much because of the title, as its true title was *Histoire de ma vie* (The Story of My Life), and the title *Mémoires* is no indication that it belongs to a fixed genre. The work owed its classification more to its depiction of events in the external world and to the fact that Casanova wrote in French, which lends a certain air of objectivity to the autobiographical material. If born autobiographers are people who, before even writing a book, live life while thinking of the manner in which they will recount it some day, Casanova belonged to a different race: he wrote his life because he was too tired to go on living it. Indeed, he insisted on the difference between himself and those who were destined to write. For him autobiography was neither a quest for the self nor a quest for an indulgent reader but rather a continuation of his quest for happiness through written memory. At first Casanova lived out the fantasy of human omnipotence—which so many partisans of the Enlightenment entertained—in the sexual mode. However, at the opposite extreme from Rousseau, instead of saying everything, Casanova amused himself by giving an account of everything that he was supposed to have seen and attempted. With Casanova autobiography takes the form of a book that one reads "with only one hand," with the added attraction of a lively wit reminiscent of the short stories of the Italian Renaissance. This innocent roué, who loved great cities and their cosmopolitanism, a man without fear, shame, complexes, or resentment, crisscrossed the Continent in every direction. He tried every profession and dabbled in every kind of knowledge and practice, including the most suspect (gambling, magic, lotteries). He frequented every milieu, tasted every kind of good fortune, and experienced every kind of reversal. Initially he owed his fame throughout Europe to his imprisonment—or, more precisely, to the tale of his escape from *i Piombi* (the famous prison in Venice, with its lead-decorated doors), which would become one of the outstanding chapters in his *Mémoires*. This *philosophe*, so proud of his liberty, was nevertheless quite at home in the ancien régime, and he sought the approval of the great. Crowned heads, princes, dukes and ministers, Church dignitaries, and the great wits of the day attracted him almost irresistibly, and he used his charm when dealing with them just as he did with the fairer sex. Having seduced all his contemporaries, male and female, obscure and illustrious (only Voltaire, whose self-esteem was wounded by Casanova, resisted him), the Venetian undertook the seduction of posterity by recounting his conquests. In addition to the material of this incredible life, he had other assets, including a buoyant style, a command of French that was clumsy to the point of being sublime, a lively wit, and a singular style that was both light and profound.

Vittorio Alfieri (1749–1803) cast his *Vita scritta da esso* (1804; The Life of Vittorio Alfieri Written by Himself) entirely in the register of the sublime—a sublime achieved by sheer effort. This Piedmontese aristocrat had no grounds for rejoicing in having been born in an enlightened time or an enlightened country and was obliged to invent an identity for himself against the grain of his epoch. The early stages of his life, which he described in the first three "Epochs" of his *Life,* dedicated respectively to childhood, adolescence, and youth, hardly presaged the evolution of the adult man recounted in the fourth and last part, *Virilità* (Maturity). In this final part, Alfieri describes himself as a victim of his moral and emotional solitude. His self-portrayal reveals his passionate character but acknowledges that he languished in a state of all but total ignorance and laziness. He was sickly, anxious, and melancholy and obstinately fled from his destiny by traveling across Europe, where he learned nothing and indulged himself in two passions that cost him dearly: thoroughbred racehorses and women of ill repute.

This almost systematic apathy, which reinforced the alienation Alfieri had experienced as a homeless orphan, paved the way for his eventual transformation when he finally found his salvation in literature. Reading rekindled in him the mortifications of the child and the frustrations of the young man, and the writing that resulted from it allowed his true passion, the love of fame, to emerge. In contrast to Rousseau, whose *Confessions* he did not deign to cite as his model, Alfieri, despite his pride, claimed to be a man like others. Nevertheless, he gave his *Vita* a unique trajectory. In other respects, however, Alfieri was like Rousseau. Alfieri too gave an anthropological purpose to autobiography, and he made much of childhood—"the man is a continuation of the child"—and of the discourse of the heart, while at the same time indulging his passion for pedagogical argument. He also presented himself, in the manner of Rousseau, as the product of his reading—although he had come to it late—and as a spiritual son of Plutarch and Montaigne. Above all, however, Alfieri defined himself by the problem of his linguistic identity, by the need to *"disfrancesarme"* (loosely, "negate my French identity") and to learn a mother tongue that he had neglected for too long and that was all but irrecoverable, except as part of the cultural inheritance that he had set out to discover in the latter half of his life. His vocation as an author was therefore preceded by his assimilation of the Italian and Latin classics—an ambition that took on the allure of a chivalrous quest and a heroic conquest. Alfieri returned to the golden age of Italian literature as Rousseau had returned to nature. Conscious of his roots, Alfieri rebelled against France as Rousseau had rebelled against civilization.

It was in the spring of 1790, in revolutionary Paris, that this *misogallo* (loosely, "anti-Frenchman"), abandoning his liberal inclinations, wrote the first draft of his autobiographical bildungsroman, which he took up again in 1798 and refined until his death. This was the first genuine autobiography to emerge from modern Italy, for Vico's *Vita* (1729; Life) was one of those stories of a career, or an extended curriculum vitae, that had been advocated by Leibniz, while the memoirs of Goldoni (in French: *Mémoires* [1787; Memoirs of Carlo Goldoni]) and Gozzi (in Italian: *Memorie inutili* [1797; Useless Memoirs]) had been true memoirs. Alfieri's personal diaries, written in French, his autobiographical poems (*Rime*), and his reflections on biography (*Del principe e delle lettere* [1786; The Prince and Letters]; *La virtù sconosciuta* [1786; The Unknown Virtue]), all paved the way for his *Vita*.

In contrast to his tragedies, Alfieri's *Vita* had a lasting impact in Europe. Madame de Staël, who read it in manuscript form in Florence at the house of the Countess of Albany (Alfieri's muse), described the experience in a letter dated 21 May 1805. It was, she explained, "a reading that captivated me to such an extent that for five days I existed only for it. . . .This man was much more admirable for his character than for his talent, and what a character, in a country where that gift is so rare!" (*Correspondance générale* [General Correspondance]). Stendhal, who made a pilgrimage to Alfieri's tomb, likened Alfieri's susceptible nature to his own and drew inspiration from an episode in the *Vita*. In his *Journal* for 21 March 1811 Stendhal refers to "Alfieri killing Élie for having pulled out one of his hairs"; in Stendhal's *Armance* (1827), Octave has similar rages. On the other hand, Goethe spoke of Alfieri with clearsighted reservations, while Friedrich Wilhelm Nietzsche, following many other commentators in doubting even the possibility of autobiographical sincerity, accused him of lying.

In England, somewhere between 1765 and 1767, the poet Cowper (1731–1800) wrote *Adelphi*, a remarkable "history of my heart so far as religion has been its object." It was published in 1816. This history of a conversion is fascinating for the clarity and simplicity of its style, as well as for what might be called the involuntary sincerity with which Cowper recounts his obsessions and terrors, his states of alienation, his attempts at suicide, and then his fervor for the biblical God, his dreams, visions, and ecstasies. Cowper's narrative, full of pathos but without a trace of self-indulgence, is admirably clear in representing the delirium of a lost soul and seems to prefigure the writings of Thomas De Quincey or Gérard de Nerval.

David Hume's *My Own Life* (1776) is even shorter than Cowper's book. Like Vico's before it, and Gibbon's after it, this autobiography revolved around the question of finding out: How did I become the author of my works? Hume characterized this text, written in the year of his death and intended to serve as an introduction to the collected edition of his works, as a "funeral oration for myself," and its brevity flaunted his vanity, just as the conspicuous display of sincerity had done for Rousseau.

The historian Gibbon (1734–94), who considered himself a disciple of Hume, tried to combine sincerity and brevity in his *Memoirs of My Life and Writings* (a patchwork assembled in 1796 by Lord Sheffield from six autobiographical drafts). He did not succeed, however, in completely concealing his well-known vanity. Nobody took further than Gibbon the will to organize one's life around a single work, in his case *The History of the Decline and Fall of the Roman Empire* (1776–88), and he traced that work's origins back to the precocious passion for reading that emerged during his childhood as a sickly orphan. The stylistic mastery of the historian of Rome (who began his literary career with an essay written in French) clearly stood the autobiographer (who claimed to be writing naturally, and without rhetorical artifice) in good stead.

Two solemn passages in Gibbon's *Memoirs* in which he describes, respectively, the moment of the conception of his masterpiece in Rome, "amidst the ruins of the Capitol," and then its completion more than 20 years later in Lausanne, where he had expatriated himself, were destined to become famous. On the other hand, there is the equally unforgettable (but comic) passage in which he describes the sole occasion on which he experienced the desire to set up a home (a whim inspired by Mademoiselle Curchot, who later became the wife of Jacques Necker and the mother of Madame de Staël). This amorous episode was cut short because his father vetoed such a mismatch. "I sighed as a lover, I obeyed as a son," Gibbon recalls. Friedrich von Schlegel mentions this episode in his *Gespräch über die Poesie* (1800; Dialogue on Poetry and Literary Aphorisms), in which he refers to Gibbon's autobiography as a book that he found "infinitely cultivated and infinitely amusing." However, the diary that Gibbon kept for 30 years shows, as often happens, the limits of the autobiographer's sincerity. The so-called act of filial submission is described there as an escape from a "dangerous and artificial girl" who had "opened my eyes upon the character of women and will serve me . . . as a preservative against the seductions of love." Infinitely cultivated, this rich and sceptical cosmopolitan was a true man of the Enlightenment. Gibbon congratulates himself on the "bounty of Nature, which cast my birth in a free and civilized country, in an age of science and philosophy, in a family of honourable rank, and decently endowed with the gifts of fortune," and is conscious of the fact that he could have been born a slave, a savage, or a peasant. All too happy to keep his place among the elite European intellectuals, Gibbon shared the attitude of his compatriot Edmund Burke toward the "disorders of France," expressing the view that the ideas of the *philosophes* should never have been put into the hands of the "blind and fanatical" multitude.

The Prelude, the autobiographical poem by Wordsworth (1770–1850), is much closer to Rousseau and to a certain idea of liberty. The first version was written in 1798, during Wordsworth and Coleridge's stay in Germany. Conceived as a history of the poet's mind and intended to serve as the prologue to *The Recluse*, a great epic poem that never went beyond the planning stage, *The Prelude* is a philosophical autobiography in free verse. Wordsworth chose poetry to express a visionary experience of the self and the world that radically transformed the very ground rules of autobiography. For this romantic, nature was no longer the antidote to civilization; it was a reservoir of "visionary gleams" and revealed to the poet a more profound, anonymous, and universal self. Here, there is virtually nothing empirical about the "I" of the author—there is no character, no psychology: this "I" is an Other and all others, an allegory of humanity itself, or a romantic counterpart of Hegel's *Weltgeist*. Wordsworth relates his experience of revolutionary France in the sublime tone of the observer, and uses a sort of novel in verse, *Vaudrecour and Julia*, for the story of his passion for Annette Vallois, a young woman from Orléans by whom he had a daughter. Thus, what he said of a French friend in Book IX, lines 304–308, of the 1805 version, can be said of him:

He thro' the events
Of that great change wander'd in perfect faith,
As through a Book, an old Romance or Tale
Of Fairy, or some dreams of action wrought
Behind the summer clouds

Coleridge's statement, in the famous Chapter XIV of *Biographia Literaria* (1817), that Wordsworth's poetic strength consisted in giving the charm of novelty to the things of everyday life, can also be applied to *The Prelude*. It may be added that as a result of the transformation of lived experience into a "supernatural" vision, the very nature of the autobiographical project was called into question; it is thus not surprising that Wordsworth's vast undertaking has had few followers in the genre of autobiography.

The Private Life of the Late Benjamin Franklin was more significant for the later evolution of the genre. When it first appeared in an abridged French version in 1791 it was immediately hailed as offering an alternative to the Rousseauist paradigm. Franklin, the typical "self-made man," describes to his son how he had become one of the leading men of his age and how he had invented his own morality and his own rules of conduct. Brought up on Bunyan, Plutarch, and Daniel Defoe, this author, who wrote most of his recollections during his stay in Paris, established the tradition of "pragmatic autobiography." For Max Weber, Franklin, who never sought to bare his soul to the reader, was a prototype of the Protestant and capitalist ethic and an incarnation of practical reason, and his *Life* ought to replace both Thomas à Kempis's *De imitatione Christi* (1441; The Imitation of Christ) and Bunyan's *The Pilgrim's Progress* (1678) in the preferences of the Western public.

Stories of the Marginalized and the Obscure

The potential for emancipation that autobiography, more than any other literary genre, offers can most fully be appreciated—albeit in a different way than in the great canonical texts—in the narratives of the lives of obscure people who came out of the shadows to claim the right to recount their distressing stories and to present them to the general public, just as Rousseau did in his *Confessions*.

It was especially around 1789 that the autobiographies of several former outcasts of society appeared, including those of the pauper Uli Bräker (1735–98), the Jew Maimon (1754–1800), and the freed slave Olaudah Equiano (ca. 1745–ca. 1801). These astonishing individuals almost give the impression of being the "primitives" of literary history. Although they had read Rousseau, the idea of emulating him never occurred to them, for they never displayed or cultivated their differences as individuals, focusing rather on their experiences as members of a different social class. Far from aspiring to the status of a singular soul, they spoke in the name of their social position, whether national or ethnic. The genius expressed in their texts is collective rather than individual: the genius of the people in the work of Bräker, who was Swiss; that of the Jews of eastern Europe in the work of Maimon; and that of Africans in the work of Equiano. Given the obvious disadvantages of their literary and linguistic training, these authors could hardly claim originality as writers. Bräker was a completely self-taught "Sunday writer," yet throughout his life he kept a diary, totaling 4,000 pages, and he used it as the basis for his *Lebensgeschichte und Natürliche Abenteuer des armen Mannes im Tockenburg* (The Life Story and Real Adventures of the Poor Man of Tockenburg). Maimon, a Polish-Lithuanian Jew, taught himself German and never wrote it correctly, while Equiano needed friends to correct his respectable but often defective English. Nevertheless, each of these writers had a tone, and therefore a style, that suited him, and each was able not only to interest his readers with the documentary value of his evidence and to fascinate them with the colorful richness of his adventures but also to move them with the "naive" expression of his sensibility.

Of these three autobiographers, Bräker was the only one who could express himself in his mother tongue. His style retains the extraordinary vivacity of spoken language and the accent of his native land. His *Lebensgeschichte* was one of those books that revealed to the public not only the condition of the poor but also their sensibility; he teaches us that the so-called simple hearts also have passions, contradictions, and a "modern" sophistication, however strong their Christian faith or their regional roots. This apparently old-fashioned text contains certain traits that herald the romantic art of Stendhal (in the description of the Battle of Lowositz and the Swiss picaro, or rogue, who deserted from the Prussian army), Machado de Assis (in the way in which the chapters are divided, and in their brevity and intensity), and Italo Svevo (in the story of Bräker's marriage).

Jewish autobiography, whether written in Yiddish or German, also developed in the age of the Enlightenment, and as a result of it. Its major representative, Maimon soon left his native Poland, where he had distinguished himself as a precocious rabbi in order to join the *Haskalah* (the Jewish Enlightenment in Berlin) and Moses Mendelssohn's circle. However, this "Jewish Faust," whose fortunes attracted the attention of Kant, Goethe, and Schiller, did not succeed in settling anywhere, nor did he make the social ascent for which he seemed to be destined by his prodigious gifts. Following Rousseau's example, Maimon prided himself on the frankness of his heart, claiming that: "Openheartedness is a main feature of my character." He also boasted of his indomitable intellectual curiosity, but he would never have dreamed of taking pride, as Rousseau did, in his lack of social graces or of boasting of his occasional moral lapses. This scholarly and rebellious man, who wrote commentaries on the great philosophers from Maimonides to Kant, was as much a "disgraceful barbarian" as a philosopher conscious of his own worth. A forceful critic of a certain rabbinical obscurantism and a staunch defender of the religion of reason that he believed could be found in Maimonides (for him the most important Jewish prophet), the free-thinking Maimon never managed to make himself acceptable either among the Maskilim, the community of enlightened Jews, or in Protestant society. Thanks to Moritz, who corrected the inaccuracies in Maimon's use of German, *Salomon Maimons Lebensgeschichte von ihm selbst geschrieben* (Salomon Maimon: An Autobiography) was published in 1792. The work is the colorful and naive account of a turbulent life that resembles many other works in this epoch, such as the memoirs of Aron Gumpertz and Lazarus Bendavid (to cite only examples from the *Haskalah*). Yet Maimon's *Lebensgeschichte* also contains a uniquely tragic quality. Enthusiasm for the Enlightenment did not provide this Eastern Jew with a viable identity, but, on the contrary, it made him into a thinker torn between two worlds.

The Interesting Narrative of the Life of Olaudah Equiano or Gustavus Vassa, the African: Written by Himself, which appeared in two volumes in London in 1789, is an exceptional and paradigmatic book from the age of the European Enlightenment. This "true history" of implausible incidents was the first political autobiography of a black African and was intended to mobilize the English-speaking public for the abolitionist cause. Born in 1745 or 1746 in what is now eastern

Nigeria, with Ibo as his mother tongue, Equiano was captured at the age of 11, transported to America on a slave ship where atrocious events occurred, was sold and sold again, and had his name changed several times. Yet thanks to his lively intelligence and to the assistance of several whites, he learned to speak, read, and write the language of his masters, and he rapidly assimilated their culture. Having succeeded in buying his freedom at the age of 21, he became a merchant and an entrepreneur, but above all a campaigner against the slave trade in both the New World and the Old. Generally straightforward and moderate, Equiano knew how to exploit pathetic images on occasion and how to use irony that is sometimes gentle and sometimes scathing. Having affirmed that his experience of the Christian religion and of a nation that exalted the dignity of human nature had largely compensated him for the loss of his homeland, he turns to the question of his own identity, in the following passage from Chapter I of his book:

> Did I consider myself an European, I might say my sufferings were great: but when I compare my lot with those of most of my countrymen, I regard myself as a *particular favourite of Heaven,* and acknowledge the mercies of Providence in every occurrence of my life.

Equiano described himself as an "unlettered African" and professed a complete lack of literary ambition, but he displayed a fine eloquence whenever he set out to promote what he called "the interests of humanity." In addition, in order to recall his childhood, of which he had no precise personal memories, he followed the example of the accounts of voyages in that period, just as he drew on Defoe's *Robinson Crusoe* (1719) to give form to the account of his own life. Equiano's autobiography, in which the word "I" encompasses an immense "we," was enormously successful in its author's lifetime. There were eight editions in Britain and one in America, and ten more were published after 1801 (the year in which it is believed he died), including translations into Dutch and German. Today Equiano's book is regarded as a classic example of the African slave narrative and the Old World itself seems to want to discover, or rediscover, this founding text of African literature, published in London long ago at the author's expense. The first French translation was published in 1987.

No less memorable than these three books are other autobiographies in which the spirit of the Enlightenment breathes, and runs out of breath. A notable example is the *Life of Theobald Wolfe Tone . . . Written by Himself and Continued by His Son, with His Political Writings, and Fragments of His Diary.* Published in two volumes by William Theobald Wolfe Tone in Washing-ton, D.C., in 1826, it is the autobiography of the great Irish patriot who served in the French army under Hoche and appealed to the French to support the cause of his people. Another such work is *Schubarts Leben und Gesinnungen: Von ihm selbst im Kerker aufgesetzt* (1791–93; Schubart's Life and Opinions: Drawn Up by Himself while in Prison), the unfinished memoirs of the unfortunate Schubart (1739–91), who ends by recanting the republican opinions for which he became a martyr. Yet another is Johann Gottfried Seume's *Mein Leben* (1808–10; My Life), the sober and bitter autobiography of a writer and traveler who abandoned 18th-century optimism but remained loyal to ideas of liberty, and whose background as a commoner made him one of those who wrote history from below. The English actor and playwright Thomas Holcroft (1745–1809), who translated works by Pierre-Augustin Caron Beaumarchais and the memoirs of Baron Trenck into English, belongs in the same category. The *Memoirs of the Late Thomas Holcroft,* an autobiography of childhood that prefigures Charles Dickens, was published in 1816 by William Hazlitt (himself the author of an autobiography, *Liber Amoris* [1823; Book of Love]). Hazlitt added to the memoirs of his friend a biography of Holcroft in which he quoted Holcroft's journal and his letters at length.

Russian literature also provides several examples of autobiographies influenced by the Enlightenment, such as the *Mémoires de l'impératrice Catherine II* (1859; Memoirs of Catherine the Great) of Catherine II, but especially *Moe vremya* (1813; My Times), the autobiography of G.S. Vinsky, a Ukrainian nobleman, to which Turgenev drew attention in 1845. For Vinsky, the reading of Buffon, Voltaire, and, above all, Rousseau was influential; he attributed a special role to childhood and even to the prenatal state, claiming to follow the example of Laurence Sterne's novel *Tristram Shandy.* Banished and demoted from his aristocratic rank following a financial scandal, Vinsky was naturally opposed to those in Russia who condemned out of hand both the *philosophes* and the French. Another Russian autobiographer, Denis Ivanovich Fonvizin (1744–92), presented himself as a somewhat ambivalent follower of Rousseau in his own *Confession sincère de mes actes et pensées* (Sincere Confession of My Acts and Thoughts). In this examination of conscience in four parts—childhood, youth, maturity, and old age—Fonvizin sought to display Christian contrition and did not dare to express the pride of the modern individual. On the other hand, enemies of the Enlightenment, such as Bolotov or G. Dobrynin, also produced autobiographical works. Between 1789 and 1816 Bolotov, who inaugurated the golden age of Russian literature, wrote a voluminous autobiography, *Zhizn i prikliucheniia Andreia Bolotova: Opisannye samim* (1870–73; The Life and Adventures of Andrei Bolotov, Written by Himself). The title itself indicates Bolotov's debt to the picaresque tradition—as well as to the French and British traditions of memoirs—in this valuable testimony of a landowner who introduced the apple into Russia, but who also insisted that the Encyclopedists and *Encyclopédie* be censored and banned and that the Freemasons be persecuted. In his *Istinnoe poviestvovanie ili Zhizn Gavrilla Dobrynina* (A True Narrative; or, The Life of Gavriil Dobrynin), Dobrynin (1752–1824), an Orthodox priest and a leading government official, also engaged in polemics against the "famous or rather infamous Jean-Jacques Rousseau" and ridiculed his Russian imitators, such as Fonvizin.

In the 19th century Aleksandr Pushkin's vigorous condemnation of autobiography (in a letter to P.A. Viazemsky, November 1825), in which he set poetic truth against Rousseau's type of sincerity, did not prevent Russians brought up on the French of the 18th century from devoting themselves to the practice of autobiography. In this respect, the trilogy *Byloe i dumy* (My Past and Thoughts) of Alexander Herzen, that passionate lover of revolutionary Paris, was exemplary.

Pedagogical Russian autobiographies that are closer to Rousseau's *Émile* than to his *Confessions* include *Zivot i prikljucenija* (Life and Adventures) by Dositej Obradovir, published in Leipzig (1783–88). This work was the sole and vibrant appeal of Obradovir, a defrocked Serb monk and priest (1739–1811), to his compatriots to follow his example and embrace the civilization of the Enlightenment. This writer wanted to bring the science and philosophy of the West to serve the national heritage, using his mother tongue to foster the emancipation of his people. With a limitless faith in the power of *Bildung*, the narrator of this *Life* resembles the protagonist of a bildungsroman (with an undeniable sense of humor typical of the picaro) when—in the wake of the desire for knowledge instilled in him by his reading and his travels—he demonstrates how to become liberated from the secular tutelage of the Church. A brilliant popularizer, Obradovir succeeded in creating a Serb literature, of which his autobiography would remain the prototype.

Autobiography and the Novel

Autobiography is both close to and distinct from such related genres as memoirs, intimate journals, and letters, but its relationship with the novel is highly paradoxical. Many if not all autobiographers could have given their books titles such as that used by Freiherr von Knigge in 1781: *Der Roman meines Lebens* (The Novel of My Life). For example, the *Vida* (Life) of Diego de Torres Villaroel (1673–1770), published between 1743 and 1758, reads like a picaresque novel,

in part because his was a picaro's life. The son of a bookseller, he tried every profession in the course of his wanderings, including village bullfighter, dance master, confidence trickster, and then teacher of mathematics, royal astrologer, priest, and who knows what else. But the *Vida* is also picaresque because this writer from Salamanca was a disciple of Francisco Gómez de Quevedo, whose *El Buscón* (1626; The Life and Adventures of Don Pablos the Sharper) served as his model. It is uncertain whether or not Torres Villaroel's *Vida* was a belated picaresque novel of the golden age of Spain or an autobiography of the Enlightenment, otherwise unknown in 18th-century Spain. Similar doubts have troubled historians of Slavic literature, who wonder whether Obradovir wrote the first autobiography or the first novel in Serbo-Croat.

This problem hardly concerned those Enlightenment autobiographers who made no secret of their affinities for the novel, and especially the picaresque novel. On the other hand, the militant advocacy of authenticity and sincerity, such as was embodied by Rousseau, went hand in hand with an antiromantic pose. That pose, it should be noted, did not prevent Rousseau and his followers from borrowing several narrative procedures from the novel, whether picaresque or not. This was why Schlegel described the link between genres that Rousseau considered incompatible as a chiasmus: for Schlegel, Rousseau's *Confessions* was an excellent novel, while his *Nouvelle Héloïse* (1761; Julie; or, The New Héloïse) was a rather mediocre one; Gibbon's *Memoirs of My Life and Writings* contained a comic novel, and so on. Conversely, Schlegel declares in his *Gespräch über die Poesie*: "the best element in the best novels is nothing else than a more or less shrouded self-confession [on the part] of the author."

Novelists, for their part, assimilated autobiographical writing. Some wrote pseudo-autobiographies or novels in the first-person voice, from which certain autobiographers in turn drew inspiration. Novelists in this vein included Courtin de Sandraz, the abbé Prévost, Alain-René Lesage, and Pierre-Carlet Chamblain de Marivaux in France; Defoe in England; and Johann Gottfried Schnabel and Christophe Martin Wieland in Germany. Other novelists inserted accounts of nonfictional lives into their novels. Thus, Tobias George Smollett included the scandalous autobiography of Frances Anne Vane, under the tantalizing title "The Memoirs of a Lady of Quality," as Chapter 88 of his novel *The Adventures of Peregrine Pickle* (1751). Goethe ennobled and purified his *Wilhelm Meisters Lehrjahre* (1795–96; Wilhelm Meister's Apprenticeship) by inserting as its sixth book the "Bekenntnisse einer schönen Seele" (Confessions of a Beautiful Soul), a monument to the memory of Susanna Katharina von Klettenberg (1723–74), a Pietist lady who had been a friend of his mother. Contemporaries took these confessions to be autobiographies, pure and simple, although Goethe constructed an autobiographical text based on the conversations and letters of this "beautiful soul."

Among the other kinds of symbiosis between the novel and autobiography, there were the various experiments of Jean Paul Richter (1763–1825). His *Konjekturalbiographie* (Conjectural Biography) fulfilled his plan "to write a novel on my future destiny," giving the preface the date of a carnival day in 1799. In another project Richter sought to alternate novel and autobiography by opposing a more or less authentic "I" with the hero of a comic novel, the Quixotic apothecary who would be the protagonist of *Der Komet* (1820–22; The Comet). Finally, the tone of his real autobiography, the fragmentary *Selberlebensbeschreibung* (1818; Autobiography), strangely resembles that of his great humorous novels and its form is also reminiscent of the art of the novelist. The narrator presents the stages of his biography in the form of lectures, assuming the role of "professor of his own history."

Many writers circumvented or distorted the autobiographical pact. For example, Mary Wollstonecraft (1759–97) left us a fragment of a hybrid text, *Mary, a Fiction*, written in 1787. In the preface, which reflects the influence of Rousseau, she asserts that "those compositions only have power to delight . . . where the soul of the author is exhibited, and animates the hidden springs." Stendhal was also fascinated by Rousseau but was anxious to avoid his grandiloquence and to relieve the blandness of autobiographical writings with a "sauce of charlatanism." In his *La vie de Henry Brulard* (The Life of Henry Brulard) Stendhal kept only the initials of his real name (Henri Beyle), thus allowing doubt to persist as to the novelistic character of his protagonist.

It fell to Goethe to take the inherent contradictions in the genre of autobiography to their logical extreme, and to invent a genuine alternative to Rousseau's *Confessions* that was literary, rather than pragmatic (as Franklin's had been). He did so in *Aus meinem Leben: Dichtung und Wahrheit* (Truth and Fiction Relating to My Life), written between 1811–14 and 1831. The "I" in Goethe's work, instead of proclaiming, exhibiting and analyzing its singularity in great detail, plays a much more unassuming role by simply giving a serene account of the organic evolution, or "entelechy," of a man who grew like a vigorous plant in the soil of his homeland, his age, and indeed the history of the whole of humanity. Goethe brought about an *Aufhebung sui generis* (unique synthesis and elevation) of the spirit of the Enlightenment; its antithetical aspect would raise generations of liberals against him. When Goethe said that his complete works were so many "fragments of a great confession," he was reminding his readers that the monopoly on truth is not reserved to intimist literature and that all the genres can work toward the same goal and serve the same cause—which for him was emphatically not that of an individual in search of his own difference.

However, Goethe's autobiographical paradigm would prove just as inimitable as Rousseau's. *Dichtung und Wahrheit* was the last of the classic autobiographies that continued to haunt those autobiographers who dreamed of eclipsing Rousseau's *Confessions* by the radicalism of their prose. For example, the failure of Charles Baudelaire's *Mon cœur mis à nu* (My Heart Laid Bare) in the mid–19th century can no doubt be attributed, at least in part, to the poet's desire—inspired by Thomas De Quincey's *Confessions of an English Opium-Eater* (1822) and by a remark in Edgar Allan Poe's *Marginalia* (1846)—to make Rousseau's book fade into insignificance.

DOLF OEHLER

See also Pietism

Further Reading

Fernández, James D., *Apology to Apostrophe: Autobiography and the Rhetoric of Self-Representation in Spain,* Durham, North Carolina: Duke University Press, 1992

Lejeune, Philippe, *Le pacte autobiographique,* Paris: Seuil, 1975

Lejeune, Philippe, *On Autobiography,* translated by Katherine Leary, Minneapolis: University of Minnesota Press, 1989

Man, Paul de, "Autobiography as De-Facement," *Modern Language Notes* 94 (1979)

Mascuch, Michael, *Origins of the Individualist Self: Autobiography and Self-Identity in England, 1591–1791,* Stanford, California: Stanford University Press, 1996; Cambridge: Polity Press, 1997

Matthews, William, *British Autobiographies: An Annotated Bibliography of British Autobiographies Published or Written before 1951,* Berkeley: University of California Press, 1955

Misch, Georg, *A History of Autobiography in Antiquity,* 2 vols., translated by E.W. Dickes, London: Routledge and Paul, 1950 (original German edition, 1907)

Morris, John N., *Versions of the Self: Studies in English Autobiography from John Bunyan to John Stuart Mill,* New York: Basic Books, 1966

Nussbaum, Felicity A., *The Autobiographical Subject: Gender and Ideology in Eighteenth-Century England,* Baltimore, Maryland: Johns Hopkins University Press, 1989

Olney, James, editor, *Autobiography: Essays Theoretical and Critical*, Princeton, New Jersey: Princeton University Press, 1980

Olney, James, editor, *Studies in Autobiography*, Oxford and New York: Oxford University Press, 1988

Pascal, Roy, *Design and Truth in Autobiography*, Cambridge, Massachusetts: Harvard University Press, and London: Routledge and Paul, 1960

Sheringham, Michael, *French Autobiography: Devices and Desires: Rousseau to Perec*, Oxford: Clarendon Press, 1993

Shumaker, Wayne, *English Autobiography: Its Emergence, Materials, and Form*, Berkeley: University of California Press, 1954

Spacks, Patricia Ann Meyer, *Imagining a Self: Autobiography and Novel in Eighteenth-Century England*, Cambridge, Massachusetts: Harvard University Press, 1976

Spengemann, William C., *The Forms of Autobiography: Episodes in the History of a Literary Genre*, New Haven, Connecticut: Yale University Press, 1980

Starobinski, Jean, *Jean-Jacques Rousseau: Transparency and Obstruction*, translated by Arthur Goldhammer, Chicago: University of Chicago Press, 1988 (original French edition, 1957)

Stauffer, Donald Alfred, *The Art of Biography in Eighteenth-Century England*, Princeton, New Jersey: Princeton University Press, 1941

Weintraub, Karl Joachim, *The Value of the Individual: Self and Circumstance in Autobiography*, Chicago: University of Chicago Press, 1978

Automaton

Automatos in Greek means "that which acts by itself." In the Aristotelian vocabulary, the word indicates any phenomenon that is "spontaneously" produced by nature. The meaning of "self-propelled device," which was unknown in antiquity, was introduced into the French language by François Rabelais during the Renaissance. In most dictionaries, "automaton" is a "term of mechanics" and in its literal sense the word denotes animals, which followers of philosopher René Descartes regarded as pure machines. More generally, however, the term is applied to any being or object that has "the principle of its own motion within itself" and has an energy source that is coextensive with the very purpose of the action. This definition is applicable to any self-propelled mechanism, from watches to rotating spits, including weight-driven clocks, snuffboxes, music boxes, mechanical instruments, and android dolls. In addition, most dictionaries mention that, figuratively, the word may denote certain human beings "lacking a will of their own," generally referring to underprivileged social groups, factory workers, or members of an army. It was in this sense that Jean-Jacques Rousseau characterized the peasants of the upper Valais as "near automatons," and Thomas Hobbes referred to "that great Leviathan they call the State" as an artificial man. In most dictionaries the making of mechanical dolls that imitate the movements of living human beings remained a division of watchmaking. The *Encyclopédie*, however, was innovative in granting a special entry to the word "android," then unknown outside francophone countries. Thereafter the original significance became outdated as the term took on the specialized meaning of machines that imitate the motion of living bodies.

The best makers of automatons in the 18th century lived in France, Britain, and Switzerland. In particular, the brilliant inventions of the French engineer Jacques de Vaucanson (1709–82) were an entirely new starting point for automatons and for mechanical music. Bernardino Baldi (1553–1617), the author of the first philosophical essay in this field, attributed the infatuation with automatons to the fascination produced in the viewer by a machine operating without the aid of an apparent energy source such as water, a horse, or the wind. In the 18th century, automatons continued to astonish, and they fascinated magicians as well. Rare and costly marvels, automatons traveled far and wide, entering every princely court, where they were a source of entertainment and were shown to distinguished visitors. However, the cultural fascination with motion during the 18th century placed the automaton in a new light. If Vaucanson's duck was surprising because of its anatomical realism, it no longer owed its success to the concealment of machinery in its body, but rather to the fact that it permitted the curious to observe its mechanical insides, now openly exhibited in every detail. The cam cylinder, James Watt's centrifugal governor, the musical comb, and even the rubber that Vaucanson used in creating robots with flexible bodies all contributed to giving life to more and more sophisticated "beings," whose graceful gestures left the grotesque gesticulations of their ancestors, the clock-tower puppets, far behind.

However, the development that revolutionized interest in automatons in the 18th century was the completely new association established by mechanistic biology between human beings and machines. The "mechanization" of the natural sciences had been advancing for some 50 years, but it was not until about 1700 that the mechanistic model triumphed in biology. If a watch could be considered a small version of the great universe, then birds, bees, and swallows were all merely complex automatons. Where earlier naturalists had seen in these flying, singing objects the perceptible expression of universal harmony, now they were interpreted as nothing more than the meaningless sounds of an impressive music box. Hermann Boerhaave, a professor of medicine in Paris, saw nothing but levers, cords, pulleys, joists, screens, reservoirs, and bellows in the human organism. Everything was merely matter and motion. Nature was uniform and continuous; its laws were the same everywhere and species differed only in the degree of complexity of their mechanism. Thus, Julien Offroy de La Mettrie in *L'homme machine* (1748; Man, a Machine) declares that man "is to the monkey . . . as the planetary pendulum of Huygens is to a watch by Julien le Roi"; and that "if Vaucanson needed more skill to make his flute player than his duck, he would have needed even more skill to make a structure that speaks: a machine that can no longer be considered an impossibility, especially in the hands of a new Prometheus." Nature and artifice were being merged, and Boerhaave's metaphors were becoming a reality. In 1744 Le Cat, the chief surgeon of the Hôtel-Dieu in Rouen, made the plan for an automaton that would have "breath, circulation, quasi digestion, secretion . . . a heart, lungs, liver, and bladder, and may God forgive us, all that follows from these. But it will have fever, it will be bled and purged, and it will resemble a human being too closely" (see Doyon and Liaigre). In 1732 a lack of money forced Vaucanson to abandon the anatomy courses offered at the Jardin du Roi (French Royal Botanical Garden) in order to become a showman of automatons. The impact of his *flûteur* (flautist) exhibited in 1738, his duck, and his drummer (1741) on the scientific community was tremendous. Voltaire spoke of a rival for Prometheus and in the *Encyclopédie* the words "android" and "automaton" became synonymous with "Vaucanson." "Android" was used as a

description of the mechanism of the flautist and the word "automaton" described the duck and the drummer. Until then, no automaton had truly played its instrument. Through the movement of fingers, lips, jaw, and tongue, the flautist produced ascending and descending tones along with the pinches, glissandos, and tremolos of an experienced player. The duck, with a truly lifelike anatomy, could stretch its neck to take seeds from a hand, swallow them, and eventually give them up, wholly digested, through the normal channels. The drummer modulated rigadoons and minuets played on the Provençal flute, a difficult instrument with three holes, the tones of which depended on the force of the breath and the half-closing of the holes.

The second half of the century saw these scientific androids multiply into a variety of species that Alfred Chapuis classified according to four functions: speaking, drawing or writing, walking, and playing an instrument. The most perfect automatons were made by the Austrian F. von Knauss (1724–89), who was, among other things, the creator of four talking heads. His creations offered a sphere that was a meter in diameter, on the side of which was seated a goddess who could write in pen with an unimaginable refinement, texts of approximately 100 characters in every known language. The watchmaker Pierre Jaquet-Droz perfected the genre of automatons that wrote or drew. His *écrivain* (writer), created in 1770, held a goose quill and was able to move its hand across a page in any direction to shape letters; it would take ink, carefully form its letters, observing downstrokes and upstrokes, and in so doing modify the pressure on the pen. The names of Henri-Louis Jaquet-Droz (Pierre Jaquet-Droz's son) and of his collaborator Jean Frédéric Leschot were associated with two masterpieces that accompanied their designer on his tours through Europe: a *dessinateur* (draftsman) that "knew" how to trace the profiles of Louis XIV and George III with extraordinary delicacy, and a female musician endowed with jointed hands, which could work the 24 keys of a harmonium and reproduce instrumental music in every detail. At the beginning of the century the artificial reproduction of the human voice had been no more than a legend to which credence was given through the myth of the talking heads of Albertus Magnus and through the research carried out by both Athanasius Kircher and Father Marin Mersenne. In 1700, however, Dodart had explained phonation through an aerodynamic doctrine in which an important role was attributed to the narrowing of the glottis. The abbé Noël-Antoine Pluche, in his *La mécanique des langues et l'art de les enseigner* (1751; How Languages Operate, and How To Teach Them), saw the lips and the glottis as nothing more than cords tightened by pegs. At the same time that research was begun on the phonetic models of primitive language, and speculations were made about vowels, the construction of a talking machine was considered a possibility. The early efforts proved to be monosyllabic, but Van Kempelen's talking head expressed itself in Latin, Italian, and French and was able to respond to several questions.

At the end of the 18th century the mechanisms animating automatons were no longer breaking new ground. Attention was focused more and more on motors that multiplied the strength of a single man by a thousand. Automatons were no longer a challenge to the discipline of mechanics and became either items of curiosity for a nostalgic elite or a type of toy that amused children up to the middle of the 20th century.

BRENNO BOCCADORO

See also Originality

Further Reading

Démoris, Réné, editor, *La machine dans l'imaginaire (1650–1800)*, Villeneuve d'Ascq, France: Université de Lille III, 1982

Doyon, André, and Lucien Liaigre, *Jacques Vaucanson, mécanicien de génie,* Paris: Presses Universitaires de France, 1966

Gallingani, Daniela, *Miti, macchine, e magie: Intrecci letterari e ipotesi scientifiche nell'età dei Lumi,* Bologna: CLUEB, 1996

Klein, Gérard, *Histoire des machines,* Paris: Livre de Poche, 1974

La Mettrie, Julien Offroy de, *Man, a Machine,* translated by Gertrude Carman Bussey, revised by Mary Whiton Calkins, Chicago: Open Court, 1927 (original French edition, 1748)

Losano, Mario G., *Storie di automi: Dalla Grecia classica alla Belle Époque,* Turin: Einaudi, 1990

B

Balkans

A Turbulent Sociopolitical Region

"The Balkans" is a useful but relatively vague term used to designate the easternmost of the three peninsulas of southern Europe. An indication of the size of the Ottoman Empire, the name "Balkan" is of Turkish origin and supplanted the Slavonic and Bulgarian expression *Stara Planina* (old mountain) while retaining the meaning of "mountain." Reference to the Balkans as a specific area came into everyday use toward the middle of the 19th century, when it came to denote a shifting geopolitical region that lacked a general appellation. In the 18th century, the standard term was "European Turkey," and one would look in vain for "the Balkans" in Bruzen La Martinière's *Grand dictionnaire géographique et critique* (1726–39; Great Geographical and Critical Dictionary) or in the *Encyclopédie.* On the other hand, in the article "Turquie" (Turkey) in the *Encyclopédie,* one finds the term "Rumelia" for the European part of the Ottoman Empire. According to Georges Castellan, "Rumeli" was a territorial whole, the old Turkish name for the Balkans, alongside "Anatolia" for the Asian part (see Castellan). Geographically, the Balkan region covers several mountain chains: the Pindus (*Pindos* in Greek), the Dinaric Alps to the west, the Rhodopes in the center and the southeast, the Carpathian Mountains, the Alps of Transylvania, and the Balkan Alps to the northeast. (In modern atlases, "the Balkans" means the European part of Turkey, Bulgaria, Greece, Albania, Romania, Yugoslavia in its truncated form comprising Serbia and Montenegro, the former Yugoslav republics of Macedonia, Bosnia-Herzegovina, and part of Croatia. Following the breakup of Yugoslavia in 1991, countries such as Slovenia and Croatia no longer wish to be identified with this geopolitical region but with that of central Europe.)

During the Enlightenment all these countries, with the exception of Turkey proper, were under foreign domination, to which the different ethnic entities adapted in varying degrees. It would be pointless to go over the political geography according to the redrawing of borders over the years, but the great differences among populations and lifestyles were readily apparent to travelers during the age of the Enlightenment. Split between the Ottoman Empire, the Habsburg empire, and, to a lesser degree, Venice, this region suffered not only from poorly defined borders but also from a lack of unity as a state. The Adriatic Sea, also known as the Gulf of Venice, washed the eastern shores of that republic's possessions, which also included the islands of the archipelago and the Peloponnesian peninsula (formerly Morea), which was handed over to the Turks in 1718. The historian may encounter parallel names, particularly for southeastern Europe, so it becomes legitimate to wonder where to locate the outposts of western Europe in relation to the East. From the end of the 17th century, what is generally referred to as Greater Europe managed to expand at the expense of the Ottoman Empire, which had attained its maximum growth on European soil during the 16th and 17th centuries and which was still a respected state, its government, above all, uncontested. Niccolò Machiavelli and Jean Bodin had both viewed Turkey as a strong state (spread over three continents) and did not count it among their examples of tyranny. However, as its conquests diminished in number Turkey became more and more vulnerable. The 18th-century European imagination thus took hold of the concept of Asian despotism, applying it to the entire region where an increasingly weak government was attempting to enforce changes that had already taken place in those countries bordering European Turkey. This form of despotism, Turkish rather than enlightened—to quote Voltaire, "There is something Turkish about outlawing the printing press"—was subjected to multiple attacks as it traversed long alternating periods of relaxation and severity. One should recall that from the time of Theodosius and the division of the Roman Empire in 395, a permanent dislocation had existed in the region, from the Pannonian plains through Bosnia to the Adriatic. The native populations of this European Turkey—Slavs, Romans, Greeks, Albanians, Jews, and others—were subjected to contradictory influences and to continual Islamization. Conversion to Islam often meant an improvement in living conditions, and it was not unusual for two religions to be practiced side by side in the Balkans. The Ottoman Turks were also favorably disposed toward the Orthodox Church, over which they could keep a tight control because the celebrated Greek Academy of the Patriarchate, heir to Byzantine teachings, was located in Constantinople (now Istanbul). Thus, in the eyes of the West, all adherents to the Orthodox religion were Greek, whether they were Greek, Serbian, Romanian, or Bulgarian.

For the various peoples of the Balkans, exposure to the Western Enlightenment came first by way of Constantinople and Saint Petersburg. Under Peter the Great (1672–1725), Russia was modernized and assumed the right to keep an ever closer watch over the Ottoman possessions, taking upon itself the responsibility to awaken the minds of the inhabitants. However, it was in the heart of the Empire, in Constantinople, that one could truly speak of an opening to Western influence, with the Tulip Age, the reign of Ahmed III (1703–30), which was brutally interrupted by an uprising against "Frankish mores." Eloquently described by Lady Mary Wortley Montagu in her *Turkish Embassy Letters* (her meeting in Belgrade with the enigmatic Ahmed Bey, originally from Bosnia, is a fine illustration), this opening seems to have coincided with a momentary laxness in Islam and with the rise of the Bektashi sect. The Bektashi were converts from affluent local families, relatively open to Western influences, and they practiced a milder version of Islam that took hold in the conquered territories, facilitating conversions as well as the regular recruitment of janissaries, who were more at ease in this willingly heterodox sect. In the heart of the Balkans, where Bosna-Saraï (now Sarajevo) was already one of the most beautiful cities in the Empire, few things changed, but the situation was quite different on the fringes.

The Emergence and Diversity of the Balkan Enlightenment

Without wishing to oversimplify ongoing profound changes, a number of generalizations can safely be made for the period up to the 1830s, leaving aside certain details in order to focus on the points of convergence. Foreign, secular domination was a unifying factor. Although they did not profess an ecumenical spirit, the two churches, Orthodox and Catholic, here served to relay the new Western ideas. During an initial phase (1700–30) there were obvious signs heralding change among the elite, who wished to keep in step with their European peers and did not display any evidence of a clear patriotic feeling for their own region. In a second phase (1730–1770/1780) it is possible to identify the signs of Westernization (synonymous with progress in general). Sometimes these signs were superficial, but they nevertheless allow us to see how new institutions (such as schools) were set up and networks of exchange (dissemination of books, adaptations of foreign works) were created. An increasingly acute sense of belonging to a nation, hitherto either unknown or unacknowledged, made people aware of their past and their cultural heritage. In a third phase (1770–1821/1830) this national consciousness, initially linked to the need for education, became the key element of an indispensable apprenticeship aimed at establishing political independence.

The peoples of the peninsula—the majority of whom were Turkish subjects and, for the most part, Christians—came under varying influences. From Venice to Constantinople, from Vienna to Buda to Ragusa (now Dubrovnik), from Kiev to Saint Petersburg, the sociocultural space was tightly controlled. With the exception of the elite, who, among these people under Turkish domination, could think in terms of the nation-state? And to which state would they belong? The Moldavian prince Dimitri Cantemir (1673–1723), who can be considered one of the enlightened monarchs of Europe, was educated in the famous academy in Constantinople but ended his life in Moscow, after very difficult times when he was a virtual hostage in the Ottoman capital. A polyglot, an Islamist, and a distinguished historian, Cantemir was elected a member of the Berlin Academy in 1714. His works include a description of Moldavia, from which he was forced to exile himself for a long period of time, and a study of the origins of Romanian, his native language. He is best known, however, for his *Incrementa atque Decrementa Aulae Othomanicae* (History of the Ottoman Empire), a major study composed while he was in Russia and translated into English as early as 1735. Notable literary figures among the first generation, who had virtually no influence in their native lands owing to the absence of any institutional support, included the Benedictine monk Anselmo Banduri (1671–1743), who "was an honor to Ragusa, his homeland," according to the chevalier de Jaucourt in the *Encyclopédie* article "Ragusa." A Byzantologist and renowned numismatist,

Banduri completed his education, primarily in Greek studies, under the direction of Jean Mabillon and Bernard de Montfaucon and composed Volumes 33 and 34 of the *Corpus Parisien* (Parisian Corpus) of Byzantine antiquities, the *Imperium Orientale* (The Byzantine Empire), published in 1711. Banduri became a member of the Académie des Inscriptions et Belles-Lettres (Academy of Inscriptions and Letters) in 1715 and was librarian to the Regent of France when he died. While he was a credit to the Republic of Ragusa-Dubrovnik (a subordinate state of the Ottoman Empire), Banduri did little to enable the republic to profit from his enlightenment and seems to have taken have little pride in his Slavic origins.

Among Greek literary figures, who were relatively more numerous than those of other ethnic backgrounds and who were educated in the best schools of both the East and the West (Russia and Constantinople), the intense intellectual activity of Eugenios Voulgaris (1716–1808) deserves mention. Born in Corfu, which was then under the Venetians, Voulgaris taught the philosophy of Gottfried Wilhelm Leibniz and Christian Wolff in Ioannina, published a work of logic in Leipzig, translated several works by Voltaire, was directly influenced by the *Traité sur la tolérance* (1763; A Treatise on Toleration), and finally tried his hand at translating John Locke into Greek. Although he was working for the good of his country, Voulgaris was accused by his detractors of neglecting the interests of his people by living abroad, largely in Russia. Finally, there was Constantinos Mavrocordatos (1711–69), one of the best-known representatives of the Greek Phanariots, who were masters of the Danubian principalities from 1709 to 1821. A convert to French reformist ideas, Mavrocordatos tried to defend the interests of his subjects and even to improve the conditions of their servitude. Prince Cantemir, the Benedictine Banduri, and the venerable Voulgaris, through their social status and their different activities, are all examples of individuals whose work, sometimes unintentionally, helped to build social and cultural bridges between the Orient and the West. Their knowledge of Greek and Arabic, and of Byzantine and Ottoman culture served as useful links between the two worlds, but had only a slight effect upon the inhabitants of their respective homelands.

The years from 1730 to 1780 were marked by a wave of renewal that had a wider influence on the multinational populations of the empire. There were three goals of note: to educate the people, to open up to reform because reform would bring prosperity to all, and to build a national consciousness. Many schools were opened under the influence of patriotic enthusiasm; the education available in these schools did not always correspond to a modern education but it served to lay the groundwork for future progress. The "Latin"

or "Latinist" schools in Transylvania and in Vojvodina (which became part of the Habsburg empire at the end of the 17th century, but under Hungarian administration) were an example of rapid westernization that did not necessarily bring progress through practical utility. In the "Latinist school" or "Slavo-Latinist School" of Karlowitz (Sremski Karlovci, the heart of "Hungarian Serbia"), founded in 1731 with the help of the Academy of Kiev, classes were taught in both Latin and German; the authors studied included Cato, Aesop, Marcus Tullius Cicero, and Ovid. The instruction in this school was intended for the Orthodox clergy, who also learned a language that had fallen into disuse, Church Slavonic, instead of using their own language. In the new political configuration on which the clergy depended, Latin became the language of administration and science and was an essential part of the education of every aspiring intellectual. After 1750 Walachia and Moldavia, similar in spirit to the Latinist schools of Transylvania, caught up very quickly. The renewed teaching of Latin in these two vassal provinces of the Ottoman Empire led to a gradual renaissance of studies in philology and history, which in turn fostered the nascent Romanian identity that still felt threatened by Greek civilizing influences. A similar resistance to the omnipresence of the Greek language in the Balkans was apparent in the work of Father Paisij (1722–89), who, having lived in the monastic communities of Mount Athos and in the Bulgaro-Serbian monastery of Hilendar, attempted to formulate the basic elements of a patriotic education in his History of the Slavo-Bulgarian People (1762). Paisij insisted upon the use of the Bulgarian language and conveyed love of country to his readers, advising them to be proud of their glorious history and to resist the temptation to seek their own identity within Greek culture. In his opinion, authentic values were to be found in the rustic life of the Bulgarian peasantry. The work circulated in manuscript form until 1844. The number of copies (more than 60) was proof of how widespread this mode of cultural dissemination was in the Balkan region, often owing to the absence of printing presses with Cyrillic characters. Handwritten texts passed from hand to hand were a way to recreate, in emblematic form, the link between traditional and learned culture.

Moreover, there was no clear dividing line between those works considered to be popular literature and those belonging to the domain of scholarly literature, thanks to some interesting crossovers. Classical texts were well represented through authors of antiquity and the European Middle Ages and were used as obligatory cultural references. These works included Aesop's *Fables*, *Le roman d'Alexandre* (12th century; The Romance of Alexander), and various Greek and Latin texts. Contemporary works inspired by the classics served a similar purpose, such as Fénelon's *Les aventures de Télémaque* (1699; The Adventures of Telemachus) or Jean-François Marmontel's *Bélisaire* (1767; Belisarius), which were printed in numerous vernacular translations. The Serbian translation of *Bélisaire* dates from 1777, the Romanian one from 1782, and Hungarians read the novel in their own language as early as 1769. In addition to the taste for classical works or for those devoted to a glorious past, a new practical and critical spirit ensured the publication of practical books (dealing with housekeeping instruction, agriculture, etc.) that tended to supplant the numerous sacred works that had been prevalent up until then. M.A. Relkovic (1732–98), originally from Slavonia (which was recovered from the Turks in 1699) and an officer in the Empress Maria-Theresa's army, inaugurated a syncretic genre that combined references to mythology and to Georgian poems with a taste for the decasyllable of popular verse, thereby creating a work that was very popular with the public and that celebrated the benefits of both work and education. The *Satir iliti divlji covik* (1762; The Satyr; or, The Wild Man), written in a Croatian dialect of Serbo-Croat, was so fulfilling to readers desperate for practical texts that it was adapted into the Slavonian dialect in 1793 and 1807. Further examples of cultural exchange within the region are the numerous translations into Romanian of works of general education, and collections of fables by the father of the Serbian Enlightenment, Dositej Obradovic (1742–1811).

However, the main effort in education was devoted to the reconstruction of a respectable past, a reference point that was indispensable to all these peoples who, far too often, had to rely on cartoon-like popular prints representing traditional life to portray their history. These images were frequently culled from a collective memory of great deeds and were founded, for the most part, in heroic epics. Thus, the commendable work of compilation carried out in the 1780s by monks such as the Serb J. Rajic (1726–1801) or the Bulgarian Spiridon of Gabrovo served to record the past of various Slavic peoples. The need to rethink the past where facts were concerned was far less pronounced among the Greeks, and the Phanariot D. Katartzis (1730–1807) provided an early example of personal reflection on the origins of the Greek nation, one that went contrary to Western historiography. Rhigas Velestinlis (1757–98) and Adamantios Koraïs (1748–1833) enabled the Greek people not only to discover those ideas that were popular in Europe during the Enlightenment but also to admire the example of the French Revolution and to anticipate the benefits of the victories of Napoleon's armies. Velestinlis's project for a Balkan federation did not come to fruition: he died a national hero, even a Balkan hero, in Belgrade, which was then a Turkish city. Koraïs advised his compatriots to follow the example of the enlightened West, denouncing the role of the clergy who were, in his opinion, ignorant but all-powerful. He died in Paris.

Early in the 19th century came the Serbian and Greek uprisings: the first Serbian uprising under Karageorge (1804), the second under Milos Obrenovic (1815), then the Greek revolution of 1821, followed by Greek independence in 1826. The major accomplishments of the French Revolution had found fertile ground. Other peoples would have to wait longer for independence. The Albanian renaissance had only just begun, and the famous remark of Naum Vegilharxhi (1797–1854) could be applied to all those who had found their most noble ideals in the Enlightenment: "Nothing is more beautiful for a people and for a language than to have their own literature." By 1800, the peoples of the Balkan region had become conscious that they belonged to a state, to a nationality and even to a nation, but they had not yet become nationalists.

A Plurality of Cultural Worlds

During the Enlightenment Europe had grown considerably but was no longer, as it had been during the classical era, a Christian Europe set in opposition to an Islamic Orient. The shimmering East that had attracted many observers eager to study non-European societies now seemed closer than it once had: it began at the Balkans. Boucher de La Richarderie, in his *Bibliothèque universelle des voyages* (1808; Universal Travel Library), was probably right in his claim that "no country in Europe, not even Italy and Switzerland, has received as many visitors of all classes as European Turkey." Admittedly, considerable diversity remained from one region to the next, meaning that the accounts left by travelers were not particularly reliable for these account depended greatly on the localities the authors had visited. Nevertheless, sincere interest tinged with good intentions and scientific curiosity enabled Western visitors to learn more and more about European Turkey, since in most cases that is where they traveled. It was also becoming apparent how much latitude the Turks gave the Christians to practice their faith. After Lady Mary Wortley Montagu, it was the comte de Bonneval who became the greatest champion of the Orient, to such a degree that he eventually converted to Islam in 1729; this greatly assisted the Turks in their quest for military and strategic modernization.

In his article in the *Encyclopédie* Jaucourt discusses the different oriental mentalities, which varied from one region to another: "The Turks of Asia greatly prize their tranquility; those of Albania, however, and other parts of Illyria, find an active and laborious life more to their taste." The Bektashi, for example, glorified work. Such notions might be compared to the various images of the "wisdom of the East" picked up by travelers to Constantinople and briefly sketched in the last pages of Voltaire's *Candide* (1759). Refusing to see only ignorance and decline among the Turks, Jaucourt remarks that they "have among them no scholars who lack a profound knowledge of the Turkish language as well as Persian and Arabic" and that "if they do not publish many works, it is so that they will not prevent their copyists, of whom there are a great many, from earning a living." The philosopher-observer saw this region in all of its disconcerting variety but, for lack of deeper knowledge, took only a superficial interest in it. The man of the Balkans, in a felicitous phrase of the Enlightenment, could feel at the same time Albanian and Venetian, Montenegrin and Dalmatian, Catholic and Muslim in his loyalties, not as a matter of choice but according to the alternating needs and moods of his rulers. One such man was Stjepan Zanovic (1751–86), a Catholic Slav of the southern coast who wrote in French and was a staunch Voltairean and who explained his difficult allegiances to anyone who cared to listen. Zanovic called himself a Turk but felt at ease only when far from the Balkans. Strategists and politicians were of course quick to realize the importance of what was at stake in the region. Revolutionary France, from 1793 onward, was interested in the Balkans (and in Bosnia in particular), hoping to find a way to thwart the Austrian influence there.

GABRIJELA VIDAN

See also Islam; Orient and Orientalism

Further Reading

Castellan, Georges, *History of the Balkans: From Mohammed the Conqueror to Stalin,* Boulder, Colorado: East European Monographs, 1992 (original French edition, 1991)

Clogg, Richard, editor, *Balkan Society in the Age of Greek Independence,* London: Macmillan, and New York: Barnes and Noble, 1981

Georgescu, Vlad, *Political Ideas and the Enlightenment in the Romanian Principalities, 1750–1831,* Boulder, Colorado: East European Quarterly, 1971

Henderson, G.P., *The Revival of Greek Thought, 1620–1830,* Albany: State University of New York, 1970; Edinburgh: Scottish Academic Press, 1971

Hroch, Miroslav, *Social Preconditions of National Revival in Europe: A Comparative Analysis of the Social Composition of Patriotic Groups among the Smaller European Nations,* Cambridge and New York: Cambridge University Press, 1985

Jelavich, Charles, and Barbara Jelavich, editors, *The Balkans in Transition: Essays on the Development of Balkan Life and Politics since the Eighteenth Century,* Berkeley: University of California Press, 1963

Kitromilides, Paschalis M., *Enlightenment, Nationalism, Orthodoxy: Studies in the Culture and Political Thought of South-eastern Europe,* Aldershot and Brookfield, Vermont: Variorum, 1994

Les Lumières et la formation de la conscience nationale chez les peuples du sud-est européen, Bucharest: Association Internationale d'Études du Sud-Est Européen, 1970

Stoianovich, Traian, *A Study in Balkan Civilization,* New York: Knopf, 1967

Sugar, Peter F., *Southeastern Europe under Ottoman Rule, 1354–1804,* Seattle: University of Washington Press, 1977

Sugar, Peter F., and Ivo J. Lederer, *Nationalism in Eastern Europe,* Seattle: University of Washington Press, 1969

Warnier, Raymond, "La découverte des pays balkaniques par l'Europe occidentale de 1500 à 1815," *Cahiers d'histoire mondiale* 2, no. 4 (1955)

Ballistics

Ballistics is the study of the motion of projectiles. This study engenders two kinds of problems: those related to the analysis of the trajectory described by a projectile, known as "exterior ballistics," which today belongs to the field of classical mechanics; and those related to propulsion—for instance, the propulsion of a ball in the barrel of a cannon, which is known as "interior ballis-tics," and which today falls into the domains of chemistry and thermodynamics. Galileo Galilei (1564–1642) is usually considered the founder of the science of exterior ballistics—the study of the trajectory described by a projectile. In the Fourth Day of his *Discorsi e dimostrazioni matematiche intorno a due nuove scienze* (Dialogues concerning Two New Sciences), published in

Leiden in 1638, Galileo expounded his theory of the parabolic motion of projectiles. In that presentation, the Italian scientist completely overturns the traditional interpretations based on Aristotle's distinction between "natural motion" (that is, the motion of bodies toward their natural place, such as the center of the Earth) and "violent motion" (that is, motion that needs external intervention in order for it to be counteracted, and particularly to counteract its natural motion). In Aristotelian theory, supplemented by the work of Niccolò Tartaglia (c. 1500–57) among others, the trajectory is split into three parts: between the two rectilinear parts (the oblique one, which corresponds to the projectile's initial violent motion, and the vertical one, which corresponded to its natural final motion in its fall), there is a middle phase, a sort of curvilinear "connector-link." This theory comprises a complicated sort of assemblage of motions that are intrinsically different from one another.

Rejecting the distinction between violent motion and natural motion (although that distinction persisted in treatises on artillery up to the beginning of the 18th century), Galileo proposed that the fall on the inclined plane possesses the same properties as the vertical fall, even though the "acceleration" of the former diminishes with the angle of inclination. Finally, on a horizontal plane, the motion is uniform. Therefore, when the moving object reaches the extremity of this plane, its uniform and rectilinear motion (which, given his understanding of the principle of inertia, Galileo calculated by mathematical approximation) combines with the motion of the fall, and the moving object thus describes a parabolic trajectory. However, this solution does not take into account the resistance caused by air; the true trajectory of a projectile cannot be a parabola. Aware of this difficulty, Galileo suggested that this resistance causes a certain deformation of the trajectory: "As for perturbation due to the resistance of the medium, it is most important, and yet, because of the variable forms it assumes, it is impossible to reduce this perturbation to fixed laws."

The science of ballistics developed precisely out of the process of establishing these "fixed laws." At the same time, artillery experts had the opportunity to construct tables of satisfactory projections based on the theory. The realization of these goals, however, did not occur until the very end of the 18th century, following the work of Benjamin Robins (1707–81) and Leonhard Euler (1707–83).

In 1683, in Paris, François Blondel (1618–86), a member of the Académie Royale des Sciences de Paris (Royal Academy of Sciences), published his *Art de jeter les bombes* (The Art of Launching Bombs), which had a clear purpose: the application to military science, and more specifically to artillery, of the chief findings in parabolic ballistics established during the first half of the 17th century by Galileo, Evangelista Torricelli (1608–48), and Father Marin Mersenne (1588–1648). Blondel's book had a cool reception among the artillery specialists for whom it was primarily intended. For instance, it is significant that in his *Mémoires d'artillerie* (Artillery Reports), published in Paris in 1697 and again in 1707, Surirey de Saint Rémy categorically rejected the excessively scholarly works of Blondel and therefore those of the ballistics experts of the 17th century. Moreover, Surirey's conservatism led him to promote the most traditional laws of firing, those used by the king's bombardiers. This very guarded attitude toward Blondel's book was quite typical. B. Forest de Belidor reinforced this attitude in his *Bombardier français* (French Bombardier), published in Paris in 1731:

> The Académie Royale des Sciences . . . applied itself to perfecting the art of launching bombs, and F. Blondel, one of its members, wrote a book about it in 1683. . . . The little use that has been made of it hardly corresponded to what [the great geometricians] must have hoped . . . seemingly they have had the misfortune not to be understood by those for whom they had undertaken the work.

A similar situation occurred in England after the publication in London in 1674 of Robert Anderson's book, *The Genuine Use and Effects of the Gunne*, which, like Blondel's book, became a reference work restricted solely to parabolic ballistics. Anderson's book was not able to arouse any greater interest among the practitioners of the art. A solution to the problem of the nonparabolic trajectory of a projectile in a resistant medium therefore became a pressing matter. Yet that was only a first step: if the findings were to be useful to artillerymen, it was equally necessary to discover how to determine the velocity of projection of the missile—a velocity that depended on the way in which combustion occurred inside the barrel. The problems that had to be solved therefore concerned both interior and exterior ballistics.

After a few insignificant attempts, Sir Isaac Newton returned in 1684 to his study of the trajectory described by projectiles in resistant medium, in a treatise, *De motu* (On Motion), that laid the groundwork for the composition of his *Principia Mathematica Philosophiae Naturalis* (1687; Mathematical Principles of Natural Philosophy). In Problems 6 and 7 in *De motu*, Newton treated, respectively, the case of uniform rectilinear motion and the case of varying ascending and descending motion, using the hypothesis that resistance is proportional to velocity. Then, on the basis of these results, he tackled the question of oblique motion. Other hypotheses regarding the laws of the resistance of the medium would be envisaged in the first three sections of Book II of his *Principia*. In particular, Newton examined the motion of projectiles in mediums where the law of resistance is proportional to the velocity, then to the square of the velocity, then finally, to a combination of the two. In Section I he dealt with the law of linear resistance in the three types of motion: in uniform rectilinear motion, in vertical motion, and in oblique motion by means of a synthesis of the preceding two. In Section II he moved on to the study of the quadratic law. First, he dealt with uniform rectilinear motion, then with vertical motion, but only after he had introduced the famous preliminary proposition or Lemma II, whose algorithmic style stresses that the methods of pure infinitesimal geometry do not suffice to solve certain problems in the science of motion. He then avoided addressing the difficult problem of the oblique shot by posing what today is called the inverse ballistic problem. In Section III Newton examined only rectilinear motion and vertical motion.

From around 1675 to 1680, Christiaan Huygens (1629–95) undertook a study of the same questions as part of his research conducted at the Académie Royale des Sciences in Paris. However, he published it in Leiden only in 1690, in his *Discours de la cause de la pesanteur* (Discourse on the Cause of Gravity), which appeared after his *Traité de la lumière* (Treatise on Light). The introduction by Gottfried Wilhelm Leibniz (1646–1716) of the new methods of differential and integral calculus, in two "Mémoires" (Reports) published in 1684 and 1686 in the *Acta Eruditorum* (Annals of Scholars), led both Leibniz and Pierre Varignon (1654–1722) to apply these new mathematical methods to some aspects of their studies of the motion of projectiles. Between 1707 and 1711, in the collected *Mémoires* of the Académie Royale des Sciences, Varignon published a series of 12 often very long reports concerning the motion of projectiles in resistant mediums. His results are organized according to a general formula that can be written without excessive modernization as follows:

$$\frac{d^2x}{dt^2} = \frac{du}{dt} = -k\mathrm{F}(u) + \mathrm{f}(t)$$

where $\mathrm{F}(u)$ represents the resistance exerted by the atmospheric medium in proportion to the velocity u; $\mathrm{f}(t)$ represents the acceleration of the initial motion; and k represents a ballistic coefficient. With this formula Varignon solved the bulk of the problems in what was known as "rectilinear ballistics" (uniform motion; vertical motion). The questions of oblique propulsion and of curvilinear ballistics were much trickier, in particular in cases where the resistance was no longer simply pro-

portional to the velocity. Jean Bernoulli (1667–1748) provided one of the most important solutions during a violent polemic with John Keill (1671–1721), regarding the quarrel over whether Newton or Leibniz had first discovered differential and integral calculus. In two "Mémoires" published in 1719 and 1721 in the *Acta eruditorum,* Bernoulli gives the solution to the ballistics problem in which the resistance exerted by the medium when the propulsion is oblique is equivalent to the *2n* power of the velocity.

Theoretical ballistics underwent a profound change at that time, in the sense that during the course of the 18th century it slowly came to be of use to artillerymen. As mentioned above, this change was essentially the work of two men, Robins and Euler. The former published *New Principles of Gunnery* in London in 1742, a work that constituted the primary treatise on experimental interior and exterior ballistics. His experimental method was based on the use of the ballistic pendulum, in which the mechanical effect of a ball striking a compound pendulum made it possible to find the ball's velocity at the moment of impact. The ballistic pendulum thus provided the means of clearly separating the fields of interior and exterior ballistics, since the instrument enabled researchers to establish the value of the initial velocity—which was the ultimate goal of interior ballistics and the starting point for exterior ballistics.

At the request of King Frederick II of Prussia, Robins's work was quickly translated into German by Euler, as early as 1745, with Euler adding a lengthy mathematical commentary to his translation. Over the following years, he then pursued his own work on the mathematical solution of equations of motion, within the framework of ballistic theory. In 1753 he published his decisive text, written in French, in the *Mémoires de Berlin,* published by the Berlin Academy of Sciences: "Recherches sur la véritable courbe que décrivent les corps jetés dans l'air ou dans un autre fluide quelconque" (Research on the True Curve Described by Bodies Projected into the Air or into Any Other Fluid).

Thanks to the work of Robins and Euler, considerable progress was made in both exterior and interior ballistics. In contrast to what was seen at the end of the 17th century, exterior ballistics received a generally favorable response from artillerymen in the 18th century. One of the reasons for their approval was that during that century practitioners of this art greatly increased their technical competence. This improvement can be attributed above all to the emergence of the various schools of artillery and military engineering, which were capable of training highly qualified military engineers. Thus, a discipline emerged in the second half of the century that united the most advanced mathematical research, often very sophisticated experimental apparatuses, and a preoccupation with the rapid application of technology. A certain modern conception of scientific work was in the process of being born.

MICHEL BLAY

See also Army; Fortification; Mechanics, Analytic

Further Reading

Blay, Michel, *La naissance de la mécanique analytique: La science du mouvement au tournant des XVIIe et XVIIIe siècles,* Paris: Presses Universitaires de France, 1992

Charbonnier, Prosper Jules, *Essais sur l'histoire de la balistique,* Paris: Société d'Éditions Géographiques, Maritimes et Coloniales, 1928

Dugas, René, *Mechanics in the Seventeenth Century: From the Scholastic Antecedents to Classical Thought,* translated by Freda Jacquot, Neuchâtel: Éditions du Griffon, and New York: Central Book, 1958 (original French edition, 1954)

Hall, Alfred Rupert, *Ballistics in the Seventeenth Century: A Study in the Relations of Science and War with Reference Principally to England,* Cambridge: Cambridge University Press, 1952

Truesdell, Clifford Ambrose, *Essays in the History of Mechanics,* Berlin and New York: Springer-Verlag, 1968

Ballooning

Jean Starobinski closes his essay *L'invention de la liberté* (1964; The Invention of Liberty, 1700–1789) with a discussion of a painting by Francesco Guardi, *L'ascension d'un ballon sur le canal de la Giudecca à Venise* (Ascent of a Balloon over the Giudecca Canal in Venice). For Starobinski this picture symbolizes the triumph of the Enlightenment: a victory of will and knowledge over the ponderousness of matter and tradition, but also a triumph of celebration and pleasure over serious-mindedness. Hot-air balloons had taken Europe by storm, and by the end of the century they had become a symbol of a new mastery over nature and a tangible sign of modernity made accessible to the public in the form of a spectacle. The French word for balloon, *montgolfière,* is derived from the family name of Joseph-Michel Montgolfier (1740–1810) and Jacques-Étienne Montgolfier (1745–99), who were the sons of a paper merchant near Lyon. Recent discoveries that had made it possible to distinguish "different kinds of air"(gases), and thus to measure their densities, led the Montgolfier brothers to inflate paper-covered canvas "globes" with hot air. In June 1783 they presented at Annonay a device that they called "diostatic" or "aerostatic." The discovery interested scientists such as Faujas de Saint-Fond and Jacques Charles, who, on the Champ de Mars in August 1783, launched a hydrogen-filled balloon made of silk coated with a rubber-based varnish to make it airtight. Demonstrations by the Montgolfier brothers were repeated before members of the Académie Royale des Sciences and before the French king Louis XVI and his court at Versailles. Next, Jean-François Pilatre de Rozier attempted manned flights using captive balloons. Then, on 21 November 1783, Pilatre de Rozier and the marquis d'Arlandes flew some six miles in a free-floating balloon. Jacques Charles and his mechanic, Noël Robert, followed suit on 1 December 1783. In January 1784 Joseph de Montgolfier, recently ennobled by Louis XVI, ascended with several passengers at Lyon.

In Volume 10 of the *Tableau de Paris* (1788; Panorama of Paris), Louis-Sébastien Mercier comments on the public's reaction on 1 December 1783:

> Once you have witnessed this spectacle, there is nothing left to see in terms of a vast assembly, surging and shifting. Two hundred thousand people, arms raised to the sky in surprise, admiration, astonishment, and joy, some weeping with fright for the dauntless physicists, others falling to their knees, choked with surprise, terror, and emotion.

Success gave rise to competition and conflict, all the more intense because the high costs involved in fabricating balloons meant that subsidies or subscriptions were necessary, and entrepreneurs were eager to exploit public expectations. The royal government and the members of the affluent classes showed their interest through their financial contributions. The princes Thurn und Taxis financed a *Luftmachine* (air machine) that never flew over Augsburg but nevertheless galvanized the German public during its construction and trial runs. In fact, the fashion spread across all of Europe and even to Mexico and the United States. However, the first accidents made the fragility of these devices quite clear. On 15 June 1785 Pilatre de Rozier and Pierre-Ange Romain were killed while attempting to cross the English Channel. François de Zambeccari, a pioneer of flights in England and then in Italy, burned to death in his balloon in 1812. Jean-Pierre-François Blanchard, who had turned professional balloonist after successfully crossing the Channel, perfected the parachute. According to Mercier, it was Blanchard who "without blanching, showed man at his proudest, on the eagle's route across the plains of the sky and crossing over the seas' tumultuous strait, 34 times the fortunate victor over the perils surrounding him."

The French Revolution exploited the new invention for its public celebrations and as a means of military observation. Under the Empire a project was established, on paper, for 100 balloons to be used in an invasion of England. These balloons were referred to as *montgolfières* or, alternatively, as *thilorières* after Thilorier, who had devised the plan. While practical exploitation of the invention remained limited and its use in scientific experiments, as foreseen by Saussure, did not materialize, it had a significant impact on the cultural imagination of the time. The heavens, which had always been reserved for the Almighty, seemed to be undergoing a sort of domestication, as the lightning rod reduced the dangers of thunderstorms and balloons enabled people to move about in the air. The most fanciful flights that had been dreamed of by novelists such as Cyrano de Bergerac now seemed possible. However, the symbolism of the invention of balloons cannot be separated from the phenomenon of fashion and high society. The balloon also belonged to the world of spec-

tacles, of aesthetic pleasure. Patrick Wald Lasowski associates "this escape from the Earth, this transgression of all laws, this detachment of a body toward the sky" with a libertine ideal of lightness, radiance, and mental prowess. Since England appeared to be less interested than France in ballooning experiments, the *montgolfières* came to embody a particularly French charm or frivolousness, reflected in the *Correspondance littéraire* of December 1783:

> Les Anglais, nation trop fière
> S'arrogent l'empire des mers;
> Les Français, nation légère,
> S'emparent de celui des airs.

(The English, with customary pride of place / Would rule the seas, all seven; / The French, admittedly a lighter race, / Would rather soar in heaven.) Aesthetically, the experience of the aerial panorama suited the taste of the times for mountainous summits and landscapes. Both art and literature abounded with "bird's eye view" or images that seemed to be captured "in flight": the very act of seeing expressed a will to seize and master a larger reality.

MICHEL DELON

Further Reading

Clement, Pierre-Louis, *Montgolfières (Hot Air Ballons)*, Paris: Tardy, 1982

Faure, Michel, *Les frères Montgolfier et la conquête de l'air,* La Calade and Aix-en-Provence, France: Edisud, 1983

Gillispie, Charles Coulston, *The Montgolfier Brothers and the Invention of Aviation*, Princeton, New Jersey: Princeton University Press, 1983

Banking. *See* Credit and Banking

Barbarian and Savage

Overview

The Impact of Voyages of Exploration

The concept of "barbarians" was born in ancient Greece and there obtained its first significant meaning, to which the age of the Enlightenment made constant reference. The contrast between Greeks and "barbarians," which is found in the works of Herodotus and Thucydides, in particular, and was taken up again by Roman writers, specifically Tacitus, had its roots in the Greek civilization's sense of superiority over other cultures and in the acknowledgment of a difference in linguistic competency. "Barbarians" were those who had not mastered the Greek language or who used it very imperfectly. Thus, the "Barbares" (Barbarians) article in the *Encyclopédie* (1751–65) states that the Greeks considered all "peoples having neither the politeness of the Greeks nor a language as pure and as prolific as theirs" to be "barbarians" and adds, "in this respect, the Romans imitated them, for they, too, called every other people 'barbarian' with the exception of the Greeks, whom they recognized as a learned and civilized nation. It is rather like us French ourselves, who see everything that is different from our own customs as crude." The concept of "barbarians" was invested with a radically new meaning in the wake of European explorers' first voyages to the New World and their discovery of the sea routes to Asia in the 15th century. At first numerous authors associated the notion of the barbarian with the word "savage," which originated in Italian and was etymologically based on the Latin word *salvaticus* (inhabitant of the woods). The *Dictionnaire de Trévoux* (1771; Dictionary of Trévoux) gives the name "savage" to persons or peoples who are "wild and unapproachable; who have not been tamed," specifying that "it is also used for nomadic peoples who have no settled dwellings, religion, law, or discipline. . . . Almost all America was found to be inhabited by *savages*. Most *savages* are cannibals. *Savages* go naked and are hirsute, being covered with hair." Thus, from the 16th through the 18th century, authors reinstated these terms inherited from antiquity, within a completely new geographic framework—that of the Americas, Africa, and the Indian and Pacific Oceans—and associated them directly with European plans for conquest and colonization. The entries for "savage" and "barbarian" in 18th-century dictionaries attest to this association with conquest, as they reestablish the meanings these terms had been given by Greek and Latin authors and integrate the discovery of peoples overseas. The article

"Barbare" in the 1753 edition of the *Dictionnaire de Trévoux* takes this term to mean a "foreigner who comes from a distant country, who is savage, impolite, cruel, and who has customs far different from our own," thereby closely associating the two concepts of "savage" and "barbarian." The article also designates Teutons, infidels, Muslims, Tatars, and Turks as "barbarians," individuals who demonstrate particularly cruel and inhuman behavior (Medea; a tyrannical father or prince). However, the peoples of the Americas appear as the very incarnation of savage and barbarian peoples in the modern era: "The Savages of America are extremely *barbarian*."

At the same time, the age of discovery gave birth to a powerful desire to acquire knowledge about the colonized peoples known as "savages" and provoked philosophical, political, and anthropological thinking regarding them. This determination to describe the mores and customs of indigenous peoples, their languages, their housing, and their economic life, was motivated both by an undeniable fascination with these peoples on the part of the authors and the public and by very pragmatic considerations aimed at improving the government and economic and military exploitation of colonized countries and peoples. This double motivation permeates innumerable stories of the colonies, including the *Historia general de las Indias* (1552; General History of the Indies) by Lopéz de Gomára, translated into French in 1584, or the *Histoire naturelle et morale des îles Antilles de l'Amérique* (1658; A Natural and Moral History of the West Indies) by Jean-Baptiste Du Tertre; geographic and anthropological works, such as the *Naukeurige beschrijvinge der Africanische gewesten* (1668; Description of Africa) by the Dutchman O. Dapper, translated into French in 1686, and the *Les moeurs des sauvages américains, comparées aux moeurs des premiers temps* (1724; Customs of the American Indians Compared with the Customs of Primitive Times) by Father Joseph-François Lafitau, which appeared in several Dutch and German translations; and a great many of the accounts of travelers and explorers of the 16th through the 18th centuries, such as those by Christopher Columbus, Jacques Cartier, and Robert Challe (1690–91) in the Americas or by P.-F.-X. Charlevoix in the East Indies (1744). The pragmatic objective of certain writers found its most elementary and crude expression in the wording of documents issued by colonial administrations relating to the census or to the education and employment of the colonized populations, such as the *Recensement général fait au mois de novembre 1708 de tous les sauvages de l'Acadie . . . Récapitulation à la fin de la quantité d'hommes et de garçons capables d'aller à la guerre* (General Census Taken in the Month of November 1708 of All the Savages of Acadia . . . Followed by a Summary of the Number of Men and Boys Capable of Going to War). Through this documentation, the French colonial administration in Canada sought to assess the military and economic power of the subjugated Indians.

From the 16th century onward, the philosophical, political, and anthropological discourses with regard to "savage" peoples were filled with often radically critical appraisals of colonial expansion and its practices. The work of the Spanish bishop Bartolomé de las Casas, particularly his pamphlet *Breve relación de la destrucción de las Indias* (1542; The Devastation of the Indies: A Brief Account), translated into French in 1579 and continually republished during the age of the Enlightenment, was a direct attack on the inhuman nature of the Spanish conquest. In the name of Christian values that assume the basic equality of all people, the pamphlet demanded a policy of religious education of the Indians; this vision was in part realized in the Jesuit colonies in Paraguay. The *Comentarios reales de los Incas* (1608–09; Royal Commentaries of the Incas) by the Inca Garcilaso de la Vega, translated into French in 1633 under the title *Histoire des Incas rois du Pérou* (History of the Inca Kings of Peru) and reprinted in 1704 and 1727, had a considerable influence on Enlightenment writers' understanding of Inca civilization. The *Comentarios* demonstrated that the indigenous cultures of the Andes, far from being savage and barbarian, constituted advanced civilizations comparable to those of Europe.

Michel Eyquem de Montaigne, whose work is deeply marked by the traumatic experience of the Wars of Religion in France (1562–98), reverses the traditional hierarchy established between "civilized peoples" and "barbarian peoples" in the chapters "Des cannibales" (On Cannibals) and "Des coches" (On Vehicles) in his *Essais* (1580–95; Essays). He bases his judgments on extensive readings of travel accounts and on his experience of an encounter in Rouen with North American Indians: "We may well call them 'barbarian' where rules of reasoning are concerned, but not where it concerns ourselves, who surpass them in every kind of barbarity." Montaigne's introduction of a fundamentally critical perspective with regard to the colonial conquest and his idealization of the Noble Savage who embodies a more humane, more egalitarian, and happier society than does civilized man exerted a considerable influence upon the thinking of the Enlightenment. This is reflected in the countless translations of his work and the commentaries upon it, in all the major European

languages, as well as the continual reprints in France, where at least 13 new editions were published between 1724 and 1801.

Enlightenment Figures

The *Dialogues curieux entre un voyageur et un sauvage de bon sens, qui a voyagé* (1703; Curious Dialogues between a Traveler and a Savage with Common Sense, Who Has Seen the World) by the baron de La Hontan—a French officer of Protestant origins who had served in Canada between 1683 and 1693—pick up on Montaigne's vision and expand it by way of personal experience. Through a series of conversations—fictional, although grounded in reality—between a baron with the same name as the author and a Huron chief named Adario, who has traveled in Europe, La Hontan presents the laws, the forms of sociability, and the moral code of Huron society. He constantly compares them to French customs, which generally appear to be more heavily imprinted with superstitions, less reasonable and less adapted to the natural needs of mankind.

Denis Diderot, in his *Supplément au voyage de Bougainville* (1774; A Supplement to Bougainville's Travels), pursues a similar goal when, through fictitious dialogues between the inhabitants of Tahiti and the French traveler comte de Bougainville, he compares the far more liberal and rational mores and political principles of the inhabitants of Polynesia to those of the European conquerors, who are superior only in military matters. The words Diderot puts in the mouth of an old Tahitian man, as he speaks to Bougainville in the name of his people, take on a virulently anticolonial tone:

And you, leader of the bandits who obey you, remove your ship from our shore immediately—we are innocent; we are happy; and you can only harm our happiness. We follow the pure instinct of nature, and you have tried to erase the character of our souls. Here everything belongs to us, but you have been preaching to us about a difference between "mine" and "yours," a difference we do not understand.

Diderot's text can be related to the anticolonial discourse of the end of the 18th century—particularly the *Histoire philosophique et politique des établissements et du commerce des Européens dans les deux Indes* (1770; A Philosophical and Political History of the Settlements and Trade of the Europeans in the East and West Indies), which he had coauthored; to Louis-Sébastien Mercier's *L'an 2440: Rêve s'il en fut jamais* (1771; Astraea's Return; or, The Halcyon Days of France in the Year 2440: A Dream); to the work of the abbé Grégoire; and, finally, to utopian literature, in which the character of the "noble savage" occupies a central role, becoming the idealized antithesis of Western civilization. This is true, for example, of Marivaux's *L'île des esclaves* (1724; The Island of the Slaves), P. de la Roche-Tilhac's *Histoire des révolutions de Tahiti* (1782; History of the Revolutions in Tahiti), and *Omai; or, A Trip round the World* (1785) by the Scotsman John O'Keefe. J.G. Schnabel's utopia, *Insel Felsenburg* (1731; The Island of Felsenburg), associates motifs taken from Daniel Defoe's *Robinson Crusoe* (1719), in which the "savage" remains a secondary and dominated character, with the vision of a utopia located on exotic and blissful islands.

From the beginning of the 18th century onward, the enhanced prestige of "savage" societies led to a transformation in the vocabulary referring to peoples and civilizations outside of Europe. To the dominant terms "savages" and "barbarians" were added *indigènes* (natives) and *habitants* (inhabitants) in French, and "natives" in English. Especially among French travelers to North America from the end of the 17th century and through the 18th, the terms *nation* or *nations sauvages* came into general use, implying the existence of complex and well-developed forms of governments and cultures and an egalitarian vision of human societies based on the concept of natural law. Thus, Colonel Jean de Champigny, in his *État présent de la Louisiane, avec toutes les particularités de cette province d'Amérique* (1776; Present Condition of Louisiana, with All the Distinctive Features of this American Province), speaks of the "Natchez nation as the most respected in all Louisiana, and the most worthy of being so regarded, because of its enlightened state and the large number of people that it includes."

Parallel to the invention of the character of the "noble savage" and the criticism of civilization for which it was the mouthpiece, a philosophy of history was developed, from the middle of the 18th century onward, that centered around the opposition between "civilization," on the one hand, and "barbarians/savages," on the other. The term *civilisation*, first coined in 1756 by the comte de Mirabeau and appearing for the first time as a dictionary entry in the *Dictionnaire de Trévoux* in 1771, indicated an advanced evolutionary stage of human societies attributed to the influence of the Enlightenment. Disseminated in the English-speaking world from the 1770s onward and in Italy (as *civilizzazione*) after the 1780s, *civilisation* found its German equivalent in the modern sense in the term *Kultur*, the antonym of *Wildheit* (savagery) and *Barbarei* (barbarism). However, the term *Kultur* more specifically emphasizes the cultural peculiarities of each nation, and the divisions between popular culture and the culture of the elite, to the detriment of the universal common traits emphasized by the notion of *civilisation*.

The major pronouncements on this vision of the course of history opposing "barbarism" to "civilization" are to be found in Christoph Adelung's *Versuch einer Geschichte der Kultur des menschlichen Geschlechts* (1782; Toward a History of the Civilization of the Human Species) and Johann Gottfried von Herder's *Ideen zur Philosophie der Geschichte der Menschheit* (1784; Outlines of a Philosophy of the History of Man) in Germany; Adam Ferguson's *Principles of Moral and Political Science* (1792) in Britain; Thomas Paine's *Rights of Man* (1792) in the United States; as well as the abbé Raynal's *Histoire philosophique et politique des établissments et du commerce des Européens dans les deux Indes* (1770; A Philosophical and Political History of the Settlements and Trade of the Europeans in the East and West Indies) and Volney's *Les ruïnes ou Méditations sur les révolutions des empires* (1791; Ruins; or, Meditations on the Revolutions of Empires); and, above all, the marquis de Condorcet's *Esquisse des progrès de l'esprit humain* (1793; Outlines of an Historical View of the Progress of the Human Mind). Condorcet attributes a vanguard role to revolutionary France and the United States:

> But if everything tells us that the human species must not fall back again into its former barbarism . . . we still see the Enlightenment occupying only a small space on the globe. . . . Must every nation one day come closer to the state of civilization reached by those peoples who are the most enlightened, the most liberated, the most free of prejudices, the French and the Anglo-Americans?

This passage from Condorcet's *Esquisse des progrès de l'esprit humain* also indicates the expanded meaning of "barbarian" and "savage" at the end of the 18th century, notably in the context of the French Revolution. At that point in time, and even quite predominantly so in the literature of revolutionary pamphleteering, these terms indicated the political abuses of the ancien régime, particularly of criminal jurisprudence—considered by Friedrich Melchior von Grimm, as early as 1765, to be the "barbarity of our regime." The partisans of the Counter-Revolution were also stigmatized as "barbarians" and "vandals" in the speeches of Maximilien Marie Isidore de Robespierre. In his report of January 1791 on French regional languages and dialects, Barère described the latter as "barbaric jargon." Critics and adversaries of the Revolution, such as La Harpe, the vicomte de Bonald, and François René de Châteaubriand resorted to the terms "savages" and "barbarians" to designate specifically those responsible for the Terror and the September massacres, in particular Jean Paul Marat, Robespierre, and Couthon.

Conceptualizing the Other

The desire for knowledge in the age of the Enlightenment that, as far as the colonial world beyond Europe was concerned, culminated in the *Histoire des deux Indes*. This extensive encyclopedia of the European expansion overseas by Raynal and his collaborators (Diderot, among others), expresses a fundamentally ambivalent attitude toward "savage" societies. On the one hand, the goal of understanding their functioning and their mentality was clearly present, in a fashion that closely resembles the questioning characteristic of modern ethnology. Such an approach endeavors to discern, behind a human nature postulated as fundamentally uniform, the infinite differences in the "customs" of peoples inhabiting the globe. It was in this spirit that Voltaire wrote his *Essai sur les moeurs et l'esprit des nations* (1756; An Essay on Universal History, and the Manners and Spirit of Nations), thereby taking the first steps toward a comparative cultural history. At the same time, the anthropological and philosophical ideas that framed this desire for knowledge constituted one of its major restrictions. The figure of the "noble savage," both in utopian discourse and in the work of La Hontan and Diderot, as well as the concept of "natural society" in Jean-Jacques Rousseau's work, are essentially figures that project Western philosophical and anthropological ideas. The philosophy of history established during the second half of the 18th century around the barbarism/civilization dichotomy contributed to the reinforcement of this tendency. Concerned with the welfare of Indians and blacks, men such as Henri Grégoire in France and Samuel Johnson in England postulated the basic equality of "savage" societies and the so-called "civilized" ones. These champions of equality demanded the abolition of forced labor, of slavery, and of the slave trade and showed great intellectual curiosity for the customs, the languages, and the artistic members of those societies according to the conceptions of the Enlightenment. Thus, in his major work *De la littérature des nègres* (1808; On the Cultural Achievements of Negroes), which was translated immediately into German and English, Grégoire salutes the first black and Creole writers and scholars—such as Phyllis Wheatley in the United States, Ignacio Sancho and Olaudah Equiano in England, or Anton Wilhelm Abo in Germany—as dazzling proofs of the intellectual capacities and the perfectibility of blacks and Indians. His work ends with a violent attack on the European legitimization of colonial expansion: "For three centuries now, Europe, considering itself Christian and civilized, has been relentlessly torturing the peoples it calls "savage" and "barbarian" in America and Africa." Thomas Jefferson, an American politician and philoso-

pher, and incidentally a friend and translator of Volney, outlines in his political speeches and his *Notes on Virginia* (1782) an enlightened policy toward the conquered Indian societies, which he saw as children belonging to an earlier stage in human evolution, whose customs and ways of thinking one had to know in order to be better able to educate them.

Faced with this overriding tendency, the age of the Enlightenment was nevertheless able to generate, albeit in a fragmentary fashion, a desire to conceptualize members of other cultures without transforming them into innocent victims, projected and idealized figures, or pupils to be educated and disciplined. The seeds of this desire can be found in the work of Montaigne and in some Canadian travel narratives, such as Gabriel Savard's *Le grand voyage au pays des Hurons* (1621; The Great Journey to the Land of the Hurons), which was reprinted in the 18th century; they can also be found in Benjamin Franklin's *Remarks on the Savages of North America*, written in 1783 while he was in Paris and immediately translated into French and Italian. Franklin's starting point is the principle of a difference that is not hierarchical but qualitative between the "civilized" societies and the societies the Europeans considered as "savage." He strongly encourages the impartial examination of the customs of different nations. Georg Forster, who accompanied James Cook on his second voyage around the world (1778–80), left detailed descriptions of the customs and the environment of the indigenous societies of the Pacific in his travel journal. However, it was undoubtedly Herder—particularly in his essay *Auch eine Philosophie zur Geschichte der Menschheit* (1774; Yet Another Philosophy of History for the Education of Humanity) and through his idea of a *Kultur* that is unchangeable and specific to each nation—who laid the epistemological groundwork for an understanding of "savage" societies free of any political or educational influence, an influence that in Enlightenment Europe was directly linked to an enlightened vision of progress and civilization.

HANS-JÜRGEN LÜSEBRINK

See also Civilization and Civility; Cosmopolitanism; Idolatry; Sociability

Further Reading

Michel, Pierre, *Les barbares, 1789–1848: Un mythe romantique,* Lyon, France: Presses Universitaires de Lyon, 1981

Mouralis, Bernard, *Montaigne et le mythe du bon sauvage, de l'antiquité à Rousseau,* Paris: Bordas, 1989

Barbarian and Savage

Representations

Artists of the Enlightenment understood the terms "barbarian," "savage," and "primitive" very differently from explorers and philosophers. As used by artists, distinctions in meaning among the terms were not readily apparent and there was some overlap among categories. Moreover, in artists' work the underlying philosophical message tended to blur, superseded by more descriptive concerns. Emerging from a different culture—that of images—artists thus used a different discourse, even when their work was intended to illustrate a book or a philosophical text.

Advances in navigational methods during the Enlightenment made it possible for ships to venture to distant seas, and as a result explorers became acquainted with almost the entire world and its inhabitants. Conflicting relationships between Europeans and "savages" began to fade with the dawning of greater understanding. The image still persisted of the blood-thirsty, cannibalistic savage belonging to an inferior, nearly animal species, but this bestiality revealed to Westerners their own latent savagery. This theme stands out in Francisco de Goya's scenes of savagery, four paintings created between 1800 and 1805, two of which are thought to represent the martyrdom of the missionary fathers Brébeuf and Lallemant at the hands of the Iroquois in 1649.

The new understanding of such peoples as the natives of Central and South America, who had been considered savage in the 17th century but were no longer because of their forced conversion to Catholicism, is clearly reflected in the iconography of the period. They became "other people," different from Europeans. This shift is exemplified in the drawings made by Noël during the expedition of the abbé Chappe d'Auteroche to California (1768–69), showing Native Americans from Mexico and Baja California. The presence of the cross in three of the drawings makes it clear that we are dealing not with savages but with human beings. However, they are represented as examples of "types" of people—like the "true Indian woman"—rather than as individuals. For further information about the identity of those portrayed, the handwritten diaries of Chappe d'Auteroche, who was concerned about the fate of the Native Americans, is a more reliable source than the book published by Cassini, who was much more biased against them. The conversion of indigenous American peoples became a common pictorial theme (as in Scheffler's work on Father José de Anchieta's mission to Brazil, in the Jesuit church at Dillingen, Germany).

Several factors influenced the emergence of a better understanding of "the savage" in the second half of the 18th century and the beginning of the 19th. Naturalists and artists set out on scientific missions to record the ways and customs of the peoples they encountered, as well as the natural and geographic history of the countries they visited. These expeditions brought to light exotic modes of human life that transformed the European conception of the world. They also resulted in the birth of a new science, anthropology, the first stirrings of which can be clearly discerned in the notes and drawings of explorers and artists. Anthropology was no longer the study of the human body—as Denis Diderot describes it in his article "Anatomie" (Anatomy) in the *Encyclopédie*—but the science of humanity. All too often, to 18th-century Europeans those representations merely suggested a distant paradise of happy people who, unburdened by law, king, or god, showed it was possible to live in a state of natural morality. Nevertheless, those images continue to represent people as objects rather than as human beings capable of thought. Although the human figure is represented the most often, artists also attempted to capture the indigenous environment. Almost all artists represented the dwelling of the savage—that is, the hut or cabin made of leaves and branches, which they associated with the notion of a primitive life centered around the hearth. Huts appear in the work of Le Prince; in that of Captain Cook's draftsman John Webber (*Hut of the Kamchadales*); in that of Duché de Vancy (*Costumes des habitants de la baie de Castries* [Costumes of the Inhabitants of the Bay of Castries]); and in the work of Daniell, who depicted African huts. Interest in the indigenous environment is also evidenced by the inventories of objects found in travel narratives and drawings, which resemble the descriptions and plates of the *Encyclopédie*. Draftsmen represented a full range of domestic objects, tools for fishing and hunting, religious objects, and so on. We must consider these images as the first recorded testimony of the history of these peoples.

Over time, the iconography of the savage was transformed and humanized. Artists were increasingly aware of humanity's convergences and differences, and these were captured in a variety of ways. The images fall into two groups. The first contains drawings made during expeditions. The other group comprises drawings made in Europe, based either on direct testimony or on the imagination. Such images were most often intended as illustrations for travel narratives (see the illustrations to the *Histoire générale des voyages* [1746–89; General

History of Travels], by Antoine Prévost). This second group promotes the general image of an exotic and utopian world inhabited by the "noble savage," a figure who also makes a frequent appearance in the work of philosophers and historians. Obviously, the first group of images, based on direct observation in the course of expeditions, is the more interesting in terms of documentary value. However, the second category also captures our interest insofar as it reflects contemporary sensibilities: draftsmen were supposed to create an iconography in the vein of Jean-Jacques Rousseau's "noble savage" living in a permanent golden age, without concerning themselves with reality.

As one would expect, the images drawn in the field vary according to the places and circumstances of the expedition during which they were made. With the increasing scope of explorations the "savage" was no longer simply the black slave or the American Indian. He became Oceanian, Asian, or African. Images of blacks changed considerably over the course of the 18th century. No longer represented solely as subjugated slaves, they gradually took on the stature of separate beings endowed with feelings, represented not as examples of a type but as individuals. Jean-Baptiste Pigalle sculpted the features of Paul, black servant of Desfriches. Joshua Reynolds (1770) and John Singelton Copley (1777–83) painted the heads of African men. In the painting *Négresse* (1800), Marie-Guilhelmine portrayed a black woman as her equal during the brief period when slavery was temporarily abolished in the French territories (1794–1802). These works all attest to the changing attitudes of Europeans toward blacks.

Nevertheless, the blacks of Africa were still rarely studied, despite Michel Adanson's investigations in Senegal as well as official reports. Draftsmen attached to expeditions were primarily concerned with representing the countries visited rather than their inhabitants. It was not until the beginning of the 19th century that Africans become an object of anthropological study. This began with Daniell's drawings, made during an English expedition to the Cape Colony, depicting Hottentots, who in many later studies were called Korah or Bushmen. By contrast, violent actions by Africans appear more than once in works of art related to Napoleon Bonaparte's Egyptian campaign (Anne-Louis Girodet's *Révolte du Caire* [Revolt in Cairo]), and these depictions recall Goya's scenes of savagery in their bloodthirsty spirit.

Native North Americans were most frequently represented in England and France, since both countries maintained colonies on that continent. Europeans had been familiar with the indigenous peoples of North America for a century, and they were thus less frequently described by explorers. Images of them predominated in literature and the arts, even the decorative arts, particularly after the American War of Independence. Although still idealized—as symbols of humanity unburdened by law—Native Americans had acquired the status of true human beings capable of feeling. Several works show them face to face with death. Joseph Wright of Derby's *The Indian Widow* (1785), inspired by Adair's *The History of the American Indians* (1775), weeps dignified tears for her dead husband, oblivious to the beauty of the natural scene surrounding her. Le Barbier's *Couple d'Indiens canadiens pleurant sur la tombe de leur enfant* (1781; Canadian Indian Couple Weeping over the Tomb of Their Child) celebrates parental virtues, particularly maternal devotion, which were recognized traits of Native American societies. This sentimentality finds its apogee in Girodet's *Funérailles d'Atala* (1801; Atala's Funeral), which was inspired by François-René de Chateaubriand's 1801 novel *Atala*, and in which allusions to race are all but lost among references to antiquity. The Indian was portrayed in the process of becoming the white man's friend, capable of goodness toward him; Borel's drawings, inspired by St. John de Crèvecoeur's *Letters from an American Farmer* (1782), provide an example. One of the drawings shows a "savage" and his dog rescuing a European child who had been lost in the woods and returning it to its parents. The Indian's deferential attitude and the idea of freedom associated with the American territories emerge as clear themes in Benjamin West's *Death of General Wolfe,* in which the artist places a tattooed Cherokee in traditional costume in the foreground, kneeling in front of the dying man. This figure was inspired by Charles Townshend's monument, designed by Robert Adam and housed in Westminster Abbey.

South American Indians, also long known in the West, held the attention of naturalists exploring the continent's natural riches, such as the silver mines of Potosí. The Jesuit Paucke completed a large illustrated survey of the indigenous people of Paraguay (*Hin und Her* [1769–80; Back and Forth]), but Dobrizhoffer considered the Abipons "useless bipeds" (*Geschichte der Abiponer* [1783; History of the Abipons]). Explorers of the 18th century refuted some of the extravagant claims of their 16th-century predecessors, who had seen monsters in profusion in South America. Nevertheless, all of them noted the gigantism of the newly discovered Patagonians and commissioned pictures of them for their travel narratives (Byron and Pernety). Explorers also noted the goodness of the people of these regions who approached them, including the inhabitants of Tierra del Fuego and the Pescherais. South American Indians also figured in the literary world. Le Barbier's illustrations for Jean-François Marmontel's *Les Incas* (1777; The Incas; or, The Destruction of the Empire of Peru) clearly show the difference between North American Indians, who were considered civilized, and South

American Indians, who were still veiled in a fascinating blend of passionate legend and newly emerging knowledge of South America's ancient civilizations.

The peoples of the Pacific constituted the greatest anthropological revelation of the 18th century. The publication of the travel narratives of Captain Cook (*Cook's Voyages* [1773–94]), the comte de Bougainville (*Voyage autour du monde* [1771; A Voyage round the World]), and the comte de La Pérouse (*Voyage de La Pérouse autour du monde* [1797; A Voyage round the World]) heightened interest in the Pacific islanders, who were studied in the field and took on tremendous resonance in the European imagination. Drawings brought back from circumnavigations of the globe made it possible to approach these peoples in a more scientific manner, even if their external appearance was not always understood. During Cook's first voyage (1768–71) the naturalist Sydney Parkinson drew different indigenous types, focusing on hairstyles and in particular on tattoos, the ritual nature of which escaped him, but which intrigued him nonetheless. These drawings confirm that the European artist's perception of the indigenous people, who seemed to belong to a golden age, differed significantly from that of the philosopher or naturalist. In these Pacific islanders, devoid of all the artifices of modern civilization, artists found the nobility of the peoples of classical antiquity. Their vision was conditioned by the training they had received in the academies of art. They continued to draw their models in static poses, often standing, with low vegetation in the foreground and a landscape in the background. Seemingly, artists always referred back to the great models of antiquity, and they showed little respect for the natural proportions of what they drew. The frequent use of draperies further underscores the tendency to reframe the figures in terms of antiquity. It thus becomes difficult to see true "savages" in artists' representations. Piron, a member of the expedition led by Antoine-Raymond-Joseph de Bruni d'Entrecasteaux, gives a man from Admiralty Island the pose and proportions of Polykleitos's *Doryphoros* (Spear-bearer), disregarding what one assumes would have been the model's actual physical characteristics. The most telling example of the framework of antiquity imposed on the conception of the "savage" is Reynolds's portrait, painted in London, of Omai, a young Oceanian brought back by one of Cook's officers. The subject is draped in a white tunic that gives him the air of an ancient orator, and only his tattooed hands indicate his origins. John Zoffany's depiction of the *Death of Captain Cook* (1779) at Karakooa Bay shows how much the idea of antiquity dominated the artistic mind: the *Dying Gaul*, now in the Capitoline Museum, served as model for Cook, while the pose of the *Discoboulos* (Discus-thrower) may be found in one of his assassins.

Similarly, depictions of women were modeled on the figures of François Boucher and his imitators, as well as on contemporary fashion plates. The fact is particularly apparent in the drawings of Duché de Vancy, who sailed with La Pérouse, especially in the drawings that represent Europeanized indigenous women. Groups are represented in various ways. John Webber, the draftsman on Cook's third voyage, was enchanted with the atmosphere of nocturnal scenes in Tahiti, and the dreamlike quality of his drawings comes close to the work of the visionary William Blake. Duché de Vancy, in his *Monuments de l'île de Pâques* (The Monuments of Easter Island) depicts the island as a kind of Arcadia where islanders and French officers and sailors are united in brotherhood. Piron gave his *Pêche des indigènes au cap de Diémen* (Natives Fishing at Van Diemen's Cape) an air of antiquity reminiscent of Renaissance representations of Diana bathing. In his *Danse à l'île d'Amboine* (Dance on the Island of Amboyna), the influence of Roman frescoes is evident as much in the draped figures as in the use of color. Such figures were subsequently reproduced in engravings, including those of Grasset de Saint-Sauveur, which were extremely successful and thus contributed to the knowledge of "the other" among Europeans during the Enlightenment.

The very end of the 18th century and first years of the 19th witnessed an evolution in representations of indigenous people, even though some works still reverted to a neoclassical aesthetic. Artists accompanying expeditions had been exposed to new ideas and their vision became more realistic. They began to take a more documentary approach. Petit, on Captain Nicolas Baudin's expedition to Australasia, used techniques associated with the revolutionary era in his drawings of inhabitants of Van Diemen's Land (Tasmania): the sky is washed in blue, there is little vegetation, and the subject is placed in the foreground in what is meant as a natural pose. He emphasizes the exceptional in his subjects—hair dyed red, tattoos, shell necklaces—but most importantly he attempts to invest them with a life of their own by making them smile. As a result, the subject is no longer a type but a human being capable of feeling.

If American Indians and Oceanians were considered "savages," the term was also used for other peoples who might more properly have been considered primitive. They included inhabitants of Siberia, as well as the Alaskan Inuit encountered by Cook and La Pérouse. In his *Voyage en Sibérie* (1768; Journey in Siberia), Chappe d'Auteroche presents the peoples he encountered in the course of his travels to the eastern regions of Russia: Tatars, Kalmuks, Votiaks, and Samoyeds. Le Prince, who was to illustrate the volume and who had lived in Russia for several years, imitated the drawings of the Russian Vosilyev and a variety of academic sources. He created an entire iconography of these primitive peoples, who may strike us as brutal, rather than merely barbaric, when they are shown engaged in corporal punishments. They live in huts heated by wood fires and eat what they can fish or hunt, in something that approaches a state of nature. This vision of a primitive Russia roused the ire of Catherine II, who wished to portray her empire as a modern state. The primitive side of these peoples nonetheless emerges in some of the plates of Peter Simon Pallas's *Voyages en différentes provinces de l'empire de Russie, et dans l'Asie septentrionale* (1788–95; Journeys in Various Provinces of the Russian Empire and in Northern Asia).

Several cases of "savages" living in Europe were reported during the 18th century, but the people in question were primitives living in an undeveloped state of humanity far from civilization, in forests or on mountains. The figure of a savage found in the mountains of Germany is the subject of a drawing by Dietrich. The creature is hairy and his head is almost like a satyr's, but he holds a snuffbox in his right hand and rests his left on the pommel of his sabre. The vacillation between the desire to see a true savage and a concern to render him more civilized is evident. In 1767 Peter Falconet presented a similar subject in London, a portrait of *Peter the Wild Boy*. The figure resembles a hirsute old man, dressed in a huge coat and eating roots, than like a savage.

It seems that for artists of the 18th century the notion of barbarism was both limited and imprecise. For many the barbarian was symbolized, as he had been since the Renaissance, by *Dacia in Tears* and by the figures of Dacian prisoners found in many buildings in Rome. The examples of Farnese and Cesi appear more than once in engravings by Giambattista Piranesi. All these images were the work of artists who worked in Rome and can be found in decorative motifs and sculpture as well. Goths, Visigoths, Ripuarians, the Franks of Germany, and Anglo-Saxons were barbarians, according to the *Encyclopédie,* but ancient peoples, including Dacians, Parthians, and Armenians, were also included in the term. Both art theorists (such as Claude-Henri Watelet) and artists used the terms "Goth" and "Gothic" in a pejorative sense to characterize works they considered unrefined and worthy of little attention. A few themes from the repertory of history painting are associated with these peoples. For example, Hallé painted Scilurus, king of the Scythians, giving his sons his parting advice and showing them, through the symbol of the fasces, that their union will render them invincible (*Salon*, 1767). The episode is related in Plutarch's *Moralia* (Morals), but the artists nonetheless clothed the Scythians in animal skins.

The discovery of national antiquities stimulated an interest in the origins of Europeans themselves. Artists began to depict a golden age of man living in harmony with nature in Switzerland and in mountainous locations untouched by civilization. The people who inhabited such scenes, however, were not considered primitive. On the contrary, they evinced a high moral awareness, celebrated by artists in paintings on the theme of open-air feasts that brought together entire communities to honor the memory of their ancestors (Vigée-Lebrun and König's *Fête des bergers à Unspunnen* [1808; Shepherds' Feast at Unspunnen]). With the publication of the *Voyages pittoresques et romantiques dans l'ancienne France* (Picturesque and Romantic Journeys in Old France), Europe rediscovered its Roman and Gothic heritage, and this renewed interest provoked a fashion for paintings on medieval subjects, known as troubadour paintings. The end of the century also witnessed the birth of an interest in texts from the northern countries. James Macpherson's *Fingal* (1762), *Temora* (1763), and *Works of Ossian* (1765) were presented as translations of Celtic texts. These evocations of the bards of the past—"sublime savages"—played an important role in the introduction of new themes in history painting at the beginning of the 19th century (Gérard and Girodet, *Ossian*). Turks, on the other hand, remained models of exoticism throughout the 18th century, and it was not until the Greek War of Independence that they acquired the status of "new barbarians" in the eyes of painters and poets—as may be seen in Eugène Delacroix's painting *Massacres de Scio* and in the writings of Lord Byron.

MADELEINE PINAULT SØRENSEN

See also Africa; Physiognomy; Travel

Further Reading

Honour, Hugh, *The Image of the Black in Western Art*, Houston, Texas, Cambridge, Massachusetts, and London: Menil Foundation, 1989–; see especially vol. 4, *From the American Revolution to World War I* (1989)

Joppien, Rüdiger, and Bernard Smith, *The Art of Captain Cook's Voyages with a Descriptive Catalogue of All the Known Original Drawings of Peoples, Places, Artefacts, and Events and the Original Engravings Associated with Them*, 3 vols., New Haven, Connecticut: Yale University Press, 1985–87

Smith, Bernard, *European Vision and the South Pacific, 1768–1850: A Study in the History of Art and Ideas*, Oxford: Clarendon Press, 1960; 2nd edition, New Haven, Connecticut: Yale University Press, 1985

Baroque

The French word *baroque* is derived either from the Portuguese word *barroco,* used as early as the 13th century to describe an irregular pearl, or from *in baroco,* which was a neutral term in 13th-century Scholastic logic. When Renaissance thinkers, among them Michel Eyquem de Montaigne, settled their differences with this logic, *baroco* became a pejorative term, meaning "ridiculous formalism." It was not until the Enlightenment that the meaning of the word was gradually broadened, as were its synonyms "bizarre" and "capricious."

Enlightenment attachment to reason, nature, truth, and antiquity led to a critical revision of the philosophical and aesthetic concepts that marked the period from the end of the Renaissance to the middle of the 17th century. This is the period we now call "baroque," with its prelude in mannerism and its epilogue in late baroque. In the mid–18th century, European artistic life was totally immersed in the "revival of antiquity and fine taste," that is, the aesthetic rules of antiquity, the Renaissance, and French classicism. This new movement, initiated at the Académie des Beaux-Arts (Academy of Fine Arts) in Paris, was influenced by Enlightenment ideals and the dogmatic efforts of Johann Joachim Winckelmann's circle to create a "neoantique" style, but the movement also remained attached to Roger de Piles's defense of color in the controversy over the relative merits of drawing and painting. This was the period when the notion of the baroque began to be used specifically to criticize forms of expression that ignored the "classical rule." The term "baroque" thus took on, with some rare but important exceptions, a pejorative meaning.

France

A baroque pearl suggests irregularity, impurity and strangeness, and the word "baroque" became a synonym of "strange" or "bizarre." This meaning of the term "baroque" can be found as early as entries dating to 1701, in the *Mémoires* (1829; Memoirs) of the duc de Saint-Simon: "What a baroque idea to have the abbé Bignon replace Monsieur de Tonnerre." It was not until 1740, however, that the *Dictionnaire de l'Académie Française* (Dictionary of the Académie Française) included this figurative meaning: "*Baroque* also means, figuratively, irregular, bizarre, uneven. A baroque mind. A baroque expression. A baroque figure." At the end of the 1740s the term "baroque" was being used to describe all the anticlassical forms of art endangered by the "revival of antiquity and fine taste." "Baroque" appeared as a synonym of "bizarre" and "capricious"

but also of "uneven," "artificial," "affected," and "in bad taste." The term was used mainly in painting and architecture but gradually slipped into the vocabulary of literary criticism, where synonyms such as "bizarre" were most common.

The most prominent and tolerant proponents of the "revival of antiquity," such as Charles Nicolas Cochin, used the term "baroque" and the synonyms "bizarre" and "capricious" in their criticism of the architectural registers of the late baroque or of the affected elegance of the rocaille style, with its characteristic wavy lines. Cochin and his entourage, among them the comte de Caylus, considered rocaille style or "French taste" to be a mannered development of the architectural vocabulary of the 17th century, particularly as represented by G. Guarini. In *Le voyage d'Italie* (1758; The Trip to Italy), Cochin describes Guarini's Dome of San Lorenzo in Turin as showing "the most bizarre sort of imagination." In his ironic criticism of the rocaille style in his "Supplication aux orfèvres, ciseleurs, sculpteurs en bois" ("Plea to Silver- and Goldsmiths, Engravers, Wood Sculptors") in the *Mercure de France* (December 1754) Cochin calls the style's convoluted ornaments "baroque shapes." Nevertheless, Cochin's circle remained faithful to Roger de Piles, who defended the colorists and argued that the "fine taste" of Gianlorenzo Bernini and Borromini was in fact rooted in antiquity, so it did not bear traces of the late baroque's overdone ornamentation. It was mainly artists such as Cochin, who had lived in Italy, who referred to the rocaille style or "rococo taste" as "baroque taste."

However, writers also mentioned Italian art in their travel journals. For example, Charles de Brosses, like Cochin, defended the ideals of the Enlightenment, "the revival of antiquity," and the masters of color. In his *Lettres familières écrites d'Italie en 1739 et 1740* (1869 edition; Familiar Letters Written from Italy in 1739 and 1740), Brosses highlights the similarities among the "baroque" (in the sense of "late baroque"), the "rocaille style," and "Gothic taste," all representing an "extravagant manner"—as opposed to the "simple fine taste" and "magnificence of the grand manner" typical, in his opinion, of antiquity and classicism but also of the Roman baroque (Bernini and Borromini). He bases this criticism on the Palazzo Doria Pamfili, a monumental baroque palace in Rome, with its exuberant late baroque facade (1734): "Recently, in an attempt to create a new order, new constructions have been added to the Pamfili Palace, decorated with lilies and rooster heads, in . . . Gothic, if not even more barbarian, taste."

With regard to Italian criticism of the "French mode," Brosses says that the "baroque" and the

"Gothic" typify the decorative accumulation of the rocaille style:

> Italians criticize us, saying that in France, with regard to fashion, we revive Gothic taste; that our fireplaces . . . are twisted and turned as if we had lost the use of circles and squares; that our ornaments become the height of baroque. . . . I do not claim to excuse this ridiculous baroque.

In his *Voyage d'un Français en Italie fait dans les années 1765 et 1766* (1769; The Voyage of a Frenchman in Italy in the Years 1765 and 1766), Joseph-Jérôme le Français de Lalande follows the abbé Gougenot and Cochin in using the word "baroque" to criticize the extravagant trompe-l'oeil perspectives of the Stupinigi hunting lodge near Turin, designed by the architect and decorator F. Iuvara: "Something as baroque as [these effects] may be seen simply as an architect's dream or folly that would never have been dared in a palace, but was thought to be able to brighten a country house." Lalande also thought of "baroque" as a synonym for "strange," as is clear from his description of the Salvator Rosa painting of Saint Cosmas and Saint Damian in the Church of San Giovanni dei Fiorentini in Rome: "However, we must consider baroque this idea of a man tossed into a corner of the painting, with only his legs showing, the rest supposedly being outside the painting." In fact, this pictorial register is now considered to be a typically baroque feature.

Toward the middle of the 18th century the word "baroque" lost its pejorative meaning in the description of rocaille ornamentation in the architecture and decorative arts of the period. L. Duvaux, in his *Livre-journal* (1749; A Journal-Book), describes "a baroque base in bronze, gilded with ormolu, trimmed with branches and Vincennes flowers, for a sleeping woman," and a writer for the *Mercure de France* (June 1751) comments that "the base [of a new centerpiece] is oval, outlined in a pleasant baroque." Roger de Piles and Cochin were so influential in their defense of the colorists that up until the end of the century, severe criticism of the anticlassical art of the 17th century was the exception that proved the rule. The reappearance of Nicolas Poussin's famous words "Caravaggio came to destroy painting," in F.-M. de Marsay's *Dictionnaire abrégé de peinture et d'architecture* (1746; Abridged Dictionary of Painting and Architecture), does not reflect the opinion of the time. In painting, "baroque taste" and its synonym "capricious," meaning "in bad taste," were used only with regard to certain approaches—especially in drawing and composition—that were clear-cut departures from "classic good taste." Pernety's *Dictionnaire portatif de peinture, sculpture et gravure* (1757; Portable Dictionary of Painting, Sculpture, and Engraving) gives the following definition:

> *Baroque*, that which does not follow the rules of proportion, but of caprice. May be said of taste and drawing. The figures in this painting are baroque; the composition is in a baroque style, which is to say that it is not in good taste. Tintoretto always had something singular and extraordinary in his paintings: there is always something baroque about them.

In the *Dictionnaire de Trévoux* (Dictionary of Trévoux), Pernety's definition is boiled down to: "In painting, a picture, a figure in baroque taste, where the rules of proportion are not respected, where everything is represented according to the artist's caprice." From the mid–18th century onward, several French architectural theorists used the word "baroque" and the synonyms "bizarre" and "capricious" to express quite severe criticism of both "Roman baroque" and of the marked rupture of late baroque architecture with the canon of classical antiquity. M.-A. Laugier, whose point of view on neoclassical architecture was influenced by the concept of rationality and the empirical approach of the Enlightenment (Sir Isaac Newton, Voltaire, Denis Diderot), believed that the "architecture of antiquity," as opposed to that of Borromini and Bernini, was perfectly suitable to inspire French architects in their search for the sublime. In Laugier's *Essai sur l'architecture* (1753; Essay on Architecture), Roman edifices designed by Borromini are given as typical examples of architecture that is "extravagant" and does not follow "any rule but caprice." Laugier asserts that unlike works influenced by "Gothic taste," Borromini's buildings are dominated by "all sorts of bizarre peculiarities" and "baroque ornaments." However, these same buildings, which today we classify as "late baroque" with their rocaille patterns, were criticized most severely by Laugier and his commentators (for example the architect C.Q. Guillaumont). In his *Remarques sur un livre intitulé "Observations sur l'architecture de l'abbé Laugier"* (1768; Comments on a Book Entitled "Observations sur l'architecture de l'abbé Laugier"), Charles de Brosses qualifies the Palazzo Doria Pamfili as "a masterpiece of bad taste," because it is spoiled by "a bizarre, extravagant taste." This is precisely the expression that, with the word "capricious," is most often used as a synonym for "baroque taste."

By the end of the 1730s, these two synonyms for "baroque" were appearing in criticisms of baroque architecture. In the *Dissertation historique et critique sur les ordres d'architecture* (1738; Historical and Critical Essay on Architectural Orders), A.-F. Frézier rebukes Borromini and his successors for their "bizarreness" and "bad taste." In the *Livre d'architecture* (1745; The Book of Architecture), G. Boffrand resumes the attacks on "fashion" and "bizarreness" because they "disfigured all parts of an edifice"—Guarini's Church of the Théatins in Paris and "the works of Borromini in Italy"—and because "bizarreness is accepted in the name of genius, as if producing a monster were a sign of fertility." C.-F. Roland le Virloys's *Dictionnaire d'architecture* (1770; Dictionary of Architecture) sums up what various architects thought of the baroque: "Baroque describes things that have an irregular shape." In the *Encyclopédie méthodique* (1788; Methodical Encyclopedia), Quatremère de Quincy clarifies his precursors' criticism of "baroque taste" and raises the frequently used synonyms "capricious taste" and "bizarre taste" to the level of independent "art terminology." However, unlike his predecessors he gives an image of a three-stage rocket, with "the baroque" as the extravagant, exuberant final stage:

> *Bizarre.* Term in architecture that expresses a taste contrary to accepted principles . . . whose sole merit is in the very novelty that constitutes its vice. *Capricious* taste makes an arbitrary choice among known forms. . . . Bizarre taste is what affronts those forms. . . . Borromini and Guarini were masters of the bizarre genre.

The baroque, in architecture, is a shade of the bizarre: it is, so to speak, a distillation or, in the eyes of some, a misuse of the bizarre. As severity is to sober taste, the baroque is to the bizarre, that is, the superlative form of it. The idea of the baroque suggests the ridiculous taken to excess. Borromini "gave the grandest models of bizarreness." Guarini was "the master of the baroque." His Cappella della Santa Sindone (Chapel of the Holy Shroud) in Turin was "the most striking example of baroque taste." For Quatremère, inspired by Winckelmann, Greek antiquity was a period in which the significant force specific to a certain genre and a certain art was keenly felt. He was particularly opposed to the baroque's stated refusal to distinguish genres, and especially the dematerialization of sculpture, the assimilation of sculpture with painting, and the confusion between sculpture and architecture. It is precisely in the Cappella della Santa Sindone that the decomposition of classical rules and the unity of the arts is pushed to the extreme.

Jean-Baptiste Rousseau was the first to use the term "baroque" to speak of musical traditions after 1600, in which the language of forms echoed baroque taste in painting and architecture. A poem inserted in a letter dated 17 November 1739 refers to "distillers of baroque chords that enchant so many fools"—for example, Jean-Philippe Rameau (*Oeuvres* [1820;

Works]). Voltaire cites these words in the *Catalogue de la plupart des écrivains français* (1753; Catalog of the Majority of French Writers). Jean-Jacques Rousseau uses the word "baroque" with the same meaning. In his *Lettre sur la musique française* (1753; Letter on French Music), he observes that "the Italians claim that our melody is flat . . . and we in turn accuse theirs of being bizarre and baroque." Rousseau is the only writer in 18th-century France to recall the Scholastic origin of the term "baroque," in his *Dictionnaire de musique* (1768; Dictionary of Music):

> *Baroque.* Baroque music is that in which the harmony is confused, overcharged with modulations and dissonance, the song is hard and unnatural, the intonation difficult, and the movement constrained. It would seem that this term comes from the *baroco* of the Logicians.

Italy

In Italy the Scholastic term *in baroco* was used longer than anywhere else. It was not used as an adjective until Domenico Caracciolo spoke of *discorsi barocchi* toward the end of the 18th century. After the anti-Scholastic polemic, the term *in baroco* took on a pejorative meaning. It referred to the overdone and the artificial and so was inspired by the French word *baroque*, used in the invectives against anticlassical art and architecture. It became a synonym of *bizzarro,* the expression most often employed by critics—for example by E. Pinzi in *Dell'architectura* (1775; On Architecture): "Borromini was certainly a most bizarre, twisted architect." The architect Francesco Milizia, who made the connection between the philosophy of the Encyclopedists and the architectural theories of Vitruvius, Laugier, and Winckelmann, was the first Italian to use the word "baroque" as an art term. In his *Dizionario delle belle arti* (1788–94; Dictionary of Fine Arts), he uses it to clarify his criticism of the exaggerated lines of Italian anticlassical architecture: "Baroque (*barocco*) is the superlative of bizarre, the excess of the ridiculous. Borromini, we read, goes in for the delirious, but Guarini, Pozzi, and Marchione in the sacristy of Saint Peter's in Rome go in for the baroque."

Milizia was certainly inspired by Quatremère's article on "the baroque," as demonstrated by the striking parallel between the essential positions of their entries on that subject. The same is true for Milizia's article on bizarreness, which seems almost a summary of Quatremère's article on this art term. However, articles about artists such as Bernini, Borromini, and Guarini in Quatremère's dictionary are clearly influenced by Milizia's more subtle criticism. In *Memorie degli architetti antichi e moderni* (1768; The Lives of Celebrated Architects, Ancient and Modern), Milizia tones down the notion of "anticlassical" features applied by his contemporaries and simply qualifies those features as "bizarre":

> Traces of the bizarreness of Borromini can be seen in the San André delle Frate Church (Rome). . . . Of all the architects who adopted the bizarre style of Borromini, none was as excessive as Father Guarini. . . . The same style can be observed in all these buildings (for example, the Chapel of the Holy Shroud), that is, there is a decided taste . . . for exaggerated curves. His designs are bizarre.

Milizia, widening the perspective for his criticism of 17th-century "baroque" Italian architecture, compares Borromini to "Seneca for prose and Marini for poetry." In his article on Borromini, Milizia forthrightly declares: "Borromini in architecture, Bernini in sculpture, Pietro de Cortona in painting, Cavaliere Marini in poetry are the plague of taste." At the end of the century, Italian literary criticism, oriented toward classicism, targeted Marini because of his complicated caprices and his unexpected, bizarre conceptual combinations; he was often compared to Borromini. Milizia certainly took as his model *Dell'entusiasmo delle belle arti* (1769; On Enthusiasm in the Fine Arts) by Saverio Bettinelli, who was inspired by Voltaire and Muratori; he was opposed to all the great artists and writers who were animated by excess "enthusiasm," because it had "capricious and bizarre" effects. Milizia chose exactly these examples: the poetry of Marini, the architecture of Borromini, and the painting of Caravaggio.

Germany

Criticism of the literature now known as German baroque—for example the poetry of Lohenstein—had already appeared at the beginning of the Enlightenment. The figurehead was Johann Christoph Gottsched, who expressed his classically oriented criticism with the word *Schwulst* (bombast), defined as follows by Johann Georg Sulzer in the *Allgemeine Theorie der schönen Künste* (1774; General Theory of the Fine Arts): "This bombast is unquestionably one of the most grievous offenses committed against good taste and is especially highly repugnant to people whose mindset is a bit more sophisticated." In the mid–18th century, when the philosophical and aesthetic ideas of the French Enlightenment were in full force, the French word *baroque* in the sense of "bizarre" was increasingly predominant in German cultural life and became a synonym for *Schwulst*. As in France, "baroque" was used primarily to refer to "taste" that broke with "classical rules." The notion of *barock* and its synonyms was used first by

aestheticians and artists who supported the "revival of antiquity" and also in Winckelmann's circle. Sometimes the French expression *goût baroque* (baroque taste) was used, particularly in the controversy over 1600s anticlassical art and over "rocaille." In *Betrachtungen über den wahren Geschmack der Alten in der Baukunst* in *Neuer Büchersaal der schönen Wissenschaften und freien Künste* (1747; Observations on the Genuine Taste of the Ancients in Architecture, in New Library of Belles Lettres and Liberal Arts), the German architect F.A. Krubsacius refers to classical Greek architecture and sculpture as the sole source of inspiration that could relieve contemporary architecture of the luxuriance of *Grillen- und Muschelwerks* (insect and shell motifs). However, he cites a very few artists (for example the sculptor J. A. Nahl the Elder) who did not abandon all "conformity with nature." According to Krubsacius, Nahl knew "how to combine earnestness with decoration so successfully that his taste, above all others, deserved to be called genuine baroque taste."

In his essay "Untersuchung vom Ursprunge, Wachstume und Verfalle der Verzierungen" (Research into the Origin, Growth, and Decline of Ornament) in a 1759 issue of the periodical *Das Neueste aus der anmuthigen Gelehrsamkeit*, Krubsacius explains that Nahl's work also revealed this form of ornamentation that, as it degenerates, becomes *Hirngespinsten* (phantoms): "It is so grotesque, so exotic, so Chinese, or in baroque taste—in short, it is so very much in fashion." Krubsacius was one of the rare aestheticians of his period to distinguish two different forms of *goût baroque*, one of which was harmonious enough to be accepted by "classical taste" and the other which completely betrayed the sacred principles of antiquity. In Germany too, *goût baroque* became a neutral synonym of the "rocaille style." Jacob von Stählin used the term in 1785 when referring to Nicolas Pineau, creator of asymmetrical ornamentation: "Pineau . . . one of the original inventors of baroque taste—who preferred the very latest and most often baroque decoration in wood-carving" in the Naryshkin Palace, Saint Petersburg (*Aus den Papieren Jacob von Stählins* [1926; From Jacob von Stählin's Papers]). Winckelmann played a crucial role in the condemnation of turn-of-the-17th-century anticlassical art and architecture, which for him were marked by "corruption of taste" and corresponded in poetry to the work of Marino: "J. Arpino, Bernini, and Borromini were in painting, sculpture, and architecture what the cavaliere Marino was in poetry: they all abandoned Nature and Antiquity" (*Geschichte der Kunst des Altertums* [1764; The History of Ancient Art]). Winckelmann himself did not use the term *goût baroque* in his *Anmerkungen über die Baukunst der Alten* (1762; Remarks on Ancient Architecture), but it was used by H. Jansen in his French translation of this work

(*Remarques sur l'architecture des Anciens* [1783]). In the late baroque style of decoration "created in stone for the duke of Caravita in a garden he had near the royal palace" at Portici, visitors were said to encounter "everything ever produced by the most bizarre, most baroque imagination"—the last two adjectives being the French translation of Winckelmann's expression "the most absurd scroll ornamentation," which marks "the most loathsome monument to the corruption of taste." Winckelmann, like his French counterparts, judged the exuberant late baroque and rococo art severely. Borromini was held responsible because he was the one who introduced this *Anmerkungen* (bad taste).

However, in the anonymous Letter to Herr Winckelmann regarding "Thoughts on the Imitation of Greek Works in Painting and Sculpture," (1756; French translation by M. Charrière, as *Lettre à M. Winckelmann à propos des réflexions sur l'imitation des oeuvres grecques en peinture et en sculpture* (1756; Letter to M. Winckelmann concerning Remarks on the Imitation of Greek Works in Painting and Sculpture), Winckelmann's attack against Roman baroque and "rocaille" is rejected in the name of the demand for artistic freedom expressed by *le goût baroque*. Referring to a dictionary definition of the term, the author of the anonymous letter states:

> Our artists do not transgress any law prescribed in the realm of art when they invent new ornamentation, which, throughout time, has been arbitrary. . . . A nation that has recently liberated itself from the shackles that once beset its society taught us this freedom in the artistic realm. This way of working was called "baroque taste," probably because of a word used to designate pearls or teeth that are not all the same size (*Dictionnaire étymologique* [1750; Etymological Dictionary], note on *baroque* written by M. Menage).

Supporting Winckelmann in his attack on the baroque, Rafael Mengs uses one of the synonyms for "baroque"—"capricious"—in his *Lettre de M. Mengs sur l'origine, les progrès et la décadence des arts* (Letter from Mr. Mengs on the Origin, the Progress, and the Decadence of the Arts): "Pietro de Cortona indulges in caprice and Borromini was extravagant to the extreme."

In the works of Gotthold Ephraim Lessing and members of his circle, who were inspired by French Enlightenment philosophy and by the French and German movements favoring a return to antiquity, different variations of the French use of "baroque" occur together with the earlier form, *barokisch*. Lessing most often uses the latter in a neutral sense because individu-alized, irregular depictions—for example "a baroque expression" (*barokische Ausdruck*—are part of "a more natural portrayal of human life" (as admirably shown by William Shakespeare) and are thus related to Greek drama, although it differs from the French classical tradition (Wieland's *Agathon* [1766; The History of Agathon]; quoted in *Hamburgische dramaturgie* [1767–69; Hamburg Dramaturgy]). Lessing, like the French, also uses the word "baroque" as a synonym for "rocaille style." Thus, when translating a passage from *De la poésie dramatique* (1758; On Dramatic Poetry) in which Diderot affirms that "a man of taste" always lives in a room where there are "no knick-knacks; hardly any gilding; simple furniture," Lessing writes "Nichts Barokes; wenig Verguldung; die Möbeln schlecht und recht" (Nothing baroque; little gilding; simple and honest furniture), in *Das Theater des Herrn Diderot* [1760; The Theatre of Monsieur Diderot]). An article in the *Briefe die neueste Litteratur betreffend* (26 July 1759), published by Lessing's friend and collaborator Friedrich Nicolai, sums up the work of Krubsacius (1759), in which the terms "rocaille" and "baroque taste" are closely related, as they are in Lessing's work. This article marks the point at which members of Lessing's circle broke with overdone rocaille and the latter phases of 17th-century anticlassical art. In *Harlequin* (1761; Harlequin; or, A Defense of Grotesque Comic Performances; in *Kleinere Schriften* [1843; Short Writings]), which Lessing had described in the *Hamburgische Dramaturgie,* Justus Möser includes in his defense of *Groteske-Komische* (grotesque comic) what he calls the "baroque taste" of Teniers and Jacques Callot:

> The style of distortion, or the so-called baroque taste, certainly has its beauty, but it does not belong in temples or other works that are meant to last into eternity. Only someone like Bartas, the prince of French poets, would be able . . . to convey the greatness of creation in burlesque verse.

Möser concludes that "the baroque taste requires dissimilar parts in order to be complete," because it includes the comic. In German literary criticism, *der Barockgeschmack* (baroque taste) refers most often to a lack of both taste and classical restraint. An anonymous writer states in *Gelehrte Neuigkeiten* (1750; Learned Novelties) that "baroque taste has driven even German poets so far that they hang their lyres no longer on upright trees, nor even according to the law of gravity." In the *Briefe die neueste Litteratur betreffend* (1764; Correspondence on the Latest in Literature), F.G. Resewitz asks, "When will our writers develop a taste that is more orderly, more consistent? When will their taste stop being so baroque?" Johann Gottfried Herder, meanwhile, states: "This man has shaped his body for many years according to baroque taste; he has apparently imparted this very taste to his own soul." (*Sämmtliche Werke* [1775; Collected Works]). In the refined, ironic German rococo poetry, the terms *barock* or *barockisch* appear either in connection with "baroque taste"—the art of Bernini for example—in which baroque forms serve to trace the profile of each individual—or else in the description of scintillating elements of rocaille, in nature or in decoration. In Wieland's comic poem *Der neue Amadis* (1771; The New Amadis), one of the characters, Blaffardine, is described as *barockish* and as "a marble sculpture in the style of the great Bernini," who of course does not have "Greek contours." "From below, he [Blaffardine] resembles Rubens's best nymphs; from above, he is ideal for scaring away birds." In a slightly ironic, learned note, the reader learns that Winckelmann battled against this "modern Phidias" (Bernini) because Bernini's style had too much *Schwulst*.

In the rococo poems of F.W. Zachariä, the term *barock* also refers to exuberant, sparkling rocaille forms in nature or in artistic ornamentation. Thus, in *Verwandlungen* (1754; Metamorphoses) he asserts that: "The snail's spiral house and colorful seashells in baroque style decorate the cliff walls"; and in *Der Phaeton* (1754; Phaeton), he writes: "Aurora became jealous that her antiquated vehicle could not compare with this Phaeton. The artist portrays the whole thing in baroque taste. The body is a gilded seashell." In sum, the German conception of "baroque taste" is somewhat more nuanced than the *Encyklopädisches Wörterbuch* (1793; Encyclopedic Dictionary) would lead one to believe, with its assertion that "baroque taste in the visual arts means the same as a corrupted taste, where the artist does not order his work according to the rules of correct judgment."

Britain

The term *barocco* appears in such 18th-century British reference works as Ephraim Chambers's *Cyclopaedia* (1728) or the *Encyclopaedia Britannica* (1788)—only with the meaning of the "Scholastic term" mentioned above. The figurative meaning of the word "baroque" or "baroque taste," as used on the European continent, is found only in English translations of foreign works, such as Henry Fuseli's translation of the aforementioned anonymous letter criticizing Winckelmann's *Gedanken über die Nachahmung der griechischen Werke in der Malerei und Bildhauerkunst* (1755; Reflections on the Painting and Sculpture of the Greeks). Synonyms for "baroque"—for example "capricious"—are found mainly in architectural criticism, notably in Colin Campbell's harsh evaluation,

inspired by Andrea Palladio, of the baroque style in Rome in *Vitruvius Britannicus* (1717–25): "The Italians . . . employed capricious Ornaments, which must at last end in the Gothick. . . . How affected and licentious are the Works of Bernini and Fontana? How wildly Extravagant are the Designs of Borromini?"

Spain

"The revival of antiquity," and the coherent criticism of the baroque that followed from it, took root strongly in Spain when Rafael Mengs was named to the Academy of Madrid in 1763. This honor came in recognition of his lectures on the art of antiquity and with the support of his admirers, especially G.M. de Jovellanos and A. Ponz. The Spanish did not use the term "baroque" in their criticism of the baroque. Most of them—for example, Ponz in *Viaje de España* (1772–94; Travels in Spain)—used the expressions *churrigueresca* or *gusto churrigueresco*, terms derived from the family name of three baroque architects, the Churrigueras. Others, such as Jovellanos, used the expressions *estilo riberesco* (Riberesco style) or *borrominesco* (Borrominesque). Spanish criticism of the baroque was clearly inspired by that of neighboring countries, as shown in this summary by J. Ortiz y Sanz, in *Elogio de la Arquitectura* (1804; In Praise of Architecture): "Unfortunately Guarini, Pozzo, Borromini, and their pernicious followers were fruitful in this depraved taste, as were our Salamancan, Jusef Churriguera and his two sons." Spanish critics of the baroque (for example Jovellanos) also drew on literary parallels, especially the plays of Lope de Vega.

Conclusion

The term "baroque" maintained its polemical meaning up to the mid–19th century, when analyses of baroque art and baroque style by, among others, Jakob Burckhardt and J. Falke (1855 and 1866) appeared. However, it was only after the publication of the significant work by Wölfflin, *Renaissance und Barock* (1888; Renaissance and Baroque), that the word "baroque" truly became a term for a precise style or "general concept" free of all pejorative connotations. In the same period, the synonyms "bizarre" and "capricious" lost their standing as terms of art and "rocaille style" became an independent notion.

ELSE MARIE BUKDAHL

See also Architecture; Rococo

Further Reading

Kurz, Otto, "Barocco: Storia di una parola," *Lettere italiane* 12, no. 4 (October–December 1960)

Martin, John Rupert, *Baroque,* New York: Harper and Row, and Westview Press, and London: Allen Lane, 1977

Tapié, Victor Lucien, *The Age of Grandeur: Baroque Art and Architecture,* translated by A. Ross Williamson, New York: Praeger, 1960; 2nd edition with new bibliography, 1966 (original French edition, 1957)

Wellek, René, "The Concept of Baroque in Literary Scholarship," *The Journal of Aesthetics and Art Criticism* 5, no. 2 (December 1946)

Beautiful

Anyone who looks into the history of speculations about the beautiful is at once struck by the inability of this key term to express an exclusively aesthetic value. Moreover, the Latin word *bellus* (from which are derived the Italian *bello,* the French *beau,* and in a more complicated way, the English "beautiful") is a diminutive of *bonus* (good). The word indicates the modesty or the mediocrity of a possession (talent, intelligence, or culture) but also the true smallness of an object (of a baby bird, a child, etc.) or else its affective value. In each of these cases, it indicates less a "full-blown goodness" than its "foretaste," as Pierre Monteil demonstrates in *Beau et laid en latin* (1964; Beautiful and Ugly in Latin). From its Latin meanings the word inherits all sorts of usages—servile, caustic, or admiring—that are difficult to reconcile. In the 17th century, the French *beau* (beautiful, fine, good, true, real, etc.) qualified "anything that approaches a certain perfection: that which is polite, honest, wise, virtuous, fortunate, glorious," according to César-Pierre Richelet's dictionary. But its usages extend to rhetorical figures, such as the antiphrase, the concession, or the hyperbole. Thus in French one could say: "J'irai vous voir un beau matin" (I shall go to see you one of these fine days); "nous avons beau nous ménager" (however much we tried to go easy); "jouer beau jeu" (to play a fine game); "avoir le commandement beau" (to be a fine leader); "avoir une belle peur" (to get a real fright).

Faced with such imprecision of meaning, the aim of Enlightenment thought on this issue, insofar as its culmination is to be found in Immanuel Kant's criticism, was to isolate or give autonomy to its aesthetic value. In that sense, the redefinition of the beautiful was closely tied to the attempt to found aesthetics as a science. It must be remembered moreover that Kant felt obliged to restrict himself to a critique of the faculty of aesthetic judgment. He asserted the impossibility of founding a science of the beautiful and in the third "Critique" of his *Kritik der Urteilskraft* (The Critique of Judgment)

he limits himself to an adjectival use of the word "aesthetic," which is a striking paradox if he is the one credited with the success of the noun. Defining the beautiful thus involves explaining the essence but also of the useful aspects of the beautiful; offering literary criticism but also art criticism; a philosophy of art but also a history; a consideration of artistic technology, and above all, a general anthropology. These heterogeneous viewpoints engaged in meditations on the beautiful—with all their attendant terminological fluctuations—attest to the liveliness of the debate over this aesthetic category at the time. We should recall that it fell to the Enlightenment, to Alexander Baumgarten, to coin the noun "aesthetics"; to La Font de Saint-Yonne and Denis Diderot to inaugurate direct criticism of the art exhibited at the Salons; to Johann Winckelmann to develop a systematic history of art; and to Kant to provide the foundations of a theory of taste.

The 18th century's chief originality was to ensure the privileged connection between the beautiful and art, evident in the expression sanctioned at that time: "fine arts" (*Beaux-Arts, belle arti, schöne Künste*). The term was already in use in the works of André Félibien and Giovanni Pietro Bellori. In the 18th century it also became a category, as demonstrated not only by the publication of Jacques Lacombe's *Dictionnaire portatif des beaux-arts* (1752; Portable Dictionary of Fine Arts), or by Canon Bonsi's *Trionfo delle belle arti* (1767; Triumph of Fine Arts), but also by the founding, in Venice in 1756 and in France in 1816, of academies of fine arts: the Accademia delle Belle Arte and the Académie des Beaux-Arts respectively. Moreover, the term *belles-lettres* was eclipsed by this new designation that had become nearly all-encompassing, as shown for instance by the definition of aesthetics as the "philosophy of the fine arts," as proposed by Johann Georg Sulzer in his entry "Esthétique" (Aesthetics) in the *Théorie générale des beaux-arts* (1771; General Theory of Fine Arts). The term "fine arts" is picked up again in the *Supplé-*

ment of the *Encyclopédie*. What can explain the training of such a favorable spotlight on the visual arts?

Doubtless the humanist heritage was too weighty for poetry to be considered under the single category of *beau* (the beautiful); and in the eyes of the public, music was not yet the art par excellence that it was to become during the romantic period. Two underlying theses emerge from the new term of "fine arts": On the one hand, whatever their ultimate ends might be, the arts had rallied under the banner of the beautiful and subsequently under the banner of pleasure. Thus, Charles Batteux presented the fine arts as "arts of pleasure," distinct from the mechanical or "useful arts." On the other hand, what is beautiful falls primarily under the category of the arts and not under that of nature or applied science.

In the history of the convergence of the beautiful and of art in the 18th century, the chief objective was first to promote the eminence of the plastic arts (arts that "soiled the hands," and therefore akin to the crafts) by emphasizing their affinity with poetry and music through reference to the classical doctrine of *ut pictura poesis* (as in painting, so in poetry): this objective reached its culmination in the work of Batteux. At the turn of the century, on the other hand, more emphasis was placed on the specificity of the arts. Recognition of the dangers of obsession with appearances, and awareness of the originality of genius and of the irreducibility of the sublime to the beautiful, had resulted in casting suspicion on any speculation that was not based on a thorough study of the effects and the means of each defined form of art. Edmund Burke or Gotthold Ephraim Lessing—whose *Laokoon* (1766; Laocoön: An Essay upon the Limits of Painting and Poetry) was not translated into French until the 19th century—played a decisive role in the formation of these views. But doubtless it was in France, and especially thanks to Diderot, that it was understood most clearly that the problem consisted of bridging the gulf between the metaphysicians of the beautiful, inspired by the ideas of René Descartes, and the artists and critics, who were less concerned with the beautiful than the quality or the excellence of a work. At the beginning of the century, in an evocation of the "beauties" that sparkle in poems or picture, the abbé Jean-Baptiste Dubos put these criteria into perspective: "It is not enough for poems to be beautiful (*pulchra*); they must be pleasing," he reminds his readers, quoting Horace. His statement suffices to show that the special union between the thought of the beautiful and the aesthetic value of the works rested on a problematic foundation, even though the idea of a potential victory of art over nature had already long been familiar.

Alongside the newly established solidarity of the concepts of the beautiful and of art, there was a relative but undeniable shift of interest with regard to the spectacle offered by nature: beauty was no longer everyone's sole focus. In addition to the beautiful, reflecting a northern European sensibility, the rough-hewn, the unkempt, the sublime, and the picturesque were promoted to the rank of aesthetic values. Moreover, when "imitation of nature" was mentioned, it was primarily a reference to man. Even though the landscape had been making steady inroads into Western art from the 16th century onward, for some time the expression and the splendor of the human body would nonetheless remain the emblem of triumphant beauty. Art was not to extricate itself easily from the "subject." In the 18th century, while ideas of an essential difference between natural beauty and artistic beauty might well be in the air, their alliance continued to arouse the keenest feeling for the beautiful, while mediation by the classical played a decisive role in the choice of the human body as the meeting point of the perceptible and the ideal, of the natural and the artistic.

The Classical Heritage: From the Idea to "Inner Form"

Although Plato won renown for giving dignity and universal value to the beautiful, raised to the level of Idea, his theory of true knowledge had led him to lock the arts into the option of simple imitation or of futile rivalry with philosophy. Paradoxically, his theory of Ideas nevertheless became the pivot point of speculations about artistic creation and criticism. It was a reversal that had its origins in classical antiquity and did not come to full realization until the Renaissance, as Erwin Panofsky has shown. Plato's theory of Ideas could well have entered into conflict with his theory on the imitation of nature, which was the keystone of the artistic renewal, if the latter had not already been conceived as "beautiful nature"—that is to say, nature in a state of perfection that it never attains empirically but that can be reconstructed from scattered, incomplete elements. The distinctive characteristic of art was not therefore to create the beautiful but to banish the obstacles that prevent us from recognizing and appreciating it. It is a process in which an increasingly essential role is played by the concept, the form in action, the *exemplum* (type) or the *modelo* (model). And so it is that, from the middle of the 16th century, in a Florentine context in Giorgio Vasari's works, and at the beginning of the 17th century in those of Federico Zuccari, the Idea had lost its meaning of ideational content to signify the imaginative faculty, the artistic project, the *disegno interno* (inner form). This shift explains the prerogatives of drawing or design over color, which had a closer connection to the physical senses.

Anthony Ashley Cooper, third earl of Shaftesbury (1671–1713) an early theorist of aesthetics, successfully assimilated this entire heritage. Taking into account the quirks of the Platonic Idea as well as the originality of the Italian theory of art, he elaborated a philosophy encompassing all the forms of the beautiful, which he ranked according to their degree of proximity to the mind that produces them (and therefore the one that appreciates them). An activation of all the powers of the mind presides over the discovery of the supreme beauties of nature and especially over the discovery of the beauties of wild and empty places whose melancholy we fear. Thus, visible beauty yields to "mysterious, hidden beauty," while the latter borrows at times from the sublime its initial frightening and disturbing aspect.

But how can one simultaneously take into account the appearance and the reality of the beautiful? "The beautifying not the beautified, is the really beautiful," writes Shaftesbury. Fénelon writes in a similar vein in the same period: "The beautiful that is nothing but beautiful is only half beautiful." In other words, the beautiful must be so active that it overflows from the object so as to make beautiful not only its actual medium or support but also the rest of the world. The challenge therefore consists in relating established beauty to beauty in the making, abandoning the domain of appearances. From the "dead forms," incapable of engendering new forms, the gaze must shift toward the "forms that form," to those that possess "intelligence, action, operation," and, finally, toward that universal genius that moves the universe and which is both nature and liberty: the "form of the forms that form." Genius will then become a "Second Creator," a rival of Zeus; and imitating nature will first consist of forging from it an "inner model," or "inner form," characterized by its unity and rhythm.

However, the elegance of such a solution is far from compatible with a mode of thought that was more inclined to skim the surface of the world, a mode of thought that introduced distinctions without yet knowing in what register to modulate them, and that sometimes sought originality for its own sake. Thus the principle of empathy with universal genius would be replaced by a "sixth sense," which would by some miracle tune in to the beautiful; and as for beauty conceived as the presenter of a kind of unique truth, it was to yield to a beauty of simple appearances, more or less illusory or deceptive, more a symbol of luxury than anything. Such concepts, however, would be merely caricatures of a powerful trend of thought whose merit was the desire to wipe the slate clean in order to reexamine the meaning of words in the light of newly acquired experience. Thus it was that, in the first half of the 18th century, the conflict between empiricists and Cartesians came to the forefront, apparently without taking into account the classical heritage that Shaftesbury had so masterfully assimilated into his theories.

Idealism or Empiricism

However elementary a meditation on the beautiful might be, it has to look in two directions at once: first, toward the object, or rather, toward the idea of that object, whose provenance, content, and status it is important to distinguish; second, toward the observing subject, or rather, toward the collection of physiological and discursive traces of the viewer's own affective modalities: a presentation of both the beautiful and the pleasure it provides. The Enlightenment strove to reveal beauty's strictly aesthetic character, which at that time was dubbed "taste" and often promoted to the rank of "love." The truth slowly emerged: neither subject nor object was readily accessible, but the ways in which they were constituted were revealed in a game whose rules seemed less and less declarable a priori. This truth was irrefutable since it turned out that the cleverest ways of getting involved in the game consisted of modifying, implicitly or not, the deal of the cards.

In Alexander Gottlieb Baumgarten's work there is a very interesting version of idealism. Aspiring to found under the name of aesthetics a "science of sensual knowledge," conceived as "a metaphysics of the beautiful," but also as "a lower-level gnoseology," or "a logic without thorns," Baumgarten credits aesthetic representations with clarity, since each one of them possesses at least one characteristic that individualizes it and suffices for its recognition. However, he denies them distinction so as not to compare them with philosophical representations. These confused perceptions were to be conceived, following Gottfried Wilhelm Leibniz, as "the result of the impressions that the whole universe makes on us." According to Baumgarten, the whole universe, and not merely one of its fragments, is what the beautiful presents to us.

In France pure idealism was a myth invented for polemical purposes. One could follow Giambattista Vico and accuse the Cartesians of having raised the value of clear and distinct ideas to the point of founding the culture of the *ingenium* (the "innate nature" of the thing) through exercises of a purely mathematical kind, but one can hardly reproach Descartes for having failed to consider suspect the appeal of the union of the senses and the imagination. Does he not catch a glimpse of the specificity of aesthetics when he asserts that the feelings caused by the ugly and the beautiful—which he calls the feelings of horror and of pleasure—are those "that deceive the most, and against which one must be most careful"? His justification is that "what reaches the soul through the senses strikes it more strongly than what is represented to it by reason." One may conclude that "Descartes never speculated on anything but the true: Malebranche added to it the good and he wrote a treatise on morals; Father André tried to add to it the beautiful," an attempt that Victor Cousin supposedly brought to completion. Thus, Emile Krantz gallicized the working out of a trinity thenceforth held as classic.

Indeed, in Father Yves-Marie André's works one encounters a typology of the visibly beautiful that has the undeniable advantage of clarity. As a Cartesian, he follows Malebranche in rejecting the doctrine of the free creation of eternal truths. He also assumes the existence of an innate idea of the beautiful that inclines us to like regularity, order, proportion, and symmetry—a liking that places, so to speak, a "compass in our eyes." Alongside this essential and uncreated beauty, he allows nonetheless for a beauty of divine origin. Mindful of the recent debate between Charles Le Brun and Roger de Piles on the preeminence of drawing or color, André denies God credit for the invention of geometry in order to grant him that of "natural color," a veritable magic that André sees as triumphing over the greatest ideas on coloration invented by man.

What became then of aesthetic pleasure? It was a necessary effect of the ideas of geometric beauty and of beauty as a divine creation, a contingent effect, but still an effect. Diderot borrows André's phrasing in his own entry, "Beau" (Beautiful), in the *Encyclopédie*. "But tell me, is a thing beautiful because it pleases, or does it please because it is beautiful? There is no problem; it pleases because it is beautiful. I think so as you do." I think so: both Diderot and Father André doubtless remember the separation that could occur between feeling and idea to which the Calvinist minister Crousaz had drawn attention: Sometimes ideas and feelings are in agreement, and an object deserves the epithet beautiful in a double sense. Sometimes, on the contrary, ideas and feelings are in opposition, and then the same object pleases and does not please: in one respect it is beautiful, and in another it lacks beauty.

Doubtless intellectual pleasure and sensual pleasure did not necessarily go hand in hand in the eyes of Father André, but finally ideal beauty won out over sensual beauty and aesthetic pleasure presupposed the assent of the mind. From such a viewpoint, either the question of pleasure remained superfluous, or else the pleasure under discussion was already merely a very sublimated pleasure.

The abbé Dubos stood at the opposite extreme of Cartesian thought. As early as 1719 he adopted the viewpoint of the spectator and, well ahead of his times, proposed an aesthetics of reception. Meditating on the nature, the meaning, and the impact of the pleasure furnished by art, he notes the contradictory character of a "pleasure that often resembles affliction," but he feels confident in asserting that "man in general suffers even more from living without feelings than his feelings make him suffer." Therefore, the "artificial feelings" engendered by art would have the double merit of keeping men from boredom—that vacuum of sensation that ultimately triggers anguish—and from the real suffering caused by the "evil consequences" of their feelings. Dubos is therefore inclined to reassert all the virtues of the Aristotelian theory of catharsis: art's prime function is to affect our emotional states so as to make them bearable. Therefore, when it comes to the question of deciding on the "merit" or "excellence" of a work of art, Dubos affirms unhesitatingly the superiority of the "sentimental path" over the path of reason, for in it there is no need for either rules or guidance. One should also trust public opinion more than that of people in the profession. To justify the feeling of the presence of genius, Dubos evokes a "sixth sense," which in contradictory fashion he conceives as both a mechanical organism and as a faculty enlightened and instructed by the repeated exercise of comparison. This sixth sense is primarily an organ belonging to a physiologically and sociohistorically determined elite. It is not simply, as it was later to become in Kant's thinking, a presupposition that allows one to represent to oneself, as objective, the subjective necessity of universal assent. Pleasure that rises to the height of passion, passion that is controlled in artifice, this sixth sense that seems to be some kind of sensualized reason—all determine aesthetic value. But it is never said that these features precede reason: a harmony is created between value, on the one hand, and feeling and judgment, on the other, which mirror each other with regard to the value.

If a theory could be found in the 18th century that made aesthetic pleasure the cause of the idea of the beautiful, aesthetic pleasure would thus be compared with physical pleasure and beauty reduced to the agreeable, while the ties between the aesthetics of the beautiful and of the moral would break. In 1748 Morelly did indeed identify beauty with the "light, keen shock" of pleasure that it gives us, in order to elaborate a purely physical theory of beauty. But Burke is certainly the one who went the furthest into the idea of a hedonistic "origin" for the idea of the beautiful: an origin he sometimes calls the "efficient cause" to distinguish it clearly from the ultimate cause. Following Sir Isaac Newton, Burke claims in effect to explain the how, not the why. He can only make positive pleasure the cause of the beautiful to the extent that he contrasts positive pleasure with a relative pleasure or charm, which comes from a distancing of displeasure: relaxation and physical repose are then distinguished from the violent organic reactions that accompany the formation of the sublime thought. Elsewhere, Burke goes so far as to deny any solution of continuity between the nature of feeling and the nature of vision. Not only does the beautiful belong to the lower order of senses, but touch acquires a privileged status. "Smoothness" is a value that pervades every domain, the ancestor of that "tactile quality" to which Berensen was to attribute every sensation of vital force or comfort. To the absence of roughness of a surface, to its plushness, would correspond the softness and gaiety of color, the clarity and regularity of certain sounds, not to mention the richness of flavors or the elegance of a perfume. "Softness is the beauty of taste": such is the phrase that sums up the aesthetics of the beautiful according to Burke. Inevitably Chardin's favorite exhortation comes to mind, which Diderot quoted: "Softness, nothing but softness!" In short, the pleasure of the beautiful was not an empty expression: "The presence of beauty inspires love as naturally as the application of ice or fire produces ideas of cold or heat . . . Beauty is, essentially speaking, a quality of the body which acts mechanically on the human mind by means of the senses." This concept was to cause a major problem in Kant's theory, since Kant took from Burke the principle of the distinction between the sublime and the beautiful. For Kant, in effect, the beautiful pleases (*gefällt*) but gives no pleasure (*nicht vergnügt*), its principle is not that of the agreeable. Based on which principle then ought one to consider beauty's distinctiveness from the sublime?

Kant: From Silent Beauty to Expressive Beauty

One cannot reduce Kant's theory of the beautiful to the admirable definitions of the analytics of the beautiful that developed what could be called a negative aesthetic. The immense primary effort made by Kant, in the tradition of Socrates, Francis Hutcheson, and Burke, is to seal off the essence of the beautiful from its supposedly contingent elements; in other words, to think of beauty as an absolute, independent of any other associations. For, if there certainly exists a beauty of the enjoyable, of the useful, of the moving, of the good, of the true, there still ought to exist a unique beauty, accessible by dint of ruling out these contingents: (1) Exclusion of practical and material interests: Far from luring one's inclinations or forcing one's respect, the beautiful is a favor that one enjoys in the sphere of meditation. The adoption of a strictly aesthetic viewpoint—supposing that it could be upheld—is thus marked by a feeling of disinterest with regard to the existence of the object as such, but not with regard to its representation. (2) Exclusion of the concept: Judgment of the beautiful cannot claim the objective universality of a judgment in full knowledge of the facts. The beautiful pleases without benefit of a concept: in other words, it becomes by right, and only by right, the object of universal assent, each individual postulating the universal communicability of its impression on the senses. (3) Exclusion of any defined end: One cannot justify the beautiful either by the perfection of its concept or by the exercise of a power (emotional, utilitarian, or

moral). "The perfection of sensory knowledge" is not what constitutes beauty, despite Baumgarten's assertions. It must be admitted; pure beauty does not rely on any concept; it is free and mute. By the same token, the expression "intellectual beauty" is incorrect, since the beautiful gives itself to the ear and the eye and is not reconstructed, as we suppose it to be. Exclusion of every defined end does not, however, equal the exclusion of every finality, a fact witnessed as much by the stimulation of our senses as by our desire to perpetuate the pleasure we feel. The beautiful is, in effect, less the promise of happiness than a happiness of the moment, whose enjoyment we try to prolong. (4) Exclusion, finally, of lack of conditions: One cannot attribute to aesthetic judgment any objective necessity whatsoever. Its necessity is always conditional, since one should make sure that the present case is properly subsumed under a principle of universal assent, which is merely presupposed.

In Kant's "Deduction" the illusion that consists of melding finality and conception of an end is clearly apparent. The problem presented in the "Deduction" is to legitimize the use of the concept "beautiful" with regard to natural forms. How do our aesthetic judgments reach the object via a pleasure felt to be universal and necessary through such judgment a priori? Kant does not regard this reaching of the object as a piece of knowledge: he aims solely to legitimize a priori the universality of a demand for assent in the encounter with objects whose form pleases in the absence of any interest in them, in their concept, or in their end, as analytics had shown. The essential point is therefore to understand that the beautiful reveals itself in the feeling of a felicitous exercise of our faculties. This pleasure constitutes neither the cause nor the effect of the representation; it accompanies it as an awareness of the harmony of the representative state. It is neither a passive pleasure (sensual enjoyment), nor an active pleasure (moral fulfillment), nor a negative pleasure (joy in recognizing the existence of a supernatural principle and a power), but a positive pleasure extracted from the perceptible world by meditation.

Kant's real contribution is therefore that of having stripped the beautiful of everything that was simply its accessory. After emptying all content from the essence of the beautiful by means of continual kenosis, what remains? Nothing, or almost nothing, only a pure myth of the beautiful, if one goes by the examples provided (flowers, foliated scrolls, musical improvisation), nothing but an indefinable favor whose universal recognition is merely postulated, an enjoyment produced by self-love, since it is the simple feeling of the unforeseen harmony of one's faculties.

The whole problem lies then in grasping how Kant moves from free and silent beauty, distinct from every perfection, to beauty conceived as "the expression of aesthetic Ideas." For Kant it is without doubt a matter of satisfying two contradictory demands: analytic rigor leads him to distinguish the pure from the impure and to create "abysses" that look unbridgeable, while his taking of human interests into account prompts him to devote less study to stable objects than to the centers of attraction and repulsion, which allows orientation and a passage over. Was it not Kant's second objective to understand the dynamics that let the beautiful play such an important role in our lives as a "vehicle" if not as the birthplace of theoretical knowledge and of practical necessity? Kant invents a third type of Idea: the Idea that is neither theoretical nor practical, but "aesthetic."

The aesthetic Idea seems an additional contradiction (*in adjecto*), since for Kant the essence of the Idea is its inability to accept intuition. Would Kant reach the point of restoring intellectual intuition in the sense sought by Friedrich Schelling? Absolutely not. Because no concept could possibly prove adequate for him, Kant recalls Baumgarten's confused notion. Nevertheless, the aesthetic idea "makes one think a great deal," "leans toward something which lies outside the limits of experience," "tries to draw near a presentation of the concepts of reason," and confers upon perceptible forms "a perfection of which no example exists in nature."

The beautiful is the "expression of aesthetic Ideas." Kant does not say that the beautiful is an Idea—far from it. The function of the beautiful is to present the Ideas in a way that makes them unforgettable without nonetheless providing us with the appropriate concept: beauty expresses, but does not imitate, the Ideas. Indeed, it is not a second and visible copy that it furnishes, it is a visible and hitherto uncommunicated message, produced by a faculty of the senses that is no longer passive but endowed with energy: the imagination, which is "the originating source of new forms of intuitions," even becomes a rival of reason. Kant has forgotten neither Shaftesbury's "inner form," produced by the second "creator," a veritable "Prometheus," nor the criticism of the theory of imitation developed by Burke and Lessing. It is striking to see him thus converge with a whole humanist current of thought, represented in the first part of the 18th century by Vico, who, without feeling the need to refer to the work of art, had managed to raise the imagination to the rank of a creative force by which man creates himself and creates his world.

In this way the fine arts attain an unexpected eminence. It has become common to cite Kant's praise of natural beauty, enjoyment of which constitutes a "distinctive sign of the goodness of the soul." It has become common to cite his denunciation of artistic use of special effects, repeating his evocation of the song of the nightingale. But the phrase in Section 49 has been for-

gotten: "The poet ventures to make perceptible the Ideas of reason . . . in a perfect form of which there exists no example in nature." The fine arts are doubtless only an opaque and unreliable screen for projecting Ideas, but nothing can replace that screen. Kant does not doubt the role of the imaginary and its essential promotion in art.

The Prestige of the Beautiful

Kant's definitions of the beautiful seem to us emblematic of the thought of the Enlightenment in that they are capable of uniting a radical distrust with regard to the beautiful and a sudden awareness, constantly increasing, of its importance in the destiny of individuals and societies. Doubtless an unmediated or direct relationship with the Absolute was always suspect and the enjoyment of stabilized forms was nourished by a certain challenge to knowledge. As Kant writes: "Taste hampers intelligence. I have to read and reread Rousseau until the beauty of the expression no longer disturbs me; it is only then that I can grasp him through reasoning." But however ambiguous that vehicle of the true and the good, why neglect this sovereign instrument of instruction? How could one not see that the beautiful constitutes the best bonding for a society, the beautiful that is the preferred tool of an age to which we owe the invention of "the art of reciprocal communication of ideas between the most cultured and the most ignorant classes" or, what is more, "the adaptation of the development and the refinement of the former classes to the natural simplicity and originality of the latter"? Today, when the adjective "aesthetic" is a natural synonym for "beautiful," aestheticism is thought of in an even more formal way than Dubos, Burke, or Kant, each in his own way, conceived it. But to admire aestheticism while at the same time stigmatizing it, as if it is a sin against the intelligence, is to adopt, at the opposite pole to the romantics, the attitude of the Enlightenment.

It is true that the 18th century managed to stress another method of access to the Absolute—a partially negative but direct way—by making the sublime not the serendipitous gift of the beautiful but a form of vertigo that destabilized the environment, dissolved one's routine outlook, and made one aware of a superior causality at the moment of its action. Behind the euphoria of the beautiful lurked, in effect, the distress of the self, conscious of both the blandness of daily routine and of its powerlessness to enhance it. When the beautiful throws its dazzling veil over my eyes and enters my life in order to open it up, when the beautiful denies itself to the point of borrowing the traits of the ugly, then there appears what the Enlightenment called "the sublime." This is the other side of the coin—the beautiful is now suspect, less for its gentleness than for the difficulty inherent in experiencing it.

BALDINE SAINT GIRONS

See also Aesthetics; Art Criticism; Ideal; Sublime; Taste; Ugliness and Deformity

Further Reading

Addison, Joseph, et al., *The Spectator,* 8 vols., London: Buckley and Tonson, 1712–15; reprint, edited by Donald F. Bond, 5 vols., Oxford: Clarendon Press, 1965

Alison, Archibald, *Essays on the Nature and Principles of Taste,* London: Robinson, and Edinburgh: Bell and Bradfute, 1790; reprint, Hildesheim, Germany: Olms, 1968

Burke, Edmund, *A Philosophical Enquiry into the Origin of Our Ideas of the Sublime and Beautiful,* London: Dodsley, 1757; reprint, edited by Adam Phillips, Oxford and New York: Oxford University Press, 1990

Gerard, Alexander, *An Essay on Taste: With Three Dissertations on the Same Subject by Mr. De Voltaire, Mr. D'Alembert, F.R.S., and Mr. De Montesquieu,* London: Millar, 1759; reprint, New York: Garland, 1970

Gilpin, William, *Observations on the River Wye and Several Parts of South Wales, Relative Chiefly to Picturesque Beauty,* London: Blamire, 1782; reprint, Oxford and New York: Woodstock Books, 1991

Hobson, Marian, *The Object of Art: The Theory of Illusion in Eighteenth-Century France,* Cambridge and New York: Cambridge University Press, 1982

Hogarth, William, *The Analysis of Beauty: Written with a View of Fixing the Fluctuating Ideas of Taste,* London: Reeves, 1753; reprint, edited by Ronald Paulson, New Haven, Connecticut: Yale University Press, 1997

Kames, Henry Home, *Elements of Criticism,* 3 vols., Edinburgh: Millar, London, and A. Kincaid and J. Bell, Edinburgh, 1762; reprint, 2 vols., New York: Garland, 1971–72

Lee, Rensselaer Wright, *Ut Pictura Poesis: The Humanistic Theory of Painting,* New York: Norton, 1967

Pratt, Samuel Jackson, *The Sublime and Beautiful of Scripture, Being Essays on Select Passages of Sacred Composition,* London: n.p., 1777

Panofsky, Erwin, *Idea: A Concept in Art Theory,* translated by Joseph J.S. Peake, Columbia: University of South Carolina Press, 1968 (original German edition, 1924)

Saint Girons, Baldine, *Fiat lux: Une philosophie du sublime,* Paris: Quai Voltaire, 1993

Webb, Daniel, *An Inquiry into the Beauties of Painting,* London: Dodsley, 1760

Bible

While there can be no doubt that the Bible was still the most widely read book in Europe in the 18th century, its status nonetheless changed radically, becoming in many respects comparable to what it is today. There were three major effects of Bible reading: first, the reappropriation of the Bible by the mass of believers; second, a greater understanding of its text, context, and history; and finally, the dissemination of this new awareness beyond the confines of theology.

In this respect as in others, the European Enlightenment initially owed much to Baruch Spinoza's *Tractatus theologico-politicus* (1670; A Theologico-Political Treatise); to the remarkable works of the Protestant Orientalists of the 16th and 17th centuries; and to the polemics that issued from the Council of Trent—the debate between Jacques-Bénigne Bossuet and Richard Simon being the most interesting for us here because it set the course for almost all research into the biblical text. Finally, two great translations of the Bible helped to shape entire new cultures: Martin Luther's translation, which was first subjected to cautious questioning in the 18th century; and the Authorized Version (the King James Bible), which, after 1760, acquired a prestige that it would long retain.

The varieties of German Pietism, along with the *Haskalah* among Jews, offer the best examples of the reappropriation of the Bible by believers. The sacred texts that religious orthodoxy had monopolized in the service of Tridentine, Lutheran, or rabbinical dogma made a new and direct appeal to believers in their own languages, without any authoritarian and unequivocal mediation. Halle was the center from which Bibles were the most widely distributed, particularly through the work of Baron Hildebrand von Canstein. Philipp Jacob

Spener, the founder of Lutheran Pietism, had already shifted the focus of Christianity toward a greater understanding of Scripture through collective reading in the *collegia pietatis* (colleges of piety), relegating academic theology to second rank. August Hermann Francke brought the Bible to everyone. Thanks to the Cansteinsche Bibelanstalt (Canstein Bible Foundation), established in 1710, and to new technical processes, Francke succeeded in mass-producing Bibles and, above all, in drastically reducing their price. Eighty thousand copies of the Bible and 100,000 copies of the New Testament were printed between 1712 and 1719. By 1812, 2 million copies of the Bible had been printed in more than 380 editions, as well as more than 1 million copies of the New Testament bound with the Psalms, and 100,000 copies of the Psalms coupled with Ecclesiastes.

Europe during the Enlightenment was a world of book collectors. In Germany, Josias Lorcke, Georg Wolfgang Panzer, and Johann Melchior Goeze owned thousands of volumes. Charles Eugene, duke of Wurttemberg, founded an immense library in Stuttgart in 1765 and personally purchased 5,000 Bibles for the collection. At around the same time, there were more than 30,000 Bibles in Wolfenbütel. In France, Cornulier, a jurist from Rennes, owned 12 editions—almost as many as Dortous de Mairan, who succeeded Bernard Le Bovier de Fontenelle as permanent secretary of the Académie Française. A catalog of the Bibles in the Bibliothèque Nationale de France has just been completed, which will allow comparisons with its English and Italian counterparts; and sales catalogs, postmortem inventories, and the study of bookplates will teach us a great deal about the presence of Bibles in libraries.

Between 1780 and 1783, toward the end of a life spent in service of the Jewish Enlightenment, Berlin philosopher Moses Mendelssohn published a German translation of the Pentateuch printed in Hebrew letters, with a wholly traditional commentary in Hebrew. He sought to return the reading of sacred texts to the center of Jewish life, and he also aimed to help Jews to learn German so that they might integrate themselves into society. Mendelssohn's work on biblical texts began with a commentary on Koheleth in 1770 and culminated in the translation of the Bible and the Psalms into German (1783), with a dedication to the poet Karl Wilhelm Ramler. German-Jewish Bibles had long assured the dissemination of the Torah. For example, in central Europe there were several hundred editions of the *Tseenah Ureenah,* also known, for women, as the *Waybertaytch,* a translation into Yiddish with commentary. These were offered for sale by thousands of peddlers.

To reappropriate the Bible meant not only owning it but also understanding it. At least one translation of the Bible, in whole or in part, appeared in Europe every year of the 18th century, in every religious denomination, and in every format. The situation varied from country to country. In England and the Protestant areas of Germany, the Bible already existed in translation whereas in the Catholic countries, the printing and reading of the Bible in the vernacular was not permitted until Pope Benedict XIV's decree of 13 June 1757. In Halle it was of course Luther's Bible that was used, although often without his glosses and prefaces. At Berleburg, a mystic Bible (1726–42) prolonged a movement already developed by Zinzendorf. In opposition to this, the Wolffian philosopher Johann Lorenz Schmidt, who had translated Spinoza, published his version, the famous Wertheim Bible, in 1735. The most celebrated and popular version of the Bible was that of Johann David Michaelis, the great Orientalist of Göttingen, who published the Old Testament in 13 volumes with commentaries "for nonscholars" (1769–83). German Catholics were forbidden to use Luther's text and had to accept the Vulgate of Popes Sixtus V and Clement VIII, which had been made canonical by the Council of Trent. Nevertheless, many German Bibles were published for use by Catholics, notably in Mainz but also in Augsburg (1723), Constanz (1751), Nuremberg (1763), and Fulda (1778). Biblical studies were promoted by Martin Gerbert and Eusebius Amort; and the prince of Hohenlohe-Waldenburg-Schillingsfürst commissioned a Bible from the priests of the Order of Teutonic Knights, which appeared in 1763 in Nuremberg. The most widely used version seems to have been that of the former Benedictine monk Heinrich Braun (Augsburg, 10 volumes, 1788–97). Finally, mention must be made of the Bible Circle of Ingoldstadt, which found a highly effective leader in Johann Michael Sailer.

From Melanesia to the various Eskimo populations, the Society for the Propagation of the Gospel in Foreign Parts, founded in 1701, printed translations of the Scriptures into languages that were among the most difficult for Europeans, the least known to them, and often poorest in words. Publication under such circumstances was challenging: for example, the Bible center in Halle sent printing blocks to Tranquebar in southeastern India so that Bibles could be printed there. England saw the notable development of translations into contemporary style (by D. Mace and E. Harwood), as well as the translation of the Catholic Rheims-Douai Bible at the end of the 16th century. The latter was revised by R. Witham (1730) and Richard Challoner (Old Testament, 1750, 1763; New Testament, 1738; then regularly from 1749). John Wesley translated the New Testament in 1755, and the King James Bible was revised for the first time in 1762.

Catholics in 18th-century France continued to read the translation of the Bible by Le Maistre de Sacy (New Testament, 1667; Old Testament, 1672–95), of which 34 editions, published between 1701 and 1790, can be found in the Bibliothèque Nationale (of these, nearly one-third date from before 1740). Nor should we neglect the translation by Nicolas le Gros (Amsterdam, 1739) or, of course, the translations of the New Testament by Richard Simon (Trévoux, 1702) and Dom Jean Martianay (Paris, 1712). A special place should be reserved for the enormous Commentaire Littéral (Literal Commentary) by Dom Calmet (Paris, 1707–16), which Voltaire plundered. Protestants in France depended upon versions of Scripture printed outside the country, such as Daniel Martin's Bible (Amsterdam, 1707), or those of Charles Le Cène or Ostervald (Neuchâtel, 1744), not to mention New Testaments published by Jean Le Clerc (Amsterdam, 1703) and Beausobre-Lenfant (Amsterdam, 1718). Despite prohibitions imposed by the Inquisition, translations were also produced in Spain. There was Anselmo Petite's Valladolid New Testament (1785) and, above all, the complete translation of the Bible by Father Felipe Scio de San Miguel (Valencia, 1790–93). Finally, Italy owed to Antoine Martini a fine translation (New Testament, 1769–71; Old Testament, 1776–81). Martini became archbishop of Florence in 1781, and it was in that city that he published a second edition (1782–92). Let us also recall the Italian version of Le Maistre de Sacy's work, published in Venice between 1775 and 1785.

Modern biblical criticism was invented in Europe in the 18th century, the offspring of the 17th-century movement that was itself born from Renaissance humanism and the Reformation. It was in Germany, where the universities were particularly efficient and offered an effective counterweight to the churches, that this new discipline arose. The two great advances made during the period were, first, the discovery that the Pentateuch had not been written by Moses himself; and, second, the situating of the biblical text within the history of the cultures of the Middle East. New concepts also emerged that are still in use today—myth, legend, source texts—and that considerably transformed exegesis. In *Jura Israelitarum in Palestinam* (1711; Laws of the Israelites in Palestine), Witter points out that the Pentateuch contains two different forms of address for God and that these indicate two distinct narrative levels. Without having read Witter's book, Jean Astruc, physician to Louis XV, arrived at the same conclusion and in 1753 published his *Conjectures sur les mémoires originaux* (Conjectures on the Original Memoirs)—the title refers to the documents that Astruc thought Moses had used in composing the Book of Genesis. Le Clerc and Simon had certainly been aware of the different names of God but had not gone so far as to construct a theory of "documents."

Textual criticism also made a breakthrough. It was necessary first of all to uncover a reliable source text. Benjamin Kennicott offers one in his *Vetus Testamen-*

tum Hebraicum cum Variis Lectionibus (1776–80; Hebrew Old Testament with Variant Readings). He had read 615 manuscripts collected from all over Europe, and the list of scholars acknowledged in the book provides an overview of European biblical scholarship that must be carefully read. Giovanni Bernardo De Rossi, professor of Oriental languages at Parma, consulted 731 manuscripts and published his *Variae Lectiones Veteris Testamenti* (1784–88; Variant Readings of the Old Testament) at almost the same time as Michaelis's *Supplementa ad lexica hebraica* (1784–92; Supplement to the Hebrew Lexicon). A comparison of these works by Kennicott and De Rossi with Charles François Houbigant's *Biblia Hebraica* (1743–54; Hebrew Bible) suffices to show how far behind France was in this area. In addition to his translation of the Old Testament mentioned above, Michaelis published *Mosaisches Recht* (1770–75; Commentaries on the Laws of Moses; abridged translation published in Bordeaux, 1785) and took a great deal of interest in objects from the biblical and Oriental world. He also demonstrated the crucial role of Egypt in understanding historical context. The idea was established that the Bible was not just a set of texts but also a body of knowledge that must be understood without preconceived opinions. Michaelis was the last to attempt to reconcile religious orthodoxy and the Enlightenment, carried by the belief that one could convince scholarly critics by using their own arguments.

For Hermann Samuel Reimarus, who was known to the 18th century solely for the celebrated *Fragmente*, excerpts from *Apologie oder Schutzschrift für die vernünftigen Verehrer Gottes* (Fragments from Reimarus Consisting of Brief Critical Remarks on the Object of Jesus and His Disciples As Seen in the New Testament) published by Gotthold Ephraim Lessing between 1774 and 1778, absolutely nothing remained of the sacred, and he contended that the Bible should be read in the same way as Homer or Pliny. Not only did he reject the attribution of the Pentateuch to Moses, but he also denied that this text and its authors had been capable of transmitting a revelation. Reimarus was the first to make this break, yet it is possible to overestimate his importance. After all, the complete text of his *Apologie* was not published until 1972.

Johann Salomo Semler, a professor at Halle from 1752, originated the free practice of biblical exegesis with his *Abhandlung von freier Untersuchung des Canons* (1771; Treatise on the Free Examination of the Canon). Building on the scholarship of Richard Simon, who had shown that the Old Testament is the product of a complex history, Semler made a clean break between the absolute *Wort Gottes* (word of God) and the relative and human *Schrift* (writing or Scripture) and asserted that no dogma could or should prevent scholarly work on the latter.

Finally, Johann Georg Eichhorn—who was born in 1752, studied at Göttingen, and then taught there from 1788 to 1827—brought together all the biblical learning accumulated during the 18th century. A scholar without peer, Eichhorn was also a humanist, akin to the baroque polymaths in his curiosity about everything. For example, he published an *Allgemeine Geschichte der Cultur und Litteratur der neueren Europa* (1796–99; General History of the Culture and Literature of the New Europe) and launched a *Repertorium für biblische und morgenländische Litteratur* (1772–86; Repertory of Biblical and Oriental Literature), which was followed by his *Allgemeine Bibliothek der biblischen Litteratur* (1787–1801; General Library of Biblical Literature). He succeeded in reconciling Semler with Johann Gottfried von Herder (whose contributions are discussed below) and also in combining the most sophisticated criticism with an emphasis on the poetic and the intuitive. Systematizing Witter and Astruc, Eichhorn showed that the Old Testament contains three types of sources: Elohist, Yahwistic, and addenda. Nevertheless, like Herder, he believed that he was studying the adolescence of humanity. It was Eichhorn who established the legitimacy of the concept of myth, which was to flourish in subsequent biblical studies. Even the Catholic scholar Alexander Geddes, brought to Germany from Britain by Johann Severin Vater, accepted the idea, if not of "documents" then at least of "fragments," an idea that has become the conventional wisdom today.

One might describe in similar terms the enormous progress in the exegesis of the New Testament, often by the same writers. It too would show that, particularly among the Pietists, scholarly knowledge was not a seedbed of atheism—as is supposed by French culture that has misread Joseph Ernest Renan—but, on the contrary, such knowledge reinforced belief. In 1734 Johann Albert Bengel, the great Pietist of Wurttemberg, published a *Novum Testamentum Graecum* (Greek New Testament) in Stuttgart, which was followed by a commentary (*Gnomon Novi Testamenti. . . .* [1742; New Testament Word Studies]) and a posthumous translation into German (1753). The thousands of variant readings that he listed contributed to a greater understanding of the Bible, "which alone can save." The same idea can be found in the work of Johann Jakob Griesbach, a professor at Halle and then at Jena, and the learned editor of a *Novum Testamentum Graece* (1775–77; New Testament in Greek) that sets out 352 variants of Robert Estienne's standard text. Griesbach used 500 manuscripts as well as a "synopsis" of Matthew, Mark, and Luke. In his highly technical works, he demonstrated how Mark alternates between following Matthew and Luke, a theory that has been received anew in the 20th century. Johann August Ernesti's *Insti-*

tutio Interpretis Novi Testamenti (1761; Training in the Interpretation of the New Testament) continued to be read up until the beginning of the 19th century. Michaelis's translation of the New Testament appeared between 1788 and 1790 (with commentaries from 1790 through 1792), although the introduction dated from 1750; Eichhorn's New Testament translation was published between 1804 and 1827.

This account of the increasing dominance of the critical method should not leave the impression that it was universally accepted. This was far from the case, and not only for confessional reasons. Mendelssohn remained very far behind the scholarship of his time, even though he encouraged it. There was also a tendency—broadly revived in our own time—to pay more attention to the poetry of the text, to its own specificity, and to its grounding in a culture that was not exclusively scholarly, a tendency represented above all by Robert Lowth and by Herder.

Between 1741 and 1750 Lowth, who was professor of poetry at Oxford, gave 34 lectures in Latin on the "sacred poetry of the Hebrews," publishing them in 1753 under the title *De Sacra Poesi Hebraeorum* (Lectures on the Sacred Poetry of the Hebrews; English translation, 1787; French translations, 1812, 1839). Reissued with voluminous notes by Michaelis in Göttingen (1758–61), these lectures had a great impact throughout Europe, for Lowth stated bluntly that Greek and Roman poetry can offer nothing that equals, or even comes near to, the quality of Hebrew poetry. He analyzed at length its rhetorical procedures, metaphors, allegories, and parables, demonstrating that Hebrew poetry is metrical and that its phrasing obeys an explicit parallelism. Lowth's exegesis greatly influenced Herder's *Vom Geist der hebräischen Poesie* (1782–83; The Spirit of Hebrew Poetry)—it is striking that the epithet "sacred" has disappeared from this title. Herder had described an authentic Hebrew humanism, and the obvious genius of ancient Israel, in his *Älteste Urkunde des Menschengeschlechts* (1776; The Oldest Document of the Human Race) and had produced a translation, with commentary, of the Song of Solomon, the *Lieder der Liebe* (1771–78; The Song of Songs). In these works he compared the Bible with Kleist and John Milton and developed a comparative poetics in order to understand it. It was necessary, Herder believed, to pass over technical arguments and return to intuitive, and largely romantic, exegesis, recognizing the rights of emotion. According to Herder, one must rediscover the naïveté of the heart in order to become receptive to the *Luft des Ursprungs* (air of the origin). The prophets were "the speaking and breathing soul of prehistory." For Eichhorn too, as we have seen, the prophets were part of the adolescence of humanity. Herder was a theologian who occupied high-ranking positions in the Church in Buckeburg and then in Weimar, where he became a friend of Johann Wolfgang von Goethe, and he was a biblical scholar like his master, Johann Georg Hamann. Herder went beyond the history of exegesis, exemplifying the impact of the Bible outside theology.

Indeed it is the biblical traces in 18th-century culture that are the most striking and best known. There is no sphere in which they cannot be found, sometimes hidden but often quite obvious to whomever wishes to recognize them. The examples of Johann Sebastian Bach and George Frideric Handel are obvious, but theatre, opera, poetry, painting, and architecture all found in biblical texts a stock of ideas, plots, and characters. Jean-Baptiste Greuze's painting *Le grand-père lisant la Bible* (Grandfather Reading the Bible) shows the Bible's presence and importance in family life. Its omnipresence in daily life during the 18th century is confirmed by the work of anthropologists who have documented the presence of the Bible under the bed of a young woman giving birth, on the cakes that Jewish schoolchildren ate, and even in the hands of the buried. It was hidden in women's hair, and fragments of it were inscribed on the lintels of doors. It has long been known that the authors of both literature (Voltaire, Jean-Jacques Rousseau, Denis Diderot) and philosophy (Christian Wolff, Immanuel Kant) reworked parts of the Bible. Voltaire read it, quoted it, and commented on it again and again. Rousseau's Protestant education ensured that he was familiar with it, while Diderot rediscovered Christian humanism in the Bible. The abbé Mallet, who wrote many articles on the Bible for the *Encyclopédie,* also borrowed from Dom Calmet. It was Diderot, however, who wrote the articles "Jésus-Christ," "Juifs" (Jews), "Philosophie mosaïque" (Mosaic Philosophy), and, above all, "Bible." Less polemical than Voltaire and less emotional than Rousseau, he relied mainly on secondhand documentation. In contrast, Protestant ministers during the Enlightenment often knew Hebrew and had known biblical culture since childhood, the German *Aufklärung* being more religious than the French *siècle des Lumières.*

In Europe the 18th century marked the end of the sacralizing and totalizing interpretations of the Bible, which had become a book like any other. However, the study of the Bible made unprecedented progress, which was shared fairly rapidly by everyone. Of course the Protestant, Catholic, and Jewish cultures each had their own separate Bible, but they communicated, debated, exchanged, and learned from one other. Indeed, these groups confronted together the development of both modern science and secularization, which spared no one. Yet the Bible was nonetheless present in the cultures of 18th-century Europe—sometimes in the form of remote traces, but already widely disseminated—and it exerted a unifying influence among the European nations, continuing to structure the greater part of the lives and works of the men and women of the period.

DOMINIQUE BOUREL

See also Catholicism; Judaism; Pietism; Protestantism; Theology, German

Further Reading

Belaval, Yvon, and Dominique Bourel, editors, *Le siècle des Lumières et la Bible,* Paris: Beauchesne, 1986

Cotoni, Marie Hélène, *L'exégèse du Nouveau Testament dans la philosophie française du dix-huitiéme siècle,* Oxford: The Voltaire Foundation at the Taylor Institution, 1984

Greenslade, Stanley Lawrence, *The Cambridge History of the Bible,* 3 vols., Cambridge: Cambridge University Press, 1963; see especially vol. 3, *The West from the Reformation to the Present Day*

Laplanche, François, *La Bible en France entre mythe et critique, XVIᵉ–XIXᵉ siècle,* Paris: Albin Michel, 1994

Norton, David, *A History of the Bible as Literature,* 2 vols., Cambridge and New York: Cambridge University Press, 1993; see especially vol. 2, *From 1700 to the Present Day*

Reventlow, Henning, Walter Sparn, and John Woodbridge, editors, *Historische Kritik und biblischer Kanon in der deutschen Aufklärung,* Wiesbaden, Germany: Harrassowitz, 1988

Bibliophilism

The word *bibliophilie* (bibliophilism) did not enter the French and English languages until the 19th century. However, the 18th century saw the creation of the French word *bibliophile,* first attested in 1740, as used by Charles de Brosses and included in the *Dictionnaire de l'Académie Française* (Dictionary of the Académie Française) in 1798. Can we deduce that bibliophilism, the love of books considered as collectible objects, was an invention of the age of the Enlightenment? In fact, the principal libraries that had been established in earlier centuries knew nothing resembling pure bibliophilism. The most elegant ones, such as Cardinal Mazarin's or Colbert's, were contained within larger artistic collections, in which books were not the most important items. Others—the library of Jacques-August De Thou being the best example—had been established by humanists or scholars avid for new knowledge and anxious to procure for themselves the best tools of their trade. They were the products of a passion that was more philological, or scientific, than truly bibliophilic.

It is clear that the spread of literacy, the growth in the production of books, the development of the book trade, and the changes in mentality that characterized the 18th century brought about a multiplication and diversification of libraries. While books became visible signs of social success, the classical ideal of the gentleman, without falling into the trap of pedantry or the excesses of erudition, had an important part to play in the advancement of culture. Gone were the days when members of a certain decorous nobility could boast of never having read a single book. Alongside scholarly or strictly professional libraries, a thousand libraries, large and small, came into existence in the main cities of Europe and among all the affluent classes. In varying proportions that are difficult to evaluate, their holdings reflect a concern for culture, a need for distraction, and a desire for prestige.

The fact that the majority of these libraries avoided specialization and retained an encyclopedic range is revealed by estate inventories (sources that are difficult to systematize) and especially by printed auction catalogs, a genre that underwent an explosive growth: from around two to three per year from 1700 to 1710, to more than 100 in 1785. Rare indeed are libraries in which the five traditional classes of the old book trade (theology, jurisprudence, the arts and sciences, literature, and history) are not represented. Seemingly, it is not in this random mix that true bibliophiles are to be found.

However, it should be noted that the spectacular development of libraries coincided with a no less remarkable increase in the number of bookplates, to such an extent that the 18th century is considered the "golden age of bookplates." Their production, which involved painters, draftsmen, and engravers, adhered to strict conventions, but the grace and creativity of their forms are still admired by connoisseurs today. All snobbery aside, the fact remains that the number and quality of these marks of ownership cannot be explained without reference to a certain attachment to the objects that they marked: that is, the books.

It should also be noted that some of the encyclopedic libraries described above grew in a way that neither the thirst for culture nor the glory of prestige can fully explain. Some of these libraries are said to have contained 30,000, 50,000, 70,000, 100,000, or even as many as 230,000 volumes. Such collections required an enduring perseverance in acquisition, efficient support in managing them, ample resources at all levels, and, over and above all these characteristics, a genuine passion for books.

Collectors' tastes continued to develop throughout the century and embraced a wide range of objects: paintings, drawings, and prints; tapestries, porcelain, weapons, and jewels; medals and coins; ancient inscriptions, which had already been sought after in earlier centuries, but were now joined by fossils; shells and crystals from the Alps; stuffed animals and herbaria of dried plants; not to mention astrolabes, telescopes, and other scientific instruments. Cabinets of natural history and physics replaced the former "curiosity cabinets," but the enthusiasts who created these collections continued to be known by the lovely name of the *Curieux* (curious ones)—and it was this same name that contemporaries also gave to bibliophiles.

It was to these *Curieux,* and not at all to "men of letters," that Guillaume-François de Bure the Younger addressed the seven-volume work he published in Paris, between 1763 and 1768, under the title *Bibliographie instructive ou Traité de la connoissance des livres rares et singuliers* (Instructive Bibliography; or, Treatise on the Knowledge of Rare and Singular Books). This survey of all the knowledge of a bookseller who specialized in old books shows that in France bibliophilism had come of age and had its own market, rules, models, and traditions. Bure's compendium includes the names of the most active *Curieux* of this period: the comte de Lauraguais, Navy paymaster Sainte-Foy, the duc de La Vallière, and, above all, Louis-Jean Gaignat, to whom the work was dedicated. It also reveals which items the bibliophiles prized the most highly: books printed on vellum, copies in large format, limited editions, works that had remained in manuscript form, and so on.

Bure had his French customers in mind. However, nothing would be more misleading than to assume that Enlightenment bibliophilism was exclusively French, or Parisian. A rapid survey of the century's leading bibliophiles clearly demonstrates the international scope of the phenomenon.

In the Netherlands the first catalog for a public sale of books had been printed in 1599, for the library of Marnix van Sint Aldegonde, and there were some astonishing bibliophiles there during the age of the Enlightenment. Among their precursors was Isaac Le Long, whose library, broken up in Amsterdam in 1744, included an almost complete collection of Bibles, Psalters, catechisms, and liturgies of the Dutch churches; a rare set of incunabula illustrated with wood-block prints; and an exhaustive collection of manuals of mathematics, accounting, and calligraphy published in the Netherlands. The next generation produced two men who were both bibliophiles and historians of printing: Gerard Meermann, whose book *Origines typographiae* (Origins of Typography) dates from 1761, and who is represented today by just a small part of his prestigious collections in the Museum Meermanno-Westreenianum in The Hague; and Johannes Enschede, a printer in Haarlem and a great lover of xylographic pamphlets, "Costeriana," and other incunabula. Another noteworthy example is the Amsterdam merchant Peter Anthony Crevenna, an astonishing man who in 1776 afforded himself the luxury of publishing a catalog of his collection of books. Its sixth and final volume contains special sections on manuscripts, incunabula, and the publications of Aldus Manutius and his heirs, the Giunti, the Estiennes, the Gryphes, the Plantins, the Elzeviers, Joseph Comino, and John Baskerville. Its preface is the first, naive confession of a man haunted since early youth by "the passion for books."

In Great Britain the library of Robert Harley and his son Edward is noteworthy for the quality of its manuscripts (all now held by the British Museum), its 50 books printed by William Caxton, and its other incunabula. Fifty Caxtons were also to turn up at the sale in 1776 of the collections of the eccentric John Ratcliffe, a candle merchant turned bibliophile. Meanwhile, Horace Walpole had become famous for his private press and for the neogothic architecture of his library at Strawberry Hill. The library of Dr. Richard Mead, a leading light in medicine and a faithful patron of arts and literature, is particularly astonishing because of its size: in the end it contained more than 100,000 volumes, and their sale, in 1754–55, lasted for a total of 56 days. In the following generation, Major Thomas Pearson, who died 1781 at the age of 41, played a pioneering role in bibliophilism by assembling an exhaustive collection of the works of old English poets. The duke of Roxburgh, at his death in 1804, owned the most sumptuous library in the West. The bibliophilism of the 19th century was to experience its golden age in Britain, and it was no accident that Reverend Thomas Dibdin provided, in his *Bibliomania* of 1811, the indispensable manual, or more exactly the Bible, of the bibliophiles.

In the 17th century the German-speaking countries had had a model of the pioneering and consummate princely bibliophile in the person of Augustus, duke of Brunswick-Wolfenbüttel. His example was followed, belatedly, not by Frederick II of Prussia, who was more a philosopher than a bibliophile, but, on a very modest scale, by Charles Eugene, duke of Württemberg, who was consumed by a passion for the Bible and, from 1765 onward, went on *Bibelreisen* (Bible journeys). In 1784 he purchased the 5,000 Bibles that had been collected by the Danish pastor Josias Lork, and eventually he established a Bible fund in Stuttgart that is still the richest in Europe today. In Vienna in 1712, Eugene of Savoy created a dazzling library of 15,000 volumes, and then had it installed in his residence at Belvedere. It was supplemented by Blaeu's *Great Atlas* in 64 folio volumes and by a princely collection of 60,000 engraved portraits. In the same period, Zacharias Conrad von Uffenbach, a leading citizen of Frankfurt, decided to devote his life to books. He traveled around Europe in search of rare items and in 1729 published a catalog of his library. He was one of the first to take an interest in autograph letters and succeeded in collecting more than 65,000 of them in his portfolios.

Other celebrated bibliophile include Cardinal Domenico Passionei, whose collection of more than 60,000 volumes ended up in the Biblioteca Angelica in Rome; Samuel Teleki, a Hungarian count; the Polish bishop Josef Andreas Zaluski, whose library contained 11,000 manuscripts and 230,000 books at his death in 1774; Empress Catherine II of Russia, who purchased Voltaire's and Denis Diderot's libraries and had them sent to Saint Petersburg; the Danish scholar Arni Magnusson, who assembled old Icelandic manuscripts just in time to rescue them; and Benjamin Franklin, Philadelphia's leading bibliophile.

It may appear that bibliophilism was a very masculine passion, but in France several women became known for the quality of their libraries over the course of the 18th century: the comtesse de Verrue during the Regency, the marquise de Choiseul-Meuse somewhat later, not to mention Madame de Pompadour.

Bibliophilism was a very urban passion and was strongly associated with the largest urban centers. Nevertheless, there were bibliophiles in the French provinces. In Dijon, Président Bouhier collected more than 30,000 books and manuscripts, which were dispersed during the Revolution. Carpentras inherited the valuable library of Monseigneur d'Inguimbert, while

Aix-en-Provence received the prestigious collection of the marquis de Méjanes. Even so, Paris remained the true capital of French bibliophilism. The library known as the Bibliothèque de l'Arsenal originated with the acquisition of a dozen Parisian collections by the marquis de Paulmy, a true prince among bibliophiles, between 1755 and 1785. His library of 60,000 volumes was then merged with another 40,000 volumes from the last of the three or four libraries created in succession by the duc de La Vallière. From the chancellor Daguesseau and the comte d'Hoym, to the abbé Jean-Joseph Rive and Marie-Joseph Chénier, bibliophiles of every stripe succeeded one another in Paris throughout the century. Some of them were known for the size of their collections. The library of the maréchal-duc d'Estrées, sold in 1739, comprised 70,000 volumes, while the books collected by the "king's doctor," Camille Falconnet, numbered 50,000 when they were sold in 1763. The collections of other bibliophiles attest to interests that prefigure the infatuations of the 19th century, including, to cite just two examples, the "Gallic antiquities" of Jean-Pierre Imbert Châtre de Cangé and the romances of chivalry collected by Charles-Jérôme Cisternay du Fay.

However, if one had to characterize the bibliophilism of the Enlightenment with a single attribute, one would have to cite its lack of specialization. Daniel Mornet points out in his pioneering study, published in 1910, that the libraries of the century of the *Encyclopédie*

were never specialized collections. Incunabula, illustrated books, first editions, and examples of printing at the Aldine, Estienne, and Elzevier presses were already being sought after, but no collector was exclusively interested in such items. It was left to the 19th century, the true golden age of bibliophilism, to explore to a dizzying degree all the specializations that the world of books could offer.

JEAN-DANIEL CANDAUX

See also Books and Reading; Library

Further Reading

Blechet, Françoise, *Les ventes publiques de livres en France, 1620–1750, répertoire des catalogues conservés á la Bibliothèque nationale,* Oxford: Voltaire Foundation, 1991
Masson, André, *Le décor des bibliothèques du Moyen Age à la Révolution,* Geneva: Droz, 1972
Ricci, Seymour de, *English Collectors of Books and Manuscripts (1530–1930) and Their Marks of Ownership,* Cambridge: Cambridge University Press, 1930
Vernet, André, editor, *Histoire des bibliothèques françaises,* 4 vols., Paris: Promodis—Éditions du Cercle du Librairie, 1988–92; see especially vol. 2, *Les bibliothèques sous l'Ancien Régime, 1530–1789,* edited by Claude Jolly, 1988

Body, Representations of

How was the word "body" understood during the Enlightenment? The range of concepts encompassed by the term was singularly broad, rich, and confused. The French term *corps* is derived from the Latin *corpus.* The polysemy of the word was at the time quite bewildering: although the *Encyclopédie* devoted more than ten pages of Volume IV to the entries "Corporation," "Corporéité" (Corporeality), "Corpus," and "Incorporation" and gave a great deal of room to recent scientific discoveries and to theories on the parallels between the microcosm and the macrocosm, or between the human body and the social body, its authors also conceded, as the chevalier de Jaucourt wrote in one entry, that "it is impossible to prove the existence of bodies." This declaration does not mean that Jaucourt had abandoned his materialist approach to the universe of

forms, but rather it indicates his belief that the polysemy of the word was all too likely to fragment its meaning into so many representations and definitions that it would be pointless to list them all. However, this semantic richness did not discourage other contributors to the *Encyclopédie* from using the term *corps.* Instead, the authors gave their opinions on the theological, political, social, metaphysical, physical, chemical, medical, literary, juridical, architectural, military, artisanal, and anatomical meanings of the term and its etymological relatives, ranging from "Corporal: liturgical term; sacred cloth that is used during Mass and which is spread beneath the chalice, so that one might decently place thereupon the body of our Lord Jesus" to "Corpulence: term of anatomy; shape and volume of the body."

The extreme usefulness of the word "body" in the age of the Enlightenment is no doubt evident in this encyclopedic overview. In all the major European languages, "body" was a kind of catch-all term, a word that said everything and whose range of meaning had never been so broad. This conceptual breadth reached its apogee in enlightened Europe before very quickly being called into question. In fact, Enlightenment thinkers were no doubt the last to establish so many connections among the different registers or disciplines in which representations of the body were used. The social and professional structures of the different European countries were conceptualized in terms of a hierarchy of bodies (the word "corporation" had this meaning most European languages, as did the organization of most European societies into "orders" or "estates"). The metaphorical image of the political community was derived from the traditional religious view of the universe, in which harmony emanated from the mystical body of Christ. Similarly, secular representations of the political body in the 18th century encompassed the notion of a community of the faithful gathered around the spiritual guide. Corporeal metaphors were also frequently used in philosophical and political debates concerning the proper administration of the polity. Finally, scientific images and essays established the human body as a standard for all knowledge. The meaning of the word "body" drew upon all of these sources, and crossovers in usage gave it exceptional prominence. In philosophical writings, pamphlets, learned treatises, newspapers, and private correspondence, the word "body" invaded European thought throughout the Enlightenment; it worked as a framework for both knowledge and description because its different metaphorical levels were capable of describing the entire world, visible and invisible.

A pamphlet dating from February 1789, *Le plus fort des pamphlets* (The Strongest Lampoon of All) suggests a few of these possible metaphors, assembled in a useful way for those who sought to forge constitutions:

What is the basis of a monarchical government? It is neither a headless body, as in Poland, nor a head without a body as with the Turks, but the following: in France the king is the head of the state, the military is its hands, the magistrates are part of the head; they are the mouth, the eyes, the ears; they are the organs of the brain, which is the king. The king is also the heart and the stomach, and the magistrates are the viscera. Great men are the trunk that envelops the viscera; the people are the arms, the thighs, the legs, and the feet. That is the body of the state. Determine accordingly what should be the functions of the monarch-brain-heart-stomach. It is certain that the health of the

political body can only result from a harmonious relationship among all the parts; that if there is the slightest congestion, the slightest lack of communication, then disorder sets in, fever breaks out, and sickness can lead the body to disintegrate altogether.

It was this strange language, blending fairly precise anatomical designations with an analogical reference to the functional relationships between the organs, that gave the word *corps* a very large range of meanings. This language was based upon the fiction of a "political body" or a "social body" whose harmony and balance must be preserved by a just hierarchy and the good complementary workings of the vital organs. The rich corpus of medical-political writings inspired by Vesalian anatomical science set forth a very coherent system to explain both the body and the organization of society. These writings also offered an abundant source of metaphors (the body attacked by illness, followed by the intervention of doctors and the eventual cure). The conflation of the king with the head, for example, was an image found all over Europe. The organicist view of the monarchy as a political body placed under the command of the royal *caput* (head) had been theorized by Thomas Hobbes in his *Leviathan* (1651), a work that was highly influential in shaping the ideas of the European Enlightenment. Hobbes laid down the conditions of legitimacy under which the individual owed obedience to the sovereign and, in the same way, to any political body, corporation, municipality, or parliamentary assembly. Pierre Manent observed, "a new corporeal idiom of the legitimacy of the monarchy within the framework of the nation had to be found: Hobbes formulated it." This "capital" authority was again recalled Louis XV's "Flagellation" speech delivered to the Parlement of Paris on 3 March 1766: "The rights and interests of the nation, which some have dared to make into a body separate from the monarch, are necessarily joined with my rights and interests, and rest in my hands alone."

The languages of the enlightened Europe were fraught with a certain tension with regard to the various meanings of the word "body," which could, all by itself, describe each individual—physically, medically, from head to foot, both outside and inside. The word could also serve to metaphorically connect multiple social communities: craftsmen, merchants, the inhabitants of the same town or the same locality, administrators, orders, estates—all those who were allowed to assemble and "form a body." Finally, "body" could provide a coherent image of the political system as a whole, as a political, religious, and monarchical model of the organization of the state. However, this powerful organicist metaphor was open to contradictory interpretations. Ambiguity in meaning was particularly prevalent at the very end of the 18th century—indeed, the discourse of the French Revolution hinged on the term's potential ambivalence. Along with the desire for transparency, for rationalization—attempts to reduce the tangle of the bodies that had fragmented the old society into zones of privilege, restriction, and darkness—there was a corresponding need to use a word with widespread connotations and with an unequaled ability to evoke and persuade. The "body" was therefore a key word of the Enlightenment on two levels. First, it could be applied to a number of far-reaching and complementary fields. Second, it was a pivotal word that embraced political, social, and cultural organization of the old society, and that, eventually, enabled the new society to tell its own story—to put together a chronicle of its own origins and "birth." At the end of the 18th century, the corporeal metaphor was thus extended even further to describe the condition of one political system, its demise, and then the birth of another, an all-powerful nation with an omnipotent popular sovereignty—all principles deemed worthy of representation in terms of the unity of life itself.

We should no doubt attribute the omnipresence of the metaphor in descriptions of both the ancien and the nouveau régimes to the fact that this image, better than any other, managed to bind together what was told and what was known, the senses and knowledge. Representations of the body made it possible to associate three different areas of debate about society. First of all, there were definitions of the *individual*: the body was the very unity of living individuality. All scientific research undertaken during the Enlightenment had contributed to this interpretation of the category of the living: that which has a constituted body was considered to be alive. Scholars from the comte de Buffon to Marie-François-Xavier Bichat chose the human body or, sometimes, the animal body, the very stuff of study and experiment, rather than the soul, to calibrate their interpretations of the microcosm and the macrocosm.

Thus, the second level of the metaphorical debate, the *human community,* defined as the organism uniting all individualities, was also represented as a corporeal whole. To fit this social entity into a logic of corporeal understanding was to compare the management of the community—either as history or as the organization of a society or of a state—to the scientific management of the body. Different individuals were cells, different human associations were organs, and those responsible (for history, for society, for the state) commanded and ruled those organs, playing the role of doctors. The corporeal metaphor offered to statesmen and intellectuals of the Enlightenment the vision of an organic ordering

of the human community, and therefore a scientific claim to observe and organize that community.

Finally, each body was immersed in a universe of bodies: the notion of body was in essence a pluralistic one, integrated into an idea of *universal nature,* of the infinitely large as much as of the infinitely small, of the visible as much as of the invisible. In this way, the corporeal metaphor for society was lined to both the singular individual-body and the pluralist universe-body, in relationships that were both homogeneous and complex. The universe, the human community, and the individual all found meaning in the corporeal representation. At the same time, owing to historical context and the work of scholars who decided to explore the body rather than the soul, all three areas—the individual, society, and the natural universe—became the objects of knowledge as well as a conceptual framework. Narrative and knowledge were tightly imbricated in this logic, which was both political and scientific. Once established—through repeated taxonomy, experimentation and dissection—as the primary object of knowledge about individuals, the community, and nature, the concept of the body enabled enlightened statesmen and scholars to write a metaphorical narrative about harmony or social upheavals, using knowledge itself as a weapon.

ANTOINE DE BAECQUE

See also Citizen

Further Reading
Baecque, Antoine de, *The Body Politic: Corporeal Metaphor in Revolutionary France, 1770–1800,* translated by Charlotte Mandell, Stanford, California: Stanford University Press, 1997 (original French edition, 1993)
Foucault, Michel, *The Birth of the Clinic: An Archaeology of Medical Perception,* translated by A.M. Sheridan Smith, New York: Pantheon Books, and London: Tavistock Publications, 1973 (original French edition, 1963)
Foucault, Michel, *Discipline and Punish: The Birth of the Prison,* translated by Alan Sheridan, New York: Pantheon Books, and London: Lane, 1977 (original French edition, 1975)
Melzer, Sara E., and Kathryn Norberg, editors, *From the Royal to the Republican Body: Incorporating the Political in Seventeenth- and Eighteenth-Century France,* Berkeley: University of California Press, 1998
Stafford, Barbara Maria, *Body Criticism: Imaging the Unseen in Enlightenment Art and Medicine,* Cambridge, Massachusetts: MIT Press, 1991

Books and Reading

Books in 18th-Century Europe

The geography of Enlightenment Europe, a cosmopolitan space where ideas and knowledge circulated freely, coincides with the geography of the book. Paris, London, Geneva, Amsterdam, Venice, Leipzig, and Berlin were simultaneously the great cities of publishing and the capitals of European culture. Availing of multiple channels, passing through harbors, by road, or inside peddlers' bags, the trade in books marked a community of spirit that extended north to Scandinavia, east to Catherine II's Russia, and as far as Greece to the southeast. Aided by the use of a language common to the intellectual elite—French having replaced Latin—the success of great books rapidly became international and established cross-border intellectual and ideological solidarity among the European elite.

This said, the diffusion of ideas in print in 18th-century Europe was neither uniform nor homogeneous. In contrast to regions that were tolerant and highly productive in book publishing, there were also sectors of resistance, control, and censorship. The book routes reveal the political, religious, and cultural fault lines in a Europe where states reacted very differently to the progress of the publishing trade, to the emancipation and secularization of thoughts and texts, and to the dissemination of new forms of writing. Before examining the concept of the "European book of the Enlightenment," it will thus be necessary to give a rough outline of the geography of European books.

A first division appears between northern and southern Europe. The former, comprising England, the United Provinces of the Netherlands and Switzerland, all Protestant countries, produced books that were actively exported, while the Catholic regions to the south—Italy and Spain—imported more than they produced. Since the 17th century, southern Europe had been affected by the progressive shifts of publishing centers to the north. Meanwhile, the Inquisition impeded the progress of intellectual life within the Spanish monarchy, and ecclesiastical and secular forms of censorship began to compete with each other in the Italian states. At the crossroads of these two sections of Europe, France found itself in a favorable situation.

Paris enjoyed intellectual prestige owing to the influence of French writers and was thus also a great center for the export of books in the 18th century. Talented engravers and typographers worked for a limited number of booksellers and printers, who were selected by those in power thanks to a system of permissions and privileges that provided them with a virtual monopoly. Highly protected but also heavily controlled, members of this select coterie made fortunes—for example, by publishing the great erudite Benedictine works of the Regency (1715–23), or the *Almanach royal* (Royal Almanac), the privilege to which Laurent d'Houry handed over to Le Breton, his grandson—at the expense of the provinces, which were forced to resort to either piracy or clandestine publishing. Yet the highly restrictive limits imposed by censorship and its climate of political intolerance led to the creation—outside of France—of an international publishing network that specialized in French writings. From Berlin to London and from Amsterdam to Geneva, the activity of this network was such that, between 1750 and 1800, over half of all books in French were probably published outside of France. From the 1740s on, a clandestine and subversive philosophical literature filtered into the country (see Darnton), greatly facilitated by the activity of peddlers who traveled throughout France.

Immediately after the revocation of the Edict of Nantes (1685), the rather liberal and tolerant intellectual climate of the Republic of the United Provinces attracted a segment of the educated French Protestant elite who had opted for exile. The influx of distinguished minds brought heterodox works such as Pierre Bayle's *Dictionnaire historique et critique* (1697; An Historical and Critical Dictionary) to this dynamic yet long-established publishing center. These books were then distributed all over Europe. In Amsterdam and in university towns such as Leiden or Utrecht, visitors were doubtless struck by the large number of bookstores where readers could buy books from France, Germany, and eastern Europe or from England, to which the Seven Provinces were closely tied. A shared intellectual dynamism brought England closer to the Republic, where censorship had been renounced at the end of the 17th century. In 1709 the Copyright Act definitively abolished both book censorship and the privilege granted in perpetuity to the booksellers, and established a modern notion of literary property. These measures favored the freedom of expression and an astonishing publishing boom. England saw an intense circulation of the written word in all its forms (books, newspapers, tracts, leaflets, political ballads) during the second half of the 18th century.

Because of its fragmentation into many small states, Germany found itself in a complex situation. Following the Seven Years' War (1756–63), the output of the publishing industry rose dramatically, increasing tenfold from the beginning of the century; this spectacular development marked a time when literature written in German was making its presence felt in opposition to Latin. Northern Germany dominated both the production of books and the book trade itself. The Leipzig book fair replaced that of Frankfurt, thanks to bookseller Philipp Erasmus Reich, who settled in Leipzig in 1764. In Berlin, meanwhile, his colleague Nicolai served the German and European Enlightenment market for books.

In the Mediterranean region, Italy had lost rank as a great power in publishing, with the exception of a few cities such as Venice and Naples. Fragmented into a dozen states, lacking both a homogeneous book policy and a unified library network, Italy reflected a variety of separate local situations. The nobility played a crucial role in the dissemination of books. For example, in Siena after 1770, the political action of Grand Duke Ferdinand III of Tuscany directly contributed to the printing of Enlightenment texts, but he acted in order to keep a greater hold over people's minds. Since religious and secular censorship were vigorous, aristocratic patronage remained essential for the publication and dissemination of books and periodicals in Italy.

In Spain the age of the Enlightenment corresponded to a growing apathy in the book trades. There were political, religious, and economic causes for this decline: relentless censorship and the role of the Inquisition contributed to the financial and technical decline of book professionals. This situation led many Spanish authors to publish elsewhere: in Venice, Antwerp, Lausanne, Geneva, Lyon, and Paris. Finally, around 1763, the regime relaxed its attitude toward printers; this created a publishing renaissance and an increase in the number of Spanish translations of French works. Nonetheless, the Inquisition, which Voltaire described as the "customs officers of thought," remained vigilant through the use of the Index.

And yet, the great mobility of the European book trade in the age of Enlightenment made light of national proscriptions and thus tied the arms of censorship. The publishing addresses given in books were never reliable: Parisian publishers printed "Amsterdam," "London," or "Geneva" on their title pages, while others marked Paris as their center of activity. In 1748 Montesquieu's *De l'esprit des lois* (The Spirit of Laws) appeared with a Geneva printer's address although it had been printed in Rouen. Under the influence of clandestine distribution networks of forbidden or counterfeit books, the outlines of Europe's book geography became blurred as the borders between states were easily breeched. A country where censorship existed, such as France, became a target for centers specializing in piracy—the duchy of Bouillon or Neuchâtel, for instance—which set up their presses on its doorstep and flooded it with unauthorized publications. Legal in some states and illegal in others (which might well be contiguous), piracy also affected—albeit in different ways—linguistic regions that were divided into several states, such as Italy and Germany. States in southern Germany and Austria, with the official protection of their sovereigns, pirated books written in German coming from the more intellectually active North. In Italy piracy was practiced unscrupulously from one state to the next. This was the case for Carlo Goldoni's works, which were first published in ten volumes in Florence between 1753 and 1757 and then shortly thereafter legally pirated in Bologna, Turin, Naples, Venice, and Rome (see Renato Pasta in Bödeker). Paradoxically, piracy helped to unify separate German entities culturally before they were united politically—but at the expense of Germany's authors, booksellers, and printers.

Access to Books: Reading and European Readers

The main reading public in the 18th century, as in previous centuries, comprised members of the elite, who were the only ones able to receive forbidden books for their libraries without risk. The prestige of books was such that whenever princes commissioned portraits of themselves, they liked to be shown surrounded by books. Madame de Pompadour, for instance, had *La Henriade* (1723; The Henriade) and *De l'esprit des lois* painted into the portrait of her created by Maurice Quentin de La Tour. The monarchy paid very close attention to its libraries and sometimes purchased the library of admired authors. For example, Catherine II purchased Voltaire's collection.

In addition, an altogether different readership emerged in Europe during the age of the Enlightenment, born of literacy campaigns initiated earlier by the Reformation and then by the Counter-Reformation. Rates and levels of literacy were very unequal between the two religious areas: Amsterdam (with 85 percent of the men and 64 percent of the women literate in 1780), Sweden, Scotland, England, and Germany were clearly ahead of Spain, Portugal, southern Italy, or Russia (with 90 percent illiteracy in 1850). Nevertheless, European countries shared common traits in terms of establishing reading institutions and forms of literature meant for the larger public.

As literacy spread across Europe from the 16th century onward (with the aid of expanded educational networks), the most important stakes were religious issues, for learning how to read meant, above all, learning how to read the texts of the "true" religion. The Bible, usually Latin, frequently served as a reader. This was the case in France, for example, even though innovations were introduced by the "Christian schools" of Saint Jean-Baptiste de La Salle at the turn of the 18th century, with French replacing Latin, and the adoption of a new educational approach whose goals were geared to social purposes. The fact remains that for most Europeans, full literacy was difficult to achieve. Even in the most literate countries, such as Sweden, people rarely learned to write once they learned to read. This compartmentalized instruction was in keeping with certain pedagogical treatises that discouraged writing for children of the lower classes (Philipon de La Madeleine, *Vues patriotiques sur l'éducation du peuple* [1783; Patriotic Views on the Education of the People]).

Since the 17th century, the network of European books had expanded with the development of peddlers' routes that allowed for the distribution of relatively inexpensive works to a broad public. Rural areas, as well as cities, were brought into contact with books. Every country created its own publishing specialties: English peddlers, after stocking up in London, would crisscross the land offering ballads, pamphlets, and almanacs, while humorous books and accounts of trials and executions also met with great success. In Italy pious plays, often written in verse, were commonly distributed, as well as almanacs, popular engravings, tales of chivalry, books for teaching reading, and devotional works. From the 17th century onward there began to develop a profusion of collections adapted to this new public. These collections included the French *Bibliothèque bleue* (Blue Library), the Castilian *pliegos sueltos* (loose pages), English chapbooks, and, in the countryside of northern Italy, almanacs with calendars used essentially as "weather guides" (see Lodovica Braida in Chartier, 1995). Indeed, these collections were mixed assortments of great thematic richness, in which literary and popular traditions were combined. These texts often reproduced adaptations or summaries of famous works rewritten and adapted with explicit typography—titles, abridgments, pictures, divisions into chapters and paragraphs—for less skillful readers, who would read only intermittently and aloud.

In urban areas, places for reading multiplied, making an ever-growing output of printed matter accessible to more people. On the one hand, well-stocked bookstores with diverse collections rich in novelties allowed customers to find what they were looking for without having to place orders. For those who wanted to read without buying, there were lending libraries ("circulating libraries" in England, *cabinets littéraires* in France, *Leihbibliotheken* in Germany), and reading societies ("book clubs" or "subscription libraries," *chambres de lecture*, *Lesegesellschaften*), and certain coffeehouses made books and periodicals available to their customers.

Book ownership began to increase in the 18th century, but with disparities along the same religious lines noted above. In 1750 the three cities heading the list were Protestant: Tübingen, Speyer, and Frankfurt, in which roughly 80 percent of households owned books (i.e., books were found in inventories after death). In Paris, during the same period, that figure was only 22 percent—even lower than in the provinces—but books owned tended to be the same as in Protestant areas: the Bible and devotional books.

Generally speaking, books gradually began to come into daily life during the Enlightenment, gaining entry into the private parts of the house, sometimes even entering the bedroom. Over time, reading itself was practiced differently, more often in a silent encounter for the individual alone. The act of reading thus tended to become a personal and private experience. The age of the Enlightenment thus marked a decisive stage in the slow process of privatizing the practice of the written word, which established one of the modern relationships of the individual to the world (see Chartier in Ariès and Duby, vol. 2).

What Is a Book?

The positive definition that opens the long article "Livre" (Book) in the *Encyclopédie* expresses the confidence that the men of the Enlightenment felt with respect to this form of disseminating knowledge as an *asile de la vérité* (sanctuary of truth):

> A piece of writing composed by an intelligent person on a given point of knowledge for the instruction and amusement of the reader. A *book* may also be defined as a composition by a man of letters, made to communicate to the public and to posterity something he has invented, seen, experienced, and assembled, and that must be of fairly considerable length in order to fill a volume.

And the *Encyclopédie*, under the direction of Jean le Rond D'Alembert, was intended to be the apogee of all that books represented. The concept of the book as explained in the *Encyclopédie* included the traditional purposes assigned to works of the mind—to instruct, to entertain, and to inform the public, but in a context of opening and renewing thought:

> The goal or the design of *books* is different according to the nature of the works: some are made to show the origin of things or to display new discoveries; others to push a science to its highest degree; still others to clear the mind of wrong ideas and to establish the ideas of things more precisely, etc.

The *Encyclopédie* article proposes an inventory of all possible books, out of a strange concern with taxonomy, including some that did not even exist—"promised" books and "imaginary" books. The inventory even includes curiosities such as the Tatar books supposedly discovered in 1721 in Russian, which were very long, had almost no width, and were written in white ink on black bark, as if they were a negative of Western culture. What should be done in the face of this diversity, this "prodigious multitude of books"? At the risk of succumbing to bibliomaniacal madness a possibility suggested in the *Encyclopédie* article "Bibliomanie" (Bibliomania), in which libraries were referred to as the "madhouses of the universe," it was imperative that a method be invented to sort out bad books from good ones and to ascertain "the best book in each genre of literature." Almost a third of the article "Livre" is devoted to a definition of such criteria.

Faced with this teleological, material, and normative conception of books, Immanuel Kant, at the end of the century, provided another definition based on the legal status that should be given to books, in "What Is a Book?" (1796):

> A book is a piece of writing (whether handwritten or typeset, composed of many or few pages, is of little importance here) that presents a speech someone gives to the public by means of visible linguistic signs. He who speaks to the public in his own name is the *writer*. He who gives a public speech in writing in the name of another (the author) is the *publisher*.

Right from the outset, a parameter appears here that is absent from the definition presented in the *Encyclopédie*: the author of the book. Does the book belong to anyone? The Enlightenment answered both yes and no. On the one hand, ideas belong to all of us, so—according to such thinkers as the marquis de Condorcet and the abbé Sieyès—no single person can claim to have an exclusive right to, or a "literary ownership" of, a work that holds the thinking of humanity. On the other hand, even though Denis Diderot defended the position that an author has intellectual ownership of his work in his *Lettre sur le commerce de la librairie* (Letter on the Book Trade), he considers books as merchandise that an author can sell to a bookstore owner and to which he thereby renounces all rights. Kant, on the other hand, responds that books contain two distinct authors' rights: the commercial right, which can be relinquished to a bookstore owner, and the author's moral right of inalienable ownership of his thoughts (Jocelyn Benoist; see "Introduction" in Benoist).

The theoretical debate among French and German Enlightenment thinkers on literary property and authors' rights was responsible for a final shift in the status of books. In order to legitimize the indissoluble right of the author to his work, defenders of literary property began to characterize books not only by the ideas they contained but also by the uniqueness of their expressive form and by the originality of their style (see Chartier, 1994). A threshold had been broken: aesthetic appreciation allowed the connection between a book and its author's subjectivity to be sealed, and that forged a new understanding of "works of the mind."

Evolution of Forms, Revolution of Texts

Eighteenth-century people respected the book as an object. Without necessarily being book lovers, they were sensitive to the material aspect of the book and, thus, before settling down for their read, they would appreciate its features of elegance and legibility, the quality of the paper, and the beauty of the engravings. For this reason the Enlightenment witnessed a series of formal evolutions in the art of bookmaking. New fonts made their appearance: the *romain du roi* (King's Roman) in France, Baskerville in England, Bodoni in Parma, and so on. In France, around 1700, the engraver Philippe Grandjean designed a font for the royal print shop on the king's orders. Starting out with rigorous geometric constructions, the *romain du roi* font was created—a tall and narrow font in which the straight line prevails over its cursive counterpart. Its thorough aestheticization marked the break between manuscript and engraved letters, a sign that the printed book had taken on an aesthetic and intellectual autonomy compared to other forms of the written word. Grandjean's font design also influenced John Baskerville of Birmingham, who created the font (Baskerville) that Pierre-Augustin Caron de Beaumarchais was to buy for his edition of the *Oeuvres* (Works) of Voltaire. In France, from the reign of Louis XVI (1774–93) to the coronation of Napoleon I (1804), the Didot font predominated. The contrast between the black of the ink and white vellum glorified antique-style writing and the affirmation of social order (see Martin).

Over the course of the 18th century, the arrangement of the typographical spacing in books changed. First of all, the half-title page was standardized as a book's first page. This seemingly modest development, conceived to protect the title page physically, concealed an important conceptual change. In fact, the half-title was "very much the true title page": it carried only the title, without any promotional information that identified the work as a piece of merchandise, and this "changed the book, from material object, into a pure title, thus an intellectual subject" (see Laufer in Martin, Chartier, and Vivey, vol. 2). On the inside of the book, increasing the number of paragraphs lightened the page. This was the "definitive triumph of white spaces over black ones" (see Martin). The texts gained in clarity, and reading speed could therefore be increased.

Illustration and the art of bookbinding enjoyed one of their most glorious periods during the Enlightenment, especially in France, where great artists, painters and engravers, collaborated to illustrate famous works.

For example Jean-Baptiste Oudry and Charles-Nicolas Cochin worked together to illustrate the *Fables* of La Fontaine, as did François Boucher and Laurent Cars to produce illustrations for the comedies of Molière. These artists revived the relationship between text and image; in contrast, during the 17th century allegorical dialogue had encouraged competition between text and image on the page. Whether it was a decorative vignette complementing a literary work or a plate explaining and completing a scientific book, the creative talent of the 18th-century illustrators gave the image back its grace (as exemplified by Claude-Joseph Dorat's *Les baisers* [1770; The Kisses], illustrated by Charles Eisen), its informative power, and its autonomy (as the plates of the *Encyclopédie* plainly attest). The improvements in engravings on copper and the invention of colored print gave pictures a refinement and a precision from which a great number of scientific works benefited, especially botanical and anatomical description.

Formats evolved less markedly. The folio continued to be reserved for dictionaries and collections of erudite texts, while scholarly works of history, philosophy, and medicine were usually bound in the quarto format. The smaller sizes, octavo and duodecimo, were used for the publication of most literary works. Clandestine publishers showed a particular preference for this format, for obvious reasons. During the 18th century the bookseller Cazin introduced the 18° and 24° formats, modeled on books published by the Elzevier family in the Netherlands, for poetry and light novels, which met with great success. The popularity that these easily hidden and transportable, miniaturized books enjoyed was an indication of the evolution of a reading practiced that was more secret and solitary, to be enjoyed outside of libraries.

"The Bible is the *Book* par excellence," proclaims one of the first sentences in the article "Livre" in Antoine Furetière's *Dictionnaire* (1690; Dictionary). This sentence is the primary context in which Furetière uses the word "Bible" in that article; the sentence was cut from the *Encyclopédie* article, and a reference to the Bible appears only later on in the entry. This downgrading from one reference work to the next coincided with the thematic development in the production of books during the 18th century, both in France and in other countries such as Germany. Edifying and religious books first declined and progressively disappeared, while fiction, literary texts, and scientific works took their place. In France, for example, religious books still accounted for one-third of printed production in 1730, but by 1750 this category had decreased to one-fourth and finally, to one-tenth by 1780, while works in the category "Arts and Sciences" doubled between 1750 and the Revolution. In Germany the process of secularization began after 1740, when theological books dwindled in the face of the growing demand for literary works. Dictionaries, encyclopedias, scientific collections, travel accounts, novels—the dissemination of new texts in Europe began what Roger Chartier (see Chartier in Bödeker) has described as the vast exchange movement that belatedly but radically dissolved the sacred aura of printed production, dominated by religious books during the high tide of the Counter-Reformation, and that devoted itself more and more to all those books in which new relationships between man, nature, and the social world were invented.

Functions of the Book during the Enlightenment

At the height of the Revolution, Condorcet extolled books and the emancipatory powers of ideas in his *Esquisse d'un tableau historique des progrès de l'esprit humain* (1794; Outlines of an Historical View of the Progress of the Human Mind):

> Finally, has printing not liberated the people's learning from all political and religious chains? . . . This learning, which every person can acquire in silence and solitude through books, cannot be corrupted universally: it is enough that there be one free corner of the Earth where presses can be loaded with paper.

It was tempting, in revolutionary France, to celebrate the role that books played in the maturation of 18th-century minds. At that time, this idea spread throughout Europe, and in Russia, Catherine II closed private printing shops and increased the number of censorship bureaus in the fear that "Jacobin ideas" would enter her realm. In reality, the influence of books on thoughts or actions was far less immediate than it was thought to be, taking the French Revolution as a prime example. Countering the idea that books made the Revolution, Chartier reminds us that the works of the *philosophes* and copies of the *Encyclopédie* were part of émigré libraries, and argues that the Revolution was instead the history of books that failed to find their public (see Chartier).

On the other hand, the generosity of the *philosophes'* project to enlighten humanity was tempered, on the part of some Enlightenment thinkers, by reluctance on the part of some to spread literacy to the masses. Why teach the poor how to read? As Voltaire wrote in the preface to his *Dictionnaire philosophique* (1764; Philosophical Dictionary): "The common people do not read at all; they work six days a week and on the seventh they go to the tavern."

The link between the book and the Enlightenment is thus not as obvious as one might think. The fact remains, however, that the Enlightenment owed its international influence to books and also to handwritten manuscripts, which were used to disseminate knowledge when secrecy was required (see Jochen Schlobach in Moureau)—when it was impossible to print a book or when it had to be copied by hand so that its contents could be disseminated. During the course of the century books made possible the spread of knowledge of science and modern thinking, advances in national literatures (in Germany, Italy, Spain), the codification of spelling systems (France), the linguistic unification of politically fragmented regions (Germany, Italy), and the emergence of European readerships that increasingly made it a habit to subscribe to collections (see Valentino Romani in Petrucci, 1993).

The book was not the only form to ensure this success of the written word —periodicals played a fundamental role—but they were its driving force, its most prestigious incarnation, the consummate form of literary and scientific communication. A growing multitude of texts gravitated toward the book, both in manuscript form or printed form, whether ephemeral or durable in character. The book encompassed these texts, contributing to the evolution of thought, sensibilities, and practices in 18th century Europe. In this way, books elicited and shaped a new reading public, a phenomenon that Kant considered to be decisive in the history of the *Aufklärung,* which he defined in terms of the public use of reason, "the way one uses reason as a *scholar* before the *reading* public" (see Kant in Benoist). Thus, Kant called for new uses for reading and new ways to read, which were less respectful of a book's authority and more attentive to its messages, more liberated and critical. Horace's motto *Sapere aude* (Dare to be wise), which Kant used as a watchword for a century that wanted to know and understand, makes sense in the context of this "major" relationship between the Enlightenment and books: the ideal no longer consisted of books that "contain understanding for me," books that think in the place of their readers. Rather, the ideal relationship between books and readers was one in which books encouraged readers to use their reason in the unfettered exercise of their faculties.

NATHALIE FERRAND

See also Bibliophilism; Censorship; Clandestine Literature; Illustration; Library; Newspapers and Journalism; Peddler

Further Reading

Ariès, Philippe, and Georges Duby, editors, *A History of Private Life,* 5 vols., Cambridge, Massachusetts: Harvard University Press, 1987–91; see especially vol. 3 (original French edition, 1985)

Benoist, Jocelyn, editor, *Qu'est-ce qu'un livre? Textes de Kant et de Fichte,* Paris: Presses Universitaires de France, 1995

Bödeker, Hans Erich, editor, *Histoires du livre: Nouvelles orientations,* Paris: IMEC Éditions, and Maison des Sciences de l'Homme, 1995

Cavallo, Guglielmo, and Roger Chartier, editors, *A History of Reading in the West,* Oxford: Polity Press, and Amherst: University of Massachusetts Press, 1999 (original Italian edition, 1998)

Chartier, Roger, *The Cultural Origins of the French Revolution,* translated by Lydia G. Cochrane, Durham, North Carolina: Duke University Press, 1991 (original French edition, 1990)

Chartier, Roger, *The Order of Books: Readers, Authors, and Libraries in Europe between the Fourteenth and Eighteenth Centuries,* translated by Lydia G. Cochrane, Cambridge: Polity Press, and Stanford, California: Stanford University Press, 1994 (original French edition, 1992)

Chartier, Roger, editor, *Histoires de la lecture: Un bilan des recherches,* Paris: IMEC Éditions, and Maison des Sciences de l'Homme, 1995

Darnton, Robert, *Edition et sédition: L'univers de la literature clandestine au XVIIIe siècle,* Paris: Gallimard, 1991

Martin, Henri-Jean, *The History and Power of Writing,* translated by Lydia G. Cochrane, Chicago: University of Chicago Press, 1994 (original French edition, 1988)

Martin, Henri-Jean, Roger Chartier, and Jean-Pierre Vivet, editors, *Histoire de l'édition français,* Paris: Promodis, 1983–; see especially vol. 2, *Le livre triomphant: 1660–1830,* 1984

Moureau, François, editor, *De bonne main: La communication manuscrite au XVIIIe siècle,* Paris: Universitas, and Oxford: Voltaire Foundation, 1993

Petrucci, A., "Pratiche de scrittura e pratiche di lettura nell'Europa moderna," *Annali della Scuola normale superiore di Pisa, Classe di lettere e filosofia* 23, no. 2 (1993)

Botany. *See* Classification; Jardin du Roi (French Royal Botanical Garden); Natural History

---

Boudoir

Previous centuries had seen the transformation of the Italian *studiolo* into the *cabinet* (or study), a place of retreat that gradually became more ornate and, eventually, luxurious. To a greater degree than the bedchamber, which at that time was still also used as a space for hospitality and sociability, the classic *cabinet* offered privacy and was dedicated to meditation, study, or grooming. The *Encyclopédie* defines it as a "room intended for study," "for private business," or for collections of valued objects but adds that: "the word *cabinet* also refers to rooms where women dress, pray or take their afternoon rest, as well as to other rooms intended for activities that require contemplation and solitude."

Jacques François Blondel, the author of the article on *cabinets,* seeks to distinguish among the various types of *cabinet,* including the boudoir, according to their shape and decoration. The boudoir, through the specialization of space and the individualization of life, thus became a place that was specifically feminine and amorous. The word *boudoir* was defined in dictionaries, first in 1740 in the *Dictionnaire de l'Académie Française* (Dictionary of the Académie Française), which regards it as colloquial: "a small *cabinet* to which one retires when one wishes to be alone." A few years later, the *Dictionnaire de Trévoux* (1752; Dictionary of Trévoux) defines it as "a small cubbyhole or very small *cabinet,* near the bedchamber, apparently thus named because of the custom of retiring there in order to be alone and to sulk (*bouder*) in private when one is in a bad mood." It was not until 1835 that the Académie Française defined *boudoir* as an "elegantly decorated *cabinet* for the specific use of women" and removed the reference to its colloquial tone. The word also passed into English, German, and Italian (in the latter language as *buduar* or *budoar*).

Despite the occurrence of the word *boudoir* in a 1735 novel by Mouhy, the term was slow to find its way into literature. The word is not used, for example, in Claude Crébillon's novel *Le sopha* (1742; The Sofa). In the course of the narrative the eponymous sofa is housed in a series of *cabinets,* ranging from its first appearance in "a *cabinet* separated from the rest of the palace" and too well decorated to be a simple oratory, to its last in "a *cabinet* decorated with an extreme magnificence and a great deal of taste," which constitutes "the temple of languor" and "the true seat of pleasure." Similarly, the word *boudoir* never appears in Jacques de La Morlière's novel *Angola* (1746), in which the hero enters "a *cabinet* in the remote depths of the apartment, more sensually furnished" than anything that he had seen up until then. The *cabinet* finally becomes a *boudoir* in *Le hasard du coin du feu* (Fortunes at the Fireside), which Crébillon did not publish until 1763; the action takes place "in one of those small, remote rooms that are known as boudoirs." Bastide includes two boudoirs in *La petite maison* (1758; The Little House)—places "that it is useless to name to the woman who enters them, for the mind and the heart understand in harmony there"—and he enumerates the elements of the decor, the purpose of which is to arouse whoever entered. The plot ends in a boudoir that is supposed to have irresistible charm.

In a treatise that reworks fiction, *Le génie de l'architecture ou l'analogie de cet art avec nos sensations* (1780; The Genius of Architecture; or, The Analogy of This Art with Our Sensations), Nicolas Le Camus de Mézières describes the boudoir (after first defining the salon and the bedchamber) as follows: "The boudoir is regarded as the seat of sensuality; it is there that a woman seems to concoct her plans, or yields to her desires." He also defines its decoration (mirrors and recesses), paintings ("amorous and pleasing scenes from fable"), lighting (candlelight softened by gauze), furniture (a daybed or an ottoman), and colors (white and blue). Above all, he defines its circular shape, corresponding to the female body and reminiscent of acts of love. Sometimes he varies the idea of its enclosed space by giving the boudoir openings into gardens. He thus treats the boudoir not only as a place but also as a mechanism for extending space through the use of mirrors, for saturating that space with allusions and stimulations, and for giving the body a suggestive setting. Amorous gestures themselves cease to be simply natural, becoming charged with cultural references and social signs. This is emphasized by the title of this work by Le Camus de Mézières, for the Enlightenment the boudoir was a place of experimentation, in which the definition of human beings could be tested by the objects that surrounded them and acted on their senses.

At the same time, however, the boudoir was a worldly place, in which the people of the Enlightenment dissipated their efforts and exhausted themselves in social ostentation and momentary delights. During the second half of the 18th century the boudoir was an obligatory element in fashionable apartments, and in the *petites maisons* that encouraged less and less clandestine love affairs, and it played a role in the modernity celebrated by Voltaire in *Le mondain* (1736; The Worldly Man), a modernity that was besotted with luxury, that preferred refinement to magnificence and the convenience of the small to the discomfort of the large, and that demanded "small apartments" alongside the apartments meant for display and prestige. In *Le salon de 1767* (The 1767 Exhibition), Diderot criticizes the paintings of François Boucher and his imitators as "little pictures, little ideas, frivolous compositions suitable for the boudoir of a fashionable little mistress in the little hideout of a little dandy." The boudoir became an allegory of French libertinism, of an art of allusion and subtle provocation, and in the term worked as a catchword in titles of collections of licentious stories, such as *Les passe-temps du boudoir ou recueil nouveau de contes en vers* (1787; The Pastimes of the Boudoir; or, New Collection of Verse Tales) or *Les offrandes à Priape ou les boudoirs des grisettes, contes nouveaux et gaillards* (1794; The Offerings to Priapus; or, The Grisettes' Boudoirs, New and Ribald Tales), as well as in the titles of two plays, one by Carmontelle and the other by the marquis de Sade. In Carmontelle's play, a lecherous old uncle contrives a "new boudoir, decorated with mirrors, pleasant paintings, and precious and fashionable furniture" for the purpose of seducing a young girl, but it is the nephew who benefits from the space and marries the heroine. In Sade's play, the "*cabinet* furnished with as much good taste as magnificence" is a place of pretense, in which the lovers play out a comedy of studious retreat for the husband who observes them while believing himself to be incognito. Like the *petite maison*, the boudoir was shot through with contradictions—between sentiment and luxury, intimacy and ostentation, the secret and the public.

As a mark of aristocratic prestige and libertinism, the boudoir inevitably figured in the polemics of the Revolution. Pamphlets opposing the royal court portrayed the boudoirs of Queen Marie-Antoinette and her favorite ladies as places of feminine excess and counterrevolutionary perversity. The narrator of *La Messaline française* (1790; The French Messalina) becomes the lover of the duchess de Polignac and of the queen, after being the lover of the princess de Hénin who, in order to seduce him, takes him into her boudoir. This initiation opens up to him the secret feminine spaces of Versailles. *Le boudoir de la duchesse de P*** [Polignac]* (1790; The Duchess of Polignac's Boudoir) also presents a princess delirious with lust, led into the whirl of transgression. It is no surprise that during the years of the Revolution Sade did not manage to stage *Le boudoir,* which featured a mythical hoax from the period of the ancien régime. He took his revenge by publishing *La philosophie dans le boudoir* (1795; Philosophy in the Bedroom), which distorts Enlightenment pedagogy and revolutionary radicalism into a lesson in polymorphous voluptuousness, as well as in a scurrilous pamphlet, "Français, encore un effort si vous voulez être républicains" (Yet Another Effort, Frenchman, If You Want a Republic). The *cabinet* meant for studying doubles as a place of orgy; philosophical reflection and aesthetic contemplation are conflated with sexual orgasm.

At the beginning of the 19th century, *Les veillées du couvent* (Evenings in the Convent), an anticlerical fiction attributed to Mercier de Compiègne, portrayed "a small, somber *cabinet,* surrounded with leafy trees and quite well provided with statues, paintings, and pretty furniture," which is called a boudoir by the young woman who shuts herself up in it with her confessor. Here the reference is to a garden cottage, devoted to clandestine love affairs. *Das Paradies der Liebe* (1801; The Empire of the Nairs; or, The Panorama of Love)—originally written in German by the British writer James H. Lawrence and translated by him into English in 1811—tells of the fate imposed on women at the four corners of the world. This image of the boudoir was perpetuated in the 19th century as a memory of the libertinism of the ancien régime, but the representation was sometimes made more agreeable by a new exoticism. The semicircular boudoir that shelters the amours of Paquita and Marsay in Honoré de Balzac's novel *La fille aux yeux d'or* (1835; The Girl with the Golden Eyes) has a Turkish divan, curtains of Indian muslin, and Persian carpets—an ambiance that inspires "sensual, indecisive, irresolute ideas." In Victor Hugo's *Les misérables* (1862; The Miserables), Marius's grandfather, being a man of the 18th century, keeps a boudoir, "a little room for lovers' trysts hung with magnificent straw draperies spangled with fleurs-de-lys and flowers." While the Goncourt brothers poured out evocations of the interiors of the great ladies and courtesans of the 18th century, in his *Albertus* (1833) Théophile Gautier translates the characteristics of the boudoir into the vocabulary of his own time—"comfort, elegance, and wealth"—and Baude-laire uses the phrase "a boudoir for men" to refer to the new space of bourgeois worldliness, the smoking room, in his *Petits poèmes en prose* (1867; Short Prose Poems).

MICHEL DELON

See also Decoration; Furniture; Libertinism; Miniature

Further Reading

Eleb, Monique, and Debarre-Blanchard, Anne, *Architectures de la vie privée: Maisons et mentalités, XVIe–XIXe siècles,* Brussels: AAM, 1989

Pardailhé-Galabrun, Annik, *The Birth of Intimacy: Privacy and Domestic Life in Early Modern Paris,* Philadelphia: University of Pennsylvania Press, 1991 (original French edition, 1988)

Perrot, Philippe, *Le luxe: Une richesse entre faste et confort, XVIIe–XIXe siècle,* Paris: Seuil, 1995

Bouffons, Quarrel of the

Between 1752 and 1754 a fierce debate over the question of the relative merits of French and Italian opera provoked a schism among French philosophers and music lovers. Friedrich Melchior von Grimm's *Lettre sur Omphale* (1752; Letter on Omphale) is often cited as the opening salvo in the hostilities. Yet, before the start of the Quarrel proper, peace reigned for almost a year after Grimm's publication, which in retrospect seems more like an epilogue to the earlier feud between the supporters of Jean-Philippe Rameau, "the Ramistes," and those of Jean-Baptiste Lully, "the Lullistes," than the prologue to a new debate. This said, the confusion came about because of the close similarities between the majority of the arguments expounded in Grimm's *Lettre sur Omphale* and those of the looming Quarrel.

In his protest against the restaging of André-Cardinal Destouches's *Omphale,* first performed with success in 1701, Grimm contrasts the dated idiom of lyric tragedy in the vein of Lully with such contemporary works as those of Rameau and the "Neapolitan school." Weary of the want of feeling, the wandering modulations, the sad and sluggish monotony of French recitative, Grimm praises the poignancy, clarity, and harmonic vitality of "Italian music." Citing Giovanni Battista Pergolesi, Baldassare Galuppi, and the Neapolitan school, he refers doubters to Jean-Jacques Rousseau's arguments in the "Recitative" entry in the *Encyclopédie.* Pergolesi's name, ranked alongside those of Johann Adolf Hasse, Georg Freidrich Handel, and the Neapolitans, turns up again in the *Lettre à M. Grimm* (Letter to Monsieur Grimm) published by Rousseau as a refutation of the remarks of an anonymous adversary who favored lyric tragedy. While Grimm had hailed Rameau's talents, Rousseau digresses expansively about the merits of that composer's theoretical writings, thereby adding yet another discordant note to the conflict. Overembellished harmony and complex intellectuality—two clichés borrowed from Raguenet and exploited by the nationalist party to show the inferiority of Italian sonatas—are now terms applied to Rameau. "Without anyone having read him," he is accused of having encouraged bad composers "to write harmony before their ears and experience have taught them to recognize the right one" (see Launay).

In the summer of 1753, without any inkling of what awaited him, Eustachio Bambini and his theatre company crossed the Alps en route to Rouen. In fact, this was not the troupe's first tour; they had already performed twice at the Paris Opéra. The first time, on 7 June 1729, a certain amount of acclaim had greeted the intermezzo, *Bajocco e Serpilla o vero il marito giocatore e la moglie bacchettona* (Bajocco and Serpilla; or, The Gambler and His Sanctimonious Wife [libretto by Romagnesi; music by Sodi or by Pietro Auletta]). But the 16-year gap separating this tour and the next is a reliable enough measure of the oblivion into which the new genre had fast fallen. In 1746, for the first time in France, the troupe made up of Luigi Riccoboni, Madame Monti, and Scapin had performed *La serva padrona* (The Maid as Mistress), which sank without a trace, having been overshadowed by a less interesting work that shared its program, *Le Prince de Salerne* (The Prince of Salerno). In 1751, on the other hand, the climate proved more favorable. Louis XV had just ceded to the city of Paris the exclusive rights to the Opéra. Lyric theatre left its home at the court. Armed with financial autonomy and faced with a different audience, the Opéra took on a new look.

This difficult period was above all a crisis of expansion, the most decisive crisis since the death of Lully. Ludovico Ariosto's heroes and the other gods of antiquity who continued to haunt the Pantheon of the Opéra had had their day. Their hieratic psychology had begun to seem like a relic of a vanished era. In an attempt to inject new life into the genre, spectacle, ballet, and music were given a greatly enhanced prominence. Having been joined by Lully in a marriage of convenience, the musical arts now divorced each other. Already violated in the multifarious episodic fables—the allegories on "The Elements," "The Ages of Man," and "The Seasons"—the principle of unity of dramatic action now gave birth to the opera-ballet, which began to vie for the public's favor at the Opéra. Rameau's music provided an effective antidote, but its content was too condensed and its audiences were too frivolous. Grimm and Rousseau, meanwhile, made a great commotion about Pergolesi and the Neapolitans. During the summer of 1752 the inspectors general of the Opéra, bent on exercising their rights, enticed the company of the Bouffons to the capital. On 1 August 1752 Pergolesi's *La serva padrone* opened a run of 150 performances, including 13 Neapolitan opera buffas, intermezzi, and *pasticci,* all given at the Opéra during a season that lasted 20 months. *La serva* padrona (1733), already 20 years old, now aroused the enthusiasm of a select public happy to discover at last the novelty it had refused to recognize in Rameau's *Platée* (1745). But in contrast to the favorable opinions propagated in the partisan press, a more general acclaim was slow in coming and the audiences remained wary. A critic for the *Mercure de France* complained in the September 1752 edition that the profusion of effects confused him, that certain ariettas pleased none but "a handful of connoisseurs," and that it was only thanks to some cuts that the piece managed to appeal to a part of the audience. Rousseau himself acknowledged that the performers were "execrable, and that the orchestra, very poorly trained at that time, mutilated as if wantonly the works it performed" (see Reichenburg). Three weeks later the *Giocatore ossia Serpilla e Bajocco* began to rival the success of *La serva padrona,* which was dropped from the program after 12 performances. For almost 20 months a series of new intermezzi followed each other at the rate of one per month, some achieving more success than others. Moreover, the methods of performing these intermezzi, staged as interludes or epilogues to the lyric tragedies, introduced a pleasing stylistic contrast. Audiences began to compare genres that were in fact the incomparable.

Apart from the baron d'Holbach's publication of his *Lettre d'une dame d'un certain âge sur l'état présent de l'opéra* (1752; Letter to a Lady of a Certain Age on the Present State of Opera), which drew no reaction, the first phase of the Quarrel unfolded orally, at the Opéra, in discussions arising from the performances, and in salons. At a date that is difficult to determine, two sides gathered under the boxes of the respective sovereigns, whose opposite tastes had become known: the Francophile "King's Corner" and the Italophile "Queen's Corner." In the first camp thronged the wealthy, the highly placed, and the ladies: the monarch, his mistress, Philidor, Rameau, and a host of literary men clustered around Élie-Catherine Fréron; the Navy commissioner, Cazotte; the royal censor, Pidansat de Mairobert; the copyist and officer of the king's household, Coste d'Arnobat; and the cellist and theorist Blainville. In the second camp were arrayed the French *philosophes* and the people of taste and feeling (such as La Poplinière) orbiting around Grimm, Rousseau, Denis Diderot, and the *Encyclopédie* and its friends. Jean le Rond d'Alembert, who had just finished his popularization of Rameau's ideas, avoided the attention that publication of sensational pamphlets would bring him. "They claim that I head the Italian faction, but I have no taste for excess," he wrote on 22 December 1752 to Madame Du Duffand. Voltaire, sceptical, prescient, and a friend of Rameau, attended only as a spectator. "Are you for France or for Italy? I am, Sirs, for my own pleasure," he remarked. Busy working on his public reply to Leonhard Euler, Rameau gave no sign of involving himself personally. Diderot joined the fray by writing three anonymous pamphlets, and although he did not reject French music outright, he did not hide his preference for Italian music. On 9 January 1753, in order to thwart the Bouffons, Madame de Pompadour commissioned an opera from Jean-Joseph Cassanéa de Mondonville, who hurriedly composed *Titon et l'Aurore* (Titon and Dawn).

A few days later the intervention of the press triggered the Quarrel proper. Around 15 February 1753, *Le petit prophète de Boemischbroda* (The Little Prophet from Boemischbroda), a character sprung fully formed from Grimm's fertile imagination, announced to the French people their redemption through Pergolesi, and he included among his reproaches the threat of transforming the Opéra (using its formal title of the Académie Royale de Musique) into a wasteland. A flood of satiric pamphlets, some wittier than others, followed this publication. Forgetting at times the topic under discussion, the pamphleteers argued with passion and drew comparisons even more passionately. On 25 January, in his *Réponse du coin du roi au coin de la reine* (A Reply from the King's Corner to the Queen's Corner), Mairobert de Pidansat drew a parallel between Lully's monologue from *Armide* (1686) and Rinaldo di Capua's *La donna superba* (The Haughty Lady). Diderot countered by inviting his opponent to prove by comparison of the *Le médecin malgré lui* (1666; The Doctor in Spite of Himself) with *Polyeucte* (1642) and of *Monsieur de Pourceaugnac* (1669) with *Athalie* (1690) "that Molière's farces are bad because Racine's and Corneille's tragedies are good" (see Launay).

This challenge indicated the dead end that the debate had reached: the comparison of genres. In *Au petit prophète de Boemischbroda* (January 1753; To the Little Prophet from Boemischbroda), Diderot tries to heighten the tone of the debate by suggesting that the two sides compare—limiting themselves "strictly to the notes"—the music from *Armide* and a similar scene (*Sesostri*) from *Nitocris* by Domingo Miguel Bernabe Terradellas, an Italian composer of Spanish ancestry. Although Diderot provides no answer, he nonetheless invites supporters of Italian music to prove that

> compared to those from *Nitocris,* the scenes from *Armide* are nothing but a listless droning, a melody without fire, soul, vitality, or genius; that the French composer owes everything to his librettist, while, in contrast, the Italian librettist owes everything to his composer (see Launay).

February saw the publication of about a dozen pamphlets: a comedy by Boissy, *La frivolité* (Frivolity), in which Madame Favart could be heard parodying La Tonnelli; four poems by Caux de Cappeval—*L'anti-scurra ou préservatif contre les bouffons* (The Anti-Scurra; or, Protection against the Bouffons), *La réforme de l'opéra* (The Reform of the Opéra), *Épître aux bouffonistes* (Epistle to the Bouffonists), and *Réflexions lyriques* (Thoughts on the Opera)—in which the Encyclopedists are blamed for provoking the Quarrel; Diderot's pamphlet *Au petit prophète;* and Rulhière's *Jugement de l'orchestre de l'opéra* (Judgment on the Orchestra of the Opera), where one reads that the philosopher-geometricians are "to music what a man who knows that a mixture of blue and yellow makes green is to painting" (see Launay).

On 6 March, *Les trois chapitres ou la vision de la nuit de mardi gras au mercredi des cendres* (The Three Chapters; or, The Vision of the Night of Shrove Tuesday to Ash Wednesday), a pastiche of Diderot's *Au petit prophète,* ushered the Quarrel into a new phase. Transported "in spirit" from his attic in Prague to the Paris Opéra, the little prophet had attended the triumph of the premiere of Rousseau's *Le devin du village* (1752; The Village Soothsayer), first performed at the court in Fontainebleau on 18 October. Dazzled by the simplicity, dramatic truth, melody, accompaniment, and the power of Rousseau's ideals worked out in his *Le devin du village,* the prophet bitterly regrets having broken violin and bow, sacrificed in a moment of despair after having "played minuets other than his" (see Launay). In the fall of 1753, after the fiasco of *Il paratoja* (The Sluice-gate), adapted from Nicolò Jommelli's *L'uccellatrice*

(The Lady Swindler), the Bambini troupe's popularity waned. At the same time, the argument stagnated. Trying to fire up the desire for a return match, in his *Lettre d'un symphoniste* (1753; Letter from a Symphonist) Rousseau accused the orchestra of having engineered *Il paratoja*'s failure. The instrumentalists at the Opéra burned the author of this text in effigy and steps were taken to ban his entry to the building.

But it was only the unforeseen violence of Rousseau's *Lettre sur la musique française* (Letter on French Music), published in November, that had the force to spark things off again. Rousseau's letter is a historically slanted reevaluation that sees the present position as the division into two parts of an original unit. His recital of the degenerative diseases of Western music, his accusatory description of French prosody, his theory of melodic unity—heard in the pure homophony of the neo-Neapolitan style—and his note-by-note analysis of the famous monologue from *Armide,* all lead to the thesis of the utter impossibility of music in the French tongue.

From that moment the hitherto flimsy excuse of a season of intermezzi took a back seat in the Quarrel, leaving the extravagances of both the *Lettre* and its author exposed to the fire of counterarguments. Replies of uneven quality showered forth, but none of the objectors managed to refute the *Lettre*'s arguments (as Rameau would do the following year in his *Observations sur notre instinct pour la musique* [1754; Observations on Our Instinct for Music]). In February 1754, even though a restaging of *Platée* might have managed to reverse the situation, an edict from the king put an end to the season. Rousseau and the Encyclopedists exited the stage firmly convinced of having had the last word. At the theatre of the Comédie-Française, the cast of Patu and Portelance's *Les adieux du goût* (Farewell to Taste) alternately mocked both the French and the Italians; at the theatre of the Comédie-Italienne, *Le retour du goût* (The Return of Good Taste), staged by Chevrier on 25 February, declared a victory signaled by the troupe's departure. Given a month's extension at the request of the duchesse d'Orléans, the performances ended on 7 March 1754 with the failure of the *Viaggiatori* (The Travelers). But the storm still raged on.

Rousseau's denial of the very possibility of French music had been enough to rile Rameau himself. As revealed in a letter from the composer's son, C.-F. Rameau, his father's analysis of the monologue from *Armide,* published in the *Observation,* should be regarded as a reply to the *Lettre sur la musique française,* which he had taken as a personal attack. The Bouffons had left Paris. The *Lettre*'s ardor inflamed the vengeful spirit of the *Encyclopédie*'s enemies who, in the musical domain, had rallied around Rameau. And so it was the turn of *Erreurs sur la musique dans* "*l'Encyclopédie*" (Errors about Music in the "Encyclopédie") to attack the articles dashed off in haste by Rousseau. Stung to the quick, the editors announced in the preface to Volume VI their plans for a dictionary to be prepared by Rousseau with the intention of deflecting the barbs directed at him.

Historians who have tried to analyze the causes and results of this affair have often resorted to terms of classification belonging properly to musicology. It has become commonplace to mention the crisis in French opera, the conflation of genres (encouraged in bad faith on all sides), or even the impact of the most readily recognized components of the Neapolitan style. Yet the most disturbing aspect of this strange affair lies precisely in the almost incidental nature of the strictly musical field in this literary debate. For instance, it is often stated that the Quarrel was started by repeated performances of *La serva padrona*. But, aside from the fact that this statement should be turned on its head—since the Bouffons' presence in Paris was the result of a difference of opinion rather than its cause—a quick check of the chronological milestones shows the lack of foundation for this hypothesis. The Italians had performed for six months before the *philosophes* even thought of wielding their pens; the trading of insults stopped spontaneously the following year, one month before the end of the performances on 7 March 1754; and when the Quarrel's volcanic activity was at the height of its intensity, Pergolesi had not featured on the playbill for almost five months. All things considered, it would be a distortion to attribute the infatuation with a 40-year-old genre of opera to purely aesthetic considerations. The spur to the debate was not some quality inherent in the new genre. Had that really been the case, the Bouffons could not have failed to trigger the Quarrel during their two earlier tours. In 1729 and 1746, the novel freshness of the intermezzi had gone unnoticed without generating any desire on the part of the *philosophes* to reform lyric theatre. By 1752 the situation had changed. The repertory was the same, the feats of the troupe—rather mediocre ones, it seems—did not owe their success to the charm of its members but to the intrigues and eloquence of their advocates. It all boils down to a coincidence of events, the conditions for which converged for the first time at that precise moment in history. Unbeknownst to them, the Italians rose to the rank of symbols of thrilling creativity, genius, and melodiousness, and ended by conforming to the clichés of a conflict that concerned the history of ideas at least as much as it did the history of political and artistic doctrines.

In January 1753, at the exact moment when the pronouncements of Grimm's little prophet had inspired an avalanche of pamphlets, a sharp break between the Jansenists and the Jesuits shook monarchic absolutism. Unsurprisingly, this schism was quickly transposed onto the controversy surrounding the Opéra, a symbol par excellence of royal ritual. By calling his little prophet "Jesuitical," Grimm was the first to substantiate this hypothesis. D'Alembert confirms it in *De la liberté de la musique* (On Freedom in Music; cited in Launay): "In some people's book, Bouffonist, Republican, Frondeur, Atheist (not to forget Materialist) are just so many synonymous terms." It would therefore be wrong to stress the frivolity of the audiences or boredom with lyric tragedy. There is reason to doubt whether the history of French musical theatre would have had a different outcome if the Bouffons had not come to perform in Paris. At the Opéra, lyric tragedy continued to predominate in the repertory for nearly 20 years; attempts to reform the *opéra comique* did not produce immediate results, and in 1759 D'Alembert complained that, unlike other countries, France had not yet adopted the new idiom. However, the real contribution of the Quarrel lies in its foregrounding of the essence and specificity of lyric tragedy. Until that time musical drama had been looked at with reference to spoken drama, using methods appropriated from literary criticism. The Quarrel led Rousseau to consider the opera as an autonomous genre, as a species apart, and led Diderot to invite the comparatists to stick strictly to the music, without taking into account the work of the librettists Philippe Quinault and Pietro Metastasio.

BRENNO BOCCADORO

See also Music; Opera; Opera, Comic; Vaudeville

Further Reading

Launay, Denise, editor, *La Querelle des Bouffons: Texte des Pamphlets,* 3 vols., Geneva: Minkoff Reprint, 1973

Oliver, Alfred Richard, *The Encyclopedists as Critics of Music,* New York: Columbia University Press, 1947

Reichenburg, Louisette Eugénie, *Contribution à l'histoire de la "Querelle des Bouffons,"* Paris: Nizet et Bastard, 1937

Bourgeoisie, Professional

In the 18th century the professional bourgeoisie consolidated its position as one of the leading groups among the commoners. Despite an increase in their numbers, the working bourgeoisie certainly comprised a smaller group than that of the bourgeois of independent means. The importance of the professional bourgeoisie is better measured in terms of social influence than in pure numbers. Proof for this conclusion can be found in the French term of praise used to describe the best professionals in medicine, law, and education: *talents*.

This expression, specific to the Enlightenment, contrasts with the mocking criticism directed at lawyers, doctors, and others in the 17th century—a ridicule that, although greatly curtailed, had not disappeared altogether from 18th-century discourse. The designation *talent* suggests a new honorable status, preceding what would become a social category held in high regard in the 19th century. The roots of this change, more clearly defined and more rapid in England and France than in Prussia or Russia, are to be found not only in objective developments but also in people's ways of thinking. Given the changes in their knowledge and practice, and the public importance of their activities, some members of the working bourgeoisie were now seen as men of learning, as competent, responsible men. They played an active and willing part in the institutions of culture and power, where they had much to do with the construction of the public sphere. Moreover, public opinion validated their usefulness and education: talented people embodied merit, a new criterion in the hierarchization of society, which coexisted with the criterion of birth—without supplanting it—and could justify a rise in social status.

Useful Professionals

The professional bourgeoisie had a number of roles to play consistent with the growing and changing needs of a more service-oriented society. This social class was therefore useful, if not indispensable, in managing private as well as public affairs, thanks to its pool of knowledge and specialized competence. The usefulness of the professional bourgeoisie was a fundamental underpinning of its high standing in public opinion.

The legal profession was omnipresent, in both towns and the rural areas. The majority of the professional bourgeoisie were lawyers who, unless they were magistrates in a lower court, devoted the greater part of their time to drawing up petitions and statements for their clients rather than actually pleading cases. On the eve of the Revolution there were more than 500 legal professionals in Paris, in addition to the lawyers of the

Conseil du Roi (King's Council); there were approximately 100 lawyers in the major provincial cities and 20 to 30 in the smaller ones. In England there were 400 lawyers registered at the Inns of Court. However, lawsuits did not increase proportionally to the number of lawyers, and as a result the less fortunate among them sank into poverty. From the sovereign courts to the lowest level crown courts, lawyers endeavored to distinguish themselves from ancillary legal practitioners such as prosecutors, bailiffs, and clerks, who were not ranked and whose functions were considered inherently demeaning. Notaries, whether royal or seignorial, pursued their activity in a fairly independent manner. Although present at the important moments of civilian life, they also spent a considerable, if not greater, amount of time working for the credit system. Many trained jurists found employment in the king's civil administration, or they served a private institution or patron. Some were subdelegates of an *intendant* (magistrate), secretaries of a justice of the peace, or treasurers for the Ferme Générale (General Tax Farms); others were secretaries or accountants for noblemen. In England economic growth and the increasing wealth of the population eventually gave rise to new professions. Some attorneys specialized in financial and commercial disputes; others acted as brokers, charged with the investment of private capital, which contributed to the development of the banking industry.

Medical professionals were far less numerous than men of law; in England they were doctors, surgeons, and even apothecaries. Whether they worked independently, for a hospital, or in the service of a great aristocrat, men in the medical profession sought primarily to respond to the needs of city dwellers and the nobility. Thanks to limited yet striking advances in medical science—such as the smallpox inoculation in France or the improvements in obstetrics in England—physicians had put a great deal of distance between their profession and those of healers and other quacks. The best professionals also taught simultaneously in the universities.

Thus, the conditions under which these professions were practiced varied greatly. The choice of whether to work independently or in the service of a private or public institution, or even to work for a patron, was rarely made freely. The theoretical preference for the exercise of an independent profession was often superseded by material constraints. A patron provided a secure and comfortable material situation as well as the protection that made it possible to put up with being a quasi servant. Thus, a position as a tutor was a coveted one among promising young "persons of talent," who expected their protector eventually to find them a more advantageous position; or a young professional might be able to hold several positions at once and thus be assured of sufficient revenue. The variety of ways in which these persons of talent could take part in society finally led others to look more closely at the interests or even the ideologies those persons represented and upheld in the exercise of their profession.

Public opinion in the 17th century had been quick to denounce personal interest, particularly financial interest, as the professionals' only motivation, regardless of the effectiveness of the service they performed or any ideological consideration. During the Enlightenment, however, both reality and the perception of the interests of the professional bourgeoisie became more complex. Social advancement, financial gain, and the exercise of power were indisputable aims, but they were not incompatible with a sense of duty and responsibility in the practice of one's profession. In other words, production-based culture to some extent gave way to a service-oriented culture—service to the client or the patron, of course, but, above all, service to the public good. Indeed, as cultural intermediaries, the skilled bourgeoisie could affirm that they were vested with a mission of public interest. Thus, Félix Vicq d'Azyir and François Quesnay were appreciated for their activities on behalf of public health, the results of which first affected members of the royal family and the court, and later the cities.

As for the work of the lawyers, it followed varied and often contradictory patterns throughout the century. In the countryside, when they represented rural communities in conflicts that pitted those communities against the nobility, lawyers sometimes went beyond their role by leading the lawsuits that were brought. The lawyers of sovereign courts affirmed for the first time their unwavering solidarity with the magistrates when there were strikes among the judiciary triggered by the Jansenist controversy: the unity of the judicial corps seemed at that point obvious and indispensable if the oppression of the monarchy were to be resisted. Then, during the second half of the century, lured by the ideas of the *philosophes* and at times influenced by Voltaire, some lawyers used legal reports to arouse public opinion. Lawyers were then seen as defenders of justice, of the oppressed, and of civil liberties, against magistrates accused of barbarity. Other lawyers, on the contrary, would intervene as "watchdog(s) of the established ideology" (M. Vovelle, *Les intermédiaires culturels* [Cultural Mediators]). For example, Jacob-Nicolas Linguet, an attorney engaged in the financial administration, defended the monarchy in his pamphlets. Backlash against Linguet's pamphlets had repercussions for all of the professional bodies, contributing to the new perception that the value of a man's role in society was not a given, but something earned through

the utility of his acts, particularly if those acts turned out to be beneficial to the public.

Men of Knowledge

During a century in which educational issues were the subject of passionate debate, public opinion began to reflect a new awareness that the professional bourgeoisie was useful because of the knowledge it possessed. This knowledge could be acquired through study, whether certified by a diploma or not, and then by a more or less formal apprenticeship.

Students of a profession were given their general education in school. They studied the humanities alongside young noblemen, learning Latin, mastery of oral and written expression, and logic. The number of years spent in school varied according to two criteria: the wealth of the parents—unless there was a scholarship to compensate for a student's lack of funds—and the activity for which a young man was destined. Those who would become notaries and minor legal officials, for example, and who did not need a university degree to practice their profession left school fairly quickly to work in the service of a bailiff, prosecutor, or notary for several years before they could set off to practice in their own name. English attorneys and apothecaries completed a true apprenticeship.

Those young men who envisaged a career in a liberal profession (lawyers and doctors) or in the university were obliged to complete their secondary studies before going on to university. The education available in the faculties of law and medicine was not conducive to assiduous study: the programs were often archaic and the conditions corrupt. Thus, to become a bachelor and then a *licencié* of law was often a mere formality. The future lawyer then completed a two-year training period as an "observer-lawyer," attending hearings and conferences, before he could be registered with the bar and then begin to exercise his profession. As for the student of medicine, if he were in Paris, he would spend more time taking courses at the Jardin du Roi (French Royal Botanical Garden) or the Collège du Roi (Royal College) than at the medical faculty, unless he went to Montpellier or Leiden, whose universities offered a more modern education.

This theoretical and practical education in law or medicine formed the basis of knowledge and savoir-faire that a professional would later perfect, enrich, and modernize not only through practice but also through reading: a proof of this fact was the preponderant amount of shelf space given to works of jurisprudence and law in legal offices and to medicine in medical offices. At the end of the century the medical professions also benefited from the new institutions created by the state to encourage the progress and spread of medical science, institutions such as the Société Royale de Medecine (Royal Society of Medicine) in France or the Josephinium in the Holy Roman Empire.

Nor were the activities and culture of the talented men of the 18th century limited to the professional sphere alone. At the beginning of the century, their libraries typically may have contained only a few volumes, many of which were classics or works on religion, but these were soon supplemented by history and even geography books, and, above all, plays and novels. Enthusiasts of moralizing comedy and drama, the professional bourgeoisie regularly attended the theatre and concerts. This growing appetite for culture was accompanied by the professional bourgeoisie's active participation in the intellectual life of the century. "Persons of talent" were present in the new structures of social life that were blossoming in the towns, the academies, and the Masonic lodges. These individuals mixed with merchants on some occasions—and with noblemen at all times—and their relative importance varied with the extent of the openness of the local society. Egalitarian customs, basing distinction upon merit rather than on birth, were slowly beginning to erase social divisions: educated commoners and noblemen shared the same culture and merged into an elite based on shared knowledge rather than on class. This lack of differentiation was apparent primarily in France and England (in Prussia the gap between the middle class and the aristocracy remained wide). Occasionally members of this new, knowledge-based elite would publish or participate in the writing of works; thus, a good number of lawyers and doctors (such as the chevalier de Jaucourt) collaborated on the *Encyclopédie*. Professional bourgeois also found themselves serving alongside the nobility as local, or even national, political authorities. Members of the professional bourgeoisie gained entry into municipal councils or maintained their foothold there—as in Frankfurt, for example, where doctors and jurists could associate with the aristocracy in the administration of the city. The power they enjoyed was often more symbolic than real, but their participation in municipal affairs did consolidate their presence among the urban elite. In England, working members of the middle class made up the largest bourgeois element in the House of Commons, although they were hardly united in their political goals. Finally, in France in 1789, working bourgeois were similarly well represented among the editors of the *cahiers de doléance* (book of grievances) and among the representatives of the Third Estate in assemblies at every level. They could be found next to the nobility not only in the halls of academe but also in the halls of power. They shared with the aristocracy the same general culture, from college to the academies, and they shared power—at least in theory—on the local level. However, those who belonged to the elite by merit and those who belonged by birth did not merge to create a new aristocracy.

Merit, a Narrow Channel of Social Mobility

The professions exercised by men of talent—legal positions such as prosecutor and bailiff; surgery; and medicine—usually entailed loss of status and could not therefore be practiced by the offspring of the nobility. There were two major exceptions, however. In England physicians had been considered gentlemen since the 17th century, and the profession of barrister was proclaimed to be noble because of its independence. Being a barrister thus entailed no diminution in status, which explains the fact that this profession was temporarily practiced by those young members of the landed gentry who were the country's future magistrates.

Moreover, the professional bourgeoisie was a social group that had opportunities for limited, but real, upward mobility. Indeed, a small number of these talented professionals were ennobled. Merit alone was rarely rewarded; to attain nobility, it had to be associated with fame and influential connections, particularly at court (letters patent conferred nobility upon 35 physicians from 1724 to 1786, and upon only half as many lawyers). Wealth was another means of attaining ennoblement (lawyers were elevated primarily by the purchase of a position as secretary to the king). However, commoners were barred from certain institutions—for example, lawyers could not join the magistrature of the sovereign courts and professional bourgeoisie were excluded from the officers' ranks in the army—and such exclusions tended in the second half of the century to impede this social ascension.

Meanwhile, the professional bourgeoisie was accessible "from bottom up," as gifted children from the ranks of artisans or even the peasantry could gain admission to the professional ranks. A parent's savings, the generosity of a benefactor, or a scholarship might enable a gifted child to pay for his studies. His ambition would often be crushed, however, by established institutions controlling the access to traditional professions: these guardians of conservative values, rewarded birth, ritual, and connections over ability. The legal profession was therefore theoretically barred to children of "mechanical" origin. This exclusionary practice gave rise to a number of incidents, particularly in the second half of the century, involving the Ordre des Avocats Parisiens (Paris Bar Association), which, following the example set in Rennes, excluded children of modest origins from its ranks for fear that their poverty would further widen the social gap between the bar and the magistrature. In the same manner, the only physicians allowed to practice in and around London were those who were members of the Royal College of

Physicians, which admitted exclusively those practitioners who had studied at Oxford, Cambridge, or Dublin, even though the best medical schools were in Leiden, Edinburgh, and Glasgow.

Professionals were therefore recruited primarily from the middle classes. To a degree, the prestigious professions seemed to be essentially self-perpetuating (as various "dynasties" of lawyers, officers of the law, or physicians attest), but some professionals originally came from the merchant class or the leisured middle class. Marriages were arranged on this same social level, rarely extending to the aristocracy. The income to be earned from professional activity was considerable if the practitioner was famous, or if he had a generous patron and could supplement the income from his land or his estate. Such an income allowed for a modest or even comfortable—but rarely opulent—standard of living and enabled these bourgeois professionals to give as much care to their children's education as to their own style of dress.

During the age of the Enlightenment, the professional bourgeoisie was virtually omnipresent in the social, cultural, and political life of both urban and rural areas. The unity of this class did not depend on a convergence of interests or the ideas that members of the class upheld, for the care taken to preserve the distinctions within the bourgeoisie and the defense of personal interests prevented any such unity. On the other hand, this bourgeoisie was a collective incarnation of new values. Contrary to the image of the man who is respected for his ancestors, the talented man presented the image of a person who is perfectible through education and valued for his social usefulness—thus, such men paved the way for a more open society. They reconciled, without shame, culture and professional practice, private and public lives, and proclaimed themselves to be gentlemen, just like the nobility.

LAURENCE CROQ

See also Orders and Classes; Work

Further Reading

Barber, Elinor, *The Bourgeoisie in 18th-Century France,* Princeton, New Jersey: Princeton University Press, 1955

Gelfand, Toby, *Professionalizing Modern Medicine: Paris Surgeons and Medical Science and Institutions in the 18th Century,* Westport, Connecticut: Greenwood Press, 1980

Porter, Roy, *English Society in the Eighteenth Century,* London: Allen Lane, 1982

Roche, Daniel, *Le siècle des Lumières en province: Académies et académiciens provinciaux, 1680–1789,* Paris: Mouton, 1978

Bureaucracy

The rise of bureaucracy constitutes a determining factor in the development of the modern state. The intensity and the modalities of bureaucracy varied from state to state: it was a major phenomenon in France and in Prussia but it was more limited in Russia, Spain, and England. Across the board, however, bureaucracy resulted in part from the marginalization of the forms of administration that were either nonbureaucratic or had only limited bureaucratic elements: regional assemblies, municipal bodies, and territorial lords were divested of all or part of their powers. Admittedly, some exceptions remained, particularly in England, but the overall pattern is undeniable. In France bureaucracy took charge of the traditional responsibilities of these institutions as well as the monarchy's new spheres of intervention, especially that of finance, thus becoming the main instrument for the preparation and application of royal decisions. Bureaucratic structures developed in private and public administrations: in the departments of the comptroller general, in tax farms, and in the turnpike companies in charge of main roads.

According to Pierre Rosanvallon, bureaucracy is characterized by the centralization, standardization, and rationalization of administration (see Rosanvallon). The first two processes, in contrast to the third, were already well advanced at the beginning of the 18th century. As for democratization—"the institution of representative government, the submission of administration to the orientations of the general will, and the transparent exercise of authority"—it was virtually nonexistent. Indeed, the pejorative neologism "bureaucracy" expressed this very deficiency. Attributed to Vincent de Gournay in Friedrich Melchior von Grimm's *Correspondance littéraire* (1764), the term was finally recognized in the *Dictionnaire de l'Académie* (Dictionary of the Académie Française) in 1798. The word was used to denounce government by clerks as a counterpoint to ministerial despotism and to condemn bureaus, practitioners of bureaucracy, and their practices, while demanding both the limitation of their power and public accountability of their activities.

Limited Centralization and Standardization

In those monarchies deemed absolutist, the authority of the monarch as head of the administration was transmitted, following a strict hierarchy of command and execution, to certain administrative agents. These were either individuals, as in France, or councils, as in Prussia. In France the administrative divisions of the central government were the Directoire Général des Finances, Guerre et Domaines (General Directory of Finance, War and Property), and various collective ministries: Affaires Étrangères (Foreign Affairs), Justice, and Religion. The 17 regions were in the hands of Chambres Régionales de Guerre et des Domaines (Regional Chambers of War and Property).

This centralized model was only partially implemented, first and foremost because the central power did not always have obedient and effective intermediaries at its disposal. For example, the lack of financial means and of personnel restricted the real influence of the central administration in Russia to the capital city, Saint Petersburg, until the reforms of Catherine II. In Spain the monarchy imposed its basic measures with difficulty, even after the appearance of the *intendentes* (administrators) who were decidedly less powerful than their counterparts with the same title across the Pyrenees. In England the lords lieutenant belonged to the great families of the earldoms that they administered, and their independence from the central authority, like that of the justices of the peace at the parish level, was incontestable. In Prussia the local administration, by virtue of its inertia, often sabotaged the orders of the monarch. However, the independence of the local or regional bureaucracy was not necessarily negative, especially where it was infused with spirit of initiative, as was the case with the *intendants* in France. Furthermore, some centers of local and regional power retained administrative attributes that monarchs were either unable or did not wish to suppress. Along with the privileges and customs of the cities and the provinces, these local and regional authorities constituted obstacles to the interventions of the bureaucrats. For example, the powers of the *intendants* were limited, or even contested, by the estates in Brittany, Provence, and Languedoc, and even more so by the superior courts. They would have been even more so if the provincial assemblies of the 1780s, which were conceived in a spirit of decentralization, had been successful. In Prussia the local administration of the countryside was in the hands of the great landowners.

Ultimately, monarchs lost more and more decision-making powers. Some of them, such as Louis XV, accepted this trend, but others, such as Frederick II of Prussia, opposed it and insisted on making all decisions, even those that were purely routine, fearing above all that the ministers would make decisions for him. Catherine II regretted that the highest level of her administration did not take enough responsibility or initiative. Indeed, independent of a monarch's personality, the extent of royal intervention, the concern for effectiveness, and the specialization of functions made it difficult for the monarch to have knowledge about every case in question. The monarch therefore made fewer decisions in royal council, more often making decisions on an individual basis in conjunction with one of his ministers. The ministers could also make collective decisions, as in the general directory of Prussia, where the five heads of sections voted and took collective responsibility for decisions; or simply among themselves, as, for example, the French comptroller general with the *intendants* of finance; or individually, with their head clerk in the secrecy of private chambers. When decisions were made without deliberation, the advice of the clerks who prepared the files often had a significant impact on the consent of a minister who was less knowledgeable of the details of the matter. The marquis d'Argenson denounced this practice: "The details confided to ministers are immense. Nothing is done without them . . . and if their knowledge is not as extensive as their power, they are forced to leave everything to their clerks, who become the true masters." Thus, the essential content of the rulings made by the royal council, especially on finance, was decided outside the council itself, which tended to be no more than a judicial fiction.

The Birth of the Civil Servant

Throughout Europe recruitment for the bureaucracy took place for the most part among the aristocracy, who monopolized the higher posts. This situation was as much justified by the education they often received as by prejudice in favor of their noble birth and by the need for officials to have sufficient personal standing to hold the authority endowed in the name of the monarch. Civil service to the state was sometimes complementary to military service. Members of the Spanish *intendencia* were essentially military men of the lesser nobility. Frederick II recruited a good part of his administration from among the military nobles, but also from among commoners. In Russia, where the nobility was more integrated into the state than anywhere else, the monarch expected the nobles to spend their careers alternating between civil and military service. The bourgeoisie were generally confined to the lower echelons. Thus, under Louis XV, commoners provided a large majority of the head clerks of the ministries; they were sometimes ennobled at the end of their careers.

There were varying requirements regarding education. Faculties of law provided a certain amount of theoretical knowledge, which was then completed and broadened within the institutions themselves. In theory, a future *maître des requêtes* (receiver of petitions) in France would have studied law for three years and then worked for six years in one of the royal courts. In Prussia such officials had to spend two years as examiners with local or central tribunals before serving in an appellate court for five years, and finally become assessors after a quite thorough written and oral examination. There was, however, one innovation that is less interesting for its true impact than for the modernity of the ideas that underpinned it: the first French school of administration, the Académie Politique, was founded in 1712 in order to train future diplomats, but it did not survive the death of its director, Yves de Saint-Prest, in 1719. Recommendation, either through family connections or through a network of associates or clients, remained the definitive key to integration into the bureaucracy, at whatever level. Thus, the *maîtres des requêtes* were all related to each other.

In concrete terms, administration was in the hands of officers and commissioners who were, respectively, the ordinary and extraordinary agents of the monarch. The officers, as proprietors of their posts, were fairly independent, and often they were not very diligent in performing their tasks; they filled the older institutions, in particular the high courts. Offices conferred honor on their holders in every country; in France officers were able to grow rich and could be ennobled. Commissioners had duties limited by their letters of commission, which could be revoked at any moment. Their more vulnerable status and the greater docility that resulted from it made them the main instruments of administration during the Enlightenment. Nevertheless, the contrast between officers and commissioners should not be overestimated. Many commissioners held offices in addition to their commissions. In France the monarch always chose members of the Conseil d'État (Council of State) and the *intendants* from among the *maîtres des requêtes*, who were officers; and the subordinates of the *intendants* were often chosen from among the officers of Justice or Finance.

Strictly speaking, officers and commissioners could be characterized as civil servants only if they derived their power less from their personal status and their local family connections than from their functions and their service to the state. Thus, in England the administrators of counties and parishes could not be so charac-

terized, since the monarch was forced to designate the lords lieutenant from among the great families in each region and to appoint the justices of the peace—who exercised their functions without pay—on the advice of the lords lieutenant. In contrast, the great administrators in Russia and France moved around a lot: the "careers" of civil servants often led them from minor to major offices before they ended up on the Council of State.

In addition, bureaucrats had above all to be attached to a function and not to a patron—yet this seemed a priori incompatible with the personal relationships that were the basis of recruitment in every country. In fact, personal interests and interpersonal solidarity always played an important role, but administrative personnel benefited from greater stability, independent of their "recruiter," as a result of the competence that they acquired with experience. Thus, an *intendant* stayed for an average of five years in the same province at the start of the 18th century and for ten years at the end, and the careers of some of Louis XV's officials continued until the First Empire. In England the employees of ministries, recruited by officers and salaried workers as a result of fees received from the public, remained in the same positions even if their "patron" left. They received regular remuneration, on a scale commensurate with seniority, and sometimes bonuses, which assured a comfortable living; they also received a retirement pension. According to Daniel Roche's *La France des Lumières* (1993; France in the Enlightenment), the bureaucracy, a body of professionals with recognized competence, "became an estate."

The absence of clear and precise distinctions among areas, interests, and private and public relations, as much at the level of recruitment as in the functioning of the administration, did not prevent the evolution of practices and mentalities. Moreover, legal functionaries appeared during this period among technical personnel. Some historians have claimed that the first civil servants in France were the maritime commissioners, who were appointed to their official function in 1670. More commonly, however, the engineers of the Ponts et Chaussées (Bridges and Roads Ministry) are cited as France's first civil servants; they assumed their official function in 1747. These engineers were actually recruited by a competitive examination and trained at the central civil engineering school in Paris. They benefited from life-long employment and enjoyed a career characterized by advancement according to seniority or by individual merit; they received salaries and could obtain a pension upon retirement, either for themselves or for their widows. They were also subject to certain constraints: residence at their place of work, obedience, professional secrecy, and selection of a spouse from a "good" family.

Standardization of Working Methods

The work of the bureaucracy was increasingly subject to the limits of time and place: the appearance of precise schedules, as in the French Secrétariat des Affaires Étrangères (Secretariat of Foreign Affairs), and the concentration of certain personnel in office buildings. Independent of the clerk's routine work, the methods of handling information were over time standardized and simplified, which enabled the bureaucracy to base its measures on real knowledge of people, wealth, and territory, or to encourage the initiative of competent personnel or institutions.

Archives were enriched by papers that were considered more as administrative documents than as personal possessions, but they also sometimes included donations or acquisitions, as at the Sécretariat des Affaires Étrangères. Far from being a dead record, archives were regularly consulted. Excerpts were taken from them and precedents or useful formulations were sought. Correspondence brought in its share of regular information to the different echelons of the administration. The correspondence between the comptroller of finances and the *intendants,* for example, enabled the central power to be regularly informed about the condition of the provinces, in the absence of annual reports. Meticulous surveys were launched, with general fiscal or military objectives. These were addressed (very often on the initiative of the comptroller general) to the *intendants,* who passed them on to their subordinates, if not to respond directly to them, then at least in order to assemble the necessary information. They could also be sent to scholarly institutions, such as the Académie Royale des Sciences. They requested general information, such as the state of opinion or statistical data. Regular statistics did exist, but these remained an exception. Thus, on the initiative of the abbé Terray, demographic changes in the French population were evaluated annually starting in 1770, using the methods introduced by Messance. The information obtained enabled the administration to conceive of a future that would not be a return to a golden age: the management of territory, public health policy or the supply of wheat, the standardization of laws, etc. Furthermore, administrative science became a goal everywhere in Europe. *Kameralistik,* the "science of the management of the state," was a subject taught in the Prussian universities beginning 1727, and in France the first treatises were written on it, even if they remained incomplete, following the example of Auget de Montyon.

Toward a Better Definition of Responsibilities

As the weight of administration increased, confusion over responsibilities became endemic. At times the overlapping of jurisdictions sparked bitter tensions, such as those between the high courts and the *intendants* in France. The accumulation of executive and judicial functions was also a general phenomenon. They were exercised as much by the French *intendants* as by the English justices of the peace.

Some measures were taken to limit the powers of the various offices, in line with Montesquieu's ideas on the separation of powers. Thus, in England, the law required a growing number of civil servants to choose between their offices and membership in Parliament if they were elected to the House of Commons. At the very end of the century Prussia separated the administrative authority of the regional chambers from their judicial authority. Above all, the growth of the workforce was accompanied by a more rational organization and a specialization of tasks. (The importance of this growth needs to be put in perspective; for example, the bureaus under the comptroller general never employed more than 150 people before the beginning of the Revolution.) Within the ministries in France, tasks were distributed among bureaus by geographic sector or by subject. The ministers had one or two personal secretaries, and in each bureau, directed by a head clerk, a senior clerk supervised the work of the ordinary clerks. In the provinces, each *intendant* surrounded himself with competent staff members, 20 at most: a personal secretary, a general subordinate to whom he delegated his powers in his absence, and other subordinates who were each in charge of a portion of territory and under whose orders the clerks worked.

The increase in the power of the bureaucracy was all the greater because it was sometimes uncontrolled. Internal dysfunctions or conflicts with those being administered, such as decisions made by incompetent persons, corruption, or the nonapplication of orders, were dealt with differently in different states. In Prussia the administrators were supervised by the king, who threatened them, made inspections, intimidated them, and hired spies; administrators there could be judged by a special jurisdiction. In England in 1786, a commission set up by Parliament denounced the wrongs of which the administration had been accused for a very long time: sinecures, whose functions were exercised by substitutes, and the remuneration of administrative services by fees that encouraged officers to dedicate themselves only to well-paid tasks. The abolition of sinecures and the transformation of officers into employees took place over a period of 50 years.

French bureaucracy was without doubt the least controlled, since its authority was supposed to issue directly from the king. Of course, it was criticized by the high courts but also by ministers, such as Argenson (who famously claimed "the clerks are running the store") or, later, Jacques Necker, who reproached the *intendants* for their absenteeism and their omnipotence. An article in the *Encyclopédie méthodique* (1788; A Methodical Encyclopedia) summarized the grievances of the public on the eve of the Revolution. It denounced the concentration of executive and judicial powers in the hands not of the king but of ignorant clerks who did not have the confidence of the public. The article also demanded the tyranny to which those clerks subjected the citizens in the name of the interests of the state. The *Encyclopédie* expressed the desire for an administration in the service of the public that would transmit and execute laws automatically. The debate on the democratization of the bureaucracy was thus broadened.

LAURENCE CROQ

See also Finance; Intendancy System; Parlements, French; State

Further Reading

Mousnier, Roland, *The Institutions of France under the Absolute Monarchy, 1598–1789,* 2 vols., Chicago: University of Chicago Press, 1979–84; see especially vol. 2, *The Organs of State and Society* (original French edition, 1974–80)

Mousnier, Roland, *La monarchie absolue en Europe du Ve siècle á nos jours,* Paris: Presses Universitaires de France, 1982

Rosanvallon, Pierre, *L'État en France de 1789 à nos jours,* Paris: Seuil, 1990

Rosenberg, Hans, *Bureaucracy, Aristocracy, and Autocracy: The Prussian Experience, 1660–1815,* Cambridge, Massachusetts: Harvard University Press, 1958

C

Calendar, French Revolutionary

Next to 14 July 1789, the most famous date in the whole history of the French Revolution is undoubtedly 9 Thermidor Year II, when the Terror collapsed with the precipitous fall of Maximilien Marie Isidore de Robespierre. It is one of the few events (18 Brumaire Year VIII, Napoleon's coup d'état, being another) still referred to in terms of the calendar then in effect, which in significant ways symbolized the Revolution itself.

The new calendar was one of a number of radical reforms introduced by the revolutionary government. Because its design was intended to exemplify the principle of reason, this calendar was as much an educational tool as a political one. Indeed the project was assigned to the Comité d'Instruction Publique (Commission on Public Instruction). Whereas the redesigning of the nation's territory put more or less isometric, geographically denominated *départements* in the place of the old provinces with their autonomous traditions and rights, the revolutionary calendar reallocated the very conceptualization of time. Its pattern, like that of the sweeping changes in weights and measures, would be, insofar as possible, metric.

First and foremost, the new calendar was created to displace that of the Church, in which every day celebrated a saint and a plethora of feast days sanctioned suspension of labor. The Revolution, which marked a new social era, furnished both the means and the occasion for supplanting the Common Era. It had been a frequent patriotic gesture since 14 July 1789 to date significant events following that moment as belonging to a new system of social chronology, the years of Liberty. But was 15 July a better date for beginning Year I than 4 August 1789, which could stand for the era of Equality, or, three years later, 22 September 1792, the birth of the Republic?

The report brought to the floor of the Convention by Gilbert Romme on 19–20 September 1793 stressed the intention of abolishing the Christian Era and with it its every token in the Gregorian calendar:

> The Common Era began among an ignorant and credulous people, and amid turmoil foreshadowing the imminent fall of the Roman Empire. For 18 centuries it served to fix in time the progress of fanaticism; the degradation of nations; the scandalous triumph of arrogance, vice, and nonsense; the persecutions and aversion to which virtue, talent, and philosophy were subjected under cruel despots or allowed in their name. . . . The Revolution has given a new temper to Frenchmen's souls; it daily moulds them to republican virtues. Time is opening a new book to history; and in the new progression, majestic and simple like equality, it will engrave with a new and bold burin the annals of regenerated France.

The committee proposed to mark point zero of the new era as the date of the founding of the Republic, 22 September 1792. In this way the monarchical phase of the Revolution would be clearly categorized as a merely preparatory phase for the new, Republican dispensation. But there would be no "before," as in the Christian calendar; rather than counting backward from Year I, Common Era dates would be retained up to and including 21 September 1792.

Throughout the report, Romme's grandiose rhetoric, like that of Fabre d'Églantine a month later, purported to endow these decisions with a momentousness of almost cosmic scale. Thus, the passage into a new era was happily echoed in and symbolized by the simultaneous occurrence of the autumnal equinox:

Thus did the sun illuminate at once the two poles and, successively, the entire globe on the same day on which, for the first time, the torch of liberty that will one day illuminate the whole human race shone in all its purity on the French nation. Thus did the sun pass from one hemisphere to the other on the same day on which the people, victorious over the oppression of kings, passed from monarchical to republican government.

The committee proposed replacing the Gregorian months of irregular length with 12 equal months of 30 days. Instead of seven-day weeks, each month would have three ten-day *décades,* which was more compatible with the decimal model. Each day would bear the name of a revolutionary symbol: *niveau* (level), *bonnet* (Phyrigian cap), *cocarde* (cockade), *pique* (pike), *charrue* (plow), and so on. "Everything that recalls the religious era, all the names and applications of the calendar would be abolished." The five-plus days unaccounted for in this 360-day paradigm would be added on at the year's end as festival days belonging to no month, to be called as a group *épagomènes,* but each with its own distinctive name. This new calendar was the arm of militant reform, much more politically charged than the metric system itself. Beyond substituting a new nomenclature, it would actually revolutionize time, most significantly by upsetting the timeless regularity of the seven-day week in which religious traditions were so vested. There would be no more Sundays, no more seventh day of rest, and civil servants would be forbidden to take a day off except on the tenth day (called *repos* [rest]).

Further, the hour units would be revised. Round decimals could not be imposed on a year. It was impossible to manipulate the basic figure of 365π days, fixed by nature itself, but nothing prevented the dividing of the day into ten parts, and each part again into ten, and so on. The old 24-hour day would subsequently give way to one with 100,000 parts (instead of 86,400 seconds), but not until the beginning of Year III, to allow time for the manufacture of the new timepieces this new departure would require. The Convention adopted the new calendar in principle on 5 October, specifying that its application should begin the very next day, which, for the time being, would be referred to, somewhat awkwardly, as the 15th day of the first month in Year II. A decree of 2 January 1793, which had started Year II on 1 January, was rescinded, and the beginning of each new year was permanently set at midnight preceding the true autumnal equinox at the Paris meridian.

When it came to nomenclature, however, it was not so easy for the assembly to reach an agreement. One tendency was toward strong patriotic didacticism, as in the committee's own proposal to label the months with icons of the Revolution itself, such as *République,* *Unité, Fraternité, Liberté, Justice, Égalité, Régénération, Réunion, Jeu de Paume, Bastille, Peuple,* and *Montagne.* On the floor other suggestions were put forward, such as civic virtues and the names of great statesmen and champions of liberty. Others favored a nonpolitical nomenclature (signs of the zodiac, for example) in order to give the calendar a universal appeal and favor its adoption outside of France. The matter was entrusted to a commission of four: Fabre d'Églantine, Marie Joseph Chénier, Jacques-Louis David, and Gilbert Romme.

Fabre d' Églantine brought the commission's proposals to the Convention on the third day of the second month (24 October). The report began once more by denouncing the old system at length: "The priests had assigned to each day in the year the commemoration of a putative saint; catalog of this sort was neither useful nor methodical; it was a repertory of lies, deceit and charlatanism." The commission also broadly eschewed explicitly political terminology in favor of names that would glorify labor and nature, particularly in connection with agriculture. The days of the week acquired simply ordinal names derived from Latin: *primidi, duodi, tridi . . . décadi,* but as days of the year they were also assigned, the better to eradicate the memory of saints' days, 360 individual names corresponding to animals, plants, minerals, or tools, "the real and effective gifts of nature," characteristic of the French countryside. The five extra days at the end of the year, however, would be reserved for a national celebration and would be called *Sanculottides,* thus enshrining the glory of the *sansculottes* (common man), who had made the Revolution what it then was. Every four years, the 366th day would be called *Franciade* in honor of France's gift to the world.

New names had been coined for the months, which would mirror nature itself. These Latinate terms evoke physical features of the seasons, each of which would have its own characteristic suffix: thus, the names of the autumn months would be *Vendémaire* (Harvest), *Brumaire* (Fog), and *Frimaire* (Cold); the winter months would be called *Nivôse* (Snow), *Pluviôse* (Rain), and *Ventôse* (Wind); spring would include *Germinal* (Rebirth), *Floréal* (Flowers), and *Prairial* (Meadows); and, finally, the summer months would be named *Messidor* (Harvest), *Thermidor* (Heat), and *Fructidor* (Fruit).

Numerous other naming schemes were proposed, some bearing on the naming of the annual *sansculottides.* Robespierre, eager to install in France a sort of civil religion, would have liked every *décadi* to celebrate a civic virtue. Only seven, however, were prescribed in the final decision, which was not made until the following year. One of them (the festival of liberty) would be set in honor of Robespierre's own execution (10 Thermidor); the others would be the festivals of youth (10 Germinal), marriage (10 Floréal), recognition (10 Prairial), agriculture (10 Messidor), and the aged (10 Fructidor). There would be four other patriotic celebrations: the foundation of the Republic (1 Vendémaire), Bastille Day (14 July 1789), the fall of the monarchy (10 August 1792), and the execution of Louis XVI (21 January 1793), the old dates still being retained for all dates prior to Year I of the Republic.

This official calendar was adopted with considerable enthusiasm and widely observed for the first couple of years. Some aspects of the new system, however, were never successfully popularized, most notably the ten-hour day. Few decimal watches were even made. Despite sporadic attempts to enforce its use, there was also much reluctance to shed comfortable patterns regulating time, and for many, Sunday stubbornly persisted, for rest if not for Mass. The calendar was retained but quickly faded under the Napoleonic regime, as habits in most places were allowed to revert gradually to the old system, and Gregorian almanacs with saints' days crept back into common use. When the churches reopened, Sunday quite visibly returned. The Revolutionary calendar was finally abolished on 1 January 1806. It had been, as Mona Ozouf says, "an extremely ambitious project of very modest duration" (see Ozouf).

PHILIP STEWART

Further Reading

Baczko, Bronislaw, "Le calendrier républicain," in *Les lieux de mémoire,* edited by Pierre Nora, Paris: Gallimard, 1984

Baczko, Bronislaw, *Utopian Lights: The Evolution of the Idea of Social Progress,* translated by Judith L. Greenberg, New York: Paragon House, 1989 (original French edition, 1978)

Guillaume, Jacques, editor, *Procès-verbaux du Comité d'instruction publique de la Convention nationale,* 6 vols., Paris: Imprimerie Nationale, 1891–1907; new edition, 9 vols., Paris: L'Harmattan, 1997; see especially vol. 2, 1894; reprint, vol. 4, 1997

Kennedy, Emmet, *A Cultural History of the French Revolution,* New Haven, Connecticut: Yale University Press, 1989

Lawrence, John, *The Patriot's Calendar for the Year 1794: Containing the Useful English Almanack, The Decree of the French National Convention for the Alteration of Style, the Interesting Report of Fabre D'Eglantine on That Subject . . . ,* London: Bew, and Ridgway, 1794

Ozouf, Mona, "Calendrier," in *Dictionnaire critique de la Révolution française,* edited by François Furet and Ozouf, Paris: Flammarion, 1988

Canal

In the West, the construction of canals for navigation between two waterways was an innovation of the 17th century, principally in the Netherlands, northern Italy, and France. Because of poorly maintained roads, transportation by river was already important in the Middle Ages for inland trade over long distances. Until 1750 most European shipping operations were carried out on inland waterways, with boats transporting heavy goods such as iron or salt, but also more manageable freight such as wine or grain. Channeling techniques were thus first developed in Europe as a means to improve the navigability of the river system.

During the Renaissance, advances in geometry enabled engineers to design diversions that allowed vessels to bypass dangerous stretches. The new bypass channels retained water by means of the extreme length and flatness of their courses or, failing that, they were fitted, after 1528, with the first locks. In the 16th and 17th centuries Dutch and Paduan engineers used their knowledge of rivers to extend the natural routes of navigation. It was at this point that the Frenchman Adam de Craponne conceived of a "junction canal," an artificial waterway that united two rivers by crossing at a watershed. Around 1550 Craponne designed a diversionary waterway between the Durance and the Rhone. He had hoped to render it navigable, but when the work was finished in 1558 it was in fact incapable of carrying boats. In spite of this disappointment, Craponne handed down a number of major projects for navigable canals. His visionary message was well received by the monarchy, and in 1575 the crown permitted the citizens of Rennes to canalize the Vilaine between their own city and Messac, the outlet for navigation in the direction of the Atlantic. As Henri IV and

Figure 1. Canals and navigable waterways in France in 1815.
Source: *Un canal—des canaux—*, Paris: Picard, 1986; *Atlas de la Révolution française*, fascicle 1, *Routes et communications*, edited by Serge Bonin and Claude Langlois, Paris: Éditions de l'École des Hautes Études en Sciences Sociales, 1987.

the duc de Sully dreamed of public works to bring about religious peace, the Briare Canal took shape between 1604 and 1638, linking the Loire with the basin of the Seine. Finally, during the reign of Louis XIV, the complex work on the Canal du Midi (Canal of the South), also known as the Deux-Mers (Two Seas) Canal, was completed between 1666 and 1670. Linking

Agde with Toulouse by way of the Lauragais region, the Canal du Midi was designed by Pierre-Paul Riquet of Béziers, with the help of Dutch engineers.

In spite of this feat, Vauban judged that French projects did not provide the desired results. In 1699, in his *Mémoire pour la navigation des rivières* (Report on River Navigation), he suggested using Dutch techniques

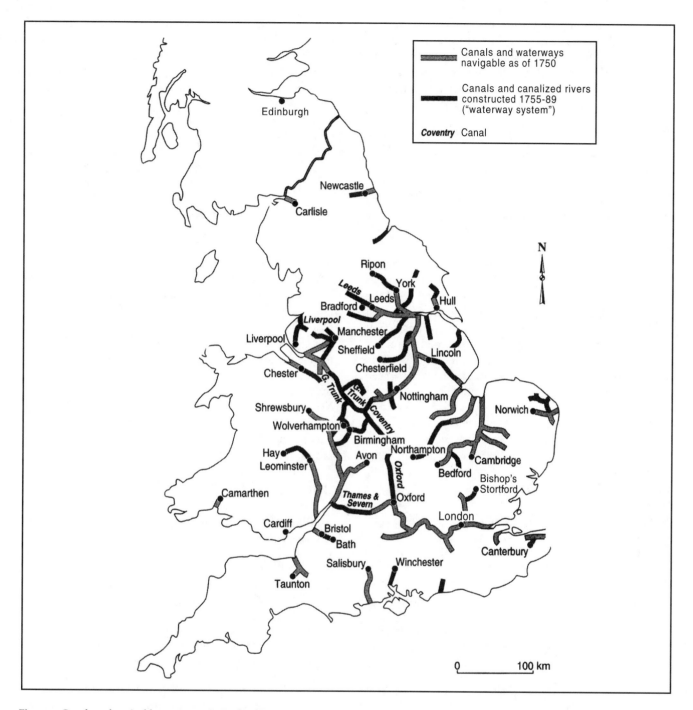

Figure 2. Canals and navigable waterways in England in 1789.
Source: Paul Langford, *A Polite and Commercial People: England, 1727–1783*, Oxford: Clarendon Press, and Oxford and New York: Oxford University Press, 1989; Rex Pope, *Atlas of British Social and Economic History since c. 1700*, London: Routledge, and New York: Macmillan, 1989.

on all the upper reaches of waterways. He also campaigned for lateral canals and numerous junctions between basins. Vauban's program was first put into practice in the north of France, where the fortifications commissioner kept a close eye on defensive construction. Between 1692 and 1753 numerous short canals

were constructed around Calais and Lille. This border zone was thus in line with the Dutch model, with constructions that expanded the river basins but did not adequately link them.

Until the death of Louis XV, canal construction elsewhere in France remained limited. During the ministry of Fleury, from 1723 to 1738, the financier Crozat contributed to the cutting of a junction between the Oise and the Somme, from Fargniers to Saint-Quentin. At Choiseul's initiative, the Neufossé Canal, from Saint-Omer to Lys, was opened in 1771, forming a Y-shaped link between Dunkirk, Douai, and Lille.

Under Louis XVI, a short stretch of the Givors Canal was completed, allowing coal to be transported from Rive-de-Gier to the Rhone. Next, in the 1780s, a sudden burst of activity took place owing to the determination of Calonne, the comptroller general, who increased the head tax for canals. In consequence some grandiose plans were in the works in 1789: the Central Canal from Châlon to Digoin (completed in 1793), the Burgundy Canal from Saint-Jean-de-Losne to Migennes (completed in 1832), and the Nantes-Redon Canal between the Erdre and the lower Vilaine (completed in 1838). The Burgundy Canal was intended to augment capacity to provide supplies to Paris from upstream, while the Nantes-Redon Canal was designed to relieve coastal shipping during maritime wars. The Central Canal was part of an industrial experiment: it served the steelmaking and metalworking complex at Creusot, inaugurated in 1784.

Despite the ambitious proposals of the closing years of the ancien régime, by 1789 there were still only roughly 600 miles of canals in France, in disconnected courses. In 1822, when Becquey's plan projected the building of 6,000 miles of canals, the French total was no more than 720 miles. The first Empire was able to build 113 miles, notably in 1810, when the Saint-Quentin Canal connected Paris to the coal mines of Valenciennes and the port of Anvers. Nevertheless, at the time of the fall of Napoleon the inland water traffic of France was still dependent on the rivers, which provided 4,300 miles of waterways that were navigable in all seasons.

With its overblown expectations, France established itself as the pioneer of junction canals until 1750. During the 18th century imperial Russia merely sought to improve navigation on the Volga. From 1799 to 1810, however, it constructed a link from the Volga to the Baltic known as the Mariinskaia Soudokhodnia Sistema (the South Sea System). Aside from the diversionary waterways around Berlin, Germany began constructing artificial junctions only after 1815, with the Main-Danube Canal. In 1811 the town councilors of the Rhineland even complained that their shipping trade was being reduced by the convoys of carts that directly linked Bremen and Hamburg with the rest of the country. Belgium, meanwhile, was initiated into the art of canal building during the Napoleonic regime, when a route between Mons and Condé on the Scheldt was opened.

During the second half of the 18th century, as economists lauded the usefulness of canals, England's canal-building energies surpassed those of France. In 1750 English boats still used only 990 miles of rivers to travel back and forth between the hinterland and the coastal shipping ports, but from 1750 to 1790 England added 2,217 miles of waterways organized in a network. This transformation, a part of the Industrial Revolution, continued until 1830, eventually linking the waterways with all the major centers of mining and manufacturing. The network chiefly handled heavy goods such as salt, kaolin (china clay), coal, and iron. The waterborne transportation of coal contributed to the emergence of steam engines in industry.

Mine owners were highly influential in the opening of shortcuts on the waterways. With the support of specially created corporations, they enlarged their markets by linking their pits with major cities such as Birmingham, Liverpool, Manchester, and Sheffield. In 1755 the first such corporation was authorized by Parliament to transform the small Sankey River into a canal in order to furnish Liverpool with coal. However, the real impetus to development came between 1759 and 1761, when the duke of Bridgewater had a canal cut between Manchester and his coal mine at Worsley. The work was costly, since it included a tunnel and a bridge; it was financed by various shareholders, including speculators, landowners, and middle-ranking entrepreneurs. The duke was so successful that beginning in 1763 he embarked on a further stage of construction to create a "Grand Trunk Canal" from the Mersey to the Trent. Because this extension crossed a region of mines and earthenware channels, the managers of all these concerns promptly subscribed for the 580 shares in the new project. Bridgewater's initiative sparked an upsurge in canal building. Despite a slowdown during the American War of Independence, 3 million pounds sterling was devoted to canals from 1760 to 1790. Because the profits from navigation tolls were good, canal stocks were very healthy between 1790 and 1802: with the investment of 10 million pounds sterling, the network was extended to 2,683 miles. As a result, the Wolverhampton Canal was connected to the Grand Trunk, linking Bristol, Liverpool, and Hull. After a hiatus during the Napoleonic Wars, work started again from 1815 to 1845. By then England had 3,470 miles of canals compared with France's 2,325.

Despite its density, the English network lacked cohesion owing to inexperience: England had no history of state oversight and coordination of canal-building. In France, 17th-century canals had been relatively standardized by official architects; those of the 18th century carried the academic stamp of the engineers of the Ponts et Chaussées (Bridges and Roads). In contrast, the English dug canals feverishly, without a coordinated plan. These canals were awkward, for they differed in size and were vulnerable to bad weather. As a direct consequence, English industrialists turned to railroads after 1830.

JEAN-MARCEL GOGER

See also Fortification; Transport Systems

Further Reading

Burton, Anthony, *The Canal Builders,* London: Eyre Methuen, and Newton Abbot, Devon, and North Pomfret, Vermont: David and Charles, 1972; 3rd edition, Cleobury Mortimer: Baldwin, 1993

Un canal—des canaux—, Paris: Picard, 1986

Geiger, Reed G., *Planning the French Canals: Bureaucracy, Politics, and Enterprise under the Restoration,* Newark: University of Delaware Press, and London and Cranbury, New Jersey: Associated University Presses, 1994

Hadfield, Charles, *British Canals: An Illustrated History,* London: Phoenix House, 1950; 7th edition, Newton Abbot, Devon, and North Pomfret, Vermont: David and Charles, 1984

Langford, Paul, *A Polite and Commercial People: England, 1727–1783,* London: Guild, and Oxford: Oxford University Press, 1989

Maistre, André, *Le canal des deux mers, Canal royal du Languedoc, 1666–1810,* Toulouse: Privat, 1968

Pinsseau, Hubert, *Histoire de la construction de l'administration et de l'exploitation du Canal d'Orléans de 1676 à 1954,* Paris: Clavreuil, 1963

Pope, Rex, editor, *Atlas of British Social and Economic History since c. 1700,* London: Routledge, and New York: Macmillan, 1989

Rolt, L.T.C., *The Inland Waterways of England,* London: Allen and Unwin, 1950; 2nd edition, 1979

Ward, J.R., *The Finance of Canal Building in Eighteenth-Century England,* London: Oxford University Press, 1974

Capitalism

In *Les jeux de l'échange* [The Wheels of Commerce]), Volume 2 of his monumental study *Civilisation matérielle, économie et capitalisme* (1979; Civilization and Capitalism, 15th–18th Century), Fernand Braudel follows in the steps of Edwin Deschepper's thesis *L'histoire du mot capital et dérivés* (1964; The History of the Word "Capital" and Its Derivatives), and shows that: (1) Although the term "capital" first appeared in the 12th century, meaning funds or a stock of goods and/or money, it was used far less frequently in the 18th century than "funds," "capital funds," "wealth," "advances," or similar terms, whether in French or in other languages. (2) "Capitalist" and its equivalents ("moneyed man" in English, for example) had a more restricted meaning than is the case today, and were almost always somewhat derogatory when used to refer to those who held or handled capital or money. (3) The word "capitalism" was unknown in the 18th century (and, strictly speaking, even at the time Karl Marx was writing). The word only gained currency in the 1840s, when it was used by French socialists in the sense of an exclusive appropriation of capital or in the sense of an economic and social regime dominated by that appropriation. The post-Marxist vulgarization of Marxism lent the term acceptance, justifying its appearance in

dictionaries as a word referring to an economic and social regime, or a structure whose motivating force is the indefinite expansion of the accumulation of capital in the hands of the private owners of that same capital.

Of course, the absence of the word does not mean the absence of the thing itself. François Quesnay's *Le tableau économique* (1758; The Tableau of the Economy) and Adam Smith's *An Inquiry into the Nature and Causes of the Wealth of Nations* (1776) provide theoretical models of economic, social, and even political structures that are thoroughly and indisputably capitalist. These writers, who thought of themselves as scientists, saw in the reality of their times the materials and, at least in outline form, the structures that enabled them to conceive these models. Quesnay focused on the domain of agricultural production, while Smith concentrated on industrial production. Marx himself derived his ideas from both Quesnay and Smith. He saw the intersection of the capitalist "agricultural" and "industrial" revolutions taking place in Britain during the second half of the 18th century, as the passage from the adolescence to the full maturity of capitalism, a system that had begun to emerge in the 16th century and would thoroughly characterize the 19th century. One need not be a Marxist to share this vision of history:

until recently, and even to some extent today, this account has essentially been the received wisdom in academic circles. Thus, the movement that, on an economic and social level, affected Europe during the Enlightenment would, in the final analysis, only become comprehensible through subsequent historical events.

Braudel's approach, which is that of a historian of "modern times" (defined as the 16th–18th centuries), does not propose a radical alternative to the received wisdom, but his work does constitute a significant departure that facilitates understanding of the empirically observed economic reality of the 18th century. For Braudel, a market characterized by the unceasing transmutation of goods or services into their monetary values, and vice versa—that is to say a market economy—has existed from time immemorial, extending back in time well beyond the modern period (there was capitalism in antiquity). The market economy was initially tenuous and then became progressively more dominant: capitalism, which characterizes economic activities whose ultimate goal is the infinite maximization of capital goods invested (in monetary form) in factors of production that, in combination, constitutes a system able to produce a greater value than that which was initially invested. From its origins, and still into the 18th century, capitalism was especially "at home in the sphere of circulation," although it did not exclusively characterize that sphere: "it had little interest in traditional exchanges, in the short-range market economy." Rather, as Braudel writes in *Les jeux de l'échange*, capitalism occupied a "high rank" in mercantile society, constituting

> a world apart, different from and indeed foreign to the social and economic context surrounding it. And it is in relation to this context that it is defined as "capitalism," not merely in relation to new capitalist forms which were to emerge later in time. In fact capitalism was what it was in relation to a noncapitalism of immense proportions (*The Wheels of Commerce*, translated by Siân Reynolds [1979]).

This model, Braudel argues, applies particularly to the realms of agricultural and industrial production.

One can generally share this point of view, while nevertheless discerning that Braudel's long-term approach fails really to specify the place that the 18th century occupies within the long-term history of capitalism. Was there, during that century, an evolution in the relationship between capitalism and noncapitalism?

If, for the sake of creating a useful analogy, one attempts to represent mercantile capitalism as it was born or reborn in 12th-century Italy, as a capitalism based on "harvesting"—trafficking goods, whether European or non-European, produced in a framework of economic and social structures that capitalism did not create—one might then, using the same analogy, characterize 18th-century European capitalism as a movement based on clearing the land. From the 16th century onward, European mercantile capitalism—in the form of a state-sponsored organization of trade with the Spanish American empire or chartered companies and myriad small and adventurous private enterprises—expanded its "harvesting" territory to the four corners of the globe. From the second half of the 17th century, mercantile capitalism was directly or indirectly responsible for the implantation of methods of production that to today's historian seem typical of the 18th century. Outside of Europe, these methods involved the great landed estates and plantations worked by slave or quasi-slave labor. Within Europe, this mode of production was protoindustrialization, which came from capital provided by urban merchants, traders, and dealers and the labor of rural members of the population dominated by urban merchants. However, a growing European population, with its increasing demand for food supply, encouraged those farmers who could do so to turn resolutely toward a market economy—a phenomenon that, with its intensity and the range of its geographic field of action cuts right through Braudel's model of capitalism. In each of these cases, capitalism spread beyond its native soil so to speak, beyond towns, and more specifically, ports, and began to revolutionize the economies of rural societies.

Thus, rural economies were reorganized, not marginalized: the time had not yet come in which capitalism would connote enormous factories and immense proletarian suburbs in the collective imagination. In addition to the domination of city over countryside, owing to the draining of land revenue and a (small) surplus of agricultural production, capitalist reasoning began to be imposed on an ever-increasing portion of the countryside's production. As Pierre Deyon expresses it:

> Almost all of the industrial capitals of the 16th and 17th centuries . . . saw a movement of their trades and workshops out into the countryside. This happened in Leiden and Delft, to the benefit of the Veluwe and the Drenth valleys; in Venice, to the benefit of its hinterland; in Lille, to the benefit of Roubaix; in Krakow, to the benefit of Andrichow; and in Amiens, Valenciennes, Zurich, and Gand, also to the benefit of the neighboring countryside. This evolution was brutal for the weavers and artisans of these cities, but it generally protected the interests of commerce and the ascendancy of the cities. Its tradesmen maintained control over production in the countryside and a monopoly over the distribution of finished goods.

In this way, vast protoindustrial centers expanded, from Ireland to the London region through Lancashire and the West Riding; from the west of France to Picardy and Flanders; from Westphalia to Saxony, Bohemia, and Silesia; from the Languedoc to Catalonia. A new organization of territory was slowly emerging into a network of greater trade and exchange, and Franklin Mendels has shown that agricultural production could, in turn, be affected by these transformations and be incorporated into a movement of specialization and modernization.

However, there was also evidence of capitalist behavior among producers themselves, as they bypassed established trade networks, raised capital and turned to the market for their own sake, and thus became entrepreneurs. Several types of capitalists can be identified.

Although manufacturers had multiple sources of assistance (both financial and legal) through public power, the essentially capitalist nature of 18th-century manufacturing is undeniable. For example, in 1786 the Conseil du Roi (Royal Council) renewed the *privilège* (permit) granted to the royal glass factory of Saint-Gobain. The renewal of the permit guaranteed (theoretically) protection from competition, made the glass works exempt from indirect taxation, and also exempted its labor force from the royal *corvée* (forced labor) and the militia. Nevertheless, the factory was unquestionably capitalistic with its unceasing capacity for technological innovation, its attention to the needs of the market (which in turn led it toward mass production), its rational personnel management, and its concern—under pressure from shareholders—for profitability. Also capitalist, without a doubt, was the medium-sized calico factory established in Zwickau in 1787, by privilege of the elector of Saxony (actually a very modest privilege, since there was a competitor in the very same city and there was always the risk that others would settle beyond the two-league limits of the protected zone). The cotton industries of Normandy and Orleans belonging to the British industrialist John Holker were also indisputably capitalist; Holker managed to obtain land from the French government as well as a position for himself as inspector general of manufactures, and he brought about the first integration of textile machine production and cotton fabrics.

In the 18th century there were numerous examples of small, medium-sized, and large businesses in which the "boss" had absolute freedom: not only in Britain but also in Gand, in Mulhouse (cottons and calicos), in Geneva and the Swiss Jura country (watchmaking), in the flatlands around Barcelona (cotton), in Piedmont and Lombardy (silk, cotton, wool, and spin-off manufacturing such as the hat industry), and Sedan (wool).

In France the "boss" was an important figure in the silk mills, paper factories, foundries, metallurgical industries, and, of course, calico factories, all prototypes of the adolescent-stage "factories." These "bosses" came from far more diverse social backgrounds than was long believed. We should not neglect that singular figure from the other end of Europe in this catalog: the great Russian landowner, overlord of vast estates and thousands of "souls," who might later become a foundry owner because his land was rich in minerals and timber. His workers, and even the overseers of his enterprises, often remained serfs. What these landowners had in common was that, like merchants and traders, they had sought and found the necessary capital on their own initiative, from their savings, from their family circles and relations, or by borrowing. They also sought and found technicians and managers, and they participated closely in the lives of their factories; they studied the market by means that would not be unfamiliar to the 20th century, and they even advertised. For example, the Montgolfier brothers, papermakers in Annonay advertised using the balloon of their design, the *montgolfière* (a stroke of genius). Other manufacturers, such as Oberkampf, publicized their wares by mailing catalogs and samples. Once they had a commercial service, this type of factory had a tendency to subordinate the merchant, who became a mere intermediary, whether wholesaler or distributor, between the producer and the consumer.

Thanks to their large production capacity, major agricultural proprietors and farmers (the French *laboureurs*), whether growers or livestock producers, were now able to speak on equal terms with grain merchants or livestock dealers, or even to have the merchants and dealers beholden to them. Such entrepreneurs could even bypass the traders and deal directly with the major purchasers: hospitals, garrisons, the royal court, the great houses of noblemen, and shipowners. The Physiocrats conceived of an ideal type, resembling the agronomist-landlords of Norfolk (the most famous of whom was Charles, Second Viscount Townshend of Raynham, known as "Turnip" Townshend) or the farmers of the French plain, recently studied by Jean-Marc Moriceau. Although eastern Europe was dominated by agriculture, its great estates, given over to the export of wheat to the West, were no less capitalist.

The penetration of capitalism in 18th-century Europe can also be understood from another point of view, that of the consumption of merchandise following the channels opened up by trade. With the exception of the grain traders of ancient Rome, who supplied markets with products from distant lands, and the traders who met consumers' demand for salt, the capitalist traders of antiquity, the medieval period, and even the first two centuries of "modern times" had only a limited market for consumption: a small minority whose purchasing power was derived from land revenues (proprietary, seigniorial, or fiscal). To cite a European example, the Dutch East India Company, a model capitalist company born of the "great discoveries," depended upon the spice trade for its prosperity, and spices were consumed only by the urban upper and middle classes. In Africa and Asia, European exports of luxury and quasi-luxury products, or even wrought iron and weapons, depended upon a market that was even more tenuous. Then, beginning in the middle of the 16th century, populations newly settled in Latin America began to call for a more diverse range of agricultural and industrial products. Beyond this development, which continued to grow throughout the 18th century and was of prime interest to France and Britain—through the intermediary of their "import-export" houses, founded by their agents in Cadiz and Lisbon—the rapid population growth in the Indies and in the 13 colonies of North America provided new outlets for the expansion of the European economy. It is a well-known fact that the textiles spun and woven in the French villages of the Maine or the Dauphiné (hemp, cotton, wool, linen-cotton mixtures) often ended up as clothing worn by slaves in the New World.

There was also a strong tendency, both in the cities and, to a considerable degree, among the upper echelons of rural societies of northwestern Europe, to increasingly consume products that were the mainstays of imperial trading later refined by a manufacturing process: coffee, sugar, soap, cotton textiles, and, in particular, painted or calico cloth. Monographs based on estate inventories speak volumes in this regard: they have revealed to researchers the secrets of chests and cupboards, as have the more impressionistic but complementary testimonials found in literature. One thus learns that the feminine demand for calico was socially widespread—to such a degree that, in 1701, a decree by France's King Louis XIV prohibited its use for clothing children and servants. In 1727 the inspector of factories for the region of Champagne wrote, in a letter to the comptroller general, that

> it is astonishing . . . to see the amount of printed cloth that is worn in this town [Provins] as well as in the town of Sens. In both of these towns, all the women wear this cloth, from judges' wives to servants and even children (as quoted by Serge Chassagne, *Le coton et ses patrons* [1991; Cotton and Cotton Manufacturers]).

The scarcity of sugar and soap in Paris and London in 1792 and 1794, due to the slave revolt in Santo Domingo and the naval war waged by France, Spain, and Britain in the West Indies, provoked riots reminiscent of those that had once resulted from grain shortages. Strictly speaking, there was nothing in the 18th century, not even the most basic consumer products such as bread, that did not owe something to international trade. In any given year there might be a shortage of local grain, and the poor people of Paris would unwittingly consume bread made from the flour of wheat ripened in Poland.

The historian's use of the word "capitalism" has been overdetermined by the Marxist mythology of the stages of history (Braudel himself concludes his magnum opus with a comprehensive dialogue with this mythology) to such an extent that even today, one cannot overlook the problems posed by the obstacles (objective) and resistances (subjective) to the penetration of capitalist reasoning and structures in European society as any whole at a given moment in history, including the 18th century.

It would be wrong to reduce capitalism to economic liberalism (both theoretical and practical), since market capitalism coexisted quite happily with mercantilism. To succumb to this error would lead one to view see adversaries of the free grain trade (including Jacques Necker and Denis Diderot!) as anticapitalists. In fact, there was hardly a trace of conscious or organized anticapitalism during this time, other than the kind expressed by guilds and commercial leagues and their sometime political defenders (including the *parlements* in France). The primacy of the profit motive was explicitly subordinated to concern for the quality of the goods' use-value. The accumulation of capital was not an economic aim in itself but rather a means to attain notability, and the preservation of their existing markets was enough to keep the manufacturers happy. Capitalism had already bypassed and isolated the corporatist archipelago by the 17th century in Britain and the United Provinces of the Netherlands, and in France by the 18th century. This was yet another reason why capitalism migrated beyond city walls.

On the other hand, contrary to the received wisdom of 19th-century historians, who tended to be hagiographers of the Third Estate, the seigniorial structure and the existence of the aristocracy were not in themselves incompatible with capitalism. When the Physiocrats tried to rally landowners likely to create advances in production, they were thinking first and foremost of the lords and their domanial reserves. Some lords responded. Others, and sometimes even these same lords, with their rights, their *banalités* (feudal monopolies), their seigniorial justice, and other privileges, became industrial leaders of considerable importance, above all in those instances where industry was still linked to the land (as in the production of iron and steel). In the 18th century one could simultaneously be a lord, concerned with obtaining one's due and continuing to demand that chores be done, while also calculating, like any managing director today, whether it was more productive to have the tasks done manually by a greater number of workers or by machine with a lesser number; or still yet, whether one should hire or fire officers of the domain, depending on the economic situation. This combination was in evidence, for example, in the ledgers of a president of the Parlement of Dijon. It is apparent that huge estates with a servile labor force could easily transform themselves into agricultural enterprises geared toward a world market, or into other powerful new industries.

However, it is also true that the great majority of noblemen in continental Europe did not want to become capitalist entrepreneurs, or did not know how to, even though they had the opportunity to do so. This observation does not imply that these nobles did not contribute, unwittingly or otherwise, to the early accumulation of capital through their investments. It is at this particular level, where opportunities for investment were competitive, that the problem of the obstacles in the development of 18th-century capitalism can be found. The economic profit, and even more importantly, the symbolic profit expected from various types of income, from the purchase of public offices or lands from which one did not initially expect any profit, obviously diverted a considerable proportion of private savings away from capitalist enterprise. More remarkably still, it is well known that in continental Europe, with the exception of the northwest, the original capitalists—shipowners, industrialists, bankers—quickly became "feudal" (alternatively, one could say that they had become landed or independently wealthy gentry) by the second or third generation, reproducing the model followed by the Medici family. The determining factors in such cases were thus sociocultural ones rather than socioeconomic ones.

FRANÇOIS HINCKER

See also Credit and Banking; Industrialization; Nobility, Commercial

Further Reading

Braudel, Fernand, *Afterthoughts on Material Civilization and Capitalism,* translated by Patricia M. Ranum, Baltimore, Maryland: Johns Hopkins University Press, 1977
Braudel, Fernand, *Civilization and Capitalism, 15th–18th Century,* 3 vols., translated by Siân Reynolds, London: Fontana, and New York: Harper and Row, 1979–84 (original French edition, 1967–79); see especially vol. 2, *The Wheels of Commerce,* 1979

Caricature

In 1751 the *Encyclopédie* defined "caricature" in these terms:

This word is the Gallicized version of the Italian *caricatura* and is what one otherwise refers to as a *charge* (exaggerated portrait). It applies principally to characters rendered grotesque or extremely disproportionate either in whole or in part, by a painter, sculptor, or engraver, in order to entertain and amuse. Calot excelled in the genre. But the burlesque in painting is the same as it is in poetry: it is a sort of debauchery of the imagination, and one should not indulge in it except as a form of diversion.

This short entry, by showing the origins of the genre, questioning its forms and its aims, and then situating it in the artistic hierarchy, raises a number of essential issues regarding the place of caricature in the 18th century.

In French and English, as in German, the word *caricatura* and its equivalents had long carried an Italian connotation that disappeared as the genre became accepted and widespread throughout Europe, particularly in the last third of the 18th century. In England as early as 1715, Jonathan Richardson the Elder noted that painters took delight in the caricature of faces (*Essay on the Theory of Painting*). However, the concept (sometimes spelled "caracatura") did not really take root until the 1740s, obliging artists such as William Hogarth to distance themselves from a term that was considered pejorative and a practice that was scorned. Following the example offered by Gotthold Ephraim Lessing, who railed against the genre in the name of ideal Beauty (*Laokoon* [1766; Laocoön; An Essay upon the Limits of Painting and Poetry]), Johann Lavater, a physiognomist from Zurich, rejected caricature because it made reality uglier, and reality was the work of God. However, he nevertheless acknowledged the didactic usefulness of these distorted creations, as he compared them, in his *Physiognomische Fragmente* (1775; *Essays on Physiognomy*), to a glass that was both magnifying and revealing.

The success of the genre in the age of the Enlightenment is also evident in the first texts specifically devoted to caricature. In 1762 Matthew and Mary Darly, who were artists, engravers, and publishers in London, brought out a collection of caricatures together with a text explaining the principles of the genre: *A Book of Caricaturas . . . with the Principles of Designing, in That Droll and Pleasing Manner.* In 1789 Francis Grose published *Rules for Drawing Caricaturas: With an Essay on Comic Painting* (translated into French in 1802). In 1792, in the *Journal du people,* J.-M. Boyer-Brun published a short "Histoire des caricatures de la révolte des Français" (History of the Caricatures of the Revolt of the French). Collections, critical texts, and manuals multiplied throughout the 1760s in England, offering proof that the satiric print had become an autonomous, codified genre, dependent upon its own standard procedures. These publications also pointed to the existence of an increasingly specialized market (as exemplified by the Darlys' flourishing trade from 1750 on). Indeed, the second half of the 18th century saw the true genesis of modern caricature, linked to the emergence of a public opinion increasingly shaped by illustrated print media that had wide circulation and chronicled newsworthy events.

Because etching was a relatively rapid process, it became the privileged medium for the satiric print. Woodcuts were occasionally used to circulate imitations of successful caricatures in the provinces. Print runs could vary from a few hundred to thousands of copies. William Hogarth, for example, had to work the copper plate on which he had etched the caricatured portrait of Lord Lovat (1746) several times in order to achieve a print run of 10,000, which was utterly exceptional in numerical terms. Comical prints existed in all sizes, from the playing-card format (launched by the amateur artist George, Fourth Viscount Townshend of Raynham, in 1756) to Hogarth's major series. Such works, although quite modest in price (six pence, as a rule, then double or triple that amount depending on the size and whether they were hand-tinted using watercolors), were nevertheless not affordable to the common people, who had access to the satiric coverage of events through storefront displays. As a writer for the *Constitutional Journal* protested in 1745, "On every street corner, along every avenue . . . in windows and on displays, one sees for sale pamphlets with very pretentious titles and the most impure images, the sight of which would cause Messalina to blush." Caricatures could indeed be found in coffeehouses, where they were the source of much discussion. They were available not only through merchants' window displays but also in the form of albums or portfolios, which one could rent. From the 1780s on, William Holland and S.W. Fores held permanent, paying exhibitions in their establishments, which were described as "a complete history of caricature: political and domestic, past and present." Preserved in albums, framed on walls, or simply used as wall covering, caricatures had thus become one of the new elements of contemporary social life.

English Synthesis of Dutch and Italian Elements

The rise of caricature reached its peak at the time of the French Revolution, and England, at a crossroads between the Dutch and Italian traditions, played a pioneering role. Beginning in 1695, the year in which Parliament refused to renew the Licensing Act of 1664, England enjoyed an exceptionally liberal regime, which set it apart from most other European countries. There was no advance censorship. Seizures and trials were rather rare compared to the volume of production, which varied in direct proportion to the political situation in the country and abroad, since caricature was a form of pamphleteering and journalistic activity. Before the 1720s, however, the satiric print in England was primarily a Dutch import (R. van Hooghe), until the influx of foreign artists and engravers (Boitard, Vandergucht, Gravelot, and others) and the growing interest of English artists (such as George Bickham the Younger), working together with publishers, made it a truly national specialty, according to the abbé Le Blanc in his *Lettres . . . concernant le gouvernement, la politique et des moeurs des Anglais et des Français* (1745; *Letters . . . on the Government, Politics, and Some Morals of the English and the French*).

Borrowing from the Dutch, the English satiric print adopted the practice of the broadside: a large plate was carefully etched and engraved by burin, filled with characters and action that were explained by a detailed text generally printed below the scene depicted. Most often, these complex images were intended for a sophisticated audience, for these loose sheets derived from the emblematic tradition and made abundant use of the repertory of allegory and fable. From the Italians, English caricature borrowed the technique of physiognomic deformation and simplification, a technique developed during the Renaissance by such artists as the Carracci brothers and Leonardo da Vinci (several grotesque portraits by the latter had been engraved by Wenceslaus Hollar in the middle of the 17th century). In the 18th century, English visitors to Italy became familiar with the genre, particularly in Venice, where they could see the works of Tiepolo, Marco Ricci, A.M. Zanetti, and others. Between 1736 and 1747, Arthur Pond, an English engraver and merchant, produced a facsimile series of drawings entitled *A Set of Caricaturas,* which consisted mainly of reproductions of works by Italian artists (two sketches inspired by the French artists La Fage and Antoine Watteau were the exceptions). The collection included primarily caricatures by Pier Leone Ghezzi (1674–1755), the leading specialist in the genre. Ghezzi frequented the royal houses of Europe, making scores of caricatural physiognomies that were much sought after. In 1750 his sketches were also published by M. Oesterreich in Germany, where they were carefully preserved; they fetched very high prices upon the death of the artist.

From the middle of the century onward, European caricature took two divergent formal directions. One approach—of Dutch and, later, Hogarthian inspiration—favored carefully executed programmatic works that avoided excessive deformation and were designed to be read as satires. The other, Italian in its inspiration, reversed the predominance of text over image and put forward sketches that were deliberately inaccurate, whether graphically or anatomically. This tendency was represented by amateur caricature, which became fashionable first among the British, then the European aristocracy. The countess of Burlington took to the practice, as did Henry William Bunbury, George Moutard Woodward, and George, Viscount Townshend, a career military officer and future viceroy of Ireland, who played an important role in the history of the genre by introducing the portrait into English political caricature. These amateurs did not themselves do the etchings; that technical task was left to the likes of James Gillray, Isaac Cruikshank, and many others. A number of dilettantes were regular patrons of the Darlys' establishment, and the Darlys, in their preface to a collection of caricatures, invited "ladies and gentlemen" to send their drawings to be executed in copper "for their own amusement, or for publication."

Consequently, Hogarth did everything he could to distance himself from a genre associated with amateurism and bad taste. In 1743 he published a plate entitled *Three Characters—Four Caricaturas,* which contrasts three portraits inspired by Raphael with four faces (five, if one counts a graffito) inspired by Ghezzi, Annibale Carracci, and da Vinci. His aim was to define a genre that would be situated midway between historical painting and caricature, dubbed "comic history painting." Following Hogarth's example, George Bickham the Younger (1706?–71), artist, engraver, and publisher, condemned all shocking representations, in his *Essay on Drawing* (1747), while he himself created the most exaggerated caricatures. The case of James Gillray (1756–1815), a member of the Royal Academy, who divided his time between the practice of virulent caricature and that of reproduction engraving and meticulous portrait painting, sheds light on the dilemma of the car-

icaturist, who, like the illustrator, tried to exchange the illegitimate side of his trade for the respectability of an artistic profession.

Themes, Traditions, and Political Uses

From an iconographic point of view, satiric prints can be divided into several categories that often overlap. During the 17th century, moralizing caricatures had attacked the particular follies of the era: fashion and extravagant social behavior. One thinks, for example, of the English "macaroni," conceited young men who had just come back from the obligatory grand tour of the Continent and who were the subject of much ridicule in the 1770s, or of the satire of mesmerism in France. Caricature could also make use of more diverse iconographic traditions, from popular imagery to the learned language of the emblematic tradition; such elements could be quoted or parodied, addressing an audience with varying degrees of education and reliant upon the glosses and descriptive captions that accompanied the prints. The iconography of a world turned upside down, of madness or death (see the work of Gillray or Daniel Chodowiecki), could be combined with the artifice of animal fables, as was the case in *Aesopus in Europa* (1701–02; Aesop in Europe), a periodic series of Dutch pamphlets, illustrated by R. van Hooghe, about the crisis over the Spanish succession. Until 1750 political caricatures portrayed national identities (expressed by visual stereotypes derived from emblems) or reintroduced confessional antagonisms, within the tradition that began in the Reformation period. In France caricatures played a role in the quarrels that opposed the power of the king to that of the Parlement. At times, caricatures could be used to launch a general attack on the corruption surrounding the rulers of the world; at others, they could target personalities, such as John Law and his disastrous economic "system." New social characters, such as the connoisseur, the art critic, and the *philosophe* (Voltaire, above all), were mocked, for more and more frequently the satiric prints portrayed individuals (see the famous caricatured portrait of the liberal journalist and politician John Wilkes made during his trial in 1762). Indeed, during the last third of the century, beginning in Britain, caricatures served the interests of specific political causes and individual ambitions. The controversy that arose over Hogarth, because of his theoretical works and his institutional positions, led to a personal struggle fought in the arena of public opinion, with caricatures as weapons. Later, Prime Minister William Pitt, exposed to the attacks of the pamphleteers, would reply by enlisting artists of his own, distributing pensions and official posts to J. Sayer and even to Gillray.

The French Revolution gave rise to an unequaled quantity of caricatures, despite the burden of censorship that was omnipresent on the Continent and was only briefly lifted in France. Awareness of the political effectiveness of satiric prints certainly did not begin in 1789, but never before had the discourse on the public impact of images taken such a reasoned and institutionalized form. The message of the Committee of Public Safety of 12 September 1793 was clear. Its aims were political and didactic, as the people had to be educated by giving them new symbols of identity. The deputy Jacques-Louis David was summoned to use his artistic talents in order to "multiply the engravings and caricatures which might awaken the public spirit and bring an awareness of the perfidy of the enemies of liberty and of the Republic"—an obvious allusion to the penciled assaults of British snipers. Whether revolutionary or counterrevolutionary, caricatures revived nationalist themes: the opposition between an emaciated sansculotte and a John Bull resplendent with well-being enjoyed great success in England, while the European menagerie was newly stocked with the French cock, the British bulldog or lion, and the Russian bear or imperial eagle. Caricatures made ample use of theories of physiognomy, deforming faces and bestializing external features. As they kept abreast of social and political struggle, they displayed an unequaled violence, illustrating severed heads, impaled bodies, and crushed monsters, striking the crudest of sexual and excremental chords.

By the end of the century the English model was predominant, above all with Hogarth's work, which was reviewed in French in 1746 and in German by Georg Christoph Lichtenberg in 1794, and was partially reproduced in Lavater's work in the 1770s. Daniel Chodowiecki, regarded as the Hogarth of Berlin, nevertheless sought to achieve a certain distance from his English precursor. He worked in a smaller format for illustrated books and especially almanacs. His satires, principally moral and social, used subtle irony and addressed a cultivated public. In the German-speaking regions, Augsburg (with J. Göz), Nuremberg, Basel, and Leipzig were centers of a satiric production that was rather favorable to liberal ideas, whereas several counterrevolutionary almanacs were published in Giessen, Koblenz, Cassel, and Göttingen. Chodowiecki had a counterpart in Switzerland, B.A. Dunker, the illustrator of the sarcastic *Tableau de Paris* (1787; Panorama of Paris) by Louis Sébastien Mercier and author of the *Moralisch-Politischer Kurier*, which was hostile to the Revolution. By 1800, however, the models had changed. Now Rowlandson, Gillray, and Cruikshank were frequently emulated on the Continent. In short, the English example, a synthesis of Italian caricature and the Dutch satiric print, gave the genre its methods, its aesthetic, and its iconography, all in the space of a few decades. The English model garnered a public following on which specialists, artists, and publishers could now rely. In other words, it established the basis of modern caricature.

PHILIPPE KAENEL

See also Art Criticism; Engraving; Grotesque; Physiognomy; Satire

Further Reading

Döring, Jürgen, *Eine Kunstgeschichte der frühen englischen Karikatur,* Hildesheim, Germany: Gerstenberg, 1991

George, Mary Dorothy, *English Political Caricature: A Study of Opinion and Propaganda,* 2 vols., Oxford: Clarendon Press, 1959

Grand-Carteret, John, *Les mœurs et la caricature: En Allemagne, en Autriche, en Suisse,* 2nd edition, Paris: Westhausser, 1885

Kunzle, David, *The Early Comic Strip: Narrative Strips and Picture Stories in the European Broadsheet from c.1450 to 1825,* Berkeley: University of California Press, 1973

Langemeyer, Gerhard, editor, *Bild als Waffe: Mittel und Motive der Karikatur in fünf Jahrhunderten,* Munich: Prestel, 1984

Paulson, Ronald, *Hogarth: His Life, Art, and Times,* New Haven, Connecticut: Yale University Press, 1971; abridged edition, 1974

Castrati

Although the practice of castration, whether for medical, judicial, social, religious, or even erotic reasons, goes back to the earliest antiquity, the mutilation of young boys in order to prevent their voices from breaking seems to have first occurred in the Eastern Roman Empire, and then in medieval Spain, where such castrati sang in Catholic ceremonies. The practice of using castrati ensured that in choral music, the highest musical parts could be sung without resorting to women, who were traditionally banned from singing in churches (because of Saint Paul's injunction that women should be silent in church).

Once authorized by a Papal Bull issued by Sixtus V in 1589, the use of castrati in church choirs spread from Rome to other areas throughout Italy, and the practice was eventually justified by theologians. It later expanded beyond the sacred sphere and entered secular musical arenas, where the rising popularity of castrati mirrored the development of opera and the vogue of baroque music throughout Europe. The boys, who often came from the poorest regions of southern Italy, were chosen for the quality of their voices. Before they reached puberty, their testicular ducts were ligated. The castrati then underwent a long and strict apprenticeship in the Neapolitan conservatories or the singing schools that were opened later in Bologna. They were trained in the techniques of vocal virtuosity, and after about ten years of study they embarked on stage careers—which were often brilliant—as sopranos or contraltos in Italy or elsewhere in Europe.

Once they had achieved fame on the Italian peninsula, many castrati were invited abroad, where they aroused the same enthusiasm as in their homeland. For example, Nicolo Grimaldi (1673–1732), known as Nicolino, departed in 1708 for London, which became one of the principal centers of Italian opera outside Italy; Francesco Bernardi (1685–1759), known as Senesino, sang in Dresden and London; and Antonio Maria Bernacchi (1685–1756) was his rival in the latter city. The most famous castrato was undeniably Carlo Broschi (1705–82), known as Farinelli, who came from an affluent social background and may have been castrated for medical reasons. He performed before Emperor Charles VI in Vienna and later in London, ultimately finding a choice audience and a passionate admirer in the person of Philip V of Spain, for whom he became a confidant and adviser. Gaetano Majorano (1710–83), known as Caffarelli, had vocal qualities comparable to Farinelli's but was his complete opposite in terms of temperament and paraded his caprices and demands across Europe. Gaspard Pacchiarotti (1740–1821) traveled as far as Saint Petersburg to perform, and allowed William Beckford to persuade him to come his mansion, Fonthill, to sing an operetta that Beckford had composed. Stendhal, who once visited Pacchiarotti, called him "the last of the Romans."

The enthusiasm aroused by these singers did not prevent enlightened opinion from being shocked by the very idea of castration, which was judged to be inhumane. Charles de Brosses refers ironically in Letter 51 of his *Lettres d'Italie* (1739–40; Letters from Italy) to "these gentlemen castrati . . . very pretty and very conceited fops who do not produce their effects for noth-

ing." Yet he admits that one could become accustomed to their voices and learn to appreciate them. In *The Present State of Music in France and Italy* (1771), Charles Burney complains of the number of castrati he has met on his tour of Italy and contends that the beauty of their singing does not at all justify the cruel operation they have undergone. However, during a visit to Bologna, he did not neglect to call on the "celebrated Signor Farinelli . . . the greatest musician of this century, and, perhaps, of all ages and of every country." In his *Dictionnaire de musique* (1768; Dictionary of Music), Jean-Jacques Rousseau denounces "those barbaric fathers who, sacrificing nature to fortune, hand their children over for this operation, in order to please voluptuous and cruel people who dare to seek out the singing of these unfortunates." According to Rousseau, the castratis' technical feats are ruined by the lack of warmth and passion in their singing. However, it is a "vile castrato," the singer milord Édouard, who reveals the beauty of Italian opera to the hero of Rousseau's *La nouvelle Héloïse* (1761; Julie; or, The New Héloïse). In this novel, aesthetic perfection seems to be a matter of sublimation, and artifice can reunite with nature. The editors of the *Supplément* to the *Encyclopédie* (1776) seconded Rousseau's opinion with a violent diatribe that relegates castrati to the past: "What cowardly cruelty to mutilate our fellow creatures, in order to provide, in temples and theatres, falsetto voices that could please only a shamefully depraved taste. The love expressed in public by miserable beings who were incapable of feeling it had become nothing more than a ridiculous and soulless farce." The *Encyclopédie* praises Pope Clement XIV's decision to rescind his predecessor's authorization for castration. This measure also corresponded to a change in taste that occurred during the last three decades of the 18th century. The popularity of opera seria and its sopranos began to wane, with audience preferences shifting toward the more "natural" music of the opera buffa, which allotted the best roles to women singers. Wolfgang Amadeus Mozart and Christoph Willibald von Gluck, both of whom wrote parts for castrati in their early works, eventually abandoned such parts, with Gluck rewriting for women the roles he originally intended for castrati.

Ultimately, in a kind of last performance of a career, castrati came to represent almost mythical characters in an Enlightenment Europe that was entirely devoted to refinement and pleasure. At the end of both his life and the century, Casanova, in his *Histoire de ma vie* (1826–38; The Story of My Life), reconstructs this baroque sense of adventure. In Book 7, Chapter 11, he recounts his meeting in Rome with a virtuoso, a favorite castrato of Cardinal Borghese: "One saw at once that this was a mutilated man, but on stage, dressed as a woman, he took fire . . . the magic worked, and one had to fall in love with him, or be the most negative of Germans." In the 19th century, while castrati continued to sing in the Sistine Chapel and in several great choirs in Rome, Farinelli became the main character in John Barnett's opera *Farinelli* (1839) and appeared in Auber and Scribe's opera *La part du diable* (1843; The Devil's Share). Various writers have imagined fictional characters based on romantic historical figures: for instance, Vernon Lee re-creates an incident in the life of Antonio Vivarelli in "An Eighteenth Century Singer" (*The Fortnightly Review*, December 1891) and Dominique Fernandez brings to life Porporino in the pages of *Porporino ou les mystères de Naples* (1974; Porporino; or, The Secrets of Naples). In 1994 Gérard Corbiau's film *Farinelli*, was a hit in Europe. Corbiau produced an imitation of the castrato's voice by mixing the voices of a countertenor and a soprano. The film reopened the debate about the operas composed for the castrati, specifically regarding whether the roles ought to be rewritten and interpreted by disguised female singers, by falsetto singers mimicking the high notes, or by those exceptional countertenors whose voices are capable of reaching very high notes. This issue, which is both technical and aesthetic, leads to the broader problem of whether one can perpetuate and comprehend a culture when living in a completely different social context.

MICHEL DELON

See also Opera

Further Reading

Barbier, Patrick, *The World of the Castrati: The History of an Extraordinary Operatic Phenomenon*, London: Souvenir, 1996 (original French edition, 1989)

Fritz, Hans, *Kastratengesang: Hormonelle, konstitutionelle und pädagogische Aspekte*, Tutzing, Germany: Schneider, 1994

Heriot, Angus, *The Castrati in Opera*, London: Secker and Warburg, 1956

Mamy, Sylvie, *Les grands castrats napolitains à Venise au XVIIIᵉ siècle*, Liège, Belgium: Mardaga, 1994

Catholicism

Catholicism was omnipresent in the societies of the ancien régime, expressed in the grandiose pomp of numerous religious festivities as well as in daily Masses. The Church was active in education and in providing aid to the sick and the poor. Emphasis has often been placed on the homogeneity of Catholicism, which can be explained by the marked dominance of the Jesuits, but it should not be forgotten that the Enlightenment saw a number of reform movements that shattered this homogeneity. The influence of these movements is difficult to discern and to describe precisely: some advocates of reform forged alliances and then separated, and their loyalties, agendas, and objectives changed frequently.

In France as elsewhere, Catholicism in the age of the Enlightenment was saturated with Counter-Reformation ideals that had arisen from the Council of Trent and the desire for a renewal within the Church. However, while the changes initiated by the Council had been put into practice systematically throughout the kingdom, they were carried out in a Gallican spirit. The training of the clergy was improved and the number of seminaries was increased. Nevertheless, the Jesuits did not achieve total domination, and other orders, such as the Oratorians, the Sulpicians, the Lazarists, and the doctrinaires continued to be active. Demonstrations of piety and religious customs were reduced strictly to the essentials, and a spirit of sobriety displaced baroque display. French Catholicism was, as R. Reinhardt put it, a "classical" Catholicism.

Depending on the country, the different areas of Christian and ecclesiastical life were distinguished by specific characteristics. Counter-Reformation Catholicism was less homogeneous in France than it was elsewhere. Proponents of reform fairly rapidly rejected the unifying yoke of the Jesuits. This was particularly the case, for example, when it came to helping the sick, an area in which serious dissensions quickly arose among the clergy, magistrates, and physicians, and in which the state and city governments played an ever-increasing role. While the secular priests were valued by the people for the quality of their training and their pastoral work (see Loupès), the same could not be said of the regular clergy or the theologians. Anticlerical sentiment rose throughout the era.

Jansenism (of which only the polemical aspects are addressed here) arose from the debate surrounding the works of Cornelius Jansen (1585–1638). At first it was a dispute only among scholars, but it spread like wildfire through the Church in the 18th century. The term became a partisan adjective, used by the opponents of the movement. At the root of the problem was the question of the mode of reform to be adopted in modernizing the Church, a matter of equal concern to people on both sides of the argument. The goal of the Jesuits, who enjoyed a great deal of respect at all levels of the clergy, as well as among the lay population and the religious communities, was the unity of the Church, from doctrine to pastoral practice. In contrast, those who were labeled Jansenists were characterized by their diversity and their tendencies toward intimism or even mysticism. They saw themselves as reformers of the Church and as rehabilitators of piety as practiced by the early Christians, and were particularly drawn to the thought of Saint Augustine of Hippo. Overall, they were brought together by their aspirations to piety and by the fact that they were more interested in ecclesiastical discipline and personal asceticism than in doctrine. By returning to the Scriptures, which they translated into French, scholars sought to bring the Bible to those who had not mastered ancient languages. The age of the Enlightenment inherited this heated quarrel from the 17th century, and at the beginning of the 18th century the influence of the Jansenists, who held important positions at court and in public life, was growing; they had a marked presence in the Netherlands, but above all in northern France and Lorraine. Their opponents eventually applied the term "Jansenist" to any theological divergence and to any opposition either to Jesuit theology or to the policies of the Vatican and of Versailles. Having already eliminated the Huguenots with the revocation of the Edict of Nantes (1685), the royal government perceived the "Jansenists," as yet another threat. Judging it necessary to put an end to the problem, it had a new condemnation of Jansenism issued. Finally, the papal bull *Vineam Domini* in 1713 outlawed the doctrines of Jansenius and of Father Pasquier Quesnel. Yet the quarrel went on: the history of the French Church in the 18th century is the history of the democratization of the reform process.

The condemnation of 101 propositions by the papal bull *Unigenitus* of 1713 split the French Church in two, but theological debate became secondary while attention was turned to the spectacular manifestations of the "convulsionaries." The coercive methods used by the Church, with the support of the state, drove many believers away and caused a decline in religious practice. The quarrel partly explains the weakening of Catholic apologetics and the diminishing of religious life. The Jansenist reform movement remained strong in the Netherlands and Lorraine and, later on, in the Habsburg empire.

This antagonism between Jesuits and Jansenists should not be confused with the question of Gallicanism. The Jansenists did indeed distinguish themselves by their sharp aversion to the Roman Curia and did not disdain the idea of a council or a degree of independence for bishops—all ideas influential in the Gallican movement. Many Jansenists, however, did not approve of the principle of the king's right to oversee the Church in France, which Gallicanism supported. This very principle was used against the Jansenists by their adversaries, who tried to compel the monarch to guarantee the unity and purity of the faith within his realm, according to custom. The opponents of Jansenism supported the royal government in order to use the monarchy as a weapon in their struggle against the movement and the "devout party."

The movement known as Gallicanism had various purposes, not exclusively concerned with relations between the universal Church and the Church in France, or even with those between the pope and the bishops. The *Déclaration des quatre articles sur la puissance ecclésiastique et la puissance séculière* (1682; Declaration of the Four Articles on Ecclesiastical Authorities and Secular Authorities) affirms that all temporal power—and therefore the power of the monarch—is derived directly from God, whence the rejection of pontifical power located at an intermediate level between God and the king. In this declaration the pope is accepted as the spiritual leader of the Church but is regarded as being subordinate to universal councils. He is recognized as having a certain decision-making power in questions of belief, but his decisions are not considered to be immutable; moreover, they must win the ratification of the Church as a whole. These arguments were not restricted to France, but it was there that they carried the greatest weight. The French Church felt the repercussions from them and sided with those favoring the traditional rights of the king and the bishops, while courageously preserving a certain degree of independence. The king appointed the bishops, the higher ranks of the regular clergy, and the abbots of the principal monasteries of the major orders, and in the northern part of the realm he even had certain rights to be represented whenever an episcopal throne became vacant. The southward expansion of this principle drew protest from two bishops, whom the pope hastened to support. The king and a large proportion of the clergy, regarding the matter as a strictly internal issue, opposed him. Fundamentally, it was a question of whether the Church in France could be conceived as a national church with two heads without the respective rights of the king and the pope being specified. If the king was to have the same rights in every part of his territory, the expansion of his prerogatives to the south of the country was legitimate. On the other hand, these traditional prerogatives presented an obstacle to the universal Church and its aspirations to a greater degree of independence. This dispute, coming on top of the conflict between the Jesuits and the Jansenists, contributed to the deterioration of the Church's image in France.

This deterioration was intensified by a third controversy, likewise originating in the 17th century and continuing into the 18th: the issue of quietism. Father Fénelon had taken up a position against Bishop Bossuet and in favor of Madame Guyon, who was accused of spreading quietist ideas in her works. Fénelon had at that time seen excerpts from her *Explications des maximes des saints sur la vie intérieure* (1697; The Maxims of the Saints Explained, concerning the Interior Life), which had been condemned by Rome, at Louis XIV's request and on the initiative of Bossuet himself. After that, any reference to a mystical experience was regarded as suspect, and mystical literature disappeared almost entirely from France during the 18th century. Mysticism itself was not completely eradicated, but it stagnated. The adoration of the Sacred Heart, for example, took place mainly during late-night vigils. Like the other two quarrels, the conflict over quietism, as perceived above all in educated circles and manifested in personal quarrels, damaged the reputation of the Church and of its members.

In 18th-century France, just as in other European countries, the Jesuits faced growing hostility in ecclesiastical and political circles, culminating in their suppression in 1764. The Society of Jesus was resented for its dependence on the absolute monarch, to the point of being identified with him, for its rejection of all forms of democracy, and for being rooted in feudal conservatism. The Jesuits, who acted as spiritual directors to sovereigns, as well as tutors to princes and future politicians, were perfectly at home in the monarchical mold. When France—and above all the court—took a step in the direction of Jansenists in the high courts, the Jesuits could not maintain their position. In a period when national feeling was being consolidated, they were accused of being agents of the papacy, a foreign power, of handing the Church over to the arbitrary power of princes, and of encouraging favoritism and confraternal solidarity. Once again, such internal disputes over a religious order made the population weary of ecclesiastical procedures and reinforced the growing hostility toward the Church.

In contrast to the German-speaking countries, France experienced virtually no ecumenical tendency. Febronianism, for example, which prospered in Germany, found no support in France. Of all the national churches, that of the Holy Roman Empire was the most directly dependent upon Rome. The Curia could intervene directly in its affairs much more easily than anywhere else. Conditions were therefore suitable for the development of an episcopal movement, which was solidly resisted elsewhere. The efforts of German episcopalism went unnoticed in Gallican France. Under the ancien régime, the bishops always had a bad public image. Often the sons of high-ranking nobles, and remaining loyal to the court and their own origins, they led the life of powerful lords. Along with the other high-ranking ecclesiastics appointed by the royal government, the bishops thus reinforced the Church's already deep roots in courtly and feudal structures. As Philippe Loupès explains:

> In the 18th century the Church gave the impression, and not only to its enemies, of being paralyzed by conservatism, inertia, and money. Some might call this image simplistic, but there was more to it than that. In the age of the Enlightenment, the Church was penalized by the shortcomings of the papacy, the negative effects of the religious quarrels that culminated in the suppression of the Society of Jesus, and the frequently negative image of the French clergy.

In Spain and Portugal the Church was wealthy and owned large amounts of land and real estate. It enjoyed significant privileges and uncontested political and religious authority, and wielded considerable political influence over affairs of state. An Enlightenment movement existed, but its representatives were all Catholics. For the most part the bishops were subject to the monarchy—without detriment to pastoral activities—but royal decrees were not always strictly followed. Members of the lower clergy were often characterized by their limited education, their greed, and their attachment to worldly things. In Spain the Jesuits dominated public education, and this prominence exposed them to criticism. They were accused of working in direct contact with Rome and of stirring up opposition to the king. Their political and social control, in conjunction with the theological quarrels in which they participated, made them unwelcome. The debate over the Society of Jesus extended into the Iberian Peninsula, first to Portugal, where the Jesuits' property was seized and they were expelled or imprisoned in 1759. The Jesuits were expelled from Spain in 1767. After the accession of the Bourbons to the Spanish throne, the state intervened in Church affairs with increasing frequency, partly in order to curb the augmentation of privileges and the growing influence of the papacy over the Church in Spain.

In those countries that were under the British crown—England, Wales, Scotland, and Ireland—Catholics were subject to changing attitudes on the part of the state and its officials, but there was one constant: penal repression was becoming less and less common. However, it was only after 1782 that the first true Catholic churches could be built in Ireland. Traditional prayers and pilgrimages survived, and Irish Catholic spirituality was modernized through a blending of the old and the new. Among the English-speaking bourgeoisie, it was expressed in a severe, fear-ridden morality. Indeed, Irish Catholicism was traditionally austere and was enduringly marked by its persecutions. In England and then in Scotland, Catholics were fully emancipated at the end of the 18th century.

Catholicism in the Holy Roman Empire may be summarized, in general terms, by reference to the episcopalism of the imperial Church, to "Josephism," to a belated form of Jansenism, and to the *Aufklärung* (the German Enlightenment). Episcopalism, following on from the *gravamina* (grievances) of the early Middle Ages and the events that shook the German-speaking world in the 16th and 17th centuries, rose up in opposition to the failure to respect the Concordat of Vienna, as well as to the encroachment of the papacy upon episcopal autonomy and Rome's interference, through its nunciatures, in the Church of the Empire. The efforts to shake off this control sometimes pushed beyond the freedoms guaranteed by the Concordat of Vienna, and the example of the Gallican freedoms was cited more and more often. The movement was given its legal and theological basis by Johann Caspar Barthel (1697–1771) and Georg Christoph Neller (1709–83). Barthel opposed the Jesuits and the Roman Curia with the "plain speaking of a German." He described the prerogatives of the German Church and of the metropolitan archbishop of Salzburg, whom he recognized as primate, as these had developed historically, and he defended these prerogatives against the claims of the Curia. Attributing the same objective to the imperial government as to the religious authorities, he concluded that it was difficult to determine their respective competences and that it was their duty to assure harmony between Church and state.

In Trier, Neller had been in contact with the auxiliary Archbishop von Hontheim, best known for his *De statu ecclesiae et legitima protestate romani pontificis* (1763; On the Status of the Church and the Legitimate Power of the Roman Pontificate), which he published under the pseudonym Justinus Febronius. This work, which makes reference to French theologians, to Van Espen, and to the canonical school of Würzburg, deploys historical examples in an empirical attempt to restore the primate to the honorific preeminence the office had enjoyed in the first eight centuries of Christianity. According to Justinus Febronius, the bishops are the successors of the apostles by divine right and not simply representatives of the pope, who therefore has no right of jurisdiction within their dioceses. It is in the state's interest to bring the pope's prerogatives and all the undertakings of the Curia under its control. The book enjoyed considerable success and the movement that

resulted from it was named Febronianism. Later, however, factions formed within the movement.

In 1769 the leaders of the Church in the Holy Roman Empire signed the *Gravamina* of Koblenz, a text that expounds their grievances against the endless wrangling of the nunciatures and the interference of the Holy See in the election of bishops. The Curia, seeking to preserve its right to intervene through its intermediary, the nuncio, showed some readiness to make concessions on the question of the relations between Church and state, in particular on the matter of the use of Church funds for state purposes. At the Congress of Ems in 1786, the prince-bishops responded with a program of reforms for the imperial Church that amounted to a declaration of war on the institution of nunciatures. Emphasizing the autonomous nature of their authority, the bishops demanded the abolition of various exemptions and the elimination of the nunciature. However, Emperor Joseph II gave only reluctant support to these demands. Furthermore, some bishops feared that the demands in fact exaggerated the authority of the metropolitan, and so, looking to their own personal political interests, one after another the archbishops finally abandoned their demands. In the end, the questions were resolved in the wake of the French Revolution and of the secularization of the ecclesiastical states.

The main current that marked Catholicism in the Habsburg territories was Josephism, in which several movements and interest groups came together: the state administrators of the Church, late Jansenism (*Spätjansenismus*), and the Catholic branch of the German Enlightenment. Over the course of the 18th century Rome's concerns in Germany brought the papal state into conflict, not so much with the emperor in his role as head of the imperial Church, as with the various territories of the Empire, which were being converted into modern states. These quarrels led to regular interventions by the bishops and by the nunciates in the territories in question.

Because of its numerous privileges and properties and the legal disputes that resulted from them, the Church appeared to many to be a state within the state. The relative economic weakness of Catholic countries could be attributed to the large number of nonworking days, processions, and pilgrimages. The state, which intervened ever more extensively in the affairs of the Church, in Bavaria as well as in the Habsburg territories, sought to suppress the power of the Church and to acquire sovereignty over decision-making. This was not a matter of instituting a program purely inspired by the Enlightenment or of eradicating the Church, but rather of positioning the Church within a clearly limited sphere of activity and, additionally, of tapping its financial potential for the state's benefit. At an earlier period,

Empress Maria Theresa had tried to use the Church's revenues to set up new parishes and to fund the training of priests, in order to suppress crypto-Protestantism.

Although some of the reforms envisaged were never realized, financial control of all the institutions of the Church was established, and the number of religious festivals was reduced. Joseph II's religious policies were not very different from his mother's, although his regulations were more detailed. In addition, he imposed his plans more rigorously and with less consideration for the Empire as a whole. It was Joseph who, by adjusting the frontiers of the dioceses to fit those of the sovereign lands, prepared the ground for the replacement of the ancient imperial constitution and the secularization and autonomy of the lands under the Habsburg crown. He also contributed to the suppression of many monasteries, chiefly those of the contemplative and mendicant orders, whose assets were integrated into religious funds that were used for training priests. In this area too, state control was manifested through the establishment of general seminaries. The confraternities that had developed from the craft guilds, with their spirituality tainted by superstition and fanaticism, were also dissolved. Their assets and privileges were transferred to a charitable association that provided a form of social assistance. Religious toleration in the spirit of the Enlightenment was on the rise, and Joseph II eventually granted freedom of private religious worship to Lutherans, Calvinists, and the Greek Orthodox Church. He also granted them rights as city dwellers, which placed them on almost equal footing with Catholics. This edict of toleration was also applied in the ecclesiastical states.

Josephism put into practice some of the ideas of late Jansenism, a reformist movement that perhaps had connections with the Jansenism of Lorraine through Emperor Francis I of Lorraine. Late Jansenism inclined toward a more inner-directed spirituality and a stricter morality, rejecting the baroque pomp of processions, pilgrimages, and other external manifestations of piety; instead advocating sobriety in pursuit of the spiritual life of the Church.

The principles of Enlightenment philosophy, also taken up by Josephism, contributed in practice to the simplification of procedures, to the management of states, and to the organization of work in accordance with principles of efficiency and economic profitability. When it came to supporting the national economy, the prince-bishops displayed the same inclinations as secular rulers: in their states too, public health and education were overhauled, while manifestations of baroque piety gave way to a more sober spirituality that made an impact on the lives of individuals. The *Aufklärung* of the German-speaking Protestant territories was sometimes imitated, but more often it was adapted in a form that was specific to Catholicism. The results could be

seen in the reforms of worship and of spirituality but also in teaching and in the Catholic theology of the end of the 18th century. The gap between the Catholicism of France and that of the German-speaking territories widened during the age of the Enlightenment.

In Italy small groups of learned men appeared, influenced by the Jansenist circles of France and Utrecht, so that it is possible to speak of Italian Jansenism. Some of these Italian intellectuals, such as Ludovico Antonio Muratori or Cardinal A.M. Quirini, held high rank. These groups, with structures that varied from state to state, moved away from the baroque Scholastic tradition and the theology and spirituality inspired by the Jesuits, and returned instead to Augustinianism. They received the support of various Italian rulers, including Peter Leopold, archduke of Tuscany, who carried over into his administration a number of the reforms of his older brother, Joseph II. The changes that the Italian Jansenists had in mind were adaptations of Gallicanism and regalism to the conditions of their own country. In 1786 the diocesan synod of Pistoia adopted the Gallican articles, but the national synod of Florence rejected them by an overwhelming majority the following year. In a country that was completely under Catholic influence, the movement paved the way for the *Risorgimento* by encouraging people to seek religious solutions that seemed even more Catholic than those of the Roman Curia.

In Poland the partitions and eventual elimination of the country struck a severe blow against the Church, but Catholicism remained a link among Poles. However, all the enlightened reforms that had been started before the partitions were suppressed.

PHILIPP SCHÄFER

See also Anti-Enlightenment; Apologetics; Bible; Clergy: Catholic; Clergy: Regular and Secular; Fanaticism; Jansenism; Jesuits; Parlements, French; Providence

Further Reading

Almond, Philip C., *Heaven and Hell in Enlightenment England,* Cambridge and New York: Cambridge University Press, 1994

Batley, Edward Malcolm, *Catalyst of Enlightenment, Gotthold Ephraim Lessing: Productive Criticism of Eighteenth-Century Germany,* Bern and New York: Lang, 1990

Bernard, Paul P., *Jesuits and Jacobins: Enlightenment and Enlightened Despotism in Austria,* Urbana: University of Illinois Press, 1971

Brockliss, L.W.B., *French Higher Education in the Seventeenth and Eighteenth Centuries: A Cultural History,* Oxford: Clarendon Press, 1986; New York: Oxford University Press, 1987

Brumfitt, John Henry, *The French Enlightenment*, London: Macmillan, 1972; Cambridge, Massachusetts: Schenkman, 1973

Chinnici, Joseph P., *The English Catholic Enlightenment: John Lingard and the Cisalpine Movement, 1780–1850*, Shepherdstown, West Virginia: Patmos Press, 1980

Haakonssen, Knud, editor, *Enlightenment and Religion: Rational Dissent in Eighteenth-Century Britain*, Cambridge and New York: Cambridge University Press, 1996

Jedin, Hubert, and John Dolan, *History of the Church*, 10 vols., London: Burns and Oates, 1980–81 (original German edition, 1962)

Loupès, Philippe, *La vie religieuse en France au XVIIIᵉ siècle*, Paris: SEDES, 1993

McIntosh, John R., *Church and Theology in Enlightenment Scotland: The Popular Party, 1740–1800*, East Linton: Tuckwell Press, 1998

O'Connor, Thomas, *An Irish Theologian in Enlightenment France: Luke Joseph Hooke, 1714–96*, Blackrock, Dublin, and Portland, Oregon: Four Courts Press, 1995

Young, B.W., *Religion and Enlightenment in Eighteenth-Century England: Theological Debate from Locke to Burke*, Oxford: Clarendon Press, and Oxford and New York: Oxford University Press, 1998

Censorship

Censorship and toleration: these two issues, although closely intertwined, were applied in quite different realms during the Enlightenment. Toleration raised primarily theoretical problems. The debate over its true value—whether it was a sign of cowardice or a recognition of otherness, whether persecution was a duty or a crime—was constantly influenced by an underlying examination of both what was intolerable and what sorts of behavior and discourses were incompatible with religious faith or life in society. Censorship was primarily an institutional question, based on historical and legal interpretations by the ruling authorities. For centuries the word *censure* (censorship) was used very broadly in France. For Antoine Furetière, compiler of the 1690 *Dictionnaire universel* (Universal Dictionary), it could just as well designate advice or rebuke from one's superior as the condemnation of books. The definition was gradually narrowed down until finally, in the 18th century, the term *censure* was exclusively restricted to measures taken to prevent the printing of a text or to eliminate a published book.

Legislation implemented in 18th-century Europe was the result of numerous conflicts between the different authorities who believed they had both a right and a duty to define and practice censorship; such conflicts were particularly acute between church and state. The Catholic Church, a self-designated guardian of orthodoxy, asserted its duty to teach divine revelation and its right to prohibit all dissenting propositions. Beginning at the time of the invention of the printing press, popes strove to control the dissemination of humanist ideas.

In order to forestall the development of critical thinking and the propagation of heresies, the Church demanded that all books be read and examined before publication. Many of the Protestant churches were also intransigent and sought to establish controls over published works. However, none of these religious institutions could act without the support of secular authorities, as the state alone wielded effective means of enforcement, such as the ability to confiscate books and penalize authors, printers, and distributors. Meanwhile, the dissemination of religious heresies was certainly not the main worry for political authorities, who were far more concerned about the propagation of subversive ideas that threatened the security of the state. Opposite the theological figure of the censor, the guardian of orthodoxy, stood the Roman figure of the censor, the guardian of morality and civic sense. In reality, dark conflicts and complex power struggles were hidden behind the official alliances of the different authorities apparently united to censor books. When monarchs officially instituted censorship, they were quite careful to assert their autonomy in making decisions and pronouncing judgments; they had no intention of simply taking orders from religious authorities.

Such conflicts resulted in a complicated tangle of institutions, where books could be subject to a whole series of different kinds of censorship. The following paragraphs present, in outline form, the principal institutions involved in censorship, the specific powers at their disposal, and the effectiveness of the measures employed.

Political Censorship

There were two main types of political censorship in the 18th century—"preventive" censorship (that is, censorship prior to publication) and postpublication condemnation—and both could be applied to any given work. Systems of preventive censorship were in operation in most of the absolute monarchies. In France this power was exercised by the state *librairie* (publishing office), which was answerable directly to the chancellor and consequently to the king. Censors were charged with examining manuscripts to verify that they did not contain any passage that was harmful to religion, the political order, or public morality. When the text was not entirely acceptable, the censors would suggest "attenuations." If the work contained nothing objectionable, the publishing office delivered a permit with an official seal, sometimes accompanied by a royal *privilège* granting the publisher exclusive rights to print the work. However, many works were presented that could not be officially approved, even though the government had no reason for prohibiting them. Early in the 18th century the publishing office set up a new category, that of "tacit permission." Books that received tacit permission were also examined by a censor, but they were published without any sign of official approval; the name of a foreign publisher was usually cited on the title page, although quite often the books were in fact published in France. The government, without acknowledging it, thus became an accomplice to false publishing practices. This reliance on semiofficial permits is a good indication of the difficulties involved in organizing a system of censorship prior to publication. Censors never knew how far they should go in prohibiting books, and their reports were often filled with anguished comments on the hidden poison that a text might spread. Moreover, despite the preventive censorship and rejection of many books, the publishing office was rarely called on to examine truly subversive or libertine works. Authors, perfectly aware of the censorship rules, were not so stupid as to submit a manuscript that had no chance of being published, that would constitute a dubious mark on their reputation, and that might be confiscated. Instead, they resorted to clandestine publishing channels and, in defiance of all regulations, published texts that had undergone no official examination.

Preventive censorship was characteristic of absolutist regimes—it was not practiced in England, for example—but all European countries practiced postpublication censorship in the 18th century. Condemnation was publicly pronounced, officially published, and enforced with practical measures to prevent the dissemination of a text. Entire editions would be seized, and if the book were particularly scandalous a copy might be torn up and solemnly burned in public. In France such ceremonies often took place at the foot of the grand staircase of the main courthouse in Paris. Sales were prohibited and the printer, booksellers, and sometimes the author were penalized. Such condemnations were all the more frequent in that they could be pronounced by the royal Conseil d'État (Council of State) as well as by various other official courts: *parlements* (high courts), sovereign councils, magistratures, and seneschal's courts. The basic difference between the two types of censorship was that preventive censorship was secret, while post-publication condemnation was public. In the first case the censor's reports were buried in the archives of the government publishing office, whereas post-publication decrees were widely published, announced by newsmongers, and posted "wherever needed." Preventive censorship was carried out in secret and was effective only to the extent that the public was unaware of its effects. Post-publication censorship was spectacular, notorious, and widely discussed. Public opinion in France and Britain was particularly susceptible to the high drama provided by post-publication censorship. In France decrees by the *parlements* included lengthy accusations that were authentic counterlibels and excited commentaries, all the more passionate in that they often revealed disputes between sovereign courts and the government. In Britain these condemnations involved court cases with obvious political dimensions and, as in the Wilkes affair, the bans stoked intellectual discussion and resulted in extensive public debate. All the other European states regularly resorted to measures of condemnation, even if the procedures were less spectacular. Voltaire's quarrels with Frederick II are sufficient proof that enlightened despotism, though it may have been more favorable to the *philosophes* than was absolute monarchy, did not admit any and all forms of freethinking. Large publishing houses, such as the Société Typographique de Neuchâtel or Cramers, were careful not to print works that were too compromising, particularly erotic literature. (This did not prevent them from supplying their correspondents with such books, which they procured from small publishers.) Following the publication of the baron d'Holbach's *Le système de la nature, ou, Des lois du monde physique et du monde moral* (1770; The System of Nature; or, The Laws of the Moral and Physical World) by the Société Typographique de Neuchâtel, that establishment's directors were dismissed by the authorities of Neuchâtel.

Religious Censorship

Religious authorities were also able to censor books. Although they usually acted after publication, some religious orders exercised a form of preventive censorship by requiring their members to obtain prior approval from superiors before publishing texts. For example, all works written by Jesuits were controlled by their provincials. Two major types of censorship were practiced. In the first of these, doctrinal censorship, theologians listed the culpable statements in a work and "qualified" them—that is, they explained how these statements were incompatible with the dogmas of the faith because they stated or approached heresies, were written in ambiguous terms that might offend pious readers, or might produce harmful effects by introducing a schism or subverting the ecclesiastical hierarchy. This activity remained purely theoretical. Theologians could qualify a statement but had no means of sanctioning imprudent or impious readers of these heresies. In contrast, the second type of censorship granted some ecclesiastics the right to declare specific spiritual punishments, such as excommunication. In Catholic countries this power was first exercised by the bishops, who regularly published instructions in their dioceses to warn the congregation against the dangers of evil books. Such episcopal instructions were often accompanied by prohibition against reading the works, under penalty of excommunication. In addition to such instructions, applicable only within the limits of the diocese or ecclesiastic province where they were delivered, there were papal briefs and decrees of the Roman Inquisition that applied to all Catholics. This is how the Index of works prohibited by the Church came to be constituted. Although these bans were immediately enforceable in all the countries of the Inquisition (notably the Papal states, Spain, and Portugal), in some states prohibitions were subject to review by secular authorities. In France a papal brief could not be accepted unless it was registered by the *parlements,* and this registration was not just a formality. The magistrates were uncompromising about the freedom of the Gallican Church and refused to allow the publication of any brief that could even slightly threaten that freedom. Although Protestant countries showed greater toleration than their Catholic counterparts in matters of the printed word, reformed churches also resorted to forms of censorship, pronounced by their synods. For example, the Consistory of the Walloon Church of Rotterdam summoned Pierre Bayle, following the publication of his *Dictionnaire historique et critique* (1697; An Historical and Critical Dictionary), and gave him an extensive memorandum noting all the changes he would have to make in the second edition. Bayle had to rewrite the article "David," eliminate obscenities, and give a more critical account of the arguments of the Manicheans, Pyrrhonians, and atheists. At a time when religion played an essential role in society, the means of pressure that churches could exert were hardly negligible. A person who was excommunicated was not only denied the

sacraments; that individual could also be refused the right to enter a church and might even be banished from society.

Multiple Censorship

Since various kinds of censorship delivered different judgments and punishments, in many cases these could be compounded without the least incompatibility. There were cases where all the authorities joined together in fierce combat against the same book. What looked like a holy coalition of religious and secular authorities might well conceal a struggle between various forces, each seeking to show that its own role was indispensable and each asserting its own importance by showing up the inadequacy of previous acts of censorship. The treatment meted out to Claude-Adrien Helvétius's *De l'esprit* (Essays on the Mind and Its Several Faculties) is an excellent example. The book was published in Paris in the summer of 1758, with approval and a publishing *privilège,* after examination by a royal censor. Just before it was put on sale, the director of the state publishing office discovered that it contained subversive material and submitted it to a second censor who called for corrections. These corrections were not sufficient, and as soon as the book reached the market it created a scandal. Publication was immediately suspended, copies of the book were seized, and a decree of the Conseil d'État revoked the *privilège* and prohibited circulation of the text. As a result of these measures, it was absolutely illegal to sell the book. However, this did not prevent other censors from belatedly joining the fray. The archbishop of Paris delivered a pastoral letter condemning *De l'esprit* and prohibited the reading of it under penalty of excommunication. The Parlement de Paris condemned the book to be burned and demanded that Helvétius disavow his work. The pope published a brief prohibiting the text's publication or translation in perpetuity. The Sorbonne, in an extensive doctrinal act of censure, detailed all the hidden poisons it contained. This surfeit of censorship reveals not so much the utter darkness of the subversive propositions of Helvétius, as the obscure rivalries among the different authorities joined against him and seeking to assert their prerogatives by condemning his work. Each new censor rushed to highlight the indispensable nature of his own action, implicitly demonstrating the inadequacy of previous measures.

However, there were other cases where several conflicting acts of censorship were applied to a work. This could occur when one authority felt threatened by an act of censorship on the part of a rival, or in instances when several authorities went to war against one another, exchanging blows through censorship. Such conflicts could result in a labyrinthine accumulation of censorships. On 23 August 1723 the Parlement de Toulouse issued a ruling canceling a decree of the Roman Inquisition delivered against a pastoral instruction of the bishop of Rodez, condemning a treatise written by a Jesuit. During the 1750s a long controversy brought the Parlement of Paris into conflict with the bishop of Troyes, with the magistrates ordering suppression of the bishop's instructions, while the prelate prohibited reading of the court's decrees. Here, censorship was an instrument of political combat and led to broad dissemination of controversies.

The effectiveness of these different sorts of censorship was quite limited throughout the 18th century and never seriously hindered the circulation of Enlightenment philosophy or libertine texts and erotic novels. However tight the surveillance, censored books were either printed illegally or imported. With improved technology, printing could be done on small, quiet, easily hidden presses, while clever smugglers developed highly effective networks of distribution. Moreover, even in absolute monarchies such as France, where surveillance was quite strict, secular authorities had to make concessions and allow books to be printed even when they did not approve of them. The political interests of the French government were in total conflict with its economic interests: if too many publications were prohibited, then national policy indirectly favored foreign publishers.

The institution of censorship itself also seemed to have ambiguous effects. It has often been argued that censorship does not really prevent the circulation of works, and that prohibition actually functions as a form of indirect publicity. In fact, Maria Theresa prohibited the publication of the Catholic Church's Index in Austria precisely to avoid these potentially perverse effects of censorship. She considered that simply reading the list of condemned titles could be harmful to her subjects, making them curious to read works whose existence they would be better off not even suspecting. It should be stressed that this type of analysis of the perverse effects of censorship makes no distinction between preventive and post-publication censorship. Prepublication censorship was a covert activity known only to the government and officials of the publishing office. Even if it were only partially effective, at least it never gave indirect publicity to prohibited works or suppressed material. As for post-publication condemnations, they were as much a tool of political publicity as an instrument of suppression of books or authors. Different authorities used these condemnations as a way of strongly asserting their power, reinforcing their position in pronouncements published through indictments and "instructions" (lengthy and widely distributed official texts in which the authorities clearly set forth the theses that they sought to defend). During the Enlightenment, censorship was not just a means of hindering free thought; paradoxically, it also offered an incomparable instrument for the dissemination of certain political theses.

BARBARA DE NEGRONI

See also Books and Reading; Clandestine Literature; Newspapers and Journalism

Further Reading

Darnton, Robert, *The Literary Underground of the Old Regime,* Cambridge, Massachusetts: Harvard University Press, 1982

Darnton, Robert, *The Corpus of Clandestine Literature in France, 1769–1789,* New York: Norton, 1995

Darnton, Robert, *The Forbidden Best-Sellers of Pre-Revolutionary France,* New York: Norton, 1995; London: Harper Collins, 1996

Malesherbes, Chrétien-Guillaume de Lamoignon de, *Mémoires sur la librairie et sur la liberté de la presse,* Paris: Agasse, 1809; reprint, Chapel Hill: University of North Carolina, Department of Romance Languages, 1979

Myers, Robin, and Michael Harris, editors, *Censorship and the Control of Print: In England and France, 1600–1910,* Winchester: St. Paul's Bibliographies, 1992

Negroni, Barbara de, *Lectures interdites: Le travail des censeurs au XVIIIᵉ siècle, 1723–1774,* Paris: Albin Michel, 1995

Chance and Necessity

"There are few matters on which philosophy, whether ancient or modern, has been brought to bear as much as on this one." In fact, the abbé Morellet's assertion in the article "Fatalité" (Fate) of the *Encyclopédie* reveals a transformation in 18th-century theological debate on chance and necessity that, around 1750, engendered renewed interest in these venerable concepts. This interest can be explained by the success of the materialist and atheist doctrine of "Necessity," and also by the spread throughout Europe of Cartesian rationalism and the doctrine of optimism—doctrines at the heart of Christian philosophy. The debate in no way concerned "chance" as something truly indeterminate: the "contingency" of the Scholastics was defined less by the absence of a cause than by the absence of logical necessity. Although those who believed in free will accepted the idea of an event without a cause, Christians and atheists alike believed "chance" to be the subjective designation for an unknown, unforeseeable cause that affects an individual either for good or for ill (hence the meanings of "luck" and "fate" that were common from this time onward). The polemic thus pitted those who equated "chance" with "blind Necessity" against those who attributed it to "Providence."

Why did this debate about necessity take on such importance during the Enlightenment? In the past, notions of necessity, in forms such as "Fate" in astrology, "Destiny" for the Greeks, or "Fortune" during the Middle Ages, had not been admitted into the realm of theology. Quarrels about the nature of grace and free will, rekindled during the Reformation and then by the Jansenists, did not prevent each group from maintaining room for some principle of freedom, whether in the form of the Molinists' free will or the Augustinians' notion of divine arbitrariness. Christian philosophers who accepted Cartesianism limited its legitimacy to physics. Although Baruch Spinoza formulated a doctrine of radical necessity, the limited spread and the unorthodoxy of his philosophy allowed Christians to reject it as an "absurd monstrosity." Sir Isaac Newton's discoveries played a more decisive role since they imposed the concept of nature's submission to universal laws and inspired research into the "necessary causes" responsible for apparently irregular phenomena. (In cosmology this task fell to Pierre-Simon Laplace, to whom the formulation of modern determinism has been retrospectively attributed.) However, Newton's followers also defended the concept of human or divine freedom. Gottfried Wilhelm Leibniz, in particular, revived the debate, since he was accused of introducing the doctrine of necessity into the very heart of Christianity. While claiming to oppose *fatum stoicum* (Stoic fate) and *fatum mahometanum* (Muslim fate) in his (*Theodicea* [1710; Theodicy]), Leibniz defends a form of *fatum christianum* (Christian fate) that turns out to be as deterministic as Spinoza's concept of necessity. Leibniz rejects free will and portrays a God who seems to be constrained *necessarily* to choose the best of all possible worlds, a world in which all events are predetermined to contribute to the best and in which the future is already contained in the present. This is a predeterminism analogous to Laplace's determinism.

In 1724, in order to stigmatize those who championed the doctrine of Necessity or "fatality"), Father Castel invented the term "fatalism" (and, for the same reasons, "optimism," in 1737). With the advance of optimism in Europe, deism was denounced as a doctrine that leads to Spinozism; refutations of fatalism became more and more common. In 1755 Prémontval published *Du hasard sous l'empire de la Providence, pour servir de préservatif contre la doctrine du fatalisme moderne* (On Chance and the Influence of Providence as Safeguards against the Doctrine of Modern Fatalism). François-André Pluquet criticized all the doctrines concerning fate from antiquity onward in his *Examen du fatalisme* (1757; Examination of Fatalism). Some contributors to the *Encyclopédie* defended Christian free will or freedom as defined by the deists; others defended the fatalism of Leibniz, Christian Wolff, or the atheists. The polemic invaded the field of literature, from Voltaire's *Zadig ou la destinée* (1748; Zadig; or, The Book of Fate) to the philosophical novels of the marquis de Sade. Fatalism became a fashionable theme: in 1769 Jacques de La Morlière published *Le fatalisme, ou collections d'anecdotes, pour prouver l'influence du sort sur l'histoire du coeur humain* (Fatalism; or, Collections of Anecdotes to Prove the Influence of Fate on the History of the Human Heart). In 1771 the *Dictionnaire de Trévoux* (Dictionary of Trévoux) accepted the word "fatalism," which was in use in most European languages by that time. Under the influence of the theories of Immanuel Kant and the positivists, scientists abandoned the term "fatalism," with its moral connotations, as well as "necessity," which had originated in metaphysics. They preferred to speak of "determinism," often conflating it with "finalism." "Fatalism" at that point assumed its modern meaning as a passive attitude (optimistic or pessimistic) based on "the sophistry of lazy reasoning" that Leibniz claimed to have refuted: if every event is necessary, it is pointless to believe in free will or in useful action. The keenest analysis of fatalism, of its metaphysical connotations and of the paradoxes it creates for atheist ethics and politics, is found in *Jacques le fataliste et son maître* (1778; Jacques the Fatalist and His Master). In this work, Denis Diderot demystifies the traditional uses of the ideas of chance and Providence in fictions.

As the 18th century progressed, the concept of necessity played a role in several areas of knowledge. Physicists continued to look for causal explanations of events that were apparently due to chance. Christian thinkers attributed these causes to Providence, and deists to a watchmaker God or to a well-organized natural world, while atheists such as the baron d'Holbach saw necessity as a way to refute finalism. The concept of necessity was more problematic in history and in the social sciences, since it either tended to negate the importance of individual actions or to come up against the problem of a small cause producing a large effect (a recurring theme for Blaise Pascal and Voltaire). Posterity has hailed Montesquieu as a precursor of sociology because he attributed the complexity of social phenomena to an ensemble of interconnected causes. Finally, after the Reign of Terror, the debate about historical necessity became the focus of interpretations of the French Revolution, with the conceptualization of "circumstances," research into past causes of the events or, in the case of those arguing against the concept of necessity without finality, an explanation of the Revolution through a fatalism dictated by Providence.

Was "chance," then, merely a derogatory term used in the 18th century to designate an event whose cause is unknown to the individual who experiences its effects? On the contrary, we should recall that "chance" also became the conceptual tool of a science meant to master the unforeseeable by formulating laws of probability and to control the uncountable with the use of statistics. When Pascal formulated the concept of "mathematical hope," he contributed to a reevaluation of games of "chance" (the French word *hasard* is from the Arabic *az-zahr*, a game of dice), games previously condemned by theologians; in part, his work derived from a legal tradition that had been stimulated by the development of large-scale trade and insurance contracts. Whether it was a question of "bets" in a game, or a religious question such as his own famous "wager," Pascal's conversion of "chance" into a mathematical concept was not an imperfect form of science, limited to concrete applications, but instead one of the major advances in knowledge closely linked to the problem of human decision making in the face of uncertainty. This transformation of the concepts of hope and prudence was accentuated during the Enlightenment by the effects both of empiricism and of the rationalization of economic and administrative practices. Although the calculation of probability as developed by the Bernoullis, the comte de Buffon, Jean le Rond D'Alembert, Thomas Bayes, Laplace, and the marquis de Condorcet was more mathematically abstract, it remained a practical theory concerned with observation, demography, and insurance.

The metaphysical and epistemological debate on the nature of "chance" continued to inform the theoretical differences among mathematicians, from the partisans of "subjective chance" to those of "objective chance": is everything linked, or is the causal series responsible for a truly independent particular event, as La Placette affirmed in 1714 in his *Traité des jeux de hasard* (Treatise on Games of Chance), more than 100 years before Antoine-Augustin Cournot? However, the transformation of "chance" into probability was concerned first and foremost with action. Condorcet was not part mathematician and part politician. His work presents a philosophy of economic and political practices, as evidenced in his *Tableau général de la science qui a pour objet l'application du calcul aux sciences politiques et morales* (1795; General Sketch of Science, Having As Its Object to Apply Arithmetic to Political and Moral Sciences). In his publication of an "Essai pour connaître la population du royaume" (Attempt to Determine the Population of the Kingdom) with Dionis du Séjour and Laplace (in the *Mémoires de l'Académie* [1786–91; Memoirs of the Academy]), Condorcet continued the work that members of the Académie Royale des Sciences (French Royal Academy of Sciences) were doing for the state by developing a "statistical method." When he proposes, in the *Esquisse d'un tableau historique des progrès de l'esprit humain* (1795; Outlines of an Historical View of the Progress of the Human Mind), the establishment of insurance against old age "by confronting chance with itself," he is not entering into the debate on necessity and Providence but into the Enlightenment struggle against the vicissitudes of individual and collective life.

LAURENT LOTY

See also Optimism and Pessimism; Probability Theory; Providence

Further Reading

Baker, Keith Michael, *Condorcet: From Natural Philosophy to Social Mathematics,* Chicago: University of Chicago Press, 1975

Brian, Éric, *La mesure de l'État: Administrateurs et géomètres au XVIIIᵉ siècle,* Paris: Albin Michel, 1994

Coumet, Ernest, "La théorie du hasard est-elle née par hasard?" *Annales* 3 (May–June 1970)

Loty, Laurent, "La genèse de l'optimisme et du pessimisme (de Pierre Bayle à la Révolution française)," Ph.D. diss., University of Tours, 1995

Loty, Laurent, *L'anti-fatalisme: Aux origines de l'optimisme et du pessimisme,* Paris: Albin Michel, 2001

Pomian, Krzysztof, "Le déterminisme: Histoire d'une problématique," in *La querelle du déterminisme,* edited by Pomian, Paris: Gallimard, 1990

Charity

According to Voltaire, it was the abbé de Saint-Pierre "who made the word *bienfaisance* [charity] fashionable." With a certain solemnity, Voltaire dedicated the last verses of his seventh *Discours en vers sur l'homme* (1734; A Verse Discourse on Man) to exalting, not so much the word *bienfaisance,* as what it should mean to his contemporaries. Voltaire's homage underscored the importance of the introduction of this word into the language of the Enlightenment. (Actually, *bienfaisance* was medieval in origin and Voltaire had attributed it to Guez de Balzac in another work.) Father Cerruti, the author of the discourse *Les vrais plaisirs ne sont faits que pour la vertu* (Real Pleasures Exist Only in Relation to Virtue), lists among the forms of virtue that he wished to reconcile with Christianity "a sentiment of benevolence and humanity, like that which animated the great Theodosius." But it is plausible that the notion of benevolence had become a new weapon in the polemic that pitted the Enlightenment *philosophes* against the Church. The article "Bienfaisance," which appears in the *Supplément* to the *Encyclopédie,* declares:

> It is virtue that leads us to do well by our neighbor, the daughter of kindliness and the love of humanity. God, nature, and reason invite us to do good: God, by his example and his essence, which is bounty; nature, through the sense of pleasure in the soul of the benefactor, a sense that is renewed as the benefactor contemplates the object of his good deeds; reason, by the interest we must take in the fate of the unfortunate.

The Supreme Being, nature, and reason—the triad fostering this new concept—inscribed it within the nonreligious ethic of the Enlightenment as a secular replacement for the Christian notion of charity. The new concept was applied to an anthropology and a cosmology different from those endorsed by the Church. Even in its allusions to a Supreme Being or a God, a new vocabulary was being forged to pave the way for the social and political transformations sought by Enlightenment thinkers.

Charity was among the "theological, Christian, and supernatural virtues" emphasized by Roman Catholicism, together with "faith and hope," according to the article on "Vertu" (Virtue) in the *Dictionnaire de Trévoux* (Dictionary of Trévoux), which—not surprisingly—did not include an article on "Bienfaisance." Like Saint Paul, Voltaire preferred charity over the other two cardinal virtues, considering them to be chimerical and of little use to other people. In his article "Vertu" in his *Dictionnaire philosophique* (1764; Philosophical Dictionary), Voltaire defines virtue as "charity toward your neighbor." As for man himself, he is "neither benevolent nor malevolent." Voltaire waxes ironic with respect to the "cardinal and theological virtues" and dismisses the "emotional virtues" of the theologians. The *philosophes* delighted in mocking the uselessness of acts of piety and worship that characterized the reclusive life of the monasteries, often targeted by Voltaire and Denis Diderot. Good deeds done for one's neighbor were the only ones that counted in the new morality. For example, the article "Des lois" (On Laws) in Voltaire's *Dictionnaire philosophique* includes the story of a princess who deserved to be queen of France because she was "charitable." In the sixth interview of the article "Catéchisme chinois" (Chinese Catechism), a disciple of Confucius declares, "the true virtues are those that are useful to society, such as fidelity, magnanimity, charity, tolerance, etc."

As in the celebrated polemic of his *Lettre à D'Alembert* (1758; *Letter to M. D'Alembert on Theatre*) concerning public spectacles, in *Émile, ou, De l'éducation* (1762; Émile; or, Concerning Education) Jean-Jacques Rousseau criticizes in a general way "the sterile and cruel pity that is content to complain of evils it could remedy." He contrasts such pity with "active benevolence" aimed at bringing peace and happiness to others. To be effective, this virtue must be truly active, as the adjective implies; "active charity" thus includes a pedagogical dimension that will perfect Émile's education:

"His active charity will soon give him insights that, with a harder heart, he would never have acquired." The young man is brought up according to the precepts of the morality of feeling: "In the interest that he takes in all unfortunates, the means of ending their miseries are never a matter of indifference to him." Although the formative, modern character of Rousseau's active charity inverts the relationship between education and charity that appears in the article "Bienfaisance" in the *Supplément* to the *Encyclopédie,* there is no real contradiction when Rousseau writes: "An education whose principles do not engender charity, however brilliant it might otherwise be, is sadly lacking; only the quality of charity carries within it the whole range of moral duties."

In his *Code de la nature; ou, Le véritable esprit de ses lois* (1755; Code of Nature; or, The True Spirit of Its Laws), the utopian philosopher-historian Morelly emphasizes the concept of charity relative to a Supreme Being whose form remains undefined except in terms of this essential virtue:

> I say (1) that, in the natural order, the idea of *charity,* whether *active* or *passive,* precedes all other ideas and even that of divinity; (2) that this idea, better and far more surely than contemplation of the universe; is the only one that elevates men to the level of a god; (3) that charity gives us a notion of divinity that is truly worthy of the grandeur of its object.

In Morelly's view, charity is not an attribute of the Supreme Being, but rather the only necessary condition for man's existence. Establishing a link between cause and effect, Morelly adds that "the idea of divinity does not become corrupted in man except to the degree that benevolence declines." Morelly also advocates the abolition of property ownership.

Gabriel Bonnot de Mably seems to be touching upon a paradox when he casts suspicion on "the benevolence [that] deserves to occupy one of the first ranks among the subordinate virtues." In fact, Mably argues that the role of charity in society could be a negative one: "In corrupted times, charity too often becomes nothing but a shameful business." Further, Mably opposes "that perfidious charity that is all the more dangerous because it wears the mask of virtue," as well as "true charity" that risks becoming suspicious. Was the philosopher-historian thinking of the abuse of patronage during the decadent period of the

Roman republic? Mably urges his reader to be wary of charity in his *Principes de morale* (1784; Principles in Ethics) in the name of morality, asking "Which is the greater vice, an ingratitude that implies a soul of bronze, or that ridiculous and stupid gratitude that, making us the slave of our benefactor, leads us to serve as the instrument of all his faults and vices?"

The morality of interest understood as the morality of sentiment favored the role of charity, but this new notion did not escape a thorough and critical examination by the baron d'Holbach in Section II of his *Morale universelle* (1776; Universal Ethics), where he argues that "charity is a habitual inclination to contribute to the well-being of those to whom our destiny binds us, in order to deserve their good will and appreciation. Thus, charity cannot be disinterested or devoid of motives." Holbach bases his case on Seneca's definition of kindness, adding that "to be just, charity must address itself to the public good, and reward virtue." The same applies to the sovereign whom Holbach addresses in *Éthocratie ou le gouvernement fondé sur la morale* (1776; Ethocracy; or, Government Founded on Ethics): "Your charitable soul aspires to a glory that is both greater and purer, so as to dry the tears of the unfortunate, heal at the bosom of peace the wounds done to the State, and happily establish morals there."

In his *Catéchisme du citoyen français ou la loi naturelle* (1793; The French Citizen's Catechism; or, Natural Law), the comte de Volney affirms that the character of natural law is "to be equally charitable toward all men, by teaching them all the true means of becoming better and happier." In *Paul et Virginie* (1788; Paul and Virginia), Bernardin de Saint-Pierre aptly expresses his view on the subject when he writes: "Charity is the happiness of virtue; there is nothing greater or more certain on Earth."

JACQUES DOMENECH

See also Virtue

Further Reading

Crocker, Lester G., *Nature and Culture: Ethical Thought in the French Enlightenment,* Baltimore, Maryland: Johns Hopkins University Press, 1963

Domenech, Jacques *L'éthique des Lumières: Les fondements de la morale dans la philosophie française du XVIIIᵉ siècle,* Paris: Vrin, 1989

Mauzi, Robert L., *L'idée du bonheur dans la littérature et la pensée françaises au XVIIIᵉ siècle,* Paris: Colin, 1960

Chemistry

Chemistry by means of visible operations resolves bodies into certain crude principles, such as salts, sulfurs, etc., but physics by delicate speculation acts upon those principles just as chemistry does upon bodies. . . . The spirit of chemistry is more confused, more constrained; it more resembles mixts, in which the principles are intermingled with one another; the spirit of physics is clearer, simpler, and more acute; it finally gets to the origins of things, while the other does not reach their end.
—Bernard Le Bovier de Fontenelle (1699)

This judgment, issued by the first permanent secretary of the Académie Royale des Sciences de Paris (French Royal Academy of Sciences), can be seen as a kind of challenge that would later be taken up by the chemists of the 18th century. By the end of that century, chemistry was recognized as an independent science, legitimate and triumphant, and it enjoyed great social prestige by virtue of its benefits to the public and its many applications in workshops and factories.

How do we account for the rise of chemistry during the 18th century? The traditional answer is to attribute it to the revolution brought about by Antoine Laurent de Lavoisier. Had he not put chemistry on solid experimental and quantitative foundations, and had he not replaced imaginary entities with solid facts? When we attribute the advance of chemical science to the exploits of a single individual, who came on the scene toward the end of the century, we are led to view all previous chemistry as a hodgepodge of empirical practices and of knowledge that was more or less convoluted, obscure, or erroneous. However, this emphasis on Lavoisier results in a paradox: Enlightenment chemistry has often been described as a field "in waiting" for a revolutionary hero who would transform its destiny, but any such retrospective interpretation may have been inspired by the very words of the participants themselves. It was Lavoisier who viewed and carried on his work as a "revolutionary" enterprise, and his contemporaries—disciples as well as adversaries—were quick to adopt and propagate that viewpoint. Further, an image of the founding of modern chemistry as an abrupt departure is reinforced by the inaccessible style of the works of earlier chemists. We may have difficulty following scientific accounts that seem to be muddled and are often unable to understand them because the vocabulary that is used to identify substances and the operations performed on them seems primitive.

However, historians who have taken the trouble to enter the world of these texts tell another story altogether. Those who have attempted to rediscover the chemical practices underlying the texts give us a far richer and more complex picture of the chemistry of the Enlightenment. By the middle of the century, chemistry had already emerged as a progressive and autonomous science, not created by Lavoisier but rather crowned by his "revolution."

The difficulty—and also the inherent interest—of the history of the sciences in the age of the Enlightenment is that the people involved were both the producers and the narrators of the story. Chemists of the 18th century understood the science they practiced in the context of a history that was already marked by revolutions. The theme of revolutions in science (as distinct from scientific revolutions) brings with it contrasting images, depending on whether it is oriented toward the past or the future. In the introduction to his *Dictionnaire de chimie* (1766; Dictionary of Chemistry), which remained authoritative until the end of the century, Pierre Joseph Macquer presents chemistry as having a lengthy history punctuated by a series of revolutions. In chemistry, the "renewal of the sciences" at the turn of the 17th and 18th centuries was brought about by Joachim Becher, "who seems to have seen in a single glance the immense multitude of chemical phenomena," and especially by Becher's disciple Georg Ernst Stahl (1660–1724), who had formulated a general theory described by Macquer as "the most reliable guide one could have for undertaking chemical research" (*Dictionnaire de chimie*). In Diderot's *Encyclopédie*, the article "Chimie," written by Gabriel-François Venel, also evokes the figure of Stahl as the Newton of chemistry, the author of a coherent system that unified the discipline. However, Venel declares that chemistry is waiting for a "new Paracelsus," an audacious, skilled, and enthusiastic chemist who would bring about a "revolution that would put chemistry on the level it deserves." On the one hand, then, 18th-century chemists referred to Stahl in celebrating a revolution that had already taken place, hailed as the dawn of modern chemistry. On the other hand, they still awaited a revolution that, with "noisy ostentation" and a few arguments, would denounce the prejudices afflicting chemistry and enhance its social image. Revolutions in both doctrine and public relations: these two images projected by the chemists of the 18th century suggest ambivalent views of chemistry in the age of the Enlightenment. It was a science that was self-assured and triumphant, a self-proclaimed rival and not a mere servant of physics; at the same time, however, it was a science that was somewhat disdained, lacking recognition and legitimacy. To what extent would this dual image shed new light on it's the evolution of chemistry during that period?

Chemistry as Science and Art

By 1700 chemistry was already a discipline, in the sense of being a subject that was taught. Chemistry courses and textbooks had been developed in Europe during the 17th century. Although this training essentially centered on the preparation of specific substances for use in medicines or the trades, chemistry was thus already an established field of knowledge by the beginning of the 18th century. To understand the composition of substances found in nature and the practical arts: such was the goal generally attributed to chemistry, making it a focal point of interest for a number of trades, including apothecaries, physicians, mineralogists, metallurgists, glassmakers, and dyers.

The profession of chemist did not exist in the modern sense. However, we could define chemists by their use of the laboratory, a common feature of these different practitioners. Since the time of the alchemists, the laboratory had been transformed from a cramped space for solitary work into a space that was open and airy (but generally private), where experiments were conducted for both exploratory and demonstrative purposes. The equipment still resembled that of the alchemists in that the furnace remained the principal instrument, varying according to the sort of combustion required (slow, rapid, intense, etc.). Enlightenment chemistry remained an art of fire; in fact, the theoretical interpretation of combustion shaped chemical doctrine. The notion of phlogiston, or the principle of fire, elaborated at the beginning of the century by Stahl, provided the basis for the organization of contemporary chemical knowledge into a coherent system for classifying chemical reactions. Since Stahl's ideas were spread by means of translation and instruction throughout much of Europe around the middle of the 18th century, phlogiston theory was one of the consensual bases upon which an international community of chemists was founded.

However, in addition to the traditional procedures carried out with fire or heat—distillation, evaporation, use of the double boiler, and so forth—chemists had developed techniques for extraction or analysis of substances in solution, whether by filtration, precipitation, or crystallization. These new laboratory procedures, just as demanding and painstaking as those of fire, pertained to the study of salts. To devotees of Paracelsus, salt, in the singular, was a principal constituent of all substances. At the end of the 17th century, all substances that were readily soluble in water were called "salts" and were characterized by their taste, by color indicators showing them to be either acid or base, and by the deposit that they left at the bottom of a retort after distillation. In 1702 Wilhelm Homberg, a member of the Académie des Sciences, distinguished three kinds of salts: alkaline salts, which are fixed; acid salts, which are volatile; and "medium" salts, which are half fixed, half volatile. These "medium" salts were to furnish chemists with a new field of research into substances in solution. This research was accompanied by a shift of interest from the development of theoretical principles to concrete chemical reactions.

Nonetheless, courses and treatises defined chemistry as the science whose objective is to determine the nature of the principal constituents of substances. This study, like that of reactions in solution, required not only costly instruments but much skill and technique. For maintaining a constant temperature or increasing it very gradually, chemists of the 18th century rarely had access to a thermometer. To control chemical reactions or identify substances, they relied mostly upon their own senses. The tools of their trade—sight, smell, taste, touch—had to be refined and sharpened through long experience in the laboratory. This commonsense empiricism, a source of contempt for the Academician Fontenelle, suited the purpose of chemists intent on affirming the identity of chemistry in contrast with mechanics. Venel's article "Chimie" in the *Encyclopédie* proudly invokes Becher, who characterized chemistry as "a fool's passion" requiring wealth, patience, and obstinacy. The article defines the chemist as "an artist" whose "thermometer is in his finger tips," who masters his field at the cost of long experience and repeated manipulations. The manual and more or less artisanal aspect of chemical practice—previously an obstacle to its academic acceptance—is deftly transformed into a source of originality and even nobility: recognized as a science, chemistry also remains an art. According to Venel's article, chemistry has in its body "a dual language, popular and scientific."

Thus promoted by the great editorial enterprise of the *Encyclopédie*, chemistry became a fashionable curiosity. Guillaume-François Rouelle's courses at the Jardin du Roi (Royal Botanical Garden) in Paris, for example, were frequented not only by future chemists such as Macquer and Lavoisier but also by the marquis de Condorcet, Anne-Robert-Jacques Turgot, Jean-Jacques Rousseau, and Denis Diderot. Some of the chemists of the Académie des Sciences became involved in industry as advisers in the manufacture of dyes, or even as manufacturers themselves, although in France chemistry was associated more with culture than with industry.

In the countries of northern Europe, the tension between the artisanal practice of chemistry and the ideal of an academic science was resolved in a different manner. In 1718, at the University of Leiden, Hermann Boerhaave practically apologized for introducing science that was crude and rough, like its symbols of fire, smoke, and ashes. However, as the rise of mining and metallurgy mobilized the talents of chemists, who were seen as advancing the economic development of their countries, chemistry progressed at the universities based upon its reputation as a useful science. This was reflected in the marked increase in the number of posts for professors of chemistry at schools of medicine in Germany. Stahl had already taught chemistry at the University of Halle from 1694 to 1715; there were three professors in 1720 and 20 in 1780. In Sweden, chemistry was promoted to the rank of a university discipline with the double identity of a science that was both pure and applied. The categories of "pure" and "applied," introduced in 1751 by Johann Gottschalk Wallerius, a chemist from Uppsala, are doubly noteworthy. By treating chemistry as a fully fledged science, of which the arts were merely applications, the chronological order of the development of the field—from a skilled trade into a science—was reversed; the trades were thereafter seen as dependent upon the science. By virtue of its impact on economic production, chemistry was deemed worthy of development and cultivation in university teaching.

Chemistry was actively involved in various movements that marked Europe during the Enlightenment, including cameralism and encyclopedism. In just half a century (from about 1710 to 1760), it had won both encyclopedic and academic status. Was this legitimization the result merely of professional strategy, or did it correspond to an actual transformation of the body of chemical knowledge?

Affinities and Salts

An initial consideration shows the difficulty of defining chemistry as a discipline in the age of the Enlightenment. Chemists, studying the three kingdoms of nature (animal, plant, mineral), were forced to share their territory with other sciences—physics, mineralogy, botany, and zoology, for example. They could therefore define their science only through a particular relationship to the natural world. They seem to have seized upon a special attribute that was highly prized in the society of the Enlightenment: utility for the public interest.

That did not resolve the ambiguity of the encyclopedic status of chemistry, however. To the extent that it was seen as a discipline under the banner of utility, chemistry was difficult to integrate within the ambitious theoretical program of natural philosophy. This explains the complaints of such scientists as Venel and Macquer concerning the poor image of their science among the public. At the start of the century, Fontenelle envisioned chemistry's eventual integration into Cartesian mechanics. The success and renown of a chemist such as Nicolas Lemery, who endeavored to interpret chemical reactions in terms of corpuscles—soft and patterned, smooth or rough, hooked or pointed—made it

seem that he was on the right track. A still more promising future opened up with Newtonian mechanics. Newton, in the 31st query of his *Opticks* (1704), had offered chemists an organizing principle and a line of inquiry by treating affinity as a particular case of universal attraction. Yet this program, when taken up and defended half a century later by the illustrious naturalist the comte de Buffon, was no more tempting to chemists than the dynamism of the Croatian scholar Rudjer Josip Bošković. Rather, it was to be more from laboratory practice that they would forge the concepts from which, little by little, a definition of their discipline would emerge.

In order to give a theoretical account of affinities, most chemists had chosen to give the concept of affinity a status that was essentially operational, a tool for organizing their empirical knowledge, classifying substances, and predicting their behavior. In 1718 Étienne-François Geoffroy had published a "Table des différents rapports observés entre les différentes substances" (Table of Various Relationships Observed among Various Substances), which was based on a series of experiments in displacement. Experiments in displacement conducted in a systematic manner by Torbern Bergman on thousands of substances resulted in tables of affinity published in his *Dissertation sur les attractions électives* (1785; Essay on Elective Attractions) and a new concept of affinity. This was not an essential attribute that could define an isolated substance, such as reflectivity, or the dryness and humidity that characterized Aristotle's elements; it was simply a relationship defined in a comparative manner, measured by displacement reactions.

This orientation toward a knowledge of relationships was concurrent with the experimental study of salts, which distanced chemists from mechanist speculations about corpuscles and enabled them to introduce theoretical innovations. Little by little, Homberg's "medium salt" came to designate a "neutral salt," a salt in which an acid is closely bonded to an alkali or a metal, in a proportion sufficient to saturate the base. They characterized it in operational terms: if we add a little acid, then the effervescence stops or the salt no longer changes the color of the indicators. The chemist had the practical possibility, through experimentation, of decomposing a salt and then reconstituting it. For example, in 1736 Henri Louis Duhamel managed to obtain fixed alkali from sea salt and demonstrated that by adding marine acid to that alkali he could reconstitute the sea salt. In short, a material obtained by extraction from a natural substance could be created in the laboratory. The chemistry of salts slowly but surely eroded the traditional notion of a chemical substance. The natural origin, the place from which it was extracted, characterized less a substance than the path by which it was obtained. The constituent principles (salt, sulfur, mercury) no longer sufficed to account for a natural substance's particular characteristics, because the study of medium salts had demonstrated the interchangeability of the bodies known as "principles." For example, the causticity of certain substances that Meyer attributed to a special caustic ingredient, called *acidum pingue*, is redefined in Macquer's *Dictionnaire* as "a tendency to combine," because of the nonsaturation of certain bases.

Finally, the relationship between neutral salts and the acids and bases that formed them led to the redefinition of a key concept in chemistry: the mixt. If Stahl was generally perceived as the founding hero of chemistry in the 18th century, it was not only for his theory of phlogiston but also for a distinction that was important to his successors. According to Stahl, the specific phenomenon of chemistry is "mixtive union"—not to be confused with aggregation, a purely mechanical union that merely reflects the general properties of homogenous matter defined by mass and movement. The mixt, in contrast, unites heterogeneous constituents into a homogenous substance that changes properties when it is decomposed. Only the chemist could carry out the analyses of mixts and the characterization of their properties. In the middle of the 18th century, chemists, determined to assert the specificity of their discipline in opposition to mechanics, revived that distinction. Together with the chemistry of neutral salts, the distinction undermined the archaic notion of properties inherent in "principles." The article "Mixte et mixtion" (Mixt and Mixtion) in the *Encyclopédie* emphasizes that the properties of each of the constituent principles disappear—or, at least, are "masked" or "suspended"—and make way for a new substance with different properties. It goes on to add that a mixt is characterized by the fact that the constituent principles combine in fixed proportions. Thus, the quantification of constituents, initially developed in the study of the formation of neutral salts, would gradually become an important objective of chemistry, to the point of constituting a new branch, stoichiometry, or the study of the proportion of the elements, founded by Jeremias B. Richter.

Gases and Measurement

The development of quantitative experiments marked the end of the century, in part as a response to practical problems confronting chemists. At the same time, these experiments facilitated chemistry's integration into the larger scientific culture of the Enlightenment. How to identify a host of new substances by analysis: such was the sort of problem that led chemists to make increasingly frequent use of scales, and with ever-greater precision. The salts, then new metals (cobalt, nickel, etc.), and especially gases—collected in an apparatus contrived by Stephen Hales—seemed to defy the qualitative and sensory methods so familiar to chemists. The need to account for gases absorbed or emitted in the course of chemical reactions, as in certain physiological phenomena, opened a new field of investigation in the 1760s. This "pneumatic chemistry" was designated as revolutionary from the 18th century onward.

The impetus for the study of gases came from Great Britain. In Edinburgh, where he was preparing a medical thesis on *magnesia alba* (carbonate of magnesium, then used as a purgative), Joseph Black, a student of the famous Scottish professor William Cullen, submitted the air given off by effervescence (when he poured a little acid on *magnesia alba*) to various chemical tests. Using this method, he identified "fixed air" (carbon dioxide) and showed that it is the same as that given off during the respiration of an animal. An invisible substance "fixed" in a compound: here was a concept that presented a host of problems. How did it become fixed in bodies, how was it absorbed or released? Black addressed these questions by concentrating on heat. Not really knowing the nature of heat, he decided to study the relationships between two measurable entities: the quantity of heat and the temperature. He designated the heat fixed in the interior of bodies as "latent heat."

While he was more interested in displacements and fixation than in the gases themselves, Black directed his research toward gases in order to isolate and identify them by means of a battery of tests. In 1764 David MacBride showed that fixed air differed from atmospheric air and that it asphyxiated animals; and Henry Cavendish showed that fixed air is a product of the combustion of coal. Joseph Priestley, who had studied fixed air emitted by fermentation vats in a brewery in Leeds, defined its characteristic properties: it does not sustain combustion; it is unfit for animal respiration but suitable for plants, which have the power to render it breathable again; finally, it seemed capable of healing certain illnesses, such as scurvy and respiratory ailments. The latter led Priestley, seeking a way to administer it in liquid form, to invent artificial sparkling water. In Germany, England, Italy, the Netherlands, Switzerland, Austria, and elsewhere, scientists were enthralled with this "fixed air" and discussed it earnestly: was it good or bad to breathe, healthy or harmful?

The collection of gases yielded spectacular results. In 1766 Henry Cavendish isolated and identified the hydrogen emitted by metals eaten away by an acid, and named it "inflammable air" because it had the property of burning. Karl Wilhelm Scheele, a Swedish apothecary, isolated a dozen new gases, notably acids, including chlorine, which he identified as "dephlogisticated" marine acid, "fire air," thought to be capable of absorbing phlogiston (known today as oxygen), and *air corrompu* ("corrupt air") that was impure and unhealthy for animal respiration (probably what is known today as nitrogen). The champion of the field was Joseph Priestley, who isolated and characterized a number of gases: gaseous hydrochloric acid, ammonia, sulfurous gas, hydrogen sulfide, hydrogen phosphate, ethylene, nitrogen, which he named "phlogisticated air," and oxygen, which he named "dephlogisticated air." From our perspective, such a record of achievement should have toppled the doctrine of the four elements, which made air a unique principle: but not at all. These new "airs," considered to be derivatives of elementary air, did not directly threaten the traditional concept. On the contrary, phlogiston, until then invisible and hidden, gained an empirical reality once it could be plausibly identified as Cavendish's "inflammable air" in its nearly pure state.

How, then, did Lavoisier manage to overturn this chemical tradition based upon the four principal elements? Since Lavoisier had doubted the role of phlogiston in combustion and calcination since 1772, his work was often presented as an ongoing methodical program to debunk phlogiston theory. Lavoisier himself encouraged this view when he delivered the final blow to that doctrine in 1785, and allowed his concept to be christened the "antiphlogiston theory." However, if we are careful not to let hindsight distort our view of Lavoisier his intellectual pathway to that point appears to have been simultaneously more ordinary and more complex. Lavoisier was neither the only chemist nor the first to criticize phlogiston, which had already been vigorously attacked. In 1772 he did not yet have the means—or even the intention—of discrediting it. If one considers the entirety of his work, as embodied in some 50 dissertations read at the Académie des Sciences in the 1770s and 1780s, we find that Lavoisier also worked on a great variety of subjects particularly concerned with gases. Unlike many of the multitude of chemists devoted to the study of "airs," Lavoisier did not isolate or discover any gases. However, he distinguished himself by his determination to repeat the experiments of his English colleagues, using his own methods and submitting them to the judgment of his scales. He did not discover oxygen, which had already been isolated and identified by Priestley, as "dephlogisticated air," and by Scheele, but, having replicated the experimental reduction of *mercury* per se (oxide of mercury), he reinterpreted the results in a radically different manner. He saw not just one more specimen in a collection of different gases, but a component of atmospheric air. Thus, the experiments of combustion and reduction became

analytic tools. Lavoisier also distinguished himself by his concern for advancing theoretical interpretations of his experiments. Alternating continually between experiment and theory, he ventured hypotheses on combustion, the nature of acids, the gaseous state, respiration, and perspiration, so that each of these phenomena came to be seen as a piece of the whole. The concept of air as a state, and no longer a substantial principle, played a major role in the elaboration of his theories. If the solid, liquid, or gaseous state of a body could be explained by the quantity of caloric it contained, air lost its essential function as a principle. The notion of caloric also furnished an argument against phlogiston, since it could explain the production of heat or light in combustion: the combination of a fuel with oxygen liberates the caloric combined with oxygen in the air.

We see, then, that Lavoisier did not really reject the old notion of principles. Even though the imponderable caloric could be measured by the calorimeter, Lavoisier's oxygen played the traditional role of a principle analogous to phlogiston: an omnipresent component endowed with a particular property—the acidity to which it owes its name—and an agent of chemical reactions. And yet he mobilized considerable financial, technical, and human resources to deprive water of its status as a principle. Lavoisier wanted to make the decomposition and recomposition of that element into an historic event, and the behest of a commission on ballooning, he was invited to study how to produce hydrogen on a large scale. He staged a formal experiment of analysis and synthesis that lasted two days in February 1785.

Reforms in Chemical Nomenclature

Determined to overturn the theory of principal elements, Lavoisier proposed in the 1780s an alternative theory designating the element as the "end term attained by analysis." Although it was by no means new, this definition made sense in the context of the *Méthode de nomenclature* (Method of Chemical Nomenclature) published by Louis-Bernard Guyton de Morveau, Lavoisier, Claude- Louis Berthollet, and Antoine-François de Fourcroy in 1787. This reform of the language, which finally precipitated the break with the phlogiston theory, took place within the framework of a project for a revised nomenclature undertaken by several chemists, notably Macquer, Bergman, and Guyton de Morveau. In 1782, as editor of the "Dictionnaire de chimie" (Dictionary of Chemistry) in the *Encyclopédie méthodique* (Methodical Encyclopedia), Guyton de Morveau had outlined a reform of chemical nomenclature by gallicizing Greek terms. The general principle was that the name would reflect the composition of a substance and, for simple bodies, their most characteristic property. In cases that were uncertain or contentious, Guyton, persuaded that language is a matter of convention, proposes an arbitrary or neutral name. The project— taken up by Lavoisier and his disciples just as they were launching their assault on the phlogiston theory—was to be resumed and retooled in accordance with Lavoisier's doctrine positing oxygen as the principle of combustion and acidity. Faithful to Étienne Bonnot de Condillac's philosophy, Lavoisier declared that it was "natural logic" that governed the new designations. From Condillac's *La logique* (1780; Logic), Lavoisier borrowed the precepts that to remake a language is to remake the science; and that analysis—understood to work in both directions, from the complex to the simple, and from the simple to the complex—is the only method capable of keeping us from error and prejudice. A language based upon this "natural logic" was, therefore, much more than a mere vocabulary; and a "method of naming" was more a program than a finished structure. Finally, whatever their degree of composition, compounds were always considered to be binary.

The new nomenclature, which remains the basis of today's language of chemistry, was initially perceived as a weapon in the war against the phlogiston theory and caused a lively controversy. Nonetheless, despite reservations and the criticisms directed at certain denominations ("oxygen" because it was doubted that all acids contained it, and *azote,* which means "unsuitable for animal life," because in fact most gases do not support animal life), the new nomenclature was adopted virtually intact and was taught throughout Europe by 1800. This rapid triumph was due not only to a vigorous promotional campaign conducted by Lavoisier and his circle but also to the fact that the need for reform and its directive principle—from simple to complex—were the subject of broad consensus. Moreover, beyond Lavoisier's "revolution," the dualism of compound names, entirely in harmony with the chemistry of salts and displacements, formed a "bridge" between the chemistry of the 18th century and the electrochemical dualism of the 19th.

In 1789 Lavoisier published his *Traité élémentaire de chimie* (Elements of Chemistry), generally considered as the first modern chemistry textbook. Addressing "beginners," it purports to develop concepts of chemistry based upon facts. In proceeding from the simple to the complex, Lavoisier undertakes to reorganize all of chemistry—both in theory and practice—in the hope of enabling chemists to complete their training in two or three years. However, like his colleagues Fourcroy and Jean Antoine Chaptal, Lavoisier was unable to realize that goal. To be sure, he imbued chemistry with an analytic logic that serves to distance it from natural history;

but in identifying analysis as the goal of chemistry, Lavoisier neither overturned nor renovated the *entire* discipline. Not only did he leave the chemistry of salts untouched, but he excluded as irresolvable the question of the constituent elements of matter and, as being too complicated for beginners, the study of affinities.

Lavoisier did not "found" modern chemistry, but rather contributed to changing the status of chemistry during the age of the Enlightenment. Condillac's philosophical patronage placed chemistry within a general cultural movement, and quantitative methods, as well as the growing role of measurement and precision, significantly transformed laboratory procedures in chemistry, aligning those procedures with those of experimental physics. A chemist adopting Lavoisier's approach would no longer need the "keen eye" of an artist. He had access to thermometers, a calorimeter, gazometers, hydrometers, and, especially, precision scales. The demand for measurement was not new either, but Lavoisier pushed it further than most of his contemporaries because he could afford to have sophisticated instruments made and because he participated in the dominant culture of the time, notably at the Académie des Sciences, which tended to make measurement the criterion of all scientific judgment.

BERNADETTE BENSAUDE-VINCENT

See also Académie Royale des Sciences de Paris; Affinity; Corpuscle; Gas; Heat; Mineralogy; Phlogiston; Remedies; Science: Collections; Thermometry

Further Reading

Bensaude-Vincent, Bernadette, *Lavoisier: Mémoires d'une révolution,* Paris: Flammarion, 1993

Donovan, A.L., *Philosophical Chemistry in the Scottish Enlightenment,* Edinburgh: Edinburgh University Press, 1975

Donovan, A.L., editor, *The Chemical Revolution: Essays in Reinterpretation,* Philadelphia, Pennsylvania: History of Science Society, 1988

Duhem, Pierre, *Le mixte et la combinaison chimique: Essai sur l'évolution d'une idée,* Paris: Naud, 1902; reprint, Paris: Fayard, 1985

Holmes, Frederic Lawrence, *Eighteenth-Century Chemistry As an Investigative Enterprise,* Berkeley: Office for History of Science and Technology, University of California at Berkeley, 1989

Hufbauer, Karl, *The Formation of the German Chemical Community, 1720–1795,* Berkeley: University of California Press, 1982

Meinel, Christoph, "Theory or Practice? The Eighteenth-Century Debate on the Scientific Status of Chemistry," *Ambix* 30 (1983)

Metzger, Hélène, *Les doctrines chimiques en France du début du XVIIᵉ à la fin du XVIIIᵉ siècle,* Paris:

Presses Universitaires de France, 1923; reprint, Paris: Blanchard, 1969

Metzger, Hélène, *Newton, Stahl, Boerhaave et la doctrine chimique*, Paris: Alcan, 1930; reprint, Paris: Blanchard, 1974

Stengers, Isabelle, "Ambiguous Affinity: The Newtonian Dream of Chemistry in the 18th Century," in Michel Serres, editor, *A History of Scientific Thought,* Oxford and Cambridge, Massachusetts: Blackwell, 1995

Childbirth

The 18th century saw the advent of profound changes in delivery practices as well as the beginnings of obstetrics as a science. Traditionally, childbirth had taken place among women, under the direction of a midwife. Often illiterate, the midwife was generally an older woman who was trained on the job and whose reputation was built on her successful assistance in several difficult deliveries; she knew how to recite the baptismal rites correctly and enjoyed the trust of the village. Very few midwives, referred to in French as *sage-femmes* (literally, "wise women") had received any formal training. At the beginning of the century there was only one school of midwifery in Europe, the Maternité at the Hôtel-Dieu in Paris, which trained about a dozen midwives every three months; under the direction of a senior midwife, the trainees acquired hands-on experience by attending the deliveries of poor women who came to the Hôtel-Dieu to give birth. This training was highly prized and even attracted foreigners, but it was restricted to a small, select group—roughly 20 women a year, then about 50 after the reform in 1735—who went on to practice in the affluent neighborhoods of cities.

In France, Germany, and England since the 16th century, medical literature, written entirely by men, had criticized midwives' exclusive control over the event of childbirth. Little by little, physicians and surgeons refined their understanding of anatomy and granted themselves the right to intervene in the traditionally feminine and hitherto off-limits space of the birthing room. In the 18th century the critics of midwifery became increasingly virulent in support of the populationist ideal, which emphasized "saving" mothers and infants, too often the victims of the "incompetence," "errors," and "prejudices" of these "coarse and ignorant women." As Raulin put it in 1770: "Every day, they cost the lives of mother and infant simultaneously, because of their lack of the knowledge that is necessary and requisite to save them." The most virulent denunciation of the midwives was an anonymous pamphlet published in Languedoc in 1782, the *Requête en plainte présentée à nos seigneurs des États du Languedoc par les enfants à naître contre les prétendues sages-femmes* (Petition of Complaint Presented to Our Lords of the Estates of Languedoc on Behalf of Unborn Children against the So-Called Wise Women), written in the name of the fetuses, doubtless by Jean-François Icart, a physician from Castres:

> We have no certainty of coming into the world. We tremble as we risk showing ourselves in it, as we are continually mistreated by certain women who are known as midwives. . . . They bruise us, flay us, tear us without pity; often, they treat us even worse: they decapitate us, they give us black eyes, they break our limbs, they tear us to pieces.

Clearly, the physicians had numerous complaints against the midwives: pressure to finish quickly caused them to act violently, pulling heedlessly at whatever presented itself, whether a head, an arm, or a foot. In difficult deliveries, they often believed, wrongly, that the infant was dead, and in order to remove it from the mother would unhesitatingly pull it to pieces with hooks. In the case of France, this bad opinion of midwives was confirmed in practice by the outcome of two inquiries conducted by the comptroller general in the *intendances* in 1737 and 1786. Parish priests and physicians were required to evaluate the level of training and the quality of care provided by the midwives in their communities. Their complaints, which were fairly widespread, attest both to negligent attitudes and to lethal inexperience on the part of midwives.

In this context, two complementary trends developed: a push for the use of the services of obstetricians and the introduction of courses on delivery for midwives. The movement that incited men to take an interest in "the art of delivery" went back to the 16th century but it had taken nearly 100 years to overcome resistance based on the antiquated idea that it was "indecent" for them to practice it. From 1650 onward, physicians or surgeons were called with less reluctance to the bedsides of affluent women; in this they followed the example given by Louis XIV himself, who in 1663 called one of them to assist Mademoiselle de La Vallière in giving birth. From the beginning of the 18th century, a small-town obstetrician such as Mauquest de La Motte, who practiced at Valognes in the Cotentin peninsula, had patients at all levels of society (although it is true that in this period Normandy was a province that was particularly open to innovation). The obstetrician's ability to overcome prejudices and establish his reputation depended on his success in deliveries that were known to be difficult and were referred to as "unnatural." In the 18th century a true science of childbirth developed from two sources: an updated understanding of anatomy that made it possible to establish a precise typology of presentations and positions; and clinical observations that provided precise measurements of the pelvis and the uterus. These scientific advances culminated, at the end of the century, in the first statistical series compiled by the major hospitals, such as the Maternité de Port-Royal in Paris. It was after 1730 that obstetrics truly came into its own as a science, with a generation of enterprising men led by Levret in France and Smellie in Britain. They constituted a real "Europe of obstetricians" through their very close international contacts: young practitioners were trained by undertaking obstetric "grand tours." The teaching hospital at Strasbourg, created in 1728 by the surgeon Jean-Jacques Fried, was a model that was often imitated, notably in Vienna and Edinburgh, and these newly formed practitioners tirelessly circulated, met, and corresponded with one another. All of enlightened Europe's learned societies were enthralled by the great debates that shook the world of obstetrics: should physicians avail of the "instruments" (forceps and levers) invented simultaneously in France and England at the end of the 17th century? The French made frequent—and sometimes inappropriate—use of them, driven by their determination to replace midwives, who practiced with bare hands. By contrast, following a great public campaign in the 1760s that criticized excessive interventionism, the English became cautious and aware of the harmful side effects of such instruments. Trained midwives such as Elisabeth Nihell of London led the fight in England against the misuse of instruments. Another fundamental debate, which was particularly lively in France in the closing years of the century, concerned the legitimacy of recourse to cesareans or symphysiotomies, particularly when the mother's pelvis was too narrow as a result of rickets. At the time, such operations were a last resort. They were crude and were often performed rashly—with no thought for the disastrous aftereffects of the operation—by very celebrated

surgeons, such as Baudelocque or Sigault, who wanted to win glory for themselves by salvaging the most desperate situations. Colleagues such as Sacombe, who were more attentive or more concerned for the health of their patients, were harshly critical of their peers in these cases.

These theoretical debates did not impede the growing use of obstetricians by all women who could afford their services, mainly in cities. For example, researcher Jacques Gélis has reconstructed Pierre Robin's clientele of from 1770 to 1797 in the city of Reims. Obstetricians gained ground first and foremost because mothers wanted safer deliveries. Skilled physicians trained in the new science of obstetrics and provided with lifesaving instruments appeared to be more competent than the old midwives who had bad, or very little, training. As recorded in the *Encyclopédie,* it became a commonplace to say, "a surgeon delivers better than a midwife."

At the same time that the practice of obstetrics was taking hold throughout Europe, training courses for midwives also developed. These courses were one of the foundations of the public health policies established in the second half of the century in the context of "populationist" ideals. In order to promote population growth—and thus increase the human resources of the country—it became urgent to save the lives of more mothers and newborns. From this time onward, the Church itself, under the impetus of Pope Benedict XIV, was concerned with saving bodies as much as souls. In France, under the aegis of the comptroller general, Madame Du Coudray, a midwife who had been trained in Paris, initiated the organization of traveling courses in delivery techniques, which lasted from 1759 until the French Revolution. Teaching materials, adapted for students who were often illiterate, were relatively new: simple manuals, organized as questions and answers and known as "catechisms," and above all "demonstration machines"—mannequins made of wicker, leather, and cloth that represented a woman's pelvis and were accompanied by several flexible dolls that could be put in every position inside the mannequins, so that the students could practice. After Madame Du Coudray's tenure, local surgeons paid by *intendances* and trained in the new methods continued the teaching. The students, recruited in the provinces with the help of parish priests, were generally young, between 20 and 35, and were open-minded. They came to the cities for several weeks, underwent intensive but essentially simulated training with the "machines," and then returned to their villages where they became responsible for deliveries. They were aware that they were practicing a real profession and expected to be paid accordingly, which had not been the case for the former midwives whose function had in fact been equivalent to domestic service, meagerly compensated in kind. Some villagers resisted the new-style midwife and continued to call in the traditional midwife; ferocious jealousies were sometimes unleashed between the two women, to which some parish priests were helpless witnesses. Nevertheless, between 1760 and 1794, a total of more than 10,000 new midwives were trained in France, which must have made thousands of births a bit less dangerous.

The training courses in delivery that were implemented throughout enlightened Europe can be classified into two main types. The French model, financed from public funds and controlled by municipal or state authorities, was implemented in northern Italy, Switzerland, and Germany. The English model, in contrast, was based on private courses organized by famous obstetricians; training took place on site at small hospices of 20 to 80 beds, in London, Edinburgh, Dublin, and other cities, and was financed by support from wealthy and philanthropic individuals.

Between the beginning and the end of the century, for many women in cities and large towns and even in particularly open-minded rural areas, the conditions of childbirth changed. Women still gave birth at home, but instead of the uneducated midwives of the past, there was a trained midwife or an obstetrician present. It became commonplace to air out the birthing room instead of sealing it up, and to ask needless spectators to leave, eliminating the noisy involvement of the *commères* (chattering neighbors) of earlier times. The mother-to-be was no longer allowed to walk around, stand, sit, or squat while waiting to give birth. Instead, she had to remain lying on her back, the position that was the most "decent" but was also the most conve-

nient for the obstetrician or the midwife. In difficult cases, instead of placing her trust in the traditional amulets and prayers, the mother now trusted in the dexterity of the skilled man, equipped with instruments so different from the old midwives' hooks, who promised to deliver her baby safely and quickly.

The process of childbirth thus entered the realm of medicine during the 18th century, with the intervention of personnel trained at the bedside of expectant mothers. The division of labor between two types of specialists dates from this same period. The midwife could perform only normal deliveries using her bare hands; in cases of "unnatural" deliveries (those with complications) she had to call in the physician, who alone had the privilege of intervening with instruments. The next stage of this shift toward medical technology occurred in the 20th century, with the transition from giving birth at home to delivering the child in a hospital.

MARIE-FRANCE MOREL

See also Children

Further Reading

Gélis, Jacques, *La sage-femme ou le médecin: Une nouvelle conception de la vie,* Paris: Fayard, 1988
Gélis, Jacques, *History of Childbirth: Fertility, Pregnancy, and Birth in Early Modern Europe,* translated by Rosemary Morris, Cambridge: Polity Press, and Boston: Northeastern University Press, 1991 (original French edition, 1984)
Laget, Mireille, *Naissances: L'accouchement avant l'âge de la clinique,* Paris: Seuil, 1982

Children

Childhood was one of the most fashionable topics in Europe during the 18th century. Taking up, in a secularized form, the optimistic concept of the child that had been developed by the Church since the end of the Middle Ages, Enlightenment thinkers—especially Jean-Jacques Rousseau, in *Émile, ou, De l'éducation* (1762; *Émile; or, Concerning Education*)—insisted on the natural goodness of the small child and recommended an education that would respect the child's personality and natural inclinations without artifice or constraints. Moreover, the fear of depopulation and the resulting emergence of the populationist ideal placed some very concrete problems of motherhood and child rearing on

the agenda. In this context, there were numerous works, in every genre, devoted to the "preservation" or "physical education" of children. These works were produced by the same intellectuals who frequented the academies and scholarly societies of the period: administrators, engineers, doctors, philosophers, and members of the clergy. The most notable works were translated and enjoyed a wide circulation. In addition to *Émile,* several other French books, including works by Desessartz, Ballexserd, and Raulin, went through numerous editions and translations abroad, and all of Europe took part in the elaboration of theories about early childhood. In Britain the most prominent authors were Harris, Cadogan, Underwood, Armstrong, and Buchan; in Germany, Zückert, Frank, Faust, and Hufeland; in Sweden, Rosen von Rosenstein; and in Italy, Baldini. The century's bestsellers were translated into at least three European languages.

For those states that began to institute health policies, the issue of children's health was one of the primary targets. Once born, children had to be kept from dying, for one in four did not live beyond their first year and only one in two reached adulthood. In order to "save" children, these states had to direct families, and above all mothers, to observe numerous physical prescriptions, expounded in the works cited above. These directives included breast-feeding by the mother alone, washing diapers and bathing the child daily, eliminating the custom of swaddling, and practicing inoculation. These new techniques—called "medicinal" (M. Brouzet, 1754), "corporal" (Desessartz, 1760), or "physical" (Ballexserd, 1762)—could be put into practice only within the narrow confines of the nuclear family. The "new" mothers and fathers who read these works on the medicalization of early childhood care and who applied the new ideas were generally themselves the offspring of the lower nobility or the upper bourgeoisie. For these parents, the health of their children became a constant concern, as is evidenced, for example, by the family correspondence of General De Martange, the Rolands, and the marquis de Bombelles. These families, for whom the "discovery of childhood" was a reality, were the pioneers of the movement for the medicalization of daily life that began in the 18th century and has continued into our own times.

Pleas in favor of maternal breast-feeding dominated the literature on the "preservation" of infants. It was not a new topic. One of the founding texts on the subject, a work dating from the end of the fourth century A.D. but still frequently cited during the 18th century, was a moralizing speech by Favorinus of Arles to a mother from the noble classes. Favorinus insisted it was the duty of every mother to give her child the milk that nature had destined for him or her. The specifically medical reasons put forward by 18th-century treatises were more original, as authors contended that failing to breast-feed could expose the mother and to her child to serious disorders. Advocates of breast-feeding held that a mother who let her milk dry up risked being poisoned by the effects of "resorbed milk," but, in contrast, a mother who breast-fed would enjoy good health and would even experience physical pleasure when she nursed. In addition, a mother had no right to deprive her infant of the benefits of colostrum, the first, very thin milk whose wholesome properties the physicians of the Enlightenment had recently rediscovered after centuries of neglect. The implication, then, was that mothers should begin breast-feeding their babies very soon after birth. Numerous instructive manuals aimed at mothers, in particular the widely circulated manuals by Madame Le Rebours and by Desessartz, detailed the practical aspects of breast-feeding, explaining how to prepare the nipples from pregnancy onward, how to satisfy the infant on demand, how to wean the infant from the moment when his or her teeth began to grow, and how to avoid becoming pregnant while nursing—a task that required explaining to the husband that his conjugal rights were outweighed by the health of the baby.

A minority of authors—such as Van Helmont, Brouzet, and Vandermonde—challenged the views of those advocating maternal breast-feeding in all cases. Sometimes, they argued, the milk of a mother who was overworked or weak would not be good for her baby. It would be better to feed these babies with gruel and moistened bread, although that must be done under the close supervision of a specialist, for the physician's skill could bring about an improvement in the infant's health. This position was an entirely theoretical resolution of the opposition between art/artifice and nature that so preoccupied Enlightenment thinkers. Other very common themes of medical discourse included the condemnation of gruel, which at that period was given to babies during the first weeks of life in order to "condition" the baby's stomach and accelerate growth. Physicians demonstrated that gruel was indigestible and a source of fatal "obstructions." The condemnation of swaddling was equally virulent. Far from helping to train the soft body of the infant, swaddling was deemed a constraint that prevented the harmonious growth intended by nature.

The influence of this medical discourse on maternal practices was limited to the elite. Some women of the upper classes, having read *Émile*, undertook to raise their children "à la Jean-Jacques," breast-feeding their babies themselves, bathing them every day, and dressing them in light clothing without swaddling. Yet this fashion did not last long, even though some philanthropic individuals, anxious to promote population growth, succeeded in founding institutions, in Lyon and Paris, for the purpose of giving subsidies to the mothers of poor families so that those mothers could breast-feed their own babies instead of placing them with a wet nurse.

The Role of Wet Nurses

In reality, the paradox was that, in the very period of the "discovery of childhood" (see Ariès), there had never been so many infants placed with wet nurses. In this regard, the situation in France was exceptional. In the 18th century wet-nursing was no longer practiced exclusively by noble and bourgeois families, but rather by people of all classes in the large cities. Parisian statistics are the best known. According to estimates by police lieutenant Lenoir in 1780, each year only 1,000 out of 21,000 newborns were breast-fed by their mothers. Two thousand babies born into the wealthier classes were placed directly by their parents in the homes of wet nurses in the close suburbs who were paid between 10 and 25 livres a month. Other infants were sent all over the Parisian basin, sometimes at several days' traveling distance from the capital, to women who were paid between five and eight livres a month. The newborns sent to the countryside remained there for one or two years, depending on their parents' financial resources. Why was this practice so popular? Traditionally, the wealthier classes wanted the woman to return to her social role as soon as possible after giving birth. Breast-feeding a baby on demand was totally incompatible with such a woman's social functions. The newborn was regarded as an uninteresting little "thing," and breast-feeding was seen as a domestic chore.

The motives of parents in lower social positions in the 18th century were somewhat different. In contrast to customs a century earlier, women often worked in collaboration with their husbands in small shops or stalls, and this sort of labor seemed less and less compatible with breast-feeding and the daily rearing of an infant. The women probably also took into account the new idea of the distinctive nature of urban life. Women in the city wanted to act more "civilized" than those in the countryside. City dwellers lived in a more artificial world and could easily imitate the nobles and upper bourgeoisie in dress, language, and customs. For the urban masses of the age of the Enlightenment, therefore, wet-nursing was a status symbol, a way to show that they belonged to an urbanized society and were superior to the rustic peasants who constituted 80 percent of the population and continued to breast-feed their own babies. A final, more "modern," reason for sending infants to out-of-town wet nurses was the awareness on the part of parents of the dangers of polluted city air. The rapidly growing popular quarters of the cities were often unsanitary, and their "miasmas" were regarded as dangerous for babies. By sending their newborns into the countryside, where they could breathe clean air and feed on the healthy milk of robust peasant women, parents gave their children a good start in life.

The use of out-of-town wet nurses by new-style city dwellers would have been impossible on such a large scale if the French provinces had not been overpopulated, a fact that forced many women from the lower peasantry to come to the city to find babies in need of their services. The pay peasant women received for wet-nursing permitted their families to live just above the poverty level. The dominance of cities, which had become richer overall, over country districts, which were overpopulated (particularly in France), explains the glut of wet nurses that doubtless encouraged a proportional demand for their services.

The practical aspects of wet-nursing are well known, for this activity was highly regulated, at least in Paris. Ever since the Middle Ages, there had been bureaus staffed by women known as "recommenders," who recruited wet nurses in the provinces and kept registers. There were four bureaus in 1715, the year of the first great royal declaration regulating their activities. From 1769 on, a single bureau, located on the rue Neuve Saint Augustin and controlled by the lieutenant general of police, held a monopoly on placements in the capital. Before coming to the city, a wet nurse had to ask her parish priest for a certificate "of good life and moral values," mentioning the age of her last child. In principle, the prospective wet nurse should have begun lactating between seven months and two years before she applied for a position.

On the journey from the countryside to the city, a wet nurse was accompanied by a male or female intermediary known as a "runner." Once in Paris, she stayed at the bureau while waiting to be hired by a father whose wife had just given birth. The wet nurse's return trip to her village with the Parisian baby, still accompanied by her "runner," was made by cart, by horse-drawn barge on the Seine, by donkey, and often on foot for the final kilometers. This journey often proved harmful or fatal to the babies, as is evident from the number of deaths of Parisian babies recorded in parishes situated along the major roads.

In her village, the wet nurse was paid every month by her "runner," who collected the money from the parents in the city and kept a register of placements. Visits by the parents were very rare, except in the cases of wealthy families, for distance was an insurmountable obstacle for most. The wet nurse's local supervisor was the parish priest, who was responsible above all for her morality and her piety rather than her hygiene or her capacity to breast-feed. The only "tools of the trade" that the administration required a wet nurse to own were a fireguard—for many infants suffered accidental burns in the fireplace—and a cradle, so that she would not lay the baby in her own bed and risk suffocating it. In reality, however, many wet nurses were too poor to afford these two items and in any case could not see the need for a cradle, since from their point of view the baby would be warmer and better nourished if he or she slept with the wet nurse. At the end of the ancien régime a few rare inspectors made limited supervisory tours. In other cities, such as Lyon, the oversight of wet-nursing was even more rudimentary.

In the 1770s, despite the anxiety of the police lieutenant, Prost de Royer, no bureau controlled the placements, which were arranged haphazardly in the squares and marketplaces.

Even when it might have been chosen for the good of the baby, wet-nursing produced a high rate of infant mortality. Babies placed with wet nurses were roughly twice as likely to die as those breast-fed by their mothers. The causes of this higher rate of mortality are obvious. They included exhaustion from traveling; the difficulties of adapting to a stranger's milk during the first weeks of life; the lack of hygiene in the peasants' often-squalid houses and even the lack of milk, when the wet nurse, despite the rules, took in several infants in order to earn more, or when she was pregnant. On the other hand, there were also good wet nurses with ample supplies of milk and warm affection, who successfully cared for several infants. When it was time for the children to return to their parents, generally after two years, the separation from the maternal figure of the wet nurse could lead to a new trauma for the children—a fact that apparently caused the parents of those times little anxiety.

The human costs of wet-nursing were emphasized by Enlightenment thinkers, whose writings relentlessly condemned the "vices, errors, and prejudices" of "mercenary" wet nurses. The nurses' milk, the writers claimed, was bad and often soured by excessively harsh labor; they did not have enough milk, and therefore they force-fed the babies with indigestible gruel; they wrapped the infants in cruel swaddling clothes, hung babies up by a peg, and, out of laziness, never washed them. Babies left unsupervised were victims of fire, water, or domestic animals that smothered or devoured them. As the Italian Baldini stated in 1784: "Infinitely more infants perish because of abuse by wet nurses than for any other reason." This brutal condemnation mirrored the condemnation of midwives who were deemed to be so inexpert that they killed both mothers and babies; both criticisms seem to demonstrate the widening of chasm separating scholarly medicine from popular practice. The women of the countryside followed traditional child-rearing practices for infants, while the men of science, newly arrived in the traditionally feminine domain of childcare, did not understand the specific reasons for those practices.

Elsewhere in Europe wet nurses were not unknown, but they were restricted to the wealthiest families, who most often employed them as resident staff in their homes. In Italy and Germany unmarried mothers were preferred as wet nurses because there was no need for concern about their husbands. In England residents of the City of London also placed their babies in the countryside, but to a much more limited extent than in Paris.

The Abandonment of Children

Institutions specializing in the reception of foundlings were first established in Europe at the end of the Middle Ages, beginning with the major cities of Italy—including Milan, Florence, and Naples—in the 14th and 15th centuries. In France, such institutions emerged later: it was not until after 1639, thanks to the energetic activity of Saint Vincent de Paul, that hospices specializing in the reception of abandoned infants were created in Paris and then in other major French cities. The 18th century saw a dramatic rise in the numbers of abandoned children. In Paris, for example, the number of abandoned children rose from 312 in 1670 to 7,676 in 1772. By the end of the ancien régime, some 25,000 children were abandoned among the 1 million births each year throughout France. The number of abandoned children also increased in nearly all the other major European countries. England, Belgium, the Netherlands, Portugal, Spain, Russia, and Bohemia were among the nations that had founded specific institutions to shelter foundlings.

Contemporaries wondered whether the increase in child abandonment was not the result of the very existence of foundling hospitals, which encouraged the parents of legitimate children to abandon them, as some found these places a convenient means to have their children raised at the expense of the state. The debate on this issue was particularly lively in Germany, where a dispute over the foundling hospitals unfolded. Those who supported the establishment of such institutions insisted that they prevented infanticide, but their opponents, citing the French example, argued that the hospitals incited abandonment. These opponents prevailed temporarily. Only a few German institutions, at Cassel and Hamburg, received a very limited number of orphans, while in some major German cities there were also institutions that supported poor children but did not allow parents to remain anonymous.

London presented an equally interesting example of the management of foundlings. For several decades (1739–81), the English capital had only one foundling hospital. Its belated creation enabled its administrators to avoid repeating the errors they saw being committed on the Continent. Infants were admitted in small numbers, and wet nurses were meticulously chosen and regulated. In 1756, 67 percent of the infants returned alive from their wet nurses. But for four years, from 1756 to 1760, admissions were more liberal and anonymous, and the numbers of abandoned babies rose so alarmingly—14,934 infants were admitted in 46 months—that the system became overloaded. As a result, large numbers of infants died and the administrators had to impose barriers and controls. The institution itself had to close its doors in 1781 as a result of financial difficulties, since donors had been alarmed by the immorality that, in their view, accompanied the ease of with which parents could abandon their offspring.

In fact, the care of foundlings posed a moral problem for 18th-century thinkers. A large proportion of found-lings were illegitimate, and many asked if these infants should be saved at the risk of encouraging moral depravity. In France the response of administrators, inspired by the demographic ideology, was clear: what-ever the parents' lack of virtue, all foundlings should be received and helped to live so these children would later be "useful" to the state, whether as peasants, soldiers, or settlers in distant lands. Some of the hospices even facilitated anonymous abandonment by installing *tours* (revolving devices, also used in Italy, that allowed the youngsters to be passed through a wall without the "donor" being seen).

However, not all foundlings were born as a result of illicit and shameful liaisons. The causes of abandon-ment are known for one-third of all abandoned babies in Paris in the 18th century, thanks to the notes or marks showing identity attached to their clothes. These marks have come down to us in the entry registers of the hospices in the form of little ribbons, medals, figu-rines, notes, or pieces of cloth, and they were the last links between infants and their families. Most of the instances in which children were abandoned wearing identification marks were necessitated by the parents' extreme poverty, a point that was often expressed in moving terms in the notes. Often these notes invoked the mother's or the father's love, the heartbreak that abandonment entailed, and the wish to retrieve the baby when times were better. These records show that abandonment was not always a total rejection of the infant; in some cases it might be, but in those instances anonymous and easy reception at the hospice was a lesser evil, for it probably prevented infanticide.

Yet, despite the good reputation of the hospices, the fate of the foundlings of Paris was tragic. Crammed into a hospice for their first few days while a wet nurse was being found, they were then taken to the provinces, often far away, for the hospitals could only pay the cheapest, most distant, wet nurses. Most of these infants (80 percent) died before their first birthday. Early in the 18th century the rare survivors were usu-ally taken back to the city, but later they were increas-ingly raised in the countryside, where they lived the rest of their lives as peasants. Despite the hopes expressed in those little notes, in reality very few children were reunited with their parents after several years—only three or four such reunions were arranged each year in Paris at the end of the 18th century.

For all its tragedy, this "massacre of the innocents" did produce some positive results in the long term. For a century the foundlings were used as subjects for all kinds of experiments. Some physicians believed that it was possible to eliminate the need for wet nurses' milk by perfecting artificial nourishment. Over the course of the 18th century experiments in feeding foundlings diets based on animal milk, moistened bread, gruel, or rice water were carried out repeatedly in various estab-lishments, both in capital cities and in the provinces, as well as in hospitals in London and Dublin. All these experiments ended in the deaths of most of the children. By the end of the century it had become clear that the most ignorant wet nurse was worth more than the most attentive physician.

Foundlings were also used to help improve identifi-cation of a certain number of childhood diseases. These included thrush, against which the traditional soothing agents and expectorants had little effect; "hardening of the cellular tissue" (now known as neonatal sclerosis, a condition that can kill hypothermic premature babies), for which physicians recommended warm wraps; and syphilis, which in Paris was treated at the Vaugirard hospice, specifically founded in 1780 to care for babies born with venereal diseases.

In any case, many babies died in the hospitals before they would normally have gone to wet nurses in the countryside. Physicians, who had increasingly turned toward clinical medicine, were able to perform autop-sies that permitted them a better understanding of the causes of their death. It is no coincidence that the author of the first treatise specifically devoted to the clinical care of childhood diseases, Charles Michel Bil-lard, had been an intern at the foundling hospital in Paris. In the preface to his famous *Traité des maladies des enfants nouveau-nés* (1826; Treatise on the Illnesses of Newborn Children), Billard acknowledges that he could not have made progress without the thousands of observations made and the autopsies he had been able to conduct there.

On a somewhat more empirical level, it was during the age of the Enlightenment that children began to be protected by inoculation against smallpox, even though the great campaigns launched in the middle of the cen-tury had not yet convinced all parents of the safety and effectiveness of vaccination. Debate over the justifica-tions for this practice troubled the best scholars for sev-eral decades. Overall, one can observe over the course of the 18th century a modest accumulation of small medical advances. These advances, along with improved nutrition for mothers, partly explain the small but perceptible drop in infant mortality in France by the end of the ancien régime.

MARIE-FRANCE MOREL

See also Education, Instruction, and Pedagogy; Fatherhood; Hospital

Further Reading

Ariès, Philippe, *Centuries of Childhood: A Social History of Family Life,* New York: Knopf, 1962 (original French edition, 1960)

Fildes, Valerie A., *Breasts, Bottles, and Babies: A History of Infant Feeding,* Edinburgh: Edinburgh University Press, 1986

Fildes, Valerie A., *Wet-Nursing: A History from Antiquity to the Present,* Oxford and New York: Blackwell, 1988

Gélis, Jacques, Mirielle Laget, and Marie-France Morel, editors, *Entrer dans la vie: Naissances et enfances dans la France traditionnelle,* Paris: Gallimard, 1978

Morel, Marie-France, "Théories et pratiques de l'allaitement en France au XVIIIᵉ siècle," *Annales de démographie historique* (1976)

Sussman, George D., *Selling Mother's Milk: The Wet-Nursing Business in France, 1715–1914,* Urbana: University of Illinois Press, 1982

China

As early as the 16th century, Italian missionaries had begun to pave the way for China's entry into the world community, but it was not until the 18th century that the mysteries of this ancient and previously isolated culture became a preoccupation for Europeans. The idea of a wise and knowledgeable China played a crucial role in the propaganda of the Enlightenment, notably with respect to the issues of deism and enlightened despotism, and particularly in France, as is apparent from the significant number of works whose titles indicate interest in China.

Over time, China's influence on the cultural imagination of the Enlightenment shifted according to the following general pattern. From 1685 to around 1750, the questioning of European civilization resulted in unconditional admiration for China. After 1760, at a time when the Jesuits had been expelled from France and when philosophers and economists were seeking to create a social science that could serve as a basis for politics and morality, interest in China was sustained by the Physiocrats and by scholarly works. By that time, however, enthusiasm for China was no longer unanimous, and the "Sinophiles" were joined by the "Sinophobes."

From the turn of the 17th century on, thinkers affected by a "crisis of consciousness" had access to a variety of sources that contributed to the myth of the *bon chinois* (good Chinese): travel accounts embellished with falsehoods and legends, the narratives of merchants, and, most significantly, the narratives of the French Jesuits. The Jesuits had long had a near monopoly on publications about China, from Father Lecomte's *Nouveaux mémoires sur l'état présent de la Chine* (1696; New Memoirs on the Present State of China) up to Father du Halde's *Description géographique, historique, chronologique, politique et physique de l'empire de la Chine et de la Tartarie chinoise* (1735; Geographic, Historical, Chronological, Political, and Physical Description of the Chinese Empire). Du Halde also played an essential role in the Jesuits' *Lettres édifiantes et curieuses.*

The earliest documented shift toward a negative presentation of China occurred in the last part of the 17th century, with the narrative of Domingo Fernandez Navarrete. This trend toward a negative image of China is also discernable in Lorenz Lange's *Journal de la résidence . . . à la cour de Chine, dans les années 1721 et 1722* (1726; Journal of a Residency . . . at the Court of Peking, during the Years 1721 and 1722) and, most notably, in George Anson's *Voyage round the World in the Years 1740–1744*—published in England in 1745 by Richard Walter and translated into French in 1749—which emphasizes Chinese dishonesty. The final phase of interest in China rested on such contributions as Cornelius de Pauw's *Recherches philosophiques sur les Égyptiens et les Chinois* (1773; Philosophical Dissertations on the Egyptians and Chinese), M. Démeunier's work *L'esprit des usages et des coutumes des différents peuples, ou Observations tirées des voyageurs et des historiens* (1776; The Spirit of Usages and Customs of Various Peoples; or, Observations Drawn from Travelers and Historians), Father Amiot's *Mémoires concernant . . . l'histoire des Chinois* (1776–89; Memoirs Concerning . . . the History of the Chinese), Father Mailla's *Histoire générale de la Chine* (1777–85; General History of China), and Pierre Sonnerat's *Voyage aux Indes Orientales et à la Chine* (1782; Journey to the East Indies and China).

The first French Jesuit mission in Peking was established in 1685, but *La science des Chinois* (The Science of the Chinese), a French version of Father Intorcetta's

Sinarum Scientia, had already appeared in 1673. It was followed in 1687 by *Confucius Sinarum Philosophus* (Confucius, Chinese Philosopher), which gave Europeans access to the three main books of Confucianism in translations by Father Couplet and other Jesuits. The information contained in these works, which Saint-Simon referred to as "deceitful accounts," was fragmentary, reflecting the need to defend the missionaries' particular practice of evangelization. The Jesuits held that it was possible to combine Christianity with Confucian doctrine and Chinese ceremonial, since the former was a moral doctrine, not a religious code, and the latter was neither superstition nor idolatry, but a civic practice.

This kind of opinion, definitively condemned in 1742, sparked the "quarrel over rites," which went beyond the realm of theology to touch on philosophy and history, by way of three central and outstanding problems: Confucian doctrine, the worship of ancestors, and the Chinese terms for translating the word "God." The main themes derived from these primary issues were, first of all, the antiquity of Chinese culture, which contradicted biblical chronology; second, the atheism of the Chinese (that is to say, their idea of God throughout history), and finally, the morality of the Chinese and the government of the mandarins. For Enlightenment thinkers, the competitions through which the Chinese entered the mandarinate were a consecration of both a social hierarchy based on merit and the institutionalized rapport that existed between the literate class and the emperor.

The Myth of China

These hotly debated issues are well represented in the texts of the principal *philosophes,* with their image of a deistic, spiritual, and tolerant China. Pierre Bayle expressed his admiration for Chinese atheism in his writings, and maintained consistent interest in China from 1685 on, including the imperial edict authorizing the Jesuits to enter the country. In contrast, Gottfried Wilhelm Leibniz, in his *Lettre sur la philosophie chinoise à Nicolas de Remond* (1714; Discourse on the Natural Theology of the Chinese), inquires into the great length of the history of China, in the belief that an understanding of that history might make it possible to retrace of the history of humankind and to discover the principles of natural religion. In his view the atheism ascribed to the Chinese is actually a projection on the part of their modern commentators, while "the true religion is enclosed within the classic books." The Chinese, he observes, believe in substances separate from and outside of matter—even though they do not recognize those substances as spiritual. *Li* is not only distinct from *qi* (matter) but produces it; *li* is the rule and phys-

ical principle of corporeal things, as well as the moral principle of virtues, customs, and other spiritual things. It therefore corresponds to the European idea of the Divinity. Further, argues Leibniz, the Chinese are superior to Europeans in morality and in the conduct of the state, and "it is necessary for us to send for these political sages to teach us the *art of governing* and all their natural theology, which they have carried to such a height of perfection" (Leibniz, *Novissima sinica* [1697; News from China]).

It is in Voltaire's works that the myth of Chinese superiority appears in its purest form. In numerous writings, including several articles in his *Dictionnaire philosophique* (1764; Philosophical Dictionary), the "quarrel over rites" gives him the pretext for comparing Christian fanaticism to Chinese tolerance. In his *Le siècle de Louis XIV* (1752; The Age of Louis XIV), Voltaire explains how the initiatives of the papal court ended up discrediting Christianity and leading the Chinese, who had tolerated the Christian faith under Emperor Kangxi, to ban it as soon as Yongzheng succeeded him in 1724. Although the Jesuits also made errors and ended up fomenting trouble within the imperial family, Voltaire's text presents many positive aspects of their role. Their skill as mathematicians led to their reception at the imperial court and they were the only people in Europe to know how to interpret Chinese ceremonies. Voltaire's attitude is compatible with his support for his former masters' thesis positing a basis of natural religion among the Chinese. Voltaire thinks that their simple religion consists in adoring the Supreme Being and is based on the cult of justice, which derives from filial respect, and therefore from a paternalistic organization of the state, which respects natural law. Voltaire expounds the same ideas in his *Essai sur les moeurs et l'esprit des nations* (1756; An Essay on Universal History, and the Manners and Spirit of Nations). For Voltaire, Confucius is the perfect deist philosopher, and it is important not to confuse him with other founders of religions but rather to compare him to Epictetus, for "he [Confucius] only recommends virtue; he preaches no mysteries."

With his arguments in favor of Chinese antiquity—not only antiquity in the absolute sense, which implied the rejection of biblical chronology, but also the antiquity of Chinese religion, morality, philosophy, and sciences—Voltaire prolonged to a fairly late date the Sinophilia that had been inspired by the Jesuits. He entered the debate again with his *Lettres chinoises, indiennes et tartares à Monsieur Paw* [sic], *par un Bénédictin* (1776; Chinese, Indian, and Tartar Letters to Monsieur Pauw, by a Benedictine), in which he states his support for the Dutch scholar Pauw, notably on the issue of the origins of Chinese characters. From Athanasius Kircher's *China . . . illustrata* (1667; China

Illustrata) to Joseph de Guigues's *Mémoire dans lequel on prouve que les Chinois sont une colonie égyptienne* (1758; Memoir in which It Is Proved That the Chinese Are an Egyptian Colony) and John Turberville Needham's *De Inscriptione Quadam Aegyptiaca* (1761; On Egyptian Inscriptions), it was in fact believed that these pictograms and ideograms were derived from Egyptian hieroglyphs. Even in terms of language, then, China seemed to the *philosophes* to be both the contemporary nation that had the longest history and a nation that had been able to preserve the signs of its antiquity. The "primitive" character ascribed to the Chinese language also involved the tones that characterize its pronunciation and which, according to the proponents of sensationalist philosophy, were residual indications of a language of actions. Étienne Bonnot de Condillac in particular, in his *Essai sur l'origine des connaissances humaines* (1746; Essay on the Origin of Human Knowledge), discusses Chinese as an example of the prosody of the first languages, which were song-like in character because the natural cries of early human beings had evolved into distinct sounds through a multiplication of the inflections of the voice. According to Denis Diderot, in his article "Chinois" (Chinese) in the *Encyclopédie,* both the multiplication of tones rather than words and the absence of an alphabet are strong arguments against the alleged wisdom of the Chinese.

Chinese Despotism

To complete the range of favorable attitudes toward China one must invoke the Physiocrats, who cited the Chinese example to support the priority of agriculture and the "natural" foundations of the economy, property, and political order. The information provided by the Jesuits, previously exploited by Étienne Silhouette in his *Idée générale du gouvernement et de la morale des Chinois* (1729; General Idea of the Government and Morals of the Chinese), was augmented after 1765 by the *Correspondance scientifique et littéraire de Pékin,* edited by Bertin. François Quesnay wrote his *Despotisme de la Chine* (1767; Despotism of China) and was nicknamed "the Confucius of Europe" by the abbé Nicolas Baudeau. Others distanced themselves from these theories, including Anne-Robert-Jacques Turgot in his *Questions sur la Chine adressées à deux Chinois* (1764; Questions on China Addressed to Two Chinese Men).

The idea of "legal despotism," a term coined by Paul Pierre Mercier de La Rivière, had various origins, including Book XIX, Chapters XVII through XIX of Montesquieu's *De l'esprit des lois* (1748; The Spirit of Laws). In the course of these chapters Montesquieu

contrasts the positive characteristics of the institutions of the Chinese with their dishonesty in trade, which is connected to the demands of "their precarious lives." Montesquieu's opinion is therefore nuanced—"not all moral vices are political vices"—although it already tends toward a critical view of China. His reflections are derived mainly from Father du Halde, whose work he tries to explicate, but his other sources include legends and propaganda. Because of its prosperity and the wisdom of its laws, Montesquieu contends, China has a special place in relation to the other empires of Asia. However, the Chinese government is based on despotism and therefore—in line with the distinction among the "three governments" established in Book III, which restricts virtue to republics—its "principle" is fear.

In Book VII Montesquieu introduces the example of China in connection with the question of luxury, which he regards as pernicious for China because that nation's high fertility rates, a consequence of the climate, make it necessary for the country to concentrate effort on feeding its inhabitants (Book VIII). In Book XIV he cites the practical character of Chinese laws as an example of their wisdom, as illustrated by the fact that the legislators contrived to resist the influence of the climate. This practical aspect is manifested in rituals, which, according to Montesquieu, are a combination of religion, law, customs, and manners, bound together by respect for fathers (Book XIX). The decline of filial piety, and of the ceremonies that expressed it, would mean the weakening of the social structure and the state organization based upon veneration for fathers. This idea gave Montesquieu the key to his interpretation of despotism in China. The rituals, he argues, regulate Chinese customs much better than would torture; the synthesis that they represent guarantees continuity throughout the endless complexities of successive dynasties. The same is true for Christianity, which Montesquieu contrasts with the customs of China.

Elsewhere, in Book VIII, Montesquieu makes a connection between the wisdom of the Chinese emperors and the fear of revolts, which is not counterbalanced by hope for an afterlife. These revolts, in a country so affected by famine, arise naturally and are associated with local brigands, who are a serious threat to the throne. In Book VII Montesquieu sketches, in the manner he introduced in his analysis of the troglodytes, the "metahistorical" parable of the 22 dynasties, each of which began in total virtue and ended in idleness and corruption, until a usurper founded a new dynasty.

European Sinophobia

For a review of attitudes that were entirely hostile to the Chinese we must begin with Diderot. As a counterpoint to his short *Encyclopédie* article titled "Chine," which mentions the principal recognized merits of the culture, the article "Chinois (philosophie des)" (1753; Chinese, Philosophy of the), deliberately written against the Jesuits, sums up the various issues touched on by Enlightenment thought and expresses Diderot's distrust for the Sinophilia of the age. From the outset he emphasizes the contradictions in the evidence of the supposed antiquity of China, owing to the unreliability of the texts and their translations. Consequently, he argues, Chinese philosophy, science, and religion are closer to fable than to historical credibility. The information concerning Confucius and the cult surrounding him is no more reliable. Furthermore, Diderot reminds his readers of the idolatry, atheism, and superstitions introduced by Buddhism ("the sect of Foe"). He sets forth and analyzes Chinese principles on the origin of things and all "subsequent science," remarking that Chinese culture would hardly have developed since the Middle Ages if it had not been for "certain changes that were apparently introduced through exchange with our [European] scholars." The Jesuits had cited the welcome given to these scholars as proof of the high regard in which science was held in China, but was it not merely proof of the more advanced state of science in Europe? In describing Chinese sacrifices to spirits, Diderot concludes that these spirits are conceived as entirely material and that "there is nothing truly immortal except *li*." Thus, he ends up comparing Chinese philosophy to that of Spinoza and applies the same analytic approach to illustrate the morality of Confucius, which was "superior to his metaphysics and his physics."

Diderot characterizes the Oriental spirit as lazy and "circumscribed by essential needs." Consequently, in his view, neither the literature nor the art of China can compare with the products of European genius. In the *Salon de 1767* (1767 Exhibition), Diderot repeats the same criticisms, this time in opposition to the fashion for chinoiserie, spurred by Madame de Pompadour among others. A condemnation of the Chinese virtue of "saving face" by the "philosopher of energy," can be found among other themes in the conversations at Grandval with "Father Hoop" in Diderot's letters to Sophie Volland. Apart from these conversations, his strongest attack is contained in the abbé Raynal's *Histoire philosophique et politique des établissements et du commerce des Européens dans les deux Indes* (1770; A Philosophical and Political History of the Settlements and Trade of the Europeans in the East and West Indies). There Diderot reviews the problems that he believes invalidate the myth of China constructed by the Jesuits. Some of these issues, such as overpopulation and the abandonment of children, persist even today. Diderot also cites lack of progress in the arts and sciences, corruption, depravity, and despotism among the factors that belie the myth of Chinese superiority. He mocks the civility of the Chinese and links their activity to necessity rather than to wisdom. In his view, admiration for China is the result of both inadequate information and a "reverence for past times and distant countries" where human intelligence founders.

Diderot's friends maintained the same negative attitudes toward China. The baron d'Holbach published his *Recherches sur l'origine du despotisme oriental* (The Origin and Progress of Despotism in the Orient, and Other Empires of Africa, Europe, and America) in 1761, and in *La morale universelle, ou Les devoirs de l'homme fondés sur sa nature* (1776; Universal Morals; or, The Duties of Man, Grounded in His Nature) he attacks the despotism of Confucius. In one number of his *Correspondance littéraire* (15 September 1766; August and October 1773), Friedrich Melchior von Grimm attacks the cult of China in France. Despite his appreciation of imperial justice in his article "Économie politique" (1755; Political Economy) in the *Encyclopédie*, Jean-Jacques Rousseau essentially shared Diderot's position. Rousseau's doubts about the progress of the arts, sciences, and morality in China, expressed in his first *Discours sur l'origine et les fondements de l'inégalité parmi les hommes* (1755; Discourse on the Origins of Inequality among Men), were reinforced after he read George Anson's *Voyage,* which he borrowed from Madame d'Épinay in 1757. In *La nouvelle Héloïse* (1761; Julie; or, The New Héloïse) Rousseau's doubts give way to an invective against the Chinese, who are "literate, cowardly, hypocritical, and fraudulent," "abundant in signs and sterile in ideas," ceremonious and dishonest. From the perspective of the marquis de Sade, China's otherness provided the most perfect demonstration of moral relativism. In particular, he was all too attracted by the idea of infanticide—a topic mentioned in the pamphlet "Français, encore un effort si vous voulez être républicains" [1795; Yet Another Effort, Frenchmen, If You Want a Republic], in *Justine; ou Les malheurs de la vertu* [1791; Justine; or, The Misfortunes of Virtue] and *La nouvelle Justine; ou Les malheurs de la vertu* [1797; New Justine; or, The Misfortunes of Virtue], and in the *Histoire de Juliette sa soeur; ou, Les prospérités du vice* [1797; Juliette]). Similarly, in *La philosophie dans le boudoir* (1795; Philosophy in the Bedroom), Sade admires the cruelty with which the Chinese abandon unwanted infants "like the results of digestion," so that all are able to work and make themselves happy.

MARA CAIRA-PRINCIPATO

See also Civilization and Civility; Cosmopolitanism; Dialogue; Jesuits

Further Reading

Broc, Numa, "Voyageurs français en Chine: Impressions et jugements," *Dix-huitième siècle* 22 (1990)

Cohen, Huguette, "Diderot and the Image of China in Eighteenth-Century France," *Studies on Voltaire and the Eighteenth Century* 242 (1986)

Guy, Basil, *The French Image of China before and after Voltaire,* Geneva: Institut et Musée Voltaire, 1963

Reichwein, Adolf, *China and Europe: Intellectual and Artistic Contacts in the Eighteenth Century,* translated by J.C. Powell, London: Kegan Paul, Trench, Trubner, and New York: Knopf, 1925 (original German edition, 1923)

Citizen

The term *citoyen* (citizen) was not commonly used during most of the 18th century. In this regard, as in a number of others, the French Revolution marked a watershed: the term was overused, and "citizen" thereby became an everyday term in political and social life. Prior to that, the use of the word "citizen" in the 18th century was limited to the context of the history of Greek and Roman antiquity or the realm of politics, where it designated either the inhabitants of Geneva—as Voltaire recalled when he wrote in *Le sentiment des citoyens* (1764; The Feeling of Citizens), a pamphlet criticizing the views of Jean-Jacques Rousseau and presented as the work of a Genevan—or, more rarely, inhabitants of the Netherlands or Great Britain. Thus, the word "citizen" initially had a historical meaning, designating a political and social status belonging to the past, without necessarily expressing nostalgia or judgment. Moreover, its use with reference to the Dutch republic or the British monarchy showed that the nature of the regime to which a citizen was subject mattered less, perhaps, than his awareness of his place relative to the political community and institutions.

Without entering into the subtleties found in dictionary definitions of "citizen" at the beginning of the century, we can accept that it referred to an inhabitant of a town or city, and more specifically of a city in antiquity. The first edition of César-Pierre Richelet's dictionary states, "this word is properly used in speaking of the ancient Greek and Roman citizens, and it indicates that they enjoyed the rights of city-dwellers." The definition in the 1694 edition of the *Dictionnaire de l'Académie* (Dictionary of the Académie Française) is almost the same. Postrevolutionary dictionaries such as the *Nouveau vocabulaire français d'après l'Académie, Wailly, et Noël et Chapsal* (1818; New French Vocabulary According to the Académie, Wailly, and Noël and Chapsal) define the term by stating, for example, that "the name of citizen, in a strict and rig-

orous sense, is given to an inhabitant of a free state who has the right to vote in public assemblies and who partakes of the sovereign (meaning power or sovereignty)." Thus, without succumbing to the retrospective illusion of truth, it is possible to grasp the semantic and ideological development of both the word and the concept of the citizen in the intellectual and linguistic practices of the 18th century. By tracing this development, the Revolution's impact on the use of the term becomes more understandable.

According to the chevalier de Jaucourt's definition in the *Encyclopédie*, a citizen is "a member of a free society of several families, who shares in the laws of this society, and who exercises his rights." One can distinguish two types of citizens, original and naturalized (categories that can be traced back to Greek and Roman examples and to the contradictions in the political life of Geneva, although Jaucourt does not mention this in the article). He then sets out the definitions of the term according to Thomas Hobbes, who had made no distinction between citizens and subjects. In Jaucourt's view, clearly, such distinctions did exist; the subject was not, or not necessarily, a citizen, because the "citizen obeys only laws, while the subject obeys the sovereign." Jaucourt adds that

the name of citizen applies neither to those who live in subjugation nor to those who live in isolation; it follows, therefore, that those who live absolutely in the state of nature, like sovereigns, and those who have completely renounced the state, such as slaves, cannot be regarded as citizens.

In fact, in this article Jaucourt presents fairly clearly the tensions within the semantic field of the word "citizen." That field was split between, on the one hand, a general, archaic usage that referred to bourgeois law and the liberties of the inhabitants of free cities, and that was essentially rooted in the model of the cities of antiquity, and, on the other hand, theoretical reflections taken directly from Aristotle and Hobbes, emphasizing the distinctions between subject and citizen, or between citizen and slave, as well as the nature of the citizen's rights and duties and his participation in sovereignty. On the level of concepts rather than that of words, everything seemed to revolve around the notion of a free society, which appeared to be the only society capable of including citizens.

Rousseau's article "Économie politique" (Political Economy) in the *Encyclopédie* gives a full account of the freedom that is a necessary condition for the existence of citizens. In this article, written during the winter of 1754–55 and published in November 1755 in Volume V of the *Dictionnaire des sciences et des arts* (Dictionary of Sciences and the Arts), Rousseau tries to define the status and role of the citizen. Taking up the "organicist" metaphor of the body politic, he shows that the sovereign power is represented by the head, while the activities that produce wealth and goods are represented by the mouth and the stomach, and that the citizens are "the body and members that make the machine move, live, and work." In a pithy formula, he contrasts the citizen, defined essentially as a member of the body politic, with membership in informal and formal associations: "One can be a devout priest, a brave soldier, or a zealous physician, and yet be a poor citizen." This contrast is a valuable one because it allows Rousseau to classify the forms of belonging to a social and political body. He writes: "Warriors, citizens, men, when they want to be; the common people or the rabble, when they so please." The article tries to define the citizen as one who enjoys rights and freedoms guaranteed by the public power, but also as one who loves his duties. By being citizens, the members of society constitute themselves as a people; by ceasing to be citizens, they are no more than rabble.

This form of adherence of the citizen to public life—his "civic responsibility," to use a more modern term—had already been highlighted by Montesquieu in *De l'esprit des lois* (1748; The Spirit of Laws), in which Montesquieu unites the citizen with democracy to such an extent that the word "citizen" is not used in the chapters on aristocracy, monarchy, or the despotic state and is contrasted with the "individual" (in aristocracy), the "subject" (in monarchy), and "the slave" (in the despotic state). Montesquieu adds the right to vote as a fundamental element in the definition of the citizen. This theoretical approach is clearly derived from the typology of governments inherited from Aristotle and Jean Bodin, and it contributes in turn to the historical thinking in Montesquieu's *Considérations sur les causes de la grandeur des Romains et de leur décadence* (1734; Considerations on the Causes of the Grandeur and Dec-

adence of the Romans). The word "citizen" appears in the first chapter of this work, in connection with the growing city, in the most direct sense of belonging to the city, but Montesquieu then infuses the word with political meaning: the citizen is one who observes the laws, not through fear but through a passionate adherence. All things considered, however, the term is used less than one might hope, as if this image of the citizen had gradually become incompatible with the conflicts that opposed patricians to plebeians. Yet Montesquieu takes care to state that it was in the nature of Rome to have political divisions when he recalls that "what is called unity in a body politic is a very equivocal thing." In this respect, the analysis of the causes of Rome's decline in the *Considérations* can be reduced to the history of the loss of "the spirit of citizens"—that is, as much to institutional changes in the status of Romans as to the abandonment by the citizens themselves of their privileged relation to the law. It is therefore no accident that Montesquieu uses the term "citizen" very frequently in Books XI, XII, and XIII of *De l'esprit des lois*, which discuss political liberty, for if there is no citizen in a free state, there is also no citizen who feels a responsibility to maintain that same liberty, regarded as the supreme good. Thus, Montesquieu exalts the citizens of the Roman republic and of Sparta, but he adds certain requirements: there can be no citizenship without frugality and equality. In *De l'esprit des lois* he insists on the rigors of being a citizen. Enrichment, the taste for pleasures, luxury, and the desire to establish differences are all far from the spirit of citizenship, as is an education that fails to prepare children to devote themselves to the state and to respect their duties even to the point of forgetting their rights.

Rousseau's *Du contrat social* (1762; The Social Contract) provides a clearer and more definite explanation of the terms defined or suggested in his article "Économie politique" or in Montesquieu's analyses. Rousseau no longer draws the sharp contrast that he once had between subject and citizen, who now appear to be complementary:

> As for the associates [participating in the social contract], they take the collective name of the *people,* but they are known in particular as *citizens* when they participate in the sovereign authority, and as *subjects* when they submit to the laws of the state.

Citizenship defines the social being, over and above the regime to which the citizen is subjected. A citizen participates in the general will: whether alienated in dictatorships, necessary to the process of the social contract, or recognized within democracy, the social being is always a citizen. These extremely complex theses advanced by Rousseau were to play an important role during the Revolution. In Rousseau's work citizenship appears as a right and the social body is constituted of citizens, regardless of the form of government.

It is well known that throughout his life Rousseau attached importance to his status as a citizen of Geneva, even when his conflicts with Geneva or the Protestant churches were at their most bitter. This importance is highlighted in Rousseau's correspondence, and in the proud affirmation with which *Du contrat social* opens. It is signed on the title page by "Jean-Jacques Rousseau, citizen of Geneva": "Born a citizen of a free state, and a member of the sovereign. . . ." In fact, this passage represents a feeble echo of his proud and skillful statement of his position in the dedication of his *Discours sur l'origine et les fondements de l'inégalité parmi les hommes* (1755; Discourse on the Origins of Inequality among Men), which Rousseau addresses to the members of the Council in his native city, identifying himself (as always) as a citizen of Geneva. He also presents himself as a "virtuous citizen" (which, if we are to believe his statement, is close to the position of Montesquieu, restated as a pleonasm), and, by playing upon a rhetorical supposition ("If I had been able to choose the place of my birth"), he defines Geneva in such a way as to pride himself on being the ideal figure of a citizen. Is there not in this evocation the ideal of an openness of the citizens to one another and to the city? Geneva, whether as dream or as reality, is the state where

> nobody would have been forced to commit to others the functions with which he was charged: a state where all the individuals knew one another, and neither the obscure maneuvers of vice nor the modesty of virtue could have escaped the gaze and judgment of the public, and where this gentle habit of seeing and knowing one another, turned love of the fatherland into love of the citizens, rather than love of the land.

Thus, Rousseau defines an ideal Geneva where the people merge with the sovereign, where the government is obviously democratic and citizens submit to the laws, and where, finally, each citizen is also a legislator, even when he has to delegate to the magistrates part of his right to make laws. Whether or not this was the real Geneva, whether or not Rousseau was dreaming and flattering, hardly matters here. This ideal of citizenship is as much a moral ideal as a political and social one. Equality does not have the harshness lent it by the ancient model, as in Montesquieu's *De l'esprit des lois*, but is closer to the openness of hearts and amorous emotions in Rousseau's *La nouvelle Héloïse* (1761; Julie; or, The New Héloïse) or the recollections of popular festivals in his *Lettre à D'Alembert* (1758; Letter to

M. D'Alembert on Theatre). So defined, citizenship is synonymous with happiness: it is a type of harmony rediscovered from the society of families that had succeeded the state of nature. Thus, Rousseau writes: "My dear fellow-citizens, or rather my brothers, since the bonds of blood as well as the bonds of the laws unite nearly all of us." Here, the vision of the citizen is a product as much of fiction as of political analysis, and it has the imprecision, charm, and fragility of the former. Distancing himself from the examples of the past, such as that of Plutarch, whose works he had read and whom he evoked in this same dedication, Rousseau rejects the conflation of citizen and warrior. His republic seeks to be peaceful and its male citizens seek to be upstanding paterfamilias, united with its female citizens, whose right of citizenship Rousseau recognizes, which was quite an uncommon attitude at that time. However, the republic is merely ephemeral and the citizen is threatened by human passions: ambition, violence, the desire to possess. Citizenship is hard to learn, for human beings are not made to be free: a responsible liberty would worry them. Time is therefore both a necessity for the establishment of citizenship, and a threat that weighs upon it. One cannot become a citizen without tradition, but time is democracy's worst enemy. Readers will have recognized here all the paradoxes inherent in the Rousseauist approach.

It is difficult to find among Rousseau's contemporaries an equivalent to the dream of citizenship that haunted his thought and legitimized the positions that he took in his *Lettres écrites de la montagne* (1764; Letters Written during a Journey in the Mountains) and in *La lettre à Christophe de Beaumont, archevêque de Paris* (Letter to Christophe de Beaumont, Archbishop of Paris). When Diderot distanced himself from the reformist projects he had suggested to Catherine II, he opted for the lively anarchy of the savages of Tahiti, and it is not easy to identify, in his *Le neveu de Rameau* (1772; Rameau's Nephew), which model of citizenship Rameau and his adversary the *philosophe* are discussing. Was the idea of citizenship possible for someone who proposes that every form of social behavior necessarily contradicts one of the three codes (religious, natural, and civic) by which the actions of individuals are to be judged?

Based on the title and the date of publication of his work *Des droits et des devoirs du citoyen* (On the Rights and Duties of Citizens), which was written in 1758 but not published until 1788, some have hailed Gabriel Bonnot de Mably (1709–85) as the ideologist of citizenship as defined by those who lived through the Revolution. It is true that his analyses of Roman and Greek governments in earlier works—*Parallèle des romains et des français par rapport au gouvernement* (1740; Parallels between the Romans and the French in

Relation to Government), *Observations sur les Grecs* (1749; Observations on the Greeks), and *Observations sur les Romains* (1751; Observations on the Romans)—exalt the citizenship of antiquity, which he contrasts with the alienation of those subjected to either monarchs or feudal oppression. Leaving aside the critical use that he makes of it, Mably's analysis of the societies of antiquity is not different, in any respect, from that of the historiography of his day, and he borrows from Charles Rollin (1661–1741) and Vertot (1655–1735), historians of the ancient world who are now forgotten. It would doubtless be historically inaccurate to accept the view of Mably that prevailed during the Revolution. Nevertheless, one can deduce, from Mably's ambiguous republicanism and his demand for equality, which is clearly present in *Les entretiens de Phocion sur le rapport de la morale ou de la politique* (1763; Phocion's Discussion of the Relationship of Morality and Politics), a radically new definition of the citizen and of citizenship. Despite the use of the word "citizen" in one of his titles, Mably rarely uses the word in his writings and most often applies it imprecisely. A passage from his *Observations sur l'histoire de France* (1765; Observations on the History of France) will show both the extended meanings that the word could have and the absence of new connotations that its use generated:

> At first, equality was needed to unite the citizens of the whole society, and the distinction between nobles and commoners could only be the result of several events and several revolutions, of which the vanity of some citizens took advantage to attribute special prerogatives to themselves and form a separate class.

Although we should not be deceived by hindsight reconstructions of "truth," we can affirm that the end of the ancien régime presented symptoms of change where perhaps they were least expected. Let us recall that Louis-François de Bourbon, prince of Condé, who opposed absolute government on behalf of the rights of the feudal aristocracy and who spoke in favor of a mythical French constitution that would the powers of the king, had himself been called the "Citizen-Prince." It is as if the word "citizen" referred, from this time on, to the defense of liberties and to a necessary opposition to a power that was judged to be excessive. As Jean Fabre has quite remarkably shown, such ambiguities shaped this prince's relationship with Jean-Jacques

Rousseau, whom he would later protect (see Fabre). Another and still more innovative symptom was the publication, under the editorship of the abbé Nicolas Baudeau from April 1765 to April 1768, and then under that of Pierre-Samuel Dupont de Nemours from March 1768 to March 1772, of the *Éphémérides du citoyen ou chronique de l'esprit national,* a periodical that defended the ideas of the Physiocrats. The citizen appears in it as one who corrects "the errors of the people and revives ancient truths": "citizen" was therefore the new word to designate the *philosophe*. Then, little by little, it came to designate the readers of good will who, out of their sense of civic responsibility, wrote to the periodical to put forward experiences, reforms, and judgments on the affairs of the day. Citizen thus became synonymous with those who embodied that public opinion to which the age began to attach such importance. The entry of this figure of the citizen into the cultural imagination is significant. One must be careful not to subscribe to a reductive belief in a relationship of cause and effect between all these signs and the meaning that the word "citizen" took on once the Revolution came; however, one can accept that the word had multiple meanings, that it was used more frequently as the 18th century progressed, and that it was applied to the contemporary world. In other words, language reflected a source of intellectual unease, and also a way, barely perceived and still ambiguous, of expressing a transformation of the political sphere.

JEAN MARIE GOULEMOT

See also Body, Representations of; Civilization and Civility; Happiness

Further Reading

Chaussinand-Nogaret, Guy, *Le citoyen des Lumières,* Brussels: Éditions Complexe, 1994

Fabre, Jean, "Jean-Jacques Rousseau et le Prince de Conti," in *Lumières et romantisme: Énergie et nostalgie de Rousseau à Mickiewicz,* by Fabre, revised and expanded edition, Paris: Klincksieck, 1980

La Cour Grandmaison, Olivier, *Les citoyennetés en Révolution, 1789–1794,* Paris: Presses Universitaires de France, 1992

Waldinger, Renée, Philip Dawson, and Isser Woloch, editors, *The French Revolution and the Meaning of Citizenship,* Westport, Connecticut: Greenwood Press, 1994

City

Planning

It was an immense city with clean, broad, and well-aligned streets; the air seemed as healthy as in the countryside; the houses of private individuals were built for comfort, with none of those grandiose exteriors that pride in wealth affects among us and that serve only to arouse indignation or jealousy. Pomp and magnificence were reserved for public buildings, which, in accordance with an architectural taste different from ours, and perhaps also simpler and nobler, marked the greatness of the genius who had undertaken them.

—Stanislas I (1752)

The author who thus evoked the discovery of a utopian city, in *L'entretien d'un Européen avec un insulaire du royaume de Dumocala* (1752; The Conversation of a European with an Islander of the Dumocala Kingdom), was none other than Stanislas Leszczynski, former king of Poland (Stanislas I), duke of Lorraine and Bar, father-in-law of Louis XV, and the selfsame genius who, while publishing his philosophical works, presided over the building of his new capital city, Nancy. Stanislas was undoubtedly one of the living symbols of Enlightenment city planning. This enlightened prince sustained the ideal of absolute monarchy by continuing a tradition of monumental architecture inherited from the 17th century. And yet, at the same time, he gave free reign to the benevolent *philosophe* within himself to create an ideal urban space, characterized by harmony among buildings and squares, civic function and a diversified society.

Sensitivity to the idea of progress shaped the municipal mentality of the Enlightenment, transcending the traditional aims of pragmatic political activity—that is, to produce buildings that were either useful or prestigious. Once an enlightened monarch had perceived that the urban populace beyond the confines of his court formed a public, he had to begin taking account of the set of urban images expressed—or called into question—by that public's quest for new identities. It fell to the monarch to understand and facilitate the recognition and appropriation of areas or places reserved for this public. Consequently, the sovereign had to share the symbols of power and show clearly that as "the father of the people," he endorsed a certain degree of equality. To the order-related virtues that had legitimized the rationalist perception of the classical city of the 17th century, the 18th century added a pedagogic virtue: the art of well-being and civic responsibility,

both integral to the self-image of the city dweller, could be taught through the physical and plastic image of the city. This image, in contrast to the ambience of the court, had to create a balance among the various factors that shape identity, ranging from identification with social, professional, or intellectual activities to patriotic attachment to the locality, the nation, and so forth.

Physical Form and Moral Improvement

Our cities are still what they were, a mass of houses piled up pell-mell, without system, without economy, without design. Nowhere is this disorder more obvious and more shocking than in Paris. The center of this capital city has hardly changed at all for 300 years. One still sees the same number of small, narrow, tortuous streets, which exude nothing but squalor and filth, and in which the excessive number of carriages causes never-ending congestion. . . . Paris, overall, is anything but a beautiful city.

Here, in his *Essai sur l'architecture* (1753; Essay on Architecture), Father Marc-Antoine Laugier, the most enlightened architectural theorist of the age, expresses the same damning critique of the disorder and squalor of Paris that Montesquieu, Voltaire, Jean-Jacques Rousseau, Pierre Patte, Louis-Sébastien Mercier, and many others made in similar terms. Arthur Young cast a foreigner's gaze upon France at the end of Louis XVI's reign, a period that, despite some remarkable exceptions (Bordeaux, Nantes, and Nancy) and numerous building projects, did not yet display the dazzling spirit of progressive urban civilization. In Rouen, for example, Young observed: "the merchants have good reason to possess houses in the countryside, so that they can withdraw from this badly built, ugly, smelly, and confined city, where one finds only filth and industry." This tendency of city dwellers to dream of life among fields, noted by an Englishman who lived in a land of sumptuous country houses and recently expanded pre-industrial cities, is symptomatic of the search for a balance between nature and the urban agglomeration; this search gave an impetus to the varied urban improvement projects that arose out of the functionalist critiques of Enlightenment thinkers.

Although in material terms, as built environments, the cities of the ancien régime fell within the competence of architects and engineers, those cities were nonetheless understood primarily as living organisms that had become ossified over the course of history. In the mid–18th century the urban landscape began to be denounced for its physical defects: overcrowded housing, dilapidated and dangerous structures, congested traffic, inconvenient and inadequate public buildings, polluted air, lack of running water, accumulations of refuse, and so on. In combination, the lack of civic sense, insecurity, pauperism, and depraved morals inherent in cities seemed to render municipal magistrates incapable of carrying out their duties with respect to policing, road maintenance, and finance, entangled as they were in a chaotic web of rival administrations that were expected, often in vain, to launch initiatives.

The moral tableau of urban life required the development of an understanding of how to manage cities and the districts on their outskirts. Urban spaces, which had expanded through demographic growth as a result of immigration, were no longer envisaged as inevitable accumulations of buildings—mere juxtapositions of residual free spaces within an anarchic traffic network—but as living entities. If the dream of aesthetically pleasing urban space were to be realized, proper hygiene and comfort would have to be introduced to these sickly and graceless bodies; city planners would have to seek out the beauties that can be found in architecture or, in the form of landscapes, in nature. Such an approach had already been outlined during the Italian Renaissance and had then been developed in 17th-century Europe, which witnessed the proliferation of "capital cities" and "fortified places"—those concrete symbols of absolutism. The baroque period thus saw the creation of several new cities laid out with a reassuring symmetry, inspired by the plans of Roman walled cities and manifesting a preference for opening up rectilinear main routes designed to rectify or extend those cities' medieval centers. Rome and Turin continued to make a strong impression on visitors and those who provided training in design. Alongside treatises on architecture (which had been flourishing since Leon Battista Alberti wrote his works on that subject), utopian narratives, such as Thomas More's *Utopia* (1516) or Tommaso Campanella's *La città del sole* (1602; The City of the Sun), had introduced a visionary element and, no doubt, a measure of political optimism, which gave a softer edge to the geometric, and all too often militaristic conceptions of city planners.

Before the beginning of the 18th century, those who planned cities had no experience of open cities in times of peace. With the growth of populations and the worldwide expansion of trade, notions of utopia emerged, and, with their suggestions for future planning procedures, the utopians paved the way for Enlightenment reflections on progress and on territory

and its political control. The very idea of long-term planning was undoubtedly the first, and perhaps the most important, contribution that Enlightenment thought made to efficient city design. During the 18th century, as urban planning found its expression and realization across Europe and even in the Americas (for example, in Pierre Charles L'Enfant's plan for Washington, D.C.), the theme of utopia was incorporated into literary works, including Pierre-Alexis Delamair's *Le songe et le réveil d'Alexis Delamair, architecte à Paris* (1731; The Dream and Wakening of Alexis Delamair, Architect in Paris); Morelly's *La Basiliade* (1753; The Basiliad) and *Le code de la nature; ou, Le véritable esprit de ses lois* (1755; The Code of Nature; or, The True Spirit of Its Laws); and Mercier's *L'an 2440: Rêve s'il en fut jamais* (1771; Astraea's Return; or, The Halcyon Days of France in the Year 2440: A Dream). The great social and economic prophecies set forth in such texts would not be realized until the 19th century.

It was only at the end of the 19th century that the word *urbanisme* (city planning) was coined to designate a new cognitive, practical, and prospective discipline concerned with the development, management, and planning of cities. Throughout the 18th century, the political, administrative, and legal aspects of city life and its concomitant structures were generated by various entities—the police force, the ministries of roads and finances, and architects—but there was no single word capable of expressing the idea of city planning. Nevertheless, the expression *l'embellissement de la ville* (beautification, or improvement, of the city), which was widely used in specialized works, in the titles of specific projects, and in the press, summed up the ambition to develop on a broad front and over the long term an art of building cities that reflected changing values and lifestyles.

Today the Enlightenment concept of urban beautification is too often perceived as a supplementary artistic element, an added-on architectural embellishment, on the part of city magistrates and architects strongly influenced by the monumental art of the 17th century. However, the stylistic and architectural reforms of the 18th century, analyses of behavior during the period, and the evolution of those cities that underwent the greatest changes during that period all indicate that by around 1750, urban planning was not merely a matter of touching up and improving cities, with an additional trimming of aesthetic symbols to reflect an ideology of ostentation. Only the 20th century's perspective on art—so radically different from the venerable belief in art as a language that defined the moral objectives of the liberal arts in the 18th century—can explain the errors made in many studies of classical city planning and its development up to the time of the French Revolution. The role of the imagination during the 18th century—mediating between pleasure, on the one hand, and social, national, or cultural identification, one the other—must be taken into account, in line with a methodological approach that respects both the era's own definition of art and the received ideas that observers and participants had about urban life. For example, an understanding of urban behavior needs to be correlated with the study of emblematic or symbolic iconography. The latter found expression in statuary and architectural design, of course, but was just as evident in festivals, rituals, and displays involving the use of natural elements, such as water, air, greenery, and light. The fireworks displays and ephemeral temples of Louis XV's reign, the amphitheater of the Federation, and the mountain honoring the Supreme Being during the Revolution were all expressions of a desire for beautification. Through rituals conducted by the authorities, the public, and the people, the temporary decorations of such festivals served as the symbolic expression of dreams or proposals in the field of city planning.

Jean-Claude Perrot, an astute analyst of urban political economy, has observed that 18th-century cities developed in accordance with appearances, not on the basis of any profound reforms that would modify those cities' status or their social and political role: "The 18th century was concerned, not so much with structures, as with reflection on urban functions. The main theme of debate was that of beauty and utility" (see Perrot). The dialectic between the beautiful and the useful dated back to antiquity and had been rekindled during the Renaissance, when Alberti, and then Andrea Palladio, discussed cities as if they were great houses and great houses as if they were cities. The discussion was extended to encompass villas, or country houses, considered as places that people not only inhabited but also used for production and for leisure. By the 18th century, Carlo Goldoni's contemporaries were using country houses as places to enjoy on vacation.

The dialectic between city and countryside compelled the *philosophes* to consider the practice of incorporating nature into the public spaces of cities (improved riverbanks, courtyards, and promenades), as well as propositions for landscaped environments in private spaces (townhouses facing onto gardens that were visible from the street, amusement parks, and, in Great Britain, squares and terraces). Works of art—landscape paintings, urban vistas, and architectural follies—shaped the vision of city dwellers. English and German art lovers had views of their capital cities painted by celebrated Venetian artists. Giambattista Piranesi magnified and popularized the splendors of Rome in his engravings. At the Salon in the Louvre, Hubert Robert and Joseph Vernet exhibited paintings of monumental vestiges of the past, such as the *Maison carrée de Nîmes* (Square House of Nîmes) and the *Pont*

du Gard (Bridge on the Gard River); a royal commission resulted in a series of resulted in a series of panoramic "portraits" of the *Ports de France* (French Harbors), celebrating the prosperity that France was enjoying due to peace and the dynamism of foreign trade. Bordeaux, and later Nantes, were among the cities that were physically transformed by intensive city planning under Louis XV and Louis XVI.

Conceiving and Constructing the Civic Landscape

The recognition of the importance of unencumbered spaces—symbolized by the notion of "scenic viewpoints"—was among the greatest contributions of Enlightenment urban reform. Such "clear" spaces freed cities from the confines of their ramparts and made them seem less congested; these spaces provided views through facades, introduced the attractions of passages through arcades and colonnades that articulated people's movements, allowed air to circulate, and provided light. They made use of fundamental compositional elements of the neoclassical style, which placed a premium on planned incorporation of clear spaces within and around structures, rather than on formal walls that emphasized or separated interior or exterior areas without articulating the space between them. Jacques Gondoin said of his early neoclassical masterpiece, the École de Chirurgie (School of Surgery) in Paris (1769–80), referring in particular to the transparent effect of the portico in its façade: "I wanted to produce an effect with an aspect that not only would be arresting but also inviting to those who saw it." A certain sensualism is revealed in this psychological intention, so clearly formulated by the architect. The physical and mental (moral) hygiene of the city was put into effect through changes in the relationships among the distribution of architectural elements, harmony, and ornamentation. Decoration, related to architectural symbolism, became a standard condition in contracts for even the smallest improvement projects.

Enlightenment theorists conducted a wide-ranging debate about the conditions in which this newly conceived city planning geared toward civic progress and well-being ought to be accomplished. According to the Physiocrats, it was the duty of the state to plan improvement and beautification projects and to implement them throughout the kingdom. While an agrarian civilization might tolerate cities, city dwellers should not enjoy privileges that were "contrary to the natural order and the rights of the nation" in the administration of those cities. (see Petit-Dutaillis). In France the *intendants* (provincial magistrates) were given far-reaching powers over city planning; it was they who administered the relevant finances under the direct control of the ministers and the king's council. The reforms undertaken by the duc de Choiseul and the controller-general Laverdy (1764) and then by Anne-Robert-Jacques Turgot (1775) displayed an acute awareness of the changes that needed to be made, not only for the sake of financial stability and the reduction of inequalities but also in order to extend the civic responsibilities of municipal authorities and citizens. These reforms did not succeed, while the royal policy of monumentalism survived until after Charles-Alexandre de Calonne became chief minister (the General Tax Farmers' Building in Paris, designed by Claude-Nicolas Ledoux, was built between 1785 and 1789).

Most of the European monarchies ruled by the "enlightened" princes followed the French model to some extent, particularly in their capital cities. However, city planning based on private initiatives prevailed over central planning on the part of the monarchy in Great Britain (which was in the midst of an urban revolution), in the United Provinces of the Netherlands (which were highly urbanized before the middle of the 17th century), and in certain cities in the Rhineland that experienced high levels of immigration. Furthermore, the private investments and speculation in real estate that characterized the entrepreneurial capitalist society of Great Britain developed in France as well, notably in Paris and in the major ports and commercial centers. Architects applied a strict uniformity of style to the facades of apartment buildings on new lots, marked by their dependence on public urban monuments and on space set aside for trade or leisure. For example, the streets and houses built in Bath beginning in around 1725 represented an ideal image of the modern city, and were greatly appealing to Continental travelers in the grip of Anglomania.

There was a proliferation of texts and regulations on the administration of cities, aimed at promoting practical city planning. Such texts included Nicolas De La Mare's *Traité de la police* (1738; Treatise on the Police), Mellier's *Code de la voirie* (1753; Road Maintenance Code), the numerous royal ordinances and declarations issued in France between 1724 and 1783, the edicts and projects of Catherine II and Frederick II, and the series of Building Acts for London (starting in 1667, consolidated in 1774). In France major private planning projects were proposed or carried out, such as Louis de Mondran's plans for Toulouse (1754), Pierre de Morand's plans for Lyon (1766), and the projects that Jean-Joseph-Louis Graslin realized in Nantes (beginning in 1779), while, as Jean-Louis Harouel has pointed out, "the scope of the embellishments realized during the 18th century stands in contrast to the almost constant destitution of the royal finances and the meager resources of most of the cities" (see Harouel). Frederick II and Stanislas Leszczynski personally funded the facades of the monumental squares that they had con-

structed in Berlin and Nancy, respectively. Architects praised the achievements of monarchs in their treatises—such as Patte's *Les monuments érigés en France à la gloire de Louis XV* (1765; Monuments Erected in France to Louis XV's Glory)—but they also urged the administration to demonstrate a more coherent policy, more perseverance, and more humanitarian views, as in Patte's *Mémoires sur les objets les plus importants de l'architecture* (1769; Reports on the Most Important Objects of Architecture) and Ledoux's *L'architecture considérée sous le rapport de l'art, des moeurs et de la législation* (1804; Architecture Considered in Relation to Art, Morals, and Legislation). The latter work summarizes Ledoux's 30-year career, which was filled with public building projects.

Meanwhile, the *philosophes* themselves reflected on the virtues of civic pride. The dialectic between public and private responsibilities was accompanied by an always imperfect balance between the interests of private individuals and the aesthetic demands of city planning. When a fifth royal square was about to be laid out on a site donated by Louis XV, to whom the square was to be dedicated, Voltaire protested in his essay *Des embellissements de Paris* (1749; On the Improvements to Paris):

> The king, by his greatness of soul and his love for his people, wanted to contribute to making his capital worthy of him. Yet, after all, he is no more the king of the Parisians than of the people of Lyon or Bordeaux; each metropolis should support itself. Does a private individual need an order from the council to alter his house?

Cities needed markets, fountains, hospitals, schools, theatres, and commercial exchanges. It was argued that prisons should be constructed in a more functional and dignified manner (John Howard, *The State of the Prisons in England and Wales* [1777]), and that cemeteries, abattoirs, and pollution-producing industries should be banned from city centers. Air and light were to play beneficial roles, thanks to wider, rectilinear streets, as well as courtyards and tree-lined promenades. All that was needed was proper planning and the initiation of new projects by passing new laws: posterity would be responsible for continuing the enhancements that had been conceived for future generation's well-being. In the end, civic action would flourish in an entrepreneurial economy that drew its profits from luxury. This widely held idea found expression in the French provinces. For example, when C.-J. A. Bertrand, an architect from Besançon, won a prize in a competition for essays about the improvements to that city, conducted by its academy in 1770 at the instigation of the *intendant* Lacorée, Bertrand remarked: "It is not always pride that raises palaces, but wisdom that embellishes the city by encouraging emulation, industry, and love of labor, and, so to speak, changes stones into bread."

In contrast to this fine optimism, one of the obsessions of the age was to reduce the expansion of excessively large cities, which aroused fear. Before Rousseau, Mercier, Nicolas Rétif de La Bretonne, or Ledoux, Montesquieu had denounced the danger of the megalopolis:

> Place people where there is work, not pleasure. In a monarchy, the capital city can grow in two ways: either because its inhabitants draw the wealth of the provinces into it (this is the case in a certain maritime nation) or because the poverty of the provinces sends them there—in which case, if one does not keep an eye on the provinces, the whole country will also be ruined.

In France the policy of the *intendants* showed that the absolute monarchy had understood the validity of Montesquieu's position. Finally, in contrast to Voltaire's viewpoint, Montesquieu observed in his *Cahiers, 1716–1755* (Notebooks, 1716–1755) that civic pride should be based on a strong image of centralized power:

> It is above all a great capital that forges the general spirit of a nation; it is Paris that creates the French: without Paris, Normandy, Picardy, and Artois would be as German as Germany; without Paris, Burgundy and the Franche-Comté would be as Swiss as the Swiss; without Paris, Guyenne, Béarn, and Languedoc would be as Spanish as the Spanish.

The Patriotic Image of Power, Trade, and Leisure

The demographic, architectural, and territorial expansion of 18th-century cities was not inevitable. Instead, that expansion resulted from the political and economic management of assets (the "fruits of the Earth," inherited assets, and goods exchanged and produced), which was accompanied by a slow change in the collective mindset. Eventually, the relationships between city and nature or between city and countryside, mentioned above, drew attention to the role of nature in communal spaces in terms of planning and amenities. Views of the surrounding landscape (for example, views of the city from a tree-lined site specifically designed for that purpose) and the ideal arrangement of places for walking (covered walkways, courtyards, avenues, the Champ de Mars, and other public gardens) symbolized the attachment of the city to the kingdom and placed it in relation to France as a whole.

Throughout Europe tree-lined promenades and royal squares, two principal improvements introduced by absolute monarchies, were then developed in the spirit of the Enlightenment and adapted to suit different regions, according to the character of a given city and its need for amenities. Noteworthy examples include the royal squares, esplanades, and "points of view" over rivers and vegetation in Bordeaux, Paris (in what is now the Place de la Concorde), Montpellier, Nancy (the Parc de la Pépinière and the Place de la Carrière Verdoyante), Brussels, Copenhagen, and Lisbon. Commercial activities were deliberately located at some remove from the squares and esplanades in Paris, Brussels, and Copenhagen, whereas in Lisbon and Reims business was conducted in the presence of a statue of the monarch. In those parks and plazas where trees and the supply of running water were most abundant (such as the Jardin de la Fontaine in Nîmes, the Place du Peyrou in Montpellier, the Parc de Blossac in Poitiers, and the Jardin Public in Bordeaux), domesticated nature contributed to the industrial and economic activities of the city: its water supply, nursery gardens, areas for raising silkworms on mulberry trees, and so on.

According to Pierre Lavedan, space "had been a royal privilege; the 18th century did not need to invent it, it simply popularized it" (see Lavedan). The concentric model, used first in Versailles and then in Paris, explains the particular contribution of France to the domain of city planning. Mythically protected by its circle of forts and citadels, with the limits of its territory having been marked by the military engineer Sébastien Le Prestre de Vauban, France was able to breathe more easily under Louis XV, and the monarchy took care to make this known through a policy of building monuments that were both useful and prestigious—a policy without precedent in modern times. Statues of the king indicated the virtual presence of the sovereign in the provincial capitals as well as in Paris. Louis XV, who loved to be represented symbolically as a peacemaker and as the father of the people, softened and humanized the royal image bequeathed to him by his predecessor. The sculpture by Jean-Baptiste Pigalle on the pedestal of the statue of the king in Rheins, *Le Citoyen heureux, La Félicité du peuple* (The Happy Citizen, The People's Bliss [1761–65])—in place of the traditional slaves or trophies—sums up Enlightenment thinking on the patriotism inspired by a sense of urban identity. (See also La Font de Saint-Yenne's *L'ombre du Grand Colbert* [1752; The Shadow of the Great Colbert] and Maile Dussaussoy's *Le citoyen désintéressé* [1767; The Disinterested Citizen]).

Improvement projects throughout France were entrusted to the Ponts et Chaussées (Corps of Bridges and Highways) and the Génie Civil (Corps of Engineering) and monitored by the *intendants,* who had at their disposal, thanks to the Académie Royale d'Architecture (Royal Academy of Architecture), a sort of permanent council of state architects, many of whom worked in the provinces themselves. Improvements proceeded by way of imitation. As Antoine Picon (see Picon) has expressed it:

> For the engineer, France was a sort of royal garden in which projects were carried out, in a way that edifices would be distributed around a park. . . . From one engineer's plan to another, one finds the same obsession with Versailles and its avenues.

Taking his cue from Paris, where immense radiating or diagonal avenues had been opened up between Les Invalides and Montparnasse and in the Champs-Élysées, following the demolition of the city walls at the end of Louis XIV's reign, Marc-Antoine Laugier called for similar improvements to be made elsewhere: "A city should be thought of like a forest. . . . Someone like Le Nôtre must draw plans for it. . . . Let us apply this idea and ensure that the design of our parks serve as a model for our cities." The plans for expanding Nantes, Bordeaux, Marseille, Nîmes, and Dijon, among scores of other examples, show that the city was no longer perceived simply as a large house. It had become a place for walking, accessible to all. The presence of the king (in the form of statues) and the profusion of mascarons—evoking the seasons, the continents, the elements, or mythology—that decorated the facades in affluent neighborhoods are strong indications that, by the middle of the 18th century, the Enlightenment city had achieved full respectability. Later, a neoclassical emphasis on proportion, elegant simplicity, and orderly sobriety would replace the excesses of rococo imagery.

In other countries where the sovereign resided in the capital city (even while owning palaces in the countryside), the symbols of power were expressed through regular street plans, whether radiating or on a grid, which articulated the new cities, connecting palaces, parks, public buildings for administration or culture, and uniform residential districts. This model is evident, for example, in Berlin, with its theatre and the Forum Fridericianum; in Potsdam, with the palace of Sans-Souci; in Kassel, with the Friedrichsplatz and the Huguenot quarter of Oberneustadt; in Karlsruhe; and in Mannheim.

After the Great Fire of 1666, Christopher Wren made plans for a complete reconstruction of London in the French style, but the royal government did not implement them, and the tradition of private improvement and beautification projects continued in the capital city itself as well as in the districts surrounding it. Building took place independently from district to district, but standardized facades ensured a degree of harmony, enhanced by the proliferation of squares and other areas set aside for greenery. Bath, a health resort inherited from the Romans, became the archetype of the rapidly expanding city. Open to its surroundings, its streets follow the topography of the natural landscape—meandering roads, the Royal Crescent, the Circus, and several other circles—and its facades were richly laid out by John Wood the Elder and his son John Wood the Younger between 1727 and 1786. London and Edinburgh took inspiration from Bath, but on a much larger scale. Imposing public buildings, hospitals, city halls, law courts, and university buildings punctuated new urban landscapes that were strictly classical in style. It was in the 18th century that banks and stock exchanges began to announce their presence with frontages that resembled temples.

While Europeans were discovering the charms of Vauxhall Gardens (which might be considered a sort of permanent middle-class fair, devoted to concerts, balls, games, coffeehouses, and exhibitions), theatres and opera houses became the type of building commission most sought after by architects who undertook building works or created new districts. Victor Louis's new Palais-Royal in Paris, which featured boutiques under its arcades and was located in an area of luxury and leisure activities, was inspired by British city planning. However, many other theatre or market districts, such as the Halle au Blé (grain market) in Paris or the Grands Hommes district of Bordeaux, illustrate the system advocated by Laugier, in that they integrated authentic elements of the new city planning into a network that extended or remodeled old city centers. Later, the new Comédie-Française (now the Odéon theatre) and the large, temple-like theatres in Bordeaux, Nantes, and Marseilles, along with Frederick II's opera house in the Forum in Berlin, became models for the rest of Europe and would remain so until the late 19th century. Theatres, those new centers of Enlightenment, were superbly set apart on monumental squares, providing a radiant setting for sociability and cultural activities.

The new ways of thinking about cities were disseminated through salons, libraries, academies, Masonic lodges, schools, and the burgeoning museums. These innovative notions also found expression through the press, which commented profusely on building plans and projects. As for the reasons that justified the recourse to Greek and Roman models (to the point where the modern city was identified as a "new Athens"), they were clearly stated by the great architect Germain Boffrand as early as 1745. In his view, the concept of urban beautification is legitimized by the shared practice, or pleasure, of the liberal arts:

> All those buildings capable of containing great gatherings of people, constructed magnificently, and that continue to astonish us even in a ruined

state, gave the architects of that time grand and frequent opportunities to deploy their talents, to cultivate and improve their art every single day, and to establish principles for that art. These principles became more firmly entrenched among a free people accustomed to seeing superb and beautiful buildings, and incapable of tolerating the mediocre, unlike other nations, where such games, exercises, and spectacles were not the custom, and where the art of architecture was employed only in the construction of private houses and solely for the necessities of life.

DANIEL RABREAU

See also City: Urbanization; Demography; Migration

Further Reading

Harouel, Jean-Louis, *L'embellissement des villes: L'urbanisme français au XVIIIe siècle*, Paris: Picard, 1993

Lavedan, Pierre, *Histoire de l'urbanisme*, 3 vols., Paris: Laurens, 1926–52; 2nd edition, 1952–66; see especially vol. 2, *Renaissance et temps modernes*

Perrot, Jean-Claude, *Génèse d'une ville moderne: Caen au XVIIIe siècle*, 2 vols., Paris: Mouton, 1975

Petit-Dutaillis, Charles, *The French Communes in the Middle Ages*, translated by Joan Vickers, Amsterdam and New York: North-Holland, 1978 (original French edition, 1947)

Picon, Antoine, *Architects and Engineers in the Age of Enlightenment*, translated by Martin Thom, Cambridge and New York: Cambridge University Press, 1992 (original French edition, 1988)

City

Urbanization

For a long time, discourse about urban centers relied on "fossilized" juridical and historical definitions of the city. The fortifications, the antiquity of the city, and the privileges of the citizenry constituted the many myths surrounding the urban condition and the many identifying cultural symbols for urban communities. Demographic growth (both in cities and in rural areas) during the Enlightenment, upheavals in the "world economy," and the general return of dynamism subsequent to the difficulties of the 17th century were accompanied by the development of categories for the analysis of urban phenomena. This development, perceptible in French geographic literature from Piganiol de La Force's *Description de la France* (1718; Description of France) to Hesseln's *Dictionnaire universel de la France* (1771; Universal Dictionary of France) is even more evident in the realm of political economy. From Alexandre Le Maître—author of *La métropolitée ou de l'établissement des villes capitales* (1682; The Metropolis; or, On the Establishment of Capital Cities)—who was among the first to define the urban condition in economic terms, up to Adam Smith and his *Inquiry into the Nature and Causes of the Wealth of Nations* (1776), a dynamic and functionalist conception of the city progressively emerged. In fact, 18th-century urban development was based on an increased polarization of urban networks and functional differentiation among cities. Certain functions, such as politics, shipping and commerce, and leisure activities, proved capable of promoting rapid rates of growth. The first point to be appreciated about urban growth in the 18th century is its selective character. The second characteristic of the Enlightenment period from the point of view of urbanization is no doubt qualitative rather than quantitative. Despite the diatribes of the moralists, who despised the "perverted city," the 18th century saw the affirmation of the values and influence of urban civilization, the center of innovations, the crucible of social relations among members of the wealthy, cultured and powerful elite.

Contrasts and Variety in the European Cities of the 18th Century

During the Enlightenment the cities of Europe underwent a revival, experiencing a phase of growth after the fluctuations, or even quasi stagnation, that had marked the 17th century. In 1700 the urbanized population of the Continent represented, with some variations according to different estimates, around 10–11 percent of the total population (assuming a threshold of urbanization fixed at 5,000 inhabitants). In 1800 this proportion supposedly slightly exceeded 12 percent of the total. However, this general statement conceals contrasting regional developments that include a shift of the economic heart of Europe toward the north since the 17th century (to the detriment of the south) and an opposition between the western regions of the Continent, which were more urbanized, and the eastern regions, which had great difficulty in closing the gap with the West. Around 1700 there were 11 European cities whose population exceeded 100,000 inhabitants: nine of them were in western Europe, and only two in the east (Vienna and Moscow). England experienced the highest level of urbanization in the 18th century: in 1800 nearly one-fourth of the English population (23 percent) was urban. By contrast, the opposite trend prevailed in Spain, where the level of urbanization fell from 12–17 percent to 11–13 percent between 1700 and 1800. The progress of eastern Europe was slow: Austria-Hungary and Russia continued to bring up the rear in urban development in Europe, their levels of urbanization in 1800 being respectively on the order of 6–7 percent and 5–7 percent. However, while the 18th century consolidated the growth of the cities of western and northern Europe, there was also some redistribution. For example, the urban center of gravity of the Holy Roman Empire was displaced toward the East as a consequence of the revival of colonization and the political ascent of Prussia and Austria. Despite the growth of the total European population (excluding Russia), which rose from 102 million to 154 million between 1700 and 1800, the Continent presents a general image of urban stagnation or regression in certain zones that had long been strongly urbanized, such as the Austrian Netherlands or the United Provinces.

Further, while the second half of the century laid the foundations for the formidable urban expansion of the contemporary era, more plainly in England than anywhere else, the rhythms of growth were subject to variation within individual countries. France, for example, underwent a phase of slow urban growth between 1650 and 1750; a period of clear acceleration followed, up until the reign of Louis XVI, when the country entered a phase of slower growth, the prelude to the urban decline of the revolutionary period. This chronology is fairly consistent with the general fluctuations in conditions and reflects the very great sensitivity of the urban population to economic variations. Overall, the hierarchy of European cities was hardly altered during the century. London and Paris remained the two largest cities throughout the 18th century, while some reordering linked to differences in urban dynamics took place else-

where: Rome, Venice, and Milan lost their places in the urban hierarchy in favor of Vienna and Berlin. This panorama illustrates the increase in spatial polarization. Growth favored cities that had dominant political functions—national capitals—and those that were in a position to become part of the vast trading networks.

Aspects and Conditions of Urban Development

The demographic development of cities provides an initial sign of urbanization. Our assessment of the phenomenon remains dependent upon the uneven quality of available sources. Fiscal sources, parish registers, and records of citizenship allow us to grasp the impact of migration, while the archives of hospitals and law courts allow us to measure the obstacles to urban integration and to approximately gauge the often quite large "floating population." The interconnection of these diverse archives allows us to define the specific traits of urban societies, based on the traditional demographic regime: first, significantly elevated death rates, particularly infant mortality rates, and endemic deficiencies in the natural demographic balance; second, a high proportion of unmarried people; and finally, a population that was fundamentally mobile. These traits were modified by the size and activity of the cities and by their population density. No doubt, the second and third of these traits partly explain the rise in the rates of illegitimate births in 18th-century cities, in contrast with rural areas that appeared to be more "sober." Thus, the excessive infant mortality rates, which were always greater in the large cities, ranged between 230 and 450 percent. Certain fatal practices, unevenly represented across Europe, such as the placing of infants with wet nurses in nearby country districts, accentuated the demographic deficit of the cities, even though the fertility of city dwellers was stimulated by the absence of maternal breastfeeding. More than epidemics and famines, which over time had become less frequent and less severe, it was poor sanitary conditions, the lack of city planning, and overcrowding that accounted for the omnipresence of death. The number of unmarried city dwellers (clerics and domestic servants, who could account for up to 10 percent of an urban population) depended on the size and function of a given city. This celibacy, combined with the traditional demographic restraint of late marriage (at around 25 years of age), was a dead weight on the demographic dynamism of the cities. Further, the 18th century saw the spread of an urban Malthusianism from the comfortable classes down to the general population. In Rouen, for example, reproduction rates were theoretically cut in half over the course of the century.

In France, Britain, Switzerland, and the Holy Roman Empire, as in Mediterranean Europe, the reproduction and growth of urban populations was therefore dependent on migrations. Everywhere, migrants were primarily recruited from the region surrounding the cities. The recruitment area of the cities depended on their size, their influence, and therefore their power of attraction. Migrants tended to be country-bred people, women, and, in general, unskilled workers. From farther off there came a more skilled male labor force, and the latter's migration to the large cities was accomplished in stages through intermediary cities. Volunteerist population policies, based on appealing to specialized workers and/or giving a liberal welcome to persecuted minorities, could also contribute to determining the range of the recruitment area. Thus, the growth of Berlin benefited from migrations of French Calvinists, Viennese Jews, and Protestants from Bohemia. Similarly, the vigorous urban and industrial growth of England was fueled by long-range migrations from Ireland and Scotland; these immigrants crowded into the cotton towns of Lancashire or into London.

Two models have been defined to describe the preindustrial urban framework and to bring to light the forces driving its development. The first, the "continental" model, gives political power a central role in the organization and development of this framework. The concentration of administrative institutions and offices can account for the growth of the capital cities in the 18th century: the example of the *Residenzstadt* (residence city) of the Holy Roman Empire, imitated at Versailles and sometimes created from nothing (as in Mannheim, Karlsruhe, or Berlin) is a telling one. The restructuring of cities in the Empire was detrimental to traditional merchant cities such as Cologne, but benefited those competitive cities that succeeded, in the wake of a confirmed political or residential function, in developing their commercial, financial, or industrial functions as well. Some of these cities were all too obviously single-purpose settlements and proved to be fragile when the court departed from them (Versailles in 1715 and 1789, Mannheim in 1778). The assignment of this role as driving force in urban dynamics to politico-administrative or even military functions can lead to a fairly close correlation, as in the kingdom of France, between the hierarchy of cities and the framework of power. Nevertheless, the French example shows some imbalance between the demographic hierarchy and the urban administrative framework. Such imbalances existed, for instance, in Lyon or Marseille, the second- and third-ranked cities of the kingdom, which were cities with dominant economic functions and therefore energizers of urban growth. Generally speaking the cities' capacity for expansion was determined by their ability to structure their commercial space and develop their functions as warehouses.

Other factors included cities' ability to dominate trade through a concentration of capital and enterprises, their modernization of transportation networks, their mastery of administrative functions and the management of information.

More specifically, the "maritime" model of development made commercial capitalism the principal agent of differentiation and ranking among cities. One could cite the growth of the French ports (Bordeaux, Nantes, and Marseille) that captured the trade with the "sugar islands," the growth of the ports on the Andalusian coast (Cadiz), the longer established growth of Amsterdam, and also that of London, as a market for consumer goods, a national warehouse, and a port for colonial trade. In a certain number of cases (London, Bristol, Marseille) commercial expansion in turn fueled the industrial expansion of the city.

Just as political and commercial functions contributed to urban dynamism, so industrial development could be the main source of urbanization. While craft and manufacturing activity played a role of some importance in the cities of modern Europe, protoindustrialization usually took the form of a relocation of industry from cities to the countryside, which was free from the supervision of the guilds and which offered lower labor costs. The adaptation of cities to "the challenges of the world economy"—the appeal of colonial markets, the development of local "consumer societies"—determined the growth of some urban organizations and the stagnation or decline of others, such as Valenciennes or Cologne. However, protoindustrialization did not result in a total separation of cities and industrial enterprise. The cities remained the centers of decision-making and also retained control of the specialized activities that required significant amounts of capital and costly equipment. Wherever the conditions for an economic takeoff were created, there instead emerged a new organization of economic space, controlled by city dwellers but based on a synergy between the city and a rural "industrial region."

While industrial growth presented few examples of mushrooming cities, the development of bathing and thermal resorts in England (Bath, Brighton, and others) represented a new example of urban development centered on the exploitation of a leisure activity. Factors conducive to this type of development included the presence of great urban centers close by, a well-developed transportation system, an aura of fashionable appeal inspired by great celebrities or by the royal court, and the social expansion of certain recreational pursuits. The impact of this type of growth was still limited on a pan-European level, but it nevertheless illustrates the wholesale adoption of the values of urban civilization.

The Enlightenment in the Cities

The prestige of cities was expressed through the splendors of the cityscape, through the cultural advantages of city dwellers, and through specific forms of social relations. The material growth of cities created the problem of urban planning on a large scale and no longer only in isolated and emblematic forms, such as royal squares. "Creative fires" (London in 1666, or Rennes in 1720), natural catastrophes (Lisbon's earthquake, 1755), or large-scale rebuilding by princes encouraged new conceptions in city planning. In addition to aesthetic and architectural considerations, from this time onward it became important to look after the well being of the inhabitants. It was particularly necessary to manage spatial and demographic expansion and the circulation of people and goods. Port cities, for example, sought to integrate the port with the rest of the urban fabric by constructing new quays and highways, but apart from Amsterdam, where a rational renovation of the port involving concentric, semicircular canals that enclosed new districts of the city as they developed, successful ventures in planning and urban development were rare. However, functionalism promoted an organic and biological vision of the city dweller, which encouraged a greater sensitivity to the quality of the environment on the part of administrators, architects, and physicians. Considerations of public health explain the removal of cemeteries to the outskirts of cities toward the end of the 18th century, as well as the general spread of a practical and utilitarian form of city planning (lighting, paving of streets, garbage collection, fire prevention and, water supply measures). However, there were variations in the timing of such policies: the United Provinces had played a pioneering role since the middle of the 17th century.

Cities also enjoyed cultural progress, linked to the concentration of elites within their walls, and the wealth of scholarly and university facilities that resulted. Higher levels of literacy characterized cities everywhere, by contrast to the countryside, even though industrial cities lagged behind the others because of the hiring of child workers at early ages, or because of denominational variations such as those between Protestant and Catholic countries. The circulation of printed matter was carried out on a much larger scale in cities, and there were various possibilities for access to written materials through libraries and reading rooms. The leisure pursuits of the elites gave rise to new urban facilities, such as theatres or concert halls, that housed permanent companies and that were also the object of the speculative operations of merchants and real estate agents. Finally, enlightened forms of social relations flourished in the cities, which functioned as "theatres of witty minds" and showcases for the professional bourgeoisie. Cities were the home of the aristocratic salons of France, which were imitated throughout Europe; the provincial academies of the time of Louis XV; the more "bourgeois" circles of the Masonic lodges or the coffeehouses, which spread from England even into the Holy Roman Empire; or the more political associations exemplified by the English "clubs." This cultural framework reproduced the hierarchies, definitions, and contrasts of urban Europe. The first academies in the French provinces met in cities that had administrative functions and more than 25,000 inhabitants; the milieu of the *Aufklärer,* the enlightened men of the Holy Roman Empire, was quite closely identified with the milieu of the senior civil servants who resided in the princely cities. The spread of certain innovations, such as coffeehouses or provincial newspapers, followed the hierarchical networks of administration or trade and depended on the development of lines of communication. Toward the end of the 18th century, Adam Smith set out to examine how English cities contributed to the "improvement of the country districts." With some lags in time and variations from region to region, the cities of Europe played an essential role in the modernization and differentiation of European societies by ensuring the spread of ideas and innovations, by inducing changes in lifestyles, by promoting the emergence of new needs, and by organizing the modern market economy.

VINCENT MILLIOT

See also City: Planning; Demography; Migration

Further Reading

De Vries, Jan, *European Urbanization, 1600–1800,* London: Methuen, 1984

Hohenberg, Paul, and Lynn Hollen Lees, *The Making of Urban Europe, 1000–1950,* Cambridge, Massachusetts: Harvard University Press, 1985

Civilization and Civility

Usage

Civilisation (civilization), like *bienfaisance* (charity), was one of the most famous political and social neologisms created prior to the French Revolution. As the modern meaning of "act of civilizing" became entrenched, the older, legal meaning of the term—"to make a criminal case civil"—rapidly fell into disuse. The first modern definition of the term appears in the 1771 edition of the *Dictionnaire de Trévoux* (Dictionary of Trévoux), a Jesuit-produced dictionary of language that purported to be "universal." The *Dictionnaire de Trévoux* cites as the first known occurrence of the term in French, with the meaning "act of civilizing," a passage from *L'ami des hommes ou Traité de la population* (1756; The Friend of Men; or, Treatise on Population), without mentioning the passage's author, the marquis de Mirabeau, the eventual founder and guarantor of militant Physiocracy: "Religion is without doubt the first and most useful restraint on humankind; it is the primary source of *civilization*. It endlessly preaches and reminds us of fraternity, and softens our hearts."

Obviously, the Jesuit authors of the *Dictionnaire de Trévoux* and their order had a vested interest in such a definition. In fact, in the passage cited, Mirabeau was elaborating on Montesquieu's arguments in Books XXIV and XXV of *De l'esprit des lois* (1748; The Spirit of Laws), where Montesquieu considers the effects of religion from the viewpoint of the social benefits it affords: it leads to gentler mores, brings men together, and establishes useful prohibitions and duties. In short, religion is a beneficial "social fact" and little more.

Tracing the gradual changes in the word's meaning in the works of its inventor (Mirabeau) enables us to make two observations. First, the term was not originally included in the linear conception of progress, which, in an outrageous oversimplification, is sometimes said to have originated in speech by the young Anne-Robert-Jacques Turgot at the Sorbonne in December 1750: "The total mass of the human race, alternating calm and agitation, good and evil, proceeds slowly but surely toward greater perfection." In fact, even the famous 19th-century dictionary compiler Emile Littré mistakenly attributed usage of the term "civilization" to Turgot, confusing Turgot's ideas with those of his editor and commentator, Pierre-Samuel Dupont de Nemours. To a degree, the notion of civilization must be considered separately from the very old theme of the progress of the human mind. The distantly "cyclical" notion of history in which the term appears in Mirabeau's works is quite compatible (but not assimilable) with the *Discours préliminaire* (Preliminary Discourse) of the *Encyclopédie,* or even with Voltaire's conception of *siècles* (ages), which refers to something quite different from the traditional theme of the mind's progress. The second observation is that we are dealing with "civilization" understood as a discriminating *condition* rather than as the result of a *process*. The notions of pluralism or a hierarchy of civilized nations had not yet emerged, but we can discern a vision of humanity with complex implications. The very definition of the act of civilizing is in fact problematic as a concept: only the driving force is given.

We must therefore empirically trace as closely as possible the expansion of the term and the development of the concept, initially limiting our consideration to the word "civilization" itself. It already appears in the 1770 first edition of the *Histoire philosophique et politique des établissements et du commerce des Européens dans les deux Indes* (A Philosophical and Political History of the Settlements and Trade of the Europeans in the East and West Indies), by the abbé Raynal and Denis Diderot, where the term is applied to a "species of degraded, degenerate men" whose minds are "not very advanced for the arts of civilization." In this context, the term encompasses the comforts of life in a society that has civilized mores and the capacity for intellectual inventiveness. "Civilization" appears in 1782 in Louis Sébastien Mercier's *Tableau de Paris* (Panorama of Paris), and it is easy to see why he had no reason to include it in his *Néologie ou vocabulaire de mots nouveaux, à renouveler ou pris dans des acceptions nouvelles* (1801; Neology; or, A Vocabulary of New Words, to Be Redefined or Considered in New Meanings). Mercier's use of the term in *Tableau de Paris* is interesting because of his association of civilization with perfectibility. "Civilization is almost perfected here," he writes in Chapter LXII, referring even more to an optimal balance than to progress. Moreover, Mercier associates civilization with the arts, thus integrating the Encyclopedists' perspective: "Is that where the progress of civilization and the arts was to lead?" Echoes of Jean-Jacques Rousseau's first important essay, *Discours sur les sciences et les arts* (1750; A Discourse on the Sciences and the Arts) are apparent, where the "virtual" place of the concept of civilization must already be studied not in itself but with regard to imminent new occurrences of the term.

However, in our view, a more essential step was taken in the last edition of the opus attributed to Raynal, where Diderot's use of the word "civilization" with reference to Russia is decisive (as we will see, the marquis d'Argenson also employed the term for the example of Russia and the activities of Peter the Great). The last edition of Raynal's work strongly connects the civilization of mores to the organization of civil society (as understood in that period) and the exercise of political power. It also associates the old term *policé* (ordered) with the new "civilized." Although that perspective may seem "archaic" and still quite far from that of the marquis de Condorcet, it brings together in a significant way the notion of civilization and that of a liberty that requires time to become thoroughly integrated into the social fabric.

> The emancipation—or, to call the same thing by another name—the civilization of an Empire is a long, difficult project. Before a nation has confirmed by habit a lasting attachment to this new order of things, a prince may, by clumsiness, laziness, prejudice, jealousy, predilection for former practices, or a spirit of tyranny, annihilate or abandon all the good brought about in the course of two or three reigns. And so all the lasting evidence attests to the fact that the civilization of states was more the work of circumstances than the wisdom of sovereigns. All nations have oscillated between barbarity and an ordered state, from an ordered state to barbarity, until unforeseen causes led them to an equilibrium that they can never perfectly maintain (*Tableau de Paris*, Chapter XIX).

This text appeared in 1780, and in our view it is of only secondary importance that it was written around 1775. There was at that time no notion of absolutely decisive or irreversible progress.

The type of conceptual innovation announced in this passage help to forge the meaning that appears in Snetlage's *Nouveau dictionnaire français* (New French Dictionary), two decades and a revolution later, in 1795:

> The act of civilizing, or the tendency of a nation to polish or rather to correct its mores and usages by holding in civil society an active, luminous, morality, that is loving, and abounding in good works. (Every citizen of Europe today has joined this final battle for civilization—a civilization of mores.)

The precise moment of revolutionary expansion can be discerned in this passage, but this is not its most significant aspect. As is always the case, the dictionary entry helped bring the term back into use, and also revealed a semantic territory related to a form of philanthropic cosmopolitanism very different from Mirabeau's concept of "fraternity." Without turning to "History" or holding to lexicographic calculations, two important moments should be noted. In 1791, prior to Condorcet's introduction of the idea of a civilizing process (now canonical in the tradition of the French Republic as it is taught) into a revitalized philosophy of intellectual history and education of the human race, the comte de Volney had already helped to shape that concept by relating it to little-known aspects of the historical thought of the French Enlightenment, taking into consideration and attempting to go beyond the notion of decadence. In *Les ruines ou Méditations sur les révolutions des empires* (1791; Ruins; or, Meditations on the Revolutions of Empires), Volney draws a close connection between civilization and the very definition of progress; indeed, civilization, a universal objective, commands progress. Now, however, progress is understood as a synthesis of human mores and triumphant intellectual fulfillment: "Above all, for three centuries the Enlightenment has flourished and propagated; civilization, favored by fortunate circumstances, has made notable progress: even obstacles and abuses have been turned to its advantage." In *Les ruines* the majestic term "civilization" implies mores, ways of living—everything that fosters material and moral perfection (including the various forms of "commerce" as defined by Montaigne). Volney holds that if China offers the spectacle of an "aborted civilization," this is due to a combination of "abnormalities" only partially attributable to the thwarted possibilities of Enlightenment expansion; despotism is combined with major cultural defects that make the Chinese a "nation of automatons."

The term "civilization" is almost unknown in the language of the French revolutionary orators who were busy laying the foundations of regeneration, but it triumphs and reveals all its historical possibilities in Condorcet's text of 1795, with a potential influence far beyond that of earlier works. Condorcet's *Esquisse d'un tableau historique des progrès de l'esprit humain* (1795; Outlines of an Historical View of the Progress of the Human Mind) was distributed officially as gospel after Thermidor, before the Ideologists brought out the fossilized vulgate, reestablishing the Enlightenment-Revolution continuity. The work also entered into a historical systematization with a promising political future. Large portions undoubtedly date from the 1780s, but what matters, as is the case with Diderot's thought, is the emergence of the idea of a public realm. There are three types of occurrence of the word "civilization" in the *Esquisse*. First, the terms refers to any state in the development of the human species once its members have formed societies: "The first state of civilization in which the human species has been observed is that of a very small society of men living from hunting and fishing." In its second usage, the term sometimes seems close to what modern anthropologists call "culture," without reference to a level of knowledge.

Finally, and most classically, the term is used to refer to the development of the arts and sciences, and life in society. In the later instance, it designates—often in association with such terms as "progress," "degrees," or "perfection"—both a process and its fortunate outcome, even before the *Esquisse* opens onto a perspective of indefinite development:

> We have come to the point in civilization where the people profit from the Enlightenment, not only through services received from enlightened men but also because they have learned how to make it a sort of patrimony, and use enlightened ideas to defend themselves against error, to foresee or satisfy their needs, protect themselves from the evils of life, or lessen those evils with new pleasures.

Used in this sense, civilization is associated (sometimes to the point of redundancy) with the mastery of knowledge, in a sense that is not the most "modern" and that fits into the type of historiography of the mind invoked earlier in this essay, a type exemplified by the ideas of René Descartes and Bernard Le Bovier de Fontenelle. As Condorcet writes in the *Esquisse*:

> We will find in the experience of the past, in the observation of progress made thus far by science, by civilization, in the analysis of the advancement of the human mind and the development of its faculties, the strongest reasons to believe that nature has not set a term to our hopes.

Sometimes, albeit rarely, the word "civilization" does not refer to a fundamental, irreducible dichotomy—civilized versus barbarian—but rather to a sort of intellectual, ethical, and political epiphany. Within a framework marked by tension, there occasionally emerges an awareness of individual autonomy and success in intellectual emancipation that marks a chronological break, in which the random element is acknowledged, in the *Esquisse,* in the word "crisis":

> We will see how this painful stormy passage from a coarse society to the state of civilization of free enlightened peoples is not a degeneration of the human species but a necessary crisis in its gradual advancement toward absolute perfection.

Origins

We must now turn to the historical and social context for the appearance of this "neologism." Ideally, its appearance could be linked to a very particular time and circle, but physiocratic philanthropy turns out to

be a rather tight circle. Let us restrict our consideration to the simpler project of semantic study. Within what (textual) limits did the word "civilization" evolve? In his notes, Émile Benveniste mentions an occurrence of the term in English in the writings of Adam Ferguson, the friend of the Scottish philosopher David Hume (see Benveniste), but the first works of the philosopher-historian postdate Mirabeau's *L'ami des hommes*. Research in this field should be pursued one day when adequate data is available. Here we will limit ourselves to tracing the term's evolution in French, linking the verbs *civiliser* (to civilize) and *se civiliser* (to become civilized) to "equivalent" terms (allowing for the necessarily critical view of this notion of equivalence) prior to the word "civilization," to suggest a line of interpretation of the appearance of the concept and the word.

(1) Voltaire did not use the term "civilization," but he had a very clear idea of the process of becoming civilized—of what *se civiliser* means: "How slowly, with how much difficulty is the human race civilized and society perfected!" he proclaims in *Essai sur l'histoire générale* (1756; An Essay on Universal History). In the final version of this text, *Essai sur les moeurs et l'esprit des nations* (1756; An Essay on the Manners and Spirit of Nations), this idea recurs: "It takes many centuries for human society to perfect itself." In this context, Voltaire actually means to denounce the barbarity of the 17th-century wars against the Turks. He establishes connections among the ideas of progress in the "arts," the "humanization" of the species, and the development of social regulations that as far as possible exclude violence. In a way Voltaire is closer to the positions of Diderot and Raynal than to that of Mirabeau. Moving on to occurrences of the word "civilize" in the same work, we find the same configuration: "We have seen how the Crusades exhausted Europe of men and money, and did not civilize it" (*Essai sur les moeurs*). In the 1770 edition of the *Histoire des deux Indes*, a similar use of "civilize" occurs, opportunely enabling us to trace the connection between this occurrence and the inaugural use of "civilization" by Mirabeau, which is compatible with Voltaire's views on religion: "Among this people of wise men, all that connects and civilizes men is religion, and religion itself is nothing but the practice of social virtues."

However, as has been pointed out (and as those knowledgeable about Condorcet's influence on posterity would surely expect), in the Tenth Epoch outlined in the *Esquisse* Condorcet introduces not a meaning for "civilize" and "be civilized," but instead a context or a situation:

> Can there be any doubt that the wisdom or the senseless divisions of European nations, seconding the slow but unfailing progress of their colonies,

will not soon produce the independence of the New World? And then, as the European population grows rapidly on this immense territory, will it not have to civilize or eliminate, even without conquest, the savage nations that still occupy vast regions?

Of course, this absorption and annihilation of the New World is proclaimed as basically generous, the fulfillment of an ancient finality that is not exclusively Christian or Catholic. The unity of the human species, by way of pedagogical propagation instead of Stoic or imperial unification, is resolutely substituted for the dread of corrupting pure sociability or destroying generous energy that haunts the Diderot of the *Supplément au voyage de Bougainville* (1774; A Supplement to Bougainville's Travels), or the address to the Hottentots in the *Histoire des deux Indes*. Fortunate colonies! "These vast countries will offer him [the colonist] abundant populations who seem only to be waiting for us to bring them the means to be civilized, find brothers among the Europeans, become our friends and disciples." What this ideology conceals is the problem posed to the Enlightenment and formulated in note IX of Rousseau's *Discours sur l'origine et les fondements de l'inégalité parmi les hommes* (1755; Discourse on the Origins of Inequality), of the fracture within the process of civilization, from colonial murder to solitude in social alienation. Rousseau raises this issue with a reference to Ovid: "*Barbarus hic ego sum quia non intelligor illis* . . Clearly, we need to go back to the long-standing common usage of the adjectival past participle "civilized" and the entrenched opposition between civilized nations (civilized peoples) and savage nations (barbarian peoples). This dichotomy obviously refers back not just to mores and manners, to the absence or presence of political organization with an explicitly legal base or admissible in the language of the Romanized West, but also, just as in the ancients' distinction between barbarian and nonbarbarian, to the form and use of language. Montesquieu writes of Alexander the Great's "civilizing" influence in India: "He forbade the Ichthyophages to live on fish; he wanted the shores of that sea to be inhabited by civilized nations" (*De l'esprit des lois*). At issue here is the creation of needs in order to lead to a society of trade. Voltaire says of the conquering flights of the Gauls, barbarians incapable of recording the meaning—if any—of their adventure: "No monument remains in our land of these emigrations, which were similar to those of the Tartars. It only proves that the population was very abundant but not civilized" (*Essai sur l'histoire générale* [An Essay on Universal History], foreword, in the *Essai sur les moeurs et l'esprit des nations* [1756; An Essay on the Manners and Spirit of

Nations]). When Volney ascribes to the Chinese an "aborted civilization," he claims, following a tradition of his time, that it is in part due to their "poorly constructed language." It is then but a short distance to the concepts of "universal language" and "universal grammar."

(2) Bloch and Wartburg had long given *police* (order) and *policer* (to order) as "equivalents" of "civilization" and "to civilize." This seems relevant to our discussion. In *Histoire de l'empire de Russie sous Pierre Grand* (1759; Russia under Peter the Great), Voltaire writes of the Spanish, with their widely varied origins: "When nations are mixed this way, they take a long time to become civilized, and even to shape their language: some become orderly sooner, others later." Perhaps it would be better, however, to focus on various forms of differentiation. The French word *police* goes back principally to the Greek *politeia*, in its general sense, which encompasses both the idea of citizenship and that of the republic or body politic. Those notions can be broadened to designate a type of philosophy of the purposes of social organization, as attested by two examples given by Montesquieu in *De l'esprit des lois*: "People who live under good order are happier than those who roam the forests without chiefs or rules"; "natural freedom [is] the aim of the order of savages." The notion of order applies to forms of social control both within and outside the structures that organize power. In the same text Montesquieu writes: "the creation of censors takes away from the consuls that part of the legislative power that regulates the mores of citizens and the momentary control of various state bodies." The same cluster of meanings is to be found in works by Voltaire and Claude-Adrien Helvétius. Noteworthy here is the crossing of semantic fields of "order" and "orderly" that contributed to the emergence of civilization. Going from Montesquieu to the *Histoire des deux Indes*, one notes a development of the syntagmas "ordered peoples" or "ordered nations" toward a conflation of "ordered" with "civilized." Initially, this development was not systematic, which is why one cannot refer to a simple entity "order-ordered," much less to a continuity between "order-ordered" and "civilization-civilized." In *Réflexions sur la monarchie universelle* (1734; Reflections on a Universal Monarchy), Montesquieu points out the politically achieved perfection of the body of "ordered" peoples: "Now that all ordered peoples are so to speak the members of a great republic, power comes from wealth." Raynal's *Histoire des deux Indes*, by comparison, presents a far broader range of conditions:

Perhaps also the mores of orderly peoples are more detrimental to the health of savages than their climates, if it is true, as has been claimed, that philosophers themselves were the cause of the deaths of the Laplanders that they took with them.

In fact, linguistic history took rather a peculiar turn in French. Jean Starobinski has clearly demonstrated how the "equivalence" in meaning underscored by Bloch and Wartburg must have been extended and understood in ways other than by reference to the *polis* and the *politeia*, because of a strange phonetic-semantic attraction in French between *police* and *policer,* on the one hand, and *polisser/polir/politesse* (*polisser:* "to polish"/"politeness"), on the other, with numerous occurrences by the end of the 16th century (see Starobinski). The result was a kind of guiding semantic thread, in which are stranded together forms of mastery of manners, mores, and language, along with the structures that embody these elements (time and tradition, the culture of arts and letters, life at the royal court, communication between the sexes), eventually leading to institutionalization of the "civil." Dictionaries attest to this, including the successive editions of the *Dictionnaire de Trévoux* during the 18th century. Charles Pinot Duclos gives the most sensitive analysis in *Considérations sur les moeurs de ce siècle* (1750; Considerations on the Morals of This Century):

Men owe each other consideration, because they all owe each other recognition. They reciprocally owe each other a politeness worthy of them, made for thinking beings, and varied by the various sentiments that should inspire it. . . . Even if we do not possess those qualities announced by the graces, we will have those announced by the honest man and citizen; we will not have to resort to falseness.

Duclos's remarks obviously go beyond good manners to focus on the conditions of existence in civil society. No mere matter of superficial contamination, contact with politeness produces something more profound, and therein lies its link to the concept of civilization. In *Considérations sur le gouvernement ancien et présent de la France* (1764; Considerations on the Past and Present Government of France), the marquis d'Argenson writes with regard to the key example of time: "Politeness has suddenly attained immense power; the immensity of that power has been neglected out of disdain for barbarity." At issue here is political power as it relates to progress in the "arts of arms and laws." In 1784 an unknown editor replaced the word "politeness" with our new concept ("civilization has suddenly attained immense power"). The substitution may signify that the former meaning of politeness had become obsolete; clearly, politeness was now to be distinguished

from intelligent civility. Montesquieu expresses it beautifully: "Politeness flatters the vices of others, and civility keeps us from bringing out our own; it is a barrier that men erect between themselves to keep from corrupting themselves" (*De l'esprit des lois*). However, that did not prevent some vacillation and the possibility of a reversal of the terms. When Helvétius distinguishes two forms of "worldly usage," one of them a purely empty code and the other an authentic social usage beyond manners, the advantage does not go to civility. Nevertheless, he posits that the word "politeness" requires a qualifying adjective for clarity: "This usage is as different from the true usage of the word always based on reason, as civility is from true politeness" (*De l'esprit* [1758; Essays on the Mind and Its Several Faculties]). The ambiguous status of politeness, whether derived from increasing alienation from court society, the prestige of primitive ingenuousness, or new incarnations of the Spartan myth, imposed a shift in meaning.

(3) Thus, it is clear that in the end we must go back to the words that are derived from "civil," as they pertain to the moral realm. The adjective has dual connotations, referring both to that which is politically organized—also called civil society, and to that which in law regulates relations between citizens (not to be confused with the organization of powers). In *De l'esprit des lois,* Montesquieu clearly demonstrates the correlation of civil law with the political realm, writing "civil law looks at each citizen, as on the whole city, with a mother's eyes." In the realm of mores, which was at the time both linked and opposed to the legal realm, the civil as a cultural value is manifested in *civilité* (civility), a term famous since Erasmus and the crucial term of what Norbert Élias has called the civilization of mores (see Élias). However, occurrences of the term "civility" are too rare to develop these positions fully. From Jean Baptiste de La Salle to Toussaint L'Ouverture, worldly Christians and moralizers of social exchange used the term "civility" in the sense of Montesquieu's "barrier" of politeness, to designate that form of moral and social virtue in which self-respect and respect for others are juxtaposed. We will doubtless have to wait for further studies of the relationship between public and privates spheres before "civility" can be definitively situated in the same semantic field as "civilization." Revolutionary catechisms, as Roger Chartier has shown, are highly suggestive in this regard (see Chartier).

The semantic landscape whose background has been sketched out here should be clarified from three points of view. First, in the West the appearance of the term "civilization" is indeed related to the expansion and general value of "civility": civility understood as in the "civilization of mores" defined by Élias (in fact, the syntagma is already found in Snetlage). A progressivist ideology of the development of the human mind, knowledge, and organization, could only have come to be embodied in the word "civilization" in a society that had in fact transcended the old society, ordered by monarchical discipline, in which the conditions of existence for "civilization" had been spawned. In societies characterized by monarchical discipline, according to Élias, interiorization of multiple constraints in social life and relations between individuals was accepted. This interiorization goes along with conceding the monopoly on legitimate violence to the state, according to the thought of Max Weber. Second, we believe that this civilizing "civility," where rationality and a renewed sense of the unity and dignity of the human species find their place, would be inconceivable without a transformation of the notion of *civis* and a rejection of the couplet *police/politesse* once their potential had been exhausted. Originally, as Benveniste recalls in the *Vocabulaire des institutions indo-européennes* (1969; Indo-European Language and Society), the *civis* was not the subject or citizen (two entities whose differences would remain uncertain for some time) but the "fellow-citizen": "the designation applied, originally among themselves, by members of a group holding native rights." The birth of "civilization" is also inscribed in this field of divergent meanings. The beginning of Rousseau's *Émile, ou, De l'éducation* (1762; Émile: or, Concerning Education) for instance, provides more than one instance of such ambiguity. In his treatment of the Spartan mirage, Rousseau brings into convergence the concept of the "reasonable" citizen and that of the member of the fatherland. The *civis* of civility respects in himself an image of man and thus respects himself, but he founds another type of community where conventionalized or even contractual individualism stands as a value even beyond the legal sphere. The appearance of the term "civilization" marks a new convergence of questions about the progress and education of the human race, and on the nature of social ties and constraints, arising from fundamental changes, in the last three centuries, in that part of French society that is not culturally immobile. Third, and finally, one cannot ignore the moment at the beginning of the 1930s when the question of this term was historically and theoretically posed. Two different lines of inquiry emerged. First, there was the German distinction between "culture" and "civilization," as expressed at a certain time by Thomas Mann himself, which demanded development of an alternative position. Second, the field of

anthropological study changed, and with it the meaning of the nature/culture dichotomy in the framework of a different education of humanity, in a direction that would be developed up until the writings of Claude Lévi-Strauss, where again two meanings of the term "civilization" enter into a critical relationship: "civilization," as understood in the Enlightenment, and "civilizations," as this term would be used from Wilhelm von Humboldt to Arnold Toynbee for organizing differences. To this one must add some other circumstances that have led to the questioning of the meaning and limits of the civilizing process.

GEORGES BENREKASSA

See also Barbarian and Savage; Conversation; Cosmopolitanism; Europe; History, Philosophy of; Police; Sociability

Further Reading

Benveniste, Émile, "Civilization: A Contribution to the History of the Word," in *Problems in General Linguistics*, translated by Mary Elizabeth Meek, Coral Gables, Florida: University of Miami Press, 1971 (original French edition, 1966)

Chartier, Roger, "Civilté," in *Handbuch politisch-sozialer Grundbegriffe in Frankreich, 1680–1820*, edited by Rolf Reichardt and Hans-Jürgen Lüsebrink, vol. 4, Munich: Oldenbourg, 1986

Élias, Norbert, *The Civilizing Process*, 2 vols., translated by Edmund Jephcott, New York: Urizen Books, 1978; reprint, 1 vol., Oxford and Cambridge, Massachusetts: Blackwell, 1994 (original German edition, 2 vols., 1939)

Pagden, Anthony, "The 'Defence of Civilization' in 18th-Century Social Theory," *History of the Human Sciences* 1 (1988)

Pagden, Anthony, editor, *The Languages of Political Theory in Early-Modern Europe*, Cambridge and New York: Cambridge University Press, 1987

Philosophy and Culture: Proceedings of the XVIIth World Congress of Philosophy, 5 vols., edited (vols. 2–5) by Venant Cauchy, Montreal: Éditions du Beffroi and Éditions Montmorency, 1986–88

Starobinski, Jean, "The Word 'Civilization,'" in *Blessings in Disguise; or, The Morality of Evil*, by Starobinski, translated by Arthur Goldhammer, Cambridge: Polity Press, and Cambridge, Massachusetts: Harvard University Press, 1993 (original French edition, 1989)

Clandestine Literature

Clandestine literature has been an object of study ever since 1912, when G. Lanson discovered a number of manuscript copies of "philosophical" or anti-Christian texts in French municipal libraries (see Lanson). In 1938 Ira Owen Wade carried out a systematic survey in France, benefiting from Norman Lewis Torrey's research on Voltaire's library at Saint Petersburg; Wade offered an inventory of 104 texts circulated between 1700 and 1750 (see Wade). In 1978 Miguel Benitez resumed this research and discovered a significant number of hitherto unknown copies; a new inventory was published in 1980 for a conference at the Sorbonne. Clandestine literature at that point emerged from the shadows, boasting 130 titles and a substantial increase in the number of extant copies. Further advances came in 1988, with a new inventory by Benitez, listing 148 titles (see Benitez, 1988), and in 1996, with the publication of a collection of his studies: the new inventory listed 257 titles with copies spread throughout Europe (see Benitez, 1996). Clearly, clandestine philosophical literature has not yet revealed all its riches. This literature raises questions for specialists in philosophy and the histories of ideas, religion, apologetics, and literature, as well as for those studying printing, censorship, and the distribution of texts. The gradual discovery of the wealth of *clandestina* has been accompanied by more thorough studies in the field of the history of ideas. The classic image of Enlightenment philosophy, reduced to a handful of prestigious texts, is no longer sufficient: clandestine literature forces us to read between the lines and discover the true intellectual context that informed the thoughts of the great *philosophes*.

This proliferation of studies has brought with it a new problem. The studies focus on the clandestine philosophical literature of the 16th, 17th, and 18th centuries, but what connection is there between Jean Bodin's *Colloquium heptaplomeres* (Colloquium between Seven Learned Men) and the baron d'Holbach's *Histoire critique de Jésus, fils de Marie* (A Critical History of Jesus, Son of Mary), or between Geoffroy de La Vallée's *Fléau de la foi* (Scourge of Faith) and Julien Offroy de La Mettrie's (*L'homme machine* [1748; Man, a Machine])? There is a great danger of anachronism here. One must beware of reading the history of ideas a posteriori as a steady march toward the Revolution, since this approach would obviously distort the interpretation of texts. There are nonetheless some perceptible currents, common points, and continuities between one century and another: the clandestine philosophers of the age of the Enlightenment felt that they were building on a long tradition of criticism of religion and the Church. Indeed, this critical stance was the meaning of "philosophical" during the Enlightenment: a text was "philosophical" to the extent that it was based, either implicitly or explicitly, on principles hostile or foreign to Catholic orthodoxy. For this reason, Socinian texts or Jansenist pamphlets should not be considered as "philosophical," although we should still be aware that clandestine philosophical texts draw on others that represent the whole range of possible positions concerning orthodoxy.

In this sense, the clear boundary between orthodoxy and heterodoxy is blurred. Some philosophers were believers without knowing it; and some believers, sometimes unwittingly, adopted positions that placed them on the side of heresy and heterodoxy. The fragmentation of the Protestant churches and sects had brought into view a whole range of uncertainties and tentative positions. Recent research on Baruch Spinoza and the Dutch Collegiants illustrates the influence of religious thought on modern rationalism; conversely, the evolution of Catholic apologetics shows the influence of the *philosophes,* to the extent that the apologists employ rational arguments more suited to the "God of the *philosophes*" than to the "God of Abraham, Isaac, and Jacob." The "inner light" of conscience and the philosophical Enlightenment strengthened one another.

The issue of the circulation of texts raises similar problems. The Bastille Archives hold the works of very few clandestine philosophers—no more than a dozen who wrote between 1653 and 1789—but they reveal the whole range of proscribed beliefs and the full weight of censorship. The successive waves of Huguenots (beginning in the 1680s) and Jansenists (from the 17th century on, but in particular after the publication of the papal bull *Unigenitus*) are readily traced; peddlers and printers of political, religious, erotic, or obscene pamphlets were arrested throughout the 18th century. Philosophical writings therefore relied on the same channels of distribution as did these other clandestine writings. Antireligious criticism was spread by specialists in the underground distribution of political pamphlets and, in the religious sphere, by the distribution of Marrano and Protestant writings from the "Refuge" (Great Britain and the Netherlands). The history of the distribution of clandestine philosophy, which was European in scope, is thus connected to the histories of the book and of censorship.

Clandestine texts were published throughout the 18th century; a complete listing can be found in Benitez's 1996 inventory. It is important to recognize that these publications reflected the vagaries of the history of ideas: the printed version did not enjoy a privileged status. Holbach and Jacques-André Naigeon specialized in editions that radicalized the ideas of the author. Their publications met the propagandistic needs of the moment; thus, they transformed the deist Robert Challe (1659–1721) into an atheist, materialist philosopher-soldier. Holbach's translations of the works of the English deists and of extracts from Orobio de Castro's *Prevenciones* responded to the same demands: the accuracy of the translation was subordinated to the requirements of the publishers' own philosophical propaganda.

A fundamental lesson to be drawn from the clandestine distribution of philosophical writings lies in the coexistence of both manuscript and printed versions of a single text. The manuscript, of course, preceded the printed version, but the manuscript survived after printing, and was still circulated after the publication of the text, or rather, of a version of the text. Manuscripts allowed modification of the text, whereas printing fixed its meaning. Consequently, it is possible to follow the evolution of thought through the various versions. The field of clandestine literature is in this respect a favorite one for scholars who are interested in *la critique génétique*, or the comparative study of successive versions of texts: variants are no longer seen simply as errors, points of infidelity to the original text, but acquire the status of testaments to a changing, collective thought-process expressing a living history of ideas. A prime example of the complex relationships between printed texts and manuscripts is offered by *La parité de la vie et de la mort* (The Parity of Life and Death), a multiple text published by O. Bloch (1993), of which two printed versions and two very different manuscript versions are known.

Clandestine philosophical literature reflects the major currents in the history of ideas and reveals their anti-Christian scope. For example, in 1659 that magisterial compendium of ancient thought, the *Theophrastus Redivivus* (Theophrastus Revived), was assembled, a vast manuscript collection that presents the classical heritage in the form of selected extracts from ancient authors on the great themes: the gods, the world, the soul, religion, hell, death, and life according to nature. It is an anthology of freethinking drawn from the works of the ancients, but modern influences are also discernable. From the same period come the different versions of Savinien de Cyrano de Bergerac's *Autre monde* (1657; Voyages to the Moon and the Sun) and the writings of Isaac Lapeyrère; several manuscripts reflect the debates about Cartesianism and a dozen texts join in the debate over Spinozism. Thus the clandestine philosophical literature of the late 17th and early 18th centuries was born from the intellectual context defined by the rivalry between the great systems of René Descartes, Pierre Gassendi, Thomas Hobbes, Nicolas Male-

branche, Baruch Spinoza, John Locke, and, later, Gottfried Wilhelm Leibniz. Michel Eyquem de Montaigne and Pierre Bayle were inexhaustible sources of quotation. Approximately 20 texts were translated directly from the English deists, whose public debates had a bearing on the evolution of freethinking in France. John Toland, Anthony Collins, Matthew Tindal, Bernard Mandeville, Charles Blount, Middleton, Henry Bolingbroke, and even Thomas Woolston fueled the writing of the clandestine philosophers, as did the Marranos Isaak de Troki and Orobio de Castro.

These modern influences allow us to view the clandestine philosophical debate from the perspective of the history of the conflict between Montaigne's Pyrrhonism and the rationalism propounded by Descartes and Malebranche. In terms of apologetics, this conflict appears in the methodological rivalry between reasoned demonstration and historical proof. The apologists themselves were only rarely aware of the contradictions existing between these two methods. Indeed, as the clandestine rationalists emphasize, if the evidence provided by reason is a certain criterion, what need do we have of revelation? If human reason is a reliable guide, divine reason should conform to it. Hence, biblical history, the story of a jealous and tyrannical God whose actions are incompatible with our conception of the justice, goodness, and wisdom of an infinitely perfect Being, was nothing more than a story told by a primitive and wretched people, as in *La Moïsade* (The Story of Moses and His People). The history of religions was that of a political imposture, as in the *Traité des trois imposteurs* (Treatise on the Three Impostors). A text such as César Chesneau Dumarsais's *Examen de la religion dont on cherche l'éclaircissement de bonne foi* (1705–10; Examination of Religion, Whose Explanation Is Sought in Good Faith) attests to the process through which Malebranche's Christian rationalism was transformed into philosophical anti-Christian rationalism—into "Enlightenment" philosophy. A similar rationalism characterizes Robert Challe's *Difficultés sur la religion proposées au P. Malebranche* (1710, 1767; Religious Issues Submitted to Father Malebranche): Challe does not believe in God, he "knows" him; faith is "annihilated" by reason, which rejects any religion founded upon facts, any "artificial" religion. In this sense, clandestine philosophy drew conclusions from the rivalry between Pyrrhonism and rationalism that defined the 17th-century crisis in Christian philosophy.

The first clandestine treatises of the 18th century were written in response to the systems proposed by the great philosophers of the previous century. "Amateur" philosophers leapt into the fray and constructed systems of their own. For example, toward the end of his life Yves de Vallone (1666/67–1705), a canon of the church of Sainte-Geneviève who converted to

Protestantism in 1697 and was exiled to the Netherlands, composed *La religion du chrétien* (The Christian's Religion), a treatise on naturalist pantheism strongly influenced by Spinoza. On 13 August 1715 Jacques Delaube, a knight and feudal lord of Bron (near Lyon), sent to Reinier Leers, the famous Dutch publisher of Bayle's *Dictionnaire historique et critique* (1697; Historical and Critical Dictionary), his *Réflexions morales et métaphysiques sur les religions et sur les connoissances de l'homme* (Moral and Metaphysical Reflections on Religions and Human Knowledge). Delaube's text is an examination of conscience in which the author rejects the doctrine of the Fall as a fallacious "law of the bipeds" and proposes, on the basis of Malebranche's occasionalism, a spiritualist pantheism in which God is everything and everything is spirit. Challe composed his *Difficultés sur la religion proposées au P. Malebranche* between 1710 and 1720. This clandestine treatise begins with a "first notebook containing that which opened my eyes," continues with a fierce indictment of revealed, "artificial" religions as well as a systematic examination of the Christian faith in particular, and concludes with a "system of religion based metaphysically upon natural reason": it was France's first systematic treatise on deism. In the Ardennes, Jean Meslier (1664–1729), an obscure parish priest at Étrepigny, covered his copy of Father Fénelon's *Démonstration de l'existence de Dieu* (1713; A Demonstration of the Existence and Attributes of God) with marginal notes; Meslier also composed the *Mémoire* (Memoir) that appears in his own *Pensées et sentiments* (Thoughts and Feelings). This philosophical testament, which was discovered only after Meslier's death, constitutes a powerful materialist and "communist" system. The first wave of clandestine philosophy in the 18th century was thus made up of treatises by often obscure amateurs who knew the great systems and developed philosophies of their own. Each of them produced a kind of philosophical examination of conscience bearing the influence of the great 17th-century philosophies. These provincial amateurs—that is, from outside of Paris—were the heirs to the traditional ambitions of philosophy.

At the same period, but at the heart of the intellectual life of Paris, the first transformation of clandestine philosophy got under way. In January 1686 Bernard Le Bovier de Fontenelle launched his *Relation de l'île de Bornéo* (1686; Depiction of the Island of Borneo) in Bayle's *Nouvelles de la République des Lettres*; Fontenelle's *Entretiens sur la pluralité des mondes habités* (1686; Discussions on the Plurality of Inhabited Worlds) appeared the same year. A series of short treatises on particular topics followed—*Du bonheur* (1714; On Happiness), *L'origine des fables* (1724; The Origin of Fables), and the *Histoire des oracles* (1687; The His-

tory of Oracles)—while a *Traité de la liberté* (1743; Treatise on Freedom), a *Traité des oracles* (Treatise on Oracles), and a *Traité des miracles* (Treatise on Miracles) circulated surreptitiously in manuscript. *Réflexions sur l'argument de M. Pascal et M. Locke concernant la possibilité d'une autre vie à venir* (Reflections on Mr. Pascal and Mr. Locke's Idea on the Possibility of Another Life to Come), a clandestine critique of "Pascal's wager" and an affirmation of the philosophical bliss reserved for a small elite, can also plausibly be attributed to Fontenelle, while his *Fragments de la république* (Fragments on the Republic) were probably the preparatory notes for *La république des philosophes, ou histoire des Ajaoiens* (The Republic of Philosophers; or, A History of Ajaoians), not published until 1768. Fontenelle thus modernized the model of Montaigne's *Essais* (1580–95; Essays) and François La Mothe Le Vayer's *Petits traités* (Short Treatises). As a philosopher, Fontenelle limited his ambitions, set his sights clearly, and developed his ideas from the margins of the great systems.

Henri de Boulainviller, for his part, outlined an *Essai de métaphysique* (Essay on Metaphysics) and scrupulously annotated his readings of Spinoza; but Boulainviller too took his inspiration from La Mothe Le Vayer's example when he composed his *Histoire des opinions des anciens sur la nature de l'âme* (History of the Conceptions of the Ancients on the Nature of the Soul), and followed Locke's example when producing a brief *Petit discours chrestien de l'immortalité de l'ame* (1647; Treatise on the Immortality of the Soul). Most of all, Boulainviller's *Lettre d'Hippocrate à Damagète* (Hippocrates's Letter to Damagetes), published in 1700, served as a model to the following generation. In this fictional letter, Hippocrates relates Democritus's discourse on the mysteries of nature, on religions and sects, and on the existence of God. "You cannot take one step in the study of nature without finding a miracle," he writes; the idea of divinity is too abstract for the common man and religions have had to "introduce mysteries, invent facts, put forth doctrines, impose laws, establish a moral code." According to the *Lettre*, it is at this price—that is to say at the price of their truthfulness—that these religions are useful to social order.

Other young philosophers linked to the Académie des Inscriptions et Belles-Lettres (Academy of Inscriptions and Letters) were following the same movement. All produced short treatises whose philosophical ambitions are restricted to the radical critique of some Christian articles of faith and some episodes in the history of its establishment. Nicolas Fréret produced his *Lettre de Thrasybule à Leucippe* (1766; Letter from Thrasybulus to Leucippus); Jean Lévesque de Burigny wrote an *Examen critique des apologistes de la religion chrétienne*

(Critical Examination of the Apologists of the Christian Religion; published in Nicolas Fréret, *Oeuvres complètes* [1775; Complete Works]) and collaborated with Thémiseul de Saint-Hyacinthe on other works. Between 1705 and 1710 Dumarsais produced his *Examen de la religion*. He followed this very widely circulated text with *Réflexions sur l'existence de l'âme et sur l'existence de Dieu* (Reflections on the Existence of the Soul and on the Existence of God) and with another little treatise in which, drawing on a little-known text by Samuel Werenfels, he offers a definition of the *Philosophe* (Philosopher).

We shall not list here all the authors of the numerous little treatises similar to those mentioned above. For one thing, many attributions remain in doubt: indeed, confusion over authorship is characteristic of the next phase in the history of *clandestina*. Once a small corpus of clandestine treatises had accumulated, it became easy to put together new treatises by borrowing relevant passages from one text or another. Plagiarism had become a very common method of composition. Bayle was a favorite victim: the case of the 13th of Voltaire's *Lettres philosophiques* (1734; Philosophical Letters) is well known. Along the same lines, the marquis d'Argens proved to be a tireless and unscrupulous compiler: all his works are filled with quotations from Bayle. Some minor figures in the history of freethinking, such as Dupré de Richemont (whose file can be found in the Bastille Archives), specialized in providing extracts from Bayle. The same method of composition was clearly used to produce *L'âme matérielle* (The Material Soul), assembled after 1724 by an unknown compiler: this is an exemplary collection of quotations torn from their original contexts in works by Malebranche, Bayle, Guillaume Lamy, Jean Leclerc, the baron de La Hontan, and others.

The relationships between this latter manuscript and the *Sentiments des philosophes sur la nature de l'âme* (The Philosophers' Feelings on the Nature of the Soul), as well as the *Essais sur la recherche de la vérité* (Essays on the Search for Truth), are currently under study by scholars. Although the precise relationships among the texts have not yet been definitely established, it is certain that the authors either copied one another or relied on a common source. Suffice it to say that plagiarism had become a mode of production and that clandestine philosophy at this stage of its evolution was characterized by a patchwork technique.

A manuscript that may be the work of the marquis d'Argens, from the time of his collaboration in Rotterdam with Prosper Marchand, offers a choice example. Under the title *De la conduite qu'un honnête homme doit garder pendant sa vie* (On the Line of Conduct a Gentleman Should Follow throughout His Life), the compiler offers a long extract from Dumarsais's *Examen de la religion*, followed by a host of short quotations from Bayle's *Dictionnaire historique et critique* (1697; Historical and Critical Dictionary) and *Oeuvres diverses* (Miscellaneous Works), stitched together into a line of argument that is an utter betrayal of Bayle's thought, a rationalist hijacking of the Protestant philosopher's Augustinian moralism. The technique of quotation had become an art of misappropriation.

Made up of quotations deftly lifted from their contexts, the manuscripts themselves were in turn widely pillaged. For example, the last chapter of the manuscript *De l'examen de la religion* (On the Examination of Religion) was incorporated by Lévesque de Burigny into his *Examen critique des apologistes de la religion chrétienne* (Critical Examination of the Apologists of the Christian Religion). The *Analyse de la religion chrétienne* (Analysis of the Christian Religion) seems to consist of an abridged version of the *Examen*. Another work, the *Doutes sur les religions révélées* (Doubts on Revealed Religions), published in 1767 and 1792, also plunders the *Examen* while adding two *Dialogues entre un Indien et l'Église* (Dialogues between an Indian and the Church) of uncertain origin.

Great confusion thus reigns with regard to attributions, and it is often alleged that clandestine literature was the work of a social group or coterie and could be attributed to nobody in particular. This is true of some of the cases already mentioned, but these examples are not necessarily the rule and should not be taken as a reason for abandoning research in this field. The discovery of an author gives a new meaning to a text, as demonstrated by the examples of Fontenelle, Challe, Meslier, Dumarsais, Boulainviller, Fréret, Delaube, Abraham Gaultier, the Lévesque brothers, and many others. One encounters the great *philosophes* (Fontenelle, Voltaire, Diderot, Boulanger, La Mettrie, Holbach), well-known authors (Boulainviller, Challe, Dumarsais, Fréret, Lévesque de Burigny, Benoît de Maillet, Mirabaud, Saint-Hyacinthe), and virtually unknown figures (Lau, Antoine-François de Fourcroy, Yves de Vallone, Gaultier, Jacques Delaube, Raby d'Amérique, Cupis de Camargo), as well as a multitude of amateur philosophers and innumerable anonymous intermediaries, copyists, bookseller-printers, and peddlers. Clandestine literature thus allows us to glimpse certain behind-the-scenes events of the Enlightenment.

Clandestine philosophy, identified as such by its mode of dissemination, is not a single entity. It would be impossible to reduce this body of texts, even considering only the 18th-century manuscripts, to an unequivocal philosophy. Moreover, the complexity and diversity of clandestine philosophy foreshadowed the similar characteristics of Enlightenment philosophy proper, which was permeated by often contradictory currents of rationalism and scepticism, deism, naturalism, pantheism, materialism, and so forth. The very definition of this corpus in terms of its critical attitude regarding Christianity ensures that the texts will contain systematic critiques of the Bible, dogma, and the clergy. Drawing on all available sources, these thinkers denounced the errors of religion—its false conception of God, its ignorance of the mechanisms of nature, the muddled and ridiculous proofs, the tricks and maneuvers of priests (denounced as "priest-craft")—and concluded that "the Church is nothing but a society of men."

This conclusion had important consequences for the question of religious toleration. Indeed, the persecutory fanaticism of believers was an additional proof that religions were not of divine origin. According to these philosophers (*Difficultés sur la religion proposées au P. Malebranche*; *Examen critique des apologistes de la religion chrétienne*, Chapter VII), religions in general, and the Christian religion in particular, had spread because of the strength and violence of their persecutions and had then taken over the minds of the people. Religious imposture was seen as fundamentally political: Machiavelli, Gabriel Naudé, Hobbes, and Vanini were plundered in order to prove that religion should be understood as nothing but a tool in the hands of a prince, which could be wielded to control the ignorant populace. Political control of religion allowed rulers to avoid conflicts that would have disturbed the public order. This maxim was interpreted with the help of Hobbes: several religions in a single state were not to be tolerated, since they would inevitably come into conflict. Heresy—religious deviancy—was thus revealed as a source of political disorder, which a wise prince would make it his business to eliminate. The imposition of religious intolerance was a political duty of the prince who wished to ensure domestic peace. Thus, the clandestine philosophers, as a political tenet, rejected the very toleration that had been denied to them.

The same conclusion was reached in the psychological analysis of the causes of error. Among the small number of enlightened thinkers, philosophy was conceived as the denunciation of error in the name of the evidence provided by reason. The waverings of conscience appeared as so many refusals to "see clearly," and the philosophers turned back upon the apologists the accusation of which they themselves had been the target for centuries: their opponents, they asserted, were of "bad faith."

ANTONY MCKENNA

See also Books and Reading; Censorship; Deism; Peddler

Further Reading

Benítez, Miguel, "Matériaux pour un inventaire des manuscripts philosophiques clandestins des XVIIᵉ et XVIIIᵉ siècles," *Rivista di storia della filosofia* 3 (1988)

Benítez, Miguel, *La face cachée des Lumières: Recherches sur les manuscrits philosophiques clandestins de l'âge classique,* Paris: Universitas, and Oxford: Voltaire Foundation, 1996

Berman, David, *A History of Atheism in Britain: From Hobbes to Russell,* London and New York: Croom Helm, 1988

Berti, Silvia, Françoise Charles-Daubert, and Richard H. Popkin, *Heterodoxy, Spinozism, and Free Thought in Early Eighteenth-Century Europe: Studies on the "Traité des trois imposteurs,"* Dordrecht, The Netherlands, and Boston: Kluwer, 1996

Betts, C.J., *Early Deism in France: From the So-called "Déistes" of Lyon (1564) to Voltaire's "Lettres philosophiques" (1734),* The Hague and Boston: Nijhoff, 1984

Bloch, Olivier, editor, *Le matérialisme du XVIIIᵉ siècle et la littérature clandestine,* Paris: Vrin, 1982

Bloch, Olivier, editor, *Spinoza au XVIIIᵉ siècle,* Paris: Méridiens Klincksieck, 1990

Champion, J.A.I., *The Pillars of Priestcraft Shaken: The Church of England and Its Enemies, 1660–1730,* Cambridge and New York: Cambridge University Press, 1992

Darnton, Robert, *The Corpus of Clandestine Literature in France, 1769–1789,* New York: Norton, 1995

Darnton, Robert, *The Forbidden Best-Sellers of Pre-Revolutionary France,* New York: Norton, 1995; London: HarperCollins, 1996

Hunter, Michael, and Wootton, David, editors, *Atheism from the Reformation to the Enlightenment,* Oxford: Clarendon Press, and Oxford and New York: Oxford University Press, 1992

Kors, Alan Charles, *Atheism in France, 1650–1729,* Princeton, New Jersey: Princeton University Press, 1990

Lanson, G., "Questions diverses sur l'histoire de l'esprit philosophique en France avant 1750," *RHLF* 19 (1912)

Love, Harold, *Scribal Publication in Seventeenth-Century England,* Oxford, Clarendon Press, and Oxford and New York: Oxford University Press, 1993

McKenna, Antony, and Alain Mothu, editors, *La philosophie clandestine à l'âge classique,* Paris: Universitas, and Oxford: The Voltaire Foundation, 1997

Rétat, Pierre, *Le "Dictionnaire" de Bayle et la lutte philosophique au XVIIIᵉ siècle,* Paris: Les Belles Lettres, 1971

Spink, John Stephenson, *French Free-Thought from Gassendi to Voltaire,* London: Athlone Press, 1960

Toland, John, *Nazarenus,* London: Brown, Roberts, and Brotherton, 1718; edited by Justin Champion, Oxford: Voltaire Foundation, 1999

Torrey, Norman Lewis, *Voltaire and the English Deists,* New Haven: Yale University Press, and London: Oxford University Press, 1930

Van Bunge, Wiep, and Wim Klever, *Disguised and Overt Spinozism around 1700,* Leiden: Brill, 1996

Wade, Ira Owen, *The Clandestine Organization and Diffusion of Philosophic Ideas in France from 1700 to 1750,* Princeton, New Jersey: Princeton University Press, and London: Oxford University Press, 1938

Wade, Ira Owen, *Voltaire and Madame du Châtelet: An Essay on the Intellectual Activity at Cirey,* Princeton, New Jersey: Princeton University Press, and London: Oxford University Press, 1941

Class. *See* Orders and Classes

Classicism

In two books that have become classics of literary criticism in France, René Bray and Henri Peyre standardized the definition and image of French classicism. Through his very detailed historical analysis, *La formation de la doctrine classique in France* (1927; The Formation of the Classical Doctrine in France), Bray made a powerful contribution to the establishment of the idea of French classicism as a doctrinal system of norms based on rationalism, a moral system, and the principle of imitation of the ancients, this system being defined by general rules (verisimilitude, propriety), as well as by more specific rules for each literary genre. Peyre answered his own question, *Qu'est-ce que le classicisme?* (1933; What Is Classicism?), by summarizing its "fundamental traits," a method that had the advantage of opening the subject to comparative and interdisciplinary approaches and to critical consideration of the history of the terminology. If we limit ourselves for the moment to the image of classicism that has been lastingly influenced by these books, we can clearly see that the French literature of the 18th century was profoundly influenced by the aesthetic of the classical age.

However, as the terminology of international research indicates, matters become more complicated when we attempt a definition of "classicism" with respect to other national literatures or other disciplines, such as the history of art, architecture, or music. The French word *classicisme* combines two important meanings that are usually distinguished from one another in other languages. For example, German has both *Klassik* and *Klassizismus: Klassik* designates a period of literary glory—perhaps the 17th century in France, but also the *Weimarer Klassik,* the literature of Johann Wolfgang von Goethe and Friedrich von Schiller around 1800; *Klassizismus,* in contrast, is defined as an aesthetic, a style that imitates a period regarded as classic, whether a phase of antiquity or of modern times. In France, Britain, Spain, and Italy, initially in the history of art, the ambivalence of the notion of classicism necessitated the creation of the term "neoclassicism" and its equivalents to refer, as far as the 18th century is concerned, to what German calls *Klassizismus.*

Conceptual Ambivalences

Since the 19th century, European classicisms have been set up as canons; however, because the history of civilizations has followed paths that diverge from country to country, these canons are too diverse to permit an overall view. Given these conceptual ambivalences, it is useful to distinguish two uses of the word "classicism," one typological and the other referring to a historical period. As a typological category, "classicism" or "classic" can be applied to the "complementary phenomenon of mannerism in every period" (see Schulz-Buschhaus). In this sense, classicism is characterized by the following stylistic and discursive elements: equilibrium between extremes; harmony and balance; an ideal of semantic clarity (the rhetorical virtue of *perspicuitas*); an acceptance of a normative poetics that is either neo-Aristotelian or neo-Horatian; a critical restriction to models worthy of imitation (*imitatio veterum*); and respect for the distinctions between styles and genres. In contrast, as a term for a historical period, "classicism" or the "classical era" refers to a period that has been canonized by regional or national historiography because of the superiority or exemplary nature of its artistic and literary productions. "Classicisms" are therefore controversial concepts that are constantly being delegitimized or relegitimized. Today the coherent constructs that provided the basis for rigid definitions of "Louis XIV classicism" (see Stenzel) or "the legend of German classicism" (see Grimm and Hermand) are being dismantled.

For each of the European classicisms—the *Siglo de Oro,* the Augustan Age, the *Deutsche Klassik,* and so on—we will highlight the connections between typology, choices inherited from tradition, and references to antiquity, on the one hand, and canonization and subsequent normativity, on the other. Moreover, we need to compare each nation's classicism with that of the others. By bringing the various classicisms together—an approach still neglected in studies in this field—we can evaluate the connections between classicism and the Enlightenment in each country. Ultimately, the Enlightenment can be viewed, depending on the specific and geographical context, as the result, the precondition, or the opposite of "classicism."

History of the Term and the Concept

The adjective "classical" originated in the canonization of certain authors by the philologists of Alexandria. In Roman fiscal law, *classicus,* which was contrasted with *proletarius,* designated the class of people who did not pay any taxes. In his *Noctes atticae* (Attic Nights), Aulus Gellius, who transferred this notion into rhetoric, recommends consultation of a "classic"—meaning an earlier literary authority—in order to learn about proper linguistic usage (*latinitas*). The first models to be considered "first class" were those of classical antiquity. It is interesting to note that in the modern period, the legacies of antiquity that were chosen as models varied according to different national classicisms. The "pre-baroque classicism" of 17th-century Germany, French classicism, the English Augustan Age, the "enlightened

classicism" of Johann Christoph Gottsched, and revolutionary neoclassicism favored Roman antiquity and its republican or imperial civilization. In contrast, Gotthold Ephraim Lessing, Johann Joachim Winckelmann, and the authors of German classicism in general found their models in ancient Greece. Their rejection of classical Rome resembled their rejection of French classicism: they departed from an overtly political environment in order to move into a moral and human context. This paradigm shift in the evaluation of the models of antiquity is particularly well illustrated in the contrastive reassessment of Virgil and Homer that occurred during the modern period, through the positions adopted by Joseph Justus Scaliger, the debate over Homer, and the writings of Lessing.

However, since the Renaissance, many modern writers have also been called "classic." In his *Art poétique* (1548; Poetic Art), Thomas Sébillet recommends "the reading of the good and classic French poets" in order to perfect imagination and judgment. In German, as in other languages, the label "classic" was applied to a larger group than that of the ancient authors alone. Christian Fürchtegott Gellert (1769) saw in such German Enlightenment writers as Gottsched, J.E. Schlegel, Gärtner, and Rabener "the classic authors of our nation." In 1771 Johann Georg Sulzer applied the term *classisch* to those authors of his own nationality "among whom reason has been developed to a high level" and characterized every advanced rational culture as having *Classicität* (classical qualities).

The adjective *classique* appeared in French much earlier than the noun *classicisme.* The latter term did not appear until the beginning of the 19th century, when it was used to designate French literature of the 17th century, in contrast to romanticism. In contrast, the adjective *classique* was already being used by the humanists of the Renaissance, albeit with reference to the models of antiquity. In his *Causeries du lundi* (1850; Monday-Chats), Charles Augustin Sainte-Beuve refers constantly to the distinction that Aulus Gellius had made when defining a classic writer: "A writer of value and distinction, a writer who counts, whose work stands out, and who is not lost in the crowd of proletarians."

Philosophy of the History of Classical Apogees

The conception of classicism as the summit of culture is a product of the cyclical theory of history. It appeared in 18th-century historiography, at the heart of the then-common pattern of history unfolding through phases of origin, progress, perfection, and decadence. The classical era in France was viewed as one of the four great "ages" of universal history by Charles Perrault, Dominique Bouhours, the abbé Dubos, and Voltaire. In this sense, the "age of Louis XIV" was compared to the classical age by being expanded through literature to all the manifestations of culture. In the humanist tradition, historiography considered each privileged era in a given country as a representation of universal culture. This French claim to universality basically excluded the coexistence of several classicisms in different nations. The revival of literature in Italy and then in France had initiated the modern period, a new cycle for which France was seen as perfection incarnate. The Quarrel of the Ancients and the Moderns reflected this new assurance, this certainty that modern classicism was equal or even superior to the classicism of antiquity.

In the 18th century a number of historians remained attached to a vision of the glorious age of Louis XIV, and, following what had been done with the ancients, they elevated the great authors of that age to the rank of models. The *Encyclopédie* declares that one can equally "give the name of classic author to the good writers of the age of Louis XIV and of this age." However, the use of the word *classique* was still limited to the sense of an elegant and correct style. Authors needed to respect the rules of classical doctrine to a degree that was measured by their adherence to the aesthetics of imitation. They compared themselves to their great predecessors and often concluded that, despite the incontestable progress achieved in other domains, there was an encroaching decadence in literature. In *Des causes de la corruption du goût* (1715; On the Causes of the Corruption of Taste), Madame Dacier denounced this trend, thus initiating a new stage in the Quarrel of the Ancients and the Moderns. Her accusation of decadence became a sort of rallying cry for Voltaire, La Harpe, and many of their contemporaries.

Other countries in Europe also distinguished exceptional periods in their cultures, although they did not refer to them as "classical." In Italy the term predictably remained limited to Roman antiquity; it could not be applied to the era of Dante, Petrarch, and Giovanni Boccaccio, which was celebrated as a revival of antiquity. For Spain the undeniable flourishing of literature in the 16th and 17th centuries has traditionally been called the *Siglo de Oro* (Golden Period) or *Edad de Oro* (Golden Age), and even those historians of literature who nowadays oppose the assumption that Spain had no Renaissance or Enlightenment hesitate to call that period "classic." Indeed, despite the works of Baltasar Gracián, Lope de Vega, and Pedro Calderón de la Barca y Henao, the literature of Spain in this period lacked the homogeneity of a literary doctrine—and a corresponding anthropology—that seems to constitute a classic era. In England, if the reign of Elizabeth I (1558–1603) is regarded as an apogee, it is so considered in literature above all because of Shakespeare's works; but that era left its marks on music and on an artistic style that are called "Elizabethan." Today the adjective "classical"

sometimes designates the period known as the Augustan Age (1660–1760), while "neoclassicism" is applied to the second half of the 18th century.

Classical French language and literature had a strong impact on Germany—as well as on other European countries—in the 18th century, and this influence seemed to confirm the universality of French classicism. Gottsched, in particular, called for the imitation of French models, although it is true that his purpose was to enrich literature in the German language. Gottsched's preference for the German language contrasted with the views of partisans of Aulic culture, such as Frederick II of Prussia, who accepted the thesis that French was superior and who wrote in that language themselves. From the 1770s on, however, the authors of the Sturm und Drang movement upheld an original and national literature and opposed the imitation of classical models. The leading representatives of German classicism, in Weimar, lived during the time of general discussion throughout Europe about classical and romantic literatures, and they themselves defined the adjective "classic" at the very moment when the noun "classicism" was making its appearance.

German Classicism

The term *Klassik*, which did not come into use in the history of German civilization until the second half of the 19th century, designates the period of efflorescence of German literature from 1786, when Goethe departed for Italy, until 1805, the year of Schiller's death. The period was centered on their friendship, which started in 1794 and which is revealed in their correspondence. However, by emphasizing these two figures as almost a Castor and Pollux, this concept suggests a fallacious unity. The use of the term *Klassik* presents a simplistic view of the whole heterogeneous spectrum of German literature during this period and glosses over, or effaces, the diverse currents then in coexistence: a delayed Enlightenment, German Jacobinism, a delayed cult of sensibility, and the dawn of romanticism. Further, the "anti-classicists," such as Heinrich Wilhelm von Kleist, Friedrich Hölderlin, and Jean Paul, but also the majority of the authors read by German speakers at the time when their classicists were writing—Cramer, Albrecht, Grosse, Johann Spiess, August Friedrich Ferdinand von Kotzebue—can be placed at a tangent to the line traced by the Germanist doctrine of literary periods.

If, as criteria of classicism, one takes versification (poetry as linked discourse, in contrast to the prose of the modern era), separation of genres (in contrast to the hybridization and disappearance of categories that characterize romanticism), and reference to antiquity (classicism as the normativity of classical mythology, as opposed to the romantic "new mythology"), then only a few works deserve to be included in the canon of German classicism, or rather of the Aulic classicism of Weimar. Such works include Goethe's versions in verse of *Iphigenie auf Tauris* (1787; Iphigenia in Tauris) and *Torquato Tasso* (1790), his epic *Hermann und Dorothea* (1797; Hermann and Dorothea), his *Römische Elegien* (1795; Roman Elegies), and his *Venetianische Epigramm* (1796; Venetian Epigrams), along with Schiller's great historical poems, such as *Die Götter Griechenlands* (1788; The Gods from Greece), *Die Künstler* (1789; The Artists), and *Die Spaziergang* (1795; The Walk), his treatises on aesthetics from the first half of the 1790s, such as the *Briefe über die ästhetische Erziehung des Menschen* (1793–95; Letters on the Aesthetic Education of Man), and his tragedies from the second half of that decade and later, including the trilogy *Wallenstein* (1798–99), *Maria Stuart* (1800; Mary Stuart), *Die Jungfrau von Orleans* (1801; The Maid from Orleans), *Die Braut von Messina* (1803; The Bride of Messina), and *Wilhelm Tell* (1804; William Tell).

Schiller's plays best exemplify the image of German classicism that crystallized in the 19th century. Goethe's *Faust* (1806), and also his cycle of *Unterhaltungen deutscher Ausgewanderten* (1795; Recreations of the German Emigrants) and his *Wilhelm Meisters Lehrjahre* (1795–96; Wilhelm Meister's Apprenticeship) have only ever been considered within the context of European romanticism, while *Die Leiden des jungen Werthers* (1774; The Sorrows of Young Werther) has always been considered a preromantic work. Furthermore, the works of Goethe's and Schiller's youth, as well as those of Goethe's later years—*Die Wahlverwandtschaften* (1809; The Elective Affinities), *Wilhelm Meisters Wanderjahre* (1821–29; Wilhelm Meister's Travels), and the *West-östlicher Divan* (1814–16; West-Eastern Divan)—tend to explode this narrow conception of classicism, replacing it with broader chronological images such as those proposed in Heinrich Heine's *Kunstperiode* (period of art), H.A. Korff's *Goethezeit* (age of Goethe) or in Wilhelm Dilthey and H. Nohl's *deutsche Bewegung* (German movement).

In contemporary Germany, which is separated from the Germany of Weimar by Buchenwald, the normative character of the concept of classicism has been called into question, most recently during the 1960s. At present, critics agree in acknowledging that it was above all its reception by posterity that gave this period of German classicism its unified character. Goethe and Schiller did not regard themselves as classicists: it was only later, in the literary historiography of the 19th century, that the idea of a classical epoch in the proper sense was established. The distinction between the national classicism of Germany, on the one hand, and Enlightenment thought and aesthetics, on the other, did

a great deal to help institutionalize the notion of a properly classical epoch. The idea of a specifically German classicism was itself to play an important role in the history of German literary ideas, through such dichotomies as classicism/romanticism or rationalism/irrationalism. In contrast, contemporary research tends to reintegrate the German *Klassik* within the framework of European classicism by thinking of *Klassik* in a comparative way; such research also tends to bring *Klassik* back into the synchronous context of the literature of Europe at the turn of the century; and, finally, from a diachronic perspective, this research works to reintegrate *Klassik* within the tradition of the *Aufklärung*.

Toward a Typology of European Classicisms?

It is doubtless not a coincidence that it should be in Germany, where the *Klassik* did not aspire to universality, that there is today a tendency to adopt a comparative approach to national "classicisms." According to some recent work, every "classicism" is characterized by a gap between, on the one hand, its normative ambition, which is necessary in order to promote one period or one style, and, on the other hand, the relative nature of its location and its historical moment. Classicism also implies a canonization that is more or less accepted by those who come after it. In the case of Greek and Roman antiquity and French classicism, this criterion was indeed fulfilled in the 18th century. The classical norm has to do with a style (simplicity and purity) and an aesthetics (harmony of forms) but also an anthropology (the ideal of the gentleman) and an obvious connection with the political system, whether as a manifestation and legitimization of power, as in France in the 17th century, or as a cultural compensation for political weakness, as in the classicism of Weimar. Clearly, the reception of classicisms in their respective countries helped to establish and legitimize national identities.

However, these attempts to define the common elements in various classicisms should not lead us to forget the substantial differences resulting from historical conditions. For example, German classicism, which emerged late in comparison to that of France, renounced the principle of mimesis and proclaimed the autonomy of art. The 18th century, which in many respects might be considered as an era of cultural flourishing in several European countries, forms a period of transition between the normative aesthetic of classicism and the historicism of the 19th century.

The normative content of classicism was to be substantially called into question only by romanticism, although it was during the 18th century that Diderot,

Lessing, and, above all, the Sturm und Drang movement in German-speaking countries began to diverge from classicism. It is somewhat ironic that the German *Klassik* implied that classicism was dead: the Alexandrine was replaced by Shakespearean blank verse and imperial Rome gave way to the Greek polis. In the process of canonization, homogenization and selection were carried out both by way of certain aesthetic principles and via the historical and philosophical structures that were linked to them. These principles were developed at the end of the 18th century, in reaction to the crisis of the Enlightenment, which was perceived as a "loss of the middle ground." Classicism appeared to provide norms and meanings during a period of semantic erosion. In particular, after the French Revolution and the coalitions, which, according to contemporaries on the other side of the Rhine, brought nothing but "chaos," the German-speaking world favored "order, the prime generator of culture" (see Vosskamp). Some of the fundamental concepts underlying this movement have turned out to be so fertile that they still serve, long after their genesis, to satisfy a need for normativity: aesthetic autonomy, the concept of *Bildung* (aesthetic education), the notion of the symbolic. However, other concepts that German critics have often regarded as originating in the German movement should in fact be placed back within their European context, in the British and French Enlightenments above all: the idea of humanity and the perfectibility of the individual, the concept of philosophy of history. Similarly, certain aesthetic norms, such as the rules of the separation and purity of literary genres, owe more to the tradition of French classicism than is sometimes admitted. However, in the same way that the conceptual field of European classicisms is reduced to classical doctrine and thereby simplified, the theory of a classicism of harmonization tends to conceal the complementary attributes that were also present in 18th-century discussions on aesthetics: genius, the sublime, enthusiasm, disorder.

Initially, the use of the term "classicism" and its cognates to designate a historical period was based on literary criteria, but the word was then extended to every realm of cultural life. In the case of music, "classical" is commonly used today in a very broad sense, contrasting with contemporary or "worthless music," yet music historians also refer to "the classicism of Versailles" (from Jean-Baptiste Lully to Jean-Philippe Rameau) or, more commonly, the "Viennese classics" (Joseph Haydn, Wolfgang Amadeus Mozart, Ludwig van Beethoven). Because, unlike in literature, classical music lacks a fundamental connection to antiquity and cannot be defined theoretically, it is perfectly possible for an English musicologist to speak of "romantic classicism."

JOCHEN SCHLOBACH AND CARSTEN ZELLE

See also Ancients and the Moderns, Quarrel of the; Antiquity; Architecture; Ideal; Siècle; Tragedy; Ugliness and Deformity

Further Reading

Bray, René, *La formation de la doctrine classique en France,* Dijon: Darantiere, 1927; reprint, Paris: Nizet, 1983

Grimm, Reinhold, and Jost Hermand, editors, *Die Klassik-Legende,* Frankfurt: Athenäum, 1971

Honour, Hugh, *Neo-classicism,* London: Penguin, 1968

Nies, Fritz, and Karlheinz Stierle, editors, *Französische Klassik: Theorie, Literatur, Malerei,* Munich: Fink, 1985

Pauly, Reinhard G., *Music in the Classic Period,* Englewood Cliffs, New Jersey: Prentice Hall, 1965; 3rd edition, 1988

Peyre, Henri, *Qu'est-ce que le classicisme?* Paris: Droz, 1933

Schulz-Buschhaus, Ulrich, "Klassik zwischen Kanon und Typologie: Probleme um einen Zentralbegriff der Literaturwissenschaft," *Arcadia* 29 (1994)

Stenzel, Hartmut, *Die französische "Klassik": Literarische Modernisierung und absolutistischer Staat,* Darmstadt: Wissenschaftliche Buchgesellschaft, 1995

Vosskamp, Wilhelm, editor, *Klassik im Vergleich: Normativität und Historizität europäischer Klassiken,* Stuttgart: Metzler, 1993

Classification

The inventory and ordering of the three kingdoms of nature was begun in antiquity by Aristotle, neglected by his medieval and 17th-century successors, and revived in the 18th century. As the founder and master architect of classification in the 18th century, the Swedish physician Carl von Linné, who wrote as Carolus Linnaeus (1707–78), is the emblematic figure among European naturalists during the Enlightenment. His *Systema naturae* (A General System of Nature), published in Leiden in 1735 when Linnaeus was 28, divided all minerals, plants, and animals known to date into classes, orders, genera, and species. Linnaeus's mineralogical classification earned him recognition only among specialists, and the progress made in chemistry from 1780 on quickly revealed the weaknesses of his system. His classification of the plant kingdom, however, aroused the enthusiasm of botanists. Linnaeus divided all plants into 24 classes, depending on the number and placement of their stamens. These classes were in turn subdivided into different orders according to certain characteristics of their pistils. This classification system, known as the "sexual system," was therefore based, like the systems in Newton's physics, upon the strictest possible application of a single principle, easily observable and virtually universal. Linnaean botany enjoyed immense success almost everywhere in Europe, above all in England and also in the Netherlands. Pope Clement XIV ordered that it be taught in the Papal States. Only in France did the system fail to achieve unanimous support. Instead, the botanists of the Jardin du Roi (French Royal Botanical Garden) and of the Académie Royale des Sciences, particularly Michel Adanson (1727–1806), Bernard de Jussieu (1699–1777), and his nephew Antoine-Laurent de Jussieu (1748–1836), favored a method for classifying plants founded on the examination of a large number of characteristics—if not the greatest possible number—arranged more or less hierarchically. This method was called "natural" because it sought to account for the affinities among plants. In this respect it was the opposite of the Linnaean system, which is based upon the examination of reproductive organs alone and which arbitrarily groups together plants that often do not resemble one another; for this reason the Linnaean system was criticized by some as "artificial." The debate between the "artificialists" and the "naturalists" was one of the richest in the history of the natural sciences in the 18th century and even through the first half of the 19th.

The zoological classification published by Linnaeus in 1735 in his *Systema naturae* also represents a milestone. Six major families in the animal kingdom were distinguished: quadrupeds, birds, amphibians, fish, insects, and worms. Each of these was subdivided into different orders depending on morphological characteristics chosen more or less arbitrarily: teeth for quadrupeds, beaks for birds, and wings for insects, for example. Linnaeus was the first scientist to study humans just like any other natural object, and he classified them among animals, as "anthropomorphous quadrupeds," alongside apes and sloths. However, to temper the scandalous implication of his purely zoological approach to the problem of the place of humans within the natural system, Linnaeus, in his definition of the genus *Homo,* invoked the Socratic injunction to "know thyself." For him, humans were created with an immortal soul, in the image of God, and were the only creatures with reasoning minds enabling them to praise their Creator. Moreover, despite their fragile constitution, they ruled over all other creatures. Linnaeus considered humans to be the ultimate purpose of Creation, for whose sake everything else was created. Linnaeus's recourse to theological, moral, and physiological criteria attest to his difficulties in finding a zoological definition for humans that would nonetheless distinguish them from other animals.

Linnaeus's adversaries went to great pains to emphasize the contradictions of his approach. Julien Offroy de La Mettrie, undoubtedly Linnaeus's first critic and the popularizer of his work in France, gives in his *Ouvrage de Pénélope* (1748; Pénélope's Work) an ironic treatment of the supposed relation between the human quadruped and the horse, and Denis Diderot also expresses his indignation in *Pensées sur l'interprétation de la nature* (1753; Thoughts on the Interpretation of Nature). Linnaeus finally decided in 1758, for the tenth edition of his *Systema naturae,* to place humans at the head of the primates and to give them the name *Homo sapiens,* which has been used ever since.

Linnaeus was convinced that he was a new Adam and refused to be discouraged by the abundance of living things. He believed that everything had its assigned place in the world. His classifying enterprise was inaugurated by *Systema naturae* and was continued in numerous other books, in particular in the *Genera plantarum* (1737; Genera of Plants), in which over 900 genera of plants are described; the *Philosophia botanica* (1751; Philosophical Botany) , in which Linnaeus lays down the theoretical foundations for a reform of botany; and the monumental *Species plantarum* (1753; Species of Plants), which lists over 5,800 species. All these works are a hymn to the great wisdom of God the Creator, who sees to the perfect organization of natural things. Linnaeus was not alone in finding a theological dimension in the wonders of the natural world. This physico-theological perspective was founded mainly by English scholars such as John Ray (1628–1705) and William Derham (1657–1735), early 18th-century authors whose popular works show how everything in Creation testifies to divine power. In their wake came the naturalists of the European continent and the entomologists in particular, such as Jan Swammerdam (1637–80), René Antoine Ferchault de Réaumur (1683–1757), and Pierre Lyonet (1707–89), who saw the tangible mark of the Creator's wisdom in the anatomy and the behavior of the living creatures they studied.

In addition to classification, Linnaeus attached a great deal of importance to the naming of nature's creatures. From 1745 to 1749, he made progressive improvements in the binomial nomenclature of species known today as the Linnaean nomenclature. He used it systematically for the first time in 1753 with plants, in the *Species plantarum,* then with animals in 1758, in the tenth edition of the *Systema naturae.* Heather, for example, would henceforth be called *Calluna vulgaris,* the cricket would be *Gryllus campestris,* and the dog would be *Canis familiaris.* With the exception of a few naturalists such as the Frenchman Adanson or the Swiss Albrecht von Haller (1708–77), the Linnaean nomenclature found an immediate and enthusiastic following, particularly in the Netherlands and Austria. Antoine-Laurent de Jussieu introduced it at the Jardin du Roi in Paris in 1774, and it is still in use today by the international scientific community.

Classification and a strictly codified nomenclature are the pillars of Linnaean science. During the second half of the 18th century, this approach attracted numerous scholars in Europe and won broad acceptance in light of the philosophical work of Étienne Bonnot de Condillac. By giving natural history a precise scientific vocabulary for the first time, Linnaeus indeed achieved what John Locke's French disciple saw as the ultimate perfection for a science: a language that ensured that if one knew the language, one would know the science. Jean-Jacques Rousseau was one of Linnaeus's most fervent partisans in France: "I read you, I study you, I meditate upon you, I honor you, and I love you with all my heart," Rousseau wrote to Linnaeus on 21 September 1771. In *Fragments pour un dictionnaire des termes d'usage en botanique* (Botany, a Study of Pure Curiosity: Botanical Letters and Notes toward a Dictionary of Botanical Terms), written in 1774 and published in 1781, Rousseau vigorously defends Linnaeus against Haller and Adanson and rejoices that Linnaeus's binomial nomenclature has been adopted at the Jardin du Roi. Imbued with the taxonomic ideas of Linnaeus and the philosophy of Condillac, the baron Guyton de Morveau (1737–1816), Torbern Olof Bergman (1735–84), and Antoine Laurent de Lavoisier (1743–94) completed the reform of chemical nomenclature from 1780 on.

Félix Vicq d'Azyr (1748–94) and Constant Duméril (1774–1860) did the same for anatomy, and Philippe Pinel (1745–1826) for diseases. The mineralogists and crystallographers Louis Romé de L'Isle (1736–90), René Just Haüy (1743–1822), and Abraham Gottlob Werner (1750–1817) followed the same path. The influence of Linnaeus's work of classification and nomenclature also influenced the classification of crimes proposed by the English philosopher and jurist Jeremy Bentham (1748–1832).

The success of Linnaeus's taxonomy in Europe during the age of the Enlightenment must not, however, obscure the debate that arose at the same time, particularly in France, as to whether a classification of living creatures was necessary and legitimate. Entomologist and physicist Réaumur, in his *Mémoires pour servir à l'histoire des insectes* (1734–42; Memoirs for a History of Insects), holds that, if it were the task of a naturalist to know and distinguish every species of insect, his memory would soon be overloaded with useless information. He was convinced that species that were distinguishable only by minor differences in color or wing shape were better left combined. This casual attitude with regard to classification was shared by the abbé Jacques François Dicquemare (1733–89), who declared in 1775 that a new species of animal he had discovered could be classified "wherever one wants." Going beyond these pragmatic concerns, the comte de Buffon (1707–88), the director of the Jardin du Roi in Paris and the principal opponent in France of Linnaeus's ideas, asserts in his *Discours sur la manière d'étudier et de traiter l'histoire naturelle* (1749; Discourse on How to Study and Approach Natural History) that classification is in no way the foundation of science. At best, according to Buffon, it is simply a dictionary, for the order to be followed is as arbitrary as alphabetical order. For Buffon, classifying systems like those elaborated by Linnaeus are only "scaffolding" to gain access to science and not science itself. This was also the opinion of Pierre-Louis Moreau de Maupertuis, who writes in his *Lettre sur le progrès des sciences* (1752; Letter on Progress in the Sciences) that only the study of general processes in nature would enable natural history to claim the status of true science. While he essentially shared the view of his two predecessors, the marquis de Condorcet, in his *Éloge de M. de Linné* (1779; In Praise of M. Linnaeus), nonetheless asks that classifying systems not be scorned.

In fact, the entire project of Linnaean classification was felt to be doomed to failure because of the continuity of nature. Buffon believed, along with most of his contemporaries, that all natural beings formed an uninterrupted chain, ordered according to a hierarchy, from raw matter (minerals) to angels and immaterial substances, by way of plants, animals, and humans. This concept of a *scala naturae,* of a great chain of being, is already present in the writings of Democritus, Plato, and Aristotle. In the Middle Ages and the Renaissance, it had acquired a truly theological significance: as God is omnipotent, he has created a world that is as rich as possible and left no gaps in Creation. Gottfried Wilhelm Leibniz, in the last years of the 17th century, shed some light on the subject through his work on infinitesimal calculus. His gradualist conception of nature led him to formulate, in his *Nouveaux essais sur l'entendement humain* (1704; New Essays concerning Human Understanding), the axiom, often repeated since, that *natura non facit saltus* (there are no leaps in nature). In 1745 Charles Bonnet (1720–93), a Swiss pioneer of experimental zoology, dared to draw a continuum of natural beings that, in keeping with Leibniz's philosophy, he organized in order of increasing perfection. Beginning with "the subtlest matters," followed by the four elements of traditional chemistry (fire, air, water, and earth), it rose progressively through the mineral kingdom to asbestos. Lithophytes and corals then provided a link to the vegetable kingdom, which then merged with the animal kingdom through sea anemones and polyps. Then came insects, shellfish, snakes, fish, birds, quadrupeds, and finally humans, immediately after the orangutan. Certain spaces were left blank to allow for the discovery of new intermediary forms. In his *Contemplation de la nature* (1764; Contemplation of Nature), Bonnet suggests a new continuum, or rather a sort of stairway, on which man occupies the highest step with his head in the clouds, suggesting that he is merely a transition toward the angels and God. Thanks to Bonnet, the natural continuum became a very popular topic among authors such as La Mettrie, Buffon, Maupertuis, Diderot, Kant, and Rousseau. Only Voltaire, in the article "Chaîne des êtres créés" (Chain of Created Beings) in his *Dictionnaire philosophique* (1764; Philosophical Dictionary), shows hostility toward this image of nature because it recalls the ecclesiastical hierarchy leading from the Capuchins to the Pope.

Paradoxically, Linnaeus did not deny the idea of the continuity of nature. As a result, his classification work did encounter certain obstacles. There was, first of all, the problem of the definition of life: where was the border between the world of the inert and the living? Certain parts of living beings, such as skeletons, shells, or calculi, are made up of mineral elements. The existence of what the naturalists of the era called "zoophytes," such as sponges, as well as the debate over the true nature of the polyp or the freshwater hydra, which reproduce by budding, also showed that the distinction between plant and animal is not always easy to establish. The ancient controversy over whether corals are stones, plants, or animals was definitively resolved in

favor of animals in 1725 by Jean André Peyssonnel (1694–1759), but his work was not published until 1752, a fact that further illustrates the difficulties of classification. Only the delicate issue of the passage from animals to humans, in the context of the debate over whether animals have souls, could potentially reconcile the classifiers and their adversaries. Indeed, many partisans of continuity, inspired by Buffon, gave humans a special place in the great chain of being, and the realization of these "intermittences" in nature was the source of overt tensions among them.

The question of classification in the age of the Enlightenment, beyond the quarrel over whether it was "artificial" or "natural," was thus one of the continuity or discontinuity of nature. Proponents of the idea of nature's fullness denied the existence of set distinctions between the different natural bodies that would enable the classifiers to establish systems and methods. This view led them to ask the fundamental question for naturalists concerning the reality of species: are the clearly distinct species on which Linnaeus's classification is based merely arbitrary divisions invented by man to facilitate his labor in ordering nature, or are they objective realities? In a word, are species produced by nature or by the naturalist? For Linnaeus, there could be no doubt: species truly exist within nature, and they were created by God at the beginning of the world, with morphological characteristics that enable one to tell them apart. To classify them is therefore a legitimate undertaking and is equivalent to finding the blueprint of Creation. Linnaeus was convinced that he had been chosen by God to fulfill this mission. However, the Linnaean perspective was far from general among his contemporaries. Buffon may have accepted the reality of species, which he defined physiologically for the first time in his *Histoire naturelle générale et particulière* (1749–89; Natural History, General and Particular), but he rejected the reality of genera, orders, and classes. Diderot perceived the novelty of Buffon's definition of species and included it in 1755 in his article "Species" in the *Encyclopédie.* Condillac, following Locke, argues in his *Logique* (1780; Logic) that it would be an error to imagine that there are species and genera in nature simply because they exist in our way of thinking. For him, there are only individuals in nature. His nominalism would later be shared by Jean Baptiste Lamarck (1744–1829), the founder of transformism.

Linnaeus is the central figure in the history of classification in Europe of the Enlightenment. Through his work, systematic ordering and nomenclature became the foundations of natural science. From this point of view, he set the tone for his century and made a very important contribution to the triumph of Condillac's ideas in France. Paradoxically, however, Linnaeus, who died in 1778, the same year as Rousseau and Voltaire, was not a part of the Enlightenment. Linnaeus's scientific work was proof of his attachment to Aristotelian logic, and his five taxonomic levels—class, order, genus, species, and variety—refer back to the categories of Scholastic philosophy. For Linnaeus, the essence of the plant resided in its reproductive organs. Nature, according to Linnaeus, must conform to pre-established rules. Unlike the French authors of the period, who sought to discover an order existing *in* nature, Linnaeus's ambition was to reveal, behind the apparent confusion of the world, the sovereign order *of* nature, attributable to divine power.

PASCAL DURIS

See also Garden, French Royal; Natural History; Science: Collections; Species

Further Reading
Broberg, Gunnar, "*Homo Sapiens*: Linnaeus's Classification of Man," in *Linnaeus: The Man and His Work*, edited by Tore Frängsmyr, Berkeley: University of California Press, 1983; revised edition, Canton, Massachusetts: Science History, 1994
Duris, Pascal, *Linné et la France (1780–1850)*, Geneva: Droz, 1993
Heller, John Lewis, *Studies in Linnaean Method and Nomenclature*, Frankfurt and New York: Peter Lang, 1983
Larson, James L., *Interpreting Nature: The Science of Living Form from Linnaeus to Kant*, Baltimore, Maryland: Johns Hopkins University Press, 1994
Stafleu, Frans Antonie, *Linnaeus and the Linnaeans: The Spreading of Their Ideas in Systematic Botany, 1735–1789*, Utrecht: Oosthoek, 1971

Clergy

Catholic

The numerical strength of the clergy in the 18th century varied significantly among the different countries of Europe: between 1.5 and 2 percent of the population in France and Spain were clerics, but only a tenth of that ratio in Poland. Within the European clergy as a whole, the ratio of secular to regular clergy (those attached to monastic orders) also varied greatly according to region. For example, in Spain some provinces had three times as many seculars as regulars, while monks and nuns were in the majority in others. Political and economic analysts have long distinguished between the high clergy and a low clergy comprised of parish and other priests. This two-tiered model today seems oversimplified, at least with respect to France. Recent scholarship tends to describe the clerical body in France as a relatively continuous hierarchy, in which most of the canons and parish priests comprised a sort of middle clergy at an intermediate level between, on the one hand, the prelates, their immediate entourage, and the members of prestigious chapters and, on the other hand, the large numbers of curates and unbeneficed priests (i.e., those without fixed parochial assignment). As regards Europe as a whole, however, the extremely varied circumstances of the different clergies and the consequent diversity of research approaches mean that we must make do with the conventional, two-tiered descriptive model.

Catholic ecclesiology, in which the bishops are seen as the successors of the apostles, lent the episcopate a special status. In most countries the bishops were mainly or exclusively noblemen; such was the case in Italy, for example, where there were numerous small dioceses. The few exceptional commoners had completely disappeared from the ranks of the episcopate in France by the 18th century. Elsewhere, the situation ranged from that of Spain, where bishops were often drawn from the minor nobility, to Austria or Germany, where the episcopate was closely linked to the upper aristocracy. These differences resulted in part from the method by which bishops were appointed. In France and Spain bishops were appointed by the crown, whereas in Germany or Austria they were chosen by very aristocratic chapters whose members elected bishops drawn from their own social milieu (many of these chapters required that a candidate for the episcopate have 16 quarterings of nobility before he could join their ranks). From the outset, the career path of bishops would have separated them from the ordinary clergy: the former received their education at an elite seminary—for example, in France at Saint-Sulpice—or at a university where they earned degrees, thus placing themselves intellectually above the common priesthood. Wherever circumstances did not allow local training, future bishops pursued their theological studies in Rome. A Roman education was the norm, for example, for Polish bishops. In contrast, many future Austrian bishops attended the Collegium Germanicum. Once they had completed their studies, very few future bishops in Europe were first obliged to take a parish ministry. In France the future prelate would have joined a bishop's immediate entourage right away; in Spain or Austria a seat in a prestigious chapter was the best interim position.

The path taken by the potential bishop was one of the factors that determined the quite variable status of chapters in the organization of the Church. Comparative studies on this topic remain to be done. In Austria bishops came from a background equal in prestige to the aristocracy of ancient lineage: the episcopate came from the powerful chapters, in which the title of canon was almost as exalted as that of bishop. Being a canon could also be just as remunerative as being a bishop—for example, in certain Spanish chapters whose revenues exceeded those of bishops in the poorest dioceses. In France, by contrast, bishops were selected more on the strength of family ties, patronage, and connections at court than as a result of connections within the Church. Apart from the most important chapters, membership in them was seen as a goal in itself—as a guarantee of a relative and variable degree of affluence—rather than as a springboard for career ambitions.

As princes of the Church, of almost universally noble origins, bishops had a share in public responsibility and political power. In the Germanic countries they participated directly in the power of the state. The most striking example is the German *Reichskirche* (imperial clergy), comprised of 65 prelates and abbots, simultaneously heads of states leaders and of dioceses, who sat in the imperial Diet and who in the 18th century formed the principal force of resistance to the ambitions of the great rival dynasties. In the hereditary Habsburg states, many bishops participated in the assemblies (which drew a third of their administrators from the episcopate), while in Hungary bishops were by right members of the Diet. On the other hand, in France the very centralized political structure did not permit bishops to hold such power, except on an individual basis. However, bishops dominated the assembly of the clergy, which, although it convened only once every five years, maintained permanent bodies and made the First Estate—the clergy—the only order in France with a collective organization. French bishops were also fully integrated into the seigniorial system, some even holding alongside the title of bishop that of count or duke,

acting in that aristocratic capacity to collect taxes and administer justice.

This participation in civil power took on a much more modern character with the increasing employment by the state of the hierarchical network of administratively experienced bishops and parish priests, the progressive growth in this direction being facilitated by changes that had taken place in both political and religious realms. During the Enlightenment, the state showed a growing interest in social organization and intellectual progress, and thus in fields such as social assistance or education, which overlapped with the Church's traditional areas of involvement. Moreover, the ideal of the bishop as a spiritual role model for his clergy and flock had waned with the decline of mysticism and was supplanted by the dominant model of the bishop good administrator, himself touched by the Enlightenment spirit.

Conversely, state control of the episcopate raised the problem of relations with Rome, whose authority over the bishops had long been weakened by the development of national absolutism. This control varied from country to country. In France, where the Gallican forces were particularly vigilant, decisions from Rome had to be recorded by the *parlements* (high courts), and French bishops did not go to Rome for formal visits *ad limina* ("to the thresholds" of the popes). In this regard, the second half of the 18th century was characterized in a number of countries by a new strengthening of the state's power over the senior clergy. For example, in Spain after the concordat of 1753, bishops opposed to the sovereign's ecclesiastical policy were repeatedly harassed or even forced to resign. In essence, the policy of the Enlightenment sovereigns was no different in its principles from absolutism by divine right: the aim of the ruler was still to limit as far as possible Rome's interference, which was accepted only when it came to the assistance of the state. However, royal policy wedged its way into new areas, reflecting the determination of states to control their subjects' ideological education. Joseph II's creation of general seminaries and proseminaries, staffed by masters appointed by the state and employing state-established curricula, was only the most spectacular example of an attitude that could be found in a number of the Holy Roman Empire's Catholic states.

At the same time, Rome and the state generally joined forces to prevent any movement of resistance against Church discipline; this alliance, which transcended the tactical or political differences of the moment, explains the common struggle of the popes and the French ruling powers against the rebellion of Jansenist bishops and priests. Heir to the conciliarist movement of the late Middle Ages, the episcopal doctrine in its radical form (which accorded Rome a merely honorary primacy over the other bishops) was revived in the southern Netherlands (now Belgium and Luxembourg) by the canonist Van Espen, author of the *Jus Ecclesiasticum Universum* (1700; Universal Church Law). It was, however, in the special circles of the German prince-bishops—those veritable sovereigns traditionally opposed to the centralism of the Roman Curia—that the episcopal doctrine appeared in its most extreme form. Febronianism, which denied the bishop of Rome any authority beyond his own diocese and restricted power to the Church collectively, came into being officially in 1763, when Justinus Febronius, assistant bishop of Trier, brought out his *De statu Ecclesiae et Legitima Potestate Romani Pontificis* (On the Status of the Church and the Legitimate Power of the Roman Pontificate). The success of this work—it was translated into numerous languages, and 16 of the 26 German bishops refused to publish a papal condemnation of it—proves that a current hostile to Roman centralization persisted in spite of the dominant forces that were striving at that time to promote an "infallible" papal supremacy.

The authority of the prelates over the parish clergy had increased greatly since the Council of Trent, which had strongly emphasized the hierarchical nature of the Church. Even in those places where the bishops did not participate by right in the mechanisms of state, this authority was upheld by the ruling power, which had its own means of controlling the episcopate. In France the Edict of 1695 confirmed the bishops' jurisdiction over religious houses and reinforced the authority of the prelates over parish priests. However, in this relationship between the state and the episcopate, the concerns of the bishops were in practice accorded less attention during the last decades of the century. In so far as possible, meanwhile, bishops sought to ensure their power and influence over their clergy against any temptation toward decentralization. Beginning early in the 18th century, in order more completely to control the training of the clergy, many French bishops had moved the teaching of theology—which until then had largely been provided by the colleges—into seminaries, where the duration of studies steadily increased.

However, clerical opposition to the power of the bishops also existed, and it was clearly not by chance that this resistance was most in evidence in France, where the clergy was sufficiently educated to judge itself entitled to oppose its bishops, even over problems of jurisdiction. During the late 17th century and throughout the 18th there were several instances in which "Richerist" ideas were revived (most notably by Pasquier Quesnel). Named after an early 17th-century syndic of the Paris theology faculty, the Richerist view held that there was no sacramental difference between bishops and priests. Those who defended this view argued that parish priests—and priests in general—should take an active part in the running of their dioceses and have voting rights in the synods. As late as 1786 two parish priests from Lorraine presented the Church as an egalitarian society whose hierarchy was in no way a matter of divine right but rather the result of a diversity of functions. The *cahiers de doléance* (books of grievances) show that this opinion, albeit in clearly less extreme forms, was widespread among the French clergy of the Enlightenment period.

In Europe more generally, the lower clergy—those who were in contact with the faithful—remained extraordinarily diverse two centuries after the Council of Trent. Clerical training was very sound in France, where every priest had at least studied at a diocesan seminary, most of which were run by a few large orders (Sulpicians, Lazarists, Eudists, etc.), whose role was fundamental. However, French-style seminaries, as they had developed from the time of Louis XIII, remained in the minority in Europe as a whole. Far from being simple boarding schools for a few poor scholarship pupils, as the Council of Trent had envisioned, these seminaries were intended to supply the parishes with a body of competent personnel. Such seminaries were nonexistent in Italy, where the bishops lacked the wherewithal to create the establishments that they would have liked. Similarly, most Spanish priests, whose ignorance astonished nonjuring French priests exiled under the Revolution, received only an empirical and haphazard training. Despite the efforts of Charles III from 1766 onward, Spain at the end of the 18th century still had only 45 seminaries, most of which were small. The intellectual gap between the higher and lower clergy was thus geographically variable, a fact that probably had consequences for relations between these two levels of clergy.

The differences between the higher and lower clerical ranks were not merely qualitative but quantitative as well. Both of these factors contributed to the more general problem of adapting the clergy to the supervision and instruction of the faithful, as required by the Council of Trent. For historical reasons, certain areas of central Europe that had been Christianized or reconquered at a late date were organized into vast bishoprics with few priests: each diocese of Lower Austria as well as those of Bohemia contained on average 500,000 to 800,000 inhabitants, and in Bohemia at the end of the 17th century, 20 percent of parishes had no priest. This shortfall in parochial personnel did not always result from a shortage of clergy, however. For example, in Spain at the end of the 18th century, only 22,000 priests out of a total of 60,000 were actually devoted to the service of a parish. As in 16th-century France, in Spain there were too many priests in the towns and too few in the country parishes, especially in the poorest rural areas (mostly situated in the south); exactly the same situation prevailed in Portugal. In Italy too, there was an abundance of very poorly trained priests, incapable of serving a parish and having no ambition to do so, being content to eke out a living in the service of aristocratic families or by taking charge of a few of the countless charitable foundations established by pious laymen. The laity, meanwhile, complained of the shortage of priests. Whatever the reason, the scenario resembled that of the Middle Ages, when the role of the priest consisted more of interceding with God by means of prayer than of teaching and guiding the people.

One of the objectives of Enlightenment bishops was therefore to make the priests themselves, and their distribution and numbers, more compatible with that essential role of the parish ministry. In recently reconquered Hungary, the number of priests rose spectacularly over the course of the century. In France the great majority of unbeneficed habited priests (i.e., those without parishes) had already been greatly reduced in numbers before the 18th century, especially in the countryside, and the bishops had endeavored to match their numbers to the availability of training and funds. This process was developed in two ways: through the requirement that a parish priest support his own curates, on the one hand, and the progressive reorientation of worship toward parish churches rather than the chapels and private oratories, on the other. The same policy was imposed by Joseph II in Lombardy, where the number of ordinations fell by 53 percent between 1782 and 1792, while the number of priests decreased by 11 percent over the same decade. Even in the kingdom of Naples there was a 25 percent decrease over the last 30 years of the 18th century.

Changes in the number of priests were equally dependent on the economic and social status accorded to the clergy. In Bohemia Joseph II awarded the secular clergy the assets of both the Jesuits and those religious orders eliminated in 1782, and he gave the parish priests a fixed annual revenue. These changes cannot be explained, however, merely in terms of episcopal or state policy; in certain regions in Spain and Portugal, poverty helps to explain why those regions lacked priests, who were simply unable to support themselves in those areas. Nor can one exclude the effect on the priesthood of changes in public opinion, which seem likely to have been a factor in 18th-century France. Up until 1730 the level of ordinations there had been high, and it was no doubt at this point that the image of the priest was at its most prestigious among the social groups from which the clergy were recruited. From that date on, studies at the diocesan or regional level reveal trends that, although divergent, sooner or later resulted everywhere in a drop in vocations. In 1768 the director of the seminary at Bordeaux, estimating that the diocese was 60 curates short, observed, "we can hardly hope any longer that the other dioceses will continue to help us, given that the shortage is beginning to be felt in every church in France." The social basis of recruitment was changing too: a slight rise in the figures for several dioceses at the end of the ancien régime, which the interruption of the Revolution makes it impossible to interpret with certainty, seems to indicate two shifts in vocations—from the urban elite to the lower middle class and from the towns to the countryside—that foreshadow the 19th-century pattern of recruitment. The evolution of the composition of the clergy, analyzed in terms of the French example, remains the product of a set of political, economic, social, and, of course, cultural factors.

JEAN QUÉNIART

See also Catholicism; Clergy: Regular and Secular; France; Secularization and Dechristianization

Further Reading

Callahan, William J., and David Higgs, editors, *Church and Society in Catholic Europe of the Eighteenth Century,* Cambridge: Cambridge University Press, 1979

Plongeron, Bernard, *La vie quotidienne du clergé français au XVIIIe siècle,* Paris: Hachette, 1974

Quéniart, Jean, *Les hommes, l'église et Dieu dans la France du XVIIIe siécle,* Paris: Hachette, 1978

Clergy

Regular and Secular

Before the Council of Trent, the Catholic Church had been characterized, particularly in the countryside, by the mediocrity of its parish clergy. In contrast to these secular priests, most of whom, apart from a few living in urban centers, hardly ever preached or taught, the regular clergy—that is, those belonging to religious orders—played a dominant role in the fields of prayer, learning, and preaching. The two Reformations had resulted in a twofold shift: the abolition of religious orders in all the Protestant churches, with whose ecclesiology they were incompatible; and significant transformations on the Catholic side, in the shape of the reform of numerous ancient orders, and the creation of new orders and congregations, which, for the most part, were oriented toward different forms of pastoral activity, such as missions, teaching, and good works. This was to some extent a pastorship born of emergency, which would be gradually replaced by that of a secular clergy better prepared for the job. The Council of Trent and the diocesan reforms were strongly marked by this desire to turn the parish clergy into the main agent of the recruitment and education of the faithful.

However, this evolution was still a long way from being complete. In 18th-century France the role of the parish clergy had become central; yet this development was by no means so advanced elsewhere. Apart from specific historical reasons such as those affecting Hungary, which had been devastated at the end of the 17th century, the establishment of a network of parishes dense enough to provide effective supervision of the population, and the installation in these parishes of a competent clergy, depended largely on economic and social structures and on the availability of proper training. The secular clergy in Spain, which composed 1.5 percent of the country's population, was very unevenly distributed geographically, leaving both priests without parishes and unfortunate parishes without priests. The situation was similar in Portugal, where the southern part of the country was badly underserved, even though the clergy made up 5 to 6 percent of the population in some towns. In Austria, 20 percent of parishes lacked a priest. Archaic conditions still existed in Eastern Europe: diocesan seminaries, for example, did not appear in Poland until the first half of the 18th century. There, as in Hungary, the clergy only represented between 0.1 and 0.5 percent of the Catholic population.

The position of regulars within the clergy as a whole, their role, and their vitality therefore varied greatly from region to region. In France the ancient male orders were undergoing a severe decline; and, while the female congregations and orders devoted to teaching or charitable work maintained varying levels of activity, the mere fact that few new houses were founded clearly indicates the Counter-Reformation's loss of impetus. In Spain and Portugal, on the other hand, monks and nuns were more numerous than secular priests, especially in the southern part of the peninsula: in Seville 60 percent of clerics were regulars. In Italy the number of regulars continued to rise until midcentury. While the strength of the monastic revival in Hungary was linked to its reconquest, numerous houses were also founded in Poland. In short, the presence and role of the religious continued to be crucial at the fringes of the Counter-Reformation. However, the examples of Austria and Poland show that the most dynamic orders were those that devoted themselves to an apostolic role in the world, such as the Piarists or the Jesuits.

In this context, the Enlightenment's hostility to the regular clergy was the outcome of multiple factors whose importance varied according to the order concerned and from one geographic area to another. Ancient orders devoted to prayer and contemplation, or even to study, were met with an incomprehension of their vocation, which was, admittedly, quite unfathomable in the case of those declining monasteries that housed only a few monks. The Enlightenment could shed no light on values that remained hidden away in the obscurity of the cloister. From the marquis de Sade's *Dom Bougre, ou le portier des Chartreux* (1748; Dom Bougre; or, The Doorman to the Carthusian Monastery) to Diderot's *La religieuse* (1760–80; The Nun) and Matthew Gregory Lewis's *The Monk*, published in 1795, the 18th century witnessed the rebirth—expressed with varying degrees of literary talent—of an antimonastic vein that went far beyond traditional anticlericalism, revealing a violent hostility toward these monks who had withdrawn from the world.

Furthermore, "reasonable" religion had no need for socially useless monks whose wealth, in some cases enormous in proportion to the number of beneficiaries, could have been used for all manner of charitable works. The attitude widely displayed in France in 1789 in the *cahiers de doliances* (registers of grievances) was one that was fully conscious, whatever the arguments against tithes, of the necessity of maintaining parish priests. Because of their supposed uselessness, however, the wealth and resources of the monks who, to quote the *cahier* compiled by the shoemakers of Laval, "live in splendor, idleness and indolence . . . [and] mock the people's poverty with their wealth," were an object of unanswerable criticism.

Nonetheless, this same *cahier* reveals a significant division of opinion concerning the regular clergy:

> The monks known as mendicants are supported by society, which is required to feed them by its alms. This burden has been cheerfully borne while we have seen them taking responsibility for the instruction and edification of the people. Today, these bodies are composed of members for the most part ignorant, idle, and, in consequence, useless to religion and society. The same arguments may be applied to the nunneries. Only those whose nuns are destined to educate young girls are of any usefulness.

This distinction between "uselessness" and "usefulness" in fact applied on two levels, religious and social. In France the authority and quality of the parish priesthood had put an end to the age when regular clergy played a central and dynamic part in pastoral work. On the other hand, the mendicant orders remained popular in places where, as in Italy and Spain, they continued to compensate for the inadequacies of the secular clergy by their mission work and teaching, and so remained in close contact with the populace.

Thus, in those areas where they had no further usefulness on the religious level, religious orders could only be appreciated in terms of their social usefulness. This social utilitarianism, together with a desire for rationalization, inspired the reforms carried out by various countries in the second half of the 18th century. In France in 1766, following the work of the Commission des Réguliers (Commission on the Regular Clergy), all religious houses containing fewer than nine monks were amalgamated. In 1782 Queen Maria I of Portugal prohibited the foundation of new religious houses; five years later she compelled any young person wishing to enter an order to obtain royal authorization. Between 1765 and 1790 the number of religious houses in Lombardy and Tuscany was reduced by a third; and in 1783, in Joseph II's Austria, the contemplative orders—amounting to more than 400 establishments—were secularized.

In reality, it was on the secular clergy that 18th-century states sought to base their religious policy, as far as local conditions allowed. The reasons were primarily philosophical. For example, the Jesuits' control over whole areas of intellectual life was no longer accepted: in line with this view, Maria Theresa reformed the commission for the censorship of books in Vienna, forcing the Jesuits in 1752 to share their authority with secular priests and laypeople. In France, following the acerbic criticism meted out to monastic education, secular priests also took over in most of the schools run by the Jesuits after the latter were expelled in 1762. Political considerations worked to the same end: states preferred a secular hierarchy of clerics—over which for the most part they strengthened their hold during the 18th century—to religious orders under the control of a distant and foreign authority. The Enlightenment ideal of government entailed cutting down the regulars to their socially useful elements, with preference given to a well-controlled secular clergy: this was Joseph II's policy and it would also be that of Napoleon Bonaparte.

JEAN QUÉNIART

See also Catholicism; Clergy: Catholic; Jesuits; Secularization and Dechristianization

Further Reading

Callahan, William J., and David Higgs, editors, *Church and Society in Catholic Europe of the Eighteenth Century*, Cambridge: Cambridge University Press, 1979

Cloth

Europeans discovered cotton during the Crusades and imported it—in the form of thread—through Mediterranean ports. For a long time its use was limited to the manufacture of stockings or mixed fabrics, in warps of wool, flax, or hemp (dimity, fustian). The protoindustrial regions that gradually came to specialize in cotton were in northern Italy, around Milan and Cremona; in southern Germany, around Ulm and Augsburg; in Switzerland, around Basel and Schaffhausen; in Champagne, around Troyes; in Beaujolais, around Lyon; and in Lancashire, around Manchester.

The trade of the great East India Companies (the Portuguese from 1501, the British in 1600, the Dutch in 1602, the Danish in 1616, and the French in 1664)

introduced new types of cotton fabric into European markets. Some were white, such as the coarse *garas* from the Surate region, the finer *bétilles, casses, guinées,* and *percales* from the Coromandel coast, and the very fine *adatais, hamans,* and *sanas* from Bengal. Others were various types of "painted cloth," partially colored with metallic mordants that permanently fixed dyes in the places where they were applied, either with a brush (painted cloth) or with woodblocks (printed cloth). These soon came to be known in Europe by the generic names of "Indians" or "chintz" (from the Sanskrit word *tchit,* "stained"). These new fabrics were brought back in great quantities after 1660, when the Restoration in Britain and the Treaty of the Pyrenees helped to revive business. They rapidly met with an immense success, as both the diary of Samuel Pepys in London and Molière's *Le bourgeois gentilhomme* (1670; The Would-Be Gentleman) in Paris indicate.

Unhappy with the competition from the East, which seemed all the more unfair because it came from "infidel countries" and contributed to the antimercantilist exportation of cash, makers of cloth and silk united in demanding that these new fabrics be banned. In October 1686, after the death of Jean-Baptiste Colbert, France became the first country to prohibit not only the importation of "Indians" but also their manufacture—except in Marseilles, because of the free status of the port—and even the "wearing and use" of them. Later reaffirmed many times, through 7 edicts and 35 rulings of the Council, this protectionist policy served only to encourage fraud and the establishment of smuggling routes, notably from Nice and Savoy. Enforcement of the policy under the authority of the *intendants* was cumbersome and socially selective, and it did nothing to prevent the development of a taste for "Indians" in French society. In fact, the policy only added to the profit of the neighboring countries that imported or produced the fabrics.

The British Parliament was subjected to pressure from cloth manufacturers, who went so far as to organize a raid on the warehouses of the East India Company in 1680. Parliament subsequently adopted a more nuanced policy. In 1700 Britain forbade only the importation of painted fabrics, leaving as a loophole the possibility of importing white cloth, which had been printed on since 1676 in London. Then, after the South Sea Bubble, from 1721 to 1774 it forbade printing on cotton cloth but not on linen, in order to encourage domestic production. After 1735 it was forbidden to print on the mixed fabrics known as "Siamese." The British production of "Indian" cloth was thus able to continue to grow, with a geographic redistribution of textile mills from London to regions such as Lancashire and Ireland where the labor force was less demanding.

The growth in demand, both domestic and foreign, favored research into timesaving production techniques that were then adopted on the Continent. One of these techniques was printing with a copper plate, analogous to engraving. It was initiated in 1752 in a mill established near Dublin by a merchant from London. Another technique was printing with a mechanical roller. It was patented by the Scotsman Andrew Bell in 1783 and adopted the following year by a mill in Lancashire and five years later by Christophe-Philippe Oberkampf in Jouy.

In 1728 the Spanish monarchy, encouraged by the example of Britain (which was also imitated by Prussia), issued an edict prohibiting foreign cotton fabrics, whether Asian or European, in order to reserve the domestic market for its own nationals, above all in Catalonia. The Catalonian market had been growing since the middle of the 17th century. An investigation into the distribution of cotton in that principality in 1732 counted 12,679 pieces of imported "Indian" cloth, of which three-fourths were in the capital, Barcelona, the place from which the wine and brandy that were the source of the province's wealth were exported. The mercantilist commitment to privileges for entrepreneurs favored the creation of factories. J.K.J. Thomson has traced their chronology and geographic distribution, which was characterized by a strong concentration in the area of the New Port in Barcelona (see Thomson). The first Spanish mill to make "Indian" cloth was opened in Barcelona in 1736, with the second opening in 1741. Ten mills were active in 1749, 29 in 1768, and 113 in 1786. The return of the ban on foreign cotton fabrics in 1768, after premature attempts at liberalization in 1742–43 and in 1760, encouraged the spread of cotton weaving to Catalonia and even to Cadiz and Ávila. But for a long time, cotton, imported from Malta and then from the West Indies, continued to be spun manually on spinning wheels. For reasons that have not yet been fully explained, the first mechanical loom was not introduced until 1785, in Barcelona, and the first water frame, constructed by British mechanics recruited by the Spanish embassy in Paris, did not appear until January 1790, and even then this innovation had no immediate consequences.

In the middle of the 18th century, what Depitre has called the "quarrel over painted cloth" erupted in France. The liberals grouped around the *intendant* of commerce, Vincent de Gournay, claimed it was necessary to permit the production and use of white and printed cotton fabrics. Their arguments seemed irrefutable. The economist Véron de Forbonnais estimated that the domestic consumption satisfied by foreigners, despite the ban, was worth 16 million livres a year. He added the demand of "the sugar islands, where the hot climate does not permit women to wear silk, because it lasts too short a time, or woolen fabrics, because they are too heavy." He concluded that "it would be a great advantage for the kingdom if it could provide itself with these two objects."

Since the end of the 17th century the making of "Siamese" cloth and handkerchiefs had also been developed in Normandy, around Rouen, and in Beaujolais, around Villefranche. This production called for increasing quantities of cotton, which the Caribbean colonies and metropolitan ship owners provided. All were naturally ready to increase the supply. The first great mill for the spinning and weaving of cotton, conceived on the model of a barracks, had been founded at Nantes under the Regency precisely in order to support this trade. It therefore required only a political decision, which the monarchical state took ten years to make.

Finally, in September 1759, under the brief tenure of Comptroller General Silhouette, France authorized the free manufacture of printed cloth within the kingdom and protected the national output of white cloth with a 20 percent duty. In 1752, during the ten years of the "quarrel over painted cloth," the Council authorized the creation at Angers of a factory for printing linen cloth on the British model. In 1755 it authorized the production of cloth "dyed in reserve"—that is, dyed cold in a vat of indigo prepared in iron sulfate, with white spaces "reserved" on the cloth by a coating of wax (a process more commonly known in English as resist dyeing or *batik*). Astute cloth makers in Rouen, Nantes, Orange, and Paris rapidly took advantage of these two loopholes, and thus provoked new complaints from the wool lobby.

Even before the legal abolition of the ban, about 15 scattered factories or "protofactories" already existed. These examples of the new industrial mode of production employed dozens of salaried workers of both sexes. They also recruited from abroad—or bribed away from their competitors—the technicians who were indispensable to the launching of the new industry. Oberkampf, hired by Cottin as a colorist at the Arsenal in July 1758, was the best known of these technicians. Under collective names or in joint stock companies, the mills accumulated capital that far exceeded that of the traditional dyers. The capital of Wetter and Co. in Orange reached 600,000 livres in 1757, and that of the bankers Gayet and Mongirod of Sèvres had reached more than 1 million livres by 1762, according to Oberkampf's partner at Jouy.

The government's decision led to a significant wave of new enterprises: 63 were created from 1760 to 1769, 45 from 1770 to 1779, and 47 from 1780 to 1789. They arose in circumstances that clearly favored the advent of new entrepreneurs, competent young men who in France were often outsiders because of their birth, religion, or language. Many of these young entrepreneurs succeeded in establishing family enterprises in France. The rigor of the "Indian" cloth industry spurred the protoindustrial processing of cotton, leading to the introduction of the first mechanical looms at Rouen in 1773 and the first water frames at Neuville in 1780. Although Louis XVI's France was not as mechanized as Britain, the French were well aware of the technical and social innovations of their rivals.

SERGE CHASSAGNE

See also Capitalism; Exclusivity System

Further Reading

Chassagne, Serge, *Le coton et ses patrons: France, 1760–1840,* Paris: Éditions de l'École des Hautes Études en Sciences Sociales, 1991

Thomson, J.K.J., *A Distinctive Industrialization: Cotton in Barcelona, 1728–1832,* Cambridge and New York: Cambridge University Press, 1992

Turnbull, Geoffrey, *A History of the Calico Printing Industry of Great Britain,* Altrincham, Manchester: Sherratt, 1951

Coffeehouse

From Coffee to the Coffeehouse

Coffee first arrived in Europe between 1570 and 1650, but it was not until the end of the 17th century that its consumption became truly widespread. Unlike chocolate or tea, which were first imported at roughly the same time as coffee beans, coffee gave birth to an institution, a place set aside especially for its consumption and named after the beverage itself. Prior to the establishment of coffeehouse, there had been only taverns or cabarets that served mediocre wine, and the appearance of coffee can be interpreted as a sign of the times: the beverage was considered a stimulant both for mind and body, and it gradually came to signify the triumph of refinement and elegance.

The first London coffeehouse was reportedly founded in 1652 in St. Michael's Alley, Cornhill. More were quickly added, and by 1663 the government required that coffeehouses be licensed. Early on, London cafés came to be places where business was conducted as well as sites for conversation and circulation of news-sheets. Late in the 17th century the coffeehouses clustered in the area around the Royal Exchange; Lloyd's, a famous shipping and insurance society, grew out of a coffeehouse by that name on Lombard Street. Charles II attempted to have the cafés closed in 1775 because of their presumed role in fostering sedition, a gesture repeated by William III in 1688. By 1739, however, coffeehouses greatly outnumbered taverns in London. In the 18th century, coffeehouses were the place where "every kind of mercantile business was transacted: cargo and ship insurance, finance, stock exchange transactions, and the buying and selling of commodities, ship properties, and miscellaneous goods of every description" (see Lillywhite). Numerous English writers were known to favor if not hold court at a particular coffeehouse, for example, John Dryden at Will's and Joseph Addison and Sir Richard Steele at Button's. Cafés also served in effect as post offices.

In Paris coffeehouses were initially humble storefronts set up in the more lively quarters of the city, such as at the Foire Saint-Germain or on the rue de Buci. Use of the term "café" to denote a place devoted to the consumption of coffee came later; at any rate the term did not make its way into official documents, and it does not appear in the decrees of the French royal council governing the sale of coffee, sorbet, or chocolate. Mention is made of "establishments where coffee is sold" or even of the *maison de café* (literally, coffeehouse), such as the one founded in Paris in 1672 by an Armenian named Pascal. In 1690 Antoine Furetière's *Dictionnaire* proclaimed the existence of nearly 3,000 *cabarets de caffé* (coffeehouses) in London—a figure that may be somewhat inflated. César-Pierre Richelet's *Dictionnaire* (1693) defines a café as: "a place in Paris where coffee is consumed." The latter *Dictionnaire* specifies that one can drink all sorts of beverages in a café, including tea and chocolate.

The Parisian coffeehouse owed some of its success to the genius of a native of Palermo and former waiter at the Café Pascal, Francesco Procopio, who set up a café called Le Procope in 1689 on the rue des Fossés-Saint-Germain. Le Procope launched the era of prestigious cafés that were luxuriously decorated with mirrors, tapestries, crystal chandeliers, and marble tables. It was no mere coincidence that Procopio located Le Procope directly opposite the premises where the Comédie-Française had set itself up only a year earlier, for the rise of the café was, in fact, linked to the development of the theatre. Theatrical performances were a perpetual topic of café conversation, and indeed those performances sometimes seemed to be continued or replicated in the setting of the café. Le Procope attracted the literary and theatre crowd even before it became the meeting place of the Encyclopedists or the emblem of the philosophical spirit of the 1750s. For example, in Denis Diderot's dialogue *Le neveu de Rameau* (1805; Rameau's Nephew), the Nephew leaves the Café de la Régence to go to the nearby opera house. Sébastien Mercier, at the end of the century, still associated a quarter past five in the afternoon, the time of day when all the carriages were rushing off to the theatre, with the time when the coffeehouses began to fill up. On the days on which performances were given (battle days!), the café served as army headquarters, packed with its own "troops" of warriors and literati.

The café was also a place for games (cards, checkers, chess), and a place where one would listen to *nouvellistes* (journalists), whom Alain-René Lesage mocks in *La valise trouvée* (1740; The Found Suitcase), but whose presence was a guarantee of success for the café owner. Alongside Le Procope, the most famous cafés of the 18th century were those that bordered the paths in the Luxembourg Gardens and the gardens of the Palais-Royal, the private estate of the duc d'Orleans (there were seven such café's on the eve of the Revolution, with just as many located on the nearby rue Saint-Honoré). This fact is important: in these gardens there were no uniformed police officers, which may explain the extreme freedom of expression and libertinism that reigned in these cafés. When the discussion began to take on too "philosophical" a drift, the speakers would try to divert the attention of spies by the use of coded phrases, which delighted those in the know. For example, in discussions about religion, God was called *Monsieur de l'Être* (Sir Being), religion was *Javotte*, and the soul was *Margot*.

The evolution of the café as an institution during the 18th century corresponded to the emergence of both a literary and a political public sphere. As a place for open debate on new themes, the café in some ways resembled clubs (such as the famous Entresol), free assemblies (such as the Société du Caveau), or even Masonic lodges. The café did, however, differ from these new social venues by the more diverse nature of its clientele. Unlike the salons or academies, the café was open to everyone and therefore was perceived as a school for intellectual growth and freedom. A refuge for the indigent, for poetasters who would leave their garret rooms to find warmth in winter around the stove, the café did not represent anyone in particular, nor did anyone need an introduction or sponsorship.

No particular deference, therefore, needed to be shown the café owner. Throughout the 18th century the cafés of Paris would play host to all the impoverished writers as well as to gifted speakers who could deliver an anecdote in a tone halfway between that of a man of the world and that of a man of letters. As early as 1695, Jean-Baptiste Rousseau described the people one usually met in cafés in a play entitled *Le caffé* (The Café):

> There are five or six of you, who, as long as you can spend the entire afternoon here singing songs and speaking nonsense, telling a story about some man, or relating the adventures of some woman, or chronicling the scandals of the human race, you care nothing for anything else.

Cafés Find Their Way into Literature

The 18th century, with Le Procope and its philosopher patrons, inaugurated the era of literary cafés. In England the coffeehouse also became a place where a spirit of conversation and debate ruled. In Italy the coffeehouse lent its name to one of the leading organs of enlightened Italian thought, *Il caffè*, a periodical founded in 1764 by Alessandro and Pietro Verri. It is interesting to note the close ties that bound the café and men of letters: just as the café opened its doors to artists, the artists in turn repaid the café in kind by enthroning it in literary fiction, novels, and dramas, as well as intellectual exchanges. Might the café have encouraged a certain type of discourse? And how would the café be honored by literature?

Initially a simple atmospheric setting over the course of the century, the coffeehouse became for many a philosophical stage. In Carlo Goldoni's *La bottega del caffè* (1736; The Coffee House), the café was merely a backdrop for a lively portrayal of daily life. For Voltaire, in *Le café ou L'ecossaise* (The Café; or, the Scottish Woman), a comedy dating from 1760, the café, while still an eponymous place, became a picturesque setting for an ideological struggle. As the century wore on, this "refuge for knaves and layabouts"(as Jean-Jacques Rousseau mercilessly described it) became a place where derision, cynicism, and scepticism found a foothold in literature and flourished. Among the dreamers, gamblers, and wastrels were to be found those "gutter intellectuals" in pursuit of literary glory, wielding harangue and paradox as they followed the example of Diderot's *Le neveu de Rameau*, enlivening their discourse with a smattering of heretical remarks. One of the central themes of the discourse on the café was that of idleness: not the idle leisure of aristocrats or the *otium cum dignitate* (dignified leisure) of philosophers, but an inactivity that took on an increasingly negative connotation as work emerged as a bourgeois value.

Louis-Sébastien Mercier, for example, in the *Tableau de Paris* (1787; Panorama of Paris), describes how in the Caveau, one of the cafés of the Palais-Royal, "other idle sorts bandied about those unproductive or literary questions that have become hackneyed."

The other essential theme of this café literature was immoderation. The café was the place where society's conventions where left in the cloakroom—where the polite, urbane conversation of the salons gave way to other forms of verbal communication. In *Les entretiens des cafés de Paris et les différens qui y surviennent* (1702; The Conversations in Parisian Cafés and the Disputes Which Arise There), the comte de Mailly showed how a discussion could end in fistfights, in which mirrors were broken and "coffee pots were knocked over." It was, moreover, a commonplace of the 18th century to associate debate (philosophical or literary) with the coffeehouse. Montesquieu set the tone in Letter 36 of his *Lettres persanes* (1721; Persian Letters), and many others would follow his example. Here, for example, is what one can read in Letter 15 of *Les lettres iroquoises* (1752; The Iroquois Letters), by Maubert de Gouvest:

> I went to the café yesterday, which is the custom of these people. Two philosophers sitting next to me were arguing about the shape of the Earth. It is flat on both sides, said one; it is the shape of a melon, said the other; and thereupon the argument became heated.

Another example of exaggeration, in *Le neveu de Rameau,* is the thundering voice of *Lui* (Him), deafening the philosopher-narrator and all the other patrons of the café. It was no doubt the setting itself that made such great triviality possible. In the civilized exchanges of worldly conversation as it was conducted in the salons, the tone of one's voice was controlled by a whole code of etiquette: excess of any kind (verbal or nonverbal) was forbidden in classical rational discourse. In *Le neveu de Rameau*, the Nephew's shouts and gestures constituted both indecent and apparently irrational behavior and such an outburst could surely take place nowhere else than in the overfamiliar space of a café. With *Le neveu de Rameau*, the café became the ironic setting for an impure philosophy. The realistic fiction about the dialogue heard in the coffeehouses—which was the setting for a different social and cultural reality, a space of greater freedom but also a new source of social tension—was certainly related to the transformation of philosophical discourse in the 18th century.

STÉPHANE PUJOL

See also Civilization and Civility; Conversation; Food; Song

Further Reading

Caraccioli, Louis-Antoine, *Les entretiens du Palais-Royal*, Utrecht: Buisson, 1786;

Carrière-Doisin, A. *Le café littéraire; ou, La folie du jour*, Paris: Leroy, 1785

Fosca, François, *Histoire des cafés de Paris*, Paris: Firmin-Didot, 1934

Lillywhite, Bryant, *London Coffee Houses*, London: Allen and Unwin, 1963

Pellissery, Roche Antoine, *Le caffé politique d'Amsterdam; ou, Entretiens familiers d'un François, d'un Anglois, d'un Hollandois, et d'un cosmopolite sur les divers interêts economiques et politiques de la France, de l'Espagne et de l'Angleterre*, 2 vols., Amsterdam: s.n., 1776

Collections and Curiosities

Denis Diderot condemned collectors as *amateurs* or *curieux:* "in painting, a *curieux* is a man who amasses. . . . Those who pursue this activity are never connoisseurs, and it is this that often renders them ridiculous." This statement resembles the view formulated in the *Dictionnaire de l'Académie* (first edition, 1694; Dictionary of the Académie Française): "curiosity: passion, desire, eagerness to see, to learn, to possess rare things." It is also close to the views expressed by Nicolas Boileau-Despréaux and René Descartes. The similarities between the two definitions might lead one to believe that during the 18th century, the culture of curiosities was immobile and dulled by ancient and fanciful dreams of gathering a *theatrum mundi* (theatre of the world).

In fact, after 1710 (to use an approximate starting point) the cartography of curiosities was organized and ordered, although recent research by Schnapper has shown that neither the contrast between the *Wunderkammern* (cabinets of marvels) of northern Europe and the cabinets of the Mediterranean, advocated by Schlosser, nor the transition, dear to Michel Foucault, from circular display to arrangement in the form of a painting, was as clear or as rapid as historians might wish (see Schnapper). Different types of objects were strictly separated in Du Molinet's curiosity cabinet at Sainte-Geneviève, and three leading German treatises on curiosities—Quiccheberg's *Inscriptiones* (1565; Inscriptions), Valentini's *Museum museorum* (1704–14; Museum of Museums), and Neickel's *Museographia* (1722)—insisted on the necessary separation and classification of *naturalia* and *artificialia,* in order not only to look at objects but also to study them. From then on, works of art were set apart. Dezallier d'Argenville, in his "Lettre sur le choix et l'arrangement d'un cabinet curieux" (Letter on the Choice and Layout of a Curiosity Cabinet), which appeared in the *Mercure de France*

in 1727, still envisaged a collection of curiosities but recognized selectivity as a necessary principle: "Our cabinets have become universal . . . but natural inclination leads us more toward one science over another. . . . Others among us, Sir, lean more toward painting."

Among the collections that are known to us from sale catalogs (a printed genre that developed in London beginning in 1690 and in the Netherlands in 1710), most contained either paintings and drawings or curiosities, with some exceptions such as those of Jan Six (sold in Amsterdam in 1702) or of Elihu Yale (sold in London in 1721–22). According to the lists drawn up by Hirsching and Meusel in Paris and Bologna, the situation was similar in Germany at the end of the 18th century, although collections of books, paintings, or fine series of medals were frequently found among the nobility. Moreover, collections of antiquities could be found throughout France, from Aix en Provence to Paris, from Montpellier to Lyon, while artistic collections were concentrated in the capital. The study of such collections is more complex than it might appear, as Schnapper has demonstrated. Some decorative objects, such as porcelains, were collected, and traveled from the curiosity cabinet to the table before ending up, as Impey points out, on the wall. On the other hand, contemporary French painting received more support from patrons, for the purpose of decoration, than from collectors. In contrast to the situation in Italy, collections were not generally inherited in France: they were most often sold when their owners died, even if no handwritten list confirming the sale has remained. Moreover, the contrast between noble and bourgeois collectors was hardly clear-cut. Financiers, along with the high aristocracy and Le Nôtre, shared a taste for northern European paintings, small bronzes, and porcelain. By approving the tastes of the elite, Louis XIV gave an added impetus to French collecting. In 1721 Philippe d'Orléans, who had come to power as regent in 1715, bought Queen Christina of Sweden's collection in Rome, using Pierre Crozat as an intermediary.

The situation in Italy around 1730 may appear to have been extremely varied, but in fact it was fairly uniform. In Rome two cardinals, Pietro Ottoboni and Silvio Valenti Gonzaga, established considerable collections, but they did not succeed in reviving the tradition of collecting and patronage that had characterized the pontificates of the Borghese and Barberini families. The ruling families of Genoa had established their collections at the beginning of the 17th century by commissioning canvases from Peter Paul Rubens and Guerchin. From around 1680 to 1730 these families issued numerous commissions to local artists, but only for decorative purposes: the paintings were to cover walls in the same way that frescoes did or that tapestries had in earlier times. In 17th-century Bologna, collections were controlled by leading merchants who relied on market structures to put the canvases of Guido Reni and Guerchin into circulation across Europe. In the 18th century, in contrast, collections became the prerogative of the nobility, who thus assured the late flowering of the Bolognese school of painting. In two generations (1680–1740), the number of great masterpieces in the palaces that the nobility had just built or renovated rose from 8 to more than 40, and canvases by Bolognese artists formed 90 percent of the collections. However, the pictures as a whole received more attention as objects than as paintings. Paintings were placed in richly sculpted and gilded frames, each costing one-fourth of the total price, that conferred a certain majesty upon the works, and the pictures were usually displayed in salons. In cases where a collection had artistic value because of the presence of works by old masters or foreign painters—such as the Boschi or Aldrovandi collections—the paintings were hung in a gallery, arranged in a triumphal manner.

In Venice the scope of most of the collections established by the nobility, with the exception of the collection amassed by Zaccaria Sagredo (1654–1729), did not go beyond the end of the 17th century, and even the newly ennobled preferred to focus only on older paintings. As a result, contemporary painting served a predominantly decorative function except among two new types of collectors: foreign residents such as British consul Joseph Smith or Marshal Schulenburg; and the bourgeois elite, which included Anton Maria Zanetti the Elder and Matteo Pinnelli. Sometimes these new collectors also specialized in the minor genres of painting. These two types of collectors also coexisted in other major Italian urban centers, such as Brescia, Padua, or Verona (although Venetian art was refused outright in that city), while the elites of minor cities, such as Rovigo, showed definite interest in contemporary Venetian and Bolognese art.

The culture of curiosities first evolved among the antiquarians, thanks to Scipione Maffei (1675–1755), who in 1732 published his *Verona illustrata* (Illustrated Verona). Abandoning a virtually exclusive interest in the rare objects, epigraphs, and medals of antiquity, this new breed of numismatists affirmed the principle of historical continuity through medieval coins. Among archeologists, the focus gradually shifted to the study of large-scale statuary and figurative monuments. From then on, texts were used to improve one's understanding of images and objects. For Maffei, monuments were historical evidence as well as expressions of taste, but for the comte de Caylus (1692–1765) they were linked above all to the history of art. In Caylus's collections of antiquities, the man of "things" gradually surpassed the man of letters. This infatuation with ancient sculpture explains the new collections that were formed in Rome (the Albani collection) and in England (the collections of the duke of Norfolk and Horace Walpole), in part because of the excavation of the Villa Hadriana and archeological sites in Campania but also because of the active influence of Gavin Hamilton.

Nevertheless, Caylus represented an older notion of the connoisseur of painting, who knew how to appreciate what Roger de Piles would have termed the subtle concepts in a painting, and who could account for the beauty of a work, because of his "understanding of the principles of painting." A painting, according to Nicolas Poussin, should be read; it was a narrative. However, such knowledge was also power. The connoisseur, demonstrating his refinement by means of a beautiful collection cabinet, was also in a position to provide guidance for artists. (Diderot rejected this idea and advocated a naturalistic and emotional aesthetic.) The connoisseur alone knew how to judge the merits of a painting, as the dealer Gersaint, for one, conceded. Such expertise was the privilege of an elite that used the salon as its place of social gathering.

However, Gersaint contrasted the connoisseur with the *curieux*, who was less interested in the historical arrangement of pictures or objects than in their manner or brushwork. The predominance of *curieux* in Paris in the 1750s can be explained by the swelling ranks of collectors in the city: some 150 collectors were active between 1700 and 1720, while this figure increased to 500 in the second half of the century (see Pomian). Other factors involved include the change in the social composition of collectors, with the disappearance of the *noblesse de robe;* and the increasing number of auctions for which catalogs were compiled by Mariette or Rémy, from less than one per year until 1730, to 15 each year between 1761 and 1770.

Without doubt, the worthiest example of the *curieux* was Blondel d'Azincourt, who came from the old established nobility and wrote his book *La première idée de la curiosité* (The First Idea of Curiosity) in 1749. For him, the pleasure of the *curieux* was a social privilege: "There are two types: the pleasure that one derives from seeing the cabinets of other enthusiasts, and that of ownership. The latter gives complete satisfaction." Such pleasure is based not on the reading of paintings, which brings the delight that Poussin desired, but on the brilliance of the painter's work: "A painting should be generally pleasing, it should have a great impact. . . . It should shine with finesse . . . [with] stimulating and agreeable subjects." Consequently, Blondel d'Azincourt acknowledged his preference for Flemish paintings, rather than "dubious and mediocre" Italian paintings "that present only sad subjects." Pictures had to be hung in an arrangement that created a pleasant overall visual effect, and French genre paintings of the 1770s imitated the small pictures of northern Europe.

The new attention paid to what the dealer Rémy called the "finesse of the brush," which contrasted with both the "finesse of ideas" emphasized by Roger de Piles and with Dezallier d'Argenville's notion of the "pictorial writing" of each painter, explains the growing importance of attribution, since from this time onward collectors no longer bought pictures simply because they liked the works themselves. Collectors were more interested in the names of the artists who had painted them. This fundamental change also explains the abrupt shift in the nature of sale catalogs beginning in the 1750s and the emergence of a new type of connoisseur, the dealer in paintings (see Pomian).

This development was not only a topic of discussion but was also true in practice, as is shown in the display of the collections of members of the Parlement of Paris. Around 1710, collections were fairly well distributed among the members of the *noblesse de robe* and, like their libraries, the collections of these nobles sustained a humanist culture. Collections were placed in galleries and were organized around narratives, such as Guido Reni's "Labors of Hercules" or Poussin's "Sacraments," and their attribution was incidental. By the end of the century, all the great collectors systematically asked dealers to evaluate their pictures, which had become works of art, and to compile catalogs of the works. Collections were thus one of the privileges of an educated and worldly elite set apart by their fortunes. Works in which one could see the hand of the artist (such as in northern European paintings, sketches, or drawings) were the most highly prized and were hung in private rooms, such as studies or bedrooms. Henceforth, collections were no longer parts of an inheritance linked to a family, but personal possessions; they no longer comprised mere paintings, whether originals or copies, but

works of art that were bought and sold and provided a pleasant delight.

However, the growing importance attached to the skill and the name of the creator, rather than to the narrative being represented, implied new rules, both for hanging paintings and for the small world of curiosities. In 1747 the abbé Le Blanc criticized the "tapestry effect" of hanging too many paintings together in the Salon and expressed a desire that the works be hung in isolation, so that each could be appreciated better. In 1748 Louis Petit de Bachaumont, a prominent French lawyer, advised Frederick II of Prussia to avoid hanging his paintings by subject and to arrange them according to artistic schools instead. In 1792 Watelet and Lévesque implored amateurs also to be connoisseurs: collectors should not jumble up their paintings but should hang them in a manner that would allow the works to be compared. In 1770 three leading collectors—the abbé Terray, Le Peletier de Mortfontaine, and Grimod de La Reynière—followed the example of Lalive de Jully and, often advised by the dealer Lebrun, they devoted a gallery of a Parisian home to the contemporary French school.

This Enlightenment approach to hanging paintings, with its obvious pedagogical purpose and its close relationship to the ideas advocated by scholars, also spread to the princely galleries of Germany. Hirsching wrote in 1786 that "collections are intended for education, for the training of an enlightened mind, and for good taste," and Mechel wrote in 1781 that "such a collection, immensely rich and of a public nature, is intended more for education than for a fleeting pleasure."

Carlo Lodoli (1690–1761) of Venice, the teacher of Francesco Algarotti, collected examples of architecture in his garden in order to reveal the styles and technical innovations of various periods, and the paintings in his gallery were classified according to schools, "in order to show the progression of the art of drawing from its revival in Italy up to the time of Titian and Raphael." The collector Tommaso degli Obizzi (1750–1803), a worthy successor to Scipione Maffei, was in fact a historian interested in the things of the past. On his behalf, Canova sought out ancient marble statues in Rome, and Visconti cataloged his collection, describing primitive works as well as medals and porcelain vases.

Collections specializing in antiquities were increasingly common by the end of the century, a fact that suggests collectors were willing both to pay close attention to individual objects and to display them in an educational manner as, for example, Felice Maria Mastrilli's collection of antique vases in Naples. Previously, vases had been placed side by side, as in a *Wunderkammer*, or above the shelves of libraries, as emblems of knowledge and tradition, either following the examples of ancient busts (the noble family Caraffa) or serving a purely decorative function. Mastrilli's preferred arrangement was to place the vases on brackets projecting from the wall, thus emphasizing the vases' curvature and lines. As in museums in later periods, this mode of display highlighted the individual object; it also paved the way for a systematic approach to display and to classification, and it fostered the development of a new discipline, classical archeology. Attention was thus shifted from manufactured objects, those types of *artificialia* worthy of cabinets of curiosities, to objects considered as works of art.

The development of the collections of Cardinal Alessandro Albani (1692–1779) tells the same story. His first two collections included one that was bought in its entirety by Pope Clement XII in 1733; together, the collections provided most of the objects displayed in the Museo Capitolino. These collections contained pieces that had been extensively restored and a series of portraits, many of which were misidentified. However, his third collection, intended for the Villa Albani, showed the influence of Johann Joachim Winckelmann in its chronological arrangement and its informative character. Bartolomeo Cavaceppi limited himself to authentic archeological restorations. Winckelmann cited the chronological arrangement of his collection of drawings as a model of how to illustrate the history of art.

In the course of the emergence of a new breed of collectors, from educated collector-patrons to amateurs interested in curiosities and then to true connoisseurs, collecting itself was transformed, both with respect to the objects collected and its methods of presentation. The increasing number of printed descriptions pertaining to collecting included not only catalogs but also tourist guides such as those for Bologna or Paris. In many cases such publications gave collecting a status that was as much public as private. Cardinal Albani's collection in Rome greatly influenced Johann Wolfgang von Goethe and Visconti and served as a model for the Museo Pio Clementino. In Paris the dealer Lebrun, with his vast experience in private collections, advocated a didactic arrangement of paintings for the new museum in the Louvre. This great museum was therefore not the fruit of the "art of liberty" but a result of the history of curiosity.

OLIVIER BONFAIT

See also Antiquity; Dilettante; Etruscan; Museum; Painting

Further Reading

Bailey, C.B., "Conventions of the Eighteenth Century *Cabinet de Tableaux*: Blondel d'Azincourt's 'La première idée de la curiosité,'" *The Art Bulletin* (September 1987)

Bonfait, O., "Les collections des parlementaires parisiens du XVIIIᵉ siècle," *Revue de l'art* 73 (1986)

Howard, S., "Albani, Winckelmann, and Cavaceppi," *Journal of the History of Collections* 4, no. 1 (1992)

Lyons, C., "The Museo Mastrilli and the Culture of Collection in Naples, 1700–1755," *Journal of the History of Collections* 4, no. 1 (1992)

Pomian, Krzysztof, *Collectionneurs, amateurs et curieux, Paris–Venise, XVIᵉ–XVIIIᵉ siècle,* Paris: Gallimard, 1987

Schnapper, Antoine, *Collections et collectionneurs dans la France du XVIIᵉ siècle,* 2 vols., Paris: Flammarion, 1988–94

Colonialism

Like its equivalents in other languages, the French word *colonialisme* was recently coined. It was unknown in the 18th century, even though the colonial phenomenon is acknowledged in the title, *L'anticolonialisme au XVIIIᵉ siècle* (1951; Anti-Colonialism in the Eighteenth Century), of G. Esquer's book of excerpts from Guillaume-Thomas Raynal's *Histoire philosophique et politique des établissements et du commerce des Européens dans les deux Indes* (1770; A Philosophical and Political History of the Settlements and Trade of the Europeans in the East and West Indies). Cognate terms began in France with the word *colonie* in the 14th century; *colonisation* appeared in the 17th century, and then came *colonial,* a noun used to refer to the colonial farmers. After 1830, with the conquest of Algeria, the words *coloniste* and *anticoloniste* came into existence in connection with colonization by settlement (see Lacouture and Chagnollaud). The words *colonialisme* and *anticolonialisme* relate to the conquest and exploitation of a territory under the direction of a dominant minority with essentially economic aims (during the 18th century), and then to the desire for power in the service of capitalism (in the 19th and early 20th centuries). The term *colonialisme* was coined before 1914 among those who were hostile to the colonial endeavors of the Third Republic: it appears in the 1910 edition of the *Larousse mensuel illustré*. The opponents of colonialism believed the state had moved from colonization to imperialism (see J. Bruhat in the *Encyclopaedia universalis* [Universal Encyclopedia]). From its origins the French word *colonialisme* carried a pejorative connotation that does not exist in British usage: British colonization, at least before the conquest of India, had first and foremost been colonization by settlement.

Forms of Colonialism

The concept of colonization was for a long time infused with humanist culture in the form of images of the colonies of antiquity, principally those of the Greeks (see, for example, "Vauban et les colonies" [Vauban and the Colonies] and François Louis Véron de Forbonnais's article "Colonies" in the *Encyclopédie*). The image of the ancient colonies persisted, with some variation from country to country, in the case of settlers' colonies, which existed only in the relatively temperate zones. Canada's Quebec and eastern Ontario, and Acadia (now Nova Scotia), which together made up New France, were royal colonies that in principle welcomed only Catholics; the British colonies of New England were refuges for religious minorities. The numerical superiority of the New England population over that of the French Canadian settlements was one of the causes of the British victory in the Seven Years' War, also known as the French and Indian War (1756–63).

The other European colonies around the world were of distinct types. Those in the Indian Ocean constituted a separate case, beyond the invisible border that ran through the Cape of Good Hope, between two colonial realms. Colonization in that area was purely mercantile, based on trading posts that were often fortified. The exception was the Dutch East Indies because of its monopoly on spices.

The realities of colonialism were revealed in Spanish and Portuguese America and, above all, in the West Indies (the Antilles). There a colonialism of intensive agriculture was the rule, mainly under British and French domination (the Dutch, the Danes, and the Swedes, used their colonies more for commercial purposes). The exclusivity policy, a specific form of mercantilism specifying that cultivation of the land would be for the sole benefit of the colonizing power, was in effect. The land was divided into what the French called *habitations* and the British "plantations." An abundant slave labor force, made up of black Africans acquired in the slave trade, worked the land. In the closing decades of the 17th century, agriculture developed in the direction of large landholdings and a quasi monoculture, that of sugar, the cultivation of which required abundant labor.

Every country imposed prohibitions on trading by foreigners, varying in rigor with time and place. In principle, each of the colonial powers also prohibited colonists from engaging in any activity requiring the processing of tropical products, in order not to compete with the industries of the colonizing country. The colonies were obliged to sell their staple products only to the metropolitan power and had to purchase from it whatever they might need. Prohibitions against smuggling and interlopers were very unevenly enforced. The French traded with Dutch colonies (notably the island of Saint Eustatius in the Caribbean), with British colonies, and even, officially but tacitly, with the Spanish territories that are present-day Trinidad and Venezuela—but in a restricted way, in order to avoid becoming a source of conflict with Madrid. Because of the inferiority of their navy, the kings of France had to suspend every form of exclusivity at the beginning of each war and reaffirm it when peace came: the letters patent issued in April 1717 and October 1727 became the basic rule throughout the 18th century.

Colonists versus Colonial Policy

Because of the many nuances that differentiated the European powers, home governments reacted in different ways to violations of policies by colonists. While Robert Walpole's Britain practiced "benign neglect," the kings of France rigorously suppressed revolts by the colonists, such as the *Gaoulé* of Martinique in 1717, in which the colonial administrators were recalled to France, or the revolts of Santo Domingo against the Compagnie des Indes (French Indies Company) in 1722–23 and against the reestablishment of the militia in 1766–67. After 1765 the Choiseul administration and his chief official for the colonies, Jean Baptiste Dubuc, the "Great White Creole" of Martinique, opted for a policy of "mitigated exclusivity," which in practice opened up the possibility of numerous exemptions and measures of toleration until Castries tried to apply it more strictly in 1784. The colonists, above all those of Santo Domingo, tried to take advantage of the outbreak of the French Revolution in order to obtain economic liberty and active autonomy, failing to foresee the explosion of the slave revolt.

In 1713 Spain agreed to allow Britain to introduce black slaves into Spain's colonies. After the Seven Years' War, Britain, in contrast to France, wanted to control and tax the trade of its colonies in North America for financial reasons. Twelve years later that policy led to the American Revolutionary War.

From Colonialism to Anticolonialism

In *De l'esprit des lois* (1748; The Spirit of Laws), Montesquieu explains the rules and rationale of the exclusivity system as follows:

> It has been established that the metropolitan power alone can trade in its colony, for the important reason that the purpose of founding the colony was to expand trade and not to found a city or a new empire. . . . This is still a fundamental law in Europe, that all trade with a foreign colony is regarded as a pure monopoly punishable by law.

For his part, the count of Revillagigedo, viceroy of New Spain, wrote in 1794 that Mexico

> is a colony that must depend on its mother country, Spain, and must pay in return by certain profits in exchange for the benefits that it receives in being protected by Spain; it must . . . make sure that their interests are mutual and reciprocal, but they will cease to be so from the moment when here [in Mexico] there is no longer any need for either manufactures or natural products from Europe.

Anticolonialism

Anticolonialist sentiment emerged in opposition to strict and centralized domination by the colonial powers, governors who were sometimes despotic, and economic monopoly in the colonies. Anticolonialism also sometimes encompassed condemnations of the slave trade and slavery. In the case of Britain, which undertook the conquest of an empire in India, the Methodists and William Wilberforce fought against the slave trade.

In France this current of thought was articulated in Raynal's monumental *Histoire des deux Indes*. The work includes a summary, documented from the best sources, describing the process of the appropriation of the world by the European powers and condemning the conquest and subjugation of native peoples. Raynal also criticizes the prohibition on colonies processing their own products and trading with others apart from their parent countries. Within the framework of the theories of Vincent de Gournay, Raynal advocates freedom of trade for the colonies, and he notes that the colonists had no interest in defending themselves, as in Guadeloupe in 1759 or Martinique in 1762. As Raynal writes of colonists in the 1780 edition of his work:

> It does not matter to this greedy and calculating person whom he receives his laws from, provided that the harvest continues to be gathered: it was to enrich himself that he crossed the seas . . . Does the mother country, which so often abandons him after tyrannizing him, or cedes him in war, or perhaps sells him during peace, deserve the sacrifice of his life?

JEAN TARRADE

See also Africa; Exclusivity System; Latin America; Migration; North America; Slavery

Further Reading

Lacouture, Jean, and Dominique Chagnollaud, *Le désempire: Figures et thèmes de l'anticolonisme*, Paris: Denoël, 1993

Tarrade, Jean, *Le commerce colonial de la France à la fin de l'Ancien Régime: L'évolution du régime de l'exclusif de 1763 à 1789*, 2 vols., Paris: Presses Universitaires de France, 1972

Color

With regard to a scientific understanding of color, it might be argued that the Enlightenment began in 1671, the year when Sir Isaac Newton published his first paper on the analysis of light in the *Philosophical Transactions* and when Philippe de Champaigne, by way of an academic lecture on Titian, triggered the famous debate about color.

For Newton the decomposition and recomposition of white light into seven basic colors was a crucial experiment. A model of experimental science, this experiment was conducted with a relatively simple arrangement of interacting prisms and led to the corpuscular theory of light, which eclipsed the wave hypothesis put forward around the same time by Robert Boyle. Newton's theory made a strong impression on contemporaries, including Voltaire, who presented it enthusiastically in his *Lettres philosophiques* (1734; Philosophical Letters). However, the theory also immediately aroused vociferous opposition, notably the arguments—over which Newton claimed to have lost sleep—of Gaston Pardie, Christiaan Huygens, and Robert Hooke. Eventually, the theory was corrected in various ways, up to Jean-Paul Marat's contribution in his *Notions élémentaires d'optique* (1784; Elementary Notions in Optics). Nevertheless, Newton's experiment had laid the foundations for a scientific treatment of colors, which found expression in the emergence of devices for measuring colors, notably Tobias Mayer's double pyramid (1745), Le Blond's trichromatism (1756), and Johann Heinrich Lambert's colored pyramid (1772).

Newton's theory dispelled the fantasies of an earlier discourse, which had originated in the theological evaluation of light. Starting from light's contrast with darkness, this earlier paradigm had understood colors to be the result of a degradation of white by black and went on to link colors not only to the symbolism of religious ritual but also to the theory of the four elements. This view had been advocated by Leon Battista Alberti, among others. He associated red with fire, blue with air, green with water, and gray with earth but did not further pursue this classification. The crucial point is that, before Newton, color had been included in the theorization that had taken hold of the domain of optics and, through the scientific treatment of the question of perspective, made it possible to place arts such as painting in the ranks of the liberal arts.

Champaigne's denunciation of color as "beautiful, superficial brilliant," a diabolical means of deceit and illusion, was related to this prescientific discourse, and in his case its religious aspect was tinged with Jansenism. In this regard, the Académie Royale de Peinture et de Sculpture (French Royal Academy of Painting and Sculpture) inherited the debate about whether *disegno* (design) or *colore* (color) should be accorded primacy in painting. This debate had been provoked most notably by the success of those masters of color, Giorgione and Titian, and it had been exalted by Paolo Pino (who dreamed, along with Tintoretto, of combining the drawing of Michelangelo with the color of Titian), and by Lodovico Dolce, who ranked Titian even above Raphael. However, Giorgio Vasari saw drafting as the master art, "the form or idea of all natural objects," thus merging graphic outlines with aesthetic forms and relegating color to a secondary status as matter or chance. At the same time, by playing on the term *disegno* itself as if it meant *segno di Dio* (sign of God), Vasari referred to a manual practice, to the outlining of a painting and to the plan, to the drawing that made

painting a *cosa mentale* (process of the mind). Thus, drawing was conceived as a matter of invention and, in a spiritual sense, as an expression of feelings. It could therefore claim a "nobility" that was very necessary to that the Académie Royale de Peinture et de Sculpture, which had been founded in order to exorcise the specter of mere craftsmanship and "daubing." To cite the term used by Fréart de Chambray in 1662, the application of color was only a "mechanical" activity.

However, even though the "idolaters" of color were sometimes attacked before 1671, the enemy where Chambray and Abraham Bosse were concerned was to be found much more often among the "libertine" mannerists in painting and among the followers of Michelangelo. Moreover, a number of fundamental texts showed an obvious interest in color. These included André Félibien's commentary (1663) on Charles Le Brun's *Les reines de Perse* (The Queens of Persia), as well as the series of lectures that Félibien published in 1668—in particular, Bourdon's lecture on *Les aveugles de Jéricho* (The Blind Men of Jericho)—and their preface, in which Félibien provides a personal version of Nicolas Poussin's theory of modes, in which the harmony of colors has a new and decisive place.

The vehemence of the quarrel launched by Champaigne's lecture of 1671 was caused by a variety of factors that did not help to resolve any of the issues that could strictly be called pictorial. Le Brun's tyrannical attitude was applied to imposing a body of doctrine on artists at a time when a royal decree had just compelled them to enter the Académie Royale de Peinture et de Sculpture. There was an element of personal opposition in the stance of Pierre Mignard, who refused to declare himself a colorist. There was also some uneasiness among painters at being integrated into a state institution committed to celebrating the glory of the monarch. The question of color crystallized a range of opposing ideas, which were often expressed with great hostility. One thing is certain: to a much greater extent than drawing, color evaded the grasp of discourse, by means of which an orthodoxy could be imposed, and for that very reason color was suspect.

In Champaigne's somewhat ambiguous reference to color as a form of beautiful brilliance that was merely superficial—by which he compared colors to "beautiful bodies," with drawing representing their soul—he brought together two criticisms that had been made about color and that reflect a matter/mind dichotomy. On the one hand, color was associated with the material realm, both in terms of the artist and what was represented in the work of art. On the other hand, color was seen as a conduit to the mind through seduction of the senses. Even more than in Blanchard's formal reply in 1672, arguing for the equality of drawing and color (a scandalous proposition for an academy in which drawing was dominant), the true response came in Roger de Piles's *Dialogue sur le coloris* (1673; Dialogue on Color). In this text Piles distinguishes color, the material of coloration, as the art of arranging colors, in which the science of light and shade is followed. He thus upholds the necessity of making the "right choice" and makes the artist responsible for being an "arbiter" of nature and not nature's "slave." Above all, however, he makes a frontal assault on the question of illusion as the objective of an art whose very purpose as an art is *tromper les yeux* (to deceive the eyes). It is from this point of view that Piles justifies the "cosmetic beauty" for which Peter Paul Rubens had been so strongly criticized, making himself Rubens's champion from then on. Piles then turns his attention from the relationship between the painting and the object it represents to the effects that this representation aims to produce, notably "surprise" and response to a "call" that the picture provokes from the viewer. This is a theme that Piles was to develop further in his *Cours de peinture par principes* (1708; A Course in Painting Based on Principles), in which he reminds his readers of the concern that the painter has with the viewer, with both his body and his desire. And this is what Félibien had in mind, even though he was theoretically on the side of the "Poussinists," when, in his fifth discussion (1679), he wonders whether the specific task of the painter does not lie in this *trompe-désir* (providing an illusion for desires), rather than in the exhibition of that painter's talent for large-scale compositions. Perhaps the painter is one who gives life to this game of illusion, by repeating the act of the Creator, rather than following the semiotic grid of the passions suggested by Le Brun. Thus, in retrospect, Piles justifies his very free translation (to say the least) of Dufresnoy, in which "The Procuress" who personified "Chromatics" was described as the "ultimate perfection of painting."

Color, regarded as painting's specific feature, became the object of a process of spiritualization and intellectualization. The theory of genius supported such an approach: the fact that color eluded discourse was perhaps the mark of an inestimable and inexplicable gift of nature, as well as the mark of a keenness of mind that was infinitely superior to rationalizing reason. Further, the fact that the painter was more concerned with the effect that his painting produced than his relationship to nature, whether visible or ideal, justified the importance of the thing as a whole, thereby allowing for a certain autonomy and artistic license with regard to the object being represented.. (It was in the name of "figurability" that Le Brun defended the superiority of drawing.) Here, the argument reached a dangerous point, for if the dogma of the imitation of nature excluded the conception of a nonfigurative art, then the idea of a harmony of color, relatively independent of

the subject, could help to undermine the twin hierarchies of genres and subjects. This was well demonstrated by Félibien in 1679, when he distanced himself from historical painting, thus expressing himself in a way that was much better than either everyday language or the emerging specialized language about painting, because his view served as a vehicle for the idea of the affective values of colors. It was no accident that throughout this period, the theme of painting as "music for the eye" was obsessively repeated, whether conveyed through the ideas of concert or harmony—in other words, by reference to an art that did not involve direct imitation of nature.

The debate over color ended in 1699 when Jules Hardouin-Mansart, the superintendent of buildings, nominated Piles as adviser and leading thinker of the Académie. Evaluating Piles's impact is a delicate matter. Certainly, no one today would deny the importance of coloration, at least not in a direct way; but the colorist convictions that Piles expressed in 1708 were framed within a unified whole that also included the theory of the beauty of nature, as well as the tribute paid to antiquity and to rules. Thus, Piles's views on color did not seriously shake up the world of painting. Certain colorist options won out, not by way of critical texts but rather through the paintings of Charles de Lafosse, Boullongne, and Nicolas de Largillière, artists who were dedicated to portraiture or to a pleasing vision of antiquity at some remove from history, as well as through the creation of the category of *fêtes galantes* by Antoine Watteau, and through the reception of Jean-Baptiste-Siméon Chardin in 1728. Moreover, many of the most remarkable unpublished academic lectures by Jean-Baptiste Oudry, François Desportes, and Largillière examined the subject of color.

One must look to the artists and those who were close to them—such as the comte de Caylus, Charles-Nicolas Cochin, or Dandré-Bardon in his treatise of 1765—to find attention being paid to *le faire* (technique) and to the effects of the materials with which the colorists had been preoccupied. The dominant liberalism did not prevent occasional indirect attacks. In 1719 the abbé Jean-Baptiste Dubos, who had no intention of reviving the quarrel over color and who recognized that Titian's talent also required imagination, nevertheless drew a contrast between color, on the one hand, and expression and poetic composition, on the other. He made the preference for the former or the latter into a question of sensory "organs": how could one fail to see that one person's "voluptuous eyes" are certainly not equivalent to another's "all too sensitive heart" in a system that suggests that the true purpose of art is to touch the viewer?

This tendency to aim at touching the viewer became more pronounced when, with the appearance of the literary genre of the "Salons" in 1747, men of letters assumed the status of art critics. These writers contributed to the revival of historical paintings and argued in favor of an art that could elevate the soul. This was certainly not an attack on color, but it was indeed Le Brun's criteria that La Font de Saint-Yenne adopted in order to eliminate the annoying questions that the crisis of 1671 had doubtless imperfectly expounded. Denis Diderot, who always declared the primacy of ideas over their execution, might well devote a chapter to color in his *Essais sur la peinture* (1796; Essays on Painting) where he proclaimed that color gives life and is a matter of flesh, which was nothing other than the reigning doctrine at the time. It is all too clear that Diderot's purpose in presenting this image of the genial and enthusiastic colorist was to annex colorism to the great painting about which he dreamed. This imaginary figure allowed Diderot to avoid asking himself if there were not some connection between, for example, the success of Chardin, whom he admired without reservation, and the modesty of the genre that that painter chose. There was nothing left for Diderot to do but return to the notions of perfect imitation and harmony and to style the artist "a great man," but none of this was sufficient to fill the theoretical vacuum in which the colorist ventures of Watteau, Chardin, and Jean-Honoré Fragonard were taking place, and which was perhaps not unrelated to the scarcity of colorists that Diderot deplored.

Did the painter perhaps make contact through color with a fundamental harmony of the universe, all the more desirable because its divine aegis hardly seemed trustworthy? What was needed was someone half-mad, with often confused notions, in order to bring this colorist fantasy into existence. In the 17th century, Athanasius Kircher had imagined an objective and necessary one-to-one correspondence between sounds and colors, and it was under his influence that Father Louis Castel constructed and imagined his famous "ocular harpsichord" in his *Optique des couleurs* (1740; Optics of Colors). This instrument, which inspired such dreams among his contemporaries—notably Diderot, in his *Lettre sur les sourds et les muets* (1751; Letter on the Deaf and Mute)—comprised a system of colored fans or ribbons that unfurled a true music of colors before the viewers' eyes. The ocular harpsichord was an attempt to put the resources of knowledge and modern technique—

for Castel also experimented with dyeing—at the disposal of a resurrection of the old mystical and symbolic discourse on colors. However, anything capable of producing wonder can also arouse fear. It fell to Jean-Jacques Rousseau, at the end of his *Essai de l'origine des langues* (1763; On the Origin of Language), to speak of the horror he experienced from the mechanical effects that the colors and their harmony produced, concerning the threat that a soulless art posed to feelings, and regarding an impact, to which the subject could attach no meaning. Thus, in an anachronistic or even somewhat primitive manner, Rousseau indicated that the danger represented by color, as being connected with the body, had lost none of its virulence. (Le Brun had earlier referred to painters who lost themselves in "the Ocean of Color.") The neoclassicism of the late 18th century made this hostility explicit: in the *Dictionnaire des Beaux-Arts* (1792; Dictionary of Fine Arts), J.-J. Levesque discusses chiaroscuro in the article "Couleur," and when homage is paid to the Italian schools of painting, Venice is symptomatically forgotten.

One could cite, in comparison to and in contrast with Rousseau's reaction, the passion for colors that seized Johann Wolfgang von Goethe on the battlefield of Valmy in 1792 and led him to write his *Die Farbenlehre* (1808–10; Theory of Colours). This treatise rejects the scientific sterilization induced by Newton, and it appeals to Kircher—as well as to the body of ancient discourses on color—while working out the relationships of contrast that give rise to harmony (for example, the relationship among complementary colors). Goethe undertakes a recharging of meanings, from a perspective that is no longer rigorously scientific but is aimed at reinterpreting the effects of color in relation to the subjects that perceive them. In a sense, he seeks to rehumanize colors and to remind his readers of the "great happiness" that human beings feel "when seeing color."

RENÉ DEMORIS

See also Art Criticism; Drawing; Optics and Light

Further Reading

Brusatin, Manlio, *A History of Colors*, translated by Robert H. Hopcke and Paul Schwartz, Boston: Shambhala, 1991 (original Italian edition, 1983)

Comedy

Perhaps it would be preferable to use the plural term "comedies" with respect to the 18th century, for the genre encompassed extremely varied forms. In the 18th century the French term *comédie* could designate all kinds of theatrical performances, whatever genre they belonged to. Comedy could carry the message of the Enlightenment, but it also brought together all the adversaries of the movement. The genre evolved considerably over time, but it also demonstrated the permanence of the structures that had originated in ancient comic traditions; it was sensitive to fashion, and, at the same time, it retained a certain anthropological consistency. Comedy was fortunate enough to have escaped from the iron laws of Aristotle's *Poetics,* and therefore from the excessively strict control of the academies. The evolution of comedy did not take place along just one trajectory: the genre had its most significant development in France and in northern Italy, yet England and Germany also produced some comedic masterpieces.

Paradoxically, the Enlightenment neglected the model of the critical comedies established in the first half of the 18th century. Despite its truly singular character, Pierre-Carlet de Chamblain de Marivaux's work blazed a trail that was not followed. Yet Marivaux devised forms that were amusing and free, insolent and rational, without being argumentative in tone. In Paris the fairground theatres created a sort of complicity between the comic spectacle and its spectators that reflected a rebellious attitude toward the institutional, academic, theatrical, and even police authorities. These fairground venues had developed flexible, free forms that were socially caustic and truly comical. The Comédie Française was certainly stuffier, but such works as the plays of Florent Carton Dancourt, Jean-François Régnard, and Charles Rivière Dufresny, or Alain-Renè Lesage's *Turcaret* (1709), developed forms that, in each case, were as capable of conveying Enlightenment philosophy as of telling a story. The need to preserve an image of social and moral respectability (particularly crucial when it came to combating Jansenism or the Catholic Church, which violently condemned theatre), the political calculations involved in forging an academic career, and other, similar concerns meant that Enlightenment writers spurned certain forms of comedy. Further, the social and political impact of comedy was perceived to be quite different from that of a text that could be read in the solitude of one's study.

Throughout the century it was commonly believed that the theatre exerted significant and immediate effects linked to an excessive (potentially dangerous) accumulation of energy in any public gathering. The *philosophes* felt compelled to adopt cautious forms that counterbalanced audacity with seriousness and moralism. The works of Philippe Néricault Destouches and Pierre Claude Nivelle de La Chaussée were their chosen models—touching and romantic plays that abandoned the satire of manners in favor of the pursuit of moral examples. To view comedy in terms of its relation to Enlightenment therefore comes down to neglecting an entire facet of 18th-century comedy: the evolution of drama. In Italy, the rivalry between Carlo Goldoni's comedy and that of Carlo Gozzi is somewhat analogous to the situation in France, despite the distinct differences between the two playwrights, not the least of which was that Goldoni also chose to make people laugh. In France only Pierre-Augustin Caron de Beaumarchais achieved a synthesis of the various traditions and innovations of the 18th century, succeeding in creating an Enlightenment comedy that was truly funny, and even he managed it only in *Le barbier de Séville* (1775; The Barber of Seville) and *Le mariage de Figaro* (1784; The Marriage of Figaro).

Indeed, it is as if the comedies that made people laugh—and these were largely confined to the boulevards during the second half of the century—really were regarded by Enlightenment thinkers as sources of resistance to their message. It is true that around 1760 the *philosophes* were targets for comedy, notably in Charles Palissot's *Les philosophes* (1760; The Philosophers). Similarly, the revolutionaries were wary of comedy and were vindicated in this attitude by the political behavior of the comic actors at the Théâtre de la Nation, most of whom did not rally to the Revolution. More generally, one can trace a growing distrust of laughter itself, which is explicitly expressed in Jean-Jacques Rousseau's *Lettre à D'Alembert* (1758; Letter to M. D'Alembert on Theatre), as well as by Louis-Sébastien Mercier and Nicolas-Anne-Edmé Rétif de La Bretonne. It seemed to them that laughter engendered a distance, often a cruel distance, between the spectator and the character, who thus ceases to be a representation of someone resembling us and instead becomes a representation of otherness. They believed the influence of exemplars, communicated through sensibility, was more useful to the project of moral reform than was the punishment inflicted by laughter.

The Enlightenment had a real loathing for satire, at least in the theatre, and a new conception of dramatic comedy took shape, notably through the defense and illustration, by Gotthold Ephraim Lessing and Mercier, of nonderisive laughter. Voltaire sensed the danger of comedies that were utterly devoid of humor. Refusing to oppose one set of emotions to another, Voltaire wrote *Nanine; ou, L'homme sans préjugé* (1749; Nanine; or, The Man without Prejudice), hoping to "make the spectators move imperceptibly from pity to laughter." Following his example, authors sought to use smiles and complicit laughter, rendered innocent by sympathy and tenderness. This was indeed a way of renewing comedy, but at the price of blurring the boundaries that separated genres. The success of both Goldoni and Beaumarchais in this type of comedy is indisputable.

Comedy, then, became a matter of proportion: every gradation was possible, from lighthearted comedy to "serious comedy" and to drama. Several "comedies" were given different generic designations in successive editions, for example, Denis Diderot's *Le fils naturel* (1757; The Natural Son) or Michel-Jean Sedaine's *Le philosophe sans le savoir* (1765; The Philosopher in Spite of Himself). With Sedaine, Mercier, and Lessing, the history of comedy merges with that of drama. Such plays as *Le philosophe sans le savoir,* Richard Brinsley Sheridan's *School for Scandal* (1777), or Lessing's *Minna von Barnhelm* (1763) were early incarnations of the bourgeois comedies that would be developed in the 19th century by Picard, Auger, Delavigne, and Eugène Scribe. A balance could be struck in a number of ways by mixing comic, serious, and sentimental elements. Serious characters could be combined with farcical characters as in *Le barbier de Séville* or in *La mère coupable* (1792; The Guilty Mother). Alternatively, lighter episodes could be inserted into a serious drama, as in Charles Collé's *La partie de chasse d'Henri IV* (Henry IV's Shooting Party). Further, the serious could be made humorous by the use of witty remarks, as in *Le mariage de Figaro.* As Beaumarchais wrote, one could ground "a comic plot . . . in the pathos of drama" (*La mère coupable*).

Beaumarchais's and Goldoni's complex handling of the comic heritage warrants some discussion. Initially, Beaumarchais treated his writing for the serious theatre, such as *Eugénie* (1767), as separate from the *parade,* a pseudo-popular form that allowed him to experiment within the conventions of traditional and popular comedy. In a later period, he developed comic stereotypes he could use in *Le barbier de Séville,* a comedy that was strikingly original. Some scholars have claimed that this comedy was written as a *parade,* although there is no evidence of this; it is known that an "interlude," *Le sacristain* (ca. 1765; The Sexton), is the first draft of the play. In any case, the basic framework of the plot was certainly taken from traditional sources: the old fool who loves his ward and whose intentions toward her are thwarted by a younger lover. Beaumarchais humanizes these stereotypes, giving them a social and human content that reinvents them. The traditional doctor-fogey becomes a troubling character, an intelligent and

desperately jealous man. Later, in *Le mariage de Figaro,* Beaumarchais brought about a true revolution in comedy, daringly integrating dramatic elements with the spirit of the Enlightenment in a unique piece of theatrical art for which there was no precedent. *Le mariage de Figaro* uses laughter for the creation of subtle and complex personalities that defy stereotypes and become images of individuals.

Goldoni, moving toward French-style high comedy, gradually eliminated the stereotypes of the commedia dell'arte, replacing them with character types that, in their development, would be quite capable of successfully representing what Diderot called "conditions." Goldoni completely exploded the stereotype of the valet, changing his characterization and assigning him a different place within the dramatic action. Everyday people enter his comedies through the varied conditions of their social activities. There are domestic servants, of course, but also porters, gondoliers, members of the petty bourgeoisie, and other plebeians who work and therefore are moral, and who use the various speech patterns of 18th-century Venice. Goldoni was an astute reader of French and Spanish literature, which he adapted rather than imitated, and he created a profoundly national theatre through the regional specificity of Italy itself, using the Tuscan dialect but above all the Venetian dialect. However, he and his new comedy came into conflict with the forces of tradition, which had hailed Gozzi as a writer of genius, and his exile in Paris brought him only minor success. Like Beaumarchais, Goldoni affirmed the dignity of the common people, but unlike Beaumarchais, Goldoni did not care to cross swords with the nobility (whose members, with a few exceptions, were often reduced in his theatre to playing bit parts).

Goldoni thus resolved the tensions within comedy, where the pursuit of realism persisted alongside the use of formal conventions and moral objectives. In truth, it was precisely the notion of realism that was missing from the debates of the period, which further underscores the innovative aspect of Goldoni's work. Nevertheless, one can perceive the idea of realism in a sketchy form in the debates around the notions of "verisimilitude," "imitation," "illusion," and the "natural." These and other terms in the debates were too deeply marked by Cartesian rationalism to find a place within a new aesthetic thought linked to other philosophical components of the Enlightenment. Dorval's advice, in *Entretiens sur "Le fils naturel"* (1757; Discussions on "Le fils naturel"), is to "move closer to real life." For Diderot real life is endowed with value—social and philosophical value, of course, but also aesthetic value, in that that realism represents an alternative to the conventions of the theatre and is deduced from paintings or novels. In this sense the pursuit of a realistic effect was incompatible with comic stylization, and burlesque realism would find itself condemned. Diderot's work on Goldoni's play *Il vero amico* (1750–51; The True Friend) attests to this mentality: in adapting the play for *Le fils naturel,* Diderot retained only what served his purposes, simplifying the plot and eliminating every trace of farce.

In Goldoni's comedies, real life is not just scenery within which stylized comic characters develop: it is part of the action and it is expressed through the characters. What is more, real life makes demands upon the characters and becomes an activating force. In *La locandiera* (1753; The Mistress of the Inn), for example, Mirandoline subordinates her desire to the demands of real life, and for the sake of real life she renounces that desire, in a disappointing compromise. It is precisely at this point that laughter bursts forth, resulting from the awareness of the reality that is opposed to the dreams, the illusions, and the hopes of the characters. The beauty of dreams is affirmed by laughter at the very moment when those dreams must be renounced; and laughter recalls—in the midst of disillusionment and renunciation—the nobility of ambition and desire.

Thus, the moral impact of Goldoni's comedies did not arise from any form of preaching, even though, like fables, they often end with a couplet, addressed to the audience that emphasizes the moral of the story. Goldoni's morality, like that of Beaumarchais, was profoundly related to its social context. *Est-il bon? Est-il méchant?* (1777; Wicked Philanthropy), the only one of Diderot's plays that allows for laughter, represents a departure from the mode of lay preaching—a sure indication of the maturation of his ideas about the theatre. The taste for paradox and play with dialogue, which he

had experimented with outside the theatre up until then, brought Diderot the least debatable of his successes. It was only when Enlightenment morality was brought into play as a source for comedy—unattached to any moralizing dogmatism—that it truly nourished the genre. Only cynicism, ambiguity, paradox, and contradiction could succeed in bringing Enlightenment morals to life within comedy, on its margins. This is why we are still attached to Goldoni, Diderot, and Beaumarchais. All three of them, at least in some of their works, were able to free themselves from the pharisaism of the Enlightenment, to rediscover moral sincerity, and to renew their ties with the *vis comica* (comic energy). In any event, a real study of 18th-century European comedy remains to be done—precisely because the genre is concealed behind the screen of the Enlightenment.

PIERRE FRANTZ

See also Commedia dell'arte; Fairground Theatre; Opera, Comic; Pantomime; Parade; Vaudeville

Further Reading

Gaiffe, Felix Alexandre, *Le rire et la scène française,* Paris: Boivin, 1931

Goldzink, Jean, *Les Lumières et l'idée du comique,* Fontenay aux Roses, France: École Normale Superieure Fontenay/Saint Cloud, 1991

Muir, Kenneth, *The Comedy of Manners,* London: Hutchinson, 1970

Pomeau, René, *Beaumarchais,* Paris: Hatier-Brown, 1956

Styan, J.L. *Restoration Comedy in Performance,* Cambridge and New York: Cambridge University Press, 1986

Commedia dell'arte

The term *commedia dell'arte* ultimately prevailed over such others as *commedia degli Zanni, commedia di buffoni, commedia di maschere, commedia all'improvviso, commedia a braccio,* or *commedia a soggetto* to describe the comic theatre, characterized by the use of stock characters and improvisation, that developed in Italy beginning in the 16th century. By an irony of fate, the origin of the expression, at least so far as written evidence reveals, can be traced back to Carlo Goldoni, the comic theatre's blacksheep son, who used the plural form, *commedie dell'arte,* in his manifesto

on comedy, *Il teatro comico* (1750; The Comic Theater), in which he contrasts the *commedie dell'arte* with character comedies. The plural further shifted the perspective: should one interpret the term *commedie dell'arte* as reference to a "genre" of comedy (popular theatre) or simply as a "genre" (type) of performance? Finally, one additional designation, the *comédie italienne,* which proved in the end to be as descriptive as the preceding terms, made its way into the French language with the permanent settlement in Paris of an Italian troupe in 1653.

Historiography of the second half of the 19th century and the beginning of the 20th century further complicates the matter. The postromantic movement—ushered in by the work of Maurice Sand (George Sand's son) *Masques et bouffons* (Masks and Clowns), which was published in 1860 and prefaced by the novelist herself, and followed in the 1880s by the more extensive studies of Edmondo De Amicis and Stoppato—emphasized the tradition of popular comedies. Later, during the period from 1910 to 1930, when a new understanding of the theatre was being sought, actors tended to disregard the commedia dell'arte except from the angle of the actor's skills, his "art." More recently an attempt has been made to reconstruct the fragmented reality of this fascinating theatrical experience, which continues to be "reborn" and in which carnivalesque masks, mimes and buffoons, stereotypical figures from popular comedy, and characters from more sophisticated and erudite forms of comedy are intermingled.

Although information on the first commedia dell'arte performances given within the duchies of northern Italy has been handed down only piecemeal, it is known that the three types of characters of the *commedie degli Zanni*—the Old Man, the Servant, and the Lovers—were quickly split up into additional characters. The first Bergamask Zanni, the clever Brighella, was now joined by a second, more playful Zanni, who was more creative but also lazier and often beaten: Harlequin, in short. The Venetian merchant, sometimes a brave man, sometimes miserly and ridiculous (Magnifico and later Pantalone), was seconded by the Doctor, a Bolognese lawyer or physician who was a caricature of the pedant. The doubling of the pair of lovers only added excitement to the already complicated plots, which included cross-dressing, ambiguities, and games of secrecy. The codification of the characters was emphasized by the masks worn by the Old Men and Servants, and by the fixed colors of their costumes: red and black for the Old Man, green and white for the Servant, black for the Doctor, and multicolored for Harlequin. Actors specialized in a single role for which they possessed *zibaldoni* (text fragments) and *concetti* (soliloquies) of love and jealousy. They adapted these fixed elements to the "framework" or "script," the subjects of which were inspired by the erudite comedies of the Renaissance and flavored with elements from the Spanish romantic comedies. The Zanni added the *lazzi,* mimed actions and brief comic scenes, whose generally short form specified in the outline ("Arlechino fa lazzi" [Harlequin performs *lazzi*]) clearly illustrated its repetitive nature but also the expectations and complicity of the audience. Outline sketches, *zibaldoni,* and *lazzi* thus represent the three levels of comedy referred to as "improvised": the first defining the situation in which the discourse will develop, the second indicating what the actor must say

or do, and the third being the comic ornamental part, which was left to the discretion of the Zanni of the day. The improvisation appeared to be limited in fact to the verbal or gestural level and was not considered a continual invention. However, even if it is a regular part of his repertory, improvisation requires the actor's inventive spirit, or, rather, his "art." Such is the conclusion of the treatises that contrast "improvised" comedy with "premeditated" (entirely scripted) comedy, but in a comedy where "improvisation" and "premeditation" are ultimately perceived as two opposite specializations of the actor, even two different approaches to acting.

Beginning at the end of the 16th century, several companies were put together according to an established model of ten or twelve actors who were assigned roles, that is, two Old Men, two Zanni, four Lovers, one Captain, and one Servant. Within a short period of time, they appeared on stages not only in Italy but all over Europe. The names of the companies, which were based on the model of the Academies—the Gelosi (jealous ones), the Confidenti (trusted friends), the Uniti (united ones), the Fedeli (faithful ones), the Accesi (ardent ones)—were intended to emphasize membership in a well-defined group, a school. These companies were not a passing fashion but an enduring attraction that survived until the middle of the 18th century. Thanks to the iconography that has been passed down to us, it is possible to trace their European path: from the frescoes in trompe l'oeil in the castle of Trausnitz in Bavaria, where actors improvised a comedy along the Narrentreppe, and the naive drawings of Menaggio, gardener to the governor of Milan; from the engravings of Jacques Callot, published in Naples, and those of "Het Italiaans Toneel," published in Amsterdam; from the "Scènes comiques" of Claude Gillot and the *Départ des comédiens-italiens en 1697* painted by Antoine Watteau; and finally, from Giovanni Battista Tiepolo, who takes us through the streets of Venice, haunted by countless Pulcinellas.

Even though the commedia dell'arte companies encountered the great moments and the great names of the European theatre on their route—Shakespeare, Molière, Lope de Vega—the duration and breadth of the commedia dell'arte phenomenon make it difficult for us to evaluate its contribution. It is important to distinguish between the simple visit by a touring company, called in to entertain the courtiers, and continuous or repeated stays in a country that could last until the content of the commedie dell'arte had been assimilated into the local culture, but also with the possibility of rejection or resistance.

In the second half of the 16th century, the first traveling troupes appeared onstage within the compass of various European courts, at Vienna and Linz, Blois and Paris, Seville and Madrid, Windsor and Reading. From providing pleasant amusement to the courts, the Italian actors quickly gained a more prominent position that ultimately coincided, all over Europe, with the era in which comedy was seeking its way and during which a deep interest in the actor's art was developing.

On the European path of the commedia dell'arte, France occupies a unique position, with the permanent settlement in Paris of *comédiens-italiens* (troupes of Italian actors) at two separate times. The nature of the performances inevitably evolved during the first long residency, from 1653 to 1697, owing to its duration and its almost institutional character. The traditional balance between plots and comic elements, between verbal lyricism and *lazzi,* tended to break down, just as the harmony of the group disintegrated as leading roles became privileged. This was the era of Fiorilli-Scaramouche and of Biancolelli-Harlequin. Further, the use of scenes in French, and thereby the introduction of topical satire, broke up the mosaic of the characters' individual peculiarities and dialects—Venetian, Bergamask, Bolognese, Neapolitan. During the Italian actors' second period of residency in Paris, beginning in 1716, which was to become permanent and which would become true assimilation into France (in 1723 the Italians became "patented royal actors"), their evolution followed an almost identical path as the first settlement, but with each phase passing more quickly than before. In fact, beginning in 1718 the actors from the Parma troupe, directed by Luigi Riccoboni, performed J. Autreau's *Le naufrage au Port-à-l'Anglais* (The Shipwreck at Port-à-l'Anglais) in French. In that performance, the transition to the other language was apparently carried off smoothly thanks to a twist in the plot: a group of Italians are shipwrecked and forced to make themselves understood by the local population, who, as it happens, are French. The Harlequin character continued his *lazzi,* "items open to debate" as Gherardi called them, but the comedy was oriented toward conversation, in accordance with the taste of the time; the only missing ingredient was Pierre-Carlet de Chamblain de Marivaux. In 1720 the Italians performed *Arlequin poli par l'amour* (1720; Harlequin Refined by Love), the title of which is the first indication of the development of the Harlequin character. Marivaux, who was to collaborate for 20 years in the repertory of the *Comédie-Italienne,* followed on with *La surprise de l'amour* (1722; The Surprise of Love), in which Harlequin is still a valet but is no longer the grotesque counterpart of his master, as he had been at the time of the first duels between Zanni and Magnifico. Harlequin's outfit loses its crudeness and becomes the gracious costume painted by Watteau. Although the "little brown-haired boy," as he is referred to by the author of *La double inconstance* (1723; Double Infidelity), retains a black mask and continues to perform his mimes, his "Italian tricks" (capers and acrobatics), he increasingly becomes the "master of love."

Even though the assimilation into French style constituted an incomparable phenomenon, a variety of other types of appropriation took place in other European countries: national popular characters took on traits of the Harlequin character; actors adopted techniques from the Italian style of acting. In Austria not only was the Italian *maschera* associated with the traditional Hanswurst, but actors such as Gottfried Prehauser blended Italian comedy with Germanic comedy. Elsewhere, as in England, the Italian influence showed mainly in the acting style of the players, and it gave a strong impetus to pantomime.

Paradoxically, it would be the success of the characters/actors, of all the European Harlequins, that would challenge and weaken the traditional commedia dell'arte. There was an ever-increasing tendency to conflate commedia dell'arte with pantomime and farce, or more generally, with what was referred to at the time as "low" comedy. It was for this reason that in Germany the theatrical reform of Johann Christoph Gottsched eliminated Harlequin and Hanswurst first of all. In France the contributor of the "Comédie" entry in the *Encyclopédie* mercilessly condemns "Italian comedy":

> A people that has long since based its honor on the fidelity of women, and on cruel vengeance for the shame of being betrayed in love, had to provide plots that were perilous for the lovers and that entailed servants' scheming. Moreover, this nation, with its pantomimes, has given rise to this mute acting that—sometimes by a lively, amusing expression, but more often by grimaces that make man resemble a monkey—alone supports the plot, which is devoid of art, of meaning, of wit, and of taste.

These lines can obviously be traced back to the negative image of Italy echoed by the *Encyclopédie* and confirmed by the political reference contained in the continuation of the article: "What characterizes Italian comedy even more distinctly is the blending of national values that the communication of the jealousy among the little Italian states stirs their poets to create." Further, the *Encyclopédie* contributor expresses surprise that the "actors still manage to keep going" in Paris, while in their own country, Molière was being played in Italian. Indeed, it was another paradox that the worst enemies of commedia dell'arte were found within its own ranks: first Riccoboni, and later Goldoni. The ambition of these two men of the theatre was "to elevate the script to the level of a character comedy" and to "throw away the mask" of the actor, literally and figuratively. Their aims applied to comedy as a genre and also entered into the debate over the "feeling" of the actor, and they were therefore central to a current of thought that shook European theatrical life. Only Venice welcomed the final faithful troupe and the last author, Carlo Gozzi, until a decree by the Cisalpine Republic banned the commedia dell'arte in 1801. From then on, all that remained for the *maschere* was to blend into the shadows of Carnival.

MICHÈLE SAJOUS D'ORIA

See also Comedy; Fairground Theatre; Opera, Comic; Parade; Vaudeville

Further Reading

Attinger, Gustave, *L'esprit de la commedia dell'arte dans le théâtre français*, Paris: Librairie Théâtrale, 1950

Molinari, Cesare, *La commedia dell'arte*, Milan: Mondadori, 1985

Commerce. *See* Trade

Confraternity

Beginning in the Middle Ages, Christianity began to be characterized by its many and varied religious associations. Some associations provided mutual aid and charity; others, the craft confraternities, grew out of the need to unite practitioners of the same profession under the protection of a patron saint. These latter organizations brought together believers who were attracted to the great devotional practices espoused by the Catholic Church, such as the rosary or the holy sacrament. In fact, all Christians concerned about salvation found a reason for hope in the strong unity of believers, whether living or dead. The merits and indulgences obtained by some could, they thought, be of benefit to others. The Christian confraternity was therefore, according to Gabriel Le Bras's definition, a form of spiritual mutualism that rested entirely on the doctrine of the communion of saints (see Le Bras).

This traditional justification for confraternities was considerably reinforced and expanded by the Council of Trent (1545–63). The council's solemn affirmation of the existence of Purgatory, of the necessity of doing good works as a condition for one's own salvation as well as for that of the deceased, and of the value of the indulgences granted by Rome made the confraternities, more than ever before, chosen places where people worked toward salvation. When the confraternities of the Good Death or the Agony of Christ were founded in the 17th century having the spiritual consolation of the dead as their principal objective, they were immediately

quite successful, and continued to be so throughout the 18th century, in France as well as in the Rhineland and in other areas of the German-speaking world.

However, by the time of the Enlightenment, the confraternities had long been conceived primarily as instruments for the spiritual improvement of Christians. In spite of their various names, confraternities functioned according to increasingly similar rules that had to be approved by the bishop of the diocese and also by the Roman authorities, who granted letters of indulgence. In 1539 the Confraternity of the Holy Sacrament was founded at the Church of Santa Maria sopra Minerva in Rome, with the purpose of promoting the veneration of the holy sacrament on the altar. The same purpose guided the Penitents of the Gonfalon (Banner) founded in Lyons in 1578. Consequently, attendance at Mass, not only on Sundays but also during the week, became one of the obligations of every member of such confraternities. Following the example of the Marian congregations that had been founded by the Jesuits for their students in 1563, frequent confession and communion, morning and evening prayers, and daily examinations of conscience soon became additional obligations. What was unique to the Jesuit colleges did not take long to spread outside their walls. As early as the 1580s, we find references to academic congregations of former Jesuit students, whether laymen or priests. Other townspeople joined in the assemblies in order to participate in their devotions. Thus there developed congregations of bourgeois, nobles, artisans, journeymen, and even merchants and lawyers, each with its own chapel, where members assembled every Sunday and on feast days to engage in acts of piety and to be instructed by their leaders.

These congregations met with considerable success. At the end of the 17th century there were 4,000 members of such congregations among the 55,000 inhabitants of Antwerp, 2,000 among 45,000 inhabitants in both Cologne and Lille, and 2,000 among the 5,000 inhabitants of Fribourg in Switzerland. In the middle of the 18th century in Nancy, which had a population estimated at between 22,000 and 23,000, ,there were 1,500 members of such groups distributed among the city's various districts and guilds. Within the larger context of their parishes or neighborhoods, as well as within their professions, the confraternities functioned as smaller units that watched over their members' conduct, supervised recruitment, and emphasized the example members were to set for everyone, above all for Protestants wherever they were present in the cities (such as Strasbourg and Augsburg) or in neighboring districts.

Many confraternities were established to honor the rosary, the holy sacrament, or the "good death," inspired by the example of the Marian congregations. Based in the parishes, and open to women as well as to men—and even to whole families—the confraternities were easily accessible to the faithful. In the 18th century they brought together considerable numbers of people, sometimes even entire parishes. The high points of the year for these confraternities were Lent, when a preacher chosen by the members gave religious instruction; their association's own feast days; and one Sunday each month, when the members as a whole took communion together. The instruction that was provided during these assemblies was reinforced and augmented by printed material. During the 18th century countless booklets were published within this context to provide Catholics with guides for following the Mass, as well as anthologies of hymns and common prayers, brief catechisms, and books of hours or meditations. The confraternities were instruments for the dissemination of Tridentine Catholicism and were also a means of educating worshipers. In addition, the practical management of these associations, which benefited numerous foundations over the years, often gave rise to fierce competition. The stakes were high since, like the parochial councils, the confraternities had close ties to city councils and rural communities. Moreover, recruitment methods used by these various assemblies were quite similar.

In the 1730s, the confraternities began to undergo important changes. They had been established mainly in cities since the beginning of the 17th century. The great missions of the following century were undertaken throughout entire regions, as teams of preachers systematically visited villages and hamlets. Preachers would stay in a given village for two weeks or more, and would leave only after they had established a confraternity there designed to extend the spirit of the mission. In some cases, missions were modeled on the churches of the religious orders that had come to preach or that were already influential in the region, such as the Penitents in the south of France, or that had been recommended by the bishops, such as the Confraternity of the Holy Sacrament.

Alternatively, some missions, such as those of the Confraternities of the Sacred Heart, sought to establish new practices that might stimulate the devotion of the villagers. A Spanish Jesuit, Father Pedro Calatayud, systematically visited the villages of Andalusia between 1740 and 1760 to teach the peasants how to honor the Heart of Jesus. In Italy this new devotional practice was encouraged by popes Benedict XIV and Clement XIII. However, it was above all in France, and more particularly in Provence and Lorraine, that the Sacred Heart confraternities were most influential. In Provence the bishop of Marseilles, Monseigneur de Belsunce, dedicated the city to the Sacred Heart after the plague of 1720. In Lorraine the Jesuits and Stanislas Leszczynski, the new duke and former king of Poland, played decisive roles in the missions of the Sacred Heart. In all, 1,088 confraternities dedicated to the Sacred Heart were founded across Europe between 1700 and 1770 (see Rosa).

Another group of confraternities, those of the Christian Doctrine, had a completely different character, and also became widespread during the Enlightenment. The confraternity was established by an Austrian Jesuit, Father Ignaz Parhamer, who was inspired by the much earlier pedagogical experiments of Saint Carlo Borromeo and César de Bus. Parhamer set out to form "cathechistic missions," which were in fact the equivalent of modern 8- to 15-day seminars for instructors. These instructors were men and women who were responsible for teaching doctrine and prayers to those living in cities and especially in the countryside. Once the preacher had departed, the adults who were invested with a mission would organize themselves into a confraternity. Each person would be responsible for instructing a portion of the village population. Women, young girls, and also couples would take on the role of catechists, both within their own homes and outside them. Members of the confraternity also had to present themselves as model Christian families. A new form of Catholic activity had been born. In Austria alone, more than 15,000 "examiners" became active over a period of just three years (1754–57), and the movement spread in no time into Hungary, southern Germany (particularly Bavaria), the Rhineland provinces, the Austrian Netherlands (now Belgium and Luxembourg), and northern France.

As these new confraternities proliferated, the earlier confraternities founded during the period of the Tridentine Counter-Reformation continued their own activities. Granted, in some areas of the Parisian Basin and upper Brittany the older confraternities no longer demonstrated as much vitality as they once did, and occasionally they aroused the suspicion of the civil and religious authorities who feared their spirit of independence in relation to the diocesan clergy. Church leaders also accused them of resisting enlightened religion, pointing out their practice of devotions and traditional rites during their festivals in honor of agrarian or regional patron saints, or even during the high points of the liturgical calendar, such as Holy Week, Easter, or Pentecost. In France the *parlements* carried out investigations in order to abolish any religious association that had not been canonically established with the authorization of the bishops. In the Holy Roman Empire, the administration of Joseph II had similar concerns. Yet despite this opposition, new confraternities, and indeed the older ones, such as those of the Virgin, the Holy Sacrament, or the Good Death, continued to thrive during the 18th century in German-speaking regions and in central Europe (see Dompnier; Froeschlé-Chopard, 1994), as well as in Lorraine and Alsace. In the former diocese of Strasbourg, 38 percent of the confraternities that existed at the time of the French Revolution had been founded between 1751 and 1789. In southeastern France and in the region around Lyon, the movement for the creation of religious associations lasted at least until about 1750 and even later in some areas. However, recent studies, notably of the Dauphiné, have revealed a profound change that occurred during the 18th century. In order to remain in existence, the Penitents, well known for their respect for tradition and their concern for autonomy in relation to the parishes, were forced to accept the parish framework and adopt statutes imposed on them by the bishops. Thus, the Penitents became the Penitents of the Holy Sacrament, subject to the parish priest in every respect.

Rather than speak of the decline of the entire range of confraternities during the Enlightenment, we should emphasize the significant transformation they underwent. This general transformation was sometimes manifest through internal change over time, as in the case of the Penitents, but it also occurred following the demise of older associations and their replacement by new groups that were better adapted to the religious sensi-

bility of the time (the Sacred Heart), or were more sensitive to the concern of enlightened individuals for a dissemination of knowledge (the Christian Doctrine). In the evolving nature of all these cases one found new ways of conceiving and living religion, concepts which the confraternities helped to spread among the populations of Europe. The dominant impression conveyed is one of an extraordinary flexibility, a constant adaptation to the times and to circumstances. Though attacked for their uselessness and their attachment to the "extravagant" devotions of the past, the confraternities proved to be effective charitable institutions, assuming responsibility for the distribution of food to the poor (through *bouillons des pauvres,* or soup kitchens) and for other good works. Accused of undermining the authority of the parish priest, the confraternities nonetheless acted as pressure groups wherever a priest was lacking, in order to get one appointed. When there could be no priests, during the Reign of Terror, confraternities often served as substitutes in the disorganized parishes, as in the case of the Charities of Perche and the Confraternities of the Sacred Heart in Lorraine.

Fundamentally, the names or the statutes of the confraternities no longer truly mattered; instead, the qualities of those who were enrolled in them were of greatest importance. By the end of the century, most members were often involved in other societies as well; they did not relinquish either the spirit or the activities of those societies when they put on the sackcloth of the penitent or lit their candle as a member of the Congregation of the Blessed Virgin. There were many members of confraternities—whether congregants or penitents—who were also zealous Freemasons, and some were among the founders of the revolutionary clubs. Perhaps, moreover, their experience of in world of confraternities was valued in societies devoted to the propagation of modern ideas. On the other hand, there was the famous Congrégation, a group of active counterrevolutionaries that developed out of a small association of Christian students founded in Paris under the Consulate (1799–1804) by Father Delpuits. In this case, the religious institution itself can hardly be held responsible for its political consequences. (The same could be said of the Cappelle Serotine (Chapels of the Night)—founded in Naples by Alfonso di Liguori on behalf of artisans and shop-owners—which were accused of being Jacobin clubs at the beginning of the Neapolitan Revolution.) During the 1790s, no matter how strongly the confraternities asserted their religious and even spiritual purpose—in terms that were even stronger than those in the past—each of their members had his or her own personality, which the confraternities had to take into account. Nevertheless, these long-established associations, revitalized in the 18th century, contributed to the education of individuals, leading them to a better understanding of themselves and to a better awareness of others. It was no doubt in this sense that the confraternities participated, however unintentionally, in the Enlightenment movement.

LOUIS CHÂTELLIER

See also Catholicism; Jesuits; Pietism

Further Reading

Châtellier, Louis, *The Europe of the Devout: The Catholic Reformation and the Formation of a New Society,* translated by Jean Birrell, Cambridge and New York: Cambridge University Press, 1989 (original French edition, 1987)

Châtellier, Louis, *The Religion of the Poor: Rural Missions in Europe and the Formation of Modern Catholicism, c.1500–c.1800,* translated by Brian Pearce, Cambridge and New York: Cambridge University Press, 1997 (original French edition, 1993)

Coreth, Anna, *Pietas Austriaca: Ursprung und Entwicklung barocker Frömmigkeit in Österreich,* Munich: Oldenbourg, 1959; 2nd edition, 1982

Desan, Suzanne, *Reclaiming the Sacred: Lay Religion and Popular Politics in Revolutionary France,* Ithaca, New York: Cornell University Press, 1990

Dompnier, B., "Les missionnaires, les pénitents et la vie religieuse aux XVIIe et XVIIIe siècles," in *Les confréries de pénitents, Dauphiné-Provence: Actes du colloque du Buis-les-Baronnies, Octobre 1982,* Valence: Gregoire, 1988

Flynn, Maureen, *Sacred Charity: Confraternities and Social Welfare in Spain, 1400–1700,* Ithaca, New York: Cornell University Press, and London: Macmillan, 1989

French, K.L., "Maidens' Lights and Wives' Stores: Women's Parish Guilds in Late Medieval England," *The Sixteenth Century Journal* 29, no. 2 (1998)

Froeschlé-Chopard, Marie-Hélène, *Espace et sacré en Provence, XVIe–XXe siècles: Cultes, images, confréries,* Paris: Editions du Cerf, 1994

Froeschlé-Chopard, Marie-Hélène, and Roger Devos, editors, *Les confréries, l'eglise et la cite,* Grenoble: Centre Alpin et Rhodanien d'Ethnologie, 1988

Gutton, Jean-Pierre, "Confraternities, Curés, and Communities in Rural Areas of the Diocese of Lyons under the Ancien Régime," in *Religion and Society in Early Modern Europe, 1500–1800,* edited by Kaspar von Greyerz, London: German Historical Institute, and Boston: Allen and Unwin, 1984

Le Bras, Gabriel, "Les confréries chrétiennes: Problèmes et propositions," in *Études de sociologie religieuse,* by Le Bras, vol. 2, Paris: Presses Universitaires de France, 1956

Mikulek, J., J. Meznik, and J. Panek, editors, "Religious Brotherhoods in Baroque Bohemia," *Historica* (1995)

Rosa, M., "Regalità e 'douceur' nell' Europa del 1700: La contrasta devozione al Sacro Cuore," in *Dai Quaccheri a Ghandi: Studi di storia religiosa in onore di Ettore Passerin d'Entrèves,* edited by Francesco Traniello, Bologna: Mulino, 1988

Tackett, Timothy, "The West in France in 1789: The Religious Factor in the Origins of the Counterrevolution," *Journal of Modern History* 54 (1982)

Tackett, Timothy, *Religion, Revolution, and Regional Culture in Eighteenth-Century France: The Ecclesiastical Oath of 1791,* Princeton, New Jersey: Princeton University Press, 1986

Terpstra, N., "Confraternities and Mendicant Orders: The Dynamics of Lay and Clerical Brotherhood in Renaissance Bologne," *The Catholic Historical Review* 82, no. 1 (1996)

Tüskés, Gábor, and Éva Knapp, *Volksfrömmigkeit in Ungarn,* Dettelbach, Germany: Röll, 1996

Vauchez, André, "Ordo Fraternitatis: Confraternities and Lay Piety in the Middle Ages," in *The Laity in the Middle Ages: Religious Beliefs and Devotional Practices,* edited by Daniel E. Bornstein, translated by Margery J. Schneider, Notre Dame, Indiana: University of Notre Dame Press, 1993 (original French edition, 1987)

Conversation

A Golden Age of Conversation

The French Spirit

When Immanuel Kant, at the end of the 18th century, sought to define the specificity of the French nation in a systematic manner, in his *Anthropologie in pragmatischer Hinsicht* (1798; Anthropology from a Pragmatic Point of View), the first word that he penned was "conversation." The character of a people, declared the German philosopher, is defined less by the form of its government, or the geography or climate of the country, than by a certain turn of mind, a common culture that is historically determined and almost unalterable. It was no accident that French had become "the universal language of conversation." It was because the nature, the "character," of the French people had determined it:

> The French nation is distinguished from the others by its taste for conversation; from this point of view, it is a model for other nations. It [France] is *courteous,* above all with regard to strangers who visit the country, although it is now passé to adopt the manners of the *court.*

Thus, Kant directly links conversation to the politeness of the "manners of the court." The moral attributes of the French people owe much to the old ideal of aristocratic civility, even though that ideal is perceived as an archaic relic. Kant's use of italics (*courteous/court*) recalls the social and political origin of conversation. Although he declares that he does not wish to base his *Anthropologie* on considerations of a historical order, he explicitly connects the taste for conversation to a way of living that developed in monarchic societies.

This conclusion had already appeared in David Hume's analysis of conversation in an essay entitled *Of the Rise and Progress of the Arts and Sciences* (in *Essays, Moral and Political* [1742]). Through his sociological aesthetic, Hume raises the question of forms of government and their connections with culture. After demonstrating that politeness and civility are the products of courts and monarchies, the Scottish philosopher asserts the superiority of 18th-century culture. In his essay *Of Civil Liberty,* Hume insists on the role played in this flowering by the development of conversation, which is expressed brilliantly in France: "There is no nation that has so perfected this art, the most agreeable of all, the art of society and of conversation that they commonly call *savoir-vivre* [the art of living]." For Hume, this French version of the Attic ideal is the corol-lary of the refinement of the arts and sciences, and the urbanity that distinguishes civilized nations.

The view of manners held by these two philosophers, one German and the other Scottish, was shared by almost all French Enlightenment thinkers except Jean-Jacques Rousseau. His *Discours sur les sciences et les arts* (1750; Discourse on the Sciences and Arts) inveighs vehemently against the corruption of morals and the decadence of taste associated with the progress of arts and technology, without explicitly addressing the question of conversation. In this text it is the art of pleasing, and politeness more generally, against which Rousseau rails. For him, politeness is the smiling and deceptive mask of vice. However, Rousseau soon turns in other texts to criticism of conversation, for politeness and conversation go together. Through them, the whole trajectory of a civilization is put on trial. As Marc Fumaroli has aptly remarked: "Rousseau, although he despised arts and literature, was well aware that this collective masterpiece of artistic and aristocratic conversation was the living heart of the civilization that he condemned" (see Fumaroli). Thus, in Rousseau's *La nouvelle Héloïse* (1761; Julie; or, The New Héloïse), Saint Preux describes to Julie the effects of the subtle poison that is Parisian conversation. Over and above conversation, that fireworks display of the mind, Rousseau primarily rejects the system of the gentlemen and the rehabilitation of traditional civility. Although he agreed with his contemporaries that the 18th century was the golden age of this culture of conversation, he deplored this fact, rather than rejoicing as others did.

Sites for Conversation

In the classical age the notion of conversation encompassed both an art of living and an art of speaking. The modern sense of the word "conversation," as used by Antoine Gombau de Méré or by Voltaire, resulted from a slippage in meaning and semantic contamination. The slippage in meaning came first, for the Latin word *conversatio* did not refer to the exercise of speech but rather to a fondness for society. Up until the 17th century, "conversation" retained a meaning (reflected in the dictionaries) of social association: that is, the set of attitudes and habits in which a community immerses itself. The semantic contamination followed, as the word *conversatio* entered everyday language in competition with an older term, *sermo,* which more specifically designated an exchange of words. Among the humanists of the Renaissance, *conversatio* became synonymous with the *sermo convivialis* (convivial exchange of words) of the ancients and then took on the modern sense of an interaction among literate people. During the second half of the 17th century, this amicable but studious recreation became a form of social relaxation, as the fashion of the salons spread into court society—a practice that until then had been the prerogative of the erudite and the scholarly. At the same time, participation in these salons was a way in which educated men and gentlemen displayed their accomplishments and recognized those of their peers. These gatherings were a part of the trend toward making education available to general public, given impetus by the Cartesians. This movement toward a more universal education was encouraged by the new ideal of the knowledge appropriate to a gentleman, who was presumed to possess at least a nodding acquaintance with science. Conversation was a means for such a gentleman to procure this necessary and adequate average level of culture, since it corresponded perfectly to the dogma of classical aesthetics: *docere et delectare* (to instruct and to delight). From that point onward, friendly conversation seems to have become the opposite of intellectual contention and to have broken away from the model of the erudite discussion dear to the humanists, as well as from the dogmatic quarrels that were increasingly associated with the schools.

In the 18th century a change occurred in this model, although the mode was not rejected. Indeed, for Hume the trend initiated in the previous century was not sufficient. The scholarly and the profane, the learned and the worldly should be united in conversation, and the numerous literary salons were its radiant focus. The meeting places of all the cosmopolitan intellectuals of the Enlightenment, the French salons flourished at least up until the time of the First Empire. There is no need to stress the centrality of the salons throughout the 18th century: it is enough to note that during that century conversation became a true social institution through the salons. The provincial academies were another cultural arena in which conversation enjoyed a prominent place. In contrast to participants in the salons, the members of these academies were exclusively masculine, erudite, and scholarly. Whereas the conversation of the Parisian salons continued to be characterized by *otium* (leisure) and did not break radically with the passions of an active life, the conversation of the academies stood apart from the collective bustle of the city. The *otium studiosum* (studious leisure) of the learned seemed to require a place suitable for contemplation, a rural retreat far from the tumult and business of the world. The setting in the academies, places of serious conversation, thus stood in contrast to the frivolous atmosphere of the salons. The

former preserved the independence of the man of letters, the scholar, and the philosopher, in comparison with the worldly circles, which were also circles of power. And yet, the open atmosphere found in the salons, the social groups, and the coffeehouses is crucial to understanding the emergence of a new notion in the 18th century, that of public opinion. This new type of Republic of Letters did not burden itself with any learning in order to decide matters of taste and intellect, or to reach conclusions about religious and political subjects. Indifferent to distinctions of class, gender, or nationality, the conversation of the Enlightenment had all the traits of an ideal republic, and its influence and authority extended throughout Europe. Through its civilized tone and a shared code of good manners, conversation showed a facility and liberty of thought that was seductive even to philosophers.

A Written Genre, an Oral Genre

For the humanist tradition, writing originated as speech, and this tradition tended to erase the differences between oral and written expression. This idea was still held in the 17th century, but it took on a different meaning. Live speech was domesticated, and conversation became a literary genre, an art with its own laws and paradigms. Nevertheless, theoreticians of gentility played on the effect of this gray area between the written and spoken language, and in one of his *Conversations* (1669), the chevalier de Méré makes the marshal de Clérambault say: "I do not know whether it is necessary to write as one speaks or to speak as one writes." In the 18th century, conversation was undeniably a rhetorical model and such genres as letters or dialogue necessarily claimed to follow it, for the sake of a naturalistic aesthetic.

This oral or literary exercise also developed as an extension of a theoretical train of thought, and a theory of conversation came into existence quite rapidly: the presentation of such a theory might appear in the form of an autonomous discourse, as in the writings of Jean de La Bruyère or Méré; more often, however, the theory would be incorporated into the emerging corpus of the treatises on civility. For almost a century, in fact, few works of *savoir-vivre* failed to devote one or more chapters to conversation. All by themselves, they defined a collection of commonplaces in which one could find both the rules of a social ethic and a series of rhetorical topoi. However, while the 17th century emphasized respect for a code of propriety, the 18th century was more interested in the subjects under discussion. From then on, the gentleman was a philosopher, and his conversation was evidence of this fact. As César Chesneau Dumarsais brings out in the *Encyclopédie,* the "gentleman who wishes to please combines a reflective and sound intellect with mores and social qualities." This was why Enlightenment thinkers did not abandon the normative perspective of the 17th-century theoreticians when approaching the topic of conversation. The reflections of the men of the Enlightenment were numerous and expressed in the most diverse genres: discourse at the Académie Française, eulogies, poems, and articles in periodicals.

In the middle of the century, the abbé Nicolas-Charles-Joseph Trublet, friend and biographer of Bernard Le Bovier de Fontenelle, published his "Pensées sur la conversation" (Thoughts on Conversation) in the *Mercure de France*. In this work Trublet develops a series of precepts about conversation that are in harmony with the sentiments of his contemporaries. His remarks bear a close resemblance to the definition of *esprit* (cleverness) that Voltaire would give in the *Encyclopédie*: for the abbé, conversation is indeed the expression of Voltaire's "ingenious reason." A place therefore exists for reasonable conversation, between *bel esprit* (wit), which is rare, and *faux esprit* (false wit), which is not rare enough. It should be added that for Trublet the pleasure of a conversation comes from the fact that it reinforces the social bond. Because conversation arose initially from the "need for company," its strictly intellectual value is subordinated to its social function.

The abbé Morellet, another abbé described as an "Encyclopedist," was to be equally in tune with the times in rehabilitating the old classical maxim of pleasing and instructing. In the second half of the century, he wrote an *Éloge de Mme Geoffrin* (In Praise of Madame Geoffrin), the muse of all the *philosophes,* entitled *De la conversation* (On Conversation), in which he recalls that "the two principal purposes of conversation are to entertain and instruct others." In particular, he gives a list of the "vices that spoil conversation," including despotism, or a dominant attitude (a shortcoming that had already been execrated by Montaigne); pedantry; and a contradictory or quarrelsome tone.

A synthesis of these opinions is found in *Combien les lois de la conversation sont précieuses et combien elles sont négligées* (How Precious the Rules of Conversation Are, and How Neglected As Well), a discourse by Jean Henri Samuel Formey, a member of the Berlin Academy. Writing in response to a "subject proposed by the Académie des Jeux Floraux [Academy of Floral Games] for the year 1746," Formey singles out the three rules, which, in his view, necessarily govern the practice of conversation: "a principle of instruction," "a social bond," and "a source of pleasure." This catechism of the exchange of words was flexible enough not to displease anyone and was a notable inspiration for the didactic and pedagogic efforts of the Enlightenment.

Conversation as a Model for the Enlightenment

An Ethical Model

The notion of conversation as a genre can finally be understood as an intersection between a historic series of texts practicing the same style of writing and a cultural practice. Above and beyond a simple literary problematic, a whole philosophy of exchange was under discussion. Contrary to the bitterness of the scholastic quarrels, conversation in the Enlightenment offered cheerfulness, badinage, and liberty. This ludic dimension expressed the necessary intellectual detachment that the *philosophe* had to display toward his own system. Against anathemas and inquisitions, against all the "formalistic pedants," the *philosophe* believed it was better to respond with mockery. This point is made in *Characteristicks of Men, Manners, Opinions, Times* (1711), a fine essay by the earl of Shaftesbury in which he exhorts the authors of dialogues to make good use of pleasantries and wit. This English philosopher advocated an alert and vivid discourse, inspired by the conversation of gentlemen. For Shaftesbury, playfulness is a mark of the liberty and civility that ought to reign in books as well as in real conversations. This ethical prescription is accompanied by pragmatic arguments. A work with a magisterial and solemn tone puts off its readers because, in Shaftesbury's view, "pedantry and bigotry can bury the best of books." In his *Apologie de l'abbé Galiani* (1770; Apology of Galiani), Denis Diderot similarly rejects the dogmatic tone, preferring what he calls "inquiring" dialogue. In response to Morellet, who had published a refutation of Ferdinando Galiani's *Dialogues sur le commerce des blés* (1768; Dialogues on the Wheat Trade), Diderot writes that he prefers "chatting" to scholastic "quarrels." The model outlined here is still that of family conversation ("you are still on the school benches and the abbé is on the sofa"). For Diderot, as for Shaftesbury, philosophical dialogue ideally is not conducted in the manner of the "pedagogues" but rather in a "conversation . . . cheerful but not frivolous," such as that of Cléobule in Diderot's *La promenade du sceptique* (1747; The Sceptic's Walk).

The role that women played in disseminating the Enlightenment's mood of cheerfulness and pleasure has often been emphasized. Eighteenth-century feminine salons were places where worldly badinage was mixed with the reflections of the philosophical avant-garde. It is in literature that one can best grasp the influence of these "modern Aspasias." A work such as Fontenelle's *Entretiens sur la pluralité des mondes* (1686; Conversations on the Plurality of Worlds) claims to "treat philosophy in a manner that is not at all philosophical," on the model of the conversations of the salon. The banter of the philosopher and the beautiful marquise transforms Copernican astronomy into a "happy" system, in which scientific reflection is effortlessly unfolded in a high-society style.

A Philosophical Model

For the men and women of the 17th and 18th centuries, the mastering of knowledge, the learning directed toward what we now call "culture," did not take place only through books. There were many, even in the ranks of the *philosophes* themselves, who challenged the exclusively bookish mode of learning. Some said that a conversation was worth as much as a book; others added that it was worth more. In the *Encyclopédie* Jean le Rond D'Alembert rejects both views, for "a conversation must no more be a book than a book should be a conversation." Nevertheless, one recalls a remark by a theoretician of language, Laurent Bordelon, for whom "conversation is the great book of the world, which instructs us in how to use other books; without it, science is unsociable and displays no charm. Study augments natural talents, but conversation puts them to work." This statement is not just a society version of the acquisition of knowledge and experience. Bordelon applies a criterion of "appeal," in conformity with the principle of pleasure defended by the age; study and conversation are nonetheless presented as complementary. The conversation of the Enlightenment thus appeared as the object of new aims. Conversation now had a cognitive value, permitting a person to verify his or her own experiences by submitting them to the test of the discernment and judgment of others. Thus, Bordelon remarks that "the most erudite men perfect their knowledge considerably in this exchange because they have occasion to uncover and resolve many of the difficulties that one could never discover by making suggestions to oneself in one's study."

This emphasis on communication as essential to knowledge acquisition was accompanied by a certain self-reflexive awareness. As a vector of knowledge, conversation had the virtue of problematizing the instruction acquired through the study of books. As a civilized ritual, conversation thus became a true *polissage* (labor of polishing). Shaftesbury himself had said that politeness was a product of liberty. "It is through this gentle *collision* that we polish each other" (*Characteristisks*). "Collision" here is not a simple play on words. The metaphor of the file that smoothes and refines, which Bordelon borrowed from Montaigne, defines quite well the function of conversation for the men of the 18th century: contact between two minds must spark light, as flint sparks fire. In the conversation of the Enlightenment, politeness did not exclude divergence of opinion, and the interlocutor represented the moment of necessary contradiction. The dialogue of ideas did not just reject the model of purely worldly conversation; it also simultaneously appeared to be an elegant way of resisting the temptation of system, and this mode of thinking suited Diderot as much as Voltaire, Hume as much as Shaftesbury. By this means, they could display a double rejection of dogmatism, both in form and in idea. On the other hand, this enhancement of dialogue represented a moment of a larger epistemological reflection: because it encouraged all forms of experience and dissemination of knowledge, the philosophy of the Enlightenment found in conversation the model of a practice that was as elegant as it was useful.

A Poetic Model

As Diderot remarked, the general tone of Montaigne's *Essais* (1580–95; Essays), with their "leaps and gambols," was also that of conversation. This valorizing of the rambling and the discontinuous, this celebration of *quicquid in buccam venit* (whatever comes out of your mouth), was the beginning of a poetics from which the 18th century would benefit. The play of digressions, the variety and freedom of propositions that were the marks of conversation, first found a literary equivalent with Fontenelle, whose *Entretiens sur la pluralité des mondes* justifies the importance and the number of his digressions by "the natural freedom of conversation." Similarly, Diderot's literary practice attests to his taste for conversation, his rejection of the linearity of written discourse. In a famous letter addressed to Sophie Volland, the *philosophe* writes of the bizarre "circuits" of conversation, "the imperceptible links that have drawn such disparate ideas together" and then formulated a "principle of liaison" among them. Likewise, Galiani explains the method to be followed in reading his *Dialogues sur le commerce des blés:* "those who take the trouble to *link* my ideas will perhaps figure out the goal of the work." In his essay on conversation, Morellet develops Diderot's intuition and connects it to a complete system: "Conversation lives by the *liaison of ideas*. It is because everything is more or less close together in nature or in people's thoughts that the mind makes progress, that it moves forward from one idea to another, and from two ideas to a fully conceived proposition." For Diderot, however, this theory has more radical consequences. In comparing conversation to the movement of dream or madness, his letter to Sophie Volland calls René Descartes's discourse on method into question. Seeking the truth *in* and *by* conversation, Diderot undermines the doctrine of clear and distinct ideas. However, it is in the three dialogues of *Le rêve de D'Alembert* (1769; D'Alembert's Dream) that the association between conversation, dream, and madness theorized in the letter to Sophie Volland is made truly concrete. A crucial difference separates Diderot from all the other apologists of conversation. Among the theoreticians of the 17th century, liberty and negligence had been positioned within a perfectly codified rhetorical system, inspired by the *ordo fortuitus* (chance order) of the Romans. In contrast, *Le rêve de D'Alembert* is the poetic and philosophical staging of a disorder that revealed itself to be an order. The text is poetic because the interweaving of the dream and Diderot's commentary creates a distinctive polyphony; it is philosophical because the diversity of species conceals the profound unity of nature and of living things. The paradox of the *Rêve* is that it entrusts the responsibility for establishing the linkage and the logic of the ideas to a fundamentally rambling form of expression. Diderot's theory of conversation explains the tone and the style of a work that is in sharp contrast to the linearity of traditional philosophical discourse. The notion of conversation forms a bridge between Diderot's aesthetic thought and his philosophical thought. Having been "free" in the opinion of the classical theoreticians, conversation becomes "libertine" with the writing of Diderot's *Le neveu de Rameau* (1805; Rameau's Nephew). For the 18th century, this "libertinism of conversation" was equaled only by the libertinism of ideas.

It is clear that conversation posed problems that were as much aesthetic as philosophical. The fundamental reason for this was no doubt connected to the fact that the practice of conversation was marked by the constitutional polarity in classical aesthetics between pleasing and instructing. We must remember that this polarity was, at least in theory, never considered an opposition but a complementarity. In reality, when reading texts, one is often amused by this balancing art: conversation sometimes moves toward pleasure, sometimes toward philosophy. However, it is necessary to recognize that the people of the Enlightenment made an effort to think about this opposition in dialectical terms. Through the reciprocal gaze of the worldly and the learned, the initiated and the profane, the *philosophe* and the general public, reflection on conversation was conducted within the framework of a questioning of the means and ends of knowledge.

This model barely outlived the Enlightenment: "it was Voltaire's fault," to quote from Victor Hugo's *Les Misérables* (1862), or, rather, it was the French Revolution's fault. The new social order marked the disappearance of a leisured society. It also corresponded to another division of knowledge, by which the relations between science and philosophy, and between philosophy and literature, were profoundly changed. After the Revolution, the autonomy of the fields of knowledge made it difficult to bring the different domains and modes of expression together. On the other hand, one can witness, beginning in the second half of the 18th century, a renewed questioning of the concept of civility: "it was Rousseau's fault." In his view, worldly sociability was the seat of sophistry and lies. One could object that Rousseau's position, however exemplary it was, was hardly representative of the interest in conversation that the age displayed. From Pierre Marivaux to Voltaire, from Diderot to Madame de Staël, the people of the French Enlightenment loved this witty and talkative self-image. However, by condemning the principal mechanism of worldly relations, Rousseau revealed a certain number of conflicts that had long been brewing in the Republic of Letters. Setting himself in opposition to the model of amiable and civilized conversation in the French manner, Rousseau undermined, in a certain sense, the ideal of communication held by the people of the Enlightenment. For these reasons, no doubt, and despite the salons of the Restoration, things would never be as they had been before. After the golden age of conversation, the 19th century would therefore be the golden age of nostalgia.

STÉPHANE PUJOL

See also Civilization and Civility; Coffeehouse; Dialogue; Essay; Salon

Further Reading

Fumaroli, Marc, *Le genre des genres littéraires français: La conversation,* Oxford: Clarendon Press, and New York: Oxford University Press, 1992

Fumaroli, Marc, "Otium, convivium, sermo: La conversation comme 'lieu commun' des lettrés," *Bulletin des Amis du Centre d'Études Supérieures de la Renaissance,* supplement no. 4 (1992)

Pujol, Stephane, "De la conversation à l'entretien littéraire," in *Du goût, de la conversation et des femmes,* edited by Alain Montandon, Clermont-Ferrand, France: Association des Publications de la Faculté des Lettres et Sciences Humaines de l'Université Blaise-Pascal, 1994

Sermain, Jean-Paul, "La conversation au XVIIIᵉ siècle: Un théâtre pour les Lumières?" in *Convivailité et politesse: Du gigot, des mots et autres savoir-vivre,* edited by Alain Montandon, Clermont-Ferrand, France: Faculté des Lettres et Sciences Humaines de l'Université Blaise-Pascal, 1993

Corpuscle

Four terms were closely related in the 17th and 18th centuries: "corpuscle" (small body), "molecule" (small mass), "particle" (small part), and—not to be overlooked—"atom" (Greek for "indivisible"). However, the future held very different destinies for these terms. Ever since 1860, when chemists convened the celebrated Congress of Karlsruhe to attempt to standardize the words and symbols they would employ, the distinction between "atom" and "molecule" has remained fixed: the term "atom" refers to the constituent parts of molecules—the entities between which chemical bonds take place. The term "particle" has kept its general meaning but is also associated today with "elementary particles"—the "ultimate" constituents of matter, precisely those constituents that the term "atom" traditionally designated in a privileged (but not exclusive) way. As for "corpuscle," no discipline has standardized its meaning.

One exception to the last statement can be found in the "wave/corpuscle" duality (usually expressed today as the wave/particle duality), which characterizes not only photons of light but all particles, in the sense understood by quantum mechanics. But in this case, the term "corpuscle" does not designate an entity in itself; it is a reminder of the fact that when photons or electrons are submitted to measurement techniques that treat them as small bodies in the classic sense, capable of collisions that result in transfer of energy, experimental data reveal exactly the behavior one would expect from individual "corpuscles." Nonetheless, the photon and the electron are not "corpuscles," since when experimental techniques deal with the question of their propagation, interference phenomena are produced, making it possible to attribute a wavelength to the quantum entity. In other words, "corpuscle" here refers to the old, corpuscular theory of light that Newton defends in his *Opticks* (1704); while the term "particle," which Newton uses to define the "small parts" that make up matter, has managed to shed its past nuances in order to designate "all" the entities introduced by high-energy physics.

Much as one would like to find profound reasons for this divergence of terminological destinies, it seems there are none. The terms "molecule," "atom," and "particle," although they have outlasted their cousin the "corpuscle," are all used inconsistently today when one considers their etymologies. "Molecule," which etymologically involves mass, is used in connection with the exploration of the complex structures that make up the compounds of organic chemistry. The atom is far from being the ultimate, indivisible constituent it was traditionally presumed to be: it has a struc-ture; it is subject to spontaneous or violent decomposition; and it can survive only in environments that are "warm," but not too hot. "Elementary particles" are no longer defined as "parts" in the sense of being constituents of a discrete whole. That assumption was still implicit in the prewar conception of electrons, protons, and neutrons composing the atom. Today, however, particles are identified relative to their interactions and to the energy required for their detection. They refer much more to the past—to the genealogy of matter—since their characterization is related to the progressive cooling of the universe. Thus, the possible unification of electromagnetic interactions with weak and strong nuclear forces would imply the existence of extraordinarily massive "bosons," the mass being measured by the energy required to "materialize" them. In fact, it would require 10^{15} GeV, a quantity of energy that could be found in the first moments of the universe (10^{-35} sec), before the rupture of symmetry between interactions that is posited by unified theories.

The history of these terms, which reveals that they were not treated consistently, is replete with anecdotes. The fact that 19th-century chemists revived the word "atom" was an especially unforeseeable development. If there was one thing that the "atomists" or "corpuscularists" of preceding centuries had avoided, it was the use of the term "atom" to characterize entities possessing chemical properties. John Dalton was the first to ascertain—from the fact that chemical compounds always combined in certain proportions—the properties of discrete entities or elements, each with a characteristic weight. He decided to ignore the complicated speculations on the structure of matter in which his predecessors had indulged since Boyle and Newton. Holding that these elements could not be transformed into other elements by any human influence, Dalton chose "atom" as the most eloquent term to affirm that claim.

Dalton's atom caused a digression that lasted a century in the controversies and speculations about the structure of matter. The term "corpuscle," until then a candidate for a respectable scientific destiny, did not survive that digression. Indeed, Dalton's "atomic hypothesis" created a scandal. It was sometimes rejected as speculative, sometimes accepted as a useful fiction, but it imposed the word "atom" upon chemists and then upon physicists, who later became capable of interpreting in their own terms the agents and transformations studied by chemists. One must go back beyond Dalton, to the 17th and 18th centuries, in order to grasp the problems inherent in the term "corpuscle."

We speak indiscriminately of "atomism" or "corpuscularism" to characterize doctrines that challenged the order of established knowledge in the 16th and 17th centuries. In fact, neither the Cartesian philosophical discourse on "small, moving, figured bodies" nor the theological arguments enabling atomism to pass from the status of a doctrine smacking of atheism to one deemed authentically Christian had need of this distinction between atoms and corpuscles. Cartesian discourse was concerned with distinguishing that which pertains to matter (primary or geometric properties) from that pertaining to the perceiving mind (sounds, odors, colors, etc.). Theologians were concerned with demonstrating that submissive matter better reflects the almighty power of God the Creator than do beings having autonomous form and endowed by pagan Aristotelianism with their own power of reason. On the other hand, distinctions became necessary when the partisans of atomism confronted the question of qualities that are difficult to relate to perception alone since they characterize the bodies that chemists transform. The question of knowing "what it is that causes gold to be gold," shared by alchemists and the *testatores* (assayers) who put the alchemists' gold to the test, had long been answered not by qualities of perception (yellow, shiny) but by what must be called intrinsic qualities, such as resistance to the action of acids.

The question of the intrinsic qualities of matter was all the more interesting because it was also thorny from the standpoint of Aristotelian physics: it was the problem of the mixture, characterized by the appearance of new substances endowed with new properties. Are the forms of the substances that enter the mixture preserved but weakened (Avicenna), or are they destroyed to the advantage of a new form (Thomas)? For the atomists, the question was that of the potential distinction between "atoms" and the qualitatively differentiated units of matter (sulfur, mercury, salt). The chemist-physician Daniel Sennert believed that the latter are the *prima mixta*, primordial mixtures more accurately called corpuscles than atoms. These atoms, unobservable and inaccessible to the operations of the chemist, are the *minima naturae*.

What impact would this "corpuscular" interpretation have on chemistry? Robert Boyle opted for scepticism, calling into question all the categories of the chemistry of elements or constituents. If atoms form a matter that is "catholic and universal," homogenous and devoid of qualities, then bodies as qualitatively differentiated must be produced by the "different textures" of that matter. From that, it follows that not only are the elements themselves not indestructible (lead could be transformed into gold), but different methods of separation (damp process, dry process, hot or low fire) can bring about different changes of texture. The

chemist, according to Boyle, must renounce the general categories explaining his procedures, in order to adhere to the most precise operative identifications possible.

Newton also held that the differentiated matter of chemists corresponds in fact to hierarchical structures, aggregates in which particles combine to create other particles. But the forces of attraction that, according to him, maintain those aggregates permit a more precise meaning to be given to the differentiated qualities of chemical bodies. Newton's *Opticks* proposes operations of "displacement," in which one body replaces another in its association with a third, as a measure of the relative attraction of the first two for the third.

The idea of seeing a chemical compound as a "combination," and the reaction as a process of dissociation and reassociation—that is, as a displacement—is "corpuscular," in Sennert's sense, and would be adopted by all the 18th-century chemists, while "affinity tables" were constructed that ordered the bodies according to their capacity to displace one another. Furthermore, the reversibility of combinations, set forth by Sennert as proof of the corpuscular theory—the fact that a series of reactions could make a substance disappear (gold dissolved in *aqua regia,* for example) then manage to recuperate it in its "primitive state" (*reductio in pristinum statum*)—would become in the 18th century the standard procedure for characterizing a "pure" substance, independently of its origin. Salt extracted from seawater, for example, is identical to the substance produced in the laboratory using the alkali derived from that salt. Correspondingly, the ancient and extensive nomenclature of bodies, most often indicating their discoverer or origin, became obsolete. In 1787 the *Méthode de nomenclature chimique* (Method of Chemical Nomenclature) of Antoine-Laurent Lavoisier and his colleagues legitimized treating a compound as a combination.

The concept of combination, which implied the corpuscular idea, dominated chemistry from then on—although without explaining exactly what a corpuscle is. In the article "Chimie" (Chemistry) in the *Encyclopédie,* Venel proposes, contrary to the Newtonians, to name "corpuscles" the sole agents, qualitatively differentiated, in the chemical combination or "mixture"; and he opposes corpuscles to the "molecules" that build "mechanical" aggregates. Thus, the notion of "corpuscle" finally acquired a positive definition, corresponding to the singularity of the chemical combination that created a homogenous body from heterogeneous bodies.

Perhaps it was because the term "corpuscle" reflected the problem of the contrast between chemical bonds and interactions of a mechanical type that it did not have a scientific future. The fact that Dalton's "atom" replaced "corpuscle" without much resistance signaled the defeat of the "chemistry of the Enlightenment," a chemistry that had rivaled physics as being the best platform for thinking about matter. The controversy among 19th-century chemists no longer concerned the difference between aggregation and combination, but rather the legitimacy of positing invisible "entities" beyond observable regularities. One word was as good as another to refer to such entities, since their scientific legitimacy posed far more problems than their properties. The word "atom" emerged victorious.

ISABELLE STENGERS

See also Affinity; Chemistry; Optics and Light

Further Reading
Dijksterhuis, Edward Jean, *The Mechanization of the World Picture*, Princeton, New Jersey: Princeton University Press, 1986
Meinel, Christopher, "Early 17th-Century Atomism: Theory, Epistemology, and the Insufficiency of Experiment," *Isis* 79 (1988)
Thackray, Arnold, *Atoms and Power: An Essay on Newtonian Matter-Theory and the Development of Chemistry*, Cambridge, Massachusetts: Harvard University Press, and London: Oxford University Press, 1970

Correspondence

Overview

Within the collective European memory, two quite distinct series of correspondence are most often associated with the age of the Enlightenment. The first of these is the actual correspondence between writers, thinkers, artists, and scholars, such as Voltaire and Jean-Jacques Rousseau, Immanuel Kant and Wolfgang Amadeus Mozart, or collections of letters by Charles-Nicolas Cochin, Charles Bonnet, and Horace Walpole. The other type of correspondence that readily comes to mind is that found in epistolary novels, which often consist of excerpts from fictitious correspondence written by such characters as Pamela, Julie, Clarissa, Usbek, Werther, Merteuil, or Jacopo Ortis. Whether authentic or fictitious, these letters allow us to listen to the voice of another time—the golden age of letter writing—as though they were addressed to us.

However, these two types of correspondence do not tell the entire story. In some sense, bodies of letters written by historical figures, understood as "correspondences," are a secondary product we create when we publish them. Meanwhile, scholars have tended to isolate epistolary novels and to devote a disproportionate amount of attention to them as a genre. In fact, alongside these two categories, the 18th century witnessed a proliferation of hybrid epistolary practices, including memoirs, travel writings, gallant heroic epics, devotional tracts, essay letters, broadside letters, prank letters, newspapers in letter form, and letters to newspapers—all those miscellaneous minor works that, with occasional exceptions, have been neglected by a literary history too narrowly focused on established genres, and that belong to the same broad, genre-spanning category of "works in letter form."

We would do well to remember how, in *Lettres sur la postérité* (Letters on Posterity), Denis Diderot celebrated another major invention after that of printing: the postal service. He invited, and foresaw between the two, a dynamic exchange of information, knowledge, and processes, in which the constraints of space and time, inertia, ignorance, and death would be broken through the resistance of men against nature—in short, through culture (Letter to Falconet, January 1766). One day, feverish and inspired, Diderot imagined a way to liberate "the energy of the species." It consisted of "a correspondence that would extend to all the parts of the human race." All that this utopia of total instantaneous communication lacked in order to become a reality, according to Diderot, was a "common idiom": "Were this idiom to be accepted and fixed, notions would immediately become permanent, the distance represented by time would disappear, places would be contiguous, liaisons would be made between all the inhabited points in space and time, and all living, thinking beings would communicate" ("Encyclopédie" entry of the *Encyclopédie* [1755]). This was for all intents and purposes an Enlightenment version of communication by Internet. A more modest synergy between the postal services and the press was in fact established in Paris in 1772: the Bureau d'Abonnements Littéraires (Literary Subscription Bureau), a private initiative, purchased books and sent them postpaid to even the most distant provinces to members who ordered them. How many letters to the addressees must have been sent along with those books! In order to reconstruct, more than two centuries later, an improbable ideal "correspondence" between the Enlightenment and its era, we must try to imagine the entire epistolary economy of circulation that joined letters to literature and literature to letters.

The Epistolary Order

Culturally, socially, and politically, Europe was to remain for several more decades an oral space structured around the Book (the Bible), where epistolary channels were the most significant conduits of communication and power. Order was maintained through letters and their attendant structures: couriers, postal services (ranging from barely adequate to perfect in terms of their organization), and exchanges, including the first bilateral postal agreements (for example, one signed in 1720 between Spain and France). Emanating from the prince to his administrators or his subjects, letters could take the form of public or private edicts or decrees, letters of entitlement or secret missives, or letters of credit, naturalization, derogation, abolition, nobility, respite, pardon, forgiveness, etc. Letters were dispatched from ministers to officers of the crown, from magistrates to those under their authority, from merchants or bankers to those they referred to as their "correspondents." Everywhere, and under a variety of names, letters ordered, defended, decided, and authorized.

In Catholic countries, following the established protocol, popes addressed constitutions, bulls, and briefs to princes. The ancient practice of the *bullarium*—a series of papal bulls issued from Rome—was organized into an essentially epistolary system in the 18th century. Mandates and pastoral letters were sent from prelates to priests and congregations. The Jesuits, leaders in the evangelization of nations, contributed to this major epistolary category with their famous *Lettres édifiantes et curieuses* (1702–76). Today, these epistles are relegated to the status of ethnological documentation; however, they in fact pertained to "relations" and "states" instituted with the foundation of the Order, and they thus constitute valuable evidence of publicly expressed power and perceived necessity.

Conversely, the Jansenists were limited to the dissidence of their "minor letters" and other "news" that offered testimony and ministry; these texts were copied and distributed by way of clandestine circuits. The sphere of public order was relatively simple in Protestant areas, which were already more focused on immanent relationships at the human level. These relationships were a source of unity for the Reformed Church, but they were also crucial to the organization of powers, social development, and economic expansion. In Geneva, letters of exchange were more important than reprimands from the consistory, while the illustrious Dr. Tronchin managed the nerves and stomachs of an international set of rich and noble patients through the medium of the postal service.

What was termed "political" correspondence, made up of instructions, commissions, and negotiations, circulated among the royal courts of Europe. Exemplified by the 19th-century publication of the monumental *Politische Correspondenz* (1879; Political Correspondence) of Frederick II of Prussia, the expression "political correspondence" persists even today in the nomenclature used in diplomatic repositories. Particularly in France, the power the monarch enjoyed in his person was symbolized in three different types of letters: the *secret du roi* (the king's secret) designated diplomatic exchanges between the great powers; the *cabinet noir* (shadow cabinet) was a missive that could break all other secrets; and the *lettre de cachet* (sealed letter), a royal warrant for imprisonment without trial (which was thus, by definition, unanswerable). Such authoritarian epistolary practices were more or less common to all major European countries and were functions of the state in strong regimes. Already much curtailed in England, these practices became reprehensible to the Enlightenment spirit, as a public affront to new rights being instituted—the rights of private individuals, who were citizens and not subjects. The *cabinet noir* was eliminated in France by the Constituent Assembly of 1789, but it was reestablished as the "Research Committee" employed in tracking the counterrevolutionary correspondence of "émigrés." In the name of citizens' rights, the Convention published a duly authenticated "selection" of such letters in 1792. Pushing this logic of revelation to extremes, the *Mémoires historiques et anecdotes de la cour de France* (1802; Historical Memoirs and Anecdotes of the Court of France), attributed to the abbé Soulavie, finally exposed to all eyes the carefully engraved, most intimate form of the *cachet du roi* (royal seal)—namely the one imprinted on his love letters (a gift of the hated Madame de Pompadour to the weakling Louis XV)—and the shame of an ancien régime indifferent to the public welfare. The work was ironically dedicated to the "sovereigns of Europe" for their edification.

Model Letters

Under these conditions it was absolutely crucial for writers to master the epistolary form, including letters written in a spirit of criticism, complaint, or opposition. The petitions, remonstrances, and grievances in the ultimate crisis of 1789 were still lodged in the form of letters. For courtly letters, business letters, social letters, or letters of recommendation, the appropriate style could be learned or acquired through practice. A protector, prosecutor, or director of conscience consulted his colleagues by letter, giving rise to a flourishing market for letter-writing manuals called *secrétaires* (secretaries). These profane and worldly heirs of the medieval *ars dictaminis* gave instructions, in all languages, on the typology, pragmatics, and art of this highly regulated form of communication, with examples drawn from ancient and classical "epistolaries." The model of politeness *à la française,* codified and urbane, remained in force in the upper echelons of society throughout Europe. The letter-writing manuals printed in Paris and Lyon were reprinted, with or without modification, in Berlin, The Hague, or London, and could be found in all public and private libraries at the time. The acquisition of social graces, literary culture and epistolary usage were thus closely interrelated. Only moral education was excluded from this acquired skill: in his notebooks, *Mes pensées* (1716–55; My Thoughts), Montesquieu included a copy of a childhood letter written without a model, inspired solely by an instinct of honor.

The long-term evolution in epistolary style can be observed in relation to the ancien régime, or to former courtly tastes. By 1730 the styles of Jean Louis Guez de Balzac, dubbed "the great letter-writer of France" during the classical era, and his contemporary, the poet and epistolarist Vincent Voiture were definitely outmoded. Thereafter, to compliment a woman, one might invoke Madame de Sévigné, considered the exemplary stylist and correspondent, and write, "You are the Sévigné of . . . " ("of Germany," "of the north," "of this country," etc.). Marie de Rabutin-Chantal, marquise de Sévigné, lived and wrote during the 17th century, but her letters were not circulated in the salons of the time and became known only when they were published in 1725. Following Sévigné's example, authorities in the matter would recommend a "natural, familiar" style. After 1760 they even encouraged the "personal" turn of phrase, but only, according to the guides, "to a certain point," thus leaving the ultimate education of the letter-writer to the family. Between 1750 and 1780 one of the most highly appreciated manuals was Samuel Richardson's *Familiar Letters* (1741), a laboratory for his novels, and written in the same modern, moral, practical spirit. Richardson's was the only foreign manual deemed worthy of being translated into French; it was also translated into German and Dutch. But new, sometimes bilingual, manuals furnished more direct instructions and models, as "commerce" was no longer merely epistolary. A French-Spanish bank manual and *Modern Letters in French and English* (1769) came out at the same time. In 1771 an anonymous reader of the *Année littéraire* denounced all this "ceremonial of our French letters" which he found "posturing and fanciful." As if to prove his point, the author ironically ended his own "letter" with a postscript, in direct violation of the manuals.

The changing epistolary styles—more informal and less given to codes, compliments, and set phrases—capture and reflect concomitant changes and new patterns in social representations. Such changes must doubtless have been the product of the "imaginary democracy" that would be analyzed by Alexis de Tocqueville and whose fluidity emerges in Voltaire's correspondence. But these stylistic changes also reflect the simplification of aristocratic usage and the cultural accession of a bourgeoisie that had greater access to the art of writing and the pleasure of reading, as well as a general need for easier communication. It was common after 1770 to see newspaper advertisements for "epistolary lessons" given at home, while the illiterate classes could always turn to a public scribe. By the end of the century the old schematized, obsolete models, embalmed in their glory, went into the *Bibliothèque Bleue* (Blue Library), a collection of small, blue-bound volumes compiling various forms of popular provincial literature, published in Troyes by Nicolas Oudot and disseminated by peddlers. The time of Republican use of the informal second-person singular pronoun *tu*—a time of "theeing" and "thouing"—was at hand, a time when people addressed each other as "Citizen." And the Restoration did not bring back all of the forms of the old days. Madame de Genlis laments in the "Billet" (Note) article of the *Dictionnaire des étiquettes* (1818; Dictionary of Etiquette): "The old protocol is abolished." Philipon de la Madelaine's *Modèles de lettres sur différents sujets* (1761; Models of Letters on Various Subjects), a reasonably classical manual written in an average style, was given official status in 1804 in the imperial education system and reprinted repeatedly up to 1871.

Semper ego auditor tantum? (Will I Then Always Be Reduced to Listening?)

Writings in epistolary form addressed to a broad public, designated as "letters," abounded during the Enlightenment: from 1716 to 1760 there were 2,000 published in French alone. These writings formed an overwhelming mass of formidable heterogeneity. In the great majority of cases they were neither fiction nor correspondence in the modern sense of the terms. Rather, they consisted of works dealing with facts and ideas: in other words, in other words, they encompassed "literature" as it was understood at that time, meaning history, knowledge, erudition, criticism, and discussion. The very expression "philosophical letter," quite common up until 1750, implies this broad intellectual open-mindedness. Today, we would probably consider these writing "essays" or "manifestos," but in the 18th century the word "letter" was used uncritically throughout the larger discourse devoted to presentations or reviews. In duration and density, the essential phenomenon was the conventional, generic "letters." Some of these texts were famous and have become classics, including Voltaire's *Lettres philosophiques* (1734; Philosophical Letters); Diderot's *Lettre sur les aveugles* (1749; Letter on the Blind) and his *Lettre sur les sourds et muets* (1751; Letter on the Deaf and Mute); and Rousseau's more controversial *Lettre à D'Alembert* (1758; Letter to D'Alembert on Theatre), his *Lettre sur la Providence* (Letter on Providence), which he addressed to Voltaire, and his *Lettres écrites de la montagne* (1764; Letters Written during a Journey in the Mountains). There were "soldier's" letters written by Francesco Algarotti, letters "Upon History" by Viscount Bolingbroke, and those "Zur Beförderung der Humanität" (On the Promotion of Humanity), by Johann Gottfried von Herder, among others. At one time or another, all the great debates of the century, whether open or suppressed, were rehearsed in such "letters": the means of knowledge, the progress of humanity, the truth of religions, the interests of the state, taxation of the clergy, freedom of conscience, inoculation against smallpox, the "commercial" nobility, the grain trade, the public education system, and even the status of the *philosophes* who were the instigators and often the agitators of all those debates. Thus was created a vast epistolary forum constitutive of the Enlightenment. Barbey d'Aurevilly one day petulantly went so far as to coin the word *épistolature* (a pejorative hybrid of "epistle" and "literature") to criticize those heretical usurpers, a laity who wished they were prelates.

Formal variation in letter writing was organized within two systems that were initially opposed to one another but eventually became all but interchangeable, testifying to the underlying ideological tensions and dynamics of their history. The first of these, an extremely old model, assumed that the letter would treat a subject of common interest; this model also implied the presence of a mute, attentive addressee and an expert scribe who was more or less prolix, sure of himself, and sure of being read. This was the apostolic letter, a letter of truth and authority, the underlying model for all letters in the Christian tradition. "Dogmatic" or "spiritual" letters, such as those of Godeau (1713), Jacques-Bénigne Bossuet (1746), and Father Lafitau (1754), were still being published, but their number declined over the course of the 18th century as demand or need decreased, and their style evolved with the times. In 1757 an abbé from Olonne broached the theme of "how to make everything work for your spiritual advancement." Religious authorities were then compelled to incorporate a more defensive position against the audacity of "freethinkers" who went against sacred truths and spread the uncontrolled products of profane thought—supposed new "truths" about man, life, and the world. Doctrinal letters, in short, had to adapt to the changing times. In a devout "epistle" published anonymously in the heat of the battle, the criminal author of the *Lettres philosophiques*, "M. de V." (that is, Voltaire), is called "frenzied." But 20 years later, serious efforts were made to "analyze" and "refute" these letters as well as Montesquieu's *Lettres persanes* (1721; Persian Letters) as well as the marquis d'Argens's *Lettres juives* (1736; Jewish Letters). This gave rise to Gauchat's *Lettres critiques ou, Analyse et refutation de divers écrits modernes contre la religion* (1755–63; Critical Letters: Analysis and Refutation of Various Modern Writings against Religion), which are curiously tailored to the taste of the day: reasoned, familiar, informal, and extremely witty. Soret and Gauchat were modern defenders of the faith who took the risk of having their works mocked as a "novel" (see Voltaire's *Candide* [1759]).

The second type of letter secretly undermined the first, contested it, turned it around, and subverted it. Initially clandestine, this second model eventually prevailed because it was driven by conviction and an internal, autonomous initiative. The Latin epigraph of the *Lettre d'un citoyen zélé* (1748; Letter from a Zealous Citizen) could serve as an example of this commitment: "Will I then always be reduced to listening?" In this letter, the young Diderot (at the time anonymous and, in fact, unknown) suggested, to the antagonistic corps of doctors and surgeons, reconciliation based on simple common sense, which did work for a short time. An ordinary patient dared to address the arrogant mandarins, breaking the silence, ending the passivity and the submission, speaking up or writing in the name of public welfare. Astonishingly, Diderot took the epigraph from the epistle in which Saint James advises timid Christians in the missionary apostolate: "Become doers of the Word, and not hearers only, deceiving your own selves" (James 1:22). In this appropriation of Scripture, Diderot thus replaced the love of the Word, or the "letter" (who knows?), with the service of men, claiming to incarnate it in a different way, in faith that had finally become humanized.

For the new apostles there was the new epistle: Voltaire, "patriarch" of the new church of Reason, would play on it with his "fraternal letters"—sometimes ending in *Écrelinf* (a coded contraction for *Écrasez l'infâme,* meaning "Crush the infamous")—that spread throughout the best Parisian philosophical circles and circulated in the European network of Friedrich Melchior von Grimm's' *Correspondance littéraire.* Such letters generated a feeling of mutual understanding, a collective force acting on history, with the notable examples of the pompous missives by princely supporters that quickly found their way into public "papers": the letter of Catherine II inviting Jean le Rond D'Alembert (who declined) to oversee the education of her son (1763), or that of Frederick II subsidizing the Pigalle statue of Voltaire (1770). This was no longer the patiently woven network of exchanges maintained in an ideal, unselfish spirit and known for two centuries as the "Republic of Letters. " That entity had unraveled under the pressure of international competition, professional specialization, and ideological conflict. A reverse image of a "correspondence" of combat and subversion appears in the "Zzuéné" entry, transcended by its oblique function, on the last page of the *Encyclopédie*. An offensive strategy was obviously at work here. By means of letters informed solely by personal conviction, Diderot had defied Father Berthier, the powerful director of Jesuit publications; Voltaire had castigated the devout factions and their pettifogging bishop, Monsignor Biord; and Rousseau had criticized Christophe de Beaumont, archbishop of Paris.

The Invention of Authorial Correspondence

Voltaire was the only writer who put himself in a position to act on a more directly political question at the heart of the most Christian of monarchies. By taking up his pen, in his later years, on behalf of the illiterate serfs of Saint Claude, archaically subject to the monks, and by writing and rewriting (however vainly) their *Requêtes au roi* (Petitions to the King), Voltaire was questioning the social order itself, from top to bottom. We would call him the first self-proclaimed "public writer," the first "intellectual." This renown led to the extraordinary innovation of including an author's correspondence in his complete works, as if the entire body of publishable letters inevitably formed a part of a comprehensive collection of that writer's published work.

At first this phenomenon of collecting an author's complete correspondence was unique to Voltaire, but it was later extended to other "great writers"—to the point of becoming a distinctive sign of their greatness. The posthumous edition of Voltaire's works, known as the Kehl edition (1785–90), was a major event in the history of epistolary literature, a turning point in the long evolution of the status and function of letters. Eighteen of the 70 volumes of the enormous collection, a veritable paper mausoleum erected to the champion of the Enlightenment, displayed first Voltaire's "general correspondence," furnished in original form or in copies by his correspondents themselves (more than 300 of them), who thereby became contributors to the monument. But the three most "remarkable private correspondences" of Voltaire were reserved for later: the

letters the *philosophe* exchanged with Frederick II, Catherine II, and D'Alembert. Alongside the two royal dialogues, at the end of a banned edition published beyond the borders of France, the correspondence with D'Alembert reiterated, in a different way, the newly established idea that literature possessed intrinsic autonomy and authority. There were more than 4,500 letters in all. Never before had the collective voice of his own era been gathered around an author, brought to him in his lifetime, then carried on beyond his death, answering to and for his work—*corresponding* with that work.

Madame de Sévigné was the first "epistolary author," but the classic model of "the man and his work"—the founding principle of the modern literary institution—was based on the example of Voltaire (who was lionized by the first "Voltaireans"), and more precisely on the example of Voltaire's letters. The "man" (the writer) attested to the literary work, of course, but even more importantly, in the old sense, "Man" (mankind) was manifested within, and attested to, *by* the author's works. "Human letters" were thus finally separated from "divine letters," and "literature" was set apart from "Scripture." This ultimate consecration of Voltaire with an *Ecce homo* (Behold Man), which surprises us today, is formulated by Condorcet in the strange *Avertissement* (editors' notice) that introduces the *Correspondance générale*, which was contemporary with Rousseau's *Confessions* (1782):

> These letters where he [Voltaire] appears completely, where he reveals to his friends his weaknesses, his shifting humor, his terrors and his courage, are the best reply that can be made to his numerous enemies. We do not find in them an ostentatious confession written for the public, where the author shows himself as he wants to be seen; we find the man himself as he was in all the moments of his life, as he allows himself to be seen, seeking neither to show nor hide himself.

Here, in this vast portfolio of correspondence during the Enlightenment, is proof of the general phenomenon of the secularization of writing. The period saw a shift from religious interests to the right to know and the duty to act; it witnessed the appearance of the new postulate of the eminent importance of human things. And in this new space of literature among men, where the letter represented a commitment, even a public commitment, the stirrings of responsibility for multiple meanings in writing can be discerned.

ANDRÉ MAGNAN

See also Correspondence: Literary; Novel; Republic of Letters

Further Reading

Altman, Janet Gurkin, *Epistolarity: Approaches to a Form,* Columbus: Ohio State University Press, 1982

Altman, Janet Gurkin, "The Letter Book as a Library Institution 1539–1789: Toward a Cultural History of Published Correspondences in France," in *Men/ Women of Letters (Yale French Studies 71),* edited by Charles A. Porter, New Haven, Connecticut: Yale University Press, 1986

Day, Robert Adams, *Told in Letters: Epistolary Fiction before Richardson,* Ann Arbor: University of Michigan Press, 1966

Magnan, André, "Le Voltaire inconnu de Jean-Louis Wagnière," *L'infini* 25 (1989)

Magnan, André, "Le Voltaire de Kehl," *Europe* 761 (May 1994)

May, G., "La littérature épistolaire date-t-elle du XVIIIe siècle?" *Studies on Voltaire and the Eighteenth Century* 56 (1967)

Versini, Laurent, *Le roman épistolaire,* Paris: Presses Universitaires de France, 1979

Correspondence

Literary

In the history of 18th-century literature, the expression "literary correspondence" has a fairly precise meaning that is distinct from its general definition as an exchange of letters having literary content or taking place between people of letters. The term designates a particular type of intellectual communication in Europe during the Enlightenment. Literary correspondence was born—and later vanished—with the ideal of the enlightened prince, the sovereign who not only wanted to model his court and society on French language and culture in general but who was often sympathetic toward the ideas of France's *philosophes* as well. The first literary correspondent of this type was Nicolas-Claude Thieriot (1697–1772), who wrote letters to Frederick II of Prussia beginning in November 1736. The genre flourished between 1750 and 1775 and lost its influence after the French Revolution, even though the *Correspondance littéraire* of Friedrich Melchior von Grimm and Heinrich Meister, the best-known example of the genre, continued until 1813.

The term was already used in this specific sense in the 18th century. In the 1730s, for example, Anfossy referred to Jean Bouhier's erudite letters as "literary correspondence." In a memoir dating from 1748, when a replacement was being sought for Thieriot after his fall from favor, precise indications were given on how to "carry on a Literary Correspondence in a proper manner with the king of Prussia." In a letter from Fréron to d'Hémery dated 26 May 1753, Denis Diderot is described as a "literary correspondent" whom "Prince Henry, brother of the king of Prussia, has chosen." The letters regularly addressed to Karlsruhe were explicitly considered as a "literary correspondence" by both the authors and the subscriber, who wrote back to one author on 13 May 1757: "Monsieur Morand, I am very pleased with your literary correspondence." Grimm himself often spoke of the "literary correspondence" requested of him, or which princes honored with their attention. In La Harpe's writings the expression occurs quite frequently; his 1801 publication, under the title *Correspondance littéraire,* of the letters he had sent to Russia from 1774 onward helped ensure the term's continued use. The success in the 19th century of three editions of Grimm and Meister's *Correspondance littéraire,* which may be considered, as Gustave Lanson has pointed out, a "model of the genre," established the term once and for all.

In addition to "correspondence" or "literary correspondent," there were other ways of referring to this type of communication: one might also speak of literary newsletters, literary newspapers, or literary commerce or exchange. The correspondents themselves were referred to as literary peddlers or agents, or even brokers of literature. These loanwords from the world of commerce to designate the activities of the literary correspondent clearly suggest a function that was both economic and social. Grimm himself considered the posting of literary news to be "a branch of commerce," and his subscribers were his "customers" (meaning his clients or purchasers).

In the 18th-century system of intellectual communication, literary correspondence was situated somewhere between the scholarly letter in the humanist tradition (Desiderius Erasmus), which presupposed an exchange between two correspondents, and the periodical, which had become an important means of disseminating information in the European Republic of Letters beginning in the 17th century. Literary correspondence shared certain features with periodicals: letters were sent "periodically" (monthly or bimonthly, sometimes even weekly); they were paid for (at a considerable rate, varying from 600 to 1,500 livres per year); they adhered to a certain length agreed upon ahead of time between the correspondent and the subscriber (but which might vary depending on the news available); they conformed to a certain standardized structure (generally a long in-depth article followed by lists of new publications and theatrical performances); and, finally, they contained information that was relatively impersonal. On the other hand, literary correspondence shared certain characteristics with private letters: these missives were handwritten, almost always executed by a copyist, and they were sent to an individual, which meant they could not be sold in bookshops.

As a genre, literary correspondence had other characteristic traits. Subscribers were aristocrats, most often even the sovereigns of foreign countries. Grimm chose his subscribers exclusively among princes. Despite offers of generous remuneration, he refused subscriptions from literary circles or even "individuals of high and illustrious birth." For him, the principal reason for limiting his subscription to sovereigns was the absolute discretion of the recipient, which he relied on to preserve his freedom of judgment in relation to both political power and public literary criticism. Pierre-Samuel Dupont de Nemours established a literary correspondence early in 1773—after the *Éphémérides du citoyen ou chronique de l'esprit national* (The Citizen's Calendar; or, A Chronicle of National Spirit) had been banned—while complaining that "the new restrictions placed upon books printed in France leave no freedom at all" and that men of letters and their protectors were forced to "return to manuscripts." Literary correspondents knew, indeed, that by ordering their subscriptions, their princely subscribers hoped to hold a kind of monopoly on information from Paris, the cultural center of Europe—and for the more enlightened among them, from philosophical circles.

To a great extent, the princely subscribers respected the discretion Grimm and other literary correspondents demanded of them and were able to prevent those of their friends who read their correspondence from sharing it with others (Johann Wolfgang von Goethe and Johann Gottfried von Herder, for example). From the point of view of the princes, the aura of exclusivity imparted by the manuscript form and regular expedition by diplomatic courier merely provided external confirmation of the privileged content—which alone would have sufficed to explain the recipient's choice of this type of subscription (since a good number of worthwhile printed newspapers were in circulation at the time).

The exclusivity and, more to the point, freedom from censorship and public opinion in the genre of literary correspondence facilitated the first endeavors to create new literary criticism in the modern sense of the term. Basically, the subscribers expected from the contract not only to be kept informed about literary works, paintings, and theatre or opera performances but also to be guided in their choice of reading or purchases. The newspapers of the 18th century, faced with the huge and rapid increase in the number of books—a trend the *philosophes* criticized—in a way supplemented books themselves, which were often expensive. These newspapers offered fairly lengthy descriptions of the books' contents accompanied by long "excerpts." The titles of a whole series of periodicals that include descriptive words such as *universelle et historique* (universal and historical), *choisie* (selected), *anglaise* (English), *germanique* (Germanic), etc. are a good illustration of that particular function. From literary correspondence, however, the subscriber expected not only information but also selective criticism. Writing about Grimm in the introduction to his 1854 anthology of the *Gazette littéraire,* Charles-Augustin Sainte-Beuve underscores this new element:

> In Grimm's time, it was still common usage to refer to the articles one wrote about books as "Extraits" (excerpts), and these excerpts, authorized and consecrated by the example of the *Journal des savants,* often went no further in fact than a dry and exact summary of the work: "Under the pretext of giving the substance, they offered only the skeleton." Grimm was not in favor of such heavy, routine criticism, which often read like the minutes of a meeting. Good writings, in his opinion, must not be known solely through excerpts, but must be read: "Poor writings need nothing more than to be forgotten. A good policy would be to allow journalists not to speak about a work, good or bad, unless they have something to say about it." His purpose in his pages was to examine and rectify, and that should be the purpose of all journalists. Grimm was something of an innovator in this respect, and he truly situated newspaper criticism where it ought to be.

Often, in fact, the criticism of a literary work, a painting, or an opera in literary correspondence incited subscribers to have the book, the libretto, or the work of art in question sent to them from Paris. Royal libraries and art collections (such as those bought by Catherine the Great for the Hermitage) testify to this social role of literary correspondence and the influence it exerted.

Thieriot might be considered the first literary correspondent of the type described here. He sent his letters to Frederick II from November 1736 until 1748, at the price of 1,200 livres a year (the sum agreed on, but which he often had to ask for, because the king was irregular in his payments). In exchange for this considerable sum Thieriot had to report on literary news, send books and various merchandise, contact the great writers (for example, Bernard Le Bovier de Fontenelle) in Frederick's name, convey letters to third parties, and so on. Voltaire, who had introduced Thieriot into the circles of the king of Prussia, was himself one of the favorite subjects of the correspondence; everything Voltaire published was of interest to the king. This correspondence has only been published in a very fragmentary way to date, and most of it seems to have been lost. No letters at all have been preserved from the second period of the epistolary activity between Frederick and Thieriot, from 1766 until the latter's death in 1772.

The samples that remain from the first period of the correspondence between Thieriot and Frederick illustrate eloquently that the method of literary correspondence was indeed an offshoot of personal correspondence. Thieriot's letters are rather short (between one and four pages long), filled with rhetorical apostrophes and forms of courtesy; Frederick's replies are also fairly personal in tone. They mingle worldly literary and military news with reports on errands; analysis and criticism of literary works are practically absent. In the end, what remains a fairly harsh judgment of this first correspondence seems quite justified. Grimm wrote, for example, in 1773: "Thieriot was not a man of letters: he was a sort of literary peddler" (see Grimm). In 1748 Frederick chose Baculard d'Arnaud as Thieriot's successor. Unfortunately, there is no record of that correspondence. When Thieriot resumed the correspondence in 1766 he had apparently modified the format of his dispatches: "This is a literary page, etc., for His Majesty, whom I address, as ever, in the manner of the Italians, in the third person." He sent his missives every week (whereas the rhythm of the first period had been irregular): "I herein enclose half a dozen notices, as succinct and clear as I can make them, of all the works of the history of philosophy and of belles lettres that gained distinctions, and I finish with an article on selected verses."

The evolution of Thieriot's correspondence reflects the origins of the genre. Letters in a personal style, addressed to a recipient who responds by articulating his or her desires and feelings, gave way to something that was predominantly impersonal, devoid of any trace of the epistolary form. A similar evolution can be seen in Guertoy's correspondence, addressed to Prussian princes in 1752–53, and in Pierre de Morand's (1757). In these cases, too, the first letters still bear the trace of the personal epistle ("you" for the recipient, for example), which would subsequently disappear.

The impersonal nature of the correspondence became necessary once a literary correspondent had more than one recipient. This was the case for the abbé Raynal, who sent his *Nouvelles littéraires* to Gotha, Darmstadt, and Saarbrücken. When he began his correspondence for Gotha, in 1747, he still seemed, quite naturally, to favor the epistolary format. However, as he sought and found other correspondents, for purely economic reasons, he soon had to abandon that format in order to adapt his dispatches to the "form of a gazette." Henceforth, personal information, which was necessary at the start of the subscription, was sent separately from the standardized post. Grimm and other literary correspondents proceeded in the same manner. With Raynal's literary newsletters and Grimm's pages (in which, it would seem, Diderot and Raynal played a role at the beginning), the genre of literary correspondence was established, and its format, with a few variations, was set.

Several major series of literary correspondence stand out in the history of the genre. First among these are the correspondences of Grimm (1753 to March 1773) and Meister (April 1773 to 1813), which were without doubt the richest and the closest in spirit to the Enlightenment. During the period of glory of this series, around 1771–72, the subscribers included royalty from throughout Europe: Catherine the Great of Russia, the duchess of Saxony-Gotha, the queen of Sweden, the countess of Nassau-Saarbrücken, the duke of Zweibrücken, the king of Poland, and the future emperor, the archduke Peter Leopold of Tuscany.

For Grimm, the son of German pastor in Regensburg, this correspondence was the means of raising his social status and achieving a remarkable material success. In 1771 he wrote to Caroline, countess of Hesse-Darmstadt, that his enterprise was earning him nine thousand livres, "of which I must deduct roughly three thousand livres for copy and office expenses" (*Correspondance inédite* [Unpublished Correspondence], letter dated 20 July 1771). In 1769 Grimm became counselor to the legation and plenipotentiary minister of the duke of Saxony-Gotha at Versailles. He was made a baron by the court in Vienna in 1772 and entered the service of Russia in 1777. He was fully aware of his mission as a proponent of the Enlightenment and of the "advantage, which is of no small consideration, of having the right to speak twice a month to all the enlightened princes and princesses of Europe." Beginning in 1774 Heinrich Meister of Zurich took over from Grimm but was not as successful, although he did publish a number of texts by Diderot, including some of the most important ones, particularly after his departure from Paris in 1794.

The second major series of note was addressed from Paris to the margrave Caroline Louise of Baden-Durlach by, in succession, Pierre de Morand, Antoine Maillet-Duclairon, Claude Pougin de Saint-Aubin, and Jean-Louis Aubert, from 1757 to 1783. This correspondence is now also a source of information for those doing research on the 18th century. It was composed in a much more traditionalist vein than the writings of Raynal or Grimm, in terms of both literary criticism and philosophical ideas. Depending on the subscriber's wishes, this correspondence regularly consisted of

> a small catalogue raisonné of all newly published books and pamphlets, an exact notion of fine arts and performances, and . . . some of those pleasing little tales that appear every day, and bits of poetry on the era that are not printed.

Also of significance were two important literary correspondences addressed to the court at Saint Petersburg: that of La Harpe (from 1774 to 1791), which is fairly well known, and that of Blin de Saint-Maur (from 1782 to 1791). The latter is of particular interest for its accurate reflection of the progressive politicization of public opinion from 1788 on—to such a degree that the correspondence lost more and more of the literary content that was meant to be the basis of the genre.

Research into literary correspondence has enjoyed a revival in recent years. Long-published correspondences, such as those of Thieriot, Raynal, Grimm, Meister, La Harpe, Favart, and Suard, have aroused renewed interest. Additionally, since 1987 a new series of *Correspondances littéraires érudites, philosophiques, privées ou secrètes* (Erudite, Philosophical, Private, or Secret Literary Correspondences), edited by Henri Duranton, François Moureau, and Joachim Schlobach, has endeavored to bring out or describe previously unpublished texts by Pierre Rousseau (sent to Mannheim), Raynal and Chompré, Jacques-Élie Gastelier, Claude Pougin de Saint-Aubin and Aubert, Antoine-Claude Briasson and Nicolas-Charles-Joseph Trublet. Previously unpublished letters by Grimm, La Harpe, Guertoy, Morand, Maillet-Duclairon, and Blin de Saint-Maur are scheduled for publication in the same series.

Together with the advances made by research into the world of 18th-century publishing, the publication of primary sources, largely unknown until now, will allow for greater in-depth study of the complex system of intellectual communication in the age of the Enlightenment, be it printed or handwritten. Apart from its documentary value for scholars of the 18th century, literary correspondence is a reflection of a particular European constellation—a very precise moment in history when rulers and writers of the French language who subscribed to the ideas of the Enlightenment were mutually attracted, for greatly differing subjective reasons. Literary correspondence, together with the French-language press and publications that could be found in every country, bears witness to the extraordinary impact of French culture throughout Europe in the 18th century. No similar phenomenon seems to have existed in other countries or other languages during that era.

JOCHEN SCHLOBACH

See also Correspondence: Overview; Newspapers and Journalism; Republic of Letters

Further Reading

Bray, Bernard, Jochen Schlobach, and Jean Varloot, editors, "La 'Correspondance littéraire' de Grimm et Meister (1754–1813)," *Actes et colloques* 19 (1976)

Funck-Brentano, Frantz, *Les nouvellistes*, Paris: Hachette, 1905; 3rd edition, 1923

Funck-Brentano, Frantz, *Figaro et ses devanciers*, Paris: Hachette, 1909

Grimm, Friedrich Melchior, Freiherr von, *Correspondance littéraire*, edited by Maurice Tourneux, 16 vols., Paris: Garnier, 1877–82; reprint, Nendeln, Liechtenstein: Kraus Reprint, 1968

Krieger, B., "Die literarischen Korrespondenten Friedrichs des Grossen in Paris: Thierot, d'Arnaud, Morand und Grimm," *Hohenzollern-Jahrbuch* 16 (1912)

Moureau, François, editor, *De bonne main: La communication manuscrite au XVIIIᵉ siècle*, Paris: Universitas, and Oxford: Voltaire Foundation, 1993

Schlobach, Jochen, editor, *Correspondances littéraires inédites: Etudes et extraits, suives de Voltairiana*, Paris: Champion, and Geneva, Slatkine, 1987

Cosmopolitanism

Louis Réau has characterized the 18th century as "the century of cosmopolitanism" (see Réau). This judgment, confirmed by numerous documents from the period, can be applied to every part of Europe that came under French influence—from Naples to Copenhagen, and from Saarbrücken to Saint Petersburg—although the meaning of the term "cosmopolitanism" varied, and the motives of those who called themselves world citizens were not always the same. Antoine Furetière's *Dictionnaire universel* (1690; Universal Dictionary) did not yet include the term *cosmopolite* (cosmopolitan) but defined it indirectly in the entry "Patrie" (Homeland) by referring to the Stoic tradition: "A philosopher is everywhere in his own homeland." The *Dictionnaire de Trévoux* (1721; Dictionary of Trévoux) defined a cosmopolitan as "a citizen of the universe" and "a person who is nowhere a foreigner." This definition was founded upon belief in the universality of human nature. However, interest in humankind in general did not necessarily imply openness to the whole world, as "general interest" might instead mean ignoring the diversity of human beings. The perception of otherness could imply toleration or even active brotherliness, or it could lead to a Manichean view. The notion of otherness could just as easily represent sceptical indifference as curiosity or a thirst for the exotic. The *Dictionnaire de l'Académie Française* (1762; Dictionary of the Académie Française) reflected the distrust cosmopolitanism sometimes aroused, describing a cosmopolitan as someone "who adopts no homeland at all" and who "is not a good citizen." These dictionary definitions suggest that attitudes toward cosmopolitanism changed over the course of the 18th century.

From Narcissism to Cosmopolitanism

Owing to the political and cultural hegemony of France under Louis XIV and even under Louis XV, Versailles and Paris became "the model for foreign nations." Yet the assumption of the "universality" of the French culture and language—an idea that underpinned the marquis Caraccioli's *L'Europe française* (1776; French Europe) and was still evident in 1786 in the attitudes of the comte de Rivarol and the Berlin Academy—was only partially related to cosmopolitanism. On the one hand, the advocates of French classicism gladly merged their model with the universalism dear to the Enlightenment. This allowed them to judge other nations according to their own criteria or, in their translations of foreign works, to make cuts and corrections for the sake of clarity or French taste. Such "beautiful but unfaithful" translations were as much an expression of

the narcissism of the French as of their curiosity about the foreign. On the other hand, with the notion of progress, the concept of universalism—the idea that human beings are always and everywhere the same—was stripped of its historical dimension. By accepting that mentalities are conditioned by climate and history, the idea of progress necessarily legitimized the contrast between the civilized and the barbaric, and it was taken for granted that French civilization remained the standard by which other cultures would be measured. For missionaries this contrast between "civilized" and "barbaric" was often linked to that between Christians and pagans. There was sometimes a danger that otherness would be misunderstood, or that the curiosity inherent in cosmopolitanism would be stifled.

Thus, at the outset, the 18th century was scarcely more cosmopolitan than the 17th. Nevertheless, through such periodicals as the *Journal des savants* or the *Acta Eruditorum*, which gave accounts of whatever "in Europe" appeared to be "worthy of [the] curiosity of men of letters," the Republic of Letters had at its disposal an instrument that could broaden the national horizons of its members, even though Latin was rapidly giving way to French or to other vernacular languages, and the perspective of these published accounts was marked by ideology. In the *Mémoires de Trévoux* (1725), the Jesuits denounced the Protestants, the Jansenists, and then the *philosophes*, while Pierre Bayle displayed his scepticism in the *Nouvelles de la République des Lettres* (1684). Huguenots, such as Basnage in the *Histoire des ouvrages des savants* (1687–1709) and Beausobre in the *Bibliothèque germanique*, adopted a heterodox perspective. There were also contacts with foreigners that resulted from the exile of such men as Anthony Hamilton and Viscount Bolingbroke from Britain, and Charles de Marguetel de Saint-Denis de Saint-Évremond, the baron de La Hontan, and Voltaire from France. Thus, despite divergences in opinion, the Republic of Letters became truly pan-European phenomenon. In the *Mercure de France* (1750), Beausobre, like Bayle, declared that "the wise man must be a Cosmopolitan . . . his sole homeland must be wherever good sense and reason reign, and his compatriots, like him, are attached to the pursuit of truth."

The scholarly periodicals were aimed exclusively at specialists, but their cosmopolitan orientation was extended by way of other periodicals and moralistic weeklies that were intended for the middle classes and contained travel narratives and even missionary reports. The *Spectator*, for example, referred to China and the Orient; a writer for the Hamburg *Patriot* (1724–26) recounted recollections of his own voyages to distant lands; and one citizen of Berlin even gave his daily the title *Der Weltbürger* (1741; The World Citizen), for he considered "the whole universe as his homeland and all men as his brothers." In these daily publications, patriotism—whether it was based on English nationalism or on German or Italian regionalism—found an entirely natural complement in cosmopolitan humanism.

One of the first manifestations of European cosmopolitanism was the "grand tour," which took European aristocrats—notably from England—to the Low Countries, France, Switzerland, and Italy. According to the *Encyclopédie,* by leading these travelers to "examine the mores, customs, and genius of other nations, their dominant taste, their arts, their sciences, their manufactures, and their commerce," the grand tour broadened the young aristocrats' horizons, enriched their knowledge and experience, and cured them "of national prejudices." Of course, these journeys were restricted to the wealthy elite, but over the course of the 18th century the bourgeoisie eventually came to imitate the nobility. Béat de Muralt of Switzerland led the way in exploring England; after 1730 Anglophilia became a factor in intellectual emancipation, only to degenerate among the French into Anglomania. For the Germans, meanwhile, interest in England and English culture became a factor in their national emancipation. Scores of young Frenchmen—more or less representative of the manners of their country—swarmed over Europe, but they were too ethnocentric to take an interest in their surroundings and were no more cosmopolitan than the European Francophiles who catered to them.

Indeed, one must distinguish between Francomania and Francophilia. Francomania implied contempt for one's own language and culture; it did not signify a cultural transfer but rather the substitution of the French model for one's national model. This was seen, among other cases, in the examples of Frederick II, king of Prussia, who wrote in French, and the European noblemen who often felt closer to the aristocracy or even the bourgeoisie of France than to their own compatriots. In contrast, Francophilia signified a desire for self-enrichment through knowledge of the courtesy, good taste, lively wit, and literature of France. Christian Thomasius, Horace Walpole, Galliani, Petoefi, and Christoph Martin Wieland all drew inspiration from French culture. In this sense, Francophilia could be the mark of a limited cosmopolitanism, unaccompanied by any interest in other countries.

Comparisons to Other Civilizations

The 18th-century European public had access to an abundance of documentary sources. These included accounts of voyages and reports by explorers, trading companies, and missionaries, notably in the collections edited by Thomas Astley (1743–47) and the abbé Prévost (1746–89). Such writings confronted Europe with the diversity of human types, which the comte de Buffon sought to explain in his *Histoire naturelle de l'homme* (1749–89; Natural History of Man), and with the diversity of mentalities and laws, to which Montesquieu devoted his *De l'esprit des lois* (1748; The Spirit of Laws). At first some of the Jesuits' *Lettres édifiantes et curieuses* (1702–76) discussing the Levant, the Americas, the Indies, and China adopted an apologetic tone, but these reports also brought forth considerable information on the mores, customs, beliefs, and institutions of the countries where missionaries were active, and this helped to broaden the horizons of Europeans. The change in worldviews over time can be seen clearly by comparing Jacques-Bénigne Bossuet with Voltaire. Bossuet's *Discours sur l'histoire universelle* (1681; A Discourse on the History of the Whole World) remains confined to the Judeo-Christian and classical worlds, while Voltaire's *Essai sur les moeurs et l'esprit des nations* (1756; An Essay on Universal History, and the Manners and Spirit of Nations) breaks out of the straitjacket of biblical chronology and places China at the beginning of universal history.

The differences among peoples had been regarded as secondary until this point, but they now appeared to some to be essential. On the one hand, people were simply categorized according to the region in which they lived, following the ancient climatological triad of the North, South, and Temperate Zones. On the other hand, following Buffon, the peoples of the earth were described according to the theory of four races, marked by differences of color and corresponding to the four known continents. However, both these theories also favored Eurocentrism, and the theme of essential difference between the civilized and the barbaric was given a new lease on life in the form of a contrast between the intelligent and the stupid, the beautiful and the ugly (see Meiners).

Two images, more than any others, drew the attention of the European public and gave rise to myths: the "Indians" of America and "New France," who were seen as typical examples of the savage, and China. Father Joseph-François Lafitau (1724) and Father P.-F. de Charlevoix (1744) saw native Americans as beings who were simultaneously good and cruel, as did the abbé Raynal, who exploited this image to denounce slavery in his *Histoire philosophique et politique des établissements et du commerce des Européens dans les deux Indes* (1770; A Philosophical and Political History of the Settlements and Trade of the Europeans in the East and West Indies). Others, such as Father Hennepin (1704), found Native Americans stupid, ignorant, ferocious, idolatrous, and lascivious, going so far as to claim they were cannibals. In contrast, La Hontan

(1703), the comte de Bougainville (1772), and Denis Diderot (1773) contributed to the spread of the myth of the noble savage, so dear to the whole of Europe. In their view, the Native Americans and the Tahitians were better, more adept, stronger, and more sensible than Europeans, and they practiced a natural religion. "Born free" and equal, these noble savages were also happier than civilized people, who were alienated by unnatural conventions, institutions, and morality. This myth reversed the relationship between the civilized and the barbaric: the true barbarian was no longer the savage but the civilized human being. It was with Jean-Jacques Rousseau's *Discours sur les sciences et les arts* (1750; Discourse on the Sciences and Arts) that the change of paradigm took effect: nature, not civilization, should be used as a criterion. Although these two images of the savage were antithetical, both were nonetheless Eurocentric, for neither the critique of barbarism nor the apology for the noble savage considered indigenous peoples on their own terms. In both cases indigenous populations were judged in contrast to European civilization, either to exalt European superiority or as an idyllic, alternative model that exposed the flaws of "civilization."

China, on the other hand, forced Europe to recognize another civilization. The Jesuits, appreciating the sheer length of Chinese history and the morality and virtues of its government, helped erase some of the land's otherness, notably by glossing over the differences between Christianity and Confucianism. No other Far Eastern country received such attention from the educated European public. Relying on information from the Jesuits, Gottfried Wilhelm Leibniz, an avid cosmopolitan, regarded Chinese civilization as equal to that of Europe and hoped for fruitful scientific exchanges between the two. Christian Wolff (1721) placed Confucius on the same level as Moses and the Greek philosophers in order to prove that reason could be a foundation for morality without recourse to revelation. However, Father du Halde (1735) transmitted a quite different image of China, and Montesquieu reproached the missionaries for becoming apologists for the Chinese government and forgetting that honor and virtue were unknown to a people "who cannot be made to do anything unless they are beaten with sticks."

For Montesquieu, as for Raynal, China was no more than a "despotic state" (*De l'esprit des lois*). On the other hand, between 1734 and 1777 Voltaire repeatedly presented China as a model and its emperor as the prototype of the enlightened ruler. Voltaire pointed out that Cam-Hi had proved to be indulgent and open to the sciences of Europe, while his son Hon Ching surpassed "his father in his love for the laws and the public good." After all, Cam-Hi had issued the edict of toleration, which favored Christianity; and his son had

revoked it only because the Christians had shown themselves to be intolerant. In the writings of Voltaire and those who followed in his footsteps, cosmopolitanism thus became a weapon against the despotism and intolerance of European governments.

The fascination with China that Leibniz shared with the Jesuits (despite their religious opinions) provides evidence of a cosmopolitan spirit, as well as of a concern to promote cultural exchanges. However, most of those who were indebted to the Jesuits—Wolff, Montesquieu, Voltaire, Rousseau, the baron d'Holbach, Raynal, and Johann Gottfried von Herder—put their cosmopolitanism at the service of their respective ideologies. In *De l'esprit des lois*, Montesquieu, who in other ways was sincerely cosmopolitan, never refers to China except to prove the appropriateness of his principles, even though he invokes the theory of climates to explain some deviances. Much the same is true of Wolff, who put the wisdom of Confucius at the service of his rationalism in order to liberate morality from the tutelage of theology.

Essentially, 18th-century cosmopolitanism existed in two forms. In one, there was a curiosity about whatever was other, or exotic. At its best, this attitude was accompanied by an acceptance of otherness (as exemplified by the Jesuits). The other type of cosmopolitanism was an expression of dissatisfaction with respect to Europe, in which the non-European was put forward as a model against which the homeland could be criticized in order to encourage reforms. This was the approach taken by Voltaire, Raynal, and many other *philosophes*. In his *Lettres persanes* (1721; Persian Letters), Montesquieu opts for a third way, which is the exact opposite of ethnocentrism and narcissism. He portrays a foreigner observing the acts and gestures of France from a naive perspective and finding strangeness in what appears familiar to the natives. In this way, Montesquieu reveals the inconsistencies and absurdities that custom had made respectable. This satirical genre was highly successful and therefore capable of teaching Europeans to grasp the relative nature of their own criteria. To the extent that travelers compared the mores of the countries they visited with those of their own, this type of account devoted more or less space to information about the Far East. From this point of view, Oliver Goldsmith's periodical, *The Citizen of the World* (1762), deserved its title.

The Rise and Decline of Cosmopolitanism

Cosmopolitanism was in fashion between 1730 and 1760. It was fostered by Freemasonry, which, beginning in 1722 with James Anderson's *The Constitutions of the Free Masons*, enjoined Masons to regard foreigners as brothers. According to Ramsay and the duc d'Antin, the purpose of Freemasonry was to form over time a great universal republic based on equality and fraternity. According to Claude-Adrien Helvétius, in *De l'esprit* (1758; Essays on the Mind and Its Several Faculties), the more nations became "enlightened," the more they would open themselves up to one another. Never before had the periodicals of Europe taken such an interest in foreign literature. Examples can be found in periodicals such as the *Journal étranger* (1754–62), *L'année littéraire* (1754–89), and the *Magazin der italienischen Künste und Litteratur* (1782–92).

Except when Voltaire and the *philosophes* put forward a political or religious countermodel (as with their championing of China, Catherine II, or Frederick II), cosmopolitanism had no political dimension and was compatible with patriotism, even for the Physiocrats. In contrast, with the resurgence of national politics following the Seven Years' War and the American Revolution, cosmopolitanism entered a crisis because patriots took offense at the sight of the *philosophes* eulogizing the philosopher on the throne who was also the enemy of France. Like Charles Palissot and de Belloy, Rousseau attacked "those who claim to be Cosmopolitans, [and] who . . . pride themselves on loving everyone so as to have the right to love no one" (*Du contrat social* [1762; The Social Contract]). Later, in 1771, Rousseau deplored the leveling effect of European cosmopolitanism on the grounds that it erased national differences. Meanwhile, Gotthold Ephraim Lessing castigated French adventurers, but in *Ernst und Falk* (1778–80; Masonic Dialogues) and *Nathan der Weise* (1779; Nathan the Wise) he deplored the fact that human beings confuse the accidental and the essential by showing pride in their nationality when they should instead seek to overcome their national and religious prejudices in order to consider one another members of one great family. Herder, Wieland, Immanuel Kant, and the classicists of Weimar distanced themselves from the excessively political cosmopolitanism of some of the

Encyclopedists and their German disciples, but were prepared to work toward the perfecting of humanity. These writers advocated a slow and organic evolution of the alliance of European nations. Cosmopolitanism then gave way to the armed messianism of the French Revolution, which reduced otherness to a schematic choice between liberty and slavery.

GONTHIER LOUIS FINK

See also Chemistry; Republic of Letters; Salon

Further Reading

Duchet, Michèle, *Anthropologie et histoire au siècle des Lumières: Buffon, Voltaire, Rousseau, Helvétius, Diderot*, Paris: Maspero, 1971

Fink, Gonthier-Louis, "Le cosmopolitisme: Rêve et réalité au siècle des Lumières dans l'optique du dialogue franco-allemand," in *Aufklärung als Mission; La mission des Lumières* [bilingual German-French edition], edited by Werner Schneiders, Marburg, Germany: Hitzeroth, 1993

Hazard, Paul, "Cosmopolite," in *Mélanges d'histoire littéraire, générale et comparée, offerts à Fernand Baldensperger*, vol. 1, Paris: Champion, 1930; reprint, Geneva: Slatkine Reprints, 1972

Meiners, Christoph, *Grundriss der Geschichte der Weltweisheit*, Lemgo: Meyerschen Buchhandlung, 1786

Réau, Louis, *L'Europe française au siècle des Lumières*, Paris: Michel, 1938

Schlereth, Thomas J., *The Cosmopolitan Ideal in Enlightenment Thought: Its Form and Function in the Ideas of Franklin, Hume, and Voltaire, 1694–1790*, Notre Dame, Indiana: University of Notre Dame Press, 1977

Todorov, Tzvetan, *On Human Diversity: Nationalism, Racism, and Exoticism in French Thought*, Cambridge, Massachusetts: Harvard University Press, 1993 (original French edition, 1989)

Counterpoint

The commonly held view that the 18th century witnessed the replacement of a linear conception of music by vertical harmony involves an oversimplification that is unacceptable, even in the context of Jean-Philippe Rameau's theories. Music theory distinguishes at least two forms of counterpoint, one of which existed before

the Enlightenment and continued unaltered throughout the period. In fact, the 18th century merely confirmed the distinction, which had begun with the crisis of 1600 in Renaissance stylistic unity, between Palestrinian counterpoint—or *stylus gravis* (serious style)—and the *stile moderno* (modern style)—or *seconda prattica* (second practice). Rather than transform and adapt counterpoint to the basso continuo, all the writers of the period sought to retain the rigor of the *osservato,* Palestrinian style as a second language, a "sacred" companion to the modern-style or *luxurians* (florid) counterpoint, which was a vehicle for theatrical and spontaneous expression.

The period began with Johann Joseph Fux's *Gradus ad Parnassum* (1725; Steps to Parnassus: The Study of Counterpoint), which definitively laid down the rules of strict counterpoint by replacing baroque imitations in the style of Palestrina's Masses. The *Gradus* was not the product of an original mind, but its pedagogical value made it the starting point for modern teaching. By arranging difficult points in "steps," Fux crystallized the doctrine of five "species" that had been formulated by Angelo Berardi: a single subject in rounds enters into counterpoint with notes of the same length, then with increasingly rapid ones, until a "florid" mixture of all the preceding rhythmic figures is achieved. A gulf of two centuries separated contemporary practice, notably that of Bach, from this *stylus gravis,* which was similar to academic drawing in that it was highly codified. However, from around 1680, composers were no longer obliged to choose between these two languages, as a third option began to open up, a free counterpoint rich in figures (referred to variously as "florid," "common," "comic," or "theatrical"), resulting from a synthesis of the *oratio* (the theatrical imitation of emotions by dramatic speech) and the *harmonia* (basso continuo).

Like poetry and the theatre, counterpoint was drawn into the Quarrel between the Ancients and the Moderns. What was at stake in the battles between Giulio Cesare Arresti, Maurizio Cazzati, Marc'Antonio Ziani, and Giovanni Paolo Colonna, on the one hand, and Archangelo Corelli and Liberati, on the other, was whether to grant autonomy to this type of harmonically saturated counterpoint, which some writers regarded as an empirical practice with no rational method. This freer form of counterpoint, having been revived by Cazzati and brought to a certain level of perfection by Archangelo Corelli, maintained its level of energy throughout the first three decades of the 18th century. It found interpreters of renown in such figures as Agostino Steffani, George Frideric Handel, Antonio Caldara, Fux, and Giovanni Bononcini, before reaching its apogee in the work of Johann Sebastian Bach.

"Luxuriant" or "florid" counterpoint was defined by the reintroduction of tonality into contrapuntal thought. Tonal harmony, combined with counterpoint, succeeded in absorbing most of the dissonant intervals that the basso continuo of the early baroque had not been capable of integrating. Some writers continued to devote separate chapters to counterpoint and to the fig-

ured bass, while others tried to abolish the distinction. With the intention of reconciling his harmonic thinking with counterpoint, Charles Masson reduced the modes to the major and the minor (*Nouveau traité des règles pour la composition de la musique* [1699; New Treatise of Rules for Composing Music]). Rameau himself thought of the tonal unity of chords as the result of a regulated alternation of sound qualities that succeeded one another over time. From this time forward, the destinies of counterpoint and harmony became one. The linear conception was retained for as long as it succeeded in holding in check the vertical tendency of the figured bass, as it did for Corelli and Johann Sebastian Bach. But it was eventually dissolved into pure homophony, when harmony came to absorb the last remnants of the polarity between melody and figured bass. Rameau's work of systematization merely accelerated this process.

Up to this point, basso continuo and counterpoint alike ignored the inversion of intervals, which was regarded as equally "fundamental." Demonstrating that most inversions were no more than three aspects of the same chord, Rameau arranged all of them along a virtual theoretical line, the fundamental bass. Independent of real writing, this ideal line eventually opened up new possibilities for voice leading. With its subsequent clarification of the texture of modulations, the fundamental bass could only encourage the stylistic upheaval that occurred around 1730, in "Neapolitan" opera as well as in the newly developing genres of the sonata and the symphony. Opera composers began to envisage the possibility of a musical dialectic that could express all the elements of the drama—intrigue, conflict between characters, dialogue, and the unfolding of the action at the present moment—by means of a conflict between the sound forms developing over time. All the innovations required for the realization of this ideal—periodic phrasing, pure homophony, the definition of vast areas of tonal stability—sooner or later came into conflict with the density and static equilibrium of contrapuntal writing. Pure homophony, which triumphed in "Neapolitan" opera and among the symphonists of the Mannheim School, eliminated the independence of the voices and reduced the last remains of the polarity between melody and fundamental progressions to a homogeneous whole. The proliferation of formulas for realizing the fundamental bass (i.e., creating music without actual thematic value), formulas that were increasingly adopted in order to dilute the colorful density of the harmonic progressions of the late baroque, had a corrosive effect on linear voice leading.

This process of development in the late baroque, which was determined by a purely musical logic, corresponded, on the aesthetic level, met with hostility from the *philosophes.* Their discussion of the value of counterpoint—a crucial episode in the Quarrel between the Ancients and the Moderns—centered on the parallels between French music and Italian music, parallels that were repeatedly drawn within French aesthetics. In his *Comparaison de la musique italienne et de la musique françoise* (1704–06; Comparison of Italian Music and French Music), Jean-Laurent Le Cerf de La Viéville draws a contrast between the "ancient," "natural," and moving simplicity of Jean-Baptiste Lully's music and the "scientific" contrapuntal complexity of Italian sonatas. Fifty years later, drawn into the controversy between his own supporters and those of Lully, Rameau replaced the Italians and the contrapuntal science of his precursors with his knowledge of harmony as the latest innovation. Yet the clichés remained unchanged, and the confusion between harmony and counterpoint was more fashionable than ever. In the terminology of the *Encyclopédie*, in which the *philosophes* tried very hard to dissociate music from mathematics, the word "counterpoint" is often used as a synonym for "science," "complexity," and "artifice" and is thrown into conflict with the movements of the soul, melody, and sincere feelings, which are inexpressible in words. Jean-Jacques Rousseau opposed this acoustic "trompe-l'oeil," which divided the semantic unity of the poetic text into a polyphony of meaning, and in doing so he revived an old debate that the theorists of opera had taken from Plato. According to the article "Fugue" in his *Dictionnaire de musique* (1768; Dictionary of Music), fugues are "gothic and barbarous" creations of a bygone order, products of the idle speculations of the Dark Ages, and they "generally make music more noisy than pleasant." Similarly, in the article "Canon," Rousseau declares that canons have no merits apart from "taking a lot of trouble to write."

These ideas, conveyed by the just developing historiography of music, found echoes elsewhere in Europe. In his *Essay on Musical Expression* (1752), Charles Avison praises the melodic inventiveness of Nicola Porpora, Bononcini, and Giovanni Battista Pergolesi but condemns the contrapuntal excesses of Palestrina, Thomas Tallis, Gregorio Allegri, Giacomo Carissimi, and Agostino Steffani. In Germany, where the crisis of 1600 had not truly taken place, pure music was being fully developed and constructivism was a part of musical practice. Relations between the upholders of the past and the proponents of the new ideas were particularly strained in Germany. In 1745 Johann Adolph Scheibe used his periodical to attack the composer whom many regard as the greatest musical master of all time, comparing the colorful density of Johann Sebastian Bach's style to that of the baroque poet Daniel Casper von Lohenstein, who was renowned for his pompous language, rich in images and with vague meaning but colorful effects.

Eventually, Joseph Haydn, Wolfgang Amadeus Mozart, and Ludwig van Beethoven took the initiative and reconquered the past after mastering the present. The history of counterpoint resulted in books summarizing its principles such as Johann Philipp Kirnberger's *Kunst des reinen Satzes in der Musik* (1774; The Art of Strict Musical Composition) and the *Gründliche Anweisung zur Composition* (1790; Fundamentals of Composition) by Beethoven's teacher Johann Georg Albrechtsberger. Such musical summaries were part of Father Giovanni Battista Martini's library, where the young Mozart studied counterpoint by using the exercises assembled and arranged in their historical order in Martini's *Esemplare o sia saggio fondamentale pratico di contrapunto* (1774–75; Examples of Celebrated Composers of Fundamental Practice of Counterpoint).

BRENNO BOCCADORO

See also Harmony and Melody; Music

Further Reading

Chailley, Jacques, *Traité historique d'analyse musicale*, Paris: Leduc, 1951

Dahlhaus, Carl, *Studies on the Origin of Harmonic Tonality,* translated by Robert O. Gjerdingen, Princeton, New Jersey: Princeton University Press, 1990 (original German edition, 1968)

McHose, Allen Irvine, *Contrapuntal Harmonic Technique of the Eighteenth Century,* New York: Appleton-Century-Crofts, 1947

Counter-Revolution

The Counter-Revolution, which came into being in 1789, was in large part the heir to the Anti-Enlightenment and to various other major trends such as historical conservatism, enlightened despotism, and integral absolutism (see Godechot). In its most radical form, the counterrevolutionary doctrine condemned not only the principles, acts, forces, and consequences of the Revolution, but also the main philosophical concepts of the Enlightenment, which it regarded as the deplorable cause of the catastrophe. The concrete effects of counterrevolutionary doctrine followed a fairly straightforward sequence, being manifested initially in the political sphere and then in armed conflict. The theoretical arguments of the Counter-Revolution, in contrast, were put forward at various times, originally in England, Switzerland, and Germany, and later taken up in émigré circles. The theoretical Counter-Revolution was complex from the outset, reflecting a range of different opinions, concepts, ideological and political perspectives, and attitudes toward the Enlightenment. Yet, despite their differences, counterrevolutionary theorists were united in their outright rejection of the abstract conception of man that was the basis of both the revolutionary notion of a constitution and the belief in man's right to take charge of his destiny and reshape the course of history. Similarly, counterrevolutionary thinkers were unanimous in their resolve to understand the causes and the progress of the Revolution, and they all tried to predict how it would end.

In the first phase of the French Revolution, none of the proponents of the Counter-Revolution disputed the need to reform the French monarchy (see the royal declaration of 23 June 1789); even the Revolution's most resolute opponents sought at first to defend the ancien régime—although not its abuses. A decisive shift came when the Third Estate declared itself the National Assembly. This democratic turning point transformed the very nature of sovereignty, and the Counter-Revolution could now be born. The first aristocratic emigration, following the flight of the comte d'Artois, who was quickly joined by monarchists such as Jean-Joseph Mounier and Trophime-Gérard de Lally-Tollendal, sparked off a series of counterrevolutionary schemes and maneuvers that proved ineffectual in both military and, as far as the immediate future was concerned, political terms. Counterrevolutionary ideas, in contrast, were immensely influential and even decisive throughout the 19th century, and they articulated a fundamental hostility to the modern world.

Elements of counterrevolutionary philosophy can be found in the flood of pamphlets and newspaper articles that were inspired by the first important debates in the Estates General, as well as in the comte de Rivarol's articles in his *Journal politique national* and in the writings of the comte de Ferrand, who, in 1790, was one of the first to put forward a conspiracy theory involving the duc d'Orléans, Jacques Necker, and the marquis de Lafayette. The notion of a conspiracy had already been adumbrated and combined with providentialist theory by the abbé Augustin Barruel in 1789. Some years later, in his *Mémoires pour servir à l'histoire du jacobinisme* (1798; Memoirs for a History of Jacobinism), Barruel took the conspiracy theory even further, denouncing the plotting of *philosophes* and Freemasons. Mention should also be made of such deputies as Jacques-Antoine-Marie de Cazalès and Montlosier, who in 1791 the published his *De la nécessité d'opérer une contre-révolution en France* (On the Necessity of Carrying Out a Counter-Revolution in France). Extreme views were also expressed by the comte d'Antraigues, the abbé Maury, and Mirabeau-Tonneau. In his *Des principes et des causes de la Révolution en France* (1790; On the Principles and Causes of the Revolution in France), Gabriel Sénac de Meilhan provided an objective analysis of the exhausted state of the monarchy, arguing that the spread of Enlightenment ideas beyond the social circles in which they could be truly understood was one of the causes of the upheaval. François-René de Chateaubriand's position, outlined later in his *Essai sur les révolutions* (1797; An Historical, Political, and Moral Essay on Revolutions, Ancient and Modern), is complex and richly suggestive. By comparing a series of different revolutions, Chateaubriand developed a cyclical conception of history based on a law of perpetual change; like its predecessors, the French Revolution had been driven by a mysterious urge to build and destroy. Human history, he argued, is nothing more than the force of events. Rejecting politics, Chateaubriand extolled the flight from civilization. The individual's inner self is tormented by the forces that trouble societies; existential malaise is a product of history. It is necessary to endeavor to recapture primitive freedom in relation to nature. In this respect, the *Essai* prefigures Chateaubriand's *Le génie du Christianisme ou beautés de la religion chrétienne* (1802; The Genius of Christianity; or, The Spirit and Beauties of the Christian Religion), his novel *René* (1802; René), and the tenets of romanticism.

London and Geneva: Burke and Mallet du Pan, or the Liberal Counter-Revolution

Edmund Burke's *Reflections on the Revolution in France* (1790) was the first genuinely counterrevolutionary interpretation of recent events to achieve international prominence. The work was immediately translated into French and went through 11 editions in less than a year. Already famous as the author of a book on the sublime (1757), this Irish-born Whig member of Parliament condemned the Revolution in the form of an answer to those in England who had drawn a parallel between English history and the course of events across the Channel. In the name of conservative liberalism, Burke contrasted the wisdom of the English Revolution of 1688—which had restored the nation to itself—to the madness of the French Revolution, its voluntarist dizziness, its ideal of a tabula rasa, and the dictatorship of reason. For Burke, politics consists of a series of practical adjustments within a real society, a society built upon custom and made up of individuals guided by their own interests. In this society individual differences are settled by the state in the light of a constitution fashioned over the centuries and representing the heritage accumulated by successive generations. The French Revolution, in contrast, was based on the notion of the abstract individual; it was therefore incapable of creating anything that would last. Burke rejected the principle of the sovereignty of the nation based on belief in the inherent right of human beings to participate in the political process. According to Burke, this belief, along with the dogma of equality, is the source of democratic utopianism. If rights exist, they are those of people, such as safety. If there is a contract, it concerns each nation, is consolidated over time, and reflects the original contract between God and humankind. The state appears, therefore, both as a hierarchical reality and as a form of mediation between private interests and that hierarchy, which since it is both natural and supernatural, will endure. It is not hard to see why the German romantics were attracted to such a philosophy.

A very different counterrevolutionary thesis was developed by Jacques Mallet du Pan. An advocate of compromise during the Geneva revolution of 1782, Mallet later moved to Paris, where he became the political editor of the *Mercure de France* from 1789 through 1792. He was highly critical of the indivisibility of the Declaration of Rights, which he thought would give rise to unavoidable excesses. Viewing the October Days of 1789 as the first manifestation of "the force of events," Mallet distinguished between, on the one hand, the legitimate revolution that had been made necessary by the collapse of an exhausted monarchy (see Sénac de Meilhan) and that would lead to a new balance of political power, and, on the other hand, the social revolution that constituted a threat to property. As a true son of the Enlightenment, Mallet continued to place his trust in reason and human perfectibility—principles he believed had been corrupted by revolutionary folly and the monstrous logic of events. His *Considérations sur la nature de la Révolution en France et sur les causes qui en prolongèrent la durée* (Considerations on the Nature of the Revolution in France and on the Causes That Prolonged It), published in 1793 when he was in exile, earned Mallet a position as adviser to several European monarchs. Although he was close to the monarchists, he did his utmost to advocate the implementation of a constitutional monarchy in France.

Toward Romanticism: Counterrevolutionary Germany

It was in Germany, perhaps, that the arguments surrounding the French Revolution became the fiercest, fed as they were by criticisms of the *Aufklärung* (the German Enlightenment), by the first stirrings of romanticism, and by the influence of Burke. With its notion of the *Volkgeist* (spirit of the people), Johann Gottfried von Herder's antirationalist thought, developed notably in his *Ideen zur Philosophie der Geschichte der Menschheit* (1784–91; Outlines of a Philosophy of the History of Man), provided a whole battery of concepts for the German theorists opposed to universalism. For Herder, the rehabilitation of prejudices and religion goes hand in hand with relativism and historicism. Drawing upon Gottfried Wilhelm Leibniz's model, Herder described cultures as collective individuals, which, paradoxically, took him to the heart of the Enlightenment problematic.

Other philosophers and commentators also made fundamental criticisms. Even before Burke's *Reflections on the Revolution in France* became known, Friedrich Heinrich Jacobi, for whom the truth of rationalism lay in the philosophy of Baruch Spinoza, had opposed the principles of legal humanism; he believed it was absurd to posit any rational basis for the notion of universal law (*Lettre à La Harpe* [5 May 1790, unfinished and unpublished at the time; Letter to La Harpe]). In June 1790 Justus Möser published in the *Berlinische Monatschrift* an essay entitled "Über das Recht der Menschheit, als den Grund der neuen Französischen Constitution" (On the Rights of Man as the Basis of the New French Constitution), in which he drew contrasts between the abstract individual and real people living within a mutually dependent, hierarchical order, and between Reason and the weight of History. In his *Politische Betrachtungen über die Französische Revolution* (1790; Political Considerations on the French Revolution), Ernst Brandes, no doubt influenced by one of Burke's House of Commons speeches tailored to support his own thesis, rejected the idea of a constitution based on abstract speculation and proposed the English constitution as a model. Brandes did, however, judge that the Revolution had been necessary because of the abuses of royal power. In 1793 Brandes's friend August Wilhelm Rehberg published a collection of his own articles, written since 1790, under the title *Untersuchungen über die Französische Revolution* (Research on the French Revolution). Taking a position close to Burke's, Rehberg carried over into the political sphere the philosophical criticisms to which the *Aufklärung* had been subjected, notably by Friedrich Heinrich Jacobi and Moses Mendelssohn. Rehberg held that humanity is only conceivable in terms of succeeding generations, in that any contract involves both the past and the future. He thus opposed constitutions and extolled the experience of those who conduct public affairs as a result of the unequal capacities of individuals.

Burke changed the German theoretical landscape. Brandes followed directly in his wake with *Über einige bisherige Folgen der Französischen Revolution in Rücksicht auf Deustschland* (1792; On Several Consequences of the French Revolution with Respect to Germany). Other direct followers were Rehberg and the translator Friedrich von Gentz, who was known as "the German Burke." Johann Gottlieb Fichte took up the defense of the French Revolution in his *Beitrage zur Berichtigung der Urteile des Publikums über die Französische Revolution* (1793; Considerations Meant to Rectify the Judgment of the Public on the French Revolution).

Burke's thought had a double influence on German philosophy. For the proponents of the historical school of right, when combined with the irrationalist theses of Herder and Justus Möser, Burkean philosophy was a rich source for German romanticism, which would become in part a revolt against the modern world. At the same time, traces of his thinking can be found in Georg Wilhelm Friedrich Hegel's philosophy of right, in which the defense of tradition, together with a critique of contractualism, is transformed into a new theory of Reason in History, in which Hegel defines law in opposition to custom. Burke therefore played a role in the development of German idealism.

Burke's translator, Gentz, who later became an adviser to Prince Metternich, had begun by supporting the Revolution. While his thinking has much in common with anticonstructivist historicism, Gentz remained faithful to the notion of human progress and therefore cannot be considered a true follower of German romanticism. One might even speak of a "Gentzian" model that recognizes the principle of the rights of man as having political significance and influence; for Gentz, the revolutionaries' error had been to elevate them into social rights since, following Immanuel Kant, a distinction must be made between right and morality. The "Gentzian" view reaffirms the ideal of a rationalization of society and refuses to endorse a historicism that negates human freedom.

The Theocratic Counter-Revolution: Bonald and Maistre

The French theocrats, who took virtually nothing from Burke's philosophy, set out to refute not only the Revolution but the whole concept of a constitution as a contract drawn up between society and the government in power. Although frequently linked because of their radical positions, the vicomte Louis de Bonald and Joseph de Maistre in fact held quite different views. In his first and most fundamental book, *Théorie du pouvoir politique et religieux démontrée par le raisonnement et par l'histoire* (1796; Theory of Political and Religious Power As Proved by Reasoning and History), the émigré Bonald, after an introductory discussion of the origins and nature of the revolutionary phenomenon, reconstructs the history of power and traces the lines of force that organize society, focusing on factors of cohesion and decline. He argues that divine revelation has conferred on social man—as opposed to the abstract individual—a primitive type of law embodied in language. History is articulated around Christ's mediation, which is the true basis for the constitution. This renders any constitution or declaration based on abstract reasoning illegitimate. History, of which absolute monarchy founded on divine right represented the culminating point, had achieved a state of harmony between a stable power and a hierarchical, organic society composed of human beings defined by their social relations. To undo the constitution is to undermine order. The causes of the Revolution were at once religious (the Reformation), intellectual (the philosophy of the Enlightenment), and socioeconomic (increased trade and money, disruption of the social structure). The Revolution could either instigate a genuine restoration or set in motion a catastrophic cycle of events that would lead to the Apocalypse. Bonald's theory is meant to be all-encompassing, and within its complex organization of concepts (constitution, conservation, nature) and principles of integration (society, power, religion), it also defines literature as "the expression of society."

Joseph de Maistre, a subject of the king of Sardinia who had emigrated in 1792, worked out a providentialist interpretation of the French Revolution. His *Considérations sur la France* (Considerations on France), published in Switzerland in 1797, together with later works such as *Du Pape* (1811; The Pope) and *Les soirées de Saint-Petersbourg* (1821; Saint Petersburg Dialogues), had throughout the 19th century an immense influence that is still not adequately recognized. According to Maistre, "Providence is never more palpable than when a higher force, replacing the actions of men, acts alone. This is what we see at this time." Maistre brought to counterrevolutionary thinking a visionary dimension, and he asserted that the

Revolution might seem an incomprehensible cataclysm, but the blood shed because of it would lead to a regenerated future. Like Bonald, he was sympathetic to Jacques-Bénigne Bossuet's conclusions in the *Discours sur l'histoire universelle* (1681; A Discourse on the History of the World), but he gave them a weight of meaning that was at once dazzling, dramatic, and poetic. Taking up a suggestion that had been made by Louis-Claude de Saint-Martin and other illuminists, Maistre defined the Revolution as a punishment decreed from on high, all the more terrible in that France, though corrupted by evil, "exercises over Europe a veritable magistracy." Paradoxically, the exemplary violence of the Revolution, which devoured its own children, contributed to the greatness of France by provoking an unavoidable Counter-Revolution, which, "in contrast to the Revolution," would unfold according to the divine will. From this point, Maistre built up a "metapolitics" that has been described as a modern *episteme* in direct line with the Western Christian tradition. Outside this Christian vision of history and order, there can be nothing but the nonbeing of chaos. Only the temporal power of a monarchy based on the unquestionable authority of divine right and the spiritual sovereignty of the pope can secure social and individual happiness. Since the Reformation, the West had been undermined.

While not endorsing Bonald's organicist sociology, Maistre shared with him a concern to restore a dogmatic religion that would defend the religious and political principle of authority—an authority that necessarily took precedence over liberty. In Bonald's phrase, the Declaration of the Rights of Man should be replaced by a Declaration of the Rights of God. No rejection of the Enlightenment could be more absolute than this phrase, which brings together Maistre, the theorist of the mystery inherent in the legitimacy of sovereign power based on transcendence, and Bonald, for whom the essential weapon was analytic reasoning.

On Counter-Revolution and Its Influence throughout Europe

Although these various counterrevolutionary theoreticians turned their attention toward France in particular, they also influenced their own countries and Europe as a whole. Thus, in Spain and Italy, French counterrevolutionary thinking fed the reaction against the Enlightenment—a reaction that played an important role in the political history of the two nations.

Burke's *Reflections on the Revolution in France* is the most important work in this respect. This counter-revolutionary guide divided English opinion. The Tories and some of the Whigs saw themselves in Burke's statements, but the radical Whigs violently attacked his positions, using the criticisms of either Mary Wollstonecraft or MacIntosh. William Godwin, Jeremy Bentham, and James Mill also joined the battle, as well as Thomas Paine, who published his *Rights of Man* in 1791. Pierre Manent, the French specialist in liberalism, has interpreted the English debate as the symbol of future conflicts between the "right" and the "left" that would divide societies tending toward liberalism, insofar as the "right" and the "left" remained within the system of liberal representation, the former leaning toward conservatism and the latter toward progressivism.

Burke's impact in France was less certain than in England or Germany, at least in the period immediately following publication of his *Reflections*. Maistre and Bonald read him, but although they praised the strength of his work, they did not find a deep common ground between Burke and the essential points of their own doctrine. During the 19th century the seminal importance of Burke's work slowly became apparent. Hippolyte Taine, in particular, found in Burke's writings the confirmation of political and social naturalism, which Taine held up against abstract idealism and the metaphysics of the French Revolution, and which influenced his *Origines de la France contemporaine* (1876–91; Origins of Contemporary France).

The entirely negative picture of France painted by Burke irritated even those members of the monarchist right who wanted an English-style monarchy. Nascent French liberalism was unable to accept Burke's fundamental conservatism, which some used in order to deny any liberalism on his part, as though traditionalism and liberalism were antagonistic to such a degree. While they were in agreement with Burke in viewing the French Revolution as the starting point of another history, 19th-century liberals tended to claim the Revolution as an inaugural and founding event. Liberal historians, from François-Pierre-Guillaume Guizot to Alexis de Tocqueville, interpreted the French Revolution as a necessity (as did the famous fatalist school invoked by Chateaubriand), including the Revolution's surpassing of the primary objectives of the Estates General. On the one hand, there was an apologia for continuity, on the other hand, a demand for a radical break. A misunderstanding thus arose between French liberalism and British theory. In contemporary French liberal thinking, Burke's positions were nevertheless increasingly taken into account.

However, Bonald's ideas, which at first disturbed the ultraroyalists, found their way, through positivism, into the fascistic doctrine of Charles Maurras and Action Française, thus influencing the emergence of the modern political "right" in France (see Sirinelli). Bonald's ideas were also one of the sources of modern political sociology. Maistre's positions can still be found in mystical interpretations of the French Revolution, as well as in literature.

GÉRARD GENGEMBRE

See also Anti-Enlightenment; Prejudice

Further Reading

Beik, Paul Harold, *The French Revolution Seen from the Right: Social Theories in Motion, 1789–1799,* Philadelphia, Pennsylvania: American Philosophical Society, 1956

Burke, Edmund, *Reflections on the Revolution in France,* London: Dodsley, 1790; edited by Conor Cruise O'Brien, Baltimore, Maryland: Penguin Books, 1968

Butler, Marilyn, editor, *Burke, Paine, Godwin, and the Revolution Controversy,* Cambridge and New York: Cambridge University Press, 1984

Cobban, Alfred, *Edmund Burke and the Revolt against the Eighteenth Century: A Study of the Political and Social Thinking of Burke, Wordsworth, Coleridge, and Southey,* New York: Macmillan, and London: Allen and Unwin, 1929; 2nd edition, London: Allen and Unwin, and New York: Barnes and Noble, 1960

The French Revolution and the Creation of Modern Political Culture, vol. 3, *The Transformation of Political Culture, 1789–1848,* edited by François Furet and Mona Ozouf, Oxford and New York: Pergamon Press, 1989

Gengembre, Gérard, *La contre-révolution, ou, l'histoire désespérante,* Paris: Imago, 1989

Godechot, Jacques, *The Counter-Revolution: Doctrine and Action, 1789–1804,* New York: Fertig, 1971; London: Routledge and K. Paul, 1972 (original French edition, 1961)

Hampsher-Monk, Iain, *The Political Philosophy of Edmund Burke,* London and New York: Longman, 1987

Klinck, David, *The French Counterrevolutionary Theorist, Louis de Bonald (1754–1840),* New York: Lang, 1996

Lebrun, Richard A., *Joseph de Maistre: An Intellectual Militant,* Kingston, Ontario: McGill-Queen's University Press, 1988

Popkin, Jeremy D., *The Right-Wing Press in France, 1792–1800,* Chapel Hill: University of North Carolina Press, 1980

Roberts, James, *The Counter-Revolution in France, 1787–1830,* New York: St. Martin's Press, and London: Macmillan Educational, 1990

Sénac de Meilhan, Gabriel, *Des principes et des causes de la Révolution en France,* London and Paris: s.n., 1790; edited by Michel Delon, Paris: Les Éditions Desjonquères, 1987

Sirinelli, Jean-François, editor, *Histoire des droites en France,* 3 vols., Paris: Gallimard, 1992

Sutherland, D.M.G., *France, 1789–1815: Revolution and Counterrevolution,* London: Fontana, 1985; New York: Oxford University Press, 1986

Court, French Royal

In Enlightenment France the royal court was no longer characterized by the splendors of the system of Louis XIV. However, despite the changes it had undergone, the court continued to show a certain vitality during the 18th century. The dictionaries of that era enable us to understand how contemporaries saw the court. César Pierre Richelet's dictionary (1690) presents the court as "the place where the prince is . . . where the sovereign makes his residence." At the same time, the term also refers to "the prince and his courtiers, the body of courtiers. All the people of quality and wit who make up the court of the prince. The court is subject to his will." The *Dictionnaire de Trévoux* (1740; Dictionary of Trévoux) reveals an approach that is not fundamentally different:

[The court] refers to the place where the sovereign is, and his following. In this sense, the court is composed of princes and princesses, ministers, lords, and officials attached by their position with relation to the sovereign. . . . The word "court" is especially taken to mean the king and his council. It is in this sense that one speaks of waiting for, and receiving the orders of, the court.

However, the entry adds, "'court' can also be taken to mean the air or manner of life of the court."

These definitions, which are fairly representative of their time, show the range of the term and also underline the contradictory perception of the whole. Mindful of such contradictory attitudes, Trévoux cites the opinions of several well-known authors:

"It is at court that the passions are excited and conspire against innocence" (Fléchier). "Deceitfulness passes for a virtue at court" (Arnauld). "The court is an excerpt of the whole kingdom: everything in it that is pure and fine is to be found there" (Saint-Évremond). "Note that there is indeed a difference between a man or woman at court and a man or woman who is a member of the court. A woman at court is usually a scheming woman. A woman of the court is one whose birth or employment attaches her to the court" (Bouhours). "The mind of a woman of the court is more active than that of a peasant woman" (Port-Royal).

The court thus appears to have been a space in which multiple elements intersected. It was, of course, a physical space because it was a place. It was a social space marked by various forms of interpersonal relations, and where different cultural transactions took place. Finally, it was a political space, its institutional and symbolic dimensions structured by the practices that it authorized. As the physical center of various social and political conflicts, the court was an arena in which the stakes could be very high.

First and foremost, the court existed in one place, the château of Versailles. The fixing of this location at a relatively late point in history reflected Louis XIV's wish to establish the court in a space with specific features (which he gradually completed). The king envisioned Versailles as an aesthetic analogue of his political system. At the center of the model was the royal bedchamber, the essential locus of representation and the physical and metaphorical heart of an ensemble that was gradually put in place during the reign of Louis XIV. This ensemble included the château itself, the ancillary buildings that accommodated the courtiers, the gardens used for royal festivals, and the new town that was built up around the château.

During the 18th century certain architectural modifications were effected at Versailles, reflecting contemporaneous social and political changes. New forms of sociability arose, leading to the creation of smaller, more intimate spaces; these smaller spaces, in turn affected court etiquette. The royal bedchamber remained at the heart of the system, but it lost its importance under Louis XV, who preferred to conduct his affairs in the château's *petits appartements* (small chambers), in which a different form of sensibility was expressed. The traditional "mechanisms" of courtly etiquette were preserved, but they became less effective and essentially became, at least in part, a kind of machinery operating in a vacuum.

As a social space, the court provided permanent housing for different groups situated in varying degrees of proximity to the core group made up of the king and his close relatives. Next came *la maison du roi* (the royal household), which included the households of the princes of the blood, together with the officials who provided for the sovereign's various needs and numerous members of the staff—servants, craftsmen, and other specialized workers. This latter group was indispensable to the daily functioning of the court as a whole, and it also allowed the court to function as an essential economic component in the trade of luxury goods and other rare items. Finally, the court extended to the nobility, for whom immediate proximity to the sovereign was essential. Nobles flocked to the palace, trying to obtain lodging there and to secure a role in the various ceremonies that marked the major events in the monarch's day.

Originally little more than an organizing framework for the daily life of the king, the court was gradually transformed into a power structure that exercised political and social control. This political dimension of the court arose from the interconnections between the royal household and the nascent apparatus of the state. Although the strengthening of royal power and the emergence of an absolutist state brought about a clearer separation between these two entities, the political function of the court did not diminish in importance. Increasingly, the court functioned as a vast network of bonds of dependency, a centralized system in which the sovereign played an essential role. The king held a monopoly on fiscal and military power, and therefore all state functions relating to the exercise of such power were ultimately answerable to the monarch. His decisions and even his everyday gestures played an essential role in the development and spread of political and social norms. The king's personality constituted a primary element in the system, and his responsibility in the workings of the system as a whole was enormous, both in the form that system took at the zenith of courtly power, under Louis XIV, and later, with some modifications, under Louis XV and Louis XVI.

The court became a mode of political regulation of the social body, expressed through rituals and symbolic practices that made increasing demands upon the courtiers. Being in the king's entourage no longer sufficed to ensure one's position at court; courtiers were required to respect and integrate the new norms of behavior that the sovereign established. Court etiquette was the expression of this imposed discipline. Together with its attendant pomp and circumstance, court etiquette served as the most visible sign of the primary role of the sovereign and of his power. However, etiquette was also a sign of certain restrictions that were imposed on the sovereign; he created rules that were valid for all, and, at least in part, he also had to respect them. Any decision the king made to change the rules was a sign of his sovereign power, a means of rendering the system active and making it into a mode of government and regulation, but he had to be careful not to make changes that would overtly transgress the rules that he himself had set. The entire ceremonial system formed an unstable social structure that reacted to the slightest tremor and that had to be continuously monitored and brought under control. Changes in etiquette, which manifested a desire to civilize and control the mores of the court, could proceed only by successive small changes if such changes were not to cause a profound upheaval in the equilibrium of the structure as a whole.

The refinement of the rules for life at court was part of the process that Norbert Élias, referring to the curia (a medieval king's court), has called the "curialization" of the noble elite (see Élias, 1983). This process was already well advanced in the 18th century, and it entailed some seemingly contradictory developments. Profound changes occurred within the aristocracy, which was affected by an increasingly extensive redistribution of its functions and the integration and rapid growth of new social classes. The changes also entailed the loss of aristocratic military and economic independence and a general decline of the "duty to revolt" that had characterized the early modern period. Eventually, the aristocracy wished to regain a certain degree of autonomy, within the framework of an acceptance of this loss of independence, and this desire led them to contest the absolutism of the king. Summing up its history, one may say that the French royal court was an entity with many potentialities. Established in the 16th century, it attained maturity in the 17th century, and during the 18th century it entered a period of reorganization and change.

One important aspect of the court's development in the 18th century was its relative lack of openness. Until the beginning of the century Versailles had remained quite accessible, and in the age of Louis XIV the congestion there had been legendary. Versailles had been open to the whole world, and one could see courtiers rubbing shoulders with simple onlookers, common tradespeople, and even people "of dubious morality" (who could rent swords at the gates of the court of honor and thus obtain the right to enter the interior of the palace).

Under new regulations introduced in 1732 and 1759, the palace was not physically closed off, but restrictions were imposed in the form of etiquette. "Honors of the court"—that is, opportunities to be officially presented to the king—were limited to members of the 462 families who could claim nobility prior to 1400, or others who were exempted from this requirement either by royal favor or because the family heads exercised certain responsibilities. The participation of the nobility in court life became more selective, and only a limited number enjoyed the privilege of being in the king's immediate entourage. Even though presence at court remained the ideal for a large part of the nobility—in particular the lower- and middle-ranking nobility of the provinces—the honors of the court became, more than ever, a criterion for discrimination within the aristocracy. There were those who had the right to be presented at court because of the authenticity of their title, and others who tried to slip in by using a wide variety of stratagems. For example, the baronne d'Oberkirch, who had been presented to the king once as a special favor, hoped to obtain a second presentation based on the titles she actually held.

The regulations of 1759 thus contributed to the closing of the court and were a reaffirmation of the supreme authoritative status of the monarchy. These regulations were integrated into the perpetually unstable edifice of court society, and by generating mechanisms of inclusion/exclusion they reinforced the tensions that existed both within the nobility and on its margins. The regulations also led to the development of various personal or family strategies to obtain presentation to the king and to land a secure position within court society. Satisfying the formal conditions for presentation before the king was not always sufficient, and other means of gaining access to the honors of the court became crucial. This implied infiltrating the networks of relationships that made access possible. Court coteries became more and more important, and the memoirs of contemporaries—such as those of the duc de Luynes, the comte de Tilly, the baronne d'Oberkirch, and the duc de Croÿ—emphasize the growing role of the networks that aspiring persons had to join if they wanted to fulfill their ambitions. There were the official networks, comprising the offices and positions of the princes and dignitaries who were close to the king, and unofficial networks made up of the king's ministers and mistresses. Madame de Pompadour, for example, wielded her authority for nearly 20 years. The coteries that allocated power were also at the center of a major financial redistribution. This redistribution of wealth took a number of forms, from the royal pensions that the most highly placed could expect to receive—such as the 91,000 livres paid to the baron de Breteuil in 1789—to more devious routes, such as the discreet payment of gratuities, which were made on more specific occasions but were just as substantial. The image of the king as granting and dispensing riches remained a powerful reality, and a direct link was maintained between the court nobility and the sovereign.

The emergence of a more "closed" court was accompanied by another change that was geographic, social, and cultural. While a sizeable fraction of the nobility remained attached to the court and its prestige, other nobles began to move from the court to the city, where private aristocratic residences played an increasingly prominent role. The privatization of the framework of daily life that appeared under Louis XV—a sign of an internal crisis at the court itself—help ensure that the court rituals of the preceding period were preserved intact. The urban and Parisian aristocracy, excluded from enjoying the honors of the court and keeping company with the king, increasingly tended to withdraw to the nearby capital and to seek other locations for socializing. The court was no longer the central model for life in elite society.

This shift toward the city was also perceptible on the cultural level. The court remained a cultural model, first and foremost because it was a place that actually shaped culture. Under Louis XIV festivals and spectacles were intrinsic parts of the process through which the court was constituted, and this tradition continued into the 18th century. The court was therefore partially involved in introducing the status of the "intellectual" attached to the world of letters, the theatre, or music. At the same time, artistic controversies could emerge at court. For example, during the Quarrel of the Bouffons, which divided partisans of traditional French opera and Italian *opera buffa,* the court appeared as a bastion of traditional values, in contrast to the taste for novelty and Italian culture so prevalent among Parisians and devotees of the Enlightenment.

A distinct cultural shift was thus taking place, and by the end of the 18th century the court at Versailles often had to make do with following trends that had been set in Paris. A center of creativity and novelty during the 17th century, the 18th-century court French court gradually lost its trend-setting function. Some of the reasons for this shift involved the personalities of the sovereigns and their declining taste for spectacles, but the roots of the phenomenon went deeper. The age of the Enlightenment witnessed an overall secularization of the content of culture. People became more open to the idea of novelty (as in the case of music, for example), and a new, more contentious mindset emerged that, at least in part, prevented the king and his entourage from remaining the sole arbiters of culture. In effect, cultural authority was shifting from the court to other places and other groups. Over the course of the 18th the century, therefore, in different spheres, the court was, paradoxically, both a model and a social structure in crisis, which was tending to lose its role as a reference point.

Even as the court's centralist role as a social, cultural and political model was beginning to wane in France itself, that type of model was taking hold in other countries. Throughout Europe, states were established in which monarchs imposed their power along the same lines as French absolutism. Louis XIV and his court appeared to be the best embodiment of royal magnificence and served as a model for all the European rulers. The component of personality within an absolute monarchy was accentuated by the role of the great families, such as the Bourbons in France and Spain and the Habsburgs in the Germanic sphere of influence.

Courts inspired by the French model were established throughout Europe. The phenomenon appeared in Paris, Vienna, and Madrid; it also flourished in northwestern Europe: in London, for example, where the house of Hanover reinforced the institution, and in Copenhagen and Sweden. The new monarchies that were established over the course of the century were well accustomed to moving from one place to another. For example, the elector of Brandenburg became king of Prussia in 1701, and in 1720 the duke of Savoy became king of Sardinia and made Turin the seat of a court. In Italy and Germany, the numerous sovereign principalities viewed the court as a way to establish themselves and to display the power of their princes.

These new courts adopted almost all aspects of the French model. The organization of space was one of the main concerns, and French artists made numerous journeys to facilitate the construction of French-style princely residences. Cities fell into disfavor with rulers, who could more easily rebuild according to their own wishes in the countryside. Several "pseudo-Versailles" were built, following the example set by Frederick II (who had both a Trianon and a Versailles in his palaces at Sans-Souci and Potsdam). The court of Versailles was imitated in all its particulars, including its architecture, its parks, its composition, its ceremonies, whether military or festive, and its etiquette. The court lifestyle of Versailles was also imitated. That lifestyle often involved a whirlwind of distractions, and the courts of Berlin and Turin sometimes appeared to be exceptional because they were places where work was actually done. New forms of sociability were developed around court receptions and the pleasure of conversation. Manners became more refined, and, with the creation of academies, cultural concerns were strengthened. In short, the French cultural model as a whole was disseminated throughout Europe. Aristocratic society throughout the Continent assimilated patterns of behavior, codes of "politeness," and a set of disciplines and constraints. Such conventions and constraints were a part of the "court rationality" that constituted one of the crucibles from which modern man would emerge.

JEAN DUMA

See also Dance; Luxury; Nobility; Theatre and Staging

Further Reading

Cattani, Marco, and Romani, Marzio Achille, *La corte in Europa*, Brescia, Italy: Grafo Edizioni, 1983

Dewald, Jonathan, *The European Nobility, 1400–1800*, New York: Cambridge University Press, 1996

Dickens, A.G., editor, *The Courts of Europe: Politics, Patronage, and Royalty, 1400–1800*, New York: McGraw-Hill, and London: Thames and Hudson, 1977

Élias, Norbert, *The Civilizing Process*, 2 vols., translated by Edmund Jephcott, Oxford: Blackwell, and New York: Urizen Books, 1978–82 (original German edition, 1939)

Élias, Norbert, *The Court Society*, translated by Edmund Jephcott, Oxford: Blackwell, and New York: Pantheon Books, 1983 (original German edition, 1969)

Revel, Jacques, "The Court," in *Realms of Memory: Rethinking the French Past*, vol. 2, *Traditions*, edited by Pierre Nora, New York: Columbia University Press, 1997 (original French edition, 1992)

Roche, Daniel, *France in the Enlightenment*, translated by Arthur Goldhammer, Cambridge, Massachusetts: Harvard University Press, 1998 (original French edition, 1993)

Credit and Banking

To speak of credit is to speak of expectation. The most typical instrument of credit during the Enlightenment was the bill of exchange, a security representing a debt with a limited term. The person drawing up the bill gave an order to the payer to dispense a certain sum on a predetermined date to either a designated beneficiary or an endorser.

Bills of exchange were both necessary and adequate to the needs of the times. The commercial capitalism that reached the height of its development in the 18th century cannot be understood without considering bills of exchange, which resolved all the problems raised by the transfers involved in exchange and payment of funds. Indeed, the quality of the services that bills of exchange offered was obvious. By creating and negotiating a bill of exchange, payment could be deferred, and when endorsed these bills could be circulated and used to regulate commerce everywhere. This was possible because the bills offered several indispensable features: partial transfers, compensation by way of juggling the books (which the Germans referred to as "book money") and discounting, which offered the possibility of immediately mobilizing short-term bills. Finally, various types of arbitrage—whether simple or mixed (commercial paper and metal)—for a variety of account types created a whole range of speculative financial opportunities. This is the form in which credit existed during the 18th century. Further, one could operate without difficulty or risk, for the bill of exchange was a means of payment that was entirely controlled throughout its brief existence: at the time of issuance, depending on its maturity and according to the specific case (the face value received being recorded as such in accounting) and duration (being payable on sight on the day it was presented or on the due date); during its circulation (by the renewal of the issue at each endorsement); and ultimately in its value, for, depending on the validity of the signature, a bill of exchange could even be refused.

As a result of all these features, the 18th-century bill of exchange appeared to be the perfect instrument of Western capitalism and was in widespread use at every level of business. Thanks to the bill of exchange and the possibility of transferring funds, there existed a pan-European unity of commerce and banking. Who, precisely, used these indispensable instruments of credit? Because bankers were far and away the principal agents for bills of exchange, it is important to distinguish among the various types of bankers. In France the merchant bankers of the great urban centers were very different from the bankers of Paris, who were close to the great financiers and to the monarchy. Merchant bankers such as the Roux brothers, in Marseille, or Claude Aimé Vincent in Lyon, divided their operations between trading and banking. They were involved in the commerce of precious metals; making constant and diverse use of commercial instruments such as discounts, credit, and arbitrage, and guaranteeing financial support for other enterprises, notably manufacturing. In Marseille, around the end of the 17th century, merchant bankers were known as "boutique bankers." In Paris, it is important to differentiate between state bankers and private bankers. State bankers—including, for example, all those at the Caisse d'Escompte during the ministry of Jacques Necker, or Le Couteulx et Compagnie after 1776, were closely connected with the business affairs of the monarchy. Private bankers were certainly also in contact with those involved in speculation, but they insisted on maintaining true independence. Private banking establishments included the Banque Mallet, Le Couteulx et Compagnie before 1776, and Greffulhe Montz et Compagnie.

Alongside these merchant and private bankers, national banks in the modern sense did exist, in forms that varied from country to country, but in fact these banks were neither necessary nor sufficient, for in the Europe of commercial capitalism, that economic space without borders, merchants and bankers truly did not need central national banks.

In France there was an enduring mistrust of such specialized institutions. In 1672, when Louis XIV's minister Jean-Baptiste Colbert suggested to Arnoul (who was the head of the galleys in Marseille) that creating a bank would be "advantageous to the trade of the inhabitants of that city," the people's hostility was so great that the proposal never got off the ground. For the 18th century, one need only recall the tribulations of the Banque Générale. This private company was established in Paris in 1716 by the financier John Law. It had a capital of 6 million livres, which were distributed in 1,200 shares, each worth 500 livres, and was endowed with a 20-year royal charter. The Banque Générale accepted deposits of cash and discounted commercial paper; it also issued bills payable on demand or to the bearer, which could be reimbursed in the bank's own *écus* (a money of account), thus removing the risk of monetary depreciation by providing a guarantee to the depositor that the amount reimbursed would be identical to the amount at the time of issue. The company was renamed the Banque Royale in 1718 and became a bank for business, trust operations, and monopoly concessions, but it collapsed at the end of 1720. Although perhaps overly severe, the judgment of the Swiss advocate Riliet was not without entirely without foundation: "Law has not given you a bank, and that is precisely the crime he is guilty of committing against you; he has insidiously and treacherously misnamed the state's promissory notes as bank notes."

In fact, bank notes played a very limited role in the economic life of the 18th century. The first two attempts to issue them—the monetary bills of the end of Louis XIV's reign and then Law's bills—had detrimental results and were not repeated. Businessmen had no confidence in bills guaranteed by a state that was burdened with debt. It was not the paper itself that was the problem but rather the origin of the guarantee. Although there was the claim placed at the bottom of a bill of exchange, "with the signature of so-and-so you can sleep peacefully" (an expression in use at the time),

the same was not true of the mark of the central government on a bill. In fact, the creation and acceptance of a state bank within an absolute monarchy, such as France, appeared to be impossible.

Unlike the bank of 1727 that was linked to the Compagnie des Indes, and the Banque du Pouvoir of 1767, which was in the hands of a group of financiers, the purpose of the Caisse d'Escompte, founded by Panchaud in 1776 and then relaunched by Necker in 1778, was to reduce interest rates on money, not in order to support trade but, above all, to lighten the burden of the public debt. The Caisse d'Escompte obtained results, albeit after an initial period of difficulty. The total value of bills in circulation rose to 100 million livres in 1786; discounts reached their record level of 483 million livres in 1788. However, there were some important restrictions. The bills were circulated only within the geographic limits of Paris. The volume of discounts was low (4.25 billion livres in 17 years, or an annual average of 250 million livres) in relation to the demand for circulation within the kingdom, at a time when the annual requirements of a single large commercial institution rose to several billion. Furthermore, not all of the discounted paper was of commercial origin; a significant portion of it was made up of *billets des Fermes* (notes issued by the Tax Farms) and reassigned notes with short-term maturities. Their double dependence—on the central government and on the leading bankers of Paris—was clearly apparent. The Caisse d'Escompte was indeed, as Guy Antonetti called it, "the bankers' bank," and not a bank for the merchant bankers (see Antonetti).

The Amsterdamsche Wisselbank (Bank of Amsterdam), founded in 1609, was a municipal bank with the world as its backdrop and enjoyed connections with international merchant banking. It provided more or less permanent support for the finances of the city, as much through its loans to the municipal treasury as through the direct payment of its revenues; it also frequently backed the Compagnie des Indes. But, above all, it rendered a wide range of services to trade through the remarkable flexibility of its rules (that allowed for partial transfers by putting receipts for deposits in kind into circulation, and through compulsory payments of expired bills of exchange, written to the credit of current accounts, domiciled in Amsterdam and denominated in florins. Under its statutes, the Amsterdamsche Wisselbank did not practice discounting, and as a result it did not offer credit based on discounted bills. Further, the advances that it granted in the form of receipts against deposits of precious metals did not cover the total value of the security. Within the framework of a self-contained city, the Amsterdamsche Wisselbank provided its clients with the facilities of a center for postal checks. However, both in practice and in principle, the bank operated in the margins of the vast currents of exchange and the operations that these currents brought about: trading, discounting, and credit.

The real center of these large-scale activities was not the banks but the stock exchange, where transactions took place either directly, banker to banker, or indirectly, through the mediation of brokers. To a very large extent, therefore, the Dutch merchant bankers also formed part of the economy of the bank.

The Bank of England, founded in 1694, has been called "the sole prototype of the public bank of the future, the bank of discounting, circulation, and credit" (see Lüthy). One important feature of the Bank of England was that its credit was created by issuing bills and that the volume of these bills in circulation was no longer required to be equal in value to real assets. Another innovation was that its assets included a commercial portfolio that was larger than its cash holdings. Two statutory arrangements arose from this: interest was set at four percent to attract depositors, and a very favorable discount rate was granted to clients who had deposited their funds with the bank. As a result, deposits increased and the portfolio ballooned in size. The bank profited from discounting by basing fiduciary circulation on it. This in turn led to a crucial problem: the economic impetus provided by discounting and bills. For the merchant bankers, the role of the bills seems to have been secondary, but the innovative nature of the practice of discounting is obvious, for it was a daily operation, affecting both "inland" and foreign bills. However, the Bank of England received only those bills that had been drawn on the London market in sterling, and it did not put them back into circulation. It therefore differed from the Amsterdamsche Wisselbank in several respects. The Dutch institution received only expired bills of exchange, which as a result could not be discounted, while the Bank of England accepted them at maturity and realized them immediately against the standard debits. The Bank of Amsterdam did not have a portfolio, while the Bank of England's portfolio expanded with bills offered every day. Thus, the Bank of England took the crucial step of linking banking practice to portfolio management, albeit with one important restriction. London bankers seeking foreign bills of exchange did not go to the Bank of England, which did not hold any. Instead, as was the case everywhere else, they turned to a stock exchange, in this case the famous Royal Exchange, the true center of international exchange transactions. The inevitable result was that the Bank of England discounted only a small fraction of the bills of exchange received in London. This gave rise to a real weakness in the discounting operations of the institution and relegated it to a marginal role, at best, in the worldwide exchange markets.

The Banque de Saint-Charles was established in Spain in 1783, in a country whose economic conditions did not allow it to take much advantage of the benefits of credit. The bank therefore presents some distinctive characteristics. It undertook discounting, issued bills, and supplied the armies. Most of its directors were French, most notably François Cabarrus of Bayonne, who had obtained the support of the Spanish minister of foreign affairs, Florida Blanca. According to its founder, the Banque de Saint-Charles was to be a fund "intended to discount all bills of exchange drawn on Madrid, at a rate of four percent." However, the total annual discounts were never very high, reaching 12.5 million livres compared to 165 million pounds in London and 483 million livres in Paris. At first, its main activity was speculation on its own shares, but it very quickly developed another important source of revenue: the monopoly on the export of cash and silver, to the primary benefit of such Parisian bankers as Le Normand, Pierre Lalanne, Le Couteulx, and Vandenyver. These bankers, in association with each other and with Cabarrus, formed what Lüthy terms "a privileged syndicate of importers of piastres" to supply the French Mint (see Lüthy).

Ultimately, for the great centers of international trade at the high tide of commercial capitalism that epitomized the age of the Enlightenment, the nature of banking structures and techniques did not differ a great deal, in spite of undeniable superficial differences. Indeed, the discernable disparities among them are far outweighed by their similarities: the high volume of commerce and the density of the international payments that commercial flows could sustain; the control of business at this level by an aristocracy of wealth that included merchants, merchant bankers, and bankers within a flexible hierarchy; the ubiquitous uniformity of methods and techniques of payment; the spontaneous regulation of all these payments; and the relatively late implementation—not in their creation, but rather in their effectiveness—of very similar institutional structures for clearing and rediscounting. Thus, the Bank of England—"the Old Lady of Threadneedle Street"—and the young Caisse d'Escompte had much in common at the end of the 18th century. This implies that there was not, and that there could not have been, a gap in banking practices between countries that had reached similar levels of economic development. To infer delayed development in banking practices by reference to official banks, which played a marginal role, makes little sense. Such inferences are perhaps even specious if, in their relationship with economic life, these institutions played roles that were almost identical from one country to another. A more accurate assessment, then, would be to acknowledge that the 18th century, with its economy driven by commercial capitalism, provides the most complete example of European unity in the realm of business and banking.

MARCEL COURDURIE

See also Exchange

Further Reading

Antonetti, Guy, *Une maison de banque à Paris au XVIIIe siècle: Greffulhe Montze et cie, 1789–1793*, Paris: Éditions Dujas, 1963

Carrière, Charles, *Négociants marseillais au XVIIIe siècle: Contribution à l'étude des économies maritimes*, 2 vols., Marseille: Institut Historique de Provence, 1973

Carrière, Charles, et al., editors, *Banque et capitalisme commercial: La lettre de change au XVIIIe siècle*, Marseille: Institut Historique de Provence, 1976

Lüthy, Herbert, *La banque protestante en France, de la revocation de l'Édit de Nantes à la Révolution*, 2 vols., Paris: S.E.V.P.E.N., 1959–61

Rebuffat, Ferréol, and Marcel Courdurié, *Marseille et le négoce monétaire international (1785–1790)*, Marseille: Chambre de Commerce et d'Industrie, 1966

Criticism

In the literary world of the 18th century, criticism occupied a central and widely recognized place. As Kant puts it in the preface to the *Kritik der reinen Vernunft* (1781; Critique of Pure Reason), "our century is truly the century of criticism." The particular importance of criticism stemmed partly from the influence of the German Protestant tradition and partly from the fact that the French *philosophes* progressively adopted a concept of philosophical criticism. Its role within the larger framework of 18th-century thought was determined by a combination of René Descartes's rationalism, John Locke's empiricism, and Gottfried Wilhelm Leibniz's idealism.

The word itself was derived—by way of the Latin *critica*—from the Greek verb *krinein* (to separate, judge, or accuse) and the corresponding noun *krisis* (decision). For Aristotle the term had two distinct meanings. In a general sense, it referred to the natural faculty of judgment, while at a more fundamental level it meant ethical and practical judgment. The aim of this distinction was to establish a close link between logic and rhetoric, a link that would be essential for the Stoics, as well as for 17th- and 18th-century philosophy. Cicero also distinguished between two aspects of criticism, namely the *ars inveniendi,* or philological aspect (*grammatica*), which focused on the study of texts, and the *ars iudicandi,* or logical aspect (*critica*). In the Middle Ages the notion of criticism fell into disuse, mainly because at that time literature was often transmitted orally, but also because the medieval mind-set was still reluctant to face the conflict of opinions that is inherent in criticism. In the 15th and 16th centuries the ancient notion of criticism was revived independently in philology and logic and was eventually introduced into the field of aesthetics.

As far as philology was concerned, the classical term appears to have come back into favor toward the end of the 15th century in works such as Angelo Poliziano's *Sylvae* (1492). Whereas in ancient world "grammarians" were authorized to make judgments only about secular texts, the "critics" of the Renaissance did not hesitate to make pronouncements about all kinds of texts. This extension of their purview meant they could discuss the Bible, thus calling into question the monopoly of the clergy with regard to scriptural exegesis. The Reformation in turn encouraged scholars to examine biblical texts critically and to call into question the texts' authority, which led to a freer treatment of theological and philosophical sources and even to the possibility of making value judgments about classical antiquity. In 1548 Ramus (otherwise known as Pierre de la Ramée) renewed the classical tradition in the field of logic. He drew a distinction between *iudicium* (logical analysis) and *inventio* (topical science); from this distinction it followed that analysis, then synonymous with criticism, could be applied equally well to the fields of logic, grammar, and rhetoric. The concept of criticism thus became, in the words of Kurt Röttgers, "the doctrine of practical logical analysis, a sort of metalogic" of judgment (see Röttgers).

The aesthetic dimension of criticism was first defined by Julius Caesar Scaliger in his *Poetices libri septem* (Poetics in Seven Books) of 1561. Scaliger's comparison of Roman and Greek literature is based on value judgments that only philologists (and not grammarians) were qualified to make.

In the 16th century the use of the term *ars critica* to refer both to philological judgments about a text—such as judgments relating to grammar, history, and aesthetics (*ars inveniendi*)—and to judgments of a philosophical nature (*ars iudicandi*) became increasingly prevalent in the fields of rhetoric and philology. The various conceptual aspects of "criticism," as practiced in the previously mentioned disciplines, were eventually merged into a single, all-embracing analytic system that could be applied to all branches of human knowledge. The primary aim of the *ars critica* was to establish the real meaning of a text and to recover its original intention. In this sense, criticism developed along the lines set by Descartes's methodical discussion of historical criticism, according to which texts were evaluated in the light of the realism of their representation.

According to Francis Bacon, the only way to reach the truth is by way of a critical path that allows the mind to acquire knowledge by means other than those of traditional representation. The critical transmission of knowledge involves the editing of canonical authors in corrected editions, critical interpretation of commentaries on their work, and comparisons to other authors. In *The Proficience and Advancement of Learning* (1605), Bacon proposes that students should be advised on what to read and that they should receive better grounding in how to read. The philological method thus became a model that could be followed in all areas of learning. Locke's immensely influential *Essay concerning Human Understanding* (1690) summarizes the critical methods that were to be the basis of all future scientific inquiry. Pierre Bayle's *Dictionnaire historique et critique* (1697; An Historical and Critical Dictionary) is the paradigm of Lockean "historical and biographical criticism." His critical method, which embraces every branch of knowledge and of history, is placed in the service of reason. For Bayle the spirit of criticism is fundamentally negative and destructive, but it nevertheless serves the cause of truth.

The middle of the 17th century witnessed the growth of two new variants of the philological tradition: biblical criticism and art criticism. The former became known as *critica sacra* (sacred criticism) after the book of that name written in 1650 by the French Protestant Louis Capellus, to which the Catholic Richard Simon replied in his *Histoire critique du Vieux Testament* (1678; Critical History of the Old Testament). During the Enlightenment, biblical criticism became a discipline in its own right, with the dual task of simultaneously taking into account and questioning the intangibility of authority. Thus, Baruch Spinoza's rational interpretation of the Bible was based on the logical approach of Cartesian analysis. Similarly, it was Cartesian logic that would give birth to the methodology of historical-critical exegesis. One of the best-known 18th-century

examples of this tradition is the work of Hermann-Samuel Reimarus (1694–1768), extracts of whose radical criticism of the Church and the Bible were published by Gotthold Ephraim Lessing between 1774 and 1777.

Around the turn the 17th century, the word "criticism" itself began to appear in the various national languages. The French *critique* was first recorded in 1580, the English *criticism* in 1607, while the German *critique* was borrowed from French in 1688. The first edition of the *Dictionnaire de l'Académie* (1694; Dictionary of the Académie Française) defines *criticism* in very general terms as "the art of judging any work produced by the human mind." Zedler's German *Universal-Lexicon* of 1733 was the first 18th-century dictionary to recognize the concept's wide range of meaning: "*Critic*. This word, in the widest sense, refers to every kind of judgment." After a very general definition of criticism as "the art of judging," Louis Moréri's *Le grand dictionnaire historique* (1759; The Comprehensive Historical Dictionary) goes on to make a further distinction between three kinds of criticism of similar status—aesthetic, philological, and historical. Jean-François Marmontel's "Critique" (Criticism) entry in the *Encyclopédie* gives a much more modern and universal definition of the concept, using such phrases as "an enlightened examination," "an equitable judgment of products of the human mind," and "the tribunal of truth"—in other words a form of judgment that can be applied equally to the sciences, to art, and to technology. For Giambattista Vico criticism was the very foundation for the study of every science and every art. In his own philosophy, Vico tried to combine the methods used in specific fields of study with the methods criticism.

During the Enlightenment, criticism became an organ of public opinion, with an increasingly political bias. Once the criteria of moral judgment were applied to the affairs of state, it was but a short step to political criticism. Critics began claiming that they expressed the public interest; they knowingly took sides and were prepared to attack any and every text, work of art, or institution. Their targets included the Church, the state, and society itself. The philological element of criticism was thus progressively pushed into the background while the political and philosophical aspects became increasingly predominant—so much so, in fact, that the word *critique* came to refer to the *philosophes'* criticism of the state of the nation in France and indeed came to be one of the Enlightenment's key expressions.

With Immanuel Kant the concept of criticism took on even wider meanings, affecting its role at three distinct levels. In the first place, the field in which criticism might appropriately be used—originally limited to discussion of classical and biblical texts—was expanded to include assessments of society as a whole ("the criticism to which all should be submitted"). Second, the function of criticism changed, and texts would no longer be judged merely according to their authenticity but rather on how well they agreed with the ideas of the Enlightenment. Finally, the subjects that criticism might treat would subsequently include reason itself. Kant's first mention of criticism occurs in connection with his reflections on aesthetics and logic. The field of aesthetics, which is essentially a critique of taste, is closely linked to that of logic, which is a critique of reason, and the rules that are operative in one field can therefore always be used to elucidate problems in the other.

In his work of the 1760s, Kant draws a distinction between logic and criticism, moving the latter concept closer to metaphysics, where it refers to the examination of cognitive possibilities. Criticism becomes the basic function of rational thought and the main criterion by which we can judge the products of human reason. In his *Kritik der Urteilskraft* (1790; Critique of Judgment)—which he originally intended to entitle *Kritik des Geschmacks* (Critique of Taste)—Kant draws a distinction between transcendental criticism, which raises the question of the possibility of making a priori judgments, and criticism as the mere expression of judgment about works of art, based on empirical rules of taste. From a philosophical standpoint, this second activity has no cognitive function. Around 1790 Kant began to see differences between *Kritik* and *Kritizismus,* the latter term referring to the doctrine that warns us to beware of any metaphysical principle and be prepared to subject the possibilities and limitations of every form of knowledge to critical examination.

Literary Criticism

By the late 17th century the notion of criticism in France had become increasingly identified with poetics, and the criteria of literary criticism were based entirely on classical rules. The close link between literature and the notion of criticism can still be seen in the entry for "Critique" in the *Dictionnaire de Trévoux* (1740; Dictionary of Trévoux): "The art of judging philosophical opinions may be called 'philosophical criticism'; but by 'criticism,' what we normally mean is 'literary criticism.'"

Of the many volumes devoted to the study of poetics that appeared between the 16th and 18th centuries, the majority were concerned primarily with Aristotle's *Poetics*. Humanist scholars developed a critical method according to which, in order to avoid categorical and premature judgments, a critic should not praise a work excessively or denigrate it too harshly; nor should he read it out of context. In France literary criticism, in the strict sense, developed side by side with the doctrine of classicism. It was this parallel that underlay the Quarrel of the Ancients and the Moderns, since those who were on the side of the moderns advocated that the same criteria should be applied to ancients and moderns alike. From the end of the 17th century onward, similar criteria were being applied to both literature and the visual arts. In his *Réflexions critiques sur la poésie et la peinture* (1719; Critical Reflections on Poetry and Painting), the abbé Dubos reflects on the possibilities and limits of any critical evaluation of a work of art when that evaluation is based on criteria involving the feelings of the viewer. In Dubos's view, literary criticism must take into account the empirical and sensationalist aspects of Locke's theory of human understanding.

Beginning around 1720, normative literary theory derived from classical models was gradually replaced by a more challenging form of practical criticism based on literary commentary. It was criticism applied to literary works, rather than abstract theory, that would help to form the reader's taste. Denis Diderot sums up this link between literature and criticism in his *Salon* (Exhibition) of 1767: "Genius creates the beauties of a work; criticism notices its defects; the first requires imagination, the second, judgment." Like Dubos, Diderot argues that the value of a work of art should not be determined by normative rules; instead, critical judgment should originate in the enthusiasm and the passions aroused by the work itself.

In the 17th century, French literary criticism had functioned essentially according to a normative system of rules, and the slightest infringement of these rules was vigorously condemned. At the same time, the rules themselves often gave rise to polemical exchanges that were totally lacking in objective criteria. In the 18th century the doctrines themselves came increasingly under attack, and, as the claims of subjective judgment began to be recognized, more and more critics questioned the very principle of aesthetic rules. The historical dimension of criticism was given greater weight, and there was a steady growth of interest in foreign literatures. English writers such as William Shakespeare, John Dryden, Alexander Pope, Jonathan Swift, Daniel Defoe, and Henry Fielding became well known on the Continent through translations, despite the obvious gap between their works and the rules of classical poetics. In Holland a group of European journalists launched a *Journal littéraire* in 1713, the preface of which sets out to define their role as critics: "We believe that such caution [not to decide on the merits of a book] is both excessive and useless; so we have determined to state plainly to the reader whatever we find good or bad in a book."

The 18th century thus witnessed the birth of a new kind of author: the critic. His task was to educate and cultivate the reader's taste and to explain causal relationships. The definitions proposed by Diderot and Voltaire are representative of the many that could be cited. For Diderot, in *Discours sur la poésie dramatique* (1758; Discourse on Drama), the critic was "a man who felt able to teach those who felt able to teach the public." In his entry "Critique" in the *Dictionnaire philosophique* (1764; Philosophical Dictionary), Voltaire holds that "a good critic is one who possesses great knowledge and taste, yet is without prejudice or envy. Such a combination is hard to find."

In England Pope, in his *Essay on Criticism* (1711), aimed to establish the precepts of critical theory and portray the "true" critic against a background of the history of literary theories. As a result, the philosopher-aesthete joined the ranks of the poet-critics, and literature about literature grew in importance and in scope. The earl of Shaftesbury's aesthetic system, situated midway between literature and philosophy, was taken up again in the 18th century by Henry Home. In *Elements of Criticism* (1762), Home takes issue with the dichotomy that distinguishes between two forms of criticism, one methodical and abstract, the other pragmatic, in the sense of giving free reign to certain faculties. Instead, Home urges the critic to strive for a happy medium between abstract thought and concrete faculties.

According to the German theorist Johann Christoph Gottsched, a critic is a philosopher whose judgments are based on precise rules, rather than arbitrary taste. His loyalty to the principles of classical poetics, clearly stated in his *Versuch einer kritischen Dichtkunst vor die Deutschen* (1730; Attempt at a Critical Poetics for the Germans), aroused the hostility of the Swiss school (Johann Jakob Bodmer and Johann Jakob Breitinger) in the 1740s. On the other hand, Lessing's *Laokoon* (1766; Laocoön; An Essay upon the Limits of Painting and Poetry) comes out strongly against a criticism based on purely rational principles. The critic's judgment must coincide with the practice of the genius, but what matters above all is the latter's aesthetic product rather than some philosophical aesthetic system. However, fully conscious of the dangers of a blend of classical rules and enthusiasm, on the one hand, and a purely empirical method devoid of criteria, on the other, Lessing endeavored to make connections between the aesthetic aspect of criticism and its philological and historical roots.

It was, however, Alexander Gottlieb Baumgarten's *Aesthetica* (1750–58; Aesthetics) that would eventually establish aesthetics as an academic discipline in its own right, worthy of being numbered alongside other branches of philosophy. Like criticism before it, aesthetics became a subdivision of logic. For Baumgarten, aesthetics was concerned with any judgment based on the reactions of human sensibility, whereas the task of criticism, in the wider sense of the term (including criticism of knowledge), was to give rulings with regard to intellectual products. Thus a pair of interdependent critical disciplines appeared in Germany. Once this connection between logic and criticism was firmly entrenched, the way was open for Kant's notion of criticism.

PETRA GEKELER

See also Aesthetics; Genius; Taste

Further Reading

Achache, Gilles, "Critique," in *Les notions philosophiques: Dictionnaire*, edited by André Jacob, Paris: Presses Universitaires de France, 1990

Barthes, Roland, *Criticism and Truth,* translated by Katrine Pilcher Keuneman, Minneapolis: University of Minnesota Press, 1987 (original French edition, 1966)

The Cambridge History of Literary Criticism, Cambridge and New York: Cambridge University Press, 1989– ; see especially vol. 4, *The Eighteenth Century,* edited by H.B. Nisbet and Claude Rawson (1997)

Fleming, Richard, and Michael Payne, editors, *Criticism, History, and Intertextuality,* Lewisburg, Pennsylvania: Bucknell University Press, 1988

Jackson, James Robert de Jager, *Historical Criticism and the Meaning of Texts,* London and New York: Routledge, 1989

Kunneman, Harry, and Hent de Vries, editors, *Enlightenments: Encounters between Critical Theory and Contemporary French Thought,* Kampen, The Netherlands: Kok Pharos, 1993

Leitch, Vincent B., *American Literary Criticism from the Thirties to the Eighties,* New York: Columbia University Press, 1988

Roger, Jérôme, *La critique littéraire,* Paris: Dunod, 1997

Röttgers, K, "Kritik," in *Geschichtliche Grundbegriffe: Historisches Lexikon zur politisch-sozialen Sprache in Deutschland,* edited by Otto Brunner, Werner Conze, and Reinhart Koselleck, vol. 3, Stuttgart, Germany: Klett, 1974

Simpson, David, editor, *The Origins of Modern Critical Thought: German Aesthetic and Literary Criticism from Lessing to Hegel,* Cambridge and New York: Cambridge University Press, 1988

Wellek, René, *A History of Modern Criticism: 1750–1950,* 4 vols., London: Cape, 1955; revised and expanded edition, 8 vols., 1994

D

Dance

In his *Réflexions sur l'opéra* (Reflections on Opera), published in 1741, Rémond de Saint-Mard asks: "Do you not find . . . that dance is given too much of a range?" Should dance be a simple prelude to the opera, structurally linked with it, or should it take on the dignity of a fully autonomous performance? This question was widely debated in the 18th century and was linked to another debate, which was just as impassioned, concerning the intrinsic nature of dance. Should dance be a display of technical virtuosity, stripped of any meaning that would explain it, or should it aspire to the imitative and representational characteristics that, according to contemporary theorists such as Charles Batteux, were appropriate to all forms of art? In the final reckoning, the intrinsic character of dance was analyzed in light of two lines of inquiry. The first was the presumed origins of dance in the acrobatic and gymnastic performances of tightrope dancers and acrobats of antiquity. The other approach stressed the potential of dance, as a visual form, to support verbal evocations and explorations of the passions by means of gesture and controlled movement. This latter aspect was considered an important component in the training of future preachers and lawyers, as a way to impart to them the eloquence needed for practice in the pulpit or at the bar.

In the 18th century, historians of dance often noted that both Aristotle and Plato had debated the subject of dance and mentioned the role it played in the performance of Greek tragedies and religious ceremonies. Ménestrier, the author of a work on both ancient and modern ballet (1682), argued that in modern Spain and Portugal dance still fulfilled a spiritual function in churches and processions. He noted that ballets had been made part of ceremonial worship for Jews and Christians as well as for pagans. A work on dance wrongly attributed to Lucien offered the depiction of passions as the purpose of dance. Writers often cited the Roman rhetorician Quintilian's opinion that orators could benefit from studying this art (seen as distinct from the vulgar clowning of tightrope walkers and pantomime artists).

As an art that had been "purified" and provided with fixed rules, dance could be considered to have a rightful place in a good education. At the Louis le Grand Jesuit college, a *grand ballet* was presented once a year, generally as an interlude during a tragedy. The Jesuit ballets were not, as some have believed, mainly pedantic spectacles consisting of an allegorical presentation of characters inspired by rhetorical figures or grammatical terms, such as Supine or Solecism. The performances were in fact much closer to models taken from society, perhaps encompassing a religious theme, similar to the propagandist content of many of the Latin tragedies performed by the students. While dance served a professional purpose by providing future preachers and legal orators with training in physical eloquence, its social role in the secular world was equally clear. The importance of physical training in education had been emphasized since the Renaissance, and physical grace was an aspect of the "civility" on which the high society of the 18th century prided itself. No court in Europe could exist without its French dance master.

In France, before the creation of the Opéra in Paris, "society" dance had been restricted to the royal court. The participants in these court ballets were nonprofessionals: members of the royal family and of the aristocracy (Louis XIV himself had enthusiastically participated). In 1661, anxious about the lack of competent dancers for this type of function, the king founded the Académie Royale de Danse (Royal Academy of Dance); its members often became stars in the productions put on by the Opéra. There was a corresponding decline in court ballet. In the 18th century, serious dance continued to be limited to the Opéra, and the repeated attempts of the Comédie-Française to obtain official permission to include ballets in its own dramatic productions were opposed by the exclusive royal *privilège* (permission) enjoyed by the Opéra. There was, however, a genre of "comedy-ballet," which included Molière's *Le bourgeois gentilhomme* (1670; The Would-Be Gentleman).

Meanwhile, the Académie Royale de Danse was busy teaching dance as an art form that involved well-defined rules and precepts. In fact, the artistic status of dance, in contrast to the vulgar clowning done at fairs, was judged to be obvious because of its institutionalized character. According to Voltaire, "dance is an art, for it has rules," and the tragedian Clairon believed that the codified nature of dance established a fundamental distinction between it and theatrical plays. Although numerous 18th-century writers emphasized that blind obedience to rules could never lead to excellence and insisted that feeling was an essential quality for a dancer, they still frequently declared that rules should not be neglected. Thus, nearly all commentators mentioned the choreographer Beauchamps's establishment of the five fundamental dance positions and noted that all the other steps derived from them.

At the same time, the codified characteristics of dance were often criticized, both because they led to an excessive uniformity in execution and because they favored an exaggerated emphasis on technique at the expense of expressiveness. Commentators rejected the entrechat and the cabriole as being nothing other than displays of virtuosity, isolated spectacles that meant nothing and required the dancer to be merely "a well-articulated puppet." The traditional link between dance and the awakening and exploration of passions was threatened by such a pressing concern with the simple mechanics of execution. In contrast, Saint-Mard argued it was necessary that the steps of a dance should correspond to the action and mood of the piece as a whole.

This argument raises a crucial point. The requirement that dance should be an organic unity, rather than a collocation of separate, distinct effects, led naturally to the need for the whole piece to have a subject. A dance piece should contain a story, and its "meaning" should be transmitted to the public by means of eloquent gestures and expressions. Denis Diderot, whose theory of drama strongly influenced the ballet master Jean-George Noverre, remarked, "dance is thoroughly bad because one barely suspects that it is a sort of imitation." Diderot and other writers thought that the lack of expressiveness of the traditional style and the resulting boredom that audiences had to endure (a constant theme in their writings) could be corrected by associating dance with pantomime, which, once masks were abandoned once and for all in 1773, included facial expressions. According to Jean-Jacques Rousseau's *Dictionnaire de musique* (1768; Dictionary of Music), the allemande, the saraband, and other dances ought to be banished from the lyrical stage because they imitated nothing. Meanwhile, Ménestrier stated that the ballet reproduced in its movements "the actions of human beings, their affections, and their mores." Louis de Cahusac, in his treatise *La danse ancienne et moderne* (1754; Ancient and Modern Dance), declared that it would be desirable to institute "ballets of action," but it was left to Noverre to fully develop this notion. He wrote in his *Lettres sur la danse et sur les arts imitateurs* (1760; Letters on Dance and Imitative Arts) that each ballet should contain an exposition, a core, and a denouement.

The participation of the audience had to be encouraged, first and foremost, by maximizing the visual attractiveness of the whole piece. This was in line with the then-current idea that the principal mode of perception is vision. According to Noverre, ballet masters should acquire the painter's ability to mix colors in order to create contrasts, to arrange the figures in the scene, to dress them in various ways, and to give them character and expression. He contended that one of his first ballets, *Les fêtes chinoises* (The Chinese Celebrations), had failed because of its visual uniformity. As lessons in composition, he recommended the study of the canvases of the great painters. As far as the disposition of the ballet dancers on the stage was concerned, the enthusiasm of the 18th century for "beautiful disorder" placed a higher value on asymmetry than on rectilinear regularity and was in accordance with the disapproval expressed by Noverre for blind obedience to choreographic rules. In his *Réflexions critiques sur la poésie et sur la peinture* (1719; Critical Reflections on Poetry and Painting), the abbé Jean-Baptiste Dubos declared that dance was a living painting, to which Noverre added that dance was superior to painting because it also involved movement.

In their *Mémoires pour servir à l'histoire des spectacles de la foire* (1743; Memoirs for a History of Shows Held at Fairs), the Parfaict brothers mentioned the "animated paintings" dancers formed "by their steps, their bearing, and their gestures" in the *Ballet de l'amour et de la jalousie* (Ballet of Love and Jealousy) of 1729. The theory of the tableau that Diderot developed in his *Entretiens sur "Le fils naturel"* (1757; Discussions on "Le fils naturel") was echoed in the *Lettres sur la danse,* in which Noverre argued that such living paintings were superior to conventional paintings because only the former had the ability to depict a sequence of events. Noting that the ballet showed successive states, Noverre added that one could compare it to pictorial sequences, such as the series painted by Peter Paul Rubens for the gallery of the Palais du Luxembourg, which showed Marie de Médici and the birth of her son Louis XIII. Yet Noverre differed from Diderot in accepting, as part of the structure of ballet, the coup de théâtre, which Diderot's theory excluded from drama in favor of the tableau. Compan's *Dictionnaire de danse* (1787; Dictionary of Dance) encouraged the geniuses of dance to begin their presentation of a "grand action" by extracting from it all the elements capable of providing a tableau. The ideal ballet was seen in terms of a linked sequence of pictorial compositions, in which each group and each character should adopt positions and execute movements different from those performed by all the others.

The case made by theoreticians such as Noverre for compositional integration amounted to saying that ballet was truly autonomous, that it was not at the service of a larger performance (an opera), but that it had its own inherent explanation and justification. Diderot's *Entretiens* put forward some reforms to be introduced into the theatre, including the need "to reduce dance to the form of a true poem, to be written and to be separated from every other imitative art." Nevertheless, Bauchaumont's *Mémoires secrets* for 1776 disapproved of Noverre's efforts to accustom his audience to ballets independent of any supporting musical performance. Bauchaumont maintained that the correct function of ballet was still to serve as an accessory to an ensemble piece, the opera. Yet there were many complaints that ballets in operas were merely boring interruptions, totally irrelevant to the action. Rousseau freely admitted this prejudice in *Du contrat social* (1762; The Social Contract): "Watching dancing bores me." In his *Dictionnaire de la musique* he declared that ballet was "a bizarre sort of opera in which dance is hardly any better placed than in other settings, and it did not have any better effect." Rousseau further argued that, in most of these ballets, the separate acts were based on different subjects and were linked together solely by "some connection foreign to the action." In *La nouvelle Héloïse* (1761; Julie; or, The New Héloïse), he conceded that ballet was the most brilliant part of an opera but complained of being very irritated by ballet's lack of relation to the plot. He declared that the mixture of music (French, not Italian!), of "marvels," and of dance at the Opéra was the most tiresome spectacle imaginable. Friedrich Melchior von Grimm, meanwhile, noted that the only thing rendering the boredom inspired by French opera tolerable was that it was constantly interrupted by dances with no connection to it.

This desire for integration also suggests a desire for a certain degree of naturalism. Clearly, the vaguely formulated "imitation of nature" that 18th-century theorists thought to be artistically desirable did not signify the abandonment of all exaggeration. The constraints of communication without words necessitated some embellishment of the presentation. However, serious dance was judged to be truly distinct from the extreme displays of the pantomime of the fairgrounds and the boulevard theatres, which had to attract audiences through less sophisticated means. Noverre followed the anti-academic Diderot, exhorting ballet masters to take inspiration from the life of the streets in order to find models of characterization and movement liberated from the affectation of academic routine. The "ballets of action," like some contemporary dramas, were judged to be eminently suitable for representing mores—that is to say, ordinary customs—rather than the elevated conditions of court society. It seems, however, that in the final reckoning Noverre, like Diderot, did not succeed in painting truly convincing portraits of everyday life in the majority of his works. He was totally revolutionary in theorizing the ballet of action, but in practice the form remained as bound up with the novelistic tradition as Diderot's "dramas," and its success was ephemeral.

Despite all the interest during the 18th century in the expressive possibilities of silence (through gesture, movement, and facial expression), many theorists remained convinced that verbal eloquence was superior. Much as it might awaken the audience's ability to project, the mute activity of dancers could hardly appear to be anything more than a "sketch" that was hopelessly difficult to interpret and that was only weakly linked to the art of narration. According to Baron, "a talking ballet" could never communicate with the ease of the most mediocre of orators (see Baron). The greatest strength of dance lay in the link between its grace and the rhythm of its harmony, its presentation of the relationships between the characters (which for Diderot was the source of beauty), and its supreme theatricality. It married ritual and expression, but in a very special way.

ANGELICA GOODDEN

See also Court, French Royal; Energy; Opera; Pantomime

Further Reading

Baron, Auguste Alexis Floréal, *Lettres et entretiens sur la danse ancienne, moderne, religieuse, civile, et théâtrale,* Paris: Dondey-Dupré, 1824

Krüger, Manfred, *Jean-Georges Noverre und das "Ballet d'action": Jean-Georges Noverre und sein Einfluss auf die Ballettgestaltung,* Emsdetten: Lechte, 1963

Noverre, Jean Georges, *Lettres sur la danse et les arts imitateurs,* Paris: Librairie Théâtrale, 1952

Peyronnet, P. "Le théâtre d'éducation des Jésuites," *Dix-huitième siècle* 8 (1976)

Winter, Marian Hannah, *The Pre-Romantic Ballet*, London: Pitman, 1974; Brooklyn, New York: Dance Horizons, 1975

Death

The age of the Enlightenment faced the issue of death in conditions that, objectively speaking, had hardly changed by comparison with earlier centuries. Although the 18th century was marked by a general growth in the European population (according to very plausible estimates, it rose from 92 million in 1700 to 145 million in 1800), contemporaries believed the population was shrinking and remained unaware of the real situation until the final quarter of the century. This growth in population took place within demographic structures that were almost unchanged. Not only birthrates, but also infant mortality rates, remained high all over Europe: on average, as in the past, one infant in four did not reach the age of one year. Certain changes did occur with respect to adult deaths: life expectancy for 20-year-olds increased slightly. This first, tentative fall in long-term death rates cannot be explained either by improvements in agriculture, which remained very limited, or by medical progress. Some important discoveries in anatomy and in physiology were certainly made by Giovanni Battista Morgagni, Marie-François-Xavier Bichat, René-Antoine Ferchault de Réaumur, and Joseph Priestley, but the art of healing had made practically no progress. Instead, it was the diminishing frequency and attenuation of major crises of mortality that were responsible for the fall in adult mortality. Owing to improvements in the distribution and preservation of the available grain, the great and devastating famines that resulted from bad harvests gave way to food shortages that were less frequent and less severe. The plague disappeared, with the last epidemic striking Marseille and Provence in 1720. Epidemic diseases such as dysentery or smallpox continued to ravage Europe, but beginning in the 1770s, authorities in many countries, moved by a new concern for public health, began to implement preventive and sanitary measures that helped to reduce the impact of these diseases. The conjunction of famine and epidemic, so formidable earlier in European history, became much less frequent. The last major crisis of this type in Europe occurred in the years 1740 to 1742.

Although great crises of mortality were rarer and less deadly than in the past, death remained a tangible presence in daily life. In a French parish with around 1,500 inhabitants, the bell would toll, on average, once a week to announce publicly the death of a parishioner. The next day the funeral procession would make its way from the home of the deceased to the church and the cemetery, once again to the sound of the death knell. In such conditions everyone was on intimate terms with death, which was not concealed. On the contrary, it was often organized as a spectacle: for example, those who had been condemned to death were executed in public, in the presence of a large crowd. Most people hoped for the opportunity to die at home surrounded by all their relatives. Far from being kept away from the deathbed, children, even very young ones, were present, and when it was their father who was dying, they received his blessing and the expression of his last wishes. Death was both familiar and also, as Philippe Ariès puts it, "domesticated." For Europeans who adhered to Roman Catholicism, death still formed part of a Christian conception of life and of its final purposes, according to which the main business of each person was to secure his or her own salvation, avoiding the torments of hell and receiving the reward of the happiness of heaven. In such a context it was incumbent upon each individual to live each day as if death might come at any moment. From this perspective, a sudden death without the ministrations of a priest was especially to be feared. If that occurred, one risked coming before the Sovereign Judge unprepared and without having received absolution for one's sins. Partially mitigating this was the belief in Purgatory, which had been solemnly reaffirmed by the Council of Trent in the face of Protestant denials, and which offered an escape from the agonizing uncertainty about whether one would attain heavenly bliss or be damned for all eternity. Purgatory was understood to be a transitory place of purification for those souls who were not yet worthy of reaching heaven but did not actually deserve hell. This belief also had the effect of strengthening the link between the living and the dead, since it was thought that the living, far from being of no use to the dead, could reduce the deceased's time in Purgatory through their prayers, just as the saints in heaven were believed to intercede with God on behalf of those living people who addressed them.

Such were the themes constantly taken up and elaborated by preachers as well as in the numerous devotional works concerned with death and the necessary preparations for it. Some of these texts were aimed at an educated readership, such as Caraccioli's *Tableau de la mort* (1761; Picture of Death), which was read throughout Europe. Others, pamphlets with evocative titles such as *Faut mourir* (Got to Die) or *Pensez-y bien* (Ponder It Well), were geared toward a larger public and sold by peddlers. The teachings of the Church—which conceived of death as a simple transition from this vale of tears into eternity and which emphasized not only the crucial importance of this journey but also the necessary solidarity between the living and the dead—were assimilated into popular culture. Popular culture, however, integrated that teaching into a more complex set of beliefs and practices, some of which—omens, phantoms, and ghosts, for example—elicited mistrust or hostility from the clergy.

These popular beliefs were in part responsible for the campaign launched in midcentury, in France and in neighboring countries, against the danger of premature burial. In his *Dissertation sur l'incertitude des signes de la mort et l'abus des enterrements et embaumements précipités* (1742; Essay on the Uncertainty of the Signs of Death and the Abuse of Hasty Burials and Embalmings), the writer Jean-Jacques Bruhier took numerous examples of ghosts from 16th- and 17th-century collections of extraordinary and marvelous tales. He claimed that most of these ghosts were not souls returning to Earth from Purgatory, to demand prayers, but simply the victims of apparent death, presumed to be dead for one reason or another, then cured and recalled to life without any miracle, by the power of medicine alone, by the workings of nature, or by patience, waiting for nature to be restored to its former condition by itself.

Bruhier thus emphasized the danger of premature burial, but, in seeking to exorcise the legitimate fear it could arouse, he paradoxically gave credence to that fear, reinforced it, and spread it among a large public that had hardly felt it before. He replaced the traditional Christian fear of death and judgment with a secularized and immediate fear of apparent death during which one might be buried alive. This fear inspired a whole subgenre in the preromantic sensibility of the second half of the 18th century. In some of the tales in his *Nuits de Paris* (1788; Parisian Nights), Nicolas-Anne-Edmé Rétif de La Bretonne provides good examples of this morbid taste for the macabre and for tales of live burials. Nevertheless, despite its ambiguities, the campaign initiated by Bruhier led to the introduction of concrete preventive measures in France in the 1770s.

These included police ordinances imposing a delay of 36 hours between apparent death and burial, the transfer of urban cemeteries outside city walls, and measures that promoted appropriate aid for the drowned.

Protestants—whether Lutherans, Calvinists, or Anglicans—shared the same vision of death as Roman Catholics except on one point, which was certainly a crucial one: the belief in Purgatory. For Protestants, the death of a believer—that is, the death of a person who had been saved by faith—was understood as the moment when that individual attained glory and eternal bliss. Between the elect and the damned there was no room for the just who were not yet sanctified. The very idea of Purgatory was unknown in Protestant theology. Nevertheless, the problem of salvation and the expectation of death did not result in anguish, for each individual might discern certain inner signs that proved he or she was among the elect: first of all, faith in the Gospel, which was the source of light and peace; and second, the depth of the moral transformation produced by a faith that had been truly lived.

The *philosophes* were unanimous in rejecting the "good death" as Christians defined it and in denouncing the triumph of the forces of darkness in the terrorizing discourse of the Catholic Church in particular. Any one of them could have subscribed to Fleuriot de Langle's remarks of 1784:

It is necessary henceforth to dismiss from our bedsides these men in black, these bands, these surplices, these images, these torches, and funerary preparations, which conjure, evoke, and call upon death; which multiply the horror that it causes and the evil that it does, twice, thrice, a hundred times; and which often, in the end, kill people by the fear of death.

For the *philosophes* a "beautiful death," according to Sylvain Maréchal, was not that of a Christian, who, "on his deathbed, trembles like a criminal at the approach of the Supreme Judge," but that of the man without God who leaves the stage "proud of his existence, accountable to nobody but only to his own conscience." Voltaire, for his part, expressed admiration for Madame de Pompadour, who "died as a *philosophe*, without any prejudice, without any trouble, while old fogies die like fools" (it hardly matters here that the reality was somewhat different). In the area of literature, the death of Julie in Rousseau's *La nouvelle Héloïse* (1761; Julie; or, The New Héloïse) appears as a model of a "beautiful death," serene and unostentatious.

However, beyond denouncing Christian death and its meaning, the *philosophes* found themselves confronted with the necessity of understanding and accepting the final reckoning. Its inevitability was obvious but also, in the eyes of some *philosophes,* necessary. The marquis d'Argens formulated the idea of death's necessity in these terms: "Those who have died before us have made way for us; can we refuse, without injustice, to do the same for those who must come after us?" Such declarations did not make the idea of death any less troubling. One cannot help but sense a profound distress behind Voltaire's statement that "Man loves life and knows that he will die." In these conditions the only recourse was to resign oneself to the inevitable; however, for many *philosophes,* notably Voltaire, resignation did not exclude perseverance, or even stubbornness, in struggling against everything that was avoidable. Overall—setting aside the nuances that reflect individual temperaments—what the *philosophes* wrote about death bears a curious resemblance to certain aspects of Christian teaching. Life is riddled with so many evils that one can speak of death only as a life that is better than life, according to the pertinent analysis of Robert Favre, who added: "Even when one compares [death] to a refuge, a port where one can enjoy repose, it is the other world that the imagination seeks to enjoy, in the absence of any other explicit belief."

Whether considered as the end of life or as the great beyond, death fascinated the thinkers of the Enlightenment, to the point that some approved of suicide. Reflection on suicide became very important in the 18th century, initially in England, where the physician George Cheyne's book *The English Malady* appeared in 1733. In this book suicide is described as something peculiarly British. In fact, as Georges Minois demonstrates, the publicity given to this type of news item in the British press, which was much freer than the press on the European continent, tended to increase the phenomenon of suicide among Britons. In any case, spectacular suicides, particularly those that affected the aristocracy, were immediately known and discussed in France and throughout the rest of Europe. Montesquieu, for example, made a connection between this "English malady" and the insular climate of that country. In France, legislation against "homicide of oneself" was confirmed by the great criminal law of 1670: the corpse was to be put on the rack and thrown in the dump, and the suicide's goods were to be confiscated. In that country, the authorities, notably those of the Church, attributed the rise in suicides to the propaganda of the *philosophes.* When the abbé Prévost coined the term *suicide* on the model of *homicide* and *régicide,* he did so in order to denounce and condemn the act thus designated (1734; Le pour et le contre [For and Against]). However, while all the *philosophes* agreed in demanding the abolition of the shaming legislation against those who committed suicide, they differed in their assessment of the act itself. Some, such as Maupertuis or La Mettrie, saw cowardice in it, while others, including Montesquieu, defended the right of every person to dispose of his own life. (Montesquieu did, however, express a number of reservations.) In the article "Suicide" in his *Dictionnaire philosophique* (1764; Philosophical Dictionary), Voltaire took up most of the arguments in favor of suicide but ironically concluded: "An almost certain means of not giving in to the craving to kill oneself is to have something to do. . . . It is the idle who kill themselves." Later, he wrote: "Suicide is not in itself reprehensible, but it is a madness; amiable people do not kill themselves." On the other hand, for Chamfort, who killed himself in 1794, "to live is a sickness, death is the remedy." The suicide of the young English poet Thomas Chatterton in 1770 aroused deep emotion throughout Europe, and this sentiment is echoed in Johann Wolfgang von Goethe's *Die Leiden des jungen Werthers* (1774; The Sorrows of Young Werther). The success of that work was so great that it prompted Madame de Staël to write: "Werther has caused more suicides than the most beautiful woman in the world." In fact, several hundred "philosophical" suicides counted for little when compared to the thousands of self-inflicted deaths, in the countryside as well as in the cities, that had far more to do with poverty-induced despair than with unhappiness in love. In reality, suicides for the more mundane reasons were no more or less numerous than they had been before this time, or than they would be in the 19th and 20th centuries.

The Enlightenment *philosophes* were haunted by the quest for happiness in life on earth, to be realized through progress. Yet this observation should not allow us to forget that they did not shirk the challenge of thinking about death. In this area as in others, they did their best to take up the challenge by opposing the "light of reason" to the "darkness of fanaticism," the "beautiful death" of the wise man to the "good death" of the Christian.

FRANÇOIS LEBRUN

See also Demography; Protestantism; Tomb

Further Reading

Favre, Robert, *La mort dans la littérature et la pensée françaises au siècle des Lumières,* Lyon: Presses Universitaires, 1978

Flinn, Michael Walter, *The European Demographic System, 1500–1820,* Brighton, Sussex: Harvester Press, and Baltimore, Maryland: Johns Hopkins University Press, 1981

McManners, John, *Death and the Enlightenment: Changing Attitudes to Death among Christians and Unbelievers in Eighteenth-Century France,* Oxford: Clarendon Press, and New York: Oxford University Press, 1981

Milanesi, Claudio, *Morte apparente e morte intermedia: Medicina e mentalità nel dibattito sull'incertezza dei segni della morte, 1740–1789*, Rome: Istituto della Enciclopedia Italiana Fondata da Giovanni Treccani, 1989

Minois, Georges, *Histoire du suicide: La société occidentale face à la mort volontaire*, Paris: Fayard, 1995

Vovelle, Michel, *La mort et l'Occident: De 1300 à nos jours*, Paris: Gallimard, 1983

Dechristianization. *See* Secularization and Dechristianization

Decoration

Interior decoration of the home was an important aesthetic concern throughout the 18th century. The first decades of the century were marked by the growing influence of the French style; the enduring Italian heritage provided the sole source of resistance to this expansion of "French fashion." Beginning in the 1750s, however, a vigorous classical reaction occurred throughout Europe. This marked the emergence of a new stylistic community, preparing the way for the establishment of neoclassical supremacy. In this way, interior decoration reflects the general evolution of the arts in the 18th century.

The Evolution of Styles

Theories differ regarding the origins of the decorative style that emerged in France at the beginning of the century. Kimball has emphasized the importance of the last phase of the construction carried out for Louis XIV around 1700 at Marly and at Versailles, under the direction of Jules Hardouin-Mansart, with Pierre Le Pautre playing a predominant role (see Kimball). The influential role played, in later phases of the construction, by artisans who were foreign or trained outside of France, notably Oppenordt and Meissonnier, has also been emphasized (see Roland Michel). In any case, a new conception of interior decoration began to emerge at the end of Louis XIV's reign; as it gradually developed, this new conception would be manifested at the level of both overall organization and ornamental details. As newly conceived, decoration per se was no longer the focal point of facades, where the use of columns, statues, and large pediments declined. Focus shifted from those elements to the use of *mascarons,* cartouches, shells, or military motifs, which were placed around openings or on projecting points, in the service of a new type of architecture that emphasized the interplay of lines.

The use of decorative elements was thus essentially moved indoors, where rooms—now smaller—were arranged in a more refined layout. In this context, decoration transformed the home into a jewel box covered with the increasingly invasive vegetation of rocaille ornamentation. New principles of interior decoration were slowly established. Although respect for symmetry remained systematic in the disposition of basic elements (fireplaces, doors, windows, and wood paneling), after 1730 symmetry was often abandoned in the composition of ornamental details or the design of panels. The desired effect was one of a balanced combination of asymmetrical elements. Fireplaces were reduced in size and mirrors were placed on the wall areas once graced by paintings, which were in turn relegated to the area above the doors. Reliance on the traditional architectural orders was abandoned, as was the use of the old-style, compartmentalized paneling, in order to create a sense of vertical unity that was further underscored by lowering the archivolts. Initially concentrated at the center and at the extremities of panels or cornices, where it served to mask architectural joints, ornamentation moved on from there to take over whatever free space remained. Finally, embellishment was integrated with figurative decoration in the form of cartouches or small scenes ensconced in arabesques. Decorative themes drawn from classical mythology gradually fell from favor and were replaced by motifs featuring children at play, pastoral scenes, chinoiserie, and menageries. These themes reflected the spirit of the times, which was resolutely devoted to the related themes of play, seduction, exotica, and childhood.

These shifting trends in interior decoration are also marked by a profoundly ambivalent relationship between the ornamental repertory and nature. In a movement imbued with natural realism, boughs, rocks, shells, and animals were added to the traditional repertory (ovum, acanthus leaves, grotesque masks, lattice-work, finials, cascades, and trophies). Inversely, however, the desire to bend these natural motifs to the fantastic wishes of their creators and to the necessities of decorative effect, which became more and more exuberant, prompted increasing stylization. Alongside increasingly contorted cartouches, hybridization—the emergence of forms that could be characterized as neither mineral nor vegetable—was to triumph. This taste for hybrids had been inherited from classical arabesque, which, at the start of the 18th century, had infused the new style with a sense of freedom from structure.

Hybridization brought about the creation of a repertory of forms that resist analysis. The originality and strangeness of these forms drew violent criticism of an art judged unacceptably irrational and unnatural. In fact, critics were making themselves heard as early as the end of the 17th century. The comte de Caylus, Pierre-Jean Mariette, and the abbé Leblanc were the first to condemn the "modern style" and to call for a reformation of taste. Such critics influenced the Direction des Bâtiments du Roi (Royal Buildings Administration), an entity directed by relatives of Madame de Pompadour beginning in 1745. The future marquis de Marigny, who was a brother of the king's mistress and who had been designated to succeed his uncle Tournehem as director of the Bâtiments du Roi, was sent to Italy from 1749 to 1751 to study the ancients. He was accompanied by the abbé Leblanc, the architect Jacques-Germain Soufflot, and the engraver Charles-Nicolas Cochin. Upon his return in November 1751 Marigny assumed his new post in the Bâtiments du Roi. In December 1754, in his *Supplique aux orfèvres* (Petition to Goldsmiths), Cochin vehemently attacked the rocaille idiom of the artists then in vogue and placed decoration at the center of aesthetic debate. Thus, from midcentury on, the climate appears to have favored the development of a new formal repertory that stressed reviving "the natural"—meaning order and simplicity, as exemplified by great examples from the 17th century and antiquity.

The search for a style to fill the vacuum left by critical condemnation of the rocaille style cannot be reduced to a simple rediscovery of antiquity. During its initial phase in the 1750s, this search was basically a restoration of the "good taste of the past century."

Jacques-François Blondel certainly thought of it in this way. An admirer of Perrault, François Blondel, and François Mansart, Jacques-François Blondel held opinions close to those of Cochin and the marquis de Marigny, both of whom distrusted the exaggerations of enthusiasts of antiquity. From 1760 on, however, rejection of modern style and a reluctance to simply return to the Louis XIV style prompted exploration of more varied aesthetic directions. Antiquity, as a political and moral mirror, was charged with new polemical force. Recent excavations at Herculaneum and Pompeii had satisfied the curiosity of amateurs and artists alike with indications of how the interiors of Roman houses were decorated. In addition, the first archeological findings of Greek remains were published. "Greek" style, the first of the ancient styles, triumphed immediately after the end of the Seven Years' War (1763). Aesthetic developments during this period were astonishingly rich, and the conventional sequence of rocaille style followed by a period of transition, and then by neoclassical style, provides only a very rough approximation of those developments.

However, two major trends can be discerned. The first of these, a radical trend, centered on the adoption of an entirely new ornamental repertory and is exemplified by the decor created in 1757 by Robert Le Lorrain (1715–59) for the furniture of La Live de Jully, a space used for top-level diplomatic functions. Heavy festoons, wide fluting, lion muzzles and paws, and Greek frets and friezes form an austere setting that breaks completely with the preceding style. These designs were severely criticized by Cochin, who objected to their massive appearance.

The second, alternative, trend was classical variation on the art of the first half of the 18th century. This tendency can be seen in the decor conceived in 1752–53 at the Palais-Royal for the duc d'Orléans by Pierre Contant d'Ivry (1698–1777). Symmetry reigns in the disposition of the ornamental elements, which are treated with a degree of naturalism. Palm leaves, shells, and boughs are mixed with smoking incense burners in the antique style. Flexibility of line still animates the whole, but it is the traditional architectural orders that give rhythm to the rooms and structure the decor, just as they did in the classical architecture of the 17th century. The richness of the era stems from the fact that artists could exploit their capacity for innovation in their choice, treatment, and juxtaposition of motifs, as well as in the organization of the decor as a whole.

In general, this "return to antiquity" reversed the trend that had marked the beginning of the century. The traditional architectural orders returned, as did the clear delineation of decorative panels and respect for architectural line. The traditional repertory of classical decorative motifs returned as well, including vases, incense burners, torches, quivers, column bases of oak or laurel leaves, ovolos, pearls, Greek scenes, friezes, and rosettes. "Egyptian," "Greek," "Etruscan," and "Pompeian" motifs abounded. Inspired by recent archeological discoveries, each of these motifs gave birth to a style, or rather a trend, of the same name. Among these trends, the "Etruscan" and "Pompeian" styles, in particular, actually owed much to the revival of interest in the classical arabesque, which regained its integrity after having been rather brutally mishandled by ornamental artists of the 1730s and 1740s. Appreciated for its lightness and finesse, the arabesque once again covered surfaces, demonstrating its inexhaustible adaptability and aesthetic potential. Alongside the arabesque, sphinxes, griffins, sirens, and chimera drew on their status as ancient motifs in order to avoid being expunged from the new style in the name of reason and nature. Finally, the flower, especially the rose—displayed in crowns, bouquets, garlands, and semicircles—appeared as the true signature of the occasionally precious naturalism that predominated at the end of the century, just as the motif of the shell had embodied the unbridled naturalism of the preceding century.

Architects and Building Sites

The first wave of new construction in Paris coincided with the end of the reign of Louis XIV and continued during the Regency. Gilles-Marie Oppenordt (1672–1742), the regent's architect, decorated the Palais Royal (1716–21), the Hôtel d'Assy (1720), and the Palais du Temple (1721). Antoine Vassé (1681–1736), sculptor at the Bâtiments du Roi was the other important name of that time. His decoration of the gallery of the Hôtel de Toulouse (1719) still exists. The Condé family's favorite decorator was Jean Aubert (died 1741), who worked on apartments in the château de Chantilly (1718–22).

The 1730s saw the triumph of Nicolas Pineau (1684–1754) and Juste-Aurèle Meisonnier (1695–1750) and, with them, the "picturesque" style. Pineau worked on the hôtels Rouille (1730), de Villars (1732–33), de Roquelaure (1733), and de Mazarin (1735). Meisonnier, the designer of the king's bedroom and chambers, created extremely free designs (the chambers of the maréchal Bielensky's chambers in 1734, the private apartments of the baronne Besenval's apartments, and the princesse Czartoriska's salon after 1735). Pineau was a sculptor and Meisonnier a goldsmith by trade—an indication that master craftsmen, rather than architects, dominated interior decoration during that decade. During the same period the architect Germain Boffrand (1667–1754) provided a much more stable version of rocaille (for example, the salons in the hôtel de Soubise, 1735–40). A noticeable decline in private

building sites took place at the middle of the century, reaching its lowest point during the Seven Years' War (1756–63). The role played by Contant d'Ivry at this time has already been discussed.

A second period of intense activity followed the Peace of Paris, with the emergence a new generation of artists. The time had come for architects to reclaim the art of decoration. Claude Nicolas Ledoux (1736–1806) was one of the first to gain recognition with his work on the hôtels Hallwyll (1766), d'Uzès (1769), Montmorency (1769), and Guimard (1770). François Joseph Belanger (1744–1818), a popular architect during the 1770s, created and directed a cohesive team that included the painter Dusseaux, the ornamental artist Dugourc, and the sculptor Lhuillier—artisans whose talents blended seamlessly. Specializing in antique-style decoration inspired by the arabesque, Boulanger worked for the comte de Provence, the comte d'Artois, the duc de Brancas, and the duchesse de Mazarin. Alexandre Brongniart (1739–1813) built and decorated the hôtels Montesson (1769), Monaco (1774–77), Bourbon-Condé (1781), and Masserano (1787). Evidence of this extraordinary period of expansion, which continued until the Revolution, can be seen in the works of Jean François Thérèse Chalgrin at the hôtel de Saint-Florentin (1763), Mathurin Cherpitel (died 1809) at the hôtel du Châtelet (1770), Étienne-Louis Boullée (1728–89) at the hôtel de Brunoy (1773), and Pierre Rousseau (1751–1810) at the hôtel de Salm (1784).

The decoration projects carried out for Louis XV (1710–74) followed their own unique path. This was essentially the result of the personality of the king's first architect, Ange Jacques Gabriel (1698–1782), who, beginning in the middle of the 1730s, played a dominant role in these projects. Throughout the reign of Louis XV, Gabriel retained the king's confidence. In addition, and unlike his predecessors, Gabriel was a prolific designer who conceived and directed the execution of his own designs. Gabriel enjoyed independence and authority derived from both the king's support and the firm touch of his own talent, and he used all these assets in the service of an art nourished by tradition, open to external influences yet always aspiring to moderation and elegance. The decoration of the king's private apartments (1738) appears very sober in comparison to Pineau's work of the same period. Gabriel's work was relatively conservative, and this explains why there is no need to look for any shift toward a conservative classicism in his subsequent projects (the new council chambers at Versailles in 1755–56 and the dauphin's library, 1755). Gabriel's art shifted toward classicism only late in his career—a shift that can be discerned in the decor of the Petit Trianon (1768) and of the king's furniture storehouse (1772), and especially of Louis XVI's library (1775) where, working for the young sovereign at the end of his career, Gabriel's style appeared totally revitalized.

Gabriel's successor, Richard Mique (1728–94), worked essentially for the queen, whose interior chambers he completely renovated at Versailles around 1780. Mique practiced a light and charming version of the antiquity-inspired styles. At this time major distinctions were no longer being made between the styles used for royal buildings and buildings belonging to individuals. The royal court no longer eschewed architectural fashions—having long since ceased to be their point of origin.

Europe

Throughout the first half of the century the spread of the art of French decorators in Europe ran up against the vitality of the Italian tradition. Italy continued to export fresco artists, stucco artists, and architects. That nation's traditional virtuosity in the treatment of light, composition, and structural complexity—inherited from Gianlorenzo Bernini, Borromini, and Guarini—continued to develop during the time that French architects and designers were working toward freedom from the conventions of decoration. Furthermore, great painted decoration, so sorely neglected in France in the 18th century, actually reached its apogee in other European countries. Pellegrini, Tiepolo, Amigoni, and Giaquinto decorated palaces and homes in Spain, Germany, and England. German rococo is an extraordinary example of the fusion of elements from the French and Italian styles. The blend of styles is particularly evident in the religious domain, but the residence of Wurzburg, built from 1720 to 1744 by Neumann, decorated by Tiepolo, and for which Boffrand and Robert de Cotte were consulted, is the best example of this astonishing synthesis. A similar stylistic idiom, with minor variations, is evident in the palaces of Schleissheim and Nymphenburg, the imperial residence in Munich, works directed by Josef Effner (1687–1745) and then by François Cuvilliés (1695–1768) for the Bavarian electors, as well as in the extensions of the castles of Charlottenburg and Sans-souci, works by Georg Wenceslas Knobelsdorff (1699–1753) for Frederick II. French and Italian practitioners worked on the same building sites in Spain and in Russia. Marked by Pozzo's move to Vienna, a school of fresco decorators flourished in Austria. Its most famous representative was Franz-Anton Maulbertsch (1724–96).

Beginning in midcentury, an international neoclassical movement began to flourish, with Rome playing an essential role in training designers. Beginning in the 1740s, young architects rubbed shoulders there with Giambattista Piranesi (1720–78). Originally an architect, Piranesi undertook the publication of collections of motifs for the use of decorators as well as views of ruins, which contributed to the resurgence of interest in antiquity. N.H. Jardin, G.P.M. Dumont, J.L. Legeay, L.J. Le Lorrain, C.L. Clerisseau, M.J. Peyre, and E. Petitot were the French decorators who came under Piranesi's influence; many of these men traveled throughout Europe. Legeay worked in Berlin for Frederick II, Petitot worked in Parma for the daughter of Louis XV, Jardin moved to Copenhagen in 1754, and Le Lorrain moved to Saint Petersburg in 1758.

The same year, Robert Adam (1728–92), one of the artists closest to Piranesi, returned to London. Through his many projects, Adam was in the vanguard in his integration of recent archeological findings related to the decoration of the private home. Thanks to him, England, which, under the sway of the most diverse currents—from Palladianism to neo-Gothic—had been profoundly original but until then not very influential, would become a powerful creative focus in the field of decoration. Men like Ledoux and Belanger, who did not travel to Italy, opted instead to cross the English Channel in the 1760s. This fact marks a shift in values that extended far beyond the domain of decoration.

FRÉDÉRIC DASSAS

See also Antiquity; Architecture; Baroque; Furniture; Miniature

Further Reading

Gruber, Alain Charles, editor, *The History of Decorative Arts: Classicism and the Baroque in Europe,* translated by John Goodman, New York: Abbeville Press, 1996 (original French edition, 1992)

Kimball, Fiske, *The Creation of the Rococo,* Philadelphia, Pennsylvania: Philadelphia Museum of Art, 1943

Roland Michel, Marianne, *Lajoüe et l'art rocaille,* Neuilly-sur-Seine, France: Arthena, 1984

Découpage. *See* Silhouettes and Découpage

Deformity. *See* Ugliness and Deformity

Deism

Deism is generally defined as the belief that God, having created the world, no longer exerts any influence on its workings. Such a belief implies a natural religion common to all humankind. The deist God is often compared to a watchmaker who, having made a watch and wound it, leaves it to function by itself.

The terms "deism" and "deists" are often assumed to have been coined by analogy with "atheism" and "atheists" (see Gawlick). Deism has attracted considerable scholarly interest, at least since Gotthard Victor Lechler's *Geschichte des englischen Deismus* (1841; History of English Deism). Troeltsch saw deism as "the religious philosophy of the Enlightenment" and therefore "the source of all modern religious philosophy" (*Gesammelte Schriften* [1898; Writings on Theology and Religion]). Troeltsch's reference is to a late manifestation of the movement and not to the "deists" first mentioned in a text by Pierre Viret, where the term refers to a heterodox group in Lyon (1564). Pierre Bayle, in the article "P. Viret" in his *Dictionnaire historique et critique* (1697; An Historical and Critical Dictionary), calls Viret's text the birth certificate of deism. Generally conceived as a religious movement that accepted the idea of God but regarded revelation as superfluous—sometimes going so far as to deny it— deism came to stand for the idea that "natural religion" was sufficient. Deism rapidly spread throughout Europe, although it was never institutionalized and never acquired a fixed doctrine. The movement remained undefined and difficult to discern; we have only sparse evidence of its existence, doubtless because it was dangerous to adhere to deism publicly.

Beginning in the 18th century, and even with its earliest inception, deism was often likened to a current of physico-theology that propagated the idea of the world as a machine functioning without its maker's intervention. Although it is generally accepted that this basic idea already existed in the second half of the 16th century and that it survived until around the middle of the 18th century, the history of deism is riddled with gaps and lacunae. There have been attempts to define it by listing a number of recurring themes, such as the rejection of the idea that any single religion had a monopoly on truth; the placing of different forms of sincere piety on an equal footing; the sense of a profound commonality of thought among reasonable minds who worship God; the belief in the existence and adequacy of an original, natural, and reasonable religion; and a corresponding liberation from dogmatic traditions. The last and most important of these recurring themes was the rejection of Christology and the dogma of the Trinity, which brought Deism close to Socinianism and neo-Arianism. The name "freethinkers" (coined by Anthony Collins in 1713), by which the adherents of the movement later called themselves, was an appropriate one. However, trying to define deism exclusively as free thought makes one aware that Immanuel Kant's classification does not reflect all of the historical facts in this case. There is a general consensus that, after making its first appearance around 1560, deism is, strictly speaking, the movement that flourished, between around 1660 and 1730, especially in England, where it was refuted by Edward Stillingfleet (1635–99) in his *A Letter to a Deist* (1697) and defended by Charles Blount (1654–93), John Toland (1670–1722), Anthony Collins (1676–1729), and, above all, Matthew Tindal (1657–1733)]. This brand of deism, transmitted through widely divergent opinions, spread to France, where it principally influenced Voltaire and Jean-Jacques Rousseau, and to Germany, where it influenced Samuel Reimarus.

A closer examination of these hypotheses reveals some fundamental problems. For example, if deism was inseparably linked to the thesis of the sufficiency of natural religion, it cannot have appeared until after 1650. Before that date both theoretical discourse (Jean Bodin) and historical accounts considered "natural religion" as no more than a primitive phase prior to the first divine revelation. It is imperative here to make the distinction between natural religion and natural theology. Natural theology proceeds from the hypothesis of a natural knowledge of God; it is therefore "philosophical" in the sense that it is an "essential theology" (an idea put forth by Panetius and Varro and later taken up by Thomas Aquinas and Moses Maimonides, among others). It was only at the end of the 17th century, in a climate of violent controversy, that a truly active natural religion emerged, against which its detractors held up revealed religion as the sole path to salvation.

It is also important to give nuance to the claim that the terms "deism" and "deist" were coined by analogy with "atheism" and "atheist." While "atheism" seems to have been established around the end of the 16th century (see Barth), it is likely that "deism" did not appear until around 1660 (see Emerson in Lemay; Betts; and Sullivan). After Viret's original use of the term "deists"—with all the negative connotations the term would carry for many people who used it after him—it was adopted by those in Lyon who believed in God but not in the consubstantiality of Jesus and God, nor in the immortality of the soul. In tracing their roots to Stoicism and Epicureanism, Viret revealed the flimsiness of his knowledge on the subject. What is surprising is that the term "deists," which originally designated one group of people, remained in use for so long. A century later there were still numerous references to "deists," both in the singular and in the plural (Blount [1695]; Humphrey Prideaux [1696]; Charles Leslie [1697]; Stillingfleet [1697]; Johann Heinrich Zedler [1734]; and, finally, Gotthold Ephriam Lessing, in *Von der Duldung der Deisten* [1777; On the Toleration of the Deists]). It was thus a long time after the initial phase in Lyon that such Englishmen as Blount (1705) began to call themselves "deists." Today, there are strong arguments showing that the differences between the "deists" of the 16th century (concentrated in Lyon and the south of France) and those English intellectuals of the late 17th and early 18th centuries were such that there can be no question of continuity between the two, except in name.

The first deists—the groups in the south of France—may have originated in Italy, but some researchers propose to trace their roots back to Lyon or to Poland. Along with offshoots in Germany and Poland, these early heterodox groups were often also known as *Trinitistes* (anti-Trinitarians) or *Arriani* (Arians). What is certain is that the groups in southern France called themselves "deists" (as is proved by Viret's text and by diocesan records) and, above all, that they rejected the Trinity. It was on this account that they became known as *Novi Arriani* (New Arians). Moreover, they probably believed neither in divine Providence nor in its manifestation through the direct intervention of God in the world.

We must conclude that these anti-Trinitarian "deists" had no direct link with the rationalist, naturalist, or freethinking movement that would later emerge. Over the course of the 17th century the terms *deistae* or *déistes* disappeared so thoroughly that, according to Betts, there is no sign of deist thought to be found between 1630 and 1670. We can therefore state that the first deists did not fire the starting gun for the Enlightenment. On the contrary, they remained attached to the principles of Christianity (as had Arius and Michael Servetus) and they wished to remain loyal to its origins—even though they were charged with heresy for rejecting the dogma of the Trinity, claiming it to be a belated product of analyses by the church fathers. In fact, since they did not adhere to the principle of natural religion that would later be a constitutive element of deism, it is most accurate to avoid the term "deism" when referring to this earlier phase.

It seems to be more appropriate, then, to see the "deists"—to adopt a usage that was still common at the turn of the 18th century—as a new movement that emerged toward the end of the 17th century, and whose members had only a vague idea of what the first deists had been like. Zedler and Bayle were not pioneers. In his *Traité de la vérité de la religion chrétienne* (1684; Treatise on the Truth of the Christian Religion), Jacques Abbadie had already loosely categorized "orders of deists" (but, we emphasize, he did not yet define "deism"). According to Abbadie, the deist orders were characterized by a conception of God, that: (1) was "bizarre" (without any further qualification); (2) held that God has no knowledge of events in the world; (3) held that God does not look after the world; (4) held that God has given men a "religion" born out of natural feelings.

According to current research, the word "deism" was given its first—albeit still somewhat vague—definition by Blount, who referred to himself a "deist." It is not known what led him to choose this term. Numerous contacts between England and France, often made through refugees, presumably spread the word "deist" to England; its first appearance in English apparently dates from 1621 (in Burton's *Anatomy of Melancholy*). The term "deism," meanwhile, first appeared around 1682, referring more precisely to a position contrary to "revealed religion." Deism was therefore regarded as the alternative to, or rather the antithesis of, revealed religion. It was a natural religion in its own right, a rejection of revealed or supernatural religion.

Even if we restrict the use of the term to this later phase, deism remains a vague concept, particularly when it is used as a standard for assigning one author or another to the movement. One would certainly no longer attribute its origins to Reginald Peacock, making of him the "first deist author," as Warner called him in 1756, nor, despite John Leland's arguments at about the same time, would one include Lord Herbert of Cherbury among the deists (see Leland). Despite these exceptions it remains all but impossible to draw up a precise list of deist writers. A number of suggestions have been made, but with widely varying results (see Sullivan). Nevertheless, it is possible to trace the beginnings of deism to Blount and to include Tindal, Toland, and Collins among deist writers, even though neither Toland nor Collins described themselves in such terms (Toland's case in particular has its ambiguities). But like deism itself, which remains largely indefinable, these three authors are difficult to categorize; to specify the characteristics of deism is more a matter of convenience than of genuine analysis (see Sullivan).

Without question, Lord Herbert of Cherbury and his five notes on the knowledge of God ([*De veritate* [1624; On Truth]) must figure in any attempt to define deism. Cherbury contends in this work that God exists; that human beings must venerate him, practice virtue and piety, and repent their sins; and that they will be rewarded in the hereafter. In themselves, these rules do not present a fundamental critique of traditional religion or constitute a revolutionary innovation. In fact, they represent a long-established tradition, that of *theologia naturalis* (natural theology), which does not correspond to a *religio naturalis* (natural religion)—either in Cherbury's writings or in the writings of anyone else. *Religio* had always been considered one of the moral virtues and therefore belonged to the natural realm or natural reason. Cherbury's innovation—like that of his rival René Descartes—consisted in investigating the conditions of knowledge with a view to securing reliable access to truth, which was a characteristic procedure of the early modern era. Thus, although he sometimes virulently condemned the abuses of the Church and presented himself in later debates as a defender of natural religion, Cherbury's reflections were not primarily concerned with theology one way or the other.

Given the reservations set out above, we can no longer include Arthur Bury (1624–1713) among English deist writers, even though he regarded Jesus as the precursor of all reasonable deists. In contrast, Blount can reasonably be considered a deist (he called himself one), since he gave himself the mission of combating the religious domination of the clergy and promoting freedom of conscience, and since he. wanted religion to be considered a form of ethics (*Latitudinarius orthodoxus* [1697; The Orthodox Latitudinarian]). Without trying to portray John Locke (1632–1704) as a

full-fledged deist, one cannot discount his influence on the generation that followed Blount. Seeking to harmonize revelation and reason, Locke highlighted the rational character of religion in his *Reasonableness of Christianity* (1695). One must also count Toland among the deists, as he denied that revelation has any priority over reason and set out to remove mystery and irrationality from Christianity in his *Christianity Not Mysterious* (1696). Tindal, for his part, proposed an original critique of the Bible, making revelation into a restoration of natural religion in his *Christianity as Old as Creation* (1730). Since revelation is no more than a reaffirmation of religious and moral principles that already existed in natural religion, he argued, biblical statements are necessarily reasonable and morally good. Finally, Collins insisted on the positive designation of "freethinkers," which he used as a synonym for "deists." For Collins too, faith finds an adequate foundation in reason, and if natural religion has waned that is the Church's fault. Meanwhile, the violently anti-ecclesiastical wing of deism may be represented by such names as Thomas Morgan (1680–1743), Thomas Cubb (1690–1747), and Peter Annet (1693–1769).

Counterreaction and opposition to the deist critique of the Bible was mainly concentrated in three camps: apologists, including the Cambridge Platonists Leslie (1650–1722), Prideaux (1648-1724), author of *A Letter to the Deists* (1696), and Stillingfleet; rationalists, including Samuel Clarke (1675–1729) and Richard Bentley (1662–1742); and finally those for whom Christianity itself was the archetype of natural religion, such as William Whiston (1667–1757), Thomas Woolston (1670–1733), Robert Boyle (1627–91), Joseph Butler (1692–1757), and George Berkeley (1685–1753).

David Hume (1711–76) was not really a deist in the strict sense of the word, but rather an empiricist. As for Voltaire, he was more a representative of the philosophical spirit of the Enlightenment. Reimarus (1694–1768) could be classed among the deists by virtue of his rigor, since he concentrated above all on a critique of Christian traditions based primarily on the Bible. Clearly, biblical criticism constituted an important element of deism.

In the final analysis, what we can call deism in the strict sense—that is, English deism—can only be described chronologically and geographically, for its essential aspects are found less in the works of Cherbury than in those of Spinoza or, especially, Uriel da Costa. Even the idea of a watchmaker God, so typically deist, belonged to a much older tradition, found as early as the writings of Nicolas Oresme (c. 1320–82). We are left, then, with a vague idea that had imprecise outlines and lexical usages that were hardly standardized. The terms "deist" and "theist" were sometimes interchangeable, and even Toland occasionally likened deism to atheism, even as he called himself a "pantheist."

ERNST FEIL

See also Apologetics; Atheism; Chance and Necessity; Clandestine Literature; Optimism and Pessimism; Protestantism; Providence; Secularization and Dechristianization

Further Reading

Barth, Hans-Martin, *Atheismus und Orthodoxie: Analysen und Modelle christlicher Apologetik im 17. Jahrhundert*, Göttingen, Germany: Vandenhoeck und Ruprecht, 1971

Betts, Christopher J., *Early Deism in France: From the So-called "Deists" of Lyon (1564) to Voltaire's Lettres Philosophiques (1734)*, The Hague and Boston: Nijhoff, 1984

Feil, Ernst, "Die Deisten als Gegner der Trinität: Zur ursprünglichen Bedeutung und speziellen Verwendung des Begriffs 'Deistae' für Sozinianer," *Archiv für Begriffsgeschichte* 3 (1990)

Gawlick, G., "Deismus," in *Historisches Wörterbuch der Philosophie*, edited by Joachim Ritter, vol. 2, Basel: Schwabe, 1972

Grell, Ole Peter, Jonathan I. Israel, and Nicholas Tyacke, editors, *From Persecution to Toleration*, Oxford: Clarendon Press, 1991

Leland, John, *A View of the Principal Deistical Writers of the Last and Present Century . . .*, London: Dodd, 1754–55

Lemay, J.A. Leo, editor, *Deism, Masonry, and the Enlightenment: Essays Honoring Alfred Owen Aldridge*, Newark, New Jersey: University of Delaware Press, and London and Cranbury, New Jersey: Associated University Presses, 1987

Rupp, E. Gordon, *Religion in England, 1688–1791*, Oxford: Clarendon Press, and New York: Oxford University Press, 1986

Sullivan, Robert E., *John Toland and the Deist Controversy: A Study in Adaptations*, Cambridge, Massachusetts: Harvard University Press, 1982

Demography

The age of the Enlightenment brought a growing awareness of European population statistics. The registration of births, marriages, and deaths was by then almost universal, except in the Russian empire and the Balkans. At times states intervened to regulate registrations—for example, in France in 1736. That same year, the Swedish Parliament ordered parish ministers to submit regular statistics of births and deaths and collated these numbers into national figures, which were initially kept secret. France followed this example in 1772. In 1754 Sweden again took the lead: using data provided by its ministers, the nation was able to introduce the first modern-type census, breaking down the population by age and sex.

Other states did not go beyond the simple system of counting the populace, although some—including Austria and Spain—refined their methods. France rejected the idea of a national census, but attempts were made to assess the population by applying a "universal multiplier" to the mean annual birthrate (which resulted in an underestimate of the population). In 1753 the English Parliament categorically rejected plans for a census. Thornton, member of Parliament for York, believed that it would have a disastrous effect on the liberty of the English. It was not until the French Revolution that the idea of the census finally took hold in Europe.

Despite the absence of official figures, historians working with the available data and using the techniques of historical demographics have been able to reconstruct the population statistics of several large countries, including France and England. Researchers have also been able to establish, with some margin for error, the distribution of the European population at the beginning and at the end of the 18th century (Figures 1 and 2). According to these estimates, around 1700 the European continent had a population of about 120 million, some 55 million of whom lived in northern and western Europe (west of the Oder). In other words, at that time Europe was home to 16 percent of the total world population, which has been estimated at 730 million.

In terms of the national boundaries of the period, the kingdom of France had the largest population (20 million), followed by the Spanish possessions in Europe (15 million), the empire of the Tsars (14 million), the

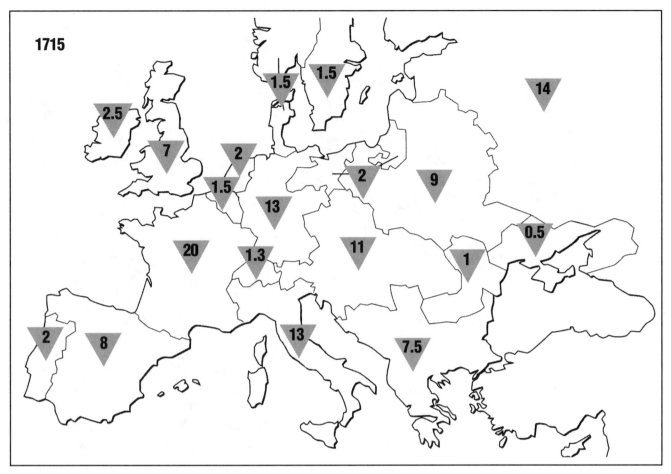

Figure 1. Distribution of the European population in 1715, in millions.
Source: Colin McEvedy and Richard Jones, *Atlas of World Population History*, London and New York: Penguin, 1978.

Austrian territories (11 million), the Turkish possessions in Europe (9 million), the kingdom of Poland (9
million), and the future United Kingdom of Great Britain (over 9 million including Ireland). As a result of the
treaties of Utrecht and Rostatt, these figures were modified in favor of Austria. In terms of today's boundaries,
France (with 22 million) would still be ahead, followed
by the Commonwealth of Independent States (CIS [the
European portion of the former Soviet Union, minus
the Balkan states]; 19 million), Italy (13 million), Germany (13 million), Spain (8 million), Great Britain (7
million), and Poland (6 million). The Balkans had a little more than 6 million inhabitants, and Scandinavia 3
million.

These populations were largely rural. Towns and cities played a major role in politics, commerce, society,
and culture, but the level of urbanization—that is, the
proportion of the population living in cities—did not
exceed 10 or 11 percent except in a few countries, such
as the Netherlands and England. The largest city on the
Continent remained Constantinople (now Istanbul)
with 700,000 inhabitants. London (575,000 residents)

and Paris (530,000) vied for second place. (The debate
as to which of those two cities was actually the larger
had prompted research into political arithmetic even
before the end of the 17th century.) Far behind Constantinople, London, and Paris came Naples (with
270,000 inhabitants), Lisbon (188,000), Amsterdam
(172,000), Rome (149,000), Venice (144,000), Moscow (130,000), Milan (124,000), Palermo (113,000),
Madrid (110,000), and Vienna (105,000).

Over the course of the 17th century, population
growth in Europe had been very modest (around 20
percent). This slow growth rate resulted from an unfavorable climate (the "little ice age") and from widespread wars, which had devastated huge tracts of
central and eastern Europe. The three apocalyptic
scourges of plague, famine, and war resulted in
extremely high mortality rates.

Bubonic plague appeared in Europe in the 14th century and continued to break out in one place or another
every year until 1670, after which point it became possible to contain the disease to a great extent, at least in
the middle and west of the Continent, by the use of

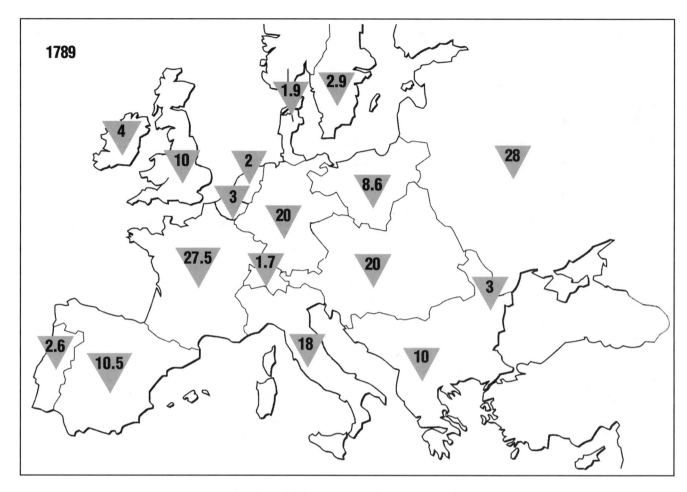

Figure 2. Distribution of the European population in 1789, in millions.
Source: Colin McEvedy and Richard Jones, *Atlas of World Population History,* London and New York: Penguin, 1978.

cordons sanitaires (quarantine lines). Subsequent epidemics still erupted on a regional scale, in central Europe in 1679–80, Poland and the Baltic countries in 1708–10, Provence in 1720–21, and Russia in 1770–74. In the 18th century the plague remained endemic only in the Balkans. However, other diseases took its place: in particular, dysentery, typhoid, miliary fever, and smallpox. These diseases returned periodically, following cycles connected both to weather conditions and to the proportion of the population immunized. Bad periods, identifiable here and there throughout Europe from the mortality statistics, included 1709–10, 1718–19, 1739–43, 1772, and 1785. Each country had its own periods of high mortality, however: England in 1712, 1720, and 1728–30; France in 1747, 1779, and 1782–83; Sweden in 1757, 1763, and 1790, and so on. Meanwhile, in 1707–08 and 1784–85, Iceland suffered smallpox epidemics, which struck its unimmunized populace without warning and carried off between a quarter and a third of the population. Medicine was powerless to prevent these scourges. Science could describe illnesses but not cure them. Inoculation was

used against the smallpox, but informed opinion remained sceptical, as demonstrated by the famous debate between Bernoulli and Jean le Rond D'Alembert at the Académie Royale des Sciences des Paris (French Royal Academy of Sciences) in 1760. Only at the very end of the 18th century did Edward Jenner perfect an effective system of prevention—vaccination.

It is hard to be precise about the impact of mortality during the Enlightenment because it varied greatly from one region and from one period to another. A major study by the French Institut National d'Études Démographiques (National Institute of Demographic Studies) has revealed that as a result of the terrible rate of infant mortality—around one child in four—life expectancy in France did not exceed 25 years between 1740 and 1749. By the end of the century, however, it had risen to 30 years. Turning to England, Wrigley and Schofield cite some significant fluctuations: the average life expectancy rose from 27.9 years in 1731 to 38.2 years in 1776. Life expectancy in Sweden stood at 33 years for the period 1757–63. Taken as a whole, there was slow and irregular progress, which should perhaps be linked to the improvement in the global environment (after the "Maunder Minimum" [1645–1715], solar activity returned to normal for the rest of the 18th century).

Despite the very high mortality rates, population levels were maintained throughout the century except in cities, where overcrowding favored contagion. In Stockholm, for example, according to the figures for 1755–63, mortality rates by age group were more than double those of the rest of the kingdom of Sweden for men and women, young and old alike. The disparity was greatest for men between 40 and 50 years old, for whom there were 49.2 deaths per 1,000 in the capital as compared to 18.4 in the provinces. The disparity was smallest for women between 60 and 70 years old, for whom there were 69 deaths per 1,000 in the capital and 44.9 in the provinces. As a result, the natural balance of population in the cities was almost invariably negative, and city populations were only maintained through the continual influx of young people from the countryside.

Most migrations centered on the cities, the role and sizes of which grew during the 18th century. Each city had its own migratory "pool," the geographic extent of which depended on the city's size, on communication facilities, and on competition from other cities. J.-P. Poussou explains that

these pools consisted of several communities that in a sense comprised a given city's "private reserve"; within this geographic zone that city consistently attracted more immigrants than any other city. The key point is that these pools were not merely permanent (or nearly so) but still to a large extent impermeable. . . . Moreover, being of similar size, the demographic pool areas were mutually almost impenetrable. The map of the kingdom of France was thus divided in the mid–18th century into a number of large demographic pool areas—in proximity to Lille, Paris, Rouen, Lyon, Nantes, Bordeaux, Marseilles, etc.—none of which overlapped. The result of this division was to leave gaps, zones where the attraction of the cities was felt only in a very limited way.

The tide of migration to the cities consisted mainly of servants, almost all from the neighboring countryside. The percentage of the population employed in domestic service in European cities ranged from 8.8 percent (Antwerp, 1755) to 25.3 percent (Berne, 1764). These migrants very young (18 to 30). More than half moved back to their villages to marry once they had accumulated some savings, a good quarter of them set up house in the city, and the rest remained in service or moved on. Those who failed to find work as servants fell into poverty, crime, prostitution, or begging. It is estimated that during the 18th century these migrations involved between 300,000 and 400,000 young Europeans every year.

The cities also took in entire households, as well as a certain number of widows, from their migratory pool zones. In times of crisis streams of impoverished people made their way to the cities in search of relief. On such occasions the authorities combined assistance with policing. They aimed either to send the poor back to their home parishes or to contain them. Generally speaking, the phenomena of vagrancy and of begging grew considerably during the 18th century, while remaining by definition very hard to measure. The level of this floating population probably varied, according to time and place, between 1 and 5 percent. Many of the vagrants were country people who had been cast out of the city. Cities played a role in redistribution, for they sent back a proportion of their immigrants after a few years and sent on a flood of emigrants to other cities or abroad. (In Rouen, for example, only about 20 percent of the emigrants were originally from that city.) In Jean-Pierre Bardet's striking expression, the city was not only a *mouroir* (a place to die) but also a *passoire* (strainer) (see Bardet and Dupâquier).

Over time the pattern changed. Immigration took place over longer distances and assumed a political and cultural scope that cut across the traditional migratory pool areas. At the same time, movement between cities intensified: in relative terms, strictly urban population movement exceeded that of the rural population. Geographic mobility also took the form of seasonal migrations. In most of the mountain regions of Mediterranean Europe, the severity of the winters forced the livestock-keeping populations to retreat to the valleys and even to travel over the neighboring plains. Known as "transhumance," this custom of moving herds of cattle or sheep about was especially significant in Spain and the southern Alps. In the already overpopulated regions of central Europe, the northern Alps, and the Massif Central, the length of the cold season forced the men to migrate temporarily to supplement their resources. There was an increased tendency toward specialized production in every region—and indeed, sometimes every valley. Lastly, the intervals between agricultural tasks were filled with brief migrations, often over short distances, for harvesting or grape picking. These seasonal migrations, which can still be thought of as "regular," shaded imperceptibly into migrations that lasted a number of years and which could be temporary or lifelong. Such longer-term migrations sometimes resulted in permanent uprootings, especially since death often turned a migration that was originally intended to be temporary into a "permanent" one.

Very little is known about these internal migrations except for those that took place in countries such as

Sweden, where parish ministers recorded arrivals and departures. The degree of mobility involved seems to have varied greatly from one country to another: the English and the Swedes appear to have been very mobile, the French very sedentary. Not that this sedentary nature excluded comings and goings in the context of everyday life—quite the opposite. Peasants traveled some distance almost every day—at least from the start of spring—to tend their own vines or fields or those of other people. Every week a good number of peasants went on foot, on horseback, or by cart to buy and sell at the market in the neighboring village or town. From time to time they traveled within the surrounding area in order to take part in local festivals or pilgrimages. They often visited their relatives, perhaps five or six miles distant, for baptisms, weddings, or funerals. Finally, they courted young women from nearby villages, often marrying and settling there, without ever losing sight of the church spire of their home village. Their children often entered domestic service some distance away, but only until they could accumulate some savings. This "regular" mobility does not really contradict the overall sedentary model; indeed, one might even say that rural societies could not have functioned without it. By the same token, seasonal and temporary migrations, far from being a prelude to departure, helped to make it possible for families to remain in one place by allowing a multitude of poor peasants to obtain the means of subsistence.

Permanent migrations thus involved only a minority of 18th-century peasants. However, although migration had only a slight impact on the zones of departure (where they helped to reduce overcrowding), they had a considerable one on the zones of arrival, because immigrants there multiplied into veritable population colonies. The most massive instance of colonization in Europe was that of the eastern provinces of the Austrian empire and the southern provinces of the Russian empire. In 1763 Maria Theresa granted colonists substantial benefits, including cash advances and exemption from taxes, and sent agents to the major German cities to recruit immigrants. In 1768 the lands of the Banat region were surveyed and divided into plots of approximately 45 acres per colonist. Ten years later a census of the area recorded about a hundred new villages and over 50,000 people. The regions north of the Black Sea, meanwhile, had been recolonized beginning in the first half of the century by small numbers of Russian peasants. The great influx began in 1751 with the arrival of foreigners, mostly Serbs.

The largest colonization at that point was that of the Ukraine proper, whose repopulation was effected partly by the distribution of lands, partly by the enforced transfer of inhabitants, and partly by voluntary settlement on the part of refugee peasants. Between 1724 and 1796 the population of the black-earth region of the Russian Steppes grew by 123 percent in the center and 126 percent in the east and south. The increase reached 226 percent in the province of Azov, and 380 percent in Voronezh. Foreigners made up a significant proportion of the new inhabitants: 23,000 Germans were counted in 1775, and over 40,000 in 1806. Even natives of Alsace and Lorraine took part in this new *Drang nach Osten* (eastward expansion), in spite of the ban on leaving the kingdom of France. Between 1768 and 1786 a total of 3,579 Alsatians settled in Hungary and 599 settled in the Galician region of Poland. More than 2,500 people emigrated from Lorraine to Banat between 1744 and 1757, followed by more than 12,000 emigrants between 1763 and 1774, and another 4,000 between 1782 and 1787.

These rural colonization movements amounted to international migrations. Seen in this light, they can be compared to the settling of Europeans in America, with that phenomenon's well-known consequences for world history. Without delving too deeply into the whole question, it can be noted that in 1700 there were a mere 300,000 English and French settlers in North America, whereas in Latin America there were already a million Iberians. The 18th-century wave of emigration of some 400,000 people essentially created a balance between the populations of the two American continents. In 1800, after the annexation of Canada, the population of Anglo-Saxon North America included about 4.5 million Europeans, while there were some 4 million Europeans in Latin America. The total population of persons of European descent in the Americas was ten times that of the number of original immigrants, thus proving again one of the most important laws of the history of population: the occupation of new territories results not from a huge influx of nonnative people but from a natural growth within the new territory itself because conditions there favor a high birthrate.

European emigration is only one aspect of the regulatory mechanisms that allowed the populations of the past to avoid implosion or explosion. In order to survive, every social group must have institutions, customs, and principles that serve both to ensure the replenishment of its population after crises and to limit population growth. Otherwise, the group might become extinct or experience an expansion that would bring the group into conflict with its neighbors. These were the institutions and models that Thomas Robert Malthus would attempt to categorize in 1803, just after the century of Enlightenment, in his second *Essay on the Principle of Population*. In this essay, which seeks to justify the general theory he had conceived five years earlier, Malthus distinguishes between repressive curbs such as war, slavery, and the abandonment of children, on the one hand, and preventive curbs such as abortion, infanticide, polygamy, and late marriage, on the other. But why speak of "curbs" when, as we have seen, the populations of the past were exposed to all manner of destructive scourges? The reason is that these past populations also had a formidable power of reproduction: a girl marrying at 16, and giving birth every other year, could in theory have 12 to 15 children over the course of her reproductive life. Even allowing for the death of half these children before reaching marriageable age and for the breaking-up of partnerships by the death of one or other spouse after 12 or 15 years, such a population would increase fivefold in less than a century.

In eastern Europe, where girls married very young (see Hajnal in Glass and Eversley), the spacing out of births, linked to a prolonged period of nursing, constituted the main curb on population growth. It also appears that the average age of women at their last pregnancy was not very high. However, the annual growth rate, which had only reached 2.2 per 1,000 in the 17th century, rose to 4.5 per 1,000 in the first half of the 18th century and to 6.7 per 1,000 in the second half of that century. The explanation for this population growth is that land was abundant in this region, which had been freed from the Mongol yoke and Ottoman domination, and the great landowners were ever willing to grant land to new couples in order to increase the number of their serfs. A similar situation existed in Ireland, where the British landlords favored the splitting up of holdings with the aim of clearing more land for agriculture and intensifying speculative grain cultivation. From then on, thanks to dairy products and the potato, a tiny plot would be sufficient to support a family. Thus the population of the island, which in 1725 was under 3 million, reached 4 million in 1780 and 5.2 million in 1800. Casting off all demographic curbs, Ireland was heading toward catastrophe, providing a belated but tragic illustration to the theory that Malthus was to formulate for the first time in 1798.

In the rest of western Europe, by contrast, the institution of marriage ensured the regulation of population. The proportion of single people was relatively high (6 to 12 percent), and the birthrate outside wedlock very low, because of the stigmatization of illegitimate births. In the countryside illegitimate births rarely exceeded 1 to 2 percent of total births, while in the cities they reached 5 to 10 percent. To a large extent the higher urban rate of illegitimate births was a result of the influx of unwed mothers who came from the countryside to give birth secretly. Moreover, marriage typically took place very late in western Europe. Whereas in eastern Europe four out of five women were married before their 20th birthday, in the west the opposite was true. In France the average age of women at their first marriage was around 22 at the start of the 17th century, 24 at the start of the 18th century, and 26 during the reign of Louis XVI, which lasted from 1774 until 1792. In England, Sweden, Germany, and Belgium the average age at marriage for a woman was around 25, with a similar upward trend over time.

The postponement of marriage seems to have begun as a cultural phenomenon, although it tended to increase as the marital market became crowded. And because late marriage cut women's childbearing period by ten years or so, the birthrate was considerably lowered. To quote P. Chaunu, deferred childbearing was "the contraceptive weapon of classical Europe." It can only be understood in the context of a wider system, combining religious imperatives (forbidding conception out of wedlock), models of family structure (one couple to a household), and economic forces (the question of whether or not the distribution of property would allow the establishment of new farmsteads). So, in the old agricultural civilizations of western Europe, the concept of tenure played a role analogous to that of territory in animal societies. Young people were deprived of the right to have sexual relations until they had inherited from their parents or worked as domestic servants and saved enough money to establish themselves by their own means. This self-regulating system allowed populations to recover very rapidly after periods of high mortality, but it was much less effective at limiting population growth, at least in sufficient time.

The European population boom picked up markedly in the 18th century. The annual growth rate, which had stood at a mere 1.5 per 1,000 in the previous century, rose to 3.3 between 1700 and 1750, and then to 5.1 in the second half of the century. This rate of growth varied greatly from region to region. Over the course of the 18th century it reached 75 percent in eastern Europe, 43 percent in western Europe, and 40 percent in southern Europe. The chronology of growth was also highly variable. In southern Europe population growth was greatest during the first half of the century, while in eastern Europe the population increased progressively. In northwestern Europe the rise in population was initially slight (France was traumatized by the crisis of 1709–10, and England was badly affected by the high mortality of 1719), but then growth accelerated rapidly beginning in 1745. This surge cannot be explained by changes in birth and marriage rates. In countries where the rate of legitimate births has been scientifically measured (such as Sweden and France), not only did it fail to increase, but there was a slight but discernable falling-off of the rates by age-group over the last third of the century. The percentage of unmarried people and the average age at first marriage rose in all the western countries except Ireland and England. Since there was hardly any immigration into Europe the only possible explanation is, as we have seen, a fall in the death rate.

The growth of the European population had very diverse effects, being somewhat positive from the economic perspective and somewhat negative from the social point of view. The increase in the number of mouths to feed gave rise initially to a market imbalance: demand exceeded supply, and prices rose everywhere. As a result, producers made profits and were able to invest in the storage and distribution of grain or in the introduction of new crops. Conversely, the mass of consumers suffered from the price increases, especially in the cities. There were food riots. In France the "flour war" of 1775 foreshadowed the upheaval of 1789. Young people had difficulty establishing themselves. Vagrancy, begging, and unemployment all increased as families were obliged to spend the bulk of their budgets on food. Finally, demographic pressure helped to destabilize society and, on a European scale, the entire established order. What then was the picture at the end of the 18th century with respect to the surge in population? In 1800 the European continent numbered around 180 million inhabitants, or 50 percent more than a century earlier. Europe's share of the global population had risen from 16 percent to 19 percent. The ranking of European nations by population had not been overturned, even though countries had enjoyed very different levels of growth. The French Republic, having extended its dominion over the Netherlands, the left bank of the Rhine, Switzerland, and northern Italy, was the most populous nation, with 45 million citizens. The European portion of the Russian empire contained 36 million subjects, the Austrian Empire had 24 million inhabitants, and the United Kingdom of Great Britain (together with Ireland, which had joined the United Kingdom that same year) had 16 million. Spain had 10.5 million, European Turkey had 10 million, and the Kingdom of Prussia, 9 million.

Given the instability of borders during the period, this hierarchy means little. In terms of present-day borders, the CIS takes the lead with around 34 million inhabitants, France (29 million) is in second place, Italy (19 million) comes third, Germany (18 million) fourth, the United Kingdom (12 million) fifth, and Spain (11.5 million) sixth. Compared to 1700 levels, the population in 1800 had more than doubled in Ireland, Hungary, and Romania; it had risen by between 50 and 80 percent in Great Britain, Scandinavia, Belgium, Poland, Russia, and the Balkans; and it had grown by between 30 and 50 percent in all the other countries except the Netherlands, where it had remained stable. The urban percentage of the population hardly varied over the century, since population growth in the countryside was as great as that in the towns. Nonetheless, there was a discernable trend toward an increased concentration of population in and around large towns. The number of towns with more than 20,000 inhabitants rose from 141 to 221, and the number with more than 100,000 rose from 13 to 22. London, with 861,000 inhabitants, was now the largest city in the world, and second place was contested between Paris (547,000) and Constantinople (570,000). Next came Naples (430,000), Moscow (238,000), Lisbon (237,000), Vienna (231,000), Saint Petersburg (220,000), Amsterdam (201,000), and Adrianople (present-day Edirne, Turkey; approximately 200,000). The 12 remaining cities of more than 100,000 inhabitants were Dublin, Lyon, Marseille, Milan, Venice, Rome, Palermo, Madrid, Barcelona, Copenhagen, Hamburg, and Berlin.

The most surprising fact is that the evident growth in the European population, which should have been blindingly obvious to contemporary observers, was denied by many intelligent commentators, in France as much as in England. Most economists and philosophers were of the opinion—and attempted to persuade their readers—that Europe and the entire world were becoming depopulated. The French were the most determined: considering population as an index of, rather than a factor in, economic prosperity, they assumed the postulate that the population must inevitably be falling because the kingdom was badly governed! For this they blamed luxury, the decline in morals, and also ecclesiastical celibacy. This absurd notion of depopulation probably originated with the incorrect calculations of Justus Lipsius and Isaak Vossius (1685) concerning the population of ancient Rome. The fallacy had been taken up in 1696 by the pastor William Whitson, who in his *New Theory of the Earth* had attempted to demonstrate that population had risen in a geometric progression until the Flood but had fallen sharply since antiquity. Montesquieu popularized the idea of depopulation in his *Lettres persanes* (1721; Persian Letters). In his *Réflexions sur la propagation de l'espèce humaine* (Thoughts on the Propagation of the Human Species), published in *Mes Rêveries* (1757; My Musings), the maréchal de Saxe again took up the theme, as did, most notably, Robert Wallace, who in 1753 published *A Dissertation on the Numbers of Mankind in Ancient and Modern Times, in Which the Superior Populousness of Antiquity Is Maintained*. This work was translated into French the following year by the chevalier de Jaucourt, author of the articles "France" and "Mariage" (Marriage) in the *Encyclopédie*.

David Hume, who had become aware of Wallace's thesis even before its publication, set about refuting it in an essay entitled *The Populousness of Ancient Nations*, which appeared in the second edition of his *Political Discourses* (1752). But Wallace maintained his position and indeed hardened it, with the result that the idea of depopulation was thereafter accepted as the only politically correct one. The marquis de Mirabeau adopted it in all seriousness in his *L'ami des hommes* (1756–58; The Friend of Men). Voltaire demonstrated its absurdity to no avail in his *Dictionnaire philosophique* (1764; Philosophical Dictionary), and the abbé Raynal attempted to destroy it in his *Tableau de l'Europe* (1774; Sketch of Europe). No one even bothered to respond to these writers. The abbé Expilly, however, who had published comparative statistics of baptisms, marriages, and burials in France for the periods 1690–1701 and 1752–63, was so thoroughly persecuted that he was unable to complete the publication of his *Dictionnaire géographique, historique et politique des Gaules et de la France* (Geographical, Historical, and Political Dictionary of the Gauls and of France). In 1766 Pierre-Samuel Dupont de Nemours took issue not only with the method but with the very interest of the study: "It is calculations of prosperity, of reviving wealth, and above all of disposable wealth that are of real interest for the nation and the state, not mere calculations of population." It was only with the French Revolution and Malthus's first *Essay on the Principle of Population* (1798) that the fear of depopulation gave way to that of overpopulation.

This fruitless argument over population at least had some beneficial effects on the development of political arithmetic. Emerging in England during the reign of Charles II, with Graunt and Petty, this new science appeared as a coherent project to express economic, demographic, and social facts in mathematical form. In the 18th century, political arithmetic prevailed decisively over statistics of the German type (represented by the work of G. Achenwall and L. von Schlozer). The German statistical method had been limited to qualitative descriptions and inventories of the factors of political power and its practitioners only reluctantly allowed the use of tables. Like a nova, after shining for a moment over all of Europe, German statistics disappeared from the scientific scene. About the only trace this method left behind was the name "statistics," which the political arithmeticians would unscrupulously take over at the beginning of the 19th century. The English (Short, Chalmers, Blake, and Price) remained very much in evidence, but they were henceforth in competition with the Dutch (Kersseboom and Struyck), the Germans (Sussmilch and Bielfeld), the Swiss (Muret), the Swedes (Wargentin and Nicander), and above all the French (Expilly, Messance, Moheau, and Laplace). In 1778 the *Recherches et considérations sur la population de la France* (Research and Reflections on the Population of France) appeared, probably written jointly by Auget de Montyon and his former secretary Moheau. The avowed aim of these authors was to measure the population of a city or a state in the absence of a census and to draw lessons from these population statistics.

In order to understand the success of political arithmetic, it is not enough to consider the ideology and practices of the world of commerce; we must also bear in mind the passion of science, the "mania for measuring everything," the development of exchanges between scientists (stimulated by the various academies throughout Europe and facilitated by the use of French as a common scholarly language), the improvement in the quality of data, and also the ideological backdrop of the debate over depopulation. This debate challenged biblical chronology and the very idea of Providence, resulting in the heavy involvement of Protestant ministers, who were eager to integrate scientific observations into their religious universe. The statistical regularity that they noted in demographic phenomena seemed to them the best proof of the existence of a divine order (the title that Sussmilch gave to his work, published in Berlin in 1741). Astronomers also intervened heavily, but their contribution was mainly concerned with perfecting the mortality table, conceived by Graunt in 1661 and put into concrete form by Halley in 1693. In the Netherlands Kersseboom and Struyck solved the problem for closed populations. In England Simpson attempted to do the same for an open population. In France Deparcieux clarified the fundamental distinction between average life span and probable life span and went on to produce a masterly critique of the data (1746). In Germany Euler laid the foundations for the mathematical analysis of populations. In Sweden Wargentin produced the first classic mortality table, based on knowledge of the age distribution of deaths, on the one hand, and of the population, on the other (1766).

Thus, during the Enlightenment the tools of political arithmetic were forged, its concepts refined. That science would pass these tools and concepts on to the discipline that would soon become known as statistics, until the appearance (1855 in French and 1880 in English) of the term "demography."

JACQUES DUPÂQUIER

See also Agriculture; Children; City; Exchange; Medicine; Migration; Peasantry; Physiocracy

Further Reading

Bardet, Jean-Pierre, and Jacques Dupâquier, *Histoire des populations de l'Europe*, 3 vols., Paris: Fayard, 1997–99
Dupâquier, Jacques, and Michel Dupâquier, *Histoire de la démographie*, Paris: Librairie Académique Perrin, 1985

Glass, David Victor, *Numbering the People: The Eighteenth-Century Population Controversy and the Development of Census and Vital Statistics in Britain,* Farnborough, Hampshire: Heath, 1973

Glass, David Victor, and David Edward Charles Eversley, editors, *Population in History: Essays in Historical Demography,* London: Arnold, and Chicago: Aldine, 1965

McEvedy, Colin, and Richard Jones, *Atlas of World Population History,* London and New York: Penguin, and New York: Facts on File, 1978

Reinhard, Marcel R., and André Armengaud, *Histoire générale de la population mondiale,* Paris: Montchrestien, 1961; 3rd edition, by Reinhard, Armengaud, and Jacques Dupâquier, 1968

Denmark

In the age of the Enlightenment Denmark and Norway constituted a single, composite kingdom that also included Iceland, Greenland, and several German-speaking duchies. The kingdom had been unable to prevent Sweden from breaking away, expanding at its own expense, and finally imposing Swedish hegemony in the Baltic. Nonetheless, while avoiding armed conflict, Denmark-Norway remained vigilant in the defense of its territorial interests against Sweden's ambitions, as well as those of Russia and Prussia. Thus, it gained recognition of its rights to the duchies of Schleswig and Holstein. The regime, although nominally an absolute monarchy, was evolving toward increased liberty. Christian VI (1730–46), influenced by pietism, was succeeded by Frederick V (1746–66), who was weaker in character than his predecessor, and Christian VII (1766–1808), whose madness quickly led to his removal from power. During the two latter reigns, real power rested with the royal cabinet and ministerial colleges, which together assured the economic development of the country. Until the crisis of 1770 the dominant figures in government were A.G. Moltke and Johann Hartwig Ernst, Count Bernstorff, minister of foreign affairs. The creation of commercial companies and banks was accompanied by a policy of industrialization and liberalization of agriculture. While the new manufactories, faced with competition from both traditional crafts and foreign industries, were unable to create a market, agrarian policy inspired by the Physiocrats managed to assure the transition from great, feudal properties to the constitution of a free peasantry. The influence of Physiocracy—evidenced, for example, by the appearance of the Royal Economic and Agricultural Society (1769) or the *Danmarks og Norges Oeconomiske Magazin* (1760; Economic Magazine of Denmark-Norway)—fostered the joint development of economic modernity and the Enlightenment.

The affirmation of the Enlightenment in Denmark was marked by tensions between divergent models: radical reforms imposed from above or slower and more consensual transformation of minds and institutions; importation of foreign experiments or elaboration of a national model; fidelity to the Pietist tradition or acceptance of a secular rationalism. The crisis of 1770 brought these antagonisms to a head. A German physician, Johann Friedrich Struensee, became the lover of Queen Caroline Mathilde, was named to the cabinet, had Bernstorff dismissed, and acquired powers enabling him to impose in a few months a complete reform of both the state and the country. Freedom of commerce, industry, and printing was decreed; the organization of government was rationalized; and the administration of justice was made more humane. Such a program, while consistent with Enlightenment philosophy, reflected the will of only a small, Germanic group and soon ran into opposition from the aristocracy and the Church, as well as the resistance of popular opinion. The Queen Mother, Juliane Marie, and Crown Prince Frederick led the counteroffensive. Struensee was arrested and put to death in 1772. This experiment in the brutal application of an enlightened—but alien—policy was followed by a period of conservatism and national introspection, personified in the tutor and later secretary to the crown prince, Ove Hoegh Guldberg (1731–1808), who headed the government. Some modest reforms resumed in the 1780s, in particular at the initiative of Andreas Peter, Count Bernstorff, a nephew of the minister of foreign affairs during the 1750s and 1760s, Johann Hartwig Ernst, Count Bernstoff (see above). Freedom of printing was reestablished, free circulation of agricultural products permitted, religious freedom adopted, and serfdom abolished, as well as the slave trade in Denmark's colonies in the West Indies. The difference between the two approaches to implementing Enlightenment ideals, illustrated in Denmark, was a matter of both the pace and the conception of society.

The new philosophy developed at first in imitation of foreign models. A German-speaking nobility that had been installed at the royal court opened Denmark to German influences. French influence, probably less in evidence than in Sweden, was nonetheless real. A French periodical even appeared in Copenhagen, *La spectatrice danoise ou L'Aspasie moderne* (The Danish Spectator; or, The Modern Aspasia). English literature was also read and imitated. A national-language developed, of which the *Danske magazin* is a notable example. Academies and societies were founded, such as the Royal Scientific Society of Denmark (1742), the Society for the History and Language of the Fatherland (1744), the Literary Academy for History, Antiquities, and Language (1753), and the Society for the Pure Sciences (1763). Ludvig Holberg's (1684–1754) *Dannemarks og Norges beskrivelse* (1729; Description of Denmark and Norway) and his *Dannemarks riges historie* (1732–35; History of the Kingdom of Denmark) were rooted in the national past and written in Danish. Holberg enjoyed success throughout Europe with a fantastic novel composed in Latin, *Nicolai Klimii iter subterraneum* (1741; The Journey of Niels Klim to the World Underground), and some comedies inspired by Molière. The novel and comedies alike criticize the ponderousness of dogmatic philosophy and traditional society. Outside Copenhagen the other center of cultural life was the Academy of Sorø where, teaching alongside German professors, were the anthropologist Jens Kraft (1720–56), author of a study on the mores of primitive peoples and the development of the human mind, the jurist Jens Schielderup Sneedorff (1724–64), and his successor, Ove Hoegh Guldberg, who became tutor to the crown prince and headed the government after the downfall of Struensee. The question of the nature of the kingdom, whether it was essentially Danish or supranational, was a recurring theme in the chronicles and histories of the country. The French Revolution renewed the antagonisms between prudent reformism and radicalism but also between German and French influences. Peter Andreas Heiberg (1758–1841) and Malthe Conrad Bruun (1775–1826) left for Paris, while the poet Jens Immanuel Baggesen (1764–1826) perpetuated German-Danish interaction.

In the artistic domain, a Royal Academy of Fine Arts was organized in Copenhagen on the Parisian model. The sojourn of several artists in Rome, and their association with Anton Rafael Mengs and Johann Joachim Winckelmann, led to the Danish school's becoming one of the poles of European neoclassicism. Asmus Jakob Carstens (1754–98) stripped representation of all color and depth and his asceticism led him to simple design, the abstract diagram. In 1795 his one-man exposition in Rome was greeted as both a revolutionary act and the foundation of a new movement. Johannes Wiedewelt (1731–1802) led a parallel quest in the plastic mode, sculpting funerary monuments that returned to simple forms such as spheres, columns, and pyramids. Finally, Bertel Thorvaldsen (1768–1844) established himself as the Canova of the North, even more enamored of archaism, heroism, and grandeur than his Italian contemporary. Danish art of the 18th century ended in a radicalism of form and a passion for rigor of line.

MICHEL DELON

See also Sweden

Further Reading

Bohnen, Klaus, and Sven Aage Jørgensen, *Der dänische Gesamtstaat: Kopenhagen, Kiel, Altona*, Tubingen: Niemeyer, 1992

Hovde, Brynjolf Jacob, *The Scandinavian Countries, 1720–1865: The Rise of the Middle Classes*, 2 vols., Boston: Chapman and Grimes, 1943

Jeannin, Pierre, *L'Europe du nord-ouest et du nord aux XVIIᵉ et XVIIIᵉ siècles*, Paris: Presses Universitaires de France, 1969

Tønnesson, Kåre, "Le cas danois de despotisme éclairé," *Annales historiques de la Révolution française* (1979)

Despotism, Enlightened. *See* Monarch, Enlightened

Devil

It is generally agreed that official doctrine on the Devil did not encounter any obstacles until the 18th century, and that it was the Enlightenment that, by relegating the Devil to the realm of imagination, inaugurated a veritable critical era concerning this belief. Up until the late 17th century, Christian theology and art had cultivated New Testament demonology, enriching it with numerous cultural variants. But after the Enlightenment both Catholic and Protestant theology dealt less and less with questions of demonology, which were largely taken over by ancillary religious groups such as occultists, satanic sects, connoisseurs, and collectors of curiosities. Abandoned by the Church, the Devil became, on the one hand, the subject of fringe religiosity, while on the other hand, he was transformed into a literary theme wreathed in aesthetic prestige. It may therefore be useful to investigate how the thought of the period came to sketch out a new demonology; what part the *philosophes* played in elaborating this new perspective; and what exactly we have inherited from the Enlightenment.

Can we really accept without reservation the idea, so proudly proclaimed by the *philosophes*, that their age had decreed the death of the Devil in the collective consciousness, thanks to the victory of the *philosophes* themselves in the fight against superstition? The decline of traditional demonology in Europe has indeed been interpreted as a consequence of the flourishing of rationalism, of methods of scientific analysis, and of a widespread enlightened spirit. However, given the fact that the doctrine of the Devil has a dogmatic and theological core that cannot be reduced to the level of superstitious beliefs, can one simply declare that the Devil slunk away as reason emerged and the Enlightenment spread? (Voltaire, for example, did precisely that when he proclaimed: "There has never been a more universal empire than the Devil's. Who dethroned him? Reason.") The problems that the elimination of the Devil posed for Christianity should be taken into account, however "enlightened" that ban may have been. These are the guiding considerations of our reconstruction of the Enlightenment's portrayal of the Devil.

The interest that the churches took in demonology had faded during the course of the 17th century, especially in light of the diminished importance of the phenomena associated with diabolical obsession. The cultural and social elites had become sceptical about Satan's showy manifestations, and the public authorities were no longer willing to punish the crimes of dealing with the Devil. The sources of the Enlightenment concept of demonology and the arguments used to undermine belief in the Devil sprang from the thought of the libertines, Aristotelians, and naturalists who,

throughout the 17th century, had expressed their scepticism about demons, witchcraft, and possession. Another source was the activity of inquisitors engaged in the struggle against witchcraft, which, based on the legal and medical thinking developed during the periods of the witch-hunts, sought above all to treat the intervention of the Devil in human affairs as a matter for discussion. Yet another factor that shaped 18th-century demonology was the trend toward a more thorough exegesis of Scripture, supplemented by a direct knowledge of cultures not mentioned in the Bible. The new hermeneutic—which was chiefly Protestant—came to see the cases of demonic possession in Scripture as nervous disorders or mental problems, and it provided a "scientific" foundation for isolated expressions of an alternative mode of thought about the Devil that had been expressed only cautiously until then: that dreams, hallucinations, and mental illness played an essential role in the phenomena attributed to diabolical activity. To interpret such manifestations as illusions was to confirm a naturalistic explanation that caused a shift in thinking about the Devil. If he had been until now the inseparable traveling companion of human beings, his disappearance from the modern world relegated him to the domain of theological and scriptural debates. This restriction of his domain removed the Devil from everyday life and turned him into a subject reserved for the speculations of specialists. This transition from the public to the private domain, from the general to the particular, characterizes the Enlightenment's consciousness of the Devil.

The issue of the Devil, his existence and his powers, was a controversial one during the 18th century. The *philosophes* and their opponents—that is, enlightened theologians and defenders of Church tradition, and physicians, and jurists—turned demonology into a battlefield. In this controversy, the issues at stake were wideranging, from propaganda for the *philosophes* to the renewal of the Christian faith, from the desire to defeat superstition to the perceived need to safeguard the prophecies of the Book of Revelation itself. If this debate produced a rapid transformation of belief, it also stimulated a rediscovery and revalorization of the diabolical supernatural long before the rebirth of romanticism. The *philosophes* and the partisans of traditional belief were therefore not the only forces on the field. As with many other concepts, the simplification of demonological thought in the 18th century was the result of the propaganda by the *philosophes*. This propaganda was aimed at depicting an intellectual battleground neatly divided into two opposing camps, with those who challenged the existence of the Devil being considered enlightened thinkers, and those who maintained a belief in his existence, regarded as stalwarts of obscurantism. But Enlightenment demonology concealed a cultural reality that was more nuanced and complex than that depicted by the *philosophes*. In fact, 18th-century demonology found itself engaged in a debate that aimed at redefining belief in the Devil in order to mitigate the severer aspects of that belief. This was obviously not the same as getting rid of Satan altogether. The Devil was just one chapter in the enormous indictment that the *philosophes* prepared against revealed religions, but the Devil also figured in the Church's campaign against the religious superstitions embedded in popular belief. The debate involved a reexamination of both dogma and the prophecies made in the Book of Revelation, and it contributed to a revised understanding of the transcendent, the miraculous, and the supernatural.

According to the *philosophes*, the Devil offended the critical sense. The teachings about him, as well as the stories associated with him, were held to be absurd. The fanaticism he aroused could not be reconciled with any aspiration to happiness. Many thinkers therefore ridiculed the Devil, representing him as a curious case of religious alienation or a regrettable product of ignorance, a pathetic bit of debris from the Dark Ages. Indeed, the *philosophes'* demonological discourse strongly emphasized the notion that the Devil was a figure from the past, incompatible with the modern world. But theological thought also found it appropriate to destroy the archaic model of demonic chaos, the phantasmagoria of the categories and subcategories of demons. Theologians sought to sweep away a history of the Devil that was made up of terrifying details and of disturbing zoomorphic or anthropomorphic images, while aiming, in general, to condemn the imagery that had traditionally been associated with the Devil. This imagery, for all its popular character, was nevertheless sanctioned by a science of demonology that had been solidly constructed over the centuries by way of Scripture, writings of the Church fathers, accounts from the desert, catechisms, rituals, inquisitors' manuals, and records of the witch-hunt trials. It was an imagery that represented the weakest link in a chain of beliefs. As such, it was an easy target for the derision of the *philosophes*, who considered its elimination to be a matter of urgency. Moreover, for many thinkers—notably Nicolas Malebranche, Balthasar Bekker, and Ludovico Antonio Muratori—the struggle against Satan represented a sort of defense of religion. To attribute too much power to the Devil was an insult to God, and diabolical magic was the sign of a corrupted religion that could be purified only by the reinstatement of God and the Devil in their metaphysical roles. It is necessary, therefore, to take note of a whole range of attitudes and perspectives between the extreme positions held by the *philosophes*

and by those who advocated unquestioning adherence to traditional belief. These wide-ranging views attest to the prestige that official demonological theology still enjoyed and to the still-powerful impact of the Devil on people's imaginations.

Interest in the diabolical was motivated by different factors, ranging from a metaphysical disquiet to a wish to inspire a more serene religious feeling free of satanic anxieties, and to the curiosity of folklorists that was tinged with varying degrees of scepticism. Several demonological conceptions grew out of an enlightened Christianity that, while it confirmed the official theology, declared itself opposed to the excesses of the official stance. This enlightened Christian perspective was represented by numerous laymen and churchmen, the supporters of a naturalistic approach that took full account of psychopathological analyses of the phenomena of obsession and demonic possession without denying the reality of the Devil. Conscious of the ambiguous nature of the figure of Satan, the advocates of this "third way" submitted the demonological tradition to rigorous examination in order to rethink the role of the Devil, while denouncing at the same time the risks that this operation entailed: dethroning Satan could mean undermining the supernatural as the basis of all religion, thus undermining the foundations of the whole edifice and overturning a world of certainties and values. This third way made a real impact on Enlightenment demonology. It pushed the debate forward, raising problems that are still discussed today and profoundly altering the image of Satan, in a metamorphosis that concerned his images, forms, and relationships but not the foundations of his existence. There is no doubt that the presence of the Devil became less of an obsession, a less troubling matter; he was no longer seen as being composed of the corporeal substance with which medieval images or the summae of the Renaissance and the 17th century had endowed him. Satan still sometimes occupied center stage as the yardstick and definition of evil, appearing in a variety of shapes derived from the oldest traditions, but he was certainly not the only image of evil. The demonological discourse of the Enlightenment backed the spiritualization of the Devil, whom it aimed to transform into a philosophical figure—a fleshless form representing the visible translation of cosmic or moral evil. Countering the overconfident attitudes and sarcasm of the *philosophes*, several thinkers noted the presence of an uncontrollable demonic energy active within the twists and turns of the subconscious, in the depths of nature and in the body of society. These thinkers set out to show the continuity and universality of the belief in the Devil through all his various incarnations, to bear witness to the vitality of an authentic and profound conception of an essentially demonic being.

The demonological discourse of the Enlightenment was able to triumph easily over a traditional doctrine that was weak in dogmatic content. Both the Catholic and the Protestant worlds have always shown acute sensitivity to the powers of evil. The Devil has played a decisive role in the interpretation of cosmic and human history: without him there would have been no fall of humanity, no suffering or death, no incarnation or redemption. It fell to dogmatic theology and apologetics to prove the Devil's existence, but the official magisterium (teaching) of the Church addressed only a limited number of points on this matter. Where Satan was the subject of doctrinal definition, it was solely in order to reject dualistic speculations: demons were created by God, they were originally good, they are not capable of creation, they encourage human beings to sin, they exercise a degree of domination over humanity, the punishment that they suffer is eternal, and so on. Theologians were therefore entirely at liberty to discuss many subjects, such as the nature of demons, their role in the fall of Adam and Eve, hell, or the forms of demonic activity among human beings. Being based on a different consciousness and on a more acute perception of the frontiers between the real and the imaginary, the normal and the extraordinary, 18th-century demonology managed to prune and edit the literary elements and mythical images within the tradition. Thinkers addressed the problem of the relationship between the Devil in Christianity and the demons of other religions, and they traced the influence, and the dangers, of Manichaeanism in the doctrine about the Devil. In examining the teachings of the Church fathers, these thinkers made distinctions between what should be considered as valuable evidence for the magisterium of the Church, being based on the biblical Revelation, and what, in contrast, was no more than an echo of the cultural milieu in which such ideas and writings had taken shape. They also detected, in the inclusion of the Devil among the forces that rule the world, the traces of an archaic ritual linked to an animistic conception of the universe.

Accordingly, Enlightenment thinkers saw the ancient belief in the Devil as based on the legacy of paganism, on the influence of heretical doctrines of primitive Christianity, and on an erroneous exegesis of the Bible. Although the Devil posed a threat to monotheism, Pierre Bayle argued, he had nevertheless been fostered in the bosom of religion because he discharged God of any responsibility for evil. In Voltaire's view, the exegetical error had taken root with the Church fathers, had been consolidated in ecclesiastical and monastic institutions, and had been reinforced by the actions of judges. For other thinkers, notably Malebranche and Muratori, the concept of the Devil was the result of ignorance, and Satan was made responsible for any phenomenon whose cause could not be understood. The *philosophes* maliciously suggested that the clergy had promoted popular ignorance out of self-interest, since the power to drive out demons gave them greater credibility. Montesquieu held that the Devil played a role in society: human beings need both hope and fear; for believers the Devil is a threat, a vigilant eye that prevents them from sinning. However, the Devil was also a convenient alibi for sinful human nature, from which he removed responsibility. Finally, the importance of the Devil had increased because people talked about him too much: silence was therefore the most effective strategy for fighting him.

Our knowledge of the views of the Devil prevalent during the age of the Enlightenment comes from many sources. To begin with, demonological "knowledge" was codified in theological and philosophical works that recast questions about Satan in terms that were rigorously historical and anthropological. Two works in particular deserve to be mentioned: *De Religione Veterum Persarum* (1690; On the Religion of the Ancient Persians), by the Englishman Hyde, and *De betowerte Wereld* (1691; The Enchanted World), by the Dutch Protestant minister Bekker. Both of these works are veritable gold mines of arguments for those who want to exercise their critical powers on the topic of Satan. We should also cite the Europe-wide debate on Manichaeanism provoked by Bayle's accusations against the Christian doctrine of the Devil in his *Dictionnaire historique et critique* (1697; An Historical and Critical Dictionary), particularly the articles "Manichéisme" (Manichaeanism) and "Marcionites." Bayle's ideas were refuted by William King, in his *De Origine Mali* (1702; On the Origin of Evil), and by J.C. Wolff, in his *Manichaeismus ante Manichaeos et in Christianismo Redivivus* (1706; Manichaeism before Manichaeus and Revived in Christianity), among others. Nevertheless, Bayle's views received forceful confirmation in the most erudite work on the subject, *L'histoire de Manichée et du Manichéisme* (1739; The History of Manichaeus and Manichaeism) by the French Protestant minister Isaac de Beausobre. Among the *philosophes* Voltaire stands out for the relentlessness, as well as the consistency, of his interest in the Devil, expressed, above all, in the *Essai sur les moeurs et l'esprit des nations* (1756; An Essay on Universal History, and the Manners and Spirit of Nations) and the *Dictionnaire philosophique* (1764; Philosophical Dictionary).

Many works aimed to disabuse the credulous, to combat the traditional belief in the Devil, or to limit the scope of that belief. A whole tradition in this line stretched from Malebranche's *De la recherche de la vérité* (1674; Treatise concerning the Search after Truth) to Muratori's *Della forza della fantasia umana* (1745; On the Power of Human Imagination), from Daniel

Defoe's *The Political History of the Devil, Ancient and Modern* (1726) to the abbé Bergier's *Dictionnaire de théologie* (1789; Dictionary of Theology).

Numerous texts were devoted to the examination of the most famous cases of witchcraft, or the most extraordinary manifestations of the diabolical supernatural, such as the witches' Sabbath, incubi and succubi, or werewolves. Some of these texts went back to the notorious instances of demonic possession of the 17th century. For example, Nicolas Aubin's *Histoire des diables de Loudun* (History of the Devils of Loudun) was reissued in 1716, 1737, and 1752. Others drew on contemporary events, which continued to provide opportunities for analyzing this phenomenon and the role that the Devil had played in it. These included Girolamo Tartarotti's *Del congresso notturno delle lammie* (1749; On the Witches Sabbath) and Scipione Maffei's *Arte magica dileguata* (1750; The Art of Magic Dispelled). Francis Hutchinson's *An Historical Essay concerning Witchcraft* (1718) made a significant contribution toward dealing the deathblow to the intellectual case for the existence of witchcraft. The writings of physicians, such as Friedrich Hoffmann's *De Potestate Daemonum in Corpora* (1713; On the Power of Demons in Bodies) or François de Saint-André's *Lettres sur la magie* (1725; Letters on Magic), helped to create an authentic pathology of the diabolical realm of fantasy, while journalists, in publications such as Joseph Addison's *Spectator* and the *Mémoires de Trévoux,* continued to announce the current existence of witchcraft and the emotion that it still aroused.

The Illuminati, such as Emmanuel Swedenborg, the "prophet of the North," or Louis-Claude de Saint-Martin, revitalized the world of darkness with their investigations into the negative principle and the problem of evil. Scholars did their best to take stock of an unlimited subject: Dom Calmet's *Dissertations sur les apparitions des anges, des démons et des esprits* (1746; Essays on the Apparitions of Angels, Demons, and Spirits) contains numerous chapters on the Devil, while Lenglet-Dufresnoy's *Recueil de dissertations anciennes et nouvelles sur les apparitions, les visions et les songes* (1752; Collection of Old and New Essays on Apparitions, Visions, and Dreams) gathers together every bizarre tradition about infernal spirits. A major source of information on Enlightenment views of the Devil is the literature on superstitions: indeed, the Prince of Darkness formed part of the arsenal deployed against these superstitions. Father Le Brun's *Histoire critique des pratiques superstitieuses* (1702; Critical History of Superstitious Practices), reissued in 1733 along with the abbé Thiers's *Traité des superstitions* (Treatise on Superstitions), lists a number of such superstitions relating to the Devil.

As for fiction, we might wonder which changes in values affected the figure of the Devil when he moved from the realm of theology and religious speculation into that of fiction. Over the centuries the interest aroused by manifestations of diabolical magic had created a stock of picturesque images that diabolical literature could draw on. Yet, the satanic imagination of the 18th century was sober, few concessions being made either to the Devil's conventional physical attributes or to his extraordinary exploits. The gap between diabolical literature and demonological theology was not so wide as one might think. From Alain-René Lesage's *Le diable boîteux* (1707; The Devil upon Two Sticks) to Matthew Gregory Lewis's *The Monk* (1796), the 18th century was punctuated by a myriad of devils. Even before the Fausts of Klinger and Johann Wolfgang von Goethe, John Milton's successors and Friedrich Gottlieb Klopstock's *Der Messias* (1748; The Messiah) ensured the continuity of Christian fantasy, and the diabolical characters in "Oriental" tales prefigured William Beckford's *Vathek* (1786; The History of the Caliph Vathek). A large audience was rapidly won over by a new-style embodiment of evil—half-serious, half-playful—symbolized by Biondetta, the androgynous and amorous devil in Cazotte's *Le diable amoureux* (1772; The Devil in Love), which allowed readers to envisage relations between human beings and the powers of darkness. Thus, at a time when the Devil was losing both his monstrous physical shapes and his unlimited powers and his ability to cause obsession, he simultaneously acquired a new seductive power—that of his transformation into a malicious instigator of transgressions, a refined master of disguise, and a subtle manipulator of the arts of eroticism and fascination.

NADIA MINERVA

See also Evil, Representations of; Witchcraft

Further Reading

Forsyth, Neil, *The Old Enemy: Satan and the Combat Myth*, Princeton, New Jersey: Princeton University Press, 1987

Grudin, Peter D., *The Demon-Lover: The Theme of Demoniality in English and Continental Fiction of the Late Eighteenth and Early Nineteenth Centuries*, New York: Garland, 1987

Kelly, Henry Ansgar, *The Devil, Demonology, and Witchcraft: The Development of Christian Beliefs in Evil Spirits*, Garden City, New York: Doubleday, 1968; revised edition, 1974

Kelly, Henry Ansgar, *Towards the Death of Satan: The Growth and Decline of Christian Demonology*, London and Dublin: Chapman, 1968

Messadié, Gérald, *A History of the Devil*, translated by Marc Romano, New York: Kodansha International, and London: Newleaf, 1996 (original French edition, 1993)

Milner, Max, *Le diable dans la littérature française de Cazotte à Baudelaire, 1772–1861*, 2 vols., Paris: Corti, 1960

Minerva, Nadia, *Il diavolo: Eclissi e metamorfosi nel Secolo dei Lumi: Da Asmodeo a Belzebù*, Ravenna: Longo, 1990

Niderst, Alain, editor, *Le diable*, Saint-Genouph, France: Nizet, 1998

Rudwin, Maximilian Josef, *The Devil in Legend and Literature*, Chicago and London: Open Court, 1931; reprint, La Salle, Illinois: Open Court, 1989

Russell, Jeffrey Burton, *Mephistopheles: The Devil in the Modern World*, Ithaca, New York: Cornell University Press, 1986

Russell, Jeffrey Burton, *The Prince of Darkness: Radical Evil and the Power of Good in History*, Ithaca, New York: Cornell University Press, 1988

Dialogue

Dialogue as a literary genre—as distinguished from the spoken exchanges between characters in drama or fiction—appears to have originated in ancient Greece, where it was used as a philosophical strategy by Plato and as a form of irony by Lucian. The genre was popular in the Renaissance and the 17th century, but it was the 18th century that witnessed the full flowering of dialogue as a literary form. A veritable flood of dialogues appeared during the Enlightenment, extending the possibilities of the genre in various directions. Most often the dialogue was used for didactic purposes, as a fictional device that enabled the writer to avoid both the dogmatism of a formal treatise and the apodictic tone of a systematic proof. The writer's strength (or weakness) lay in the skill (or lack of skill) with which he managed to create true-to-life characters in a believable context.

In Italy the dialogue had been used extensively during the Renaissance, and in the 17th century the great Galileo Galilei took it up again in two major works—*Dialogo sopra i due massimi sistemi del mondo, tolomaico e copernicano* (1630; Dialogue concerning the Two Chief World Systems, Ptolemaic and Copernican) and *Discorsi e dimostrazioni matematiche intorno a due nuove scienze* (1638; Dialogues concerning Two New Sciences)—as a means of asserting the merits of the Copernican world view, which he shared, in contrast to traditional Aristotelianism. The spokesman for Aristotle in Galileo's dialogues, symbolically enough, was named Simplicio. Unfortunately, no further noteworthy dialogue writers would appear in Italy during the age of the Enlightenment. Instead, the genre was developed to its fullest extent in England and France during that time.

A flood of political dialogues appeared in England in the aftermath of the 1688 Revolution, just as they had proliferated in Germany after the Reformation. However, writers of philosophy in England would make the greatest use of the form during the 18th century. Unlike his great idol Plato, Anthony Ashley Cooper, 3rd earl of Shaftesbury, never wrote dialogues himself, but as early as 1711, in his *Characteristicks of Men, Manners, Opinions, Times,* he advised other philosophers to do so, even as he warned them of the inherent difficulty of the genre, which consists of allowing the reader to be the sole judge of arguments that must be objectively reported:

> The two sides of the debate must appear natural and just as they are. . . . Be careful not to endow the sceptic who represents your own point of view with arguments that are too strong, or with a particularly witty turn of phrase. . . . Make sure that your opponent has all his wits about him and that his ingenuity and his artistic sense are evident to the reader.

When Denis Diderot came to write his biting satire "of partisan pamphlets and new-style theological essays," he would recall these admirable principles as well as Shaftesbury's emphasis on the need for unity of character (in the interlocutors portrayed).

George Berkeley, bishop of Cloyne (1685–1753), had no such methodological scruples. When he published his *Three Dialogues between Hylas and Philonous* in 1713, shortly after his arrival in London, he gave the work a subtitle that states explicitly that the purpose of these dialogues is "plainly to demonstrate the reality and perfection of human knowledge, the incorporeal nature of the soul, and the immediate providence of a Deity, in opposition to Sceptics and Atheists." Hylas is portrayed as a strict and stubborn believer in the existence of material substance, who is finally led to share the immaterialist point of view of his adversary. Philonous claims that matter does not exist independently from the mind; bodies exist, but only insofar as they are perceived; therefore, whatever is corporeal is in fact an idea—"esse est percipi." Berkeley's idealist, subjectivist, and phenomenalist system assumes the primacy of the mind, with divine Providence as its sole support.

Berkeley's three dialogues are brilliantly argued, but their style is closer to that of propaganda than that of open discussion. The dialogues were unfavorably received in England, and Diderot would later discover in them embarrassing objections to his own philosophy. Berkeley was less inspired in the seven dialogues of *Alciphron; or, The Minute Philosopher,* which he wrote between 1728 and 1730, during his stay in Rhode Island, and published in London in 1732. The dialogues are in fact a diatribe against the English freethinkers (or "minute philosophers") Anthony Collins, Shaftesbury, and Bernard Mandeville, whom the dialogues scornfully dismiss in what Berkeley took to be a definitive rebuttal, using the theory of vision to prove the existence of God.

In his *Enquiry concerning the Principles of Morals* (1751), David Hume adopted a radically different strategy. As originally conceived, the *Enquiry* concluded with an astonishing dialogue that undercuts all of the conventional answers regarding questions of morality. The narrator listens to an account given by his friend Palamedes of a journey to the land of Fourli and the time he spent there in the company of an unusual companion, Alcheic. The latter behaves in a manner that defies all accepted standards of behavior: he is in love with a boy; he kills his dearest friend; he offers no resistance when he is thrashed by another friend; and, finally, he hangs himself—to universal applause and admiration. Echoing Denis Vairasse's *Histoire des Sévarambes* (1677–78; The History of the Sevarites or Sevarambi), Hume also alludes in passing to communities governed entirely by women—a common practice among the ancient Britons. In fact, Hume's Palamedes uses the device of the imaginary voyage to evoke the customs of the Greeks, whose social and moral conventions ran totally counter to our own, as the many references to ancient texts make clear. In this way, the storyteller believes he has proved beyond all doubt "that an Athenian man of merit might be such a one as with us would pass for incestuous, a parricide, an assassin, an ungrateful, perjured traitor, a monster whose name alone would invoke horror, not to mention his rusticity and ill-manners." But it is the author-narrator, not Palamedes, who has the last word and is able to put forth his case for utilitarian relativism:

Your representation of things is fallacious. You have no indulgence for the manners and customs of different ages. . . . There are no manners so innocent or reasonable but may be rendered odious or ridiculous if measured by a standard unknown to the persons.

It is Hume's conviction that "all the rules regarding marriage conform equally to the laws and to natural principles, but they are not all equally favorable to the good of society." Palamedes answers that he only wanted to convince the narrator "that fashion, vogue, custom, and law were the chief foundation of all moral determinations." From this exchange, the narrator is able to conclude that principles are universal and immovable, but that everything else is variable, with the sole proviso that the moral quality thus defined should be useful and agreeable to the person who possesses it or to others. It is not hard to imagine the general outcry that this relativist thesis provoked among right-thinking people. Neither Claude-Adrien Helvétius nor Diderot would take scepticism any further than the Scots philosopher, whose most daring ideas were reserved for posterity. The remarkable *Dialogues concerning Natural Religion,* which revealed the full originality of Hume's thought, were published by friends in 1779, three years after the author's death.

Other English writers who used the dialogue form had styles that were more prudent and more conventional than was Hume's. In his three-volume *Moral Philosopher,* published anonymously between 1738 and 1740, Thomas Morgan attacked Anglican orthodoxy in a dialogue between Philalete (a Christian Deist who speaks for the author) and Theophanes (a Christian Jew). In 1759 Richard Hurd published his *Moral and Political Dialogues* in which a group of well-known modern characters (including Joseph Addison, Sir Kenelm Digby, and John Arbuthnot) discuss, among other things, the policies of Queen Elizabeth. Henry Home, Lord Kames, established a set of rules for successful dialogue in his *Elements of Criticism,* first published in 1762. Home underscored the suitability of the genre for the expression of feelings but also insisted on the need to have each interlocutor express feelings in a manner consistent with his character.

In France the dialogue had an even greater vogue than in England. It was in widespread use in the 17th century, notwithstanding Pellisson's derogatory comment about "that little-known and rarely practiced genre"—a remark that, admittedly, dates from 1655. Toward the end of the 17th century, Bernard Le Bovier de Fontenelle published his *Dialogues des Morts* (1683; Dialogues of the Dead) and the *Entretiens sur la pluralité des mondes* (1686; Conversations on the Plurality of Worlds), in which his anthropological scepticism alternates with his faith in scientific progress. The cause of the moderns was brilliantly championed by Charles Perrault in his *Parallèle des Anciens et des Modernes* (1688–97; Parallel between the Ancients and the Moderns). The Jesuit priest Dominique Bouhours dealt with matters of taste and (aesthetic) *je ne sais quoi* in his *Entretiens d'Ariste et d'Eugène* (1671; Conversations of Aristo and Eugene) and in *La manière de bien penser dans les ouvrages de l'esprit* (1687; The Arts of Logick and Rhetorick). The two dialogues by François-Armand de Salignac de La Mothe Fénélon, *Dialogues sur l'éloquence* (Dialogues on Eloquence) and *Dialogues des morts* (Dialogues of the Dead), also date from this period, although they were not published until 1712 and 1718, respectively. Barnard Lamy's *Entretiens sur les sciences* (Conversations on the Sciences) appeared in 1684, shortly after Roger de Piles's *Conversations sur la connaissance de la peinture et sur le jugement qu'on doit faire des tableaux* (1677; Conversations on the Knowledge of Painting and How Paintings Should Be Assessed), in which two characters named Pamphile and Damon, after a visit to the royal picture galleries, take a stroll in the Tuileries gardens to discuss the validity of aesthetic judgments.

The early years of the 18th century saw the appearance of several dialogues devoted to a wide range of moral issues, focusing in particular on the legitimacy of pleasure. Among them were Baudot de Juilly's *Dialogues entre MM. Patru et d'Ablancourt sur les plaisirs* (1701; Dialogues between Messrs. Patru and d'Ablancourt on Pleasure), Rémond de Saint-Mard's *Nouveaux dialogues des Dieux, ou Réflexions sur les plaisirs* (1711; New Dialogues of Gods; or, Reflections on Pleasure), N. Dupuy's *Dialogues sur les plaisirs, sur les passions, sur le mérite des femmes et sur leur sensibilité pour l'honneur* (1717; Dialogues on Pleasure, the Passions, and the Merit of Women and on Their Sensitivity to Matters Related to Honor). The first of these dialogues was concerned with the philosophical aspects of pleasure; the second dealt with a wider range of related problems; and the third took up the broad question of the nature and status of women, issues that had been raised at the end of the 17th century in works such as J.B. de Crues's *Les entretiens de Théandre et d'Isménie sur la prééminence du sexe* (1689; The Conversations of Theandra and Ismenia on the Preeminence of the Fair Sex) and Guyonnet de Vertron's *Entretiens d'un abbé et d'un cavalier sur la liberté des dames françaises* (1693; Conversations between a Priest and a Gentleman on the Freedom of French Ladies) and *Conversations sur l'excellence du beau sexe* (1699; Conversations on the Excellence of the Fair Sex).

In 1704 Jean-Laurent Lecerf de la Viéville used the dialogue form in his *Comparaison de la musique italienne et de la musique française* (Comparison between Italian and French Music). Viéville admitted that the nature of his characters—people of quality who could hardly be expected to be learned—had caused him some concern, but he felt justified in using them because of the truth that was contained in their conversations. The former officer and explorer Louis-Armand de La Hontan dealt with much more explosive material in his *Dialogues curieux entre un voyageur et un sauvage de bon sens, qui a voyagé* (Curious Dialogues between the Author and a Savage with Common Sense, Who Has Seen the World), published in 1703 on his return from Canada. La Hontan's aim was to combine documentary information about North America with an attack on European civilization. His eloquent spokesman, Adario, is scathingly critical of the habits, judicial system, acquisitiveness, and restlessness of the colonial settlers. In 1705 the defrocked priest Nicolas Gueudeville used La Hontan's *Dialogues curieux* to fashion a radically subversive dialogue of his own, in which he excoriates, in succession, royalty, other French institutions, the notion of property, and Christianity, whose dogma and views on sexual morality he finds unacceptable. The violence of Gueudeville's denunciation of French civilization lent credence to the theme of the noble savage for many years.

Telliamed, ou Entretiens d'un philosophe indien avec un missionaire français (Telliamed; or, Conversations between an Indian Philosopher and a French Missionary), by Benoît de Maillet, inspector of public buildings for the Mediterranean region, was also probably written in the early years of the century, although it was published posthumously in 1748. In this dialogue Maillet advances the hypothesis that human life must have originated in the sea and that man had only gradually grown accustomed to living on Earth—a notion that must have seemed preposterous to his contemporaries and which elicited sarcastic comments from Voltaire. The author's scientific pretensions went hand in hand with the attitude of a *philosophe,* since he clearly intended to prove that the account of the Creation in Genesis was nothing more than a fable.

Like Maillet, Nicolas-Malebranche made no attempt to see both sides of the question in his *Entretiens d'un philosophe chrétien et d'un philosophe chinois* (ca. 1707; Conversations between a Christian Philosopher and a Chinese Philosopher). The conversation centers on the practices of the Jesuit missionaries in China, within the larger context of the debate over whether Chinese rituals were necessarily heretical, but the primary target was the philosophy of Baruch Spinoza, who at the time was regarded as an atheist. Malebranche's Chinese philosopher does little more than raise objections, which are immediately demolished by the Christian's closely argued and complex dialectic. In such instances, the dialogue form is merely a pretext, with no other function than to superficially enliven an argument that is fundamentally magisterial, didactic, and strongly coded.

A more subtle, nuanced use of dialogue can be found in the *Dialogue de Sylla et d'Eucrate* (Dialogue between Sylla and Eucratus), which the young Montesquieu intended to present to the "club de l'Entresol." Probably written around 1724, it was not published until 1745. Closely related from the outset to Montesquieu's *Considérations sur les causes de la grandeur des Romains et de leur décadence* (1734; Considerations on the Causes of the Grandeur and Decadence of the Romans), the work deals with the question of dictatorship and, at a deeper level, the nature of absolute power.

The confrontation is a rather unusual one. Montesquieu portrays the Roman general Sulla refusing the dictatorship—although it lay well within his grasp—and explaining to one of his admirers the reasons for this action. Sulla has previously instituted a strong government to combat the anarchical freedom desired by his subjects, but since he loves risk and danger, he despises his subjects for offering him no resistance. The lesson of this particular dialogue is somewhat ambiguous, but Montesquieu does clearly show the danger of a state ruled by a superman capable of striking terror in the hearts of his subjects, thus paralyzing all political life and creating a climate of violence and a break in the social order, with consequences that cannot be predicted. Ultimately, Sulla's true desire is to restore the freedom of the aristocracy, thereby reinstating the political order he has unwittingly destroyed by the exercise of arbitrary and absolute power.

Later in the century—and similarly concerned with political theory—there appeared the *Entretiens de Phocien sur les rapports de la morale et de la politique* (1763; Conversations with Phocion on the Relations between Ethics and Politics), written by the abbé Bonnot de Mably, Condillac's elder brother, who presents the dialogues as the translation of a Greek text (which is clearly apocryphal). Advocating equal ownership of common property, while at the same time stressing the need for a strong government to uphold moral and religious standards and combat the excesses of individual freedom, Mably develops in these dialogues a radical socialism not unlike that of Jean-Jacques Rousseau. Benjamin Constant would later denounce this political scheme as the very essence of antiliberal thought and despotic tyranny.

Because the political climate during the Enlightenment was hardly conducive to open discussion of such topics, most authors of dialogues selected less controversial themes. When the abbé Pluche cast in dialogue form *Le spectacle de la nature, ou Entretiens sur les particularités de l'histoire naturelle qui ont paru les plus propres à rendre les jeunes gens curieux et à leur former l'esprit* (1732; Nature Displayed: Being Discourses on Such Particulars of Natural History As Were Thought Most Proper to Excite the Curiosity, and Form the Minds of Youth), he had no other ambition than to write a work of popular science. In fact, Pluche's dialogue became one of the best sellers of the day, doubtless because he managed to reconcile orthodox religious views with an account of physics and the natural sciences that could be understood by the general reader. In the chevalier de Méhégan's *Dialogue entre Alcippe et Oronte* (Dialogue between Alcippe and Oronte), set in a garden between the mountains and the sea, the conversation touches upon wisdom, solitude, and the role of the writer in society. Wealth and prejudice, the vanity of society life, the possibility of happiness far from the madding crowd, the virtues of reading, and, above all, the concept of the writer in the service of virtue and truth are among the themes evoked in the dialogue. Méhégan's *Dialogue* culminates in a "philosophical" vision of history, as "vice and ignorance walk hand in hand with virtue and enlightenment." Following Voltaire's lead, Méhégan's work was in its own way an attempt to answer Rousseau's *Discours sur les sciences et les arts* (1750; Discourse on the Sciences and Arts).

On a quite different note, the anonymous *Dialogues sur l'âme, par les interlocuteurs en ce temps-là* (Dialogues on the Soul, by the Interlocutors of the Time) published in 1771 from a manuscript that dates from around 1755–60, questions the immateriality of the soul, arguing instead for an intransigent brand of materialism. A conversation between a Christian, a Sadducee, and a "plain and simple" *philosophe* completely undermines the basic tenets of Christianity. Of the many clandestine manuscripts that circulated during the 18th century, *Dialogues sur l'âme* appears to be the only one that was cast in the form of a fictional dialogue.

It was in the same period, in the years after 1750, that the two great masters of the dialogue genre, Voltaire and Diderot, began to exploit the form in earnest. The dialogue would prove the perfect weapon for Voltaire's ideological polemics and his war against Catholicism. Diderot had used dialogue as early as 1747, in *La promenade du sceptique, ou les allées* (The Sceptic's Walk), but he was careful not to seek for his work any notoriety that would bring him into conflict with the authorities.

Voltaire's first dialogue was written during his stay in Potsdam. Ostensibly recording the conversation between *Un philosophe et un contrôleur général des finances* (A Philosopher and a Chief Inspector of Public Finances), the dialogue's sole purpose was to set down in very didactic terms the author's ideas about economics. Voltaire's first openly militant philosophical dialogue was *Marc-Aurèle et un Recollet* (1752; Marcus Aurelius and a Recollet Monk). The philosophically minded emperor comes back to Earth and is astonished to find that the Capitol has been taken over by unknown priests. He subsequently learns about the fall of the Roman Empire, the rise of Christianity, the Inquisition, and the triumph of theology over philosophy. Finally, having been excommunicated by the Recollet friar, the emperor has no alternative but to rejoin "the Being of beings."

The strategy used here is the one to which Voltaire would remain faithful in subsequent dialogues. In the battle between two points of view, one of the adversaries invariably starts with an advantage, since the author is always looking over his shoulder to ensure a successful outcome. Should the opponent fail to concede graciously, attention is quickly drawn to the ineptitude of his opinions and the absurdity of his language. Voltaire's is a closed form of dialogue—militant in tone, with the dice loaded from the outset—which is nevertheless capable of charming and seducing readers because of Voltaire's masterful command of rhythm and his subtle and effective use of irony, paradox, and pastiche. It is a form that does not lend itself to lengthy developments that would bore the reader. Brevity is of the essence. Longer developments are therefore broken up into short sections of a few pages and in some cases a single page.

Thus conceived, the dialogue fit perfectly with the strategy that Voltaire would adopt in his other works written after 1750. His dialogues were aimed at a different audience than that of his theatre pieces and his poetry; presumed readers of the dialogues also read the *Dictionnaire philosophique* (1764–65; Philosophical Dictionary). In the *Dictionnaire,* several entries are cast in the form of conversations: "Les 4 Cathéchismes" (The Four Catechisms), "Dieu" (God), "Fraude," "Liberté" (Freedom), "Liberté de penser" (Freedom of Thought), "Nécessaire" (Necessity), and "Papisme" (Popism). The comic element is often in evidence, and such articles could easily figure among Voltaire's facetiae. *Un plaideur et un avocat* (A Litigant and a Lawyer) points out the absurdities of French jurisprudence. *Mme de Maintenon et Mlle de Lenclos* (Madame de Maintenon and Mademoiselle de Lenclos) deals with happiness, power, and inner freedom. The discussion of chance and necessity in *Un Brahmane et un Jésuite* (A Brahmin and a Jesuit) concludes that we should resign ourselves to "the chain of destiny." The subject matter of the two dialogues in *Lucrèce et Posidonius* (Lucretius and Posidonius) did not lend itself to comic treatment. The case for an intelligent Creator is successfully argued by Posidonius-Voltaire, easily triumphing over Lucretius's materialist atheism. The final advice to the reader is that "we should feel our powerlessness, recognize a Supreme Being, and beware of systems."

Un sauvage et un bachelier (A Savage and a Young Man) deals with the relationship between nature and society from an anti-Rousseauist perspective. Religious intolerance is criticized in *Ariste et Acrotal* (Aristos and

Acrotal), while *Lucien, Erasme et Rabelais* (Lucian, Erasmus, and Rabelais) depicts the three sages taking a friendly stroll in the Elysian Fields and conversing about their common mission to "disabuse others" by ridiculing error. Madame de Pompadour's dressing room is the setting for *Les Anciens et les Modernes* (The Ancients and the Moderns), in which the marquise, Cicero's daughter Tullia, and a duke who thinks and speaks like Voltaire discuss the Quarrel of the Ancients and the Moderns and its corollary, the notion of progress. The conversation in *Le chapon et la poularde* (The Capon and the Fattened Chicken) consists of a lamentation over human barbarism, torture, and cannibalism, with a conclusion that is both comic and tragic. *Un caloyer et un homme de bien* (1764; A Greek Orthodox Monk and a Wealthy Man) criticizes the revealed religions of Judeo-Christian origin, denounces fanaticism, and presents the case for natural religion. *Le douteur et l'adorateur* (The Sceptic and the Worshipper) treats the same topic, with some bitter comments on miracles and Saint Paul, whom Voltaire holds responsible for Christianity's distortion of Jesus's wise morality. The tone is even more scathing in the *Conversation de M. l'Intendant des menus en exercice avec M. l'abbé Grisel* (Conversation between the Acting Steward and the Abbé Grisel), which focuses on the Church's attitude toward actors and, in particular the case of Mademoiselle Lecouvreur. Voltaire defends the theatre and the profession of acting against a cynical and avaricious abbé, with some characteristically pointed remarks about the intolerance and abuses of the clergy. The legal system, incarnated in an absurdly stupid character named Croutef, is pilloried in *André Destouches à Siam* (André Destouches in Siam). Incoherent laws arbitrary justice, horrifying tortures, and the ridiculous system of venal offices are systematically denounced.

L'ABC, a dialogue written in 1768, reveals a more serene side of Voltaire's wit. It consists of 17 conversations between A, an English liberal; B, a Dutch republican; and C, an aristocrat from the south of France. For once, Voltaire does not hide behind one of his characters but allows the debate to range freely, pragmatically adopting in turn the point of view of his three interlocutors on a variety of subjects, from Montesquieu's *De l'esprit des lois* (1748; The Spirit of Laws) to theocracy, and from religion to the right to make war. The final word is given to A, who professes to be a "citizen of the world" and claims that the pursuit of happiness is mankind's first duty.

Despite its title, the *Relation du bannissement des Jésuites de la Chine, ou l'empereur de la Chine et frère Rigolet* (1768; How Jesuits Were Banished from China; or, The Emperor of China and Brother Rigolet) is also a dialogue, and, indeed it is one of Voltaire's most brilliant contributions to the genre. The emperor Yong-Cheng summons Brother Rigolet, a Jesuit convert, to inform him of the imperial decision to expel all the Christian missionaries from China. After initially professing to admire Christian dogma and rituals in order to fool his naive interlocutor, the Chinese emperor changes tactics and makes Christianity the target of his scorn and anger. The comic effects here depend on a wide range of innuendos, with frequent recourse to the absurd. Rigolet's simplistic faith is no match for the emperor's eloquence, which pushes the mockery of the Christian liturgy and the doctrine of Incarnation to its most extreme, as Yong-Cheng concludes: "You have eaten and drunk your God." The violence of this text, although frequently concealed beneath its humor, ranks it alongside Voltaire's most aggressive diatribes against "the infamous," such as *Examen important de Milord Bolingbroke* (1767; A Thorough Examination of Milord Bolingbroke).

Turning now to the dialogues of Diderot, the genre appears in a completely different light. Diderot's themes have little in common with those of Voltaire. More important, the relationships between the participants in Diderot's dialogues, and between the participants and the author, are strikingly original. Abandoning the Greek model that had been established by Plato and Lucian, Diderot gives the form a radically new purpose. Instead of answering questions, the function of Diderot's dialogues is to raise them—in other words, to set down in dramatic form the problems and unanswerable issues encountered in his own philosophical enquiries. With such a technique, there is no room for easy victories, one-sided competitions, or the manipulation of language for the purpose of demonstration. Diderot's interlocutors are genuinely complex, living characters in their own right, rather than mere puppets to be manipulated by the author, and it is doubtless this quality that explains why his dialogues have been so successfully adapted for the stage in our own time. Diderot himself has a speaking part in these dialogues, in which the alternation of voices is of paramount importance. His *Apologie de l'abbé Galiani* (Apology of Galiani), written in 1770 in reference to the *Dialogues sur le commerce des blés* (1768; Dialogues on the Wheat Trade), contains in essence an apologia for the dialogue form:

No other literary form is as well suited to research and the art of persuasion—research because it is by doubting that one becomes sure of things, and persuasion because dialogue throws passion off the scent. . . . Dialogue is the best method of teaching: how else do master and pupil relate, if not by endless conversation? . . . If the air of impartiality in these *Dialogues*—so necessary to charm and seduce and involve the reader—strikes you as proof of indifference, so much the worse for you. You must have too much pride and too

little taste. While the abbé's mind was engaged in an inquiry, yours was already made up in advance. You are still squatting on your school bench, while he relaxes on the couch. . . . What are these dialogues, in short? Nothing less than a comedy.

From such statements it is clear that Diderot wishes to dissociate himself from the Platonic model and other traditional forms of dialogue. In his hands, the dialogue is still capable of teaching, but it is neither authoritative nor scholastic. It is based on doubt and proceeds by inquiry. Its author, rather than possessing truth a priori, is in search of answers. In this sense, Diderot's method can properly be defined as heuristic. Refusing to play the role of guide or master, his aim is to awaken minds that are too set in their ways. He sets out to disturb peace of mind and is bent on upsetting every form of intellectual complacency, his own included. *Le neveu de Rameau* (1805; Rameau's Nephew) is typical of this strategy, even though only part of the text is cast in dialogue form. In the opening pages, the reader encounters the Nephew (Jean-François Rameau), a cynical eccentric whose purpose in life appears to be to challenge accepted ideas: "He is like a grain of yeast that ferments. . . . He shakes and stirs us up . . . discloses the worthy and unmasks the rascals. It is then that the sensible man keeps his ears open and sorts out his company." The Nephew's role is to break "that tedious uniformity that our education, our social conventions, and our customary good manners have brought about." In the Nephew's mind, the dialogue in which he and the author are engaged is a relentless attack on received wisdom, whether about genius, politics, happiness, education, or money. Neither the philosopher's own values nor the idea he has of his role are spared in this general onslaught: "You think the same happiness is meant for all. What an idea! Your conception presupposes a sentimental turn of mind. . . . You call your quirks virtue, or philosophy." In the Nephew's view, the way to be happy is "to drink good wines, gorge on choice food, tumble pretty women, sleep in downy beds—outside of that, all is vanity." The narrator-*philosophe* is forced to admit that, on many points, his interlocutor speaks the naked truth: "There is some truth in almost everything you have said. . . . How does it come about that in your silly head some very sound ideas are all muddled up with extravagant ones? . . . There are things that have been said which one thinks to oneself and acts upon, but which one never says." The Nephew is simply more frank and more logical than others and "thus often profound in his depravity." Moreover, Diderot endows the Nephew with exceptional musical sensibility, and the author admires the liveliness of his mind as much as the frankness of his speech. The dialogue with the Nephew explores issues with which Diderot found himself grappling. In many instances the Nephew's objections are identical to Diderot's own thoughts concerning Thomas Hobbes or the social comedy. This fact explains why there could be no explicit conclusion to such a dialogue. When it comes to an abrupt end, the two speakers are still clinging to their respective positions.

Diderot perfected his technique in the three dialogues included in the book usually referred to by the title of the second of them, *Le rêve de D'Alembert* (1769; D'Alembert's Dream). The narrator-*philosophe* expounds his materialist views, based for the most part on the natural sciences, to a sceptical Jean le Rand D'Alembert; while sleeping, the latter has a dream in which matter, once endowed with sensibility and memory, becomes capable of movement and thought. A certain Dr. Bordeu lends weight to this evolutionist hypothesis by referring to the most recent discoveries in medicine, while Julie de Lespinasse asks questions that would naturally occur to a layperson unfamiliar with scientific literature or the latest experiments. The third dialogue opens up the discussion to the paradoxical consequences of the new materialism within the realm of morality. Once again, Diderot gives the impetus to his discourse by expressing doubt, by putting ideas to the test, and by a calculated risk-taking made more acceptable by the hypothetical nature of the entire exercise. With consummate artistry, Diderot created in *Le rêve de D'Alembert* an entirely new kind of dialogue, both philosophical and scientific, based on an astonishingly subtle system of rhetoric.

The *Entretien d'un philosophe avec la Maréchale de* * * * (1776; Conversation between a Philosopher and Lady de * * *) consists of a conversation about the existence of God between two equally sincere, honest, and frank speakers, Diderot and the maréchale de Broglie. Both speakers express themselves with complete spontaneity; the maréchale is "beautiful and as pious as an angel" and regards unbelievers as so many gallows birds, while Diderot persists in his right to deny the existence of God—without, however, giving way to the "mania for proselytism." He has no desire to deprive others of a hope that makes them happy, adding "I recognize that everyone has a right to their opinions, provided I am allowed to hold on to my own." The importance of this respect for the opinions of others, however different from our own, is underlined by the fact that the maréchale is a charming and sympathetic character; Diderot even gives her the last word—"Fie on you, you naughty hypocrite"—as they discuss how to behave during our final moments on Earth. The dialogue thus ends on a note of friendship and lighthearted banter.

The *Entretien d'un père avec ses enfants* (1770; Conversation between a Father and His Children) is also based on a true story, in this case drawn from Diderot's experience in his parents' home in Langres. The central issue is the clash between written law and natural justice, or the letter and the spirit of the law. Do we have the right to destroy or disregard a will that disinherits a poverty-stricken family of country folk in favor of a well-to-do and avaricious Parisian bookseller? Behind the legal hairsplitting, there lies a difficult moral problem. The opinions of various people are solicited, and each one has a different point of view, all based on the soundest principles. The young Diderot believes that charity should prevail over legalism. His father disagrees, contending that no individual, however well-intentioned, has the right to place himself above the law; it is healthy in any society that individuals should not share the common opinion, but to break the law is to open the door to every kind of abuse. The final scene ends on this note, as the wise old father sends everyone off to bed. Once again, the problem is addressed in open debate among sincere people who have opinions that are both sensible and susceptible to change—qualities that may well be a reflection of Diderot's own character if we may trust the account that Madame d'Epinay gave to the abbé Galiani of the first such discussion at which she was present.

Diderot turned from legal issues to questions of everyday morality in the *Supplément au voyage de Bougainville* (1774; A Supplement to Bougainville's Travels), with its very explicit subtitle, *Dialogue entre A et B sur l'inconvénient d'attacher des idées morales à certaines actions qui n'en comportent pas* (Dialogue between A and B on the Disadvantages of Linking Moral Ideas to Certain Actions Which Are Devoid of Them). The sexual mores of Western Christendom are unfavorably compared to the happier ways of the inhabitants of Tahiti, which were rapidly corrupted by the arrival of Christianity. Should we, therefore, reject our own code of behavior and return to nature? As in the previous *Entretien d'un père avec ses enfants*, Diderot refuses to open the door to disorder and anarchy: "We must speak out against meaningless laws until they are reformed, but in the meantime, we must obey them . . . . There is less danger in being crazy among the crazy than in being wise all alone." The philosopher has no right to undermine society, but he does have the right and the duty to work for reforms by alerting the public to abuses in the system. Voltaire's remark about Lucian—"reading his dialogues, it is always tempting to add comments of our own"—could apply equally well to Diderot.

As for the three dialogues contained in *Rousseau juge de Jean-Jacques: Dialogues* (Rousseau, Judge of Jean-Jacques: Dialogues), written between 1772 and 1776, it is highly questionable whether they actually belong to the dialogue genre as it is being discussed here. Rousseau himself claimed to have "chosen the dialogue form as it seemed the most appropriate to express the two sides of the case" (*Oeuvres auto-biographiques* [Pléiade edition, 1959; Autobiographical Work]). However, there is no real conflict between Rousseau and his interlocutor, the Frenchman. The work actually consists of a long apology on Rousseau's own behalf, periodically interrupted by a character who is supposed to represent ill-informed public opinion and who reiterates the various accusations against Rousseau made by the *philosophes*. Rousseau justifies his behavior through a strange psychological passage, and denounces at great length the plot of which he was the victim, as well as the role of the "evil-doers."

When compared to such masterpieces, which only became known to the public in the 19th century, most of the other dialogues written during the Enlightenment naturally appear somewhat lackluster, although they are not without interest. Mention should certainly be made of *Le génie du Louvre aux Champs-Elysées* (The Genius of the Louvre at the Champs-Élysées), a series of dialogues on painting by La Font Saint-Yenne, published in 1756. Also noteworthy is the marquis de Sade's *Dialogue entre un prêtre et un moribond* (1782; Dialogue between a Priest and a Dying Man), which paradoxically combines an atheistic materialism derived from the baron d'Holbach with Voltairean wit. In Sade's dialogue, the final word is given to the dying man, who declares to the priest: "Give up your idea of another world, it doesn't exist; but don't give up the idea of being happy in this world." After this reflection, the dying man spends his last hours happily in the arms of "six women more beautiful than the day." The seven dialogues contained in Sade's *La philosophie dans le boudoir* (1795; Philosophy in the Bedroom) are closer to theatre and to the dialogical novel in the manner of Crébillon than to the dialogue genre as such.

Finally, notwithstanding the chronological limits of this survey, Joseph de Maistre's remarkable *Soirées de Saint-Petersburg* (Saint Petersburg Evenings), written around 1802 but only published in 1821, deserves to be included in any discussion of the dialogue form. De Maistre—a visionary with a penchant for the esoteric, and a fervent Catholic but also a Freemason—was the most redoubtable opponent of Enlightenment ideas and, alongside Edmund Burke, the most eloquent spokesman for counterrevolutionary thought. Through the voice of a Russian senator, de Maistre railed against rationalism and its spokesmen, Francis Bacon and Voltaire, while glorifying divine Providence, the value of sacrifice, and the sacred role of the executioner. The concept of original sin lay at the core of his political thought.

There was no comparable proliferation of dialogues in Germany, but those that were written there were of outstanding quality. Of the Berlin group of *Aufklärer*, special mention should be made of the Jewish deist Moses Mendelssohn. An admirable example of the tolerant and generous-minded intellectual of the day, Mendelssohn wrote several dialogues in the Platonic mode, among which the most remarkable, *Phädon, oder über die Unsterblichkeit der Seele* (1767; Phaedon; or, The Death of Socrates), is an eloquent defense of religious idealism. Between 1778 and 1780, Gotthold Ephraim Lessing published the admirable *Ernst und Falk: Gespräche für Freimaurer* (Lessing's Masonic Dialogues), in which he expressed his confidence in a future society in which minds are free and without national or religious prejudice, and men are united in their humanist faith and their practical wisdom, a world that the two speakers seem to embody. Wolfgang Amadeus Mozart's opera *Die Zauberflöte* (1791; The Magic Flute) would be the noblest, even if indirect, expression of Lessing's ideas.

However, the most important German dialogue of this period was the brief but quite astonishing one written by the fideist philosopher Friedrich Heinrich Jacobi, based on an actual encounter with Lessing. It contains a detailed account of the conversation Jacobi had on 5 July 1780 with his illustrious colleague. Jacobi is shocked to discover that Lessing admires Spinoza's *Ethica* (1677; Ethics) and thinks of himself as Spinoza's intellectual heir. Because Spinoza's thought was commonly identified with atheism at the time, the appearance of Jacobi's *Über die Lehre des Spinoza in Briefen an den Herrn Moses Mendelssohn* (On the Teachings of Spinoza in His Letters to Mr. Moses Mendelssohn) in 1785 caused a considerable scandal. However, the passage of time has cleared up the misunderstanding on which the ensuing polemics were based, and Jacobi's brief essay can now be seen as one of the finest texts produced in Germany during the Enlightenment and a genuine masterpiece of the dialogue genre.

ROLAND MORTIER

See also Ancients and the Moderns, Quarrel of the; Conversation

Further Reading

"Le dialogue, genre littéraire: Émile Zola: La littérature et les arts au XVIIᵉ siècle," *Cahiers de l'Association internationale des études françaises* 24 (1972)

Egilsrud, Johan, Le *"Dialogue des morts" dans les littératures française, allemande et anglaise (1644–1789)*, Paris: L'Entente Linotypiste, 1934

Guellouz, Soûad, *Le dialogue*, Paris: Presses Universitaires de France, 1992

Hirzel, Rudolf, *Der Dialog: Ein literarhistorischer Versuch*, 2 vols., Leipzig: Hirzel, 1895; reprint, 1986

Merrill, Elizabeth, *The Dialogue in English Literature*, New York: Holt, 1911; reprint, New York: Franklin, 1970

Mortier, R., "Pour une poétique du dialogue: Essai de théorie d'un genre," in *Literary Theory and Criticism Festschrift Presented to René Wellek in Honor of His Eightieth Birthday*, edited by Joseph B. Strelka, vol. 1, Bern and New York: Peter Lang, 1984

Mortier, R., "Variations on the Dialogue in the French Enlightenment," *Studies in Eighteenth-Century Culture* (1986)

Purpus, E.-R., "The Plain, Easy, and Familiar Way: The Dialogue in English Literature (1660–1725)," *Journal of Literary History* 17 (1950)

Roelens, M. "Le dialogue d'idées au XVIIIe siècle," in *Histoire littéraire de la France, 1715–1794*, edited by Roland Desné and Pierre Abraham, vol. 5, Paris: Éditions Sociales, 1976

Voltaire, *The Best Known Works of Voltaire: The Complete Romances, including Candide, The Philosophy of History, The Ignorant Philosopher, Dialogues, and Philosophic Criticisms*, New York: Blue Ribbon Books, 1927; reprint, 1940

Dictionary

In the 1750s observers noted the trend—indeed the "craze"—of putting everything into dictionaries. The first dictionary of dictionaries appeared in France in 1758 (Durey de Noinville, *Table alphabétique des dictionnaires* [Alphabetical Table of Dictionaries]). The continuous growth in popularity of the alphabetical format constitutes one of the major editorial and cultural phenomena of the 18th century. Infused, by way of 18th-century "encyclopedism," with a new dimension and a modern meaning, the dictionary format continued to increase in popularity and use during the 19th century. As dictionaries of all types and genres proliferated, this format proved to be remarkably adaptable. The dictionary thus allows us to trace and understand the massive accumulation of new knowledge during the Enlightenment, as well as the development of methods for the organization and communication of that knowledge.

The vigorous growth that gave dictionaries and encyclopedias a place of central importance in the history of European publishing is easily documented. Although it is very incomplete, the chronological inventory of dictionaries in France established by Bernard Quemada shows that after a period of stagnation that lasted until the 1740s (when only about 30 new titles appeared every decade), there occurred a period of rapid growth, during which 80 to 120 new titles appeared every decade (see Quemada). The revolutionary years brought a brief downturn in the production of dictionaries, but growth in that field subsequently resumed and continued unabated. This phenomenon was considerably strengthened by the large number of new editions and by the expansion in size—sometimes by an enormous amount—of these same new editions. Encyclopedias grew in size to an even greater extent. There were, for example, 24 editions of Louis Moréri's *Grand dictionnaire historique, ou Le mélange curieux de l'histoire sacrée et profane* . . . (Great Historical, Geographical, and Poetical Dictionary; Being a Curious Miscellany of Sacred and Profane History . . .) between 1674 and 1759 (from one to ten volumes in folio); nine editions of Pierre Bayle's *Dictionnaire critique et historique* (An Historical and Critical Dictionary) between 1697 and 1741 (from two to four or five volumes in folio); nine editions of the *Dictionnaire de Trévoux* (Dictionary of Trévoux) between 1704 and 1771 (from three to eight volumes in folio); and ten editions of Ephraim Chambers's *Cyclopaedia; or, An Universal Dictionary of Arts and Sciences* . . . between 1728 and 1752. The total encyclopedic output far surpassed all established limits in the volume of publication. Chambers's *Cyclopaedia* had only two volumes in folio. Johann Heinrich Zedler's *Grosses vollständiges* (Universal-Lexicon), published in Leipzig and Halle between 1732 and 1754, contained a total of 68 volumes in octavo, including four supplements. G. Pivati's *Nuovo dizionario* (New Dictionary), published in Venice from 1746 to 1751, had ten volumes in folio. Finally, Denis Diderot and Jean le Rond D'Alembert's *Encyclopédie*, taken in its totality between 1751 and 1780, with its 17 volumes of text, 11 volumes of plates, 5 volumes of supplements, and 2 volumes of indexes, comes to 35 volumes in folio. Still higher numbers were reached, although over longer periods of time, with the *Encyclopédie méthodique* (A Methodical Encyclopedia), which consisted of 158 volumes in quarto of text and 51 volumes of plates between 1782 and 1832, and the *Oekonomische Encyklopädie* (Economic Encyclopedia), which was made up of 242 volumes published from 1773 to 1858.

Projects of this size required an increasing number of collaborators (more than 135 in Paris for the text of the *Encyclopédie*), as well as considerable capital, powerful publishers, and entrepreneurs who were willing to take a risk. Scholarly studies by Jacques Proust, John Lough, and Robert Darnton have related the history of the *Encyclopédie* to the successful speculation of the Parisian bookseller Le Breton and his associates. Later editions of the *Encyclopédie*, as well as the *Encyclopédie méthodique*, depended on the publishing empire of Charles-Joseph Panckoucke, the "Atlas of booksellers." Drawing from materials in the archives of the booksellers' guild of Neuchâtel, Darnton has described the bitter battles waged at the time. He has also brought to light the extraordinary dissemination, in France and in the rest of Europe, of these collections, which became less expensive as their format decreased in size. Works of lesser scope also ensured substantial profits for their publishers: it was claimed that the bookseller Coignard married off one of his daughters with each edition of Moréri's *Grand dictionnaire*.

Without question, the dictionary in all its forms was one of the cultural products most in demand and the most fought over in the publishing world during the 18th century, and these works were produced and marketed throughout Europe. Dictionaries whose publication was illegal in France (including those of Antoine Furetière and Bayle) were printed in Holland or Switzerland and then sold in France through clandestine channels. Translations and later editions ensured the wide distribution of dictionaries throughout a market characterized by transfers and reciprocity arrangements—which were especially notable when works of monumental size were involved.

There were six new editions or reprints of the English translation of Moréri's *Grand dictionnaire* from 1694 to 1727, eight new print runs of the German translation of that work from 1709 to 1747, and one in Spanish as late as 1753. Four English editions of Bayle's *Dictionnaire* appeared from 1709 to 1741–44. The *Philosophical Dictionary*, an English translation of Voltaire's *Dictionnaire philosophique*, was published in 1765, followed by three other translations in Great Britain and the United States by the end of the century. Inversely, Thomas Dych's *New General English Dictionary* was translated into French and reprinted several times. What eventually became the *Encyclopédie* was originally conceived of as a translation of Chambers's *Cyclopaedia*. Four Italian editions of the latter were published in Naples, Venice, and Genoa from 1747 to 1775. The Paris *Encyclopédie* also did very well in Italy,

where the Lucques and Livourne editions reproduced it, with a few added notes, in its original folio format between 1758 and 1779. In Germany, along with Chambers's work, the *Encyclopédie* inspired G. Kuster's 24-volume *Deutsche Encyclopädie* (1778–1804; German Encyclopedia). In Switzerland the *Encyclopédie* appeared in a completed and corrected edition published by Fortunato Bartolomeo de Felice (58 volumes in quarto, 1775–80) in Yverdon. Finally, in Russia more than 500 articles from the *Encyclopédie* were published separately in Moscow and Saint Petersburg between 1767 and 1805. Data collected by Frank A. Kafker and researchers working with him have shed light on these exchanges, which slowly created, reinforced, and consolidated a communal encyclopedic culture (see Kafker, 1981; 1994).

The period's enormous production of alphabetically organized reference works was not a clear-cut, unequivocal phenomenon. It has often proved all too tempting to view all literary production of the period through the lens of encyclopedism, implicitly interpreting various genres as emanations of that phenomenon when in fact they are not. Compilers of 18th-century dictionaries found that the conventional division, in dictionaries, between "words" and the "things" to which they refer did not do justice to the more complex historical reality of the classical era. In his article "Dictionnaire" (Dictionary) in the *Encyclopédie*, D'Alembert adds [historical] "facts" to the categories of words and things, thus giving to the historical dictionary a status equal to that of the lexical dictionary as well as to that of the dictionary of "arts and sciences." This three-part conception had in fact solidly established by the end of the 17th century, with the publication of, Moréri's *Grand dictionnaire historique*, the *Dictionnaire de l'Académie Française* (Dictionary of the Académie Française), and Thomas Corneille's *Dictionnaire des arts et des sciences* (Dictionary of Arts and Sciences). Only by taking into account this three-part model can we understand the interrelationships and traditions of knowledge in the realm of the dictionary and assign to them their proper place and function within the culture of the period. It should be stressed that the three-way division did not preclude the inevitable influences of one area of knowledge on another; the production of dictionaries was thus a lively, creative, and sometimes unpredictable activity. Furetière's *Dictionnaire* (1690) had already provided an intermediary form between the dictionary of "words" and that of "things," giving birth to the "universal dictionary." The *Dictionnaire de Trévoux*, which at first was a copy of Furetière's compilation and which remained successful for a long time, is the best example of such a work. Bayle's *Dictionnaire critique et historique*, an unusual and paradoxical variation on the historical dictionary, served to reinvigorate that genre and extend its vitality within the "Republic of Letters." Bayle turned the historical dictionary into a forum for free discussion and an instrument of philosophical criticism and debate, paving the way for the ideological and polemical use of the "Dictionnaire" article in Diderot's *Encyclopédie* and in Voltaire's *Dictionnaire philosophique,* originally conceived as a reference work that could conveniently be carried on one's person.

The terms "encyclopedia" and "portable" designate two formats that are in all respects opposites of one another. They represent the two extremes of another typology that was both editorial and intellectual. Alongside the great dictionaries and monumental encyclopedias that generally appeared in the folio format (because of its readability, its aura of seriousness and erudition, and its suitability for large libraries), we should stress the importance of the multitude of specialized dictionaries. Many of these retained the in-folio format (including the geographic, biblical, casuistic, and commercial dictionaries) but many others were heavily influenced by the general trend toward reduction in size (as in the dictionaries of physics, chemistry, and natural history). As relative newcomers to the dictionary format, the sciences lent themselves to simplification and digesting, thus responding particularly well to the popularizing ambitions of the compilers of dictionaries. Perhaps more important still were the small dictionaries, often referred to as "portable," that proliferated after 1740 in octavo or duodecimo format. In these small volumes everything was put into dictionary form in the most indiscriminate and sometimes most unconventional way. These smaller dictionaries were devoted to subjects such as gardening, fashion, passions, virtues and vices, food, anecdotes, portraits, proverbs, and mineral water. Dozens of prefaces boasted that women and youths could take these works with them into the country and consult them with ease.

The desire or the claim to master a language, a field, or all fields of knowledge, which inspired the overwhelming and systematic use of works in alphabetical order, is inseparable from the epistemological and ideological situation in which this desire was born. Certain cultural choices were implied in the format that was adopted. The scandal of Furetière's dictionary did not lie simply in the dictionary's attack on the honor and privilege of the Académie Française, but also in the way the compiler treated language. The dictionary revealed a fundamental divergence from previous practices with respect to breadth and appropriateness of vocabulary. It questioned the social and normative value and suitability of language by including popular and technical words. The 18th century was responsible for a considerable body of work that brought up to date both vocabulary and definitions in all linguistic areas. In France the successive editions of the *Dictionnaire de l'Académie Française,* the *Dictionnaire de Trévoux,* and also Diderot's numerous *Encyclopédie* articles—which aimed at creating a philosophy of language by means of definitions—are fascinating documents for those interested in either the study of the evolution of language or critical reflection on language itself. Other European nations also attempted, sometimes under the aegis of a national academic institution, to identify, standardize, and clarify lexical usages. Samuel Johnson's *Dictionary of the English Language* (1755) deserves to be mentioned because of its recognized status as a monument of the English language. Whereas Nathan Bailey, in his *Universal Etymological English Dictionary* (1721)—which remained the standard dictionary used throughout the 18th century—collected any and all words, Johnson wanted to do for the English language what the Académie Française had done for the French language. He wanted to preserve the purity of English and standardize its usage; his greatest fear was contamination from the influence of French. The crowning success of Johnson's undertaking, which made it a major English reference work, was the desire for lexical orderliness. But Johnson also deserves credit for his willingness to accept popular and dialectical words, and he should be recognized for a very new method of creating citations and especially for his highly polished art of definition, exactness, and precision, which distinguished him from all his predecessors.

The historical dictionary, which would return to favor at the beginning of the 19th century in the form of universal biographies, was the perfect product of the "Republic of Letters"—the community of Europeans who considered themselves scholars, critics, or *curieux* (amateurs motivated by intellectual curiosity). In his "Discours préliminaire" (Preliminary Discourse) to the *Encyclopédie,* D'Alembert treats the historical dictionary with barely veiled disdain, casting it back into the distant past. In its place, he envisions a "dictionary of reason in the arts and sciences" that will accompany and crown a certain level of maturity of the human mind. Refusing the process of mere accumulation by "memory," this ideal, "reasoned" dictionary will reflect in its perception of the world a structure of the sciences and of the mind. It will take takes a complete inventory of experiences, practices, and techniques, offering offer radically new possibilities by adding a methodical element to the use of alphabetical order and cross-referencing. This dictionary will have the express aim of outlining and filling in the entire tree of knowledge, and it will aspire provide an effective method for acquiring knowledge and perceiving connections. This "encyclopedic" fervor, even more than critical audacity and reformist propositions, embodied the organizing spirit of the Enlightenment and affected all alphabetical production at the end of the century.

The prospectus for the abbé André Morellet's *Nouveau dictionnaire de commerce* (New Dictionary of Trade), which was never published, grew to become a larger volume in which he asks, "How may one create a theory in a dictionary?" There was no compilation so mediocre that it did not have such pretensions. Encyclopedic fervor thus lent new impetus to the movement toward bringing to light new discoveries in scientific knowledge, and toward more and more voluminous compendia. Panckoucke's *Encyclopédie méthodique* (A Methodical Encyclopedia) is certainly, as Darnton remarked, "the supreme encyclopedia of the Enlightenment."

But the Enlightenment dictionary developed other, more subtle and perhaps more enduring strengths: the freedom and playfulness with which it was written, its ability to create paradoxes and to subvert convention, and even the typographical beauty it occasionally offered to the reader. Bayle's *Dictionnaire* owed its extraordinary success in the 18th century not only to its eminently "philosophical" content but also to its sense of freedom, the tone—even outright bizarreness—of its "commentary" and its style, and to everything else that made it an unclassifiable work, lending itself to all interpretations and to all uses. Both Diderot, in certain articles of the *Encyclopédie* (for example, in "Jouissance" [Pleasure]), and Voltaire, in his *Dictionnaire philosophique* as well as in the *Questions sur "l'Encyclopédie"* (1771; Questions on the "Encyclopédie"), demonstrate the potential for personal and aesthetic expression of this short format. The folio dictionary, on the other hand, in its most prestigious and expensive form, graced with both engravings and great typographical complexity and beauty, can stand as a monument to the culture of the book. The engravings of Chambers's *Cyclopaedia*, within the space of a few foldout pages, offer the spectacle of baroque disorder. The 2,900 plates of Diderot and D'Alembert's *Encyclopédie* are stunning in their impeccable execution; they hold the interest of the historian of customs and professions, as well as that of the analyst of relationships between text and image. However, these engravings can also inspire a fascinating, almost visionary grand tour through the quasi fantastic world of representation.

PIERRE RÉTAT

See also Eclecticism; Encyclopedia; Essay

Further Reading

Collison, Robert, *Encyclopaedias: Their History throughout the Ages,* New York: Hafner, 1964; 2nd edition, 1966

Darnton, Robert, *The Business of Enlightenment: A Publishing History of the Encyclopédie, 1775–1800,* Cambridge, Massachusetts: Belknap Press, 1979

Kafker, Frank A., editor, *Notable Encyclopedias of the Seventeenth and Eighteenth Centuries: Nine Predecessors of the Encyclopédie,* Oxford: Voltaire Foundation, 1981

Kafker, Frank A., editor, *Notable Encyclopedias of the Late Eighteenth Century: Eleven Successors of the Encyclopédie,* Oxford: Voltaire Foundation, 1994

Lough, John, *Essays on the Encyclopédie of Diderot and D'Alembert,* London and New York: Oxford University Press, 1968

Lough, John, *The Encyclopédie,* London: Longman, 1971

Lough, John, *The Contributors to the "Encyclopédie,"* London: Grant and Cutler, 1973

Proust, Jacques, *L'"Encyclopédie,"* Paris: Colin, 1965

Proust, Jacques, *Diderot et l'Encyclopédie,* Paris: Colin, 1967; 3rd edition, 1995

Quemada, Bernard, *Les dictionnaires du français moderne, 1539–1863,* Paris: Didier, 1967

Tonelli, Georgio, *A Short-Title List of Subject Dictionaries of the Sixteenth, Seventeenth, and Eighteenth Centuries as Aids to the History of Ideas,* London: Warburg Institute, 1971

Dilettante

The word "dilettante" refers to a person who devotes himself to an art or a science for pleasure and out of personal interest, but it can also describe an amateur, a connoisseur, a collector, or a virtuoso. In a pejorative sense, it describes someone who practices an art or a science with a certain nonchalance, without possessing the necessary knowledge or aptitude, and in order to pass the time, or someone who has mastered an art or a science only from a technical, theoretical, or subjective point of view.

Whereas in the 17th century "virtuosos" were, for the most part, of noble birth and distinct from specialized artisans by virtue of their diversified but highly codified taste, bourgeois dilettantes in the age of the Enlightenment concentrated on specific matters that corresponded to their interests and aptitudes. In particular, dilettantism brought a significant social and didactic flair to the realm of the plastic arts, although its impact was less through artistic production than through a torrent of writings about art. In England, for example, dithyrambs addressed to painters were held in high regard. These verses, most of which appeared anonymously in reviews, were collected by Horace Walpole and published after his death under the title *Anecdotes of Painting in England, 1760–1795*. Although the classical Horatian doctrine of *ut pictura poesis* (as in painting, so in poetry) would remain incontestably important, a number of authors conspicuously distanced themselves from rococo in favor of a rediscovered simplicity, a nascent sensitivity to color, and, above all, a strong interest in moralizing and patriotic subjects. In general, their writings displayed a less dogmatic, sometimes liberal attitude that set these texts fundamentally apart from 17th-century literature on classical art. In this respect, a special role was played by the Society of Dilettanti, founded in London in 1734–36, a society of wealthy men who influenced the taste of young archeologists and artists by way of travels in Italy and Greece. The Society of Dilettanti was followed later by independent societies of artists who opened their studios to the public. The role played by dilettantes in the development of taste, by commissioning and collecting works, acting as patrons, and providing ideas, was first and foremost a social phenomenon (see Dobai). The same role was also played in exemplary fashion on the continent of Europe, even though the preliminary conditions were somewhat different.

In 18th-century France, artistic life was also determined by the Académie Royale de Peinture et de Sculpture (Royal Academy of Painting and Sculpture), a very hierarchical scholarly institution based on the model of the royal court. Ever since the Académie's foundation, dilettantes had been admitted to membership under such titles as *académicien honoraire* (Honorary Academician), *conseiller amateur* (Amateur Counselor), or *connaisseur de premier ordre* (Connoisseur of the First Order), and as connoisseurs and collectors they devoted themselves to improving taste. A number of dilettantes won fame as writers of treatises, including Giovanni Pietro Bellori, Roger de Piles, the comte de Caylus, Pierre-Jean Mariette, and Claude-Henri Watelet. In his capacity as receiver general of the royal finances, Watelet had the means and time to devote his leisure hours to drawing, gardening, literature on art, and travel. In addition, he was the coauthor, with P.Ch. Lévesque, of the article "Amateur," published in the Académie's *Dictionnaire des arts de peinture, sculpture et gravure* (Dic-

tionary of the Arts of Painting, Sculpture, and Engraving) in 1792. Academies of painting awarded the title "amateur" to members "who are not artists by profession but who are connected with art by their taste and their knowledge." In his article, Watelet compares the advantages and disadvantages of dilettantism. In his view, the decisive factors are "a sincere love of the arts" and knowledge, which is indispensable if one is to be able to make proper judgments. As for theory, Watelet recommended the writings of artists capable of describing their works in clear terms, such as Leonardo da Vinci, Giovanni Paolo Lomazzo, Giorgio Vasari, Nicolas Poussin, and Coypel. He also declared that it is necessary continually to deepen one's knowledge by studying the masterpieces held in collections. Finally, Watelet recommended that the knowledge obtained in this way should be put into writing.

Johann Georg Sulzer made a clearer distinction, in the preface to the first edition of his *Allgemeine Theorie der schönen Künste* (1771–74; General Theory of Fine Arts), between the "amateur" and the simple *curieux* (interested person) or dilettante who makes the fine arts a game or a pastime." The 1772 version of Sulzer's book, which was edited by Johann Wolfgang von Goethe, opened up a critical discussion of 18th-century dilettantism. The resulting interpretations of the word, both positive and negative, are still valid today.

The main argument of literary critics rested on the contrast between the connoisseur and the artist. Goethe, himself an active artist when he edited Sulzer's book, categorically rejected the idea of a connoisseur who theorizes solely in accordance with philosophical rules; rather, he expected that a "true theory" would provide the practical instruction of the great masters. In contrast to the connoisseur—to whom the dilettante, who does nothing but derive pleasure passively, corresponds at a lower level—the active artist stimulates "true" amateurs, who want to imitate him, into active production. As Goethe put it, "man does not learn or enjoy anything, without becoming immediately productive." In Goethe's reflections on the problem of dilettantism, these four figures—connoisseur, artist, amateur, dilettante—were at the core of the typology that he maintained up to the artistic conception of his old age.

A little later, Goethe began to take an interest in the psychology of students, whose early efforts in art were centered on perfection. As a student, the dilettante thus obtained a legitimate and assured place in the realm of art, being the living proof of the first stage in a program of development in three phases that Goethe had set out in his essay "Die Einfache Nachahmung der Natur, Manier, Stil" (The Simple Imitation of Nature, Manner, Style) after his travels in Italy in 1789. Goethe was fascinated by the idea of a vast didactic and critical treatise on dilettantism. Between March and May 1799, in collaboration with Friedrich von Schiller and J.H. Meyer, he outlined various models and notes that attempted to define the phenomenon of dilettantism, in its psychological, sociological, historical, and comparative aspects, within the framework of the classical cultural program of Weimar. What is striking is that the discussion spilled over to take in the arts of dance and horticulture, which were valued by dilettantes. Also remarkable was the attempt to distinguish clearly the advantages and disadvantages of dilettantism for both society and the individual. Members of the Weimar circle adhered to the basic precept that "dilettantism is more innocent, and even more formative, in those arts where the subjective already in itself plays an important role," that is, in dance, music, and lyric poetry. In other arts—dramatic poetry, drawing, painting, sculpture, architecture, gardening, the theatre—for which there are objective norms, dilettantism, in their view, is detrimental. The Weimar group therefore attempted to oppose the absorption of the notion of art by the subjective aesthetics of romanticism. They did this by reasserting the idea of art as being subjected to rules that the self-taught dilettantes were entirely unable to respect, apart from some exceptional cases. According to the Weimar classicists, the true strength of dilettantes was still their intense enjoyment of, and respect for, works of art, and it was here that their social usefulness was to be found. However, there was also a risk that the dilettantes themselves might confuse their penchant for imitation with artistic originality.

BERNHARD VON WALDKIRCH

See also Artist; Collections and Curiosities; Drawing; Painting; Taste

Further Reading

Dobai, Johannes, *Die Kunstliteratur des Klassizismus und der Romantik in England,* 4 vols., Bern: Benteli, 1974–84

Goethe, Johann Wolfgang von, *Essays on Art,* translated by Samuel Gray Ward, Boston: Munroe, 1845

Goethe, Johann Wolfgang von, "Über den Dilettantismus" (1799), in *Gedenkasugabe der Werke, Briefe und Gespräche,* edited by Ernst Beutler, Zurich: Artemis, 1950

Kemp, Wolfgang, *Einen wahrhaft bildenden Zeichenunterricht überall einzuführen: Zeichnen und Zeichenunterricht der Laien, 1500–1870,* Frankfurt: Syndikat, 1979

Sulzer, Johann Georg, "General Theory of Fine Arts (1771–74)," in *Aesthetics and the Art of Musical Composition in the German Enlightenment: Selected Writings of Johann Georg Sulzer and Heinrich Christoph Koch,* edited by Nancy Kovaleff Baker and Thomas Christensen, Cambridge and New York: Cambridge University Press, 1995

Walpole, Horace, *Anecdotes of Painting in England [1760–1795] with Some Account of the Principal Artists; and Incidental Notes on Other Arts,* edited by Frederick W. Hilles and Philip B. Daghlian, London: Oxford University Press, and New Haven, Connecticut: Yale University Press, 1937

Watelet, Claude Henri, and P.Ch. Lévesque, *Dictionnaire des arts de peinture, sculpture et gravure,* 5 vols., Paris: Prault, 1792; reprint, Geneva: Minkoff Reprints, 1972

Doubt, Scepticism, and Pyrrhonism

The terms "Pyrrhonian" and "sceptic" originally referred to a Greek school of philosophy, founded in the third century B.C. by the Academicians, of which Pyrrho was one of the most famous theorists. Practicing a method of observation and study that led to generalized doubt, the Pyrrhonians showed that it could not be ascertained whether acquiring any reliable knowledge was possible; they defined philosophy as a purgative that eliminated everything, itself included. The wise man ought to live without dogmatism, conforming to appearances, obeying his natural inclinations, and the laws and customs of society. After their rediscovery in the 16th century, these arguments played an essential role in the development of a critical philosophy, from Michel de Montaigne to the learned freethinkers, and from Pierre Bayle to the Enlightenment *philosophes.* For these authors, there was no question of creating a history of scepticism and Pyrrhonism by differentiating the Academicians' theses from those of the Pyrrhonists; the two terms "scepticism" and "Pyrrhonism" were generally taken as synonyms. The article "Pyrrhonienne" (Pyrrhonist) in the *Encyclopédie* states that

"Pyrrho was the first to practice this pusillanimous and doubting philosophy, which is named Pyrrhonist after him, and also after his sceptical nature." The Enlightenment *philosophes* reworked the sceptics' arguments, learned lessons in method from them, and thus acquired the intellectual tools that enabled them to analyze metaphysics or the various sciences, as well as morality or politics. In this way the *philosophes* developed a modern scepticism whose aims differed in many ways from those of the ancient Greeks.

This body of criticism functions primarily through the practice of doubt. Like René Descartes, the Enlightenment *philosophes* regarded doubt as the only means of radically challenging the prejudices that upbringing and society have inculcated in us and the illusions that constantly deceive us. For Descartes, however, doubt had been a means of reaching truths that could not be questioned: the doubting mind never stopped searching for what might be immune to doubt. Once sensory knowledge and mathematical truths had been challenged, once the hypothesis of an evil spirit that took pleasure in endlessly deceiving us had been raised, the certainty of Descartes's *cogito* ("I think, therefore I am") surfaced as an absolutely undeniable truth, providing the fixed point on which he could raise the whole structure of the *Méditations philosophiques* (1641; Meditations on First Philosophy). In contrast, from the time of Bayle's writings until that of Denis Diderot's, the Enlightenment *philosophes* used doubt in a purely critical way, as a means of destroying prejudices. Far from seeing doubt as a departure point for the reconstruction of the world, they used it to emphasize the inadequacies of human reason and the vanity of certain metaphysical speculations.

For Enlightenment thinkers, doubt was primarily a critical tool that made it possible to denounce errors, prejudices, the illusions to which men fall victim, and the machinations employed in order to dominate them more effectively. In publishing his *Dictionnaire historique et critique* (1697; An Historical and Critical Dictionary), Bayle wanted to compose a dictionary of errors—to collect all the falsehoods that had been written throughout the history of humankind and to expose their origins. Lazy scholars recopy errors because they have not checked their sources; biased writers twist incidents to fit their ideologies; fawning historiographers try to win a prince's favor by embellishing his portrait; deceitful monks fabricate miracles and apparitions in order to attract pilgrims and thus reap substantial profits for their convents. The establishment of an indubitable historical truth was not what interested Bayle: the articles in his *Dictionnaire* sum up the main incidents of a person's life in a few lines executed with broad brushstrokes. The essential part of his text is found in the notes (very often devoted to a minor point), which ana-

lyze legends, superstitions, popular beliefs, absurd theories, and vague polemics. By wandering through the thickets of Bayle's notes, by comparing certain articles, and thus bringing together the polemics that the author scattered throughout his text, the reader learns how to interpret and how to practice a critical method. The *Encyclopédie* uses the same strategy. The most subversive passages in its text often lie hidden in seemingly innocent articles. Only the collation of scattered elements or the reconstruction of an apparently contradictory line of argument makes such subversive passages understandable. Forced to interpret, the reader becomes to some extent the authors' accomplice. The marvelous and extraordinary could not stand up to this generalized doubt, this apprenticeship in mistrust; Enlightenment scepticism provided radical antidotes to naïveté and credulity. When Bernard Le Bovier de Fontenelle wrote his *Histoire des oracles* (1687; The History of Oracles), he showed how spectacular phenomena, thought to be miracles, in fact had rational explanations. Although amazed spectators might think that a child had grown a gold tooth and might listen to the most fanciful explanations about this phenomenon, the philosopher was able to denounce the trickery and peel off the thin film of gold leaf that had been cleverly affixed to a normal tooth. This challenge to the supernatural made it possible to denounce finalistic explanations as well as recourse to the mysterious designs of Providence. Behind these scientifically absurd theories lay political interests: provoking terror had made enslavement possible, and manipulation of the credulous was used to achieve domination. From politicians to spiritual directors, a good many men had established power over others by preventing them from developing any kind of critical ability. Henceforth, natural explanations would replace supernatural explanations of superstition. Man was not surrounded by mysterious and incomprehensible forces that only bizarre ceremonies could appease; he was simply prey to fear and ignorance and had allowed himself to be taken in by impostors who sought to dominate him. The scepticism of the Enlightenment was first and foremost a tool for intellectual liberation, a way of teaching men to think for themselves, to dare to use their own understanding, to reject intellectual submission and subordination.

However, this critical task was not limited to targeting the deceit practiced by priests and kings, the pseudoscientific speeches of charlatans, or the false arguments of astrologers. It went much further by questioning man's very ability to construct true knowledge, to produce genuine proofs, and to establish a scientifically based order. The proofs offered by scientists and metaphysicians alike may belong to the same category of imposture. In order to realize their critical task, the sceptics employed the deconstructive procedures of various philosophical systems, without of course falling into the gross contradiction of building a new system to replace them. That is why it is impossible to sum up sceptical philosophy, or present it as a dogmatic collection of theories. It is, however, possible to analyze its methods and critical concepts. Throughout the Enlightenment, various arguments were used in order to question the pretensions of scientists and metaphysicians; even if one author used them in a particular way, the same arguments frequently turn up in the writings of others, as if the sceptic philosophers had banded together in the same struggle against dogmatism and employed complementary strategies. In his *Dictionnaire,* Bayle consistently practices a method of comparing philosophical systems, showing how they are mutually destructive and never succeed in producing an irrefutable argument. According to the *Encyclopédie* article "Zénon" (Zeno), Note G, although the various philosophical sects triumph as long as they are on the attack, demolishing their opponents, they allow themselves to be demolished once they are on the defensive. Far from being outdated, the arguments of the ancient Greeks seem to become ever more relevant. Modern physics has not demolished Zeno of Elea's theses about the impossibility of motion; it has, on the contrary, given them a new legitimacy, as one reads in Note I of the article "Zénon":

> By means of this sample of the problems that can be encountered when discussing a vacuum, my readers can easily understand that Zeno would be in a much stronger position today than he was in his own day. It can no longer be doubted, he would say, that if all space is filled, then motion is impossible. This impossibility has been proved mathematically. He would take care not to argue against these proofs, he would admit their irrefutability, he would apply himself to the sole task of showing that a vacuum is impossible, and he would make a laughingstock of his adversaries. Whichever way they turned, he would keep them on the run, and by deploying these dilemmas he would force them into one impasse after another. He would cut the ground from under their feet wherever they wanted to retreat, and if he did not force them to hold their tongues, at least he would oblige them to admit that they knew nothing, that they did not understand what they were saying.

Bayle compares human reason to Penelope, who unravels during the night what she has woven by day. In other words, man cannot reach any absolute certainty. All Bayle's examples of the uncertainties of human reason and the inadequacies of science are supposed to lead his readers metaphorically to perform Penelope's

work themselves; scepticism cannot be taught dogmatically without becoming contradictory, it must be practiced. In his *Pyrroneioi hypotyposeis* (Outlines of Pyrrhonism), Sextus Empiricus piles up a series of arguments that are contradictory and difficult to follow, the objective being to exhaust the reader and make him realize that doubt is the only solution. Many of the notes in Bayle's *Dictionnaire* play a similar role, brilliantly juxtaposing philosophical and metaphysical systems in order to confront the reader with insoluble dilemmas.

The task of deconstructing human knowledge, which Bayle disseminates throughout the notes in his *Dictionnaire,* was completed systematically by David Hume in the first part of his *A Treatise of Human Nature* (1739–40). Analyzing the theory of causality, Hume shows that the relation between cause and effect is not based on any preconceived or a priori proof; it is simply created empirically through habit. We say that the sun warms stone because our experience has regularly shown us that the temperature of a stone rises when placed in the sun. But we have no innate idea of such a phenomenon, no preestablished knowledge of it, and we are totally incapable of providing any proof of it. The whole of the Cartesian concept of mathematical physics is impugned; mathematics is not composed of clear and distinct ideas that provide an absolute model of truth, it consists only of abstractions fabricated out of sensory experience; it provides man with intellectual tools but not a touchstone of knowledge. The proposition "The sun will not rise tomorrow," although it is highly improbable, is not impossible: nothing allows us to prove its falsehood. The willfully provocative character of the last example is aimed at making readers react, at forcing them to think and take an active role. Hume regularly practices a challenging philosophy, explaining to his readers that if they do not agree they have only to find a counterargument. Such criticism of science and metaphysics shows the vanity of definitive research. Like Newton, Hume reveals causes without claiming to go back to first principles, writing in Book I, Part I, Section IV of his *Treatise:*

> Nothing is more requisite for a true philosopher, than to restrain the intemperate desire of searching into cause, and having established any doctrine upon a sufficient number of experiments, rest contented with that, when he sees a farther examination would lead him into obscure and uncertain speculations.

Such a critical approach leads one to reject the dogmatism of single theories. In the same way, Diderot introduced into philosophy a fundamental role for pluralism. Diderot's dialogues often bring together several characters who express widely divergent points of view without any single truth emerging from their conversation. In opposition to the whole of Plato's Socratic method, or maieutics, which leads Socrates's questioner to understand which intelligible idea lies hidden beneath the diversity of sensory appearances, to progress from diversity of opinions to the uniqueness of truth, Diderot shows the value of several simultaneous points of view. In *Le neveu de Rameau* (1805; Rameau's Nephew), "He" says to "Me": "The important point is that you and I exist, and that we are you and I." Plurality is the important point; critics have shown how in this text the most audacious and subversive theses are upheld by the character of the Nephew. Primarily, this pluralism performs a polemical function; against the dogmatism of the churches, Diderot's scepticism gives lessons in toleration. By making an unbeliever engage in a dialogue with a staunch believer in his *Entretien d'un philosophe avec la Maréchale de **** (1776; Conversation between a Philosopher and the Marchioness of ***), Diderot does not aim to substitute an atheist catechism for a Catholic one. It is precisely because he does not seek to convince the Marchioness that he can expose the dangers of a missionary zeal that has recourse to persecution. Like Montaigne, Diderot observes humanity's diversity of customs and habits and refuses to think about them in terms of a universal norm; he dismantles hierarchies so as to take plurality into account. *La promenade du sceptique* (1747; The Sceptic's Walk) introduces us to a sort of regional philosophy, where man's varied lifestyles seem like so many strolls in a garden. The work describes three main paths: the Rose Path, whose sweetness and perfume lends itself to amorous adventures, sensuality, and libertinism; the Thorny Path, where asceticism is thought to be the only way to salvation and where people rival each other in their quest for self-mortification; and Chestnut Alley, where books, shade, tranquility, and silence reign. The sceptical philosopher is capable of acknowledging this diversity instead of thinking about human life strictly in terms of the intellectual pleasures he is able to enjoy. Philosophy is thus seen no longer as a journey but as a stroll: it is not a matter of seeing philosophy as an initiation test, as a way of making discoveries or progress; the stroll has no end other than itself. It is undertaken without maps or compasses, governed simply by the pleasure that it provides.

However, Enlightenment scepticism cannot be reduced to a purely critical activity. It also addressed the question of the philosopher's task, and the way in which he must govern his moral and political behavior. At the end of the first part of the *Treatise of Human Nature*, Hume shows that the philosopher, having recognized the limits of reason and of man's incapacity to acquire an undeniable base of knowledge, is overcome by an attack of black melancholy and feels himself doomed to spend his life on a lonely rock. However, all a man has to do is enjoy himself with friends, and such metaphysical speculations will seem ridiculous. There is truly a natural sociability in man, which can only be observed empirically and which leads Hume in the second part of his book to perform the task of reconstructing ethics and politics. Although human action cannot be founded on absolute principles, nor on an absolutely proven order, a plausible order can nonetheless be sought; without claiming to extract a priori values, beneath the diversity of human customs lie certain general principles of approval or disapproval that can be discovered.

Although the basis of values was purely empirical in the case of many sceptical philosophers, in certain instances it could also rest on revelation. Scepticism and fideism are far from being incompatible: to demonstrate the weaknesses of reason is a way of humiliating man and teaching him to surrender himself entirely to faith. When Bayle expounds Pyrrhonian arguments in a particularly brilliant way, when he denounces with irony the contradictions of theologians, he is quick to add that this is his way of demonstrating the necessity of revelation. However, these texts remain equivocal; revelation can be considered just as much the outcome of sceptical philosophy as an alibi for self-protection; the *Encyclopédie* article "Pyrrhonienne" remarks that

> among the modern *sceptics,* some have sought to decry philosophy in order to lend authority to revelation; others, in order to attack it more surely by damaging the solidity of the base on which it must be established.

It is therefore not surprising that the sceptics regularly suffered from a very bad reputation, or that they have been accused as often of intellectual weakness as of subversion or of libertinism, and even been described as self-styled freethinkers. The relevance of their criticisms, the pleasure and irony that emanate from their writings, their wish to make their readers acquire intellectual autonomy, and their struggle against dogmatism and obscurantism could hardly fail to be offensive to the adversaries of the Enlightenment.

BARBARA DE NEGRONI

See also Eclecticism; Secularization and Dechristianization

Further Reading

Popkin, Richard H., *The History of Scepticism from Erasmus to Spinoza,* Assen, The Netherlands: Van Gorcum, 1960; revised and expanded edition, Berkeley: University of California Press, 1979

Drama

During the second half of the 18th century new dramatic forms developed throughout Europe. These new forms either called into question the traditional genres of tragedy and comedy, while remaining on their margins, or transformed those genres from within. Some writers claimed to have invented a new genre, while others characterized their plays as simply adaptations of previously accepted forms. The sheer diversity of the names given to these new theatrical forms reveals the inchoate character of the alternative to classical tragedy that eventually came to be called in French the *drame*. (While it is a cognate and indeed the only available translation, the English word "drama" lacks the historical specificity of *drame*.) The evolution of the *drame* can best be understood as a dynamic process rather than as a stable form. Nevertheless, the *drame* is a form that can be found in the development of comedy and tragedy. Its trajectory may be traced in the exchanges between different national literatures, but, paradoxically, drama was reinvented within the boundaries of each country, resulting in, among other things, the foundation of a "national" theatre in German-speaking lands and the development of Goldonian comedy in northern Italy.

Some indication of the problematic character of the drama, which was both ill-defined and hegemonic, can be seen in the terms used to describe it. Gunnar Von Proschwitz has traced the term's etymology. The French word *drame* had its origins in the Latin plays performed in colleges. These performances were known as "dramas" from the 16th century onward. The abbé Prévost included the word *drame* in his *Manuel lexique* (1750; Lexical Manual) and in the *Dictionnaire de l'Académie française* (1762; Dictionary of the Académie Française), where he defined it as "a theatrical piece, either tragic or comic." Mercier emphasized that *drame* was the "collective word, the original word, the proper word." *Drame*, like *pièce* (play), which was sometimes used, therefore had a neutral meaning that was independent from comedy or tragedy. Other terms were formed by the addition of adjectives to the names of the traditional genres. For example, "comedy" could be either "serious" or not, while "tragedy" could be qualified as "domestic" or as "bourgeois" or used without any adjective at all. The term "comedy" was not only applied to theatrical pieces that were meant to cause laughter but could also simply designate plays that were not tragic. Similar fluctuations in meaning are found in other languages, but the term "drama" was most often used to describe a work that was serious in tone.

The qualifying terms that accompanied "drama" have given rise to a great deal of confusion. The expression *drame bourgeois* (bourgeois drama) was rarely used in the 18th century; that category was brought into service chiefly in the 19th century when there was, in effect, "bourgeois comedy," and it rapidly became common to speak of "bourgeois" or "domestic" tragedy in order to emphasize the contrast with heroic tragedy. The qualifier "bourgeois" referred not so much to a sociological definition of a class as to the private lives of citizens—especially those who lived in cities. Bourgeois drama could thus present protagonists who were nobles, kings, or even heroes in the mythological sense, but they were depicted in private or family settings. For example, D'Orbesson, the father of the family in Denis Diderot's play *Le père de famille* (1758; Father of a Family), is a nobleman viewed in just this way. But even when the central characters in bourgeois dramas belonged to the bourgeoisie, it would be a mistake to imagine that that they were presented as conquering heroes, reflecting the historical role of the bourgeoisie as a class. Bourgeois characters were often seen as crushed and powerless, enclosed within their domestic settings, victims of court intrigue—like the unfortunate members of the Galotti family in Gotthold Ephraim Lessing's play *Emilia Galotti* (1772). The events to which bourgeois characters are subjected, and even their eventual heroism, have a moral dimension.

Moreover, the undeniable social content of the bourgeois drama led to a schematic identification with the play's implied audience. For example, Félix Gaiffe defines *drame* as "a spectacle directed at a bourgeois or popular audience, presenting a touching and moral portrayal of their own milieu" (see Gaiffe). However, this definition did not always apply, as several plays of this type were created within the salons of the nobility.

Forerunners of the drama may be found in many different countries. In France such precursors include the comedies of Destouches and Marivaux, the "tearful comedy" of La Chaussée, and the comedies of Voltaire; in Italy comparable examples include the comedies of Carlo Goldoni; the dramatic form was foreshadowed, in Germany, in the plays of Johann Christoph Gottsched and Christian Fürchtegott Gellert, and in England, in the London presentation of Lillo's *The London Merchant* (1731) and *George Barnwell* (1731).

In France it was Diderot who gave the *drame* as a genre a kind of official birth by publishing in 1757 his comedy *Le fils naturel* (The Natural Son), accompanied by *Dorval et moi* (Dorval; or, The Test of Virtue) and *Entretiens sur "Le fils naturel"* (Discussions on "Le fils naturel"), and then, one year later *Le père de famille* and the *Discours sur la poésie dramatique* (1758; Discourse on Drama). In these works, the Encyclopedist provided both the theory and the model for the *drame*; these plays, along with the theoretical texts that accompanied them, acquired a reputation as the founding manifestos of a new genre, and their publication occurred at the height of the ideological, philosophical, and social conflict between the *philosophes* and the anti-*philosophe* movement; indeed, the *drame* itself was very much part of that conflict. The drama thus appeared as a genre peculiar to the Enlightenment, which would spread its philosophy far and wide. The principal themes of the Enlightenment, including the struggle for religious toleration, the fight against social prejudices, and militant moralism, could be found within dramas. From this point of view the most successful model of the philosophical drama was Lessing's *Nathan der Weise* (1779; Nathan the Wise). Yet the explicit philosophical messages of Diderot's dramas were deemed both harmless and uncontroversial. The attacks to which they were subjected focused on their strictly literary and formal aspects. In essence, Diderot's opponents wanted to undermine him by accusing him of having plagiarized Goldoni. Charles Palissot and Fréron, in particular, raged against the new genre, while, in the other camp, the entire clan of Encyclopedists rallied around their leader. Other plays appeared in the wake of Diderot's works, including *drames* by Jean Sedaine, Louis Sébastien Mercier, Fenouillot, Falbaire, Pierre Augustin Caron de Beaumarchais, Jean Pierre Clans de Florian, and Madame de Genlis. These works were often accompanied by impassioned theoretical treatises, such as Mercier's *Du théâtre* (1773; On Theater) and Beaumarchais's *Essai sur le genre dramatique sérieux* (1767; Essay on Serious Drama). In 1755 Lessing published the play *Miss Sara Sampson,* identifying it as a *bürgerliches Trauerspiel* (bourgeois tragedy), and in 1767–68 he published the critical articles that would be compiled as *Hamburgische Dramaturgie* (Hamburg Dramaturgy). In these critical pieces, he expressed himself strongly as a follower of Diderot in order to attack the French style of classical tragedy. The popularity of the drama was spread and lasted even beyond the Revolution, with some high points and some relative eclipses offset by success in the provinces. In the 19th century the influence of the drama can be seen in the melodramas and bourgeois comedies of such writers as Casimir Delavigne, Eugéne Scribe, and Augier. The new genre spread into Italy between 1772 and 1778 and even to Russia, where it influenced the works of Lukin and Fonzivin, but it is in Germanic literature that one finds the most striking examples of the genre, in works by Lessing and by writers associated with the Sturm und Drang movement.

Drama was made up of a certain number of characteristics, all duly highlighted by its theorists. In the first place, it involved breaking away from the traditional opposition between the social connotations of comedy and tragedy. The characters and types found in comedy were derived from humanity in general, whether bourgeois or other people in private life, and were portrayed in a contemporary situation that was designed to "make people of taste laugh." The protagonists of classical tragedy were people in high places, such as kings, princes, or military leaders, placed in situations that magnified their sufferings and put them into conflict with their destiny. Drama depicted bourgeois characters (or others in private settings) in serious or even tragic situations in order to inspire pity and fear among the spectators. From comedy, drama borrowed the social condition of its characters, and from tragedy, it took the nature of the action. Drama thus appeared as an "intermediate" genre that corresponded to the development of bourgeois class-consciousness in the 18th century.

Such is the description that is generally put forward. However, the notion of drama as an intermediate genre presents a certain number of difficulties—even to its theorists. First of all, problems arise from the status of the characters depicted. It is hard to conceive of a protagonist who is halfway between a comical character and a tragic hero, in terms of historical or legendary individuality: what middle ground could there be between Theseus and Brutus, on the one hand, and Harlequin and Molière's Miser, on the other?

Drawing on Diderot's reflections on the nature of dramatic characters, Lessing drew attention to the fact that the individuality of tragic heroes is an illusion, since the writer is only drawn to the heroes because of their exemplary dimension and has given them a new status as characters in a fable. It was therefore necessary that characters in tragedy be as generalized as those in comedy. And so it was pointless to invent an average character, since all the traditional distinctions between tragic heroes and ordinary people had disappeared. Beaumarchais affirmed that it is the mother and not the queen who touches us in Voltaire's tragic heroine Merope, thus bringing tragic heroism to the level of ordinary humanity. Marmontel's reasoning was the same. He held that the character should be a synecdoche of humanity. Tragedy itself was reduced to being a variety of *drame*. Diderot proposed to replace "character" with a key concept in his system of theatrical writing, the "condition" (financier, merchant, or judge) and the "relationship" (such as father of the family or illegitimate son). In fact, however, Diderot put only the latter into his own work. In summarizing the program of dramatic reform in his *Entretiens sur "Le Fils naturel"* Dorval suggests that "the condition of a person ought perhaps to be substituted for the characters in all genres." Diderot declared that since comic characters are "marked by their principal traits," it was impossible to re-create in the theatre "the little differences that are noticeable in people's natures." Comic stylization is contrary to a realistic representation of people and their characters, which is to say, their individuality. Such stylization stands in the way of the nuances that make each bourgeois individual both a universal type and an infinitely individual subject. More and more, this obstacle led writers to perceive only a single, universal human condition and to erase the former distinctions between tragedy and comedy. From its former intermediate position between tragedy and comedy, drama thus came to dominate the entire realm of writing for the theatre.

Diderot's concept of "condition" opened another door for the genre, that of social realism or at least of a questioning of the relationship between individuals and society. Following his lead, writers such as Sedaine, Mercier, and Madame de Genlis all proposed a gallery of "conditions," comprising portraits of characters belonging to bourgeois or petit bourgeois life in their professions, whether major or minor. These ranged from the great merchant and shipper Vanderk in Sedaine's *Le philosophe sans le savoir* (1765; The Philosopher in Spite of Himself), to the vinegar maker in Mercier's *La brouette du vinaigrier* (1775; The Barrel-Load of the Vinegar Merchant), and even to the destitute man in Mercier's *L'indigent* (1772; The Distressed Family). Unfortunately, moralism all too often stifled or oversimplified the conflicts between individuals and their condition.

The insistence on a moral message—within the framework of a simple fable in which society punishes the unfortunate villain—removed any tragic dimension from a drama such as Lillo's *The London Merchant* (which, in Diderot's view, was one of the English models of the genre, along with Moore's *The Gamester*). Benjamin Constant remarked later that dramatists had always missed an essential tragic motivation, the impact of society on passions and character. Yet, while this reflection is very pertinent in the context of French or English literature, it can hardly be applied to the Sturm und Drang playwrights. Lenz's *Der Hofmeister* (1774; The Tutor) or his *Die Soldaten* (1776; The Soldiers), written 60 years before Büchner, provided a remarkably well-developed and profound denunciation of a society that both defines and crushes the individual. This was a hopeless conflict, for in addition to the detailed denunciation of a specific society, Lenz expressed a deep pessimism about the social contract, which he perceived as a bond that literally denatures mankind. In a less profound way, Friedrich von Schiller's dramas *Die Räuber* (1781; The Robbers) and *Kabale und Liebe* (1784; Intrigue and Love) portrayed a similar conflict but placed it in the context of a struggle for freedom against a perverse and unjust society.

All these texts must be understood in terms of a quest for new dramatic effects. Between terror and pity (the effects of tragedy) and laughter (the effect of comedy), a whole range of emotions was opened up to exploration. Paradoxically, it was necessary not to weaken but to reinforce and revitalize emotion, to render it universal, to create among the spectators a sense of civic community. Whereas the classical French system conceived only an incompatibility between comic emotion and tragic emotion, dramatists such as Beaumarchais, Florian, and Goldoni were now seeking the marriage of laughter and sensibility. They had found their model in the comedies of Terence, in which horror and tenderness are combined with enthusiastic celebration of models of virtue. However, such mixtures of frank comedy, despair, terror, and pity gave rise to certain misgivings on the part of dramatic theorists. In France especially, these theorists recoiled from what they felt to be outlandish extremes in Shakespeare's plays, yet Shakespeare's work held a powerful fascination for both French and German writers. A play such as Lenz's *Der Hofmeister*, although presented as a "comedy," freely and audaciously mixed parody, derision, the grotesque, and horror. The French remained decidedly on the safe side of such bold experiments.

In reality, playwrights and dramatic theorists alike were searching for the renewal of emotion by way of a new conception of dramatic illusion. All the criticisms that they aimed at classical genres were organized around this theme. Coups de théâtre, monologues, recitations, asides, the absence of unity in the dramatic performance, and the conventional settings and costumes seemed to them to destroy the dramatic illusion that they sought. Diderot's ideas were significant in this regard. He conceived dramatic illusion on the model of painting and wanted to replace coups de théâtre with tableaus. He sought to contain the performance within the enclosed sphere of the stage, which should be completely separated from the auditorium by a "fourth wall," which was invisible but invincible. The spectacle, no matter what its genre, should radically deny the existence of the spectator. The spectators should look upon the dramatic tableau in the same way they behold a genre scene in a painting.

As a result, the effectiveness of drama was inseparable from the reforms that all these writers called for. The efforts of Voltaire and Diderot, of such painters and designers as Philip James Loutherbourg in Britain, the Slotzes in France, and Desprez in Sweden, and of such actors as Garrick, Lekain, Mademoiselle Clairon, Molé, and Talma all pointed in the same direction: the quest for visual coherence within the spectacle, conceived on the model of painting. Dramatic writing was strongly influenced by this ideal. Diderot, Mercier, Sedaine, and Beaumarchais investigated those theatrical moments when characters move within their ordinary circles and their everyday occupations, or pause in striking dramatic postures. As a result, dramatic action was more or less modified. Many years before Büchner, Lenz composed plays as a succession of relationships between characters linked not by a perceptible plot but by a more deeply hidden coherence and design.

These conceptions alone permitted the drama to tackle history without reducing it to conspiracies in palaces. The French showed themselves to be very cautious in this regard—for example, Mercier's most daring works, such as *La mort de Louis XI* (1783; The Death of Louis XI), and *Philippe II* (1785), were never performed. But Goethe, with his *Goetz von Berlichingen* (1773; Goetz of Berlichingen), and Schiller, with his *Die Räuber* and his trilogy *Wallenstein* (1798–99), gave this movement achievements that bear witness to the ambition of German theatre. As Lenz strongly emphasized, this was a theatrical method that broke with the Aristotelian conception of action, which the classical model of tragedy had imposed as a vision of history.

Unlike the German-speaking countries, France did not adopt this sort of drama, this "national tragedy," although many writers called for it. France's different path is perhaps explained by the fact that the nation had long been politically unified and the elite had faith in a cultural hegemony that, perhaps, was more imaginary than real. It is also possible that academic punctiliousness, and the search for success through tragedy, definitively impeded the French quest for a national form of tragedy. The Germans achieved it to the extent that they developed a culture of resistance and opposition to the French model, a culture that referred to a myth of the people that was very foreign to French theatre. In his *Anmerkungen übers Theater* (1774; Notes on Theater), Lenz clarified the German approach by writing:

Thus, to define the contours of our tragedy with more precision than has been done up until now, and by analogy with our religious conceptions and our whole way of thinking and acting, we must give up taking Aristotle as our starting point. To find our own starting point we must consult the popular taste for the past and for our country, which still remains today, and will always remain, the popular taste.

More than a new genre, the drama was therefore a movement of renovation that affected all of the serious theatre of Europe in the second half of the 18th century. Its link with the Enlightenment, which characterized it at its birth, was weakened by the end of the century, and the forms to which it gave birth would become linked to other ideological configurations. Sturm und Drang drama and French melodrama alike bear witness to the Enlightenment as a turning point.

PIERRE FRANTZ

See also Comedy; Tears; Theatre and Staging; Tragedy

Further Reading

Bevis, Richard W., *English Drama: Restoration and Eighteenth Century, 1660–1789*, London and New York: Longman, 1988

Didier, Beatrice, *Beaumarchais, ou, la passion du drame*, Paris: Presses Universitaires de France, 1994

Gaiffe, F., *Le drame en France au XVIIIe siècle*, Paris: Armand Colin, 1910; reprinted 1970

Lamport, F.J., *German Classical Drama, Theater, Humanity, and Nation, 1750–1870*, Cambridge and New York: Cambridge University Press, 1990

Niesz, Anthony J., *Dramaturgy in the Drama: From Gryphius to Goethe*, Madison: University of Wisconsin, 1977

Rougemont, Martine de, *La vie théâtrale au XVIIIe siècle*, Paris: Champion, 1988

Drawing

During the second half of the 18th century, drawing underwent many changes—changes in how it was taught, in its techniques, and above all in its status. As an alternative form of human writing, it became the reflection of its author, and it was expected to reflect the artist's sensibility as well as the truth of nature. The primacy of drawing was recognized in all domains of art: architecture, painting, sculpture, engraving, and the applied arts. During this period, drawings were endowed with a new status as complete works of art. They were no longer merely sketches or drafts for paintings or sculptures, but were considered works in themselves, destined either for the personal use of the artist or for the use of whoever commissioned or collected them. This new status was reflected in several different categories, including that of portrait drawings which came to be regarded as highly as portrait paintings, as well as that of landscape drawings framed flush with the composition, without a matte, under glass. Such drawings were listed in catalogs and inventories as "pictures in gouache" or "drawings painted in gouache." Drawing no longer followed the hierarchy of genres used in the academies, in which history painting was considered the highest form. The category of drawing, in contrast, included landscapes, and few artists drew historical scenes except as preliminary studies for paintings. Like engravings, drawings gradually appeared as a form of art in the Salons and became objects to be collected and traded. Certain artists specialized in drawing and as a result produced only a limited number of paintings.

The classification of drawings according to the "Trois Écoles" (the three schools) was always used in catalogs to refer to Italian, Northern European, and French styles of drawing. In fact, however, this notion of national schools is problematic, since many artists traveled all over Europe, and drawing was precisely the technique that allowed an artist to note all the influences to which he was particularly subjected while traveling. Some landscape drawings made in the cosmopolitan city of Rome were very similar to each other, yet they could have been done by artists from different countries. The situation was much the same in Paris, where many foreign artists drew in the same style as the French. Nevertheless, certain schools had their peculiarities or preferences; for example, British artists composed landscapes in watercolor. Artists claimed the status of free men, and this conception of artistic freedom took on its full meaning in the first years of the 19th century, making classification according to national schools all the more problematic.

Drawing was taught in schools; it was considered one of the disciplines that every well-educated young man should master. Students learned the rudiments of perspective and landscape drawing, as well as the correct way to handle the pen and colors. Artistic instruction was provided in drawing schools and academies. Access to the Académie Royale de Peinture et de Sculpture (Royal Academy of Painting and Sculpture) in Paris was restricted to young men who already had practical experience in art (this training was not available to young women). In the academies, one studied models taken from life or from casts of celebrated antiquities, such as the *Laocoon* or the bas-reliefs of Trajan's Column. This style of training was often criticized, notably by Denis Diderot and later by Antoine Quatremère de Quincy. Six exceptional students of painting and architecture were chosen each year to receive three additional years of training at the École Royale des Élèves

Protégés (Royal School for Privileged Students), which existed from 1748 to 1775. The most outstanding students could continue receiving instruction at the Académie de France (Royal Academy of France) in Rome, where they had the opportunity to spend three or four years studying antiquities and old masters, draped figures, and, little by little, landscapes. In the second half of the 18th century, there was new interest in disseminating knowledge throughout all levels of society. Drawing played an important role in the provincial academies that were created, following the Parisian model, by amateurs or professional artists. It was in the 18th century, too, that a large number of European academies were established, many of them based on the French model. The teachers at the academies in Copenhagen, Saint Petersburg, and Stockholm were French, as were the models—engravings and drawings by old masters—that circulated in those cities. Teaching methods were codified and virtually identical in all these institutions.

Another group of institutions, which were linked to the artistic professions and intended for young male students, were the free schools of drawing. These schools reflected a socioeconomic concern with improving the applied arts. With this goal in mind, a "Projet pour l'établissement d'écoles gratuites de dessin" (Proposal for the Establishment of Free Schools of Drawing) was published in the *Mercure de France* in 1746 by Ferrand de Monthelon, who opened a "school of practical mathematics and drawing" in Rheims in 1748. This was followed by several more free schools of drawing in the provinces, including the one created by Quentin de La Tour in his hometown of Saint-Quentin in 1782. The École Royale Gratuite de Dessin (Royal Free School of Drawing), established in 1766 under the direction of Jean-Jacques Bachelier, was intended for the "use of elementary schools for the improvement of the mechanical arts." Its students were divided into three major categories that were related to the professions: architecture, stonemasonry, perspective and mathematics; the human face and animals; and flowers and ornaments. The program was not intended to produce artists, but to prepare young men for their future trades or professions. The course was rounded off with geometry, which was taught in each category. Drawing also formed part of the syllabus at the military engineering schools—the École Royale du Génie (Royal School of Engineering) in Mézières and the École Royale des Ponts et Chaussées (Royal School of Bridges and Highways)—where the engineers became true artists; and at the École Polytechnique (Polytechnical School), where both technical and artistic drawing was taught. Drawing played a political role during the Revolution through the bureau of draftsmen created by the Committee of Public Safety in 1793; its mission was to make a visual record of all the technical equipment of the Republic (now in the industrial portfolio of the Conservatoire National des Arts et Métiers [National Conservatory of the Arts and Professions]). Some private schools were also opened, either by artists, such as François Boucher or Joseph Marie Vien, or by connoisseurs, such as the duc de La Rochefoucauld and his brother in law, the duc de Chabot, who created the Académie La Rochefoucauld, where Eschard and Hubert Robert occasionally taught. Similar schools were opened in other countries, including the one in Geneva that was run by Robert Subeyran. In the second half of the 18th century, alongside this formal instruction, many pedagogical texts on drawing were published, written by artists or theorists. These texts were aimed above all at amateurs, although they closely followed the principles then in vogue in the academies. The most celebrated of these works was Jombert's *Nouvelle méthode pour apprendre à dessiner sans maître* (1740; new edition, 1755; New Method to Learn Drawing without a Master), which served as the model for the chapter "Dessein" (Drawing) in the *Encyclopédie*. Some books on anatomy were also published, notably by Gautier-Dagoty (1773), Jacques Gamelin (1779), and Süe (1787).

The techniques used by the artists of the 17th century continued to be used during the 18th century, but they became more diversified, and artists often combined them. Artists attached a great deal of importance to technique, and some artists purposely created the same composition using a variety of techniques. White paper was the most widely used material, but dark-colored, gray, beige, or blue paper continued to be highly valued. Some artists experimented with their paper (for example, Desfriches's paper tablet). Pens were used to sketch scenes from life and for architectural and technical drawings. Brown wash drawing was quite popular among artists, who used it in different ways, almost dry or very diluted (Jean-Honoré Fragonard, Giovanni Battista Tiepolo, and landscape artists). Ink and wash were often mixed (Giambattista Piranesi). Drawings made *aux trois crayons*—a technique involving red, black, and white pencil—remained popular (Jean-Étienne Liotard). Drawings made using *sanguine* (red chalk), which had been in use for a long time, became much more widespread in the 18th century. This medium was adopted in studios all over Europe and for a variety of studies (Edme Bouchardon, Jean-Baptiste Greuze), as well as for the genre scenes and portraits that were so highly valued by connoisseurs (François Boucher). Charles-Joseph Natoire, the director of the Académie de France in Rome, used red chalk mixed with *pierre noire* (a type of black chalk), along with brown or black ink and wash for landscapes. It was during his tenure as director that landscape became an important subject in the Académie's curriculum. This development resulted in the use of red chalk in the drawings of the many views of Rome and its environs by those enrolled in the Académie, such as Jean-Honoré Fragonard and Hubert Robert. One advantage of both red chalk and *pierre noire* lay in their ability to be counter-proofed, thus permitting the production of several copies of a single drawing, albeit in reverse and often of a lower quality than the original. With the rise of neoclassicism, red chalk fell into some disfavor among artists, as neoclassicism valued line above every other aspect of drawing; neoclassical artists used pen and ink, and above all *pierre noire* (Jacques-Louis David), sometimes highlighting in white (Pierre Paul Prud'hon).

The major innovation in drawing in the 18th century involved the use of color and the adoption of two media: gouache, which had long been used in topography and for natural history drawings; and watercolor, employed on a much more limited scale. Both techniques were used for landscapes more than for any other subject and were in demand among all connoisseurs and travelers. Gouache was the medium favored by the artists of the Naples school, the *védutistes* (scenic painters) working in Rome, and other landscape artists (including Moreau the Elder). A water-based paint, gouache was sometimes diluted with water or mixed with *aquarelle* (watercolor). Watercolor became overwhelmingly fashionable in Britain around the 1750s, and it eventually spread to the European continent. Paul Sandby pioneered the use of the watercolor medium, and was followed by numerous British artists—Thomas Gainsborough, Thomas Girtin, Cozens—for whom it became almost the single medium of expression. J.M.W. Turner used watercolor in his landscapes, as well as in abstract pieces. British artists who worked exclusively in watercolor were not allowed to exhibit at the Royal Academy, and in 1804 they created the Water Colour Society, which was followed by a rival association in 1807. In France the word *aquarelle* made its first appearance as a drawing technique at the Salon of 1776 and then appeared as the subject of an article in the *Encyclopédie méthodique* (1791; Methodical Encyclopedia). Watercolor was associated with the education of young women, who practiced it both in the princely courts of Europe and in the homes of the bourgeoisie; above all it was associated with amateurs. It was essentially in landscape that watercolor was able to display all its qualities of luminosity, transparency, and freshness of color, and it became a synonym for the outdoors, as well as the ideal technique for traveling draftsmen. The effects of sky, clouds, snow, ice fields, and water could be accurately depicted, thanks to colors that could be diluted with water.

Watercolor was linked to the world of discoveries, whether faraway—for example, on the shores of Tahiti

(John Webber)—or closer to home, as in the Alps (John Robert Cozens). Every artist used watercolor, whether in Italy (Francesco Guardi), in Switzerland (Abraham-Louis-Rodolphe Ducros, Kaisermann), in Germany (Jakob Philipp Hackert, Caspar David Friedrich), in the Netherlands (Cornelis Troost), or in France (Robert, Moreau). Watercolor was also linked to the world of feeling, in that its more or less fluid consistency allowed the artist to render all the variations found in the subject being represented, even the depths of his or her soul (Henry Fuseli, William Blake). Some artists used watercolor for portraits or illustrations (Saint-Aubin, Blake). Watercolor supplanted gouache, which was considered to be too dry, in drawings of natural history subjects (Schouman, Ehret, the Redoutés, Van Spaendonck).

Color was just as important in the art of pastel portraiture, which was introduced by Rosalba Carriera. Following her example, pastels were favored by portraitists such as Perronneau, who was both a painter and a pastelist; and, above all, by Quentin de La Tour, who used only pastels—for example in his portrait of Madame de Pompadour (now in the Musée du Louvre in Paris)—and by artists who took up portraiture and pastels at the same time, such as Jean-Baptiste Siméon Chardin. These artists all appreciated the qualities of pastels, notably the rapidity of execution that they allowed, and the wealth of possibilities in their colors. The fixing of pastels, previously a difficult procedure, was improved by applying the *Méthode pour fixer le pastel* (1780; Method for Fixing Pastel) developed by Loriot and published by Renou.

With the increased prosperity of European society, the art of miniatures—whether on enamel, ivory, or vellum, circular or rectangular, showing one figure or several figures—achieved unprecedented popularity. Overall, the typology of drawing was widely varied, depending on who made these works and on the circumstances of their creation. Travel notebooks were sometimes covered with annotations or long texts giving details of the journey; there were *livres de raison*, books in which artists accumulated their own drawings and those of other artists; and individual drawings, some mounted and some not.

The subjects taken up by the artists also varied widely and generally mirrored those dealt with by painters. Drawing, like painting, encompassed every genre. This was especially true since drawings were often preliminary studies for paintings: subjects from ancient and modern history, mythology or religion, various portraits, natural history plates, etc. These works reflected the sensibility of the period. Drawing was influenced by writings on art, such as those by Johann Joachim Winckelmann, as artists tried to reconcile the incompatible demands of beauty and truth, art and life. The artists who pursued this unattainable ideal gave

primacy to the line, leading to a strong revival of structured compositions and historical subjects (David, Antoine-Jean Gros, Théodore Géricault, artists of the northern school, and the German painters). Drawing, more than in any other art form, was marked by a return to the themes of antiquity and a preference for morbid subjects—a trend that is also discernable in preromantic literature.

The art of landscape was dominant in the drawings of the second half of the 18th century, oscillating between realism, the picturesque, and the pursuit of the sublime as advocated by Immanuel Kant. At the end of the century some artists in Britain (Jones and Cozens) and in France (Valenciennes) tried to render reality in its most fleeting state, prefiguring photographic experimentation. The sky, clouds, and water thus became subjects for drawings. The topographic tradition was continued with large-scale, broad panoramas of cities and landscapes, drawn with the aid of the camera obscura. The horizons of draftsmen were also broadened by travel. British and Dutch travelers were often accompanied on their grand tours by artists (Ducros), and the portfolios that they assembled then became the basis for the publication of large volumes illustrated with occasionally picturesque archeological and topographic plates (Robert Adam, *The Ruins of the Palace of Diocletian*, [1764]). The drawings made by artists taking part in voyages around the world or in military campaigns were engraved and printed in accounts of voyages (such as those of James Cook, the comte de La Pérouse, or Antoine Raymond Joseph de Bruni d'Entrecasteaux) or in accounts of scientific expeditions (Niebuhr and the *Description de l'Égypte*, 1809–22; Description of Egypt). Artists also provided drawings that were used to illustrate "picturesque voyages," in which landscapes played an important role.

Daily life in the 18th century can be rediscovered through drawings, thanks to the "little masters" of the art. Eighteenth-century Paris is restored in Saint-Aubin's partially completed drawings, as well as in his rapid sketches, and it is essentially through drawings that the French Revolution and its consequences elsewhere in Europe unfold before our eyes, from the *Serment du Jeu de Paume* (Oath Sworn at the Jeu de Paume) drawn by Jacques-Louis David, to Bonaparte's Italian campaign. There was an enormous vogue for using drawings as illustrations, as a result of the growth of publishing and of connoisseurs' interest in illustrated books. Their demand was met by didactic volumes (encyclopedias), religious texts (missals and breviaries), works of natural history (Buffon), novels (Ariosto), and fables (La Fontaine, in the 1763 edition sponsored by the Fermiers Généraux [General Tax Farmers]). Some artists specialized in such illustrations (Gravelot, Eisen, Cochin). Among architectural drawings, there is a distinction between plans that were related to specific commissions and the many architectural fantasies that followed in Piranesi's wake. Piranesi, it should be noted, set himself apart from his highly technical predecessors with his exuberant imagination and his penchant for the fantastic. There were also a great many collections of decorative models.

People from various social and intellectual milieus collected drawings. In the catalogs of their collections, which display an immense diversity of taste, one finds both "first impressions" and drawings executed for their own sake, without any connection to future works. Such collections belonged to emperors or empresses (Catherine II of Russia), to kings (the kings of France, George III of Britain), to princes (Prince Eugen in Vienna), or to private individuals (Pierre Jean Mariette). Diplomats assigned abroad assembled some fine collections (comte Tessin, the Swedish ambassador in Paris; Joseph Smith, the British consul in Venice). Other individuals assembled their collections over the course of their travels (the comte d'Orsay, Richard Payne Knight); while other collections were formed by artists (Desfriches, Pâris) and connoisseurs (Atger,

Robien, Veyrenc). Some collectors classified their collections (Lagoy), stamped their seals (Mariette) or initials (Desfriches) on had them placed on a personalized mounting. The 18th century was also a period in which many people discovered the pleasures of drawing or of being a connoisseur, such as Mariette and certain British lords.

MADELEINE PINAULT SØRENSEN

See also Collections and Curiosities; Color; Grand Tour; Illustration; Miniature; Picturesque

Further Reading

Benhamou, Reed, *Public and Private Art Education in France: 1648–1793*, Oxford: Voltaire Foundation, 1993

Birembaut, A., "Les écoles gratuites de dessin," in *Enseignement et diffusion des sciences en France au dix-huitième siècle*, edited by René Taton, Paris: Hermann, 1964

Roland, Michel Marianne, *Le dessin français au XVIIIe siècle*, Fribourg, Switzerland: Office du Livre, 1987

Dream

To what extent did the ambiguous definitions of the word *rêve* (dream) in the *Encyclopédie* reflect ideas about dreaming as it had been understood during the ancien régime, and to what extent did those definitions transform received ideas on the topic? Which of the new elements associated with dreaming during the 18th century were passed on to later centuries?

Many of the popular works that proliferated in the 17th century reused (and sometimes distorted) ideas from Greco-Roman or Arab sources, including the works of authors such as Valerius Maximus, Macrobius, Apollonius, Alexander, and Artemidorus. As a result, the interpretation of dreams was linked to numerous supposed "sciences" such as physiognomy, astrology, and magic. These systems of belief—which were often used in combination—were accorded legitimacy as highly ritualized keys to possible interpretations of the future.

At the start of the 18th century, Father Le Brun in his *Histoire critique des pratiques superstitieuses* (1701; Critical History of Superstitious Practices), continues to speculate about the potential uses of dreams while at

the same time casting doubt on their prophetic function. In particular, following up suggestions made in the 17th century, Le Brun introduces a new category of interpretation that posits the existence of a "motor" in the imagination—a "spring" that sets dream activity in motion and even, in extreme cases such as nightmares, gives dreams a component that is implicitly both pathological and physiological.

The *Encyclopédie*'s Approach

Le Brun's attribution of a dual function or nature to dreams reappears in the *Encyclopédie*. Dreams materialize during sleep, which the *Encyclopédie* calls "a state that man needs in order to sustain, repair, and reassemble his 'machine' [body]." In fact, dreams are so enigmatic, so difficult to discuss, that the *Encyclopédie* devotes two separate entries to defining them and describing their meaning and function. These entries are entitled "Songe" (Dream), excerpted from Jean-Henri-Samuel Formey's *Essai sur les songes* (1746; Essay on Dreams), and "Rêve" (Dream; Dreaming), which in turn is divided into two sections. The entry "Rêve" relates dreams to metaphysics (and partly overlaps with the entry "Songe"). It argues that dreams serve to give people "the inner feeling of ourselves" and at the same time they give the dreamer the possibility of observing everyday things in a state of "delirium" (which today we might call "disorientation"). In contrast, the second section of the entry "Rêve" relates the topic, however paradoxical it may seem, to medicine. Dreaming is defined as a "malady" denoting a specific condition of the body and the ailing soul. Moreover, dreams are also presented in their long-established role as "symptoms." This role had been assigned to dreaming since the era of Lomnius and Hippocrates, and dreams had gained more and more acceptance as a subject of medical studies, which focused on analyzing the specific factors that most influenced the body and produced perceptible changes in it.

In the 18th century, the French word *songe* (dream) was a term that belonged as much to the domain of metaphysics as to that of physiology. It was defined as an apparently bizarre phase of the soul, which was at the mercy of sensations that were independent of external objects. In his *Essai sur les songes,* cited above, Formey assumes an a priori distinction between the soul and the body, but he accepts that dreaming is a faculty of the soul—a soul that feels sensations without possessing a real knowledge of them and that imagines objects without forming specific impressions of them. Formey nevertheless maintains that the physiological component of dream states prevails—to the point that he prefigures the theory of vibrations (well before Denis Diderot and David Hartley). Just as precociously, he sets forth a theory of the association of ideas, which was he calls the "law of the imagination," describing its role as setting the flux of dreams in motion. This law is basically inactive during waking states but shows its elusive, incoherent, and anarchic character during its operation in dream states.

From a reading of these two entries in the *Encyclopédie,* it can be inferred that dreams and dreaming form part of dialectical relationships—both during waking states and in dream states—between body and soul, imagination and sensation, and reality and nonreality. These relationships constitute the more or less explicit framework for the arguments in these entries. These themes were interesting enough to gain the attention of 18th-century philosophers and writers in France and elsewhere, and they indicate a point of view that increasingly based its axioms on empirical foundations.

At first, the writers of the entry "Rêve" in the *Encyclopédie* seem to consider the "soul" to be an entity that gives impetus to the imagination and to dream states. However, the writers then temper this position by including the interference of the bodily state, which

"alone determines the perception of dreams." In fact, the body's role is deemed so essential that the state of health of the "dreamer" has as much influence over the production of dreams as the uncontrolled activity of the imagination. The *Encyclopédie*'s entries find neither a winner nor a loser in the rivalry to determine the possible supremacy of the soul or body in the realm of dreams—the body being regarded as a veritable dream-producing "machine." However, when imagination and sensation are coupled as rivals, the sensations prove to be slightly superior to the imagination in provoking dreams. Thus, the entry "Rêve" states, "an ordinary act of the imagination is always connected with a sensation that precedes it, without which it would not exist." A little further on, the entry states, "every dream begins with a sensation and carries it on through a series of acts of the imagination." This assertion conforms to the most classical rules of the analogy. Because sensations coincide with the impressions prompted by external objects (which are often identified with physical problems), sensation, the veritable "mother" of dreaming, determines the type of dreaming. Finally, one can infer from the *Encyclopédie* that dreams and dreaming are "arbiters" of reality—a reality that is apparently difficult to discern and to define, for it slides away and becomes confused with nonreality in the transition from the waking state to the dream state.

In 18th-century France, Germany, and Russia, dreams were often associated with the realm of the visionary: they were regarded as a form of clairvoyance and a glimpse into the future, as can be seen in the works of Nicolas Rétif de La Bretonne, Mercier de Compiègne, Louis Sébastien Mercier, and Aleksandr Nikolayevich Radishchev. "Oneiromancy" does not appear in the pages of the *Encyclopédie*'s two dream entries, but these entries clearly borrow from Lucretius's *De rerum natura* (On the Nature of Things) as well as from the works of René Descartes. Thus, one finds traces of Lucretius's journey toward a "naturalistic" and "mechanical" conception of dreaming, which could determine the possibility of "seeing equally well with the eyes of the body or those of the soul" and also the possibility of combining, just as indiscriminately, the "truth of the real with the lie of dreaming." On the problem of the interchangeability of dreaming and reality, the writers of the two entries borrowed from Descartes the idea that a dream can be an extension of reality, as well as a realm in which all capacity for judgment is suspended.

As for the analysis of sensations, such an important topic in the *Encyclopédie*'s entries, the two entries on dreams evoke the notion that sensations are the "motors" of ideas, recalling John Locke's emphasis on the illusory character and falseness of dream states. Similarly, the interchange between reality and dreaming and the extension of the one into the other recall Gottfried Wilhelm Leibniz's ideas, which emphasize even more firmly than Locke the "heuristic" role of reason, the supreme guarantee of the truthfulness of the images in dream states.

Diderot's Contribution

These issues are addressed in *Le rêve de D'Alembert* (1769; D'Alembert's Dream), in which Diderot reaffirms the difficulty of distinguishing the experience of dreaming from the experience of lived reality and in which he insists on the role of the sensations that invariably "have an effect" on both states. The entries "Sensation," "Imagination," and "Sommeil" (Sleep), as well as the entry "Rêve" from the *Encyclopédie*, reappear in Diderot's *Éléments de physiologie* (1778; Elements of Physiology), where all these topics are regarded as "phenomena of the brain." Furthermore, like the *Rêve de D'Alembert,* the *Éléments* shows the influence of the theories of Albrecht von Haller, the leading physiologist of time, and it also attests to Diderot's increasing conviction that biology, rather metaphysics or introspection, should be given priority. Diderot had completed his studies of "physiology" by reading Théophile de Bourdeu's *Recherches anatomiques sur la position des glandes et sur leur action* (1742; Anatomical Research on the Position of Glands and on Their Action), which incorporates Haller's position, centered on anatomy, into the study of the mechanisms of secretion.

Jean-Paul Marat, author of *De l'homme* (1775–76; On Man) and a fierce advocate of a clear separation between the body and the soul, also influenced Diderot, who had been tempted by a monistic conception of the universe, on all the issues relating to the nervous system. However, Julien Offroy de La Mettrie was the true source of inspiration for Diderot and the other Encyclopedists with respect to their opposition to animist theories and their support for sensationalist theories. First through his *L'homme-machine* (1747; Man, a Machine), then through his *L'homme plante* (1748; Man, a Plant), and finally through his *Histoire naturelle de l'âme* (1745; The Natural History of the Soul), La Mettrie influenced not only the opinions expressed in the entries in the *Encyclopédie* but also Diderot's views in *Éléments de physiologie* and *Le rêve de D'Alembert.*

However, La Mettrie's thinking contained contradictions, as is evidenced in particular by his position in the debate against the soul. La Mettrie was not convinced enough of the nonexistence of the soul to embrace a "materialist philosophy in the strict sense" and, being to some extent a disciple of modern empiricism, he proposed the justification of his thesis on the nonnecessity of the soul through experiment. In *L'homme-machine* in particular, despite his finding any suggestion of meta-physics repugnant, La Mettrie hypothesizes the presence of an *énormon*—a principle that is located within the brain, the source of the nerves, through which the brain exerts its will over the rest of the body. Only a few lines farther on, although he insists once again on the mechanical character and materiality of human beings, La Mettrie himself gives humans back their subjectivity. He does so not so much because he emphasizes the dependence of the soul on the more general conditions of existence (nutrition, physiological state, etc.) but rather because he reevaluates the one psychic function that does not lend itself to an exclusively mechanistic interpretation: namely, the imagination, which is active even in dream states and which is the unique form of knowledge capable of constructing a society, a state of happiness, and a civilization.

Charles Bonnet's influence on Diderot was as important as La Mettrie's. In his *Essai de psychologie* (1755; Essay in Psychology) and his *Essai analytique sur les facultés de l'âme* (1760; Analytical Essay on the Faculties of the Soul), Bonnet postulates that every action and sensation of the soul is produced by the movements of nervous fibers. However, he could not understand the illogicality of dream states, whose cause he finally attributes to the fortuitous meeting of external perceptions and the very weak inner perceptions. For Bonnet, the strangeness of the dream state arises because of the individual's inability to act and have control over the faculty of attention; during sleep the soul is no more than a simple spectator of fortuitous movements of the brain. The comte de Rivarol, too, in *De l'homme* (1797; On Man), reaches the conclusion that the consciousness of self is completely lost during sleep, even when one is dreaming. In short, Diderot's theory about dream states and memory is heavily permeated with Bonnet's theoretical elaborations.

It is no accident that according to Diderot in *Éléments de physiologie*, "disjointed" dreaming should be derived from the tumultuous movement of *brins* (strands), some of which make one hear speech, while others arouse desire, and still others evoke images. It was perhaps as the result of these notions that Diderot allowed himself to be seduced by the charm of classification. And so he moves on to discuss the dreams of the young, which transform their original state of innocence into obscure desires, vague uneasiness, and melancholy moods of which they do not know the causes. For this reason also, Diderot establishes a strict affinity—a perhaps gratuitous similarity—among dreaming, delirium, and madness, and he rather hastily equates "reasoned delirium" with "steady dreaming." He writes that even the transition from wakefulness to sleep is nothing but a "little attack of delirium," through which one can return to one's proper state only by use of the memory. This particularly innovative hypothesis arises from the assumption that there is no difference between dreamed experience and lived experience; the same hypothesis appears again in the *Encyclopédie* entry "Somnambule" (Sleepwalking).

As Lester Crocker has observed, one can discern in Diderot's *Éléments de physiologie,* even if only in limited form, the idea that consciousness of one's self, which requires the aid of memory, differs from consciousness of being, which requires constant attention to sensations (see Crocker). It would be arbitrary to claim that a psychological theory of dreams, in the strict sense, emerged in the 18th century. Nonetheless, it is certain that, principally thanks to the theories of physiologists and "mechanists," attention began to be paid to dream states—to the "structures, instincts, and predispositions" that inform behavior and individual character.

In France in the mid–18th century, mechanistic ideas were increasingly influential, thanks primarily to the *Encyclopédie,* and also to Diderot's *Le rêve de D'Alembert* and *Éléments de physiologie.* Mechanistic theories also became prevalent in Britain and Germany, often inspired by visits back and forth among or by translations of their works. La Mettrie, for example, translated several texts by Hermann Boerhaave. Hartley's *The Observation of Man* (1749) and Haller's renowned *Elementa Physiologiae Corporis Humani* (1757–66; Physiological Elements of the Human Body) both explore the phenomena characteristic of dreaming. Hartley identifies them with the imagination, and Haller regards them as very largely created by reason. Nonetheless, for Hartley, ideas and impressions received during the day, such as a person's mood and the association of their ideas, may determine the content of dreams, yet they cannot explain their bizarreness and incoherence, nor their repetitive and fragmentary nature. Haller draws attention to the way in which all dreams, being dependent on chance associations, come from a combination of ideas and suggestions characterized by diverse sensations. It must be emphasized, however, that both Hartley and Haller tried to provide physiological explanations for these associations, as well as for these sensations.

Order and disorder characterize dreaming, but each instance of a dream's appearance has a physical origin determined by the varied movements of the nervous system. The concept of a nervous system is perhaps the truly innovative feature of Diderot's theories, in contrast to the sources from which he worked and also in opposition to the approach adopted by the baron d'Holbach in his *Système de la nature, ou Des lois du monde physique et du monde moral* (1770; The System of Nature; or, The Laws of the Moral and Physical World), in which Holbach continues to attribute the production of dream states to chance but sees this pro-duction as "calculable" and foreseeable as long as the activity of memory does not intervene. Haller's account, in contrast, is indebted to Diderot's work in that memory constructs and lays down sediments of amorphous material in what today would be called the unconscious. These sediments occasionally are stirred up again, independently of the will of the individual.

Finally, we might also cite certain German scholars who operated in a cultural climate that was dominated by physiological theories throughout the 18th century (apart from such dissenters as Heinrich Nudow, who writes in his *Materialen* [1791; Materials] that the soul acts and continues to act during dreaming). The dominance of physiology is evidenced, for example, by Johann August Unzer's view of dreaming as being an excess of *Nervensaft* (nervous fluid) and by L.H. Jacob's opinion that dreaming is a condition programmed by nature, put forward in *Grundriss der Erfahrungsceleche* (Manual of Psychology). In contrast, for Melchior Adam Weickard (1742–1803), the author of the *Philosophicien Arzt* (1775–77, 1782; Philosophical Doctor), the sensations that he calls "actions of the fancy," true dreams in the waking state, still remain the "springs" of dreaming. However, it was not until after the appearance of *Le rêve de D'Alembert* that the theory of stimuli was also adopted in Germany. As a result, some German writers also affirm that, independently of the will and reason, one could acquire self-knowledge through dreaming. Therefore, dreams themselves began to be written down and published for the first time in the form of accounts of the self "in front of a mirror." These appeared in numerous German periodicals, such as the *Anthropologischen Journal* (1803–04) and the *Psychologischen Magazin,* on the model of what *The Spectator* was already doing in Britain. It was only beginning in the first decade of the 19th century that dreaming began to be considered in Germany as a concrete form not necessarily linked to a concept, and that memory and recollection were recognized by Mauckart (among others), as having the function of reconstructing the associations of ideas and images grouped together by fantasy in dreaming.

Johann Gottlob Krüger—the author, from 1754 onward, of a collection of 157 dreams (*Traüme* [Dreams])—nevertheless adumbrates some of the above hypotheses (just as Diderot had). Krüger was following up the conclusions of a pupil of Georg Ernst Stahl, the scholar Joachim Becher (1635–82), who had maintained that dreams, even more important than their function as predictors of the future, could be used to gain knowledge about human beings. Krüger undermines the old belief that linked dreams to superstition and the convictions of those who thought that dreams arose from inferior forms of the soul and were barely credible products of fantasy. For Krüger, a physician who practiced a pragmatically oriented philosophy known as *Weltweisheit* (worldly wisdom) and based his thought on the laws of nature and poetry, dreams are a means of getting to know humanity and even an inexhaustible "medium" of poetry.

This overview of the concept of dreaming in the 18th century serves to highlight the importance of Diderot's innovative ideas. During this period thinking about dreams and dream states meant, above all, directing one's attention to an intermediate domain in which neither philosophy nor official medicine had yet developed adequate categories of interpretation, a territory that increasingly favored "knowledge of the self." It was impossible, throughout the entire course of the 18th century, to establish a definitive interpretation of dreaming for a number of reasons. The term "dream" itself was an inclusive one, encompassing many meanings and approaches, such as the suggestive, dreamlike images in the paintings of Henry Fuseli and Francisco de Goya, which so accurately evoke "the maladies of the soul constantly at the mercy of boredom and anxiety." In addition, it was difficult to define the boundaries between the sensationalist and mechanistic hypotheses that explained dreaming as a natural phenomenon. As a result, ideas about dreaming remained in an unresolved state, encompassing, on the one hand, views that favored the magical nature of dreaming, and, on the other, scientific investigations aimed at analyzing the body and its activities.

DANIELA GALLINGANI

Further Reading

Crocker, Lester Gilbert, "L'analyse des rêves au XVIIIe siècle," *Studies on Voltaire and the Eighteenth Century*, vol. 23, Geneva: Institut et Musée Voltaire, 1963

Cullen, William, *Institutions of Medicine*, Edinburgh: n.p., 1770

Formey, Jean-Henri-Samuel, "Essai sur les songes," in *Mélanges philosophiques*, Leiden: s.n., 1754

Haller, Albrecht von, *Primae Linae Physiologiae*, Edinburgh: Drummond, and Kincaid and Bell, 1767

Liebeault, Ambrose Auguste, *Du sommeil et des états analogues*, Paris: Masson, 1866

Dynamics

The term "dynamics" first occurred in the work of Gottfried Wilhelm Leibniz, where "dynamic science" referred to the science of the forces or powers that move bodies. The term was introduced into the Latin and French languages in a remarkable way, appearing in the titles of three of Leibniz's scientific works: *Dynamica de potentia* (1689–90; Dynamics of Power); *Specimen dynamicum* (Dynamic Examples), published in part in the *Acta Eruditorum* in 1695; and the *Essai de dynamique* (Essay on Dynamics), written between 1699 and 1701. The feminine noun form of the term in French—*la dynamique*—was fixed in 1752, in the third edition of the *Dictionnaire de Trévoux* (Dictionary of Trévoux). In that work, "dynamics" is defined according to Leibniz's terminology as the science of the forces or powers that move bodies. The term was taken from the Greek word *dynamis*, which means "power" and is derived from the verb *dynamai*, meaning "I can."

The appearance of the term in Leibniz's writings marked the emergence of both a new conception of the science of motion and of a new way of treating problems in mechanics. The science of motion, or mechanics, was conceived in terms of forces rather than in terms of quantities of movement, as had been the case for René Descartes. This new conception was developed on the European continent under Leibniz's influence and, simultaneously, in England, under the influence of Sir Isaac Newton, who published his *Principia Mathematica Philosophiae Naturalis* (Mathematical Principles of Natural Philosophy) in 1687. The term "force," introduced notably in Definitions 3 through 8 of the *Principia*, allowed Newton to construct a science that could be defined a priori as dynamics. However, Newton himself did not use the term "dynamics" either in the first edition or in those that followed in 1713 and 1726, because Leibniz's usage of the word referred to something more than a conception of the science of motion in terms of forces. It signified the emergence of a new approach to the science of motion using a mathematical tool that Leibniz had perfected between 1684 and 1686, namely, differential calculus.

The science that Leibniz named "dynamics" arose from the application of differential calculus to mechanics. By 1687 Newton had acquired the method of fluxions, which had similarities to Leibniz's calculus, but he did not use that method in the *Principia*. Newton preferred to employ the method known as "first and last reasoning," a process of calculation that, despite its essentially geometric character, suggested the formation of the derivative of a function for a given value of the variable. This point is important if we bear in mind that, as stated above, the science of dynamics arose from the application of infinitesimal calculus to the science of motion. It was perhaps because Newton remained attached to a geometric method of calculus for mathematizing the science of motion, and not to a method of analysis of infinitely small units, that he could not see the point of using a new word—"dynamics"—to designate his new conception of the science of motion in terms of forces. One could certainly rewrite the *Principia* in terms of differential calculus, but that would constitute an interpretation of Newton's text. Leibniz, on the other hand, very quickly grasped the point of applying the new calculus to the science of motion, signaling the introduction of new mathematical procedures into mechanics by the use of the term "dynamics."

Nevertheless, Leibniz was far from having definitively constructed a new conceptual framework for mechanics. His work in mechanics is dispersed among various minor texts; he wrote no systematic work equivalent to Newton's *Principia*. The conceptual framework of the science of dynamics had to wait until Pierre Varignon translated the *Principia* in terms of differential calculus at the beginning of the 18th century, and this construction was the work not of one scholar but of a community of scholars. One could list those who laid the foundations—Galileo, Leibniz, Newton, and Christiaan Huygens (who took an interest in the important problem, for dynamics, of centers of oscillation)—and those who subsequently built on those foundations, including Varignon but also Jacques, Jean, and Daniel Bernoulli; Alexis-Claude Clairaut; Leonhard Euler; and Jean le Rond D'Alembert. Finally, there were the codifiers, including the comte de Lagrange and Pierre-Simon Laplace. This list shows that the science of dynamics was essentially created during the 18th century—as is confirmed by the article "Mécanique" (Mechanics) in the *Encyclopédie*. In this article, D'Alembert describes the stages in the constitution of a science of mechanics and states that we owe "to the geometers of this century the theory of dynamics."

D'Alembert's Definition of Dynamics

D'Alembert stands out among these scholars as the only scientist in the 18th century to exclude from mechanics the consideration of forces inherent in bodies in motion. He dismissed such forces as "obscure, metaphysical entities that are capable only of spreading darkness over a science that in itself is clear" (*Traité de dynamique*

[1743, 2nd edition, 1758; Treatise on Dynamics]). Yet, at the same time, he was the only 18th-century writer to give the title *Traité de dynamique* to a treatise on mechanics. Varignon had written a *Nouvelle mécanique ou statique* (New Mechanics; or, Statics), which was published posthumously in 1725. The Bernoullis and Euler wrote several treatises on mechanics and dynamics without using the term "dynamics" in any of their titles, apart from Daniel Bernoulli's *Hydrodynamica* (1738; Hydrodynamics), which discusses the specific topic of the dynamics of fluids.

The title of D'Alembert's treatise might be read as an echo of the titles of Leibniz's works from 1692 and 1695 (*Specimen dynamicum* and *Essai de dynamique*). But as we shall see, this echo also represented a correction of Leibniz's usage of the term. By giving his treatise the title *Traité de dynamique*, D'Alembert emphasized two points. In one sense he followed in the tradition of the problematization of the science of motion in terms of differential calculus. But by excluding consideration of the forces inherent in bodies in motion, from the preface of the treatise onward and to the greatest degree possible, he showed that he was both Leibniz's heir and his critic. In fact, D'Alembert sought to return to the Cartesian concept of quantities of motion: that is, a dynamics of effects and of effectively produced motions. He tried to remove from mechanics the metaphysical and ontological dross that, in his view, resulted from the badly directed usage, and the vague, obscure meaning, of the term "force." What he sought through his reworking of the meaning of the term "dynamics" was to give mechanics the status of a mathematical science: in other words, a science with the highest possible degree of certainty. According to D'Alembert, only the use of a mathematical method could guarantee the exactness of mechanics, itself conceived as a part of mathematics in the *Traité de dynamique*.

The justification of the title, which is included in the preliminary discourse of the treatise, appears in a precious portion of the text that indicates the usual 18th-century meaning of the term—the meaning from which D'Alembert sought to distance himself. However, when analyzing this passage, we should note another important point that confirms our notion of D'Alembert as standing apart from other scientists of his day, both in the meaning he conferred on the word "dynamics" and in his refusal to regard it as a science of forces, in the manner of Leibniz. This point is D'Alembert's resolution of the dispute over *forces vives* (literally, "living forces," or, in today's terminology, "kinetic energy"). In the preface to his treatise, D'Alembert emphasizes the inanity of this dispute by showing the scientific equivalence between the respective positions of the Cartesians and the Leibnizians in their treatment of the problems of mechanics. He reduces the dispute to a squabble over words and, more precisely, to the problem of defining the measurement of the force engendered by a body in motion. The Cartesian approach measures the force of the body in motion by the absolute quantity of the obstacles, whereas the Leibnizian approach measures it by the sum of the resistances. The Cartesian approach corresponds to cases of equilibrium, so the force in question can be represented by the momentum, that is, the product of the mass and the velocity. The Leibnizian approach corresponds to delayed motion and the force is represented by the *force vive,* that is, the product of the mass and the square of the velocity. D'Alembert concludes that the dispute is completely useless for mechanics, which, properly understood, functions with the aid of purely mathematical procedures and without raising questions about the nature of forces—mysterious entities created by the metaphysicians of mechanics to complicate things.

The Title of D'Alembert's *Traité de dynamique*

The following is the passage in which D'Alembert justifies the title of his treatise:

> This name, which properly signifies the science of the powers or causes of motion, may appear at first sight to be inappropriate in this book, in which I envisage mechanics as the science of effects rather than as the science of causes. Nevertheless, as the word *dynamique* is much used among scholars nowadays to signify the science of the motion of bodies acting on one another in any manner at all, I have considered it my duty to preserve the term, to announce to geometers, in the very title of this treatise, that the main purpose that I propose for it is to improve and augment this part of mechanics.

D'Alembert explains that he has distorted the meaning of the term, which seems strange in view of the great care that he pays to definitions (and, as a corollary, to abuses of language) and the fact that he has placed this distortion in the title of the treatise. He puts forward two reasons in defense of the title. The first is an argument ad hominem: scientists use the word "dynamics" to signify the science of the motion of the bodies acting on one another in any manner at all. Who were these scientists who, D'Alembert claims, have revised the meaning of the term (The justification of the title is included in the first edition)? The article "Dynamique" in the *Encyclopédie* can clarify the issue for us. D'Alembert (the author designated by the letter "O" in the *Encyclopédie*) recalls the first meaning of the term—"'dynamics' properly signifies the science of the powers or causes of motion, that is, the science of the forces that

set bodies in motion" and adds, "Monsieur Leibniz was the first to use this term to designate the most transcendental part of mechanics, which deals with the motion of bodies as being caused by motive forces that are simultaneously and continually active."

This distinction confirms that the term "dynamics" did indeed refer to a new branch of mechanics, established through the application of differential calculus to the problems of mechanics, which D'Alembert calls "the most transcendental part of mechanics." The language of the article "Dynamique" is perfectly clear: with Leibniz there emerged a new terminology, which led, for example, to the renaming of Descartes's "mechanical curves" as "transcendental curves." This change in terminology stemmed from the discovery of differential calculus, which permitted the conceptualization of exponential or cycloid curves.

In the next section of the article "Dynamique," D'Alembert pinpoints another meaning of the term "dynamics"—"widely used by geometers for several years"—in which the word designates "the science of the motion of bodies acting on one another in any way whatsoever, whether pushed or pulled by means of some body placed between them, and to which they are attached, such as a thread, an inflexible lever, a plane, etc." This definition of the word seems to reverse the relationship of the part to the whole and to make mechanics part of dynamics. It also suggests that problems of percussion, such as the problem of centers of oscillation, for example, also belong to the science of dynamics—something that is confirmed in the remainder of the article. D'Alembert goes on to point out that this problem was the first to have been resolved by the new dynamics, which he associates with the names of Huygens, Jean and Daniel Bernoulli, Euler, Clairaut, Montigny, and d'Arcy. It seems that we have here the answer to our question. These are the scientists who, according to D'Alembert, understood the word "dynamics" to mean not the science of the powers and causes of motion but the science of moving bodies acting on one another in any manner at all. Through the choice of the title for his treatise, D'Alembert was aligning himself with those scientists and announcing his intention to contribute to the progress of dynamics through new applications of differential calculus to the problems of "mechanics."

However, this meeting of minds on the meaning of the word "dynamics" seems problematic when one considers the respective works of the scientists of the first half of the 18th century. They did not all have the same conception of dynamics, as is obvious in their approaches to the dispute over *forces vives.* In fact, nearly all of them opted for Leibniz's sense of the term "dynamics," meaning the science of powers and forces (as ratified by the *Dictionnaire de Trévoux* in 1752). In the context of 18th-century science, D'Alembert was something of a lone warrior, reviving and using the Cartesian critique of the notion of power or force, refusing to recognize the notion of force as an operational concept in dynamics, and focusing exclusively on the effects produced, rather than on the causes of the motions of bodies. Scientists were fundamentally divided over the meaning and function attributable to the notion of force, and their disagreements were echoed in the various definitions of the word "dynamics." Thus, D'Alembert's first reason for claiming that he is merely accepting a new but current usage of the term seems highly contentious. By giving to the science of the motion of bodies acting on one another in any manner at all the label of "dynamics," he was in fact seeking, above all, to universalize his own usage of the term. This intention clearly emerges from his anti-Leibnizian and antimetaphysical position, which he expresses in his rejection of dynamics conceived as the science of forces.

As he explains in the preface to the *Traité de dynamique,* D'Alembert's second reason for using the word *dynamique* in the title of that work is that he wants to make it clear to the geometers that the main purpose of the treatise is to extend and perfect the application of differential calculus to the science of the motion of bodies acting on one another in any manner at all. However, in presenting this second reason, he returns in a curious way to a conception of dynamics as a part of mechanics. It follows from this that the purpose of choosing this title was to impose a certain conception of mechanics, as a science of effects and not of forces or causes, and at the same time to gain recognition of the contribution of differential calculus to this science. In this way, D'Alembert plays on two meanings of the word: a first meaning in which "dynamics" is a synonym for mechanics as the science of the motion of bodies acting on one another in any manner at all; and a second meaning in which "dynamics" designates the transcendental part of mechanics that arises from the application of infinitesimal calculus to the problems of the motions of bodies. The purpose of the choice of title then becomes clear: it was not so much to bring it into conformity with the usage of the time, nor to clarify the purpose of the treatise, but rather to systematize the principles of mechanics and dynamics, in one and the same book, according to considerations of effects and not of causes or forces.

D'Alembert thus indicates that he wants to unify mechanics while placing the emphasis on the new branch called dynamics, in order to reconcile those scientists who were divided over the question of *forces vives.* He shows that the concept of force in general can be apprehended within mechanics as a secondary or derivative concept. Moreover, the subtitle confirms the intention of the title and indeed announces the two parts of the treatise. The first part deals with the laws of equilibrium and of motion, while the second part deals with dynamics in the strict sense. A single principle takes on the role of general principle in the second part: that is, in dynamics. This principle, which would serve as the basis for the whole development of analytic mechanics, allows D'Alembert to effect the unification of kinetics and dynamics. By way of D'Alembert's Principle, it becomes possible to consider the general case of a mechanical system that evolves while remaining subject to constraints. D'Alembert shows that, because the constraining forces are in equilibrium at each instant, there must be an equivalence (or, if one prefers, an equilibrium) between the real forces that import to the system the motion by which it is animated and the forces that would be necessary for the system to have this motion if the constraints did not exist. By stipulating that this equilibrium takes place at each instant, the scientist is able to eliminate the constraining forces, whose form is generally unknown, and reduce the problem of dynamics, so to speak, to a problem of equilibrium. D'Alembert regards this principle as a general principle of dynamics allowing him to resolve any problem in dynamics by means of equations and thus realize the systematic mathematization of mechanics. This procedure also had the very great advantage, in D'Alembert's eyes, that it does not depend on any bad or obscure metaphysics, for, as he notes in the article "Dynamique," "it takes into consideration in the motion only what is really there, that is, the space traversed and the time taken to traverse it, and makes no use either of actions or of forces."

Lagrange, a disciple of D'Alembert, took up the same principle. In his *Mécanique analytique* (1788; Analytic Mechanics) he emphasizes the fundamental and productive character of the principle declaring: "One of the advantages of this approach is that it immediately provides general equations that contain the principles or theorems known under the names of conservation of energy, surfaces, etc." From that time onward, dynamics ceased to concern itself with the basis and nature of forces and became, as D'Alembert had wished in his *Encyclopédie* article, "a purely analytic matter."

VÉRONIQUE LE RU

See also Force; Mechanics, Analytic

Further Reading

Alembert, Jean Le Rond d', *Traité de dynamique,* Paris: David, 1743; revised and enlarged edition, 1758; reprint, Sceaux, France: Gabay, 1990

Jammer, Max, *Concepts of Force: A Study in the Foundations of Dynamics,* Cambridge, Massachusetts: Harvard University Press, 1957

Le Ru, Véronique, *D'Alembert philosophe,* Paris: Vrin, 1994

Newton, Isaac, Sir, *Sir Isaac Newton's Mathematical Principles of Natural Philosophy and His System of the World,* 2 vols., translated by Andrew Motte in 1729, revised by Florian Cajori, edited by R.T. Crawford, Berkeley: University of California Press, 1934 (original Latin edition, 1687)

Truesdell, Clifford A., *Essays in the History of Mechanics,* Berlin and New York: Springer, 1968

E

Earth, Shape of the

In 1668 the Académie Royale des Sciences de Paris (French Royal Academy of Sciences) decided upon a mission whose conclusion would allow them to obtain a more precise estimation of the Earth's radius, given the hypothesis that it was spherical. To do so it would be necessary to measure the length of an arc of the terrestrial meridian. This figure would help in establishing more reliable ephemerides for navigation (which was rapidly expanding), for cartography, and for geography. In 1670, having used triangulation to determine the length of an arc of meridian on either side of the Observatoire de Paris (Paris Observatory), from Malvoisine in the south to Sourdon in the north, the abbé Jean Picard found a length of 57,060 *toises* (69.1 miles) for an arc of 1 degree. Thus, he concluded, the length of the pendulum of a clock that beats once per second must be shortened as one moves from north to south. In 1672 the astronomer Jean Richer, in Cayenne, did indeed shorten this length by 2.7 thousandths. "Gravity" at the equator was seen to be weaker as a result. The reduction of the length of the pendulum substantiated the theory of the flattening of the planet—a phenomenon that had already been observed with large planets such as Saturn and Jupiter.

Christiaan Huygens and Sir Isaac Newton had been working on this problem since the beginning of the 1680s. Huygens agreed with Newton that the measurement of gravity at the equator should be reduced by 1/289, thus admitting the flattening of the planet, but the figure he suggested to account for the flattening of the planet was very different from that calculated by Newton: 1/578 instead of 1/230. For Huygens, centrifugal force, a consequence of a given circular movement, was sufficient to explain gravity. In 1690 he wrote in his *Discours de la cause de la pesanteur* (Discourse on the Cause of Gravity):

The gravity of bodies consists of the effort, made by fluid matter [made up of very small and agitated particles] that turn in a circular motion around the center of the Earth in every direction, to move away from the center and to push in its place all those bodies that do not follow the same movement.

Meanwhile, the idea of action at a distance that had been postulated by Newton in 1687 opened the way to a great deal of research, some of which was complementary to his theory, some of which was contradictory. For Newton the force of attraction between two bodies was inversely proportional to the distance separating their centers.

In 1691 J.G. Eisenschmid presented the debate between Newton and Huygens in a little book where the expression "shape of the Earth" appeared for the first time. But by comparing the different values of the degrees obtained in various locations, to "make them coincide," Eisenschmid concluded that the Earth was "oval" and its polar axis was longer than its equatorial diameter. Meridians had an elliptical shape, as Cassini I stressed in 1701, when delivering his latest findings to the Académie des Sciences. Cassini's measurements did indeed seem to support Eisenschmid's suggestions. But, Cassini added, it was necessary to know the value of the degrees of meridian over greater expanses. And this changed the nature of the problem.

Here it is necessary to trace the history of the first calculations of the meridian in France, for the results of those calculations were at the origin of the greatest scientific controversy of the 18th century, the conclusion of which would mean the total victory, half a century later, of Newton's theory. Picard died in 1683 without having been able to fulfill his major ambition—to chart a map of the kingdom through triangulation. However, he had improved the instrumentation necessary for such an undertaking, adding quadrant telescopes and considerably improving geometers' levels with angular sectors. He had also taken the precaution of defining a universal standard of measurement, the length of a clock's second pendulum in Paris, which, compared to the *toise* of the Grand Châtelet, allowed him to define that *toise*. The Châtelet *toise* would be the reference for all measurements relative to the size of the Earth.

Cassini I took over Picard's work in 1693 and in 1700–01 pursued it as far afield as Mont Canigou in the Pyrenees. In 1713 his son Jacques published a table of degrees of meridian quadrants, diminishing from the south to the north. The arguments given for the shape of the Earth were uncertain, he said; therefore it was preferable to make use of indisputable measurements. He suggested a lengthening of 1/262. In 1718 Jacques returned to the calculation of the meridian line to the north of Paris as far as Dunkirk. His measurements confirmed his earlier results. French scientists, as a result, knew the length of 3 arcs of longitude, subtending a total angular amplitude of 8 degrees. The account of this lasting Cassini family enterprise was published in 1720, in Volume II of the *Histoire de l'Académie royale des sciences pour 1718, avec les mémoires* (History of the Académie Royale des Sciences for the Year 1718, with the Memoirs). The arc of 1 degree to the south of Paris measured 57,097 *toises* (69.2 miles), to the north it measured 56,960 *toises* (69.0 miles). Picard's value for the arc had been intermediary. The length of the unit arc really did diminish as it went further north.

A firm believer in Cartesianism, Jacques Cassini enjoyed an excellent reputation as a practicing astronomer. In 1720 it was fairly easy to find the minutes of an angle using portable instruments. The instruments could be read with a magnifying glass, and with practice one could estimate the size of angle within a third of a minute (roughly 20 seconds) of accuracy. Using fixed instruments, such as the vertical sector, the angle could be estimated to within seconds, but various potential sources of error made it impossible to achieve a precision of less than 10 seconds of arc with any confidence. But an error of 10 seconds of arc per degree of median latitude corresponds to a distance of about 150 *toises* (0.18 miles) on the surface of the Earth.

Cassini I's suggestion in 1701 may have inspired research on the effects of central forces, but this was not something that came from authorized academic circles. At the end of the 17th century further study was devoted to Huygens's centrifugal force and to the curves of movement subjected to central forces, and, as a corollary, to the problem of gravity. Pierre Varignon's theoretical work would dominate this period as well as the beginning of the 18th century, when he published in

succession his *Mouvement et forces centripète, centrifuge et pesanteur* (1700; Movement and Centripetal, Centrifugal, and Gravitational Forces), *Sur les forces centrales* (1701; On Central Forces), *Forces centrales et pesanteur* (1706; Central Forces and Gravity), and *Mouvement en milieu résistant* (1707; Movement in a Resisting Medium). For each of these treatises Varignon used the methods of differential calculus of the marquis de L'Hospital, whose *L'analyse des infiniments petits* (1696; The Analysis of Infinitesimals) was strongly inspired by the teachings of Johann Bernoulli. It was L'Hospital's work, written for specialists, that had the greatest influence in the field of centrifugal force and the physics of vortices. For, according to René Descartes, planets are sent spinning around the Sun by the vortex, which is made of ethereal matter that offers no resistance. The Earth has its own vortex, which pulls the Moon around it, and so on.

Advanced mathematical research attempted to reconcile the vortex model with what had been observed. The Académie remained strongly influenced by the school of Nicolas Malebranche who, inspired by Huygens, had modified the status of the vortex. Thus, when Cassini went about publishing his findings, the Académie was already deeply involved in the very painstaking experiments that sought to prove the legitimacy of the vortex system.

Beginning in 1719, another leading authority, Dortous de Mairan, a disciple of Malebranche, also played an important role in defending the vortex theory. In 1722 he posited the theory that the Earth is an oblate spheroid that must have been much more elongated at the beginning of time and that, under the effect of centrifugal force, has lost its elongation. By 1720, the groundwork for the idea that the Earth is not perfectly spherical had been laid. The new theory was confirmed by experimental observation which, when added to the revelation of the deficiencies of the theory of attraction, combined to, create a climate of intense intellectual activity. Members of the Académie even began to consider the vortex theory as the only one that could explain elongation, whereas attraction could only lead to a flattening of the Earth. The publication of a revised and amended edition of Newton's *Principia* influenced the research carried out in France at the end of the second decade of the 18th century on central forces.

In the 1720s the Académie began to give a prize, every other year, for work related to the movement of planets. The Académie would reaffirm its very Cartesian standpoint by systematically awarding the prize to a disciple of the vortex theory (Mazières in 1726, Bulffinger in 1728, and J. Bernoulli in 1730). In 1732 the debate was so passionate, both within and outside the Académie, that the prize was not awarded. In 1734 it was again given to the Bernoulli brothers, Daniel and

Johann II. At the same time, the subjects of the prizes during the decade 1724–34 stimulated the research of the Academicians themselves. In 1728 Privat de Molières published a work entitled *Lois générales du mouvement dans les tourbillons sphériques* (General Laws of Movement in Spherical Vortices). Using Malebranche's little vortices, he sought to give a better response to "Mr. Newton's" objections. The debate continued in 1729. Malebranche's system attained a satisfactory degree of plausibility thanks to the support of Dortous de Mairan, who, in fact, would succeed in explaining, the following year, the rotation of a planet on its axis; this phenomenon was due to the imbalance created by a heterogeneous distribution of the different weighty parts. Thus, in the early 1730s, although accepting certain propositions borrowed from Newton, an important faction of the Académie des Sciences rejected with "horror" the idea of an "occult" force of attraction.

In this context a eulogy of Newton was published in 1729, in the volume *Histoire de l'Académie des sciences de Paris avec les mémoires pour l'année 1727* (History of the Académie des Sciences de Paris, with the Memoirs for the Year 1727). Bernard Le Bovier de Fontenelle, the Académie's permanent secretary, paid homage to Newton while at the same time praising Descartes. Fontenelle held that the very idea of attraction could be dangerous, for in becoming familiar with it, a person "is exposed to the danger of believing that he understands it." This praise summed up the objections that the proponents of vortices would raise against Newtonianism, a fashion that was imported into France from across the Channel and spread by the help of two men in particular: Pierre-Louis Moreau de Maupertuis, from within the Académie itself, and Voltaire. At the Académie, Maupertuis found the support of a young prodigy, Alexis-Claude Clairaut, and of a high-level spokesman, Bouguer.

By the end of 1731 all the protagonists were in place. Maupertuis, whose visit to London in 1728 had profoundly changed his ideas about mechanics, had the benefit of a pension from the Académie. The young Clairaut was granted a waiver of the age requirement and was admitted to the Académie as an adjunct mechanic on the 14th of July. In September Bouguer, too, finally fulfilled his ambition to enter the Académie. A lukewarm Cartesian, not yet a Newtonian, and by nature somewhat cautious, Bouguer would manage to keep to the abstract level of a general principle, without forcing reality—that is, the reality of the vortex—to conform to it. As soon as he entered the Académie, Bouguer found himself deeply involved in several issues, including the one that interests us here—the shape of the Earth. His first contribution was to study the curvilinear movement of bodies in a medium where every-

thing is in motion. All through his text, gravity was defined as a central force *G*, which was either inherent in the body or produced by another much more subtle fluid. He presented the phenomenon in mathematical terms without preferring one hypothesis over the other, using formulas that were adjustable to each of the theories by giving particular values to certain coefficients. But the conclusion was ambiguous because Bouguer would not commit himself.

This attitude was fairly representative of a faction of the new generation of scientists, something against which Maupertuis reacted quite strongly. Certain phenomena and Newtonian theory, he said, had too much in common to allow continued equivocation. A physical cause must be taken into account. The *Discours sur les différentes figures des astres* (Treatise on the Different Configurations of Celestial Bodies), which Maupertuis published in 1732, was destined to bring the polemic into the public arena. He compared the two systems and showed the superiority of the theory of attraction. Here is where the Newtonian studies really began. The debate became impassioned. All through 1733 Maupertuis tried to convince his fellow academicians; over a period of weeks, he read treatises on the laws of attraction, and on the shape of the Earth, whereupon strict Cartesians replied to these issues, also for weeks on end. The most persistent of the Cartesians was the abbé de Molières, whose vortex theory required ever more additional hypotheses. One can imagine the stormy sessions at the Académie where the speaker was interrupted on more than one occasion by his detractors.

Meanwhile, the task of measurement continued, in particular the measurement of arcs of latitude, begun in 1730. In June 1733 the Paris–Saint-Malo line was finished and then, in 1734, the line that ran east to Strasbourg. The results again confirmed Cassini's thesis. The public followed the debates. Voltaire had called upon Maupertuis to help him with his *Lettres philosophiques* (Philosophical Letters), which were published in 1734. Letters 14, 15, and 16 detail the two competing systems, giving the advantage to the English system. In the 14th letter Voltaire writes:

> A Frenchman who arrives in London finds things much changed, in philosophy as in all the rest. He had left behind a full world: he finds it empty. In Paris one sees a universe composed of vortices of ethereal matter; in London, one sees nothing of all that.

French national sentiment had been insulted; this was an issue where the honor of the kingdom was at stake: research must continue. On 23 December 1733 Godin, a reputable astronomer, offered to go and make observations from the equator. The viceroyalty of Peru was chosen. The following year Maurepas, the minister of the navy, began the necessary diplomatic procedures with the Spanish authorities. On 16 May 1735 a team set sail from La Rochelle, among them three members of the Académie: Godin, Bouguer, and Charles-Marie de La Condamine.

In 1734 and 1735 the most popular subject of debate at the Académie was without a doubt the problem of the shape of the Earth. Maupertuis and less illustrious scholars struggled fiercely with Cassini II. In 1734 Cassini had to defend himself against attacks in the *Journal Littéraire*. In 1735 the quarrel reached its climax. When Maupertuis sought to win him over, Cassini's response drew not only on his intelligence but also on his skill in astronomical measurement—a domain where Maupertuis still had no experience. Maupertuis finally suggested organizing an expedition to the polar circle. On 2 May 1736, accompanied by Clairaut, Maupertuis set off for Finland, which was then a dependency of the kingdom of Sweden. Three weeks later the scientists were ready to get to work.

With the help of Anders Celsius and the participation of the Swedish army, the team reconnoitered the terrain and set up camps. The Torne River, at the end of the Gulf of Bothnia, ran in a roughly north-south direction and was suitable for their purposes. The chain of triangles extended over roughly 60 miles, between the town of Tornis in the south and that of Kittilä in the north. The measurement of angles was completed without any major difficulties on 2 September 1736. In the meantime the astronomical measurements were begun. The team's stay was pleasant and the French received a magnificent welcome. Maupertuis was much in demand and spent most of his evenings at receptions. Measurements were carried out on the pendulum during winter. In the springtime the final verifications were made and then the instruments were packed away. The scientists' aging vessel was shipwrecked on the Swedish coast; fortunately, they managed to save the equipment. In November 1737, at the Académie Royale des Sciences, Maupertuis triumphantly announced that the length of the degree of meridian at the polar circle was superior to those obtained in France; the Earth was flatter at the pole by 1/174 degree. Voltaire celebrated the event in his own way, composing Alexandrines, then immortalized the voyage in his philosophical tale *Micromégas* (1752; Micromegas). Maupertuis had come back with two Sami women. The society pages were full of anecdotes about the expedition.

After Maupertuis's return, doubt was cast upon Cassini's meridian line. Cassini II had continued his triangulation of France after 1733. This work aimed to complete a geodesic network covering the entire kingdom, and it was in any case independent of the con-

tested theory since the calculations would be made with Picard's sphere. Thus, the work continued. In 1739 Cassini de Thury, known as Cassini III, along with the abbé La Caille, returned to the measurement of France's meridian line with more accurate triangles and a new, more precise quadrant. (The micrometer could give a reading to within half a second of arc and an error in the measurement of the arc would not exceed a few seconds. Personal error, due to the observer, was often much greater.) Meanwhile, Le Monnier returned to the astronomical measurement of the arc. In 1744 Cassini publicly recognized his ancestors' errors; his results, this time, coincided with those of Maupertuis.

The same year, Bouguer became the first to return from the Peruvian expedition. He had been absent for nine years, missing nine years of debate at the Académie Royale des Sciences and enduring nine years of hell in the Andes. After Maupertuis's success in Scandinavia in 1737, the leader of the Peruvian expedition had received a letter from the Académie telling the team members to come back, but the idea of returning without results was unthinkable. Forgotten by their country, the scientists had decided to carry on all the same, on their own. Very early on, quarrels broke out among members of the team and two groups were formed: Godin and the two Spanish officers, on the one hand; Bouguer and La Condamine, on the other. Local difficulties compounded internal difficulties. Members of the expedition often fell ill from tropical diseases. Years were lost in fruitless efforts. It took the incredible tenacity of these men to complete their observations, often at altitudes higher than 10,000 or even 20,000 feet, in the oppressive heat of the valleys, in the thick, stubborn fog, or in the intense cold of the mountains. Often their signals were destroyed by a superstitious local population, thus ruining their work. Once again they would drag themselves and their heavy equipment up rugged paths to start all over. Godin's chain of triangles stretched over 180 miles from the north of Quito to the south of Cuença, and for Bouguer and La Condamine, along the plain of Tarqui, covering an arc of meridian of roughly 3 degrees.

The geodesic measurement was finally completed in 1739. Astronomical measurement began to be completed in 1743. Then Bouguer and La Condamine split up. Bouguer arrived in Brest in June 1744. La Condamine, who had decided to go down the Amazon, disembarked in Amsterdam in November, only to read in the newspapers about the glorious success of his fellow team member: The Earth was found to be flatter at the poles, which confirmed Maupertuis's observations. A disagreement broke out between the two former companions of this major, difficult expedition, only ending with Bouguer's death in 1758. Godin had stayed behind in Quito but returned to Spain several years later. He never obtained permission to return to France, and his work was lost before it could be published.

However, in 1744 the theoretical problem had taken on new dimensions. Clairaut, upon his return from Lapland, concentrated his efforts on the study of the Earth's shape. He proposed an elegant solution in his work dating from 1743, *Théorie de la figure de la terre* (Theory of the Shape of the Earth), derived from hydrostatics according to Newton's principles. Clairaut determined the Earth's flatness by measuring gravity, what we would nowadays call "gravimetry," deducted from a seconds pendulum. Two observations were enough if one knew the equatorial radius. The measurement for the flattening was somewhere between $1/274$ and $1/303$. In the context of an elliptical shape, the measurement of the arc of meridian taken 2 by 2 led to values of flattening that differed widely from one another and that were outside of the proposed interval. Doubts were then cast upon the Lapland degree. A revision of the calculations was imperative, in the course of which some negligence in the manipulation of the sector came to light. In addition, Bouguer's readjusted calculations gave a flattening of $1/215$ degree closer to Newton's value. A new verification of the *toise* that had served both expeditions was undertaken, and Picard's baseline in Juvisy was remeasured. All the same, the discrepancies that were found only got worse with subsequent measurements, including La Caille's determination of the degree of meridian at the Cape in 1750 and that of Boscovich and Maire in Italy in 1753.

As measurements were ever more numerous, the heterogeneity of the degrees of meridian became more and more obvious. It seemed almost impossible to attribute a shape to the Earth. Local irregularities popped up in a very noticeable way. The influence of rocky masses upon the direction of the plumb line had been noted by Bouguer in Chimboraço in 1737 and was also noted by Boscovich with the influence of the Apennine range during his expedition. The comte de Buffon was the first to speak of it in *Histoire de la terre* (History of the Earth), which was first published in 1744 and revised in 1746. Jean le Rond D'Alembert touched on the problem theoretically several times. He wrote a synthesis for the *Encyclopédie* in 1756. A few doubts arose over the formula of attraction, but the essence was not called into question; attraction was accepted by younger genera-

tions. Thereafter, the issue ceased to be a fashionable topic. Work on the terrain continued without arousing any debate; results were improving and became progressively more precise. In 1787 Cassini IV, Pierre-François-André Méchain, and Legendre repeated the work of their predecessors, using Borda's circle and improving triangulation measurements.

By seeking to establish a universal standard of measurement that would depend on no single nation or era (the 10-millionth part of a quadrant of the terrestrial meridian), the French Revolution put the shape of the Earth back on the agenda. The measurements that had been conducted throughout the 18th century were judged insufficient, and Delambre and Méchain were appointed to measure France's meridian line in 1792. The methods of calculation were new, as were the instruments. The 18th century had come to an end. Pierre-Simon Laplace would show that an accurate figure for the flattening could be obtained from the unequal values for the latitudes and longitudes of the Moon. The results would coincide with the values obtained from the arcs of meridian. This lunar method was one of the most striking proofs of the validity of universal gravitation. For Laplace the difficulties involved in the voyages of the 18th century had been out of proportion to the scientific benefits that had been obtained.

DANIELLE FAUQUE

See also Geography; Mathematics; Newtonianism; Science: Dissemination and Popularization; Weights and Measures

Further Reading

Brunet, Pierre, *L'introduction des théories de Newton en France au XVIIIᵉ siècle, avant 1738,* Paris: Blanchard, 1931

Greenberg, John L., *The Problem of the Earth's Shape from Newton to Clairaut: The Rise of Mathematical Science in Eighteenth-Century Paris and the Fall of "Normal" Science,* Cambridge and New York: Cambridge University Press, 1995

Lacombe, Henri, and Pierre Costabel, editors, *La figure de la terre du XVIIIᵉ siècle à l'ère spatiale,* Paris: Gauthier-Villars, 1988

Eclecticism

The word *éclectisme* (eclecticism) comes from the Greek verb *eklegein*, which means "to choose." In the age of the Enlightenment this word's meaning was a great deal stronger than it is today. Eclecticism did not consist simply of a lack of an exclusive taste, but also implied taking the best ideas from various systems, to the extent that they could be reconciled. In the entry "Éclectisme" in the *Encyclopédie*, Denis Diderot offers a beautiful definition of the eclectic as

> a philosopher who tramples upon prejudice, tradition, antiquity, universal consent, and authority—in short, upon anything that subjugates the minds of the masses. It is anyone who dares to think for himself, who goes back to the clearest general principles in order to examine and discuss them, accepting only what is based on the evidence of his own experience and reason. From all the philosophies that he has analyzed, without respect or partiality, the eclectic makes for himself an individual and domestic philosophy that belongs to him. I speak of "an individual and domestic philosophy" because the eclectic's ambition is not so much to be the tutor of the human race, as to be its disciple; not so much to reform others, as to reform himself; not so much to teach the truth, as to understand it. The eclectic is not at all a person who plants or sows, but a person who gathers and sifts.

In contrast to the sectarian, who embraces the teachings of a philosopher, the eclectic does not recognize any master at all. In contrast to the syncretist, who always reasons in the terms of a philosopher of whom he is the disciple, the eclectic is never inspired by any single philosophical system. What interests Diderot is the method that the eclectic uses. In its dependence on the autonomy of reason, on the criticism of prejudices, and on toleration, that method offers a fundamental instrument of intellectual liberation; in its capacity to assemble and organize truths, it permits the advancement of knowledge.

The primary characteristic of eclecticism is its capacity to take an interest in a great variety of domains of knowledge. The eclectic not only traverses the range of philosophical systems but also knows how to bring together those elusive kinds of knowledge that are in danger of being forgotten and are often not even recognized. The value that was placed on eclecticism in the 18th century was profoundly linked to the extension of the domains accessible to reason. By providing a rigorous foundation for physics and mechanics, René Descartes had shown that human beings could make themselves masters over nature, and so science was defined as a domain that could be completely mastered by reason. However, the Cartesian method, that model of rigor and order, could only embody the sciences by eliminating whatever was extrascientific. Analytic geometry could not study certain curves that were characteristic of mechanics; physics rejected all specific analysis of living things that were regarded as irrational; and science eliminated history, which was not part of the order of certain knowledge.

In contrast, during the age of the Enlightenment, the field of application of reason was extended, thus constituting an immense diversity of forms of knowledge. Blaise Pascal made probability into a mathematical concept by theorizing the calculation of chance. And so, far from being purely contingent, the future became calculable; uncertain events appeared as eventualities of which the possibility could be determined with certainty. By writing his *Dictionnaire historique et critique* (1697; An Historical and Critical Dictionary), Pierre Bayle showed how a rigorous method could be established in historiography. Historical events were not beyond the scope of rationality but could be interpreted and were framed within a logic. Even the distortions to which history could be subjected were explicable. Bayle also showed how the field of historiography could be enlarged by writing lives of the infamous in parallel with those of the celebrated and by supplementing the narrative of great events with studies of the daily life of ordinary people.

By analyzing human superstitions, Bernard Le Bovier de Fontenelle, David Hume, and others showed that one could find rational explanations for irrational beliefs. In order to justify their absurd practices, superstitious people provide incoherent theories that rely on finalist reasoning, but their behavior can be completely and rationally explained, and the true causes can be brought to light. Those causes are the fear and ignorance of the future that make people lose all lucidity, as well as the deceits and impostures of the charlatans who exploit these natural terrors in order to derive considerable political and economic benefits from them.

Gottfried Wilhelm Leibniz sought to reunite the forms of human knowledge. For that purpose, it was not enough to be interested in philosophy and established knowledge. It was equally necessary to study the elusive forms of knowledge transmitted by oral tradition, which were often neglected and misunderstood. An encyclopedia of knowledge would have to be complemented by a theatre of all the trades, bringing together all the forms of practical knowledge used in the various arts. Leibniz was interested in children's games as well as craft secrets, the skills of mariners as well as those of hunters. Taking pride in avoiding any glib contempt, Leibniz offered a model of the eclectic philosopher, capable of finding knowledge in all the domains of human life.

Diderot and Jean le Rond D'Alembert's undertaking of the *Encyclopédie* was clearly based on a similar perspective. Calling on a multitude of collaborators, and taking as much of an interest in the sciences as in the arts and crafts, these two editors sought to assemble the diversity of forms of human knowledge. Their eclecticism had profound connections with their critique of the absolute model of mathematics. For them, human knowledge could not be deduced from a set of theoretical principles, and there were forms of knowledge, each appropriate to a given practice, that could only be acquired empirically. In the entry "Arts," Diderot writes ironically and provocatively that "the elements of the geometry of the Académie Royale des Sciences are nothing but the simplest and least complex among the elements of the geometry of the shops." He thus brings into question the traditional hierarchy of liberal and mechanical arts, rejecting the scorn with which the latter was treated. Against the monarchy of the Académie, he opens the way to a republic of the sciences.

For Diderot it was therefore indispensable to gather the knowledge and experience of those who practiced crafts, and who often operated solely by instinct, without even being aware of the importance of their practical understanding. In the *Prospectus* for the *Encyclopédie,* Diderot compares himself to Socrates, performing in the workshops "the difficult and delicate task of making minds give birth." This was also the reason for the fundamental role played by the plates in the *Encyclopédie.* Far from being simply decorative or illustrative, they serve an essential theoretical purpose. Each plate not only offers aid to the imagination but also supports reflection, and in many cases seeing a machine is indispensable to understanding how it functions and the things that it produces.

However, even this diversity in the forms of knowledge was not sufficient to establish a basis for eclecticism in the age of the Enlightenment. What was essential to all the projects cited above was the work that was done to organize this knowledge in order to perceive the connections among these various forms and to find method and system within them. In this regard, several different models of eclecticism can be distinguished.

First of all, there are sceptical eclectics, such as Bayle. At first reading, Bayle's *Dictionnaire* can appear to be an immense compilation of a mass of quotations in complete disarray, juxtaposing instead of constructing, and practicing digression instead of organization. Nevertheless, the labyrinth of footnotes and the accumulation of commentary do not indicate that the text lacks any guiding thread. On the contrary, these elements form parts of a polemical and antidogmatic project. Bayle was inspired by Montaigne, and like the latter's *Les Essais* (1580–95; The Essays), Bayle's *Dictionnaire* is a coat of many colors, a hodgepodge that has been clumsily assembled. The digressions are the sign of a sceptical philosophy. They express in the form of the text the inability of human beings to establish an absolute order of knowledge. They permit Bayle to describe the various images of humanity without articulating them to any universal standard and to think through the contradictions of philosophical systems without resolving them by means of a synthesis. In such an enterprise, quotations play a fundamental role. By quoting a text, Bayle displaces what is at stake in it, alters its perspective, and shows its limitations by confronting it with other texts. Quotations become weapons of polemic. For example, Bayle cunningly takes pleasure in copying obscene passages from the Fathers of the Church. Instead of laboring at the task of reconciling all his authorities in a vague syncretism, Bayle uses quotations to provide evidence for the ways in which their arguments can be reciprocally and mutually destructive.

However, eclecticism could also seek to produce a systematic organization of knowledge, as with Leibniz's proposal for a universal set of characters and an "alphabet of human thoughts." In order to create a true encyclopedia of knowledge, Leibniz sought to establish a universal language that would not only facilitate communication among the learned but also make the logical relations among concepts clear. Such a philosophical language implied that he would have to find a natural expression for each idea that could indicate its logical components and become a formula for it. To this end, Leibniz sought a set of characters, inspired by ideograms, that would express concepts and make their composition and their relationships obvious and visible. As a complement, he envisioned an alphabet of human thoughts that would train people to break down each thought into primitive ideas and simple concepts, just as one breaks down a number into its prime factors.

Through this work Leibniz succeeded in integrating the entire body of knowledge acquired by humanity into his philosophy. All known truths were demonstrated by being reorganized according to their simple and obvious principles. All the partial knowledge discovered by human beings took on meaning and value by appearing as so many elements of the Leibnizian system. In the case of Leibniz, eclectic philosophy amounts to a great enterprise of integration. Those ideas that Leibniz criticizes are treated less as errors than as partial truths, and their importance is made apparent as soon as they are located within his universalist system.

Finally, the work of the Encyclopedists offers a third model of eclecticism. By recruiting a large number of collaborators, Diderot and D'Alembert made it obvious that no single person could master and expound the ensemble of human knowledge. Yet this does not mean that the *Encyclopédie* is merely a juxtaposition of articles or that the contributors were content simply to enumerate bits of knowledge. The *Encyclopédie* is an analytic dictionary in which the articles are put together in two different orders: alphabetical order, used solely for convenience, and encyclopedic order, which allows the relationships between the topics covered to be presented methodically. For this purpose, the system of cross-references is crucial. In the *Prospectus* Diderot comments on the work of the editors as follows:

In the course of our work, the only operation that required a degree of intelligence was to fill the gaps that separated two sciences or two arts, and to pick up the threads at those points where some of our colleagues relied on others for certain articles.

Eclecticism in this case permitted a true communication of the Enlightenment.

BARBARA DE NEGRONI

See also Doubt, Scepticism, and Pyrrhonism; Encyclopedia

Further Reading
Billard, Jacques, *L'éclectisme*, Paris: Presses Universitaires de France, 1997

Education, Instruction, and Pedagogy

Questions about education were among the principal topics of interest for Enlightenment philosophers. It is therefore in philosophical texts, above all, that fundamental concepts about education were expounded, with "education" referring here both to moral education and to instruction, or the acquisition of intellectual knowledge. Pedagogy was not yet an entirely distinct discipline in the 18th century; the theory of education and instruction was a branch of philosophy and theology.

The main pedagogical principles of Enlightenment philosophy were formulated in England in the 17th century. John Locke provides their basis in *Some Thoughts concerning Education* (1693). This work is permeated with an undeniable optimism about education, boldly stating that nine out of ten individuals—whether good or bad, skilled or not—are what they are solely because of their education. In Locke's frame of reference, education is private, dispensed by a tutor—an education for the perfect "gentleman." Although education might be valuable for everyone, it needs to take the individuality of each pupil into consideration.

In this "enlightened" spirit, Locke establishes a hierarchy of objectives for instruction, giving first place to virtue or morality, defined repeatedly as the governing of the passions by reason. A corollary of virtue is the trait—characteristic of Locke's thinking—of practical wisdom, the faculty of being able to reflect upon all the problems of life, particularly those of a practical nature.

The third place in the hierarchy is occupied by "good breeding"—good conduct and good manners—based on sincere respect for oneself and for others. Knowledge and learning do not make their appearance until the fourth place.

The basic principles of the Enlightenment may also be found in Locke's recommendations to tutors. Not only what they teach, but also their behavior toward their pupils, must show an enlightened attitude. Physical education should be aimed at toughening the pupil and encouraging simple living. Corporal punishment is proscribed, while providing stimulation through play is encouraged, for it is by playing that one learns best. Teachers should disregard all old-fashioned theories; teaching should focus on practical exercises and examples, in order to train the mind through experience and the formation of habits. Finally, Locke declares his conviction that one can guide children better by lavishing respect and love upon them than by inflicting punishment and whippings.

In France pedagogical thinking was centered on three themes. They are defined in César Chesneau Dumarsais's "Éducation" entry in the *Encyclopédie*: to nourish, to raise, and to instruct. These imply three educational objectives: the health and proper development of the body, the training of the mind, and moral education, which encompasses the individual's behavior, conduct, and social qualities. Education cannot be too highly prized, for it is important to humanity in three ways: first of all, it benefits individuals themselves, so that they can be useful to society and can find esteem and prosperity within it; second, education aids individuals' families, which they should support and honor; and finally, it supports the state, which harvests the fruits of the education of its citizens, the members of its society. Education is therefore the greatest good that parents can pass on to their children.

Claude-Adrien Helvétius and Voltaire shared Locke's beliefs, and they both insisted on the power of education, thus illustrating the pedagogical optimism of the Enlightenment. In his *Remarques sur les pensées de M. Pascal,* the 39th of his *Lettres philosophiques* (1734; Remarks on the Thoughts of Monsieur Pascal, in Philosophical Letters), Voltaire opposes Blaise Pascal by affirming that everything can be instilled into human beings and that it is education that gives rise to morality, virtue, and piety. Similarly, Helvétius, the author of *De l'esprit* (1758; Essays on the Mind and Its Several Faculties) and *De l'homme, de ses facultés intellectuelles et de son éducation* (1772; On Man, His Intellectual Faculties, and His Education), argues that "education can do everything."

What specific forms of education did the Enlightenment *philosophes* identify? Jean-Jacques Rousseau's three categories—the education "of nature," that "of things," and that "of man" (*Émile, ou, de l'éducation* (1762; Émile; or, Concerning Education)—arise out of the general discussion among *philosophes* concerning education. The first category is aimed at children's internal development of senses and faculties; the second focuses on the acquisition of experience by way of objects in the external world; and the third consists of the tutor teaching children how to use their faculties for learning on their own. In contrast to Locke and Helvétius, for whom the nature of the pupil is very largely malleable, Rousseau sees in human nature, with its senses and faculties, the element that is in control in the educational process. For Rousseau, such an approach to education is superior to learning that is merely receptive or molded by one's surroundings.

During the Enlightenment there was another, almost more important distinction in the area of education: namely, that between "private" education, dispensed by a tutor, and "public" or "national" education. Again, it is to Rousseau that we owe these well-known formulations. The *philosophes* supported the idea of a secular education, which could be either private or public, based on human reason, in opposition to education dominated by the spiritual and placed under the supervision of the Church—for example, the Jesuit colleges. Private education by a tutor was profoundly in keeping with the spirit of the age, which was enamored of individualism and concerned about the happiness and virtue of each man. The ideal of public education, on the other hand, went along with the thought of those political writers who hoped for a community of free and equal human beings, a "new" society of good citizens.

In France several proposals for public education appeared on the eve of 1789 (those of Louis-René de Caradeuc de La Chalotais, Anne-Robert-Jacques Turgot, and Rousseau), and the French Revolution developed these into plans for national education (by Gracchus Babeuf, the marquis de Mirabeau, Charles-Maurice Talleyrand, the marquis de Condorcet, and Louis-Michel Lepeletier). Two tendencies may be singled out. Condorcet called for a more "liberal" approach in which public instruction is to be responsible only for the education of the intellect, leaving moral, religious, and philosophical education in the hands of the family. On the other hand, Rousseau and Lepeletier championed a more "social" approach aiming to include ethical and religious matters in national education. It was hoped that this "social" approach would improve the integration of the citizens into the community and their identification with the state.

In matters of education and instruction, Enlightenment philosophy pursued objectives that were directly linked to the enlightened view of humanity and that were inherited from the tradition of antiquity: reason and virtue, as opposed to the excesses of the Church and of metaphysics. However, the Enlightenment set itself apart from the pure intellectualism of the ancients (notably Plato and the Stoics), which could still be sensed in the works of René Descartes and Baruch Spinoza, by suggesting that what is required for education, what determines the morality and virtue of human beings, is no longer reason and knowledge alone. Education must also cultivate free will, which must be raised to a moral desire, a moral sense (as the earl of Shaftesbury and Francis Hutcheson the Elder understood it), and moral awareness (Rousseau).

Unlike the Stoics or the moralists of the 17th century, Enlightenment thinkers no longer opposed the passions to reason. Accordingly, the purpose of education was not to make reason dominant by eliminating the passions but, on the contrary, to find in the passions the building blocks of human morality. Shaftesbury still proclaimed the reign of reason, which he supported by promoting the social passions and keeping the selfish passions under control, repressing only those passions that are against nature. Later, however, the passions, anchored in self-love, were fully rehabilitated and presented as the motors of human activity and its achievements.

Even in the intellectual domain, moral reason, which is aware of values and ideal norms and makes moral judgments, was regarded as being accompanied by other faculties. These included, above all, practical and technical wisdom, with its understanding of causation and its creative knowledge, which human beings need in order to deal with the world. They also included the critical spirit of scepticism toward religious fervor or metaphysical speculation, a spirit that sees through the pretensions of society and does not accept any tradition without first examining it. Immanuel Kant's educational objective—the attainment of maturity by humanity—involved not only understanding but also courage and decisiveness of will.

Finally, following from the Enlightenment's image of humanity and its educational objectives, the age put a strong emphasis on the pleasure that morality and reason can procure. Shaftesbury insisted that the finest moral sentiments are the surest means of enjoyment for the individual, while Rousseau established the principle that action and enjoyment of one's existence are the two main attitudes toward which education should guide the individual. Julien Offroy de La Mettrie, who occupied an extreme position on this point, saw in the quest for pleasure the supreme accomplishment of human life, and he believed that one can devote oneself to this quest without having to relate it to virtue. It is in reaction to this inherent hedonism that Kant emphasized moral rigor and opposed the philosophy of happiness.

Materialism—whether anthropological, as with La Mettrie, or cosmological and atheistic, as with the baron d'Holbach—also had consequences for the definition of the objective of education, as morality and reason lost their religious foundations and became inherent values. A purely earthly happiness, a simple pleasure in existing, became the greatest good for mankind.

A new image of the child was also developed during the Enlightenment, propagated by Rousseau, who stoutly defended childhood and its entitlement to be considered a wholly distinct stage of life. In the 17th century, children had still largely been treated as miniature adults, but Voltaire, Denis Diderot, and Helvétius all emphasized the idea that children are morally and sexually innocent. Children fascinated men of the Enlightenment. They were seen as naturally good and free from the stain of original sin. Accordingly, it was argued that education should not repress their natural state, but, on the contrary, should try to encourage it. Children were not to be influenced directly, trained intellectually, or educated morally. They were expected to carry out their own experiments under the guidance of a tutor. Their first duty was self-preservation, and it was posited that they should not be expected to be altruistic and should certainly not be forced into altruism by pedagogical means. The basic objectives of education—to acquire, for example, the ability to act and to enjoy existence—were also applied to children. As for the higher objectives, morality and reason, it was asserted that they are developed during childhood through the realization of partial objectives: good sense and then spirituality, self-awareness, and finally altruism.

These same objectives, organized around the new view of humanity during the Enlightenment, were also supposed to determine the selection of subjects to be taught. Locke had already turned away from the traditional instruction of the *collèges* (secondary schools), which was still overwhelmingly dominated by the study of classical languages and literature (especially Latin) and remained under the sway of Christian view of humanity. Given the "secularization" of educational objectives, Voltaire, Diderot, Louis René de Caradeuc de La Chalotais, and Jean le Rond D'Alembert, as well as Holbach and Rousseau, drew the same conclusions as Locke in their proposals for programs of learning. If enlightened education was to be, above all, civil and not spiritual (Diderot), it was clear that antiquity, Latin, and rhetoric could no longer remain dominant but had to be replaced by disciplines that would help modern individuals to orient themselves within the world and even to gain control over it. Those disciplines were primarily mathematics and the natural sciences—physics and astronomy in particular—but also included economics and law.

The teaching of languages was still justified by men of the Enlightenment, but instead of Latin, which was dominant in the Catholic Church and in the world of scholarship, the communicative dimension of native languages was emphasized. The disciplines of the ancient trivium, including rhetoric, were relegated to a secondary role, while the importance of history, presented primarily as a repository of moral examples, and of geography gradually increased. All these developments are fully illustrated, with special reference to universities, in Diderot's *Plan d'une université pour le gouvernement de Russie* (1775; University Project for the Government of Russia). Physical education gained support among the *philosophes* and the Encyclopedists, less as an amusement for children than as physical effort directed at maintaining good health and at preparing for any eventuality—a view in contrast to the refined attitude of court society.

In Germany Christian Wolff had a distinctive influence on pedagogical theories. His practical philosophy was aimed essentially at leading individuals toward happiness and general well-being by stimulating them to improve themselves and to participate, as much as possible, in the improvement of every other human being. It is in this sense that the philosophy of the *Aufklärung*, the German Enlightenment, conceived the school and its objectives, taking up Wolff's idea that the individual must contribute to the general welfare. According to Wolff, the state has no other purpose than to enable humanity to attain the most precious moral good, the improvement of the self, and to contribute to the moral improvement of others and of the community. The state must see to it that its people achieve moral excellence, which is possible only if their wills are guided by a clear understanding of good and evil.

A practical reform of the school system, based on these foundations and imbued with this new spirit, was introduced in Germany on the initiative of a group of educators. These innovators, whose publications began to exert their influence around 1770, were known as the Philanthropists. Their best-known representative was Johann Bernhard Basedow, who founded a boarding school, the Philanthropinum, in Dessau in 1774, but the group also included Christian Gotthilf Salzmann, Joachim Heinrich Campe, Ernst Christian Trapp, Friedrich Eberhard von Rochow, and the Swiss educator Isaak Iselin. Aspiring to link reason with nature, they achieved a synthesis between, on the one hand, the orientation of the Enlightenment toward what is perceived by the senses, is usable and useful, and procures pleasure, and, on the other, Rousseau's ideal of nature.

Gotthold Ephraim Lessing's thinking went far beyond the range of Wolff's philosophy of schooling to spread the spirit of the Enlightenment to various domains of cultural life (poetry, art criticism, and others). It was Lessing who originated the idea of the "education of the human race." He argued that humans evolve according to a divine plan of education, passing through several stages of moral and religious training, with the last stage representing the performance of duty for its own sake. Lessing combined ethical, religious, and philosophical themes in a synthesis that went beyond Enlightenment philosophy in the strict sense of that term.

FRITZ-PETER HAGER

See also Civilization and Civility; Children; Fatherhood; Grand Tour; Technical Instruction; Women Writers and Feminism

Further Reading

Bollenbeck, Georg, *Bildung und Kultur: Glanz und Elend eines deutschen Deutungsmusters*, Frankfurt: Insel, 1994

Bowen, James, *A History of Western Education*, 3 vols., London: Methuen, 1972–81; see especially vol. 3

Hager, Fritz-Peter, *Wesen, Freiheit und Bildung des Menschen: Philosophie und Erziehung in Antike, Aufklärung und Gegenwart*, Bern: Paul Haupt, 1989

Snyders, Georges, *La pédagogie en France aux XVIIe et XVIIIe siècles*, Paris: Presses Universitaires de France, 1964

Egyptomania

The Enlightenment mentality played an important role in sparking greater interest in Egypt. Relatively early on, various publications made readers aware of all that Egypt had brought to the Western world. These publications also helped to establish Egyptian civilization as being among those common roots of Europe from which historians of the day hoped to derive some transcendent ideal. As a result, Egyptian art became one of the important artistic sources of the age, although its original function was altered to suit the needs of the time. The European Enlightenment turned to Egypt as a source of inspiration for new ideas in scientific research as well as in artistic creation.

Earlier studies, notably those of the Jesuit Father Athanasius Kircher, had presented a mystical and distorted image of Egypt. In the first half of the 18th century this false image was replaced by a fresh vision derived from three essential sources of information. First, travelers to Rome found Egyptian artifacts (notably sphinxes and obelisks) and other relics of Roman Egyptomania, such as those commemorating Antinoüs. In 1710 archeological digs in Rome unearthed the statue of Queen Touia in the vineyard of Verospi Vitelleschi. Several obelisks, including those of the Quirinal, the Piazza della Trinità dei Monti, and the Piazza di Montecitorio, were discovered and re-erected. And in 1748 Pope Benedict XIV opened a small Egyptian museum in the Palazzo Nuovo to house the Egyptian and Egyptian-style works that had been unearthed during the excavation of Hadrian's villa. Second, the publication of illustrated works of serious scholarship such as the Benedictine Bernard de Montfaucon's remarkable *L'antiquité expliquée et représentée en figures* (1719; Antiquity Explained and Illustrated), itself very typical of the spirit of the Enlightenment and paving the way for later archeological studies, added to the enthusiasm and fed this new passion. The comte de Caylus's *Recueil d'antiquités*

égyptiennes, étrusques, grecques, romaines et gauloises
(A Collection of Egyptian, Etruscan, Greek, Roman,
and Gallic Antiquities), published between 1752 and
1767 was equally well received. Finally, travel literature, illustrated by an increasingly realistic iconography,
was growing in popularity. Besides the publications of
Paul Lucas (1714–20) and Benoît de Maillet (1753),
Richard Pococke's *Observations on Egypt* (1743) and
Frederik Norden's *Voyage d'Egypte et de Nubie* (published in Copenhagen in 1755; Travels to Egypt and
Nubia) contained remarkable descriptions that were
based on personal observations. Such texts remained
standard reference works until the publication of Dominique Vivant Denon's *Voyage dans la Basse et la Haute
Égypte pendant les campagnes du général Bonaparte*
(1802; Travels in Lower and Upper Egypt, during the
Campaigns of General Bonaparte in That Country).

However, there existed at the same time a fanciful
iconography (especially in the works of Johann Fischer
von Erlach and Louis-François Cassas) that, when
added to forms derived from Roman Egyptomania,
tended to muddle the Egyptian sources from which
18th-century artists drew their inspiration. This confusion led in turn to various expressions of a new sort of
Egyptomania, which rapidly began to influence all fields
of art. The publication of a widely circulated series of
Egyptian-style engravings by Giambattista Piranesi, collectively entitled *Diverse maniere di ardonare i cammini*
(1769; Different Manners to Adorn Fireplaces) and
accompanied by a preface entitled "Apologetic Discourse in Favor of Egyptian and Tuscan Architecture,"
was immensely influential. At the same time, interest in
Egypt spurred the development of specialized collections such as those of Albani and Borghese in Italy;
Lord Sandwich, Lord Charlemont, and Thomas Herbert in England; and the comte de Caylus in Paris. The
study of mummies continued to fascinate connoisseurs
of Egyptian antiquities, especially in England, where the
scientific study of ancient Egypt emerged, notably on
the initiative of the Egyptian Society, founded in London in 1741.

Against this background of ever more rigorous and
scientific activity, discussions arose concerning the
place, role, and importance of Egypt in the development
of Western civilization. Caylus was one of the first
experts to stress the aesthetic qualities of Egyptian art,
while Annibale Albani and his younger brother, Cardinal Alessandro Albani, were daring enough to adopt the
new view of Egyptian civilization as being on a par with
those of Greece and Rome. Anxious to clarify this issue,
in 1785 the French Académie des Inscriptions et Belles-
Lettres (Academy of Inscriptions and Letters) organized
a competition entitled "Egyptian Architecture Considered with Respect to Its Origin, Its Principles, and Its
Taste, and Compared in the Same Respects with Greek

Architecture." The winner, Quatremère de Quincy, provided the essential points of his thesis three years later
in the *Encyclopédie méthodique* (A Methodical Encyclopedia); the essay did not appear in its entirety until
1803.

Egyptomania in the strict sense—the reuse of ancient
Egyptian themes in the art of the Enlightenment—flourished throughout the 18th century in response to several factors. Not least among these was the ancien
régime aristocracy's pronounced taste for ancient Egyptian art, which held for them a profound charm as well
as an underlying mystery: astonishing architectural
forms, a whole pantheon of zoomorphic symbols, and
arcane hieroglyphs. The notion of a return to nature
and the European taste for Anglo-Chinese gardens
encouraged the display of obelisks, pyramids, and
sphinxes. Sphinxes and Egyptian lions began to appear
at the entrances of private mansions, while every fashionable interior across Europe reflected an Egyptianate
touch: sphinxes, obelisks, and heads adorned with the
characteristic *nemes* (pharaoh's striped headdress) decorated furniture and objets d'art. Once this fashion had
taken root, under the influence of Marie-Antoinette in
France, Egyptomania became all the rage and soon
spread to all the European courts (notably those of
Charles III of Austria-Hungary, Frederick II of Prussia,
Gustavus III of Sweden, and Catherine II of Russia).
Meanwhile, in the years preceding the French Revolution, visionary architects began to exploit these new
forms whose popularity seemed assured by their gigantic proportions, their hermetic symbolism, and their
sheer novelty. However, the architects seldom saw the
realization of their monumental creations (pyramids
and enormous tombs), except for ephemeral versions
erected for Revolutionary celebrations.

Another factor that explains the popularity of Egyptomania was its connection with Freemasonry, which
officially drew its vital energy from ancient Egyptian
sources. Egyptian influence was reflected in the decor of
the lodges, as well as in the mansions or landscaped
gardens of the liberal aristocracy associated with the
movement. In Paris, for example, an obelisk and a pyramid grace parc Monceau; the pyramid of Maupertuis is
also noteworthy in this regard. Mozart's Masonic opera
Die Zauberflöte (1791; The Magic Flute), for which the
first edition of Emanuel Schikaneder's libretto is illustrated with an Egyptian-style frontispiece, constitutes
the high point of enlightened Egyptomania.

Political discourse offered its own interpretations of
all the new documentary evidence concerning Egypt.
Caylus, for example, saw the timeless and monumental
quality of Egyptian art as an ideal reflection of an
enlightened monarchy. Infused with such a notion of
utopia, Europeans of the second half of the 18th century were nevertheless torn between two attitudes

toward Egypt: one that saw Egypt as a country that was exemplary in all respects, to be taken as a model; and one that considered Egypt a monstrous creation that was to be shunned. The French Revolution brought an end to this ambivalence. It is conceivable that if the revolutionaries were going to use Egyptian monuments in the organization of their mass assemblies it would have been in order to exploit the monuments' political significance as symbols of the absolute power of the pharaohs, symbols that were to be destroyed as such, in the same way that the symbols of royalty and feudalism had been destroyed. But that was not the case: the utopian view, reinforced by strong interest in Egypt, prevailed. Antiquity seemed to offer an example of an ideal purity to a people who wanted nothing more to do with the buildings that had been erected by royal dynasties since the Gothic age. The Fontaine de la Régénération (Fountain of Regeneration), built in Paris on the ruins of the Bastille for the celebration of 10 August 1793, probably constituted one of the most perfect examples of the spirit of the Enlightenment: Reason, Nature, and Mankind are celebrated side by side in perfect harmony beneath the gaze of a pseudo-goddess Isis crowned with a *nemes* and wearing a pharaonic loincloth. The soldiers and scholars who took part in Bonaparte's Egyptian expedition were all imbued with this idealized image, which was at least in part responsible for Bonaparte's choice of Egypt for a military campaign. This utopian image, blended with the Napoleonic myth, sustained Egyptomania for the greater part of the 19th century.

JEAN-MARCEL HUMBERT

See also Archeology; Freemasonry

Further Reading

Baltrusaitis, Jurgis, *La quête d'Isis: Essai sur la légende d'un mythe,* Paris: Perrin, 1967

Curl, James Stevens, *Egyptomania: The Egyptian Revival, a Recurring Theme in the History of Taste,* Manchester: Manchester University Press, 1994

Humbert, Jean-Marcel, *L'Égyptomanie dans l'art occidental,* Paris: ACR, 1989

Humbert, Jean-Marcel, editor, *L'Égyptomanie à l'épreuve de l'archéologie,* Paris: Musée du Louvre, 1996

Humbert, Jean-Marcel, Michael Pantazzi, and Christiane Ziegler, *Egyptomania: Egypt in Western Art, 1730–1930,* Paris: Réunion des Musées Nationaux, and Ottawa, Ontario: National Gallery of Canada, 1994

Iversen, Erik, *The Myth of Egypt and Its Hieroglyphs in European Tradition,* Copenhagen: Gad, 1961

Electricity

Science as Spectacle

On the eve of the French Revolution, the writer and dramatist Louis-Sébastien Mercier wrote in his *Tableau de Paris* (1781–89; Panorama of Paris): "The reign of literature is over; physicists are replacing the poets and novelists; the electrical machine has taken the place of the stage play." In fact, the close of the 18th century marked the high point of frictional electricity, in terms of its public success as much as its scientific achievements. The electrical machine was a prized piece among the collections of princes, great noblemen, and wealthy bourgeois, used for demonstrations and varied entertainments. Its cost alone—nearly a thousand livres for the machine owned by the duc de Chaulnes, which can still be seen at the Musée des Arts et Métiers (Museum of Arts and Trades) in Paris—was indicative of its owner's interest in the sciences. Sometimes as much a work of art as a scientific instrument, with its glass disk or cylinder, its gleaming copper accessories, and its carved wooden wheel, an electrical machine put on a show that no witness could forget.

More often than not, its effects were made still more spectacular by the addition of a battery of Leyden jars. Named for the city of Leiden, where its effects were discovered in 1746, the Leyden jar, simply a bottle covered on the inside and outside with metallic foil, made possible the accumulation and storage of electricity. The discharges created inside the electrical machine by the high voltage caused by the rubbing of a large glass disk, made to rotate by means of a wheel, produced sparks that could be several feet long, and which erupted with an awesome noise like musket fire. At Versailles the abbé Jean-Antoine Nollet made 180 royal guards forming a human chain in the Hall of Mirrors jump simultaneously. In Berlin Ludolff astonished the king of Prussia by igniting alcohol with his finger. At Wittenberg Georg Matthias Bose performed "electrical beatification," creating a halo around a subject's head by means of a metal band stuck with prongs and hidden in the person's headdress. In Philadelphia Benjamin Franklin devised the "magic painting," which would give a violent electric shock to anyone who dared to touch the king's gilded crown. Other effects included the appearance of evanescent luminous drawings on glass panels, the dancing of lightweight puppets, a little house struck by lightning, electric whirligigs, chimes, planetariums, sprays of luminous plumes, the electric kiss, and so on.

Even when presented to an audience of enthusiasts, however, demonstrations of electricity were not simply intended as fashionable entertainment. For some, following Denis Diderot's lead, the instruments of experimental philosophy bore witness to the greatness of the sciences and showed man harnessing the forces of nature according to his will. For others, such as John Wesley in England or the abbé Noël-Antoine Pluche or René-Just Haüy in France, the reproduction of natural phenomena—lightning and the aurora borealis in the case of electricity—and an explanation of their causes were above all proof of the power, beauty, and order of God's creation. However, all were keen to distinguish the effects produced by the physicist from the seemingly miraculous tricks of charlatans. In the physics laboratories of the scientific lecturers, the electrical machine allowed the principal properties of electricity to be taught through demonstrations and experiments. The idea was both to astound and to explain. Nor was the general public left out—for a shilling, a few talers, or a few sous they could experience the surprising effects of the magic fluid produced by a "pocket machine" at fairs and traveling sideshows. Thus was electricity first experienced by means of the senses: not only through blinding visions and deafening explosions, but also in the form of sensations resembling cobwebs or a light breeze on the skin, pinpricks, and even the smell of phosphorus.

At the same time, electricity was one of the major developments in experimental physics during the 18th century and the field most widely explored by the most varied cast of characters. Professors of physics (such as Nollet, Alessandro Volta, or Bose), along with naturalists (such as Lamarck or the comte de Lacépède), physicians (such as Jean-Paul Marat or Luigi Galvani), churchmen (such as Wesley in England, Divis in Bavaria, or Pierre Bertholon at Lyon), philosophers (such as Montesquieu, Voltaire, or Madame du Châtelet), and amateurs (such as Franklin) all competed for the prizes offered by the academies for electrical work, conducted experiments (Voltaire ordered physics instruments worth over 10,000 livres from Nollet), and

advanced their hypotheses. By the end of the century, physicists had more or less reached a consensus on the interpretation of electrical phenomena. They had a law for the variation of electrical force over a distance, as well as a method of measuring that variation and instruments sensitive enough to detect low voltages. Combined with the interest in finding parallels between "electrical fluid" and "nervous fluid," electrical research culminated in 1800 with the Italian physicist Alessandro Volta's perfection of a new means of producing electricity that replaced friction machines: the battery. It produced a much weaker voltage, but its operation was continuous, which facilitated the opening up of new perspectives, particularly in the field of chemistry. As a practical by-product of these theoretical and experimental advances, 18th-century "electricians," as those who studied electricity were called, gave European and North American civilization an effective protection against lightning for buildings and ships, with the development of the lightning rod. These scientists suggested that electricity might play an important role in other atmospheric or terrestrial phenomena, such as earthquakes or volcanic eruptions. Finally, they raised hopes by suggesting that a number of illnesses, in particular paralyses, could benefit from the application of medical electricity.

The Development of Qualitative Experimental Skills

At the beginning of the 18th century, however, electricity was considered to be an insignificant phenomenon, a mere curiosity of nature among so many other as yet unexplained natural curiosities: the attraction of light objects by amber and certain other objects (glass, resin, precious stones) when these were rubbed. The 17th century's main contribution had been to distinguish the properties of electricity from those of magnetism. Unlike the latter, electricity up until the middle of the 18th century was hardly linked to any technology or theoretical system at all. Nor was it widely associated with natural phenomena because, prior to the 1700s, no connection was made between lightning and the unspectacular behavior of amber. In contrast to mechanics, optics, or astronomy, the study of electricity was the study of artificial phenomena, created in the laboratory by means of manmade artifacts. Experiments on frictional electricity (dubbed "static" electricity in the 19th century to distinguish it from the "dynamic" electricity produced by a battery) were—as the 18th-century electricians noted—highly sensitive to material conditions. Atmospheric humidity was the most significant factor, but also wind direction, exterior temperature, the composition of the bodies used, their color and shape, the nature of the experimental table and of the ground, even the experimenter's breath, all affected the phenomena—as if the apparent inconsistency of the phenomena themselves were not enough.

Another essential peculiarity of electrical experiments, up until the 1780s, was their qualitative nature. The intensity of the effects produced by an electrical machine could, to some extent, be monitored by the number of turns of the wheel or the length of an indicator spark, but experiments on the interactions between electrified bodies remained entirely dependent upon the shrewdness of the observer. The search for a quantitative monitoring instrument inspired a great deal of electrical research in the second half of the century. The generic and original term for this instrument in the middle of the century—"electrometer" rather than "electroscope"—bears witness to this desire for quantitative measurement. However, there was considerable disagreement as to what the various instruments were actually measuring. Whenever the length of a spark or—another standard approach—the angle formed by two charged, hanging wires as they repelled each other were noted, the answer to the question "what is being measured?" was also required. This was not really possible until the very end of the century, once the three key concepts of voltage, charge, and capacitance had been developed. The "capriciousness" of the experiments, to use the physicists' expression, the precariousness of their quantitative control, meant that to attain experimental mastery of the phenomena required rigorous training. By definition, an experiment must be able to be replicated, and scientists of the era were liable to be required to do so on demand. The demonstration of experiments was in fact one of the essential roles of the scientific academies and societies established in the major European cities at the end of the 17th century.

In 1705 Francis Hauksbee, the demonstrator for the Royal Society of London (then under the presidency of Sir Isaac Newton), studied a phenomenon spectacular enough to be well suited for public experiments. When a mercury barometer is shaken in a darkened room, bluish phosphorescence can be seen passing through the vacuum inside. By showing that this phenomenon was electrical in origin (due to the friction of the mercury against the glass), Hauksbee brought electricity out from the margins of science. Indeed, from that moment on, for almost a century, electricity went hand in hand with light and thus with "fire." Exploring next the effects of friction by means of a glass ball turned by a wheel, or a glass tube, rubbed in either case with a piece of woolen cloth—devices that became standard— Hauksbee managed to produce evidence of a genuine repulsive force exerted by the glass upon some light objects and, in a delicate experiment, to distinguish this repulsion from a simple recoil following upon an attraction. He also observed, to his great astonishment, that

the electrical effect continued to be felt through a thick glass screen, while the majority of other substances— even paper or the lightest muslin—blocked it. References to astonishment, strangeness, and incomprehension are common in the annals of electricity in the 18th century.

At the beginning of the 1730s two experimenters, Stephen Gray, a member of the Royal Society who was familiar with Hauksbee's experiments, and Charles-François de Cisternay Du Fay, a member of the Académie Royale des Sciences de Paris (French Royal Academy of Sciences), defined the essential points of the electrical properties of different bodies and of the consistency of their interactions. Gray showed that a hemp rope, a metal wire, or the human body could transmit electrical attraction at a distance, allowing the electrical effluvia to escape, in contrast to silk threads, resin, or glass. Du Fay created a generalized model of this difference of behavior, classifying all objects into one of two distinct categories that John Theophilus Desaguliers named "conductors" and "electric objects per se." The second group (the insulators), which could be charged by simple friction, were in themselves a natural source of electricity. The first group (the conductors or "nonelectric" bodies) could not be charged by friction. However, as Du Fay demonstrated, they could be charged— something that up until then no one had succeeded in doing—provided that they were hung from silk threads or placed on a block of resin before they were brought into contact with the rubbed glass. With this new possibility of charging all objects, including metals and liquids, electricity appeared to constitute a universal property of matter. After much research, Du Fay pronounced these "simple rules" of electricity. First, a charged body will attract any uncharged body, transmit electricity to it, and then repel it. Second, there are two types of electricity: "vitreous" electricity produced by friction on glass and "resinous" electricity produced by resin; a body charged with one of the two types will attract any body charged with the other type and repel any body charged with the same type. The underlying order of the chaotic dance of light bodies around glass tubes and pieces of resin had finally been discerned.

In an attempt to clarify the role of air in electrical phenomena, several physicists conducted experiments in a vacuum. Controversial and uncertain results concerning this question of the action of electricity in a vacuum recurred throughout the century. Despite the improvements made to the vacuum pump, notably by Hauksbee for his own in vacuo electrical experiments, the vacuum was never perfect and the electrical effects were complex. The development of new electrical machines by the Germans Christian August Hausen, Bose, and Johann Heinrich Winkler revitalized the field of electrical experimentation. In the 1740s they revived

Hauksbee's glass globe, abandoned 30 years earlier in favor of tubes because of the danger of implosion, and intensified its electrical effect by employing cushions, instead of the experimenter's hands, to rub the ball as it rotated and by adding a horizontal metal rod suspended by silk threads in front of the ball, which it brushed against at one end so as to collect the effluvia (what we would today refer to as electrical discharge). Beginning in 1745, a number of technical refinements regarding the nature of the cushions, the electrical insulation of the various parts, and the electricity collection mechanism made the electrical machine into a reliable instrument. The only notable development thereafter was the replacement in 1766 of the globe by a disk, brought into use by the English manufacturer Jesse Ramsden, again with the intention of reducing the risk of accidents.

Du Fay's young assistant, the abbé Jean-Antoine Nollet, who was to become a successful lecturer and instrument maker and who devoted more of his energies to scientific pursuits than to religion, was one of the many who were eager to build an electrical machine. While Nollet became one of the most enthusiastic exponents of electrical entertainment, it was his explanatory system that made him "Europe's foremost electrician." Certainly, however, he would not have been able to invent the Leyden jar (or condenser), an indispensable device that led to the overturning of his theory, since to do that it was necessary to break one of Du Fay's strict rules. That achievement instead came about through the work of amateur enthusiasts—the German canon Ewald Georg von Kleist and, independently, the wealthy Dutchman Andreas Cunaeus. Attempting to charge the water in a bottle, they held the bottle with one hand, instead of placing the vessel on an insulating stand in order to prevent the effluvia from escaping to the ground through the glass and the experimenter's body. When, with their free hand, they touched the iron rod immersed in the water and connected to the electrical machine, they experienced a violent shock. News of this "terrifying experiment" from the professor of physics at Leiden University, Pieter van Musschenbroek, in January 1746, gave rise to a rash of duplications, marked by blackouts, temporary paralyses, chain discharges, luminous discharges in a rarefied gas, and so on. It was discovered that the power of the discharge could be increased still further by replacing the water with lead shot or metal foil stuck to the inside of the bottle, covering the outside of the vessel in the same way, reducing the thickness of the glass, and, finally, connecting several bottles. Moreover, the bottle retained its capacity to produce discharges over several hours, or even several days. However, attempts to explain the mechanism of the "lightning bolt" were thwarted by the supposed transparency of glass to elec-

trical emissions, a hypothesis assumed in order to explain the action of electricity through a glass screen. The problem of the electrical behavior of glass was added to that of the vacuum.

Diverse Interpretations

The Leyden jar brought about an explosion of different theoretical interpretations. The hypothesis of the emission of electrical effluvia by electrified bodies, first advanced at the beginning of the 17th century by William Gilbert, was predominant until the mid-18th century. Did not electrical attraction disappear when a screen was put in the way, unless it was made of glass? Did not Hauksbee's "threads of light" radiating from his glass ball, and the luminosity emanating from the metal rods materially show the path of the effluvia? Could not the very essence of these effluvia be felt on the skin in the form of the "electric wind"? Without mass (since they did not increase the weight of a charged body), able to escape from glass and set into motion by friction, the effluvia formed a subtle and highly penetrative emanation and pulled with them whatever matter they encountered on their way. Electrical repulsion was thus easy to explain. Attraction posed more difficulties and various mechanisms were suggested: effluvia returning to their point of origin and pulling along light bodies on their way; rarefaction of the air around the charged body drawing in more distant air and light objects; reflection of the effluvia onto nearby bodies; vortical or linear movements; and so on. A host of authors came forward and complex mechanisms were proposed involving air, electrical atmospheres, particles of "fire," and vibrations. Ultimately, Nollet's "complete theoretical system" predominated in France and Germany until the 1770s. It presumed a simultaneous double current of "affluent" and "effluent" effluvia. Whatever the details of the proposed mechanisms, all were based on the effects of contact between electrical matter and ordinary matter. Those who took up Newton's and Leonhard Euler's hypothesis of a "subtle ether" filling all space—whose vibrations could explain electrical effects—were few.

What was the situation as far as the nature of electrical matter was concerned? As the article "Feu électrique" (Electrical Fire) in the *Encyclopédie* clearly shows, the substance of the effluvia was commonly likened to that of fire and light. Yet the nature of this fire was open to discussion: was it or was it not identical to ordinary fire? Was it or was it not associated with a sulfurous substance? In any event, the presumed uniqueness of electrical matter caused Du Fay's hypothesis of two types of electricity—one vitreous and the other resinous—to be abandoned. The differences in the behavior of glass and resin were then attributed to differences of intensity and not of kind. The Englishman Robert Symmer, however, revived the concept of two electrical fluids in 1759, with some success. This qualitative natural philosophy, which explained known phenomena within a mechanistic framework, certainly had little predictive value, but theoretical divergences provided a stimulus to experimental justification. Besides, even more markedly in electricity than in other areas of natural philosophy, theoretical paradigms did not always dictate experimental practice.

Franklin's approach was quite different. He applied the accountant's logic he had developed in the course of his business career. An American amateur, knowing little of European Cartesian theories, he constructed a radically new system of interpretation. In his view, all electrical phenomena could be understood in terms of an electrical matter to be found, like water in a sponge, in every body in its natural state. In a charged body, there was either more or less than the normal quantity of this electrical matter, and the body was thus "positively" or "negatively" charged. The great strength of Franklin's system, as compared to Nollet's, was its ability to explain the operation of the Leyden jar. It did so using two revolutionary assumptions: the impermeability of glass to electrical matter and the action of electricity at a distance. According to Franklin's theory, the particles of electrical matter repel one another at a distance, while electrical matter and ordinary matter attract one another. When the bottle is "charged" or "discharged," Franklin claimed, there is merely a displacement of electricity. More generally, electrical matter remains constant in the course of the various physical operations. This "electrical algebra" disconcerted his contemporaries. Abstract, and indifferent to the actual nature of electricity (fire, ether, or light) and to the mechanism of its action, Franklin's theory implied the conservation of electrical matter. His experiments in support of his theory quickly convinced English-speaking and Dutch electricians. However, the theory involved obscure points such as the presence of electrical atmospheres and remained incapable of explaining various phenomena such as the repulsion between two bodies that had both lost electrical fluid. The argument between the supporters of Nollet—who was performing many experiments to oppose the electrical permeability of glass and other hypotheses put forth by Franklin—and the "Franklinists" raged across Europe and the United States. Nollet's *Lettres sur l'électricité* (1753; Letters on Electricity) offered a response to Franklin's letters to Peter Collinson in his *Experiments and Observations on Electricity* (1752). With the lightning conductor coming into use in Europe, however, Franklin's reputation went a long way to gain acceptance for his theory.

"Fire from the Sky" and "Vital Fluid"

While the analogy between electric sparks and lightning was first made at the beginning of the 18th century, the absence of experimental proof made the nature of lightning a question asked in vain by the academies. Having established that a metal point discharges a charged body smoothly and without sparks, Franklin proposed to draw fire down from the sky using a long vertical metal rod. The experiment, soon to be famous and reproduced all over Europe, was carried out near Paris in 1752 at the instigation of the comte de Buffon, who, being an opponent of Nollet, hoped to support Franklin's theory. Soon afterward, Franklin succeeded in conducting electricity from a kite in order to charge a Leyden jar, which then reproduced all the known properties of electricity. While this demonstration of the similarity between the electricity from the sky and ordinary electricity convinced the natural philosophers, his proposal to protect buildings using a metal rod, no longer insulated but connected to the ground by a conductor, caused widespread controversy. Not only peasants but also academic and religious authorities expressed hostility to the lightning rod as an affront both to God and to common sense. Was there not indeed a risk of attracting lightning to the building rather than averting it? For every Voltaire, who was one of the first to install the diabolical object (on the roof of his château at Ferney), or Maximilien Robespierre, who advocated it before the courts, or Cesare Bonesana Beccaria, professor of physics at the University of Turin, who saw to it that Italy was the first European country to be so equipped, how many Benjamin Wilsons were there advocating the spherical lightning rod or Nollets denying that Franklin's invention had any usefulness to the public?

There was another relationship between electricity and natural phenomena that seemed logical to many physicists, physiologists, and physicians: might not the "electrical fire" be linked to the process of life? At the beginning of the century, the vitalist conception of electricity, opposed to a mechanistic and materialistic view, was still close to alchemy, but a succession of experimental efforts gave substance to this conception. After all, Nollet and others had shown that electricity encourages seed germination and animal metabolism; the torpedo fish produces electricity within its organs; and, above all, the Leyden jar had a violent effect on the muscles and sensory organs. Some, such as Divis, went so far as to construct a "theology of electricity," in which "electrical fire" was supposed to have constituted the light of the first day of the divine creation, the universal fire present in all bodies, a life principle of divine origin that made the development of life on Earth possible. Electrical experiments could reveal God's secrets in Nature.

More pragmatic were the many scientists who were content to limit themselves to researching electricity's therapeutic virtues. Electricians set themselves up as physicians to treat paralysis, migraine, deafness, blindness, and so on. While condemned by the scientific authorities of Paris at the same time as Franz Anton Mesmer's "animal magnetism," medical electricity nevertheless helped popularize the hypothesis of the analogy between electrical fluid and nervous fluid. This hypothesis was put into concrete form when Luigi Galvani, professor of anatomy in Bologna, announced in 1791 that he had discovered a form of electricity specific to living organisms, "animal electricity." However, the contractions in frogs' legs that he attributed to a discharge of this animal electricity between the nerve and the muscle were attributed by the physicist Volta to the contact between two different metals that connected the nerve and muscle. The controversy between supporters of animal electricity and defenders of metallic electricity led to ten years of contradictory experiments before Volta invented his electric cell.

The Quantification and Mathematization of Electricity

Mathematicians viewed electrical phenomena from another angle. For them, the triumph of Newtonian mechanics, with its explanation of the solar system, made it the model for all physical explanations. The Baconian sciences—electricity, magnetism, heat, light, and chemistry—had been quantified very little and subjected to mathematics still less. During the latter half of the century, a tension developed between a minority of scientists who, following Jean le Rond D'Alembert, maintained that experimental physics should model itself on mechanics and therefore be based on mathematical laws and the majority who, like Franklin, objected to the excessive use of mathematics, arguing that it distanced the natural philosopher from nature and gave him too much confidence in abstract formulas that were largely incomprehensible to the layman. In 1759 Aepinus, an astronomer at the Academia Scientiarum Imperialis Petropolitanae (Imperial Academy of Sciences of Saint Petersburg)—and therefore a mathematician—abandoned Franklin's concept of atmospheres surrounding charged bodies and but developed much further Franklin's idea of the distant action of electricity. Aepinus even carried out calculations about these electrical forces operating from a distance, without forming any hypothesis as to their mode of action, and made several predictions based on deduction that were later confirmed. With Johann C. Wilcke, he also accounted for the bothersome phenomenon of electrostatic induction (the charging from a distance of a neutral body by a charged body), which interfered with

experiments. The Eulers, father and son, also attempted calculations to explain what they called "subtle ether," but without success. By the 1780s the Franklinists' concept of electrical atmospheres, like the concept of effluvia promoted by Nollet's supporters, no longer seemed so obvious. Moreover, no result had succeeded in resolving the question of the single or dual nature of electrical fluids, despite much experimental research, in particular on the branching of sparks. A mood of positivism reigned that favored the introduction of mathematics.

First, however, it was necessary to clarify what the instruments were measuring and to define theoretical entities that could be quantified and compared with experimental results. Volta, Henry Cavendish, and Charles-Augustin Coulomb, all of whom expressed a new insistence on precise measurement, were the major figures in this development, which was still continuing at the end of the century. Innovation centered on the "combination of calculation and experiment" advocated by Coulomb. Thus, Volta, defining equality of "tension" (today called "voltage") by an identical angle of displacement between the two straws in his electrometer, and the "charge" (or quantity of electricity) by the number of revolutions given the machine, suggested a proportional relationship between these two quantities by means of a third: the "capacity" of the body to store electricity.

The other direction for mathematical work concerned electrical force. Taking up Aepinus's theory, Cavendish split up the electrical force between two charged bodies mathematically into an infinity of elementary forces acting between particles of electrical matter—a mathematical approach comparable to that used in mechanics. In 1771 he showed that as the distance between the particles increased, this elementary force decreased by a factor of less than the cube of the distance. His experimental demonstration of the decrease as $1/d^2$ was unpublished, like the majority of his work; so it fell to the military engineer Coulomb to advance a proof of it using his torsion balance, a device of unprecedented sensitivity. However, the delicacy of his experiments, his mathematical presuppositions, and his belief in the existence of two fluids meant that his findings were slow to gain acceptance outside Paris. With Volta, Cavendish, and Coulomb, the study of electrostatics at the turn of the century turned away from the question of the nature of electricity in favor of researching the mathematical laws governing electrical phenomena. This shift in focus meant leaving behind the amateur enthusiasts whose successes had brought the study of electricity into prominence.

CHRISTINE BLONDEL

See also Force; Heat; Magnetism; Physiology

Further Reading

Gillmor, C. Stewart, *Coulomb and the Evolution of Physics and Engineering in Eighteenth-Century France,* Princeton, New Jersey: Princeton University Press, 1971

Hackmann, Willem Dirk, *Electricity from Glass: The History of the Frictional Electrical Machine, 1600–1850,* Alphen aan den Rijn: Sijthoff and Noordhoff, 1978

Home, Roderick Weir, "Introduction," in *Aepinus's Essay on the Theory of Electricity and Magnetism,* by Franz Aepinus, translated by Peter James Connor, Princeton, New Jersey: Princeton University Press, 1979 (original Latin edition, 1759)

Home, Roderick Weir, *Electricity and Experimental Physics in Eighteenth-Century Europe,* Aldershot, Hampshire, and Brookfield, Vermont: Variorum, 1992

Pera, Marcello, *The Ambiguous Frog: The Galvani-Volta Controversy on Animal Electricity,* translated by Jonathan Mandelbaum, Princeton, New Jersey: Princeton University Press, 1992 (original Italian edition, 1986)

Priestley, Joseph, *The History and Present State of Electricity, with Original Experiments,* London: Dodsley, 1767; reprint, 2 vols., New York: Johnson Reprint, 1966

Sigaud de La Fond, M., *Précis historique et expérimental des phénomènes électriques depuis l'origine de cette découverte jusqu'à ce jour,* Paris: Rue et Hôtel Serpente and Imprimerie de Demonville, 1781; 2nd edition, Rue et Hôtel Serpente, 1785

Eloquence

The ancients divided eloquence into three genres: deliberative, demonstrative, and judicial. In the modern period, eloquence stopped being perceived according to these genres and their specific discursive functions (persuasion or dissuasion, praise or blame, and accusation or defense, respectively) and came to be identified with important aspects of social life, while also becoming a fixture of certain institutional practices. Accordingly, three main divisions were established: "eloquence of the pulpit" (religious), "eloquence of the bar" (judicial), and "eloquence of the rostrum" (political). From the point of view of aesthetic theory, eloquence referred only to the art of oratory, but in fact it encompassed all branches of literature in the 17th century. In "Des ouvrages de l'esprit," (On the Works of the Mind), Chapter 1 of *Les caractères* (1688; The Characters), Jean de La Bruyère observes, "it [eloquence] can be found in conversation and in every genre of writing. It is to the sublime what genre is to a work's parts." That shift toward a broader meaning still obtains, since today eloquence does not refer to any particular literary genre or form of discourse, but rather to facility in speech or language in general, with an emphasis on its expressive character. The 18th century, an age of transition, stood at the crossroads of these various ideas about eloquence.

Enlightenment thinkers undertook to trace the history of eloquence as part of a broader ideological project. The eloquence of antiquity, to which Enlightenment authors invariably referred, was judged favorably but was considered a lost art. In writings of the modern period it was a commonplace to reiterate the causes of this "decadence." In 1630 a translation by Giry of Cornelius Tacitus's *Dialogus de oratoribus* (Dialogue on Orators) was published under the title *Dialogue des causes de la corruption de l'éloquence* (Dialogue on the Causes of the Corruption of Eloquence). In reaction to this pervasive notion of decadence, 17th-century writers proposed their own important models of eloquence—models that Enlightenment thinkers do not appear to have found altogether satisfactory. The 18th century thus witnessed a reevaluation and, simultaneously, a redefinition of eloquence. A process of secularization of the art of oratory, with academic discourse gradually taking the place of the eloquence of the pulpit and the bar, was complemented, toward the end of the century, by a new interest in political eloquence.

Eloquence and Morality in the Classical Age

Thinking on the topic of eloquence originally focused on an ancient debate about rhetoric. Here is it necessary to explain how rhetoric and eloquence relate to each other, particularly since the terms were often confused or used interchangeably. According to 17th-century theorists, rhetoric was the art of speaking well, and eloquence the result of applying that art. As Bernard Lamy observes in *La rhétorique ou L'art de parler* (1675; Rhetoric; or, The Art of Speaking), "the same difference exists between eloquence and rhetoric as between theory and practice." This formula was often repeated: by Brulart de Sillery in his *Réflexions sur l'éloquence* (1700; Reflections on Eloquence) and, above all, by Denis Diderot, in his article "Rhétorique" (Rhetoric) in the *Encyclopédie*. Eloquence was thus part of a general critique of rhetoric that extended from antiquity into the 18th century. Plato had accused rhetoric of playing sophistic games and condemned it in the name of truth and morality. That double condemnation, although displaced, may be found again among the moderns.

Cartesian philosophers were the first of the moderns to revive the critique of rhetoric. Following in Plato's footsteps, they focused not on the art of oratory per se but rather on poetic language in general and its place in learned discourse. At the heart of their inquiry lay the problem of whether philosophy required ornament to be understood. This was an important debate at the end of the 17th century, when rhetoric came under siege by the development of scientific discourse—a fact that was not without consequence for intellectual writing in general, which was expected to be *more geometrico* (in geometric fashion) from that point onward. Without completely renouncing that ambition, Enlightenment philosophers made certain concessions motivated by pedagogical concern. From the works of Bernard Le Bovier de Fontenelle to those of Jean le Rond D'Alembert, the use of imagery and figures of speech was permitted in theoretical discourse, provided that any excesses that might undermine a rationalistic approach were avoided. In his "Rhétorique" article in the *Encyclopédie,* Diderot comes to the conclusion that "even in philosophy, no matter how austere, one looks for refinement, and not without reason: eloquence is to the sciences what the sun is to the world; the sciences are but shadows if those who write of them do not know how to write."

However, it is undoubtedly in the work of Madame de Staël at the turn of the 19th century that one finds the most original conception of the relationship between eloquence and truth. Taking a stance against the traditional opposition between philosophy and eloquence, between reasoning and feeling, she defends the paradoxical idea that everything that is eloquent is true: "That is to say that in a plea for a bad cause, reasoning is false; but eloquence properly understood is always founded on truth. It may be easy to err in the application or consequences of that truth, but in such cases, any error lies in the reasoning." This argument rests on an anthropological postulate very dear to Enlightenment thinkers: that feeling inclines men to be good. To cite Madame de Staël once again: "Since eloquence always requires the movements of the soul, it addresses itself only to human sentiment, and the sentiments of the multitude always tend toward the good" (*De la littérature* [1801; The Influence of Literature upon Society]).

Theologians soon took up the debate on eloquence and truth, considering the issue from a resolutely moral perspective. In *Réflexions sur l'éloquence* (1700; Thoughts on Eloquence), a collection of texts by Brulart de Sillery, François Lamy, and Antoine Arnauld, the topic of eloquence lies at the heart of a theological controversy concerning the use of figurative speech (tropes) in eloquence at the pulpit. The three writers essentially take up the Cartesians' objection and transpose it to the realm of apologetics: although the divine word, they concur, is distinctly different from geometric truth, can it withstand the use of eloquence in sermons? In other words, is it possible to attain spiritual elevation by means of appealing to the senses? Yes, says the orator Bernard Lamy, conscious of the limitations of the human mind ("men ordinarily are capable of understanding only those things that enter the mind by way of the senses"). Wrong, retorts the less tolerant Benedictine François Lamy, in whose view eloquence interferes with the intelligibility of the divine word. The Jansenist Arnauld chooses to couch his defense in terms of the manifestation and communication of divine truth: eloquence is good if it can contribute to the conversion of sinners. Brulart de Sillery also asks, "Is it possible to convert, or even move, without stirring up eloquence in general, and consequently the stirring imagination and all the rest, and can this be done without using tropes and figures?" In reality, the theological debate over the problem of eloquence took place in two stages. The rejection of pomp and false brilliance was forcefully articulated in the *Logique de Port-Royal* (1662; Logic; or, The Art of Thinking) by Arnauld and Pierre Nicole and in Father René Rapin's *Réflexions sur l'usage de l'éloquence de ce temps en général* (1715; Reflections on the Use of Eloquence in This Period in General, in *Oeuvres* [Works]). In this work, Rapin writes: "Generally speaking, eloquence, with its careful arrangements of words . . . rarely succeeds: people are mistrustful of everything that appears artificial and contrived." At the same time, it seemed that sacred discourse could benefit from special treatment. Acknowledgment of an elevated, figurative style—commonly called "sublime eloquence"—was based on a moral perspective. The Christian terminology used by Father Rapin in his *Réflexions sur l'éloquence de la chaire* (1715; Reflections on the Eloquence of the Pulpit, a work also included in his *Oeuvres*) reveals his conviction that the language of the passions is legitimate when its is associated with a sacred mission.

In his *Dialogues sur l'éloquence* (1718; Dialogues on Eloquence), Father Fénelon takes up the question of the relationship of eloquence to truth and virtue. He proposes a forceful new definition that was to be largely adopted throughout the 18th century. For Fénelon, eloquence is not some frivolous invention intended to dazzle men with brilliant speeches; it is a serious art form that serves morality. In one dialogue, Fenelon's characters ponder the issue:

A: What is eloquence?
B: It is the art of speaking well.
A: Does not that art have another goal . . . ?

Fénelon's immediate answer to the latter question is that "the goal of eloquence is to sway men to truth and virtue." If it is necessary to *please* the listener or the reader by using figures of speech, it is because the art of speaking well inspires justice and other virtues "by making them pleasant." Such a perspective means that the orator will play a decisive role. For Fénelon, the good orator must be both a philosopher *and* a virtuous man. He must be a philosopher because the orator's profession, like philosophy, is "devoted to instruction and the reformation of public mores." There is so much as stake with eloquence that "only the philosopher can be a true orator." This statement, which is compatible with other Enlightenment ideas, takes up Plato's ideas from the *Gorgias* and its critique of "rhetors." Fénelon's position also infuses with new meaning the traditional dialectic between persuading and convincing. In accordance with the rationalist credo of his time, Fénelon rejects the notion of persuasion without proof. However, he shows the superiority of eloquence as compared to philosophy when practical consequences are taken into account: a discourse is effective only to the extent that it touches the soul of the listener. From the perspective of Fénelon's contemporary Chancellor d'Aguesseau, revealed in his *Défense de l'éloquence du barreau* (speech delivered in 1698; Defense of the Eloquence of the Bar), it is not enough to know what is good, one must also love it. Conviction, the chancellor argues, influences understanding, whereas persuasion affects the will. For d'Aguesseau, as for Fénelon, the orator must be a philosopher and philosophy has an obligation to be eloquent.

In addition to being a philosopher, the orator must also be a virtuous man, so that eloquence may serve the public good. "Orators," Fénelon writes, "have a duty to act as defenders of the law and masters of the people, to teach them virtue." For that reason, the orator must be irreproachably virtuous, as Quintilian had insisted in his *Institutio Oratoria* (Methods of Eloquence). The orator's chief virtue, according to Fénelon, is his disinterestedness. Taking the ancient sage as his model, the orator should be distinguished by his contempt for death, material wealth, and earthly pleasures. He must show probity in all situations, thereby serving as a model for all citizens. Fénelon even dreams of an "incorruptible" orator—an ideal that the famed orators of the Revolution may have borne in mind as they dictated their principles to the nation. This moral imperative was also demonstrated by the orator's intimate relationship with truth. In this respect, the 18th century makes a clean break with the ideas of the previous century. For Arnauld, the author of the *Grammaire de Port-Royal* (1660; Grammar of Port-Royal), eloquence did not necessarily presuppose the full conviction of the orator. Recalling Saint Augustine, Arnauld declares that "the vicious are equally capable of observing the rules of eloquence to move men to falsity and injustice as the good to move them to justice and truth." Following Horace (*Si vis me flere, dolendum est / Primum ipsi tibi* [If you want me to weep, you yourself must weep first]), in the article "Élocution" in the *Encyclopédie,* D'Alembert argues that on the contrary, one cannot truly convince anyone unless one is convinced oneself. In the same vein, Jean-Jacques Rousseau writes, "I have always written timidly and badly when I was not strongly convinced myself" (*Fragments biographiques* [Biographical Fragments]). For Enlightenment thinkers, then, a truly eloquent man was incapable of deceit.

Eloquence in the Context of the Linguistic Thought of the Enlightenment

As regards literary writing in general, Rousseau's example illustrates both the disdain in which the 18th century held the rhetoric taught in schools and treatises, and the century's admiration for eloquence that was free of artifice. In the view of Enlightenment thinkers, the ideal eloquence was natural. In his article "Éloquence" for the *Encyclopédie,* Voltaire states that "eloquence is born before rhetoric, in the same way that languages are formed before grammar." In the article "Élocution," D'Alembert observes that eloquence is less a skill acquired through constant practice than a talent and a natural gift. In the words of Blaise Pascal, "true eloquence disdains eloquence." Such beliefs explain the general conviction that reading good books was preferable to reading rules of rhetoric. In the words of Bernard Lamy, in his *Art de Parler* (1676; Art of Speaking): "one benefits much more from reading an eloquent piece than from learning precepts by heart." Voltaire defends the same idea in his *Essai sur la poésie épique* (1727; Essay upon the Civil Wars of France and Also upon the Epic Poetry of the European Nations from Homer down to Milton).

Eloquence during the classical period was situated within a system of genres. In the 18th century its popularity was connected to the development of the demonstrative genres: academic discourses and eulogies gradually replaced the grand funeral orations of the age of Louis XIV. The Enlightenment *philosophes* also invented the new genre of the "historical eulogy." Voltaire produced an original model with his *Éloge historique de la raison* (1775; Historical Defense of Reason). In the 17th century, by contrast, the panegyric and the funeral oration occupied the foremost place in French eloquence, while the academic eulogy was granted secondary importance. People were familiar with the *Oraisons funèbres* (Funeral Orations) by Bishop Bossuet (1689) and Bishop Fléchier (1672–90), which Voltaire still admired, as well as the *Sermons* composed by Louis Bourdaloue (1707–34) and Massillon (1745), and Pélisson's *Panégyrique de Louis XIV* (In Praise of Louis XIV), which had made a tremendous impression in its own time. In the 18th century the death of a prince was no longer commemorated only by a bishop delivering a pompous funeral oration, but rather by men of letters using the more sober form of the eulogy. Thus, when the dauphin died in 1765, no fewer than 22 funeral orations were presented, but it was the *Éloge du Dauphin* (Oration for the Dauphin) by Léonard Thomas that captivated the contemporary audience. Thomas was the most gifted and most lavishly rewarded practitioner of the academic eulogy of his time, which earned him a place in the Académie Française. This honor did not prevent Diderot from writing an extremely negative evaluation of the *Éloge du Dauphin* or from proposing a countereulogy to feed public debate. At the same time that efforts were being made to reform the traditional oratorical genres (for example, in Thomas's *Essai sur les éloges* [Essay on Orations]), the Encyclopedists launched a serious critique of those genres. Voltaire, who also composed a *Panégyrique de Louis XIV* (1768; In Praise of Louis XIV) and later, as a somewhat gratuitous stylistic exercise, an *Éloge de Louis XIV* (1774; Oration for Louis XV), observed more than once that the oratory of the 17th century reached a summit of perfection that would be difficult to equal. This was evidently not the opinion of Louis-Sébastien Mercier, whose *Tableau de Paris* (1781; Panorama of Paris) contains the observation that

all the literature of the previous century is infested not only with the most contagious adulation but also with the most false and ridiculous ideas, and we do not perceive anything in those vaunted models of eloquence but idle words and insufferable jargon, even if we have not become accustomed to substantial, modern works, in which an elevated reason speaks, moves, and convinces.

This critique turns on two different arguments. First, there is the role of philosophy, which imposed a specific tone and use of language, in the creation of modern eloquence. In the article "Éloge académique" (Academic Eulogies) in the *Encyclopédie*, the chevalier de Jaucourt defines the content of that type of discourse in the following terms:

Above all, philosophical reflection must be the soul of this kind of writing; it [philosophical reflection] is sometimes artfully and succinctly worked into the oration and sometimes developed in individual pieces, forming points of light that illuminate the rest.

In his *Défense de l'éloquence du barreau*, Chancellor d'Aguesseau had already requested that eloquence and philosophy be reconciled, on the grounds that "it took a Plato to create a Demosthenes." For Madame de Staël, progress in eloquence followed closely on the heels of progress in philosophy: "In the same way that new thoughts develop from new feelings, advances in philosophy will furnish new means to eloquence." In his essay entitled *Of Eloquence* (1742), the Scottish philosopher David Hume nevertheless points out a shortcoming in the new empire of reason: the triumph of common sense and moderation, along with the rejection of rhetorical artifice and pathos in favor of rational demonstration, were partly responsible for the decline of modern eloquence. As intellectual language was refined, there was the risk that a gap would develop between saying and doing.

In addition to this argument about form, Hume advances an argument about the content of eloquence: like Diderot, he suspects that the disorder and monstrous crimes of antiquity created an atmosphere conducive to eloquence. This suspicion that there might be a close connection between eloquence and passion helps us to understand the second aspect of the critique of the oratorical genres. In his article in the *Encyclopédie*, Voltaire takes it as a given that eloquence is born of the passions: "Nature makes men eloquent at moments of great interest and great passion." In his *Essai sur l'origine des langues* (1781; Essay on the Origin of Languages), Rousseau goes all the way back to the invention of speech, which, he argues, stemmed not from need but from passion. That is why, he explains, the first language must have been figurative. We should note in passing the 17th- and 18th-century interest in the eloquence of savage peoples: from the writings of Father Joseph-François Lafitau to those of the baron de La Hontan, from ethnologic transcriptions to literary fictions, we find a vast reverie about the energy of the languages of Native American peoples, which were thought to be close to primitive language. Diderot provides a wonderful example of this current of thought in the old man's harangue in the *Supplément au voyage de Bougainville* (1774; A Supplement to Bougainville's Travels).

In its most radical consequences, the link between eloquence and the passions led some Enlightenment thinkers to call into question the classical aesthetic. From the perspective of defenders of classicism, literature demanded a respect for codes; it was considered an art requiring submission to the most rigorous rules and constraints. In the view of numerous writers of the 18th century, by contrast, literature should convey emotion in an immediate way. It is revealing to trace the emergence of this new aesthetic ideal. Schematically, one might say that in the course of the 17th century decorative rhetoric (the art of speaking well) was supplanted by functional rhetoric (the art of moving and persuading). Later, following Bernard Lamy's lead—after all, Rousseau rewrote his *Essai sur l'origine des langues* while rereading Lamy's *L'art de parler*—functional rhetoric was in turn supplanted by a rhetoric of the passions. As Ernst Cassirer rightly notes, Hume and Diderot both espouse an aesthetics of sentiment, a development that may be linked to advances in the philosophy of sensation. In the view of both writers, eloquence must be sublime and passionate, as it was for the ancients, rather than rational and argumentative. In his effort to revive the eloquence of antiquity, Hume points to the expressive power of language—its "force"—to sway the opinion of audiences (*Of Eloquence*). Diderot revisits this idea frequently, demanding that oratory have more energy, more enthusiasm. Commenting on Jean-François La Harpe's *Éloge de Fénelon* (1796; In Praise of Fénelon), he denounces "a style that flows but does not roil, that does not tear at its banks and carry off trees, men, and houses. It does not disquiet us, shatter us, throw us headlong into tumult and confusion." In contrast to such intensity, the aesthetic of the passions also authorized a form of mute eloquence, which D'Alembert calls "eloquence of silence, the energetic and sometimes sublime language of the passions" (*Réflexions sur l'art oratoire* [Reflections on the Art of Oratory]). In other words, from Pascal to Saint-Just, eloquence could also appear in the guise of an economy of rhetorical means. Even in the discourse of the revolutionary assemblies there were those who manifested a taste for laconic polish, a love of decisive and trenchant formulas. From Aristotle to the Enlightenment, then, rhetoric had come full circle: the 18th century reaffirmed the ancient postulate that viewed the passions as the key to the art of oratory. But for writers such as Diderot, leaving the classical system behind also authorized every sort of audacity. Genius could not be confined to a body of precepts, to a series of rules that

must be respected. As an autonomous creative force, genius spread its wings in a violent and passionate eloquence.

The Role of Eloquence in 18th-Century Political Thought

During the 18th century men and women of letters were resolutely engaged in the quarrels and debates of their time. A leitmotif running through all contemporary works was that eloquence should allow all citizens to achieve full self-realization. In short, eloquence was seen as the indispensable instrument of the legislator: "Clothed in all the charms of eloquence," Mercier remarks, "the law will soon be carved in the hearts of all." Armed with this idea, Enlightenment thinkers from early on sought to understand the connection between forms of government and the development of eloquence. The notion of a close link between liberty and eloquence has a long history, and is expressed, for example, in Tacitus's *Dialogus de oratoribus* (Dialogue on Orators) and in Pseudo-Longinus's *Peri hypsous* (On the Sublime). This theme reappears in the works of Fénelon, D'Alembert, Voltaire, Hume, Diderot, and Rousseau. In the chapter entitled "Rapports des langues aux gouvernements" (Relationship between Languages and Governments) in his *Essai sur l'origine des langues,* Rousseau shows how eloquence is necessarily constrained under tyrannical governments, sometimes to such an extent that it becomes useless: "one needs neither art nor figures of speech to say, 'because it pleases me.'" Saint-Just makes the same point in chilling terms: "Have you seen orators under the royal scepter? No. Silence reigns around a throne." This is why Madame de Staël opens the chapter on eloquence in *De la littérature* with this strong statement: "In free countries, where the will of the nation decides its political destiny, people seek out and acquire the highest degree of influence to shape that will; and the foremost tool of influence is eloquence." A notable exception to this chorus of favorable opinions was Condorcet, who viewed eloquence as "the germ of a destructive corruption" (*Rapport sur l'instruction publique* [1792; Report on Public Education]).

The 18th-century critique of the oratorical genres thus took on a political dimension. The rejection of flattery is a recurrent theme in theoretical reflections on oratory. In his *Essai sur les éloges,* Thomas deplores excessive and unmerited panegyric, which had become "the scourge of the people by corrupting their princes." Hume disapproved of the speeches given on the occasion of admission to the Académie Française: "Having no worthy subject to discourse upon, they are forever being thrown into nauseating torrents of panegyric and flattery."

In Rousseau's work, the criticism of flattery is part a larger critique that rejected society's *politesse* (conventions of refinement) altogether. Like Diderot (whose *De la poésie dramatique* [1758; On Dramatic Poetry] includes the observation, "the more civilized a people is, the more refined, the less poetic its ways"), Rousseau does not limit his rejection of refinement to stylistic matters. His first important essay, *Discours sur les sciences et les arts* (1750; Discourse on the Sciences and Arts), links the development of the arts and sciences to the enslavement of subjugated peoples. In the *Essai sur l'origine des langues* Rousseau reiterates the same idea, transposing it into in the realm of language. For some authors, refinement was a "feeling for the nuances of language," but for Rousseau, as for Mercier, it encouraged an art born of ambition, flattery, and lies.

The revolutionary period more clearly exposed the oppositions between the classical aesthetic and the ideals that supplanted it in the course of the 18th century. From the perspective of the counterrevolutionaries, the Revolution embodied a plebeian culture, a culture of vandalism and vulgarity, built on the ruins of the ancient patrician civilization. It was no accident that the partisans of the classical aesthetic were also those people who were the most reluctant to admit the failings of the ancien régime. In their theoretical works on the subject, writers such as the comte de Rivarol and La Harpe underscored the value of good taste, beautiful language, and elegance and denounce the "fanaticism" of revolutionary language (La Harpe, *Du fanatisme dans la langue révolutionnaire* [1797; On Fanaticism in Revolutionary Language]). At the other end of the spectrum, authors such as Mercier wanted language to express a new energy—even to the point of welcoming neologisms: "Today, people ask only for sweet and fluent words, for grace and softness in language . . . It would be much better to remember words that are infrequently used or even to invent new ones." In opposition to the "softness" that Mercier deplored, men of the Enlightenment often preferred fiery eloquence: when Robespierre pronounced his approval of Rousseau, he invoked "his [Rousseau's] masculine and true eloquence that paints the charms of virtue in the colors of flame." In practice, however, such political and aesthetic polarities were not always clear-cut: one famous orator of the Counter-Revolution, the abbé Maury, author of *Principes d'éloquence* (1785; Principles of Eloquence), stood out precisely because of his violent and popular style, while the pompous rhetoric of Robespierre often elicited mockery from his colleagues.

It should be stressed that the linguistic research of the 18th century helped to pave the way for revolutionary eloquence. In the *Histoire philosophique et politique des établissements et du commerce des Européens dans les deux Indes* (1770; A Philosophical and Political History of the Settlements and Trade of the Europeans in the East and West Indies) by the abbé Raynal, Diderot tries his hand at producing an example of political eloquence worthy of both the orators of antiquity and the savages of the New World fighting for their freedom. The vehement tone of his polemic and his use of prosopopoeia and harangue turn historical discourse into an immediate call to arms. The innovations introduced by such writers as Voltaire, Diderot, Mercier, the marquis de Sade, stimulated the emergence of a new rhetoric. While the Constituent Assembly of 1789 was still dominated by traditional eloquence, Legislative Assembly of 1791—especially owing to the Jacobin presence—abandoned the old mechanical rhetoric in favor of a reinvigorated art of oratory. "In that time," according to the royalist Desmarais, "the language of Racine and Bossuet vociferated about blood and carnage; it roared with Danton; it howled with Marat; it hissed like a serpent in the mouth of Robespierre. But it remained pure."

The stakes were particularly high in the debate over eloquence during the 18th century. This was undoubtedly because the orator, like the legislator, was the figure that embodied the aspirations of all men of letters. In the words of Chrétien-Guillaume de Lamoignon de Malesherbes in his acceptance speech to the Académie Française:

> In an enlightened age, in an age in which every citizen can speak to the nation by way of its emotions, those who have the talent to instruct men and the gift to move them—men of letters, in short—play the same role among the dispersed public audience that the orators of Rome and Athens played among the assembled people.

The transition from belles lettres to the modern notion of "literature" involved the abandonment of traditional, normative eloquence in favor of a more unbridled eloquence. Nonetheless, the classical aesthetic did not entirely disappear. For the contemporaries of Voltaire and Diderot, the idea of natural eloquence was not incompatible with the existence of specific genres such as the panegyric or academic discourse. Despite these new models, however, the complaint about the "decline" of eloquence returned periodically in the 18th century: first at the dawn of the Enlightenment, when the art of oratory was still in mourning for the eloquence of antiquity, and later at the time of the Revolution, when those who wished for a return to the classical aesthetic struggled against an escalating aesthetic of the passions. The latter conflict, however, had a positive effect: when historical conditions were finally again favorable to the cultivation of deliberative eloquence, the eternal nostalgia for a golden age ended up producing a form of public speech that reinvigorated political discourse.

STÉPHANE PUJOL

See also Apologetics

Further Reading

Aulard, F.-A., *L'éloquence parlementaire pendant la Révolution française: Les orateurs de l'Assemblée constituante,* Paris: Hachette, 1882

Aulard, F.-A., *L'éloquence parlementaire pendant la Révolution française: Les orateurs de la législative et de la convention,* 2 vols., Paris: Hachette, 1885–86

Barthes, Roland, "L'ancienne rhétorique/Aide mémoire," *Communications* 16 (1970)

Fumaroli, Marc, *L'âge de l'éloquence,* Geneva: Droz, and Paris: Champion, 1980

Starobinski, Jean, "Rousseau et l'éloquence," in *Rousseau after 200 Years,* edited by R.A. Leigh, Cambridge and New York: Cambridge University Press, 1982

Empiricism

One can rather easily identify a broad philosophical current in the age of Enlightenment that it is appropriate to call "empiricism." Its origins are to be found in the work of Francis Bacon (1561–1626), notably in the *Novum Organum* (1620) and its praise of induction, as well as, more generally, in the opposition to the Cartesianism of English authors such as Thomas Hobbes (1588–1679) or French authors such as Pierre Gassendi (1592–1655).

John Locke (1632–1704), in his famous *Essay concerning Human Understanding* (1690), founded the empiricist current of thought, which largely dominated both the English and French Enlightenments. It was characterized by the refutation of innate ideas and the affirmation of the primacy of experience in the scientific method. However, it was not until the publication of Immanuel Kant's *Kritik der reinen Vernunft* (1781; Critique of Pure Reason), with its discussion of the thesis and antithesis within each of four pair of logical propositions, that the term *Empirismus* explicitly came to designate a type of philosophical doctrine. The *Encyclopédie* gave only the ancient meaning for empiricism: "a practice of medicine founded solely upon experience." Initially, the doctrine gained its identity through opposition to the major post-Cartesian metaphysical systems of Nicolas Malebranche, Baruch Spinoza, and Gottfried Wilhelm Leibniz and, more generally, through opposition to what was identified very early on as "rational philosophy," rather than through references to the authors of antiquity who had developed themes related to empiricism, such as Aristotle, Epicurus, or Lucretius.

In rational philosophy, "empirical," which is an adjective, refers to an inferior form of knowledge or a form of nonreflective activity: Leibniz maintained that "in the majority of our actions we are merely empirical." Leibniz's disciple Christian Wolff (1679–1754), who popularized dogmatic rationalism, contrasted *cognitio historica* (historical knowledge) to *cognitio philosophica* (philosophical knowledge, or knowledge through reason), in his *Philosophia rationalis sive logica* (1728; Rational Philosophy; or, Logic). Here *historica* is synonymous with *empirica*. This dichotomy is also found in the *Neues Organon* (1764; New Organon) by Johann Heinrich Lambert (1728–77) and in Kant's *Logik* (1800; Logic). Thus, Wolff contrasted his *Psychologia empirica* (1732; Empirical Psychology), a science that establishes through experience the principles explaining what occurs in the human soul, with his *Psychologia Rationalis* (1734; Rational Psychology), a science that establishes all the possibilities arising from the notion of the human soul. In fact, this second work seeks to explain the elements described in empirical psychology. The development of empiricism proceeds through a critique of reason's claim to go beyond experience; Kant retained this aspect of the doctrine and, although he gave empiricism its name, he intended to go beyond it with transcendental idealism.

Experimental Method

The mathematical physics of Galileo and René Descartes emphasized the use of abstract and rational principles. This emphasis found a perfect expression in the idea that science can be reduced to a synthetic discourse, *more geometrico*, following an order of reason, from first causes or first principles, that the cognizant subject discovers in the depths of understanding. In the 17th century, many scholars—the physician Thomas Sydenham (1624–89), who inspired Locke; Robert Boyle (1627–91) and the Royal Society; Sir Isaac Newton himself—rejected speculations that is not supported by facts: Rational evidence does not outweigh certainty. In writing his *Éloges* (Eulogies) of scholars for the Académie Royale des Sciences de Paris (French Royal Academy of Sciences), Bernard Le Bovier de Fontenelle (1657–1757) constantly praised the experimental method. In his *Pensées sur l'interprétation de la nature* (1754; Thoughts on the Interpretation of Nature), Denis Diderot does not hesitate to claim that " by now time has overturned almost all the edifices of rational philosophy." In Mangogul's dream in Diderot's novel *Les bijoux indiscrets* (1748; The Indiscreet Jewels), rational philosophy is the realm of hypothesis that collapses when experience makes its appearance. "Observation gathers facts," Diderot contends in *Pensées sur l'interprétation de la nature,* "reflection combines them; experience verifies the results of the combination."

Yet Diderot was not an empiricist; in his opinion "experimental philosophy" was a question of method and not a theory of understanding. This method was discussed throughout the century. In 1770 the Society of Sciences of Haarlem set the following question for a competition: "What is required in the art of observation, and to what degree does this art contribute toward perfecting understanding?" Jean Senebier (1742–1809) won the prize with a practical, if not very original, manual entitled *L'art d'observer* (1755; The Art of Observing, which was republished with additions as the *Essai sur l'art d'observer et de faire des expériences* [1802; Essay on the Art of Observing and Conducting Experiments]). For empiricism, conceived as a philosophical doctrine, the importance of the experimental method resides in the question of its extension. To be an empiricist is to maintain that all knowledge of reality without exception depends upon it. David Hume (1711–76), in his *Dialogues concerning Natural Religion* (1779), goes so far as to propose an experimental theist, in the character of Cleanthes.

Étienne Bonnot de Condillac (1714–80) further developed the theoretical consequences of this empiricist position in the most powerful work of philosophy of the Enlightenment, the *Traité des systèmes* (1749; Treatise on Systems). A system is nothing more than the arrangement of the different aspects of an art or a science into an order where they all offer mutual support and where the last will be explained by the first. The value of a system, therefore, depends upon its principles, which can be abstractions, hypotheses, or facts. Systems founded on the first two types of principles (the major metaphysical systems of the neo-Cartesians) are illusory. The only legitimate systems are founded upon

facts, such as Newtonian physics. In *Traité de l'art de penser* (1775; Treatise on the Art of Thinking), as well as in *Logique* (1780; Logic), Condillac returns to the experimental method, having recourse, where necessary, to the history of sciences (the discovery of atmospheric pressure by Evangelista Torricelli). He takes up the watchword already mentioned in passing in the *Essai sur l'origine des connaissances humaines* (1746; Essay on the Origin of Human Knowledge), the analytic method, which proceeds through the composition and decomposition of ideas. Above all, he clearly exposes the consequences of the experimental method for the ontology of knowledge. Knowledge can only expand within the sphere of our experience, where we meet the testimony of fact; beyond that point, we can know nothing, and reflection can only give birth to chimeras. The *Traité des systèmes* had already pointed this out: it is a natural tendency of the mind to link together abstract principles and to arrive at discoveries "which are the work of *pure understanding* [and] . . . truths which are entirely spiritual," Condillac contends. "Observe the human mind, and you will see in each century that everything is system, among the people as among philosophers."

This was the first formulation of what became, for Kant (who never cited Condillac), the "transcendental illusion" of reason. While Kant allowed that concepts without intuition (without empirical content) are empty, transcendental idealism consists of equally allowing the opposite and maintaining that intuitions without concept are blind. In this way he preserved a favored position for understanding and reason. If the claims of pure reason are unfounded, so are those of pure experience. Kant proposed a synthesis between rational philosophy and experimental philosophy, while preserving innateness in the adulterated form of the formal constitution of human understanding, and the role of abstract principles as ideas that regulate its functioning. For Condillac empiricism did not negate rationality: his theory of understanding suggested a genesis of it.

Empiricists did not even deny the preeminence of mathematics, in degree of certainty, over knowledge of the physical world, but this was precisely because mathematics offers no knowledge of the objective world. For Hume, mathematics concerned only the relation of ideas; Condillac explained the value of mathematics through the way it is constituted and the rigor of its semiotics (algebra is the one and only well-made language). The essence of empiricism is to recognize that the boundaries of our experience are the limits of our knowledge. From that point on, there are only two ways in which to envisage the value of knowledge according to objective criteria: to consider the exactness and the completeness of that knowledge, as Condillac specified. Knowledge is exact when all its elements correspond to facts; it is complete when all facts correspond to elements of knowledge. All knowledge must be exact (which eliminates abstract metaphysics), but not all our knowledge can be complete: although mathematics and theories of understanding are complete, physics can never be, because unlike understanding, the world is infinite. For empiricists, the truth was more a question of semantics than of syntax; they preferred truth as equivalence over truth as coherence, as propounded by Kant.

Theory of Understanding

The tabula rasa is not the primary dogma of empiricism; what is primary is the refutation of innate ideas. Nor is this refutation merely a piece of abstract theory: it results in a reversal of the way in which understanding is conceived. The idea is to apply the experimental method to understanding, no more and no less. In *A Treatise of Human Nature* (1739–40), Hume explains clearly that the goal is to found a new science that will be for the mind the counterpart of what Newton had done for nature. Hume sees in the concept of the association of ideas the equivalent of universal gravitation. In his treatise *De l'esprit* (1758; Essays on the Mind and Its Several Faculties), Claude-Adrien Helvétius (1715–71) declares his intention to imitate the method of experimental physics. Following from the rejection of innate ideas, one now has to observe the development of the mind and be alert to the information and facts provided by the thoughts of children or of other peoples. The discussions initiated by William Molyneux (1656–98), who presented Locke with the problem of knowing whether a blind man who suddenly regained his sight would be able to identify the objects he saw, took an indisputably empirical turn. The experiment involving a reduction of cataracts in a man born blind (1728) only accentuated the direction the debate was taking. If the facts seemed to contradict innateness, all that remained to explain knowledge was to admit that it was a result of a flow of information procured by our senses. In *An Essay towards a New Theory of Vision* (1709), then in *A Treatise concerning the Principles of Human Knowledge* (1710), popularized in *Three Dialogues between Hylas and Philonous* (1713), George Berkeley (1685–1753) accepts this theory, which—going beyond Locke—not only limits knowledge to sensation but also reduces human beings themselves to sensation.

Many of the philosophers of the Enlightenment were confronted with the problem of explaining how cognition appears in the mind; their theory of understanding had to confront the difficult question of the origins of abstract and general ideas. Their answers varied: Condillac, following Locke on this point, described a process of abstraction, as did a majority of authors; Berkeley and Hume favored the association of particular ideas. All of these philosophers had recourse to a genetic theory of the mind, a theoretical form that was the great innovation of empiricist thought. In this approach thinkers often placed emphasis on the role of signs, making language central to the theory of knowledge. One cannot stress too much the novelty of the problems engendered by the empiricist conception of understanding. In his second work, *De l'homme, de ses facultés intellectuelles, et de son éducation* (1772; On Man, His Intellectual Capacities, and His Education), Helvétius wonders if "the present inequality of minds" is determined by an inequality of organs, or by differences in education. He provides an answer by noting that humans do not all share the same desire to learn and that it is by chance that they find themselves in "different positions." Empiricism eventually led to discussion of the mind as placed in the context of society and history, an approach defended by the marquis de Condorcet (1743–94) in the *Esquisse d'un tableau historique des progrès de l'esprit humain* (1795; Outlines of an Historical View of the Progress of the Human Mind).

The Empiricist Doctrine

Empiricism can be reduced to a few simple theses: the primacy of sensory impressions; the correspondence of the impression and the idea; the possibility of reducing all complex ideas to simple elements. This radical breakdown to the particular runs into a few difficulties (for Hume, for example, time and space cannot derive from a particular impression), which can be resolved by making the stages in the development of reason or ideas more complex. In short, the thesis of empiricism is that reason does not arise directly. For Hume, it was founded in the principles of the imagination (contiguity, resemblance, causality), and imagination could no longer be viewed as something wild and unchecked and so could no longer be reviled by rationalism; for Condillac, empiricism was founded on the faculty of analogy that guides the construction of our ideas. Our ethical activity itself depends not on abstract rational principles but on a moral sense (Hume) or on feelings of pleasure and displeasure. In the preface to the *Nouveaux essais sur l'entendement humain* (1704; New Essays concerning Human Understanding), not published until 1765, Leibniz accepts Locke's (and Aristotle's) principle that there is nothing in the mind that was not originally in the senses, but he adds *"nisi intellectus ipse"* (except the intellect itself). It is difficult to do without a ghost in the machine. Along with the senses, Locke accepts reflection as another source of ideas. In *Émile, ou, De l'éducation* (1762; Émile; or, Concerning Education), Jean-Jacques Rousseau allows for innate ideas in order to preserve human liberty. For the Dane Johannes Nikolaus Tetens (1736–1807), in his *Philosophische Versuche über die menschliche Natur und ihre Entwicklung* (1777; Philosophical Investigations on Human Nature and Its Development), *Selbsthätigkeit* (spontaneity) is the primary faculty. The question of the spontaneity of understanding, taken up by Kant, was one of the weapons to be used against empiricism: To ensure the independence of the mind, one must imagine a faculty that is innate as well as mysterious.

The solution proposed by Hume or Condillac is much more profound. The natural relationships that, for Hume, organize the flow of sensations and their associations are not substantial entities in the way that Leibniz's intellect is; according to Hume, these relationships are forces that can be evaluated by their effects and for which an ontological hypothesis is no more imaginable than it was for Newton and gravitation. According to Hume, through their unconscious and unstoppable activity, the natural relationships give birth to philosophical relationships that the subject of knowledge can manipulate at will. The same problem is treated in a semiotic fashion by Condillac in his *Essai:* when we enter into contact with the world, we have sensations aroused in us by the appearance of analogous things, at the whim of circumstances (the circumstances being the accidental signals for the sensations); repetition will cause us, one day, to evoke our sensations at will, for they will have become the "arbitrary" signs (depending on the arbiter) of things. Self-organization ("custom" for Hume; "habit" for Condillac) gives birth to the embryo of a mind, which will henceforth develop out of a conscious activity and whose reality is totally functional.

Hume and, to an even greater degree, Condillac carried empiricism to its fullest: in their theories, traditional human faculties lose all substantial reality and are not excluded from the general process of development applicable to knowledge. These were the theoretical givens that were progressively abandoned by the Ideologues as they became a major part of French intellectual life and discussion. Antoine-Louis-Claude Destutt de Tracy (1754–1836) gave volition an essential role in his *Traité de la volonté et de ses effets* (1815; Treatise on the Will and Its Effects), the fourth volume of *Éléments d'idéologie* (Elements of Ideology), begun in 1804 with a first volume, *L'idéologie proprement dite* (Ideology Proper). Maine de Biran (1766–1824), after his dissertation *L'influence de l'habitude* (1802; The Influence of Habit), went on in his *Essai sur les fondements de la psychologie et sur ses rapports avec l'étude de la nature* (1812; Essay on the Foundations of Psychology and on Its Relations with the Study of Nature) to research the primitive fact of the innate senses: effort alone is the true foundation of psychology; effort implies two terms and the consciousness of their distinction; the nature of effort is hyperorganic.

One can understand that some retreated fearfully from empiricism, given the boldness of the ideas put forth. The Scottish common sense school struggled constantly to limit the consequences of Hume's doctrine, and Kant remarked that this doctrine seemed to deprive morality and religion of all their power. In contrast to his *Treatise of Human Nature,* Hume's *Inquiry concerning Human Understanding* (1748) insists less on natural relationships and the association of ideas than on an analysis of causality. The idea of necessary connection loses all objective foundation. The question of necessity was the last point shared between rationalism and empiricism. For Leibniz, innateness was not the affirmation of an immediately transparent cognitive content, present unto itself: even the principle of identity and that of contradiction can fail to be known in an explicit way. Their necessity is nonetheless recognized reflexively: it is the necessity of relationships that justifies innateness. Kant understood the concept of necessity perfectly: His task was to preserve the necessary aspect of scientific knowledge. He invented the extraordinary artifice of distinguishing between foundation and origin: experience is the origin of our knowledge (a question of fact), experience is not the foundation of knowledge (question of right); for the foundation to preserve its necessity, it must reside in the constitution of the human mind on which phenomena depend. One must of course distinguish between right and fact, but what empiricism attests to is that right is nothing but fact: right is not the fact on which right can legislate, but it is subject to an origin and a history.

The glory of empiricism is to renounce the absolute. The assurance of scientific knowledge is a question of exactitude, not of necessity. Does that position automatically imply materialism, as "right-thinking" people proclaimed? Helvétius was a materialist, as were the Englishmen David Hartley (1705–57) and Joseph Priestley (1733–1804). Materialism, where the theory of understanding is concerned, consists of identifying the operations of the mind with those of the brain. That is what the baron d'Holbach (1723–89) does in *Le système de la nature, ou Des lois du monde physique et du monde moral* (1770; The System of Nature; or, The Laws of the Moral and Physical World). Knowledge is a reasonable possibility, not a necessity. In *Siris* (1744), Berkeley, an advocate of immaterialism, maintains that phenomena are merely appearances in the soul and cannot be explained by mechanical causes. Condillac readily accepted that the soul or the mind are realities distinct from matter. Empiricism is first and foremost a theory of what the French call *l'esprit*—in the sense of "the mind," as opposed to "spirit"—which leaves open the question of the mind's relationship to the brain.

SYLVAIN AUROUX

See also Idea; Ideology and Ideologues; Imagination; Materialism; Medicine; Physics, Experimental; Sensationalism

Further Reading

Auroux, Sylvain, *Barbarie et philosophie*, Paris: Presses Universitaires de France, 1990

Bennett, Jonathan Francis, *Locke, Berkeley, Hume: Central Themes*, Oxford: Clarendon Press, 1971

Malherbe, Michel, *La philosophie empiriste de David Hume*, Paris: Vrin, 1976

Smith, Norman Kemp, *The Philosophy of David Hume: A Critical Study of Its Origins and Central Doctrines*, London and New York: Macmillan, 1941

Encyclopedia

The 18th century was the age of general encyclopedias intended for a broad spectrum of readers who were hungry for knowledge accessible in their own language. Unlike the "partial" encyclopedias of earlier periods, the 18th century saw the publication of encyclopedias that covered all branches of learning, thus making a broad spectrum of knowledge available to everyone. The alphabetical arrangement of the articles—the description of a plant might be followed by a discussion of a point of theology—put encyclopedias in the same category as dictionaries; at the same time, they facilitated the dissemination of knowledge that was accessible to a general audience. The exclusion of certain topics, such as biography, and the inclusion of other, more popular ones suggests that the primary aim of Encyclopedists was to produce works that were, above all, lively. The Encyclopedists' use of plates, a feature that dictionaries lacked but that encyclopedias always included in order to illustrate the material treated in the text, reveals their strong pedagogical preoccupation. A rapidly expanding book trade, the collaboration of a number of enterprising booksellers, and the enthusiastic response of a number of segments of society all contributed to the success of these encyclopedias.

The encyclopedic movement was dominated by two major undertakings in French and English, respectively: Jean le Rond D'Alembert and Denis Diderot's *Encyclopédie, ou Dictionnaire raisonné des sciences, des arts, et des métiers* (Encyclopedia; or, A Reasoned Dictionary of Sciences, Arts, and Trades) and the *Encyclopaedia Britannica*. These projects were preceded by several dictionaries published in England, specifically John Harris's *Lexicon Technicum; or, An Universal English Dictionary of Arts and Sciences* (1704; further editions in 1708, 1710, and 1736; Supplement in 1744); Thomas Dyche's *New General English Dictionary* (1735); and, above all, Ephraim Chambers's *Cyclopaedia; or, General Dictionary of Arts and Sciences* (1728; republished in 1738, 1739, 1741, 1742, 1746, 1751–52; Supplement, 1753; further editions, 1778–1802). In fact, Chambers's work may be regarded as the model for the *Encyclopédie*, since at the outset the *Encyclopédie* was supposed to be simply a translation of it. Italian translations of the *Cyclopaedia* were published in Naples, Venice, and Genoa. Published in two volumes with the articles arranged in alphabetical order, Chambers's *Cyclopaedia* drew on earlier sources for both the text and its 20 plates.

The Paris *Encyclopédie*

The *Encyclopédie* consisted of 17 volumes of text and 11 volumes of plates. The first 7 volumes of text were published in Paris by Briasson, David, Le Breton, and Durand between 1751 and 1757; the remaining 10 volumes appeared in 1765, under the imprint of Samuel Faulche and Company, Neuchâtel. The work was based on the English models cited above but also on the work published by the Académie Royale des Sciences de Paris (French Royal Academy of Sciences). Rather than propagating erudite learning in the manner of their 17th-century predecessors, the editors were interested in a more practical knowledge, even if the compilation methods remained traditional.

The publication of the *Encyclopédie* was rather eventful and took place in three distinct phases. The first, from 1747 to 1752, was largely devoted to the gathering of material and editorial organization. Volumes I and II appeared in June 1751 and January 1752, respectively. This first phase was brought to a close by the scandal surrounding the abbé de Prades's articles, some of which were deemed subversive or heretical—a scandal that led to the banning of the *Encyclopédie*. The second phase, from 1752 to 1759, saw the publication of Volumes III through VII and was characterized by extremely strained relations among the booksellers, the Parlement of Paris, the Church, and the king's executives. In January 1759 the Parlement revoked the *Encyclopédie*'s *privilège* (permit to publish), originally granted in 1746, and condemned the work, along with Claude-Adrien Helvétius's book *De l'esprit* (1758; Essays on the Mind and Its Several Faculties). The final years (1759–72) were relatively calm, as the project was brought to a close. Despite the official ban on the work itself, a new *privilège* was granted to the booksellers for the volumes of plates that were to accompany the text. However, this final phase of publication was not without its difficulties. There was the affair of the plates "plagiarized" from the Académie des Sciences by the *Encyclopedie*'s engravers. In addition, the printer Andre-François Le Breton took it on himself to censor texts he found too daring. However, thanks to a tacit agreement, Volumes VIII through XVII—printed in France but with a Neuchâtel address on the title page—appeared in 1765. A lawsuit on behalf of a disgruntled subscriber, Luneau de Boisjermain, brought the turbulent publication history to a close.

The editorship had initially been offered to the abbé Gua de Malvès, but in 1747 it was entrusted to D'Alembert and Diderot. Diderot would remain sole editor after D'Alembert's resignation in 1757. The introductory texts of the *Encyclopédie*—the *Discours préliminaire* (Preliminary Discourse) setting out the aims and organization of the work, the *Avertissement* (Foreword) that prefaced Volume III, and the various *Éloges* (Eulogies)—were all written by D'Alembert. He was also responsible for roughly 1,600 articles signed with the symbol "O," most of which dealt with the exact sciences. Diderot's role in the production of the *Encyclopédie*, both as editor and author, was paramount. In addition to authoring approximately 5,250 articles signed with an asterisk and 5,000 unsigned ones, he added material to articles by other contributors when those pieces seemed inadequate. The nature and the extent of his contribution varied from volume to volume, according to the subject matter. As an author, he was primarily interested in three main topics: arts and technology, the history of philosophy, and—in Volumes I through V—synonyms. Diderot employed a consistent working method: using earlier sources, such as another dictionary or a more specialized treatise, he would either copy out entire paragraphs or sum up the essential information in a single sentence. His wide and varied vocabulary contributed to easy understanding.

Another major contributor was the chevalier de Jaucourt. Beginning with Volume II and continuing on through XVII, he wrote no fewer than 17,395 articles, on a wide range of subjects, from the natural sciences and geography to biblical criticism, morality, ancient history, and numismatics. The baron d'Holbach's contribution—which also began with Volume II—consisted of 425 signed articles dealing mostly with the earth sciences and a large number of other entries, both signed and unsigned, devoted to political and religious questions. Those articles were among the most outspoken entries in the *Encyclopédie* (for example, "Prêtres" [Priests] or "Représentants" [Representatives]). The other collaborators, more than 135 strong, came from varied social and intellectual backgrounds. They included Parisians, provincials, and foreigners chosen either for their professional knowledge or their personal expertise. Not all of these authors were chosen at the same time. In the early years, members of the clergy and friends of Diderot and D'Alembert predominated. As the project gathered momentum, famous names—such as the comte de Buffon, Louis Daubenton, Charles-Marie de La Condamine, Charles Pinot Duclos, François Quesnay, Jean-Jacques Rousseau, and Anne-Robert-Jacques Turgot—became associated with it. Civil engineers (Perronet, Voglie, Delacroix, and Viallet) made an important contribution, and the team of writers also included merchants and manufacturers.

The publishers chose a folio format for the *Encyclopédie*. The articles were arranged alphabetically in double columns, with an indication of the category to which they belonged. The author's name or his symbol (such as Diderot's asterisk) generally appeared at the end of each article. An elaborate system of cross-references was devised by the coeditors to show the relationships that existed among the different subjects treated. This system, in effect, enabled several authors to cover the same topic under different headings, encouraging the expression of a wide variety of opinions. On the other hand, the use of digressions in certain articles gave authors a way of denouncing ideas that they felt were too risky or unorthodox. According to D'Alembert's *Discours préliminaire*, the *Encyclopédie* should

> explain as completely as possible, the order and structure of human knowledge: as a Reasoned Dictionary of Sciences, Arts and Trades, it must contain the general basic principles, as well as the most essential details that make up the body and substance of each science and each art, whether liberal or mechanical.

D'Alembert and Diderot developed this point of view in their respective articles entitled "Dictionnaire" and "Encyclopédie." The different branches of knowledge were classified according to the system devised by Francis Bacon. It was based upon an individual's three fundamental faculties of memory, reason, and imagination, which became the bases for subsequent division into further categories and subcategories of knowledge. The category of memory encompassed all branches of history (sacred, ecclesiastical, civil, ancient, or modern), natural history, work, and the use of natural resources (arts and trades). In the category of reason were found philosophy (the science of God) and the human sciences. Fine arts were treated under imagination. Diderot and D'Alembert made few changes to this Baconian model. The chief goal of the *Encyclopédie* was to place the maximum amount of knowledge in the hands of the maximum number of readers. This concern to spread knowledge within the framework of categories was not without some problems: some articles could be judged to be too long or too short; others had inadequate references or were copied practically verbatim from existing sources.

From the start the *Encyclopédie* met with an enthusiastic response, as well as with vigorous criticism from many quarters. The editors' chief error, according to their critics, was to have systematically opposed all forms of authority. Religious circles, notably the Jesuits, waged a bitter campaign against the publication, finding certain articles on theological questions heretical, others dealing with Christianity overly critical, and those treating other religions unduly tolerant. D'Alembert's article "Collège" (Secondary School), which was highly critical of Jesuit methods of education, aroused a storm of protest. The article "Autorité politique" (Political Authority), which was unsigned but undoubtedly written by Diderot, disparaged the authority of the state and power in general, but it did not question the authority of the crown. The affair of the plagiarized plates, mentioned above, which brought the editors into direct conflict with the Académie des Sciences, was merely a pretext, behind which lay a much deeper issue. Most Academicians cared very little about the plates that had been engraved for René-Antoine de Réaumur; their real objection was that the *Encyclopédie* was threatening the intellectual hegemony of the Académie des Sciences whose authority previously had been unchallenged.

In addition to a handful of major critical articles, the publication as a whole is remarkable for the wide range of subjects treated: there is no greater testimony to the insatiable curiosity of the thinkers of the Enlightenment. At the same time, however, the *Encyclopédie* has inherent weaknesses. It could hardly be original: it would have been impossible for the editors to gather all of human knowledge and present it in a new light. Their dependence on earlier works, including that of Chambers, was inevitable; copying existing texts and images was a common practice at the time. Borrowing from other sources resulted in questionable choices, both of texts and of illustrations, and the inclusion of much out-of-date information. Geography, natural history, and the mechanical arts received excellent treatment, whereas the articles dealing with history and art were relatively weak.

The 11 volumes of plates, entitled *Recueil de planches, sur les sciences, les arts libéraux, et les arts mécaniques, avec leur explication* (Collection of Plates on Sciences, Liberal Arts, and Mechanical Arts, with Explanations) were published in Paris between 1762 and 1772. They are of crucial importance for the understanding of much of the text of the *Encyclopédie*—the many entries dealing with the arts and trades, anatomy, surgery, the pure and natural sciences, military sciences, and the fine arts. Diderot oversaw the publication of the illustrations, issuing instructions to the engravers and making corrections if the plates seemed unsuitable to him. In this area he and his collaborators were equally dependent on earlier publications. With the exception of a few drawings made by renowned engravers such as Boissieu or by specialized calligraphers or engineers, most of the plates were made by illustrators already established in the Parisian book trade. Charles Nicolas Cochin was responsible for the famous frontispiece.

The *Supplément*, the *Table*, and the Geneva and Neuchâtel Editions

The bookseller Charles Joseph Panckoucke was responsible for four parallel supplementary projects to the *Encyclopédie*, although his name was not openly linked to any of them: the *Supplément* and the *Table analytique* (Analytic Table) volumes, the Geneva folio edition, and the Geneva and Neuchâtel quarto editions. The history of these overlapping publications is extremely complex.

The *Supplément* was published in Bouillon by Pierre Rousseau's Société Typographique, under the supervision of Jean Baptiste René Robinet. The format is similar to that of the Paris edition, with identical typeface and the same alphabetical arrangement of entries. The four volumes of the *Nouveau dictionnaire des arts et des sciences* (New Dictionary of Arts and Sciences) were published in Paris and Amsterdam in 1776 and 1777, followed by a volume of plates, also in 1777. The editorial team for the *Supplément* was small; it included D'Alembert and several new collaborators, such as Michael Adanson, Daniel Bernoulli, the marquis de Condorcet, and Joseph Jerome de Lalande. There was an emphasis on exact science and medicine. Certain articles reflected contemporary issues and drew on the latest research (Condorcet on mathematics, the baron

Guyton de Morveau on crystallography); others were not original and were simply copied from earlier publications. The references were often identical to those in the Paris edition; in some cases, errors in the Paris version were corrected. The index or *Table analytique* was compiled by Pierre Mouchon and published in Paris and Amsterdam in 1780. It summarized all the volumes of the *Encyclopédie*.

The history of the Geneva folio edition runs parallel to that of the *Supplément*, with which it is closely linked. Panckoucke's initial idea was simply to reprint the Paris edition, but this was not allowed by authorities, which led to a complications. The first three volumes were seized by the police and held for several years; Volumes IV and V of the text, and the first volume of plates, were published in Geneva in 1771, followed by Volumes I, II, III, and VI through IX, as well as the second volume of plates in 1772, and by Volumes X through XVII of the text in 1773. There were eventually 11 volumes of plates instead of the 8 planned. Circumstances proved favorable to the Geneva edition. From 1774, with the accession of Louis XVI and the ministry of Turgot, it was allowed to circulate freely. The Geneva edition is often mistaken for the original.

The quarto edition variously called Geneva, Pellet, and Neuchâtel bore the Geneva bookseller Pellet's name on the title page; in fact it was printed at Lyon and in Switzerland. It was immensely successful and came out in a second edition, which was in fact just a reprint. A "third" edition came out in Neuchâtel with the imprint of the Société Typographique. Pirated copies of the quarto edition appeared in Avignon, Lyon, Nîmes, and Toulouse, but the energetic Panckoucke was largely able to stamp out the competition. The three versions, sometimes called the "Pellet" versions, of the *Encyclopédie* incorporate texts originally published in the *Supplément*. These quarto editions, which appeared between 1778 and 1789, consisted of 39 volumes, including 3 volumes of plates. Six volumes of *Tables*, similar to those that Pierre Mouchon had prepared for Panckoucke but adapted to the quarto format, were published by Amable le Roy in Lyon in 1780–81. The text in the Pellet editions was both corrected and augmented from previous works. The Société Typographique's foreword explained why the Neuchâtel edition was superior to the Geneva quarto. Both had far fewer plates than the original Paris edition; however, in the edition put out by the Société Typographique, plates for articles dealing with arts and trades were replaced by more detailed descriptions in the body of the text. For articles that had appeared in different versions in the Paris folio and the *Supplément*, whichever one seemed to have been "better treated" was chosen for inclusion.

Other Editions of the *Encyclopédie*

The Lucca folio encyclopedia was the earliest of the European reprints of the *Encyclopédie* to appear. This 28-volume work was published in Lucca, Italy, between 1758 and 1776, thanks to the initiative of Ottaviano Diodati, and it received support from prominent citizens of Lucca and the town senate. Since the Lucca folio edition reproduced the Paris edition, its publication history was equally checkered: Volumes I through VII appeared in 1758–60; VIII through XV from 1765 to 1770; XVI through XVII in 1771; and I through XI of plates (identical to the Paris edition) in 1765–76. Diodati added notes, made corrections and additions to entries that seemed inadequate, and, in some cases, substituted or even refuted certain texts.

The Leghorn (Livorno, Italy) folio encyclopedia was edited by Giuseppe Aubert and dedicated to his patron, Peter Leopold, archduke of Tuscany (the future emperor Leopold II of Austria). It is a reprint of the Paris edition, with notes taken from the Lucca folio and with additions made by Aubert. The 33 volumes appeared between 1770 and 1779 (I through XVII from 1770 to 1775, the five volumes of the *Supplément* in 1778 and 1779, Volumes I through XII of plates from 1772 to 1778).

The Bern and Lausanne (Switzerland) octavo edition was published in 1778 by the Sociétés Typographiques of Lausanne and Berne, publishers who had a longstanding reputation for issuing pirated editions of French books. Its more manageable format and substantially lower price (less than half that of the quarto edition) explain its success; it sold particularly well in Germany and was reprinted. The entire series was made up of 36 volumes of text (1778 onward) and 3 of plates (1780–81).

The *Encyclopédie d'Yverdon* was published from 1770 to 1780 under the editorship of Fortunato Bartolomeo de Felice, an Yverdon (Switzerland) publisher of Italian and Catholic origin who had converted to Calvinism. His declared intention was not just to reissue the Paris *Encyclopédie* but to "improve" and complete it. In fact, he completely transformed it. While retaining the alphabetical classification, he made additions and corrections and removed articles that were "of purely national interest" and those devoted to foreign languages. He had signed a contract with Panckoucke, which explains why some of the contributors to the *Encyclopédie d'Yverdon* also worked on the *Supplément*. However, the majority of Felice's collaborators were of Swiss background and were Calvinist, antiCatholic, antimaterialist and, for the most part, opposed to the spirit of the Paris *Encyclopédie*. The *Encyclopédie d'Yverdon* consists of 42 volumes of text (1770–75), a 6-volume *Supplément* (1775–76), and 10 volumes of plates (1775–80). Most of the plates were copied—in reduced format—from the Paris edition, although some were original.

Panckoucke's *Encyclopédie méthodique, ou par ordre de matières, par une Société de gens de lettres* (Methodical Encyclopedia, Organized by Subject Matter, by a Society of Men of Letters) was a project taken up by Panckoucke after it was started by a Liège bookseller. The idea was to rectify the weaknesses of the Paris edition; errors were to be corrected, additions and cuts made, and new articles inserted. The alphabetical arrangement of articles, which had been widely criticized, was abandoned in favor of a thematic organization, comprising in effect 26 mini-*Encyclopédies* that were meant to encompass the entire range of knowledge. Within each of these mini-*Encyclopédies,* however, the alphabetical classification is retained. Each volume has *Tables* and *Tableaux* (Charts) in which the most important facts concerning the topic under discussion are summarized. The system of cross-references of the Paris *Encyclopédie* was abandoned. The relationships among different subjects and different articles were neglected in this new system of classification. As for the text itself, Panckoucke retained only a small amount of the original material. Aside from some members of Diderot's team, most of the contributors were new. In the early years, Panckoucke's brother-in-law Suard played several roles at once, as author, proofreader, translator, and censor. Collaborators were chosen for their professional status rather than their real abilities; many were members of various royal academies. The legal profession, virtually absent from the Paris edition, was well represented; on the other hand, the *philosophes* were fewer in number. Scientists were given preferential treatment. The *Encyclopédie méthodique* ran into all sorts of financial and technical problems. Initially put out by Panckoucke in Paris and Plomteux in Liège between 1782 and 1792, the vast undertaking was continued by Henri Agasse, Panckoucke's son-in-law, from 1792 until 1832. Instead of the 42 volumes of text and 7 of plates originally planned, the *Encyclopédie méthodique* eventually comprised 157 volumes of text and 53 of plates; 5,943 of the illustrations were engraved under the direction of Robert Benard.

Responses to the *Encyclopédie*

The story of the *Encyclopédie* also includes the critical response that it provoked. The best known of these was Voltaire's *Questions sur l'"Encyclopédie" par des amateurs* (1770–72; Questions on the "Encyclopédie" from the Uninitiated), which reprinted several articles from the 1769 edition of his *Dictionnaire philosophique* (Philosophical Dictionary) and which was frequently

reprinted in its turn. The "amateurs" or "uninitiated" in question refuted many of the statements made in the *Encyclopédie;* at the same time, Voltaire took the opportunity to criticize Holbach's *Système de la nature, ou, Des lois du monde physique et du monde moral* (1770; The System of Nature; or, The Laws of the Moral and Physical World).

Many projects related to the *Encyclopédie*—such as reprints, revisions, abridged versions, and translations—failed to materialize. A prospectus for a new edition was published in Nice in 1771, but nothing came of it. However, some publications that consisted of partial reprints (or selections) were produced. They included the *Encyclopédie augmentée de l'histoire des hommes illustres* (1768; Encyclopedia in an Edition Enlarged with the History of Great Men); Joseph de la Porte's *L'esprit de l'"Encyclopédie" ou choix des articles les plus curieux, les plus agréables, les plus piquants de ce grand dictionnaire* (1768; new edition in 1798–1800; collected and ordered by M. Hennequin, edited by R. Ollivier, 1822, 15 volumes; The Spirit of the "Encyclopédie"; or, A Selection of the Most Curious, the Most Pleasant, and the Most Surprising Articles of This Great Dictionary); and the *Histoire générale des dogmes et opinions philosophiques depuis les plus anciens temps jusqu'à nos jours* (1769; General History of Philosophical Dogmas and Views from the Most Remote Times to Our Day). As early as 1752, there were plans for an English translation; a prospectus entitled *The Plan of the French Encyclopedia* appeared that year, together with an English version of D'Alembert's *Discours préliminaire*. This project was never realized, as was the case with similar schemes announced by Sir Joseph Ayloffe and Samuel Leacroft. There were also plans for German and Italian translations. In some instances, as in the case of the Russian version, partial editions were published. Translations of the *Encyclopédie méthodique* came out in Spain and in Florence—the latter under the continued patronage of Archduke Peter Leopold—while pirated editions appeared in Padua, Venice, Milan, Nice, and Liège. The spread of such publication projects all across Europe shows that the impetus behind the *Encyclopédie* was not simply a matter of financial gain, even though some of the publishers made a great deal of money out of such enterprises; rather, it came out of a profound need in European culture of the time.

Encyclopedias in Other Languages

For their part, the British had the *Encyclopaedia Britannica; or, A Dictionary of Arts and Sciences Compiled upon a New Plan,* sponsored by "a society of gentlemen of Scotland." It was produced by William Smellie (future secretary to the Society of Antiquaries of Scotland), the engraver Andrew Bell, and the printer Colin Macfarquar, all natives of Edinburgh. Fascicles of the first edition began to appear in 1768; the first volume was complete in 1769, the second in 1770, and the third in 1771. It contained 2,459 pages and 160 plates engraved by Bell. The publication of the *Encyclopaedia Britannica* probably accounts for the fact that the *Encyclopédie* had less influence in English-speaking countries than in other countries where French was spoken in educated circles. The Edinburgh editors adopted a quarto format, with the text set in double columns. Articles were arranged alphabetically, and the plates were incorporated into the text. The arts and sciences were treated in separate sections, under page-wide, large-type headings: philosophy, mathematics, mineralogy, natural history, medicine, anatomy, surgery, agriculture, and so on. Several new editions followed, including that of James Tytler (1778). The editions were usually followed by supplements; for example, those of George Gleig (3rd edition, 1801–03) and James Millar (4th and 5th editions, 1810 and 1817). Abraham Rees produced a revision of Chambers, entitled *Cyclopaedia; or, An Universal Dictionary of Arts and Sciences* (five volumes, 1778–88), which he later expanded to 45 volumes as *The New Cyclopaedia; or, An Universal Dictionary of Arts, Sciences, and Literature* (1819–20); this edition had 39 volumes of text, of which the last was an *Addenda and Corrigenda,* and 6 volumes of plates, including one on natural history.

There was a considerable vogue for encyclopedias in Britain, as evidenced by the large number that were produced at the end of the 18th century and the beginning of the 19th, both in London and in Edinburgh. Invariably announced as "dictionaries of arts, sciences, and literature," they were usually the collective work of "societies of gentlemen," whose opinions frequently contradicted one another. They included *The New Royal Cyclopaedia, and Encyclopaedia; or, Complete, Modern, and Universal Dictionary of Arts and Sciences* by Henry Boswell, Felix Stonehouse, and others (3 volumes, 1788); and the *Encyclopaedia Londiniensis* of John Wilkes (24 volumes, 1797–1829). The first American encyclopedia, *Encyclopedia; or, A Dictionary of Arts, Sciences, and Miscellaneous Literature,* was published in 1798 by Thomas Dobson (18 volumes with 542 plates) in Philadelphia.

Among the many German encyclopedias, the earliest was Johann Theodor Jablonski's *Allgemeines Lexicon der Kunste und Wissenschaften* (1721; 1748–67; General Encyclopedia of the Arts and Sciences). It was followed by the *Grosses vollständiges universal Lexicon* (The Large Complete Universal Encyclopedia) of J.A. Frankenstein and P.D. Longolius (1732–50; supplement by C.G. Ludovici, 1751–54). The *Deutsches Encyclo-*

pädie oder allgemeines Real-Wörterbuch aller Künste und Wissenschaften von einer Gesellschaft von Gelehrten (The German Encyclopedia; or, A General Dictionary of All the Arts and Sciences for an Association of the Learned) was published by H.H.G. Köster and J.F. Roos in 23 volumes, including one of plates (1778–1807). This work contained a system of cross-references that facilitated access to a wider body of knowledge; as with the Paris *Encyclopédie* and the English-language encyclopedias, the contributors frequently expressed contradictory opinions. Some of the works that appeared in this period were of a more specialized nature, such as Johann Georg Krünitz's *Oeconomische Encyklopädie oder allgemeines System des Staats-, Stadt-Haus und Landwirthschaft* (1787–91; The Economic Encyclopedia; or, A General System of National, Regional, and Local Economies) and its successor, the *Oeconomisch-technologische Encyklopädie* (Volumes 47 to 72, 1796–98; Volumes 73 to 221, 1798–54; Economic and Technological Encyclopedia). In the 19th century, several major German-language encyclopedias were published, notably that of Friedrich Arnold Brockhaus, the *Allgemeine Deutsche Real-Encyklopädie für die gebildeten Stände* (1819–20; General German Encyclopedia for the Learned Classes), frequently reprinted and with many supplements. In Vienna, the *Neuestes Conversations-Lexicon, oder allgemeine deutsche Real-Encyclopädie für gebilde Stände* (Newest Conversation Encyclopedia; or, A General German Encyclopedia for the Learned Classes) was published in 19 volumes between 1825 and 1856. The encyclopedia movement touched almost every country in Europe in the form of major and minor publications, some of which had a distinctly national character.

MADELEINE PINAULT SØRENSEN

See also Dictionary; Newspapers and Journalism; Republic of Letters; Technical Instruction

Further Reading

Becq, Annie, editor, *L'Encyclopédisme,* Paris: Aux Amateurs de Livres, 1991

Darnton, Robert, *The Business of Enlightenment: A Publishing History of the Encyclopédie, 1775–1800,* London and Cambridge, Massachusetts: Harvard University Press, 1979

Hardesty, Kathleen, *The Supplément to the Encyclopédie,* The Hague: Nijhoff, 1977

Kafker, Frank A., editor, *Notable Encyclopedias of the Seventeenth and Eighteenth Centuries: Nine Predecessors of the Encyclopédie,* Oxford: Voltaire Foundation, 1981

Kafker, Frank A., editor, *Notable Encyclopedias of the Late Eighteenth Century: Eleven Successors of the Encyclopédie,* Oxford: Voltaire Foundation, 1994

Kafker, Frank A., and Serena Kafker, *The Encyclopedists as Individuals: A Biographical Dictionary of the Authors of the Encyclopédie*, Oxford: Voltaire Foundation, 1988

Lough, John, *The Encyclopédie in Eighteenth-Century England and Other Studies*, Newcastle upon Tyne, Tyne and Wear: Oriel Press, 1970

Lough, John, *The Encyclopédie*, London: Longman, and New York: McKay, 1971; reprint, Geneva: Slatkine, 1989

Lough, John, "Encyclopédie," in *Dictionnarie universel des littératures,* edited by Beatrice Didier, vol. 1, Paris: Presses Universitaires de France, 1994

Pinault, Madeleine, *L'Encyclopédie*, Paris: Presses Universitaires de France, 1993

Energy

The idea of energy typified the break from classical thought that took place in Europe in the second half of the 18th century. This idea belonged to a new definition of language, of nature, and of human beings; these were no longer considered in terms of essence, but rather in terms of evolution, and were henceforth approached less from an analytic point of view and more from a global and dynamic understanding of them.

The idea of energy can be traced back to the writings of Aristotle. In the *Metaphysics,* he pairs *energeia* with *dynamis* in order to explain movement, based on the opposition between the possible and the real, between power and action. Aristotle's notion deals with reality and accomplishment, whereas energy in the modern sense designates power that can potentially effect work. As seen in *Nicomachean Ethics, energeia* (behavior, activity) is morally coupled with *ethos* (aptitude, manner). Finally, the passages of the *Rhetoric* that concern energy are fraught with uncertainty in that *energeia* (vivacity, the liveliness of a style) is sometimes confused with *enargeia* (clarity, the ability to reveal). These various Aristotelian meanings of energy were very widespread throughout the West, through latinization of the terms. In the vocabulary used by philosophers, *dynamis* became *potentia* and *energeia* became *actus.*

The word *énergie* in French sometimes referred to occult qualities or hidden virtues, but its usage was rather rare. In consequence, the term remained relatively untouched and was thus ripe for success as a new word in the 18th century. While *puissance* (power) and *acte* (action) were losing their value as terms of the former metaphysics, energy emerged as a new idea. In 1779 Madame Du Deffand wrote that the word *énergie* "has come into style and that nothing is written any more without using it." The term had undoubtedly remained in the specialized vocabulary of rhetoric.

However, because classical rationalism advocated an equivalence between words and things, languages were compelled to refine this equivalence in order to become more precise and, above all, clear; *energy* was still suspected of carrying a magical residue that would cause the word to be part of the thing, thereby sharing an essential power with it. Rationalism could not ignore the role played by sensitivity, emotion, and heart in linguistic exchange, but this role remained secondary to the drive toward rationality and semantic precision. The emotional dimension was emphasized only as part of a paradox or when exploring semantic limits.

The notions of the sublime and of *je ne sais quoi* (something indescribable) provide two examples of such exploration of boundaries. Yet the polemics triggered by these notions show just how much they threatened to shake the organization of classical thought when they surrendered their marginal status and became more widespread. *Je ne sais quoi* refers to the extrarational outer limits of communication, to everything that makes an art object or a person appealing or enticing for reasons that we cannot understand; it is a religious or aristocratic principle, for only the sacred or the social hierarchy can allow the rational norm to be transgressed in this way. The *Entretiens d'Ariste et d'Eugène* (1671; Conversations of Aristo and Eugene) by Father Bouhours shocked the upholders of strict rationalism. Without indulging in finalism, by searching for some form of romanticism in the *Entretiens,* one can at least show where the idea of energy would call into question classical rationalism from within.

The second borderline notion is that of the sublime—that which comes from God or from a power that exists beyond individual reason. When the aristocratic principle of *je ne sais quoi* and the religious principle of the sublime shed their quality of privilege and exclusivity, when they became widespread, then classical rationalism was subverted. These notions then belonged to the new sensationalist model of communication, according to which exchange involves sensitivity and is gauged in terms of emotional and energetic impact.

This model is championed in the *Lettre sur les aveugles* (1749; Letter on the Blind) and *Lettre sur les sourds et les muets* (1751; Letter on the Deaf and Mute), in which Denis Diderot dismantles the dominance of clear vision in the name of experimental trial and error and strength of expression. Similarly, Jean-Jacques Rousseau in his *Essai de l'origine des langues* (1763; On the Origin of Language) offers a historical and geographical interpretation of the contrast between clarity and energy. In James Harris's *Hermes* (1751) and in John Horne Tooke's *Epea Pteroenta; or, The Diversions of Purley* (1786), the energy of language is symbolized by Hermes or Mercury. Harris and, later, Wilhelm von Humboldt turned classical language into creative action, and tabular visibility into historical dynamism.

In parallel fashion, the fine arts went from the universality of the principle of imitation and of the pictorial model to the new principle of strength and to the distinction between the arts of space (painting, sculpture) and the arts of time (music, poetry). In his *Salons*, especially that of 1767, Diderot offers the model of a critique that seeks to do more than simply describe the works that it presents, that perceives the works as more than a simple reproduction of palpable reality. Under the banner of energy, Diderot relates human creativity to the major cycles of universal dynamism. The German philosophers theorized the dimension that in Diderot's work remained on the level of intuition and metaphor. The task of defining art as a force and as energy fell to the Leibnizian circles at the Berlin Academy and in particular to Johann Georg Sulzer, who, in 1765, delivered to the Academy a report on energy in the fine arts. This lecture is developed further in his *Allgemeine Theorie der schönen Künste* (1771–74; General Theory of the Fine Arts) and also inspired the articles for the *Supplément* to the *Encyclopédie*. This was this same theoretical movement that introduced *aesthétique* as a French neologism and defined art as energy. The abbé Charles Batteux attempted to reduce the fine arts to a single principle; this was rejected by Gotthold Ephraim Lessing, who, in *Laokoon* (1766; Laocöon: An Essay upon the Limits of Painting and Poetry), places poetry and painting in opposition in order to free them both of the mimetic imperative.

Music, which does not represent palpable reality, increasingly became the model of artistic activity; it was able to give shape to an ideal or even to create another world. Other artistic forms such as dance, architecture, and landscaping also laid claim to energy. Dance broke free of realistic representation and aimed at a concentration of gesture to affect the spectator. Architecture returned to basic forms of nature, pure forces capable of influencing both individuals and the future of society. Garden designs, which had been considered in terms of spatial effect and visibility, were henceforth founded on duration and movement; at every turn, they provided a surprise and a new effect. It was no coincidence that the adjective "romantic" was borrowed from English to describe French landscape and the art of gardens.

The modern concept of literature emerged in conjunction with the transition from a linguistics based on clarity to a linguistics based on expression; in the realm of aesthetics, there was a concomitant shift from imitation to creation. Whereas the belles lettres were defined by reference to codes and to a hierarchy of forms, literature was characterized by authenticity and originality. Seeking to transcend hackneyed models, decorum, and social norms, literature returned to a basic force, that of popular legends, or primitive mythology. Through its yearning for an original energy, literature opened the door to the future.

Central to the aesthetic debates of the Enlightenment, the idea of energy was also at the heart of the philosophical tension between materialism and spiritualism. The word "energy" designated the autodynamism of matter, thus establishing a materialist monism. The term can be found in John Toland's *Letters to Serena* (1704), and later in the baron d'Holbach's *Le Système de la nature, ou Des lois du monde physique et du monde moral* (1770; The System of Nature; or, The Laws of the Moral and Physical World), and in other writings by those in his circle. Gottfried Wilhelm Leibniz had abolished the essential difference between rest and motion. The materialist thinkers drew a distinction between visible, external movement, and invisible, internal movement. Diderot took up this distinction between inert sensibility and active sensibility in order to explain matter in motion versus living matter. In these texts, energy tends to be posited as an intrinsic property of bodies, but the idea of phenomena connected to exchange and change also appears.

The scientific concept of energy that emerges in the works of Thomas Young, Nicolas-Léonard Sadi Carnot, and William John Macquorn Rankine assumes that there is a triple continuity between action and reaction, movement and work, and heat and work. Carnot's first principle asserts that the conservation of energy in an isolated system and the transformation of energy from one state to another are equivalent in terms of energy. His second principle shows the loss of one part of the energy that changes into heat. Energy, which Aristotle had conceived as actualization, thus became virtual.

The semantic success of the word undoubtedly also explains how, by extension, it could designate human force or will. Just as virtue could refer to a referred moral norm or even to *virtu,* to virile nature, and just as the term *character,* which referred a type and a temperament, eventually came to designate personality or originality, so too *energy* became specific to man who was breaking away from simple determinism, imposing his creativity, leaving his mark on his surroundings. Human beings were defined less by their birth than by their work; the whole of humanity was defined less by its nature than by its potential. The idea of energy thus overturned all the normative structures and preestablished hierarchies. It blurred the arbitrary contrast between those of noble and those of modest birth, between virtue and vice (imposed by dogma), and between pleasure and suffering. Energy could be engaged by an elitism that justified the prerogatives of the strongest, or by a revolution that claimed rights through merit and work. It could emerge in immoralism, or indeed a certain kind of sadism, that identified energy with aggressiveness and crime; or in a new social morality free of the old hypocrisies. The idea of energy contributes to an understanding of the Enlightenment's shift toward romanticism, the transition from analytic thinking to synthetic thinking, from classical rationalism to dialectic logic—or, in still other terms, from Nature to History.

MICHEL DELON

See also Aesthetics; Architecture; Dance; Dynamics; Force; Materialism; Mechanics, Analytic; Music

Further Reading

Bethge, Wolfgang, *Das energische Prinzip: Ein Schlüsselbegriff im Denken Friedrich Schillers,* Heidelberg: Carl Winter, 1995

Carnall, Geoffrey, "The Quest for Energy," in *The Mid–Eighteenth Century,* by John Everett Butt, edited by Carnall, Oxford: Clarendon Press, and New York: Oxford University Press, 1979

Delon, Michel, *L'idée d'énergie au tournant des Lumières (1770–1820),* Paris: Presses Universitaires de France, 1988

Dixon, B. Lynne, *Diderot, Philosopher of Energy: The Development of His Concept of Physical Energy, 1745–1769,* Oxford: Voltaire Foundation at the Taylor Institution, 1988

Jost, Leonhard, *Sprache als Werk und wirkende Kraft: Ein Beitrag zur Geschichte und Kritik der energetischen Sprachauffassung seit Wilhelm von Humboldt,* Bern: Haupt, 1960

England

England was a much applauded nation in the 18th century, yet highly puzzling too. It was in many respects the envy of the Continent. Religious toleration and freedom of speech had largely been secured, thanks to the constitutional settlement following the Glorious Revolution of 1688–89, which had expelled the Roman Catholic and would-be absolutist James II (1633–1701) for a more constitutional monarch, William III (1650–1702). The mixed constitution, in which the powers of the monarch were legally balanced against the people represented in Parliament, avoided the extremes of despotism and democracy and secured the freedom of the individual and of property. England's fluid, dynamic social system was admired by those who condemned the ossified "feudalism" that was conspicuous in, for instance, Spain or Poland. England was highly inventive in the sciences and was developing a national literary tradition, while economic freedom and a thriving bourgeoisie aided commercial development and industrialization. The ideal of progress celebrated by the *philosophes* in many respects found its embodiment in England.

Yet commentators, at home and abroad, also found much to deplore. England's parliamentary politics appeared factional and corrupt; public spirit was markedly deficient. Neither monarchy nor Parliament was prepared to fund those grand programs of building and culture that were the glories of Bourbon Versailles or Habsburg Vienna. England had few profound thinkers to match Immanuel Kant (1724–1804) abroad or even Scotsmen such as David Hume (1711–76) or Adam Smith (1723–90). Hence, England wore a somewhat enigmatic air, and the English were a puzzle: wealthier and enjoying greater liberty than their continental fellows, yet (it was said) notoriously melancholy (suffering from the "English malady") and given to suicide. The question of the English Enlightenment thus involves a historical paradox.

Throughout the 18th century, *Aufklärer* (enlightened ones) of all nations revered English government, society, and opinion as the acme of Enlightenment. Anglophiles celebrated the British constitution, law, and freedom, the open weave of English society, its religious toleration and its prosperity. In his significantly titled *Lettres philosophiques, ou Lettres anglaises* (1734; Philosophical Letters; or, English Letters) Voltaire asserts that:

> The English are the only people upon Earth who have been able to prescribe limits to the power of kings by resisting them; and who, by a series of struggles, have at last established that wise government, where the prince is all powerful to do good, and at the same time is restrained from committing evil; where the nobles are great without insolence, though there are no vassals; and where the people share in the government without confusion.

A popular Paris comedy of the 1760s depicted the Anglomaniac who had "Hogard" and "Hindel" (William Hogarth and George Frideric Handel) on his lips, drank only tea, read nothing but William Shakespeare and Alexander Pope, and proclaimed: "The teachers of mankind have been born in London, and it is from them we must take lessons." Many aspects of English thought were eagerly taken up on the Continent. Deism sped to France through the writings of John Toland, Matthew Tindal, Anthony Collins, William Wollaston, and Thomas Woolston and also through texts by those scions of aristocratic natural religion, the earl of Shaftesbury and Lord Bolingbroke.

Moral benevolism also flowed to the Continent from English sources: John Locke and Shaftesbury, Joseph Addison and Richard Steele. Denis Diderot's lifelong passion for *virtu* began when he translated Shaftesbury. Other *philosophes* admired Alexander Pope's *Essay on Man* (1745), while Jean-Jacques Rousseau approved of Addison. Nor was exporting less brisk in the natural sciences, where Sir Isaac Newton's physics flooded into France through many channels, not least Voltaire. Likewise, in practical knowledge, the great *Encyclopédie* itself arose from a scheme to translate Ephraim Chambers's *Cyclopaedia*.

English letters exerted considerable fascination too. Daniel Defoe's *Robinson Crusoe* (1719) took Germany by storm—by 1760 more than 40 continuations had appeared—and English bourgeois sentimental drama and novels ravished European hearts: "O Richardson, Richardson, man unique in my eyes," apostrophized Diderot, "thou shalt be my reading at all times!"

Abundant contemporary evidence thus proves the importance of English developments to the Enlightenment. Yet major Enlightenment historians of varied nationalities—Ernst Cassirer, Georges Gusdorf, Peter Gay, and so on—have tended to play down the English contribution. Cassirer's *Die Philosophie der Aufklärung* (1932; The Philosophy of the Enlightenment) omits David Hartley, Bernard Mandeville, Thomas Malthus, Joseph Priestley, Thomas Paine, Bolingbroke, Jeremy Bentham, Erasmus Darwin, Samuel Richardson, and Defoe.

There are three main reasons why historians have tended to downplay the significance of the Enlightenment in England: the assumption that the Enlightenment must necessarily have been essentially *French;* the idea that it must have been *atheistic;* and the notion that it must have been politically *revolutionary.* If we, however, forget these anachronistic prejudices, we can begin to see the real nature of the Enlightenment in England.

Certainly, England produced no text comparable to Kant's *Kritik der reinen Vernunft* (1784; Critique of Pure Reason). But why should systematic theorizing be the touchstone of Enlightenment? The real intelligentsia was not chair-bound but worked in the marketplace, or what Jürgen Habermas has called the public sphere. Ideas were soon seen as a trade, produced for a wide popular readership. "It was said of Socrates," wrote Addison,

> that he brought philosophy down from heaven to inhabit among men; and I shall be ambitious to have it said of me, that I have brought philosophy out of closets and libraries, schools and colleges, to dwell in clubs and assemblies, at tea-tables and in coffeehouses.

Forming a coffee-table philosophy, English opinion was concrete, practical, entertaining. And writers occupied many niches.

The cardinal fact is that in England, and in England almost uniquely, the realization of Enlightenment hopes was not thwarted by the existing order of state and society. Quite the reverse was the case. In England after 1688–89, the constitution itself incorporated central Enlightenment demands, such as personal freedom under *habeas corpus,* representative government, religious toleration, and the sanctity of property. Furthermore, neither censorship, economic regulation, nor unbending social proprieties prevented the affluent, articulate, and ambitious from chasing their own personal Enlightenment goals, such as free speculation or the pursuit of wealth or happiness. In England the educated and propertied who espoused Enlightenment rationality did not need to storm barricades, for by application of intellect alone they could succeed within the rules of the game.

Hence, the Enlightenment in England was marked by its pragmatism. Foreign visitors marveled at the busyness, practicality, and resourcefulness of England's thriving hive. The Swiss-American Louis Simond proclaimed that "the English are great in practical mechanics." Characteristically, English religion was esteemed for being oriented toward deeds, not words. "Religion in England," wrote the abbé Prévost, "in towns, and even in the smallest villages finds its expression in hospitals for the sick, homes of refuge for the poor and aged of both sexes, schools for the education of the children."

On the other hand, enlightened Englishmen felt contempt for Continental backwardness. Finding peasants in the Palatinate "poor and wretched," Mrs. Montagu chorused the Enlightenment contrast between them and their "princes so magnificent." The novelist Tobias Smollett lamented:

> such signs of poverty, misery, and dirt, among the commonalty of France, their unfenced fields dug up in despair, without the intervention of meadow or fallow ground, without cattle to furnish manure, without horses to execute the plans of agriculture, their farmhousemen, their furniture wretched, their apparel beggarly; themselves and their beasts the images of famine,

and he drew the predictable Enlightenment conclusion: "I cannot help thinking they groan under oppression."

The point is that this pragmatism did not result from a traditional attachment to the good things of this world. It was a philosophy of expediency, an art of living well, integral to the liberation and the limitations prescribed by English Enlightenment consciousness, following Locke's notion that "our business here is not to know all things, but those which concern our conduct." The Enlightenment sanctioned the pursuit of happiness, and to this end Englishmen set about manufacturing a consumer society of objects and opportunities and also the practical skills needed to manage a capitalist economy taking off into industrial growth.

A key dilemma faced enlightened Englishmen: how could one create a society that allowed individuals to pursue life, liberty, wealth, and happiness, but that nevertheless possessed the stability required to preclude anarchy? The English Enlightenment had certainly come riding in on the wave of rampant assertions of rights. Lockean liberal individualist prescriptions became definitive for enlightened minds. Each man best knew his own interests, which drove his quest to maximize happiness. "Virtue is the conformity to a rule of life," explained the Reverend John Gay, "directing the actions of all rational creatures with respect to each other's happiness; . . . obligation is the necessity of doing or omitting any action in order to be happy." "Whatever is expedient," wrote the Reverend William

Paley, glossing Alexander Pope, "is right." The rightness of self-interest meant that, in Joseph Priestley's words, "it is most advisable to leave every man at perfect liberty to serve himself, till some actual inconvenience be found to result from it."

In practice, egoism also had a free run. The arguments from Locke to Jeremy Bentham for private property and laissez-faire bore fruit in economic liberalism, the freedom of capital. In a parallel way, it has recently been argued that it was Enlightenment England that saw, among the gentry and professional classes, the first flowering of affective individualism: greater freedom of choice in spouses and a degree of emancipation for women from male dominion, as well as more freedom for children from the paternal rod. Writers and artists won freedom from the straitjacket of the patron. "How sweet this bit of freedom really is!" exclaimed Joseph Haydn in 1791, on one of his visits to London. "I had a kind prince, but sometimes I was obliged to be dependent on base souls. I often sighed for release, and now I have it in some measure."

This liberation from the past, from tradition, from the judgment of society, elders, and peers could be dared because optimism was programmed into Enlightenment consciousness. Faith grew regarding human nature: Locke taught that man was not flawed by original sin; what Priestley called man's "endless cravings" produced progress; man could educate himself; knowledge was limitless. Optimism arose about nature: Newton's universe, like the society envisioned by the political economists, was composed of individualistic atoms, yet its sum was a harmonious and glorious economy, which, through science and technology, man had a right to dominate. And an optimism developed about the divine order: God's rational benevolence dissolved the theodicy problem; evil was an illusion once the invisible hand had not only dictated that self-love and love of society were the same but also made progress the result of selfishness. Private vices were, as Mandeville argued, public benefits. Egoism was therefore natural, because self-interest could be enlightened. In Shaftesbury's sanguine formulation: "The wisdom of what rules, and is *first* and *chief* in nature, had made it to be according to the private interest and good of every-one, to work towards the general good." Or, in Frederick Eden's more bourgeois terms, "the desire of bettering our condition . . . animates the world [and] gives birth to every social virtue."

Thus encouraged, 18th-century Englishmen seized the chance to express themselves, to indulge their feelings, to escape from the traditional disciplines of custom and Calvinism. Acquisitiveness, high living, sexual and emotional exploration, social climbing, and the delights of fashion were freed from the moral and religious restraints of guilt, sin, and retribution. Parental authority toward children was relaxed. Humanitarianism awakened sympathy toward lunatics and animals, and campaigns to emancipate slaves. Enlightened elites had to reassure themselves, however, that subjective emancipation, humanitarianism, and the relaxation of formal discipline could, in practice, be won without social collapse. The Civil War (1642–46) had scarred the mind. The challenge flung down by Hobbes stated that if man were utterly individualistic, the Leviathan alone could curb his excesses.

The special quality of the social ethics of the English Enlightenment lay in demonstrating how to make the world safe for egoism—how order could be sustained within an individualistic ethic. And solutions expressed in sermons, manuals of conduct, and periodicals had to reckon with two special features of English society. First, having abolished absolutism, Enlightenment elites were confronted with a boisterous and assertive plebeian voice. Elites could not directly suppress the masses but must negotiate with them. Madame du Bocage did not mince words: "In France we cringe before the great, in England the great cringe before the people."

Second, England's free-market economy, licensed by Enlightenment individualism, was growing by means of rising consumption throughout the social spectrum. With the growth of service industries, and the commercialization of leisure and knowledge, an expanding middle class could newly influence matters in the cultural preserves of the traditional elite. "It is evident," observed Madame Roland, "that man, whatever he may be, is here reckoned something, and that a handful of rich does not constitute the nation."

In these circumstances, with assertive claims for freedom passing down the social order, Enlightenment opinion mapped out two strategies for socializing egoism within a stable social fabric. The first lay in embracing inclusiveness. The pioneers of the Enlightenment were propertied elites, yet they expounded a universal ideology. Reason was—potentially—a comprehensive attribute, including even women. The best bid for harmony was to assimilate as many sections of society as possible within enlightened values, to welcome all who qualified themselves for admission by their industry, rationality, civility, or wealth. Stability might be won through hegemony: through the universality of the law, mobility on the basis of merit and patronage, the minimalization of formal civil disabilities, and capitalization on rising expectations. Other, unenlightened, people were to be stigmatized. Religious fanatics, obdurate criminals, and the idle and undeserving poor threatened the consensus, and so they were subjected to what became severe social discipline. However, in a society that set little store by blood and still less by predestination, few were excluded on the grounds of birth alone.

In fact, there were two main tactics for comprehension. One lay in paternalism. The threatening glare of the destitute, the mad, the sick, and the fallen could be bought off by a humanitarian generosity that confirmed rank even as it palliated suffering. Enlightened sentiment—rather than exclusively Christian piety—swelled a spring tide of voluntary charitable foundations of schools, hospitals, dispensaries, asylums, and reformatories. The beauty of philanthropy lay in enhancing among the elite feelings of the superiority of their own sensibility.

The other mode of assimilation lay in social *openness*. Foreigners observing "the Quality" were struck by their choosing to mingle with the people. The Prussian Pastor Moritz was surprised that in England "officers do not go in uniform but dress as civilians." The coffeehouse was a special place, said Prévost: "What a lesson to see a lord, or two, a baronet, a shoemaker, a tailor, a wine merchant, and a few others of the same stamp poring over the same newspapers. Truly the coffeehouses . . . are the seats of English liberty."

Bath, that most genteel and enlightened of the resorts, was open to anyone with money in his pocket, so long as he kept to the rules enforced by that enlightened despot of etiquette, "Beau" Nash. As Smollett describes it, through his dyspeptic character Matt Bramble,

> every upstart of fortune, harnessed in the trappings of the mode, presents himself at Bath, as in the very focus of observation—Clerks and factors from the East Indies, loaded with the spoil of plundered provinces; planters, negro-drivers, and hucksters . . . agents, commissaries, and contractors . . . usurers, brokers, and jobbers of every kind; men of low birth, and no breeding . . . all of them hurry to Bath, because here without any further qualification, they can mingle with the princes and nobles of the land . . . Such is the composition of what is called the fashionable company at Bath; where a very inconsiderable proportion of genteel people are lost in a mob of impudent plebeians.

Many Englishmen were able to share Enlightenment aspirations for amusement, social emulation, the pursuit of taste, novelty, and fashion. Enlightenment culture created an enviable world within reach of the masses. John Newbery sold improving children's books for those

> Who from a State of Rags and Care,
> And having Shoes but half a Pair;
> Their Fortune and their Fame would fix,
> And gallop in a Coach and Six.

The Enlightenment creed of self-improvement and progress offered incentives to the lower orders to turn themselves bourgeois. Money became the universal language of social commerce.

This open market in possessive individualism created common goals in what seemed, especially to foreigners, a society dangerously lacking traditional formal discipline and the spirit of subordination. And this drive toward inclusiveness informed other facets of the English Enlightenment mind. Whereas militant French *philosophes* represented the world in contending opposites—light versus dark, body versus soul, humanity versus priestcraft—and whereas Immanuel Kant's critical philosophy bifurcated into profound dualisms, English thought went for comprehension: individual and society, trade and gentility, conscience and self-love, science and religion, Locke's sensations and reflection, and notably Priestley's monistic fusion of matter and spirit. The tragic paradoxes of Stoic humanism and the otherworldly solutions of Augustinian Christianity were abandoned for faith in man's progressive ability to remold—even perfect—himself and surmount dichotomies.

Faced with the Enlightenment dilemma of how to prevent hedonistic liberty from turning self-destructive, one bid for order thus lay in the progressive equilibrium resulting from the mechanics of open market forces. The other lay in establishing a rational framework of cosmic order and moral imperatives. History appeared a saga of rudeness and barbarity tempered by despotism. Seventeenth-century fanaticism had resulted in full-scale civil war and a king beheaded. Enlightenment opinion sought to replace barbarism with a civil and political order. These required civility and politeness. But how could men lead happy lives in harmony with each other? Not through traditional certainties, such as the Christian dogmatics whereby righteousness had wielded the sword. Rudeness had to yield to a new moral order of refinement. In "Sur les presbytériens"(On Presbyterians) in *Letters philosophiques*, Voltaire claimed that he could see this filtering down into social practice in England's "free and peaceful assemblies":

> Take a view of the Royal Exchange in London, a place more venerable than many courts of justice, where the representatives of all nations meet for the benefit of mankind. There the Jew, the Mahometan, and the Christian transact together as though they all professed the same religion, and give the name of infidel to none but the bankrupt. There the Presbyterian confides in the Anabaptist, and the Churchman depends on the Quaker's word. And all are satisfied.

This passage confirms that the market made Enlightenment cooperation possible by undermining confessional divides. Money was the new cult. But in showing men content, and content to be content, Voltaire reveals a revolution in the idea of the *summum bonum* ("highest good"), a shift from an ethic of righteousness that was transcendental and religious to a selfhood that was psychological and personal. The Enlightenment translated the cosmic question "How can I be good?" into the pragmatic "How can I be happy?" and opened the gates for a new psychology of personal and social adjustment.

Individual and social adjustment paved the highway of cultivation. Pursuit of refinement was not a petty obsession with punctilio; it was the last-ditch therapy for chronic social conflict and personal frustration arising from ignorance, family tyranny, isolation, or spleen. Refinement could be taught by education—and, after Locke, pedagogy stressed "learning in the uses of the world." Refinement was also to be learned by practice.

Above all, the refinement of self was to be directed toward sociability. Solitude—in Samuel Johnson's opinion, "certainly one of the greatest obstacles to pleasure and improvement"—brought on hypochondria and boorishness. The scholar immured in his study succumbed to pedantry and spleen.

To be a rational gentleman, a fellow had to be sociable, or, in Johnson's phrase, "clubbable" (and Johnson's own club contained the leading minds of the day—Edmund Burke, Joshua Reynolds, Adam Smith, Oliver Goldsmith, Edward Gibbon, Thomas Percy). Clubs, Masonic lodges, tavern meetings, coffeehouses, and friendly societies flourished in the name of company, fellowship, and credit, free republics of rational society. And in urging sociability, Enlightenment writers codified the art and science of pleasing. Human nature was malleable. Men must cheerfully conform and accommodate. Good breeding, discreet charm, and conversation were the polish that reduced social friction, "contributing as much as possible to the ease and happiness of those with whom you converse." "We polish one another," wrote Shaftesbury, "and rub off our corners and rough sides by a sort of amicable collision." A rational art of ease, good humor, sympathy, restraint, moderation, sobriety, and culture, based upon knowledge of human nature: this was the key felicific technology pioneered by the English Enlightenment.

Thus, the Enlightenment in England sought patterns of conduct that would embody order. But social harmony also had to be seen to be anchored in the larger order of nature. All English natural philosophers affirmed the rational cosmos. Theologians found natural religion, moralists natural law. Christian providentialist natural theology, and deism too; the static chain of being and Erasmus Darwin's evolutionism; uniformitarian natural law and theories of change; universal human nature and the infinite perfectibility of man—all these beliefs offered some universal and objective underpinnings to the social frame. "Cease then, nor *order* Imperfection name," declared Pope:

All Nature is but Art unknown to thee;
All Chance, Direction, which thou can'st not see;
All Discord, Harmony not understood,
All partial Evil, universal Good:
And, spite of Pride, in erring Reason's Spite,
One truth is clear, "Whatever is, is Right."

The distinctive dilemma of the English Enlightenment was the need to achieve individual and group fulfillment within the familiar social frame. Unlike elsewhere, the central concern was not absolute power, but rather private and voluntary activities. With their constitution assured, English thinkers were less interested in providing comprehensive theories of the cosmos or speculations on the biology of man but were more concerned with a praxis of man in society. In the short term, this preoccupation succeeded. The idioms of liberty, interest, and consensus won many converts. Eighteenth-century England retained a general equilibrium while undergoing rapid local change.

In the slightly longer term, the hopes of Enlightenment ideologues for creating a stable, though free and fluid, society were jeopardized by the increasingly open social ruptures late in the century—these class conflicts being the consequence of the Enlightenment's endorsement of possessive individualism. From the time of John Wilkes, and despite the parliamentary reform movement and English Jacobinism, Enlightenment ideology began to break into contradictory fragments, and the conjuring trick of juggling dynamic individualism with social stability tumbled to the ground. And once Enlightenment libertarian rhetoric was appropriated by "rights of man" radicals such as Paine, the hope that freedom and order would march progressively together was destroyed.

Yet, in the long term, the Enlightenment ideology had burrowed very deeply under the skin. By providing a secular legitimization for free-market capitalism, it continued to inform Victorian "self-help" liberalism and modern defenses of the open society. In proclaiming individual progress through reason, it conjured up a meliorist, gradualist future that immunized radicals against ideologies of class war and fraternal socialism. Owenism, phrenology, secularism, and Fabianism are all legacies of the English Enlightenment. Élie Halévy's thesis perhaps needs supplementing: might it have been the Enlightenment that rendered England proof against the French—and all subsequent—Revolution? The peculiarities of the English are not least the product of the peculiarities of the English Enlightenment.

ROY PORTER

Further Reading

Porter, Roy, "The Enlightenment in England," in Roy Porter and Mikuláš Teich, editors, *The Enlightenment in National Context,* Cambridge and New York: Cambridge University Press, 1981

Porter, Roy, *English Society in the Eighteenth Century,* London: Allen Lane, and London and New York: Penguin, 1982; revised edition, London and New York: Penguin, 1990

Redwood, John, *Reason, Ridicule, and Religion: The Age of Enlightenment in England, 1660–1750,* London: Thames and Hudson, and Cambridge, Massachusetts: Harvard University Press, 1976

Spadafora, David, *The Idea of Progress in Eighteenth-Century Britain,* New Haven, Connecticut: Yale University Press, 1990

Engraving

The 18th century witnessed profound changes in the art of engraving, affecting the various processes involved, the design of the prints, and the way they were marketed. The prints were ranked according to a twin hierarchy of techniques and genres. Popular woodcuts and playing cards were at the lowest end of the scale. More often than not, they were colored and engraved along the grain of the wood. Their coarse style set them radically apart from the delicate finish and shading preferred by high society. With a few exceptions, xylography was neglected. In France J.-B.M. Papillon promoted that art form through his *Traité historique et pratique de la gravure sur bois* (1766; Historical and Practical Treatise on Engraving on Wood Engraving). Papillon's English pupil John Baptist Jackson tried to revive wood engraving in two or three colors through his *Essay on the Invention of Engraving and Printing in Chiaroscuro* (1754). In addition, engraved decorations by Choffard were included in some prestigious publications. But no significant advance was made in xylography until the 1790s, when Thomas Bewick developed the more precise and versatile technique of engraving across the grain of the wood, which would dominate illustration during the 19th century. Bewick's work was published in his *General History of Quadrupeds* (1790) and then his *History of British Birds* (1797–1804).

In contrast to wood engraving, copperplate engraving was both prestigious and widely used. Indeed, from the 17th century onward, engraving with the burin continued to be the preferred technique because its precision and finish allowed larger print-runs than etching. Eventually, etching came to compete with copperplate engraving, but the former also came to the latter's aid, as most copper plates were etched before being completed with the burin. Occasionally, etching was rigorous enough in its execution to be on a par with copperplate engraving, following the advice of Abraham Bosse in his treatise of 1645, which was frequently translated and also reissued in French during the 18th century. In some contexts, etching was prized because it could be executed almost as quickly as drawing. However, nothing could have been more foreign to the craftsmen using the traditional burin, whose task was to represent the "character" or the "spirit" of the sculpture or picture that was to be reproduced, and who made it a point of honor to display their skill through the virtuosity of their cutting and cross-hatching.

Etching was one of the main instruments of the revolution in printmaking that took place in Europe around the middle of the 18th century. Indeed, the immense vogue for drawing—which was associated with the genius, the hand, and the personal style of the individual artist—encouraged graphic reproduction in all its forms. In 1780 Le Prince, the inventor of the aquatint, asked, "Does not the provision of a method of reproducing the first impulses of the imagination, with all the spirit of the original, render a service to the arts?" Various different styles of printmaking emerged and flourished at this time, involving the use of pencils (1759), washes (1766), pastels (1769) and water colors (1772), all applied by the intaglio process, which combined engraving (with points, gravers, matting tools and multipointed awls) with etching (in which acid is painted onto the plate and eats into the surface through various porous varnishes). Using the techniques of aquatint, *manière noire* (black style), soft varnish, and stippling, engravers scratched their plates, cross-hatched them, riddled them with points, or washed them, in an effort to simulate the subtle textures and soft gradations appropriate to the various techniques of drawing.

The vogue for reproductions also stimulated research on color, which was either applied by hand on proofs struck off in black or inked by depositing all the desired tints onto the plate with a dabber. Jacques Christophe Le Blon, inspired by the writings of Sir Isaac Newton, invented the principle of chromolithography by using matrices inked with the primary colors yellow, blue, and red (*Coloritto* [1722]). It was with this method that Le Blon printed the portrait of Louis XV in 1739. The technique was adopted and further developed by the Frenchman Gautier-Dagoty, who published his *Lettres concernant le nouvel art de graver et d'imprimer les tableaux* (Letters concerning the New Art of Engraving and Printing Pictures) in 1749. However, this method posed serious technical problems concerning the location and proportions of the colors, and it did not replace hand coloring, which remained common until the end of the 19th century.

In addition to the treatises and manuals that were published in Europe to patent and explain these inventions and improvements, there were numerous publications devoted to engraving and engravers. To begin with, there were directories of artists, ancient and modern, which had titles such as *dictionnaire* (dictionary) or *notices* (notices) in French and *Handbuch* (handbook) or *Verzeichnis* (catalog) in German. Such works included texts by P.-F. Basan (1767), Thomas Martyn (Cambridge, 1770), J.K. Füssli (Zurich, 1771), Strutt (London, 1785–86), and Huber (Leipzig, 1787). Other works were oriented toward history, such as Abraham von Humbert's *Abrégé historique des origines et des progrès de la gravure* (1752; Historical Treatise on the Rise and Development of Engraving), or toward aesthetics, such as William Gilpin's *Essay upon Prints* (1768), which was frequently reissued and translated. In general, these works were compilations of lists of engravers, technical and historical explanations, aesthetic reflections, and practical advice intended to satisfy a diverse readership of artists and connoisseurs. Such concerns are illustrated by the title of the *Raisonirendes Verzeichnis der vornehmsten Kupferstecher und ihrer Werke zum Gebrauch der Sammler und Liebhaber* (1771; Catalog Raisonné of the Most Renowned Copper Engravers and Their Works, for the Use of Collectors and Connoisseurs) by J.K. Füssli, the father of the celebrated Swiss painter and engraver Henry Fuseli, who emigrated to London. The older Füssli's foreword sets out the issues in contemporary engraving in a characteristic manner, insisting on the usefulness of prints for didactic, pedagogic, and documentary purposes. André Félibien had made the same point earlier: "There is no one, in whatever condition or profession he may be, who cannot derive a great deal of benefit from them [prints]" (*L'idée d'un peintre parfait* [1707; The Idea of a Perfect Painter]). Similarly, the article "Gravure"

(1757; Engraving) in the *Encyclopédie* underlines the usefulness of prints "for the general communication of the arts and of knowledge," a conception that would occupy a central place in the republican ideology that arose from the French Revolution.

Füssli also regretted the dominance of French and, more particularly, English taste in the question of "finish." Engraving was indeed a matter of national specialties. London and Paris became the two main centers of the market for prints in the 18th century. The rivalry between the two cities, which influenced the attitudes of European artists and intellectuals, was at once economic, political (particularly during the Revolution), and aesthetic. English prints saturated the European market, thanks to the English government, which subsidized their export while taxing Continental prints. Many engravers had to conform to the smooth "English" style, obtained on copper plates stippled or worked on with the *berceau,* a multipointed awl.

Füssli draws a revealing contrast between the specialized engravers of reproductions—users of the burin who "are little more than simple mechanics"—and the great artist, whose hand is freed by the very nature of etching, which is "almost the same as drawing." While pointing out the superiority of the engraver's burin for portrait and the advantages of the etching needle for landscapes, Füssli situates the two techniques within a hierarchy of genres, dominated by history paintings and portraits. Two principles of classification are thus brought into opposition, one appropriate to the burin and promoted by academic institutions, the other associated with etching and based on the Neo-Platonic notion of "genius" or "originality."

A similar opposition is found in the chapter entitled "On Originals and Copies" in Jonathan Richardson's *An Essay on the Theory of Painting* (1728). Richardson notes the inferiority of engravings, and even "original" etchings, to the drawings and pictures of the masters. The article "Gravure" in the *Encyclopédie,* while pointing out the freedom granted by etching in comparison with copperplate engraving, remains conservative. Its author values these "sketches full of spirit and fire" but judges them to be "inaccurate and not very pleasant works," for they are the products of the "infinite number of engravers" who have appeared and have made these "imperfect works with which we are inundated." This text thus raises two issues that surfaced in the 18th century. First, the "de-professionalization" of prints was encouraged by the development of relatively easy techniques such as etching. Second, the proliferation of printed images, especially illustrations, provoked criticism among contemporaries, above all in literary circles. Louis Sébastien Mercier summarized the situation in his *Tableau de Paris* (1781; Panorama of Paris) by stating, "There is a ridiculous abuse of engraving nowadays." Not only were prints invading books, they also were being displayed everywhere in the cities, on storefronts, and on the walls of houses. (From the 1720s, it was even fashionable to cut up engravings, affix them to walls, and varnish them.) Prints were also spilling out of the cases of connoisseurs, who were becoming ever more numerous and ever more avid for rare proofs. In the 18th century their demand for prints encouraged the development of commercial and speculative strategies on an unprecedented scale.

Genres and Their Markets

The national, aesthetic, and professional polarities that informed practices and discourses coincided with, and sometimes intensified, the debates over issues of genres and techniques. For example, the pieces accepted by the Académie Française were normally executed in copperplate and were limited to historical subjects and portraits. As in the 17th century, portraits remained one of the principal genres for prints, but with the difference that in the 18th century small portraits of the bourgeois began to appear alongside portraits of the elite. In Britain, portraits formed an essential part of the output of engravings. Genre engravings were plentiful in the print market, although they made little impact compared to that of popular and institutional prints. Prominent among these genre engravings (and similar to what were known as engravings *en petit* [in miniature]), were the vignettes that were flooding the market in many types of books, including novels, volumes of poetry, travel literature, and almanacs. In addition, single engravings became extremely popular, and were used for all kinds of everyday purposes, including notices, invitation cards, bookplates, fans, and caricatures.

Landscapes also flourished, particularly in countries where tourism was developing. In Switzerland, notably in Winterthur, Bern, and Zurich, such engravers as J.L. Aberli, A. Zingg, and G. Lory the Elder specialized in line etchings or watercolored aquatints depicting Alpine scenery. In Italy, especially in Rome, innumerable artists, both Italian and immigrant, made their living from the English who were taking their grand tours, as these artists directed their work toward these visitors' pictorial and archeological expectations. Engravers sometimes formed workshops, such as A.L. Ducros, a Swiss engraver, and Giovanni Volpato, a Roman by adoption, who produced great watercolored line etchings. Many collections of published engravings depicted ancient sites, modern townscapes, frescoes, or paintings. Such collections were an Italian specialty, and in Rome they were monopolized by the Rossis (or de Rubeis), a family of dealers who eventually gave their immense collections to Pope Clement XII to form the Calcographia Camerale, the papal collection of engravings. The genre also attracted masters of the Venetian style of free etching. These included such great names as Giovanni Antonio Canaletto (*Vedute* [Scenic Views], 1740–43), Giambattista Piranesi (*Carceri* [Prisons], 1750; *Antichità Romane* [Roman Antiquities], 1756), and Tiepolo.

Other collections of engravings displayed the contents of major art collections. These engravings thus contributed to the dissemination of aesthetic conventions and the development of a more documentary approach to the history of art, an influence felt throughout Europe, but centered on Italian masterpieces, particularly those of Venice, Florence, Rome, and London. Venetian collections included the *Descrizione di tutte le pubbliche pitture della città di Venezi* (1733; Description of All the Public Paintings of the City of Venice) and *Della pittura veneziana* (1771; On Venetian Painting) by A.M. Zanetti. The Florentine collections included those by A. Scacciati (1766) and S. Mulinari (1774, 1778, and 1782), and a notable Roman collection was Gavin Hamilton's *Schola Italica Picturae* (1773; The Italian School of Painting). Other collections were published in London by C. Rogers (1778) and by J. Chamberlaine (1786–1812); in Dresden (1753–59) and Düsseldorf (1778); in Vienna, notably A.J. von Prenner's *Theatrum Artis Pictoriae* (1728–37; Theater of the Pictorial Arts); and, of course, in Paris, where Pierre Crozat undertook the publication, in two volumes, of his sumptuous *Recueil d'estampes* (1729–42; Collection of Prints). Crozat's volumes contain reproductions of pictures and drawings belonging to the king and to various collectors, including Crozat himself. The texts were written by great connoisseurs, dealers, and collectors, such as Pierre Jean Mariette and the comte de Caylus. In the same period, J. de Julienne, the director of the Gobelins factory and a great admirer of the work of Antoine Watteau, commissioned the engraving of 350 copperplate prints based on the artist's paintings, which were also published in two volumes (1726–28).

The taste for reproductions is also indicated by the fact that these plates were executed by the best engravers of the period, including J. and B. Audran, Boucher the Younger, Cochin the Elder, F.-B. Lépicié, Laurent Cars, and C. Vanloo. Reproductions also became one of the specialties of Arthur Pond of London, who was a portraitist, an engraver, a dealer, and a publisher. Closely associated with Mariette, and also with Richardson, some of whose collection of ancient drawings he reproduced, Pond printed an album entitled *Prints of Drawings of the Best Masters* (1740) and a *Collection of Early Caricatures,* which appeared in Britain in the 1740s. Similarly, C. Ploos Van Amstel published 46 reproductions of ancient drawings in the Netherlands in 1765. The cosmopolitan Venetian engraver and con-

noisseur A.M. Zanetti published a set of around 20 chiaroscuro engravings based on his own vast collection of ancient drawings. He dedicated it to the prince of Liechtenstein but also to his friends, including Mariette, Crozat, and the British consul Joseph Smith. Even more important, however, Zanetti destroyed the plates after making the prints.

These enterprises, notably those of Crozat and Julienne, which amounted to exhibitions of works of art, were hardly disinterested, for engraving undeniably increased the value of the originals. Julienne sold his Watteaus shortly after the printing of his collection, which thus served as a large catalog for the sale. Such lavish publications characterized the patronage exercised by wealthy collectors of the day, and these works were closely associated with the negotiations carried out by the dealers, who played a leading role in the history of engraving in the 18th century. In London, for example, John Boydell launched the ambitious Shakespeare Gallery, where he exhibited a collection of paintings, specially commissioned from leading English artists and subsidized by the sale of reproduction prints. In Paris P.F. Basan (1723–97), whose father was a wine merchant but who was himself an engraver, a publisher, an appraiser, and an art editor, promoted Dutch and Flemish engravings of the 17th century. He also reissued prints by Rembrandt and Teniers, taken from the original copper plates. Using his personal contacts to gain access to the magnificent collections of the duc de Choiseul, Crozat, and Poullain, Basan edited a *Dictionnaire des graveurs* (1767; Dictionary of Engravers) and organized the sales of collections from major workshops (Bouchardon, Slodtz, Wille), as well as private collections. The auctioning of Mariette's collection in 1776 lasted for a year and brought in the enormous sum of 350,000 livres.

The Status of Engravers

Engravers were divided into three main groups, according to their degree of "professionalism." Among the least committed were obviously the dilettantes, most of whom were to be found among the aristocracy. Marquises, counts, knights, abbés, and even Madame de Pompadour practiced etching, producing small-scale works of their own invention on lighter subjects.

The second group of engravers was made up of painters who provided the designs for engraved illustrations. They occasionally took up the burin to make etchings of their own but generally regarded that aspect of their work as decidedly secondary. Following the examples of Tiepolo and Francisco de Goya, they called their attempts at engraving "caprices" or "fantasies." They were the "painter-engravers," to borrow the term used in an important catalog of their work by

A. Bartsch, begun in Vienna at the end of the 18th century and published between 1803 and 1821.

The work of the painter-engravers has been highlighted by historians to the detriment of the third category, the true professional engravers, who very often were copperplate engravers by training. These professionals included Drevet, Johann Georg Wille, Le Bas, V. Vangelisti, Demarteau, R. Strange, Francesco Bartolozzi, and M. Pitteri. In the 18th century, engraving was often a family business that involved teamwork. Leading families of engravers included the Cars, the Cochins, and the Drevets in France; the Morghens and the Longhis in Italy; and the Ridingers, the Rugendases, and the Preisslers in Germany. One engraver might specialize in portraits, while another specialized in landscapes, one in copperplate and another in etching, and so on. The younger family members benefited simultaneously from the experience of their elders and from learning how to handle the presses and heavy materials. They were also able to study the collections of engravings kept in the workshops, which encouraged some of them to open stores and become dealers. Apprentice engravers who did not belong to such dynasties or clans spent years in workshops, preferably in Paris or London, which were the main centers of recruitment, training, and production. Engravers who worked in Paris included Roslin, Hall, Wertmüller, and Lavreince (Lafrensen) from Sweden; Schenau, Kraus, and the Willes (father and son) from Germany; Demarteau from the Austrian Netherlands; and Jean-Étienne Liotard and Freudenberger from Switzerland. J.-G. Wille and Le Bas had at least 30 pupils. Bartolozzi had a brilliant career in England and was appointed engraver to the king. Bartolozzi had been born in Florence and trained in the Venice workshop of Johann Wagner (himself a native of Germany and a former pupil of Cars). Bartolozzi acquired a Europe-wide reputation by becoming a master of stippled engraving. In 1773, when around 300 engravers were active in London, he had nearly 50 pupils in his workshop there.

After their apprenticeship, engravers generally remained in the service of their masters for some years, gaining a reputation of their own by association with him and benefiting from commissions. The profession could be very lucrative, especially for those heads of a workshop who engaged in ancillary activities as publishers, dealers, brokers, or appraisers. Collections of engraved plates could also earn income for the engraver. Some engravers published their own catalogs. Demarteau, for example, engraved an order number at the bottom of each of his works, referring to a printed list of those that were for sale. As for price levels, the engraver R. de Launay charged from 1 livre to 16 livres, and engravings that reproduced pictures by Boucher, Watteau, or Chardin fetched similar prices. Engravers also made use of publicity. New prints were frequently advertised in the press (for example, in the *Mercure de France*), appeared on dealers' shop front; or were exhibited in public (for example, at the Society of Artists in London or the Salon in Paris). Everywhere, however, the markets in prints were supervised by political or religious authorities, who gave engravers temporary privileges and insisted that proofs be deposited with them.

The conditions in which engraving was practiced varied according to the prestige of the engraver. Piranesi, for example, became his own printer and publisher in 1761 and, as such, exceptionally, was exempt from customs duties on the paper that he imported. Conditions varied from country to country, as is shown by the juridical, economic, and social pretensions of the artists. William Hogarth used particularly aggressive commercial tactic. Around 1720 he printed a "trade card," offering his services as a copperplate engraver and etcher, but he soon came up against the monopoly of the dealers, whom he described as "pirates." In 1734, in order to succeed in his struggle against exploitation and illicit copying, Hogarth helped to launch a petition to Parliament under the title "The Case of Designers, Engravers, Etchers, etc." This led to the enactment in 1735 of a law on copyright, which, however, was to be of little use to the many artists who were paid by the job.

In addition to commissions and profits from sales, whether direct or through dealers, some artists were given royal offices and pensions that increased their incomes and their prestige. In France the best artists aspired to the honors of that country's Académie Royale de Peinture et de Sculpture (Royal Academy of Painting and Sculpture). These artists started by being "recognized," and then, at last, they were "accepted," as were A. and P. Drevet, J. Audran, de Poilly, Tardieu, the Cochins (father and son), Cars, Lépicié, Le Bas, Schmidt, Surugue, Dupuis, Wille, Demarteau, Moitte, and others. However, engravers continued to be regarded as artists with a lower status than painters, sculptors, and architects. In England the Royal Academy, founded in 1768, excluded engravers, judging their profession to be too close to the mechanical arts. As is suggested by the title of a work on prints by R. Donnie, *Handmaiden to the Arts* (1758), engraving remained, more than anything else, ancillary to painting, sculpture, and architecture.

In quantitative terms, what would later be regarded as "original" prints formed only a very small proportion of those produced. Metal engraving served the interests of contemporary artists, such as Boucher, Chardin, and, above all, Jean-Baptiste Greuze, who was associated with a team of engravers composed of J.-J. Flipart, R. Gaillard, J. Massard, and J.-C. Levasseur.

On Greuze's own admission, the group's reproductions made 300,000 livres for him. The business was managed by his wife, who took care of publicity through newspapers; distributed advertisements, eulogies, and review slips; and attracted customers by diversifying the states of Greuze's prints. For example, the print entitled *The Spoils of Kings* was sold for 36, 24, or 16 livres, depending on whether it was complete, lacked the engraver's address, or had the point badly placed in the inscription. Greuze himself signed the back of each proof, although it was not until a century later that signing on the front or using artificial means to limit the number of proofs came into general use.

In many ways, then, the production of metal engravings during the Enlightenment prefigured what would follow in the 19th century. Indeed, the debates over reproduction and originality, the legitimacy and autonomy of this artistic practice, and the question of the hierarchies of genres and techniques heralded the economic, professional, institutional, and aesthetic issues that were to become particularly acute in the age of mechanical reproduction.

PHILIPPE KAENEL

See also Aesthetics; Antiquity; Caricature; Collections and Curiosities; Illustration; Painting; Printing

Further Reading

Adhémar, Jean, *Graphic Art of the 18th Century*, London: Thames and Hudson, and New York: McGraw-Hill, 1964

Calabi, Augusto, *La gravure italienne au XVIIIᵉ siècle*, Paris: Van Oest, 1931

Carlson, Victor I., and John W. Ittmann, *Regency to Empire: French Printmaking, 1715–1814*, Baltimore, Maryland: Baltimore Museum of Art, and Minneapolis, Minnesota: Minneapolis Institute of Arts, 1984

Courboin, François, *L'estampe française: Graveurs et marchands: Essais*, Brussels and Paris: Van Oest, 1914

Delteil, Loys, *Manuel de l'amateur d'estampes du XVIIIᵉ siècle*, Paris: Dorbon-Aîné, 1910

Mason, Lauris, and Joan Ludman, compilers, *Print Reference Sources: A Select Bibliography, 18th–20th Centuries*, Millwood, New York: Kraus-Thomson Organization, 1975; 2nd edition, revised and enlarged, Millwood, New York: KTO Press, 1979

Enlightened Despotism. *See* Monarch, Enlightened

Enlightenment, Representations of

The Enlightenment was not a system and cannot be reduced to any single philosophy or "ism." It was represented through metaphors and mottoes that were open to shifts in meaning and interpretation. The founding image is that of light—French speakers refer to *les Lumières*, in the plural, and German-speakers to the *Aufklärung*. The primal experiences of night and day have always been given arbitrary values, light being associated with the positive and darkness with the negative.

The metaphor of light had earlier referred to the light of divine truth and supernatural understanding before shifting its meaning to emphasize natural light—that is, both human reason and the knowledge that light makes possible. The very title of a posthumous dialogue by René Descartes defines this natural light's purpose: *La recherche de la vérité par la lumière naturelle* (1701; The Search for Truth by Natural Light). Natural light here appears to be a torch, responsible for dispersing the shadows of ignorance and error.

Nicolas Malebranche adopted the same title as Descartes—*La recherche de la vérité* (The Search for Truth)—but in Malebranche's preface the image of light appears in a plural form: "The mind must judge everything according to its inner lights, without listening to the false and confused evidence of its senses or its imagination." For Malebranche the inner lights of reason cannot but be in harmony with the supernatural light of revelation.

In his *Commentaire philosophique sur ces paroles de l'Évangile: Contrains-les d'entrer* (1687; Philosophical Commentary on These Words of the Gospel: Compel Them to Enter), Pierre Bayle states that in cases of an apparent clash in interpretation, "the clear lights of Reason" must provide moral reference and intellectual certainty; no dogma can justify violence. For Bayle the anteriority of natural light is consistent with the divine order; however, for his less religious successors, natural light could claim to replace light that was deemed supernatural.

The uses of the metaphor of light varied from country to country. In France, where anticlericalism developed in opposition to official Catholicism, light became the equivalent of independent human reason, and everything that continued to represent religion was rejected as being related to darkness and obscurantism. In England and Germany, which were more influenced than France by Protestant traditions, the image of the "light of the world" or "God's candle" emphasized the link between philosophy and religion. The transition from *lumière* (light) in the singular to *lumières* (lights) in the plural conformed to classical French usage, which used the singular to designate the abstract principle (reason) and the plural to designate its concrete realizations (forms of knowledge). However, in France this transition represented a radical shift from a transcendent and vertical perspective to an immanent and horizontal one. To borrow a term used by Jean le Rond D'Alembert in his *Discours préliminaire* (1751; Preliminary Discourse) to the *Encyclopédie*, the Encyclopedists entered a "labyrinth" of light and shadow guided only by their reason and the trial and error methods of experimentation.

The pluralization of the *Lumières* (Enlightenment) reflects the relativity of the men of the 18th century as well as our own desire for objectivity with respect to them In France the word *Lumières* was sufficient to characterize the atmosphere of the period, a movement of sensibilities and ideas. In Germany, from the second half of the 18th century onward, an abstract intellectual approach was defined with a neologism: *Aufklärung*. In England, too, a neologism—"Enlightenment"—was employed, although this term was introduced much later than the German one. At the end of the 18th century, speakers of Italian used the words *lumi* and *illumi-*

nati, while Spanish speakers used *luz* and *ilustrados* (meaning, in both cases, "light" and "the enlightened," respectively). The neologisms *Illuminismo* in Italian and *Ilustración* in Spanish—both meaning "Enlightenment"—came later. The definition of the Enlightenment covers many things: an image and a slogan of the period, with their necessary vagueness; an effort of reflection and rigor a posteriori; a historically dated sentimental commitment; and a retrospective task of historiography, with variations according to the languages and cultural climates.

The metaphor not only determined a series of contrasts—between obscurity and clarity, sleep and lucid wakefulness—but also involved a range of intermediate images of false or dangerous lights. Striving to coin an image that would evoke his mistrust of a rationalism that had been cut off from its moral roots, and true to his role as inside critic of the Enlightenment, Jean-Jacques Rousseau explains in a note in his *Discours sur les sciences et les arts* (1750; Discourse on the Arts and Sciences) that "according to an ancient fable, a satyr wanted to kiss and embrace fire the first time he saw it, but Prometheus cried out to him: 'Satyr, you will weep for the beard on your chin, for it [fire] burns when one touches it.'" The frontispiece of the *Discours* is an illustration of this note. Along with the whole of his philosophy, Rousseau's image has been taken over as a weapon against the Enlightenment whenever it was seen as a party, a political force, or a subversive movement. The comte de Rivarol reinterpreted Rousseau's frontispiece by rewriting Prometheus's warning to the satyr: "It was therefore necessary to cry out to him: 'Come no nearer, for light burns.' And that was the gist of the warning. Our philosophers have therefore thrown light at our satyrs, without thinking that it burns." The distinction between light and heat raises the issue of the relationships between reason and history, intellectual progress and social change, philosophy and action.

With her views shaped by her experience of the French Revolution and the Empire, Madame de Staël denounced, in *De l'Allemagne* (1810; Germany), the radicalization of an Enlightenment philosophy, which had turned against both religion and tradition: "Minds have rushed to their destruction: thus, the lights have changed into a fire, and philosophy, that irritated enchantress, has burned down the palace in which she displayed her wonders." In Madame de Staël's view, critical reason had lost those moral and religious reference points that alone would allow it to become a source of reform.

Conversely, another series of images generated by the metaphor of Enlightenment evoked a light that was useless, cold, and ineffective. In a letter to Christian Jacob Kraus, responding to Immanuel Kant's famous article

Was ist Aufklärung? (1784; What Is Enlightenment?), Johann Georg Hamann makes numerous ironic and derogatory remarks. Hamann writes that he prefers "a clear and healthy human eye" to "eyes illuminated by the moonlight of an owl-eyed Athena" and a blazing sun to "blind illumination." He goes on to state that "the Enlightenment of our age is no more than an Arctic light . . . a cold lunar light, a sterile light, incapable of illuminating the idle understanding or of reheating the timid will." In contrast to reason alone, which is nothing but a reflection, a passive light, Hamann puts forward inner truth and faith, which are transcendent and active lights.

In fact, Kant's reply to the question *Was ist Aufklärung?*, posed by Zöllner in the *Berlinische Zeitschrift,* makes less use of the metaphor of Enlightenment than of contrasts between minority and coming of age, wardship and independence. Kant sets out to restrict the public and private uses of reason, to bring into harmony individual critical rigor and the duty of obeying the law. He thus postulates a meeting between individual reason and *raison d'État* (reason of state).

However, at the heart of his analysis lies his suggestion of a motto for the Enlightenment: *Sapere aude* (Dare to be wise), which, like the metaphor of light, leaves his text open to this phrase's history and its various meanings. In Horace's *Epistles* this phrase refers to the imperative of wisdom and could be loosely translated, as Madame Dacier suggested, by the French phrase *ayez le courage d'être vertueux* (Dare to be virtuous). Pierre Gassendi was seemingly the first to transform this traditional moral injunction into what Franco Venturi has called "a conscious appeal for free investigation" (see Venturi). Virtue, which requires conformity to a norm, was replaced by a dynamic of critical reason. Boldness was understood to require energy, impetus, and rejection. Horace's phrase was taken up by Hugo Grotius and then served as a motto on a medal struck in Berlin in 1736 in honor of Gottfried Wilhelm Leibniz and Christian Wolff by the Society of Aleothophiles, which proclaimed in its statutes its trust in reason and in the necessity of extending reason's use. The heads of Leibniz and Wolff form a Janus figure below a bust of Minerva. Both Minerva and the motto can also be found in several German engravings from the second half of the 18th century, as well as on the medal commissioned in 1765 by King Stanislas Augustus of Poland in honor of the pedagogue Stanislas Konarski, who reformed the Polish education system and promoted scientific knowledge. Such evidence suggests that Kant had succeeded in changing a moral precept into an ethic of reason; obedience into a critical reaction.

Another Enlightenment motto was launched by *Le philosophe* (The Philosopher), a work attributed to César Chesneau Dumarsais and first published in 1743 in *Nouvelles libertés de penser* (New Freedoms of Thought). Dumarsais defines the philosopher in terms of his faith in reason and his sense of social duty. For Dumarsais the question is not one of linking individual with political reason, as with Kant, but of linking individual reason with social solidarity. "Our philosopher, who knows how to share his time between solitude and companionship with his fellow man," Dumarsais writes, "is full of humanity."

In Terence's comedy *Heauton timorumenos* (The Self-Tormenter), the character Chremes knows that he is a man and that only mankind takes an interest in the good or bad fortune of his neighbor: *Homo sum, humani nihil a me alienum puto* (I am a man; I regard nothing human as foreign to me). This line from the above play might be a warning against every form of pride that would lead us to exclude ourselves from the human condition: I am a man, and I share in all the weaknesses of humanity. However, knowledge and recognition of our limits can change this weakness into strength. Awareness of the identical nature of all human beings, of a law of compassion that unites all people, becomes the basis for a morality and a political stance. In the entry "Amour-propre" (Self-Love) in the *Encyclopédie,* the abbé Yvon writes that "the property of being human, common to us all, is the cause of that general benevolence that we call humanity: *homo sum* . . . " To the philosopher falls the task of proclaiming this humanity and of putting it to work within society. Dumarsais's essay was essentially plagiarized by Voltaire and the *Encyclopédie* and spread throughout the literature of the second half of the 18th century, whether this literature was strictly philosophical or a broader vehicle of the new sensibility. Terence's phrase characterized the project of the *Encyclopédie,* which sought to gather together all the forms of human knowledge. According to D'Alembert, Francis Bacon

> would have been able to say, like that old man in Terence's drama, that nothing that concerned humanity was foreign to him. The knowledge of nature, morality, politics, economics, all seem to have been among the resources of this luminous and profound mind.

Terence's phrase also characterized the social awareness of the militant *philosophes* who undertook to change the world, and it defined aesthetic creation, based on the interest taken by the artist and then by the spectator in the complexity of human reality.

Terence's line served as an epigraph for moral essays, reformist and political pamphlets, and treatises on aesthetics, but it was also quoted by theologians and Christian novelists who were critical of the *philosophes.*

In the *Philosophie de Kant* (1801; Kant's Philosophy), Charles de Villers turned the line against the French *philosophes*. In Villers's view they were guilty of monopolizing the concept of humanity and of confusing universal values with national or even merely worldly principles; in other words, the Parisian Enlightenment had announced no more than *Gallus sum* (I am a Frenchman). Whenever the Enlightenment failed to pay due attention to differences and contradictions, its universalism was in danger of being reduced to the defense of individual interests—that is, it risked turning into its opposite.

The characterization of the Enlightenment by such metaphors and mottoes helped to maintain its diversity and imprecision and to counter the temptation to provide a strictly conceptual or historical definition of it. However, the Enlightenment continues to be unified in a militant or polemical way, its plurality being reduced to thesingle cause that is either defended or condemned. While the history of ideas and of sensibilities prohibits us from drawing a clear line between Enlightenment and Anti-Enlightenment, the reality of political conflicts has defined parties, alliances, and confrontations. Thus, in its quest for legitimacy the French Revolution constructed continuities and claimed to be following theoretical models, retrospectively creating a certain continuity between the Enlightenment and itself, and reconciling Voltaire with Rousseau under the dome of the Panthéon. Saint-Just remarked that, in addition to these two founding fathers, "the 18th century should be placed in the Panthéon." The entire century was unified under the banner of Philosophy and according to the perspective of the Revolution.

In the 19th century an early form of liberalism defended the joint legacy of philosophy and the Revolution. From the so-called Kehl edition of Voltaire to Naigeon's edition of Denis Diderot, a missionary zeal brought about the publication of the complete works of Enlightenment thinkers, a proselytism that was not incompatible with respect for the actual words of the thinkers or with linguistic scruples. Similarly, the Counter-Revolution united a destructive and subversive philosophical movement under the banner of conspiracies, secret societies, and Masonic lodges. In a more conceptual sense, Georg Wilhelm Friedrich Hegel and other German idealists regarded the Enlightenment only as a negative and critical phenomenon that had to be surpassed through the establishment of positive values. While some treated philosophy and the Revolution as single entities, others sought to establish distinctions, to separate the good seed from the bad, whether on chronological grounds (as between a moderate first half of the 18th century and a radicalized second half, or between the main body of the century and its final decade); or on

explicitly ideological grounds (as between good philosophy, which was respectful of religion, and harmful philosophy, which was anticlerical and materialist); or on grounds of national interest (as between French philosophy and British or German philosophy).

The theorists of the 19th century were led to propose theories about the Enlightenment and the Revolution by their concern to understand their own time. Karl Marx defined the Enlightenment as the philosophy of the bourgeoisie, which, hampered in its symbolic legitimacy and expansion by the feudal structure of the ancien régime, discovered the bases for its seizure of power in ideas of juridical equality and liberty. The 18th-century currents of materialism, utopianism, and Rousseauism provided elements for critical thought about the dominant order when, having secured its domination, the bourgeoisie ceased to be a revolutionary force and became conservative. Such radical ideas would permit Marx and others to go beyond the Enlightenment and individualism.

In a more specifically French context, Alexis de Tocqueville regarded the Enlightenment as a current of thought that had arisen among the elite—the nobility and the upper bourgeoisie—when they were confronted by the political and administrative centralization of the monarchy. The French Revolution had been born of their demands but then evolved under the influence of the violence of the common people. The Revolution confirmed the disappearance of the ancien régime, which the declaration of the modern state had already placed on the agenda. Tocqueville emphasized continuity whereas other historians and polemicists continued to be obsessed by the Revolution's break from the past. The theoretical models of the Enlightenment as either bourgeois philosophy or elite thought have served as hypotheses for subsequent historical studies discussing the categories of social order and class in 18th-century Europe, the unity and diversity of the Enlightenment, or the place and function of ideas in historical development.

In the 20th century the pressures of current reality continued to influence research and reflection and to crystallize syntheses and interpretations. In 1932 *Die Philosophie der Aufklärung* (The Philosophy of the Enlightenment) by Ernst Cassirer, a professor at the University of Hamburg, was published in Tübingen, and in the same year, he published a substantial article, "Das Problem Jean Jacques Rousseau" (The Question of Jean-Jacques Rousseau), as well as a series of studies on Johann Wolfgang von Goethe. The following year, after Adolf Hitler became chancellor, Cassirer resigned his post and went into exile. *Die Philosophie der Aufklärung* is an attempt at synthesis from a Kantian and liberal point of view, as well as an act of faith in reason and the values of free thought at the time when fascism, intolerance, and the irrational were on the rise. Although Cassirer's book was not translated into some European languages until much later, his analyses had a decisive influence on others' views of the 18th century.

Conversely, *Philosophische Fragmente* (1944; Philosophical Fragments, later published as *Dialectik der Aufklärung* [1947; Dialectic of the Enlightenment]) by Theodor Adorno and Max Horkheimer denounced a form of reason that, in the logic of its development and its mastery of reality, had ended by denying itself, by organizing the mechanical dehumanization of society, and by administering totalitarian states. In the view of Adorno and Horkheimer, the *Aufklärung* (German Enlightenment) was not the philosophy of the 18th-century Enlightenment in the strict sense but a much larger movement of rationalization. Nevertheless, it encompassed the age of Voltaire, and for these two theorists the position occupied by the marquis de Sade in this polemical panorama is revealing. According to them, Sade's *Histoire de Juliette* (1797; Juliette) shows the true face of a philosophy that became the Terror when it involved itself in the modernization of the economy and of society. The assumption that reason, nature, and progress are identical is turned on its headThe Cold War and the rivalry between the two ideologies of liberalism and Marxism, both claiming the heritage of the Enlightenment, spurred some studies and findings but the era also produced some syntheses that were politically outdated. In *An Age of Crisis: Man and World in 18th-Century French Thought* (1959) and *Nature and Culture: Ethical Thought in the French Enlightenment* (1963), Lester G. Crocker argues that inherent in the French *philosophes'* criticism of the Christian tradition are the risk of nihilism and, ultimately, the threat of every sort of terror. Once again, Sade is invoked in order to put the 18th century's faith in nature on trial, and the Enlightenment is indicted for having fathered the various totalitarianisms of the 20th century. In contrast, Peter Gay considers the whole of Europe in *The Enlightenment: An Interpretation* (1966; Volume I: *The Rise of Modern Paganism*, and Volume II: *The Science of Freedom*). In Gay's view the Enlightenment initially sought to be critical and was mistrustful of the past and tradition; it elaborated a "science of freedom" that culminated in the American Declaration of Independence and the birth of a homeland for liberalism.

Most of these syntheses appear to be trapped in a double dilemma—whether to assimilate Enlightenment philosophy to the Revolution or to consider the 18th century to be without a revolutionary future; whether to identify with the values of the Enlightenment or to denounce its illusions. In recent works, authors express a perceptible desire to question the past in order to answer the questions of the present, but they also seek to escape from this double dilemma. In *Strukturwandel der Öffentlichkeit* (1962; The Structural Transformation of the Public Sphere), Jürgen Habermas defines the concept of *Öffentlichkeit* as "publicity" or the "public sphere," which founded an authority that was independent of religion and royal power and which enhanced the channels for sharing and debating ideas. To enlighten is to publish, to make public, to integrate individuals into a community that is capable of elaborating and expressing opinion and to postulate a continuity of individual opinions in order to form a public opinion.

Contemporary studies in social history, the history of cultural practices, and the history of ideas exploit these viewpoints. From a philosophical point of view, Michel Foucault rereads Kant's text, which does not define the present in relation to a history or a future, but purely negatively, in relation to the past (see Foucault). For Foucault the motto *Sapere aude* resounds as a call placing oneself on the outside, to give up one's commitment. The rejection of a minority and dependent position implies the continual reactivation of critical awareness. Foucault applies this rigor to the Enlightenment itself, denouncing all forms of blackmail and such simplistic alternatives as the choice between either recognizing oneself in the Enlightenment or rejecting it. Criticism belong to that part of the Enlightenment which can only define itself within its own historical relativization and self-questioning. More generally, the critical attitude implies avoiding the choice between being inside or being outside. Enlightenment man is ever at the edge.

The international institutionalization of research on the 18th century and the increasing number of associations, groups, and publications concerned with the Enlightenment should not obscure the problems posed by the very definition of the Enlightenment and by the burden of representations that have organized its categorization and interpretation. Researchers are always pulled between the past and the present, between the isolation of the past as such and the anachronism that assimilates it into the present, and between detachment and commitment, as well as between announcing guiding hypotheses or engaging in the nearsighted groping for knowledge in archives and texts. The arguments of Adorno and Horkheimer and the invectives of Crocker have degenerated into journalistic debates, and the end of the Cold War has been followed by a revival of debate about most of the concepts of the Enlightenment. Meanwhile, both the work of the scholars specializing in the 18th century and studies by those who do not accept that label are reflecting such trends as the enlargement of the corpus, the growing number of noncanonical authors being studied, and the investigation of regions of Europe that were long neglected by historians. Thus, contemporary authors are contributing to the continuous displacement of the frontier between the Enlightenment and the non-Enlightenment—in other words, they are contributing to the transformation and redefinition of the Enlightenment itself.

MICHEL DELON

See also History, Philosophy of; Progress; Reason

Further Reading

Adorno, Theodor, and Max Horkheimer, *Dialectic of Enlightenment,* translated by John Cumming, New York: Herder and Herder, 1972; London: Allen Lane, 1973 (original German edition, 1944)

Cassirer, Ernst, *The Philosophy of the Enlightenment,* translated by Fritz C.A. Koelln and James P. Pettegrove, Princeton, New Jersey: Princeton University Press, 1951 (original German edition, 1932)

Crocker, Lester G., *An Age of Crisis: Man and World in Eighteenth-Century French Thought,* Baltimore, Maryland: Johns Hopkins Press, 1959

Crocker, Lester G., *Nature and Culture: Ethical Thought in the French Enlightenment,* Baltimore, Maryland: Johns Hopkins Press, 1963

Delon, Michel, "'Homo sum, humani nihil a me alienum puto': Un vers de Térence comme devise des Lumières," *Dix-huitième siècle* 16 (1984)

Foucault, Michel, "Qu'est-ce que les Lumières?" in *Dits et écrits: 1954–1988,* by Foucault, vol. 4, Paris: Éditions Gallimard, 1994

Gay, Peter, *The Enlightenment: An Interpretation,* 2 vols., New York: Knopf, and London: Weidenfeld and Nicolson, 1966

Habermas, Jürgen, *The Structural Transformation of the Public Sphere: An Inquiry into a Category of Bourgeois Society,* translated by Thomas Burger, London: Polity Press, and Cambridge, Massachusetts: MIT Press, 1989 (original German edition, 1962)

Klein, Wolfgang, and Waltraud Naumann-Beyer, *Nach der Aufklärung? Beiträge zum Diskurs der Kulturwissenschaften,* Berlin: Akademie Verlag, 1995

Mortier, Roland, "Lumière et Lumières, histoire d'une image et d'une idée," in *Clartés et ombres du siècle des Lumières: Études sur le XVIIIe siècle litterature,* by Mortier, Geneva: Librairie Droz, 1969

Ricuperati, Giuseppe, "Le categorie di periodizzazione e il Settecento, per una introduzione storiagrafica," *Studi settecenteschi* 14 (1994)

Roger, Jean, "La Lumière et les Lumières," *Cahiers de l'Association internationale des etudes françaises* 20 (1968)

Venturi, Franco, "Sapere aude," in *Europe des Lumières: Recherches sur le XVIIIe siècle,* by Venturi, Paris and The Hague: Mouton, 1971

Enthusiasm

In its original sense the ancient Greek word for "enthusiasm" meant a divine transport, a sacred delirium, or, literally, the presence of a god within an interpreter. The word then took on the more literary meaning of poetic exaltation at a moment of inspiration. Plato made a theoretical connection between these two meanings in his dialogue *Ion,* in which Socrates states that poets and musicians are guided by a divine force that actually possesses them. As a result the poet is simply a kind of resonance chamber. In order to create, the poet must alienate his own personality ("be outside himself") and no longer make use of his reason. Plato makes the poet sacred, only to abase him immediately afterward: the poet speaks a language that comes from elsewhere, making him a medium rather than a creator; strictly speaking, he has no personal poetic gift. He expresses

himself in a trancelike state that resembles delirium and is similar to the oracular utterances of the Pythia at Delphi. Plato thus reconciles his admiration for poetry with his distrust of rhapsody, which explains why he seeks to exclude poets from his ideal republic.

Such a derogatory conception of poets could not prevail for long. Poets would soon be regarded as *vates,* types of magicians or prophets, superior and privileged beings who are sometimes, when in a state of enthusiasm, favored by a divine spirit. This latter opinion is expressed in Ovid's verse in *Fasti VI, 5:* "Est Deus in nobis, agitante calescimus illo" (There is a god in us, by whose stirring we are inflamed). Renaissance thinkers constructed their theories of poetics based on this concept and wrote of *furor poeticus* (poetic madness). Some of the odes by the 16th-century poet Pierre de

Ronsard's contain curious, premonitory expressions of this view: "I am aroused by frenzy, / My hair stands up in terror."

The 18th century did not succumb to such exaltation. The classicism of the 17th century had repeatedly emphasized the importance of technique and of literary labor, which was gradually defined as the imitation of great models. During the "philosophical" century, the primacy of poetic expression was abandoned in favor of the idea that works of literature should stimulate and liberate the intellect. The idea of a sacred delirium or divine transport began to assume a negative connotation by association with the delirium of religious fanaticism.

This negative association is evident in the meaning that 18th-century French gave to the noun *enthousiaste* (enthusiast), which was almost always synonymous with "visionary" or "fanatic." As late as 1787, the abbé Féraud implied the latter meaning when he defined the word in his *Dictionnaire critique* (Critical Dictionary), although he also commented on the term's history: "It is strongly in fashion today, but it has been given a less odious sense." The expression *enthousiaste de* (enthusiastic about)—as in Jean-Jacques Rousseau's phrase "a people enthusiastic about their liberty"—did not carry any pejorative nuance and was synonymous with "deeply affected by."

As for the term *enthousiasme* itself, in the 18th century its definition varied somewhat from dictionary to dictionary. According to the *Dictionnaire de Trévoux* (Dictionary of Trévoux), the word refers to "a prophetic or poetic frenzy that transports the mind, that kindles and elevates the imagination, and that makes people say amazing and extraordinary things." The dictionary produced by the Académie Française shows more reserve, defining *enthousiasme* as an "extraordinary movement of the mind, caused by an inspiration that is, or appears to be, divine or by which a poet, an orator, a man who works with his genius, is elevated in some way or another above himself." Féraud does not choose either of those two meanings of the word; instead, he merely gives a number of examples, such as "prophetic enthusiasm," "noble enthusiasm," "the enthusiasm of eloquence, or of poetry," "he is seized with enthusiasms; he speaks only through enthusiasm; to enter into enthusiasm." Féraud also mentions the verb *enthousiasmer*, which he defines as being the equivalent of "to ravish with admiration," although he comments that *enthousiasmer* "is used more often to criticize than to praise." In the 18th century, therefore, the semantic field of "enthusiasm" was fairly contradictory due to its double usage, which was both religious and literary.

In England Samuel Johnson proved to be particularly critical with regard to the term's original meaning and rather lukewarm toward its derived meaning. In his *Dictionary of the English Language* (1755), Johnson distinguishes three meanings for "enthusiasm":

(1) A vain belief of private revelation, a vain confidence of divine favor or communication. *Enthusiasm* is founded neither on reason nor divine revelation, but rises from the conceits of a warmed and overweening brain. (2) Heat of imagination; violence of passion; confidence of opinion. (3) Elevation of fancy; exaltation of ideas.

Johnson then cites an example taken from John Dryden's preface to *The Satires of Decimus Junius Juvenalis* (1687) in which "enthusiasm" is glossed as an "extraordinary emotion of soul which makes it seem to us that we behold those things which the poet paints."

In French, synonyms for "enthusiasm" were derived from various areas of culture. Mythology provided equivalents such as "divine frenzy, divine fire, prophetic frenzy, divine flame, divine inspiration, to invoke one's muse"; metaphoric meanings included "ray of light, intoxication, verve, ecstasy, to be outside oneself"; and psychology was the source of meanings such as "transport or activity of the soul, emotion, delirium, madness, insane ardor, rage." These latter, psychological meanings were linked to Socrates's suggestion in *Ion* that the state of enthusiasm is analogous to madness (*mania* in Plato's text) or to paranoia.

In the French classical aesthetic this irrational and uncontrollable element played a secondary role. Art was to obey rules and to be created in a state of complete lucidity. The vaunted poetic delirium was no more than a fiction or an imposture, whose effects were in any case blameworthy. In his *Art poétique* (The Art of Poetry), Nicolas Boileau-Déspreaux concedes that the true poet doubtless feels "the secret influence of heaven," but this prior influence must immediately be subordinated to the empire of reason:

Love reason then; and let whate'er you write
Borrow from her its beauty, force, and light.
Most writers mounted on a resty muse,
Extravagant and senseless objects choose;
They think they err, if in their verse they fall
On any thought that's plain or natural ("Boileau's
Art of Poetry," translated by William Soames, in
The Art of Poetry, edited by Albert S. Cook,
1892)

The return to emotion and sentiment, an important aspect of the 18th century, was manifested in a return to the idea of inspiration, but without any divine or prophetic connotation. The expression *feu divin* (divine fire) remained in common use but it was no more than a figure of speech. The source of inspiration was no longer divine, but instead inhered in the genius of the artist. In the Enlightenment's climate of secularization, attention came to be focused on the personality of creative individuals and on the powers with which nature had endowed them. According to Charles Perrault the poet's soul "is illumined by itself," and this view is echoed in the abbé Batteux's *Cours de Belles-Lettres* (1753; Course on Belles-Lettres):

> There are . . . favored moments for the genius when the soul, inflamed as if by a divine fire, imagines the whole of nature, and spills onto objects that spirit of life that animates them, those touching traits that seduce or delight us. This state of the soul is called "enthusiasm," a term that everyone understands well enough and that almost no one defines. The ideas that most authors give of it appear to arise rather from imaginations astonished and struck by enthusiasm itself than from minds that have thought or reflected. Sometimes it is a celestial vision, a divine influence, a prophetic spirit; sometimes it is intoxication, ecstasy, joy mingled with distress and admiration, in the presence of the divine. Do they intend, with this grandiloquent language, to elevate the arts and to hide the mysteries of the Muses from the profane? As for us, who seek to clarify our ideas, let us reject all this allegorical splendor that offends us. Let us consider enthusiasm as a philosopher considers great men, without any regard for the vain show that envelops and conceals them.

Enthusiasm was, therefore, no longer a mysterious influx, a sudden irruption of the sacred. It was psychologized and secularized by being definitively reduced to the imagination and emotion—that is, to a person's inner being. The abbé Dubos even orients the concept toward physiology when he bases it on "the quality of the blood . . . combined with the favorable disposition of the organs." For him, the creative process is situated within a state of grace in which the artist's imagination transforms his perception of the real and reveals to him a secret world hidden behind appearances. "It is enthusiasm that possesses poets," Dubos says, "when they see the Graces dancing in a field in which ordinary people perceive only livestock." In his *Cours de peinture par principes* (1708; A Course in Painting Based on Principles), Roger de Piles takes a somewhat similar view when he defines enthusiasm as "a transport of the mind that makes one think of things in a sublime, surprising, and convincing way." A little later Piles explains the connection between enthusiasm and the sublime:

Although the true is always pleasing, because it is the basis and foundation of all forms of perfection, the true is often insipid when it is isolated. But when it is combined with enthusiasm, the true transports the mind into a state of admiration mixed with astonishment; it violently ravishes the mind, without allowing it any time to return to its normal state. I have included the sublime in the definition of enthusiasm because the sublime is an effect and a product of enthusiasm. Enthusiasm holds the sublime as the trunk of a tree holds its branches, which it spreads out in various directions; or rather, enthusiasm is a sun, the heat and influence of which cause noble thoughts to be born and lead them into a state of maturity that we call sublime.

It is notable that enthusiasm produces the sublime rather than the beautiful, the latter seeming to be more the province of artists who work sedately and according to rules.

Claude Buffier renounces any rational explanation of enthusiasm in his *Traité philosophique et pratique de poésie* (1728; Philosophical and Practical Treatise on Poetry). He writes:

But what is this enthusiasm about which there is so much talk? Is it something that cannot be said? If it could be defined it would be within the grasp of our reasoning, but its character is such as to make itself felt but not at all to make itself understood. It is real and hardly depends on anything but the imagination; it pleases and one cannot say why; it evokes approval and applause; and when one seeks to justify it to oneself, one gets tangled up. It is something happy, noble, sublime, transcendent that places the poet at the perigee of glory, and the reader at the height of rapture.

The most paradoxical article on enthusiasm is certainly the one that Voltaire devoted to the concept in his *Dictionnaire philosophique* (1765; Philosophical Dictionary). Voltaire is wary of the original meaning of the term, which is too close to a state of delirium or trance. He recalls that it originally signified "an emotion in the entrails, an inner agitation," with a strong physiological component that can assume the nature of paroxysm—for instance, in the case of the Delphic priestesses, whose contortions, Voltaire notes, had a sexual character. The immoderate nature of this frenzy, its very intemperance, is close to fanaticism and is therefore highly suspect: "The spirit of faction is marvelously prone to enthusiasm; there is no faction that does not have its wild-eyed zealots. Enthusiasm is above all the lot of misunderstood devotion." (Incidentally, François-

René de Chateaubriand echoes this opinion in the preface to *Atala* [1801].) Since an irrational and uncontrolled enthusiasm is unreasonable, Voltaire goes on to develop the idea—a fairly paradoxical one at first glance—of a reasonable enthusiasm. Thus, in his own way, he attempts a compromise between the traditional vision of poetry and the new spirit of the Enlightenment. He writes:

> The rarest thing is to combine reason with enthusiasm. Reason consists of always seeing things as they are. Whoever sees objects double while intoxicated is thus deprived of reason. . . . How can reason govern enthusiasm? At first a poet designs the layout of his picture; and reason holds the pencil. If, however, the poet wants to animate his characters, and imbue them with passions, then his imagination is stirred and enthusiasm becomes active; he is like a bolting horse; but the path of his flight is traced according to rules.

One danger still looms: "giving oneself up to the bombastic, the overblown, and the nonsensical."

Voltaire's article can be understood more readily when one knows that he wrote it in response to an entry by Louis de Cahusac in the *Encyclopédie*. In a letter to Jean le Rond D'Alembert dated 15 November 1756, Voltaire expresses the profound reservations that are echoed in his article in the *Dictionnaire philosophique*. Cahusac's entry seemed to him to be long-winded and yet incomplete:

> There is no need for such a long discourse to teach that enthusiasm must be governed by reason. The reader wants to know where the word comes from, why the ancients devoted it to divination, poetry, eloquence, and the zeal of superstition; the reader wants examples of this secret transport of the soul that is called enthusiasm; then it is possible to say that reason, which presides over everything, must also guide this transport.

It is true that Cahusac, a man of the theatre and the opera who did not know much about literary theory, is discernably muddled in his description of this condition. He writes:

> One generally means by enthusiasm a type of frenzy that takes hold of the mind and masters it, that inflames the imagination, elevates it, and makes it fertile. It is said to be a transport that makes people say or do extraordinary and surprising things; but what is this frenzy . . . what is this transport, and what is the cause that produces it? These are the points, it seems to me, that we

should have been taught, and about which the least information has been given. . . . Frenzy is nothing but a violent fit of madness, and madness is a lack of or a distraction of reason: thus, when one has defined enthusiasm as a frenzy or a transport it is as if one has said that it is a redoubling of madness and therefore eternally incompatible with reason. However, it is reason alone that gives birth to enthusiasm; it is a pure fire that reason lights in the moments of its greatest superiority. Of all the operations of reason, enthusiasm is always the most sudden and the most animated. Enthusiasm implies an infinite multitude of combinations. . . . Enthusiasm is, if I may say so, the masterpiece of reason.

The most harmonious article on the subject of enthusiasm can be found in an unexpected place in the *Encyclopédie,* in the entry "Éclectisme" (Eclecticism), written by Denis Diderot. This long entry primarily discusses thinkers with whom Diderot felt intellectually compatible, from thinkers of ancient Greece to Nicolas Malebranche. Diderot mentions, among others, the figure of Porphyry, a disciple of Plotinus, whose temperament oscillated between enthusiasm and melancholy. This is Diderot's opportunity for a brilliant digression:

> I shall remark in passing that it is impossible to produce anything sublime in poetry, painting, eloquence, or music without enthusiasm. Enthusiasm is a violent impulse of the soul by which we are transported into the midst of the objects that we have to represent. We see then an entire scene flash into our imaginations as if it were outside ourselves; and indeed, it is outside ourselves, for as long as the illusion lasts, all the beings actually present are wiped out and our ideas are brought to life in their place. It is only our ideas that we perceive, and yet our hands touch bodies, our eyes see animated beings, our ears hear voices. If this condition is not one of madness, it borders on it. This is why considerable common sense is required to balance enthusiasm. Enthusiasm enthralls only when the minds of listeners have been well prepared and controlled by the power of reason; this is a principle that poets must never lose sight of in their fictions, and that eloquent men have always observed in their oratorical flights. If enthusiasm predominates in a work, it injects into all its parts something of the gigantic, the incredible, and the enormous . . . and discourses mingle the insane with the sublime; some people are carried away to acts of bizarre heroism, which show the grandeur, power, and disorder of the soul all at once. Enthusiasm takes a

thousand diverse forms. One man sees the heavens open above his head, another sees hell open up beneath his feet: the first believes himself to be in the midst of celestial spirits, he hears their divine concerts and he is transported by them; the second speaks to the furies, he sees their lighted torches, and he is struck by their cries; they pursue him; he flees from them in terror.

Diderot displays a still more intense fervor in the second *Entretien sur "Le fils naturel"* (1757; Discussions on "Le fils naturel") where the theme of enthusiasm seems to plunge him into the emotional state that he describes rather than defines. He is concerned with expressing the internal process that unfolds in the mind of a creator—a true irrational possession in which it seems as if the artist is seized by a power that disturbs and overwhelms him. Such a state obviously is beyond any logical analysis or clear definition:

Enthusiasm arises from a natural object. If the mind has seen this object from striking and diverse angles, it is preoccupied, agitated, and tormented by it. The imagination is stirred, the passions are moved. One is astonished, touched, indignant, incensed by turn. Without enthusiasm, either the true idea does not present itself at all or if, by chance, one comes across it, one cannot pursue it. . . . The poet feels the moment of enthusiasm: it comes after he has reflected. It makes itself known to him by a shudder that starts in his chest and passes, delightfully and rapidly, to the extremities of his body. Soon it is no longer a shudder, but a powerful and permanent warmth that fires him, makes him breathless, consumes him, and slays him; but it gives life and soul to everything that he touches. If this heat increases, the specters in front of him multiply. His passion is elevated almost to the level of frenzy. He cannot experience any relief except by pouring out a torrent of ideas that press upon one another, collide with one another, and chase one another.

Over the years Diderot's thought underwent a marked evolution. In the *Paradoxe sur le comédien* (1769; Paradox on the Actor), he puts forward as an ideal model the artist who proves capable of controlling his soaring sensibility. In his *Pensées détachées sur la peinture* (1776–81; Detached Comments on Painting) he returns again to the notion of enthusiasm, bringing to bear some new thoughts that take into account the importance of this art form. He writes:

Genre painting does not lack enthusiasm, but there are two types of enthusiasm: that of the soul

and that of the art. Without the first, the conception is cold; without the second, the execution is weak: it is their combination that makes a work sublime.

Nevertheless, Diderot persists in exalting the intoxicating sensations that arouse in him grandeur and mystery. He states:

The great landscape artist has his own particular enthusiasm: it is a type of sacred terror. His dens are dark and deep, his craggy rocks menace heaven; mountain streams roar down from them. . . . Man passes through the enormities of demons and gods. . . . It is in this situation that the philosopher, whether seated or walking slowly, retreats within himself. When my gaze falls on this mysterious imitation of nature, I tremble.

In contrast to Diderot, Séran de La Tour is wary of lyrical tirades on enthusiasm. In *L'art de sentir et de juger en matière de Goût* (1762; The Art of Feeling and Judgment in Matters of Taste), he renounces grandiose terms and sets out to find reasonable and natural explanations of the phenomenon by reducing it to the normal operations of the mind. He analyzes enthusiasm at the moment of the creative impulse as an intense mental effort, an attempt to reconcile the beauty of an image with the difficulties of representing it. He adds:

it seems that the various operations of the soul in a state of enthusiasm are made more comprehensible by the explanation that I have just given than by the grandiose terms, such as "divine frenzy," "ray of light," or "transport of the soul" with which most of those who have addressed this topic have thought to convey it. It is as if they responded to the question why it is night by saying, because it is not day.

In his *Dictionnaire des arts de peinture, sculpture et gravure* (1792; Dictionary of the Arts of Painting, Sculpture, and Engraving), Claude-Henri Watelet makes enthusiasm one of the principal characteristics of young artists. He writes:

The vivid impressions that arouse enthusiasm and that beauty inspires must therefore be regarded as infinitely favorable omens in those young artists who are susceptible to them; such impressions sustain their zeal, encourage emulation, and stir their souls.

Watelet also warns against false or simulated enthusiasm, which he considers as ridiculous as hypocrisy.

Finally, in Volume II, he eventually adopts Voltaire's idea of a reasonable and clearly formulated enthusiasm:

> Listen to a man who is truly smitten and inspired by the perfection of the object that he loves. However enthusiastic he may be, he expresses his various transports clearly; the expressions, the turns of phrase, and the emphases in his speech are as varied as his feelings, but they always express something that we understand; in short, he is interesting, and he communicates his impressions.

In his *Éléments de littérature* (1787; Elements of Literature), which was a standard reference for a long time, Jean-François Marmontel creates a direct link between enthusiasm and imagination, and in doing so he makes use of the usual metaphors of intoxication, frenzy, and delirium. The superior operation of the genius in a state of enthusiasm consists of creating a perfect illusion of the real, as much for himself as for others. In Volume II he writes:

> It is this final degree of illusion that one calls enthusiasm . . . for one can then regard the imagination of the author as the theatre in which the picture is painted or the action is performed, and one can consider his soul to be the spectator who surrenders himself to the illusion and is profoundly affected by the passions that animate the scene. Thus, it is as if, in these moments, the man of genius is two people and resembles the sculptor in the fable, simultaneously the deceiver and the deceived.

In England the earl of Shaftesbury suggested a balance between the mystical and aesthetic senses of the term. In his *Letter concerning Enthusiasm* (1708), Shaftesbury severely criticizes the mental disturbances caused by the combination of intense faith with the rigors of persecution among the Calvinist refugees who had escaped from the Cévennes. In contrast, for Shaftesbury enthusiasm is also the name of an impulse that is at once aesthetic and moral and that impels the artist toward the beautiful and the good. He holds that "every admiration, every healthy love is enthusiasm; the intoxication of poets, the sublime of authors, the fire of musicians, the ecstasy of virtuosos—all are forms of enthusiasm." The same approach was adopted by all the members of the group known as the Cambridge Platonists.

In the German-speaking world it was more often a question of enthusiasts than of enthusiasm, and the first term was used to criticize the *schöne Seelen* (sensitive souls) who often took a false and morbid pleasure in this heightened state. Christoph Martin Wieland compared *Schwärmerey* (exaltation) and true enthusiasm, to the difference between sickness, on the one hand, and health and life, on the other. Under the influence of Shaftesbury, the Swiss school (including Johann Jakob Bodmer and Johann Jakob Breitinger) and the poet Friedrich Gottlieb Klopstock endowed enthusiasm with entirely positive value. Immanuel Kant's attitude on this issue was fairly ambiguous. He associated enthusiasm with a strongly felt notion of good, but he distrusted its variability and questioned its capacity to truly ascend to the sublime. This distrust was generally shared by German critics, who were very sensitive to the immoderate aspects of an exaltation that they judged to be close to a psychological and physiological derangement and that increased the number of those claiming to be "visionaries." According to these German thinkers, unhealthy and often erotic elements were mixed with aesthetic and moral pretensions.

In Germany as elsewhere, neither the principle of enthusiasm nor its effects were truly accepted until the publication of the famous chapter on enthusiasm in the final part of Madame de Staël's book *De l'Allemagne* (1810; Germany). She says:

> For literary nations, enthusiasm is everything. . . . This disposition of the soul has strength, despite its sweetness. . . . The storms of the passions subside, the pleasures of self-esteem fade away, enthusiasm alone is unchanging; in a word, it is inseparable from happiness and from enlightenment.

ROLAND MORTIER

See also Artist; Beautiful; Criticism; Genius; Inspiration; Melancholy; Originality; Sublime

Further Reading

Knabe, Peter-Eckhard, *Schlüsselbegriffe des kunsttheoretischen Denkens in Frankreich von der Spätklassik bis zum Ende der Aufklärung*, Düsseldorf: Schwann, 1972

Knox, Ronald Arbuthnott, *Enthusiasm: A Chapter in the History of Religion, with Special Reference to the XVII and XVIII Centuries*, New York and Oxford: Oxford University Press, 1950

Tucker, Susie I., *Enthusiasm: A Study in Semantic Change*, Cambridge: Cambridge University Press, 1972

Epicureanism

There are numerous references to Epicureanism in countless texts produced during the age of the Enlightenment. They appear in several of the great debates of the period—including debates on Creation, nature, happiness, and pleasure—and they often crystallize strongly held but antithetical ideological positions. The Greek philosopher Epicurus was one of the most-cited names of the age of the Enlightenment. For example, Julien Offrey de La Mettrie's *Système d'Épicure* (1751; System of Epicurus) and the abbé Batteux's *Morale d'Épicure* (1758; The Morality of Epicurus) appeared in the same decade. The adjective "Epicurean" also frequently occurs in moralistic writings of the age, with a wide variety of connotations. However, in contrast to the well-defined schools of Epicurean thought that emerged in the second half of the 17th century with the works of Pierre Gassendi or Charles de Marguetel de Saint-Denis de Saint-Évremond, it is not easy to identify schools of Epicurean thought in the 18th century. Accordingly, we must consider the functions of all these references and the various degrees of consistency among them.

The rediscovery of Epicurus began in Italy at the start of the 17th century and was propagated in France with François La Mothe Le Vayer's *Quatre dialogues faits à l'imitation des anciens* (1630; Four Dialogues Made in Imitation of the Ancients) and Gassendi's treatise *De Vita et Moribus Epicuri* (On the Life and Manners of Epicurus), completed in Latin in 1634 and published 13 years later. In 1659 the rare fragments of Epicurus's works were translated into French for the first time in *Le Xe livre de Diogène de Laërce contenant la vie et la doctrine d'Épicure* (The Tenth Book of Diogenes Laertius, Comprising Epicurus's Life and Doctrine) by Michel de Marolles and the abbé de Villeloin.

Epicurus's thought was disseminated first in Parisian intellectual circles, but it gradually spread throughout enlightened Europe, enjoying a particular vogue in England between 1650 and 1725. Epicurean doctrine influenced the thinking of John Locke, Thomas Hobbes, and Baruch Spinoza, among others. This rediscovery initially entailed a rehabilitation. Numerous texts, such as the entry "Épicurisme" (Epicureanism) in the *Encyclopédie,* began with a reminder of the unjust calumnies that had been heaped upon the philosopher and his followers. Every work thus addressed the problem of reconciling the distinct and antithetical images of Epicurus—as sage or depraved man—handed down in Western culture. Enlightenment thinkers took up the task of explaining and analyzing Epicurean thought, and of discussing the morals of the philosopher, through long debates about the double meaning of the Latin word *voluptas,* which could mean either "sensual pleasure" or "spiritual tranquility." As Pierre Bayle writes in his *Dictionnaire historique et critique* (1695; An Historical and Critical Dictionary):

> It was easy to read bad meanings into the teachings of this philosopher and to frighten off good people with his use of the term *volupté* [the French form of the Latin *voluptas*]. If only his explanations had been included when speaking about the term, people would not have made such a fuss.

A century later Epicurus had been restored to favor, giving other thinkers the opportunity to mount a more philological critique, as when Savérien, in his *Histoire des philosophes anciens* (1770; History of the Ancient Philosophers), reproaches Epicurus for his unacknowledged plagiarism of Democritus and Aristippus.

Nevertheless, it is doubtful that the 18th century had gained a thorough understanding of Epicurean philosophy. The earliest excavations at Herculaneum, begun in 1752, unearthed the papyruses containing Epicurus's great treatise *On Nature,* as well as treatises by his disciple Philodemus. However, these texts could not be unrolled, they were not published until a century later, and even today they have been only very partially deciphered. *De rerum natura* (On the Nature of Things) by Lucretius was translated several times (by Marolles in 1650 and 1677, and by Des Coutures in 1685) and was quoted constantly by Enlightenment thinkers, but their knowledge of Lucretius's Greek sources was only secondhand, derived essentially from the texts of his Latin commentators, notably Diogenes Laertius.

This fact explains why, for Enlightenment thinkers, Epicureanism was less a set of fixed dogmas than a storehouse of varied arguments that writers could use in ways that were just as varied. For example, La Mettrie used his *Système d'Épicure* to expound his own ideas. Similarly, it is highly symptomatic that Georges Schmit, in *De la philosophie et des philosophes* (1760; On Philosophy and Philosophers), cites the example of the "schools of the philosophy of Epicurus, formed in France at the beginning of this century" to illustrate the independence of thought of his time, free of the control of the universities and their systems.

The fact that the actual content of Epicureanism was open to debate explains the essentially polemical uses made of this philosophy during the 18th century. In a large number of debates Epicureanism was invoked to justify antagonisms whose ideological foundations are often difficult to trace. When La Mettrie addresses himself to "modern anti-Epicureans," it is clear that he is referring to Christian moralists opposed to earthly pleasures. In contrast, the praise of Greek philosophers by the highly moralistic Samuel August André David Tissot in *L'Onanisme* (1760) is more complex. In Tissot's text, the same opprobrium is directed against those who despised Epicurus in ancient times—the Stoics—and "those who claim to be his modern disciples, who know nothing about him except his name, and who abuse it disgracefully to lend authority to infamous systems that he would have abhorred." Epicurus's name was thus continually being bounced between vices and virtues, *ataraxia* (detached tranquility) and sensuality, and moderation and excess.

For many, the image of Epicureanism retained its magnetic power to repel, although Horace's topos of "Epicurus's swine" clearly fell out of favor during the Enlightenment. That image belonged above all to the 17th century, as exemplified in Garassus's satires (1623–24) against Théophile de Viau's circle. Garassus wrote of "our Epicureans, who . . . make verses when they are in the taverns and eat like pigs," referred to "our young sodomites and Epicureans," and declared in agreement with Sganarelle that "you see in my master Don Juan . . . a swine of Epicurus, a veritable Sardanapalus." During the Enlightenment such negative references were made only anecdotally, as an element in a portrait, as in Denis Diderot's description, in his *Salon de 1769* (The 1769 Exhibition) of the painter Francesco Casanova as "a fat Epicurean who is a little libertine."

The presence of Epicureanism at the heart of the theological debates of the 18th century was far more fundamental. In 1750 La Mettrie wrote *Les animaux plus que machines* (Animals, More Than Machines) in order to appease the anger of the Church following the appearance of *L'homme machine* (1747; Man the Machine). Feigning offense, La Mettrie asks: "Does not this brazen evocation of the system of Epicurus, in a time as enlightened by religion as our own, cry out for vengeance?" Two schools of Christian thought must be distinguished here. The first, following Gassendi, sought to reconcile Epicurean morality and Christianity in the figure of the gentleman (the abbé Trublet); the second, in contrast, wanted to accentuate the differences between Epicurean and Christian doctrines. Thus, in his *Nouveau système du microcosme* (1727; New System of the Microcosm), Edme Guyot uses the label "new Epicureans" to designate disciples of René Descartes who had substituted the arbitrary power of blind chance for the divine order. The marquis d'Argens and Charles Noblot adopted much the same approach.

However, it is Charles Batteux's *Morale d'Épicure* that best expresses the deep distrust that 18th-century Christians generally felt toward Epicurean thought. Batteux challenges the modern praise of Epicureanism and stresses the necessity of warning the young against

"a doctrine contrary to the essential principles of society and religion." Clearly aware of the upheavals then taking place within Western thought, Batteux considers Epicureanism one of the disguises of the Evil One, one of the weapons used by libertines to deny Creation, divine order, and the immortality of the soul:

> One arrives at this final conclusion: Epicureanism, materialism, Stoicism, Stratonism, Spinozism, atheism—all these means are only slightly different from one another, all these sects, at the point where they meet, make common cause.

This revealing amalgam of "isms" shows how, during the Enlightenment, Epicureanism was endorsed or rejected less on its own terms than for the implications that could be ascribed to it, less as evidence of the past than as the premise for a future that some saw as distressing, and others, as glorious.

Indeed, the Epicureanism of the Enlightenment had less to do with the art of living than with ideological engagement. Reacting against the spiritualization of Epicurus's teachings, Saint-Évremond had developed a worldly Epicureanism that celebrated the lively pleasures of youth rather than the indolence and tranquility of a "sick and languid Epicurus," as Saint-Évremond put it in *Sur la morale d'Épicure* (1670; On the Morality of Epicurus). This version of Epicureanism reached its apogee during the Regency, with Chaulieu, Rémond de Saint-Mard, and Pison in the abbé Prévost's *Aventures de Pomponius* (1724; Adventures of Pomponius), before it gradually faded away.

During the Enlightenment the philosophy underlying this morality of the good life gave rise to a large number of aesthetic theories that contested the Stoicism of the 17th century and offered a counter model, based on an exploration of sensibility, of an aesthetics of sensory stimulation (for example, the abbé Dubos's *Réflexions critiques sur la poésie et sur la peinture* [1719; Critical Reflections on Poetry and Painting], Levesque de Pouilly's *Théorie des sentiments agréables* [1749; Theory of Pleasurable Feelings], and La Mettrie's *Art de jouir* [1751; Art of Pleasure]). This aesthetic Epicureanism was firmly rejected by the *Aufklärung* at the end of the century (especially by Baumgartner and Gotthold Ephraim Lessing). However, it can be argued that in the broader scheme of things, worldly Epicureanism gave way during the 18th century to a celebration of free thought. Bayle devotes the bulk of his article "Épicure" to the purity of the philosopher's morals—to the detriment of the philosopher's physics—in order to support his idea of a virtuous atheist society. The same approach can be found in *A Discourse of Freethinking* (1713) by the English writer Anthony Collins, who includes Epicurus among the saints that adorn the chapel he celebrates. The 1800 article "Épicure" in Sylvain Maréchal's *Dictionnaire des athées* (Dictionary of Atheists) is one of the most developed references and is linked to other articles through the recurring adjective *épicurien*. Voltaire, in contrast, never departed from an admiration for Epicurus the physicist, "a great man, for his time," but nevertheless maintained a clearly sceptical attitude toward his philosophy.

This almost elegiac cult celebrating Epicurus's atheism—so different from the indifference toward the gods the philosopher had professed—must be contrasted to the somewhat less uniform celebrations of his morality. The concept of a negative happiness rooted in the idea of repose attests to the Enlightenment's indebtedness to antiquity in general and to Epicureanism in particular. More often than not, however, the debates tended to elide the differences between Epicureanism and Stoicism, even those initiated by the boldest of thinkers, above all Diderot in his *Essai sur les règnes de Claude et Néron* (1779–81; Essay on the Reigns of Claudius and Nero). In this vein Rousseau's heroine in *La Nouvelle Héloïse* (1761; Julie; or, the New Héloïse), professes a completely disembodied and almost ascetic Epicureanism: "To refrain in order to enjoy, that is the philosophy of the wise, the Epicureanism of reason." Even La Mettrie's desire for pleasure is inseparable from a fear of its costs. In *L'anti-Sénèque ou discours sur le bonheur* (1751; The Anti-Seneca; or, Discourse on Happiness), La Mettrie declares that, while "[I am] enough of a Stoic with regard to suffering, illness, calumny, and so on, I am perhaps too much of an Epicurean when it comes to pleasure, health, and praise." In the *Système d'Épicure*, he writes: "Such are my plans for life and death, that in the course of the former [life] and until my last breath, [I am a] voluptuous Epicurean, but at the approach of the latter [death] I am a firm Stoic." For La Mettrie, as for others, Epicureanism was most often detached from any precise philosophical reference and was thus just as often reduced to a rationalization of egotistical and cynical individualism.

Most of the 18th-century debates on Epicureanism bring us back to the question of reconciling individual pleasure with collective happiness. This explains both the interest this philosophy elicited and the stumbling blocks it inevitably encountered. Epicurus's atomistic physics was unacceptable to Christian thinkers in that it denied the divine order, but these same thinkers were at least as critical of the absence of any social or humanistic dimension in Epicurean morality. From the theological point of view, Epicureanism was a strictly individualist philosophy that authorized vice and replaced divine judgment of the soul in the hereafter with conformity to the greatest number here below. Thus, Noblot writes in *L'origine et les progrès des arts et des sciences* (1740; The Origin and Progress of the

Arts and Sciences): "If one found oneself in a state where vice was rewarded and virtue punished, it would be necessary, according to Epicurus, to prefer vice to virtue." Batteux, for his part, writes in *La morale d'Épicure*: "Epicurus can be turned in whatever way suits him. In his system, everything is for the wicked people and against the good." Logically enough, these attacks conclude with the same accusation that would be launched some years later against Rousseau's philosophy: Epicureanism reduces human beings to a level below that of animals, or in the Cartesian version of the critique, to the condition of automatons.

This condemnation of the philosophies of Epicurus and Rousseau under the same heading is hardly accidental. Both philosophies contain the idea that the misfortunes of human beings result from their loss of connection to their own natures. For Epicurus this premise justifies choosing to withdraw from society, while for Rousseau it constitutes the very foundation of his republican ideal: the quest for individual comfort acquires an additional, social dimension. In *L'idée de nature en France dans la première moitié du XVIIIᵉ siècle* (1963; The Idea of Nature in France in the First Half of the Eighteenth Century), Jean Ehrard has interpreted this dual perspective (which can also be found in the thought of Montesquieu and Charles Pinot Duclos) as representing a social shift in how people read Epicureanism:

> Aristocratic Epicureanism [that of Saint-Évremond or La Fontaine] became less idle and less egoistical. The "new man" found his happiness in activity and in the social virtues. Virtuous pleasure, serious happiness: Epicurus had become bourgeois.

Here one finds all the ambiguity that characterized references to Epicureanism during the Enlightenment, whether it was being caricatured by its detractors or distorted by its followers. Epicureanism was used both to legitimize the aspiration to collective happiness and, and the same time, to vindicate that concern for the self from which modern individuality was born in the 18th century.

In closing, we cite two examples of very individualized references to Epicurus from the age of the Enlightenment. The first comes from the comte de Buffon. In 1777, on death's door, he wrote a self-portrait intended as an epitaph, to which he gave the title "La mort de l'Épicurien" (The Death of the Epicurean). His reference to the sage who "is sparing in his consumption even as he increases his enjoyment of it" fits in with the mythology of modest genius that Buffon tirelessly constructed about himself. La Mettrie called himself "Epicurean," but here Buffon proclaims himself "*the*

Epicurean," the genius who isolated himself from his fellow men for the good of humanity and died in peace, certain that his work would soon be completed by others. By way of a second, and final example we should consider ways in which Epicurean philosophy was twisted in the subtle sophistries of the marquis de Sade's libertine characters such as Bandole, who fathers and drowns children and is described as the "great enemy of pomp and sumptuousness, absolutely according to the principles of Epicurus." Here, the philosophical principle is only valid and meaningful in so far as it increases the enjoyment of murder: thanks to his frugality, "Bandole enjoyed the best of health, and his women enjoyed an astonishing freshness; they produced offspring like egg-laying hens." This cynical rendition is of course a far cry from the philosophy of Epicurus, or even the sugarcoated versions of it left to posterity. Yet Sade, too, was the product of an age that appropriated many philosophies for its own purposes and that saw in Epicureanism not so much a school of thought as an ideal mirror to reflect its own doubts and inconsistencies.

JEAN-CHRISTOPHE ABRAMOVICI

See also Atheism; Materialism

Further Reading

Annas, Julia, *Hellenistic Philosophy of Mind*, Berkeley: University of California Press, 1992

Clay, Diskin, *Lucretius and Epicurus*, Ithaca, New York: Cornell University Press, 1983

Frischer, Bernard, *The Sculpted Word: Epicureanism and Philosophical Recruitment in Ancient Greece*, Berkeley: University of California Press, 1982

Hicks, Robert Drew, *Stoic and Epicurean*, New York: Scribner, and London: Longmans Green, 1910; reprint, New York: Russell and Russell, 1962

Menzel, Walter, *Der Kampf gegen den Epikureismus in der französischen Literatur des 18. Jahrhunderts*, Breslau, Germany: Priebatsch, 1931

Mitsis, Phillip, *Epicurus' Ethical Theory: The Pleasures of Invulnerability*, Ithaca, New York: Cornell University Press, 1988

Osler, Margaret J., editor, *Atoms, Pneuma, and Tranquillity: Epicurean and Stoic Themes in European Thought*, Cambridge and New York: Cambridge University Press, 1991

Equality and Inequality

A look back on the 18th century in light of that famous slogan of the French Revolution, "Liberty, Equality, Fraternity," would seem obviously to lead to the conclusion that the notion of equality played a fundamental role in Enlightenment thought, and that it both paved the way and provided a rationale for revolutionary demands. Clearly, however, one can arrive at this conclusion only by way of a fictitious and almost entirely erroneous reconstruction, against the grain of the facts.

It is true that in the 18th century, utopias were still sometimes imagined as egalitarian societies, but in fact this viewpoint was less common than has usually been supposed. The portrayal of the African kingdom of Butua, the utopia of evil and extreme inequality imagined by the marquis de Sade in his *Aline et Valcour* (1788; Aline and Valcour), illustrates this fact. Indeed, utopian societies themselves were usually strongly hierarchical, as in Father Fénelon's *Aventures de Télémaque* (1699; The Adventures of Telemachus), Guillaume Grivel's *L'île inconnue* (1783; The Unknown Island), and in many other examples. In

some cases, utopias were soaked in blood, as in the abbé Prévost's *Philosophe anglais, ou, Histoire de M. Cleveland, fils naturel de Cromwell* (1731; The Life of Mr. Cleveland, Natural Son of Oliver Cromwell). Other utopias were based on an authoritarian paternalism, in the style of the island of Tamoé in Sade's *Aline et Valcour*. Indeed, equality was so far from being a necessary component that the French translators of Thomas More's *Utopia* (Nicolas Gueudeville [1715 and 1730]; revolutionary activist Thomas Rousseau [1780 and 1789]) made it a point to remind their readers of the work's egalitarian aspirations. This fact had been largely forgotten in the translators' own time, as had the work's condemnation of the existence of "thine and mine," defined as the source of every evil. Still more evidence that this insistence on equality was not the unanimous opinion of those who favored utopias is found in *Les voyages imaginaires* (Imaginary Travels), published under the direction of the lawyer Garnier in 1788, on the eve of the Revolution.

The aspiration to equality was not quite dead and buried, however, as Denis Diderot's *Supplément au* voyage de Bougainville (A Supplement to Bougainville's Travels) reminds us, albeit somewhat ambiguously. The work seems to have been almost entirely marginal to the Enlightenment as Diderot never published the text of the *Supplément*. The *Mémoire* (1864; Memoir) of Jean Meslier (1664–1729), a parish priest who advocated a form of agrarian communism, was reduced at the hands of Voltaire to a denunciation of religion. This was not simply a question, as has been assumed a little too hastily, of the wealthy Voltaire reacting against Meslier's ideas. There is evidence that the demand for equality was far from the norm in the 18th century, and, indeed, the idea seemed, paradoxically, somewhat archaic.

In this context, several examples of texts advocating egalitarianism should be mentioned. *Le vrai système* (The True System) by Dom Deschamps (1716–74), was conceived in the circle of the Argensons. However, despite Deschamps's genuine compassion for the difficulties existing in his day, the real depth of his commitment to equality is uncertain, and in any case the text remained unpublished for 200 years. Even if Morelly's *Code de la nature* (1755; The Code of Nature) is added to the list—a work that posterity, following Gracchus Babeuf and Jean-François de La Harpe, long attributed to Diderot—the impact of egalitarian ideology remained insignificant during the period.

Generally speaking, the call for equality, where it existed, arose out of the denunciation of inequality as the source of all social and moral disorders. Writers advocated a model of authoritarian monarchical government (one is tempted to see in this a reflection of enlightened despotism)—a monarchy that would eliminate the aristocratic class in order to provide itself with a powerful administration that would impose the rules of a strict communal life on its subjects. In Eldorado—described in Chapters XVII and XVIII of Voltaire's *Candide* (1759)—money has disappeared (Candide and Cacambo do not pay for the meal that they eat in the public inn), the Church does not exist, and everything is available in abundance; however, nothing in the text allows us to conclude that a genuine egalitarianism is the rule there. In fact, the splendor of the king's palace and the status accorded to the elderly sage who advises the travelers give us grounds for doubting that it is. On the other hand, the most radical passages in the baron de La Hontan's *Dialogues curieux entre l'auteur et un sauvage de bon sens, qui a voyagé* (1703; Curious Dialogues between the Author and a Savage with Common Sense, Who Has Seen the World) denounce the unjust and triumphant inequality of the European monarchies while vehemently exalting the moral and rational egalitarianism of Native American societies. These passages were written by Gueudeville, one of the translators of

More's *Utopia* mentioned above, who was also the author of a fiercely antimonarchical text, *L'esprit des cours* (1699–1710; The Spirit of the Courts). This is the proof that, on the subject of equality, utopias give apparently contradictory lessons. Moreover, to use utopian texts as evidence for the existence of a unanimous Enlightenment demand for equality is to forget the nature of utopias themselves. The volumes of the *Encyclopédie méthodique* (published from 1782; Methodical Encyclopedia) that are devoted to "Economics" remind us that utopias were products of political experimentation, which one should obviously take care not to confuse with political programs.

The overwhelming majority of the writers of the period did not wish to be egalitarian, as is shown by their commentaries on the experience of the Jesuits in Paraguay, who had organized the Guarani Indians according to a strict ideal of communal life. Voltaire explicitly criticizes this ideal in his *Essai sur les mœurs et l'esprit des nations* (1756; An Essay on Universal History, and the Manners and Spirit of Nations) and ridicules it in Chapter XV of *Candide*, which concerns a baron who is both Cunégonde's brother and the Jesuit colonel of a strange native community. Perhaps the presence of the Jesuit priests would have doomed any experiment, even an egalitarian one, to criticism from the *philosophes*. But then, what explains the *philosophes'* unanimous condemnation of the Moravian Brothers who, under the leadership of Thomas Munzer, attempted, at the height of the Reformation, to organize Jerusalem the Golden—a terrestrial Jerusalem—subject to the precepts of the Gospels, and who aspired to a fraternal society, which was to end in anarchy, fire, and blood? In Chapter CXXXI of the *Essai sur les mœurs*, entitled "Des Anabaptistes" (On the Anabaptists), Voltaire, who took his information about the Moravians from Louis Moréri's *Dictionnaire historique* (Historical Dictionary), denounces the ill-fated consequences of their egalitarian dream:

> They developed that dangerous truth that is in every heart, which is that all men have been born equal, and that if popes had treated princes as their subjects, the lords themselves were treating peasants like animals. . . . They claimed the rights of human beings, but they championed them like wild beasts.

The egalitarianism of the English Levelers of Oliver Cromwell's time, and that of the Anabaptists several decades before, were both linked in the memory of the Enlightenment to nightmarish and bloody visions. As Voltaire writes in Chapter CLXXX of the *Essai sur les mœurs et l'esprit des nations*:

They called themselves Levelers, a name that indicated that they wanted to place everything on the same level and to recognize no master above themselves, whether in the army, the state, or the Church.

So, in fact, there was no earthly paradise, for which one would still harbor some nostalgia, but rather the sad reality of a chaotic, cruel, and tortured world, subject to the brutal appetites of the masses or to the ruthless severity of those who held property and power. Voltaire was impressed by the fraternity of the Quakers in their Pennsylvania colony, but the texts he devoted to the subject contain no allusions to any form of equality. Everything seemed to indicate that colonization, if it were well organized, procured a wealth that was unequally distributed, as was demonstrated by the uprising of the insurgents and the loss of Canada, and confirmed by the abbé Raynal's analysis in the *Histoire philosophique et politique des établissements et du commerce des Européens dans les deux Indes* (1770; A Philosophical and Political History of the Settlements and Trade of the Europeans in the East and West Indies).

Like many of his contemporaries, Voltaire believed that inequality was inherent in the nature of human beings and in the way the world functioned. There is no one who does not wish to give orders to one's neighbors or who does not dream of depriving the neighbors of their possessions. The fable of the Troglodytes in Letters XI to XIV of Montesquieu's *Lettres persanes* (1721; Persian Letters) offers a perfect illustration of this sad assumption. Montesquieu evokes the natural savagery of human beings, stating, "All the individuals agreed that they would not obey anyone any longer, and that each would see to his own interests alone, without taking the interests of others into account." That development led to the reign of egoism and the passions. If one of the Troglodytes fell in love with his neighbor's wife, he immediately abducted her. If two Troglodytes joined forces in order to steal from their weaker neighbors, one of them, "tired of sharing what he could have all to himself, killed the other and became the sole master of the field. His domination did not last long: two other Troglodytes came to attack him; he was too weak to defend himself and was slain."

The fable of the Troglodytes, a narrative of the misfortunes caused by absence of virtue and surrender to the brutal violence of the passions, also shows the dramatically harmful results of the rejection of hierarchy and property. The same lesson applies to relationships among nations. After the conversion of the Troglodytes to justice and virtue, Montesquieu notes that "such prosperity was not viewed without envy; the neighboring nations assembled and, using an empty pretext, they resolved to steal their livestock."

Thus, although it seems somewhat paradoxical, both the Christian view of humanity and the atheist view were in agreement that inequality was inevitable, either because of original sin or because of the essential egoism of human beings. In addition to the fable of the Troglodytes, we could also consider Thomas Hobbes and his *Leviathan* (1651), or the utilitarian doctrines developed by Bernard Mandeville in *The Fable of the Bees* (1714–29). In their views, human beings are fatally driven toward inequality by their natural malice, their hedonistic desires, and their vanity. When man is a brute toward other men, society is necessarily inegalitarian, either because the strong oppress the weak or because an authoritarian government imposes itself in order to ensure the survival of a humankind otherwise doomed to perish as a result of its own natural violence.

On a less intellectual level, Voltaire encouraged participation in trade, praised the London and Amsterdam Stock Exchanges, and rejected both a Pascalian withdrawal from the world and the paralyzing anguish of metaphysics, and in all of these positions he endorsed a society based on profit, where personal gain typically prevailed over the general interest. Although Voltaire and Rousseau did not share the same values, they both thought that work and property were the driving forces of historical and social development. In Letter VIII of his *Lettres philosophiques* (1734; Philosophical Letters), Voltaire suggests that Britain's achievement of political liberty and its elimination of oppression by an exploitative nobility were due to trade and to the labors of the most useful part of the nation. However, while Rousseau saw in property the very source of the general unhappiness of humanity, Voltaire perceived in it the liberating movement of progress. In opposition to Blaise Pascal, Voltaire made competition and the aspiration to social advancement into the driving forces of human activity.

Nevertheless, it cannot be denied that during the Enlightenment there was a real nostalgia for primitive equality, whether religious, philosophical, or political. Travelers' reports repeatedly underscore the happy and simple communal life of the "Indian" tribes. However, Voltaire obstinately insisted on distancing himself from this idyllic view of the pre-Columbian world by recalling the authoritarianism of the Aztecs, the human sacrifices that they offered to the Sun God, and the continual wars that tore their empire apart. Voltaire did not believe in the myth of the egalitarian origins of humanity. His views were in contrast to a vague religiosity that conceived of the possibility of a communal paradise, without sexuality, without work, and without property.

His views were also in contrast to those of Montesquieu, who for the sake of his argument mythologizes the republican egalitarianism of Sparta and Rome in the first few books of *De l'esprit des lois* (1748; The Spirit of Laws). Montesquieu recognized all the while that frugality and equality, the principles of democratic government, belonged to the distant past, as was shown by the corruption in the commercial Netherlands of his own day and by the decadence of Rome, which he himself described in *Considérations sur les causes de la grandeur des Romains et de leur décadence* (1734; Considerations on the Causes of the Grandeur and Decadence of the Romans).

The entry "Égalité" (Equality) in Voltaire's *Dictionnaire philosophique* (1764; Philosophical Dictionary) is an unambiguous text. Voltaire does not describe human beings as aspiring to equality or to the communal life, but rather as universally (and naturally) rejecting subordination and the constraints of hierarchy. No one wants to be subordinate, everyone wants to be dominant. All humans naturally desire what their neighbors have. Subordination is the consequence of the simple fact that no one can be self-sufficient. In this text Voltaire argues:

> All human beings would therefore necessarily be equal if they had no needs. The wretched poverty attached to our species subordinates one person to another; it is not inequality that is a real misfortune, but dependency. It matters very little whether such a man is addressed as His Highness or another as His Holiness, but to serve either one is hard.

For example, a cook who works for a cardinal resident in Rome would himself like to have the services of a cook: He too would like to be a cardinal. He has no dreams of equality but rather nurses an irresistible desire for inequality, which he does not want to see exercised at his own expense. Some would say that Voltaire's realism was the cynicism of a wealthy man who belonged to a social and intellectual elite. The entry provides the clearest expression of the *philosophe*'s pessimistic view of humanity:

> On our unhappy planet, it is impossible for men living in society not to be divided into two classes, that of the oppressors, that of the oppressed; both classes have a thousand subdivisions, and these thousand also have their various nuances.

This passage helps to explain Voltaire's strong and ironic rejection of Rousseau's ideas. Reconciliation between the two philosophies is impossible.

It should also be observed that the theme of social advancement is prevalent in 18th-century novels. These novels are peopled with upstart peasants of both sexes, as in Pierre Marivaux's *Le paysan parvenu* (1734–35; Up from the Country) and the chevalier de Mouhy's *La paysanne parvenue* (1735–36; The Virtuous Villager). The contrast between the deserving commoner Figaro and the corrupt Count Almaviva in Pierre-Augustin Beaumarchais's *Le mariage de Figaro* (1784; The Marriage of Figaro) has no connection at all with any demand for equality; rather, it is related to an ideology of merit. It is not so much the class system that is called into question in this work but its foundations, which are considered to be illegitimate. Figaro does not advocate a strict equality but a hierarchy in which his intelligence, his practical knowledge, and his talents will guarantee him his participation in the power structure. The relatively common mistake of interpreting the text as a demand for equality arises from the critique of inequality that Figaro delivers. In Beaumarchais's *La mère coupable* (1792; The Guilty Mother), Figaro denounces revolutionary measures and the new usages of patriotic language, behavior that shows that this spirited servant never shared in a call for equality.

Rousseau begins his *Discours sur l'origine et les fondements de l'inégalité parmi les hommes* (1755; Discourse on the Origins of Inequality) by distinguishing between two types of inequality:

> one that I call natural or physical, because it is established by nature, and consists of a difference of age, health, bodily strength, and qualities of the mind or of the soul; and another that one might call moral or political inequality because it depends on a sort of agreement and is laid down, or at least authorized, by the consent of men. This latter comprises the various privileges that some people enjoy to the prejudice of others, such as being richer, more honored, more powerful than others, or even being able to compel obedience from others.

The whole of the *Discours* comprises a demonstration that there is no inherent relationship between what Rousseau calls "natural" and "political" equality:

> Even less can one discover whether there is any necessary connection between the two forms of inequality, for that would mean asking, in other words, whether those who issue commands are necessarily better than those who obey them and whether physical and intellectual strength, wisdom, and virtue are always found in the same individuals, in proportion to their power or their

wealth. These are questions that should perhaps be raised among slaves within earshot of their masters, but they do not suit reasonable and free people who are seeking truth.

Natural inequality, which Rousseau therefore does not deny, has no social consequences so long as there endures a state of nature in which abundance is the rule and in which human beings live in isolation. It is through the division of labor—beginning in agriculture and then in metallurgy—that physical inequality comes to play a role:

> The division of land was a result of its cultivation, and the first rules of justice followed once property had been recognized. . . . Things could have remained equal in this situation if talents had been equal, and if, for example, the use of iron and the consumption of commodities could always have been exactly balanced; but, there was nothing to maintain proportion, which was soon destroyed; the strongest did the most work; the most skillful made better use of their own work; the most ingenious found ways of reducing their work; laborers needed more iron, smiths needed more wheat, and while they did equal amounts of work, one earned a great deal while the other had difficulty surviving. In this way, natural inequality spread imperceptibly.

Physical strength thus wins for its owner the power of accumulation, a preponderant role in trade, the possibility of theft, and the subjection of the weakest to the strongest. It is at this point that what Rousseau calls "the state of civil war" begins, a war in which the powerful, using their strength and whatever it has allowed them to accumulate, tear one another apart and are subjected to harassment by the weak, who join forces in an attempt to oppose the strongest. "Nascent society gave way to the most horrible state of war," Rousseau asserts. Not only do humans become unequal because of the difference in the goods that they produce or accumulate, but the society of families that follows the isolation of primitive humanity readily allows for comparisons to be made and superiority to be evident. The embryonic social organization is based on competition and the desire to supplant and dominate. "Being and appearing became two different things." The establishment of the right of ownership, which had become the de facto state of affairs, is legalized henceforth. The evolution of labor and natural inequality lead to this state of affairs. One sentence from Rousseau's *Discours* has become famous: "The first person who, having enclosed a piece of land, thought to say, *This is mine*, and found people who were

simple enough to believe him, was the true founder of civil society."

The inequality of wealth becomes ever greater from then on: The rich grow ever richer and the poor become poorer through a process of pauperization that is described in the second part of the *Discours*. The political organization adopted by civil society develops from a freely accepted obedience to wise magistrates by men whose society is still structured around their families, into servitude imposed by tyrants. Rousseau declares that

> it is at this point that all individuals once again become equal, because they are nothing. As subjects have no law other than the will of the master, and the master has no rule other than his own passions, notions of goodness and principles of justice flourish once again.

This is not a matter of a return to a primitive state of affairs, but rather of an ironic perversion of these origins.

Rousseau did not always remain faithful to his radically modern ideas. Romantic fiction allowed him to imagine compromises and types of moderate "inequality," such as the society of Clarens in his *La nouvelle Héloïse* (1761; Julie; or, The New Héloïse). Further, in his relations with the prince de Conti or the maréchal de Luxembourg, Rousseau kept up the illusion of a relationship that respected differences but, being based on free choice, was egalitarian. The fact that he freely wrote to the prince de Conti revealed his desire to keep up this relationship, because it was free from any political or economic dependence. What may appear to be hard to explain or an incomprehensible blindspot on Rousseau's part is easier to understand in the light of his *Du contrat social* (1762; The Social Contract). Indeed, through the establishment of the contract of association and delegation, individuals are defined, by way of a process that the 20th-century theorist Louis Althusser has shown to be complex and theoretically clever: they possess fragments of a divided sovereignty, of which they are simultaneously the donors and the beneficiaries. This concept, which makes possible both the surrender and affirmation of liberty of the self, allows for equality among individuals—even if only at times.

However, the discussion of equality does not end with Rousseau. A study of protests against inequality that is limited to literary texts and that takes care not to confuse them with calls for equality will show that such protests against inequality clearly became increasingly fierce over the years. One such protest appears in Figaro's monologue in Act 5, Scene 3 of Beaumarchais's

Le mariage de Figaro, in which the servant reproaches his master for having received every social benefit at birth, without truly deserving them. Some masters deserve to be servants and some servants to be masters. Once again, the call is for reversal of status within an inegalitarian ideology and not a call for equality: Figaro contends that the authority of masters in modern society should be legitimized by their merit or works. One can trace a tradition that runs from Frontin in Alain-René Lesage's *Turcaret* (1709), who ended up taking the place of his master, to Figaro, through the ambiguous disguises of Marivaux's servants or to the fantasies Marivaux created in *L'île des esclaves* (1724; The Island of Slaves) and *L'île de la raison* (1727; The Island of Reason). This 18th-century carnival version of the "world turned upside down" reveals dissatisfaction with society and an aspiration to a more just legitimization of power, wealth, and authority.

One should not be surprised to find in the marquis de Sade a view that is paradoxically close to Figaro's view. The libertines possess power and authority and exercise their power in all its excess. That power is their legitimate possession, however, because they are made worthy of it by their knowledge, their lack of illusions, their knowledge of human nature, their free acceptance of the body as it is (a machine made to desire and enjoy), and their rejection of religious illusions and the mists of metaphysics. Their victims are weak and isolated and deserve to be victims. While Justine abandons herself to subjection and condemns herself to death, her sister Juliette joins the gang of libertines and masters. Léonore, a character in *Aline et Valcour,* is coldhearted, free from religious belief, lucid about what is at stake in the world; she ends up victorious. In contrast, the virtuous are duped and condemned to perish: Not one of them escapes—neither Aline, nor her mother, nor Sainville. At the end of a long process of development, which Rousseau seemed to have interrupted in writing the *Discours,* this declaration from Sade's heroes made a dramatic reappearance: power belongs to those who are strong in body and in mind.

One has to conclude with the picture of an age that was divided in some ways. It was unanimous in its hostility to equality, which, in its view, did not belong to this world. Ironically, this allowed men of the Enlightenment to rediscover the old Christian idea of equality in the face of death. Rameau's Nephew, in *Le neveu de Rameau* (Rameau's Nephew), published posthumously in 1805, refers to this notion when he says:

At the last moment, everyone is equally wealthy: both Samuel Bernard, who leaves 27 million in gold as a result of theft, pillage, and bankruptcies, and Rameau, who will leave nothing; Rameau, for whom charity will provide the cloth that will

enshroud him. A dead man does not hear the ringing of the bells. It is in vain that a hundred priests chant themselves hoarse on his behalf, and that he is preceded and followed by a long line of flaming torches.

The same idea informed Christian sermons.

At the same time, some people were demanding equality by right during the Enlightenment period. The Société des Amis des Noirs (Society of Friends of the Blacks), for example, called for an end to slavery. Following a tradition that went back to François Poullain de la Barre (1647–1723), others asserted the natural equality of men and women; variations on this idea were passed on by Father Fénelon, in his *Traité de l'éducation des filles* (1682; Instructions for the Education of a Daughter); by Marivaux, in *La vie de Marianne* (1731–38; The Virtuous Orphan; or, The Life of Marianne); and by Pierre-Ambroise-François Choderlos de Laclos, in *Les liaisons dangereuses* (1782; Dangerous Liaisons), through the powerful character of the marquise de Merteuil, as well as in Laclos's response to a question from the academy at Châlons-sur-Marne about the education of women.

It must be acknowledged that libertine radicalism, from Laclos to Sade, was fundamentally opposed to the very idea of equality. The libertine belongs to the race of masters, and the creatures who are subject to his pleasures are so many slaves—without any defense. Sade's *Les cent-vingt journées de Sodome* (The 120 Days of Sodom) provides a perfect illustration of the division of libertine society into tormentors and victims, the strong and the weak, although this division is not the novel's most essential point. Sade's narrative offers a leisurely and detailed picture of libertines and their victims in its portrayal of convents given over to depraved monks, of the castle of Sielling in which libertines and victims are both confined and bound, and of the regulations of the Société des Amis du Crime (Society of the Friends of Crime), an organization governed by a strict hierarchy. It is as if, with a foreknowledge of the events to come, Sade's philosophical discourse was turning itself into a powerful affirmation of the right to inequality for the strong: it was reconstructing, in a proud and denunciatory manner, through the practice of libertinism, the *habitus*—that is, the mental and physical traits—of an aristocratic society.

JEAN MARIE GOULEMOT

See also Natural Law and the Rights of Man; Property

Further Reading

Delaporte, André, *L'idée d'égalité en France au XVIIIe siècle,* Paris: Presses Universitaires de France, 1987

Eroticism

No attempt will be made here to propose yet another definition of eroticism, since to do so in the context of the Enlightenment would run the risk of anachronism. In French the word *érotisme* first appeared in the early years of the 19th century, while the adjective *érotique*, from which it is derived, was rarely used during the Enlightenment. By the same token, the corresponding adjectives in other European languages ("erotic" in English, *erotico* in both Italian and, later, Spanish) do not turn up in dictionaries until the final decades of the 18th century.

In the early years of the Enlightenment the term "erotic" had a specifically medical meaning, linked to the idea of excessive love and delirium. The term seems to have retained this meaning until the 1760s when *érotomanie* (erotomania) came to be used in its place. In the years that followed, the French *érotique* gradually came to designate a literary genre, equivalent to "romances" or "love tales" in English and to *Liebesgedichte* in German. However, if we look more closely it appears that *érotique* was an imprecise generic designation, since it was used to refer both to highly respectable works such as Claude-Joseph Dorat's *Réflexions sur le poème érotique* (1759; Reflections on the Erotic Poem) and to pornographic ones, such as the "erotic" plays written by Delisle de Sales for the prince d'Hénin, or what the marquis de Sade, in his personal notebooks, defined as the "genre of simple eroticism, without words."

The present article will not address the question of pornographic works, but rather will focus on the immense profusion of forgotten texts that deal with love in the age of the Enlightenment. These texts form a legitimate object of study because love was more than just a literary theme in European culture. It was a standard for judging the degree to which a society was "civilized." At the dawn of the Enlightenment, love continued to be associated with a certain aristocratic and French refinement, a view that the 18th century would increasingly call into question.

Erotic works in this age-old tradition were particularly in vogue in the opening decade of the 18th century and again in the 1750s; most readers today would find them virtually unreadable. They were based on a different conception of literature than ours: one focused less on producing serious works than on creating texts designed to be short-lived and for the moment. Erotic literature was often published in the form of small, portable volumes that could be read (or that the owners could pretend to read) in social settings. In reconsidering such erotica, we must imagine the social activity that surrounded their use and that was in harmony with the text: the burst of laughter, the tapping of a fan, the whispering. This type of erotic work represented the very essence of the frivolous in literature—such books were written for women and perceived as disposable consumer products. In one of them we read: "A tale of love must indeed be horribly written and difficult to digest if, having begun life in the bookseller's store, it ends up at the dairy or the grocer's. In any case, one buys such books without being too concerned about the expense" (*Les doux et paisibles délassements de l'amour* [1760; The Sweet and Peaceful Relaxations of Love]).

As an aristocratic product, works of eroticism were supposed to espouse the improvement of morals, which is why Madame de Staël gave them a place as one of the few genres that contributed to the process toward the perfectibility of literature. Throughout the 18th century, this type of erotic work aspired to a poetic style that would come as close as possible to expressing both authentic feelings and delicate morals. Such works sought to reject two aspects of the past: the cold abstractions of chivalrous love and the unseemly excesses of "Gallic" coarseness. As a result, the line between this genre of erotic writing and that of the eclogue, or pastoral genre, was a very fine one. Apart from similarities of setting (shepherds, nature in springtime), the theorists of the pastoral, from the abbé Dubos to the abbé Genest, stated that the style of erotic writing must avoid both the realistic coarseness of the peasant and the artificial affectation of the courtier. Both traditions—the erotic and the eclogue—can be seen as part of a wider movement on the part of the Enlightenment writers to reconcile conflicting elements of their cultural traditions, by proposing a form of happiness that would satisfy both the demands of the heart and the demands of reason.

Criticism of preciosity (an overly refined and affected style) did not begin with the Enlightenment but originated in the previous century; the criticism was aimed less at a social phenomenon than at an aspect of sophisticated discourse. The canonical texts of 17th-century gallantry—such as Honoré d'Urfé's *L'Astrée* (1607–27; Astrea) (or at least its "precious" expurgated version) and Madeleine de Scudéry's *Artamène; ou, Le grand Cyrus* (1649–53; Artamenes; or, The Grand Cyrus) and *Clélie* (1654–60; Clelia)—were invariably proscribed as symbols of artificiality and coldness. In his *Art d'aimer* (1775; The Art of Love), Pierre Bernard, who was known as Gentil-Bernard, could not find words strong enough to condemn those "concoctions of pastoral puerilities and romantic favors" and their "frivolously convoluted sentiments" that reduced love to a "silly

and glacial esteem." Such quasi-metaphysical idealiza-
tions of feelings appeared, in fact, to be incompatible
with the cult of the self on which the whole of the 18th
century was focused. When an Enlightenment writer
spoke of the heart, he referred first of all to his own: "I
do not give a fig about other people's intrigues," the
abbé Chayer proclaims in *L'amour décent et délicat, ou
le beau dans la galanterie* [1760; Decent and Delicate
Love; or, The Beautiful in Gallantry). "I am not at all
moved, as the Scudérys were, by the sugar-coated
heroes like Cyrus the Great and several others. . . . I am
often busy with my own loves."

It seems, however, that this ban on the old-fashioned codes of chivalry went unheeded by authors of
erotic texts during the Enlightenment. When they tried
to return to Greek and Roman models of erotic
romances, they could not escape from the weight of
aesthetic conformism, following the same patterns
that had been brought back into fashion by Montesquieu and his *Le temple de Gnide* (1725; The Temple
of Gnidus): Set in a naturalistic background that is
represented through stereotypically erotic images
(shaded riverbanks, cool groves, and humid grottoes),
nymphs, shepherds, and satyrs are depicted as mingling around a temple that is inevitably dedicated
either to Venus, Love, or Hymen. Yet, within the tradition of 17th-century romans à clef allusions are always
understood: the allegorical figures in poems are
equally at home in Paris or on Cythera. *Le temple de
l'amour* (1752; The Temple of Love) goes so far as to
specify in a note that the satyr depicted in the poem is
a statue in the garden of the Tuileries—"the god Pan,
near the entrance on Saint Honoré." During the same
period in England, a different literary device linking a
conventional genre with eroticism was in vogue. *Ero-
topolis, the Present State of Betty-Land* (1684) and
other works consisted of allegories of the female body.
Thomas Strelser was a master of this genre, which
happily and bawdily distorted the French "cartes du
tendre" (the 17th-century guide to the "Country of
Love"). Strelser came close to writing *fabliaux*—an
old genre of rather coarse tales in his erotic allegories,
rejecting any idea of literary "delicacy."

Another complaint commonly leveled against the
eroticism of the 17th century, its social elitism, had
equally little effect on 18th-century literary practice.
Although 18th-century poets often dreamed of a "natural" society, free from conventions and labels, they
were quick to turn their eclogues into eulogies of marriage. Although marriage was supposedly no longer of
interest to these writers (as, for example, in *Le temple
de l'hymen* [1759; The Temple of Marriage]), it
remained the only triumphant conclusion to the frolics
in the grove. Similarly, reminders of social propriety
were inevitably used to temper emotional lyricism.

Gentil-Bernard repudiated one by one all the cold erot-
icisms of the past, but when he came to define his own
work, he was far from giving free rein to the effusions
of the heart. Instead, he himself became a censor: "This
new poem demonstrates the art of submitting love to
the proprieties, to duties, to morals. . . . It does not
propose to stifle nature at all, but rather, to teach such
love as a gentleman would wish to feel." References to
nature were no less ambiguous for the erotic writers of
the Enlightenment than they were for the thinkers of the
age; such references seemed to be less a rejection of
the socially privileged sphere in which the texts circulated than of its singularly rigid and obsolete forms.
However, as in the literature of gallantry, there was an
ambivalence about desire, which writers tried to disguise and monitor, resulting in writing that was as artificial as the babbling of the *précieuses* ("precious"
women writers).

In contrast, the eroticism of the Enlightenment seems
coherent in its systematic rejection of coarseness and
obscenity. It found a common purpose in the rejection
of all the forms of libertine writing, attacking that
genre's excesses (the "filthy paintings" of debauchery)
as well as its hypocrisies (the "dishonest veils"). The
types of literature rejected were less the pornographic
novels of the period, which belonged to a completely
separate genre of literature, than the poems glorifying
the "attributes" of love. Such odes rejoiced in using the
suggestive words that had been banished by preciosity;
the Venetian Giorgio Baffo and Alexis Piron excelled in
this genre during the Enlightenment. In contrast, many
poems about love sought to transcend the mere physical: "You will not find in this poem," wrote Gouge de
Cessières, " those excessively free depictions, or allusions, that suggest only too well that which should not
be said, nor any half-veiled ambiguities" (*L'art d'aimer*
[1745; The Art of Love]). While libertine writers sought
to flatter the "base instincts" of their readers, erotic
poets claimed to make their readers share in the enthusiasm of pure feeling. Gouge de Cessières saw an illustration of this in the energy of the great thinkers: "Here,
you will find love," he concluded, "such as has been felt
by Descartes and Newton, or by yourselves." Such a
comparison may be surprising but it reveals the complexity of Enlightenment sensibility. In many poems
that sing of pure love, such as "Le lendemain" (The
Day After) in the chevalier de Parny's *Poésies érotiques*
(1778; Erotic Poems), sexuality was not so much denied
as displaced, removed to a different sphere—sexuality
was sometimes the point toward which the whole text
gradually tended; sometimes it was present in a sweetly
recollected moment.

Nevertheless, it must be noted that writers sometimes failed to carry out to the letter their aspirations.
In the 18th century, writers on the arts of loving often

followed the ancient tradition of combining the sweetness of feelings with the bodily pleasures of the table. The union of Venus and Bacchus, extolled in all the "Bacchic" odes of the century and celebrated by the English poet Dashwood in his very Rabelaisian *Medmenham Abbey,* remained loyal to a masculine imaginative tradition in which women are reduced to the status of objects. In Blanchet's *Les réclusières de Vénus* (1750; Venus's Keepers), women start out as mute and consenting lovers and end up as experienced prostitutes. Misogynist fantasies of mastery, often thought to be found only in libertine writing, were also worked into love poems in various ways. Sometimes the theme was introduced in the form of classical pictorial motifs; for example, the text might describe vigorous satyrs or priapic swans, as in Carné's *L'univers perdu et reconquis par l'amour* (1758; The World Lost and Reconquered by Love). Such allusions, which were perfectly transparent to 18th-century readers, account for the difficulty that critics had in distinguishing between obscene texts, which were only easy to identify by virtue of their clandestine dissemination, and "simply" erotic or licentious texts. Pierre Bayle and Julien Offroy de La Mettrie insisted on the differences between them, but Malesherbes, that legislator of the book trade, admitted to being perplexed: "It would certainly be better to suppress them, if one could," he wrote, referring to erotic texts, "but what would be the certain rule or the fixed boundary in this respect? This is where the difficulty lies" (*Mémoires sur la liberté de la presse* [1759; Memoirs on the Freedom of the Press]). In a dramatization of the judgment of authors on Parnassus, written in 1739 by Gachat d'Artigny, the character Baillet extends every extenuating circumstance to licentious authors: "They say that they sing of infatuations in verse, or of loves, but chaste loves; which is to say, it seems to me, that those are loves that make light of the reader's modesty." In the literature of the French Enlightenment, there was no clear definition of what eroticism was, and the real-life world of bookselling reflected this lack of clarity: it was not unusual in this period to find modest odes to love added to collections of forbidden novels, as a purely commercial ploy to increase the size of the volume.

In the 18th century, therefore, the French model of refined and delicate eroticism remained a prisoner of its traditions. As a result, it found itself increasingly out of line with modern sensibilities, or those that were proclaimed as modern. It is clear that, beginning in the second half of the century, sensitive souls were turning to the literatures of northern Europe. Erotic verse became a specialty of British writers (from Edmund Spenser in the 16th century to Alexander Pope in the 18th), but above all of writers in German. The latter include Friedrich Gottlieb Klopstock, Christoph Martin Wieland (*Anti-Ovid, oder die Kunst zu Lieben* [1752; The Anti-Ovid; or, The Art of Love]), and the Swiss writers Albrecht von Haller and, especially, Salomon Gessner, whose works were translated by Denis Diderot and Anne-Robert-Jacques Turgot. In 1759 Dorat became one of the first to recognize this superiority, in his *Réflexions sur le poème érotique,* written as a preface to his rather vapid *Tourterelles de Zelmis* (Zelmis's Turtledoves). In seeking to explain the talent for erotic verse that belonged to the English- and German-speaking nations, he suggested "that in those countries men are more focused, more in touch with themselves; they nourish in silence the sensibility that evaporates in our circles, and seek out nature in the sanctuary of solitude." The frivolity of the French, celebrated by some writers as the essence of sociability (Boudier de Villemert, *Apologie de la frivolité* [1750; Apology of Frivolity]), was contrasted with the greater closeness to nature that characterized the German soul. This idea occurred frequently in François Métra's *Correspondance littéraire et secrète* (1775–93; *Literary and Secret Correspondence*) and in commentaries on erotic novelties. In the final quarter of the 18th century, the comparison became a commonplace, with some writers in German-speaking countries coming to denounce it as overly simplistic. The same idea was also at the center of the change in aesthetic values that took place after the French Revolution, notably among Madame de Staël's circle of friends at Coppet.

In 1806, seven years before the aesthetic synthesis contained in Staël's *De l'Allemagne* (Germany), Charles de Villers wrote a very elaborate study that was formally directed against French eroticism, entitled *Sur la manière essentiellement différente dont les poètes français et allemands traitent de l'amour* (On the Essentially Different Manner by which French and German Poets Deal with Love). In order to demonstrate the superiority of the Germans over the French, Villers made use of a familiar critical tradition, the theory of climates, formerly used to legitimize the supposed superiority of both Western culture and the classical way of thinking. In contrasting the German, who is "more inclined to the internal enjoyment of feeling," with the Frenchman, who is more directed toward "the world and exterior objects," Villers was simply restating the century-old contrast between the gentleman and the libertine. As we have seen, French poets had rejected the metaphysical abstractions of chivalrous love; Villers turned the argument around in order to demonstrate the greater sensibility that was to be found on the other side of the Rhine:

Most Frenchmen entrust to their poetic crucible the elements taken from the sensual and material reign of love, from the passionate attraction of pleasure and enjoyment. In contrast, our German neighbors have almost always chosen the elements of their poetry from what is most holy, most ideal, most mystical in love.

At the end of this rather obvious analysis, Villers dismissed as part of the barbarism of the past not only the French gaiety so often praised by the Enlightenment but also the aesthetic and political coarseness of the French Revolution. The ground was thus well and truly prepared for the prudishness of the 19th century, when numerous "obscenity" trials would condemn, without distinguishing among them, all the forms of eroticism of the Enlightenment, from the most pornographic to the most mannered.

JEAN-CHRISTOPHE ABRAMOVICI

See also Love; Orient and Orientalism

Further Reading

Fischer, Carolin, *Éducation érotique: Pietro Aretinos "Ragionamenti" im libertinen Roman Frankreichs*, Stuttgart: M and P, 1994

Gournay, Jean-François, editor, *L'erotisme en Angleterre: XVIIᵉ–XVIIIᵉ siècles: Études*, Lille, France: Presses Universitaires, 1992

Villers, Charles de, "Sur la manière essentiellement différente dont les poètes français et allemands traitent de l'amour" in *L'"Érotique comparée" de Charles de Villers*, by Edmond Eggli, Paris: Gamber, 1927

Wagner, Peter, *Eros Revived: Erotica of the Enlightenment in England and America*, London: Secker and Warburg, 1988

Wagner, Peter, editor, *Erotica and the Enlightenment*, Frankfurt and New York: Lang, 1991

Zanger, Abby E., *Writing about Sex: The Discourses of Eroticism in Seventeenth-Century France*, Lexington, Kentucky: L'Esprit Créateur, 1995

Essay

While one may assert that the essay as a genre was extremely popular throughout Europe during the Enlightenment, one must always keep in mind that the term could refer to extremely diverse projects and types of writing. For both authors and readers of the era, the essay was a familiar but ill-defined mode of expression. This lack of definition may be observed in the diverse titles used for essays. Many works were explicitly entitled *essais* (essays) but the characteristics that are usually associated with the genre can often also be applied to *discours* (discourses), *enquêtes* (inquiries), *considérations* (considerations), *pensées* (thoughts), and even *lettres* (letters) of the period. What is more, the essayists employed a great diversity of styles and compositional methods. Most essays were in prose but some were in verse, such as Alexander Pope's *Essay on Man* (1733–34). They could be both serious and formal in tone, and highly structured, such as the didactic texts of "popular philosophy" that Christian Garbe gathered in his *Popularphilosophische Schriften* (1796; Writings in Popular Philosophy); others were rhapsodic, formless, and idiosyncratic, as evidenced by the satiric verve of Gasparo Gozzi's *Osservatore veneto* (1761–62; Venetian Observer). There was also great diversity of formats and modes of publication. Essays typically consisted of a few pages published periodically in a newspaper; the majority of what were called "essays" at the time came out in this form, the most celebrated being of course Joseph Addison and Richard Steele's review, *The Spectator* (1711–12). On the other hand, a series of short articles might be gathered together to make a book, sometimes of impressive dimensions, as in the case of Benito Jerónimo Feijóo y Montenegro's nine-volume *Theatro critico universal* (1726–39; Universal Critical Theater). Yet again, an individual essay might itself be several hundred pages long: for example, Voltaire's *Essai sur les moeurs et l'esprit des nations* (1756; An Essay on Universal History, and the Manners and Spirit of Nations), which he expanded from one edition to another. Finally, the essays of the Enlightenment period offered to the reader a vast range of content, resulting from their authors' widely diverging intentions. Some writers—for example, the earl of Shaftesbury in his *Characteristicks of Men, Manners, Opinions, Times* (1711)—chose the essay form to express a philosophy that, while it dealt with abstract questions, deliberately avoided metaphysical jargon and scholastic quibbling. Others, such as Christoph Martin Wieland in *Der teutsche Merkur* (1773–1810; The German Mercury), used the genre as a way of applying their poetic, dramatic, or narrative skills to the treatment of themes taken directly from everyday life. Still others, such as Nikolai Novikov in his *Truten'* (1769–70; The Drone), considered the essay to be a convenient tool with which to criticize the government in power or make partisan comments on the contemporary scene.

Given such diversity, it is by no means certain that 18th-century theorists understood the essay to be an independent genre in its own right. The encyclopedias and dictionaries of the period (Ephraim Chambers's *Cyclopaedia,* Denis Diderot and Jean le Rond D'Alembert's *Encyclopédie,* and the dictionaries of the Académie Française and Samuel Johnson) do mention it as such, frequently with reference to its origins in the writings of Montaigne, but very few contemporary treatises or manuals of rhetoric or composition discussed techniques of essay writing, although Johann Bernhard Basedow did in his *Lehrbuch prosaischer und poetischer Wohlredenheit* (1756; Manual on the Art of Writing in Verse and Prose). On the other hand, these techniques were often reviewed in the context of analyses of more traditional topics, such as the Attic mode—there are detailed comments on Addison's style in Hugh Blair's *Lectures on Rhetoric and Belles-Lettres* (1783)—or the epistolary genre studied by Friedrich Andreas Hallbauer in his *Anweisung zur verbesserten Teutchen Oratorie* (1728; Instruction for Improving German Oratory). While such texts help us to understand the genre, they often seem oversimplified and, as it were, remote from their subject.

For theoretical reflection on essay writing, we need to turn to the writings of the essayists themselves. Some of the most pertinent comments are to be found in various essays about the essay: for example, in two texts entitled "On Essay Writing," one by David Hume (in *Essays, Moral and Political* [1741–42]), the other by Vicesimus Knox (in *Essays, Moral and Literary* [1778]), or again, in the first issue of Pietro Verri and Cesare Bonesana de Beccaria's *Il caffè* (1764–66). That it should be the essayists themselves who theorized about the genre, rather than literary critics, is itself highly significant and reflects the fact that, as a literary form, the essay was always the site of a lively inventiveness. More than in any other type of writing, no doubt, from its earliest modern manifestations in the writings of Montaigne and Francis Bacon—both of whom chose the term "essay" precisely because of its flexibility—essay writers persistently claimed their right to reinvent the rules of the genre by taking the most extreme formal liberties.

For this reason, no attempt will be made here to pinpoint the essential features of essay writing or summarize its customary formal characteristics. Rather, by examining the form from a series of different points of view and, more particularly, by considering its stylistic, sociological, and epistemological status, we shall try to focus on what the essay enabled Enlightenment writers to express that could not be said in other literary forms, while underlining the tensions (and paradoxes) that are inherent in this highly problematic and unstable genre.

Composition and Style of Essays

In the broadest terms, the essay may be characterized as a collection of formal strategies designed to seduce the reader. If the term was used and valued by 18th-century writers, it was by implied contrast to other forms of expression that were felt to be too ponderously formal or technical, such as the *traité* (treatise) or, by the same token, *principes* (principles). By calling his book an "essay," the author was entering into a contract with his readers, making a promise that they were to be instructed without being bored. In the case of highly formal types of essays, the label is nothing more than bait held out to the reader, with little or no connection to the composition or style of the book in question; one would be hard put, for example, to discover any formal differences between Étienne Bonnot de Condillac's *Essai sur l'origine des connaissances humaines* (1746; Essay on the Origin of Human Knowledge) and his *Traité des sensations* (1750; Treatise on Sensations). However, the promise of a lighter kind of reading was often kept, and in such cases, the essayist did everything possible to catch and keep the reader's attention, with short lively texts that had apparently been composed in a single moment of inspiration and that consequently could be read in a single sitting, requiring no previous knowledge. Some essays treated a single topic; others would be packed with bizarre digressions or a combination of random thoughts and anecdotes, spiced with witty sayings or illustrative allegories, the entire exercise being alternately serious and satiric in tone. Needless to add, essays were always written in the vernacular, Latin—the language of the Church—being strictly avoided. Every stylistic feature contributed to this strategy of pleasing the reader. As Knox notes in his *Essays:* "A book's format, its size and its weight all deserve our attention, since they may contribute to its influence."

The classic formula of pleasing the reader in order to instruct him thus took on new formal dimensions. This inventiveness is especially apparent in the redefined relationship between authors and readers, as illustrated by the opening line of Pierre de Marivaux's *Spectateur français* (1721–24): "Reader, I would not wish to deceive you; you should know it in advance, it is not an author that you are about to read." What was an author, exactly, in this context? A figure who imposed his authority by writing in a style that was at once pedantic and intimidating. An essayist, on the other hand, was simply a human being who relied on human nature alone to communicate with other human beings, sharing with them his experience in order to spur their interests. Given that the essayist defined both himself and his reader by reference to the same human nature, his style of writing assumed a mutual trust and a shared complicity. Consequently, the essay writer felt free to expose his thoughts as they evolved during the creative process, inviting the reader to become his collaborator, whether sympathetically or otherwise: thus, the typical asides or solemn invocations addressed to the reader, the challenges and confessions of doubt, the successive and contradictory versions of the same idea, the anticonformist provocations or disarming admissions of inaccuracy or missing information. All of these stylistic devices imply the figure of an intelligent, open-minded, and active reader.

As a final point regarding style, we should note two inherent tensions that created stylistic problems for writers in this genre. In the first place, the desire to please while simultaneously instructing seems to pull the form in opposite directions. This tension is at its most acute in the works of the *philosophes,* who chose the essay form to express their elaborate and hard-to-digest philosophical systems in order to reach a wider audience. Hume's *Philosophical Essays concerning Human Understanding* (1748) and Immanuel Kant's brief *Was heiszt sich in Denken orientieren?* (1786; What Does It Mean to Orient Oneself in Thought?) are thus every bit as complex as the learned treatises whose ideas they were supposed to popularize, even more so, perhaps, in that the philosophical arguments are of necessity condensed into a few pages. Works such as these push the genre to the limits of its possibilities, by overloading it with material that it is ill-suited to express. A second tension may be observed between the essayists' belief in their right to exercise great stylistic freedom and their adherence to a tradition that, for all its flexibility, nonetheless tended to follow certain well-established models. This latter tension is particularly noticeable in the case of periodical essays. Following the immense success of *The Spectator* and its translations into other languages, imitations sprang up all over Europe. Despite some modification on the part of imitators to adapt Addison and Steele's stylistic inventions to new contexts, the end result was the replication of a more or less common model.

The Social Status of the Essay

The purpose of the essay, then, was to please in order to teach. But to what end, exactly? What was ultimately at stake in the growth of the genre was its social impact. Literature, in this new secularized form, would henceforth constitute a power, the effects of which would be felt in every sector of society. As a new figure on the social scene who claimed the right simulta-

neously to inform, to moralize, and to reason with and politicize the reader, the essayist hoped to exercise the greatest possible influence on a readership that, under the pressures of various economic and political factors, was rapidly acquiring power in the form of public opinion. It was this sense of purpose that enabled Enlightenment essayists to tackle an immense range of subjects that, by their variety and topicality, constitute a portrait of the entire social spectrum: the mechanics of government, the latest social customs, the activities of public enemies and benefactors, the censure of old prejudices, and the praise of new technology were all equally grist for the essayists' mill, and the occasion for descriptions, commentaries, and even—if and when required—proposals for reform. As an example of these noble ambitions and proof of the lofty aims of the essayists, consider the case of Catherine the Great, who published her own essays—not unnaturally, on apologetics: "Notes relatives à l'histoire russe" (Notes Relating to Russian History), in *L'Interlocuteur des amis de la langue russe* (1783–84; The Interlocutor of the Friends of the Russian Language). This desire to influence society was often accompanied by a certain self-importance; in the essays of the period, explicitly or implicitly, one frequently encounters the assumption that society *needs* essays, that it does solicit them on account of their beneficial effect. Explanations for this supposed need took many forms, from the most pompous declarations—in his *Frusta letteraria* (1763–65; Literary Scourge), Giuseppe Baretti grandly presents himself as the spokesman for a supposed public reaction against the barbarism and immorality of modern Italian literature—to the kind of market survey that takes a detailed look at the familial and economic situation of potential readers. As Knox explains in his *Essays,* "What are people likely to read if not essays, in the odd half-hour available to them between the inevitable interruptions by chattering children, importunate visitors, or the pressures of business?"

In their desire to understand society and articulate the role that they saw themselves playing in it, the essayists thus built up a picture of society that, while it fell short of a coherent social theory, nevertheless constituted a more or less wide-ranging imaginative representation of social life. In this respect, the essay is similar to the dialogue, in that both genres take as their model the notion of polite conversation as it was practiced in the salons, clubs, and coffeehouses of the age, a form of sociability that was highly valued by 18th-century society. Hume, for example, describes himself in his *Essays* as "an ambassador from the land of knowledge arriving in the land of conversation." Quite apart from the fact that essays were typically written in an informal style that was itself reminiscent of conversation, the essayists who wrote for periodicals frequently used the device of a fictional discussion club, a strategy that allowed them to express various different points of view and give equal weight to all sides of an argument. The title of the abbé Prévost's newspaper *Le pour et le contre* (1733–40; For and Against) illustrates this desire to reach that consensus of opinion that is necessary for social harmony. In *The Spectator,* by a careful distribution of characters, Addison and Steele managed to represent the main elements of English society of the day, notably personified in the Whig merchant Sir Andrew Freeport and the Tory landowner Sir Roger de Coverley. If these essays may indeed be said to offer an authentic representation of social life, it is because they assume that social and political disagreements among the fictional characters are capable of being resolved in the series of polite conversations that take place under the benevolent gaze of Mr. Spectator, that ideal arbiter who is above party interests and who serves as a metaphor for the desirable resolution of similar conflicts among readers, a process that their reading of *The Spectator* was intended to facilitate. If the essayists took polite conversation as their model, it was because they saw in it an ideal process through which men and women could learn to live together in harmony, an expression of that civility that alone makes it possible to reconcile the differences that threaten to disturb the social order. In their celebration of this ideal, the essayists were thus making a much greater claim for the genre than that of mere after-the-event social utility or the expression of a reformatory zeal; in their view, the essay functioned as nothing less than a basic socializing force in society.

However, two tensions inherent in such an ambition need to be pointed out. In the first place, it may be asked to what extent the imaginative representation of society developed in the essays of the day allowed them to have an impact on that society. Is the ideal of a polite sociability, even when it does not run directly counter to reality itself, not likely to be contaminated by more powerful, rival systems of representation, such as political or religious beliefs, or various kinds of prejudice? When Marivaux, frustrated by the difficulties of bringing the public round to his point of view, provocatively and deploringly asks in *L'indigent philosophe* (1727; The Destitute Philosopher), "Are there any readers in the world? I mean people who really deserve to be called readers," it is the public just as much as the essay form that is being put on trial. A second kind of tension derives from the fact that the essayist is required to plunge into the heart of society but at the same time stand apart from it by taking a detached, not to say eccentric, position that alone guarantees his critical independence. In this regard, the eponymous characters that are mentioned in various newspaper titles and refer to this independent stance are particularly revealing. One thinks immediately of *The Spectator,* of course, but

also of José Clavijo y Fajardo's *El pensador* (1762–67; The Thinker), Friedrich Samuel Bock's *Der Einsiedler* (1740–41; The Hermit), Marivaux's *L'indigent philosophe* (Reasoning Beggar), Justus van Effen's *Le misanthrope* (1723), and even James Boswell's *The Hypocondriack* (1777–83). As we can see, the essay claimed to occupy a position that was at one and the same time at the very core of society and almost completely outside it.

Epistemology of the Essay

For all the above-mentioned stylistic and sociological reasons, 18th-century essayists tended to think of themselves as spokesmen for a commonsense point of view that was easy for the public to understand and accept. However, behind this assumption there lay an epistemology that was just as diffuse, but also just as real as the idea of society to which we have alluded. To begin with, it should be recalled that, in the eyes of educated 18th-century readers, the notion of "essay" was inevitably associated with John Locke's *Essay concerning Human Understanding* (1690). In his preface, the English philosopher specifically links the genre to the empiricist nature of his inquiry. It is this Lockean connection between essay writing and empiricism that explains why many authors adopted the title "Essay" for philosophical works that totally lacked the stylistic features that we associate with the genre, such as the previously mentioned essay by Condillac or, again, D'Alembert's *Essai sur les éléments de philosophie* (1759; Essay on the Elements of Philosophy). Moreover, both the etymology and the original meaning of the word "essay" refer, of course, to the notion of experiment, as the relevant articles in the *Encyclopédie*—"Epreuve, Essai, Expérience (gram.)" (Test, Essay, Experiment [Grammar]), as opposed to "Essai (littérat.)" (Essay [Literature])—remind us. Although the meaning of the term "empiricism" needs to be specified, since it has been connected to "experiment" in many different ways, many essayists can indeed be described as empiricists—if for no other reason than the fact that empiricism has been so closely associated with common sense. However, even if we accept that the essayists took the concept of experiment as their starting point, it does not follow that they adhered strictly to the empiricist position, as can be seen in the case of Gotthold Ephraim Lessing, who nevertheless asserts, in his *Abhandlungen über die Fabel* (1759; Studies on Fables), that "the general only exists in the particular and can only be intuited in the particular." Thus, while the epistemology of the essay may not be described as totally empiricist in spirit, its general tendency is to begin with particulars and only then move on to generalities. For example, Lessing's *Wie die Alten den Tod gebildet* (1769; How the Ancients Represented Death) opens with an analysis of a particular Greek participle and concludes with a general discussion of religion among the ancients and among Christians. The real distinguishing feature of the epistemology of the essay is its opposition to the systematic method embodied in the treatise, which essay writers criticized as being obscure and too far removed from concrete reality.

This preference for particular experiences and concrete examples may be discerned in the way that essayists organized their discourse, with accessibility for the reader always taking precedence over the systematic ordering of knowledge. In this respect, the essay shared the same goals as the dictionary. However, whereas the latter achieved accessibility by the artificial and arbitrary arrangement of subject matter in alphabetical order, essay discourse followed the more natural and legitimate order dictated by the association of ideas as they occurred spontaneously in the mind, an order subsequently rearranged according to the degree of formality desired by the author or the demands of logical cohesiveness. Such a juxtaposition of subject matter, whether between essays in a series or within a single text, therefore presupposes an epistemological postulate that the natural association of ideas guarantees their authenticity and their interest. As Marivaux observes, in the first issue of the *Spectateur français:* "When the human mind is stimulated by random circumstance or the chance encounter with objects, does it not produce more sensible, less bizarre ideas than when engaged in the artificial exercise of composition?" For authors in the empiricist tradition, then, the composition of essays may be properly described, in the fullest possible sense of the term, as a form of experimental writing, in which the writing itself constitutes the experiment by means of which the subject matter treated is given form.

We may conclude by mentioning two concerns that are peculiar to the epistemology of the essay. In the first place, the 18th-century essayist was faced with the classic problem encountered by all thinkers who attempt to reach general truths from particular cases. The very mass of observations that he accumulates may prove an obstacle when it comes to organizing them into a coherent and self-conscious system of knowledge. This problem is reflected in the fact that when collections of essays were republished, the text was often rearranged in chapters grouped by subject matter—this was the case with the 1767 edition of Gozzi's *Osservatore veneto*—or, at the very least, by the addition of a table of contents, as in the 1728 edition of Marivaux's essays. In the second place, because the essay identified in the natural association of ideas a criterion of value, it tended to focus on the site of such associations, namely the individual self, which acquired a privileged epistemological status. Following the example of Montaigne, many essayists used the genre more as an exploration of the self than as a means to analyze the suurounding world. In his discussion of the French essayists in *Characteristicks,* Shaftesbury complains that "everything that is being written these days seems to take the form of memoirs." Epistemologically speaking, then, the essay seems to have had two aims, often fruitfully combined: the constitution of the object of study and the investigation of the observing subject.

MICHAËL BIZIOU

See also Conversation

Further Reading

Bleznick, Donald W., *El ensayo español del siglo XVI al XXX,* Mexico: Ediciones de Andrea, 1964

Butt, J., and G. Carnal, "Essays, Letters, Dialogues, and Speeches," in *The Oxford History of English Literature,* vol. 8, Oxford: Clarendon Press, 1979

Dobrée, Bonamy, *English Essayists,* London: Collins, 1946

Fraser, Theodore P., *The French Essay,* Boston: Twayne, 1986

Küntzel, Heinrich, *Essay und Aufklärung,* Munich: Fink, 1969

Walker, Hugh, *The English Essay and Essayist,* London and New York: Dutton, 1915

Etruscan

Over the course of the 18th century, Italians developed as part of the study of antiquity an interest in Etruscan civilization. The rediscovered Etruscan past represented for the Italian states, and particularly for the Grand Duchy of Tuscany, an ancient cultural identity, one preceding that of the Romans. The recognition of such ties was later extended to other regions, from Venezia to the south of Italy, when many of the archeological sources (especially epigraphic ones) discovered in the south were also interpreted as being "Etruscan." In fact, the entire century was marked by "Etruscomania," which A. Momigliano criticizes as "the sickness of Italian culture," but which was also echoed, albeit more weakly, elsewhere in Europe.

The beginning of this "mania" was spurred by the publication of *De etruria regali* (On Royal Etruria) by Thomas Dempster, professor of Roman law at the University of Pisa from 1616 to 1619. Although the work had been commissioned by Cosimo II de Medici a century earlier, the manuscript was not yet printed when Sir Thomas Coke bought it in 1716 during his grand tour in Italy. With financing from Coke, it was finally printed in Florence between 1723 and 1724 and began to be circulated in 1726. The edition was enriched with *Explicationes et conjecturae* (Explanations and Conjectures), prepared by Filippo Buonarrotti, and had more than 80 engraved plates. This brought it into line with the model proposed some years earlier by Bernard de Montfaucon in his *L'antiquité expliquée et représentée en figures* (1719; Antiquity Explained and Illustrated).

The publication of *De etruria regali* provoked a vast movement of ideas that were reflected in academic dissertations, in archeological excavations, and in the materials selected for private and public collections. The Accademia Etrusca (Etruscan Academy) in Cortona, founded in 1728 by the Venuti brothers played a central role in this movement. The Livorno edition of the *Encyclopédie* devoted an entry to the Accademia Etrusca, which welcomed as members such leading specialists in Italian antiquities as Ludovico Antonio Muratori (1728) and Scipione Maffei (1730), who were well known throughout Europe, as well as Montesquieu (1739), Voltaire (1745), and Johann Joachim Winckelmann (1760).

The chief archeological excavations were at Volterra, Chiusi, and Perugia, the former Etruscan cities that had endured into the modern era, but excavations also extended to the Tuscan countryside and to the painted tombs at Corneto (Tarquinia) in the territories of the Papal States. Illustrated volumes were published to reach the general public, extending interest in the excavations beyond the self-contained circle of the academies. Three volumes are noteworthy: *Museum Etruscum* (The Etruscan Museum), published between 1737 and 1743 by Anton Francesco Gori, who was the principal promoter of Etruscan studies in Florence; *Museum Veronense* (1749; The Verona Museum), which was indebted to Maffei, for his provision of some Etruscan antiquities; and *Museum Cortonense* (1750; The Cortona Museum), published by Francisco Valesio, Antonio Francisco Gori, and Rodulphino Venuti. In addition, there is the *Picturae Etruscorum in Vasculis* (1765–75; Pictures of the Etruscans on Vases) by G.B. Passeri, which was published with Winckelmann's

approval and was devoted to decorated ceramics, a genre that was identified as Etruscan.

The land-owning nobles of Florence, Volterra, Sienna, and Perugia began to collect Etruscan artifacts even before public collections had been gathered for educational purposes. These private collections preceded those in the museums of Volterra and Sienna and even the "Etruscan Museum" in the Uffizi Gallery. In addition, these private collections fed a market in which non-Italian amateurs participated. The non-Italian collectors included Baron Philipp von Stosch, whose collection of engraved stones was cataloged by Winckelmann in Florence (1758–59), and the comte de Caylus, who used Italian intermediaries to augment his collection, which was later integrated into the king's collection (see *Recueil d'antiquités égyptiennes, étrusques, grecques, romaines, et gauloises* [1752–67; A Collection of Egyptian, Etruscan, Greek, Roman, and Gallic Antiquities]).

Etruscan studies extended into the field of historical linguistics, starting with an essay, *Degl'Itali primitivi* (On the First Italians), which Maffei attached to his *Istoria diplomatica* (1727; Diplomatic History). A critique of this essay appears in the *Bibliothèque italique* (Italian Library), published in Geneva, and was translated into Latin by Johann Georg Lotter at Augsburg. At the center of this academic debate is a long text engraved on the bronze tables of Gubbio in the Umbrian language. Maffei believed the language of the text to be of "Etrusco-Hebraic" stock, a view not very far removed from what had been inferred by the Italian linguists of the 16th century. However, and not without controversy, Louis Bourguet, a Neuchâtel scholar and editor of the *Bibliotheqùe Italique*, triggered further discussions about this text by theorizing in detail about the types of writing in ancient Italy.

While the publication *Universal History,* which first appeared in London in 1736, accepted without question the results of the Etruscan infatuation that began in Italy with the publication of *De Etruria regali*, a philologist Nicolas Fréret, secretary of the Académie des Inscriptions et Belles-Lettres (Academy of Inscriptions and Letters) developed his own theory on the origin of the Etruscans in 1753. Based on his personal reading of ancient sources, Fréret held that the Etruscans had entered Italy from the north. This theory was disputed and even rejected in Italy, but Barthold Georg Niebhur would revive it at the beginning of the 19th century.

In Tuscany, at the heart of the debate, the antiquarians, whose ideas did not always benefit the advancement of knowledge, endeavored to consider the outlines of the Etruscans' political organization in relation to the systems highlighted by Montesquieu. According to Giovanni Maria Lampredi, in his *Saggio sulla filosofia degli antichi Etruschi* (1756; Essay on the Philosophy of the

Ancient Etruscans), Etruria was not the land of kings that the courtier Dempster had depicted but, rather, a country of autonomous republics united in a federation, as described by Livy. This political structure favored the free growth of the fine arts. A similar vision inspired the first book of Carlo Denina's *Rivoluzioni d'Italia* (1769; Revolutions of Italy) and the chapter on Etruscan art in Winckelmann's *Geschichte der Kunst des Altertums* (1764; The History of Ancient Art). The latter combined the forms of aesthetic appreciation developed by Caylus, who had already put forward his own theory of the development of art among the Etruscans, and a model derived from Montesquieu of a "nation" dominated by liberty and encouraged by the various republics. This situation explained the number and the quality of the links between the Etruscans and other peoples and the Etruscans' artistic flowering, which was placed chronologically between those of Egypt and Greece. Thus, in line with a schema based on the biological cycle of "nations," copies of archaic Greek statues were situated along with those of Etruscan origin in an interpretive grid that made little sense, in terms of philology.

Christian Gottlob Heyne (1729–1812), one of the "masters" of Göttingen, offered a more scientific reconsideration of these problems. In several essays written between 1772 and 1774, he became one of the first to argue that philology, the study of antiquities, and the history of art were all connected. The numerous amendments he brought to Winckelmann's theories stemmed mainly from his historical vision of the whole culture. This vision had the merit of highlighting two components in Etruscan figurative arts: a "historical" element, and a "Pelagian" Greek—and therefore protohistoric—element. It also took into account what these arts represented, including their ideal forms and their acceptance of Greek mythology. Heyne's work gave rise in Germany to a scholarly current that led to the writing of

the first "modern" monograph on Etruscan civilization, Karl Otfried Müller's *Die Etrusker* (1829; The Etruscans), despite Niebhur's cutting judgment on this field of ancient studies.

In Italy Luigi Lanzi (1732–1810), a Jesuit trained in Rome, became director of the Uffizi Gallery after the suppression of his religious order in 1775. Trained as both a classicist and a scholar of neoclassicism, Lanzi was equally concerned with Etruscan antiquities and inscriptions and with the history of Italian art. He favored a pragmatic and experimental method, which he applied to works of art, classified according to regional schools (in his *Storia pittorica della Italia* [1795–96; The History of Painting in Italy]), and to Etruscan inscriptions, which he encouraged the gallery to buy. Lanzi was responsible for almost completely deciphering Etruscan writing and for developing a preliminary outline of the phonetics and grammar of the language. He succeeded in his work by relying less on the etymological and deductive methods that had previously been used than on an internal analysis of the texts and on comparison to the formulas of Latin inscriptions. His *Saggio di lingua etrusca* (1789; Essay on the Etruscan Language) received the unconditional approval of academic circles in Göttingen, Paris, and Vienna. It was no accident that its publication date also coincided with the beginning of a renewed interest in Etruscan studies.

MAURO CRISTOFANI

See also Archeology; Collections and Curiosities; Museum

Further Reading

Cristofani, Mauro, *La scoperta degli Etruschi: Archeologia e antiquaria nel 700*, Rome: Consiglio Nazionale della Ricerche, 1983

Europe

In 1935, in the midst of a difficult period that drove many intellectuals to raise questions about the identity of Europe, Paul Hazard proposed a time and a place that were to become an interpretive category still in use today: the crisis of European consciousness during the classical period. Like all such historiographical constructs, the time and place defined by Hazard created more problems than it solved, but it identified a profound transformation that foreshadowed another typically European cultural adventure, the Enlightenment. Hazard was the first to suggest that the irruption of "symbolic foreigners" contributed to the breakdown of the majestic stasis of classicism, of that "age of Louis XIV," which Voltaire, significantly, had seen as one of history's four periods of apogee.

These foreigners, represented in various ways, confronted Europe with the problem of complex otherness and diversity in the political, ethical, and religious realms. The Jesuit periodical *Lettres édifiantes et curieuses* (1702–76; Edifying and Curious Letters) did not simply introduce Chinese mandarins to France and the rest of Europe, thereby provoking curiosity and acerbic religious debates, they also gave rise to a desire, for historiographic knowledge, as well as complex economic proposals. The symbolic Chinese sages were accompanied by chivalrous Arabs, who in Henri de Boulainviller's opinion became metaphors for a long-lost aristocratic and feudal liberty, and by Turkish spies and Persian travelers, whom Montesquieu invented after encountering Chinese "others" in Paris. The process of transforming the wild savage into the noble savage was another way of raising questions about the significance of Europe itself. If we examine this same time and place today, we cannot help but identify some of the elements that round out a notion of Europe during the Enlightenment.

First, the Ottoman empire was decreasingly perceived as a threat to Christendom following its last great effort, the siege of Vienna in 1683. The European press considered the siege a moment of great interest, although various audiences reacted in profoundly different ways. The idea of a Crusade had sparked greater enthusiasm in Rome, Vienna, Venice, and Warsaw than it did in Paris, London, and Amsterdam, yet it was precisely in those latter cities that the official culture, as well as the unsanctioned and clandestine cultures, developed a profound appreciation of Islam, just as the strengthening of the Habsburg empire to the East was redefining the borders of eastern Europe.

Another factor that contributed to a developing European identity was the impetuous entrance of Peter the Great's Russia into the European context. This was a painful process, for it redefined the balance of power not only in the East but also in northern Europe, undermining Swedish ambitions to become a great power, threatening Poland's identity, and contributing to the crisis of the Ottoman empire.

A third set of factors were those related to the ongoing modification of the tradition of a balance of power, which had been created during the Renaissance with respect to the Italian states and then exported to the rest of Europe. In truth, national perspectives played a fundamental role behind the scenes of this balancing process. The tradition of natural law was the source not only of the culture of guarantees that led to the theory of a *jus publicum europaeum* (European public law) but also of the plans that appeared through-

out the 18th century for perpetual peace, in the words of the abbé de Saint-Pierre (Charles-Irénée Castel) as well as those of Jean-Jacques Rousseau and Immanuel Kant.

The idea of a Europe already had to contend with England's desire for naval hegemony, with France's ambitions on the continent, and with the territorial plans of Prussia. From the Peace of Westphalia (1648) to the Peace of Utrecht (1713), what the diplomats called the *theatrum europaeum* (European theatre) had tried to use the principles of national law and moral philosophy elaborated in the 17th century by Grotius and others, and to create as a body a balance that would no longer apply only within its own territories but also govern its relationship with the rest of the world. The crisis of European consciousness that thus emerged during the Enlightenment not only reflected an expanded and varied reality but also forced the development of a new idea of Europe upon foundations more solid than those shaken by the Reformation—of a far distant religious unity. The crisis encouraged—and later transformed—the notion of a European *res publica literaria* (Republic of Letters).

In this sense, symbolic foreigners came not only from other continents of the time but also from the past, and they served to reshape the fundamental archetypes of European civilization. For example, the links among Judaism, the classical civilizations, and Christianity were called into question by the reappearance of the myth of the learned Egyptians, Moses's teachers and therefore the fathers of Western culture—or at least of Hermeticism, one of the components of Western culture that Christianity had tried to conceal.

It is difficult to avoid the impression that during the time of crisis during which the Enlightenment originated, Europe was defined above all by contrasts. Europe still lacked a self-defining term such as "civilization," one that it certainly needed, and, significantly, the word was coined in the course of the 18th century. Viewing itself as an essential and creative part of the Old World, which was designated as such only after the discovery of the Americas, Europe used its otherness to develop a critical self-awareness. This was Montesquieu's approach in the *Lettres persanes* (1721; Persian Letters), although he would take another direction in his more mature work, *De l'esprit des lois* (1748; The Spirit of Laws). It was no accident that this latter work appeared after Montesquieu had truly traveled and experienced the political customs and models of various lands. On this journey, he had encountered the work of an original thinker who, in many respects, swam against the tide of the age: Paolo Mattia Doria.

In 1709 Doria tried to define "civil life," and in his later works he argued that the mercantilist model and the ideology of the economists were irreparably corrupting European society. Like his friend Giambattista Vico, who had explored the proud myths of the *antiquissima sapientia italica* (most ancient Italian wisdom) during the same period, Doria expressed an uneasiness and a critical attitude with respect to the type of modernity that was developing. Robert Shackleton has shown that Montesquieu was familiar with Doria's first meditation. In contrast, it is more difficult to establish such a link between Vico's idea of Europe and that of the author of *De l'esprit des lois*. In any event, Vico contributed to the philosophical discovery of the Middle Ages as barbarism "returned," which was perhaps not very far from the belief that the origins of European liberty were found in German forests.

As Federico Chabod has emphasized, Montesquieu puts forth the theme, already sketched by Aristotle, of the difference between a territory dominated by a demand for liberty and another territory, that of Asia, which tends all too naturally toward servitude (see Chabod). This was the archetype of Asiatic despotism that would be so much debated in the 18th and 19th centuries. For Montesquieu the theme of liberty became essential. Voltaire had already made an initial and powerful contribution to this theme with his *Lettres philosophiques* (1734; Philosophical Letters), which, significantly, were also presented as being "English," and not just because Voltaire wrote them in London. For Voltaire the theme of liberty was the fruit of an encounter between economic ideology and toleration. Montesquieu offered Europe the British constitution as an already achieved, and therefore concrete, example of a balance among the three powers (executive, legislative, and judicial) as a source of liberty.

It is difficult to discern a precise idea of Europe in Voltaire's prolific output. If we limit ourselves to the best-known works, it must be said that the *Histoire de Charles XII* (1731; History of Charles XII) takes note of the end of Swedish hegemony in the North and of the emergence of a new power that was henceforth necessarily regarded as European: Russia. The *Lettres philosophiques*, in turn, illustrate a model of liberty and religious toleration the author would wish to prescribe for Europe. Through a study of the reforming energy of such a model, *Histoire de l'empire de Russie sous Pierre le Grand* (1759; Russia under Peter the Great) places a favorable emphasis on the significance of Russia's entrance into Europe, which Voltaire had already evoked in the reconstruction of the mainly military (and therefore not philosophical) adventures of Charles XII. In his more mature works of historiography, Voltaire made a significant contribution to the enrichment of the idea of Europe. For example, by defining periods of apogee, he implicitly outlined, through great syntheses, a history of European civilization. This history encompassed the age of Pericles, the Roman Peace of Augustus, the Italian Renaissance, and finally the classicism of 17th-century France. Through this historical journey, Voltaire implied that the nascent Enlightenment had less to do with Louis XV than with the free and tolerant England described in the *Lettres philosophiques*.

One may wonder which Europe was emerging in the *Essai sur les moeurs et l'esprit des nations* (1756; An Essay on the Manners and Spirit of Nations), Voltaire's great attempt at universal history. It is clear that Voltaire was reacting to the strictly Christian Eurocentrism of his principal predecessor, Jacques-Bénigne Bossuet, whose *Discours sur l'histoire universelle* (1681; A Discourse on the History of the Whole World) was the last great affirmation of the Augustinian theory of history. According to Bossuet, the central position of the Judeo-classico-Christian tradition left no room for other civilizations. There was no place in this Gallican bishop's majestic reconstruction for either symbolic foreigners or for the disquieting opening up of exegesis. Barring the way to Baruch Spinoza also meant sacrificing Richard Simon, who sought not only to renew Christian biblical hermeneutics but also to open up a courageous dialogue with Greek Orthodox culture.

In opposition to Bossuet's model, Voltaire evoked civilizations different from European civilization for two purposes: to combat a tradition that ultimately forced Europe to be tied to *Christianitas* (Christendom) and to criticize the errors of the European model. Nevertheless, in Voltaire's paradigm the idea of European superiority over the ways of life on other continents remained intact, albeit profoundly secularized. A rejection of the biblical narrative forced Voltaire to retain from libertine thought the polygenetic hypothesis of humanity, with all its disconcerting ambiguities, including the accentuation of racial differences. In any case, Voltaire's vision of the Middle Ages is so rich in components "external" to Europe, such as the Byzantine and Arab worlds, that his work can be regarded as one of the first great historiographic reconstructions of the genre. This is certainly quite far from the tenacious stereotype found during the romantic period, of an Enlightenment as a condemnation of the medieval past.

Universal histories are important sources in which to measure the change in the idea of Europe. Both parts of the two-part English *Universal History*, the section on antiquity (1730–42) and the modern part (1758–64), can be studied from this point of view. The publication dates are significant, for the authors in each period were concerned with different problems. The first part originated in the closing stage of the protracted crisis of European consciousness, when the traditional superiority of sacred history over profane history was fading away. It was no accident that the *Universal History* was proposed by George Sale, an unorthodox Islamicist who translated the Koran into English. Along with

Henri de Boulainvillers, Sale became one of those who promoted Muhammad's image in Europe in the 18th century. In the collectively authored *Universal History,* there is no historiographic awareness of the Middle Ages, which are displaced to form an appendix to the ancient world and then reappear as the origin of modernity. The "modern part," which was composed at the time of the Seven Years' War and at the height of English colonial power, takes on a special significance here. As he first analytic outline of the history of the territories the European countries—notably England—were actively conquering, the *Universal History* is not only Eurocentric but overtly favorable to colonialism. The thesis sustained in its pages is that Europe had an incontestable right to dominate other continents—and it should be noted that "Europe" is used as a synonym for England.

In this regard it should also be noted that one of the main authors, John Campbell, along with Lord Bute's spokesman, Tobias Smollet, had a great deal of knowledge not only about the policy of expansionism but also about the economics of colonialism. Campbell was a passionate supporter of the East India Company and subsequently of English rights in the American colonies that were in the meantime preparing for rebellion. Campbell was a Scotsman who dreamed of a "Great Britain"—which would encompass not only his own homeland but also Ireland—as a great naval, commercial, and colonial power.

The *Universal History* is particularly significant because it was translated into nearly every European language over the course of the century. Although the content of its adaptations varied as they were aimed at different audiences, the work in effect united an impressive number of European readers through the same historiographic stereotypes, as is suggested by its five English editions (including two pirate editions in Dublin), two French translations, one German translation, and five Italian editions. David Ramsay used the *Universal History* as a model for an "Americanized" universal history. However, the most important edition was the German version. Its 31st volume gave rise—through such historians as August L. Schlözer, Johann C. Gatterer, and Johann G. Meusel—to a new *Allgemeine Weltgeschichte* (General World History), which was less shaped by the English colonial model and more focused analytically on the territories of northern and eastern Europe.

The abbé Raynal took this procolonialist model sharply to task in his *Histoire philosophique et politique des établissements et du commerce des Européens dans les deux Indes* (1770; A Philosophical and Political History of the Settlements and Trade of the Europeans in the East and West Indies), which indicted most of the various types of European colonialism, from that of the Spanish and Portuguese to the English, while sparing, and even occasionally defending, the "rational" and state-directed colonialism of France.

Alongside the procolonialist model, The abbé Prévost's *Histoire générale des voyages* (1746–89; General History of Travels) appears as an interesting case study both for the idea of Europe and for the rifts within it. Prévost initially based his work on an English model, the work of John Green, which, from a French point of view, had two serious limitations—its insular perspective and its rigid Protestantism. In his French translation Prévost undertook from the outset not only to correct these elements but also to assert the superiority of his own cartography over British efforts in the same field. In this rivalry, which coincided toward the end with the Seven Years' War, Prévost was the victor, owing to his greater flexibility. Green abandoned his work, while the French version proved worthy of the label "general" because of its capacity to describe all the continents by way of the various types of European voyages, not only those of Dutch, English, and French merchants but also those of missionaries and diplomats. Protestant prejudice led Green to make ironic remarks about the *Lettres édifiantes,* without displaying any understanding of them; in contrast, Prévost was profoundly aware that these types of voyages had provided new images and therefore new knowledge of China, India, and the Americas.

The various editions and translations of the *Histoire générale des voyages* in turn reveal the rifts within Europe. The Protestants recognized themselves in the pirated Dutch edition by Pierre d'Hondt, who restored Green's text. Meanwhile, the Spanish, Italian, and German editions reflected Prévost's version, although the Spanish translators not only cut out all the allusions to the "Black Legend" of Spanish colonialism but also inserted passages explicitly defending the Spanish colonial model. After Prévost's death, the *Histoire générale des voyages* was continued by the same people who were collaborating on the *Histoire des deux Indes,* and it reflected other tensions among European rivals, particularly those relating to the competition between England and France in the Pacific; to the discovery of Australia and Oceania; to the competing voyages of the comte de Bougainville and Cook; and, finally, to the exploration of Siberia by Russia, a new and much-feared component of the all-powerful Europe. In opposition to the assessment of European civilization implied in Voltaire's work, James Roberson's presented another important evaluation in *View,* which precedes his monumental history of the emperor Charles V.

The rebellion of the American colonies brought about a new and complex crisis in English and European consciousness, suggesting in the 20 years preceding the French Revolution an ideological space that was henceforth Atlantic rather than just European. It is therefore somewhat disconcerting today to read in *Recherches philosophiques sur les américains, ou mémoires intéressants pour servir à l'histoire de l'espece humaine (1768; A General History of the Americans, of Their Customs, Manners, and Colours)* the indictment Cornélius de Pauw derived from the comte de Buffon to support Pauw's belief in the inferiority of the New World. Even for so convinced an anticolonialist as Raynal, there was no doubt about the inferiority of the New World. This belief, which Raynal also derived from Buffon, provoked the good-humored irony of Benjamin Franklin, who, proposed to an assembled group a comparison between the physical presence of his daughters, born on a continent where everything was necessarily corrupted and inferior, and Raynal's own small stature. The Académie de Lyon even managed to entice its audience of European intellectuals to reflect upon the significance of Christopher Columbus's discovery and to determine whether that discovery should be considered a misfortune or an opportunity for Europe and for human civilization in general.

The many negative responses to the Académie's question revealed a profound uneasiness, a phase of deep crisis, as the equilibrium that had temporarily made synonyms of "philosopher," "patriot," "cosmopolitan," and "European" was being upset. In order to understand this crisis, we must take a step back and consider the ideas of Rousseau. Indeed, that great Genevan did not simply bequeath to the 18th century his demystifying critique of the model of European civilization based on property, luxury, inequality, and individualism; he also reinforced the idea of the homeland with his frontal attack on the cosmopolitan ideology of Voltaire and the *Encyclopédie*.

The *Encyclopédie* entry "Europe," written by the chevalier de Jaucourt, was no more than a confirmation, based on Montesquieu's *De l'esprit des lois*, of the superiority of the Continent, which had a smaller area and population than many others but was much more creative in the realms of the arts, the sciences, and political institutions. Under the same heading, the *Encyclopédie méthodique* (Methodical Encyclopedia) contained a much more complex and dramatic article in its geographic section, which was published in three volumes from 1783 to 1788, the years immediately preceding the French Revolution. The author of this article, which replaced Jaucourt's, was Nicolas Masson de Morvilliers, a barrister at the Parlement of Paris, and an avid reader not only of Raynal but also of Rousseau. The portrait that emerges from Masson de Morvilliers's text is generally quite different from that which Jaucourt had derived from Montesquieu. No longer a land of liberty contrasted with Asiatic despotism, Europe was presented as overwhelmed by discord, by its leading

powers' spirit of conquest, and by the total absence of any laws of international justice. Each state acted according to its own interests, and in their conflicts the small states were nearly always crushed. The examples were obvious, from Corsica to Poland.

Masson de Morvilliers wondered whether the peoples who were constantly being dragged into these wars between nations had at least some reason to be satisfied with their internal administrations. Who were these European peoples whose fate might be envied? Certainly not the indolent Spanish, with their priests, their prejudices, and their poor administration. Nor the Portuguese, who were "as ignorant as they were superstitious" and were under the tyrannical protection of both their clergy and England. Nor was there any reason to envy the lot of the Prussian "in his military slavery," or that of the Germans, who were oppressed by too many masters. Poland was the victim of the despotism of the nobility, nobles, Denmark and Sweden had governments that consumed the resources of their peoples, while in Russia barbaric splendor coexisted with a system of servitude. The Italian states were also areas of dramatic contrasts between the poverty of their inhabitants and the palaces of the aristocracy. This denunciation did not spare France, where the repellent opulence of the cities sentenced the unfortunate peasants to poverty and hunger. A positive Europe did exist for Masson de Morvilliers, who saw it in Switzerland, the Netherlands, and Britain, industrious countries where liberty and just laws reigned, where people knew their rights, and where an agreement of all wills tended toward the general good. Patriotism, which could exist only where there was a homeland, was indeed possible in these countries.

Following these pages full of echoes of "republicanism" and of Rousseau, Masson de Morvilliers turned back to the problem of Europe's confrontation with other continents. It was acknowledged that in Europe people were less enslaved and consequently less miserable than in other parts of the world. The arts and sciences in Europe delayed the progress of slavery. Nevertheless, the outlook remained pessimistic: because all monarchies could tend only toward despotism, the Netherlands and Britain were also threatened, and despotism in those countries would bring about the end of liberty in Europe. One difference above all others seemed to prove definitively Europe's superiority over other civilizations—the other civilizations had not been able to set down roots in regions other than those in which they originated. Europe was able to construct a history that included the histories of all peoples.

Two years later, in 1784, Masson de Morvilliers wrote the article "Pologne" (Poland), passionately denouncing the dismemberment that the great powers imposed on that grand but fragile country. In 1788 the *Encyclopédie méthodique* devoted two articles to Russia, both written by François Robert, who made a distinction between European Russia, civilized in the time of Peter the Great, and Asiatic Russia. Events in Poland, in particular the role of the Russian Empire there, had a tendency to influence the great intellectual witnesses of the age. For example, Edward Gibbon's *History of the Decline and Fall of the Roman Empire* (1776–78) is not only one of the masterpieces of Enlightenment historiography but also a vivid documentation of the tensions and problems that an English and European intellectual could perceive in the decade leading up to the French Revolution.

Two works written in this same context indicate that the heritage of Vico survived, albeit transformed, into the final phase of the Enlightenment: Gaetano Filangieri's *La scienza della legislazione* (The Science of Legislation) and Mario Francesco Pagano's *Saggi politici* (1791; Political Essays). Filangieri's work is one of the great books that transformed the teachings of Montesquieu and Cesare Bonesana de Beccaria through the courage to generalize, Masonic geometry, and a sense of prophecy. In Filangieri's time Europe witnessed the crisis of England, which was no longer the England described by Voltaire and Montesquieu. From then onward Europeans would also observe the disturbing consequences of American liberty, which initiated a process that could involve other countries, including Spain and France, even though they had sympathized with the revolt of the colonies against England. Europe also became aware, with some disquiet, of the presence of Russia. In Pagano's work, Vico's teachings are profoundly transformed through confrontations with the naturalist models of Buffon and, most importantly, Boulanger. In relation to Europe, one sees here the appearance, undoubtedly for the first time in Italy, of the term *civilizzazione,* a translation of the French neologism *civilisation* used by Boulanger and the marquis de Mirabeau. For Pagano, Europe was a continent in which the middle classes, allied to the monarchies, had learned how to vanquish the feudal system. However, while enlightened absolutism and the possibility of reforms constituted reasons for optimism in the first edition of Pagano's book (1783–85), they were cited as reasons for a contrite admission of failure in the next edition (1791–92), in which the danger of catastrophe and the prospect of utopia both figured as possible destinies for Europe.

With the French Revolution the relationship between what Heinz Gollwitzer has called the *Europabild* (picture of Europe) and *Europagedanke* (thought about Europe) changed once again. Cosmopolitanism was recast in models of equality and fraternity, seen as valid for all the citizens of the world. In reality the Jacobin model, engaged in a war against all the states of the ancien régime, tried to construct, irresistibly and almost

self-critically, an ideology of the "great nation" of France, destined to be perceived as a violent usurper by cultures that, one by one, were not so much liberated as conquered. In 1910 Paul Hazard himself reconstructed an example of the creation of a culture by antithesis in his first major work, *La révolution française et les lettres italiennes* (The French Revolution and Italian Literature), in which the origins of Italian romanticism are traced back to the resistance to French models imported by revolutionary propaganda.

For us, as for his contemporaries, Edmund Burke also offers an early example of a rethinking of the idea of Europe based on an anti-French and, more importantly, anti-revolutionary conception. He depicts a Europe where England, preparing to lead the struggle against the "great nation" [France], upholds its own tradition, which, in the face of Jacobin violence, remains the only instrument capable of guaranteeing liberty. The most significant transformation of the *Europabild* would be realized through Napoleon's enterprise, which for 15 years succeeded in constructing on a Europe-wide scale a political and administrative experiment that was not only original but also largely multinational. However, Napoleon's Europe would be defeated by the nation, to which romantic culture, notably in Germany, would offer the most organic and enduring of ideologies, effacing the cosmopolitan ideals of the Enlightenment or restricting them to secretiveness.

GIUSEPPE RICUPERATI

See also Civilization and Civility; Colonialism; Translation

Further Reading

Anderson, Matthew Smith, *Europe in the Eighteenth Century, 1713–1783,* London: Longman, and New York: Holt Rinehart and Winston, 1961; 3rd edition, London and New York: Longman, 1987

Anderson, Matthew Smith, *Historians and Eighteenth-Century Europe, 1715–1789,* Oxford: Clarendon Press, and New York: Oxford University Press, 1979

Chabod, Federico, *Storia dell'idea di Europa,* Bari: Laterza, 1961; 10th edition, 1991

Doyle, William, *The Old European Order, 1660–1800,* Oxford and New York: Oxford University Press, 1978; 2nd edition, 1992

Guerci, Luciano, *L'Europa del settecento: Permanenze e mutamenti,* Turin, Italy: UTET, 1988

Hazard, Paul, *The European Mind: The Critical Years, 1680–1715,* translated by J. Lewis May, New Haven, Connecticut: Yale University Press, 1953 (original French edition, 1935)

Hazard, Paul, *European Thought in the Eighteenth Century, from Montesquieu to Lessing,* translated by J. Lewis May, London: Hollis and Carter, and New

Haven, Connecticut: Yale University Press, 1954 (original French edition, 1946)

Im Hof, Ulrich, *The Enlightenment,* translated by William E. Yuill, Oxford and Cambridge, Massachusetts: Blackwell, 1994 (original German edition, 1993)

Jüttner, Siegfried, and Jochen Schlobach, editors, *Europäische Aufklärung(en): Einheit und nationale Vielfalt,* Hamburg: Meiner, 1992

Venturi, Franco, *The End of the Old Regime in Europe, 1768–1776: The First Crisis,* translated by R. Burr

Litchfield, Princeton, New Jersey: Princeton University Press, 1989 (original Italian edition, 1979)

Venturi, Franco, *The End of the Old Regime in Europe, 1776–1789,* 2 vols., translated by R. Burr Litchfield, Princeton, New Jersey: Princeton University Press, 1991 (original Italian edition, 1984)

Williams, E. Neville, *The Ancien Régime in Europe: Government and Society in the Major States, 1648–1789,* London: Bodley Head, and New York: Harper and Row, 1970

Evil, Representations of

Evil was fascinating to the people of an age that rehabilitated human nature and had faith in the goodness of that nature. According to tradition, humanity had been handed over to the control of the Evil One. In *Paradise Lost* (1667) John Milton had expressed poetically the power of the Devil and his influence over the destinies of human beings. Thomas Hobbes made the break with all religious explanations concerning the aggressiveness of human beings, accounting for it by relating it to their limitations, their fears, their impotence, and their lack of reason. In the state of nature, man is without doubt a brute to other men, but social and political organization permits humans to escape from this primal violence, to establish a rational order. In the entry on "Hobbisme" in the *Encyclopédie,* Denis Diderot applauds such a definition of evil:

In Hobbes, the evil person is a robust child: *malus est puer robustus.* Indeed, evil is as great as reason is weak and the passions are strong. Suppose that a six-week-old infant had the stupid judgment of that age, with the passions and the strength of a man of 40 years. It is certain that he would strike his father, violate his mother, and strangle his wetnurse.

Diderot believed that, thanks to the progress of the Enlightenment, human beings could pass from blind aggressiveness to a collective equilibrium. This conception of an originally evil nature, corrected by reason and society, competed with the idea of the natural goodness of human beings, obscured or led astray by superstitious illusions and the violence of those who would arrogate power over their equals. In the latter conception, the evil person is not so much an egoistic infant as an impostor who has deceived his fellows or a tyrant who has imposed himself upon them.

The personality and writings of Jean-Jacques Rousseau underline the contradiction between the vision of a naturally good human being, corrupted by an unjust and inegalitarian society, and that of a human being who is naturally violent but capable of being socialized. The issue became a point of contention between Rousseau and his friends the Encyclopedists, who identified moral progress with intellectual and economic development. In *Le fils naturel* (1757; The Natural Son), Diderot exorcises every temptation to misanthropy by making his character declare that "man is good in society and is only evil when he is alone." Rousseau reacted strongly against this declaration, responding to it in the seventh of his *Rêveries du promeneur solitaire* (1782; Reveries of the Solitary Walker): "I have become solitary, or, as they say, unsociable and misanthropic, because the most savage solitude seems to me to be preferable to the society of evil people." However, these opposing visions of humanity could lead to the same denunciation of religious imposture and social injustice. Some insisted on the danger of every intolerant faith, others on the danger of a continuously increasing inequality, and both groups could join in criticizing the existing order. In his *Essai sur les moeurs et l'esprit des nations* (1756; An Essay on Universal History, and the Manners and Spirit of Nations), Voltaire sets out the blood-soaked history of a humanity delivered over to evil advisers. He seems fascinated by the long succession of massacres and exterminations, while maintaining the perspective of a rationalization of life among individuals and among nations.

Evil was thus relativized, secularized, and socialized. It could even be reduced simply to a fashion. The chevalier de Jaucourt's entry "Méchanceté et méchant" (Evil and the Evil Person) in the *Encyclopédie* presents evil as a perversion of French worldliness:

It is a kind of malicious gossip, spread with pleasure and in a style of good taste. It is not enough to do damage, it is necessary above all to be amusing; without an amusing tone, the most evil discourse rebounds more on its author than on the person who is the subject of it.

Jaucourt goes on to say that "today, evil is reduced to an art," which is directed above all at the foreigners who place themselves at risk in the salons of Paris. This is illustrated in Gresset's comedy *Le méchant* (1747; The Evil One), which presents Cléon, a seducer without scruples who is ready to mingle social privilege with intellectual elitism. Cléon proclaims his egoism by stating: "Fools are put down here for our trifling pleasures." He limits evil to a simple amusement: "Everyone is evil, and no one is: / One receives, and one takes, one is more or less square." The character Cléon can be linked to a succession of libertines, from Claude-Prosper Jolyot de Crébillon's character Versac in *Les égarements du coeur et de l'esprit* (1736–38; Aberrations of the Heart and the Spirit) to Lovelace in Samuel Richardson's *Clarissa* (1747–48). These characters both build up their desires into aristocratic privileges and analyze their right to be predators. In all the European novels written in imitation of Crébillon and Richardson, evil is embodied in a blasé courtier who seduces naive, bourgeois, provincial, and devout women. Often he is an aristocrat who exercises the mythical *droit du seigneur* (the aristocrat's legal right to sexual possession): he slides from seduction to the pleasure of losing the women who allowed themselves to be taken, to the pleasure of inflicting suffering on others. From gossip and persiflage—at that time, a new (French) word used to designate verbal wickedness—the evil libertine passes to violence and to moral and physical atrocities.

At the end of the 18th century the marquis de Sade constructed his entire oeuvre on the conjunction between worldly libertinism and a metaphysic of evil nature. A radical atheist, Sade declared that his nature was such that he needed to destroy in order to guarantee his own permanence, and sometimes—through one of his characters—he even claimed to be a supreme being of evil. Sade's libertines abandon the social proprieties and deny that society is founded on any principles other than general competition and aggression. Human beings are only distinguished from animals by the reflective character of their wickedness. All morality is a system of illusion to deceive the weakest and the most naive. The contrasting behavior of the two sisters Justine and Juliette shows that virtue is destined to misfortune and vice to prosperity.

The socialization of a concept of evil that, by tradition, fell within the domain of theology also led to the aestheticization of evil and its absorption into dialectic. The seducers of the type of Versac or Lovelace claimed to represent an aesthetic of aristocratic life and to transform their acts of violence into works of art. The title character in Diderot's *Le neveu de Rameau* (1805; Rameau's Nephew) applauds the worst crimes of the renegade Avigon, who is responsible for the ruin and then the death of a Jewish merchant, as if those actions were a theatrical performance: they are "the sublime of evil." Diderot tolerates even greater evil on the part of the Nephew, who discusses a crime "as a connoisseur of painting or poetry examines the fine points of a work of good taste," and who thus helps to liberate aesthetics from its moral implications. In Britain seducers and criminals could proclaim Milton's Satan as a model of dark grandeur who was to be admired. At the end of the century, Gothic novels in England, *romans noirs* (black novels) in France, and novels of terror in Germany conferred an ambiguous value upon criminals while the revolutionary violence of the Terror suggested a satanic explanation of events to some counterrevolutionaries. Seducer or terrorist, the perpetrator of evil could become the bearer of forbidden desires, of repressed social demands, and of a different system of values. He or she was thus implicated in a dialectic of history and became a central figure in literature.

MICHEL DELON

See also Devil; Drama; Novel, Gothic; Libertinism; Passions; Persiflage; Virtue

Further Reading

Pellisson, Maurice, "La mode de la méchanceté: Une maladie morale au XVIIIᵉ siècle," *La nouvelle revue* 36 (15 October 1905)
Sckommodau, Hans, "'Il n'y a que le méchant qui soit seul': Zu den Anschauung der französischen Aufklärung über Menschenhass und Weltflucht," *Romanistisches Jahrbuch* 1 (1947–48)

Exchange

Denis Diderot and Jean le Rond D'Alembert's *Encyclopédie* gives two definitions of the word *échange* (exchange). The first involves a history of the exchange of goods (including barter); the second evokes an exchange between persons, generally the offspring of two financiers, each of whom learns a different business practice from the other. This suggests that in terms of 18th-century semantics, the word "exchange" had more to do with a problematic of the equivalence of roles, employment, and services than with an evaluation (measurement and price) of the goods exchanged. Further, the *Encyclopédie* treats money as a commodity and puts forward the act of measuring as an effect of the thing being measured. The Physiocrats and the liberal politician and economist Anne-Robert Jacques, baron de Turgot, sought to understand the mechanisms of the circulation of money and of credit within a critique of political voluntarism. They represented economic forces not so much as instances of decision but as agents or factors of an organization. Le Trosne, in *L'ordre social* (1776; The Social Order), defines the state itself as administration. The abundant literature of the economic journals supports this view.

The theme of exchange was not limited to economic goods, but was applied to knowledge, to institutions, and even to human beings. For example, in relation to the art of legislation Montesquieu, in Books XXVI and XXIX of *De l'esprit des lois* (1748; The Spirit of Laws), speaks of the transfer of the laws of one political system to another, of a place to another, and of a time to another. For example, within despotism, where there are no laws, religion in fact plays the role of a "depository of laws." The deformation that laws undergo in the course of such a transfer demonstrates that laws have no value in isolation but are dependent on systems.

The search for equivalents or functions introduced a line of thought concerning the notion of service. To define the nature of a thing by its role or its functions was to adopt the experimental method advocated by Francis Bacon and John Locke, who are cited by François-Louis Véron Duverger de Forbonnais in the article "Espèces," (Coins) in the *Encyclopédie,* or by Sir Isaac Newton. As a corollary of this method, the exchange of participants creates the function of the spectator—not only the English periodical *The Spectator* but also the theme of the spy or the traveler, Marana or Montesquieu. Accordingly, there are not only exchanges of goods for money or of currencies for other currencies; things other than commodities are also exchanged, as are human beings in a division of labor. In these mechanisms of exchange, the persons involved are conscious of the fact that money enters only as a factor and not as the measure of the exchange.

Witold Kula has shown how signs and measurements were subject to criticism as things in their own right, following the dialectic of the measuring and the measured in the phenomenon of evaluation. Money is a sign like any other and is therefore subjected to criticism by Locke, in *Some Considerations of the Consequences of the Lowering of Interest, and Raising the Value of Money* (1691), and by Ferdinando Galiani, in *Della moneta* (1751; On Money). As Charles de Brosses considered an economy of linguistic signs, so Forbonnais imagined a physics of the circulation of cash.

The critique of measurement produced another line of questioning that concerned the ways in which economic actors represented themselves in making their demands—for example, in the case of the famous problem of the freedom of circulation of grain, in the request for a regulation of granaries and the circulation of wheat (see Gauthier and Ikni). Florence Gauthier shows how these representations formed part of the movement of commodities and cash. Galiani, in his *Dialogues sur le commerce des blés* (1770; Dialogues on the Trade in Wheat), raised the issue in terms of the time that it takes to transmit information from one grain-market to another, or from one province to another. This line of inquiry, which takes into account the actors as factors in the phenomenon, inverts the physiocratic problematic of public instruction.

Exchange as Determined by the Division of Labor

Jean-Pierre Séris draws attention to the double meaning of the English word "trade"—profession and commerce—in his *Qu'est-ce que la division du travail? Ferguson* (1994; What Is the Division of Labor? Ferguson). He writes:

> The division of labor, before the "celebrated apotheosis" that Smith reserves for it, marks the unforeseen intersection of three perspectives: (1) the mercantilist perspective of maximizing profit; (2) the English moral perspective, which tends to give credence to the principle of the reversal of effects, or of the axiological disparity between effects and causes, a principle according to which there is no place for the "social virtues," which are, in fact, unnecessary; (3) the technological perspective, with its objective of operative efficiency through the maximizing of output and economy of effort.

In *An Inquiry into the Nature and Causes of the Wealth of Nations* (1776), Adam Smith designates labor time as the source of value resulting from the reduction of intervals of labor by assigning a single task to each operative. (See Karl Marx's analyses of fragmented labor in Chapters I and XIV of *Das Kapital* [Capital]). In contrast, Delaire's entry "Épingle" (Pin) in the *Encyclopédie* does not describe the standardization of the labor force but ascribes the differentiation of the operatives' tasks to the system of machinery. In Jean-Jacques Rousseau's *Discours sur l'origine de l'inégalité* (1755; Discourse on the Origins of Inequality) one finds an institutional critique of these technical systems. Rousseau distances himself from Locke and the Physiocrats in order to criticize civil society as the end of all society, as well as the division of labor between the city and the countryside, between agriculture and manufacturing, arising from the civil law implied in the ownership of land. This critique leads him to reflect on the economic and political price of services. By generalizing this problematic, Rousseau concludes, for example, that the price of ancient democracy was slavery.

Rousseau's declaration that "Man is born free but everywhere he is in chains" must be interpreted literally. Slavery was a reality. Slaves formed an inexhaustible labor supply; they were the true raw material of labor. Whereas in Europe labor time was calculated according to Smith's method of reduced intervals, in the colonies labor time was offset by the sheer numbers of slaves. It was perhaps slavery that enabled Bernard Mandeville and Adam Ferguson to conceive of that featureless "man without qualities," the ideal worker. Slavery thus taught them to consider human beings simply as labor power, in the same category as the other powers that a machine stockpiles and consumes, such as the wind, sea currents, or the power of animals, a theory proven by the steam engine and its "horsepower." This "black gold" made fortunes not only for the planters but also for manufacturers, for cities such as Bordeaux or Nantes, and for nations. Linguet, in his *Théorie des lois civiles* (1767; Theory of Civil Laws), shows that the wealth of society is founded upon the inexpensive services of this "human coinage," whether the slaves of ancient times, the slaves of modern times, day laborers, or workers. He makes his point in a sort of monogram, evoking a Dutch maidservant who drinks her coffee from a porcelain cup made in China: how many workers died so that she could do this?

The price of services overturned the argument of the Physiocrats about the land being the only producer of wealth. The Physiocrats divided society into three classes: landowners; laborers, men whose labor produced more value than their wages represented; and men engaged in manufacturing, transportation, and navigation, whose wages were equal to their labor, indicating the "sterility" of their services. (See François Quesnay's *Tableau économique des physiocrates* [1758; Economic Picture of the Physiocrats], reissued in *François Quesnay et la physiocratie* [1958; François Quesnay and Physiocracy].) This underestimation of the price of jobs and services had beenpreemptively criticized, so to speak, by the mercantilists, by Melon in his *Essai politique sur le commerce* (1734; Political Essay on Trade), and by John Law. However, the Physiocrats took into consideration the mobility of the population, as a function of markets and treaties, and the division of labor in manufacturing.

Diderot, in his *Supplément au voyage de Bougainville* (1774; Supplement to Bougainville's Voyage), speaks of the Tahitians before they were swindled into slavery by underhanded legislators, economists, and chaplains. He presents the ideological form of a thesis on population as wealth in the image of the freedom of their customs and their love of children. However, the most characteristic population studies were undertaken from the dual perspective of physical theology, as in William Derham's *Physico-Theology; or, A Demonstration of the Being and Attributes of God in His Works of Creation* (1713), and political arithmetic, as in Sir William Petty's *Essays on Mankind and Political Arithmetic* (1676). Jon Elster makes the case that Gottfried Wilhelm Leibniz's harmony of divine calculation corresponded to a true economic calculation, and there was a convergence between the calculation of the optimal form and statistical laws. Discussions of population in terms of numbers, whether expressed in tables of death rates and birthrates or drawn from the civil registers of the state, reflected the application of a method practiced by all those who drew up numerical tables for other purposes—navigation, insurance, or finance, for example. The interesting point about this method, which reduced the importance of individual intentionality and subjectivity, is that it could not be attacked by the theologians because such reduction was in no respect a natural history of the soul or an ethics in Baruch Spinoza's sense. The laws that this method clarified were those of a divine order and were nothing less than a questioning of the moral order (see Johann Peter Süssmilch's *Die göttliche Ordnung in den Veränderungen des menschlichen Geschlechts* (1741; The Divine Order in the Alteration of the Human Race).

In the entry "Esclavage" (Slavery) in the *Encyclopédie*, the chevalier de Jaucourt refers to Montesquieu's statement in *De l'esprit des lois*, "all men are born free," to condemn slavery in the name of natural law. After tracing the history of the diverse forms of slavery in antiquity and modern times and showing its impact on the division of labor, Jaucourt recalls the abolition of serfdom in France in 1315, stating:

It is therefore directly contrary to the law of nations and to nature to believe that the Christian religion gives to those who practice it the right to reduce to servitude those who do not, in order to render its propagation easier. Nevertheless, this was the way of thinking that encouraged those who destroyed the Americas to [commit] their crimes.

Jaucourt is clearly referring here to the *Code noir* (Black Code) and to the edict of 1685 cited in the article "Esclave" (Slave), which is signed "Mallet and A."

The *philosophes* vented their indignation by publicizing the price of indigo, tobacco, and sugarcane and the atrocity of the slave-trading vessels in trade between Africa, the West Indies, and Europe. In his book *Le code noir, ou le calvaire de Canaan* (1987; The Black Code; or, Canaan's Martyrdom), L. Sala-Molins looks at the implications of religion, economics, and humiliation in the process of enslavement. The French Civil Code that was subsequently put in place ostensibly compensated for economic exploitation by providing instruction in the Catholic faith. Its provisions on concubinage, marriage, inheritance, and giving evidence, and its ban on the participation of slaves in assemblies and in trade, all demonstrate that slaves were regarded as being under the guardianship of the law rather than subjects of it. Slaves were nonetheless regarded as persons in some sense: they could be charged with civil and criminal offenses and subjected to a narrow range of penalties, from whipping and branding to mutilation and death. It should be noted that masters were not permitted to sell or exchange their slaves in France. They had to send them to the colonies to be traded and put to work. There was even a prohibition on anyone removing slaves from the control of their masters in order to free them. The state was the ultimate authority in judging the use of slaves. The system of buildings in which sugarcane was cultivated recalls the administration and development of territory by the Jesuits in Paraguay, except that the Jesuits were careful to avoid the appearance of servitude among the natives.

Exchange as the Circulation of Currency and Commodities

In his study *Or et monnaie dans l'histoire* (1974; Gold and Currency in History), Pierre Vilar examines the increase in the means of payment that avoid the movement of cash, such as systems of credit and insurance. In particular, in relation to the trade in precious metals, he explores the differences in the exchange rates between the European markets, and between domestic and international circulation. These differences underlie his explanation "of the regulatory and redistributive role of the Bank of Amsterdam and the Amsterdam market in relation to the stocks of metals used in large-scale trade" until the early 18th century. Vilar demonstrates that the mercantilist theses of Thomas Mun and Sir Josiah Child were directly linked to colonial development, and discusses the way in which the Bank of England was established as an organ of credit that would replace the goldsmiths' exchange. In an article on J.J. Savary and his *Dictionnaire universel de commerce* (Universal Dictionary of Trade), Jean-Claude Perrot explores the epistemology of the economic theory developed in a family chronicle written by a Benedictine monk, based on the application of scholarship to business affairs (see Perrot). Exchanges of documents replace transfers of funds; documents in different locations replace the actual transportation of currency, which itself had replaced the actual transportation of commodities; and economics is confronted with the problem of value based on displacement and representation.

One finds the history of currency written in different versions. There is the history of the mints where money was produced, which raises such issues as the transportation of goods in the form of signs, in contrast to barter; the knowledge of how these signs were established, their relationship to an authority that guaranteed their value or varied it in order to impose taxes on subjects, and therefore also the form of consent that was invested in them; the consequent critique of enforced circulation and the various methods for the appreciation of coinage by which monarchs reduced their debts; the markets in gold and other precious metals; all the objects, such as bills of exchange, that could play the role of money; banks and credit; and the creation of the great companies that entered into contracts with states. Charles Joseph Panckoucke addresses all these issues in the *Encyclopédie méthodique* (1780; Methodical Encyclopedia). The writings of Galiani and Turgot show how economic actors viewed the Quarrel of the Ancients and the Moderns with reference to credit and identify the traces of Scholasticism and theology among the magistrates who were expected to forbid usury and protect traditional society.

However, there is another history of money (as seen, for example, in Court de Gebelin or, again, in the Jaucourt article cited above), both of which enumerate in an anthropological fashion the materials, forms, and functions of money in different geographical regions. Forbonnais pursues the analyses developed in his *Traité des éléments du commerce* (1754; Treatise on the Principles of Trade) in two entries in the *Encyclopédie*, "Circulation des espèces" (Circulation of Currency) and "Commerce" (Trade). He begins with the history of money in France, where the issuing of coins was a right held by the crown, and cites royal ordinances. He distinguishes between the real and the intrinsic value of currency, which depends on the size of the coins and the quantity of metal in them, and on their imaginary monetary value. He thus presents a historical study of the circulation of money as a function of the arbitrary decisions of kings and the scarcity of currency. In his view, the value of money depends neither on the arbitrary will of the monarch (contrary to Boizard's thesis) nor on the consent of the people (contrary to Locke's thesis). Next, Forbonnais embarks upon a general theory of money as a representation of value, from the point of view of "natural" circulation, meaning when there is a perfect balance between money and commodities, continually dividing them up among all the inhabitants of the country, and when there are no borrowers.

However, if the supply of money is "tightened," for example due to the threat of war, and it becomes necessary to recall it in trade, it is the interest on the money that determines who owns it. Compound circulation arises, then, from the unequal competition between commodities and their signs: further supplies of money can come only from working in the mines or from foreign trade. Forbonnais writes:

> Wherever money is no longer a simple sign attracted by commodities, it has become in part the measure of them, and because of this characteristic it attracts them reciprocally. Thus, every increase in the supply of money, perceptible in circulation, begins by increasing its function as a sign before increasing the volume of those signs. That is to say, before new money raises the prices of commodities, it attracts a larger number into trade than was there before. Finally, however, this volume of signs will be increased by being composed of old and new supplies, whether of commodities, or of their signs.

Regarding the volume of signs compensated by the speed of circulation, Pierre Vilar (see above) cites a text by Adam Smith; one could also cite Quesnay on this issue. With some degree of optimism, Forbonnais describes how

> the volume of signs reestablishes a kind of equilibrium with the volume of commodities, encourages the labor of workers, and develops the consumption of all the classes of people that are useful to the state, in other words, all those who work.

Physical Space as a Factor

Pierre Dockès reminds us of Marx's observations on Sir James Steuart's *An Inquiry into the Principles of Political Economy* (1767) and the division of labor

between the city and the countryside. Following Cantillon's *Essai sur la nature du commerce en général* (1775; Essay on the Nature of Trade in General), he stresses the importance of cities as centers of manufacturing, residences of landowners and *rentiers* (individuals living off private income), sources of expenditure, and centers of communication, as well as the concentration of the labor force, the transportation of raw materials and manufactured products, and the existence of markets.

The Physiocrats objected to the feudal organization of territory into places that were subject to different jurisdictions and tried to homogenize economic "space" just as René Descartes approached physical space in geometric terms. In Volume IV of *Das Kapital,* Marx denounces their attempt to think of administration on the model of physics as a historical mystification. However, one might also wonder whether this attempt was not in fact an extension of the debate between Cartesian physics and Newtonian physics (see Markovits). Looking at the phenomenon of market fairs, Turgot criticized the idea of organizing space around centers. In those places where feudal institutions were less active, Petty, following Cantillon, took an interest in the concentration of cities and "in a limited economic channel in which all activities would be localized at a single point, or in a restricted location, in one city where everything would be produced, consumed, imported or exported." In polemical fashion, other economists, such as Galiani, increased the number of models for the organization of space, differentiated locales, and imagined a local causality governed by factors that were not only geographic and economic but moral and institutional. The placing of physical and moral factors on the same level determined space as a system; the location, or the organization of places, determined the movements of commodities and people; the place, in its turn, appeared as a sort of machine.

The epistemology of economic exchange was thus dominated by three main themes. First, there was the problem of scale. Demography, then in its infancy (John Graunt, Peter Süssmilch, W. Kersseboom), integrated the new mathematical disciplines in order to address the phenomenon of cities and the flow of their populations. There was also a growing awareness of the changing scale of economic forces: the state and the large companies, and the state's concession of commercial monopolies to individuals or companies—for example, the slave trade and the Spanish *asiento*. Second, the exchange of commodities and the exchange of labor (wage-earners and slaves) were placed on the same level, and distances were integrated into the calculation of norms—for example, the means of evading the control of the Spanish exchanges, or smuggling aboard slave-trading vessels.

(In passing, one could link this philosophy of exchange with the philosophy of censorship and the politics of bookselling.) Third, there developed twin discourses of the divine order and the natural order, in which political arithmetic was combined with physical theodicy. The analysis of places that were pathways, easier channels (costs), and the statistical analysis of populations led to moral considerations of public health. A social morality was put in place, a science of the social nature of human beings, which—unlike most of the tenets of Encyclopedists—incorporated the dogmas of providentialism.

The economists' initial treatment of the notion of exchange led to reflections on the phenomena of markets and credit. Some political philosophers attempted to decipher a model of the marketplace within the Hobbesian system of rivalry. One may wonder what impact the economists' method of investigating coinage and credit made on the interpretation of the phenomena of belief and religion. Hume and Smith, for example, used the concepts of political economy to analyze society and the natural history of beliefs. One may still wonder where the philosophies of Kant and Hegel might find the weapons with which to respond to this historical anthropology and, against the natural history of human beings, rescue the cause of the spiritual.

FRANCINE MARKOVITS

See also Credit and Banking; Demography; Physiocracy; Political Economy; Trade

Further Reading
Dockès, Pierre, *L'espace dans la pensée économique du XVIᵉ au XVIIIᵉ siècle*, Paris: Flammarion, 1969
Elster, Jon, *Leibniz and the Development of Economic Rationality*, Oslo: Chair in Conflict and Peace Research, University of Oslo, 1975
Gauthier, Florence, and Guy-Robert Ikni, editors, *La guerre du blé au XVIIIᵉ siècle: La critique populaire contre la libéralisme économique au XVIIIᵉ siècle*, Montreuil, France: Éditions de la Passion, 1988
Kula, Witold, *Measures and Men*, translated by R. Szreter, Princeton, New Jersey: Princeton University Press, 1986 (original Polish edition, 1970)
MacPherson, Crawford Brough, *The Political Theory of Possessive Individualism: Hobbes to Locke*, Oxford: Clarendon Press, 1962
Markovits, Francine, *L'ordre des échanges: Philosophie de l'économie et économie du discours au XVIIIᵉ siècle en France*, Paris: Presses Universitaires de France, 1986
Perrot, Jean-Claude, "Le premier dictionnaire d'économique politique en langue française," *Revue de synthèse* 49 (1980)
Sgard, Jean, editor, *Dictionnaire des journaux, 1600–1789*, 2 vols., Paris: Universitas, 1991

Exclusivity System

The term *exclusif* (not usually translated by scholars, but loosely equivalent to "exclusivity policy") refers to the juridical system that regulated the economic relations between France and its colonies in the Americas under the ancien régime. The system was established within a framework of mercantilist doctrines and practices developed in western Europe in the 17th century. The 1651 Navigation Acts adopted by England under Oliver Cromwell constituted a concrete model for French policy in this area. It was along the same lines that Jean-Baptiste Colbert laid the foundations of the French colonial system in the 1660s and that letters patent, issued in April 1717 and October 1727, reorganized that system in an enduring form around its essential core, the policy of exclusivity.

According to the 18th-century letters patent, the exclusivity regime comprised a set of "laws prohibiting foreign commerce," based on the mercantilist principle that "the colonies must exist only for the sake of the mother country," in order to contribute to the development of that country's assets. "A commercial colony is a province whose cultivation society has overseen with the aim of enhancing the total national output," and this premise justified the creation of a commercial monopoly. As Montesquieu quite clearly asserts in *De l'esprit des lois* (1748; The Spirit of Laws): "It has been established that the mother country alone can trade with its colony, and this for the very good reason that the purpose of establishing [the colony] was to extend commerce."

The monopoly was delineated in the following concrete ways, as set out in a 1766 memorandum calling for (1) "the exclusive use of goods from the mother country carried in its vessels," including that essential factor of production, slaves, brought from the coasts of Africa solely by slave-trading ships from the mother country;

(2) "the direct transportation to the mother country, in its own vessels, of all the products of the colonies," with the corollary that the re-exportation of colonial goods to foreign countries could not be conducted except from ports of the mother country; and (3) "the prohibition on manufactures that the mother country possesses," a prohibition so extensive that it included a ban on the establishment of sugar refineries on the islands that produced the sugar, reflecting the far-reaching logic of the asymmetric division of labor that restricted processing activities to the mother country.

The monopoly on the commerce of the islands was initially held by a single company, the Compagnie des Indes Occidentales (French West Indies Company) founded by Colbert in 1664 with support from Parisian financiers. This unmanageable monster was dissolved soon after, in 1674, but until 1716 the slave trade, the crucial element in the system, remained the prerogative of privileged companies—the Compagnie de Guinée (Company of Guinea) and the Compagnie du Sénégal (Company of Senegal)—that were even less effective. Beginning in the Regency the colonial trade, having been reorganized, ceased to be the absolute privilege of a handful of inefficient companies. Under the terms of the "classic" exclusivity policy, it became a privilege shared by traders in the main ports of the kingdom, whose numbers rose from 13 in 1717 to nearly 20 in 1789. From that point onward these merchants developed a greatly enhanced and dynamic drive to trade with the colonies. On the average they paid a modest fee of 3 percent of their colonial revenues to the Domaine d'Occident, but this was reduced by half in the case of revenues from the slave trade.

However, this relaxation of the exclusivity policy was only "liberal" in appearance. From the point of view of the other essential partners in the trade—the colonists or, more precisely, the Creole aristocracy that owned the plantations—the unilateral and asymmetric character of the monopoly regime remained unchanged. Throughout the 18th century the plantation owners continually contested the foundations of a system that proved itself incapable of sustaining adequate supplies of food and slaves and of absorbing some colonial products, such as *tafia* (a low-quality rum). The exclusivity system also placed the colonies under the control of traders from the mother country by blocking the incentive of foreign competition.

Opposition to the exclusivity system was initially manifested in practice, through the development of endemic fraud and omnipresent double-dealing. Illegal trade with foreigners was facilitated by the proximity of islands that were under foreign domination and by the tolerance, or even connivance, of colonial authorities influenced by Creole landowners. Alongside the illicit trade with the Dutch and the English, one can observe

the growing importance of Anglo-American colonies in North America in such activities. Their involvement was stimulated by the merchants of New England, who were well placed to provide the French islands with timber, flour, and cod at competitive prices, in exchange for the *tafia* and molasses the mother country did not want. This bypassing of the exclusivity policy by an endemic illicit trade increased every time a naval war broke out and paralyzed relations with the mother country, a phenomenon that reached its peak during the Seven Years' War. It was coupled with a renewed questioning of the foundations of the policy.

Perhaps unsurprisingly, no opposition to the policy was voiced in Paris. Exclusivity had received the intellectual support of Montesquieu, who was from Bordeaux, and of the *Encyclopédie* itself. In the entry "Colonies," François-Louis Véron de la Forbonnais writes: "If the colony maintained trade with foreigners, [that would be] a theft committed upon the mother country . . . Restraint of trade in this case is not therefore an affront to freedom of commerce." Accordingly, the policy was criticized by those whose interests were directly damaged by it—the colonists who owned the plantations. Demands for at least a partial opening of the islands to foreign trade became increasingly stronger, since such an opening would satisfy the colonists' need for supplies, notably of slaves, at the best prices and facilitate the circulation of colonial goods by increasing their value in line with the enlargement of the markets for them.

In this clash of doctrines over the exclusivity system, the group favoring the interests of the colonists could rely on the growing power of the Physiocrats' "liberal" ideological critique of mercantilism. Some of Physiocrats, such as Pierre-Samuel Dupont de Nemours, relayed their arguments, in a somewhat muted way, when the great public debate on the topic began in 1765–66.

The colonists, organized into a veritable lobby group, also gradually succeeded in making themselves heard even by the royal government, above all through the duc de Choiseul, who wanted to adapt the system to the new realities created by the Seven Years' War. In 1764 Choiseul named Jean-Baptiste Dubuc, a planter from Martinique, to the post of head of the Bureau des Colonies. Dubuc had a decisive influence on the development of state policy, which from then on was led to arbitrate, for better or worse, between the contradictory positions that placed the traders of the mother country in open conflict with the colonial planters. At the end of what became a veritable national debate lasting two years, Dubuc was cunning enough to propose a compromise formula to the government. His *exclusif mitigé* (qualified exclusivity policy) was made concrete by a decree of July 1767, which—while it reiterated the principles of exclusivity—nevertheless made a legal breach in the system. The decree authorized the creation of two *entrepôt* (intermediary) ports—the Carénage on St. Lucia for the Windward Isles, and the Môle St. Nicolas on Santo Domingo—where foreign ships could dock from then onward to bring timber, livestock, and hides and to load up with syrup and *tafia*. Despite the fairly restrictive provisions of this 1767 decree, "qualified exclusivity," which was interpreted broadly by the colonists and by the colonial authorities, permitted a significant relaxation of the mother country's commercial monopoly, in line with the wishes and the interests of the planters. In this ambiguous, mitigated form, reflecting the unstable compromise imposed by the royal government on the two opposed interest groups in this area, the exclusivity system was prolonged up until the French Revolution, although Castries made one final adjustment to it after the American War of Independence. The decree of August 1784 increased the number of colonial ports open to foreign ships from two to seven and broadened the range of products for importation.

The problem of exclusivity laws disturbed business and government circles alike throughout the century and thus revealed both the growing contradictions of a colonial regime bound in the straitjacket of an archaic and stifling monopoly system and the pretenses of an ideological debate around a false "freedom" of commerce. In fact, this debate was conducted between two interest groups, neither of which questioned the true foundations of the system—that is, the economic system of slave plantations. The system was jointly defended by those who owned the slave-trading ships and by the colonists who owned the plantations. The "liberating" explosion of the slaves on Santo Domingo in 1791 would cause the whole system to disappear by destroying the social framework of the plantation, which was essentially the foundation of the exclusivity system.

ANDRÉ LESPAGNOL

See also Colonialism; Exchange; Ports; Slavery

Further Reading

Tarrade, Jean, *Le commerce colonial de la France à la fin de l'Ancien Regime: L'évolution du régime de l'exclusif de 1763 à 1789*, Paris: Presses Universitaires de France, 1972

Exhibitions. *See* Collections and Curiosities; Museum; Painting: Exhibition of

F

Fable

Overview

During the Enlightenment the verse fable underwent a spectacular evolution. Roughly 150 collections of French fables were published, many of them substantial in size. A great number of these followed the format canonized during the 17th century by Jean de La Fontaine's popular verse fables, comprising 12 books of approximately 20 fables each published between 1668 and 1694. In addition, pieces from the pens of several celebrated authors, including Voltaire, were published in various ephemeral periodicals and poetry collections.

From the last quarter of the 17th century the work of La Fontaine inspired a remarkable crowd of emulators, initially in his own country (including Antoine Furetière, Madame de Villedieu, and, above all, Eustache Lenoble). In the 18th century the trend took on an astonishing momentum throughout Europe. Since the verse fable was an essentially imitative genre, the movement was characterized by complex networks of influence and cultural exchange. The movement can be roughly divided into two periods: fables published before 1760 and those published later.

Before 1760 earlier French influence dominated the production of fables. In France itself, Antoine Houdar de La Motte, in 1719, and Louis Lebrun, in 1722, sought to set themselves apart from their famous predecessor by attempting to combine the poetical form inherited from La Fontaine with more rigorous moralizing and didactic aims that seemed to them to justify the invention of new subjects. Richer, a talented but inferior imitator, set out to exploit that part of the legacy of the classical Greek fabulist Aesop that La Fontaine had neglected. Ardène, in an important preliminary discourse of 1747, reflected on the formulas most likely to recapture the manner of La Fontaine; Pesselier in 1748 transformed the apologue into a sharp observation of worldly society. Outside of France, the Englishman John Gay explored the possibilities of the satiric apologue (1726 and 1733); he owed as much to the great French classical fabulist as to the "modern" La Motte (whose collection had been translated into English in 1721). The German Lichtwer was a great Francophile and took his inspiration—but often in a sentimental vein—from the Aesopic tradition and from La Fontaine. Lichtwer's compatriot Christian Fürchtegott Gellert set edifying moral tales in verse (1746 and 1748), a tendency to which Moore also lent distinction in Great Britain. Again in France, the abbé Aubert, who was considered in his time to be the successor to La Fontaine, sometimes illustrated, as in his works of 1756 and 1760 the strong pull of the moral tale on the apologue.

After 1760 the French influence remained strong, and enthusiasm for fables spread to other countries in Europe. In Italy, Passeroni methodically versified the bulk of the Aesopic legacy—without being able to avoid the influence of La Fontaine, which also colored Pignotti's work of 1779. Pignotti was also a great reader of the Englishman Gay, with whom he shared a certain long-windedness. His compatriot Bertola, on the contrary, preferred to seek inspiration in the German Gellert, whose methods he analyzed in a long *Saggio sopra la favola* (1788; Essay on the Fable). In Spain in 1781, Samaniego pillaged both La Fontaine and the author of *The Beggar's Opera* (1728) for satiric and anticlerical pieces that revealed his familiarity with

Voltaire's work, while in 1782 the more original Yriarte adapted the fable to the requirements of literary debate.

In Sweden, Gyllenborg displayed his considerable poetic talent in his imitations of La Fontaine. In Poland, Ignacy Krasicki favored a satiric tone in his works of 1779 and 1802. The Russian Khemnitzer, writing in 1779, felt the influence of both the French master fabulist and the German Gellert. French poets very quickly became acquainted with the works of their European counterparts through translations, particularly those published as excerpts in the *Journal étranger,* or complete prose translations (Gay was translated by Madame de Kéralio in 1759, Lichtwer by Pfeffel in 1763, Gotthold Ephriam Lessing by d'Antelmy in 1764, and many pieces by Lichtwer, Gellert, Lessing, Gleim, Schlegel, and Friedrich Hagedorn appeared in Huber's *Choix de poésies allemandes* [1766; Selection of German Poems]). Verse translations were also plentiful. Gay's works were translated into verse by de Mauroy in 1784, and Gellert's fables appeared in a verse translation by Madame de Stevens in 1777; Binninger's *Choix des plus belles fables qui ont paru en Allemagne* (Selection of the Most Beautiful Fables That Have Been Published in Germany) appeared in 1782. Hoping to renew an inspiration that for too long had been dependent on Aesop and La Fontaine, the new French fabulists borrowed shamelessly from foreign authors, adapting them to La Fontaine's poetic mold. They even plundered the works of the German Lessing, who had written a collection of *Fabeln* (1759; Fables), published with an appendix of three speeches that sought to show poetry as inimical to the apologue's moral purpose.

The verse fable formed a crossroads where pedagogy, politics, and narrative intersected. Three clergymen—Grozelier, Barbe, and Reyre—were writing pedagogical verse fables at roughly the time when Jean-Jacques Rousseau, in *Émile, ou, de l'éducation* (1762; Émile; or, Concerning Education), was attacking the pedagogical use made of La Fontaine's *Fables.* Other writers, including Imbert and Claude-Joseph Dorat, were publishing political fables, while still others were concentrating on narrative, including Le Monnier and Jean Jacques Boisard, the undisputed record holder for verbosity with his *Mille et une fables* (1777; A Thousand and One Fables). Then, on the eve of the Revolution, the verse fable reached an equilibrium with the works of three writers: the duc de Nivernais (1796), who drew from the continental sources as well as from Oriental and classical sources; Le Bailly (1784), whose collection was expanded under Napoleon I and the Restoration; and, above all, Jean-Pierre Claris de Florian (1792).

Although he is no longer widely read, Florian is still considered second only to La Fontaine and his case is

particularly illuminating. Florian produced only 120 fables altogether: 9 were borrowed from Gay, 4 from Lichtwer, 4 from Gellert, 3 from Lessing, and 11 from Yriarte. Others were clearly drawn from classical sources, from the Indian fabulist Bidpai, from earlier French authors, and from Father Desbillons, a contemporary fabulist who wrote in Latin. (Desbillons had played a considerable role in making foreign apologues known, for he was one of the first to translate apologues into a language that could be read by all intellectuals.) The rest of Florian's work, although not the bulk of it, seems to have been invented. All in all, his work, which does preserve a perfect unity of tone, is in reality little more than a sort of synthesis of earlier influences, from ancient Greece to classical France and from Great Britain to Spain by way of Germany. Florian even borrows elements from a Provençal fabulist. The morality of Florian's tales is cautiously conservative, and politics are limited to scratching the surface of the excesses of those who were expected to be enlightened despots. His poetic expression is clearly in the mode of La Fontaine; his moralizing and "sensitive" tale is often developed at the expense of the dryness of the Aesopic apologue, but he still leaves room for satiric caricature. Relatively speaking, Florian's work resembles the collection of a La Fontaine who had not been reduced to taking his topics from Phaedra and Aesop or from the Indian fables of Bidpai, but of a La Fontaine who had foreign predecessors worthy of providing him with material.

If one were to speak of fables throughout Europe in the age of the Enlightenment, France would be both the driving force, through the universal influence of La Fontaine, and the culminating point, through the country's capacity to assimilate the production of foreign authors—a trend that would continue well into the next era. It is difficult, however, to situate the production of the fabulists in the literary and ideological evolution of the Enlightenment. By virtue of its moralizing character and its ancient origins, the genre was more conservative than progressive, and its practitioners were first and foremost imitators and traditionalists. The approach of a fabulist such as La Motte, who, closely linked to Father Fontenelle and Pierre Bayle, claimed the fabulist's right to engage the philosophical spirit, remains quite marginal. La Motte's few imitators, such as Dorat and Imbert, emerged principally for topical reasons because the times (the 1770s) had undoubtedly approved new ideas, and these writers did not hesitate to transform the apologue into a political tribunal in which to preach toleration or the overthrow of tyranny. More often, a moderate, middle-of-the-road opinion was discernible in the fables, at least in France. Most of the fables were severe with regard to the petty foibles of the human animal and cautious in matters of religion and politics. Some fabulists aggressively satirized the *philosophes*. In fact, the *philosophes* were the favorite target of the abbé Aubert because of the religious scepticism he attributed to them. In short, the fable of the age of the Enlightenment was not very open to enlightenment, even if it illustrated, in its own way, the didactic frenzy of the era.

JEAN-NOËL PASCAL

See also Satire; Tale

Further Reading

Hassauer, Friederike, *Die Philosophie der Fabeltiere: Von der theoretischen zur praktischen Vernunft: Untersuchungen zu Funktions- und Strukturwandel in der Fabel der französischen Aufklärung*, Munich: Fink, 1986

Janssens, Jacques, *La fable et les fabulistes*, Brussels: Office de Publicité, 1955

Pascal, Jean-Noël, *Les successeurs de La Fontaine au siècle des Lumières (1715–1815)*, New York: Lang, 1995

Fable

Critique

To understand why the critique of fables developed during the 18th century, one should consider the role played by the libertine scholars of the previous century. Those scholars applied the rules of historical criticism to different religious traditions, including ancient paganism. The same impulse that led Baruch Spinoza and Richard Simon to look critically at how sacred texts developed also pushed them to question the veracity of pagan fables. This critique of fables, therefore, had a double edge. First, it was part of the historical examination of diverse beliefs, which resulted in the formation of a genuine science of mythology as early as the beginning of the 18th century. At the same time—as sceptical minds gradually came to view religious history as a "tissue of fables"—this critique of fables implicitly led back to the critique of religion.

From an aesthetic point of view, in the Quarrel of the Ancients and the Moderns, the critique of fables supported the argument of the moderns, who questioned whether the literature of antiquity was as worthy of renown as its fierce advocates, the partisans of the Ancients, claimed. By dismissing fables as filled with exaggeration and erroneous stories, modern writers worked toward the triumph of rationalism as well as toward the demystification of preconceived ideas. However, the critique of fables did pose problems for Enlightenment scholars, who were sometimes put into a bind by their own convictions. They faced difficulties over at least two burning questions. The first was how to do away with fables, fiction, and imagination when they are a necessity nestled in the hearts of all men and women. The second question was how to include fables within the purview of philosophy and still retain the Platonic triad according to which Beautiful equals Good, which equals Truth. Let us assume, for the moment, that they would determine either that the fable could be incorporated in their philosophical approach or that it could not.

A Fundamental Change

During the 18th century the term "fable" often acted as a synonym for "myth." The word was used to designate genealogies, adventures, metamorphoses, and all other kinds of stories about pagan deities and heroes, such as the tales of Hesiod, Ovid, and other popular writers. Throughout the classical period, knowledge of fables was a necessary part of the education of a gentleman. The student encountered fables in the important ancient texts that teachers assigned in school, and fables were depicted and admired in royal palaces or private homes—not only in paintings but also in the operas and tragedies performed there. Charles Rollin, whose *Traité des études* (1726; Treatise on Studies) was an authoritative text on education for half a century, considered a knowledge of fables to be a must for understanding literature. For the chevalier de Jaucourt, who devoted an article to the subject in the *Encyclopédie*, fables were the antecedents of the arts. He said, "It is impossible to ignore them without blushing, at a certain point, at one's lack of education." As the modern critic Jean Starobinski has stated, knowledge of fables was necessary to read the entire cultural world (see Starobinski). At the same time that it offered the key to the aesthetic world, the knowledge of fables acted as a sign of social distinction.

However, the use of mythological motifs had long had critics. Before the Ancients and Moderns clashed, some satirists, who were tired of seeing ancient legends pompously feeding the heroic ideal, triggered the debate by composing burlesque epics, or parodies, such as Charles Dassoucy's *Ovide en belle humeur* (1650; Ovid in a Good Humor) and Paul Scarron's *Virgile travesti* (1652; A Parody of Virgil). In the 18th century the young Pierre-Carlet de Chamblain de Marivaux continued in the burlesque vein, publishing *Homère travesti* (1736; A Parody of Homer).

In the 18th century the critique of fables could also be detected in the changes within French opera. In *Platée* (1745), Jean-Philippe Rameau and his librettist, Jacques Autreau, severely rejected the ancient world by depicting Mount Olympus as teetering in the marshes. In this opera the voices of the mythical heroes were replaced by frogs croaking and donkeys braying. It was a fierce attack on the study and imitation of antiquity, which was prevalent in the culture of the time. Both the musical innovations and the daring libretto of the opera indicate the death of tragedy in music as it had been created by Jean-Baptiste Lully.

To further evaluate the role of fables, one has only to compare the treatment of the fable in literature to its use in the arts in the 17th and 18th centuries. Mythology was a constant source of inspiration for the artists of the *Grand Siècle* (17th century), and its use was encouraged by the royal family. Royal personages had themselves depicted as identifiable gods and goddesses. For example, in the gilding of the Versailles, the queen mother was shown as Cybele, holding the Earth, and the queen was Juno, accompanied by a peacock; the king appropriated the best roles, including those of Jupiter, Apollo, Mars, and Hercules. This recourse to mythology must not be seen, however, as a mere demonstration of flattery on the part of the artists toward their rulers. It was a matter of representing the monarchy as the political manifestation of a cosmic order. The Sun King's feat was to revive a system of symbols that were losing their force of inspiration and that had already been criticized by historians in the 17th century. Countering a rationalist and critical movement that reduced the fable to playing a purely decorative role, the Versailles monarchy sought to reinvigorate mythological imagery for political ends. However, in the 18th century, at the same time that Christianity and the monarchy were being criticized, fables were being slowly demystified. From the 16th to the 18th century, there was, therefore, a fundamental change in the way

mythology was understood. On the whole, this change can be interpreted as part of the transition from a "symbolic" mindset to a "critical" one.

An Emerging Science of Mythology

As Starobinski has pointed out (see Starobinski), it is important to distinguish the *fable*, which uses mythological motifs, from *mythology*, defined as historical and critical texts that seek to develop knowledge about myths. He argues, "the fable poeticizes the world, mythology questions its origins." Although mythology and the fable derived from approaches that were fundamentally different from one another, the study of mythology considerably affected how fables were represented in the 18th century. In particular, three movements formed in literature and the history of ideas.

The first of these movements involved a resolutely critical attitude toward fables. In the "Achilles" article of his *Dictionnaire historique et critique* (1697; An Historical and Critical Dictionary), Pierre Bayle highlights the contradictions observed in the different versions of fables. "I would say in passing that the fiction of the ancients would be slightly more tolerable than it is if they had made the effort to not contradict each other so much." Bernard Le Bovier de Fontenelle spearheaded the critique of fables, publishing, in 1684, *De l'origine des fables* (On the Origin of Fables). Fontenelle begins by challenging the Platonic idea that fables are allegories for truth, an idea that would be developed by the advocates of a symbolic interpretation. "The makers of Fables were not people who knew of morality or physics, nor did they discover the art of disguising such things in borrowed images." The sentence that summarizes his treatise *De l'origine des fables* is famous: "Let us not seek anything else in fables but the history of the errors of the human mind." Fontenelle seemed to attack only popular superstition, but he laid down the basis for a more radical critique when he observed that "men are always inclined to these kinds of stories." In reality, what the author of *De l'origine des fables* was attempting to show was how most peoples had transformed fable into religion. As opposed to the rational historians or specialists in mythology who followed, Fontenelle did not so much aim to construct the history of fables as he did to list the reasons for the emergence of fables. He thus explained the mechanisms of belief, including ignorance, wonder, and the tendency to explain the unknown through the known. Fontenelle put forward many psychological reasons similar to those that David Hume developed in *The Natural History of Religion* (1757). This sceptical attitude toward fables eventually led certain authors to atheism. The equation "fable equals religion," which Fontenelle implicitly coined, was later adopted by such materialist thinkers as the baron d'Holbach. It was also ultimately embraced by such revolutionary writers as Pierre Sylvain Maréchal, who, in 1794, published a piece that was significantly titled *La fable du Christ dévoilée* (The Fable of Christ Unveiled).

In the face of this radical critique, two less spectacular, more scholarly approaches to fables can be distinguished—one that can be called allegorical and the other historical. They are, nevertheless, equally important to the history of ideas in the 18th century. In his *La mythologie et les fables expliquées par l'histoire* (1738; Mythology and Fables Explained through History), the abbé Banier refers to both approaches when he contrasts the allegorical approach which he criticizes, with the historical approach, which he advocates. For him, the former can be traced back to the Platonic philosophers, who "pressed into this view by apologists of the Christian religion whose goal was to prove the absurdity of Paganism through the absurdity of Fables that acted as its base. These apologists affirmed that the fables were but allegories hiding great mysteries."

In reality, far from being the privilege of the *philosophe* alone, allegories were also used by numerous theologians. Faithful to the Renaissance mind-set, certain Christian writers continued to see the expression of secret knowledge in fables. Convinced that fables should be interpreted symbolically, they strove to draw close parallels between sacred antiquity and pagan antiquity. At first denounced as absurd signs of idolatry, pagan fables gradually emerged as the veiled revelations of Christian truths. The value of fables as metaphorical vehicles for truth, articulated in Pierre-Daniel Huet's *Demonstratio Evangelica* (1679; Demonstration of the Gospel) was employed in various ways in the 18th century. Huet used his method to extract "proof" of the factual character of the Old Testament—by showing that ancient populations had received Moses's teachings and that traces of this remained in their mythology. The deists, on the other hand, steered the argument to favor natural religion, which knew only divinity. The Jesuit missionary Father Lafitau, who defended symbolism as the key to all religions, rejected Huet's theory as one likely to promote atheism. In his work *Les moeurs des sauvages américains comparées aux moeurs des premiers temps* (1724; Customs of the American Indians Compared to the Customs of Primitive Times), Lafitau nonetheless retains the comparative method that Huet developed, in order to prove that the religions of all the world's populations shared a common foundation. According to Lafitau, the savages of the New World did not have a single custom, belief, or rite that was not also found in antiquity.

The other approach is the one upheld by the abbé Banier. For the author of *La mythologie et les fables*, fables have a true connection to history. To study fables is first and foremost to study the religious system of paganism. By questioning the origin and development of religious representations, the abbé Banier's writing subjects fables to both historical and critical analysis. At the same time, it decidedly legitimizes mythological science. In the "Fable" article he wrote for the *Encyclopédie*, the abbé is considerably more polemical than in *La mythologie et les fables*. Following in Fontenelle's footsteps, Banier strongly emphasizes the negative sources of fables and the role of priests "who changed a barren cult into another, more lucrative one." Fontenelle's approach was also furthered by the rationalist deism of Charles de Brosses, whose work *Du culte des Dieux fétiches* (1760; On the Worship of Fetish Gods) aims to show that creation myths are imaginary responses to metaphysical concerns. Refuting the allegorical system, which he named "figurism," Brosses backs up his thesis with linguistics and, especially, the study of etymology. In contrast to Holbach, he does not stop at the point of saying that fetishism is a false cult; instead, he goes on to show its function and meaning. Furthermore, he modifies what was then the commonly accepted historical scheme, according to which the deterioration of beliefs and religion took man from Revelation to superstition or polytheism. In Brosses's view, polytheism is the universal religion for "primitive" societies. In order to have a clear idea of divine perfection, intellectual and material conditions must first come together. Therefore, the Revelation could not occur without the aid of historical development.

In the face of these major schools of thought, Voltaire's position is complex. When examining the question of mythology, Voltaire seemed to dissociate himself from his *philosophe* friends. Instead of condemning the allegorical reading of fables, Voltaire gave it some credit. In the "Fable" article in his *Dictionnaire philosophique* (1764; Philosophical Dictionary), he asks, "Are not the oldest of fables clearly allegorical?" The "Allegorie" article in the same *Dictionnaire* is, however, more reserved, and Voltaire reminds the reader that the Church Fathers used this method of exegesis on the Scriptures.

In fact, the issue of allegory does not provide a clear dividing line between the position of the Enlightenment *philosophes* and that of the representatives of the anti-Enlightenment: the stance an individual took depended on the viewpoint from which he looked at the issue. Even though Banier's historical interpretation gradually became popular, the allegorical interpretation was still favored by many in the 18th century, including both orthodox thinkers and the *francs-tireurs* (independents).

Aside from the critique of fables, it has often been noted that the Enlightenment and the French Revolution produced their own arsenal of symbols and allegories. However, it must be emphasized that during the intervening years the status of the allegory changed pro-foundly, in contrast to the period from the end of the Renaissance and during a part of the *Grand Siècle,* when allegory could be understood as an interpretative technique that, following the example of philosophical discourse, aimed to produce knowledge about the world. During the Enlightenment, allegories ultimately came to be seen as mere metaphors, merely ornamental examples concealing no special secrets.

A New Philosophical Fable

In the 18th century the use of fables clashed with the endeavors of historians who wanted to promote a ratio-nal historiography, stripped of the love for romance and of the credulity that had traditionally filled the world. Voltaire's *Essai sur les moeurs et l'esprit des nations* (1756; An Essay on Universal History, and the Manners and Spirit of Nations) can be seen as an attempt to restore history at the expense of fables. Throughout the text, the word "fable" always appears in opposition to "history," except in discussions of ancient history. And so, Chapter LII of the *Essai* is titled "Des premiers peo-ples qui écrivirent l'histoire et des fables des premiers historiens" (On the First Peoples Who Wrote the His-tory and Fables of the First Historians). Understood negatively as an imagined story without a concern for truth, the fable competed against history. The conclu-sion of the *Essai* speaks clearly on this point: "In all nations, history is deformed by the fable, until finally philosophy comes to enlighten men."

The Enlightenment *philosophes* wanted to show that the fable was developed as a substitute means of dis-course, often replacing a pure and simple explanation of the real. But the fable was not necessarily the result of an inability to produce a discourse based on reason. It could also be the consequence of an aesthetic choice, if not a philosophical one. In *De Sapienta Veterum* (1609; On Ancient Wisdom), a work devoted to the interpretation of ancient myths, Francis Bacon affirms that fables "act to cover and veil, but also to clarify and illustrate." In *Les aventures de Télémaque* (1699; The Adventures of Telemachus), Father Fénelon draws on the fable as a pedagogical tool for a moral and highly political end. In *The Fable of the Bees* (1714–29), Ber-nard de Mandeville proves to be a moralist, even if the intention of the fable is indeed rather puzzling.

Through the use of fable, tales such as Jonathan Swift's *Gulliver's Travels* (1726) and Voltaire's *Micromégas* (1752) illustrate critical reflection on the relativity of beliefs and customs. In stories such as Vol-taire's *Taureau blanc* (1774; The White Bull) and Hol-bach's oriental tale of *Le bon sens, ou, Idées surnaturelles opposées aux idées surnaturelles* (1772; Common Sense; or, Natural Ideas Opposed to Super-

natural Ones), the fable seems to be working toward its own destruction, or on destroying what made reading it possible—that is, credulity. If such fables deserve "philosophical" as an adjective, it is not only because their purpose is to teach but also because they force the reader to be sceptical when coming face to face with the fantastic elements in the tale. Yet, if a story like *Taureau blanc* can be understood as a distancing from the fable by means of a fable, with a religious polemic as its underlying purpose, Voltaire's tales also show a pen-chant for fantastic elements similar to those found in ancient tales of metamorphoses. Like the Huron in Vol-taire's *L'ingénu* (1767; The Pupil of Nature) after he had been civilized, the author may have exclaimed, "I love the fables of philosophers, I laugh at those of chil-dren, and I hate those of impostors." In his short essay *De l'origine des fables,* Fontenelle does more than emphasize the ever-fresh temptation of myth; he also grants it aesthetic legitimacy: "The things about which reason is first undeceived do not lose any of their charm with respect to imagination." One might say that through the fable Enlightenment thinkers could use their scientific imagination and create a world made according to their measure.

For several Enlightenment writers, the fable signified anything but a divorce from reason. This perspective had been adumbrated in the 17th century in the work of Jean-Pierre de Florian, a brilliant fable writer in the style of La Fontaine. Florian opens his book *Fables* (1668) with an important allegory about Truth, who appears stripped, decrepit, and ill, and Fable, who is richly decked in fake diamonds. At the end of a futile argument, Truth and Fable decide to walk together in order to guarantee a more universal success for them-selves. Raymond Trousson has underlined the impor-tance in the 18th century of certain ancient myths, including the myth of Prometheus (see Trousson). The role myths played in developing the German *Aufklärung* remains to be analyzed. The rationalist movement that affected different Enlightenment think-ers did not mean myth was dead—quite the opposite. In its secularized form, adapted to the cultural outlook of European philosophers, myth made a strong comeback well before the romantic era. Neoclassical aesthetics, which harbored this new function for fables or myth, serves as proof for this resurgence.

There is certainly no better topic than fables for dem-onstrating how the Enlightenment thinkers undertook the formidable work of critically examining the tradi-tions people followed and the values they held. The problematics of the potential value of fiction, which lies at the heart of the critique of fables, is indeed only grad-ually approached through a process of critical analysis of the origin and progress of religions, of the methods of history, and of the nature of the human mind. It would be wrong to see the critique of fables simply as a triumphant movement of a reason that was self-confident of its powers and incapable of contradicting itself. Besides encouraging the formation of new knowledge (mythology, the history of religions, ethnology, and literary fiction), the critique of fables brought the *philosophes* back to a haunting truth: humans are naturally drawn toward the fable and the imaginary. And even if reason ultimately triumphed, this not so much because its advocates acknowledged a temporary defeat in the face of the tricks of imagination, but instead because reason itself forced them to recognize the power, beauty and appeal that fables held for the imagination.

STÉPHANE PUJOL

See also Idolatry

Further Reading

Albouy, Pierre, *Mythes et mythologies dans la littérature française*, Paris: Colin, 1969

Feldman, Burton, and Robert D. Richardson, *The Rise of Modern Mythology, 1680–1860*, Bloomington: Indiana University Press, 1972

Manuel, Frank Edward, *The Eighteenth Century Confronts the Gods*, Cambridge, Massachusetts: Harvard University Press, 1959

Pomeau, Rene, *La religion de Voltaire*, Paris: Librarie Nizet, 1956

Starobinski, Jean, "Fable et mythologie aux XVIIᵉ at XVIIIᵉ siècles," in *Le rémède dans le mal: Critique et légitimation de l'artifice à l'âge des Lumières*, by Starobinski, Paris: Gallimard, 1989; as "Fable and Mythology from the 17th to 18th Centuries," in *Blessings in Disguise; or, The Morality of Evil*, translated by Arthur Goldhammer, Cambridge: Polity Press, and Cambridge, Massachusetts: Harvard University Press, 1993

Trousson, Raymond, *Le thème de Prométhée dans la littérature européenne*, 2 vols., Geneva: Librairie Droz, 1964; 2nd edition, 1976

Fairground Theatre

As places where crowds gathered, fairs in the commercial towns of Europe inevitably attracted troupes of traveling players. Especially in Germany the wandering troupes that performed at the princely courts also made their appearance when the great markets or fairs were held in Frankfurt, Cologne, and Leipzig. In England there had been theatrical performances at fairs since the 16th century. In Italy, France, and Spain, charitable confraternities often took advantage of the festive environment of fairs to hire out their halls to theatrical troupes. In France the monks of Saint Lazare and the priests of the Mission, like the priests of Saint Germain des Prés, hired out plots of land for the fairs of Saint Laurent and Saint Germain (to name only the two principal fairs). The fairground was quickly covered with pretty wooden stalls, to be used for all sorts of trade. Featuring various attractions and spectacles, including dancers, acrobats, and puppets, the fair of Saint Germain took place from 3 February to Passion Sunday, while that of Saint Laurent was held from 9 August to 29 September (with minor variations over the years).

Beginning in around 1640, troupes of actors set up shop at fairs and developed a theatrical "trade" that attracted large audiences of diverse social origins. Nobles and bourgeois mingled with artisans, shopkeepers, and the common folk. The actors performed in small wooden theatres known as loges. These permanent stages came to characterize the French tradition of fairground theatre and partly explain the unique development of this cultural genre.

In 1678 the acrobats in Alard troupe and Vondrebeck's troupe joined forces to produce a combined show. Their particular blend of acrobatics and dialogue was tolerated for a while by the authorities. However, once the entertainment developed into a genuine, distinct type of spectacle rivaling those of the elite theatres, the fairground theatres became victims of frequent persecution—which only spurred the performers on to find ingenious new ways of circumventing authority. In 1699 fairground shows were banned; the harassment continued. When plays with dialogue were banned in 1704, the players responded by singing or acting out monologues instead. In 1709 the performers were forbidden to sing and, in 1710, even forbidden to speak, so they performed pantomimes, or "mute plays," lowering printed signs from the flies, or having the audience sing couplets set to well-known tunes for which the lyrics were distributed with the entry tickets. When their wooden theatres were demolished, the performers immediately rebuilt them. Thus, with the active and amused complicity of the spectators, the performers at fairs resisted attack by reinventing themselves so successfully that by the opening decades of the 18th century, the fair was the leading center of theatrical creation in Paris. From 1697 onward, fairground theatres drew in the audiences of the Comédie-Italienne, which had been expelled from France on grounds of irreverence. This development served to encourage the fairground players all the more strongly in re-creating and Gallicizing character types from the Italian commedia dell'arte, such as Harlequin and Punchinello, which from then on were mixed with French character types such as Pierrot. The Comédie-Italienne, when it was reestablished, was increasingly hybridized, including French as well as Italian material.

In 1724 the principal fairground theatre was renamed the Opéra-Comique. This term, which had appeared several years earlier, designated a new genre that was based precisely on the blending of songs and dialogue. Indeed, the Opéra-Comique displayed more common sense than the elite Comédie-Française, for the Opéra-Comique decided to relax enforcement of its *privilège* (permit including exclusivity rights) and allow the wandering troupes pay a fee in exchange for relative tolerance. Both Monet, in 1752, and then Charles-Simon Favart, in 1758, retained the name Opéra-Comique for their theatre. In 1762 it merged with the Théâtre-Italien.

Over time the fairground theatre became an institution. In 1752, on the initiative of Monet, a very beautiful theatre was built at the fair of Saint Laurent. Graced with interior decoration by François Boucher, the new theatre would serve for a long time as an architectural model, and it was a far cry from the original wooden trestles. Beginning in 1759 some fairground troupes, in order to perform in the intervals between fairs, set themselves up in theatres built on the boulevards that had been opened up by the removal of the city's fortifications. This use of permanent structures became typical, even though the spectacles continued at the fairs up until the Revolution. The most famous permanent facilities were the Théâtre des Associés, the Théâtre des Variétes-Amusantes, the Ambigu-Comique, and Les Grands-Danseurs du Roi, where Nicolet's troupe was a great success; its main attraction was a performer known as "le Petit Diable" (the Little Devil), a *sauteur*, or tightrope walker, who was renowned throughout Europe.

As early as 1712, these theatres called on the services of good, even great, writers. They included Alain-René Lesage, who wrote *Arlequin, roi de Serendip* (1713; Arlequin, King of Serendip), *L'école des aments* (1716; The Lovers' School), *Les beaux de Merlin* (1721; Merlin's Waters), and *La tote noire* (1721; The Black Head); Dominique Fusilier, who wrote *Arlequin et Scar-*

amouch endangers (1710; Arlequin and Scaramouche as Grape-Pickers), *Arlequin baron allemand, ou le triomphe de la folie* (1712; Arlequin, German Baron, or the Triumph of Folly), *Le rémouleur d'amour* (1722; The Knife-Grinder; or, On Love), and *Les comédiens corsaires* (1726; The Corsair Comedians); D'Orneval, author of *Arlequin, gentilhomme malgré lui* (1816; Arlequin, Gentleman in Spite of Himself); and Alexis Piron. These playwrights worked alone or in collaboration with one another. Later they were followed by Pannard, Favart, Fagan, and Thomas Gueulette. Piron succeeded in transforming the monologue into a totally polyphonic work in his memorable and astonishing play *Arlequin-Deucalion* (1722). These authors' association with the fairground theatres coincided with the beginning of the theatres' evolution toward a greater artistic and moral dignity, and eventual institutionalization. This evolution did not, however, prevent the development of *parades* (short slapstick sketches played outside of theatres to attract paying customers), such as those of Gueulette, which had scatological or obscene content. Authors such as Jean Vadé and Favard gave to the grotesque, with its popular origins, the charm of naive genre paintings, which appealed to a very large audience. Vadé's plays, such as *La fileuse* (1752; The Spinner), *Les troqueurs* (1754; The Swappers), and *Les racoleurs* (1758; The Touts), renewed the genre of the opéra comique, drawing on the popular language of Paris by stylizing a certain number of distinctive pronunciations, errors, and incorrect liaisons. Several years later, Dorvigny, in *Janot, ou Les battus paient l'amende* (1779; Janot; or, The Losers Pay the Bill), and Beaunoir, in *Jérôme Pointu* (1781), gave their little comedies a dimension of cruel but ambiguous social satire.

Such plays were based on a wide variety of plots that originated in popular culture, such as farces, folktales, or Italian sketches, or that parodied subjects borrowed from elite culture, as in Vadé's *Les Troyennes en Champagne* (1755; The Trojan Women in Champagne). The dramatic power of these plays was based on effects that sometimes belonged to the repertoire of the magician, such as apparitions, disappearances, magic tricks, or special effects. However, the surprise effects were offset by critical distance, wit, or comedy: the strings were all too visible. With its parodies and rapport of complicity with audiences, fairground theatre developed a rebellious culture that took aim at well-established cultural institutions, with the Comédie-Française and the Académie Royale de Musique (Royal Academy of Music) as its favorite targets.

The performances of the actors, which combined different traditions and played them off against each other, were no more inhibited by the restrictive canons of elite theatre than by the style of the street performers who had preceded the development of fairground theatre.

The *poissard* (vulgar) style developed an imaginary, fishwife language from the jargon of Paris's market-place, Les Halles. There were also interactions with the Italian and English traditions. The fairground panto-mime that had originated in the traditions of the com-media dell'arte served as the model for English pantomime, and, in return, English performers such as Mainbray performed at fairs in France.

A space for artistic freedom was thus opened up in the dramatic life of Paris. The boulevard theatres were able to accommodate all the productions of a new genre, which had been rejected by the official theatres for precisely that reason. It was on the boulevards that drama, pantomime, opéra comique, vaudeville, and, later, melodrama all found their audiences. Those the-atres were the forerunners of a genuine entertainment market that was eventually given legal status by the law on the freedom of theatres, passed in January 1791.

PIERRE FRANTZ

See also Actor; Comedy; Commedia dell'arte; Fairs and Markets; Opera, Comic; Pantomime; Parade; Parody; Theatre and Staging; Vaudeville

Further Reading

Attinger, Gustave, *L'esprit de la commedia dell'arte dans le théâtre français,* Paris: Librairie Théâtrale, 1950
Campardon, Émile, *Les spectacles de la foire,* 2 vols., Paris: Berger-Levrault, 1877; reprint, Geneva: Slatkine Reprints, 1970
Vénard, Michèle, *La foire entre en scène,* Paris: Librairie Théâtrale, 1985

Fairs and Markets

"The word 'fair' comes from *forum,* public place, and was originally a synonym of 'market.' In some respects it still is: both words signify a gathering of merchants and buyers in a specified place and time." This definition, given by Anne-Robert-Jacques Turgot in the article "Foire" (Fair) in the *Encyclopédie,* is similar to that found in all 18th-century dictionaries. As the definition reveals, the institutions of the market and the fair date back to antiquity and designate both the voluntary gathering of buyers and sellers to conclude "markets" (that is, contracts) and the time and place where this activity takes place. The two institutions differ from one another, however, in frequency and geographic scope: Savary des Bruslons affirms in his *Dictionnaire de Commerce* (1741; Dictionary of Trade) that "the market differs from the fair in that the market ordinarily concerns only a town or a particular place, whereas a fair covers an entire province, or even several."

Turgot attributes this difference to the privileges and franchises enjoyed by "large fairs, where the products of part of Europe are brought together at great expense, and which seem to be a gathering place for nations." By emphasizing the discriminating criterion of size, Turgot meant to criticize the implicit fiscal policy that ham-pered "the natural course of trade" in ordinary times, and to plead for free trade. "Large fairs," he concludes, "are never as useful as the inconvenience that they involve is harmful." He thus accepts the notion of a hierarchy between the "major" merchandise fairs, which, according to Fernand Braudel, in the 18th cen-tury remained "essential tools for widespread com-merce . . . within the center of the larger mercantile way of life," and the more tenuous world of rural or smaller-scale fairs, which did not enjoy any franchise agreement and more closely resembled the markets (see Braudel). However, by criticizing the privileges of the fairs, Tur-got places indirect emphasis upon a trait shared by both institutions: fairs and markets were both under the authority of the monarch, and their creation was directly linked to the desire to encourage trade and the monetarization of the economy, a prerequisite for an increase in fiscal pressure, direct or indirect.

The fact remains that fairs and markets, while essen-tially of the same nature, constituted two distinct forms of periodic commerce. Markets were held weekly, or even several times per week, and their aim was to sup-ply cities and towns. According to Braudel, who cites Adam Smith, markets represented "the greater part of known trade" between cities and the countryside. Mer-chandise consisted primarily of foodstuffs and perish-able items. Fairs followed a different rhythm: they were held once a month at most, but more often only annu-ally or once each trimester. There were no fresh or agri-cultural products on offer, and most of the trade was in finished products, raw materials, or livestock. Fairs could be held in the city or the countryside. Consequently, the participants were also different, as were the social and cultural roles of the two types of gathering. Savary writes that "some believe that the word *foire* derives from *a Feriis,* a Latin phrase signifying feasts, for in olden times fairs in France were almost invariably held in the places where feast days were celebrated, and where churches were consecrated." He could have added: on feast days. Unlike markets, fairs were frequently associated with celebrations for patron saints. Such celebrations were in and of themselves an opportunity for entertainment and merrymaking, a venue for theatre and festive performances, a place to enact a fantasy of abundance in times of scarcity, and a delight for the senses. Even more so than at the markets, fairs were places where, in addition to commercial relations, intense networks of nonmercantile exchanges were woven.

From Open Markets to Private Markets

The network of markets in Enlightenment Europe remains poorly known. The available studies are mainly selective or regional, except for those concerning England and France. By the 17th century England and Wales were endowed with a dense network of market towns slightly greater than the French market network in the 18th century. Each city served an average area of around 64 square miles (that is, of a radius of roughly 4.5 miles) and a population of between 6,000 and 7,000 people. In France these figures could reach around 77 square miles for a radius of influence of five miles and a population of up to 11,000. These figures are only rough estimates, for the pattern varied from region to region, and above all they cannot account for the behavior of the populations or the actual areas covered by the distribution of goods, which could vary by as much as 100 percent. In 1740, in the Toulousain region in southern France, certain markets were spread over parishes as far apart as 15 to 19 miles. In any case, the presence of a market was a good indicator of both the basic level of urban life and the concentration of other secondary or tertiary activities. Truly rural markets were rare therefore, although in Enlightenment France 63 percent of the market towns had fewer than 2,000 inhabitants and, as in England, these towns were the epicenters of the rural areas they served.

While the majority of the markets reflected local interests and responded to various necessities of exchange between town and country, there was nonetheless a trend toward specialization. This occurred not only in major towns, with the emergence of multiple weekly markets and, increasingly, neighborhood markets, but also in smaller towns within each region: markets dealing in grain, livestock, horses, onions, or

textiles were proof of the increasing tendency toward a division of labor. Increased specialization of activities also affected the physical organization of the marketplace. The reconstruction or extension of covered markets was accompanied by a stricter delimitation of the plots assigned to each type of product, as in the Leadenhall Market in London or Les Halles in Paris, although trade tended to sprout up spontaneously around the allotted space. These were places of intense social life where strong feelings could be aroused among the people, so municipalities kept markets under close surveillance. Prices, quality, and quantities were regularly checked and recorded, weights and measures were verified, and hygiene conditions were inspected.

For all their vitality, open markets accounted for a smaller and smaller proportion of trade. The rise of shops in towns, and the growing role of merchants who could purchase goods directly from suppliers as roads networks were improved, indicated a growing private market where new forms of exchange replaced the traditional encounter between producer and consumer. This trend marked the arrival of commerce on a larger scale—a development welcomed by liberal elite. Many consumers had reservations, since for them the public market was a concrete place where "fair prices" could be agreed on. The most vulnerable producers were also sceptical about private markets; they viewed the expansion of market networks as a means to escape the "tyranny" of market logic and as a chance to make maximum profits from their own production. Although monarchical administrations had diverse and conflicting attitudes toward markets, the fact remained that in England and in France, policies were conducive to the development of a dense and carefully planned network of markets to ensure security, a steady flow of goods, and public access to commerce.

Country Fairs

On the whole, fairs were a rural, agricultural phenomenon. Both in England and in France, every marketplace was also a fairground, but many towns or villages that held fairs had no markets. By 1789, three quarters of the 4,264 fairgrounds registered in France belonged to parishes of fewer than 2,000 inhabitants, and more than 40 percent had fewer than 1,000. Most of the fairs were devoted to the sale of agricultural products—oil, wine, wax, honey, and cheese, along with raw materials such as silk, linen, hemp, or wool, and, above all, livestock: oxen, horses, donkeys, pigs, sheep, and goats. In certain areas livestock fairs accounted for three quarters of the annual gatherings. At other fairs, local artisans sold their products: textiles, timepieces, toys, small carpentry, and so on. In return, the fairs offered seed, tools, forging iron, construction materials, nails and hardware, and, above all, everyday utensils and clothing.

The calendar of these country fairs followed the rhythm of the farming and grazing calendar but also took into account the imperatives of transportation—which was difficult and dangerous in winter—and of the religious calendar. There was a marked decrease in the number of fairs in winter, during Lent, and at harvest time; the busiest periods were during May and September. Fairs also had an additional role as "hiring grounds," labor markets where contracts for hiring farmhands were made and wages were settled.

For those who attended the fairs, however, the main attraction was the presence of peddlers and itinerant or semi-itinerant merchants who worked throughout a radius of 12 to 19 miles and who offered an array of "merchandise of all kinds" in varying quantities. Itinerant merchants' proportion of sales, in cases where it can calculated, rarely exceeded 10 to 20 percent of the total. The fair, in its literal and figurative meaning alike, was a feast, a break in the "confined circle of ordinary exchange" and in the monotonous cycle of work and days. The presence of entertainers, charlatans, dancers, and wandering musicians made it a joyful and noisy place, and occasionally, a place of drunkenness and disorder—anathema to the clerics who unsuccessfully denounced the chaotic blending of the religious and the profane.

The Transformation of Large Mercantile Fairs

The festive and popular atmosphere of country fairs also reigned at the "major rendezvous." Savary notes that "although it is not the essence of these mercantile assemblies to have actors, tightrope walkers, tumblers, puppeteers and other such people, hardly a single fair of any considerable size is without a good number of them." All the major European fairs attracted a considerable nonprofessional public. "The nobility of Languedoc always travel in great numbers to the fair at Beaucaire," Savary continues, "and the Norman nobles to the fair in Guibray; but that is nothing in comparison to the gatherings of princes and lords in Germany at the three fairs in Leipzig, or the two fairs in Frankfurt am Main." By carriage or on foot, for the wealthy or the humble, the fair was an "outing," a "distraction," at least as much as it was a place to do one's shopping. In and of itself, a fair was a spectacle for the whole community, whether it was held in the depths of the countryside, as in Guibray and Beaucaire, where it was spread out under colorful awnings or in wooden barracks, or, as at the fair at Saint Germain, in sumptuously furnished loges, "beneath a strong piece of carpentry" and equipped with lights, wells, or even a chapel.

Nevertheless, the most famous venues, such as Lyon, Antwerp, Genoa, or Naples, depended economically on the activity of the mercantile elite. Turgot, as noted above, explained their existence by the franchises and privileges, arguing that these alone could compensate for the expense of transporting goods from one country to another. "Free fairs" were rare occurrences, but they did indeed ship and receive goods "duty free," that is, entirely or partially free of customs duties, drafts, toll fees, and so on. Nevertheless, they were subject to inspection by fair organizers and representatives of the merchants' guilds, who verified quality and enforced conformity to any applicable production regulations. Apart from the princely protection enjoyed by foreign merchants, the main advantage was the existence of a special jurisdiction qualified to rule on quarrels and suits that could arise between merchants during the fair, regarding goods, obligations, or payment—a system of "in-house" justice that was discreet, quick, and efficient. The security of the venue made it a privileged place for the circulation of credit, and certain fairs, such as those of Lyon, Plaisance, or Geneva were essentially payment and exchange fairs where letters and bills of exchange were negotiated. The majority, however, remained fairs where goods were physically present. Among them, textiles (including raw materials) occupied a dominant role, but ironmongery, horses, groceries, and hardware were always on offer.

Initially, these were wholesale markets that helped establish contacts among tradesmen and with producers—the "manufacturers," as Savary calls them. During the age of the Enlightenment the most concentrated part of production, whose quality was the most consistent, was often shipped directly—a trend further facilitated by the expansion of road networks, particularly in northwestern Europe. Direct shipping explains the nearly universal decline in the cosmopolitan nature of the gatherings, with the exception of the very specialized fairs, such as the book fair in Frankfurt. Fairs thus became main place for merchants to unload the most geographically and technically heterogeneous goods, usually of the most mediocre quality. In parallel fashion, there was a marked increase in the number of retailers coming to take in new stock; the proportion of retailers and semi-wholesalers among all sellers gradually increased, and along with it the ratio of public attendees to sellers. From a wide-ranging instrument for trade, fairs were tending more and more to function as a mechanism for off-loading and redistributing the national market, although some fairs, such as those of Beaucaire and Bordeaux, were still mainly focused on the Mediterranean or colonial markets. The emergence of nationwide markets had a certain effect on the supply structure. Remainders of unsold merchandise grew more rapidly than sales figures, and this meant merchants had to offer an increasingly wide range of products to a larger body of consumers who followed fashion right down to the latest whim, but whose standards of quality varied widely.

It is difficult to make an overall assessment of the conditions affecting fairs, for circumstances were irregular and unlikely to follow a pattern. Fairs were tied to the development both of manufacturing in the hinterland and consumer markets within particular countries and across national borders. The constant rise in sales at Beaucaire was not entirely representative, but neither was the virtual disappearance of major fairs from England and the Netherlands. More appropriately, one might speak of the transformation of these traditional instruments, "a hundred times reworked," which held their place in the sweeping movement of expanded consumption and the emergence of national markets. That is how the monarchical administration in France viewed the issue during the 18th century. If the atmosphere of liberalism led more than one observer—inspector of manufacturing or steward—to note with satisfaction the sharp rise in trade outside the fairgrounds, the bureau of commerce, and later the revolutionary administration,

remained committed to establishing a dense and rationally planned network of periodic commerce, ready to support the dynamic forces of the consumer market and thus of growth.

DOMINIQUE MARGAIRAZ

See also Peddler; Trade

Further Reading

Braudel, Fernand, *Civilization and Capitalism, 15th–18th Century,* 3 vols., translated by Siân Reynolds, London: Collins, 1981 (original French edition, 1968–79)

Everitt, A., "The Marketing of Agricultural Produce," in *The Agrarian History of England and Wales,* edited by H.P.R. Finberg, vol. 4, *1500–1640,* London: Cambridge University Press, 1967

Margairaz, Dominique, *Foires et marchés dans la France préindustrielle,* Paris: Éditions de l'École des Hautes Études en Sciences Sociales, 1988

Thomas, Jack, *Le temps des foires: Foires et marchés dans le Midi toulousain de la fin de l'Ancien Régime à 1914,* Toulouse, France: Presses Universitaires du Mirail, 1993

Family. *See* Children; Fatherhood

Fanaticism

In his *Questions sur l'"Encyclopédie" par des amateurs* (1771; Questions on the "Encyclopédie" from the Uninitiated), Voltaire commented on the article "Fanatisme" (Fanaticism), pointing out that "*Fanaticus* was an honorable title; it meant 'servant' or 'benefactor of a temple.'" The word derives from *fanum* (temple; sacred place) and referred in ancient times to inspired seers and priests who celebrated the cult of Bellone and were transported into a divine frenzy. Raving in ecstatic, often violent convulsions and beating themselves with a sword or hatchet blade to the point of drawing blood, fanatics were the messengers of prophetic truths.

This venerable title took on opprobrious connotations in the 16th century, starting with Philipp Melanchthon, who expressed disapproval of the "Anabaptist fanatics" in his *Loci communes rerum theologicarum* (1521), translated by Jean Calvin as *La somme de théologie* (Summa of Theology) in 1546. Significantly, Renaudot's *La Gazette* (1661) introduced the term in the context of an English article on the misdeeds of sects during the Civil Wars. Bishop Bossuet later applied it to the Quakers in his *Oraison funèbre d'Henriette de France* (1669; Funeral Oration on Henrietta of France). Compiling a list of those responsible for the English revolution and the rule of Oliver Cromwell,

Bossuet denounced Socinians and Anabaptists, "quaking, fanatic people" who were persuaded that "all their daydreaming is inspired." By the time Bossuet was berating Father Fénelon and quietism in *Histoire des variations des eglises protestantes* (1688; History of the Variations of Protestant Churches), *Premier avertissement aux protestants* (1689; First Warning to Protestants), and the *Sommaire de la doctrine du livre intitulé "Explications des maximes des saints"* (1697; Summary of the Doctrine of the Book Entitled "Explications des maximes des saints"), "fanatic" was deemed the appropriate word to describe Lutherans, Calvinists, Anabaptists, and others who sought to pervert the power of the Roman Church and Catholic Europe.

Lexicographical orthodoxy sanctified this biased and pejorative usage. "Mad, extravagant, alienated in mind, visionary; those who imagine they are having revelations and inspirations or believe they are being transported by a divine furor"—this portrait of the fanatic appeared in the *Dictionnaire de l'Académie Française* (1694; Dictionary of the Académie Française) and was repeated in the *Dictionnaire de Trévoux* (1771; Dictionary of Trévoux). The latter even coined the verb *fanatiser* (fanaticize) at the time of the scandal of the confessional notes in 1752. The definition was scarcely revised by Sobrino's French-Spanish dictionary (1705) or Marques's French-Portuguese dictionary (1758), although it was expanded by references to Protestants. All these dictionary compilers were following in the footsteps of the *Histoire du fanatisme de notre temps* (1692; History of Fanaticism in Our Time) by Brueys, a Huguenot who had come back into the fold of Catholicism and who attacked the "prophetism" of the Calvinist convulsionaries in southern France. Borrowing the Cartesian mechanism for the framework of his thesis, Brueys identified fanaticism with a "sort of melancholy and mania" for which there were no other remedies than bloody repression; this view is reflected in the frontispiece of the collection, a cautionary illustration of a couple seized by epileptic fits before the gaze of the crowd and the threat of the executioner.

Repression, of course, was no empty word in the context of the bonfires of the Inquisition, on which the books and the souls of heretics burned for centuries. Nor was repression a meaningless concept for the Sun King (Louis XIV), who had revoked the Edict of Nantes in 1685 and whose army pursued the converts of the Dauphiné and massacred the *trembleurs* (shakers) of the Cévennes between 1702 and 1710. Any number of smaller-scale Saint Bartholomew's Day massacres found zealous promoters. In order to discredit the Calvinists of the Cévennes, Father de L'Ouvreleuil, in *Le fanatisme renouvelé* (1701–06; Fanaticism Renewed), described churches ablaze, atrocities, murder, and sacrilege. The same state of mind seems to have guided

Esprit Fléchier, the bishop of Nîmes who denigrated the rebels in his *Relation des fanatiques du Vivarais* (1715; Account of the Fanatics of the Vivarais) and the article "Fanatisme" in Alletz's *Dictionnaire théologique* (1756; Theological Dictionary), which stigmatized their "religious fury" and their "Messianic delirium." *Le fanatisme dénoncé* (1720; Fanaticism Denounced) impugned the supporters of Cornelius Jansenius by revealing the abbé d'Asfeld's liberal interpretations of papal bulls (the bull of 1713 favored persecution of Protestants), while *Le fanatisme des Quesnellistes* (1724; The Fanaticism of Quesnel's Followers) criticized the "senseless and scandalous fanaticism" of the followers of Father Pasquier Quesnel.

In response to Catholic reproaches, the Genevan pastor Turretin published a *Préservatif contre le fanatisme* (1723; Safeguard against Fanaticism), a vast theological, philosophical, and moral rebuttal of the revelations claimed by the newly "inspired." Through his condemnation of the dissidents of the Reformation, Turretin absolved the Calvinist and Lutheran Churches. Restricting fanaticism to prophetism, he exculpated Jean Calvin, who had Jacques Gruet executed and Michael Servetus burned in Geneva (1553); Philipp Melanchthon, who congratulated Calvin on this pious act; and Martin Luther, who in August 1566 had ordered that the churches and chapels of 17 Netherlands provinces be sacked and who had recommended exile for heretics. The only true fanatics afflicted with "contagious madness," argued Turretin, were Jean Tennbard, the "Anabaptists" Thomas Münzer and John of Leiden, the mystic Antoinette de Bourignon, the *illuminatus* Durand Faye (who provided the background for the collection *Théâtre sacré des Cévennes* [1707; Sacred Theatre of the Cévennes]), the Society of Friends (Quakers), and the Catholic prophets who had the support of Rome and the popes and councils who granted themselves the gift of infallibility that Turretin contested. Whether one was Catholic or Protestant, fanaticism was always defined as concerning the Other, the adversary.

Nevertheless, at the time when Bossuet was declaring war on fanatics and visiting the Pope in order to crush Fénelon's quietism, John Locke had begun to protest against persecution. In his 1689 *Letter concerning Toleration,* Locke examined the problem not in religious and theological terms, but rather as a political and civic issue that would lay the foundation for a freedom of conscience exempt from all control: "the magistrate ought not to forbid the preaching or professing of any speculative opinions in any Church because they have no manner of relation to the civil rights of the subjects." Chapter XIX of Locke's *Essay concerning Human Understanding* (1690), entitled "On Enthusiasm," deals with the philosophical dimensions of fanaticism. Whoever renounces reason and the natural revelation placed by God in man in order to replace them with the vain fantasies of an excited spirit is, according to Locke, an enthusiast. That person's belief is an illusion, a chimera; his behavior is a public danger; and his existence is madness in the realm of shadows.

Despite all this, Locke withheld toleration for atheists and Catholics. However, Pierre Bayle, who was harassed by Dutch Protestants for his moderate attitudes, his defense of freedom, and his criticism of fanaticism, celebrated virtuous atheism in his *Pensées diverses sur la comète* (1682; Various Thoughts on the Comet), comparing the peaceable Baruch Spinoza with the criminal practices of certain believers. Less audacious, the deist earl of Shaftesbury condemned the immigrants from the French Mediterranean as "hotheads," "cruel and vicious usurpers," and "bad subjects." Yet he advocated understanding and mercy, a strengthened civil society, and the restoration of reason delivered from political and religious tutelage. In his *Letter concerning Enthusiasm* (1708) Shaftesbury pointed out that the ancients had tolerated visionaries and fanatics, yet their philosophy had enjoyed complete freedom and served as an antidote to superstitious ignorance.

The need for toleration became the leitmotiv of philosophy and the central theme of fictions about Indians, Peruvians, Muslims, Persians, Chinese, and other peoples, which went hand in hand with the crusades organized against the inimical counterpart, intolerance. In *Istoria civile del regno di Napoli* (1723; The Civil History of the Kingdom of Naples), Father Giannone, in the manner of the parish priest Jean Meslier, denounced an ecclesiastical policy that was continually encroaching upon the authority of the state, accumulating wealth, multiplying abuse and atrocities, and disfiguring Christianity.

In order to "crush infamy," Voltaire entered the fray with his *La Henriade* (1723), an allegorical epic poem in which Fanaticism, the supreme plague of humanity, is for the first time personified as a monster born in the shadows of superstition which goes on to combat Toleration, the daughter of Reason and Truth engendered by the Enlightenment. Then, in *Le fanatisme, ou Mahomet le prophète* (1741; Fanaticism; or, Mohammed the Prophet), ironically dedicated to Pope Benedict XIV, Voltaire denounced not so much the founder of the Muslim faith as the extremists of the author's own country and century. Reproducing the crimes of Oedipus and characterized (in a letter to Frederick II, December 1740) as a "Tartuffe with weapons in hand", the character of Mohamed is portrayed as universally representative of all the hypocrites who violated the most sacred ties, the voice of blood, and the laws of nature. Whether in the *Traité sur la tolérance à l'occasion de la mort de Jean Calas* (1763; A Treatise on Tol-

eration on the Occasion of Jean Calas's Death), the *Dictionnaire philosophique* (1764; Philosophical Dictionary), or the *Tombeau du fanatisme* (1767; The Tomb of Fanaticism), Voltaire waged a relentless battle against "the sickness of religion" and "the plague of souls" that contaminated the weak and ignorant. In his *Avis au public sur les parricides imputés aux Calas et aux Sirven* (1771; Public Notice on the Parricides Attributed to the Calases and the Sirvens), he even coined the word *intolérantisme* ("intolerantism"). A sign of the times, the article "Fanatisme" in the *Encyclopédie* (1751), written by Deleyre and reprinted in Voltaire's *Questions sur l'"Encyclopédie" par des amateurs*, devoted 17 columns to Bossuet's neologism, a word the majority of European dictionaries had left out. Legitimized in 1718 by the Académie Française, the sulfurous notion of fanaticism hid

a blind and passionate zeal, engendered by superstitious opinions, causing one to commit ridiculous, unjust, and cruel acts, not only without shame and remorse, but even with a sort of joy and consolation. Fanaticism is nothing more than superstition put into action.

A favorite target of Enlightenment thinkers, who tended to equate zealous behavior with superstitious beliefs, the Catholic religion was also taken to task by a series of texts of Protestant inspiration. Two Dutch odes on fanaticism could not find words harsh enough to describe Châtel, Clément, Ravaillac, or the Saint Bartholomew's Day Massacre, four events regarded in the 18th century as incarnations of religious delirium. *De l'imposture sacerdotale* (On Sacerdotal Imposture), a collection of sermons, originally delivered in English and translated into French by the baron d'Holbach in 1767, makes excessive use of the word "fanaticism." A priest in *Des fourberies et des impostures du clergé romain* (On the Treachery and Deception of the Roman Clergy) justifies the advantages of the confession in this manner: "We inspire enthusiasm and fanaticism in people's hearts, and these are the true pillars of our Empire, and we are very well paid for the rage we inspire." Translated into French by Jacques-André Naigeon, the Englishman Johan Crell's *Vindiciae Pro Religionis Libertate* (1769) wrote in the same polemical vein, proclaiming that "the religious hatred of Catholic fanatics" is "the fruit of illusion and superstition grafted upon madness and weakness, with which they [the fanatics] identify, out of a habit forced upon them by odious artifices." The violence of the philosophical attacks was justified by the ongoing religious hostility inherited from the Reformation.

This persistent hostility was visible in political conflicts such as the Seven Years' War, which opposed the

Catholic powers (France, Austria, and Spain) and the Protestant countries (England, the Netherlands, and Prussia). It was also apparent in continuing discrimination and persecution: Protestants were subject to trial by the Inquisition in Spain and Portugal, practicing pastors risked death in France, Catholics were stripped of their civil rights in England, and a plan for unlimited toleration toward them alarmed even the most liberal of religious leaders, unleashing such violence that the leaders retrenched from their progressive positions (as related in the anonymous English essay *Fanaticism and Treason; or, A Dispassionate History of the Rise, Progress, and Suppression of the Rebellious Insurrections in June 1780*). All of this notwithstanding, there did seem to be a retreat from fanaticism in the 18th century. In Florence, Peter Leopold, archduke of Tuscany (later Emperor Leopold II), abolished torture and obtained the closing of certain convents; in Spain the count of Aranda, who was the president of the Council of Castile and much praised by Voltaire, ordered the expulsion of the Jesuits and the containment of the Inquisition; and in Portugal the marquis of Pombal also limited the repressive powers of the Holy Office when he was head of the government.

As an essentially religious phenomenon, fanaticism was not something that could readily become secular and profane. Nevertheless, from the beginning of the century the word tended to include all deviant beliefs and distorted views of reality. Refusing to limit the power and scope of fanaticism to consecrated religions alone, Shaftesbury borrowed from Gottfried Wilhelm Leibniz the formula "fanatical atheists" (*A Letter concerning Enthusiasm*). The abbé Chardon mused in the article "Déistes" (Deists) in the *Dictionnaire antiphilosophique* (1767; Anti-Philosophical Dictionary): "Witness Vanini, for the true idea of fanaticism is a furious zeal for insane opinions. If fanatics are, in general, the most odious of men, what are we to think of atheist fanatics?"

In support of the conviction (expressed in the article "Fanatisme") that "fanaticism produces more virtue than irreligion," the Catholic (characterized in *Questions sur l'"Encyclopédie"* as a "street corner fanatic" who might have done "great deeds one Saint Bartholomew's Day")—could draw on the example of *Émile, ou, de l'éducation* (1762; Émile; or, concerning Education). In this work Rousseau aspired to rehabilitate this "grand and strong passion that uplifts the heart of man," "causes him to scorn death," and "gives him a formidable resilience" and that needed only to be properly channeled "to achieve the most sublime virtue." He compared that passion favorably to the "reasoning and philosophical spirit" of the atheist, whose debased soul and "indifference to Good" undermine society. Going beyond mediocre personal interest, exceeding the limits

between being and appearances, the fanatic extolled by Rousseau is not an apostle of theocracy in any sense: paradoxically, his fanaticism remains tolerant. It retains something of the civic involvement of the Roman patriots Brutus and Cato so praised by Deleyre in the *Encyclopédie*. Beyond the bloodthirsty cruelty of the religious extremist, Enlightenment writers recognized the seductive nature of the extremist's energy. "I like fanatics," declared Denis Diderot in his *Salon de 1765* (1765 Exhibition), making a distinction between God's madmen and individuals animated by "strong passions" (of whom Rousseau was the archetype).

Such strong passions, whether applied to good or evil, to crime or artistic creation, showed the power of temperament. They revealed the limits of conscience and form part of a cycle of aesthetic excess that was literally fascinating. Around the same period, Linguet reversed the attitude of condemnation generally preferred by Enlightenment thinkers in his pamphlet *Le fanatisme des philosophes* (1764; The Fanaticism of the Philosophers). Expanding the notion of fanaticism to "all passions that fill and subjugate the human heart," he took his adversaries to task as "a prideful sect" and as "dogmatic enthusiasts" and exalted the virtuous ignorance of "barbarians." Also following Rousseau's lead were Father Faucher's *Observations sur le fanatisme* (1772; Observations on Fanaticism), the abbé Nicolas-Sylvestre Bergier's article "Fanatisme" in the *Encyclopédie méthodique* (1789; Methodical Encyclopedia), and François-René de Chateaubriand's *Le génie du Christianisme ou beautés de la religion chrétienne* (1802; The Genius of Christianity; or, The Spirit and Beauties of the Christian Religion). All these lexical shifts and reversals of opinion help explain the rather dubious distinction made by the marquis de Sade between good fanaticism (inspired by one's tastes and principles) and the bad fanaticism of one's persecutors (in a letter to his wife, early November 1783); his ambiguous self-portrait, tinged with irony, in which he proclaims himself to be "extreme in everything," "an atheist bordering on fanaticism" (late November 1783); and the speech by Pope Pius VI in the *Histoire de Juliette* (1797; Juliette), which presents murder as a debauched and incorrigible passion bordering on "fanaticism." Catholics or Protestants, deists or atheists, could those who created a sect around a religion or an idea be compared with fanatics, if not through their acts, then in what they said and wrote?

The Revolution and its desacralizing processions certainly favored all the permutations between the religious and the political, radically extending the semantic field of fanaticism to stigmatize the enemies of the nation. Pamphlets condemning the ancien régime proliferated. Such works included *Le fanatisme écrasé* (1790; Fanaticism Crushed), which relates the victory of Protestant revolutionaries over the retrograde Catholics at the time of the massacres in Nîmes; the *Lettre de l'abbé Rive à Camille Desmoulins, sur l'extirpation du fanatisme créé par les despotes* (1791; Letter from the Abbé Rive to Camille Desmoulins, on the Eradication of the Fanaticism Brought about by Despots), which denounces the privileges of the aristocracy and the clergy, for "if fanaticism is a crime under religion, it is a duty under freedom, and one should have fanaticism for freedom alone"; the *Feuille villageoise* (1791; Village Paper) provides a "Recette contre une ancienne maladie que les historiens appellent fanatisme" (Recipe against an Ancient Malady That the Historians Call Fanaticism); and the allegory *Le fanatisme aboli, ou le Triomphe de Léopold* (1791; Fanaticism Abolished; or, The Triumph of Leopold), which praises the merits of the "philosopher emperor." Poems celebrated the arrival of equality (*Le fanatisme tombé, ou la régénération de la France par la raison* [1793; The Fall of Fanaticism; or The Regeneration of France through Reason]); cataloged the atrocities committed by the Catholics (Monti's *Le fanatisme et la superstition* [1797, Fanaticism and Superstition]); and warned of an imminent return to the papal tiara (*Les fanatiques modernes* [1801–02; The Modern Fanatics]). Plays attacked continuing abuses of power (Ronsin's *La ligue des fanatiques et des tyrans, tragédie nationale* [1791; The League of Fanatics and Tyrants, a National Tragedy]) or mocked the prejudices of the nobility. The revolutionary years thus pushed the tensions and ambivalences surrounding fanaticism and Catholicism, aristocracy and Counter-Revolution to their peak.

Eager to clarify ideas, Immanuel Kant characterized the sight of the Revolution as "sublime" in his *Die Metaphysik der Sitten*, Part 2, *Metaphysische Unfangsgründe der Tugendlehre* (1797; Metaphysic of Morals, Part 2, The Doctrine of Virtue). The ephemeral experience of the sublime, during which imagination takes flight, resembles the certainty that humanity is progressing toward Good. With its dynamic effect upon the senses, revolutionary enthusiasm banishes weakness, selfishness, and mediocrity—while the negative finality of *schwärmeri* (fanaticism) belongs to the realm of pure delirium (*Kritik der Urteilskraft* [1790; Critique of Judgment]). Thus, in Kant's view, enthusiasm and the sublime both went against the Jacobin perception of human history during the Reign of Terror. This explains his conclusion in *Der Streit der Fakultäten* (1798; The Conflict of the Faculties): that "the pious fanatic already dreams of a just return and of the world's renewal, when the world has already perished by fire."

To her credit, in *Considérations sur la Révolution française* (1818; Considerations on the Principal Events of the French Revolution) Madame de Staël reexamined the relationship between religious fanaticism and political fanaticism. Criminal passions and the "irresistible need to kill," she contended, had merely shifted from the religious to the secular. More than a century after Pierre Bayle, Jacques Necker's daughter was advocating unlimited toleration and a freedom deeply rooted in a law-bound state. She would continue to hope for an enlightened Europe, rising once again to its feet after the dictatorial and inquisitorial deeds orchestrated by a bloodthirsty Corsican general named Napoleon Bonaparte.

PATRICK GRAILLE

See also Catholicism; Clandestine Literature; Protestantism; Toleration

Further Reading

Bianchi, Serge, "Fanatique(s)/Fanatisme (1789–95)," in *Dictionnaire des usages socio-politiques (1770–1815),* fascicle 1, Paris: Institut National de la Langue Française, 1985

Colas, Dominique, *Civil Society and Fanaticism: Conjoined Histories,* translated by Amy Jacobs, Stanford, California: Stanford University Press, 1997 (original French edition, 1992)

Schalk, Fritz, "Über fanatique et fanatisme," *Exempla romanischer Wortgeschichte* (1966)

Fate. *See* Chance and Necessity; Optimism and Pessimism; Providence

Fatherhood

In the 18th century, as during other periods, the father/child relationship within the family was subject to two kinds of influence: the weight of lasting traditions (customs, religious confession) and the pull of social and political changes such as the increasing role of the state, the need for individual autonomy, economic shifts, and demographic upheavals. It was at the crossroads of these diverse element that the images of fatherhood and familial relationships were strengthened or reworked.

Customs, Economies, and Fatherhood

The image of the father is omnipresent in creative works from the second half of the century. From Voltaire to Jean-Jacques Rousseau, from Jean-Baptiste Greuze to Georges Desmarées, fatherhood is portrayed in every possible way, from the bad father who deserves to be struck down—and through him the image of a vengeful God who punishes his children—to the compassionate, loving father seen in the privacy of the family circle, with, between the two, the father who is respected simply because he is the person to whom one owes one's existence. The playwright Heinrich Wilhelm von Kleist wrote in a letter to his sister: "The life given to us by our parents is a sacred pledge that we must transmit to our own children. This is an eternal law of nature from which the law derives its permanence."

The memories of a once turbulent son could transform such feelings of gratitude into a sense of guilty remorse. Upon his return to Langres in 1770, Denis Diderot recognized the merits of his "good parents" and confessed: "I caused my father pain and my mother suffering as long as they lived." It was but a short step from the image of the forgetful son to that of the accursed father who was sometimes forced to utter an awful curse. An abundance of literary and artistic images that alternately reveal feelings of revolt, compassion, disapproval, or complicity portrays, sometimes in exaggerated form, the range of family relationships during the 18th century.

Behind these images, the realities of family relations were governed by a demographic process affected by the rapid increase in population throughout Europe from the 1720s onward. A trend common to all European countries, this population growth was due more to a decrease in the mortality rate, both among children and adults, than to any significant increase in the birthrate. In fact, birthrates were actually often slowed owing to a trend toward marriages later in life. This improvement in life expectancy changed the entire makeup of 18th-century households. Less likely to be broken up by the premature death of a parent or by subsequent remarriages, the nuclear family became established as a norm within social life. This effect was especially noticeable in France, in the Austrian Netherlands, and in England, where nuclear family units accounted for nine out of ten households; the nuclear model seems to have strengthened the paternal role within the tight family circle.

However, the pattern was certainly not uniform, even though the model of the nuclear family could be found everywhere in Europe: in the regions around Lisbon (Corruche and Salvaterra de Magos), around Belgrade, and in Silesia. Other types of family units existed in rural areas, including multiple households, extended families, and several generations all living together. This latter arrangement was common in Corsica (accounting for one-fourth of households in 1770), in the south of France, in Emilia, and in Tuscany. Within these familial structures, the role of the father might have appeared essential, but perhaps more as the head of the household than as the manager of a patrimony, which was governed by custom. In some French provinces (Limousin, Burgundy, Nivernais), the father had the authority to favor one of his heirs or even, as in Haute Provence, to *faire l'aîné* (designate the eldest). But in many other places—for example, in the Pyrenees—fathers did not have much freedom in these matters.

Furthermore, the "English model," which spread throughout Europe, did not always bring about the same results. According to A. Burguière, the nuclear family in France often remained connected to the peasant community, with the father continuing to play a major role (see Burguière). However, in England this type of household seemed to pave the way for individualism. Perhaps the sometimes pure and simple eviction of a surviving parent after a couple was married and the encouragement of minors to leave home accentuated this trend, or at least weakened the bonds between fathers and children. It is best not to establish too systematic a correlation between different family models and the principles governing customs.

In predominantly rural societies, the father was both head of the household and head of an agricultural enterprise. He managed a domain, whether large or small, and controlled the activities of the young people who remained under his roof just as he would control other assets. This arrangement was common in Gévaudan, in Provence, in the plains of Campania, and in Poland, for example. In some regions of Switzerland (Neuchâtel) and the Ardennes, the rise of a protoindustry in textiles (prints and other fabric) reinforced the role of the father, who was also in charge of distributing the tasks among family members. However, the same type of protoindustrial configuration could also have the opposite effect. In southern Germany, Austria, the Dauphiné, and Languedoc, the development of rudimentary manufacturing activities in rural areas opened new perspectives for young men, beyond the all-encompassing agricultural economy ruled over by their fathers. Some industrial tasks, such as glove manufacturing in the Dauphiné, were taken on by women, so that fathers sometimes had to do the domestic chores. Even in peasant societies the figure of the dominant and authoritarian paterfamilias was sometimes altered as a result of new economic structures. In the Pouilles region, large-scale farming created a constant need for manpower, leading to a widespread displacement of young, unmarried agricultural workers, who were consequently freed from paternal control. The agricultural system in the Carpathian Mountains required seasonal work and residence in the mountains. Young single girls were hired (in the Tatras) as were young shepherd boys, thus freeing them from normal parental surveillance.

Practices in other pastoral economies—the annual migrations of mountain dwellers from the Grisons, the Appenzell, the Forez de Savoie, and the Tessin valleys seeking employment in the agricultural plains of Languedoc, or southern Germany, in the towns of Lombardy, or on the Mediterranean coast—also greatly modified the paternal position and reinforced the image of the absent father. Patterns that became common with the 19th-century industrial revolution were already emerging during the Enlightenment when Savoyards and masons from the Limousin came to swell the ranks of the urban workforce. Such migrations, which were usually temporary, were already creating rifts with the family structure and reinforcing the power of the mother.

The economy was instrumental in changing family relationships in other ways, as well. Rural families in Germany and England often hired out their children either as domestics with other peasants, as in the regions of Ravensburg or Salzburg, or as apprentices as in Bedfordshire or the canton of Zurich. This frequent practice of "life-cycle servant" always resulted in multiple ruptures in the fabric of technical, educational, geographic, and familial structures and represented various facets of the training of these young people from northwestern Europe. By showing their children the road to the outside world and by forcing them to adapt to it, fathers may have been admitting that they did not really have the will to dispense "educational training" that would necessarily be brutal and authoritarian. They therefore passed along part of their parental duties to others. In this respect the situation was not that different in the world of artisans, where the master tradesman who accepted boys into his workshop or store, explicitly promised to use his authority "gently,

humanely, as would a good family man," as stipulated in two-thirds of the contracts signed in Acquitaine in the 18th century. Of course some sons, such as the Parisian glassmaker J.-L. Ménétra, began their apprenticeship at their own father's side.

Fathers as Educators; Educated Sons?

The different patterns described above, with multiple social and geographic variations, emphasize how the paternal hold over his children's education might vary, and how that hold tended to weaken. With a few exceptions, the most extraordinary being Leopold Mozart's great eagerness to control the training of his child prodigy, aristocratic and bourgeois fathers, a bit like some peasant fathers, increasingly entrusted the education of their children to others. At a time when the publication of Rousseau's *Émile, ou, De l'éducation* (1762; Émile; or, Concerning Education) opened a wide debate on the subject of the ambiguous role of the father, the memoirs of noblemen, bourgeois, and artists reveal the lack of interest those fathers had in the education of their sons (or indeed their daughters, who fared even worse). For every Devernois or Jean-Victor Moreau, future generals of the Empire who were held firmly by their fathers' reins, for every merchant such as Panon Debassyns, who came from his home on the Île Bourbon (now Réunion) for the express purpose of overseeing the progress of his children's progress in the schools of revolutionary Paris, there were countless men who remained uninvolved in the face of a thankless task.

Without going as far as the father of the prince de Ligne, whose method of education consisted only of beatings and silence, many fathers left it to schools and tutors to oversee the upbringing of their children. Benjamin Constant, son of a Swiss officer, followed his father from one post to another and was taught by a series of tutors from different countries. Frederick Augustus, elector of Saxony, hired 12 different tutors for his children between 1764 and 1778. Arguably, frequent changes of this sort may be a subtle indication that in some cases, at least, the father was not really indifferent to the difficulties of this type of education.

As a matter of fact, fathers who delegated the education of their sons to others did not necessarily always abandon all control over the process. Following the example of other English aristocrats, Lord Chesterfield hired a tutor to accompany his son Philip on a long tour of the Continent in order to infuse his son's education with European culture. During that time Chesterfield maintained a lengthy correspondence with his son (more than 400 letters between 1737 and 1768). These letters were full of advice, reflections, and warnings which were intended primarily to temper the influence of his son's mentor and also to voice Chesterfield's own opinion on subjects as varied as aesthetics, the salons, and women. On the subject of women, Chesterfield wrote in 1751, "I want to speak to you as would one man of pleasure to another if he has taste and wit" (*Letters to His Son by the Earl of Chesterfield* [1774]). In abundant letters sent to school directors in Lille, who took in many children from Flanders and the Austrian Netherlands during the course of the 18th century, other fathers expressed their wishes for an education that would train perfect gentlemen of the world of commerce. To this end, it was better to master French and mathematics than Latin.

Love and Conflict

The father's more or less voluntary retreat from his children's education, his real or virtual absence, did not ultimately eliminate one of the major functions of that education: to teach obedience. In many social classes in the 18th century, this principle gave rise to frequent, and sometimes serious, conflicts in the home. The old, well-established families, though glorified by Frédéric Le Play, did not escape such conflicts. On the contrary, the system that benefited a sole heir fueled frustrations and disagreements. An analysis of the types of conflicts that occurred within families—conflicts that were always more frequent between fathers and sons—reveals two distinct categories. The first includes conflicts of interest, the son's questionable friends or dissipated lifestyle, or differences in opinion concerning the father's plans and the professional or matrimonial preferences of his children. The second category involves adolescent crises during which children ran away from home repeatedly, joined the army, or entered religious orders. Whatever form this "familial dysfunction" took, it was definitely perceived as a sign that the father had lost his honor, which he sought to regain with the help of those near him—or in spite of them. Reform schools and even banishment to islands of the Americas, which served to break those rebellious young wills, were denounced by Christian Thomasius, the jurist of Halle, and later by Rousseau in the name of natural rights. In France and Spain fathers who were loyal subjects could always call on royal justice to send recalcitrant young people to prison without trial through the expediency of a *lettre de cachet* (royal order); in a sense, private tranquility guaranteed the maintenance of public order. During the reign of Louis XV, having recourse to the official *lettre de cachet* meant that fathers, whether famous or unknown, were publicly displaying the failure of an ideal model. A father's duty to educate his children was akin to a duty toward the state; in such a context, the imprisonment of recalcitrant youngsters may be interpreted as a pedagogical measure motivated by paternal love (in a somewhat warped form).

This sentiment, which might arouse justifiable scepticism given the domestic dramas centered around coercion or inadequate education, nonetheless forms one of the elements of this complex historical look at families. The Enlightenment gave paternal love a new freedom of expression and a wide range of dissemination. In their own way, working-class fathers exhibited a real attachment to their young children, particularly when they were newborns. These feelings of tenderness may explain the ancient and unique practice of the *couvade*: after a woman gave birth, her husband took her place in the bed, where he writhed as if in labor, then pretended to breast-feed the baby, and received gifts and congratulations. The *couvade* was still a common custom in Navarre, the Tyrol, and Bavaria in the 18th century. Were these affectionate gestures that accompanied the manifestation of paternal recognition and association authentic, or merely a simulation dictated by the ritual? The practice of the *couvade* aside, fatherly affection appears gradually to have become part of accepted family behavior. Acts of violence notwithstanding, paternal love often emerged when children were undergoing a crisis. The testimony in letters or books of reason by pastors, bourgeois writers, and intellectuals in Georgian England conveys the overall sense of coherence of paternal feelings. Confronted with the illness or death of a child, profound sorrow was eloquently expressed. Arthur Young's terse admission on the occasion of the death of his 14-year-old daughter in 1797 is captivating: "I was kneeling at the foot of her bed, hopeless, when she looked at me and said, 'You should pray for me.' I told her I would. 'Do it now, she added'" (see Pollock).

Given the new social value attached to paternal love and sensitivity, the increase in numbers of abandoned children in all European cities, particularly after 1750, might at first appear contradictory. Rome, Lyon, Milan, Strasbourg, London, and Paris, all faced considerable numbers of foundlings. In Paris alone, there were 4,500 foundlings per year in the 1770s and 1780s. Regarding this phenomenon there is unanimous agreement in stressing the interconnections among the increased abandonment of babies, the relaxed control of admissions to foundling hospitals (as was the case in London after 1739), and the growing numbers of orphanages. This social movement to provide for homeless children, which was almost unknown before 1760, gained momentum during the reign of Catherine II in Moscow and Saint Petersburg, where orphanages had recently been established. But for a long time the widespread nature of the phenomenon of child abandonment was considered to be the consequence of illegitimacy and of the disintegration of social mores. Though not totally inaccurate, this explanation is inadequate. Sometimes abandonment was a consequence of the Church's campaign against infanticide and abortion, and a family's economic problems were most certainly a decisive factor. Confronted with poverty and unable to provide for their children, many parents were forced to place them temporarily in a charitable institution; they took care to leave an identifying mark on the infant's swaddling clothes. Some—possibly even the majority—of these cases of child abandonment were therefore indications of concern about rather than indifference to the child's fate.

These brief remarks should convey the complexity of family situations, and at times their contradictions, depending on the time, the place, and the community. In general, 18th-century Europe stressed an affirmation of sons, perhaps to the detriment of fathers who were sometimes absent but were nonetheless concerned about protecting the calm of the home, and who were not terribly attentive to the education of their children but were not lacking in domestic love. The French Revolution confirmed the model of victorious sons, but without seeking to destroy the family. While trying to limit paternal despotism, intellectuals of the revolutionary period sought to encourage other values and suggest other bonds based on relationships that were already in existence. The establishment of family courts, the possibility of divorce, the recognition of illegitimate children, and the acceptance of adoption were for a long time the building blocks of a fundamental social transformation in France and in the annexed territories.

ALAIN CABANTOUS

See also Children; Demography; Education, Instruction, and Pedagogy; Love; Peasantry; Sensibility

Further Reading

Burguière, André, et al., editors, *A History of the Family,* 2 vols., translated by Sarah Hanbury Tenison, Rosemary Morris, and Andrew Wilson, Cambridge: Polity Press, and Cambridge, Massachusetts: Harvard University Press, 1996 (original French edition, 1986)

Delumeau, Jean, and Daniel Roche, editors, *Histoire des pères et de la paternité,* Paris: Larousse, 1990

Pollock, Linda, editor, *A Lasting Relationship: Parents and Children over Three Centuries,* London: Fourth Estate, and Hanover, New Hampshire: University Press of New England, 1987

Stone, Lawrence, *The Family, Sex, and Marriage in England, 1500 to 1800,* London: Weidenfeld and Nicolson, and New York: Harper and Row, 1977

Trumbach, Randolph, *The Rise of the Egalitarian Family: Aristocratic Kinship and Domestic Relations in Eighteenth-Century England,* New York: Academic Press, 1978

Feminism. *See* Law, Public; Women Writers and Feminism

Festival

In the age of the Enlightenment, festivals were more than simply a topic of academic interest. Although carnivals, princely *carrousels* (carousels), royal processions, and religious ceremonies were not as popular as they had been during the Renaissance, festivals continued to elicit passionate involvement, at least among the dominant social groups. It is not by chance that the 19th century bequeathed to posterity the image of an 18th century characterized by elegance and frivolity, an image easily justified by the many descriptions of festivals handed down. From one end of Europe to the other, a class of men and women experienced the pleasure and illusion of living a life of perpetual festivity.

To understand the phenomenon of the festival, we must take into account its mythical construction. There was an ever-growing feeling among the masses that they were being excluded from the wasteful extravagance of festivals, and although festivals brought together various forms of art, the social cohesion they induced was no longer all encompassing. Adopting Roger Caillois's anthropologically based definition of the festival as a moment of social excess and frenzy (see Caillois), it can be seen that by the 18th century festivals had long since ceased to unite the social body around a ritual event capable of stirring the totality of society's energies to a fevered pitch. The efforts of the *philosophes* to promote a ritual communion of individuals resulted in a model of the patriotic ceremony, conceived as a rallying together of the community. However, the trend toward privatization of entertainment dominated the age of the Enlightenment. The 18th century marked a decisive stage in the development of a system that controlled festivities so as to prevent occasions for spontaneous, wild abandon. Although the many ways in which that control was exercised prevents one from making generalizations, one can see the progress made, for better or worse, toward festivals conceived as periods of rest and relaxation, festivals at which people no longer relieved their daily tensions and frustrations by exploiting the infinite resources of collective violence, but rather by taking refuge in the privacy of their solitude or the company of their immediate family.

The Rejection of Festivals

In the vague sense of loss of references to the community, Enlightenment critics of the festival were able to discern its essential unifying function. Beyond the range of sometimes contradictory opinions, there was the idea of a positive society, one in which bonds of community would sweep away every factor of disintegration and separation among groups and individuals. Nostalgia for this type of society motivated a denunciation of contemporary festivals as obstacles to the progress of the human spirit. No one questioned the principle of festivals or the need for them; criticism focused instead on their excessive frequency and on the way in which those who took part in them enjoyed them. The Encyclopedists' arguments included criticism of images of luxury and debauchery, statements about the wasteful expense incurred by festivals, the utopia of a union among people that was torn apart by the very notion of spectacle, and a fear of revolt and riot, from which stemmed a concern for control and regulation in the name of civil order.

Millin, Bérenger, and other enlightened writers and travelers who observed customs in Provence in the second half of the century saw in the traditional festivals the heritage of an obscurantist past that incorporated everything they opposed: idleness, expense, superstition, vice, ignorance, fanaticism, and excess. These observers associated festivals with feudalism and were disturbed by the coarseness and strangeness the festivals, their elements of depravity and popular bad taste.

In Spain the enlightened bourgeoisie—and the nobility of Catalonia, Andalusia, and the Basque provinces—protested against the vulgarity to which the Castilian nobility abandoned themselves during the *majisme* festivals. In this case, the fear that the noise and ritual behavior at festivals were vehicles of disorder was shared by the civil and ecclesiastical authorities, who had bad memories of the festival of fools and feared any loss of control at public festivals.

The Jesuit-compiled *Dictionnaire de Trévoux* (1704; Dictionary of Trévoux) specified that church festivals were of value not as spectacles but as examples and should not be pretexts for public debauchery. In Voltaire's view the excessive number of holidays was the cause of drinking binges that led to crime and filled the prisons. The idea of reworking the calendar of religious festivals to reduce the number of festivals went back to the proposals of Jean Gerson during the Councils of Rheims and Constance (1413), but a production-oriented society had only just begun to take precedence over a society addicted to festivals. The article on "Fêtes des chrétiens" (Christian Feast Days) by the economist Faiguet, in Volume 6 of the *Encyclopédie* (1756), still listed an average of 24 festivals per year in each French diocese. The *philosophes* were alarmed by such numbers and suggested the cancellation of festivals on weekdays in order to encourage work and reduce poverty. Festivals, and their licentiousness, were antithetical to the imperatives of an age in which energy was focused on practical, useful, and serious activities, an age in which time, having previously been viewed as cyclical and reversible, had come to be understood as irreversible and calculable.

This criticism of festivals, based on economic concerns and fear for the social order, was supplemented by an aesthetic repugnance, which—to quote Mona Ozouf—corresponded to a loss of the "childlike taste for illusion" (see Ozouf). After an accident on the rue Royale on 30 May 1770, which had taken the lives of several hundred spectators at a fireworks display in celebration of the dauphin's wedding, Voltaire exclaimed in a letter to Madame Du Deffand, "Is it possible that one can get oneself killed simply by going to see paper lanterns?" This incident was perceived by some pamphleteers as a presage of misfortunes to come.

Audiences became increasingly immune to displays of magic. After 1750, with Voltaire's examples of Candide dining with six dethroned kings (in his 1759 novel) and of Amazan in *La princesse de Babylone* (1768; The Princess of Babylon), most travelers became merely bored and sceptical at the Carnival of Venice. Under the cover of their masks, the Venetians protected themselves from outsiders with subtle barriers, defining a private and exclusionary recreational space that could not be shared. This exclusionary tendency was precisely what Jean-Jacques Rousseau, Denis Diderot, and Sébastien Mercier deplored about spectacles in general. For these writers the theatre was the most obvious expression of the reign of exclusion, since it could be entered only by a group favored by birth and wealth, in which individuals pursued a pleasure that left them isolated even in the midst of their peers. Women occupied the boxes at the theatre for the sake of being courted, not to share in the action on stage. The pretenses of the theatre were to be deplored because of the segregation that they encouraged.

The Intoxication of Festivals

While the culture of festivals was the subject of polemics in the name of natural morality, it was nonetheless very much a part of Enlightenment sensibility. For the nobility, even if they were enlightened, free spending was a congenital requirement. The scholarly marquis Scipione Maffei, speaking of a ball that he had given in Verona, commented "I have bankrupted myself," but "with good taste." Sensual pleasure came first, and reason was subordinate to it. For those who followed Bernard Mandeville in defending the economic role of luxury, festivals ensured the subsistence of numerous workers within a great state. In his *Lettre à D'Alembert* (1758; Letter to M. D'Alembert on Theatre), Rousseau posits that these moments of collective exhilaration have lasting social usefulness, for the people draw their energy and their motivation to work from them:

> If therefore you wish to make a people active and hardworking, give them festivals, provide them with amusements that make them love their station in life and prevent them from envying more comfortable positions. The days thus lost will increase the value of all the others.

Linked in turn to the pleasure principle, or to the work ethic, festivals were demonstrations of joy and contentment. Many of the old customs still survived in the cities and the countryside of Europe—from raucous gatherings of youth to shivarees to the ritual slaughter of scapegoats—while peace and prosperity encouraged the appearance of new rituals that became the basis of the folklore festivals to which 19th-century writers attributed a timeless origin.

In addition to discussing popular festivals, which were ignored except in order to condemn their lack of order, the contributors to dictionaries commented at length on religious festivals and also made brief references to private festivals. However, these authors appear to have been most fascinated by court festivals, in which a refined aesthetic and an art of living was developed, transforming the churches themselves into festive spaces. In the princely residences of the small German states, the castles and their parks were places of pleasure and enchantment, with operas, orchestras, and ballets, banquet halls and dance halls all located in either temporary of permanent buildings.

Festivals were nevertheless political duties, and the leisure activities of a courtier were "a continuous or almost continuous chore" (see Alewyn and Sälzle). Festivals also brought the fine arts together in order to celebrate the power of princes or to reinforce the prestige of a dynasty, as in Sweden under the reign of Count Tessin. In the outlying cities of the Austrian Empire, festivals represented the changing state of the relations between the imperial power and local social structures. However, rulers no longer wished, as they had in previous centuries, to transmute reality and create an absolute order. Through the ceremonial of festivals, they repeated conventional rituals and attempted to hold sway over their subjects by enchanting them. The representatives of power themselves became walk-on actors, "hollow men." Festivals created a paradoxical illusion in which people went incognito, spying on each other, and yet attempted to be recognized in spite of their masks. During the balls at the Paris Opéra or at the Carnival in Venice, heroes revealed themselves at the same time as they evaded the gaze of others. The result was a mute uneasiness that in paintings led from the melancholy of the *fêtes galantes* (pastoral idylls) to the disturbingly cynical vision of William Hogarth, Francisco de Goya, and Giovanni Domenico Tiepolo.

Such practices permeated the Enlightenment mentality. The venues for festivals deteriorated and diminished; the royal palaces became less popular than the pleasure houses, casinos, and gaming rooms that were devoted to the pursuit of luck and pleasure. For the aristocracy festivals came to replace the art of conquest on the battlefield as their principal raison d'être. Monarchs became more interested in commemorating peace treaties, military victories, and family events—such as births, marriages, and funerals—than in planning shows of public pomp, triumphant celebrations, joyous processions, or parades for the masses. Private enjoyment prevailed over public entertainment. At the same time, the steady professionalization of theatrical and musical spectacles led to the separation of spectators from players, even in Sweden, where until 1754 festive entertainments had been performed by the ladies and gentlemen of the court. Contrary to the theory of transgressive humor later developed by Sigmund Freud, the festivals of 18th-century revelers were restrained, and the destructive power of laughter was missing from their urbane entertainments.

Festivals under Surveillance

The sheer number of different types of festivals prevents us from setting forth a single festival model. Michel Vovelle has stated that in the period before 1789, the number of festivals in Provence did not really decline; rather the festival itself underwent a transformation (see Vovelle). In Yves-Marie Bercé's opinion, in 18th-century western Europe a multisecular repression managed to destroy the surviving remnants of the urban triumphs, the agrarian rituals, and popular religiosity alike (see Bercé). Yet Philippe Loupès has found records revealing that religious festivals had never been conducted with such fervor (see Loupès). Despite this contradictory evidence, the tendency to withdraw into more private festivals, of a less public character than in previous centuries, was sufficiently widespread that we may cautiously accept it as having been the dominant trend. The courts shut themselves up in their own worlds while the common people had decreasing involvement in displays of power, for the potential wild behavior of the masses caused too much concern. Urban carnivals continued, but, except in Rome and Venice, court masters of ceremonies and pyrotechnicians no longer played any role in them. From the courtly open-air carnivals crowded with commoners there remained only fireworks displays at which the people became distant spectators.

Since ordinary people found no great reason to delight in the festivals that their rulers provided them, the commoners served at best as props in certain displays of skill. Elsewhere, they were turned away for fear their coarseness might spoil the spectacle. The famous fistfights of Venice were suppressed after 1705, and archery societies disappeared from many European cities during the 18th century.

In contrast to the elaborate rituals that had accompanied the entrance of princes into cities during the Renaissance, ceremonies no longer mirrored the social hierarchy because they now only provided the spectacle of an elite. Wherever it existed, royal power focused festivals so exclusively on itself both the cities and the countryside were ultimately deprived of festivals altogether. The causes of this development are well known: the growth of modern states concerned with direct control over their subjects, the progress of civilized materialism, and the replacement of a religious mentality by secular logic.

Age-old solidarities were lost at different rates. Enlightenment thought was integrated into this climate of social control, of the privatization of the emotions, and of the fear of the subversive dynamic of festivals. Festivals were acceptable only if strict limits were imposed on them. Authorities began to increase the number of decrees and regulations controlling the excessive energies of carnivals and other rituals of youth, and thus sanctioned the decline of such customs.

Once limits had been imposed, festivals could once again assume a more positive role. Religious festivals took on an enlightened aspect. The codification of rituals, processions, and ceremonies allowed the bishops to exclude suspect emotional excesses permanently; faith became embedded in the matrix of local processions and family prayers. Above all, after having denounced exclusive spectacles, the *philosophes* demonstrated a certain nostalgia for festivals as moments of communal unity. In his historical romance *Les Incas* (1777; The Incas; or, The Destruction of the Empire of Peru), Jean-François Marmontel interprets the festivals of the Incas in terms of a social cohesion that they in fact did not have. According to Diderot, Athenian tragedy had transformed its audiences into a single great being. Rousseau rehabilitated the rituals that united a people, reinforced their conscious solidarity, and created a feeling of fervor simply by gathering them together. While his *Nouvelle Héloïse* (1761; Julie; or, The New Héloïse) and the *Lettre à D'Alembert* exalt the happy and spontaneous community, Rousseau's *Considérations sur le gouvernement de Pologne* (1772; Considerations on the Government of Poland) proclaims, in contrast, the necessity of using civic festivals to establish the bonds that attach citizens to their country. This pedagogical motive reintroduced a hierarchy among participants, as well as what Jean Starobinski has called an "authoritarian mass medium" (see Starobinski). The reinvented festival did not exclude constraints.

The utopia through which Enlightenment thought could be reconciled with festivals was materialized in the ceremonies of the French Revolution. There was intellectual support for these occasions, which guaranteed their existence, but disappointment loomed. Intended to mark the achievement of the festive dream of the Enlightenment, revolutionary festivals initially sought to fill the void created by revolutionary changes. By doing this, as Ozouf has shown, festivals were intended to effect a transfer of sacredness—that is, a transition from religious worship to a different form of civic-social worship (see Ozouf). These revolutionary festivals were meant to be spontaneous, but they developed in a coercive way, turning history into parody and serving to camouflage a dismal reality. Violence—perhaps the basis of every festival—achieved an inflexible and meticulous order. Should we then conclude from this that the festival that the Enlightenment had desired was a failure? In fact, in the realized dream there remains the expression of a desire that helps to determine what festivals, in all their plurality, represented in the age of the Enlightenment: less the negation of a traditional order than the celebration of an ideal order, capable of reuniting in a brief moment of self-representation the fragments of a shattered society.

GILLES BERTRAND

See also Court, French Royal; Happiness; Luxury; Mask; Night; Sociability

Further Reading

Alewyn, Richard, and Karl Sälzle, *Das grosse Welttheater: Die Epoche der höfischen Feste in Dokument und Deutung,* Hamburg: Rowohlt, 1959

Bercé, Yves-Marie, *Fête et révolte: Des mentalités populaires du XVIe au XVIIIe siècle,* Paris: Hachette, 1976

Brown University, Department of Art, *Festivities: Ceremonies and Celebrations in Western Europe, 1500–1790: An Exhibition,* Providence, Rhode Island: Brown University, 1979

Caillois, Roger, *Man and the Sacred,* Glencoe, Illinois: Free Press of Glencoe, 1959 (original French edition, 1939)

Diderot, Denis, *Paradoxe sur le Comédien, précédé des Entretiens sur "Le fils naturel,"* 1773; reprint, Paris: Garnier-Flammarion, 1967

Gruber, Alain Charles, *Les grandes fêtes et leurs décors à l'époque de Louis XVI,* Geneva: Droz, 1972

Loupès, Philippe, *La vie religieuse en France au XVIIIe siècle,* Paris: SEDES, 1993

Newman, Simon P., *Parades and the Politics of the Street: Festive Culture in the Early American Republic,* Philadelphia: University of Pennsylvania Press, 1997

Ozouf, Mona, *Festivals and the French Revolution,* translated by Alan Sheridan, Cambridge, Massachusetts: Harvard University Press, 1988 (original French edition, 1976)

Rousseau, Jean-Jacques, *Considerations on the Government of Poland,* translated by Willmoore Kendall, Minneapolis: Minnesota Book Store, 1947 (original French edition, 1772)

Rousseau, Jean-Jacques, *Julie; or, The New Héloïse,* translated by Philip Stewart and Jean Vaché, Hanover, New Hampshire: University Press of New England, 1997 (original French edition, 1761)

Rousseau, Jean-Jacques, *Politics and the Arts: Letter to M. D'Alembert on the Theatre,* translated by Allan Bloom, Glencoe, Illinois: Free Press, 1960; reprint, Ithaca, New York: Cornell University Press, 1982 (original French edition, 1758)

Santos, Maria Helena Carvalho dos, editor, *Comunicações apresentados no VIII Congresso Internacional a Festa,* Lisbon: Sociedade Portuguesa de Estudos do Século XVIII, 1992

Starobinski, Jean, *The Invention of Liberty, 1700–1789,* translated by Bernard C. Swift, Geneva: Skira, 1964 (original French edition, 1964)

Voltaire, *The Philosophical Dictionary,* London: Brown, 1765 (original French edition, 1764)

Vovelle, Michel, Mireille Meyer, and Danielle Rusa, *Les métamorphoses de la fête en Provence de 1750 à 1820,* Paris: Aubier/Flammarion, 1976

Feudalism

"**W**hat a beautiful spectacle the feudal laws are," exclaims Montesquieu in his *De l'esprit des lois* (1748; The Spirit of Laws). With this remark he recognizes the fact that feudalism, the common denominator of all European societies in the 18th century, constituted one of the foundation stones of Western private law. Since the Renaissance the term *féodalité* (feudalism), as well as its derivatives, had undergone a considerable semantic expansion. From its original limited meaning, which defined only the bonds established through the contract of a fief, it had come to designate the whole body of seigniorial relations, whatever their object and nature. This semantic process was completed by the eve of the French Revolution in 1789, and the Constituent Assembly merely gave it official legitimacy by creating, after the Night of 4 August, a Committee of Feudal Fights, with a broad authority. In a still more radical way, certain Enlightenment authors, both in France and in Germany, applied the label of feudalism, generally in a condemnatory sense, to the entire ensemble of traditional burdens commonly imposed by the monarchies of their day. The term thus acquired a predominantly political meaning, far removed from its original content. More recently, the economic concept of feudalism developed by Marxist historians has also, in many respects, further extended the term's meaning.

The Nature of Feudalism

The feudal or, more precisely, feudal-seigniorial regime of 18th-century Europe could be defined as a double juridical system encompassing ownership of a landed estate as well as partial ownership in the public authority over that estate; the subjection of individuals and the imposition of obligatory economic levies were thus integrated. In general, a lord's estate took the form of a territorial domain divided into two parts, which were quite different from each other in nature. First came the close or reserved domain, combining the residence of the lord and its direct appendages with a group of lands and forests wholly owned by the lord. He could exploit these resources personally, with the aid of servants and day laborers directed by a steward, and with the casual work of his dependents who were subject to the *corvée* (forced labor). Alternatively, he could rent out his lands on short-term leases, either adopting such common forms as sharecropping or tenancy or making more unusual contracts. The second element of the lord's domain involved subinfeudation, which distributed fiefs in exchange for "noble services" such as "fealty and homage," as well as the peasant tenures, in which land was rented out for long terms or in perpetuity. The nature of these leases to commoners could vary considerably. In those countries where Roman law applied, there were numerous variations on the ancient concept of *emphyteusis,* or long lease, with copyhold uniquely in force in England. In France it was customary to use the *bail à cens* (lease for rent), the rent being a low annual payment signifying recognition of the lord's seigniorial power. The word *cens* (quitrent) gave rise to the generic terms *censives,* referring to such leases, and *censitaires* (poll taxes), referring to the tenants. Whatever type of contract was used, the tenants were obligated to provide services to the lord, the number and kind of which could vary greatly. These services could be discharged by labor, in cash, or in kind; they could be fixed or proportionate, financial payments or purely honorific ones, regularly levied or just potentially in force; and they could take the form of economic monopolies. Among the most widespread obligations were *champarts* (the lord's proportional share in agricultural production), *corvées* (periods of forced and unpaid labor), *tailles* (tallage), *lods et ventes* (the right to tax transfers of property between people under the lord's jurisdiction), *banalités* (the obligation to use the manorial mill, oven, etc., or pay a fine), and hunting or pigeon-keeping privileges. In the eyes of contemporaries, the mass of seigniorial rights was justified by the tenants' lack of a complete right of ownership over their land. Indeed, according to the medieval theory of the "double domain," which governed this question, the tenant enjoyed only a type of extended and almost hereditary right of use, while the lord retained the right of eminent or direct domain. French jurists of the 18th century, typified by Robert-Joseph Pothier, no longer hesitated to consider the tenant as a quasi proprietor; the same could not be said of the majority of European countries, where the lord always tended to be perceived as the principal rightful owner. Of course, the greatest

infringements of the tenant's right of use were to be found in the systems of serfdom. Over and above the bundle of economic and social prerogatives just described, the lords generally also exercised local judiciary powers. In France, for example, there were more than 20,000 private jurisdictions of this kind.

Seigniorial property, far from being unitary in character, was multiple in nature. To begin with, it involved plural ownership, generally with three components—juridical, landowning, and in relation to serfs—known in German respectively as *Gerichtsherrschaft, Grundherrschaft,* and *Leibherrschaft.* These sets of rights frequently belonged to different individuals, even in a single location. Seigniorial property was also arranged in a hierarchy. Each domain was set up, through the conferring of fiefs and subfiefs, in a pyramidal structure, its summit being none other than the monarch, the supreme enfeoffed sovereign. In practice, each domain could be classified according to a scale that in France ranged from lords of the manor at the bottom to the peerage at the top, and passing through baronies, earldoms, marquessates, and duchies. Feudal titles, like military ranks, were arranged in a hierarchy and conferred an undeniable prestige on the title-holder; the elite group of dukes and other peers was surpassed in dignity only by the princes of the royal blood. The rank of lord or seigneur was a powerful indicator of honorable status, and it continued to represent a highly desirable social position. It is not surprising, therefore, that land outside of the feudal system, the *alleux* (allods) of ancient French law, were exceptional cases; many provinces even lived by the radical watchword "No land without a lord." Finally, seigniorial property was a form of property that was under challenge. In the countryside the lordship as the juridical power was superimposed on, but never merged with, two other structures: the religious domain of the parish and the social domain of the local community. The main point of friction between the villages and their lords was the possession of common lands; that is, of areas that were not cultivated, including forests, wastelands, and moors, which the groups that exploited them used collectively. In France the lords, despite their obvious legal advantages, never succeeded in completely taking possession of these lands, which continued to play a crucial supplementary role in the traditional peasant economy. Another major source of tension arose whenever a lord tried to reestablish his rights in a given locality. Estate management was the cause of so much litigation that such management had to be conducted by a whole stratum of "intermediaries," who were essential to many rural activities. They included various officials, adjudicators, and tax collectors—the lord's revenues were frequently rented out to individuals—as well as *feudistes* (lawyers who specialized in feudal law).

Feudalism in Different Regions

The nature and the burden of feudalism could vary perceptibly from country to country, and regional differences were clearly evident. First, by the 18th century the seigniorial regime in certain places—notably the Iberian and Italian peninsulas, but also England—was unusually weak or in decline. Such areas displayed three main characteristics: the complete absence of serfdom, which had disappeared much earlier; the relatively low level of feudal obligations; and the weakness of feudal tenure, which was being slowly replaced by the formation of a small number of great seigniorial estates. These in turn were either divided up among a multitude of tenants or rented out as a block to agricultural entrepreneurs. This dual phenomenon of rural expropriations combined with concentration of landownership was particularly striking in Andalusia, the Papal States, the kingdom of Naples, and Britain, where it received a considerable boost from the process of enclosure.

Other than the areas just described, feudal Europe was fundamentally divided into two distinct regions along a frontier that roughly corresponded to the Elbe River and the borderlands of Bohemia. To the east of this frontier there was a powerful seigniorial system characterized by extremely harsh conditions and universal personal serfdom, which was of relatively recent origin (it had hardly begun before the 16th century). This "second serfdom," as it has come to be known—following the terminology of Marxist historians—was based on forced labor and compulsory residence on the lord's estate. Individual peasants rarely owned land, but peasant ownership was relatively widespread within a collective framework. The best example of communal ownership available to us is the Russian village community, the *mir*. The entire system in place in eastern Europe was directly linked to a specific type of rural economy, an agrarian protocapitalism centered on latifundia (the great estates). The lord enjoyed complete possession of immense tracts of land and also wielded important legal powers. He "reigned" as a potentate, his power being all the less vulnerable to challenges because the noble elites retained a leading role in government. It appears that this system achieved its fullest flowering in Russia under Catherine II, where serfdom often bordered on slavery and involved large concentrations of people.

There was a quite different historical and social situation to the west of the Elbe. Political fragmentation was more marked. Serfdom had ancient or at least medieval origins, was less concentrated than in the east, and became significantly weakened over the years. In theory, peasants always could have recourse to arbitration by a national authority. Instead of forming a united social group, the landlords shared their ownership of land with a multitude of tenants and exercised only limited public authority (judiciary powers). Regional varieties of feudalism are almost impossible to count. In France the seigniorial "burden" on the peasantry was negligible in the Mediterranean provinces and the wheat-growing plains of the Paris Basin, but it remained significant in Brittany and in the central and eastern regions of the country. The survival of serfdom in these areas is evidenced by the widespread survival of the truly servile right of mortmain (perpetual ownership of land, usually by an institution), which probably affected at least one-third of the village communities of Burgundy and Franche-Comté in 1789. The neighboring duchy of Savoy, the abode of the most disadvantaged, experienced a significant level of emigration, which was largely due to the burden of rents (known as *servis*) and of tallage. In the Low Countries (the region known in German as the *Lage Landen*, which extended beyond the Netherlands and modern Belgium into northwest Germany), Flanders and Holland, which had hardly any lords, were in advance of Overijssel, Guelderland, the Ardennes, and Luxembourg. The latter in particular still had a large number of quite burdensome servile tenures: the *Vogteigüter*, whose owners were stripped of all their property rights by an imperial decree in 1765. In western Germany *Leibeigenschaft* (serfdom) had been reduced in Baden and Württemberg to the payment of a modest fee to the lord, but it became increasingly coercive as one moved eastward, culminating in *Gutsherrschaft*, the harsh system of subjection that prevailed in Prussia.

Changes in Feudalism in the 18th Century

The feudal world did not remain unchanged over the course of the 18th century: the "ancient oak," as Montesquieu chose to call it, swayed in the wind. Indeed, it was during this period that feudalism began, so to speak, to be put on trial, with some significant practical results. The emancipation of the peasants (the *Bauernbefreiung*, as German historians call it) can be directly correlated with the great intellectual movements of the time, primarily the Enlightenment. The first stage in the offensive against the feudal-seigniorial complex was the challenge to the remnants of serfdom, which an increasing number of thinkers regarded as a legacy of barbarism, an intolerable offense to the most basic rights of the individual. In 1719 Leopold I, duke of Lorraine, decreed the permanent abolition of personal serfdom in most of his lands. The emancipation movement slowly gained support in France, where the celebrated campaign, led by Voltaire and the young advocate Christin, against the Chapter of Saint-Claude in Franche-Comté (1770–77) eventually discredited the institution of mortmain. Meanwhile, from the 1750s onward, the

Physiocrats disseminated a new and more rational set of arguments against feudalism. These economists were tireless in their sermonizing on behalf of complete freedom of landownership, which they saw as the indispensable preliminary to any progress in agricultural production, and in their militant demands for the redemption of all remaining feudal rents. Claude-Joseph Boncerf's polemical pamphlet *Les inconvénients des droits féodaux* (1776; The Disadvantages of Feudal Rights) and Guillaume-François Le Trône's *Dissertation sur la féodalité* (1779; Essay on Feudalism) were the strongest weapons in the armory for this assault.

In August 1779 Louis XVI responded to these various forces by issuing an edict abolishing mortmain in all the lands belonging to the crown and, crucially, also eliminating the lords' right to exact personal servitude throughout the realm, even though that right was fully legitimized by custom. This apparently timid measure was actually a significant blow to French feudalism. However, the first example of the genuine elimination of seigniorial ownership came from the duchy of Savoy, which was in the hands of the relatively new kingdom of Sardinia. Through two edicts issued in January 1762 and December 1771 (the first being concerned only with serfdom), the government in Turin organized a large-scale process to enable the village communities to buy back existing feudal rents. At first this process was fraught with difficulties, but by 1792, when the territory was annexed by France, most of the communal territories had been redeemed. Aside from the abolition of the remnants of serfdom in the Republic of Geneva (1782) and the Swiss canton of Solothurn (1785), the few other examples of antiseigniorial legislation in the period before the French Revolution occurred in Italy, Germany, and Scandinavia. Empress Maria Theresa significantly lightened the burden of serfdom in force in her German and Bohemian domains, notably by regulating forced labor through letters patent issued in 1771 and 1775. Her son Joseph II completed her work between 1781 and 1785 by abolishing personal servitude in all the Habsburg lands, but he failed in his attempt to overhaul the system of feudal fees. Charles Frederick, margrave of Baden, a fervent disciple of the French Physiocrats and also influenced by Joseph II's social reforms, abolished *Leibeigenschaft* in July 1783 and organized a partial redemption of feudal rents in

1785. Another "enlightened despot," King Christian VII of Denmark, decided to regulate the system by setting up a Grand Commission on Agriculture (1786), which soon decided to overhaul seigniorial justice and, in 1788, to abolish the *stavnbaand* (the system of national serfdom). In the European hinterland other than the Habsburg territories, there were some minor advances: for example, in Prussia measures were taken against serfdom in 1719, 1763, and 1773; also, in Wallachia and Moldavia—the Romanian provinces ruled by the Ottoman Turks—the governor Constantine Mavrocordates introduced some liberal reforms (1746–49). In contrast, in some places, pressure from the powerful and conservative local aristocracy only served to reinforce the existing state of affairs. In Prussia and Bavaria, for example, the law codes issued during the 18th century prolonged the dependence of the peasants on the lords. Meanwhile, in Russia after 1783, following the failure of the Legislative Commission and Yemelyan Ivanovich Pugachev's revolt, the system of serfdom became even harsher and spread over a much wider area, notably into the Ukraine.

The second and decisive stage in the "trial" of European feudalism was initiated by the revolutionary events in France between 1789 and 1798, which brought about the brutal liquidation of the seigniorial regime, first in France itself and then, as if by contagion, in most of the neighboring countries. This process was not to be completed until late in the 19th century, certainly not before 1864, when feudalism was officially abolished in Romania and Poland.

THIERRY BRESSAN

See also Peasantry; Property; Village Communities; Work

Further Reading

Confino, Michael, *Domaines et seigneurs en Russie vers la fin du XVIIIᵉ siècle*, Paris: Institut d'Études Slaves de l'Université de Paris, 1963

Link, Edith Murr, *The Emancipation of the Austrian Peasant, 1740–1798*, New York: Columbia University Press, 1949

Mackrell, J.Q.C., *The Attack on "Feudalism" in Eighteenth-Century France*, London and Boston: Routledge and Kegan Paul, 1973

Finance

As succinctly put by Pierre Goubert and Daniel Roche, "the ancien régime lasted as long as it managed to avoid paying its debts" (see Goubert and Roche). The American War of Independence—which cost France more than a billion livres that were raised almost entirely in the form of credit—created problems that could not be resolved. For five years after the war, successive comptrollers general attempted to plug the holes in the dyke, but in 1788, faced with a deficit that exceeded available revenues, even when the debt had been paid off, the government had to steel itself and convene the Estates General. The monarchy was forced to yield to a broad current of opinion demanding that the imposition of taxes must receive the consent of the nation, a consent to be expressed through the *parlements* (the high courts of justice of Paris and of some of the provinces, which were quick to transform themselves into defenders of the people) and through the Estates, which had not met since 1614.

Although the government had only rarely succeeded in compelling expenditures and adjusting them to receipts, this was not for want of effort. Nor was this inability to balance the books the result of the absence of a budget—a conventional but inaccurate explanation. Jacques Necker's *Compte rendu au roi sur les finances de la nation* (1781; Report to the King on the Finances of the Nation) was the first French budget to be made public, but throughout the modern period there existed budget estimates that enabled the monarchy to avoid navigating blindly. The comptroller general began work in October of each year, when the royal court resided at Fontainebleau. His services included analyzing spending plans, forecasting receipts and deciding on the letters patent to be issued regarding the amount of the taille (the principal direct tax), the leasing of "tax farms" for collecting indirect taxes, and extraordinary resources reserved for times of war. There was no centralized treasury, since a multitude of funds were received and paid out; and a large part of the monarchy's expenditures were settled in the market through the system of assignments to avoid the always risky and expensive task of transporting funds. However, none of this implies the absence of a general view of state finances on the part of the comptroller general.

In the 18th century the financial state, headed by the comptroller general, continued to be strengthened and to operate more independently of the judicial state. Formerly, two councils had handled finances: the Conseil d'État Privé, Finances et Direction (Privy Council of State for Finances and Supervision)—which sat either in its capacity of Court of Appeal or in its capacity of Council of State and Finances—and the Conseil Royal des Finances (Royal Council of Finances), created after the fall of Fouquet. These councils no longer met, although they had not officially been dissolved. The various bureaus established by the Council of State and Finances had entered a phase of decline—notably the Grande Direction (Large Department) and the Petite Direction (Small Department). However, the bureau of royal demesne and *aides* (sales taxes), and that of the *gabelles* (salt taxes), the Cinq Grosses Fermes (five large tax farms), the tailles, and other taxes, continued to be more active.

Sovereign courts were bypassed, such as the Cour des Monnaies (Court of the Mint), when Calonne raised the ratio of gold to silver from 14.46:1 to 15.42:1 in 1785, and the Chambres des Comptes (Accounts Control Chamber), following the bankruptcy of the treasurers general of the army and the navy. In fact, in the closing years of the ancien régime all the government's finances were handled by a small committee comprising the comptroller general and the *intendants de finances* (superintendents of finances), of whom there were six from December 1774 onward. These superintendents—all former *maîtres des requêtes* (masters of petitions) or provincial *intendants* (magistrates)—were experienced and could enjoy long tenure of office. Even so, these influential individuals often had true power at a time when the comptrollers general were little more than silhouettes: indeed, the very word "silhouette" commemorates Étienne Silhouette, whose reign as comptroller general from 4 March through 21 November 1759 was one of the briefest of the 18th century. In the 1780s, at their unofficial weekly meetings, this unofficial committee made decisions, passed judgments, and produced a great number of decrees. The Council was no more than a fiction. The great bureaucrats who formed the unofficial committee were powerful and often envied, but they laid themselves open to criticism, for they held venal offices that were obtained through heredity (for example, the Ormesson family) or by royal favor. In 1777 Necker replaced these superintendents with a committee of legal control of finances that was linked to the King's Council. Ten years later the committee was reinstated but with only four superintendents, and the position offered salaried and revocable commissions. In 1788 the reform of the Treasury also changed the status of its *gardes* (custodians) from officers to salaried administrators. There were complaints from the sovereign courts; for example, the Cour des Aides (Court of Fiscal Appeals), in a famous remonstrance of 1775, denounced the despotism of the commissioners of finance, hidden from the "eyes of the chief of justice." But by 1789 the monarchy had completed its technocratic reform at the highest level. The executive powers had seized control of the nation's finances. From this point onward there was a financial administration with its own traditions and personnel: the comptroller general, the Treasury, scores of leading officials, and hundreds of collaborators.

Two important points must be made. The receivers in the *généralités* (tax regions) were abolished by Necker in 1780, but they were reinstated in 1781 and retained in 1788 by Loménie de Brienne. The receivers remained secure in their purchased posts that were among the most expensive in France (often costing more than a million livres). The capital that the receivers general invested in these posts was repaid at 5 percent interest; the statutory profit on the taxes that they levied was fixed at 3 percent; and they also made large amounts from the yield on public money between the moment when they banked it and the moment when they turned it over to the Treasury. For their monthly payments from the Treasury, the receivers general provided equal amounts of *rescriptions,* essentially a form of paper money guaranteed by their communities. The most powerful receivers general collected the commitments of their colleagues, which they acquired at 4 to 5 percent and lent to the government at 6 percent. Five great receivers provided half of the *rescriptions.* Thus, they acted as bankers to the Treasury, offering the state money that belonged to it by right, disposing of cash provided free of charge by the taxpayers, and being protected from risks by the fact that the basic direct tax, the taille, was an *impôt de répartition* (assessment tax), the amount of which, decided by the king, was apportioned among the commoners. It would be difficult to dream up a more comfortable situation than this post, which the state was "prepared to grant" or "forced to consent to beneficiaries of private fortunes accumulated in the shadow of the Treasury" (see Bruguière).

A similar level of corruption prevailed among the many individuals who were involved in the affairs of the king in order to collect indirect taxes. A gigantic mechanism, this network encompassed 40 *fermiers généraux* (general tax farmers), 46 directors, and 166 receivers in the Ferme Générale (General Tax Farm); 25 general registrars, 91 receivers general, and 133 specialized receivers for the *aides* (sales taxes); 25 general administrators of royal demesne, as well as 34 directors, 36 directors of control, and 50 receivers general at this level; and, at lower levels, a horde of officials, verifiers, and comptrollers, numbering 30,000 for the Ferme Générale, 6,000 for the *aides,* and 3,000 for royal demesne. These assorted administrators held the kingdom in the meshes of a net that was effective but highly unpopular. It was no longer possible for the king to convene by decree a "chamber of justice" in order to try to compel the mendacious tax farmers and their cor-

rupt partisans to return their ill-gotten gains. The last chamber of justice had been held in 1716. After that date the interconnections between the state and the moneymen were so extensive that it was not possible to envisage a break with a system that handled such enormous revenues. Tax farmers and specialists infested all the machinery of the state, took part in government alongside ministers, and made themselves indispensable to the settlement of deficits by subscribing to government loans on a massive scale. In 1741–42 the general tax farmers loaned 25 million livres at 10.5 percent for the War of Austrian Succession; in 1755 they loaned 60 million livres for the Seven Years' War; in 1768 they loaned another 72 million livres, and so on. The Ferme Générale was a pressure group, capable of resisting the attacks of the Physiocrats, the liberals, and those who advocated direct administration of finances by the state. The monarchy could no longer do without it.

The Ferme Générale was indispensable in another sense. On the eve of the Revolution indirect taxes provided more than half the resources of the state. This proportion had continuously increased over the course of the century, rising from 41 percent in 1750 to 50 percent in 1775 and then to 56 percent in 1788, while the proportion raised through direct taxes—the taille, the poll tax, and the *vingtièmes* (twentieths)—declined from 41 percent in 1750 and 1775 to 34 percent in 1788. Nevertheless, it was direct taxation that provoked the most bitter struggles between the monarchy, on the one hand, and the *parlements,* the Provincial Estates, and public opinion, on the other. Since the end of the 17th century the royal government had attempted to impose a more equitable system of taxation, which, while maintaining the taille (an outstandingly unequal tax discriminating against commoners), imposed a poll tax was imposed on all individuals regardless of their social class, their status, or the nature of their incomes.

The poll tax had been introduced in 1695, abandoned in 1698, and definitively reinstated in 1701 to cope with expenditures associated with the War of the Spanish Succession. The tax known as the *dixième* (tenth), which theoretically amounted to 10 percent of the taxpayers' income, followed in 1710; it lasted until 1717 and was then reintroduced, from 1733 to 1737 and from 1741 to 1749, to finance the Wars of the Polish Succession and the Austrian Succession respectively. In May 1749, and therefore in peacetime, the Comptroller General Machault d'Arnouville made a new departure by introducing another general tax, the *vingtième,* in the face of strong opposition from the *parlements* and those provinces that had Estates. In December 1751, however, the comptroller general had to defer imposing it on the clergy. Despite this partial failure, the new tax and the increase in the leases on tax farms combined to make the 1752 budget 23 percent higher than the budget of 1740. The monarchy enjoyed its last financial good times, and the year 1756 had a surplus budget. The outbreak of the Seven Years' War made a second twentieth necessary, although the government had to consent to receive *abonnements* (a fixed yearly contribution) from Franche-Comté and the Dauphiné instead. In 1760 Bertin imposed a third twentieth, doubled the poll tax on those who did not pay the taille, and tripled the poll tax on judicial officers. This third twentieth was abolished in 1764, and the elimination of the second twentieth was repeatedly promised and deferred, by L'Averdy in 1767, Maynon d'Invault in 1768, and the abbé Joseph-Marie Terray in 1771.

These new taxes were by no means sufficient to meet expenditures. The Seven Years' War cost France more than a billion livres in extraordinary expenditure and therefore led to numerous loans and annuities at 10 percent, which greatly inflated the public debt. By the time Louis XV died, in 1774, these charges had absorbed 40 percent of the budget. Under Louis XVI the slogan, more than ever before, was: "Neither bankruptcy nor new taxes." The American War of Independence cost a little more than the Seven Years' War had, but Necker and Joly de Fleury raised at least 75 percent of the financing for it through loans. The last budget under the monarchy, submitted by Loménie de Brienne in 1788, forecast receipts of 472 million livres, of which 288 million livres were absorbed by rents, annuities, repayments of loans, payments of interest to receivers and tax farmers, and provision for repaying anticipated loans. With 27 million livres being allocated to revenue collection, there remained only 157 million livres to cover expenditures totaling 317 million livres.

The wars were thus the main factor in the financial crisis that sparked the Revolution. More fundamentally, the situation in 1789 was the result of the state's inability to carry out a thorough reform of the fiscal and financial system. However, economists and politicians had made proposals for overhauling the system. The imperfections of the tax base and the parasitic nature of the tax collectors had been the focus of criticism even before the demand for equal taxation became a major theme in the years leading up to the French Revolution. As early as 1717 the duc de Noailles, the leading member of the council of finances in the *polysynodie,* the system of multiple royal councils under the Regency (1715–23), had set his officials to work on what he called the "graduated taille." This direct tax would be based not on arbitrary estimates by tax collectors but instead on a reasoned evaluation, according to a preset tariff, of the various sources of taxpayers' incomes, such as the lands they owned or rented, their livestock, or their professional activities. One comptroller general, Philibert Orry, revived this proposal and encouraged

the provincial *intendants* to put it into practice. Some results were obtained in the Limousin under Tourny and Turgot, as well as in Champagne. In 1776, after a long hiatus, the Paris *intendant* Bertier de Sauvigny reactivated the reform and succeeded in imposing the "graduated taille" on his *généralité.* The parishes in it were classified on a 24-step scale, according to the quality of their land, which was used to determine the level of the taille on land use, or "real taille." To this was added a taille on property, known as the "personal taille," at a rate set at one *sol* per livre (5 percent). The graduated taille encountered hostility from the whole hierarchy of financial officials, from the *élections* (tax districts) to the Cour des Aides, and was also greeted with suspicion by the taxpayers, who became reluctant to accept a tax that revealed the extent of their resources. Wherever it was successfully imposed, the graduated taille never received the support of the taxpayers, but it was nonetheless regarded as the best that the ancien régime could do in regard to the allocation of taxes. From that point onward, it was the rich, with the exception of the parish priests and the landed *seigneurs,* who paid this direct tax. Bertier de Sauvigny also undertook the reorganization of the poll tax in Paris, increasing the revenues from it by two thirds. Commendable efforts were also made by the commissioners of the twentieth, whose activities were relaunched by the abbé Terray. Despite the concession of *abonnements* to certain provinces, this general tax became the ancien régime's best income tax, technically speaking.

In the middle of the 18th century the issue of taxation was addressed in a new way by the Physiocrats, who put forward a plan for a "territorial subsidy" that would be levied on landed estates, without any exceptions, and would be equitably allocated by local assemblies. When Turgot became comptroller general in 1774, after the fall of the Triumvirate (made up of the duc d'Aiguillon, the abbé Terray, and René Nicolas de Maupeou), he asked his friend, the Physiocrat Dupont de Nemours, to work on a general program of assemblies for the parishes, the *élections,* and the provinces, whose tasks would include the allocation of taxes. Calonne and Loménie de Brienne revived the plan for a territorial subsidy in the dying days of the ancien régime. Aside from the opposition of the nobility and, even more, the clergy, who were viscerally attached to the fiscal immunity of their property, such an innovation came up against a major technical obstacle—the lack of a general land survey. Only Languedoc had land records, the famous *compoix,* which were relatively reliable and periodically revised, as a potential basis for establishing a real taille that would be fairer than the personal taille already current in most parts of the kingdom. Some attempts at surveys had been made, but they had always taken a long time and encountered complications. It had taken 30 years, for example, to survey the land in the 180 parishes of Angoumois. The provincial assembly of Berry, one of the two experimental assemblies created by Necker in 1779, gave up the attempt when confronted with the enormity of the task; but perhaps the assembly also lacked the will to enter into the secrecy of property holding. In 1780, however, when the Council issued a decree (dated 13 February) that froze the amount of the taille for that year, the assembly of Bourges, reassured that the tax would not be increased, undertook to ascertain whether communities were being taxed equitably. It organized a sampling of 24 parishes for which the revenues were precisely evaluated and compared to the amount of the taille in order to fix an average rate that could be used to correct the allocation among the parishes.

Some improvements were thus made in the fiscal system of the kingdom, but they were not enough either to establish the fiscal fairness that was increasingly being demanded or to increase receipts to match expenditures. Was the royal government genuinely willing to engage in a fundamental reform, which would have obliged the nobility and the clergy to pay in proportion to their income? Was it not the culmination of absolutism to make the king's law triumphant by imposing it on all his subjects, on clerics and nobles as well as on the members of the Third Estate? Both through acknowledged techniques and through changes to the fiscal system, there was some real progress in the sense that there was greater equality. The poll tax and the twentieths were meant to disregard the ancient and outmoded division of society into three estates; and, although the taille remained an unequal tax and was a heavier burden on the commoners of the countryside than on the cities, by 1789 it represented only 15 percent of revenues, compared to 25 percent in 1725. In contrast, indirect taxation, which was regularly increased in the budgets, was proportional to consumption and was therefore greater for the wealthy, regardless of the estate they belonged to. It also weighed more heavily on the cities than on the rural areas.

Could the royal government go any further without destroying the very foundations of a state that depended on the inequality between the three estates, the provinces, and the communities? Or would it simply allow itself to be insidiously trapped in an impasse, in which its only allies in its struggle against fiscal privileges were the supporters of absolutism, while the opposing camp had an easy time of it, exploiting to its own advantage the deep attachment of the French to their liberties, including that of approval, or disapproval, of taxation?

CLAUDE MICHAUD

Further Reading

Bosher, J.F., *French Finances, 1770–1795: From Business to Bureaucracy,* Cambridge: Cambridge University Press, 1970

Bruguière, Michel, "Les receveurs généraux sous Louis XVI: Fossiles ou précurseurs," in *Pour une renaissance de l'histoire financière, XVIIIᵉ–XXᵉ siècles,* Paris: Comité pour l'Histoire Économique et Financière de la France, 1991

Goubert, Pierre, and Daniel Roche, *Les Français et l'Ancien Régime,* 2 vols., Paris: Colin, 1984

Riley, James C., *The Seven Years' War and the Old Regime in France: The Economic and Financial Toll,* Princeton, New Jersey: Princeton University Press, 1986

Touzery, Mireille, *L'invention de l'impôt sur le revenu: La taille tarifée, 1715–1798,* Paris: Comité pour l'Histoire Économique et Financière de la France, 1994

Folk Life. *See* Popular Culture

Food

Cultural historian Lucien Febvre, a cofounder of the journal *Annales d'histoire sociale et économique,* once recalled Jules Michelet's astonishing statement stressing the impact people's diets have upon their history. In Michelet's words:

> Each group of people has special foods that create its members from day to day, that are their daily creators. For the French, from time immemorial these have been bread and soup; for the English—especially since 1760 with Blackwell's development of new breeds of livestock—this national food has been chiefly meat.

Michelet thus envisioned a comparative history of nutrition on a pan-European scale. At the Collège de France, Febvre taught the links between history and food; the *Annales d'histoire sociale et économique,* ever since its creation 1929, has continued to address those connections, notably in the work of Fernand Braudel. In France and in the rest of Europe this aspect of historiography has been dominated by a quantitative approach focused on nutrition and everyday consumption of food. Alongside the great history of publishing, cookbooks have also been of interest to those historians wishing to study nutritional practices and the culinary arts. Today, following in the footsteps of the sociologist Norbert Elias and the anthropologist Claude Lévi-Strauss, historians who study food and its consumption focus on the sociability and conviviality that take shape around meals. Such historians no longer look simply at the food and its preparation, but also at the ways in which meals are shared. In reflecting on food, Febvre liked to point out that the individual is a biological and a social being. Three historiographical topics will serve as a framework for this essay: the production and consumption of grain and wine in Europe, the preparation of various foods and the birth of gastronomy, and meals and conviviality.

Grains and Wine

The European diet was based on the consumption of grain, but it also included several other elements. Alcohol—above all wine—was also a significant source of calories. A person's food said a great deal about his social ranking, his civilization, and the culture that surrounded him.

The essence of human nutrition has always been based on plants. In Europe wheat and other grains comprised the bulk of the daily food ration of the largest number of people. Analyses of the production and consumption of grain products among the French population indicate that French soil was able to feed the population in normal years and that local and regional trade was generally sufficient to equalize the distribution of grain. During the 18th century there were very few crises involving wheat crops, and those that did occur could hardly be compared with those of previous centuries. During the famines of 1709 and 1740 and at the end of the ancien régime, international trade made up the deficit. Only England, whose agricultural activities were fully developed and which had a powerful merchant marine, was completely protected. Grains came from the less populous areas of Europe—Denmark, Ukraine, Poland, and Turkey—and from the Americas. Overall, although it was sometimes expensive, the supply of grain was hardly ever inadequate. In the 18th century French grain production was divided equally between wheat and rye: this is a good illustration of France's intermediary position between the Mediterranean countries, where wheat predominated, and the northern lands, where rye was common. In the European diet grains consumed in the form of bread provided the cheapest source of calories, being around 11 times less expensive than meat and 60 times less expensive than fish. Bread was therefore the most highly valued source of energy, especially in the Mediterranean region. Europe was not only a land of bread, but also a land of accompaniments to bread (called *campanage* in France and *companatico* in Italy), for this monotone diet made no sense except when balanced with other foods: meat, fish, vegetables, and, of course, wine.

A land of grains, Europe was also a land of wine and other alcoholic drinks. Wine, produced almost entirely in southern Europe, was distributed throughout the Continent. Two contradictory trends coexisted within viticulture. One was aimed at the moderate production of *grands crus* (great vintages) and the other at the mass production of ordinary wines. Coarse varieties of high-yield grape vines were commonly found in the vineyards that supplied the capital cities, around Naples, Rome, and Paris. The harsh, usually red wines made from such grapes had low alcoholic content and they were not very expensive. They were made available to the poorer members of society in the taverns, inns, and cabarets surrounding the capital cities. As the price of wine varied in inverse proportion to that of bread, wine and brandy became complements to the normal diet. Many 18th-century sources cite examples of workers who drank two to three liters of wine every day in order to get their work done. Playing the same role as these inexpensive wines, beer was the drink of choice in northern Europe, where it was consumed in abundance even though drinking it often meant doing without bread, since beer was made from grain. Luxury beers, such as the "small" beer imported from Leipzig by the Dutch, were just as highly esteemed as the great wines reserved for the tables of courtiers and wealthy connoisseurs, including burgundies in France and port and bordeaux in England.

Most diets, from those of princes to those of the poor, provided an adequate number of calories, mainly in the form of grains for those living at the bottom of the social scale, and from increasingly varied food sources as one rose higher in the social hierarchy. Families spent the greatest portion of their budgets on food, and that percentage became huge among the poorest classes. Except in periods of famine, which were rare in the 18th century, people ate as much as they needed. Nevertheless, during this period there were deficiencies in every diet, notably of calcium and vitamins, and this resulted in short stature, rickets, and various other deformities. In general, people ate in quantity but not in quality. Cooking, or the "art" of preparation, served to break the monotony of food and to mitigate nutritional deficiencies by adding various seasonings. Artful preparation provided some people with the chance to correct nutritional imbalances or simply to "eat their fill," while to others it offered the delicacy of the most refined, varied, and unusual dishes.

Cuisine and Gastronomy

The exclusive consumption of grains led to the preparation of a variety of grain-based foods, including various types of bread, soups, gruels, and porridge. Simple soups were the mainstay of peasant households, where cooking was not the art that it became in refined homes.

In the cities bakers produced numerous types of bread, including white bread made from pure wheat flour (for the rich) and dark bread made from rye flour (for the poor). They sold their breads in shops or in marketplaces. In the 1760s a baker's apprentice in Paris freely proclaimed that "to change your bread is to change your life"—a perfect illustration of the social hierarchy of food consumption. Travelers commented on the great lightness and delicacy of the white breads made in the capitals of western Europe—Paris, Rome, and Madrid—and they frequently criticized the heaviness of the rye breads of northern and eastern Europe. The consumption of white bread was less of a social issue in cities, where it was available to almost everyone. Social distinctions were made instead according to the size and weight of the bread. In Paris, Bologna, and Rome the authorities guaranteed the supply of bread to preserve social peace. In times of scarcity urban authorities allowed only one type of bread to be made, brown bread—known today as *pain de campagne* (literally, "country bread"). This injunction served to prevent bakers from making only white bread for the rich, thus depriving the poor of their pittance.

Peasants in rural areas, always ready to avoid their landlords' levies, preferred not to have their grain ground in the lords' mills or baked in communal ovens. In some regions of France and Portugal, as well as in northern England and Scotland, peasants ate wheat gruels, porridge, or puddings. Such practices remained common in some provinces until the 19th century (the novelist George Sand was not above occasionally eating porridge in her house at Nohant). When the inhabitants of the countryside ate bread, it was inevitably as an accompaniment to soup.

Soup was the main dish—indeed often the only dish—of peasant meals. It contained green vegetables (usually cabbage or lettuce), root vegetables (carrots, turnips, or rutabagas), legumes, and, rarely, meat, sometimes in the form of salt pork. The soup was prepared in a pot or a kettle and heated over the fire. The popular expression *vivre à pot et à feu* (to live by pot and fire) perfectly illustrates the simple lifestyle of these people who lived on *pot-au-feu* (stew). The fire crackling in the hearth symbolized the family life centered around it, for here simmered the restorative soup that revived the workingman. Broth, which was sometimes fatty, was served over slices of stale bread placed at the bottom of earthenware bowls or plates. It was followed by cheese eaten with the remainder of the bread, and fruit. Soup was the only potable nonalcoholic beverage—safe because it had been boiled at length. Peasant cuisine was distinguished from the cuisine of the bourgeoisie and nobility by its long cooking times and by its focus on soups and stews—on the laborer's broth so disdained by the lord. The lord, in turn, preferred roasts and other meats cooked rare. The preparation of meat was the true subject of most cookbooks of the time.

The rules of cooking, which were elevated to an art form during the Renaissance, were set down in books that set the stage for controversies and for a rapid development in culinary practices. In France, more than anywhere else, cooking became a vehicle of social competition, primarily due to the importance of court society and to that nation's great social disparities. In the 18th century cooking became dissociated from ostentatious quantitative displays in favor of what appeared to be the height of luxury: refinement. However, there were indeed some diners in earlier times who were more concerned with the quality of their food and drink than with the quantity of it. This priority became the norm in the 18th century, when high society worshiped at the altar of good taste and refinement and avoided gluttony at all costs. The voracious appetite of Louis XVI, which resembled that of his ancestor Louis XIV, was no longer acceptable. Only toward the end of the 18th century did the chevalier de Jaucourt, in the *Encyclopédie*, and later still, Grimod de La Reynière, in *L'almanach des gourmands* (1803-12; The Gourmands' Almanac), rehabilitate gourmandizing by comparing it to epicurism. The epicure was able to recognize good food, "tasty morsels," and good wine, and consumed them only for pleasure and not for nourishment.

The epicurean quest for sensual pleasure and good taste at all costs caused many devotees of fashion to lose their heads—and their money. This fashion, which even ruled on which bread should be eaten, exercised a true dictatorship over people's eating habits. Complex and erudite recipes—for example, for dishes mixing numerous ingredients, such as bread with five spices—were highly valued because they were greatly pleasing to the senses of taste and smell.

Initially, cookbooks were associated with court society, but they were very quickly adopted by the middle classes, especially by those who wanted to "follow Parisian ways a little." Bourgeois economizing was contrasted to the extravagance of the nobility, and bourgeois simplicity became the height of fashion. The bourgeoisie constituted a social class that was favorable to the emergence of a theory—and a literature—of gastronomy and moderation. *La cuisinière bourgeoise* (1746; The Bourgeois Cook), the bestseller in this genre, was written by Menon to honor "new, simple and good, dishes." Nevertheless, let us follow the path indicated by Michel de Montaigne: "One must look not so much at *what* one eats as at *whom* one eats it with. . . . For myself, there is nothing so sweet, nor a sauce so appetizing, as that which comes from society."

Food and Conviviality

In the *Gorgias* Plato defined cuisine as the knowledge of how to create good cheer, pleasure, and compliments. Cooking a meal necessarily led to a sharing of it, to eating in the company of others, among "connoisseurs." According to Jean-Louis Flandrin, the act of preparing food was similar to religious sacrifice or to the act of love. To eat or drink in a group beyond the framework of one's family was traditionally regarded as the very symbol of sociability. Let us now look at the differences between meals taken within families and those shared with a group.

In the 18th century long-standing migratory patterns provided the cities with a labor force for industry, trade, and domestic work. As a result, large numbers of people lived in very sparsely furnished conditions and had few cooking utensils at their disposal. The temporary and decrepit lodgings these workers occupied had only one or two rooms and were not always equipped for cooking. For lack of time and means, therefore, migrant laborers ate in cafés or brought food from the shops back to their rooms. They obtained bread from bakers and soup from resale street vendors, including the *regrattières d'arlequins* (women who sold a wide variety of leftovers within every price range).

In all European cities the food industry was one of the most important areas of economic activity. Depending on their incomes, consumers dealt with one intermediary or another, or directly with growers and merchants in the streets, in the shops, or in the markets or fairs. A family life centered on the meal and the hearth was rare among the urban working classes. The men were often absent, running around the city with their friends. In the 19th century the bourgeoisie, who could no longer tolerate seeing the outrageous behavior of the poor, attempted to impose on their workers their own way of life—one centered on the family meal. By teaching the wives of working men how to be good housekeepers and how to look after their homes, the bourgeois elite thought it could induce the men to return home, instead of wasting their money on getting drunk. In the 18th century, however, the urban masses essentially lived outdoors and went home only to sleep. The peasants were also busy outdoors working the land, but they returned in the evenings to eat at home, even if they first stopped at an inn. Peasants and the bourgeoisie derived the same pleasure in being at home for meals, even though their conceptions of life and the family differed.

We have just pointed out the strong connections among dwellings, ways of living, and food. For some people, the outside world was an annex to their lodgings (as, for example, the taverns were for the masses), but for others the public realm was a place of social display separate from the private sphere. Taverns, inns, and other eating and drinking establishments could be found in every city and village in Europe, and they were a part of everyday life for millions of people. Patrons could eat and drink anywhere at any hour. The decor of such establishments varied from the sordid to the luxurious, depending on their location and their regular clientele. People would gather around a table with a pitcher of beer or a jug of wine and would eat to prevent drunkenness. Village inns and taverns were violent places, often frequented by criminals and rabble-rousers, but they were also familiar places where the clientele had its little habits and where people could be with members of their family as well as coworkers.

In contrast to the warm, boisterous atmosphere of cabarets and taverns, cafés were orderly and civilized places, and they encouraged a different kind of solidarity. Cafés were frequented by all social groups, but they were bourgeois places, made tepid by the attitudes and ways of life reflected in a relatively serene ambience. People went into cafés to play checkers, to read newspapers, or to listen to debates while partaking of café au lait and rolls. At the end of the century fashionable cafés in France doubled as restaurants. In England taverns most resembled the institution of the restaurant as it would later develop.

In Paris during the Revolution, the chefs who had worked for the exiled nobility set up shop on a large scale around the Palais-Royal, a favorable location at that time owing to the influx of politicians. The chefs emerged from their previous indifference, and their establishments competed to attract diners. Meals meant the sharing of pleasure in good company and enabled people to savor the joys of being included in a group. This sociability, of course, was shaped by the time and the place in which it developed. The "triumph" of the monarchy, which gave rise to immense popular festivals, is a good example. As with Jesus Christ and his disciples, the communion between the monarchy and the people took on a material form in the sharing of bread and wine, which were distributed in abundance. When financial difficulties arose, shrinking budgets substituted bonfires for fireworks, and marriage dowries for the poor bitterly replaced the abundant food and fountains of wine. Once these Rabelaisian festivals had faded away, the link between the monarchy and the people became weaker. Social peace was to be bought not only at the cost of daily bread and wine, but also at the cost of festive offerings.

JEAN-MICHEL ROY

See also Children; Coffeehouse

Further Reading

Braudel, Fernand, *Civilization and Capitalism, 15th–18th Century*, 3 vols., translated by Siân Reynolds, London: Fontana, and New York: Harper and Row, 1979–84 (original French edition, 1967–79); see especially vol. 1, *The Structures of Everyday Life: The Limits of the Possible*

Camporesi, Piero, *The Magic Harvest: Food, Folklore, and Society*, translated by Joan Krakover Hall, Cambridge: Polity Press, 1993 (original Italian edition, 1989)

Flandrin, Jean-Louis, *Chronique de Platine: Pour une gastronomie historique*, Paris: Jacob, 1992

Kaplan, Steven L., *Bread, Politics, and Political Economy in the Reign of Louis XV*, 2 vols., The Hague: Nijhoff, 1976

Kaplan, Steven L., *Provisioning Paris: Merchants and Millers in the Grain and Flour Trade during the Eighteenth Century*, Ithaca, New York: Cornell University Press, 1984

Marenco, Claudine, *Manières de tables, modèles de moeurs*, Paris: Éditions de l'E.N.S.-Cachan, 1992

Mennell, Stephen, *All Manners of Food: Eating and Taste in England and France from the Middle Ages to the Present*, Oxford and New York: Blackwell, 1985; 2nd edition, Urbana: University of Illinois Press, 1996

Mennell, Stephen, "The Sociology of Food: Eating, Diet, and Culture," *Current Sociology* 40 (1992)

Montanari, Massimo, *The Culture of Food*, translated by Carl Ipsen, Oxford and Cambridge, Massachusetts: Blackwell, 1994 (original Italian edition, 1993)

Force

The fundamental notion of force enables us to describe the action of one body on another, and to study fields, such as electromagnetic fields, since in the case of the latter a force is defined at each point in space. The definition of a force has two parts. The first, which is purely mathematical, indicates that force acts as a vector, that is, it has a certain intensity, its norm, and acts in a given direction; in a certain sense, it thus obeys the law of the parallelogram as demonstrated by Sir Isaac Newton. The second part of the definition enables us to measure of a force in units. These units are often units

of gravitational force (weight), and the measurement is made by means of a scale.

Newton was the first to present an abstract concept of force, bringing together phenomena as disparate as gravity or weight, electricity, magnetism, and forces of resistance. His predecessors had already worked out the properties of specific forces, such as weight and magnetism, but they had not extrapolated a general concept specifying what is common to all forces. During the age of the Enlightenment, the vocabulary of force was not yet established and we must therefore consider many different terms. They include: *vis, virtus, potentia,* and *momentus* in Latin; *force, puissance, vertu, moment, action, effort, énergie, travail,* and *pression* in French; "force," "power," "virtue," "moment," "action," "effort," "energy," "work," and "pressure" in English; and their equivalents in other European languages. Each of these terms could cover either generally or in a specific instance what is now known as force, and vice versa: what Jean le Rond D'Alembert called "this obscure term 'force'" could sometimes indicate energy or work. The achievement of the 18th century was to distinguish and to give a precise mathematical expression to the modern notions of quantity of movement, of force, pressure, and momentum, as well as the notions of energy, power, and work. It was left to the 19th century to clarify the notions of tension and shearing.

Force of Inertia

According to D'Alembert in the *Encyclopédie,* the "force of inertia" is a "property that is common to all bodies remaining in a given state, whether at rest or in motion, unless an external cause brings about a change in them." The expression translated the *vis insita* introduced by Newton in the *Philosophiae Naturalis Principia Mathematica* (1687; Mathematical Principles of Natural Philosophy) to account for the principle of inertia René Descartes had introduced in 1644 in his *Principia philosophiae* (Principles of Philosophy), as well as the conservation of momentum. Most of the authors of the period were thinking of this $m\vec{v}$—mass times velocity—when they wrote about the force of inertia. Only Leonhard Euler objected, writing in his 1750 *Recherches sur l'origine des forces* (Research on the Origin of Forces) that

> it is very inappropriate that some people call inertia the force of inertia, for, given that the effect of inertia consists in the conservation of the same state and that the effect of forces tends to change the state of substances, it is obvious that these two effects are directly contrary to each other.

Centrifugal force, another effect of inertia, had been studied in 1659 by Christiaan Huygens. Newton had used centrifugal force as the basis for his deduction that Earth, rotating on its axis, must be flattened at the poles. Two major expeditions were launched by the Académie Royale des Sciences (French Royal Academy of Sciences). The first of these expeditions, whose participants included Pierre Bouguer and Charles-Marie de La Condamine, was to Quito, on the equator, in 1735. The other was to Lapland, within the Arctic Circle, in 1736; it included Pierre-Louis Moreau de Maupertuis

and Alexis Clairaut. The objective of the expeditions was to measure an arc of the meridian and to verify Newton's statement. Their resulting research had implications for other scientific fields, for the model used as a basis for the calculation and to find an expression for this flattening was that of a rotating liquid sphere, as shown in Clairaut's *Théorie de la figure de la terre, tirée des principes de l'hydrostatique* (1743; Theory on the Shape of the Earth, Drawn from the Principles of Hydrostatics). The subject continued to be studied for the rest of the century, until the appearance of Pierre-Simon Laplace and Adrien-Marie Legendre.

Moving Forces

"These [moving forces are] what others call 'mechanical powers.' They are the simple machines mentioned in the elements of statics" (D'Alembert, *Encyclopédie*). These "simple machines" included levers, inclined planes, screws, wedges, and pulleys and had been studied since antiquity, according to the *Mechanica* (Mechanics), a text wrongly attributed to Aristotle. Historically, studies of these simple machines had connected all their properties to Archimedes's law of the lever. In 1725 Pierre Varignon, pursuing an idea that he had put forward in 1687, challenged this more than 1,000-year-old assumption and proposed connecting such properties to the law of composition or to the law of the parallelogram of forces. One year later, Daniel Bernoulli—following in the footsteps of his father, Johann—reproached Varignon for demonstrating the law of the composition of forces by means of the law of the composition of momentum, thereby confusing two different physical quantities, both of which were vectorial and therefore obeyed the law of the composition of the parallelogram. On this occasion, Daniel Bernoulli published a very modern work in which his concern to provide a purely geometric proof for the law of the composition of forces in stasis led him to a demonstration very close to the one that is used today for vectorial composition. This demonstration was repeated and improved upon several times during the course of the 18th century, in particular by D'Alembert and by Daviet de Foncenex in 1761.

The forces of stasis, or "dead forces," were contrasted with the "living forces" of dynamics, which became the subject of a fierce debate. D'Alembert describes this controversy as a "dispute about words" in his *Traité de dynamique* (1742; Treatise on Dynamics); Euler calls it a *logomachia* (battle of words) in 1745, in an article on "the force of percussion"; and it was discussed at length by Immanuel Kant in 1747. The dispute arose because, while all those who took part in it were at least partly right, they were not all speaking of the same thing. Furthermore, when Descartes applied his law of the conservation of the "quantity of motion" (momentum), he did not take into account the vectorial character of momentum and thus obtained completely erroneous laws of impact. This error had aroused the wrath of Gottfried Wilhelm Leibniz, who had maintained (in 1698) that what was conserved was not momentum proportional to speed but the "living force" proportional to the speed squared.

Leibniz was thinking of a form of energy $\left(\frac{mv^2}{2}\right)$ when he referred to a "living force." Even though his study of the laws of impact had, by 1662, convinced Huygens that when momentum was defined vectorially it would be conserved just like energy, the 18th-century scientific community continued to debate the question in an attempt to settle the issue of whether the force was proportional to the speed or to its square. The fact that energy is a scalar quantity, while momentum and force are vectorial quantities, added to the confusion. The addition of forces according to the vectorial law of the parallelogram was accepted only with difficulty by some because it implied that the resulting force was less than the algebraic sum of the components. The dispute continued in spite of the explanation published by Daniel Bernoulli in 1726 in the first volume of *Commentarii*, papers published by the Academia Scientiarum Imperialis Petropolitanae (Imperial Academy of Sciences of Saint Petersburg).

Accelerating Force

Newton introduced the expression "accelerating force" to describe the increase in speed per unit of time as an effect of force (*Principia*, Definition VII). This led to the formulation $\vec{F} = m\vec{a}$. The first differential expression of this relationship was provided by Jacob Hermann in his *Phoronomia* (1716; Phoronomia) in the form $dc = p\,dt$ where c is *celeritas* (speed), p is *potentia* (power or force), and t is time. In 1736 Euler, by then an expert in the use of differential calculus, extended the well-understood force of statics to dynamics, stating in his *Mechanica* (Mechanics) that

in statics, where everything is assumed to remain at rest, all forces always maintain their direction. In mechanics [i.e., dynamics], as a body continually changes position, the forces that act on it continually change direction. . . . Thus, the measurement of forces in mechanics differs from statics, where they always retain the same size; in mechanics, as a force may have changed direction when a body has changed position, its size may also have changed, following a certain law.

In "Discovery of a New Principle in Mechanics" (1750), Euler also made progress in mathematical formalization. By projecting Hermann's relationship on three orthogonal planes and taking the vectorial properties of its elements into account, Euler obtained three equations: $2M\,ddx = P\,dt^2$, $2M\,ddy = P\,dt^2$, and $2M\,ddz = P\,dt^2$. The 2 that appears in these equations came from a definition of speed formulated by Huygens. Setting out from the conservation of energy $mgh = \frac{1}{2}mv^2$, the latter expresses speed as a function of the depth of the corresponding drop. Over the course of the age of the Enlightenment, Newton's ideas about forces gradually appeared as accepted notions, from the work of Alexis-Claude Clairaut's (1733–62) to the apotheosis of Newton's theories in Pierre-Simon Laplace's *Mécanique céleste* (1799; Celestial Mechanics). Nevertheless, some scientists such as D'Alembert remained unconvinced. For them, force was defined only by its effect—that is, by the movement that it produced. This was the "driving force" (*force motrice*), which was nothing more than the product of the mass times the acceleration or the element of speed. Lazare Carnot agreed with D'Alembert, and Joseph-Louis Lagrange maintains the same point of view in his *Mechanique analytique* (1788; Analytical Mechanics):

In general, one understands "force" or "power" to be the cause, whatever it may be, that imparts, or tends to impart, motion to a body to which it is assumed to be applied; and it is also by the quantity of the motion imparted, or ready to be imparted, that the force or power must be estimated.

This was not the point of view of other scientists of the 18th century, whose approach differed from that of 19th-century thinkers so much that at the beginning of the 20th century G. Hamel could write:

I have given the concepts of mass and force their former prerogatives [as fundamental (or a priori) magnitudes]. There is no doubt that we need these concepts, for without them there would be no mechanics. Force is more than the product of mass and acceleration, as we can see in the fundamental equation itself, since it affirms that mass times acceleration is equal to the *sum* of the forces.

Although he possessed a general concept of force, Newton had limited his definition to the movement of a point acted on by a central force and to the same movement in a resistant environment. This theory, which dominates the first two books of the *Principia*, concerns a central force of any type. It is not until the third book, "On the System of the World," that Newton specifies this central force as gravitational attraction, which corresponds to a force decreasing by $\frac{1}{r^2}$. In doing this, Newton brings together in a single theory both the parabolic movement of falling heavy objects described by Galileo and the elliptical movement of the planets described by Johannes Kepler. Newton did not have to know how force is transmitted in order to find these movements. He needed only a mathematical understanding of force and its decrease as a function of the distance from the center of attraction.

This way of considering the question aroused strong reactions against Newton's reliance on "action at a distance" and led many researchers at the beginning of the 18th century to prefer the explanation of the planetary system that Descartes had provided—that vortices of matter had swept the planets into movement. An initial confirmation of gravitational attraction came with an explanation of tides, which was the subject of a competition by the Académie Royale des Sciences in 1740. One Cartesian, the Reverend Father Cavalleri, and three Newtonians, Daniel Bernoulli, Euler, and Colin Maclaurin, shared the prize. Another important confirmation was the return of Halley's Comet in 1758, on a date forecast by Clairaut using Newton's precepts. At the end of the 18th century, Laplace inserted an addendum into his work in which he explained the phenomena of capillary motion using Newton's theory.

Electric and Magnetic Forces

These forces were mentioned by Newton, who estimated that magnetic force decreased more rapidly than $\frac{1}{r^2}$. This assertion gave rise to numerous experiments, conducted primarily by Brook Taylor and Francis Hauksbee the Elder in England and by Pieter van Musschenbroek in the Netherlands. In 1629 Musschenbroek measured the intensity of a magnetic force by means of a scale, thus showing that he was one of the first to have understood the concept of force. For weighing a magnetic force meant admitting that phenomena as different as magnetism and weight both involved forces.

In 1750 J. Mitchell stated that magnetic force decreases by $\frac{1}{r^2}$. In 1760 Daniel Bernoulli (in a lecture that was not published until 1777) and Joseph Priestley in 1766 both reached a similar conclusion with respect to electricity. We now know that to observe a decrease of this type it is necessary to isolate an electric charge or a magnetic pole by using a very long magnet. In 1720 Taylor had stressed the difficulties of such an observation if these conditions are not met by admitting that he did not know how to measure the distance between the magnet and the point where he wanted to measure the force. Should one consider the distance from this point to the center of the magnet or to one of its poles?

In 1789 Charles Coulomb obtained his law of electric and magnetic forces in the case of isolated poles or charges by comparing magnetic force with torsion force using a scale. Coulomb's law is specific to the experimental model that has just been mentioned, for the field of magnetic force is much more complex than that of gravity, which is simply central. Experiments with iron filings enable us to observe it in action. Newton's reasoning, which only took into account for the decrease of force as a function of distance, eliminated everything concerning the propagation of force and, therefore, of fields. Euler and Daniel Bernoulli grasped the importance of this and, even though they were ardent supporters of Newton's ideas on gravity, they went back to Descartes's theory of vortices to explain magnetic fields. Euler tried to apply the equations that he had developed in hydrodynamics to the "magnetic fluid" that "whirled" around a magnet.

In 1759, Aepinus (Franz Maria Ulrich Theodor Hoch) combined the phenomena of electricity and magnetism, for the first time constructing a theory of magnetism that closely paralleled Benjamin Franklin's theory of electricity. The excess or lack of magnetic and electric "fluids" was said to engender electrical charges or magnetic poles; these fluids seem to exert a force of attraction from a distance, but they do not interact. Electric and magnetic phenomena were not yet correlated.

Some writers, such as Tobias Mayer (1760) and Johann Heinrich Lambert (1766), tried in vain to find linear equations for magnetic force based on Newton's force and $\frac{1}{r^2}$. There was no complete mathematical description of electromagnetic fields until the work of Michael Faraday and James Clerk Maxwell in the 19th century.

Principle of Least Action

Euler was drawn to the idea of deducing mechanics from a single variational principle around 1751. He hoped to build on the principle of least action formulated by Maupertuis in 1744, who wrote:

> Whenever a change occurs in nature, the quantity of action necessary for this change is the smallest possible. The quantity of action is the product of

the mass of the bodies times their speed and times the space they traverse.

Maupertuis's idea in turn had been inspired by the principle adopted by Pierre de Fermat in optics. As formulated by Maupertuis—and with the level of generality he conferred on it (he even used it to deduce the existence of God) the principle of least action required some amendment. A heated debate ensued, in which Samuel König, supported by Voltaire, was pitted against Maupertuis, and in which Frederick II became involved. Euler took Maupertuis's side and restated the principle in a new form in his "Harmony between the General Principles of Rest and Motion" (1751). In this text, Euler gives the name "effort" to the quantity $\int \vec{F} \, d\vec{s}$, which Maupertuis had called "action" and which we now call the "work" of a force $\vec{F}$ during displacement $d\vec{s}$. This idea was taken up again by Lagrange in his *Mechanique analytique*.

With help from Daniel Bernoulli, Euler also used the variational principle to resolve the problem of the curvature of an elastic strip (a problem raised by Jacob Bernoulli at the end of the 17th century). Euler published his findings in the *Additamentum I de curvis elasticis* (1744; First Addendum on Elastic Curves), which is part of his *Methodus Inveniendi Lineas Curvas Maximi Minimive Proprietate Gaudentes* (1744; A Method to Find the Curves That Have a Property of Maxima or Minima). This problem confronted researchers with "elastic force," while Coulomb, in *La règle des maximis et des minimis appliquée à l'architecture* (1773; The Rule of Maxima and Minima Applied to Architecture), introduced a "cohesive force" to account for the difficulty of causing one part of a broken pillar to slide over the other part in a certain direction. These two "forces" led to discoveries relative to the mechanics of continuous mediums, and to the development of the concepts of tension and shearing investigated by Augustin-Louis Cauchy and his contemporaries in the first half of the 19th century.

PATRICIA RADELET-DE GRAVE

See also Dynamics; Magnetism; Mechanics, Analytic; Newtonianism; Physics, Experimental

Further Reading

Jammer, Max, *Concepts of Force: A Study in the Foundations of Dynamics*, Cambridge, Massachusetts: Harvard University Press, 1957
Maltese, Giulio, *La storia di "F=ma": La seconda legge del moto nel XVIII secolo*, Florence: Olschki, 1992
Radelet-De Grave, Patricia, and Jean Dhombres, "Contingence et nécessité en mécanique, étude de deux textes inédits de Jean d'Alembert," *Physis* 28 ns 1 (1991)

Fortification

To understand the nature of fortifications in the 18th century, we must first describe the system of bastions, a defensive technique that had reached its maturity, and then consider the contribution of those who were responsible for that system, recognizing that they were heirs to a prestigious tradition, who, to a large extent, still typified the traditional image of the engineer. We should also notice the early signs of a crisis in the art of the defense and attack of fixed locations, a crisis linked to the development of military strategy but also to changes in the policies of some of the great European powers, such as France. While fortifications still represented an absolute priority for Louis XIV's state, their importance declined somewhat under Louis XV and Louis XVI, as France put more emphasis on needs related to economic development. Affected by all these factors, the role of fortifications and of their engineers appears to have been decidedly complex—in line with the role of war in Enlightenment Europe, where the *philosophes* dreamed of universal peace at the same time that a new appetite for territorial conquest was being aroused.

Modern fortifications made their appearance during the wars of the Renaissance. Conceived by the Italians to counterbalance the new power of artillery, the system of bastions was rapidly mastered by French engineers. The writer Jean Errard de Bar-le-Duc categorized its essential elements in his *Fortification démontrée et réduite en art* (Fortification Demonstrated and Reduced to an Art), which first appeared in 1600. Those elements included the burial of the fortifications, the flanking of fortifications with pentagonal bastions, the use of artillery fired in enfilades, and the adjustment of the size of fortifications to the range of weapons. The system was improved by Antoine de Ville and Blaise de Pagan, and developed even further by Sebastien Le Prestre de Vauban. By the end of the 17th century, fortification was one of the few entirely systematized fields of engineering. As Errard had claimed, its principles could be completely "demonstrated" in geometric and ballistic terms. Moreover, it was a field in which experimentation and international exchange led to new developments. Indeed, the principles of fortification with bastions spread from Spain to Russia and from Sweden to the Ottoman Empire.

Rather than searching for anything fundamentally new, Enlightenment engineers improved on existing types of fortifications and explored variations on them. Thus, in France, for example, the engineer Louis de Cormontaigne modified Vauban's layouts at the time of the rebuilding of the fortifications of Metz between 1728 and 1752. Cormontaigne's rules, based on a universal method, became in their turn the basis for the courses in the attack and defense of fixed locations that were taught at the École du Génie (Engineering School) in Mézières. The improvement of fortifications also resulted from a better evaluation of their resistance to enemy assault. Combining empirical data on such resistance—data that was collected during actual sieges—with the principles of ballistics and knowledge of building techniques, engineers sought to set up the front lines in accordance with the defensive power that they wished to obtain. The emphasis they placed on the logic of ensuring the best possible defense is one of the most striking features of the mind-set of the fortification engineers.

The 300 or so French engineers who specialized in this field, and who were organized into a single corps in 1696, did not concern themselves exclusively with the attack and defense of fixed locations. Like many of their counterparts in other countries, they were also very active in cartography, as well as in major projects for the improvement of territories and cities. For example, it was an engineer of the École du Génie, Jacques-Philippe Mareschal, who planned the garden for the fountain at Nîmes. Around the same time, some of his colleagues, with their extensive knowledge of hydraulics, were building canals and aqueducts, as constructing channels, locks, and pipelines called for the same skills needed to build fortifications.

Given the scientific nature of the knowledge upon which it was based, the world of the fortification engineers was among the first to be affected by the trend of teaching technical courses in schools—a trend that swept across Enlightenment Europe. Schools of engi-

neers and officers were created almost everywhere. Not even the Ottoman Empire escaped this trend; it established a school of fortifications in 1784. Among this series of new establishments, the École du Génie en Mézières, which trained the engineers of France from 1748 onward, deserves special mention. Unlike its great rival, the École des Ponts et Chaussées (Civil Engineering School) in Paris, the Mézières school recruited students by competitive examination and offered some of the best scientific and technical training available in Europe. Indeed, in addition to offering specific instruction on the principles of fortification, the school hosted a whole series of courses given by professors and assistants of high quality. The abbé Bossut served as professor of mathematics from 1752 to 1768, and the abbé Nollet taught there from 1761 to 1770. However, the school owed its scientific reputation primarily to Gaspard Monge, the inventor of descriptive geometry, who taught at Mézières from 1764 to 1784. Monge set out to promote the application of the sciences to engineering, a point of view that he was to take further at the time of the creation of the École Polytechnique. Those who studied at Mézières included several first-rate engineers and scholars such as Jean-Charles de Borda, Charles-Augustin Coulomb, and Pierre-Louis-Georges Dubuat.

Fortification engineers, heirs to a long technical tradition and better trained overall than their counterparts in civil engineering, formed a genuine scientific and technical elite in a country such as France. However, despite the prestige that they enjoyed, doubts began to arise about the field for which the fortification engineers were responsible. Over the course of the 18th century, military strategists increasingly questioned whether fortified places, with their great costs, were really effective. The century was rediscovering the tactics of mobility as an alternative to the war of position that had characterized 17th-century battles. In his *Rêveries, ou mémoire sur l'art de la guerre* (1756; Reveries; or, Memoir on the Art of War), the maréchal de Saxe had already criticized what he claimed was the excessive number of fortified places maintained by the rulers of Europe. The comte de Guibert was even more critical in his *Essai général de tactique* (1770; General Essay on Tactics). The victories won by King Frederick II of Prussia during the Seven Years' War, thanks to the mobility of his troops, were used to back up this type of analysis. Following this conflict in which France had lost the majority of its colonies, it seemed more appropriate to reorganize the artillery and the infantry, rather than renewing the policy of fortification.

This questioning of the usefulness of fortifications was redoubled during the second half of the 18th century, as economic development took on an increasingly strategic importance. The engineers of the Ponts et

Chaussées (Bridges and Roadways Administration), who had been in charge of the construction and maintenance of roads in France under the comptroller general since 1716, were the main beneficiaries of this shift in the priorities of the monarchy. Being responsible for an infrastructure that was vital for trade, these engineers gradually took on the chief responsibility for construction projects at the expense of the engineers trained in Mézières.

The final decades of the century were marked by analysis of ways to modernize the art of fortification, both to adapt this art to the changing nature of armed conflicts and to make it, if possible, less costly. In France, the marquis de Montalembert, who was an artillery general, proved to be one of the leading advocates of this policy of modernization. Montalembert totally rejected the legacy of Vauban and Cormontaigne in the 11 volumes of his *Fortification perpendiculaire* (1776–86; Perpendicular Fortification). Based on an intensive use of artillery, polygonal layouts, and separate fortifications replacing continuous bastions, his daring proposals met with violent opposition from the corps of fortification engineers. Another artillery officer, Pierre-Ambroise-François Choderlos de Laclos, vigorously supported Montalembert in his *Lettres à MM. de l'Académie Française sur l'éloge de M. le maréchal de Vauban de 1786* (Letters to Messrs. of the Académie Française on M. le Maréchal de Vauban's Eulogy of 1786). However, the leading theorists of the corps of engineers from the École du Génie in Mézières regarded these proposals as no more than a dangerous aberration.

The conservatism of the corps of engineers with regard to fortifications stands in complete contrast with their open-mindedness in areas as varied as urban development and scientific research. Montalembert's work prefigured some of the characteristics of fortifications in the time of Napoleon, yet it made hardly any impact on the history of fortifications in France. His true heirs were in Sweden, Austria, and, above all, Germany. Indeed, the polygonal layouts and separate line of defense with which Montalembert had wanted to line the frontiers of France became standard practice in the German-speaking regions of Europe.

In the 18th century, an age of transition in which the old and the new were often inextricably mixed, the field of fortification appeared with two contradictory faces: one as an outstanding example of the new in the technical domain, because of the rigor of the wholly scientific inspiration that governed the field's operation, and the other as an area of activity marked by archaic practices, in view of the changes in the art of war and the imperatives of economic development. Similarly, the engineers responsible for fortifications were both ahead of and behind their times. These engineers simultaneously heralded the alliance of science and technology that would gradually become the norm in the 19th century, while remaining loyal to an outmoded system. They were products of the Enlightenment, but at the same time they had to defend a tradition that was threatened by that same Enlightenment. At a time when a new ideal of constant progress in science and technology was being formulated, it was no longer as easy as it had been to embody this tradition.

ANTOINE PICON

See also Ballistics; Technical Instruction; Technology; Transport Systems

Further Reading

Picon, Antoine, "Naissance du territoire moderne: Génies civil et militaire à la fin du XVIIIe siècle," *VRBI* II (1989)

Prost, Phillippe, *Les forteresses de l'Empire: Fortifications, villes de guerre et arsenaux napoléoniens*, Paris: Éditions du Moniteur, 1991

Rocolle, Pierre, *2000 ans de fortification française*, 2 vols., Limoges, France: Lavauzelle, 1973; 2nd edition, Paris: Charles-Lavauzelle, 1989

France

In the *Encyclopédie* the chevalier de Jaucourt describes France as "a large European kingdom, bordered on the north by the Netherlands; on the east by Germany, Switzerland, and Savoy; on the south by the Mediterranean Sea and the Pyrenees; and on the west by the Atlantic Ocean." This definition, based on the nation's political system and its geographic situation, is followed by some remarks on climate and economic resources, together with a brief survey of France's political, cultural, and social history. For a militant Encyclopedist such as Jaucourt, French history was characterized by a twofold, though belated, awakening: a social awakening of the nation, which, after having labored too long under the sway of tyrannical noblemen and kings, was finally being ruled by a monarchy that promised to guarantee commercial and literary progress; and a cultural awakening, thanks to which France, after centuries of ignorance and inertia, had finally joined the concert of European powers, with the French nation poised to assume the mantle of leadership.

Jaucourt's geographic description was essentially the same as the one proposed a century earlier by Louis Coulon in his *L'Ulysse français ou le voyage de France* (1643; The French Ulysses; or, The Journey through France). But whereas Coulon had invited his readers and prospective travelers to contemplate the magnificence of a country that was rich in churches, courts of law, universities, and other institutions, and in the full flower of its literary and scientific achievements, Jaucourt defined contemporary France both in relation to its darker past in order to highlight the progress that we have come to associate with the Renaissance and the Enlightenment, and in the context of a still-troubled future, in which further reforms would be needed. In Jaucourt's view the nation's "immense wealth" was as unevenly distributed as was Rome's at the fall of the Republic, and it was these inequalities that were hampering demographic growth.

Jaucourt's article creates a double opposition—on the one hand, between France and the Enlightenment and, on the other, between the writings of the *philosophes* and the monarchic system. If France aspired to become one of the centers of the European Enlightenment, the *philosophes* for their part hoped to take part in the modernization of the state that had been inaugurated by the monarchy. Both ambitions were fraught with contradictions and conflicts, yet, in Jaucourt's estimation, the causes and the solutions were not hard to find. His article concludes with cross-references to "Taxes" and "Toleration." In other words, the solutions lay in the state and in the Enlightenment.

For most of the 18th century the French monarchy held itself to be inviolable. Its carefully repeated rituals and gestures were the tangible expression of the permanence of its beliefs and values. The country was ruled by a succession of kings with the same name: Louis XIV (1643–1715), Louis XV (1715–1774), and Louis XVI (1774–1792). At least on the surface, then, this was a period of relative stability. Except for the acquisition of Lorraine and Corsica (in 1766 and 1768, respectively) and the loss of American colonies to England in 1763, France's territories remained virtually unaltered, and the nation remained largely free of the internal and external strife that had characterized its history in earlier centuries. Yet beneath this apparent calm, profound changes were underway. In less than a century France moved from the absolutism of Louis XIV to the procla-

mation of the first Republic in 1792, and from the Sun King's imposition of a single state religion to the Revolution's move toward a completely secularized society. The last decade of the 18th century, with its radical upheavals and innumerable breaks with the past, made up for a century of superficial calm and prosperity.

One example of the inner tensions of the period was the contrast between, on the one hand, France's relatively unified administration and language, which was far greater than that of the other leading nations of continental Europe, and, on the other hand, the tangle of local differences that emerged from a society divided into three "orders" and, more particularly, from the permanence of privileges and dispensations granted to the various provinces, corporations, towns, parishes, families, and individuals. An administrative structure that claimed to function rationally was inherently hostile to the introduction of new authorities and institutions inherited from different periods.

Unity and Heterogeneity

The task of modernizing France, which the monarchy had taken upon itself and which had the full support of the writers of the Enlightenment, involved gathering information about the country in order to place it under centralized control, subject to the all-powerful gaze of the king. The metaphor of the *regard* (gaze), fundamental to the very notion of Enlightenment, was just as essential to a royal authority that hoped to exert its influence throughout the land, and to be omnipresent and all-powerful, as it was to the ambition of the Encyclopedists, which was to make an inventory of the world in order to better exploit its resources and adapt it to human needs. The commanding eye of the king and the scrutinizing eyes of the *philosophes* joined forces in such institutions as the Académie Royale des Sciences de Paris (French Royal Academy of Sciences), whose task was to promote observation, gather and classify information, verify existing knowledge, and compare the lessons learned by explorers with the opinions of scientists based in France. Their work was supported by the royal geographers and by teams of civil and military engineers, the land surveyors who took measurements, made sketches, and drew up plans for the development of the entire country. Additional regional documentation was provided by the provincial academies. These efforts toward homogenization were crowned by a national land survey carried out by successive generations of the Cassini family, resulting in the publication of the first modern map of France.

Information about the state of the nation was also furnished by the king's *intendants* (magistrates); their reports served as the basis for statistical analyses that were still being used during the Revolution and the

Empire. Advances in statistical and demographic methods provided new techniques to assist in the interpretation of such data. Whether they were intended to determine tax rates or to organize military conscription, it was these statistical surveys carried out by the *intendants* under the monarchy—and continued, in a more systematic way, by their successors during the Revolution and the Empire—that enabled the central government to evaluate France's resources. Under the ancien régime the organization of the nation for tax-gathering purposes into the various administrative *intendances* and *généralités* gave a certain degree of unity to a country that was otherwise multifariously divided within itself, broken up into innumerable divisions or subdivisions, none of which overlapped or corresponded with one another. These divisions included provinces, bailiwicks, seneschalsies, *pays d'élection* (regions where taxation levels were traditionally set by elected officials) as well as *pays d'état* (those regions where they were not) (the), ecclesiastical provinces and dioceses, military jurisdictions, and law courts administered by the *parlements* (high courts).

The monarchy had begun to bring some order and unity into this administrative chaos, but the process would not be completed until later under the strong centralized governments of the Revolution and Empire, notably through the abolition of the privileges formerly enjoyed by provinces, principalities, and towns and by the parceling up of France into departments. During the Revolution the many arguments and clashes between advocates and opponents of centralization (especially between the Jacobins and the Girondins) highlighted the problem of just how far this process of unification and homogenization could and should go. In 1790 a major national survey about the status of regional languages, the *questionnaire relatif aux patois*, illustrated the government's need to understand the linguistic diversity and complexity of the country in preparation for the imposition of a single, uniform language. In this case the Revolution was simply confirming a century-long trend, as French gradually replaced regional languages and written French came to be the form of communication that all citizens were expected to master.

If the entire nation were deemed to be "visible" beneath the royal gaze , it could also be deemed to be "readable" by an enlightened public, insofar as information regarding administrative matters was made available to every educated reader rather than being confined to government circles. When Denis Diderot became interested in the development of Siberia in response to what he took to be a request from Catherine the Great, he sent a series of questions to the Academia Scientiarium Imperialis Petropolitanae (Imperial Academy of Sciences of Saint Petersburg). However, no reply was forthcoming since Catherine believed that the future of Siberia was solely her concern. Enlightenment authors continually protested this kind of state secrecy, just as they opposed the secret practices of the professional guilds and corporations. The *philosophes* were convinced that the growth of the reading public and the ever-wider dissemination of knowledge were essential if France was to become a united nation. Increased mastery over geographic space should be accompanied by increased freedom for those who inhabited that space. It is no coincidence that there was a great demand throughout this period for travel literature and related compilations, or that maps, atlases, and textbooks for the study of geography and history proliferated, including those by the abbé Lenglet-Dufresnoy, which went through many editions.

Parallel to this unified and homogenized notion of space, the 18th century witnessed a tendency to quantify and mechanically calculate time. For the men and women of Enlightenment France, alongside the rotation of the seasons and the traditional activities and festivals associated with them, there existed a different sense of time, a linear one measured by clocks and newspapers and controlled by tradesmen, engineers, and government officials. People kept time by means of precise, individual watches, rather than by looking at the sun or the sundial or listening to church bells. Two of the leading figures of the French Enlightenment grew up in families of watchmakers. Jean-Jacques Rousseau was the son and grandson of Genevan watchmakers, and Beaumarchais (born Pierre-Augustin Caron) followed in his father's footsteps by becoming a watchmaker; in fact, Beaumarchais perfected an escapement mechanism. The first of these two craftsmen, Rousseau, was to become one of the world's leading advocates of the doctrine of human perfectibility and of different models of progress. Beaumarchais, for his part, was to write plays that gave a new meaning to the principle of dramatic unity of time and that unfold with a sense of rhythm quite unlike anything hitherto seen onstage. For example, in the Beaumarchais's *Le mariage de Figaro* (1784; The Marriage of Figaro), the hero is discovered in the opening scene, measuring rod in hand, taking measurements for his future bedroom, and he makes strategic use of time throughout the play, clearly expressing these new Enlightenment values. In a similar fashion, alongside the older almanacs, periodicals began to appear and compete for the attention of readers, arousing an interest in contemporary history, which was presented as an endless cycle of cosmic, religious, and dynastic events. The endeavors of Enlightenment scholars and philosophers to understand what the past had really been like ran counter to every kind of preestablished truth.

Following up on a suggestion by Daniel Roche, we may observe a second kind of polarity that was endemic to this period (see Roche). This polarity existed between rural France, on the one hand, where continuity, self-sufficiency, and authority were the order of the day and land and tradition were considered to be the supreme values, and, on the other, a new mercantile France that was already a dominant force in the ports and in those towns that were already commercial and banking centers—a France, in other words, where energies were focused on trade, profit, and change. It would be an error, however, to describe this polarity in terms of a simplistic, black-and-white opposition between the older aristocratic mindset and an emerging bourgeois consciousness. Thanks to village schools, a slow process of acculturation was spreading throughout rural France, and notables, innkeepers, and postmasters all played their part in the gradual rise in literacy rates. Nevertheless, the new mercantile France was still a very different place from the nation of middle-class traders that Voltaire had discovered during his stay in England and made familiar to readers of his *Lettres philosophiques* (1734; Philosophical Letters). Commerce in France was a permanent compromise between privilege and free enterprise, between government controls and individual initiative. Advocates of mercantilism, Physiocracy, and liberalism argued their respective cases and even exchanged insults, without arriving at any homogeneous consensus. To varying degrees, according to region, the merchant classes were integrated into local society or became members of Masonic lodges or the provincial academies.

The real changes were taking place in towns. In a period when the overall population of France rose from roughly 21 or 22 million inhabitants at the beginning of the 18th century to around 28 or 29 million at the outbreak of the Revolution, urban population grew slowly and unevenly by about 20 percent. Paris and Versailles grew steadily in political and cultural importance, although this development was not always reflected in a rise in population. The same was true of the great regional capitals, which included the major ports (Bordeaux, where the population doubled, Marseilles, and Nantes) and, later, Lille and Lyon. Those persons who were new to urban life enjoyed many cultural advantages, but they also faced new hardships, such as the necessity of later marriages, a relatively precarious family life, and the need to foster out children to wet nurses. They also had to face new experiences that resulted from having members of different social classes living in close proximity to one another and mixing socially to a certain degree. No longer limited to the privileged few who owned books and libraries, the circulation of printed matter increased steadily throughout the 18th century, thanks to a proliferation of reading rooms and subscription libraries, from which books could be rented. Rare and sacred books, luxuriously bound for the wealthiest owners, required careful and repeated reading and were becoming a thing of the past, replaced by books that were meant to be read more quickly and by persons with wider-ranging reading habits.

If we are to trust the testimony of Louis Sébastien Mercier's *Tableau de Paris* (1781–89; Panorama of Paris), the towns themselves were evolving along the same lines as book production and reading. Consequently, towns were the subject of endless administrative, medical, and architectural discourses. Whereas the traditional town had been built around the monumental signs of religious and monarchic authority, its modern equivalent was evolving into a place that was designed for commerce and circulation and thus existed in a permanent state of flux. This evolution of the town was similar to the way in which the monumental and definitive literary work, highly charged with symbolic meaning, was giving way to periodicals and to books that reflected a rapidly evolving world, whether by their utilitarian character or by affording immediate enjoyment.

The power of Paris and Versailles was apparent for all to see. It reflected a phenomenon that was at once European—the development of their respective capitals was a necessary part of the modernization of the various European nation-states—and specifically French, because of the centralized nature of a monarchy that wished to retain absolute control of its policies intended to bring about administrative, cultural, and linguistic unification. At the court of Versailles the king could count on the support of advisers and a royal council, whose role, however, was more like that of a receiver general than a chancellor; in the provinces the monarch was represented by his *intendants*. But this centralized authority was offset by the powerful influence of the royal family and the nobility, as well as by that of the many military officers and officeholders who had purchased their positions. The history of France throughout the 18th century reflects these contradictions and the sundry inefficiencies and crises to which they gave rise. The delicate balance between maintaining the status quo and reform, between centralization and decentralization, but also between traditional values and the ideas of the Enlightenment, was constantly being modified by these basic political contradictions. The *intendant* represented the key link between the central power and the heart of the nation, between the royal will and the realities of everyday living.

The career of Anne-Robert-Jacques Turgot, who was both a contributor to the *Encyclopédie* and an employee of the state, is an excellent illustration of the impact of the conflicts in question. As an *intendant* in Limoges from 1761 to 1776, Turgot tried to pursue an enlightened policy in a region with which he was ill acquainted. Thanks to the influence of his *philosophe* friends, he became minister of finance (1774–76), where once again he tried to put in practice his philosophical principles by drawing on his local knowledge. His liberalization of the grain market led to riots and his eventual dismissal. Following Turgot, and frequently in opposition to him, Jacques Necker too would attempt to reform the administration, on principles outlined in his *Compte rendu au roi* (1781; Account to the King), but his proposals were just as unpopular as Turgot's and his enemies managed to have him dismissed. The failure of these ministers raises the question of the extent to which reform from within was possible in France under the ancien régime.

Yet some measure of reform, in addition to Enlightenment ideas, gradually spread from Paris to the provinces. The principles of free speech and open debate, as well as the proliferation of discussion groups and scholarly societies in the provinces were visible signs of the forces of decentralization. On the other hand, the nationwide acceptance of Parisian linguistic and cultural norms strengthened the process of centralization. The country bumpkin became a stock character in plays and novels; a succession of peasants and valets, often named after the region of their origin, were immediately recognizable by their dialects and by their mangling of standard French, which was by then the official language of the administration and of mainstream culture. While for practical purposes, even as late as the Revolution, the state still recognized bilingualism, the principle of linguistic homogeneity throughout France was no longer in dispute.

The two-way polarity between Paris and the provinces conditioned attitudes and became a literary theme. The best people were drawn to the capital, but at the same time, Paris was thought of as the city of illusions. A series of contrasts between town and country, between center and periphery, gave rise to the widespread belief that true values could only be found in the provinces or in the countryside. The arrival of a young provincial in Paris became a familiar literary topos that underlined the difficulty of reconciling dazzling images of the "City of Light" with the reality of its poverty and injustices. Urbanization, the centralization of government, and the increasing concentration of the nobility at court fostered the myth that the provinces and the countryside were the last refuge of authenticity, while celebrating the virtues of an impoverished and virtually unknown rural nobility.

Power and Opinion

Another manifestation of the tensions of the age was the conflict between tradition and public opinion. The king's person was the incarnation of the principle of absolute monarchy; however, an aging Louis XIV, the nonconformist regent Philippe, the duc d'Orléans, the shy, retiring character of Louis XV, and the similarly unprepossessing Louis XVI hardly corresponded to the original model of the soldier-king, or the Sun King, who had only to appear in public to impose his will on his subjects. The seriousness with which these monarchs carried out their royal duties and the affection that the people as a whole showed toward them right up until the beginning of the revolutionary crisis could not mask the fact that the dynastic and court rituals were slowly becoming emptied of their content. The king was no longer the miracle worker who cured "the king's evil" (that is, scrofula) on the day after his coronation. In 1775 those who suffered from the disease still crowded around Louis XVI to be touched, just as they had in 1722, but the traditional phrase "The king touches you, God cures you" had become "The king touches you, may God cure you." People with enlightened views did not conceal their scepticism, while the medical authorities concentrated on establishing the typology of diseases and measuring the efficacy of available treatments. The king continued to make frequent public proclamations; his own glory and God's were still celebrated in *Te Deums;* and the 17th-century tradition of ritualized "ceremonies of information" (to use M. Fogel's phrase) was still alive as a ritual, although these ceremonies became less frequent in the period from the War of Austrian Succession (1744–48) and the Seven Years' War (1756–63) to the American War of Independence (1778–83). Commercial publications were providing an alternative source of information to supplement the data ceremonially released by the crown. Moreover, there was a deep division between the notables who were privy to the government data and the ordinary people who could simply marvel as it was released to them. Given the increasing demand for better communications, it could no longer be taken for granted that it was the ordinary people's duty simply to marvel.

Painters and town planners also had a role to play in upholding the rhetoric of royalty. Instead of the heroic, legendary Louis XIV, artists were creating images of more prosaic kings in which it was possible to discern the individual behind all the pomp and ceremony. In Paris a square dedicated to Louis XV was built on the model of earlier squares named for Henry IV, Louis XIII, and Louis XIV; the possibility of a square in honor of Louis XVI was discussed. Similar squares, of regular classical proportions, were constructed in provincial towns, usually dominated by an equestrian statue of the king, as manfully in control of his mount as he was presumed to be of his subjects. In his *Tableau de Paris,* Louis-Sébastien Mercier is highly critical of Edmé Bouchardon and Jean-Baptiste Pigalle's statue of Louis XV in the square named after him: "When will our sculptors be capable of portraying something other than the pose of the king sitting on a horse, with his hand on the reins?" Walking in Paris in the futuristic world of his *L'an 2440: Rêve s'il en fut jamais* (1771; Astraea's Return; or, The Halcyon Days of France in the Year 2440: A Dream), Mercier notes that the city is still adorned with equestrian statues of various kings; but the monarchs in question look more like pacific defenders of the people than conquering heroes. What he finds especially admirable are the allegorical figures (such as "Humanity") and the statues of national leaders.

In Mercier's utopian world the admiration formerly reserved for kings goes to those who defended the cause of freedom; the heroic energy once incarnated in a single monarch has shifted to the representatives of the people, for it is they who make history. By the same token the academies and learned societies of the Enlightenment were no longer content merely to sing the praises of the king. As they saw it, their task was to record the heroism of the entire nation, independently of the fate of the Bourbon dynasty. With the coming of the Revolution the equestrian statues would be demolished and the Church of Sainte-Geneviève, which had been rebuilt in conformance with the wishes of Louis XV, would be transformed into the Pantheon, a temple to honor France's national heroes.

The situation of the king vis-à-vis the state, but also in his relations with the people, was beset with contradictory principles. The king was regarded as a moderator to whom the representatives of the various legal bodies reported in order to give him information and advice—this was how the members of the *parlements* in particular perceived their own role. However, at the same time, the king had to function as an absolute monarch, separated from the nation as a whole by the court and its rituals. Advocates of reform could therefore try to influence the intermediary bodies such as the *parlements*, which were supposed to represent the people; alternatively, advocates could appeal directly to the king, who, as the head of state, was the only person in a position to impose reforms from above. In one sense, then, the role of the king was that of a rational administrator and coordinator; in another, it was paternal, symbolic, and religious. These two facets of his role came into conflict whenever administrative or financial logic proved incompatible with the exigencies of royal ritual. The financial crisis, which increased both the national debt and the power of the financiers on whom the state depended, placed the traditionally extravagant lifestyle of the royal family and the court nobility in an extremely unfavorable light. The conspicuous grandeur that had been expected of God's representative on Earth was no longer thought appropriate for a man who, in the early stages of the Revolution, was regarded merely

as the nation's chief civil servant. The financiers who had served as scapegoats until the beginning of the 18th century, sheltering the king from the hostility provoked by excessive taxation, continued to be unpopular, but Louis XVI and his advisers were no longer able to avoid being held responsible for fiscal policy. Financiers, advisers, and monarch would all be struck down by the Revolution.

The king's position in relation to the judicial system was equally fraught with ambiguity, leading to doubt and arguments The king ruled over what Daniel Roche has called "an imbroglio of competences and jurisdictions" in which the various seigniorial courts, provostries, bailiwicks, and *parlements* were set off against one another or arranged hierarchically (see Roche). In major legal affairs, when the conscience of the entire nation became aroused—most notably, in the affaire Calas," in which Voltaire decried the failures of the judicial system that had wrongfully executed a Protestant merchant from Toulouse—Louis XV no longer appeared capable of quelling local partisanship nor of moderating the spectacular violence of public executions. For Voltaire, as for the *philosophes* as a whole, the only hope for a rational, coherent, and humane judicial system lay in the strength of public opinion. The *lettre de cachet,* by which kings had traditionally been able to intervene directly in legal matters by ordering imprisonment without trial, was no longer viewed as a possible recourse to combat what Arlette Farge and Michel Foucault have referred to as "family disorders" but rather served as an example of judicial arbitrariness, if not indeed a denial of justice. In pre-revolutionary and revolutionary France, the collective imagination focused on a Gothic castle, the Bastille, as the symbol of a royal power that was no longer perceived as the absolute and impartial guarantor of legal rights.

If the monarchy itself were no longer sacrosanct, this change could not help but affect the status of the clergy and of religion because there was no separation between Church and state in France. Since both king and clergy were increasingly perceived as necessary components in the workings of society, rather than the beneficiaries of a transcendent legitimacy, mystical reverence toward them began to give way to an evaluation of their functional utility. The clergy were respected for the tasks they performed. Consequently, the parish priest, bringing succor or alms to his parishioners, was compared favorably to the rich prelates, who incurred the same kind of disapproval as did members of the court nobility. The various privileges enjoyed by the first order, its property and wealth and its exemption from taxation (in return for the "free donation" paid annually to the state), could only be justified if the order assumed responsibility for elementary schools and social and medical assistance.

On strictly doctrinal matters, such as the need to preserve orthodox beliefs and practices, or the exclusion of Jews and Protestants, public opinion was distinctly more critical. At the same time that the state was trying to put a check on the Church's autonomy, the *philosophes* sought to reduce Christianity to a universal morality, reserving for themselves the role of mentor to the people and adviser to the king. The possibility of a Catholic Enlightenment in France was compromised, on the one hand, by the fact that Catholic theologians found it hard to think in terms of a world governed by human passions and market forces and, on the other hand, by the extreme views of certain Enlightenment thinkers who wrote openly in favor of materialism, atheism, and a secularized state. The efforts to reconcile the Church with the Revolution were similarly caught in the crossfire of two equally radical views—those of the refractory priests, who actively opposed the Revolution both from abroad and within France, and those who favored militant secularization. Catholic apologetics, under pressure from the Enlightenment, were less concerned with historical truth than with the social utility and beauty of religion, although the *philosophes* could not have predicted the rhetorical power that this shift in emphasis would give to later generations of religious writers, after the Revolution, in works such as François-René de Chateaubriand's *Le génie du Christianisme ou beautés de la religion chrétienne* (1802; The Genius of Christianity; or, The Spirit and Beauties of the Christian Religion).

This kind of change, both in the life of institutions and the behavior of individuals, was not only part of a larger change from a life founded on belief to one founded on knowledge but also was accompanied by the development of a single cultural model and the emergence of a public sphere and a public opinion. Increased educational opportunities were in line with the work begun by the Catholic Counter-Reformation, which held that more instruction was the best way to spread the Divine Word, and by the monarchy itself, which, as early as 1698 and 1724, had issued ordinances to increase the number of schools throughout the nation and for universal schooling. While the availability of schooling was unevenly distributed between town and country, North and South, and men and women, illiteracy was on the wane, as the practice of transmitting knowledge by imitation was gradually replaced by a system of learning based on common sense, individual judgment, and reading.

After completing primary school, the children of the affluent and privileged classes could be sent to the *collèges* (secondary schools) run by the various religious orders, including the Lazarists, the Jesuits (until 1760), the Oratorians, and the Doctrinarians. Some particularly gifted pupils went on to have teaching careers in these schools. The *collèges* and universities contributed to the spread of written culture, but their teaching was based on Latin and tradition. They took no steps to increase their enrollment, and in the last decades of the century they faced competition from a whole series of pedagogical innovations within new institutions that emerged in response to the demand for an education that would fit France's citizens for a changing world.

Alongside the steady growth of available printed matter, the 18th century also witnessed the creation of new places for discussion and the exchange of information, more or less independently of the time-honored social structures and state institutions. Among the latter, the great Parisian academies—the Académie Française, the Académie Royale des Sciences de Paris, the Académie de la Paléographie (Academy of Paleography), and the Académie Royale de Peinture et de Sculpture (Royal Academy of Painting and Sculpture)—were already accustomed to combining respect for their royal founder with the cultivation of their own value systems. The provincial academies, the literary societies, and the Masonic lodges were equally adept at steering a middle path between conformism and criticism and between social elitism and egalitarianism. It was those institutions that were responsible for spreading the principle of a social group based on free choice and open discussion. Parallel to the increased availability of books and newspapers, they constituted a space for collective reflection in which the participants, from more specialized beginnings, began to discuss a whole range of intellectual and political problems. The major crises that shook France during the 18th century—the Regency, the economic experiments of John Law, the conflicts between orthodox religion and Jansenism and between royal authority and the *parlements,* and (of course) the economic and fiscal crises that punctuated the final years of the ancien régime—provided ample opportunities for this newly constituted public opinion to manifest itself and learn how to express itself.

Naturally, people were only too ready to debate issues that the crown would have preferred to keep out of the public eye, but they did not always adopt a consistent stance toward traditional political institutions (such as the *parlements'* ongoing struggle against "despotism"). Such bodies were often thought of as guarantors of liberty. Nor was public opinion undivided with respect to the monarchy, which many Frenchmen believed still capable of internal transformation. Concepts such as "our native land" and "the nation," long associated with the king's person, were acquiring a strength of their own. They made sense to people independently of the monarchic system and, during the Revolution, would even be used to oppose it.

The Art of Living and the Art of Thinking

Historians still disagree among themselves about the rate of demographic and economic progress in 18th-century France, but there can be no doubt whatsoever that the average Frenchman's attitude toward life and death underwent a profound change in this period. Resigned acceptance of the natural life cycle that governed the destiny of humans, as well as that of every other living creature, was giving way to a thirst for knowledge and a desire to influence that destiny. State authorities introduced medical supervision of childbirth and took steps to prevent epidemics and promote inoculation, a first step on the road that would lead to vaccination. The Société Royale de Médecine (Royal Society of Medicine), under the direction of Félix Vicq d'Azyr, was given the task of coordinating these measures. Scientific research had a responsibility to improve the human condition. Such research was supposed to enable farmers to increase the quality and quantity of their produce or help doctors to reduce mortality rates and eradicate epidemics. The fact that a value was attached to each and every human life fostered self-awareness and personal growth; an individual was defined according to his or her merit, industry, and potential, rather than by birth or family situation. This valorization of the individual reflected a new confidence in man, in his potential for economic initiative and enterprise and in his right to use his own judgment and to exercise his freedom of political choice. Better survival rates for infants and a certain degree of freedom in selecting one's spouse were transforming the traditional notion of the family.

A number of attitudes—amply criticized and challenged today—about what constituted a "normal" family, or regarding the status of women or sexual minorities, have profoundly shaped historical research and the image we have of the past. However, there can be no disagreement about the fact that, in the period under review, relationships between husbands and wives, and between parents and children, were undergoing radical changes. Apart from the information that can be gleaned from archives and registries, there is overwhelming evidence in the literature of the day that paternal authority within the family, long considered as much an absolute as God's rule over mankind, or the king's reign over his subjects, was being questioned. Inspired by the name of the protagonist in the abbé Prévost's novel *Manon Lescaut* (1731), M. Daumas coined the term the "des Grieux syndrome" to characterize this revolt against blind paternal authoritarianism, coupled with a demand for individual affection within the family. (In Prévost's novel, the chevalier des Grieux resists his father's efforts to dictate the course of his life, while never totally accepting the notion of

an independent marriage and a complete break with his family).

Throughout the 18th century social and ideological tensions were crystallized in demands for personal freedom and the right to choose one's life partner. Paternal opposition to the marriage of individuals from different social backgrounds was a typical example of the kind of prejudice that strength of feeling alone could overcome, and so such themes became popular in novels and plays. Diderot authored two major plays concerning family relationships: *Le père de famille* (1758; Father of a Family) and *Le fils naturel* (1757; The Natural Son). In 1779, Nicolas Rétif de La Bretonne published both *La vie de mon père* (My Father's Life) and *La malédiction paternelle* (The Paternal Curse). The infamous *droit du seigneur* (a lord's legal right to sexual "possession" of his vassal's bride), symbolizing both feudalism and despotism, was the subject of several plays, including a comedy by Voltaire and Beaumarchais's *Mariage de Figaro*.

Jean Starobinski chose *L'invention de la liberté* (1964; The Invention of Liberty, 1700–89) as the title for his important essay on 18th-century literature and art. The liberty to which Starobinski refers involved many things: choosing the kind of life one wanted to lead, being creative, launching a new project, and expressing oneself. It was stimulated by stock-market speculation and was reflected in a fascination with the movement of money and in the proliferation of luxury goods and intellectual demands. The spirit of liberty assumed myriad forms, some of them contradictory. It was reflected in the luxurious lifestyle of the rich, the nonconformism of the libertine, the legal demands of the bourgeoisie, and the brutality of the Paris mobs during the Revolution. The idea of liberty was inseparable from that of equality. The latter concept was no longer the passive Christian belief according to which we are all equal before death and an all-powerful God. Rather, it was an active equality that endows every individual with common sense and a good heart.

Rationalist philosophers could take for granted that reason, like pity and sympathy, was a universal attribute. This shared belief was at the heart of scientific research, just as it explains the notoriety that surrounded the *philosophe* movement itself. A belief in universal reason also provided the justification for the expression of nonconformist views, as well as the popularity of autobiographies. The "common reader" was deemed capable of understanding the problems presented to him, even if they were of a religious or political nature, just as the ordinary reader could be moved by the experiences of other individuals as recounted in their memoirs. The success of the autobiographical genre in the 18th century reflected a number of religious, social, and aesthetic tensions and implied a threefold rejection: rejection of the need for an intermediary between the believer and his God, of a separation or fixed hierarchy between individuals, and of the traditional proprieties and codes of behavior. Parallel to the steady stream of published memoirs and autobiographies, the evolution of the art of portraiture was another manifestation of the spirit of liberty. Formerly the sole preserve of royalty and the rich and powerful, this art became available to everyone; every citizen had the right to be immortalized in paint, just as he had the right to the services of a doctor or to ways of expressing his political opinions.

The influence of the new ideas of the *philosophes* spread far beyond their immediate intellectual circles. Thanks to Bernard Le Bovier de Fontenelle, the *philosophes'* views infiltrated the salons of polite society, and Pierre Bayle made them known throughout Europe. It was these two men, both of them born in the middle of the 17th century, who, in terms of historiography, were responsible for bridging the gap between classical age of Louis XIV and the age of the Enlightenment. Fontenelle's career was at once literary and scientific, worldly and philosophical. His many essays—including *De l'origine des fables* (1684; On the Origin of Fables), *Sur l'histoire* (1766; On History), *Relation de l'île de Bornéo* (1686; Depiction of the Island of Borneo), *Histoire des oracles* (1687; The History of Oracles)—offer an analysis of popular credulity and priestly frauds, together with a scathing indictment of those who refuse to use their powers of reasoning. His *Entretiens sur la pluralité des mondes* (1686; Conversations on the Plurality of Worlds) demonstrates how much these powers are capable of accomplishing when faced with major ontological questions such as humanity's place in the universe or the end of the world. Like Fontenelle, Bayle attacks credulousness and superstition in his *Pensées diverses sur la comète* (1680; Various Thoughts on the Comet). To combat those dangers he underlined the need for relativism and a critical state of mind, both in his periodical, *Nouvelles de la République des Lettres* (1684), and in his *Dictionnaire historique et critique* (1697; An Historical and Critical Dictionary). The two adjectives that he chose to describe his dictionary give an excellent idea of Bayle's method.

The works of Fontenelle and Bayle laid the groundwork for both the aims of the new philosophy (to oppose prejudice, question tradition, examine issues in the light of strict reason, and facilitate the growth of an enlightened public) and its methods (ironical satire, publication of documents and arguments, dissemination of theoretical discussions, and popularization of scientific advances). The two pioneers also anticipated the literary forms that Enlightenment writers would use to propagate their ideas. Those forms included the dialogue or dramatization of an idea, which highlighted the open-minded research that was to replace dogmatism; the periodical press, which kept closely in touch with events as they occurred and had a direct influence on those events; and the dictionary, which undermined systematic beliefs point by point, used detail and classification as weapons of criticism, and provided the reader with the basis for a new system of knowledge.

The works of the abbé Castel de Saint-Pierre illustrate the effectiveness of the *philosophes'* critical approach when it was brought to bear on political matters. In his *Discours sur la polysynodie, ou, l'on démontre que la polysynodie, ou pluralité des conseils, est la forme de ministère la plus avantageuse pour un roi, et pour son royaume* (1719; A Discourse of the Danger of Governing by One Minister: In Which Is Demonstrated That the Most Advantageous Administration, Both for the King and the People, Consists in an Establishment of Many Councils, or a Polysynody) and *Projet pour rendre la paix perpétuelle en Europe* (1713–17; A Project for Establishing the General Peace of Europe), this prolific writer and zealous reformer paints an unflattering portrait of the age of Louis XIV, contrasting it with an imaginary (and better) Europe of the future. Behind the display of erudition and the mask of secrecy, such criticism frequently expressed radical views. Nicolas Fréret's entire career was devoted to classical and Oriental scholarship, within the confines of the Académie des Inscriptions et Belles Lettres (Academy of Inscriptions and Letters). From the safety of this position he was able to expose the mechanisms of religious alienation. Fréret was very probably the author of the *Lettre de Thrasybule à Leucippe* (1766; Letter from Thrasybule to Leucippe), a text that circulated in manuscript form before being published, in which a philosopher dissuades a young woman from taking her vows.

The doubt surrounding the authorship of this work is characteristic of the earlier phase of the Enlightenment, before the propagation of new ideas began to be orchestrated by the *philosophes*. In Dumarsais's *Le philosophe* (The Philosopher), as in *Le sentiment des philosophes sur la nature de l'âme* (1743; The Philosophers' Feeling on the Nature of the Soul), which is attributed to Mirabeau, the metaphysics and morality of Christianity were similarly subjected to systematic criticism. The story of the dissemination of these texts, which first circulated in manuscript or as clandestine publications, tells us a great deal about the history of the *philosophe* movement, as it evolved from erudite libertinage to systematic Enlightenment and from intellectual skirmishing to ideological warfare.

The propagation of philosophical thought did not, however, invariably signify acceptance of a radical point of view. The abbé Meslier, an obscure country priest from Etrépigny in the Ardennes, worked patiently for years on a *Testament* in which his atheist and communist opinions were expressed with all the fire and rhetorical conviction of a prophet. Copies of the manuscript began to circulate after his death in 1729. Later, in 1762, Voltaire published a bowdlerized version of the *Testament*, in which Meslier's atheism was transformed into anticlericalism, and the social criticism and arguments in favor of communal ownership of property were omitted.

Julian Offroy de La Mettrie, a doctor from Brittany who was obliged to flee to Holland and later took up residence in Berlin, made no effort to conceal his unconventional attitude toward the medical establishment and his lack of respect for Christian morality and spirituality. The very title of his best-known work, *L'homme-machine* (1747; Man, a Machine), rang out like a provocation. His materialism led him to an extreme form of moral relativism that both shocked and intrigued Diderot. The more militant materialists of the second half of the 18th century often defined their position by opposing La Mettrie's radicalism.

These changing attitudes and frames of reference were also reflected in new ways of looking at the past and at foreign cultures; historical and geographic relativism was simply another means to criticize traditional values. The Quarrel of the Ancients and the Moderns, which had broken out in the latter half of the 17th century but was still being waged periodically during the 18th, drew the public's attention to the problems posed by change and progress. Travel literature posed a challenge to claims about the universality of Christianity and Western ways of life. The baron de La Hontan, a poor Gascon nobleman, emigrated to Canada and later published three works based on his experiences there: the *Nouveaux voyages dans l'Amérique septentrionale* (1703; New Travels in Northern America), his *Mémoires,* and the *Dialogues curieux entre l'auteur et un sauvage de bon sens qui a voyagé* (1703; Curious Dialogues between the Author and a Savage with Common Sense, Who Has Seen the World). In the latter work, the Indian mentioned in the title turns out already to have mastered critical inquiry and reasoning.

Robert Challe, too, had visited Canada, but he also traveled widely in Europe, the Mediterranean countries, and India. In addition to his collection of short stories, *Les illustres françaises* (1713; The Illustrious French Lovers), scholars have recently unearthed other works by Challe. They include a *Journal de voyage aux Indes orientales* (1688; Diary of a Journey to the East Indies) and the *Mémoires sur le règne de Louis XIV* (written between 1716 and 1721 but not published until 1731; Memoirs on Louis XIV's Reign). Challe is now also thought to be the author of the *Difficultés sur la religion proposées au P. Malebranche* (1710; Religious Issues Submitted to Father Malebranche), the manuscript of which was frequently referred to as *Le militaire philosophe* (The Philosophical Soldier). Challe's remarkable powers of differentiation and argumentation make him one of the outstanding representatives of the earlier phase of the Enlightenment. The two best-known works of those early decades of the century—Montesquieu's *Lettres persanes* (1721; Persian Letters) and Voltaire's *Lettres philosophiques* (1734; Philosophical Letters, originally known as the *Lettres anglaises* [Letters concerning the English Nation])—both use foreign narratives as a device to criticize traditional French values. It would be quite inappropriate, of course, to liken Montesquieu's tale, which culminates in the suicide of the recluse but lacks a conclusion, to the report that Voltaire culled from his enforced stay in England; nevertheless, both works draw on a broad range of irony and stylistic effects to criticize religious, political, and intellectual prejudices. Montesquieu's Persia is simply a metaphor for French "despotism," while Voltaire presents England as the very model of an open-minded, dynamic, and tolerant nation.

Toward the middle of the 18th century, this type of criticism and the many suggestions for reform took on a new aspect when a flood of simultaneous publications and the launching of certain big collective projects drew the attention of both the authorities and the general public. In 1746 Étienne Bonnot de Condillac's *Essai sur l'origine des connaissances humaines* (Essay on the Origin of Human Knowledge) applied John Locke's empirical methods to the French situation. *De l'esprit des lois* (The Spirit of Laws), which constituted the synthesis of Montesquieu's thinking, was published in 1748. The following year saw the appearance of the first volume of the comte de Buffon's *Histoire naturelle générale et particulière* (Natural History, General and Particular), which would take more than half a century to complete. In 1750 Diderot launched a prospectus announcing his *Encyclopédie* and began accepting subscriptions for it. The publication of his own first works, the *Pensées philosophiques* (1746; Philosophical Thoughts) *Lettres sur les aveugles* (Letter on the Blind) three years later, quickly followed in 1750 by the *Discours sur les sciences et les arts* (Discourse on the Sciences and Arts) by Jean-Jacques Rousseau (who at that time was Diderot's close friend), confirmed the arrival of a new generation of *philosophes* and a new style of writing. Both the opening sentence of Diderot's *Pensées philosophiques* ("We are constantly being warned against the danger of the passions . . . yet only the passions, only the great passions can raise men's spirits sufficiently to accomplish great deeds") and Fabricius's *prosopopoeia* in Rousseau's *Discours* signaled the emergence of a style that is very different from the irony of Montesquieu or Voltaire, an emotional tone that appealed more directly to the reader.

The publication of the successive volumes of the *Histoire naturelle* and the *Encyclopédie,* followed by Claude-Adrien Helvétius's *De l'esprit* (1758; Essays on the Mind and Its Several Faculties) and major essays by Rousseau—both *Émile, ou, de l'éducation* (Émile; or, Concerning Education) and *Du contrat social* (The Social Contract) appeared in 1762—attracted widespread public notice and brought the work of the new generation of *philosophes* to the attention of religious and government authorities, who until then had been preoccupied with the quarrel between the Jesuits and the Jansenists. Despite the fact that the *Encyclopédie* was a collective project and that the works of Helvétius, Diderot, and Rousseau expressed very different (and often conflicting) points of view, it appeared to the authorities that a general attack on traditional values was being orchestrated.

The literary world became divided between *philosophes* and anti-*philosophes,* even though personal relations, ambitions, and clan loyalties frequently cut across these ideological lines. The battles were waged in the press, onstage, and in the Académie Française. The books of both the *philosophes* and their opponents were banned or censored, often simultaneously. Like the *philosophes,* government officials were sharply divided among themselves. There were those officials who were sympathetic to the forces of change and in favor of the modernization of France and others whose sole purpose was to defend religious and monarchic orthodoxy. These contradictions, which were inherent in the ancien régime, are well illustrated by the ambiguous situation of Chrétien de Malesherbes, who as director of the state *librairie* (printing office) was in sole charge of censorship but managed at the same time to be friend and supporter of Rousseau and the Encyclopedists. The *philosophes* themselves vacillated between using the influence of those who, like Malesherbes, were in positions of power and appealing directly to public opinion or the more enlightened governments of other nations.

In the 1760s and 1770s the ideological warfare became more intense. From his outpost in Ferney, Voltaire launched a series of pamphlets in defense of victims of judicial injustice (including Calas, Sirven, and the chevalier de La Barre), all of which became causes célèbres. The baron d'Holbach gathered a team of writers around him to publish clandestine manuscripts from the early decades of the century—including those of Dumarsais, Fréret, Challe, Meslier, and Boulanger—and translations of English freethinkers such as John Toland. Holbach's team was also responsible for new works, including his own *Système de la nature, ou, Des lois du monde physique et du monde moral* (1770; The System of Nature; or, The Laws of the Moral and Physical World), initially attributed to Mirabaud and which

Roland Mortier has characterized as "the Bible of materialism" (see Mortier), together with an abridged version entitled *Le bon sens* (1772; Common Sense). Diderot undoubtedly collaborated with this militant group and also had a part in crafting the extreme views expressed in the final version of the abbé Raynal's *Histoire philosophique et politique des établissements et du commerce des Européens dans les deux Indes* (A Philosophical and Political History of the Settlements and Trade of the Europeans in the East and West Indies). Originally conceived as a history of colonialism and a guidebook for French traders, this treatise contained an outspoken condemnation of slavery, the colonial system, and the absolute monarchy. Rousseau, on the other hand, having evaded arrest in Paris, broke with his *philosophe* friends and reaffirmed his faith and spiritual beliefs. Utopians, such as Morelly, and other admirers of the communism of primitive societies criticized both the ancien régime and the notion of private property. The possibility of a united philosophical front, hoped for by some thinkers and feared by others, was undermined by the tensions that existed among atheistic materialists, deists, and Christians and between adversaries and defenders of a free economy.

The Revolutionary Experiment

Despite the widespread circulation of the books and ideas that have been discussed above, it would be a mistake to think that the writers of the Enlightenment spoke with a single voice. In 1933 Daniel Mornet published a book entitled *Les origines intellectles de la Révolution française* (The Intellectual Origins of the French Revolution). Half a century later Roger Chartier urged us to focus, rather, on the Revolution's cultural origins (see Chartier). In 18th-century France the philosophy of the Enlightenment was only one factor in a much wider evolution of mental attitudes. If we are to understand the subversive impact of the *philosophes,* we should not simply look at their words in specific books. Rather, the best evidence of the power of the *philosophes* can be found in the fact that so many of their books were published, in the growth of reading and the emergence of the notion of individual judgment, and in the deconsecration of traditional authorities.

Viewed in retrospect, the violent and radical nature of the events of the French Revolution seemingly established continuity between that upheaval and the leading intellectual figures and books of the 18th century, since they could be seen as its origin, its theoretical justification, and its explanation. As a consequence the various divergent positions on the revolutionary chessboard could be traced back to ideological differences among the *philosophes.* In the 19th and 20th centuries, historians constructed imaginary genealogies linking, for example, Diderot to George-Jaques Danton and Auguste Comte, Rousseau to Maximilien-Marie-Isidore de Robespierre and the 1848 socialists, and Montesquieu to advocates of constitutional monarchy and liberalism. It should not be forgotten, however, that when the Revolution broke out, Rousseau and Voltaire had been dead for more than ten years, and Diderot for five years. Most of the Encyclopedists were no longer alive; and those who were (Jean-François Marmontel, the abbé André Morellet, and Jean-François de Saint-Lambert) showed no enthusiasm for the events of 1789; their attitude was essentially the same as that of the émigrés who elected to return to France. Even the abbé Raynal, whom the revolutionaries hailed as one of their prophets and spiritual fathers, astonished readers of his *Histoire philosophique et politique* by coming out in defense of the monarchy.

It was a later generation of intellectuals who actually took part in the Revolution. Madame Helvétius, who gathered many of them around her in her salon in Auteuil, provided a link between the Encyclopedists and those who were committed to the revolutionary cause. Both the marquis de Condorcet, who had contributed to the publication of the complete works of Voltaire, and the comte de Volney, who borrowed the first syllable of his pseudonym from the latter's name and the last from the latter's home at Ferney, became active in politics, as journalists and members of revolutionary clubs and commissions. In the midst of the revolutionary turmoil, both also found time to write. Volney's *Les ruines ou méditations sur les révolutions des empires* (1791; Ruins; or, Meditations on the Revolutions of Empires) and Condorcet's *Esquisse d'un tableau historique des progrès de l'esprit humain* (1794; Outlines of an Historical View of the Progress of the Human Mind) were parallel reflections on human progress, heralded uneasily by Volney and triumphantly by Condorcet—who nevertheless committed suicide just after finishing his *Esquisse,* in order to avoid the guillotine. Pierre-Jean-Georges Cabanis and Antoine-Louis-Claude Destutt de Tracy tried to develop and systematize the theories of Condillac and the Encyclopedists in order to constitute a philosophical system appropriate to France, as the nation emerged from the Terror. The Ideologues turned their energies to founding the great cultural and academic institutions that date from the end of the Convention and the Directory periods.

At the turn of the century the Quarrel of the Ancients and the Moderns flared up again, in the form of a battle between classicists and romantics. Historians have frequently pointed out the paradoxical reversals of positions in this particular literary conflict, noting the classical tastes of the revolutionaries, while

identifying romanticism with the counterrevolutionary cause. However, to appreciate the dangers of any hasty equation of political, ideological, and aesthetic opinions, one only needs to recall certain cases, such as how Louis-Sébastien Mercier, a virulent opponent of classicism, was at the same time, both as a journalist and a deputy, a staunch supporter of the Girondins or how, after the Terror, Madame de Staël, the first theorist of French romanticism, continued to defend Republican principles.

Around Madame de Staël, the so-called Groupe de Coppet brought together leading intellectuals of various national and religious backgrounds whose aim was to bring about a reconciliation between the Enlightenment and religion, between progress and the sense of tradition. In *De la littérature, considérée dans ses rapports avec les institutions sociales* (1800; The Influence of Literature upon Society), Madame de Staël acknowledged her debt to the Enlightenment but proposed to a nation still reeling from ten years of civil war that France should accept the achievements of the Revolution, which included a society based on free trade and the equally free exchange of ideas. Benjamin Constant began to write a work that would incorporate the basic principles of this liberal society. But, like the ideologues, both Madame de Staël and Constant were faced by the centralized administrative power being exercised by the former Bonaparte, who in 1804 had become the emperor, Napoleon I. The rationality of the Enlightenment had been replaced by the rational needs of the state; educational, administrative, and military uniformity, both within France and in the neighboring countries that came under France's control, had replaced the idea of progress. The ideals of a Francophone and Francophile Enlightenment were both extended and distorted by the European campaigns of the Republican and Imperial armies. The writers and intellectuals who were the natural heirs of the Enlightenment were either neutralized within the framework of newly created institutions or increasingly marginalized. Madame de Staël, whose *De l'Allemagne* (1810; Germany) was judged anti-French by the Imperial censors, was condemned to exile; the marquis de Sade, who had used 18th-century rationality to demonstrate the irrationality of all forms of social life, was sentenced to life imprisonment; and Chateaubriand, whose *Le génie du christianisme* had demonstrated the need to abandon Enlightenment principles in favor of a return to France's religious and monarchic roots, was obliged to spend many years of his life in foreign travel.

So when exactly did the age of the Enlightenment come to an end in France? To take 1789 as a cutoff date is to risk identifying its representatives with the ancien régime, while endorsing the *philosophes'* notion that they spoke with a single voice and recognizing the break between their faith in progress and the violence of the Revolution. Moving the date forward to the end of the 18th century does justice to the many links between the generation of the *Encyclopédie* and that of Charles Joseph Panckoucke's *Encyclopédie méthodique* (1788; A Methodical Encyclopedia) and between those who witnessed the various crises of the monarchy and the actual participants in the Revolution. Madame de Staël's *De la littérature* and Chateaubriand's *Le génie du christianisme* launched the French romantic movement; the first of these works acknowledged a debt to the Enlightenment, while the second rejected it. If, on the other hand, we stretch the end of the Enlightenment as far forward as 1815, or even 1820, then our chronology is circumscribed either by political events—the collapse of the Empire or the Restoration, with its fruitless efforts to eradicate a quarter-century of history, including the legacy of the Enlightenment—or by the accidents of literary history, which included the posthumous publication of André Chénier, the discovery of Marceline Desbordes-Valmore, and the revelation of Alphonse de Lamartine, all of which illustrated simultaneously the final stages of a sensualist, not to say materialist, vein of poetry and the rebirth of an inevitably spiritualist brand of lyricism.

Just as it was possible for historians to assimilate the French Revolution and the Empire to an Age of Revolutions encompassing most of the 19th century and extending from the earliest challenges to the monarchic system to the failure of Henry V to reassume the throne in 1873, so we might conceive of an age of the Enlightenment that began with the *Encyclopédie* and culminated in the great liberal and socialist manifestos of the 19th century, which shared with their 18th-century precursors a similar concept of history and a similar idea of progress but functioned according to an inner logic that was radically opposed to that of the Enlightenment.

MICHEL DELON

Further Reading

Chartier, Roger, *The Cultural Origins of the French Revolution,* translated by Lydia G. Cochrane, Durham, North Carolina: Duke University Press, 1991 (original French edition, 1990)

Delon, Michel, and Pierre Malandain, *Littérature française du XVIIIe siècle,* Paris: Presses Universitaires de France, 1996

Dupront, Alphonse, *Les letters, les sciences, la religion, et les arts dans la société française de la deuxième moitié du XVIIIe siècle,* Paris: Centre de Documentation Universitaire, 1963

Goubert, Pierre, and Daniel Roche, *Les français et l'Ancien Régime,* 2 vols., Paris: Colin, 1984

Mornet, Daniel, *Les origines intellectuelles de la Révolution française, 1715–1787,* Paris: Colin, 1933

Mortier, Roland, *Clartés et ombres du siècle des Lumières: Études sur le XVIIIe siècle littéraire,* Geneva: Librairie Droz, 1969

Roche, Daniel, *France in the Enlightenment,* translated by Arthur Goldhammer, Cambridge, Massachusetts: Harvard University Press, 1998; London: Harvard University Press, 2000 (original French edition, 1993)

Starobinski, Jean, *The Invention of Liberty, 1700–1789,* translated by Bernhard C. Swift, Geneva: Skira, 1964 (original French edition, 1964)

Freemasonry

The inclusion of Freemasonry under the general rubric of "Enlightenment" would have seemed distinctly odd to 18th-century readers for two reasons. First, it was by no means certain that the English word "Freemasons," the French *francs-maçons* (or *frimaçons*), the Italian *liberi muratori,* and the German *Freimaurer* were interchangeable terms any more than "Enlightenment, "*Lumières, Illuminismo, Aufklärung, Illustración* (Spanish) were, for each word occupied its own specific geographic space. While the *Lumières* in France struggled against religious intolerance from the time of the Revocation of the Edict of Nantes (1685) onward, the Enlightenment in England did not have to face that issue, while the *Aufklärung* blended well with German Pietism. Furthermore, Immanuel Kant's response to the question *Was ist Aufklärung?* (What Is the Enlightenment?)—posed by Pastor Zollner in the *Berlinishe Monatsschrift* in January 1783—became emblematic. In the preface to the second edition of his *Kritik der reinen Vernunft* [1787; Critique of Pure Reason]), Kant proposes to eradicate at one and the same time "materialism, fatalism, atheism, the faithlessness of the *freigeisterischen* (freethinkers), fanaticism, superstition." Although this proposal may have been accepted in Königsberg, it would have surprised more than one philosopher in Paris, and even some in Berlin.

The second reason that 18th-century thinkers would have found it problematic to link Freemasonry and Enlightenment has to do with Freemasonry itself, for its exact nature in that century is hard to define. Certainly, the institution established in London on 24 June 1717 was endowed with a charter authored by the Scotsman James Anderson: *The Constitutions of the Freemasons, Containing the History, Charges, Regulations, etc., of That Most Ancient and Right Worshipful Fraternity for the Use of the Lodges* (1723), which was reprinted a number of times. The charter was duly accepted as a founding document and translated into Dutch and French by Jean Kuenen in 1736 and 1741, into French by the monk La Tierce in 1742, 1745, and 1765, into German in 1741 and 1783, into Italian in 1784, and into Spanish in 1786. However, because of its limited circulation and the distortions it underwent, the charter was perceived on the European continent as a flexible text and never as an absolute and final source.

When La Tierce translated the charter, in his *Histoire des francs-maçons* (1745; History of the Freemasons), he retained those parts dealing with God and religion, as well as civil magistrates, but he drastically altered the historical portion of the original text, as well as part dealing with regulations. Similarly, as John Bartier has explained, J.P.J. Du Bois, entrusted by the Grand Lodge of London to adapt the document to the Dutch mentality, condensed the first article and introduced an authorization to smoke during meetings (see Bartier). However, Du Bois's most significant contribution was his modification of Article 2 of the English charter, which enjoined Masons to obey civil authorities, and which had evoked sharp criticism in Holland.

In France there was no hesitation about correcting Andersonian latitudinarianism; the phrase "that Religion in which all men agree" became "the Religion in which all Christians agree." According to Alec Mellor, "the common denominator [among men of faith] is no longer a transcendent and personal God, but the eternal Word, the second Person of the Holy Trinity, Christ" (see Mellor). Similarly, as André Bouton has demonstrated, at the Du Moria Lodge in 1783, the initiate was asked if he had been "baptized in the name of the Father, and of the Son, and of the Holy Spirit" (see Bouton). The Union des Coeurs (Union of Hearts), a lodge founded in Liège in 1774, went further, summarily dismissing Andersonian toleration:

Jews, Muslims, Goths, and other nations that practice only circumcision for baptism may not enter our lodge except at such time as they wash in the waters of Holy Baptism and their lives and values are spotless; whereas the English and Dutch lodges were excessively lenient and, whether because of greed or some other reason, admitted Jews, we declare our lodge closed to this infamous nation, condemned by God and Christians, and we have only contempt for those who receive them.

Not only did the lodges move away from the letter of the original document by Anderson, its spirit was no longer respected either. The English had shown the way in 1738 by turning their backs on the text of 1723, and requiring that the Mason, presented as a "true noachite" (Freemason), make Christian confession. However, this change, though it may seem important today, was inconsequential at the time because none of the Grand Lodges established at the time referred to Anderson's *Constitutions*. The lack of references to this document proves that Masonry was not a religion of the book, and it explains why it was necessary to call together members of various lodges—including Altenberg (1745), Kolho (1772), Brunswick, (1775), Lyon (1778), Wolfenbuttel (1778), Wilhelmsbad (1782), and Paris (1785 and 1786)—in order to define the nature and objectives of Masonic "science," an attempt that moreover met with little success.

The history of the *Constitutions* is checkered: it was completely ignored throughout the 19th century and then republished in Paris in 1930 by Ernest Jouin as *Livre des constitutions maçonniques* (Book of Masonic Constitutions). Jouin was the obscure publisher of the *Protocole des sages de Sion* (1920; The Protocols of the Learned Elders of Zion) and the *Revue internationale des sociétés secrètes,* a mouthpiece of anti-Semitic Freemasonry: This suggests that right-wing intellectuals had found in the long-neglected *Constitutions* a weapon to wage their own ideological battles. They used the 1877 decision by the Grand Orient of France to remove from its constitution the obligation to believe in the revealed truth and the immortality of the soul—requirements introduced in 1849—to argue that Freemasonry was going back the latitudinarian origins that had been responsible for the French Revolution, whose most tangible result had been the establishment of democratic governments, under the control of international Zionism.

In truth, the controversy over the role of the Freemasons in the events leading up to the Revolution and, subsequently, in the conduct of the Revolution is as old as the Revolution itself. The theory of Masonic responsibility was put forward as early as 1789, in *La vraie philosophie* (True Philosophy) by Chaillon de Jonville, who had been the substitute for the comte de Clermont, Grand Master of the Grand Lodge. The theory was taken up and developed in dozens of pamphlets and synthesized in Augustin Barruel's *Mémoires pour servir à l'histoire du jacobinism* (1797–98; Memoirs Illustrating the History of Jacobinism). The idea was then spread throughout Europe by John Robison's *Proofs of a Conspiracy against All the Religions and Governments of Europe: Carried on in the Secret Meetings of Free Masons, Illuminati, and Reading Societies* (1797), J.A. Starck's *Der Triumph der Philosophie in achtzehnten Jahrhunderte* (1804; The Triumph of Philosophy in the 18th Century), and Lorenzo Hervás's *Causas de la revolución de Francia en el año 1789* (1807; Causes of the Revolution in France in 1789). The myth of a Masonic conspiracy, according to which the lodges and "backstairs" lodges actively participated in the controversies of the *philosophes* and then in the revolutionary process, was denounced in a peremptory fashion in 1801 by the former constituent Jean-Joseph Mounier, a former member of the French Constituent Assembly during the French Revolution, who held that "the Freemasons did not have the slightest influence over the Revolution" (*De l'influence attribuée aux philosophes, aux francs-maçons et aux Illuminés sur la révolution de France* [1801; On the Influence Attributed to Philosophers, Freemasons, and Illuminati on the French Revolution]). Still, the myth found echoes in the works of authors who were decidedly anti-Masonic—including Nicolas Deschamps's *Les sociétés secrètes et la société, ou La philosophie de l'histoire* (1880; Secret Societies and Society at Large; or, The Philosophy of History), Gustave Bord's *La franc-maçonnerie en France des origines à 1815*, Volume 1, *Les ouvriers de l'idée révolutionnaire (1688–1771)* (1908; Freemasonry in France from the Origins to 1815, Volume 1, The Workers of the Revolutionary Idea [1688–1771]), Augustin Cochin's *La Révolution et la libre pensée* (1924; Revolution and Freethinking) and *Les sociétés de pensée et la Révolution en Bretagne (1788–1789)* (1925; Philosophy Societies and the Revolution in Brittany [1788–1789]), and Bernard Fay's *La franc-maçonnerie et la révolution intellectuelle du XVIIIᵉ siècle* (1935; Freemasonry and the Intellectual Revolution in the 18th Century). Furthermore, the myth was also spread in the works of militant Masons, such as Louis Amiable, who wrote *Une loge maçonnique d'avant 1789, la R . . . L . . . des Neuf Soeurs* (1897; A Masonic Lodge before 1789, the R . . . L . . . of the Nine Sisters), and Gaston Martin, who wrote *La franc-maçonnerie et la préparation de la Révolution* (1926; Freemasonry and the Preparation for the Revolution).

In an article that has become definitive, Albert Soboul clearly demonstrates that understanding this still-unresolved debate over the Freemasons' role in the Revolution requires that one carefully distinguish between two aspects of the problem (see Soboul). On the one hand, with regard to the remote origins of the Revolution, scholars need to specify the exact form that the Masonic intervention took and to ask to what extent the Freemasons participated in the propaganda of the *philosophes*. On the other hand, scholars must describe the attitude of the Freemasons in the years preceding the Revolution, at the height of electoral competition, in order to determine their ideological orientation and decide what may have been the Masonic "role" in the collapse of the ancien régime.

With respect to the first point, we have to accept that the Masons were orthodox in religious matters. Masonic meetings were generally followed by a Mass and, to a lesser extent, the statutes of the lodges throughout the kingdom provided for a religious service for the brothers who had passed on to the Eternal Orient. In the lodge at the time of admission, the recruit had to take an oath on the Gospel of Saint John. Furthermore, the numerous Masonic speeches that have been preserved affirm the brothers' allegiance to the religion of the monarch. This symbiosis between the Masons and the Church explains the massive presence of members of both secular and regular orders in the lodges; there were even lodges within monasteries, despite the various papal interdictions applying to Freemasonry, such as the bulls *In Eminenti* (1738) and *Providas* (1754).

Historians Maurice Agulhon and Claude Mesliand have shown that in Provence and Avignon there was a shift toward Masonry among the Penitents (see Agulhon; Mesiland). The case was significantly different in the southwest; in Toulouse, for example, the movement was less visible, as has been shown by J.-L. Boursiquot (see Boursiquot). Therefore, one could conclude that Masonic recruitment was not made at the expense of the members of Christian brotherhoods, but that these groups did lend their support to the lodges.

The connection between the Masons and the Church in France, which was perfectly understandable under a regime in which there was one predominant religion, does not, however, allow us to prejudge the "faith" of the Masons or to judge the degree to which social conformity or honest piety influenced their personal choices. Nevertheless, there is ample evidence indicating that the movement toward secularization that characterized the Enlightenment was also taking place within the lodges. Michel Taillefer has pointed out that in 1744 a lodge in Toulouse no longer required from its followers the traditional oath on the Sermon (see Taillefer). Twenty years later the Parfaite Amitié (Perfect Friendship), another lodge in Toulouse observed that Masonry had nothing to do with religion and asked if it were really necessary to oblige the brothers to attend Mass on the day of Saint John. What is more, on 31 January 1785, the Brothers of the Amis Réunis (United Friends) lodge in Paris were asked to promise to respect, at least outwardly, the religion that one professes; to avoid any joke liable to make fun of it; to refrain from any discussion of religious matters except with trustworthy people and those whom one has no reason to fear, when there is no risk of causing them harm or disturbing their tranquility; and finally, to perform as much as one's conscience will allow the religious duties that one may not miss without scandalizing others.

This declaration, recorded in the *Livre d'or* (visitors' registry) of one of the most important lodges of the ancien régime, seems to indicate that those who swore such an oath, while still practicing Christians, had ceased to be true believers.

As Daniel Ligou has shown, Masonic rituals were being progressively more secularized throughout the 18th century (see Ligou). The role of references to the Bible, or indeed to Christ himself, in the rituals diminished, while the God of the Old Testament—the God of Abraham, Isaac and Jacob—became the "Great Architect," more reminiscent of the Platonic tradition than of the legacy of Saint Augustine. This was a development that would give rise to many a contradiction.

A similar evolution occurred with regard to the political sphere. Certainly, in France as in the other European countries, loyalty to the monarch was the rule and continued to figure prominently in the specific regulations of the lodges. An apolitical stance, which was the norm during a period in which the laws did not allow any independence to associations, did not prevent Masons as a group from showing their allegiance to the Crown. Thus all the lodges in the kingdom, on every occasion, demonstrated their loyalty to the regime and, specifically, to the royal family. The first of the ritual toasts was always addressed to the royal family, and the second to the prosperity of the nation. These practices were not always disinterested, as many brothers remembered the persecutions that Freemasonry had suffered, particularly under the Inquisition. The Masons had also suffered under the administration of André-Hercule de Fleury.

However, in the last years of the ancien régime, the intrusion of politics was noticeable within the lodges. The speeches, which insistently recalled the sacred principles of liberty, equality, and brotherhood, could be seen as veiled criticism of certain aspects of governmental activity. Moreover, at the level of political action, the Masons as a group (including the Grand Orient of France, whose creation dates back to 1772–73) supported the American Revolution and called for military intervention by France on the side of the insurgents. It is significant that Benjamin Franklin was elected an elder of the Neuf Soeurs (Nine Sisters) in 1779. And in June

1782 La Candeur started a fund in view of arming a ship, *Le Franc-Maçon*. The same tendencies could be observed in internal politics; thus, while the dismissal of the *parlementaires* in 1771 met with a mixed reaction within the lodges; their return was called for unanimously, whether in Toulouse, Bordeaux, Besançon, or Paris. These comments do not mean to imply that the lodges were highly politicized on the eve of the Revolution. However, the opening up of the lodges to politics was evident in the first months of 1789, and it may not have been a coincidence that the Philathètes, members of the Amis Réunis lodge, demanded the restoration of the Paris assemblies at the meeting of the Estates General.

Following Cochin, it is often asserted that the lodges were "societies of ideas" and that in this regard they contributed, if not to the development, at least to the spread of the "program" of the Enlightenment. This idea has since been convincingly refuted by Taillefer (see Taillefer). In fact, French Freemasonry generally kept its distance from the Enlightenment movement, although a few lodges were involved. As Brother Raymond declared when challenged by Barruel:

I must confess that I was wondering how you would manage to connect the rites, ceremonies and totally religious morality of the Masons with the *philosophe* movement, since, over the last 20 years, I have had constant proof that Freemasons of every stripe, both French and foreign, censure and vigorously oppose the writing of the *philosophes;* so much so that they could be accused of being anti-*philosophes*, rather than having close links with that movement.

In reality, the vast majority of Masons in the 18th century were not very concerned with "philosophy." Should proof be required, there is massive evidence of this fact; but since the topic is still discussed, it may be useful to recall the case of the marquis de Chefdebien, who, in a largely unknown document quoted in Fabre (see Fabre), described the lodge as a place of conviviality, having nothing to do with "all these complicated scientific Masonries." The "copious and gay" banquet, Chefdebien added, was the "true climax of all these preludes" during which relatives or friends were admitted "and the company allowed itself a few innocent pranks." Finally, this "way of relaxing, which was both entertaining and respectable," concluded with some "acts of charity and of generosity" that the brothers did not forget to exercise "as Masons" and "as sensitive and well-educated men." (Nevertheless, some Continental lodges, tired of what Claude-Adrien Helvétius called the "supreme nonsense" in which most of the brothers engaged, were drawn into academic circles. Witness the Neuf Soeurs and the Encyclopédique (Encyclopedic) lodge in Toulouse as well as other examples in central Europe. The chevalier Ramsay, in his famous *Discours* (1737) to Épernay, exhorted "all the learned men and the artists in the brotherhood to come together to provide material for a universal dictionary of the liberal arts and useful sciences, excluding only theology and politics," a call that was echoed in 1772 by the abbé Robin. However, the fact remains that, as Robert Shackleton has shown, the Masons per se did not have any part in the *Encyclopédie* of Denis Diderot and Jean Le Rond D'Alembert (see Shackleton).

Nevertheless, the major themes of the Enlightenment penetrated the lodges as a generalized ideology. This was particularly evident in the choice of distinctive titles for the lodges and in the speeches given within them. Analysis of Masonic speeches makes it clear that the lexicon of the Enlightenment, organized around some key concepts, was perfectly assimilated: these speeches contend that virtue and equality are the necessary conditions for friendship, which is cemented in turn by a sense of brotherhood based on charity, the "source of true happiness." Such ideas were commonplace for "sensitive and well-educated men." And indeed, taking their cue from the Church, which until then had had a monopoly over charitable activity, the Masons increased the number of foundations and included in their specific regulations the need for the brothers to assist widows and orphans. They also established philanthropic societies, but in that regard they were not breaking new ground, as charity was now included in the secular sphere. Moreover, their latitudinarianism, formally declared in 1723, was subject to numerous modifications over the years; thus, although Jews were admitted in the early days of the English lodges, this was not the case in northern Europe, where it was required that Jews abandon their "identity," or in France. In fact, in southwestern France, the Zélée (Zealot) lodge of Bayonne was one of the few lodges to accept Jews. Furthermore, Protestants, who were behind the establishment of the Grand Lodge of London, were in principle denied admission to the lodges in France by the Statutes of 1755; in reality, however, Protestant Masons practiced their beliefs in towns where the reformed community was important, including Bordeaux, La Rochelle, Montauban, Nantes, Nîmes, and Sedan.

Finally, there was the issue of "equality," a magic word during the century of the Enlightenment and a key word for the Masons. For the brothers, equality could only be "philosophical," and it was limited to use within a lodge; it was only in anti-Masonic literature that a positive sense of equality was attributed to the Masons. The concept of equality was applicable primarily to the Masons but within clear limits, since in each city "aristocratic" lodges existed alongside "bourgeois"

lodges, which at times ignored each other and often fought each other. Aristocrats who were ready to bow submissively in the "royal art" of Masonic rituals tended to look askance at shopkeepers, tradesmen, or commoners who engaged in the same practices. It was to put an end to this democratic trend, moreover, that the comte de Clermont, grand master from December 1737 until 1771, initiated a reform of the order. According to one newspaper report, his plan was to "remove everything that was not gentlemanly or good bourgeois," and "on his advice the police arrested several persons who demanded money of newly elected members." This text, and several others, shows clearly that Masonic equality did not challenge the social hierarchy. In a speech given in Troyes, on 28 May 1787, and quoted by Henri-Félix Marcy (see Marcy), the duc de Crussol d'Uzes perfectly summarized the Masonic doctrine:

> At some mysterious level, we know that we were all born equal; and while . . . the need for public order and the respect for institutions demand that we maintain a necessary subordination between different ranks, we are no less children of the same father, and we must respect the dignity of the nature of every human being.

As a result, Ran Halévi's claim that lodges fostered the growth of a "democratic" sociability (see Halévi) seems doubtful, even though it is true that from its inception the Grand Orient introduced the principle of eligibility for masters of the lodge, and despite the fact that the lodges encouraged a certain social intermingling by taking in all those who were not too far apart in social standing. In fact, abbés were routinely elected in certain monastic orders (the Oratorians, in particular), and to a certain extent, the academies, the reading societies, and the cafés had allowed at least some connections among the elite groups, if not a complete intermingling among them. Artists and musicians were given the social status of "lay brother" in the lodges. Finally, popular entertainers and women were excluded, as La Tierce's version of the Masonic rules proclaimed: "Those who are admitted as members of a lodge should be men of good reputation; honorable and upright, born free, mature, and discreet. They must not be slaves, women, nor men living immoral or scandalous lives." However, the frequent practice of "adoptive" membership in the 18th century finally led to the inclusion of actors in the lodges. All these exclusions and reservations invalidate misconceptions arising from a retrospective interpretation of the French Revolution through the lens of the Russian Revolution.

Irrespective of one's opinion of him, Barruel, who put forward the theory of Masonic responsibility for the Revolution, continues to dictate our approach to the Masonic phenomenon during the Enlightenment. From Cochin to François Furet (see Furet), the same conceptual framework can be observed, namely, analyzing Freemasonry in terms of "conspiracy" or "driving force" and placing it at the center of the Revolution. This approach, plausible as it appears, fails to take into account the important reservation formulated by Barruel. According to him, it was not the Masons who had carried out the Revolution, but the "backstairs" lodges. As we have seen, the Masons were no more enlightened than their contemporaries; Voltaire himself, who would be admitted into the Neuf Soeurs in 1778, spoke of the "poor Freemasons" in his 1771 article "Initiation" in *Questions sur l'"Encyclopédie" par des amateurs* (Questions on the "Encyclopédie" by the Uninitiated). In Barruel's eyes the Masons had played little part in the terrific upheaval that would transform the world. He contended that the Revolution was attributable to a conscious betrayal on the part of a civil and ecclesiastical elite who, little by little, were won over to the ideas of the *philosophes,* who wanted to establish a universal republic—and, of course, to the "Chapters" that brought the citizens of that republic together.

Although the notion of a Masonic plot is hard to prove, the social environment that developed within the lodges throughout the century offered a republican model based on the ideas of liberty, equality, and brotherhood. Taillepied de Bondy, the historian of the Amis Réunis pointed out in his *Livre d'or* that

> they [Masons] wanted to form a society of friends similar to the clubs . . . in England, but which—thanks to an esprit de corps based on sincerity, equality, charity, and the practice of social virtues—created meaningful relationships between its members, strengthened by mutual respect and a familiarity with one another that was the result of the republican system of values that existed within a lodge of Freemasons.

Despite its baroque aspects, its myriad ranks and rituals, and its "parti-colored costumes," Freemasonry, because of its fondness for operating in secret, can arguably be viewed as the only institutional framework in which an underground politics capable of shattering the absolutist model, which characterized old Europe, could develop. In addition, within a divided society, Freemasonry was the developing ground for the political parties that, by way of secret societies such as the Charbonnerie, emerged in the form that would become familiar in the 19th century.

In this regard, the role of the Illuminati, who developed a radical ideology in Bavaria in the second half of the century, needs to be reevaluated. Founded by Adam Weishaupt in 1776, the Order of the Illuminati appeared as an overtly anticlerical and rationalist secret society in Catholic Bavaria, which, beginning in 1777, would utilize the resources of Freemasonry to endeavor to "grant men their liberty and original equality and to pave the way for those that lead them." Thanks to the efforts of Adolf von Knigge, admitted to the brotherhood in 1779, this plan was developed over the following years and was implemented in numerous lodges in Catholic Germany, to the point that the order could boast of having recruited 2,000 to 3,000 members—a boast that was certainly exaggerated. Differences of opinion between Weishaupt and Knigge, together with the blunders of certain leaders from Munich, led the elector of Bavaria to ban the order. However, it survived in Saxony under the leadership of Christian Bode until 1790. The Illuminati were enlightened Masons, rationalists who, along with many of the best minds of their time, thought that the Church had distorted the true religion—i.e., Christianity—and for whom, there was a "rational" religion that the "chosen few" had passed on from age to age since the Flood.

Denouncing priestly deceit, the Illuminati pushed deism, the religion of the majority of Masons in the 18th century, to its conclusion. In 1787 Bode was sent to Paris, where he met Savalette de Langes, the founder of the Philalèthes' system and organizer of the Paris lodges, and where lengthy meetings were spent trying to define "Masonic science." This meeting between the last representative of Bavarian Illuminiati and a high-ranking member of Freemasonry (and one of the founders of the Grand Orient of France) is what led some observers to conclude that Bode had exported Illuminism into France. Until quite recently, this argument was abandoned for lack of documentation. The *Mémoire concernant une association intime à établir dans l'Ordre des F.-M., pour le ramener à ses vrais principes* (Memoir concerning a Core Association to Be Established in the Order of the Freemasons to Bring the Order Back to Its True Principles) was written in 1776, but it would not be published until 1834, when it appeared in the *Mémoires biographiques, littéraires et politiques de Mirabeau* (Mirabeau's Biographical, Literary, and Political Memoirs). Still, it may well have been circulated earlier in manuscript. Greater plausibility is lent to Barruel's assertions about the Masons' role in the Revolution by the recent publication of Bode's *Journal de voyage* and a portion of his correspondence. The comte de Mirabeau, an eminent politician, was himself a Mason; he had been affiliated on 22 December 1783 with the Neuf Soeurs; and this affiliation indicates that he had been initiated earlier. The fact that Mirabeau was a member of the order is suggestive of the much wider connections that linked Freemasons throughout Europe at this time. That is not to say that the enlightened fringe of Masonic aristocracy actually conspired against the throne and the Church, but rather that a certain form of monarchy had had its day and that the chivalrous values of liberty, equality, and brotherhood, stripped of their mythological coating, had profoundly shaken the base on which the monarchy had rested for three centuries.

Beginning in the 1770s, Europe abandoned Christian eschatology: although God remained on everyone's lips, Rome ceased to be Rome. This fact became evident throughout Europe with the expulsion of the Jesuits and the complementary notion of an infiltration of Freemasonry by the Order of Saint Ignatius. Witness, too, the rapid growth of teratological lodges in this period. Illuminism (the principles and ideals of the Illuminati) was spread by the Scottish high ranks, and in a broad sense it responded to the widespread need felt—particularly by the brothers—to fill the void created by the collapse of Roman Catholicism. In short, the Masons were Christians who, since the 17th century, had been searching through the ruins of a fallen empire for new reasons to believe and hope. The meetings of various assemblies at Lyon, Wilhelmsbad, and Paris—to name only the most important—were the most tangible indication of the crisis that European Masonry experienced. The "ban," then the collapse of the Grand Lodge, and, finally, the creation of the Grand Orient of France were the most tangible signs of this crisis. Furthermore, under these conditions, it is hardly surprising that some unscrupulous brothers profited by trading royal patents, that the chevalier de Beauchaine traded in diplomas following the armies, or that talented impostors, such as Mesmer and Cagliostro, had been able to establish themselves as conveyors of occult powers (the latter posed as the founder of a type of Freemasonry in London). Just as the Hellenistic period saw the degeneration of Platonism and the appearance of numerous forms of Gnosticism, the late Enlightenment witnessed the birth of a "street-corner" Masonry, the age of charlatans and supposed prophets. It was doubtless this kind of charlatanism described by the comte de Lagrange when he wrote that Masonry was an "aborted religion."

Nevertheless, in the years preceding the Revolution, there were undeniable connections between the Enlightenment (*Lumières*) and Illuminism. Evidence of such connections can be found in the creation of an "Illuminist" lodge in 1787 by Savalette de Langes, Bode, and Langes's friends from among the Philalèthes, including Roettiers de Montaleau, who would bring about the rebirth of the order from its ashes after the Revolution. The involvement of Masonic principles in the "first" Revolution confirms the connection—inscribed on one of several plates published on 20 January 1790 by the lodge Saint-Jean du Contrat Social (Saint John of the

Social Contract) is the declaration: "Many centuries before Rousseau, Mably, and Raynal wrote about the rights of man . . . we were practicing the principles of true sociability in our lodges."

Understandably, much has been written about Voltaire's induction into the Neuf Soeurs. It was clearly significant that the champion of toleration, the adversary of superstition and the *infâme* (the "priestly imposture"), and the advocate of true justice should have become a Freemason. Some observers thought that "he had died of it." But those who admitted him did not die; they acknowledged their debt to Voltaire and his thought—a way of thinking that remains one of the strongest symbols of the Enlightenment.

CHARLES PORSET

See also Alchemy; Cosmopolitanism; Egyptomania; Guild; Illuminism; Night

Further Reading

Agulhon, Maurice, *Pénitents et francs-maçons de l'ancienne Provence*, Paris: Fayard, 1968; new edition, 1984

Bartier, John, "Les 'Constitutions' d'Anderson et la franc-maçonnerie continentale," *Revue de l'Université de Bruxelles* 11 (1977)

Boursiquot, J.-L., "Pénitents et société toulousaine au siècle des Lumières," *Annales du Midi* 88 (April–June 1976)

Bouton, André, *Les francs-maçons manceaux et la Révolution française, 1741–1815*, Le Mans, France: Monnoyer, 1958

Bullock, Steven C., *Revolutionary Brotherhood: Freemasonry and the Transformation of the American Social Order, 1730–1840*, Chapel Hill: University of North Carolina Press, 1996

Fabre, Benjamin, *Un initié des sociétés secrètes supérieures "Franciscus, Eques a Capite Galeato," 1753–1814*, Paris: La Renaissance Française, 1913

Furet, François, *Interpreting the French Revolution*, Cambridge and New York: Cambridge University Press, and Paris: Éditions de la Maison des Sciences de l'Homme, 1981 (original French edition, 1978)

Goodman, Dena, *The Republic of Letters: A Cultural History of the French Enlightenment*, Ithaca, New York: Cornell University Press, 1994

Gordon, Daniel, *Citizens without Sovereignty: Equality and Sociability in French Thought, 1670–1789*, Princeton, New Jersey: Princeton University Press, 1994

Halévi, Ran, "Les représentations de la démocratie maçonnique au XVIIIe siècle," *Revue d'histoire moderne et contemporaine* 32 (1984)

Ligou, Daniel, "Recherches sur le rite français," in *Franc-maçonnerie et Lumières au seuil de la*

Révolution française, Paris: Grand Orient de France, 1984

Ligou, Daniel, "La Bible des Maçons," in *Le siècle des Lumières et la Bible,* edited by Yvon Belaval and Dominique Bourel, Paris: Beauchesne, 1986

Marcy, Henri-Félix, *Essai sur l'origine de la franc-maçonnerie et l'histoire du Grand Orient de France,* Paris: Éditions du Foyer Philosophique, 1949

Mellor, Alec, *La charte inconnue de la franc-maçonnerie, chrétienne,* Tours, France: Mame, 1965

Mesliand, Claude, "Renaissance de la franc-maçonnerie avignonnaise à la fin de l'ancien régime (1774–1789)," *Bulletin d'histoire économique et sociale de la Révolution française* (1970)

Porset, Charles, "La franc-maçonnerie française au XVIIIᵉ siècle: État de la recherché: Position des questions (1970–1992)," in *La masonería española entre Europa y América,* edited by José Antonio Ferrer Benimeli, 2 vols., Zaragoza, Spain: Gobierno de Aragón, Departamento de Educación y Cultura, 1995

Roberts, John Morris, *The Mythology of the Secret Societies,* New York: Scribner, and London: Secker and Warburg, 1972

Shackleton, Robert, "The *Encyclopédie* and Freemasonry," in *The Age of the Enlightenment: Studies Presented to Theodore Besterman,* edited by W.H. Barber et al., Edinburgh and London: Oliver and Boyd, 1967

Soboul, Albert, "La franc-maçonnerie et la Révolution française," *La pensée* 170 (August 1973); reprint, in *Dictionnaire universel de la franc-maçonnerie,* edited by Daniel Ligou, Paris: Éditions de Navarre, 1974; 4th updated edition, Paris: Presses Universitaires de France, 1998

Taillefer, Michel, *La franc-maçonnerie toulousaine sous l'ancien régime et la Révolution, 1741–1799,* Paris: E.N.S.B., 1984

Weisberger, Richard William, *Speculative Freemasonry and the Enlightenment: A Study of the Craft in London, Paris, Prague, and Vienna,* Boulder, Colorado: East European Monographs, and New York: Columbia University Press, 1993

Function

The concept of the function evolved considerably during the age of the Enlightenment. From a simple means of representing a geometric curve, the function became a mathematical object open to a representation that the curve could, in turn, provide. This confirmation of the status of a concept that was initially transient was related to a reversal of priorities, as geometry was eclipsed by analysis. However, in order to avoid anachronism, one must qualify the word "analysis" with the adjective "algebraic," although Enlightenment mathematicians were reluctant to apply the alternative adjective "infinitesimal." In fact, the evolution of the function caused a de facto departure from algebra and thus contributed to the creation of analysis as a new discipline, which was established as such only in the 19th century. Moreover, the concept of function gave rise to the second great controversy within Enlightenment mathematics, following the Europe-wide dispute over who had been the first to discover differential and integral calculus. The dispute surrounding function began with the appearance in 1749 of a paper by D'Alembert on vibrating strings and was effectively ended in the 1780s, not because of the exhaustion of the subject but because of the participants.

The controversy over the originator of calculus was not resolved by the Enlightenment, yet it was fundamental to it, since it set in motion the alternative of determinism. On the one hand, the debate concerned the potential of mathematics to provide an integral ordering of reality. On the other, it raised the question of the position of mathematics as an ideal approximation (that is, mathematics as constituting a repertory of effective models, each in its own field, but nonetheless conceived *a priori* as incapable of expressing the variety and profusion, and therefore the fundamental irregularity, of nature). In the 19th century this question was expressed in a different way, allowing at least a nominal resolution through a conceptual contrast between a mathematics characterized as "pure" (because its objective was to reveal structures), and a mathematics described as "applied" (because it brings these structures together to describe the complexities of reality). Earlier interpretations of functions provided the historical background for this opposition, which contributed to the establishment of scientism because it liberated abstraction from its realist or presupposed justification.

For the Enlightenment, functions were mathematical representations of what the *philosophes* called "machines," a term that many of them, including Claude-Adrien Helvétius and Julien Offroy de La Mettrie, used in an anthropological framework. Although the distinction between the two notions of function was already part of history, and Enlightenment mathematics insisted on the complete autonomy of its modes of thought, the functional analogy between the two concepts is nonetheless noteworthy. In both cases, a process of reduction was at work: a machine was seen as a combination of elementary machines, not as a complex that functioned as a whole. Mechanics reduced machines to simple mechanisms; according to the analytical explanation in the *Encyclopédie,* there are three such mechanisms: the lever, the inclined plane, and the wedge. In an analogous way, functions were broken down into specific functions or *puisssances* or "powers." However, as early as 1725 Pierre Varignon had felt compelled to add, in his *Nouvelle mécanique* (New Mechanics), the "funicular machine," that is, a combination of forces stretched along lines. Such was the succession of postulations that located the same dynamic in every form of analysis, and inevitably caused disorder as much in philosophy and psychology as in mathematics. This disorder is precisely the phenomenon whose meaning Condorcet eventually attempted to determine in the name of progress.

The Reduction of Functions: A Program that Opened onto Another World

In his *Introductio in Analysin Infinitorum* (1748; Introduction to Analysis of the Infinite), Leonhard Euler indicates in a fairly technical manner the central role of the notion of function—"the object of infinitesimal analysis" (according to the preface of J.B. Labey's French translation of 1796)—and gives its definition as follows: "A function of variable quantity (*functio quantitatis variabilis*) is an analytic expression composed, in whatever manner it may be, of this same quantity and of numbers, or of constant quantities."

The adjective "analytic" in this definition is the wild card that shifts the burden of further explanation onto the examples, imprinting on the memory both the idea of a calculation $a + 3z, \dots, az + b\sqrt{aa - zz}\dots$ are functions of z and the particularly effective idea of a variable on which the function operates to obtain another variable: "The function of a variable is therefore also a variable quantity." A function cannot be dissociated from either its calculation or its result. The ambiguity lies in the need for classification that inevita-

bly arises: "Functions are either algebraic or transcendental." This division replicates that of the operations of calculus, which are assumed to correspond uniquely to each function, whether they be algebraic operations (such as addition, subtraction, multiplication, division, or extraction of roots), or transcendental operations, which, Euler writes in his preface, are "the same combinations as those preceding but repeated an infinite number of times." In the main body of the text, he avoids this contrast with that which is finite and resorts to the use of a list which arranges, as transcendental functions, "exponential, logarithmic, and countless others that integral calculus makes known." The two classes of functions are not mutually exclusive: Euler's ambition is less to demonstrate them than to unify them in a single treatment and to develop them in a complete series. A function f of the variable z is consistently written as an additive combination of terms that are whole powers of z, combinations that the eye arranges in the order $A + Bz + Cz^2 + Dz^3 + \dots$ and which required printers to adapt their techniques. The coefficients A, B, C, etc., characterize the function and express all its properties. The most notable example concerns the relations of recurrence linking the coefficients for expressing rational fractions. Because there is a decomposition of a function into simple elements, such as Dz^3 the study of functions is a form of analysis. Its method is algebraic, in the sense that there is an extension of the techniques relating to single polynomials that Descartes had described with sober elegance in his *Géométrie* (1637; Geometry), in all their richness and flexibility, under the name of "the method of indeterminates."

If such procedures of decomposition in fact encompassed the practice of infinitesimal analysis, that practice was not yet a doctrine; practical application had outpaced theory. In this case, the paradigm of the analysis of functions is the formula of the binomial associated with Newton's name. Infinitesimal analysis deals with the development of an exponential function, but the variable is contained in the base, since it is a matter of $(a + z)^\alpha$ where a is a constant, z is the variable, and the exponent α—the parameter—is as much the location of the complexity as the sign of the extension. When α is whole, the formula is simply that of a polynomial, the first powers being $(a + z)^2 = a^2 + 2az + z^2$, $(a + z)^3 = a^3 + 3a^2z + 3az^2 + z^3$, etc. Recurrences handle the coefficients, which are the subject of a magnificent summary study by Pascal relating to the arithmetic triangle. As soon as α becomes negative or fractional the polynomial is extended to infinity, since already for $\alpha = -1$ one finds that:

$$(a + z)^{-1} = \frac{1}{a} - \frac{z}{a^2} + \frac{z^2}{a^3} + \dots + (-1)^n \frac{z^n}{a^{n+1}} + \dots$$

or for $\alpha = \frac{1}{2}$

$$(a+z)^{\frac{1}{2}} = \sqrt{a+z} = \sqrt{a} + \frac{z}{2\sqrt{a}} - \frac{z^2}{8a\sqrt{a}} + \dots$$

$$+ (-1)^n \frac{1 \bullet 3 \dots (2n-3)}{2 \bullet 4 \dots 2n} \frac{z^n}{a^{n-\frac{1}{2}}} + \dots$$

Newton's formula of the binomial gives for any α whatever, whether it be irrational ($\alpha = \sqrt{2}$) or complex ($\alpha = 1 + i$), the expression $(a+z)^{\alpha}$ according to

$$(a+z)^{\alpha} = a^{\alpha}\left(1 + \alpha\frac{z}{a} + \frac{\alpha(\alpha-1)}{1 \bullet 2}\left(\frac{z}{a}\right)^2\right.$$

$$+ \frac{\alpha(\alpha-1)(\alpha-2)}{1 \bullet 2 \bullet 3}\left(\frac{z}{a}\right)^3$$

$$\left. + \frac{\alpha(\alpha-1)(\alpha-2) \dots (\alpha-n+1)}{1 \bullet 2 \bullet 3 \dots n}\left(\frac{z}{a}\right)^n + \dots\right)$$

Euler adds that the numeric validity of this expression requires a limitation of the variable z, whose absolute value must remain less than that of a. In fact, this restriction on a local level is not a significant constraint, since the techniques for changing variables listed in the *Introductio* maintain the overall intelligibility of the effective form of the series.

Euler attempted on several occasions to demonstrate the binomial and, since the example is a fundamental one, he tried to construct a progressive architecture of analysis for it. On each occasion, he failed. Sometimes he destroyed the general construction by creating a vicious circle: a theorem that had to be deduced was surreptitiously smuggled into the proof. For example, in the result of his demonstration of 1755, Euler postulated the form of the derivative of a function x^{α} that the formula of the binomial was supposed to provide. On other occasions, the technique of demonstration compelled Euler to restrict the validity of the formula to excessively specific values of α: for example, only rational values (as in his demonstration of 1774). In any case, before undertaking any calculus Euler was compelled to assume the development of the binomial in a whole series, that is, to postulate the very existence of the analysis of functions.

All these attempts helped to establish the task of analysis as such, which was then elaborated and reshaped through the multiple contributions of other scholars. Some were Euler's former students, including Franz Ulrich Aepinus (1724–1802) born in Rostock; and Abraham Gotthelf Kästner (b. 1719), a professor at Göttingen, where he taught Carl Friedrich Gauss. Oth-

ers, such as Johann Castillon (born in Tuscany but based in Utrecht and then in Berlin), or Heinrich Wilhelm Clemm (a theologian of Tübingen), were imitators of Euler. Still others were rivals: Alexis-Claude Clairaut (1713-65); D'Alembert, of course; John Colson, who was a professor at Cambridge when he died in 1760; and Thomas Simpson, a member of the Royal Society from 1746 onward. Finally, there were those who continued Euler's work, such as Abraham Robertson at Cambridge, Heinrich August Rothe in Leipzig, or Simon Guriev in Saint Petersburg.

The mathematical formalism of the Enlightenment was experimental. It placed a high value on doubt and achieved an *a posteriori* success through the decisively constructive criticism of the mathematicians of the 1820s. Thus, the young Norwegian Niels Henrik Abel, who attacked the formula of the binomial using rigorous criteria worked out by Cauchy, was driven to admit that nothing had been firmly established in the domain of the series except what Euler had assessed negatively in one of his articles on Newton's binomial theorem, *pro casibus quibus exponentes non sunt numeri integri* ("for cases in which the exponents are not whole numbers").

This particularly original and open form of mathematics came into contradiction with the genre of the textbook, creating serious distortions in relation to mathematics as it was taught, a characteristic trait of the later Enlightenment. Above all, the new mathematics permitted changes that appeared all the less like repudiations, since no dogmatism was affected. At the age of 67, Euler, who by then had a reputation across Europe, went back to one of his own books, which had appeared 20 years earlier, and declared that:

In those days, undoubtedly, I taught a demonstration drawn from the analysis of infinites, but because that analysis itself was based on our theorem, I now recognize that it must be rejected as vitiated by a *petitio principi*.

When Cauchy was compelled in 1853 to revise one of the theorems that had appeared in his *Analyse algébrique* (1821; Algebraic Analysis), he refused to consider any modification beyond a simple detail. In this opposition between two methods, the presence of vanity must not hide the underlying mathematical organization. For Cauchy, a framework for analysis existed, but it had to be reinforced by correcting structural weaknesses. For Euler, however, the very plans for the edifice to be constructed had to be worked out.

Jacques-Louis Lagrange believed that he had discovered this edifice, and he described its architecture at the very end of the 18th century in his *Théorie des fonctions analytiques* (1797; Analytic Theory of Functions).

Lagrange's work was not an act of destruction or a revolution. His goal was to pass on the whole of Euler's method of series without changing any of its techniques. The exclusions set out in the title of the book emphasize that Lagrange intends to undertake a cleansing operation: "Principles of Differential Calculus, Separated from Any Consideration of Infinitely Small or Diminishing Limits or Fluxions, and Reduced to the Algebraic Analysis of Finite Quantities." This operation was a failure, as Cauchy demonstrated 25 years later. Nevertheless, Lagrange did enrich methodology, the most accomplished example being the series of the hypergeometric function, of which Gauss made a refined study in 1813. Lagrange added the manipulation of inequalities to the polynomial structure conceived within algebra: that is, he brought into algebraic analysis the very old techniques of framing by exclusion areas, volumes, or lengths. His undeniable success was in permitting the analytic expression of what is missing from a function when the development of that function into a whole series is stopped at a certain stage—what is now called Taylor's formula with integral remainder. The fact that this formula is associated with the name of Brook Taylor (Secretary of the Royal Society from 1714 to 1718) who followed Leibniz and Jean Bernoulli in expanding an algorithmic notation based on the derivative of any whole series, is far from being a sign of the end of a general movement. The remainder, expressed by a defined integral and in a form that was recognizable even when its explicit calculation was inaccessible for most functions, was approachable. According to Lagrange, in Article 48 of the *Théorie des fonctions analytiques*: "One can find the limits of this quantity, which will suffice to determine the error that one can make when keeping to some of the first terms of the series." With the removal of integrals, estimates, and the use of ε and δ according to a terminology that would eventually become standard, analysis remained prominent for a long time. There was no longer any need to add adjectives to the term "analysis," whether "algebraic," "infinitesimal," or even "functional."

A succinct way of describing the historical movement of the Enlightenment in relation to the function is to express it as a transition from Taylor's formula as a form of interpretation—Leibniz would have called it a "blind thought"—to Taylor's formula as the limit of the field of the functions that verify it. Thus, in this context, the history of Newton's binomial theorem is just one example of this transition.

An Epistemology of Necessity

It was Leibniz who adopted the Latin term *functio* from legal terminology and applied it to mathematics, and this usage was rapidly adopted in every European language. Leibniz used the term to indicate the role of liaison that an ordinary point on a curve can perform between two lengths that are associated with it, for example its abscissa and its ordinate, the measurements of the segments, respectively horizontal and vertical, that attach it to a fixed system of rectangular axes. This accomplishment depended upon a specific type of observation, manifested in the method of marking coordinates, but Descartes's double coordinates could be replaced by others, such as the polar coordinates that Newton used. These functions are a tool that the coordinate geometry of Descartes and Fermat progressively put in place. At first, therefore, the word "function" was not intended to characterize a curve, and was certainly not an equivalent of the Cartesian equation. There was also, for example, a function of the radius of curvature at the ordinate, on which the calculus of fluxions naturally operated. Newton explains in *The Method of Fluxions* (as translated by J. Colson, from the then unpublished Latin text, *Artis Analyticae Specimina,* and published in London in 1736): "The problem is not otherwise perform'd, when the curves are refer'd, not to right lines, but to other curve-lines, as is usual in mechanick curves."

A significant inflection of the term came from Leibniz himself, who had already placed functions at the center of a new investigation in the very title of a manuscript of 1673, *Methodus Tangentium Inversa, seu De Functionibus* (Inverse Method of Tangents; or, On Functions). In this text, functions are no longer deduced from curves, but are worked out within a problematic of equations and solutions that are no longer of numbers but of functions, and these characterize curves. There is an equivalence whereby thought could privilege the curve, a phenomenological object with which the mathematician works, as well as the function and the differential equation of which it is the solution. These possibilities coexisted for many years, although in practice the geometric language of the curve predominated for expressing properties. This did not prevent Jean Bernoulli from deciding on a notation with the characteristics of a function, because it proved necessary to evoke the object that determines an equation. In his "Remarque sur ce qu'on a donné jusqu'ici de solutions de problèmes sur les isopérimètres" (Remark on What Until Now Has Provided Solutions of Problems with Isoperimeters) in the *Mémoires de l'Académie des Sciences* (1718; Reports of the Academy of Sciences), Bernoulli individualizes the object function f by labeling the variable that governs it, producing fx: "A function of variable size is a quantity composed, in whatever manner it may be, of this variable size and of constants." Bernoulli's definition, predating Euler's by 30 years, is not more general, it is simply imprecise. In the *Encyclopédie,* D'Alembert writes about the word "function" in terms of a historical progression that is in fact a conceptual genesis:

> The ancient geometers, or rather the ancient analysts, called the "functions" of any quantity x the different "powers" of this quantity, but today we call the "function" of x, or in general of any quantity whatever, a quantity, composed of as many terms as we might wish, in which x may or may not be mixed in any manner at all with constants.

Since it was not possible to circumscribe a field by a uniform operation, Euler's definition of 1748 limited the operations that were permitted for fixing a function.

Euler himself removed the constraints of this system almost as soon as they were formulated. He made this revision in response to his experience with functional equations, but the change also reflects his epistemological desire to incorporate the function into an account of necessity that was as much philosophical, in its logical form, as natural, in its realist form; finally, Euler removed the constraints because of his wish to lay deep foundations for the mathematical architecture of the future. A function became that which generally governs variation. Euler defines functions in the *Institutiones Calculi Differentialis* (1755; Institutions of Differential Calculus) in relation to cases where "quantities depend on others in such a way that if the latter are changed, the former are also changed." Thus, a function is that which measures the dependence "of one quantity on another" and therefore its determination by it. Given the idea of an "arbitrary" function, the notion of the curve in its turn was extended to include freehand curves, that is, without having the position of a point inevitably indicating the position of the following point. Euler argues for a due consideration of such a function within analysis in a programmatic article of 1767, "De Usu Functionum Discontinuarum in Analysi" (On the Use of Discontinuous Functions in Analysis), which he contributed to the *Nouveaux commentaires de l'Académie de Saint-Petersbourg*. The "law of continuity" remains, but it governs "analytic" functions—that is, those functions that can be obtained uniformly from the variable, such as the square root of a variable whose exact representation is a parabola. This law avoids erroneous definitions of a domain for a function, leaving it open for all the values of the variable. Around 1807, Fourier found difficulties in unavoidably associating such a domain with a function.

The enlargement of the field of the function, and its corollary, the division of the function into types, comprised the major defect of what K.F. Pfaff has aptly called the "functional method" of the 18th century. This method was in a direct line of descent from the Cartesian method. A function marking a dependence or possibly a cause was presented as an unknown, its determination being governed by an equation (whether a differential equation, a partial derivative, or some other type) that resulted from the very "geometry" of the problem in question. Nevertheless, "useful" solutions of this equation were manipulated as if they were "analytic" functions. There was no serious danger when the objective of mathematicians was principally a matter of discovering forms. In 1749 D'Alembert had great success with the complex waves of the vibration of strings, largely surpassing Taylor's measurements of simple wave frequencies; Lambert's expression of the logarithms for the propagation of heat in *Pyrometrie, oder, Vom Maasse des Feuers und der Wärme* (1779; Pyrometry; or, On the Substance of Fire and Warmth) was equally original. However, this essentially geometric method became defective precisely when it was used to demonstrate that one form alone was possible. Legendre was deceived in 1794 when he thought that he had "functionally" settled accounts with the ancient axiom of Euclid's parallels. Similarly, Pfaff, in his *Dissertatio Inaugurale* (Inaugural Dissertation) of 1788, wrongly concluded that he had presented the only possible form of differential calculus. Above all, this was at the heart of the dispute over vibrating strings, which thus allowed different epistemological attitudes to appear.

Those who, like D'Alembert, held that mathematics inevitably had limitations could accept that it was incapable of expressing physical reality. In contrast, Euler and others postulated that physical reality could be described by a new mathematics formatted for such a purpose, broadening its scope. Still others, notably Lagrange, focused on refinements of functional equations and attempted to rethink the adaptation of integral calculus to physics. In the 18th century, the function was one of the driving forces in the mathematical effort to understand the world.

JEAN DHOMBRES

See also Acoustics; Algebra; Geometry; Mathematics; Mechanics, Analytic

Further Reading

Dhombres, Jean G., *Nombre, mesure et continu: Épistémologie et histoire,* Paris: Nathan, 1978

Dhombres, Jean G., "Quelques aspects de l'histoire des équations fonctionelles liées à l'évolution du concept de fonction," *Archives for History of Exact Sciences* 36 (1986)

Pensivy, M, "Jalons historiques pour une épistémologie de la série infinie du binôme," *Sciences et techniques en perspectives* 14 (1987–88)

Truesdell, Clifford, *The Rational Mechanics of Flexible or Elastic Bodies, 1638–1788:*

Introduction to Leonhardi Euleri Opera Omnia, vol. X and XI, Seriei Secundae, Zurich: Orell Füssli, 1960

Youschkevitch, A.P., "The Concept of Function up to the Middle of the Nineteenth-Century," *Archives for History of Exact Sciences* 16 (1976–77)

Furniture

In the 18th century, French furniture enjoyed immense prestige throughout Europe, both because of its quality and because of the influence of French culture in general. The courts of Europe spoke French and acquired Parisian furniture, although this trend varied from country to country and from period to period. The conditions for a renaissance in the art of furniture were already in place at the beginning of the 18th century. That art flourished during the reigns of Louis XV and Louis XVI, when furniture design and craftsmanship reached its apogee. There were two types of furniture-making in the period: on the one hand, *menuiserie,* heavy, carved pieces made by carpenters from waxed, painted, or gilded wood; on the other hand, *ébénisterie,* pieces with inlayed or veneered surfaces, made by cabinetmakers. This clear-cut distinction between the two types of furniture reflects some of the inherent complexities of furniture-making crafts at that time.

Customers and Suppliers

Three elements contributed to the development of French furniture in the 18th century: society's taste in furniture, the genius of the furniture designers, and the skill of the craftsmen. A spirit of competition led the wealthy classes to decorate lavishly the new residences that they had built for themselves. Furniture was constantly being changed, as outmoded pieces were moved into second-rank apartments or less important residences. Clients wanted up-to-date furniture with innovative features, severely testing the imagination of the designers and furniture dealers. Most old furniture was not valued, except in the case of pieces designed by André-Charles Boulle (1642–1732), a cabinetmaker for Louis XIV famous for his inlay work. When furnishing their rooms, the wealthy turned to intermediaries, who were responsible for finding and coordinating the various craftsmen who made the furniture. With a few exceptions, the craftsmen who made furniture did not design it. The renaissance of the decorative arts in the 18th century was the work of designers ("ornamental-

ists," architects, and decorators) and merchants (dealers in furnishings and upholstery).

Architects and decorators were responsible for conceiving of the overall setting: the design and colors for paneling and the choice of fabrics. These designers usually were involved in the work of the carpenters and upholsterers who made the furnishings for their buildings, but they also sometimes worked with cabinetmakers, assigning locations and dimensions for certain large pieces of furniture. Smaller pieces and fashionable objects were acquired from dealers, "sellers of everything and makers of nothing," as Denis Diderot called them in the *Encyclopédie.* These importers of exotica were responsible for numerous technical innovations, such as the concept of furniture decorated with lacquer panels from the Far East or with porcelain plaques from Sèvres, and they promoted the use of porcelain with mounts of gilded bronze or silver. Their trade was one of coordination rather than fabrication: they had their ideas carried out by craftsmen whose names they were careful not to reveal and to whom they sent their designs and the materials required for making them. The desire to attract a European clientele eager for novelties gave these merchants an important role in the development of the decorative arts. Upholstery dealers played a role similar to that of dealers in objects but worked with carpenters, not cabinetmakers.

In Paris the organization of furniture production was rigidly divided. Carpenters were forbidden to do the work of cabinetmakers, and vice versa. These two crafts, with their restricted areas of activity, were nevertheless regulated by a single guild of carpenters and cabinetmakers. The carpenters were of French origin, worked in family units, and resided in the Bonne-Nouvelle quarter. The craft was passed down from father to son, and the workers formed true dynasties, such as the Foliots or the Tilliards, that endured through most of the century. Among the cabinetmakers, such dynasties were rare, since one-third of them were not of French origin. Many cabinetmakers originally came from the Low Countries and Germany, countries that had a considerable number of skilled inlayers.

These craftsmen settled in the Faubourg Saint-Antoine or in small enclaves. Other groups of craftsmen also took part in the making of furniture. For example, workers in bronze, locksmiths, and makers of inlays often joined cabinetmakers in the creation of desks, while carpenters, wood carvers, painters, gilders, and upholsterers shared in the making of chairs; the carpenters who signed the pieces were the ones who earned the least of all.

The regulations of the carpenters' and cabinetmakers' guild were very strict. The maker's mark, made obligatory in 1743, was meant to commit the craftsman to being responsible to the client. Guild officials controlled the quality of production. They made quarterly visits to the workshops and applied the guild's official seal to pieces that were correctly made; other pieces were destroyed. This very rigorous control by the guild enabled Parisian furniture to achieve a quality of construction without equal in Europe. This supremacy would cease during the French Revolution, when the guilds were abolished.

The Legacy of the Reign of Louis XIV and of the Regency

The main factors in the development of furniture in the 18th century were put in place during the reign of Louis XIV and the Regency. Louis XIV's melting down of silver furniture in 1689 prompted the development of counterparts in gilded bronze or carved and gilded wood, which were created in order to obtain the brilliance of silver at a lesser cost. The 17th century's fascination with lacquer and porcelain imported from Asia led to the establishment of workshops in Paris that sought to reproduce such objects. Finally, Boulle's innovations at the turn of the 18th century set the trends for the next several decades in the history of furniture.

Boulle caused a quasi revolution in the making of furniture by *ébénistes* (cabinetmakers), in terms of both new designs and new manufacturing techniques. The flat-topped desk with three large drawers can be attributed entirely to him, while designs for chests of drawers and cabinets also owe a great deal to him. Boulle conferred nobility upon floral inlay, and, although he did not invent the inlay work that bears his name, he developed a technique for its production that allowed for the completion of two pieces in one operation—known as the "first part" or "counterpart" technique, depending on whether the base was made of tortoiseshell or copper. Under the Regency, when colored woods were gradually substituted for ebony, Boulle was one of the first to cover his pieces with them and to use the grain of the wood to create geometric motifs. A cabinetmaker but also a sculptor, Boulle promoted the use of gilded bronze in furnishings. He used bronze in functional decorations for fireplaces and lighting, and he applied it to pieces of furniture both to decorate them and for the protection of inlays. His example was swiftly followed by Charles Cressent (1685–1768), who also had been trained as both cabinetmaker and sculptor.

There is no single carpenter whose name can be linked to the innovations in *menuiserie* during the 18th century. Sofas and daybeds had existed since the beginning of the reign of the Sun King. Chairs, including armchairs, had lower backs, which enabled let the wood to be seen, and their legs no longer had crosspieces. The fashion in women's clothes for the wide-skirted *robes à panier* (dresses worn over armatures that exaggerated the hips) launched under the Regency explains the lowering of the arms of chairs, with the columns supporting the armrests no longer directly above the front legs.

Innovations

A growing concern for comfort led to an increase in the number of pieces of furniture in use, as well as to a wider variety of types of furniture available. It also led to the creation of more comfortable seats, as well as numerous pieces of furniture designed on a more intimate scale. Furniture was no longer subject to changes as drastic as those that Boulle had imposed. Craftsmen would simply employ and improve upon the changes dating from the beginning of the century. Innovation meant the stylistic evolution of forms, as well as a greater variety in the types of furniture and their surfaces. Two great styles succeeded one another, separated by a phase of development known as the Transition. Although these styles bear the names of two kings—Louis XV and Louis XVI—their appearance did not entirely coincide with the two reigns. The two styles followed the decorative movements of rococo and neoclassicism, adopting these two movement's general lines and ornamental vocabulary. The Louis XV style that flourished between the 1730s and the second half of the 1750s was followed, from 1760 to 1775, by the Transition period, which culminated with the Louis XVI style; that in turn persisted for several years after the king's death. However, this division is an arbitrary one, for in reality the periods partly overlapped. Craftsmen, attached to their familiar ways, tended to distrust anything that was new and did not change their models except under the impetus of a major commission, although the cabinetmakers made changes a little more quickly than did the carpenters. This distrust of novelty was stronger in the provinces, which created a time lag between regional and Parisian furniture making.

In carpentry the chairs known as *chaises à la Reine*, which had flat backs and were placed against the wall, contrasted with the standard chairs known as *chaises en cabriolet,* which had curved backs and were placed in the center of a room. The upholstery of the chair could be fixed or removable. In the latter case, the upholstery was known as *garniture à châssis* and could easily be replaced when there was a change of "furnishings," that is, the ensemble of fabrics, tapestries, and carpets that decorated a room. In great homes the upholsterer would change the furnishings twice a year, in order to clean them and so the materials and colors would reflect the change of the seasons. The search for harmony between the walls and carpentered furniture involved both the wood of the chairs—so that the design and carving of furniture would match that of the paneling—and their painting or upholstery, which formed a homogeneous ensemble with the curtains and the wall hangings. Under Louis XV the opulence of gilt and silvered wood was played down in favor of the use of polychrome, with colors that were soberer and that harmonized with the upholstery. In the veneer technique pioneered by the Martin brothers, plant motifs carved and painted to look natural stood out against a pale background, but a simple two-color scheme was often preferred, in which gold or silver could be one of the colors selected. In the middle of the century the use of polychrome waned in popularity and was replaced by a gold with white color scheme. A unified white or a contrast between two types of gold became prevalent under Louis XVI, the sobriety of these colors serving to emphasize the forms. Over the course of the century, armchairs became easier to handle and more comfortable and assumed various forms. The four-poster bed was abandoned in favor of the *lit à la duchesse,* placed at right angles to the wall, or the *lit à la polonaise,* placed parallel to the wall. The form of sideboards did not evolve, except that the shapes of their bases and legs were modified by the changes of style.

In their quest for innovation, the cabinetmakers limited themselves to varying—or to combining in new ways—the major types of furniture invented before the reign of Louis XV: chests of drawers, tables, flat-topped desks, cupboards, and cabinets. There was a great variety in chests of drawers, which, according to the period, underwent variations in their shapes and in the number of drawers they had. Around 1740 Cressent discovered a way to make the traverse bars between the drawers disappear from the front of the piece of furniture. From the chest of drawers *en console,* which had very long legs and a single row of drawers, cabinetmakers derived a new type of chest, which had a crossbar or an internal shelf. The dining-room sideboard was a chest that had lost the fronts of its drawers and was differentiated from the ordinary sideboard by its depth and the number of its shelves.

The variety of tables reflected high society's quest for comfort. Each table was made to serve a specific need,

and there were four main table types: writing tables, dining tables, dressing tables, and gaming tables. The flat-topped desk evolved into other types of desks and small writing tables. The concern with hiding one's work quickly from visitors inspired several types of desks. For example, the combination of the desk and the drawing board led to the sloping desk of the 1730s and then, in 1761, to the roll-top desk created by Jean-François Oeben (1721–63) for the king, and finally to the *bonheur du jour,* a kind of stepped desk with drawers at the back and a top leaf that pulled up to act as a book rest, which was very fashionable from the end of Louis XV's reign. In the middle of the 18th century the drop-leaf desktop inside a cupboard or a cabinet was developed by combining the cupboard or cabinet with the desk/drawing board. Oeben, the king's cabinetmaker and mechanic, also invented small transformable tables, such as writing or dressing tables with sliding tops and the *table à la Bourgogne,* which could close into a night table.

The 18th century was characterized by the remarkable diversity of surfaces used to adorn furniture made by cabinetmakers, including inlay, lacquer or veneer, and porcelain. All these techniques sought to imitate painting and always reflected the concern for unity among the decorative elements in a room. Inlay of exotic woods, that true triumph of the century, was made possible by the arrival of new products on the market, the results of trade with the colonies. Depending on the fashion, either veneer or inlay was preferred. The geometric inlays that appeared with Boulle remained in vogue, but their design changed in order to fit the lines of the piece. There were butterfly wings and waves during the Louis XV period, cubes without depth and fans during the Transition, and trellises and mosaics during the Louis XVI period. Floral inlay vanished around 1690 but reappeared around 1740 in the work of Bernard Vanrisamburgh, known as BVRB (d.1766), who gave it a stylized and monochromatic aspect by using violet wood. Ten years later Oeben made floral inlay natural looking and multicolored. After around 1750, inlay was used to depict still lifes, decorative trophies, or landscapes that sometimes included human figures.

With the advent of neoclassicism, the use of wood veneers, which had previously been limited to simple pieces of furniture, was applied to high-quality pieces to provide a foil for bronze decorations. Mahogany was used by Oeben in 1752 for Madame de Pompadour's chests of drawers at the Château de Ménars. Lemon wood was used at the end of Louis XVI's reign by cabinetmakers such as Claude-Charles Saunier (1735–1807), Mathieu-Guillaume Cramer (d. 1804), and Guillaume Benneman (d. 1811).

Lacquered furniture was valued throughout the century, whether it was decorated with lacquer panels from China or Japan or, failing the genuine article, with imitations using European varnish. At first, furniture makers reused in their entirety the front panels of drawers from cabinets imported from Asia; these panels were inserted into new, Paris-made pieces lacquered in black. In the 1730s dealers conceived of taking screens and cabinets apart and planing the panels in order to fit them onto new pieces of furniture. In 1737 the first chest of drawers decorated with lacquer panels entered the royal collection. It was the work of BVRB and was supplied by the dealer Hébert for Queen Maria Leczinska.

European varnishing, which was meant to imitate lacquer but was much lighter, was also very successful, thanks to the Martin brothers, who lent their name to it. At first, the European technique was a faithful copy of Asian lacquering, on a red or black base, but around 1740 craftsmen departed from the Eastern model, breaking completely from it in midcentury and using the European technique to represent painted scenes in the manner of François Boucher, Jean-Baptiste Oudry, or Joseph Vernet. During the reign of Louis XVI furniture made of lacquered metal enjoyed a vogue because it was relatively economical to produce. The cabinetmakers Pierre Macret (1727–96), Saunier, and G.H. Lutz (1736–1812) became specialists in the technique. At the end of the century, other types of painted decoration were used on furniture. Flowers painted in oils on a maple or sycamore base decorated the furniture of Joseph Baumhauer, while flowers fixed under glass were used by Adam Weisweiler (1744–1820), Philippe Pasquier (d. 1783), and Jean-Ferdinand Schwerdfeger.

The idea of using panels of Sèvres porcelain to decorate furniture came from the dealer Poirier, who obtained a monopoly on their manufacture. The first chest of drawers to be decorated in this way was made by BVRB for Mademoiselle de Sens in 1758. This type of paneling, generally limited to small items of furniture, was used by the cabinetmakers BVRB, Roger Vandercruse, known as Lacroix or RVLC (1728–99), and Martin Carlin (d. 1785). These panels were the material of choice for small coffee tables, because it was possible to have the porcelain on the tabletop complement that of the tea service.

The revival of interest in decor from the reign of Louis XIV caused the reappearance of two types of inlay: that in the tradition of Boulle and inlay using hard stone. Étienne Levasseur (1721–98) and Philippe-Claude Montigny (1734–1800) gave a new impetus to inlay using copper and tortoiseshell, the use of which had been limited to pendulum cases since the Regency. Carlin and Weisweiler removed stone inlay panels from 17th-century ebony cabinets to decorate their furniture. Ornamentation in gilt bronze benefited from technical improvements. At first, the techniques for fixing bronze onto furniture, using nails or screws, were rudimentary or even crude. Then Oeben succeeded in disguising the settings with a system of screwed dowels. Jean-Henri Riesener (1734–1806), Marie-Antoinette's favorite cabinetmaker, gave his bronzes a chased and gilded quality worthy of the work of goldsmiths.

French Furniture and Europe

The dissemination of the French art of furniture-making occurred primarily through diplomatic exchanges, but also through the emigration of French artists and the diffusion of designs by way of engravings. Foreign rulers and ambassadors who visited Versailles and admired its royal furniture would stop off in Paris to make their purchases, while French diplomats stationed abroad took part in the spread of Bourbon art through their conspicuous consumption. In the 18th century, furniture became worthy of being given as gifts. Furniture exported from Paris to foreign courts became a source of inspiration for local craftsmen, who would either copy it exactly or interpret it according to the particular tastes of their countries.

At the court of Frederick II, Kambli and Spindler enhanced the Parisian models in order to accentuate their asymmetry, in accordance with the German fashion for rococo. The Louis XV style, transposed to England by Thomas Chippendale, was strongly influenced by chinoiserie. Cabinetmakers' pieces were often made in mahogany with more rigid lines, while gilded wood came to be carved exuberantly. Louis XVI furniture owed to England the use of mahogany, as well as the arrival on the Parisian market of dining tables and of small tables with pivoting tops. Russia was a great lover of things French but remained open to British and German influences as well. Those countries of southern Europe that had Bourbon rulers naturally came under French influence. Among the countries of northern Europe, Sweden was the most responsive to French art, ordering furniture from France and sending its cabinetmakers for training in Paris.

CATHERINE FARAGGI

See also Decoration

Further Reading

Eriksen, Svend, *Early Neo-Classicism in France: The Creation of the Louis Seize Style in Architectural Decoration, Furniture and Ormolu, Gold and Silver, and Sèvres Porcelain in the Mid–Eighteenth Century,* London: Faber, 1974

Pallot, Bill G.B., *The Art of the Chair in Eighteenth-Century France,* Paris: ACR-Gismondi, 1989

Pradère, Alexandre, *French Furniture Makers: The Art of the Ébéniste from Louis XIV to the Revolution,* translated by Perran Wood, Malibu, California: J. Paul Getty Museum, and London: Sotheby's, 1989 (original French edition, 1989)

Verlet, Pierre, *Styles, meubles, décors: Du Moyen Age à nos jours,* Paris: Larousse, 1972

Verlet, Pierre, *French Furniture of the Eighteenth Century,* Charlottesville: University Press of Virginia, 1991 (original French edition, 1956)

G

Garden

If one compares two well-known gardens, Versailles in the 17th century and Ermenonville in the late 18th century, important differences immediately become apparent. At Versailles, simple geometric, often symmetrical forms organize the space and offer impressive views. One finds temples constructed in the classical style, statues evoking Greek and Roman mythology, fountains leaping forth to create cascading pools and mirrors, and trees pruned to form cubes, or cones; the overall effect is one of supreme order, at once pleasant and majestic. At Ermenonville, in contrast, there is a lack of symmetry and geometry. The classical temples are falling down, and the artificial ruins seem deliberately primitive or Gothic. The statues represent illustrious men, one of whom is actually entombed there. The water flows naturally or forms a pond, seemingly without the intervention of any human hand, and the trees are set out in an irregular fashion and are not pruned in any way. The scene as a whole evokes feelings of contentment with nature, contemplation and a sense of solitude. Further, whereas the entire garden at Versailles is contained within a central perspective beginning at the château, the garden at Ermenonville is open to the surrounding countryside and seems to cradle Jean-Jacques Rousseau's tomb. The two gardens have contrasting relationships with the environment: in the case of Versailles, the countryside has become a garden, whereas at Ermenonville the garden has been returned to the countryside. Indeed, as regards these gardens' forms, the social climates in which they were conceived, or their relationships to their times and their locations, it is clear they are two completely contrasting—albeit extraordinary—creations.

A transformation in design principles occurred during the 18th century and was accompanied by reconceptualization of the art of gardens. Horace Walpole, the first historian of gardens, vaunted them as the equals of poetry and painting in a famous phrase: "Poetry, painting and the art of landscape gardening will always be regarded by men of taste as three sisters, the three Graces of our age, if you will, that clothe and adorn Nature." This opinion has been confirmed by the fact that gardens were painted, drawn, or even designed by painters as early as the beginning of the 18th century (Antoine Watteau, William Kent, Hubert Robert, J.M.W. Turner) and by the fact that gardens guided the elegiac, sublime, or sentimental wanderings of James Thomson, William Wordsworth, and Johann Wolfgang von Goethe. Gardens thus seemed to be a sort of avant-garde art in the discovery of nature through sensibility. The names mentioned above indicate the role England played in this movement, and this is why the French term used to describe any garden that deviates from the geometry of the baroque is *jardin à l'anglaise* (garden in the English style). Specialists, however, choose to refer to them as "picturesque" gardens (from the Italian *pittore* [in the manner of painters]), landscape gardens, or gardens "of sensibility." Yet the conventional term is not entirely misleading, for the new type of garden found a favorable climate on the English side of the Channel, owing to a convergence of factors.

Politics

Large pleasure gardens were as costly as the buildings they surrounded and, as Francis Bacon said, they were the symbol of the supreme refinement of a civilization. No change in style could be imposed without the influence of the members of the elite who used that style to promote their image and their status. Such elite circles existed in England. The rural elite had gained political prestige following the Revolution of 1688, which limited the king's power by that of Parliament. The Lords were landed gentry and the members of the House of Commons were elected by an electoral system in which the countryside was overrepresented; the fall of absolutism was followed by decentralization. The nation was becoming prosperous through its supremacy at sea, but it was administered from the countryside, and country estates became the seats of power. Lords and squires divided their time between London and the countryside; they traveled to Italy, and endowed their estates with prestigious cultural trappings that are still apparent in country homes today. The gardens at Stowe, which exalt the political thinkers of antiquity and other great figures in the national history, offered the elite a political program worthy of an imperial power, the "new Rome of the West" (John Toland). The political prestige associated with rural residences led to an idealization of the countryside's poetic climate, which lent a touch of Virgil to the greatest poem of the era, James Thomson's *The Seasons* (1726–30). It also led to a program to embellish rural estates, as suggested by Joseph Addison in his influential newspaper *The Spectator*. This program was carried out in part by Viscount Bolingbroke on his *ferme ornée* (ornamental farm) designed by Dawley, or by William Shenstone at Leasowes. The marquis de Girardin put a curious twist on the trend when he launched a program of physiocratic utopia at Ermenonville.

Once the new English style had been launched, it did indeed reach France, where the socioeconomic situation was very different but where, nonetheless, Boulainvillers and Montesquieu could rely on the nobility to block arbitrary uses of royal power. The duc de Saint-Simon was very critical of Versailles, and the poetic idealization of châteaus in French literature, from Fontanes to Chateaubriand, always emphasized their venerable presence in the countryside. Whichever side of the Channel one happened to be on, feudal ruins showed both the age of the estate and its connection with the local landscape. Walpole cited Honoré d'Urfé's novel *L'Astrée* (1607–27; *Astrea*) as one of the ancestors of the new style.

At the same time, a general affinity for nature was spreading throughout England, thanks to the anti-absolutist consensus of 1688. This movement found its strength in a latitudinarian Protestantism influenced by dissidents or former Puritans whose religion was founded on a meditative reading of the Bible and on the worshiping of the Creator within Creation/nature. The French found echoes of the Huguenot mentality in the work of Bernard Palissy (who designed gardens in which he could celebrate the famous 104th Psalm), Olivier de Serres, Boyceau, or Guillaume du Bartas (the author of *La semaine* [1678; The Week]). Du Bartas was an acquaintance of the Puritan poet John Milton, whose *Paradise Lost* (1667) was often quoted by theoreticians of the picturesque and whose unrhymed verse was used by Thomson (who himself received a Calvinist education) in his great poem of the new imaginary world of landscapes, *The Seasons*.

Epistemology

Although we may account for the growth of a certain style of garden, such an account does not explain the forms of that style. These forms would not have spread throughout Europe had they not met certain expectations and inspired creativity. They prevailed because they embodied the modernity of Newtonian epistemology.

The years between 1700 and 1730 were crucial in this regard. John Vanbrugh built Castle Howard in 1700; it is surrounded by a vast panorama that is completely different from the baroque emphasis on symmetry and order. In 1709 Vanbrugh pleaded for the preservation of the Gothic ruins at Blenheim, claiming they would "make a fine subject for a landscape architect." Two years later, in *The Spectator*, Addison associated despotism with rectilinear perspectives, and English freedom with the natural contours of the new style in gardens. Alexander Pope echoed this sentiment in his "Epistle to the Right Honourable Richard, Earl of Burlington" (1731), scoffing at ready-made symmetries and asking that the gardener "paint as he plants." Color won out over geometry, irregularity over symmetry, and by 1730 the new style was sufficiently well established for a layman to declare that gardens were now being designed "without rulers or chalk lines."

These were also the years when theories of knowledge were undergoing great changes. Newton's *Philosophiae Naturalis Principia Mathematica* (Mathematical Principles of Natural Philosophy) dates from 1687, and his *Opticks* from 1704. John Locke's principal works were published between 1690 and 1700. The debate between Newtonians and Cartesians had begun. It revolved around the nature of space, the role of time, and methods of experimentation. Newton, Locke, Boyle, and the scientists of the Royal Society in London advocated methods of investigation that were quite different from the methods employed by geometers. Their primary criticism of the Cartesians was that they "feigned hypotheses." The issue was no longer one of presenting postulates or reasoning on the basis of principles. English scientists engaged in a meticulous observation of reality and composed "histories," that is, accounts of "particulars," salient facts that were dated and situated in space, without positing any initial hypotheses or a priori reasoning. This approach was reflected in English gardens. To the same extent that 17th-century gardens were based on an a priori format, with their layouts planned over a remodeled landscape,

18th-century gardens increased their use of meandering, unpredictable paths to guide those wandering along them. Nothing was revealed in advance, and the "particulars" (the sight of a nearby church steeple, of a waterfall discovered by chance) were there to enable the visitor to "discover" his surroundings by following the steps toward a "history" that he could compose in his mind.

This liberation of forms corresponded to the mindset of the new physics. Newtonians did not believe in forces governed by simple mechanics. Attraction was mysterious. One could tell it was working, but one could not know how. The world was no longer defined in terms of pulleys, gears, and pumps. Demechanization was accompanied by a degeometrization resulting from discoveries by chemists who spoke only in terms of elasticity, expansion, transitions from solid to liquid to gaseous, and the transformation of bodies through exchanges engendered by their porosity. This was the great path that would lead to Lavoisier. Unlike geometric shapes, which are "not in Nature" (Diderot), the shapes of the new life sciences interpenetrated one another in an ongoing transformation. They underwent imperceptible changes (Newton refers to the calculation of flow as an infinitesimal calculation) in weight, shape, and nature. The faces of beings and things changed over time.

The garden of sensibility removed geometry from nature in order to partake of nature's deeper life. It espoused all of nature's rhythms, whether meteorological, historical, or celestial: Locke charted barometric pressure, precipitation, descriptions of the sky; in 1718 William Stukeley founded the Society of Antiquaries; and Bishop Burnet's *Telluris Theoria Sacra* (Sacred Theory of the Earth) defined, as early as 1690, what Buffon would later refer to as the "stages of nature." Whereas the baroque garden measured time in terms of the shadows cast by its geometric volumes, the garden of sensibility was one of an all-transforming duration, a duration evoked by the passage of sunlight and shadow on undulating lawns, by ruins, or by grottoes and boulders whose mass had "wearied time" (Jacques Delille, inscription at Mortefontaine).

Locke's Sensation Psychology

This image of unfettered nature accords the same place to time and memory as does Locke's *Essay concerning Human Understanding* (1690). In the introduction to this work, which is the foundation of modern psychology, Locke warns his reader that he has proceeded by way of the "simple method of histories," and he explains the formation of ideas as a gradual process based on sensations that recombine and diversify as one advances in age. This process implies that the organs involving the senses react to stimuli from the outside world that are in the form of particles whose impact causes either pleasure or pain, depending upon the intensity of the perceptions. In this case, Locke relies upon Newtonian physics to link the sphere of the organic to that of the emotions. The link between sensation and sentiment is established by means of the concept of sensibility, and the "physics of the soul" (Voltaire) verifies Newton's assertion that "the universe is the sensorium of Divinity" (*Opticks*).

The new style of garden was a realization, in a modeled form, of that sensorium. To follow a winding path was to watch the sun shift position, or to vary the sound of a waterfall depending on whether one was walking past a boulder or through a valley. If the path rose or fell, the shape of the panorama changed. Further, all gardens were designed to produce a particular experience of perception. According to Locke, this perception depended on two of our senses: sight and touch. His theory, which explains why there was so much subsequent interest in the blind, created a tactile imagination that reworked shapes by piercing them through, defining their edges, or rendering their contours uneven. Locke's influence largely explains why the rococo and the Gothic styles, and a Chinese influence had become prevalent in gardens, emphasizing the contrasts between the smooth surface of lawns and the roughness of ruins, the aigrettes of the pagodas and the horizontal plane of the water.

The influence of Locke's theory also explains the triumph of atmospheric perspective in the fine arts (for example, in the skies of Gelée and Cuyp, where light is diffused by the density of the air) over linear perspective, which was perceived as dated and dictated by doctrine. Locke explains, in fact, that whereas objects are beyond our reach, colors guide our eyes to judge distance. They construct space by situating objects in space. Gardeners created this effect through the introduction of new varieties of plantings (black larch, cedar of Lebanon, poplar, birch, laburnum, and exotic flowers). It should be stressed here that pleasure and pain, inseparable from all sensation, arise out of each other. A pleasure that fades provokes pain, and vice versa. The same notion can be found in gardens. Depending on whether one discovered a ruin or a pleasing landscape as one turned a corner on a path, one would see the nature of one's feelings change. A careful arrangement of perspectives and artificial ruins allowed a person to avoid abrupt or insensitive changes of emotions. The garden, a sensorial and sentimental experience, became the chosen domain of the sensitive person.

The popularity of Locke's theory of sensation psychology explains why the role of the garden became increasingly important throughout the 18th century, although in varying ways. As Locke's disciples granted a growing importance to the association of ideas, they used the spectacle of nature to create "moral scenes." According to Francis Hutcheson, a flower that withers evokes the death of a hero; an old oak, the end of an empire. This Lockean perspective enabled architects to dispense with mythological representation and paved the way for the German *Naturphilosophie* (philosophy of nature) that developed rapidly when the life sciences created an organicist conception of the expansion of beings out of a seed. This construct of *expansibilité* (expansibility) also led to the concept of *perfectibilité* (perfectibility)—two neologisms coined by Turgot— which favored the rebirth of geometry, but on a cosmic and colossal scale, in the 1780s.

History

The convergence of politics, epistemology, and psychology explained the dynamics of the garden of sensibility and the major stages of its evolution.

1700–1730

- Development in England of a "rural" style integrating views of the surrounding countryside into garden design. Two trends become apparent. The first is national and Nordic, rehabilitating the Gothic style (Vanbrugh, Hawksmoor). The second is Palladian and Italianate (Burlington, Kent, Pope); however, Palladianism may borrow architectural elements from the Gothic style.
- Vanbrugh and Hawksmoor at Castle Howard. Bridgeman at Claremont and at Stowe (with Vanbrugh and Brown). Pope at Twickenham.
- Burlington at Chiswick.
- In Pope's writings one finds neologisms such as "picturesque" (whose forms are worthy of a painter's brush) and "romantick" (whose ambiance evokes old novels).
- First appearance of *fermes ornées* (ornamental farms): Dawley (Bolingbroke).
- In France Dézallier d'Argenville's *La théorie et la pratique du jardinage* (1709; The Theory and Practice of Gardening) is still very faithful to the symmetrical garden. Reprinted in 1713, 1722, and 1747. Dufresny seems already to show an interest in asymmetry, but there is little documentation of this.

1730–1760

- In England, triumph of Brown's style, with its gentle undulations, trees arranged either alone or in copses, and serpentine paths and streams.

- At the same time, showing a more picturesque, lively style, Shenstone develops the ornamental farm (Leasowes). Shenstone is the poet who epitomizes Hutcheson's sentimental associationism.
- The rococo style, with its fantastic curves and its openwork edifices (Painswick), gains in popularity at the same time as does the Chinese style. Chambers publishes his *Design of Chinese Buildings* (1757).
- The Gothic style is established and Walpole builds Strawberry Hill (1750s).
- Blondel publishes his *De la distribution des maisons de plaisance* (1736; On the Arrangement of Leisure Houses).
- Wilhelmina, sister of Frederick II, at the Hermitage (1735) and at Sanspareil (1745) near Bayreuth.

1760–1780

- The period during which the movement becomes theoretical.
- Chambers works at Kew from 1757 until 1763.
- Shenstone publishes his *Unconnected Thoughts on Gardening* (1764).
- In France the established vogue for the Chinese style and the 1752 publication of Attiret's *A Particular Account of the Emperor of China's Gardens, near Pekin,* facilitate the acceptance of the landscape garden. In Germany rococo is a driving force in gardening. Pigage at Schwetzingen (1762).

1760	Watelet begins the Moulin Joli.
1761	Jean-Jacques Rousseau's *La nouvelle Héloïse* (Julie; or, The New Héloïse).
1765	J.F. Eysebeck at Wörlitz.
1771	Whately's *Observations on Modern Gardening.*
1772	Chambers's *Dissertation on Oriental Gardening.*
1773	Controversy between Chambers (Chinese style) and Mason (national and Gothic style).
1774	Watelet's *Essai sur les jardins* (2nd edition; Essay on Gardens). Walpole finishes his *On Modern Gardening.*
1774–79	Carmontelle at Monceau.
1775	Bélanger's voyage to England.
1776	F.L. Sckell at Schwetzingen. Goethe at Weimar. Morel's *Théorie des Jardins* (Theory of Gardens). Le Rouge begins publishing his *Jardins anglo-chinois à la mode* (20th and last volume in 1788; Fashionable Anglo-Chinese Gardens).

1777	Girardin's *De la composition des paysages* (On Landscape Gardening).
1778	Goethe visits Wörlitz.
1778	Zug begins his work at Arkadia (Poland).
1779	Mason finishes *The English Garden*. Carmontelle finishes work on the Jardin de Monceau.

1780–1800

1781	Laborde begins the publication of *Voyage pittoresque de la France* (last volume in 1796; Picturesque Travels in France). Appearance of colossal forms related to the concept of perfectibility.
1774–85	M. de Monville's *Le Désert de Retz* (The Retz Desert).
1784	Csakvar and Tata appear on maps of Hungary.
1785	Hirschfeld's *Theorie der Gardenkunst* (Theory of Gardening).
1786	Méréville Hubert Robert succeeds Bélanger at Méréville. Polemics about the picturesque: In *The Landscape* (1794), Knight attacks Brown. Price's *Essay on the Picturesque* (1794) invokes Burke's sublime. Repton defends Brown's style against the supporters of the picturesque. *Sketches and Hints* (1795).
1796	Beckford at Fonthill.

MICHEL BARIDON

See also Energy; Jardin du Roi (French Royal Botanical Garden); Landscape; Mountain; Picturesque; Ruins

Further Reading

Baridon, Michel, "Ruins as a Mental Construct," *Journal of Garden History* 5, no. 1 (1985)

Baridon, Michel, "History, Myth, and the English Garden," in *The Fashioning and Functioning of the British Country House*, Washington, D.C.: National Gallery of Art, 1989

Gothein, Marie Luise, *A History of Garden Art*, 2 vols., New York: Hacker Art Books, 1979 (original German edition, 1928)

Hunt, John Dixon, *Garden and Grove: The Italian Renaissance Garden in the English Imagination, 1600–1750*, London: Dent, and Princeton, New Jersey: Princeton University Press, 1986

Hunt, John Dixon, *William Kent, Landscape Garden Designer: An Assessment and Catalogue of His Designs*, London: Zwemmer, 1987

Hunt, John Dixon, *Gardens and the Picturesque: Studies in the History of Landscape Architecture*, Cambridge, Massachusetts: MIT Press, 1992

Hunt, John Dixon, and Peter Willis, *The Genius of the Place: The English Landscape Garden, 1620–1820*, London: Elek, and New York: Harper, 1975

Hussey, Christopher, *The Picturesque: Studies in a Point of View*, New York and London: Putnam, 1927; reprint, London: Cass, 1983

Laird, Mark, *The Flowering of the Landscape Garden: English Pleasure Grounds, 1720–1800*, Philadelphia: University of Pennsylvania Press, 1999

Ligne, Charles Joseph, Prince de, *Coup d'oeil at Beloeil and a Great Number of European Gardens*, translated and edited by Basil Guy, Berkeley: University of California Press, 1991 (original French edition, 1781)

Mosser, Monique, and Georges Teyssot, editors, *L'architettura dei giardini d'Occidente: Dal Rinascimento al Novecento*, Milan: Electa, 1990

Stroud, Dorothy, *Capability Brown*, London: Country Life, 1950

Wiebenson, Dora, *The Picturesque Garden in France*, Princeton, New Jersey: Princeton University Press, 1978

Gas

The word *Gas* (gas; in French, *gaz*) was coined by the Flemish physician and chemist Jan Baptist Van Helmont (1577–1644) to refer to invisible vapors, emanations, or spirits given off by bodies during combustion, fermentation, or effervescence, and which then mix with the air in a vast chaos. The word is a transliteration of the Greek *chaos*, the "g" arising from the Flemish representation of "ch," sounded as a guttural in that language. The word *gaz* first appeared in French in 1670 in a translation of Van Helmont's works on the principles of medicine and physics. It was adopted by Pierre Joseph Macquer and then, in 1774, by Antoine Laurent Lavoisier, who believed that it came from the archaic word *ghoast*, meaning "spirit" (*Opuscules physiques et chimiques* [1774; Opuscules in Physics and Chemistry]).

Studies of pneumatic phenomena played a major role in 17th-century experimental physics. Evoking the founding of this branch of physics in earlier centuries, Roger Côtes emphasizes the importance of such studies in his *Leçons de physique expérimentale* (1742; Lectures in Experimental Physics):

> Archimedes's hydrostatic experiments, Galileo's experiments on gravity, Toricelli's experiments on atmospheric pressure, and, finally, the experiments of the eminent Mr. Newton on light, can all be regarded as so many foundations that nothing will ever undermine.

Côtes also refers to the "works of the most learned academies" and "the discoveries of Otto von Guericke, Pascal, and Boyle."

The scientists of the age of the Enlightenment inherited the idea that air is a heavy and elastic fluid and that the atmosphere is a vast ocean that envelops our planet. The fluidity of air, they believed, caused its parts to yield to the slightest effort. Thus, bodies moved about easily in it, sounds were propagated and odors diffused. The heaviness of air caused mercury to rise in barometric tubes. The elasticity of air caused it to respond to the pressure of other bodies by compressing its volume and then expanding again when the pressure ceased. The problem of the limits to be assigned to the condensation or rarefaction of air by pneumatic machines was thus frequently raised. Many physicists thought that air's heaviness and elasticity were the sole reasons for its capacity to sustain the combustion of bodies. According to Louis Bernard Guyton de Morveau, the flame of a candle placed under a glass bell jar goes out because the heat increases so much that it causes the air's elasticity to compress the flame, thus extinguishing it. Moreover, a candle flame cannot burn in the vacuum created by a pneumatic machine because the parts of the flame, no longer held in place by the surrounding air, disperse into the vacuum created around the candle. Thus, the fire is separated from the combustible body that fuels it. In this way, as Antoine Baumé writes in Volume 1 of his *Chimie expérimentale et raisonnée* (1773; Experimental and Reasoned Chemistry), "air does not materially contribute to the combustion of bodies, it is not absorbed by them during that process; or, to state it another way, air is not destroyed by bodies when these are burned in sealed vessels." This theory contradicted Robert Boyle's hypothesis that the air contains—as Jean Le Rond D'Alembert puts it in the entry "Air" of the *Encyclo-*

pédie—a "vital and singular substance that we do not understand" and that makes air necessary for the feeding of the flame.

From what they gleaned from Boyle and Edmé de Mariotte, physicists of the time continued to assume that air is rarefied in such a way that its volume is always in inverse proportion to its weight. In 1702 Guillaume Amontons proved experimentally that an "air" that is always in the same state of condensation—that is, that always has the same volume—increases its "springiness," or elastic force, and therefore balances a weight becomes greater in proportion to its increase in heat. For these experiments, Amontons used a U-shaped glass tube with branches of unequal length, welded a hollow globe to the end of the shorter branch, and poured mercury into the tube. The "springiness" of the air trapped in the globe balanced the weight of the atmosphere and of the column of mercury that weighed down on it. Increasing the heat had the effect of increasing the "springiness" of the air in the globe. This increase was indicated by a greater difference in the level of the mercury in the tube, and Amontons inferred that the volume of the air had stayed more or less constant when it pushed the column of mercury if the globe's capacity was proportionate to the width of the tube. He noted that the "springiness" of the air was not affected when his instrument—in effect, a thermometer—was placed in water containing a large quantity of ice. He conjectured that a considerable amount of heat remained in the ice and that the air would lose "springiness" if it were deprived of heat. He was then able to determine "the extreme point of cold of his thermometer." His results, converted into centigrade, came out at −239.5, instead of −273 degrees.

There were diverse interpretations of Boyle's law over the course of the 18th century. In the *Philosophiae Naturalis Principia Mathematica* (1687; Mathematical Principles of Natural Philosophy), Newton had suggested that elastic fluids are composed of particles that exert repulsive forces upon neighboring particles; as a result, only those forces of repulsion that are inversely proportional to the distances to their centers obey Boyle's law (Book 2, Proposition 23). This demonstration assumes that the particles are arranged in a cubic lattice. In proposing this static model in which pressure is attributed to the forces of repulsion in the particles, Newton expressed some customary reservations about its use. He wrote:

> But whether elastic fluids do really consist of particles so repelling each other is a physical question. We have here demonstrated mathematically the property of fluids consisting of particles of this kind, that hence philosophers may take occasion to discuss that question. (*Sir Isaac Newton's*

Mathematical Principles of Natural Philosophy and His System of the World, translated by Andrew Motte in 1729, revised by Florian Cajori, edited by R.T. Crawford, Berkeley: University of California Press, 1934)

Moreover, when he published the second English edition of the *Opticks* (1717) Newton was not concerned with solving the problem that arose from assuming that there are repulsive forces between neighboring particles (to account for the elasticity of fluids) and yet, at the same time, postulating among these same particles extremely powerful attractive forces that are in immediate contact and that remain perceptible at very small distances (*Opticks*, Book 3, Question 31) in order to explain the cohesion of bodies and of chemical compounds. Nevertheless, during the 18th century the Newtonians generally adopted this model of elastic fluids and applied it to air, forgetting that Newton had viewed it simply as a mathematical problem. To resolve the inherent contradiction in the idea that particles exerted both attractive and repulsive forces, Rudjer Josip Bošković replaced particles with immaterial centers of forces that were attractive or repulsive depending on distance. However, most writers assumed that only attractive forces could exist among particles; they posited a mechanical cause for repulsion, located in the air surrounding the particles and not inherent in the particles themselves. Indeed, according to Anne-Robert-Jacques Turgot, if particles exerted repulsive forces among themselves these forces would be universal and would also affect the celestial bodies, yet this had never been observed. Many physicists regarded the fire that filled the interstices among air particles as the cause of repulsion, and some of them thought that only the presence of fire could make air elastic. The great authority of Hermann Boerhaave and other Dutch physicists strengthened this view.

In his *Hydrodynamica* (Hydrodynamics), published in 1738, Daniel Bernoulli suggests that elastic fluids, and air in particular, are composed of an infinite number of heavy particles that can be rapidly displaced in any direction; he further suggests that air can be compressed infinitely. When air is enclosed in a cylinder sealed with a piston, the impact of the particles on the piston balances the weight that presses on the piston. Bernoulli considers the case of a greater weight that would displace the piston and reduce the volume of air. He supposes that compression does not alter the speed of the particles and that it increases the frequency of their impact in proportion to the density of the air. Without taking into account the size of the particles, he demonstrates that the force of compression of the gas is approximately in inverse proportion to the volume occupied by the gas, assuming that the temperature is fixed, which conforms to Boyle's law. Bernoulli also thinks that the pressure of the gas can be increased, not only by reducing its volume but also by increasing its temperature, which increases the speed of the particles. Given these assumptions, Bernoulli finds it obvious that, when the temperature rises, the weight that bears down on the piston must vary with the square of the speed of the particles so that the volume occupied by the air remains unaltered. Historians might be tempted to infer that Bernoulli linked the temperature of the air to the "living force" (*vis viva,* or mv^2) of its particles, a point he did not explain and which his contemporaries did not discover. For more than a century, this theory found few adherents.

In his *Vegetable Staticks* (1727) Stephen Hales showed that it is possible to collect large amounts of "airs" by heating (and thus breaking down) many substances. Convinced that the airs collected in this way were no different from atmospheric air, he did not try to determine their chemical properties and believed they had become noxious only because vapors had infected them, making them lethal to animals and plants. Antoine Baumé still shared this opinion in 1773. Hales focused exclusively on the volume of gases collected and was astonished by the large amount of force needed to reduce them to the volume of the solids that had contained them. It seemed obvious to him that the gases contained within terrestrial substances had lost their capacity to expand. Indeed, it was inconceivable that these immense quantities of gas had been able to enter plants and become part of them if the isolated molecules of gas had been elastic. The ability of gas to expand was also deemed to be a property of fire, which appeared to be the most volatile and the least substantial of the traditional elements. In his *Chimie expérimentale et raisonnée*, Baumé admits that

> the molecules of elements, when they are isolated and detached from one another, necessarily have properties that differ from those elements themselves when they are joined in an aggregate mass. That is, an isolated molecule of air is not at all elastic; an isolated molecule of fire no longer has any effect on a body and contains no heat; an isolated molecule of water is extremely solid; and, finally, an isolated molecule of earth is also very solid and impenetrable.

These ideas inspired Joseph Black's research on the latent heat of bodies and his idea that the fire contained in certain substances loses its ability to heat those substances. Thus, to Hales and his contemporaries, the properties of air did not appear to be those of an "aeriform" state of matter but rather those of a specific chemical element, one of Aristotle's four elements.

It was not until Turgot wrote the entry "Expansibilité" (Expansibility) for the *Encyclopédie* that the possibility was conceived that air could also be liquefied by the joint action of strong compression and intense cold, or that the physical properties attributed to air—which could also be found in water vapor—must also be attributed to a state of matter.

In 1754 Black showed that Hales's "fixed air" had physical and chemical properties that were different from those of "common atmospheric air" and theorized that the two types of "air" were not one and the same. Black was describing carbon dioxide. In 1766 Henry Cavendish isolated an "inflammable air" (hydrogen). At the end of 1771 Joseph Priestley presented the results of his pneumatic experiments to the Royal Society in London, and from 1772 to 1774, he undertook various observations of the different types of "air."

Lavoisier was led to revolutionize chemistry by his reflections on Turgot's theory of vapors, British pneumatic chemistry, and the experiments that he himself had conducted—either alone or in collaboration with Guyton de Morveau, Antoine François Fourcroy, or Claude Louis Berthollet—on the combustion and calcination of metals, the nature of water, the composition of acids, and the dissolution of metals. What most concerns us here is Lavoisier's view that the various types of "air" corresponded to different chemical substances, all mixed in fiery substance he called "caloric," which, through its repulsive force, opposed the attraction of particles. Lavoisier used the word *gaz* to designate a broad class of elastic, aeriform fluids, although he made an exception in the case of atmospheric air in order to preserve the name that was "consecrated in society by ancient usage" (*Traité élémentaire de chimie* [1789; Elements of Chemistry]). One of Lavoisier's main achievements—resulting from his experiments in collaboration with Pierre Simon Laplace—was the isolation in vapor form of ether, spirit of wine, and water, in accordance with Turgot's ideas. Another of Lavoisier's important achievements was his analysis of atmospheric air, which he demonstrated to be composed of two gases, oxygen and nitrogen, one breathable, the other incapable of sustaining combustion or respiration.

Until that time physicists had restricted themselves to studying the expansion of atmospheric air exposed to heat. Then Priestley, followed by Gaspard Monge, Berthollet, and Alexandre Vandermonde in 1786, and later Guyton de Morveau and Duvernois, came to apply these studies to other gases. As early as 1787 Jacques-Alexandre-César Charles set out to determine how heat increases the elasticity of gases. According to Lavoisier, the molecules of all natural substances are in a state of equilibrium between the forces of attraction, which tries to reunite them, and the repulsion of the caloric, which fills the spaces between molecules and tends to separate them. When the attraction of the molecules is stronger, the body is a solid; if the repulsive force is greater, the molecules move apart indefinitely if it were not for atmospheric pressure. Depending on atmospheric pressure and the degree of heat, such substances are either liquids or gases. We find here the image of elastic fluids inherited from Newton, except that Lavoisier attributed the source of the forces of repulsion to caloric. Berthollet and Laplace adopted these ideas and remained faithful to them until the early 19th century.

ROBERT LOCQUENEUX

See also Chemistry; Heat; Phlogiston; Thermometry

Further Reading

Bensaude-Vincent, Bernadette, and Isabelle Stengers, *A History of Chemistry,* translated by Deborah van Dam, Cambridge, Massachusetts: Harvard University Press, 1996 (original French edition, 1993)

Brush, Stephen G., *Kinetic Theory,* 3 vols., Oxford and New York: Pergamon Press, 1965–72; see especially vol. 1, *The Nature of Gases and of Heat*

Brush, Stephen G., *The Kind of Motion We Call Heat: A History of the Kinetic Theory of Gases in the 19th Century,* 2 vols., Amsterdam and New York: North-Holland, 1975; see especially vol. 1, *Physics and the Atomists*

Brush, Stephen G., *Statistical Physics and the Atomic Theory of Matter: From Boyle and Newton to Landau and Onsager,* Princeton, New Jersey: Princeton University Press, 1983

Hankins, Thomas L., *Science and the Enlightenment,* Cambridge and New York: Cambridge University Press, 1985

Genius

By the dawn of the Enlightenment, the concept of genius had apparently lost most of the theological and mythological connotations that originally linked it to a generative divinity, to the Latin noun *genius* (guardian spirit), to demons and angels, but it was still closely associated with the procreative function implied in the Latin verb *gignere.* Consequently, the problem that the concept raised for criticism was nothing less than the awesome enigma of creation itself. Criticism developed along two axes, corresponding to a double legacy handed down from antiquity. On the one hand there was the notion of genius as expressed in the Latin *furor,* which meant a "delirium" of either divine or demonic inspiration; it meant enthusiasm in the etymological sense of the word, but also referred to mental illness. On the other hand, there was the notion of genius derived from *ingenium,* which referred to natural ability or talent, the source of invention according to Cicero. For Giambattista Vico genius was the gift of synthesis (as opposed to analysis): "that mental faculty that enables one to bring together in a rapid, appropriate, and felicitous manner things that are separate" (*De Nostri Temporis Studiorum Ratione* (1708; On the Study Methods of Our Time).

During the Renaissance, but even more so in the 17th century, in the works of Matteo Peregrini and Baltasar Gracián y Morales, *ingenium* was linked to *acumen,* which meant "piercing," in both the physical and moral sense, and could therefore be applied to any kind of sharpness or ability to penetrate. The Italian *acutezza* and the Spanish *agudezza* were similarly used to designate the highest form of human power in fields as different as art, philosophy, and politics. The chevalier de Méré, in his treatise *De l'esprit* (1677; Of Spirit), introduces a baroque vision of the world into France by placing the "spirit" above reason and raises a question that would become central for 18th-century thinkers, that of defining the mental power or the link between faculties that constituted the essence of genius. Finally, it should be recalled that the French *génie* (from the Latin *ingenium,* by way of the Old French *engin,* meaning "machine" or "apparatus") also refers to the art of engineering, in other words the ability to construct military, civil, or naval "engines," or machines.

The fundamental shift that occurred in the 18th century involved a new type of relationship between the individual, freed from considerations of race or heredity, and his own "genius." In earlier times "great craftsmen" or "illustrious authors" were recognized as possessing genius, but that was simply a way of saying that they had outstanding talent. Once these individuals were labeled "geniuses," however, the concept shifted decisively. Henceforth, genius was no longer situated outside the individual as one of his attributes; instead, it was an integral part of a fortunate being, that "second *Maker:* a just Prometheus under Jove," in the earl of Shaftesbury's much-quoted definition (1710; Soliloquy; or, Advice to an Author). It is precisely this shift, from a word used as an attribute to a word referring to an exceptional being, that would eventually allow the romantic generation to promote genius to the rank of a human ideal, thus replacing earlier models of perfection such as the saint, the knight, the courtier, or the gentleman. But how might one define the inner fiber that lies at the heart of genius? Can its essence even be communicated? And does not madness lie in wait for whoever gives free rein to his genius, rather than tailoring it to the demands of his time? Issues such as these may be summed up in a single question: can one explain the miracle of genius without blunting its piercing originality?

Toward an Anthropology of Genius

To answer this question, a purely rhetorical definition of the term will not suffice. Instead, one must look into the heart of the work of genius, at the phenomenon itself. Initially, in their reluctance to attribute genius to the influence of some unknown divinity, critics such as the abbé Jean-Baptiste Dubos were content to explain it as a fortuitous combination of the blood and the brain. But this appeal to nature soon ran into the limitations of their knowledge of physiology. Dubos admits that:

> I am suspicious of physical explanations, given the imperfections of a science in which so much is guesswork. Yet the facts that I [seek to] explain are real . . . So I must suppose that this happy configuration corresponds, physiologically speaking, to the divine spirit to which poets refer as the source of their inspiration.

There then developed a need for *in vivo* observation and the privileged role played by introspection. It is striking that the *Encyclopédie* article "Génie" (Genius), written by Jean François de Saint-Lambert but undoubtedly reworked by Denis Diderot, concludes with the following admission: "This article, which I should not have written, ought rather to have been the work of one of those exceptional men who honor our century, a man who, to understand genius, would have only needed to look within himself."

The idea that genius could only be understood from the inside is taken up eloquently by Jean-Jacques

Rousseau in the article "Génie" of the *Dictionnaire de musique:*

> Seek not, young artist, to understand *genius.* If you have it, you will feel it within you; if you have not, you will never know it . . . If you feel neither delirium nor rapture, if you see only beauty where there is bliss, how dare you ask what is genius? Mere mortal that you are, do not defile its sublime name.

In this way, a definition based on effect is replaced by one based on cause. A genius is one whose work inspires rapture in the observer (or listener); or, by the same token, a genius is one who convinces others that genius exists. Yet only a genius, in the depths of his own ingenious soul, can perceive the true nature of genius. The magic circle thus closes, in a realm far removed from those ordinary mortals who are no more capable of perceiving the sublimity of the word "genius" than of understanding the phenomenon itself.

Claude-Adrien Helvétius rejected such an elitist definition of genius; in his view, rather than being some innate faculty, genius is simply the result of good fortune or education. Genius cannot readily be separated from the mind; and, while genius may govern invention, the latter possesses no creative power in itself, and is reduced to a mere concatenation of circumstances. However attractive the out-and-out materialism of this explanation should have been to Diderot, he could not accept the trivialization of genius based on the belief that it was always possible to supplement a natural gift through interest or hard work. "Genius's tyrannical drive," Diderot was forced to admit, was completely "foreign" to Helvétius.

Since genius is first experienced as a form of constraint, ideas are, as it were, the genius's "harlots," whom he longs to bend to his sovereign will. Diderot is therefore particularly careful to keep track of the various moments of his mental as well as physical work. His *Entretiens sur "Le fils naturel"* (1757; Discussions on "Le fils naturel") thus contains a description of the creative process that is both a self-portrait and a literary manifesto. The poet quickly scans the physical world around him: "He gazes across the waters and his genius spreads out." Soon a physical tremor announces the arrival of inspiration; originating in the heart, it spreads out to the extremities and is followed by a burning that kindles his very being. It is a burning "that makes him pant, that consumes him, that even destroys him, yet brings life and spirit to everything it touches." It is almost as if, to escape this consuming flame, the poet has no alternative but "to pour out the torrent of ideas that crowd, collide, and chase each other round." Under the impulsion of such a flood,

even silence is forced to speak. To describe genius in this manner in 1757, at the very height of the Enlightenment, constituted something of a provocation. By representing the raptures of enthusiasm as a physiological phenomenon and bringing to that description, in addition to the usual mystical terms, a whole battery of chemical and medical terms, Diderot nevertheless emphasizes the most essential question of all, namely the role and status of enthusiasm in the creative act. By what mechanism is an act of vision translated into creative energy? How does the simple mirror of the mind become incandescent, like one of those polished surfaces of Archimedes that managed to destroy the Roman fleet? Descartes thought that a mirror capable of burning an object one league away was an impossibility, unless it were "excessively large." But then the comte de Buffon showed that it was possible after all and, in so doing, he may be said to have invented the emblem of genius.

From a Sense of Enthusiasm to Creative Enthusiasm

"Without enthusiasm, either true ideas do not occur, or if by chance they do, we cannot pursue them." This was the argument advanced by Diderot, who believed the ideas of the genius possessed an inherent energy, a form of energy that governed not only their birth but also their uncertain evolution. From Shaftesbury Diderot had derived this theory of an enthusiasm that followed the dictates of an inner form. Distinguishing between the playful, polytheist, and tolerant enthusiasm of the ancients and the dark, melancholic, and fanatical variety of the moderns, Shaftesbury had advocated an active enthusiasm, one compatible with wit and humor: "A poet is an enthusiast in jest, and an enthusiast is a poet in good earnest" (*Miscellaneous Reflections*). This active enthusiasm is above all a moral sense, in the English meaning of the term *moral,* that is to say with none of the ethological connotations of the corresponding French adjective *moral,* which remained closely associated with the noun *moeurs* (meaning "mores" or "customs") from which it was derived. If enthusiasm is a moral sense, then it must be guided by the creative mind, that *Geist* (spirit) whose presence is acknowledged in the German *Begeisterung* (inspiration). The latter, the source of all that is truly great in this world, is in direct contrast to *Schwärmerei,* the effusiveness that, according to Immanuel Kant, leads from exultation and extravagance to madness (*Wahnwitz*). Doubtless, there is no exact equivalent in French to the English "wit" or the German *Witz,* words that refer to the faculty that prevents enthusiasm from degenerating into vague sentimentality or from wandering off along some solitary path. On the contrary, wit frees enthusiasm for the task of producing those forms that Kant would later define as Aesthetic Ideas. Nevertheless, Diderot's scathing remarks about sensibility in his *Paradoxe sur le comédien* (1773; Paradox on the Actor) attest to the strength of a line of thinking that led Kant to question the value of even the most virtuous emotion and that culminated in Georg Wilhelm Friedrich Hegel's denunciation of those "beautiful souls" who are ruled by "the laws of the heart"—in other words, by an empty and abstract sentimentality that renders them incapable of recognizing the conditions under which ideas are made real.

However, Shaftesbury's notion of enthusiasm was not only recast by critical subjectivity. It was also enlivened by a cosmic energy that allowed subjectivity to uncover hidden forces deep within nature and to activate "the universal plastic nature." Thus, if genius became *ein Stück Natur* (a piece of nature) for Sturm und Drang writers, this was because genius was the embodiment of the technical energy of the universe. Their discovery of genius—and their adoption of the gallicism *Genie*, first suggested by Schlegel in his translation of the abbé Charles Batteux (1751)—led the Sturm und Drang movement to rebel against the established order. Rules and laws were henceforth seen only as a "corset" that stifled freedom of expression.

Thus Kant's famous definition of genius as the "innate disposition of the mind (*ingenium*) through which nature confers its rules upon art" owes much more to Shaftesbury and Gotthold Ephraim Lessing than it does to the Sturm und Drang movement. Genius, in Kant's view, is conceived not as a total absence of rules but as a source of new rules, by virtue of a necessarily exemplary originality. Moreover, Shaftesbury's concept of a "noble enthusiasm, properly directed," making no claim to penetrate the secrets of the universe, but simply giving sensible form to objects of feeling, prefigures Kant's theory of genius as a presentation of Aesthetic Ideas:

> By Aesthetic Idea, I mean an idea presented by the Imagination that is deeply thought-provoking, but which no particular thought, that is to say no particular concept, can encompass, and that no language can completely express or render comprehensible.

Nevertheless, the Aesthetic Idea "is similar" to the Rational Idea, insofar as it reaches out toward "something beyond the limits of experience." If it fails to give an adequate presentation of the Idea of Reason, it is because the gap between the presentation and that Idea is insurmountable. The essential quality of genius is not to close that gap but to reduce it symbolically. "It is in poetry," Kant adds, "that the capacity of Aesthetic Ideas can show its true measure."

Figures of Genius

The gift of genius is experienced as the result of a moment of inspiration, as if summoned forth by some guardian *genius*. The difficulty for Kant stems from the fact that the individual genius is powerless to "explain scientifically how he creates"; unlike knowledge, genius does not appear to be communicable. In fact, genius dies with the person in whom it appears. Consequently, it would be "ridiculous" to equate the work of a genius with that of a scientist; genius may dictate the rules that govern art but not those of science. In thus ascribing a limited role to genius, Kant seems entirely faithful to the spirit of the Enlightenment, with its preeminent emphasis on the authority of Reason. Despite this, the concept of genius can be regarded as a Trojan horse smuggled into the fortress of criticism. Kant is perfectly aware of this when he subordinates genius to taste: "Should these two qualities come into conflict in a work of art, and it be necessary to sacrifice one of them, it should be the quality of genius."

At the beginning of the 18th century, Giambattista Vico, like Shaftesbury, tried to assess the precise impact of genius by endowing it with polemical significance. As a paradigm of genius, instead of Shaftesbury's Promethean "moral magic" or the image of "a just Prometheus under Jove," Vico suggests Hercules, celebrated for his superhuman capacity for work, his ingenuity, and his inventiveness. A genius is first and foremost "an inventor," in the fullest sense of the term; his principal virtue is not to seek but to *find,* not only in rhetoric and poetry but also in the mechanical arts and the sciences, as well as in the field of military or political strategy. The great technical inventions that have transformed the destiny of the world are not at all the result of the analytical method advocated by Descartes. On the contrary, such inventions rely on that capacity for synthesis that allows "the rapid, appropriate, and felicitous linking of separate things." Moreover, as Vico points out in a marginal note in the *Scienza nuova* (The New Science), the capacity for synthesis is characteristically found among the ignorant and the barbaric. Genius is a "faculty of youth"; to understand this is to understand the need for both a criticism of Cartesian analysis, which Vico finds dry and sterile, and for a new vision of history. Vico thus sets out to show how primitive man, possessing only limited powers of reasoning but a vigorous imagination, was able to invent language, institutions, laws, agriculture, industry, and so on.

Having become a rival of the gods, Prometheus defies Zeus in Johann Wolfgang von Goethe's lines of 1773: "I, adore you? Why? What have you done to relieve the sufferings of the oppressed?" Thus, while Prometheus was soon to shine forth as the emblem of romanticism, Hercules tended to symbolize nothing more than the strength of hard labor. The figure of the engineer became dissociated from that of the genius, despite their common origins.

Among Enlightenment thinkers of the middle of the 18th century, Diderot clearly showed the greatest reluctance to restrict genius's sphere of activity, as evidenced by the following statement from his *De l'interprétation de la nature* (1753; On the Interpretation of Nature):

> Workers engaged in the most humble manual tasks, simply by being obliged to carry out experiments, may experience a presentiment that has all the characteristics of inspiration. They are but one step away from making the same error as Socrates, and labeling it their familiar *daimon*.

As for the great experimental physicists, can their "extravagances" be reduced to "intelligible and clear ideas"? Are not the most important scientific discoveries the result of "habits of unreason" and "dreams of a sort"? Are there not philosophers of genius who extract truth from contemplation, independently of any proof? For Diderot the gift of observation, which "sees without looking," can be assimilated to the gift of prophecy or the gift of divination, and he worries that they cannot be passed on. But in a wider sense, can we deny that certain eccentrics—even certain criminals—have their modest share of genius? Perhaps the term should be applied to anyone who rescues us from mediocrity or stems the tide of vulgarity. In short, for Diderot it is the nature of genius to strive to transcend any particular sphere of activity. Yet art must remain its chosen domain, since it is in that field alone that, under the aegis of genius, there emerges the prototype, "the model, the true line, the ideal."

Throughout the history of the concept of genius in the 18th century, thinkers insisted on asking whether the very notion of genius is not tarnished whenever it is applied to anything except a sublime act or work of art. One is tempted to propose a cybernetic model of the concept, with genius located in the sender and the sublime in the receiver. But such a polarity appears untenable. This is partly because the circle of genius—the special, ingenious quality felt and conceived by the very genius that provokes it—mirrors the circle of the sublime, which itself generates the feelings and thoughts that form it. Further, and above all, the understanding of what causes genius remains a complete mystery. It is crucial to understand what is occurring when a work of genius moves us deeply, not only in order to be able to distinguish a rare gift from mere competence, but also

to avoid extending the concept to realms where it is inappropriate. While it is difficult to avoid individualizing the sublime by giving it the features of a Homer, a Plato, a Demosthenes, or an Alexander, we can allow a work of *ingenium* to dazzle us, and yet use *genius* as a simple metaphor.

BALDINE SAINT GIRONS

See also Aesthetics; Criticism; Enthusiasm; Idea; Imitation; Inspiration; Originality; Prometheus; Pygmalion; Reverie

Further Reading

Burke, Edmund, *A Philosophical Enquiry into the Origin of Our Ideas of the Sublime and Beautiful*, London: Dodsley, 1757; reprint, edited by Adam Phillips, Oxford and New York: Oxford University Press, 1990

Diekmann, H., "Diderot's Conception of Genius," *Journal of the History of Ideas* (1941)

Dubos, Abbé (Jean Baptiste), *Critical Reflections on Poetry, Painting, and Music*, translated by Thomas Nugent, London: Nourse, 1748; reprint, 3 vols., New York: AMS Press, 1978

Duff, William, *An Essay on Original Genius*, London: Dilly, 1767; reprint, New York: Garland, 1970

Gerard, Alexander, *Dissertations on Subjects Relating to the Genius and Evidences of Christianity*, Edinburgh: Millar, 1766

Matoré, G., and A.J. Greimas, "La naissance du génie au XVIIIᵉ siècle," *Le français moderne* (October 1957)

Montagu, Elizabeth Robinson, *An Essay on the Writings and Genius of Shakespear, Compared with the Greek and French Dramatic Poets: With Some Remarks upon the Misrepresentations of Mons. de Voltaire*, 8 vols., London: Dodsley, 1769; 6th edition, London: Priestly, 1810; reprint of 6th edition, New York: AMS Press, 1966

Reynolds, Joshua, *A Discourse, Delivered to the Students of the Royal Academy*, London: Davies, 1769–91; as *Discourses on Art*, edited by Robert R. Wark, New Haven, Connecticut: Yale University Press, 1997

Shaftesbury, Anthony Ashley Cooper, *A Letter concerning Enthusiasm, to My Lord *****, London: Morphew, 1708

Shaftesbury, Anthony Ashley Cooper, *Soliloquy; or, Advice to an Author*, 8 vols., London, 1710

Warton, Joseph, *An Essay on the Genius and Writings of Pope*, 2 vols., London: Cooper, 1756–82; reprint, New York: Garland, 1974

Geography

According to Voltaire, in his *Dictionnaire philosophique* (1765; Philosophical Dictionary), "Geography is one of those sciences that will always need perfecting." In the 18th century geography meant above all cartography, and the French phrase *savoir la carte* (knowing the map) was a synonym for having a good grasp of geography. The essential function of the geographer, in the silence of his study, was to correct existing maps by using the most recent accounts of travelers. Maps and travelers' reports, then, were the twin foundations of the geography of the Enlightenment.

The Image and the "Face" (Shape) of the Earth

From the time of their establishment, the Académie Royale des Sciences de Paris (French Royal Academy of Sciences) and the Observatoire de Paris (Paris Observatory) were assigned the task of correcting the map of the world. In 1682, new methods of determining longitude enabled the Académie des Sciences to produce a revised map of France that showed the country to be smaller and also more slender than the squat shape that had been accepted under Louis XIII. At the same time, geographic "missionaries" were sent out to various points on the globe (the Cape Verde Islands, the West Indies, Guyana, for example) to determine exact longitudinal positions. Their observations, combined with those of the English astronomer Edmund Halley in the southern hemisphere, made it possible for Jean-Dominique Cassini (1625–1712), the director of the Observatoire de Paris, to have a great planisphere prepared in 1696, with the continents and the oceans correctly positioned for the first time. This new image of the world was popularized by G. Delisle (1675–1726), a pupil of Cassini's. On Delisle's 1700 world map, the very clear outline of the continents contrasts with the "blanks" that still cover most of North America and Africa, not to mention New Holland (Australia), which is barely sketched in. The Atlantic's "breadth" is noticeably diminished, while the "Great Sea" (the Pacific) is greatly exaggerated.

Around 1730 learned circles in Paris resounded with the quarrel between Cassini's followers and those of Newton over the "face," or shape, of the Earth. According to Cassini's camp, our planet was elongated toward the poles, while for the Newtonians it was flattened because of centrifugal force. The only way of settling the dispute was to measure two meridians, one below the equator, the other in the polar regions. As a result of the journeys of Charles de La Condamine and Bouguer to Peru (1735–43) and of Pierre Maupertuis and Clairaut to Lapland (1736–37), Cassini's followers acknowledged their error. However, many French people were averse to seeing the Earth given, as Maupertuis put it in Letter 13 of his *Oeuvres* (1756; Works), a "foreign face . . . a face that had been imagined by an Englishman (Newton) and a Dutchman (Huygens)."

The 18th century's finest geodesic and cartographic achievement was perhaps the detailed map of France, on a scale of 1:86,400, begun in 1750 by Cassini de Thury, also known as Cassini III (1714–84). Cassini III adopted the measurements made by his father, Jacques Cassini (1677–1756), and by his grandfather, Jean-Dominique Cassini, and after a meticulous triangulation of the territory conducted onsite by hundreds of military engineers, he was able to publish the first pages as early as 1756. The publication of the full map, in 173 pages, was completed only under the First Empire, after the project had been "nationalized" during the Revolution. Cassini's geometric but not topographic map was the first such large-scale map of a major country, and this initiative was soon imitated in the majority of European states: by the Ferraris in the Low Countries, by Weiss in Switzerland, by von Schmettau in Brandenburg (Prussia), and in England, by the Ordnance Survey, at a scale of 1:63,360.

Broadened Horizons

The world map that J.B. Bourguignon d'Anville (1697–1782) published in 1761 reflected the extent of the progress made in geographic knowledge since the beginning of the 18th century. In 1700 Delisle had been chiefly concerned with the positions and outlines of the continents, but d'Anville went to extreme lengths to fill in the blanks inside those territories. This "armchair geographer," who had practically never traveled outside Paris, was able to conjure forth a new world through the power of his critical eye and through his use of hundreds of maps and travelers' reports.

What sources did d'Anville have at his disposal? For the eastern Mediterranean, Egypt, and the Maghreb, there were works by Tournefort, Maillet, Richard Pococke, and Thomas Shaw. In China, from the end of the 17th century onward, the Jesuits had made themselves indispensable as engineers, diplomats, astronomers, and cartographers. The results of their endless wanderings appeared in du Halde's monumental work, *Description de la Chine* (1736; Description of China), the superb *Atlas* of which was compiled by d'Anville himself. In the West Indies, Father Labat and Sir Hans Sloane, the President of England's Royal Society, laid the foundations of tropical geography. In Canada, Father Hennepin had reported on Niagara Falls, while

La Vérendrye, a *coureur des bois* (fur trapper), had reached the foothills of the Rockies. The Jesuit Father Pierre Charlevoix's descriptions of the forests and the "savages" of the New World inspired several beautiful passages by Chateaubriand. In South America the naturalists Jorge Juan and Antonio de Ulloa, companions of La Condamine, were the direct predecessors of Alexander von Humboldt.

D'Anville's world map reveals that there were still some major enigmas in the field of geography. Were Kamchatka and California islands or peninsulas? Was there a vast sea in the west, symmetrical with the Hudson Bay, that would facilitate the hypothetical "Northwest Passage"? Above all, what was the truth about the famed austral (southern) continent, the descendant of the Antipodes of the ancient Greeks? In his *Lettre sur le progrès des sciences* (1752; Letter on the Progress of the Sciences), Maupertuis imagines that it is inhabited by hairy men with tails and remarks: "I would rather have one hour of conversation with them than with the finest mind in Europe." In his *Histoire des navigations aux terres australes* (1756; History of Sea Travels to the Southern Lands), Charles de Brosses states his firm belief in the existence of vast territories, which he divides into three areas: Australasia, in the southern Indian Ocean; "Magellanica," in the south Atlantic; and Polynesia, in the south Pacific. Moved by a great enthusiasm for colonization, he advised the rulers of Europe to undertake the conquest of these fabulous lands.

In order to solve these enigmas or to test these hypotheses, the great sailing ships set off around the world soon after the signing of the Treaty of Paris (1763). John Byron, Samuel Wallis, Philip Carteret, Louis-Antoine Bougainville, Yves de Kerguélen-Trémarec, the Count of La Pérouse, and their companions were scientific travelers, commissioned by learned institutions to scour the Pacific. They discovered hundreds of archipelagos, but no southern continent, apart from a small part of Australia and New Zealand. On his three voyages, James Cook brought about more progress in "physical geography" than all his contemporaries put together. On his second voyage (1772–75), he circled the southern hemisphere completely at the latitude of the Antarctic Circle, without encountering the least sign of land, and Cook was thus able to dismiss "Messieurs Buffon, Maupertuis, and de Brosses and their ingenious daydreams" (1784; A Voyage to the Pacific Ocean: Undertaken by the Command of His Majesty, for Making Discoveries in the Northern Hemisphere).

The great maritime voyages did not take precedence over explorations of the continents. On the contrary, by facilitating long-distance journeys these voyages inaugurated a new stage in the development of land exploration. One need only cite the explorations of James Bruce in Ethiopia, Niebuhr in Arabia, Anquetil-Duperron in India, Carl Pieter Thunberg in Japan, Mungo Park in Sudan, Levaillant in southern Africa, Sir Alexander Mackenzie in northern Canada, and Volney in the United States. German explorers willingly placed themselves in the service of foreign powers, particularly Russia: Pallas, Gmelin, and Steller thus undertook the exploration of the Urals, Siberia, and the Russian Far East. At the end of the century, taking advantage of France's relative withdrawal from explorations, England created strong institutions that would ensure its supremacy in the geography of the 19th century. Alongside the Royal Society, the Admiralty, and the East India Company arose the Indian Survey, whose first stage was entrusted to James Rennell, resulting in the *Bengal Atlas* (1779). In addition, the African Association was created by Sir Joseph Banks, a former companion of Cook.

From Cosmology to Physical Geography

Until the middle of the 18th century, physical geography was essentially limited to cosmology. In their studies about the origin of our planet and its surface heights and depths, most authors, whether theologians or naturalists, strove to reconcile science and religion. The "Neptunian" theories that predominated at the beginning of the century posited, at the origin of the world, a universal Ocean (which was commonly equated with the Biblical Flood). Buffon drew inspiration for his *Théorie de la Terre* (1749; Theory of the Earth) from the great British cosmologists Thomas Burnet, Bishop William Whiston, and, most importantly, John Woodward, all of whom skillfully guided science onto the paths of theology. Even though Buffon reproaches these theorists for mixing "divine science with our human sciences," he accepts, as they did, that the mountains were formed at the bottom of a primeval ocean, since "marine life forms and shells" can be found on the highest peaks.

The first writer to focus on the Earth in its present state and to provide a description rather than a history was Philippe Buache (1700–73). Trained as an architect, and a son-in-law of the geographer Delisle, Buache compared the terrestrial globe to a majestic building, of which the mountains form the scaffolding; then, in an analogy between the microcosm and the macrocosm, he likened the world to the human body, of which the mountains constitute the skeleton. In a famous report submitted to the Académie des Sciences in 1752, Buache, as a good Cartesian, defined three categories of mountains: the ranges "that encircle our globe" from East to West or from North to South; the "buckle" ranges perpendicular to these; and the small ranges that fan out "like crows' feet" from the ranges in the second category. As these mountain ranges delimit river basins, Buache established three categories of rivers, corresponding to the three types of mountains. Buache hypothesized that the durability of the "scaffolding" and the solidity of the "building" are assured by the extension of the land mountain ranges as underwater ranges that tie the continents together. Perhaps Buache's most important innovation was his proposal of a division of the Earth into natural units, into hydrographic basins, which are more stable than political units. Buache's clear and logical system enjoyed immense success in France and elsewhere in Europe. The notion of "hydrographic basins" was popularized by the German writer Gatterer in his *Abriss der Geographie* (1775; Outline of Geography), and survived in geography curricula until the end of the 19th century.

In the same year that Buache presented his theories, J.E. Guettard revealed to the sceptical scholarly world the volcanic nature of the mountains in the Auvergne. He later produced the first geological maps of France and strove to build bridges between geography and geology. The study of the ancient volcanoes of France, Scotland, and Ireland, and of the active volcanoes of Naples, the Canary Islands, and the Andes, gave a new impetus to the plutonic theory of the origin of the Earth. Thirty years after publishing his *Théorie de la Terre*, Buffon adopted the plutonic theory in his *Époques de la nature* (1779; Cycles of Nature), attributing the formation of high mountains to the "central fire" and, more specifically, to the slow cooling of the molten globe. Only the lower and younger "secondary mountains" could have been formed by water, he holds. Abandoning Neptunian catastrophism, Buffon adopts a kind of transformationism that implies cooling over a long period of time. Ill at ease with the Bible-based calculation of the age of the Earth at 6,000 years, he fixes it at 75,000 years.

A major development took place in the last quarter of the century: the "exploration" of high mountain peaks. Ramond de Carbonnières in the Pyrenees and Deluc, Dolomieu, and Saussure in the Alps measured the heights of the summits, revealed the deep structure of the massifs, and clearly demonstrated the erosive action of glaciers and mountain streams. However, the true hero of the new physical geography was an obscure priest in the Ardèche, Giraud-Soulavie (1752–1813). From his meticulous observations in the high Vivarais, Giraud-Soulavie deduced the essential role of rivers in carving out valleys and, more generally, in the shaping of terrestrial relief. The idea of the gradual action of fluvial erosion seemed so implausible at the time that, despite its being confirmed by the Scottish geologist John Playfair in his *Illustrations of the Huttonian Theory of the Earth* (1802), it did not supplant the pervasive theory of catastrophism for another century. Even more than Buffon, those who believed that geological processes continue into the present blithely leapt over the "wall of Genesis." Giraud-Soulavie, one of the originators of this approach, made the new unit of geological time one million years. He may also be regarded as the founder of botanical geography, since he first proposed the idea of "strata of vegetation" on mountains, an idea half intuited by Tournefort on Mount Ararat and by La Condamine in the Andes, and which would be brilliantly developed by Humboldt. Thus, for 18th-century geographers and naturalists, mountains truly became "Nature's laboratory."

Toward a Human Geography

Although what are now called the human sciences did not exist in the 18th century, one can find elements that prefigure ethnology, sociology, demography, and human geography in the works of *philosophes* and in travelers' accounts. Some have sought to make Montesquieu the father of the "climate theory"—that is, of geographic determinism—by pointing out his statement in *De l'esprit des lois* (1748; The Spirit of Laws) that laws are "related to the physical condition of the country; to the icy, burning, or temperate climate; to the quality of the land . . . and to the way of life of the peoples, whether they are plowmen, hunters, or herders." In fact, inspired by travelers' reports, Montesquieu contrasts savage countries, where "nature and climate are almost exclusively dominant," to civilized countries, "which are cultivated not because of their fertility but because of their liberty." Switzerland and the Netherlands, for example, are "the two worst-endowed countries in Europe," yet they are the richest and the most heavily populated. In general, Montesquieu tries to show the "perpetual victory of morality over climate or . . . other physical circumstances." For him, a "good government" is one that corrects the harmful effects of nature.

Buffon's point of view in his *Histoire naturelle générale et particulière* (1749; Natural History, General and Particular), which was published one year after *De l'esprit des lois*, is quite strictly ethnological and determinist: "Climate is the primary cause of variety in the human species." Thirty years later, in the seventh of his *Époques de la nature*, Buffon contrasts "hideous" nature, in deserts and wild lands, with nature cleansed, cultivated, and embellished by humankind. Overall, "the present appearance of the Earth owes as much to man as man owes to the Earth." Jean-Jacques Rousseau, in *Du Contrat social* (1762; The Social Contract), takes his stance in the field of political geography and demography. He believes that in each state there should be an "appropriate relationship" between the extent of the territory and the "number of people." This relationship, which today we call population density, varies according to climate, fertility, and way of life, so that mountains, being less productive, are generally less populated than coastal regions. Rousseau was perceptibly influenced in this regard by the Physiocrats and by such pioneers of demography as Expilly, Moheau, and Cantillon. In Germany the partisans of political geography and statistics, such as Achenwald or Büsching (*Neue Erdbeschreibung*, 1792; New Description of the Earth), systematically connected the territorial size of states, their populations, and their resources. Clearly, Malthus was not too far in the future.

Constantin-François Volney was an heir to the *philosophes* but also their superior in that he was a traveler, while the *philosophes* were relatively cloistered. In the East, from 1783 to 1785, Volney was struck by the contrast between nomadic and sedentary peoples and theorized that nomadism must be related to lack of water and infertility of the soil. He wondered whether this might also explain the anarchy that persisted among the Turks. As soon as "wandering tribes" find peace and security, he observes in his *Voyage en Syrie et en Egypte pendant les années 1783, 1784 et 1785* (1787; Travels through Syria and Egypt, in the Years 1783, 1784, and 1785), they settle and "change imperceptibly into sedentary cultivators." In North America, from 1795 to 1798, Volney witnessed the disintegration of the indigenous ways of life in the face of the white man's incursions. He also pondered the reasons why the nomads of Syria and Egypt made the best of their repellent environment, while the American savages stagnated on very fertile land. Both ideologists and *philosophes* thus condemned determinism, being anxious to affirm human freedom and the omnipotence of "good government" in the face of natural constraints.

Geography in Its 18th-Century Context

Geography was useful to politicians, diplomats, merchants, missionaries, and travelers, and geographical knowledge was spread throughout society in myriad ways. There were numerous treatises, manuals, and summaries of the discipline by writers such as Salmon, Hübner, Buffier, and Lenglet-Dufresnoy. Ingenious methods for teaching children were devised, such as geography in verse. Repelled by the arid style of the textbooks, the higher classes preferred travel narratives and read the *Lettres édifiantes et curieuses* (1702–76) that the Jesuits sent from China, Canada, and Paraguay.

The abbé Prévost's *Histoire des voyages* (1746–61; History of Voyages), inspired by Thomas Astley's *A New General Collection of Voyages and Travels (1745–47)*, was a bestseller. The most interested people consulted dictionaries of geography such as the one compiled by Bruzen de La Martinière, comprising ten hefty volumes, or the portable *Dictionnaire Vosgien* (Dictionary of the Vosges), aimed at "newspaper readers." Nor should we forget the atlases, the finest of which was perhaps the one published by Robert de Vaugondy in 1757.

Geography was a valuable ally of the spirit of the Enlightenment because, in addition to demonstrating human diversity, it also revealed the relative nature of customs and beliefs, and was therefore in high esteem in learned societies and provincial academies. On the other hand, geography played only a limited role in the *Encyclopédie*. Finally, operas, such as Jean-Philippe Rameau's *Les Indes galantes* (1735; Love in the Indies), and literature point to the century's marked taste for exoticism. The heroes of Daniel Defoe's *Robinson Crusoe* and Voltaire's *Candide*—which might be considered "real" geographic novels—joined company with the imaginary travelers portrayed in Jonathan Swift's *Gulliver's Travels* or Voltaire's *Micromégas*.

In June 1768 Friedrich Melchior von Grimm wrote in his *Correspondance littéraire* that "without any national prejudice, I believe that Monsieur d'Anville can be regarded as the leading geographer of Europe." In fact, many people today view 18th-century geography as a "French science." However, thanks to Humboldt and Ritter, Germany would soon take the lead. Immanuel Kant, who had taught both geography and anthropology, felt drawn to contrast history, a chronological science that situates human beings in time, with geography, a chronological science that situates them in space. He thus gave geography the epistemological status that it had previously lacked.

NUMA BROC

See also Earth, Shape of the; Geology; Map; Mountain; Travel; Volcano

Further Reading

Broc, Numa, *La géographie des philosophes, géographes et voyageurs français au XVIIIᵉ siècle*, Paris: Ophrys, 1975
James, Preston E., *All Possible Worlds: A History of Geographical Ideas*, Indianapolis: Bobbs-Merrill, 1975; 3rd edition, by Geoffrey J. Martin and James, New York: Wiley, 1993

Geology

The word "geology," already in use in its Latin form in the 14th century, first appeared in French (*géologie*) in the "Système des connaissances humaines" (System of Human Knowledge) entry in Volume I of the *Encyclopédie*, amid a number of other neologisms, as a name for the "science of the continents." Denis Diderot borrowed it from the Englishman Benjamin Martin, who first used it in 1735. The appearance of the term in French did not mark an upheaval in the history of science. Ever since Thomas Burnet's *Telluris Theoria Sacra* (1681; Sacred Theory of the Earth), which for that matter was based on a model invented by René Descartes a third of a century earlier in his *Principia Philosophiae* (1644, 1647; Principles of Philosophy), histories of the Earth had been written under the title "Theory of the Earth," and they would continue to be titled this way into the early 19th century. James Hutton, who is generally recognized today as one of the founders of geology, published his revolutionary ideas under that time-honored title in 1795, and the "Discours préliminaire" (Preliminary Discourse) to the *Recherches sur les ossemens fossiles* (Research on Fossilized Bones) that Georges Cuvier published in 1812 was translated into English in 1815 under the title *Theory of the Earth*.

Diderot's neologism has endured—perhaps its only merit. Far more indicative of advances in geology were the simultaneous attempts to coin other new terms, some of them actually more eloquent than "geology." Nicolas Desmarest (1725–1815) contributed the entry "Géographie physique" (Physical Geography) to Volume VII of the *Encyclopédie* (1757), and other authors such as Nicolas Boulanger (1722–55) wrote of "subterranean geography" in order to emphasize that the structure formed by the "layers of the Earth" extended into the three dimensions of space.

German authors, following Georg Christian Füchsel (1762), spoke of "geognosis" to designate the science that classifies "mineral masses or their various systems . . . according to their order of layering or their relative ages." Associated with the name of Abraham Gottlob Werner (1749–1817), the famous professor at Freiberg, geognosis long remained connected to the "Neptunian" conception of the history of the Earth.

The word *géologie* eventually took hold in France when Jean-André Deluc (1727–1817) used it in his *Lettres physiques et morales* (1778, 1779; Moral and Physical Letters), as did Horace-Bénédict de Saussure in the same year in Volume I of his *Voyages dans les Alpes* (1779; Travels in the Alps). In 1793, when the Muséum National d'Histoire Naturelle (National Museum of Natural History) was established in Paris, the two professorships concerned with Earth sciences were assigned

the disciplines of geology (held by B. Faujas de Saint-Fond) and mineralogy (Louis-Jean-Marie Daubenton).

Organic Remains

The object of the theory of the Earth was to reconstruct the stages in the history of our planet. In this sense, it could be called a historical science, presupposing the mastery of a key with which to read the "archives of the Earth." The first element of this key was the correct interpretation of organic remains recovered from the ground, offering evidence of the former presence of a sea or a lake, and also that of the ground itself, identified in terms of strata (consolidated deposits). Once these two concepts were made available, interpretation obeyed three rules. First, the lowest layer is the oldest and the uppermost is the most recently formed (the principle of superposition). Second, since the layers are originally laid down horizontally, those that are inclined or vertical have undergone tilting (the tectonic principle). Finally, the layers will contain different fossils depending on whether they were laid down in marine or fresh waters.

Nicolaus Steno (1638–86), a Danish scholar residing at the court of the archduke of Tuscany, had proposed these rules in 1669 in the *De Solido intra Solidum Naturaliter Contento Dissertationis Prodromus* (The Prodromus of Nicolaus Steno's [unpublished] Dissertation Concerning a Solid Body Enclosed by Process of Nature within a Solid). It was Steno who borrowed the term "strata" from medicine to designate the layers of the Earth. The *Prodromus* is an astonishingly modern work. Sadly, although he was not entirely forgotten by posterity, Steno's name was little known, as his ideas were too novel and were most often expressed in an abstract and very general form (although he did apply them successfully to the geological history of Tuscany).

For all but the keenest minds, the very question of the organic origin of fossils presented a problem. Steno had shown that the so-called snakes' tongues (*glossopetrae*) were merely the teeth of dogfish, but the strata contained more problematic forms, such as shells in the shape of sheep's horns (now known as ammonites) that resembled no living creature of the present era. It was necessary to postulate either that these animals lived at great depths or that their genus had been "lost," to use a word coined by Bernard Palissy a century earlier. Those who rejected these two explanations were forced to regard the fossils as *lapides sui generis* (stones unique unto themselves). This is what Martin Lister, a contemporary of Steno's, claimed, misled by Steno's overly thorough description of fossils, while Robert Hooke,

Steno's rival, preferred to believe that the group had become extinct. Leibniz had even suggested that species underwent transformations (1693).

The question had not yet been completely resolved when Buffon's *Théorie de la terre* (1749; Theory of the Earth) appeared, since the renowned naturalist considered it worthwhile to demonstrate anew the organic origin of fossils in his "Preuves" (Proofs). Moreover, Buffon had an equally illustrious opponent in Voltaire, who sent a "Dissertation" from Bologna in 1746 claiming that shells had been left behind by "pilgrims." Although this "Italian letter" was ridiculed, Voltaire was not entirely wrong, even if he launched his argument somewhat frivolously. When he returned to the problem in his *Questions sur l'"Encyclopédie" par des amateurs* (1771; Questions on the "Encyclopédie" from the Uninitiated), he observed that many shellfish live in freshwater. In other words, the hermit of Ferney, who was specifically considering the fossils of Swiss sandstone which had been laid down in freshwater, was merely contesting the idea that the continents were once covered by the sea.

The incursions of the sea posed no serious problems as long as people imagined that it had overrun the coastal plains. Medieval authors had used this supposition to prove the existence of the biblical Flood. Now, however, organic remains were being discovered as high up as the summits of mountains. Antonio de Ulloa (1716–95), who went with Charles-Marie de La Condamine to Peru, discovered fossils at an altitude of over 13,000 feet. The simplest way to explain this finding was to assume that the ancient (or primeval) sea had exceeded this level and had subsequently receded. Two Swedish scientists set out to measure the sea level in the Gulf of Bothnia. One was the physicist Anders Celsius (1701–44) and the other was his friend, the naturalist Carolus Linnaeus (1707–78). Observations began in 1724 and were continued after Celsius's death. They provided further confirmation of the (relative) drop in sea level, inasmuch as Scandinavia was rising at a rate of around three feet each century.

In 1744, in his *Oratorio de Telluris Habitabilis Incremento* (Discourse on the Growth of the Globe), Linnaeus used this result to explain the expansion of the fauna, beginning from one pair of each species, created on an equatorial mountain. However, Linnaeus believed in the chronology derived from the age of the Patriarchs (Genesis 5 and 11) and, at a rate of four feet each century, the fall over 6,000 years would have been less than 300 feet. Either the rate of fall or the timescale would have to be increased.

Benoît de Maillet (1659–1738), a French author from Lorraine, did attempt to adjust both the fall rate and the timescale in a work conceived during a long stay in Egypt (where he was appointed consul in 1696).

The work, using an anagram of his surname, was entitled *Telliamed, ou Entretiens d'un philosophe indien avec un missionnaire français* (1748; Telliamed; or, Conversations between an Indian Philosopher and a French Missionary). Based on a decrease in water level, his system proposed a very slow fall of approximately three inches per century. This decrease, amounting to less than one yard per millennium, required that Maillet compensate by calculating an immense time span. Furthermore, Maillet introduced two elements that remained the basis of all the Neptunian systems of that time, and that resolved two difficulties: first, that the distribution of mountains across the planet implied that in some regions sediments had accumulated to a depth of approximately 2.5 miles, while elsewhere nothing had been deposited; and second, that the highest mountain ranges contained no fossils. The strata formed within a universal ocean only in certain regions as a result of the action of currents that deposited them where mountain ranges are now to be found; therefore, the strata had not been laid down in all regions. The first deposits, when the ocean's level was very high, contained no remains of life because the depth was too great. Thus the "primeval" mountains were formed. Subsequent deposits, stratified and containing fossils, were formed on the sides of these first peaks, in several successive generations, reaching lesser heights as the waters receded. The principle of superposition was thus respected, and the highest mountains were deemed the oldest.

Two Orders of Mountains

Maillet's intuition (or luck) inhered in his distinction of the generations of mountains (although the original idea can be equally attributed to Steno, who divided the geological history of Tuscany into two phases, characterized by rocky and sandy strata). After Maillet's death, it was established that the oldest mountains were crystalline and massive (unstratified). Following the poem "Die Alpen" (1732; The Alps) by the physiologist Albrecht von Haller, Johann Gottlob Lehmann (1719–67), a physician turned mine owner, in his *Versuch einer Geschichte von Flötz-Gebürgen* (1756; Essay on the Natural History of the Layers of the Earth), translated into French by the baron d'Holbach, distinguished primeval mountains—massive, nonfossiliferous, and dating from the Creation—and secondary mountains, with strata and fossils, associated with the Flood. Guillaume-François Rouelle in France (under the designations "ancient Earth" and "new Earth") and Giovanni Arduino in Italy adopted the same division at almost the same time. The Saxon school, notably Werner, made it the basis of their geognosis.

Between the time of Maillet and of Lehmann, however, the same distinction had been drawn by another author, and in such a different context that it deserves mention here. In 1740 an Italian priest, Lazzaro Moro (1687–1764), in a work on the "marine bodies to be found in the mountains," recognized two generations of mountains, which he called primary and secondary. He did so, however, from a "Vulcanist" perspective: a first upheaval raised up the rocky, stony seabed, debris accumulated at the foot of the mountain, then a new eruption lifted up the debris and deposited it in layers. The essential point distinguishing Moro's theory from those of the previous authors was that Moro thought the raising of the mountains explained the discovery of fossils at high altitudes: the primeval ocean need no longer have been miles above its present level. Moro estimated the earlier ocean level to have been around 1,100 feet.

These two orders of mountains formed the framework of the histories of the Earth advanced toward the end of the 18th century. Those histories were the first "archives" recognized by geologists. The role of such "archives" was all the more crucial in that it was believed that no authentic history could exist without an archive. This point becomes clear if we look somewhat further back in time. Descartes and other authors of the first theories of the Earth were interested primarily in reconstructing the formation of the planet rather than its history. With only a knowledge of the laws of nature at his disposal, and speculating as to the initial state (the "vortices," or the chaos of the poets), Descartes claimed to explain the present state of the planet and its relief. The successive states through which his scenario unfolds certainly did not constitute a history, but were rather a possible means of linking the initial state and the final state of a physical phenomenon. In order to create a historical account, it is necessary, as Antoine-Augustin Cournot wrote, to look for "facts that by their nature are beyond the scope of any theoretical investigation based on the observation of present-day facts and on the knowledge of permanent laws." Such facts are only accessible in the form of archives, that is to say, of datable evidence. The fossils that characterized paleontological stratigraphy became the archives of 19th-century geologists.

The allusion to archival research appeared in the Earth sciences at the very moment when Deluc and Saussure were using the word "geology." It is unlikely that this was mere coincidence. Peter Simon Pallas (1741–1811) alluded to archives following his *Reise durch verschiedene Provinzen des russischen Reichs* (1771–76; Journey through Various Provinces of the Russian Empire"), in his "Observations sur la formation des montagnes et sur les changemens arrivés au globe" (1777, 1779; Observations on the Formation of Mountains, 1779; and on the Changes Occurring to the Globe).

These observations contain, according to Pallas, "the archives of nature." Faujas de Saint-Fond (1741–1819) followed Pallas, stating that it was the exceptions and discrepancies "in the series of events" that made it necessary to rummage among the archives of nature (1779). Buffon had said the same thing the year before in his *Époques de la nature* (1779; Cycles of Nature): the "archives of the world" are the counterpart to the headings of "civil" (secular) history. The abbé Giraud Soulavie (1752–1813) also spoke of the "annals of the physical world" (1780).

For the time being, these archives were to be found in the layers of the Earth. The principle of stratigraphy was eventually used to analyze the interiors of secondary mountains. Lehmann (1756) and Füchsel (1762) had already recognized several formations in the Post-Hercynian deposits of Germany. This research obviously presumed that such formations were uniformly present all over the globe. The object of the Neptunian theory was to establish this hypothesis. If the universal ocean, full of material in solution or suspension, had covered the entire planet, then the precipitation of these materials should have occurred everywhere to the same extent. It should therefore be enough to study one region in order to determine the "geognostic column," according to the Wernerian school. Since the master had established the order of deposits in Saxony, it remained only to verify that the same held true elsewhere.

The project was concerned primarily with mountains. During the 1770s and 1780s, explorers penetrated into the main mountain ranges of Europe: Dieudonné Dolomieu, the abbé Pierre-Bernard Palassou, and Ramond de Carbonnières ventured into the Pyrenees; Saussure and the Deluc brothers into the Alps; Pallas into the Urals; and so on. Curiously, the Neptunians were almost entirely unaware of tectonics, and it took Saussure, fine observer that he was, some time to recognize that the vertical layers of the Vallorcine pudding-stone had been lifted up after they had been deposited.

Neptune and Vulcan

At the same time that these investigations were taking place, the study of volcanic phenomena began. This study was the beginning of a great debate between Neptunians and Vulcanists. Volcanoes, of course, had been known since antiquity. Strabo had already referred to them as the cellar windows of the globe. They had certainly been active in the past. Buffon, who believed, as had been customary since Georgius Agricola (1494–1555), that volcanoes were caused by the ignition of coal by pyrites, considered that the fourth epoch of nature was that of the volcanoes.

In 1751, however, Jean-Étienne Guettard, traveling in the Auvergne with Chrétien-Guillaume de Lamoignon de Malesherbes, discovered the volcanic nature of the hills around Clermont-Ferrand. The rock of Volvic was "similar to certain rocks of volcanic areas." Guettard did not extrapolate from his observations, however, and it was Desmarest who first realized that basalt is a form of solidified lava. This was the point that inspired the debate. Werner and his students refused to believe that basalt was not of sedimentary origin. This controversy continued into the 19th century.

One article by Desmarest is a fine example of the rift that occurred around 1775–80 in the methods of the Earth sciences. In 1775 Desmarest delivered a paper "on the determination of several epochs of nature by the products of volcanoes." The title calls Buffon to mind, of course, but Desmarest's position was quite different: Desmarest considered only a few epochs, and for that purpose he began at the present time, that of the most recent and thus best-preserved volcanoes, and worked back in time to those whose lava was covered by the last marine deposits. He thus proceeded in reverse—unlike Buffon, who presented his epochs in chronological order from the formation of the Earth onward. Desmarest's limiting of the field of investigation, and the progression of his exploration from the known to the unknown, indicated a mind that questioned its assumptions and submitted its ideas to the verdict of careful observation.

Everything thus suggests the late 1770s as a cutoff point that marks the very birth of the modern science of geology. Its gestation lasted a good half-century; but it was a product of the revolutionary period. Geology is frequently characterized by its establishment of long durations of geological time, which then led to the work of Charles Lyell (1797–1875) and to the concept of ongoing or gradual causes, but the truth was not so simple. Maillet had already proposed cycles of a half-million years, and Gautier had calculated the time taken to erode a continent at 35,000 years. Moreover, Gautier's figures implied values so much higher that François Ellenberger has concluded that he was not being sincere in limiting himself to his 35,000-year estimate (see Ellenberger).

Voltaire, so mocked by the historians, writes in his *Éléments de la philosophie de Newton* (1738; The Elements of Sir Isaac Newton's Philosophy) of a cycle of 2 million years. It is also known that Buffon, who in the printed edition of the *Époques de la nature* limited the history of the Earth to a period of 75,000 years, had envisaged a period 40 times longer in his manuscript. Palassou, who was very timid on some points (and, incidentally, a priest) believed that it would take 1 million years to erode the Pyrenees, though admittedly his time frame was set in a hypothetical future. Soulavie, unhindered by religion, clashed with the abbé Augustin Barruel by positing an immense timescale.

The debates of the early 19th century between the uniformitarians and the catastrophists were not, in fact, concerned with the question of timescale—but that is another story.

GABRIEL GOHAU

See also Geography; Mineralogy; Mountain; Science: Dissemination and Popularization; Volcano

Further Reading

Adams, Frank Dawson, *The Birth and Development of Geological Sciences,* New York: Dover, 1938

Ellenberger, François, *History of Geology,* Rotterdam and Brookfield, Vermont: Balkema, 1996– (original French edition, 2 vols., 1988–94)

Gohau, Gabriel, *A History of Geology,* revised and translated by Albert V. and Marguerite Carozzi, New Brunswick, New Jersey: Rutgers University Press, 1990 (original French edition, 1987)

Gohau, Gabriel, *Les sciences de la terre aux XVIIe et XVIIIe siècles: Naissance de la géologie,* Paris: Albin Michel, 1990

Hölder, Helmut, *Kurze Geschichte der Geologie und Paläontologie,* Berlin and New York: Springer Verlag, 1989

Laudan, Rachel, *From Mineralogy to Geology: The Foundations of a Science, 1650–1830,* Chicago: University of Chicago Press, 1987

Geometry

Overview at the Dawn of the 18th Century

Geometry during the Enlightenment was to a large extent heir to the changes that had occurred in mathematics in the 17th century. In antiquity geometry referred to the general study of the dimensions and properties of figures; since then it had developed into many forms, diversifying in a number of directions in terms both of purpose and of method. It was further transformed as a result of the institutionalization of science and technology.

A new analysis was expounded by René Descartes in his *Géométrie* of 1637 and developed by his "nephews," including Thomas Fantet de Lagny, Parent, Pitot, Saurin, Philippe de La Hire, author of the *Nouveaux éléments des sections coniques* (1679; New Elements of Conic Sections), and Guisnée. Descartes's *Géométrie* incorporated algebra into geometry and classified algebraic problems and curves into categories according to the degree of the equation involved. In other words, the text marked the birth of analytic geometry. The term "analytic geometry" appears in the *Mémoires* (1708–09; Reports) by Michel Rolle of the Académie Royale des Sciences de Paris (French Royal Academy of Sciences) and also in posthumous editions of works by Sir Isaac Newton. Moreover, this new approach to geometric problems and the consideration of the properties of a curve by means of a system of coordinates owed as much to Pierre de Fermat, Thomas Harriott, and John Wallis as it did to Descartes. Even the system of squaring up, point by point or line by line, used by the perspectivists played a part in the development of this new form of geometry.

With the treatment of conic sections as projections of a circle, and the recognition of the projective invariance of the ratios of rectangles constructed on three pairs of aligned points (the involution of six points), Girard Desargues's work on conic sections, particularly in his *Brouillon project d'une atteinte aux événements des rencontres d'un cône avec un plan* (1639; Proposed Draft of an Attempt to Deal with the Events of the Intersection of a Cone with a Plane), opened the way to a redefinition of geometry as the study of an infinite space and its configurations and as the study of what Gottfried Wilhelm Leibniz called "optical or apparent" transformations, which foreshadowed the transformational geometry of the 19th century. Blaise Pascal would draw on this new definition of geometry, which appears at the front of an elementary Port-Royal geometry textbook:

(1) The subject of pure geometry is *space*, whose threefold extent is considered in terms of three different directions known as dimensions, distinguished by the names of 'length,' 'breadth,' and 'depth.' . . . It presumes that all these terms are known in themselves. (2) Space is infinite in all its dimensions and (3) immobile as a whole and in each of its parts.

A similar definition is found in the *Philosophiae Naturalis Principia Mathematica* (1687; Mathematical Principles of Natural Philosophy), where Newton writes "Absolute space, in its own nature, without relation to anything external, remains always similar and immovable."

The gap between "pure" and "applied" geometry (the "mixed disciplines" of the *Encyclopédie*) grew wider, and what was then known as "synthetic" geometry was marginalized with the developments in practical geometry (architecture, surveying, stonecutting, the design of sundials, and so on).

The flourishing of rational science against a background of secularization and institutionalization (the birth of the major academies and the progressive establishment of military schools) raised the question of the transmission of that science. The challenge to the Euclidean model, which was synthetic and based on hypothesis and deduction, and was developed in the elementary geometry texts of such writers as Alexis-Claude Clairaut and Bézout, can be traced back to the efforts of the Jansenist Antoine Arnauld and the Oratorian Bernard Lamy. The late 18th century would see a return to a somewhat modified Euclidean system—for example, with A.M. Legendre's *Éléments de géométrie* (1794; Elements of Geometry).

This development initially took a variety of forms that reflected the peculiarities of national schools. After a period of marked regionalism, science began to be internationalized. In Italy the heirs of Galileo, up until Viviani and Giovanni Alfonso Borelli, favored the synthetic approach for a time, but in France the influence of Descartes and Fermat made analytics preeminent. The efficacy of Leibniz's algorithm and its notation caused infinitesimal calculus to dominate on the European continent. Meanwhile, the English school after Francis Bacon—a school instigated by Napier and Wallis and stimulated by Isaac Barrow (who was as well versed in the geometry of the ancients as in the new analysis)—produced the figure of Newton, who was torn between the expediency of calculus and the desire to understand that field of mathematics step by step in geometric terms. International communication, brought about by Mersenne and other intermediaries of the European scholarly community, and then through academic periodicals, helped to blur these national styles and to promote the tendency toward general trends.

A generation of "great-nephews" followed in the wake of Descartes. His analysis won over many followers, in the 17th century as well as during the Enlightenment, and the image of the 18th century as being obsessed solely with the new calculus developed by Newton and Leibniz is a modern distortion of events. First, this new analysis owed much to the method of coordinates, and further, many believed that Cartesian analysis was adequate to deal with the whole field of algebraic curves (which Descartes called geometric curves), which are expressible as equations and which the master distinguished from their mechanical counterparts (such as the cycloid or any logarithmic solution of a differential equation), mentioned only in a cursory manner in a few letters. That was the view of a number of 18th-century geometers, including Michel Rolle and the abbé Jean-Paul de Gua de Malves. More significantly, what was at issue in this development of geometry was a detailed mastery of dimension and number.

Desargues had intellectual "nephews" of his own. In addition to Pascal and his *Essay pour les coniques* (1640; Essay on Conic Sections), Philippe de la Hire deserves mention. La Hire continued the projective study of conic sections and produced the first example of plane homology as early as 1673, in his *Nouvelle méthode en géométrie pour les sections des superficies coniques et cylindriques* (New Method in Geometry for the Sections of Conic and Cylindrical Surfaces). Then in 1685 he presented a synthesis based on harmonic division, which appeared as part of his major treatise *Sectiones Conicae* (Conic Sections). Also noteworthy is Jacques-François Le Poivre, who in 1704, in Paris and again in 1708, at Mons published a treatise in which curves were related by means of relief. But to consider Desargues's ideas simply in terms of conic sections is to take too narrow a view of a matter that was in the forefront throughout the 18th century, as evidenced in the interest shown in it by two of the greatest intellects at the turn of the century: Leibniz and Newton. Leibniz, for example, wrote in a letter to Huygens dated 8 September 1679: "I believe we need another strictly linear or geometrical analysis, which will explain *situm* directly, as algebra expresses *magnitudem*." In 1704 Newton would propose, in his *Enumeratio Linearum Tertii Ordinis* (Enumeration of Lines of the Third Order), an analytic classification of third-order curves, which owed much to a synthetic vision based on the work of Desargues.

Descartes's concept of algebra remained that of a geometer attached to the classical objectives of geometry—even if his analytic method set out to go beyond the ancients—and of a philosopher for whom extension and matter were one and the same. Desargues's pre-projective vision and Pascal's establishment of the concept of space displayed a more synthetic approach in both content and form, since both men were reluctant to use algebra and remained attached to a mode of exposition based on hypothesis and deduction. These apparent contradictions began to be resolved in the 18th century, for example with the treatment of curves of an order greater than two by Newton and his English and French followers, or with Clairaut's application of analytic geometry to surfaces and lines of double curvature (skew curves) in space.

Geometry in the 18th Century

In the *Encyclopédie*, Jean le Rond D'Alembert defines geometry as "the science of the properties of extension, insofar as it is considered simply as extended and represented." This definition does not mention space explicitly and is limited to speaking of extension, both as a noun and an adjective. Though it may seem enigmatic today, the definition is clarified in the *Discours préliminaire* (1753; Preliminary Discourse) to the *Encyclopédie*, in which D'Alembert distinguishes two kinds of extension: on the one hand, the "impenetrable," extension of a body, and on the other hand, extension as the location of a body, that is, the portion of space occupied by a body. Geometry, then, was the study of this second kind of extension and its relationships of form and size. Here we see that the Greek definition of geometry was joined by the concept of space as defined by Pascal and Newton.

This concept of space, which remains implicit in the entry "Géométrie" (Geometry), becomes explicit in the entry "Mécanique" (Mechanics), in which D'Alembert writes that the idea of movement "presupposes a space whose parts are permeable and immobile." The notion of space could, it seemed, be more clearly explained in terms of mechanics than in terms of geometry. As Pascal had stated a century earlier, the concept of space was linked to the idea of the void, which was a necessary condition for the existence of movement—an idea that was again adopted by 18th-century mechanists. Some time after D'Alembert, Leonhard Euler explains in his *Lettres à une princesse d'Allemagne, sur divers sujets de physique et de philosophie* (1768–72; Letters of Euler to a German Princess, on Different Subjects in Physics and Philosophy) that space "merely provides a place for bodies to occupy and fill," specifying that "such a space without bodies is termed a *void* [stressed by Euler], and a void is thus an extension without bodies."

If space were the location of geometric phenomena (bodies), the purpose of geometry was to study these bodies from the standpoint of their size and shape. Furthermore, added to the traditional objects of Greek geometry were those new objects that had been systematically studied since the previous century, namely curves. This study was made possible by the new "analytic" methods derived from the application of algebra (including infinitesimal calculus) to geometry. Geometry was thus defined by the objects it studied, and to the geometers of the empiricist 18th century, these objects remained the fruit of sensory knowledge, which is not to say that the objects were associated with empirical knowledge alone. This explains how the objects could play a part in what the Encyclopedists termed "mixed phenomena." In this light we may understand, for example, the connection that arose between the new infinitesimal study of curves, derived from the work of Newton and Leibniz, and the study of mechanics.

It was this mixed mathematics, however, that finally gave rise to the elimination of the object, eclipsed by calculus at the end of the century. Such was the achievement of the comte de Lagrange in his *Mécanique analytique* (Analytic Mechanics), which was first published in 1788. In this work Lagrange expresses what may be taken as a "profession of faith":

> No figures will be found in this work. The methods I present here call neither for constructions nor for geometrical or mechanical reasoning, but simply for algebraic operations, submitted to a regular and uniform method. Those who favor Analysis will be delighted to see that Mechanics becomes a new branch of it, and will be grateful to me for having extended its domain.

From the standpoint of the history of science, it appears that it was the need to understand mixed phenomena that led 18th-century scientists to distance themselves from empiricism in their study of the natural sciences. A comparison between D'Alembert's *Traité de dynamique* (1743; Treatise on Dynamics) and Lagrange's *Mécanique analytique* clearly illustrates this point.

Paradoxically, but perhaps significantly, it was at the moment when analytic reductionism was becoming more extreme in the work of Lagrange that the current of thought derived from perspective became fully developed in the work of Gaspard Monge (who was closely involved with both methods), and then in that of Nicolas-Léonard Sadi Carnot and Poncelet. In fact, since the time of Desargues and Pascal the perspectivist current had never really completely disappeared. It remained active in the field of perspective itself, as seen in the work of Willem Jacob 'sGravesande and Brook

Taylor on central perspective, of Guarino Guarini on multiple projections, and of Johann-Heinrich Lambert on the application of perspective to geometry, or even in the progress made toward homology by Abraham Bosse and Ennemond Alexandre Petitot by means of relief perspective. The perspectivist current is also seen in the application of conic and cylindrical projections to the properties of curves, as shown by La Hire and Le Poivre for conic sections, and by Newton, Clairaut, Gua de Malves, and Murdoch for higher degree curves.

Algebra and Geometry: A Formal Distinction?

In the classification of sciences presented in the *Encyclopédie*, two major mathematical topics appear: arithmetic and geometry. Each is given its own field: the science of numbers, on the one hand, and the science of extension (in the sense explained above), on the other. Algebra (including infinitesimal calculus) appears under the heading of "Arithmetic," although it plays a double role. It appears both as the "science of the calculation of magnitudes in general" and as a method of studying problems arising in the various sciences. Whereas, the objects of geometry and mechanics are "material and palpable," according to the *Encyclopédie*:

> The principles of Algebra are concerned only with purely intellectual concepts, with ideas that we form for ourselves through abstraction, by simplifying and generalizing primary ideas; thus these principles, strictly speaking, contain only what we have put into them, and that which is most simple in our perceptions; they are in a sense our own creation.

But this distinction did not prevent D'Alembert from proposing a nuanced system of permutations among various fields of science. He discusses not only the application of algebra or of analysis—the latter being the use of algebra to find unknown quantities—to geometry, but also the application of geometry to algebra, the application of both geometry and algebra to mechanics, the application of mechanics to geometry, and the application of geometry and analysis to physics. These combinations of applications should be viewed as indicative of the interrelationships that were developing among the various fields of science.

The Subdivisions of Geometry

Once it has defined geometry in terms of its domain of study, the article "Géométrie" describes different ways of dividing the subject up, first into elementary geometry and transcendental geometry and then into ancient geometry and modern geometry. Elementary geometry deals only with "the properties of straight lines, circular lines, and the simplest figures and solids—in other words, rectilinear figures and solids bounded by such figures." Transcendental geometry, on the other hand, is "specifically that which is concerned with all the different curves of the circle, such as conic sections and curves of a higher order." Let us note that the term "transcendental" refers here to the general study of curves and differs from Leibniz's terminology, introduced at the beginning of the century, which distinguishes algebraic curves (defined by a polynomial equation) from transcendental curves (all others). The *Encyclopédie*'s distinction appears less restrictive than that of Descartes, who wanted to limit his method's field of application, and more effective than D'Alembert's, which would nonetheless persist into the 19th century—for example, in Gergonne's *Journal*.

The second division proposed in the *Encyclopédie* distinguishes between ancient geometry, "that which does not use analytic calculus, or which uses ordinary analytic calculus," and modern geometry, "that which uses Descartes's analysis in the investigation of the properties of curves, or that which uses the new calculus."

The Curve As Instrument and As Object of Study

Descartes's systematic study of curves never progressed beyond an outline, and his extension of that study to the realm of space remained a mere plan, as it did for Fermat. Following a few specific studies by Philippe de La Hire, Antoine Parent, Jean Bernouilli, and Henri Pitot, it was Clairaut who ultimately succeeded in producing a systematic study of skew curves, in his *Recherches sur les courbes à double courbure* (1733; Research on Double-Curved Curves). In this work Clairaut defines a skew curve by the two equations of two projecting cylinders, after noting that an equation with three variables defines a two-dimensional locus—in other words, a surface—and that a curve in the third dimension requires such equations, certain combinations of which, deficient in the x, y, or z term, represent projecting cylinders. In short, it is a kind of reciprocal "duction," to use the term employed a century earlier by Grégoire de Saint-Vincent to designate a method of producing certain solids. The curve will be plane so long as there exists one such combination of the first degree. The concept of double curvature in Clairaut's work led, among other things, to that of torsion, which was fully expounded by Euler and formulated analytically by a pupil of Monge, Michel-Ange Lancret, in 1806.

Newton, with his enumeration of cubic curves, achieved a synthesis between the Cartesian approach and Desargues's ideas as early as the beginning of the 18th century. He in fact proposed a classification based

both on the consideration and the reduction of the general equation, and on the extension to the third degree of various concepts imported from the theory of conic sections, such as the concept of diameter, which became the locus of the centers of gravity of the three points of intersection of a parallel sheaf of transversal lines, that of the asymptote (three at most), possibly considered as a "tangent at infinity," and that, adapted, of the right or transversal side. Desargues' influence is particularly evident in a paragraph on the shading of curves, which essentially states that cubic curves are projections of five curves, which he calls "divergent parabolas" (having the equation $y2 = ax^3 + bx^2 + cx + d$, the separation into five cases resulting from the factorization of the right-hand side). This paragraph is somewhat oracular, inasmuch as the property is given without demonstration, and is accompanied by a conjecture as to the existence of a finite number of curves of a given higher order from which all the others may be derived by shading. The paragraph led a number of English geometers and followers of Newton, such as Colin MacLaurin and James Stirling, to review the master's enumeration, increasing it by means of his criteria from 72 to 76—a number that Gua de Malves would raise by a further two cases. Furthermore, Plücker produced a typology of 219 varieties in his *System der analytischen Geometrie* (1835; System of Analytic Geometry). The English geometers would also attempt the enumeration of higher degrees.

But the thinkers whose insights must closely resembled those of Newton, Clairaut and Nicole in two *Mémoires* (1731), the abbé de Bragelongne in various *Mémoires* during the same decade, Gua de Malves in his *Usage de l'analyse de Descartes* (1740; Uses of Descartes's Analysis), and Patrick Murdoch in his edition of Newton's treatise *Neutoni Genesis Curvarum per Umbras* (1746; Newton's Creation of Curves with Shadows). The reasoning of these writers was in keeping with the cautious spirit of Newton, who would accept the results of analytic calculus only if the working and final result were matched by a clearly explicable synthetic geometric process. Clairaut proved the theorem of the five cones of the third order by means of an ingenious substitution of unknowns in the homogeneous equation of a cone resting on a cubic curve, which foreshadowed the use of homogeneous coordinates. Gua de Malves, following in Rolle's footsteps, set out to demonstrate the correspondence between the various irregularities of algebraic representation and certain geometric attributes (double points, inflection, asymptotes, infinite branches, etc.) when they were projected from one plane to another. Murdoch approached the question from a projective standpoint, displacing the neutral plane (parallel to the plane of projection and passing through the viewer's vantage point) in parallel to itself or in rotation around the axis of the viewer. As can be seen, there were numerous approaches, ranging from the analytic to the synthetic, by way of a mixed approach that foreshadowed the methods of Monge or Poncelet. Nonetheless, this research remained relatively marginal or private, marked as it was by an attachment to synthetic geometry or to an analytic method that excluded the advances made by infinitesimal calculus, and the mathematical community was more influenced by Cramer's and Euler's calculations concerning algebraic curves.

Synthetic Geometry and Practical Geometry: A Combination Born of Circumstance

Geometry, while figurative, has always been marked by its physical origins. During the 18th century there were treatises on the sphere and on plane and spherical trigonometry, inspired by astronomical and geodesic problems and relating to a description of the terrestrial globe or the canopy of the heavens. There were also dissertations on perspective, stonecutting, and sundial design, theoretical works on the layout of fortifications and garden design, manuals of civil architecture, and collections of mathematical puzzles. In short, the 18th century abundantly continued a tradition begun during the Renaissance in response to both civil and military needs—needs that were accentuated by the proliferation of schools (chiefly military), which offered scientific training. But then this process began to be reversed because a number of practical disciplines had reached an advanced stage of theoretical development from which they would henceforth contribute to geometry itself. It is worth noting a few examples of this tendency.

Following the theoretical breakthrough of perspective in the field of conic sections, Brook Taylor developed his own axiomatic principles of perspective by systematically—and for the first time—using the geometry of incidence in space. Then Johann Heinrich Lambert solved some fundamental problems of plane geometry through the use of an appropriate perspective, such as the plotting with only a ruler of a line parallel to a given straight line, passing through a given point, with the aid of a known parallelogram on the same plane.

The work carried out by Desargues on the inchoate concept of the invariant not only induced Newton, La Hire, and Le Poivre to devise plane transformations for curves (the forerunners of our plane homologies) but it also led Abraham Bosse, in the 17th century, and thereafter, in the late 18th century, Petitot in France and Breysig in Germany to conceive geometric solutions for the creation of bas-reliefs. These results, added to the research in the field of artistic perspective, culminated

in the concept of relief perspective, that is in Poncelet's spatial homology.

Similarly, Amédée-François Frézier's advances in the field of stonecutting were among the elements of applied geometry that led Monge to develop descriptive geometry, which was itself something of a mixture between the graphic techniques used in engineering and the analysis of curves and surfaces. All these explorations led in the same direction, stretching from Lazare Carnot's theory of transversals to Jean-Victor Poncelet's projective geometry, which was developed in the first years of the 19th century.

Parallel Lines

When D'Alembert writes in his *Essais sur les éléments de philosophie* (Essays on the Elements of Philosophy) of the "scandal of geometry," referring to the question of the parallel postulate, it is not the truth of the postulate that is in doubt—D'Alembert assumes that this pronouncement—on which rests the whole of geometry, from the method used by the Greeks to calculate area to the system of coordinates—must be true. But he argues that this assertion does not belong among the axioms of geometry—"propositions evident in themselves"—and therefore it has to be proven. The scandal lies in the failure of the attempts to prove Euclid's dictum.

Such a proof was the goal of a work by Saccheri, published in 1733 with the significant title *Euclides ab Omni Noevo Vindicatus: Sive Conatus Geometricus quo Stabiliuntur Prima ipsa Geometriæ Principia* (Euclid Cleared of Every Defect; or, A Geometrical Essay in Which the Very First Principles of Geometry Are Consolidated). Saccheri continues the tradition of proofs by reductio ad absurdum that was inaugurated by the Arab geometers, although the line of transmission leading from the work of the Arabs to the European geometers of the 18th century is unknown, if indeed it exists. Saccheri bases his approach on a figure studied by Omar Khayyam in the 11th century. Taking an isosceles trapezoid with right angles at its base, what will be the values of the other two angles? They can readily be shown to be equal. Three possibilities then follow, depending on whether these angles are right, obtuse, or acute. It can readily be shown that if they are right angles, the parallel postulate is proven. Saccheri easily eliminates the possibility that the angles are obtuse, leaving only the possibility that they are acute. He is unable to show that the latter hypothesis entails a contradiction, so he concludes by declaring that "the hypothesis of the acute angle is absolutely false, since it is contrary to the nature of the straight line."

This appeal to the straight line raises the issue of the very definition of such a line. A few years later D'Alembert, after alluding to the difficulties of the theory of parallel lines, writes that the proof of the parallel postulate "would be more easily found if we had a satisfactory definition of the straight line"—an implied criticism of the classical definition, which stated that a straight line is the shortest route between two points. Thus D'Alembert's critique went beyond the single question of the parallel postulate to take up the problem of defining the objects of geometry, including the primary objects. According to Descartes, these primary objects were among the clear and evident ideas accepted by everybody, or—in Pascal's words—belonged to the class of "things so well known in themselves that we have no clearer terms with which to explain them."

There were further attempts to prove the postulate of parallel lines although we are unable to cite them all here. In 1763 Klügel published a critical study of these proofs and in doing so raised the question of whether such a proof was possible. This text was then cited by Johann Heinrich Lambert in one of the most important studies on the theory of parallel lines prior to the discovery of the non-Euclidean geometries, the *Theorie der Parallellinien* (1766; Theory of Parallel Lines). Lambert notes that the parallel postulate holds true if the fourth angle of a quadrilateral having three right angles is also a right angle. Considering such a quadrilateral, he examines the three possible cases. The fourth angle is either right, obtuse, or acute. It should be noted that this problem had been addressed in the 10th century by Abu 'Ali al-Hasan ibn al-Haytham (also known as Alhazen), although here again the connection between that work and modern geometry is unknown. Considering the consequences of each hypothesis, Lambert notes that while the hypothesis of the obtuse angle is incompatible with the primary postulates of geometry, it holds true in the case of a sphere if one considers the great circles as straight lines. The relationship between trigonometric lines and hyperbolic lines (which Lambert has introduced by comparing the analytic representations of a circle and an equilateral hyperbola) then enables him to show that the hypothesis of the acute angle is true for a sphere of imaginary radius $r\sqrt{-1}$. He is thus able to show that following the right-angle hypothesis the sum of the angles of a triangle is equal to two right angles and the postulate of parallel lines holds true, while according to the obtuse angle hypothesis the sum of the angles of a triangle exceeds two right angles by a quantity proportional to the area of the triangle. And finally follows the acute angle hypothesis the sum of the angles of a triangle is less than two right angles by a quantity proportional to the area of the triangle.

While Lambert could not prove that plane geometry implied the right-angle hypothesis, thus leaving the problem of parallel lines unresolved, he at least showed that the three hypotheses were coherent by clarifying what would come to be known as non-Euclidean geo-

metric models. In this sense he highlighted, if not non-Euclidean geometry, then at least geometric constructions distinct from Euclidean geometry. He did not go so far as to consider the possibility that conventional geometry might not satisfy the postulate of parallel lines. This would happen in the following century. But that was to require a radical reassessment of geometric concepts, as Gauss would explain in a letter of 1817 to Olbers:

> I grow more and more convinced that the necessary truth of our geometry cannot be proven, or at least not by or for human reason.. Perhaps in another existence we may obtain an understanding of the nature of space that is at present beyond our reach. Until that time we should not place geometry on a level with arithmetic, whose truth is purely a priori, but rather on a level with mechanics.

Finally, Legendre's the proofs must also be noted—both because they represent the last great attempt before the birth of non-Euclidean geometry and because Legendre set out, in the context of a return to strict Euclidean principles in the teaching of geometry (see below), to give a proof that could be included in an elementary syllabus. To this end, proofs of the parallel postulate appear in the various editions of the *Éléments de Géométrie* (Elements of Geometry), which were published between 1794 and the author's death in 1833. Moreover, shortly before his death, in response to his critics, Legendre published a memoir in which he restates his various proofs. Each of the proofs is based on an obvious truth subsequently known to be equivalent to the postulate of parallel lines. Regarding the contested assertion that any straight line passing through a point inside an angle must meet at least one of its sides, Legendre remarks: "For it goes against the nature of the straight line that such a line, prolonged indefinitely, could be enclosed within an angle."

Legendre's words seem to echo those of Saccheri. As a man of the 18th century, schooled in Enlightenment empiricism (which should perhaps be distinguished from the empiricism that Gauss, in the letter to Olbers quoted above, or Lobachevsky would invoke to explain their positions regarding the problem of parallel lines), Legendre was unable to conceive that the parallel postulate might be wrong. He had, after all, written at the beginning of his *Éléments de géométrie* that "an *axiom* is a property evident in itself. A *theorem* is a truth that becomes evident by means of a process of reasoning called *proof*."

Enlightenment empiricism once again led some geometers at the end of the 18th century to seek a more obvious postulate than that of parallel lines. There was

Laplace, for example, taking his lead from observations by Wallis, proposed a postulate based on the existence of similar figures. Here again 18th-century empiricism, for which rational knowledge was an extension of sensory knowledge, should be distinguished from post-Kantian empiricism (in the sense of a reaction to Kant), which tends toward a distinction between empirical knowledge and the rational constructs designed to make it intelligible.

New Pedagogical Concerns

The teaching of mathematics, and specifically of geometry, evolved significantly in France over the 17th and 18th centuries—an evolution that entailed some questioning of established pedagogical assumptions. The Euclidean corpus, while still relevant from an elementary standpoint, could no longer be presented in its synthetic form once the new Cartesian analysis appeared on the scene. In particular, the whole treatment of proportion and the handling of irrationality were simplified as a result of the algebraic interpretation of geometry. The first attempts to rewrite geometry according to the new order occurred in the work of Pascal and the philosophers of Port-Royal, such as Arnauld, who was closely followed by several geometers from the teaching orders, such as the Oratorian Bernard Lamy. Next, Clairaut, with his *Éléments de géométrie,* and the abbé de La Chapelle, with his *Institutions de géométrie* (Fundamentals of Geometry), tried to suggest a "natural" approach that would open the way to a reinvention, so to speak, of geometric truths. Nonetheless, at the end of the century there was a partial return to Euclidean rigor, as seen in the works of Legendre and Lacroix, which were intended for the use of the *écoles centrales* (forerunners of the modern *lycées*) established by the French Revolution. On the other side of the English Channel the Euclidean tradition, which had not received such vigorous criticism as it had in France, had remained stronger through the teachings of Simson and Playfair.

Finally, mention should be made of the importance of elementary geometry (extended to encompass the properties of the most notable curves, such as conic sections) in the syllabi of the military schools and of the entrance examinations for the *grandes écoles* (France's most prestigious institutions of higher education) set up under the ancien régime and then during the Revolution and Consulate—the Écoles Centrales (schools of engineering, arts, and sciences), the École Normale (training school for teachers and researchers) of Year III in the Revolutionary calendar (1795), and the École Polytechnique (polytechnical school). A number of mathematicians devoted themselves to writing pedagogical works, which proliferated in the second half of the century, such as the treatises by Camus, Bossut, and Bezout, and then those of Legendre and Lacroix referred to above.

RUDOLF BKOUCHE AND JEAN-PIERRE LE GOFF

See also Algebra; Astronomy; Function; Mathematics; Mechanics, Analytic

Further Reading

Bkouche, Rudolph, "La naissance du projectif," in *Mathématiques et philosophie de l'antiquité à l'age classique,* edited by Roshdi Rashed, Paris: Éditions du Centre National de la Recherche Scientifique, 1991

Bonola, Roberto, *Non-Euclidean Geometry,* translated by H.S. Carslaw, Chicago: Open Court, 1912; reprint, New York: Dover, 1955 (original Italian edition, 1906)

Boyer, Carl B., *History of Analytic Geometry,* New York: Scripta Mathematica, 1956

Le Goff, Jean-Pierre, "Un auteur méconnu: Jacques-François Le Poivre, et une oeuvre oubliée: *Le traité des sections du cone . . . ,* Mons, 1708," *Cahiers de la perspective* 6 (June 1993)

Le Goff, Jean-Pierre, "Un mémoire d'Alexis-Claude Clairaut (1713–1765): *Sur les courbes que l'on forme en coupant une surface courbe quelconque, par un plan donné de position et sur les courbes du troisième ordre* (1731)," *Cahiers de la perspective* 6 (June 1993)

Le Goff, Jean-Pierre, "*Les recherches sur les courbes à double courbure* (Paris 1731) d'Alexis-Claude Clairaut (1713–1765)," *Cahiers de la perspective* 6 (June 1993)

Germany

The *Frühaufklärung* (Dawn of the Enlightenment)

Beginning at the end of the 17th century, scholars and universities propagated a new mode of thought and action guided by rational pragmatism. During the progressive secularization that occurred in the 18th century, this new spirit, which Germans would call the *Aufklärung*, was implemented in nearly every domain, its development being shaped by a very specific religious and political context. The country had been divided by confessionalism and was slowly recovering after the 30 Years' War. In the heart of the Holy Roman Empire, the borders between the territorial states were reinforced and regional differences became more marked. Ultimately, the political fragmentation and religious fission favored the birth of an Enlightenment that took on many specifically Germanic aspects, the fruit of anti-religious and anti-ecclesiastical criticism.

Recent research into the 18th century reveals the *Frühaufklärung* (from 1680 to 1720–30) to have been a transition period between the baroque era and the Enlightenment. Although changes in Germany were initially limited to philosophy and the sciences (including natural sciences), nonetheless, these changes represented a veritable "intellectual earthquake" (see Schneiders). In the realm of philosophy, natural law was becoming conspicuously secular; its first definitions appeared in the works of Christian Thomasius and in Gottfried Wilhelm Leibniz's *Metaphysische Abhandlung* (1686; Discourse on Metaphysics). In 1687 Thomasius delivered a speech on the imitation of the French, but present-day research does not regard the *Frühaufklärung* as an emulation of French or English philosophy. From the beginning, in fact, the German Enlightenment followed a theological line, which generated a debate specifically opposed to tradition in general and to established religion in particular. Theology was largely supplanted by metaphysics, juridical science was transformed into political philosophy, and philosophy, based on method and reason, was raised to the ranks of a science par excellence.

This Enlightenment was not born at the court of the emperor of Germany, nor in the capitals and royal residence towns, but in the commercial and university towns, particularly in Leipzig and Halle. In Leipzig, host of the largest commercial fair in the country, there was no lack of wealthy merchants. The university there was open to new ideas, although the Lutheran orthodoxy kept close watch to make sure that this new enthusiasm for innovation did not become immoderate. Prohibited from teaching or publishing in 1690, Thomasius left Leipzig and moved to Prussia, where he was invited, thanks to the good offices of Samuel von Pufendorf, to participate in the creation of the University of Halle. There, at least in the beginning, Thomasius supported Pietism and its establishment in Halle; the schools and foundations set up in that city by August Hermann Francke were much-admired throughout Europe and achieved a synthesis between the Enlightenment and Pietism, despite everything that might set the two movements apart.

However, in these early days of the Enlightenment the dissemination of new ideas was not the privilege of philosophers and men of letters alone. Scientists, jurists, as well as free-thinking theologians sought the light of a "natural" and "free" rationality, and they demanded the right to utter criticism about prejudices, tradition, and authority. Those who had inspired the European Enlightenment enjoyed a wide reception: René Descartes and Francis Bacon were read; Thomas Hobbes, John Locke, Sir Isaac Newton, and Baruch Spinoza were discussed; Pierre Bayle and Bernard Le Bovier de Fontenelle were quoted. Pufendorf set the tone for the entire course of the Enlightenment by founding natural law on anthropology. From his proposition that, despite humanity's faults, society was governed by *ratio* (reason), Pufendorf developed an image of a human nature inseparable from the community. Everything that benefited the community was a precept of natural law. His two major works, *De Jure Naturae et Gentium Libri Octo* (1672; The Law of Nature and Nations) and *De Officio Hominis et Civis Juxta Legem Naturalem Libri Duo* (1673; Two Books on the Duty of Man and Citizen according to the Natural Law), laid the foundations for the vast debate on natural law that would engage the 18th century. As for the natural sciences, their rise could be felt even in poetry and philosophical methodology; theologically, it was through "physico-theology" that the natural sciences acquired their letters patent. Nature, the site of apprenticeship through sensory experience, was taken seriously, for God's word could be heard in its beauty and purpose.

Before the birth of radical biblical criticism, even before Bayle and the anti-traditionalism he expressed in his *Dictionnaire historique et critique* (1697; An Historical and Critical Dictionary), institutional religion—the established churches—had already suffered a severe blow from Gottfried Arnold and his *Unpartheyische Kirchen- und Ketzer-historie* (1699–1700; Impartial History of the Church and Heretics). Adopting a mystical and separatist position that did not altogether conform to Pietist principles, Arnold demonstrated with great scholarship that the Church had entered a period of decadence as early as the decline in devotion among the first Christians.

Both in theory and in practice, the *Frühaufklärung* bore the distinctive stamp of a vehement anti-traditionalism—thus, this movement cannot lay complete claim to the adherence of someone like Gottfried Wilhelm Leibniz, who hoped to bring about reform by allying the old and the new. A concept that Leibniz created from scratch, the monad—that is, the unity of strength and conscience, an indivisible and individual substance—made possible the hypothesis of a "preestablished harmony" of body and soul. Fundamentally optimistic, Leibniz declared that man was responsible for his world, which enabled that same world to be considered independently of God. It was in this way that philosophy became emancipated from theology; in the 18th century, theology would be replaced by metaphysics.

For his part, Thomasius endeavored to create a framework for a practical philosophy for men here on Earth, contending that the reasonable and virtuous life is not necessarily the sole preserve of scholars and philosophers. His success was undeniable, as the great number of reprints of most of his works demonstrates: his *Einleitung in die Sittenlehre* (1692; Introduction to Moral Philosophy) went through eight editions, compared to only one for its Latin translation (1706). For the educated public that was slowly emerging, these writings served as an initiation to the Enlightenment. Thomasius's entire work gravitated around his ethic of love, which posited love as the very essence of humanity: a rational love for one's fellows, a personal affection whose ideal illustration would be perfect love between man and woman. An outcome of this rational nature, communicative and capable of love, is *socialitas* (sociability). In his thinking about prejudice, Thomasius nevertheless recognized that man hinders himself through his anxiety, his nonrational love, and his tendency to cling to his prejudices. As an antidote, the philosopher advocated the courage to search out new truths for oneself. The apprenticeship of the free examination of self presupposes that one will renounce the help of others, that one will reject the usual references and apply oneself to perceiving reality through one's senses, in order to arrive at one's own conception of reality.

Christian Wolff also argued that all criticism must result first and foremost from an eclectic thought process. He adopted and amended the Aristotelian tradition, already abandoned by the Leipzig philosophers at the beginning of the Enlightenment. At the instigation of mathematician and philosopher Ehrenfried Walter von Tschirnhaus, he applied the mathematical method to philosophy. In this respect Wolff was modern, yet he was more conservative where the critical adoption of metaphysics was concerned; he became the representa-tive par excellence of academic philosophy and attracted many followers. According to Wolff, it was possible to cause knowledge to progress, antinomies to disappear, and the mind to attain truth, provided that clear concepts were used, that one principle was deduced from another, and that a strict reasoning was followed. Wolff's ambition was to incorporate the encyclopedic knowledge of his era into a universal system: his mathematical method was supposed to enable the mind to conceive all objects.

Outside of the Republic of Letters, the public of the late 17th and early 18th centuries read edifying works, when they read at all. At the turn of the century, many state civil servants still could not read. Even in 1740, when 72 percent of the titles published in Germany were in German (the remaining 28 percent were published in Latin), 19 percent of those German texts were works of edification, compared to only 6 percent devoted to belles lettres. Under such difficult conditions, the Enlightenment owed a great deal to the press. The various *Spectators*, or moral periodicals, played a particularly important role between 1720 and 1760, occupying a privileged place among the early forms of entertaining didactic material. In addition, there were popular periodicals aimed at interested laymen, soon to be followed by enlightened newspapers, which began to appear around 1750.

The *Aufklärung* and Literary Genres

In the field of literature, the decades around 1700 were a period of transition: in its reevaluation of the baroque style, the literature of the *Frühaufklärung* distanced itself from the bombastic pompousness of such writers as Daniel Casper von Lohenstein, but it did not abandon the rhetorical tradition that was the foundation of baroque poetry. Christian Weise, a primary school teacher and poet, was a typical figure in this instable period. His novels and treatises (*Politischer Nascher* [1676; Political Nibbler], *Politischer Redner* [1677; Political Orator]) propagated a new conception of politics: spreading well beyond the public sphere of the court, politics entered the private domain—moving from the collectivity of *Staatsklugheit* (public wisdom) to the confines of *Privatklugheit* (private wisdom). Action was no longer guided solely by political orientation but also by a curiosity of the mind and the senses, by the "entertainment" to be derived from new and unprecedented things, and finally by gallantry. "Gallant conduct" was the key to success in both court and town; people sought to please through their appearance, clothing, manners, and speech. Novels featuring gallantry contributed to a laxer public morality.

Whereas the novel would not achieve great popularity as the vehicle of the enlightened mind until the second half of the century, satire began enjoying a considerable following at a much earlier date. It was linked to no particular genre and could easily adapt to the form of the subject attacked: for example, that of the scholarly treatise by Christian Ludwig Liscow or of the dictionary entry by Gottlieb Wilhelm Rabener. Whether personal, general, or social, satire attempted to instruct and amend by means of the *Witz* (witty joke). From the writings of Christoph Martin Wieland to those of Adolf von Knigge, satire, in the form of character comedies or satiric sections slipped into the text of a novel, frequently irritated the censor.

The fable was the ideal genre to meet the need for moral and pedagogical stimulation so vital to the Enlightenment. As in the earlier rhetorical tradition, the fictional example was intended to convince and instruct the reader. Just as satire had done, the fable took on a more literary and aesthetic air during the 18th century; from the moralizing tone of the verse tales by Christian Fürchtegott Gellert there was a shift to the self-scrutiny of Gotthold Ephraim Lessing's prose fables. Another form of writing common to the Enlightenment was the didactic poem; sometimes called the "philosophical" or "moral" poem, it rose to the rank of a separate genre in the poetic art of the *Aufklärung*. Barthold Heinrich Brockes and Albrecht von Haller (*Über den Ursprung des Übels* [1734; On the Origin of Evil]) excelled in the genre and heralded the beginning of a specific enlightened trend in poetry.

Between 1680 and 1730, theatre in the German language was a broad mix of the classical and the new: the baroque style of heroic and pathetic tragedy gave way to the first incarnations of the bourgeois drama. If one name is inseparable from the establishment of a new German theatre and the emergence of a coherent discourse about poetry, it is that of Johann Christoph Gottsched. In the footsteps of Thomasius and Wolff, Gottsched subjected the main genres of literary culture to critical scrutiny. Translator of and commentator on the writings of several enlightened French philosophers (among his translations was that of Bayle's *Dictionnaire*), he was also a theoretician of poetic art (*Versuch einer critischen Dichtkunst* [1730; Attempt at a Critical Poetics for the Germans]), as well as a poet, linguist, and rhetorician. Thus, when the idea of a reform of the theatre was born around 1730, Gottsched immediately put that idea to work for the promotion of culture and morality, creating for this purpose a kind of tragedy whose substance was "not tragic"—the idea was, above all, to give a rational and "moral" image of the world based on a concrete example.

When Gottsched banned all emotional excess and all comedy from his reformist system, his ideas soon provoked a reaction: in the 1720s the Zurich-based Swiss school, inspired by the English and French models and led by Johann Jakob Bodmer and Johann Jakob Breitinger, rose up against this supremacy of reason, initially expressing their views in a moral periodical intended to enlighten conservative minds. This school did not abandon the principle of imitation, but it sought to free poetic art from the constraints of realism, from the reasonable and the natural, by exhorting poets not to disdain the possible and the magical. Creativity, the realm of imagination and wonder, should fascinate readers through novelty, speak to the heart as well as the mind; the poet should instruct or amuse "wittily," to be sure, but also move and "touch" the feelings. In his *Critische Dichtkunst* (1740; Critical Poetics), Breitinger adopted in its entirety the new emotional aesthetic of the abbé Dubos and related that aesthetic to the cosmic model of Leibniz's *Die Theodicee* (1710; Theodicy). Borrowing from Leibniz "the imitation of nature in the possible," and placing the emphasis on the rhetorical *movere* (the doctrine of emotion, in opposition to Gottsched's *Witz* [Wit]), this poetic art outlined an aesthetic and poetic evolution that already heralded Friedrich Gottlieb Klopstock. The similarity of Bodmer and Breitinger's positions on aesthetics—the new discipline devoted to "sensory ideas"—has been pointed out. As for Siegmund Jakob Baumgarten, the most original of Wolff's disciples, he continued to rely on his master's method but he also acknowledged a quality inherent in inferior knowledge "based upon the senses." Since poetry was a "perfect discourse of the senses" (*Meditationes Philosophicae de Nonnulis ad Poema Pertinentibus* [1735; Reflections on Poetry]), then wonder was also capable of containing poetical attributes. This new discipline was not only a descriptive science about representation by means of the senses: it also had to show how to experience life through the senses. The aim of aesthetic education was to "perfect one's sensory knowledge."

In lyrical poetry these new elements were put into practice, even before Klopstock, by Immanuel Jakob Pyra, by the *Bremer Beiträger* (1744–48), and by the Hainbund, a poetic coterie of undergraduates from Göttingen. If the perception of the world through one's senses could be conceived as *analogon rationis* (reasoning based on analogy), as a sensory representation of the world, then it was justifiable to adopt sensuality as an artistic theme and principle. Lessing, Heinrich Wilhelm von Gerstenberg, Johann Jakob Wilhelm Heinse, and Johann Wolfgang von Goethe, who had embarked on their poetic careers under the influence of rococo, were initially followers of this trend of enlightened sensationalism, which was welcomed and encouraged by an audience composed of patricians, tradesmen, students, and cultured ladies—a public Wieland had cultivated and who repaid him amply by supporting him.

To favor the development of a public forum for criticism, ostensibly apolitical methods, such as informal meetings, were also sought. Many viewed the national theatre as an instrument that was perfectly adapted to this purpose. Lessing drew up a reform plan for an enlightened, bourgeois, national theatre in his *Hamburgische dramaturgie* (1767–69; Hamburg Dramaturgy). With his penchant for detailed criticism, Lessing extended the analysis of plays and performances in order to tackle questions of mimicry, gestures, and declamation. Basing his arguments on individual examples, he was able to bring out the importance of the sociology of the audience and the theory of genres. The ethos of systematic deduction of rationalist poetic art repelled him. The highpoint of his dramaturgy is his definition of the basic principles of the theatre's functional aesthetic: therapeutic laughter in comedy, fear and self-pity reinforced by identification with the hero in tragedy. In *Emilia Galotti* (1772), as in his dramatic testament *Nathan der Weise* (1779; Nathan the Wise), dramatic conflicts, already in embryonic form in his earlier plays, were essentially conflicts between authority and freedom. Lessing condemned political violence and religious intolerance, but always through plots giving the example of an individual and his family.

Alongside Lessing in the dramatic and literary criticism spheres, or Wieland in the realm of the novel and verse narrative, Klopstock opened new ground for lyric poetry and lyricism in general. In his major epic, *Der Messias* (The Messiah) in 20 cantos, the first of which appeared in 1748 and which he reworked incessantly until the end of the century, he "psychologized" passion and rendered it divine: in order to "move" the soul of the reader, Klopstock used not only hexameters but also new stylistic and syntactic procedures, among them an audacious manipulation of space and time to produce a sense of "infinity" and abstract depth. He gained a well-deserved following. His odes and hymns speak to the heart; his expressive lyricism imbues the language with a hitherto unimagined musicality: the "flow of the words" is intended to match the impulses of the reader's soul.

The 18th century was the era of reason, morality, and feelings worthy of enlightenment. The notion of sensibility appeared about 1750, first in the form of tenderness, and was soon to pervade the moral register. The goal was to achieve a balance between the "head" and the "heart"; this collective mentality was the fruit of Pietist religiosity, which renders feelings hypersensitive, but also, and above all, it was indebted to the concept of moral sense, which came from England and Scotland. The heightened appeal to the imagination during a reading designed to arouse readers' emotions transformed the conditions of reception and the production of belles lettres.

The *Spätaufklärung* (Late Enlightenment)

In its final phase, the age of the Enlightenment was no longer so much a philosophical or literary movement as it was a moral and political one. Reformism did not spare a single sphere of public or private life. The "literary revolution" of the Sturm und Drang movement was the dynamic conclusion of the *Aufklärung,* but it also marked the beginning of a separation between literature and moral education; such was the theme of the autonomy of aesthetics postulated first by Karl Philipp Moritz in the mid-1780s, then by Goethe and Friedrich Schiller. While the Enlightenment continued its rapid development in northern and central Germany, southern Germany and Austria were more cautious about embracing its tenets. Sturm und Drang would not reach Vienna.

In Germany the *Spätaufklärung,* motivated by a concern for the general interest, practical activity, and social reform, began in the 1770s and reached its height with the moral pragmatism of the 1780s. But the debate of 1782–83, indicative of the crisis that was brewing, revealed the need for critical reflection about the Enlightenment. After the death of Frederick II, the political wind turned against the philosophers of the *Aufklärung,* particularly in Prussia and especially in Berlin. The French Revolution, and the sceptical and disapproving reception given to it in Germany, greatly helped the cause of conservatives and opponents of the Enlightenment. After the Restoration, the situation became increasingly difficult for the Enlightenment, and the movement gradually died out after 1820.

What Was the *Aufklärung?* Berlin Was Its Heart

Whether destined for failure or success, the attempts at enlightened reform (most often in the field of popular or peasant education) led to a vast debate on the Enlightenment, its nature and importance, its usefulness or its shortcomings: between 1779 and 1802 this debate in Germany gave rise to no less than 70 treatises, something observed in neither France nor England. At the beginning of the 1780s, *Aufklärung* was still essentially a synonym for intellectual, moral, and cultural progress. In Berlin enlightened minds gathered together from the most diverse origins—jurists, government clerks, theologians, philosophers, and physicians—founded a Society of the Friends of the Enlightenment, rebaptized the *Mittwochsgesellschaft* (Wednesday Society) in 1783, and devoted themselves to the "free examination of the truth in all its forms." From these weekly meetings was born, in January of the same year, the *Berlinische Monatsschrift,* published by Johann Erich Biester and Friedrich Gedike, and that periodical became the voice of the *Spätaufklärung.* In the September 1784 issue, Moses Mendelssohn published an article entitled "Über die Frage: Was heisst Aufklärung?" (On the Question: What Is Enlightenment?), where he defined the concepts of *Bildung* (education), *Kultur* (culture), and *Aufklärung*. *Bildung* is a generic concept that encompasses the two others. *Kultur* belongs to the aesthetic field (beauty in artistic and artisanal production, but also the polish of social customs), and *Aufklärung* encompasses rational knowledge and the faculty of reflection about humanity. Mendelssohn singled out in man a human vocation and a civic vocation, the latter of which depends upon one's social origins and profession. At a time when enlightened philosophers were examining the pragmatic and political aspects of their movement, he envisaged the possibility of a controversy between the "Enlightenment of man" and the "Enlightenment of the citizen" and cautiously denounced the risk of excesses, which might lead to irreligion and anarchy.

Three months later, in the same magazine, it was Immanuel Kant who would answer the question *Was ist Aufklärung?* (What Is Enlightenment?). In the spirit of criticism for its own sake that characterized the era and, to a considerable extent, bore the imprint of his three great works of criticism, Kant elevated in this essay freedom of examination to the rank of an enlightened principle par excellence. The *Aufklärung* should take as its motto *sapere aude* (dare to be wise). For Kant, freedom implies that one "must make public use of one's reason in every way." However, he limits freedom of expression to the Republic of Letters. In Prussia this republic enjoyed the liberalism of an enlightened king. Curiously, Kant makes the distinction, already criticized by his contemporaries, between the public use of reason, reserved for scholars, and the private use, which might be enjoyed by civil servants who were subjected to the principle of absolute obedience.

From the middle of the 18th century on, the ideas of the Enlightenment found in *Popularphilosophie* (popular philosophy) an important medium for popularization. Using as their starting point the hypothesis of an enlightened public who thought along a single line, the "popular" philosophers were especially attached to several principles: flexibility of language, beauty and grace of vocabulary, wealth of ideas, clarity and precision of argument. Authors such as J.J. Engel, J.G.H. Feder, Thomas Abbt, Christian Garbe, Mendelssohn, Johann August Eberhard, E. Platner, Christoph Friedrich Nicolai, Johann Georg Sulzer, C. Meiners, and Knigge dealt in their works with all aspects of social and private life, but in particular with enlightened morality. Contrary to the ethos of deduction inherent in academic philosophy, the "popular" philosophers conceived of their own ethos as a "moral doctrine based on experience." At the end of the century, *Popularphilosophie* suffered a seri-ous challenge. Kant, Reinhold, Johann Gottlieb Fichte, and later, Georg Wilhelm Friedrich Hegel—and their disciples—categorically rejected all popularization of their ideas, contending that to popularize philosophy was to distort it.

Political Enlightenment

At the end of the 18th century, Kant's notion of achieving maturity remained an ideal accessible to only a handful of privileged people. Social hierarchy prevailed, and the Enlightenment remained the prerogative of an educated middle class. Equality was constantly invoked (in the spirit of the Declaration of the Rights of Man) by the leaders of the Enlightenment, but the prevailing view was that it could not possibly be extended to the "lower rungs on the ladder." For the remaining nine-tenths of the population, the lower middle classes and the peasants, the only Enlightenment they could envisage was that "appropriate" to their status.

A number of literate people, essentially country preachers, were personally committed to educating "the people," an entity discovered during the final phase of the Enlightenment. These ecclesiastics, expressing themselves in the clerical newspapers of the era, considered their role to be that of "tutors to the people," and they regarded themselves to be equally responsible for the material well-being of their parishioners. From roughly the middle of the century onward, a number of treatises and travel tales reflected the growing interest of the enlightened economic press in the household and agricultural economy; questions were raised about the practical application of natural sciences and studies were undertaken of the daily life of the peasantry. Between 1742 and 1780, 500 gazettes and newspapers devoted to these issues were created, 100 of which were published by economic societies, and 100 others directly addressed rural society.

As for women, they were largely overlooked in the emancipation of humankind—that great idea of the Enlightenment. "Assistants" to men, women were subordinate in their work and in their persons. A few voices were raised, however, to demand an equality that went beyond that which women had already obtained in their lifestyles through education. Political and private equality were now demanded. It was time, commentators declared, to put an end to the humiliation of women, who spent their lives in the guardianship of men, and to demand for them both human rights and a citizen's rights. Some women did achieve emancipation by means of education and culture. Pietists and pedagogues such as Francke and Johann Bernhard Basedow became advocates of women's rights. Reading and studious isolation were the weapons these women wielded as they set out to conquer the intellectual and cultural world of men, and these tools enabled them also to start to think about themselves. Sophie von La Roche's works are a good illustration of female emancipation attempted simultaneously from "below" and "above."

The Jews, another social group on the fringes of this strongly hierarchical society, had even fewer rights than Christian women. Considered by the community to be foreigners—in the best case, regarded as "protected Jews"—members of the "Jewish nation" were tolerated by princes only because they served the rulers' economic and fiscal interests. In Germany Jewish emancipation in the spirit of the Enlightenment began in 1781, under the impetus of C.W. Dohm (a Prussian state counselor and a friend of Mendelssohn), whose work *Über die bürgerliche Verbesserung der Juden* (Concerning the Amelioration of the Civil Status of the Jews) sparked a public debate. Calling for access to education for the Jews, Dohm also aimed to enhance their social condition by drawing them away from commerce and into crafts and agriculture.

Beginning in 1750 Germany witnessed the establishment of associations whose members were not exclusively scholars. In addition to Masonic lodges, patriotic societies of general interest were founded, with the aim of democratizing access to new knowledge, to useful and applicable discoveries. It was the heyday of reading societies. Certain groups—the Bavarian Illuminati, for example—sought to open the way to Enlightenment through political power. The most radical among these people established popular societies and Jacobin clubs, such as the Mainz Society of Friends of Freedom and Equality (1792), but such "extremist" organizations would, in Germany, be short-lived. The common aim of all these groups was to bring about a "discursive" society, in which an autodidactic education was acquired through contact with kindred spirits, and in which enlightened principles were propagated through debate, lectures, newspapers, and literary prizes.

Bookstores and the Press

In the 18th century, bookstores still served as both publisher and shop and offered a wide range of books. By the 1770s Germany had a fairly dense network of publishing houses (roughly 220 bookstores); a growing number of works were published; and print runs of 1,000 copies were typical for most new publications. Between 1770 and 1780, 22 million books were available in the bookshops. This "deluge" of new titles was accompanied by a burgeoning of the press, with more and more titles in every specialized area. People complemented their newspaper reading with specialized journals; criticism became more subject-specific, with Nicolai, Lessing, and Mendelssohn laying down the principles of literary criticism. Berlin became the "capital" for criticism, being the city of the *Bibliothek der schönen Wissenschaften und der freyen Künste* (1757–65), of *Briefe, die neueste Litteratur betreffend* (1759–65), and of Nicolai's *Allgemeine Deutsche Bibliothek* (1765–1805), which reached 265 volumes. In 1788, however, Minister Wöllner's edict on censorship threatened the critical journals, among other publications, and for a time the production of such journals shifted to the town of Stettin.

By the 1770s the "scholarly journal," which consisted purely of reviews, had had its day. Beginning in 1772 Johann Heinrich Merck, Herder, and Goethe called for a necessary critical analysis in the *Frankfurter Gelehrte Anzeigen;* then Berlin's monopoly on criticism began to disappear with the birth in Jena/Halle of the *Allgemeine Literatur-Zeitung* (1785–1849). Literary debate spread beyond this critical press; new journals, such as Wieland's *Der teutsche Merkur* (1773–1810) or Boie and Dohm's *Deutsches Museum* (1776–88), gave a forum for expression to authors and even to the youngest among them. These new literary newspapers thus won public appreciation for their articles on political history.

Jacobin Literature

The term "Jacobin," which is not quite accurate (most of the authors were Girondins), designated pro-revolutionary literature, which hoped for a German revolution; questioned the legitimacy of violence and the best form the state could take; stood up for the rights of man; and criticized religion and the Church, the nobility, and despotism. Discussions on public law in the 17th and 18th centuries, the constitutional monarchy in England, and the revolutions in France and America were central themes in this literature. Between 1789 and 1806 revolutionary writing flourished in the major imperial cities, where authors enjoyed the liberal attitudes of the existing societies and relatively relaxed censorship standards. Nevertheless, revolutionary commitment remained limited to philosophy and literature. A new type of writer was appearing, who was more of a journalist, a reasoning and opinionated author. Changes in Europe quickly became known thanks to numerous translations and the exchanges of travel accounts. Authors such as Joachim Heinrich Campe, Georg Forster, Knigge, August Lamey, Georg Friedrich Rebmann, Friedrich Christian Laukhard, and Konrad Engelbert Oelsner all sought to condemn feudal traditions in their accounts of journeys to Paris, their political appeals, their pamphlets, poems, novels, and—during the brief life of the Republic of Mainz—their Jacobin dramas. They published political journals. After the Jacobins came to power in 1793, however, those authors lost a large portion of their readership.

The Protestant Enlightenment

At the end of the century, the Enlightenment stepped up its attacks on religious dogmatism. Wolffianism still sought a compromise between revelation and reason, and beginning in the 1740s an eclecticism had developed, seeking to ally Wolffian formalism with individual Pietist devotion; from the eclectic viewpoint, a difference could exist between dogma as taught to theologians and the principles preached to the faithful. Baumgarten, Johann Friedrich Wilhelm Jerusalem, and Johann Joachim Spalding advocated the incorporation of empirical religious subjectivity into theology. From the 1780s on, revealed ideas were interpreted as purely reasonable ideas, and revelation by Scripture became practically useless. Neologists such as Spalding and Jerusalem broke with the Lutheran dogmatic tradition. The Christian religion had become the religion of reason and was henceforth to be the instrument of propagation of a practical morality that would help man to fulfill his destiny. Based on an enlightened theological anthropology, neologism set its sights on the doctrine of original sin. This refusal to admit that doctrine is striking evidence of the "optimistic" anthropology that marked the era. The historical and critical method adopted by the neologists dealt a decisive blow to the hitherto uncontested authority of the Bible, and it was against this blow to its authority that Lessing was protesting when he complained that he could no longer differentiate, in this view of Christianity, between reason and Christian thought. By publishing the *Fragmente* (Fragments), excerpts from *Apologie oder Schutzschrift für die vernünftigen Verehrer Gottes* (1774–78; Apology; or, Written Defense for the Reasonable Worship of God), written by the Hamburg Orientalist Hermann Samuel Reimarus, Lessing scandalized the orthodox Lutherans as much as he scandalized the neologists. The themes set out by Reimarus (deist toleration; the links among reason, history, and revelation; and research on the life of Jesus) led to a heated debate between Lessing and Johann Melchior Goeze, the head pastor of Hamburg; this theological quarrel poisoned the last years of Lessing's existence. In *Nathan der Weise*, he used the theatre as a forum after he was prohibited from publishing other pamphlets against Goeze.

Herder did not affiliate himself with any particular theological trend. Like Johann Georg Hamann, he saw in the Scriptures the poetry and the mother tongue of humankind and wanted a "human" reading of it. Taking his inspiration from the historical biblical criticism of Johann Heinrich Martin Ernesti (Leipzig), Johann Salomo Semler (Halle), and Johann David Michaelis (Göttingen), Herder joined Hamann in attacking the literal theology of Michaelis. In his *Älteste Urkunde des Menschengeschlechts* (1776; The Oldest Record of the Human Race), Herder interprets the Book of Genesis as the most ancient document, as the eternal divine revelation. He discovers in the biblical texts the primitive poetry of a shepherding people in his *Vom Geist der hebräischen Poesie* (1782–83; The Spirit of Hebrew Poetry), and in *Gott, einige Gespräche* (1787; God: Some Conversations), he dares to make an apologia for Spinoza—a philosopher who also interested Lessing in the last years of his life. Finally, in *Christliche Schriften* (1796–97; Christian Writings), devoted to the Gospels, Herder warns against the risk of confusing these four texts with one another and insists on their individuality, each evangelist having painted his own portrait of Christ.

At the end of the century, the theologians of the Enlightenment, after a series of remarkable creations, finally accepted the fact that their discipline could no longer be the mother science that led to all others, and as a result they began to remodel their discipline.

The Catholic Enlightenment

The German *Aufklärer* (men of the Enlightenment) were almost all Protestant. In the Catholic territory (Rhineland, Westphalia, southern Germany, and Austria), it was primarily among the regular and secular clergy that the spirit of the Enlightenment found its followers—but this development did not occur until after 1763, when, by comparison, nearly two generations of Enlightenment thought had elapsed in Protestant Germany. The Catholic movement was linked to internal trends within the Church, such as Italian Catholic reformism or late Jansenism, which fought against the pomp and ritual on which the Church based its power. The contradiction between reason and revelation did not upset the Catholics as much as the Protestants, and anti-ecclesiastical and antireligious criticism among Catholics was generally more moderate and accompanied by proposals for reform. Between 1750 and 1780 Wolff's philosophy acquired a significant status in the universities and Catholic lyceums, and after the 1780s Kant's teachings also made an entry into those institutions (except in Cologne and Paderborn). From 1740 on, voices, timid at first, began to be raised in Catholic Germany against traditional doctrine and the near-monopoly of the Jesuits over university instruction. The dissolution of that order, decided by the Church as a whole in 1773, can be considered one of the first successes of this particular movement of the German Enlightenment. New universities were founded during that period in Münster (1780) and Bonn (1786). The episcopalism of the Empire, which became Febronianism after 1763, was linked to reformism and the religious policies of the Catholic sovereigns. Beginning in 1760 a polemical attack against monasticism and convents rocked ecclesiastical circles; it spread to Austria after 1780. Under the watchful eye of the Catholic *Aufklärer,* the prince-bishops were in a delicate position, but some of them did nevertheless reform education, particularly in the primary schools (for instance, in the Electorate of Cologne, in Münster, Mainz, Trier, Würzburg, Bamberg, and Salzburg). Joseph II, who came to the throne in 1765, launched a global reform of the Church in Austria, and by the end of the century a convergence of the Protestant and Catholic Enlightenment could be observed. After the deep rift caused by secularization of 1803, the Catholic Enlightenment was able to blossom out fully (research has hardly focused yet upon the role of the University of Würzburg as the center of the Catholic Enlightenment, on the activities of J.H. von Wesenberg, Johann Michael Sailer, and G. Hermes, or the Catholic *Aufklärung* itself). At the beginning of the 19th century, however, the Enlightenment eventually gave way to a conservative ultramontanism.

The Austrian and Bavarian Enlightenment

The Austrian Enlightenment, which came quite late, was largely transmitted through the Freemasons. It was fashionable, in Vienna and the rest of the country, to belong to a lodge. The Freemasons had established a sort of experimental society without national, religious, or social barriers; but its activities were hampered by the "Freemason patent" decreed by Joseph II in 1785. To promote their reforms, Maria Theresa and her son had relied first of all on the scholarly tradition of the religious orders, in particular of the Jesuits, which were supposed to unite the Latin tradition with enlightened rhetoric and morality. Under the influence of that tradition, the language of morality and example held sway for a long time, appearing nevertheless alongside short forms of mock-epic journalism: local sketches and satiric characters. Epistolary satires were very successful between 1780 and 1787. Using these elements and drawing from the local drama tradition, authors also produced novels, sometimes in dialogue form. Travesties of the epic form were also highly appreciated; authors sought to define their social role between fiction and polemics, political engagement and usefulness to society. The literature of the Austrian Enlightenment, essentially antiauthoritarian and irreverent, attacked the Church, the clergy, the religious orders, and the veneration of the saints but did not conspire against faith. These trends are particularly well chronicled in L.A. Hoffmann's critiques attacking sermons (1782–84), where seriousness is combined with satire, mockery, and linguistic criticism, and in Aloys Blumauer's *Glaubensbekenntniß eines nach Wahrheit Ringenden* (1782; Confession of Faith for Those Struggling toward

Truth), which expresses doubt but not disbelief. Although men of letters had begun by supporting Joseph's reforms, after 1785 they attacked the authority of the emperor and of the state. Joseph certainly appreciated Lessing and Wieland, but his views were colored, as had been the case for Frederick II, by the French literature of 1740–70. In his *Beobachtungen über Österreichs Aufklärung und Literatur* (1782; Observations on the Enlightenment and Literature in Austria), Aloys Blumauer notes that the "grandeur of our state, colossal in many ways, contrasts strikingly with its literary diminutiveness."

In Bavaria prior to the 1760s, the class that generally made up the substratum of the enlightened public, the bourgeoisie, was largely nonexistent, even in the capital. Until the end of the 1770s, the region also lacked any newspapers likely to draw readers to the ideas of the Enlightenment. The market was dominated by a late-baroque literature, patriotic panegyrics, and pious works (sermons, books of miracles and prayers, edifying literature). As in Vienna, satirical sermons made an appearance, mocking commonplace beliefs and the rhetoric of sacred sermons. However, such people as Fronhofer, Zaupser, or Westenrieder were hardly successful in adapting the trends that came from the north or the center of the Germanic world or in adopting the virtuous sensitivity of Gellert or the lyrical functional aesthetic of Klopstock. Under Maximilian III Joseph (1759–77), no continuous evolution took hold, and, even under Charles Theodore, a philosopher as important as Westenrieder remained isolated and oppressed instead of being recognized. This handicap imposed upon the greatest writer of the Catholic *Aufklärung* was indicative of the relations between Catholicism and the literary Enlightenment.

Reaction against the Enlightenment

Whereas older research pointed to Hamann and Herder as the heralds of the German antiphilosophical party, recent studies have shown that the two writers' conceptions were merely in the line of the "Germanic" trend of thought of the early 20th century, which was marked by a rejection of the Western Enlightenment and which, as a result, acclaimed any Germanizing opposition. It is primarily in Hamann's work that one finds a violent criticism of Kant's positions. Hamann argued that it is wrong to want to dictate to others what is reasonable, and it is even worse to seek to impose that notion upon them by force. Hamann and Herder applied the principle of emancipation to the *Aufklärung* itself by asking for the right to be free of any desire for total emancipation. They unmasked the authoritarianism of the Enlightenment, which professed to be anti-authoritarian; they flushed out the prejudice of the held-to-be-true that was so dear to Enlightenment thinkers and the illusion in those thinkers' faith in the infinite perfectibility of humankind. What Hamann criticized in particular was Kant's conviction that one could explain the unexplainable in human existence. For Hamann, as for Herder, it was by making reason its supreme principle that the Enlightenment ensured its own downfall, particularly as this assumption had never been clearly justified. These accusations thus threw light on the Enlightenment itself: they cast light on its limitations, its tendency to favor the formation of small groups, to monopolize the truth, and to indoctrinate people's minds. Herder expressed his rejection of the theory of perfectibility in a number of metaphors. He referred to the great universal histories of Voltaire, David Hume, or Isaak Iselin as "novels"; he reproached the enlightened century for lacking "warmth! blood! humanity! life!" To those who said they wanted to support virtue and happiness, he replied that they might end up obtaining the opposite; whereas this era had claimed to be "the most enlightened century," he contended that, at the most, it had the vision of a mole where knowledge was concerned. What he condemned most forcefully, therefore, was not the program of the Enlightenment in itself but rather its false pride, its hardening of the heart, its absolutism.

GERHARD SAUDER

See also Monadism; Philosophy, German; Pietism

Further Reading

Sauder, Gerhard, *Empfindsamkeit*, Stuttgart, Germany: Metzler, 1974– ; see especially vol. 1, *Voraussetzungen und Elemente*, 1974
Schneiders, Werner, *Die wahre Aufklärung: Zum Selbstverständnis der deutschen Augklärung*, Fribourg, Switzerland: Alber, 1974
Schneiders, Werner, *Hoffnung auf Vernunft: Aufklärungsphilosophie in Deutschland*, Hamburg, Germany: Meiner, 1990

Germany and the Holy Roman Empire

The various states of Germany, most often referred to in the 18th century under the collective singular, Germany, were linked by a complex political and legal structure, the *Heiliges Römisches Reich deutscher Nation* (Holy Roman Empire of the German Nation). Diplomats referred to the Empire as the "Germanic corpus." Whatever the designation chosen, as a geopolitical entity 18th-century Germany did not count among the powers that shared out the world among themselves, and it was particularly not significant in the world across the oceans. According to the abbé Raynal, who began his history of Germany in 1770, Germany had few ports, and even these were bad. The Germans had thus been reduced to watching with jealousy or indifference as its ambitious neighbors grew rich from the spoils of the sea and the East and West Indies. From the end of the 30 Years' War, Germany was more often an object of European policy than a player, serving as a middle ground around which political powers maneuvered or, worse, as a battlefield. The latter fate befell it at least three times during the century before the French Revolution: the War of the Spanish Succession (1701–14), the War of the Austrian Succession (1740–48), and the Seven Years' War (1756–63), whose outcome had consequences worldwide.

The Holy Roman Empire

Chosen by a collegium of eight or nine princely electors, the emperor at the head of the Empire played the role of *administrator imperii* (administrator of the empire), rather than *dominus imperii* (lord of the empire). Since 1438 a Habsburg had always been selected. The only brief exception to this dynastic monopoly occurred in the period following 1740, when the Habsburgs of Austria had no male heir to be crowned. Prince Charles Albert of Bavaria (of the House of Wittelsbach) had himself elected Emperor Charles VII in 1742, but upon his death in 1745 the crown returned to the Habsburgs, in this case to Francis of Lorraine, the husband of Maria Theresa. The Habsburgs would retain the crown until the end of the Empire in 1806.

Since 1563 the elections and coronations had been held in Frankfurt-am-Main following an unchanging ceremony, which was eloquently described by Johann Wolfgang von Goethe in *Aus meinem Leben: Dichtung und Wahrheit* (1811–22; Truth and Fiction Relating to My Life). On such occasions, the emperor took an oath to uphold a certain number of "electoral capitulations," by which he undertook to respect the autonomy and privileges of the princes over whom he was sovereign.

These capitulations condemned him to almost complete political impotence. The most "visible" institutions of the Empire were the Imperial Chamber of Justice in Wetzlar, the Imperial Court Council in Vienna, and the permanent Diet in Regensburg.

These institutions were the subject of much fascination, because of their exceptional complexity, but they were also mocked. Samuel von Pufendorf decried them as monstrous, whereas Montesquieu, with a bit more disinterest, equated the spirit of monarchy with war and aggrandizement, and that of a republic with peace and moderation. The Empire defied definition. The *Encyclopédie,* having noted the difficulty of "finding the correct term," rallied to the notion of "mixed republic." Once the taxonomic obstacle had been overcome, the Encyclopedists turned to the regulating mechanisms of "public peace" instituted by Maximilian I at the Diet of Worms in 1495. Raynal devoted a considerable number of pages to the subject in his *Histoire philosophique et politique des établissements et du commerce des Européens dans les deux Indes* (1770; A Philosophical and Political History of the Settlements and Trade of the Europeans in the East and West Indies). He insisted upon the long history of the German system, noting that the institutions had perpetuated an original system of independence and federation or, as he put it, of "separation of nations yet of political union." He even suggested that this "public peace" could well serve as a model for a united, pacified Europe. However, the constitution of the Holy Roman Empire was also ridiculed. It was criticized for its impotence and the quasi inertia of its institutions, as in the *Encyclopédie:* "In the Diets of the Empire, resolutions are arrived at with unbearable slowness, making the state ridiculous in the eyes of other nations, for whom German ponderousness has almost become proverbial." In contrast, the capacities for reform of modern, enlightened monarchies were praised, although the *Encyclopédie* also denounced the ambiguous application of the concept of liberty to the Empire:

This much-vaunted liberty of the Germanic corpus is nothing more than the arbitrary exercise of power, enjoyed by a small number of sovereigns; the Emperor is incapable of preventing them from oppressing the people and trampling them underfoot; they are counted as nothing, although it is in the people that the strength of a nation resides.

Such criticism should be tempered, however. The imperial law courts—notably the one in Vienna—did actually "work": a decision handed down in 1771, for example, ruled against the duke of Württemberg and in favor of his parliament. Moreover, despite its archaic aspects, the Holy Roman Empire held a sort of patriotic

and poetic prestige in national memory. The authors of Sturm und Drang literature in the 1770s made the Empire fashionable, and honorable once again; certain jurists (such as Johann Jakob Moser) became its staunch defenders, and this feeling of patriotism for the Empire lasted until the end of the century. In the 1780s the very person who had done the most to shake the foundations of the Empire's territorial and institutional equilibrium, Frederick II, proclaimed himself its loyal defender during the episode of the League of Princes (1785). The league, it is true, was directed against plans for territorial redistribution, pursued obstinately, although unsuccessfully, by Emperor Joseph II. The redistribution would take place later on, during the vast Napoleonic "regrouping of lands," but the millennial Empire would not survive the ravages.

Although the Germany of the Holy Roman Empire was not a presence in the European political scene, two dynasties concurrently expressed aspirations toward such a presence, while they vied to be the hegemonic force in German politics. The duality that constituted German reality until 1871 was born in the 18th century. The first dynasty, that of the Habsburgs, united the territories of the southern and Catholic flank of the Empire to the territories of central Europe, Moravia, Hungary, and the Balkan territories, as well as northern Italy and, in the northwest, the Austrian Netherlands. The second dynasty, that of the Hohenzollerns, ruled over a kingdom that was also far-flung, from Königsberg in eastern Prussia (beyond the borders of the Holy Roman Empire) to Cleves on the Rhine, a realm with a strong Slavic component, but where absolutist centralization was stronger than in Vienna. The Hohenzollerns challenged the preeminence of the Habsburgs, not without success, particularly after Frederick II's accession to the throne. The "leftover" princes of the "third" Germany (whether ecclesiastical or lay) tried to live and survive between the two powers, playing to one or the other, or more often playing off one against the other, depending on their own interests of the moment and their other alliances outside Germany. After the Peace of Westphalia, two foreign powers, France and Sweden, were guarantors of the treaties; Russia joined France and Sweden during the 18th century. For its part, England had dynastic links to the Holy Roman Empire through the House of Hanover.

The Habsburg States

The pluralism of the states of the Habsburg dynasty (federated by personal union), as well as the southern and Balkan tropism that marked the history of that dynasty from the end of the 17th century onward, ensured that the Empire, where the Counter-Reformation had long held sway, would not be at the forefront of the

Enlightenment during the 18th century. The shock that followed the loss of Silesia, conquered by Frederick II, provoked a salutary rise in national awareness, placing the dynasty on the path to modernization and reform. Maria Theresa—well advised by her ministers (first Christian August von Haugwitz, then Wenzel Anton von Kaunitz)—had preserved the cohesion of her states during the Silesian wars and launched a series of administrative, social, and economic reforms. Moreover, to regain Silesia, the Habsburgs once again entered the diplomatic game of western Europe, whence the "reversal of alliances" that preceded the Seven Years' War. Joseph II pursued and accelerated the reforms when he succeeded his mother in 1780. Would Vienna wrest the title of capital of the *Aufklärung* from Berlin? It was a question that political journalists, at any rate, were asking at the beginning of the 1780s. The reforms long advocated by men of the Enlightenment followed at a regular pace: edicts on toleration toward non-Catholic confessions and toward Jews, an edict on freedom of the press, the suppression of serfdom, a reform of the penal code, the quasi abolition of capital punishment, and so on. The Catholic version of the Enlightenment seemed capable of catching up with the Protestant version. However, the second half of Joseph II's reign was less brilliant; it met more setbacks than successes. The perhaps too-hasty reforms often brought on contradictory challenges, but they inspired enough opposition to make one doubt the reforms' validity: this was the case in Hungary and in Brabant. Leopold II was obliged to revoke some of the reforms. Finally, at the end of the century, the clash between ideology and the military during the French Revolution was to shuffle the cards once more. The enlightened period, after the death of Leopold II (1792), was followed by a phase of reaction, led by Francis II. The quickly unmasked "plots" by a handful of "Viennese Jacobins" in 1793–94 attested, for the last time in the century, to the political hopefulness that Joseph's Enlightenment had aroused and the impossibility of fulfilling those hopes.

Prussia

Prussia was the last to arrive in the concert of Europe, but from 1740 on it was a noisy participant. Voltaire's friend and the author of *L'Antimachiavel* (1741; The Refutation of Machiavelli's "Prince"; or, Anti-Machiavel), Frederick II used the military instrument wrought by his father, the "Sergeant-King" Frederick William I, to enlarge his territory from 120,000 to 195,000 square kilometers, while the population doubled during the same period to reach 5.4 million inhabitants. This Protestant power stood up to the rest of the world during the Seven Years' War. Its sovereign then transferred the energy once applied to waging war

toward working for peace. He developed the capital, Berlin, and took a series of measures aimed at modernizing and rationalizing his government. He launched a series of studies to prepare a civil code (which would come into force in 1795). He developed the educational system, protected the arts and sciences, and attracted world-renowned scholars to his Academy. However, as far as German patriotic sentiment was concerned, Frederick was in an awkward position. Too enthralled with French culture, he could not grasp the "progress" of German letters. Even in 1780, he was still unsure that German literature had a future, a fact that explains the ambivalence felt by people such as Johann Gottfried von Herder or Gotthold Ephraim Lessing toward their king. After his death in 1786, anti-Enlightenment "reaction" grew during the reign of his successor, Frederick William II, and momentarily reinforced the prestige of Vienna. Berlin remained the showplace of the *Aufklärung,* however, with its enlightened administration, its journals that were read throughout the country, and its salons, opened by the Jewish bourgeoisie. Berlin's position as the leading city of the *Aufklärung* no doubt explains why the marquis de Mirabeau made a lengthy stay there in the years preceding the French Revolution.

The "Third" Germany

It would take too long to describe the "leftovers" of the Empire or to establish a list of leaps of progress made by the Enlightenment, as did certain journalists at the end of the 18th century. All the regions, in a sort of inter-German spirit of competition, gradually experienced an economic and cultural upsurge. Of particular interest was the progress in Bavaria, Saxony, Hanover (with its university at Göttingen), the Palatinate, the duchy of Württemberg, the margravate of Baden, and some of the imperial free cities, such as Hamburg, Frankfurt, or Augsburg.

It remains an undeniable fact that Germany had accumulated a certain number of structural handicaps, the legacy of its social, political, and religious history. To the multiplicity of divisions, ranks, classes, and estates common to all feudal societies was added the almost infinite variety of regimes in force within its boundaries, from absolute monarchies—where, in some cases, there were parliaments endowed with more or less symbolic power—and ecclesiastical or secular principalities, all the way to urban republics. These political and administrative divisions, which were fragmented into more than 300 entities, provoked caricature and irony, frequently aggravating the religious divisions that were frozen into institutions by the *corpus evangelicorum* (body of Evangelicals) and the *corpus catholicorum* (body of Catholics) in the Diet of the Empire at Regensburg. The only compensation was that the multiplicity and diversity of rules and regulations made it easier, or less perilous, to indulge in criticism.

Germany had no capital city. As a result, there was no urban concentration (220,000 inhabitants in Vienna at the end of the 18th century, 180,000 in Berlin) that might have accelerated a "civilizing process" like that seen in England (London had 1 million inhabitants) or France (600,000 residents in Paris). The ideal of the national theatre, which was pursued in Germany throughout the century but never attained, attests to the fact that Germany's cultural development was affected by this lack of a capital. Germany was often perceived as a cultural province. However, several elements did help to compensate for the absence of a center for German culture: the existence of universities, which generated an intellectual life (Göttingen, notably, founded in 1737, but also Halle, Leipzig, Königsberg, Strasbourg, and so on) and which gave rise to great philosophers (Christian Thomasius, Christian Wolff, Immanuel Kant), and the presence of major national literary and political periodicals, beginning in the second half of the century (Christoph Friedrich Nicolai's *Allgemeine Deutsche Bibliothek,* Professor Schlözer's *Briefwechsel,* Christoph Martin Wieland's *Der teutsche Merkur,* Dohm and Boie's *Deutsches Museum,* Friedrich Gedike and Johann Erich Biester's *Berlinische Monatsschrift,* etc.), with their networks of correspondents and a readership spread throughout Germany, including many members of the numerous reading societies. In addition, there was the constantly renewed activity of secret societies throughout the last third of the century, from the Strict Templar Observance to the German Union, by way of Bavaria's Illuminati. Here as elsewhere, these societies played a fundamental role in progressively discrediting the ruling powers, and their participation in the process of the ideological and cultural homogenization of the elite was far from negligible. Finally, a major element contributing to the cultural growth of the federation—one that would become increasingly influential as it took its place in the European cultural landscape—was German literature. Supported by an ever-expanding market for printed matter and with the help of numerous publishing houses (prefiguring the empire of the book studied by Frédéric Barbier), this literature contributed to the renaissance of a national consciousness, while assuring Germany's cultural recognition (see Barbier).

Germany and the Germans as Seen by the French

The road to this recognition was a long one. A brief historical overview of the cultural relations between France and Germany over the century illustrates the perceptible evolution of views. Initially indifferent to, and even scornful of, German cultural production, French observers came to express fascination and admiration with regard to Germany. Around the turn of the 18th century, the French were disdainful of Germans, a position fed by national prejudice. In his *Entretiens d'Eugène et d'Ariste* (1673; Discussions of Eugène and Ariste), Father Dominique Bouhours was the first to chronicle this attitude. He hastily assimilated the Germans with the Muscovites and denied them any aptitude for wit. For Bouhours, wit was utterly incompatible with "the rough temperament and huge frames of the men of the North." This prejudice was shared: the duc de Saint-Simon, introducing the Palatine princess, described her as a

> princess of a bygone era, attached to honor, virtue, rank, and grandeur; inexorable where propriety is concerned . . . very German in all her ways and frank, oblivious to any consideration or delicacy toward oneself or toward others, sober, antisocial and not without fantasies.

This indifference mixed with disdainful incomprehension toward the Germans lasted for a rather long time. Even in 1735 the adjective "German" could be an outright insult, meaning vulgar, brutal, unsociable, and sometimes drunken. Philibert-Joseph Leroux, the author of the *Dictionnaire comique, satyrique, critique, burlesque, libre et proverbial* (1718; A Comic, Satirical, Critical, Burlesque, Free, and Proverbial Dictionary), cited the above meanings of the word, although he deplored them.

During his journey to southern Germany, Montesquieu offered an unsympathetic portrait: "Germans who are hardly quick and alert in their youth, grow supremely dull in old age"—a comment that proved the banality of such stereotypes. Another significant text demonstrating that France and Germany were out of touch in the 1740s is that of a Huguenot author, Éléazar de Mauvillon. He undertook to compare and contrast the two countries in a work entitled *Lettres françaises et germaniques ou réflexions militaires, littéraires et critiques sur les Français et les Allemans* (1740; French and German Letters; or, Military, Literary, and Critical Reflections on the French and the Germans). Significantly, he noted the Germans' almost pathological readiness to take offense without even asking himself from where the notion came: "they do not want to concede anything to any other nation." He did not limit himself, however, to calling attention to their prickly nationalism. Praise was not altogether absent from his work, and he even seemed to adopt some of the Germans' own stereotypes. He wrote, for example, of their admirable candor. The choicest pieces, however, are the chapters devoted to language and literature, that is, to the domain where the French believed themselves to be definitively superior and therefore authorized to judge others without the slightest effort of understanding or empathy. Here resurfaces the inevitable criticism of the German language, forever unsuitable, according to Mauvillon, for poetry or literature. He conceded that the language could make some progress. There was, after all, a society of scholars in Leipzig who were continuously working to perfect it; but he doubted that they could "change its rough, barbarian nature." Germany, reduced to an utter foreignness, possessing an imperfect linguistic instrument, could therefore never hope to have good poets. Reiterating the faults already stigmatized by Bouhours, he also argued that Germans have no wit. Finally, Mauvillon also held that it was characteristic of Germany not to have produced from its own sources a single dramatic work. The cultural evaluation was totally negative; it was also totally unfair, for in 1740 significant efforts had already been made with a view toward the renewal of German letters, and there were already some promising successes.

These lengthy considerations, coming more than a century after Bouhours, reveal less about the constancy of German characteristics than about the durability of French prejudice. Mauvillon went to Germany in order to confirm the stereotypes he had already formed before his trip. His work did not arouse much interest in France, but it did, however, leave its mark upon Germany. The author's positive remarks did not efface or make up for the more unpleasant ones, all the more so because they were uttered in a tone of scientific certainty. Mauvillon, an erudite anthropologist, seemed to base his assertions upon a scrupulous and objective observation of German reality, although his work lacked the most elementary sense of social or anthropological perspective or proportion. The chapters dealing with language and literature elicited a very strong reaction, and their author was vehemently reproached for his "Bouhourian" attack on German literature.

French indifference was also the result of the fact that France's cultural and political model during this entire period was not Germany but England. Voltaire and Montesquieu crossed the Channel in search of their political models and philosophical references. In the imagination and ideas of the French during the first half of the century, Germany did not occupy the first or even second place: it was quite simply absent altogether—even if some of its merits were recognized, by Mauvillon first of all, in certain philosophical, scientific, or military domains; and even if, symptomatically, the abbé Dubos resorted to the use of a German word, *Heimweh*—which he gave the odd spelling *hemvé*—to "designate the instinct that tells us when the atmosphere in which we find ourselves is not as beneficial to our constitution as the one that an inner instinct causes us to desire." This was proof that this much-criticized language had its

resources all the same, even in the very subtle domain of the soul's activity.

However, soon after the middle of the century, references to Germany began to emerge in French discourse. The same literature that had been deplored for its sterility was eventually perceived in a positive way in France. The presence in Paris of mediators—Germans who were well rooted in literary or artistic circles, such as the editor of the *Correspondance littéraire*, Friedrich Melchior von Grimm, as well as the painter and engraver Johann Georg Wille—and the birth of *Le journal étranger* (1754), which provided regular news from the German "Republic of Letters," brought about a change in people's attitudes. From the 1760s on, Albrecht von Haller's poems about the Alps and Salomon Gessner's idylls were appreciated in France. Readers who had wearied of rococo refinement and the corrupt world of the court or the city (in short, of civilization) found that the unspoiled nature evoked in these poems let them dream. Jean-Jacques Rousseau and his criticism of civilization were linked to this concept of a return to nature. There was no need, moreover, to set off on a quest for some faraway exoticism. Nature, unchanging and good, could be found close at hand. One could even specify its location, within the bounds of Germany and Switzerland. "O happy people, O gentle Germany," exclaimed the poet Antoine de Cournaud in his enthusiasm for poetic idylls.

In 1768 the fashionable author Claude-Joseph Dorat ventured a prophecy: "Today the German muse prevails. O Germany! Our fine days are gone, and yours are just beginning." In 1773, traveling through Germany on his way to Saint Petersburg, Denis Diderot seemed to confirm Dorat's presentiment: "The Germans are advancing, and we are slipping backward, and if they had had a capital they would already have overtaken us." The abbé Raynal, in his *Histoire des deux Indes,* reiterated the alleged inadequacy of the German language for literature and poetry, but, in speaking of the situation of literature in Germany, he felt obliged to disprove the allegation:

Its shortage of writers seemed to point to a country where fine arts, poetry, and eloquence could not blossom. But, suddenly, there was an explosion of genius, and original poets in a number of genres came forward in sufficient numbers to rival other nations.

This view acknowledged Germany's decisive entry into the European cultural landscape. There was nothing surprising, therefore, about Napoleon having read Goethe's *Die Leiden des jungen Werther* (1774; The Sorrows of Young Werther) several times over, as he told the author during their famous meeting in Erfurt.

Between 1760 and 1770, moreover, German music, with the school in Mannheim, had attracted noticeable attention in Paris. In fact, it was perhaps the 1780s that witnessed the birth of what would be known as the "German mirage," which would reach its pinnacle with Madame de Staël's *De l'Allemagne* (Germany), published in 1810. Henceforth, and for a long time to come, Germany would be the intellectual benchmark for French thought.

JEAN MONDOT

See also Nation

Further Reading
Barbier, Frédéric, *L'empire du livre: Le livre imprimé et la construction de l'Allemagne comtemporaine, 1815–1914*, Paris: Éditions du Cerf, 1995
Espagne, Michel, and Michael Werner, editors, *Les relations interculterelles dans l'espace franco-allemand (XVIIIᵉ–XIXᵉ siècle)*, Paris: Éditions Recherche sur les Civilisations, 1988
Mondot, Jean, Jean-Marie Valentin, and Jürgen Voss, *Allemands en France, français en Allemagne, 1715–1789*, Sigmaringen, Germany: Thorbecke, 1992

God

In addition to an atheist wing, the Enlightenment had a deist or theist camp (the necessary distinctions between the last two terms will be discussed below). Let us first consider the deist/theist camp, in which, in his early days, Denis Diderot stood alongside Voltaire and Immanuel Kant. In a brilliant—perhaps too brilliant—passage in his *La pensée européenne au XVIIIᵉ siècle* (1935; The European Mind, 1680–1715), Paul Hazard describes this camp in negative terms. If he worshiped any deity, Enlightenment man worshiped only "an unknown God, an unknowable God," what remained after a series of "subtractions," a God deprived even of his name, or very nearly: "Among all the possible titles, he [the man of the Enlightenment] gave him [God] only the vaguest and most honorable, and called him the Supreme Being."

Two objections can be raised to this terse epithet. First, in the 17th century "Supreme Being" was a perfectly orthodox "divine name." It can be found, for example, in such Catholic writings as Cardinal Pierre de Bérulle's *Discours de l'état et des grandeurs de Jésus* (1623; Discourse on the State and Glory of Jesus), in Father Bourgoing's *Les vérités et excellences de Jésus-Christ Notre Seigneur* (1636; The Truth and Excellence of Jesus Christ Our Lord), and in Saint Jean Eudes's *Le royaume de Jésus* (1637; Jesus's Kingdom). Thus, there was never a time during the 18th century when Enlightenment man had a monopoly on the term "Supreme Being." Second, in his *Pensées philosophiques* (1746; Philosophical Thoughts), Diderot defines his philosophical reconceptualization of God in wholly positive terms, as is shown by his famous injunction "Élargissez Dieu" (Broaden God). Seen from this angle, "broadening God" entails breaking the narrow bounds of tem-

ples, sanctuaries, and enclosed orders and putting an end to the ethnic privilege of a "chosen people" and to the spiritual privilege of the Church—in short, as modern sociologists would say, "detribalizing" God.

In his *Sermon des Cinquante* (1751; Sermon of the Fifty), Voltaire invokes the "God of all the planets and of all beings," an expansion that parallels the one that cosmology had undergone, a transition from a "closed world," as Alexandre Koyré puts it (see Koyré), to an "infinite universe." Similarly, broadening God meant liberating him from his role, a petty one after all, of a personal lifeguard. In the dialogue entitled "Providence" in Voltaire's *Questions sur l'"Encyclopédie" par des amateurs* (1771; Questions on the "Encyclopédie" from the Uninitiated), a metaphysician reminds Sister Fessue that God governs the world through a "general Providence." He states:

If Ave Marias had caused Sister Fessue's sparrow to live for a moment longer than it was supposed to live, those Ave Marias would have violated all the laws set in place by the Great Being for all eternity; you would have upset the universe; you would have needed a new world, a new God, a new order of things.

Seven years earlier Voltaire had said much the same in his entry "Grâce" (Grace) in the *Dictionnaire philosophique* (1734; Philosophical Dictionary): "The Eternal Being is never guided by specific laws, as base human beings are, but by his own general laws, which, like him, are eternal." In the above two texts, Voltaire thus gives a radical turn, at the expense of miracles, to the theme of "general laws," which he had borrowed from Nicolas Malebranche (see Alquié). God abandons his role of casual lifeguard and becomes—or again becomes—"the eternal Geometer" (*Sophronisme et Adélos* [1776; Sophronisme and Adelos]). God is in no way diminished but is raised—or returned—to a higher rank. Here too there is a broadening of the horizon.

Consequently, the Voltairean God of the Enlightenment, the eternal Geometer, is also the "great architect of the world" (*Dialogues d'Evhémère* [1777; Dialogues of Euhemerus]). On a cosmic scale, he has regulated mathematically the courses of the star, and the contemplation of the heavens brings to good Parouba's lips in the *Histoire de Jenni ou le Sage et l'Athée* (1775; Young James; or, The Sage and the Atheist) the phrase "The heavens declare God," recalling the line *Coeli enarrant gloriam Dei* (The heavens declare the glory of God) from the biblical Psalm. In Voltaire's *Dialogues entre Lucrèce et Posidonius* (1756, Dialogues between Lucretia and Posidonius), we are told that God has assembled living machines upon the Earth:

> One would have to have seen human beings and animals being born from the womb of the Earth, cereals without seeds, and so on, to dare to affirm that matter alone gives itself such forms; as far as I know, no one has seen this operation: therefore, no one is required to believe in it.

What then is one to think of man? A radical follower of Malebranche's doctrine on this point, Voltaire considers that "God takes the place of our soul" (*Dialogues d'Evhémère*); this "apsychism" (if we may coin this term) unexpectedly grafts the "vision in God" onto Voltairean anthropology. In the ethical field, his *Poème sur la loi naturelle* (1756; Poem on Natural Law) credits the universal moral law to God:

> I cannot not know what my master has ordained;
> He has given me his law, since he has given me being.
> Without doubt he has spoken, but to the universe:
> He did not dwell in the deserts of Egypt;
> Delphi, Delos, Ammon were not his refuge;
> He did not hide himself in the lairs of the sibyls.
> Morality, uniform in every time and place,
> Speaks in the name of God to endless ages.

But does the Voltairean God of the Enlightenment solve the eternal problem of evil? We have to admit that on this point the philosopher's apsychism plays a nasty trick on him. In the entry "Théiste" (Theist), inserted into the *Dictionnaire philosophique* in 1765, Voltaire certainly asserts that the Supreme Being "punishes crimes without cruelty and rewards with kindness virtuous actions," but he is unable to explain "how God punishes, how he favors, how he pardons." If the soul-substance does not exist and therefore cannot outlive the body, the courtroom of the Rewarder-Avenger would be empty, for there would be no just soul to be rewarded and no guilty soul to be sentenced or pardoned. Could it be that Voltaire, the "Fourth Impostor," is professing a double doctrine? Some late texts allow us to glimpse a way out. For example, in the *Dialogues d'Evhémère*, Euheremus says to Callicrates:

> If God has placed within the reasoning animal called man an invisible, impalpable spark, something less tangible than the elemental atom that was known to the Greek philosophers as a monad, and if this monad was indestructible, if it was the monad that thought and felt inside us, then I would no longer see anything absurd in saying that this monad could exist, could have ideas and feelings, when the body of which it is the soul has been destroyed.

We can now turn to the famous tirade from the *Épître à l'auteur du livre "Des trois imposteurs"* (1769; Epistle to the Author of the Book "The Three Impostors"):

> This sublime system is necessary to man.
> It is the sacred bond of society,
> The first foundation of holy equity,
> That reins in villainy and gives hope to the just.
> If the heavens, deprived of his august imprint,
> Could ever cease to manifest him,
> If God did not exist, it would be necessary to invent him.
> Let the wise man adore him and kings fear him.
> Kings, if you oppress me, if your arrogance disdains
> The tears of the innocent, which you cause to flow,
> My avenger is on high; learn to tremble.

One might conclude that the impalpable monad, which Voltaire borrows for the occasion not from the Greeks but from Gottfried Wilhelm Leibniz (in a fine vindication for the man who was the butt of Voltaire's sarcasm in *Candide* [1759]), would present only a limited target to the wrath of the Celestial Avenger.

Other texts from the same period suggest some simpler solutions. God's power, however great it might be, may be limited nonetheless (*Dialogues d'Evhémère*):

> He is truly the sole power, since it is he who has shaped everything; but he is not extravagantly powerful. . . . Each being is circumscribed within its nature; and I dare to think that the Supreme Being is circumscribed within his.

Even clearer is the theme of the *Lettres de Memmius à Cicéron* (1771; Letters from Memmius to Cicero): "Good exists, therefore God is good; evil exists, therefore this evil does not come from him. How then should I envisage God? As a father who has not been able to promote the well-being of all his children." The Great Architect of the world has had to take his materials and his location into account. A passage in *Sophronisme et Adélos* that is unique in Voltaire's writings finally exculpates the Supreme Being by developing a theory of earthly retaliation:

> There is no reason to accuse God of injustice because the hells of the Egyptians, of Orpheus, and of Homer do not exist. . . . There is certainly a more inevitable punishment, in this world, for villains. And what is it? It is remorse, which never relents, and human vengeance, which rarely fails. I have known very wicked, atrocious men; I have never seen a single one of them who was happy.

Voltaire was hostile to all forms of incarnation, yet he still pleaded God's case, although in a non-mythological way.

As for whether this was deism or theism, Voltaire replaced the former term with the latter when in 1751 he changed the title of his text *Du Déisme* (1742; On Deism) *Discours sur le Théisme* (Discourse on Theism). Hence, we may conclude, with Theodore Besterman, that Voltaire regarded the two notions as identical; or if not, that after some reflection he judged the second title to be better suited to the text, in which one reads such statements as "deism is a religion that is widespread within all religions" and "God has deigned to establish a relationship between himself and mankind." Silhouette, in his preface to Warburton's *Dissertations* (1742), had in fact defined the theist as "the man who combines the worship of one religion with belief in God." The entry "Théiste" in the *Dictionnaire philosophique* would also use the word "worship": "To do good is [the theist's] worship; to submit to God is [the theist's] doctrine." There is a reciprocal relationship between God and man. General Providence and the gift of the social instinct come from God to man; submission and worship come from man to God. To cite the *Sermon des Cinquante* once again:

> O God of all the stars and of all beings, the only prayer fitting for you is submission, for what can be asked of him who has ordained everything, foreseen everything, and linked everything together since the origin of all things? If, nonetheless, one may present one's needs to a father, preserve in our hearts this very submission, keep your religion pure.

This request is in fact an exhortation that man addresses to himself. The submission of man to God is essential, but we should emphasize that submission is not simply resignation, for worship pervades it and magnifies it. Voltaire's theism is directed at the God of philosophers and the learned—a point that will surprise no one, although we should note that Rousseau's view converges with Voltaire's at more than one point, over and above their well-known differences.

Rousseau, like Voltaire, was a theist. In *La profession de foi du vicaire savoyard* (The Creed of a Priest of Savoy) in *Émile, ou, De l'éducation* (1762; Émile; or, concerning Education), the interlocutor sees in the Vicar's feelings nothing but "theism or natural religion, more or less," and the Vicar replies: "You see in my exposition nothing but natural religion. It is somewhat strange that one should require any other!" The Vicar's Christianity cannot, therefore, be distinguished substantially from pure theism.

Like Voltaire, Rousseau rejects the notion of prayers that ask for things, but Rousseau's rejection is even more radical in its form than Voltaire's, since the Vicar says about God: "I am moved by his favors, I bless him for his gifts, but I do not pray to him." Not of course, that the Vicar is ignorant about worship and praise: "The more I try to contemplate his infinite essence, the less I can conceive it; that essence exists, and that is enough for me; the less I can conceive it, the more I worship it." This worship is expressed as: "Being of Beings, I am because Thou art; meditating constantly about Thee raises me to my source." Even more of a purist than Voltaire, the Vicar does not speak here of "prayer," yet this *is* a prayer nevertheless, in the pure tradition of Fénelon. When Rousseau expresses himself in this way, is he perhaps echoing the *Fiat* (Let it be done) of the Gospels, the *Explications des maximes des saints sur la vie intérieure* (1697; The Maxims of the Saints Explained, concerning the Interior Life) or the *Sermon des Cinquante?* Without seeking to probe the secrets of the heart, or to overstate the paradox, the historian can only point out this thematic convergence.

Finally, the attitudes of Voltaire and Rousseau, those "fraternal enemies," are also similar with regard to miracles. Rousseau doubted their factuality and objected to their use as a method of religious proof. To quote the Vicar again:

> It is the unalterable order of nature that best reveals the Supreme Being; if there were many exceptions, I would no longer know what to think about him, and, for my part, I believe too much in God to believe in so many miracles that are so little worthy of him.

Given these convergences, it will be no surprise that Voltaire incorporated many pages from *La profession de foi* into his *Recueil nécessaire* (1765; Necessary Collection), placing them, aptly enough, next to his own *Sermon des Cinquante*.

Should we therefore nominate Rousseau's Savoyard Vicar as parish priest of Voltaire's refuge at Ferney? Most definitely not. In addition to their differences of emphasis and tone, a rift opens up between Rousseau and Voltaire whenever they refer to Jesus. Voltaire rejects the Incarnation, whereas the Vicar proclaims, "the life and death of Socrates were those of a wise man, but the life and death of Jesus were those of a God." To this phrase Voltaire added a marginal note: "Do gods die?" In his *Profession de foi des théistes* (1768; Profession of Faith of the Theists), he compares Jesus, the "Israelite theist," to Socrates, the "Athenian theist." At the moments of his greatest respect, Voltaire even calls Jesus the "Socrates of Galilee" and "the first of the theists" (*Homélies prononcées à Londres en 1765* [Homilies Given in London in 1765]). However, in *Dieu et les hommes* (1769; God and Men), he also disparages Jesus as a "rustic Socrates." For Voltaire, Jesus in no way represents a super-Socrates. Yet perhaps the rift between Voltaire and Rousseau was not so deep. As Henri Gouhier pointed out in *Les méditations métaphysiques de Jean-Jacques Rousseau* (1970; The Metaphysical Meditations of Jean-Jacques Rousseau), Rousseau wrote in his *Discours sur l'économie politique* (Discourse on Political Economy) that "in his position between Caesar and Pompey, Cato seems a God among mortals," a statement that, by its rebound effect, could put the Vicar's enthusiastic expressions in a different perspective.

In *La profesion de foi du vicaire savoyard,* the God of the Enlightenment is a Christian God, or seems at least, but he was to lose this confessional cloak in *Du contrat social* (1762; The Social Contract) by becoming the dogma of the "Civil Religion":

> The existence of the powerful, intelligent, benefi-cent, and providential Divinity, the life to come, the happiness of the just, the punishment of the wicked, the sanctity of the social contract and the laws: these are the positive dogmas.

There is nothing specifically Christian in these minimal criteria: this God, duly stripped of all confessional trap-pings, was waiting for a historic opportunity to rise to the status of God of the State. His opportunity came in France on 21 Prairial Year II (8 June 1794), when the first (and only) Festival of the Supreme Being was cele-brated. As president of the Convention, Maximilien Marie Isidore de Robespierre was the official orator and could believe that a new era had begun. But it was an ephemeral victory and, like many victories, it was fol-lowed by a defeat. Less than two months later, the events of 9 Thermidor (27 July) put an end to the reign of this pontiff and discredited his God along with him. Nemesis threatens gods as well as human beings.

Before leaving the subject of the theist side of the Enlightenment, let us consider Kant's testimony. Where, in his view, did the difference lie between theism and deism? Neither Voltaire nor Rousseau, both of whom had died in 1778, could have known, even indirectly (neither of them read German), the contents of Kant's *Kritik der reinen Vernunft* (Critique of Pure Reason), which was published in 1781. On the other hand, Kant knew the gist of their work, and on this question of the-ism and deism he summarized their teaching. Distin-guishing the blind causal agent, the *Urwesen* (original being) from the free causal agent, the *Höchstes Wesen* (Supreme Being), Kant draws the following dividing line: the deist "under the name of God . . . imagines only a cause of the world," whereas the theist "imag-ines an author of the world." In Kant's view, then, "the deist believes in a God, while the theist believes in a *liv-ing* God" ("Die transzendentale Dialektik," in *Kritik der reinen Vernunft* [Transcendental Dialectic, in Cri-tique of Pure Reason]; parallel text in Section 57 of *Pro-legomena zu einer jeden kuenftigen Metaphysik* [1783; Prolegomena to Any Future Metaphysics]). This typo-logical presentation of theism, conceived in terms of its specific difference, certainly would not have suited either Rousseau or Voltaire.

Initially, it might seem that the atheist camp of the Enlightenment need not detain us for long: why dwell at length on an admission of an absence? In fact, things were not so simple: God reappeared, in unexpected forms, at least three times in the viewpoints about nature, which in principle had been set free from his tutelage.

When Diderot wrote *Le rêve de D'Alembert* (1769–74; D'Alembert's Dream), he had completed his philo-sophical conversion, or, rather, his deconversion, put-ting the deism of his *Pensées philosophiques* far behind him. In the later text, the idea of God, burdened with too many contradictions, has become a useless instru-ment. The Being is nothing more than "an immense ocean of matter," and "there is no longer more than one substance in the universe, in man, and in animals." Since sensitivity is a general property of matter, "stone too must possess sensitivity." Trusting the "Eelman" Needham, Diderot accepts "spontaneous generation" and takes part, in his mind, in a perpetual Genesis: life "is but a continuum of actions and reactions." In short, there is "nothing in the whole of nature that does not suffer or enjoy."

Won over by this lyricism, was the reader, already adrift on this boundless ocean, no longer ruled by any

Neptune? What would surprise the reader most was that Diderot introduced a new divinity in the unexpected form of an ugly spider (but then gods are given to metamorphosis). "Who has told you," Diderot asks, "that this world does not also have its brain, or that a spider, large or small, does not dwell in some remote corner of space, and whose filaments are attached to everything?" To be sure, "this type of God would be material, within the universe, a part of the universe, subject to vicissitudes, he would grow old, and would die." This digression into myth stops at this point and Diderot is careful to note, through Bordeu's words, that this type of God is "the only one conceivable," thus relegating the immaterial God of theology to the realm of the unreal and inconceivable. In other words, if the reader does not believe in the Spider, he must believe still less in the God of the catechism. Let us not mistake this fantasy for a concept. It is enough to say that Diderot, being a great artist, has grafted this arachnid God onto our Western realm of fantasy.

The historian of ideas would like to add two observations of his own. Firstly, the image of the spider literally obsessed Diderot before he wrote *Le rêve de D'Alembert*. It turns up as all-purpose image whenever a coordinating agent is needed: in the entry "Asiatique" (Asiatic) in the *Encyclopédie*, in the *Lettre sur la vie et les ouvrages de M. Boulanger* (1766; Letter on the Life and Works of M. Boulanger), and in the *Salon de 1767* (1767 Exhibition). Secondly, the theme of the world as a "great animal," which originated with the Stoics, had been adopted by libertine thinkers in the 17th century. For example, in "Discours du philosophe lunaire" (Discourse of the Lunar Philosopher) in *États et empires de la lune* (1657; States and Influences of the Moon), Cyrano de Bergerac wrote: "Picture the universe, therefore, as a great animal, with the moon and the stars as other animals within it, serving in their turn as worlds for other peoples, such as ourselves."

Another deity conceived by a materialist and located on the fringes of a materialist system is the "Being supreme in wickedness" who forms the keystone of "Saint-Fond's System" in the marquis de Sade's *Histoire de Juliette* (1797; Juliette). Indeed, through his resentments and fantasies, Sade presents this cruel minister, Sartine, as being antithetical to his own materialism and that of the principal Sadeian heroes, who are all rigorously atheist and even anti-theist. In the third dialogue of Sade's *La philosophie dans le boudoir* (1795; Philosophy in the Boudoir), Dolmancé, as a worthy disciple of baron d'Holbach, proclaims that nature is self-governing and self-propelling:

If matter is active and moves through [chemical] combinations that are unknown to us; if, in the end, nature alone, because of its energy, can cre-

ate, produce, and balance so many stars in the immense plains of space . . . what need is there to search for an agent outside all of this?

If God existed, the text continues, he would be no more than "an inconsistent and barbarous being, creating a world one day and repenting of its construction the next" (there is an obvious allusion here to the biblical Flood). Madame Delbène, Juliette's governess, specifies when addressing the priests: "This action that you believe you can separate from it, this energy of matter: there is your God" (*Histoire de Juliette*). God is therefore nothing but a name given mistakenly to the energizing properties of matter. The system of Saint-Fond (one of Sade's fantasy spokesmen) contradicts the marquis's other fictional mouthpieces on one crucial point. Saint-Fond tells Clairwil and Juliette: "Far from thinking like you, I accept a Supreme Being, and even more firmly the immortality of our souls. But your pious people, charmed by this opening, should not go beyond that to imagine that they have made a convert out of me." Let us consider the specifics of Saint-Fond's system.

God, "supreme in wickedness," the "Supreme Being of evil deeds" and "center of evil and ferocity," loves, values, and performs only evil. Served by "evildoing molecules" (the demons of the poets), he sows suffering and destruction everywhere. The wicked, who return at death to the "center of wickedness," have little to fear, for their vices and crimes in this life have made them resemble the evil molecules that welcome them into the other life, and they merge into them without pain: "The more vices and crimes a man has displayed in this world, the less he will have, as a result, to acquire in the center of wickedness, which I regard as the raw material making up the world." The fate of the good will be quite the opposite: "As virtue is in opposition to the system of the world, all those who have acknowledged it will be certain to endure, after this life, incredible tortures, owing to the difficulty that they will have in returning to the bosom of evil."

A quasi-chemical law that Sade does not spell out favors the bonding of homogeneous elements and excludes the bonding of contrary elements. Moreover, a law of attraction (which, on the other hand, Sade does spell out) requires that victims put to death by a given form of torture be subjected, by the evil molecules, to a type of welcoming torture identical to what they had undergone in this world. Naturally, this can only stimulate the zeal of their tormenters. Apparently, Sade constructed this scenario by systematically inverting Christian dogmas about life after death. "The Being supreme in wickedness" may have come, lexically speaking, from Manichaeanist doctrine, but Sade may also have coined the term himself. We should recognize that this myth, which Clairwil considers "bizarre," avoids one of the contradictions of traditional theology, which makes devils, themselves sinful and damned, into executors of divine justice.

As for the "evil molecules," there is no mystery about their lexical origin: Sade named them this in reference to the comte de Buffon's "organic molecules." In the *Histoire de Juliette*, Noirceuil speaks of "the organic molecules that compose us"; they are undeniably material in nature. Is it not logical that the demons, their victims, the "center of evil," and the God of evil himself should gradually become material bodies? In that case, Saint-Fond's system would be compatible with the materialism inherent in Sade's heroes who are worthy of the name. The only remaining difficulty would be to justify Saint-Fond's use of the word "soul." The immortality of the soul mentioned above would then fall into the same category as the "indestructible monad" conceived by Voltaire for eschatological purposes.

Our third Enlightenment atheist in the closing years of the Second Enlightenment, contrasting with Sade but not, perhaps, with Diderot, is the wise and learned Pierre-Jean-Georges Cabanis. It was during the Empire, around 1806 or 1807, that Cabanis wrote to Fauriel his *Lettre sur les causes premières* (Letter on Primary Causes). (He was to die in 1808 and the *Lettre* was not published until much later.) As a perennial *Aufklärer* (enlightener), Cabanis dismisses in this letter the idea of an infinite power exceeding the sum of all existing forces: "The mind cannot even imagine a power not limited by its own nature, by the circumstances under which it operates, by the results that it must produce, or by the ends that it must reach." As Voltaire had said, "God is not extravagantly powerful." In the same spirit, Cabanis refuses to anthromorphize the kindness and justice of the first cause, to shape by thought "a being situated outside the universe, yet present in every part of matter," a type of "colossal man, endowed with all the characteristics of prudence and strength, to whom, nonetheless, one attributes nearly every human foolishness and the basest of passions." If indeed "such is the Supreme Being that is proposed for human worship," writes Cabanis, "one must have made very little use of one's powers of reason, or else have a strange reliance on the madness and credulity of men." On the other hand, in his *Lettre* Cabanis adopts as his own the hypothesis of an intra-cosmic "willing intelligence," concentrated in certain places:

It is not contrary to reason to suppose that the universe as a whole is organized in such a way that all its parts are mutually sympathetic, that there are partial centers, as in other organized bodies, where intelligence is gathered and produces more perceptible effects, and likely for the same reasons, a common center where all the impulses culminate and are perceived.

Whether unforeseen or all too foreseeable, this is another embodiment of the Stoic theme revived earlier by Diderot. Less than a century later, Renan compared the universe to a pearl-bearing oyster in his *Examen de conscience philosophique* (1892; Examination of Philosophical Consciousness). It appears that, in 1806-07, the image of the "great animal" was not entirely extinct. Is this the case even today? Perhaps, but who knows? In any case, whether on the theist/deist or the atheist side, the age of the Enlightenment had given mankind more than one idea of God.

JEAN DEPRUN

See also Atheism; Deism; Mechanism; Mysticism; Nature; Prometheus; Providence; Theology, German

Further Reading

Alquié, Ferdinand, *Le cartésianisme de Malebranche,* Paris: Vrin, 1974

Hazard, Paul, *The European Mind, 1680–1715,* New Haven, Connecticut: Yale University Press, 1952; London: Hollis and Carter, 1953 (original French edition, 1935)

Klossowski, Pierre, *Sade My Neighbor,* Evanston, Illinois: Northwestern University Press, 1991; London: Quartet, 1992 (original French edition, 1947)

Koyré, Alexandre, *From the Closed World to the Infinite Universe,* Baltimore, Maryland: Johns Hopkins Press, 1957

Mathiez, Albert, *The Fall of Robespierre, and Other Essays,* New York: Knopf, and London: Williams and Norgate, 1927; reprint, New York: Kelley, 1968 (original French edition, 1927)

Vovelle, Michel, *The Revolution against the Church: From Reason to the Supreme Being,* Columbus: Ohio State University Press, and Cambridge: Polity Press, 1991 (original French edition, 1988)

Government. *See* Authority, Government, and Power

Grammar

European Enlightenment thinkers were interested in diverse aspects of language and languages: their structure, their historical relationships, their "moral" and philosophical qualities, the methods used to teach languages, their function in society, and their role in science and literature. Philosophers, grammarians, and the society of "gentlemen" all agreed on the importance of language as the vehicle of human thought, an instrument of analysis and power, and a condition of socialization. Various disciplines or schools of thought that focused their attention on languages flourished in the 17th and 18th centuries. There was the comparative study of languages, the construction of artificial languages, (unilingual) lexicography, stylistics and rhetoric, and a philosophy of language that focused on the origin of language and on the relationship between language and thought (see Droixhe; Ricken; Robinet; Swiggers).

A grammatical description of languages, which was central to these disciplines, established an outline of linguistic macrostructures and provided lasting, reliable, general knowledge based on empirical foundations. Antoine-Isaac Silvestre de Sacy, writing at the end of the century, expressed the humanitarian impact of grammar in the preface to his *Principes de grammaire générale* (1799; Principles of General Grammar), written for his son:

> Thus will you become accustomed to well-conceived general principles, the various branches of each realm of knowledge that you must thenceforth acquire, and you will assume the good habit of connecting your ideas, combining them, connecting consequences to principles, effects to causes, and thus soundly judging your own opinions and those of others with whom you will live in society. May the heavens bless these first efforts of your father to train your mind and heart and render you one day worthy of the eternal Author of your being, and the noble destiny to which He calls you, to seek to ensure your own happiness by contributing to the happiness of your fellow man.

In the classical age in France, grammar was assigned the cognitive (and ethical) role of providing the human subject with rules for a complete and orderly expression of his thoughts. To understand this role, a look at the development of the study of grammar up to modern times will be helpful.

Definition and Function of Grammar

"General grammar," which emerged in the 17th century as a reaction against school grammar texts and the works of purists who amassed countless ad hoc rules and conceived of language learning as a simple process of rote memory, brought together the art of speaking and the art of thinking, connecting them with the concept of the sign. According to the Port-Royal *Grammaire générale et raisonnée* (1660; General and Reasoned Grammar):

> Grammar is the art of speaking. To speak is to make thought explicit by way of signs, that men did invent for this purpose . . . Now we must study that which is spiritual in [speech], which gives man one of the greatest advantages over all other animals, and which is one of the greatest proofs of his reason. It is the way we use it to signify our thoughts, the marvelous invention of composing from 25 or 30 sounds an infinite variety of words, which are unrelated in themselves, unrelated to what goes on in our minds, but which do not fail to reveal to others all our secrets, to reveal to those who cannot penetrate within, all that we conceive of, and all the varied movements of our soul. Thus can one define words, distinct and articulate sounds that men have made into signs to signify their thoughts.

The semiotic link of representation and expression posited between language and thought confers on grammar the methodological status of that which formulates the general, rational principles of a mechanism of noetic-linguistic transposition. As the understanding and description of this transposition improved, there was a corresponding improvement in grammatical description and a perfection of the process of cognition. Thus grammar was integrated into a current of thought, influenced by René Descartes and Nicolas Malebranche, in which the notion of method was predominant.

In the 18th century both philosophical and pedagogical interest in the methodic or systematic aspect of grammar led to a far-reaching theoretical reflection that placed grammar squarely within a general epistemology of the sciences, a theory of knowledge, and a philosophical anthropology. A grammatical science was formulated during the Enlightenment, one focused on the organizing principles of language systems and their relationship to thought. This interest in explanation of linguistic structures by way of universal principles created a separation between general or philosophical grammars and practical manuals (see Buzzetti and Ferriani, editors; Chevalier, 1971 and 1979; Foucault; Rosiello).

General grammar with a philosophical bent was primarily a French discipline. In comparison with 17th-century grammar, it had a broader empirical basis, used terminology that distinguished between form and function, and appealed to the rationality of language in general (instead of the "particular reasons" of specific languages). This general grammar of the 18th century was initiated in the first half of the century by a few French grammarians who developed a theory of sentence construction and of the contents of parts of speech. The brilliant scholar and teacher Claude Buffier was the first to orient grammatical analysis toward a semantic and syntactic concept of the clause in his *Grammaire françoise sur un plan nouveau, pour en rendre les principes plus clairs et la pratique plus aisée* (1709; A French Grammar Presented in a New Way So As to Make Its Principles Simpler and Its Use Easier). Father Buffier proposed a new theory of sentence structure and showed that the distinction of different parts of speech according to the traditional outline was in fact relative. Another innovator, the abbé Gabriel Girard, formulated a grammatical typology of languages, in *Les vrais principes de la langue françoise* (1747; The True Principles of the French Language), in which languages are divided into three categories: "analogous" languages, such as the modern Romance languages; "transpositive" languages, such as Latin or the Slavic languages; and "mixed" or "amphilogical" languages, such as Greek or German. Girard also developed a model of grammatical analysis based upon the distinction between seven semantic and syntactic functions: subjective, attributive, objective, terminative, circumstantial, conjunctive, and adjunctive. This analytic model was combined with a theory of two *régimes:* the constructive and the enunciator (see Seguin).

Buffier and Girard formulated a conception of grammar as an empirical discipline designed to explain the structure of language viewed as a system of representation. The three terms "structure," "system," and "rep-resentation" are essential for an understanding of the aims of general grammar in the 18th century, as opposed to the particular grammars that lacked a universalist scope. "Structure" refers to the organization of a language as an edifice constructed throughout time. "System" is a way of qualifying a language as a hierarchy of forms and a set of categories. "Representation" refers to the function of a language and the mode of functioning of languages. In his *Hermes; or, A Philosophical Inquiry concerning Language and Universal Grammar* (1751), the English philosopher-grammarian James Harris defined language as "a system of articulated sounds, which are signs or symbols of our ideas, primarily those which are general or universal." In his *Grammaire* (1775; Grammar), Étienne Bonnot de Condillac (author of a *Traité des systèmes* [1749; Treatise on Systems]), defined grammar as "a system of words that represent the system of ideas in our mind, when we want to communicate them in some order and with the relationships that we perceive."

As a system of signs, grammar, being both a description and the object of description, belongs in the *organon* of the sciences. Therefore, if its definition and function are to be understood it must be placed back among the arts and sciences. Denis Diderot and Jean le Rond D'Alembert's *Encyclopédie* and the *New Royal and Universal Dictionary of Arts and Sciences* (1769–71) are invaluable resources on this subject. The English *Dictionary* clearly distinguishes between grammar as descriptive and normative text, and grammar as a fact (that is, the art of speaking properly and the systematic knowledge of universal principles): "Grammar is the same in all languages, as to its general principles, and notions, which it borrows from philosophy to explain the order and manner wherein we express our ideas by words." The *Dictionary* also emphasizes the function of language as representation: "the art of speaking properly; that is, of expressing one's thoughts, by signs mutually agreed on for that purpose." Diderot and D'Alembert, inspired by Francis Bacon's classification (*Novum Organum* [1620]), conceived of grammar as pertaining to logic, the object of which is reason. Reason, in turn, along with memory and imagination, comprises the three spheres of human knowledge. More specifically, logic has three functions: (1) it must study the formation of ideas, how they are conceived, and the possibilities of their being combined to form a judgment; (2) it must study the means of retaining ideas; and (3) it must study the means of communicating ideas. Grammar must be situated theoretically with regard to this last function, communication, defined as "the science of the instrument of discourse" (*Encyclopédie,* "Explication détaillée du système des connoissances humaines" [Detailed Explanation of the System of Human Knowledge]). Discursive content is distinguished from the qualities of discourse, which pertain to rhetoric. Discursive content exhibits a rationality that is founded in man, a rational being, and in the history of languages, which testifies to a long-term refinement of thought through thinking, a rational purification of languages (see Foucault; Robinet; Swiggers, 1984 and 1986).

Grammatical Categories and Functions

The status and function of grammar formed a subject of theoretical interest that only concerned philosopher-grammarians; this reflection presupposed the conjunction of theories of ideas, language, and knowledge. For the philosopher-grammarians, the object of the study of grammar was the word in its function as image of thought. Consequently, grammar should proceed from an analysis of thought, following the laws of logic. This formally analyzed content is what languages, as systems of arbitrary signs, "translate" into a linguistic form. Linguistic symbolization respects two types of principles: eternally valid universal principles related to the nature of thought; and free, historically variable conventions unique to a given language. The difference between general grammar and particular grammars is set along these lines. General grammar is a "science" oriented toward a search for universal properties in all languages; particular grammars are arts that describe the structure of a specific grammatical system.

In the 18th century both general and particular grammars were centered on the word, seen as the hinge unit between sounds (or "letters"), which were the material elements, and the sentence (or "phrase"), which was a combination of words expressing a complete thought. The word, understood as the sign of a complete idea, was defined as a sonic segment that, by convention, communicated content. Although most particular grammars (normative or didactic) were organized from the smallest to the largest units (from description of sounds/letters to parts of speech to syntax), the grammarians of the *Encyclopédie* (Father César Chesneau Dumarsais and later Nicolas Beauzée) instead constructed "a tree-like "system of grammar." Beauzée presents a detailed grammatical chart in his "Système figuré des parties de la grammaire" (Outlined System of Parts of Grammar) in the article "Grammaire." Grammar includes orthography (the study of letters, diacritical signs, and the use of types of letters) and orthology, subdivided into lexicology and syntax. Lexicology is subdivided into three branches: the "material" of words, the "value" of words, and the "etymology" of words. The subdivision of the study of words includes phonetics and prosody, morpho-syntax, and an etymological explanation leading into a history of cultures and ideas, at least in Turgot's ambitious view

(in the article "Étymologie" [Etymology]). The morpho-syntactic branch, covering the value of words, is a study of classes of words organized according to the totality of ideas constituting the meaning of words (see the article "Mot" [Word] in the *Encyclopédie*). The classification is based on a combination of formal grammatical criteria, logical and semantic criteria, and discursive (or pragmatic) criteria. It makes a distinction between affective words (interjections) and enunciative words, the latter being divided into four classes of declinable words: nouns and pronouns, words that designate determined objects; adjectives and verbs, words that designate indeterminate objects; and three classes of undeclinable words (conjunctions, words of discursive liaison, and two types of "suppletive" words, adverbs and prepositions, the latter implying a double connection, to an antecedent and to a consequent term) (see Swiggers, 1984 and 1986).

The second branch of orthology is syntax, which was highly esteemed by Enlightenment grammarians. The central object of syntax is the phrase, whose "form" and "matter" were studied by the philosopher-grammarians. The "matter" is all of the parts of speech that compose the phrase: logical parts (the functions "subject," "attribute," and "copula," along with the mid-17th century discovery, of the "complement") and grammatical parts ("words required by the enunciation & the language spoken to constitute the whole of the logical parts" [the article "Grammaire"]). This "matter" must be organized by a form, or a particular arrangement of the parts of the phrase. The formal organization of the phrase corresponds to three structural principles: concord, case, and construction. The first two principles occur on a morpho-syntactic level because they mark a syntactic relationship by a particular inflection, agreement, or relationship of determination; the third principle occurs on a syntactico-syntactic incidence because it concerns a syntactic relationship marked by a particular arrangement of words in a simple or figurative construction (see Chevalier, 1968 and 1979; Swiggers, 1984).

Grammar as a theoretical subject in the 18th century was basically a construct of the grammarians of the *Encyclopédie*. Their thought was based on earlier grammatical tradition, particularly 17th-century general grammar, which had already considered the raison d'être of various classes of words, studied their notional content, and offered reasoned explanation of the combination of words in phrases (expressing "judgments"). This thinking was systematized and expanded during the 18th century. All grammatical concepts were analyzed to establish their hierarchy; research was extended to the categories of different languages; the study of grammar was ultimately combined with a reflection on the status of language, its origin, and the origin and development of human knowledge. Grammatical concepts were redefined from a functional and comparative perspective. This global study brought out the interrelationships of these concepts as elements in a system (see the "Système figuré des parties de la grammaire" [Figurative System of the Different Parts of Grammar] in the *Encyclopédie;* and the "Tableau méthodique pour la Grammaire" [Methodic Table for Grammar] in the *Encyclopédie méthodique: Grammaire et littérature* [1782–86; A Methodical Encyclopedia: Grammar and Literature]). In his *Dictionnaire grammatical de la langue françoise* (1761; Grammatical Dictionary of the French Language), which covers the fields of orthography, pronunciation, prosody, and "grammatical rules," the abbé Féraud stands out as a technician of grammatical terminology (see Auroux, 1979; Bartlett; Swiggers, 1986).

Grammatical Theory, Descriptive Grammar, and Linguistic Thought

Grammar in the 18th century was constructed as a theoretical object inscribed within a theory of signs. Elaborated by the Encyclopedists, this theory of grammar drew on the empiricism of Bacon and the philosophical principles of Newtonian science; the Cartesian component was gradually replaced by the sensationalism of Condillac. The notion of a universally identical reason was maintained but its composition was completely separated, through analysis and the abstraction of sensations, from any suggestion of innateness. In a significant exception to this trend, Pierre-Louis Moreau de Maupertuis's *Réflexions philosophiques sur l'origine des langues et la signification des mots* (1748; Philosophical Reflections on the Origins of Languages and the Meaning of Words) postulated the existence of "planes of ideas," differing from one people to another, thus opening the way to 19th-century anthropological and linguistic comparativism. Condillac considered the study of grammar as nothing less than the study of the methods used by human beings to analyze thought. For the ideologues (Domergue, Antoine-Louis-Claude Destutt de Tracy, F. Thurot, the comte de Volney), grammar invested with philosophical content became the introductory discipline of a theory (and encyclopedia) of knowledge, as well as of a social ethic.

The universalist ambitions of this theory of grammar were all the more easily upheld because the theory maintained a static view of languages and a nondiscursive approach to language. The French movement had two currents: the first approach, represented by Dumarsais and Beauzée, was more grammatical and produced general grammar (connected to a rhetorical theory); the second approach, exemplified by Condillac and Destutt de Tracy, was more epistemological and proposed a method for analyzing simultaneously the art of speaking, the art of writing, and the art of thinking. In effect, this latter approach functioned as the basis of an all-encompassing "ideology." Universalist theorization in Germany, most often labeled "philosophical," was inspired by Gottfried Wilhelm Leibniz and to an even greater extent by Christian Wolff. Proponents of this current such as Canz (1737), Carpov (1743), and Panzer (1747), drawing on their background in Hebrew studies, were primarily interested in the connection between language(s), thought, and reality. In England 18th-century philosophical grammar was not particularly inspired by the ambitious projects of artificial languages or by the pasigraphy undertaken in the 17th century. Most notable was the persistent influence of the Port-Royal *Grammaire générale et raisonnée* (translated into English and integrated, for example, in the *Grammar of the English Tongue* [1711], attributed to John Brightland but in fact compiled by Charles Gildon), until the publication of Harris's treatise, mentioned above, which was of Platonic and Aristotelian inspiration, with an innovative view of the nature of classes of words (see Auroux, 1983; Land; Michael; Ricken, 1990; Weiss).

Alongside this movement of theorization, there was a great deal of activity related to grammatical description backed by the development of language teaching in the 18th century. For France, three genres of writing on grammar can be distinguished: (1) practical grammars—elementary grammars, grammars for instruction or for consultation intended for the general reader, and contrastive grammars; (2) "reflective" grammars—works directly inspired by general, reasoned, philosophical grammars that aimed to explain the principles that govern the structure of a language; and (3) synthetizing and normative grammars—lexical grammars that formed a bridge between practice and reason and included the elements of practical grammars while broadening the documentary base using the style of "observations" or "remarks about the language." The latter type is exemplified by the *Traité de la grammaire françoise* (1705; Treatise on French Grammar) by the abbé Regnier-Desmarais, the second type by Buffier's *Grammaire françoise* and Girard's *Vrais principes* (both mentioned above). The best examples of the first and most widely represented type are Pierre Restaut's *Principes généraux et raisonnés de la grammaire françoise* (1730; General and Reasoned Principles of French Grammar); Noël-François de Wailly's *Grammaire françoise ou Principes généraux et particuliers de la langue françoise* (1754–63; French Grammar; or, General and Specific Principles of the French Language); and, later, François-Charles Lhomond's *Élémens de la grammaire françoise* (1780; Elements of French Grammar). These three works initiated the current of "scholastic grammar." Authors engaged in grammatical description generally maintained close ties with the theorizing current, even in some books of a practical nature. Examples of this category from England include an elementary work, *Rudiments of the English Grammar* (1761), and a philosophical treatise on the structure and "qualities" of languages, *Course of Lectures on the Theory of Language, and Universal Grammar* (1762), both by Joseph Priestley (see Chevalier, 1971 and 1994; Swiggers, 1984 and 1994).

However, it should be stressed that grammar in the 18th century was related to significant linguistic studies, both empirical and theoretical. Among the major accomplishments of this Enlightenment linguistics, the following should be mentioned: (1) the analysis and explanation of synonyms—this philosophical and lexicological branch was initiated by Girard's *La justesse de la langue françoise* (1716; The Precision of the French Language) and his *Synonymes françois* (1736; French Synonyms), and pursued by Beauzée (1769) and Roubaux (1785); (2) the development of a typology of languages, also by Girard, in *Les vrais principes* (mentioned above), which inspired Adam Smith's essay (1761) on the genius of languages and inspired the myth of the "clarity of French" (Rivarol, 1784), and the controversy over the natural (because it is "analytic") order of French (see Ricken, 1978); (3) reflections on the origin of language, which evolved from mythical and philosophical hypotheses (Giambattista Vico, Johann Georg Hamann), through philosophical and cultural theories (Rousseau, Johann Gottfried von Herder, Aleksandr Nikolayevich Radishchev), into vast historical reconstructions, drawing on the "(re)discovery" of Sanskrit and leading to the comparativism of the romantic period (for example, Lord Monboddo's *Of the Origin and Progress of Language* [1773–92]); and (4) etymological research, sometimes conveying Cratylian ideas (Charles de Brosses and Antoine Court de Gébelin), but armed with an extremely reliable set of criteria in Turgot's article "Etymologie," and affirmed in relation to the Romance languages (P.-N. Bonamy) and the Teutonic languages (J. Ihre; see Droixhe, 1978).

By the end of the 18th century, all the elements had been assembled for a complete comparative grammar. Father Coeurdoux (1768, an essay presented in 1785) and William Jones (1786) had indicated striking similarities between Sanskrit, Latin, Greek, and modern European languages. The relationships among Finno-Ugric languages had been demonstrated by János Sajnovics (1770) and Sámuel Gyarmathi (1799). The historian A.L. Schlözer had designated the family of Semitic languages (1781). However, the blossoming of this comparative grammar was thwarted by the universalist, ahistorical, philosophical grammar patiently developed during the age of the Enlightenment, which

was a faithful reflection of that era's epistemological ideal: to discover a coherent unifying principle subtending diverse facts (see Aarsleff; Swiggers, 1992).

PIERRE SWIGGERS

See also Eloquence; Idea; Language; Sensationalism; Words, Abuse of

Further Reading

Aarsleff, Hans, "The Eighteenth Century," in *Current Trends in Linguistics,* vol. 14, *Historiography of Linguistics,* edited by Thomas A. Sebeok et al., The Hague: Mouton, 1975

Auroux, Sylvain, *La sémiotique des Encyclopédistes: Essai d'épistémologie historique des sciences du langage,* Paris: Payot, 1979

Auroux, Sylvain, "General Grammar and Universal Grammar in Enlightenment France," *General Linguistics* 23 (1983)

Bartlett, Barrie E., *Beauzée's Grammaire générale: Theory and Methodology,* The Hague: Mouton, 1975

Buzzetti, Dino, and Maurizio Ferriani, editors, *La grammatica del pensiero: Logica, linguaggio e conoscenza nell'età dell'illuminismo,* Bologna, Italy: Il Mulino, 1982

Chevalier, Jean-Claude, *Histoire de la syntaxe: Naissance de la notion de complément dans la grammaire française (1530–1750),* Geneva: Droz, 1968

Chevalier, Jean-Claude, "La grammaire générale et la pédagogie au XVIIIᵉ siècle," *Le français moderne* 39 (1971)

Chevalier, Jean-Claude, "Analyse grammaticale et analyse logique: Esquisse de la naissance d'un dispositif scolaire," *Langue française* 42 (1979)

Chevalier, Jean-Claude, *Histoire de la grammaire français,* Paris: Presses Universitaires de France, 1994

Droixhe, Daniel, *La linguistique et l'appel de l'histoire (1600–1800): Rationalisme et révolutions positivistes,* Geneva: Droz, 1978

Foucault, Michel, *The Order of Things,* London: Tavistock, 1970; New York: Pantheon Books, 1971 (original French edition, 1966)

Land, Stephen K., *From Signs to Propositions: The Concept of Form in Eighteenth-Century Semantic Theory,* London: Longman, 1974

Michael, Ian, *English Grammatical Categories and the Tradition to 1800,* Cambridge: Cambridge University Press, 1970

Ricken, Ulrich, *Grammaire et philosophie au siècle des Lumières: Controverses sur l'ordre naturel et la clarté du français,* Villeneuve-d'Ascq, France: Université de Lille III, 1978

Ricken, Ulrich, et al., *Sprachtheorie und Weltanschauung in der europäischen Aufklärung: Zur Geschichte der Sprachtheorien des 18. Jahrhunderts und ihrer europäischen Rezeption nach der Französischen Revolution*, Berlin: Akademie-Verlag, 1990

Robinet, André, *Le langage à l'âge classique*, Paris: Klincksieck, 1978

Rosiello, Luigi, *Linguistica illuminista*, Bologna, Italy: Il Mulino, 1967

Seguin, Jean-Pierre, *L'invention de la phrase au XVIIIe siècle: Contribution à l'histoire du sentiment linguistique français*, Louvain, Belgium: Peeters, and Paris: Société pour l'Information Grammataiale, 1993

Swiggers, Pierre, "La grammaire dans l'‘Encyclopédie’: État actuel des ‘études,’" *Beiträge zur romanischen Philologie* 20 (1981)

Swiggers, Pierre, *Les conceptions linguistiques des Encyclopédistes: Étude sur la constitution d'une théorie de la grammaire au siècle des Lumières*, Heidelberg: Groos, and Louvain: Leuven University Press, 1984

Swiggers, Pierre, *Grammaire et théorie du langage au dix-huitième siècle: "Mot," "temps," "mode" dans l' 'Encyclopédie méthodique,'* Lille, France: Presses Universitaires de Lille, 1986

Swiggers, Pierre, "Seventeenth- and Eighteenth-Century Europe," in *International Encyclopedia of Linguistics*, edited by William Bright, vol. 2, Oxford and New York: Oxford University Press, 1992

Swiggers, Pierre, "Joseph Priestley's Approach of Grammatical Categorization and Linguistic Diversity," in *Perspectives on English*, edited by Keith Carlon et al., Louvain, Belgium: Peeters, 1994

Weiss, Helmut, *Universalgrammatiken aus der ersten Hälfte des 18. Jahrhunderts in Deutschland: Eine historisch-systematische Untersuchung*, Münster, Germany: Nodus, 1992

Grand Tour

The "grand tour" was an initiation, a journey that allowed young Anglo-Saxon gentlemen to enlarge their knowledge of social and political practices in various countries on the European continent and to immerse themselves in classical culture in Italy. Father Richard Lassels, who traveled through Italy as a chaperone for young English nobles five times between 1637 and 1668, is said to have been the first to use the term "the grand tour." In the preface to one of the many editions of his guidebook *The Voyage of Italy,* first published in 1670, Lassels states that one must make the grand tour of France and of Italy in order to truly understand Caesar and Livy. Subsequently reference was made to the grand continental tour, which included at least Italy (as far as Naples) and France, but often encompassed Flanders, the Netherlands, Switzerland, and the German-speaking lands as well.

As a social institution, the grand tour developed in England around the middle of the 17th century. It was fixed within a rigid framework in the second half of that century, and then, having become fashionable, generated numerous derivative forms that more or less followed the pattern throughout the 18th century. The grand tour was a specific type of instructional journey, always oriented from north to south, with a return to the point of departure; it was initially intended for the sons of the aristocracy between the ages of 16 and 20, thus marking the end of their formal studies. The journey obeyed strict rules, notably that a young man was never to set off on his grand tour alone but was to be accompanied by a tutor, sometimes referred to as his "bear-leader." The educational value of the young man's experience depended to a large extent on the tutor. Ideally, the tutor was a serious, respectable, and mature man, with natural authority and a dignified personality. As well as being a teacher, mentor, and guide, he was responsible for supervising the morals and religion of his pupil. The most affluent young men traveled with an entire entourage, including a "governor," who was responsible for overseeing and organizing the practical details of the journey, a physician, several valets, and sometimes an artist, who was there to make souvenir sketches of the places visited.

The whole tour through western Europe took about three years (although there were shorter grand tours) so that the young man might acquire a good knowledge of languages and could study the diverse forms of government of the lands that he visited. The customary itinerary began in France (18 months), went on to Italy (10 months), and, on the way back home, included the German-speaking lands and the Low Countries (5 months); one might also spend 3 additional months in Paris in order to practice "noble manners" there one last time. Originally, the grand tour was essentially restricted to urban Europe—a tour from city to city following a set itinerary derived from guides and anthologies aimed at travelers. Unlike explorers, who searched, those who went on the grand tour, found. They verified with their own eyes what they had learned from their textbooks, or had seen mentioned in their tourists' guidebooks. The grand tour was never a matter of traveling in order to break away, but an educational experience in which return was implicit.

The Cosmopolitan Grand Tour in the Age of Enlightenment

While the grand tour, strictly speaking, was a formative journey intended for young British aristocrats from the second half of the 17th century onward, when one looks at the travel literature of the period it appears that the subject deserves a closer and more in-depth investigation. The rigid, conventional institution of the grand tour was criticized, notably by the English themselves, from the beginning of the 18th century, in caricatures, in newspaper articles, and elsewhere. In his *Sentimental Journey through France and Italy* (1768), Laurence Sterne even speaks of "the whole army of peregrine martyrs . . . young gentlemen transported by the cruelty of parents and guardians." Moreover, soon the term "grand tour" was no longer applied exclusively to the formative journeys of young English nobles but also to those of the Dutch, German, French, Swedish, and Russian aristocracy.

The ideal age for setting out on the grand tour was a subject of constant debate, as was its educational value. Some strongly denounced the social conservatism of this aristocratic institution; others, embodying this very conservatism, feared that the grand tour helped to corrupt the young. While the Enlightenment *philosophes* were happy to defend the usefulness of such formative journeys, Beat Louis de Muralt of Switzerland declared in *Lettres sur le voyage* (1725; Letters on Traveling) that they were mechanisms for corrupting the natural ingenuousness of his young compatriots.

Alongside the development of the grand tour, there was also a radical change in the practice of foreign study. During the general restructuring of the education of European ruling classes in the 17th century, the English aristocrat, the German *Kavalier,* and the French *honnête homme* (gentleman), felt that a period of study at a university or a religious secondary school in Italy was an indispensable addition to their curriculum vitae. This phenomenon was gradually incorporated into the classic initiation rite of the grand tour and affected

every nation in Europe. Subsequently, those who were destined to join the ruling class were expected to complete their training by traveling abroad. The Scots economist Adam Smith held that the mediocre quality of the two universities in England was one reason why the grand tour was endowed with such a reputation for the education of gentlemen. And, again, it was in order to compensate for the narrowness of the routine book learning dispensed by universities that Father Fénelon, in his *Télémaque* (1699; Telemachus), offered an imaginary formative journey to his young pupil the duc de Bourgogne, who was forbidden to travel abroad because of his princely status. Earlier, Baudelot de Dairval had highlighted the educational advantages of foreign travel in *De l'utilité des voyages* (1686; On the Usefulness of Travels), and Francis Maximilien Misson in the dedicatory epistle of his *Voyage d'Italie* (1691; Voyage to Italy), had evoked the usefulness as well as the pleasure that could be derived from a long journey. In the *Encyclopédie* the chevalier de Jaucourt devotes almost the whole of his article "Voyage" (Travel) to educational journeys, even though travel was not restricted to young aristocrats in training.

The voyages of scholars and businessmen, who were little inclined to follow a set itinerary imposed by tradition, gradually altered the routes of the grand tour and broadened its strictly cultural horizons. As a result, there was a gradual movement over the course of the 18th century toward less-traditional grand tours inspired by the desire to discover more about, in particular, the arts, sciences, and technology, and more oriented toward the enjoyment of travel and living in a different culture. Although tutors remained in favor among the aristocracy, it became increasingly common to see young men who set out on grand tours simply in the company of a companion—such as Horace Walpole and Thomas Gray in 1739—on the highways of Europe. The English historian Edward Gibbon even argued that the grand tour should not be limited to the privileged alone and that every cultivated person should be able to travel abroad. Although such travels had been restricted to men up until this time, several women took part in grand tours, including Madame Du Boccage, Lady Mary Wortley Montagu, and Hester Lynch Piozzi (known to readers of Samuel Johnson's works as Mrs. Thrale).

Nevertheless, the grand tour was very expensive and continued to be limited to the wealthy classes. Only a minority of artists and scholars could take part, doing so as a result of patronage or through opportunities to participate in the activities of their clients. The accounts of journeys published in the 18th century reveal how those who went on the grand tour moved within the circles of "polite society." Such travelers were to be found everywhere that gentlefolk met, from concert halls and theatres to scholarly or academic societies, as well as in Masonic lodges, salons, and curio shops. Between 1773 and 1783 Jean-François Séguier of Nîmes, a member of the Académie Française, was visited by nearly 190 English travelers on the grand tour. Such visits to celebrated intellectuals were also a duty. Like many other travelers, James Boswell spoke at length with Jean-Jacques Rousseau and Voltaire during the Swiss leg of his journey through Europe.

Over the course of the 18th century, the highways of Europe were improved for strategic and commercial reasons, while the increasingly efficient performance of postal systems encouraged the movements of travelers and contributed to the "discovery" of "new" regions, in particular the Netherlands, Scandinavia, and Poland; Spain, in contrast, continued to be excluded from the grand tour. The greatest "discoveries," however, were those of the mountains of Savoy and the cantons of Switzerland. In the past, these Alpine regions had been places that travelers passed through en route to Italy when they did not want to sail from Nice to Genoa or from Marseille to Livorno. Now the Alps became destinations in themselves, in particular for English and German travelers, who exhibited a taste for landscapes that had formerly been unknown or unappreciated. The spectacular waterfalls, canyons, cliffs, and irregularly shaped peaks inspired a nascent fascination for the sublime and picturesque aspects of nature, in line with aesthetic values that came into fashion beginning in mid–18th century. The countless guides to Switzerland, published in every language, revealed this new interest in the landscape as well as in the people who lived there. Take, for example, Baron von Zerlauben's *Tableaux topographiques, pittoresques, physiques, historiques, moraux et politiques de la Suisse* (Topographic, Picturesque, Physical, Historical, Moral, and Political Depictions of Switzerland), which was published in five volumes in Paris by Jean-Benjamin de la Borde between 1780 and 1788. The work contains more than 270 engraved plates, and its title alone is a clear indication of the diversity of the new interests in the age of Enlightenment.

Italy: The Ultimate Destination of the 18th-Century Grand Tour

The main French traveling routes continued to be heavily used, with a preference for roads to Paris, Versailles, the chateaus of the Loire valley, Dijon, Lyon, and Provence. However, during the age of the Enlightenment there was a perceptible reorientation of the grand tour that made Italy preeminent in the itineraries of the travelers. In 1711 the earl of Shaftesbury, a philosopher, published *Characteristicks of Men, Manners, Opinions, and Times,* in which he instructed the new

generation in the unity of morals and taste, the connection between the good and the beautiful. From then on, the acquisition of "good taste" was an essential ingredient in the education of young British gentlemen—and good taste could only be acquired in Italy. These ideas were developed by the painter Jonathan Richardson, who defined the rules of enlightened connoisseurship and, in 1720, published a guide to the monuments and works of art that were to be seen and studied if one wished to become truly cultivated.

Charles Nicholas Cochin, the architect Jacques-Germain Soufflot, and the abbé Leblanc, who were sent by Madame de Pompadour to help influence the taste of the future marquis de Marigny on his grand tour, from 1749 to 1751, accompanied their young protégé on a voyage that had been meticulously planned in order to form his taste in the "grand manner." Their journey is described in Cochin's *Voyage pittoresque d'Italie* (1756; Picturesque Voyage in Italy), in which the main topic is the art and architecture of the peninsula. Italy also occupied a dominant position in German travel literature in the 18th century, no longer simply as the land of antiquity but also as a place of mild climate, enchanting landscapes, and, above all, of the arts, aspects that heralded the Sturm und Drang movement (see the accounts of Italian travels by Johann Volkmann and by the Goethes, both father and son). The main focus of aristocratic travel was thus increasingly oriented toward the arts. For those who spent time on the grand tour frequenting the opera houses and concert halls in every important city, music clearly played a special role, yet the fine arts were by far what interested the most.

Although visits to monuments, ancient ruins, and palaces were part of the obligatory program, travelers also wanted to acquire objects en route that would allow them, once they had returned home, to display the tangible signs of their cultural power, which was so necessary to preserve their status as aristocrats. Medals, cameos, sculptures, and archeological artifacts (or copies sold as such) began to decorate the stately homes of the travelers. The wealthiest had their portraits painted next to famous monuments. Between 1760 and 1780, no fewer than 250 gentlemen had their portraits painted by Pompeo Batoni in Rome. Others purchased views of the countries they had visited. These souvenirs, put on display in their residences, reminded visitors that they had enjoyed the privilege of journeying to the sources of the civilized world.

Published texts regarding travel played a decisive role in forming a collective mentality, and these writings influenced the grand tour itself. Ever since the *Mirabilia* (wonder books) of the Middle Ages, there was an endless proliferation of travel guides intended for pilgrims and travelers on their way to Italy. In his *Bibliothèque universelle des voyages* (1808; Universal Travel

Library), Boucher de La Richarderie lists close to 3,000 works published in the 18th century alone. A study of the most famous guides, or of those that were most frequently reissued, allows us to see the main lines in the developing interests of travelers, the routes they followed, and the places they visited most often; but it also compels us to notice how certain stereotypes were constantly reproduced from one guidebook to the next.

The numerous translations of travel guides made during the 18th century reveal how increasingly cosmopolitan the grand tour had become during that time. The standard text used as a vade mecum in the first half of the century—not only by English travelers but also by Montesquieu, who had a great deal of respect for it—was Joseph Addison's *Remarks on Several Parts of Italy* (1705), reprinted in 1718, 1726, and 1733; a French version was published in 1722. Maximilien Misson's *Voyage d'Italie* (1691) enjoyed the same success, going through six editions in French until 1743 and five in English until 1739, and was translated into Dutch (1704) and German (1713). This guide, issued in four small volumes, was a favorite of Montesquieu, Brosses, Gibbon, and Goethe, to cite only its best-known readers. In addition, authors of works regarding Italy included in the *Encyclopédie* drew extensively from Misson's guide when writing their articles. Joseph-Jérôme de Lalande's *Voyage en Italie* (1769; Voyage to Italy), which was more systematic, came to replace Misson during the final decades of the 18th century. Lalande's work, which was published in seven volumes with a supplementary volume of maps, was a true best seller all over Europe, due to its encyclopedic nature.

There was a definite change in the most popular destinations of the grand tour during the 1770s, when Venice and Florence lost ground to Rome and Naples. The Italy of the grand tour had long excluded the Mezzogiorno, the Abruzzi, Sicily, and Sardinia. Archeologists were instrumental in bringing about a "rediscovery" of these southern regions. Up until 1770 few travelers had ventured farther south than Naples, but the beginning of archeological excavations at Pompeii (1738) and Herculaneum (1748), the rediscovery of Paestum, and the new fashion for the Sicilian Doric that was linked to these events led "civilized" Europeans to recognize in these ruins the roots of their own culture. The passion for antiquity became a point of reference for the cosmopolitan sensibility of travelers.

We owe to Winckelmann's friend Baron Johann Hermann von Riedesel the first complete guide to southern Italy and Sicily, the *Reise durch Sicilien und Gross-griechenland* (1771; Travels through Sicily and That Part of Italy Formerly Called Magna Graecia), which was translated into French in 1773. Along with Patrick Brydone's *A Tour through Sicily and Malta* (1773; translated into French in 1775), Riedesel's book initiated the fashion for visiting Sicily. *Le voyage pittoresque, ou Description des royaumes de Naples et de Sicile* (1781–86; The Picturesque Voyage; or, Depiction of the Kingdoms of Naples and Sicily) by Dominique Vivant-Denon and the abbé de Saint-Non remains the most accomplished of the publications, establishing the synthesis of the tradition of the grand tour with that of archeological expeditions. The care given to the illustrations—engravings based on signed works by the best landscape artists of the day—makes this an invaluable and admirably documented work. Along with Jean-Pierre-Laurent Hoüel's *Voyage pittoresque des Îles de Sicile, de Malte et de Lipari* (1782-87; Picturesque Voyage to the Islands of Sicily, Malta, and Lipari), these folio volumes, aimed at enlightened connoisseurs, represent a magnificent homage to Italy by Enlightenment France.

The term "grand tour" has often been misused to indicate any journey to southern Europe, whether for business or pleasure, undertaken by artists, bankers, or princes; but these types of journeys were merely secondary derivatives of a venerable institution. As a formative journey for young aristocrats, the grand tour was increasingly rare after the French Revolution and came to a symbolic end in 1841, with Thomas Cook's first package tour.

PIERRE CHESSEX

See also Drawing; Education, Instruction, and Pedagogy; Ruins

Further Reading

Burgess, Anthony, and Francis Haskell, *The Age of the Grand Tour,* London: Elek, and New York: Crown, 1967

Burke, J., "The Grand Tour and the Rule of Taste," *Studies in the Eighteenth Century* (1968)

Hibbert, Christopher, *The Grand Tour,* London: Weidenfeld and Nicolson, and New York: Putnam, 1969

Mead, William Edward, *The Grand Tour in the Eighteenth Century,* Boston: Houghton Mifflin, 1914; reprint, New York: Blom, 1972

Sutton, Denys, *Souvenirs of the Grand Tour,* London: Wildenstein, 1982; 2nd edition, revised, 1983

Grotesque

The term "grotesque" dates from around 1480, when strange frescoes discovered in Nero's Domus Aurea (Golden House) in Rome were dubbed in Italian *grottesche,* doubtless because of the subterranean location—or grotto—in which they had been found (see Harpham). These odd paintings, whose only charm lay only in what Montaigne called "their variety and strangeness" (*Les essais* [1580–95; Essays]), present a hodgepodge of plant, animal, and human forms in an ornamental style that was to become very popular during the Renaissance (see Dacos; González de Zárate). The monstrous shapes of Hieronymus Bosch and Pieter Brueghel were called "grotesque"; Raphael placed grotesques alongside scenes from the Old Testament in his decorations of the loggias of the Vatican; and, as Andre Chastel has observed, Montaigne resorted to the French word—in the form *crotesque*—to "justify the free and capricious formula of the essay" (see Chastel). According to Chastel's account, from the 16th century onward, the ebullient grotesque style spread throughout the West, presenting itself as the antithesis of a mode of representation in which norms were defined by "a view of space in perspective" and a "characterization of types." The grotesque style, in contrast, was characterized by a "negation of space" and a "fusion of types," "weightlessness of forms" and the "outrageous proliferation of hybrids." However, the grotesque as a movement of artistic "liberation" that capsized the established order (see Kayser) permeates the whole history of Europe, as evidence of either collapsing social structures or, conversely, cultural efforts toward a regeneration of humankind and of the collectivity (see Korthals Altes).

In his *De architectura* (On Architecture), Vitruvius, the engineer of the Augustan Age, had already issued a decisive verdict against such "absurd and disjointed scenes" whose literary counterpart—illustrated, for example, by Ovid's *Metamorphoses*—rested on enduring Greco-Roman tradition of criticism and satire. It is not surprising, given the vogue for the grotesque at that time, that César-Pierre Richelet's *Dictionnaire françois* (1680) gives the concept of the grotesque a much broader definition than simply the decoration of ancient grottoes: "Amusing, with an amusingly ridiculous element. Grotesque man. Grotesque young woman. Grotesque look. Grotesque face. Grotesque action." Similarly, the 1694 edition of the *Dictionnaire de Académie Française* defines the term as follows:

Figuratively, it means ridiculous, bizarre, eccentric. A grotesque outfit, this speech is really grotesque, a grotesque facial expression.—*Grotesquement* [grotesquely], adverb. In a ridiculous and eccentric manner. Dressed grotesquely, dancing grotesquely—Bizarre, weird, eccentric, capricious.

Dictionaries took their examples of the art of the grotesque from painting (Jacques Callot and Diego Rodriguez de Silvay Velázquez) or from literature (Rabelais, Cervantes, Shakespeare, Francisco Gómez de Quevedo y Villegas, Paul Scarron, and Cyrano de Bergerac), all with the general connotation of "comic" or "burlesque." It should be emphasized that such examples do not contest the parallel development of ornamentation toward the spirited and voluptuous forms of the rocaille style.

The *Dictionnaire de Trévoux* (1704; Dictionary of Trévoux) and the 1725 edition of Antoine Furetière's *Dictionnaire universel* (Universal Dictionary) focus above all on the figure of Callot and on the commedia dell'arte and its characters, as typical examples of the aesthetic of the grotesque. Denis Diderot, in his *Discours sur la poésie dramatique*, 1758; Discourse on Dramatic Poetry), and Justus Möser, in his *Harlekin oder die Verteidigung des Groteske-Komischen* (1761; Harlequin; or, The Vindication of the Grotesque-Comic), both expand upon the European "comic-grotesque tradition" of the farce. In Chapter VI of his *Discours*, entitled "Du drame burlesque" (On Burlesque Drama), Diderot states that "an excellent farce is not the work of an ordinary man. It requires an eccentric gaiety; its characters are like Callot's grotesques, in which the chief features of the human face are preserved." The triumphant nonchalance of Antoine Watteau's paintings, the whimsical tone imparted by chinoiserie and arabesques (decorative forms derived from the grotesque but lacking its brutality), the amusing tone of caricatures, and the gaiety of farces were among the many elements invoked as the grotesque was adapted to suit the exquisite tastes of the age of the Enlightenment. And yet, this concept of the grotesque underwent such a pivotal transformation in the 18th century that it is considered today to be the impetus for the modern aesthetic (see Todorov; Bozal Fernández).

From its birth as a decorative style to its comic and burlesque flowering in literature and painting, the grotesque aimed to appear incongruous. This effect of incongruity could be the result of the disproportion or distortion found in satire, the passion of the vices and failings, or the surprise of unexpected responses; invariably, it was achieved using conventional elements as a foil for distorted ones. In the classical tradition, the purpose of such distortion was to demonstrate the goodness or the truth of a given state of affairs. As a corollary of this principle, comedy was regarded as a way of looking at the world that was in contrast to seriousness but within its frame of reference. The comic was therefore not autonomous but regarded as the negative form of something else, to which it had to be linked. Thus conceived, the grotesque had been considered a legitimate "style" prior to the 18th century. However, the coherence of the classical principles collapsed with the progressive elaboration of the notion of taste—for example, through Joseph Addison's theories on "the pleasures of the imagination" in *The Spectator* (1712). Incongruity could be achieved when it was based on the established opposition of the beautiful and the comic—comic in the sense that Karl Friedrich Flögel still gave it in 1788 in his *Geschichte des Grotesk-Komischen* (History of the Grotesque-Comic), that is, ugly, vulgar, crude, and vile. However, grotesque incongruity lost all meaning as soon as the beautiful/comic opposition was overwhelmed by the existence of "several beauties" (as Addison put it), ranging from beauty as it was traditionally regarded to picturesque beauty and sublime beauty.

This development in aesthetics gave the comic two quite different meanings from the 18th century onward: its traditional meaning, as the effect of stylistic distortion, and a new meaning, as an autonomous aesthetic category that makes possible a different way of contemplating the world. This is the grotesque as defined in the modern sense by Valeriano Bozal Fernández: "I mean by *grotesque* the kind of distortion produced by an attitude or an angle on things such that this distortion reveals their inner nature, and goes even further by revealing that the latter is in fact their only real nature" (see Bozal Fernández). In this sense, the grotesque, as an aesthetic category, is different from satire and caricature, in that those genres distort only in order to correct or to moralize and thus refer back to some notion of perfection. The negativity in satire and caricature is merely an instrument of reform, for the person or thing ridiculed tends to be corrected as a result. Therefore, satire and caricature had an ostensible purpose in Enlightenment Europe, so long as optimism endured and enlightened men believed that reform was possible. But with the ebb of the Enlightenment, hope gave way to scepticism toward the canons and to mistrust of reason. In a world where everything was going wrong and where the ridiculous was the norm, the grotesque as a way of expressing life's uncertainties was to enjoy an unprecedented ascendancy.

Well before Victor Hugo or Théophile Gautier, European literature chose the path of the strange, and European painting became "capricious" before it became romantic. The Spanish, who did not have a good reputation in a Europe that was perhaps a little too enlightened, were to take the lead in "illuminating" the shadowy path of the grotesque, which had been a familiar part of their culture for some time. The "exuberant imagination" that Flögel attributed to the Spanish was the reason for their preponderance over "all the other European peoples" in matters grotesque. Kayser became interested in the grotesque after visiting the Madrid's Museo del Prado (Prado Museum), where he saw Velázquez's dwarfs and *meninas* (maids of honor), Francisco de Goya's *Saturn* and his *Caprichos* (Caprices), surrounded by paintings by Bosch and Brueghel, with their hellish images, which made a greater impact on him than the tales of Edgar Allan Poe. Indeed, Spain had a cultural history that was essentially based on comedy, particularly in literature, as the enlightened treatise writer Ignacio Luzán emphasized in his *La poética* (1737; Poetics). The famous exponents of Spanish comedy included Cervantes, Felix Lope de Vega, Quevedo, and Pedro Calderón de la Barca, the author of *En esta vida todo es verdad y todo mentira* (1770; In This Life, Everything Is Truth and Everything Is a Lie), a play in a grotesque tone that was adapted by Pierre Corneille as his *Héraclius* (1647) and translated by Voltaire as *L'Héraclius espagnol* (The Spanish Héraclius). As Luzán posited, picaresque writings are the *jocosos*, that is, the laughably ridiculous pillars of the national literature of Spain. Recommended by Father Feijoo and described by Juan Sempere y Guarinos in his *Discurso sobre el gusto actual de los españoles en la literatura* (Discourse on the Current Taste of the Spaniards in Literature), contemporary French literature wielded great influence in 18th-century Spain. However, the most notable works of fiction in that country at that time must be classified as grotesque: for example, Diego de Torres Villarroel's *Visiones y visitas con Don Francisco de Quevedo* (1728; Visions and Visits with Don Francisco de Quevedo) and Father Isla's *Historia del famoso predicator Fray Gerundio de Campazas* (1758; History of the Famous Preacher Friar Gerundio of Campazas, alias Zotes), among others. In short, Spain was a country where the grotesque was the refuge of the hidden face of this *ilustrado* (enlightened) age, a realistic place where there would appear what Father Isla called, in the preface to his *Fray Gerundio,* "ridiculous, exotic, and eccentric individuals."

Cultivated in a forward-moving Spain, which was nonetheless still in search of the bizarre, the taste for the grotesque extended to the rest of Europe by the time of the waning of the Enlightenment. That taste was spread through paintings, particularly those by Goya and Henry Fuseli (who spoke of Nero's Domus Aurea in his lecture "De l'état present de l'art" [On the Present State of Art]). It was also spread through strange literary works, rationalized fantasies, such as those of Nicolas-Anne-Edmé Rétif de La Bretonne, Robert Martin

Lesuire, Jan Potocki, and William Beckford. These writings form a bridge between the age of reason and the age of the Gothic novel. The grotesque as a category of modern aesthetics may therefore be defined by reference to the fancifully outlandish works of the aforementioned Spanish writers and painters as well as to the works of these other Europeans active around the end of the century.

The territory of the grotesque, true to its semantic origins, is the subterranean: the grotto (or variations on the grotto, configured as closed spaces: the brothel or the labyrinthine passage, for example). Its time is night. The grotesque is inhabited by nocturnal animals, wild beasts, or creatures symbolizing the ridiculous, such as bats, donkeys, and lynxes (which, because of their piercing eyes, are linked to the night); hybrid beings, such as those depicted in the ornamental motifs of the grotesque's origins; monstrous beings, including dwarfs, giants, and deformed or simply disguised figures; witches and their "rational" alter egos, the *celestinas* (lovers' go-betweens); devils and their "rational" alter egos, monks and inquisitors; phantoms and visions in general, and their "rational" variants, the living dead and animalcules; and, automata (although the latter were generally attributed to the grotesque in the 19th-century machine age, they were already markedly present at the end of the age of the Enlightenment, the age of mechanical inventions).

The style of the grotesque is humor. The grotesque aesthetic does not condemn the world that it represents but limits itself to observing the fragility of the frontiers between the human and the animal, the passionate man and the monster, the beautiful and the ugly, good and evil (see Barrena and Vásquez). The first step in this demonstration of the impotence of the logical and natural vision of the world consisted in unveiling the false appearances of human beings. Thus, the young noblewoman in Goya's *Galán con maja,* a drawing in his *Album de Madrid* (Madrid Album) becomes the prostitute in one of his *Caprichos.* Similarly, Spinacutta, who appears to be noble in Lesuire's *Seconde suite de l'aventurier français contenant les mémoires de Cataudin, Chevalier de Rosamène* (1784; Another Sequel to the French Adventurer, including the Memoirs of Cataudin, Chevalier of Rosamène), is unmasked by a miraculous fire, revealing a face "more diabolical" than that of "Satan plunged into holy water." While appearances are often deceptive, a new perception, as piercing as the eyes of a lynx, allows one to glimpse the true face, the reflection of the soul, the monstrous beings that inhabit the world—and Enlightenment Europe—in greater numbers than generally acknowledged. These "monstrous" beings include black men and women in Lesuire's *Aventurier français* (French Adventurer) and its three *Suites* (1782–88; Sequels); eunuchs and dwarfs in Beckford's *Vatheck, conte arabe* (Vathek, an Arab Tale [written in French, but first published in English in Paris in 1786]) and in Potocki's *Manuscrit trouvé à Saragosse* (1804–15; Manuscript Found in Saragossa); hunchbacked and toothless old women in Goya's *Caprichos* (the old flirt in *Hasta la muerte* [Until Death], and horrible goblins in the artist's *Duendecitos* [Little Goblins]); Lesuire's automatons; and diabolical combinations of all these beings, such as Potocki's "dwarf with a bluish face and a wooden leg." The grotesque is essentially an affirmation that the animal has not been eliminated from humanity, however civilized it might be; for evidence, one has only to open the windows, as do the heroes in Lesuire's work and in Rétif's *La découverte australe* (1781; The Southern Discovery), to see all sorts of animals in human shape, as well as men and women in animal shape, moving "grotesquely" around, generally in either a downward or an upward direction (see also Goya's *Capricho* entitled *Subir y bajar* [Rise and Fall]).

What are these grotesque beings that people the artistic visions of the somber twilight of the Enlightenment? Behind these faces of Satan that they multiplied infinitely, Fuseli and Goya dared to paint the very essence of the nature that human beings carry hidden within themselves, as can be seen in Fuseli's *The Nightmare,* or in many of Goya's *Caprichos,* where the Devil himself is depicted. One of the finest examples of this personification occurs in Goya's most famous *Capricho: El sueño de la razón produce monstruos* (The Sleep of Reason Brings Forth Monsters). If the night plays these evil tricks upon us, the day does not contradict it: Lesuire's and Goya's monks supposedly represent the diurnal, "real" image of the Devil. Only laughter, induced by the grotesque, can save us from madness, from the loss of reason that the incursion of nocturnal nightmares into daytime reality threaten to provoke in us.

Goya's *Capricho, ¿Dónde va mamá?* (Where Is Mama Going?) depicts a witch being escorted to a sabbat, protected from the sun by a cat holding a parasol, for she is so fat that she must set out by day, before all the other witches, in order to arrive on time. Such humor will stay by our side during our candlelit walk through the grotesque, whether it arises from the pen of Rétif and his weird beings; from the Briton Beckford or the Pole Potocki, with their taste for "arabesques"; from the "escathologies" of Lesuire and Goya; or from that precursor of Picasso, Fuseli.

LYDIA VAZQUEZ

See also Aesthetics; Monster; Physiognomy; Satire

Further Reading

Bakhtin, M.M., *Rabelais and His World,* translated by
    Helene Iswolsky, Cambridge, Massachusetts: MIT
    Press, 1968 (original Russian edition, 1965)
Barrena and Vásquez, "La beauté hideuse des corps ou
    la dégénérescence du 'corps naturel' au tournant des
    Lumières," *Queste* 7 (1994)
Bozal Fernández, Valeriano, *Goya y el gusto moderno,*
    Madrid: Alianza Editorial, 1994
Chastel, André, *La grotesque,* Paris: Le Promeneur,
    1988
Dacos, Nicole, *La découverte de la Domus Aurea et la
    formation des grotesques à la Renaissance,* London:
    Warburg Institute, 1969
González de Zárate, Jesús María, "El grutesco en el
    mundo antiguo y moderno," *Boletín del Museo e
    Instituto Camón Aznar* 33 (1988)

Harpham, Geoffrey Galt, *On the Grotesque:
    Strategies of Contradiction in Art and Literature,*
    Princeton, New Jersey: Princeton University Press,
    1982
Iehl, Dominique, *Le grotesque,* Paris: Presses
    Universitaires de France, 1997
Kayser, Wolfang J., *The Grotesque in Art and
    Literature,* translated by Ulrich Weisstein,
    Bloomington: Indiana University Press, 1963
    (original German edition, 1957)
Korthals Altes, L., "Du grotesque dans l'oeuvre de
    Michel Tournier," *Revue des sciences humaines* 232
    (1994)
Todorov, Tzvetan, *The Fantastic: A Structural
    Approach to a Literary Genre,* Cleveland, Ohio:
    Press of Case Western Reserve University, 1975
    (original French edition, 1970)

Guild

Historians use the term "guild" (in French, *corporation*) to designate an association of specialist artisans or merchants who join together to regulate their craft and defend their interests, thus constituting an economic group with a quasi-public legal status. In the 18th century various terms described these groups: in French, *jurande, corps,* or *communauté d'arts et métiers* (*corporation* was not used until late in the century); in English, "guild," "craft," or "trade"; in Flemish, *ambacht* and *guelde*; in German, *Zunfte, Handwerk,* or *Innung;* in Spanish, *gremio;* and, in Italian, *arte* or *mestiere.* All of these words refer to a production system characteristic of the preindustrial urban world—one of stalls, small stores, and workshops. This was a world made up of both wholesale and retail merchants and of journeymen and apprentices, generally working alone or in pairs under the authority of a master craftsman who owned a small workshop. In contrast to manual laborers, who had no official status, craftsmen held an intermediate position in the social hierarchy, between the elite—the nobility and the upper bourgeoisie—and *le petit people* (the common people)—unskilled manual laborers (such as day laborers, domestic servants, and paupers). The craftsmen insisted on the prestige and dignity of the "mechanical arts," by analogy with the "liberal arts." Technical mastery thus won them social rank through their incorporation into a recognized professional group.

The origins of the guilds are uncertain, but they can be traced back to the trend toward city charters in the 12th and 13th centuries, when the elite among the merchants and the craftsmen contributed to both the achievement of municipal autonomy and the definition of the rights of city dwellers. These organizations of skilled men were one of the pillars of municipal power, and in the 18th century their upper levels remained an essential component of the urban oligarchies. Guilds were therefore as much political structures as economic or trade groups. They reflected the overall social organization of the ancien régime as an "association of trade corporations," composed of organic collectivities defined by their specific privileges and by a certain degree of self-organization. Traditional society was an unequal and hierarchical arrangement of recognized groups, protected from arbitrary decrees by their "liberties," under the tutelage of the reigning sovereign; guilds were only one specific example of this general pattern.

Guilds As Self-Managed Bodies

The phenomenon of guilds was therefore in keeping with an image of the social world based on privilege above all. Guilds were bodies that had been officially chartered. They were endowed with a juristic personality, commercial monopolies, and prerogatives of a public nature, which allowed them to control their craft. They could own property, act in court cases, use a seal and coat of arms, and they paraded by right in grand processions or official ceremonies, in positions assigned to them by protocol. In the cities where they operated, the guilds' collective monopoly meant that they essentially determined the laws of their particular craft: in order to work in an "incorporated" craft, a craftsman had to join the appropriate guild. To do so it was necessary to complete an apprenticeship lasting several years and then to be received into the guild as a master, either by creating a "masterpiece" or by paying an entry fee. The journeymen—those who were not masters—constituted the labor force of the workshops and were paid regular wages, but they were members of guilds only in a passive sense, as they had no voice in the guild's deliberations. The day-to-day management of the trade was undertaken by guild representatives, who were elected at periodic general meetings. In France these representatives were known as *gardes, syndics, esgards,* or simply *jurés* and constituted the *jurande*—that is, the administration of the guild. (By a process of metonymy the word *jurande* also came to designate the whole guild.) The *jurande* and its equivalents in other countries managed the guild's common resources, saw to the application of the rules and the discipline of the workers, controlled admission of new master craftsmen, arbitrated internal differences, ensured order within the trade, and represented the guild in dealings with the authorities. The *jurande* also defended the guild's prerogatives and, above all, its local commercial monopolies, against any encroachment by external competitors, whether by individual entrepreneurs or nearby guilds.

Based on shared privileges, this communal existence was strongly shaped by ideology: the craft claimed to be a moral community, founded upon its particular profession. All of a guild's members, supposedly being parts of the same whole, were considered to have not only reciprocal duties but also a common obligation to their "art." In short, their esprit de corps assumed a profound moral unity, reinforced by the guild's religious counterpart, the devotional and charitable confraternity, which was both a symbol of the group's cohesion, affirmed by a solemn oath, and a pledge of brotherhood, centered on the cult of the guild's patron saint and this saint's annual feast day. This dual nature made the guild an association of men sharing simultaneously a collective legal personality and a sworn spiritual brotherhood. A guild member committed himself to his trade for life, which even included his funeral, a ceremony representing the ultimate show of guild solidarity.

Conversely, the guild was also a restrictive institution. Each member had to submit to visits and inspection by representatives of the managing body, who checked the quality and "honesty" of the work or the products as well as the strict observation of the guild's rules. The counterpart of these controls was the guarantee of equal competition within the trade and equal access to the market for all members. Contrary to any entrepreneurial individualism, the spirit of the guild was based on a "moral economy," on the assumption that competition was to be practiced on equal terms within the limits of collective rules defined by the practitioners themselves. However, the guilds conceived of this competition only under the umbrella of their collective monopolies. Their statutes focused particularly on controlling access to the trade, regulating entry into apprenticeships, and, above all, acceding to the rank of master, the latter power being especially significant because each of the already qualified masters was anxious to retain for himself an adequate portion of the market. This regulatory power was the source of their adversaries' accusations of the guilds' Malthusianism and of their monopolizing stance. Instruments of self-management and self-regulation, the guilds also sought to provide collective protection of their members, namely the masters.

Instability in the World of the Guilds

A myth has long reigned about craftsmanship, with its reassuring image of warm intimacy inside the workshop, with the master and his journeymen working side by side, united by their shared love of fine work. The reality of the situation was harsher because the world of the guilds turned out to be marked, in every respect, by an acute sense of rank. Among the various guilds there was a hierarchy of social values accorded to the various trades, and even within the same guild the richer masters were more influential than the less affluent. Guild democracy was largely a myth, if not the prerogative of a small core group. In fact, the journeymen could only hold subordinate positions in that community. Only the masters held seats at the guild meetings, and their workers had to obey them completely. The relationship between wage payers and wage earners amounted to a form of domestic discipline. The status of journeyman was supposed to be only a transitory phase, a preliminary to gaining the rank of master. The theoretical pattern of the craftsman's career did not generally make provision (except in certain trades) for journeymen to grow older, get married, and have a life outside the master's house. In fact, however, the masters' ethos of exclusivity, which limited entry into their ranks and reserved most places for the sons of masters already installed, led to the existence of a permanent wage-earning class: many apprentices never became masters but remained workers for their entire lives.

Such stagnation in the wage-earning classes did not necessarily equate with stability. On the contrary, the skilled labor force was generally noted for its mobility. The cities of Europe formed a vast labor market in which journeymen moved around without much regard for borders or religious affiliations, in response to the reputations of certain promising urban centers and the possibilities of recruitment or support. Largely related to regional or local specializations, this mobility facilitated the exchange and circulation of skills as workers continually sought to improve their techniques. In Germany, mobility was institutionalized by rules that, in most trades, required a craftsman to undertake a *Wanderzwang* (tour) of three or four years, following three or four years of apprenticeship, before he could accede to the level of master. This period of wandering, which did not follow any predetermined route, was viewed as a final stage in the training of the craftsman, a time for him to find a city where he could establish his business. In France mobility did not have the same obligatory nature; but in those crafts where it was practiced, the tour of the country was organized in a more restrictive fashion since the number and the sites for stopovers were strictly legislated. The most common path was a vast hexagonal circuit south of the Seine, passing through Paris, the Rhône valley, Provence, and Languedoc, and continuing along the western Atlantic coast.

In addition, mobility served as a form of labor regulation. There was an increasing tendency in many countries to close crafts to new entrants, the effect of the Malthusian policies on admission to the rank of master. This restriction had two consequences. First, the period of the journeymen's wanderings increased as they waited for the opportunity to set up shop, an event that was slow to occur. This prolongation of the tour, which was accompanied by longer periods of unemployment, helped to control the growing congestion in the labor market, as jobs were divided up among larger numbers of workers on the move, notably in Germany. In tandem, the group of lifetime journeymen, who were often married, became larger. These developments led to a certain bifurcation in the labor force. On the one hand, there were young, mobile journeymen who took on temporary employment. On the other, there were older workers who formed the stable and permanent core of the workshops.

Finally, voluntary mobility was also a tool in the hands of the workers, who would move in response to regional conditions of employment and prices and exploit the regional differences in wage levels in their search for better-paid positions. In England, where the guild system was more flexible than elsewhere, there was no obligatory tour, nor was there a masterpiece to be completed, but mobility—known as "tramping"—was widely practiced by all those who lacked the means to open a shop upon completion of their long appren-

ticeships. (The length of apprenticeships had been fixed at seven years ever since the enactment of the Statute of Artificers in 1563.) Recent research has shown that in France, outside the organized tours, there was a veritable Brownian motion within the skilled labor force, with workers endlessly changing employers and cities, depending on what they were offered and the terms proposed. Qualification as a journeyman was a pledge of freedom for a worker, often assuring him a powerful position in the labor market.

Other Workers' Associations

As the prospect of becoming masters became more remote, journeymen settled into the role of wage earners and formed various types of autonomous workers' organizations. The most highly structured were the French *compagnonnages*. Condemned by the religious and civil authorities in 1645 and 1655, the *compagnonnages* became clandestine and took on the character of secret societies. They even had codes of esoteric customs analogous to those of Freemasonry, including initiation rituals, passwords, and rules of conduct. A whole range of symbols was borrowed from the biblical legend of the construction of the temple of Jerusalem in the time of King Solomon. This ritualized behavior provided a means of social distinction and affirmation: the shared code of honor, with all its constraints, united the group in a spirit of exclusiveness.

The *compagnonnages* were interprofessional associations, mainly in the building trades, and involved the practice of the tour. They protected their members in all their laborious wanderings, thanks to their networks of *cayennes*—inns that welcomed members in each city and formed the focal points of the system of mobility. By organizing themselves into employment bureaus for the wandering journeymen, the *compagnonnages* attempted to control the labor market. In cases of conflict with the masters, their ultimate weapon was the boycott. During a boycott a city would be declared "off limits," and the *compagnonnage* would forbid all the workers in the craft in question to work there. In France three unions competed jealously in what amounted to fratricidal quarrels: the Dévorants, or "children of Master Jacques"; the Gavots, or "children of Solomon"; and the Bons Drilles, or "children of Father Soubise," often fought over control of the cities on the tour.

The picturesque history of these associations should not lead us to overlook other forms of workers' organizations that were local and based on single trades. The journeymen's brotherhoods were often on the workingman's counterpart to the guilds that were controlled by the masters of their trade. These fraternities stood for solidarity, and at first their purpose resembled that of mutual aid societies, particularly in the United Provinces (the Netherlands). Above all, the trade fraternities were a sign that the journeymen were reclaiming the corporate spirit, with its related professional pride and code of honor. These values, however, were turned against the masters, who were accused of corrupting the values of the trade by imposing wages that were too low or working conditions considered to be violations of tradition. With their more or less formal structures, the workers' fraternities were the medium for protest movements, organizing plots that repeatedly disturbed the world of the craftsmen. Many strikes began in one workshop or on one street but spread and became organized thanks to cabarets and inns—rallying points where the workers' meetings could be held, where mail was received from fellow workers living in other cities, and where information was exchanged.

Throughout Europe guild authorities and forces of order tried to bring the journeymen back under the control of their rules, but without any real success. The great strike by the journeymen shoemakers in Augsburg in 1726 was without doubt the most serious strike ever experienced in the Holy Roman Empire, and it led to the publication in 1731 of the *Reichshandwerksordnung* (the Imperial Ordinance on Guilds), which banned strikes and assemblies, prohibited all clandestine correspondence between groups of workers in different cities, and attempted to limit the mobility of the labor force. In order to be hired, a journeyman would have to submit a *Kundschaft* (ticket of leave) signed by his previous employer. The same measures were decreed in France in 1749 and repeatedly reaffirmed in later years. However, neither this parroting of regulations nor the attempt in 1781 to introduce a mandatory worker's record book, which served as a certificate of good conduct, could manage to control the rebellious journeymen, whose honor had been offended. Finally, in central Europe the workers' wanderings were viewed as contrary to the needs of the modern state and of effective domestic order. The obligatory tour was abolished in the Empire in 1772 and in Prussia in 1784, but its practice on a voluntary basis survived. At the end of the 18th century it really seemed that the guild model had exhausted its abilities to control labor and to maintain social order. Even worse, it seemed that the guild, having been an instrument of control, had been turned into medium for the "spirit of intrigue" among the workers. Some therefore believed that it offered nothing but drawbacks.

The End of the Guilds?

In the 18th century there was no lack of critics to denounce the guilds' archaic nature. The strongest criticisms came from the liberals, who accused the guilds of keeping prices artificially high by preventing free competition. The ultraconservatism and Malthusianism of these institutions, described as overly rigid and crippled with debt, blindly hanging onto their privileges, appeared to hamper economic and technical progress. In the name of respect for the natural order, the advocates of liberal individualism proposed the reshaping of society, based on individual competition and the disappearance of intermediate organizations. In France, however, Anne-Robert-Jacques Turgot's attempt to abolish the guilds failed in 1776. They were finally eliminated by decree in 1791.

In other European countries, criticism of the guilds was less radical and often limited solely to the economic aspects. German cameralism expressed itself in an inclusive national political economy, without pretensions to social reform. The reformers who inspired enlightened absolutism turned out to be ambivalent in their attitude: they wanted to reform the guilds and make economic freedom more general, but they were not willing to disrupt the social order by doing so. This approach often succeeded in considerably reducing the influence of the guilds, while placing them under the direct control of the state in order to adopt them. Such reforms were partially realized, without too many difficulties, in Italy in the 1770s, but Emperor Joseph II failed in his attempts in the Austrian Netherlands. The reforms implemented from 1784 onward were abandoned in 1787, when a new imperial edict appeared to open the way to a reorganization of the whole political system, reducing local autonomy. The edict thus provoked an outcry. In Spain the prerogatives of the *gremios* were gradually reduced by Charles III and Charles IV.

The example of England shows that the guilds were capable of evolving. Far from "declining," as is so often said, many merchant corporations, such as the Livery Companies of London, gradually transformed themselves into less formal but equally active groups of employers, expressing the sociability of both the elite and middle-class merchants. At the same time, the communities of craftsmen relaxed their attempts at economic control, without thereby losing their political influence in local life. In short, the guilds became just another kind of association in an era when clubs and societies of every type flourished in the cities of England. From being examples of restrictive control, they became voluntary groups promoting cross-consultation and cross-fertilization.

Such a development leads us to modify the conventional picture of a rigid, set-in-its-ways corporative world. Recent historiography invites us not to take too literally the standard texts, with their view of a massively "incorporated" world, and their idealized perception of an institution that was itself ordered while also giving order to the urban social milieu. Reality was much more diverse and more flexible. The world of the trades was infinitely malleable, and all crafts were not institutionalized to the same degree. Even in those cities organized by guilds, there always existed alongside them "free" sectors with "false workers" plying their trade outside the guilds. There were often as many conflicts and variations within a guild as between the guild and the free sector. Furthermore, it appears that capitalist initiative most often adapted quite easily to the supposed constraints of the guilds. Entrepreneurs and wholesalers knew how to use the communal framework when necessary for their own advantage. Contrary to popular belief, the guilds did not prevent industrial development. The image of a reductive opposition between two types of economic organizations must be replaced with a model of a variety of regulatory institutional forms, exploited by the people involved in ways that were both voluntary and conflicting. Similarly, one must distinguish the practical plying of a trade from the associative form that claimed to be identified with it. For example, in Turin, around 1730, it was the merchants, not the tailors, who managed the tailors' guild. Because they had lost their influence in the municipality, the merchants simply tried to play the card of guild privilege in order to regain political influence. Such examples show that the institutions known as guilds could cover some very diverse realities.

As a result, the inevitability of the abolition of the guilds becomes obvious only in hindsight. The need to combine forces in order to be heard is actually as necessary for economic agents as is freedom of movement.

Although the abolition of guilds became common practice across Europe throughout the 19th century, there continued to be a need for other forms of regulatory and self-managing institutions.

PHILIPPE MINARD

See also Industrialization; Technical Instruction; Work

Further Reading

Black, Antony, *Guilds and Civil Society in European Political Thought from the Twelfth Century to the Present,* London: Methuen, and Ithaca, New York: Cornell University Press, 1984

Dobson, C.R., *Masters and Journeymen: A Prehistory of Industrial Relations, 1717–1800,* London: Croom Helm, 1980

Kaplan, Steven, and Cynthia Koepp, editors, *Work in France: Representations, Meaning, Organization, and Practice,* Ithaca, New York: Cornell University Press, 1986

Leeson, Robert Arthur, *Travelling Brothers: The Six Centuries' Road from Craft Fellowship to Trade Unionism,* London: Allen and Unwin, 1979

Rule, John, *The Experience of Labour in Eighteenth-Century Industry,* London: Croom Helm, and New York: St. Martin's Press, 1981

Sonenscher, Michael, *Work and Wages: Natural Law Politics and the Eighteenth-Century French Trades,* Cambridge and New York: Cambridge University Press, 1989

Truant, Cynthia Maria, *The Rites of Labor: Brotherhoods of Compagnonnage in France,* Ithaca, New York: Cornell University Press, 1994

H

Happiness

"Happiness is a new idea for Europe!" In proclaiming *le bonheur* (happiness) before the French National Assembly on 3 March 1794, Louis-Antoine-Léon Saint-Just used a word that was enjoying great success while encompassing all the contradictions of the times. Saint-Just followed this declaration with an extremely strict decree against the enemies of the French Revolution, within the context of the bloody post-Revolutionary period known as the Reign of Terror: "Europe must understand that you no longer want a single unhappy person nor a single oppressor anywhere on French territory; may this example flourish all over the world; may it propagate happiness and the love of virtues." The "unhappy" person referred to here is the poor individual, the enslaved man, the victim of an unjust social system. The happiness that Saint-Just was invoking is collective, social, and political—the common good rather than individual well-being. It corresponds to the first article of the 1793 *Déclaration des droits de l'homme et du citoyen* (Declaration of the Rights of Man and of the Citizen): "The goal of society is the common happiness." However, the age of the Enlightenment also called for individual fulfillment and personal happiness.

The idea of the pursuit of happiness marked a break with the tradition that had placed the highest value on the salvation of the soul or the glory of the prince. Now, before being true followers of a religion, or the subjects of a monarchical authority, human beings were seen first and foremost as individuals and members of a human collectivity. The meaning of their lives was thus no longer found beyond those lives, in death and the Last Judgment, nor in devotion to a larger cause. Human life acquired intrinsic meaning in the "here and now," even though life was also sometimes deemed to be integrated into a higher religious or social order. The mentality of the Enlightenment, particularly in France, replaced transcendent values with immanent values (happiness contrasted with salvation) and focused on societies and individuals rather than on dynasties and hierarchies (happiness contrasted with honor and glory). Countless treatises were written on the subject, from the abbé de Saint-Pierre's posthumous *Des moyens de vivre heureux* (Ways to a Happy Life), to Louis de Beausobre's *Essai sur le bonheur* (1758; Essay on Happiness), Madame Du Châtelet's posthumous *Réflexions sur le bonheur* (1806; Reflections on Happiness), and Jean-Baptist-Claude Delisle de Sales's *La philosophie du bonheur* (1796; The Philosophy of Happiness). Despite some conceptual weaknesses, such essays are representative of the ideal of the period.

Enlightenment discourse made individual happiness a legitimate concern and revived the notion of pleasure in both philosophical and social terms. In an earlier period religious salvation and aristocratic honor had been imposed through the mortification of the flesh or the acceptance of a heroic death. Empiricist philosophy connected the development of individuals with their sensory activity, with the distinction between pleasurable and unpleasant sensations, with each person's quest for the satisfaction of his or her own interests. The pursuit of pleasure led to knowledge of the world, as well as to its exploitation and transformation. The notion of the individual's right to self-assertion and fulfillment became current at a time when infant mortality rates were declining, when suffering from famine and epidemics among the poor was decreasing, and when the privileged classes were enjoying greater comfort or luxury. From this period onward, birth and death became more private experiences, rather than strictly ritualized public spectacles. Ideally, the goals of medicine, education, and morality were to attenuate suffering and ensure good health and satisfaction for each and every person. Borne along by these social transformations and economic progress, the notion of enjoying life suffused literature and art. Real life was then reflected in illustrations and speculations. In *Le Mondain* (1736; The Worldly Man), Voltaire praises without shame an existence that seems entirely devoted to the satisfaction of the mind and the senses. Music and art also vaunted the pleasures of love and sensuality. An aristocratic art of living, refined by the worldliness of the French court, spread beyond the narrow circles of power and crossed the borders of France to spread throughout Europe.

This portrayal of pleasure did not preclude an investigation of the other negative side of pleasure: ennui (boredom) and restlessness. Robert Mauzi has pointed out the contradictions in the idea of individual happiness: it could refer either to a brief moment or a length of time; it could imply a variety of sensations and feelings that could be evaluated, or a permanent state of harmony attained once and for all (see Mauzi). Does happiness reside in one's life or one's consciousness, in movement or in repose? Should the perception of existence be sharp or soft, intense or lasting? Voltaire sums up the dilemma in a famous expression in *Candide* (1759): man is forced to live "in the convulsions of restlessness or the lethargy of boredom."

At the beginning of the 18th century, in his *Réflexions critiques sur la poésie et sur la peinture* (1719; Critical Reflections on Poetry and Painting), the abbé Dubos presented the individual as torn between "restless passions" and the "boredom of indolence." The Iroquois in Maubert de Gouvest's *Les lettres iroquoises* (1752; The Iroquois Letters) ironically describes Europeans as being trapped either by "the boredom of living" or by "the restlessness of not living enough." At the close of the century Sénac de Meilhan in *L'émigré* (1797; The Emigrant) and Senancour in *Oberman* (1804) cited Voltaire and wondered about the possibility of "a middle state between lethargy and convulsion." For those two authors ideal happiness would lie in the reconciliation of introspection and extroversion, of qualitative reflection and quantitative accumulation of experience.

The issue of happiness reveals certain tensions within Enlightenment thought. For the followers of Cartesian rationalism, happiness was related to knowledge and progress was ensured by the growth and dissemination of knowledge. But Jean-Jacques Rousseau drew a distinction between happiness and knowledge. The savage, in harmony with himself and with the natural setting in which he lives, spontaneously experiences a happiness that is denied to the civilized, cultured man, who is increasingly removed from his natural reflexes. Whereas for some thinkers ennui prompts activity and serves as a basis for progress, Rousseau viewed ennui as the result of man's increasing distance from his natural state. Since humanity cannot return to its origins and history cannot reverse its direction, the only solution is to establish a society based on egalitarian and fraternal foundations that would guarantee a social happiness much akin to that of primitive times. Rousseau himself pursued a wrenching and very personal path, rediscovering his own inner nature through solitude. In Rousseau's work, happiness is experienced spontaneously by primitive man, constructed socially in the city of *Du contrat social* (1762; The Social Contract), and reinvented beyond suffering in *Les confessions* (1782) and the *Rêveries du promeneur solitaire* (1782; Reveries of the Solitary Walker).

Nature, which Enlightenment thinkers invoked as a guarantee of happiness, thus appears as both primal and dynamic, as a stable model and as an ideal that prods human beings toward endless self-transformation. The rural pastoral ideal was seen by some as an embodiment of the maternal nature that provides humanity with the elements of its happiness, while others looked to the future for a guarantee that social inequalities and injustice would be overcome through technical advances and by the rationalization of collective life. Happiness was thus variously ascribed to country-dwellers, who can avoid the temptations of debauchery and luxury; to merchants, who participate in economic production, that is, in economic and demographic progress; or to philosophers, who participate in the spread of knowledge. As Pierre-Augustin Caron de Beaumarchais proclaims at the end of *Le mariage de Figaro* (1784; The Marriage of Figaro), "Thus wise nature / Leads us, in our desires / By pleasures to her purpose." This play, which ten years before the Revolution had exposed the social contradictions and the difficulties inherent in an attempt to harmonize the various claims of rights to happiness, portrays nature as a conciliatory power. Just as the important Enlightenment concept of perfectibility reflected each individual's natural tendency toward progress, "natural" sociability would eventually guarantee the convergence of individual interests.

This sociability was expressed minimally in the precept that people should not do unto others what they themselves would not wish to suffer, and maximally in the identification of one's happiness with that of others. In the euphoria of his early years Denis Diderot, as a disciple of the earl of Shaftesbury, tended to equate happiness with virtue. As he grew older, the *philosophe*—who had hoped to be a new Socrates—became less certain of this conviction and came to see virtue as a personal sacrifice. In the name of values superior to the individual—no longer honor and religion, but the city and posterity—Diderot turned away from facile happiness that seemed too much like immediate pleasure.

Diderot stigmatized selfish hedonism, as portrayed in the character of Rameau's Nephew in his work of the same name (*Le neveu de Rameau* [1772]). Individuals were to sacrifice themselves to a power greater than they, and individual happiness was to bow before collective happiness, but who was to embody this collectivity and become its spokesperson? Common happiness, public contentment—these expressions gave rise to many debates and contradictions. Francis Hutcheson the Elder and Jeremy Bentham settled on the greatest happiness of the greatest number of people as their political ideal. Chastellux built his treatise *De la félicité publique* (1772; An Essay on Public Happiness) on this principle, contrasting a general prosperity pertaining only to empires with public contentment, which belonged to individuals. The "greatest number" represented a majority, which was not to be confused with the totality of the social body. When Saint-Just proclaimed that happiness was a new idea for Europe, he was not referring to the public welfare as identified with a monarch, or to the welfare of people as private individuals. Instead, he was referring to the happiness of the citizen who identifies with the public interest: a utopian formula that, for the enemies of Saint-Just, was extreme. At the end of the century the marquis de Sade

directly countered Enlightenment optimism. He too referred to nature, but to a cruel and destructive nature in which the individual could only find happiness in the unhappiness of others. Sade's libertine protagonists reinforce their pleasure by comparing it with the suffering of their neighbors and then, in a higher degree of cruelty, by causing this suffering. The Enlightenment, an age of happiness, explored the whole realm of human consciousness and social relations: it drew up a typology of maladies of the soul, gave "sadism" its name, and, during the Revolution, tested the full spectrum of the politics of happiness.

MICHEL DELON

See also Epicureanism; Liberalism; Luxury; Police; Utopia

Further Reading

Biondi, C., et al., editors, *La quête du bonheur et l'expression de la douleur dans la littérature et la pensée françaises: Mélanges offerts à Corrado Rosso*, Geneva: Librairie Droz, 1995
Mauzi, Robert, *L'idée du bonheur dans la littérature et la pensée françaises du XVIIIe siècle*, Paris: Colin, 1960

Harmony and Melody

Trying to imagine in spatial terms time and pitch, and the graphic disposition of notated music, has given credence to the common belief that the relationship between harmony and melody implies the superimposition of two classical orthogonals of musical space: the horizontal, or diachronic dimension of melody and time, and the vertical, or synchronic dimension of the chord. Based on this conception, harmony is to the chord what melody is to counterpoint. However, even a cursory reading of the theoretical sources reveals a more complex reality.

The original meaning of "melody" in ancient Greek referred to the parts or members of an animated being and, by extension, to the articulation of elements of musical syntax within the harmonic system: sounds, intervals, tetrachords, structures, modal octaves, and tones of transposition. Revived by the Renaissance humanists, this concept of melody survived intact throughout the baroque era and reappeared, with altered emphases, in the writings of most of the 18th-

century theorists of music. However, the semantic field of the word "melody" had become enormous. The word could refer to a vocal or an instrumental melody, whether or not combined with a poetic text, in accordance with the Platonic trinity of oration, harmony, and rhythm; the ordered arrangement of notes and the scale (Lorenz Christoph Mizler von Kolof, Johann Adolph Scheibe, and Christoph Nichelmann); the aesthetic effect of songs and of "sounds that succeed one another in a manner agreeable to the ear" (Sébastien de Brossard, Friedrich Wilhelm Marpurg, Béthizy, and Jean le Rond D'Alembert); an affective quality, endowed with a psychic power (Johann Mattheson, Meinrad Spiess, Johann Philipp Kirnberger, and Johann Nikolaus Forkel); or a series of sounds "ordered according to the laws of rhythm and modulation" (Jean-Jacques Rousseau).

Around 1730 the emergence, within the "preclassical" style, of incisive, periodic, and symmetrical phrasing, integrated with the working out of the musical theme, encouraged a great deal of theoretical reflection on the metric and rhythmic values of melodic thought, which was known in the German-speaking world as *Prosamelodik*. The best-known example of this theorizing dates from 1739 and appears in the writings of Mattheson, who shows how a minuet of 16 measures can be broken up by "periods," "colons," and "semicolons," using categories taken from the ancient meters proposed by theorists of plainsong.

Brossard's definition of harmony refers to the combination of several sounds heard simultaneously. By contrast, Jean-Philippe Rameau, Rousseau, and D'Alembert all make a distinction between the chord and harmony, since the latter does not necessarily imply a vertical conception. In his *Éléments de musique* (1752; Elements of Music), D'Alembert states that "the mixture of several sounds heard simultaneously is called a 'chord'; harmony is, strictly speaking, a series of chords that please the ear as they occur in succession." Indeed, tonal coherence always results from a correlation of several mutually reinforcing parameters, combined according to the laws of resonance: the progression of fundamental sounds, the use of chords, the resolution of dissonances, and the degrees of the musical scale. The quality of the tonic is not only the point at which all the mathematical relationships of the tonal system converge but also the point at which melodic dissonances are simultaneously resolved in a closing cadence: the seventh and the third of the "dominant tonic" are compensated by the contrary motion to the third and the tonic (see Dahlhaus, 1990).

The role allotted to such fundamental successions does not imply the recognition of a syntactic value in the linear progression of the parts, still less its interference in the composition of chords. The campaign that Rameau led against this conception was intended to integrate into the society of sounds those dissident elements that still evaded the jurisdiction of the harmonic series. Indeed, it was the melodic progression of the parts that justified the presence in the accompaniment of "false" intervals that had little conformity with resonance. This viewpoint led to inversions of a single chord being regarded as isolated elements.

Within a polyphonic construct in which a decisive role was allotted to melodic values, this aggregation was a consequence of the progression of the parts, rather than its cause. The "harmony of intervals" implied by this viewpoint could be taken to be a theory of the chord and its inversions. More often than not, what was assumed to be a chord was nothing more than a "mixture," brought about by means of a temperament of more or less heterogeneous sound elements endowed with a specific character. The idea of a common fundamental had no place in this viewpoint. Gioseffo Zarlino, who was Rameau's standard of reference for assessing the novelty of his own ideas, regarded all the intervals being used as equally "fundamental." The difficulty of establishing a single principle of causality among sounds precluded the possibility of any inversion: the fourth GC was the complement of the fifth CG, and not its double; the "slack" and plaintive affect of the minor sixth EC had nothing in common with the third CE, *allegra et incitata*. In the chord of the sixth EGC, accepted in basso continuo, one could see either an interval, or a harmony between the sixth and the third that had the same qualities in relation to that of the fifth and the third, or a secondary form of the perfect chord with the fundamental as its "base" (see Dalhaus, 1990). Musicians were familiar with the connection between these intervals.

Since 1600 the modern notion of the chord, implicit in the continuo, which displays the median parts in a single figuring, had appeared in the writings of Giovanni Maria Artusi, Henricus Baryphonus, Johannes Lippius, Thomas Campion, the marquis de Saint-Lambert, and Roger North, among others. However, it was Rameau who succeeded in integrating the rational description of this phenomenon into a coherent system. The principle of resonance, prefigured in the works of René Descartes and Father Marin Mersenne and demonstrated by Sauveur in 1700, confirmed the physical reality of the monochordist ideas put forward in Rameau's *Traité de l'harmonie* (1722; Treatise on Harmony), that "high-pitched chords are contained in low chords, but not vice versa." From then on, it was impossible to confuse the sounds being generated with those that generated them: in the sixth EC, it is the high note that produces the low note, and not the other way around.

Abandoning the monochordist approach in favor of this new "compass of the ear," Rameau set out to conquer the wilderness that the theorists of the basso continuo had been unable to colonize in a rational way. A common denominator was established among all the families of chords related to each single series of harmonic sounds, reducing the number of combinations in use by one-third. The possibility of annexing the melodic functions of the scale to one of the three bodies of sound based on the fourth, first, or fifth degree of the mode—the subdominant, the tonic, and the dominant (FAC, CEG, GBD in the key of C)—thus made it possible to subordinate all the parameters of composition to an implied theoretical line, the fundamental bass, independent of the real bass, the basso continuo.

From this point onward, musical discourse developed on two different levels—one that was strictly theoretical and maintained a rigorous analogy with resonance, and another that was a sort of sensitive meeting point for sonorous, real compositions, giving the melodic imagination carte blanche. On the one hand, the freedom to explore this empty surface, in every direction, contributed to the later liberation of melody, as the last vestiges of linear polarity were fused in a single current of sound. At the same time, however, no one—neither Mattheson, Rousseau, D'Alembert, Francesco Geminiani, nor even the divine Giuseppe Tartini—could avoid any longer thinking of melody as the consequence of a progression of fundamental sounds.

The optical instruments developed by Rameau were amazingly up-to-date, and they received immediate and concrete confirmation with the dissolution of the polarity between melody and basso continuo upheld in the Neapolitan school—whose style, paradoxically, was held to be exemplary by the Encyclopedists. With a clearer representation of the orthogonals, and with purer and more direct lines, resonance set new limits on the arborescent arabesques of baroque melody. The forest of musical sounds submitted to the pruning shears of Reason, which transformed the luxuriant vegetation of baroque musical rhetoric into a garden in the French style. Rich in dissident melodic elements, the republic of harmony was transformed, little by little, into a monarchic regime. From the metaphysical point of view, Rameau's harmony is a pyramidal structure, simple at the summit and complex at the base, the only difference being that the One was in the base and the Many in the treble. For that reason, Rameau theorized that harmony had preceded melody: "while we are exerting ourselves to find the path that one part must take compared to another, we often lose sight of the one we had chosen. . . It is therefore harmony that guides us, not melody" (*Traité de l'harmonie*).

Just as harmony implied reason and mathematical objectivity, so too the first opposition (between harmony and melody) led to another, relatively subtle analogy: melody is to harmony what genius is to rules. Here, we reach the core of the 18th-century aesthetic debate about whether beauty is judged by rules or by appreciation of its gracefulness. Is the character of a melody an objective property of the elements of musical syntax, or is it rather an irreducibly subjective psychological value? Is the affective quality of a melody coextensive with the components that convey it, or does it have more to do with an abstract relationship established through an ineffable arrangement of its parts? Finally, does the meaning of music lie in the domain of scientific knowledge, or is meaning the business of genius?

Historians of ancient music were well aware of the opinion favored by Aristoxenus's followers. Thus, the author of the *Dialogue de Plutarque sur la musique* (1733; Plutarch's Dialogue on Music) states, "harmonics is not qualified to examine [song]." From this standpoint, notes, intervals, and the scale are to music as letters, syllables, and the elements of discourse are to grammar. By contrast, the distinctive feature of the *melos* (melody) is that it is a form that is superior to the mixture of parts, being a matter of a logical synthesis that is difficult to describe, and that varies from one example to another. The author of the *Dialogue de Plutarque sur la musique* quite naturally extrapolated from this remark the notion of "genius": "It is not the business of harmony to adapt every genre and every mode . . . to such and such a type of singing poetry. That is for the taste and the genius of the poet-musician to decide."

With just twelve notes Jean-Baptiste Lully managed to write hundreds of different melodies, each with its own character, and, just as one hesitates to conflate the meaning of a poem with its syntax, so too one avoids tracing the distinctive qualities of a melody simply to its constituent elements. Rousseau notes in Volume V of his *Fragments détachés* (Loose Fragments), in *Oeuvres complètes* (1995; Complete Works), that "there is as great a distance from counterpoint to composition as there is from grammar to eloquence." The counterclaim was that science could be applied to syntax and to the practice of its applications, as Rameau points out in his *Erreurs sur la musique dans l'"Encyclopédie"* (1754; Errors about Music in the "Encyclopédie"): "When a laborer uses a lever to lift a weight, he does it without knowing Descartes's theory of mechanics. Must we conclude that the laws of simple machines are of no importance?"

Nevertheless, one might deem the program that Rameau had set out in his *Traité* of 1722 more ambitious:

It is true that a skillful musician can conceive of a beautiful song that fits in well with the harmony; but where does this happy knack come from? Cannot nature have had something to do with it? Undoubtedly, if, in the opposite case, nature has withheld this gift from [the skillful musician], how can he succeed? Then, it perhaps comes about by following the rules.

Fifteen years later, in *La génération harmonique* (1737; Harmonic Generation), Rameau states that

nothing can do without them [the rules] except these elements which might depend on taste. . . . However, at the same time it is good to warn them that everything that has been imagined in music, and everything that might be imagined in the future, is directly drawn from the fundamental bass prescribed in this article, and that it is impossible to produce anything good or pleasant in this art that is not a necessary consequence of it.

In principle, academicism had been able to escape this impasse by means of a marriage of convenience, following the adage *nulla die sine linea* (no day shall pass without producing a line [of music]). According to Malcolm's *Treatise of Musick* (1721), melodic invention implies certain rules, an ear attuned to the "commonplaces" of the great musicians, and—above all—a great deal of "genius." By contrast, according to Rameau, the composer abandoned by the muses could compensate for his lack of a "gift" by studying.

The first public response to the latter assertion came from Mattheson. In 1725, in the second volume of his periodical *Critica Musica* (1725), he accused Rameau of seeking to rationalize to an excessive degree (*vernünftteln*) a science that was hardly exact. The emergence of this debate in the pages of this periodical—the first influential organ of modern musical criticism—was to assume great historical importance. Indeed, the irreducibly subjective character of melody was to music what taste was to the critical instinct. As the direct expression of the personality of an individual genius, melody became an ambiguous entity relegated to the fringes of reason and of the harmonic system. French and Italian writers referred to ornamental dissonances, unintegrated into the body of sound, as "notes of taste." German writers translated this term as *manieren,* the word that their humanist predecessors had adopted to describe irreducibly subjective personal styles. The quality of a melody was too complex to be predictable and therefore resisted analysis. However, if reason lost its way, taste—a "quasi-reason" located halfway between the senses and the intellect—could still serve as a compass. The whole problem of academicism lay in this paradox: although melody was the expression of an irreducibly personal psychic structure, it was nonetheless allotted absolute aesthetic values.

Music was confronted with the problem of normativity in connection with melodic writing, just as art criticism was confronted with the problem of rationality in connection with appreciative judgment. The paradoxical result was an acceptance of a measure of value that was both normative and incommunicable. The problem had already been raised by the theorists of natural magic, who had resolved it by developing a concept of a "hieroglyphic" art, incommunicable and yet charged with meaning. The very same notion was to reappear, in secularized form, in Diderot's discussion of the amount of meaning in pure music. The history of music theory in the 19th and 20th centuries is characterized by its oscillations between a view of melody as something that can be explained in a rational way and a perception of melody as something that cannot be debated.

This paradoxical ambiguity is embodied in the writings of Mattheson himself, who devoted a whole treatise to melodic composition, the *Kern melodischer Wissenschaft* (1737; The Core of Melodic Science).

Irritated by the fact that one could distinguish "harmony from melody," Mattheson attacks Rameau's argument that "it would be all but impossible to provide reliable rules in this domain." The conflict expanded alongside the growth of a specialized periodical press. In Germany, Scheibe objected to Bach's contrapuntal science. In 1751 the columns of a leading newspaper were given over to the debate between Charles Henri de Blainville, the abbé Raynal and Rousseau on the one side, against J.A. Serre on the other. The latter's critics accused him of wishing to undermine the third mode, recently discovered by Blainville, by subjecting it to harmonic analysis.

It was during this period that Encyclopedist hagiography disseminated the example of the Italian musician who creates beautiful melodies in a state of ecstasy, without starting from the fundamental bass. Some Italians, such as Geminiani, were sufficiently versed in musical theory to challenge Rameau. Tartini was also singled out because of his complete theory of differential sounds, an experiment in which Rousseau believed he had found a physical demonstration of the anteriority of harmony (discussed in the article "Harmonie," *Dictionnaire de musique* [1768; Dictionary of Music]).

Rousseau's mystic theological interpretation is representative of the psychological aspect of the debate. The polarity between the feeling of having been deprived of a state of simple, unsullied, Edenic innocence and the desire for a reconciliation corresponded to a whole series of binary oppositions, such as melody/harmony, nature/artifice, unity/multiplicity, and genius/conventions, which Rousseau transformed into a psychodrama of the senses and the intellect. Concealed behind this facade of sensualism are the elements of a neo-Platonic theory of Ideas in which harmony, the division of the Idea in counterpoint, and the divorce of the arts in opera can only reproduce the same primeval dichotomy between an essence and its deformation within a phenomenon. Fugues and counterfugues, produced by skill and the conventions, exert only a mechanical effect, which is restricted to the soul's material shell. Romances sung "in unison" pierce the heart directly and, just as the imagination recognizes the ideal circle in the circle that can be traced by hand, such romances are safe from contingencies and are immune to deformation in the hands of the unskilled performer. Finally, melody has a social dimension to the extent that it can reflect the character of a milieu, a group, the genius or soul of a people—just as taste does. In the draft version of his *Principe de la mélodie* (Principle of Melody) Rousseau responds to Rameau as follows:

If there is a natural melody derived from harmony, it must be the same for all human beings, because harmony, having its source in nature, is the same in every country in the world. Yet the songs and airs of each nation have their own character because they all have imitative melodies derived from the different accents (*Oeuvres complètes* [Complete Works], Volume 5, 1995)

When its time came, ethnomusicology, in an embryonic form in Rousseau's writings, would produce the idea of normativity in melodic analysis.

BRENNO BOCCADORO

See also Counterpoint; Music; Opera

Further Reading

Dahlhaus, Carl, *Die Musiktheorie im 18. und 19. Jahrhundert,* Darmstadt, Germany: Wissenschaftliche Buchgesellschaft, 1984

Dahlhaus, Carl, *Studies on the Origin of Harmonic Tonality,* Princeton, New Jersey: Princeton University Press, 1990; Oxford: Princeton University Press, 1991 (original German edition, 1967)

Shirlaw, Matthew, *The Theory of Harmony,* London: Novello, 1917; reprint, New York: Da Capo Press, 1969

Siegmeister, Elie, *Harmony and Melody,* Belmont, California: Wadsworth, 1965

Heat

In the *Cyclopaedia* article on heat, translated in 1753 by Jean le Rond D'Alembert for the *Encyclopédie,* Ephraim Chambers compared heat to the effect of fire. Influenced by John Locke's "metaphysics," his definition of heat begins with sensation:

> Heat in us is properly a sensation, excited by the action of fire; or it is the effect of fire on our organs of feeling. Hence it follows, that what we call heat is a particular idea or modification of our own mind, and not any thing existing in that form in the body that occasions it. Heat, says Mr. Locke, is no more in the fire that burns the finger, than pain is in the needle that pricks it. In effect, heat in the body that gives it, is only motion; and in the mind, only a particular idea. (*Encyclopædia Britannica,* 1771)

At around the same time, the abbé Jean Antoine Nollet stated in his *Leçons de physique expérimentale* (1757; Lectures in Experimental Physics) that it was not known

> whether fire is a simple, stable substance that produces heat, conflagration, and dissolution of bodies by its presence or by its action, or, instead, if its essence consists solely of motion or fermentation of the so-called "inflammable" parts.

The latter opinion claimed few remaining supporters, and those who did support it generally attributed either to the ether or to subtle matter the movement they believed to be the essence of fire. Such attributions, according to Nollet, brought the two ideas "substantially closer together."

A generation earlier, Francis Bacon and then Sir Isaac Newton had reasoned that heat was an internal motion of the smallest particles of bodies, while Robert Boyle thought heat to be the motion of the matter of fire. In his "Suite des essais de chimie" (Series of Essays on Chemistry), published in the *Mémoires de l'Académie de Sciences* of 21 April 1705, Wilhelm Homberg expressed his belief that the elementary principle of heat, or sulfur, thought to be a simple chemical ingredient preexisting in all bodies, was actually fire. Most Dutch physicists shared this opinion, as did Louis Lemery (the son of Nicolas Lemery), when he wrote his "Conjectures et réflexions sur la matière du feu et de la lumière" (Conjectures and Thoughts on the Matter of Fire and Light), and when he published an article in the *Mémoires de l'Académie de Sciences* (13 November 1709). In his *Physices elementa mathematica* (1720–21; Mathematical Elements of Physics), Willem Jacob 'sGravesande suggested that fire was part of the composition of all objects, that it was contained in them and could be separated from them if it were set in motion by rubbing the objects against each other. According to 'sGravesande, the heat in a hot body was actually movement of its parts caused by the body's innate fire, and a body was not perceptibly hot until its degree of heat exceeded that of our sensory organs; he believed it was the increased agitation in our bodies that stimulates in our mind the idea of heat. Lemery not only posited that fire was contained within objects, he also theorized that it was evenly distributed everywhere, in empty spaces and even in the imperceptible spaces between particles of matter. He based his proposition on Boyle's experiments, which had shown that liquids such as oil of vitriol (sulfuric acid) become extremely hot when partially melted pieces of ice are dropped into them. 'sGravesande also reasoned that if the idea of heat arose from the irregular motion of fire, the idea of light should come from the linear motion of this same fire. Similarly, Nollet compared "wheel axles (that) get hot by friction" and the electrified steel rod that gave off "plumes of fluid electricity" [sparks], and he deduced that "the substance of electricity and that of fire [were] essentially the same thing." These conjectures, according to which fire, light, and electricity, considered in principle, were one and the same substance were widely adopted, albeit with some variations. They were founded less on experimentation than on the very common idea that "nature produces beings sparingly but multiplies their properties profusely" (*Leçons*, Volume 4).

However, the work that became the standard reference on the subject was the "Deigne" (Treatise on Fire) that Hermann Boerhaave included in his *Elementa chemiae* (Elements of Chemistry), which, published in Latin in 1732 (and in English in 1735), were as highly valued as Newton's *Opticks* (1704). Boerhaave sought to clarify the idea of fire, looking at all the signs by which its presence is generally recognized. First, there must be a sensation of heat, which is nonetheless an imprecise and subjective sign that does not allow the amount of fire to be determined; the second clue to the presence of fire was light, although a very hot body might produce no light, and one bright light—moonlight—produces no heat at all. Melting, boiling, combustion, and the chemical combinations and decompositions of bodies could all be invoked to prove the presence of fire, yet how could the nature of fire be determined on the basis of such variable and unpredictable effects?

Instead, Boerhaave proposed the expansion of heated bodies as the sign of the presence of fire. In volume 2 of his *Elementa* he maintains as a given that "in all phenomena in which this increasing rarefaction takes place, there is a proportionate quantity of fire that is the cause of it," and he asserts that this provides a means to discover the nature of fire. He is inclined to believe that fire is a substance, one that "while not known, has within itself the ability to penetrate any substance, solid or fluid, and cause it to expand" by impeding the forces of attraction these small parts of matter exert upon one another. Boerhaave thus found a way to determine the smallest increases or decreases in fire by observing the slightest variations in the volume of a fluid in a hermetically sealed glass. Does this theory suggest that the thermometer reading is a function of the amount of heat contained in the thermometric fluid? On the verge of arriving at that conclusion, Boerhaave hesitated and conducted further experiments that led him to entirely different conclusions. He observed that, by means of friction, a great deal of fire could be derived from the coldest of objects. And since he could not accept that the friction creates fire, he had to accept that fire is always present in every part of space. Placing a thermometer into a vacuum glass or onto a piece of gold, the most solid substance known, he discovered the same degree of heat and cold in both of them, provided they had remained at the same temperature over a long period of time. This discovery contradicted "(ordinary) experience, which tells us plainly that iron is colder in winter than a feather is" (*Elementa*). Ultimately, Boerhaave noted that up until that time he had not observed any substance in nature that attracted and accumulated heat: there was no magnet of fire.

From these three categories of findings, Boerhaave deduced that fire was not only present in every of space but that it was also equally distributed in every substance, from the most rarefied to the most solid. Using the analogy of a metal bell that creates powerful vibrations in the air when it is struck, Boerhaave reasoned that "if two dense, hard and very elastic bodies are struck together with force and speed, all their parts are at every moment tightly compressed, and because those parts are rigid they strongly resist this compression. Hence in each part of these bodies there exists a very rapid and powerful motion of contraction and expansion." It was therefore evident, according to Boerhaave, that fire was contained in the pores of the body and was violently compressed and released within them. Further, because fire seemed to be the most elastic of all substances, it was likely that movement greatly increased its force and motion. Thus, fire was a substance that

once created, exists forever and in the same quantity. However, through all its actions it undergoes various changes affecting its motion, its rest, its regrouping, its dispersion, and its direction, so that sometimes it is apparent to our senses and at other times not.

Fire thus sometimes gives us a sensation of heat and at other times of that of cold. According to this theory, inflammable matter is not different from other matter because it contains a greater quantity of fire but simply because its specific parts are naturally lend themselves more readily to the action of fire when that action has been stimulated. We should note that Boerhaave did not set experimental physics in opposition to various "physics systems." Instead, he borrowed from various models in order to explain observable phenomena, referring to fire corpuscles and the small bits of matter inspired by Pierre Gassendi's atoms or Wilhelm Gottfried Leibniz's monads, Newton's theory of attraction, or René Descartes's motion of fire as matter.

In spite of Boerhaave's great authority, the idea that fiery matter is uniformly distributed throughout the physical world was generally received with suspicion. In his *Leçons,* Nollet notes: "It is commonly believed that some kinds of matter contain more fire than others . . . and that opinion is very probable: it is at least extremely appropriate for making sense of the rapid inflammability that distinguishes some substances from others." However, it was the work of Joseph Black, a professor of chemistry at the Universities of Edinburgh and Glasgow, that provided the strongest challenge to Boerhaave's ideas. Beginning in December 1761 Black undertook to explain why ice melts so slowly when heat is applied, why the temperature of the melting ice does not change no matter how much heat is applied to it, and why, similarly, the temperature of boiling water remains constant no matter how much heat is applied. An initial experiment indicated that if equal quantities of water and ice were heated similarly, the ice took 21 times longer to increase its temperature by seven degrees on a Fahrenheit thermometer. From this observation, Black deduced that there were 140 degrees of heat that the thermometer was not indicating. To be better assured of this hidden "reserve" of heat, Black mixed equal quantities of hot and cold water and established that the temperature of the mixture was the exact average of the temperatures of the hot and cold water, a finding that supported what Nollet discovered at almost the same time: "The first (the hotter one) shares equally with the second the excess amount of heat that it has" (*Leçons*). These results contradicted those of Boerhaave, who had found that the temperature of the mixture was half of the difference between the temperatures of the two amounts of matter prior to mixing, and who claimed that the amount of heat common to both parts was lost in the mixing process. Black then demonstrated that when ice is melted in an equal quantity of water at 176 degrees Fahrenheit, the resulting mixture is approximately the temperature of melting ice and that thus a considerable amount of heat disappears that the thermometer does not indicate. Black called that heat "latent heat." He conducted similar experiments on boiling water and found that here again evaporation absorbs a large quantity of heat. From this, he concluded: "I imagined that, during the boiling, heat is absorbed by water, and enters into the composition of the vapor produced from it, in the same manner as it is absorbed by ice in melting, and enters into the composition of the produced water" (1803; *Lectures on the Elements of Chemistry*).

Black understood latent heat as the heat generated in the process of combination. In the years 1762–65 he undertook a series of experiments on the temperature of mixtures of various liquids at different temperatures. Black established that by taking equal masses of two liquids, the resulting temperature was higher or lower than the average temperature, depending upon which of the two liquids was hotter. Thus, by mixing equal parts (by weight) of water and whale oil, he could establish that the quantity of heat exchanged that raised the temperature of the water by one degree decreased the temperature of the whale oil by two degrees if the whale oil was the hotter of the two, and vice versa. It followed that the heat capacity of water was twice that of whale oil, and that equal weights of different substances absorbed differing quantities of heat in order to have equal temperature change.

Black's research, which he presented in his chemistry lectures at the University of Glasgow, was continued there by William Irvine and Adair Crawford. Their efforts also inspired the work of Johan Carl Wilcke in Stockholm. Making reference to those studies, João Jacinto de Magalhães, a Portuguese scientist living in London, introduced the expression "specific heat" to designate the quantity of absolute heat that each element possesses. Antoine-Laurent de Lavoisier and Pierre-Simon Laplace adopted the expression but gave it a different meaning, defining the "heat capacity" or "specific heat" of a substance as the ratio of the respective quantities of heat necessary to raise the temperatures of equal masses of this substance and of water by the same number of degrees.

Laplace conceived of measuring the heat released by an object by placing it in the center of a sphere of ice; the amount of heat was measured by the weight of the melted ice. Lavoisier designed and had two "calorimeters" built on this principle, and, between 1782 and 1784, the two scientists jointly conducted several series of experiments to determine the specific heat and the latent heat of various substances. They also determined the first combustion heats, and inaugurated research in physiological chemistry by determining the heat released by respiration. The results of these various calorimetric experiments still had to be interpreted. In their *Mémoire sur la chaleur* (Memoir on Heat), published in 1783, Lavoisier and Laplace set forth the two opinions on the nature of heat that had polarized physicists:

A number of [scientists] think of heat as a fluid diffused throughout nature, and by which bodies are more or less permeated according to their temperature and to their specific ability to retain it. . . . Other scientists think that heat is only the result of the invisible motions of the constituent particles of matter. We know that even the densest bodies are filled with a great number of pores or tiny empty space . . . to oscillate freely in all directions, and it is natural to think that these particles are in a constant agitation which, if it increases to a certain point, can break them apart and so decompose the bodies. It is this internal motion, according to these scientists we are speaking of, that constitutes heat. (Lavoisier and Laplace, *Memoir on Heat*, translated by Henry Guerlac, New York: Watson Academic, 1982)

The *Mémoire* develops the implications of each of these theories to demonstrate that both are consistent with observable phenomena. The total amount of perceptible heat is conserved in the simple mixture of two substances:

This is evident, if heat is a fluid that tends to reach equilibrium, and also if it is only the *vis viva* (living force) which results from the internal motion of matter, then the principle in question is a consequence of the principle of conservation of *vires vivae*.

It is natural to assume that Lavoisier, the chemist, would draw all his conclusions from the first hypothesis—he was personally convinced that heat was a fluid, which he called *calorique* (caloric). It is also natural to assume that Laplace, the geometer, would draw all *his* conclusions from the second hypothesis. (Historians commonly think that he then preferred the second one, but later, in Arcueil, Laplace in fact opted for the caloric hypothesis). The amount of heat absorbed in a phase change (melting or vaporization) or when several substances are combined was interpreted similarly in both cases: either a portion of the caloric was combined with one or more substances and became imperceptible to the thermometer, or else "the molecules of one or more substances undergo the action of forces of attraction that can change the quantity of their living force." However, with respect to phase changes, this theory was not the only way to interpret latent heat. Irvine, along with Crawford and then John Dalton, reasoned that latent heat is the effect of a sudden change in the specific heat of a substance during a phase change. They therefore believed that only perceptible heat exists. They further hypothesized further that the specific heat of a substance in a given state is the same at all temperatures. Thus, the absolute quantity of the heat of a substance is proportionate to its specific heat. It was

therefore possible to determine the absolute quantity of heat contained in substances and to define the value of absolute zero—a total lack of heat in a given substance or object. The readings of a mercury thermometer would therefore lead to the exact measurement of caloric contained within an object. The mathematical method used to determine "real zero of temperature" was simple, but it should be noted that there was little agreement among the findings stated for various substances; for many scientists these findings seemed to contradict the assumptions on which these calculations were based.

At the end of the century, Benjamin Thompson, Count Rumford, believed he had refuted the caloric theory. He submitted as evidence the fact that when cannons were bored, the friction created heat; he judged that this phenomenon could only be possible because heat was motion. The argument was scarcely convincing at a time when friction was the only means to obtain fluid electricity. Thus, at the end of the century, concepts of temperature and heat had been completely differentiated, and a new science, calorimetry, was emerging. The idea that heat was a fluid was the view most commonly held. Before being refuted, this notion proved rich in possibilities, as is evident in the works of the Société d'Arcueil and the accomplishments of Nicolas Clément, Charles-Bernard Désormes, Nicolas-Léonard Sadi Carnot, and Émile Clapeyron.

ROBERT LOCQUENEUX

See also Chemistry; Gas; Phlogiston; Thermometry

Further Reading

Duhem, Pierre, "Les théories de la chaleur," in *L'évolution de la mécanique*, by Duhem, Paris: Joanin, 1903; reprint, Paris: Vrin, 1992

Fox, Robert, *The Caloric Theory of Gases: From Lavoisier to Regnault*, Oxford: Clarendon Press, 1971

Hoefer, Ferdinand, *Histoire de la physique et de la chimie*, Paris: Hachette, 1872

Mach, Ernst, *Principles of the Theory of Heat: Historically and Critically Elucidated*, Dordrecht, Germany, and Boston: Reidel, 1986 (original German edition, 1896)

McKie, Douglas, and Niels H. de V. Heathcote, *The Discovery of Specific and Latent Heats*, London: Arnold, 1935; reprint, New York: Arno, 1975

Hero, Representations of

Like other traditional concepts, the notion of the hero, a venerable artistic theme since antiquity, was subjected to criticism by the philosophical minds of the Enlightenment. The basic challenge was to find a way of reconciling the mythic dimension of the hero with the new discourses on society and the citizen. In the 17th century the art academies had succeeded in enforcing the supremacy of history painting, a genre centered on the ancient gods and heroes. During the reign of Louis XIV, propaganda on behalf of the French monarchy had reclaimed the image of the victorious conquering hero (Charles Le Brun), while educated connoisseurs sought to contemplate the virtuous hero of neo-Stoical morality (Nicolas Poussin). Louis XIV thus commissioned *Les batailles d'Alexandre* (Battles of Alexander) from Le Brun in order to make a symbolic appropriation of the legendary glory of the conqueror. Louis XV continued to encourage great paintings with this purpose in mind: Charles-Joseph Natoire was commissioned to paint the *Histoire de Marc-Antoine* (1741; The History of Marc Antony); Jean-François de Troy, to paint the *Histoire de Jason* (1743; History of Jason); and Carle Van Loo, the *Histoire de Thésée* (1745; History of Theseus).

However, from the late 17th century onward, critics charged that the control over the status of hero exercised by the absolute monarchy and the aristocratic ideal was excessive. As Jean de La Bruyère puts it in *Les caractères* (1680; Characters): "It seems that the hero has only one skill, that of making war, and that the great man is one who has every skill. . . . Perhaps Alexander was no more than a hero, while Caesar was a great man." In a letter to Frederick the Great, dated 26 May 1742, Voltaire criticizes the way in which the 17th century had reduced history to a cult of masters and princes:

> I have little love for heroes, they make too much
>   noise.
> I hate these conquerors. . . .
> Seeking death wherever they go and dealing it
> To 100,000 of their fellow men.
> The greater their blaze of glory, the more
>   detestable they are.

These ideas were taken up by the chevalier de Jaucourt when he came to write the entry "Héros" in the *Encyclopédie*. He includes a condemnation of the warrior hero and a eulogy for the great man whose guiding principle is not success but virtue.

In his *Discours sur la vertu la plus nécessaire au héros* (1782; Discourse on the Virtue Most Necessary to the Hero), Jean-Jacques Rousseau argues that the hero's virtue should be moral strength. In his view, while the sage, the statesman, the citizen, and the philosopher possess admirable virtues, and work together for the benefit of humanity, only the hero can change the way things are by his actions. Rousseau writes that it is in "the character of the hero to take to the highest level the virtues that make him"—that is, to attain the sublime.

The conception of heroism in the age of the Enlightenment cannot be separated from the new moralizing fervor that suffused literature and the arts. In England in the 1730s and 1740s, the ancient idea that society could be reformed by example and demonstration inspired William Hogarth's prints and Samuel Richardson's novels. In France 20 years later, Jean-Baptiste Greuze, who painted touching scenes of village life, and Jean-François Marmontel, the author of *Contes moraux* (1755–59; Moral Tales), successfully pursued the same idea, but the prestige of history painting and classical literature remained unscathed. In line with the wishes of the monarchy, which granted prestigious commissions, the heroes of antiquity and the Bible continued to dominate the exhibitions at the Académie Royale de Peinture et de Sculpture (Royal Academy of Painting and Sculpture) in Paris.

From the middle of the 18th century onward, a large number of writers condemned the chivalrous and pastoral mythology depicted in the paintings of François Boucher and his imitators, regarding it as evidence of artistic and moral decadence. After a visit to the Salon in 1753, La Font de Saint-Yenne, a pioneer of art criticism who was on good terms with the *parlementaires*, exhorted painters to find forms of "animated expression" that would raise the soul "above the senses and remind it of its primordial dignity by examples of humanity, generosity, grandeur, courage, contempt for danger and even for life, passionate zeal for honor and the safety of the fatherland, and above all the defense of religion." According to Saint-Yenne, artists should renounce the monstrous implausibilities of fable and seek their subjects in the annals of antiquity and of the nation. The valorization of ancient art and its aesthetic principles, eventually adopted as points of reference in neoclassicism, had an effect on artists' choice of imagery. Instead of moments in which the plot of a narrative was depicted, artists became interested in scenes that invited the spectator to engage in moral meditation, be it a scene in which the hero prepared to be tested or a denouement that displayed his humanity. As a result, the notion of the hero was enriched with a new psychological dimension. Like the age of the Enlightenment itself, the hero developed feelings.

In France in 1764 Charles-Nicolas Cochin, the secretary of the Académie de Peinture who provided the frontispiece for the *Encyclopédie,* devised a plan for decorating the royal palace of Choisy, in which the exemplary hero was situated at the center of official art. The cessation of the Seven Years' War had created a climate of optimism, and Cochin judged that it was in some cases reasonable to depict the generous and humane actions of good kings, which have contributed to the happiness of their subjects. Having been commissioned to paint four pictures, Cochin chose not to depict the traditional four seasons or four elements. Instead, he took his subjects from the lives of the Roman emperors Augustus, Trajan, Titus, and Marcus Aurelius. This philosophical project was carried out, but ten years later Louis XV, who found Cochin's pictorial pedagogy too austere, preferred to look at Boucher's graceful nudes. The moral imperative asserted by the *philosophes* also encountered serious opposition. Some objected to the relegation of the visual attractiveness of pictures to a secondary status beneath that accorded to their subjects, since giving primacy to the latter meant that artistic creation ignored a whole range of human experiences. In his *Salon de 1765* (1765 Exhibition), Denis Diderot advocates a morality of energy: "I do not hate great crimes, mainly because beautiful paintings and fine tragedies can be based on them; besides, they bear the same energy as great and sublime actions."

In his *Fragments de philosophie morale* (1767; Fragments in Moral Philosophy), Marmontel strongly objects to this approach:

> Some people have been impressed by the surprising energy of mind or soul in great crimes, as in great virtues. Vivid imaginations have seen in the explosion [of this energy] no more than a prodigious development of forces of nature, or a magnificent picture that deserves to be painted. In admiring the cause, they praise the effects; thus, the tyrants of the Earth become heroes.

Despite all these ambiguities associated with ways of looking at works of art, artists continued to be drawn irresistibly to the theme of the exemplary hero. Throughout the 18th century, scenes of ancient virtue continued to pour out of the studios of such painters as Gavin Hamilton, who was British but resided in Rome, Heinrich Füger in Austria, André Lens in the Austrian Netherlands, and Johann Heinrich Tischbein in Germany.

In France between 1776 and the Revolution, the comte d'Angiviller, Louis XVI's director of works, ensured a steady flow of royal commissions to numerous artists. The monarchy was then under fierce attack from the Parisian *parlementaires,* as well as from the *philosophes.* With a certain nostalgia for the 17th century, it expected to derive political advantage from the artistic preeminence of French painters and sculptors. Accordingly, the comte d'Angiviller gave painters who belonged to the Académie de Peinture a series of ancient and modern subjects that he considered "appropriate to reanimate virtue and patriotic feelings," and he commissioned sculptors to make statues of great Frenchmen. His program was not motivated by a desire to glorify heroic acts; instead, it sought to eulogize the grandeur of the soul as expressed through such traits as religious piety, disinterestedness, and firmness.

The positive hero invoked by the monarchy was required to occupy a position somewhere between the innocent and the sage and was thus exposed to attack. There was a major contradiction between the antiheroism of the Enlightenment project and the artistic forms that were expected to realize that project. The artists of the Académie de Peinture found it difficult to satisfy the monarchy's wishes, while the critics, with Diderot in the lead, reacted sarcastically to the banality and theatricality of the works displayed at the Salons. In the *Dictionnaire des arts* (1792; Dictionary of the Arts), Pierre-Charles Lévesque, an advocate of antiquity, recalled the harmful effect of this failure:

> The heroic style must contain a large element of the ideal, but all is lost if theatricality enters the picture. The theatrical is no more than an imperfect representation of the natural person, while the heroic should rise above the human.

In the eyes of the critics, the use of figures, expressions, and gestures based on the commonplace made the fine action represented in these paintings seem meaningless. Artists were sometimes more concerned with the dramatic possibilities of a narrative than with its exemplary nature. The darkness of intrigue, the effects of style, and the nuances of feeling obscured the lessons of history. Consider, for example, the depiction of Brutus, the Roman consul who avenged Lucretia, put an end to the tyranny of Tarquin, and founded the republic. Since the Renaissance, European humanists had been fascinated by this hero who had decreed the death of his own sons because they had betrayed their country. French revolutionaries followed Voltaire (*Brutus* [1730]) in adopting the Roman as the embodiment of patriotic devotion, but the reservations expressed by Plutarch, who found Brutus's paternal severity excessive, were not forgotten. In 1789 the painter Jacques Louis-David exhibited a picture that showed Brutus after his return to his family as a man racked by remorse, seated in shadow near a statue of Rome, the divinity to whom he had sacrificed his sons. This scene does not evoke the transparent morality of the Enlightenment but rather the crime novel, with its conventional figure under extreme duress.

In France it was difficult to imagine a form of heroism that did not demand some sacrifice of personal interest for the public good. In Britain, however, starting most notably with David Hume's *A Treatise of Human Nature* (1739–40), it was accepted that virtue should be interpreted more broadly and be extended into the realm of private life. In short, British thinkers achieved a reconciliation of the heroic and the human. They concluded that even a man who did not become a warrior or a statesman could still contribute to the improvement of society by exercising his moral faculties within his family and among his friends. This notion of domestic heroism was also given artistic expression. The ideal of virile stoicism put forward by the earl of Shaftesbury at the beginning of the 18th century gave way to a celebration of gentler, more temperate passions, as in Daniel Webb's *An Inquiry into the Beauties of Painting* (1760). Virtuous heroines such as Agrippina, the widow of Germanicus, often provided occasions for the spectator—usually male—to cultivate his sensibility. More generally, the aristocratic conception of virtue was rejected by British society, which, being based on commercial relations, required its citizens to cultivate less-elitist values. Instead of reinforcing existing social divisions as in France, the representation of exemplary acts became a firm foundation for sentiments of patriotic pride and communal sympathy. It was necessary to accept that heroic figures known to their contemporaries were more capable of arousing admiration and emotion than the ancients were, and that the stories of individuals found in the press made a stronger impression on the public than the abstract formulas of ancient texts. From the 1760s onward, painters reflected this trend by representing celebrated heroes—most often military figures—as they really were, engaged in private acts, particularly acts of charity. Nevertheless, artists were careful to maintain an explicit connection between their compositions and the grand tradition. The masterpiece in this genre, which rarely surpassed the level of mere anecdote, was *The Death of General Wolfe,* exhibited by Benjamin West in London in 1771. This painting depicts Wolfe's moving death at the moment of victory over the French on the battlefield of Quebec City in 1759; the scene is modeled after the Lamentation of Christ.

The creation of London's Royal Academy in 1768 impeded further innovation in England. The influential theories of the Academy's president, Sir Joshua Reynolds, who gave his support to the conventional grand manner and to subjects taken from ancient history, were developed within the academic tradition that had been codified in France. Reynolds encouraged artists to dedicate themselves to an outstanding example of heroic action or heroic suffering.

One of the most original aspects of the program of artistic commissions under Louis XVI was the inclusion of subjects taken from the history of France, although, unlike those in England, the commissioned subjects had no connection with contemporary reality. The comte d'Angiviller commissioned paintings that honored loyalty to the crown (represented by such military figures as the seigneur de Bayard and Bertrand du Guesclin) and patriotic sacrifice (the burghers of Calais, Jeanne Hachette). Ménageot's *Death of Leonardo da Vinci,* exhibited at the Salon of 1783, was a tribute both to the king as a patron of the arts and to an artist who deserved the admiration of those in high places. Like the story of the Greek painter Apelles, to whom Alexander gave up his mistress, this modern subject painted by Ménageot heralded the romantic eulogy of the creative genius, who would supplant the traditional hero in the 19th century. The historical character who appeared most often in the pictures commissioned by the monarchy was Henri IV, the embodiment of the benevolent king who was close to his people. However, this paradoxical and ambiguous figure was given a different, unheroic interpretation by those who supported the rights of the *parlements* (high courts) against the crown—they used the example of Henri IV to highlight the failings of the reigning monarch.

Reality burst in upon the arts in France only after the Revolution of 1789. Public opinion reacted strongly against the homage that the arts had rendered to such famous men as Jacques Necker, the marquis de Lafayette, and Jean-Sylvain Bailly, and even against a conqueror of the Bastille who was distinguished by his courage. David's *Serment du Jeu de Paume* (Oath of the Tennis Court), a picture intended to fulfill his ambitious plan to commemorate the collective heroism of the representatives of the nation, fell victim to the instability of politics. Some of the heroes of 1789 had become traitors to the patriotic cause by 1791. The cult of great men, which led to the installation of the marquis de Mirabeau and Voltaire in the Panthéon in 1791, and then of Jean-Paul Marat and Rousseau in 1794, withstood the erosion of time with only slightly more success. Mirabeau and Marat were "depantheonized" as soon as they fell from favor.

During the Revolution, the cult of heroes became principally a cult of the dead. The supreme sacrifice tended to replace accomplishments as the criterion of appreciation. The martyr for liberty gradually supplanted the great man. David painted Lepeletier and

Marat, deputies assassinated in 1793, while other less-celebrated "martyrs" were often represented as icons of this new cult. However, military actions continued to call for traditional depictions of heroism, although such depictions were subjected to democratic pressure, just as the organization of the army was. The trend in favor of admitting citizens to the status of heroes reached its peak in 1794, with the publication and extensive dissemination of the *Recueil des actions héroïques* (Collection of Heroic Deeds), a series of pamphlets commissioned by the Comité d'Instruction Publique (Commission of Public Instruction), an organ of the Convention. The descriptions of republican patriotism in these pamphlets were intended to raise the morale of the nation in wartime. In a report on this initiative, Henri Grégoire, one of the deputies in the Convention, recommended that these pamphlets should depict popular heroes in a sober manner:

> An account of magnanimous acts should present them in all their simplicity, relying on history, not oratory. . . . Indulgence in words or thoughts would destroy feeling, for the sublime resides in things as they are and does not need to be adorned.

Moreover, according to Grégoire, the Republic needed to break away from the ostentation and exclusive mentality of the aristocratic tradition. By a series of examples aimed at avoiding uniformity, he recommended that each account of a heroic act be accompanied by remarks on disinterestedness or filial piety. The pamphlets were not to honor only men but also women, children, and the elderly, and not only individuals but also groups and communities of citizens. Some deputies worried that this transformation of living people into heroes could lead to political abuses.

Under the influence of the democratic movement, artists were drawn to certain specific subjects. One of these was the largely fictional tale of the heroine known as the grocer of Saint-Milhier, who had succeeded in driving away the brigands of the Vendée by threatening to blow up a keg of gunpowder. Numerous engravings were made depicting this woman of the people, who was willing to die with her children in order to resist the counterrevolutionaries. Another was the 13-year-old child who joined the Republican army in the Vendée and died in December 1793. His youth was a guarantee of his moral purity, in an age when the Terror was destroying all landmarks. At the same time, the fact that the boy had supported his mother with his meager wages made him a paragon of filial affection and patriotic devotion. In order to endow this vision with dra-matic presence and represent his martyrdom, David adopted the nudity and gracefulness of the ephebus, a figure that had become one of the symbols of the ideal of republican liberty and civic virtue under the influence of Johann Joachim Winckelmann's theories about ancient art. The painter Bara had to display an example to citizens of how beautiful it is to die for one's country. However, in placing the feminine beauty of the murdered adolescent in the service of pathos, the artist annoyed Robespierre, whose politics had developed out of a hatred of sexuality that went beyond the puritanism of the Jacobins. Robespierre's fall from power on the ninth day of Thermidor in the Year II (1794) and the success of the Republic's armies rapidly brought an end to this experiment in state propaganda on the theme of popular heroism. Around 1799, when the nation was being mobilized in response to the threat of invasion, there were representations of collective heroism, such as the inhabitants of a town taking up arms against the enemy besieging it. The traditional cult of the military hero reappeared, benefiting the generals who had been victorious on the battlefield before the theme became focused on Napoleon Bonaparte. Official ideology and strategy no longer had any use for eulogies of the ordinary soldier or the man of the people but represented instead a view of the human condition that implied an end to the era of heroism in action.

The political situation in France did not permit the full expression of this idea, cherished by the romantic generation, but in England and Germany it found clear expression in the arts. Joseph Wright of Derby's *Dead Soldier* (1789) pays homage to the anonymous hero, his face pressed into the ground while the battle rages on in the background. Despite Wright's concession to the sentimentalism of the period—the widow holding her baby in her arms and weeping for her husband—the painting raises the dignity of the scene to the level of history. It is as if the unknown man has a right to an elaborate backdrop, recalling the traditional trappings of the funerals of the great, while his gun, lying forgotten on the spot, figures as an attribute of his glory.

During the occupation of Dresden by Napoleon's troops (1813–14), Caspar David Friedrich painted a symbolic landscape in which a crow announces the imminent death of a French soldier lost in the snow, surrounded by tall fir trees, as mournful as the cries of the bereaved. Napoleon kept the myth of heroism alive a little longer in France than elsewhere, but the disillusionment of the rising generation was ready to manifest itself in 1815.

PHILIPPE BORDES

See also Painting; Prometheus; Virtue

Further Reading

Aulard, François-Alphonse, "Le recueil des actions héroïques," in *Études et leçons sur la Révolution française*, vol. 8, Paris: Alcan, 1924

Bonnet, Jean-Claude, *Naissance du Panthéon: Essai sur le culte des grands hommes*, Paris: Fayard, 1998

Crow, Thomas E., *Painters and Public Life in Eighteenth-Century Paris*, New Haven, Connecticut: Yale University Press, 1985

Locquin, Jean, *La peinture d'histoire en France de 1747 à 1785: Étude sur l'évolution des idées artistiques dans la seconde moitié du XVIIIᵉ siècle*, Paris: Laurens, 1912; reprint, Paris: Arthena, 1978

Rosenblum, Robert, *Transformations in Late Eighteenth-Century Art*, Princeton, New Jersey: Princeton University Press, 1967

Solkin, David H., *Painting for Money: The Visual Arts and the Public Sphere in Eighteenth-Century England*, New Haven, Connecticut: Yale University Press, 1992

Triomphe et mort du héros: La peinture d'histoire en Europe de Rubens à Manet: Une exposition, Milan: Electa, and Lyon: Musée des Beaux-Arts de Lyon, 1988

History, Philosophy of

If one discusses the 18th century's philosophy of history, one implies that a form of thought truly existed in that century that today can be described as a philosophy of history—however, this idea certainly cannot be taken for granted. One reason for caution in positing an Enlightenment philosophy of history is the epistemological incompatibility of history and philosophy. A second reason is the semantic distinction between the terms "historical" and "philosophical" made by two men at opposite extremes in the history of classical thought: René Descartes (*Regulae ad directionem ingenii* [Rules for the Direction of the Mind]) and Immanuel Kant (*Kritik der reinen Vernunf* [1781; Critique of Pure Reason]). It is interesting, however, to note that in his *Idee zu einer allgemeinen Geschichte in weltbürgerlicher Absicht* (1784; Idea for a Universal History with a Cosmopolitan Intent), Kant did cautiously write of "discovering in the absurd progress of human events a plan of nature." This notion is equivalent to sketching a philosophy of history on the level of meaning, not on that of truth or objectivity, to developing a view in line with his *Beantwortung der Frage, Was ist Aufklärung?* (1784; Response to the Question: What Is Enlightenment?), a view that would take into account the development of historical knowledge in the 18th century.

An additional reason to doubt whether a "real" philosophy of history could have possibly been created before the arrival of the post-Kantians would be that, according to Michel Foucault, the classical theories of knowledge presupposed a fixed order of historical events and accepted only a fully explanatory version of those events; it was only in the 19th century that man's historicity was recognized and the concept of historicism emerged (see Foucault). Nevertheless, if one takes into account Alexandre Koyré's work on the history of the sciences or Thomas Kuhn's thinking on "the structure of scientific revolutions," along with the 18th-century texts attesting to the awareness that the period's thinkers had of their place in history and their desire to define this place and to learn from it, it seems clear that Enlightenment thinking was profoundly informed by a renewed view of human historicity. In other words, the Enlightenment did not occur without remaking or reinventing the meaning of history.

The emergence of a new conception of history in the 18th century can be attributed primarily to the scientific revolution whose principal leaders and interpreters were Galileo and Descartes. The new conception of history attempted to express the consequences of the Copernican revolution and, by extension, to apply to the "human sciences" the intellectual tools and method used by the inventors of a new cosmology and a new physics. The idea of an advance in knowledge and the related idea of a real beginning or renewal of philosophy were clearly in Descartes's mind. These ideas recur, in clearer form, in the writings of Bernard Le Bovier de Fontenelle, who, in his *Digression sur les Anciens et les Modernes* (1688; Digression on the Ancients and the Moderns), for example, speaks of truths made accessible by the discovery of the "true philosophy." The realm of myths (still called "fables" at the time) and that of history would henceforth lend themselves to a genealogical study that would shed light on the origins of knowledge, which was conceived as being continually transformed until it produced, after a last qualitative leap, objective knowledge. Fontenelle was author of *Entretiens sur la pluralité des mondes* (1686; Considerations on the Plurality of Worlds) and became secretary of the Académie Royale des Sciences de Paris (French Royal Academy of Sciences), acting in his role as editor of the *Mémoires de l'Académie des Sciences* (Reports of the Academy of Sciences) as a historian of recent science and of the science to come. Thus, he can be thought of as the inventor of the idea that his successors continued to call the "history of the human mind." This history of the mind refers to a narrative account of the development of knowledge, or even, in its best examples, a history of epistemology, which the 18th century constantly rewrote.

When the new celestial mechanics of Sir Isaac Newton (*Principia Mathematica Philosophiae Naturalis* [1687; The Mathematical Principles of Natural Philosophy]) and the infinitesimal calculus of Gottfried Wilhelm Leibniz and Newton became known, the method of using examples, as well as the key role of mathematics and the sciences most closely derived from mathematics, was strengthened and seemed destined to provide definitive models in other areas. A reading of Voltaire's *Éléments de la philosophie de Newton* (1737; The Elements of Sir Isaac Newton's Philosophy) makes it clear that, for that philosopher, as for his contemporaries, the Newtonian system provided not only a solid basis for accurate astronomy and physics but the foundations of a general philosophy as well. These mathematical milestones required a reorganization of the methodology of knowledge. In fact, the history of this mathematical rationalism can be traced until the end of the 18th century, as far as the marquis de Condorcet, a mathematician and philosopher, and Pierre-Simon Laplace and the comte de Lagrange (both scientists).

This does not mean that the preeminence of those who were called—occasionally with derision—the "geometers" was always guaranteed. Proof of the interest aroused by the stakes of scientific progress and the direction of its development can even be found in Denis Diderot's prophecy in his *Pensées sur l'interprétation de la nature* (1753; Thoughts on the Interpretation of Nature): "We are approaching," he writes, "the moment of a great revolution in the sciences." He declares that mathematics will soon be honored only as a monument to a bygone period, and that henceforth "experimental philosophy" will prevail, entirely oriented toward the history of nature and the life sciences. Based on this certainty of the coming reorientation of minds, Diderot went on to found a biological philosophy of generation, from which, as author of the *Rêve de D'Alembert* (1769; D'Alembert's Dream) and *Éléments*

de physiologie (1774–78; Elements of Physiology), he deduced a complementary history of man in nature. Beginning in the early 1760s, the century's authors began to develop a preference for writing histories of nature, histories that, while they offered moral or metaphysical views that were scarcely compatible with a rationalist history, nonetheless seem in their inspiration and views to descend from models derived from the geometric paradigm.

The theorized awareness of scientific progress was logically accompanied by a systematic reflection on its causes, indicators, and future. Accordingly, it became necessary to focus on the conditions and modalities of invention and on the more or less obscure progression of new truths, which, whether as a result of slow maturation or sudden intuition, presented increasing opportunities to ponder developments in collective thought and the nature and workings of individual genius. It therefore seemed necessary to conceive of a historical sociology of knowledge in an increasingly obvious relationship with political philosophy. At the same time, it became customary not to advance a theory, whatever its purpose, without reconstituting the historical background of the question treated, in line with the methods sanctioned by the Académie des Sciences and presented in its *Mémoires*. Scientists began writing the histories of their own sciences: for example, Jean-Étienne Montucla's *Histoire des mathématiques* (1758; History of Mathematics) or Jean-Sylvain Bailly's *Histoire de l'astronomie* (1775; History of Astronomy). Even the lives and works of these scientists were inspired by a something akin to historical reflection on the occasion of academic eulogies. Bowing less to official rhetoric than to a concern for the truth, this genre, completely restructured by Fontenelle, who was remarkably aware of the individual genesis of knowledge, was perpetuated through the century thanks to Grandjean de Fouchy, Dortous de Mairan, Jean le Rond D'Alembert, and Condorcet.

An important consequence of the historicization of scientific knowledge concerned the various disciplines considered to be dependent on mathematics and physics to varying degrees. On the one hand, all these disciplines tended to be inspired by the rational method, definitively demonstrated by the latter sciences to be effective, while, on the other hand, they planned to tighten their bonds with the founding sciences. The advancement of any given scientific discipline was measured in terms of its degree of rationalization. That criterion was particularly noticeable in the evolution of chemistry, since Antoine-Laurent de Lavoisier and the comte de Fourcroy presented themselves as authors and witnesses of a revolution that had incorporated into their science a way of reasoning essentially different from the one that preceded it. This requirement for rationalization, which was thenceforth part of the spirit of the age, meant that the 18th century witnessed the creation of autonomous sciences, such as mineralogy, and saw the emergence of generalized standards of method and verification. The same was true in the field of natural history, although it was not until the chevalier de Lamarck's work at the end of the century that the idea of the transformation of species took shape, ending the uncertainties (for instance, the questioning of Buffon's ideas) and the hypotheses (for example, Diderot's brilliant views) that had impeded natural history's emergence as an autonomous discipline. However, biology and medicine had trouble ridding themselves of obsolete concepts and practices.

The same impetus toward rationalization affected the sciences that were soon to be known as the "human" sciences. This evolution in thinking is perfectly exemplified by the abbé Jean Terrasson's declaration, in *La philosophie applicable à tous les objets de l'esprit et de la raison* (1754; Philosophy Applicable to All the Objects of the Mind and of Reason), that the human mind progresses at the same pace in the natural sciences and in literature: "My principal aim is to transfer to belles lettres this spirit of philosophy that for a century has caused such progress to be made in the natural sciences." He posits that "philosophy" consists of "opting in human doctrines for examination over prejudice and for reason over authority." Step by step, as the tree of science conceived by Francis Bacon and redesigned by the Encyclopedists branched out, learning seemed to achieve unity, and the same principles were applied in fields that had seemed to preclude them. The identifying feature—and illusion—of the age of the Enlightenment was that epistemological theory and the historical view verified and complemented each other in terms of the achievements that they had determined, whereas the authors of those achievements supposedly embodied the method and the spirit of the times, synthesized into what was called "true philosophy." It was by virtue of this basic convergence between the evolving discourses of epistemology and history that collaboration between the sciences and literature began to be powerfully advocated. Montesquieu, following Antoine Houdar de La Motte, had already suggested such collaboration in his speeches to the Académie de Bordeaux (Bordeaux Academy). In his great unfinished poems, "Hermès" and "L'Amérique" (America), André Chénier celebrates the undreamed-of wedding of poetry and Newtonian science.

Thus illustrated, the marriage of the sciences and the arts, under the stern eye of a critical and rational philosophy, obviously implied some kind of parallelism (albeit improbable from any angle) between their respective histories. The central and mobilizing theme of Enlightenment thought was that concurrence had finally been achieved, or was at least on the way to being achieved. The idea arose from a blatant voluntarism; it also depended on an absolute confidence in the eschatology of reason. Now, nothing could be better for confirming these views than the discovery, in the past and the present, of signs of an assured future. In the 17th century, Catholic France had remained faithful to the Judeo-Christian view of history that had been expressed in Bishop Bossuet's *Discours sur l'histoire universelle* (1681; Discourse on the History of the Whole World). Father Thomassin and Bishop Pierre-Daniel Huet continued to believe that all known forms of civilization and culture derived from the doctrine of truth passed to man through the word of God; Father Joseph-François Lafitau still held this belief, as can be seen in his *Moeurs des sauvages américains comparées aux moeurs des premiers temps* (1724; Customs of the American Indians Compared to the Customs of Primitive Times).

Various factors precipitated the reshaping of universal history: the scientific opening up of the whole of time and infinite space; comparative sociology and ethnology (disciplines that had not yet found names); the narratives of travelers and missionaries; encounters with other peoples, particularly in China and India, whose chronology contradicted biblical chronology (already roughly handled by biblical scholars, following the example of Baruch Spinoza in his *Tractatus Theologico-Politicus* [1670; A Theologico-Political Treatise]); and, finally, the revelation of pre-Columbian cultures. This reshaping prompted authors to give history a truly human orientation—an orientation that would be confirmed precisely by the very visible development of technology and the sciences. Montaigne had clearly questioned the fate imposed on the American Indians by Europeans, and that question remained central to the problematics of the Enlightenment. The answer clearly involved the very conception of history, as shown, for example, by the 20th-century anthropologist Claude Lévi-Strauss's praise of Jean-Jacques Rousseau for having challenged the progressivist thesis of the Encyclopedists. It was not too difficult for those who considered recent advances in science and philosophy decisive to portray man's long progress toward perfection: they called this adventure the "history of the human mind," and priority was given to demonstrations of such progress in the acquisition of knowledge and the related development of a theoretical discourse. The rewriters of history traced a line of this sort from Fontenelle to Condorcet, and even those who denied the benefits of this progress and the utility of the new knowledge had to give thought to the hypothesis of a quantitative increase in knowledge and a more exacting rationalization of modes of thought. Rousseau begins by accepting the Enlightenment's diagnosis in his *Discours sur les sciences et les arts* (1750;

Discourse on the Sciences and Arts), if only to denounce the harmfulness of these arts and sciences and the unhappiness of man struck by the curse of intellectualism. None of the *Aufklärer* (the thinkers of the German Enlightenment) described with such rigor, logic, and precision as Rousseau (although he did not bother with strict verification of historical facts) the despairing march of humanity toward a state in which it turns it back on its fundamental values for the sole benefit of illusions of the mind. The counterhistory in Rousseau's *Discours sur l'origine et les fondements de l'inégalité parmi les hommes* (1755; Discourse on the Origins of Inequality) and his *Essai de l'origine des langues* (1763; On the Origin of Language) is not the least masterly form of philosophy of history, and it is no doubt the analysis that best does justice to the state of so-called primitive or savage man, and as a consequence, to the characteristics of these societies where some element of the primitive is preserved under the nomenclature of the "natural."

Things were different for believers in progress of the mind, who were forced to construct an entirely different historical schema. They elaborated upon commonplace notion already highlighted by Pascal in his *Fragments d'un traité du vide* (1647, printed in 1779; Fragments of a Treatise on the Void): "The entire succession of mankind through the course of so many centuries should be envisaged as a single man who still exists and learns continually." Fontenelle, in his *Digression sur les Anciens et les Modernes,* returns to this image of humanity compared to a single individual with a childhood, youth, and age of virility, but who could not be given an old age.

When it became necessary to translate this comparison into terms of an events-based history, the 18th century reverted to the type of periodization that the modernist minds of the previous century had partly developed, themselves prolonging a way of thinking familiar to François Rabelais's novel *Gargantua* (1534). The course of the history of the mind was very schematically set out as follows. First, there was the blossoming in Greece, then in Rome, of the admirable culture of antiquity, whose only defect was to indulge in idealist metaphysics and rhetoric, and whose scorn of the sciences and of concrete experience prevented it from developing, and therefore from resisting the brute force of the barbarians. Western humanity was then buried for more than ten centuries in a darkness that was neither unproductive—since the texts of antiquity were saved and, since technical progress was paving the way for future great discoveries—nor totally opaque—since a few great minds came into the world during this period, and since breaks in the clouds and sunlit clearings could be glimpsed there: for example, the reign of Charlemagne (as presented in Montesquieu's *De l'esprit*

des lois [1748; The Spirit of Laws]) or the 13th century, the equivalent of a pre-Renaissance.

With the Renaissance, modern times actually began. The renewal of arts and letters preceded the scientific revolution, but some adjustments of the chronology made it possible to turn an expanded 16th-century watershed era into a miracle in which the invention of printing played a very significant role. Because it disseminated new truths and helped to prevent regressions in a culture that despotism and religious dogmatism could have kept mute, printing was seen as the sign of a real revolution in the history of the mind. Different historians would introduce complements and variants into this schema, aiming in particular to emphasize the shortfalls in the thought of the ancients, or to reveal the merits of the underappreciated Middle Ages (for example, the role played by Arab thought as a way station for preserving and transmitting the Aristotelian heritage).

This conception of history was not as perfunctory and biased as one might imagine: it stimulated authentic research, provided a framework for the development of historical knowledge, and provoked productive debates. In this regard, two works generated by the urgent concern to master the history of the mind merit particular mention. First, Voltaire's *Essai sur l'histoire générale et sur les moeurs et l'esprit des nations* (1756; An Essay on Universal History, and the Manners and Spirit of Nations), the title of which was changed in 1765 to *Essai sur les moeurs* (Essay on Manners) and which was at that point given a preface aptly entitled "Philosophie de l'histoire" (Philosophy of History). The significance of this history and the chronological structure adopted by Voltaire is especially evident in the supplementary section entitled "Chapitre des arts" (Chapter on the Arts). Second, it was thanks to Condorcet, mathematician and direct heir of the Encyclopedists, that this methodical view of history received its most polished form: the ten epochs in his *Esquisse d'un tableau historique des progrès de l'esprit humain* (1794; Outlines of Historical View of the Progress of the Human Mind) take humanity from the emergence of the first social groups to a final and decisive revolution that has only a few obstacles to overcome before creating the definitive happiness of the species based upon the Enlightenment's guarantee. According to Condorcet, the historical view

must present the order of these changes [in human societies], explain the influence that each moment exerts on the one that follows it, and thus show in the changes that the human species has undergone, by being unceasingly renewed over the vast length of the centuries, the journey that it has made and the steps that it has taken toward truth and happiness.

This progress, described thus by the philosopher with an optimism that defies the revolutionary tribunal, prefigures the positivist view in Auguste Comte's history.

This idea of a progressivist history, verifiable (according to Condorcet and his predecessors) by the history of the sciences as much as by the history of peoples and successive forms of civilization, was only really conceivable if the "human mind" was constructed over time and equipped with its own knowledge and its acquired truths (rather than having received them from a supernatural authority or of having discovered knowledge and truths preformed within itself). These historians were indebted to John Locke for this idea of the genesis of the mind. According to Voltaire in his *Lettres philosophiques* (1734; Philosophical Letters), after "so many thinkers [who had] written the 'fiction of the soul,'" Locke, in his *Essay concerning Human Understanding* (1690) "makes an unassuming history of it." Voltaire's main intention was to use Locke as a critic of classical rationalism and the thesis of innate ideas, and as the founder of a strict empiricism. It is true that Locke's genetic psychology—which, beginning with a tabula rasa, explains the development of knowledge by means of the recording of perceptions and the formation of ideas—set out to provide a foundation for the sciences and authorized a new epistemology. This is certainly how Father Claude Buffier, in his *Traité des premières vérités* (1717; Treatise on Primary Truths) understood it when, before Voltaire, he linked the establishment of fundamental certainties, and therefore of authentic sciences, to the geometric method.

Until the end of the century, Lockean sensationalism continued to serve as a basis for philosophical constructions, as far as the "ideologues"—loyal heirs to the *philosophes* in this regard—particularly in Pierre-Jean-Georges Cabanis's *Rapports du physique et du moral de l'homme* (1802; Relations between the Physical and the Moral in Man). It also became necessary to study the interpretation of sensationalism given by Étienne Bonnot de Condillac in his *Essai sur l'origine des connaissances humaines* (1746; Essay on the Origin of Human Knowledge) and his *Traité des sensations* (1754; Treatise on Sensations), as well as the further development of this treatise by David Hume and in Scottish philosophy more generally. To measure Locke's influence and to understand how it could justify a history of the human intellect, it suffices to read specific texts by three authors: those passages in the comte de Buffon's *Histoire naturelle de l'homme* (Natural History of Man)—"Des sens en général" (On the Senses in General), in the third volume of the *Histoire naturelle générale et particulière* (1749; Natural History, General and Particular)—in which Buffon attributes to a fictitious first man the narrative of his opening up to the external world through the senses, then the development within

himself of reflection; Diderot's rewriting of those passages in his *Lettre sur les sourds et les muets* (1751; Letter on the Deaf and Mute), prior to Charles Bonnet's *Essai analytique sur les facultés de l'âme* (1760; Analytic Essay on the Faculties of the Mind); and, above all, those texts by Condillac in which he counters Buffon's prose epic with his own allegory of the statue.

It was logical that this genetic concept of the mind should be translated into innovative educational methods: for example, Morelly's *Essai sur l'esprit humain ou principes naturels de l'éducation* (1743; Essay on the Human Mind; or, Natural Principles of Education) and, later, Rousseau's *Émile, ou, De l'éducation* (1762; Émile; or, Concerning Education), but also, in an entirely different spirit, inspired by purely materialistic logic, the works of Claude-Adrien Helvétius, about which Diderot and the baron d'Holbach made scathing comments. Diderot and Holbach pointed out the social and political uses that could be expected from genetic psychology: the forming of minds leads to the forming of opinion and thus prepares the way for easily deducible changes in society and institutions. This reasoning explains why Voltaire, anxious to shelter "philosophy" from any accusation of subversion, denounced such radical systems. As soon as Enlightenment thinkers had adopted this progressivist history, they were confronted with the question of the dissemination of truth. After the reticence of the libertine Fontenelle, Montesquieu and, naturally, the Encyclopedists concluded that it was their duty to enlighten the people. Diderot professed that it was inconceivable and would be harmful to separate the dissemination of "enlightenment" from general education. To counter reservations on the part of Voltaire and Louis-René de Caradeuc de La Chalotais, Condorcet wrote his *Réflexions sur cette question: S'il est utile aux hommes d'être trompés?* (Reflections on the Question, Whether It Is Useful for Men to Be Deceived), and, during the Revolution, his *Mémoires sur l'instruction publique* (Memoirs on Public Education).

Another subject, closely related to the preceding ones, was the role of the writer: the definition of the *philosophe* included the obligation to make oneself useful to society. The principles advanced in theoretical texts were thus confirmed by the contents of the works, the stated ambitions of the authors, and the obvious purpose of those works such as dictionaries and catechisms that were intended to propagate good morality and true philosophy, as well as to teach people to criticize religious and political traditions. The mission of the writer was presented as if it came within the scope of the development of contemporary history.

In order to measure the historical spirit's hold on the 18th century, its first and most striking manifestation must also be kept in mind: the debate on the progress of arts and letters. This debate, which continued throughout the 18th century up to Condorcet and then to Madame de Staël's *De la littérature* (1801; The Influence of Literature upon Society), went through two particularly lively phases: the Quarrel of the Ancients and the Moderns, between 1687 and 1694, and the quarrel about Homer around 1714. The first, somewhat ambiguous episode of the debate was heralded by the question of the epic genre: should epics that imitated the ancients and exploited the resources of mythology be replaced by entirely Christian epics? Other themes of the Quarrel turned on the political, even philosophical ideology of the antagonists, such as Jean de La Bruyère and Fontenelle.

However, Charles Perrault, although crediting the French monarchy at its zenith with the superiority of the works of art and literature produced by the moderns, as well as the decisive advances in scientific disciplines, clearly sketches a nonlinear conception of history: by designating the age of Louis XIV as a zenith, a later decadence had to be admitted. This outline of a cyclical pattern to history, marked at unforeseeable intervals by the appearance of "ages" propitious for the flourishing of genius in all disciplines, was passed on, by way of the abbé Jean-Baptiste Dubos, to Voltaire. Such a thesis required ingenious justifications from those who proposed it, in the form of geographic data, climatic influences, historical circumstances, political regimes, or changes in the temperament of peoples. These reasons were proposed individually or in combination to explain what could be attributed to chance, if not to Providence. A problematic was worked out, using old arguments but engendering investigations into historical causality throughout the century, as exemplified by Diderot's *De la poésie dramatique* (1758; On Dramatic Poetry). Such investigations were also inspired by the thinking of the philosophers of antiquity. The determination to describe the course of history as a degradation of primitive ideals led Madame Dacier (in her *Des causes de la corruption du goût* [1714; On the Causes of the Corruption of Taste]) and her allies in defending Homer to counter the modern Houdar de La Motte with a coherent conception of their own regressive determinism.

In the midst of this fermentation of ideas, Father Fénelon and Montesquieu had to explain why the Gothic was barbarous. Montesquieu also had to explain why Italian painting had reached its peak in the 17th century, and Voltaire had to reconcile his obsessive fear of decadence in arts and letters after the *Grand Siècle* (the 17th century) with his belief in the law of progress. He therefore dreamed of correcting literary masterpieces—those of Pierre Corneille, among others—in which the language and even the form had become outdated.

Thinking in other countries followed the same lines and was sometimes remarkably broad in scope. Giambattista Vico, in *Principi di una scienza nuova* (1725; The New Science of Giambattista Vico), turns his gaze back toward ancient Italy and "rehabilitates tradition and precritical common sense against the pretensions of reason," thereby becoming one of the representatives of the anti-Enlightenment. Vico was also the precursor of those who, through their conviction that the science of history was more rigorous than the physical sciences, helped to found the "human sciences."

Also basing himself upon national traditions, Johann Gottfried von Herder countered French taste and the idea of the rationalist mind with what he called a "new philosophy of history." In contrast, Gotthold Ephraim Lessing developed his theory of the arts and invented the new German theatre in the spirit of the "Enlightenment"; yet like Herder and, after him, Friedrich von Schiller, Lessing showed himself to be concerned about "the education of the human race." From the above examples, it can be seen to what extent 18th-century reflections on the origins of languages (Rousseau), the development and solidarity of the arts, the sources and nature of poetry (Edward Young), and aesthetics in general (the earl of Shaftesbury, Hume, Diderot, Edmund Burke, Kant), could maintain links with the invention of a philosophy of history.

Taking only French literature into account, one can measure the consequences of a modernist belief in the evolution of genres and, first and foremost, in the abandonment of classical canons. Theatre in particular attests to the desire to bring the stage into tune with evolving thought. Foreshadowed by Fontenelle and theorized and illustrated by Diderot, Louis-Sébastien Mercier, and Pierre-Augustin Caron de Beaumarchais, drama sought to reflect the contemporary world, to depict the modern mind and modern manners. The same could be said for the handling of dialogue and the poetics of prose. Preference was given to short texts, gathered together in dictionaries, catechisms, or collections, such as Nicolas-Anne-Edmé Rétif de la Bretonne's *Les nuits de Paris* (1788; The Parisian Nights) or Mercier's *Tableau de Paris* (1781–88; Panorama of Paris). Poetry, meanwhile, was in decline, languishing under the weight of the era's theoretical philosophizing.

The reason for doubting whether a real philosophy of history was created in the 18th century lies in the fact that any synthesis of the virtual components of a history unified in its significance was at that time usually considered inconceivable or harmful. In the middle of the century, the "Discours préliminaire" (Preliminary Discourse) of the *Encyclopédie* provided the most remarkable and most symbolic attempt at a synthesis. In the "Discours," D'Alembert proceeds in two phases. He begins by "examining, if we can use the term, the genealogy and line of descent of our collected knowledge, the causes which must have given rise to it, and its salient individuals." This first phase entails a reconstruction, on Bacon's model, of the tree of sciences. D'Alembert then suggests "the historical exposition of the order in which our forms of knowledge succeeded each other." This exposition entails a history of the sciences and of the "geniuses who contributed to spreading the light among human beings" since the Renaissance. The historian makes a crucial point at the outset: "When one considers the advances of the mind since that memorable period, one finds that these advances were made in the order that they naturally had to follow." The advancement of learning had thus supposedly embraced what Diderot refers to as the "metaphysical" logic of the development of the mind—the progress of humanity's collective mind being the equivalent of the progress of the individual from childhood on. This systematic rationalism lends weight to 20th-century critical theorists Max Horkheimer and Theodor Adorno's objections to the radicalism of the Enlightenment (see Horkheimer and Adorno). However, when it comes time to draw conclusions about the arts and letters, D'Alembert is indecisive. He laments the damaging effects of that abuse of the philosophical spirit that has made the literature of his own century inferior to that of the preceding century, although he extols Voltaire for his universality, Jean-Philippe Rameau as a philosopher-musician, and finally registers his objection to Rousseau's attack on literature.

Following D'Alembert's example, many other thinkers refused to believe that a general progress swept the human sciences forward, that this progress was evident in artistic disciplines (except to the extent that it facilitated theoretical reflection), or that it actually influenced morality. On the contrary, many thinkers—such as Madame Dacier and the partisans of the ancients, and later, following Rousseau's example, others such as Father Lefranc de Pompignan—linked the corruption of morals to the ascendancy of the new philosophy. Without any deep-seated bias, but by virtue of their experience and reflections as writers who were intransigent about their liberty and art, such authors as the marquis de Vauvenargues or Marivaux criticized and worked out their own models of mental progress. Both of them had more faith in the contribution of the "sciences of the mind," whose products were not subject to any continuity and could only be evaluated in relationship to historical knowledge. It could be said about these sciences that historical reflection was truly enriched by the refutation, in the name of the independence of art and the singular genius of the writer, of a unifying and uniformly progressivist view of human history.

Even Voltaire—however enchanted he may have been with the progress of philosophy and however convinced he might episodically appeared to have been of philosophy's effectiveness (for instance, in the struggle for toleration)—never stopped believing the course of concrete history to be a succession of crimes and misfortunes. As a disciple of Pierre Bayle, Voltaire was not ready to admit any clear meaning in the events that punctuate his account of the history of the world—or at least he did not want to despair of humanity and went on recounting their abominable odyssey. From this twofold decision there would result, not a philosophy of history but a historian's philosophy: to continue writing history in order to make oneself capable of writing it differently. Buffon's efforts lent this conclusion a new meaning, of which Voltaire and especially Diderot were clearly aware: the history of humanity could only be illuminated by being absorbed into the history of the physical universe, that of the Earth and the kingdoms of nature. In a sense, the "systems of nature" of the second half of the 18th century adopted a plan that had the merits of making a place for the sciences of observation and of not condemning to obsolescence every ancient form of thought.

Another intellectual benefit that could be gained from the debate over the meaning of history was that the complexity of the fields of study, and of the determinisms in question, was demonstrated. It became permissible, or even recommended, to mistrust a logic of ineluctable progress. It was therefore necessary, no matter what the cost, to continue to philosophize, as did Diderot or Rousseau, in the wake of criticisms of a rationalism that was radical, as would be said later, only because it was incomplete.

If one wanted to extract a "philosophy" of history peculiar to the thinkers of the age of the Enlightenment, it would be that independently of theologies and metaphysics, human beings had to think of themselves as fully and exclusively historical beings, reaching an awareness of what they were and of the responsibility of this totally human history. This "philosophy" of history would also reveal—and this is not of secondary importance—that thinkers of the age of the Enlightenment, although they were grounded in classical philosophies, nevertheless had excellent reasons not to yield to the temptation of historicism.

JEAN DAGEN

See also Ancients and the Moderns, Quarrel of the; Barbarian and Savage; Counter-Revolution; Progress; Siècle; Terror

Further Reading
Cassirer, Ernst, *The Philosophy of the Enlightenment*, translated by Fritz C.A. Koelln and James P. Pettegrove, Princeton, New Jersey: Princeton

University Press, 1951 (original German edition, 1932)

Dagen, Jean, *L'histoire de l'esprit humain dans la pensée française de Fontenelle à Condorcet*, Paris: Klincksieck, 1977

Delon, Michel, *L'idée d'énergie au tournant des Lumières (1770–1820)*, Paris: Presses Universitaires de France, 1988

Foucault, Michel, *The Order of Things: An Archaeology of the Human Sciences*, London:

Tavistock, and New York: Pantheon Books, 1970 (original French edition, 1966)

Horkheimer, Max, and Theodor W. Adorno, *Dialectic of Enlightenment*, translated by John Cumming, New York: Herder and Herder, 1972; London: Verso, 1979 (original German edition, 1944)

Vyverberg, Henry, *Historical Pessimism in the French Enlightenment*, Cambridge, Massachusetts: Harvard University Press, 1958

Holland

At the Peace of Utrecht in 1713 the United Provinces found themselves on the side of the victors. However, since the Republic had been ruined by the War of Spanish Succession, it could no longer play a leading role in international politics. On the domestic front, the political system, which had been in existence since the 17th century, and which constituted an exception in a Europe dominated by powerful monarchies, was still in place. Sovereignty was vested in the Estates-General, the seven provinces thus forming a federation. Within the Republic, power was divided. On the one hand, there were the old patrician families, whose interests were embodied in the person of the grand pensionary. As in the previous century, these rich burghers held positions of influence in the political and social realms, and determined the code of values by which Dutch society lived. Order, respectability, material success, and a peaceful family life were the principal features of the Dutch conception of happiness, and an appreciation of Enlightenment views would fit in well with these values.

On the other hand, there was the stadtholder, who was supported by the nobility, the Calvinist Church, and the ordinary people of the towns. His position was somewhat ambiguous, since he answered to the Estates-General while at the same time retaining some of the rights of the former sovereigns. The fact that the stadtholderate was held by an individual descended from the House of Orange helped strengthen his position—because of his ancestry, the stadtholder was generally regarded as a source of unity in a state that lacked a central power.

There were advantages to this kind of loose federation. Although often deficient at the national level, the governmental structure gave considerable autonomy to the provinces and towns—so much so, indeed, that the

efficiently run local governments protected the country from anarchy. The absence of a central authority also contributed to freedom of expression and toleration, the latter quality being enhanced by the fact that Calvinism, while the official religion of the Republic, never became a state religion. The other virtue of the political system was its flexibility. In 1702, when William III died without leaving a direct heir, the Estates-General did not retain his position, thus inaugurating a period without a stadtholder. This situation lasted until 1747, when, under the threat of French invasion, the title was restored. The nation as a whole calmly accepted these alternations, which they regarded as natural and inherent in the Dutch way of doing things.

During the course of the 18th century, however, there were calls for political reform. The criticism was aimed principally at the regents, who were accused of holding several posts at once, not to mention embezzlement and nepotism. The rich burghers and the enlightened middle classes felt excluded from positions of power, despite their abilities. The malcontents pinned their hopes on William, the heir to the Frisian branch of the House of Orange (1711–51). In 1729 William strengthened his position by becoming stadtholder of Friesland, Gelderland, Groningen, and Drenthe. In 1734 he married Anne, the daughter of George II of England, and subsequently exploited this English connection to the full. His chance came with the War of Austrian Succession (1740–48); in 1747, under the threat of attack by France, the Dutch Estates-General reestablished the stadtholderate and declared it hereditary. The ensuing Peace of Aix-la-Chapelle (1748) set the final seal on the Dutch Republic's loss of power, and the provinces thus remained neutral during the Seven Years' War (1756–63). Despite this eclipse, Holland still had a role to play on the political chessboard of Europe; Louis XV and Louis XVI did everything they could to keep the United Provinces neutral and to use them as a bulwark against England, laying the groundwork for an alliance that eventually became official with the Treaty of Fontainebleau in 1785.

In terms of the history of Holland, the brilliance of that country's golden age has tended to overshadow developments there during the 18th century, traditionally characterized by historians as a period of decline. Economically, the country was stable, but the role of mediator, which had brought such wealth to the Republic in the previous century, had become less profitable, as other nations no longer required its services. Overseas trade remained important—the Dutch East India Company was fabulously rich—and external trade amounted to 120 florins a year for each inhabitant (as opposed to 60 florins for England, and 35 for France). The skilled trades, industry, and fishing were indeed on the decline, but agriculture—notably the export of tobacco, madder-dye, and fruits and vegetables—was booming. The financial sector was still healthy, and there was a considerable growth in foreign loans. Despite various crises (for example, in 1763 and 1772–73), Amsterdam was still a major center for gold trading and the movement of capital. The Republic's ongoing role as banker to the rest of Europe meant that economically, and even politically, it was still a power to be reckoned with in international relations.

The real decline of Holland dates from the time of the fourth Anglo-Dutch War of 1780–84. The disastrous consequences of that war led the publicists of the day to revive one of their favorite themes, the idea that moral decadence lay at the root of economic and political decadence. The would-be reformers refused to accept the United Provinces' new role as a small, neutral (and insignificant) nation; even as they focused on specific abuses, the reformers were dreaming of restoring the Republic to its former glory. Their aspirations, which for a while had been pinned on William IV, were soon disappointed. William was not really committed to reform, being more interested in consolidating his own power with regard to the oligarchy of regents. But neither he nor his son William V was in a position to play the stadtholder's traditional card, which had been to influence foreign policy, since the Republic no longer played a decisive role in international affairs. Moreover, neither by training nor by family tradition was either of the stadtholders disposed to become an advocate of reform.

Their contemporaries criticized their inertia. The most outspoken criticism came from the Patriots, a party composed of men from different social backgrounds and with different interests, but united in their desire to reform the political, social, and cultural system

of the Republic. One of their leaders, Johan Derk van der Capellen (1741–84), published a *Brief aan het volk van Nederland* (Letter to the People of the Netherlands) in which he proposed, among other things, the setting up of a "popular" government, which would put an end to the system of co-option in local councils. Between 1785 and 1787, we may even speak of a prerevolutionary situation. The trend toward democracy began in Utrecht in 1786 and spread to other towns, where local governments loyal to the House of Orange were replaced by Patriots. However, the stadtholder gathered his supporters and took control of the situation. In 1787, with the help of the Prussian army, the Patriots were routed. Many of the latter fled to the neighboring Austrian Netherlands and to France, where they contributed to prerevolutionary agitation. But the Orangist restoration was short-lived. When the French (revolutionary) armies invaded the Republic in 1794–95, the Patriots regained control and set up the Batavian Republic (1795–1806) in which most of the aims of 1787 were realized, including the creation of a single nation based on a strong central government, the democratization of political power, and a more just society.

"Nowadays, light comes to us from the North." Paul Hazard has emphasized the fact that from 1680 to 1715—the period of incubation for the great intellectual upheavals of the 18th century—light and Enlightenment indeed came down from the North. Hazard also pointed out the crucial role of Holland as a haven—"The refugees' great ark," in the words of Pierre Bayle, who, with Baruch Spinoza and Grotius, must be regarded as one of the main precursors of the Enlightenment. And it was a fact that ever since the 16th century, the ideal of Christian humanism propounded by Erasmus—an ideal shared by both the patrician regents and the "dissidents" (the non-Calvinist Protestants)—had created a climate of toleration that favored the acceptance of new ideas.

This atmosphere, fostered by commercial interests and the need to balance the claims of various religious groups, meant that the Republic was particularly well suited to play the role of intellectual mediator. Books that were banned everywhere else in Europe were published in Holland, while newspapers and gazettes—notably French-language ones—prospered. Dutch publishers dominated the book trade throughout the first half of the 18th century, and Holland became the European capital for the publication of scholarly periodicals. French-born foreigners were extremely active there. For example, Prosper Marchand (1678–1756) was one of the key figures in Dutch publishing. Many journals, including the various *Bibliothèques* (collections of small-format books) published by the Swiss-born theologian Jean Leclerc (1656–1736), followed the pattern set by the *Nouvelles de la République des Lettres,* which Pierre Bayle had launched in 1684. The Dutch intellectual networks were made up of journalists and scholars alike. Thus, for example, the renowned physicist Willem Jacob 'sGravesande (1668–1742) was a coeditor and a brilliant collaborator of both the *Journal littéraire* and the *Journal de la République des Lettres.* Such periodicals were open to the discussion of religion, and they made room for heterodox opinions. They also played a leading role in introducing English ideas and culture to the Continent.

Dutch science and technology also made remarkable progress in this period. Newtonian physics found its way into Dutch universities, and in order to understand it, Voltaire himself went to Leiden in 1737 to hear 'sGravesande's lectures. Dutch scientists were pioneers and innovators in many fields, including microscopic science (Nicolas Hartsoeker [1656–1725]), botany, medicine, and chemistry (Herman Boerhaave [1668–1738] and Pieter van Musschenbroek [1692–1761]). Rejecting René Descartes's theory of innate ideas and his deductive method in favor of English experimentalism, such men laid the foundations of 18th-century scientific methodology. Following Sir Isaac Newton, they used the study of nature to support their religious aspirations.

This attempt to reconcile faith and reason by appealing to science took the form of a physico-theology, of which the most representative figure was Bernard Nieuwentyt (1654–1718). His book *Regt gebruik der werelt beschouwingen* (1715; The Religious Philosopher; or, The Right Use of Contemplating the Works of the Creator) posits a reconciliation between the new naturalist philosophy and an optimistic image of God. The argument between the respective claims of natural theology and revealed theology, initiated in the previous century, was taken to its logical conclusion, in the 18th century in the work of Johan Lulofs (1711–68). In his *Primae Lineae Theologiae Naturalis* (1756; Primary Lineage of Natural Theology), Lulofs, who succeeded 'sGravesande in Leiden, expressed his confidence in the autonomous power of reason and saw no grounds for a conflict between reason and the revealed truth of Christianity.

Toward the middle of the century, this physico-theological synthesis was taken even further by Christian von Wolff, who popularized the ideas of Gottfried Wilhelm Leibniz. Physico-theology even began to find favor with orthodox Calvinists, whereas it had hitherto appealed mainly to the "dissidents." A reformed pastor, J.F. Martinet (1729–95), published his *Katechismus der Natuur* (1777–79; Catechism of Nature), a highly successful work of popular science intended for young (and not so young) readers, in which he defended "philosophy"—that is, the study of the natural sciences—

against the many Calvinist believers who saw in such study a threat to their faith. The success of the *Katechismus* created widespread interest in the principles of physico-theology, while at the same time encouraging its many readers to become actively involved in the natural sciences.

The possibility of a harmonious fusion of reason and revealed religion was characteristic of the Dutch Enlightenment. It is evident even at the level of vocabulary, since the key terms used to describe the movement—*Verlichting* (Enlightenment) and *verlicht* (enlightened)—retained their original religious connotation of "illuminated by divine light." It is this religious aspect that explains the Dutch intellectuals' reservations with regard to Spinoza and his followers—all those who, like the prominent journalist Jean Rousset de Missy (1686–1762), represented much more radical (though largely clandestine) opinions. And while works by the French *philosophes* were printed, translated, and sold in Holland, it was the German disciples of Christian Wolff, men such as Jean-Henri-Samuel Formey and Johann David Michaelis, who, in the wake of John Locke and Newton, were most influential there, doubtless because the themes those Germans discussed, like those of the "popular philosophers" (such as Martinet), appealed to the Christian side of Dutch Enlightenment mentality.

The spread of knowledge, another Enlightenment trademark, was greatly facilitated in Holland by a relatively high rate of literacy, with periodical literature always to the fore. In addition to the French-language journals already referred to, Pieter Rabus (1660–1702) created the *Boekzaal van Europe* (1692–1702), the first learned periodical to be published in Dutch, with moderate and Newtonian leanings. In addition to these learned journals, Justus van Effen (1684–1735) launched a series of "Spectators" based on the English model and intended for a much wider audience. Effen is a typical representative of the ambivalent position of the Dutch intellectuals of this period: simultaneously highly cosmopolitan and yet sympathetic to national values. In his youth, he wrote for the newspapers published by French expatriates and founded several French-language papers of his own—*Le misanthrope, La bagatelle,* and *Le nouveau spectateur françois*—which served as media for Enlightenment ideas, notably those of Newton and Locke. In 1731 Effen abandoned French to found the first Dutch-language *Spectator,* the *Hollandsche Spectator* (1731–35). While it dealt with many topics (including language, literature, religion, and society), the main focus of the paper was on national identity and the need to protect it against harmful foreign influences, together with the related theme of the decline of standards resulting from moral corruption. The *Hollandsche Spectator* was immensely successful and was widely imitated in the second half of the century.

Efforts such as these to spread knowledge throughout society led directly to an interest in educational theory. Locke's ideas on education were widely disseminated, both in the various Spectators and in more specialized works, such as W.E. de Perponcher's *Instructions d'un père à son fils* (1774; Directions from a Father to His Son) and *Onderwijs voor kinderen* (1782; Teaching for Children). Throughout the 18th century Locke remained the undisputed authority in this field, whereas Jean-Jacques Rousseau's *Émile, ou, De l'éducation* (1762; Emile; or, concerning Education) had a more mixed reception. Many of the great names of Dutch literature took an interest in education. Hieronymus van Alphen (1746–1803), a leading figure in the Dutch Christian Enlightenment, wrote a pioneer work of poetry entitled *Kleine gedigten voor kinderen* (1782; Short Poems for Children) in which he makes a genuine attempt to penetrate the child's universe.

Educational theory is also a central concern in the work of Elizabeth Wolff-Bekker (1738–1804) who was also sympathetic to the Christian Enlightenment. Unlike Alphen, a loyal Orangist who opposed the Patriots, Wolff-Bekker had democratic sympathies, which led her to settle in France after the failed revolution of 1787. In 1779 she published *Proeve over de opvoeding* (Essay on Education), a work intended for mothers, in which she expressed her optimistic views on childhood and the virtues of education. Her famous epistolary novel, *Historie van Mejuffrouw Sara Burgerhart* (1782; Story of Miss Sara Burgerhart), written in collaboration with Agatha Deken and with a preface underlining its specifically Dutch features, gave great prominence to a theme that would recur in her later work, namely the links between the education of the young and the ongoing debate in 18th-century Holland between the rival claims of reason and revealed religion.

Another important factor in the dissemination of knowledge was the role played by the academies and learned societies. The century was well advanced before their influence began to be felt, since the oldest among them—the Hollandsche Maatschappij der Wetenschappen (Academy of Sciences of Haarlem)—was not founded until 1751. This relative delay can be explained by the decentralized structure of the Republic and the universities' exclusive control of scientific research until around 1740. However, the popularity of physico-theology, the growth of a sense of national identity, together with an increasingly literate public led the elite in power to establish several learned societies. Alongside those with semiofficial status, such as the one in Haarlem and the Maatschappij der Nederlandse Letterkunde (Society of Literature of the Netherlands) founded in Leiden in 1766, smaller literary and scientific societies as well as various reading circles sprang up everywhere.

In the late 1770s a number of reform societies were set up, the most famous of which was the Maatschappij tot Nut van 't Algemeen (Society for Public Welfare). Founded in 1784 by the Mennonite pastor J. Nieuwenhuyzen (1724-1808), its aim was to give those who were politically disenfranchised the opportunity to express themselves on matters of social policy. Reaching out to educate the poorer classes of society, this association was remarkably successful. In 1800 it had more than 3,500 members. Mention should also be made of the Teylers Stichting, a foundation established in 1778. This organization gave M. van Marum (1750–1837), the director of the Museum of Physics and Natural Sciences, the opportunity to champion the theories of Antoine-Laurent de Lavoisier, thereby giving a new sense of purpose to Dutch research in chemistry. These various groups were representative of a process of intellectual and civic emancipation that was affecting increasingly large sectors of the population. They were influential in the development of revolutionary ideas, the effect of which was felt in the reforms introduced by the Batavian Republic.

The growth of a sense of national identity did not lead to the disappearance of Dutch intellectual cosmopolitanism, since many leading figures, while playing an important part in the cultural life of the Provinces, were at the same time members of the European Republic of Letters. Elie Luzac (1721–90), for example, who was descended from a French expatriate family and was active as a bookseller-printer and publicist, maintained a large network of international contacts that included Huguenots living in England, the Swiss writer Charles Bonnet (whose works he published), and—above all—Samuel Formey, the permanent secretary of the Academy of Sciences in Berlin, with whom he had an extensive correspondence. Luzac was also a regular contributor to Formey's *Bibliothèque impartiale* from 1750 to 1758.

Luzac was an active member of the large Huguenot community that had spread throughout Europe; by their opposition to every sort of fanaticism but also to scepticism, this group was representative of the moderate strain in Enlightenment thought. Thus, his *Nederlandsche Letter-Courant* (1759–63) characteristically kept Dutch readers in touch with French philosophical trends, while at the same time criticized ideas that seemed to him too radical. Luzac's efforts mirrored those of the international community of liberal Protestants as a whole, and in the 1770s they would take a distinctly political turn, as he was an outspoken adversary of the Patriots.

There was widespread fear among liberal Protestants that the principles of moderate Enlightenment would be pushed into the background by the winds of radical change blowing in from France. Isaac de Pinto (1717–87), a Portuguese-born Jewish banker and man of letters, was, like Luzac, sympathetic to the Orangist cause and a typical example of Dutch cosmopolitanism. He was acquainted with the leading figures of the European Enlightenment—including Voltaire, Diderot, Adam Smith, and Hume—and contributed to both national and international debate on political economy. Pinto's arguments in favor of state loans and paper money in his *Traité de la circulation et du crédit* (1771; An Essay on Circulation and Credit) sets him apart from mainstream Dutch economic theory, which was more concerned with the decline of trade and ways of combating it. In Pinto's view, competition with other European nations was an unavoidable fact of life. The Dutch should concentrate on what they did best, namely finance.

In the field of philosophy, the most distinguished figure of this period was Frans Hemsterhuis (1721–90). Hemsterhuis, who chose to write in French, can be situated at the meeting point between English neo-Platonism and Dutch Cartesianism. Princess von Gallitzin helped to translate and popularize the work of this "Dutch Socrates" in Germany. While rejecting materialism and atheism, Hemsterhuis was also opposed to orthodox Christianity. Instead, he favored natural religion with a distinctly pantheistic flavor, as is seen in his concept of "the soul of the world" in *Aristée* (1779; Aristea). Hemsterhuis's praise of enthusiasm and imagination in *Alexis* (1787; Alexis) anticipates the theory of inspiration and the notion of the poet as seer and prophet, which would be fundamental to romanticism. Madame de Staël expressed a widely held view when she wrote in *De l'Allemagne* (1810; Germany): "Three thinkers were the main precursors of Kant: Lessing, Hemsterhuis, and Jacobi. The Dutch philosopher Hemsterhuis was the first to express the generous ideas on which the new German school is based."

Another representative of Dutch cosmopolitanism, although of a later generation, was the novelist Belle van Zuylen, who, upon her marriage, became Isabelle de la Charrière (1740–1805). She left Holland in 1771 and settled in Switzerland. Fluent in several languages, she preferred to write in French. Initially sympathetic to the new ideas, Charrière wrote in support of the Dutch Patriots in 1787 and followed the events of the French Revolution with keen interest, but as a strong opponent of every kind of violence and fanaticism, she was disillusioned by the Terror. Already as a young woman, she had shown considerable talent as a letter writer. In Switzerland her literary career was launched in 1784–85 with the publication of the *Lettres neuchâteloises* (1784; Letters of Neuchâtel), *Lettres de Mistress Henley* (1784; Letters of Mistress Henley), and *Lettres écrites de Lausanne* (1785; Letters Written from Lausanne), a series of short epistolary novels that manage to be both natural and subtle. In addition to her successful career as a novelist, which continued until 1799, Charrière wrote plays, political pamphlets of considerable journalistic skill, and an impressive number of letters. Her letters were addressed not only to major literary figures, such as Benjamin Constant, but to a series of young men and women whom she undertook to educate, displaying all the pedagogical zeal that was so characteristic of her age.

Rijkloff Michaël van Goens (1748–1810), a contemporary of Charrière's, was one of the most cosmopolitan Dutchmen of the time. Goens was a genuine child prodigy, and at the age of 18, he held the chair of Oratory, History, and Greek at the University of Utrecht. He was a founding member of the Society of Literature at Leiden, and, in a series of three essays (1765–66), he opened up several new paths for Dutch literary criticism. He introduced the public to Ossian and Gessner, treated Rousseau as the most genuinely innovative mind of the age, and argued that the expression of feeling and the creative imagination were more important in art than reason or academic rules. Goens was violently attacked by orthodox Calvinists and in 1776 resigned his chair to pursue a career in politics. When the Patriot revolution occurred in 1787, his well-known and outspoken sympathy for the Orangist cause led to his exile. Goens went to Switzerland and later settled in Germany where, as we know from his voluminous correspondence, he became close to such men as Jean le Rond D'Alembert, Denis Diderot, Christoph Martin Wieland, Salomon Gessner, Moses Mendelssohn, Friedrich Heinrich Jacobi, and Melchiorre Cesarotti. While no longer participating directly in Dutch cultural life, van Goens may still be regarded as one of those figures who made an important contribution to the literature of his native land by opening it up to the new currents of thought that were circulating in Europe at the end of the 18th century.

MADELEINE VAN STRIEN-CHARDONNEAU

Further Reading

Jacob, Margaret C., and W.W. Mijnhardt, editors, *The Dutch Republic in the Eighteenth Century: Decline, Enlightenment, and Revolution*, Ithaca, New York: Cornell University Press, 1992

Velema, Wyger R.E., *Enlightenment and Conservatism in the Dutch Republic: The Political Thought of Elie Luzac (1721–1796)*, Assen/Maastricht, The Netherlands: Van Gorcum, 1993

Holy Roman Empire. *See* Germany and the Holy Roman Empire

Hospital

The definition of the word *hôpital* (hospital) in Antoine Furetière's *Dictionnaire universel* (1690; Universal Dictionary) conveys both the double meaning that the term carried and the duality of the social reality it described: "Hospital, Charitable, pious place where the poor are taken in and cared for. The general hospital is where all beggars are taken in. The *hôtel-Dieu* [house of God] is the hospital for all sick people." This linguistic and institutional double meaning was common to many European countries; in Germany, however, a *Krankenhaus* referred exclusively to sick people. Depending on its vocation, a hospital would take care of either poor people who were healthy or the ailing poor. The term *hôtel Dieu*, which originally referred to the Parisian institution on the Île de la Cité founded in the ninth century by the Notre Dame chapter, was often used in France to designate hospitals that treated the ailing. However, many institutions reserved for sick people used the denomination *hôpital* rather than *hôtel-Dieu*. Various names were used in France and in other European countries for places where vagabonds, beggars, and other able-bodied poor people were confined: "general hospital" or simply "hospital," "hospice," "poorhouse," "lockup," or "prison." Whatever the term used, both the general hospitals created in France in the 17th century (such as the Hôpital Général de Paris [General Hospital of Paris], founded in 1656) and the poorhouses established in the 18th century were responses to a political choice to "keep poor people in confinement." However, there was quite a gap between political will and reality. In almost all European countries, attempts were made to lock up, voluntarily or forcibly, all healthy and sickly beggars and vagabonds, as well as abandoned children and "lost girls and women," but this was an endless task that could never really be accomplished. Although it is at times difficult to make a clear distinction between the different types of hospitals, this article will be limited to the definition of a "hospital" as a place that takes in sick people, most of them indigent. (The admission to hospitals of people with means, who received special services at their own expense, was a widespread exception to the usual practice of admitting the poor.)

Various factors prevent an accurate quantitative evaluation of the hospitals in 18th-century Europe. Information about France drawn from the papers of a Parisian surgeon, Jacques Tenon (1724–1816), shows the geographic distribution of *hôtels-Dieu* in 1789, with much greater density in northern and eastern France than in the west and southwest. However, these statistics are somewhat misleading because all institutions were counted on an equal basis, regardless of important differences in size and capacity. To cite just one regional example, in 1762 Anjou had 20 hospitals with a total of 717 beds, including 315 beds at the *hôtel-Dieu* in Angers, 50 in Château-Gontier, 42 in Saumur, and 310 scattered among 17 other institutions, with an average of 18 beds per hospital. In large or medium-sized cities, there were typically large hospitals with hundreds of beds, while most often one found small institutions with a few beds in the small towns or villages. In fact, the number of beds is itself an imprecise indication of the number of persons admitted to a given hospital, for, even into the 18th century, one hospital bed might hold two or, in dire situations, three patients. Furthermore, there was a quick turnover because hospital stays were brief: either the patient died shortly after admission or he was declared cured and quickly discharged. In his *Voyage médical en Italie fait en l'année 1820* (Medical Journey through Italy Made in 1820), Louis Valentin, a doctor from Lorraine, portrays the situation in Italian hospitals. Written too late for it to be considered a true representation of hospitals in the 18th century, this account is nonetheless revealing. Valentin notes that every major city had at least one or two hospitals, if not more (10 in Naples, 9 in Rome), each with several hundred beds—for example, the Santa Maria Nuova in Florence had 1,200 beds. In medium-sized cities, such as Padua, Leghorn, or Pavia, there was 1 hospital with 200 to 300 beds. There were many other hospitals scattered all over Italy, but most observers considered them to be unsatisfactory.

Despite several attempts at reform in the 16th and 17th centuries, particularly in France and England, the institutional structure of European hospitals during the Enlightenment remained extremely varied, and, in general, it was poorly adapted to new needs. Institutions founded by generous pious benefactors in the Middle Ages were often still managed according to the provisions of their original charte, even though the Council of Trent had in some cases authorized a reallocation of funds to meet new demands. The same type of stagnation characterized the various types of administrations. Again in conformity with a provision of the Council of Trent, bishops nevertheless managed here and there, in cases where episcopal oversight was not among the provisions of the founding charter, to broaden their visiting rights in all the *hôtels-Dieu* of their diocese and, moreover, to insist on being present or represented on the boards of directors of these institutions, especially when the accounts were presented. In some countries, notably in France, this ecclesiastical interference came up against the will of the king, who tried to intervene and impose some order on the finances and inner workings of the *hôtels-Dieu*. Finances were a general problem for these institutions. The *hôtel-Dieu* obviously did not earn income from the patients who were almost always poor (with the rare exceptions mentioned above); instead, revenues came from real estate bequeathed by the founder of the institution. This income often dwindled over the centuries, while expenses kept increasing. In the best of circumstances, new donations would prevent the institution from deteriorating or disappearing. However, attempts by civil authorities to impose uniform standards and to rationalize regulations and budgets met with all sorts of resistance, largely due to prevailing attitude of religious respect toward these pious foundations.

Beyond financial and administrative problems, medical conditions in these hospitals left much to be desired. Observers from all countries described the same deplorable conditions: two or three patients to a bed; beds crammed together in stuffy, decrepit wards; filth and poor sanitation; surgical operations performed in dreadful conditions, often right in front of other patients; few or no modern treatments, even by the standards of the time, when the art of healing was in its infancy. There were, of course, exceptions—the hospital founded by Madame Necker in the Saint Sulpice parish of Paris in 1778, or the Santa Maria de Vita hospital in Bologna, which "brought joy to the heart" of the Englishman John Howard who visited it in 1783—but they were few and far between. The general situation was unsatisfactory, owing in large part to the persistent, radical difference in both the training and practice of doctors and surgeons. The doctor was a scholar trained at the university, who learned his science from books; the surgeon was a manual worker trained on the job, who performed bleedings, lanced

abscesses, and set fractures according to the doctor's prescription. Medicine was one of the seven liberal arts; surgery was a mechanical art. In the course of his university studies, the future doctor received a purely theoretical education, without putting it into practice "at the patient's bedside," which would have enabled him to visit the hospital. In fact, most doctors were not the least bit interested in hospital practice either during their studies or later when they went into practice. Hospital work was left to staff surgeons functioning under the vague and often theoretical direction of a slightly less indifferent doctor and to the nuns or monks who ran the institution.

There were some signs of progress in the 18th century, beginning in the United Provinces and Italy. The great Dutch doctor Herman Boerhaave (1668–1738), a professor at the University of Leiden, who taught that "theory must bow down at the patient's bedside," had considerable influence throughout Europe, and his efforts would ultimately bring about positive results. The first steps were taken in medical colleges or academies, such as the Collège du Roi (Royal College) and the Jardin du Roi (French Royal Botanical Garden) in Paris, on the fringes of university teaching, which remained rigid and dogmatic. The Sant'Ortola Hospital in Bologna opened its training facilities to future doctors, thereby combining theoretical courses and clinical experience gained through the treatment of hospitalized patients. In a spirit of dynamism that sharply contrasted with traditional university conformism, the University of Pavia endowed two new chairs in 1780: one in surgical operations and the other in theoretical and practical medicine. The first holder of the medical chair, in 1781, was the Swiss doctor Samuel August André David Tissot, author of the widely read *Avis au peuple sur sa santé* (1761; Advice to the People about Their Health). Tissot's successor, Johann Peter Frank from the Rhineland, who took the chair in 1783, presented to Joseph II a plan for radical reform of the health system in Austrian Lombardy, calling for a merging of the professions of doctor and surgeon, an end to the separation between universities and hospitals, and a complete reorganization of the geographic distribution of hospitals in the Po Valley. However, Frank was recalled to Vienna in 1795 before he could put his plan into action. Similarly, in France in the last years of the ancien régime, there were many investigations and reform projects based on a severe evaluation of the shortcomings of the hospital system, with suggestions for radical reforms that included financial reorganization, increased participation of doctors, and the elimination of oversized hospitals. Horrified by the conditions in a great majority of these institutions, many reformers even suggested a program of home medical care to replace hospitalization.

Whatever was advocated in the specific solutions, the idea gradually developed that caring for the poor, especially the poor and ailing, was a national responsibility that must be assumed by the government. Good works and philanthropy free of all religious connections came to replace Christian charity. In France as in neighboring countries, events in the last decade of the 18th century contributed to bringing about changes. Georges Gusdorf's description of French medicine in 1789 also applies perfectly to that era's hospitals both in France and, beyond its borders, all across Europe: "French medicine in 1789 was at a standstill; only the trauma of the Revolution, which wiped out all the former institutions, was able to get it moving again."

FRANÇOIS LEBRUN

See also Children; Medicine; Surgery

Further Reading

Cosmacini, Giorgio, *Soigner et réformer: Médecine et santé en Italie de la grande peste à la première guerre mondiale*, Paris: Payot, 1992

Imbert, Jean, editor, *Histoire des hôpitaux en France*, Toulouse: Privat, 1982

Humor. *See* Caricature; Comedy; Irony; Parody; Satire

Hungary

After the Peace of Karlowitz (1699), Hungary became an autonomous state within the Habsburg empire, governed by a hereditary king. The king of Hungary, that is to say the Habsburg emperor, also reigned over the principality of Transylvania. From 1703 a war of independence was fought, under the leadership of Ferenc II Rákóczi, with the objective of maintaining the privileges and autonomy of the nobility, and the independence of Transylvania under the government of a Hungarian prince. This war ended in 1711 with the Peace of Szatmár, which did bring about the restitution of the nobles' privileges; however, the peace settlement left Hungary to total dependence on the Viennese court in military and foreign affairs and partial dependence in financial affairs.

The Roman Catholic Church (and to a certain extent the Greek Catholics), supported by the Habsburgs, dominated this religiously diverse nation, attempting by means of conversions and administrative measures to thwart the activities of Protestants and the Orthodox Church. Latin was the official language in Hungary, but the inhabitants spoke many different languages. According to the 1784 census, the population (including Croatia and Transylvania) numbered more than 9 million; 38.9 percent spoke Hungarian, 16.7 percent Romanian, 13.9 percent Slovak, 12.2 percent German,

8.9 percent Croatian, 6.7 percent Serbian, and 1.1 percent Ruthenian. Up to the early 19th century, the title *Hungarus,* given to nobles and intellectuals of non-Hungarian origin, designated a fatherland, not a nationality. Hungarian society was made up of 5 percent nobles, 80 percent serfs, and 15 percent free peasants and a small bourgeoisie. Among the 15,000 to 20,000 intellectuals, there were priests, pastors, lawyers, physicians, stewards of the great landowners, professors, and teachers.

Enlightened Absolutism

The Hungarian nobility, which had accepted the Pragmatic Sanction of 1723, broke with a long anti-Habsburg tradition to take up the defense of Maria Theresa (reigned 1740–80) at the 1741 Diet, offering *vitam et sanguinem pro rege nostro* (life and blood for our monarch). After 1765 the queen attempted to implement a number of reforms. Freemasons in the military and the bureaucracy tried to strengthen the power of the state, to impose a more profitable economic structure, to improve the efficiency of the administrative system, and to reduce the influence of the Church. To prepare the Hungarian nobility to accept reforms, in 1768 Maria Theresa created a royal guard composed of 100 Hungarians and 20 Transylvanians, in which the young men studied languages and came into contact with Enlightenment ideas.

In 1767 Maria Theresa issued a decree, the *Urbarium,* granting freedom of movement to serfs. In 1773 the Jesuit order was dissolved, and in 1777 the *Ratio Educationis* (An Account of Education) reformed the school system. Inspired with the spirit of enlightened despotism, Joseph II (reigned 1780–90) pursued this nascent reform policy. Karl Anton von Martini, Johann Heinrich Gottleib von Justi, and Joseph von Sonnenfels stimulated reforms to modernize society from the top and to reinforce government centralization. In 1781 the king eased restrictions on the press, thus weakening the absolute power of the Catholic Church. That same year, Joseph signed a decree granting religious toleration. Protestants and Orthodox, were thereafter liberated from the Catholic oath imposed since the 1731 *Carolina Resolutio* and free to perform administrative functions and so escape from the humiliations to which the Catholic Church subjected them. Also in 1781, Joseph attempted to centralize the imperial administration by replacing Latin with German, the most widespread language in the empire, but he was blocked by the joint opposition of Roman Catholics and Protestants.

The death of Joseph II was followed by a power struggle involving three camps: a nobility that has been described as "baroque" because it remained attached to the values of the past; an elite that recommended reform but resisted change in prevailing social structures; and a small group of radical intellectuals. Most of the nobles wanted to maintain their fiscal immunity and the system of serfdom. They also demanded the reform of the Diets, where they could expound their *gravamina* (grievances), and the preservation of the system of *comitats* (counties) for local administrative purposes. At the same time, the nobles accepted the authority of the Habsburgs and feudal dualism, along with the military and diplomatic restrictions that these entailed.

The "reform" nobles, influenced by Locke, Montesquieu, and Rousseau, called for economic and cultural reforms based on the idea of the social contract. Their principal representative, György Bessenyei (1747–1811), a member of the royal guard and representative to Vienna of the Protestant churches, gave a warm welcome to the *Ratio Educationis* and the decree granting religious toleration. The "Josephists" attempted economic reforms, seeking in particular to introduce new methods of agriculture. Particularly prominent among them were Karl von Zinzendorf, a friend of the marquis de Mirabeau, and aristocrats such as Count József Teleki, Baron József Podmanicky, Baron Pál Almássy, and Count Nikola Skerlec, who were all influenced by François Quesnay. Gergely Berzeviczy (1763–1822), inspired by the ideas of the abbé Raynal, Jean-Baptiste

Say, and Adam Smith, proposed the reform of customs between Hungary and the hereditary countries of the Habsburg empire in order to develop industry and commerce (*De Commercio et Industria Hungariae* [1797; On the Trade and Industry of Hungary]).

In 1790 Hungarians celebrated the return from Vienna to Pozsony (now Bratislava) of Saint Stephen's Crown, the symbol of their autonomous monarchy, as well as the coronation of the new king. The Diet became the place where the nobles expressed their nationalism. Leopold II (1790–92) used his very active police force to promote the struggle between the diverse political tendencies. His successor, Francis I, sided with the reactionary forces and avoided convening the Diet. When incidents in the Austrian Netherlands (now Belgium) and, especially, the French Revolution had brought an end to the program of top-down social reform, the Habsburg possessions still retained a feudal social and political organization, and Enlightenment ideas remained confined in the main to the spheres of culture, language, and literature at least until 1825.

The "Hungarian Jacobins" wanted to go even further. Their major figure, József Hajnóczy (1750–95), advocated a radical transformation of society, with the establishment of a bourgeois system, total abolition of serfdom, redemption of lands, taxation of nobles, the introduction of a parliamentary system, the appointment of commoners to administrative posts, a "national" education system administered by the state, and cultural development of the country (*De Comitiis Regni Hungariae deque Organisatione Eorundem Dissertatio Juris Publicis* [1791; A Public-Law Dissertation on the King of Hungary's Estates and their Organization] and *De Diversis Subsidiis Publicis Dissertatio* [1792; A Dissertation on Various Public Subsidies]). After the death of Leopold II, the "Jacobins" were influenced by Canon Ignác Martinovics (1755–95), a university professor who, after earlier collaboration with the police, founded two associations in 1793, one dedicated to the initiation of a qualified abolition of the feudal system (the Association of Reformers) and the other whose program called for a people's power (Association for Liberty and Equality). The "Jacobins" were arrested in 1794 and 1795; 42 of them were tried and seven were executed.

New ideas were disseminated to fairly broad strata of the population through the schools. In 1771 more than 50 percent of the prosperous peasantry could read and write, but the majority of the population was illiterate. The *Ratio Educationis* stimulated the development of primary education, providing for a specific number of masters and "mixed" national schools. Schoolmasters were trained in model schools based on the Prussian system. The number of secondary schools also increased; in 1785 there were 130 secondary schools in Hungary and Transylvania. Until its dissolution on charges of excessive conservatism, the Jesuit order had dominated secondary and university education. The Piarists were the only clerics who introduced new methods adapted to national realities into secondary education.

Protestant professors, who maintained close relations with Dutch, Swiss, and German universities, introduced new disciplines into the educational system. In itself, the *Ratio Educationis* thoroughly renovated the curriculum, adding history, geography, and the natural sciences to the list of requirements. In the mid–18th century the city of Selmecbánya developed an Academy of Mines that attracted interest in the Western world because of its new methods. After 1777 new chairs and an engineering institute were established at the University of Buda. After university graduation, Catholics, and especially Catholic priests, pursued further studies in Austria or Italy. The Protestants, who were influenced by certain Enlightenment ideas but also by the orthodoxy of Protestant churches, did their graduate studies in German, Dutch, or Swiss universities.

With support for publishing from the policy of enlightened despotism, newly founded presses were active in publishing textbooks, scientific brochures, and literary works. The number of books published increased from 1,720 in the period 1731–71 to 4,587 in the period 1791–1800. Whereas Latin had been the principal language of publication in the time of Joseph II, it now accounted for just 36.8 percent of published works, while Hungarian rose to 33.8 percent and German to 23.3 percent. Some bookstores organized reading rooms to present periodicals. Some bishops and aristocrats opened their libraries to the public. For example, in 1802 Count Ferenc Széchenyi made an inaugural donation of 20,000 books to the library of the National Museum. The first German newspaper, the *Pressburger Zeitung*, appeared in 1764, followed by the first Hungarian paper, *Magyar Hirmondó*, with 320 subscribers in 1780, replaced by *Hadi és más nevezetes történetek* in 1791. In 1786 the *Magyar kurir* already had 1,200 subscribers.

Peasants continued to read the Bible, psalms, pious books, almanacs, chapbooks, and other sorts of popular literature. Nobles, intellectuals, and some of the bourgeois subscribed to newspapers and bought books on legal subjects, popularizations, and literature. The enlightened nobles and young intellectuals, influenced by new ideas, were the most interested in social reform.

Movement of Ideas

The 1781 decree on toleration, unanimously saluted by "reformers" and especially by Protestants, brought in its wake a series of critical publications. For example,

Sándor Szacsvay (1752–1812), the founder of Hungarian journalism, published pamphlets against the Jesuits and nuns in 1786 and 1787. In 1790 the future "Jacobin" János Laczkovics (1754–95) translated the writings of Friedrich Trenk and Johann Rautenstrauch against Catholic Church ceremonies. After the promulgation of the 1781 decree, Voltaire was translated by Protestants such as Jószef Pétzeli (1740–92), for *La Henriade* (1723; The Henriade), *Zaïre* (1784; Zara), and *Alzire* (1789; Alzira); and Ferenc Kazinczy, the future reformer of the Hungarian language, for *Mérope* (1744).

At the same time, the Catholic Church was defended by apologists such as Balázs Alexovits (1742–96) who opposed the reading of banned books and Léo Szaitz (1746–92), who gave the meaningful title of *Igaz magyar* (The True Hungarian) to his defense of ecclesiastical power. Deism and atheism were also attacked by Protestants in Hungary and Transylvania. In 1760 Count József Teleki (1738–96), a representative of the Calvinist Church of Transylvania, published in French an *Essai sur la faiblesse des esprits forts* (Essay on the Weakness of Strong Minds). Moral questions were debated: Jean-François Marmontel's *Bélisaire* (1767; Belisarius) was published in Latin in 1771, then in Hungarian in 1773 and 1776. His translators disagreed with his conception of natural religion but accepted his ethical values. Marmontel's *Contes moraux* (1755–59; Moral Tales) were translated in 1795 by a member of the Hungarian guard, Sándor Báróczi (1759–1809), who defended the idea of natural religion and praised the author's sensitive, elegant style.

In a book published in German (*Der Mann ohne Vorurtheil* [1781; The Man without Prejudice]), Bessenyei returned to the problem of morality; following the example of Claude-Adrien Helvétius, he sought compromise between individual and public morality by his declaration that liberty is the supreme value and must be achieved through reason, and consequently by the establishment of laws. Ferenc Kazinczy (1759–1837), who was later imprisoned as a "Jacobin," in 1789 published a review entitled *Orpheus*, whose first issue dealt with the dissemination of "rational thought":

I must call this thought *Aufklärung*, Enlightenment, because some people want to adulterate it by indifferentism, with irreligion, or so-called Socratism or deism, and like Helvétius's owl they shout that the warm sun does indeed enter their dark lairs.

Kazinczy wanted to promote a "religion purified of its superstitions, a philosophy without preconceived theses." The "Jacobins" were usually deists, but some, inspired by the baron d'Holbach's materialism, adhered to a more or less utilitarian morality, as did Martinovics in a book written in French, the *Mémoires philosophiques* (1788; Philosophical Memoirs).

Language and Literature

The modernization of the Hungarian language had been on the program of the Enlightenment movement since the 1770 publication of a book in Latin by János Sajnovics, *Demonstratio Idioma Hungarorum et Lapporum Idem Esse* (Demonstration That the Idioms of Hungarian and Lapp Are the Same), which caused a sensation by classifying Hungarian among the Finno-Ugric languages. This hypothesis, confirmed by Sámuel Gyarmathi in *Affinitas Linguae Hungaricae cum Linguis Fennicae Originis Grammatica Demonstrata* (1799; Grammatical Proof of the Affinity of the Hungarian Language with Language of Fennic Origin), came up against another theory claiming a Turkish origin for the Hungarian language. In 1778 Bessenyei published pamphlets that drew attention to Hungarian culture and the modernization of the language (*Magyarság* [The Hungarian Language]): "It is through their language that nations acquire their knowledge." In 1790 he presented a proposal for an academy *Egy jámbor szándék* [A Humble Proposal]) that would not be realized until some time later.

Modern nationalism also infiltrated in historiography. The Jesuit school, with István Kaprinai (1714–85), György Pray (1723–1801), and István Katona (1732–1811), undertook a critical study of documents; Katona published a 42-volume *Historia Critica Regum Hungariae* (1779–1817; Critical History of Hungarian Affairs) in Latin. Enlightened despotism was defended by Ferenc Adám Kollár (1716–83), who upheld the rights of the kings of Hungary in ecclesiastical affairs, and by György Márton Kovachich (1744–1821), who published previously unknown texts of the *Corpus Juris Hungarici* (Corpus of Hungarian Law) and brought together historians to collect documents on the Diets (among others the "Jacobin" Karoly Koppi and the Romanian Gheorghe Tincai), thus giving prominence to the importance of the constitution and the role of the state.

Political science (in the form of German *Staatenkunde* [political geography]) was introduced at the dawn of the century by Mathias Bél (1684–1749), author of a geographic and historical description of the ten Hungarian counties (*Notitiae Hungaricae Novae Historico-Geographica* [1735–42; New Historical-Geographical Notes on Hungary]). In 1746–48 Bél's disciple Johann Georg Schwandtner published in his *Scriptores rerum Hungaricorum* (Writers on Hungarian Affairs) the *Gesta* (Acts) by Anonymous (in fact, the notary of King Béla III), a document that led to discussions about the settlement of the Hungarians in Pannonia and Dacia. The war against the Ottoman empire awakened national interest in the heroes of the Christian campaign, particularly in János Hunyadi, whose memory was celebrated by Bessenyei (1772–78), among others. Thereafter, history served not only to glorify the past but also to express a sort of criticism of the present, becoming an instrument to awaken nationalism in the 19th-century nation-state.

In the realm of technology, new releases from western Europe were disseminated in manuals and popularizations and through the reformation of public hygiene and agrarian. After the University was transferred to Buda in 1777, its press became the center of scientific popularization with the publication of works in Hungarian, German, Romanian, Serbian, Slovak, and even modern Greek, making Buda an important nerve center for technical publication for central Europe and the Balkans.

"Baroque" politics inspired some of the Hungarian literary works of the period. For instance, the novel *Etelka* (1788) by the Piarist András Dugonics (1740–1818) that attacks change imposed from the outside; *Egy falusi notárius budai utazása* (1790; A Village Notary's Journey to Buda) by Count József Gvadányi (1725-1801) treats the new fashions with irony. A "baroque" sensibility also inflects the poetry of Baron Lörinc Orczy (1718–89), who was against atheistic or deist *philosophes*. There was also a current of rococo lyricism in a libertine vein, such as the *Rhapsodies* (Rhapsodies) of Count János Fekete (1741–1803), written in French and sent to Voltaire along with numerous bottles of wine.

However, the most important representative of the Enlightenment in Hungarian literature was Bessenyei. In a political novel, *Tarimenes utazása* (The Voyage of Tarimenes), written in 1804, Kirakades, a Voltairean "savage," mocks sarcastically the vices of the society of Totoposz before adapting himself to it. Tarimenes becomes the queen's favorite and fights for her despite his forced conversion to the Roman Catholic Church, which he secretly continues to hate. Bessenyei also created, in 1792, the first Hungarian drama, *Ágis tragédiája* (The Tragedy of Agis), portraying the conflict between the king and the Spartan people, whose spokesman is an individualistic high-ranking noble. In *A filozófus* (1777; The Philosopher), Bessenyei ridicules the conservatism of a minor provincial noble. His most important disciple, János Batsányi (1763–1845), editor of the first Hungarian review, the *Magyar museum*, enthusiastically welcomed the French Revolution in *A franciaországi változásokra* (1789; On the Changes in France). Imprisoned with the "Jacobins," he subsequently contributed to Napoleon's manifesto to the

Hungarians. He later settled in France, where he tried to promote the Hungarian language and literature.

The Josephist school inspector Ferenc Kazinczy, born to a noble Calvinist family, was another important Enlightenment figure in Hungary. He made his debut as a sentimentalist and the translation of Salomon Gessner, then went on to translate Shakespeare, Friedrich Gottlieb Klopstock, Gotthold Ephraim Lessing, Johann Wolfgang von Goethe, but also Rousseau, Helvétius, and Holbach. His review, *Orpheus,* was at the center of cultural life between 1790 and 1792. After his release from prison, Kazinczy published epigrams—*Tövisek és viragok* (1811; Thorns and Flowers)—and memoirs, such as the *Fogságom naplója* (My Prison Journals). He was a major figure of Hungarian literary life and maintained an extensive correspondence. József Kármán (1769–95), another figure of sentimentalism, published the first genre novel, *Fanni hagyományai* (1794; Fanni's Legacy), a nuanced psychological description of the feelings of a young girl who is misunderstood.

The most important poet of the period was Mihály Csokonai Vitéz (1773–1805). Born into a bourgeois family in Debrecen, he began his career with Goliardian poetry written in his youth in a Calvinist school and later took a stand against religious obscurantism and serfdom in philosophical poems inspired by Voltaire, Rousseau, and Holbach. He also wrote love poems of a new sensibility close to popular poetry. In 1793 he published a play, *A méla Tempeföi* (The Sensitive Tempeföi), which is outstanding for its spontaneous dialogue. Having acclaimed the French Revolution, he later fell under the influence of aristocratic patriotism and supported the wars against France. However, his suspected relations with the "Jacobins" brought his educational activity to a halt. His travels across the country inspired a comic epic, *Dorottya* (1799), ridiculing unmarried women. He also introduced burlesque elements into an improvised farce, *Az özvegy Karnyóné* (The Widow of Karnyó). Toward the end of his life, he published another philosophical poem in which the ideas of religious leaders and *philosophes* are expounded in a historical setting in praise of natural religion. Csokonai Vitéz, who drew on foreign sources as well as Hungarian folklore, thus became the inspiration for the great Hungarian poetry of 19th- and 20th-centuries.

The first theatrical performances were given in Kolozsvár in 1790 and in Pest in 1792 and 1796. However, the majority of Hungarian and foreign plays were performed by itinerant theatre companies until the foundation of the first Hungarian theatre in Kolozsvár in 1825.

In the musical sphere, besides religious and Goliardian chants, Hungarians played *Verbunkos* (from the German *Werbung*), a sort of march to incite recruitment of soldiers. Manor houses and bourgeois homes resounded with rococo elegiac and romantic rhythms and with music by Viennese composers. At the Eszterházy palace one could hear works by Joseph Haydn, who was employed there by Prince Miklós József Eszterházy, and the music of his contemporaries was played in the castles of the nobility.

As with some literary genres, the "baroque" school dominated in painting and sculpture. Its masters were the painters Franz Anton Maulbertsch, Johann Lucas Kracker, and Stefan Dorffmeister, and the sculptors Georg Raphael Donner and Franz Xaver Messerschmidt. The baroque style predominated in churches, castles, manor houses, and the homes of the bourgeois and the more prosperous peasants. Thus, the Royal Palace of Buda, started in 1715, is in baroque style. Johann Lucas von Hildebrandt and A.E. Martinelli built the castles and churches. Some aristocrats chose the rococo style: typical examples are the castle of Gödöllő, built by Prince Antal Grassalkovich between 1744 and 1750, and the castle in Fertöd built for Prince Miklós József Esterházy between 1762 and 1786. Neoclassicism was also represented, for example by the church at Vác (1763–77) designed by J.M. Canevale or the church and the secondary school in Eger (1765–85) conceived by Jakob Fellner and Joseph Ignatz Gerl.

BÉLA KÖPECZI

Further Reading

Beales, Derek Edward Dawson, *Joseph II,* Cambridge and New York: Cambridge University Press, 1987

Haselsteiner, Horst, *Joseph II. und die Komitate Ungarns: Herrscherrecht und ständischer Konstitutionalismus,* Vienna: Böhlaus, 1983

Király, Béla K., *Hungary in the Late Eighteenth Century: The Decline of Enlightened Despotism,* New York: Columbia University Press, 1969

Klaniczay, Tibor, editor, *History of Hungarian Literature,* Budapest: Corvina, and London: Collet's, 1964

Köpeczi, Béla, *A francia felvilágosodás* (The French Enlightenment), Budapest: Gondolat, 1986

Köpeczi, Béla, et al., editors, *L'absolutisme éclairé,* Budapest and Paris: Akadémiai Kiadó/CNRS, 1985

Kosáry, Domokos G., *Culture and Society in Eighteenth-Century Hungary,* Budapest: Corvina, 1987 (original Hungarian edition, 1980)

Les Lumières en Hongrie, en Europe Centrale, et en Europe Orientale (1971–) (irregular colloquium papers)

Marczali, Henrik, *Hungary in the Eighteenth Century,* Cambridge: Cambridge University Press, 1910; New York: Arno, 1971 (original Hungarian edition, 1882)

Reinalter, Helmut, *Aufgeklärter Absolutismus und Revolution: Zur Geschichte des Jakobinertums und der frühdemokratischen Bestrebungen in der Habsburgermonarchie*, Vienna: Böhlaus, 1980

Tapié, Victor Lucien, *L'Europe de Marie-Thérèse: Du baroque aux Lumières*, Paris: Fayard, 1973
Wandruszka, Adam, *Leopold II*, 2 vols., Vienna: Verlag Herold, 1965

Hydrography and Navigation

Today the word "hydrography" is understood as the science that deals with undersea topography, marine charts, sea currents, and, more generally, the dynamics of the oceans. In the age of the Enlightenment, the training of pilots and captains was based on the acquisition of knowledge about such matters as navigating by the stars, using the compass, studying the tides, reading and preparing charts, knowing about beaches, depths, and the oceans, and maneuvering vessels correctly. The ensemble of this knowledge was known as *hydrographie*, or the "art of navigating by rules and principles." It is in this restricted, 18th-century sense of the term that we shall discuss hydrography in this entry.

The Scope of Hydrography in the Age of the Enlightenment

In order to find his bearings at sea, far from any shore, a pilot would use the compass to determine the magnetic declination and inclination at his location, and the log to work out the speed of the vessel in a given direction. Two important technical improvements were made to the compass during the 18th century: the introduction of better methods of suspension and the creation of artificial magnets. Various attempts to improve the log were proposed during the second half of the century. In France Pierre Bouguer suggested taking measurements of the force of resistance exerted by the water on a submerged heavy ball: a table of equivalence then allowed the speed of the vessel to be deduced from the force measured (1753). Others preferred to develop a log with a propeller (Foxon, 1772). However, pilots continued to use the traditional log, and the log and the compass provided very imprecise means of estimating location. As far as possible, estimates had to be corrected by observation.

The determination of latitude and longitude on the Earth's surface was based on the measurements of angles. Latitude could be measured correctly by the 18th century. The astrolabe—known in French as the *arbalestrille*, the *arbalette*, the *bâton de Jacob* (Jacob's

stick), or the *croix astronomique* (astronomical cross)—had been invented around the beginning of the 16th century and remained in use until the middle of the 18th century, the Dutch East India Company only abandoning it in 1779. The astrolabe was improved during the 17th century, and during the 18th century it became known in French as the *quartier* and in English, successively, as "Davis's quarter," the "English quarter," and the "quarter of 90."

In 1731 John Hadley presented an even more effective instrument to the Royal Society. This was the octant, which was improved and remained in use for a long time, giving heights to within 1 or 2 degrees. The vessels of the Dutch East India Company brought the octant into general use only from 1779. Meanwhile, between 1757 and 1759, the sextant was conceived by Captain John Campbell. Used like the octant, the sextant could measure one-tenth of a minute of arc and give a height at approximately six seconds. It replaced the octant on ships at the beginning of the 19th century.

The measurement of longitude, meanwhile, required more sophisticated methods, such as those of eclipses and lunar distance. Astronomical data were provided by ephemerides tables and, by the end of the century, the *Nautical Almanac*—founded by Nevil Maskelyne—and the annual French equivalent, *Additions et tables nouvelles pour la connaissance des temps de l'année V* (1797; Additions and New Charts for the Knowledge of the Seasons for the Year V), were both using his tables. The Greenwich Meridian was chosen as the reference point for these tables, which contributed to its adoption by chart makers. Borda's reflecting circle (1772) allowed a much broader range of measurements of lunar distance and considerably reduced the instrumental errors, thanks to the procedure of repeating measurements. However, the revolution in navigation that came about as a result of the introduction of marine chronometers profoundly altered the practice of determining location. In order to ascertain a ship's longitude rapidly and simply it was enough to have on board a timepiece set to the proper meridian of reference, but no navy possessed such a clock before the last quarter of the 18th century, and few even believed in a solution of this type in the early part of the century. Instead, there was a preference for developing tables of the eclipses of Jupiter's moons (James Pound) and catalogs of the stars (James Bradley). The contribution of astronomy to the needs of sailors was therefore considerable. Improvements in optical instruments came later.

During the 18th century the determination of the longitude of a location became an economic, political, and strategic issue of the first order and a crucial problem for the navies of the leading powers. In Britain the Board of Longitude, created for the purpose of developing a means of determining longitude, was presented with numerous proposals. John Harrison began his research around 1720 but it was only from 1763 that he began to be rewarded, following the first successful trials of his chronometer. In France, beginning in 1766, the Swiss clock makers Ferdinand Berthoud and P. Leroy made some remarkable timepieces.

Once a navigator had completed his calculations he used them to identify his position on a chart and to determine his course. Often he would use Mercator's projection, which was still well known and undergoing improvement in the 18th century. Some navigators, however, continued to use the simpler plane projection, as Bouguer reports. On longer voyages pilots kept two logbooks. In the first, they recorded their immediate observations; in the second, they made a clean copy of them from day to day. In France the information provided by these logbooks, which were deposited at the offices of the Admiralty, permitted the making or correcting of charts. The *Neptune françois* (The French Neptune) began publication in 1693. Beginning in 1720 a general depository of charts, plans, logbooks, and memorandums concerning navigation brought together all the information collected during various voyages. It constituted a true navigational service of a type not found in Britain until 1795. The engineer Bellin revised and commented on the charts of the *Neptune françois* in midcentury, and by 1800 the *Neptune* covered the entire globe in 11 volumes. It was at about this time that Charles-François Beautemps-Beaupré completely reformed the principles of chart making by introducing a modern and coherent approach to conducting hydrographic surveys.

We should not delude ourselves, however. Not all vessels were equipped with precision instruments for determining location, and many sailors continued to navigate by guesswork. The famous French navigator Yves-Joseph de Kerguélen was opposed to the modern methods. Oral tradition and experience remained powerful influences and, when observing location, it was rare to correct for parallax, atmospheric refraction, the depression of the horizon, the diameter of the sun, and

so on. The introduction of more scientific methods took a great deal of time. Whether in France, Great Britain, or the Netherlands, from 20 to 50 years could elapse between the appearance of an invention and its systematic use on board. The Dutch navy was not equipped with chronometers until the beginning of the 19th century, and even after that the instrument makers found it difficult to meet their requirements. Charts in the Netherlands often contained information that was more than half a century out of date. This was a somewhat extreme case, but the country, which had been the leading sea power in the 17th century, had not kept up with the significant innovations that had emerged in Great Britain and France. The treatises on navigation that were most widely disseminated in the Netherlands were reissues of works such as *Le flambeau reluisant* (1667; The Gleaming Torch) or those of Klaas de Vries (1702), which had been very successful in their day but had been overtaken by the second half of the 18th century. Translations were very common, but they did not meet the needs of instructors.

By the end of the 17th century the need for instruction in the art of navigation had been imposed on navigators, as well as on politicians, throughout Europe. In France it had been established by royal ordinances. In 1681 a major ordinance issued by Colbert created a Marine Code that served as an example to other nations. Some of the basic ideas in that code are still applied today. Among other matters, it set the conditions for instruction in navigation in France. Pupils were to be trained in drawing and had to learn applied mathematics in relation to the instruments that they were being trained to use. This national program also led to a prolific output of publications, of varying worth, for the use of sailors. Jean Bouguer's treatise of 1698 was one of the first books adapted to the program, and Bouguer's son Pierre reissued it, in a considerably augmented form, as the *Traité de navigation* (Treatise on Navigation). It became a standard source in Europe and gave rise to a number of manuals and guides. During the same period, the British learned a great deal from such masters as H. Wilson and, above all, J. Robertson, whose *Elements of Navigation,* published in midcentury, became a model for all studies in the theory and practice of navigation.

The Seven Years' War (1756–63) demonstrated the inadequacies of the French royal navy. There was a gap between instruction according to the official texts and the actual practice of navigation. A far-reaching reform was begun by the duc de Choiseul (1761–66) and continued by the marquis de Castries in the 1780s, but it was not until the ordinance of 1825 that the training programs in mathematical and navigational sciences were truly modernized. There was a far-reaching reform in the Netherlands too, under the leadership of Cornelis

Douwes, a professor at the country's nautical college, and instruction in mathematics and astronomy was taken much further. Douwes introduced rigorous but very simple methods for instructing all sailors, and his tables were added to the *Nautical Almanac* in 1771. In France the art of navigation was divided into two quite distinct branches during the Revolution. Everything that dealt with determining location was handled by the Bureau des longitudes (Office of Longitudes). Created in 1795, the Bureau was the equivalent of the British Board of Longitude, which, since its foundation in 1767, had provided the *Nautical Almanac* with forecasts for six years ahead. The navy's Depository of Charts and Plans concerned itself with whatever was linked to hydrography in the strict sense. A similar division of responsibility was adopted in a number of the other European countries. This structure worked well. By the end of the century national navies were equipped with chronometers and instruments for measuring very precise angles and could undertake unprecedentedly ambitious hydrographic work.

Navigation in Enlightenment Society

The Académie Royale des Sciences des Paris (French Royal Academy of Sciences) awarded a prize for an essay on a subject aimed at improving marine navigation every other year. In Great Britain the Royal Society was involved in placing the best astronomical data at the service of the navy. In the 18th century navigation was a field that was still being constructed, and navigators, officers, scholars, instrument makers, and numerous instructors contributed to its development. Some officers, who were more inquisitive and scholarly than others, created a naval academy at Brest in 1753 and worked on the preparation of a maritime dictionary. Captain James Cook used the most modern instruments to observe, on Tahiti, the transit of Venus, while Falconer published his *Universal Dictionary of the Marine* in 1769. The years 1768–88 constitute a glorious period, with such great voyages of discovery and exploration as expeditions undertaken by Bougainville (1766) and Cook (1768). Finally, the comte de La Pérouse's ill-fated expedition (1785), which was scientifically equipped as no other had been, completed the European discovery of the Pacific.

The closing years of the 18th century bear witness that the progress achieved in and by instruments of navigation had done more for the art of navigation than mathematics and astronomy had for a century. Following La Pérouse's research in 1791, Entrecasteaux took Beautemps-Beaupré on board for his expedition. It was during this voyage that Beautemps-Beaupré developed the hydrographic techniques that were later adopted by all the nations of the world. He published an account of these techniques in 1808 as an appendix to Entrecasteaux's narrative of the voyage. This treatise on navigation explained in particular the methods of surveying, without leaving the ship and while under sail. It combined astronomical observations with the determination of points on the Earth. Angles were measured with a reflecting circle and recorded on coastal charts made on the spot. Hydrography as we know it today had been born.

DANIELLE FAUQUE

See also Astronomy; Canal; Observatories and Instruments of Observation; Transport Systems

Further Reading

Daumas, Maurice, *Scientific Instruments of the Seventeenth and Eighteenth Centuries*, translated and edited by Mary Holbrook, New York: Praeger, and London: Batsford, 1972 (original French edition, 1953)

Sobel, Dava, and William J.H. Andrewes, *The Illustrated Longitude*, New York: Walker, 1995; London: Fourth Estate, 1996

Taylor, E.G.R., *The Mathematical Practicioners of Hanoverian England, 1714–1840*, London: Cambridge University Press, 1966

I

Idea

The Sensory Origin of Ideas As Opposed to Innate Ideas

"How should 'Idea' and other entries be treated?" asked Voltaire, who offered to write the entry for the *Encyclopédie*. Jean le Rond D'Alembert informed him that another author had already agreed to cover that topic, but Voltaire nevertheless continued to be very interested in the issues raised by the origin of ideas, and the consequences of what that origin implied at the time for the nature—corporeal or not—of human thought, the interpretation of which depended upon the presumed relations between body and soul. These issues developed into a controversy that was laden with the legacy of Cartesianism and the opposing sensationalist philosophy of John Locke, a controversy that took shape precisely around the term "idea," instead of singling out other synonyms such as "concept," "notion," or "thought."

Since ancient times, the Greek word for "idea" and then its Latin equivalent, *idea*, had been used to designate philosophical notions, among them Plato's *Idea*, which was a milestone in the history of philosophy. In his *Des principes de la connaissance humaine* (1710; On the Principles of Human Knowledge) René Descartes made *idée* (idea) a key term in his theory of knowledge and gave it a very broad definition: "In general, I consider an idea to be anything that is in our mind, when we conceive of something, however we might conceive it." The idea, then, was the first operating unit of thought. The Port-Royalist *Logique; ou, L'art de penser* (1662; Logic; or, The Art of Thinking), conceived in a Cartesian spirit, dealt in detail with ideas as the mind's first operation before the mind advanced to judgment and reasoning.

Among the objections raised against the Cartesian theory of knowledge, the hypothesis of Nicolas Malebranche, who posited that we see everything through God, gave rise to the famous controversy about ideas involving Antoine Arnauld, one of the Port-Royalist authors of the *Logique,* who consequently wrote *Des vraies et des fausses idées* (1683; On True and False Ideas). However, the sensationalist objection, already advanced in Descartes's lifetime by Pierre Gassendi, was a far more radical attack. It targeted first and foremost the Cartesian hypothesis of innate ideas, which it countered with the claim that all ideas originated in sensory experience. That argument was in turn rejected by Arnauld, who judged it to be contrary to religion, since the consequences of that hypothesis would be to make all our ideas corporeal.

Locke nevertheless pursued the sensationalist path, laying the foundations of a philosophy of experience in his *Essay concerning Human Understanding* (1690), in which "idea" is a key term. Locke even apologizes to his readers for his very frequent use of the word "idea," and when an English prelate informed him that his use of the term might be dangerous for religion, Locke defended himself by explaining that he needed a new word to designate the object of our understanding when we think. The translator of the French version, which appeared under the title *Essai philosophique concernant l'entendement humain* (1700), found it all the easier to translate "idea" by *idée* given the fact that Locke's work was a response to the Cartesian doctrine of *idées,* so that for Locke the meaning of the English term was based on the French model, even though the philosophical interpretation of Locke's term was quite the opposite.

In order to prove the sensory origin of ideas, Locke contends in his *Essay* that in all languages, the words one uses to designate the things that are not of the realm of the senses have their origin in sensible ideas. Even the Latin word *spiritus,* from which "spirit" derives, in its first meaning designated "breath" before it came to denote an abstract idea. Locke therefore posits two sources for ideas: sensation and reflection. Reflection refers to ideas that come from sensory perception. From the combination of "simple ideas" arise "complex ideas," which form an idea thanks to the words that designate them, such as the names of numbers. Finally, his considerations on the sensory origin of ideas led Locke to formulate the hypothesis that God may have conferred the faculty of thought upon a purely material being—an oft-quoted hypothesis that, despite Locke's caution in advancing it, inevitably elicited criticism. Opponents of Locke's sensationalist philosophy charged that it questioned the immortality of the soul. The *Historia Philosophica Doctrinae de Ideis* (1723; The Philosophical History of the Doctrine of Ideas), published by Johann Jacob Brucker, testified to the currency of the notion "idea" by presenting its evolution from ancient Greece to Locke and Gottfried Wilhelm Leibniz. Voltaire undertook to propagate Locke's philosophy. In his *Lettres philosophiques* (1734; Philosophical Letters), Voltaire credits Locke with having ruined innate ideas. That same year, in the chapter entitled "Que toutes les idées viennent par les sens" (That All Ideas Come from the Senses) in his *Traité de métaphysique* (1734; Treatise on Metaphysics), Voltaire gives a succinct summary of the doctrine that maintains that our first ideas, without doubt, have a sensory origin, an opinion that he continues to profess in his *Éléments de la philosophie de Newton* (1738; The Elements of Sir Isaac Newton's Philosophy); in the *Dictionnaire philosophique* (1764; Philosophical Dictionary), whose entry "Idée" was compensation for his not having written the entry in the *Encyclopédie*; and in his *Commentaire sur Malebranche* (1769; Commentary on Malebranche). In the meantime, the celebrated Prades affair, in the early 1750s, gave Voltaire the opportunity to mock the Sorbonne for having inadvertently accepted the defense of a thesis upholding the sensory origin of ideas and then condemning that thesis for impiety, thereby establishing the doctrine of innate ideas as an article of faith (despite the Sorbonne's condemnation of the author a century earlier). At the time of the Prades affair, Voltaire had the satisfaction of seeing the publication of the works of Étienne Bonnot de Condillac, whose aim was to carry on the work of Locke while offering a more consistent theory of the origin of ideas than that conceived by his English predecessor.

Idea As Sensation, Transformed into Ideology

In a letter of 1756 Voltaire invited Condillac to his home so that Condillac, working in better conditions, could write an overview of his philosophy: "There are times when you would go further than Locke, there are times when you would oppose him, and often you would be of the same opinion. It seems to me that such a book is lacking in our nation . . . " In his *Essai sur l'origine des connaissances humaines* (1746; Essay on the Origin of Human Knowledge), later complemented by a whole series of other works, Condillac had indeed gone further than Locke by assuming that even reflection developed from sensation over the course of a long process of interaction between sensations and signs in the history of humanity. Ideas and language condition each other and are the result of a progressive abstraction from sensations and from the language of action, which is a mixture of gestures and inarticulate sounds. Finally, the articulated language that gradually develops during this process makes possible the formulation of increasingly abstract ideas, as well as increasingly refined thought processes. Thought, even when embracing the most abstract ideas, is thus nothing more than "sensations transformed," thanks to the signs created and perfected by human beings themselves. The principle that assures the operation of the intellect and the imagination, the connection between ideas, also allows one, through hitherto unexplored combinations, to create new ideas.

Imbued with Locke's persistent influence, Condillac's doctrine of ideas left its imprint on the thought of a number of representatives of the Enlightenment, beginning, in France, with Denis Diderot and Jean-Jacques Rousseau. In his *Discours sur l'origine et les fondements de l'inégalité parmi les hommes* (1755; Discourse on the Origins of Inequality), Rousseau is inspired by Condillac, outlining the formation, thanks to language, of the ideas that had served to establish and maintain social inequality. It was as a sort of appendix to Jean-Henri-Samuel Formey's *Anti-Émile* (1763; Anti-Émile) that Rousseau published a *Réunion des principaux moyens employés pour découvrir l'origine du langage, des idées et des connaissances de l'homme* (Collection of the Prinicpal Means Used to Discover the Origin of Language, Ideas, and Knowledge of Human Beings), reproaching Condillac's hypothesis on the origin of ideas and of language for having opened the way to materialism. Already during the Prades affair, then at the time of the scandal over Claude-Adrien Helvétius's *De l'esprit* (1758; Essays on the Mind and Its Several Faculties), Condillac had been subjected to similar criticism in his role as Locke's successor. At the time, he therefore had good reason not to accept Voltaire's invitation.

Thus, the author of the article "Idée" in the *Encyclopédie*, who announces his subject as one of the most important in philosophy, displays a certain reserve as he avoids mention of Condillac, rejecting all the while the Cartesian hypothesis of innate ideas as well as Leibniz's modified version of the hypothesis based upon the assumption of preestablished harmony. Attributing to "idea" a significance that includes sensation—"we comprehend the word 'idea' in its broadest sense, as including both sensation and the idea itself"— this article in the *Encyclopédie* extends to the nature of ideas what the author calls the "inexplicable mystery that governs the ties between the soul and the body." This "mystery" had already been invoked in Voltaire's *Dictionnaire philosophique*, which nonetheless left no doubt as to his conviction that ideas derive from sensory perception.

The great dictionaries of the French language that were published in new editions in the course of the second half of the 18th century (César-Pierre Richelet, Trévoux) evoke in considerable detail the dispute over the origin of ideas. The different uses of the word that they record remind one that, even though it was a philosophical term, "idea" was also a word that had become commonplace, with an entire range of different meanings (opinion, project, false imagination, etc.), to such a degree that Daire's *Épithètes françaises, rangées sous leurs substantifs* (French Attributive Adjectives, Arranged by Their Substantives), published in 1759, offers more than 120 adjectives likely to qualify "idea," some of which were far from being terms of praise: "stubborn, hollow, outrageous, impertinent, obscene, ridiculous, sinister, somber ideas," and so on. However, the role of the word as a philosophical term was not over. Toward the end of the 18th century, in the marquis de Condorcet's work *Esquisse d'un tableau historique des progrès de l'esprit humain* (1795; Outlines of a Historical View of the Progress of the Human Mind), the history of the human mind is conceived as a process unfolding from the faculty of shaping and combining ideas, and the progress of those ideas making possible the evolution of human society.

Among the derivatives of "idea" or its Greco-Latin roots, such as "ideal," "idealize," "idealism," "idealist," it was "ideologist" and "ideology" that, initially, bore the imprint of Condillac's philosophy and pointed to the new currency that the word gained at the end of the 18th century thanks to the Ideologue movement. The word *idéologie* (ideology) was a creation of Antoine-Louis-Claude Destutt de Tracy, considered the leading member of the Ideologues, a group of scholars who, from the mid-1790s, had their headquarters at the Institut National des Sciences et des Arts (National Institute of Sciences and Arts), and who proposed to endow the

French Republic with a scientific program based upon the philosophy of Condillac. At the time, "ideology" meant nothing other than the "science of ideas," whose principles were to infuse education and the different domains of knowledge, granting considerable importance to the role of signs for the formation, operation, and evolution of ideas.

Through the impetus of the Ideologues' thought, in 1797–98 the Institut National des Sciences et des Arts set as a competition topic: "Determine the influence of signs on the formation of ideas." To the topic addressed in the title was added an entire range of questions that evoked the problematic issue of ideas and their signs, from the transformation of sensation to the perfection of sciences:

> Is it true that sensations can only be transformed into ideas through the intermediary of signs? . . . or, which amounts to the same question, to our first ideas essentially assume the sympathy signs? Would the art of thinking be perfect if the art of signs were taken to perfection? . . . Is there any way to correct those signs that are poorly conceived and to make all sciences equally susceptible to demonstration? (*Mémoires de l'Institut National des Sciences et des Arts pour l'an IV de la république* [Memoirs of the National Institute of Sciences and Arts for the Fourth Year of the Republic]).

At the end of the 18th century, and at the beginning of the 19th, the Ideologues wielded considerable influence well beyond the borders of France. For Louis-Gabriel-Ambroise de Bonald, as he drafted a theory of the Restoration well before 1815, Ideology was a doctrine to be resisted because to claim, as Condillac had done, that men themselves had created ideas and language, was to deny that the first human beings had "come into the world formed as men and in a state of society," and consequently to deny that the "Author of all human and social perfection" had also created society, conferring upon society all the respect due to its divine origin.

Napoleon's hatred—he could not tolerate the republicanism of certain Ideologues—contributed to the demise of the movement and of the word "ideology." Napoleon's hate-filled tirades, delivered publicly even in the Senate (*Le moniteur* [21 December 1812]), discredited Ideology as "shadowy metaphysics" impeding the knowledge of reality and of essential political action. Thus began a semantic evolution that led "ideology" far from its initial meaning as the science of ideas.

The word "idea," however, preserved its predominant meaning, the one that had held the attention of philosophers during the Enlightenment. When Daniel

Mornet, the author of *La pensée française au XVIIIe siècle* (1926; French Thought in the 18th Century), published his *Histoire de la clarté française* (1929; History of French Clarity), his analysis was divided into three parts, all devoted to the role of ideas in the sometimes problematic prominence granted in French thought to "clarity," from the Renaissance to the 20th century: "Le choix et la détermination des idées" (The Choice and Determination of Ideas), "L'ordonnance des idées," (The Organization of Ideas), and "L'expression des idées" (The Expression of Ideas).

Ideas in the Intertextuality of the Enlightenment: The Franco-German Example

The history of "idea" and its international equivalents in the intertextuality of the European Enlightenment has yet to be written. Such a history would need to take into account the fact that until the 18th century, numerous Latin texts conveyed the term "idea" from country to country, since for the Republic of Letters Latin was still the universal language. Locke's *Essay concerning Human Understanding* was one of the many 17th-century texts that testified to the progression of national languages where science was concerned, but it was still published in Latin in the 18th century. Before writing his *Essay,* which would propagate the term "idea" and its translations throughout Europe, Locke had read the texts of French authors—Descartes, Gassendi, Malebranche, Arnauld—who gave many examples of the use of "idea." Seen in this light, the reception in France of Locke's *Essay* constituted a sort of terminological homecoming. In other countries where Romance languages were spoken, the Latin tradition facilitated equivalents for the French or English term.

In Germany, the reception of the Latin *idea* or the French *idée* occurred under somewhat different circumstances, which were governed as much by the Germanic basis of the language as by the specificity of the *Aufklärung* (German Enlightenment). In fact, *Idee,* which one might have assumed was an old German word, was fully admitted into the vocabulary only during the second half of the 18th century. Yet Germany had not been ignorant of the debate about ideas—to the contrary, Ehrenfried Walter von Tschirnhaus, an important precursor of the *Aufklärung,* had already exchanged correspondence in Latin with Baruch Spinoza on the topic of the meaning of the Latin word *idea,* and on numerous occasions Leibniz had examined the problematic issue of ideas, although he wrote his texts in Latin or French. Other German authors followed his example, expressing themselves entirely in Latin or using the Latin term *idea* even when their texts were written in German. During this era, when scientific works of European renown were already being written in English, French, or Italian, the German language did not yet have at its disposal a philosophical terminology adapted to German. For the specific terminology of texts written in German, usage required authors to integrate Latin terms in a German context, even subjecting those terms to their original Latin declension.

Christian Wolff, the philosopher and scholar who gained extraordinarily widespread acceptance in Germany during the first half of the 18th century, sought to put an end to the mixture of Latin and German: he replaced Latin terminology with German words, and he wrote a number of works in *Reindeutsch* (a pure German) that was accessible to those who did not know Latin. These efforts earned Wolff the reputation of having given German science an adequate language, which was indeed one of the fundamental aims of the *Aufklärung.*

The program that Wolff devised meant that he also had to replace the Latin word *idea* with German words, instead of simply opting for the French equivalent *idée,* which some German authors had already used on occasion, and which offered the advantage of eliminating Latin declensions in the middle of German texts, while remaining close to the original Latin preferred by scholars. To replace *idea,* Wolff chose *Begriff* (concept) and *Vorstellung* (image), which were borrowed from everyday German and would allow people to differentiate the semantic extensions of *idea* and *idée. Begriff* emphasized the classifying and abstract character of a thought; in contrast, *Vorstellung* designated thought as an act of the imagination. *Begriff,* first and foremost, was of capital importance in Wolff's system, and, as a result, the use of this term eventually became an indication, for his contemporaries, that one belonged in his camp. The lengthy discussion, ongoing since Descartes, about "clear" or "obscure" ideas, "distinct" or "confused" ideas, was continued by Leibniz and many others and was echoed in Germany in the corresponding qualities attributed to *Begriff: klare* (clear) or *dunkle* (opaque) *Begriffe; deutliche* (explicit) or *undeutliche* (vague) *Begriffe.* The first German translations of the *Discours sur . . . l'inégalité* and the work by Helvétius, *De l'esprit,* illustrate that by 1756 and 1760 the use of *Begriff* as a synonym for *idea* was widespread.

Two factors then contributed to the complete integration of the French loan word *idée* into German thus creating *Idee*: the continuing presence in Germany of French and English texts propagating the word of Greco-Latin origin, and a new school of thought that was moving away from Wolff's school, and whose literary expression was found in the Sturm und Drang movement. This was the era that saw the word *Genie* (genius) become fashionable in Germany—a German word, also borrowed from French, that expressed a new vision of creative thought. Wolff too had sought to expand intellectual faculties. However, Wolff's objective was above all to elaborate methods leading to an objectification of thought and its operations, hence the emphasis placed on logic and on the deductive method, with its use of definitions and paragraphs. Yet, the thought process of *Genie* was not one that moved through a series of definitions and syllogisms, based upon *Begriff*. To qualify the intuitive thought of the *Genie*, the German word *Idee* was a perfect fit, thanks to its relative newness and its fairly indeterminate meaning, which had already caused Descartes's *idée* and Locke's "idea" to catch on.

This extended meaning gave *Idee* a dynamic nuance that *Begriff* could not express. In the title of Johann Gottfried von Herder's work, *Ideen zur Philosophie der Geschichte der Menschheit* (1784; Outlines of a Philosophy of the History of Man), to replace *Idee* with *Begriff* would be to distort the subject. Immanuel Kant also used *Idee* in a sense that emphasized its difference from *Begriff*. The latter term designated more of a result, a thought that was ready to serve as a basic element of intellectual operations; *Idee*, on the other hand, suggested the dynamic nature inherent in thought, designating less a result than the vision and approach to a problem. *Idee*, for Kant, was thus associated with the intuitive thought of the *Genie*, who immediately grasped the essence of a problem while ordinary human beings could go no further than *empirische Begriffe* (empirical ideas).

The intertextuality of the European Enlightenment thus went hand in hand with a linguistic evolution in German that reflected the need to diversify and enrich the denominations of human thought. For *Idee* did not replace *Begriff*, which had served to replace the Latin term *idea*, but was rather an additional term. *Begriff* remained indispensable to the German language and to its philosophical terminology. More than 5,000 occurrences of the word *Begriff* have been found in Kant's works, compared to 1,400 references to *Idee*. The coexistence of these two terms—*Idee* often implying a certain subjectivity, and *Begriff*, in contrast, the objectivity of a thought—has continued to this day. This coexistence differs from the corresponding semantic field in French, dominated by *idée*, which has eclipsed terms such as *notion* or *concept*; while in German, the use of *Begriff* and *Idee* is fairly equally divided. That is why, in our time, the expressions *histoire des idées*, "history of ideas," and *Begriffsgeschichte*, so familiar to researchers, do not seem to convey an identical meaning, even though they designate the same field of research, whose results have so enriched our understanding of 18th-century thought.

ULRICH RICKEN

See also Empiricism; Ideology and Ideologues; Reason; Sensationalism

Further Reading

Yolton, John W., *John Locke and the Way of Ideas*, London: Oxford University Press, 1956

Ideal

The concept of the *ideal* has been one of the great themes of Western thought: it can be traced back to Plato, who makes a distinction in *The Republic* between good or beautiful things and absolute goodness or beauty. The plurality of beautiful things, which are visible, is contained within a single Idea, known but not seen, which is the essence of beauty. Plato's Idea, as *eidos* (meaning "form") contains a visual reference (the root *vid*) that has produced paradoxical results. If, in the case of mathematics and its figures, the visible image of the square only approximates the absolute square (the Idea of the square), the metaphor of visibility nonetheless governs the concept, since the supreme Idea, the Idea of the Good, is supposed to confer truth

upon what is known, in the same way that light illuminates objects.

The history of the idea and the ideal cannot be separated from the network of commentaries on Plato's text. Erwin Panofsky's theories of art in his major work, *Idea: Ein Beitrag zur Begriffsgeschichte der älteren Kunsttheorie* (1924; Idea: A Concept in Art Theory), follow Plato, but Panofsky's work also had an implicit impact on a debate that was taking place in Germany at the time his book was published. Panofsky's work was called into question in an oblique way by Martin Heidegger in *Platons Lehre von der Wahrheit* (1931–32; Plato's Doctrine of Truth). Heidegger focuses on three aspects of Plato's doctrine that had been developed over time: the visual metaphor, the concept of art as the representation of an object, and the relationships between representation and truth and the norm. All three of these aspects were the subject of lively debate in the 18th century because they were the strong points of classicism and its revival in the form of neoclassicism. Panofsky has shown how the Renaissance generated a double imperative: to imitate reality, postulated as objective, and to make it even more beautiful.

For the theoretician Leon Battista Alberti, as for Raphael, "the idea" refers to a superhuman beauty, which in the 18th century would be called the "ideal." The obligatory reference here is the famous letter from Raphael to Baldassare Castiglione (1516), in which Raphael apparently refers to the apologue about Zeuxis, who, seeking to represent the beauty of Helen of Troy and not finding it incarnated anywhere, took the five prettiest young women from the city of Croton, determined the most beautiful feature of each, and put them together to create a perfect body. Raphael, however, while suggesting that one should compare several women, does not make a collage of them but lets himself be guided by "a certain idea" that comes into his mind. Yet he requires neither normativity nor a metaphysical foundation for his "certain idea."

This letter helped shape the construction of classical and neoclassical doctrine throughout Europe. It is cited by the art critic and theoretician of classicism Giovanni Pietro Bellori, in *L'idea del pittore, dello scultore e dell'architetto* (The Idea of the Painter, the Sculptor, and the Architect), and again, 100 years later, by Johann Joachim Winckelmann, the theoretician of neoclassicism. (Both occupied the post of papal antiquary in Rome.) Bellori's subtitle confirms the new direction taken by art with regard to the idea—the painter chooses from nature and thus creates that which is superior to nature. His treatise had an enormous influence—Bellori was a member of the Académie Royale de Peinture et de Sculpture (Royal Academy of Painting and Sculpture) in France from 1689 on. His collection, *Vite de' pittori, scultori, et architetti moderni* (1672; Lives of Modern Painters, Sculptors, and Architects), dedicated to Jean-Baptiste Colbert, was summarized in the December 1676 issue of *Le journal des savants,* and his ideas were disseminated by André Félibien in his major work, *Entretiens sur les vies et les ouvrages des plus excellents peintres anciens et modernes* (1666–88; Conversations on the Lives and Works of the Most Excellent Painters, Ancient and Modern). Bellori himself, however, seems to have been inspired by his conversations with Nicolas Poussin, and it is in those exchanges of ideas that one can discern Bellori's contribution to the development of classical doctrine. The remarks accompanying his *Vita di Nicolas Poussin*

(1672; Life of Nicolas Poussin)—in reality, most probably reading notes by the great artist himself—are pure neo-Platonism: "Painting is nothing other than an idea of incorporeal things . . . if it shows bodies it only represents their order, and the way in which things are put together . . . it is more attentive to the idea of beauty than to anything else." Yet Bellori himself conceives the idea not as something innate but as having been elaborated a posteriori, subsequent to the contemplation of nature.

However, the source of modern theories on the ideal, Bellori's conception had a more complex influence than might at first seem apparent. It introduced not only neoclassicism but also "normality" in art, in the modern, double sense of "what functions as the norm" and "what is banal." In his life of Annibale Carracci especially, where he describes the state of painting after the death of Raphael, Bellori praises Carracci for having avoided both naturalism—which, in the works of Caravaggio, for example, merely reproduces nature—and mannerism, which is based on fantasy. Closely following Bellori, André Félibien makes the same point in the sixth *Entretien* (Discussion):

Some sought in particular to imitate nature just as they saw it . . . and others failing to study the natural, letting themselves be led by the strength of their imagination, without any other model than their ideas alone, worked on the basis of the images they formed in their minds.

This double imperative was reproduced throughout the 18th century, and some of its effects led to more than a simple repetition of classicism. It made it possible to conceive an art or a literature that was neither basely naturalist nor mannered, an art that could be at once natural and normative. Denis Diderot, for example, in his *Entretiens sur "Le fils naturel"* (1757; Discussions on "Le fils naturel"), explains that in the "serious" genre—the genre that Diderot himself practiced for the theatre and recommended with enthusiasm—writers should adopt "the tone we use for serious matters." In the "dramatic system" Diderot sets forth, the serious genre is situated between the opposite poles of the comic and the tragic, or their extreme limits, burlesque and the supernatural. Examples of the serious genre would be such works as his own plays *Le fils naturel* (1757; The Natural Son) and *Le père de famille* (1757; Father of a Family), or the novel *Amelia* (1752) by Henry Fielding, which to us today seem to strive so awkwardly to produce heroes who are both real and exemplary.

Bellori's theory reached England through John Dryden and his preface to the 1695 translation of Dufresnoy's Latin poem, *De arte graphica* (1667; On Graphic

Arts). To Bellori's ideas Dryden adds certain complements: the importance of the theme—painting must have meaning, *Ut pictura poesis* (as in poetry, so in painting)—and the need for erudition: "An erudite painter must form an idea of perfect nature. He must place this image before his mind in all his undertakings, and extract as if from a repertory the aspects of beauty that will figure in his work." The ideal is therefore the product of the artist's knowledge and not a neo-Platonic form, foreign to visual experience. The painter Joshua Reynolds later annotated Dufresnoy's poem to emphasize that the rules of art teach us nothing other than a way to view nature: "Nothing can be so lacking in philosophy as the supposition that we can shape an idea of beauty or excellence outside of nature, which is or should be the source whence all our ideas flow." In the third of a series of lectures given between 1769 and 1776, Reynolds goes even further: the ideal—"idea of the perfect state of nature"—joins beauty with perfection. Yet perfect beauty is not an undifferentiated quality, common to all beings. Clearly, for Reynolds—and implicitly for Bellori—the ideal that is the norm leads to the ideal that becomes a type. Aesthetics and logic overlap: the "common form" of a species (children, for example) is capable of embodying the perfection of this form. Reynolds's ideas are in line with the notion of classifying the human race, as exemplified in the research of such anatomists as Petrus Camper or Charles Bell, who used the measurement systems developed to understand the ideal beauty of Greek statues to gauge their own specimens—European, black, or "Kalmyk" (Turkmen). For Reynolds, as for Winckelmann, the study of ancient statues helps the artist to select from the offerings of experience and reach an ideal.

Winckelmann's *Gedanken über die Nachahmung der Griechischen Werke in der Malerei und der Bildhauerkunst* (1755; Reflections on the Painting and Sculpture of the Greeks) and his *Geschichte der Kunst des Altertums* (1764; History of Ancient Art) established the ideal of beauty for the second half of the 18th century and laid the foundations for the practice of neoclassical artists. It is not without reason that the statue, with its colorless, immobile dignity, comes first in Winckelmann's view: the greatest beauty is the most indeterminate. Violent passions are banned from public monuments (*Geschichte der Kunst des Altertums*), and even statues such as the *Laocoön* exhibit "a noble simplicity and a tranquil grandeur," for although the priest's body displays the pain of death, his face expresses no *Wut* (anger) and no cry escapes his lips. Gotthold Ephraim Lessing gives a brilliant critique of this commentary in his *Laokoon* (1766; Laocoön: An Essay upon the Limits of Painting and Poetry). The ancients, continues Winckelmann (who was familiar only with Roman copies of Greek statuary), could legitimately turn to the beauty of nature, for human shapes had not yet been altered by disease or deforming clothing; the Greeks practiced gymnastics, they danced naked, they lived under regimes of freedom: "The beauty of the senses has given beautiful nature to the artist; ideal beauty has given sublime features; from the senses the artist has taken human beauty, and from the ideal, divine beauty" (*Geschichte der Kunst des Altertums*). Thus, the idea could go no further than the "more than human" proportions of the Apollo Belvedere, which does, however, place that perfection before our eyes.

Immanuel Kant develops the tension surrounding the ideal in his *Kritik der reinen Vernunft* (1781; Critique of Pure Reason). Ideas attain a completeness that experience can never attain. Situated at an even greater remove from objective reality, the ideal develops the idea, since it contains in a perfect state the qualities necessary to the idea, which it has determined in its totality. The ideal therefore exists only in the divine understanding. It is here, in this chapter on the ideal, that the influence of Enlightenment deism becomes apparent: the logical necessity assigned to reason to think the unconditioned, the ideal, is transformed into a debate about divine existence. What was for Winckelmann an undeveloped paradox about the relations among humanity, ideal proportion, and the visible becomes for Kant an imperative that reason conceive an unconditioned being that could make the thought of the absolute determination of each thing possible. In the *Kritik der Urteilskraft* (1790; Critique of Judgment), the ideal beauty determined by the concept can be applied only to humankind, for humans are the only species in nature capable of self-determination and of the ideal of perfection, by virtue of being human, and by virtue of the "humanity in their person" (while, strangely, the judgment of pure beauty is made without concept, without idea: it is a vague beauty).

In the *Kalliasbriefe* (1793; Callias Letters), Friedrich von Schiller elaborates on this curious consequence in order to equate self-determination with beauty: that which has developed for itself is beautiful, without reference to an external influence or to an end to be attained. In his *Über naive und sentimentalische Dichtung* (1795; On the Naive and Sentimental in Literature), however, Schiller ascribes this freedom to a state in cultural evolution that humankind has lost (even if certain individuals may still find it) and makes of the ideal a future for humans: "Nature has joined with man; art divides him and splits him in two; through the ideal he will return to oneness." Yet neither the ideal nor the return is ever attained.

MARIAN HOBSON

See also Aesthetics; Art Criticism; Beautiful; Classicism; Imitation; Taste

Further Reading

Fontaine, André, *Les doctrines d'art en France*, Paris: Laurens, 1909; reprint, Geneva: Slatkine Reprints, 1989

Heidegger, Martin, "Plato's Doctrine of Truth," in *Pathmarks*, edited by William McNeill, Cambridge and New York: Cambridge University Press, 1998 (original German edition, 1967)

Mahon, Denis, *Studies in Seicento Art Theory*, London: Warburg Institute, University of London, 1947

Michel, Régis, *Le beau idéal: ou L'art du concept*, Paris: Réunion des Musées Nationaux, 1989

Panofsky, Erwin, *Idea: A Concept in Art Theory*, translated by Joseph J.S. Peake, Columbia: University of South Carolina Press, 1968 (original German edition, 1924)

Ideology and Ideologues

The Ideologues were a group of intellectuals and philosophers born, for the most part, between 1750 and 1765 who constituted—according to Louis Girard in *Les libéraux français, 1814–1875* (1985; French Liberals, 1814–75)—the last generation of French Enlightenment thinkers and the first generation of liberals. This intellectual movement can be likened to a rationalist lobby that united practitioners of a multidisciplinary approach. Among the most important of the Ideologues were: the physician Pierre Cabanis (1757–1808); the writer Marie Joseph Chénier (1764–1811); the archivist and historian Pierre-Claude-François Daunou (1761–1849); the philosopher Antoine-Louis-Claude Destutt de Tracy (1754–1836); the historian, critic, and translator Claude Fauriel (1772–1844); the comte de Garat (1749–1833), a lawyer and politician; the jurist and philosopher Joseph-Marie Degérando (1772–1842); the poet and critic Pierre-Louis Ginguené (1748–1816); the intellectual Joseph Lakanal (1762–1845); the philosopher Maine de Biran (1766–1824); the politician Pierre-Louis Roederer (1754–1835); the economist Jean Baptiste Say (1767–1832); the abbé Sieyès (1748–1836); the comte de Volney (1757–1820), a geographer and historian; and Marie-François-Xavier Bichat, Pierre Laromiguière, and François Thurot. Most of the Ideologues were French, but some were Italian, and the movement's linguistic and literary theories also provoked reflection and debate in Germany.

The word *idéologie* (ideology) was defined by Destutt de Tracy—in his *Mémoires sur la faculté de penser* (1796–97; Memoirs on the Faculty of Thinking) and again in his *Éléments d'idéologie* (from 1801; Elements of Ideology)—as the science of ideas, based on an analysis of sensation; analysis of the human facilities is used to explain human knowledge. Ideology involved systematizing the tenets of Étienne Bonnot de Condillac's philosophy, which include the ultimate nonexistence of innate ideas, the importance of sensation as the source of all ideas, the definition of the thinking subject as a series of sensations and sensory transformation, and the conception of language as the basis for abstract and reflexive thinking.

Rejecting metaphysics, the Ideologues envisioned a science that encompassed human beings and their faculties, and indeed all sciences, whether they be natural, moral, or political. Before the Revolution participants in the movement met at Auteuil in the salon of Madame Helvétius. In 1789 they entered politics and participated most notably in the successive assemblies. The Ideologues endorsed the notion of perfectibility as defined by Condorcet in his *Esquisse d'un tableau historique des progrès de l'esprit humain* (1793; Outlines of an Historical View of the Progress of the Human Mind), published after Thermidor thanks to Daunou, and they used that principle as they attempted to make sense of the Revolution by interpreting it philosophically. By referring to the Declaration of the Rights of Man, and being careful to maintain harmony between individual liberty and the collective interest, the Ideologues opposed both the violent and emotional intervention of the masses in the progress of history and the terrorist leanings of the government.

Republicans by reason and by conviction (see Nicolet), the Ideologues saw the diffusion of the Enlightenment through education as the cornerstone of the true revolution. Garat proclaimed in no uncertain terms the importance of education: "The Revolution began when the enlightened thinking of philosophers became that of the legislators; the Revolution will not be over until the enlightened thinking of the legislators becomes that of the people." The Ideologues, therefore, played a decisive role in the development of the laws of Years III and IV, particularly those that created the central schools, the École Normale Supérieure (Normal School) and the Institut de France (French Institute). The École Normale, that utopia of the Encyclopedists, led Garat to say, "for the first time on earth truth, reason, and philosophy will have a seminary." Cabanis called the Institut de France a "veritable living encyclopedia," and the Ideologues filled its six sections with moral and political science. According to Gusdorf, "the Ideologues consecrate the appearance of the teacher in French culture." In this way, the ideology movement revolutionized a way of thinking by developing a pedagogy of knowledge as well as a philosophical and practical theory of knowledge. In fact, the movement offered a critique of rationalist philosophy that turned philosophy into what Pierre Machery called a "universal methodology of thought."

In this reasoned revolution, these intellectuals welcomed the dawn of a French era, and could agree with Napoleon Bonaparte when he said that "from now on, the French Republic's real power must consist in not allowing any new ideas but its own to emerge," for the Ideologues had approved of Bonaparte's coup d'Etat of 18 Brumaire before they condemned the repressive practices of the First Consul and became part of the opposition in 1802. The new epoch was to be considered an era of liberty, with liberty conceived as a practical means to ensure freedom of activity guided by self-interest and to authorize the progressive construction of individual happiness, as part of a historical process to be shaped by politics. The individual and society nurture each other, particularly through the expansion of trade. Democracy, the Ideologues held, was founded upon property.

In his *Essai sur les garanties individuelles que réclame l'état actuel de la société* (1818; Essay on the Individual Guarantees Warranted by the Current State of Society), Daunou stated that "the more a man accumulates and enriches the fruits of his labor, the more he uses his own physical and moral faculties and frees himself from the yoke of the specific wishes of other men, thus putting himself in a position in which the only laws he need obey are the general laws of society." Defined in relation to liberty, the civil equality of rights compensated for natural inequality and limited the effects of that inequality.

Although laws should exist to protect the poor, they should, nevertheless, not oppose the laws of economic science. In actuality, legislation consisted of a set of measures that benefited the middle class—called the "common" class by the Ideologues. According to Destutt de Tracy, in *Commentaires sur "De l'esprit des lois" de Montesquieu* (1819; Commentaries on "De l'esprit des lois" by Montesquieu), "the spirit of order, work, justice, and reason naturally reign" in this republican class, and therefore the class was also "distanced from all excess," thanks to its position and its direct interest. The duty of the middle class was to legislate in the name of all people. Democracy boiled down to elitism, at least as long as Enlightenment remained the attribute of this enlightened class, whose goal it was to circulate Enlightenment values and to infuse those principles into the entire social body. We can then see these Ideologues, these humanist anthropologists, as the founding fathers of a republican "ideology," in the modern, global sense of the term. Agnostic in their analytic research, they promoted a sort of pragmatic virtue.

The Ideologues circulated their ideas through the periodical *La décade philosphique, littéraire et politique,* which appeared every ten days from 10 Floréal, Year II (29 April 1794) to 21 September 1807, when Napoleon ordered its merger with the *Mercure de France.* The journal was born of the partnership of six founders: Ginguené; the poet and playwright Andrieux; the art historian playwright; Amaury Dunal; Jean Baptiste Say; Joachim le Breton, a teacher and defrocked Theatine monk and teacher; and Georges, librarian at the Natural History Museum. Men of letters and of science, the collaborators and correspondents represented political and intellectual republican circles—learned societies, institutes, and the courts. *La décade* led the Ideologues' battles with its defense and illustration of the philosophy of the Enlightenment, the idea of progress and of perfectibility, the attack on Christianity in the name of deism and with its militancy in favor of education and notably of centralized schools. The journal also helped to define a republican literature. An initial prospectus proclaimed: "All literature must so to speak be cast in a new mold. . . . Taste must be enlarged, criticism must be enlightened and expanded."

According to *La décade* the Revolution, while reinstating the roles of artist and poet in the city-state, also returned to the ancients, who were closer to nature, their regenerating force. If there was any classicism in the literary articles of *La décade* (which later made the Ideologues adversaries of romanticism), it must be interpreted as a gesture of freedom, a refusal of dogmatic rules, the definition of an aesthetic of impression, and a taking into account of the concrete conditions of writing. Such positions formed the beginnings of modern literary history. Madame de Staël's *De la littérature considérée dans ses rapports avec les institutions sociales* (1800; The Influence of Literature upon Society) bears witness to the influence of Ideological theses, as do the works of Fauriel (see Espagne).

In 1811 Ginguené published a *Histoire littéraire de l'Italie* (Literary History of Italy), in which he applies to Italy the principles he had defined in the Year VII, when, in the periodical *La décade,* he likened the history of literature to "an analytic table of the birth and progress of the various areas of literature by placing, so to speak, each major literary work in its proper historical frame, and by then deducing the precepts which, in all the genres, came into existence subsequent to the models." This perspective explains why, at the Athenaeum, Ginguené followed up La Harpe's literature course by offering a course in literary history.

GÉRARD GENGEMBRE

See also Empiricism; Idea; Language; Metaphysics; Sensationalism

Further Reading

Baker, Keith Michael, *Condorcet: From Natural Philosophy to Social Mathematics,* Chicago: University of Chicago Press, 1975

Espagne, Michel, "Claude Fauriel en quête d'une méthode ou l'idéologie à l'écoute de l'Allemagne," *Romantisme* 73 (1991)

Gusdorf, Georges, *La conscience révolutionnaire: Les idéologues,* Paris: Payot, 1978

Moravia, Sergio, *Il pensiero degli idéologues: Scienza e filosofia in Francia (1780–1815),* Florence: La Nuova Italia, 1974

Nicolet, Claude, *L'idée républicaine en France, 1789–1924: Essai d'histoire critique,* Paris: Gallimard, 1982

Staum, Martin S., *Cabanis: Enlightenment and Medical Philosophy in the French Revolution,* Princeton, New Jersey: Princeton University Press, 1980

Idolatry

At the center of the violent conflict between Catholics and Protestants that began in the Renaissance lay the question of whether idolatry originated before or after the Flood. Protestant iconoclasts in Britain, the Netherlands, Germany, Switzerland, and France condemned the "paganism" of the Roman Catholic Church, embodied in its processions, the rituals of the Mass, its superstitious beliefs, and the adoration of images, angels, saints, and relics. The reformers rejected the division of divine unity that was implicit in that unity's replacement by a host of perceptible representations. As an heir to these quarrels, the age of the Enlightenment came up against an essential metaphysical question that touched upon the fundamentals of faith and revelation and the salvation of pagans. The response to this question must be understood in context with the spread of anticlericalism and deism, scepticism and atheism.

Sharing a religious conception of a world moving toward its end as a result of the Fall and sin, Catholics and Protestants both envisioned a single religion that had originated under the rule of a single God but had since lost its initial purity and degenerated into idolatry—to be precise, into the worship of images, or, more generally, the adoration of false gods. However, it remained unclear how this passage from a primitive monotheism to polytheism could be explained. In a comparative history of religions entitled *De Veritate* (1624; On Truth), the deist Baron Herbert of Cherbury appeals to human understanding rather than revelation when he posits the omnipresence of a creative sovereign power among all peoples and in every latitude. The Cambridge Platonist Ralph Cudworth also defended the doctrine of innate knowledge, in opposition to both the materialism of antiquity and the theories of Thomas Hobbes. In Chapter IV of *The True Intellectual System of the Universe* (1678), Cudworth simplifies the question by declaring that the polytheists adored one central divinity and reduced their other gods to inferior, satellite divinities. The same thesis is defended in other works, from Father Tournemine's "Projet d'un ouvrage sur l'origine des fables" (Project for a Work on the Origin of Fables), published in the *Journal de Trévoux* (December 1702), to Don Calmet's *Dissertation sur l'origine de l'idolâtrie* (1713; Essay on the Origin of Idolatry) and the Jesuit priest Lafitau's *Moeurs des sauvages américains, comparées aux moeurs des premiers temps* (1724; Customs of the American Indians Compared with the Customs of Primitive Times). All these writers detected among the ancient peoples of the Earth various vestiges of a religion that had originally been pure, and they aimed to demonstrate that it was only the later traditions of these peoples that obscured from them the truth of the Christian Scriptures. The abbé Pluche acknowledges this idea in his introduction to the

Histoire du ciel où l'on recherche l'origine de l'idolâtrie et les méprises de la philosophie (1739; History of the Heavens, Tracing the Origin of Idolatry and the Mistakes of Philosophy). In Chapter VI of this book, the abbé sets out to address the moral dimension of the problem:

> The primary origin of evil, the true source of idolatry and of every superstition, is the abuse of the language of astronomy and of the characters of ancient writing, an abuse introduced by blind cupidity and excessive love of earthly things.

He supposes, accordingly, that the divinities of ancient Egypt had been brought to Asia and Europe by the Phoenicians.

The *Dictionnaire de Trévoux* (1743; Dictionary of Trévoux) brings together various orthodox accounts of the subject. They treat idolatrous practices as a general feature of all pagan nations, summarizing both the various manifestations of those practices (such as worship of stars, animals, and objects) and their absurd implications, including human sacrifice, profane initiation rites, and the use of incense. No matter how elaborate or well-supported manmade idols are, biblical prohibitions—particularly the celebrated Song of Solomon, which criticizes all impure forms of worship—condemn them irrevocably. The *Dictionnaire de Trévoux* supplies a long list of disparate causes for idolatry, including not only anthropomorphism, the fear inspired by religion, the charisma of false prophets, the trickery of priests, and the misreading of sacred texts but also ignorance of ancient times, lack of understanding of natural phenomena, confusion of languages, deceitful narratives of travelers, colonization, the subjugation of judgment to the senses, the unbridled imagination of artists, and so on.

The debate took a new turn with John Locke, who refuted the notion of innate ideas in his *Essay concerning Human Understanding* (1690). Pierre Bayle, too, believed that all knowledge proceeds from the senses. He was therefore able, in his *Réponses aux questions d'un provincial* (1705; Answers to the Questions of a Provincial), to be ironic about the dogmatic character of his contemporaries, while evoking the example of savages in order to undermine the principal innate ideas. In Volume II he writes, "some have written of the glorious remains of an innate idea of God, the admirable image of a creator imprinted upon the heart of man, which could not be effaced by the malice of the devil," whereas in Volume I he posits that "if we accept that the general agreement of nations is proof that something is true, it would be necessary to reject the oneness of God and embrace polytheism." In his *Continuation des "Pensées diverses sur la comète"* (1705; Continua-

tion of "Pensées diverses sur la comète"), Bayle makes the even more radical assertion that ignorance of God and atheism remain preferable to a knowledge of God mingled with blasphemies and superstitions, fanaticism and idolatry.

The barbarism of humanity in ancient times, discreetly evoked by Bernard Le Bovier de Fontenelle in *L'origine des fables* (1724; The Origin of Fables), found a revolutionary echo in the works of David Hume, including *The Natural History of Religion* (in *Four Dissertations* [1757]), in which Hume subverts the prevailing opinion identifying the primitive religion of humanity with monotheism. In the first chapter of this essay, Hume challenges the notion that pure theism may have arisen in ancient times, before the discovery of writing or development of the arts and sciences. He declares that it is highly improbable that primitive people discovered the truth in their ignorance but fell into error as soon as they acquired knowledge. Polytheism should therefore no longer be seen as the result of the degradation of an alleged primitive monotheism but as the very origin of religious belief among all the peoples of the Earth. If faith in a superior power arises from psychological motives, such as fear and hope, resulting from experiences, then the representation of the character of the gods as malevolent or benevolent reflects not so much an intellectual desire to apprehend the world as a projection of human anxieties and expectations. In divine representations Hume detects "the natural progress of human thought," which is gradually lifted from lower to higher things. In his *Origine, progrès et décadence de l'idolâtrie* (1758; The Rise, Development, and Decadence of Idolatry), Guillaume-Alexandre Méhegan adopts the same idea, which scandalized religious orthodoxy, rehabilitated paganism, and perverted the dogma of Providence as well as the idea of a primitive Arcadia, which John Toland persistently evokes in his *Philosophical Letters on the Origin of Prejudices, of the Doctrine of the Immortality of the Soul, of Idolatry, and of Superstition* (1768).

Hume's *The Natural History of Religion*, translated into French in 1759, was soon complemented by Charles de Brosses's *Culte des Dieux fétiches ou Parallèle de l'ancienne religion de l'Égypte avec la religion actuelle de Nigritie* (1760; On the Worship of Fetish Gods; or, Parallel between the Ancient Religion of Egypt and the Current Religion of West Africa). This work was overseen by Denis Diderot, who read the manuscript and modified it in the light of Hume's *Natural History*. In distant lands—Africa, Lapland, and India—Brosses found the rites that were practiced in the infancy of humanity. His theory was extremely influential. Subsequent authors saw idolatry and polytheism as deriving from the worship of stars and above all from *fétichisme* (fetishism), a term invented by Brosses on this occasion to designate the primary and universal religion. As distinct from idolatry (which usually implies a separation between a representation and what it represents, an adoration of images symbolizing divinity), fetishism results from the direct deification of things. In his *Des cultes qui ont précédé et amené l'idolâtrie ou l'adoration des figures humaines* (1805; On Earlier Cults That Have Brought about Idolatry or the Worship of Human Figures), Jacques-Antoine Dulaure pushes the argument further by situating the origins of this adoration in figures and objects created to commemorate the dead. Although influenced by Hume, Jean-Jacques Rousseau makes a distinction between polytheistic belief and the idolatrous worship inherent in such a belief in Book IV of *Émile, ou, De l'éducation* (1762; Émile; or, Concerning Education): "The manitous of the savages, the fetishes of the blacks, all the works of nature and of men were the first divinities of mortals; polytheism was their first religion, idolatry their first form of worship."

Conversely, in a long article in his *Dictionnaire philosophique* (1764; Philosophical Dictionary) and another article in the *Encyclopédie* (1765), Voltaire rejects Hume and Brosses's views of primitive polytheism and fetishism and reduces idolatry to the worship of idols. Aiming to put an end to the sterile literature that attempted to define the various notions of ancient idolatrous peoples, Voltaire draws a contrast between the natural religion of the elite and that of the "ignorant and vulgar":

It is clear that each person made a judgment according to the degree of his reason, or his credulity, or his fanaticism. It is obvious that priests associated as many divinities as they could with their statues, in order to attract more offerings. We know that philosophers condemned these superstitions, that warriors mocked them, that magistrates tolerated them, and that the people, always absurd, did not know what they were doing.

Thus, at the heart of the debate remained a criticism of an archaic past and the simpleminded present as well as a condemnation of the Catholic religion—notably the Jesuits, who were frequently accused of favoring idolatry in China. Criticism became more radical over the course of half a century, from Montesquieu's *Lettres persanes* (1721; Persian Letters), in which Rica describes the pope as "an old idol that

people praise out of habit," to the baron d'Holbach's materialist *Système de la nature, ou Des lois du monde physique et du monde moral* (1770; The System of Nature; or, The Laws of the Moral and Physical World), which celebrates the triumph of reason and associates idolatry with despotism and religious imposture. Replying to an indictment of 10 August 1770, Holbach humorously asked: "And what are our gods that we hold them shut up inside boxes for fear that the mice will eat them?"

In the confrontation between cultures, the age of the Enlightenment, which held sacred the idea of nature, looked beyond Europe and marginalized the problem of idolatry in order to give weight to the polytheistic or fetishistic origins and survivals of religion. Two perspectives seem to have been available to the West. One, turned toward the past, exploited the notion of idolatry to legitimize a colonial policy of racial supremacy. Thus, the Spaniard Juan Bautista Muñoz's *Historia del Nuevo-mundo* (1793; History of the New World) challenges the idea that the Incas had great knowledge and identifies the Indian peasants of South America as "simple and retarded." The other perspective, directed toward the future, involved reflection on spiritual needs and the specificity of indigenous customs. For example, the baron de Gérando, a progressive thinker who was a member of the anthropological Société des Observateurs de l'Homme (Society of Observers of Men), hails the study of primitive forms of worship as an ethnological necessity in his *Considérations sur les diverses méthodes à suivre dans l'observation des peuples sauvages* (1799; The Observation of Savage Peoples). Through these two perspectives, the debates on idolatry permitted a redefinition of man as, perhaps regrettably, a religious animal.

PATRICK GRAILLE

See also Barbarian and Savage; Fable: Critique; Witchcraft; Words, Abuse of

Further Reading

Bernand, Carmen, and Serge Gruzinski, *De l'idolâtrie: Une archéologie des sciences religieuses*, Paris: Seuil, 1988

David, M.-V., "Les idées du XVIIIe siècle sur l'idolâtrie, et les audaces de David Hume et du président de Brosses," *Numen* 24, no. 2 (1977)

Schmidt, Francis, "La discussion sur l'origine de l'idolâtrie aux XVIIe et XVIIIe siècles," in *L'idolâtrie*, Paris: Documentation Française, 1990

Illuminism

Illuminism claimed to be derived from an older tradition, that of theosophy, or the knowledge of God through wisdom—knowledge that was said to be timeless. However, the emergence of illuminism can be dated historically: its most important representatives wrote at the end of the 18th century and the beginning of the 19th. Illuminism must be distinguished from esotericism, hermeticism, speculative mysticism, and other movements that certainly had links with it but are too often wrongly identified with it. Illuminism bore some relation to Renaissance Neoplatonism, gnosticism, and the Judeo-Christian cabala, but one of its main inspirations was the work of the German theosophist Jakob Boehme (1575–1624), translated into French by one of the most illustrious illuminists, Louis Claude de Saint Martin (1743–1803). Contemporary with the philosophy of the Enlightenment in France and in Germany, to which it was at once friendly and hostile, illuminism was also contemporary with—and one of the hidden inspirations for—early romanticism. Illuminism often arose within Freemasonry but distinguished itself from that movement by developing its own rites of private initiation, just as it differed from all the other contemporary trends to which its irrationalist occultism and its passion for the supernatural gave rise.

Unaffiliated with any church or official dogma, standing apart from philosophies and religions—although in constant dialogue with them—illuminism held an entirely distinct place within the configuration of 18th-century knowledge. In general, illuminist discourses were expressed in mythic and symbolic language rather than in conceptual terms, even though modes of expression varied with the specific beliefs of different authors. The most important illuminists developed original systems of thought, on the basis of shared elements. Thus, nearly all of the illuminists professed a spiritual monism, which was sometimes nuanced by the theory that all creatures had to pass through the material realm, based on an emanationist conception of human origin.

The illuminists paid extremely careful attention to material phenomena, often from the point of view of the natural sciences. They conceived of the totality of these phenomena as the diverse and hierarchical manifestation of a single unity, set in motion by the existence of opposite poles of energy. They saw man as superior to all other creatures, even angels, and humanity and its development were at the center of illuminist thought. Their simultaneously tragic and optimistic interpretation of human destiny, structured around a conception of the Fall and a future "Reintegration," was often accompanied by a form of millenarianism. Man's regeneration was the illuminists' main goal, whether they pursued such external activities as the performance of rites or magic or advocated internal, contemplative works, such as the struggle to achieve the inner metamorphosis that accompanies the rebirth of God within man. This regeneration often found its logical corollary in social regeneration, expressed in various approaches that later influenced the theocratism of Joseph de Maistre (1753–1821) and 19th-century versions of utopian socialism.

The illuminists envisioned a hierarchically ordered system of mystical correspondences that exerted its effects throughout history. From such a perspective, the tragic future caused by man's Fall encompasses the entire universe. It follows that the work of regeneration has similarly cosmic effects. The whole "chain of being" is affected by humans' individual efforts. At their extreme, such efforts even have an effect on the Divine Being itself, whose creative process has been disrupted by the Fall. Man is the living image and mirror of the divinity and puts into effect the three divine powers of thought, will, and action. Depending on the author, the figure of Christ—who was very important to Karl von Eckartshausen (1752–1803), for example—may be credited with a central or more limited role in the process of creation and regeneration.

According to illuminism, reason and imagination are the chief faculties that man must bring to bear in the work of regeneration. Human reason is not just the faculty of reasoning but an inner light, fire, and energy, a portion of the divine light that sustains and rectifies this reason. Depending on the author, illumination may take the form either of instantaneous revelation or of a gradual intellectual development rather similar to the process evoked by the proponents of natural religion. Reason, replenished at the divine source and without mediation of dogma or institution, allows humanity to reestablish communication among the different "regions" of being and bring the future into alignment with a harmonious developmental process.

Imagination, unrelated to any ordinary spiritual activity, allows humans to transcend their present degenerate condition and accede—in privileged moments or with constant inner certainty—to a perception of a unified state free from temporal limits, as well as to the universal correspondences. Imagination also embodies participation in God's creative powers, in God's "magic," as Boehme put it. For certain illuminists, imagination took the form of communication with the *Sophia* (Wisdom), the primordial locus of the forms of divine manifestation. This theory of the imagination implies that certain writers will enjoy a heightened understanding of the arts.

Several illuminists, including Louis-Claude de Saint-Martin, also associated the faculties of reason and imagination with that of desire, which took on connotations of need, lack, nostalgia, and Eros. In this theory, thought is swayed by desire and guided by the will, and it finds its fulfillment in action, which is also and primarily the Word, on the model of the divine *Logos*. Saint-Martin even developed a theory of languages—as Antoine Fabre d'Olivet (1768–1825) later did—and a poetics. According to Saint-Martin, poetic speech—in the highest sense of the term, as heightened energy and feeling—acts simultaneously upon the person enunciating it, the person hearing it, and the world, transforming all. For other disciples of the illuminists, action was to be above all political. Julie de Krüdener (1764–1824) sought to inspire rulers—the Russian emperor Alexander I in particular. Russia, with its illuminist lodges and such individuals as Novikov (1744–1818), Lopushin (1756–1816), and Labzin (1766–1825), was one of the centers for the development of such political theories.

The most important illuminists were those theoreticians who sought to advance an alternative philosophy in opposition to institutionally or culturally recognized systems: thus, Saint-Martin countered materialism and Eckartshausen challenged Kantianism. In Germany many illuminists were also men of science. Franz von Baader (1765–1841) is undoubtedly one of the best examples of these *Naturphilosophen* (natural philosophers). A mineralogist and physician and an assiduous reader of Boehme and Saint-Martin, Baader produced a veritable summa of physical and metaphysical questions that played an important role in politics and religion. Friedrich Christoph Oetinger (1702–80) preceded Baader in exploiting the scientific knowledge of the age for gnostic purposes. Gotthilf Heinrich von Schubert (1780–1860), renowned above all for his *Die Symbolik des Traumes* (1814; Symbolism of the Dream), and J.W. Ritter (1766–1854) carried on the tradition.

Martínez and Saint-Martin

In France illuminism was embodied particularly more specifically in Martinism, which had an influence on all of Europe. Martinism was based on the teachings of Martínez Pasqualis (ca. 1715–79), whose Judeo-Christian esotericism, strongly influenced by the cabala, found its principal expression in his *Traité de la réintégration* (written 1770–72; Treatise on the Reintegration). This unfinished work, which was not published in the 18th century, focuses on the Old Testament, expounding sacred history in the dehistoricizing terms of typology (the theory that history is an endless repetition of central events corresponding to a creation story set in a mythic temporality) and of "recurrent prophets." These events constitute a cosmogonic system that is both topological and dramatic and is frequently expressed in terms of numerology.

"Before time," Martínez holds, God produced emanations of "spiritual beings," who had to worship him and take charge of the secondary causes. Out of pride, one of these beings, Lucifer, sought to make himself equal to God so as to produce emanations of his own. God blocked his activities and then, according to a complex process in which imagination played a major role, created "a physical universe that seemed to have material form," to confine the fallen angels. God's next emanation was Adam. A "minor" being as he was created last, Adam was nevertheless superior to all other spirits, being invested with a "glorious body" and "emancipated" by God so that he (Adam)—as a "Man-God"—could command the creation and work toward general reintegration. Seduced by Lucifer, Adam repeated his seducer's "breach of trust," but the consequences were more serious because of Adam's status and the "Word of creation" with which he was imbued. Adam created a "dark and material form" (Eve), which God in his turn also bestowed on Adam. Adam had thus become "terrestrial" and dragged the universe along with him in the process of materialization.

Symbolically, from that point on, the history of humanity has been a series of falls and reconciliations, parts of a process in which each person, each place, each detail appears as an "image" corresponding to one of the elements in the primordial drama. It is up to man to recover his original state and to reintegrate the whole of creation into the divine fullness. Although man's new state renders conditions more difficult for him, he may look for aid to the spirits of good and to Christ, who is known as the "regenerator." Once accomplished, the regeneration will abolish time, return matter to its "glorious" state, and restore the spirits—"subjected" since the Fall to the task of managing the universe and reconciling mankind—to their primordial function, the proclamation of divine glory.

For Martínez, theory is no more than a preparatory stage for an active theurgy. The work of reintegration implies an effort from the inner being but also several theurgic activities that are associated with initiation and other specific rituals. During such rituals, angelic entities are supposed to manifest themselves in the form of "passes," signs in the form of light or sound. Martínez gathered his followers, including Grainville, Willermoz, the abbé Fournié, Bacon de la Chevalerie, and Saint-Martin, into the Ordre des Chevaliers maçons élus Cohen de l'Univers (Order of Knight-Masons Elect Cohens [elected priests] of the Universe), a system of high Masonic degrees, the highest of which was named the Réau-Croix (Royal Cross). Apart from its considerable intellectual prestige and its literary influence—exemplified in the writings of Jacques Cazotte (1719–92)—Martínez's doctrine, including its theurgic aspect, influenced 18th-century Freemasonry through Willermoz.

Sometimes called the "unknown *philosophe*," Saint-Martin inherited the structures of Martínez's theosophy but distinguished himself from his exemplar by the wealth of his ideas, his involvement in 18th-century intellectual life and writings, and his gradual retreat from ceremonial theurgy. Saint-Martin aimed his work not at initiates but at all "men of desire," and his writings sought to awaken that desire, which he thought to be latent in everyone. To an even greater extent than Martínez, Saint-Martin distanced himself from mysticism, which he regarded as too passive and too concerned with personal salvation. He sought to make his works both demonstrative and "active," in the sense that they were intended to function as both a rational and a poetic process that would bring to fruition in mankind, for universal purposes, the seeds of the creative Word, which had been stifled but not eradicated by the Fall.

Saint-Martin's first works, *Des erreurs et de la vérité* (1775; On Errors and Truth) and *Tableau naturel des rapports qui existent entre Dieu, l'homme et l'univers* (1782; A Natural Depiction of the Relations That Exist among God, Man, and the Universe), already show originality in their attempt to present a rational argument, in the multiplicity of the subjects addressed, and in the broadening of the philosophical discussion, the Bible being no more than one reference among many. The New Testament occupies a more significant place in his commentary on the scriptural narrative. Unlike Martínez's work, the main purpose of Saint-Martin's commentary was not to bring about a rediscovery of a memory of the past. Saint-Martin was interested in such an archaeology of what already exists only to the extent that its vestiges could give rise to a hermeneutic study, a reactivation, and an unlimited quest, focusing man on the meaning of the destiny of being as it is contained in this history. Truth resides in man, who must "create his own revelation" through a search that completely engages his being.

However, the full flowering of Saint-Martin's thought came in three later works that established his influence: *L'homme de désir* (1790; The Man of Desire), written in a poetic style that makes it especially appealing; *De l'esprit des choses* (1800; On the Spirit of Things), a treatise on "gnostic science" that comes close to German *Naturphilosophie*; and *Le Ministère de l'homme esprit* (1802; The Agency of Human Spirit), a synthesis in which Saint-Martin sets out his philosophy of history. In these writings, Saint-Martin related his thought to the philosophical conflicts of his contemporaries, refuting materialism in a very polemical manner but not refraining from using some of the conceptual and methodological tools of the Enlightenment, with which he shared a number of preoccupations. Saint-Martin pitched his appeal to man's innate "desire for knowledge," to his experience of being lost in a universe where signs have been obscured by the Fall and where various religious and philosophical systems have resulted in nothing but false or partial interpretations. He set out to "explain things by man" and defined the only possible approach as the search for reality behind the veil of appearances, the passage from the outer world to the inner world, in order to understand, through the various layers that make up the history of the world and of humanity, the powers and destiny of man and the nature of his relations with God and the universe.

For Saint-Martin, reintegration veered toward a process of becoming, even more sharply so after the outbreak of the French Revolution, which he interpreted as a favorable sign of a new era. Man the universal healer must guide the reclamation of knowledge, in the sense of both personal reintegration and, within the framework of a divine economy in which he becomes main agent, his own mastery of the world. Such efforts are part of a divine economy in which man becomes the main driving force, to the point of acting on God himself, who must be roused from self-contemplation. Saint-Martin regarded the effects of the Fall and the necessity for human beings to live by effort to be a permanent "labor," the very condition of dialectical transcendence. However, simultaneously and with no contradiction, this optimism is tragic. Since the Fall, humanity and the universe have been held within a violent and dramatic process of becoming, marked by successive "crises" that are fruitful yet brutal.

Saint-Martin also clearly differentiated the work of regeneration from any blissful belief in ineluctable progress. The thinking and speaking subject who carries within himself the signs of human history is torn between his nostalgic aspirations to an ideal world and the disenchantment of a painful and ridiculous existence. Often obscure to himself, man looks at the world and its contradictions from a double viewpoint of potential master and stranger in a strange land. Nevertheless, this state of perpetual and painful tension endows the man of desire with the ability to capture the multiple meanings of the world in a language that is "poetic," in the strong sense of the term.

Illuminism rapidly developed a comparative orientation with the discovery of Asian literatures and in the more dubious context of Egyptomania, as exemplified by Cagliostro (1743–95), who was more renowned for the myth that he inspired than for his specific teachings.

The diverse trends of European illuminism were explored in depth in the works of Johann Caspar Lavater (1741–1801), the inventor of "physiognomy"; Johann Heinrich Jung-Stilling (1740–1817); and Johann Friedrich Oberlin, in whose writings, as in those of F.R. Saltzmann (1749–1821), the millenarian aspect of illuminism is developed. In contrast to Saint-Martin, Saltzmann insisted on the annihilation of the will as a prerequisite to man's penetration by divine illumination, which could be manifested both internally and externally through visions.

Oberlin was a great admirer of Emmanuel Swedenborg (1699–1772), the author of *De Nova Hierosolyma et Ejus Doctrina Coelesti* (1763; The Heavenly Doctrine of the New Jerusalem, as Revealed from Heaven), whose spiritual and visionary orientation was to appeal to many curious minds—he conversed with angels and described heaven and hell—and exerted an influence as far away as the Americas. Swedenborg's work helped to popularize the theory of correspondences, and he inspired the mystical school of northern Europe. In France the circle around Dom Pernety (1716–86), an alchemy enthusiast and author of a dictionary of myth and hermeticism, established the group of Illuminés (Illuminati) of Avignon. In Switzerland Nicolas Antoine Kirchberger (1739–99) who also had a passion for the various forms of illuminism, was Saint-Martin's chief correspondent, while J.P. Dutoit-Membrini (1721–93), author of *La philosophie divine* (Divine Philosophy), exemplified the relations that were maintained between quietism and illuminism. In 17th-century England there had been a full-blown school of followers of Boehme, but illuminism—and more particularly those elements in illuminist theory that involved the powers of the imagination—found expression above all in literature, specifically in the works of William Blake (1757–1827).

Across the whole of Europe, the 19th century witnessed the disappearance of the last great theorists of illuminism in the strict sense. Pierre-Simon Ballanche (1776–1847), Joseph de Maistre, Fabre d'Olivet, and even Wronski—whose importance has yet to be fully explored—did no more than integrate, to various degrees, the theories and themes of the great illuminists into works that also included other perspectives. Novalis (1772–1801) was a writer and poet first and foremost, and Friedrich Wilhelm Joseph von Schelling (1775–1854) was chiefly responsive to illuminist metaphors, which he absorbed into his own philosophical system. After 1830 illuminism as such disappeared, but it continued to inspire literature, as seen in the works of Etienne Pivert de Senancour, Gérard de Nerval, Charles-Augustin Sainte-Beuve, Honoré de Balzac, and Charles Baudelaire, among others, while it also influenced certain aspects of philosophy and politics.

NICOLE JACQUES-CHAQUIN

See also Alchemy; Anti-Enlightenment; Freemasonry; Mesmerism; Mysticism

Further Reading

Faivre, Antoine, *Mystiques, théosophes et illuminés au siècle des lumières*, Hildesheim, Germany, and New York: Olms, 1976

Le Forestier, René, *La franc-maçonnerie templière et occultiste aux XVIIIe et XIXe siècles*, Paris: Aubier-Montaigne, 1970

Waite, Arthur Edward, *The Life of Louis Claude de Saint-Martin, the Unknown Philosopher, and the Substance of His Transcendental Doctrine*, London: Wellby, 1901; reprint, as *The Unknown Philosopher*, Blauvelt, New York: Steiner Publications, 1970

Weintraub, Wiktor, *Literature as Prophecy: Scholarship and Martinist Poetics in Mickiewicz's Parisian Letters*, The Hague: Mouton, 1959

Wilkins, Kay S., "Some Aspects of the Irrational in 18th-Century France," in *Studies on Voltaire and the Eighteenth Century*, vol. 140, edited by Theodore Besterman, Oxford: Voltaire Foundation, 1975

Illustration

In their book *L'art au XVIIIe siècle* (1868–70; Art in the Eighteenth Century), the brothers Edmond and Jules de Goncourt devote a chapter to Hubert-François Gravelot, one of the most renowned illustrators of the 18th century. In the chapter, they declare that the 18th century was the age of the vignette . . . and the reign of Louis XV saw the triumph of what would later be called "illustration." Pictures filled books, spilled onto the pages or framed them, appeared at the beginning and at the end,

ILLUSTRATION   687

and ate up all the white space, as frontispieces, fleurants, initial letters, tailpieces, cartouches, complements, and symbolic borders.

Indeed, the second half of the 18th century marks a turning point in the history of books and their illustration. Simultaneous developments included a sharp decline in Latin texts and religious publications; the rise of novels and verse, books on the arts and sciences, and travel books; and the abandonment of the large formats associated with scientific literature and prestigious texts. Engraved illustrations spread through all types of printed matter, from the humblest to the most official, including ephemera (tickets, theatre passes, and invitations), almanacs, gifts, pamphlets, gallery and sales catalogs, collections of fashion plates, patterns, or motifs aimed at artists, accounts of picturesque voyages, novels and verses, birthday books, and scientific writings.

The functions of illustrations varied from genre to genre. In novels, books of verse, and printed plays, illustrations were essentially part of the narrative and were applied as faithfully as possible to the text to highlight what Gotthold Ephraim Lessing calls "the most fertile moments"—passages that best summarize what has happened and that allow the reader to anticipate what will happen next. The allegorical images that appeared in moralistic, philosophical, and historical texts were often limited to frontispieces and tailpieces. Serving as both syntheses and parallel discourses, these pieces had both programmatic and decorative significance. The informative illustrations in scientific works could reinforce the verbal discourse and analytic character of the text, as in the plates for the *Encyclopédie* (from 1762 onward), or they could complement the text by showing in a concise manner what could not easily be described, as the comte de Buffon indicates in the 36 richly illustrated volumes of his *Histoire naturelle générale et particulière* (1749-1784; Natural History, General and Particular). Many illustrated collections of antiquities and accounts of journeys presented the world as a lavish spectacle. The vignettes in alphabet books and other children's works had mnemonic, didactic, and pedagogical purposes, which can also be discerned in publications for more sophisticated audiences, such as technical manuals, moralistic works, and scholarly treatises. And what would emblem books be without engravings! One thing is certain: illustrations made readers stop and look, compelling them to be moved and guiding their imaginations by proposing an initial "reading" of the text. In short, vignettes decorated, enriched, and clarified the printed text that they complemented, but they also competed with it.

The rising number of engravings in books led the printer Charles-Antoine Jombert to codify the use of specialized terms in his *Avis aux marchands d'estampes* (1774; Notices to Engraving Dealers). He defines a frontispiece as "a print placed at the beginning of a book, opposite the title page," and a vignette as "a small print, surrounded with a light decorative border or a double line. . . . Its width is generally twice its height." He describes how "initial letters are generally accompanied by vignettes, which serve as decorations for these opening letters of chapters." According to Jombert, "the fleurant is placed on the title page of a book, in the space between the author's name and the name and address of the bookseller," while "the tailpiece, strictly speaking, is the decoration that ends a work and is therefore placed at the end of a volume, a part, a book, or a chapter."

As for the techniques of illustration, copperplate engravings almost completely supplanted xylographs, or woodcuts. However, copperplate was expensive because the vignettes had to be printed in a separate stage from the text, and complex operations had to be undertaken to align the plates correctly. As a result, a significant proportion of 18th-century illustrations took the form of separate plates, and the captions or titles for these plates were often executed in "copperplate letters," in order to reduce the number of times the illustrations had to be passed through the press. Engravings on wood were more economical at the printing stage because they could be printed at the same time as the text, but readers deemed them displeasing. Connoisseurs associated such pictures with the sometimes vulgar imagery found in popular works, to such an extent that the insertion of woodcut fleurants and tailpieces by J.-B. Papillon and N. Le Sueur in the four deluxe folio volumes of Jean de La Fontaine's *Fables choisies, mises en vers* (1755–59; Selected Fables, Rendered into Verse) shocked more than one connoisseur who had grown accustomed to the effects of copperplate.

The creation of illustrations was the work of many hands. As a general rule, an outline first had to be etched into the copper plate, either by the artist himself or by a draftsman responsible for the task. The picture was later finished with a burin by a professional engraver. These tasks were rarely undertaken by the same person, partly because of technical specialization—the use of the burin in particular was a skill that required a long apprenticeship—but mainly out of concern for efficiency. The division of labor allowed the pace of production to be accelerated in response to demand, and thus permitted printers to keep promises made to subscribers. Many specialized artists were quite adept at accommodating the fluctuating needs of booksellers and print dealers. Some of these artists, such as Gravelot or Pierre-Philippe Choffard, were engravers by training. Several, for example Charles Eisen, came from families of artists and copperplate engravers.

The profession of "vignettist" allowed draftsmen without patrons or capital to prosper. However, it was rare in France for anyone to gain recognition as an artist in what was regarded as a minor genre, so the renown earned by Charles-Nicolas Cochin (1715–90) was a brilliant exception to the rule. It is significant that Cochin, who was on good terms with the most influential booksellers and art dealers and who was elected to the Académie Royale de Peinture et de Sculpture (Royal Academy of Painting and Sculpture) by acclamation in 1751, renounced the "petite manière," or humble style. By the same token *L'almanach historique des peintres* (1776; The Historical Almanac of Painters) condemns "this dry and meager genre, never disinterested, this passe-partout of mediocre books . . . which has never been the serious occupation of a member of the Academy."

Specialization and Internationalization

Louis Réau has identified three stages in the development of illustrations in publishing in 18th-century France (see Réau). The first, from 1700 to 1750, was characterized by the occasional contributions of painters, such as Charles-Antoine Coypel or Claude Gillot; the second, up to the end of Louis XV's reign (1774), by the emergence of an elite group of book illustrators; and the last, up to 1800, by signs of decline. In France the development of illustrated books was undoubtedly stimulated by political changes. After the death of Louis XIV, the aristocracy left Versailles and moved into private residences in the capital. The private libraries created there competed with one another in making acquisitions, while a new type of high-class social life developed around the salons, which placed an emphasis on books decorated with engravings. The nobility and the upper bourgeoisie, by turns taking over the state's role as patrons, thus formed the readership and the main source of commissions for illustrated publications. The fabulously wealthy Fermiers Généraux (General Tax Farmers), for example, charged one of their number with the task of commissioning a sumptuous edition of La Fontaine's *Contes et nouvelles* (1795; Tales and Short Stories). Not content with assuming the role of publisher and bookseller, some patrons became writers and artists themselves. Notable dilettantes in the 18th century included specialists in antiquities, such as the comte de Caylus, and collectors of prints, such as Pierre-Jean Mariette. Madame de Pompadour (under Cochin's guidance), and even Louis XV in his childhood printed, drew, composed, and engraved etchings. Such people manipulated the pen, the crayon, the watercolor brush, and, above all, the purse strings. The close relationship between those who commissioned works and the artists and writers who executed them favored the active bibliophilism that characterized the age.

In response to the growing demands of an elite enamored with fine books, publishers exploited a range of techniques to create rare books and to make each volume individual. Limited editions abounded on various types of paper, using inks of different colors, and in several formats. There were series of "pure" etchings (not yet finished with the burin) and "uncovered" erotic proofs ("before [the addition of] drapes and clouds"). Prints in unfinished states were also offered. Artists busied themselves duplicating their original drawings in order to satisfy eager collectors. Luxury book sales thus depended on a speculative market: Cochin recognized its mechanisms when, encouraging subscriptions to "his" *Gerusalemme liberata* (1784; Jerusalem Liberated by Torquato Tasso), he wrote to a connoisseur as follows: "Despite the apparently frightening cost of [the volume] . . . it will perhaps come to be worth twice what it cost in three or four years time, because there are so few copies and the printing is certainly a masterpiece of typography."

Indeed, from a financial standpoint, books decorated with engravings required large investments. The risks of such commercial speculation were offset by the widespread adoption of the subscription method, but that did not prevent L.R. de Montenault, who was responsible for publishing La Fontaine's *Fables choisies* (1668–94; Selected Fables) and spent more than 100,000 écus on the first three volumes, from having to approach Louis XV to support the publication of the final folio. The publication of *Le voyage pittoresque ou description des royaumes de Naples et de Sicile* (1781–86; The Picturesque Voyage; or, Depiction of the Kingdoms of Naples and Sicily) was equally ruinous. Initially, the cost of the work—which was illustrated, most notably, by Jean-Honoré Fragonard, Louis-Jean Desprez, Hubert Robert, and P.-A. Pâris—was shared between Benjamin Laborde, Louis XV's first gentleman in waiting and a tax farmer, who was responsible for the texts and coordinated the illustrations, and the abbé of Saint-Non, who was a draftsman and engraver in his spare time. In order to control this enormous publishing enterprise the abbé had to sink his entire fortune into a "printing house" in Paris, where he could bring together the printers and the engravers; there were more than 60 specialists, including Choffard, L.-J. Masquelier, and A. de Saint-Aubin.

Nevertheless, the role of illustrations was not exclusively to confer luxury on a work. In fact, editions decorated with engravings offered some protection against piracy. The harsh reality of these economic factors is summarized in Volume 30 of *Les contemporaines* (1782; Contemporary Women). Nicolas-Anne-Edmé

ILLUSTRATION   689

Rétif de la Bretonne, the work's author and publisher, expresses the problem as follows:

> Today, I make advances for the printing of my works, my prints; these prints ruin me; but they are necessary in order to frustrate the pirates, for piracy is still more ruinous. . . . I pay my pressman, my paper supplier, my engraver, my draftsman, my binder, my stitcher, my assembler, my crocheteur: I reckon that, counting them all together, I have the good fortune to have provided livelihoods for 13 heads of families every day since around 1777. This, then, is my title as a citizen, and my glory.

The vogue for illustrations was not limited to France, although Paris, under both Louis XV and Louis XVI, largely set the tone. In Italy, Venice—one of the centers of European engraving—prevailed over Bologna and Rome in this field because publishers in these other two cities mainly issued collections of plates based on images from antiquity or the Bible. Various famous artists worked for the booksellers Zatta, Pasquali, and Albrezzi, including Francesco Fontebasso, G. Guarana, Schiavono, Giovanni Battista Piazzetta, and P. A. Novelli. Their illustrations enriched not only editions of Dante or Torquato Tasso but also the works of Jacques-Bénigne Bossuet, as deluxe products aimed at an international clientele.

The various regions of Germany also saw a revival of publishing, with different aesthetics and ideologies depending on the type of patronage. While enterprises in southern Germany, following the example of Austria, were still publishing a great many large-format scientific and religious volumes, printers in Nuremberg, Saxony, and Hamburg produced more secular illustrations and were more closely related to Paris and London, the two centers of illustration. Leipzig was the leading locale for the specialized market in illustrated books, being endowed with publishers such as M.G. Weidmann and J.G.J. Breitkopf, as well as a veritable school of vignettists that developed around A.F. Oeser. Among engravers, the brothers J.M. and J.B. Bernigeroth reproduced the "Parisian" copperplate drawings of Eisen, Gravelot, and others. Similarly, in Berlin Frederick II, that great admirer of Voltaire, established his own printing press, "Au Donjon du Château" (in the castle keep), where for his own pleasure he undertook the publication of *Oeuvres du philosophe de Sans Souci* (Works of the Philosopher of Sans-Souci). His edition of the *Palladion* (1750) was limited to just 24 copies. During the following decades, Berlin became another center, alongside Leipzig, of the publication of illustrated books in German, thanks to such brilliant and productive artists as Johann Wilhelm Meil and Daniel

Nikolaus Chodowiecki, who both enjoyed successful careers as members of the city's Kunstakademie (Art Academy). In England the publication of illustrated books was concentrated in London, where a whole constellation of immigrant artists, engravers, and draftsmen worked, including Gravelot and Henry Fuseli. Francis Hayman, a painter and decorator, was the first important English vignettist. He was devoted to Shakespeare, Milton, and other classics of English literature, as well as to successful contemporary authors such as Samuel Richardson, who was unusual among authors of the era in that he personally selected the illustrations for his novel *Pamela* (1741). Hayman was succeeded by Thomas Stothard, William Hogarth, and, later, William Blake (1757–1827), who was unique in Europe in that he not only drew and wrote but also engraved on copper, in relief, the letters and illustrations of his works, which he then hand colored and sometimes distributed.

Like England, the Netherlands welcomed political and religious exiles, notably in The Hague and Amsterdam, and these exiles produced numerous illustrated works of science and topography, along with a number of literary publications on the Parisian model. The French artist Bernard Picart, for example, settled in Amsterdam, where he trained engravers and vignettists.

I. Ibarra, Spain's most important printer in the 18th century, produced several illustrated editions of *Don Quijote* (1605; Don Quixote). The last and most luxurious of these editions (1780) received the patronage of the king. It was undertaken by the Réal Academia (Royal Academy) in Madrid and brought together most of the notable vignettists of the country, including A. Carnicero, P. Arnal, and J. de Castillo—but not Francisco de Goya, whose drawings were rejected.

Illustration also flourished in Switzerland, on the periphery of both France and Germany. Salomon Gessner of Zurich was celebrated throughout Europe. Berne was the homeland of B.A. Dunker and S. Freudenberger, who began their careers in Paris. At Winterthur, home of the prolific J.R. Schellenberg, the sumptuous volumes of Johann Caspar Lavater's *Physiognomische Fragmente* (1775–78; Physiognomical Fragments), produced by the printer H. Steiner in collaboration with Weidmann of Leipzig, were illustrated and engraved by a multitude of mainly Swiss and German artists.

The internationalization of the trade in illustrated books in the 18th century influenced a series of ventures, both modest and large-scale. Ludovico Ariosto's *Orlando furioso* (1576), for example, became one of the most frequently illustrated works, not only in Italy—four editions appeared in Venice between 1713 and 1730—but throughout Europe. About 40 editions illustrated with prints appeared in the second half of the century, the most important being the edition in two formats (quarto and large octavo) published in 1778 by the brothers Molini, who were established in London, where P. Molini was a bookseller for the Royal Academy, as well as in Paris and Florence. The text was printed by the renowned typographer John Baskerville of Birmingham, and the 47 illustrations were executed by Giovanni Battista Cipriani, a Florentine based in London, and by the French artists Moreau the Younger, Cochin, Jean-Baptiste Greuze, Monnet, Choffard, and Eisen. Also revealing is the 1759 publication by Leipzig's Weidmann of a German translation of Samuel Richardson's 1753 novel *The History of Sir Charles Grandison* (*Geschichte Herrn Carl Grandison*), which appeared in seven volumes. The first German translation of the novel (1754–55), limited to 2,500 copies, sold out rapidly. A French version followed, printed in collaboration with E. Luzac of Leiden in 1756. In the summer of 1756 Philipp Erasmus Reich, director of the Weidmann house, met Richardson in London and heard his suggestions for the subjects of the illustrations. Drawings were then commissioned from Eisen in Paris, to be engraved by J.M. Bernigeroth in Leipzig. The illustrations were completed by G. Eichler of Augsburg. The frontispiece and the 21 etchings were also sold separately, so that they could be inserted into the earlier French and German editions that Weidmann had already published.

Given the complexity of the production process for illustrated books, Weidmann, despite specializing in such projects, sometimes entrusted the burden of organizing the illustrations to third parties, usually draftsmen. In France, Cochin undertook such a project on behalf of wealthy connoisseurs who had decided to have a set of Jean-Baptiste Oudry's drawings engraved 20 years after they were made. The edition of La Fontaine's *Fables choisies* was Cochin's work in more than one sense, for he not only redrew Oudry's rough sketches, but he also chose the 42 engravers, oversaw the quality of their work, supervised the printing, and so on. Writers too would sometimes take charge of the illustrations of their works. In Venice, Carlo Goldoni offered scenes from his life to the publisher Pasquali and the illustrator Novelli, as frontispieces in the 17-volume *Delle commedie di Carlo Goldoni* (1761–78; On the Comedies of Carlo Goldoni). In 1757, Jean-Jacques Rousseau offered to take charge of the illustrations for his novel *La nouvelle Héloïse* (1761; Julie; or, The New Héloïse), but his Amsterdam publisher refused to take the financial risk, despite the fact that François Boucher was suggested as the artist. The publication went ahead with Gravelot coordinating the illustrations. Rousseau submitted to him a long text, "Sujets d'estampes" (Subjects for Prints), in which he selected the episodes to be depicted and determined their settings. The engravings were also put out as a separate

collection, ready to be inserted into the book. Rousseau, for whom the illustrations were principally a promotional medium, noted: "It seems to me that this [system of an insert] is a very appropriate method for enhancing the value of the edition by means of the plates and that of the plates by means of the edition."

Nevertheless, from the 1750s onward some voices were raised against the "mania" for vignettes and their power in the bookselling business. Engravings were attacked as being means for artificially increasing the price of books, enhancing the fame of writers who lacked literary merit, spoiling major texts that had no need of them, and exercising a harmful influence over literature by encouraging writers to produce texts that were easy to illustrate. They were also attacked for turning young talents away from great art and perverting the skills of engraving. Such criticisms formed part of a more general rejection of rococo affectations and small-scale engravings in favor of a return to the grand style, a more moral iconography that would be the work of great artists rather than of lowly draftsmen.

In France the Revolution killed the aristocratic market for illustrated books. The republican ideology reinforced the criticisms of small-scale engraving, which continued most notably in almanacs and in the genres of libertine and erotic writings (by Pierre-Ambroise-François Choderlos de Laclos, Rétif de La Bretonne, and others). The Didot publishing house in Paris, the semiofficial printers for the new regime, not only sought to distinguish the illustrations in its great and prestigious editions from "the vignettes that one commonly sees in books" (to quote the prospectus for its edition of Virgil, 1797) but also presented them as ventures imbued with a patriotic mission (to compete with the great English editions) as well as a national purpose (to provide work for artists through the patronage of the state). Jacques-Louis David, in association with Didot, directed and lent patronage to a new school of artists that was to develop a concept of monumental illustration and claim on its behalf a dignity borrowed from history painting. From this point on, the vignettes of the 18th century passed into a sort of limbo, from which they would eventually be rescued by the enthusiastic bibliophiles of the Second Empire (1852–70).

PHILIPPE KAENEL

See also Books and Reading; Drawing; Engraving; Printing

Further Reading

Fürstenberg, Hans, *Das französische Buch im achtzehnten Jahrhundert und in der Empirezeit*, Weimar: Gesellschaft der Bibliophilen, 1929

Lanckoronska, Maria, and R. Oehler, *Die Buchillustration des XVIII. Jahrhunderts in Deutschland, Österreich, und der Schweiz*, Frankfurt: Frankfurter Bibliophilen-Gesellschaft, 1932

Osborne, Carol Margot, *Pierre Didot the Elder and French Book Illustration, 1789–1822*, New York: Garland, 1985

Ray, Gordon Norton, *The Art of the French Illustrated Book, 1700 to 1914*, New York: The Pierpont Morgan Library, 1982; London: Dover, 1986

Réau, Louis, *La gravure d'illustration*, Paris and Brussels: Van Oest, 1928

Stewart, Philip, *Engraven Desire: Eros, Image, and Text in the French Eighteenth Century*, Durham, North Carolina: Duke University Press, 1992

Imagination

Imagination was long considered suspect and even condemned in European thought, on the basis of its ontological fragility, its semantic ambiguities, and its purportedly dangerous links with the emotions. It was considered an impure faculty, blurring the distinction between reality and appearance, action and perception, memory and understanding. It was denounced by most 17th-century moralists, who insisted on order, clarity, and reality. Imagination was described as "Mistress of error and falsity—and the more treacherous because she does not always play that role," and as "man's second nature" (Blaise Pascal, *Pensées* [1670; Thoughts]); "a lunatic who enjoys playing the lunatic" (Nicolas Malebranche, *Recherche de la vérité* [1674; The Search for Truth]); "often vain and puerile," contrary "to right reason" (Jean de La Bruyère, "De la société et de la conversation" [On Society and Conversation] in *Caractères* [1688; Characters]); "an erroneous and strange" capacity (*Dictionnaire de l'Académie Française* [1694; Dictionary of the Académie Française]). In short, imagination was held responsible for the worst derangements of the mind.

This negative view of imagination continued to be found in the works of many Enlightenment writers. A common tactic to discredit the convictions of an adversary was to suggest they sprang from the imagination. While "strong-minded" *philosophes* denounced metaphysical abstractions as fanciful constructions contradicted by reflection and experience, as illusions floating in unreality, their enemies denounced empiricism and materialism as fantastical systems based on the appearances of the external world and the deceptive nature of the senses. Beyond these polemics, however, both sides acknowledged the hold of the imagination on the mind and on human activities.

Imagination began to be viewed more favorably in the 18th century due to the dissemination of Cartesianism and sensationalist philosophy. According to the 17th-century philosopher René Descartes, imagination is a positive instrument for learning, in spite of its indisputably low status. Even if "imagining is nothing more than contemplating a figure or the image of a material thing," it nevertheless gives assurance of the real union of the soul and the body and of the individual's uniqueness and sentient existence (*Meditationes de prima philosophia* [1641; Meditations on First Philosophy]). In his *Traité des passions* (1649; Treatise on Passions), Descartes argues that imagination, both subordinate to and an intimate part of the intellect, might even serve as a "remedy" for "excesses of passion," redirecting its own distractions, so that we might become aware of the right road to follow.

Malebranche carries Descartes' arguments even further in the second book of his *Recherche de la vérité* (1674; The Search for Truth). He emphasizes the close link between the senses and the imagination, going so far as to suggest that they are "not separate." Studying the famous example of the mother who gave birth to a child with broken limbs after she had seen a miscreant receive a beating, Malebranche gives a psychological and physiological explanation of the phenomenon, asserting that "children see what mothers see," "hear the same cries," and "are moved by the same passions." It seems paradoxical that Julien Offroy de La Mettrie and Denis Diderot later used this example of "the beaten child" to validate their materialism, but the paradox is only apparent, in that Malebranche actually paves the way for the vitalist and mechanistic theories of the Enlightenment. He does so both through his distinction between "passive imagination" (resulting from the strong influence of "animal spirits") and "active imagination" (activated by the will) and through his subtle attempt to differentiate imagination from memory, in relation to the fact that both imagination and memory register images produced by the senses and more or less faithfully reproduce such sensory data.

Empiricist philosophy contributed to the confusion. In the theories of John Locke, who defines sensation as the most basic element of all knowledge, imagination, as the primary agent for combining, coordinating, and associating ideas and for developing networks of analogies, is barely distinguishable from memory. Christian Wolff, George Berkeley, Charles Bonnet, Albrecht von Haller, and David Hume draw no essential distinction between imagination and memory. In La Mettrie's view, imagination, producing fantasies, visions, deliriums, ecstatic states, superstitions, and fanaticism, "combines the diverse and incomplete sensations that memory recalls to the soul, and turns them into images or scenes represented by the various objects." (*Histoire naturelle de l'âme* [1745; The Natural History of the Soul]). Defining imagination as the "perception of an idea produced by internal causes resembling one of the ideas that external causes customarily engender," La Mettrie rates imagination relatively low in comparison to the power of judgment.

The Italian philosopher Giambattista Vico presents a similar view in his *Principi di una scienza nuova* (1725; The New Science of Giambattista Vico). The senses are the first step in the development of human ideas, fantasy is the second, and reason the third. Humanity successively passes through three stages that correspond to this gradation. Vico defines the first stage as "the divine period," in which humans are mute, expressing themselves through symbols; then comes the "heroic period," in which the collective unconscious and myths prevail; and finally "the human period," marking the appearance of true concepts as conceived by the intellect. Étienne Bonnot de Condillac, a proponent of associationism, speaks of "living memory, which makes present what is absent," and relegates imagination to a simple mental mechanism that merely reproduces and combines such memories (*Traité des sensations* [1754; Treatise on Sensations]). The sensationalist poet Jacques Delille clearly equates imagination with memory when he writes that it "is nothing more than a vast and faithful memory / In which objects are depicted as in a mirror." At the same time this poet gives imagination an expansive and dynamic capacity to project itself into "the future" (*L'imagination* [1806; Imagination]).

Subordinated to reason, the senses, and to memory, the faculty of imagination has no unity or identity of its own. It is passive and not responsible for the effects it might produce. This is certainly the opinion of the Italian historian Ludovico Antonio Muratori (*Della forza*

della fantasia umana [1745; On the Power of Human Imagination]) and Antoine de Pas, marquis de Feuquières, who in his *Phantasiologie, ou Lettres philosophiques à Madame de *** sur la faculté imaginative* (1760; Phantasiology; or Philosophical Letters to Madame de *** on the Faculty of the Imagination) makes a deliberate distinction between two kinds of imagination: positive imagination, which is "embellished reason," "lets itself be guided by judgment," and has agreeable effects; and negative imagination, "which has no law but its whim and which jumps thoughtlessly from one idea to another."

Voltaire explores a related duality in an attempt to liberate imagination from its traditional bonds. He enriches the classical division between passive imagination (of organic origin, common to humans and animals, "dependent upon memory," and the "source of our passions and our mistakes") and active imagination ("which links reflection and the combination of ideas with memory" and "examines objects in depth"). Active imagination is the "beautiful imagination," initiator of enthusiasm and talent. Voltaire then merges imagination (of both kinds) into a single broad mental category reminiscent of the bold theories of Pierre Gassendi and La Mettrie. In the article "Imagination" (1765) in the *Encyclopédie* Voltaire writes, "the words *perception, memory, imagination, judgment* do not indicate distinct entities at all—one with the gift of feeling, the other of remembering, a third of imagining, a fourth to make judgments." On the contrary, these abilities are neither different nor separate according to Voltaire, who eventually concludes that the motivations and operations of the mind are unknowable.

Despite their claims of ignorance, many writers in the second half of the century tended to describe the soul as a "superstructure of sensation," to use Robert Morin's expression. Imagination was seen as more indeterminate than ever, combining and (con)fusing mental activities. It was associated with artistic creation and could be the object of the most laudatory tributes. Hume viewed the imagination as the ultimate judge of all systems of philosophy and as the foundation of artistic and literary taste (*A Treatise of Human Nature* [1739]). In his poem *The Pleasures of Imagination* (1744), Mark Akenside piles up disparate images and metaphors to characterize the origin and effects of imaginative delight. In an abstract style claiming to be grand, new, and beautiful, the elegiac poet manipulates the most tangled metaphysical abstractions and sings the joys of a pastoral life and writing free from any constraint. In a somewhat more restrained mode, Claude-Adrien Helvétius showers praise on imagination by placing it at the forefront of his temple of arts (*Le bonheur* [1772; Happiness]). The following year, going beyond associationism, he defines imagination in *De l'homme: De ses facultés intellectuelles et de son éducation* (1773; A Treatise on Man: His Intellectual Faculties and His Education) as "the fairy whose power enables us to metamorphose and so to recompose objects, and to create, as it were, new creatures and sensations in the universe and within man."

Diderot's Dorval heaps praise on the faculty of imagination as well: "Here we have the capacity without which no one is a poet, a philosopher, a wit, a reasonable being, or a man" (*De la poésie dramatique* [1758; On Dramatic Art]). But it is above all in the *Lettre sur les aveugles* (1749; Letter on the Blind), the *Lettre sur les sourds et muets* (1751; Letter on Deaf Mutes), and *Le rêve de D'Alembert* (1769; D'Alembert's Dream) that Diderot examines imagination's importance and ambiguities. In the *Lettre sur les aveugles,* reflecting at length on the imaginings of a blind philosopher, Diderot demonstrates the complexity of thought based on imagination. The impassioned divagations of the blind Saunderson—who explains his materialist convictions about the hazards and hardships of life before he dies—lead into an entirely imaginary vision of a universe in constant metamorphosis, a vision beyond the ability of the absent or imperfect senses to perceive accurately.

In the *Lettre sur les sourds et muets,* Diderot reduces discourse to a "web of hieroglyphs" and concludes with the much-discussed idea that "all poetry is symbolic." This apology for suggestion, insinuation, and decipherment resembles the "evocative witchcraft" that Charles Baudelaire was to glorify a century later. In *Le rêve de D'Alembert,* traditional materialism, which always gave precedence to the influence of the physical over the moral, is approached somewhat in reverse. D'Alembert's delirium minimizes the role of pure reason by honoring the powers of the soul over the body, the triumph of unmediated convictions and fertile intuitions. Linked to genius, imagination promotes an energetic ideal of surpassing limits. Akin to the sublime, imagination is related to a new aesthetic, bringing about the downfall of classical and metaphysical certainties, because, as Saunderson puts it, "there is nothing precise in nature." Diderot thus blurs the boundaries between the real and the realm of the imaginary. Might we not consider real everything imagination offers us, since pleasure and pain, sensation and vision are experienced as entirely real in dream and delirium?

From a dream perspective closer to nightmare, the title of Jean Marie Chassaignon's first work implies that the most unbridled imagination is fed more by monstrosity than beauty: *Cataractes de l'imagination, déluge de la scribomanie, vomissement littéraire, hémorragie encyclopédique, monstre des monstres* (1779; Cataracts of the Imagination, Deluge of Scribomania, Literary Vomiting, Encyclopedic Hemorrhaging,

Monster of Monsters), spoken by Épiménide, the Inspired. This is untamed prose of rare critical violence, combining all the literary genres in an apocalyptic and cataclysmic style. Unhealthy imagination becomes a chaos of words, an obsessional accumulation of disparate references, a systematic transgression of standards and an overturning of forms, a continual surpassing of the limits of individual identity. A significant chapter (Volume I, Chapter 15) entitled "Effervescence du sang, ébranlement du cerveau, éruption des volcans de l'imagination" (The Boiling of the Blood, the Rattling of the Brain, the Eruption of the Volcanoes of the Imagination) depicts the convulsions of the suffering poet, gripped by madness bordering on clairvoyance: "Subterranean vaults burst open, unheard of objects appall my sight and congeal my blood with dread. A sea in fury heaves waves of liquid tar against me, their rage churning the foam; a dreadful comet fans out its blazing mane and heralds a thousand disasters." Imaginative caprices such as these were prudently curbed by the critical philosophy and the ideologues of the end of the Enlightenment.

Frankly denounced, then partially reinstated and positively liberated, the faculty of imagination, as elusive as ever, became the subject of new theoretical research by Immanuel Kant, who tried to defuse its subversive potential by defining it as a connective act and a principle of synthesis. He describes imagination as the "fundamental power that serves *a priori,* as the principle of all knowledge" (*Kritik der reinen Vernunft* [1781; Critique of Pure Reason]). In its reproductive capacity, "the transcendental imagination" occupies a privileged position for Kant, because it affects the relationship between a fact or a sensory intuition and its representation in the intellect. Nevertheless, Kant echoes Voltaire's admission of ignorance when he attempts to specify the primary causes and functioning of the faculty of imagination: "An art concealed within the depths of the human soul." In its productive capacity, imagination relates especially to the realm of aesthetics. In the *Kritik der Urteilskraft* (1790; Critique of Judgment), with regard to the forms of pleasure that a work of art may give an individual, Kant also explains how "imagination and its *freedom,* and comprehension and its *laws,* stimulate each other." If judgment, which is necessarily subjective as regards taste and satisfaction, remains inseparable from feeling, the inspired artist will define himself through his ability to express this universal and ideal balance between *ratio* (reason) and *phantasia* (imagination) in sensitive artistic representations.

The imagination of the sublime is more ambiguous, however, for it is the form of imagination in which pleasure appears only indirectly, as a negative form of displeasure, since the sublime is precisely that which goes beyond all imagination, in a sort of flight toward the inexpressible and the infinite. Reformulating this ultimate limit imposed on the imaginary, the Swiss critic Heinrich Meister compares two kinds of imaginative faculties in his *Lettres sur l'imagination* (1799; Letters on Imagination): one rational and moral, the other "extravagant and sublime," which he further describes in Letter VIII as being "like Phaedra's mania or Clementina's delirium, the rages of Orestes or the madness of King Lear." A loyal heir of the empiricist school and of critical philosophy, Meister examines the close relationship between imagination and sensibility before concentrating on their particular characteristics: imagination expands and develops "sensibility's impressions"; sensibility serves "as guide and regulator for imagination's greatest leaps." Finally, according to the well-known belief of the period, when imagination is applied to the arts it becomes "the source and the focus of all the other faculties of our soul." Overcoming his distrust of the illusions created by that "worthy magician," the imagination, Jean Simon Lévesque de Pouilly also acknowledges that imagination "is the union of sublime qualities that our nature does not include" and that defines "the degree of perfection" in masterpieces (*Théorie de l'imagination* [1803; Theory of Imagination]).

In an innovative, middle-ground perspective between the sensationalism and rationalism of earlier philosophers, Karl Victor Bonstetten emphasizes the selective affinities among imagination, sensibility, and ideas: "Imagination is the action of sensibility on ideas and the reaction of those ideas on sensibility or on the organs" (*Recherches sur la nature et les lois de l'imagination* [1807; Inquiries on the Nature and Laws of Imagination]). This eclectic philosopher from Bern carefully lists the specific functions of each category in his triad and how they interact in order to highlight the motivating role of imagination, a faculty that encompasses "the entire active man."

Madame de Staël presents an original, but less systematic and doctrinal explanation of the powers of imagination in a commentary on Goethe's genius (*De l'Allemagne* [1810; Germany]). Her explanation might be read as an attempt to synthesize the conceptions of the waning Enlightenment with those of nascent romanticism:

> man encloses sensations within himself, hidden powers that correspond to day, night, and storm; it is this secret alliance between our being and the marvels of the universe that gives poetry its true grandeur. The poet knows how to restore unity between the physical world and the moral world: his imagination forms a bond between them.

This harmonious balance between nature's energy and the daring nature of writing admirably suggests the inspiring character of a faculty that, with its lights and shadows, remains the mistress of all excess, as well as of all progress.

PATRICK GRAILLE

See also Aesthetics; Dream; Idea; Originality; Reverie; Sensationalism; Sublime

Further Reading

Bundy, Murray Wright, *The Theory of Imagination in Classical and Mediaeval Thought*, Urbana: University of Illinois Press, 1927; reprint, 1981

Huet, Marie-Hélène, *Monstrous Imagination*, Cambridge, Massachusetts: Harvard University Press, 1993

Marx, Jacques, "Le concept d'imagination au XVIIIe siècle," in *Thèmes et figures du siècle des Lumières: Mélanges offerts à Roland Mortier,* edited by Raymond Trousson, Geneva: Droz, 1980

Starobinski, Jean, "Jalons pour une histoire du concept d'imagination," in *L'oeil vivant*, vol. 2, *La relation critique*, by Starobinski, Paris: Gallimard, 1970

White, Alan R., *The Language of Imagination*, Oxford and Cambridge, Massachusetts: Blackwell, 1990

Imitation

Discussions of the topic of imitation in the 18th century were particularly lively in three contexts: debates on morality focused on human beings imitating each other, while the imitation of nature and of antiquity were both of interest in the fine arts. In all three cases, imitation clearly indicated a relationship between a model and its copy, but also, more subtly, their cross-influences. Although the entry on moral imitation in the *Encyclopédie* prescribes imitation of great men, it also advises that one should become one's own model. This contradictory counsel exemplifies the tensions inherent in Enlightenment thinking on imitation and helps to explain the tumult at the end of the century. The thinking of Jean-Jacques Rousseau, Denis Diderot, the marquis de Sade, William Beckford, and others on the subject of imitation challenged the conventional morality of the age, called into question the use of the general and the commonplace in the arts (a challenge offered by Jean-Honoré Fragonard, Henry Fuseli, and William Blake, in theory as well as in practice), and attempted to replace hackneyed classical references with a return to antiquity that would revive the tradition of great art without succumbing to slavish imitation (in the works of Jacques-Louis David, Antonio Canova, and Johann Wolfgang von Goethe).

In his *Confessions* (1782), Rousseau describes how he was influenced by Plutarch's *Lives,* which he had inherited from his grandfather and had read after the novels that his mother had bequeathed to him. Rousseau credits Plutarch's work with forming his own "proud indomitable character," his "free republican spirit." However, Rousseau's moral development owed less to a deliberate imitation of classical heroes than to a passionate identification with them—the same type of identification that reading novels had aroused in him: "I became the character whose life I was reading." Rousseau's education, in which the imitation of a character from a novel opened the way to moral imitation by a kind of transference, was thus founded on the paradox developed in his *Lettre à D'Alembert* (1758; Letter to M. D'Alembert on Theatre). By imitating the great and their passions, Rousseau argues, dramas elicit our sympathy and later incite us to feel the need for the same emotions.

In the notes he took in preparation for *De l'imitation théâtrale* (On Theatrical Imitation), Rousseau closely follows Book X of Plato's *Republic,* accentuating its negative judgment of works of art by condemning the emotions that they arouse even more harshly than the Greek original. In this way he points out the connection between imitation as denounced by Plato and imitation as approved by his pupil Aristotle. In Book X of *The Republic,* poets and artists are presented as variations of the sophist, apparently capable of producing everything and anything, but lacking true knowledge, engendering nothing but phantoms. In contrast, Aristotle argues in the *Poetics* that every man is imitative, to a greater degree than any other creature, and that imitation is the very basis for our initiation into social life. According to Rousseau, our reaction to comic imitation, far from broadening our moral view, serves merely to confirm the approval or aversion already inculcated by social relations, while tragic imitation manipulates our expectations by causing "sweet emotions" that will later find their object. Diderot's attempt to make virtue attractive and encourage the audience to imitate a model presented onstage is doomed to failure, for such imitation is foiled in advance by our inveterate sympathy with the passions as well as by our egotism, which pays homage to virtue without going so far as to follow it in the face of real danger.

The Aristotelian concept of imitation laid the groundwork for the anthropological perspectives that haunted the 18th century, for these anthropological implications touched on the nature of social bonds and on the difference between the natural and the artificial in human behavior. Thinkers who rejected the notion that language was a gift from God at the time of the creation considered imitation as the source of the ambivalent character of language: a given primitive reaction—for example, a simple gesture, or a cry expressing emotions—could be repeated in other situations than the one that originally provoked it. Étienne Bonnot de Condillac, for example, describes the birth of speech in this manner in his *Essai sur l'origine des connaissances humaines* (1746; Essay on the Origin of Human Knowledge). By dint of imitation, the primitive cry or gesture gradually transforms itself from a symptom into a signal or sign. At the earliest stage of language and of social life itself, the sight of suffering arouses pity:

> He who suffered because he was deprived of an object that his wants made necessary did not restrain himself from crying out: he made an effort to obtain the object; he shook his head, his arms, and every other part of his body. Another person, moved by the sight of this suffering, fixed his gaze upon the same object, and, finding feelings stir within his soul that he was not yet capable of explaining to himself, he suffered to see this pitiable person suffer.

The transference of emotion takes place above all through the eyes and by a type of communication that borders on the mimetic. For the earl of Shaftesbury and Diderot, as for Henry St. John, Viscount Bolingbroke, and Louis Jean Levesque de Pouilly, the social instinct arises from "sympathy with one's kind." As Shaftesbury puts it in *An Inquiry Concerning Virtue, in Two Discourses* (1699), "the communicative or social principle" drives us to adapt ourselves to the emotions of others. The theatre (a social genre par excellence), particularly tragedy, offers proof of this imitative participation. According to Levesque de Pouilly, plays teach us that one cannot perceive emotion in others without also sharing those feelings. This mimicry is the moral version of the "sympathetic impulses" that fascinated the great physicians and that Diderot considers in *Éléments de physiologie* (1774–78; Elements of Physiology):

The organs have the ability to mimic all kinds of emotion, which is a result of sympathy, or this mimicry can be induced by the imagination. A person laughs when he sees laughter and weeps when he sees weeping; this observation may throw some light on the emotions of the populace and other epidemic illnesses.

Whether it be the mass terror of a panicking crowd (Shaftesbury in a *Letter Concerning Enthusiasm* [1708]) or hysterical convulsions among cloistered young women, the transference of emotion and its physiological effects induce us to imitate deep within ourselves the impulses that we observe in others.

According to David Hume in his *Treatise of Human Nature* (1739), social communication is not only a conscious exchange of opinions but also a kind of mimetic transference: this (in Book II, Part I, Section XI): "When any infection is infused by sympathy, it is at first known only by its effects and by those external signs in the countenance or conversation, which convey an idea of it. This idea is presently converted into an impression, and acquires such a degree of force and vivacity as to become the very passion itself." This infection by another's passion is made possible by the identical make-up of human beings, but it is also possible because an impression that relates to a mental torment or to a real event that happens to me differs only in its strength from the impression made on me by the passion of another, or even by an illusion. In a normal, nonhallucinatory state, an impression based on reality differs only in degree from an impression inspired by art or from one's perception of the impressions of others.

Hume doubtless derived this idea from his reading of abbé Jean-Baptiste Dubos's great book *Réflexions critiques sur la poésie et sur la peinture* (1719; Critical Reflections on Poetry and Painting). According to Dubos,

The impression that an imitation makes is no different from the impression that the original object would make, except that it is less strong . . . the copy of the object should, so to speak, excite in us a copy of the passion that the object itself would have aroused in us.

However, for Dubos such an impression is not quite the same as an illusion: "The most perfect imitation has only an artificial existence; it has only a borrowed life." According to Dubos, human beings need constant emotional stimulation; they require a kind of controlled agitation. An artist should therefore try to choose subjects that are most apt to move the passions. Because we always refer our emotions to ourselves, by way of the

pain or pleasure they cause us, condition of spectatorship is at the heart of our experience of art. The etymological relationship between *im*itation and *im*age, which have a common root, is thus reactivated. A reflexive consciousness colors our reactions. As Pierre-Augustin Caron de Beaumarchais remarks, "When I see virtue persecuted . . . what great pleasure I take in that spectacle and what a beautiful moral I draw from it!" Self-referentiality allows us to take pleasure in the sight of tormented virtue's suffering, which assures us of our own safety at the same time that we can pride ourselves on our sensibility. This movement toward an amoral sensibility prepares the way for an aesthetic in the manner of the marquis de Sade.

Shaftesbury had already stressed the fact that a painter must conceive his picture as if he were a playwright: if the painter imitates, he should not imitate everyday life. In his *Einleitung in die Ästhetik* (1820s; Introduction to Aesthetics), Georg Wilhelm Friedrich Hegel states that imitation risks creating a useless copy of nature. Imitation makes memory the foundation of artistic creation and reduces art to technique. Commenting on Jean-Baptiste-Siméon Chardin, an acclaimed painter of still lifes, Diderot sighed, "If it were not for his sublime technique, Chardin's ideal would be pitiable" ("Bachelier" in *Salon de 1765* [The 1765 Exhibition]). Chardin's work also sparked Diderot's recognition that the concept of imitation may lead the artist to omit everything the painting needs: "It is not the real and true scene that one sees [in Chardin's work]; it is, so to speak, nothing but its translation" ("Deshays" in *Salon de 1763* [The 1763 Exhibition]).

However, most French critics in the 18th century were confronted with a dilemma. In fact, it was the genre painters who best displayed the resources of the art form, whereas the work of painters of historical scenes often revealed weak technique. As La Font de Saint-Yenne described a genre painting, "A seductive imitation, a freshness and a marvelous melding of colors, a suaveness of brushwork, etc." (1754). The "etc." is telling: it implies that with their banal and vulgar subjects, the genre painters remain far behind painters of historical scenes, who, working in that "grand genre," choose noble subjects and imitate what the critic abbé Charles Batteux, in *Les beaux-arts réduits à un même principe* (1746; Fine Arts Reduced to a Common Principle), calls "la belle nature" (beautiful nature). Batteux writes, "in a word, an imitation in which one sees nature, not as it is in itself, but as it could be and as one can conceive it in one's mind." The ambitious artist must not only choose imposing subjects that narrate a grandiose action; he must also avoid making an excessively exact imitation of them. This was the opinion of Shaftesbury in his *Sensus Communis, an Essay on the Freedom of Wit and Humour* (1709) and of Sir Joshua

Reynolds, who in his third of his *Seven Discourses on Art* (1778; all fifteen discourses published posthumously in 1797) delivered to the Royal Academy emphasizes that the beauty of art lies in raising oneself above the particular form, above local custom, above individual traits and details.

Imitation should generalize, it should break away from the accidental and the fortuitous, in order to approach the ideal. In the view of its partisans, imitation represents a counterweight to the license of genius: "Genius has been able to produce the arts only by means of imitation" (Batteux, *Les beaux-arts*). The concept of "imitation" drives a wedge between 18th-century art and nascent romanticism. In his sixth discourse, Reynolds gives an account of the dispute between the partisans of genius and those who believe in imitation, affirming that the genius of a painter is an asset to be measured by the dual standard of technical convention and accepted rules of representation. He argues that genius, embedded in an aesthetic and social environment, depends on imitation. In his annotations to the sixth *Discourse*, William Blake castigates Reynolds for his "idiotic" belief that genius is not innate but can instead be learned.

In the second half of the 18th century, "imitation" could mean the vulgar procedures and inauthentic methods learned in the schools, but it could also suddenly soar into the sublime, as in Diderot's description of acting: "Pure imitation, a lesson remembered in advance, a pathetic grimace, a sublime mimicry" (*Paradoxe sur le comédien* [1773; Paradox on the Comedian]). Here, the imitative talent becomes that of John Keats's "chameleon poet." The great artist is characterized by the fact that he has no fixed being of his own and by that very quality he is capable of representing the world in its vastness.

Reflections on music in particular evince a shift toward a radically subjective understanding of imitation, which opened the way to romanticism and an aesthetic based on the impressions of the listener (or spectator or reader). Whereas music had been thought incapable of imitation, especially in the first half of the 18th century, Rousseau, with characteristic lucidity, expresses the shift in a letter dated 26 June 1756: "Except for a very small number of things, the musician's art does not consist of direct depiction of objects, but of lulling the soul into a state similar to the one induced by the objects' presence." Imitation is compared here to a relationship based on analogy. In a chapter devoted to aesthetics in his *La Musique* (Music), Hegel's very subtle analyses eliminate every vestige of imitation in order to make time into the "mode of being" that music and the subject share in common. Since subjective inwardness is its "content," music presents itself as the expression of this interiority.

Like Reynolds, Goethe argues in his commentary on Diderot's *Essais sur la peinture* (1796; Essays on Painting) that *Nachbildung* (imitation) separates nature from art; and the imitation of antiquity provides the standard for this separation. In the pan-European movement of neoclassicism, Johann Joachim Winckelmann's *Gedanken über die Nachahmung der griechischen Werke in der Malerei und der Bildhauerkunst* (1755; Reflections on the Painting and Sculpture of the Greeks) expresses this paradoxical relationship best: "The only path that allows us to become great—inimitable if we can—is to imitate the ancients." Originality is achieved through the model provided by Greek culture. Jacques-Louis David, Antonio Canova, the Danish artist Købke—whatever their differences, they all incorporated this visual source of antique models into their works.

MARIAN HOBSON

See also Actor; Art Criticism; Genius; Landscape; Music; Originality; Painting

Further Reading
Becq, Annie, *Genèse de l'esthétique française moderne: De la raison classique à l'imagination créatrice, 1680–1814*, Pisa: Pacini, 1984
Crow, Thomas E., *Painters and Public Life in Eighteenth-Century Paris*, New Haven, Connecticut: Yale University Press, 1985
Hobson, Marian, *The Object of Art: The Theory of Illusion in Eighteenth-Century France*, Cambridge and New York: Cambridge University Press, 1982
Klein, Robert, *Form and Meaning: Essays on the Renaissance and Modern Art*, New York: Viking Press, 1979 (original French edition, 1970)
Nivelle, Armand, *Les théories esthétiques en Allemagne de Baumgarten à Kant*, Paris: Les Belles Lettres, 1955

Industrialization

Between the middle of the 18th century and the middle of the 19th, a dramatic shift took place throughout Europe. Faster and more regular economic growth, due primarily to powerful increases in industrial output, accompanied structural transformations of the economy, technology, society, culture, and politics, first in Britain and then on the Continent. This economic surge, generally attributed to the birth of modern industry, initially took place without major changes in the mode of production. Economic historian F. Mendels has characterized, this first stage in modern industrialization as "protoindustrial" (see Mendels). It made possible the breakdown of traditional obstacles and the start of the first phase of industrial growth.

In fact, in the 18th century, rates of industrial growth in France and Great Britain were comparable to one another and both started to rise. Nevertheless, around 1790, France's per capita industrial output remained below that of Great Britain, as a result of the initial lag of French industry at the end of the 17th century. However, in absolute terms France was still the world's leading industrial economy. The patterns of growth in the two countries began to diverge in the 1770s. In Britain industrial growth accelerated, while in France it slowed down and was eventually interrupted during the revolutionary period. The forms of industrial development in the two countries also differed, as industrialization was adapted to each nation's particular markets and social structures. In France development continued to be extensive within the framework of traditional production structures, while in Britain growth became more intensive following the birth of large-scale industry within the framework of the factory system.

Protoindustrial structures began to emerge in the 16th century. The rise of the urban bourgeoisie and the attraction of external markets opened by the explorers stimulated a considerable increase in demand for manufactured goods, particularly textiles. Productivity could hardly be increased in the absence of significant change in manufacturing techniques. Only an increase in available labor could meet the growing demand for commercial goods. This need for workers led merchants to circumvent the rules of the urban guilds by developing pools of "free" skilled labor in suburban and rural areas.

This process was accompanied by socioeconomic changes within the guild system itself. In the textile industry, the most important industrial sector, the group of master producers became more and more socially diverse. Most of the journeymen were prevented from attaining the status of master and either remained as they were or became dependent, "working for the mas-ters" in the masters' establishments or at home, in exchange for wages paid at piece rates. Deprived of the means of production—even though most of them formally owned their own equipment—and of the fruits of their labor, the workers themselves could no longer gain access to the market. The prosperous masters, therefore, became producer-merchants, performing both commercial and productive functions. Such entrepreneurs could be characterized as protoindustrial capitalists because they were owners of the means of production (fixed capital), purchasers and owners of raw materials or semifinished products (circulating capital), distributors of labor and controllers of the production process, and sellers of the finished products in the market, either in person or through a broker, earning high profits when possible.

The disintegration of the urban guild system was accelerated by the development of manufacturing in rural areas, in forms quite unlike medieval rural industry. Alongside the traditional craftsmen, whose services and proximity responded to local needs, a workforce of artisan-producers made goods intended for external markets in other regions or countries. Protoindustrial conditions were thus established. A movement of "ruralization" spread outward from the manufacturing cities, the centers of merchant capitalism where traders and merchant-producers resided. The result was the development of structures much like nebulas. For the merchant-producers, ruralization was a means of skirting the guild system and state regulations, but it also meant using a rural workforce that might or might not comprise farm laborers, might be permanent or seasonal, was flexible, cheaper, more docile, and available in abundance. This family-centered rural industry, craft-based and dispersed, procured additional resources for the peasantry and proletariat of the countryside. Mainly located in poor agricultural regions, rural industry could also be found on the outskirts of cities that served as commercial centers for rich agricultural regions.

Thus, in northwestern Europe in the 18th century a dependent workforce, dominated by merchant capitalism in the cities and in the countryside through what Mendels terms the *Verlagsystem* ("putting-out" system), gradually replaced the independent workers of the *Kaufsystem* (domestic system). In an attempt to describe this movement of rural industrialization and its role in the process of modern industrialization, Mendels has proposed the theory of protoindustrialization as a new explanation for the economic transition in the developed countries of the time. His theory accomplishes three aims: (1) it identifies a new form of industrial organization, based on the specific social relations that prefigure the capitalist mode of production; (2) it traces the genesis of protoindustrialism and the reasons for its appearance and development, in space and time; and (3) it postulates an evolutionary, continuous relationship between protoindustrialism and modern industry—a lineage that, as we shall see, cannot always be verified.

According to Mendels and P. Deyon, both proponents of this model, the protoindustrial system at the regional level is characterized by three features: (1) the development of industry in rural areas and the participation of a fragmented peasantry and rural proletariat; (2) production intended for exchange outside local markets and regulated by intermediaries and merchants; and (3) symbiosis and complementarity between rural industries and commercial agriculture, within an intraregional or interregional framework. This definition enables us to distinguish rural industry from "preindustry"—which encompassed all activities of transformation prior to large-scale industry, including the activities of urban craftsmen—and from protoindustrialism, the first stage of modern industrialization. However, epistemological and methodological difficulties arise in the definition of protoindustrial employment. Mendels bases his concept of protoindustrial employment solely on rural industry, although he does not ignore the role of the city as a commercial center.

The present article advocates a definition that is at once broader and more restrictive than that of Mendels. Such a definition must be restricted because rural protoindustrialism is associated more strongly with the rural craft economy than the agricultural economy. More often than not, for the laborers rural protoindustrialism was a principal and not simply a complementary economic activity, providing income that replaced, rather than simply supplementing, income from farming. Rural protoindustrialism could tap two sources of labor, one continuous and permanent, the other occasional or seasonal—no longer simply the latter. This emerging economy partially reproduced the division of labor between the sexes and the different stages of manufacture found in the earlier system.

Our definition of protoindustrial employment is broader than Mendels's because protoindustrialization was also an urban phenomenon. The city was not only the headquarters of the merchant capitalism that organized and coordinated protoindustrialism; it was also the site for every stage of the manufacturing process, not just for the finishing stage of a given product. Protoindustrialism was therefore both urban and rural, not exclusively rural, and the complementarity of these different locations was central to the merchant-producers' economic and social strategy. Moreover, protoindustrial social relations did not differ fundamentally between the cities and the countryside. Geographic location was less important than the organization of labor.

Thus, in the textile industry, the driving force of modern industrialization, property relations determined two fundamental social classes. One class, the merchant-producers (or producer-merchants), possessed an essentially circulating industrial capital. The size of their circulating capital might vary, but the merchant-producers always controlled workers in several different trades, whether on the merchant producers' premises or in the piece-rate workers' own homes. The size of the other class, the wage laborers and dependent artisans, increased with the trends toward concentration and proletarianization that accompanied protoindustrial growth. Although their objective interests brought these laborers somewhat closer to the merchants, the fundamentally contradictory position of these two groups in the production process made them socially distinct and could lead to antagonisms that, under the ancien régime, were articulated principally through regulation and the guild system.

With regard to the organization of labor, protoindustrial modes of production retained the characteristics of the traditional domestic economy while prefiguring certain characteristics of large-scale industry. On the one hand, protoindustrialism was characterized by relatively low levels of fixed capital, along with manual labor, dispersed, specialized workshops, and familial and patriarchal relationships. On the other hand, there was a geographic concentration of production and labor and a relatively advanced and complex technical division of labor, which was even more pronounced in luxury industries. The disappearance of traditional institutional structures and state controls following the adoption of economic liberalism, first in England and then in France, brought this mode of production closer still to the capitalist mode of production.

Protoindustrialism is distinct from a merchant mode of production, defined as a multiplicity of small independent producers who own their means of production, their labor power, and the product of their labor. The distinction between the merchant and the protoindustrial modes of production parallels the distinction established above between the "domestic system" and the "putting-out system." In the former, which was more traditional but in decline in the 18th century, the independent producer was subject only, and directly, to the market for his goods. In the "putting-out system," however, the pieceworker is subject to the vagaries of the labor market, while remaining indirectly subject to changes in the market in goods. His status, close to that of a wage laborer, is that of a "protoworker."

Protoindustrialism was not an isolated phenomenon within the social formations of the 18th century. Reaching full development in that century, merchant capitalism controlled and dominated protoindustrialism. This domination, whether in the form of the direct and immediate power of local merchants over producers or the distant, mediated power exercised by the merchant-shipowners of port cities, was coupled with exploitation. Protoindustrial exploitation takes a different form from the exploitation associated with the capitalist mode of production, for the merchants, the ultimate masters of the protoindustrial production process, did not directly receive the surplus value produced by the textile workers. However, the mechanism of exploitation characteristic of the capitalist mode of production germinated within the "putting-out system," through the labor market. The position of the merchant-producers was ambiguous. As subcontractors collecting surplus value, they were subject to the laws of the market imposed by the monopolist merchants (except when the two roles were combined in one person). The merchant-producers in turn exerted downward pressure on the wages of employees and pieceworkers, again prefiguring the production relationships within industrial capitalism.

Should a theory of protoindustrialization take into account both the independent producers in the "domestic system" and the dependent producers in the "putting-out system" or only the latter? The choice results in either a broad or a restrictive conception of the protoindustrial mode of production, with different implications in relation to the transition to modern industry.

If we accept the idea that protoindustrialization represents the first stage of modern industrialization, as a specific transitional mode of production containing the seeds of the characteristic features of the capitalist mode of production, then only the "putting-out system" offers a form of organization of industrial production that prefigures the capitalist mode in the following ways: (1) the subjugation of workers to the twin markets for goods and labor; (2) the status of workers, approaching that of wage laborers; (3) social relationships of production based on the growing separation between capital and labor and the producers' loss of control of production; and (4) structures of domination and exploitation by merchant capital.

In theory, the "domestic" and "putting-out" forms of protoindustrialization and the factory system (depending exclusively on wage labor) that succeeded them represent three distinct historical phases of industrial development. In reality, all three forms frequently coexisted in the 18th and 19th centuries within the same region or the same sector of industry. Only the dominant form provides the means to identify the dominant mode of production within a regional framework. The first and oldest form (the "domestic system") is therefore not in itself sufficient to characterize a region as protoindustrial: the "putting-out system" is indispensable.

Now that the concept has been defined, it remains to be seen whether protoindustrialization was a precondition for the industrial transition, as Mendels suggests. Many studies have focused on the characteristics of the industrial revolution. At the macroeconomic level, the factors that define a capitalist system are above all economic, involving issues of production, markets, and industrial profits. They are also sociopolitical, involving the behavior of social classes and their interrelationships, the role of institutions, and the policies pursued by the state. Finally, they are ideological and cultural. Some factors serve to promote capitalist growth while others act as impediments that actually shape innovative paths of development. The pattern of regional development engendered by modern industrialization is uneven, clustered around certain centers of development, and bears little relation to the earlier geography of industry. Engaging these facts, the theory of protoindustrialization appears to provide a new explanation of the industrial revolution in developed countries, raising issues of continuity and geographic shifts.

The theory of protoindustrialization is concerned with protoindustrial regions that actually became industrial and those that seemed capable of being industrialized but somehow failed to make the transition, setting aside those regions that remained purely agricultural and those that were industrialized without passing through a protoindustrial phase. The model developed by Mendels considers protoindustrial regions that became industrial when he makes protoindustrialization a necessary, if not sufficient, precondition for the industrial revolution. Following the example of Flanders, many regions in northwestern Europe were able to industrialize during the 19th century because they already combined several favorable factors: (1) a group of merchants or traders had formed, who were accustomed to the economy of markets and profits through their experience in international trade; (2) significant merchant capital had accumulated and was available for investment in nascent industries; (3) an abundant and replenishable labor force, assured by accelerated population growth resulting from high fertility rates (linked to marriage at a relatively early age among protoindustrial families); (4) a supply of skilled workers, semiproletarian in status and already integrated into the market economy; and (5) an established, complementary capitalist agricultural sector that could provide food staples at low prices, thus permitting the payment of lower wages and/or an increase in the purchasing power of protoindustrial workers, stimulating demand for manufactured goods, and ultimately stimulating the modernization of industrial production. Successful modern industrialization thus involved a complex dynamic of demographic, economic, and commercial growth, depending on specific social relations.

This straightforward state of affairs obtained in certain regions, but the model does not apply universally. Many regions saw intensive protoindustrialization in the 18th century but became "deindustrialized" in the 19th century—notably the regional economies bordering France's Atlantic coast. It is often not possible to establish whether this failure to complete the transition was due to factors that are part of the model or extraneous to it. The scarcity of studies on protoindustrialization does not at present permit us to give a satisfactory evaluation of competing models. As a result, it is not yet possible to conclude that there was an evolutionary relationship between protoindustrialization and modern industrialization.

In any event, the protoindustrial system reached its limits in England during the last three decades of the 18th century, under the impact of the expansion of markets. The costs of dispersing production outweighed the benefits. Industrial growth was no longer the result solely of an extension of productive capacities within the framework of an expanded protoindustrialism. This is why modern industrialization first took hold in Great Britain, where the factors favorable to industrialization first converged.

The numerous manifestations of the industrial revolution have been abundantly described. They can be schematically reduced to a range of economic, technical, social, and political changes, linked to the appearance of modern industry within the framework of a new mode of production with specific characteristics. These included, at the socio-economic level, private ownership of the means of production and of goods produced, free enterprise, competition, markets, and profits; a new organization of labor, with a concentration of the workforce in factories run by entrepreneurs who owned the means of production; the subordination and dependence of wage laborers who had only their labor power to sell; mass production organized in assembly lines and aimed at a continuously growing market, permitting economies of scale; and an increase in productivity owing to technical progress and increased intensity of labor, which reduced production costs and lowered prices. On the technological level, this new mode of production was differentiated from the traditional craft industry by the substitution of machines for simple tools and human or animal energy, mainly with the appearance of steam engines, which became a factor in geographic and industrial concentration. Investment in fixed capital became essential, to the detriment of circulating capital.

In the realm of social relations, two new social classes made their appearance and became entrenched: the industrial bourgeoisie: owners of the industrial means of production, and wage laborers who offered their labor power. These two classes established relationships that liberal analysis regarded as harmonious, since everybody had an interest in entrepreneurial development, which was, therefore, regarded as a community of interest. In contrast, Marxist analysis saw the relations between classes as necessarily antagonistic and conflictual with respect to the sharing of added value, since the income of proprietors—their profits—was necessarily realized at the expense of the income of workers, in the form of their wages. On the political and ideological level, the control of the state by the industrial and financial bourgeoisie assured the passage of legislation favorable to this form of development that guaranteed private property and free enterprise and, as a consequence, the reproduction of the two classes.

It follows that the industrial revolution that began in England in the second half of the 18th century should not be confused with a simple technical revolution or with the appearance of machines. Born out of an economy and a society in transition that prepared its way, the industrial revolution opened a new era in the history of humanity, an era of true upheaval in the way people lived and thought, first in Europe and then throughout the world.

CLAUDE CAILLY

See also Agriculture; Capitalism; Cloth; Guild; Nobility, Commercial; Work

Further Reading

Cochet, François, and Gérard-Marie Henry, *Les révolutions industrielles: Processus historiques, développements économiques,* Paris: Colin, 1995

Kriedte, Peter, Hans Medick, and Jürgen Schlumbohm, *Industrialization before Industrialization: Rural Industry in the Genesis of Capitalism,* translated by Beate Schempp, Cambridge and New York: Cambridge University Press, 1981 (original German edition, 1977)

Mendels, F., "Des industries rurales à la proto-industrialisation: Historique d'un changement de perspective," *AESC* (1984)

Verley, Patrick, *La révolution industrielle,* Paris: Gallimard, 1997

Inequality. *See* Equality and Inequality

Infancy. *See* Children

Inspiration

In the 18th century the word "inspiration," with variations in meaning, was used in connection with the spiritual domain, the intellectual domain, and even the realm of everyday life. It was commonly thought that inspiration was instilled by God or by the spirit of creation. The anonymous entry "Inspiration" in the *Encyclopédie* (1765) deals mainly with the word in the theological sense, but the last four lines of the article refer to intellectual inspiration, specifically in the context of poetry: "In order to appear *inspired,* poets invoke Apollo and the Muses whenever they begin some great work." The entry contains a cross-reference to "Invocation," which in turn refers the reader to three additional entries: "Muses," "Épique" (Epic), and "Proposition." The author of the entry "Invocation," citing Father Le Bossu, author of a *Traité du poème épique* (1675; Treatise on the Epic Poem), explains that an invocation is "a prayer that a poet addresses, when beginning his work, to some god, and above all to his muse, seeking to be inspired by them."

Inspiration had long been linked to the realm of epic poetry, as may be seen in Raphael's sixteenth-century fresco *Parnassus* (in the Stanza della Segnatura [Signature Chamber] of the Vatican), and in Nicolas Poussin's *Parnasse* (Parnassus) and his two versions of *Inspiration du poète* (Inspiration of the Poet; one version is now housed in the Niedersächsisches Landesmuseum [State Museum of Lower Saxony] in Hanover, the other in the Louvre in Paris) from the 17th century. (Marc Fumaroli has shown that the latter two Poussin works are in fact also depictions of Parnassus [see Fumaroli]). In the 18th century Charles-Nicolas Cochin created a version of the same subject in his *Poète inspiré par Apollon et les Muses* (Poet Inspired by Apollo and the Muses), which was intended as a frontispiece for the *Oeuvres* (1743; Works) of the poet Jean-Baptiste Rous-

seau. Later, Anton Rafael Mengs brought Inspiration, the Muse, Apollo, and the crowned Poet together in his *Parnassus* (1761), which he painted on the ceiling of a room in the Villa Albani in Rome.

Understandably, allusions to an essential inspiration appear most often in connection with writing and the fine arts. In those areas the word "inspiration" combines several states of mind that are often unrelated but which are directly linked to creation. Inspiration might refer to the spirit that animates a creator, regardless of his medium, or to the intuition that impels the writer or artist in a specific and well-defined direction, or to an influence experienced consciously or unconsciously. Inspiration might come by chance, without appeal to any specific memories. Thus, in his *Jacques le fataliste* (1778; Jacques the Fatalist and His Master), Denis Diderot writes that Jacques "has few ideas in his head; if he happens to say something sensible, it comes from memory or from inspiration." This spontaneous aspect of inspiration can also be found in the writings of Voltaire, who comments in a letter to the playwright Chabanais: "You will work on your tragedy when your enthusiasm commands you; for you know that it is necessary to receive inspiration and never to seek it out."

Inspiration can also develop slowly over time. In his *Description de la statue equestre que la Compagnie des Indes orientales de Dannemarc a consacré à la gloire de Frederic V* (1771; Description of the Equestrian Statue That the Danish East India Company Has Dedicated to the Glory of Frederick V), the sculptor Jacques Saly explains the process by which he created this statue. Although he describes specific features peculiar to sculpture, Saly argues that artists in all genres can experience the same progressive inspiration that allows them to complete their works. Saly's testimony is especially important in that it is a rare account of an artist's working method. He writes:

> When an artist or a poet is engaged in producing an important work, his spirit is fired, his inspiration flares up, all the faculties of his soul are aroused, ideas present themselves in profusion and collide with one another, so to speak. These ideas are all pleasing to him and he wishes that he could carry all of them out; his difficulty is to fix his attention on one of them and to determine the best, and he can hardly fail to prefer the newest. However, the poetic fire begins to give way to the realization that it is necessary to harmonize the new and picturesque with great and noble simplicity, to combine the unity of the theme with all the parts that should form it, and to link these parts in such a manner that they are analogues of the whole and all work together toward its success, and, above all, that they are based on consistent reasoning that is apparent to all. At that point, the spell wears off; the difficulties become evident and these difficulties replace any supposed advantages inspiration might bring.

Thus, after the initial inspiration the artist must revert to the material aspect of his art and transform that often-disordered inspiration into art by means of refinement and reflection. Saly agrees here with Diderot, who writes in his *Salon de 1767* (1767 Exhibition) about le Prince's *Musicien champêtre* (Village Musician) as follows:

> What, therefore, is inspiration? The art of raising a section of a veil and displaying to human beings an unknown, or rather forgotten, corner of the world that they inhabit. He who is inspired is sometimes himself uncertain whether the thing that he heralds is a reality or a chimera, whether it ever existed outside himself. At that moment, he stands at the outermost limit of the energy of human nature and of the resources of art. But how can it be that the most common minds feel these impulses of genius, and suddenly conceive what I have so much trouble rendering? The man most subject to bursts of inspiration, if his mind were more composed, would not himself be able to conceive anything resembling what I write about his mind's labor and his soul's effort.

Inspiration is thus linked to the primary process of creation, to the artist's initial thought, and therefore to the sketch of the work to be completed. Diderot was undoubtedly correct when he wrote in his *Salon de 1765* (1765 Exhibition) about Jean-Baptiste Greuze's inspiration for his *Mère bien-aimée* (Beloved Mother):

> Sketches generally possess a fire that completed paintings lack: they reveal the moment of the artist's taking wing, pure inspiration, without any admixture of the polish that reflection applies to everything; the painter's soul flows freely over the canvas. The poet's quill and the skillful draftsman's pencil look as though they are running and playing. Rapid thought can characterize [the subject matter] in a single stroke.

Here the critic agrees with the artist. Inspiration is linked to invention and to imagination, as Diderot remarks in his *De la poésie dramatique* (1758; On Dramatic Poetry): "Imagination is the gift without which one is neither a poet, a philosopher, a man of wit, a reasonable being, nor a man." As a result, inspiration is linked to the most spontaneous form of art, drawing. For many theorists (such as Roger de Piles) and for writers, drawing was, in the words of Dezallier d'Argenville, "the first flame of the imagination." Claude-Henri Watelet, in his entry "Esquisse" (Sketch) in the *Encyclopédie*, writes that "thought rapidly traced" in order "to render an idea that offers itself to one's imagination" takes hold of whatever material one has at hand. Later, in his article on the same subject in the *Encyclopédie méthodique* (1788; Methodical Encyclopedia), Watelet adds that the artist's preference must be for the quickest and easiest method "since the mind always loses some of its fire because of the slowness of the means."

Images representing inspiration are relatively rare in the works of artists, as if the moment could not be captured and rendered in all its plenitude. Inspiration does not appear in Cesare Ripa's *Iconologia* (1593; Iconology), which nonetheless devotes an illustration to *furor poetico* (poetic frenzy). On the other hand, an image of inspiration is included in Jean Baudoin's French translation of Ripa's work (1644), this time personified by a young man. It is therefore quite exceptional that Jean-Honoré Fragonard should have painted in his series of fantasy portraits (now in the Louvre), a portrait of a young man, informally referred to as "The Writer," which some critics have seen as an allegory of inspiration. This work represents a man with a quill in his hand, seated before a register, his head thrown back, his eyes gazing into the beyond. This was the way in which artists would see the image of inspiration, by pulling the model's head, so to speak, toward an irrational world while the rest of the body remains located in the real world. Although Fragonard had painted first and foremost a portrait, an illustration of this phenomenon is clearly visible in the painting *Corinne* by François-Pascal-Simon Gérard (now in the Musée des Beaux-Arts [Museum of Fine Arts] in Lyon), which was inspired by a scene from Madame de Staël's novel *Corinne; ou, l'Italie* (1807; Corinne; or, Italy). The character Corinne receives heavenly inspiration at the Cape of Messina, and this inspiration "at that moment lights up Corinne's physiognomy." The baron Gérard depicts the precise moment when Corinne turns around and receives the stigmata of inspiration upon her face. In the absence of inspiration in the strict sense, artists relied on conscious or unconscious influences. In the case of Gérard's canvas, *Corinne; ou l'Italie,* the literary model, acts as a support for the work of art, but many others found their sources in older models, whether ancient Greek and Roman, Etruscan, or medieval.

MADELEINE PINAULT SØRENSEN

See also Enthusiasm; Idea; Imagination; Imitation; Originality

Further Reading

Fumaroli, Marc, *L'inspiration du poète de Poussin: Essai sur l'allégorie du Parnasse,* Paris: Éditions de la Réunion des Musées Nationaux, 1989

Heidsieck, François, *L'inspiration: Art et vie spirituelle,* Paris: Presses Universitaires de France, 1961

Loy, John R., "Reminiscence and Inspiration: Diderot and Rousseau," in *Essays on Diderot and the Enlightenment in Honour of Otis Fellows,* edited by John Pappas, Geneva: Droz, 1974

Instruction. *See* Education, Instruction, and Pedagogy; Technical Instruction

Instruments. *See* Music: Musical Instruments; Observatories and Observation Instruments; Science: Collections; Weights and Measures

Intendancy System

The kingdoms and colonies of France and Spain and the duchy of Savoy were, at various periods in time, placed under the intendancy system, whose primary purpose was uniformly to strengthen the authority of the central government. Although the specifics of the French model were copied by some other states, the idea was espoused throughout Europe, and rough versions of the system had already appeared as early as the 16th century.

Chronology

Developed in the 16th century from the inspection tours made by royal counselors, then later by special commissioners from the Conseil du Roi (Royal Council), French intendancies took root beginning at the time of Louis XIV's personal rule. Between 1660 and 1789, the number of regions using the intendancy system rose from 23 to 32. In the colonies, intendancies were created in America during Louis XIV's reign, on l'île Bourbon (known today as Réunion) in 1766, in Pondicherry (India) in 1778, and in Saint-Louis (Senegal) in 1785. In Piedmont-Sardinia, the first "intendants for legal and administrative matters" were posted in selected locations beginning in 1679. By 1696 at the latest, intendants were firmly entrenched in Piedmont and its neighboring territories; they were equally well established in Savoy by 1717. The royal ordinances of 1723, 1729, and 1770, and the directives of 1775, gradually defined the role of the intendants and their sphere of authority.

Appointed in 1691, Spain's 21 *superintendentes de rentes reales* (superintendents of royal revenues), had prescribed districts and defined fiscal, financial, and economic authority and were the direct ancestors of the Spanish intendants of the 18th century. In 1703 Philip V decided to appoint intendants whose powers were largely inspired by those of their French counterparts: the "intendants of the army and finances" were present in every Spanish province by 1711. By 1715 only seven intendancies with a military mandate still remained. Three years later, the number of intendants rose again to 21. In 1724 the whole system was dismantled, but in 1749 the system of intendants was reinstated, to be organized meticulously in 1750 and then weakened in 1766 by the intendants' loss of the function of *corregidores* (magistrates) of the provincial capitals. The reorganized intendancy system was gradually transported to America via Cuba beginning in 1764 and to the Philippines in 1784. On the eve of the Napoleonic crisis, Spain had 26 intendancies, Spanish America had five *superintendencias* (superintendancies) and about 40 intendancies, while the Philippines had one intendancy.

Organizational Flaws

The setting of the boundaries of the intendancies followed no territorial logic: the provincial boundaries were used in Spain and Piedmont; the *généralités* or old tax districts became intendancies in France; and in the colonies, the extant administrative networks created boundaries. Except perhaps in Piedmont, no attention was paid to creating a demographic balance among the intendancies. The same conditions prevailed for the subdelegations and the *partidos,* as Spanish subdelegations were called. Everywhere, there were central bureaus run by skeleton staffs that were organized on a purely pragmatic basis. Further, remuneration was fixed and never sufficient (30,000–80,000 *reales* in Spain and 70,000–100,000 *reales* in its empire; between 5,000 and 25,000 livres in France; between 1,800 and 4,000 livres in Piedmont).

Despite appearances, the career structure was ill defined; in France there was no apparent career ladder

or hierarchy; in Piedmont each of the three ranks was divided into two classes, and in Spain each of the three ranks was divided into four classes. But, except perhaps in Piedmont, no specific professional qualifications were defined. The reason for this sketchiness was undoubtedly the advanced age of entrants into the service (about 35 years old in France, about 42 in Piedmont, over 50 in Spain), which presupposed the entrants' previous tenure in other offices (acting as royal counsel in France or exercising various official duties in Spain and Piedmont). In practice, the length of service in a post varied a great deal: six years in the French West Indies; five to seven years in Piedmont; and three to ten years in Spain, according to one's grade. In addition, the methods of subdelegation had weaknesses: appointments were made by the king in Spain, but by the intendant himself in France and Piedmont; qualifications were ill-defined and appointments were unpaid in France.

A Closed Society

For the most part, French intendants were recruited from the ranks of the upper magistracy (from among the royal counsels, royal law courts, and the nobility— often of ancient lineage—and from the ranks of the wealthy), who were united by ties of marriage, legal training, and a common cultural background. In the Piedmontese system, 42 percent of the appointees were nobles and 53 percent were legal experts. In Spain two-thirds were nobles or members of a religious order (on entry). The rarity of administrative dynasties and the great number of brief transits through the intendancy posts created, however, a certain mobility.

Gauging Administrative Efficiency

For many years now, historians of administration have limited the focus of their interest to the social aspects of the intendancy system, examining nothing other than spheres of activity. In the United States, meanwhile, scholars have tended toward the global study of the impact of state initiatives. Making allowances for subtle differences at the local level, it can be said that in all cases, the intendants' responsibilities were fiscal (taxation, litigation), legal (supervision of the law courts, dispensation of justice), military (administration), economic (reports, construction projects, incentives), administrative (financial and even political supervision of a community), and social (health, poverty, etc.), with an overall tendency to focus primarily on economic and social matters. It is impossible to present an accurate evaluation of the intendancies, even for Piedmont-Sardinia, where the intendancies seem to have exerted an especially forceful authority over the communities.

The intendants encountered many institutional or practical obstacles: such factors as their status as untenured commissioners, the provincial Estates, the law courts, towns, governors, viceroys, colonists, popular mistrust of the central government, the slowness of communications, the local recruitment of subdelegates, the lack of financial means, privileges, *fueros* (codes of laws) curbed their activities in many ways. Intendants were first and foremost information officers, executives (often disdainful of local authorities), serious and conscientious administrators. Yet whenever one tries to define their exact role—for instance with regard to economics or town planning—the intendants disappear behind a haze of powers and initiatives either imposed on the local level or emanating from the capital.

What of the perhaps mythical figure of the "enlightened" intendant? Everywhere, and especially after 1750, one can cite intendants who were open to new ideas, leaders of cultural life, fully committed to a paternalistic vision of the exercise of power, philanthropic, and even reformers. In France such figures as Montyon, Sénac, Cordier de Launay, Caze de la Bove, Bertrand de Molleville, Caumartin de Saint Ange, and many others exemplified this progressivist model. Above and beyond the wish of such men to alleviate the sufferings of the population in times of crisis (which was not simply a "philosophical" attitude), their economic activities must be studied closely. All things considered, what did men such as Anne-Robert-Jacques Turgot or d'Étigny seek to accomplish, if not to improve the material and legal environment of productivity and trade, thus favoring individual efforts? Some intendants, such as Tourny, d'Étigny, or the Spanish American intendants managed to ally themselves with intermittent but important operations. However, when scrutinized more closely, those operations reveal an extraordinary tangle of contributions and decisions that impede identification of exactly what devolved upon the king's representatives.

What would the institution's future have been if the French Revolution had not occurred? In France, just as in Spanish America or the French West Indies, the intendancy system was marked by a certain stagnation, even regression. From another angle, the system's networks served the social body quite well, opening up many possibilities. For that reason, in Spain and in Piedmont-Sardinia the intendancy system survived the Napoleonic period, and its spirit was later reborn in the French system of prefectures.

FRANÇOIS-XAVIER EMMANUELLI

See also Bureaucracy; Colonialism

Further Reading

Emmanuelli, François-Xavier, *Un mythe de l'absolutisme bourbonien: L'intendance du milieu du XVIIe siècle à la fin du XVIIIe siècle: France, Espagne, Amérique,* Aix-en-Provence: Publications de l'Université de Provence, 1981

Fisher, Lillian Estelle, *The Intendant System in Spanish America,* Berkeley: University of California Press, 1929; reprint, New York: Gordian Press, 1969

Gruder, Vivian R., *The Royal Provincial Intendants: A Governing Elite in Eighteenth-Century France,* Ithaca, New York: Cornell University Press, 1968

Morazzani de Pérez Encios, Gisela, *La intendencia en España y en América,* Caracas: Impr. Universitaria, 1966

Interest

An Impure Notion (Religion and Morality)

Originally, "interest" was a term in jurisprudence. It was associated with the Roman legal expression *id quod interest;* thus, as early as the 13th century, "interest," in French, implied *dommages et intérêts* (damages and interests)—that is, an amount owed as compensation for an unsettled debt or for damage caused. As early as the 15th century, interest also euphemistically referred to the sum debtors paid to creditors for the use of their money. This term gradually replaced the term "usury," which in the 16th century acquired the negative meaning of an excessively high rate of interest. The Judeo-Christian tradition had a particularly ambiguous stance with regard to the question of interest-bearing loans. Mosaic law forbade this practice among Jews but allowed it in trade with Gentiles. This double standard gave rise to innumerable interpretations, the technical details of which are often noted in Enlightenment encyclopedias. In general, however, the Catholic Church consistently condemned interest-bearing loans, while the Reformation saw money as indirectly productive property and deemed that the borrower had to pay for its usage in the form of interest to the creditor. In this regard, Jean Calvin's *Lettre sur l'usure* (1545; Letter on Usury) marked a milestone. Nonetheless, the question of which path to choose remained a matter of conscience, especially since the Scriptures state that one should lend without expecting something in return (Luke, VI:35). Consequently, the interest-bearing loan, no matter how favorable it may have been to trade, was still considered morally impure.

In the 17th century, this impurity also tainted the term "interest" as it was understood in the moral sense—that is, as a binding attachment to a thing or person, as already found in the work of Pierre Corneille. Thus, the definition of the word *intérêt* in Volume VIII of the *Encyclopédie* (1765) asserts from the outset that, "taken in an absolute sense," this word "denotes the vice that causes us to seek our own advantage regardless of justice and virtue." Meanwhile, according to Volume 5 of the *Dictionnaire de Trévoux* (Dictionary of Trévoux), *intérêt personnel* (personal interest) "means what is important to or suits . . . the person . . . disregarding what suits others."

This very negative meaning, which suggests all the deplorable aspects of egotism, comes from Spanish mysticism, in which Saint Ignatius of Loyola, Saint Teresa of Avila, and Saint John of the Cross interpret the term "interest" to mean reprehensible egocentrism. The contrast between pure love inspired by an imitation of Christ and self-interested love, the impurity of which must be unmasked, spread from Spanish mysticism to French spiritual literature and broadly shaped the suspicious stance of 17th-century moralists. Because the notion of self-love was more central to this debate than was the notion of interest, the *Encyclopédie* criticizes Nicole, Blaise Pascal, and especially the duc de La Rochefoucauld for "wanting to make of self-love a constantly corrupting principle," whereas it is a virtuous principle, "which is the eternal motive of our soul." Although this article denounces the incorrect usage of the word "interest" to mean a just and virtuous self-love, that usage can already be found in La Rochefoucauld's *Réflexions, ou sentences et maximes morales* (1664; Reflections; or, Moral Sayings and Maxims): "Interest, on which we blame all our crimes, often deserves to be praised for our good deeds."

When thinkers shifted from examining individual consciousness to focusing on social considerations, the idea of interest was reevaluated. In his *De l'esprit* (1758; Essays on the Mind and Its Several Faculties), Claude-Adrien Helvétius made the first systematic proposal of a notion of interest untainted by any moral impurity, from a political and not theological perspective:

> Common thinking generally restricts the meaning of this word "interest" to the love of money alone; the enlightened reader will feel that I am taking this word in a broader sense, and applying it generally to whatever might procure our pleasure, or enable us to avoid pain.

In the second discourse of *De l'esprit*, entitled "De l'esprit par rapport à la société" (On the Mind in Relation to Society), he shows how, "both in matters of morality and in matters of the mind, it is interest that dictates all our judgments." However, in 1759 the Parlement of Paris condemned *De l'esprit*. This unfortunate event helps to explain Denis Diderot's prudent tone in the article "Intérêt" in the *Encyclopédie*. Diderot explicitly laments the impurity of the word itself, the very sounds of which recall "ideas of avarice and baseness," for, in his opinion, "interest" is used instead of *amour-propre* (self-love), which was Helvétius's main point.

In England, at the beginning of the 18th century, a more positive evaluation of self-love and self-interest was offered by defenders of the ethical theory of the "moral sense." For the earl of Shaftesbury, whose *An Inquiry concerning Virtue, in Two Discourses* (1699) Diderot translated in 1745, this moral sense inherent in human nature allows a person to distinguish between good and evil as spontaneously as he distinguishes between beauty and ugliness. Hence, the individual strives toward moral beauty and, through his kindness, can encourage the well-being of all. Although Diderot rejected such unselfishness out of principle, he still defended a teleological ethic, the goal of which is the individual happiness that is necessarily connected to the happiness of all—whence his utilitarian vision of self-interest.

In his *An Inquiry into the Origin of Our Ideas of Beauty and Virtue* (1725) Francis Hutcheson the Elder systematizes Shaftesbury's theses by supposing that there are internal senses, such as a sense of beauty and, of course, a sense of morality. Although the notion of interest is not well defined in Hutcheson's work, one sees how the term "self-love" shifts toward "interest," sometimes replacing it in the third edition of the book. In the realm of ethics, Hutcheson generally asserts that the notion of self-love or interest is neutral, and he even recognizes that self-love is as indispensable to general well-being as is kindness; yet in the realm of aesthetics he opens the way for Immanuel Kant's conception of disinterested pleasure that determines the judgment of taste (*Kritik der Urteilskraft* [1790; Critique of Judgment]) by eliminating the sense of the beautiful from all interested motivation.

Interest as Stimulation (Fine Arts)

The extreme contrast in the value judgments attaching to the notion of interest is particularly palpable when one observes the meanings connected to the adjectives related to it. Although the word *intéressé* (interested) was decidedly pejorative as soon as it emerged in the 17th century, the word *intéressant* (interesting), which was accepted by the Académie Française in 1718, was, on the contrary, quite positive, since it meant "what offers interest" or is "worthy of attention." In 1765, this adjective also denoted an active principle relative to "awakened feelings" and "excited passions" (*Encyclopédie*). All of these meanings stemmed from the first sense of the Latin verb *interesse* (to interest), that is, to "take part in." In discourse on the arts, the words *intéresser* (to interest) and *intéressant* therefore indicated the intellectual and emotional participation of the spectator in the spectacle offered to him. According to the abbé Dubos, in his *Réflexions critiques sur la poésie et sur la peinture* (1719; Critical Reflections on Poetry and Painting), "a subject can be interesting in two ways. First, it is interesting in itself, and because its circumstances are such that they must affect people in general. Second, it is interesting with respect to certain people only." In other words, it piques their curiosity. For Diderot, the emotional element, which all individuals share, becomes of primary importance. In his writings, *intéresser* and *émouvoir* (to move) are synonymous. Thus, in *De la poésie dramatique* (1758; On Dramatic Art) Diderot states that "the historian wrote what happened, purely and simply . . . that which neither moves nor interests one as much as it is possible to move and to interest."

It is especially with regard to the theatre that the spectator's emotional motivation plays a major role in the concept of interest. The most powerful means ignite the passions both in tragedy and in comedy. "Fate and wickedness, these . . . are the foundations of dramatic interest." In the serious genre that Diderot invents in order to include the power of noble sentiments, the interest kindled should not be weakened by being distributed over several objects; hence one needed to respect the "unity of interest." As early as 1750 Gotthold Ephraim Lessing had already focused on this idea of unity of interest, which had first been proposed by Antoine Houdar de La Motte in his *Premier discours sur la tragédie, à l'occasion des "Machabées"* (1722; First Discourse on Tragedy, on the Occasion of the Performance of "Les Machabées"): "It is the unity of interest that is the true source of continuous emotion." Lessing refers in German to *Einheit des Anteils* (unity of

interest) in his critique of Plautus's play *Captivi* (The Captives) in the *Beyträge zur Geschichte und Aufnahme des Theaters* (1750; Contributions to the History and Reception of the Theater). However, it was not until 1767, after he had translated Diderot's work, that Lessing introduced the word *interessant* (interesting) into German in order to designate that which is appealing or captivating (*Hamburgische Dramaturgie* [1767–69; Hamburg Dramaturgy]). Like Diderot, Lessing wanted the characters of bourgeois drama to be interesting, attractive, and close enough to the audience so that, in identifying with the characters' noble feelings, the spectator would also become ennobled.

After the French word *interessant* had been adopted into German, a debate ensued in Germany on the aesthetic notion of *das Interessante* or *das Interessierende* (the interesting). In his *Allgemeine Theorie der schönen Künste* (1771–74; General Theory of Fine Arts), Johann Georg Sulzer defines the concept as "the opposite of indifference, and all that awakens our attention, piques our curiosity . . . affects us . . . [and] holds our minds in a state of suspense and expectation." All of the inner faculties of the human being have to be stimulated by art, for, according to Sulzer, the active use of these faculties is what is best in mankind. For Christian Garbe, who published his thoughts on *das Interessierende* in the periodical *Neue Bibliothek der schönen Wissenschaften und der freyen Künste* (1765–1806), it is *die Unruhe* (unease) that guarantees that a work of art will be effective; for being one of the soul's essential activities, it spreads easily and triggers a precious ethical distinction. However, no matter what name is given to inner activity, "it is no different from what the philosophers have named self-love or interest, and to which they have attributed the primary motive behind our behavior." Hence, the artist's obligation is to excite the forces of the soul by representing interesting subjects, and to direct those forces toward justice and virtue.

The success of the words "interest" and "interesting" in Enlightenment aesthetics was connected to the growing importance granted to the subjective reception of works. A relativization of the notion of beauty then followed. For Jean-François Marmontel, "poetic beauty is nothing but interest," and "the interest that is the most vivid, the most captivating, the strongest, is that of dramatic action" ("Intérêt" [Interest], in the *Supplément* of the *Encyclopédie*). By depicting gripping scenes of truth, goodness, and beauty, drama as influenced by Diderot aimed to reform both theatre and society. Yet the emphasis was placed on individual psychology within the context of the bourgeois family, which was seen as representing universal human values. This moral objective became political in the dramatic work of Louis-Sébastien Mercier in 1773. In his *Du théâtre* (1773; On Theater), although rejecting all rules, Mercier nevertheless recommends unity of interest since "it is this that draws in the spectator, that captures his entire soul, and, not allowing for any distraction, focuses all his ideas onto a single point." Instead of igniting individual emotion, interest acts here to mobilize the people by instilling such patriotic sentiments as love of freedom and hatred of tyranny. Like Helvétius, Mercier asserts that the theatre is only truly successful in republican states in which all citizens are united by a common interest, that is, affairs of state. In his opinion, the theatre hall should foreshadow the public sphere where all people gather to discuss their "true interests" and, in disregarding their personal interests, become just, against themselves, in the name of the greater good (*Du théâtre*).

An Operational Term (Politics and Economics)

The sovereign entity, whether the prince in a monarchy or the people of a republican state, must submit to interest, the goal of which is the prosperity or at least the conservation of the state itself. In 1639, the duc de Rohan expounded this political meaning of the notion of interest in *De l'interest des princes et estats de la Chrestienté* (On the Interest of Christian Princes and States). The idea conveyed by the Italian expression *interesse dello stato* (interest of state) was developed during the Italian Renaissance, at the same time as the expression *raison d'état* (reason of state) emerged in France. Consequently, political action was separated from preestablished religious or moral principles. For political action to be carried out properly, all interests involved had to be distinguished, and therefore it had to be accepted that each individual had the right to preserve his or her own interests. Such reciprocity was sufficient to found a politics of interests without having to resort to other forms of legitimizing power. In fact, legitimization in the 18th century was nothing more than the "rights of propriety" subordinated to the calculation of interests. In a political testament dated 1768, Frederick II, king of Prussia, bluntly asserts that the interests of the state must be followed blindly.

The likely conflict between private interest and public interest provoked various thoughts concerning the organization and the prosperity of nations. According to Jean-Jacques Rousseau, society corrupts human nature to such an extent that man is incapable of knowing his true interests. Man constantly compares himself to others and pursues apparent interests to gain respect of others. Therefore, man must learn "to prefer his natural interest to his apparent interest" so as ultimately to become "the most solid support of a well-ordered society" (*Du contrat social* [1762; The Social Contract]). This is why Rousseau's vision includes a legislator who will intervene, "to find the best societal rules suitable to the Nations" (*Du contrat social*). Conversely, the baron d'Holbach minimizes the conflict of interests by extolling virtue. Holbach defines interest as "the object with which each man, according to his temperament and his own ideas, associates his well-being" (*Système de la nature, ou Des lois du monde physique et du monde moral* [1770; The System of Nature; or, The Laws of the Moral and Physical World]). In pursuing one's interest, therefore, one is working toward one's happiness, but one is virtuous only when one establishes individual "interest in accordance with the interest of others." This social mediation of interest is necessary to maintain political society. Because members of a nation are bound to each other through their desires and pleasures, it is, according to Holbach, entirely to their advantage to strive toward their happiness without harming one another.

Whereas for Rousseau the desire to obtain the respect of others is alienating, for Holbach, conversely, it encourages virtue. For Adam Smith, this desire ultimately motivates man to improve his economic condition. It keeps human industry running, and, by improving their own fortunes, individuals also unwittingly advance the interests of society (*The Theory of Moral Sentiments* [1759]). Smith studies the economic aspect of the progress of societies and shows how the distribution of power in a given society depends on the way in which its members satisfy their material needs. In order to analyze the interdependence of economic phenomena, he proposes a purely operational notion of personal interest that functions as a working hypothesis. In the context of the contractual exchanges that characterize trade between people—such as barter or any other system of exchange—he starts simply from the principle that everyone seeks their own advantage and takes care of their own interests. To obtain what he wishes, a person does not first appeal to the goodwill of his contemporaries but to their self-love: "It is not from the benevolence of the butcher, the brewer, or the baker, that we expect our dinner, but from their regard to their own interests" (*An Inquiry into the Nature and Causes of the Wealth of Nations* [1776]).

As its etymology indicates—*inter esse* (to be in between)—the notion of interest stands between the well-established places of thought, between good and evil, subject and object, theory and practice, especially for Kant. Since it emerged during the Enlightenment, the term, varied and changing, has permeated a number of specific fields and remains available for use in still other new contexts.

MONIQUE MOSER-VERREY

See also Aesthetics; Happiness; Trade; Utility; Virtue

Further Reading

Habermas, Jürgen, *Knowledge and Human Interests,* translated by Jeremy J. Shapiro, Boston: Beacon, 1971; London: Heinemann Educational, 1972 (original German edition, 1968)

Moser-Verrey, Monique, "L'émergence de la notion d'intérêt dans l'esthétique des Lumières," *L'homme et la nature: Actes de la Société canadienne d'étude du dix-huitième siècle* 6 (1987)

Irony

Irony is a notion that belongs simultaneously to several fields: in rhetoric, as an antiphrastic structure of discourse; in ethics and psychology, as a posture and a moral attitude; in philosophy, as an overall vision of the world and a metaphysical principle; and, finally, in literature, aesthetics, and semantics, as a breaking of illusion. Since the time when Plato and Socrates employed *eironeia* (asking questions while feigning ignorance), irony has taken on many shapes up to modern forms that approach the absurd. Enlightenment irony represents a significant stage in the notion's history. Although it was heir to the Platonic tradition and to classical rhetoric, particularly in the works of the German romantics, 18th-century irony became an expression of one form of "modernity."

Ironic Style

In traditional rhetoric irony was first defined as a style, notably by Cicero and Quintilian. For these orators it meant the general intention to reveal a truth hidden by an obvious falsehood—a falsehood that was presented as such. Irony was therefore an oblique mode of discourse, based on stylistic figures such as the innuendo and the antiphrasis, which tend to make the hearer understand the opposite of what is said. When Voltaire, in the entry "Guerre" (War) in his *Dictionnaire philosophique* (1764; Philosophical Dictionary), evokes this scourge thus— "An undoubtedly very fine art is war that leaves the land desolate, destroys the houses, and makes 40,000 out of 100,000 men perish in an average year"—the antiphrasis in the expression "a very fine art" is clearly ironic. The style involves extreme agility and a very precise manipulation of frivolity, which allows its user to play on all the meanings of the words. Irony, which depends on construction and nuance, is the very opposite of spontaneity.

This intellectual composition is the most important factor distinguishing irony from other forms of humor. Indeed, the word "humor" (which seems to have an English origin) appears for the first time in any reference work in the first edition of the *Encyclopaedia Britannica* (1771). Humor is above all a defensive outburst against attacks from the outside world and is simply intended to mark the victory of the pleasure principle over the reality principle—as, for example, in the works of Henry Fielding (1707–54) or, somewhat later, in those of William Makepeace Thackeray (1811–63). In contrast to irony, humor is instinctive. It reaches its zenith in black humor, a form that expresses total pessimism allied to a feeling of superiority that is no less absolute. The critical distance that characterizes irony is not always underpinned by such a degree of self-confidence.

The ironic style is principally concerned with creating a discrepancy within the statement, either by means of overstatement (hyperbole) or by means of understatement (litotes). One can therefore always adopt two different readings of what is stated ironically. On one level, the statement can be identified as a serious but clumsy or faulty utterance; on another level, the ironic statement can be identified as a parody of this serious statement. The ironic style is thus an excellent method for outmaneuvering the upholders of social norms, such as censors, standards and since a naive first reading does not uncover any reprehensible idea. Accordingly, for the 18th-century Enlightenment *philosophes,* the Encyclopedists in particular, irony was a verbal weapon of choice, ranging from simple ridicule to sarcasm, and it was often deployed in the service of satire. Through its skillful manipulation of opposites, falsehoods, and mystification, irony used in traditional rhetoric already indicated the expression of an imbalance between intent and statement.

The Reign of the Equivocal

In fact, if one adopts the classical rhetoricians' approach and assumes that irony tells an obvious lie in order to permit a hidden truth to be understood, one misses irony's most subversive aspect. Everything is rendered ambiguous; every value is called into question. It would be wrong to infer that there is a "true" but hidden meaning when the whole point lies precisely in the equivocal meaning of the statement. The polemical writers of the 18th century were well aware of the explosive potential of irony, and they used it to undermine the very foundations of society. Thus, Johann Wolfgang von Goethe could make this observation about Georg Christoph Lichtenberg's aphorisms: "Wherever Lichtenberg uses a witticism, a problem is concealed." In a sense, the ironist uses deceitful forms of discourse that exist solely to be unmasked. Hence, during the age of the Enlightenment irony was closely linked with militant philosophical writings, although their authors sometimes resorted to techniques inherited from Blaise Pascal and his art of persuasion. In this respect, Pascal's *Les provinciales* (1657; The Provincials) remained a model of polemical unveiling of moral hypocrisies. Voltaire follows that model in his *Lettres philosophiques* (1734; Philosophical Letters), dedicated to the Quakers. The ironist wants to open his reader's eyes and to promote the philosophy of the Enlightenment. Even where Voltaire expresses, in the manner of Socrates, an absolute defiance of the guardians of knowledge—as in the title of his little work, *Le philosophe ignorant* (1766; The Ignorant Philosopher)—he often has pedagogical aims and seeks to stimulate the reader to think again. He wants to encourage the reader to think for himself.

Irony's important role as a philosophical weapon in the 18th century was made possible by the cultural context of the period: society was gradually freeing itself from the clutches of religion, and art and literature were acquiring a certain autonomy with regard to the moral authorities. Indeed, the influence of sensationalist theories, which recognized the primacy of feeling and the inestimable value of the ephemeral moment, was making itself felt through a subversion of values that had previously been assumed to be universal. The philosophy of the self espoused by Johann Gottlieb Fichte, which might be interpreted as a radical relativization of the real for the sake of the mind, was just one among the theoretical bases for this detached attitude. Acknowledgement of the relativity of points of view triumphed on every level. The realms in which irony could be applied were thus greatly extended, and irony played out its destructive role in full. In Montesquieu's *Lettres persanes* (1721; Persian Letters), his fictional Persians, Usbeck and Rica, introduce a detached and ironic view of the institutions of France under the ancien régime and thus articulate an essential critique of the very foundations of the social order. These fictional Persians are not content to question the details of certain blatant injustices but express a truly global critique. Here, irony

aims to destroy and unmask, but without confiding its own views or offering any concrete suggestions for reconstructing what it attacks. All the anarchic power of irony is sometimes concentrated in the form of a paradox that challenges "common sense," prejudices, and received wisdom, rejects the principle of authority, and demands the free exercise of each person's judgment.

It should be noted that irony was not used solely to attack political and social values. The libertines were happy to demythologize love itself. When Choderlos de Laclos adopts a phrase from Jean-Jacques Rousseau as an epigraph for *Les liaisons dangereuses* (1782; Dangerous Liaisons), or presents a distorted imitation of certain episodes from *La nouvelle Héloïse* (1762; Julie; or, The New Héloïse), such as the crossing of the brook, he shakes the foundations of amorous relationships in his own completely ironic style.

Irony in 18th-Century Literature

In the literature of the European Enlightenment, several forms lent themselves naturally to the use of irony. Let us draw up an inventory of them.

First of all, there was the novel of apprenticeship, or bildungsroman, the narrative of the destiny of a young and naive hero who learns by questioning wherever he goes the norms and codes of the society in which he moves. His innocence gives rise to an ironic view of society. Voltaire's two novels *L'ingénu* (1767; The Pupil of Nature) and *Candide* (1959) turn this type of irony into a veritable act of social and political criticism. Christoph Martin Wieland includes numerous satiric passages in his novel *Agathon* (1766; The History of Agathon), notably in the form of portraits. Goethe's Wilhelm Meister also exploits this vein of irony.

We have already mentioned the exotic and Orientalist trend typified by the *Lettres persanes,* which was merely the best known among a long series of disguised fictional accounts that were published in great numbers during the 18th century. It was certainly less dangerous to write about the Great Moghul or muftis than to mention the king of France or Catholic priests. The choice of a foreign setting proved to be an excellent means of revealing the absurdity of norms and conventions.

Instead of immersing themselves in a fantasized Orient or transporting their readers into the American forests, authors could also choose to create a completely imaginary country within a utopian narrative. The relativity of civilized European societies is clearly shown by the imaginary voyages into topsy-turvy worlds whose values are not the same as ours. *Gulliver's Travels* by Jonathan Swift was published in 1726 and enjoyed an immense success. Between the land of the giants and the country of the Lilliputians, man's place in the scheme of things becomes difficult to determine. Nicolas-Anne-

Edmé Rétif de La Bretonne, in his *La découverte australe* (1781; The Southern Discovery), invents a fantastic world peopled by hybrid races of lion men and snake men. He thus invites his readers to cast an ironic eye on the laws that govern our society and encourages them to imagine a truly utopian realm.

The crisis of traditional values also becomes clearly apparent in the picaresque novel, where the accidents, encounters, coincidences, and ironies of life have a special place. The picaresque genre began in Spain with Miguel de Cervantes and had its golden age in the 17th century, but it resonated throughout 18th-century European literature, especially because it expressed a fascination with confidence tricks and theatricality that was widespread at that time. One can cite, in no particular order, Alain-René Lesage's *Histoire de Gil Blas de Santillane* (1715–35; The History and Adventures of Gil Blas of Santillane), Denis Diderot's *Jacques le fataliste* (1778; Jacques the Fatalist and His Master), Hans Jakob Christoffel von Grimmelshausen's *Der abentheurliche Simplicissimus Teutsch* (1668; Simplicius Simplicissimus), and Daniel Defoe's *Moll Flanders* (1722). Each of these works displays the same ironic detachment in the face of destiny or Providence.

Finally, it should be added that Enlightenment irony worked hand in glove with the development of the genre of the novel itself. Indeed, the detached point of view of the novelistic narrator—his view, as it were from the outside, of the fates of his characters—generated an ironic style quite naturally. In the early years of the 20th century Georg Lukács, a Hungarian critic who wrote in German, made an ironic style into one of the main forms of the genre in *Die Theorie des Romans* (1920; Theory of the Novel). Irony could not be expressed so easily in the theatre, but it burst out there in the speeches of theatrical heroes in three different ways: (1) in defensive postures, when the hero utters words with double meanings that he himself does not perceive as such; (2) in a more hidden way, in the detached moral posture that the hero adopts—for example, in the theatrical works of Friedrich von Schiller (1759–1805); and (3) in an irony inherent in the dramatic situation, in what could be called the "irony of fate."

Whatever literary form is used, irony requires the readers' participation. Irony always corresponds to the element of surprise and comes into being only when the reader perceives it. An ironic book is a book that in some sense makes the reader its coauthor—a book of the type that Voltaire liked to write when he wanted "to let the reader work out the consequences for himself." The ironist relies on the reader's intelligence, critical spirit, and powers of interpretation. Parody in particular presents a very conspicuously encoded message. The ironic process, which is nothing if not active,

implies three actors: the object on which irony is being exercised; the author (or other subjectivity) who provides the ironic perception of that object; and the receptive reader or audience member who decodes the irony and reconstructs the intended meaning of the discourse by rejecting its apparent meaning. The 18th-century novel is a favored place for the use of ironic distance: the novelist sets up the conventions of the genre and reaches agreement with readers based on a realistic illusion. At the same time the novelist takes the readers aside, making them perceive the very mechanisms that activate the characters, thus clearly revealing his own authorial omnipotence. Diderot is an expert in this art of unveiling, this exercise in the deliberate undermining of illusions.

The German Romantics

In the second half of the 18th century the German romantics gave irony a wholly different status, far removed from rhetoric and social criticism, by taking it into the realm of philosophy. In fact, they revived a perception of fate that the ancient Greeks had already expressed in their tragedies: the irony of fate, dramatic irony, and tragic irony. In the works of the German romantics two types of irony can be distinguished on the literary plane: objective, or situational, irony, which can be traced in the fate of a character, and subjective irony. The latter is more radical and is expressed through the self-destructive tendencies of the subject, who is aware of the blind alley in which he finds himself and of the constant imbalance between the principle of reality and his thirst for an ideal. The poetry of Heinrich Heine (1797–1856) is profoundly marked by subjective irony. The dramas of Ludwig Tieck (1773–1853) even introduce onto the stage a fictitious audience that comments ironically on the situations that are presented. It was also through irony that German romanticism found its way to the grotesque and the marvelous, as in *Prinzessin Brambilla* (1821; Princess Brambilla), one of the tales of E.T.A. Hoffmann.

However, the German romantics went even further by elevating irony to a metaphysical principle, a way of thinking, a literary criterion and sign of recognition. Jean Paul Richter, known as Jean Paul, dedicates more than one chapter of his *Vorschule zur Ästhetik* (1804; School for Aesthetics) to the subject. The Schlegel brothers, August Wilhelm and, especially, Friedrich, were theorists and spokesmen for this literary irony. Friedrich Schlegel offers a number of inspired—even ironic—definitions of irony, such as: "Irony is really no laughing matter" (*Athenäum*); "Irony is the clear awareness of the eternal agility of abundant chaos" (*Ideen*, number 69); and (from the *Athenäum* fragments):

At its most fundamental, irony is the mood that soars over everything, that rises infinitely far above everything conditioned, above even art, virtue, and the genius of the artist; as for its form and its creation, it is the style of mimicry of an ordinary good Italian clown.

This conception of irony is thus allied to transcendental and idealist philosophy. Reality and the ideal never coincide and are even linked by an atrociously painful and irreducible conflict between two poles. Romantic and tragic irony arise from this conflict between aspiration to the ideal and the inadequacy of the real. Irony expresses endless negativity; but it is also synonymous with lucidity, which is why the romantics made irony into the supreme literary criterion and point of reference. Irony became one of the components of "modernity" in the romantics' understanding of that term, and in the one that the 19th-century poet Charles Baudelaire would later give it in France.

NICOLE MASSON

See also Parody; Persiflage; Portraiture

Further Reading
Behler, Ernst, *Irony and the Discourse of Modernity*, Seattle: University of Washington Press, 1990 (original German edition, 1997)
Knox, Norman D., *The Word Irony and Its Context: 1500–1755*, Durham, North Carolina: Duke University Press, 1961
Yaari, Monique, *Ironie paradoxale et ironie poétique: Vers une théórie de l'ironie moderne sur les traces de Gide dans Paludes*, Birmingham, Alabama: Summa, 1988

Islam

During the Enlightenment in Europe, "Islam" meant above all the Ottoman empire, which dominated the Mediterranean and Arab worlds; in 1683 this vast empire had even extended to the gates of Vienna. Although travelers such as François Bernier had ventured into the Mogul empire in the mid–17th century, and although Persia, the homeland of Montesquieu's fictional travelers in *Lettres persanes* (1721; Persian Letters), became known through the accounts of Jean-Baptiste Tavernier and Jean Chardin, 18th-century Europeans kept up relations primarily with the countries bordering on the Mediterranean. After their defeat outside Vienna, the Ottomans presented less of a threat to Christian Europe. In fact, during the 18th century the sultan grew increasingly aware of being under threat himself, while the power of the local provincial governors continued to grow at the expense of the central power in Istanbul. The balance of power in the Mediterranean slowly tipped in favor of the European states, whose trade was beginning to develop, and whose technical innovations gave them an edge over the Ottoman world. Nonetheless, the Barbary pirates continued to prey on European ships and to capture their crews and passengers. Although certain thinkers accused European governments of putting up with this state of affairs, and of appeasing those Barbary states that were useful to them as long as these states attacked the Europeans' enemies, the image of bloodthirsty pirates, reducing Christians to slavery and forcing them to convert to Islam, remained strongly rooted in the popular imagination and was carefully nurtured by the Church. This image would be exploited at the time of the conquest of Algiers in 1830.

Within the Islamic world, new intellectual currents emerged, preaching a return to strict observation of Islamic law and of the Koran and rejecting anything that could be interpreted as an innovation. In general, despite indications of interest in Europe—which was visited by a growing number of open-minded Muslims—Islamic society remained relatively untouched by intellectual developments in Europe.

For enlightened Europe, however, the Islamic world, at once so familiar and so strange, held a particular place, and interest in Islam played a significant role in European thought of the time. Certain Enlightenment thinkers took a new look at Islam, and although their attitude was ambiguous, it nevertheless contrasted sharply with the views of earlier periods. Since the Middle Ages, Islam had been the enemy par excellence, a religion that had sprung up after Christianity and presented itself as a rival to the Church. Hence, discussions about Islam and its world were inevitably confrontational and any knowledge that a European could acquire about the Muslim religion or the Arab language could only be used for polemical ends. By the end of the 17th century, however, with the waning of the threat presented by Islam, a new curiosity emerged in Europe, together with a desire to acquire real knowledge about the Islamic civilization; that desire was already evident in the works of the English Arab scholar Edward Pococke in the 17th century. Although the first French translation of the Koran by the sieur du Ryer in 1647 had continued the medieval tradition of disparagement, the Latin translations of 1694 and 1698 reflected the new, more open attitude.

Another sign of this new desire for objective knowledge was Barthélemy d'Herbelot's *Bibliothèque orientale* (Oriental Library), published by Antoine Galland in 1697. This was an encyclopedia of impressive erudition, based for the most part on Arabic sources, and it remained a very important reference work throughout the 18th century. At the same time, a great many Latin translations of Arabic works appeared throughout Europe, despite the fact that those translators who showed the greatest objectivity and who avoided a polemical stance risked being accused of lacking religion, as happened in the case of the German Arabic scholar Johann Jakob Reiske. The desire to inform was often accompanied by a wish to destroy the anti-Islamic prejudices that had until then obstructed real knowledge. Thus in 1684 Richard Simon wrote an account, "De la créance et des coutumes des Mahométans" (On the Customs and Beliefs of the Mohammedans), "so that those who travel in the Levant may free themselves of a number of prejudices they harbor against this religion" (Chapter 15, *Histoire critique de la créance et des coutumes des nations du Levant* [A Critical History of the Customs and Beliefs of the Nations of the Levant]). In 1705 the Dutchman Adriaan Reland published *De religione mohammedica* (On the Mohammedan Religion), a work that undertook to destroy certain anti-Muslim prejudices, and which David Durand, a Huguenot, translated into French under the title *La religion des Mahométans* (1721; The Religion of the Mohammedans). This same open-minded attitude was especially apparent in George Sale's English translation of the Koran published in 1734, which is accompanied by a preface attacking the distorted image of the prophet offered by Christian propagandists and which show greater understanding of Mohammed and of the Muslim religion. These works, as well as histories such as the one written by Simon Ockley (*The Conquest of Syria, Persia, and Aegypt, by the Saracens* [1708–18]), based on Arabic texts and on great scholarship, remained sources for all those who wrote about Islam during the 18th century.

Travel writing and histories, often written by people who had lived in the Muslim world, were another sign of the interest in this world and of the desire for further objective knowledge of it. Such works were published throughout the century, finding a large and receptive audience interested in knowing more about this geographically close but radically different world. An Englishman, Joseph Pitts, who had been made prisoner by Algerian pirates and converted to Islam, even described the pilgrimage he had made to Mecca in *A True and Faithful Account of the Religion and Manners of the Mahometans* (1704). Such narratives often pandered to a taste for the exotic by including very romantic stories, but they doubtless also helped to provide a less prejudiced view of the Muslim world, and they were used by thinkers such as Montesquieu.

What influence did this greater knowledge have on the 18th-century European's view of Islam? It would be a mistake to reduce the image of the Muslim world to that of the *Thousand and One Nights* or to a taste for exotic stories about harems, for Islam encompassed much more important issues, many of which lay at the very heart of Enlightenment concerns. After all, since the Middle Ages Islam had been the chief enemy of the Church, perceived only through a fog of prejudice and distortion. It is hardly surprising, then, that a questioning of Christian dogma also accompanied the rehabilitation of this rival religion and a rejection of the views of Islam propounded by Christian theologians. This is not, however, to say that Enlightenment thinkers took a unanimously positive view of the Muslim religion. It is difficult to agree entirely with Hichem Djait when he represents 18th-century Europe as being fundamentally and overwhelmingly concerned with understanding Islam (see Djait); or with Maxime Rodinson, when he writes: "The eighteenth century's view of the Muslim East was truly fraternal and understanding" (see Rodinson).

In fact, anti-Islamic attitudes inherited from the Middle Ages had not disappeared, although some Europeans made a conscientious effort to oppose them; traces of such anti-Islamic sentiment can even be found in Sale's text, despite accusations that he showed too much sympathy for Islam. The fundamental ambiguity of 18th-century attitudes is clearly revealed in the article "Mahomet" in Bayle's *Dictionnaire historique et critique* (1697; An Historical and Critical Dictionary). Bayle wavers between the traditional image of the prophet as an impostor and his own desire to criticize the intolerance shown by the Christian churches. Similarly, in the *Encyclopédie,* Mohammed appears as an impostor and a false prophet, even though the sublime morality of Islam is emphasized. Indeed, while this work reproduces certain prejudices about the Koran, it also contains more ambiguous opinions about the history of the Islamic world and about Muslims (particularly in the articles "Alcoran" [Koran] and "Mohométisme" [Mohammedanism]. It was often, in fact, the prophet himself who was the focus of attention, and even among those who showed the least hostility toward him, the image of the cunning legislator predominated.

But writing about Islam or its founder could never be devoid of ulterior motives. Enlightenment discussions on the subject were always inscribed within the contemporary European context and seemed rarely to spring from a simple desire for knowledge. Islam was in fact an important weapon in 18th-century battles over religion. Humphrey Prideaux's book *The True Nature of Imposture Fully Displayed in the Life of Mahomet* (1697), used as such a weapon throughout the century, was written to a large extent as part of the onslaught against the deists. In his introduction, as well as in his "Letter to the Deists," which was published as an appendix, the author explains that since the deists were accusing Christianity of trickery and imposture, he intends to reveal Mohammed's true deceitfulness, in order to demonstrate how different the Christian religion is from Islam. But since at the same time he denounces popery and "the Bishop of Rome," his work could also be used to supply arguments to those who attacked Christianity. Indeed, the denunciation of the "false prophet" and his imposture was a favorite weapon in denunciations of the Catholic Church. This can certainly be seen in an early 18th-century clandestine manuscript such as the *Traité des trois imposteurs* (Treatise on the Three Imposters). In this work Mohammed is portrayed, together with Jesus and Moses, as an impostor who invented a false religion. In 1732 the Italian Alberto Radicati, the count of Passerano, wrote in a similar vein *A Parallel between Muhamed and Sosem* (which in 1737 became *La religion muhammedane, comparée à la paienne de l'Industan, par Ali-Ebn-Omar, Muslim* [The Mohammedan Religion, Compared to the Pagan Religion of Hindustan, by Ali-Ebn-Omar, a Muslim]), an atheistic text that shows, by means of scholarly references to the Koran and to Arab authors, that, like the prophet, Moses was an impostor. Voltaire's play *Le fanatisme, ou Mahomet le prophète* (1741; Mahomet the Prophet; or, Fanaticism) belongs to the same tradition. His denunciation of the prophet, apparently following the line of the Medieval Church, aims in fact to discredit the Christian Church and priests. Similarly, the criticisms of Islam contained in Montesquieu's *Lettres persanes* are attacks against the Catholic Church, and perspicacious readers of the era would have understood them as such.

On the other hand, criticism of Christian fanaticism could also take the form of praise for Muslim toleration, for this toleration set an example that the Church should have followed but was far from imitating. Hence Voltaire, for example, in his *Essai sur les moeurs* (1765; Essay on Manners) could also stress religious toleration among the Turks and express a decidedly more favorable view of their own religion. This image of a tolerant Islam became almost commonplace among the critics of the Catholic Church. At the beginning of the century, the Irishman John Toland, the freethinking author of such well-known works as the *Pantheisticon* (1720) and the *Letters to Serena* (1704), also showed an interest in the Muslim world, for instance in his *Letter from an Arab Physician to a Famous Professor* 1705 or 1706), which undertook to defend Islam against Christian attacks. This work denounced in particular the intolerance and cruelty of the Christians who did not follow their own principles, compared to the evangelical gentleness and tolerance manifested by the Saracens.

Islam was similarly portrayed by the marquis d'Argens, author of several works that quite successfully imitated the model of Montesquieu's *Lettres persanes*. Argens often condemns Christian fanaticism, which he contrasts with Muslim toleration and humanity, a condemnation that does not prevent him, in other places, from denouncing the Turks and *their* intolerance when he wants to stress parallels between Islam and the Christian Church and priests.

But religious toleration was not the only issue raised in connection with Islam. Certain deists went further, seeing Islam as a natural religion close to deism itself, freed from the abuses and corruption that had invaded Christianity as well as Judaism, and which emphasized the unity of God and preached a simple morality. Such were the beliefs of the comte de Boulainvillier, whose famous *Vie de Mahomed* (1730; Life of Mohammed) presents the prophet as a great legislator and portrays Islam as resembling a sort of deism (or perhaps Socinianism). This work, which circulated in manuscript form before its publication in England in 1731, was generally read as a criticism of the Catholic religion. In England it was often the Socinians or Unitarians who showed sympathy for Islam, which was considered closer to the true Unitarian Christianity that had existed before the corruptions introduced by the Church Councils. This was the theme of Henry Stubbe's book *An Account of the Rise and Progress of Mohometanism,* written about 1671, which circulated in England in manuscript form without ever being published. It was perhaps this work that inspired Prideaux's book and it doubtless influenced John Toland. In his own *Nazarenus* (1718), Toland stresses the connection between Judaism, Christianity, and Islam and shows the latter to be close to early Christianity. A less well-known work is J. Morgan's *Mahometism Fully Explained* (1723–25), presented as the translation of a manuscript (which Morgan claimed to have bought in Tunisia in 1719) written in 1603 by a Moor from Aragon and addressed to the Moriscos. The translation was accompanied by notes and commentaries that, while adopting a cautious attitude, indicate that the translator wished to use this work to criticize certain aspects of Christian doctrine and the Catholic Church in particular.

In a similar way, Argens tended to present Islam as an admirable creation because it was nearer to natural religion and taught a refined morality. So he writes that despite its "absurdities," "I must admit that in it I find precepts worthy of the admiration of the greatest philosophers" (*Lettres juives* [1736; The Jewish Spy]). He goes on to defend the Koran, writing, "the whole of philosophy could not present a more majestic idea of the power of the Divinity." Here again, the most admirable aspects of Islam were precisely those that brought that religion closer to deism and distanced it from Christianity. A similar idea can be found later in the work of the historian Edward Gibbon, another author hostile to the Christian religion, who wrote: "A philosophic theist might subscribe to the popular creed of the Mahometans, a creed too sublime perhaps for our present faculties" (*The History of the Decline and Fall of the Roman Empire* [1776–88]). This inaccurate view of Islam betrays a wish to use any weapon at hand in the fight against the Church, rather than a real desire to understand Islam as such.

In the later part of the 18th century, interest in Islam was less closely linked to such concerns, and the wish to find out more about it seemed to correspond to more practical needs. At the same time, Islam and the Muslim world became part of the history of humanity as did other civilizations. In the view of Gottfried von Herder (*Ideen zur Philosophie der Geschichte der Menschheit* [1784; Outlines of a Philosophy of the History of Man]), Islam is just another religion whose not always harmful influence on people may be assessed. But Herder's view of the Koran and the Muslim world tends to be negative, and he above all stresses the despotism to which he believes this religion has contributed. The theme of despotism—often linked to fatalism, a characteristic that was frequently evoked and rarely seen in a positive light—was not new; Montesquieu popularized it in his *De l'esprit des lois* (1748; The Spirit of Laws). Islam is viewed in this text in terms of "Oriental despotism," whose epitome the Ottoman empire had for a long time been seen to represent. Thus, condemnation of despotism, for Montesquieu as for the comte de Volney, encompasses a condemnation of Islam, which was believed to encourage it. For Volney, the result of the spirit of the Koran is "to establish the most absolute despotism in the one who commands by means of the most blind devotion in the one who obeys" ("État politique de la Syrie" [The Political State of Syria] in *Voyage en Egypte et en Syrie* [1787; Travels through Egypt and Syria]). Thus the old hostility toward this religion was reinforced by Enlightenment thinking on the question of political institutions. In his 1770 *Histoire philosophique et politique des établissements et du commerce des Européens dans les deux Indes* (A Philosophical and Political History of the Settlements and Trade of the Europeans in the East and West Indies) the abbé Raynal launched an appeal for the conquest of North Africa by a league of European states in order to free that region from Turkish despotism and to civilize it; and the century closed with the French invasion of Egypt.

In conclusion, the curiosity and relative open-mindedness that Enlightenment thinkers showed toward Islam should not disguise the fact that this religion was always perceived through the lens of European concerns or that it was used as a weapon in disputes that involved Europe alone. Despite the efforts of numerous scholars, the European image of Islam—whether positive or negative—was always distorted, and the prejudices inherited from the Middle Ages, which had never entirely disappeared, would later resurface even stronger than before.

ANN THOMSON

See also Balkans; Orient and Orientalism

Further Reading

Daniel, Norman, *Islam and the West: The Making of an Image,* Edinburgh: University Press, 1960; revised edition, Oxford and New York: Oneworld, 1993

Djait, Hichem, *L'Europe et l'Islam,* Paris: Seuil, 1978

Grosrichard, Alain, *The Sultan's Court: European Fantasies of the East,* translated by Liz Heron, London and New York: Verso, 1998 (original French edition, 1979)

Gunny, Ahmad, *Images of Islam in Eighteenth-Century Writings,* London: Grey Seal, 1996

Hentsch, Thierry, *Imagining the Middle East,* translated by Fred A. Reed, Montreal and New York: Black Rose Books, 1992 (original French edition, 1988)

Hourani, Albert, *Islam in European Thought,* Cambridge and New York: Cambridge University Press, 1991

Netton, Ian Richard, "The Mysteries of Islam," in *Exoticism in the Enlightenment,* edited by G.S. Rousseau and Roy Porter, Manchester and New York: Manchester University Press, 1989

Rodinson, Maxime, *Europe and the Mystique of Islam,* translated by Roger Veinus, Seattle: University of Washington Press, 1987; London: Tauris, 1988

Said, Edward W., *Orientalism,* New York: Pantheon Books, and London: Routledge, 1978

Italy

Historiography: Myth and Awareness

The first difficulty encountered by the specialist of 18th-century Italy (today inevitably studied in a European context) is the stubborn tradition of the Risorgimento ("Resurgence," the movement for national identity and a political state), a historiographical myth that had its golden age in the second half of the 19th century, when the objective was to create the nationalistic concepts of Italy and Italians. It was not by chance that this viewpoint became dominant during the 1930s when nationalism, the monarchic tradition, and fascist policies of self-sufficiency transformed a culture already deeply marked by the process of unification.

Another difficulty in the interpretation of Italian history, also inherited from positivism, is that of the local nature of reforms in Italy and, more generally, the purported autonomy of Italian culture in relation to Europe. Such a perspective in effect denies any relation between the political models implemented in the peninsula and what was happening outside Italy, in order to construct an idea of the "moral and civil" primacy of Italy. This viewpoint is present in the well-documented work of Michelangelo Schipa and can also be found in that veritable gold mine of literary erudition, Giulio Natali's *Settecento* (1929; The Eighteenth Century). This approach is completely reversed in a brief study by Henri Bedarida and Paul Hazard in 1934: that study, using a comparative model of positivist origin, but open to new and more fertile inquiries, examines the scholarly documents supplied by Natali in the light of the concept of France's cultural influence (see Bedarida and Hazard). And yet the study actually represents a step backward when compared to an earlier work by Hazard—his thesis of 1910, which dealt with the relationship between the French Revolution and Italian literature. Although Bedarida and Hazard's joint work does decisively destroy myths of the totally autochthonous origins for the trends occurring in Italy, it tends to replace these with myths of dependence in relation to the cultural hegemony of France. One can find the beginnings of an ideological turning point in a fundamental work by Benedetto Croce, *Storia del Regno di Napoli* (1925; History of the Kingdom of Naples), the first volume of a major tetralogy (along with the history of Italy, the history of the baroque era, and the history of Europe), published in an era of triumphant fascism, and which made a clean sweep of Schipa's traditional claim of the completely local nature of Italian reforms in the 18th century.

In 1935 Luigi Salvatorelli advanced claims about the autonomy of the 18th century in relation to the Risorgimento from an openly antifascist and rationalist perspective. However, it fell to Franco Venturi, who defined his research program in *La circolazione delle idee* (1954; The Circulation of Ideas), to unravel this complex issue. Venturi's study became a veritable historiographical manifesto and was a forerunner of the three volumes entitled *Illuministi italiani* (1958–71; Italian Enlightenment Thinkers), as well as *Utopia e riforma nell'Illuminismo* (1970; Utopia and Reform in the Enlightenment), and above all the *Settecento riformatore* (1969–90; The First Crisis). This last work is seen today as the most complex and significant attempt to establish the nature of the Enlightenment in Italian thought. It is founded on the firm understanding that one cannot describe 18th century-Italy without taking into account the continual impact of events, choices, projects, and ideas elaborated not only in Europe but also in the vast expanses on the other side of the Atlantic.

Here we can relate only a small part of Venturi's tracing of history from the crisis of the 1730s, to the powerful surge of the Enlightenment during the 1760s, as witnessed by two specifically European although quite different institutions: the "Milan school" (with the Verris, Cesare Beccaria, the Accademia de' Pugni (Society of Fists), and the journal *Il caffé*), and the chair of political economy in Naples, held by Antonio Genovesi. A significant and somewhat related issue was the increasing prominence of the controversy over Jesuitism, with its broad international context (Portugal, South America, Spain, France) and its definite impact upon Italian centers (Naples, Parma, Venice, Rome, Florence). This period extends from the first expulsions of the Jesuits up to the definitive suppression of the order (1773) under the combined action of the Bourbon states and the *philosophes*. The second volume of Venturi's *Settecento riformatore* is a sort of extension of the first on the religious question, and the third tends to focus on the first crisis of the ancien régime (1765–76). Here, the relation between the Italian sphere and the impact of global events predominates. The crisis began with the entrance of Catherine II's Russia on the Mediterranean scene and lasted until the beginning of the American War of Independence. The next phase (1776–89) covers the fall of the ancien régime and provides an ample description of the manner in which those responsible for disseminating information in Italy (intellectuals, gazetteers, and journalists) perceived events taking place not only in Geneva, America, Venice, London, and Paris but also in Poland, Russia, or Turkey. The fifth volume, in two parts, extends to the end of the Jacobin period (with the new Napoleonic order already on the horizon) and analyzes the events occurring in what was then Italy, according to an 18th-century geography that includes Corsica, Dalmatia, and the Ionian islands. Venturi's study approaches the reforms of the 18th century by recording the defeat of the generation that lived through the crisis of European consciousness, including the Italian approach to the radical Enlightenment, which certain historical works had examined in the wake of Venturi's 1954 *Radicati* (I am referring in particular to my own study, *L'esperienza civile e religiosa di Pietro Giannone* [1970; The Civil and Religious Experience of Pietro Giannone]).

Vincenzo Ferrone gives a general overview of the beginning of the 18th century in Italy in the light of European events in his original and monumental work of 1982 entitled *Scienza, natura, religione* (The Intellectual Roots of the Italian Enlightenment: Newtonian Science, Religion, and Politics in the Early Eighteenth Century), recently translated into English. The relationship between the dissemination of scientific models (Sir Isaac Newton's theories and John Locke's philosophy) and the revival of the Italian states beginning in the last decade of the 17th century is the preeminent theme of the study. The cultural geography of Ferrone's work is vast and ambitious, stretching from the Mezzogiorno (the South) to Savoy. The work also covers less-studied regions, such as the Veneto (Venice, Padua, Verona), Bologna, Tuscany from Florence to Pisa, and, above all, Rome. It is no accident that the hero of Ferrone's work is Celestino Galiani, a monk was educated in the south but who long-time resident of Rome: Galiani was an enlightened, restless Catholic, who would come to represent an epistemological model that was far more complex than that of Ludovico Antonio Muratori, another major figure in the Italian Enlightenment. Galiani established connections between the most complex elements of European culture. His studies in the Roman monastery encompassed not only Baruch Spinoza's *Tractatus Theologico-Politicus* (1675–77; A Theologico-Political Treatise) and the first insights of English "freethinking," but above all with the approach taken by the Anglican rationalists, who through their readings of Robert Boyle were seeking an unassailable response to the breaches opened by deism and the early forms of freethinking and who, to that end, adapted to their own ends the powerful model of Newtonian science. Alongside Newton and his *Principia Mathematica Philosophiae Naturalis* (1687; Mathematical Principles of Natural Philosophy), which Galiani read with considerable insight and whose ideas he helped to disseminate, there were Locke's contributions. Locke's work had two aspects: his disturbing *Essay concerning Human Understanding* (1690), his defense of the validity of Christianity, exemplified in Locke's writings in response to John Toland's *Christianity Not Mysterious* (1696). Armed with these instruments, Galiani could

offer the nascent Italian Enlightenment not only an impeccable and sophisticated epistemological model, but also a code of ethics that could proudly proclaim itself to be a science of morality. With the conception of science as a world view, it was possible for historians to reconstruct an overall view that would, on the one hand, extend the transformation of Italian culture in its relations with Europe back to the end of the 17th century and, on the other, elude the two interpretative limitations mentioned above, that is, viewing the Italian Enlightenment from extremes of being under the influence of French cultural hegemony or being autonomous. Ferrone furthered his research in a later study, reviewing the models of knowledge available to the Italian Enlightenment—which were not only those of Cartesian rationalism or Locke's empiricism, but also the naturalism of the Renaissance, which had been long neglected and which makes more problematic the definition of the Enlightenment as the age of reason.

The books cited thus far suggest a complex chronology for the Italian Enlightenment, from the European crisis of consciousness to the end of the ancien régime: a period that extends back into the last decades of the 17th century and ends with the last years of the revolutionary period (1796–99). The beginning of the revolutionary period is sometimes said to coincide with the first formation of the Jacobin republics, sometimes with the end of the Republic of Venice, or even the disappearance of the Piedmontese state, or the dramatic fall of the Parthenopean Republic. All things considered, the very proposition of an 18th-century Italy or an Enlightenment Italy is still, in some respects, a product of an ideology based on the idea of the *Risorgimento*. The lack of political unity in the 18th century brought with it very specific responses, to such a degree that even on the cultural level one can discern areas linked by an identity that was partly a "geographical expression," where the only connection was the development of a shared literary language, and partly the myth of humanist origins, which had been invoked by Petrarch and Machiavelli.

Intellectual History and Reforms throughout the Italian Peninsula

The Spanish presence in Italy, which by the 18th century had already lasted for more than two centuries, had not created any definitive political model in the long-occupied territories. Even the lands of the Mezzogiorno, which had once been united by Frederick Barbarossa's model of a state, manifested profound differences at the end of the 17th century. In Sicily the Spanish government had been able to count on a powerful feudal nobility. The dramatic defeat of 1674 at Messina had reinforced the supremacy of Palermo, the seat of the viceroyalty and of an aristocracy used to unopposed control over its fiefs. The situation in Naples was very different: there the administrative nobility had managed effectively to counter the power of the provincial nobility, thus reinforcing a tradition of government and autonomy, to such a degree that one recent historian has characterized 17th-century Naples as a *res publica* of the legal profession. Moreover, in the Parthenopean capital, the administrative nobility and the bourgeois class crossed paths in the great academies that had renewed their ties with the naturalist tradition of the Renaissance as well as with the richness of the European intellectual heritage, from Francis Bacon to René Descartes, Pierre Gassendi, Baruch Spinoza, or Nicolas Malebranche. Assuming the heritage of the Accademia degli Investiganti (Academy of Researchers), one Spanish viceroy, Luis La Cerda, duke of Medinaceli, played the card of culture to consolidate his power by gathering together writers and thinkers who were to bring a profound renewal to what was already a remarkable literary tradition. Some, such as Giambattista Vico and Paolo Mattia Doria, took the side of the *veteres* (ancients) and brought a singular creativity to that seemingly doomed cultural position. Others, such as Pietro Giannone, transformed the Neapolitan legal tradition of jurisdictionalism into political history and plans for religious reform.

Paolo Mattia Doria, a leader within the academy, had a singular career. A noble from Genoa, he had been sent to Naples to oversee the economic interests of his family. He did not return to his homeland, thus escaping through intellectual activity the fate that was reserved for most of his class: that of being a punctilious courtier, a duelist, or a dandy. In addition to Doria's prestigious role in the academy at Naples—where he showed his interest in the art of war—the work that most certainly brought him fame throughout Europe was titled *La vita civile* (1709; The Civil Life of Paolo Mattia Doria, in Three Parts). The book openly proclaims its origins in the humanist tradition, and it apparently made an impression on Montesquieu during his stay in Naples. Doria, adapting the ideas of his favorite author, Plato, deals with the issues of the development of human society and political forms. The book, strikingly modern in tone, provides a very clear assessment of the model of Spanish domination, which had ended during the early 1700s when the south passed from the Spanish to the Austrian Habsburgs as a result of the War of the Spanish Succession. Doria had ties with one of the principal representatives of the administrative nobility, Gennaro d'Andrea (the brother of Francesco, who had been a proponent of the reform of the law), and had tried to offer his intellectual abilities to a class that had cleverly attempted to work in conjunction with the Habsburgs, pushing aside the aris-

tocrats who had nonetheless been the first to move in favor of Vienna, with the Macchia conspiracy in 1701. Eventually Doria's misadventures as a mathematician and his criticism of modernity and the existing economic ideology set him further and further apart from his contemporaries. He had one last dramatic encounter with the Bourbon regime, which in 1734 had replaced the Austrians Habsburgs in Naples, and which sought to rebuild the former "national" state around the monarchy of Charles III. Doria's proposal for government in *Idea di una repubblica perfetta* (Idea of a Perfect Republic) was incompatible with a plan of reform based on monarchical power and centralization. Thus, in 1753 the hand of the executioner condemned to the flames the republican and aristocratic utopia of this singular representative of the ancients, whose religious sentiment was nourished less by genuine Christianity than by the philosophy of Socrates and Plato.

Doria had been one of the closest and most devoted friends of Giambattista Vico, with whom he shared his allegiance to the ancients and to Plato. Vico, the son of a modest printer, had been a marginal figure in Medinaceli's academy, to which he had gained entry because of his position as a professor of rhetoric. His *Orationes* (1766; Orations) heralded a period of change, not only for the university but also for the society of the south: During this period the region witnessed the last Spanish government, with the viceroy Medinaceli and his willingness to employ intellectuals; the transition to the Bourbons of Spain; and projects of reform, which were regularly opposed by the new regime of the Habsburgs. In his memoirs, Tiberio Carafa exalts the political project of the nobility, its desire to renew, under the youngest son of the Austrian emperor, a "national" state that would accept representation of all classes. Vico devoted a work to this event, *Principum Neapolitanorum Coniurationis Anni MDCCI Historia* (History of the First Neapolitan Conspiracy), fated to remain unpublished because of the change in regime. This work defends the role of the nation, and the connection between the state and the magistrates, who represented the state against the arrogance of the aristocrats and the violence they stirred up among the popular classes. However, with the accession of the Habsburgs, Vico's role as orator led him to celebrate the aristocratic victims of the Macchia conspiracy. His speech in 1709 betrayed the distance that separated him from the projects of reform that were gaining ground in the University of Naples, in a spirit of strengthening and modernizing professional culture. Confirming his choice of the ancients, Vico opposed a university model based on professions, proposing instead a classical model of instruction based on a single master. At the same time, his choice of the ancients was confirmed in *De Antiquissima Italorum Sapientia* (1710; On the Most Ancient

Wisdom of the Italians). His efforts to move from the chair of rhetoric to the more prestigious chair of civil law led him to undertake the themes of *De Jure Universo et Uno* (On the One Universal Law), in which emerges the demand to renew—in the face of any type of scepticism—the tradition of the discipline and its interpretation. In these pages one can already find traces of his masterpiece, the *Principi di una Scienza Nuova* (The New Science of Giambattista Vico), of which the final version (after those of 1725 and 1730) was to appear in the year of his death, 1744. Vico counters the rationalist Cartesian model with a proposal for an innovative philosophy of history that reabsorbed into its "ideal and eternal" form the history of different nations. Through the encounter between philology and philosophy, which enabled him to have a deeper reading of poetry, language, institutions, and law, he constructed a theory of development in stages (the ages of brutes, heroes, and, finally, scholars) that is not linear, but rather rich in cyclical returns, including, among others, one that allows him to have an original perspective on the Middle Ages as an era of "rediscovered barbarism."

Another young intellectual, also present in Medinaceli's academy although in a very marginal role, marked his era with such a unique message that his name became a convenient synonym for describing the politics inspired by jurisdictionalism. Pietro Giannone was from the province of Ischitella and had been able to study law in Naples thanks to the largesse of an uncle who was a priest. After Giannone obtained his doctorate in law, he tried to make his way in the Neapolitan bar. His master had been the great Domenico Ausilio, a partisan of the ancients, who was also a great connoisseur of modern culture, including Spinoza. Through Gaetano Argento, who would become the political leader of the Neapolitan legal profession, Giannone was introduced to the principles of jurisdictionalism and the historical nature of law, according to a tradition that called for a positive reevaluation of barbarian jurisprudence, in comparison to the Roman code. Thus were born, in the heart of the group of young jurists who were disciples of Argento, the first ideas behind Giannone's *Istoria civile del regno di Napoli* (The Civil History of the Kingdom of Naples), printed in 1723. This work would make Giannone an intellectual of renown all over Europe, as witnessed not only by the accounts of the work in the most important journals of the era but also by the numerous translations of this work, which appeared in English (1729–31), French (1742), and German (1751–58). Giannone inaugurated a model of civil history that claimed theoretical affiliation with Jean Bodin and Bacon but could trace its roots, on a more specifically historiographical level, to the great tradition of the Renaissance (Machiavelli, Francesco Guicciardini, and Paolo Sarpi), to the Erasmian heritage of Grotius, to the Gallican culture of Pierre de Marca and above all Jacques-Auguste De Thou. Inevitably, Giannone's peers saw in this work primarily a gigantic war machine against the privileges and abuses of the clergy. This interpretation, however, runs the risk of limiting Giannone to a single aspect of his thought—an aspect that was purely polemical and critical, and the very one against which the Catholic offensive inevitably unleashed a fury that would be relentlessly renewed with each generation until the early 20th century.

In fact, Giannone's intellectual path is much more complex if one takes into account what he wrote in Vienna, particularly after he realized that he would never return to Naples to advocate the principles of jurisdictionalism. Access to the major European libraries—including the Palatine and those of Prince Eugene; Alessandro Riccardi; Pio Nicolo Garelli, the chief imperial physician; and the baron of Hohendorf—enabled him to gain exceptional knowledge of the culture of English and Dutch freethinking. Thus was born Giannone's *Il triregno* (finished by 1734, published in 1895; The Triple Crown), a complex meditation on human history as seen from the viewpoint of religion and its role as an exploiter. Libertine views, freethinking, and a certain radicalism converged to form a project that completely transformed the original jurisdictionalism. It was no longer a question of defending states against the excesses of the Church. The unmasking of the very core of ecclesiastical power had now become Giannone's task.

Through Spinoza and Toland, Giannone could demonstrate that the Jews had assigned no other aim to the covenant between themselves and God than happiness on earth. Job bemoaned the loss of his material wealth, and the idea of the immortality of the soul came to the Jews much later, through the Egyptians, as Toland, above all, had taught him. In opposition to the earthly kingdom, Jesus had preached the heavenly kingdom, giving his first disciples, in the uneasy world of the Jewish sects, the hope of its immediate realization. However, Christ had preached a simple religion, without rites or cults or ceremony, founded on the hope of complete resurrection and upon two essential virtues, faith and charity. Saint Paul had enriched this foundation, reconciling certain elements of the Pharisaic and Hellenistic traditions. In the absence of an immediate realization of the heavenly kingdom, a third kingdom, that of the popes, had gradually materialized. From the 4th century on, Christianity had modeled itself upon the institutions of the Roman Empire, adopting both its geography and its rites. The ecclesiastical hierarchy and the separation between clergy and laypeople were born. Proposed as an alternative to complete resurrection were the ideas of the immortality of the soul and the existence of a realm beyond the terrestrial, which was a legacy of paganism and included the notions of hell, Limbo, and Purgatory. The Church used these inventions to increase its power of intercession. Such are the broad lines of the work that Giannone drafted in Vienna and refined in Venice in 1735. The Inquisition had him expelled from Venice and pursued him furiously, obliging him to find a precarious refuge in Geneva. Unknown to him, he had become a pawn caught in the battle between the House of Savoy, which sought the confirmation of the 1727 Concordat, and the obstinate Pope Clement XII, who challenged the agreement made by his predecessor. Following his composition of the *Istoria civile,* his exile in Vienna, and his writing of the *Triregno,* Giannone was lured into Savoy on false pretenses and imprisoned there. He wrote the following works in detention: his autobiography; the *Discorsi sulle decche di Livio* (Discourses on Livy's Decades); the singular *Apologia de' teologi scolastici* (In Defense of the Scholastic Theologians), which has yet to be published in its entirety; the *Istoria della vita, e del pontificato di S. Gregorio Magno, Papa, e dottore della Chiesa* (1758; History of the Life and Pontificate of His Holiness Gregory the Great, Pope and Doctor of the Church); and *L'ape ingegnosa* (The Cunning Bee), a painful, dramatic, and original confirmation of his own intellectual and religious experience, which was also a way of pursuing, under prison conditions, the discourse of the *Triregno* that had been interrupted by his arrest, and the relentless search for, and destruction of, his manuscripts.

During the last years of the Habsburg viceroys in Naples, the inspired policies of jursidictionalism enjoyed the support of Vienna, particularly that of the viceroy, Count Friedrich Alois von Harrach. Under his rule, Galiani became chief chaplain. Practically speaking, Galiani assumed not only the ecclesiastical but also the cultural responsibilities of the viceroyalty. His appointment was a clear victory for the camp of the moderns, who took their inspiration from Descartes, Gassendi, and, above all, Locke and Newton. Galiani tried to translate their ideas into new institutions and drafted a bill for some extraordinarily innovative reforms of the university. He had the opportunity to carry out a large part of his program during the first phase of the Bourbon reforms, when the entire Mezzogiorno, including Sicily, was united under Charles III.

It was in this vastly transformed university that, thanks to the support of Bartolomeo Intieri—a Tuscan out of the Accademia dei Georgofili (an group involved with agrarian reform) who had taken on a role of talent seeker—another young provincial, Antonio Genovesi took the chair of political economy at Naples. There Genovesi completed his transformation from "metaphysician" to "merchant," and his chair has come to stand as the symbol of the southern Italian Enlightenment.

In the Papal States it is difficult to find anything comparable to the creativity of Naples, although Rome's cosmopolitan role, and the presence of certain great cultural and religious institutions, make this territory a very interesting one. It was in Rome that the early journalistic experiment of the *Giornale de' letterati* took place at the end of the 17th century, modeled very closely on two newspapers in France and England. As Jean Gardair has shown, the *Giornale de' letterati* enjoyed the support not only of the university in Rome but also of the Jesuits' Collegio Romano (Roman College) and the Collegio Urbano Da Propaganda Fide (College for the Propagation of the Faith). The editors of the newspaper, Francesco Nazari and Giusto Ciampini, recorded the crisis of the culture of the Counter-Reformation and sought a new cultural identity for Catholicism, finding inspiration in the great academies of the 17th century as well as Galileoism, the teachings of the Maurists (a strict order of Benedictines that engaged in important scholarship), and the new culture of the missions. The experiment of the *Giornale de' letterati* was not a straightforward one. Nazari and Ciampini eventually severed relations, and both founded their own newspapers, which ceased publication at the beginning of the 1680s. In the region between Parma and Modena, Benedetto Bacchini attempted another newspaper. Bacchini was a man of great erudition who was inspired by Galileoism and the Maurist tradition. Bacchini's newspaper survived until 1697.

Vincenzo Gravina, an important jurist and intellectual who had arrived in Rome from Naples, was to play an active role in the new cultural climate brought about by Pope Clement XI. Gravina modernized not only the teaching of law, through his *Origines Juris Civilis* (1708; Origins of Civil Laws), but also the literary theory of his era, with *Della ragion poetica* (1708; On Poetry). Ciampini and Gravina were among the founders of the Arcadia, a literary academy that became such an enormous success with its institutions, its laws, and its satellite groups that it characterized an entire period of Italian culture.

In Modena, Bacchini had the good fortune to be the teacher of Ludovico Antonio Muratori, who, along with Galiani, represented the richest and most mature embodiment of enlightened Italian Catholicism. Bacchini gave Muratori his first solid notions of religious erudition, according to the model that Jean Mabillon had confirmed in *De Studiis Monasticis* (1729; Treatise on Monastic Studies). Muratori lived in Milan as the librarian of the Ambrosiana, the library founded by Cardinal Federico Borromeo that was subsequently immortalized by the novelist Alessandro Manzoni. Back in Modena, Muratori had launched a proposal for an

Accademia d'Italia (Academy of Italy) that sought to gather writers and thinkers from every corner of the Italian world into one *res publica literaria* (literary republic). In reality, the project focused on Rome, Naples, Florence, Milan, and Venice, in addition to the smaller city of Modena, but it did not encompass Savoy, which was still caught up in traditions of war and lacking a true cultural identity. At issue were the areas of debate that were threatened by the War of the Spanish Succession. Muratori's project to establish an academy had no precise ideological character. It was based on lay and ecclesiastical traditions and accepted the central role to be played by Rome. One of Muratori's collaborators, Bernardo Trevisan, tried to move the cultural axis of the project closer to Venice. Later developments transformed Muratori into a champion of jurisdictionalism, linked to the neo-Ghibelline and imperial traditions.

Muratori's collaboration with Gottfried Wilhelm Leibniz (which soon turned into a rivalry) obliged Muratori to put the Maurist method of scholarship to the service of political writing: whence the *Antichità estensi* (1717–40; Antiquities of Ferrara), the major project of the *Rerum Italicarum Scriptores* (1723; Italian Historians), and the *Antiquitates Italicae Medii Aevii* (1738; Antiquities of Medieval Italy). After Giannone and Vico, who had set out to explore the Middle Ages in terms of polemics and philosophy, respectively, Muratori approached the same topic from a scholarly viewpoint. The *Rerum* and the *Antiquitates* were born of the collaboration between Modena and Milan, now a staunchly Habsburg city, and the Vienna of Charles VI. However, Muratori's teachings went still further: His Catholic reformism drove him to make incursions into other domains, from "plague management," to a critique of the Roman model of justice, to a definition of a common-sense, enlightened Christian conduct, as he engaged in a lively polemics against religion based on superstition. Muratori ended his career by offering not only a remarkable model of "civil history," the *Annali d'Italia* (1744; Annals of Italy), but also a complete program of reforms that he presented during the years of peace that followed 1748: *Della pubblica felicità oggetto dei buoni principi* (1749; Public Felicity as the Object of Good Principles). In the first volume of his *Riflessioni sopra il buon gusto* (1708–15; Reflections on Good Taste), which is a sort of intellectual program, Muratori had deplored the loss of the tradition of the *Giornali de' letterati*, as embodied by Nazari, Ciampini, and, especially, Bacchini. A few "bad" traditions survived, provincial and totally alien to the demands of an elevated cultural organization such as the one that he had envisaged in his youthful project for a national academy.

Three Venetian intellectuals came forward to put into action some of Muratori's teachings by establishing the journal that in 1710 became the *Giornale de' letterati d'Italia,* printed in Venice. Initially, the most active among these intellectuals was a Venetian man of letters, Apostolo Zeno, who would later move to Vienna and become a poet at the imperial court. Along with him was Scipione Maffei, a high cultivated Veronese nobleman who made his mark on Italian public opinion with the ideas contained in *Della scienza chiamata cavalleresca* (1710; On the Science of Chivalry), in which, as an alternative to the culture of war and arms—which now was no more than a pointless rhetorical activity — he recommends to nobles the pastime of study and writing. The third intellectual involved in the project was Antonio Vallisnieri, a professor at the University of Padua, who was already a scholar of renown all over Europe, with solid ties to Bologna and Rome. Behind these three principal editors there was a vast network of correspondents in the principal Italian cities. This undertaking would end after a significant and active ten-year period. The first of the journal's principals to break away was the irascible and eccentric Scipione Maffei. Caterino Zeno tried zealously to make up for the absence of his brother in Vienna, but during the second ten-year period the publication of the newspaper was increasingly neglected. On the whole, it had been a remarkable experiment, one that had made invaluable use of Jean Leclerc's model of *Bibliothèques.* The legacy of this journal was taken up by the *Novelle letterarie* in Florence, edited from 1740 by Giovanni Lami, a Tuscan scholar who preferred to work with Pierre Bayle's model (short summaries and reviews rather than excerpts of works). Lami drew his inspiration from Muratori's enlightened Catholicism, from the religious experience of Benedict XIV, and from rigorist and Augustinian ideals.

A rapid process of modernization occurred in the state of Savoy, which Muratori had considered to be outside of the *res publica literaria italiana* (Italian republic of letters) at the beginning of the 18th century. Victor Amadeus II engineered not only the passage from duchy to kingdom but also a project for government that, while based on that of Louis XIV, contained new elements. The program was multifaceted but coherent, facilitated by the relatively small size of the territory in which it was being implemented: a ruling class chosen from among lawyers and magistrates; a strong, central bureaucracy, along with representatives of the state in the provinces, who functioned like French *intendants* (provincial magistrates), and the joining of the fiscal and political spheres in a rigorous mercantile system. The reform of schools strengthened those professions that were useful to the state and also contributed to the creation of an ideal of public service; moreover, the school reforms removed secondary instruction from the former monopoly of the Jesuits and made education a duty of the state.

The reign of Victor Amadeus was marked by conflicts with the Church: initially because of the treaty with the Vaudois, and then, once he had become king of Sicily, because of what was known as the Lipari Dispute, behind which was the defense of *Liegazia*, an institution of law that gave the sovereign powers of control over the ecclesiastical domain. Even after the loss of Sicily and the acquisition of Sardinia, tensions did not decrease, but were merely transferred: to the newly acquired territorial jurisdictions, to the defense of the privileges granted by Pope Nicolas V, to the nomination of the bishops, to the fiefs that the Church possessed in Piedmontese territory, and to the ecclesiastical immunities that the mercantilism had already damaged. Victor Amadeus arrived on the scene shortly after the great Neapolitan controversy over benefices and the Comacchio conflict, which, against the Church and on the side of the Estes, was based on imperial models. Victor Amadeus knew how to use such events to give a response that was undoubtedly more pragmatic, but no less hard-line, and that caused partisans of jurisdictionalism and Gallicans to rally to his side.

The reforms of the university had brought to Turin brilliant intellectuals who had links to very significant experiments, not only in Italy but also in France. All this ferment is reflected in one personal journey of astounding creativity, representing not only a testimony to the climate of reform but also the radical and utopian direction the reforms were taking. Such was the life of Alberto Radicati di Passerano, a representative of the feudal nobility of the House of Savoy. Contact, through marriage, with Calvinist culture had made him profoundly different from his family and his class. While the nobility was hostile to the Piedmontese sovereign, Radicati had welcomed his king's reforms and considered them a starting point for a "religious reform of Italy," which he believed should come about gradually. In the eyes of this brother in misfortune to Pietro Giannone, the 1727 Concordat was a betrayal. Radicati felt threatened and fled to England, where he could work in a freethinking atmosphere. His attack on religious hypocrisy, his refusal to be threatened, his republican credo, and his democratic and egalitarian ideals made his position unacceptable even in free England. His publisher was imprisoned, and Radicati had to take refuge in the Netherlands, where his principal work was published in English translation in 1734 (*Twelve Discourses, Moral, Historical, and Political*), and later in French (1737; *Douze discours moraux, historiques et politiques*). Radicati grew close to radical sects in the Netherlands, but shortly before his death he definitively adopted Calvinism. The journey of the greatest Piedmontese thinker of the early 18th century ended in 1737, in the anonymity of the paupers' cemetery in Amsterdam. One year earlier, Giannone had been arrested and forced to recant, and he had then been held in prison in a citadel of Turin until his death in 1748. The example of these writers who shared a great moral passion—Radicati and Giannone—clearly shows the limits of the reform spirit of the House of Savoy, its wariness of creative intellectual ventures, and its tendency to suppress heroes.

The 1730s and 1740s were years of war and, on the cultural level, of suspended animation. The creativity that had characterized the first two decades of the century had been lost force. The major experiments by Vico, Giannone, Doria, and Radicati seemed to have ended in the writers' becoming victims of indifference, silence, and condemnation. The generation of enlightened thinkers who could be considered victors also died out: Celestino Galiani in Naples, Muratori in Modena, and Maffei in Verona. Through their choices, these thinkers were to influence the most positive aspects of the 1740s and the early 1750s, as witnessed by Galiani's university reforms, Muratori's debate on religious holidays and propositions for "public joy," and Maffei's writings on interest on loans and against magic.

The most significant figures of the 1750s belonged to a new generation, even if their roots were intertwined with the culture of the early 18th century of the Mezzogiorno. This was the case of Ferdinando Galiani, Celestino's nephew, who shortly after his 20th birthday entered the heart of the ongoing debate about currency. He was educated in the circles surrounding Bartolomeo Intieri, the talent seeker of genius mentioned above. An employee of Bernardo Tanucci—the reforming secretary of state in the kingdom of the Two Sicilies—the young Galiani spent the 1760s in Paris and was a passionate participant in the meetings of the baron d'Holbach's circle. Ferdinando Galiani's Machiavellian realism, and a certain cynicism borne of his diplomatic and administrative profession, doubtless distanced him from the more utopian aspects of the Enlightenment.

That was not the case for another young man, Antonio Genovesi, who was discovered by Intieri and who held the chair in political economy at Naples. Genovesi came from a modest family from the provinces. He had only been able to complete his studies because he had agreed to become a priest. His intellectual development was rather complicated. Initially a partisan of the ancients, following the examples of Doria and Vico, he later switched his allegiances to the moderns. Early on Genovesi cultivated a strong interest in theology, but his choice of authors such as Jean Leclerc and Samuel Clarke and his interest in the religious rationalism that had principally pervaded the Protestant world aroused the strong opposition of the local curia. He was ripe for conversion to a new discipline, inspired by his encounters at Intieri's. The first step in that process was an introduction to the work of the Ubaldo de Montelatici, associated with the Accademia dei Georgofili movement. The chair of political economy, for which Genovesi prepared his fundamental lectures, *Lezioni di commercio* (1765–67; Lessons in Trade), was an ideal forum for his major lessons on the philosophy of the Enlightenment. Genovesi had witnessed the great famine of 1763 and had participated in the elaboration of all the short-, medium-, and long-term measures adopted to revitalize productive sectors. His economic theories evolved from the mercantilism of his years at university to the liberalism of his mature years, while eschewing the dogmatism of the Physiocrats. Deeply involved in the most positive aspects of Tanucci's reformism, Genovesi shared the Bourbon states' strategy against the Jesuits, preparing the educational reforms that would, perhaps, be the most significant result of the polemics against the order. In this struggle for public instruction funded by the state, Genovesi rediscovered ideas that had been elaborated by Giannone and that had prefigured the main points of the new approach. One of the last struggles was fought within the Faculty of Law, to abolish the chair of canon law, which gave theoretical support to what were viewed as the privileges and abuses of the Church. Radical utopians were trained in this school, including Francesco Longano, who introduced Jean-Jacques Rousseau's ideas on democracy to the Masonic lodges. Others trained in this school were reforming realists such as Giuseppe Maria Galanti, who continued social and economic analyses.

If Genovesi's chair became the central symbol of the Enlightenment in the Mezzogiorno, Milan's Accademia de' Pugni (Society of Fists) was equally significant. During the first decades of the 18th century, the capital of the duchy of Lombardy had experienced great transformations. The Habsburg political model brought strong demands for modernization, as illustrated by the long history of census taking (a practice introduced at the end of the 1750s). Milan had no feudal aristocracy. Instead, its wealthy and often cultivated aristocracy preserved its privileges and autonomy through the Senate. However, Habsburg centralization tended to leave the aristocracy less and less room to maneuver. This motivated an entire generation of intellectuals to enter the struggle against privilege. The contrast between Gabriele Verri (senator and civil servant, and a jealous, clever guardian of autonomy in opposition to Vienna) and his sons, Pietro in particular, is typical of this change. The Accademia de' Pugni opposed the Accademia dei Trasformati (Academy of the Transformed), where Giuseppe Parini's civil and religious teachings continued to predominate. The Accademia de' Pugni

was a symbol both of controversy and of a break with the past. This was clearly manifested in the journal *Il caffè*, which Pietro and Alessandro Verri, along with a group of friends, produced for nearly two years, from 1764 to 1766. *Il caffè* represents a milestone in the development of the periodical press: the passage from the scholarly paper, such as *Novelle letterarie*, a successful publication founded by Lami, to the opinion sheet. The ideal audience was no longer the man of letters but a far vaster, more militant public, to whom was offered as a model a culture inspired by the *Encyclopédie*.

The Accademia de' Pugni and *Il caffè* both belonged to a very intense period that saw the birth of several masterpieces of the Italian Enlightenment: Pietro Verri's *Meditazioni sulla felicità* (ca. 1763; Meditations on Happiness) was an elaboration of an ethical system intended to be both secular and utilitarian; above all, Beccaria's *Dei delitti e delle pene* (1764; An Essay on Crimes and Punishments) challenged the European conscience to consider the question of justice and made the "school of Milan" one of the true centers for cosmopolitan dialogue. It was a brief and charmed period, interrupted in 1766 when Alessandro Verri and Beccaria went to Paris to meet directly with the Holbach coterie, while Pietro remained in Milan, bound by his administrative duties. Alessandro, after a stay in London, settled permanently in Rome, abandoning his involvement in the Enlightenment to become a brilliant and increasingly conservative man of letters.

These years marked the beginning of the least interesting period: The former editors of *Il caffè* had become civil servants, and the differences that had been hidden by their youthful collaboration came to light. For Alessandro Verri and Beccaria, who had chosen economic policy as their terrain for confrontation, this meant differing ideas on the relationship between utopia and reform, in light of their readings of Montesquieu and Rousseau. Whereas Verri was decidedly liberal and was evolving toward a model of society based upon a constitutionalism in which productive members also have political responsibilities, Beccaria tended to emphasize the ethical, political, and economic responsibilities of the state with regard to inequality and poverty, which he viewed as the true causes of crime and which had to be eradicated. Even greater were the differences between Gian Rinaldo Carli, from Capodistria, and the former contributors to *Il caffè*. Carli reproached Beccaria for having been too enthusiastic a proponent of Rousseau's ideas. While Alessandro Verri had become wary of the centralization practiced by Joseph II, which left little room for local autonomy, Carli became the theoretician of a form of enlightened despotism that in fact was more despotic than enlightened. Pietro Verri had tried to save at least a part of the heritage of *Il caffè*: he transferred to Milan the publication of *L'estratto della letteratura europea,* a periodical containing excerpts of European words, begun in Yverdon by Fortunato de Felice. The nature of the publication was in part that of a scholarly journal, but the militant tone of its excerpts and summary critiques made it more of a precursor to the *Giornale enciclopedico* published in Vicenza by Elisabetta Caminer, who would later prove to be a major journalist of the Enlightenment.

Among the contributors to *L'estratto* was a former Piedmontese Dominican, Giambattista Vasco, who, with his brother Francesco Dalmazzo, was to become one of the greatest reformers of the twilight of the Italian Enlightenment. The intellectual journey of Giuseppe Baretti began in Turin, with the *Frusta letteraria* (1763–65; Literary Scourge), a lively, conservative journal opposed to *Il caffé.* Baretti's opposition to the Enlightenment was linked to two factors: on the local level, the teaching of Sigismondo Gerdil, who had greatly influenced his education; and, on the international front, his adherence to Samuel Johnson's models from English society. Another Piedmontese, Carlo Denina, prior to becoming the historian of the *Rivoluzioni d'Italia* (1769–70; Revolutions of Italy), was also involved in journalism of opinion with his *Parlamento ottaviano,* a journal that was short-lived and poorly distributed and that also chronicled the limits of society in Turin. Denina's insatiable sense of curiosity, revealed by the *Discorso sopra le vicende della letteratura* (1761; An Essay on the Revolutions of Literature) and his eclectic reformism, witnessed by the unsuccessful text *Sull' impiego delle persone* (On Human Employment), neutralized his conservative education and led him in the early 1780s—thanks to the aid of the comte de Lagrange—to a chair in the Berlin Academy, the very same through which Pierre-Louis de Maupertuis, Julien de La Mettrie, and Voltaire had passed, and which Denina celebrated in *La Prusse littéraire sous Frédéric II* (1790–91; Literary Prussia).

Giambattista Vasco and his brother Francesco Dalmazzo made a choice that was clearly oriented toward the cause of the Enlightenment. Vasco was a reformer and economist, his brother a utopian and political thinker, but they often swapped roles. Francesco Dalmazzo was involved in the events in Corsica and contributed armed assistance in the fight for the freedom of the island. He was arrested, and attempted while in prison to reconcile the demands of liberty, which he had learned from Montesquieu, with the democratic teachings of Rousseau. Vasco, after a brief stint as a theology professor in Cagliari, had sought greater freedom in Lombardy, where he had at first encountered Verri's mistrust. Then he returned to Piedmont in the 1770s, when the end of the reign of Charles Emmanuel III and of the power of his minister Bogino seemed to open new

opportunities for experts in economics. He worked for many years in the finance administration in a totally secondary role. In the latter part of the 1780s, the two brothers founded one of the most remarkable journals of the last period of the Enlightenment, the *Biblioteca oltremontana.* The journal's orientation toward the world outside of Italy was reflected in the adjective *oltremontana* (beyond the mountains) in its title, as it was decidedly more oriented toward France and England, and toward Europe in general, without forgetting the lessons in freedom that were coming from across the Atlantic. The French Revolution interrupted the collaboration of the Vasco brothers and gradually transformed the journal. In 1791 Francesco Dalmazzo ended up in prison again for trying to propose, to his king and to the comte d'Artois, who was in Turin, a model of representative democracy as a solution to state crises.

No less dramatic, although different, was career trajectory of Giambattista Vasco, who in 1789 entered the scientific academy in the kingdom of Savoy to become the economic mentor of the new minister of the interior, Giuseppe Pietro Graneri. His vocation as a great reformer and admirer of the liberal economist and politician Turgot, attentive to the English model but critical with regard to the French high courts (*parlements*) and their claims to be representative, led him to oppose Vittorio Alfieri and his radical republicanism in the years that preceded the French Revolution. Giambattista Vasco could not have been familiar with such texts by Alfieri as *Della tirannide* (1777; Of Tyranny) or *Del principe e delle lettere* (1778–89; The Prince and Letters). Vasco drew his ideas about the political beliefs of the great tragic author from *Panegirico di Plinio a Traiano* (1785; Pliny's Panegyric on Trajan), whose obvious target was the philosophical sovereign and enlightened absolutism. Totally conscious of the social costs of a revolutionary solution, Vasco openly defended the possibilities of reform and wagered on a more constitutional evolution of the system. His brother's arrest left him no choice but exile; thus he headed for Lombardy where, in his youth, he had found a number of comrades who shared his beliefs. A reader of Adam Smith, Vasco led his last battles against the guilds, for the freedom of trade and for interest on loans, emphasizing the importance of productivity. He later returned to the kingdom of Savoy, which was soon to be conquered by Napoleon. The death of his brother in prison in 1794 slightly preceded Vasco's own death.

If one stops to consider the 1780s, which show all the complexities of the last crisis of the ancien régime, there are two regions that illustrate the various possibilities of Habsburg reform. The first was Lombardy, where Joseph II's grand program deepened tensions over centralism, remodeling not only society and the economy but also culture and religion and provoking the resistance of one of the great protagonists of the Enlightenment, Pietro Verri, who was nostalgic for the time of Maria Theresa. The other path was that taken by Tuscany under Archduke Peter Leopold and Scipione de Ricci, who carried out the most significant reforms (including the abolition of capital punishment) in line with a constitutional model capable of enlisting the participation of different classes. However, dramatic problems and demands for change were also present in the Church, as shown by the periodical publications linked to Rome's cultural institutions, from the *Effemeridi* to the *Antologia romana,* and to a still greater degree to the press of the Papal States, particularly the *Memorie enciclopediche* of Bologna, to which such brilliant intellectuals as Giuseppe Compagnoni and Giovanni Ristori were contributors.

However, it was in Naples, above all, that the decade preceding the French Revolution saw the creation of the most disturbing and forward-looking projects. The reforms inspired by Tanucci, which had linked the Mezzogiorno to the Bourbon strategies, had run their course, and the new court of Maria Carolina leaned toward programs akin to those of Joseph II. This was the context in which a new generation of intellectuals had been raised, one that knew Genovesi's teachings only indirectly and that was characterized by intensive participation in Freemasonry. The generation included Francesco Antonio Grimaldi, Gaetano Filangieri, and Francesco Maria Pagano. These thinkers differed on interpretations of Montesquieu and, above all, of Rousseau. While Grimaldi, an implacable realist, maintained that inequality was natural both on the physical level and on the ethical and economic levels, Filangieri tried to transform "the spirit of the laws" into a science capable of informing all areas, from economy to society and religion. His *Scienza della legislazione* (1784; The Science of Legislation) appears as a radical and well-organized plan capable of systematizing, transforming, and, at the same time, saving the ancien régime, erasing all traces of feudalism and setting up a new social opposition: the distinction between manual workers and intellectuals. Vico's philosophy of history had thus reemerged, secularized and made compatible with the philosophy of nature (Boulanger and Buffon). This is what could be seen in Pagano's *Saggi politici* (1785; Political Essays): The

first edition revealed thinking of the reformist type, while the second seemed to be waiting, as clear-eyed as it was desolate, for the catastrophe destined to shatter the ancien régime once and for all.

With 1789 and the beginning of the 1790s, the different realities in Italy clashed with the new political model born of the French Revolution. Yet again, the periodical press was the most significant and comprehensive mirror, at least until the flight of Louis XVI and the onset of the war, for through its most eloquent voices it tended to advocate a "constitutional"—thus, on the whole, rather positive—interpretation of the National Assembly. The war and the execution of Louis XVI changed this attitude of hopefulness. The "news from France" became, increasingly, the "horrible news from France." The Italy of the Enlightenment thus produced new and fiercer divisions. The possibility of reform vanished, while the ideas of utopia were gaining force. In the midst of the counterrevolutionary culture, and against that culture, a Jacobin Italy was born. Pagano, with others of his generation, would be its protagonist and its martyr.

GIUSEPPE RICUPERATI

Further Reading

Bédarida, Henri, and Paul Hazard, *L'influence française en Italie au dix-huitième siècle,* Paris: Les Belles Lettres, 1934

Capra, Carlo, Valerio Castronovo, and Giuseppe Ricuperati, *La stampa Italiana dal Cinquecento all'Ottocento,* Rome: Laterza, 1976

Carpanetto, Dino, and Giuseppe Ricuperati, *Italy in the Age of Reason, 1685–1789,* London and New York: Longman, 1987

Ferrone, Vincenzo, *The Intellectual Roots of the Italian Enlightenment: Newtonian Science, Religion, and Politics in the Early Eighteenth Century,* Atlantic Highlands, New Jersey: Humanities Press, 1995

Ricuperati, Giuseppe, "A Long Journey: The Italian Historiography on the Enlightenment and Its Political Significance," *Storia della Storiografia* 20 (1991)

Venturi, Franco, *Settecento riformatore,* Turin: Einaudi, 1969–

Venturi, Franco, editor, *Illuministi Italiani,* 3 vols., Milan and Naples: Ricciardi, 1958–65

J

Jansenism

Jansenism was not an exclusively French phenomenon, nor was it limited to the 17th century. The French term *jansénisme* first appeared in 1641, as a pejorative designation for the disciples of Cornelius Jansenius, bishop of Ypres, who advocated a return to the principles of Saint Augustine in his book *Augustinus,* published posthumously in 1640.

Jansenius taught that human beings have been fundamentally corrupt since the fall of Adam. Man the sinner is given to evil and is incapable of discerning good without the aid of God's grace. Alluding to Augustine's adversary Pelagius, Jansenius condemned as "Pelagian" the more confident vision of humanity that had arisen during the Renaissance and that was often defended by the Jesuits. Jansenius's ideas were diffused in France through one of his friends, the abbé Jean Du Vergier de Hauranne of the monastery of Saint-Cyran, but Jansenism was also linked to other currents of thought within French spirituality, such as those represented by Cardinal Pierre de Bérulle and Saint François de Sales. This devotional current was part of the triumphant world of the Catholic Counter-Reformation that had resulted from the Council of Trent. The earliest Jansenists clashed with the duc de Richelieu, condemning his policy of alliances with Protestants during the Thirty Years' War. French Jansenism enjoyed broad dissemination in intellectual circles and was associated with such illustrious names as the Antoine Arnauld family, Blaise Pascal, and Jean-Baptiste Racine. The Cistercian community of Port-Royal formed the heart of the Jansenist venture.

Louis XIV against the Jansenists

Louis XIV always detested the Jansenists. He regarded them as "republicans" and did not forgive their connections with the rebels of the Fronde. In the years following his expulsion of the Protestants with the revocation of the Edict of Nantes (1685), Louis XIV set out to annihilate this other form of opposition within Catholicism. The repressive measured peaked in severity in October 1709, when the nuns of Port-Royal were dispersed by the authorities and sent to rival convents. In the years that followed, the church and the monastic buildings at Port-Royal were razed, and the corpses in the cemetery were exhumed and thrown into a communal grave, except in those cases when the families of the deceased could transfer them elsewhere. The Jansenists were treated like the Protestants, whose churches had also been pulled down. The king destroyed and crushed those who resisted him, in France as in the Palatinate.

Many Jansenists went into exile in the Netherlands, where they came under the influence of the Protestant refugees. The Oratorian Pasquier Quesnel emerged as the leader of the new generation of Jansenists. He mixed traditional Augustinianism with a strong tradition of Thomism, some elements of Bérulle's ideas, and some "Richerist" principles. (Edmond Richer had defended the rights of parish priests against the bishops in the 17th century.) Infuriated and hoping to halt the activities of these rebels once and for all, Louis XIV appealed to Rome to issue the papal bull *Unigenitus* (1713), which left its mark on 18th-century history throughout Europe. The bull lists 101 propositions taken from Quesnel, grouped in such a way as to present those censured as summarizing Jansenism. However, the conflict came to be focused on the 91st proposition, which seemed to confer the full powers of excommunication on the pope. Like the Jansenists, many Gallican bishops were reluctant to accept this implicit affirmation of papal infallibility. Louis XIV stifled their recriminations, but the conflict was revived after his death in 1715.

The Jansenists' Hopes in the Regency

Philippe II, duc d'Orléans and regent to Louis XV (who would not reach his majority until 1723), had to negotiate. Within the framework of the collective government, Cardinal de Noailles, who was close to the Jansenists, was appointed president of the Conseil de Conscience (Council of Religious Affairs); consequently, Jansenism could count on the support of the Gallicans against the 91st proposition. This coalition went public in the appeals of 1717–18, in which bishops, parish priests, monks, and laymen "appealed" the bull of the "ill-advised" pope at a council held to protest the *Unigenitus* constitution. (In 1728 this same alliance would play a part in what has come to be known as "the legend of Gregory VII." As part of the solemn Mass celebrated in Rome, the Sacred Congregation of Rites honored Saint Gregory according to custom, but invoking the virtues of this pope necessarily led to the condemnation of his old enemy, the emperor Henry IV, a convert to Catholicism who had nevertheless signed the Edict of Nantes in 1598, thereby mandating a certain degree of religious toleration. This emperor had his defenders in Paris in the age of the Enlightenment. Pope Gregory VII, in contrast, was accused of having aspired to a theocracy that had threatened the balance of Europe and compromised peace among its states.) The notion of Christendom was no longer what it had once been. The regent was soon alarmed by the size of the opposition—the renewed appeals of the mid–1720s affected 45 dioceses and involved 7,000 people—and he sought a compromise, which he thought he had found in the accommodation of 1720. The authorities attempted to regain control over hearts and minds. A crucial episode occurred in 1727 with the condemnation of Jean Soanen, the pious bishop of Senez, at the provincial council of Embrun; the Jansenists described the event as the "plundering of Embrun." The underground periodical *Nouvelles ecclésiastiques* began publication around this time, to provide support for the persecuted "appellants" and to alert public opinion. The remarkable success of clandestine publications continued throughout the century, marking the transition of the Gallican-Jansenist alliance to a defensive position. By making the bull *Unigenitus* a law of the state, the royal declaration of 24 March 1730 sanctioned the defeat of Jansenism.

The Disintegration and Reconstitution of Jansenism (1730–50)

In these desperate circumstances, the appellants waited for a miracle. Deacon François de Pâris, a holy man of the Jansenist movement who had devoted his life to the poor of the Saint Antoine district, was buried in the cemetery of Saint Médard, and miracles reportedly began to take place on his grave. These miracles involved more or less violent convulsions in those present. Citing the "indecency" of these demonstrations as a pretext, the authorities closed the cemetery in 1732, provoking this sarcastic comment: "In the name of the king"—the formula used in *lettres de cachet*—"God is forbidden to perform miracles here!" The miraculous manifestations were continued in secret, in cellars and lofts, the convulsions experienced by participants becoming more and more spectacular. Soon, the convulsionaries began to solicit "assistance" in order to demonstrate that their bodies had been miraculously made insensitive to pain. Some of them even had themselves crucified. Among the common people, certain women prophesied and organized primitive liturgies around the bodies, which aroused curiosity and indignation and led to divisions among the appellants.

However, over and above these ostentatious outbursts, the appellant movement, on the defensive from this time onward, came into contact with physicians and, above all, with lawyers. By closing the Church to appellants, the authorities made these alliances inevitable, thereby creating a link between the issue of Jansenism and that of liberty. The first political struggles of the 18th century in France had been those of the appellants, who preceded the *philosophes* by one or two generations. The submissions of the Parisian lawyers in favor of Soanen in 1727 had been imbued with ideas close to those of John Locke and had evoked the attractiveness of a contractual monarchy: the king was described as head of the nation, the *parlements* (high courts) as the "senate," and the laws as compacts between governors and governed. Curiously enough, the Jansenists were becoming the "republicans" that Louis XIV had suspected them of being. As early as the Regency, Nicolas Le Gros had declared the inalienability of the rights of the community, while in 1737 Jérôme Besoigne, in his *Catéchisme sur l'Église pour les temps de trouble* (Catechism on the Church for Troubled Times), took a decisive step in the development of Christian politics by transposing "Richerist" ideas from the Church to the state: just as dogmatic authority rests in the whole body of the faithful, he argued, so political authority is based on the national community.

Midcentury and the Jansenist Reawakening

Around 1750 Mey and Maultrot, using the same analogical argument, saw the *parlements* as a form of national representation. The abbé Barral made the *parlements* the guardians of good government, the sole ramparts against tyranny. These new ideas were to become part of the eclectic heritage of the Enlightenment. However, it was the scandal of the *billets de con-*

fession (certificates of confession) that sanctioned the rapprochement between Jansenists and *philosophes*. Whenever someone died, a "constitutional" bishop (the *Unigenitus* was sometimes referred to as the "Constitution") would demand a certificate signed by a non-appellant priest and refuse last rites to those suspected of Jansenism; without the sacrament one could not be buried in consecrated ground. By this point in history, however, death had become a private matter, and public opinion could not understand the decisions of the constitutional clergy. The Parlement of Paris called the priests to account. In the eyes of the magistrates, religion was primarily a social function and the clergy performed a public service. Why create disorder by persecuting men and women who, although they were certainly obstinate, had not disturbed anyone and had done good to those around them? The chroniclers of the day reported that Paris awakened to find itself Jansenist; the appellant movement, which had been slowly fading away, was rejuvenated and mobilized a new generation.

Outside France, meanwhile, Jansenism was experiencing an astonishing if belated good fortune. It flourished in Austria with the support of several reforming bishops, who were especially hostile to the Jesuits and welcomed the ecclesiastical reforms introduced first by Maria Theresa and then by her son Joseph II. Jansenism also had numerous followers in Italy, where it was often merged with the Catholic Enlightenment. In Tuscany, which was ruled by Joseph II's brother the archduke Leopold II, Jansenism inspired the ecclesiastical reforms proposed by Scipione de Ricci, bishop of Pistoia and Prato. In Spain Jansenism was characterized by a similar determination to struggle against the Jesuits and to denounce the dangers of ultramontanism. The Spanish Jansenists defended the rights of the monarchy in relation to the Church and were able to attach themselves to a Catholic "third party" that desired reform.

Jansenism against Absolutism

In France Jansenists were to be found wherever there was a struggle against absolutism. The key role they played in the agitation on behalf of the *parlements* was the driving force in the revolt against Maupeou's "coup d'état" in 1771, and they scored a crushing victory over the Jesuits by inspiring the campaign that led to the latter group's expulsion from the realm in 1764. In the 1780s the Jansenists favored a form of civil toleration of Protestants, while the *Nouvelles ecclésiastiques* extolled the policies of Joseph II. The provisional alliance between the Jansenists and the Enlightenment should not mislead us, however. The Jansenists remained faithful to Augustinianism, fought Pelagianism, denounced unbelievers, and were the most vigilant

of all against Jean-Jacques Rousseau and his *Le profession de foi du Vicaire savoyard* (The Creed of the Priest of Savoy, Chapter 4 of *Émile, ou, De l'education* [1762; *Émile*; or, Concerning Education]), even though by the end of the century their thought was being influenced by Rousseau's concepts (such as the notion of the general will). Although the role that Jansenists played in working out the Civil Constitution of the Clergy (1790) has long been emphasized, they were actually divided on the issue. In opposition to Armand Camus, the abbé Grégoire, Gabriel Nicolas Maultrot, and Henri Jabineau all wanted to maintain the absolute autonomy of the Church by separating the two powers that the Constitution blithely blended within an Erastian tradition.

Jansenism had demonstrated an astonishing capacity for change. Challenging, almost in spite of itself, the imperatives of *raison d'État* (reasons of State), Jansenism was impregnated during the 1680s with the values of the Protestants who fled to Holland; but these new ideas were integrated with the typically French traditions of Gallicanism and Richerism. During the period of persecution, Jansenism was enriched with concepts and legends, heroes and martyrs, and it preserved a culture of opposition to arbitrary power and absolutism that brought it into contact with the struggles of the Enlightenment. The Jansenists were not the sinister leaders of a premeditated conspiracy against the monarchy, but it cannot be denied that they contributed to the wider movement of opposition to the ancien régime.

MONIQUE COTTRET

See also Catholicism; Jesuits; Religion, Popular; Secularization and Dechristianization

Further Reading

Cognet, Louis, *Le jansénisme,* Paris: Presses Universitaires de France, 1961

Cottret, Monique, "La querelle janséniste," in *Histoire du christianisme: Des origines à nos jours,* vol. 9, Paris: Desclée, 1997

Cottret, Monique, *Jansénismes et Lumières: Pour un autre XVIIIᵉ siècle,* Paris: Michel, 1998

Kreiser, B. Robert, *Miracles, Convulsions, and Ecclesiastical Politics in Early Eighteenth-Century Paris,* Princeton, New Jersey: Princeton University Press, 1978

Taveneaux, René, *La vie quotidienne des jansénistes aux XVIIᵉ et XVIIIᵉ siècles,* Paris: Hachette, 1973

Taveneaux, René, editor, *Jansénisme et politique,* Paris: Colin, 1965

Van Kley, Dale K., *The Jansenists and the Expulsion of the Jesuits from France, 1757–1765,* New Haven, Connecticut: Yale University Press, 1975

Van Kley, Dale K., The Religious Origins of the French Revolution: From Calvin to the Civil Constitution, New Haven, Connecticut: Yale University Press, 1996

Japan

Economic and Social History

After a century of troubles and civil wars, Japan was definitively unified with the establishment of the Tokugawa family's shogunate in 1603. The first shogun, or generalissimo, was Tokugawa Ieyasu. He set up his seat of government at Edo (now Tokyo) while, in accordance with tradition, the *dairi* (emperor) continued to live in Kyoto, a city that was then known as Miyako (or, among the Encyclopedists, "Méaco"). Although the position of shogun was officially conferred and sanctified by the *dairi*, the sovereignty of the latter was mostly symbolic and ritualistic. This fact is reflected in the chevalier de Jaucourt's entry "Japon" in the *Encyclopédie*, where he referred to the shogun as the "secular emperor" and to the *dairi* as the "ecclesiastical emperor." In reality, absolute political power belonged to the shogun.

The Tokugawa government was anxious to protect Japan from any invasion by the Portuguese or the Spanish. In 1638 it snuffed out a peasant rebellion stirred up by samurai who had converted to Christianity, and the following year the government expelled all European missionaries. For the most part these missionaries were successors to the Portuguese Jesuit mission that had arrived in 1549 with Francis Xavier. At the same time the Tokugawa government also banned Christian practices in Japan, under penalty of death. However, Japan still found it necessary to continue trade with Europe, which was as profitable for the Japanese as for the Westerners engaged in it. The country therefore maintained a purely commercial relationship with representatives of the Dutch East India Company, who for their part had prudently refrained from trying to convert the Japanese to Christianity. The Dutch were thus able to live in Japan, on Deshima, an artificial island constructed in the harbor of Nagasaki in the northwestern corner of the island of Kyushu. Aside from its exchanges with this single Western country, Japan traded only within Asia, namely with China. Thus began what became known as "the closing of Japan," although some historians have argued that in reality it was a policy of controlled opening of that country,

based on the fact that the volume of trade with foreigners increased considerably during the Tokugawa period.

Several revolts by samurai with too much time on their hands certainly occurred, as well as a few urban and rural riots, which increased in frequency during the famine of 1782–87. However, once freed from any fear of foreign invasion, together with the abandonment by the provincial lords of all armed resistance to the central government, the Japanese were able to enjoy the "Pax Tokugawa" for two and a half centuries, from 1603 until 1867. This era is known as the Edo epoch because Edo was chosen by the shoguns as the capital city.

Throughout the period the European calendar was unknown to the Japanese, and time was counted in eras, each of which usually lasted somewhat less than 20 years, depending on the will of the *dairi*. Nevertheless, it is noteworthy that in the Japanese archipelago the 18th century constitutes a real and distinct historical unit. It began with the Genroku era, which spanned the reigns of the emperor Higashiyama and the shogun Tsunayoshi. This transitional period, which stretched from 1688 to 1704, seemed to herald a new epoch. During the Genroku era the shogunate took firm root, the bourgeoisie became economically and culturally significant, literature and art prospered, and—spurred on by a thirst for novelty—ideas and customs became freer. And so the Genroku era served as a turning point from the first part of the Tokugawa period to the second.

In order to differentiate between the earlier and later halves of the Tokugawa period, some historians refer to them as, respectively, the military period and the period of civility. In contrast to the Genroku era, the end of the 18th century was characterized by the fear of a foreign threat, a fear that was felt more and more strongly by the inhabitants of the archipelago. In 1791 Hayashi Shihei, who was very sensitive to the threat, wrote *Kaikoku heidan* (A Discussion of the Military Problems of a Maritime Country), which urged the organization of coastal defenses and a powerful navy. The following year the first diplomatic mission from Russia, led by navy Lieutenant Adam Kirillovitch Laksman, arrived at Nemuro, a port on the eastern coast of the island of Hokkaido, to ask the Japanese government to establish trade relations with his country. This event was the first in a long series of European attempts at rapprochement. A century of peace, in a country closed in upon itself, was thus at the end of the 18th century about to be replaced by a period of uncertainty.

Meanwhile, 18th-century Japan was characterized by a social hierarchy headed by the feudal lords (daimyo) and their vassals (*bushi* or samurai, both words meaning "warrior") with the shogun at their head. According to Edwin O. Reischauer, this dominant class represented 7 percent of the total population of Japan, while the commoners consisted of peasants (85 percent), artisans and merchants (6 percent), and those lacking any social status or rank (2 percent) (see Reischauer). However, it was during the 18th century that the function of the samurai, which until then had consisted of military duties, gradually became more and more bureaucratic, and the warriors thus became educated civil servants. One of the most remarkable representatives of these cultured samurai, at the very beginning of the century, was Arai Hakuseki (1657–1725), a Neo-Confucian philosopher and statesman who was a personal adviser to two successive shoguns, Tokugawa Ienobu (1709–12) and Tokugawa Ietsugu (1713–16).

At the beginning of the 18th century, Japan enjoyed strong economic growth. The development of the economy was felt just as much in the countryside as in the cities. Around 1600 Kitajima Masamoto had recorded a rice harvest that yielded 257.7 million *koku* (1.3 billion bushels; the *koku* was a Japanese unit equivalent to a little over 5 bushels). One hundred years later, the output of rice was estimated at around 304 million *koku* (1.5 billion bushels). Since the amount of tax, which was levied in the form of rice by the shogunate and the feudal lords, did not change during those 100 years, its proportion of the total harvest declined from 66 percent to 28 percent. As a result of increased production, the peasants became better off with each passing year, and the resulting growth in trade gave new impetus to the national economy.

The good health of the economy, which had reached its peak of prosperity during the Genroku era, could not be maintained at the same level in the 18th century, in spite of the economic reforms attempted by the government during both the Kyoho era (1716–45) and the Kansei era (1787–93). However, since the government was now more concerned about the well-being of the people, policy makers aimed to promote trade throughout the whole of Japan. The transportation of merchandise was greatly facilitated by the existence of very dense networks of land and sea routes. Agricultural products, as well as minerals, porcelain, ceramics, silk, cotton, wool, sake, tobacco, and livestock, all circulated by these routes throughout the country.

Economic progress was also due, in part, to other changes that affected 18th-century Japanese society. Cities increased in size with the growth in economic activity during the Tokugawa period. By the end of the 18th century, the largest city, Edo, had around 1 million inhabitants, while Kyoto and Osaka each had 300,000. In tandem with this urban growth, the status of merchants improved considerably, especially after 1721, and their guilds acquired monopolistic control of sales. Thanks to commercial wealth and the rise of the commercial bourgeoisie, a new society was born and prospered, especially in Edo, Kyoto, and Osaka, but also to a lesser extent in the provincial cities that had developed around the castles of the feudal domains. A distinctive bourgeois culture thus came into being during the Genroku era. Notable members of this class include Chikamatsu Monzaemon (1653–1724), who excelled in both Kabuki (a type of Japanese theatre) and *Joruri* (the art of accompanying the manipulation of puppets with singing and accompaniment on the samisen); Ihara Saikaku (1642–93), who wrote popular fiction; Hishikawa Moronobu (died in 1694), who produced prints; and Matsuo Basho (1644–94), who composed poetic essays and haiku. This urban culture continued to develop throughout the 18th century in fiction, verse, drama, and painting.

Intellectual Life

Thanks to the solid foundation of Japanese society and its economy, as well as Japan's cultural maturity, various educational systems were put in place in the feudal lands of the archipelago. In the 17th century, formal education had been restricted to the sons of the samurai and had been undertaken by their parents, tutors, Buddhist priests, or learned samurai who were capable of teaching. In the 18th century the various fiefs made it their duty to create official schools. These institutions were so successful that by the end of the century most of the sons of the samurai, even those of lesser means, were being educated, and some schools even admitted commoners' sons. The total number of such institutions rose to 91 by the end of the 18th century, compared to the 16 that had existed in the previous century. Instruction in these schools was partly devoted to calligraphy, arithmetic, good manners, and martial arts, but they were mainly concerned with the study of the Chinese humanities, classic books on Confucianism, history, literature, and treatises on military strategy. There was also some instruction on the rudiments of Western astronomy and mathematics, as interpreted in Chinese translations or works compiled (in Chinese) by Jesuits living in China. Apart from the samurai schools, separate institutions were created to instruct the children of commoners. The main subjects taught in these schools were reading, writing, arithmetic, and those rules of polite society that were regarded to be suitable to their status.

Confucianism was the official philosophy of 18th-century Japan, having been recognized as official doctrine by the third shogun, Tokugawa Iemitsu, who ruled from 1623 to 1651. Nonetheless, the dominant philosophy among the intellectuals of the period was Neo-Confucianism, the doctrine of Chu Hsi, a Chinese philosopher of the 12th century who had reorganized Confucianism on the basis of his own metaphysics. In 18th-century Japan, where everybody was devoted, not to the values of the other world preached by Buddhism, but to the earthly values of everyday life, Arai Hakuseki, Kaibara Ekken (1630–1704), and Yamagata Banto (1748–1821) exemplified the trend toward empiricism. At the same time, two schools of philosophy appeared in Japan, both opposed to the Neo-Confucianist school. The first was the school of Wang Yang-ming (1472–1529), a Chinese philosopher who challenged Chu Hsi's teachings and emphasized the subjectivity of each individual. The government distrusted this school because its philosophy prized individual wishes more than the social order. The second school in opposition to Neo-Confucianism, called the "school of ancient learning," advocated a return to the roots of Confucianism. The philosophers of this school, notably Ito Jinsai (1627–1705), his son Ito Togai (1670–1736), Ogyu Sorai (1666–1728), and Dazai Shundai (1680–1747), promoted a philological approach to Confucian classics.

Two more independent and original philosophers lived in the shadow of these more or less renowned scholars. Ando Shoeki (1703–62) broke with Neo-Confucianism to create a philosophical system that rejected Confucianism and Buddhism. His basic tenet was what he called the "direct labor" of each individual. Miura Baien (1729–80) elaborated a philosophical doctrine that explained not only politics and economics but also astronomy, physics, natural history, and medicine. The 18th century also saw the rise of a new school of Japanese studies. Moto'ori Norinaga, for example, having studied the Japanese classics *Genji monogatari* (ca. 1001–10; The Tale of Genji) and the *Kojiki* (712; Record of Ancient Matters), claimed to have uncovered the origins of Japan on the basis of interpretations that were free of any influence either from India (Buddhism) or from China (Confucianism).

Dutch Studies

At the beginning of the 18th century the number of pioneers of "Dutch" studies, such as the astronomer Nishikawa Joken (1648–1724) and Arai Hakuseki, could be counted on one hand. In 1720, however, in order to give the Japanese access to European scientific knowledge, the shogun Tokugawa Yoshimune (1684–1751) lifted the ban on Dutch publications, except for those related to Christianity. From then on it was possible for people other than the official interpreters in Nagasaki to learn a foreign language.

In 1740 Tokugawa Yoshimune ordered Aoki Kon'yo (1698–1769) and Noro Genjo (1693–1761) to study Dutch. Soon afterward a fashion for Dutch studies began to spread among intellectuals, notably such samurai scholars as Maeno Ryotaku (1723–1803), Sugita Genpaku (1733–1817), and Otsuki Gentaku (1757–1827). According to Jacques Proust, Desiderius Erasmus, Galileo, René Descartes, and Sir Isaac Newton were introduced into Japan, and the influence of Western science was felt in many areas, including medicine, physics, and astronomy (see Proust). Copernicus's theory and the works of Ambroise Paré were introduced through translations of Dutch publications. One clear sign of this interest was the first Japanese-Dutch dictionary, compiled in 1796 by Inamura Sanpaku (1758–1811). The number of specialists in Dutch studies rose considerably, to a point where Edo became a true Republic of Letters, thus propelling Japan into the intellectual sphere of the European Enlightenment.

Japan as Seen by the Enlightenment

Most 18th-century European philosophers took an interest in the Far East, and especially in China and Japan. In the period between the arrival of Francis Xavier in Japan in August 1549 and the issuing of the decree that banned Portuguese vessels from approaching Japanese coasts in 1639, the correspondence of the Jesuits was the only source of information about the remote archipelago available to Europeans. However, after the departure of the Portuguese, Europeans were able to profit from the copious information supplied by the employees of the Dutch East India Company based at Deshima. This information was assembled in the official work describing the company's voyages, *Begin ende voortgangh van de Vereenighde Nederlandtsche geoctroyeerde Oost-Indische campagnie* (1645), compiled by Izaäk Commelin and translated into French in 1702 as *Recueil des voyages qui ont servi à l'establissement et aux progres de la Compagnie des Indes orientales*, and especially in Engelbert Kaempfer's book *Geschichte und Beschreibung von Japan* (1777–79; The History of Japan). Kaempfer, who was described by Voltaire as a "truthful and learned traveler," lived in Japan for two years.

Jean-Gaspard Scheuchzer, a Swiss physician and scholar and a member of the English Royal Society, translated into English everything that concerned Japan in Kaempfer's manuscript. This translation appeared in

London in 1727 in two folio volumes under the title *The History of Japan*. Pierre Desmaizeaux, a French scholar associated with Pierre Bayle and Saint-Évremond, and a member of the Royal Society himself, followed with a French version, which was published in the Hague in 1729 in two folio volumes. The text was later reissued in 1732 in three duodecimo volumes. It was from this version that the *philosophes,* from Montesquieu and Voltaire to the Encyclopedists, took a good deal of their information. In addition to describing his travel experiences from Batavia (now Jakarta) to Nagasaki via Thailand, Kaempfer had collected data on the geography, natural resources, history, politics, religion, arts, and technology of the Japanese archipelago, and he recounted his two visits to the court of the shogun at Edo. The French version of his book also had an appendix containing several articles taken from another of Kaempfer's works, *Amoenitatum exoticarum* (1712; On the Pleasantness of Exotic Places). These pieces outlined the natural history of tea and the manufacture of paper, explained the curing of colic by acupuncture and the use of moxibustion (the burning on the skin of moxa, a soft down resembling flax, as a caustic to heal illnesses), described ambergris (an aromatic substance derived from the intestinal secretions of sperm whales), and discussed the policy of seclusion practiced by the Japanese government. For Kaempfer, a pious Protestant, the ties that bind both society and open communication among all the nations on Earth are the will of the Creator. However, in the case of Japan, which was peaceful and happy, the policy of seclusion seemed justified. The French version also included excerpts from the diary of a Dutch official who lived on Deshima.

Montesquieu was the first person in 18th-century France to attempt to analyze Japanese society. He based his analysis on various sources, including Kaempfer's book and the *Recueils de voyage*. In Book VI, Chapter 13, of *De l'esprit des lois* (1748; The Spirit of Laws), Montesquieu refers to Japan as a nation where "extreme penalties can corrupt despotism itself." He then tries to examine how effective this severity was, concluding in Book XXIV, Chapter 14, that the harshness of the laws that Japan applied had only one purpose—to compensate for the defects of a religion without dogma and without a heaven or hell. However, Montesquieu's discussion of the country is anecdotal and fragmentary.

Voltaire offers a more detailed picture of Japan in two chapters (142 and 196) of his *Essai sur les moeurs* (1756; Essay on Manners). This work presents a history of Japan from the 14th century, when Europe first became aware of its existence through Marco Polo's account, up to the time of Kaempfer. Naturally, as a fierce defender of toleration, Voltaire expressed preference for this country where "12 religions" coexisted peacefully. In his article "Japanese Catechism" in the first edition of his *Dictionnaire philosophique* (1764; Philosophical Dictionary), the "12 religions" became "12 caterers," each using a different recipe, who lived together nonviolently, with the result that all the Japanese could live happily by visiting whichever "restaurant" they preferred.

In *Candide* (1759) Voltaire describes a Dutch sailor born in Batavia who had to walk four times over a crucifix in order to be allowed to disembark in Japan. Here Voltaire alludes to the requirement that individuals renounce Christianity in order to enter the country, describing it as having been imposed on the Dutch. In reality the Dutch were not asked to trample on the image of Christ in the ceremony known in old Japanese as *jefumi* or *efumi* but today known as *fumie*, which literally means "trampling the image." Only the Japanese had to do it at the beginning of each year in order to show that they had not converted to Christianity. In his *History of Japan*, Kaempfer had not made Voltaire's error.

In his master's thesis, Koseki Takeshi calculates that the *Encyclopédie* surveys Japan and the Japanese in 219 entries. All these entries are divided into topics, such as general information, human geography and customs, politics and jurisprudence, religions and cults, and science and technology. The most important of these is undoubtedly Diderot's entry "Japonais, Philosophie des" (Philosophy of the Japanese), which presents Shintoism, Buddhism, and Confucianism. The entry refers to Confucianism as the doctrine of "Sendosivists," a distortion of the Japanese word *sjudosju*, which means "followers of the path of Confucius." Diderot took some of his peripheral information from the entry "Japon" in Bayle's *Dictionnaire historique et critique* (1697; An Historical and Critical Dictionary), but his main source was the chapter "Philosophia Iaponensium" (Philosophy of the Japanese) by a German Protestant clergyman named Jacob Brucker of the *Historia critica philosophiae* (1744; The History of Philosophy: From the Earliest Times to the Beginning of the Present Century). Diderot translated almost word for word Brucker's text and augmented it with personal remarks that pointed out the parallels between Japanese Confucianists and French atheists, for whom he made himself the spokesperson. He valued the Japanese disciples of Confucius for their unique moral principle, the practice of the one thing that can "make us as happy as our nature allows"—virtue. This notion was dear to Diderot's heart.

Although the *Encyclopédie* provides a fairly balanced view of Japan, the analysis is limited in several ways by the Encyclopedists' use of Kaempfer as the principal source on the subject. First, when the French translation of Kaempfer's book was published in the second quarter of the 18th century, the information in that work was three-quarters of a century old, as he had returned to Europe in 1685. Second, the *Encyclopédie* did not include articles on mathematics, literature, and fine arts, all of which were already highly developed in 17th-century Japan. This failure should also be attributed to Kaempfer. A physician and a naturalist, he did not discuss those aspects of Japan that fell outside of his areas of interest. Hence the somewhat hasty conclusion of the chevalier de Jaucourt's *Encyclopédie* entry "Japon," inspired by Chapter 142 of Voltaire's *Essai sur les mœurs*. Jaucourt holds that Oriental peoples, despite their antiquity, are "no more than barbarians, or children" in matters of art.

Kaempfer's work played a decisive role in informing European views of Japan, but other books also reflected an interest in the region. For example, the abbé Raynal wrote about Japan at the beginning of his book *Histoire philosophique et politique des établissements et du commerce des Européens dans les deux Indes* (1770; A Philosophical and Political History of the Settlements and Trade of the Europeans in the East and West Indies), which was very popular at the end of the 18th century. Raynal revised this book on several occasions, in collaboration with Diderot and others. It is curious that, while Raynal explained Shintoism and Buddhism in detail, he gave no information on Confucianism, which had been so highly praised by Voltaire and Diderot. In Raynal's view, Shintoism is a form of natural religion, while Buddhism is nothing but an abominable superstition. In contrast to Kaempfer, Raynal advocated communication with the outside world in order to foster the exchange of goods and ideas. He held that it was absolutely necessary for the Japanese to allow themselves to release, through travel abroad and commercial relations, their repressed energy. Since it is the nature of human beings to communicate, he contended, the exchange of goods and ideas could only serve the well-being of the Japanese people. Raynal added that international commerce was a guarantee of peace for the world.

At the end of the 18th century, in Volume II of his *Philosophie ancienne et moderne* (1792; Philosophy, Ancient and Modern), which was part of the *Encyclopédie méthodique* (A Methodical Encyclopedia), Jacques-Andrée Naigeon borrowed from Diderot's much used article on the philosophy of the Japanese. As a result the illusion of an idealized Japan, held up as a model by Voltaire and Diderot, was thus imposed on French readers (with the notable exception of Raynal) in the second half of the 18th century.

Japan aroused curiosity not only in France but also among German philosophers. As we have seen, Diderot's entry in the *Encyclopédie* had borrowed a great deal from Brucker, who in the writing of his chapter on Japanese philosophy had himself used information from Kaempfer's *History* dealing with Shintoism, Buddhism, and Confucianism. Yet another German intellectual who was interested in Japan, half a century after Kaempfer, was Immanuel Kant, who discussed Japan in the course on physical geography that he taught at Königsberg University between 1756 and 1797. Kant described the Japanese as an angry, stubborn, cruel race that had no fear of death. He too had read Kaempfer's work, in the form of extracts from *Amoenitatum exoticarum*, which had been translated from the original Latin into German under the title *Seltsames Asien* (Asiatic Marvels).

In addition, Jean-Baptiste Du Halde, a Jesuit, had published a four-volume work entitled *Description géographique, historique, chronologique, politique et physique de l'empire de la Chine et de la Tartarie chinoise* (Geographical, Historical, Chronological, Political, and Physical Description of the Chinese Empire and Chinese Tartary) in Paris in 1735, and then in the Hague in 1736. The latter edition contained important additional information, including a summary of Kaempfer's *History*. Du Halde's book was translated into German and published in Rostock, in 1747 and 1749, in four volumes. From then on, by way of a triple translation, a summary of Kaempfer's book was accessible to German readers. The original German text was unavailable until 1777, when Christian Wilhelm Dohm published it under the title *Geschichte und Beschreibung von Japan*. This work described the Japanese mentality, their religion, their science and technology, as well as the natural resources of the archipelago.

Meanwhile, in his *Beobachtungen über das Gefühl des Schönen und Erhabenen* (1771; Observations on the Feeling of the Beautiful and Sublime), Kant remarked that the Japanese did not seem to experience the feeling of the sublime and compared them to the British, as being two insular peoples that, in his view, were characterized by courage and contempt for death. The comparison drawn between the Japanese and the British could already be found in Voltaire's *Essai sur les mœurs* and in the *Encyclopédie* entry "Japon" (which, as has already been pointed out, the chevalier de Jaucourt adapted from Voltaire). However, Kant insisted that it was pride that the two nations had in common and cited the frequency of suicide in these two island countries so distant from one another. In his *Zum ewigen Frieden* (1795; Project for Perpetual Peace), Kant approved of the Japanese policy of seclusion, which forbade access to their territory by foreigners, with the exception of the Dutch who—"similar to prisoners"—were excluded nonetheless from the social life of Japan. Kant concluded that the ban was reasonable at a time when the Western powers were undertaking the conquest of the Americas, Africa, and Asia. This stance echoes the view of Kaempfer, who had also approved of the seclusion policy. Finally, Kant, like Raynal, asserted that "the spirit of commerce is a guarantee against violence and wars, a natural guarantee of perpetual peace."

In *Anthropologie in pragmatischer Hinsicht* (1796; Anthropology from a Pragmatic Point of View), Kant mentioned Japan once again, in an anecdote describing how Japanese children, when they saw foreigners, would make fun of them by shouting "Big-eyed Dutchman!" Kant's intention was to demonstrate the need for mutual respect and to point out the absurdity of any contempt based on difference. He took the anecdote from the narrative of a voyage by the Swedish scholar Carl Peter Thunberg. A physician, botanist, and traveler, Thunberg had written *Resa uti Europa, Africa, Asia, förrättad åren 1770–1779* (1788–93; Travels in Europe, Africa, and Asia, Made between the Years 1770 and 1779), a four-volume Swedish work published at Uppsala. It contained an account of Thunberg's visit to Japan between 1775 and 1776, when he worked for the Dutch East India Company as a surgeon aboard its flagship. Thunberg's book was translated into French by Louis Langlès and published in Paris in 1796. Its contents differed a great deal from Kaempfer's work in that it contained reflections on the Japanese language, agriculture, sciences, arts, and professions, as well as on domestic and foreign trade. Thunberg recounted his meetings with Japanese specialists in Dutch studies—physicians, astronomers, naturalists—and his visit to the shogun in the spring of 1776. Thunberg also alluded to the institution of *fumie* but added that the Dutch did not have to submit to it.

Since the Netherlands had a monopoly on trade with Japan, Britain, the other great maritime power of the 18th century, was not allowed to have a direct relationship with the archipelago. However, the 1727 English translation of Kaempfer's book attracted the attention of British and Irish intellectuals. Even earlier, interest in the subject could be discerned in Part III of Jonathan Swift's book *Gulliver's Travels* (1726), "A Voyage to Laputa, Balnibarbi, Glubbdubdrib, Luggnagg, and Japan," which ends with the hero's visit to the Japanese archipelago. Swift's account evocatively emphasizes the famous ceremony of "trampling upon the crucifix." Thanks to the benevolence of the emperor of Japan, or rather the shogun of Edo, Gulliver is able to leave the country without having to reject his religion at "Nangasac" (Nagasaki). Swift thus prolonged European misunderstandings of the *fumie* ceremony.

English literature contains at least one other example of the British interest in Japan: Tobias Smollett's *The History and Adventures of an Atom* (1768), a Rabelaisian political satire. Smollett had been responsible for the "modern part" of *An Universal History, from the Earliest Account of Time* (1747–68), written in collaboration with the historian John Campbell. Smollett made considerable use of the research that had been carried out on Japan, starting with Kaempfer, in order to create an exotic setting for his thinly disguised account of typically British political realities. Recognizable portraits of William Pitt the Elder, Queen Anne, the duke of Cumberland, and many other public figures are presented in Japanese masks. The first three are transformed, respectively, into the Taycho (the great Japanese general Hideyoshi Toyotomi), the empress Syko, and Fatzman (the god of war).

For the *philosophes* of 18th-century Europe, Japan was a "virgin" land that encouraged all sorts of illusions and offered new possibilities offered to the imagination. Japan was regarded as a country in the Far East that respected freedom of conscience, and people seemed to lived there not under the yoke of religion but in accordance with purely moral precepts. These illusions clearly reflect the influence of Kaempfer, who believed that Japan had never been in a "more fortunate situation" than the one it enjoyed in the late 17th century, dominated by the shogun "Tsinajos" (Tsunayoshi), who had himself been "trained in the philosophy of Confucius." In short, Europeans perceived Japan as a country where the philosophical and moral ideas of the Enlightenment had already been achieved. The Encyclopedists needed models capable of supporting their criticisms of the political and social system, and they found in Japan an example that was all the more convenient because it was so far away. However, from the last quarter of the 18th century onward, Europeans were freed from this idealization, which was one more form of exoticism, and they began to regard the Japanese in a more objective and scientific light, as a people akin to themselves even though the Japanese lived on the other side of the globe.

HISAYASU NAKAGAWA

Further Reading

Beasley, William Gerald, *The Japanese Experience: A Short History of Japan,* Berkeley: University of California Press, and London: Weidenfeld and Nicolson, 1999

Dore, Ronald Philip, *Education in Tokugawa Japan,* Berkeley: University of California Press, and London: Routledge and Kegan Paul, 1965

Guth, Christine, *Art of Edo Japan: The Artist and the City, 1615–1868,* New York: Abrams, 1996

Kato, Shuichi, *A History of Japanese Literature,* vol. 2, *The Years of Isolation,* translated by Don Sanderson, Tokyo and New York: Kodansha International, 1991 (original Japanese edition, 1979)

Keene, Donald, *The Pleasures of Japanese Literature,* New York: Columbia University Press, 1988

Keene, Donald, editor, *Anthology of Japanese Literature: From the Earliest Era to the Mid–Nineteenth Century,* London: Allen and Unwin, and New York: Grove Press, 1955

Nishiyama, Matsunosuke, *Edo Culture: Daily Life and Diversions in Urban Japan, 1600–1868,* translated and edited by Gerald Groemer, Honolulu: University of Hawaii Press, 1997

Proust, Jacques, *L'europe au prisme du Japon: XVIe–XVIIIe siècle: Entre humanisme, Contre-Réforme et Lumières,* Paris: Michel, 1997

Reischauer, Edwin O., *Japan, Past and Present,* New York: Knopf, 1946; London: Duckworth, 1947; 4th edition, as *Japan: The Story of a Nation,* New York: Knopf, and London: Duckworth, 1970

Jardin du Roi

French Royal Botanical Garden

Numerous botanical gardens existed in Europe during the age of the Enlightenment, and several of them were already well established at that time. The first of these had been planted in Italy more than 100 years earlier during the Renaissance—in Padua and Pisa (both in 1545), Florence (1550), and Bologna (1567). Other botanical gardens were soon established in northern Europe—in Leiden (1577) and Leipzig (1580). In 1597 the Englishman John Gerard published the catalog of the medicinal plants he had cultivated in Holborn. In France itself there were precursors, such as the apothecaries' garden created in Paris in 1576 by Nicolas Houel and, most importantly, the botanical garden of Montpellier, founded in 1593 by Henri IV on the initiative of Richer de Belleval. In the 17th century the planting of medicinal species for instructional purposes increased around the faculties of medicine.

Among all the gardens existing in Europe around 1715, the Jardin Royal des Plantes Médicinales (Royal Garden of Medicinal Plants) in Paris was certainly one of the best known. Louis XIII had decreed its creation by edict in January 1626. After the acquisition of some land in the Faubourg Saint Victor in 1633, this new enterprise received its first statutes in 1635 and opened its gates in 1640. It is therefore one of the oldest of France's official scientific institutes, following the Collège Royal (1530) but preceding the Académie Royale des Sciences (1666) and the Observatoire de Paris (1672, Paris Observatory). Its first director and true founder was Guy de La Brosse (1586–1641), personal physician to Louis XIII. Its first teachers were all doctors of medicine, for like the other botanical gardens of that period, the Paris garden, mainly intended for the training of future physicians and apothecaries, offered courses in botany, anatomy, and, for the first time in France, official instruction in chemistry.

Despite its pedagogical function, the garden was under the direction of the chief royal physician rather than one of the medical professors of the Faculté de Médecine (Faculty of Medicine). Placed under the direct protection of the sovereign and established outside the university system in order to function as an institute for free research and expression, from the outset the royal botanical garden had a "modern" character that heralded the spirit of the Enlightenment. For example, it demanded no academic prerequisites that would have restricted attendance at its lectures. Moreover, instruction at the institute, which was practical in character, was entrusted to "demonstrators," and courses were taught in French beginning in 1640, even though Latin would remain the compulsory language in universities for a long time to come. Finally, and most importantly, the institute provided a forum for the dissemination of audacious scientific doctrines, such as William Harvey's theory of the circulation of the blood (from 1673), and the use of "chemical medicine," in particular emetics based on antimony. All these innovations profoundly irritated the old Faculté de Médecine in Paris, and these guardians of the tradition of the ancients were powerful because they had the exclusive right to confer doctorates. The conflict was all the more bitter because the majority of the court physicians, the garden's protectors, had received their degrees at provincial universities—often at the Faculté de Médecine in Montpellier, the rival of the Paris medical faculty and the headquarters of those who advocated the use of antimony. Quarrels proliferated, but, thanks to royal protection, disputes were generally resolved in the garden's favor. In any case, Guy-Crescent Fagon (1638–1718), a medical professor at Paris Faculté de Médecine, an instructor at the Jardin Royal des Plantes Médicinales starting in 1671, head royal physician beginning in 1693, and a member of the Académie Royale des Sciences from 1699 onward, went to some trouble to settle these conflicts.

Fagon's long service as director of the Jardin Royal des Plantes Médicinales, from 1693 to 1718, marked the end of the "medical" period in the garden's history. Fagon's tenure was also notable for at least two other developments. First, he recruited a scientific staff of great distinction: the botanists Joseph Pitton de Tournefort (1656–1708), Antoine de Jussieu (1686–1758), and Sébastien Vaillant (1699–1722) and the chemists Étienne-François Geoffroy (1672–1731) and Simon Boulduc (1652–1729), all of whom were members of the Académie Royale des Sciences. Second, mindful of the trend that encouraged dissemination of scientific ideas and knowledge, Fagon promoted the cultivation of plants from the colonies as well as those gathered during the travels of researchers to distant countries. These journeys included those of Father Charles Plumier (1646–1704) in the West Indies; Father Louis Feuillée (1660–1732) in Chile and Peru; Tournefort in the eastern Mediterranean; and Augustin de Lippi (1678–1732) in Upper Egypt and Nubia. The garden's first hothouse was constructed in 1714 to accommodate a valuable coffee plant that had been donated by the Dutch.

The new orientation initiated by Fagon accelerated under the two directors who followed him: Pierre Chirac (1650–1732) from 1718 to 1732 and Charles-François de Cisternai Du Fay (1698–1739) from 1732 to 1739. Thus, the Jardin Royal des Plantes Médicinales became, imperceptibly, the Jardin du Roi (Royal Botanical Garden) as it changed its focus from the art of healing to true natural history. Two main events are symbolic of this development. Under a royal declaration of 31 March 1718, supervision of the garden was separated from the office of the chief royal physician, and from that date onward the post of superintendent remained vacant until it was formally abolished in 1732. The garden continued to be managed by its director. Eleven years later, in 1729, the former "druggist's shop," which had gradually ceased to be a dispensary, was officially renamed the Cabinet d'Histoire Naturelle (Natural History Collection).

The spirit of the Enlightenment was first embodied at the Jardin du Roi in the imposing figure of the comte de Buffon (1707–88), who became the garden's director in 1739 and remained in the position for 50 years, until 1788. A Newtonian, an Anglophile, and a free and audacious thinker, this ennobled bourgeois typified his age through the diversity of his talents. A philosopher, scholar, writer, businessman, and master smith, Buffon wore many hats. However, he was conservative on social issues and aristocratic by temperament. Imperious and solitary, Buffon remained on the fringes of the scientific society of his time. Having rapidly fallen into dispute with the *philosophes,* he never provided to the compilers of the *Encyclopédie* the article on nature that Diderot had announced, and, although he was a member of the Académie Française and permanent treasurer of the Académie Royale des Sciences, he counted more enemies than friends in both societies. The Jardin du Roi was not enough to absorb all the energies of this industrious man, and he was in residence there for barely half of each year, preferring to avoid the salons of the capital in favor of the comfortable retreat of his château at Montbard, where he wrote his *Histoire naturelle générale et particulière* (1749; Natural History, General and Particular).

Nevertheless, the Jardin du Roi was at the heart of the activities that made Buffon one of the scientific luminaries of Europe. Having become a powerful figure during the last 20 years of his "reign," Buffon doubled the garden's surface area between 1771 and 1787, working in three stages. First, he extended the plantings successively to the south, where the rue de Buffon, which has borne this name from the start, was laid out in 1782. He then extended the garden to the east, up to the Seine, and finally to the north, up to the rue de Seine-Saint-Victor (now the rue Cuvier). Under Buffon's direction continuous works of construction and new planting profoundly altered the profile of the establishment. At the end of 1787, some months before his death, Buffon had the architect Edme Verniquet (1727–1804) undertake the building of a vast amphitheatre, which still stands today.

Buffon did not intervene much in the courses given at the Jardin du Roi. The structure of the curriculum remained much the same as before, with its division into botany, chemistry, and anatomy. Each of these three major disciplines was allocated to a pair of teachers, one of whom now bore the title of "professor," while the other retained that of "demonstrator." The respective responsibilities of the professors and demonstrators are difficult to define except in the field of chemistry, which remained clearly divided up to the end of the ancien régime. In that discipline, the professor gave the lectures and the demonstrator was responsible for experiments and preparations. However, Buffon jealously kept for himself the task of appointing the holders of the six posts whenever one fell vacant. His choices—like those of Fagon in his day—demonstrate his great perceptiveness. In the field of botany Buffon chose Louis-Guillaume Le Monnier (1717–99) and Antoine-Laurent de Jussieu (1748–1836); in chemistry, he appointed the two Rouelle brothers, Guillaume-François (1703–70) and Hilaire-Marin (1718–79), as well as Pierre Macquer (1718–84) and Antoine-François de Fourcroy (1755–1809); and in anatomy, Buffon selected Jacques-Bénigne Winslow (1669–1760), Antoine Mertrud (died 1767), Antoine Ferrein (1693–1769), Antoine Petit (1722–94), and Antoine Portal (1742–1832). During the 18th century the Faubourg Saint-Victor seemed quite far removed from the center of Paris, but the lessons of nearly all these masters attracted many people to the Jardin du Roi. Again, it was Buffon who discovered Jean-Baptiste de Lamarck (1744–1829), the future theorist of "transformationism," and acted as patron for Lamarck's earliest scientific work.

André Thouin (1747–1824), who was named "head gardener" in 1764 at the age of 17, acclimatized the rare plants and sent thousands of packets of seeds, as well as saplings, to the four corners of Europe. The collections of living plants cultivated in the garden continued to expand. In 1774 Buffon tripled the size of the school of botany and decided to reorganize it. He replaced Tournefort's methodology with a combination of the binary nomenclature developed by Carl von Linné (Linnaeus) of Sweden and the natural classification proposed by Bernard de Jussieu (1699–1777), brother of Antoine. In 1788 the school, which had expanded again by one-fourth, owned more than 6,000 plants. The most fragile specimens and those from exotic countries were housed in the orangery and in greenhouses built by Fagon, Du Fay, and Buffon. The collection of plants in the herbarium was enlarged in tandem with that of the botany school. Thus a reference collection was created and then regularly enriched, notably with the addition of two major herbariums in the early years of the century. The first of these herbariums was added in 1708 by Tournefort; the second was added in 1722 by Sébastien Vaillant, assistant demonstrator of botany, who had achieved fame in 1716 by establishing the sexuality of plants and their fertilization mechanisms. Finally, rigorously precise paintings were made of the rarest and most beautiful plant specimens for the famous collection of the Vélins, which was kept in the royal library. Following Nicolas Robert (1614–85), the post of royal miniature painter was held in turn by Jean Joubert (died ca. 1705), Claude Aubriet (1665–1742), Magdeleine Basseporte (1701–80), and Gérard Van Spaendonck (1746–1822).

Buffon, in particular, devoted special care to the collection of natural history specimens at the Jardin du Roi. Having failed to get a new building constructed for it, he reorganized at great expense the existing location and tripled its size. In 1745 he entrusted the cura-

torship of the Cabinet d'Histoire Naturelle to a fellow resident of Montbard, the physician Louis-Jean-Marie Daubenton (1716–1800), and, in order to assist Daubenton in a task that grew unceasingly, he saw to the creation of two more posts, occupied by Bernard-Germain de Lacepède (1756–1825) and Barthélemy Faujas de Saint-Fond (1741–1819), neither of whom was a physician. Because the Cabinet, open to the public for two days every week, was in a sense the display window for the Jardin du Roi, the collection was enriched extraordinarily over the course of the 18th century. Buffon maintained an active correspondence with scholars around Europe and with officials in the distant colonies, soliciting supplies and information and granting to the most enthusiastic the official title of "correspondents" of either the Jardin du Roi or the Cabinet d'Histoire Naturelle. When the first volumes of his *Histoire naturelle* appeared (from 1749), becoming an immediate and prodigious bestseller, Buffon shrewdly named in it those who had provided materials for the Cabinet. As a result, more donors presented gifts for the Cabinet in the hope of having their reputations burnished by such recognition. Even the rulers of Denmark, Poland, Sweden, Prussia, and Russia had the honor of contributing to this successful undertaking by sending the natural produce of their countries. In 1782, when Catherine II gave him a pressing invitation to come to Saint Petersburg at once, Buffon had his son take her a bust of himself that had been sculpted by Augustin Pajou.

Several important natural history collections, either purchased or obtained free of charge, came to enrich the Cabinet, notably those of Michel Adanson (1727–1806) and René Ferchault de Réaumur (1683–1757). The Cabinet also received plants brought back from various parts of the world by such travelers as Philibert Commerson (1727–73), a companion of Bougainville on his voyage around the world; Pierre Sonnerat (1748–1814), who continued the exploration of the Indian Ocean begun by Pierre Poivre (1719–86); Joseph Dombey (1742–94), who traveled in Latin America; André Michaux (1746–1803), who traveled in North America; and Charles Sonnini de Manoncourt (1751–1812), who went first to Guyana and then to Egypt and Asia Minor.

By 1780 Buffon had become a figure of international stature. As a member of academies in Berlin, London, Saint Petersburg, Bologna, Florence, Edinburgh, Philadelphia, and elsewhere, he enjoyed an extraordinary prestige outside France. And his prestige reflected on the Jardin du Roi, where the masters whom he had brought together formed a scientific pantheon of the first order, with Buffon himself at its center. At that point, no other botanical garden in Europe—not even the already celebrated Kew Gardens, founded near London in 1759—could rival the Jardin du Roi in Paris. Buffon's death, on 16 April 1788, marked the zenith of the history of the garden, and at the same time the end of an era that had been profoundly affected by his personal influence. The grandiose funeral that was conducted for Buffon, one year before the opening of the Estates General, was also, in some sense, the funeral of the ancien régime.

Buffon's successors, Auguste Flahaut de La Billarderie (1724–93), from 1788 to 1791, and Jacques-Henri Bernardin de Saint-Pierre (1737–1814), from 1792 to 1793, were the last two directors of the Jardin du Roi. In the midst of the revolutionary turmoil these men could not add much to Buffon's work, the lasting quality of which was another indication of its value. The Revolution, which was to transform so profoundly the structures and teaching of the sciences in France, respected the Jardin du Roi, which became the Jardin National (National Garden). Its activities were not disrupted even momentarily. The institute held out, and it was in response to the wishes of Jardin's own staff that the Convention issued the decree of 10 June 1793 trans-

forming the garden into the Muséum d'Histoire Naturelle (Museum of Natural History).

YVES LAISSUS

See also Classification; Natural History; Science; Travel

Further Reading

Contant, Jean-Paul, *L'enseignement de la chimie au Jardin royal des plantes de Paris*, Cahors, France: Coueslant, 1952

Crestois, Paul, *Contribution à l'histoire de l'enseignement de la pharmacie: L'enseignement de la botanique au Jardin royal des plantes de Paris*, Cahors, France: Coueslant, 1953

Laissus, Yves, "Le Jardin du roi," in *Enseignement et diffusion des sciences en France au XVIIIᵉ siècle*, edited by René Taton, Paris: Hermann, 1964

Laissus, Yves, "Les voyageurs-naturalistes du Jardin du roi et du Muséum d'histoire naturelle," *Revue d'histoire des sciences* 34 (1981)

Jesuits

While the Enlightenment did not invent anti-Jesuitism, the age did crystallize all its characteristics, condensing criticisms developed over the two previous centuries into a comprehensive rejection, in which the values embodied by the Society of Jesus were seen as the opposite of those on which the Enlightenment ideal was based. The Society represented a distillation of everything against which the *philosophes* were fighting. It was a religious order and so by nature was intolerant, obscurantist, hypocritical, and even scheming. It was a hierarchical body whose members, subjugated by their vow of obedience, suppressed a freedom that the *philosophes* were in the process of defining as inalienable. It was an institution controlled by a powerful general, upon whom it bestowed an unparalleled power, which, by reason of the educational monopoly his organization had obtained, represented a danger to the young.

In the 18th century, a century of anticlericalism, the Society found itself accused of all the faults of the Church as a whole; indeed, the characteristics that had made the Jesuits unique as a new religious order in the mid–16th century were viewed as extreme manifestations of those faults. This antagonistic view left no

room for a more qualified analysis, which would have been out of keeping with the Enlightenment approach. Hostility toward the Society, widespread among the *philosophes* (as their many writings show), was also shared by some religious circles, and by the generation of politicians who, on reaching power in the 1750s, set about suppressing the order. While none of the controversies in which the Jesuits found themselves embroiled in the 18th century originated in the age of the Enlightenment, the growing support for anti-Jesuitism among the European ruling classes of that period explains the attacks to which the Society was subjected during the 1750s.

Founded by Ignatius Loyola in 1540, the Society had enjoyed continued growth and expansion right up until the middle of the Enlightenment period. Its universal vocation, proclaimed by its founder and codified in its Constitutions, explains why, after two centuries of existence, the Society's membership in the mid–18th century was the largest it had ever been. At Ignatius's death in 1556 its numbers had stood at 1,000, rising to 8,500 by the beginning of the 17th century and to 15,500 at the time of its first centenary. Although growth had subsequently slowed, membership in the society was still increasing 200 years after its founding. In 1749 there were 22,589 members, distributed over a network of 1,180 schools, professed houses, novitiates, residences, and missions.

In addition to being numerically strong, the Jesuits enjoyed a worldwide presence through their missionary work. Since the time when Francis Xavier had traveled to Asia, visiting Goa for the first time in 1542 and Japan in 1549, Jesuit missionaries had penetrated China, where leading Jesuit mathematicians won recognition among the imperial entourage, and the New World, where they gradually infiltrated the vastness of the Amazon region. There were 213 Jesuits in Chile in 1729, 417 in Brazil in 1735, and in 1741 there were 335 Jesuits in Mexico and 566 in Peru. Moreover, in 1768 the "reductions" (supervised settlements) in Paraguay were home to 200,000 Indians, living in communal, agriculturally based villages run by the Jesuits. In total, 15.5 percent of the Jesuits were involved in the missions. In Europe they were concentrated in the Mediterranean countries. There were 1,420 in the kingdom of Naples, 1,754 in Portugal (half of whom were in missions), 3,500 in France, and 5,400 in Spain. These figures show the extent of the social, cultural, religious, political, and economic importance of the institution. Of the five assemblies stretching from England to Poland, that of Germania was the largest, involving a third of the Society's members, who ran 207 schools and 80 seminaries.

Universalism was also an apostolic policy. The Jesuits had taken on the responsibilities of preaching, conversion, confession, and education. The last two activities, partly entrusted to the numerous and omnipresent Marian congregations, undoubtedly helped to establish the Jesuits within European society and made them a force to be reckoned with. As far as the Society's importance in the educational system is concerned, the idea of the Jesuit monopoly, widely propagated by its detractors, needs to be seen in the light of the facts and modified according to the country concerned—something few studies make possible as yet. In France, for example, this "monopoly" corresponded in 1763 to just under a quarter of the educational establishments in the kingdom, where schools run by other regular clergy, notably the Oratorians, also enjoyed a certain reputation. All the same, in the cities of Europe the Jesuit colleges were prestigious establishments that attracted the elite of society—the nobles' seminary in Madrid, for example. Moreover, just when the Jesuit Fathers in Portugal were threatened with expulsion, that great enlightened despot Frederick II, friend of Voltaire, called on the Society to organize his schools.

Although its actual significance has been exaggerated, the extent and uniformity of the Jesuit educational network inspired the widespread belief that the Society was omnipresent. Education, of course, was one of the main concerns of the *philosophes,* and the development of textbooks on teaching, along with the proliferation of plans for pedagogical reform necessitated by the rise of enlightened monarchies, encouraged reformers to analyze critically the Jesuit system, which still adhered rigidly to rules drawn up in 1599, and to practices incompatible with the new ideas, particularly in the scientific field—opposition to the new experimental physics remained the order of the day in the overwhelming majority of philosophy classes.

Meanwhile, the Jesuits had effectively taken over the role of "royal confessors." In France one Jesuit after another could be found at Louis XV's side. In Bourbon Spain, Charles III discontinued the custom, but various members of the royal family maintained such confessors. In the Austrian Netherlands from 1745 to 1780, Charles de Lorraine was guided by Father Hallerstein. Contemporary observers concluded from such examples that the Jesuits had European politics under their control—though their influence was in reality no longer so pervasive.

In the general context of criticism of the Church and its institutions, the Society's fiercest opponents were to be found within the Church itself. Internal conflicts, which had pitted the Jesuits against the other orders as well as against the secular clergy, centered mainly on the problems of the missions and of Jansenism. The division that Jansenism had opened in the Catholic community weighed all the more heavily because it had made the Jansenists and the Jesuits into implacable enemies. The theological quarrel between orthodox Catholicism and Jansenism that had begun in the middle of the 17th century had become, with the publication of *Les provinciales* (1656–57; The Provincial Letters of Blaise Pascal), one of the most important cultural and moral debates of contemporary Europe. The debate on divine grace opened the way to quarrels over religious morality. (As early as 1588 the Jesuit Molina had tried to reconcile the efficacy of grace with humanity's free will in his work *De concordia liberi arbitrii cum gratiae donis* [The Harmony of Free Will with Gifts of Grace]). In the polemical fury that was characteristic of both camps, the Jesuits were labeled as laxists and as such vigorously denounced by the Jansenist rigorists. Far from bringing the rise of Jansenism to a decisive halt, the 1713 papal bull *Unigenitus* caused the quarrel to continue into the mid–18th century and to spread throughout Europe, giving rise to alliances against the Jesuits (on a temporary basis and depending on the country) between Jansenists and Gallicans, Josephists, Febronianists, regalists, or jurisdictionalists. Thus, in the midst of the Enlightenment, Jesuit spirituality had become one of the main targets of a Catholic

Church that aspired to a less ostentatious, plainer, and more rigorous form of religion.

The same kind of criticism of the Society was the central plank in the quarrel over rites—another conflict that, arising within the Church, contributed directly to the weakening of the Society during the Enlightenment period by calling into question one of the most striking aspects of the Jesuits' success. The competition between missionary orders, which began with the arrival of the Dominicans and Franciscans in China at the beginning of the 1630s, had raised the question of how to interpret the traditional Confucian and ancestral ceremonies of the Christianized Chinese. Whereas the Jesuits viewed these rites to be secular customs, the Franciscans and Dominicans petitioned Rome, insisting on the religious aspect of these Chinese customs and accusing the Jesuits of laxity in their conversions. When in 1715, by the constitution *Ex ilao die* the pope forbade all missionaries in China to make any concession to local beliefs (an ordinance confirmed in 1742 by the bull *Ex quo singulari*), he brought about the end of the policy of toleration hitherto extended toward Catholics by the emperor of China. From 1717, reprisals against the Chinese Christians became frequent, underlining the precariousness of the advances made in the previous century and ultimately signaling the end of Jesuit and Catholic expansion in China. The quarrel over rites had aroused interest in Europe through the circulation of the *Lettres édifiantes et curieuses* (1702–76) and the commentaries they inspired from the *philosophes*. The Society emerged from this controversy weakened both in its geographic base and by its image as an order in decline.

The difficulties the Society faced within the Church were not, however, the only factors behind the decline of its power during the Enlightenment. The suppression of the order began with its expulsion from a number of European countries. These expulsions were owing to economic and political problems, as the case of Portugal perfectly illustrates. The reign of Joseph I, marked by the political dominance of the marquis of Pombal and the implementation of a massive program of modernization in the country, was also distinguished by a bitter struggle against the Society. The Spanish-Portuguese colonial treaty of 1750 gave Portugal control of a portion of the Jesuits' reductions in Paraguay, exposing the Indians to the greed of the Portuguese and subjecting the missionaries to political and economic rule by the state.

The Guarani rebellion against the Portuguese and Spanish armies in 1754–56 was interpreted by the European monarchies as a Jesuit response to the threat of losing their control of these reputedly rich territories. In Portugal this interpretation was one of the pretexts for the decision in 1755 to expel the Jesuits from Para-

guay. At the same time, the attempted assassination of the Portuguese king in 1748 and the Lisbon earthquake of 1755 gave Pombal sufficient pretext to develop the theme of a Jesuit plot against the monarchy. He had already begun to wage war in earnest against the Society, banishing them from the court and putting pressure on Pope Benedict XIV in order to obtain a brief for the reform and visitation of the Jesuits in Portugal. As a result of Pombal's plot, Gabriel Malagrida (1689–1761), one of the most important figures in the Jesuit mission to Brazil and a popular preacher since his return to Lisbon, was turned over to the Inquisition and found guilty of treason and heresy. Voltaire witnessed Malagrida's execution by burning in one of the last autos-da-fé (1761). Meanwhile, in 1759 the order had been expelled from Portugal, the Jesuits shipped back to Italy, and their property confiscated.

Taken at the very time that Enlightenment ideas were prevailing throughout Europe (and chiefly in the political field), this measure opened the way to similar reactions in other countries and indeed hastened their implementation. The anti-Jesuit pamphlets that Pombal disseminated were circulated throughout Europe, thereby strengthening the hostility toward the Society that the religious controversies had already helped to spread. Louis XV's France was rocked by the affair of Father Lavalette, head of the mission in Martinique, who had taken up sugar- and coffee-growing for commercial ends and then had contracted debts in order to buy more estates. Lavalette's financial speculations collapsed when the Jesuits' cargoes were seized by English pirates (1755), leaving him with debts that he was unable to honor. This affair, complicated by the refusal of the Jesuit provincial of France to take responsibility for his subordinate's monetary difficulties (on the pretext that Jesuit establishments were financially autonomous), threw the profit-making activities of the Society into an especially negative light. The decision of the Parlement of Paris (1 April 1761) to subject the Jesuit Constitutions to scrutiny, in the hope of resolving an episode that had a bearing on relations between the spiritual and temporal spheres, reveals the extent to which attitudes toward the order had changed since its foundation.

This decision by the Parlement, which led to the condemnation of 1762, was interpreted abroad as a new victory for the Enlightenment spirit. The indictment pronounced against the Society in the Parlement of Brittany by La Chalotais was distributed across Europe, further emphasizing how much the opposition of the "Republic of Letters" to an order that represented obscurantism and intolerance helped to give an international resonance to all these initially strictly national issues. This opposition was accentuated by the protagonists in the affair themselves. As Jean le Rond

D'Alembert noted in *Sur la destruction des Jésuites en France* (1764; On the Destruction of Jesuits in France), the Jesuits

> had also discovered the secret of antagonizing deeply a class of men, apparently less powerful, but in fact more formidable than is generally suspected—the men of letters. The Jesuits' denunciations of the *Encyclopédie,* at court and in town, had stirred up against them everyone who took an interest in this work, of whom there were a great many. . . . One should never make enemies of those who, having the advantage of being read from one end of Europe to the other, can exact a devastating and lasting vengeance with a stroke of the pen.

The Society had indeed thrown its whole weight as a leading cultural organization into the fight against the new ideas. The *Mémoires de Trévoux* attest to this fact, as does the Jesuit Fathers' very limited participation in European academic circles. Compared to the general Jesuit abstention from these circles, the interest in Newtonian physics displayed by Louis Castel of the Collège Louis-le-Grand and the scientific activities of Ruggero Boscovich were rare exceptions to the general rule.

The suppression of the order in France (1764)—followed by their suppression in Spain and Naples (both in 1767) and in Parma (1769)—was based on a variety of different pretexts. In Spain the minister Pedro Rodríguez Campomanes, editor of the *Dictamen fiscal de expulsión de los Jesuitas de España (1766–1767)* (1767; Fiscal Judgment regarding the Expulsion of the Jesuits from Spain), a lengthy indictment of the Society, capitalized on the popular revolts of 1766 and the rise of a huge anti-Jesuit front to bring about the order's brutal expulsion and forced return to Rome. Over and above the differences in procedure, it is worth noting the characteristics shared by the various movements opposing the Jesuits. These efforts were often spurred, especially in Mediterranean Europe, by the accession of enlightened despots who were steeped in Enlightenment ideas and surrounded by enterprising ministers. These ministers were avid for political reforms that would free states from Church influence and would result in a program of far-reaching change—and they believed that the Jesuits represented the chief obstacle to this fulfillment. Pombal and Campomanes shared their profound anti-Jesuitism with the marquis of Tanucci in Naples, Guillaume Du Tillot in Parma, and Joseph II in Austria.

The distinctive religious context and the relative youth of their countries no doubt explain the opposite attitude displayed by those other two enlightened despots, Frederick II of Prussia and Catherine II of Russia. In these two non-Catholic countries, the question of mutual duties between state and papacy was irrelevant. In the context of a general shortage of civil servants, such posts were routinely assigned to Jesuit personnel—a situation whose political implications were not lost on the two eastern European rulers were well aware. Thus, in 1773 when Pope Clement XIV, acting under pressure from Catholic rulers, proclaimed the bull of dissolution *Dominus ac Redemptor,* Prussia and Russia became safe havens, from which the new Society began to reestablish itself in the early years of the 19th century. This papal decision not only shows the virulence of the hostility toward the order even in pontifical circles but also highlights the papacy's weakness in the face of temporal monarchies.

The most recent historical work, chiefly consisting of specialized studies, calls for a modification of views about the Society and its relationship with the Enlightenment, particularly on the subject of education. In this arena, the suppression gave rise to serious shortfalls in a number of countries, none of which was able to make good the void left by the exiles. The material consequences of the suppression amounted to the destruction of more than 600 religious houses, the expulsion of around 20,000 priests, the closing of several hundred schools, and the abandonment of entire mission territories. The last general of the old Society, Lorenzo Ricci, died at the castle of Saint-Ange in 1775, in the prison to which the papal bull had consigned him.

ANTONELLA ROMANO

See also Anti-Enlightenment; Catholicism; China; Confraternity; Dance; Jansenism; Science: Dissemination and Popularization; Theatre and Staging

Further Reading

Northeast, Catherine M., *The Parisian Jesuits and the Enlightenment: 1700–1762,* Oxford: Voltaire Foundation, 1991

Polgár, László, *Bibliography of the History of the Society of Jesus,* Rome: Jesuit Historical Institute, and St. Louis, Missouri: St. Louis University, 1967

Journalism. *See* Newspapers and Journalism

Judaism

For the Jews, who had lived as exiles in Europe for centuries, the Enlightenment proved a momentous period, marked particularly by the beginnings of two significant movements: Hasidism and political emancipation (in 1791 France's revolutionary government granted Jews political equality for the first time in that nation's history). Yet, notwithstanding such unifying moments, Jewish life in this period can primarily be characterized as a mosaic, within an overall framework of distinct communities that had little to do with one another. In some countries this diversity was quite pronounced. In France, for example, there was a population of assimilated Jews in the southeast, the so-called Portuguese merchants, who were very different from the more traditional, strictly observant Jews in Alsace and Lorraine who made up the majority of the local population. Similarly, the Berlin millionaires who emerged after the Seven Years' War or the hostesses of famous literary salons bore little resemblance to the Yiddish-speaking masses of eastern Europe. It should also be clearly noted here that Christian attitudes toward Jews varied widely, depending on whether the Christians were Catholic or Protestant, city dwellers or country folk. The Pietists and the *Aufklärung* philosophers had an entirely different view of Jews and Judaism from that held by orthodox Lutherans or militant Catholics.

There were approximately 40,000 Jews in France on the eve of the Revolution. Within the frontiers of the future German Empire there were already 70,000 Jews in the mid–18th century, and by the end of the Napoleonic Wars the Jewish population had grown to 400,000 or 500,000. However, the Jewish population in Germany hardly ever exceeded 1 percent of the total population (Jews made up 3 percent of the population in Hesse, counterbalanced by a meager 0.05 percent in Saxony). Around 1780 only a few cities—Frankfurt, Berlin, Furth, Hamburg, and Glogau—had a Jewish population of more than 1,000. Judaism at the dawn of the 18th century was largely self-sufficient and, except for a few *Hofjuden,* very few Jews had contact with the non-Jewish world. By the end of the century, however, the situation was reversed: there were very few Jews who had not encountered Christians or had dealings with them. In Prussia, as in the Netherlands in the 17th century, Jews showed that toleration could also be turned to commercial advantage. Furthermore, the secularization of European society and culture, together with the spread of the concept of natural rights, frequently led to movements to abolish forms of discrimination and humiliation that had come to be regarded as medieval.

In Tuscany the commercial skills of Jews were put to use at an early date: there were 30,000 Jews in Italy, including 7,000 in Rome. However, the popes of the Enlightenment period hardly distinguished themselves by their love of Jews. Clement XII asked Cardinal Petra to establish a code hostile to Jews. This code was reinforced by Benedict XIV, who was lax on the matter of forced baptism. But Clement XIII requested his nuncio in Warsaw to defend the Jews against an accusation of ritual murder. The most tolerant pope was Clement XIV, but his successor Pius VI fell back into the old ways, publishing an *Editto sopra gli Ebrei* (Edict on the Hebrews) in 1775. When, in 1781–82, Joseph II suggested a series of measures aimed at ameliorating the status of Jews, the papacy clearly expressed its disapproval. Catholics were not the only ones to discriminate against Jews. An attempt to pass a naturalization edict in London in 1753 was unsuccessful, and the measure was withdrawn.

The great Jewish philosopher from Berlin, Moses Mendelssohn (1729–86), was living proof for 18th-century Europeans that one could be a highly talented thinker without being Christian, as Spinoza had already shown. Mendelssohn, who in 1763 was awarded the first prize in the class of speculative philosophy at the Berlin Academy, ahead of Immanuel Kant, was the author of *Phädon, oder über die Unsterblichkeit der Seele* (1767; Phaedo; or, On the Immortality of the Soul). The book achieved great success throughout Europe and was translated into more than ten languages. Mendelssohn's German translation of the Bible, which he transcribed in Hebrew letters, aimed at teaching Jews to share the language of their host country with a view to future citizenship. His *Jerusalem, oder über religiöse Macht und Judenthum* (1783; Jerusalem; or, On Religious Power and Judaism) is the charter of modern Judaism. It shows that religious observance is not incompatible with life in modern society and also demonstrates that Judaism is a school of toleration. The *Haskalah* (Jewish Enlightenment) clearly proved that Jews could participate fully in scientific and philosophical progress of the countries where they lived. Moreover, they could be leaders in these movements, as would be the case in the 19th and early 20th centuries. The philosophers Theodor Gomperz, Marcus Herz, Mendelssohn, and later Solomon Maimon and many others were examples for dozens and then hundreds of Jews who enrolled in German universities.

Just when Gotthold Ephraim Lessing's *Nathan der Weise* (1779; Nathan the Wise) had altered the public's perception of Jews, Christian Wilhelm Dohm, a high-ranking Prussian official as well as a pure product of the *Aufklärung,* wrote *Über die bürgerliche Verbesserung der Juden* (1781; Concerning the Amelioration of the Civil Status of the Jews). The first part of this book quickly appeared in French as *De la réforme politique des juifs* (1782), and then in Italian. Although the book was officially condemned, it circulated widely in France, and its theses were disseminated by the marquis de Mirabeau (in *Sur Moses Mendelssohn sur la réforme politique des juifs, et en particulier sur la révolution tentée en leur faveur en 1753 dans la grande Bretagne* [1788; On Moses Mendelssohn on the Political Reform of the Jews, and More Particularly the Revolution Attempted on Their Account in 1753 in Great Britain]). Mendelssohn's ideas had already been extensively used by competitors in the Académie de Metz contest on the question "Is there a way to make the Jews more useful and happier in France?" The 1787 version of the question led to a prize being shared in 1788 between the abbé Grégoire, Zalkind Hourwitz, and the lawyer Thiery. This was the first time that the "Jewish question" had been treated on a truly national and even European scale rather than a regional one.

While public opinion as a whole remained indifferent, the Judaeophobia of the *philosophes*—Arthur Herzberg goes so far as to speak of anti-Semitism—has been carefully documented by B.E. Schwarzbach, R. Mortier, and F. Diaz. In fact, it consisted more of an attack against Christianity, or against all positive religions, than against Judaism as such, of which the *philosophes* were quite ignorant. Denis Diderot's observation of Jews in Holland led him to remark that "nowhere else do the Jews come so close to the condition of other citizens. They have their own neighborhood. Some are clean-shaven, some wear beards." The former "are rich and pass for being honest; you have to be on your guard against the bearded ones who are not infinitely scrupulous. Some of them are very well-educated." His *Encyclopédie* article on the philosophy of the Jews is rather superficial. In Germany, by contrast, and especially in

Prussia, almost all the pastors knew Hebrew, and Christian forms of theosophy and Kabbalah were known to exist in Würtemberg. However, if the governments Enlightenment Europe were largely favorable to the Jews, Frederick II can be cited as one example of a dangerous ambivalence. He permitted Jews to settle in his country, while strictly limiting their numbers. He used their skills and international contacts (for example, in Poland), but he detested them as people, all of which casts something of a shadow over the celebrated toleration of the philosopher-king. The Lavater affair, named for the Swiss pastor Johann Kaspar Lavater who in 1769 publicly asked Mendelssohn to convert, clearly demonstrates the limits of *Aufklärung* toleration, its "darker side." Even Johann Georg Hamann asked how a person could be a philosopher and remain Jewish. Nonetheless, the *Haskalah* left a decisive mark in the history of Western Judaism, causing a break with traditional Jewish life, exploding community structures, and undermining the power of the rabbis. A new Jewish identity took shape in Europe. This process happened more rapidly in France than in Germany, where relative economic, social, and cultural integration contrasted, from the late 18th century, with the absence of political emancipation, something that did not really occur in Germany until 1871. This new Jewish identity remains imprinted on Jewish identity today.

On the opposite side of Europe another movement started, Hasidism, which was contemporary with emancipation but not at all related to it. Still very active today in the United States and Israel, Hasidism began in southeastern Poland and Lithuania and centered on the figure of a "miraculous" rabbi, the Besht, Israel ben Eliezer Ba'al Shem Tov (1700–60). In a context of crisis (the Chmielnicki massacre and the conversion of the false messiah Shabbatai Zvi), Judaism concentrated on the lived experience of faith, on asceticism and/or ecstasy. The Kabbalah offered an infinite method of interpreting Scripture, thus retrieving it from the doctrinaire authority of the rabbis. Much of what we know about the history and ideas of the Ba'al Shem Tov has come to us from the *Shivhei ha Besht* (1814–1815; In Praise of the Ba'al Shem Tov [Shivhei ha-Besht]: The Earliest Collection of Legends about the Founder of Hasidism). Apparently born in Podolia and recognized as a master in the 1730s, he was believed to be miraculous, and few could resist his magnetism. He traveled far and wide to heal the sick, perform exorcisms, and combat evil spirits. He wanted to go all the way to Palestine. His approach to God involves prayer and ecstasy, though reading of the Torah remains central. Faith reaches God by *Devekout* (adhesion), because faith must be found in all daily acts. The community is organized around a *Tzadik* (just man), whose spiritual qualities are exceptional and are accepted as such by the group. It is the *Tzadik* who keeps sin at a distance by placing himself on the same level as ordinary men. The dreams, tales, and thought of Ba'al Shem Tov still form a mythical base of the life of Jews in eastern Europe today, especially since Martin Buber wrote in the 20th century.

It was the disciples of the Ba'al Shem Tov who gave the *logia* and systematized the doctrine of Hasidism, notably Dov Baer of Mezbireh and Jacob Joseph of Polonnoye, the latter in the famous *Toldot Ya'akov Yosef* (1780). Some, including the Polish rabbi Baruch Schick, translator of Euclid, went as far as Berlin to meet Mendelssohn. Others emigrated to the Holy Land in 1747 or 1777. Hebron, Safed, Tiberiad, and Jerusalem received European Jews.

From Statu Mare to Vilnius and from Kiev to Opatov, Hasidism was an important component of the Jewish world until 1933, structuring the lives of millions of individuals. However, Hasidism also gave rise to opposition movements within the Jewish community, notably the *mitnagdim*. Their master was Eliyah ben Salamon Zalman (1720–97), better known as the Gaon of Vilnius, who rejected charismatic authority and pseudomiracles. He too had many followers.

The outstanding event of the century for European Jewry was clearly the granting of political and legal equality by the French Revolution. The Enlightenment had demanded respect for all human beings, and an edict of toleration was published in France in 1787, recognizing the existence of "those who do not belong to the Catholic religion." The year of the Académie de Metz prize, Chrétien-Guillaume de Lamoignon de Malesherbes gathered information, received delegations, and had reports made by both Jews and non-Jews. Contrary to many have reported, he did not create a "Malesherbes Commission," but he did wish to improve the condition of the Jews as he had done for the Protestants. At the time of the Estates General Jews claimed political rights only on a limited basis. Berr Isaac Berr made a speech on 14 October 1789, but

emancipation was still proclaimed in a rather fragmentary, piecemeal way. First, the rights of the "Portuguese, Spanish and Avignon Jews" were confirmed. Then, on 27 September 1791, the entire Jewish population of the kingdom was placed on the same level as other citizens. As Simon Schwarzfuchs has noted, "the Jews [in France] were emancipated before being assimilated into the rest of the population," which is the opposite of what happened in Germany (see Schwarzfuchs).

Even before Jewish social and political integration, the Enlightenment did not view the Jews as harmful to society or as false believers who must convert. Many people came to see them as citizens identical to others. Emancipation, Hasidism, and the French Revolution profoundly changed the sense of identity of European Jews. The Revolution also changed how Europeans represented and thought about them. The promise of a harmonious symbiosis between Judaism and Europe may be considered as one of the major achievements of the 18th century. But we know today that that promise remained a utopia, one among many spawned by that century.

DOMINIQUE BOUREL

See also Bible; Migration

Further Reading

Ages, Arnold, *French Enlightenment and Rabbinic Tradition*, Frankfurt: Klostermann, 1970

Feuerwerker, David, *L'émancipation des juifs en France: De l'Ancien Régime à la fin du Second Empire*, Paris: Albin Michel, 1976

Katz, Jacob, *Out of the Ghetto: The Social Background of Jewish Emancipation, 1770–1870*, Cambridge, Massachusetts: Harvard University Press, 1973

Katz, Jacob, editor, *Toward Modernity: The European Jewish Model*, New Brunswick, New Jersey: Transaction Books, 1987

Schwartzfuchs, Simon, *Du juif à l'israélite: Histoire d'une mutation, 1770–1870*, Paris: Fayard, 1989

Justice and Prisons

The age of the Enlightenment marked the halfway point in a slow process of transformation of the judicial system and of legal thought, which extended from the closing years of the 17th century up to the middle of the 19th century. This gradual change had an impact on

judicial and penal institutions, on the laws in force and their legitimization, and on the position of lawyers and their role in society. The transformation also affected the way criminality as such was generally regarded. Michel Foucault has established 1670 and 1838 as the boundary markers of this process (see Foucault, 1975): 1670 was the year in which the royal ordinance regulating the ancien régime's system of justice was promulgated, while in 1838, France's first "modern" prison, La Roquette, constructed according to principles laid out by the English philosopher Jeremy Bentham in his *Panopticon* (1791), was opened in Paris.

Under the ancien régime, justice was fundamentally linked to the divine right of monarchy. Not only in France (through the royal ordinance already cited) but also in other European countries, justice was based on principles that were partly inherited from the Middle Ages. These principles included the nonpublic nature of criminal trials (except in Britain) as well as the practice of interrogation under torture (known in France as *la question*) to obtain proof of the role played by the accused and to force him to reveal his accomplices; the administering of *supplices* (corporal punishments carried out in public), such as the pillory, hanging, or branding, within a meticulously coded, ritualistic framework; and the particularly severe punishments meted out for any offense against religion or against the person of the monarch. This last principle was a result of the fundamental nature of justice itself, which, in the words of the article "Justice" in the *Dictionnaire de Trévoux* (1771 edition; Dictionary of Trévoux), "resides in the person of the sovereign, its administration being entrusted to the magistrates."

Several schools of Enlightenment thought subjected this entire system of justice to direct frontal attack, denouncing it as inhuman and despotic. The attack began in the 1730s but only made a significant impact on public opinion from the 1760s onward. In his *Relation de la mort du chevalier de La Barre, adressée au marquis de Beccaria* (1764; Account of the Death of the Chevalier de la Barre, Addressed to the Marquis of Beccaria), Voltaire challenges La Barre's conviction for blasphemy and, following the marquis de Vauvenargues, defines crime as "an act that offends society," adding that "this truth should be the basis of all criminal codes." In the article "Des délits locaux" (1767; On Local Offences) in his *Dictionnaire philosophique* (Philosophical Dictionary), Voltaire insists that the crimes of theft, murder, adultery, and calumny—crimes that every human society condemns—should be punished wherever they occur. On the other hand, he also insists that inequities in the punishment of such crimes must be corrected. Adopting the same approach, Montesquieu, in *De l'esprit des lois* (1748; The Spirit of Laws), establishes a correlation between the severity of penalties and the despotism of governments and explicitly calls for the relaxation of penalties, as well as for the abolition of torture.

The Italian jurist Cesare Beccaria played a leading role in the Europe-wide movement for judicial reform,

and the publication in 1764 of his *Dei delitti e delle pene* (An Essay on Crimes and Punishments) marked the beginning of an intensification of the debates about criminal justice. In this work, Beccaria takes as a given the principle that crimes should be judged and punished according to the damage that they cause to society, and makes a plea for rational punishment that would be oriented toward prevention rather than repression. Having read the works of the French *philosophes*, Voltaire in particular, Beccaria takes issue with the secret nature of criminal proceedings in most of the courts of Europe. He demands a strengthening of the defense of the accused and also calls for the abrogation of excessively long periods of imprisonment preceding trials. His compatriot Gaetano Filangieri, who was deeply influenced not only by Beccaria himself but also by Georg Ludwig Schmid von Avenstein's *Principes de la législation universelle* (Principles of Universal Legislation), lays the foundations in his influential treatise *Scienza della legislazione* (1780; Science of Legislation) for a thorough reform of the judicial system. In 1777 Gabriele Verri wrote *Osservazioni sulla tortura* (Observations on Torture) following discussions within a group of "enlightened" intellectuals associated with *Le Caffè*, a Milan periodical that was influential throughout Europe.

The chevalier de Jaucourt's article "Crime" in the *Encyclopédie* reflects the new direction taken in discussions of criminal justice following the publication of Beccaria's ground-breaking book. In contrast to entries on crime or justice in earlier French reference works, such as the dictionaries of Furetière, Trévoux, and the Académie Française, or in German and British publications such as the *Dictionarium Britannicum*, Jaucourt's article is divided into two wholly separate parts. One addresses the question from the point of view of natural law, the other from the point of view of jurisprudence. In the part concerned with natural law, Jaucourt defines "crime" as "an atrocious action . . . that directly injures the public interest or the rights of the citizen," and thus emphasizes the importance of the security of "citizens." He then sets out a new classification of crimes and formulates a whole series of principles that call into question crucial aspects of the judicial system. For example, he stigmatizes as contrary to natural law any notion of penalties involving dishonor. He regards the severity of penalties as ineffective and contrary to propriety, and also challenges the principle that "it is better to risk letting one criminal escape than to punish an innocent person."

Neither Beccaria's book nor Jaucourt's article put forward specific proposals for reforms that would abolish "abuses." Instead, they advocate a complete overhaul of the judicial system that would also shake the foundations of the political system and even its legitimacy by way of the notion of "natural law." They thus helped to politicize the debate about justice, which process was continued through numerous theoretical writings and legal memorandums. Between 1760 and 1789 French censors banned more than 100 such texts, purportedly, according to Jacobson, on the grounds of injury to the public authorities. These texts included, for example, a *Discours sur l'administration criminelle* (1767; Essay on Criminal Administration) by Michel de Servan, a young lawyer at the *parlement* (high court) in Grenoble. Servan particularly attacks the severity of the punishments ritually administered in public and asks that punishments be simply a means of preserving public morals, not political acts. A whole series of such essays and pamphlets appeared in the 1770s and 1780s. Some of these texts originated in competitions organized by provincial academies, in France as well as in Italy. Many were written by lawyers who would go on to play significant roles in politics during the revolutionary period. The most representative examples of this wave of reformist writings are Lacretelle's *Discours sur ce sujet: Assigner les causes des crimes, et donner des moyens pour les rendre plus rares et moins funestes* (1774; Essay on the Elucidation of Crimes, and on Means to Make Them Rarer and Less Lethal), the result of a competition organized by the Academy of Mantua in Italy; the abbé de Mably's *De la législation, ou principes des loix* (1774; On Legislation; or, Principles of Laws); *La théorie des loix criminelles* (1781; Theory of Criminal Laws) and *Le sang innocent vengé* (1781; Innocent Blood Avenged) by Jean-Pierre Brissot, who was honored by the Académie of Châlons-sur-Marne; G.-F. Letrosne's *Vues sur la justice criminelle* (1777; Views on Criminal Justice); and the *Discours sur le préjugé des peines infamantes* (1784; Essay on the Prejudice of Sentences Involving Exile or Deprivation of Civil Rights) by Maximilien-Marie-Isidore de Robespierre, which shared first prize with a work by Lacretelle on the same subject, in a competition organized by the Société Royale (Royal Society) of Metz in 1784.

There was apparently no equivalent to this reformist wave in any other European country in the 18th century. Over and above differences in perspective and ideology, these writings are characterized by three common traits that suggest a shared desire for change. There is a generalized and politicized view of the phenomena of justice and criminality, based on natural law. The style is often sentimental, sometimes resembling that of the pamphlets of the period, deliberately aimed at arousing and mobilizing readers. They also commonly referred to recent trials that had generated scandals toward the end of the ancien régime, from the cases of Calas, Sirven, and La Barre (1762–64) to that of the Three Roués (1785–86).

The movement for reform of the traditional legal system thus embraced a very wide range of different topics, from the questioning of the fundamental principles of law and justice to very detailed proposals relating to those new forms of punishment (forced labor, imprisonment, the guillotine) that were intended to replace such traditional public and ritualized punishments as torture, burning, and the wheel (these latter now being almost universally denounced as "barbaric" and "inhuman"). The spokesmen for this reform movement concentrated on a certain number of issues of particular interest that aroused public controversy in every European country in the second half of the 18th century, although these issues were particularly acute in France during the decades leading up to the Revolution. The main reforms that were sought included the eradication of corruption in the allocation of judicial responsibilities; the suppression of seigniorial and ecclesiastical courts; and the transformation of judicial proceedings into public events. Advocates of reform argued that the judicial system should be independent both from the executive and from the legislature, following the principle of the separation of powers that Montesquieu had introduced in *De l'esprit des lois*. There was a call for a redefinition in the ranking of crimes, notably of those felonies that were severely punished by the courts of the ancien régime, such as blasphemy, adultery, sodomy, smuggling, and every form of attack, whether verbal or physical, on the person of the king. Finally, the reformists sought the abolition of exceptional measures, mainly typified, in the case of France, by *lettres de cachet* (orders of the king) and imprisonment in the Bastille.

The radical questioning of the judicial system and its ideological underpinnings led to the establishment of a new system, a process that began in the closing years of the ancien régime but was completed only after the French Revolution and the Napoleonic era. In 1740, well before Beccaria had launched the reform movement, Frederick II had abolished torture in the kingdom of Prussia. Empress Maria Theresa of Austria had followed suit in 1776 by abolishing torture and restricting imposition of the death penalty throughout the hereditary Habsburg lands. Her successor, Joseph II, extended these measures to all the other territories of the empire, including Lombardy. Projects for reform of civil and criminal codes were compiled in Catherine II's Russia in 1769, in Prussia in 1780, in Pennsylvania in 1786; in Tuscany in 1786, and in Austria in 1788.

In France *la question préparatoire* ("preparatory" torture preceding trial) was abolished in 1781, under the ministry of Necker, while *la question préalable* ("preliminary" torture applied to those who had been condemned to death just before their execution to force them to name their accomplices) was abolished in 1788. This latter reform was one of the concrete measures decided by a commission for reform of the penal code that had been established by the royal minister Loménie de Brienne and the chancellor Lamoignon; it was widely supported by such enlightened lawyers of the period as Dupaty. The commissioners nevertheless encountered fierce resistance, notably from the Parlement of Paris, and succeeded in introducing only very limited reforms up to 1789, when reform of justice became one of the demands most fully developed in the *cahiers de doléances* (Registers of Grievances), compiled for the meeting of the Estates General that year. The demolition of the Bastille, a prison that had practically lost its function during the last few decades before the Revolution, had been envisaged as early as 1784. However, it was the Revolution that finally gave the decisive impetus to the reform of the judicial system, not only in France but in most other European countries, starting with the promulgation of the *Déclaration des droits de l'homme et du citoyen* (Declaration of the Rights of Man and of the Citizen) in August 1789. Three major innovations followed the Declaration. First, a new criminal code was introduced. (1791). Second, the guillotine (proposed in December 1789) was adopted as the most humane instrument of execution. Third, the civil code of 1804—the Code Napoléon—was promulgated and would serve as a model for numerous civil codes in central and eastern Europe. The reform movement culminated in the establishment during the first half of the 19th century of a penal system that made imprisonment the main punishment for crime. Prior to that time, prisons had been no more than places for detaining accused individuals until a judgment was made).

Alongside its institutional dimension, the judicial reform movement also had a more directly political dimension, notably in France. The *parlements,* the highest courts in the judicial system of the ancien régime, had been the only institutions capable of controlling and resisting the authority of the monarchy and the Church. Their highly politicized confrontations had included, for example, their refusal to ratify the papal bull *Unigenitus* (1713) which forbade the sacraments to Jansenists (1727–56); their imposition of a ban on the Jesuits in 1763; and their opposition to the reform of the courts proposed by the royal minister René-Nicolas-Charles-Augustin de Maupeou, who dissolved the *parlements* in 1771 and sought to replace them with institutions that would be less troublesome to the government. Up until the beginning of the 1780s, the *parlements* managed to present themselves as defenders of traditional rights against the heavy hand of absolutist power.

The most notorious legal cases of the final years of the ancien régime—the cases of Calas, La Barre, and Sirven (1762–65) and the case of the Three Roués (1785–86)—politicized public opinion in another way. Alongside writers and *philosophes* such as Voltaire (who defended the Protestant Calas), Pierre-Augustin

Caron de Beaumarchais (whose memorandums, written during the Kornmann case, had a decisive impact on his own reputation), and the marquis de Condorcet, many lawyers—including Froudière, Dupaty, Lecauchois, Delacroix, Robespierre, and, above all, Linguet—became known as spokesmen and defenders of certain accused individuals who were innocent and who, in many cases, came from the lower classes of society. The high degree of sensationalism surrounding these cases explains both the presence and the dominant role of lawyers among the deputies in the Constituent Assembly, where they formed two-thirds of the total membership, and illustrates the close connections linking the political, literary, and legal circles of the period. The legal memorandums that appeared in connection with such causes célèbres as the Collier case, in which Marie-Antoinette and Cardinal de Rohan were implicated, or the Cléreaux case, in which a servant who resisted the advances of her master found herself accused of theft and condemned to death, read like intensely moving literary melodramas. At the same time, these notorious cases helped to spread a highly political perception of social inequalities, which led in turn to a far-reaching questioning of the legal system then in force.

The reform movement, the struggles of the *parlements,* and the impact made by the causes célèbres of the 1760s, 1770s, and 1780s, together with the significant growth in litigation between peasant communities and seigniorial courts, from the middle of the century to the Revolution, all helped to transform contemporary perceptions of judicial institutions. These institutions came to be seen as being among the main supports of a political and social system that was essentially arbitrary and inegalitarian. During the 18th century the main symbol of these institutions came to be the Bastille, the royal prison founded in 1356 and used primarily for the detention of "prisoners of state" jailed by order of the king: that is, by way of *lettres de cachet.* The writings of some of its former prisoners in particular gave the myth of the Bastille an intense potency that resonated throughout Europe. There was Renneville's *L'Inquisition françoise, ou Histoire de la Bastille* (1715; The French Inquisition; or, The History of the Bastille); Linguet's *Mémoires sur la Bastille* (1784; Memoirs of the Bastille); Chapter 10 of Voltaire's *L'ingénu* (The Pupil of Nature), which is entitled "L'ingénu enfermé à la Bastille avec un janséniste" (The Pupil of Nature Jailed at the Bastille with a Jansenist); and Latude's *Le despotisme dévoilé; ou, Mémoires de Henry Masers de Latude, détenu pendant trente-cinq ans dans divers prisons d'état* (1790; Memoirs of Mr. Henry Masers de La Tude, Containing an Account of His Confinement Thirty-five Years in the State Prisons of France). The storming of the Bastille in 1789 would symbolize the gaining of liberty and the decisive break with the ancien régime. The huge sensation this event caused throughout Europe and as far away as the Americas demonstrates the power of this myth to mobilize the masses, as, for example, when the subjects of the duke of Hesse stormed the "Bastille of Cassel" and the peasants of Saxony, in 1794, attacked the prisons that they regarded as "bastilles."

Finally, the radical movement that put the traditional judicial and penal systems on trial, and its increasingly political character over the course of the 18th century, led to a brief but very intense questioning of the boundaries, relatively stable until then, between normality and deviance, criminality and innocence. An entire genre of literature developed around "social bandits" and "big-hearted brigands" such as Robin Hood in England, Cartouche and Mandrin in France, Schinderhannes in Germany, and Angelo Duca in Italy. People who had been condemned as criminals and punished with death under the judicial system of the time were transformed into popular heroes and role models in a large number of the popular serial works sold by peddlers, notably in the French *Bibliothèque bleue,* the Italian *cantastorie,* and the Spanish *Literatura del cordel.* They also appeared in works by more celebrated writers, such as Friedrich von Schiller's *Der Verbrecher aus verlorner Ehre* (1786; The Criminal from Lost Honor) or Christian August Vulpius's *Rinaldo Rinaldini, der Räuber-Hauptmann* (1799; The Life, Surprising Adventures, and Most Remarkable Escapes of Rinaldo Rinaldini, Captain of a Band of Robbers). The works of the marquis de Sade, who undertook an all but total inversion of the ancient system of values, provide the most palpable literary traces of the uncertainties that followed from this kind of upheaval. Such texts as *Les Cent-vingt journées de Sodome* (1785; The 120 Days of Sodom) exploit the meticulous mechanisms of punishment devised by the judicial system of the ancien régime, while completely reversing their meaning. The revolutionary era also saw the practice of "popular justice"; a total upheaval in notions of "crime," "villainy," "felony," and "justice" in a number of pamphlets, notably from the years 1789 to 1794; and the sudden appearance of a gulf between the norms of justice then being enforced and social representations of justice. The execution of De Launay, the governor of the Bastille, on 14 July 1789, by a crowd that had set itself up as a collective judge in the place of a system of justice now perceived as fundamentally corrupt, served as a model for the practice of popular justice. This would culminate in the Paris massacres of September 1792, in which thousands of prisoners suspected of treason and antipatriotic activities were killed. Many of the pamphlets published in the 1780s and 1790s set out not only to pass judgment on abuses, but also to determine which acts should be characterized as crimes and which people should be designated as "criminals." Pamphlets such as *Les crimes des reines de France* (1791; The Crimes of the Queens of France), *Les crimes des aristocrates* (1790; The Crimes of the Aristocrats), *Les crimes et forfaits de la noblesse et du clergé* (1789; The Crimes and Felonies of the Nobility and the Clergy), *Les crimes des parlements* (1790; The Crimes of the Parlements) or—from a counterrevolutionary perspective—*Les crimes de l'Assemblée Nationale* (1790; The Crimes of the National Assembly) bear witness to the violence, not only verbal but physical, aroused by the questioning of traditional justice on the eve of the institutionalization of the modern judicial and penal systems of France, which was itself a result of the Enlightenment movement for reform. This combination of upheaval and reform was particularly brutal in France, yet it would prove to be crucial in bringing about the reform of judicial institutions and prisons throughout most of Europe, notably through the influence of the Civil Code.

HANS-JÜRGEN LÜSEBRINK

See also Prison

Further Reading

Foucault, Michel, *Discipline and Punish: The Birth of the Prison,* translated by Alan Sheridan, New York: Pantheon Books, and London: Allen Lane, 1977 (original French edition, 1975)

Lüsebrink, Hans-Jürgen, *Kriminalität und Literatur im Frankreich des 18. Jahrhunderts,* Munich: R. Oldenbourg, 1983

Lüsebrink, Hans-Jürgen, and Rolf Reichardt, *The Bastille: A History of a Symbol of Despotism and Freedom,* translated by Norbert Schürer, Durham, North Carolina: Duke University Press, 1997 (original German edition, 1990)

Maza, Sarah C., *Private Lives and Public Affairs: The Causes Célèbres of Prerevolutionary France,* Berkeley: University of California Press, 1993

L

Landscape

Change was the only constant of landscape, as it was understood and practiced during the Enlightenment. Moreover, the notion of landscape, while not exactly marginal, was certainly not central among the concerns of that period as it is traditionally defined. However, the chronological limits that usually define the Enlightenment are not entirely relevant in this case: interest in landscape surged only after the 1760s, and it is both misguided and arbitrary to drop it from consideration at the threshold of romanticism, since it was within that movement that landscape found its way and fulfilled its potential. Linked as much to painting as to gardening, and eventually extended into the domain of literature, the concept of landscape followed a meandering path of development, and its fields of application were extremely varied.

Landscape and Painting

The French term *paysage* (landscape) is derived from *pays* (land) and can serve as a rough synonym for that word. It seems to have been applied first and foremost to a subcategory of genre painting, typified above all by the works of Robert Le Lorrain, Nicolas Poussin, and Salvator Rosa, who were endlessly cited as models in the aesthetic writings of the period. Alain Roger, puzzled by this curious semantic evolution, based his approach to the question of landscape on the definition given by the chevalier de Jaucourt in the *Encyclopédie,* which restricts the term solely to its pictorial meaning. According to Roger, if this particular meaning preceded its other meaning in the French language, that of natural space, it was because the former notion itself existed only in reference to painting in particular and to art in general. This argument seems all the more persuasive because it also applies to the English word "landscape"

and the German word *Landschaft*. Whatever it designated, then, landscape remained an aesthetic object. One could provide plenty of examples of this usage, but René Louis de Girardin's definition of landscape as a "large picture on location" in his *De la composition des paysages* (1777; On the Composition of Landscapes), provides one of the most striking and convincing.

Ambiguity in a word is often a sign of ambiguity in the thing designated. No one played on this equivocation between pictorial representation and natural space better than Denis Diderot in the "walk through Vernet" in his *Salon de 1767* (1767 Exhibition). Using a subterfuge that reverses the usual relationship between a model and its copy, Diderot turns himself into a walker, not through canvases but through a countryside and along shores that seem to present themselves directly to his sight. While this procedure refutes the notion that art is an imitation of nature and helps add movement and life to representation, it also poses the question of which comes first, the pictorial figuration or the natural space. In Diderot's fiction, natural space comes first, and yet, paradoxically, his visit to the Salon and Vernet's genius in combination evoke a nature that would not have existed without the landscapes executed beforehand by the artist. Moreover, because this "walk through Vernet" describes wanderings that are purely imaginary but presented as real, and because the walk postulates the existence of natural and authentic locations independent of any pictorial representation, it is also the result of an artifice one step beyond the artifice of the paintings.

Landscape on Site: The Art of Gardening

Gardening, to the extent that it developed in this same period, proceeded in the same fashion as the pictorial art of landscape. The creation of the parks then in vogue required considerable labor, expense, and time, and entailed the complete transformation of the original site. Yet the parks were expected to provide people with an illusion of virgin nature, since nature was admired "for effects that art cannot imitate," as Claude Henri Watelet puts it in his *Essai sur les jardins* (1774; Essay on Gardens).

Gardening had many deep affinities with landscape. In Great Britain the two types of space were combined in a single term, "landscape gardening." In France, where the equivalent term, *jardin paysager,* did not appear until 1808, many writers, following Girardin's example, spoke of *paysage* and categorically rejected the word *jardin.*

The convergence between gardens and landscapes was not accidental. Indeed, the invented space of the garden was not so much created out of a disruption of the horticultural aesthetic as installed within the pictorial tradition. Painting lent an aura of authority, loaned its methods, and even provided modes of perception to the art of landscape gardening, with its feeling of newness. The texts of the period constantly make the point: according to Alexander Pope, writing as early as 1734, "the whole art of gardening comes from landscape painting" (as cited by Martinet).

Landscape gardening stimulated a large number of writings. In France between the 1760s and 1810, at least 50 works, starting with Jean-Jacques Rousseau's *La nouvelle Héloïse* (1761; Julie; or, the New Héloïse) made the garden their central theme, though that theme is developed in a variety of ways. The genre sometimes took the form of practical manuals; at other times gardens were discussed in tourist guides, theoretical treatises, descriptive albums, and poetry, and any one text might make use of different conventions. For example, the abbé Delille's famous book *Les jardins ou l'art d'embellir les paysages* (1784; Gardens; or, The Art of Beautifying Landscapes) is a descriptive and didactic poem preceded by a long preface mingling practical advice, theoretical statements, and aesthetic reflections. The works in English in this genre are notable for their relatively early appearance, their greater volume, and the advanced aesthetic ideas they develop.

A society of refined connoisseurs was thus created, including painters, poets, architects, great landowners, and prominent members of the bourgeoisie. A passion for landscape transcended national borders, as well as professional and other social divisions. Through treatises on horticulture and through their travels, these new gardeners engaged in dialogue that sometimes became quite polemical, thereby removing geographic and linguistic barriers from their works. From the 1770s onward English-language texts on gardening were rap-

idly and almost systematically translated into French, but there were also rare examples of French works being translated into English. Girardin's book, for example, became available to a British audience in the same year it was first published in French. Christian-Cajus-Lorenz Hirschfeld, an adviser to the king of Denmark, published his *Théories de l'art des jardins* (1779; Theories of the Art of Gardening) in simultaneous French and German editions. In some respects, the prince de Ligne, a cosmopolitan individual who wrote a book entitled *Coup d'oeil sur Beloeil et sur une grande partie des jardins de l'Europe* (A Glance at Beloeil and at Many European Gardens), may serve as a symbol of this Europe of landscapes. In 1772 Catherine II of Russia went so far as to write to Voltaire:

> At the moment, I am madly in love with gardens in the English style, their curved lines, their gentle slopes, their ponds in the form of lakes, their archipelagos on dry land, and I despise straight lines and symmetrical avenues . . . In a word, Anglomania reigns over my plant mania.

The empress's remarks reflect what was to constitute an aesthetic agenda—one also present in Horace Walpole's famous description of William Kent in his *On Modern Gardening* (1774): "He removes fences and arranges for all of nature to become a garden." Enclosing walls were demolished and replaced with ditches, the famous "hahas," so called because of the exclamations of surprise they elicited from those who encountered them. Seemingly freed from the constraint of the gardener's cord, and symbols of liberty because certain gardens had served as emblems of the Whigs in Great Britain, these landscapes were nonetheless rigorously organized. In particular, they were managed in such a way as to provide the spectator with a series of scenes, each linked to an aesthetic category: the amusing, the somber, the pleasant, the terrifying, and so on. The use of technical artifices to provide visitors with carefully orchestrated views also attests to the strength of the connections between gardening and painting. Ultimately, the two became indissociable: if painting led its connoisseurs to the garden, the garden returned them to painting.

Among the many characteristics of the new parks, the decorative motif of ruins, so successful in the romantic era, has often attracted attention. As man-made artifacts, such ruins were intended to disrupt temporal order by inscribing the garden's own future, as it were, in the form of the imagined past of monuments. Nevertheless, one sometimes forgets that ruins were not to be found only in gardens during this period: unsurprisingly, they also turned up in paintings. Their presence, notably in the works of Hubert Robert, provides still further evidence of the interaction between the landscapes of gardeners and those of painters. In literary texts, they often acquired an even more disconcerting aspect.

The Power of Landscapes: The Art of Description and Aesthetic Categories

Eighteenth-century novels, poetic works, and travel accounts are full of landscapes in the modern sense of the term, that is, "a piece of land that nature presents to an observer" (as defined in *Le Robert* dictionary). These works do not seem to allude to painting or gardening so much as they evoke places that are far away or perceived as virgin territory—such as mountains or the tropics. Nevertheless, the same motifs were used to describe landscapes, from the highly refined gardens of European aristocrats to the summits of the Alps, which were often described as "hideous" or "lugubrious," and which at that time had hardly been explored. Toward the end of the 17th century John Dennis describes mountains, in one of his letters, as "the ruins of the world before the Flood." Bertin uses similar phrases to evoke the natural crater at Gavarny in his magnificent *Lettre à Parny, écrite des Pyrénées* (Letter to Parny, Written from the Pyrenees), which is also an account of a journey:

> Picture to yourself, if you can, a vast amphitheatre of perpendicular rocks, with bare and horrifying flanks that present themselves to the imagination as the remains of towers and fortifications . . . How can people still talk about the works of the Romans, those amphitheatres that travelers go to admire the ruins of in Nîmes or other cities! These monuments in which vile gladiators once fought before the eyes of an idle people can only impress those who have not seen this cirque, which is even more blind and more terrible, and in which nature, as seen by the philosopher, struggles perpetually against time.

More surprisingly, Louis-Sébastien Mercier's *Tableau de Paris* (1781–89; Panorama of Paris) includes a "Vue des Alpes" (View of the Alps) that exploits the same metaphor of "immense and magnificent ruins." No doubt it had become a commonplace. Nevertheless, the image, however conventional, implies that the most remote regions were once alive, that they are invested with the memory of a human presence in the distant past, and that they can be described by reference to discourses that may also evoke those places that are the most familiar. When Bernardin de Saint Pierre depicts

the Isle de France in *Paul et Virginie* (1788; Paul and Virginia), he too seems to make some concessions to the aesthetic of landscapes, although he transposes it to a very different locale. Nature is thus reconnected to savage and primitive qualities perceived in conventional and relative terms. Literary works used landscape to achieve various effects: to arouse fear, to simulate a pioneering spirit, or, by using models calmly prepared in advance, to eliminate all the disquiet that the savagery of nature could generate. Innovation became less a matter of discovering unknown landscapes than of depicting them and extending the practice to new objects through the art of description.

The difficulty lay in making the transition from life to writing. Diderot expresses this difficulty in his *Salons,* and Saint-Pierre also waxes eloquent on the issue, as in Letter XXVIII of his *Voyage à l'Isle de France* (1773; A Voyage to the Isle of France):

> The art of rendering nature in writing is so new that the terminology for it has not [yet] been invented. Try to describe a mountain in a way that makes it recognizable. When you have spoken of its base, its slopes, and its summit, you have said everything: but what of the variety of convex, rounded, elongated, concave and other forms! You will find only periphrases for them.

In addition, landscape defied description because its power to move the spectator had an ineffable quality. Writers were anxious to push their expressiveness further, but they ran the risk of being overwhelmed by the inadequacies of language, of suffering from that "famine of words" about which Diderot complained. Therefore the problem was how to arrive at an appropriate intensity of expression and feeling.

Moreover, literary texts variously presented landscapes as pictorial works, as natural spaces, or as simple settings (perhaps displaying, in the latter case, a kind of indifference to the object being specified). The interaction between objects that are today seen as distinct—paintings, gardens, natural places—suggests a different interpretation: that what mattered most was the spectator's point of view, and that person's relationship along with the landscape itself. Landscape's unifying principle, then, transcended specific media and lay in the modes of perception it demanded. As Marie-Madeleine Martinet has shown, this question was at the heart of aesthetic thinking about landscape in 18th-century England, where ideas derived from optics, which permitted a link between the eye and the object being contemplated, gave way to technical considerations developed over a long period. Jaucourt also shows an interest in this question, however reductive his approach may seem, when he sets out criteria for the success of a landscape in the *Encyclopédie*:

> However, this form of imitation cannot move us except in moments of melancholy, when the thing being imitated echoes our feelings. In any other condition, even the most beautiful landscape . . . holds no more interest for us than the view of a section of a frightening or pleasant country. There is nothing in such a tableau that sustains us, so to speak, and as it hardly touches us, it does not remain with us for long.

External or objective beauty is completely rejected and all the spectator retains is the emotion the tableau is capable of arousing. Jaucourt is interested only in the relationship between the landscape and the spectator, which might even be seen as a dialogue. The aesthetic he outlines in this passage is also a form of psychology.

Therefore, it should not be surprising that landscapes were categorized in terms of "characters" or that, more often than not, they were culturally situated halfway between description and psychology. In attempting to describe landscapes, horticultural treatises, novels, and poetic texts all made extensive use of such adjectives as "noble," "rustic," "magnificent," "terrible," or "voluptuous." Such lists were also indications of a certain conceptual imprecision. Nevertheless, more clearly defined categories also made their appearance, notably the "picturesque" and then the "romantic." The latter term appeared for the first time in French in the introduction Pierre Le Tourneur wrote for his 1776 translation of Shakespeare's works:

> The English word "romantic" is more felicitous and more energetic [than the French *romanesque* or *pittoresque*]. It not only contains the idea of parts grouped in a new and varied manner in such a way as to arouse the senses, it also inspires in the soul a feeling of the gentle and tender emotion that arises from the sight of these parts inspires, and joins together the physical and moral effects of perspective.

Finally, the following passage from Le Tourneur's introduction merits particular attention: "The paintings of Salvator Rosa, certain places in the Alps, several gardens and rural scenes in Britain are not at all fantastical, but one can say that they are more than picturesque: they are touching and romantic." It would be difficult to imagine a more complete synthesis: the "romantic" at last gives landscape a single identity by making a threefold reference to painting, to natural space, and to gardening. It is significant that, at the moment when a principle of coherence is found for landscape, that which exceeds the principle is also discovered. Repeatedly breaking out of its framework, landscape dispenses with its limits, only to encounter other limits that are less easily transcended.

It is intrinsic to the definition of landscape that both the word and the object are associated with both works of art and natural locations. But this is not the most important consideration. Landscape was essentially a tool, both poetic and supple, that offered models for artistic perception and influenced the direction of aesthetic theory. As it provided the basis for one of the major contributions of the Enlightenment to the domain of art, landscape also contributed, through romanticism, to the marking of the Enlightenment's borders.

SOPHIE LE MÉNAHÈZE-LEFAY

See also Garden; Mountain; Painting; Picturesque; Ruins; Sublime; Volcano

Further Reading

Andrews, Malcolm, *The Search for the Picturesque: Landscape Aesthetics and Tourism in Britain, 1760–1800*, Aldershot, Hampshire: Scholar, 1989

Birkett, Mary Ellen, "Pictura, Poesis, and Landscape," *Stanford French Review* (1980)

Gilpin, William, *Three Essays: On Picturesque Beauty; On Picturesque Travel; and On Sketching Landscape: To Which Is Added a Poem, On Landscape Painting*, London: Blamire, 1792

Hunt, John Dixon, *The Figure in the Landscape: Poetry, Painting, and Gardening during the Eighteenth Century*, Baltimore, Maryland: Johns Hopkins University Press, 1976

Thomson, James, *The Seasons*, London: n.p., 1730; reprint, Oxford and New York: Clarendon Press, 1981

Language

The age of the Enlightenment marked a fundamental turning point in the history of knowledge about language and linguistic theory. The movement to create systematic grammars for vernacular languages, which had originated during the Renaissance, had come to fruition with respect to the major European languages: these languages were the subject of a considerable number of new grammar books and dictionaries. In addition, with an eye to nationalistic competition, numerous theoretical and practical studies sought to develop the respective potential of these languages, while the role of Latin in scientific usage was steadily declining. The movement toward grammatical systematization continued with other world languages (Amerindian, Finno-Ugric, and Asian languages). With this unprecedented development of linguistic knowledge there arose the problem of discerning a unifying principle for the study of language amid the dazzle of ever-increasing diversity.

Enlightenment scholars envisaged two responses to this problem: a general grammar and, more marginally, a comparative approach to the study of languages based on historical or genetic background. In such a way, 18th-century linguists elaborated the totally novel project of a science of languages and of the language faculty. They were greatly aided in this endeavor by the publication of the *Encyclopédie* (1751–75), which contained the greatest amount of linguistic knowledge ever published up to that time. The grammatical section was overseen by César Chesneau Dumarsais (1676–1756) and then by Nicolas Beauzée (1717–99). In the article "Encyclopédie," Denis Diderot deplores the relative weakness of the sections dealing with language compared to those dealing with grammar. In the three volumes of *Grammaire et littérature* (1782–86; Grammar and Literature) for the *Encyclopédie méthodique* (Methodical Encyclopedia), Beauzée and Jean François Marmontel (1723–99) partially rectified this shortcoming. The *Encyclopédie* also set the standard for the cultural definition of what is meant by "language," identifying it as "the entire body of usage belonging to a nation to express its thoughts vocally."

The First Half of the 18th Century

Until midcentury the linguistic activity of the Enlightenment was concentrated on the production of grammatical standards for those languages that were more or less rationalized (that is, where rules were accompanied by explanations). The most significant theoretical innovation was linked to semantics. In 1694 the publication of the *Dictionnaire de l'Académie Française* (Dictionary of the Académie Française) inaugurated a new form of monolingual dictionary; it was revised four times during the 18th century (in 1718, 1740, 1762, and 1798). This dictionary was intended for the use of native speakers, and by excluding professional terms and the names of overly specific mundane objects, it no longer presented language as a nomenclature, concentrating instead on the way in which language itself works to express shared ideas.

This theoretical attitude coincided with the new concept of synonymy, which led to *La justesse de la langue française ou les différentes significations des mots qui passent pour synonymes* (1718; The Precision of the French Language; or, The Different Meanings of Words That Usually Are Thought to Be Synonyms) by the abbé Girard (1677–1748). Girard's dictionary adopts the same type of entries as the Académie's; that is, it does not seek to list the differing labels of the same object. According to this approach, a language does not contain true synonyms, and the words one takes to be synonyms are actually distinguished by nuances. The research into contextual oppositions that enable one to detect these nuances was one of the liveliest areas of inquiry of the century. Published in a new edition in 1736, Girard's dictionary was supplemented in numerous places by various authors as prestigious as Jean le Rond D'Alembert or Beauzée, and it served as a model for works about most European languages. Of these works, the study by S.J.E. Stosch (1714–96) and Johann August Eberhard (1739–1809) on German synonyms was particularly noteworthy. Dumarsais also attempted a theoretical approach to lexical semantics in his *Traité des tropes* (1730; Treatise on Tropes). Representation, like synonymy, facilitated the approach to the particularities of each language with the help of general protocols.

The Origins of Language and the Anthropological Approach

In the *Essai sur l'origine des connaissances humaines* (1746; Essay on the Origin of Human Knowledge) Étienne Bonnot de Condillac (1714–80), proposes a model for the origin of languages, and that model gave rise to a debate that culminated in 1769 with the open competition sponsored by the Berlin Academy; the prize was awarded to Johann Gottfried von Herder (1744–1803) for his treatise, published in 1772. Like Condillac's model, this treatise is founded on the idea that necessity is at the heart of social interaction. Herder advocates renouncing models such as that offered by Pierre-Louis Moreau de Maupertuis (1698–1759) in *Réflexions philosophiques sur l'origine des langues et la significa-tion des mots* (1748; Philosophical Reflections on the Origin of Languages and the Meaning of Words), which holds language to be the product of a rational activity of calculation; or Jean-Jacques Rousseau (1712–78), in the *Discours sur l'origine et les fondements de l'inégal-ité parmi les hommes* (1755; Discourse on the Origins of Inequality), and Giambattista Vico (1668–1744), both of whom believed that passion played the initial role in language formation. For Herder, the source of language is to be found in human consciousness. German idealism rendered this position more radical. In his essay *Von der Sprachfähigkeit und dem Ursprung der Sprache* (1795; On the Ability to Speak and the Origin of Language), Johann Gottlieb Fichte (1762–1814) explains the need to "deduce" the invention of language and to replace empirical description by reference to his-torical precedent.

The question of the origin of language inevitably raises the problem of the relation of language to thought. The classical conception of language-translation stated that language was the reflection of thought, but the reciprocal notion was problematic. Johann David Michaelis (1717–91) received the Berlin Academy's prize for his dissertation on the topic in *Ueber den Ein-fluss der Sprachen auf die Meinungen der Menschen* (A Dissertation on the Influence of Opinions on Language, and of Language on Opinions); published in German in 1759, it was translated into French, with numerous additions, as *L'influence des opinions sur le langage et de l'influence du langage sur les opinions*, in 1762. Con-dillac had tried to impose the idea that language is the very condition of rational thought: a well-made lan-guage makes for well-conceived science. In *Des signes et de l'art de penser considérés dans leurs rapports mutu-els* (1800; On Signs and Thought Considered in Their Mutual Relationships), the ideologue Joseph Marie Degérando (1772–1842) grants more autonomy to thought. Whatever the case, the status of language brought on a reexamination of Immanuel Kant's ideal-ism. In a short pamphlet, the *Metakritik über den Puris-mus der reinen Vernunft* (1784; Metacritique of the Purism of Pure Reason), Johann Georg Hamann (1730–88), arguing against Kant, maintains that the critique of pure reason must begin with language. Herder, in his *Metakritik zur "Kritik der reinen Vernunft"* (1799; Metacritique of the "Kritique der reinen Vernuft" [Cri-tique of Pure Reason]), notes the constitutive role of history. To grant a transcendent status to thought does not, however, exclude recognition of the empirical role of language: against a background of anti-French polemics, Fichte, in his famous *Reden an die deutsche Nation* (1807–08; Addresses to the German Nation), makes language the decisive element in the identity of a nation.

General Grammar

Although the *Grammaire de Port-Royal* (Port-Royal General Grammar) dated from 1660, it was almost never imitated, and its program was not revived until the second half of the 18th century. The initiative for that revival came from the Englishman James Harris (1709–80), in *Hermes* (1751), a treatise on universal grammar of Aristotelian rather than Cartesian inspira-tion. Harris's hostility to John Locke's empiricism is evi-dent, not only in his own work but also in that of James Beattie (*The Theory of Language* [1783]). Only John Horne Tooke (1736–1812), in his essay *Epea Pteroenta; or, The Diversions of Purley* (1786), attempted to reduce grammatical relations to etymological relations between words and to adopt an ostensibly empiricist stance.

In France the publication of general grammar books came after the *Encyclopédie*: Beauzée's *Grammaire générale* (1767; General Grammar); *Grammaire uni-verselle et comparative* 1774; Universal and Compara-tive Grammar) by Antoine Court de Gébelin (1725–84); Condillac's *Grammaire* (1775; Grammar); *Gram-maire générale analytique* (1799; General Analytic Grammar) by U. Domergue (1745–1810); *Éléments de grammaire générale* (1799; Elements of General Gram-mar) by A. Sicard (1742–1822); *Grammaire philosophique* (1802; Philosophical Grammar) by D. Thiébault (1733–1807); and the second of the four vol-umes of *Éléments d'idéologie* (1803–15; Elements of Ideology) by Antoine Destutt de Tracy (1754–1836). The discipline had a veritable scientific program at its disposal with relation to human languages. As Bauzée states in the introduction to his *Grammaire générale*, "General grammar is the rational science of the immu-table and general principles of the spoken or written word in all languages." Such an objective presupposed that grammar could be closely linked to the cognitive structure of the human mind and that this structure would be universal. The ideologues used that notion as the basis for an anthropology, to be further enriched by the philosophical analysis of language proposed by the comte de Volney (1757–1820) in 1820. They found a considerable following in Italy and Spain. In Germany A.F. Bernardhi (1770–1820), a disciple of Fichte, elabo-rated in *Sprachlehre* (1801; Teaching Language) an attempt to show that general grammar (parts of speech and sentence structure) derive a priori from Kant's cate-gories, a hypothesis that was sharply contested by pro-ponents of comparative grammar.

History and the Comparison of Languages

To view language as the universal and rational expres-sion of thought did not mean that one could not envisage a diversity of languages. In *Les vrais principes de la langue françoise* (1747; The True Principles of the French Language), the abbé Girard suggests a typology: analogue languages, which follow natural order and a gradation of thoughts (French, Italian, Spanish); transpositive languages, which because of their inflected cases follow no order but that of the imagination (Latin, Russian, Slavonic); and mixed languages such as Greek or German, which contain elements of the two other classes. Moreover, morphology plays a secondary role.

German authors, guided perhaps by their own language, took a different approach. A.B.G. Mäzke (born in 1732), in his study of word families, and Friedrich Fulda (1724–88), who, in 1776, systematically reduced vocabulary to *Urwurzeln* (monosyllabic radicals), along with a number of German authors of Greek and Latin grammar books, created the foundations of a true morphological break-down. The work of these German authors explains the success of the typology suggested by August Wilhelm von Schlegel (1767–1845)—a brother of the Sanskrit scholar Friedrich von Schlegel (1772–1829)—in *Observations sur la langue et la littérature provençale* (1818; Observations on the Provençal Language and Literature). Schlegel's work separates languages into isolating, agglutinative, and inflected categories. The reflections of Wilhelm von Humboldt (1767–1835) on the connection between the diversity of linguistic forms and thought also owe their success to the foundational work on morphology. Empirically, it seems that the recognition of linguistic families was the almost automatic result of an adequate grammatical systematization of related languages. As early as 1702, H. Ludolf (1624–1704) elaborated a genetic comparison of a great number of Semitic languages, in his *Dissertation de harmonia linguae aethiopicae cum ceteris orientalibus* (Dissertation on the Harmony between the Ethiopian Language and Other Eastern Languages). In *Affinitas linguae Hungaricae cum linguis Fennicae originis grammatica demonstrata* (1799; Grammatical Proof of the Affinity of the Hungarian Language with Languages of Fennic Origin), Sámuel Gyarmathi (1751–1830) proved that Hungarian and Finnish belong to the same family; he also extended his comparison to other Finno-Ugric languages.

An adequate knowledge of different languages is possible only when the authors can take a certain distance from those languages. In the case of the Romance languages—which, like their ancestor Latin, were well known—etymological and historical studies, which were often guided by a search for national origins, did not automatically lead to a comparative approach to grammar. The field of comparative grammar appeared only relatively late, with the *Grammaire comparée des langues de l'Europe latine avec la langue des troubadours* (1821; A Comparative Grammar of the Languages of Latin Europe with That of Troubadours) by F.M. Raynouard (1761–1836). During the last quarter of the 18th century, a certain number of works appeared that dealt with the study of humans through the intermediary of the knowledge of world's languages: *Of the Origin and Progress of Language* (1773–92) by Lord Monboddo (1714–99); Court de Gébelin's *Monde primitif analysé et comparé avec le monde moderne* (work interrupted after nine volumes had been published, 1773–82; The Primitive World Analyzed and Compared with the Modern World); *Catálogo de las lenguas de las naciones conocidas, y numeración, división y clases de éstas segun la diversidad de sus idiomas y dialectos* (1800–05; Catalogue of the Languages of the Known Nations, and the Numeration, Division, and Classes of These according to the Diversity of Their Dialects and Tongues) by Lorenzo Hervás y Panduro (1735–1809); *Mithridates oder allgemeine Sprachenkunde* (1806–17; Mithridates; or, General Linguistics) by Johann Christoph Adelung (1738–1806) and J.S. Vater (1771–1826); and *Atlas ethnographique du globe ou classification des peuples anciens et modernes d'après leurs langues* (1826; Ethnographic Atlas of the Globe; or, Classification of Ancient and Modern Peoples according to Their Languages) by A. Balbi (1782–1848). All these works were based on solid compilations.

These studies were characterized by a growth in the number of languages compiled (from 60 to more than 600), but they did not achieve a consensus of viewpoints and methods. Both the attempt undertaken by Charles de Brosses (1709–77) and that of Court de Gébelin, who was looking for a way to break down, mechanically, the diversity of languages into a collection of primitive, organically motivated words (*La mécanique des langues ou les principes physiques de l'étymologie* [1768; The Mechanisms of Languages; or, The Physical Principles of Etymology]), remained basically speculative. Affinities between Greek and Sanskrit had already been identified during the Renaissance, and now Sanskrit appeared on the intellectual horizon of the Enlightenment with the publication of a letter by Father Pons (1683–1732) on the *Grammaire des Brahmanes* (1743; The Grammar of Brahmins). Learning progressed continually up to the publication of the first Western grammar of Sanskrit, the *Sidharubam, seu Grammatica Samscradamica* (1790; Sidharubam; or, Sanskrit Grammar) by Father Paulin de Saint Barthélemy (1748–1806). The main thrust for the study of Sanskrit came from the needs of English colonialists after the French were ousted from India. On 15 January 1784 the Asiatic Society of Bengal was founded in Calcutta, and in 1788 it began to publish a series of *Asiatic*

Researches or Transactions. The first issue contained an address given by Sir William Jones in 1786. This British administrator noted that the affinities uniting Greek, Latin, and Sanskrit were such that those languages must have come from one and the same source, which probably no longer existed, and that Gothic and Celtic probably also derived from that same, now-extinct common source. Friedrich von Schlegel, in a work that was instantly famous although quite opaque—*Über die Sprache und die Weisheit der Indier* (1808; On the Language and Wisdom of Indians)—singled out Sanskrit as a particularly worthy subject of study. He desired, among other things, a "comparative grammar that would provide altogether new information on the genealogy of language, not unlike that of comparative anatomy, which has shed light upon upper levels of natural history."

The Status of Linguistic Knowledge

In 1744 Giambattista Vico, in *Principi di una scienza nuova* (1725; 3rd impression, 1744; The New Science of Giambattista Vico), developed the idea that the science of man (principally philology) was the science of the future. In a certain way, his prediction has borne fruit. However, determining what form this science of man would take remained the basic question of the Enlightenment. Philology, which was not popular among the French, eventually suggested a model. In the *Prolegomena ad Homerum* (1795; Prolegomena to Homer), Friedrich August Wolf (1759–1824) inaugurated the German philological school.

Competing with this school, even in German-speaking countries, was the nascent hermeneutic school, which was more attached to meaning than to form. The university courses taught by Friedrich Schleiermacher (1738–1834) between 1805 and 1832 were published under the title *Hermeneutik* (Hermeneutics). In 1813 Schleiermacher also published an essay *Ueber die verschiedenen Methoden des Uebersetzen* (On the Different Methods of Translation). In the second volume of *Mithridates* (1808), Vater uses the neologism *Linguistik* to designate the science that establishes the genetic groupings of languages by comparing languages. In 1819 Jakob Grimm (1785–1863) published his *Deutsche Grammatik* (German Grammar), a historical and comparative grammar of Germanic dialects. Influenced by Rasmus Christian Rask, Grimm formulated in the second edition (1822) what would later become known as "Grimm's law," but which he referred to as *Lautverschiebung* (phonetic mutation).

There are historical laws that explain the development of languages. The project of a general grammar would never be abandoned, but the dominant paradigm throughout the 19th century was that of comparative grammar. This dominance had significant consequences for the conception of language, due, no doubt, to the political situation in the German-speaking countries. General grammars left certain languages vulnerable to the arbitrariness of usage. Because of their centralized state, the French could endeavor to resolve the issue of linguistic unity by creating synchronic grammars. The Revolution, in its struggle against dialects, followed the same policy as royal absolutism. German speakers, however, because they had no such political unity, could have no such objective. The debate about usage (in the grammatical works of Adelung, for example) was founded on the necessity for the German bourgeoisie to put together a standard written instrument that would nonetheless not attempt to eradicate dialects (see, for example, Friedrich Fulda's *Ueber die beiden Hauptdialekte der Teutsche Sprachen* [1773; On the Two High Dialects of the German Language]). Grimm's *Deutsche Grammatik* was not a grammar of German in the sense intended by the Académie Française, which sought to promote a definitive French grammar. Rather, Grimm's work was a historical grammar of German dialects. Language is not the sum of the different usages current in a nation; it is the sum of the stages in its own development.

SYLVAIN AUROUX

See also Eclecticism; Grammar; Nation

Further Reading

Auroux, Sylvain, *La sémiotique des encyclopédistes: Essai d'epistémologie historique des sciences du langage,* Paris: Payot, 1979

Auroux, Sylvain, editor, *Histoire des idées linguistiques,* Liège, Belgium: Mardaga, 1989– ; see especially vol. 2, *Le développement de la grammaire occidentale,* 1992

Guilhaumou, Jacques, *La langue politique et la Révolution française: De l'événement à la raison linguistique,* Paris: Méridiens/Klincksieck, 1989

Latin America

The Enlightenment in Europe and in Latin America

In Latin America the European Enlightenment found a distant "echo of Reason." The Latin American Enlightenment, the result of the active assimilation of ideas and changes in European consciousness, is part of an intellectual continuum that developed from the colonization of the New World by the Spanish and the Portuguese. It was part of a specifically American intellectual history, in which the direct influences, not only of Spain and Portugal but also of France, Britain, Italy, and North America, were felt, albeit in a discontinuous fashion. Enlightenment ideas were adopted and adapted in Latin America, with some delay, between around 1770 and 1830, at a time when the age of the Enlightenment in Europe was already approaching its end. It is this cultural time lag of approximately half a century that essentially explains the specificity of the Latin American Enlightenment. The beginning of a *pre-Ilustración* (pre-Enlightenment) marked by the reception of *criticismo* (criticism), exemplified by the works of Spanish Benedictine monk and scholar Benito Jerónimo Feijóo y Montenegro (1676–1764), can be dated to around 1750. Its apogee coincided with the period of the French Revolution. One result of this time lag was that the generation of Latin Americans born between roughly 1750 and 1780 had the entire range of Enlightenment ideas at their disposal. The Latin American Enlightenment was thus characterized by an extreme eclecticism that evolved from an imitation of European cultural models to the emancipating formation of its own self-awareness. However, since baroque culture and the world of scholastic ideas continued to predominate in Latin America until the 1770s, traditional ideas and Enlightenment ones were superimposed, as had also been the case in the Catholic countries of Europe.

The main influences on the Latin American Enlightenment came primarily from the colonizing nations, especially in the early stages, during which a framework was established by the reformist policies of enlightened despotism. From the French Enlightenment Latin Americans took not only the works of the great *philosophes*, and vulgarized forms of Encyclopedist and physiocratic ideas, but also, at a later stage, its materialism. The British Enlightenment, and in particular the ethics and empiricism that were characteristic of it, received an especially warm welcome from Latin Americans. Similarly, the constitutional democracy and republicanism of North America had an exemplary and stimulating effect on political thought in Latin America. The Italian Enlightenment, with its attempts at political and economic reform (Gaetano Filangieri, Antonio Genovesi,

Cesare Bonesana Beccaria), also had a significant impact across the Atlantic. The Latin American Enlightenment therefore appears to have been an amalgam of heterogeneous ideas and knowledge. However, we must also take into account the fact that, until the end of the colonial era, the acquisition and possession of Enlightenment writings that had been put on the censors' index could lead to prosecution in Latin America, a fact that influenced the regional propagation and development of Enlightenment knowledge. This knowledge was disseminated above all in those regions that were turned toward Europe and maintained multiple contacts with the outside world. It was this fragmentary reception of European ideas, combined with the *Criollismo* (Creolism) of the 18th century, and the growing awareness of the specificity of the Americas—continents that were putting a more and more critical distance between themselves and their colonizers' homelands—that gave birth to the Creole Enlightenment. This movement was restricted to a small minority and was expressed less in literary, artistic, or philosophical productions than in the desire for modernization in education, the economy, and politics. It also consciously distanced itself from the image of the Americas that the European Enlightenment had constructed.

In Europe the colonial system was regarded as a system of oppression and exploitation. As a rule, the knowledge of South America that was available to Europeans at this time was incomplete, superficial, even fanciful: witness the "pre-Humboldtian" image parodied in Voltaire's *Candide* (1759). On the whole, what was true of the image that Enlightenment Europe had of Spain and Portugal was still more true of its ideas concerning their colonies. An even more pronounced obscurantism was attributed to the American colonies than was attributed to their colonizers; the colonies' alleged backwardness in matters of science and education was held to be even greater, and the negative character traits of their peoples even more glaring. The Europeans who lived in the Americas were represented as being prouder and more passionate, more fickle and more ignorant, but also more ruthless than the inhabitants of their respective homelands. The *leyenda negra* (Black Legend), to which the European Enlightenment showed itself rather sensitive, cast a shadow over the heirs of the conquistadores. Contemporary conceptions of nature, and in particular the fashionable climatic theories, also fostered the idea of a "tropicalization" of those Europeans who came into contact with the exotic world of the Americas. The strangeness of its flora and fauna and the contrasts of its natural geography, led to the belief that the South American continent was still at an early stage of development. It was seen as an immature part of the world, with environmental conditions that would rapidly lead to the degeneration of European cultural imports. As for the native peoples of Central and South America, 18th-century Europe, apart from Spain and Portugal, had only quite vague ideas about them. The ancient civilizations of the Americas, with their idolatrous religions and their sacrificial rites, were hardly capable of arousing as much enthusiasm as the Chinese or Persian worlds. Jean François Marmontel's poetic romance *Les Incas* (1777; The Incas; or, The Destruction of the Empire of Peru), which relates the destruction of the Inca empire, made no impact. The natives of the Americas did not correspond to the image, so dear to the Enlightenment, of the "noble savage," innocent and virtuous by nature. It was generally believed in Enlightenment Europe that the exploration of the South American continent had been carried out by a process of destruction, and that this process, combined with the work of conversion carried out by the religious orders, had left the natives in a stage of development corresponding to infancy. The interest shown by the public in the native reserves set up by the Jesuits, especially in Paraguay, stemmed in part from an Enlightenment polemic against the desire of the religious orders for theocratic domination, but it also reflected the fascination that the Jesuits' social programs of education exercised upon Enlightenment minds. In the 18th century the image of Latin America continued to be influenced by the comte de Buffon, the abbé Raynal, Cornelius de Pauw, and William Robertson while the refutations supplied by the Benedictine Antoine-Joseph Pernety and the Jesuit Juan Nuix, based on considerably greater knowledge, were no more widely disseminated than the isolated topographies of the padres expelled from Latin America, notably those of Mexico by Francisco Xavier Clavijero, of Chile by Juan Ignacio Molina, and of New Grenada by Filippo Salvatore Gilij. Nevertheless, these works were the catalysts for the scientific exploration of the South American continent, which culminated in the travels of Alejandro Malaspina and Alexander von Humboldt at the end of the century. The collection and handling of the latter's data was accompanied by an increasing realization of the continent's problems, especially, regarding colonial ties, in the work of the Physiocrats and the followers of Adam Smith. By its critique of mercantilism, of the policy of autarky, and, above all, of thinking in terms of monopoly and wealth, the political economy of the Enlightenment tended to reject the colonial system (notably in the writings of Anne-Robert-Jacques Turgot). After the British colonies in North America gained independence, the European *philosophes* thought that it was only a matter of time before the Spanish and Portuguese colonies in turn emancipated themselves. In its closing stages the Enlightenment maintained an anticolonialism that rested as much on moral and humanitarian scruples (the rejection of slavery) as on the idea of universal human reason (as represented by the marquis de Condorcet).

Chronology

In chronological terms the Latin American Enlightenment corresponds to the period of transition between colonial reforms and political independence (1825). Around one-fifth of the continent's population of 18 million were of European descent, among whom more than 90 percent were Creoles of Spanish or Portuguese origin. As these Creoles were excluded from the highest political functions and had to be content with posts at the lowest level of the municipal councils, they turned to economic activity and thereby became receptive to liberal ideas. By the end of the 18th century the Viceroyalties of New Spain, Peru, New Grenada (since 1739) and La Plata (since 1776) were governed from Madrid and Seville, in line with Spanish bureaucratic centralism, by the relevant Secretary of State in conjunction with the Council of the Indies. Brazil, under Portuguese administration, was governed in a similar fashion by a viceroy (1720), under the orders of the Conselho Ultramarino (Overseas Council) in Lisbon, although, to judge by its bureaucratic structure, this arrangement was less effective than the Spanish one.

Since the great majority of the population throughout Latin America had virtually no intellectual aspirations (around 88 to 90 percent were illiterate), the culture of the Enlightenment remained subject to the discretion of the state and the Church up to the end of the colonial era. The native peoples who lived in their own communities and represented between one-third and one-half of the population (depending on the region) took practically no part in the active assimilation of Enlightenment ideas, and for the most part they did not adopt the Latino-European culture. The situation was much the same for the oppressed black population, which represented around 10 percent of the population in Spanish America but more than half of the population of Brazil. Beyond a modest level of religious instruction, the education of large parts of the population was hampered by the inadequacy of the structures for general education. The monopoly of the Church in matters of education and culture formed a barrier to the philosophy of the Enlightenment and contributed to a channeling of new ideas and new knowledge. In Latin American the Inquisition, in whose activities of censorship both Church and state cooperated, did not successfully prevent the infiltration of the Enlightenment ideas that the Inquisitors judged to be dangerous.

At the same time, however, the Inquisition was able to a large extent to exclude those ideas from public life. Initially, therefore, Enlightenment philosophy in Latin America was predominantly of a type filtered by the mother countries, decreed from above, and controlled by the Church. As with the Enlightenment in Spain and Portugal, the Enlightenment in Latin America can be distinguished from its French counterpart by its close ties to Catholicism. In other words, it was an Enlightenment that did not reject the idea of God. Consequently, there was often no clear distinction between a reformist ideology that was genuinely inspired by the Enlightenment and one that was influenced by Jansenism. It was only in the wake of the revolutionary ideas of the 1790s that critical and emancipatory positions began to wield a more pervasive influence.

It was the reform policies of enlightened despotism that sparked the growth of enlightenment ideas. Bourbon reformism had reached its peak under Charles III (1759–88). Its objective was to develop socially and economically Spain's possessions in the Americas, so that they might better serve the interests and the common good of the whole empire. This objective implied an increase in the state's intervention in almost every domain. For example, both the expulsion of the Jesuits (1767) and the establishment of the Comercio libre (1777)—that is, the opening of the American markets to the main centers of commerce in Spain—were parts of this program. Fiscal control of the colonies was enhanced with the introduction of state monopolies and a more rigorous enforcement of tax collection. A series of measures was taken to ameliorate the situation of the natives. In the case of Brazil, the reformist chief minister of Portugal, the marquis of Pombal (1699–1782), initiated a policy inspired by enlightened despotism. Among other reforms, he introduced legislation aimed at modernizing the country. This process was completed after 1777 by colonial officials acting in the spirit of the Enlightenment and was extended to almost every aspect of social life. The policy of reform pursued by Spain and Portugal was not notably different in character from the programs of development and education put forward by enlightened despots in other monarchies that were seeking to catch up with more developed countries. However, in an indirect fashion, because of the criticism and opposition that these reforms introduced to the colonies, enlightened despotism also favored the spread of Enlightenment ideas and programs in Latin America. It was to the European *philosophes* that the Latin Americans turned to look for ideological support in their debates on the policies of the colonizing powers. Over and above Enlightenment principles authorized by the colonial administration, and under the influence of revolutionary ideas that were generally opposed to that administration, the social and political ideas of western European Enlightenment gained in importance. In this light, it is even possible to speak of two Enlightenment phenomena, separated by the experience of the American Revolution: a rationalist and reformist Enlightenment, on the one hand, and the revolutionary Enlightenment that Jean-Jacques Rousseau called "political," on the other.

The hypothesis that the Enlightenment played an ideological role in the independence of Latin America is still a source of controversy among scholars. Undeniably, there was no direct causal link nor a chronological succession between the two movements; however, if the process of emancipation is considered in a wider historical perspective, it is clear that they were nonetheless indissolubly connected. The high point of the reception of the Enlightenment in Latin America coincided with the beginning of the revolutions that led to independence. Whitaker even goes so far as to suggest that the independence movements helped the Enlightenment make progress, and not the reverse (see Whitaker). In 1808, when the political crisis started by the French occupation of Spain and Portugal raised the issue of independence for Latin Americans, the ideals of the Enlightenment concerning state and society were available to serve as the ideological basis of the struggle against colonial domination. By lending a revolutionary tone to the widespread criticism of colonial dependence, the Enlightenment became one of the forces that prepared the ground for the independence movement. The examples of Miguel Hidalgo y Costilla, Francisco de Miranda, Simón Bolívar, and Manuel Belgrano show the extent to which the Enlightenment agenda was present, in various forms, in the minds of the pioneers of independence. These figures embodied the sociocultural changes that had begun in the 18th century, changes in which the Enlightenment was an essential element.

In Latin America the culture of the Enlightenment was linked to a realization and appropriation by Latin Americans of their own countries and their own histories, as well as of their natural environment. New scientific thinking, as well as the reforms of enlightened despotism, both of which had set in motion a reevaluation of the colonies, sustained the interest of Latin Americans in the political, economic, and cultural situation of their own lands. The reception of the Enlightenment made the Creoles into patriots, and the way in which they interpreted and adopted the ideals of the western European Enlightenment in relation to state and society turned them into advocates of political independence. It cannot be denied that the Enlightenment thus contributed to the formation of the identity of the newly emerging nations of Latin America.

Actors and Instruments in the Propagation of the Enlightenment

There were no societies of *philosophes* in Latin America as there were in Europe, for the bourgeoisie, the substratum of the public sphere and the discourse of the Enlightenment, was not sufficiently developed in the colonies. The propagation of Enlightenment culture was essentially the work of three social categories. First, there was the administrative elite: the highly placed civil servants and the corps of officers. Then there were the higher regular clergy, including the professors of higher education. Finally, there were the professional classes, notably those who had received legal training or had a knowledge of technology or natural history. Among such representatives of enlightened despotism were the viceroys Mendinueta (1736–1825), the second conde de Revillagigedo (1738–99), and Antonio de Amar y Borbón (1742–1826) in Spanish America. Other leading civil servants included the *Fiscal* (public prosecutor) Moreno y Escandrón (1736–92) in Bogotá or the magistrate Ramirez (1777–1821) in Cuba; and in Brazil, Viceroy Vasconcelos e Sousa, founder of the Sociedade Literária (Literary Society) in Rio de Janeiro (1785), as well as the minister of the Navy and Colonies R. de Souza Coutinho, who made the seminary of Olinda at Pernambuco a center of Enlightenment education (1800). According to J.T. Lanning, only one of the seven Latin American bishops was sympathetic to the Enlightenment, but among the representatives of the "enlightened" clergy were such prelates as the archbishop and viceroy of Santa Fe, Caballero y Góngora (1723–96); the bishop of Quito, Pérez Calama (1740–92); the archbishop of Chuquisaca, F. de San Alberto (1727–1804); and, at Pernambuco, the physiocratic archbishop Azeredo Coutinho. Among members of the regular clergy, there was the Mexican Dominican José Servando Teresa de Mier Noriega y Guerra (1763–1827), author of the *Historia de la revolución de Nueva España* (1813; History of the Revolution of New Spain) and an advocate of a federal constitution; the Franciscan Liedo y Goicoechea at the University of Guatemala, one of the leading American reformers in matters of education; and P. Agostinho Gomes, a member of the society of Cavalheiros da Luz (Knights of the Light) founded at Bahia in 1797. Nor should we forget those parish priests, in many cases radically inclined, who devoted themselves entirely to the education of the people in the spirit of the Enlightenment, among them Miguel Hidalgo y Costilla (1753–1811), the hero of Mexican independence. Beyond the framework of purely pastoral instruction, many churchmen, the Jesuits in particular, helped to disseminate the knowledge and precepts of the Enlightenment and thus create the intellectual and

scientific conditions that were required for a Latin American Enlightenment culture. The first works of natural history and geography to be compiled in Latin America were written by priests, to whom the continent also owed the first botanical and mineralogical collections, as well as the first physics laboratories.

The typical Latin American *philosophe,* although often of quite humble origins, usually took up one of the liberal professions or became a teacher. Examples of such individuals would be the Peruvian doctor and physicist José Hipólito Unánue (1755–1833), a collaborator in the *Mercurio peruano* (1791–95), or the jurist José Baquíjano y Carrillo (1751–1818) of Lima, president of the University of San Marcos. There were also literary men, such as the Mexican José Joaquín Fernández de Lizardi (1776–1827) and José Joaquín Olmedo (1780–1847) of Guayaquil, a liberal deputy in the Spanish Cortes (Parliament) and poet of the independence struggle. In Buenos Aires there was Juan Cruz Varela (1794–1839), who published philanthropic and liberal patriotic writings, and also the "Jacobin" Mariano Moreno (1778–1811), who condemned the Spanish monopoly of trade in his *Representación de los hacendados*, as well as publishing the first Latin American edition of Rousseau's *Du contrat social* (The Social Contract). In Chile there was Camilo Henríquez (1769–1825), publisher of the first Chilean review, *La Aurora* (1812–13), and Juan Egaña (1768–1836), a professor of philosophy and law at the University of San-Felipe. Cuban *philosophes* included Felix Varela (1788–1853), who held the first chair of philosophy in Havana, and Francisco de Arango y Parreño (1765–1837), founder of the Consulado de Agricultura y Comercio (Agricultural and Commercial Consulate). Finally, in Brazil there were the naturalist Manuel Arruda da Cámara (1752–1810); the physician Novais de Almeida, a defender of the idea of equality, and the journalist Silva Lisboa, author of a work on the principles of political economy (1804). Members of the Creole upper class participated only to a limited extent in the Enlightenment movement, and in a rather selective and imitative way. They included A. Nariño (1765–1823), a merchant of Colombia who translated the French Declaration of the Rights of Man (1793), and J.C. del Valle (1776–1834) of Honduras, a graduate of the San Carlos University in Guatemala who went on to run as a candidate in the election for the presidency of the Central American Federation. However, it would be an exaggeration to speak of an intellectual elite. We should think, rather, of a small number of outstanding individuals carrying the message of the Enlightenment and of isolated groups with sensibilities influenced by Enlightenment culture, as may also have been found among those persons of mixed racial origins who had risen through the social hierarchy. Typical examples would include Francisco Xavier Eugenio de Santa Cruz y Espejo (1747–95), founder of the Sociedad Patriótica (Patriotic Society) of Quito (1791) and publisher of the first cultural review in that city, and J. de Deus of Bahia, who in 1798 called for a republic based on equality and liberty.

Beginning in the 1780s, the propagation of Enlightenment ideas was encouraged by the activity of *sociedades* (societies) under the surveillance of the state and the Church, although it is impossible to estimate the role that these "organizations for the public good" played, either in the intellectual realm or with respect to practical reforms. Their popularity is indicated by the founding of a number of Sociedades Económicas de Amigos del País en Espagne (Economic Societies of Friends of the Nation in Spain): a dozen of these societies were established before the end of the colonial era, although only those in Havana (1791) and Guatemala (1794) remained active for any length of time and in the period 1793 and 1820 total membership for the six most important of the societies never exceeded 700. Although literary societies, aimed at fostering the exchange of ideas through informal meetings of literary men, were rare, some *academias* (academies) were founded in this period. These were Enlightenment-style societies, dedicated to philosophical ideas and scientific knowledge that were not transmitted by the universities and *colegios* (secondary schools) since these latter institutions essentially operated along traditional lines. The "patriotic societies" that were formed in increasing numbers at the beginning of the 19th century, a period of controversial relations between the colonies and the colonizing powers, were an expression of an Enlightenment politicized by the reception of North American and French conceptions of society. In many cases, these societies also had direct relations with Freemasonry. The first lodges were founded as early as 1809, when the independence movements were emerging.

Periodicals underwent a development similar to that of the patriotic societies. From the beginning of the 18th century, these ephemeral publications often had merely imitated the press of the mother country. But between 1790 and 1810, periodical publications developed themes and ideas that were intended to fulfill the Enlightenment objective of forming public opinion. The titles of the politicized journals during the period of the wars of independence—for example, the *Casi-público*, the *Argos constitucional*, the *Peruano liberal*, and the *Americano*—are clear indications of a trend toward liberalism. One could also cite here the decidedly enlightened programs of the *Mercurio peruano* (1791–95), published by the Sociedad de Amantes del País (Society of Friends of the Nation) in Lima; the *Semanario del Nuevo Reino de Granada*, which appeared from 1808 under the direction of the engineer Francisco José de Caldas (1771–1816); or, in Buenos Aires, Manuel Belgrano's *Diaro de Comercio* (1810). In Mexico the celebrated *Gaceta*, which was founded in 1784 and supported the reforms of enlightened despotism, was replaced in 1812 by the *Pensador mexicano*, edited by Lizardi. The *Gaceta* combined literary and scientific contributions with a critique of contemporary society.

Higher education appears to have played a relatively small role in the Enlightenment movement in South America. Traditional scholarship, for better or worse, was transmitted through the 25 universities and *colegios*. There was no university in Brazil, which is why there was a preference for studying at Coimbra. While rationalism (René Descartes), empirical theories (Sir Isaac Newton), and even some elements of Enlightenment philosophy (including Condillac) were included in courses, such modernization can be traced to the reforming zeal of a few isolated professors. The Spanish reforms were not accompanied by any enlightened or uniform policy for higher education, and there was no collaboration, within Iberian culture, between enlightened absolutist authorities, on the one hand, and pedagogues seeking to transmit Enlightenment ideas, on the other. There were two exceptions to this generalization. In Guatemala, San Carlos University integrated the rational and empirical sciences into its programs of study, under the influence of the patriotic society of that province. The University of Quito experienced even greater success in reforming its educational practices, becoming the only university to open up to secular culture. At the same time, however, with regard to practical knowledge, the specialized institutions known as *colegios* or *escuelas* (some public, some private) distinguished themselves. These institutions were dedicated to useful sciences such as medicine, mathematics, or mining, and it was above all their graduates who became the agents of intellectual change.

HANS-OTTO KLEINMANN

See also Colonialism

Further Reading

Aldridge, A. Owen, editor, *The Ibero-American Enlightenment*, Urbana: University of Illinois Press, 1971
Gerbi, Antonello, *The Dispute of the New World: The History of a Polemic, 1750–1900*, translated by Jeremy Moyle, Pittsburgh, Pennsylvania: University of Pittsburgh Press, and London: Media Directions, 1973 (original Italian edition, 1955)
Lanning, J.T., "The Enlightenment in Relation to the Church," in *Studies Presented at the Conference on the History of Religion in the New World during Colonial Times*, Washington, D.C.: s.n., 1958

Shafer, Robert Jones, *The Economic Societies in the Spanish World, 1763–1821*, Syracuse, New York: Syracuse University Press, 1958

Stoetzer, O. Carlos, *El pensamiento político en la América española durante el período de la emancipación, 1789–1825*, 2 vols., Madrid: Instituto de Estudios Políticos, 1966

Whitaker, Arthur Preston, editor, *Latin America and the Enlightenment*, Ithaca, New York: Great Seal Books, 1958

Law, Natural. *See* Natural Law and the Rights of Man

Law, Public

The expression "public law" was not new to the 18th century. For many years, scholarly judicial doctrine had commented on the Roman distinction between *jus publicum* (public law) and *jus privatum* (private law), but during the Enlightenment, and above all during the last decades of the ancien régime in France, the use of the term "public law" developed in political circles and the concept was included in the debate over the nature of power. However, its meaning was always ambiguous, even as used in the writings of a single author. Public law could refer either to all or only a part of the body of rules governing the relations between states or even simply to international relations themselves. Today we use the terms "international public law" and "international relations" for the latter aspect of public law. The term "public law" eventually replaced the traditional *jus gentium* (law of nations) as defined in the 18th century by Grotius, Samuel von Pufendorf or his translator Jean de Barbeyrac, and many others.

Montesquieu used the terms *droit public* (public law) and *droit du people* (law of the people) interchangeably. In a passage about "positive" laws, he writes: "All nations have a law for their people; even the Iroquois, who eat their prisoners, have one. They send and receive ambassadors; they know the laws of war and of peace" (*De l'esprit des lois* [1748; The Spirit of Laws]). Elsewhere in the same text, in a passage on the law of conquest, Montesquieu quotes "the authors of our public law." And it is possible that he includes Gabriel Bonnot de Mably among these authors.

In 1746 Mably published the first of many editions of *Le droit public de l'Europe fondé sur les traités conclus jusqu'en l'année 1740* (European Public Law, Based on Treaties Concluded before 1740), a work presented as a "handbook of diplomatic history for the use of statesmen." In the introduction to *Observations sur l'histoire de France* (1765; Observations on the History of France), however, Mably uses the expression "public law" in analyzing and explaining the evolution of monarchical power in France:

> Until the reign of Philippe de Valois, the right to rule belonged in turn, or simultaneously, to all those who could or would seize it. If I have succeeded in tracing the consequences and sequence of these revolutions and the connections between them, their interrelated causes and effects, I have written the unknown history of our ancient public law.

In the second half of the 18th century, this particular use of the term "public law" became the most common, designating what we today call general public law.

As witness to the latter usage, Boucher d'Argis, the author of two short entries in the *Encyclopédie*, offers definitions of both *droit public* and *droit public français* (French public law). He defines public law as the law "that has been established for the common use of people considered as a political body." It differs from "private law, which is enacted for the use of each person considered individually and independently of other persons." Boucher d'Argis defines French public law as "a political jurisprudence resulting from the laws that concern the state in general." In writing of the law of the "political body" and "political jurisprudence" he was inspired by the theoreticians of natural law, who used "political law" as a synonym for "public law." These theoreticians included Jean-Jacques Burlamaqui, the author of *Principes du droit politique* (1751; Principles of Political Law), who discusses not only the principles of international law but also those of civil law.

Burlamaqui first considers "the origin and nature of civil society, sovereignty in general, and its characteristics, modifications, and essential parts," and in his discussion he refers to the seventh book of Pufendorf's *De jure naturae et gentium libri* (1672; Of the Natural Right and Law of Nations). Burlamaqui then goes on to discuss "the different laws of sovereignty with regard to foreign states, the law of war and everything connected with it, public treaties, and the law of ambassadors."

Montesquieu himself defined "general political law" as the law that "concerns every society"—that is, civil public law (*De l'esprit des lois*). Jean-Jacques Rousseau, after hesitating among several titles, published as a subtitle to his *Du contrat social* (1762; The Social Contract) Burlamaqui's title, *Principes du droit politique* (Principles of Political Law), limiting the contents of his treatise to a general theory of public law and to various forms of government. Thus for the advocates of *jus naturalis*, public—or political—law was an integral part of natural law, as Rousseau himself acknowledged when he wrote that his *Du contrat social* "should be taken into account only along with those others that deal with *natural and political law*" (*Lettres écrites de la montagne* [1764; Letters Written during a Journey in the Mountains]). It was precisely the above origin and affiliation that hindered and delayed, in France more than in the Germanic countries, the acceptance of this notion of universally valid public law, which described the construction of a state and institutions based on reason.

The general reluctance to introduce the study of public law into judicial instruction was significant in this respect. In 1745 Louis XV had created at the University of Besançon a chair of public law reserved in the first place for members of the local *parlement*. Owing to considerations peculiar to the Franche Comté, a border province joined to France for less than three quarters of a century, but also for more general reasons, among which can be counted the need to keep in France students anxious to obtain a full university education (students hitherto apt to seek such education abroad, particularly in Protestant countries), this innovation aimed to make it possible to teach simultaneously international law, national law, and provincial law. However, although a professor of public law was appointed, he was never able to begin teaching and was never replaced. The project therefore fell through and was not taken up elsewhere, the reason being that resistance to this "novelty" was strong. As the president Bouhier wrote:

A professor of public law . . . seems quite useless in a kingdom where there is little regard for such law. . . . In truth, the subject is taught in universities in Germany. But the princes themselves are obliged to educate themselves in public law to uphold their rights against the emperor or against other princes. But in France, there is no other code of law on this matter than the whim of the king.

Public law seemed, therefore, to be a construct of foreign origin as much from the standpoint of political organization as from that of geography. In his *Dictionnaire universel* (Universal Dictionary), Furetière had already defined *droit public* in such a way: "In Germany," he writes, public law is "made up of general laws that govern the Constitution and the well-being of the states, particularly of those states that belong to the Empire." Much later, in 1762, when the noun *publiciste* was accepted by the Académie Française to designate the thinker who writes about public law, it was noted, "There are in Germany great publicists." What is more, public law was viewed in France as having its origins in the political thought of the Reformation, which further emphasized its foreign status. This disparity among treatments of public law within the Europe of the Enlightenment was often pointed out to France's detriment. The marquis d'Argenson was aware of the disparity and regretted it: "We have good institutes of Roman civil law; we have decent ones of French law; but we have absolutely no institutes for general and universal public law" (*Les loisirs d'un ministre, ou essais dans le goût de ceux de Montaigne* [1787; A Minister's Leisure Time; or, Essays in Montaigne's Style]). And yet, since the 17th century, the pedagogical aim with regard to principles of governance had not been absent from the kingdom of France, but reflections about those principles had neither the same content nor the same audience as the treatises inspired by natural law.

To a greater degree than in Jean Domat's *Droit public, suite des lois civiles dans leur ordre naturel* (1697; Public Law, Following Common Laws in Their Natural Order), the abbé Claude Fleury's work gave clear proof of the above differences. Fleury was the son of a lawyer in the Conseil du Roi (Royal Council). At the end of the 17th century and the beginning of the 18th the abbé was in charge of the education, first, of the prince de Conti's children and, later, of children of the royal house of France. Fleury created for his pupils an overview of French law in which his *Droit public de la France* (French Public Law)—which would not be published until 1769, nearly a century after it was written—held a prominent place, alongside discussions of the *droit ecclésiastique* (ecclesiastical law) and the *droit privé* (private law). Following the advice of Georges de

Scudéry according to whom "it is dangerous to wish to know everything that monarchs know," Fleury regarded public law as "a mystery reserved for kings and their ministers" since "politics" should only be explained to "those who by their birth are destined for important roles." Therefore, he focused his treatise on public law on (1) "policy" (by this he meant administration), "the part of public law that is the most necessary"; (2) the finances of the kingdom, which were not, moreover, clearly distinct from those of the king; and (3) warfare on land and at sea. However, all reflections of a philosophical order on the nature of power or of a sociological order on the various forms of government were deliberately excluded from the work. In any case, the problem of sovereignty was rapidly solved. In Chapter V, the abbé writes:

> We know that France is governed by a king, that the kingdom is hereditary, and that it does not fall into female hands, by virtue of Salic law. The king does not share his power, and the queen has the right only to be respected, like any other noblewoman, but no right at all to power. All public power, that is the complete authority to command the French and make use of their persons and their goods, according to the needs of the state, resides solely in the person of the king; he is the proprietor of that power, in such a way that no one can take it from him.

Directly inspired by the *Institution au droit français* (The History of the Origin of the French Laws) by Guy Coquille and by the treatise *Des seigneuries* (On Seigniories) by Charles Loyseau, the above passage places Fleury's thought both among that of the authors of the literature of princely pedagogy and within the fold of the monarchist or absolutist movement, which found expression in the 18th century in *L'introduction à la description de la France et au droit public de ce royaume* (1752; Introduction to the Description of France and to Public Law in This Kingdom) and in *La science du gouvernement, ouvrage de morale, de droit et de politique* (1751–54; The Science of Government; A Work of Ethics, Law, and Politics) by Gaspard de Réal de Curban. The fact that Fleury's treatise was published in 1769, 90 years after it was written, was proof of the desire to strengthen the absolutist thesis and to undermine the natural law notion of public law, which was gaining support at that time. The natural law concept would spread further thanks to the objective support of the parliamentary opposition, which based its perspective on theoretical foundations that were very different from—if not contrary to—those of the natural law supporters, but which opposition was also fighting against absolutism.

This convergence of the anti-absolutist tradition and the modernity of the Enlightenment became greater in fact after 1770, in step with the conflict between the *parlements* and royal authority. The "coup d'état," or "Maupeou revolution," and the subsequent crisis were the catalyst of this increased convergence. In order to assert the political prerogatives of the sovereign courts, numerous texts were published that were not merely topical pieces but that helped to enrich, or at least to popularize, the content of the "public law of France."

The *Maximes du droit public français* (Maxims of French Public Law) is undoubtedly the most illuminating example of such occasional writings in this regard. A first anonymous and clandestine edition came out "in France" in 1772. It was the result of the collaboration of three lawyers in the Paris *parlement*—the abbé Mey, Maultrot, and Aubry. This anonymous publication was followed in 1775 by a second edition, considerably enriched and emanating from Amsterdam where another parliamentary lawyer, Blonde, was a refugee. As the title page of the new version indicated, *Maximes du droit public français, tirées des capitulaires, des ordonnances du royaume et des autres monuments du royaume* (Maxims of French Public Law, Drawn from Capitularies, Royal Ordinances, and Other Monumental Works of the Kingdom) was "twice the size of the preceding edition," and it enjoyed great public success. This heavy volume accumulated arguments of a historical nature; these arguments were sometimes a bit fanciful, evoking the golden age of a long-ago monarchy when the king's powers were limited in a number of ways. Scattered throughout were multiple textual references from the time of antiquity to the 18th century. Among the most recent, the editors of the *Maximes* made lavish use—with no fear of contradictions—of both the reprimands of the sovereign law courts, disclosure of which was traditionally forbidden, and of the works of *jus naturalis* publicists. A host of European authors were thus called on for support, from John Locke to Heineccius, by way of Pufendorf, Gerhard Noodt, Christian Wolff, and many others, with a preference for the thought of Swiss theorists of natural law—Jean de Barbeyrac, Jean-Jacques Burlamaqui, and Emmerich de Vattel. Montesquieu was also often among those cited, but the Parisian lawyers feigned ignorance of Rousseau.

From these multiple and disparate references were extracted the "maxims," or principles, of public law; these expressed themselves in the fundamental laws of the kingdom and outlined the judicial structure of a "temperate monarchy." The "positive and variable fundamental laws," which varied according to states and times, were simply mentioned as reminders. These fundamental laws concerned the devolution of the crown of France, the inalienability of the domain, and—for the authors of the *Maximes* as well as for the magistrates of the *parlements*—the permanence of public positions. Apart from this last point, there was nothing really innovative in the *Maximes*, and the absolutists themselves recognized that it was necessary for the king to submit to these important traditional rules, which had been respected for centuries.

More original to the *Maximes* was the notion of "natural and essential" fundamental laws common to all states and all times, engendered by conventions established between the monarchs and their subjects. Chapter IV of the *Maximes* states:

> Governing according to the laws of justice and equity, seeking the public good, oppressing nobody, regarding one's subjects as children to whom one is a father, being concerned only with their happiness, and refraining from all that whims, passion, or arbitrary power might inspire: these are all fundamental laws of a well-regulated government. Even the most absolute power should not evade them.

The best example of a transgression of these laws was that of the *lettres de cachet*, which, precisely, enabled the sovereign to remove recalcitrant parliamentarians, and against which letters the authors of the *Maximes* unleashed their fury. They contended that the use of those letters breached the convention made "between the king and the nation" by virtue of the fact that one of the parties had not respected its obligations. Although this conventional agreement had not been drawn up formally in writing, it was a true contract entailing reciprocal obligations and was comparable to the contract of mandate familiar to private law. As such, the contract between the ruler and the ruled could be annulled on grounds of non-execution or poor execution; it could even be annulled when its conclusion had been vitiated by an error—for example, if the people had been deceived. After annulment, the subjects would have a different relationship with their king, modifying the form of government to make it conform to natural laws, for although the nation did not always exercise sovereign power, the principle of that power still resided with the people. Therefore the authors of the *Maximes* viewed the ceremony of the coronation as the sign that the new king had been accepted by the body politic, which enabled them to claim that "the choice of the people is not contrary to the principle of inheritance of the crown" and that the adage "The king is dead, long live the king" (without interregnum) was a "modern rule against which all antiquity can testify."

But who can express the will of the nation? For many years, it was the Estates General, whose role was not only advisory. In a short note appended to the *Maximes—Dissertation sur le droit de convoquer les États Généraux* (Essay on the Right to Convene the Estates General—the Parisian lawyers maintained that in serious cases the Estates General could call their own assembly, without having to wait for the king to call them, and expressions such as the "national diet" or the "general assembly of the nation" appeared for the first time in writing. However, by a simple sleight of hand, the *Maximes* entrusted the attributions of such institutions to the *parlements* that had succeeded the Frankish Popular Assembly and would take the place of the Estates General.

Thus, the main objective of the *Maximes* had been achieved: to show that the sovereign law courts were the depositary of the laws and that they must be able to verify all new laws in complete freedom. If the king wanted to impose their registration, it was the duty of the magistrates to resist, refusing to allow the *lettres de cachet* to force parliamentarians out of the seat of their jurisdiction or prevent them from carrying out their mission. The people of the *parlement* would then remain as firm as Chinese mandarins, "martyrs to the public good," for having struggled against the arbitrariness of emperors.

Many other texts inspired by the struggle of the French magistrates were in the same vein, from the *Extrait du droit public de la France* (1771; Extract of French Public Law) and the *Tableau de la constitution française ou autorité des rois de France dans les différents âges de la monarchie* (1771; Description of the French Constitution; or, authority of the Kings of France during the Different Periods of the Monarchy) by Louis Brancas de Lauraguais, to the monumental *Théorie des lois politiques de la monarchie française* (1791–92; Theory of Political Laws in the French Monarchy) by Marie-Charlotte-Pauline de Lézardière, which, conceived and written under the ancien régime, would not begin to be published until 1790. The fact remains that, with the aim to support the most retrograde forces in France in the 18th century, such works publicized, or even popularized, concepts engendered by the most innovative trends in European thought, such as those of the social contract and the sovereignty of the nation. Thus the notion of public law, by its very ambiguity, was at the heart of the political debate waged in the years before the French Revolution. At that period, the concept was easily absorbed into that of the constitution (with which it tended to be confused), before it would be fully implemented in the Declaration of the Rights of Man and of the Citizen voted by the French Constituent Assembly on 26 August 1789.

JEAN BART

See also State

Further Reading

Büllinger, Martin, *Offentliches Recht und Privatrecht: Studien über Sinn und Funktionen der Unterscheidung*, Stuttgart: Kohlhammer, 1968

Chevrier, G., "Remarques sur l'introduction et les vicissitudes de la distinction du *jus privatum* et du *jus publicum* dans les oeuvres des anciens juristes français," *Archives de philosophie du droit* (1952)

Derathé, Robert, *Jean-Jacques Rousseau et la science politique de son temps*, Paris: Presses Universitaires de France, 1950; 2nd edition, Paris: Vrin, 1970

Lemaire, André, *Les lois fondamentales de la monarchie française d'aprés les théoriciens de l'Ancien régime*, Paris: Fontemoing, 1907; reprint, Geneva: Slatkine-Megariotis, 1975

Olivier-Martin, François, *L'absolutisme français*, Paris: Loysel, 1988

Liberalism

At first glance, the use of the term "liberalism" with regard to the age of the Enlightenment is anachronistic. The term was actually coined at the beginning of the 19th century, in the wake, it would seem, of the creation of the Spanish Liberal party (1812) inspired by English constitutionalism; it appeared in Maine de Biran in 1818 and was used in an 1819 citation in the *Oxford English Dictionary* ("Liberalism") to designate a type of doctrine that aimed to encourage the development of liberties; in 1823 its use was discussed in Claude Boiste's *Lexique* (Lexicon). The development of liberties refers both to the protection of individual freedom ("the true modern freedom," in the words of Benjamin Constant), which is in turn guaranteed by political liberty, and to the free expansion of individual freedom within an economic system based on competition. In the first instance, freedom is inseparable from security with regard to what Constant calls "private pleasures," in that this security is guaranteed by institutions; in the second instance, freedom is equated with property, understood as both unlimited appropriation and as the pursuit of one's own advantage—in short, freedom of enterprise in the broadest sense of the term. In both instances, the task of the state is to guarantee peace and prosperity to its citizens, by adopting appropriate constitutional and judicial mechanisms.

However, as is often the case, the idea preceded the word. Even before liberalism came to be framed within a precariously rooted doctrine and through a hesitant economic policy, the adjective "liberal"—deviating from its traditional application to a branch of study (the liberal arts)—was used to designate a spirit of toleration, a demand for freedom of conscience and expression, and the defense of the exercise of individual rights. In a particularly significant way during the Enlightenment, the word also came to refer to the struggle against all forms of superstition and fanaticism. In a nutshell, "liberal" came to mean a rejection of authoritarianism and arbitrariness. However, far from challenging the legitimacy of political power per se, liberalism aimed, to the contrary, to make political power the instrument of "security," through the limitation of its own power, in keeping with Montesquieu's celebrated declaration: "To prevent an abuse of power, things must be arranged in such a way that power will put a stop to power" (*De l'esprit des lois* [1748; The Spirit of Laws]). Meanwhile in the social and economic realms, the individual acquired new prominence, coming to embody initiative and a certain taste for entrepreneurship—a practice that had its roots in individual self-interest and adopted the goal of the maximum satisfaction of that same self-interest, thereby promoting, in the complex play of social relations initiated in this way, what became known as the common good. In this regard, the function of the state was defined as guaranteeing this "natural" individual disposition, by limiting the government's own intervention in the sphere of trade and by restricting itself to three main duties: national defense, "a scrupulous administration of justice," and the establishment and maintenance of institutions of public interest (see Adam Smith, *An Inquiry into the Nature and Causes of the Wealth of Nations* [1776]). The individual thus became the symbol of social mobility, a subject capable both of preserving and, if necessary, of developing his rights, but also a producer-consumer who, through his activities, would be capable, sometimes unwittingly, of contributing to the harmonious development of society. Despite the obvious points of agreement between the two doctrines, one should nevertheless distinguish, up to a point, between political liberalism and economic liberalism.

The Anthropological Base of Liberalism

As Max Weber has argued, self-love, self-preservation, self-interest, and pleasure, but also the need to act, readily sublimated in work, which in its way reveals the fundamental anxiety of human beings, are all integral to the common foundation of all "liberalisms," as well as to the break these liberalisms made from the tradition inherited from antiquity. Departing from the pre-liberal worldview, the city ceases to represent the full flowering of man's (political) nature; it is only the means to protect and fulfill the interests of individuals.

The common basis of political and economic liberalism is indeed the individual: the state, having once been master over individuals, was required to place itself at their service and become their tool (see Laski; Tawney). According to liberals, the individual is both the *archon* (ruler) and the telos of society, but it plays these roles according to certain patterns that have to be kept distinct. From what is indeed a single anthropological base (survival, self-interest, pleasure), liberalism developed along two divergent paths.

In the political domain liberalism was a descendant of the doctrines of natural law and the social contract elaborated by jurists and philosophers throughout the 17th century and revived and popularized in the 18th century by authors such as Christian Wolff, Jean de Barbeyrac, Jean-Jacques Burlamaqui, or Emmerich de Vattel. Whatever the reasons invoked—natural sociability (Grotius), the fragility and precariousness of the natural state of peace (Samuel von Pufendorf, John Locke), the war of all against all as a natural condition of mankind (Thomas Hobbes), or, later, with Jean-Jacques Rousseau, the intervention of "circumstances"—the transition from nature to civilization was always perceived as the fruit of a decision made by fearful individuals, by means of an artifice, in order to bolster their natural inclinations, and/or safeguard their existence and further their own interests. In every case, the creation and subsequent implementation of a civil state capable of regulating social relations in the best interests of all was founded upon a voluntary commitment emanating from free individuals. It should be noted, however, that the break thus made with the theological and political views, along with the replacement of divine right by popular sovereignty as the foundation of political power, did not determine a priori any specific restrictions on the choice of the form of government, which could, depending on the case, be that of a republic, a limited monarchy, an absolute monarchy, or even, for Hobbes, an unlimited sovereignty (with no specification of that sovereignty's monarchic, aristocratic, or democratic nature). Looked at in this light, political power of a liberal variety does not seem to be an inevitable consequence of a doctrinal constellation, which

did, however, set up the necessary theoretical conditions for liberal political thought.

In the economic domain, on the other hand, the principle of civil society resided in individual and "selfish" calculations of one's own interests, independently of any voluntary action and, consequently, without the obligatory prerequisite of the hypothesis of a social contract. The postulate governing the undertaking is that of the involuntary harmonization of the sum of individual interests: it stipulated that the interest of all was (and could only be) the product of the sum total of individual interests. Each individual, in pursuing his own interest and indulging in calculations that would produce his own greatest satisfaction, with no regard for the common good, thus unwittingly contributes to the realization of the greatest possible collective happiness. Later radicalized by Jeremy Bentham in his theory of utilitarianism, which held that the preponderance of egotistical instincts was the prerequisite for the continuation of the species (see Halévy), this view was first expressed in the work of the Machiavelli of economics: Bernard Mandeville's *The Fable of the Bees* (1714–29). The paradox developed in the fable, according to which "private vices cause public good," tends to separate—in a provocative manner—moral virtue from utility and to link personal interest with social virtue, by pointing out the common prosperity that could result, without any collusion, from the combination of various expressions of amoral egotism. At the same time, far from being the result of a founding social contract deliberately made among rational or judiciously calculating individuals, social organization results from a division of labor that Mandeville sees as an intermediary force in the fulfillment of the needs and the passions that everyone, idiosyncratically, seeks without respite to satisfy, as intensely as possible (see Carrive; Guéry; Séris). The specialization of labor, which masks the general mechanism of production while contributing to it in the most effective way, defines the technical version of the image of a collectivity built upon foundations that, as Adam Ferguson says in his *Essay on the History of Civil Society* (1767), "are the result of human activity, but not the result of human design." The recurrence of this theme, from Montesquieu (*De l'esprit des lois*, Book III, Chapter 7) to Immanuel Kant (the fourth proposition in the *Idee zu einer allgemeinen Geschichte in weltbürgerlicher Absicht* [1784; Idea for a Universal History with a Cosmopolitan Intent]), by way, in particular, of Smith (the famous "invisible hand"), indicates that the politico-legal stance was transforming into an economic viewpoint. If there is voluntary association, it does not necessarily happen because of a principle of society; society is the terrain of needs, desires, individual interests, trade, and utility. Thus, the "market" tended to replace the contract as the very foundation of the institution and regulation of society (even the notion of the social contract might be explicitly contested, as witnessed in the works of David Hume, then in the writings of Edmund Burke and Bentham), thereby initiating restraints on the field of influence exercised by political authority. Everything then unfolded as if this initial shift toward an economic interpretation had revealed the truth of the liberal attitude, which was still concerned with the definition of the role of the state confronted with the aspirations of individuals within civil society.

Liberalism and Its Enemies

A highly controversial doctrine, liberalism had from its beginnings identified clearly the enemies it intended to fight: despotism and mercantilism. In its political version, liberalism states the problem, in the most abrupt way possible, of the relationship between authority and freedom by determining the state's scope of intervention on the basis of its constitutional structure—hence the interest shown all through the 18th century in the constitution that had resulted from the Glorious Revolution of 1688, whether it was understood as a real innovation (Hume), as a possible model (Montesquieu), or even as a perfectible system. In the wake of Locke's *Second Treatise on Civil Government* (1689–90), the foundations of absolutism, authoritarianism, and even of despotism had to be challenged, by insisting first of all on the necessary separation of powers (legislative and executive), but above all by stipulating that the executive must be made subordinate to the legislative, to which it is accountable. More than a given type of political regime, despotism for Montesquieu is the specter that haunts all forms of government; from this point of view, the model described in Chapter 6 of Book XI of *De l'esprit des lois* seeks less to define the need for a still equivocal and problematic separation of powers than to shed light on the virtues of "moderation" in the preservation of political liberty, and in the protection of individual well-being and security. Here "moderation" designates a regulation of powers and, consequently, of the social forces that, thanks to a system of weights and counterweights, should be able to attain an equilibrium that is more ideal than concrete, with the English regime serving not as an example of the perfect realization of moderation but as the most reliable indication of what might be achieved. Gentle commerce" itself (see Larrère), through its civilizing effect, is based on the spontaneous quest for a means to counterbalance the passions that threaten to dissolve society: the relative equilibrium thus attained joins forces with the balance of powers and social forces. Moderation therefore masks a process of limitation by compensation, hovering around an ideal point of equilibrium of the forces at play. The model adopted by nascent political liberalism

was not that of the separation of powers (seen as strictly independent of the functions of the state) but of the *balance* of powers.

However, the struggle against the factional spirit could not fail to show that active solidarity among the productive elements of society would perforce find expression in the political body. The victory of moderation over factionalism thus demanded the recognition and consolidation of the plan for freedom put in place by the Glorious Revolution and by the Declaration of Rights of 1689, which, according to Hume, introduced "a new face of the constitution." Here, too, the system of "checks and balances" had to be freely deployed, far removed from the factional spirit, which would damage its workings and wear them down more quickly—although that spirit was something quite natural in other circumstances. The level-headed limitation of political power could thus have as its purpose—beyond its obvious role as guarantor of the rights of citizens—to facilitate (or, at the very least, to avoid obstructing) spontaneously initiated economic development, perceived as a factor of "refinement."

Voltaire had already seen that the "happy mixture" that characterized the English government under its new constitution and gave its citizens the greatest freedom was inseparable from economic growth: "Commerce, which has enriched the citizens of England, has contributed to their freedom, and this freedom in turn has expanded commerce; whence the greatness of the state" (Letter 10, *Lettres philosophiques* [1734; Philosophical Letters]). The attacks directed later against the British constitution (notably by Kant), on the suspicion that it was inclined toward despotism because of the corruption that the system of influence engendered, were made in the name of an ideal of limited monarchy that the said constitution claimed, precisely, to embody.

In its economic version, nascent liberalism immediately rebelled against "mercantile" policies (an adjective coined by the marquis de Mirabeau in 1783 in *Philosophie rurale, ou économie générale et politique de l'agriculture* [Rural Philosophy; or, A General and Political Economy of Agriculture] and adopted by Smith in Book IV of *Wealth of Nations*), policies put into practice by nation-states: protectionism, prohibition, commercial jealousy, and finicky regulations. This rebellion was less for reasons of morality than to denounce the ineffectiveness of the measures implemented, as well as the perverse effects that they could produce (according to the abbé André Morellet, it is at such times that "prohibition makes fraud necessary"). Because they implemented a certain number of obstacles to the progress of society in the spheres of production and trade, mercantilist policies were regarded by liberals as proof of the policy makers' deep-seated misconceptions about the conditions necessary for society's own development. On the one hand, mercantilism persisted in treating each society in isolation and establishing relations among nations based on rivalry and jealousy, effectively paralyzing each nation's growth; on the other hand, it interpreted in a purely mechanical rather than organic fashion any development that led to advancement in both social development and productivity.

To the notion of "moderation" one would henceforth have to add the notion of "laissez-faire" (attributed to Vincent de Gournay), readily adopted as a veritable slogan. Still, the apparent transparency of this slogan could be deceiving. It tended to disguise the political choices that corresponded to quite nuanced models. Nascent liberal thought—just like the medical thought with which it had united—denounced all forms of violence imposed upon the natural course of things. Abstention or facilitation would have to replace limitations and prohibitions; art, conceived as the antithesis of nature, would have to make way for nature itself, or for an art conceived as an auxiliary to nature. However, between doing nothing and doing something (however little) there was a difference, one that led to two divergent views of the way society worked. Thus, when François Quesnay stated that *il mondo va da se* (the world moves by itself), he meant that free competition would lead to the best price (which is in keeping with the interest of the different classes), if one envisages the ideal state as the means as well as the model for the circulation of goods within society, under the control of a "tutelary and sovereign authority" that guarantees the recognition of a natural order. In this instance, the freedom of the working parts is that of a machine that has been adjusted once and for all, and then placed in an ideal position inside a circulating system, where any disparity is viewed as pathogenic. Letting nature take care of things meant allowing property take care of things in its best interest, which would merge with the general interest of the nation, under the banner of natural order.

Hume and Smith reproached the Economists for this very thing, for their blindness to the spontaneity of the living body and for having sought to impose, in the name of natural order, a dietary restriction on society, the social body. In their view the solidarity that, in fact, regulates the functioning of the social body also facilitates the maintenance of society's cohesion through the necessary artifice of trade. The essential notion here is that of "repair," which joins those of "fellow feeling" and involuntary harmony. In contrast to mercantilism, this notion meant that there is no absolute loss and that compensation, through the dynamic nature of the body (individual or social), acts spontaneously at every level to reestablish relative equilibrium. In contrast to the Physiocrats, however, the notion of "repair" stipulates

that trade is not a pure and simple cycle, conceived in keeping with the ideal system of continuing return, in accordance with a strict regime; on the contrary, the greater or lesser speed of the process prevents the a priori establishment of a standard of health, the regulating principle according to which one would be asked to evaluate the level of pathology in the social body. This disparity is the natural progression of a perpetual cycle of exchanges in which an always precarious equilibrium is constantly being restored as a result of "circumstances." In other words, unlike the Physiocrats, who held that experience must fall in line with a taught and fixed standard, restricting and unrelated to the agent, the other liberalism (that of Hume and Smith in particular) stated that the standard was constructed and invented under the pressure of the environment, by the body's ability to "repair" losses. Hence, the opposite of the natural is not "the artificial," but "the arbitrary"; the split occurs not between nature and artifice, but between the disrupting artifice and the facilitating artifice, a divide that leaves room for a possible intervention by the government, within the framework of the constitution.

All of this goes to show that, contrary to a simplistic view, the two variants of nascent economic liberalism—based on what might be incompatible criteria—certainly did acknowledge a regulating role for political authority. However, whereas, in the first variant, legal despotism was expected to make certain that natural order was respected, the second variant addressed the possibility of correcting artifices that would reestablish the inner equilibrium of the social body whenever it was too directly threatened. The first variant hinged on *conformity*, the second on *invention*.

DIDIER DELEULE

See also Agriculture; England; France; Natural Law and the Rights of Man; Physiocracy; Social Contract; Trade

Further Reading

Burdeau, Georges, *Le libéralisme,* Paris: Seuil, 1979

Carrive, Paulette, *La philosophie des passions chez Bernard Mandeville,* Paris: Didier-Érudition, 1983

Deleule, Didier, *Hume et la naissance du libéralisme économique,* Paris: Montaigne, 1979

Guéry, François, *La société industrielle et ses ennemis,* Paris: Orban, 1989

Halévy, Elie, *The Growth of Philosophic Radicalism,* translated by Mary Morris, Clifton, New Jersey: Kelley, and London: Faber, 1972 (original French edition, 3 vols., 1901–04)

Larrère, Catherine, *L'invention de l'économie au XVIIIᵉ siècle: Du droit naturel à la physiocratie,* Paris: Presses Universitaires de France, 1992

Laski, Harold Joseph, *Liberty in the Modern State,* London: Faber and Faber, and New York: Harper and Brothers, 1930

Rosanvallon, Pierre, *Le libéralisme économique: Histoire de l'idée de marché,* Paris: Seuil, 1989

Séris, Jean-Pierre, *Qu'est-ce que la division du travail? Ferguson,* Paris: Librairie Philosophique J. Vrin, 1994

Tawney, R.H., *Religion and the Rise of Capitalism,* London: John Murray, and New York: Harcourt Brace, 1926; reprint, New Brunswick, New Jersey: Transaction, 1998

Libertinism

Inseparable from the Enlightenment, was *libertinage* (libertinism; freethinking) a phenomenon throughout Europe? There is, in fact, little evidence to support such a hypothesis. On the other hand, the concept of libertinism was linked to the philosophical debates and socioeconomic changes that did have an impact, to a greater or lesser degree, on the majority of European nations. Libertinism continues to be associated primarily with the France of the ancien régime, perhaps because of the numerous ideological struggles that preceded the French Revolution. Before it became a literary myth or a phenomenon of social history, "libertinism" was a word invoked for its force as an injunction.

An Ideological Weapon

From the time of the Protestant Reformation and Jean Calvin's pamphlet *Contre la secte phantastique et furieuse des libertins qui se nomment spirituels* (1544; Treatises against the Anabaptists and against the Libertines through the Age of the Enlightenment), the concept of libertinism was at the center of religious and political debates. Some of these disputes, in the Netherlands and then in France, have become well known, whereas the issues seems to have made less of an impression on the countries of southern Europe, where the repressive weight of the Counter-Reformation was felt more strongly. The various European languages bear the imprint of this divergence of cultural experience. Scholars have thoroughly documented the evolution of the French word *libertin,* which changed in meaning during the 1680s from "freethinker" to "debauchee." Alongside this slow "devaluation," of the term *libertin,* one can trace different meanings given to related words in various European languages. In the Romance languages, the original meaning of the Latin word *libertinus* (freed slave), which was contrasted with *ingenuus* (free man), was retained throughout the 18th century, alongside more clearly pejorative meanings. In Italian, Spanish, and Portuguese, *libertino* referred to a man who rejects social constraints, to the point where "libertinism" (*libertinaggio* or *dissolutezza* in Italian, *disolución* in Spanish) became synonymous with "debauchery." However, the influence of Catholicism meant that the definition of "libertinism" as a "rejection of religion" (*incredulita* in Italian, *incredulidad* in Spanish) did not appear in bilingual dictionaries until the end of the century.

In contrast, in the Germanic languages, the definition of a libertine as a "freethinker" became primary, being expressed in German by the words *Freidenker* or *Freigeist,* and in Dutch as *vrygeest.* During this period, the German word *Ruchlos* also acquired a range of meanings comparable to that of the French word *libertin.* Finally, while English translations of these words came closer to the Germanic than to the Romance languages, it should be noted that the primary meaning associated in English with "libertinism" continued to be that of debauchery—as in "lewdness" or "licentiousness"—and that the other meaning ("freethinking") was not common until the time of the French Revolution. In 1702, in the "Libertin" entry of Boyer's French-English dictionary, the author proposed as translations of the French *libertin* (explained as "freethinker in matters of religion") the somewhat unphilosophical English words "wit" and "droll," which more accurately characterize the French *plaisantin* (joker) or *bel esprit* (witty person). The misleading English words were not replaced by "freethinking" until the dictionary was reissued in 1792.

Clearly, the words "libertine" and "libertinism" had no stable meanings during the Enlightenment. This was all the more true because the connotation of atheism that had been attached to these terms was only gradually applied, with "libertines" eventually being used only to describe a Dutch sect of the 16th century (in the 1704 edition of the *Dictionnaire de Trévoux* [Dictionary of Trévoux], the *Encyclopédie,* or the 1765 edition of Johann Theodor Jablonski's French-German dictionary). Consequently, libertinism came to be evaluated rather than defined and to be not so much a concept as an expression of a system of values. As the *Encyclopédie* puts it, libertinism "stands midway between voluptuousness and debauchery." Sénac de Meilhan later established a hierarchy of forms of corruption in which the libertine was surpassed by the debauchee and the villain. Finally, in the closing years of the century, a novel by Nougaret with the subtitle *Les progrès du libertinage* (The Progress of Dissolution) depicted an ineluctable path of degeneration leading from prostitution to the pox. This lexical devaluation did not express the disappearance of ideological struggles but rather revealed their slow transformation.

Indeed, it became impossible to espouse libertinism. At the beginning of the 17th century, members of the intellectual elite had been able to proclaim themselves "libertines" in their struggle against the standardization of morality, but alliances among their adversaries rapidly increased the concept's pejorative connotations. The same struggle seems to have continued during the Enlightenment. For example, in 1747 Desmonts wrote *Le libertinage combattu par les auteurs profanes* (Libertine Philosophy Fought by Secular Authors). In reality, no one dared to proclaim himself a libertine. The word itself was violently rejected by such *philosophes* as Julien Offroy de La Mettrie, who feared that "this amiable liberty [freedom of thought] be put on trial under the odious names of libertinism and debauchery, which I deplore" (*La volupté* [1746; Voluptuous Pleasures]). Eighteenth-century German dictionaries took care to keep the word *Freidenker* free from the pejorative connotations that were associated with *Libertiner* or *Libertinismus*. The struggles of the Enlightenment *philosophes* against religious dogmas, struggles based on the ideas of John Toland, Pietro Giannone, and the French materialists, were no longer linked to libertinism. A definitive turning point seems to have been reached when the marquis de Caraccioli's *Dictionnaire critique, pittoresque et sentencieux* (1768; Critical, Picturesque and Concise Dictionary) offered a definition of the libertine as "a debauched man, not an impious one, as some dictionaries assert." It must be concluded that conflation of "atheist" and "debauchee" gave way to a general confusion about the real-world causes and effects of fiction: time and again, corrupting novels were presented as the products, or the origins, of spiritual libertinism. In 1799 Pierre Sylvain Maréchal protested against the "dirty trick" played on atheists by those who included "some of their maxims in obscene books, in an attempt to turn the contradictory characteristics of impiety and libertinism into synonyms, and to make men without God [seem the same as] men without morals." The connection had become a commonplace in French: libertinism was no longer simply a school of thought, but a debauched way of life. However, at the same time, the transformation of the libertine into a character in novels became the source of a complex myth that embodied a different and positive image.

Between Rejection and Fascination

The image of the libertine in the novel was certainly a principal one with which many 18th-century readers identified, either in their imaginations, or unconsciously. The libertine was that disturbing or attractive Other, whose character was interpreted differently by different social groups. From the aristocratic and socially elevated point of view, there was little to distinguish libertinism—a word that, according to César-Pierre Richelet in 1680, "is spoken laughingly"—from lighthearted gallantry: libertinism was excused by youth. During the Enlightenment the reaction of the aristocracy to the escapades of the wicked members of their group, from Marshal Richelieu to the marquis de Sade, was always ambiguous, oscillating between repression and caste solidarity. These were also the novelists' images of libertines, with their examples of varying degrees of paternal complicity. From the abbé Prévost's *Manon Lescaut* (1731; Manon Lescaut) to Crébillon's *Égarements du coeur et de l'esprit* (1736–38; Aberrations of the Heart and the Mind), libertinism is presented in a nostalgic light by narrators recalling the errors of their youth. Nevertheless, the relaxation of morals supposedly associated with the Regency (1715–23) led such aristocrats as the duc de Saint-Simon to evoke the specter of the degeneration of the aristocratic class and to call for a moral response. By expressing such views, these aristocrats opened the way for external attacks on the aristocracy as a whole and produced in advance the image of the debauched nobleman that would soon become omnipresent.

Gallantry perhaps became libertinism when it changed from an aristocratic entertainment into a product for consumption by the bourgeoisie. This shift occurred when the manuscript that the comte de Bussy wrote for Madame de Montglat, the *Histoire amoureuse des Gaules* (History of Love in Gaul), became a commercial success in 1665. In fact, the bourgeoisie came to identify libertinism with the aristocracy after having appropriated the principal virtues of the aristocracy along with a large part of its power. The public display of the libertine represented a threat to the private peace of the bourgeois household. In the early years of the 18th century, many works in French and German warned against the libertinism of ladies, understood as either public exhibitionism or simple flirting (Antoine Furetière). However, the hostility of the bourgeoisie was above all a matter of economics. The libertine was a spendthrift, an undisciplined person who upset the new society's rules of moderation and economy. Such bourgeois arguments thus reinforced the Christian rhetoric that stigmatized libertines for their lack of foresight: by not preparing for their futures, they were making, as it were, a bad investment. As César de Rochefort wrote in the *Dictionnaire général* (1685; General Dictionary), "one could say that they [libertines] never begin to live, for all the time that they have lived counts for nothing."

Medical writings of the Enlightenment were also concerned with economy and moderation, and they developed their own rhetoric of prudence in order to attack libertinism. Libertines did not only risk eternal damnation, they also faced suffering in old age. Furthermore—and this conclusion represents a singular paradox—libertines failed to derive any benefit from their debauchery, for the sexual pleasure that they extracted remained inferior to that of proper gentlemen. This was a reassuring image for those who criticized libertinism: the impotent libertine, doomed to be the victim of sexual disease and finding in his numerous conquests only feeble compensation for his lack of enjoyment. Procope-Couteau declares in *L'art de faire des garçons* (1748; The Art of Making [sic] Boys) that "the pleasures enjoyed by the libertine, the lover, and the philosopher resemble a number, its square, and its cube; that is to say, if the pleasure of the first were 4, that of the second would be 16, and that of the third would be 64." When it invoked the specter of degeneration, satire could even be tinged with anguish. In the final quarter of the 18th century, some alarmist medical writers diagnosed the deterioration of the human race and issued stirring appeals to those of their contemporaries who engaged in libertinism. Thus, De Lignac writes in *De l'homme et de la femme* (1777; On Men and Women):

You for whom the habit of sexual indulgence has rendered pleasure necessary, for whom libertinism and debauchery have taken the place of ecstasy, you impotent old man who still expects sensual delights! . . . If you can be useful to society, it is not by providing it with men who, in the spring of their lives, already presage old age and decrepitude.

However, such cold responses by men of the Enlightenment whose own consciences were clear, in the face of the more or less fantastical social reality of the libertine, constitute only one aspect of the bourgeois attitudes of the time. Indeed, it was this very same audience whose fascination assured the success of all the fictional representations of libertinism.

The integration of the image of the libertine into the domain of fiction had a number of consequences. In the first place, it led to the change in the meaning of "libertine" from "freethinker" to "debauchee." Philosophical libertines, whose discourse is more than merely a device for amorous conquests, appear in novels from *Thérèse philosophe* (1748; Thérèse as Philosopher), by the marquis d'Argens, and *Le nouveau Dom Bougre à l'Assemblée nationale, ou l'abbé Maury au Bordel* (1790; The New Dom Bougre at the National Assembly; or, Abbot Maury at the Brothel) to the novels of Sade, but such libertines remain in a minority. Most important, the introduction of libertines into fiction brought about a process of individualization. Before Molière made Don Juan into a legendary figure, libertinism had been perceived primarily as the behavior pattern of a group, whether that group be a sect, as it was for Calvin, or a simple brotherhood, as it was for Father Garasse. The transfer of these patterns of behavior and speech to an individualized character created the myth of the libertine, conferring a timeless image of perceived "danger" upon the realities of a specific time in history. The typology of libertine characters in French novels—the effeminate and affected petty bourgeois, the uncouth and moody libertine, the willful libertine who was an apathetic tactician—has been so extensively explored that it is sometimes confused with the historical manifestations of libertinism. Rather than repeating all the details discussed above once again, one might consider how this myth was to fare throughout Europe.

The complexity of a character such as Lovelace, the antihero of Samuel Richardson's novel *Clarissa* (1747–48), is evidence both of the popularity of French models and of the way in which those models were very quickly transformed. Over and above his extravagant cynicism, Lovelace has a sentimental and evil side, prefiguring the heroes of the Gothic novels that appeared toward the end of the century in England and Germany. These heroes are not identified as libertines, yet their behavior does conform to the libertine model, as, for example, in the case of Vathek's debauchery in William Beckford's novel of that name (*Vathek, conte arabe* [1782; Vathek, an Arab Tale]). The true change in the nature of the libertine in novels lies in the author's abandonment of the established social and historical traits of the character—Vathek, for example, is a caliph, while the eponymous hero of Matthew Gregory "Monk" Lewis's *Ambrosio; or, The Monk* (1796) lives in an Alpine setting without social ties—and in the author's adoption of a dimension of fantasy. Such changes create a certain distortion of libertine atheism, for while these new heroes do not believe in God, they nonetheless do not deny the existence of the Devil. This abandonment of realism in favor of stylization, this passage from the legend of Don Juan to the myth of

Faust, should perhaps be understood as a denial of the historical realities of the revolutions in which the spirit of libertinism was invoked.

Fear of the Common People

According to Michel Foucault, historian of "discourse," libertinism in the age of the Enlightenment was not so much a myth as the product of a new perception of the social body: "Libertinism became a sin in a new sense . . . a moral peril rather than a threat to religion" (see Foucault). In fact, libertinism assumed a new identity when it appeared on the registers of hospitals, in police reports, and in the verdicts of courts. The word was used to designate a new type of jobless and homeless pauper, subsisting on the margins of the urban population. This figure was becoming increasingly visible in all the capital cities of Europe, but primarily in Paris and London. Faced with these debauchees (in the original sense of that term), people's response was to condemn rather than to understand. For Christian moralists, idleness was a sin. For example, in his book *La science des moeurs* (1694; The Science of Morals), Courtot declares:

> if a person abuses this sort of corporal freedom, I believe that he must be called a libertine, for, strictly speaking, a libertine does not signify a sinner so much as a vagabond or a debauchee who has no place to stay, who lives without rules, who comes and goes, and whose conduct is always uncertain and uneven.

The discourse of the Encyclopedists was subtler than Courtot's view, but they shared the same vision of poverty that prevailed throughout Enlightenment Europe on all social levels. It is as if, while the image of the corrupting libertine was being individualized, the idea of an anonymous community—an idea that had once been applied to scholarly atheists—was being transferred to this "libertine and idle nation," which was now beginning to be placed under surveillance, described, and enclosed. This "popular libertinism" very quickly gave rise to its own myths. Modern cities began to be described as places as dangerous as medieval deserts; for example, in his weekly journal *Correspondance secrète*, François Métra frequently evoked somber rumors from "that vast forest we call Paris." Paradoxically, feelings of insecurity and fears of epidemics were combined with fantasies of degeneration. Under the anguished gaze of the bourgeoisie, two absolutely contradictory social realities—the debauched aristocrat and the poor vagabond—became enduringly intertwined.

Such fears were also accompanied by a more or less conscious curiosity about the ways in which the poor supposedly lived without rules. In the 18th century, literary works depicting prostitutes were immensely popular. There were almanacs that listed their names, fees, and specialties; well-intentioned proposals for reforming prostitutes, such as Nicolas Edmé Rétif de La Bretonne's *Le pornographe* (1769; The Pornographer), as well as numerous texts in English from the same period or earlier; and pornographic texts that revealed the secrets of all the forbidden alcoves, such as the *Correspondance d'Eulalie ou tableau du libertinage de Paris* (1784; Eulalie's Correspondence; or, A Depiction of Dissoluteness in Paris). *Monsieur Nicolas ou Le coeur humain dévoilé* (1794–97; Monsieur Nicolas; or, The Human Heart Laid Bare) and other works by Rétif, as well as the works of Louis-Sébastien Mercier, provide evidence, albeit of two different types, for this new curiosity about the mysteries of Paris, which was often supplemented with more or less utopian desires for reform. The purely sexual component of the libertinism of the common people was to be a recurrent theme in English and German literature and was representative of societies in which the gap between social extremes long remained significant.

During the French Revolution, the complexity of libertinism gradually gave way to a number of strongly politicized caricatures. While revolutionary pamphlets made libertinism into the stamp of a degenerate and despotic aristocracy, exiles who took refuge in other European countries launched attacks in much the same terms, denouncing the bloody debaucheries of the new men in power. According to Charles de Villers, for example, Maximilien-Marie-Isidore de Robespierre would read Sade's novel *Justine; ou Les Malheurs de la vertu* (1791; Justine; or, The Misfortunes of Virtue) in order to firm up his own intransigence. Once these battles had died away, libertinism remained a symbol of the 18th century. Nevertheless, the mythic character who had so swiftly taken hold as the emblem of libertinism was not merely French, but European: this mythic figure was a man whose life transcended all national cultures, social conditions, and different literary genres. In the final reckoning, it is perhaps in the figure of Giacomo Casanova that the libertinism of Enlightenment Europe has left its most powerful legacy.

JEAN-CHRISTOPHE ABRAMOVICI

See also Atheism; Boudoir; Evil, Representations of; Miniature; Passions; Sexuality, Representations of; Virtue

Further Reading

DeJean, Joan E., *Libertine Strategies: Freedom and the Novel in Seventeenth-Century France*, Columbus: Ohio State University Press, 1981

Delon, Michel, "Débauche, libertinage," in *Handbuch politisch-sozialer Grundbegriffe in Frankreich, 1680–1820*, edited by Rolf Reichardt and Hans-Jürgen Lüsebrink, vol. 13, Munich: Oldenbourg, 1992

Foucault, Michel, *Madness and Civilization: A History of Insanity in the Age of Reason*, translated by Richard Howard, New York: Vintage Books and Pantheon Books, 1965; London: Tavistock, 1967 (original French edition, 1961)

Foxon, David Fairweather, *Libertine Literature in England, 1660–1745*, London: Shenval Press, 1964; New Hyde, New York: University Books, 1965

Reichler, Claude, *L'âge libertin*, Paris: Éditions de Minuit, 1987

Vázquez, Lydia, *Elogio de la seducción y del libertinaje: Sequido de un, prontuario de la seducción*, San Sebastián, Spain: R and B, 1996

Weber, Harold, *The Restoration Rake-Hero: Transformations in Sexual Understanding in Seventeenth-Century England*, Madison: University of Wisconsin Press, 1986

Liberty. *See* Authority, Government, and Power

Library

Whereas 18th-century European libraries were ancient institutions that had evolved gradually under the influence of two centuries of humanistic scholarship and the emergence of a new class of book owner in the 17th century, the *cabinets de lecture* (subscription libraries) and *chambres de lecture* (reading rooms) were relatively recent phenomena that only began to emerge from 1750 onward. Aside from works bought and owned by individuals, libraries and the two types of *cabinets* constituted the three principal collective spaces for reading in Enlightenment Europe. While differing in their history, their purposes, and their operating methods, they complemented each other in providing services that responded to the diverse expectations of the community of readers. This readership included both those who made scholarly use of texts and others who were attracted to the "novelties" that the diffusion and popularization of printed matter helped to foster.

While reading rooms and subscription libraries did not require readers to have any specific competence or status other than the desire to read, along with certain financial means, two sets of factors made it difficult for the general public to gain access to libraries during the Enlightenment. First, libraries maintained a scholarly and professional conception of texts; in addition, they remained private places that owners opened only to circles of friends or initiates, and in a carefully regulated manner. Following the transformations that they had undergone in the 16th century, the elite social classes began to open the doors of their libraries to carefully chosen members of the public beginning in the second half of the 17th century. This trend was the result of a variety of initiatives by political authorities, public bodies, religious congregations, or, in some cases, universities or academies. The various motivations for their creation meant that each of these libraries had its own distinct character, but it also meant that they suffered from various inadequacies, which prompted the creation of alternative spaces for reading. Nevertheless, it is safe to say that the 18th-century library did express the Enlightenment spirit to the extent that those members of the elite who put such collections together did so not with a view to personal satisfaction, but rather to provide a community of scholars with access to knowledge. The entry "Bibliothèque" (Library) in the *Encyclopédie* describes these institutions as being "among the principal ornaments of Europe." The author of the entry then provides a detailed enumeration of the principal European libraries. He begins in Copenhagen, moves through Sweden, Poland, and Russia, before returning to the Low Countries. From Leiden he then sets off to Germany, Switzerland, and Austria, and on to Italy, describing the libraries of Rome in particular detail. He lingers in Spain before ending up in France, where he makes a distinction between private collections, on the one hand, and "public" or "special" ones, on the other.

In France, where historians of books have extensively studied the phenomenon of libraries, there is evidence that certain collections were made accessible to a limited and specialized public beginning in the 15th century. In 1429 the rector of Sélestat, Jean De Westhus, founded a parish library, the nucleus of which was a collection of manuscripts bequeathed by a humanist scholar. In 1551 the town magistrates of Amiens created a modest library of legal and historical texts. The examples of Valenciennes (1563) and Dole (1582) confirm the existence of this practice, while the Protestant library officially established in La Rochelle in 1604 was expanded through various gifts and legacies before it was confiscated by Cardinal Richelieu after the siege of 1628. The movement gained impetus from the establishment of more libraries, including those of Rouen (1634), Abbeville (1643), Roanne (1648), and Troyes (1651). This first wave was characterized by its provincial origins and its connection, in the main, with members of the clergy who entrusted the management of their patrimony to colleges, monasteries, or religious orders.

Secular libraries in France were created on the basis of foreign examples. Three great libraries were opened to the public in the early years of the 17th century: the Ambrosian Library in Milan (1602), the Bodleian Library in Oxford (1611), and the Angelic Library in Rome (1620). The first of these made a great impression on a young librarian in the service of the président de Mesme, Gabriel Naudé (1600–53), who in 1627, published a "memorandum on establishing a library." Addressed to bibliophiles and collectors within the legal profession, urging them to open their large private collections, Naudé's proposal reflected in particular the ambitions of the *noblesse de robe*, those ennobled professionals who were seeking symbols of power that could provide them with the legitimacy, competence, and seniority that the *noblesse d'épée* (nobles of the sword) already possessed by virtue of their coats of arms and their illustrious military exploits. It was in this spirit that the *noblesse de robe* purchased manuscript collections from a number of religious communities that were forced to sell them for economic reasons. In this way the ennobled professionals became the custodians of a spiritual heritage, while at the same time representing the temporal order on the basis of their legal knowledge and skill, which they deployed in the service of the monarchy. Jules Mazarin led the way by opening his library to scholars in 1644, but only on Thursdays, from morning until evening. In 1647, when his library was installed on the rue de Richelieu, access was unrestricted from 8 o'clock in the morning to 5 o'clock in the evening. In 1654 a legacy from Henri du Boucher, a lawyer of the Parlement of Paris, allowed the abbey of Saint Victor to welcome readers three days a week. The specialized library of the Ordre des Avocats (lawyers' association) was opened in 1708, following the receipt of a legacy from E. Gabriau de Riparfonds, an advocate at the Parlement of Paris. The library of the priests of Christian doctrine was opened in 1718. The King's library itself was opened in 1720, although public access to it was postponed because it was frequently relocated. The library movement spread rapidly from the 1750s onward: of the approximately 40 "public" libraries that existed in 1789, two-thirds were created after 1750. The establishment of these libraries depended upon the good will of individuals who left their collections to religious or corporate institutions. In return, such individuals would require that the collections be maintained by librarians and that the public be given access to them on a number of days determined by the testator.

The academies also contributed to the phenomenon of public libraries. Between 1736 and 1750 four academies—those at Bordeaux, Pau, La Rochelle, and Nancy—opened libraries, which were enriched by successive legacies from their members. Access to the academy libraries was initially restricted to members only, but later all four were opened to a larger, but still select, public. Legacies were sometimes based on prior negotiations, as in Pau, where a professor of law at the university bequeathed his collection in exchange for a post as librarian and a commitment from the academy that the library would be open to the public twice a week. Other systems were also being introduced. In 1732 the Pau academy issued a new rule requiring its members to contribute either 30 livres or four books to the library. In Grenoble the library was founded with subscriptions intended for the purchase of a private collection that would form the library's nucleus; the subscription plan was launched in 1772 and the library opened two years later.

Meanwhile, French university libraries, which had fallen into decay for lack of funds, their books dispersed as a result of either individual transfers or theft, were enjoying a phase of revival, benefiting from the collections of the Jesuits after the ban of that order in 1760. The renaissance of university libraries seems to have gathered strength from 1780 onward, apart from the Sorbonne, which had maintained its standards throughout this period. This renaissance occurred in response to a numb er of pressures: readers required materials for their work; donors sometimes expressed particular wishes, as at the university library in Orléans; and certain libraries, such as those at Douai and Strasbourg, were managed by the municipal authorities and therefore affected by those authorities' decisions.

The establishment of "acquisitions" budgets permitted libraries to acquire new items at public auctions, as, for example, at Caen, where 3,000 livres were spent in 1735; such public auctions increased in number from the 1750s. This practice sometimes allowed the acquisition of major collections by "public" libraries. All told, according to the *Nouveau supplément à la France littéraire* (1784), there were 18 "public" libraries in Paris, while 16 cities in the French provinces had at least one library each.

However, despite this generous allotment of libraries, many of those institutions did not meet the expectations of most readers, who were not inclined to devote a great deal of time to acquiring information, and who had a taste for publications other than scholarly works. For such readers, the increasingly numerous periodicals were appealing for several reasons. In particular, they provided access to news and fashions, and they were readable, sparing readers the tedium of more specialized texts or the drawbacks and expense of "useless books," while drawing attention to works that were considered to be "useful." However, the majority of so-called public libraries remained focused on scholarly texts, with works of theology, law, history, and classical Latin literature being predominant. Moreover, the restricted hours during which these libraries were open tended to discourage those readers for whom the pleasures of reading were associated with those of social intercourse.

Beginning in the mid–18th century, the establishment of reading rooms, variously known as *cabinets littéraires* or *magasins littéraires*, began to make up for the inadequacies of libraries. The sheer number of different names for these reading-rooms is a good indication of the ambiguity of their status. They reflected both a philanthropic discourse that barely concealed commercial intentions and a concern for profits. In France, as elsewhere, there were two main types of reading room: the *cabinet de lecture* and the *chambre de lecture*. The former, created on the initiative of booksellers to bring a little extra money into their business, rented out books and periodicals on a subscription basis. Bookstores were furnished with tables and chairs so that customers could consult dictionaries and other reference works, or allow the translation classes to be organized. At the same time, bookstores publicized the opening of their reading rooms through announcements, notices, and various other forms of advertising, and they printed catalogs of available titles. These bookstores allowed those subscribers who needed the service to borrow specially marked items without leaving home. The provision of facilities for reading within the establishment seems to have distinguished certain *cabinets de lecture* from others, which were simply lending libraries. Businesses of this type could be found all over France.

Between 1759 and 1789 there were 13 in Paris and 36 in 24 provincial cities, but the length of time that they stayed in business was extremely variable. They could also be found elsewhere in Europe, in Germany, Switzerland, and the Low Countries, and in such major cities as Geneva and Warsaw.

The success of the *cabinets de lecture* was due to the fact that they met both a need and a demand: on the one hand, the book trade itself was extremely precarious during the second half of the 18th century, and booksellers needed the revenues provided by cabinets de *lecture;* on the other hand, the well-documented delight in reading and the taste for conviviality among men of the ancien régime ensured demand. In order to survive, booksellers had to resort to such expedients as selling forbidden books, and their careers were routinely punctuated with bankruptcy, closures and reopenings, or exile. The *cabinets de lecture* gave booksellers an opportunity to pay their debts, to transform stock that they could not sell into items that could be rented, and attract a clientele who could revive sales through an interest in dictionaries, novels, and periodicals. The cost of subscriptions to these libraries was fairly consistent, generally being set at 24 livres per year, 15 livres for six months, and three livres for a month. However, for 4 to 6 sous per day, one could consult books freely from 8 o'clock in the morning to 8 or 9 o'clock in the evening. The relationship with subscribers was apparently profitable enough for some booksellers to pay willingly 800 livres for one of the bookselling licenses put on sale under the royal edict of March 1767. Further evidence of the success of this sort of enterprise may be found in Robert Darnton's study of a Metz bookseller named Gerlache, in *Bohème littéraire et Révolution: Le monde des livres au XVIIIᵉ siècle* (1983; Literary Bohemia and Revolution: The World of Books in the 18th Century). Darnton shows that Gerlache's *cabinet de lecture* brought in 3,750 livres in December 1775, while in the ten months prior to May 1777 it brought in 2,654 livres and his bookstore 3,600 livres. Gerlache had as many as 379 subscribers.

It is certain that dictionaries and periodicals functioned as means of publicity, but the content of these *cabinets* varied in importance and quality, depending on the image that the bookseller wanted to promote. A survey of seven *cabinets* in Paris and the provinces between 1764 and 1789 shows that their stock varied from 797 to 2,182 items, with the majority holding around 1,700. They contained some legal and historical texts, but the bulk of their stock comprised a large number of novels and travel books, and the arts and sciences were occasionally also well represented. The proportion of items for study relative to those intended for pleasure could be lower or higher, depending on the degree of respectability that the bookseller sought to give to his "literary establishment." Those booksellers who were less anxious about their image specialized in novels, disdaining the bad reputation that resulted from the discovery of forbidden books kept under the counter. Some *cabinets* contained texts by the *philosophes*, but booksellers tended to be more discreet about such works than they were about other genres that were currently in fashion, such as works on European history. However, since the booksellers' catalogs were subject to censorship, it is difficult to estimate how many banned books these booksellers made available to the public. The clientele of the *cabinets* included schoolboys, students, and literary people of every type, as well as members of the administrative bourgeoisie and, to a lesser extent, of the commercial bourgeoisie. The ability to take books home had a greater impact on the novel-reading female public, although it is difficult to make generalizations about the profile of the subscribers to the *cabinets de lecture,* given that so many of their loan records have disappeared.

The *chambres de lecture* were quite different institutions. They can be distinguished from the *cabinet de lectures* in that they were not-for-profit associations of individuals who liked "novelties." The *chambres* purchased books and newspapers out of common funds, and these items were either packaged and circulated among the members according to a strict order or made available at a location set aside for the purpose, such as a room rented in a city. The distinctive characteristic of these reading rooms was that they were established on the basis of legally binding statutes, which were co-signed before a notary and provided for annual elections of a treasurer, a secretary, and a management committee. The statutes also addressed the possibility of bankruptcy and subsequent conversion into a charity.

Such associations were often created by middle-class readers who wanted to break away from the social promiscuity of the *cabinet de lecture* and discover within their own association a certain conviviality among people of their own social rank. Some readers, who wanted to economize on the time and hard work involved in serious study while avoiding the pitfalls of dilettantism, were attracted to the *cabinets* by the rising number of literary works (whether for reference or for recreation), the high cost of living, and the powerful example of the academies. In an age when a single issue of a magazine could cost the equivalent of two weeks' salary for a craftsman, economizing was a particularly significant incentive for participation in a *chambre de lecture.* Membership in the most expensive of these societies also cost as much as a single copy of a review, but that membership gave a person access to six or seven periodicals.

Some of the *chambres* had a precarious existence, while others settled into regular and stable ways. The number of members varied from one place to another, ranging from around 10 to 700 in the case of Nantes. The principal activity of these *chambres de lecture* was subscribing to periodicals, but members might also partake in card games and conversation. Some *chambres* were more ambitious and, if there were urban centers or regional academies nearby, they could develop into literary societies, modeling their activities on those of learned societies. For example, some *chambres de lecture* organized reading circles and poetry contests, invited the participation of university scholars, and campaigned for the establishment of public libraries or the opening of theatres. Literary and scientific interests meant more to these groups than issues of politics or international relations. Recruitment into these associations depended to a large extent on their degree of development and on the aims of the founders. Some *chambres* attracted new members among the administrative and professional bourgeoisie. Others recruited among the aristocracy and tended to become venues for high society, with entry being based on invitation or on selection by the management.

The *chambres de lecture* were more closely linked to the academies and Masonic lodges than were the libraries or the *cabinets de lecture.* In this way, the *chambres de lecture* formed part of the growing phenomenon of places for social intercourse, alongside coffeehouses, reading circles, academies, and literary salons. However, we should distinguish between two types of *chambres de lecture:* one was directly inspired by the model of the academy, while the other more closely resembled the modern book club. Both types could be found not only in France but also in the great cities of Germany and Switzerland, such as Basel, Bern, Geneva, Zurich, Stralsund, or Schaffhausen, as well as in the cantons of Glarus and Grisons.

BÉATRICE BRAUDE

See also Bibliophilism; Books and Reading

Further Reading

Chartier, Roger, and Henri Jean Martin, editors, *Histoire de l'édition française,* Paris: Promodis, 1983– ; see especially vol. 2, *Le livre triomphant, 1660–1830,* 1984

Darnton, Robert, *Bohème littéraire et révolution: Le monde des livres au XVIIIe siècle,* Paris: Gallimard, and Seuil, 1983

Jolly, Claude, editor, *Histoire des bibliothèques françaises,* 4 vols., Paris: Promodis, 1988–92; see especially vol. 2, *Les bibliothèques sous l'Ancien Régime, 1530–1789,* 1988

Light. *See* Optics and Light

Literature. *See* Books and Reading; Clandestine Literature; Correspondence: Literary; Drama; Essay; Fable; Novel; Novel, Gothic; Poetry; Tale; Women Writers and Feminism

Love

The word *amour* (love) underwent a slow semantic evolution in France during the 18th century. The word resonates with ever-increasing emotion in the successive editions of the *Dictionnaire de l'Académie Française* (Dictionary of the Académie Française). In the first edition (1694), *amour* is defined in the rather neutral psychological terms of the times: "Sentiment of the one who loves. Affection that one has for an object that one considers as a possession." A more dynamic definition from 1778 expressly refers to sensibility: "Sentiment by which the heart is drawn to the one who seems lovable and makes him the object of one's affection and desires." The content of the word varied according to the context in which it was used: in philosophy, in literature, or to describe historical experience.

Legacy from Classicism: The Progress of Sensibility

We cannot really appreciate the change in meaning of *amour* during the age of the Enlightenment unless we first take 17th-century notions into consideration, such as the definition offered in Antoine Furetière's *Dictionnaire* (1690):

Passion of the soul that makes us (desire what is good for) someone, or (take pleasure in) something. . . . Used principally to describe the violent passion that nature inspires in young people of different sexes in order to join them together and to perpetuate the species.

The erotic meaning of the term was used most often; it rarely extended to the reciprocal tenderness that can unite a man and woman outside of sexual impulse; in such cases the word *amitié* (friendship) was used (see Saint François de Sales's, *Introduction à la vie dévote* [1609; Introduction to a Devout Life]; or, Honoré d'Urfé's, *L'astrée*, [1607–27; Astrea]). *Amour* remained suspect as a passion tainted with disorder, although the altruism of a love that goes beyond lust was already exalted: "To love is to rejoice in the happiness of the other," declared Gottfried Wilhelm Leibniz, who died in 1716.

Despite its preconceived ideas about love, the Catholic Church appeared as the only defender of love in a society where love was often dissociated from marriage, the only legitimate context recognized for sexual love. Although it was certainly wary of sexuality as an end in itself, the Church demanded voluntary consent to sexual relations on the part of both spouses, independent of parental pressure, for a marriage to be valid (Council of Trent, 24th session). According to the Tridentine Fathers, this free choice presupposed a minimum of amorous sentiment, even if it were limited to the "tender overestimation" without which the "promised ones" would not commit to each other for a lifetime, as they would incur the risk of feeling a disgust incompatible with the indissolubility of marriage. Nevertheless, there may have been a gap between the Church's stated principles and reality, as well as some further development in religious opinion on this subject. A study of ecclesiastical investigations of requests for dispensations for prohibited consanguine unions shows that love was almost never given as a justification for such requests. Arguments were based on vital necessities: to settle a family conflict, to ensure the means of survival, to find a husband or wife in spite of a moral or physical handicap, or to give a father or mother to children orphaned of one parent, and so on (see Gouesse's study in the journal *XVIIe siècle* [1974]). In contrast, in the late 18th century, half of the candidates for marriage gave love as their reason for wanting to marry, which proves that the argument had become acceptable to official circles (see Poitrineau in *Aimer en France* [1980; To Love in France]). It seems that over the course of the 18th century love as an erotic drive began to be integrated with "friendship" love between marital partners and was gradually extended to all classes of society. In fact, this "bourgeois" model (see Stewart) gradually appeared in aristocratic society (see Flandrin, 1980) as well as in "village loves" (see Fillon).

This enriched notion of conjugal love did not appear simultaneously throughout Europe. Historians generally agree that it developed early on in England (see Flandrin, 1979). Francis Hutcheson, who influenced David Hume and Immanuel Kant, based the importance of marriage on its social functions of reproduction and education, as did most philosophers of his time (see Hutcheson's *A System of Moral Philosophy* [1755]); but Hutcheson also argued that the marital union could not succeed if husband and wife did not share mutual affection. In *The Theory of Moral Sentiments* (1759), Adam Smith praises the love of one's fellow man, as the most perfect achievement of human nature, but he also shows indulgence for love's sexual form:

Of all the passions . . . love is the only one that appears, even to the weakest minds, to have any thing in it that is either graceful or agreeable. In itself, first of all, though it may be ridiculous, it is not naturally odious; and though its consequences are often fatal and dreadful, its intentions are seldom mischievous

Anglomania was certainly related to the adoption of this new concept of "love" by the French elite, with the exception of the libertine circles. But identical aspirations arose elsewhere, in the theatre of Carlo Goldoni for example, although that fact alone does not enable an extrapolation to the whole of Italy. In *L'osteria della posta* (The Post-Stage Inn), the disillusioned lieutenant says that "after all, marriage is nothing but a contract; if love enters in, it is but one more article"; however, many other characters value highly the hope of contracting a marriage based on love, including the countess in the same play and, in varying degrees, the protagonists of Goldoni's *Il burbero benefico* (1771; The Times). In contrast, the severity of mores in Russia—already found in the *Domostroj* (mid–16th century; A Book on the Organization of the Home and the Family), which established an absolute tyranny of the father and husband—endured well into the 19th cen-

tury. This brutality was found in all classes, among the aristocracy as well as, a fortiori, the ignorant masses. In the latter half of the 18th century, the Russian nobility read works by the *philosophes* and translations of the abbé Prévost's *Manon Lescaut* (1731) and Jean-Jacques Rousseau's *La nouvelle Héloïse* (1761; Julie; or, The New Héloïse), and thus inspired by French culture these nobles claimed to be "enlightened," although the Russian "Enlightenment" was more a fashion than a profound transformation of the Russian way of life and thinking. Nikolai Mikhailovich Karamzin was one of the first Russian writers to develop the character of the "gallant gentleman" and to write works reflecting a taste for French preciosity (*La pauvre Lise* [1792; Poor Lise]). In Portugal, or at least in Portuguese literature, conjugal "love" often seemed to be expressed only through the compulsory jealousy of husbands. The Bourbons' arrival in Spain brought the fashion of "gallants" and provoked profound changes in the practices of love in high society, to the detriment of fidelity and traditional ideas about honor (see Martin Gaité).

Parental love was among the other forms of love that were also developed. Furetière noted the "violence" of this type of love; Goldoni remarked upon its "power" (*Il bugiardo* [1750; The Liar]); and moralists emphasized its necessity. This sentiment remained somewhat unilateral: whereas "nature" demanded that parents love their children, society demanded nothing more than respect and obedience from children. This view endured throughout the 18th century. A passage in the article "Amour" in the *Encyclopédie* observes rather cynically that it is only "recognition [that] prepossesses in wellborn children what duty imposes. . . . It suffices to be a man, to be a good father; and if one is not a good man, it is rare that one is a good son." The ungrateful son was not just a literary theme for Jean-Baptiste Greuze; and Denis Diderot and Jane Austen celebrated their parents, but filial love was not generalized or represented as being "natural" until well into the 19th century.

Often rough in its desire to protect, parental love as conceived in the 18th century may not have changed from the conception that prevailed in the previous century, and the father—in the theatre as in real life, and particularly in noble or wealthy families—maintained the power to arrange marriages for his children. However, in the age of the Enlightenment he dared to express his feelings: "You know how much I love you," says Monsieur Orgon to his daughter Sylvia in Marivaux's *Le jeu de l'amour et du hasard* (1730; The Game of Love and Chance). In *La vie de mon père* (1778; My Father's Life), even Nicolas Rétif de La Bretonne's authoritarian father declares to his son Edmond, who had obeyed him with deference, "I have always loved you." This statement brings to mind, in counterpoint, the fathers in Molière's plays, who are usually mistrustful of, if not frankly hostile to, their children. Elsewhere, fathers started to solicit their children's opinions (including those of daughters) before concluding the marriages that they had arranged, as illustrated again by the actions of Orgon in *Le jeu de l'amour et du hasard*.

The dearth of studies on fraternal love makes it impossible for us to speak of it with any assurance. We do not know what went beyond family fidelity (whose complexity is demonstrated by the judicial archives of certain provinces), "blood fanaticism" (Goldoni), and complicity against parents, to reach, despite obvious conflicts of interest and some positive examples, a genuine and reciprocal affection between persons.

Texts of "Enlightened" Love

The articles entitled "Amour" in Volume I of Diderot and Jean le Rond D'Alembert's *Encyclopédie* and in Voltaire's *Dictionnaire philosophique* (1764; Philosophical Dictionary) are among the indispensable references for those interested in French views of love. Both texts, however, are strangely shallow. The abbé Yvon's long, dense text for the *Encyclopédie* is dominated by a somewhat moralizing rhetoric, with little or no analysis and no trace of a psychology or metaphysics of love. The initial definition bears the mark of a moderate sensualism: "Usually, there is much sympathy in love, that is, an inclination of which the senses are the source: but although they may be the source of love, they are not always of primary interest in love." Yvon then lists, in addition to the "love" of persons ("of one's fellow man," "of the sexes," "conjugal," "paternal," "fraternal and filial"), love of the world, love of glory, love of literature and science, and, in a lengthy passage, *amour propre* (love of oneself). Although essentially filled with banalities, every paragraph does in fact provide potentially new ideas. Writing 11 years before Rousseau would sing the praises of breast-feeding in *Émile, ou, De l'éducation* (1762; Émile; or, concerning Education), Yvon advocates this practice as an expression of the mother's "instinctive" love for her child. He also has a "preromantic" conception of love between men and women: "True love forbids the thought of any sensual idea, any flight of imagination that could offend the fine sensibility of the beloved. He who is capable of love is virtuous; I would dare say that whoever is virtuous is also capable of loving." This is exactly what Johann Wolfgang von Goethe's Werther would say.

Voltaire, for his part, puts forth a rather materialistic notion of love: One must refer to the physical; it is the stuff of nature that has been embroidered by the imagination: "If you want to know what love is, look at the sparrows in your garden . . . watch the bull led to the

heifer." However, observing that for most animals, "as soon as that appetite is satisfied, everything is extinguished," he admits that, "as human beings have received the gift of improving all that nature has bestowed on them, they have improved on love." Again, however, this "improvement" is manifest on the physical level: "Cleanliness, caring for oneself by making the skin softer, increases the pleasure of touch, and attention to one's health makes the organs of voluptuousness more sensitive." Contemporaries of Voltaire, such as Claude-Adrien Helvétius, supported this utilitarianism: "To love is to need," posited Helvétius. In the *Supplément au voyage de Bougainville* (1774; A Supplement to Bougainville's Travels), Diderot carries this notion over into a kind of "naturalism": "All other sentiments then enter into the sentiment of [physical] love, like metals that combine with gold: friendship, esteem . . ." On a different level, in *Grundlegung zur Metaphysik der Sitten* (1785; Grounding for the Metaphysics of Morals), Kant advocates "a practical and nonpathological love that resides in will and not in a sensual attraction, in the principles of action and not in a debilitating compassion."

A Different Kind of Love

During the age of the Enlightenment, but in total contradiction with its optimistic and rather finalized notions of a purely erotic, reproductive "love," the attraction between a man and a woman was fundamentally redefined and revolutionized through a modification of sentiments, as seen in France in Rousseau's *La nouvelle Héloïse*. Certainly, the chevalier des Grieux in Prévost's novel exemplified the "hero of love" (see G. Lély): his affair with Manon Lescaut is scandalous and tragic, moved by passion but lacking the heart, the self-mastery, and the sense of duty whose fulfillment brings peace to Julie and Saint-Preux in Rousseau's novel. Outside societal norms Julie and Saint-Preux's love nevertheless remains honorable. When Julie gives herself, she is free; once married, she is able to avoid adultery, even though her heroic drowning arrives providentially to prevent her from giving in once more. In his preface to *La nouvelle Héloïse*, Rousseau warns that the book might have subversive effects. In fact, it was influential through the deep current of thought that it stimulated throughout Europe, which was amplified in the first few decades of the 19th century.

An indispensable literary link in the evolution of the concept of love, Goethe's *Die Leiden des jungen Werther* (1774; The Sorrows of Young Werther) grew out of an exaltation of the sensitivity inherited from *La nouvelle Héloïse*. Making an impact first in Germany and then throughout Europe (in France it was translated and reprinted 15 times in 18 years and imitated several times), the book announced what might be called, without entering into critical disputes, "romantic love." Love as a "frenetic passion with no end," "the only thing in the world that makes us indispensable," reaches a degree of idealization in Goethe's work never before achieved: "[Charlotte] is sacred for me," declares Werther, "all desire goes silent in her presence." This sentiment is far from the lusty grins of Enlightenment libertines. Love again becomes something serious, which, when it is impossible, could end in voluntary or accidental death, as for the young Werther and, later, for Odile and Edward in Goethe's *Die Wahlverwandtschaften* (1809; The Elective Affinities).

MARCEL BERNOS

See also Eroticism; Fatherhood; Sensibility; Sexuality, Representations of; Virtue

Further Reading

Fillon, Anne, *Les trois bagues aux doigts: Amours villageoises au XVIIIe siècle*, Paris: Laffont, 1989

Flandrin, J.-L., *Families in Former Times: Kinship, Household, Sexuality,* Cambridge and New York: Cambridge University Press, 1979 (original French edition, 1976)

Flandrin, J.-L., "Amour et marriage," *Dix-huitième siècle* 12 (1980)

Kluckhohn, Paul, *Die Auffassung der Liebe in der Literatur des 18. Jahrhunderts und in der deutschen Romantik,* Tübingen, Germany: Niemeyer, 1966

Martin Gaité, Carmen, *Love Customs in Eighteenth-Century Spain,* translated by Maria G. Tomsich, Berkeley: University of California Press, 1991 (original Spanish edition, 1972)

Stewart, Philip, *La masque et la parole: Le langage de l'amour au XVIIIe siècle,* Paris: Corti, 1973

Luxury

In Antoine Furetière's *Dictionnaire* (1690; Dictionary), *luxe* (luxury) is defined as follows: "Unnecessary expense, excessive extravagance, whether in clothing, furnishings, or food." In complete contrast, in the *Encyclopédie* (1759) the marquis de Saint-Lambert begins his entry on the same word by declaring that "it is the use that one makes of wealth and of industry in order to ensure oneself an agreeable existence." This wide gap between extravagance and an agreeable existence signified the distance between two cultural and material worlds. Later in his article, Saint-Lambert, who was aware of this difference, contrasts pomp, or the luxury of distinction, with the quest for comforts, or the luxury of observing proper decorum, "which always tends toward the useful and never degenerates into foolish emulation." Here Saint-Lambert expresses both a normative intent and a clear awareness of the profound changes that had occurred over the course of the century—the development of material civilization, but also the transformation of sensibilities and moral values that had accompanied the "crisis of European consciousness."

Luxury had been part and parcel of the baroque state, being embedded in the logic of societies centered on monarchical courts that generated economies based on eccentric spending. In the 18th century, however, luxury was subject to a different logic, as it developed alongside the slow shift in centers of wealth from the courts toward the cities, and simultaneously stimulated and expressed a rise in consumption and the spread of a new relationship of consumers to objects.

In its own way, the sudden revival of the debate on luxury at the height of the Enlightenment is evidence—in the same way that inventories of property or macroeconomic indicators are—of the reality of the changes and the hopes, but also the disquiet and the questioning those changes and hopes engendered. Nevertheless, Enlightenment writers were capable of perceiving the relative nature of luxury, and the difficulty of determining what is necessary and what is superfluous. It is impossible to define luxury in any absolute sense, for it is related to the social norms of an age, and the adjectives *commode* (convenient) and *luxueux* (luxurious) can be understood only in relation to the individuals to whom they are applied. One might therefore construct a sociology, or a politics, of luxury as Montesquieu did, but not an economics of luxury. Accordingly, it is not surprising that, after having been the focus of a significant part of the economic debates of the century, the theme of luxury eventually ceased to interest economists.

Court Society and the Economy of Luxury

Against this background it is hardly surprising that sociologists—Max Weber, Werner Sombart, and Thorstein Veblen—were the first to attempt a general interpretation of the aristocratic economy of ostentation. Written in its definitive form in 1933 but not published until 1969, Norbert Élias's *Höfische Gesellschaft* (The Court Society) is based on a comparative approach to the absolutist princely courts, most completely exemplified by that of Louis XIV. Even today the book remains an indispensable reference tool (see Élias).

Assessing the emergence of a new social formation, court society, in which the social "self" of the individual was completely merged into the representation that he gave or that others gave of him, Élias shows how that society established an economy of luxury and ostentation, which regulated expenditure according to the requirements of rank rather than following a rational management of income. The affirmation of the absolute power of the prince was inseparable from the process of subordination of the rich and the rise of competing social groups (for example, bureaucrats and civil servants loyal to the state), and these interrelated developments consequently aggravated rivalry over status and the symbols of prestige.

The logic of distinctions determined the hierarchy and the dynamics of consumption, for which ostentation served two main purposes. By making their appearances into ornamental displays, the powerful reflected the greatness of the prince to outsiders and maintained the nobles' distance from competing classes. In turn, the propensity of these rivals to imitate the high-ranking nobility encouraged members of the latter group, who had been relieved of many of their political and administrative functions, to affirm their primacy within the social hierarchy through extravagant expenditures.

Élias's model emphasizes the political function of luxury, as well as its role in the continuation of cultural divisions. The monarch, who dispensed benefits and favors, rewarded political submission by granting the bonuses or pensions that were essential to the maintenance of rank. Moreover, the diffusion of luxury was not just a matter of a circulation from on high to those below. It reciprocally increased the demands for distinction among the rich and powerful and intensified their need to search constantly for new discriminating symbols. In this sense, the court was a laboratory for norms of good taste and the location for a new form of alienation—fashion. Luxury was no longer seen as superfluous, but as a necessity.

As instructive as it may be, Élias's model does not capture the complexity of historical reality. Indeed, many subsequently published studies have shown that the system of luxury that gave rise to this model of ruin-

ous expense was nonetheless far from responsible for causing the financial collapse of wealthy nobles. Monarchs periodically intervened in order to do what was necessary to maintain social positions, and nobles themselves were actively involved in their economic fates, as they participated in commercial ventures or in financial operations, cornered the most profitable posts, or arranged marriages that would guarantee the consolidation of incomes. This relative degree of consolidation of the elite classes was yet another symptom of the tendency for class distinctions to become blurred, as the leading members of the commercial and financial bourgeoisie began to emulate the life style of the aristocracy. Theologians and moralists castigated this confusion among the ranks, a perversion of the transparency of appearances, while the sumptuary laws sought to prevent it. The fact that these royal edicts banning sumptuary display were so frequently reissued shows that they were largely ineffectual. However, these laws must also be understood in the light of the policy of "mercantilism," which, notably in France from the time of Jean-Baptiste Colbert, was aimed at limiting imports with high added value, which put a strain on the balance of trade.

The monarchical fiscal system was organized around the objectives of self-sufficiency and the domestic exchange of value for value, alongside unequal exchange and the strengthening of comparative advantages in relation to foreign countries. In this context, luxury could be conceived only as a means of external enrichment, or as the privilege, within the domestic economy, of a narrowly defined elite, whose pomp was linked to the celebration of the greatness of the prince. In France, however, the growth of trade that began around the end of Louis XIV's reign and then the immense boost given to the economy by John Law's financial experiments, which provided incomparable opportunities for enrichment and for the reduction of debts, definitively undermined any hope of confining luxury within the sphere of the royal court. The Regency (1715–23), which brought the royal court back to Paris, inaugurated a new phase of luxury in the midst of an inflationary whirlwind.

From Luxury to Affluence

In order to understand how representations and judgments of luxury were transformed, one must first assess the material changes that affected the whole of 18th-century Europe to differing degrees and following diverse rhythms. In this regard, England seems to have been the laboratory for experiments in new attitudes and patterns of behavior.

From the 1650s onward, certain social groups with greater purchasing power, notably farmers and merchants made wealthy through colonial trade, began adapting their lifestyles and their spending habits to more closely approximate to those of the aristocracy. In the 18th century, England's economy was strengthened through a truly diversified pattern of domestic spending, based on the increased purchasing power of the affluent classes in the cities. England's development was accelerated, and it became both a model and an object of fascination for continental Europeans. The broadening of access to luxury items had an impact not only on England's foreign trade, through the demand of its trading partners for new colonial products, but also on domestic production, which partly replaced manufactured imports. It also led people to perceive their society as being more open, one in which the elite joined others in enjoying the pleasures of life. Rank and wealth were based on the use of the same material goods, which were no longer simply ostentatious objects of vain finery, but items that contributed to the comfort of everyday life. Luxury began leaning toward the useful, toward convenience, and comfort. The rational arrangement of domestic interiors and the refinement of furniture, the enrichment and diversification of wardrobes and dress codes, and a new concern for hygiene, which came to dominate food consumption and encouraged an increased use of water and soap—all these innovations demonstrate the slow displacement of luxury from the sphere of appearances alone to that of general well-being.

This movement affected the rest of Europe over the course of the century, in line with the strengthening of the Continental economies. A wiser, more reasonable, more bourgeois type of luxury appeared, and was compared by writers to the comfortable affluence of the more egalitarian societies, best exemplified by the Netherlands. The model of extravagance thus fell into disequilibrium, being shaken by an increased sharing availability of prestigious objects and contaminated by the bourgeois innovations brought about through new lifestyles. In his *Tableau de Paris* (1781–89; Panorama of Paris), Louis-Sébastien Mercier noted that "the word 'court' no longer carries any weight with us," thus indicating that the city had become the site for the transformations being pushed forward by the new elite formed through a combination of rank and wealth. Urban aggregation took the place of courtly segregation, engendering more open competition, as well as new cultural and material exchanges.

The Ideal of Earthly Happiness

Such a development could not be conceived without a revolution in perceptions, concepts, and values. Literary historians have explored the paths and the modalities of expression of this revolution through such themes as

nature, disquiet, and happiness, providing evidence for the emergence of attitudes that valued having over being, possession and enjoyment over greatness, glory, or spiritual salvation. No longer the exclusive sign of belonging to a certain class, or of social power, luxury became the manifestation of a legitimate aspiration to earthly happiness.

As an indirect result of the scientific revolution, a belief in progress and in a potential mastery of nature nourished the idea of an improvement in the human condition. Increased social mobility, as well as material and technical improvements, seemed to confirm this potential, both individually and collectively. Human beings, "from whom," according to Blaise Pascal, "God wishes to hide," sought to live their lives to the fullest in their sojourn upon Earth, for they no longer conceived it as a transitory exile. It was up to them to shape their lives for their own use and happiness. As a result, luxury became tinged with hedonism; it was no longer simply a matter of accumulation or distinctive excess, but a search for enjoyment through satiety. The need for the superfluous was felt by way of a new relationship to the world and to objects that provided security, embellishment, and reassurance. Virtue was the fruit no longer of renunciation, but of the moderate and reasonable use of goods and of the benefits those goods provided. Love of the self no longer separated the individual from the community of Christians. Instead, it contributed to the progress of civilization.

This revision of moral concerns and values gave luxury an unprecedented positive image and gradually marginalized the discourse of theologians. However slow and uneven, the growth and enrichment of a significant section of society beyond the narrow circle of merchants was evidence that such passions as cupidity, vanity, and frivolity did not conflict with the general interest. To the apologists of luxury, not only was it beyond moral condemnation, it was economically beneficial, as well.

The Quarrel over Luxury

The revival of luxury that was inscribed within the new philosophy of happiness gave rise to a major public debate in the 18th century. Throughout Europe academies and newspapers gave a great deal of attention to the quarrel, and economists and philosophers seized on the issue. Once again the impulse came from England, although the libertine critiques of Saint-Évremont and Pierre Bayle had fully prepared the ground by laying the foundations for a secular morality.

Bernard Mandeville's *The Fable of the Bees* went unnoticed when it was first published in England, as a broadsheet, in 1705, but the 1723 edition, expanded with a voluminous commentary, stimulated a fierce polemic that was played out through reviews in the press. It reached France in 1725 through hostile articles in the *Bibliothèque britannique* and the *Journal des savants*. By maintaining that private vices can be transformed into public benefits, Mandeville takes the ineradicable nature of passions into account and casts an anthropological eye on society. He also asserts that society functions automatically, that evil—which is inevitable—can have a civilizing effect, and that the passions of individuals can work spontaneously for the common good. Mandeville thus lays the axiological foundations of nascent liberal thought. The "invisible hand" of Adam Smith, who defends luxury in his *The Theory of Moral Sentiments* (1759), works in the same way.

Nevertheless, apologias for luxury continued to be made mainly by mercantilist writers. Jean François Melon's *Essai politique sur le commerce* (1734; Political Essay on Commerce), which defends the social utility of luxury as a factor in full employment and as a source of abundance, seems to have been as much of an inspiration as Mandeville's *Fable* for two texts by Voltaire, *Le Mondain* (1734; The Worldly Man) and *Défense du "Mondain"* (1736; Defense of "Le Mondain"). Voltaire provocatively and lightheartedly ridicules the myth of a golden age of virtue, in which frugality was merely a mask for destitution. Once again, we find here the arguments of classical economics, which hold that luxury enriches the state and that the spending of the rich helps the poor to live.

In contrast, at the beginning of the 1750s, physiocratic thought, which was hegemonic at that time, presented a quite different argument. Its emphasis on the role of productive investment implied a condemnation of luxury as being a sterile diversion for a sterile class. So long as France had not achieved the maximum degree of civilization, the superfluous expenditures of landowners were prejudicial to its prosperity. Regarded as a form of unproductive spending, luxury was not presented as a factor in economic growth for Anne-Robert-Jacques Turgot, or for Smith in his *The Wealth of Nations* (1776). Both moralists and social critics

came to reject luxury as the extravagant passion of an idle class. It was on this battlefield that the opponents of luxury deployed their arguments throughout the century, from Father Fénelon to Jean-Jacques Rousseau and the abbé François-André Pluquet. As Pierre Rétat has emphasized, luxury was not only an idea but also a concrete and immediate experience of inequality (see Rétat). This is eloquently demonstrated through Rousseau's introspective journeys, which culminated in his *Discours sur l'origine et les fondements de l'inégalité parmi les hommes* (Discourse on the Origins of Inequality), published in 1755.

DOMINIQUE MARGAIRAZ

See also Boudoir; Court, French Royal; Festival; Nobility; Utility

Further Reading

Brewer, John, and Roy Porter, editors, *Consumption and the World of Goods,* London and New York: Routledge, 1993

Carrive, Paulette, *Bernard Mandeville: Passions, Vices, Vertus,* Paris: Vrin, 1980

Élias, Norbert, *The Court Society,* translated by Edmund Jephcott, Oxford: Blackwell, and New York: Pantheon Books, 1983 (original German edition, 1969)

Goubert, Jean-Pierre, *Du luxe au confort,* Paris: Belin, 1988

McKendrick, Neil, John Brewer, and J. Plumb, *The Birth of a Consumer Society: The Commercialization of Eighteenth-Century England,* London: Europa, and Bloomington: Indiana University Press, 1982

Rétat, P., "Luxe," *Dix-huitième siècle* 26 (1994)

Roche, Daniel, *The Culture of Clothing: Dress and Fashion in the "Ancien Régime,"* Cambridge and New York: Cambridge University Press, 1994 (original French edition, 1989)

Sekora, John, *Luxury: The Concept in Western Thought, Eden to Smollett,* Baltimore, Maryland: Johns Hopkins University Press, 1977